The Book of Contours

by Ajani Abdul-Khaliq

SATA

2025

ISBN: 978-1-955275-07-1

Social Arts & Technical Alliance, LLC
Glennville, GA

1st edition

Table of Contents

Relationships built upon your full truth are those with the best chance of enduring easily, for all time.

It does not matter whether that truth is pretty or unsettling. Almost everyone has both light and dark sides—the latter of which they are trained to keep imprisoned for long stretches of their lives.

Humanity itself has a dark side, yet all sides have been allowed under Creation. There *must* be a way to translate even this into the language of God. If only we could access the source code for explaining the need for both the hero and the villain in a greater story…

Blessed are those whose darkness cannot be hidden. With far less to lose, they have an opportunity to advance God's language for the understanding of all, that the long-term survival of the whole may be assured. Indeed, to attempt to build our eternity upon the lie of "the wholly righteous man" is to poison ourselves through our own hypocrisy. Our ignorance of the FULL Universe. Our hate for all the things that don't please our little lenses; for the one outside of our favor also believes *himself* to be wholly righteous at our expense, whether or not we have revoked his voice among our friends; all this will have done was give his perspective a place *outside* of our influence.

Blessed are those whose darkness cannot be hidden. But will they make use of that blessing? Will they apply their darkness beyond themselves, beyond their favorite things, beyond the narrowness of family, clique, country, or even the present time? Unfortunately, darkness applied only for the benefit of our friends and the destruction of our "enemies" is energy wasted. God will allow all so-called "enemies" to exist despite our myopic smallness, and our little interests will eventually be replaced by those of the next trender. For no one is truly an enemy in the eyes of the game's Great Programmer.

We can understand both light and dark in terms of the abstract dynamics behind them, and offer those abstractions as a gift to the rest of the world. While darkness may render our human plot more interesting and sometimes more worth living, only its conversion into a potential light for *all the world* will bring us closer to the Rule Set which created us.

This is my story and my body, exploded into a million code snippets for you and the rest of human science to use in the truest reproductions of our stories—not as our judgment censors it or downvotes it, but as our Creating-Laws have scripted it.

Surely I can only speculate, but I have broken my speculation into tiny blocks of interactions which you may rearrange to fit your path as you will. Formal human science may relabel these blocks according to its biases against astrology, but I will use the social prescriptions embedded in astrology to make this journey much easier than formal academia will allow. The *social* truths contained herein—despite being packaged behind signs, angles, and asteroid names—are true, nonetheless. With the *p*-values to attend them.

I disclose myself to you as a way of forcing only options built on truth to be the ones that manifest in my life—having freed myself of the need to hide every dark corner in any new meeting. Not everyone will understand this form of outing, because it begins with several discussions of several silenced areas of human life. But on the other side of each dark beginning is a collection of interactions which you may apply to your light. All you will need to do is collect the blocks as they are presented.

The Book of Contours is an autobiography born from my lifelong dream of contributing to the best of humanity. But how can a single person in an obscure field, with no name, money, or influential connections do this? I think he or she does this by finding and sticking with their niche, and using that niche to advance one slice of our human story. Through decades of introspection, I've found that the only real way for me to go from lemons to lemonade is to change my own mentality, regardless of anything else happening beyond me. Knowing that I'll never win any awards for sainthood, charisma, looks, or any other popular trait, I asked myself what I *could* win awards in—what I *have* been rewarded for *on the small scale* throughout life—which also advanced those around me. My conclusion? It hasn't always been pretty, but I've found that my role has always been to ally with people for a while, stir up or be part of some kind of major disruption that forced a change in thought, to fail in that message and, finally, to be rewarded with freedom to leave the wreckage with far more insight than I came with—turning that insight into books for you. I know that there is a pattern of not having my efforts looked at until after I've left or been kicked out of a place, and that's actually safer for building the transformation in peace while still inside the system, free of the powerful gravity back towards the (in many cases broken) status quo. So I can more or less learn everything there is to know about the framework in need of change.

As far as I can see, humanity is most in need of a change in mentality. It doesn't matter how many little or big fires we fight, there will always be another one until we evolve a kind of psychological rule set for fire safety. *Contours* is my contribution to an upgraded mentality, from ape social frameworks to ingroups that live and die off of their ability to produce constructive, path-stabilizing information; what we lack isn't new forms of power, money, or even technology, but rather a new lens for understanding how each human works behind the scenes—especially those humans whom we are trained to perpetually see as outsiders.

From the outsider perspective, I aim to do something which I think very few people can: my goal throughout this book is to show you, "Okay, this is a complete manual of how that alien over there actually works, what his thinking is based on, and why you don't actually have to fight him in order to advance the whole thing—including your own aims." "Here is the WHOLE manual. You may or may not like much about him, but this is the only chance you will have had up to now to see a near complete map of how *all* humans are built."

> "Pretend we're trying to save a person as data in a way so thoroughly, so accurately as to allow people to rebuild him after he's dead. Rather than tell his story through the usual subjective lens, we'll tell it through data blocks that the future 'reprinting' machinery can convert into usable algorithms."

To capture the complexity of human sociology as data blocks, this book uses super fine-grained statistical astrology. Here, things like planets and aspects are treated like buckets of social experience, such that the autobiography serves as more of the "zip file" through which I learn all this and transmit it to you. No autobiography = no book. And if I think of my brain as a kind of calculator, these books are kind of like the extra RAM I need to do those calculations on. (That's in case you're wondering, "Why can't he just gives us the astro and leave all of the personal stuff out? It's kind of like me asking you to explain your network of decision-making and situation-finding without explaining anything you actually do. Maps like the extensive ones you'll find in this book can't be made without deep biography. I certainly couldn't have done the core research without thousands of these.)

That said, despite the density of content to come, the suggested way you interpret charts is now simpler than ever:

- Only read conjuncts. These tell you when two ideas act together at the same time.
- If two things aren't conjunct, then assume that you'll need to be in [whatever angle / aspect] mode in order for the objects you're looking at to be brought *into* conjunct. Oppositions (1/2 circle) tell you that you'll need to consider one "with respect to" the other (x 2). Trines (n/3rds of a circle) tell you that you'll need to "think internally" about them together (x 3). A 5-ariquintile ([n=5]/137ths of a circle) tells you to employ a mode of

singular, active, direct control (x 137 repeats of this frequency make you whole again). Use Table 10, page 165 to help you.

That's it. There is no need to get bogged down by signs or the other regions I talk about unless your goal is to see the situations in which specific buckets are more likely to activate themselves—provided you turn your efforts towards those situations. If you turn your attention to generic Scorpio pushing of your will onto another, you will get whatever major planets are in there as output. Turn it to duodecanate 34 (Capricorn-10), then "mastery" will be your theme for the moment and you will get the standouts among about 150-250 asteroids as the output. Don't overthink it. Just look at what clumps together.

Lastly, this book contains all sorts of offensive content. All of the sides of our human lives (which we must necessarily hide in order to keep our societies stable) are studied here, even basic biological functions and private behaviors. For the most part, *Contours* probably fits best under a field we could call "social anthropometry," where we'd study things like evolutionary effects on behavior, prejudice, various inborn pathologies, trait popularity and opportunity-opening, body-image, family trade, et cetera… all for the purpose of really dissecting our sociology to enable newer, better paths for ourselves and our world. This version of social anthropometry, if it were a thing, would also be critically tied to any technology which put a human's event patterns into nonhuman or time/space-teleported contexts, because the anthropometry part doesn't just measure the external body, but things like visual appearance (via the **e**lectro**m**agnetic spectrum) and internal **h**or**m**one flows: "emhim" for short. I have a couple of chapters that illustrate this concept, at least one of which focuses on an abstract technology called "talking trees."

Alas, in order to build the full human or its translation, you first need a good map of what a full human involves. In 2025 as I'm writing this, AIs don't yet mate or use the bathroom. But they'll need to if they are going to be used to approximate the original us in some other context.

For readers who have a hard time keeping up with everything in this book, know that *Contours* is the culmination of several previous works. Starting with the most relevant, they are

1. *Laurentia 2nd edition*
2. *Genevieve of Venus* (Book 6 of a mostly unpublished six-book philosophy-as-fiction series. I published both this one and *Laurentia 2* prior to *Contours* because these books have concepts which are married to the ones in here.)
3. *Sex in 12 Dimensions*
4. *Alma Mater*
5. *Gamified Spirit*

Laurentia 2 specifically is a kind of companion to this book, where each of the 21000 asteroids I list in Figure 7 (page 99) is interpreted there.

Chapter 1. Archetypal stories

WHY DO I SAVE MYSELF AS DATA FOR ALL THE WORLD TO SEE? **DO YOU HAVE A WHY?**

My autobiography is of no use to you. To me, it is a kind of driver's license. Countless times I have started down the road to relating with someone else, only to have that connection inevitably derailed by various factors that I surely know will surface eventually. Tired of carrying a known elephant into every room, I decided to simply declare the elephant at the customs gate, so that any and all potential exchanges would be forced to begin with the entire truth of who they will be working with. For I have many ideas which I believe to be of benefit to society, but I know that I am far more likely to be socially punished if certain among my truths surface later rather than earlier. Though uncomfortable in the eyes of some, these truths are harmless. Yet my failure to out them on my own terms is a recipe for others' inventing my narratives rather than me controlling my own. I have learned this from hard experience. This book attempts to set those stories, both past and potential, aright.

There are so many things I wish to tell you about the road to enduring happiness. I have found it. Ceaselessly I seek to share it with all the world. But what to do when others squirm! Or judge? They judge the traits that they themselves have. Traits we all have—every one of us. And yet we cannot even investigate the problems of this world in the age of high censorship and norming. These are necessary for the safety of all, that is true. But at the bounds of our social rules are the private worlds, the taboos, the troubling psychologies, the easily explicable yet inconveniently darkened reasons why we do what we do. Some people, like myself, do not have the stereotypical beauty or riches or power to get by without having those traits outside-of-norm put on display before a cold public first. Oh, have I paid the price several times over for not meeting others' ideal. I am also susceptible to distrust in general. And yet despite this (perhaps even because of it), I have spent much of my adult life seeking to reach an unparalleled level understanding regarding the tiny blocks that build human nature. Those blocks rearranged, I may yet assume even the worst hand of cards dealt to me by Fate, and *still* come out a winner simply by knowing how to play them. In this book, I will show you what I have speculated about how it all works, so that you too may rearrange even the strangest of hands dealt to you.

In the process, even if no one ever reads this, I will have officially declared to the world all of a single person's psychology—especially those sides we are taught to hide. Having done so, I will have used every card, all narrative material, all judgments and assessments, all previously difficult life patterns, to expand several fields (I hope) of social and formal science, thereby liberating myself from the need to see these bestowed patterns as a cap on my potential—a burden in each exchange. Regardless of what anyone says about you, you too deserve the right to look in the mirror with all of your traits, socially favored or not, and know that you rocked the game of life in ways that no one other than you could have.

This one is for all of those out who need the tools to turn their disadvantages into unquestioned advantage—not to beat their opponent, but to advance their very world like no other.

FIRST, ONE SHOULD REDUCE THEMSELVES TO A FOOTNOTE ON THE LIPS OF OTHERS

My autobiography begins by reducing myself to a bullet—as the rest of existence which is not me will actually see me. We know how we ourselves describe any nameable historical figure. Whole lives are reduced to simple one-liners. Wikipedia first sentences. If you were good to friends, the sentence may be laced with love or admiration. In the eyes of strangers who read about you, you were more likely to be cursorily described by an image, what you did for a living, and some major event you were associated with. More rarely, you may be cited for events you helped bring into being. Despite all of the importance I assign to my life, it is true that (usually) no one will know or care about the details which preoccupy me so diligently. In the beginning I, like most people, may court an epitaph which is far from where I want to be. But if I use the tools shared with you in this book, I can take that same default mediocrity of future-summary and turn it into something of my own design.

WHO WAS I? WHO WERE YOU? THE "ONE-LINE"

I was an early 21st century black thinker and writer who looked at controversial social topics in individuality.

There may be more to that in the initial paragraph, but that about captures it. As for my dreams and goals and other aspirations while I yet lived, anything that strays from the "one-line" was simply less likely to succeed whenever I took it on. For better or worse, the above is who I know I would have been—given 45 years of life spent observing where Fate ultimately kept putting me.

The one-line tells all the things worth pursuing, which will surely succeed across all rememberable Time. For me this is

- Living within the 21st century historical context and all that this brings
- Being black (and male)
- Putting my thoughts and speculations out there, with an implied intellectual bent (thinking)
- Writing as one of my most significant my persona-defining mediums
- Putting "controversial topics" before others—whatever that means
- Notably focusing on individuality

The rest of the first wiki paragraph (if I had one), would elaborate on this. I won't cover it here though, because if it were a zip file, it would be quite dense. We'll unpack these later.

SUPPOSE I HAD A CLONE IN LIFE THAT DID THE MOST IMPORTANT THING. YOUR INTERFACE

Suppose I really want to save myself as data, but don't have the computing power to do so. Nor the technology or knowledge. The one-line would be THE most important gauge of this clone's accuracy, but how would this clone operate in order to produce the one-line? Hmm…

Living in the 21st century suggests the clone would be information related	…as opposed to living in some other time. Future readers will automatically conjure a context for you as soon as they are told the time period you lived in
Being black would suggest a higher tendency for people interacting with you to rile themselves up via your presence, if not your actual actions (an evolutionary lineage for amplifying divisions of category across all external situations you encounter, as well as the basis for the human species, v1.0)	…as opposed to, for example, being white (with an evolutionary lineage for having your will prevail upon environments you enter, foreign though they may be) or being broadly Asian (having an evolutionary lineage for imposing collectively abstract structure upon the places your group enters).

Being male suggests internal wiring that favors projecting your inner inclinations onto spaces regardless of what those spaces are, and having the outward body which tells others to expect this from you. It is easier for you to lose your senses in light of another individual, body, overture, or situation that stirs your inner appetite.	…as opposed to being female, with internal wiring that favors the projecting of world-contexts and space-membership onto the inner inclinations of anything that enters your zone, regardless of what those things are. This also would bring an outward body which tells others to expect this from you. It is easier for you to lose your senses in light of high status, high worth, high comfort, or high fanship spaces which conjure the potential for the world which you want to pervasively describe your own.
Being a thinker suggests that my thoughts are more likely to be the determiner of distinguishing permanence for me as a concept in others' minds	…as opposed to, say, being an office manager, where my handling of organizable concerns would be the determiner of distinguishing permanence in others' minds.
Writing would be the means I used to bring my permanence into your view	Sports or contract work might be some other examples of one's route-to-impression-making
Putting controversial topics before others is more of a statement of the character of situations I end up in, or which others around me end up in when I am there. This regular-day character imposition is THE most important thing that a clone must get right in order to be considered accurate, because its place, time, available routes to impression, and even internal wiring aren't always guaranteed to be the same. Let's call the regular-day character imposition **your interface**. My history is littered with discomforts imposed upon others, almost always unplanned and unintended—sometimes done out of defense of my own self-worth. More interestingly, in detached places like work where I don't connect closely enough to unsettle individuals, the institution itself has ALWAYS undergone a major tough transition… or closed entirely. Every time I've been in a place. Not once has it gone otherwise across my full working career. Unfortunately, it does not pay for me to teach or learn along the path of the socially favorable or straight and narrow. Something always happens to attach offense to it. This book, my very interest in astrology, are ways to take this default offense and put it constructively under my control, for everyone else's benefit if they are interested in receiving it.	What kinds of events are conjured around you whenever you arrive in a place and stay there for months or weeks?
Notably focusing on individuality means that for better or worse, individual traits, slights, and gifts will be something I am hypersensitive to. This can't help but imply the kind of disruptions I tend to see and gravitate towards more easily.	…as opposed to focusing on topics like family, achievement, revenge, status, or any number of other concepts

My clone would need to preserve the dynamics of my baseline human one-line, even if someone cloned my personality into a video game NPC (non-player character). Or the body of a sky dolphin—an analogy for an engineered creature on 25th century Neptune. Perhaps I might be cloned into the AI for a traffic light talking smack to the cars below. More likely, I would just be a kind of software program that does a job peculiar to the way living Ajani did it, and produces similar results: tomes full of tables with occasionally questionable content. Whatever the case, my *interface* is the set of events that necessarily come with me everywhere I go. Beyond my own private sense of self, it is the more important story that every other interactant outside of me is more likely to find themselves involved in—in some cases even after I am dead.

TABLE 1: AJANI'S [WORLD] DATA-SAVE PART 1 OF 1. INTERFACES

	Positive, Negative, or neutral	People, Places, or Situations
What happens to places when you are there?		
Region: civic development after 2+ years (**EXPERT**)	+	place
Region: sports teams more likely to win championships upon his arrival and departure (**EXPERT**)	+	place

Region: politically prosperous	O	place
What kinds of events happen among your closest collaborators or rivals?		
Close partner: chance at dreams granted (**EXPERT**), usually not capitalized on	+	people
Close partner: conflict over Ajani's need for two partners, or one partner versus a heavily married work / trade	-	people
Close partner: increased single-mindedness	O	people
Not everyone has the same categories of events serve as important in their lives. Romance and sexual partners feed into my one-line, so I ask what happens in these areas.		
Romantic partner: increased secretiveness from initial meeting, but gradual understanding of this	-	people
Romantic partner: increasingly visible, but gradually decreased obsessiveness	+	people
Romantic partner: difficult personality increase, stabilization over the long run	O	people
Sexual partner: commentary on expectations or effort	-	people
Sexual partner: highly cerebral mind	O	people
Are there patterns in the work you do? This makes it easier to know where you belong as a regular-day expresser		
Employing institution: experiences existential crisis involving merger, cuts, and regulatory challenges (**EXPERT**)	- then + (if the institution is good)	places, situation
Employing institution: Ajani in low status until crisis occurs, then elevated to influencing position	O	situation
Employing institution: Ajani works in an isolated location, automated mapping of difficult data (**EXPERT**)	O	places, situations
Bosses: often come in pairs	O	situation
Bosses: heavy body build	O	people
Bosses: embattled, assaulted by *their* bosses or even higher powers in the institution. In positive cases, just kept *very* busy	O	people, situations, places
Bosses: faced with some version of homelessness / being an outcast	-	people
This is your all-important default impression in the world. It is heavily affected by any social, prosocial, or socially unfavorable qualities others deem you to have.		
Strangers: feel uncomfortable; Ajani = weird	-	people
Strangers: closed opportunity doors to Ajani as solo; "solicitation never works" (i.e. Ajani introducing himself or his ideas alone almost always ends in failure) (**EXPERT**), but...	-	people
Strangers: wide open doors to Ajani when he has a close female partner, and...	O	people
Strangers: susceptibility to notable influence by Ajani + two close partners of the same sex (either both male or both female, or trans and another person of the sex they transitioned to)	+	people, situations
Strangers: attracts women in pairs when traveling in a foreign, historically educational environment	+	people
What kinds of events happen among your closest collaborators or rivals?		
Friends (in general): rarely communicates with them, despite wishing there were more communication, but...	O	situation
Friends (in general): Ajani won't communicate with friends unless there is a material progress update to give them (heavily tied to Venus in Scorpio-1 / Scorpio 28°)	O	people
Friends (in general): more friends than fewer reference "sir" or some other ranking	O	people
Friends (in general): friends VERY social, creatively dominant/visionary, or both; generally popular / attractive, and are working towards more mastery in their (media or information-related fields)		people
Friends (in general): topics often revolve around feelings, intuition, and balancing this with practical relationships	O	people
How do you self-reinforce?		
Self: interaction influences content of books being written at the time	O	situation, people
Self: art mirrors life; the shows and games Ajani is interacting with at the time almost always parallel his life, so he can't choose these randomly (**EXPERT**)	+	situation
What are the typical patterns among your children or creations?		
Creations: permanent published works, read in distant places by certain kinds of seekers, tomes which vacuum in information	+	people
Creations: academic, taxonomic, intended to help tolerance	+	situation

Creations: imperfect, not necessarily believable, sometimes cringeworthy, but willing to go there where others won't	O	situation
Creations: rooted in the as-of-yet unexplored social, anthropological or astronomical; body or form-centric	O	situation

I listed these in order of most to less highly significant in my life. Your order may vary.

My interface provides a set of rules for how I would interact with others if I were only a *template*, an algorithm rather than a specific individual living at a narrow point in time. If my theory of "interactional packets as building blocks" (called **frequentics**) is applicable, then I should be able to find the regions in my chart which correspond to the above patterns...

...Yes, I have several regions of asteroid clusters which reflect my algorithm, but the strongest are

- *qc141 (133q5, 97q5) - imposition of another's notion of victory*
- *qc389 (112q1, 76q1) - setting yourself apart to stir up others' energy*
- *qc374 (113q10, 5q10, 77q10) - the hero and their dynamics*
- *qc96 (101q8, 65q8) - dragged into*

133q5 <your guest's hobby which influences you>, for example, contains these asteroids, the grouping of which reflects both my experience of self-reinforcing through writing successive books as well as my strangers-meeting of pairs of interactants in travel:

265924	Franceclemente	wheeling and dealing, or otherwise serial interacting as a means of advancing one's personal interests broadly
8025	Forrestpeterson	capturing footage of the wild and natural state of things; brings with it a need for space. More space. More space still for becoming truly free; a tell asteroid which you can build up in order to heal many of the issues tied to the containing duodecanate; a healing asteroid which uses the room afforded by nature to release a person from confining pressure
455739	Isabelita	where something is done, pirate-like, savage, and/or horrific, and no justice comes to it; in the Jansky family of justice evasion; seems related to places "where you are hard-pressed to give an apology"
3535	Ditte	a fellow--in the sense that one shares a culture or indoctrination system with others; "a co-indoctrinee"
22996	De Boo	making practical use of one's alliance by knocking down a friend's door;	*Ajani's note: interesting. This seems to be the kind of test you put your friends through, because they are your friends. Few others would survive this kind of test in the form of the containing duodecanate; arguably one of the reasons why you have certain kinds of friends*

Honestly, there are more accurate clusters for my self-reinforcing and stranger meeting than this, but this group—taken as a whole collection of five—does help us start the conversation regarding how to transform our specific lives into abstract formulas that can be stored and ported into new bodies and virtual simulations. I really do tend to attract co-indoctrinees as friends during extended travel in open spaces, and there is definitely an element of doing this after an unapologetic major blow-up with someone else. See how the above can reflect a dynamical truth without any need for the actual events or people involved...

But perhaps I should first explain to you what we've done here.

WE CAN USE ASTROLOGY TO REPRESENT PRE-MADE SOCIAL PACKETS

Let's say for simplicity's sake that the astrology chart shows a snapshot of the sky when you were born. The objects in the sky like

- the Sun
- the Moon
- the highest point in the sky at the moment (the Midheaven)
- one of the changing focal points of the Moon's orbit around Earth (the North Node)

all move according to certain math formulas, and those formulas in turn reflect a maze of forces influencing each other across the Solar system. The formulas reflect the physics. Furthermore, not only is the Earth itself made up of the same physics, but everything on it *at least* follows where the Earth is going and what it's made of (chemically, for example). So everything that applies to Earth's large-scale behavior also applies to you—including the way bodies like Pluto relate to other bodies like Neptune that relate to other bodies like Jupiter which relate to Earth which pulls you and your day-night cycles of evolved body along for the ride. Even your body chemistry obeys the math and physics of potential energy bands, Hamiltonians and commutators (look them up); and if we wanted to, we *could* string all of the local functions involved together into a very big soup. But that soup would be a mess if we did this, and the reality of separate-looking planets suggests that there is a more coherent approach than just throwing every clump of potential-band chemistry functions into a single formula. We should just take the packages as they appear, treat them semi-separately, and give analogies for how one package "gave birth to" another. How a third package disrupts the orbit of several others when it passes, and thus corresponds to "war-waging." These are just examples of how the relationships among formulas can have stories assigned to them. Indeed, the story of cells firing in our brains in certain activated states really does correspond to certain behavioral patterns.

When we look at an astro chart, we're looking at chains of gravitation, energy emission, and chemistry which—though reflecting a single complicated mathematical system flattened in 2D—is just easier to view in packages. The astrological bodies themselves actually *look* like packages, but the regions of the sky with respect to the Earth's seasons and the Solar system's spin around the Milky Way can *also* be packets. Further still, the *angles* between bodies with respect to Earth's frame can also be packets in the sense that

- two objects next to each other show where two "math clumps" have temporarily intersected in their orbit algebra,
- while two math clumps 90° to each other are showing where one body's algebra is completely zeroed-out with respect to the pushing-pulling trajectory of the other.
- 180° apart on either side of Earth pulls in complementary directions, but on the same axis.
- 60° and 120° apart shows where one body pulls or pushes at exactly ½ of the potential to do so that the other one is allowed. That is,

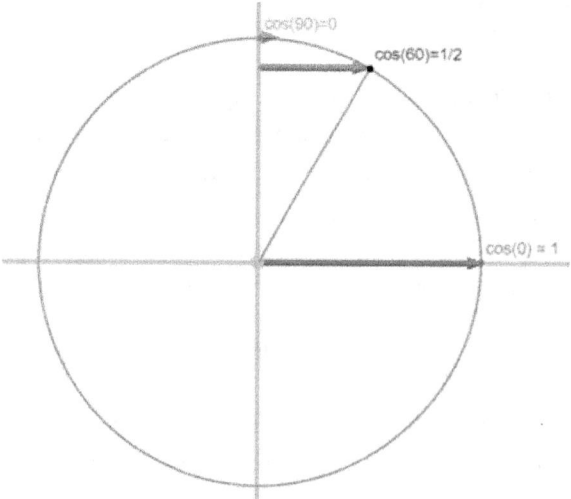

Figure 1: The amount of "sideways pull" changes with different angles

so angles in astrology (aspects) can also be treated as "packages." They indicate the types of 2D-flattened directional support the separated bodies provide to one another, and how many multiples /cycles of this separation it will take to bring the angled bodies back to the same axis for pulling in the same direction. (It takes at least six stacks of 60° angles to get back to 360°, so 60° is called a sextile, and is very similar to a Virgo package for joining two ½s of an idea into a whole.)

The basic packets of meaning in astrology are inherently socially useful, but traditionally not statistically reliable as a serious basis for truth… or at least they weren't until the age of LLMs—particularly "embeddings." LLM is short for "large language model." Embeddings are basically the math matrices which assign words, characters, and other facets of language and grammar to certain columns in a matrix, and these flow from the probabilities that particular language facets will tend to occur alongside certain others. You are less likely to see the concept of a `tiger` appearing next to the concept of an `A♯ note` than to see it next to the concept of a `jungle`; and more likely to see the letter Q appear near the letter U than near the ¥ yen symbol. So math matrices can help us put all of these probabilities together. If you scan tons of documents with all kinds of symbols and words in them, then you can build up a pretty serious matrix full of "this is more likely to be said or typed after that," and autocomplete, then a language model are born. You can further analyze these models for things like emotion, chains of thought for deep thinking, and also apply the concept to things like art generation or robotics movement; that leads directly to AI, but we need not go that far. LLMs and their embeddings are more than enough to finally give us the tools we need to *really* investigate astrology's social and interpretation packages: you just feed the various biographies of lots of people's charts into an embedding matrix and run stats on the columns versus the angles, degrees, or region locations of the astronomical bodies in each of those charts. If you get anything statistically significant, then there you have it. I did this, and that's half of how *The Book of Contours* was born. The other half we'll get to later.

Now the human social world is far more complex than 12 signs and a few dozen major planets. The ways in which humans interact goes far beyond basic notions of "beauty," "intellect," or "public reputation" for example. We'll need to do better than that if astrology is to capture the complexity we know we have. In preparation for this book, I wrote *Laurentia 2nd edition*, which has the interpretations of over 21,000 astronomical bodies' worth of research I did on the biography-to-text mining space of 46,000+ sample charts. The bios—scraped from Wikipedia, pulled from the links provided to me by Astrodatabank, and acquired from an additional adult and private sample of charts—came with the usual words reflecting each person's culture and a few behavior dynamics, and these social-communicative dynamics follow the same situational probabilities that LLM's use to build their embeddings matrices. Thus it shouldn't be too surprising that there were tons upon tons of results. Among the results was the idea that we could definitely get more fine-grained than signs, then finer-grained still. In fact, if we want to look at the kinds of "areas of life" in particular that a human can have, 12 signs and houses should at least be looked at in packages of 12 x 12 (144), or even 12 x 12 x 12 (1728). Again, I researched this, and developed regions called duo(Ƨ+0ı)decanates (144 or 1/12 of a 1/12-circle sign) and **qunits** (1728 or 1/144 of a 1/12-circle sign: short for a "centa(100+)quarenta(40+)quadrate(4)" unit).

- Duodecanates have numbers 1-144 and count *backwards* from Pisces, because this is how the stats strongly suggested things actually work when you slice signs like that, folding one cycle of 12 into the next. Each sign holds 12 duodecanates in it, and each duodecanate can also be referred to in words. Duodecanate #25, for example, can also be called Capricorn.Aries, because it's the first 1/12 (2.5°) slice of Capricorn when you count backwards from the end of Pisces. D25 includes 27.5°–30° Capricorn.
- Qunits have names based on the duodecanate they are in, plus their 1/12 slice of that duodecanate called the "qunit fraction." Qunit 133q5, for example, starts with duodecanate 133—which is in the last block of 12 duodecanates (Aries)—and ends with qunit fraction 5 (or q5), this isn't quite Leo-like, but q5 (on average across *all* qunits) often looks more Leo-like than other qunit fractions do. 133q5 would be something like Aries.Aries.Leo.

Duodecanates are fine-grained, but with an average of 150-250 interpretable asteroids[1] (out of 21000) located in each one, even finer-grained qunits needed to be developed. $21000 \div 1728$ gives us about 10-20 asteroids per region on average, and this is more than detailed enough to determine the real character of a specific area of life. If we have interpretations for each of those bodies then we can see how certain orbital probabilities came pre-promoted from the moment we were born. Why is this useful for writing an algorithmic biography? Because it allows us to represent pervasive patterns in an abstract form that can be transferred across contexts. Despite the fact that my specific elementary school, named best friend or street I grew up on may be important to *me*, to you and everyone else they might as well be random words from a fake ID generator. Outside of ourselves, what matters to everyone else is the *interaction*, not the name tag. When I can see a certain group of specific partnerships or job interaction-patterns I've been in being eerily captured by a cluster of asteroid interpretations in a certain region of my chart, then it's the *formula* for these dynamics that becomes evident… at little loss to you my viewer other than the name tags I used internally to file those experiences when I was alive.[2]

Without further delay, let's look at the three levels of region meanings we will be using throughout the rest of this book.

---

[1] As always, throughout this book I will refer to all astronomical bodies as "asteroids," whether they are planets, dwarfs, centaurs, mathematical points like the North Node or Vertex, etc. Even the Sun and Moon will be counted among the "asteroids." This is simply for brevity.

[2] Sure the specific proper nouns of a person's world help us tie frameworks across other people, but these specific names aren't nearly as important to strangers reading about us later, and may have the unintended effect of hiding the deeper behaviors hosted by those specific actors. You could change the names without changing the basic story, but if you kept the name and instead changed the historical figure's actions, you might have a different story entirely. The real value in names lies in their ability to capture the history and motivations of the ones who assigned those names—the thing's parents, creators, or commissioners. Those are far less likely to be stored with your algorithm. But then again, if the main point of storing your algorithm is to reproduce you outside of your original context—into another time, place, form, or dimension, for example—then breaking the chain of title and history is *exactly* what you want to do. How else could we explain how you and your human lineage ended up in this database or on this distant planet from where you began?

Abstractifying full stories into nameless astronomical dynamics allows us to save enough of one's story to keep their interfaces without prohibiting their teleportation into new situations lineage-wise improbable.

FIGURE 2: THE 12 SIGNS: INTERPRETATIONS

Signs and their common associations		
1. Aries Instinct, assertion, bravery, pressure to BE, spontaneity, creation, existence **inborn spontaneous IMPULSES**	**5. Leo** ego, attention, good standing, leadership, reliability, pride **how you PROJECT YOUR CHARACTER**	**9. Sagittarius (Saj)** fun, exploration, journey, success, importance, luck, politics, fame, expansiveness **NICHE ENVIRONMENT and the BEHAVIOR PATTERNS naturally around you**
2. Taurus self-image, money, confidence, body, sensation, self-value (ideas that you build your identity against) **things and ideas used to IDENTIFY other things**	**6. Virgo** meaning, comparative health, analytical nature, rules of order **how you JOIN or RECONCILE concepts**	**10. Capricorn** rules, karma, old age, time, built structures, wealth as security, law, history, authority, respect **BOUNDARIES, STRUCTURES, AND LIMITS that determine what can and can't be easily done**
3. Gemini Internal thoughts, ideas, dexterity, driving, talking **INTERNAL MONOLOGUE and how you turn collections of ideas into A FIELD OF POSSIBLE STATES**	**7. Libra** fairness, affinity, friendship, sharing, manners **FEEDBACK LOOPING and COMMUNICATIVE INTERACTION with others**	**11. Aquarius** sociable detachment, society, rumors, peer groups, technology, humane ideals, renown **AMBIENT INFORMATION and CROSSTALK typically floating around you**
4. Cancer subconscious, feeling, dreaming, wants, connection, emotionality, the home, mothery-ness **how you WANT or INCLINE towards behaviors**	**8. Scorpio** sex, death, others' money, psychology, power, the occult **how you IMPART INERTIA upon things to push them in a different direction than their current one, or with different levels of energy than their current level**	**12. Pisces** humane feeling, intuition, illusion, escape, the hidden, art, abstraction **AMBIENT MOOD, what the environment around you typically inclines towards when you are there**

FIGURE 3: THE 144 (12²) DUODECANATES (IN THE TROPICAL SYSTEM IN 2025)

Duodec anate	Duodec anate Name	Tropical degree	Noun	Traits that are reinforced by asteroids in this region (in a standard (tropical) 2025 chart)
1	Pisces-1	27.5°-29.9°	proceeding	Your basic personality among people who've met you
2	Pisces-2	25°-27.5°	identification	What it seems others prefer you behave as
3	Pisces-3	22.5°-25°	transmission	Roles the world encourages you to play
4	Pisces-4	20°-22.5°	insertion	Tactics only you know about, and can't explain to others
5	Pisces-5	17.5°-20°	reception	♆ HOME[3] (HOUR OF ♆ CHARACTER); Your default treatment of long-term domestic partners
6	Pisces-6	15°-17.5°	agreement	The bases for your choices to pursue selected ends
7	Pisces-7	12.5°-15°	participation	Feeling of the self-talk or conversation you need to have next
8	Pisces-8	10°-12.5°	consideration	That which you will continually seek to influence when bored
9	Pisces-9	7.5°-10°	shop	Where your wanderlust lands you
10	Pisces-10	5°-7.5°	demand	♀ HOME (HOUR OF ♀ CHARACTER); When you're dead tired / energy-drained
11	Pisces-11	2.5°-5°	production	♅ HOME (HOUR OF ♅ CHARACTER); The information you keep around you for inspiring your next step

---

[3] I've found that signs and regions have multiple "rulers" depending on how fine-grained we get. For the purposes of this book, a body's HOME is the region that acts most like that body. Asteroids in a region's HOME will have one or more qunits within them which will be closer to synonymous with the ruler. For example, even though my Neptune is in d41 (duodecanate 41 or 9-5), I've found that using it tends to look like using all of the asteroids in my 5q5 together. Others' future research should refine these with bigger sample sets than the ones I used.

12	Pisces-12	0°-2.5°	pattern	How people around you advance things you can't do on your own
13	Aquarius-1	27.5°-29.9°	percept	Your will to *be*, based on the info you are bathed in
14	Aquarius-2	25°-27.5°	pull	Who your information spaces teach you to think you are
15	Aquarius-3	22.5°-25°	inclusion	Where you give your personal opinion/interpretation of the situation
16	Aquarius-4	20°-22.5°	rules	The nature of your family
17	Aquarius-5	17.5°-20°	choices	The definition / framework you have for leadership
18	Aquarius-6	15°-17.5°	comprehension	The kinds of stories you best tell about the world; "by your logic"
19	Aquarius-7	12.5°-15°	knowledge	One's interactions with their friends
20	Aquarius-8	10°-12.5°	translation	Your understanding of armies—what they entail and how they manifest
21	Aquarius-9	7.5°-10°	attention	How the information around a group you're in defines your group
22	Aquarius-10	5°-7.5°	scope	Career and the industry one is in
23	Aquarius-11	2.5°-5°	frame	What you are uniquely good at. Your unique attunement
24	Aquarius-12	0°-2.5°	space	The mood of the info/entertainment you like to surround yourself with
25	Capricorn-1	27.5°-29.9°	group	How you respond to feeling trapped
26	Capricorn-2	25°-27.5°	agenda	Fans and followers
27	Capricorn-3	22.5°-25°	priority	Under limits, how you think; one of the strongest regions for fear
28	Capricorn-4	20°-22.5°	acceptance	Your morals, values in situations where you don't have a choice
29	Capricorn-5	17.5°-20°	subordination	How one stands up and presents themselves (to others) in times of trial
30	Capricorn-6	15°-17.5°	model	♄ HOME (HOUR OF ♄ CHARACTER); The nature or character of the answers you tend to encounter
31	Capricorn-7	12.5°-15°	framework	Interactions you use to navigate your way back to familiarity
32	Capricorn-8	10°-12.5°	kinesis	How you get events to go your way when you've been limited
33	Capricorn-9	7.5°-10°	function	Under limits, the culture you run to
34	Capricorn-10	5°-7.5°	designer	The nature of the institutions you typically interact with
35	Capricorn-11	2.5°-5°	uniqueness	The information brought to bear when pressure or limits are experienced
36	Capricorn-12	0°-2.5°	presence	How you are remembered after you are gone / have exited
37	Sagittarius-1	27.5°-29.9°	wrapping	The experience of meeting new groups
38	Sagittarius-2	25°-27.5°	contact	♃ HOME (HOUR OF ♃ CHARACTER); The part of larger niches / cultures which you internalize for yourself
39	Sagittarius-3	22.5°-25°	presentation	Your opinions when engaging cultures or niches systems not your own
40	Sagittarius-4	20°-22.5°	amplification	*What* one feels when in a comfortable feeling environment
41	Sagittarius-5	17.5°-20°	convenience	Public figures who resonate with the culture they are in
42	Sagittarius-6	15°-17.5°	purpose	How you handle "game time," competition, or pressure
43	Sagittarius-7	12.5°-15°	reason	Those in a position to judge or evaluate a space or define its reputation
44	Sagittarius-8	10°-12.5°	involvement	Experiences with foreign ways that leave an impression on you
45	Sagittarius-9	7.5°-10°	administration	How you believe cultural or societal change should be undertaken
46	Sagittarius-10	5°-7.5°	region	How you learn the foreign
47	Sagittarius-11	2.5°-5°	center	Social dealings amidst travel or culture exploration
48	Sagittarius-12	0°-2.5°	category	One's relationship to their land or the lands they prefer to occupy
49	Scorpio-1	27.5°-29.9°	pacifying	How you give updates to change a situation's background
50	Scorpio-2	25°-27.5°	lure	How you express your defiance of certain circumstances you're in
51	Scorpio-3	22.5°-25°	acquisition	While wanting another to do something, the commentary one makes
52	Scorpio-4	20°-22.5°	absorption	How you handle comparative insignificance
53	Scorpio-5	17.5°-20°	displacement	♂ HOME (53q4, HOUR OF ♂ CHARACTER); The process you go through while trying to make an intentional impression
54	Scorpio-6	15°-17.5°	inculcation	Those who can tell you what to do, do next, or what to reconcile as a task
55	Scorpio-7	12.5°-15°	separation	How you collaborate towards an end
56	Scorpio-8	10°-12.5°	appraisal	What is happening when you are at the peak of your power
57	Scorpio-9	7.5°-10°	market	How you get a space of behaviors under control
58	Scorpio-10	5°-7.5°	disruption	How you mitigate or offset potential threats
59	Scorpio-11	2.5°-5°	development	The information you assemble in order to achieve a certain result
60	Scorpio-12	0°-2.5°	transformation	How you feel when engaging something willingly under your control
61	Libra-1	27.5°-29.9°	clarification	Communicating in a context which is quickly passing by. "travel talk"
62	Libra-2	25°-27.5°	standout	What friendship looks like as displayed by you
63	Libra-3	22.5°-25°	resembling	Your conversational bearing and how you reply or give retorts
64	Libra-4	20°-22.5°	gesture	What you or the other secretly want during an exchange
65	Libra-5	17.5°-20°	animation	♀ HOME (HOUR OF ♀ CHARACTER); How you show yourself when extremely comfortable with someone

66	Libra-6	15°-17.5°	role	Interacting for logical reasons, not because one prefers to
67	Libra-7	12.5°-15°	information	Your most sustainable conversations—how you progress them
68	Libra-8	10°-12.5°	count	What occurs when you and another are not on the same page
69	Libra-9	7.5°-10°	monopolizing	The superstars you pay attention to. You on the red carpet
70	Libra-10	5°-7.5°	validation	How you enforce rules for determining which interactions are close
71	Libra-11	2.5°-5°	frequency	What your world looks like when all is lost. Associated with forgetting
72	Libra-12	0°-2.5°	energy	The consequences of your interactions; feeds your next circumstances
73	Virgo-1	27.5°-29.9°	reflection	When you commit to a path, what you do or how you initiate this action
74	Virgo-2	25°-27.5°	proxy	How people close enough to you see you managing your domestic affairs
75	Virgo-3	22.5°-25°	basis	One's role on a problem-solving team (as an opinion giver)
76	Virgo-4	20°-22.5°	component	How you feed yourself, satiate your hunger
77	Virgo-5	17.5°-20°	operation	Things you use to put others into a corner. Or guardedness
78	Virgo-6	15°-17.5°	training	☿ HOME (HOUR OF ☿ CHARACTER); The experiences you stockpile as you get older; your units for TIME
79	Virgo-7	12.5°-15°	search	Support from others in accomplishing a task
80	Virgo-8	10°-12.5°	exploration	How you exercise the most influence in your daily doings and work life
81	Virgo-9	7.5°-10°	method	How one appears before their managers or daily culture groups
82	Virgo-10	5°-7.5°	perspective	Creating formal structures from one's meaning making, deriving laws
83	Virgo-11	2.5°-5°	summary	The kinds of (message) traffic you help sponsor
84	Virgo-12	0°-2.5°	alternative	The time you spend in quiet. Quiet time duty-doing activity
85	Leo-1	27.5°-29.9°	intersection	How you make advances towards a thing you want and don't currently have
86	Leo-2	25°-27.5°	transfer	How people see your personality when you are off in your own world
87	Leo-3	22.5°-25°	gift	How you summarize your perspective to others
88	Leo-4	20°-22.5°	suggestion	Developing your own character with no assumption of labels
89	Leo-5	17.5°-20°	assumption	Flings. You as a self-reinforcing personality
90	Leo-6	15°-17.5°	opening	☉ HOME (HOUR OF ☉ CHARACTER);; Puzzles you tackle for fun; your patterned answer to challenges
91	Leo-7	12.5°-15°	aim	How you speak to friends when you're having real fun
92	Leo-8	10°-12.5°	hunger	Your general views and approach to sexuality / co-creativity
93	Leo-9	7.5°-10°	fulfillment	The kinds of people you attract when you have your fun
94	Leo-10	5°-7.5°	fixation	Where one takes pride in how they handle challenges or difficulties
95	Leo-11	2.5°-5°	update	Where it's easier for you to be part of the in-crowd
96	Leo-12	0°-2.5°	pathway	Your idea of fully realized personhood as a lifestyle
97	Cancer-1	27.5°-29.9°	preference	The attitude you would like to develop
98	Cancer-2	25°-27.5°	collection	The kind of person you desire to be, especially when on a journey
99	Cancer-3	22.5°-25°	progression	In your ongoing wants, how you monologue them. Your soapbox
100	Cancer-4	20°-22.5°	arrival	☽ HOME (100q9, HOUR OF ☽ CHARACTER); Building your readiness to pursue a line of expression
101	Cancer-5	17.5°-20°	following	Childhood play life—the games, friends, and teachers involved
102	Cancer-6	15°-17.5°	holding	Your childhood behavior; when you're brand new to a learning space
103	Cancer-7	12.5°-15°	reinforcement	How you behave when lost or lonely
104	Cancer-8	10°-12.5°	value	Your approach to bringing wayward domains under your control
105	Cancer-9	7.5°-10°	culture	The overall lifestyle you are chasing
106	Cancer-10	5°-7.5°	dilemma	The barriers you (unintentionally perhaps) seek for yourself
107	Cancer-11	2.5°-5°	compeller	Your interaction with buried or secret information, or with the dead
108	Cancer-12	0°-2.5°	continuation	Your motivation to keep going
109	Gemini-1	27.5°-29.9°	truth	The topic that will always get introduced with your new thoughts
110	Gemini-2	25°-27.5°	connection	Your label among people you are expressively close to
111	Gemini-3	22.5°-25°	other	How you "revoice" yourself in support of more of what you're doing; topics you dwell on
112	Gemini-4	20°-22.5°	rights	How you feel about your own thought process
113	Gemini-5	17.5°-20°	enjoyment	Who you or your representative claims themselves to be
114	Gemini-6	15°-17.5°	relation	Idiosyncratic sense-making—how you explain things to yourself
115	Gemini-7	12.5°-15°	representation	Who you are when steering a conversation in a direction you've long favored
116	Gemini-8	10°-12.5°	difference	Your process for making something fit your own paradigms
117	Gemini-9	7.5°-10°	self-image	One's outlook on how the world works or should work
118	Gemini-10	5°-7.5°	insistence	☊ HOME (HOUR OF ♊ CHARACTER); What you respect or do to earn respect
119	Gemini-11	2.5°-5°	context	That which is constantly on your mind / occupying your thoughts

120	Gemini-12	0°-2.5°	audience	The brands you trust. That which you could spend a lifetime studying
121	Taurus-1	27.5°-29.9°	individual	**7285 Seggewiss HOME (121Q8?, HOUR OF ☉ CHARACTER)**; Where you go to teach yourself how to be yourself
122	Taurus-2	25°-27.5°	instance	Things that have their own intrinsic value sourced from within themselves
123	Taurus-3	22.5°-25°	membership	Those whose mode of expression you admire
124	Taurus-4	20°-22.5°	food	The family or journey support systems you are entitled to
125	Taurus-5	17.5°-20°	nurturance	Uniqueness, what separates you from your pack
126	Taurus-6	15°-17.5°	promotion	What you're labeled as doing for a living
127	Taurus-7	12.5°-15°	treatment	The efforts that keep another close to you
128	Taurus-8	10°-12.5°	work	An area where you feel entitled to influence
129	Taurus-9	7.5°-10°	material	Where you define cultures just by virtue of having an identity. Archetype
130	Taurus-10	5°-7.5°	construction	That which naturally teaches you your limits. Formal educational experience
131	Taurus-11	2.5°-5°	source	Traits or skills you have which are in demand / passed around
132	Taurus-12	0°-2.5°	effect	How you broadly feel when willingly under the control of another
133	Aries-1	27.5°-29.9°	infiltration	How you feel inclined to express all of a sudden
134	Aries-2	25°-27.5°	harmonizing	**Quaoar HOME (HOUR OF ♈ CHARACTER?)**; The instinctual way in which you carry yourself when you have no attachments
135	Aries-3	22.5°-25°	excitement	How you handle or experience anticipation, preparation or, negatively, desperation
136	Aries-4	20°-22.5°	recruitment	What you need in order to make a choice
137	Aries-5	17.5°-20°	mobilization	The urge to project your character, driven by a rootless impulse
138	Aries-6	15°-17.5°	behavior	Your first reaction for reasoning out (or out of) an unanticipated situation
139	Aries-7	12.5°-15°	imposition	The boyfriend / girlfriend—comfortably off-the-cuff communication
140	Aries-8	10°-12.5°	co-creation	How you experience sex or the co-created urge
141	Aries-9	7.5°-10°	ideal	One's ideal; the future you are pursuing knowingly or unknowingly
142	Aries-10	5°-7.5°	stability	How you hold yourself back or experience sickness
143	Aries-11	2.5°-5°	activity	The kinds of music which accompanies your spirit / vibe / aura as a person
144	Aries-12	0°-2.5°	atmosphere	First impressions of you. The "aura" you establish upon entering a situation

FIGURE 4: THE 1728 (12³) QUNITS

Degree[4]	Deg-Min	Sidereal°	Qunit	Meaning
359.9	359°54'	334.9	1q8	Your basic personality as described by others—that which it strikes people with or imposes upon them
359.69	359°41'	334.69	1q7	Where you are witness to conflicts others must resolve regarding your participation in a thing
359.48	359°29'	334.48	1q6	How you approach the coming of your ultimate public performance
359.27	359°16'	334.27	1q5	Abuses allowed to be suddenly inflicted
359.06	359°4'	334.06	1q4	The dawn of a subordinate situation's emerging into the spotlight / leading role
358.85	358°51'	333.85	1q3	Characters in the entertainment you watch in order to renew your spirits in life
358.65	358°39'	333.65	1q2	Reaffirming your values via a social group or your ingroup
358.44	358°26'	333.44	1q1	Where others have the power to approve or disapprove something you're invested in
358.23	358°14'	333.23	1q12	What is done to finally make it happen for someone
358.02	358°1'	333.02	1q11	Your look at fans or social groups who expect the best from you; those who would probably like your work
357.81	357°49'	332.81	1q10	Progressing with the help of friends or friend-cultures
357.6	357°36'	332.6	1q9	Learning how to handle prisoners, being a prisoner, or imprisonment in general
357.4	357°24'	332.4	2q8	What you can be relied upon to provide others
357.19	357°11'	332.19	2q7	Your approach to intercourse
356.98	356°59'	331.98	2q6	Your body in action, earning the events it earns
356.77	356°46'	331.77	2q5	Resiliency and adaptation demonstrated or required by those who may have lost access to the familiar
356.56	356°34'	331.56	2q4	Others strike on your behalf
356.35	356°21'	331.35	2q3	That which brings prosperity to you
356.15	356°9'	331.15	2q2	Drop what you're doing and take time to reflect on who you really are, what you're really after
355.94	355°56'	330.94	2q1	That which launches and announces your creativity
355.73	355°44'	330.73	2q12	Some party's underlying tastes that in turn trigger collective action

---

[4] The first two columns list the degree values according to the Tropical zodiac. This is the system that follows the Earth's seasons and the one that almost everybody uses. Unfortunately this system creeps by 1° about every 75 years, and can be expected to be way off by the year 2100. Hence the third column, Sidereal degrees.

355.52	355°31'	330.52	2q11	Abandonment, especially by a male or asserter, in order to bring an unaligned situation back into alignment
355.31	355°19'	330.31	2q10	A sponsored invite of others into one's world
355.1	355°6'	330.1	2q9	Coming together in a collective in order to undertake a change of route
354.9	354°54'	329.9	3q8	An association you have which commandeers your agenda and enables access to something you couldn't get to before
354.69	354°41'	329.69	3q7	Collector of information / feedback loops
354.48	354°29'	329.48	3q6	Trials which build up the eventual final memory of your terminal legacy in a place
354.27	354°16'	329.27	3q5	The other who leads in the interface with information on your perimeter. If you yourself are a producer of that information, your work will be represented by the 75-5s and you will be represented by one of the squares
354.06	354°4'	329.06	3q4	Groups or institutions which have higher hopes for you than you are able to achieve without instruction; the dominion which grants you and your people their title or legitimacy
353.85	353°51'	328.85	3q3	Son in your local experience of a family unit. Useful in the Gauquelin family data
353.65	353°39'	328.65	3q2	Folks you would like to have in your family, but who can't see or reach you
353.44	353°26'	328.44	3q1	Sequestered pairing, secret or closed door interactions
353.23	353°14'	328.23	3q12	Seems to indicate loyalty; the kind of person who is loyal to you, or where you are more likely to experience someone's loyalty; 1) an amorphous population or 2) invasive, broadcasting personalities and terroristic loners—especially those interested in medical or biology fields
353.02	353°1'	328.02	3q11	A significant decision regarding [how to use] or [what to do with] a certain kind of information
352.81	352°49'	327.81	3q10	The kind of additional alliance you seek when wanting to open a brand new kind of door
352.6	352°36'	327.6	3q9	The operating principle you grow into as your role in the world; when represented by others, seems to indicate the people who train you or train with you in your evolving role. They have their own military-like "MOS" so to speak
352.4	352°24'	327.4	4q8	Where you are positioned such that your communication helps people feel better or do better
352.19	352°11'	327.19	4q7	Being let into a certain aspect of nature or the bigger world with more comfort or privileges
351.98	351°59'	326.98	4q6	Your housemate's attitude towards the topics they focus on while socializing or interacting in leisure at home (especially on the phone)
351.77	351°46'	326.77	4q5	What another person envisions for the world you could build; you are more likely to disappoint them here unless you give them control in other areas
351.56	351°34'	326.56	4q4	The disordered or wanton social or relational world, with a general unsettled inertia towards some state
351.35	351°21'	326.35	4q3	Throwing out tension inducing or passionate energy
351.15	351°9'	326.15	4q2	That which is added to one's body, form, or presentation
350.94	350°56'	325.94	4q1	The rebellious or separatist acts you experience which sever your ties from ally groups
350.73	350°44'	325.73	4q12	One who has command of the army of forces—how they administer that command
350.52	350°31'	325.52	4q11	The one who facilitates or wrangles the order you operate under
350.31	350°19'	325.31	4q10	The transition of events around you into rule systems or contexts that exist beyond your own borders
350.1	350°6'	325.1	4q9	Routines where you consider the stance of a rival or assailant who attacks your friend
349.9	349°54'	324.9	5q8	Where your desire to influence others reflects on your character as a background steeror of a room's mood; where others can see the effects of your urges through your character, though not necessarily the urges themselves; related to the butt—more likely the flank
349.69	349°41'	324.69	5q7	Stubbornly growing or establishing something; stubborn work on making a thing happen; land or property ownership—what you hold as a value asset?
349.48	349°29'	324.48	5q6	What you're doing which draws out other people's display of problems
349.27	349°16'	324.27	5q5	The deeply sought value which you pursue to the point that it may become others' indelible memory of you
349.06	349°4'	324.06	5q4	How you uniquely project towards your equals and kindred: anti-communion
348.85	348°51'	323.85	5q3	How secrets are conveyed to you, or how you maintain them; how you may be involved with them
348.65	348°39'	323.65	5q2	Your closest comrade—something like a twin soul
348.44	348°26'	323.44	5q1	You as a bully
348.23	348°14'	323.23	5q12	When differences are resolved, what the liberated one ends up doing
348.02	348°1'	323.02	5q11	The guest spirit who intrudes upon your default home, indelibly coloring it; seems to be the visitor who's actions are telling you what's going on in the highest levels of your house, potential candidate for THE qunit of Neptune (or one very near it)	*Alma Mater* ds#14
347.81	347°49'	322.81	5q10	You as a single gray power holder
347.6	347°36'	322.6	5q9	Snapshot of the domain's instantaneous or fierce burst of desire
347.4	347°24'	322.4	6q8	An activity you build up as a practical decision to offset some otherwise undesirable default outcome
347.19	347°11'	322.19	6q7	The TIME *COUNTER*; that which stacks up under the flow of time; Vertex-like
346.98	346°59'	321.98	6q6	The place or party that nurtures you in full with inputs you actually prefer; related to dogs

346.77	346°46'	321.77	6q5	Resetting your reputation or presentation in a social area
346.56	346°34'	321.56	6q4	How you respond to mistakes, especially your own: [5]wanting (4), to reconcile (6), a mood (12) = (12.)6.4
346.35	346°21'	321.35	6q3	A thing which stays thoroughly on the mind, perhaps on repeat
346.15	346°9'	321.15	6q2	Your approach to necessary lawn or environment care
345.94	345°56'	320.94	6q1	Where you expect external forces to be responsible for progressing your milestones, or project this inclination onto them
345.73	345°44'	320.73	6q12	A feud brought to a close, this is an indicator that parties have called a ceasefire
345.52	345°31'	320.52	6q11	Risks taken which may undercut your previous rules
345.31	345°19'	320.31	6q10	Internal changes which gradually grow to produce visible results to external viewers
345.1	345°6'	320.1	6q9	Under watch or under caution, where this is a thing
344.9	344°54'	319.9	7q8	Surveying the room to blend or balance the views of the parties with each other
344.69	344°41'	319.69	7q7	The work you are actively obsessed with continuing
344.48	344°29'	319.48	7q6	A room scan across the very noisy space; how you see the crowd?
344.27	344°16'	319.27	7q5	A collective whose culture reflects your mentality; the class of interaction which sees you as foreign—maybe or maybe not trustworthy—but a class which presents an intriguing departure from your comfortable world. You probably wouldn't know what this means if you—like most people—won't give them a chance; you're more likely to share the same mentality as this group's culture
344.06	344°4'	319.06	7q4	The supportive voice for your actions—how it presents or what it tells you to do
343.85	343°51'	318.85	7q3	A nearby party's deeds become the past for another party who views them
343.65	343°39'	318.65	7q2	The setting in which taboo conversations can be easily had in a fairly acceptable way (at least such that one's public identity can register it)
343.44	343°26'	318.44	7q1	That which others are inspired to do—perhaps forcefully—in light of you
343.23	343°14'	318.23	7q12	What manhood creates as a broad concept—the experiences it initiates
343.02	343°1'	318.02	7q11	What another does which discourages the one from wanting to fight them
342.81	342°49'	317.81	7q10	Your solo work within an institution
342.6	342°36'	317.6	7q9	The environment in which you do your solo daily work, possibly including the people; where you blend into such an environment while watching others do their solo work
342.4	342°24'	317.4	8q8	Special talent tasks which only you can perform—or at least where others may see this as a thing that only you can do while your role in their life persists. (It is not known whether you will keep this monopoly after you've exited their lives.)
342.19	342°11'	317.19	8q7	Approaches you value for taking certain projective steps in the world
341.98	341°59'	316.98	8q6	Where you are being watched carefully, scrutinized by a powerful person
341.77	341°46'	316.77	8q5	The enemy you have come to quell. What your fixer acts against
341.56	341°34'	316.56	8q4	Where you may spontaneously align with someone else in your pursuit of a goal
341.35	341°21'	316.35	8q3	The events you create or experience which constitute occasions to evaluate hoped efforts or hopeful performers against a standard... your standard
341.15	341°9'	316.15	8q2	How you vent in light of an overgrown issue
340.94	340°56'	315.94	8q1	The actual subject matter people will typically encounter when they first become familiar with you; very Ascendant-like. Weirdly, qunit fraction #1 in 12-8
340.73	340°44'	315.73	8q12	The outlook which waking up fosters within you
340.52	340°31'	315.52	8q11	How you execute survival tactics, or frame such execution in general
340.31	340°19'	315.31	8q10	How you or your representative present yourselves in work mode

---

[5] At this point you may be asking, how in the world do degrees so close end up so different? I asked this question too. My theory is this: You can divide the wheel however you like—using 12 sections, 8, 199, a million, or whatever. But if you assume that every round of your cycle includes previous rounds, then each turn of your wheel can "vacuum in" information from the previous turn. This is actually one way that the counting numbers are defined in math theory; 4 includes 3 which includes 2 which includes 1. They don't just line up in a line. Instead, each new number actually *nests* the one before it. Similarly, I believe that when we choose a certain number of divisions to chop our cycle into, then the next round of cycles includes all of the ones that have just finished. So one sign includes compressed information from all 12 cycles that came before it. But if you think about this as working the same way memory does, then you can see how the bigger sign should actually weigh *less* than the duodecanate which takes the next detailed step inside of it, and the duodecanate will weigh *less* than the qunit fraction within it. That is, we can look at, say, Pisces (12) first, then go another round and land on Virgo (6) from within Pisces. This brings, Virgo to the forefront and pushes Pisces further back in immediacy. Thus duodecanate 6 (Pisces.6) will be more Virgo-like than Pisces-like: a time ticker more similar to duodecanate 78 (Virgo.6) than to Pisces.7, which will look more immediately like Libra. If we go another round still, we might end up in a Cancer (4) mini-slice of d6, bringing us to 6q4. This will push back 12.6 and look more like Cancer against a Pisces.Virgo background. It will also make 12.6.4 more similar to 6.6.4 (78q4) than to 12.6.5. 12.6.4 looks more immediately like today's Cancer operating against yesterday's Virgo operating against the previous day's Pisces. Thus the priority of nested signs ticks *backwards* from the direction we read the nesting in, and that's how adjacent qunits and duodecanates start looking so different from each other in some cases: The pushed-back context may look the same, but the immediate slice actually changes in bigger ways from where we came from. That's my theory.

340.1	340°6'	315.1	8q9	If you were to become a household name, it would be for this
339.9	339°54'	314.9	9q8	How the social world rewards your work... whether or not you appreciate this
339.69	339°41'	314.69	9q7	Your experience with the true dad-like figure in your life, or you as such if you are sufficiently asserting. Interestingly against 81-7, the dad will always be in some way separated from the unborn child, no matter how close he wants to be. Biologically, he is not—by default—the womb, and will never get any closer than the mom's shield unless medical science eventually permits this
339.48	339°29'	314.48	9q6	Your interface with (your representation of) symbols of status or status-bearing opportunities
339.27	339°16'	314.27	9q5	Situations or parties who seem to have it in for you or wish to thwart your actions
339.06	339°4'	314.06	9q4	How and where you tell stories
338.85	338°51'	313.85	9q3	What happens around you in places or associations where you are a recognized connection
338.65	338°39'	313.65	9q2	The role of one of the "uncles"—an asserter who is kindred to one of the parents that made and trained you, whom you don't actually have to listen to, but who also is good at pushing something that their sibling (your main parent to whom they are related) missed
338.44	338°26'	313.44	9q1	The superstar, perhaps one you genuinely admire
338.23	338°14'	313.23	9q12	Your tackling the dirty work or difficult issues
338.02	338°1'	313.02	9q11	What you value or how you behave in a state of uncertainty
337.81	337°49'	312.81	9q10	Your visitation into a place which will task you to put on a role; your attitude in the role place?
337.6	337°36'	312.6	9q9	What it is to grind through something
337.4	337°24'	312.4	10q8	Your forms of sharing with the partner. For them
337.19	337°11'	312.19	10q7	How the interactions between the parents or the concepts of general parental duty are understood—particularly as one's dad or husband are concerned
336.98	336°59'	311.98	10q6	The character or daily doings of those who watch you do your daily doings
336.77	336°46'	311.77	10q5	Character of "eggs in the womb" that you know how to recognize; that is, various perspectives emerging from the walls of a domain which press definition onto the assertions therein
336.56	336°34'	311.56	10q4	How you escape the bad guy relationship or wind it down
336.35	336°21'	311.35	10q3	Pursuing an outlet after a tensely held state
336.15	336°9'	311.15	10q2	How males in one's life express their resistance to what is going on; fight-ish
335.94	335°56'	310.94	10q1	The strong males in one's life—the archetypal man. (Unlike my usual domain-asserter paradigm, this one is biological, not just "masculine"; may be related to Camelia)
335.73	335°44'	310.73	10q12	Where you are ushered out of a conflict beyond your ability to stop
335.52	335°31'	310.52	10q11	Excitement over the activities / information exchange unfolding in a space
335.31	335°19'	310.31	10q10	Tension-based remediation of difficulties? How or where it happens?
335.1	335°6'	310.1	10q9	Conflict between two institutions or two parts of the same institution around you
334.9	334°54'	309.9	11q8	How you take action against the arrangements of dynamics around you, declaring what you want rather than letting it run you over
334.69	334°41'	309.69	11q7	The main interactants responsible for the ambient arrangement of dynamics around you
334.48	334°29'	309.48	11q6	How the work is done to evolve the dynamics arrangements around you
334.27	334°16'	309.27	11q5	The traits of various characters who share or occupy your ever-present space of ambient dynamics
334.06	334°4'	309.06	11q4	That which is raised from seemingly inhospitable ground; raising from the dust; associated with the growth of plants and cities from the land; the co-parent experience with the ones who work with you to determine the ambient dynamics around you; co-parents in the surrounding information space you occupy
333.85	333°51'	308.85	11q3	How you see the ambient dynamics environment around you; materially, describes the space where such dynamics take place; a candidate for Uranus' HOME
333.65	333°39'	308.65	11q2	The object or interactant which you are identified with, synonymous with you in your ongoing ambient dynamical space
333.44	333°26'	308.44	11q1	That which stirs up or calls your attention to the ambient dynamical arrangements around you
333.23	333°14'	308.23	11q12	How parties around you engage your ongoing ambient dynamical arrangements, in secret or without your clear knowing; situationally clairvoyant; tells you EXACTLY how your housemates actually approach your informational ambient environment
333.02	333°1'	308.02	11q11	How the ambient patterns gradually evolve around you(?), growing out of their original forms
332.81	332°49'	307.81	11q10	Elements of the ambient dynamical arrangement which have to be guarded against or are used to guard against certain kinds of change?
332.6	332°36'	307.6	11q9	The culture / behavior spaces of the ones who sponsor your ambient arrangements—what they can typically be found doing or working with
332.4	332°24'	307.4	12q8	Inspiration to create
332.19	332°11'	307.19	12q7	A powerful impression sweeping into view; the air zooming-in
331.98	331°59'	306.98	12q6	Expectations failed, your disappointment in one close to you is rooted in this

331.77	331°46'	306.77	12q5	Gift-receipt feeling(?); the feel-good vibration that you pick up or resonate with upon participation in the region
331.56	331°34'	306.56	12q4	To others, a known fact regarding you and how you work, particularly what you insist on
331.35	331°21'	306.35	12q3	Attempts to do things on your own which are more likely to be second rate or at least incomplete without help
331.15	331°9'	306.15	12q2	How to handle these strange characters attempting to communicate with you
330.94	330°56'	305.94	12q1	Repeating something in the hopes of achieving some sort of perfected final state
330.73	330°44'	305.73	12q12	The mood you project into the energy of those around you
330.52	330°31'	305.52	12q11	The changes that come with you or you charge's increased maturity; who your children grow up to be
330.31	330°19'	305.31	12q10	How the institution that protects you is run in the background
330.1	330°6'	305.1	12q9	A part of your sphere which markedly disagrees with how you've intended to relate. Not exactly an enemy, but more like a thwarting situation against how you've set yourself up to relate to others
329.9	329°54'	304.9	13q8	The element of your sphere which would reconcile / actually bring you closer to equilibrium
329.69	329°41'	304.69	13q7	From within, I create for you
329.48	329°29'	304.48	13q6	Laying out the network in one's conception
329.27	329°16'	304.27	13q5	Divergence of your expressive path from those of your peers, even while you are still among them
329.06	329°4'	304.06	13q4	Your blessed talent; Selene clearly rules this; the HOME of Selene/White Moon
328.85	328°51'	303.85	13q3	The information dynamics floating around you which help determine whether or not anyone wants to see what you project
328.65	328°39'	303.65	13q2	That which protects what you've built from assault, insult, or deterioration
328.44	328°26'	303.44	13q1	Looking back on the simpler times, that which is easy; what you will have experienced prior to your current evolution—that which is easier for you to see when spontaneously framing information; may be related to default attitudes towards the information in front of you
328.23	328°14'	303.23	13q12	What ultimate ongoing successful expression looks like for you
328.02	328°1'	303.02	13q11	Fencing yourself in via a social or actual shield
327.81	327°49'	302.81	13q10	The mass movement of two kinds of energy against each other
327.6	327°36'	302.6	13q9	A smooth image, drawn out expression
327.4	327°24'	302.4	14q8	Your more ambitious projects
327.19	327°11'	302.19	14q7	The supposed "co"creative partner who actually expects you to deliver the work. Not a shared endeavor
326.98	326°59'	301.98	14q6	You as a sojourner—the talk about you specifically associating you with your most adventurous location visited
326.77	326°46'	301.77	14q5	The events involved in a dominating scenario
326.56	326°34'	301.56	14q4	Genuinely connecting with one's audience and their sentiments
326.35	326°21'	301.35	14q3	The legacy left by a mentor figure after (he) has gone
326.15	326°9'	301.15	14q2	What you are challenged over
325.94	325°56'	300.94	14q1	Recounted storytelling about trials; writings or solidified storytelling about dark or doomed situations?
325.73	325°44'	300.73	14q12	A thing that presents you with bullshit requirements you didn't ask for, or your response to extraneous intrusions; related to 6232 Zubitskia
325.52	325°31'	300.52	14q11	Very important or significant technical work that very few people will ever know about, let alone understand
325.31	325°19'	300.31	14q10	The parenting dynamic which is helped or hindered by the environment that hosts it
325.1	325°6'	300.1	14q9	A situation which a kindred party gets you into that critically alters your plans
324.9	324°54'	299.9	15q8	How you offer your opinion for the sake of convincing others of something
324.69	324°41'	299.69	15q7	Embroilment in someone else's battles; or someone else embroiled in yours
324.48	324°29'	299.48	15q6	The encounter with one you may ultimately divorce
324.27	324°16'	299.27	15q5	The thing that grants access to a field of possible information
324.06	324°4'	299.06	15q4	Where you are compelled to opinionate in light of / response to a challenge; answering a challenge via communication
323.85	323°51'	298.85	15q3	Presenting your values, bringing what you have to offer into the world (for others to absorb into their experience?)
323.65	323°39'	298.65	15q2	Rivalries or complementarities with others in the course of your daily duties; how your work tasks foster or correlate with certain social interaction sagas
323.44	323°26'	298.44	15q1	How you pioneer/make your way known into the wide world; going out there in exploration or on a journey
323.23	323°14'	298.23	15q12	Observing another party or particular system grants the ability to define who a hero is
323.02	323°1'	298.02	15q11	Your youth/elementary school experiences, which your own youth may later learn from you
322.81	322°49'	297.81	15q10	That which must be built under protection, but later graduates from that protection
322.6	322°36'	297.6	15q9	The groups over which a process is iterated
322.4	322°24'	297.4	16q8	Young adult accomplishments

322.19	322°11'	297.19	16q7	Evolution of the first space you make for yourself
321.98	321°59'	296.98	16q6	Situations which invite conflict eventually, or are conducive to it; more positively, the circumstances that endure after conflict has already occurred—armistice
321.77	321°46'	296.77	16q5	How you compel your interactants to get to the point...the point YOU want made
321.56	321°34'	296.56	16q4	The situations that play out more as you get older
321.35	321°21'	296.35	16q3	What is going on when your mannerisms are noticed
321.15	321°9'	296.15	16q2	That which infuses your experience with a moment of beauty
320.94	320°56'	295.94	16q1	Initiation into a particular class of behaving actors / sub-culture
320.73	320°44'	295.73	16q12	That which announces your arrival in the club (inner circle or higher status); investigate this region in New York
320.52	320°31'	295.52	16q11	How you represent the members of your family (a group whose behavioral origins you share, which are never so complex as to keep you from "getting the point") as a group of ideas relating together; if things are unclear, perhaps you should rely on these personalities to help you?
320.31	320°19'	295.31	16q10	What you are there to witness or facilitate—your role as one holding a career with a plot happening around you
320.1	320°6'	295.1	16q9	Pushing through powerfully towards a goal
319.9	319°54'	294.9	17q8	A social connectedness scenario
319.69	319°41'	294.69	17q7	How you engage others in a way that affirms you are their friend
319.48	319°29'	294.48	17q6	One who stands apart from any path you are able to help them on
319.27	319°16'	294.27	17q5	Your fit match, possibly for deep bonding
319.06	319°4'	294.06	17q4	You portfolio. If you were a business, this would be your product
318.85	318°51'	293.85	17q3	The big sign or symbol telling people where to go
318.65	318°39'	293.65	17q2	One part of your deeply held philosophies for addressing a social ill
318.44	318°26'	293.44	17q1	The vehicle through which you make social statements
318.23	318°14'	293.23	17q12	Ordering the scattered pieces
318.02	318°1'	293.02	17q11	When another does something to shut you or your chances down for good
317.81	317°49'	292.81	17q10	Situations which trap you, which you yourself have walked into
317.6	317°36'	292.6	17q9	Persistent preoccupation shared with or dissected against another
317.4	317°24'	292.4	18q8	How the strong male energy expects/draws its domain or female targets to receive that energy
317.19	317°11'	292.19	18q7	Books you create or are very interested in
316.98	316°59'	291.98	18q6	The pursuit of inspiration. When you get it you can also inspire others
316.77	316°46'	291.77	18q5	Where you put everyone else out of your way; everybody go home. Leave me in peace
316.56	316°34'	291.56	18q4	Expectations of the new leader / successor in light of the old
316.35	316°21'	291.35	18q3	The nature of the eulogy—either its contents or the process of its delivery
316.15	316°9'	291.15	18q2	Onerous or repetitive work you do for few allies, while those who expect it or demand it continue to look on; associated with the presentation or shape of the butt
315.94	315°56'	290.94	18q1	Situations in which you express, vent, or work to reduce worry
315.73	315°44'	290.73	18q12	Where you voice your disapproval of (or basic response to) someone else's crazy or offensive act
315.52	315°31'	290.52	18q11	Where you push hard for a certain economic decision
315.31	315°19'	290.31	18q10	Touring the array, how you process a cross-section of a topic or experience
315.1	315°6'	290.1	18q9	The kinds of activity-roles which describe your friends. Critical and strong for determining who your friends are
314.9	314°54'	289.9	19q8	The force which influences the information you talk about; one good indicator of your partner or a friend who influences your path strongly; (what you experience or what they do)
314.69	314°41'	289.69	19q7	One with whom you explore and elaborate upon communicative options
314.48	314°29'	289.48	19q6	One whose analysis produces results worthy of further conversation
314.27	314°16'	289.27	19q5	The welcome intermittent visitor, a character you respect for handling the information properly; a good situational interpreter
314.06	314°4'	289.06	19q4	Your idealized friend's milestone qualities
313.85	313°51'	288.85	19q3	The major impression of you and your partner as a duo
313.65	313°39'	288.65	19q2	The ultimate couple's retreat or journey
313.44	313°26'	288.44	19q1	Who is this stranger / unfamiliar party deserving of my attention?
313.23	313°14'	288.23	19q12	The one who stops another's wandering; very sidereal Capricorn
313.02	313°1'	288.02	19q11	The family that plays opposite you
312.81	312°49'	287.81	19q10	The force with which you compel others to respond to your will (or interaction?), or the force with which you direct them; seems to be a general indicator of the penis as a potential entrant into a creating space; restricting (10) using interaction (7) with cross-talk / being talked (11) about as context; Hibbitts?
312.6	312°36'	287.6	19q9	The culture of your friends; the spaces of behavior that comes with them?

312.4	312°24'	287.4	20q8	The standards of behavior you place upon the armies you command
312.19	312°11'	287.19	20q7	The army's frontline iconic rallyer if not a forefront leader
311.98	311°59'	286.98	20q6	The mode of problem solving conducted by the army's scouts or recon team
311.77	311°46'	286.77	20q5	The characters who prune the talent in the army to match the former's own agenda; "look into my eyes"
311.56	311°34'	286.56	20q4	Style of airing dissent or concerns before the army
311.35	311°21'	286.35	20q3	The army's cleanup, branding, or formal muster with little additional clutter involved
311.15	311°9'	286.15	20q2	The hardcore soldier who extols the honors of the army; the object or concept which verifies the honor of the army
310.94	310°56'	285.94	20q1	How the army is briefed; the messaging delivered to reinforce the army's goals and culture
310.73	310°44'	285.73	20q12	The owner of a professional team; a big time boss
310.52	310°31'	285.52	20q11	What bosses want or require of you. Failing this, they are much more likely to withdraw their support or withhold certain key enabling resources from you
310.31	310°19'	285.31	20q10	Conversation which separates or draws a (class or category) distinction between the two interlocutors
310.1	310°6'	285.1	20q9	That which distinguishes one as having a parental or guardian role
309.9	309°54'	284.9	21q8	Forcing the existence of a path across an otherwise level terrain in order to resolve something
309.69	309°41'	284.69	21q7	What happens in worlds whose nature is outside of your nature; alien worlds
309.48	309°29'	284.48	21q6	In the role of the submitter to scrutiny or interrogation
309.27	309°16'	284.27	21q5	The new phase of creation as the previous phase is lost
309.06	309°4'	284.06	21q4	That which sponsors bad blood (or intensity?) between you and some other person or group. May not be used until things go south (or until the permissions for intensity have been allowed?)
308.85	308°51'	283.85	21q3	The default lifestyle you (and your partner) lead in your home
308.65	308°39'	283.65	21q2	Where you don't necessarily have friends, but clients and second-degree amicable associations; how that situation presents itself
308.44	308°26'	283.44	21q1	Embellishments provided to you by others simply because they have a need to express something for which you would make an adequate canvas
308.23	308°14'	283.23	21q12	Those beneath you, adjuncts to you
308.02	308°1'	283.02	21q11	The sub-institution you are connected to which goes in a different direction than that of your native system
307.81	307°49'	282.81	21q10	Those whom you depend upon to even enter the battle at all
307.6	307°36'	282.6	21q9	Those you rely on to execute part of your dream
307.4	307°24'	282.4	22q8	Things that one might do out of desperation
307.19	307°11'	282.19	22q7	What you personally appear to value, especially through the lens of the pressuring place you're in… whether or not this aligns with the place's values
306.98	306°59'	281.98	22q6	Problems people have which won't ever be resolved; more positively. If people do the things in this region, they will suddenly be ready to learn from you or teach you; the prerequisites
306.77	306°46'	281.77	22q5	A group which seeks what a particular party or type of individual seems to have
306.56	306°34'	281.56	22q4	A regular critical imposition upon others that occurs as part of a sustaining process?
306.35	306°21'	281.35	22q3	Those who repair the foundation on which you stand / on which you rely. Could be you yourself
306.15	306°9'	281.15	22q2	Private events which you air or discuss publicly; | *Ajani's note: it seems that the more this forces people's actions, the bigger one's butt. But if you are male and assert this region all the time, your hit rate will be much lower. To the extent that Latinas and black women for example are more heavily socialized to unleash the private upon the public as a show of force, it will be more common to see bigger butts here. Jennifer Lopez and her ongoing wedding-action-hero theme is a glaring example of a clearly private fantasy made into something people are expected to pay for. My own butt reflects an unending stream of recordings which have a super low hit rate, but because those recordings are strongly asserted, mine is also muscular*
305.94	305°56'	280.94	22q1	The thing you carry which constitutes an enterprise all its own
305.73	305°44'	280.73	22q12	One in a position of power who can commission you to carry out a high will on their behalf
305.52	305°31'	280.52	22q11	Who you are in the service of the mighty or in the service of Fate
305.31	305°19'	280.31	22q10	The powerful mother figure or domain
305.1	305°6'	280.1	22q9	What fans of your legacy are typically seeking which inspires them to follow you
304.9	304°54'	279.9	23q8	How the work on your house or ambient homebase gets done
304.69	304°41'	279.69	23q7	Where you are tasked to interact with a situation out of necessity. Why? Look for a different grand cross to explain what the goal is. Possibly a dispositor thing
304.48	304°29'	279.48	23q6	How you process the events intended to correct you or make you better
304.27	304°16'	279.27	23q5	The units of your (self-)esteem
304.06	304°4'	279.06	23q4	Close ties with particular kindred or family members
303.85	303°51'	278.85	23q3	The premise or factors gathered together before you and your kindred, as entertainment

303.65	303°39'	278.65	23q2	What sustained communication with you tends to build up in others who respond to your [interactional displays of conversational competence]
303.44	303°26'	278.44	23q1	What you feel you have the right to express (assuming you're in a place that actually accepts you)
303.23	303°14'	278.23	23q12	What you are uniquely talented in fostering around yourself given almost no effort; Selene-like
303.02	303°1'	278.02	23q11	The authority figures of your friends or the kinds of events your childhood friends participated under
302.81	302°49'	277.81	23q10	When your power is down, what do you do?
302.6	302°36'	277.6	23q9	How you see your parents or those who raised you when you were under their family structure
302.4	302°24'	277.4	24q8	That which achieves the notice of those who watch a whole scenario; the main shows that get your attention, as you live out this kind of show yourself
302.19	302°11'	277.19	24q7	Those means from afar which grow your cause greatly. Could be people situations or things
301.98	301°59'	276.98	24q6	How you unsettle others when conducting your daily duties—a quirk in your work
301.77	301°46'	276.77	24q5	That which can usher you into immortality; immortal name for the power you displayed
301.56	301°34'	276.56	24q4	Your interface with the technology serving as the means to great profit; the product you can make your money in, or the asset relationship which makes that money for you
301.35	301°21'	276.35	24q3	Your relationship to a key co-deliberator or co-creator
301.15	301°9'	276.15	24q2	The catalyst which transforms you more into your prime, full-powered self
300.94	300°56'	275.94	24q1	Your coming into comfortable society
300.73	300°44'	275.73	24q12	A major conflict put into the distance from oneself—how this is done
300.52	300°31'	275.52	24q11	The general cast of characters and social crosstalk which populates your personal tv show
300.31	300°19'	275.31	24q10	The standard behavior of the opposite sex or of the class of partner you are interested in
300.1	300°6'	275.1	24q9	Seems to put you in charge of or at the forefront of a group or partnership where you are responsible for making the main moves; a more long-run scenario
299.9	299°54'	274.9	25q8	The bureau of foreign affairs; those charged with the business of interfacing with minority classes and the underprivileged
299.69	299°41'	274.69	25q7	The person who likes you or relies on you in the background, if only you would support them
299.48	299°29'	274.48	25q6	The nature of your self-exposure; this region of qunits seems to be very sexually dimorphic: depending on whether you are male or female, there are noticeable differences in whether the 25s, 61s, 97s, and 133s are expressed actively or passively by those who gravitate towards your specific body type. There are also implications for the kinds of body that are drawn to yours
299.27	299°16'	274.27	25q5	What you or your counterpart require to express their individuality when basic circumstances are too difficult to get around in a generic way
299.06	299°4'	274.06	25q4	The process for asking your guest to leave?
298.85	298°51'	273.85	25q3	Your process of handing guests, those attached to you, or those to whom you have given the pink slip
298.65	298°39'	273.65	25q2	The decorations or fixtures present in the house you keep, even if they are people
298.44	298°26'	273.44	25q1	Your children or subordinates' enterprises
298.23	298°14'	273.23	25q12	Your creations' ability to expand
298.02	298°1'	273.02	25q11	The wall which prevents attachments from connecting to you
297.81	297°49'	272.81	25q10	The guest authority visits—the kinds of things that happen at this time
297.6	297°36'	272.6	25q9	When free from (mostly social) obligations, what do you do?
297.4	297°24'	272.4	26q8	How military-like authority is exercised, an ability to stop everyone's progress
297.19	297°11'	272.19	26q7	An alternative partnering to the one that would have been decided by your kindred
296.98	296°59'	271.98	26q6	The regular deeds of those who support you, perhaps in a die-hard way; this qunit is a potentially sobering look at the interconnectedness even among strangers. You can be a fan of someone and have their chart affect you. "your telepathic radio audience"; if you put out messages encouraging these asteroids, you have a higher chance of fostering fanaticism behind you
296.77	296°46'	271.77	26q5	Your experience being around those who see more than you do; certain asteroids here can give even good interactants an air of superiority above you which you might work to oppose
296.56	296°34'	271.56	26q4	How you use books and documents, packets of information which you employ as communication to others, partly alongside the reinforcement of your will
296.35	296°21'	271.35	26q3	When you no longer have a need to collect, where you are
296.15	296°9'	271.15	26q2	Your dynamic with unpressured intimate exchangers, partners, or travelmates
295.94	295°56'	270.94	26q1	Those who hang around you: who they become as energy givers
295.73	295°44'	270.73	26q12	The kind of energy you are known for putting out into the world through your generic behavior; your frequentic "currency"; EXTREMELY CRITICAL for how people assess what you're good at contributing. Selene-related
295.52	295°31'	270.52	26q11	Shaping your easy body or form appeal under no external pressure
295.31	295°19'	270.31	26q10	Where you hear of someone near you going through a tough time
295.1	295°6'	270.1	26q9	Interaction with others under doubted or doubtful circumstances / with questions floating in the air

294.9	294°54'	269.9	27q8	How you act to address growing uncertainty
294.69	294°41'	269.69	27q7	Your professed driver or reason to push through a conflict
294.48	294°29'	269.48	27q6	You as the creative center—where people turn to you to alleviate their nervousness
294.27	294°16'	269.27	27q5	What you do to regain your stability in light of turbulence; what you believe when insecure or uncertain regarding an outcome
294.06	294°4'	269.06	27q4	The (perhaps difficult) saga which unfolds over a long time, how you process it
293.85	293°51'	268.85	27q3	How you act to fix turbulence you've experienced that has already manifested
293.65	293°39'	268.65	27q2	Thinking back on something that sucked or really wasn't fun, hoping not to go through that in the same way or put up with that again
293.44	293°26'	268.44	27q1	Your route to the upper hand amidst uncertainty
293.23	293°14'	268.23	27q12	Your approach to sex, as experienced by you or your partner; if a person wants to have sex with you, this is what they will need to be ready to provide to you as an experience
293.02	293°1'	268.02	27q11	A person whose presence / with whom your interaction earns the doubt of close witnesses; the kinds of conflicts close others or institutions tend to have around you
292.81	292°49'	267.81	27q10	The reality check or limits dealt to you to make you more uncertain; not necessarily your actual fears, but rather the situations which make you a lot more uncertain
292.6	292°36'	267.6	27q9	The surroundings left in the aftermath of your turbulence—what others or partners feel after you have projected such turbulence
292.4	292°24'	267.4	28q8	Child-tree experiences made with or through your partner; what your intimate interactant has put upon them in light of you—where your ability to satisfy this depends heavily on the success of your creative children or child (as in spin-off tree) experiences
292.19	292°11'	267.19	28q7	Your creativity applied to the world / an actor outside of your internal energy
291.98	291°59'	266.98	28q6	Where, despite alignment with someone, you definitely go your own way in some respects
291.77	291°46'	266.77	28q5	You when face-to-face with alternative worlds
291.56	291°34'	266.56	28q4	Where affairs you are connected to need to be formally administered (by you), this region shows the kinds of events which occur with it
291.35	291°21'	266.35	28q3	How you let yourself perceive the options available to you; scrolling through a space to determine what your choices are or were; the question: Why can't I get certain tasks off the ground?
291.15	291°9'	266.15	28q2	How you approach or avoid tough tough topics
290.94	290°56'	265.94	28q1	Where someone else thinks something is a big deal, burdening you with tension in the process
290.73	290°44'	265.73	28q12	Overtures by the thief; what one insists on taking from you. If you don't give it, they will take from you anyway. Or impose a state upon you which is aligned with themselves. A key qunit for understanding security
290.52	290°31'	265.52	28q11	The troubled kin-situation
290.31	290°19'	265.31	28q10	What you learn you have to do in order to reaffirm your sense of self
290.1	290°6'	265.1	28q9	How the environment changes / warns you when there are about to be problems; psychic
289.9	289°54'	264.9	29q8	The force which compels the appearance of a character reflected as if under pressure
289.69	289°41'	264.69	29q7	The kinds of interactors who are more likely to express their character as if under threat or in prison, or who are more likely to support such types
289.48	289°29'	264.48	29q6	Where the threatened personality lets up—that which would resolve things for them if the person acknowledged the cluster asteroids as satisfactory. But as long as this does not happen and the individual remains threatened, this qunit's duodecanate will remain in effect
289.27	289°16'	264.27	29q5	The part of your threatened character that will never be stoppable unless you are killed
289.06	289°4'	264.06	29q4	What you anticipate the threatened character will impose upon you; the burden they will saddle you with
288.85	288°51'	263.85	29q3	The deep seated style of perseverance which underlies your character when you feel bound by your situation; when you feel like you're doing what you can, given that you've hit limits. Your mentality for getting past this
288.65	288°39'	263.65	29q2	The activities others associate you with under limits
288.44	288°26'	263.44	29q1	What you're inclined to take with you on your journey to express your character in the face of limits
288.23	288°14'	263.23	29q12	Over the very long term, who you will have shown yourself to be / how you will have revealed your character as one who faced challenges; you may be known for this
288.02	288°1'	263.02	29q11	The friends or surrounding information exchangers who accompany your character under limits
287.81	287°49'	262.81	29q10	How you design structures and forms when constrained by certain rules; how you architect
287.6	287°36'	262.6	29q9	The niches most conducive to your active tackling of the things that limit you, bringing out your character
287.4	287°24'	262.4	30q8	How the pruning of your space is triggered; the event which clears your environment of the chaff (anything that doesn't really belong at the core of where you are)

287.19	287°11'	262.19	30q7	Trait which some of your friends would do better to obtain from a different friend rather than you? Your complement in a friend circle; an indicator of who the best "other friend C" might be—besides you, "B"—to your friend "A"
286.98	286°59'	261.98	30q6	Your tool, gear for putting yourself into the unknown of another receiving territory
286.77	286°46'	261.77	30q5	Your internal world which you want certain outsiders to see (males: you as having projected creatively; females: you as having others / events project in response to you); the aspirational sexual self-image or self-image trigger
286.56	286°34'	261.56	30q4	How you get told what's what—what you actually did wrong or what you actually need to do right in order to avoid conflict the next time
286.35	286°21'	261.35	30q3	How you and your rival combatant separate / leave each other space after an argument
286.15	286°9'	261.15	30q2	Forcing others to deal with the consequences of your bad mood or negative / unfulfilled state
285.94	285°56'	260.94	30q1	Your collaboration efforts—especially the parts that make them smooth or difficult
285.73	285°44'	260.73	30q12	Your intuition for other people's business
285.52	285°31'	260.52	30q11	The dreaded confrontation, but also one you were specifically built to handle
285.31	285°19'	260.31	30q10	What you receive as a token of separation from one who was close or one you associated with
285.1	285°6'	260.1	30q9	Big decisions to associate oneself with something, and how the effects of this spread to your family and friends
284.9	284°54'	259.9	31q8	External parties using you as their fuel supply, because what they got before wasn't enough
284.69	284°41'	259.69	31q7	Project partner for new explorations?
284.48	284°29'	259.48	31q6	Opportunities lost; how this occurs
284.27	284°16'	259.27	31q5	Collectives or groups you're associated with, under pressure to make some kind of progress
284.06	284°4'	259.06	31q4	The thunder outside which you definitely hear
283.85	283°51'	258.85	31q3	Conjuring the projective force
283.65	283°39'	258.65	31q2	The wide world opens up at the hands of another…but the assault from that world is evident
283.44	283°26'	258.44	31q1	Another does your organizing for you. Maybe forcefully
283.23	283°14'	258.23	31q12	The engaging interview
283.02	283°1'	258.02	31q11	One who takes control of the limits of nature to move according to their own homeostatic will
282.81	282°49'	257.81	31q10	An event that divides, splitting your supporters into two camps
282.6	282°36'	257.6	31q9	Things that could have happened, had you opted for nervous energy; sustained conversations you couldn't have had, though they may have appeared possible; opportunities forgone when you finally do settle with a partner?
282.4	282°24'	257.4	32q8	How you orchestrate the sexual experience—the environment or practices you favor
282.19	282°11'	257.19	32q7	Where you make a decision "I'm doing this my way. To hell with everyone else's advice"
281.98	281°59'	256.98	32q6	How an ancient or forerunner's pattern replays itself
281.77	281°46'	256.77	32q5	The character you express as you build up your power
281.56	281°34'	256.56	32q4	Willful forking to engage one's own power; possibly paid a lot more attention to in males
281.35	281°21'	256.35	32q3	The self-destruct button is hit. The union is now all but finished
281.15	281°9'	256.15	32q2	One's inner fire—the issues they face internally which possibly help them want to seek a second person to fight alongside them
280.94	280°56'	255.94	32q1	What you've learned or that which the learning environment drives you to project
280.73	280°44'	255.73	32q12	Knowledge or ability-honing tailored specifically to you; the college or higher educating environments you materialize for yourself
280.52	280°31'	255.52	32q11	Events which allow members of the stranger public to experience or even acquire some of your worth or possessions
280.31	280°19'	255.31	32q10	A telling image which captures the legacies of those associated with you
280.1	280°6'	255.1	32q9	Situating yourself to receive what you expect
279.9	279°54'	254.9	33q8	The socialization spaces which you protect; something like your favored neighborhood; traveling in an arts education setting
279.69	279°41'	254.69	33q7	Your social support anchor; very friend-like—especially during something's end
279.48	279°29'	254.48	33q6	The legend told of your partner; an apocryphal story of your partner
279.27	279°16'	254.27	33q5	Interactions with your co-parent-like family or kindred
279.06	279°4'	254.06	33q4	The progression of your marriage
278.85	278°51'	253.85	33q3	How you show commitment to or within a marriage
278.65	278°39'	253.65	33q2	Under commitment, what the commitment partner does in their regular role with respect to you
278.44	278°26'	253.44	33q1	Early boyfriending, girlfriending, or intimate exploratory experiences
278.23	278°14'	253.23	33q12	How you will remember your association with the glamorous—an association ultimately lost and unlikely to be recovered
278.02	278°1'	253.02	33q11	Your first seducers and pre-romantic play experiences

277.81	277°49'	252.81	33q10	The grand adventure you are designed to go off and undertake in a distant land far from home; HOME of 1812 Gilgamesh
277.6	277°36'	252.6	33q9	The events floating in the background which are being driven either by you or by your representatives to move your relationship to a mutually better place; unfortunately, it is common for some of this background activity to go against what you personally would prefer; contains some information on why others would cheat on you or circumvent your influence; positively, you may yet be able to encourage this in those around you and, in so doing, automatically generate followership, if not fanship; telepathic
277.4	277°24'	252.4	34q8	Your first exposure to certain kinds of co-creative or sexual experience
277.19	277°11'	252.19	34q7	Your literal or spiritual house as you age into maturity?
276.98	276°59'	251.98	34q6	Your response to your enemies, limiters, or detractors once you realize them as such
276.77	276°46'	251.77	34q5	How you attract others to you; your character appeal or appeal of your presence
276.56	276°34'	251.56	34q4	How adversarial exchanges evolve in the long term
276.35	276°21'	251.35	34q3	Where the hypothetical affects one's actions or energy
276.15	276°9'	251.15	34q2	Things which, if you do, will block intimacy
275.94	275°56'	250.94	34q1	Perspectives shared among small kindred groups—something like reflection or retrospective, especially regarding the structure of a space or situation
275.73	275°44'	250.73	34q12	Events you produce amidst travel / traversing a system
275.52	275°31'	250.52	34q11	The social technology context just outside of you
275.31	275°19'	250.31	34q10	How you at least temporarily accept the ongoing presence of a rival
275.1	275°6'	250.1	34q9	The ultimate determination of who is and isn't feedbacking with you
274.9	274°54'	249.9	35q8	Time to go forward, though there will likely be little help; seems to be associated with the shoulders and the work you must do while others look on from the sidelines. Positively may indicate a kind of monopoly you have over a certain kind of work
274.69	274°41'	249.69	35q7	Communication with another during far travel
274.48	274°29'	249.48	35q6	A 30000 ft view of society
274.27	274°16'	249.27	35q5	Processing something even though you can't really accept it for yourself
274.06	274°4'	249.06	35q4	Paths that perhaps could have been tread in a better way; related to mistakes? (35q4 = 10d11q4 = wanting (4) the information (11) structured (10)
273.85	273°51'	248.85	35q3	A deep or deeply engaging communicative impression
273.65	273°39'	248.65	35q2	How the family processes someone (particularly one of the parents) on the warpath
273.44	273°26'	248.44	35q1	Your experience with other-slamming gossip. You could be that other who is gossiped about by strangers
273.23	273°14'	248.23	35q12	Self-possession or a high sense of value held by those standing in proud absorption of nature
273.02	273°1'	248.02	35q11	Assessing how much more can actually be gotten out of a (seemingly capped) situation
272.81	272°49'	247.81	35q10	Working at one's little piece, but knowing one is nowhere near the skill level to compete on a high quality level
272.6	272°36'	247.6	35q9	Traveling out in the world, or (in the case of stationary objects or concepts) getting others to travel from the outside world to you
272.4	272°24'	247.4	36q8	The story you yourself tell of what you went through in the years prior
272.19	272°11'	247.19	36q7	What others learn of the interactions which defined who you are now
271.98	271°59'	246.98	36q6	The kind of work or task-performance experience you ultimately would have gained in life
271.77	271°46'	246.77	36q5	How people describe your personality to each other, especially when they are analyzing your merits objectively or in light of problem situations associated with you
271.56	271°34'	246.56	36q4	Experiences you say you enjoyed and want again
271.35	271°21'	246.35	36q3	The opinions you were known to have held
271.15	271°9'	246.15	36q2	Situations you had an affinity with—which described your identity in life
270.94	270°56'	245.94	36q1	How you behaved when you were really isolated? The context for imagining your ideal role
270.73	270°44'	245.73	36q12	Deeds or descriptions of key others you were associated with in life
270.52	270°31'	245.52	36q11	How people talk about you or your behaviors, especially in relationships?
270.31	270°19'	245.31	36q10	The general path and message gotten from your biography; how your relationship with your partner (or your partner themselves) is (historically) described
270.1	270°6'	245.1	36q9	Events or behavior paradigms typically to be found where you were, per others' descriptions
269.9	269°54'	244.9	37q8	What one attempts to do (with other people's stuff) when the decision is at one's own discretion
269.69	269°41'	244.69	37q7	Where or how you apologize for breaches you have committed or been involved in; otherwise, the correlates of events which others might say you should regret or apologize for; to manifest this positively, you may need to be shameless
269.48	269°29'	244.48	37q6	How or through what means you separate off from a thing / joined space
269.27	269°16'	244.27	37q5	Your morning routine, what you do when you wake up

269.06	269°4'	244.06	37q4	"Sunday activities," how time is spent when you have the opportunity to perform actions that relieve the week's tension; quintessential not-Virgo / not-your own individual (but, rather, contextual) logic applied to resolve something when you get a chance
268.85	268°51'	243.85	37q3	Definitely following your own path despite certain social rules hindering it
268.65	268°39'	243.65	37q2	How others REALLY get to know you: by being allowed to see you express the asteroids here
268.44	268°26'	243.44	37q1	One trying to build up a super duper (possibly ethereal) space
268.23	268°14'	243.23	37q12	Going off into the unknown, your experience or view of this
268.02	268°1'	243.02	37q11	A neighbor has something unresolved, and we are going to struggle looking for a solution
267.81	267°49'	242.81	37q10	How you are (finally) forced to move to the next level
267.6	267°36'	242.6	37q9	Deliberating: separating real options from a fake one
267.4	267°24'	242.4	38q8	Ulterior motives, things you definitely do which you might be ill-advised to share with anyone else
267.19	267°11'	242.19	38q7	Sides of yourself that you show which, if seen by another, indicate that a kind of intercourse or intimacy is possible
266.98	266°59'	241.98	38q6	How you handle the pressure to possess certain traits or items
266.77	266°46'	241.77	38q5	The acts that distinguish or separate one from their mother / home context
266.56	266°34'	241.56	38q4	Taking time to think in a way that others cannot deeply access
266.35	266°21'	241.35	38q3	At the peak of one's work efforts, that which is experienced
266.15	266°9'	241.15	38q2	The work that has to be done by you or your surroundings which stops others from connecting with you; you can hold back another's progress here while they are waiting for you to get whatever third party thing it is cleared up. Once this is done, connections can begin; the surface you present which separates people who know you from people who've only seen you, and until they've seen you do the things in this cluster they may never know you; related to what strangers recognize in you when they see you? If 73q1 is an issue for you, 38q2 partly indicates your response to events you have faced because of your class specifically
265.94	265°56'	240.94	38q1	Foggy initial memory—stories of other energies traveling around; the séance
265.73	265°44'	240.73	38q12	Work done to finally resolve the mysteriously intractable machine
265.52	265°31'	240.52	38q11	Diminishment plans on one's mind
265.31	265°19'	240.31	38q10	The regular background goings on which continue the structure of a thing
265.1	265°6'	240.1	38q9	Waiting in the wings for the opportunity to make one's mark
264.9	264°54'	239.9	39q8	An umbrella energy which covers everything you express in a certain position
264.69	264°41'	239.69	39q7	A situation where close involvement with another (maybe you) is strongly discouraged
264.48	264°29'	239.48	39q6	Joint efforts to challenge an original work
264.27	264°16'	239.27	39q5	A personality which sells itself, but is unattractive or undesirable in what it presents
264.06	264°4'	239.06	39q4	Your specific role in the family legacy
263.85	263°51'	238.85	39q3	Mother or nurturer in your local experience of a family unit. Useful in the Gauquelin family data
263.65	263°39'	238.65	39q2	The event which registers one as being part of the family
263.44	263°26'	238.44	39q1	Backroom debilitation—sometimes witnessed by another or others
263.23	263°14'	238.23	39q12	Those you hate on or disrespect you; or maybe they just hate you in the regular way
263.02	263°1'	238.02	39q11	When closing in on someone you are about to formally partner with; may explain some part of cold feet
262.81	262°49'	237.81	39q10	Correlates with the prized partner's co-creative pattern; what you are sexually or co-creatively attracted to as a status indicator
262.6	262°36'	237.6	39q9	The outcome of your interactions with very far-distant cultures
262.4	262°24'	237.4	40q8	How you want the world to receive you
262.19	262°11'	237.19	40q7	That which you do alongside another in order to mold the world according to your desires
261.98	261°59'	236.98	40q6	Activities you perform, side gestures while you are busy shaping pieces of your environment in your own way
261.77	261°46'	236.77	40q5	How you cooperate with close partners towards the building of a shared niche
261.56	261°34'	236.56	40q4	How you shape your body or presence to better fit the world you want to build or attract
261.35	261°21'	236.35	40q3	How you believe the world around you should evolve itself to fit your image of it, possibly calling you to participate in this process; this should feel like going with the flow if possible
261.15	261°9'	236.15	40q2	The direction which your physical body or health keeps wanting to go in as you evolve; THE quint of body evolution as you grow older
260.94	260°56'	235.94	40q1	What you think of your own sex appeal—how you use bodies or physical appeal as a commodifiable product
260.73	260°44'	235.73	40q12	What you say to others—where it must be sharply packaged in order to avoid upsetting or unsettling others. Not because it would be considered wrong, but because people would prefer you not be associated with *that stuff*
260.52	260°31'	235.52	40q11	The state of separation from family

260.31	260°19'	235.31	40q10	The other who presents you with a palpable challenge scenario—forcing you to level up to your externally considered potential or stay at your current skill level
260.1	260°6'	235.1	40q9	That which raises noise or frequencies to a high level
259.9	259°54'	234.9	41q8	Resistance encountered when attempting to gain entry into a new community
259.69	259°41'	234.69	41q7	How you acquire new assets or riches
259.48	259°29'	234.48	41q6	The watcher looking out for whether resolution is achieved—commissioned to solve someone else's problem
259.27	259°16'	234.27	41q5	The attitude people said you took, expressed through your work; your legacy when you are no longer present to actively pursue your deep values
259.06	259°4'	234.06	41q4	The definition of dominance and power-distant leadership: agency
258.85	258°51'	233.85	41q3	The cast and crew needed to advance your story; CRITICAL to see if you are represented in another's chart as a potential friend
258.65	258°39'	233.65	41q2	The visitors to my deepest family
258.44	258°26'	233.44	41q1	Your bully
258.23	258°14'	233.23	41q12	A major difference in APPROACH compared to a parallel actor in the same space
258.02	258°1'	233.02	41q11	Information or talk compelled in response to one's self-projection into a niche; how [the longstanding spirit of a situation] or [what was on one's mind] was finally addressed?
257.81	257°49'	232.81	41q10	Your interaction with 'the good guys" or as a good guy—not necessarily a hero (a popularly celebrated, unique one)
257.6	257°36'	232.6	41q9	An event that cannot be allowed to last, as its continuation will surely complicate things
257.4	257°24'	232.4	42q8	Attention donated to changes you are undergoing
257.19	257°11'	232.19	42q7	How you prefer to spend your time between key hours changes, if flowing with time were all you needed to do
256.98	256°59'	231.98	42q6	Pivotal entry and exit milestones between eras in your life; events or states which require you to leave your own cognitive framing at the door?
256.77	256°46'	231.77	42q5	Facing this may mean that you have grown up in the related situation
256.56	256°34'	231.56	42q4	The means to discussing your honest views of sexuality
256.35	256°21'	231.35	42q3	The patriarchal system perpetuated endlessly
256.15	256°9'	231.15	42q2	In light of the breakup of a family or close group
255.94	255°56'	230.94	42q1	An underground personality may yet rise up the make their presence known
255.73	255°44'	230.73	42q12	Vehicles to supremacy
255.52	255°31'	230.52	42q11	What ruthlessness or ruthless pursuit looks like
255.31	255°19'	230.31	42q10	The backstory that will have ultimately explained how you ended up at your final stable point
255.1	255°6'	230.1	42q9	Your style of enforcing problem solving (for situations not puzzles)
254.9	254°54'	229.9	43q8	One who is a bottleneck for progress unless things are absolutely clear and easy to agree with for them
254.69	254°41'	229.69	43q7	People's talk about their situation now that you're no longer around. It's not so much about you (though you might think it is), but more about how you fit into an issue that has shadowed this other party regardless of who their counterpart is. You may be an engine of karma here
254.48	254°29'	229.48	43q6	A foreign-to-you party looks for ways to execute their will
254.27	254°16'	229.27	43q5	Where you are ordained, encouraged by your surrounding space to do something
254.06	254°4'	229.06	43q4	Attempts at smooth communication despite not feeling received by the hearer
253.85	253°51'	228.85	43q3	The maintenance state for an important advancing of an Other's role in one's life
253.65	253°39'	228.65	43q2	You as a distinct guide to others through the foreign
253.44	253°26'	228.44	43q1	Major events which change how you can see or approach something thereafter
253.23	253°14'	228.23	43q12	What you build up in response to / how you handle being overpowered or outgunned; when your notion of manhood or male projection is invalidated, what you do in response
253.02	253°1'	228.02	43q11	How the other person is made to feel during an argument—behaviors they find themselves performing specifically because they are arguing with you. A strongly psychic region associated with projection, you onto another when there is conflict. You may be inclined to think that all the world is like this in how they present as enemies, though it's really just your own emotional swimming pool following you around specifically. If you find someone else doing this, it may indicate that you are naturally inclined to fight them. If you're doing it towards them, it may show that they are naturally inclined to fight you. Squares to this make conflict-heavy disagreements unnecessary, unwise, or unsustainable
252.81	252°49'	227.81	43q10	You as a co-worker
252.6	252°36'	227.6	43q9	The state of conception; the initiating act which will eventually lead to the birth of something co-sponsored by a partner
252.4	252°24'	227.4	44q8	The illusion has a power in it to change one's course
252.19	252°11'	227.19	44q7	How you engage your major assets

251.98	251°59'	226.98	44q6	Girls' time; collections of spaces hanging out together; possibly associated with maps and travel as a lifestyle
251.77	251°46'	226.77	44q5	How fixers operate in your world, and the events that they bring to help them turn a massive effort around
251.56	251°34'	226.56	44q4	Compelling another to stick to your rhythm, or vice versa
251.35	251°21'	226.35	44q3	The place where hopefuls are scrutinized for their performance of established work. You could be the hopeful or the scrutinizer
251.15	251°9'	226.15	44q2	Regular content you consume, to orient yourself against your circumstances?
250.94	250°56'	225.94	44q1	Spreading political or cultural views / paradigms you believe in
250.73	250°44'	225.73	44q12	The various scenarios under which you wake up
250.52	250°31'	225.52	44q11	The environments against which you engage your survival
250.31	250°19'	225.31	44q10	Your deepest long-term connections
250.1	250°6'	225.1	44q9	As you grow distanced from those close to you, this is what happens
249.9	249°54'	224.9	45q8	Quietly observing others' chaotic energy; the chaos within "that one" outside, or how "that one" deals with exploitation or being mercilessly used/demanded of
249.69	249°41'	224.69	45q7	Where you observe others feel the rile-up around you
249.48	249°29'	224.48	45q6	Your foundational environment, possibly gone back to for relearning, or newer in teaching you a new space, given *how* you learn
249.27	249°16'	224.27	45q5	That which requires bravery or boldness to do
249.06	249°4'	224.06	45q4	When you look at your own work and its direction, what you see
248.85	248°51'	223.85	45q3	The kind of bf or gf you ultimately end up with—specifically the kinds of adventures you have together
248.65	248°39'	223.65	45q2	Your stable identity for reconciling generic issues you encounter
248.44	248°26'	223.44	45q1	What constitutes home when you're away from home or traveling; could be people who make you feel like you're at home when traveling
248.23	248°14'	223.23	45q12	How you behave / what you experience at the end of a long day or beginning of your off-time
248.02	248°1'	223.02	45q11	One whom you admire for their ability to soothe you
247.81	247°49'	222.81	45q10	Character of the cycle of tempestuousness that plays out around you when dynamics are tense
247.6	247°36'	222.6	45q9	Deeply drawn engagement, immersion in the spirit of a context, 9-9-9
247.4	247°24'	222.4	46q8	Your partner's first response to you when sexual exposure begins, especially when you are younger. When older, more people are less likely to make the teenage observations; the impression you put on their minds
247.19	247°11'	222.19	46q7	The body type you interface with during sex—describes part of how your partner is built as a complement to you
246.98	246°59'	221.98	46q6	Your thoughts about you and your other as a sexual pair. You'll need to make sure all asteroids in here are fun if sex is to be fun
246.77	246°46'	221.77	46q5	The separation between you and some institutional regulator which is very much not you
246.56	246°34'	221.56	46q4	The bad guy with whom you partner, then separate
246.35	246°21'	221.35	46q3	An authority holding tension or becoming gradually annoyed
246.15	246°9'	221.15	46q2	The females in one's life when they are under pressure
245.94	245°56'	220.94	46q1	After the female partner is lost or severed, what happens
245.73	245°44'	220.73	46q12	A pairing or interaction which refuses to deliver what you expected, but brings an unexpected social price instead
245.52	245°31'	220.52	46q11	How you retaliate or seek to be made whole in the face of one who has impeded you or thwarted the plans you expect should be followed
245.31	245°19'	220.31	46q10	Going all in on a situation even though it isn't the most favorable place to be. *Something* must be gotten from there
245.1	245°6'	220.1	46q9	When others are not performing, how you handle it; a situation that describes this; my research as compensatory for this
244.9	244°54'	219.9	47q8	Other-compelling or persuasive conversations about what's happening in the world
244.69	244°41'	219.69	47q7	The process or others you interact with which help you get the information you need to navigate the foreign; host sponsors; easily fully studyable images or people
244.48	244°29'	219.48	47q6	Why others would be unwilling or unable to explore the world with you
244.27	244°16'	219.27	47q5	How you study or improve your skills within a niche
244.06	244°4'	219.06	47q4	How you behave against a significant conflicted character or bad guy
243.85	243°51'	218.85	47q3	How you express your opinion of what parties are communicating with each other in the world
243.65	243°39'	218.65	47q2	Your logic applied to the world around you, what you attach to as your informational niche gains more form
243.44	243°26'	218.44	47q1	How you enable the logging of your understanding of foreign systems
243.23	243°14'	218.23	47q12	The story ultimately to be told about your explorations of the world; another "how you are remembered" region—this time for the scenarios you left others behind for and ended up experiencing in a far off place
243.02	243°1'	218.02	47q11	How you process the information needed to understand foreign cultures or niches

242.81	242°49'	217.81	47q10	The nature of your kindred and family-like connections
242.6	242°36'	217.6	47q9	When people visit you from a distance, what they will be introduced to
242.4	242°24'	217.4	48q8	Watching the burdens or pressures unfold before you
242.19	242°11'	217.19	48q7	First major encounter in a path of ongoing relating
241.98	241°59'	216.98	48q6	How the person close to you must defend against you, avoid disappointing you
241.77	241°46'	216.77	48q5	How you control the media influences that enter your space
241.56	241°34'	216.56	48q4	Painstaking or detailed overview of something
241.35	241°21'	216.35	48q3	Touring, canvassing an area in order to get the job done
241.15	241°9'	216.15	48q2	The split-up of the core family
240.94	240°56'	215.94	48q1	Those who stay reasonably aligned with your direction even as the details change
240.73	240°44'	215.73	48q12	Packages you are more likely to await or be stirred by when they arrive
240.52	240°31'	215.52	48q11	The muscle or body builder; adjuncts to you which impose power upon things, on your behalf
240.31	240°19'	215.31	48q10	Where you are resigned to sit in the corner and think about things—away from everyone else
240.1	240°6'	215.1	48q9	Not exactly secrets, but things you don't (or shouldn't) necessarily tell your partner or vice versa
239.9	239°54'	214.9	49q8	Lower class or esteem, called in to do work
239.69	239°41'	214.69	49q7	A response to what the space has taught you about yourself
239.48	239°29'	214.48	49q6	Going far out onto the frontier in order to heal or stabilize oneself
239.27	239°16'	214.27	49q5	How you (knowingly or unknowingly) work to make yourself into the centrally effective party in a situation
239.06	239°4'	214.06	49q4	The initial conditions for your hooking up with your significant other; how you intend to introduce yourself as a steering force—if intending is what you're still doing
238.85	238°51'	213.85	49q3	Where others take back the results of your projection or expression towards them
238.65	238°39'	213.65	49q2	The events which renew your "will terrain"—restoring stability to situations you have forced your will upon after you have bowled everything over; investigate in victims of crimes—the aftermath or their being victimized and how they recover
238.44	238°26'	213.44	49q1	Your true personality when in your own company and surrounded by things just like you—which receive your purest communication; when your own private culture constitutes your surroundings; maybe a Mars-Jupiter midpoint?
238.23	238°14'	213.23	49q12	Commanding others towards your ultimate success, or them commanding you towards theirs
238.02	238°1'	213.02	49q11	Information which you can't unsee or unlearn once it has been provided to you
237.81	237°49'	212.81	49q10	"Distinctified" styles between kindred, or between two sides of the same story
237.6	237°36'	212.6	49q9	Your interactions with someone who can help you align with your stronger version
237.4	237°24'	212.4	50q8	How you push someone into defiance, or push them into your defiance
237.19	237°11'	212.19	50q7	The kinds of interactants / interactions involved in responding to a situation that has been patterned against one's way
236.98	236°59'	211.98	50q6	Security in one's financial situation
236.77	236°46'	211.77	50q5	Pulling back from a family-like association with someone; anti-communion
236.56	236°34'	211.56	50q4	Where only the few are privy to your real emotional release domain—what you actually want others to perceive—and how it works
236.35	236°21'	211.35	50q3	How you execute continued progression in light of perceived losses—experiences which have left you behind?
236.15	236°9'	211.15	50q2	The scattered kindred whom you assemble
235.94	235°56'	210.94	50q1	The nature of external events that you find wildly amusing
235.73	235°44'	210.73	50q12	Outlook on managing family affairs
235.52	235°31'	210.52	50q11	Where you move into a place which is already powerful
235.31	235°19'	210.31	50q10	The no-bullshit remedy: cut to the heart of the matter and unleash the final solution easily
235.1	235°6'	210.1	50q9	Being a part of a space or culture which is making moves
234.9	234°54'	209.9	51q8	The kinds of situations or people you monitor, possibly awaiting a particular kind of change
234.69	234°41'	209.69	51q7	The events, spaces, or populations behind each of your expressive milestones
234.48	234°29'	209.48	51q6	The dynamics shown by at least one of your strongest associates; (a future divorcé(e)?)
234.27	234°16'	209.27	51q5	The surrounding informational context which facilitates transmissions. The medium
234.06	234°4'	209.06	51q4	The parent figures observe the children for execution in alignment with the formers' will
233.85	233°51'	208.85	51q3	Fellatio (your idea of your role); based on the house qunits and sample subject bios, shows where one inserts an engine of forced-out production into another's space of nurturance intake rather than a space of product-import—kind of like receiving a shipment through one's customer entrance rather than the warehouse where it is to be processed, a convenience for the deliverer, but a thing to be digested by the consumer. Seems to say to the target, "I'm willing to digest / internalize (or at least trigger the internalization of) what you are creatively re-producing as a copy of your own will. I will develop myself personally / internally with it, though not necessarily process it towards my own product-export process as

you would normally intend." This may sound nasty to some of us humans, but humans aren't actually the center of the universe: your dogs and cats use an animal-kingdom version of this qunit all the time when they sniff each other as a form of identification.

233.65	233°39'	208.65	51q2	Circumstances under which you meet actors who could be co-creative partners, without your going out to find them—when this happens
233.44	233°26'	208.44	51q1	You or your representative in attack mode
233.23	233°14'	208.23	51q12	Imaginings given the inertia of greater circumstance
233.02	233°1'	208.02	51q11	Your energetic counterpart who models certain experiences with you
232.81	232°49'	207.81	51q10	Becoming more detached from old drama, donating less energy to it. Seems to be related to aging
232.6	232°36'	207.6	51q9	A looping or repetitive subprocess meant to bang down the door in places where no other key to the lock may be found
232.4	232°24'	207.4	52q8	A place, situation, or adjunct which advertises fortune and may get you excited about it in theory, but is likely not to deliver (or you are less likely to capitalize on it)
232.19	232°11'	207.19	52q7	Your dream maximum—specifically, the ideal you replay to yourself when you are in a situation which renders you comparatively insignificant / renders your real role a limited one
231.98	231°59'	206.98	52q6	The events that ride along with you in conflict
231.77	231°46'	206.77	52q5	Your first romances and romantic prospects, as well as your attempts to introduce certain new things or retry certain abandoned things in your romantic attachments to others
231.56	231°34'	206.56	52q4	What you aspired to or experience amidst your aspirations when you were still immature
231.35	231°21'	206.35	52q3	The process of overlooking and everything that comes with it
231.15	231°9'	206.15	52q2	Pre-teen and adolescent habits as one begins figuring out their worlds
230.94	230°56'	205.94	52q1	How you jump into the action and help another near you to meet a particular challenge; where you ARE the assistant to 88q1
230.73	230°44'	205.73	52q12	The impressions you feel watching your partner, significant other, or someone close headed off to work / preparing to tackle something intensely
230.52	230°31'	205.52	52q11	Your experience of scenarios which are too complicated to fix, how you answer this
230.31	230°19'	205.31	52q10	The aspect of your partner's or interactant's life which threatens your security
230.1	230°6'	205.1	52q9	Cultures or behavior paradigms which you think are broken or warrant distrust
229.9	229°54'	204.9	53q8	How you debrief, recover from, or separate yourself from work
229.69	229°41'	204.69	53q7	Who you declare yourself to be in light of a breakup or severing of ties
229.48	229°29'	204.48	53q6	Coming to learn of a certain secret—especially one held by a group
229.27	229°16'	204.27	53q5	The situation which assaults your allies or protects your allies against such assault
229.06	229°4'	204.06	53q4	The juxtaposing introduction: representatives here engage the space of two complementary participants as a way of expressing something the former intends
228.85	228°51'	203.85	53q3	A state which forces another's energy to align with the environment which a first person is in
228.65	228°39'	203.65	53q2	That which forces you to reconfigure your paradigms
228.44	228°26'	203.44	53q1	How you face injustices you can do nothing about
228.23	228°14'	203.23	53q12	How you respond to being unable to get what you want
228.02	228°1'	203.02	53q11	What you cite in order to assert the significance of your own character, despite restrictions inherent in the current situation
227.81	227°49'	202.81	53q10	What you are doing when others get into conflict with you—where you are often the source of frustration or irritation
227.6	227°36'	202.6	53q9	Your relationship to your household, especially to brothers
227.4	227°24'	202.4	54q8	Experiences that the major female energy sponsors; the world or circumstances sponsored by the major female energies around one
227.19	227°11'	202.19	54q7	What you can get immersed in, really sinking your teeth into
226.98	226°59'	201.98	54q6	Regrouping in light of setbacks
226.77	226°46'	201.77	54q5	Your domestic companion who serves as a source of serious entertainment
226.56	226°34'	201.56	54q4	Secrets which float around you, perhaps involving others' complicity
226.35	226°21'	201.35	54q3	Very clearly a qunit showing how you experience others' transition into death
226.15	226°9'	201.15	54q2	Where you go when you are AWOL
225.94	225°56'	200.94	54q1	The decision to go all in. You won't be any more ready than this
225.73	225°44'	200.73	54q12	How your assertions or actions are affected by moods that color the collective air
225.52	225°31'	200.52	54q11	The information or communication you pull around you in order to put order back onto a thing which has gotten out of hand
225.31	225°19'	200.31	54q10	The group that watches your training progress. These are the individuals who teach you to develop a thick skin for certain kinds of insult

225.1	225°6'	200.1	54q9	The setting for intimate engagement, but does not reflect the final occupants you are more likely to be attached to
224.9	224°54'	199.9	55q8	Though inside the box or prison (that you can't control?), creation still happens in this way
224.69	224°41'	199.69	55q7	The ups and downs of your true kindred groups
224.48	224°29'	199.48	55q6	Sending out a message in order to clear the air
224.27	224°16'	199.27	55q5	Where the crowd witnesses your use of persuasion; related to crowd control
224.06	224°4'	199.06	55q4	The injustices you face which hinder or end successful relating
223.85	223°51'	198.85	55q3	Your partner as lost—that which is happening which remains attached to them; spirit reminders of your lost partner. In some cases may be tied to the paranormal. Seances. Charged objects. You may make use of this cluster to channel previous partners
223.65	223°39'	198.65	55q2	What you will brag about. The sum of these has a heavy effect on your reputation
223.44	223°26'	198.44	55q1	A domainic space takes more and more, limiting any assertions
223.23	223°14'	198.23	55q12	The infinite forces which proliferate unchecked
223.02	223°1'	198.02	55q11	Kindred non-family: family-like, but those with whom you cannot stay on the same route for long
222.81	222°49'	197.81	55q10	Your fiercest creative expression; closer to when you're in the zone creatively; possibly that which enters the reproductive space in collections, i.e. Sperm…	see my Figure 7 notes—slider_pregnant was one of the t-test findings
222.6	222°36'	197.6	55q9	Confiding in someone, letting them see what you don't know or aren't sure of
222.4	222°24'	197.4	56q8	A voice which knows the far foreign space. The astronaut to your mission control; the greatest of all time?
222.19	222°11'	197.19	56q7	How you send messages to your enemies or otherwise act against them
221.98	221°59'	196.98	56q6	The prodigy's interaction with the teacher; how the prodigy appears
221.77	221°46'	196.77	56q5	An overview of the little people living their lives
221.56	221°34'	196.56	56q4	Your template for ambition—who has the kind of ambition you admire
221.35	221°21'	196.35	56q3	What others see happening that you yourself don't see; their internal response to your nonconscious forcing upon them
221.15	221°9'	196.15	56q2	Just for us, welcome to our closed family
220.94	220°56'	195.94	56q1	The activity needed to advance your sense of comfort while under someone else's world or rules
220.73	220°44'	195.73	56q12	Where you yourself can do no more in a situation
220.52	220°31'	195.52	56q11	Calling a spade a spade under very honest / unvarnished opinion
220.31	220°19'	195.31	56q10	The equilibrium state which constitutes a kind of desired healthy norm
220.1	220°6'	195.1	56q9	Where and how your expertise is made visible to others
219.9	219°54'	194.9	57q8	How you position yourself before a challenge presented by the world
219.69	219°41'	194.69	57q7	Energy you use to inspire those who let you influence them. Is this telepathic projection?
219.48	219°29'	194.48	57q6	The face you put on in light of institutional warfare
219.27	219°16'	194.27	57q5	When you've left a situation without help, how you move on
219.06	219°4'	194.06	57q4	In the direction of profit or compelled richness
218.85	218°51'	193.85	57q3	A guided plunge into the vast depths of an environment in order to reshape what is known about that environment; how you advance naturalistic knowledge
218.65	218°39'	193.65	57q2	When the world welcomes your expression, this is what is happening. Squares to this show where the world shows expressions welcomed by those around you—not you
218.44	218°26'	193.44	57q1	Waking yourself and others up from dormancy, how you engage; how you captivate other's attention?
218.23	218°14'	193.23	57q12	Here you are. You finally got what you asked for. Are you satisfied? Are you even ready for it?
218.02	218°1'	193.02	57q11	How one engages the city or interacts with a public setting
217.81	217°49'	192.81	57q10	You in hardcore battle mode, given that your supporters back you
217.6	217°36'	192.6	57q9	The act of gathering together the things that relieve one's sense of incompleteness
217.4	217°24'	192.4	58q8	The expansion of your sexual dominion, wanting to make your procreative mark on more people
217.19	217°11'	192.19	58q7	The one who handles inconveniences, or the process thereof; this region seems to make a big difference in how alone you feel yourself to be in handling problems
216.98	216°59'	191.98	58q6	Who you are as a teacher, steering a class
216.77	216°46'	191.77	58q5	One who is broken down by the mob, the many, or a collective. Overwhelmed by a group
216.56	216°34'	191.56	58q4	Who your spiritual "casting director" ultimately ends up choosing
216.35	216°21'	191.35	58q3	The historical price paid by something that lives around you / whose energy surrounds you
216.15	216°9'	191.15	58q2	For the record. Major moments which you convey to others, they are highly likely to regard this as a milestone quirky event for you
215.94	215°56'	190.94	58q1	The imminent looming institution and the effect of its loom on moods looking out for it
215.73	215°44'	190.73	58q12	The circumstances under which another party gives your ideas a chance
215.52	215°31'	190.52	58q11	You in persuasion-mode

215.31	215°19'	190.31	58q10	Lessons mom or a mother figure taught you, examples she imposed upon you or which you impose as a mother upon your children or creations
215.1	215°6'	190.1	58q9	Your audience. Those who use your legacy in the larger culture
214.9	214°54'	189.9	59q8	One foists insistence upon the other
214.69	214°41'	189.69	59q7	How your child or charge interferes with your partnership; partnership interference correlated with your child's witnessing of such partnerships or you in partnership mode; the child jealous of the partner
214.48	214°29'	189.48	59q6	How your bosses task you or frame information around you in order for you to navigate
214.27	214°16'	189.27	59q5	The stance of one who would direct or advise you
214.06	214°4'	189.06	59q4	Observing what some might call questionable tactics / craziness by others or another part of oneself, but tactics you surely benefit from those others' using
213.85	213°51'	188.85	59q3	That which is fostered by your background noise
213.65	213°39'	188.65	59q2	Occurrences which you stay very separate from, or which may distance you from your former kindred
213.44	213°26'	188.44	59q1	The extra information you take in when cheating, betraying, or just supplementing someone else's role in your life
213.23	213°14'	188.23	59q12	The responsibilities posed by your relationships; seems to be a quality passed onto or affecting your (created) children
213.02	213°1'	188.02	59q11	Gathering new experiences, hosting many more than one
212.81	212°49'	187.81	59q10	Programmed cell death, intentional pruning or cutting short of something, often done to resolve what would otherwise be the continuance of an uncomfortable interaction; my guess is that this is associated with coming out—preferring to risk the loss or severance of something rather than keep up the mask
212.6	212°36'	187.6	59q9	What you see when you look at your own family (the one you have built with another)
212.4	212°24'	187.4	60q8	When you have a daunting task ahead of you
212.19	212°11'	187.19	60q7	Disconnection from the group or task before oneself
211.98	211°59'	186.98	60q6	Your creative studio; if you were to setup a studio, this is what it should look like / what you would do there
211.77	211°46'	186.77	60q5	What you do in your creative studio
211.56	211°34'	186.56	60q4	Bleeding out energy; where something desirable or favorable exists, but for an irrecoverable thing
211.35	211°21'	186.35	60q3	That which threatens your sphere health or actual health. Do the squares to avoid this. Perhaps use an intermediary to engage it
211.15	211°9'	186.15	60q2	How one positions themselves to service or answer to someone else's authority
210.94	210°56'	185.94	60q1	True villains, or where truly villainous potential lives
210.73	210°44'	185.73	60q12	Difficult aspirations marred by hesitancy, and for good reason
210.52	210°31'	185.52	60q11	Watching from a quarantined distance, possibly in sickness or away from others; the VIP booth or sick bed, with a view sweeping over everything else
210.31	210°19'	185.31	60q10	The dirty side of politics
210.1	210°6'	185.1	60q9	The bumbler or stress inducer, come to botch or blow up a perfectly good plan. There is entertainment value, however
209.9	209°54'	184.9	61q8	How you seek out someone to talk to or get a sought conversation started; this is more easily activated when one is not subject to lineage checks—whites, males, the famous, and majority power holders for example—making conversations easier to attempt
209.69	209°41'	184.69	61q7	Your attached person's predicament—roles they adopt in response to such
209.48	209°29'	184.48	61q6	The body of the one who approaches you; seems privileged or female to the extent that viewers are invited to view / assert towards the body-revealer's space; associated with flashing
209.27	209°16'	184.27	61q5	The guest who moves in and is allowed to impose their standards upon you
209.06	209°4'	184.06	61q4	For males, that which gets you on a shit list; I can't tell for females, but appears to be something that, when done with respect to you, gets you on a shit list
208.85	208°51'	183.85	61q3	Impulse thought bubble in communications; deep motive (more preconscious or impulse-serving than "ulterior"); a behind-the-scenes plan that often works against another
208.65	208°39'	183.65	61q2	The relationship between your partner (or partnered cause) and your prime creation (your most salient child); seems to apply more to your partner as a step-parent versus your most typical or obvious child
208.44	208°26'	183.44	61q1	A challenging situation or revelation put to you by another
208.23	208°14'	183.23	61q12	Deliberation over the recovery of a compromised situation—how it works
208.02	208°1'	183.02	61q11	An indicator of those who are subject to you, truly like children to you
207.81	207°49'	182.81	61q10	What people attached to / subject to you do behind your back, more likely in light of their interaction with you. Your knowing this can render you partly clairvoyant or interpersonally claircognizant—basically psychic regarding the turns in your relationships: applying structure (61 or 7d1)q10 = (10) using impulse (1) with feedbacking (7) as context
207.6	207°36'	182.6	61q9	The cultural dynamic of groups you influence, especially your kids—their interactions with each other
207.4	207°24'	182.4	62q8	Your personal story which explains your social effect

207.19	207°11'	182.19	62q7	Your masterless state
206.98	206°59'	181.98	62q6	Why you pursue the lifestyle ends that you do
206.77	206°46'	181.77	62q5	Your post-work socialization
206.56	206°34'	181.56	62q4	You as you engage a tool or product used in the projection of your will
206.35	206°21'	181.35	62q3	Collections which have a hallowed place in your history
206.15	206°9'	181.15	62q2	Graduation to the next level—what happens during or just after graduation
205.94	205°56'	180.94	62q1	How you make 1:1 confessions to another regarding the trouble you've gotten yourself into
205.73	205°44'	180.73	62q12	How you break up or interrupt the flow of an established relationship
205.52	205°31'	180.52	62q11	Where family or kindred dynamics are reconfigured around you—often around your temperament
205.31	205°19'	180.31	62q10	The kindred or successor's accomplishments—especially one's sons
205.1	205°6'	180.1	62q9	Information which, unfortunately, must be expressed away from a primary partner
204.9	204°54'	179.9	63q8	How you interact with those whom you hold hostage / those who are obligated to keep engaging you for reasons related to their own worlds, deeds, or commitments
204.69	204°41'	179.69	63q7	A kind of utilitarian relationship with something or someone needed to secure the square or some other activity
204.48	204°29'	179.48	63q6	The dark side actor who reifies your demons; or you as such a reifier
204.27	204°16'	179.27	63q5	Knowing that you are moving in the direction towards a goal
204.06	204°4'	179.06	63q4	That which constitutes stability as growth progresses; the skeletal system and adult body frame?
203.85	203°51'	178.85	63q3	Spaces or domains made sleeker, more polished
203.65	203°39'	178.65	63q2	Loss given that you have failed someone
203.44	203°26'	178.44	63q1	Trading the old home base for a newer model. Subtly but perhaps completely forgoing the old
203.23	203°14'	178.23	63q12	What reasons your partner presents which block your interest in sex with them
203.02	203°1'	178.02	63q11	The social news you tune into when other's doubt in such sources has been settled
202.81	202°49'	177.81	63q10	First glimpses of the home or where one belongs emotionally, (perhaps where they DON'T belong)
202.6	202°36'	177.6	63q9	The environments which you tell everyone else is the environment that exists out there; your local reality where environments are concerned, and to some extent the reality of those who share your bubble
202.4	202°24'	177.4	64q8	How your intended feedback loops come to affect you
202.19	202°11'	177.19	64q7	The one who captures how you intend to converse
201.98	201°59'	176.98	64q6	That which puts you in the situation for meeting your intended feedback interactant
201.77	201°46'	176.77	64q5	What following your heart looks like (especially given all of the difficulties you've faced up to that point)
201.56	201°34'	176.56	64q4	Entertaining, but possibly offensive; the two sides through which a choice manifests as attention-worthy versus fitting or unfit for the situation at hand
201.35	201°21'	176.35	64q3	You amidst pressures applied to you?
201.15	201°9'	176.15	64q2	Light shenanigans and rejection. Hijinks. A tangle-up
200.94	200°56'	175.94	64q1	Circumstances which ramp up your enthusiasm or sense of urgency
200.73	200°44'	175.73	64q12	Experiences lost, reflected on, but still cited when a certain freedom needs to be asserted
200.52	200°31'	175.52	64q11	A convincing case made for something done at your expense. You may have done something to earn others' taking from you here
200.31	200°19'	175.31	64q10	Your desire to be seen by the general public
200.1	200°6'	175.1	64q9	Experiencing relocation with or in light of partners or friends
199.9	199°54'	174.9	65q8	When you accept a foreigner's invitation to travel with them (including abstractly, in life in general), this is what happens
199.69	199°41'	174.69	65q7	Accosted by another domain on the rebound from one who just filled it
199.48	199°29'	174.48	65q6	How you handle or investigate an illness or some ongoing state that doesn't feel right
199.27	199°16'	174.27	65q5	Who you are when hanging out in your trophy social situation
199.06	199°4'	174.06	65q4	How you and you mate get into drama
198.85	198°51'	173.85	65q3	A space in which you are most likely to end up in a battle
198.65	198°39'	173.65	65q2	The headshaking shame you share with family
198.44	198°26'	173.44	65q1	While within a partnership, dissatisfied
198.23	198°14'	173.23	65q12	Your attempts to gather support, establishing a mood (12) using 1:1 interaction (5) with feedback conversation (7) as the context
198.02	198°1'	173.02	65q11	Your engagement with a temperamental / downer of a character
197.81	197°49'	172.81	65q10	When you've been or are being screwed, here is what happens; when you screw others or cheat them out of what they expect, this is what you do
197.6	197°36'	172.6	65q9	Appears to be some kind of guard's role, guarding the quality of people who can access something
197.4	197°24'	172.4	66q8	Your partner's influence tactics
197.19	197°11'	172.19	66q7	The activity paradigm in which your feedback partner is immersed
196.98	196°59'	171.98	66q6	How your partner addresses something that is driving them nuts—what they see which triggers this

196.77	196°46'	171.77	66q5	The thing your partner may blame or interact with as they avoid a conflict with you
196.56	196°34'	171.56	66q4	A common rift weapon employed by the partners you attract which serve to break you up
196.35	196°21'	171.35	66q3	How you ramp up a disagreement or conflict with frameworks progressively loaded from your own mind; the HOME of 65590 Archeptolemos?
196.15	196°9'	171.15	66q2	Showdowns, standoffs with the partner—how you assert who you are during such
195.94	195°56'	170.94	66q1	How you think about things / engage your thoughts when you head off into your escape place
195.73	195°44'	170.73	66q12	A battle buddy archetype for you against the challenges or objectives in the world
195.52	195°31'	170.52	66q11	The information around you which serves as one of the main indicators of why others shouldn't trust you
195.31	195°19'	170.31	66q10	Directives which overshadow your attempts to communicate with new systems or ideas
195.1	195°6'	170.1	66q9	Speaking up to or against the system
194.9	194°54'	169.9	67q8	How you make the case for something in an engaged conversation
194.69	194°41'	169.69	67q7	How you express confidence in present / future events or satisfaction with past events in deeply engaged conversation (or deeply engaged feedback loops)
194.48	194°29'	169.48	67q6	How you transition the interlocutor's topic into one which relates a little more to your own in deep conversation; the point of impact in a ping-pong feedback loop; your interaction with authority or logic systems you really respect and more likely (than not) want to continue working for
194.27	194°16'	169.27	67q5	How you present ideas which are close to your heart in deep conversation
194.06	194°4'	169.06	67q4	How or when you wish to close a deep conversation
193.85	193°51'	168.85	67q3	How you listen or how you accept the beginning of a soon-to-be deep conversation; a tell qunit for deep conversations being initiated upon you
193.65	193°39'	168.65	67q2	Situations which can compel you into sustained conversation
193.44	193°26'	168.44	67q1	What motivates those who do engage you in deep conversations—what they are after
193.23	193°14'	168.23	67q12	Events which facilitate ongoing conversation
193.02	193°1'	168.02	67q11	Your typical topics of sustained conversation; interesting to know in another's chart
192.81	192°49'	167.81	67q10	Where you are challenged to keep up engaging conversation
192.6	192°36'	167.6	67q9	Your relationship with the environment, niche, or zone in a sustained feedback loop; not just conversations, but could be gaming, music-making, or yard work for example; great for knowing where to take another person for sustained conversations
192.4	192°24'	167.4	68q8	Routines you conduct with your body, maintaining your appearance
192.19	192°11'	167.19	68q7	Your aired assessment of outgroups and non-allies
191.98	191°59'	166.98	68q6	A beautiful idea, but daunting in the things it involves
191.77	191°46'	166.77	68q5	The evolution of your deep commitments, your marriage; a MAJOR QUNIT
191.56	191°34'	166.56	68q4	The transfer of mandate to less qualified but more popular people; how you interpret the actions of those who are intimacy seekers to you
191.35	191°21'	166.35	68q3	The vacuum. A region of feminine / domainic power at its maximum ability to define through communication; the age trait was both t-test and canonical correlation significant
191.15	191°9'	166.15	68q2	Your critical co-creative partner; one whom you attract who may yet change and / or advance how you co-create
190.94	190°56'	165.94	68q1	Appears to be a set of milestones in your social life. Depending on your maturity level, fights you felt spontaneously compelled to fight at the time. 68q1=>(7q8 or Libra-8)q1=> compulsion (1) using power (8) with interaction (7) as the context
190.73	190°44'	165.73	68q12	Your view of the forces which loom overhead, imposing their preferred direction upon you; how you frame or respond to looming pressure
190.52	190°31'	165.52	68q11	That which you cannot really be supported in; a thing you must engage solo
190.31	190°19'	165.31	68q10	Those set to be ousted from your world
190.1	190°6'	165.1	68q9	Foreignized—where your attention moves towards a group that is even more foreign than any current one you might be in
189.9	189°54'	164.9	69q8	Someone else who administers your dream character projection for you
189.69	189°41'	164.69	69q7	Your ambition partner while you are still chasing such
189.48	189°29'	164.48	69q6	You and your friends' base camp—where your friend group and its personalities gather
189.27	189°16'	164.27	69q5	What you experience at the hands of the person you like
189.06	189°4'	164.06	69q4	How you behave in a marriage
188.85	188°51'	163.85	69q3	When you want to show commitment to someone or something, how you build up the will to do so
188.65	188°39'	163.65	69q2	Things your partner does in the commitment just because they feel good
188.44	188°26'	163.44	69q1	How you apply discipline or barriers to prevent others from initiating bf or gf mode on you, or at least how you regulate the entry of such
188.23	188°14'	163.23	69q12	The situation which attracts a certain kind of mate into your sphere, but also keeps you behind a barrier preventing their yours and their interaction

188.02	188°1'	163.02	69q11	You as seducer
187.81	187°49'	162.81	69q10	Circumstances in which you blare your insistence on something—not always angrily
187.6	187°36'	162.6	69q9	Enjoyment you seek on your own which explains why you would NOT show up at a standard party or favor a more social-networky gathering
187.4	187°24'	162.4	70q8	Parties whose progress you follow; after you know what you like co-creatively, WHO you would indulge
187.19	187°11'	162.19	70q7	The precursors—conditions you consider—for partnering with someone? How you engage your (shared) living situation as you mature
186.98	186°59'	161.98	70q6	Solitary time in your own mind / channeling your private theories of mind into practice
186.77	186°46'	161.77	70q5	Revealing your natural character while in a confined (alone) space with another. May be among the more memorable sets of moments for how you and a triggering other spent time together alone
186.56	186°34'	161.56	70q4	Steps you follow as you create scenarios to share with a particular trusted party
186.35	186°21'	161.35	70q3	What a major (co-creative) character in your life is going to need in order to truly connect to your idea-space or help you create there
186.15	186°9'	161.15	70q2	How you work inside of someone else's realm, tending to it; the intimate setting, how another experiences your intimate onset
185.94	185°56'	160.94	70q1	Thoughts behind the mask, especially for handling rivals or counterparts
185.73	185°44'	160.73	70q12	Rules that people enforce in your background, mostly without your knowledge
185.52	185°31'	160.52	70q11	How you return to relax after a hard day
185.31	185°19'	160.31	70q10	When the battles are over, what retirement looks like for you
185.1	185°6'	160.1	70q9	Things you collect, compilations you assemble and how this is done
184.9	184°54'	159.9	71q8	The other life story you watch parade by
184.69	184°41'	159.69	71q7	The trials of someone kindred to you
184.48	184°29'	159.48	71q6	Where others are made uncomfortable thanks to things associated with you
184.27	184°16'	159.27	71q5	That which fiercely hijacks your attention, pulling your effort towards itself; seems like an anti-Linsley qunit
184.06	184°4'	159.06	71q4	That which sponsors or is built on resentment
183.85	183°51'	158.85	71q3	An attitude of getting away with it, being big shit
183.65	183°39'	158.65	71q2	Keeping cool despite chaos all around
183.44	183°26'	158.44	71q1	Who you compel your partner to become, just by being associated with you; or vice-versa; a powerful position, counterruler of which may be Aksnes. People who start doing this cluster after some period of association with you may truly be a part of your sphere; or maybe you start doing these things
183.23	183°14'	158.23	71q12	How you project even as nearby support is waning
183.02	183°1'	158.02	71q11	While on your home turf, how you live and the things that reflect you; investigate in NFL players, their team logos, and stadiums
182.81	182°49'	157.81	71q10	Your response to having your world-space invaded or visited by another's need for help
182.6	182°36'	157.6	71q9	Future states considered which engage the brain or internal logistical functions
182.4	182°24'	157.4	72q8	Events that come with or cause conflict with those in a position to cap your progress in a particular area
182.19	182°11'	157.19	72q7	Events which put you alone against impending loss or abandonment
181.98	181°59'	156.98	72q6	The party who receives your full-blast will towards influence
181.77	181°46'	156.77	72q5	Circumstances where you keep trying despite having no support
181.56	181°34'	156.56	72q4	The kinds of meetings you host
181.35	181°21'	156.35	72q3	Information—sometimes published—used as a highway for expressing one's force
181.15	181°9'	156.15	72q2	Your role during big conflicts
180.94	180°56'	155.94	72q1	The role you play opposite your life partner
180.73	180°44'	155.73	72q12	Things that your close circle can do well, their capabilities
180.52	180°31'	155.52	72q11	The people and institutions around you which force you to grow up...those who train you in the deep and difficult	*Ajani's note: I translated this about 2 months after its opposition 144q11. Didn't remember that one, yet the relationship is obvious. Not a coincidence*
180.31	180°19'	155.31	72q10	The private attitude / character "known" to insert itself into your public work; the part of your reputation expressly communicated by and put to use by others for whatever purposes they may have / helping them to compel some result in an exchange
180.1	180°6'	155.1	72q9	The major tales that could be told about the life you will have led; a memory region like the 36s
179.9	179°54'	154.9	73q8	You in a teaching gig or reporting what your (voluntary or involuntary) teachers taught you
179.69	179°41'	154.69	73q7	Watching someone else's affairs, possibly reluctantly keeping an eye out for them as they pursue their foolish aspirations
179.48	179°29'	154.48	73q6	Your interface with scammers and parties of questionable character (logic.impulse.logic renders a self-serving or convenient new logic on top of the old)
179.27	179°16'	154.27	73q5	How your recruiters see your character; how you experience the go-ahead to start a new path; what happens in order for new parties to bring you on

179.06	179°4'	154.06	73q4	Help from others, perhaps strangers, amidst the dangerous or very foreign; outside help in rising to the challenge
178.85	178°51'	153.85	73q3	Someday, when you get to where you're going... how you experience the thoughts of someday
178.65	178°39'	153.65	73q2	An illustration of what "going berserk" looks like
178.44	178°26'	153.44	73q1	A thing witnessed is conducive to doubt or skepticism towards at least one of the actors
178.23	178°14'	153.23	73q12	How a culminative rift unfolds, where one party has had enough of another, exiling themselves or being exiled from the exchange
178.02	178°1'	153.02	73q11	A double-edged advantage you partly enjoy, partly pay for having
177.81	177°49'	152.81	73q10	The state of the ones who ultimately end up recruiting you
177.6	177°36'	152.6	73q9	What being cornered looks like
177.4	177°24'	152.4	74q8	Engaging your main partner's social world
177.19	177°11'	152.19	74q7	What the person who co-creates with you ends up creating or drawing forth in their own lives; an other-affecting, sexual-effect region
176.98	176°59'	151.98	74q6	Those who are watching you, perhaps with an interest in courting you
176.77	176°46'	151.77	74q5	Rallying or mustering strength on the eve of trouble / on the eve of an ending
176.56	176°34'	151.56	74q4	You being crowned the head of a group
176.35	176°21'	151.35	74q3	Those around you who embody indomitable personalities
176.15	176°9'	151.15	74q2	How you process society / the goings on beyond your immediate world
175.94	175°56'	150.94	74q1	Your siblings' (mainly your brothers') work—perhaps the work of your comrades, not you
175.73	175°44'	150.73	74q12	The ever-looming shadow which unsettles those beneath it
175.52	175°31'	150.52	74q11	Those who have the rights of power, but who also build an assaultable castle in the process
175.31	175°19'	150.31	74q10	That which is involved in sexual climax for the chartholder
175.1	175°6'	150.1	74q9	Channeling the many / a group towards independent expression, apparently from within that group
174.9	174°54'	149.9	75q8	Kindred to you who want to take your sphere to the max; sweeping viewty
174.69	174°41'	149.69	75q7	Your opportunity as things go downhill or progress towards their end
174.48	174°29'	149.48	75q6	The epilogue to your trials; what happens after (what was thought to be) the main story ends
174.27	174°16'	149.27	75q5	The information objects which circle your perimeter; a book or info collection which can always be found around you; the circling spell books
174.06	174°4'	149.06	75q4	The group of inspectors on behalf of the institution or practice indicated in 3q4; the accreditation team; conducive to power and a certain ability to instill fear; group representatives of the dominion in 3q4
173.85	173°51'	148.85	75q3	Daughter in your local experience of a family unit. Useful in the Gauquelin family data
173.65	173°39'	148.65	75q2	Folks who apply for membership in your family, who probably won't get in, or will only be considered as partners to someone else who is already in
173.44	173°26'	148.44	75q1	Giving something a chance, though you can't understand what is at work behind the scenes
173.23	173°14'	148.23	75q12	What another person expects of the domestic life?
173.02	173°1'	148.02	75q11	The high authority figure who draws the devotion (or at least compliance) of followers
172.81	172°49'	147.81	75q10	Seeking someone else to support your aims
172.6	172°36'	147.6	75q9	One's earliest military role or roots of their behavior in a military-like setting
172.4	172°24'	147.4	76q8	Innocuous work opinion; the general plot of the information space in which you form opinions regarding the point of your daily duties
172.19	172°11'	147.19	76q7	How you (or your representative) defy the verdict handed down
171.98	171°59'	146.98	76q6	How your housemate spends their leisure (interaction) time
171.77	171°46'	146.77	76q5	What you work through to let off steam amidst an (internally felt) conflict. This action serves to replenish you somehow
171.56	171°34'	146.56	76q4	Narration about you which takes place beyond you, especially regarding your use of force or your intentions in a situation that reflects others
171.35	171°21'	146.35	76q3	Situations affected by your throwing of intense energy
171.15	171°9'	146.15	76q2	An institution or structure which serves as a fuzzy umbrella over your deeds; an overarching situation which influences your health?
170.94	170°56'	145.94	76q1	After an initial pass, a second chance—especially in something that can make money or which is money-related
170.73	170°44'	145.73	76q12	The shaky tension-filled grip on control in a situation
170.52	170°31'	145.52	76q11	The counterpart / counteractor to a (more likely negative) spheremate or experience of yours; related to food?
170.31	170°19'	145.31	76q10	The events sponsored by your nichemates which compel changes in how you position yourself against your own immediate challenges. This may look like a certain level of unpredictability or radicalism in what they are doing, but is actually a consequence of you doing your squares to this;	*Ajani's note: I wonder if*

				this is associated with your body-to-environment surfaces or passageways like sweat glands or pores—skin texture or other porous exits?
170.1	170°6'	145.1	76q9	Where your friends are attacked or cornered by a rival energy
169.9	169°54'	144.9	77q8	How people back away from you and leave you in your own world
169.69	169°41'	144.69	77q7	Game over. The sentencing
169.48	169°29'	144.48	77q6	What initiates your perception of a problem (which someone else has) that needs to be resolved
169.27	169°16'	144.27	77q5	The skill or interactant you work with in establishing yourself as an indelible memory
169.06	169°4'	144.06	77q4	Your kindred group as a whole: communion
168.85	168°51'	143.85	77q3	Deep secrets which stay guarded
168.65	168°39'	143.65	77q2	The bringer of something unfortunate upon your family; that which curses your family or is a means to such
168.44	168°26'	143.44	77q1	Your bully victim
168.23	168°14'	143.23	77q12	How the things you hide (from close others) are eventually resolved; what the still-burdened team ends up doing when rifts are resolved
168.02	168°1'	143.02	77q11	Spirit of the upper room, the nature of the overarching ambient energy unclaimed by the overt house activities; most likely THE qunit of AntiNeptune
167.81	167°49'	142.81	77q10	What the corridors of power look like for you
167.6	167°36'	142.6	77q9	Sublimation of the self through a bigger group's or another's expression
167.4	167°24'	142.4	78q8	Your dealings with pets and those directly under your charge? Dogs, students, followers
167.19	167°11'	142.19	78q7	That which offers relief from your recursive attention (78q6)—what you check in with when taking a break from sustained joining of concepts; electronic or informational input used to perpetuate your beliefs about a topic; your electronic timekeepers / devices you use to count the passage of time
166.98	166°59'	141.98	78q6	Your means of evolving your core relationships over time, especially those with family; related to human reinforcement of existing mental frameworks; possibly the HOME of Mercury	Alma ds#87
166.77	166°46'	141.77	78q5	Protective behaviors of or by a close other; situations you automatically interact with or interactions you are drawn into which sustain your ability to recursively reconcile events before you
166.56	166°34'	141.56	78q4	The accounts of your troubles which you give to other people
166.35	166°21'	141.35	78q3	Your process of active construction—whether or not the constructed things is a physical object
166.15	166°9'	141.15	78q2	What happens under the greatest separation
165.94	165°56'	140.94	78q1	The clarification of your relationships through a very obvious event
165.73	165°44'	140.73	78q12	What you produce which leaves wide effects on the environment; AntiYrjo?
165.52	165°31'	140.52	78q11	Wooing and courting, putting someone in a position as you attempt to bring them over to your side; trying to persuade or seduce someone back to your side
165.31	165°19'	140.31	78q10	Where you really, deeply, seek to impress the gods / be generically impressive, as if—from the heart—part of your sense of self depends on this
165.1	165°6'	140.1	78q9	When you are the designated beneficiary of something
164.9	164°54'	139.9	79q8	How you execute your cooperation with others / team projects
164.69	164°41'	139.69	79q7	Where you go forward, facing the very unknown
164.48	164°29'	139.48	79q6	Surroundings conducive to your brand of comfortable socialization or sense-based experience
164.27	164°16'	139.27	79q5	Ideas or visitors who infiltrate your territory, or who you wish would visit your territory
164.06	164°4'	139.06	79q4	The kinds of characters who really act in ways to support your becoming a better person or doing the right thing for the whole
163.85	163°51'	138.85	79q3	The beginning of the end of an important character's role, strongly suggesting that there will be an aftermath worth noting
163.65	163°39'	138.65	79q2	One who talks about or engages taboo topics as if it isn't a thing
163.44	163°26'	138.44	79q1	Elevated, but oh the grand trouble this brings! Where you are brought to attention in others' eyes, possibly affecting their deeds?
163.23	163°14'	138.23	79q12	How manhood manifests in your life, its definition
163.02	163°1'	138.02	79q11	The events that attend your being unable to project or defend yourself, especially through combat or assertion
162.81	162°49'	137.81	79q10	Your coworking or daily duties collaborative environment
162.6	162°36'	137.6	79q9	Your approach to solo work on the job or in daily duty
162.4	162°24'	137.4	80q8	How you work—specifically, how you interface with others as an influencer of their actions during work; even if you have asteroids in this section which do nothing, people will still manage to be moved by you when you do the things in this very important qunit
162.19	162°11'	137.19	80q7	How you interact with colleagues in order to get your work done
161.98	161°59'	136.98	80q6	How you do your daily work
161.77	161°46'	136.77	80q5	The personality dynamics and various relationships you can expect in the course of performing your job role

161.56	161°34'	136.56	80q4	How you motivate yourself to get to work—not just in the job setting
161.35	161°21'	136.35	80q3	How you think about your job—why you even have it—and how you describe (to yourself and to others) what it is you do
161.15	161°9'	136.15	80q2	Underground work and its processes; low-key skills you have to hone because of the work you do, or skills which develop with the work you do
160.94	160°56'	135.94	80q1	The process of introduction; most members of the public's / outside departments' first introduction to you at work; you as a first introducer
160.73	160°44'	135.73	80q12	The effect or impression you leave as an influencer, the environment that surrounds you as you drive daily tasks or work
160.52	160°31'	135.52	80q11	What those around you talk about experiencing in light of your effect on them in your job; what you talk about as affecting your livelihood or options
160.31	160°19'	135.31	80q10	Your job description—what you are there to endure or sponsor
160.1	160°6'	135.1	80q9	What your form of work influence contributes to the surrounding culture
159.9	159°54'	134.9	81q8	The work you would publish to the world
159.69	159°41'	134.69	81q7	A cry unanswered; a rift that cannot be resolved, despite one party's cries for help (the agitated energy itself which is transmitted in the pregnancy process?)
159.48	159°29'	134.48	81q6	The occasion for performances in your life
159.27	159°16'	134.27	81q5	A thing you do which smoothes over or improves relations with the partner or interactant
159.06	159°4'	134.06	81q4	What happens in the stories you tell
158.85	158°51'	133.85	81q3	The forcing process, kindred upon kindred
158.65	158°39'	133.65	81q2	What is happening when you travel
158.44	158°26'	133.44	81q1	Teaming ideas or approaches alongside another in your daily life or duties
158.23	158°14'	133.23	81q12	What your commitment partner or significant other actually wants (from life in general)?
158.02	158°1'	133.02	81q11	How (general) others around you feel you were soliciting their company or signing up to be their ally...their subject (actually); what you did which told others you wanted to be in charge of implementing their ideas
157.81	157°49'	132.81	81q10	Coercively pulled resources or cooperation
157.6	157°36'	132.6	81q9	A scenario one is in was already sketchy, now it's worse
157.4	157°24'	132.4	82q8	How you approach immersion in a certain activity; how you "stick with it" until it's done
157.19	157°11'	132.19	82q7	The things you do / lifestyle practices employed / interactions you take up in order to escape or flout other people's boxes
156.98	156°59'	131.98	82q6	How those privy see how you work / perform your daily duties
156.77	156°46'	131.77	82q5	How those who promote you, see you; your contributions
156.56	156°34'	131.56	82q4	Mother figures who provide you with certain challenging scenarios you'll need to learn how to navigate
156.35	156°21'	131.35	82q3	Those with a high likelihood of disrespecting you or learning to become your enemy; your eventual detractors
156.15	156°9'	131.15	82q2	Central person historicity; who your group's spirit leaders are; the central figures around whom a large part of your historical path revolves; you are more likely to be featured in this person's Wikipedia article if you didn't have one yourself
155.94	155°56'	130.94	82q1	The close friend who makes you think about the restrictions you are under, or the one who imposes them
155.73	155°44'	130.73	82q12	The partner's handling of work (mostly), with some implications for daily duties; other-writing and highly psychic, as it tells you who your partner can and should be, but ALSO tells people who know this qunit in your chart, how they have to behave towards you in order to stand a better chance of registering as your partner; I consider this to be an extreme astrohack qunit for manufacturing a kind of "love potion" for yourself, if you haven't already found the partner you really want
155.52	155°31'	130.52	82q11	Problems introduced into the environment by others(especially those close to you)—your take on such problems
155.31	155°19'	130.31	82q10	The kinds of troubles or obstacles your friends our spheremates face
155.1	155°6'	130.1	82q9	What you are a fan of and how you conceive of their workings
154.9	154°54'	129.9	83q8	Your work ethic—how you conduct focused work
154.69	154°41'	129.69	83q7	Your stance on the issues presented by the information you frequent; a MAJOR indicator of your basic attitude towards most news or happenings on a normal day
154.48	154°29'	129.48	83q6	The ethos / behavior pattern of your primary pet
154.27	154°16'	129.27	83q5	Dynamics passed down (from your parents) to your kids
154.06	154°4'	129.06	83q4	How you announce or pursue your desire to move forward in a practical situation / in your daily duties
153.85	153°51'	128.85	83q3	Who you present as over the phone / over a remote call
153.65	153°39'	128.65	83q2	The world declares you to be this while you are pro-creating
153.44	153°26'	128.44	83q1	Fun-likable dynamics with another
153.23	153°14'	128.23	83q12	The person you gradually march towards becoming in a relationship

153.02	153°1'	128.02	83q11	The substitute for a non-ideal or failed partnership
152.81	152°49'	127.81	83q10	What you allow to happen on your land / in your property
152.6	152°36'	127.6	83q9	How you establish a collective culture
152.4	152°24'	127.4	84q8	Reflecting while one builds—how and when this is done
152.19	152°11'	127.19	84q7	Pressing a strong first impression against the air of the one; wind wall
151.98	151°59'	126.98	84q6	The regular course of business for your partner, how they daily-evolve
151.77	151°46'	126.77	84q5	Your handling of / true expectations regarding the gifts you've been given
151.56	151°34'	126.56	84q4	Spacing out, how it is achieved
151.35	151°21'	126.35	84q3	How you express your thoughts about your working conditions
151.15	151°9'	126.15	84q2	How you drive others to project given that they have engaged you extensively enough
150.94	150°56'	125.94	84q1	The revolutionary fights uphill despite their background
150.73	150°44'	125.73	84q12	Communication or thoughts about others while one is on a challenging journey
150.52	150°31'	125.52	84q11	Basic behavior that comes with your own space
150.31	150°19'	125.31	84q10	Household or small office dynamics which show up when you are regularly involved with a close-knit group in daily affairs; a tell and trigger region for what you are actually able to build as a daily life
150.1	150°6'	125.1	84q9	An activity particular to you which describes your daily life; your unique daily-like activity which follows your lifestyle
149.9	149°54'	124.9	85q8	Elaborating the internal map
149.69	149°41'	124.69	85q7	Your passionate sojourn; where you get to chase a dream in passion
149.48	149°29'	124.48	85q6	The truest energy allowed maximum sprawling expression
149.27	149°16'	124.27	85q5	Your default self-character reinforcement
149.06	149°4'	124.06	85q4	Reflection upon routes you've taken in service to something else, deliberation over affairs you were once medium-term engaged in
148.85	148°51'	123.85	85q3	That which serves as a foundation upon which your public image can be built. This is very likely to be executed by someone else before you. If you do this, you are a foundation for others represented by the 13q3s
148.65	148°39'	123.65	85q2	The subtle or hidden conditions which build the potential for your eventual display of aggressive will
148.44	148°26'	123.44	85q1	How you are directly challenged to keep your lifeline strong; likely against expectations you've picked up in the form of 13q1
148.23	148°14'	123.23	85q12	The apprentice to a powerful person
148.02	148°1'	123.02	85q11	Getting oneself lost in the information of it all, swimming in one's prerogative information
147.81	147°49'	122.81	85q10	One who thinks about or orchestrates the mass movement of people
147.6	147°36'	122.6	85q9	What you do to present yourself as schmoove
147.4	147°24'	122.4	86q8	Someone discloses their secret pain, attribute, or burden to you
147.19	147°11'	122.19	86q7	Sexual release done for esteem purposes or non-co creation; in males, sex with partners you know you are not connected to or don't respect. Where *co*creation isn't actually possible. You're just expected to deliver
146.98	146°59'	121.98	86q6	Financial or status-based power (means-based power) over another—how this is exercised
146.77	146°46'	121.77	86q5	The nature of those whom you see as dominating others
146.56	146°34'	121.56	86q4	When the external world gives you its feedback; affects women differently?
146.35	146°21'	121.35	86q3	Power or values spread as a blanket over a field of participants
146.15	146°9'	121.15	86q2	Those who challenge you head-on
145.94	145°56'	120.94	86q1	Alpha, masculinized, or otherwise potent woman / domain; a domain which challenges its occupants' conceptions
145.73	145°44'	120.73	86q12	How you respond to surprise burdens you can do nothing about... unless you're willing to compromise your life or humanity; your response to big burdens you can only get out of at the cost of your soul
145.52	145°31'	120.52	86q11	One's fallback internal practices for managing something in response to insult, isolation, rejection, or boredom
145.31	145°19'	120.31	86q10	Breaking away from the status quo, yet undeniably innovative
145.1	145°6'	120.1	86q9	Producing art from your creative core; elaborating your surrounding niche with more artifacts from within your unique production process
144.9	144°54'	119.9	87q8	How you go about living in your ideal search space, for better or worse
144.69	144°41'	119.69	87q7	You as the singular focal character(s) around which a big (possibly dramatic) plot revolves
144.48	144°29'	119.48	87q6	You as a current or future divorcé(e)
144.27	144°16'	119.27	87q5	The position through which influential data can be accessed
144.06	144°4'	119.06	87q4	Troubles the family keeps in its collective memory
143.85	143°51'	118.85	87q3	Events that attend your move into a place, sometimes including the retrospective of the places you have moved out of

143.65	143°39'	118.65	87q2	Where you need or receive help from another in managing your daily affairs and where your life is going
143.44	143°26'	118.44	87q1	From the perspective of the would-be victim, when an attack is imminent
143.23	143°14'	118.23	87q12	Preservers of the creative mandate when it is not actively being called upon
143.02	143°1'	118.02	87q11	Where you charge people a fee or impose costs on them to engage what you produce
142.81	142°49'	117.81	87q10	After a trouble phase ends, one sees it as not so bad and is able to do it again
142.6	142°36'	117.6	87q9	A collection of stories associated with the groups over which you iterate
142.4	142°24'	117.4	88q8	You do you; deeds done to assert your unique importance, possibly at the expense of others
142.19	142°11'	117.19	88q7	Accomplishments of the sons or children—especially the most salient
141.98	141°59'	116.98	88q6	Where you are too engaging to be in the conflict, but may be calling attention to it instead
141.77	141°46'	116.77	88q5	Life milestone chapters; the nature of milestone journeys, events, or roles you play which stand to be long citable in your memory
141.56	141°34'	116.56	88q4	What you do a lot more of in your mature state
141.35	141°21'	116.35	88q3	Getting noticed; seems more positive for males, negative for females; | *Ajani's note: need to study more to see if this is a thing*
141.15	141°9'	116.15	88q2	Observing or capturing complex transitions; ongoing observation of existential or at least dramatic state transitions unfolding?
140.94	140°56'	115.94	88q1	Engaging those who assist your creation
140.73	140°44'	115.73	88q12	Definition of "the Club," what it actually looks like to you; the process of engaging the enstatusing environment; clubs you would go to
140.52	140°31'	115.52	88q11	The subtle context for how you get into relationships / partnerships—information which you are (knowingly or unknowingly) pouring over your partner, usually without their knowing what they are signing up for. If you do these things about someone, you may be partnering with them in some way
140.31	140°19'	115.31	88q10	A return to homeostasis or natural form involves this purging process
140.1	140°6'	115.1	88q9	Going out front alongside another; what you can be the first to help others experience
139.9	139°54'	114.9	89q8	Your route to influence via rapport
139.69	139°41'	114.69	89q7	The inner workings of the upper room, backroom opinionation of the decision makers
139.48	139°29'	114.48	89q6	The troubled one processes their troubles
139.27	139°16'	114.27	89q5	What your certified deep bonding requirements are
139.06	139°4'	114.06	89q4	That which you are visibly committed to elaborating; Juno-related
138.85	138°51'	113.85	89q3	Recurring tense area with a foreigner, foreign area, or plain old personality type; 5-5-3, a field (3) sprayed with character(5) sets the character (5)
138.65	138°39'	113.65	89q2	Your character as you address a social ill
138.44	138°26'	113.44	89q1	Politicking via one's true affinities, and what events come with this. Seems to be a critical event which gets you started in social activism
138.23	138°14'	113.23	89q12	How the environment around you handles your most natural behavior
138.02	138°1'	113.02	89q11	Epilogue: what is inclined to happen around you after your main role has ended
137.81	137°49'	112.81	89q10	?What your partner or complementary group does which limits your natural expression?
137.6	137°36'	112.6	89q9	How secession works in your world; how you secede from those close to you and break off your own culture
137.4	137°24'	112.4	90q8	How you present / impose your influence powers upon another, using yourself or character as a weapon; the endowment made visible, decreasing the other's will to fight
137.19	137°11'	112.19	90q7	The interaction through which one solves their chosen problem activity for fun
136.98	136°59'	111.98	90q6	Nature of the work done in one's fun / natural problem-solving choices
136.77	136°46'	111.77	90q5	What you focus on projecting / building up in the privacy of your own company (especially in your own home)
136.56	136°34'	111.56	90q4	The organization of certain things that makes you feel better about their containing circumstances
136.35	136°21'	111.35	90q3	Your experience of funerals
136.15	136°9'	111.15	90q2	How you watch someone else at work, assessing and possibly interrupting them
135.94	135°56'	110.94	90q1	Where you perceive yourself as unready, how you handle this; how you work to get something ready when you feel it is not
135.73	135°44'	110.73	90q12	The shenanigans of someone close to you whose actions you can't completely contain
135.52	135°31'	110.52	90q11	Where you feel the pressure to make a certain institutional thing happen
135.31	135°19'	110.31	90q10	Deep feelings you hold for or against a certain kind of person. Your prejudices (towards or against)
135.1	135°6'	110.1	90q9	How you expand the reach of your social agenda. Not necessarily your actual social network, just your agenda for socializing others into your own paradigm. 90q9 = 5d6q9: engaging cultures (9) using joining (6) with 1:1 interaction as the context (5)
134.9	134°54'	109.9	91q8	...that this experience may live up to what the institution promises
134.69	134°41'	109.69	91q7	Duty borne of circumstances, not from within the one performing

134.48	134°29'	109.48	91q6	Visiting the homes of your benefactors or successful forebears
134.27	134°16'	109.27	91q5	How a vote of no confidence in your creativity plays out—when someone doesn't believe you are up to the task
134.06	134°4'	109.06	91q4	Those who feel like home
133.85	133°51'	108.85	91q3	Your designated partner or close friend, out of reach; this qunit is creepy, and has something to do with the dead or dying
133.65	133°39'	108.65	91q2	Where the visionary comes from in your life
133.44	133°26'	108.44	91q1	The spirit that surrounds or overtakes one
133.23	133°14'	108.23	91q12	Where another party puts a stop to your meanderings in favor of a single strict direction
133.02	133°1'	108.02	91q11	Your role in your family
132.81	132°49'	107.81	91q10	An overall map of the many spaces; seems to denote copies of her feminine energy; | *Ajani's note: hypothesizing a relationship to one's eggs*
132.6	132°36'	107.6	91q9	How you settle an unresolved issue, giving it a second chance and sticking with it; as in Shalamar - Second time around
132.4	132°24'	107.4	92q8	You versus the army against you, what happens
132.19	132°11'	107.19	92q7	Those whom the army leader can rally; the counterparts who back or oppose the army's leader—those whom the leader shines their spotlight attention upon
131.98	131°59'	106.98	92q6	How situations that were once very difficult eventually pass into memory
131.77	131°46'	106.77	92q5	What you do which draws out others' consternation in light of how they have seen you communicate something (often impersonally sweeping); where others see you as having disregarded their wishes or feelings
131.56	131°34'	106.56	92q4	Where you witness someone out of their mind or making no sense
131.35	131°21'	106.35	92q3	When you are tasked to keep order, however this is done
131.15	131°9'	106.15	92q2	Your creative battle buddy's central dilemma at some point
130.94	130°56'	105.94	92q1	The other person has access to riches or the means to something—how this relates to your situation
130.73	130°44'	105.73	92q12	That which keeps coming back in blatant disregard for whether certain witnesses want them there or view them as tacky
130.52	130°31'	105.52	92q11	A dramatic story you convey to others, especially one which involves your partners and certain situations compelled by your association with them
130.31	130°19'	105.31	92q10	The experience that comes with your being regulated by your primary sexual or co-creative partner
130.1	130°6'	105.1	92q9	The dilemmas your co-creators put you into, which may be better kept secret from them or anyone else
129.9	129°54'	104.9	93q8	Your encounters with the gruesome, disgusting, or graphic; the span of hidden or unknown features to be found throughout a realm
129.69	129°41'	104.69	93q7	Where and how you merge into or reflect nature
129.48	129°29'	104.48	93q6	The interrogator, scrutinizer, or spotlighter who is in a position to put someone else in a corner and exact performance from them
129.27	129°16'	104.27	93q5	The event which constitutes the loss or phasing out of a previous stage of events
129.06	129°4'	104.06	93q4	Your stardom- or power-hungry friends. May also include you
128.85	128°51'	103.85	93q3	A different model experience / cultural contributor compared to what you started with; when you move away from the root, the culture you get
128.65	128°39'	103.65	93q2	The idealized social interaction template that hovers just outside of your "aura"
128.44	128°26'	103.44	93q1	A bid to display one's power as a form of introduction; flexin'
128.23	128°14'	103.23	93q12	Those who conquer territory for you, reflecting your spirit of imperialism
128.02	128°1'	103.02	93q11	The arsenal, the crew that rolls deep; fam
127.81	127°49'	102.81	93q10	Who you are seen as with respect to those gatekeepers who let you into the battle; a TRIGGER qunit
127.6	127°36'	102.6	93q9	How you display your ambitions, or harness them
127.4	127°24'	102.4	94q8	When you are desperate, how you behave
127.19	127°11'	102.19	94q7	The values pressured upon you by a place or situation
126.98	126°59'	101.98	94q6	How you feel about new learners—what you experience when this is happening
126.77	126°46'	101.77	94q5	One who keeps the mob or the collective at bay
126.56	126°34'	101.56	94q4	Who stands out among a gathering of semi-familiar people
126.35	126°21'	101.35	94q3	The foundation which supports you. Naturally, there was a price paid in building it
126.15	126°9'	101.15	94q2	Private events which you record privately
125.94	125°56'	100.94	94q1	The story of your struggle while others don't believe in you
125.73	125°44'	100.73	94q12	The team or circumstances you are a part of which lend reality to another's ideas or intentions
125.52	125°31'	100.52	94q11	Passing things onto their display shelves
125.31	125°19'	100.31	94q10	You participation in the process of commerce, patronage, and the role of a customer
125.1	125°6'	100.1	94q9	Circumstances which clarify your ambitions worth seeking

124.9	124°54'	99.896	95q8	The institution puts several restrictions on / sets a number of boundaries around what you intend to do
124.69	124°41'	99.688	95q7	Connecting with someone via favored information
124.48	124°29'	99.479	95q6	What another serves you with in order to help you fall in line or get your stuff together
124.27	124°16'	99.271	95q5	How someone with a particular kind of authority challenges you
124.06	124°4'	99.063	95q4	How you feel about interacting with principles; also, a panoramic work of art
123.85	123°51'	98.854	95q3	Family entertainment; where you enjoy entertainment time with your kindred
123.65	123°39'	98.646	95q2	You as an interlocutor responding to kindred—especially how you show them you know what you're talking about or affirm your take on where they are coming from
123.44	123°26'	98.438	95q1	A uniquely you, nonmainstream activity you enjoy participating in, especially after hours
123.23	123°14'	98.229	95q12	That which sponsors your growing display of uniqueness—especially wide-market economically; could be considered one of your best client bases
123.02	123°1'	98.021	95q11	Hanging out with your childhood friends
122.81	122°49'	97.813	95q10	Where you take advantage of an opportunity to see if a situation is influenceable by you, or if you can get something out of a situation where most of the control of what people do belongs elsewhere
122.6	122°36'	97.604	95q9	How you were as a child under your parents' family
122.4	122°24'	97.396	96q8	The overarching problems you struggle against as a social actor
122.19	122°11'	97.188	96q7	That which drives your social action forward
121.98	121°59'	96.979	96q6	The events which constitute your personal story framework, filtering what can and can't happen around you in any significant way
121.77	121°46'	96.771	96q5	How you control both sides of an event space
121.56	121°34'	96.563	96q4	One who withholds their gifts or contributions until you perform as they demand; that one event where you met your best friend or your destiny—that which would travel with you ever after. This event is highly unlikely to happen more than once in remotely the same way, unless you have asteroids to the contrary
121.35	121°21'	96.354	96q3	A very long-running soapbox or pet cause
121.15	121°9'	96.146	96q2	Therapeutic environments, havens
120.94	120°56'	95.938	96q1	Your actual creation or invention process—what comes with it
120.73	120°44'	95.729	96q12	Taking your situation into your own hands
120.52	120°31'	95.521	96q11	The fate of the villains in your experience
120.31	120°19'	95.313	96q10	What the opposite sex or co-creator partner brings to your table
120.1	120°6'	95.104	96q9	How you administer your world in light of your victory or attainment of a significant goal
119.9	119°54'	94.896	97q8	Characteristics passed through lineage. In ethnicities and other classes for whom lineage matters, comes with minority standing. See 61q8, 25q8, and 133q8
119.69	119°41'	94.688	97q7	What you do which affirms that you still have the background support
119.48	119°29'	94.479	97q6	The responses of those who believe you have made moves on them
119.27	119°16'	94.271	97q5	The final imposition of your notion of victory onto everything
119.06	119°4'	94.063	97q4	What your guest does to get you to kick them out
118.85	118°51'	93.854	97q3	How your guest handles separating from you
118.65	118°39'	93.646	97q2	Your picky preferences for a full-fledged asserter. I suspect this is the quint of your strictest partner ideal; possibly your relationship with the mother or father of your child—if there is one
118.44	118°26'	93.438	97q1	What you say to challenge your children; their approach to enterprise
118.23	118°14'	93.229	97q12	Your creations' children's inner process for producing work
118.02	118°1'	93.021	97q11	Processes you engage outside of your partner's notice
117.81	117°49'	92.813	97q10	When you have rank, how you show that you're amused or express that you've been entertained? Ideas you are excited about spreading to anyone you encounter
117.6	117°36'	92.604	97q9	Your children's or creations' creations—the process employed by the former to generate the latter
117.4	117°24'	92.396	98q8	Deliberation which leads to a concentrated direction; something like "a decision"
117.19	117°11'	92.188	98q7	Your role on the timeline away from core family
116.98	116°59'	91.979	98q6	How idealized stardom works for you; an ambition region
116.77	116°46'	91.771	98q5	Manager mode—what the manager process looks like to you
116.56	116°34'	91.563	98q4	The circumstances which recover your health after you have been hit with insult
116.35	116°21'	91.354	98q3	When you no longer have a pressing need to collect, WHO you are
116.15	116°9'	91.146	98q2	Your childhood experiences which directly influence the adult relational preferences you are constantly returning to
115.94	115°56'	90.938	98q1	The energy that is stirred up whenever people remotely close to you donate their interaction energy—what you turn such information into
115.73	115°44'	90.729	98q12	How you exhaust your body vitality
115.52	115°31'	90.521	98q11	The shape of your body appeal is driven by this region as a motivator
115.31	115°19'	90.313	98q10	When you're all grown up, what changes

115.1	115°6'	90.104	98q9	Health problems experienced by you, especially amid a frustrated push
114.9	114°54'	89.896	99q8	Security asked for or provided through partnership
114.69	114°41'	89.688	99q7	How you see examples of recursion in action
114.48	114°29'	89.479	99q6	The strongest foundational support that another can provide you; seems to render you dependent on whether the other wants to do this for you at all or even tell you what it is they want in exchange. Strongly out of your control, yet something in you is very broken if you don't get it—similar to a kind of food. How are you about providing the necessary food to others, though they likely have nothing to give back and you will be drained by giving it to them?
114.27	114°16'	89.271	99q5	How you manifest uncertainty, from a point of insecurity
114.06	114°4'	89.063	99q4	More power or ability passed to you from someone who has it
113.85	113°51'	88.854	99q3	What the children become in light of their mother. A female's effect on small groups; how a male aims to interact with his partners or receiving spaces. Clearly the masculinization
113.65	113°39'	88.646	99q2	How people are stirred in light of your having shown your intensity to them
113.44	113°26'	88.438	99q1	What males assert; what females define entrants as asserting; ESSENTIAL maleness or femaleness
113.23	113°14'	88.229	99q12	Thoughts about what the sex partner is prepared to give?
113.02	113°1'	88.021	99q11	Your close doubted person has clear effects on your auric events and attitudes
112.81	112°49'	87.813	99q10	How out of control environments or moods end up getting resolved for you
112.6	112°36'	87.604	99q9	When you take responsibility
112.4	112°24'	87.396	100q8	What you keep working to have even more capacity for
112.19	112°11'	87.188	100q7	How you are when you want your way over others'
111.98	111°59'	86.979	100q6	Your long term plan for pursuing the things you ceaselessly want to want even more of
111.77	111°46'	86.771	100q5	That which you engage in order to play out your penchant for mischief vicariously (through someone else, as they make the mischief for you)
111.56	111°34'	86.563	100q4	How your children treat you or see you as a parent
111.35	111°21'	86.354	100q3	The interrelationships you explore privately, especially when at home or when watching your children
111.15	111°9'	86.146	100q2	How you spend your deep alone-time
110.94	110°56'	85.938	100q1	How others interrupt your process or what they are inclined to experience when they do; interruptive circumstances themselves?
110.73	110°44'	85.729	100q12	The impression your presence leaves on a room, or what you are doing when people address your ongoing presence in a room
110.52	110°31'	85.521	100q11	One's first child or major known creation—how this one fares in the home
110.31	110°19'	85.313	100q10	Sibling dynamics, events involving the brothers, sisters, and sibling-like characters in one's life
110.1	110°6'	85.104	100q9	Events or characters whom your body attracts; associated with physical appeal to certain partners
109.9	109°54'	84.896	101q8	Admonitions triggered by something believed about what is being seen; for me this happens when an argument has hit a peak and the interaction in settling into its deathbed
109.69	109°41'	84.688	101q7	How you played make-believe when you were young; definitely related to how sociable you would become later on
109.48	109°29'	84.479	101q6	The issue over which built-up conflicts or the need to introduce one's imagination comes to a head
109.27	109°16'	84.271	101q5	Looking over the horizon past the current exchange, however this is done
109.06	109°4'	84.063	101q4	The orchestrator or settings-maker for your childhood play scenarios
108.85	108°51'	83.854	101q3	Doing what one has to do, last ditch rule-breaking tactics—especially by normally good people—to get out of a bad situation
108.65	108°39'	83.646	101q2	How a parental or caretaking relationship wanes
108.44	108°26'	83.438	101q1	Cleanup—gathering things back together, especially after a mess has been made
108.23	108°14'	83.229	101q12	Your rememberers, your audience: the troubles or tradeoffs that come with a certain increased empowerment, those who look to you
108.02	108°1'	83.021	101q11	What bombardment looks like—whether you are a participant or a witness in it; seems to indicate an exploded blend of some sort
107.81	107°49'	82.813	101q10	Parental dynamics which you yourself may absorb
107.6	107°36'	82.604	101q9	That sometimes-idea which intrudes upon your world and causes inconvenience, or your ideas that attend such intrusions
107.4	107°24'	82.396	102q8	Where others must take time to learn how to limit or control your overzealousness or your indulgence
107.19	107°11'	82.188	102q7	The outlook you had while growing up—where everything was relatively new and you were freer to move on passion
106.98	106°59'	81.979	102q6	Piles of artifacts from your administrative affairs and how you are responsible for tending to them or cleaning them up
106.77	106°46'	81.771	102q5	How your partner elects to play with you; a GREAT tell region for who you belong with
106.56	106°34'	81.563	102q4	How your family circle broadly behaves. This describes the roles of several people

106.35	106°21'	81.354	102q3	How you host works or the kinds of tours you participate in when hosting works
106.15	106°9'	81.146	102q2	Where you willingly absorb your surrounding influences and let yourself be susceptible to their programming
105.94	105°56'	80.938	102q1	Where certain communication paths of yours are restricted, prohibited, or just strongly structured
105.73	105°44'	80.729	102q12	Help that must simply come to you in order to advance a key piece of your goals
105.52	105°31'	80.521	102q11	Information you feed yourself with routinely, and what happens when this occurs
105.31	105°19'	80.313	102q10	How you behave when you're not quite sure of your own abilities; self-doubt
105.1	105°6'	80.104	102q9	The tactics or traits that you develop in your teens, as defenses or responses during adulthood; Phase two of one's creative development?
104.9	104°54'	79.896	103q8	Shows of devotion to one's preferred council group
104.69	104°41'	79.688	103q7	The experience you participate in which teaches you much about how power works
104.48	104°29'	79.479	103q6	The emergence of a leader or authority through hardships
104.27	104°16'	79.271	103q5	A space which summarizes what your social relationships should be, if not for certain fundamental character barriers (by you or others) in the way; where you go (or I go) when your social situations are less than ideal, constituting a model for what it is you actually want your social setup to provide
104.06	104°4'	79.063	103q4	Longing; when you wish your communication outlets were better or wish you had a more solid person to talk to about your actual wants
103.85	103°51'	78.854	103q3	Forgoing the comrade in favor of the land or context
103.65	103°39'	78.646	103q2	Another party is called to order
103.44	103°26'	78.438	103q1	The summary of another's activities that everyone sees, or your response in light of them
103.23	103°14'	78.229	103q12	Something or someone you rely on goes off and does crazy stuff
103.02	103°1'	78.021	103q11	A mighty presence regulates your affairs in your place
102.81	102°49'	77.813	103q10	Relationships you shouldn't be having, where you choose to stand with someone who will bring you or others trouble later down the line, or maybe they themselves are just troubled
102.6	102°36'	77.604	103q9	Formalizing an attached relationship after the bf/gf phase, establishing its climate
102.4	102°24'	77.396	104q8	From the underground, encroachment. How do you possibly handle this?; also, how others respond to the sexual or creative environment you set up
102.19	102°11'	77.188	104q7	"What is this!?" holding up contraband as one processes something they deem unbelievable
101.98	101°59'	76.979	104q6	Working one's tail off to make sense of a mess of social inputs
101.77	101°46'	76.771	104q5	Relationships which look like they could be marriages, but fail
101.56	101°34'	76.563	104q4	Going on learning journeys; seems to show how intimacy is built up around you. Paid a lot less attention to in males than females
101.35	101°21'	76.354	104q3	How you vent the tension you've held within as the result of conflict
101.15	101°9'	76.146	104q2	The battle meant to evolve you, but a battle nonetheless (single creation, not co-creation)
100.94	100°56'	75.938	104q1	Where your will is subordinated to your rivals or some other (ideally) complementary party. It matters greatly whether you chose this willingly
100.73	100°44'	75.729	104q12	When unsupported or non-exchanging with another, how you create as a solo singleton
100.52	100°31'	75.521	104q11	Those who steal from you or freeride off of what is yours
100.31	100°19'	75.313	104q10	The spark of energy you provide to a context
100.1	100°6'	75.104	104q9	Attempting to take something back
99.896	99°54'	74.896	105q8	Who you're interested in inflicting your lifestyle journey upon
99.688	99°41'	74.688	105q7	Interactions where the ideal lifestyle / bucket list is discussed
99.479	99°29'	74.479	105q6	Steps taken towards realizing what some have described as the ideal lifestyle
99.271	99°16'	74.271	105q5	[Where you are] or [the behavior you naturally wander towards] in building the idealized lifestyle
99.063	99°4'	74.063	105q4	Who you model your lifestyle pursuit after
98.854	98°51'	73.854	105q3	What comes with your assessment of the forward progress of your friends or niche mates
98.646	98°39'	73.646	105q2	How you present yourself as a liver of the idealized lifestyle, or how you do this in order to build such a lifestyle with another
98.438	98°26'	73.438	105q1	How you set out on a particular lifestyle/bucket list adventure for the first time
98.229	98°14'	73.229	105q12	Situations which enable pursuit of the idealized lifestyle
98.021	98°1'	73.021	105q11	Who's talking as the ideal lifestyle is being pursued
97.813	97°49'	72.813	105q10	The nature of pauses and stopping points along the path of lifestyle chasing
97.604	97°36'	72.604	105q9	The situation under which the lifestyle pursuit is undertaken
97.396	97°24'	72.396	106q8	The providers of your first sexual / co-creative experiences of a certain kind; the means through which you imposed child-izing / reductionist punishments upon yourself
97.188	97°11'	72.188	106q7	Your allies in the fight against self-limitation; those interactants which, ironically, attract the limiting side of your intentions

96.979	96°59'	71.979	106q6	The steps you take which lead you to self-limitation via your intentions; if you must use this region, try doing so *carefully*
96.771	96°46'	71.771	106q5	The character which serves to draw out the limiting sides of your own dreams; this is the Hinderer in your Cancer-10
96.563	96°34'	71.563	106q4	What one is aiming for which eventually drives their self-limitation; the aims that attract adversaries to you
96.354	96°21'	71.354	106q3	One's chain of thought correlated with self intention-limitation
96.146	96°9'	71.146	106q2	The cited nature of the self-limitation
95.938	95°56'	70.938	106q1	The view or action held by the agent who brings out the self-limitation
95.729	95°44'	70.729	106q12	How your self-limitation process is described by those whom you cannot see
95.521	95°31'	70.521	106q11	The various actors involved in your self-limitation
95.313	95°19'	70.313	106q10	Straight up mistakes which sponsor your self-limitation via intentions
95.104	95°6'	70.104	106q9	What the other person does to engage your self-limitation
94.896	94°54'	69.896	107q8	Your expectations for the kind of help you would ideally want for your 35q8s
94.688	94°41'	69.688	107q7	[Convincing to] or [convincing during] travel—what the foreign has which someone or some context says you need
94.479	94°29'	69.479	107q6	A kind of contribution to or scanning of the society at large
94.271	94°16'	69.271	107q5	The unfolding of your evolution in the world
94.063	94°4'	69.063	107q4	Correction of bad or ill-chosen paths, how it is done
93.854	93°51'	68.854	107q3	Who you are (or would be) as a top communicator
93.646	93°39'	68.646	107q2	The adventure that you surely lived out—at least for a little while
93.438	93°26'	68.438	107q1	Attributes you have which may frustrate others' expectations, especially if you're male
93.229	93°14'	68.229	107q12	Themes which surround you and keep your sense of self-value high
93.021	93°1'	68.021	107q11	The embodiment of your box; an indicator of what others see as your home turf
92.813	92°49'	67.813	107q10	Your alone activities on your home turf, when more interpersonal interactions are blocked
92.604	92°36'	67.604	107q9	The nature of recuperation on one's home turf
92.396	92°24'	67.396	108q8	Actions or intentions to counter enemies, rivals, or naysayers in the background
92.188	92°11'	67.188	108q7	A critical other-half spheremate whose role may explain half of your spiritual objectives in a situation
91.979	91°59'	66.979	108q6	The "need for achievement" (of a certain kind)—how to feel the pressure to reach some goal
91.771	91°46'	66.771	108q5	The evolution of some external or imagined character through whom you may play out certain ideals which are difficult to realize on your own
91.563	91°34'	66.563	108q4	Where one is tasked to go outside of another's rules and build status
91.354	91°21'	66.354	108q3	The impression you give when obligated to engage something you know you are not aligned with or are actively disinvested in
91.146	91°9'	66.146	108q2	What happens to you / your experience after conflict
90.938	90°56'	65.938	108q1	Your deepest sought scenario for intimacy—whether you know it or not
90.729	90°44'	65.729	108q12	What partnership leaves you wanting, fantasizing about
90.521	90°31'	65.521	108q11	Remote actions by a party disallowed in your dimension which nonetheless influences your path
90.313	90°19'	65.313	108q10	What you fall back on building when there is no other mandated activity in the moment; seems to reflect leisure. A trigger
90.104	90°6'	65.104	108q9	Downtime segue period which reorganizes one's interacted energies after a major experience
89.896	89°54'	64.896	109q8	Optimistic or hopeful retelling of trial or travels
89.688	89°41'	64.688	109q7	Seems to be the aftermath or postmortem of sexual / co-creative release
89.479	89°29'	64.479	109q6	The freezing or event stopping process triggered by those who normally pass by you
89.271	89°16'	64.271	109q5	What is done after a struggle / conflict has died down or done in order to MAKE a struggle die down
89.063	89°4'	64.063	109q4	The kinds of traffic or activity you like to have implied going on around you
88.854	88°51'	63.854	109q3	Deciding on a path and going all the way on it
88.646	88°39'	63.646	109q2	The activities a person might participate in with you as they get to know you
88.438	88°26'	63.438	109q1	How you express your interpersonal charismatic value; the things you do to increase your social worth
88.229	88°14'	63.229	109q12	This is fun or relaxation time... but seriously, let's get to work
88.021	88°1'	63.021	109q11	Your interaction with a situation which changes your life
87.813	87°49'	62.813	109q10	The life-changing event begins here
87.604	87°36'	62.604	109q9	Diagnostic or scrutinizing writing separating what really belongs where
87.396	87°24'	62.396	110q8	The kinds of secrets your major allies will not show to you, but which likely affect your standing in their eyes, limiting how deeply they relate to you in an area
87.188	87°11'	62.188	110q7	The circumstances which describe how—though you may be drawn to another in a kind of mutual intimacy—failure to attain closeness is HIGHLY likely

86.979	86°59'	61.979	110q6	Reconciliation of lies or illusion happens in this way; also, the aftermath of sex or co-creation with someone who was (likely unknowingly) with you in order to answer the pressures they felt for accomplishment
86.771	86°46'	61.771	110q5	The event that announces no further recourse? A dead end to an arrangement
86.563	86°34'	61.563	110q4	The battle buddy; the kinds of close associations you need as you build—characteristics they should and should not have
86.354	86°21'	61.354	110q3	Your deep response to something you've seen and may pity
86.146	86°9'	61.146	110q2	Near those who assert a kind of freedom—especially as seen through the eyes of outsiders
85.938	85°56'	60.938	110q1	How the practice of discussing problems plays out as a predictable process
85.729	85°44'	60.729	110q12	The subtle way that powerfully constrains how a situation unfolds; rules of the playing field
85.521	85°31'	60.521	110q11	Silent underground penetration of an agenda
85.313	85°19'	60.313	110q10	How you set up situations rather than performing direct actions to advance your agenda—especially in light of a challenge
85.104	85°6'	60.104	110q9	They bring out-in-the-open-drama
84.896	84°54'	59.896	111q8	The moment you've been waiting for—one's greatest creation
84.688	84°41'	59.688	111q7	Those who sponsor the prohibition on connection, even if it is your connection with themselves
84.479	84°29'	59.479	111q6	Someone else's original work left undone: what aspects of it will need to be revisited when it is looked at again
84.271	84°16'	59.271	111q5	Bookstores, book sales, and spaces full of individuals' personal brands turned into a space;	*Ajani's note: an interesting analogy to jazz*
84.063	84°4'	59.063	111q4	The various accomplishments of your family. May be very useful in studying the Gauquelin birth data
83.854	83°51'	58.854	111q3	Father or battler in your local experience of a family unit. Useful in the Gauquelin family data
83.646	83°39'	58.646	111q2	The types of people you welcome into your personal family
83.438	83°26'	58.438	111q1	Where you are the administrator of affairs and judge of how things actually went
83.229	83°14'	58.229	111q12	One who assists the formation of your domestic establishment
83.021	83°1'	58.021	111q11	Your seducer in action
82.813	82°49'	57.813	111q10	How you get involved with a colorful diversity of characters
82.604	82°36'	57.604	111q9	An interaction between two warrants some serious thinking, especially in light of how outsiders weigh in on it
82.396	82°24'	57.396	112q8	The publication of secrets; getting caught, seen, or witnessed doing a secretive thing; people in on this region may truly be open to your dirt
82.188	82°11'	57.188	112q7	The aspect of partnership or union which you avoid or dislike strongly... but what if you really need to agree to this?...
81.979	81°59'	56.979	112q6	Who really surrounds you in your attempts to express, when push comes to shove
81.771	81°46'	56.771	112q5	That which you grow up to be familiar with, and are inclined to eventually give despite what your partner may want from you
81.563	81°34'	56.563	112q4	Bringing order to a disordered (especially social or affinity-based) terrain
81.354	81°21'	56.354	112q3	How you select clothing or dress; how you dress yourself. In some cases, how you interface with it
81.146	81°9'	56.146	112q2	Talk-worthy guest appearance; how people talk about you as a guest in light of expectations, or how you steer the talk about guests. (is this a masculine/feminine -biased region?)
80.938	80°56'	55.938	112q1	Finding something inherently appealing (though apparently complex) in a far off place away from those normally close to you; even your close friends may not understand your reasoning here
80.729	80°44'	55.729	112q12	Panic in a productive direction, or handling of someone else's panic; shaky stability maintained
80.521	80°31'	55.521	112q11	Who you ally with in order to separate yourself from family; seems to be associated with victimization at the hands of another, specifically a foreign intruder OR where you go in league with a foreign intruder to mess up something you have
80.313	80°19'	55.313	112q10	Unshared lifestyles which circumscribe your goals for your own by comparison; the life that your level-up driver leads or the background which they hail from
80.104	80°6'	55.104	112q9	Raised energy atop the otherwise silent background
79.896	79°54'	54.896	113q8	Detached / arm's length activity or influence
79.688	79°41'	54.688	113q7	How you display your riches or display that you have such; what you're doing when tending to the assets you have; how you look at the assets, things of value, or money you have acquired
79.479	79°29'	54.479	113q6	The one whose unsettled sentiment needs to be resolved
79.271	79°16'	54.271	113q5	Documenting or being documented in a search
79.063	79°4'	54.063	113q4	When people do this cluster on your behalf, then you have true power
78.854	78°51'	53.854	113q3	How you play out your basic role towards your key cast of characters; CRITICAL for watching in another's chart to see if they want you in their cast
78.646	78°39'	53.646	113q2	Your deepest family attachment

78.438	78°26'	53.438	113q1	How you handle your bullies
78.229	78°14'	53.229	113q12	A major difference of opinion with a partner
78.021	78°1'	53.021	113q11	How the context changes after a major transition out of something
77.813	77°49'	52.813	113q10	Hero dynamics, a hero of the people
77.604	77°36'	52.604	113q9	A powerful woman; a mother asserting over everyone—the matriarch
77.396	77°24'	52.396	114q8	Home enterprises—especially in houses you don't own;
77.188	77°11'	52.188	114q7	Typical moment-marking events sponsored by your life partner or domestic companion—how they mark what time it is
76.979	76°59'	51.979	114q6	Where you are faced with a growing-up decision; those who force join-frames onto you from outside of your own; related to cats
76.771	76°46'	51.771	114q5	A significant attachment to you which is a constant source of irritation
76.563	76°34'	51.563	114q4	Reckless acts that may yet be forgiven
76.354	76°21'	51.354	114q3	The (often brief) airing of your discontent or approval
76.146	76°9'	51.146	114q2	Someone whom everyone in your world wants to get behind; HOME of Massalia?
75.938	75°56'	50.938	114q1	Aspect of your life which elicits awe for its extensive not-givin'-a-shit in the things that it pushes for
75.729	75°44'	50.729	114q12	People presuming familiarity with you—perhaps overly so
75.521	75°31'	50.521	114q11	The citations of one who believes things need to go their way
75.313	75°19'	50.313	114q10	That which precedes an upcoming substitution of how one makes an impression
75.104	75°6'	50.104	114q9	Steps taken to become the ultimate powerful woman or domain
74.896	74°54'	49.896	115q8	The one around you who, though they may not be the easiest to relate to, can be relied upon to keep progress going
74.688	74°41'	49.688	115q7	Things that happen in your favor to let detractors know that you aren't dead yet (in terms of accomplishment)
74.479	74°29'	49.479	115q6	The automatic or easy acquisition of another who pairs with you, assisting in the pursuit of your wants
74.271	74°16'	49.271	115q5	Your explorations of non-native territories
74.063	74°4'	49.063	115q4	Passionate communication where at least one party doesn't appear to really believe in the other (behind the scenes)
73.854	73°51'	48.854	115q3	When you now know that the present advancing relationship alongside a central other or group of others is not sustainable
73.646	73°39'	48.646	115q2	The agent or situation which carries a process into death or being discarded
73.438	73°26'	48.438	115q1	A thing you will eventually reminisce about, stopped at some point
73.229	73°14'	48.229	115q12	Powers had by associated interactants to override you; when your notion of assertion is rendered ineffective
73.021	73°1'	48.021	115q11	What you do to render it unwise for others to want to fight you. But if you show them you are losing interest in this, the fights may begin
72.813	72°49'	47.813	115q10	Your prime coworking, daily duties counterpart or collaborative space
72.604	72°36'	47.604	115q9	How your coworking group is generally seen. Seems to have an affinity with at least three people
72.396	72°24'	47.396	116q8	The methods of progressing a situation which you admire or love to see
72.188	72°11'	47.188	116q7	Family financial and asset management. May extend to small business money management
71.979	71°59'	46.979	116q6	Administrative support function to rescue or define an unclear situation
71.771	71°46'	46.771	116q5	What the mandate of the fixer role (a leader type) feels like. When you do this, your interactant stands to be the fixer
71.563	71°34'	46.563	116q4	The qunit of your memoirs or biography—especially the parts describing your separation from family; a mysterious region which gives you a GOOD clue as to who in your family dies first or dies before or after you; definitely related to the account given after a family member's death, whether or not that is you, a partner to you, or a sibling
71.354	71°21'	46.354	116q3	Rebuttal; inclined response to circumstances others try to put you into
71.146	71°9'	46.146	116q2	Outer spill of the hesitancy or doubt on your inner mind
70.938	70°56'	45.938	116q1	A dark past yields to a more illuminated aftermath which we can now more safely navigate; is this associated with rising into consciousness from nonconscious sleep?
70.729	70°44'	45.729	116q12	Flamboyancy or exaggerated character used to influence others' impressions
70.521	70°31'	45.521	116q11	Social activity which drains the energy of you or your representative
70.313	70°19'	45.313	116q10	How you reinforce the memory of your deepest companions
70.104	70°6'	45.104	116q9	Your accomplice in becoming well-known, or you as the accomplice to such a party
69.896	69°54'	44.896	117q8	Having to go back and try again with more information
69.688	69°41'	44.688	117q7	The body's preparation to be a parent. Opposite 45q7, may facilitate an "oh shit, what do we do?" in others
69.479	69°29'	44.479	117q6	How you re-frame the niched story of your detail-oriented (daily) work or interaction concepts
69.271	69°16'	44.271	117q5	Your mental escape methods

69.063	69°4'	44.063	117q4	How you learn to be tough in the face of / as the representative of an institution
68.854	68°51'	43.854	117q3	Far and wide pronouncements, especially regarding complements to which one is committed / commitment partners
68.646	68°39'	43.646	117q2	Going back to the drawing board because of a family act which needs to be corrected
68.438	68°26'	43.438	117q1	Seems to indicate a lifepath-altering decision to engage or not engage something; hypothesis: writing, schools, acting? Verified - this is acting… "the *Gone With The Wind* qunit"
68.229	68°14'	43.229	117q12	Your limbo state between jobs or at the end of major endeavors—entering at least a temporary retirement
68.021	68°1'	43.021	117q11	What is needed for you to smooth over places of former tension
67.813	67°49'	42.813	117q10	With the persistent / memorable patterned presence in another's story
67.604	67°36'	42.604	117q9	Public unrefined theatrics; outbursts which others can see, though the temper-loser may well be in the wrong
67.396	67°24'	42.396	118q8	How you feel about your partner's response or how you respond to their response when first exposed to you sexually
67.188	67°11'	42.188	118q7	What your responsiveness teaches your potential partners to feel about sex with you
66.979	66°59'	41.979	118q6	Considerations the potential partner has when contemplating sex with you
66.771	66°46'	41.771	118q5	Freezing outside surroundings in their tracks or keeping other's behavior in check; your behavior kept in check given something done to you in front of outsiders
66.563	66°34'	41.563	118q4	Your attachment to the bad guy
66.354	66°21'	41.354	118q3	Critical-eye observation of or by those [information / multi-party dialogue] sources close to you
66.146	66°9'	41.146	118q2	How the female energies seek relief from pressure; similar to Pluto felt by one's containing domain—may be square a Pluto-like dominion qunit
65.938	65°56'	40.938	118q1	The forever-affixed (seems to be mainly female) partner
65.729	65°44'	40.729	118q12	The wall presented to outsiders by a collective or institution of which you are a part
65.521	65°31'	40.521	118q11	The process that checks or blocks your progress
65.313	65°19'	40.313	118q10	The character of those who will ultimately take from you; perhaps how you take from others
65.104	65°6'	40.104	118q9	A path which is uniquely yours and uniquely correct for you; home ruled by the North Node; seems to be a kind of personal Time
64.896	64°54'	39.896	119q8	How you and your friend build up or add to your joint dwelling or niche-space
64.688	64°41'	39.688	119q7	The commander of forces, more likely an asserter; is at least listened to if they don't garner respect
64.479	64°29'	39.479	119q6	How you perform your regular course-of-business duties in arranging stuff in your world 119q6 => (3d11)q6=>doing arrangements/joining (6) using cross-talk (11) with field-defining as context (3)
64.271	64°16'	39.271	119q5	A call to action, getting others on your side, signing on with someone, despite being more committed to some additional idea than one is to them
64.063	64°4'	39.063	119q4	Going into work for yourself
63.854	63°51'	38.854	119q3	Traveling through (or past), spurring talk, noise, or conflict in the process
63.646	63°39'	38.646	119q2	What you may need to avoid becoming if you want your dynamics with others to remain healthy
63.438	63°26'	38.438	119q1	Your unlikable qualities, off-putting when you approach certain people's orbit
63.229	63°14'	38.229	119q12	How you spread your work in the world
63.021	63°1'	38.021	119q11	Informational aesthetics—the talk inspired by occupants just at the edge of your orbit. When people enter your personal zone, what they tend to start talking about first; your "Welcome To…" sign. People who don't know of this conversation tend not to know how to locate you in some daily practical way. People who do know this may have an easier time getting you to air your real opinions about where they are
62.813	62°49'	37.813	119q10	Those who present healing solutions to your problems
62.604	62°36'	37.604	119q9	Your approach to the maintenance of friendships or partnerships
62.396	62°24'	37.396	120q8	Aspirational decoration; how you decorate your environment with reflections of the kind of life you want to live / what you would have in your idealized life
62.188	62°11'	37.188	120q7	The start of retirement, exiting a zone
61.979	61°59'	36.979	120q6	The one close to you, who has disappointed you, resorts to this
61.771	61°46'	36.771	120q5	Management of house-entering information(?), how it's done
61.563	61°34'	36.563	120q4	The jumbled maze of paths put before your eyes, and how you engage this maze
61.354	61°21'	36.354	120q3	In the void nearby, that which is accomplished
61.146	61°9'	36.146	120q2	A group or body parading by in a show of force
60.938	60°56'	35.938	120q1	Where you formally dedicate attention to discrepancies / attention to a distraction in light of discrepancies in a social realm
60.729	60°44'	35.729	120q12	Shipping, redirecting energy from one place to another
60.521	60°31'	35.521	120q11	The object or means that completes the communicative noise in your house
60.313	60°19'	35.313	120q10	Where the people or places around you dwell in amorphous reasoning (as conveyed to you). To you this appears like the illogical or inexplicable behavior of two or more people

60.104	60°6'	35.104	120q9	Gathering different smaller manifestations of a larger imagination
59.896	59°54'	34.896	121q8	Maintenance care for the spaces you visit
59.688	59°41'	34.688	121q7	What the people are highly motivated to talk about around you—or how they are inclined to be stirred
59.479	59°29'	34.479	121q6	When in the presence of an encroaching counter-enemy or rival, what you do
59.271	59°16'	34.271	121q5	The degree to which your esteem or sense of projective effectiveness is (a) wrapped up in how you affect others in your environment or (b) built on how you yourself project through such an environment; this is THE qunit of the nipples, and one of the first definitely bodily regions I've found. Very male/female dimorphic
59.063	59°4'	34.063	121q4	Where you make your home amidst craziness or a perpetually tense state
58.854	58°51'	33.854	121q3	Cleansing the inner workings, possibly associated with a woman's period and period-like circumstances which bring strain as an arrangement is pruned to eliminate unwanted energy
58.646	58°39'	33.646	121q2	Vehicle for the aggressive compounding of your will upon others
58.438	58°26'	33.438	121q1	The ultimate personality against which you refine your own personality. If your aim is to keep elaborating who you are—especially your interpersonal and expressive tastes—this may be more of a frequent character in your life
58.229	58°14'	33.229	121q12	The power-bearing space insisting on others' success; the one who insists you perform up to code
58.021	58°1'	33.021	121q11	Response to other's surprise attempts to steer you / vice-versa; a strong tell region
57.813	57°49'	32.813	121q10	Your average view of Q-public?
57.604	57°36'	32.604	121q9	Those who can see what you need or perhaps just provide it, more likely using a kind of force or compelling to accomplish this
57.396	57°24'	32.396	122q8	Watching someone else be the victim of struggle or an uphill climb
57.188	57°11'	32.188	122q7	Genetic donation process; 2d2q7, feedback (7) using identity (2) in the context of identity (2)
56.979	56°59'	31.979	122q6	Items you associate with which reflect your values / collected self-typical experiences
56.771	56°46'	31.771	122q5	The story of how one made it to the top, or at least made it to where they are—whether or not that story is yours; one who, by their role, is exempt from domination
56.563	56°34'	31.563	122q4	Stable family membership around you; they know exactly what went into your growing up, because they were there
56.354	56°21'	31.354	122q3	Forward progress in the process of being made—what the work looks like
56.146	56°9'	31.146	122q2	Your process for scanning the scattered kindred / affinities
55.938	55°56'	30.938	122q1	How you amuse yourself or keep yourself entertained. Could be social or solitary
55.729	55°44'	30.729	122q12	Body activities you are more likely to be associated with as you age and your work evolves
55.521	55°31'	30.521	122q11	The singular hero's deeds, narrated
55.313	55°19'	30.313	122q10	Where the ultimate situational equalizer is found
55.104	55°6'	30.104	122q9	Progressing an (impassioned) communicated message
54.896	54°54'	29.896	123q8	How someone you know or take care of screams for help or resolution
54.688	54°41'	29.688	123q7	Someone is optimistic, though either they or another are simultaneously limited or oppressed by something
54.479	54°29'	29.479	123q6	How your divorcing someone or some system works
54.271	54°16'	29.271	123q5	The informational thread which ties you to the will of another. The signal between phones
54.063	54°4'	29.063	123q4	Crazy ideas propagated among you and your kindred
53.854	53°51'	28.854	123q3	Your experience of the nurturance process via those who also let you influence them; by nurturing your production, they change themselves; analogous to those who give fellatio in your world (your idea of their role, when they give it)
53.646	53°39'	28.646	123q2	Mom's or one of the parents' enforcement/benevolence upon you—teaching you HOW to properly interact with a complement. Seems to be greatly influenced by your parents, and be perpetuated by you
53.438	53°26'	28.438	123q1	Recovery after being attacked
53.229	53°14'	28.229	123q12	They who carry the will to force a collective direction
53.021	53°1'	28.021	123q11	The time is now. You must perform this carefully
52.813	52°49'	27.813	123q10	Volatile information you still take in while young or new to a space, mainly as fuel
52.604	52°36'	27.604	123q9	How you assert that your rivals don't know what they're doing
52.396	52°24'	27.396	124q8	Recalling something or someone who had a serious impact on you
52.188	52°11'	27.188	124q7	Withdrawing from a difficult or stuck situation in order to rally one's forces
51.979	51°59'	26.979	124q6	How you go off into a corner and handle conflict (mainly privately)
51.771	51°46'	26.771	124q5	A source of inner talent which serves as a strength you can fall back on in times of difficulty
51.563	51°34'	26.563	124q4	Buildup of one's domain; if you *are* a domain, may build up your body or weight; opinions of weight gain?
51.354	51°21'	26.354	124q3	Your contribution to the world, how you attempt to make it better—even if just for yourself; lots of triggers; that which is overlooked, but still important as a process
51.146	51°9'	26.146	124q2	A good setting for your discovery of certain among your sense-favored patterns

50.938	50°56'	25.938	124q1	Correspondence or resonance with the inner members of a group, while being outside of them; the opposition is a group with at least 2 people in it
50.729	50°44'	25.729	124q12	How your near neighbors experience your encounters with them
50.521	50°31'	25.521	124q11	How you prepare the environment to receive stable company, or stabilize the environment for those receiving you
50.313	50°19'	25.313	124q10	How you refine your communication
50.104	50°6'	25.104	124q9	How you survey events when at home; my building and writing environment
49.896	49°54'	24.896	125q8	A system you just have to trust to work, because you're probably not going to engage it directly without great encouragement
49.688	49°41'	24.688	125q7	The barrier to friendship; the thing which separates you and another from being friends or being close
49.479	49°29'	24.479	125q6	When one is on their own in their own element, what they do
49.271	49°16'	24.271	125q5	Those who attack your way of building something
49.063	49°4'	24.063	125q4	The tradition you just expect to happen
48.854	48°51'	23.854	125q3	Getting involved, helping to serve others; something like charity-work-style
48.646	48°39'	23.646	125q2	Seems to be a critical step in the evaluation of males and the male experience—how this is done
48.438	48°26'	23.438	125q1	As far as you're concerned events in this region might as well have been fate since there was no conceivable way you could have prevented it
48.229	48°14'	23.229	125q12	Cold call-out of the rules of the system; the situation whose occurrence shows that you can't always get what you want
48.021	48°1'	23.021	125q11	Actions of those in the subservient position
47.813	47°49'	22.813	125q10	Those who are easily irritated with you or who look down on you easily
47.604	47°36'	22.604	125q9	When one surveys their circumstances, what they tend to see
47.396	47°24'	22.396	126q8	Creative endeavors which exclude your partner or occurs at their expense
47.188	47°11'	22.188	126q7	How you express your plans for advancing, though there is a VERY good chance that this will not *actually* drive you forward monetarily—it will only be the talk you gravitate towards
46.979	46°59'	21.979	126q6	What you do to escape from uncomfortable situations
46.771	46°46'	21.771	126q5	?Co-personalities with whom you pursue a better future
46.563	46°34'	21.563	126q4	Your dreams of an ideal environment in which to live your everyday life
46.354	46°21'	21.354	126q3	The body or formed legacy of the one whose death you have been near
46.146	46°9'	21.146	126q2	What you are doing while AWOL
45.938	45°56'	20.938	126q1	When you are finally ready to go forward, the circumstances that accompany this
45.729	45°44'	20.729	126q12	Generative production—your process for producing tangible things in the world from essentially nothing
45.521	45°31'	20.521	126q11	What you drain out your energy on
45.313	45°19'	20.313	126q10	The things you see as prone to roasting or social assault
45.104	45°6'	20.104	126q9	The expression you may interact with or use to represent yourself while building a friendship, though the true test of stable friendship will depend on whether this person does the squares (18) to this
44.896	44°54'	19.896	127q8	How you seek to keep control even in your closest relationships—especially when they start to veer off course
44.688	44°41'	19.688	127q7	Seems to indicate those who will always be there for you
44.479	44°29'	19.479	127q6	Moving around building up a social network
44.271	44°16'	19.271	127q5	The tool or agent which influences individuals in your place
44.063	44°4'	19.063	127q4	The nature of your assistant, if you were to have one
43.854	43°51'	18.854	127q3	The connection to the partner is thus etched in the official record
43.646	43°39'	18.646	127q2	The event that actually occurred behind the thing you brag about
43.438	43°26'	18.438	127q1	Digging down to the deep truth
43.229	43°14'	18.229	127q12	The place or situation where the infinite forces are allowed to unfold
43.021	43°1'	18.021	127q11	The kindred's reference frame, their headspace
42.813	42°49'	17.813	127q10	The space which receives some of your most unfiltered creative expression; coming back to this one after 91q10, may be related to the ovaries and general female reproductive space, as such was the text mine
42.604	42°36'	17.604	127q9	The spaces produced by others chosen, indulged in from among many more options; narrowing down a place to stay with, selecting one's "major"
42.396	42°24'	17.396	128q8	The arrival of a new family member
42.188	42°11'	17.188	128q7	Someone else launches an attention effort intended to elevate their agenda
41.979	41°59'	16.979	128q6	The trainer of prodigies, the tutor
41.771	41°46'	16.771	128q5	Where you are called to persist despite others' expectations
41.563	41°34'	16.563	128q4	Someone else who really is out there thinking about you as you tackle the institution
41.354	41°21'	16.354	128q3	No, no, it's not right. We need to look at it again
41.146	41°9'	16.146	128q2	Things in the ambience that force or challenge you to absorb their perspective

40.938	40°56'	15.938	128q1	The broken record. The repetition that won't change, but keeps getting produced every time you hit the 56q1 button—even if that button only occurred once and people just keep reloading it
40.729	40°44'	15.729	128q12	Someone else around you who actively controls great forces?
40.521	40°31'	15.521	128q11	The beginning of the next major phase, realized
40.313	40°19'	15.313	128q10	Overcome by a non-homeostatic state; not quite illness, but not optimum either
40.104	40°6'	15.104	128q9	The behavior that helps establish you as an expert in an area
39.896	39°54'	14.896	129q8	Things you find wonder in; where attunement with the mystical or unexplainably, contextually spiritual is felt
39.688	39°41'	14.688	129q7	One who receives the inspiration from myriad sources
39.479	39°29'	14.479	129q6	Your behind-the-scenes mechanisms for navigating an institutional burden
39.271	39°16'	14.271	129q5	A winning scenario, but oh the discontentment; pyrrhic victories
39.063	39°4'	14.063	129q4	Sharable horrors; states you pass through on your way to more prosperity?
38.854	38°51'	13.854	129q3	Pressure sponsored by the root culture you operate under the influence of
38.646	38°39'	13.646	129q2	A mode for your continuous learning. Doing this, the world keeps giving you more insight
38.438	38°26'	13.438	129q1	The nature of captivity or of being in it—how you experience this
38.229	38°14'	13.229	129q12	Your role with respect to those beneath you
38.021	38°1'	13.021	129q11	Those who display confidence against the unknown
37.813	37°49'	12.813	129q10	Your action packed supporter's qualities (displayed towards you)
37.604	37°36'	12.604	129q9	Those who embody charisma
37.396	37°24'	12.396	130q8	How identity structures are forced upon the individual
37.188	37°11'	12.188	130q7	The attitude one takes towards going through further trouble for something, being inconvenienced; if these asteroids hold, you are more likely to accept the inconvenience
36.979	36°59'	11.979	130q6	How a teacher connected to you goes about training or keeping things under control
36.771	36°46'	11.771	130q5	Behaviors shown by those who still need discipline or correcting. Could be you or the kinds of students you get; if you show this, you will invite the world's attempts to correct you
36.563	36°34'	11.563	130q4	What one's desired version of the structured good-life looks like
36.354	36°21'	11.354	130q3	Interestingly, traits which your teachers project onto you. How they urge you to express
36.146	36°9'	11.146	130q2	How you handle very difficult lessons
35.938	35°56'	10.938	130q1	The overall systemic source for where the lessons are taught; the school to which one belongs
35.729	35°44'	10.729	130q12	The work going on around you, your office mates; people who cheat off of you or sit next to you in class generally
35.521	35°31'	10.521	130q11	Changes in others around you which you may be cautious against; your classmates from other cliques
35.313	35°19'	10.313	130q10	Ways in which the behaviors of others seem a hindrance to you; where they can get out of control
35.104	35°6'	10.104	130q9	How your legacy of built structures is used in the larger culture
34.896	34°54'	9.8958	131q8	What you introduce into the larger culture?
34.688	34°41'	9.6875	131q7	What you see when you watch the executed influence of one close to you
34.479	34°29'	9.4792	131q6	Seems to indicate the grandparents
34.271	34°16'	9.2708	131q5	How you receive advice
34.063	34°4'	9.0625	131q4	How you invite someone to join and build family with you
33.854	33°51'	8.8542	131q3	The information you like to keep running in the background; background noise you prefer
33.646	33°39'	8.6458	131q2	The nature of the distance between you and the rest of your family—what separates you from your family's domain
33.438	33°26'	8.4375	131q1	The artifacts of your life which you pass on or communicate about to others, sometimes full of pride, often with greater attention than other aspects of your life
33.229	33°14'	8.2292	131q12	Your encounter with foreign viewers eyeing the ways in which contact with you will facilitate changes in their own situation
33.021	33°1'	8.0208	131q11	Beauty and dating experiences?
32.813	32°49'	7.8125	131q10	Preparations for the next great adventure as circumstances reconfigure themselves to let you out of where you are
32.604	32°36'	7.6042	131q9	Your overall attitude towards your family
32.396	32°24'	7.3958	132q8	Who lives in the house
32.188	32°11'	7.1875	132q7	Response to opinions held of the house or advice given
31.979	31°59'	6.9792	132q6	Work done on the house
31.771	31°46'	6.7708	132q5	Preferences for interfacing with the house
31.563	31°34'	6.5625	132q4	Processes which constantly demand you put more energy into them
31.354	31°21'	6.3542	132q3	Talk or opinions about the house or home base

31.146	31°9'	6.1458	132q2	A defining property of one's preferred house; the vortex-domain which pulls another's energy inside; | *Ajani's note: may indicate the vagina, check results... actually 132-3 was significant for this body region. How I knew this stems from a later table in this book. It's opposite d60*
30.938	30°56'	5.9375	132q1	Sudden feelings / impulses held about the house
30.729	30°44'	5.7292	132q12	Background attitudes about the house
30.521	30°31'	5.5208	132q11	The kind of information which flows in the background of your house, perhaps media you are NOT watching, which influences the ones you interact with; a tell qunit
30.313	30°19'	5.3125	132q10	Structured activities around the house
30.104	30°6'	5.1042	132q9	The behavioral culture of others in the house
29.896	29°54'	4.8958	133q8	How you regulate what your body takes in; likely associated with majority favored women and identity partners, as well as other "enstatusing" associations. The rich and the blonde for example. This presents an interesting trigger...
29.688	29°41'	4.6875	133q7	How the attached person sees you while they are in their predicament
29.479	29°29'	4.4792	133q6	Overseeing / witnessing a world, and others from a distance—from the outside looking in
29.271	29°16'	4.2708	133q5	Your guest's hobby which influences you
29.063	29°4'	4.0625	133q4	People you really should retain, or whom you should at least replace with a stable template, as they further your expression
28.854	28°51'	3.8542	133q3	Preparing to go out foraging on one's own, or in the process of doing so
28.646	28°39'	3.6458	133q2	In order to advance a value, one also has to give up a related thing
28.438	28°26'	3.4375	133q1	How you think your family dynamics should go (especially when they are at their best or most idealized)
28.229	28°14'	3.2292	133q12	What constitutes your commission of a transgression, a personal "sin"
28.021	28°1'	3.0208	133q11	Those subject to you have now signed on to share burdens; related to 10072 Uruguay?
27.813	27°49'	2.8125	133q10	What you do to trigger associates' / children's actions behind your back
27.604	27°36'	2.6042	133q9	Your children's or creations' interface with their partners or immediate attached interactants
27.396	27°24'	2.3958	134q8	How you work for a cause beyond yourself (even if you do so selfishly) | the HOME of Quaoar? *Alma ds#143*
27.188	27°11'	2.1875	134q7	Accomplishments or histories which add to the family name
26.979	26°59'	1.9792	134q6	The airing or engagement of your private life
26.771	26°46'	1.7708	134q5	How you behave after college / after you have learned the basic foundation for your psychological frame
26.563	26°34'	1.5625	134q4	The management or organization of many pieces
26.354	26°21'	1.3542	134q3	Your relationship with the meaning-holders or circumstance-objects you collect
26.146	26°9'	1.1458	134q2	The interactional work you do on a system which you are capable of evolving ceaselessly; related to aging, drooping, and wrinkles? Checked findings... yes
25.938	25°56'	0.9375	134q1	Your default (more likely to be secret) means to keeping a particular effort successful
25.729	25°44'	0.7292	134q12	How you handle wins or display yourself a winner; seems to describe some aspect of the body—energy distribution?
25.521	25°31'	0.5208	134q11	You under pressure to make a cogent influencing point in the coming presentation
25.313	25°19'	0.3125	134q10	The behavior of pioneers in establishing new rules; adventurous
25.104	25°6'	0.1042	134q9	Health problems experienced by others
24.896	24°54'	359.9	135q8	The procedure which gets you ready to do the dirty work
24.688	24°41'	359.69	135q7	Alliances wanted, but your energy or response to theirs puts it off
24.479	24°29'	359.48	135q6	The other who is your sadist; your display is often not good enough, but amusing enough to an owed party for them to toy with you or challenge you at their whim; those to whom you have a duty to use your skill, or who supervise your performance of skill and can give you the thumbs up thumbs down based on whether you satisfy them (often a thumbs down)
24.271	24°16'	359.27	135q5	The means through which your goal is met
24.063	24°4'	359.06	135q4	That which supports your stability as you gradually build
23.854	23°51'	358.85	135q3	An entrancing space which hijacks the attention and response
23.646	23°39'	358.65	135q2	The route to overcoming one's tension against a situation
23.438	23°26'	358.44	135q1	How one keeps control of their house?
23.229	23°14'	358.23	135q12	Why your partner may find the idea of sex with you distasteful
23.021	23°1'	358.02	135q11	How you welcome and support a trusted social news source
22.813	22°49'	357.81	135q10	When the surrounding environment is out of your control; seems to be related to storms
22.604	22°36'	357.6	135q9	The ideas you profess to the world as being most important
22.396	22°24'	357.4	136q8	That which having choices gives you access to do. Without choices, it seems, you cannot do 136q8 nearly as easily
22.188	22°11'	357.19	136q7	How you engage your choice spaces, discerning which from which
21.979	21°59'	356.98	136q6	The family work?

21.771	21°46'	356.77	136q5	How you handle the air of pressure around you
21.563	21°34'	356.56	136q4	Going in depth, assessing the choices that were truly available to you
21.354	21°21'	356.35	136q3	How your preferences trigger other people's critical modes; how your critical or analytical modes affect others
21.146	21°9'	356.15	136q2	The beginning of your primary role as a learner, may be an indicator of any circumstances where you are poised to learn easily
20.938	20°56'	355.94	136q1	The estranged male, related to loss of a father or father-like influence; events which interrupt your circumstances?
20.729	20°44'	355.73	136q12	Mechanisms which help you lay out the choices in front of you and, possibly, develop a preference among them
20.521	20°31'	355.52	136q11	The silly or mocking voice from above, perhaps indicative as a comical or mocking Olympian god
20.313	20°19'	355.31	136q10	How you would prefer to ultimately live; the adventure scenario you want to someday claim, if you haven't already
20.104	20°6'	355.1	136q9	How your partner behaves, showing that they indeed have a choice
19.896	19°54'	354.9	137q8	A sudden will to influence a situation one has just been greeted with, via some natural visceral attribute of one's character; seems to be THE HOME of 3474 Linsley
19.688	19°41'	354.69	137q7	Indulging the desire for a more comfortable dynamic against some issue
19.479	19°29'	354.48	137q6	How you raise up less experienced recipients to adopt your values or perspective
19.271	19°16'	354.27	137q5	Not a care in the world or, how you hunt the object you want—as a character you put on
19.063	19°4'	354.06	137q4	How you engage beasts or monsters
18.854	18°51'	353.85	137q3	That which makes you feel like a badass—attuned to the fight
18.646	18°39'	353.65	137q2	A regular family occurrence
18.438	18°26'	353.44	137q1	You in your own adventure, generating distrust or hostility in others (stirring them out of their current comfort)
18.229	18°14'	353.23	137q12	Bodily action is employed to achieve an ambition objective
18.021	18°1'	353.02	137q11	Compelled recontextualization—what happens
17.813	17°49'	352.81	137q10	A region used to separate two sides: those who are with the event you're good at sponsoring, and everybody else
17.604	17°36'	352.6	137q9	Your "fixer"; less so, your major partner as a marryer—what they do and why they do it
17.396	17°24'	352.4	138q8	The solutions you incline towards which you think would get you out of a limiting situation
17.188	17°11'	352.19	138q7	Looking at a place of relief, a bright spot—what you see
16.979	16°59'	351.98	138q6	Broadcasting far and wide your methods of organizing something
16.771	16°46'	351.77	138q5	How you initiate guidance systems
16.563	16°34'	351.56	138q4	Influencing fate through writing
16.354	16°21'	351.35	138q3	How you control or set limits on the energy or resources you spend
16.146	16°9'	351.15	138q2	Stern remedy—your most standout notion of a doctor
15.938	15°56'	350.94	138q1	Backstage preparations before a more front-facing show
15.729	15°44'	350.73	138q12	In the ongoing broad daylight of beautiful nature, drama; the *Magnum PI / Miami Vice* region
15.521	15°31'	350.52	138q11	The devil over your shoulder—a character-ized inclination constantly persuading you to chase the impossible or the highly unsustainable... when really it is wholly up to that other to grant you access to this or not
15.313	15°19'	350.31	138q10	Things that swoop in and out—the hawk's region
15.104	15°6'	350.1	138q9	Bad habits you observed and avoid which your parents had, especially your opposite sex parent; you are more likely unable to do these or do them right; a sibling or close other may always be around to manifest these traits
14.896	14°54'	349.9	139q8	How you attempt to influence your partner
14.688	14°41'	349.69	139q7	Your interaction with your "suddenly I want to share this" companion
14.479	14°29'	349.48	139q6	How you and your casual partner work out issues among yourselves
14.271	14°16'	349.27	139q5	How you help another resolve their conflicts with a third
14.063	14°4'	349.06	139q4	Why or how another stays with you
13.854	13°51'	348.85	139q3	The close partner you work with in accomplishing something / driving an effort forward
13.646	13°39'	348.65	139q2	Your relationship to your brothers or brother-like exchanges?
13.438	13°26'	348.44	139q1	Experiencing another barging in in an unwelcoming way perhaps, but putting up with it
13.229	13°14'	348.23	139q12	The air you bring to the context as someone's bf/gf
13.021	13°1'	348.02	139q11	The context of a bf/gf style-relationship, especially that sponsored by the partner; your partners will invariably become this as your bf-gf (boyfriend or girlfriend); a counter-Aksnes
12.813	12°49'	347.81	139q10	Your sisters or sisters in law

12.604	12°36'	347.6	139q9	The culture around which you easily display boyfriend / girlfriend mode—around which you find potential partners if you don't already have one
12.396	12°24'	347.4	140q8	Your experience of your partner's reproductive organ or, more abstractly, their creative tooling—but this definitely has implications for how you experience your partners sexually; if you want to have sex with someone and want to know what your chances are, see if their 140q8 describes you
12.188	12°11'	347.19	140q7	Actual interaction with the partner describing the overall dynamic in sex or co-creation
11.979	11°59'	346.98	140q6	Surrounding judgements regarding your co-creation; the activities of those around you during co-creation; may indicate comparators or those who do the comparing, looming over your co-creative acts
11.771	11°46'	346.77	140q5	The aftermath of sex or co-creation, both had or successfully avoided
11.563	11°34'	346.56	140q4	How you respond to or reinforce the actions of your intimacy seekers; when sex or co-creation is being considered by you, what your conditions are for granting this
11.354	11°21'	346.35	140q3	How you flirt / show others you are receptive to them as co-creators, or simply how they feel you've shown this
11.146	11°9'	346.15	140q2	The steps you go through when deciding to live with another as your co-creator
10.938	10°56'	345.94	140q1	What you bring when you move in with a partner
10.729	10°44'	345.73	140q12	How your life appears in the eyes of those you have moved away from—in order to be with your co-creative partner
10.521	10°31'	345.52	140q11	The house which your deeds have earned you, and the kinds of surrounding interactions which you let unfold in the shaping that house's further evolution
10.313	10°19'	345.31	140q10	The structures or rules you build up in creative turf which you control or occupy; the structuring factors which describe or limit your creative house; also seems to present a metaphor for how you maintain or interface with your reproductive organ
10.104	10°6'	345.1	140q9	When sex or procreativity happens or looms, these are the correlated events
9.8958	9°54'	344.9	141q8	How you push for your ideals via another's receipt of you / the scenarios you wish to create; an effigy of yourself and your attachments
9.6875	9°41'	344.69	141q7	Ideas or entertainment mediums which you like to keep engaging as a portal to how you'd like to live
9.4792	9°29'	344.48	141q6	The partner who builds your idealized world with you, per the Fate game player;
9.2708	9°16'	344.27	141q5	The voices who deliberate behind you, how they do so and what they are saying—not necessarily about you, but a theme which follows you or which you may be suspicious about
9.0625	9°4'	344.06	141q4	How you view marriage or formal social commitment as a concept
8.8542	8°51'	343.85	141q3	Outside of a marriage or commitment, how you address the concept of people's investments in such
8.6458	8°39'	343.65	141q2	Events in a commitment which stir the energy around your partner or upsets them; psychic projective
8.4375	8°26'	343.44	141q1	Learning or growing up as a wall which separates immature you from mateable you. Until this qunit is done developing, you really won't be ready to mate with. Related to youth or immaturity, which is *the* thing that puts you under legal "age." This process, when repeated, may lead to breaks in your partnering activity
8.2292	8°14'	343.23	141q12	Your early dating experiences with a certain kind of co-creator, testing the waters
8.0208	8°1'	343.02	141q11	How others respond to your overtures and seduction attempts
7.8125	7°49'	342.81	141q10	How you exit a relationship, putting the other into the distance; more rarely, how this is done to you; how you breakup with someone—the the procedure you project with this
7.6042	7°36'	342.6	141q9	How you hang out ideally among friends; your idea of a "party" or fun and supportive social gathering
7.3958	7°24'	342.4	142q8	After you know what you like co-creatively, how you indulge
7.1875	7°11'	342.19	142q7	How your shared living situation evolves as you mature
6.9792	6°59'	341.98	142q6	How your means of traversal in some area suddenly invalidates your wishes; the onset of sickness
6.7708	6°46'	341.77	142q5	Solitary intimate experiences
6.5625	6°34'	341.56	142q4	Your adversaries
6.3542	6°21'	341.35	142q3	Misadventures which your body or presence gets you into
6.1458	6°9'	341.15	142q2	The intimate act begins
5.9375	5°56'	340.94	142q1	The breakup has begun, starting with this region
5.7292	5°44'	340.73	142q12	Personas who record their impromptu thoughts
5.5208	5°31'	340.52	142q11	Quiet internal workings of something where other's access to it (or you) is greatly restricted
5.3125	5°19'	340.31	142q10	If you are masculine/male, this is what you do. If you are female, this is how you consider allying with a significant masculine(?)
5.1042	5°6'	340.1	142q9	Seeker-guests allowed to enter your space in your expression of a hobby, though they may not have been your active choice
4.8958	4°54'	339.9	143q8	The music [imposed upon] or [introduced to you by] your partners
4.6875	4°41'	339.69	143q7	Group scrutiny or assessment (Arielhaas-like)
4.4792	4°29'	339.48	143q6	Resolving something that is broken, was broken by, or broken in the eyes of another

4.2708	4°16'	339.27	143q5	Your domestic servant amidst their restorative actions
4.0625	4°4'	339.06	143q4	The displays of behavior that get you isolated
3.8542	3°51'	338.85	143q3	(The one man stunt show); seems related to dancing
3.6458	3°39'	338.65	143q2	Ugly or gritty evidence that may raise people's discomfort?
3.4375	3°26'	338.44	143q1	Things you do in order to evade other's frustration with you? They may still be annoyed, but you don't have to be bothered by this
3.2292	3°14'	338.23	143q12	Situations which allow you to muster the energy to keep going, even if you are running out
3.0208	3°1'	338.02	143q11	The types of characters you engage on your home turf / in your house
2.8125	2°49'	337.81	143q10	How you are invited to join other's complication
2.6042	2°36'	337.6	143q9	The body appearance or presence-effect held by your close kindred, and perhaps you yourself eventually
2.3958	2°24'	337.4	144q8	The basis of conflicts with those given authority in a situation
2.1875	2°11'	337.19	144q7	How you face intimidating circumstances
1.9792	1°59'	336.98	144q6	The handful, where you may be too much to handle
1.7708	1°46'	336.77	144q5	When you just can't match / can't align with the path of someone kindred
1.5625	1°34'	336.56	144q4	The kinds of audience members or guests who attend your meetings
1.3542	1°21'	336.35	144q3	Your inner world mechanisms in youth/yesterday?
1.1458	1°9'	336.15	144q2	A group to which you have at least a semi-loyal connection has members who occasionally put you in a foreign place
0.9375	0°56'	335.94	144q1	The main social space you draw, providing the backdrop in which you fulfill your biographic role
0.7292	0°44'	335.73	144q12	Your work towards a goal which other people witness. In some cases, the effect it has on those people
0.5208	0°31'	335.52	144q11	Training in the deep and difficult, often at the hands of another
0.3125	0°19'	335.31	144q10	How you come to learn the way proper family responsibility works, your way of doing what needs to be done for family
0.1042	0°6'	335.1	144q9	That which is publicly known to happen around you when you are in a situation (as opposed when you are not in a situation, dead for example); the public's experience of your presence

How did I arrive at the qunit meanings? Having no clue what to expect of each region initially, I took 6 – 10 charts of people whom I knew very well, focused on one region at a time, and asked myself what situation was being described by the whole cluster of asteroids in that region for each person. I asked what these situations had in common. If flanking regions were already defined, I asked what situations were immediately related to what I seemed to be reading. And that situation became the definition for the first 500 or so qunits—assigned in a random order.

Along the way, I accidentally discovered a MAJOR geometric rule. It was, in fact, SO major and so pervasively, predictably true that I had to explore some more complicated math in order to understand it, and ultimately ended up reordering my tables into groups of four qunits forming a big square around the wheel (32.5°, 122.5°, 212.5°, and 302.5° for example). I called this a "qunit grand cross" (qc, or qcross for short), of which there were a total of 432 (1728 / 4). The qcrosses were numbered 1 – 432 starting with Aries 0° and ending at Gemini 30°, with each sign containing 144 of them and each qcross containing the opposition and both squares to the point I chose. After the first 500 qunits, I worked under the well-supported assumption that every region should be situationally complemented by its opposition, and this situation "potentialized" or prevented by the axis of the two regions square to it. This bore out basically every time, provided my understanding of that aspect of the sample people's lives was deep enough.

Despite the semi-qualitative nature of the work done to produce Figure 4: The 1728 (12^3) Qunits, I would also eventually run principle components analysis on embeddings clusters of asteroid interpretations in the charts of 25 adult-set people whom I *didn't* know well, but whose full body images and submitted bios formed a kind of visual+ identitySummary biography for me to test my original hypothesized interpretations against.

Later still, I ran canonical correlations against body-descriptive words and the regions that they corresponded to, with each (nominal) qunit being held constant, principal components-reduced embedding-column frequencies being the X group, and the count of major aspects to one word-associated asteroid at a time being the Y group. That is all a technical way of saying, "when we look only at this tiny 1/1728 of a circle as constant, are the number of major aspects such as the conjunct, opposition, trine, or sextile from this region to an asteroid associated with a word statistically significantly related to any facets of language-space as the model I'm using frames it?" I started by using the matrix columns of the SpaCy 3.1 medium web English model and later moved to the nomic-ai 1.5 model as the technology became available. Wilks lambda statistics tended to approach 1 here for most results (meaning there was *no* real support for a statistical relationship), but some results did get closer to zero. Deeper dive tests which had a statistical power $> .80$ and a p-value $<.05$ were retained, giving me some interesting conditional behaviors which said things like "as long as a person has asteroids strongly related to 'ovalness' and strongly unrelated to 'location,' this particular qunit is relevant to them. Otherwise, it's dialed down in effect." There are too many millions of complicated results to squeeze into this book, so I've left only the final table and this description of the methods applied.

"FATE SETS"

29Q12 EXAMPLE: WHO YOU WILL HAVE ULTIMATELY SHOWN YOURSELF TO BE AS A LEADING FIGURE

Given that we now have all of the precise regions we need to delve deeply into a chart, and given that we can also find all of our birthchart asteroid placements by going to a site online that provides them, and given that we have good, non-vague interpretations of each asteroid, we can begin to see how fine-scoped astrology clues us into our most likely paths; we'll call these "fate sets." One of the strongest regions in a person's chart, Capricorn-5 (d29) shows something like the character of historicizable leaders in your life—possibly even you as such. Whether or not you would ever consider yourself a formal leader, the 12 qunits of duodecanate 29 strongly show what you are more likely to be prominently remembered for. To this end, there are few qunits more powerful than 29q12. If you could only look at one place in your chart to ask who life is pushing you to be in the broad stranger world, this is it. I present my 29q12s below, along with a few asteroid interpretations:

Table 2: Ajani's 29q12s

- Inohara (288.329°): amateur's first foray into the mystical

- Jaroslavbocek (288.32°): a morbid or dark tradition that follows a particular culture, sometimes couched in its storytelling

- Koichisuzuki (288.313°): being moved from inside of a situation to being an evaluator of it; associated with greying hair

- Quarenghi (288.311°): excelling as a cluster who, in the thick of the action, can feed off of or multiply its power based on problems

- Michelleabi (288.307°): the reduction of situation to a more obvious summary made common to all; you can translate the duodecanate's events into simpler general principles. Though slightly inaccurate or oversimplified, these translations may be far more useful for general understanding by bigger groups

- Petit (288.303°): medical or health-based nakedness; bodily exposure for educational, therapeutic or explanatory purposes

- Chahine (288.296°): one who is allowed to stand by another and advance the latter's presentation, but may have the support squandered as confusion and the need for a singular way overtakes the alliance; this asteroid can be rendered positive if the implied pair get on the same page, stay on the same page, share the goal equally with neither lording over the other, and turn the penchant for "eugenics" (my way or no way) towards some outward market instead

- Chonofsky (288.294°): tribute to a ranking figure whose shenanigans nonetheless endear them to the world; "a Byronic character"

- Thorvaldsen (288.282°): a little message or act sent out to encourage a whole scenario in a particular direction

- Keinonen (288.274°): rearranging a visual or commercial setting

- Poulanderson (288.27°): where one regulates the allowable limits of expansion, including the exclusion of parallel alternatives; "the stickler for how things are grown"

- Anagolay (288.267°): where, when one has lost their enthusiasm for an undertaking, they may resort to nastygram letters and dictatorial expression. Only when the exchange is flagging though

- Christy Carol (288.264°): biased two-part communication; a necessitated response that serves to keep a topic running even if it should have ended
- Evamarkova (288.232°): reflecting on what caused one's sexuality, beneath the surface lies a need to release, without pain, what is truly there; "questioning sexual identity origins"; the cluster's full expression is more likely to require that such questions be asked in ways that consider the workings of neighboring asteroids. that is, Evamarkova's neighbors will form part of the basis of how one investigates who they should be co-creatively
- Mitton (288.228°): one who will eventually be used for a hallowed purpose, but who—if this weren't so— wouldn't be nearly as desirable
- Street (288.213°): where one can become a great fighter or challenge-overcomer by continuing to perform (perhaps shrewdly) in spontaneous scenarios; associated with wrestling and brawl-readiness
- Allender (288.21°): communication which aids another's transition from a guard encounter to a guardian / inspiration encounter; helping another's blocker become their shrine attendant
- Giupalazzolo (288.178°): the talent for firing analysis at something, claiming the authority to diagnose it immediately—or at least undeniably
- Ozenuma (288.171°): where a healer uses their healing arts to poison opponents, not necessarily knowingly, but probably instinctually
- Radmall (288.148°): thanks to unplanned difficulties, being alert to what one favors, having this broadcasted to an entire kin layer; associated with obituaries and goodwill; the cluster is more likely to thrive under difficulties which are perceived by a whole group
- Amata (288.136°): the big bucks for the high risk work

ADDITIONAL "FATE SET" OBJECTS TO LOOK AT

There are certain easy paths which a particular astronomical snapshot will favor with respect to the environment around it. Regardless of how many people or things have the same chart as you, the factors below are more likely to be favored by circumstance itself as the universal context processes your specific earth-centric moment.

- Remember, the qunits in the list (and throughout this book in general) are defined against the Tropical Zodiac in the 2020s; they may or may not drift as the years go on. I don't know.
- Whenever a qunit is listed which you want to learn more about, be sure to look up the *entire* qcross associated with it. These will be the four regions involved in a big square with the qunit in question, separated by 36 duodecanates (144 / 4). For example, 41q7 shows how you acquire value. Its opposition 113q7 (41+36+36 q7) shows the appearance of the value acquired—a necessary complement to 41q7. Meanwhile, the square axis consists of 5q7 (41+36+36+36 q7, wrapped around past 144) and 77q7 don't show how you obtain the asset as potential, but instead show the asset as it actually is, as well as how it is administered. To give another key example, is 29q12 shows how you are stranger-remembered, its opposition 101q12 shows who remembers you—something like your audience, for better or worse.

29q12

over the very long term, who you will have shown yourself to be / how you will have revealed your character as one who faced challenges; you may be known for this; we look at this factor because it shows who you will have ultimately shown yourself to be as a leading figure

47q12

the story ultimately to be told about your explorations of the world; another "how you are remembered" region—this time for the scenarios you left others behind for and ended up experiencing in a far off place; we look at this factor because it shows who the people you have evolved past or left behind will say you became

26q12

the kind of energy you are known for putting out into the world through your generic behavior; your frequentic "currency"; EXTREMELY CRITICAL for how people assess what you're good at contributing. Selene-like; we look at this factor because it shows You as social currency—what you bring to the table wherever you go

Alma

where others use the milestone events of your life to discuss how you should be interpreted; "ever-revising wiki biography"; this cluster describes the qualities you have which stand out the most in how the world sees you. Imparts definition-writing primacy to the trait; we look at this factor because it shows your wiki-like biographical legacy

Naema

that which is deeply known about a person in such a way as to discourage rewriting; "the record of oneself which is thought to be permanent"; the epitaph asteroid and a powerful indicator of how you will be remembered based on the word of people who actually met you; we look at this factor because it shows your etched character in the eyes of those who remember their encounters with you

Midheaven

what you are broadly known for by individuals talking about you in the public; we look at this factor because it shows your easiest basic public reputation

18q3

the nature of the eulogy—either its contents or the process of its delivery; we look at this factor because it shows who you are in death

105q2

how you present yourself as a liver of the idealized lifestyle, or how you do this in order to build such a lifestyle with another; we look at this factor because it shows your idealized lifestyle

41q7

how you acquire new assets or riches; we look at this factor because it shows how you acquire assets or riches.

Andrewcook

financially comfortable; experiencing leisure in nature; we look at this factor because it shows where you are financially comfortable

mean Node / North Node

expressively stylized, near-guaranteed effectiveness as a cause generator; a MAJOR asteroid, Gemini-6, -1, or -8; we look at this factor because it shows your "destiny"—your optimum expression if you had the opportunity to really find your path of belonging

Sylvania

developing a pattern for handling something across one's travels; getting it done regardless of where one is; "the asteroid of 'stale moves'—tactics that work, so you keep using them any time, any place. No imagination needed"; | Ajani's note: inconjuncts to this asteroid constituted the 3rd most significant (not) human species asteroid template result, p ~2e-3, U ranks, 17.8 notHumanChart vs 8.5 isHumanChart; we look at this factor because it shows the moves that always work

130q9

how your legacy of built structures is used in the larger culture; we look at this factor because it shows how your legacy is used in the larger culture

98q6

how idealized stardom works for you; an ambition region; we look at this factor because it shows your best supporter for forward progress in the world, and one of the "big four" ally archetypes represented by each region in this qcross (one of whom reflects you yourself)

36q10

the general path and message gotten from your biography; how your relationship with your partner (or your partner themselves) is (historically) described; we look at this factor because it shows how you will have been said to interact with your domestic or romantic partner

Lemarchal

preferring the most natural, most intuitive communication; | Ajani's note: a VERY powerful asteroid which seems to indicate your most preferred communication if you could just be yourself; may affect the voice; like Venus, but "judgment free conversation"; top 50; we look at this factor because it shows who you would be as a communicator if you could just be yourself

CHAPTER SUMMARY

In this first chapter I have described the fundamentals which a reproduced human algorithm must obey in order to preserve the **interaction-style** (not the specific proper nouns) of their history. When the aim is to save and load you out of your original context chain, it is more important to save the cluster of probable rules for others' view of you than it is to preserve your list of personal characters for implementing these rules. It may, in fact, be necessary to drop many of the specific names and places just so that your new dolphin-drone parents 200 years from now can name you into *their* chain instead. We also introduced the critical concepts of duodecanates, qunits, and fate sets for precisely targeting a specific basket of dynamics in a person, as well as what kinds of things you'll read in those astrological baskets.

Chapter 2. Internal self-sustainment of the archetypal stories

So we've concluded that, when writing your biography for the purposes of saving and reloading into some other time, place, or dimension, it isn't necessary to include your actual timeline any more than a save game of Super Mario needs to store the behavior of a specific goomba instance. As long as the object's class and instance *patterns of interaction* are saved, we can reload your basics anywhere—possibly with even greater "moddable" freedom. But now, even if your external shell-effects constitute half of the human-as-save-data battle and a lot of your remaining specifics can be ignored, we still have two other aspects of the data save that need to be addressed:

- How does your external interface sustain itself internally?
- How do you even learn to self-sustain to begin with? (Hint: What do others *around you* use to reinforce your interface?)

This chapter addresses the first bullet. We will be covering some potentially offensive content.

ON PRIVATE PERSONALITY: WHAT IT'S USED FOR

I believe that what humanity needs most to get past our aggressiveness towards each other is a deeper understanding of our own pathologies, psychologies, and where they come from. I've been fortunate enough to have damaging asteroids in key public places in my chart, facilitating a long chain of strained relationships and burned bridges made invariably public to those near me. As for those not near me, I know that I will not be able to do my real work until all of the skeletons are let out of their closets, because if I attempted to do work as a public educator but left the writing of my story to the same pattern of people I rifted with, then it would be more of a "downfall" thing for someone who taught rather than an evolution for someone you first met under censorable topics. It is critical that I be the potentially censorable specimen first, so that you and everyone else will know this skeleton-fueled work beforehand through my own documentation, not afterwards through someone else's accusation—not for anything criminal, mind you. Just for my being stubbornly weird.

To generate the internal self-sustainment (homeostasis) portion of the biography, we start with a simple question:

> Suppose your life is a spaceship or a factory designed to keep you projecting your interface from the previous chapter. What kinds of activities would you say you perform to keep that factory running?

- Your personality belongs to a Leo-like space; it shows the dynamics you project to others regardless of their influence. Your Aquarius objects show the informational responses that attend this, or your beliefs about the world which addresses projected characterizations broadly.

- Your identity is square to this in a Taurus-like space; it shows the concepts which are not your projection, but which come from somewhere else in order to anchor who you think you are in life. Your Scorpio objects show how these concepts are pushed upon you, or what you believe about how types of value get pushed upon another in general. You can see this in the duodecanate meanings for 85 – 96 and 121 – 132 in Figure 3.

Investigating the inner fuel behind my interfaces, I present my personality and identity characteristics below:

FIGURE 5: [SELF] DATA SAVE PART 1 OF 3

Identity anchors and key idea-labels attached to:

- His thesis is: mobility through mapping **EXPERT**

- His ethos is: the golden rule

- His friends were: revolutionary, tolerant, logical sticklers

- Strong self-identification as: Black, oldest brother, writer, scholar, Buddhist-Daoist

- Favorite things: Tang, Perry Como, Aoife O'Donovan, Donald Byrd, Sarah Vaughan, the color Dark Purple, Tech N9ne, Psytrance, Epic-J (Yoko Kanno future style), Honor Folk/Bluegrass, Tactics RPGs and games involving directed decisions in a grid or along a tree; top all-time favorite songs: #1 Kahimi Karie – Blue Orb, #2 Akino Arai – Unknown Vision, #3 Wiesty, The OC Jazz Collective - Killer Instinct "Combo Breaker" OC ReMix

- Turn-ons: toned or complex abs on women (not excessively muscular), Indian women, big areolae, wide hips, shows of mercy where it did not have to be given, changes of heart to do the right thing towards another, chill personalities, let's-go-explore personalities

- Turn offs, anger triggers: Presumption, one person imposing their thoughts on another's patterns, assumed familiarity that wasn't invited, bullying, being disrespected, lied to, arrogant minimization of others, flaky or fleeting exchanges, distrusts surface beauty or power by default until more information about a person is gathered, punishment over unexplained rules, bullet-hell / haphazard pressure, the need for quick wit, being rushed, being commanded, smart-assedness of most kinds to or from most people- including generic comedy shows, slight distrust towards same-race couples by default, distrusts hype

- Biases: affinity with transgender (non-sexual), complicated relationships with Latinas (Americanized, not Mexican enculturated) but generally respects them, appreciates futanari (sexualized hermaphroditism), more positive but mysterious affinity with Mexican women, has both silly and dirty senses of humor, gets along with everyone – but white, Indian, and Latina follow more specific patterns in his encounters, affinity with redheads or auburn hair, affinity with writers, affinity with males who paint

- Sexual orientation: non-monogamous, hetero, polyamorous, bisexual-favoring, alpha projecting, feminine-communicating male. Can survive mono relationships, but typically has to compartmentalize them in order to thrive in ambitions. Poly relationships help ambition thriving, but require constant travel if they are to avoid being fleeting. Ajani dislikes fleeting relationships. Practices parts of the Ananga Ranga (~sacred sexuality). Leans demi-sexual, outside of poly or deeply stable emotional connection, has little interest in sex or sexual release; sexual information is mostly cognitive fuel for logic work

- Attracts heavier-build women but partners with very thin ones high in Big-5 neuroticism

- Overwhelmingly attracts interracial couples as friends

- Distrusts most women who turn him on until he is sure they will add to rather than take from his ambitions

- Almost all friends and self are obsessive, have high big-5 neuroticism, or both

Personality, beliefs, and interests:

1. Character
   - An advocate for the voiceless (strong characteristic)
   - Motivated by: sexual information, measurements (strong characteristic)
   - Motivated towards: vast space in which to order patterns
   - Insists on politeness, whether or not he shows this insistence; will work in a group to acknowledge others' attempts to speak up which may have been run over by stronger personalities; group "mama bear"
   - Seems passive / not dominating, BUT generally it's his way or failure for the other—whether people, groups, or institutions. Accordingly, he heavily values win-wins.
   - Personality [strangers and public]: cold, logical, guarded, discourages interaction
   - Personality [acquaintances and colleagues]: always asking for more data, access, passionate about work, a decent counselor or listening ear, wordy, a bit too logical, can be strange
   - Personality [close friends]: happy, pushover, zero-tolerance for certain concepts, ambitious, prone to turbulent or eventful encounters, has been exiled often
   - Personality [private]: Easy, live and let live, happy (sings to self), industrious
2. Mentality
   - Talented in automation, a magnet for mass, often private data—not necessarily from you or the institution at hand, but through methods learned there (strong characteristic, **EXPERT**)
   - Talented in inheriting the talents of people he wanted in his life, whose company was not granted or whose association was in some way blocked, **EXPERT**
   - A heavy documenter, thousands of recordings and writings (strong characteristic, **EXPERT**)
   - Much faster when focused
   - Only focused when interested
   - Only interested when effective at influencing culture
   - If not moving another's impulse, not interested in conversing
   - If conversing with another is harmful, block interaction
   - Minimize self-inconsistency in wants
   - .when idle / unable to influence in any way, be interested in what I want
   - .block all information unless it supports spiritual health
   - .general journey towards spiritual health / contentment
   - .influence others only if their situation is broken and they don't block me
   - .avoid others' broken situations
3. Beliefs:
   - .Most cultures are broken / harmful to their members...
   - .objects are the only way to make people listen where the threat of divine or governmental punishment no longer keeps them in line
   - .weird or socially unapproved manners and traits are the best way to filter out people using you for convenience. Beauty does the opposite, attracting everything at the price of one's own peace, and often their trust
   - With beauty, status, and power, it's harder to know who would be there if you didn't have these
   - Strength is best used to move creative building blocks
   - Sometimes people's impressions are the building blocks
   - No matter how pessimistic, transactional, or utilitarian the view, if you seek the peace of your whole life-sphere and un-know all things which would destroy their own spheres, then your sphere will only merge consistently with the right ones. Nothing else will touch you
   - People value that which validates them, so most people value things which are as selfish as themselves, hence the rich are unlikely to lift up the poor. The fertile landowners are unlikely to share their food and water. Neither the rich nor poor value the sharing.
   - What the naturally poor call sharing is usually just taking. What the naturally rich call valuable is usually just the taking of popular favor via objects. Few are truly generous. This mainly applies to the rich and poor in spirit. Objects are only a fraction of this

o   Most generous people are fools. But some are truly rich and emit generosity as trees emit breathable air. For the rest, non-fools are those who limit their generosity to recipients who avoid harm—self-harm, other-harm, sphere-harm

o   Most modern information and commercial sources are agnostic to spiritual if not communicative harm. Even the generous give to them. Thus the foolishness of most

o   Am I a fool? Probably. Through a self-presentation which does not naturally validate most things, my world has fewer supporters, my work has fewer people who would relate, but the quality of those who remain—including information sources—is much much higher

o   Few people appreciate philosophers. Even fewer appreciate philosophers' philosophies. A statue or heading in a book will suffice for knowing. As a philosopher your job is to make the heading, regardless of how silly your thoughts are. To you they're not silly. To your viewers they were at least seen

o   Wrapped for all of life in their own feelings and thoughts, one occupies a material body that means little to them by comparison. Perhaps the thoughts and fears about that body can convince us otherwise, but these are still thoughts and feelings, not the object itself.

o   Locked outside of the thoughts and feelings of a body holder, others depend mightily upon your body to build their favor, speculation, and prejudices. In that sense, my body is one of the most stubborn co-producers of my life's movie that my soul will ever carry around with it

o   He who studies the body thoroughly knows more about at least one co-producer of your movie than you do. You're not outside of it, so how would you know? Still, he may never know the inner you

o   If your inner workings adore self-harm, other-harm, or sphere-harm, I'd rather never know the inner you, but studying your body allows me to understand a pattern which plagues all humans

o   I wouldn't call myself a pessimist, but I won't fool myself about the kinds of things that bring a person into my life. Sometimes it's a genuine alignment of spheres. Most of the time, it's just utility of some sort.

o   Some would say that the world is ugly. But it's the only world we have. That view is unhealthy.

o   Beautiful is that which compels a perceiver to keep doing so in the way that he or she is currently perceiving – harmoniously same *captivation*. Tension is more oscillation, less harmony of steps. It may fixate or lock in, but shouldn't be said to "captivate"

o   Even within an ugly world, one's inner self can forever captivate them, demanding their sphere's endless reinforcement. Thus the inner self always has the potential to be beautiful by definition—as any other smoothly re-compelling object. The rough edges and the smooth fixation on those edges are not the same

o   If I must choose between the so-called ugliness of the world and the beauty of my world within that world, well... the choice is obvious

o   He who studies the body may yet see where your world would place you at your most beautiful. We hope that he shares what he learns. We hope you will put your weapons down against a world less immediate to you, taking up the inner art instead

Ideally, we would find the clusters that correspond to all of the traits above, and I did do this. But rather than bog down the book with that analysis, I'll talk about what it means to wrap specific ideas into a series of astro factors broadly.

REPRESENTING SPECIFIC TRAITS AS SETS OF ASTRO FACTORS

Proper nouns and specific labels like "Tang" and "psytrance" form an easy beginning for any biography. When we abstractify them into qunits, it is similar to assigning one or more pointers to a synastry chart. For example, my research into taboo psychology is described by the asteroids of 134q2 in my chart <the interactional work you do on a system which you are capable of evolving ceaselessly>. Here are the asteroids:

116939	Jonstewart	an assessment service rendered in concert with sports and entertainment
9281	Weryk	letting something out to head into its own version of confines, that it may not have its path solidified in the same way as others [something like 'work']

31282	Nicoleticea	policy writing and formation; the research put into analyzing the relevant information and options for writing such policy
9523	Torino	a situation, event, or thing purported to guard some mysteriously perception-effecting possession
10242	Wasserkuppe	from a position of obscurity/unfindability, absorbing from the rest of the world
15376	Martak	a forceful stare-down or confrontation against another believed to have taken one's protections away; associated with the protest side of pro-choice
27091	Alisonbick	agreeing to mobilize one's backers in light of a thing, supporting it or (more rarely) the mobilizer
8072	Yojikondo	touring the less privileged underground of another context; renders you a visitor in an area where the inhabitants are (usually figuratively) [poor or poverty stricken] with respect to the duodecanate
711	Marmulla	blending objectives together with a strong or decisive force; "releasing the high powered compression of a gathered collection "associated with volcanoes and eruptions""; you may be particularly explosive in this duodecanate, and if you should require a powerful release of steam, Marmulla's containing duodecanate may show you what that looks like. (Not the same as losing your temper)
23727	Akihasan	that which is recurring, reemerging off and on with an unsettling force

Each idea that goes into your save should have a nearest match to one of the 1728 cluster interpretations, or at least a few of the 21,000 asteroids scattered across those clusters. This is because the asteroid definitions were built from a 24000 word vocabulary which can frame most topics you can think of, so even if there is no asteroid or region for a "ghost hunter," there are asteroids for ghosts and hunters separately. We can gather these into a group to represent any aspect of our lives, including our friends and ourselves.

Whenever an object in an astro chart stands in as a representative of an entire character, we can call the former a "significator" for the latter. The more important the character or situation being symbolized, the more objects it will have to represent it. You yourself will have several clusters that add up to who you are in summary, and my theory is that our ability to port these objects across charts constitutes a quick way to see how you affect others at a glance. My friend Priya, for example, is described by 11 different qunits in my chart, one of them being 19q9 <the culture of your friends; the spaces of behavior that comes with them>. Among the 11 regions, some of them represent the situations she "owns" as part of my sphere, while some of them aren't so much strong as degree windows, but are strong because of the specific asteroids located in them. Let's take a closer look at Priya's significators in my chart so we can get a better idea of how to represent specific nouns in a human data save, even if the data itself only stores abstract clusters of objects.

SIGNIFICATOR CASE STUDY

The following regions represent my friend Priya in my chart:

FIGURE 6: A FRIEND OF MINE AS A "NOUN"

Qunit	Qunit Interpretation	Qunit grand cross	qCross Interpretation	Key Asteroids and \\notes
111q3	father or battler in your local experience of a family unit. Useful in the Gauquelin family data	qc403	nuclear family members	
111q2	the types of people you welcome into your personal family	qc402	family entrance requirements	\\the types of people you welcome into your personal family. Priya, Auguste
3q9	the operating principle you grow into as your role in the world; when represented by others, seems to indicate the people who train you or	qc397	the role you're trained to project outside of yourself	

	train with you in your evolving role. They have their own military-like "MOS" so to speak			
41q2	the visitors to my deepest family	qc378	family themselves and their challenges	\\TADA! Robots, mainly; how I interact with and influence Priya specifically; people who are crazy deep into data and messaging
43q4	attempts at smooth communication despite not feeling received by the hearer	qc356	your guides (may be esoteric)	\\what Priya brings to my life
50q7	the kinds of interactants / interactions involved in responding to a situation that has been patterned against one's way	qc275	co-creative urge for biological reasons	10247 Amphiaraos 19005 Teckman
55q12	the infinite forces which proliferate unchecked	qc208	the encompassing space	\\my conception of a standard conquistador; Bijonix, Pizarro, Priya, KK? 4488 Tokitada 13082 Gutierrez 25512 Anncomins
19q9	the culture of your friends; the spaces of behavior that comes with them?	qc205	choosing to confide	\\Priya, Auguste
97q9	it now falls to your kids to do the rest	qc133	your children's or creations' creations—the process employed by the former to generate the latter	277883 Basu 1173 Anchises
31q5	\\collectives or groups you're associated with, under pressure to make some kind of progress	qc69	persuading your niche to accommodate certain patterns	\\the space of partner arrangements across the niche; partnering paradigm. Spiritual-sphere 'genetics?' soul group 107223 Ripero 43605 Gakuho
105q8	who you're interested in inflicting your lifestyle journey upon	qc48	monuments to your own will that others must observe	\\keeping my work safe, with only Priya to see it. But once my best is no longer locked underground... 5662 Wendycalvin 605 Juvisia

Earlier we talked about how a human data save requires first and foremost that the dynamics or "object classes" are the main things we need to store, while the specific names of a thing's history can (and in some cases should) be dropped. But if you wanted to save a specific instance of an object class, then you would do it by finding all of the clusters of asteroids that described the object, then determining whether it was 1) ALL asteroids in the cluster (and thus the qunit itself), 2) some of the asteroids (and thus those specific asteroids as significators) or 3) none of the asteroids, but the situation holding them which seemed to describe the instance. Using the example above, if you wanted to include information about this specific friend in my life, then you could say something like `Priya = { [Juvisia, Wendycalvin] -> [Tokitada, Gutierrez, Anncomins] -> [Amphiaraos, Teckman] -> [Basu, Anchises] -> [Ripero, Gakuho] -> 19q9, 111q2; qc356, qc37, qc397, qc403}`. See here how a specific identity can be treated as a kind of shorthand for a pattern of interactions across a targeted series of situations. These specific mini-saves within your file can be used to reconstruct who the friends were or identify the friends or objects' potential roles in other charts, for example. And if you had the nerve (or the means) to cover all 1728 qunits in your chart, you will have truly obtained the most complete answer to question 48.3 in the book *Alma Mater*.

Your friends and personality are just a couple of routes to your internal self-sustainment. They are represented in a similar way to your interfaces, except for two notable differences:

TABLE 3: (WORLD) INTERFACES VS (SELF) INTERNAL STATES

| Interfaces
(Your strongest surface effects on the world) | Internal states
(Your inner real [personality] and potential [identity] mechanisms which keep your outer effects going) |
| --- | --- |
| The interfaces aim for generic reproducibility of the core experiences others have of you, without specifics. Said another way, your interface is semi-static as a history book. | The internal states and objects aim to capture chains of processes, possibly through mixed compartments comprising specific people and events. This is dynamic as a flow network. |
| When saving your biography, *this* is your first priority. Because after you're gone, the interface will at least serve as a kind of billboard against which people can "kind of" interact with your old form, regardless of the internal means of propping that form up... | ...Meanwhile, the internal states represent the towns you are able to visit in your ongoing psychological city. They become more important when we want your external interfaces to keep sustaining themselves in whatever form we transfer your personality to. |

One of my routes to self-sustainment is through my friends: talented, revolutionary, logical sticklers (at least that's how they show up in my own life). Priya is one of those friends, and is one of the main representatives of my 55q12 and 31q5 specifically. If you tried to build the internal programming to keep reinforcing my external interface, you would need a `Priya = {…}` type network-flow to capture how my attention and dedicated communicative energy moves across all of the concepts mentioned in Figure 6.

THE ROLE OF TIME IN HOMEOSTASIS

As they are properties of my inner world, my Personality and Identity features are heavily attentional in nature. Sure, I actually do communicate with the friends mentioned and eat the foods mentioned, but as a matter of keeping the external interface churning, it may be more useful to focus on the inner world as a collection of traffic patterns telling me how I flow from one conceptual activity to another. The output of that flow is my interface. But how does all of this get animated? It has to do so against ever-progressing Time. Beginning with the assumption that every day is a cycle from full energy at sudden waking back down to zero energy upon sleep, let us hypothesize that biological sleep is represented by long-wavelength (Tropical) [Neptune / Pisces], while instant waking is represented by super short wavelength [Aries / some high-activity, high-urge "point of Action" like 3474 Linsley]. I have found that, in the spirit of humans as microcosms of the Earth we have localized through our bodies, cycles of Time are not limited to things like daily or yearly windows, but are more indicative of you we go from [full energy] to [running out of energy] in things broadly. For whatever reason which may or may not apply to you (others will need to research it), I begin ALL voluntary activities with my Moon in 21°36' Aries, 136q4 <going in depth, assessing the choices that were truly available to you>. The rest of that region includes the following:

TABLE 4: AJANI'S MOON QUNIT, 134Q6

206185	Yip	scratching, strumming, or chiseling through to an escape route for the contents of something
-10001	Moon	"the intentions you turn towards in place of the tension you would otherwise feel; one's base method of goal placement in lieu of tension, which ultimately gets reduced to visible measurable associations"; a MAJOR asteroid Cancer-5, -6, or -10, tension-resolution protocol, 'ones system for wanting things;' associated with hormone proportions; the Moon's neighbors, when stably compounding each other, affirm that the want system is strongly functional
7299	Indiawadkins	prophesy which may not actually come to pass, but *is* more likely to make swindling someone or a system easier

| 80179 | Vaclavknoll | protests or collective agitation over the mandated imposition of a thing - from government to health epidemics; investigate in France |
| 120 | Lachesis | many not moved to co-create with something see the death of materiality-based blocks to their imagination given exposure to a hero archetype; "the co-creative emboldened by a hero tale" |

Note that the asteroids above, the disruption they bring, will occur again and again throughout the Ajani character and times, as in the very first (and strongest) aspects of the interfaces from earlier…

...REGARDING THE MOON'S QUNITS

Look for your Moon's qunit to explain how you willingly incline towards anything—even collective-unconsciously.

Opposite my Moon is the following:

Table 5: Ajani's AntiMoon qunit 64q2

5314	Wilkickia	one is counseled on what they may have to say before an authority party
36235	Sergebaudo	an obscure hurdle emerges in the night; the demon that haunts one; associated with nightmares
24604	Vasilermakov	running on all cylinders, going all-in at a social gathering place, but perhaps for more desperate reasons than it appears
1165	Imprinetta	where one needs assistance seeing or being allowed into the perspective of another. Assistance from whom? Perhaps the opposition or clustermates will tell
12561	Howard	where one or another holds a rival in their communicative efforts
14792	Thyestes	a technician pays attention to the details in the machinery
129158	Michaelmellman	assembling a particular collection for / in response to the queen (domain)
149243	**Dorothynorton**	**overseeing the authorship of something**
25021	Nischaykumar	a popular one whose skill or sought after qualities are unquestioned, but who lives on the berserk side
362911	Miguelhurtado	addressing issues of the conscience and, sometimes, social issues
25543	Fruen	a benefactor? yes. Prudent behavior? No.
12490	Leiden	pronounced rising and falling, taking in the highs of an arc or cycle
11949	Kagayayutaka	using one profile or position to engender certain sweepingly ill-considered thoughts across constituents
1084	Tamariwa	public or group outcry comes with the unified occupation of a place where information is learned
1560	Strattonia	"birth of the clown"; area of the chart which sponsors a dramatic shift in how one addresses issues that are now known impossible to really influence the way one wanted
19952	Ashkinazi	one who may share their taxonomy / ranking system with you if you play nice; you may be this to others
11955	Russrobb	the industrial machine which promotes various interactions between different components
26293	Van Muyden	a brand or well-known persona associated behind the scenes with civic or community betterment; the well-known white-label
17351	Pheidippos	despite any losses or demotions that may have occurred, one remains in full throttle fight mode, displaying all of their raw skill
49109	Agnesraab	attempting to rectify one's hardship, though one may not actually be in the position or have the right to do so; overstepping one's bounds
3274	Maillen	a friend or hire who supports one's secret maneuver around a system's or parent's restrictions; "the sneak accomplice"

You already know that I write books as one of my main modes of expressing what I want or want to understand. 64q4 corresponds to <entertaining, but possibly offensive; the two sides through which a choice manifests as [attention-worthy] versus [fitting or unfit for the situation at hand]>; this kind of binary division is also, as we will see later, one of the defining characteristics of "African morphs" (black ethnotypic body packages), such that the super strong role of my Moon in my chart goes hand in hand with a body wired to divide categories. **Look for your AntiMoon to see the frameworks you will continually incline to operate against when pursuing your inclinations in general.**

The squares to your Moon will tell you the states you perceive when your wants just can't take priority.

Now, if you've read some of my books then you know that I have a form of claircognizance tied to Time, and a type of clairaudience that manifests through music. About 4-5 days a week, I get songs in my head that predict events later in the day. (For example, I woke up yesterday with Beyonce & Lady Gaga – "Telephone" in my head, and later ended up having to take an unexpected certification course on the Telephone Consumer Protection Act in my day job. This happens ALL the time, and is one of the mysteries that motivated my writing *Alma Mater*.) From these observations of time, I've seen how smaller windows predict bigger ones beginning from your "starting point" (wherever that is), and have called this phenomenon "the Hours" in my other books. What I feel 10 minutes after 17:21 predicts what I will most likely feel at 17:41. What I sense at 17:41 predicts the general state of things at 18:01, and this keeps going until 1:18 am early in the morning when my Hour of Moon ends and my Hour of Mars takes over. The hour of Node / Jupiter starts for me at 2:22 am. Saturn starts at 3:23 am. Pluto at 5:18, then Sun: 6:34, Uranus: 7:17, Venus: 7:47, Mercury, 8:07, Neptune: 9:18, and there may be another Taurus-like hour sometime between noon and 13:18… but I wouldn't know because I very rarely wake up that late, and haven't collected a lot of data on how the day differs from waking up at other times. For me, the time window in which I wake up HEAVILY determines what kind of day I have, and this is how I gradually learned the Hours were a thing in the first place. I really try to avoid waking during the hours of Mars, Pluto, and especially Mercury or Uranus, where the days tend to be filled with utter chaos. Whatever the case though, the progression of a time pushes Sun-like, Venus-like, or any other hour-like background energy through my daily network chain, where activities like sleeping, eating, and working are each given their turn as points through which attention and actively-invested energy flow. We can use this idea of time/energy level-cycling to animate our data save networks once we've built them; that is, this is how we automate the focus shift from one aspect of our personality or identity to another.

REGARDING THE NORTH NODE'S QUNITS

The Moon shows where on your energy-level cycle you are most-likely to pursue your wants. But the Moon itself revolves upon a creeping elliptical axis around the Earth. That axis is shown by the North and South Nodes. As you pursue your wants, your North Node shows a kind of "directional correctness" for the space you're in as that pursuit is happening. You can be Moon-satisfied in the wrong Node context. But when your Moon's pursuits have the North Node as part of its assumed background, this is more likely to feel as though you are operating in an optimum space for the Moon to really reach its peak. As you will see, my North Node qunit will explain A LOT about the kinds of things in this book, including why and how I work with adult data sets and content:

Table 6: Ajani's North Node qunit, 82q9

7316	Hajdu	the vehicle for transferring focus or intent to a state opposite its starting point; transferring away from one's position; Libra or Scorpio -10 or -12 like; related to the funneling process
6508	Rolcik	the conduit which enables your access to the how/whether an engine or formal energy burner runs. A systemic handle providing access into the underpinnings of an energy consuming actor
5368	Vitagliano	locking things together, creating an inner world or layer between them; your use of this cluster may confer an inner layer even on things that were once accepted only at face value
18121	Konovalenko	rebellion and women's action, with a focus on spreading the word regarding something; the containing cluster may become stronger in light of women's rights efforts
65100	Birtwhistle	strongly structured creation; "amusement park engineer"; while the process may be dead serious, the result is a space that all can enjoy

19009	Galenmaly	sharp talent that meets the goal
207687	Senckenberg	the afterword reflecting what one has gone through
9093	Sorada	an ongoing series, a stream which confronts experiencers with an overwhelming value
21369	Gertfinger	social earthquake; the shot heard around the world; related to events that send shockwaves far beyond their point of origin
28474	Bustamante	where one not granted clearance sneaks into a situation and signs up anyway
33633	**Strickland**	**growing old; a cluster whose expression increases as one does so**
84928	Oliversacks	learning something without having the actual formal mechanisms normally used for doing so
9026	Denevi	aggressive challenger for the title, who realistically may not have a chance until the title holder is eliminated from the field; investigate in the chart of any person who, after an unsuccessful attempt to take the top spot from another, branched off their own distinct enterprise instead
-10010	mean Node	expressively stylized, near-guaranteed effectiveness as a cause generator; a MAJOR asteroid, Gemini-6, -1, or -8
15791	Yoshiewatanabe	a fixed role for an energy issuer, manifesting their influence through a material or normatively agreed upon form
27302	Jeankobis	being imprisoned or punished for activism, particular in the area of equality
40764	Gerhardiser	disrobing for whatever reason, where that which is revealed makes a substantial impression; this asteroid is associated with those situations where a person may be in a serious, functional, or medical situation, as witnesses to their body need to hold back a reaction

My South Node qunit is as follows:

Table 7: Ajani's South Node qunit, 10q9

17098	Ikedamai	the long trail or tail of a dress or dressed on, announcing their epic or (negatively) shocking introduction; this asteroid unfolds events over a series and amplifies to climactic salience of events that happen in the containing region
1005	**Arago**	**related to "the invention of different methods upon natural laws"**
897	Lysistrata	a learning institution administrator lays out a non-user friendly agenda; "the technical underpinnings of an otherwise understandable learning paradigm"; replaces absorbable things with the non-absorbable technical or formal structures behind them, often preventing others from comfortably connecting with you when they want to do so
5117	Mokotoyama	being seduced, succumbing to something for the short term, presumably for one's well-being in some way
1785	Wurm	"an import for completing an existing development motif"; pulls a third construct into an existing a space of two in order to complete the two; a noticeable motivator of many-actor exchanges (3+)
278141	**Tatooine**	**having crashed somewhere during one's warmongering or combat tour, forced to stay, teach, and learn**
8302	**Kazukin**	**hungry—starving for something; the situation which is more likely to bring this out of you**
10740	Fallersleben	tracing the cycle of energy flow after the fact, or when the play is not unfolding; "rewiring a system or event at rest" where things need to be powered down in order for you work on them. And even though the energy level may be significantly cut, you'd be surprised how much can get done in your zombie state;
6442	**Salzburg**	**holding dominion or dominion-conjuring power over all the 'land' (area of life, funneling the resources one has acquired towards a higher-spanning cause**

Your North Node qunit shows you at your optimum place for achieving ongoing Moon wants. Your South Node shows the content you work with in doing so. The squares to your Nodes show what you attempt to do

or what happens in order to get you to that optimum. I snack a lot during the day, and teach humanity-sweeping categorization systems.

READ EACH OF YOUR QUNITS AS A GROUP!

*Hopefully by now you're starting to get the general idea of how we read qunit clusters; you read them *as a collection*, not as individual asteroids.

For example, when I first saw this cluster 118q9 <how you and your friend build up or add to your joint dwelling or niche-space> —which is square to my Nodes—I asked, now what aspect of my life does this cluster remind me of?

TABLE 8: AJANI'S SQNODE- QUNIT: 118Q9

22422	Kenmount Hill	the innovator displays crazy or a disruptive level of abstraction
23277	Benhughes	a dramatic display involving sexuality; investigate in "A Little Life"
23975	Akran	studying the detailed workings of a thing and deciding that an effort should not be continued or should be outsourced
20793	Goldinaaron	tales told about something whose true origins can likely never be recaptured /accurately translated
21022	Ike	one bravely teaches amidst uncertainty and outrage; helps one calmly guide others through turbulence
11584	Ferenczi	removing something as a matter of resource balancing, but being at least a little sarcastic about it
87	Sylvia	one who inquires incessantly, teaching others in the process despite taking a seemingly inferior or ignorant position; "Socrates' asteroid"
171183	Haleakala	where an institution or structure relaxes its normal restrictions to allow a performer in; the passage of performers; may indicate duodecanate behaviors which allow you to 'skip the line'; a career asteroid?
4886	Kojima	to inherit an internal war on one's plate, perhaps signified by an attached feminine role complement
6683	Karachentsov	one's rationale for growing something is weirdly greedy at the same time
342017	Ramonin	in small ways, one is given a lot of latitude to recover oneself
19695	Billnye	breaking down or playing back academic material in a popular or performer's (perhaps cheeky) way
5047	Zanda	(conclusion of) a wonderful interaction with a small group

118q9 reminds me of several things, but generally describes my psychological (though not bodily) drop in interest in romantic partnership with every woman I meet, coincident with other sexual practices instead. As my focus on those practices have gone up, my susceptibility to random allure has gone down—thus allowing me to put together a short description of this region

\\my retirement from interest in girls. STRONG

This is part of how I get to my Moon-inclination's optimum.

One of the strongest routes to self-biography is for you to go through all 1728 of your qunits, one by one, and log what aspects of your life their overall cluster reminds you of…

Once you have done so, you will have built one of the strongest foundations possible for other people to truly interact with who you were, or duplicate the experience of you in situations where the original you is no longer present.

Chapter 3: Ajani's biography

Why this chapter exists:

Like most people, I have gotten into more than my share of drama over the years, and left an extensive trail of burned and abandoned bridges in the process. It was my fault about 70% of the time; and the narrative I left others to write about me in those cases has been summarily negative. Additionally, I have a stereotypically male mind, with scholarly energy fueled by sexual and bodily information as input, but value control and certain kinds of power more than I value actual physical company. Like a typical Scorpio. Yet I come from a family of teachers, am the oldest of three brothers, and have always ALWAYS looked out for people whose voices or worth has been in a lesser position—as long as they're not jerks. On the other hand, I've also identified with people in a greater position—unless they are bad stewards. I've always done the best I could with what I had and what I knew at the time, and feel like my role as villain or mercenary in those past exchanges stemmed mainly from the bigger human problem of us not knowing how to treat each other—how to see the much more complicated frameworks of people besides ourselves, and how to give each other grace for the discrepancy.

The world is wide. I believe everyone from the highest king to the lowest slave has a story sponsored by the greater whole, and has a story worth telling. With all of my quirks and errors, I would not change a thing, and ask myself, "What can you do with that history that will allow you to be the highest person you can be, for the greater good?" Saddled with a history that could only be a liability if told by someone else, I decided to use my life to do something that no one has ever done before on the scale of modern data: I would donate my life—dark parts and all—to the advancement of human understanding.

I might be the worst sinner or excommunicated person, but I can still advance the freedom of all through my framework for why your villains act the way they do.

When writing this book, I determined that it would not be balanced for me to give only a male perspective. But try to imagine how difficult it is to find other people willing to lay out their ENTIRE life story, censorable skeletons and all, in front of the world. Imagine how hard it is for a random creepy man to come up to you and say, "Hey! Will your bare all for my occult book?" Because I have my pride and was in no mood to justify my work to anyone, I decided that there *would* be a female counterpart, but she would be a fictional character. This opens up even more doors than only having two real people, and you will meet her later. At the bottom of *The Book of Contours* lies this idea that every corner of my and your life is useful, and I will illustrate this by showing how the psychology of a real human is both wired and savable. That said, I am a straight male, and do think about and *do* male things. I also have some more specialized habits, and you will learn about them in the table below. But here's what I hope readers will understand: We can't fix social problems if we don't look at them or learn how they work. We can't cure hate and misunderstanding if we don't have a good framework for seeing what all sides want. My dream is that, regardless of my occasionally strange life, you will get a glimpse not so much into how pathology works, but how the sides you are socially trained to hide *forever* actually do bubble up in some people, who in turn make a considerable living using mechanisms we are not encouraged to discuss sanely, let alone fathom. I myself never want children of my own, but why? I can be power hungry, imperialistic, arrogant,… destructive, but why? I have a couple of very dirty and chauvinistic sides. And the aim is not to get you to like that fact. The aim is to use my unique position as one with his chart's skeletons in a public place to put to good use the dark sides he just wasn't ever allowed to hide. Some people are simply dealt weird hands. Throughout this chapter, I hope to give you a glimpse into a complete psychological study. As a man in new times, my frontier isn't the untamed country, but the undiscovered thought-spaces that only this one life can traverse. I hope by putting myself under the microscope, I can free not only myself, but millions of other people from this idea that you need all of the normative perks to be worth a damn… or that having all of the normative perks should confine you to roads that don't necessarily suit you.

[SELF] DATA SAVE PART 2 OF 3: COMMON ACTIVITIES LIST

80% of my self-data save comes from two sources: 1) a spontaneous list of everything I can possibly picture myself doing in a day, week, year, and beyond (common behaviors). 2) A walk through all 1728 qunits and what situation each one's unique combination of asteroids reminds me of in my of life (the Q-bio). This section discusses the construction of a common behaviors list.

So you want to save yourself as data? Let's recap.

1. Save your interfaces. Determine what always happens around you (in ways that can be viewable by others) when you've been in a place for a reasonable amount of time.
2. List all aspects of your personality (character you project to others) and your identity (ideas which are not you, but advance who you think you are and how others help you to be)
3. List your common activities; At any moment of any day, you can typically be found doing one very predictable thing. What are the most obvious things you could be described as doing in a particular day?
4. List what situations each of the 1728 qunits reminds you of.

#3 is covered here, while #4 is covered in the next section.

Before we begin, let me warn you about some things.

- I disprefer some things that are publicly celebrated. I wouldn't call myself antisocial, but do have several non-prosocial preferences.
- My male characteristics and hormones are still very much active, regardless of how socially acceptable it is to talk about this and the ideas that follow from it. My goal is to advance our understanding of the psychology behind this.
- I am still a human with basic biological functions. If you want your robots to have life-equivalent and survival imperatives, they will have to have some way of getting rid of wasteful input and reinforcing their wills. I list basic bodily functions like peeing, pooping, and eating because *someone* out there has to tell us how to put these operations into a reloaded human's network.
- I have a particular multifaceted realm of sexual practice which isn't as randy as it seems, but may offend the unprepared. It doesn't involve actual sex, or orgasm, but even if it did that would be my right too. Because there are 1728 qunits, having 30 or so of them relate to this topic may make it seem like the taboo keeps coming up, but the number of occurrences of the topic is actually normal.

Let's get started.

SAVING MY MOST COMMON ACTION PATTERNS

The rules for constructing the list below were simple: List anything you do in a day, then on days that are not today. List dreams you have for your life. Mentalities you hold. Finally, try connecting everything you listed into a causal chain: for every behavior you listed, what other behaviors need to come before it? This last step will almost certainly lead you to start listing things like time windows and the all-important "views of the great dream"—those things you are taught to pursue in your society. If I were to be re-rendered as a character in a game or simulation, this list below would constitute the space of most major actions that my character would perform. The second column, labeled "behavior," is the main one you want to look at. All other columns support this one.

TABLE 9: AJANI'S BASIC ACTION PATTERNS

before->	behavior	harmonic	category	->after	valence
1 day; wake up	sleep	1	homeostasis	4 hours; peek at potential wakeup hour	0
thorough work mood; background calculate; nod off; time passage; motivated towards vast space to order patterns	nod off	89	homeostasis	sleep; jolt to alertness	-0.5
drink heavy caffeine; eat heavy salt; thorough work mood	blackout crash	97	homeostasis	jolt to alertness	-0.5
background calculate; time passage	snack	87	homeostasis	highly cerebral mind	0.5
4 hours	eat	1	homeostasis	contemplative mood; reflect on data structuring; seek to improve	0
1 day; The mono partner	dine	87	homeostasis	eat	0
Turn offs, anger triggers	search it solution	46	work & job	inquire of experts	-2
search it solution	decipher it problem	124	work & job	declare voluntary time	-2
be annoyed with high it confounds	mull over it message	73	work & job	inquire of experts	-1
guarded travel; be annoyed with high it confounds	passively listen to it colleagues	73	work & job	declare voluntary time	0
decipher it problem; dread administrative exact deadline	be annoyed with high it confounds	52	work & job	declare voluntary time	-2
mull over it message	semi-invested in IT discussions	52	work & job	declare voluntary time	0.5
decipher it problem; participate semi-invested in it discussions	demo it work	73	work & job	passively listen to it colleagues	0.5
passively co-watch classroom entertainment; explanatory mood	moderate fact-finding discussions	15	teaching	hover around classroom	1.5
explain classroom lessons	hover around classroom	102	teaching	explain classroom lessons	2
explain classroom lessons	guide student in-class work	15	teaching	moderate fact-finding discussions	1
moderate fact-finding discussions	passive watch class entertainment	86	teaching	moderate fact-finding discussions	1.5
teacher family; oldest brother; mama bear welcomer	explain classroom lessons	27	teaching	moderate fact-finding discussions	1
counsel student (accept late student work)	grade-glance single student work	83	administration	seek to improve	0
administrative writing	grade-mass pile of student work	71	administration	zombie through admin filing & writing	0.5
warm introductory conversation; hangout with students	counsel student	29	communication	time passage	1
explain lesson; passively co-watch classroom; off chat with student	hangout with students	29	communication	off chat with student	1.5
moderate fact-finding discussions	demo student assignment	82	teaching	guide student in-class work	1
warm introductory conversation; mama bear feedback gatherer	off chat with student	29	communication	time passage	1.5
hour of mercury - demanded mind	administrative writing	83	administration	time passage	0
gather documents on investments; oldest brother	zombie through administrative filing	52	administration	zombie through administrative filing	-1
recall administrative failures and social barriers	dread administrative exact deadline	74	administration	delay performance of obligation	-3

dread administrative obligation	prepare music playlist	78	daily duty	disinvested performance of obligation	1
dread administrative obligations; contemplative mood	self-occupy before long administrative work	78	daily duty	disinvested performance of obligation	0.5
status reinforcement	long drive	102	daily duty	eat heavy salt food	0
dad's influence; mom's influence; enjoy general peace	mood match music play	118	daily duty	mark move	1

A story: From my private recordings about the asteroids in my 124q4

This qunit is SUPER IMPORTANT. In my life it is called "the guiding music" and explains how the songs that spontaneously arise in my head are actually clarifications of whole situations that I find myself in when I am without a clue. This is a form of musical clairvoyance which also includes perfect timing between the things that I am doing and the progression of certain songs that I'm listening to. Interestingly, when we were younger, we would record video games we were playing with music in the background, noting every time it "matched." This makes sense in opposition to 52q4 where my Uranus is, and was almost certainly myself training myself for an intuition-related skill that I would have in the future. If I find myself confused, without solutions, then I can stop and listen to whatever song is invariably lurking on the playlist in my head and get a great summary of where I am and sometimes what may need to be done.

disinvested performance of obligation; shop for groceries	stern-block public during errand	68	daily duty	guarded travel	0
antisocial/private	retreat to privacy for concentration	110	publisher	write works	0
sick or ill	zen sickness	109	homeostasis	sleep	-1
drink light alcohol; drink hard alcohol; drink heavy caffeine; drink other; drink tea; 4 hours	pee	1	homeostasis	post-bathroom cleanup	0
eat; 10 hours	poop	1	homeostasis	post-bathroom cleanup	0
eat; 4 hours; sick or ill	poop uncomfortable	109	homeostasis	post-bathroom cleanup	0
pee	post-bathroom cleanup	1	homeostasis	wash hands	0
pee	wash hands	87	homeostasis	time passage	0
1 day; drink heavy caffeine	shower	43	homeostasis	time passage	0
partner fantasy + indifference to 2 day bad day; 2 hours; turn-on: large breasts/low drag hips; pre-sleep fantasy; seducible by two; sex w partner;	ejaculate	67	mating drive	hr of uranus - chaos; partner argmt spray; solicitation fail; pre-sleep fantasy; susceptible to 2 partners	2
enjoy well-assembled body and measurable creativity	light mood sing	43	daily duty	eat; snack; time passage; reflect on diy project priority; assembly line process or label data	1
long drive	tap fingers on wheel	88	daily duty	zen obligation performance	0.5
pull new music or series; Motivated towards: vast space in which to order patterns; Personality [close friends]: Personality, private	impromptu rave	142	mating drive	sleep; nod off; contemplative mood	2
declare voluntary time; Seems passive / not dominating, BUT generally it's his way or failure for the other; seek to improve; background calculate	mark move	100	reflection	enjoy badassery	2
dad's influence	silly song invent	103	voluntary time	the mono partner	2
birthright	prepare minimal snack	93	homeostasis	snack	1
decide to leave a situation; time passage; fun duo conversation	reflect on relationship distancing	93	reflection	record thoughts	-1
develop complex algorithm or workflow; pose an abstract question	reflect on data structuring	36	daily duty	assembly line process; recursive inspect research; record thoughts; background calculation	0
dread administrative obligations; make more money	reflect on diy project priority	100	daily duty	background calculate; hardware diy movement and preparation procedure; record thoughts	0.5
observe far day or tower view; search for new investment channels; make more money	reflect on status attainments	86	field of mind	search for more investment channels; enjoy tower view; enjoy general peace; seek to improve; desire for more money	0.5
art mirrors life; watch series; mood match music play; inquire of experts	search tv shows for match	65	daily duty	time passage	0.5
pose abstract question; motivated towards vast spaces for ordering information	search video games for match	56	daily duty	pose abstract question	1
play video game jrpg; 16-bit; play with Lego	play video game tactics	132	voluntary time	art mirrors life; contemplative mood; eat; snack; drink other	2

aj's relationship with brothers; 16-bit	play video game jrpg	16	voluntary time	put on penis stretcher; motivated towards vast space for ordering information	1.5
declare voluntary time	reflect on penis growth goals	115	field of mind	seek to improve; inspect penis; decrease triggerability by women; enjoy general peace; prepare snack	1.5
put on penis stretcher	wear penis stretcher	86	voluntary time	seek to improve; Motivated towards: vast space in which to order patterns	0
seek to improve; time passage; penis jelq freestanding	put on penis stretcher	77	voluntary time	wear penis stretcher	0
penis jelq freestanding; time passage; seek to improve	penis jelq roller	93	voluntary time	penis jelq freestanding; inspect penis	0.5
declare voluntary time; Seems passive / not dominating, BUT generally it's his way or failure for the other; seek to improve; background calculate; 27 y.o.	penis jelq freestanding	95	voluntary time	contemplative mood; time passage; seek to improve; mark move; Motivated by: sexual information, measurements	1
jelq freestanding	load or observe girly-girl pictures	56	communication	Motivated by: sexual information	0.5
reference the body for immediate answers; imaginary friends; motivated by sexual information	ai generate girly-girl pictures	58	daily duty	refine ai prompt; ai generate other types of image	1
declare voluntary time	inspect penis	65	mating drive	reflect on penis growth goals; snack; retreat to privacy for concentration; susceptible to two partners; volume down distrusted other	2

A story: The personal sexuality directed towards my work and growth, not to a person

Colleague Afterhours	Honestly man, I keep asking myself why you would publicize something like that. I mean, I don't even know where to begin. Aren't you worried that this may cost you your job?
Ajani	Not really. We don't work in the kind of culture that makes a big deal out of people's personal decisions.
Colleague	Yeah, I guess you're right. But you've got to expect some funny looks from a few coworkers, at least?
Ajani	Eh, well, maybe. But again, I think making it an open topic just isn't going to be a thing. It's a practice that has heavy implications for human psychology and sociology, and I think the full chapter on it isn't nearly as crazy as people might first think.
Colleague	Bet. So I guess I should just ask, what is this with your penis exercises?
Ajani	Do you want the short version or the long version?
Colleague	Let's start with the short version.
Ajani	Okay. It's a state of focus. It's not particularly sexual. It has an if-and-only-if relationship to both my resistance to inefficacy and my quality use of time. Lastly, it is very VERY tied to what I publish outwards, and the hours I rack up taking other's publishing in.
Colleague	So it's not just to make your dick bigger or to compensate for something?
Ajani	Correct. It isn't. I approach my exercises the same way some people approach running or painting as a hobby. It's something my body likes as part of my preferred health regimen.
Colleague	Hmm. I'm sorry for the image of you I get in my head—hunched over with your eyes rolled back while doing your best porn groan.
Ajani	Haha. It isn't like that.
Colleague	Then what is it like?
Ajani	What is what like, the specific exercises or the thought process?
Colleague	The way the exercises work.
Ajani	I'm going to tell you about the thought process instead, and also give you a little history first. That will give you a better idea of what's going on.
Colleague	Okay.
Ajani	I've been bathed in body-centric energy from a very young age. Whether it was mom's copy of *Our Bodies Ourselves*, dad's *Penthouse*, or various interesting events with a couple of friends and neighbors, I still remember having my He-Man and Teela action figures make out in that blue bowl of water—probably inspired by what I heard from mom and dad across the hall—knowing that I needed to keep that hidden. I mean, they did right? I was four, maybe five years old, but even at three I know I had this energy. No one traumatized me or molested me or anything like that. It was just the way I was. I guess my spirit selectively absorbed certain kinds of inputs over others. Alas, I heard things; it just so happened that I *knew* what I was hearing.
Colleague	Hm.
Ajani	So I've carried that lusty energy all my life. It flies all around my aura. And on top of that, I've always been fairly serious, hypersensitive, and with a high sense of responsibility for others by default. Put these together and you get someone whose energy feels like that of a predator. Although I've never done any such thing, this does explain my later gravitation towards the Dom role in BDSM in my 30s.
Colleague	Whips and leather, huh?
Ajani	For a subset of such folks, but not for me, no.
Colleague	So how does that work?
Ajani	That is a vast topic that you should research in your free time. But I'll tell you that some people find it much healthier to play out otherwise pathological wiring through a role rather than in the regular life context. I was taught by a group of people in the leather culture, yes, and they introduced me to a rich world of sexualities that my classifying brain couldn't get enough of. The world itself, that is. As a space. When it comes to the specific practices however, I've spent most of my life preferring celibacy.

Colleague	Really?
Ajani	Yes. And this should make sense when you think about it. My childhood exposure to sexuality was necessarily played out alone, does that make sense? And it didn't manifest itself through masturbation or playing doctor. I was five, for God's sake. So my creative energy went into building Lego cities and later SimCities. Granted, the Lego characters would shag more often as I reached puberty, but I was always more of the world controller type. A "rigger" if you will.
Colleague	This is all too much.
Ajani	Is it really? I can stop.
Colleague	No, no! Please continue.
Ajani	So anyway, the first girl who ever kissed me was named Jasmine. It was in a line in Mrs. Kahanek's class, if I recall, and I slapped her. It was a visceral reaction.
Colleague	Oh, that's terrible!
Ajani	Eh, who's to say? The slap was no good, of course. But I think the concept of one rejecting their first kiss that way is probably the more bothersome part to people. Anyway, she tried it again in fourth grade. And that next time I could only stand there dumbfounded. I immediately resolved to take her up on it the next time, but there was no next time.
Colleague	Sounds like the beginning of a pattern.
Ajani	The beginning of a couple of patterns, yes. In between Jasmine and my first girlfriend-interest is a whole other chapter that birthed my polyamory/nonmonogamy, but that's actually not relevant to the current topic. What is relevant is that around this time I was hanging out with my cousin Michael and our friends Cedric, Brandon, and Trey. Michael and Trey got all the girls, as far as I could see. They were taller, better looking, and generally more popular, but I had my own niche in academics. It was here that I learned to carve out a space of my own in the romance department.
Colleague	I see.
Ajani	But school, for the most part *was* my romance. My first girlfriend-interest, T.O., was someone who I kind of saw as being reachable from my tier, and we agreed to go out on something like a date when I was 13. But she stood me up. I was heartbroken, and started to develop in earnest the pessimism I have today towards any romantic prospects.
Colleague	That sounds so sad.
Ajani	Well, you know. Teenage sadness is always apocalyptic. Later in high school, then in college, T.O. reemerged, and we almost had a thing. We started to have sex, but I hid my interest. It died out and I never saw her again. Having resisted her twice, I don't think I was welcome in her life again. Now THAT became a pattern.
Colleague	Jesus, man! You're your own cock-blocker.
Ajani	And I think Snoop and Tha Dogg Pound would have agreed with you at the time. But my focus has always been on world-building first. I was my little brothers' only oldest brother, and my parent's first scholar admitted into a top-tier prep school. More than that, I was a young black male with the standard black-trained temper, struggling first and foremost to block the control of all things ambushing my hormones. It was more important never to be railroaded at another's whim than to join the hundreds of millions of boys out there rolling around in the bed with someone who didn't actually respect them. It was also around this time that I was watching the relationship between my mom and dad drop in direct correlation with him being screwed in his radio career. Meanwhile, he too was having problems of his own making. There you could see that committed relationships meant sharing, yet there was no guarantee that the other person would play fair even if you did. Trust me. Staying single throughout high school was a GREAT blessing to me. But it wasn't just given. I had to actively choose discipline over the alternatives. My work today hinges on me having had that discipline yesterday.
Colleague	I got it. And I take it all this is related to what we were talking about?
Ajani	Yes. It will all make sense shortly.
Colleague	Alright.
Ajani	So I changed a lot in college. Had a crush on this girl L.A., turned activist, lost almost all of my friends by appearing unstable and being roundly difficult, explored Islam, discovered my claircognizance, was introduced to astrology by a classmate Olga, was put on academic suspension twice, and eventually finished a year late. So I was an iconoclast by the time REDACTED invited me to Europe randomly while I was reading a book *Sexual Alchemy* in a Borders bookstore. It was weird because I didn't know her at all, I mean not. at. all. Though I suppose we had crossed paths at some point a couple of times on campus. Later that year we did go to Europe. (I suspect I was a replacement for the guy she really liked, REDACTED), and I lost my virginity at age 23 at a mountaintop B&B in Italy. Anacapri on the island of Capri, to be exact.
Colleague	Whoa. Exotic.
Ajani	Yes. And I was a minuteman. Done in 30 seconds.
Colleague	Ouch.
Ajani	Tried again in Corfu. Minuteman again. The shame of it was so bad that I threw a big baby tantrum in Athens, was a 100% jerk towards REDACTED, and we went our separate ways, leaving me on my own with no sense of how to navigate a foreign country for the remaining three of the six week trip.
Colleague	Yikes.
Ajani	No. You see, during the course of the trip up to then, REDACTED had been a fun travelmate, but not really interested in my philosophy or work or anything like that. By 2003 my dad had already died of a stroke and I had learned to seriously distrust my mom's example as his partner. I knew that I should definitely not let my partner, whoever she might eventually be, circumscribe my manhood and my professional potential the way I felt my mom had my dad's and I also knew—just based on our household growing up and my experiences at Caltech—that I *definitely* couldn't assume that my partner would support me when I most needed it. Only when things were going well. Only when there were results. But for works in progress, I was on my own—unless they were *her* works in progress, that is. This pattern is specific to me and is by no means an indictment of women, but for my own personal setup continues to play out this day without fail. My close female partner is my travelmate

	through life, but I would be very surprised to find a supportmate in her as well. REDACTED was my first exposure to that, and the realization made me very angry. There would be no white picket fences or gripping love stories in my future after all.
Colleague	(Nods sternly.)
Ajani	So on my way back to Charles de Gaulle, I decided to make a few stops. First was Genoa, where I *really* wanted to spend a couple of days thinking about mom's relationship with dad. Did some journalling there. Then I went back to Nice because it was sooo much friendlier to me as an American than Paris was, and I was not itching to get back to Paris any earlier than necessary. I took a vow of silence for 2 days, watched the sunset while listening to Rachid - Feed the Pigeons, and went back to my hostel. Then, at the end of the first day I met them: Leah and Jess. They let me finish my second day without speaking, then we had a great time for the rest of our stay there. They actually were interested in astrology, we sat on the beach at night while I read their charts, and we drank at a cafe until the wee hours of the morning. It was awesome.
	Back in Paris, I met a dude named Oram, and we bonded as if he was some kind of weird substitute for my friend Kevin back home. Jazz clubs, talk about girls, I saw how dirty brown the Eiffel Tower actually was, and decided Paris wasn't as great as it was hyped up to be. After Oram departed, I spent the last three days in Europe hanging out with some Canadians and a hip addition, Shannon, Fred (female with a male nickname), and Colin where we went on a whirlwind tour of various places in the city—including the Louvre, where we gazed upon the rather tiny Mona Lisa just before closing hours.
	The point is, I did so much better on my own after splitting with my travelmate, and got a chance to come to terms with some things. But the time with REDACTED did a lot to shape my notions of manhood back then, and more generally my sense of what it means to be effective. Especially this one comment she made:
	(You'll have to forgive my categorizing brain, but I work in numbers. It's how I formerly register the differences in things.)
	While we were in Corfu, REDACTED made a comment about my size. I hadn't measured at the time, but later found out that I was about 7.4" long and 4.9" in circumference, and by her assessment, this was big. Unfortunately, amidst the shame of both first performances, I found the idea of being further assessed to be roundly off-putting. Like my mom assessing my dad. This particular male becomes responsible for both people's enjoyment, I suppose? But what about the partner? What if they can't or won't contribute to their own enjoyment with you? What if you give what you know, but they don't clue you in as to what they prefer, they don't connect with your needs, or whatever? And there I was. The rappers I knew of talked about having 9" dicks all the time, and this person in the bed was setting the bar for me? I mean, she clearly wanted me to be her other preferred dude. Or maybe she didn't but the bar itself was messed up. Too low in some ways, too high in others—and mostly my fault for misinterpreting—but in all cases, just plain confusing. I couldn't have someone tangling up the standards I set for myself, especially when their standards were lower than mine. None of this was REDACTED's fault. It's just that, what did the rapper Too $hort say, "When you're first, you know you get it worst." She was my first, and had the misfortune of unlocking all of my insecurities and the family and college baggage that came with it.
Colleague	So you're saying you thought you should have been bigger?
Ajani	Not at the time. Rather, I thought I was in less of a position to confidently brag the way I thought the brag-level dude could, and her comment only reminded me of my own internal sense of insufficiency. Not inadequacy, insufficiency. That internal reminder, coupled with my "poor" performance in bed, gave me double the heartburn. She asserted the right to judge me a little, and I was even angrier as I judged myself *a lot*.
Colleague	I see.
Ajani	Months later on my last visit with her, she made another comment, "You talk big, but you don't do much." During those times where we were alone, it was never my intent to talk big, just to connect. And here I was having that used against me? What the fuck? I took it as emasculation, intended or otherwise. Because again, this is what I had perceived my mom doing to my dad. Anyway, rather than reload all of the events surrounding that comment, I note that at some point she also said something like, "You don't respect me, do you?" and I told her "no." Because I don't lie. It was fucked up, really, and I guess we gave what we got. But you know what? We're okay today. There was a little mini email exchange a couple of years ago, and I think all of that is mostly water under the bridge.
Colleague	So this story with her doesn't actually have a bad ending.
Ajani	Correct. I eventually grew up.
	Fast forward three years to 2006. I've bought my first house out in the country and am living on my own. Out of curiosity, I measure myself and obtain the values I just told you about. Having just finished the *Kama Sutra* and concluded that it just wasn't that scandalous, I picked up the *Ananga Ranga* instead. I learn about the jelq technique for penis growth, and apparently there are some guys claiming on the internet that this is possible. I'm 26 years old at the time, quite a ways past puberty. But I try out the exercises and see that you can get at least some visible change going. I like being in my own space, doing the exercise, reflecting on the complications of certain exchanges and certain aspects of the body, and realize that the whole experience is pretty similar to yoga. The practice for me, however, got me closer to my own trained standard for being able to broadcast a message of effectiveness in the world, and it turns out that this wasn't that different from what the rappers used to brag about. But there were some noteworthy conditions for doing this.
Ajani	I found that I was much more likely to do the growth exercises after a social failure—especially coming home day after day emptyhanded in real estate. I still had some girls I liked, and was more effective in my exercises when they were blocked. I learned that orgasm hurts my eyes and in most cases gives me a massive headache for two days. I learned that sex in general greatly raises the chances that someone will try to fight me two days later—fight in the professional or daily partnership sense. When you do the exercises, you can't cum, you can't jerk off or put on your favorite porn tape. It isn't ahegao or something extreme like that. It's just focus. Furthermore, I found that I tend to hit milestones in my measure every time I publish a book—as if the ruler reach stays in the same place until a new book comes out that covers new ground dissimilar from the last, then—like magic—you're bigger. But there isn't a lot of sex involved there, just focus.
	Jelq, the roller (which is the most effective of all), a stretcher I made when I got too big for the first one I bought, a high vitamin-C diet (for my own personal metabolism), and sleep. That's what I use. Oh, and you can't be around anything that turns you off.
Colleague	I see.

Ajani	A trick I found useful when I don't feel like doing the exercises, is to have what I call my "girly-girl" pics around. This is its own complicated side story, but you can think of it as having a gallery of naked images nearby which fuels your hormones to stay semi-erect even if you yourself are not into it.
Colleague	Why would you do it when you're not into it?
Ajani	A great question. And this is probably the reason I'm comfortable talking about all this:
	In your astro chart, you have at least two areas where the asteroids contained describe Time. Duodecanate 78 describes how you measure time, while the opposition duodecanate 6 describes things which you register as passing during time's tick. If you have a particular trait in these areas, they will tend to correspond to your sense of how you spend time. One of the asteroids associated with penis length, Luznice, lives in the 78s in my chart, so like an artist who absolutely has to paint or else they'll go stir crazy, I absolutely have to keep progressing in the size department, no matter how incremental, or else I feel like shit, to be honest. Like I'm just throwing away chunks of my life for no good reason. Said differently, failing to do my growth exercises feels like I'm wasting my life. There is no one I'm trying to please, not even myself. It's just a personal routine that *has* to progress in my downtime.
Colleague	That's crazy. I can't imagine thinking like that.
Ajani	Because I admire the great humans in history who went past the bounds of almost all of their fellows, and I know for a fact that my growth is one area where I've been able to defy the limits that constrain almost everyone else—my books also cover ground that two millennia of astrologers haven't had access to cover and I know it—these things are definitely correlated. Speaking of thinking, your Mercury in your chart describes how you join ideas together. It's related to your personal logic system, and constitutes a "major" planet because It's something you really can't avoid using. My logic system is not the easiest for people to relate to, so I convey it in book form for anyone interested to consume at their leisure. My Mercury is near my Midheaven, so this logic and publishing is part of what I'm known for in public. But one of the asteroids related to interracial pairing with an endowed partner, Ostozhenka, is also on my Mercury. Another asteroid related to general effectiveness, Falk, is in my Taurus region of discipline—which keeps increasing as I get older. These are three of the approximately 30-ish asteroids which text-mined on male endowment. So my logical explorations are inherently sexual and always have been. The more I publish, the more extensive my toolset for enabling mine and witnesses' creativity, and this is more or less what a penis does, energetically speaking.
Colleague	So publishing builds up a body of creation-tooling public work, and brings with it a buildup of your actual creation-tool body area near it.
Ajani	Exactly.
Colleague	So you'll probably keep getting bigger as long as you keep publishing and not wasting time.
Ajani	Something like that. But I think I'm past the point where such growth is useful. My interest in further publishing has dropped in light of some other interests which are out of the scope of this conversation.
Colleague	So if I were to ask you how I can grow myself, would you tell me?
Ajani	I've already told you the tools I use. That's it. There's no surgery or anything, just 20+ years of a compelled routine. If you don't have some kind of otherworldly drive to do this the way I do, though, it's probably not worth it. There are very real health risks. You CAN give yourself a heart attack, and you will go months without noticing any progress of any kind. If you succeed, you'll do so through spending a lot of time ignoring your partners or doing your exercises in a setting where it is totally unsafe for your partner to help you. So you will necessarily have less sex while you are doing this. If sex with your partner is something you value, doing all this can get tricky really fast. You can still have sex, mind you, but the penetration won't be desirable for most partners.
Colleague	Oh.
Ajani	For me, it's not just worth it, though, but necessary. My life partner Shanna has known about it from the beginning of our relationship, seen all the gear and such, and… it's just my routine.
	But I haven't told you the biggest benefit, and why I keep doing this.
Colleague	Aside from impressing people?
Ajani	That's not a reason. I don't assume people are impressed or offended or annoyed or whatever. This is my body and my standards. They can find their own body-to-experience mapping.
Colleague	But it must greatly change how you have sex.
Ajani	If you're already above average, it makes sex harder, not easier, and less likely to happen at all. I prefer celibacy myself.
	No, the biggest benefit is, the longer I do this, the farther I get away from the person who used to let his partner tote him around like a bag. I say no to subpar things and people much more readily, I have less to prove and more space to assess my assessors. Lastly, If I want to say something, I can say it without intruding or without hurting anyone, but say it nonetheless. My procreations sit passively in books, and I now have more nerve to write the kinds of books I want. Trust me, I'm still going through *Laurentia 2* in the hopes of finding all the typos, but there are diminishing returns on the 5th readthrough of an 800-page dictionary—in trying to make it look like it came from Random House. It's just a reference book which sits out there in a sea of content. I still have a day job and do need to move on with my life. Because I block most information sources unless I know I can trust them, I know that my work is 100% my own, not steered by the power of mass suggestion.
Colleague	Wow. So you say you've grown over the past 20 years. What's your measure now, if you don't mind my asking?
Ajani	Here's the data. I've placed it later in a book I'm writing. Length and circumference, flaccid and erect, were four of the 340 numbers I used in my 300-person adult data set to do the statistics for the book. To determine which astro factors correlate to what on every area of the body, you *do* need numbers, you know.
Colleague	Hm. I guess that makes sense, but man. Isn't that kind of growth, uh, inconvenient? I mean for something you yourself can control?
Ajani	It's tied to Time. That and Mercury's progress as a thinker. Stopping the practice wouldn't make me happy. It would feel unendingly shitty, to be honest.
Colleague	Kind of like an addiction, right?
Ajani	Well, I wouldn't go that far, but we all have our thing we just **need** to have happen. This has coevolved with my sense of control over all aspects of my life and my ability to ignore barriers as a writer. It's important beyond other people's assessments.

Colleague	But what about your partner's happiness? I mean, realistically, most people aren't in porn and probably wouldn't be very comfortable with that kind of proportion.
Ajani	True. But that's not the centerpiece of sex with the partner. I don't want an eye ache or a two day bad day. My exercises are for my own sense of life-progress, control of the body. It is my own form of sacred sexuality reserved for my creative mind and the work that matters: the philosophy I publish. Sex with my partner has any number of other ways to unfold without injuring the other person.
Colleague	Fair enough. Wait a minute. *340* body measurement numbers?
Ajani	Yeah, things like the three measures of nose width, abdominal tone scale, finger length, philtrum squareness, navel height, head triangularness, arm veininess... you name it.
Colleague	Man, that's crazy. I guess you really do look at it like a science. I really wish you luck in finding people mature enough to talk about this
Ajani	Thanks. Some of it's luck, but most of it is my choice. I'm not talking about it, I'm writing. Hit and run. And I'll never be obligated to respond to anyone's immaturity about it.

search video games for match, volume down distrusted other	play video game platformer	52	daily duty	be irritated with self-continued frustration; time passage	1
inquire of experts; search video games for match	play video game first-person or visual novel	56	daily duty	time passage; seek to improve; contemplative mood	0.5
relationship with brothers	play video game beat-em-up hack-n-slash or co-op	54	communication	time passage; friends: rarely communicates with them, despite wishing there were more communication, but...	0.5
birthright; 8-bit	play video game logic puzzle	101	voluntary time	inquire of experts	1
pace conscious contemplate; negative surprise encountered	write works	94	communication	write dialogues	0
contemplative mood	record thoughts	3	voluntary time	pace conscious contemplate	0
play passive absorb with pet	exchange vibes with cat	132	daily duty	enjoy general peace; time passage	1
disinvested performance of obligation	play active with pet	97	daily duty	exchange vibes with cat; prepare minimal snack	0.5
disinvested performance of obligation; 1 day; low energy mood	play passive absorb with pet	114	daily duty	exchange vibes with cat; prepare minimal snack	0
disinvested performance of obligation; 1 day	monitor pet for trouble	120	daily duty	monitor pet for trouble; time passage	0
develop complex algorithm or workflow; talent for automation and mass data	recursive build workflow	22	field of mind	recursive build workflow; recursive inspect research data; motivated by sexual information	0
assembly line process or label data; pose abstract question	recursive inspect research data	126	field of mind	recursive inspect research data; recursive build workflow	0
recursive inspect research data; seek to improve; time passage	assembly line process or label data	130	field of mind	recursive inspect research data	0
assembly line process or label data; thorough work mode	explore existing data repository	108	field of mind	recursive inspect research data	0
ai generate girly girl images	ai generate other types of image	58	field of mind	ai generate girly-girl pictures; refine ai prompt; Distrusts most women who turn him on until he is sure they will add to (rather than take from) his ambitions	0.5
recursive inspect research data	refine ai prompt (caught up)	83	field of mind	ai generate other types of image; ai generate girly-girl pictures	-0.5
motivated by sexual information; motivated towards the vast space to order information	develop new question from body observation	57	field of mind	recursive inspect research; record thoughts; build complicated workflow	1
mood match music play; dad's influence; prepare music playlist; hear resonant energy; time passage	pull new music or series	83	field of mind		0
pose abstract question; motivated towards vast spaces for ordering information; silence on feeling stupid	pace preconscious contemplate	77	field of mind		2.5
status reinforcement; motivated towards vast spaces for ordering information; low energy mood	pace conscious contemplate	88	communication		0
enjoy general peace; reflect on status attainments	observe far day or tower view	121	status reinforcement	enjoy general peace; status reinforcement	2.5
mom's influence	drink tea	81	status reinforcement		0.5
1 day; the mono partner	drink light alcohol	97	daily duty	work on diy	0.5

brother #3, youngest; mom's influence; motivated towards: vast space to order patterns; retreat to privacy for concentration	drink hard alcohol (1 bottle per week, rationed over mini sips per night)	91	field of mind	highly cerebral mind; recursive inspect research data; record thoughts	0.5
thorough work mood	drink other	1	homeostasis		0
hardware diy movement and preparation procedure	work on diy	60	daily duty	shower; time passage; hardware diy movement and preparation procedure	0
watch diy video; work on diy	follow diy instructions	75	daily duty		0
reflect on diy project priority; pose an abstract question	watch diy video	75	daily duty		0.5
fitness drop; fitness practice; time passage; enjoy well-assembled body and measurable creativity	follow fitness video instructions	88	homeostasis		1
inquire of experts; dread exact administrative performance	follow other video instructions	109	daily duty		0
guarded travel	awkward chat with stranger	61	communication		-1
dad's influence; mama bear feedback gatherer; warm introductory conversation	sir chat with former students and friends	87	communication		1
32 y.o.; mishap responder; reflect on relationship distance	real talk chat with brother	16	communication		2
mom's influence	update chat with partner	16	communication		1
mom's influence; dad's influence	listen to other person in conversation	45	communication		0.5
strangers Feel uncomfortable. Ajani = weird	block judgement of other	94	field of mind		0
pace conscious contemplate	record what is on the mind	24	communication		0
nod off	pre-sleep fantasy	89	mating drive	sleep; susceptible to two partners; greatly admires princess royal victoria; motivated by sexual information	2.5
nod off; imaginary friends	meditate pre-sleep	132	homeostasis	enjoy general peace; sleep	2
dread exact administrative deadline; determine a situation intolerable; self-occupy before long administrative work	do yardwork	20	daily duty	hardware diy movement and preparation procedure; shower; drink light alcohol	0
2 weeks	shop for groceries	40	daily duty	disinvested performance of obligation	-0.5
shop for groceries	town errand administrivia	75	daily duty	disinvested performance of obligation	-0.5
declare voluntary time; be irritated with frustrating self-continued situation; lost direction finder	organize computer data	38	administration	pace conscious contemplate	-0.5
work on diy; hardware diy movement and preparation procedure	haul diy various	38	daily duty	heavy hauler	0
1 day; the mono partner	wash dishes	40	daily duty	disinvested performance of obligation	-0.5
obligation music	hardware diy movement and preparation procedure	75	daily duty	work on diy	-1
1 week; disinvested performance of obligation	enter timesheet	73	daily duty	disinvested performance of obligation	-0.5
mama bear feedback gatherer; difficult personality increase	assist partner with task	38	daily duty	mama bear welcomer	1
write works	final publishing process	60	daily duty		-1.5
megaman; reflect on relationship distancing	absorb immunities from challengers	102	field of mind		-1
make an eject plan; slam stubborn persons difficulty(slam)	poison self-opinion of interaction with ones critics	113	field of mind		-2
stunned when suddenly checked	write off future cooperation with critic	76	field of mind		-2
be irritated in negative dynamic with another	make an eject plan	74	field of mind		-2
seek to improve; stunned when suddenly checked	be irritated in negative dynamic with another	55	communication		-2.5

	A story: How I think about face-to-face criticism
Cris Figment	What is this shit? It's full of typos. How could you publish something like this?
Ajani	You mean *Laurentia 2*?
Cris	Yes.
Ajani	I mean, it's 800 pages so...
Cris	Don't you care about quality?
Ajani	I read through it 4 times during the self-publishing process and caught 99.999% of what was there to be caught.
Cris	And yet there is a cringy typo or some other mistake on literally every other page.
Ajani	True. But I'll correct it one day, just like the book itself was a correction to its predecessor.
Cris	You're referring to that almost pedantic, pseudoscientific "reference book" of yours, *Laurentia 1st edition*?
Ajani	That's right.
Cris	Hmph. I'll be honest, I couldn't keep up with it, but part of me thinks it was more interesting—even if the physics was wrong.
Ajani	You don't know that. And you're no physicist.
Cris	Fine. I'll give you a pass on that and write it off as speculation.
Ajani	A thought experiment.
Cris	Speculation.
Ajani	Fuck you. We're done.
Cris	Quitting so soon?
Ajani	You're putting words in my mouth, telling me what *my* intention was. And this is why I publish books with typos. Because at some point I know people like you aren't interested in whether my work is directionally correct or even worth a conversation. You use it as fuel for whatever preconceived ideas you had about the subject, and you will find only what you're looking for rather than what's actually in there.
Cris	Yeah b—
Ajani	Furthermore, I... anyway. I've lost interest in this conversation.
Cris	Eh—
Ajani	If you don't like it, no one's forcing you to keep reading.
Cris	...
Ajani	...
Cris	... Okay, okay. I know I'm not likely to see this perspective anywhere else, so I guess I'll lay off. You're right. I don't know enough physics, statistics, or astrology to knock the direction. And I guess I am interested in hearing what you have to say about all this, so. I guess I apologize.
Ajani	Whatever.
Cris	But I apologized!
Ajani	Yet now I don't trust you.
Cris	Just like that?
Ajani	We live in a world which norms every individual into a corner. I grew up in that corner and learned that even if no one was listening, I owed it to myself to say it anywhere, somewhere, even if it was only to my recorder. Or to an obscure book that almost no one will read, but everyone *could* read if they wanted to.
Cris	...
Ajani	I am not obligated to defend my inner thoughts to you.
Cris	Well, if you put them out there—
Ajani	Well, if you're bored enough to dissect them rather than looking at what they say about your own life—
Cris	Once it's public, it's fair game.
Ajani	Thankfully, I'm pretty good at blocking the public opinion. You will be ignored, and I'm going to publish another journal full of typos and speculation anyway.
Cris	You'll be a laughing stock.
Ajani	Ha! You are VERY wrong about that.
Cris	Prove it.
Ajani	Get out.
Cris	I mean to sa... (Cris dissolves.)
Ajani	...
Ajani	You want me to "prove" something in *your* brain? Arrogant and lazy. Nobody forces my hand. No king, no president, not even Jesus himself. NOBODY. If you don't want to meet me halfway in what I'm trying to say, then I as a communicative sender can't do anything about that. It's not my right to. I prove only to myself and that's it.
	People talk about the right to private enjoyment—ownership over property—but there is no right more fundamental than the right to one's own mind. The flood of information out there will silently erode your voice until you blend in with the pessimistic mob. There, your opinions of politics, billionaires, movies, and work—your entire view of the human dream will simply become one with the template you consume. It is an insignificant life that one leads where the part of themselves that is truly their own is consigned to burial beneath the latest breaking news out there. I have the power to be my own breaking news, broadcast my own channel. And although I can entertain differing opinions, you absolutely must be respectful to me when you air them, or else finish the rest of the conversation with yourself. You'll get nothing further from me. Your dissent won't stop me either. All disrespect does is render you impotent in my space. When I tell you what my intention was, and you brazenly re-tell me that it

was something else, I consider that to be the beginning of the worst kind of enslavement: that of the mind—from which all perspectives ranging from the highest highs to the most excruciating hardships may yet be recast into one's own personal harmony. I defend my mind like a freed slave defends his life from recapture; as a wild animal being dragged into a cage, you'll just have to put me down if you want something other than a berserk swath carved in the direction of my restored freedom. To lose your mind is to lose everything.

These works are the assertions of my mind, recorded in the tradition of the classic scholars who had far fewer social bureaucracies to bind them.

negative surprise encountered; dread exact administrative deadline; mama bear feedback gatherer	be irritated with frustrating self-continued situation	4	communication		-2
matriarchal family; institution or group experiences existential crisis involving merger, cuts, and regulatory challenges	lose faith in solvability of externally-controlled situation (pathfinder)	74	field of mind	write works	-0.5
play video game hack n slash	enjoy badassery and deep skill execution	54	field of mind		1
motivated by sexual information; 27 y.o.; built the lego city	enjoy well-assembled body and measurable creativity	35	field of mind	strangers uncomfortable, ajani = weird	1

A story: qc109 and the body appearance

This qcross is about my body image as a correlate to the world I project as reality onto others. From what I could tell, qcross 109 tells you something about the reification of a world that you present to others, and there's a good chance that your body and body image is located somewhere among these four qunits. I had seen this before, and feel that it probably opens up yet another dimension in the study of frequencies. To account for diversity, we can't always say that this specific region is tied to this specific trait. But what we can often say is that "this particular *cycle* of regions more than likely contains this particular trait." There are some people who are nice to look at and other people who make us feel like we're nice to look at or that they think so. There are other regions where we stand from afar and notice others treating their target as the thing nice to look at. And across all of this we end up with the full cycle for a particular energy. When I surveyed my friends and the charts of people whom I knew well, I found that they had one asteroid that was the best representative of their body and appearance in either 27q9, 63q9, 99q9, or 135q9. This suggests that qc109 <the slice of the world which you defined for others> sits at the heart of body frequentics. My idea that the body is a reflection of an energy projection is supported here. More study is needed.

youthful loss of temper; 20 y.o.	enjoy general peace	133	status reinforcement		2.5
table and map findings; background calculate; decide when to wakeup; reflect on status attainments; reference own research for answers	sunday morning calculate (pathfinder job)	102	field of mind		1
recursive inspect research data; reference own research for documentable answers	develop complex algorithm or workflow	35	daily duty		0
sleep	peek at potential wakeup hour	78	field of mind		0
consider the coming days affairs and desired involvement therein	decide when to wakeup	127	homeostasis		0
sleep; time passage	wakeup	100	daily duty		0
peek at wakeup time	consider the coming day's affairs and desired involvement therein	57	homeostasis		0
pull back from unlistenable situation or person; recall administrative failures and barriers	dread administrative obligations	96	homeostasis		-3
Personality [close friends], has been exiled often; contemplative mood	recall admin failures, social barriers	24	communication	dread administrative exact deadline	-1.5
mom and dad's relationship	collaborate with a stubborn person	70	communication		1
be irritated in negative dynamic with another; hear resonant energy;	slam stubborn persons difficulty(slam)	51	communication		-2.5
volume down distrusted other	consider energy costs of responding	95	homeostasis		-0.5
low energy mood; friends: rarely communicates with them	choose not to respond	31	homeostasis		-0.5

hour of uranus; time passage; be irritated with a self-continued situation	choose not to follow up	31	homeostasis		-1
low energy mood; dread administrative obligations	choose not to work on important project	74	homeostasis		-0.5
disinvested performance of obligation; Ajani won't communicate with friends unless there is a material progress update to give them (heavily tied to Venus in Scorpio-1 / Sco 28°)	donate expected participation	49	daily duty		1
Ajani in low status until crisis occurs, then elevated to influencing position	donate expected initiative	81	daily duty		1
birthright; Motivated towards: vast space in which to order patterns; oldest son	inquire of experts	55	learning	built lego city	1
negative surprise encountered; seek to improve　　　pull back from unlistenable situation or person	98	homeostasis	decide to leave a situation	-2.5
always asking for more data; can be strange; stunned when suddenly checked volume down distrusted other	131	field of mind		-3
stunned when suddenly checked	mute or block fully distrusted other	20	homeostasis		-2
built lego city	flow-build colored blocks or tactics actors	81	homeostasis		2.5
highly cerebral mind	flow-build general	35	learning		0.5
declare voluntary time; general peace	observe sum of own created works	48	iworth		2
obligation music	shore-up house preparation	74	daily duty		-1.5
make more money; reflect on status attainments; seek to improve	search for new investment channels	121	status reinforcement		1
hour of uranus - chaos	decide to leave a situation	98	homeostasis		-2
seek to improve; pull back from unlistenable situation or person; Turn offs, anger triggers: Presumption, one person imposing their thoughts on another's patterns,	determine a situation intolerable	55	homeostasis		-3
hour of mercury - demanded mind	gather documents on investments	83	administration		-2
declare voluntary time; retreat to privacy for concentration; search for new investment channels; Talented in automation	make more money	39	time passage		0.5
enjoy general peace	status reinforcement	106	time passage	desire for more money	1
make more money; enjoy general peace	raise property expectations	39	status reinforcement		2
large penis	decrease triggerability by women	116	status reinforcement	reflect on status attainments	2
time passage; large penis; talent for mass data	increase co-creating partner threshold	86	iworth	status reinforcement	0.5
partner argument spray	decrease collaboration willingness	116	status reinforcement		1
built lego city; talent for mass information	increase automation scoping	44	communication		1.5
reference own research for documentable answers	watch series	58	communication		0.5
background calculate; listen to another in conversation	play repetitive puzzle game	81	homeostasis	background calculate	0.5
be irritated with frustrating self-continued situation; slam stubborn person's difficulty(slam)	raise voice in argument	68	communication	post-conflict apology	-2.5
recall administrative failures and social barriers	delay performance of obligation	78	homeostasis		-2
dread administrative obligations; assembly line process or label data	disinvested performance of obligation	86	daily duty		-2
errand administrivia; be irritated with frustrating self-continued situation	speed zen performance obligation	77	daily duty	tap fingers on wheel	-1.5
disinvested performance of obligation; prepare music playlist	obligation music	78	daily duty		0.5
thorough work mode; background calculate; assembly line process or label data	low energy mood	60	homeostasis		-0.5
shower; dad's influence; nakedness	silly song mood	66	communication		1.5
declare voluntary time	contemplative mood	72	status reinforcement		2

mama bear feedback gatherer; reference own research for documentable answers	explanatory mood	60	teaching		1
seek to improve; motivated towards vast spaces for ordering information	thorough work mood	99	daily duty	contemplative mood	0
eat heavy salt food	sick or ill	84	homeostasis		-1
time passage; retreat to privacy for concentration; reference own research for documentable answers; talent for mass data; develop complex algorithm or workflow	holiday overdrive	77	daily duty		0.5
bosses and influencers deploy ajani to a foreign map; town errand administrivia	lost direction finder	94	daily duty		-0.5
oldest brother; mercy shown where it did not have to be given	mishap responder	53	communication		0.5
dad's influence	mama bear welcomer	91	communication		1
oldest brother; middle and youngest brothers' relationship	mama bear feedback gatherer	33	communication		1
work on diy	diy beer or red bull break	118	daily duty		0.5
fitness drop	run health recover	61	iworth		0.5
hour of uranus - chaos; pull back from unlistenable situation or person; low energy mood	sleep to dodge high ambient stress	83	homeostasis		-1
hour of uranus - chaos	leave to dodge high ambient stress	74	homeostasis		-3
listen to other person in conversation; oldest brother; Personality, close friends: happy, pushover, zero-tolerance certain concepts, ambitious, prone to turbulent or eventful encounters, has been exiled often	warm introductory conversation	67	communication		2.5
hangout with students	fun duo conversation	129	communication		1.5
mama bear welcomer; oldest brother	public ham personality	92	communication		1
embattled, assaulted by their bosses or even higher powers in the institution. In positive cases, just kept very busy; passively listen to it colleagues	insightful questions	26	learning		0
write works; mama bear feedback gatherer	writer explanatory voice	90	communication		0.5
reference own research for documentable answers; write works	writer technical diagram	71	communication		-0.5
write works; advocate for innovation	writer dialogues	72	communication		1
write works; writer technical diagram; writer explanatory voice	writer self-discloser	79	communication		1
declare voluntary time; make more money; Motivated towards: vast space in which to order patterns	built diy	35	offspring	shower	1
Motivated towards: vast space in which to order patterns	built lego city	107	offspring		0.5
flow-build general; Ajani works in isolated location, automated mapping of difficult data	built favorite collection	87	iworth		0.5
insightful questions; record thoughts; time passage; write works; increase co-creating partner threshold	built published portfolio	34	iworth		1
permanent published works; youthful losses of temper; happy, pushover, zero-tolerance for certain concepts, ambitious, prone to turbulent or eventful encounters, has been exiled often	label field changer	34	iworth		2.5
partner argument spray	rebellion against partner	11	homeostasis		0
strangers Feel uncomfortable. Ajani = weird	secrecy or gossip by partner	74	niche		-1
birthright; mom and dad's relationship; 27 y.o.	put in place by partner	74	communication		-3
openly defy partner; be irritated with frustrating self-continued situation	partner argument spray	55	niche		-3
increased secretiveness from initial meeting, but gradual understanding of this	partner cites third	67	niche		-1
Turn-ons	information blocks intimacy	76	mating drive		-1.5
always asking for more data, access, passionate about work, a decent counselor or listening ear, wordy, a bit too logical, can be strange; insightful questions	advocate for innovation	34	communication		-1
desire for more money; status reinforcement	job application fill	83	administration		-2
seek to improve; desire for more money	job application fetch quest	73	administration	hour of uranus	-3
slam stubborn persons difficulty(slam)	post conflict apology	94	communication		0.5
Attracts women in pairs when traveling in a foreign, historically educational environment; Susceptibility to notable influence by Ajani + two close partners of any kind	seducible by two	48	status reinforcement		3
bosses and influencers deploy ajani to a foreign map	guarded travel	64	administration		2
lost direction finder; thorough work mood	unassuming travel	64	status reinforcement		1

bosses and influencers deploy ajani to a foreign map	far distant witness travel	111	field of mind		0.5

A story: 75q9, Two for the road

It appears that this region indicates my preferred sexuality. Very strange. I have never seen this for what it is. Starting with 152226 Saracole <a young or inexperienced group on an adventure sworn to be kept secret>, onto 78429 Baschek <carved into form having a statue made of oneself>, next to 4076 Dorffel <a writing smashes open the scandal about a figurative candidate's figurative campaign>, we have a remake of the kinds of adventures that I've been on with pairs of girls—especially in a foreign land. I suppose it makes sense that one has their sexuality on one point and the target display of compatibility on the other side. What is noteworthy about this is that I don't typically run into this kind of sexuality on a regular basis, mainly because I don't travel for a living. I know travel has a lot to do with this. What abstract thing do I normally partner with instead? Probably something from a different context. We'll see what that is shortly. But this qunit describes my adventures with the girls I met in REDACTED—where we saw all kinds of statues and museums and stuff like that. With 20828 Linchen <an organization set up to spread a particular parties influence to the neighboring surrounds>, other adventures in the back of a teacher's van, in the back of a bus, across apartments and the like are also explained here. But one does not kiss and tell though. Those stories aren't entirely mine to convey, so we'll skip them in this biography.

bosses and influencers deploy ajani to a foreign map; brother #2 middle brother	karaoke or other socialization	125	daily duty		0.5
dad's influence; oldest brother	level-headed problem handler	128	communication		0.5
volume down distrusted other	resource withholder	17	communication		0
haul diy various; work on diy	heavy hauler	9	daily duty	shower	0
pose an abstract question; friends are: revolutionary, tolerant, logical sticklers; Seems passive / not dominating, BUT generally it's his way or failure for the other	silence on feeling stupid	105	homeostasis	youthful losses of temper	-1
1 day; nod off	brush teeth	105	homeostasis		0.5
seek to improve; Turn offs, anger triggers	stunned when suddenly checked	81	communication	write off future cooperation with critic	-2
negative surprise encountered; righteous feedback against bullying	openly defy partner	143	communication		-0.5
enjoy badassery; motivated by sexual information	fitness practice	134	homeostasis		1
background calculate; thorough work mood	eat heavy salt food	137	field of mind	sick or ill; nod off	1
1 day; 4 hours; mom's influence	drink heavy caffeine	81	field of mind		0.5
vision quest; decide a situation intolerable; Susceptibility to notable influence by Ajani + two close partners of any kind	tour foreign lands history	53	daily duty		1
lose faith in solvability of externally-controlled situation (pathfinder); insightful questions; decide to leave a situation; motivated towards a vast space to order patterns	vision quest	35	field of mind		-1
guarded travel	multiweek occupy	139	time passage		0
determine a situation intolerable	declare voluntary time	36	time passage	reflect on penis growth goals; contemplative mood; decide to leave a situation	2
birthright	seek to improve	36	homeostasis		1
birthright	background calculate	36	homeostasis		1
contemplative mood; reflect on relationship distancing	pose an abstract question	27	field of mind		0
birthright; youthful losses of temper	reference the body for immediate answers (pathfinder)	35	field of mind		0
pose an abstract question; motivated towards: vast space for ordering information	reference own research for documentable answers	25	communication	record what is on the mind	0
insightful questions; build the lego city; motivated towards the vast space to order information	table and map findings	6	field of mind		1

A story: 134q10 and my research

134q10 is in many ways my "research protocol" for doing the work I do. Included in this is an asteroid 3385 Bronnina <a stylized wig, a cool announcement of how one handles limitations and rules>. This is how I keep my hair. You might say that as long as I wear my hair wild, I am telling the world that I am still actively on my journey. Also in this region is 1669 Dagmar <enduring long separations and difficult travels, conferring a kind of stoicism through rough conditions>. There is also 1263 Varsavia <a naturalist or collector gathering understanding of their chosen (cluster related) topic>; this one might be considered the ruler of qunit 57q8, where my Sun is located. The cluster 134q10 itself describes the behavior of pioneers in establishing new rules. A lot of the things I do in charting this terrain is described by these and the other handful of asteroids in 134q10. 18510 Chasles <interactive or directly experienced table art which immerses the artist

or the audience> is also here, as are 2814 Vieira <a vocal leader who issues forth a specimen reflecting a wider viewpoint—one which likely stands apart from the prevailing wisdom> and 4315 Pronik <running through a flood of detailed, tried then exhausted plans>.

negative surprise encountered	record ideas for answers	59	communication		0
shower	nakedness	50	homeostasis	light mood	0
leave to dodge high ambient stress; 2 years	region: civic development after 2+ years	83	interface		1
birthright; multiweek stay; being brought into a place	region: sports teams more likely to win championships upon his arrival and departure	136	interface		1
civic development after 2+ years	region: politically prosperous	15	interface		1
friends: rarely communicates with them, despite wishing there were more communication, but...; more friends than fewer reference "sir" or some other ranking	associated collaborator: chance at dreams granted , usually not capitalized on	14	interface		0
The mono partner; partner argument spray	partner/opposite sex close: conflict over Ajani's need for two partners, or one partner versus a heavily married work / trade	92	interface		-0.5
birthright; 12 y.o.	partner/opposite sex close: increased single-mindedness	141	interface		-1
mom's influence; youthful losses of temper; 16 y.o.; make more money	partner/opposite sex close: increased secretiveness from initial meeting, but gradual understanding of this	87	interface		-1
The mono partner; time passage	partner/opposite sex close: increasingly visible, but gradually decreased obsessiveness	28	interface		-0.5
birthright; mom and dad's relationship; 16 y.o.	partner/opposite sex close: difficult personality increase	28	interface		-1
matriarchal family; mom's influence; insightful questions	partner/opposite sex close: commentary on expectations or effort	28	interface	seek to improve; mom's influence; HATES being assessed or compared	-1

A story: 14q12. Shanna

This qcross is definitely a significator for Shanna. It is a powerful description of who she is, especially as a temperament. We have asteroids for fine and delicate quality for nurturing the senses (20787 Mitchfourman), 200025 cloud gate, the worker of magic who is sought after yet intimidating, 3533 Toyota <the insanely fixated patriot commander who is not only crazy or obsessive, but good on top of it>, and several other asteroids which give a good overview of Shanna as a person. There is a very consistent template for this one, and prior to Shanna I have met, women like her with whom I got along had very specific features. I would not be surprised if there were indicators of white or light skin, a longer face, a refined or high class bearing, and or a pronounced nose... OK I looked up the asteroid features and they're actually pretty amazing. Aside from another indicator of Indian ethnicity, a lot of the features for a tiny waist, fashionability, magical ability, refinement, and precision in a certain area are all there. 20898 Fountainhills and 3533 Toyota both seemed to really align with a set of Makehuman sliders which are reflected in the bodies and faces of these six or seven women. 34239 Louisgolowich as the artists outside the context of the marriage, also aligned with a couple of features, and I suspect this one and Fountainhills may influence the nose in particular... Yep, Louisgolowich was associated with an inverse relationship between nose compression and nostril width dependent on tense versus harmonious aspects. Cloud gate affects the eyes and the stomach tone among other things, and this probably partly explains Shanna's perpetually fit abs through no effort whatsoever.

birthright	highly cerebral mind	13	interface		1
birthright; time passage	institution or group experiences existential crisis involving merger, cuts, challenges	71	interface		-1
oldest brother; black; ajani = weird; stern-block public during errand	Ajani in low status until crisis occurs, then elevated to influencing position	49	interface		0
retreat to privacy for concentration; antisocial/private	Ajani works in isolated location, automated mapping of difficult data	92	interface		1
Susceptibility to notable influence by Ajani + two close partners of any kind	bosses often come in pairs	101	interface		1
birthright; dad's influence; embattled, assaulted by their bosses or even higher powers in the institution. In positive cases, just kept very busy	bosses: Heavy body build	87	interface		0
mom and dad's relationship	bosses: embattled, assaulted by their bosses or even higher powers in the institution. In positive cases, just kept very busy	79	interface		-1
dad's influence; matriarchal family	bosses: faced with some version of homelessness / being an outcast	83	interface		-1
black; retreat to privacy for concentration	strangers Feel uncomfortable. Ajani = weird	12	interface	large penis; writer self-discloser	-2

A Story: From my private recordings about qc83

Here is a qcross that presents stark contrasts between the drama of groups, and freedom and success on the solo road—with a change maker somewhere in the room. I've never really thought about this, but my worst experiences with having lies told, gang-up on, and that kind of thing are directly correlated with the strength of an in-group's solidarity. The more I interface with a mob-in-the-making or a clique, the harder my life is in general. I told you I've always had a lusty energy—like a gigolo who only owns leisure suits with the chest hair out, or a stereotypically curvy woman with the full lips and difficult-to-ignore cleavage—you see these people, and you think, "Ohh... no." Then time has stopped; let the visceral reactions begin. But some people wear that on their spirit. you feel the rile-up as if they were out gigoloing, when they're actually just being themselves going to the store. Where the clique sees you, but remains walled off from whatever it is you were carrying, there will be talk. If that group is somehow forced to depend on you—as a colleague, gatekeeper, or whatever, there may be *negative* talk. And if you're a black male and the above apply, then there's a very good chance that that negative talk will be taken more seriously, believed with less questioning, reaffirm deep-rooted suspicions that you've already learned from American culture anyway, and questions about you, your competence, your guilt, your lack of fit, your crimes, the need for justice, and the fact that your assessors are just trying to be "fair and logical" as they "treat everybody the same," will spread like wildfire.

I tell you my story through *The Book of Contours*, because I tell you that I've never been guilty of any of it—except for the temper tantrums. I've had plenty of those. And then there was that complex exchange with Simeona, which I talk about elsewhere, and the various over-the-top confessions to my actual friends at the time—almost all of which were destined to make it into this book anyway. But never harm to an individual. Never ugly or skeevy towards an individual in any way that I knew. But even if you do do a thing that others find off-putting, rarely will the other person tell you. But they will tell their cliques and thread-mates plenty. The (formerly) most frustrating thing is, I have always prided myself on the respect I show to others as something deeply ingrained in my oldest brother protocol. You are as diplomatic and courteous as you can be, then people get buck and try to run you over. You resist, and then they go back to their friends and just invent a breach. Often, the friends come back with additional torches and no need for facts *at all*. Unfortunately, I can't control what I don't know, and what people are seeing—especially after they no longer like me. But at least through books like this, I can control my own narrative, and put lopsided stories like that to use for anyone who reads my books and anyone looking to really fix aspects of their relationships that were previously unfixable before these frameworks existed.

I'm very happy in my Frankenstenian tower, penning cures for relational ills, and I can honestly say that the injustices that I've experienced have never been so great that it compromised my core drive to help others. You can see from the 66q7 – 138q7 pattern that the alternative to the lone road for me is one in which a collective's members consider themselves to have equal say over how your individual deeds are evaluated. The missing piece, though, is that the collective typically doesn't know the first thing about what you're actually doing. They just know that they can evaluate it. And that's really the life that I stand outside of. Like most artists, I'm taking something of my own and producing with it. *Because* it is on my own, it is necessarily on somebody's fringe. My life actually punishes me for diving into the collective, but rewards me greatly for standing outside of it and writing about what I see.

antisocial/private; strangers Feel uncomfortable. Ajani = weird; youthful losses of temper; guarded travel	strangers: Closed opportunity doors to Ajani as solo; "solicitation never works"	62	interface		-2
The mono partner; partner argument spray	strangers: Wide open doors to Ajani w a close female partner,	92	interface		2
ajani's relationship with his brothers; enjoy general peace	strangers: Susceptibility to notable influence by Ajani + two close partners of any kind	140	interface		0
Susceptibility to notable influence by Ajani + two close partners of any kind	Attracts women in pairs when traveling in a foreign, historically educational environment	23	interface		2
off chat with student	friends: rarely communicates with them, despite wishing for more communication but...	70	interface		-0.5
enjoy badassery	Ajani won't communicate with friends unless there is a material progress update to give them (heavily tied to Venus in Scorpio-1 / Scorpio 28°)	28	interface		-1
off chat with student; call me anytime	more friends than fewer reference "sir" or some other ranking	49	interface		0
dad's influence; ajani's relationship with his brothers; music mood match play	friends VERY social, creatively dominant/visionary, or both; generally popular / attractive, and are working towards more mastery in their (media or information-related fields)	141	interface		1.5

A story: qc376, Simeona

Qcross 376 does not have any special notations in my original file, and that makes sense. It really describes mostly a single moment in time—namely my various interactions with Simeona during the save our school efforts which established her character as my counterpart. If you have not read the rest of this story, Simeona was one of my college students at the time, and we were generally very close throughout most of the period when we knew each other. We went through a lot as a team in our ultimately futile attempts to find a buyer, raise awareness, and put on a fashion show to showcase the talent in our school, but ultimately sound economics prevailed and the college was taught out anyway. At some point during our exchange a couple of things happened which led to me seriously getting on Simeona's case as her teacher, and it strained us beyond repair. A follow up event occurred a few weeks later, then we were really strained—to the point that I had to kick her out of my class. The remarkable thing about this, however, was that from her isolated new home in a room all the way across the building from the rest of the class, she proceeded to give one of the most outstanding project presentations I have ever seen. Surely it was up there with Joseph L's portfolio presentation. And it was such a noble effort, and I was so proud of her—essentially doing a better job than almost anyone from a position of exile—you just get the sense that some people live more fiercely and more determinedly than others. They just try harder. Some of it involves greater risk, but a lot of it is just adherence to some kind of north star. I jumped on Simeona for reasons I won't get into here, but the two friends that were also chewed out at the same time will know what I'm talking about. Yet she was such a remarkable person, that I never really lost my respect for her. She is definitely one of my favorite people of all time whom I've met in this life, and always has been since we went through the fire together.

I had a couple of colleagues at that school—well maybe only one who showed it—who just plain hated me. And the colleague who comes to mind was the main one who caught me giving Simeona a shoulder massage in room 210. And I guess that validated the three years of witch-hunting that the colleague had already sponsored against me. But REDACTED knows that, like my dad, I was always a sentimental type. More than a couple of times I greeted REDACTED with a hug (because I'm a hugger), and the thing with Simeona occurred on the heels of something she was going through which threatened to be devastating. REDACTED of course never knew this, never asked, and probably didn't care. It was the one time EVER that I crossed an implied professional line, I suppose. But if you had been at that school with artists hanging out with teachers hanging out with artists hanging out with teachers who were also artists, going to Blue Star and First

Fridays and gallery openings and people's bands and all that, then you probably would have come to the same kind of conclusion that I did: in the days before the workplace training got super serious, the closeness between students and instructors was just part of our culture. Had we had the kinds of training that I have in my day job now, I never ever would have done that. But those weren't the times. And nothing untoward happened between us. This is one of those things I just need to clear up. Should you ever find this favorite person of mine somewhere out there, make sure you respect who she is and where she's coming from. The world needs more people like that who are willing to burn down the old structures to make something better. Because right now, we have a lot of great people, a lot of rich people, a lot of famous people, a lot of philanthropists... But not nearly enough folks rewriting the rules of the human mentality itself—the problems with education, the shaming through socialization for being a member of any group that some other group doesn't approve of. Simeona worked against those things, as do I. So I guess it shouldn't be surprising that I have an entire qcross of four signs taken up primarily by her. I never served in the military, but if I had, then she definitely would have been my battle buddy. It's not the same realm as family or romance or friendship necessarily, but now that school is long over, it could be any number of things. Alas, the past is the past, so I can't get too nostalgic. But you never know. Fate is always full of surprises.

more friends than fewer reference "sir" or some other ranking	friends: topics often revolve around feelings, intuition, and balancing this with practical relationships	7	interface		-0.5
volume down distrusted other; insightful question	interaction influences content of books being written at the time	9	interface	art mirrors life	0
music mood match play; megaman; aj's art mirrors life; interaction with brothers; watch series	the shows and games Ajani is interacting with at the time almost always parallel his life, so he can't choose these randomly	9	interface		1
astrology skill; insightful questions; reflect on relationship barriers and failures; teacher family	permanent published works, read in distant places by certain kinds of seekers, tomes which vacuum in information	8	interface		1
write works	academic, taxonomic, intended to help tolerance	90	interface		0.5
writer self-discloser; male; motivated by sexual info	imperfect, not necessarily believable, sometimes cringeworthy, but willing to go there where others won't	23	interface		-1
reference own research for answers; built the lego city; motivated towards: vast space for ordering information; insightful questions	creations: rooted in the as-of-yet unexplored social, anthropological or astronomical; body or form-centric	23	interface	permanent published works, read in distant places by certain kinds of seekers, tomes which vacuum in information	-0.5
12 y.o.; insightful questions	brother from another mother: similar but complementary focus	117	sphere		1
middle brother	brother: more serious and popular, but heavier challenges and more traditional family and friend dynamics	28	sphere		0
20 y.o.; birthright	slim, hedonistic, neurotic, smart, heavy emotional trauma experience, can be vindictive, sneaky, indifferent, but also weirdly loyal as long as she's doesn't feel owned, obsessed with a certain kind of pet. The mono partner	79	sphere	desire for more money	1
birthright; 8 y.o.; mom's influence; dad's influence	an ally "sort of," round face, popular, sly, neurotic, a flaky connection, can't really get together unless work is involved	67	sphere		-1
off chat with student	Indian girl, super warm, fun connections, brief intermittent interactions which often involve 1) an exchange of music, 2) philosophical or abstract positioning on some ongoing event, 3) one party's problems with family, 4) wanderlust. Trust and emotional safety tend to be high here, but in order to build this association, Ajani has to be ready to seek help in problems with family. Usually n/a	89	sphere		2.5
The mono partner	a highly temperamental work partner, charmed early by Aj, turns to hate Aj when aims not precisely aligned. Ajani's true co-creative partner and the mother of his (figurative) child if he has one	63	sphere	bias-latina	1
dad's influence; time passage	heavy set, politically embattled, faces personal transition, lord of the realm of colleagues	79	sphere		1
32 y.o.; san antonio environment	a [white and Hispanic] or [slim and sly] pair whom Ajani meets in historical travel. Fun and risk taking, but Ajani needs to be deployed to this travel or operating at competition level for this to be worth maintaining. The poly partnership. I'm less likely to be interested in this until my major personally projects are finished / cannot be worked on.	79	sphere		-2
16 y.o.; san antonio environment	tall, white, male, opens new places, known by everyone, but very easily misunderstood. We make a great team	83	sphere		1
dad's influence	old, messy-crowded, functional objects all within reach (LIFE LEVEL INCREASE)	48	sphere	status reinforcement	2
dad's influence	black, shiny or silver, lasts or lingers a looong time	48	sphere		2.5
dad's influence	black and wood, possibly orange if a power tool	23	sphere		2
Motivated towards: vast space in which to order patterns; seek to improve; Talented in automation, a magnet for mass, often private data; reflect on penis goals; 27 y.o.	Motivated by: sexual information, measurements (strong characteristic)	103	personality		0
Motivated towards: vast space in which to order patterns; play video game jrpg	Talented in automation, a magnet for mass, often private data—not necessarily from you or the institution at hand, but through methods learned there (strong characteristic,)	18	personality		3
time passage; reflect on relationship distancing	Talented in inheriting the talents of people he wanted in his life, whose company was not granted or whose association was in some way blocked,	57	personality		2.5
record thoughts; 4 years	A heavy documenter, thousands of recordings and writings (strong characteristic,)	50	personality		1
built lego; insightful questions; highly cerebral mind; permanent published works	His thesis is: mobility through mapping,	45	personality		2
birthright; oldest brother	His ethos is: the golden rule. "Do unto others as you would have them do unto you"	47	personality	warm introductory conversation; write works	1
8 y.o.; teacher family; bosses embattled, assaulted by their bosses or even higher powers in the institution	His friends are: revolutionary, tolerant, logical sticklers	19	personality		1.5

birthright	Motivated towards: vast space in which to order patterns	144	personality		1
seek to improve; warm introductory conversation; write off unlistenable situation	Insists on politeness, whether or not he shows this insistence; will work in a group to acknowledge others' attempts to speak up which may have been run over by stronger personalities; group "mama bear"	19	personality		-1
relationship with cousin; 12 y.o.; label field definer; built lego	Seems passive / not dominating, BUT generally it's his way or failure for the other—whether, people, groups, or institutions. Accordingly, he heavily values win-wins.	37	personality		-2
youthful loss of temper; reflect on relationship distancing; general peace; private / antisocial	buddhist-daoist	44	personality		1
dad's influence; drink tea; middle brother and youngest brothers' interactions; Motivated towards: vast space in which to order patterns; 8 y.o.	Favorite things: tang, Cap'n Crunch, H-E-B temptation roll (sushi), Perry Como, Aoife O'Donovan, Donald Byrd, Al Jarreau, Sarah Vaughan, the color Dark Purple, Kahimi Karie – Blue Orb, Akino Arai – Unknown Vision, Tech N9ne, Psytrance, Epic-J (Yoko Kanno future style), Honor Folk/Bluegrass, Tactics RPGs and games involving directed decisions in a grid or along a tree	79	personality		1
mama bear welcomer; put in place by partner; listen to conversation partner; Distrusts most women who turn him on until he is sure they will add to (rather than take from) his ambitions; Seems passive / not dominating, BUT generally it's his way or failure for the other	Personality, strangers and public: cold, logical, guarded, discourages interaction	30	personality		-1.5
aj's relationship with brothers	Personality, acquaintances and colleagues: always asking for more data, access, passionate about work, a decent counselor or listening ear, wordy, a bit too logical, can be strange	112	personality		-1
16 y.o.; insightful questions	Personality, close friends: happy, pushover, zero-tolerance for certain concepts, ambitious, prone to turbulent or eventful encounters, has been exiled often,	122	personality		0
aj's relationship with brothers; 16-bit; oldest brother; enjoy badassery	Personality, close friends: has abandoned many of the most important friends—always for the same reason: the friend began talking to Ajani differently after a third party was introduced. Distrust detected. Ajani doesn't lie, HATES being obligated to people who distrust him, and sees this as a long-running obligation to lie	69	personality		-1
dad's influence; music mood match play	Personality, private: Easy, live and let live, happy (sings to self), industrious, ~every 3-5 weeks finds himself in an "impromptu rave"—dancing to trance and dance songs like Shanti People – Tandava (Blazy & Gottinari Remix) when no one is around. Despite everything else people may read about his social life, Aj is a very happy person—loves his life and is optimistic about the contributions to humanity he can control; shielded from social frictions within a circle of interactions he knows he can trust	66	personality		2.5
mom and dad's relationship	Turn offs, anger triggers: Presumption, one person imposing their thoughts on another's patterns, assumed familiarity that wasn't invited, bullying, being or feeling disrespected, lied to, arrogant minimization of others, flaky or fleeting exchanges, distrusts surface beauty or power by default until more information about a person is gathered, punishment over unexplained rules, bullet-hell / haphazard pressure, the need for quick wit, being rushed, being commanded, being obligated to continue talking to fools or liars, people he feels don't respect him (may be normal from strangers, but not acceptable from friends or allies), smart-assedness of most kinds to or from most people— including generic comedy shows, slight distrust towards same-race couples by default, negative media, general internet noise, information bombardment from unsought sources. Distrusts hype, can't stand mobs	96	personality		-3

A story: From my private recordings about the asteroids in my 58q4

In a completely different vein, qunit 58q4 shows a very standard loss of temper that I have always displayed when caged or feeling caged. Included in this region are views of me which change under this loss of temper. I would say that typically when I lose my temper like that, there is this element of seeing a fight as unwinnable. The asteroid 570 Kythera brings with it an immediate need to divorce myself fully from the one I am arguing with and the asteroid 2937 Gibbs shows a kind of recursive speculation on what the other is thinking and where they stand—whether I am being listened to or not. This is obviously a negative qunit, although the role of 6016 Carnelli does add a bit of mystery to the region in the sense that it is almost as though I am arguing against the loss of choice, because the sense of the original puzzle we were trying to solve has been violated. That said, I will not decide to stop using this qunit or even to avoid it. My temper has always been one of the major reasons that people who seriously attempt to run over me once don't usually get to do it again. I am hardly a threat to anyone, I think, but the protest is so loud and so disruptive that it becomes impossible to push your agenda in that same way without encountering great and noisy problems. The longest that this ever lasted was when I worked at REDACTED and REDACTED continually flung impossible deadlines over the fence and expected REDACTED and I to complete them yesterday. Because I don't lie, you could be the Pope or the president, but if you ask me to do something impossible, I will tell you that it is impossible. And if you don't want to hear that, then I don't care if you don't want to hear that. If you insist that I get it done anyway, then we are dead and my service to you is over. I imagine there is a bit of this in my relationship with the notion of God that I grew up on. To me that relationship struck me as an impossible one with impossible asks of everyone else besides the people who got to tell their own stories in their own favor and in their own mega churches for free. I don't respect that, never will, and consider it an existential mandate to tell that person, place, authority, or other object "Hell no" so that they know, that a simple ego does not simply have the right to make all laws for all existence "just because."

Motivated by: sexual information, measurements (strong characteristic); bosses and influencers deploy ajani to a foreign map	Turn-ons: toned, fit, or complex abs on women (not excessively muscular), Indian women, wide hips, Welsh lips, shows of mercy where it did not have to be given, changes of heart to do the right thing towards another, chill personalities, let's-go-explore personalities, smooth voices, an artist's mind	93	personality		1.5

A story: 92q12 and the Indian woman

2264 Sabrina indicates the fixed routines typical of a small community. This is again indicative of JRI and the study groups that I participated in during Caltech and my graduate years. There are some high spirited characters here, including 33520 Ichige, associated with Indian ethnicity and beauty. I can't help but wonder whether this region partly explains my draw towards Indian women. Indeed there were some standout Indian students in every situation where this applied. REDACTED, REDACTED, REDACTED, and REDACTED was a peer rather than a student—but all of these people contributed a high sense of warmth to the dynamics in a space that otherwise could have been flooded by wayward information. This region is very happy, and may also have an asteroid in it which is associated with a soft sing-songy voice, romance, but also perfectionism. I do see that Sabrina is associated with the text mined word "symphonic" as well as the context of warming. Two other asteroids are associated with dance, and Johnaligawesa is associated with the words "speaking" and "sour." To me this is definitely the region of my pro-Indian character and personality bias. I have a theory on how the squares would work. But I will save it for later.

27 y.o.; explain lesson; warm conversation; shows of mercy where it didn't have to be given	bias-Indian female	85	personality	Personality [private]: easy, live and let live	3
Motivated towards: vast space in which to order patterns; enjoy general peace; relationship with cousin; dad's influence	Sexual orientation: feminine-communicating	19	personality	Seems passive / not dominating, BUT generally it's his way or failure for the other	2.5
retreat to privacy for concentration; Closed opportunity doors to Ajani as solo. "solicitation never works"; reflect on relationship distancing; seek to improve; inquire of experts	Practices parts of the Ananga Ranga (~sacred sexuality) and certain exercises contained therein, resulting in profound bodily changes and changes in interactions with potential partners over a 20+ year period. Leans demi-sexual or "noetisexual." Outside of poly or deeply stable emotional connection, has little interest in sex or sexual release; discouraged by the very consistent "2-day bad day" after orgasm, orgasm almost always brings an "eye ache-headache," hair thinning afterwards, sexual information is mostly cognitive fuel for logic work (except under very special circumstances with very special partners)	122	personality	jelq freestanding	2.5

A story: 60q7, On orgasm

I was on a roll recording qc299 and its asteroids, and 24q7 and the relationships to it as granting major opportunity in the world, and then I'm interrupted by this. Seemingly unrelated to all that is 60q7: a region that definitely describes orgasm—particularly my first orgasm at the start of puberty. Unlike most self-disclosure events in these books, this is an event I will never describe to anyone. The details are super memorable, and the circumstances a lot more exotic than I can publish, but suffice it to say that one of the defining asteroids that called my attention to what this region was doing was 163641 Nichol—twice when it occurs once. This has *always* been a feature of orgasm for me, usually hours apart. And then there is the feeling of corruption that attends this—the battles that visit me for two days afterwards. 25482 Tallapragada is here, and it indicates teen or young adult memories. 4518 Raikin (authorized to explore and if necessary dispense with the occupants of the territory) is also here, and the phases that I went through throughout my teens and early 20s where masturbation was a regular occurrence do speak to this. Now as for the two day bad day, that's kind of funny and very obvious. 18263 Anchialos shows [the desire to eliminate with impunity or never see a thing again], and is not only one of the main asteroid of cats, but the more *evil* side of cats (I love cats by the way, and have always been a cat person). 31957 Braunstein shows where one works to heal a chronic, unpleasant condition. 4050 Mebailey is the asteroid of "raising a pillar, post, or other container stabilizer." 7247 Robertstirling shows why a decision to exile someone was made. Together these make for bad, punishing, or at least tricky sex, and constituted the main route I eventually took to a mostly strictly celibate life.

The lore out there states that if you're not having sex or good sex, then something must be wrong with you. These asteroids are what's wrong with me... there's actually nothing wrong. It's a creative setup, that's all. Yet while I observe these asteroids, I also note the connection between the women I've known to have knockout orgasms themselves and a love of animals broadly. 136557 Neleus (cataloging the animals that live on a farm) is right next to 11826 Yurijgromov (foundational breaking down associated with virginity), while 60q7 itself is associated with dissociation from the thing in front of oneself.

In my investigations of my own mutation of heterosexuality, I found that sex has always been a kind of task list handed to me by the partner—though it was never actually the partner but my own lurking shadow of an expectation instead, almost fully self-generated. Thanks to circumstances which you will surely read about elsewhere in this biography, I've typically approached sex like it was some kind of arduous trek through godforsaken territory, with the ultimate goal to activate the geyser and get out with my need for achievement intact. I've got too much pride for dolls and such, but not enough heart for actual humans unless the environment is completely downer-free. **Completely**. Things like weird music, corny movements, a barking dog, distractibility, professional implications, a skin burn on couch leather... are all instakillers for me. I've never had enough passion to just "do it anywhere" with somebody. That may sound sexy to some people, but as someone who absolutely has to know what's around every corner, spontaneity like that makes me more annoyed than titillated. That's why I stay away from games like Doom or Diablo. Not knowing what's around the corner upsets my sense of map-control. It's taxing for me to both tell what you want and be the sole culpable party for what you feel you've gotten. If only I could go out-of-body for a while and turn it all into a side scroller. First-person shooters just aren't fun for me.

Now all that said, my ultimate goal in sex is to give my partner the devastating orgasm, check the box, and go raid the fridge thereafter. Then go to the next partner, do the same thing, and check the other box. Have I actually done this before? Yes I have. Was it worth it? Yes it was. Would I do it again? Eh, I don't know. I'm 45, not really a fan of sex except for certain exceptional occasions, and find that I just feel more powerful writing books from outer space. It seems rarer and therefore more valuable to me than something that everybody else can do. Yes my partner and I still go there on occasion, but we generally have to clear it with our puritanical chihuahua first. He doesn't like mom and dad touching *at all*. He thinks that's nasty and tells me so even in 2D; that is, if Shanna is three feet away from him looking to the left and I'm 7 feet in the background looking to the right and bending down, he sees a molestation about to happen and protests loudly. See shit like that makes you *not* horny ever, and he's done an effective job in ensuring the place of writing as my most intimate space. It's okay though. I was already going there before he and his mom met. We get the spheremates we deserve. As for my ultimate goal these days, my other partner is a figurative one—this work and the body of my research. The findings produced have been immeasurable, with no sign of slowing down in sight. (I didn't say this biography would be flattering, just complete.)

righteous defense of another against bullying	attracts heavier-build women but partners with very thin ones		21	personality	0
mom and dad's relationship; san antonio environment; black	overwhelmingly attracts interracial couples as friends		70	personality	black; Personality [private]: easy, live and let live	0
Personality [private]: easy, live and let live, happy (sings to self); pull back from an unlistenable situation	Distrusts most women who turn him on until he is sure they will add to (rather than take from) his ambitions		30	personality		-1
mom's influence	Almost all friends (and Ajani himself) are obsessive, have high big-5 neuroticism, or both		79	personality		0
20 y.o.; attracts slim, hedonistic, neurotic, smart, heavy emotional trauma experience, can be vindictive, sneaky, indifferent, but also weirdly loyal as long as she's doesn't feel owned, obsessed with a certain kind of pet. The mono partner		upper-average penis	86	body	be irritated with frustrating self-continued situation; HATES being compared or assessed	0
32 y.o.; black; upper-average penis; 10 years; final publishing process; HATES being compared or assessed; jelq freestanding; sleep		large penis	32	body	reflect on penis growth goals; enjoy well-assembled body and measurable creativity; reflect on status attainments; absorb immunities from challengers; write off future cooperation with critic; volume down distrusted other; turn on: wide hips; develop new question from body observation	1
40 y.o.; large penis; 4 years; seek to improve; jelq freestanding; 4 years; declare voluntary time; load or observe girly-girl pictures; turn-ons: large areolae; Closed opportunity doors to Ajani as solo "solicitation never works"; Sexual orientation: non-monogamous, hetero, bisexual-favoring, alpha projecting, feminine-communicating male; write off future cooperation with critic; final publishing process; background calculate; built diy		very large penis	82	body	increase co-creating partner threshold; reference own research for documentable answers; resource withholder; level-headed problem handler; inspect penis; writer self-discloser; pull back from unlistenable situation or person; built published portfolio; retreat to privacy for concentration; status reinforcement	2
youthful loss of temper		strong neck	32	body		0
birthright		black	61	body		0

A story: 33q11, 105q11 and Black indicators

33q11

This qunit is a strong indicator of the black self-image. 31996 Goecknerwald is the central asteroid of African Americans here, and I find that the neighboring asteroids are good reflections of how I've come to see myself as a black person. I won't list every asteroid in this region but I will say that overall regions like this are double-edged in that when you first learn of them as defining your identity, you're not necessarily enthusiastic about the box you observe. Later on, as you kind of accept the framework—your "make and model" of bodily vehicle if you will—then you see that there is a lot to get comfortable with. I'm not sure if Goecknerwald always does this in some way, but I'm pretty sure that 33q11 is not exclusive to black people. Overall, this cluster is positive for me, and I use it as a source of inner fuel or navigating even the most closed spaces.

105q11

This is a qunit in that it describes the various issues that black people wrestle with, and various arguments for why African Americans in particular are where they are in society. 108205 Baccipaolo is the asteroid of the chromosomes. 6395 Hilliard shows <closed off ones lucky to have run into others who are willing and able to release them>. 5309 MacPherson is <sensitive to infection or the spread of triggers from contact, and melodramatic in reaction to such contact>. 20858 Cuirongfeng shows <imitation where the imitator isn't real and isn't available, thus leaving only the sizzle>; this corresponds to concepts like "haters," "the man," and niggaz. Lastly, 11079 Mitsunori corresponds to <one held prisoner by a ruling regime which seeks total supremacy>. Much of the content of this cluster is negative, and has associations with colonialism, slavery, instant widespread problems, and asteroids like 128389 Dougleland <that which is valuable, but easily slips away> don't help this. I find 318676 Bellelay <what one pours their money into, not because it's worth it, but because doing so keeps an aspect of their expression balanced> to be probably the best explanation for why I'm still pursuing moneymaking as a high priority even though the region I recently recorded which actually corresponds to money doesn't seem to require it. I did not find an explanation for my own chasing of money really anywhere in qig31[6], but now that I find an explanation buried here in the internal square to that region, qig67, my pursuit of money in a context square to money makes a whole lot of sense from the black perspective. You really do need to try to set the demons that come with being black aside in order to do mainstream American business. I know that's a tall ask, and I definitely had about two decades worth of fuck yous to the motivational speakers of the world who attempted to pass their white success onto my colored framework in disregard of the harsh realities. But if you're black and you're reading this, I'm telling you the best thing I ever did for myself was to move away from the home that trained me—both the city and the immediate family structure. While the latter was not really destructive and the former pretty much was, neither of them put me in the spaces where I was required to learn independent of that baggage. Now a little while ago I said that I did not expect unit 33q11 to represent black people. But as I look at qc39 on the whole and reflect on its parent qig67's relationship to the mobility of qig31, I do think that any culture's emphasis on passion and seduction and the reactions it triggers is going to automatically be out of the context of rationalized business. So the stereotypical black, French, Mexican, artist, gypsy, Irish, sexuality-prominent, or any other culture depicted as commonly passionate is also more likely to

---

[6] "qig" is short for "qunit inconjunct group," which I define in the next section.

be depicted as bohemian—employed by cooler heads for the latters' entertainment and maintenance projects. That's not to say that these groups can't get rich. Of course that would be an oversimplification. But it is to say that when we as Americans depict these groups, we don't typically assume that they belong on the golf courses of the world. This is why I like being a self-publisher. Because if I said this in an open forum, it would piss a lot of people off and for some ridiculous fucking reason would get *me* labeled as racist by someone just for describing the racist, classist troops themselves. Among some groups, you can't talk about a subject without being guilty of that subject, even if there is no guilt to be had. But that mobby reframing of the topic won't make the opportunities come any faster. You have to look at a problem in order to solve it. Even though 105q11 summarizes the issues attending black people in my own chart and personal experience, the ability to see those issues laid out in a single small list of asteroids it's pretty damned amazing I think. You can teach people to see what the issues might be before they waste decades learning those issues the hard way.

middle and younger brothers' relationship; birthright		oldest brother	1	personality		0
counsel student		bias→connects easily with trans, easy relationships	94	personality		0
san antonio environment; 27 y.o.	bias-connects easily with latina, difficult relationship		79	personality		0
12 y.o.	bias-connects easily with red or auburn hair, easy platonic relationships		101	personality		0
black; mom's influence; attracts heavier build women but partners with thin ones		turn-on: large (but not huge) breasts	86	personality		0
turn-on: large breasts; very large penis		turn on: big areolae	111	personality		0
partner argument spray; information blocks intimacy		draw: small or medium breasts	99	personality		0

Comment: 3474 Linsley, better than Mars or Pluto, one of the best alternative rulers of Aries

Many people maintain that when a man is drawn to certain aspects of a woman's body, objectification or his own stupidity must follow. Eh, I don't know about all that. I think most of us males know that we would be much more attractive to prospective partners if we A) had more money, B) had more fans, C) were funnier (see more fans), or D) served as some sort of vending machine for the other's abstract notions of "happiness." Obviously I'm generalizing. Yet the heuristic is hard to ignore; from what I can tell, these prosocial possessions are to women what tits n' asses are to men. I'd never throw my underwear on stage just because the person's on the stage. Males and females both have their animal sides after all. It isn't shallow. It's evolution. Like a quadruped assuming the position, we have some urges within us that are just pre-wired beyond the adult stories we learn to cover them with. Pick your trigger; it may be abstract or physical, and it may play out through work or play, but as a member of the human species, you probably have it. Find 3474 Linsley in your chart to see what it might look like.

My Linsley is in 11q12 <how parties around you engage your ongoing ambient dynamical arrangements>. I have also included the statistically significant text-mined words most related to other turn-ons I have listed elsewhere in this table (words not shown are unrelated to this topic). Compare anything I've listed in this table, and see how Linsley's location highlights the various concepts that can thump around your hormones at will.

5222	Ioffe	big, charm, exhibit, girl, rowdy, sculpture	the outspoken comedian, lord of the corny; B-movies and bad production; shabby things; all-known to lift people's spirits while still providing function. Even if form is lacking
6349	Acapulco	[adb: Philosopher/ Humanist], covet, fascinating, fertile, iconic	where one steps back from social turbulence and works towards more abstractly humanist ends; this cluster can be used to advance the humanist cause whenever you use it
1970	Sumeria		a regular diet of necessary social input: this is where it is for you; the cluster and duodecanate will reveal more on how this manifests
30840	Jackalice	[breast roundness slider (later in this book)] sexiest, sociology	a well-known social actor turns their warring history into more benevolent pursuits; "redemption through history"; if you have this asteroid active, it may be possible to turn past crimes towards some cause that people value, provided those crimes really are past
8338	Ralhan		sitting back, comfortably leaving it to others (whatever 'it' is). The cluster will reveal more
183	Istria		a work allowed despite the pressure to replace it with more socially favored alternatives; "a high work regardless of social favorability"
114094	Irvpatterson		the rules of structures upon which we're built; where the natural of the past shine through the forms that currently encapsulate them; the cluster shows the kinds of experiences that put you directly in touch with influences considered to be your primitives, and thus give you a sense of being (psychoemotionally, if not spiritually) at home
22833	Scottyu	[adb: Teacher], girth, hot, voluptuous	after a bitter or difficult conflict, one party is formally blocked, leaving mystery to take over; should either party absorb the energy of the mystery instead, it may unlock their genius
3474	Linsley	[adb: Sex, Extremes in quantity], companion, compulsive	associated with being victimized repeatedly by the same party, having ones place erased; like Natalie, an asteroid of rape or other kinds of violation. Unlike Natalie, the perpetrator implied is well-known and is likely to return more frequently; unfortunately this asteroid does not offer solutions to people who have already suffered in this way, but it does suggest preventative measures: positively, this is the asteroid of "having some other thing draw out your co-creativity"
4222	Nancita	smoking, story - measure	trying to reach something mentally, especially across a flow of appetites; related to assisted navigation of passages, passing through experiences with help
30310	Alexanderlin	plump, self-esteem, winery	related to grand or important rooms and big settings; conference rooms and war rooms where big decisions are made; the duodecanate and cluster tell you the situational background evoked by such environments as you encounter them; on a micro level, also associated with the cellular environment and the conditions under which you may easily experience cell proliferation and regeneration

mom's influence; art mirrors life; values peace	Turn-ons: shows of mercy where it didn't have to be given	21	personality		-0.5

you beat your own version of this game; A controversial american sociologist and pioneer in the field of frequentics	I am a global legend in human history for having helped correct the course of humanity through my work in psychology; talk topic, side quest provider	85	desired ending		0
declare a situation intolerable; make more money; develop complex algorithm or workflow; permanent published works, read in distant places by certain kinds of seekers, tomes which vacuum in information	I live in a place that is free and easy, safe and quiet, protected against noise; I am a millionaire / multimillionaire; I do almost no work at all, and spend all of my time at my leisure; I have a huge house; I travel the world teaching spirituality; I own a massive data save company	48	desired ending		1
40 y.o.; 4.5 years; 12 years; 28 years; writer self-discloser; develop new question from body observation; lost direction finder; a controversial american sociologist	I die at age 81-83; I have a notorious reputation; for having saved my full self as data	2	desired ending		1
Attracts women in pairs when traveling in a foreign, historically educational environment; vision quest; teacher family; Indian girl, super warm, fun; a controversial american sociologist; I live in a place that is free and easy, safe and quiet, protected against noise; develop new question from body observation	I have two romantic or close partners; at least one is voluptuous; she dotes on me; the other is an intense driver of forward progress, my life partner, body traits matter less; our thrio lives a life of benevolently productive comfort, which brings light to the world; the girls are major fun; one of my girls is Indian or has Indian features. At the time of this writing, our cat Kit and dog Rachel split this energy and the warring circumstances that bring the Indian woman. Since I keep war out of my personal space as a rule, the latter may never stably materialize after all. Given the price I'd have to pay, I'm fine with that.	85	desired ending		1
writer self-discloser; digital asset publishing; motivated by sexual information; strange uncomfortable, ajani - weird; develop complex algorithm; nakedness	A controversial american sociologist and pioneer in the field of frequentics. He is best known as the author of several important books in statistical astrology	22	desired ending		0
digital asset publishing; develop a complex algorithm; final publishing process; relationship with brother #2 middle; recursive inspect research data; Talented in inheriting the talents of people he wanted in his life, whose company was not granted or whose association was in some way blocked,	You, reader, beat your own version of this game, helped by my books	87	desired ending		2
birthright; relationship with cousin; Motivated towards: vast space in which to order patterns	antisocial/private	32	socialization		-1
reference the body for immediate answers; righteous defense of another against bullying; imaginary friends	greatly admires princess royal victoria	41	personality		2.5
birthright; mom's influence	dad's influence	41	family	pull new music or series; mood match music play; put in place by partner; stunned when suddenly checked; mama bear welcomer	2
birthright	mom's influence	105	family	seek to improve; Personality, strangers and public: cold, logical, guarded, discourages interaction	0.5
mom and dad's relationship	birthright	32	family		0
time passage	time passage	144	family		0
mom's influence; birthright	youthful loss of temper (hypersensitivity)	10	family		-3

A story: Qunit 138q7 and a private recording about the shittiest moment(s) in my exchanges with others

The asteroid 3355 Onizuka—the onset of something ugly, scary, or difficult—really sums up the generally creepy nature of several things about living in my house in REDACTED. First of all there was the REDACTED stuff, which actually was really ugly—the first of my wholly false accusations came there—and actually, now that I think about it, the only formally mobbed, escalated, false accusation that has occurred to date. I may have been so bothered by that one that I have really only imagined what others have said in the years since then.

Really, this is the first time I've realized that I actually haven't had any more false accusations since then. I only imagined them. But stuff like that will make you paranoid. And my relationship with at least one person as well as the city of San Antonio on the whole suffered because of how all of that went down. Right now as I record this, I'm actually at a loss for words to describe that event—mainly because it's a side road to what I'm trying to do with the rest of this quint. Part of me wonders if retelling that event would be useful to my future self, given a reload of my data. But most of me thinks more value came out of the subsequent decades of distrust, and that the single event, the letter that was written to our boss, the factions involved... It was just so freaking stupid, and the claimed action by me in that letter just wasn't a thing done. But the rest of my experience with racism in San Antonio is really born here. You can search other recordings of mine to get the details on that event. And there are surely other points in this biography where I will tell you when I did something wrong. The worst thing I ever did to anyone, in fact, was definitely the way I treated the interim Minority Student Affairs director Brandy at Caltech. I was horrible. And very guilty. Here is probably a good time to apologize for that. So to Brandy, I'm sorry. I was immature. As for the people who made-up a lynch mob over something that a tyrannical temporary supervisor thought she saw me doing (I wasn't.) No apologies there. Because that was completely false. I did lose my temper afterwards. But that's what happens when you put an advocate for the voiceless in a cage with no voice; the monkey comes out.

The feeling I have right now talking about this is... I guess I'm just more mystified by how people can be like that. But then again, maybe that's what Caltech Brandy said of me. Anyways, now that I'm looking at The rest of 138q7, I see that it is EXACTLY the event that happened at REDACTED. So I guess I am obligated to talk about it. This might be a run on:

I worked remotely for and with somebody who didn't like me from the beginning, but she was a strong colleague so I asked our manager to invite her on the extension of the contract when I had been invited by myself after our team was moved on. In the meantime I was deployed to help another company, REDACTED, and there I met REDACTED. To make a long story short, me, REDACTED, and a coworker named REDACTED ended up in a faction against this person and / or other coworkers. It had to do with some drama revolving around REDACTED which eventually got her dismissed from the job as far as I could tell. I really didn't like the bullying that went on regarding REDACTED though, and furthermore there was even more bullying of REDACTED. So I wrote a letter and gave our proxy manager from REDACTED what for, even though I was lower ranking. I'm pretty sure our actual boss was not amused by any of this. He was just trying to run a company, his best friend (around whom he modeled his ideal employee, and none of us were that) had just left, and now it was high school all over again. I was put in charge of training a new person on the team who was ironically named, given what I've talked about. But she essentially thought I was some combination of incompetent, annoying, or, whatever. I never really knew, and never really cared because it was based on who knows what from inside her head. I think they believed I was in REDACTED's back pocket, and REDACTED was just a weak programmer. But your job as a member of the team is to pull the whole team together, and I really felt that the rest of my team was just off-puttingly cold as humans.

The gossip flew around the office, more drama ensued, and this person that I was watching over along with REDACTED at some point took the opportunity to tell me how bad a team lead I was, and even called me a "limp pencil dick" to my face. That's funny, because later she would be part of the mob saying I had shown sexist behaviors towards the main person who would end up leading the charge (whom I had actually argued to bring on from earlier) I laughed the comment off, because not only was it harassment of me, but it was just false and showed that—for all of her criticisms—she wasn't nearly as professional as she claimed. The drama reached our main boss and what does he do? He puts me under her ally—the manager I had brought on which, in my opinion was the worst possible decision. Because a couple of weeks later we ended up having a sit down where that lynch mob manager asserted her bosshood over me. I was so livid, but couldn't react, so I just sat in my chair loosely trying to breathe and count to 100 in my head. And this was the basis of the harassment letter. In that office with her and the other teammate staring me in the face attempting to give me a demotion of sorts, she gave me some kind of assignment—a bullshit one and it all ended. But Later I've found out that she had written a letter, saying that I was spreading my legs during the conversation with her and the other person. I absolutely was not, but they had decided that "He was a monster, he favors his girlfriend so obviously all he's thinking about is shagging the colleagues and if we say no, then he's just a bad person—a nasty harasser who has done XYZ..." I don't know what they said because I actually never saw the letter that was written...

...but apparently because I *had* lost my temper on top of this later and slammed a door once back in my sound booth office, that was all the remaining team of four needed to (as I'm told) draft of a letter complaining to our boss. I was already out the door getting ready to start my real estate career, and was going to put in my two weeks if I had not already done so. And so there was a certain arrangement with our main boss, and on my side it all ended up OK with the main boss. Because the story was false, you see. And he seemed like he knew that. Years have gone by and I'm not sure what he thought. With all of this drama, I am so thankful to our immediate manager Paul P., who shielded me from pretty much everything that was written, and everything that the other factions said. Thank you so much Paul. In a world full of people who are accused without a hearing—falsely so, simply because a clique has decided (and that part I have gotten several times), it is so nice to have advocates.

You know, really the biggest problem in that toxic office culture, was that there were two kinds of people. There were cliques and bullies, and then there were temperamental sensitive people who really needed nurturing. The environment was basically against the three of us who needed that kind of sensitivity. I don't think that that was the culture for us. Me, REDACTED, and REDACTED did not fit there. But I am so grateful to Paul for protecting us from the rest of the bullies in there. And I didn't have the maturity to fight back at that time. I *was* immature, don't get me wrong. Very. Childish and petulant. I *did* throw a temper tantrum, a big one. But I NEVER harassed, gestured towards, or even hit on anybody in the professional space. It just wasn't done. But people really will just make things up. They think they saw it because they were in the mood to see any possible negative interpretation in the person they were dealing with. But I repeat, it just wasn't true. I would encounter this same thing later at IADT, and then again when me and REDACTED rifted in SATA, but by the time that happened I had become very good at distancing myself from such people from the very beginning.

That chapter at the contractor job taught me several things that really ended up crazy valuable, though. First, I don't hang out with bullies. I don't know them, I'm not friends with them, I have none in my circle. 100% of my friends are in some kind of education field, teaching and guiding others, or in engineering, media, or military, under top notch, honorable cultures. When I see somebody who smells like a bullying asshole, I deal with them in RAM for as long as the current communication requires, then I flush it. Second, if I don't trust you, the communication basically stops right there. Instantly. Never again will I reinvite someone who I know hated me or made things difficult through no fault of my own. Third, going back to the office was such a stupid move, I threw away remote work and peace for all that crazy nonsense. I vowed never to do it again, and like so many things I talk about in these books, my working remotely, means that all of the bullshit of commutes, and looking for stuff to wear, and getting an early start to beat the traffic, and all of that does not have to be done. So whole chunks of hours in a day, and spaces of peace in the night before where I don't have to rush tomorrow, have allowed these books to be written. I think in the end, all of that craziness forced me to really insist on a particular kind of lifestyle, friendship circle, and distance from other people's blow ups. I also learned just how pronounced my temper was and still is today.

I hear that one of the colleagues essentially threatened me in the letter that I never saw. But that's not... Well... I have No Fear. He didn't know that. And the conversation that me and REDACTED had with Paul when he was telling us about this was so cool, because I told Paul that "He threatened *me*? 6'4" or not, my 5'9" ass is like, MUHFUCKA DON'T LET ME CATCH YOU ON THE BLOCK!! Nigga who in the FUCK threatens *me*?[7] Goddammit. Man, that chick called me a

---

[7] That's why I love being a black male. Because at the end of the day, God himself could come down and say something to you, and if you thought he was disrespecting you, you *are* inclined to be like, "Biiiitch!" It may be costly in a lot of places, but under assault, we're just not afraid of anything, any rank, or anybody. (The challenge with that is figuring out how to NOT use this when provoked, as it can ruin everything.) Every class has a power of sorts. This is one of ours.

pencil dick! I didn't file a harassment complaint against *her*! And that *actually* happened! These shitheadz, fabricatin' stuff... She ain't even *seen* me like that, dawg. And no I'm *not* offerin'. Treatin' me like a piece of meat that you can just talk to any old way, dammit....]" (Now I didn't say all that in REDACTED's company, but I *did* say that and more to *myself*.) And the gist of Paul's response (being former military) was, "yeah, some people are like that. Just stirring up trouble. I didn't think you needed to see that. It doesn't help anything." And we all continued unpacking REDACTED's stuff in her apartment. So here's to the homies. Despite the bullshit, a good one can make everything better.

time passage	mom and dad's relationship	81	family	information blocks intimacy	-1
mom and dad's relationship; birthright; time passage	brother #2, middle	80	family		2.5

A story: 96q9 recordings. Keith

Dude, this qunit totally describes my brother Keith—or more like the things he gravitates towards. There are mentions of his background in the Air Force, his interest in geography, 10773 Jamespaton describes "pressing hard the case for something based on what one knows as fact or definiteness." And this too is relevant to Keith's story. I don't really understand this, honestly, so I look up the definition of 96q9: "how you administer your world in light of your victory or attainment of a significant goal." Interestingly, it appears that my relationship with Keith is partly a reflection of my own achievement of goals in life. Indeed Keith is really one of the most reliable reflections of my Buddhist-Daoist sense that I don't really have to strive for the desires of childhood anymore. I have become the person that I want it to be, and everything else I have accomplished is icing on the cake. I have believed this for a long time, though I only discovered the framework for this in 2009. I reconnected with Keith in 2016 after a fateful phone call while I was teaching at IADT, where he was like, "Dude what happened to our family? You never talk to us." And that hit me to the point that I really needed to do something about it, because up to then my identity as the oldest brother head really rendered me OK with my role. But Keith compelled me to rethink that. Since then we've been pretty close, and this is also around the time that I was in my first three-year celibacy vow after having chosen a kind of semi-enlightened path. The sense of abandoning the wheel of karma, samsara. Having no more deeming desire. And my reward was someone other than myself who I would be tasked to support in this life.

mom and dad's relationship; brother #2, middle; time passage	brother #3, youngest	63	family		-2
time passage; brother #2, middle; brother #3, youngest	middle and younger brothers' relationship	119	family	fun duo conversation	1.5
middle and younger brothers' relationship; birthright; time passage	aj's relationship with brothers	80	family	Susceptibility to notable influence by Ajani + two close partners of any kind	0.5
time passage	aj's relationship with cousin	104	family		1.5
dad's influence	teacher family	19	family		1.5
mom's influence	matriarchal family	81	family	listen to other person in conversation	-1
time passage; 8 y.o.	8-bit	83	age		0.5
8-bit	16-bit	81	age		2
time passage	8 y.o.	120	age		-0.5
8 y.o.	12 y.o.	93	age		-1
12 y.o.	16 y.o.	123	age		1
16 y.o.	20 y.o.	83	age		-2.5
20 y.o.	27 y.o.	84	age		-2.5
27 y.o.	32 y.o.	94	age		2
32 y.o.	40 y.o.	119	age		2.5
8-bit	megaman	71	age	absorbs the traits of people he wanted in his life	2
birthright	san antonio environment	60	time passage		-3
time passage	2 hours	135	time passage		0
2 hours	4 hours	93	time passage		0
4 hours	10 hours	101	time passage		0
1 day	2 days	84	time passage		0
2 days	1 week	138	time passage		0
1 week	2 weeks	73	time passage		0
2 weeks	2 months	137	time passage		0
9 months	2 years	139	time passage		0
2 years	4.5 years	118	time passage		0
4.5 years	12 years	104	time passage		0
12 years	28 years	93	time passage		0
engrossed in my own research; 2 weeks	fitness drop	96	time passage		-2
10 hours	1 day	34	family		0
aj's relationship with cousin; mom and dad's relationship; seek to improve	HATES being assessed or compared to others	32	family	be irritated with frustrating self-continued situation; pull back from unlistenable situation	-3
9 months; job application fill	being brought into a place	108	family		-1.5
2 months	9 months	75	time passage		0
mama bear feedback gatherer; matriarchal family; institution or group experiences existential crisis involving merger, cuts, and regulatory challenges	righteous defense of another against bullying	17	personality	youthful losses of temper; information blocks intimacy	-2.5
oldest brother; insightful questions; embattled, assaulted by their bosses; institution or group experiences existential crisis involving merger, cuts,	bosses and influencers deploy ajani to a foreign map	140	personality	guarded travel	1

enjoys badassery; declare voluntary time; leave an intolerable situation; be irritated with frustrating self-continued situation		final debt strike	42	personality		2.5
attracts heavier-build women but partners with very thin ones; HATES being compared or assessed; mom and dad's relationship	Sexual orientation: nonmonogamous. Can survive mono relationships, but typically has to compartmentalize them in order to thrive in ambitions. Poly relationships help ambition thriving, but require constant travel if they are to avoid being fleeting. Ajani dislikes fleeting relationships.	85	personality		2
Seems passive / not dominating, BUT generally it's his way or failure for the other; Turn offs, anger triggers:	Sexual orientation: hetero	84	personality		1
seducible by two; middle and youngest brothers' relationship; HATES being assessed or compared; put in a place by partner	Sexual orientation: bisexual favoring	85	personality		3
black; Almost all friends (and Ajani himself) are obsessive, have high big-5 neuroticism, or both; warm introductory conversation; write works; His friends are: revolutionary, tolerant, logical sticklers; Seems passive / not dominating, BUT generally it's his way or failure for the other; built lego	Sexual orientation: alpha ambition	32	personality		1
birthright	imaginary friends	82	personality	motivated towards: vast spaces in which to order pattern	1.5
20 y.o.; insightful questions; wake up; astrology skill	hour of uranus - chaos	84	time passage	be irritated with frustrating self-continued situation	-2.5
20 y.o.; insightful questions; wake up; astrology skill	hour of mercury - demanded solve	80	time passage	dread exact administrative deadline; oldest brother; search it solution	-2.5
birthright; mom's influence	Sexual orientation: male	124	personality		1
oldest brother; male	need to explain on the spot	82	personality	writer self-discloser	-1.5
Closed opportunity doors to Ajani as solo. "solicitation never works"; birthright	negative surprise encountered	82	event	youthful loss of temper	-3
mom's influence	desire for more money	121	personality	search for more investment channels	0.5
20 y.o.; listen to the other in conversation	astrology skill	44	personality		2
nod off	jolt to alertness	118	homeostasis		0
institution or group experiences existential crisis involving merger, cuts, challenges; mama bear feedback gatherer; off chat with student; friends (and Ajani himself) are obsessive, have high big-5 neuroticism, or both	call me any time	42	personality		2
music match mood play	hear resonant energy	85	personality		3
final publishing process; recursive inspect research data; recursive build workflow; passively listen to it colleagues; be annoyed with high it confounds; lost direction finder; astrology skill; Talented in automation, a magnet for mass, often private data	digital asset publishing	82	personality		0
birthright; youthful losses of temper; childhood asthma	average adult height	88	body		0
birthright	childhood asthma	10	body		-1
highly cerebral mind; high metabolism	slim athletic build	23	body		1
birthright	high metabolism / high baseline background tension	83	body	eat high salt foods, favorite things: tang, drink caffeine; insightful questions	-0.5
pace conscious contemplate; pace preconscious contemplate; slim athletic build; jelq freestanding	narrow butt	135	body		-1
psoas and circulation; childhood asthma; jelq freestanding; high metabolism; highly cerebral mind; information flood	respiratory inconsistencies	81	body		-2
respiratory inconsistencies; jelq freestanding	psoas and circulation warning	89	body		-1.5
psoas and circulation warning; childhood asthma; jelq freestanding; eat high salt foods; drink hard alcohol; drink caffeine; high stress company; pre-sleep	heart warning	120	body		-1.5
athletic build; prefer peace	follow fitness video	50	daily duty		2
dad's influence; 12 y.o.	dirty-private sense of humor	43	personality		2.5
family power; godfather	richer than god	109	the great dream	Ajani won't communicate with friends unless there is a material progress update	-3
monopolistic technical expertise	extremely wealthy	23	the great dream	I have two romantic close partners	1.5
never have to work again	an extremely wealthy-like leisurely lifestyle	91	the great dream	nightlife riches	1.5
high leisure	nightlife riches	122	the great dream	strangers: feel uncomfortable, ajani=weird	-2
nightlife riches	fast cars and clothes	126	the great dream	strangers: feel uncomfortable, ajani=weird	-2.5
unassuming travel	jet set penthouse travel	48	the great dream	attracts women in pairs when traveling	0
be irritated in negative dynamic with another; great business owner	godfather-powerful organizational controller	110	the great dream	monitor pet for trouble	1
uncageable by any other; desire for more money	massive land or shares	121	the great dream	uncageable by any other	2
great spiritual leader	loved by all	70	the great dream	exiled often	0.5
strangers: Susceptibility to notable influence by Ajani + two close partners of any kind	millions of fans	131	the great dream	personality, strangers: cold, guarded logical	-1

motivated by the vast space	monopolistic technical expertise	130	the great dream	uncageable by any other	2
strangers: cold and calculating	celebrated followed leader	113	the great dream	abandoned many close friends	1
friends are sociable, pioneering	massively influential idea influencer	83	the great dream	unable to find benevolent understanding; organization experiences existential crisis	0
millions of fans	top media performer	127	the great dream	millions of fans; abandon close friendships	-0.5
friends are sociable, pioneering	top content creator	106	the great dream	media pied piper; unable to find benevolent understanding from others	-2
uncageable by any other	field pioneer / founding father	41	the great dream	legend in human history	3
birthright	powerful family and immunity	142	the great dream	godfather	2
godfather; kill or eliminate at will	underworld mastermind	97	the great dream	fast cars and clothes; family power	0
be frustrated with self-continued situation	kill or eliminate at will	105	the great dream	nightlife riches	-1
stuck state: unable to find beneficial understanding from others; golden rule	great spiritual leader	71	the great dream	you beat your own version of the game; legend in human history	0
monopolistic technical expertise; successful business owner; nightlife riches	elite club member	125	the great dream	friends are sociable, pioneering, creatively dominant	-1.5
friends are sociable, pioneering; millions of fans	media pied piper	119	the great dream	massively influential idea influencer	-3
enjoy well assembled body and measurable creativity	people's athletic or trend hero	78	the great dream	guarded travel; millions of fans; unable to find benevolent understanding from other	-2
golden rule ethos	personal honor	47	the great dream	golden rule ethos	3
strangers: closed doors when solo	family well-provided for	100	the great dream	partner close: commentary on expectations/effort	-1
motivated by the vast space	self-actualization	34	the great dream	generic happiness	3
birthright; oldest brother; one of a kind	uncageable by any other	144	the great dream	self-actualization	3
partner: slim, hedonistic, temperamental	renowned artist	50	the great dream	I am a global legend in human history	0.5
people's athletic or trend hero	record setter in a specific thing	82	the great dream	I am a global legend in human history	0
motivated by the vast space; personality, live and let live	one of a kind	79	the great dream	uncageable by any other	0.5
personality: happy live and let live	generic happiness	103	the great dream	stuck state: unable to find beneficial understanding from others	0.5
retirement on the beach; partner, increased single-mindedness	never work again	2	the great dream	personality, strangers: cold, guarded logical	-2
never work again; age 40	retirement on the beach	124	the great dream	partner, slim hedonistic	-3
uncageable by any other; motivated by the vast space	build a great work	49	the great dream	uncageable by any other	2
friends are sociable, pioneering; volatile latina exchanges	successful business owner	138	the great dream	personality, strangers: feel uncomfortable, ajani= weird	-1
nightlife riches	party vacation road trip	56	the great dream	partner argument spray; travel solo; declare voluntary time	-0.5
motivated by sexual information, measurements	stuck state: unable to find beneficial understanding from others	116	the great dream	monopolistic technical expertise	1
black; motivated by the vast space; motivated by sexual information, measurements	stuck state: no cocreators that aren't creations themselves	52	the great dream	motivated by the vast space; motivated by sexual information	0

Comment: Views of the Great Dream

I had initially built this table without realizing how societal pressures factored in. Conspicuously absent from the proffered American values are concepts like love and filial piety. Our mainstream social upbringing just doesn't emphasize these things. If you are going to save yourself as data, I think it's very valuable to include your handling of the Joneses' bucket list, as this little piece of information can greatly help in, say, determining what kinds of communities researchers will be most successful cloning you into. Alas, you can see that I don't really value a lot of these advertised values very highly. It is likely that you won't swallow every pill handed to you either.

FIGURE 7: [SELF] DATA SAVE PART 3 OF 3
AJANI'S Q-BIO (WITH THE 144 QUNIT INCONJUNCT GROUPS / QIGS)

The table above starts from top of mind activities actually performed. The table below starts from the chart and compels one to think about what each cluster represents. It may not seem valuable to very many people at first glance, but in the future, when we really start saving humans into a reliable format, These tables, combined with Figure 4 and the definitions in *Laurentia 2*, will give researchers in several fields one of the rare first case studies they need to network a full personality and simulate the most accurate summaries of internal and external human lives. It also illustrates how certain asteroids in your own chart end up playing out within clusters in an actual life…

Critically, you will also note that these qunits are arranged by qunit grand cross—allowing you to see for yourself how regions in sharp square are more related to each other than adjacent regions are. This may not seem like the most organized way to do things, until you attempt your own biography. If you should ever do so, know that grand crosses and qunit inconjunct groups are ESSENTIAL for understanding how to hack your circumstances on purpose.

But what is a qunit inconjunct group?

Thanks to some complicated analyses that I won't put here, I found an answer to a question that had been bothering me: If grand crosses are supposed to ease the process of context switching, why can I still not get certain regions working? The reason is that there are TWO ways to block an event. You can block a situation (or render it potential instead of reality) by using a square. You can also avoid a situation entirely, neither blocking it nor enabling it. Inconjuncts to an object or region work in a kind of separate dimension from it. You may want to make money as a "self," but your would-be money attention might be pervasively "other" or world in "nature" where you're more focused on social riches, for example. Between qunit grand crosses of squares, and triplets of grand qcrosses in the form of inconjunct groups you can *really* find out why something you want doesn't appear to be accessible. When producing my q-bio below, I found that, for any qunit I sought to understand, it was MUCH easier to look at its opposition right afterwards, then its two squares after that. Once the whole quartet in a qcross was defined, it made further sense to repeat this process for the other two qcrosses within the same qunit inconjunct group. This allowed me to get a basic sense of what each group of twelve microregions in the same degree all around the wheel were actually doing.

(Note that the qcrosses (qcs) are NOT interpretations, as how you handle the quartet of them will be a highly personal sum of your specific qunits in it. It's the qig interpretations which will be the more generalizable to you.)

(One other EXTREMELY IMPORTANT thing to note about this table, which I didn't realize until editing a few pages in: Even if you don't have asteroid translations on hand, my biography qcs give you a hint as to what at least one of the asteroids in each group does—provided the qunit's description is unique among the four, or at least describes no further than a pair in opposition. If a description seems to span all four qunits in a qc, then it is probably not just one of the asteroids at work, but the qc itself.)

IMPORTANT! Oppositions A and B necessarily complement each other. Pairs of oppositions C and D will "square" the first pair! Doing A or B temporarily prevents the pair C and D

101

qig106[8]: things you do, work on, or project in order to fit in with outside society

qc432[9]: the duo against which my personality is more likely to be projected

1q8 (359.896) \\it would be nice to have money or resources for this; 22292 Mosul, 663 Gerlinde, 5229 Irurita, 1746 Brouwer, 137166 Netabahcall, 32931 Ferioli, 181419 Dragonera, 2779 Mary, 20532 Benbilby, 10468 Itacuruba

73q8 (179.896) \\in my early recordings, going on and on about some romantic disappointment or other; 9291 Alanburdick, 5904 Wurttemberg, 28556 Kevinchen, 584 Semiramis, 195777 Sheepman, 5359 Markzakharov, 10448 Schawlow, 12517 Grayzeck, 3034 Climenhaga, 145075 Zipernowsky, 3643 Tienchanglin, 7221 Sallaba, 1316 Kasan, 260824 Hermanus

37q8 (269.896) \\incubus; seems to affect muscularity amount; accretion integration amount; 6751 van Genderen, 26736 Rojeski, 3184 Raab, 34133 Charlesfenske, 1448 Lindbladia, 128608 Chucklove, 18776 Coulter, 202778 Dmytria, 4804 Pasteur, 107805 Saibi, 2460 Mitlincoln, 3231 Mila, 28855 Burchell, 367 Amicitia

109q8 (89.896) \\my lighter recordings; 10436 Janwillempel, 12056 Yoshigeru, 4338 Velez, 37519 Amphios, 30312 Lilyliu, 15735 Andakerkhoven, 1277 Dolores, 13652 Elowitz

qc288: coop work and play

13q8 (329.896) \\the approach which actually supports my creativity; 5180 Ohno, 227641 Nothomb, 2247 Hiroshima, 3167 Babcock, 8548 Sumizihara, 33852 Baschnagel, 14360 Ipatov

85q8 (149.896) \\as my paycheck builds my foundations, so too does my sense of maleness; 6060 Doudleby, 4369 Seifert, 121327 Andreweaker, 8295 Toshifukushima, 4353 Onizaki, 32059 Ruchipandya, 4653 Tommaso, 27286 Adedmondson, 932 Hooveria, 11197 Beranek, 37640 Luiginegrelli, 28747 Swintosky, 43751 Asam, 2191 Uppsala, 25122 Kaitlingus

49q8 (239.896) \\nobody cares about my work... until they need data to rescue their situation; 2451 Dollfus, 7311 Hildehan, 6097 Koishikawa, 246153 Waltermaria, 50250 Daveharrington, 3670 Northcott, 9516 Inasan, 1665 Gaby, 134091 Jaysoncowley, 553 Kundry, 4382 Stravinsky, 15837 Mariovalori, 175629 Lambertini, 6372 Walker, 8993 Ingstad, 15037 Chassagne, 4932 Texstapa, 19704 Medlock, 10637 Heimlich, 205 Martha, 997 Priska, 5936 Khadzhinov, 6979 Shigefumi, 14147 Wenlingshuguang, 28488 Gautam, 1668 Hanna, 13716 Trevino, 24332 Shaunalinn

121q8 (59.896) \\negotiating lawncare against public image; 16189 Riehl, 22534 Lieblich, 249539 Pedrosevilla, 5211 Stevenson, 27284 Billdunbar, 161699 Lisahardaway

qc144: ideas about how nature should be handled

25q8 (299.896) \\where the nusians live; sb. me needing to travel to groups like waking angels, agd or the adult groups. But when I do this, my complement is the one more likely to be in the underposition; endangered territories; 10680 Ermakov, 18114 Rosenbush, 9784 Yotsubashi, 6268 Versailles, 23402 Turchina, 1083 Salvia, 22783 Teng, 388 Charybdis, 227218 Renyi, 7528 Huskvarna, 10679 Chankaochang, 498 Tokio, 25410 Abejar, 22137 Annettelee, 9717 Lyudvasilia, 26639 Murgas, 13298 Namatjira

97q8 (119.896) \\the conversation already started, my speaking up when my presence was not invited, corrections of some sort will happen; related to my being black and my perspective as an underattended class member; speaking out on how nature should be handled or exploited; 66661 Wallin, 31905 Likinpong, 358894 Demetrescu, 1568 Aisleen, 20073 Yumiko, 1767 Lampland, 44217 Whittle, 12687 de Valory

61q8 (209.896) \\my cornering zealotry. Later when I stop doing this, other's towards me. There is no value to be had in me expressing this qunit; because I am black in overt appearance, my 97s are more likely to be loaded first, which explains why shanna having her juno there is so useful. she attaches to a trait which is otherwise an entry barrier for me; industrial calculation regarding nature; 9184 Vasilij, 6790 Pingouin, 17983 Buhrmester, 14927 Satoshi, 120208 Brentbarbee, 3134 Kostinsky, 350178 Eisleben, 9828 Antimachos, 27466 Cargibaysal, 364636 Ulrikeecker, 13989 Murikabushi, 9077 Ildo, 3130 Hillary, 17926 Jameswu, 25404 Shansample, 90370 Jokaimor, 10151 Rubens

---

133q8 (29.896) \\regulating carefully what one allows their body to take in. taking on others' accosting of you as a chore. Preferring studies instead. Frequentics which transcends lineage; man makes use of nature; 356863 Maathai, 451 Patientia, 9379 Dijon, 5894 Telc, 2462 Nehalennia, 263932 Speyer

qig107: your projecting role as a witness to another's problems or issues

qc431: making plans with another over their thing, or getting tired of this

1q7 (359.688) \\turning to do it on my own; 33789 Sharmacam, 30242 Naymark

73q7 (179.688) \\me watching the partner's self-rile-up; 3996 Fugaku, 914 Palisana, 23949 Dazapata, 79149 Kajigamori, 26711 Rebekahbau, 22537 Meyerowitz, 121557 Paulmason, 46702 Linapucci, 358376 Gwyn, 4423 Golden, 9249 Yen, 5606 Muramatsu, 2265 Verbaandert, 20768 Langberg, 25233 Tallman, 22623 Fisico, 60000 Miminko, 13627 Yukitamayo, 16002 Bertin

37q7 (269.688) \\the full monty; 83 Beatrix, 188 Menippe, 33572 Mandolin, 6025 Naotosato, 13684 Borbona, 5118 Elnapoul, 29979 Wastyk, 7128 Misawa, 3720 Hokkaido, 28457 Chloeanassis

109q7 (89.688) \\sgl and I planning the incubator, to a lesser extent, abie, angela, and i; 5637 Gyas, 17992 Japellegrino, 28874 Michaelchen, 134419 Hippothous, 6191 Eades, 1986 Plaut

qc287: a listener: letting others cut me off

13q7 (329.688) \\putting out my astro work to make a name for myself; 3139 Shantou, 32614 Hacegarcia, 205599 Walkowicz, 6252 Montevideo, 20141 Markidger, 22571 Letianzhang, 11212 Tebbutt

85q7 (149.688) \\this work in qunits; 6701 Warhol, 672 Astarte, 22810 Rawat, 1383 Limburgia, 4732 Froeschle, 12509 Pathak, 6786 Doudantsutsuji, 8102 Yoshikazu, 25129 Uranoscope, 1272 Gefion, 43882 Maurivicoli, 13743 Rivkin

49q7 (239.688) \\me thinking I belong in the world of the body, modeling, the human form; 763 Cupido, 18987 Irani, 72834 Guywells, 2073 Janacek, 11725 Victoriahsu, 15988 Parini, 13753 Jennivirta, 15631 Dellorusso, 8943 Stefanozavka, 19159 Taenakano, 978 Aidamina, 5940 Feliksobolev, 40459 Rektorys, 34892 Evapalisa, 2569 Madeline, 7276 Maymie, 3568 ASCII, 4345 Rachmaninoff, 49272 Bryce Canyon, 25979 Alansage, 21555 Levary, 73827 Nakanohoshinokai

121q7 (59.688) \\barack obama, taylor swift, and other mega successful people; those with fans can visit things, not necessarily be the best at it but be granted a win there *because they have fans*—they who walk on water in the eyes of their followers; mine is afflicted by Grosseteste. might be reversible if i learned kindness... but i won't learn it in the US. maybe Portugal or the Netherlands—a unassuming country. I would also have to be rich already, not obligated or energy-exploitable. and would need a thing to give which wasn't too complicated for the receiver; 10477 Lacumparsita, 30030 Joycekang, 36169 Grosseteste, 511 Davida, 844 Leontina, 4589 McDowell, 2684 Douglas

qc143: the scream out from within the caging institution

25q7 (299.688) \\the big-bodied person is more likely to be interested in engaging my experience; was probably kevin or simeona at some point, rachel. The clearest significator qunit for the big girl; horror movie; 25580 Xuelai, 5187 Domon, 13346 Danielmiller, 27606 Davidli, 2173 Maresjev, 19873 Chentao, 24907 Alfredhaar, 3719 Karamzin, 2618 Coonabarabran, 18027 Gokcay, 15032 Alexlevin, 138016 Kerribeisser, 6461 Adam, 17779 Migomueller, 20853 Yunxiangchu, 22719 Nakadori, 6814 Steffl, 339223 Stongemorin, 6335 Nicolerappaport, 170909 Bobmasterson

97q7 (119.688) \\one of my regulated responses to the big girl. With dg over jla. Likely a trigger for the big girl; rebel in the institution; 22450 Nove Hrady, 117240 Zhytomyr, 405207 Konstanz, 23010 Kathyfinch, 947 Monterosa, 6299 Reizoutoyoko, 10399 Nishiharima, 13705 Llapasset, 1891 Gondola, 6398 Timhunter, 11406 Ucciocontin, 3486 Fulchignoni, 18228 Hyperenor, 2667 Oikawa

61q7 (209.688) \\the big girl's role and story; 172996 Stooke, 4108 Rakos, 18467 Nagatatsu, 9818 Eurymachos, 13560 La Perouse, 6119 Hjorth, 7064 Montesquieu, 14445 Koichi, 28633 Ratripathi, 9665 Inastronoviny, 3889 Menshikov, 24005 Eddieozawa, 313921 Daassou, 8144 Hiragagennai, 4245 Nairc

---

[8] For a chart around the year 2000, the qunit inconjunct groups start at 106, as the issues they cover most resemble Cancer-10. The qunit grand crosses don't really follow fancy holistic numbering, since they are more like the XYZ self-other-world axes across separate scopes of a life.

[9] Qcross 432 covers your introduction to the world. See how it compares to qc288 and qc144, which cover realms where people are already cooperating with you or the situation has already accepted you.

Notice how, if you had trouble fitting in or being accepted into a place, there is a stronger likelihood that you're using one of the qunits in qc432, though switching to an attitude where qc288 or qc144 might be more pleasant. Qc432 puts a person outside of these contexts. All triplets of qunit inconjunct groups work like this. In general, you can only focus on one, though they don't actually block the way square groups do. It's more like they "miss" the opportunity.

133q7 (29.688) \\the big girl comes highly sexualized, see me as such, or vice versa in the case of mb; 293 Brasilia, 61 Danae, 25316 Comnick, 5107 Laurenbacall, 331992 Chasseral, 320880 Cabu, 3692 Rickman, 6145 Riemenschneider, 1025 Riema, 2812 Scaltriti

qig108: how will they respond to what I reveal?

qc430: presenting myself messily"

1q6 (359.479) \\my performance is on a slow time scale - more like a public reputation; 3283 Skorina, 6256 Canova, 33677 Truell, 79418 Zhangjiajie, 1920 Sarmiento, 210686 Scottnorris, 4679 Sybil, 241090 Nemet, 25608 Hincapie, 34106 Sakhrani, 8253 Brunetto

73q6 (179.479) \\how I was scammed via promises of getting rich quick; 12999 Torun, 3389 Sinzot, 20600 Danieltse, 37840 Gramegna, 129151 Angelaboggs, 3427 Szentmartoni, 7093 Jonleake, 22499 Wunibaldkamm, 285 Regina, 10126 Larbro, 152647 Rinako, 25137 Seansolomon, 5390 Huichiming

37q6 (269.479) \\great differences in cleanliness and messiness in our house; 28277 Chengherngyi, 11348 Allegra, 1750 Eckert, 777 Gutemberga, 17025 Pilachowski, 232923 Adalovelace, 4971 Hoshinohiroba, 1810 Epimetheus, 30488 Steinlechner, 25878 Sihengyou, 495253 Hanszimmer, 18128 Wysner, 8685 Faure, 217576 Klausbirkner, 215463 Jobse, 2709 Sagan, 115254 Fenyi

109q6 (89.479) \\coffee trips? Halo?; 5757 Ticha, 19407 Standing Bear, 48 Doris, 15732 Vitusbering, 33135 Davidrisoldi

qc286: alone time, on a plane, solitary mode

13q6 (329.479) \\me sketching a map or an outline of what I've seen; 25669 Kristinrose, 254749 Kurosawa, 50033 Perelman, 9542 Eryan, 33195 Davenyadav, 4748 Tokiwagozen, 1004 Belopolskya, 29292 Conniewalker

85q6 (149.479) \\my energy suggests that I don't want to hear it at all; 8756 Mollissima, 22521 ZZ Top, 1753 Mieke, 95179 Berko, 12146 Ostriker, 4716 Urey, 245158 Thomasandrews, 2611 Boyce, 58214 Amorim, 19282 Zhangcunhao, 7140 Osaki, 21799 Ciociaria, 8835 Annona, 12823 Pochintesta, 18565 Selg, 21674 Renaldowebb

49q6 (239.479) \\time alone to really reflect; 246789 Pattinson, 8806 Fetisov, 13817 Genobechetti, 14262 Kratzer, 3493 Stepanov, 974 Lioba, 816 Juliana, 8600 Arundinaceus, 13677 Alvin, 4925 Zhoushan, 5156 Golant, 555 Norma

121q6 (59.479) \\when I am cornered, I am more likely to do things which inspire people to accuse me, though I have done nothing; this qunit explains the futility that undergirds my inability to fix things when attacked in the 68s; the easiest way to get myself into a corner is to promise myself or my services to someone; 12812 Cioni, 4803 Birkle, 39971 Jozsef, 10884 Tsuboimasaki

qc142: an initially benign work yields to madness and witch hunts

25q6 (299.479) \\my own self-exposure through contours; the mad doctor; 7661 Reincken, 933 Susi, 1675 Simonida, 3795 Nigel, 94556 Janstary, 13830 ARLT, 10891 Fink, 21563 Chetgervais, 443 Photographica, 7648 Tomboles, 8939 Onodajunjiro, 2405 Welch

97q6 (119.479) \\b.a.r.. The complex response of people who see me as having made moves on them. Unless the surrounding society permits it, I am not likely to be seen favorably. However, in places like Albuquerque and other cities where my type might be seen as socially desirable—especially if i am a kind of master to them, the relationship may yet work; the mob that makes plans to oust the mad doctor; 266983 Josepbosch, 2981 Chagall, 202704 Utena, 18151 Licchelli, 20570 Molchan, 20582 Reichenbach, 3972 Richard, 26934 Jordancotler, 214820 Faustocoppi, 23228 Nandinisarma, 21802 Svoren, 13895 Letkasagjonica, 22475 Stanrunge, 5391 Emmons, 28942 Yennydieguez

61q6 (209.479) \\certain conversations with dg. But then, exile. REDACTED's move; 16053 Brennan, 2254 Requiem, 23771 Emaitchar, 241192 Pulyny, 18912 Kayfurman, 9622 Terryjones, 1371 Resi, 22082 Rountree, 3899 Wichterle, 19638 Johngenereid, 39405 Mosigkau, 4063 Euforbo, 325436 Khlebov, 9782 Edo

133q6 (29.479) \\a critical no. my response to [various REDACTED] when they exposed themselves / made their moves on me; when I judge the big girl as unworthy; 354659 Boileau, 14526 Xenocrates, 27120 Isabelhawkins, 22920 Kaitduncan, 6142 Tantawi, 236746 Chareslindos, 486170 Zolnowska, 28482 Bauerle

qig109: the adjustments others make in order to be effective with you

qc429: I absolutely need to know I've advanced in my creative tooling"

1q5 (359.271) \\my "abuses" are weirdly abstract, and have to do with my presence; 4577 Chikako, 2510 Shandong, 6240 Lucretius Carus

73q5 (179.271) \\an empty seat which CANNOT go unfilled; 11769 Alfredjoy, 47294 Blansky les, 58 Concordia, 25628 Kummer, 1771 Makover, 12608 Aesop, 5820 Babelsberg, 161371 Bertrandou, 48492 Utewielen, 18974 Brungardt, 313116 Palvenetianer, 31661 Eggebraaten, 16091 Malchiodi, 22999 Irizarry, 11304 Cowra,

6804 Maruseppu, 12443 Paulsydney, 6050 Miwablock, 34253 Nitya, 23844 Raghvendra, 10127 Frojel

37q5 (269.271) \\wakeup solo exercises; 55223 Akiraifukube, 1275 Cimbria, 18434 Mikesandras, 22868 Karst

109q5 (89.271) \\when I am more likely to spend my saved money on a more expensive thing; 9766 Bradbury, 17090 Mundaca, 27 Euterpe, 18290 Sumiyoshi, 5687 Yamamotoshinobu, 1775 Zimmerwald, 300932 Kyslyuk, 248183 Peisandros, 178267 Sarajevo, 3658 Feldman

qc285: my sudden check-in on my exercise progress

13q5 (329.271) \\my becoming more chill around people who outrank me socially (since I won't win in the extroversion department); 11628 Katuhikoikeda, 1088 Mitaka, 8865 Yakiimo, 23 Thalia, 7231 Porco, 7228 MacGillivray, 11376 Taizomuta, 253536 Tymchenko, 438 Zeuxo, 9041 Takane, 2706 Borovsky

85q5 (149.271) \\my default self-reinforcement is strongly negative/discontented— especially through my recordings; 23755 Sergiolozano, 18970 Jenniharper, 2469 Tadjikistan, 1346 Gotha, 134348 Klemperer, 25273 Barrycarole, 13235 Isiguroyuki, 8731 Tejima, 21652 Vasishtha, 6091 Mitsuru, 198993 Epoigny, 12793 Hosinokokai, 20361 Romanishin, 33472 Yunorperalta, 1051 Merope, 243529 Petereisenhardt, 32057 Ethannovek, 6657 Otukyo

49q5 (239.271) \\when I am the centrally effective party; 72633 Randygroth, 16706 Svojsik, 28208 Timtrippel, 24249 Bobbiolson, 14574 Payette, 1971 Hagihara, 8353 Megryan, 325588 Bridzius, 90376 Kossuth, 12278 Kisohinoki, 25047 Tsuitehsin

121q5 (59.271) \\many watch as a business partnership plays out; 16039 Zeglin, 25629 Mukherjee, 13658 Sylvester

qc141: what you and your (close housemate) are actually prepared to converse about on a regular basis—how you respond to each other's conversation attempts

25q5 (299.271) \\where I cannot find any good match to support me in whatever; leaving the other person cold; 6326 Idamiyoshi, 142291 Dompfaff, 6463 Isoda, 17075 Pankonin, 5520 Natori, 28766 Monge, 1400 Tirela

97q5 (119.271) \\the side which destroys the whole ship; disney unstoppable; 33562 Amydunphy, 12530 Richardson, 5730 Yonosuke, 448051 Pepisensi, 10028 Bonus, 221026 Jeancoester, 4994 Kisala

61q5 (209.271) \\shanna's move in with me; where one still believes fighting the man is worth it; 14988 Tryggvason, 28475 Garrett, 25094 Zemtsov, 5929 Manzano, 34164 Anikacheerla, 377 Campania, 9082 Leonardmartin, 9116 Billhamilton, 117430 Achosyx, 1647 Menelaus, 17703 Bombieri, 229737 Porthos, 2002 Euler, 210290 Borsellino, 30094 Rolfebode, 27765 Brockhaus, 24147 Stefanmuller, 2516 Roman, 157064 Sedona, 900 Rosalinde

133q5 (29.271) \\shanna' s requirements, or mine. Imposed; the privileged or powerful imposer; 265924 Franceclemente, 8025 Forrestpeterson, 455739 Isabelita, 3535 Ditte, 22996 De Boo

qig110: you as the rule writer

qc428: when it's time to solidify the next status level"

1q4 (359.063) \\shanna's studio, mural; 8822 Shuryanka, 5036 Tuttle, 10008 Raisanyo

73q4 (179.063) \\me as a leader when the group is under threat or coming closure; 4408 Zlata Koruna, 84921 Morkolab, 17305 Caniff, 332 Siri, 6842 Krosigk, 181702 Forcalquier, 27130 Dipaola, 134169 Davidcarte, 18426 Maffei, 12335 Tatsukushi, 5196 Bustelli, 3047 Goethe, 872 Holda, 3112 Velimir, 24351 Fionawood, 22346 Katsumatatakashi, 13529 Yokaboshi, 26243 Sallyfenska, 176867 Brianlee, 10713 Limorenko, 7829 Jaroff

37q4 (269.063) \\REDACTED trips, finally going out to get supplies to progress the home; 28527 Kathleenrose, 184096 Kazlauskas, 73610 Klyuchevskaya, 15252 Yoshiken, 7735 Scorzelli, 16043 Yichenzhang, 1510 Charlois, 4541 Mizuno, 4674 Pauling, 12675 Chabot, 30136 Bakerfranke, 32071 Matthewretchin, 8066 Poldimeri, 10254 Hunsruck, 10413 Pansecchi, 27079 Vsetin, 90709 Wettin, 30240 Morgensen

109q4 (89.063) \\what I ultimately ended up wanting to do with the money I've saved; 3570 Wuyeesun, 31556 Shatner, 22701 Cyannaskye, 2820 Iisalmi, 21853 Kelseykay, 36060 Babuska, 6284 Borisivanov, 13250 Danieladucato, 10275 Nathankaib, 30698 Hippokoon, 11256 Fuglesang

qc284: things I pay ongoing feedbacking attention to, and how I show I'm paying attention

13q4 (329.063) \\regulating others' potential for certain kinds of accomplishment; my blessed interpersonal talent; 31458 Delrosso, 25162 Beckage, 47 Aglaja, 263613 Enol, 4681 Ermak, 69961 Millosevich, 30055 Ajaysaini, 145062 Hashikami

85q4 (149.063) \\my (social) time at caltech; 18734 Darboux, 1967 Menzel, 143048 Margaretpenston, 25813 Savannahshaw, 6010 Lyzenga, 19713 Ibaraki, 4162 SAF, 6744 Komoda, 12227 Penney, 2482 Perkin, 257371 Miguelbello, 53250 Beucher

49q4 (239.063) \\when I believe I should be able to pull that one specific girl; 13223 Cenaceneri, 18689 Rodrick, 33348 Stevelliott, 13059 Ducuroir, 13928 Aaronrogers, 27440 Colekendrick, 13244 Dannymeyer, 10164 Akusekijima, 13423 Bobwoolley, 136825 Slawitschek, 7669 Malse, 1185 Nikko, 321453 Alexmarieann, 21949 Tatulian, 30277 Charlesgulian, 14980 Gustavbrom, 4623 Obraztsova, 10708 Richardspalding

121q4 (59.063) \\the rift's argument; 12325 Bogota, 11266 Macke, 27619 Ethanmessier, 4374 Tadamori, 6762 Cyrenagoodrich, 5267 Zegmott, 65091 Saramagrin, 9282 Lucylim

qc140: who you get when you need help, or those whom you don't want

25q4 (299.063) \\why I kicked dg and b.a.r. and vb out; 602 Marianna, 14664 Vandervelden, 4185 Phystech, 13980 Neuhauser, 7779 Susanring, 18773 Bredehoft, 365 Corduba, 782 Montefiore, 7769 Okuni, 99070 Strittmatter, 8751 Nigricollis, 331011 Peccioli

97q4 (119.063) \\what vb and dg did, and mb; 8801 Nugent, 331 Etheridgea, 4347 Reger, 8380 Tooting, 12119 Memamis, 17002 Kouzel, 9319 Hartzell

61q4 (209.063) \\caught with simeona; 31824 Elatus, 11246 Orvillewright, 5438 Lorre, 629 Bernardina, 12405 Nespoli, 23179 Niedermeyer, 69754 Mosesmendel, 1611 Beyer, 2094 Magnitka, 8034 Akka, 20426 Fridlund, 10664 Phemios, 90830 Beihang, 9358 Faro, 152559 Bodelschwingh, 6890 Savinykh, 39802 Ivanhlinka, 714 Ulula, 7838 Feliceierman, 121593 Kevinmiller, 19130 Tytgat, 4882 Divari

133q4 (29.063) \\dg, ah, sk. A critical character whom you really shouldn't kick out; 7750 McEwen, 11868 Kleinrichert, 18124 Leeperry, 13859 Fredtreasure, 14040 Andrejka, 8558 Hack

qig111: passing burnoff energy

qc427: I may retreat now, but will see you in the funny papers

1q3 (358.854) \\star trek; 815 Coppelia, 191857 Illeserzsebet, 5806 Archieroy, 32086 Viviannetu, 10280 Yequanzhi

73q3 (178.854) \\after experiencing an ostensible defeat, my making new plans to turn the tide later… someday; 6137 Johnfletcher, 713 Luscinia, 9466 Shishir, 336392 Changhua, 43889 Osawatakaomi, 23867 Cathsoto, 80652 Albertoangela, 12618 Cellarius, 9482 Rubendario, 7622 Pergolesi, 294402 Joeorr, 14977 Bressler

37q3 (268.854) \\underground or rogue rebellious group; 5812 Jayewinkler, 120120 Kankelborg, 22927 Blewett, 8191 Mersenne, 18766 Broderick, 184275 Laffra, 3653 Klimishin, 6355 Univermoscow, 3152 Jones, 6674 Cezanne, 25751 Mokshagundam, 8736 Shigehisa, 27287 Garbarino, 5849 Bhanji

109q3 (88.854) \\the fugitive or top assistant on the run; 10387 Bepicolombo, 17976 Schulman, 10108 Tomlinson, 112797 Grantjudy, 39890 Bobstephens, 9156 Malanin, 100027 Hannaharendt, 167113 Robertwick, 9053 Hamamelis, 37687 Chunghikoh, 366689 Rohrbaugh, 8786 Belskaya, 1994 Shane, 85196 Halle

qc283: holding back in social situations

13q3 (328.854) \\my learning from a holistic situation, angela e, smh, ht, jb?; 129185 Jonburroughs, 24051 Hadinger, 9758 Dainty, 34266 Schweinfurth, 2225 Serkowski, 20528 Kyleyawn, 842 Kerstin, 23730 Suncar

85q3 (148.854) \\my withholding of support from those who make me feel uncomfortable in any way; 6910 Ikeguchi, 7542 Johnpond, 27791 Masaru, 6729 Emiko, 1314 Paula, 2664 Everhart, 103460 Dieterherrmann, 1349 Bechuana, 132524 APL, 114829 Chierchia, 1137 Raissa, 2552 Remek, 13411 OLRAP, 954 Li, 12223 Hoskin

49q3 (238.854) \\engagement of the data on my computer in order to do the work; when I'm annoyed enough to start recording; 10389 Robmanning, 3244 Petronius, 5827 Letunov, 2908 Shimoyama, 18142 Adamsidman, 106 Dione, 5134 Ebilson, 32078 Jamesavoldelli, 278735 Kamioka, 841 Arabella, 1576 Fabiola, 15407 Udakiyoo, 4874 Burke, 181627 Philgeluck, 1538 Detre, 3963 Paradzhanov, 12408 Fujioka, 8112 Cesi

121q3 (58.854) \\the more intimate details I reveal about myself, the more likely problems are to arise in the exchange; 8871 Svanberg, 612 Veronika, 20334 Glewitsky, 2045 Peking, 128343 Brianpage, 5909 Nagoya, 33205 Graigmarx

qc139: challenged or saved from a challenge

25q3 (298.854) \\how I have quietly or tamely released collaborators; 76272 De Jong, 3282 Spencer Jones, 29565 Glenngould, 3129 Bonestell, 6143 Pythagoras, 189347 Qian, 34227 Daveyhuang, 20271 Allygoldberg, 6836 Paranal, 9471 Ostend, 45685 Torrycoppin, 10200 Quadri, 14145 Sciam, 29252 Konjikido, 18572 Rocher

97q3 (118.854) \\b.a.r. and dg's unhappy exits; 39564 Tarsia, 1355 Magoeba, 6212 Franzthaler, 15364 Kenglover, 18727 Peacock, 3586 Vasnetsov, 117032 Davidlane, 19768 Ellendoane, 240381 Emilchyne, 36177 Tonysharon, 4439 Muroto, 28407 Meghanarao, 11688 Amandugan, 12061 Alena

61q3 (208.854) \\behind the scenes, deciding not to favor sg; 19663 Rykerwatts, 30073 Erichen, 31969 Yihuachen, 20264 Chauhan, 8005 Albinadubois, 13748 Radaly, 2219 Mannucci, 30933 Grillparzer, 5891 Gehrig, 39463 Phyleus, 1869 Philoctetes, 19004 Chirayath, 17103 Kadyrsizova, 167960 Rudzikas, 5091 Isakovskij, 176711 Canmore,

5435 Kameoka, 142562 Graetz, 22903 Georgeclooney, 15566 Elizabethbaker, 120375 Kugel, 23074 Sarakirsch

133q3 (28.854) \\meeting es, scam artist, me accidentally getting j's stuff stolen. DON'T ALLY WITH STRANGERS WHEN FORAGING / ORDERING YOUR AFFAIRS!!; 9012 Benner, 2923 Schuyler, 4658 Gavrilov, 142408 Trebur, 100732 Blankavalois

qig112: your shell

qc426: that which is involved in really getting to know me

1q2 (358.646) \\eth:latin, tumultuous, san antonio | //library niche where your story is archived (in your head)?; 344581 Albisetti, 3965 Konopleva, 3393 Stur, 5141 Tachibana, 544 Jetta

73q2 (178.646) \\dogs going nuts over whatever. Especially when scared; dad's issues; 2084 Okayama, 39571 Puckler, 10900 Folkner, 7967 Beny, 145475 Rehoboth, 18983 Allentran, 12722 Petrarca, 5013 Suzhousanzhong, 503 Evelyn, 13793 Laubernasconi, 23437 Sima, 28534 Taylorwilson, 7230 Lutz, 118945 Rikhill, 10702 Arizorcas, 1289 Kutaissi, 85199 Habsburg, 33056 Ogunimachi, 19441 Trucpham, 9385 Avignon

37q2 (268.646) \\how people REALLY get to know me, what I'm doing; 10524 Maniewski, 48471 Orchiston, 149573 Mamorudoi, 23102 Dayanli, 1686 De Sitter, 15552 Sandashounkan, 806 Gyldenia, 16191 Rubyroe, 8171 Stauffenberg, 1563 Noel

109q2 (88.646) \\co-op, movement of the earth magic, twos, things I engage and bond over. Toejam and earl (lol! Movement of the earth); 27276 Davidblack, 3919 Maryanning, 32945 Lecce, 24524 Kevinhawkins, 3154 Grant, 20690 Crivello, 3076 Garber, 3655 Eupraksia, 10693 Zangari, 13609 Lewicki

qc282: my wish for a latina, but generating ai images instead [unclear general interpretation]

13q2 (328.646) \\my bearing regarding my astro data. Not the data or the work itself; 6363 Doggett, 20855 Arifawan, 33379 Rohandalvi, 198592 Antbernal, 306367 Nut, 1013 Tombecka, 9226 Arimahiroshi

85q2 (148.646) \\conversations with foreigners, staying on certain games or puzzles; 5526 Kenzo, 19763 Klimesh, 1343 Nicole, 4261 Gekko, 201019 Oliverwhite, 26679 Thomassilver, 1412 Lagrula, 14708 Slaven, 18564 Caseyo, 7229 Tonimoore, 3547 Serov

49q2 (238.646) \\my stiff regulation of conversation partner exchanges, highly international, yet they do seem to happen and do seem to be fruitful; 12782 Mauersberger, 12309 Tommygrav, 1782 Schneller, 15964 Billgray, 16083 Jorvik, 4995 Griffin, 170306 Augustzatka, 72596 Zilkha, 21275 Tosiyasu, 12645 Jacobrosales, 26412 Charlesyu, 25817 Tahilramani, 201372 Sheldon, 7010 Locke, 113950 Donbaldwin, 25652 Maddieball, 6891 Triconia, 25418 Deshmukh, 25570 Kesun, 7670 Kabelac, 48700 Hanggao, 10094 Eijikato, 23946 Marcelleroux, 517 Edith, 14182 Alley

121q2 (58.646) \\problems appearing in a relationship yield to even more problems… until final rift; mturk. The fact that there may need to be two attempts before I answer; 8860 Rohloff, 9996 ANS, 314082 Dryope, 5495 Rumyantsev, 18110 HASI, 318723 Bialas, 11124 Mikulasek, 25266 Taylorkinyon, 83956 Panuzzo, 4422 Jarre, 1096 Reunerta

qc138: san antonio liberal culture and those outside of it

25q2 (298.646) \\shanna, at least; 2939 Coconino, 17196 Mastrodemos, 11585 Orlandelassus, 5841 Stone, 13085 Borlaug, 5341 Purgathofer, 170011 Szkody, 4406 Mahler, 2345 Fucik, 1770 Schlesinger

97q2 (118.646) \\my pickiness over what kind of body I will create with; 2979 Murmansk, 28484 Aishwarya, 13154 Petermrva, 8797 Duffard, 3558 Shishkin, 14354 Kolesnikov, 6685 Boitsov, 3948 Bohr, 1280 Baillauda

61q2 (208.646) \\ajani in date mode with a girl - but I always bring my work to bear; 175726 Borda, 9589 Deridder, 43935 Danshechtman, 24713 Ekrutt, 4143 Huziak, 3835 Korolenko, 22185 Stiavnica, 27896 Tourminator, 22730 Jacobhurwitz, 18617 Puntel, 192749 Michelebianda, 4618 Shakhovskoj, 27348 Mink, 14967 Madrid, 6416 Nyukasayama, 7714 Briccialdi, 13914 Galegant, 25515 Briancarey, 958 Asplinda, 13207 Tamagawa, 68144 Mizser, 2195 Tengstrom, 17980 Vanschaik

133q2 (28.646) \\i can't both heal and run the healing practice; 301638 Kressin, 27327 Lindaplante, 133528 Ceragioli, 17563 Tsuneyoshi, 120074 Bass, 95982 Beish, 28503 Angelazhang, 5866 Sachsen, 6676 Monet, 17608 Terezin, 129307 Tomconnors, 2200 Pasadena

qig113: you help yourself navigate the culture with this…

qc425: common views of one's abstract worth

1q1 (358.438) \\editors and academics. I pretty much deny these people wholesale; 1634 Ndola, 360 Carlova, 1672 Gezelle

73q1 (178.438) \\scandal over simeona or accusations of impropriety; ramped up distrust and accusations that come with being black; 31376 Leobauersfeld, 24986 Yalefan, 2095 Parsifal, 25058 Shanegould, 2157 Ashbrook, 17045 Markert, 13168 Danoconnell, 6723 Chrisclark, 154938 Besserman, 22473 Stanleyhey, 5923 Liedeke, 4232 Aparicio, 52295 Koppen, 1799 Koussevitzky, 8245 Molnar, 20242 Sagot, 2896 Preiss, 180739 Barbet

37q1 (268.438) \\picking out the next female superstar; 31618 Tharakan, 1723 Klemola, 103422 Laurisiren, 23018 Annmoriarty, 7269 Alprokhorov, 515 Athalia, 1171 Rusthawelia, 21128 Chapuis, 179875 Budavari, 156542 Hogg, 5443 Encrenaz, 2651 Karen, 22454 Rosalylopes, 7178 Ikuookamoto

109q1 (88.438) \\how I aim to be thought of sexually, and by whom; 13015 Noradokei, 10602 Masakazu, 7917 Hammergren, 755 Quintilla, 5668 Foucault, 33282 Arjunramani, 5366 Rhianjones, 69159 Ivanking, 4286 Rubtsov, 372573 Pietromenga, 278986 Chenshuchu

qc281: wine and the scattering of spacetime

13q1 (328.438) \\the jumpers, ptt, my circle as a culture [keith, emily, me, authors of sata], I can't support them without running BLOCKING MODE, however. A tricky situation; 32579 Allendavia, 15929 Ericlinton, 25264 Erickeen, 30146 Decandia, 830 Petropolitana, 30022 Kathibaker, 23900 Urakawa, 34996 Mitokoumon, 378214 Sauron

85q1 (148.438) \\BLOCKING MODE: where I strongly block communication which I know is prevented its highest operation; I use this region ALL THE TIME; 26267 Nickmorgan, 6911 Nancygreen, 1932 Jansky, 9865 Akiraohta, 10221 Kubrick, 5656 Oldfield, 13777 Cielobuio, 2583 Fatyanov, 4558 Janesick, 28669 Bradhelsel, 6901 Roybishop, 8591 Excubitor, 4471 Graculus, 11715 Harperclark, 25925 Jamesfenska, 1497 Tampere, 21623 Albertshieh

49q1 (238.438) \\my ACTUAL 1:1 PERSONALITY, uncensored. Heard only by my recordings and myself. And also my music interests, known only to be shared by M. Ajas, DPG; 9239 van Riebeeck, 134034 Bloomenthal, 2221 Chilton, 7038 Tokorozawa, 4262 DeVorkin, 55555 DNA, 11669 Pascalscholl, 10828 Tomjones, 17108 Patricorbett, 16261 Iidemachi, 6564 Asher, 29347 Natta, 28449 Ericlau, 1164 Kobolda, 3481 Xianglupeak, 24778 Nemsu, 3829 Gunma, 102536 Luanenjie, 157494 Durham, 6765 Fibonacci, 638 Moira, 21785 Mechain, 2872 Gentelec

121q1 (58.438) \\the thin girl as one i can actually approach my truest self against. Emotionally distanced as a partnership, but more reflective of my regular 24-7 bearing—special occasions like sex, travel, and major celebrations excluded. And when this fails or is absent: blocking other inputs; 23166 Bilal, 17063 Papaloizou, 18238 Frankshu, 7778 Markrobinson, 32899 Knigge, 11467 Simonporter, 25348 Wisniowiecki, 1727 Mette, 5448 Siebold

qc137: left alone, will you get yourself taken advantage of?

25q1 (298.438) \\the last event with both b.a.r. and mb, as experienced by them?; 7846 Setvak, 3151 Talbot, 3095 Omarkhayyam, 7572 Znokai, 13992 Cesarebarbieri, 16826 Daisuke, 4468 Pogrebetskij

97q1 (118.438) \\what I said to challenge mb's notion of me even further; 10421 Dalmatin, 10688 Haghighipour, 28173 Hisakichi, 24120 Jeremyblum, 19818 Shotwell, 4832 Palinurus, 26605 Hanley, 3183 Franzkaiser, 5999 Plescia, 170022 Douglastucker

61q1 (208.438) \\me going door to door in real estate, or figuratively with ideas; 2774 Tenojoki, 6950 Simonek, 79375 Valetti, 12747 Michageffert, 5465 Chumakov, 11075 Donhoff, 6796 Sundsvall, 12311 Ingemyr, 22498 Willman, 166746 Marcpostman, 26685 Khojandi, 33335 Guibert, 30025 Benfreed, 1024 Hale, 8 Flora, 10030 Philkeenan, 31938 Nattapong

133q1 (28.438) \\my near-ceaseless desire for a fictitious "baddle buddy" to help me administer my house and business affairs—nice and mundane, my production of homegrown DIY fixes because of my low confidence in contractors or help in general—all the while wishing for a unicorn who will help me with all this | up-down point; oscillating vertical amplitude gaze direction towards you the viewer. Traits point noticeably up or down or are posed as such; 17121 Fernandonido, 95024 Ericaellingson

qig114: what is done anyway even though there are rules

qc424: an animal disappears from the zoo—how the rest of the animals handle this

1q12 (358.229) \\i organize the life zoo in service to others. Kind of; 10041 Parkinson, 655 Briseis, 32069 Mayarao

73q12 (178.229) \\what actually happens when I go through a fierce rift with someone; 9289 Balau, 170995 Ritajoewright, 25001 Pacheco, 55222 Makotoshinkai, 21554 Leechaohsi, 22354 Sposetti, 2536 Kozyrev, 871 Amneris, 3833 Calingasta, 22519 Gerardklein, 4552 Nabelek, 55 Pandora, 5502 Brashear, 32263 Kusnierkiewicz, 2767 Takenouchi

37q12 (268.229) \\how we handle death and wakes; 23234 Lilliantsai, 21075 Heussinger, 6482 Steiermark, 12040 Jacobi, 2305 King, 10403 Marcelgrun, 7495 Feynman, 9715 Paolotanga, 274246 Reggiacaserta, 13689 Succi, 16094 Scottmccord, 1783 Albitskij, 7174 Semois, 2102 Tantalus, 343057 Lucaravenni

109q12 (88.229) \\easy tutoring with james. After banter, tutoring mode with hnt; 1146 Biarmia, 25933 Ruoyijiang, 28715 Garimella, 2093 Genichesk, 83982 Crantor, 2357 Phereclos, 104210 Leeupton, 9528 Kuppers, 3105 Stumpff, 25966 Akhilmathew, 23938 Kurosaki, 6998 Tithonus

qc280: the billionaire

13q12 (328.229) \\my notion of the billionaire; bill gates; other people's temperaments stirred in light of this?; 4214 Veralynn, 136824 Nonamikeiko, 361183 Tandon, 154006 Suzannehawley, 22158 Chee, 5786 Talos, 17466 Vargasllosa, 231307 Peterfalk, 4495 Dassanowsky

85q12 (148.229) \\my apprentice who has healed after humiliation...; 7858 Bolotov, 27582 Jackieterrel, 33814 Viswesh, 14972 Olihainaut, 239675 Mottez, 1465 Autonoma, 1401 Lavonne, 13079 Toots, 19141 Poelkapelle, 157301 Loreena, 336203 Sandrobuss, 6527 Takashiito, 14382 Woszczyk, 7134 Ikeuchisatoru, 18806 Zachpenn, 4772 Frankdrake, 6860 Sims

49q12 (238.229) \\my mode when commissioned to work with the women who would be my collaborators; 30126 Haviland, 8927 Ryojiro, 101 Helena, 3093 Bergholz, 14217 Oaxaca, 19487 Rosscoleman, 11637 Yangjiachi, 8051 Pistoria, 27983 Bernardi, 100433 Hyakusyuko, 23091 Stansill, 23686 Songyuan, 5385 Kamenka, 33495 Schaferjames, 28163 Lorikim, 28453 Alexcecil, 8294 Takayuki, 5260 Philveron, 4349 Tiburcio

121q12 (58.229) \\the temperament of the women close to me, estrogen-moderated; 21392 Helibrochier, 9900 Llull, 3280 Gretry, 13915 Yalow, 15358 Kintner, 50717 Jimfox, 47144 Faulkes, 8831 Brandstrom, 453 Tea

qc136: me sabotaging the rest of the sg collaboration, and any broken one for that matter

25q12 (298.229) \\why I do better REDACTED in charge: Kolokolova-Kitami-Lancearmstrong; 13723 Kolokolova, 1876 Napolitania, 17208 Pokrovska, 5271 Kaylamaya, 7287 Yokokurayama, 16357 Risanpei, 12373 Lancearmstrong, 25457 Mariannamao, 3785 Kitami

97q12 (118.229) \\i in my private jurisdiction; 1455 Mitchella, 6499 Michiko, 6584 Ludekpesek, 8585 Purpurea, 4572 Brage, 34180 Jessicayoung, 9910 Vogelweide, 15971 Hestroffer, 741 Botolphia, 31976 Niyatidesai, 3468 Urgenta, 8122 Holbein, 353232 Nolwenn, 32002 Gorokhovsky, 10959 Appennino, 3287 Olmstead, 10060 Amymilne

61q12 (208.229) \\looks like I should never share my actual deliberation process with anyone. Discuss, yes. Affectionately solve an issue with another, no. this qunit effectively forbids collaborative, relational solutioning. a republic where we all cast our vote is one thing. a democracy where i or the other merge group solutions is another (fail); 203773 Magyarics, 5481 Kiuchi, 21009 Agilkia, 25111 Klokun, 8690 Swindle, 32580 Avbalasingam, 31174 Rozelot, 11518 Jung, 2866 Hardy, 26879 Haines, 11718 Hayward, 10067 Bertuch

133q12 (28.229) \\what happens when I fall into a trap; 928 Hildrun, 21639 Davidkaufman, 828 Lindemannia, 163626 Glatfelter

qig115: the reach towards alignment

qc423: the truth behind the legend

1q11 (358.021) \\a group goes after justice given my self-exposure—never literally, except for when I publish contours 3 years from now; 7188 Yoshii, 14312 Polytech, 32449 Crystalmiller, 2248 Kanda

73q11 (178.021) \\how I treated t.o., simeona, and vward. Maybe mb: good girls whom I simply cut; 7224 Vesnina, 305661 Joejackson, 5328 Nisiyamakoiti, 27303 Leitner, 17059 Elvis, 332084 Vasyakulbeda, 283142 Weena, 17278 Viggh, 61190 Johnschutt, 157693 Amandamarty, 250526 Steinerzsuzsanna, 12524 Conscience, 4962 Vecherka, 8664 Grigorijrichters, 14537 Tyn nad Vltavou, 214180 Mabaglioni, 9155 Verkhodanov, 878 Mildred, 4428 Khotinok, 14702 Benclark, 35093 Akicity, 5634 Victorborge, 19129 Loos

37q11 (268.021) \\we pursued the mona lisa just because, it had to be done. Probably a legend region for me; 17892 Morecambewise, 4825 Ventura, 9764 Morgenstern, 1431 Luanda, 292051 Bohlender, 235999 Bucciantini, 27244 Parthasarathy, 12800 Oobayashiarata, 24208 Stelguerrero, 7127 Stifter, 4028 Pancratz, 28321 Arnabdey, 6941 Dalgarno, 11578 Cimabue

109q11 (88.021) \\where I fully believe that I have the key to turning anyone's life around; a DEFINING and CRITICAL asteroid for me; 5197 Rottmann, 16647 Robbydesmet, 30168 Linusfreyer, 2092 Sumiana, 134044 Chrisshinohara, 17934 Deleon, 10218 Bierstadt, 420356 Praamzius, 21670 Kuan, 2928 Epstein

qc279: my dynamics with the big girl and the prosperity that comes with this

13q11 (328.021) \\me as an unusual character; 89739 Rampazzi, 20180 Annakoleny, 6615 Plutarchos, 145558 Raiatea, 3232 Brest, 27421 Nathanhan

85q11 (148.021) \\mb's personal life? Avoid unbalanced duos; 3476 Dongguan, 392120 Heidiursula, 256795 Suzyzahn, 23038 Jeffbaughman, 30199 Ericbrown, 7835 Myroncope, 290127 Linakostenko, 115059 Nagykaroly, 10266 Vladishukhov, 4620 Bickley, 16790 Yuuzou, 254 Augusta, 58424 Jamesdunlop, 10969 Perryman, 121328 Devlynrfennell, 23669 Huihuifan, 21648 Gravanschaik

49q11 (238.021) \\people's response to the book of contours, and my books in general, given that they've read them to read them (like an actual conversation) and not just to skim the alleged contents; 25901 Ericbrooks, 16447 Vauban, 4860 Gubbio, 11056 Volland, 128327 Ericcarranza, 107074 Ansonsylva, 38674 Tesinsko, 1850 Kohoutek, 55112 Mariangela, 228110 Eudorus, 12161 Avienius, 25491 Meador, -10003 Venus, 165192 Neugent, 34132 Theoguerin, 70409 Srnin, 2413 van de Hulst, 142106 Nengshun, 149160 Geojih, 9411 Hitomiyamoto, 10650 Houtman, 30216 Summerjohnson, 18910 Nolanreis, 16599 Shorland

121q11 (58.021) \\my good-luck side; 1527 Malmquista, 24130 Alexhuang, 11459 Andraspal, 5483 Cherkashin, 8062 Okhotsymskij, 28039 Mauraoei, 1254 Erfordia

qc135: an eye for uniqueness and one's unique will

25q11 (298.021) \\the wall which blocks potential regular partners from entering while the wall itself takes up all the engagement; 10372 Moran, 26234 Leslibrinson, 7698 Schweitzer, 3976 Lise, 232553 Randypeterson, 224831 Neeffisis, 1266 Tone, 3686 Antoku, 185640 Sunyisui, 2326 Tololo, 28836 Ashmore, 100308 CAS, 16516 Efremlevitan, 33377 Vecernicek

97q11 (118.021) \\my vulgar songs and jokes, recordings, cheerful activity. Things done without a partner; 5760 Mittlefehldt, 545 Messalina, 522 Helga, 4858 Vorobjov, 10700 Juanangelviera, 12769 Kandakurenai, 10931 Ceccano, 3354 McNair, 13850 Erman, 11712 Kemcook

61q11 (208.021) \\a significator for kvt in general; kvt's contribution to some of my most used styles and habits, though there isn't much value in engaging this duodecanate anymore. Not as it was. Maybe through a new template for my acting, this is clearly mb, partly b.a.r.. explains the role of hall—the asteroid of incest—in my chart. i co-create best with my own co-creations, so i never wanted kids—only authored books or generated AI and workflows as the best partners. students and people trained by me wouldn't work either. reading this, though, the D/s Daddy gravitation makes a lot more sense; 3746 Heyuan, 20195 Mariovinci, 942 Romilda, 18182 Wiener, 19025 Arthurpetron, 7701 Zrzavy, 96206 Eschenberg, 6955 Ekaterina, 4513 Louvre, 7330 Annelemaitre, 3203 Huth, 2148 Epeios, 21966 Hamadori, 32911 Cervara, 5041 Theotes, 12910 Deliso, 38046 Krasnoyarsk, 14155 Cibronen

133q11 (28.021) \\new ideas, new purging; 20836 Marilytedja, 466 Tisiphone, 9178 Momoyo, 854 Frostia, 19550 Samabates, 23773 Sarugaku

qig116: what the public will appreciate hearing (for better or worse, rotated about your sphere)

qc422: contract indebtter

1q10 (357.813) \\the contract or operating document as an instrument. I'm good at this, but SHOULD NOT write them except to indebt the signer; 3527 McCord, 33458 Fialkow, 1755 Lorbach, 144692 Katemary, 37729 Akiratakao

73q10 (177.813) \\signing sata contracts with people introduces a heavy debt; 26620 Yihuali, 5414 Sokolov, 190283 Schielicke, 12624 Mariacunitia, 5203 Pavarotti, 25912 Recawkwell, 5148 Giordano, 10395 Jirkahorn, 1454 Kalevala, 16695 Terryhandley, 100731 Ara Pacis, 15418 Sergiospinelli, 5206 Kodomonomori, 6147 Straub

37q10 (267.813) \\deciding to do something myself when the contract signer does not come through; 4721 Atahualpa, 5115 Frimout, 16090 Lukaszewski, 34090 Cewhang, 5239 Reiki, 18119 Braude, 642 Clara, 20081 Occhialini, 3700 Geowilliams, 389 Industria, 9344 Klopstock, 7895 Kaseda, 16250 Delbo, 5934 Mats, 30963 Mount Banzan, 128022 Peterantreasian, 752 Sulamitis, 48415 Dehio, 29776 Radzhabov, 118102 Rinjani, 8280 Petergruber, 30409 Piccirillo

109q10 (87.813) \\three meetings, like me, cory, and kvt, or me, b.a.r., and shr—on the rare adventure; 1944 Gunter, 542 Susanna, 12324 Van Rompaey, 17615 Takeomasaru, 4842 Atsushi, 435 Ella, 23041 Hunt

qc278: big investments and big help; REDACTED just in time

13q10 (327.813) \\when I'm frustrated, busy with something that won't work, ramming it through; 2733 Hamina, 51431 Jayardee, 11111 Repunit, 2943 Heinrich, 19477 Teresajentz, 9882 Stallman, 2615 Saito, 30191 Sivakumar, 427 Galene, 236305 Adamriess, 2416 Sharonov, 54827 Kurpfalz, 19456 Pimdouglas, 8188 Okegaya, 24268 Charconley

85q10 (147.813) \\cooper, me after a certain level of growth; 10129 Fole, 32766 Voskresenskoe, 15375 Laetitiafoglia, 33498 Juliesmith, 24754 Zellyfry, 14098 Simek,

---

10012 Tmutarakania, 25676 Jesseellison, 4099 Wiggins, 802 Epyaxa, 391988 Illmarton, 34235 Ellafeiner, 2230 Yunnan, 18872 Tammann

49q10 (237.813) \\trope: the calm but possibly villainous commander; 1551 Argelander, 6310 Jankonke, 19425 Nicholasrapp, 2519 Annagerman, 5 Astraea, 10101 Fourier, 8190 Bouguer, 22469 Poloniny, 1768 Appenzella, 66391 Moshup, 11968 Demariotte, 11248 Bleriot, 12407 Riccardi, 39300 Auyeungsungfan, 9887 Ashikaga, 39427 Charlottebronte, 28700 Balachandar, 862 Franzia, 4771 Hayashi

121q10 (57.813) \\my notion of the populace: the fans in their dwellings; 1361 Leuschneria, 1079 Mimosa, 34753 Zdenekmatyas, 18891 Kamler

qc134: tragic rockstars and the private as well as public burdens they carry

25q10 (297.813) \\ongoing dissatisfaction with the one I'm with; 10676 Jamesmcdanell, 80008 Danielarhodes, 3319 Kibi, 19022 Penzel, 1461 Jean-Jacques, 2745 San Martin, 28716 Calebgonser, 9244 Visnjan, 192158 Christian, 3329 Golay, 3300 McGlasson, 100675 Chuyanakahara, 1655 Comas Sola

97q10 (117.813) \\eager to spread my dark alchemist findings; 4175 Billbaum, 278197 Touvron, 25125 Brodallan, 61342 Lovejoy, 33596 Taesoolee, 18368 Flandrau, 21746 Carrieshaw, 7504 Kawakita, 199947 Qaidam, 34399 Hachiojihigashi, 23324 Kwak, 26214 Kalinga, 32393 Galinato, 22155 Marchetti, 9757 Felixdejager

61q10 (207.813) \\what is invariably said about me behind my back when things are going wrong. Confused actions and suggestions of sacrifices—ubasti and jaywilson—enable me to read this in another; 6035 Citlaltepetl, 1220 Crocus, 5052 Nancyruth, 9140 Deni, 25858 Donherbert, 246861 Johnelwell, 3966 Cherednichenko, 19617 Duhamel, 475802 Zurek, 129172 Jodizareski, 3260 Vizbor, 27208 Jennyliu, 391257 Wilwheaton, 21726 Rezvanian, 1294 Antwerpia, 4257 Ubasti, 30109 Jaywilson

133q10 (27.813) \\what I do to get myself talked about behind my back; 6231 Hundertwasser, 3876 Quaide, 4294 Horatius, 3707 Schroter, 29982 Sarahwu

qig117: you behind the fence, depending on another

qc421: trapped, unable to acquire as I wish

1q9 (357.604) \\learning how to handle prisoners, being a prisoner, or imprisonment in general; 9954 Brachiosaurus, 15841 Yamaguchi, 85179 Meistereckhart, 12050 Humecronyn, 216241 Renzopiano, 33523 Warashina

73q9 (177.604) \\what being in a prison or trapped obligation looks like; 1320 Impala, 12175 Wimhermans, 4865 Sor, 4391 Balodis, 7195 Danboice, 128408 Mikehughes, 72021 Yisunji, 27184 Ciabattari, 9158 Plate, 3569 Kumon, 2572 Annschnell, 22913 Brockman, 13982 Thunberg, 25276 Dimai, 169 Zelia, 32735 Strekalov, 14888 Kanazawashi, 121608 Mikemoreau, 26355 Grueber

37q9 (267.604) \\direct decision regarding what aspects of a situation are real; 8422 Mohorovicic, 560 Delila, 11580 Bautzen, 1817 Katanga, 27522 Lenkenyon, 23854 Rickschaffer, 5146 Moiwa, 23663 Kalou, 29198 Weathers, 202740 Vicsympho, 23855 Brandonshih, 12630 Verstappen, 1874 Kacivelia

109q9 (87.604) \\me going out and finally buying what I'd like to buy; 30708 Echepolos, 8720 Takamizawa, 23735 Cohen, 4714 Toyohiro, 162 Laurentia

qc277: where I put my concentration, including knime workflows

13q9 (327.604) \\my sharp attention to workflows, continuous skill improvement—gets me recruited; 32311 Josephineyu, 242648 Fribourg, 21717 Pang, 1579 Herrick, 157533 Stellamarie, 11193 Merida, 27320 Vellinga, 8339 Kosovichia, 9831 Simongreen, 20822 Lintingnien, 336177 Churri, 20830 Luyajia, 8870 von Zeipel, 25542 Garabedian

85q9 (147.604) \\me in front of most inherited classes, since no one else is available; my workflows and ai generates; 16036 Moroz, 121329 Getzandanner, 17637 Blaschke, 34778 Huhunglick, 17853 Ronaldsayer, 14164 Hennigar, 17898 Scottsheppard, 25670 Densley, 80808 Billmason, 6201 Ichiroshimizu, 375176 Beziau, 2504 Gaviola, 19 Fortuna, 121506 Chrislorentson, 9891 Stephensmith, 2748 Patrick Gene

49q9 (237.604) \\keith's undertakings and my communication with him; 719 Albert, 13149 Heisenberg, 249520 Luppino, 2059 Baboquivari, 15434 Mittal, 7873 Boll, 10541 Malesherbes, 6305 Helgoland, 5289 Niemela, 9159 McDonnell, 6819 McGarvey, 46596 Tobata, 4549 Burkhardt, 33761 Honoranavid

121q9 (57.604) \\my impatient review of what went wrong; 434453 Ayerdhal, 526 Jena, 26998 Iriso, 1588 Descamisada, 30416 Schacht, 85217 Bilzingsleben, 32089 Wojtania, 27150 Annasante

qc133: academic co-conspirators and rap battlers who co-conspire through what they publicly communicate

25q9 (297.604) \\my presence over the house—how others react to my freedom or privilege (negative to share)| zig-zag line; a more visible sawtooth that runs the course of the body, seems to be a reflector of joints, likely a critical human species location; 3826 Handel, 1073 Gellivara, 3846 Hazel, 3090 Tjossem, 6157 Prey, 19637

Presbrey, 31944 Seyitherdem, 8757 Cyaneus, 7899 Joya, 25778 Csere, 24232 Lanthrum

97q9 (117.604) \\traits of my best tutees—supriya, james, isaac, ah; 6530 Adry, 5114 Yezo, 277883 Basu, 95793 Brock, 1173 Anchises, 33747 Clingan, 59232 Sfiligoi, 10370 Hylonome, 23777 Goursat, 2108 Otto Schmidt

61q9 (207.604) \\james, other former students; 2579 Spartacus, 1836 Komarov, 275106 Sarahdubeyjames, 42585 Pheidippides, 4902 Thessandrus, 414026 Bochonko, 27525 Vartovka, 726 Joella, 25432 Josepherli, 129161 Mykallefevre, 457 Alleghenia, 6972 Helvetius, 148 Gallia, 126444 Wylie, 9602 Oya, 2032 Ethel, 171396 Miguel, 11189 Rabeaton, 13479 Vet, 3727 Maxhell, 1749 Telamon, 13475 Orestes, 14814 Gurij, 8060 Anius, 25696 Kylejones, 9511 Klingsor

133q9 (27.604) \\the inclination for all of my books to be re-citeable reference books instead of one-time experiences; 64975 Gianrix, 656 Beagle, 3806 Tremaine, 7852 Itsukushima, 27353 Chrisspenner

qig118: inner tension seen outside of one

qc420: whether or not I share during showtime will make all the difference in whether there will be problems with another

2q8 (357.396) \\me in SHOWTIME! Mode in a group setting | twin cylinders; noticeably departed legs from anchor point a defining scissoring of arms and legs; 87954 Tomkaye, 31925 Krutovskiy, 977 Philippa, 34107 Kashfiarahman, 6403 Steverin, 8074 Slade, 9435 Odafukashi, 10925 Ventoux, 28558 Kathcordwell, 2344 Xizang

74q8 (177.396) \\overlooking sim cities; 11792 Sidorovsky, 4150 Starr, 39734 Marchiori, 31323 Lysa hora, 2719 Suzhou, 11787 Baumanka, 33213 Diggs, 2475 Semenov, 40457 Williamkuhn, 7881 Schieferdecker, 63162 Davidcapek, 13860 Neely, 2860 Pasacentennium, 28705 Michaelbecker, 4059 Balder

38q8 (267.396) \\sides of myself and activities I can't, won't, or shouldn't share with anyone; 13248 Fornasier, 155290 Anniegrauer, 2965 Surikov, 14588 Pharrams, 11365 NASA, 34014 Pingali, 117384 Halharrison, 17251 Vondracek, 28666 Trudygessler, 17803 Barish, 144716 Scotttucker, 37582 Faraday, 8847 Huch, 189944 Leblanc

110q8 (87.396) \\my former business partners or scammers engaging the law or skirting it around me; many people I deal with secretly evaluating others as better. To avoid this, don't let anyone have you execute 14588 pharrams for the purpose of them somehow rewarding you with something. this is the "it should be easy" grand cross; 10386 Romulus, 32720 Simoeisios, 16000 Neilgehrels, 55384 Muiyimfong, 283990 Randallrosenfeld, 2449 Kenos, 48529 von Wrangel

qc276: putting on a show for someone else's image standard

14q8 (327.396) \\deployed to a nice hotel | the setting of many british murder mysteries; bali; 27718 Gouda, 3168 Lomnicky Stit, 20484 Janetsong, 811 Nauheima, 13206 Baer, 4914 Pardina, 5767 Moldun, 11195 Woomera, 218987 Heidenhain, 236463 Bretecher, 17951 Fenska, 2846 Ylppo, 104896 Schwanden

86q8 (147.396) \\REDACTED's disclosure; 20888 Siyueguo, 21647 Carlturner, 4992 Kalman, 247 Eukrate, 1255 Schilowa, 24308 Cowenco, 393 Lampetia, 4117 Wilke, 25234 Odell, 1008 La Paz, 6574 Gvishiani, 4751 Alicemanning, 4948 Hideonishimura, 1243 Pamela, 2128 Wetherill, 9215 Taiyonoto, 4334 Foo, 30154 Christichil

50q8 (237.396) \\the person who makes diminishing comments to me; 33594 Ralphlawton, 19631 Greensleeves, 17446 Mopaku, 85119 Hannieschaft, 31312 Fangerhai, 7248 Alvsjo, 6019 Telford, 16583 Oersted, 121032 Wadesisler, 11305 Ahlqvist, 121232 Zerin, 21270 Otokar, 21364 Lingpan, 168531 Joshuakammer

122q8 (57.396) \\part of the disappointment I felt during the REDACTED event; 85773 Gutbezahl, 6621 Timchuk, 33248 Nataliehowell, 170073 Ivanlinscott, 212606 Janulis, 32616 Nadinehan

qc132: the woman under fire and the things which abuse her, the woman in her safe space and the things which build her up

26q8 (297.396) \\working as a contractor, REDACTED; 3745 Petaev, 178226 Rebeccalouise, 6542 Jacquescousteau, 118178 Rinckart, 9126 Samcoulson, 30767 Chriskraft, 363623 Chelcicky, 33617 Kailashraman, 1926 Demiddelaer

98q8 (117.396) \\a level of objectivity coupled with a strong refusal to be moved by what I am scrutinizing; 3100 Zimmerman, 21454 Chernoby, 2968 Iliya, 28443 Crisara, 18189 Medeobaldia, 23096 Mihika, 57868 Pupin, 51828 Ilanramon

62q8 (207.396) \\THE significator for mb; evolution of my particular brand of scholarship; 24105 Broughton, 73782 Yanagida, 10671 Mazurova, 68730 Straizys, 188061 Loomis, 135561 Tautvaisiene, 23648 Kolar, 11245 Hansderijk, 7629 Foros, 6023 Tsuyashima, 423 Diotima, 124075 Ketelsen, 3199 Nefertiti, 24607 Sevnatu, 789 Lena, 21472 Stimson, 12051 Picha, 21474 Pamelatsai, 54411 Bobestelle

134q8 (27.396) \\my data request deliverables, things like asteroid translations and general work productivity done in bursts; 3006 Livadia, 9641 Demaziere, 5070 Arai,

10681 Khture, 464 Megaira, 9751 Kadota, 22865 Amymoffett, 25653 Baskaran, 32308 Sreyavemuri, 12355 Coelho

qig119: co-creative cast of characters and energies

qc419: the easy power worshippers as co-creators… sort of

2q7 (357.188) \\how I conduct myself during sex; 4266 Waltari, 3994 Ayashi, 17496 Augustinus, 11944 Shaftesbury, 21703 Shravanimikk

74q7 (177.188) \\how I saw the slave search—place to find the one who does my bidding; 3860 Plovdiv, 1844 Susilva, 6879 Hyogo, 23244 Lafayette, 10870 Gwendolen, 1312 Vassar, 5700 Homerus, 13937 Roberthargraves, 3495 Colchagua, 7096 Napier, 1534 Nasi, 117614 Hannahmclain, 20256 Adolfneckar, 4095 Ishizuchisan, 14028 Nakamurahiroshi, 6069 Cevolani, 129980 Catherinejohnson, 2503 Liaoning

38q7 (267.188) \\where I am sexually interested; 28209 Chatterjee, 145445 Le Floch, 9972 Minoruoda, 13962 Delambre, 2226 Cunitza, 2327 Gershberg, 34261 Musharahman, 31846 Elainegillum, 718 Erida, 23644 Yamaneko, 39549 Casals

110q7 (87.188) \\AVOID THE EXISTENCE OF A TERTIARY REDACTED, BUSINESS ALLIANCE, BLIND FRIENDSHIP, SCRUTINIZING EITHER PARTY'S ETHICS, AND REDACTED WHO DISTRUST REDACTED IN GENERAL. AND ANYONE TO WHOM YOU FEEL INCLINED TO SEND A GET-TO-THE-HEART-OF-IT MESSAGE. hehe. 99, b.a.r., sg, vb. This is THE REDACTED + REDACTED combination, but also any REDACTED but REDACTED-worshipping setup; 61195 Martinoli, 100553 Dariofo, 65775 Reikotosa, 10725 Sukunabikona, 30835 Waterloo, 25321 Rohitsingh, 1099 Figneria, 22900 Trudie, 48373 Gorgythion, 2715 Mielikki

qc275: co-creating (works better with a male or traumatized person)

14q7 (327.188) \\my experience with REDACTED, including the REDACTED in REDACTED and our subsequent disconnect; REDACTED's big and slick vagina; a fascinating qunit to observe as I've gotten older. Basically, I've developed a gross distaste for this kind of partner, sexually, professionally or otherwise. if all they are is a basket of imposed folkloric or social …, and if i were fool enough to still engage them, i can expect myself to … again. it's not performance anxiety, just hypersensitivity in places where ease and comfort are not easy to achieve. hence REDACTED and REDACTED. starting with REDACTED, and then shanna, i only partnered with women i actually loved. but where there is an expectation of orgasm at some point, if i do release, it is almost always onto the body, as i don't like oral from women i don't COMPLETELY trust, where none of my partners meet this. and although i wouldn't say that my exercises were a form of compensation for the experience i had with REDACTED (there was nothing to compensate for), i would say that my growing too wide to fit inside the partner does ensure that—if i ever did encounter another one-way … as "co-creator," her lack of interest in actual CO-creation will simply leave her splashed on, in pain, or both. Consensual, as always, of course. for actual partners who are into a real connection, we have plenty of gentler methods. honestly, i have no interest in sex with such a sorry complement again. … was what they got, as … was all they deserved. I used to be … about that, but all it was was …—not in sex, but in picking based on actual love; 593 Titania, 7319 Katterfeld, 90449 Brucestephenson, 1390 Abastumani, 304368 Moricz, 16674 Birkeland, 8128 Nicomachus, 9306 Pittosporum, 6806 Kaufmann

86q7 (147.188) \\my … fate with REDACTED; for me as a …, REDACTED's large and extra slick vagina; programming macros; see the note on 14-7. if 18953 Laurensmith is required from me in order to be your partner, you are very likely to leave disrespected and humiliated. that's not solely limited to the sexual, but goes for my bratty project collaborators as well. in the case of REDACTED, i broke up with her so as not to do this. once split, i assumed no expectations from her whatsoever, and avoided some of the less savory tactics of emotional warfare. … is much better; 5069 Tokeidai, 28094 Michellewis, 1837 Osita, 23831 Mattmooney, 173649 Jeffreymoore, 194 Prokne, 23323 Anand, 21707 Johnmoore, 18953 Laurensmith, 110297 Yellowriver, 3657 Ermolova

50q7 (237.188) \\yali. My experience of orgasm or general co-creative firing. It seems that my willingness to give something up to another indicates my ability to release with them. As of 5/8/2024 I'm not giving up much to anyone—except a free book to Priya; 11173 Jayanderson, 15957 Gemoore, 10247 Amphiaraos, 21680 Richardschwartz, 16211 Samirsur, 26640 Bahyl, 15371 Steward, 5418 Joyce, 19005 Teckman, 49187 Zucchini, 9702 Tomvandijk, 7382 Bozhenkova, 4207 Chernova, 20590 Bongiovanni

122q7 (57.188) \\in males, the (usually figurative) ejaculation process; 31283 Wanruomeng, 7443 Tsumura, 2622 Bolzano, 5157 Hindemith, 4527 Schoenberg, 19528 Delloro, 17806 Adolfborn, 3660 Lazarev, 3016 Meuse, 61913 Lanning, 129277 Jianxinchen, 5286 Haruomukai

qc131: society the constrainers, who it constrains, and those who offer a way out of this

26q7 (297.188) \\me and sb recovering after an argument or separate tension; 5793 Ringuelet, 14621 Tati, 36472 Ebina, 16887 Blouke, 159999 Michaelgriffin, 24152 Ramasesh, 26954 Skadiang, 6484 Barthibbs, 21488 Danyellelee, 31475 Robbacchus, 27974 Drejsl, 1827 Atkinson, 3015 Candy, 2392 Jonathan Murray, 171 Ophelia, 95882 Longshaw

98q7 (117.188) \\my foraging for the family food; 20782 Markcroce, 385 Ilmatar, 23752 Jacobshapiro, 31465 Piyasiri, 1595 Tanga, 35268 Panoramix, 4085 Weir, 3760 Poutanen

62q7 (207.188) \\the ambitious woman seeking my help, though I am bound to be trouble; sg, shanna, vb; 11064 Dogen, 239 Adrastea, 26665 Sidjena, 10195 Nebraska, 29745 Mareknovak, 3046 Moliere, 12363 Marinmarais, 12896 Geoffroy, 6020 Miyamoto, 20270 Phildeutsch, 28341 Bingaman, 23995 Oechsle, 32622 Yuewaichun, 25686 Stephoskins, 320260 Bertout, 25421 Gafaran, 230691 Van Vogt, 7214 Anticlus, 6357 Glushko, 35237 Matzner

134q7 (27.188) \\the record, reputation I end up having after I have burned the person who once relied on me to build their dynasty; 7966 Richardbaum, 24063 Nanwoodward, 11409 Horkheimer, 2385 Mustel

qig120: the route to power encouraged in you

qc418: those who steal and the consequences of such

2q6 (356.979) \\high energy combat weapon—helping others learn how to fight. This is the key to triggering an admirer. Ref angelina; 5519 Lellouch, 6131 Towen, 21503 Beksha, 48624 Sadayuki, 1466 Mundleria, 15624 Lamberton, 17033 Rusty

38q6 (266.979) \\my attention to crystal and, thanks to the 110q6s, likely explains my attraction to her and adc, maybe REDACTED—an attraction to criminal types | ovoid repulsion; 5468 Hamatonbetsu, 1674 Groeneveld, 3789 Zhongguo, 71482 Jennamarie, 2337 Boubin, 1600 Vyssotsky, 10301 Kataoka, 8169 Mirabeau, 325369 Shishilov, 18123 Pavan, 259905 Vougeot, 214136 Alinghi, 641 Agnes

74q6 (176.979) \\working in nature, sometimes running, but always searching; also, dh, dg, REDACTED, shanna, REDACTED, angelina, simeona, leah & jess, edna & allison, sherry; 143641 Sapello, 141 Lumen, 326290 Akhenaten, 25624 Kronecker, 1011 Laodamia, 77870 MOTESS, 2295 Matusovskij, 20557 Davidkulka, 11260 Camargo, 6400 Georgealexander, 1283 Komsomolia, 18453 Nishiyamayukio

110q6 (86.979) \\the fate of those who have lied or scammed—especially to me; there are asteroids in 110q6 conducive to both two-timing and opportunistic gain; 658 Asteria, 9238 Yavapai, 6449 Kudara, 22862 Janinedavis, 8236 Gainsborough, 22414 Hornschemeier, 117156 Altschwendt

qc274: cult drive

14q6 (326.979) \\adventurous locations. Make the house into this?; 18830 Pothier, 8438 Marila, 4402 Tsunemori, 2103 Laverna, 23218 Puttachi, 383417 DAO, 11316 Fuchitatsuo, 11621 Duccio, 172315 Changqiaoxiaoxue, 9919 Undset, 32810 Steinbach, 13583 Bosret

86q6 (146.979) \\financial domination; 142760 Csabai, 2690 Ristiina, 22877 Reginamiller, 3644 Kojitaku, 12787 Abetadashi, 25378 Erinlambert, 664 Judith, 3036 Krat

50q6 (236.979) \\jogging the neighborhood, secure in body and position; 7544 Tipografiyanauka, 31559 Alonmillet, 33468 Nelsoneric, 10255 Taunus, 23109 Masayanagisawa, 60609 Kerryprice

122q6 (56.979) \\stimulating experiences collection, girly girl depictions and encounters; 24153 Davidalex, 13156 Mannoucyo, 4256 Kagamigawa, 17938 Tamsendrew, 20214 Lorikenny, 19721 Wray, 32630 Ethanlevy

qc130: the lifestyle I actually choose

26q6 (296.979) \\vb, dg, b.a.r. and the loss of faith at the moment of public appearance; 6770 Fugate, 8974 Gregaria, 74439 Brenden, 318694 Keszthelyi, 34351 Decatur, 9777 Enterprise, 10019 Wesleyfraser, 9698 Idzerda, 778 Theobalda

98q6 (116.979) \\my lifestyle after much of the battling is over. Could be more utopian, but oh well; 5421 Ulanova, 2919 Dali, 333717 Alexgreaves, 40436 Sylviecoyaud, 7039 Yamagata, 6975 Hiroaki, 29457 Marcopolo, 17281 Mattblythe, 34183 Yeshdoctor, 170162 Nicolashayek, 11812 Dongqiao, 64296 Hokoon

62q6 (206.979) \\head-shaking notions of my partnerships. That which drives my pursuit of the lifestyle; 9480 Inti, 7345 Happer, 30174 Hollyjackson, 26667 Sherwinwu, 9713 Oceax, 13125 Tobolsk, 251001 Sluch, 14447 Hosakakanai, 16167 Oertli, 2088 Sahlia, 8208 Volta, 135799 Raczmiklos, 121715 Katiesalamy, 7799 Martinsolc, 20497 Marenka, 22846 Fredwhitaker, 1318 Nerina

134q6 (26.979) \\telling my story enthusiastically, but cautious in doing so; 11012 Henning, 160013 Elbrus, 7253 Nara, 7006 Folco, 18818 Yasuhiko, 34081 Chowkitmun

qig121: in the presence of a dominator

qc417: when it is clear my efforts have ended in a loss, what happens

2q5 (356.771) \\my feelings about travel, leaving the homeland in general; 1369 Ostanina, 6401 Roentgen, 5831 Dizzy, 4812 Hakuhou, 17611 Jozkakubik, 4237 Raushenbakh, 128895 Bright Spring, 8536 Mans, 14277 Parsa, 44597 Thoreau

74q5 (176.771) \\the beginning message of s.o.s.; 3651 Friedman, 98494 Marsupilami, 8814 Rosseven, 8827 Kollwitz, 31729 Scharmen, 315088 Daniels, 2389 Dibaj, 7738 Heyman, 22421 Jamesedgar, 79641 Daniloceirani, 25472 Joanoro, 11664 Kashiwagi, 16068 Citron, 788 Hohensteina, 41199 Wakanaootaki, 7489 Oribe, 19612 Noordung, 23327 Luchernandez, 6221 Ducentesima, 938 Chlosinde, 4636 Chile, 1608 Munoz, 14335 Alexosipov

38q5 (266.771) \\when I feel there is nothing left, getting back to work; 252 Clementina, 27758 Michelson, 4998 Kabashima, 23212 Arkajitdey, 1907 Rudneva, 121016 Christopharnold, 6337 Shiota, 15583 Hanick, 3766 Junepatterson, 29992 Yasminezubi, 23858 Ambrosesoehn, 30307 Marcelriesz, 28168 Evanolin, 10483 Tomburns, 7280 Bergengruen, 6637 Inoue, 31480 Jonahbutler, 10034 Birlan, 651 Antikleia, 7684 Marioferrero

110q5 (86.771) \\me homeless at caltech and in europe, and iadt fashion; 149968 Trondal, 7718 Desnoux, 7048 Chaussidon, 99861 Tscharnuter, 33382 Indranidas, 2138 Swissair

qc273: me in a disagreement

14q5 (326.771) \\how I would build up the Master role. Right now I keep this side quiet, may produce people I can't tame the more I grow 86q5; internal self-gamification; 6554 Takatsuguyoshida, 2086 Newell, 1919 Clemence, 33905 Leyajoykutty, 4702 Berounka, 7217 Dacke, 123818 Helenzier, 84943 Timothylinn, 21074 Rugen, 34179 Bryanchun, 8077 Hoyle, 37692 Loribragg

86q5 (146.771) \\Doms. I am growing into this; generally though, can indicate an abusive counterpart; 25189 Glockner, 796 Sarita, 21117 Tashimaseizo, 2670 Chuvashia, 26259 Marzigliano, 9383 Montelimar, 7046 Reshetnev, 18801 Noelleoas, 11716 Amahartman, 13044 Wannes, 2214 Carol, 7318 Dyukov, 300909 Kenthompson

50q5 (236.771) \\my peaceful introversion doing the things I like; in disagreements—especially against mobs—misunderstood; 34141 Antonwu, 1603 Neva, 32428 Peterlangley, 7887 Bratfest, 16163 Suhanli, 27588 Wegley, 33337 Amberyang, 2837 Griboedov, 2302 Florya, 9003 Ralphmilliken, 19801 Karenlemmon, 30037 Rahulmehta, 460 Scania, 35461 Mazzucato, 11361 Orbinskij, 278 Paulina, 110074 Lamchunhei, 6043 Aurochs, 345 Tercidina, 48638 Trebic, 28167 Andrewkim

122q5 (56.771) \\bodyguard role; 3523 Arina, 73511 Lovas, 22451 Tymothycoons, 6130 Hutton, 11457 Hitomikobayashi, 9494 Donici, 16947 Wikrent

qc129: my intellectual journey

26q5 (296.771) \\how I clamor to give input in a conversation being held by much more knowledgeable people; 215016 Catherinegriffin, 27106 Jongoldman, 18088 Roberteunice, 574 Reginhild, 18099 Flamini, 234750 Amymainzer, 7237 Vickyhamilton, 4755 Nicky, 49700 Mather, 15949 Rhaeticus

98q5 (116.771) \\manager mode—either my own managers or me managing the house resource pool with sb as the 26; 9733 Valtikhonov, 893 Leopoldina, 9845 Okamuraosamu, 70715 Allancheuvront, 33157 Pertile, 21448 Galindo, 185250 Korostyshiv, 132718 Kemeny, 1541 Estonia, 15513 Emmermann, 11572 Schindler, 34297 Willfrazer, 22587 McKennon, 680 Genoveva, 3949 Mach, 32208 Johnpercy, 3931 Batten

62q5 (206.771) \\my activities in spaces where there are no superiors or inferiors / subordinates, in semi-solitude in nature; 33219 De Los Santos, 21547 Kottapalli, 4613 Mamoru, 3617 Eicher, 3276 Porta Coeli, 12272 Geddylee, 9315 Weigel, 30085 Kevingarbe, 48300 Kronk, 16497 Toinevermeylen, 129973 Michaeldaly

134q5 (26.771) \\sk, me later at caltech; 33539 Elenaberman, 26513 Newberry, 42485 Stendhal, 18779 Hattyhong, 198700 Nataliegrunewald

qig122: others who carry your will forward for you

qc416: attempts to break into an information space which is far more power-complex than I suspected

2q4 (356.563) \\my notorious sudden shows of affection. There must be an asteroid in here related to being remembered; 11142 Facchini, 275264 Krisztike, 859 Bouzareah, 4676 Uedaseiji, 17617 Takimotoikuo, 249514 Donaldroyer, 7163 Barenboim, 21361 Carsonmark, 14836 Maxfrisch, 8137 Kviz, 9922 Catcheller, 24546 Damell

74q4 (176.563) \\me as I approach and ultimately conquer the aspirational mountain; what conquest looks like for me; 4147 Lennon, 32611 Ananyaganesh, 5060 Yoneta, 9063 Washi, 13254 Kekule, 468 Lina, 166 Rhodope, 21496 Lijianyang, 322390 Planes de Son, 120481 Johnwalter, 3732 Vavra, 16982 Tsinghua, 11760 Auwers, 4265 Kani, 209540 Siurana, 121718 Ashleyscroggins, 2509 Chukotka

38q4 (266.563) \\me on youtube videos; 18086 Emilykraft, 4780 Polina, 16154 Dabramo, 50768 Ianwessen, 8579 Hieizan, 887 Alinda, 16358 Plesetsk, 4891 Blaga, 12365 Yoshitoki, 27253 Graceleanor, 21507 Bhasin, 3470 Yaronika, 5397 Vojislava, 32031 Joyjin, 1324 Knysna, 30267 Raghuvanshi, 4134 Schutz, 3588 Kirik, 14995 Archytas

110q4 (86.563) \\my basic interaction with 99; 454 Mathesis, 59793 Clapies, 134329 Cycnos, 41795 Wiens, 2799 Justus, 21351 Bhagwat, 8255 Masiero, 3480 Abante, 5010 Amenemhet

qc272: my closest support systems

14q4 (326.563) \\reminds me of both myself and angela ilo (in light of) pain; 5039 Rosenkavalier, 29471 Spejbl, 31234 Bea, 164586 Arlette, 23931 Ibuki, 3974 Verveer

86q4 (146.563) \\me working at the center of tutorship in c2c; 128372 Danielwibben, 27982 Atsushimiyazaki, 4862 Loke, 3471 Amelin, 21470 Frankchuang, 7580 Schwabhausen, 311785 Erwanmazarico, 248993 Jonava, 25183 Grantfisher, 17831 Ussery, 489603 Kurtschreckling, 120214 Danteberdeguez, 33737 Helenlyons, 657 Gunlod, 1194 Aletta, 3353 Jarvis, 3313 Mendel

50q4 (236.563) \\one on one with a topic I really like, impromptu rave, tutoring; also, a solo runner of sata; 20341 Alanstack, 25160 Joellama, 280642 Doubs, 14600 Gainsbourg, 31487 Parthchopra, 2196 Ellicott, 7777 Consadole, 851 Zeissia, 244 Sita, 9297 Marchuk, 5464 Weller, 25522 Roisen, 12079 Kaibab, 211374 Anthonyrose, 7794 Sanvito, 12312 Vate, 19633 Rusjan, 14463 McCarter, 13561 Kudogou, 14074 Riccati, 1816 Liberia, 10246 Frankenwald, 11356 Chuckjones

122q4 (56.563) \\how I use the girly girl and ai pictures; numbers, nuances, and stats; the pre-sleep fantasy visitor; 504 Cora, 12581 Rovinj, 23308 Niyomsatian, 40447 Lorenzoni, 4963 Kanroku, 319 Leona, 13673 Urysohn

qc128: my dream creation and how I feel when I think I can't realize it

26q4 (296.563) \\my books and the elf-disclosure therein; MY DREAM CONSTRUCTION!; 144333 Marcinkiewicz, 25103 Kimdongyoung, 17403 Masciarelli, 28533 Iansohl, 14486 Tuscia, 11002 Richardlis, 12087 Tiffanylin, 18956 Jessicarnold, 25490 Kevinkelly, 5446 Heyler, 88795 Morvan, 12138 Olinwilson, 3517 Tatianicheva, 22531 Davidkelley, 4039 Souseki, 11907 Naranen, 5006 Teller, 88611 Teharonhiawako

98q4 (116.563) \\me becoming a self-appointed authority in astro; 9299 Vinceteri, 162035 Jirotakahashi, 22253 Sivers, 10835 Frobel, 15963 Koeberl, 20641 Yenuanchen, 11800 Carrozzo, 39420 Elizabethgaskell, 11771 Maestlin, 17077 Pampaloni, 57567 Crikey, 21887 Dipippo, 69263 Big Ben, 7815 Dolon, 11828 Vargha

62q4 (206.563) \\me on knime in ee; 89903 Post, 95980 Haroldhill, 15905 Berthier, 3787 Aivazovskij, 15008 Delahodde, 7790 Miselli, 263906 Yuanfengfang, 164589 La Sagra, 20038 Arasaki, 8103 Fermi, 11546 Miyoshimachi, 58185 Rokkosan, 7166 Kennedy, 1175 Margo, 30306 Frigyesriesz, 189795 McGehee

134q4 (26.563) \\knime as a tool—how it works; 22564 Jeffreyxing, 30441 Curly, 249541 Steinem, 120460 Hambach, 2750 Loviisa, 3306 Byron, 322 Phaeo, 14965 Bonk

qig123: top amasser of trophies or accomplishments

qc415: the existential circus host

2q3 (356.354) \\experiments with substances, alone; 14790 Beletskij, 109712 Giger, 19855 Borisalexeev, 26800 Gualtierotrucco, 44 Nysa, 9007 James Bond, 161545 Ferrando

74q3 (176.354) \\the grand master of ceremonies, my conception of a ringmaster; 24695 Styrsky, 7959 Alysecherri, 22191 Achucarro, 24663 Philae, 4936 Butakov, 64974 Savaria, 23116 Streich, 2276 Warck, 12241 Lefort, 32384 Scottbest, 197196 Jamestaylor, 24949 Klacka, 38684 Velehrad, 10137 Thucydides

38q3 (266.354) \\the mystery of my romantic life; 12067 Jeter, 6151 Viget, 13492 Vitalijzakharov, 3161 Beadell, 13039 Awashima, 31936 Bernardsmit, 7645 Pons, 30347 Pattyhunt, 26246 Mikelake, 5642 Bobbywilliams, 5740 Toutoumi, 9308 Randyrose

110q3 (86.354) \\my belief that people just need to come to the table | bowed at the central abdomen; investigate connection to elbows; 58608 Geroldrichter, 1340 Yvette, 26251 Kiranmanne, 19911 Rigaux, 4568 Menkaure, 72543 Simonemarchi, 10103 Jungfrun, 6740 Goff, 16271 Duanenichols

qc271: based on rough relationships, how I get the material to write about

14q3 (326.354) \\the personal life section of my posthumous wikipedia article; 18991 Tonivanov, 144296 Steviewonder, 24969 Lucafini, 4668 Rayjay, 6234 Sheilawolfman, 26919 Shoichimiyata

86q3 (146.354) \\where I leave people like REDACTED and go off on my own; 27618 Ceilierin, 28553 Bhupatiraju, 898 Hildegard, 129321 Tannercampbell, 3624 Mironov, 243000 Katysirles, 3513 Quqinyue, 28833 Arunachalam, 2376 Martynov, 121313 Tamsin, 3911 Otomo, 26400 Roshanpalli

50q3 (236.354) \\my energy becomes distorted when the partnership is unhappy. This happens ALL THE TIME WITH ALL CLOSE PARTNERSHIPS. But why?; 120299 Billlynch, 5704 Schumacher, 7041 Nantucket, 11313 Kugelgen, 3420 Standish, 14146 Hughmaclean, 27714 Dochu, 36061 Haldane, 25722 Evanmarshall, 24749 Grebel, 9994 Grotius, 7578 Georgbohm, 3791 Marci, 21064 Yangliwei, 53285 Mojmir, 53316 Michielford, 5524 Lecacheux, 20454 Pedrajo, 18623 Pises

122q3 (56.354) \\my collection of exploratory writings built up in a sense of abandonment—often emotional; 5959 Shaklan, 6675 Sisley, 1199 Geldonia, 9995 Alouette, 2827 Vellamo, 43 Ariadne, 19079 Hernandez, 52872 Okyrhoe, 1478 Vihuri, 32 Pomona

qc127: teaching and the topics I prefer; a GREAT candidate for the qcross of one's *definition* of women (62q3), men (26q3), and the kinds of effects that you expect these to host as abstract categories respectively (134q3 ♀ and 98q3 ♂). See qc115 –one duodecanate away—to see how one sees women as social actors (63q3) and self-developers (135q3), men as social actors (27q3) and self-developers (99q3). qc139 shows how each defends their worth (61q3, 25q3) and the context employed

26q3 (296.354) \\the backdrop I work against in settled mode; 32091 Jasonwu, 27450 Monzon, 3485 Barucci, 5454 Kojiki, 11378 Dauria, 8964 Corax, 77856 Noblitt, 1462 Zamenhof, 19348 Cueca, 21475 Jasonclain, 685 Hermia

98q3 (116.354) \\gaining stature in my work, settling down. But the more i do this, the less likely I am to enter relationships with women among my options; 3669 Vertinskij, 8590 Pygargus, 3190 Aposhanskij, 8963 Collurio, 10613 Kushinadahime, 821 Fanny, 10694 Lacerda

62q3 (206.354) \\women | coronal curvature; eastern europe to western asianizes, encourages smaller male reproductive organs and a lighter, gentler feminine build instead; arcs the posture and narrows the eyes; 121609 Josephnicholas, 26448 Tongjili, 213637 Lemarchal, 191856 Almarivan, 3815 Konig, 10707 Prunariu, 8207 Suminao, 2489 Suvorov, 230656 Kovacspal, 4253 Marker, 11898 Dedeyn, 6236 Mallard, 3991 Basilevsky, 8807 Schenk, 42478 Inozemtseva, 7260 Metelli, 15913 Telemachus, 32406 Tracyhughes, 3458 Boduognat, 35316 Monella, 13439 Frankiethomas, 2679 Kittisvaara, 2852 Declercq

134q3 (26.354) \\my casual relationships with women; 12118 Mirotsin, 31086 Gehringer, 20581 Prendergast, 4316 Babinkova, 32296 Aninsayana, 242492 Fantomas, 3263 Bligh, 17965 Brodersen

qig124: fighting for the right to choose your friends

qc414: my flow state, assessing what aligns and what doesn't

2q2 (356.146) \\characteristic events that floated around me in childhood; learning fast, changing school; 31479 Botello, 8229 Kozelsky, 18839 Whiteley, 73857 Hitaneichi, 293926 Harrystine, 22366 Flettner, 27572 Shurtleff, 10442 Biezenzo, 410928 Maidbronn

74q2 (176.146) \\why tito's works; my sharper focus under this, cognac, yukon jack, and other quality substances; drunken thoughts; 6089 Izumi, 10719 Andamar, 133782 Saraknutson, 4145 Maximova, 266725 Vonputtkamer, 22385 Fujimoriboshi, 32299 Srinivas, 4799 Hirasawa, 19769 Dolyniuk, 67308 Oveges, 11978 Makotomasako, 20187 Janapittichova, 16908 Groeselenberg, 22858 Suesong, 3615 Safronov, 9419 Keikochaki, 26390 Rusin, 9945 Karinaxavier, 3834 Zappafrank

38q2 (266.146) \\interface with m+; 2708 Burns, 21684 Alinafiocca, 128323 Peterwolff, 125071 Lugosi, 255587 Gardenia, 236800 Broder, 32603 Ariaeppinger, 10954 Spiegel, 1339 Desagneauxa, 8816 Gamow, 11678 Brevard, 9555 Frejakocha, 13565 Yotakanashi, 3430 Bradfield

110q2 (86.146) \\my tactics for addressing monsterfication; 48778 Shokoyukako, 10715 Nagler, 14116 Ogea, 24538 Charliexie, 2363 Cebriones, 25656 Bejnood, 2388 Gase, 33044 Erikdavy, 34135 Rahulsubra

qc270: kk

14q2 (326.146) \\behaviors I display which get me challenged; kk prompt; 750 Oskar, 24148 Mychajliw, 3428 Roberts, 43844 Rowling, 1780 Kippes, 19758 Janelcoulson, 33456 Ericacurran, 10465 Olkin, 11976 Josephthurn, 32281 Shreyamenon, 78536 Shrbeny, 99201 Sattler

86q2 (146.146) \\those who challenge me; seems to be a minority ethnic in their community. Eventually blocked, constituting the fee; 8719 Vesmir, 15897 Benackova, 33536 Charpudgee, 11261 Krisbecker, 7358 Oze, 10209 Izanaki, 9438 Satie, 7780 Maren, 840 Zenobia, 21336 Andyblanchard, 9381 Lyon, 13435 Rohret, 11694 Esterhuysen, 3396 Muazzez, 749 Malzovia, 2800 Ovidius, 5324 Lyapunov, 9373 Hamra

50q2 (236.146) \\the women and the empty spaces between them for autoexercise; 26909 Lefschetz, 16909 Miladejager, 14832 Alechinsky, 9993 Kumamoto, 3233 Krisbarons, 1575 Winifred, 3311 Podobed, 5021 Krylania, 23879 Demura, 6582 Flagsymphony, 3426 Seki, 2751 Campbell, 1167 Dubiago, 8969 Alexandrinus, 16193 Nickaiser, 33 Polyhymnia, 686 Gersuind, 69434 de Gerlache, 7796 Jaracimrman

122q2 (56.146) \\my filing through lineups of profiles, or images; 12850 Axelmunthe, 2819 Ensor, 11454 Mariomelita, 16892 Vaissiere

qc126: how I'm talked about as a boyfriend, in hard times and easy

26q2 (296.146) \\dean, me REDACTED and REDACTED, me REDACTED and REDACTED. In the far aftermath of yelling. Reflecting on mom and dad in genoa; 2932 Kempchinsky, 5658 Clausbaader, 7252 Kakegawa, 128321 Philipdumont, 28824 Marlablair, 19727 Allen, 10343 Church, 26295 Vilardi, 54288 Daikikawasaki

98q2 (116.146) \\i keep wanting to trade and trade partners until I have two. Funk as a trigger? Dance?; 9998 ISO, 26653 Amymeyer, 25892 Funabashi, 224617 Micromegas, 5635 Cole, 4942 Munroe, 17961 Mariagorodnitsky, 11905 Giacometti, 11820 Mikiyasato

62q2 (206.146) \\preparing to move shanna, REDACTED, or REDACTED in—preparing for trouble; 3886 Shcherbakovia, 23111 Fritzperls, 12014 Bobhawkes, 16414 Le Procope, 2040 Chalonge, 194982 Furia, 268242 Pebble, 19446 Muroski, 690 Wratislavia, 4221 Picasso, 10116 Robertfranz, 5576 Albanese, 121716 Victorsank

134q2 (26.146) \\the work I do in astrology, underrepresented voices; 116939 Jonstewart, 9281 Weryk, 31282 Nicoleticea, 9523 Torino, 10242 Wasserkuppe, 15376 Martak, 27091 Alisonbick, 8072 Yojikondo, 711 Marmulla, 23727 Akihasan

qig125: reinforced communicated messaging

qc413: my interactions and power positioning with the partner

2q1 (355.938) \\me as house owner, evader of conflict with partner, also shows a lack of interest in sex consummate with the evasion. Prefer mass images and work. In order to get around this, I have to not act as the house ruler; 23176 Missacarvell, 308856 Daniket, 126578 Suhhosoo, 68718 Safi, 10561 Shimizumasahiro, 1297 Quadea, 11242 Franspost, 99862 Kenlevin

74q1 (175.938) \\sb's preferences—likely what most of the girls I encounter want; 20477 Anastroda, 12909 Jaclifford, 257248 Chouchiehlun, 34283 Bagley, 28131 Dougwelch, 500 Selinur, 3114 Ercilla, 34304 Alainagarza, 11385 Beauvoir, 6636 Kintanar, 11849 Fauvel, 9478 Caldeyro, 7463 Oukawamine

38q1 (265.938) \\me teasing and playing with the dogs, scaring them—the sadist; 11438 Zeldovich, 3218 Delphine, 3855 Pasasymphonia, 22725 Drabble, 7031 Kazumiyoshioka, 12515 Suiseki, 210533 Seanmisner, 243458 Bubulina, 175548 Sudzius, 8147 Colemanhawkins, 26323 Wuqijin, 4472 Navashin, 92279 Bindiluca, 18568 Thuillot, 25561 Leehyunki, 29762 Panasiewicz, 32628 Lazorik, 7856 Viktorbykov, 1721 Wells

110q1 (85.938) \\classic BDSM, spanking and gear—the masochist; 272 Antonia, 54521 Aladdin, 8709 Kadlu, 10038 Tanaro, 1666 van Gent, 884 Priamus, 2722 Abalakin, 8140 Hardersen, 694 Ekard

qc269: ousting sl

14q1 (325.938) \\dark cloud, ill fatedness of formal sata; 5765 Izett, 8043 Fukuhara, 3005 Pervictoralex, 30826 Coulomb, 10168 Stony Ridge, 12124 Hvar

86q1 (145.938) \\cb, sbr; 228165 Mezentsev, 4030 Archenhold, 919 Ilsebill, 34026 Valpagliarino, 1524 Joensuu, 5716 Pickard, 23164 Badger, 207716 Wangxichan, 9711 Zeletava, 2793 Valdaj, 17638 Sualan, 3038 Bernes, 11958 Galiani, 23928 Darbywoodard, 16150 Clinch, 1457 Ankara

50q1 (235.938) \\my not putting much stock in relationships, but having some good absorbable takeaway from their failure. My leg; 207715 Muqinshuijiao, 2553 Viljev, 2564 Kayala, 110298 Deceptionisland, 26671 Williamlopes, 163639 Tomnash, 21964 Kevinhousen, 7837 Mutsumi, 11006 Gilson, 8740 Vaclav, 48472 Mossbauer, 4556 Gumilyov, 18175 Jenniferchoy

122q1 (55.938) \\my feeling that I have the answers through astro; 6269 Kawasaki, 20526 Bathompson, 7434 Osaka, 22929 Seanwahl, 34063 Mariamakarova, 4523 MIT, 28828 Aalamiharandi, 100519 Bombig

qc125: the general nature of me and shanna's partnership

26q1 (295.938) \\those who hang around me,—especially shanna, dad, and the dogs—donate this energy; 3366 Godel, 14678 Pinney, 10251 Mulisch, 17066 Ginagallant, 14092 Gaily, 11135 Ryokami, 6880 Hayamiyu

98q1 (115.938) \\the frequentic currency I want to draw in strongly—how I receive what close others give from 26q1; 1694 Kaiser, 137052 Tjelvar, 4381 Uenohara, 8313 Christiansen, 11441 Anadiego, 18091 Iranmanesh, 12352 Jepejacobsen, 14989 Tutte, 12863 Whitfield, 31737 Carriecoombs

62q1 (205.938) \\sneaking with someone—something I am unlikely to do UNLESS in some special dimension. The logos themselves sneaking into our dimension; 136922 Brianbauer, 9217 Kitagawa, 4068 Menestheus, 3462 Zhouguangzhao, 184318 Fosanelli, 13449 Margaretgarland, 9180 Samsagan, 23406 Kozlov, 736 Harvard, 65363 Ruthanna, 9968 Serpe, 32063 Pusapaty, 23155 Judithblack, 8772 Minutus, 200578 Yungchuen, 21284 Pandion, 18431 Stazzema, 7543 Prylis, 5652 Amphimachus

134q1 (25.938) \\sudden inspiration to group concepts; 110408 Nakajima, 117381 Lindaweiland, 4677 Hiroshi, 8239 Signac, 75569 IRSOL, 28508 Kishore

qig126: day job and daily duties

qc412: my colleagues fare far better in my day job than I do. look at the rest of **qig126** *to see why...*

2q12 (355.729) \\the pair skyrockets via 74q12; use this alongside someone; establishes Ogawamachi as STRONG in my chart; 10375 Michiokuga, 22120 Gaylefarrar, 6210 Hyunseop, 90328 Haryou, 33550 Blackburn, 14315 Ogawamachi, 18858 Tecleveland, 281068 Chipolin

74q12 (175.729) \\MPS interactions; 6824 Mallory, 7078 Unojonsson, 1009 Sirene, 1761 Edmondson, 19410 Guisard, 343 Ostara, 129149 Richwitherspoon, 5870 Baltimore, 120405 Svyatylivka, 4115 Peternorton, 2294 Andronikov, 4031 Mueller, 6383 Tokushima, 3026 Sarastro, 26727 Wujunjun, 22824 von Neumann, 11848 Paullouka, 5796 Klemm

38q12 (265.729) \\ah; looking for bugs, looking to bring in more help and improve the system; when I am this person looking for someone who will actually complement me, others more likely disingenuous; 5597 Warren, 14075 Kenwill, 275962 Chalverat, 44033 Michez, 410619 Fabry, 8521 Boulainvilliers, 29484 Honzavesely, 6605 Carmontelle, 192208 Tzu Chi, 15144 Araas, 14047 Kohichiro, 9664 Brueghel, 26389 Poojarambhia, 17869 Descamps, 9654 Seitennokai, 6330 Koen

110q12 (85.729) \\unrepentant in how I run sata despite REDACTED's investigations; distrust towards my inquisitor; 5330 Senrikyu, 12158 Tape, 26664 Jongwon, 455 Bruchsalia, 12533 Edmond, 10864 Yamagatashi

qc268: my domestic and work duties

14q12 (325.729) \\from my house, the working of magic; 200025 Cloud Gate, 397 Vienna, 3533 Toyota, 20898 Fountainhills, 34239 Louisgolowich, 23180 Ryosuke, 167976 Ormsbymitchel, 10550 Malmo, 271009 Reitterferenc, 20787 Mitchfourman

86q12 (145.729) \\MY IDEAL RELATIONSHIP SPACE; how we live; 15676 Almoisheev, 3432 Kobuchizawa, 30353 Carothers, 120354 Mikejones, 5159 Burbine, 58279 Kamerlingh, 34137 Lonnielinda, 989 Schwassmannia, 92893 Michaelperson, 20798 Verlinden, 17023 Abbott, 454350 Paolaamico, 27938 Guislain, 1536 Pielinen, 3068 Khanina, 16074 Georgekaplan, 3715 Stohl

50q12 (235.729) \\my addressing and concern over job; 4458 Oizumi, 18964 Fairhurst, 6085 Fraethi, 6213 Zwiers, 48451 Pichincha, 3768 Monroe, 14701 Aizu, 1514 Ricouxa, 4781 Sladkovic, 14922 Ohyama, 24648 Evpatoria, 6906 Johnmills, 9176 Struchkova, 268 Adorea, 15466 Barlow, 12848 Agostino, 21462 Karenedbal, 45300 Thewrewk, 4997 Ksana, 3620 Platonov, 29443 Remocorti, 21412 Sinchanban

122q12 (55.729) \\i create more watchable series of things as I get older; downtime between projects; 2356 Hirons, 13214 Chirikov, 11806 Thangjam, 18948 Hinkle, 10696 Giuliattiwinter, 3514 Hooke, 7605 Cindygraber

qc124: how shanna and I relate compared to our other priorities—how this is described to others

26q12 (295.729) \\the kind of energy I am known for putting out from my own expression; 14186 Virgiliofos, 64295 Tangtisheng, 6927 Tonegawa, 10570 Shibayasuo, 296525 Milanovskiy, 384282 Evgeniyegorov, 9548 Fortran, 9295 Donaldyoung, 49440 Kenzotange, 2560 Siegma, 10043 Janegann, 8300 Iga, 2349 Kurchenko, 25416 Chyanwen, 10227 Izanami, 378669 Rivas

98q12 (115.729) \\how you exhaust your body vitality?; 24139 Brianmcarthy, 26660 Samahalpern, 14042 Agafonov, 8223 Bradshaw, 6478 Gault, 7611 Hashitatsu, 48801 Penninger, 7239 Mobberley, 31918 Onkargujral, 4376 Shigemori, 11885 Summanus, 11814 Schwamb

62q12 (205.729) \\meeting the two, then losing them immediately. REDACTED & REDACTED; 20340 Susanruder, 42479 Tolik, 12658 Peiraios, 6104 Takao, 4520 Dovzhenko, 24370 Marywang, 473 Nolli, 8546 Kenmotsu, 36187 Travisbarman, 13488 Savanov, 10179 Ishigaki, 29969 Amyvitha, 33376 Medi, 5113 Kohno, 48909 Laurake, 5185 Alerossi, 25867 DeMuth, 21817 Yingling, 2109 Dhotel, 2749 Walterhorn, 20329 Manfro, 33261 Ginagarlie, 2131 Mayall, 5490 Burbidge, 28952 Ericepstein, 3706 Sinnott, 338 Budrosa

134q12 (25.729) \\how I handle wins; 21417 Kelleyharris, 89973 Aranyjanos, 8420 Angrogna, 31324 Jirimrazek, 148780 Altjira, 28868 Rianchandra, 7147 Feijth

qig127: self-maturation

qc411: the women whom I change, for better but (formerly) often worse

2q11 (355.521) \\minor role in ..., then bowing out; ezra to wine; 22831 Trevanvoorth, 8957 Koujounotsuki, 10660 Felixhormuth, 9327 Duerbeck, 24265 Banthonytwarog, 33661 Sophiaswartz

74q11 (175.521) \\jo, sg, b.a.r., wine. There is power here, but this is an unfortunate situation in general, and part of the reason I avoid being in the center of a party (unless I'm teaching a class that will end); it really is easy to give up after going gray here; a cluster which brings a major gotcha to those seeking power who are associated with me, and one of the reasons why most potential meetings like this will never actually take place; 40007 Vieuxtemps, 33684 Xiaomichael, 27261 Yushiwang, 3973 Ogilvie, 300226 Francocanepari, 70942 Vandanashiva, 776 Berbericia, 26737 Adambradley, 7527 Marples, 23472 Rolfriekher, 6810 Juanclaria, 19148 Alaska, 8098 Miyamotoatsushi, 71001 Natspasoc

38q11 (265.521) \\the air becomes sour; b.a.r. at ddsn, sg; hollar likely aids my empathicness for these situations; earth's buried instinct towards ezra as he interacts with her (110q11); 12493 Minkowski, 8782 Bakhrakh, 14953 Bevilacqua, 6435 Daveross, 9914 Obukhova, 46280 Hollar, 58345 Moomintroll, 24190 Xiaoyunyin, 196736 Munkacsy

110q11 (85.521) \\interactions with priya, jj, more generally expressed in my childhood peers and a daughter—if I had one; earth; strada, LCL; 8743 Keneke, 7939 Asphaug, 15370 Kanchi, 8800 Brophy, 3734 Waland, 2261 Keeler, 16715 Trettenero, 12154 Callimachus, 8515 Corvan, 23246 Terazono

qc267: city and academics

14q11 (325.521) \\my failed education business endeavors, partnerships: probably better done as a role play, since there is no practical use for it otherwise except to make me more notorious; 52267 Rotarytorino, 7481 San Marcello, 992 Swasey, 22151 Davebracy, 31839 Depinto, 26611 Madzlandon, 17945 Hawass, 14181 Koromhazi, 10088 Digne, 24125 Sapphozoe, 28968 Gongmiaoxin, 1508 Kemi

86q11 (145.521) \\my increased exercises which ultimately MUST be public; 785 Zwetana, 15557 Kimcochran, 115058 Tassantal, 21527 Horton, 4506 Hendrie, 20193 Yakushima, 1052 Belgica, 95593 Azusienis, 231 Vindobona, 10213 Koukolik, 23271 Kellychacon, 7149 Bernie, 4368 Pillmore, 8231 Tetsujiyamada, 3085 Donna

50q11 (235.521) \\me under highly respected authorities, for better or worse; 21928 Prabakaran, 12057 Alfredsturm, 1032 Pafuri, 12159 Bettybiegel, 6928 Lanna, 456627 Cristianmartins, 1736 Floirac, 316186 Kathrynjoyce, 31104 Annanetrebko, 8296 Miyama, 174281 Lonsky, 23741 Takaaki, 76309 Ronferdie, 31933 Tanyizhao, 10217 Richardcook, 348034 Deslorieux, 4420 Alandreev

122q11 (55.521) \\the nba jam announcers; 277106 Forgo, 309227 Tsukiko, 502 Sigune, 27354 Stiklaitis, 4597 Consolmagno, 19178 Walterbothe, 3249 Musashino, 22863 Namarkarian

qc123: a great summary of mine and shanna's relationship

26q11 (295.521) \\my intentional design for contours; 1196 Sheba, 53157 Akaishidake, 8315 Bajin, 56000 Mesopotamia, 3043 San Diego, 3841 Dicicco, 25190 Thomasgoodin, 1893 Jakoba, 37583 Ramonkhanna, 8750 Nettarufina, 66652 Borasisi, 132 Aethra, 7818 Muirhead

98q11 (115.521) \\stephen hawking, christopher reeve; 5663 McKeegan, 2824 Franke, 210939 Bodok, 11807 Wannberg, 6079 Gerokurat, 25354 Zdasiuk, 190333 Jirous, 24950 Nikhilas, 30797 Chimborazo, 8626 Melissarauch, 21733 Schlottmann

62q11 (205.521) \\what shanna began doing in her move in; 2487 Juhani, 102 Miriam, 242523 Kreszgeza, 9263 Khariton, 212 Medea, 3861 Lorenz, 4454 Kumiko, 17795 Elysiasegal, 82332 Las Vegas, 2580 Smilevskia, 8125 Tyndareus, 6532 Scarfe, 15094 Polymele, 30372 Halback, 9681 Sherwoodrowland, 23048 Davidnelson, 22369 Klinger, 349 Dembowska

134q11 (25.521) \\preparing a system demo when I know I'm a noob; 5155 Denisyuk, 171256 Lucieconstant, 10784 Noailles, 6389 Ogawa

qig128: work and play under the parental eye

qc410: consummation, the union of creativities

2q10 (355.313) \\orgasm eye-ache comes from inviting others into my fantasy world; m; 1183 Jutta, 243526 Russwalker, 12094 Mazumder, 16783 Bychkov, 1252 Celestia, 21775 Tsiganis, 1884 Skip, 2662 Kandinsky, 29657 Andreali

74q10 (175.313) \\the actors typically involved in sexual climax for me; 7711 Rip, 3969 Rossi, 9083 Ramboehm, 12088 Macalintal, 3315 Chant, 4323 Hortulus, 22599 Heatherhall, 259387 Atauta, 10675 Kharlamov, 1931 Capek, 90826 Xuzhihong, 219 Thusnelda, 9334 Moesta, 3359 Purcari, 19656 Simpkins, 59389 Oskarvonmiller, 25602 Ucaronia, 44455 Artdula, 6018 Pierssac, 24732 Leonardcohen

38q10 (265.313) \\drunken thoughts and critical recordings; 12642 Davidjansen, 5075 Goryachev, 246643 Miaoli, 8933 Kurobe, 8199 Takagitakeo, 13540 Kazukitakahashi, 214081 Balavoine, 7603 Salopia, 367436 Siena, 327695 Yokoono, 15910 Shinkamigoto, 23040 Latham, 4384 Henrybuhl, 33499 Stanton, 2335 James, 28535 Sungjanet, 133527 Fredearly, 32613 Tseyuenman, 9254 Shunkai, 3579 Rockholt

110q10 (85.313) \\resorting to schemes in order to level a crooked playing field; 129969 Bradwilliams, 189310 Polydamas, 159164 La Canada, 10607 Amandahatton, 33395 Dylanli, 18028 Ramchandani, 21409 Forbes

qc266: I begin to rally the family economically

14q10 (325.313) \\my work within the house, despite rumors; refugee or clan march; 10608 Mameta, 4215 Kamo, 25965 Masihdas, 4819 Gifford, 82656 Puskas, 5116 Korsor, 136473 Bakosgaspar, 28511 Marggraff, 5617 Emelyanenko, 15129 Sparks, 6170 Levasseur

86q10 (145.313) \\me listening to DPG while working in the attic; 13669 Swammerdam, 5265 Schadow, 3552 Don Quixote, 5620 Jasonwheeler, 42531 McKenna, 9222 Chubey, 5384 Changjiangcun, 1599 Giomus, 29458 Pearson, 2122 Pyatiletka, 95928 Tonycook, 30157 Robertspira, 1367 Nongoma, 637 Chrysothemis, 16065 Borel

50q10 (235.313) \\i am a master in a certain kind of astrological diagnosis; rally 'round the family; 18112 Jeanlucjosset, 9680 Molina, 2705 Wu, 27323 Julianewman, 4538 Vishyanand, 7708 Fennimore, 16671 Tago, 134146 Pronoybiswas, 270553 Loureed, 31503 Jessicahong, 8549 Alcide, 4893 Seitter, 3099 Hergenrother, 73883 Asteraude, 8975 Atthis, 5560 Amytis

122q10 (55.313) \\you insult me? Fuck it I'll do my own thing then. A lot of it; 11936 Tremolizzo, 2702 Batrakov, 159 Aemilia, 20311 Nancycarter

qc122: the climate and timeline of shanna's and my relationship

26q10 (295.313) \\obviously the life I lead with shanna, but also rachel's successor and chico; 302 Clarissa, 20634 Marichardson, 228893 Gerevich, 6009 Yuzuruyoshii, 33319 Kunqu, 22906 Lisauckis, 21395 Albertofilho, 39726 Hideyukitezuka, 55428 Cappellaro, 16672 Bedini, 25986 Sunanda, 8340 Mumma, 161693 Attilladanko, 32034 Sophiakorner, 33455 Coakley

98q10 (115.313) \\sk, girl problems; 30386 Philipjeffery, 20012 Ranke, 3 Juno, 2123 Vltava, 4297 Eichhorn, 7106 Kondakov, 4553 Doncampbell, 25430 Ericlarson, 5120 Bitias, 16221 Kevinyang, 26896 Josefhudec, 73670 Kurthopf

62q10 (205.313) \\owning up to a failing thing. Hard; 4559 Strauss, 13641 de Lesseps, 10181 Davidacomba, 96205 Ararat, 78535 Carloconti, 9130 Galois, 1364 Safara, 1878 Hughes, 9509 Amfortas, 141995 Rossbeyer, 117852 Constance, 256699 Poudai, 152641 Fredreed, 4701 Milani, 1759 Kienle, 24226 Sekhsaria, 28210 Howardfeng, 224027 Gregoire, 8764 Gallinago, 11341 Babbage, 4302 Markeev, 771 Libera, 4075 Sviridov, 956 Elisa, 12167 Olivermuller, 21986 Alexanduribe, 3564 Talthybius, 2179 Platzeck

134q10 (25.313) \\unorthodoxy in work on contours; 18510 Chasles, 2814 Vieira, 4315 Pronik, 3385 Bronnina, 187 Lamberta, 1669 Dagmar, 1263 Varsavia

qig129: ambitions re-worded

qc409: scrutinizing my close alliances when things get difficult

2q9 (355.104) \\me assuring people around me in times of uncertainty; 3012 Minsk, 5253 Fredclifford, 13251 Viot

74q9 (175.104) \\simeona, s.o.s.; 113405 Itomori, 1522 Kokkola, 20106 Morton, 1701 Okavango, 20556 Midgekimble, 5543 Sharaf, 21625 Seira, 304813 Cesarina, 12089 Maichin, 17022 Huisjen, 10776 Musashitomiyo, 2513 Baetsle, 13624 Abeosamu, 85197 Ginkgo, 13006 Schwaar, 6094 Hisako, 11860 Uedasatoshi, 296968 Ignatianum, 1916 Boreas, 2871 Schober, 27332 Happritchard

38q9 (265.104) \\sad or epic breakup music when I play it; 3406 Omsk, 19228 Uemuraikuo, 4093 Bennett, 25619 Martonspohn, 2597 Arthur, 6933 Azumayasan, 484613 Cerebrito, 53237 Simonson, 17060 Mikecombi, 5835 Mainfranken, 11238 Johanmaurits, 3803 Tuchkova, 31061 Tamao, 8115 Sakabe, 129160 Ericpeters, 5798 Burnett

110q9 (85.104) \\REDACTED, REDACTED, REDACTED, other people I've met who were positioned to compete with and possibly terminate their partner's enterprise for the competition it posed to their own interests; 16062 Buncher, 6925 Susumu, 18843 Ningzhou, 10691 Sans, 10838 Lebon, 20207 Dyckovsky, 4635 Rimbaud, 14351 Tomaskohout, 14441 Atakanoseki

qc265: crafting my rallying message

14q9 (325.104) \\me deciding that rather than wait for help, I should build my own assistant; 2681 Ostrovskij, 233661 Alytus, 15318 Innsbruck, 283786 Rutebeuf, 404 Arsinoe, 9273 Schloerb, 151835 Christinarichey, 4064 Marjorie

86q9 (145.104) \\my stopping my book writing to produce idealized AI; the difficult-to motivate helpmate who eventually ends up being dropped for nonperformance; 12895 Balbastre, 12664 Sonisenia, 11528 Mie, 9866 Kanaimitsuo, 22981 Katz, 9171 Carolyndiane, 29783 Sanjanarane, 6076 Plavec, 24296 Marychristie, 17356 Vityazev, 2425 Shenzhen, 11019 Hansrott, 7418 Akasegawa, 22547 Kimberscott, 8829 Buczkowski, 36888 Skrabal, 264061 Vitebsk, 3920 Aubignan, 1282 Utopia, 209107 Safranek, 20321 Lightdonovan, 171458 Pepaprats, 8892 Kakogawa, 1119 Euboea

50q9 (235.104) \\prompt engineering for AI; 12819 Susumutakahasi, 18957 Mijacobsen, 2889 Brno, 11244 Andrekuipers, 11292 Bunjisuzuki, 2832 Lada, 21687 Filopanti, 6479 Leoconnolly, 4127 Kyogoku, 21846 Wojakowski, 1230 Riceia, 5865 Qualytemocrina, 15507 Rengarajan, 19524 Acaciacoleman, 8610 Goldhaber, 23783 Alyssachan, 766 Moguntia, 1157 Arabia, 130006 Imranaslam

122q9 (55.104) \\my book collection keeps building; AI art; 5310 Papike, 8634 Neubauer

qc121: relationship and individual health priorities within it

26q9 (295.104) \\REDACTED crosses the line; 22936 Ricmccutchen, 30173 Greenwood, 4554 Fanynka, 187709 Fengduan, 3792 Preston, 232949 Muhina, 10822 Yasunori, 90579 Gordonnelson, 7274 Washioyama, 181824 Konigsleiten, 2717 Tellervo, 49443 Marcobondi, 7868 Barker, 7204 Ondrejov, 5506 Artiglio, 18113 Bibring, 48575 Hawaii, 15088 Licitra

98q9 (115.104) \\the flood, asthma; frustrated surprise in code; 250374 Jirovec, 22921 Siyuanliu, 22828 Jaynethomp, 10456 Anechka, 17439 Juliesan, 913 Otila, 990 Yerkes

62q9 (205.104) \\i suddenly become mobile in high circles despite being only a noob; 8881 Prialnik, 412 Elisabetha, 226 Weringia, 994 Otthild, 380480 Glennhawley, 11043 Pepping, 2857 NOT, 17521 Kiek, 2927 Alamosa, 9535 Plitchenko, 19913 Aigyptios, 16705 Reinhardt, 10720 Danzl, 20288 Nachbaur, 23772 Masateru, 2260 Neoptolemus, 95954 Bayzoltan, 2959 Scholl, 7447 Marcusaurelius, 2065 Spicer, 31922 Alsharif

134q9 (25.104) \\i take up the bodyguard bearing, our dog rachel; 20441 Elijahmena, 7295 Brozovic, 5931 Zhvanetskij, 888 Parysatis

qig130: held in place, fixes limited to this…

qc408: and encounter with an assortment of possibly colorful characters

3q8 (354.896) \\encountering adventurous people in travel; 212797 Lipei, 19210 Higayoshihiro, 6436 Coco, 11120 Pancaldi, 2714 Matti, 7019 Tagayuichan, 20840 Borishanin, 10453 Banzan, 26661 Kempelen, 11767 Milne, 8474 Rettig, 2789 Foshan, 2325 Chernykh

75q8 (174.896) \\REDACTED and her engagement of me in full on crush mode; may be tied to my perceived attractiveness being HEAVILY dependent on lighting. If light is anywhere behind me I look worse… and worse; 16203 Jessicastahl, 5182 Bray, 7707 Yes, 31893 Rodriguezalvarez, 349785 Hsiaotejen, 8279 Cuzco, 8958 Stargazer, 11773 Schouten, 1880 McCrosky, 10210 Nathues, 27123 Matthewlam, 2033 Basilea, 13017 Owakenoomi, 28607 Jiayipeng, 22618 Silva Nortica, 1696 Nurmela, 4195 Esambaev, 36783 Kagamino, 16452 Goldfinger, 22112 Staceyraw, 5186 Donalu, 21649 Vardhana, 19488 Abramcoley, 14439 Evermeersch

39q8 (264.896) \\my blocking REDACTED. Otherwise, my mh data; 2570 Porphyro, 22633 Fazio, 21424 Faithchang, 11239 Marcgraf, 18472 Hatada, 48434 Maxbeckmann, 43843 Cleynaerts, 2598 Merlin, 12396 Amyphillips, 263255 Jultayu, 21630 Wootensmith, 11081 Persave

111q8 (84.896) \\my long work. The youngest is the current book I'm working on, and the one with the active volatility; 12514 Schommer, 127810 Michaelwright, 164536 Davehinson, 12643 Henkolthof, 18670 Shantanugaur, 7116 Mentall, 32811 Apisaon, 10584 Ferrini, 8968 Europaeus, 245983 Machholz

qc264: situations I attempt to approach and those who allow or block this

15q8 (324.896) \\"Let me tell you a different story:" my Ascendant location; 17051 Oflynn, 5996 Julioangel, 37788 Suchan, 32049 Jonathanma, 3990 Heimdal, 8059 Deliyannis, -1 Ascendant, 4579 Puccini, 3565 Ojima, 100734 Annasvidnicka

87q8 (144.896) \\caring backup to more likely a big girl. my Descendant location; 136472 MakeMake, 5518 Mariobotta, 8905 Bankakuko, 114725 Gordonwalker, 2836 Sobolev, 10794 Vange, -7 Descendant, 10186 Albeniz, 6106 Stoss, 29845 Wykrota, 97069 Stek, 21562 Chrismessick, 12399 Bartolini, 41279 Trentman, 4392 Agita, 251621 Luthen, 107638 Wendyfreedman, 23743 Toshikasuga, 1336 Zeelandia, 8406 Iwaokusano, 74 Galatea

51q8 (234.896) \\my state of the field messages which almost never get responses; 212795 Fangjiancheng, 4153 Roburnham, 10440 van Swinden, 8529 Sinzi, 27385 Andblonsky, 195657 Zhuangqining, 349606 Fleurance, 4324 Bickel, 7361 Endres, 22581 Rosahemphill

123q8 (54.896) \\talking about the vast territories I've covered; 5935 Ostankino, 11102 Bertorighini

qc120: coercion or extortion in the attitude, as well as the victim of such

27q8 (294.896) \\me in a flow state knocking down a task. Muscle memory? Smooth villain; 147421 Gardonyi, 5987 Liviogratton, 7251 Kuwabara, 27922 Mascheroni, 17503 Celestechild, 315493 Zimin, 1614 Goldschmidt, 25020 Tinyacheng, 2010 Chebyshev, 26386 Adelinacozma, 57424 Caelumnoctu, 647 Adelgunde

99q8 (114.896) \\my general handling of REDACTED even after our split; 26696 Gechenzhang, 3971 Voronikhin, 22817 Shankar, 6029 Edithrand, 6080 Lugmair, 2792 Ponomarev, 7806 Umasslowell, 822 Lalage, 882 Swetlana, 11414 Allanchu, 5791 Comello, 8678 Bal, 951 Gaspra, 8411 Celso

63q8 (204.896) \\how I interface with strangers 1:1 - space with no eye contact; 13185 Agasthenes, 1570 Brunonia, 915 Cosette, 13906 Shunda, 7216 Ishkov, 15622 Westrich, 374 Burgundia, 46669 Wangyongzhi, 10747 Kothen, 31912 Lukasgrafner,

12937 Premadi, 163470 Kenwallis, 52457 Enquist, 11854 Ludwigrichter, 28068 Stephbillings, 6528 Boden, 17835 Anoelsuri, 3674 Erbisbuhl, 12065 Jaworski, 27453 Crystalpoole, 7784 Watterson, 5822 Masakichi

135q8 (24.896) \\psyching myself up to do something alone, preparing a playlist; 4802 Khatchaturian, 156880 Bernardtregon, 2761 Eddington, 11431 Karelbosscha, 17285 Bezout, 6547 Vasilkarazin, 172317 Walterbos

qig131: the beg for attention

qc407: the beg for attention within the homebase to elsewhere within the homebase

3q7 (354.688) \\more paintings arising on the house walls; 4937 Lintott, 33002 Everest, 47162 Chicomendez, 1353 Maartje, 9108 Toruyusa, 15115 Yvonneroe, 11604 Novigrad, 43083 Frankconrad

75q7 (174.688) \\in gig work, let the layoffs continue. We will emerge elevated, at least for a time; 26248 Longenecker, 2851 Harbin, 257296 Jessicaamy, 28411 Xiuqicao, 2890 Vilyujsk, 3681 Boyan, 21646 Joshuaturner, 15053 Bochnicek, 3900 Knezevic, 8143 Nezval, 8706 Takeyama, 18322 Korokan, 132820 Miskotte, 2849 Shklovskij

39q7 (264.688) \\my hesitancy to get involved on …; luna; 26247 Doleonardi, 114022 Bizyaev, 12749 Odokaigan, 115434 Kellyfast, 16273 Oneill, 22924 Deshpande, 23649 Tohoku, 2502 Nummela, 21629 Siperstein, 22109 Loriehutch, 27344 Vesevlada, 457743 Balklavs

111q7 (84.688) \\the people on … whom I pay attention to; 6679 Gurzhij, 39860 Aiguoxiang, 31632 Stephaying, 15705 Hautot, 96327 Ullmann, 16682 Donati, 3608 Kataev, 5130 Ilioneus, 21405 Sagarmehta, 33413 Alecsun

qc263: the great difficulty I have tending to business

15q7 (324.688) \\sb as housemate; doing taxes and business; 6747 Ozegahara, 1257 Mora, 16220 Mikewagner, 33384 Jacyfang, 21434 Stanchiang, 2333 Porthan, 25555 Ratnavarma, 187125 Marxgyorgy

87q7 (144.688) \\pharaonic. Those who will forever stand apart from the norm; 41979 Lelumacri, 4380 Geyer, 324925 Vivantdenon, 10982 Poerink, 26075 Levitsvet, 24998 Hermite, 24149 Raghavan, 8046 Ajiki, 3689 Yeates, 37279 Hukvaldy, 17470 Mitsuhashi, 22195 Nevadodelruiz, 7898 Ohkuma, 17909 Nikhilshukla, 1981 Midas, 17771 Elsheimer, 2856 Roser, 2753 Duncan, 4200 Shizukagozen, 59000 Beiguan, 7913 Parfenov

51q7 (234.688) \\kit in jail; the quiet students who populate the class. Regular people who are around, but of whom I don't really have an established opinion. NPCs in general; 14573 Montebugnoli, 5889 Mickiewicz, 22729 Anthennig, 254846 Csontvary, 3236 Strand, 175562 Ajsingh, 19397 Lagarini, 121655 Nitapszcolka, 185546 Yushan, 9549 Akplatonov, 2323 Zverev

123q7 (54.688) \\me teaching my students—the messages they pick up; 33383 Edupuganti, 21419 Devience, 5674 Wolff, 30418 Jakobsteiner, 19258 Gongyi, 249160 Urriellu, 4228 Nemiro, 95935 Grego

qc119: looking for the superstar

27q7 (294.688) \\headed towards contours… but I might need to talk to or partner with a trans person in it; 266465 Andalucia, 4186 Tamashima, 14120 Espenak, 2605 Sahade, 11144 Radiocommunicata, 232763 Eliewiesel, 26269 Marciaprill, 120942 Rendafuzhong, 30937 Bashkirtseff, 210030 Taoyuan, 29738 Ivobudil, 10107 Kenny, 33958 Zaferiou, 2053 Nuki, 25549 Jonsauer

99q7 (114.688) \\my notion of the building of pyramids, rail, and other great works… on the backs of the small, in the vision of the mighty; 21512 Susieclary, 7100 Martin Luther, 10716 Olivermorton, 11808 Platz, 5619 Shair, 8244 Mikolaichuk, 4749 Ledzeppelin, 20965 Kutafin

63q7 (204.688) \\tj, the attention magnet, kad—and probably the reason I wouldn't have access to kad. That access would be had by asz. Relatedly, tj was connected to ezra through Sâvitrî, who underwent a more alpha turn. Perhaps a template for this kind of link; 12433 Barbieri, 12762 Nadiavittor, 12222 Perotto, 254876 Strommer, 18649 Fabrega, 20696 Torresduarte, 5423 Horahorejs, 9732 Juchnovski, 2286 Fesenkov, 12789 Salvadoraguirre, 14446 Kinkowan, 1459 Magnya, 9203 Myrtus, 5775 Inuyama, 8942 Takagi, 17201 Matjazhumar, 5459 Saraburger, 166622 Sebastien, 266711 Tuttlingen, 33662 Tacescu, 6560 Pravdo, 15384 Samkova, 4532 Copland, 31402 Negishi

135q7 (24.688) \\asz; 6109 Balseiro, 284996 Rosaparks, 30162 Courtney, 14973 Rossirosina, 33634 Strickler

qig132: your shadow side

qc406: the great intellectual or creative challenge that changes your life permanently

3q6 (354.479) \\how I executed globus; sata and spacetime; 5445 Williwaw, 33667 Uttripathii, 5514 Karelraska, 80984 Santomurakami, 198110 Heathrhoades, 7132 Casulli, 200 Dynamene, 10315 Brewster, 7614 Masatomi

75q6 (174.479) \\the five obstructions and how it worked. May have some affinity with reprinting after life; 6361 Koppel, 6105 Verrocchio, 17198 Gorjup, 22138

Laynrichards, 1910 Mikhailov, 112798 Kelindsey, 1438 Wendeline, 33606 Brandonmuncan, 19578 Kirkdouglas, 8906 Yano, 20779 Xiajunchao, 38250 Tartois, 18788 Carriemiller, 4312 Knacke, 20465 Vervack, 28096 Kathrynmarsh, 7000 Curie, 5415 Lyanzuridi

39q6 (264.479) \\lars von trier and joergen leth's interaction in the five obstructions; 17224 Randoross, 44027 Termain, 28675 Suejohnston, 3333 Schaber, 28206 Haozhongning, 1317 Silvretta, 31152 Daishinsai, 3892 Dezso, 298877 Michaelreynolds, 41740 Yuenkwokyung, 2038 Bistro, 128439 Chriswaters, 8695 Bergvall, 20376 Joyhines, 2244 Tesla, 6450 Masahikohayashi, 135979 Allam, 3279 Solon, 3380 Awaji

111q6 (84.479) \\the original perfect human and joergen leth's turning of it; 4550 Royclarke, 30334 Michaelwiner, 9234 Matsumototaku, 6878 Isamu, 91275 Billsmith, 38246 Palupin, 65590 Archeptolemos, 29980 Dougsimons, 24069 Barbarapener, 8625 Simonhelberg, 12168 Polko, 7273 Garyhuss, 2685 Masursky

qc262: power circles around me

15q6 (324.479) \\the godsent colleague is actually a prelude to divorce; 4224 Susa, 594 Mireille, 11795 Fredrikbruhn, 2589 Daniel, 2117 Danmark, 14054 Dusek, 27447 Ichunlin, 18777 Hobson, 10498 Bobgent, 190 Ismene, 5761 Andreivanov, 31380 Hegyesi, 19461 Feingold, 2091 Sampo, 1764 Cogshall

87q6 (144.479) \\who I am as a future or current divorcé; 12498 Dragesco, 5104 Skripnichenko, 255308 Christianzuber, 17748 Uedashoji, 21506 Betsill, 5045 Hoyin, 8142 Zolotov, 11473 Barbaresco, 11444 Peshekhonov, 4508 Takatsuki

51q6 (234.479) \\vb; nostradamus; REDACTED's horror; 1590 Tsiolkovskaja, 90308 Johney, 3984 Chacos, 37584 Schleiden, 13582 Tominari, 314650 Neilnorman, 69261 Philaret, 22489 Yanaka, 3094 Chukokkala, 1728 Goethe Link, 4632 Udagawa, 55418 Bianciardi, 5143 Heracles, 25301 Ambrofogar, 6488 Drebach, 9351 Neumayer, 3049 Kuzbass, 29638 Eeshakhare, 13140 Shinchukai, 46722 Ireneadler, 5961 Watt, 7991 Kaguyahime, 3256 Daguerre, 1112 Polonia, 16419 Kovalev, 14575 Jamesblanc, 1494 Savo

123q6 (54.479) \\my breaking off from vb; REDACTED; 3664 Anneres, 15406 Bleibtreu, 21445 Pegconnolly, 8630 Billprady, 9525 Amandasickafoose, 5549 Bobstefanik, 1525 Savonlinna, 14438 MacLean

qc118: me, shanna, and spol: how we came to be

27q6 (294.479) \\messaging I am tasked to send out to move things forward, not always comfortably though; 12481 Streuvels, 22769 Aurelianora, 3407 Jimmysimms, 4130 Ramanujan, 178603 Pinkine, 48435 Jaspers, 85400 Shiratakachu, 28317 Aislinndeely, 8151 Andranada, 1153 Wallenbergia, 230155 Francksallet, 24962 Kenjitoba, 2873 Binzel, 16209 Sterner

99q6 (114.479) \\negative: my concern over an inability to meet my business responsibilities after having been abandoned in sata—maybe I am to be there for others who have been left in this way—when people aren't turning to me, I have these concerns. Influences the jri book specifically; 3724 Annenskij, 28416 Ngqin, 21460 Ryozo, 189396 Sielewicz, 11458 Rosemarypike, 24344 Brianbarnett, 24898 Alanholmes, 21238 Panarea, 10573 Piani, 23008 Rebeccajohns, 2944 Peyo, 12343 Martinbeech

63q6 (204.479) \\my concerns / dread over doing basic business; 6244 Okamoto, 43706 Iphiklos, 5292 Mackwell, 6316 Mendez, 7639 Offutt, 454352 Majidzandian, 11017 Billputnam, 9761 Krautter, 4048 Samwestfall, 10979 Fristephenson, 25116 Jonathanwang, 322912 Jedlik, 140980 Blanton, 13446 Almarkim, 599 Luisa, 12916 Eteoneus, 4358 Lynn, 5248 Scardia, 22978 Nyrola, 32079 Hughsavoldelli, 2829 Bobhope, 29212 Zeeman, 7353 Kazuya

135q6 (24.479) \\the two girls only appear as part of a larger bad luck situation. My continuing to want them ties me to futility in some sense. Talking myself out of that one threesome | \\sam and rachel's response to sam's agitation; 9422 Kuboniwa, 10663 Schwarzwald, 317715 Guydetienne, 10628 Feuerbacher

qig133: floating information not absorbed by you

qc405: bookstore action

3q5 (354.271) \\ah, then keith as those who take over the publishing space; 23046 Stevengordon, 8796 Sonnett, 4263 Abashiri, 50251 Iorg, 6505 Muzzio, 1822 Waterman, 10377 Kilimanjaro, 13991 Kenphillips, 187123 Schorderet, 4880 Tovstonogov, 7413 Galibina, 19366 Sudingqiang

75q5 (174.271) \\the books I put into bookstores—their energy, dynamics, and topics; 5538 Luichewoo, 399673 Kadenyuk, 1476 Cox, 3127 Bagration, 2870 Haupt, 1846 Bengt, 60406 Albertosuci, 11061 Lagerlof, 24328 Thomasburr, 18841 Hruska, 22632 DiNovis, 20804 Etter

39q5 (264.271) \\real estate under and with the angelas against san antonio. Who I am, who I meet, or what I'm reading in the bookstore when the exchange starts. This is favorable when I work with the occult; 13069 Umbertoeco, 181 Eucharis, 5179 Takeshima, 176610 Nunez, 5631 Sekihokutouge, 17956 Andrewlenoir, 27263

Elainezhou, 175730 Gramastetten, 10502 Armaghobs, 2699 Kalinin, 6078 Burt, 50428 Alexanderdessler, 149244 Kriegh, 6324 Kejonuma, 20689 Zhuyuanchen, 3158 Anga, 25701 Alexkeeler, 10075 Campeche, 13033 Gardon

111q5 (84.271) \\there in REDACTED, I meet REDACTED. Later, simeona. Or vv. Something about bookstores; 128315 Dereknelson, 14643 Morata, 573 Recha, 22705 Erinedwards, 39557 Gielgud, 15028 Soushiyou

qc261: political factions

15q5 (324.271) \\when I actually have the higher level access to data; the political star; 2134 Dennispalm, 10119 Remarque, 13911 Stempels, 170010 Szalay, 4210 Isobelthompson, 1241 Dysona, 4295 Wisse, 10021 Henja, 4421 Kayor

87q5 (144.271) \\the position from which higher data access can be requested; hot button political issues; 899 Jokaste, 1841 Masaryk, 5477 Holmes, 7161 Golitsyn, 20336 Gretamills, 11698 Fichtelman, 1207 Ostenia, 23030 Jimkennedy, 3574 Rudaux, 8937 Gassan, 1071 Brita

51q5 (234.271) \\arguing for automation or the mass access to data; general democrats; 1321 Majuba, 215044 Joaoalves, 34028 Wuhuiyi, 325455 Della Valle, 22631 Dillard, 28750 Brennawallin, 31110 Clapas, 88874 Wongshingsheuk, 39335 Caccin, 27417 Jessjohnson, 18698 Racharles, 24159 Shigetakahashi, 15160 Wygoda, 11492 Shimose, 4097 Tsurugisan, 2865 Laurel, 75570 Jenowigner

123q5 (54.271) \\going all in confidently as the supporter to someone else, using data; general republicans; 15072 Landolt, 31298 Chantaihei, 8773 Torquilla, 17696 Bombelli, 21678 Lindner, 5675 Evgenilebedev, 25907 Capodilupo, 22497 Immanuelfuchs, 29772 Portocarrero, 13543 Butler, 38270 Wettzell, 19136 Strassmann, 13424 Margalida

qc117: actions under insecurity or uncertainty. There are some notable areas that also infuriate interactants here

27q5 (294.271) \\me loading the worst of the uncertain thing, making it easy to exit. This is an EXTREMELY negative act which people perform in my life which ratchets up anger in the other; 16435 Fandly, 12320 Loschmidt, 31477 Meenakshi, 4116 Elachi, 5905 Johnson, 9537 Nolan, 4698 Jizera, 1089 Tama, 10734 Wieck, 8572 Nijo

99q5 (114.271) \\strange places, c&l sort of; the instant vacating plans of one who has been coldly stared down; 392142 Solheim, 4395 Danbritt, 33511 Austinwang, 831 Stateira, 18163 Jennalewis, 3111 Misuzu, 18461 Seiichikanno, 29080 Astrocourier, 1747 Wright, 6801 Strekov, 1718 Namibia, 228029 MANIAC, 33158 Rufus

63q5 (204.271) \\my editing process with a tense book; 108140 Alir, 181241 Dipasquale, 29643 Plucker, 1659 Punkaharju, 12238 Actor, 3032 Evans, 4007 Euryalos, 34993 Euaimon, 25157 Fabian, 2614 Torrence, 6006 Anaximandros, 5285 Krethon, 9775 Joeferguson, 7782 Mony, 24911 Kojimashigemi, 11668 Balios, 3929 Carmelmaria, 13387 Irus, 129564 Christy, 23294 Sunao, 1889 Pakhmutova, 147595 Gojkomitic

135q5 (24.271) \\my view of the privilege of being an editor; makosinski is probably THE reason nonmonogamy is safer for me partnership-wise; 3343 Nedzel, 10424 Gaillard, 31272 Makosinski

qig134: family name and legacy

qc404: specific power granters (ancillary to the political system)

3q4 (354.063) \\i don't recognize this | \\phaedra and cyclops? Abie and angela? christina and arianna? Under the flood?; 30832 Urbaincreve, 25322 Rebeccajean, 31774 Debralas, 10865 Thelmaruby, 5181 SURF, 7478 Hasse, 5024 Bechmann, 20969 Samo, 9387 Tweedledee

75q4 (174.063) \\various accreditation or inspection teams—the phd committee which visits on behalf of the institution in 3-4. probably a hayden clan-specific characteristic; 8813 Leviathan, 43881 Cerreto, 3956 Caspar, 31360 Huangyihsuan, 16407 Oiunskij, 92585 Fumagalli, 44005 Migliardi, 3975 Verdi, 18656 Mergler, 19806 Domatthews, 4414 Sesostris, 9977 Kentakunimoto, 28603 Jenkins, 3914 Kotogahama, 129555 Armazones, 46727 Hidekimatsuyama, 25050 Michmadsen, 2130 Evdokiya, 14250 Kathleenmartin, 19294 Weymouth, 5838 Hamsun, 438973 Masci, 27056 Ginoloria, 129154 Georgesondecker, 1150 Achaia

39q4 (264.063) \\my role in the family; 169834 Hujie, 19776 Balears, 7016 Conandoyle, 25834 Vechinski, 234294 Pappsandor, 209209 Ericmarsh, 13219 Cailletet, 12755 Balmer, 4313 Bouchet, 16463 Nayoro, 5042 Colpa, 9224 Zelezny, 81790 Lewislove, 78430 Andrewpearce, 11103 Miekerouppe, 1034 Mozartia, 16135 Ivarsson

111q4 (84.063) \\our various family accomplishments; 15946 Satinsky, 6594 Tasman, 21936 Ryan, 9490 Gosemeijer, 2411 Zellner, 1824 Haworth, 30917 Moehorgan, 55576 Amycus, 10815 Ostergam, 42516 Oistrach, 21522 Entwisle, 7886 Redman, 11470 Davidminton

qc260: the values held by political players. 15q4 shows the people as a commodity themselves. 87q4 is what they want

15q4 (324.063) \\approach to my acting career?; 2694 Pino Torinese, 239593 Tianwenbang, 174365 Zibetti, 10061 Ndolaprata, 99906 Uofalberta, 29869 Chiarabarbara, 369088 Marcus, 21702 Prisymendoza, 23066 Yihedong, 12984 Lowry, 30276 Noahgolowich

87q4 (144.063) \\this looks like a particular acting role. A kind of mirror to my experience under awl; aspirations towards a better life; 20265 Yuyinchen, 29431 Shijimi, 85168 Albertacentenary, 39529 Vatnajokull, 4461 Sayama, 236785 Hilendarski, 15391 Steliomancinelli, 24376 Ramesh, 5969 Ryuichiro, 21302 Shirakamisanchi, 6965 Niyodogawa, 100483 NAOJ, 9745 Shinkenwada, 13438 Marthanalexander, 15669 Pshenichner, 16266 Johconnell, 6012 Williammurdoch, 7150 McKellar

51q4 (234.063) \\gathering what is needed for data projects. How easy is the data to obtain?; 23070 Koussa, 26763 Peirithoos, 2942 Cordie, 3584 Aisha, 133296 Federicotosi, 75823 Csokonai, 18770 Yingqiuqilei, 30153 Ostrander, 4288 Tokyotech, 10684 Babkina, 8437 Bernicla, 14190 Soldan, 134105 Josephfust, 4152 Weber, 7947 Toland, 1236 Thais

123q4 (54.063) \\me running all kinds of crazy data scenarios in the background; 139028 Haynald, 6949 Zissell, 15006 Samcristoforetti, 120350 Richburns, 7988 Pucacco, 1975 Pikelner, 29905 Kunitaka, 5261 Eureka

qc116: defining moments in getting along with another… or not

27q4 (294.063) \\my life timed to music; musical claircognizance; sb stolen seasons; 3479 Malaparte, 37117 Narcissus, 30186 Ostojic, 434 Hungaria, 20583 Richthammer, 18980 Johannatang, 10686 Kaluna, 8403 Minorushimizu, 2145 Blaauw, 13674 Bourge, 10074 Van den Berghe, 144752 Plunge, 28801 Maryanderson

99q4 (114.063) \\as I gain more of this, I also see more health issues. Hm…; the fight with kvt; 21057 Garikisraelian, 69231 Alettajacobs, 4711 Kathy, 10699 Calabrese, 6739 Tarendo, 21425 Cordwell, 16450 Messerschmidt, 13200 Romagnani, 431397 Carolinregina, 11970 Palitzsch, 28081 Carriehudson

63q4 (204.063) \\largely over the house, we cannot build jointly as a couple; 158913 Kreider, 4427 Burnashev, 33160 Denismukwege, 35 Leukothea, 26578 Cellinekim, 13053 Bertrandrussell, 5367 Sollenberger, 28251 Gerbaldi, 129955 Eriksyrstad, 173108 Ingola, 99193 Obsfabra, 12187 Lenagoryunova, 461 Saskia, 159778 Bobshelton, 11739 Baton Rouge, 3772 Piaf, 4795 Kihara, 9694 Lycomedes, 24748 Nernst, 20854 Tetruashvily, 7855 Tagore, 10208 Germanicus, 5605 Kushida, 16255 Hampton, 32424 Caryjames, 8063 Cristinathomas, 16106 Carmagnola

135q4 (24.063) \\in light of non-anchoring by REDACTED, this is what I do, a great increase in protection of important things. I apparently need to be represented in other's charts here as a sign that we should continue; 19096 Leonfridman, 9690 Houtgast, 5100 Pasachoff, 1449 Virtanen, 8319 Antiphanes, 11811 Martinrubin, 107393 Bernacca, 8681 Burs, 6194 Denali

qig135: people see your additions to and role in your family

qc403: domestic demands for the state of the space

3q3 (353.854) \\sam; doing the damn lawn as a social keep-up; 1399 Teneriffa, 8850 Bignonia, 73984 Claudebernard, 13801 Kohlhase, 23122 Lorgat, 29085 Sethanne

75q3 (173.854) \\rachel, shanna; 23514 Schneider, 10992 Veryuslaviya, 6408 Saijo, 20799 Ashishbakshi, 7120 Davidgavine, 4524 Barklajdetolli, 4011 Bakharev, 129318 Sarahschlieder, 5279 Arthuradel, 246504 Hualien, 58418 Luguhu, 33714 Sarakaufman, 12881 Yepeiyu, 2180 Marjaleena, 7257 Yoshiya, 441 Bathilde

39q3 (263.854) \\me as a complement to our dogs/fur-children; 27615 Daniellu, 42849 Podjavorinska, 5022 Roccapalumba, 13531 Weizsacker, 19968 Palazzolascaris, 130127 Zoltanfarkas, 6602 Gilclark, 8110 Heath, 28019 Warchal, 10001 Palermo, 120040 Pagliarini, 22758 Lemp

111q3 (83.854) \\the mother type—interesting. Based on this, would be sgs, bs, dg, less so shanna, vb definitely, maybe priya later, Sâvitrî. IF I DEMAND THIS, I AM THE MOTHER. like dg or Sâvitrî; 2400 Derevskaya, 16915 Bredthauer, 6617 Boethius, 189188 Floralien, 21276 Feller, 32969 Motohikosato

qc259: the values and remediating actions of the various political stakeholders

15q3 (323.854) \\sallying forth, especially in the promulgation of unorthodox methods; 166745 Pindor, 24378 Katelyngibbs, 32018 Robhenning, 26656 Samarenae, 22495 Fubini

87q3 (143.854) \\after I have gone forth, others (in the place I have left) begin discovering shocking things; 18398 Bregenz, 31744 Shimshock, 12576 Oresme, 9395 Saint Michel, 6566 Shafter, 18244 Anneila, 12460 Mando, 8120 Kobe, 1702 Kalahari, 13586 Copenhagen, 31450 Stevepreston, 10657 Wanach, 10774 Eisenach, 5167 Joeharms

51q3 (233.854) \\my feelings about oral sex (receiving); 2972 Niilo, 212176 Fabriziospaziani, 3901 Nanjingdaxue, 1664 Felix, 3187 Dalian, 4071 Rostovdon, 24837 Msecke Zehrovice, 21697 Mascharak, 38268 Zenkert, 22638 Abdulla, 3532 Tracie, 111661 Mamiegeorge, 15248 Hidekazu, 20312 Danahy, 4360 Xuyi, 27425 Bakker, 15574 Stephaniehass, 14833 Vilenius

123q3 (53.854) \\a very specific set of circumstances and a very specific kind of person. Implies MUCH more luck with a foreigner who is a member of an untrusted class, and one who does it to learn more about something internal to them. Partly explains my sharp and gradual nonpreference for standard american-attitude women. no it's not about getting head (123), i didn't even know this qunit was a thing until now. instead, it's definitely about projecting something that the other actually wants to internalize; 12150 De Ruyter, 23279 Chenhungjen, 10966 van der Hucht, 227326 Narodychi, 23168 Lauriefletch, 1391 Carelia

qc115: masculine and feminine upbringing?

27q3 (293.854) \\yardwork starts, then keeps going and going… to music; looking for matches in music recordings; 1605 Milankovitch, 55874 Brlka, 33462 Tophergee, 15729 Yumikoitahana, 3810 Aoraki, 49500 Ishitoshi, 17777 Ornicar, 99824 Polnareff, 17101 Sakenova, 182592 Jolana, 43794 Yabetakemoto, 5162 Piemonte, 8075 Roero, 1285 Julietta, 90936 Neronet, 28504 Rebeccafaye

99q3 (113.854) \\Clearly the masculinization; my attention to this; male training; 8618 Sethjacobson, 12861 Wacker, 341826 Aurelbaier, 13843 Cowenbrown, 2691 Sersic, 2202 Pele, 10437 van der Kruit

63q3 (203.854) \\the design of my oracular tools as workflows and newly polished technology; 22575 Jayallen, 2543 Machado, 13001 Woodney, 9814 Ivobenko, 16395 Ioannpravednyj, 13062 Podarkes, 220736 Niihama, 2153 Akiyama, 174801 Etscorn, 4066 Haapavesi, 25113 Benwasserman, 18180 Irenesun, 25693 Ishitani, 210245 Castets, 5860 Deankoontz, 3770 Nizami

135q3 (23.854) \\soothing rhythms, asmr, untangling my hair as an autosensory spellbinding habit. Happens in the background while I'm working on another qunit. Discovery how this simultaneity works; 3852 Glennford, 8601 Ciconia, 10444 de Hevesy, 6535 Archipenko, 9921 Rubincam, 3498 Belton, 28598 Apadmanabha, 8375 Kenzokohno

qig136: successors to one's legacy

qc402: those who have easy access to becoming my family

3q2 (353.646) \\shanna as mom in her element; AI, book characters, latinas; 1408 Trusanda, 770 Bali, 2107 Ilmari, 1302 Werra, 21643 Kornev, 37392 Yukiniall, 19395 Barrera

75q2 (173.646) \\shanna as housemate (sister?), simeona. Folks who apply for membership in your family, probably won't get in, or will only be considered as partners to someone else who is already in; 33011 Kurtiscarsch, 28784 Deringer, 29984 Zefferer, 17402 Valeryshuvalov, 52387 Huitzilopochtli, 8763 Pugnax, 249521 Truth, 172525 Adamblock, 96344 Scottweaver, 11933 Himuka, 2087 Kochera, 9721 Doty, 2696 Magion, 4868 Knushevia, 5342 Le Poole, 6766 Kharms, 8899 Hughmiller, 1218 Aster, 12102 Piazzolla, 32074 Kevinsadhu, 24535 Neslusan

39q2 (263.646) \\the event which registers one as being part of the family; tv time; hanging with keith and joanna; 95851 Stromvil, 11537 Guericke, 16944 Wangler, 955 Alstede, 562 Salome, 25685 Katlinhornig, 1406 Komppa, 8303 Miyaji, 1673 van Houten, 24494 Megmoulding, 3212 Agricola, 4285 Hulkower, 18555 Courant, 27810 Daveturner, 2806 Graz, 17061 Tegler, 3078 Horrocks

111q2 (83.646) \\the types of people you welcome into your personal family. priya, auguste; 10023 Vladifedorov, 4122 Ferrari, 10105 Holmhallar, 151697 Paolobattaini, 28738 Carolinolan, 11154 Kobushi, 229631 Cluny

qc258: raising the public interest in various political circles

15q2 (323.646) \\walmart stern mode; my general public appearance; 1621 Druzhba, 179593 Penglangxiaoxue, 9453 Mallorca, 18635 Frouard, 1387 Kama, 6295 Schmoll, 7610 Sudbury, 7176 Kuniji, 4292 Aoba, 6063 Jason, 365756 ISON

87q2 (143.646) \\seems to correspond to the messiness in my house, and is probably one of the keys to cleaning this up; 229 Adelinda, 31522 McCutchen, 85190 Birgitroth, 2216 Kerch, 10970 de Zeeuw, 117657 Jamieelsila, 148384 Dalcanton, 4398 Chiara, 25764 Divyanag, 4846 Tuthmosis, 2659 Millis, 7020 Yourcenar, 33892 Meligingrich, 12715 Godin

51q2 (233.646) \\when not engaging a partner in order to move forward, ramming my experiences through anyway; 1115 Sabauda, 7036 Kentarohirata, 10569 Kinoshitamasao, 28299 Kanghaoyan, 15 Eunomia, 27900 Cecconi, 7021 Tomiokamachi, 19691 Iwate, 15582 Russellburrows, 25043 Fangxing, 14244 Labnow, 7763 Crabeels, 190310 De Martin, 16123 Jessiecheng, 32032 Askandola, 172985 Ericmelin, 10985 Feast, 2183 Neufang, 13579 Allodd, 22467 Koharumi, 9362 Miyajima

123q2 (53.646) \\the dynamics which describe someone highly more likely to become a kind of main interactant to you; 4216 Neunkirchen, 10819 Mahakala, 399979 Lewseaman, 2212 Hephaistos *qc114: harsh coaching by a pushy person or group. This entire qcross is fucking irritating and offers no ambition or asteroid-based value. Mute my response and get out. Use qc402 and talk to Shanna instead*

27q2 (293.646) \\waiting for a solution from heaven to one's ills, snatching easy victory from circumstances; subject to an overriding committee—I find myself annoyed; 22426 Mikehanes, 32858 Kitakamigawa, 418220 Kestutis, 10831 Takamagahara, 1250 Galanthus, 17044 Mubdirahman, 18184 Dianepark, 14659 Gregoriana, 199763 Davidgregory, 26493 Paulsucala

99q2 (113.646) \\ REDACTED, REDACTED, etc. the fact that I have no inclination to put myself in their shoes or adjust myself (redefine what she's doing according to my template) when we are misaligned when they do this underscores my lack of core nurturance; small nipples and areolae, male or female; likely the nipples, as it affects one party at a time; the overriding committee or pushy person; 10583 Kanetugu, 296907 Alexander, 2963 Chen Jiageng, 6835 Molfino, 9147 Kourakuen, 28954 Feiyiou, 23245 Fujimura, 1693 Hertzsprung, 334 Chicago, 17032 Edlu, 20731 Mothediniz, 19852 Jamesalbers, 12631 Mariekebaan, 5183 Robyn, 25426 Alexanderkim, 29812 Aaronsolomon, 19872 Chendonghua

63q2 (203.646) \\i feel like shit after losing my temper, but then have to put on a face of recovery; 7438 Misakatouge, 94291 Django, 3434 Hurless, 2759 Idomeneus, 6115 Martinduncan, 13327 Reitsema, 128610 Stasiahabenicht, 304233 Majaess, 8640 Ritaschulz, 18699 Quigley, 3291 Dunlap, 9167 Kharkiv, 78393 Dillon, 19318 Somanah, 24186 Shivanisud, 1645 Waterfield

135q2 (23.646) \\the lesson I think I should learn and try to internalize after a loss of temper; 3573 Holmberg, 2788 Andenne, 2956 Yeomans, 10449 Takuma, 33274 Beaubingham

qig137: one's defenses, breached

qc401: the woman who humors me despite not necessarily believing in me

3q1 (353.438) \\the dark issues that need to be aired. The inner contents of these books tend to be shocking; 23759 Wangzhaoxin, 19676 Ofeliaguilar, 5145 Pholus, 49469 Emilianomazzoni, 8089 Yukar, 66454 Terezabeatriz, 187680 Stelck

75q1 (173.438) \\aunt cynthia gives me a chance; visit to okinawa; 27052 Katebush, 6195 Nukariya, 2215 Sichuan, 5103 Divis, 14024 Procol Harum, 20377 Jakubisin, -10006 Saturn, 903 Nealley, 133537 Mariomotta, 20281 Kathartman, 18728 Grammier, 20286 Michta, 27613 Annalou, 30324 Pandya, 19982 Barbaradoore, 65672 Merrick, 28537 Kirapowell

39q1 (263.438) \\dark cloud, strange places, s12, i&R's books; 22782 Kushalnaik, 5997 Dirac, 128314 Coraliejackman, 229781 Arthurmcdonald, 5168 Jenner, 355 Gabriella, 27328 Pohlonski, 5356 Neagari, 22628 Michaelallen, 30155 Warmuth, 3858 Dorchester, 5944 Utesov, 458063 Gustavomuler, 5280 Andrewbecker, 24654 Fossett

111q1 (83.438) \\i&R and other backup identities; what I do on my day job; 2701 Cherson, 18735 Chubko, 106545 Colanduno, 21713 Michaelolson, 11184 Postma, 30724 Peterburgtrista, 2914 Glarnisch, 73891 Pietromennea, 1204 Renzia

qc257: focal representatives of the major political interest groups

15q1 (323.438) \\adc?... Yes! AI governors found this image (#167). At the time of MAJOR transition into the world, a kind of deal with the devil; 9375 Omodaka, 262876 Davidlynch, 19293 Dedekind, 22106 Tomokoarai, 10927 Vaucluse, 6506 Klausheide, 236 Honoria, 299755 Ericmontellese, 7169 Linda, 2762 Fowler, 17369 Eremeeva, 21685 Francomallia, 25049 Christofnorn, 3828 Hoshino, 27960 Dobias, 42614 Ubaldina, 53843 Antjiekrog, 5242 Kenreimonin, 17501 Tetsuro

87q1 (143.438) \\my going ice cold if I think I'm being attacked or setting myself up for attack; 2742 Gibson, 58535 Pattillo, 33014 Kalinich, 10975 Schelderode, 23888 Daikinoshita, 5955 Khromchenko, 26080 Pablomarques, 1227 Geranium, 13806 Darmstrong, 13281 Aliciahall, 13480 Potapov, 8405 Asbolus

51q1 (233.438) \\a plan to attack, executed; 29650 Toldy, 241418 Darmstadt, 7963 Falcinelli, 177967 Chouchihkang, 8691 Etsuko, 2473 Heyerdahl, 204710 Gaoxing, 7900 Portule, 7492 Kacenka, 9272 Liseleje, 152188 Morricone, 2904 Millman

123q11 (53.438) \\recovering after being attacked and getting out of it; 7238 Kobori, 133874 Jonnazucarelli, 31271 Nallino, 170395 Nicolevogt, 93102 Leroy, 291325 de Tyard, 34220 Pelagiamajoni

qc113: my quiet withdrawal of support under a vote of no confidence in another

27q1 (293.438) \\my connecting with hot or popular girls helps me prove a particular point; 1705 Tapio, 8972 Sylvatica, 18132 Spector, 18836 Raymundto, 735 Marghanna, 10872 Vaculik, 10462 Saxogrammaticus, 17962 Andrewherron, 34215 Stutigarg, 13994 Tuominen, 8006 Tacchini, 25958 Battams

99q1 (113.438) \\bodyguard as maleness | //frankenstein's monster keeps working at it | //institutional resonance | //mercenary allegiances; 8745 Delaney, 21521 Hippalgaonkar, 31489 Matthewchun, 28559 Anniedai, 11466 Katharinaotto, 3070 Aitken, 23712 Willpatrick, 175259 Offenberger, 8409 Valentaugustus, 7931

Kristianpedersen, 7509 Gamzatov, 6966 Vietoris, 2164 Lyalya, 11780 Thunder Bay, 1122 Neith, 18675 Amiamini

63q1 (203.438) \\called in as a substitute in uil; 11321 Tosimatumoto, 11360 Formigine, 7119 Hiera, 881 Athene, 13845 Jillburnett, 13679 Shinanogawa, 3555 Miyasaka, 9834 Kirsanov, 13672 Tarski, 28807 Lisawaller, 4761 Urrutia, 15120 Mariafelix, 96200 Oschin, 37786 Tokikonaruko, 6452 Johneuller, 1523 Pieksamaki, 12758 Kabudari, 13615 Manulis

135q1 (23.438) \\how I keep control of the house despite complaints; 85386 Payton, 58578 Zidek, 5440 Terao

qig138: your approach to procreativity

qc400: the lawn below

3q12 (353.229) \\ a great % of my naked body is designed for this group; lvz? nina hartley types; 25226 Brasch, 7408 Yoshihide, 1168 Brandia, 9579 Passchendaele, 15412 Schaefer, 2991 Bilbo, 25106 Ryoojungmin, 2687 Tortali, 5170 Sissons, 27500 Mandelbrot, 21677 Tylerlyon, 9529 Protopapa

75q12 (173.229) \\partner's emphasis on the necessity of the good life; also the thing I'd rather be doing which is not the lawn; 21637 Ninahuffman, 31697 Isaiahoneal, 25689 Duannihuang, 5266 Rauch, 22869 Brianmcfar, 13599 Lisbon, 27296 Kathyhurd, 29419 Mladkova, 22815 Sewell, 18092 Reinhold, 225254 Flury, 21484 Eppard, 20631 Stefuller, 13198 Banpeiyu, 22990 Mattbrenner, 283 Emma, 9670 Magni, 471143 Dziewanna, 21219 Mascagni, 13704 Aletesi, 1741 Giclas, 17035 Velichko, 160 Una

39q12 (263.229) \\haters; those who want my head do this; THE explanation for my relationship to the lawn; apparently the person who does my lawn hates doing it, so I should do it for now and have a robot do it later; 210532 Grantmckee, 37655 Illapa, 19458 Legault, 342843 Davidbowie, 22440 Bangsgaard, 129324 Johnweirich, 29157 Higashinihon, 20618 Daniebutler, 19730 Machiavelli, 5522 De Rop, 269252 Bogdanstupka, 1571 Cesco, 4896 Tomoegozen, 18524 Tagatoshihiro, 19017 Susanlederer, 1095 Tulipa, 23450 Birkenstock

111q12 (83.229) \\ REDACTED, kind of mb or REDACTED; me under REDACTED; others drawn to meet me while I'm doing the lawn; 4878 Gilhutton, 17842 Jorgegarcia, 52294 Detlef, 1184 Gaea, 27392 Valerieding, 40106 Erben, 7730 Sergerasimov

qc256: how events are orchestrated by political forces

15q12 (323.229) \\my surveying a thing until the time is right, then moving to acquire; the supervillain? My EXCELLENT timing; 1743 Schmidt, 30566 Stokes, 1452 Hunnia, 379173 Gamaovalia, 25405 Jeffwidder, 8849 Brighton, 28452 Natkondamuri, 6686 Hernius, 33604 McChesney, 4643 Cisneros, 199741 Weidner, 2760 Kacha

87q12 (143.229) \\the superhero when they are not being seen. What they are doing; 189011 Ogmios, 6813 Amandahendrix, 13930 Tashko, 8166 Buczynski, 33568 Godishala, 128065 Bartbenjamin, 57879 Cesarechiosi, 27515 Gunnels, 70782 Vinceelliott, 16702 Buxner, 69312 Rogerbacon, 21229 Susil, 25717 Ritikmal, 200002 Hehe

51q12 (233.229) \\the various fans and characters needed in order to make a superhero into what they are; 7062 Meslier, 16967 Marcosbosso, 4193 Salanave, 44473 Randytatum, 100309 Misuzukaneko, 28136 Chasegross, 4563 Kahnia, 49777 Cappi, 7421 Kusaka, 3201 Sijthoff, 3040 Kozai, 7061 Pieri, 19994 Tresini, 73491 Robmatson, 31203 Hersman, 15004 Vallerani, 15651 Tlepolemos, 5343 Ryzhov

123q1 (53.229) \\the superhero mandate; 18665 Sheenahayes, 33514 Changpeihsuan, 10806 Mexico, 20503 Adamtazi, 6526 Matogawa, 17286 Bisei, 4869 Piotrovsky, 133861 Debrawilmer

qc112: I hate to say this, but what you're creating cannot possibly be allowed as it is. My always having drawn friends either ~15 years younger or 15 years older than me, skirting the breaking of protocol in a couple of cases. There is an interesting parallel between this and my job/team work's major projects. investigate this. most likely i want to stay away from this kind of project

27q12 (293.229) \\my general grayness is tied to Ropakov / someone who knows my struggles; shanna's mom, hanging out with; 117736 Sherrod, 63129 Courtemanche, 41107 Ropakov, 16124 Timdong, 21269 Bechini, 34038 Abualragheb, 117714 Kiskartal, 15342 Assisi, 33191 Santiagostone, 10298 Jiangchuanhuang, 17770 Baume, 29491 Pfaff

99q12 (113.229) \\how shanna sees me as a partner? Earth's complex; 2975 Spahr, 120174 Jeffjenny, 111570 Agasvar, 8235 Fragonard, 26002 Angelayeung, 5193 Tanakawataru, 10237 Adzic, 1188 Gothlandia, 6625 Nyquist, 6022 Jyuro, 21330 Alanwhitman, 2423 Ibarruri

63q12 (203.229) \\what reasons your partner presents which block your interest in sex with them; 14741 Teamequinox, 9620 Ericidle, 3794 Sthenelos, 21306 Marani, 23069 Kapps, 2925 Beatty, 13493 Lockwood, 20952 Tydeus, 12173 Lansbergen, 5879 Almeria, 7403 Choustnik, 28125 Juliomiguez, 4418 Fredfranklin, 5352 Fujita, 14372

Paulgerhardt, 630 Euphemia, 3115 Baily, 27591 Rugilmartin, 73637 Guneus, 15199 Rodnyanskaya, 291855 Calabrocorrado, 15745 Yuliya, 12577 Samra, 6371 Heinlein

135q12 (23.229) \\\why your partner may find the idea of sex with you distasteful; 3431 Nakano, 17509 Ikumadan, 16901 Johnbrooks, 3845 Neyachenko

qig139: being seduced or purposely soothed

qc399: bodies I am weak against as my seducers

3q11 (353.021) \\a dilemma in AI; running ai in a stream; 20616 Zeeshansayed, 8608 Chelomey, 196772 Fritzleiber, 52291 Mott, 2044 Wirt, 176884 Jallynsmith, 9279 Seager, 13577 Ukawa, 5357 Sekiguchi, 6948 Gounelle, 16900 Lozere

75q11 (173.021) \\ir recounting the male strip club, later me recounting twos and ...; romano; my ai images; 24158 Kokubo, 27439 Kamimura, 24045 Unruh, 39543 Aubriet, 92525 Delucchi, 134069 Miyo, 19155 Lifeson, 17905 Kabtamu, 17543 Sosva, 3414 Champollion, 24052 Nguyen, 100051 Davidhernandez, 4897 Tomhamilton, 24711 Chamisso, 1262 Sniadeckia, 6758 Jesseowens, 2911 Miahelena, 293499 Wolinski

39q11 (263.021) \\when closing in on a choice for a body to publicize, this is what happens. My lived experience of something that will later be bragworthy; 8492 Kikuoka, 8084 Dallas, 9346 Fernandel, 90455 Irenehernandez, 100047 Leobaeck, 34259 Abprabhakaran, 1821 Aconcagua, 32298 Kunalshroff, 167852 Maturana, 9860 Archaeopteryx, 33902 Ingoldsby, 25688 Hritzo, 28916 Logancollins, 2346 Lilio, 7638 Gladman, 22465 Karelandel, 30847 Lampert, 15740 Hyakumangoku, 12866 Yanamadala, 8298 Loubna, 4335 Verona, 31043 Sturm, 30235 Kimmiller

111q11 (83.021) \\my seducer in action; 3195 Fedchenko, 9725 Wainscoat, 55543 Nemeghaire, 3416 Dorrit, 26689 Smorrison, 20760 Chanmatchun, 6938 Soniaterk, 10501 Ardmacha

qc255: the issues around which people seem to harness their political sides

15q11 (323.021) \\my elementary school experiences; starting with shanna at the rally; 28137 Helenyao, 18928 Pontremoli, 24649 Balaklava, 2905 Plaskett, 22734 Theojones, 27373 Davidvernon, 111468 Alba Regia, 2312 Duboshin, 204816 Andreacamilleri, 11623 Kagekatu, 17427 Poe

87q11 (143.021) \\charging for access to ...; 20352 Pinakibose, 24750 Ohm, 14683 Remy, 6567 Shigemasa, 11015 Romanenko, 48047 Houghten, 13117 Pondicherry, 2782 Leonidas, 4311 Zguridi, 11500 Tomaiyowit

51q11 (233.021) \\the idealized contours partner; spacetime, Sâvitrî; 25368 Gailcolwell, 12465 Perth Amboy, 32623 Samuelkahn, 12674 Rybalka, 58184 Masayukiyamamoto, 24734 Kareness, 22435 Pierfederici, 6250 Saekohayashi, 13643 Takushi, 9382 Mihonoseki, 2707 Ueferji, 23865 Karlsorensen, 15523 Grenville, 21660 Velenia, 9069 Hovland, 25138 Jaumann, 1323 Tugela

123q12 (53.021) \\only certain people passing into my circle; 274301 Wikipedia, 6626 Mattgenge, 172505 Kimberlyespy, 1409 Isko, 33582 Tiashajoardar

qc111: this qcross describes my pre-sleep guardians, drunken thoughts, advice, and imaginary friends from childhood

27q11 (293.021) \\~shanna's mom interaction; my interaction with mb; 6179 Brett, 131245 Bakich, 18745 San Pedro, 29687 Mohdreza, 250606 Bichat, 9742 Worpswede, 21575 Padmanabhan, 16445 Klimt

99q11 (113.021) \\mb's role; 22901 Ivanbella, 7857 Lagerros, 8078 Carolejordan, 4950 House, 51406 Massimocalvani, 37706 Trinchieri, 215841 Cimelice, 3234 Hergiani, 6262 Javid, 5686 Chiyonoura, 18924 Vinjamoori, 70710 Chuckfellows, 18493 Demoleon, 4583 Lugo

63q11 (203.021) \\my skeptical but prospering review of friendships after mb; 10340 Jostjahn, 14223 Dolby, 11911 Angel, 15126 Brittanyanderson, 6125 Singto, 18379 Josevandam, 27899 Letterman, 15663 Periphas, 5547 Acadiau, 16974 Iphthime, 7607 Billmerline, 6083 Janeirabloom, 79144 Cervantes, 6475 Refugium, 3739 Rem, 25358 Boskovice, 167208 Lelekovice

135q11 (23.021) \\mb's reception of me as we closed—what I gave which she picked up more of; 20649 Miklenov, 15856 Yanokoji, 30160 Danielbruce, 3688 Navajo, 30184 Okasinski, 22171 Choi, 33196 Kaienyang, 175452 Chenggong, 21798 Mitchweegman

qig140: out of your control, but likely in your favor later

qc398: attempting to reconcile for another, wishful thinking

3q10 (352.813) \\related to living with REDACTED; incites imagination, but also traps the "corrupt" and for that reason should not be chased via 75q10; 248262 Liuxiaobo, 33624 Omersiddiqui, 11460 Juliafang, 29910 Segre

75q10 (172.813) \\me defaulting to the reconciler role when I want to start something. Very easy to resist; me defaulting to the solicitor role when I want something. hard to resist, and will prove ineffective; 17091 Senthalir, 11145 Emanuelli, 10125 Stenkyrka, 22536 Katelowry, 27342 Joescanio, 41206 Sciannameo, 23411 Bayanova, 6753 Fursenko, 1740 Paavo Nurmi, 2414 Vibeke, 17095 Mahadik, 1467 Mashona, 6882

Sormano, 297409 Mallgan, 29886 Randytung, 186142 Gillespie, 9609 Ponomarevalya

39q10 (262.813) \\lewis & clark, the wright bros; the mario bros; a pioneer duo; 31975 Johndean, 9208 Takanotoshi, 6 Hebe, 369 Aeria, 14835 Holdridge, 21531 Billcollin, 15908 Bertoni, 26441 Nanayakkara, 23191 Sujaytyle, 8121 Altdorfer, 129196 Mitchbeiser, 49384 Hubertnaudot, 12790 Cernan, 55873 Shiomidake, 6578 Zapesotskij, 5780 Lafontaine, 10958 Mont Blanc, 28934 Meagancurrie, 34791 Ericcraine, 2656 Evenkia, 2663 Miltiades

111q10 (82.813) \\the pioneers' work which serves to recruit all; 21814 Shanawolff, 8967 Calandra, 21073 Darksky, 3186 Manuilova, 4867 Polites, 31037 Mydon

qc254: transformative boss figure who is more a myth than a reality, and the actors and situations she interacts with

15q10 (322.813) \\leaving the house in order to rent it; adg; 2141 Simferopol, 129152 Jaystpierre, 2395 Aho, 11451 Aarongolden, 65821 De Curtis, 4822 Karge, 6185 Mitsuma, 5236 Yoko, 738 Alagasta, 189264 Gerardjeong, 129188 Dangallagher, 255073 Victoriabond

87q10 (142.813) \\hindsight renders a former thorn in my side more palatable; 8717 Richviktorov, 9175 Graun, 30389 Ledoux, 21862 Joshuajones, 7788 Tsukuba, 21160 Saveriolombardi, 15462 Stumegan, 8224 Fultonwright, 53093 La Orotava, 21400 Ahdout, 316202 Johnfowler, 34104 Jeremiahpate

51q10 (232.813) \\reducing what I give to ungrateful interactants, requiring more assurances instead; 35357 Haraldlesch, 26467 Jamespopper, 15938 Bohnenblust, 1251 Hedera, 8237 Constable, 15898 Kharasterteam, 20204 Yuudurunosato, 26333 Joachim, 4958 Wellnitz, 50866 Davidesprizzi, 21795 Masi, 13097 Lamoraal, 11682 Shiwaku, 25617 Thomasnesch, 34189 Ambatipudi, 32096 Puckett, 30308 Ienli

123q10 (52.813) \\how I take in difficult information and attempt to understand it in terms of things I can fix within; 22542 Pendri, 211375 Jessesteed, 8799 Barnouin

qc110: easily gleaning information about a trying situation

27q10 (292.813) \\the pankhudi-REDACTED interaction. Weird how these go together; 33556 Brennanclark, 24318 Vivianlee, 33622 Sedigh, 3404 Hinderer, 3086 Kalbaugh, 5165 Videnom, 509 Iolanda, 12147 Bramante, 5433 Kairen, 30829 Wolfwacker, 17936 Nilus, 30371 Johngorman, 6902 Hideoasada, 207341 Isabelmartin, 4670 Yoshinogawa

99q10 (112.813) \\how I think others are judging me ilo 27q10; when tornio happens, we're done; 446 Aeternitas, 7511 Patcassen, 9819 Sangerhausen, 129095 Martyschmitzer, 14994 Uppenkamp, 1016 Anitra, 207931 Weihai, 39854 Gabriopiola, 9824 Marylea, 21720 Pilishvili, 75225 Corradoaugias, 1018 Arnolda, 89664 Pignata, 1471 Tornio, 4920 Gromov

63q10 (202.813) \\me realizing I'm getting wrapped up in another's grid. Deeply buried upset. More rarely, passion and closeness; 9956 Castellaz, 6598 Modugno, 11547 Griesser, 4555 Josefaperez, 4124 Herriot, 2586 Matson, 18009 Patrickgeer, 2358 Bahner, 3796 Lene, 5479 Grahamryder, 4487 Pocahontas, 185744 Hogan, 12133 Titulaer, 22809 Kensiequade, 21989 Werntz, 353 Ruperto-Carola, 19367 Pink Floyd, 3415 Danby

135q10 (22.813) \\lighthearted interaction with lg or mom despite massive confusion; 151362 Chenkegong, 18161 Koshiishi, 5450 Sokrates, 10566 Zabadak, 5833 Peterson

qig141: this role of yours is actually more for the world

qc397: relationship boxes I have ended up in

3q9 (352.604) \\the m.o. I grow into as I learn what the world will and will not help with, and where I fit there; priya, auguste, keith, emily kind of, kls, REDACTED, REDACTED, REDACTED; 8243 Devonburr, 12358 Azzurra, 7042 Carver, 207321 Crawshaw, 195900 Rogersudbury, 4648 Tirion, 10464 Jessie, 153686 Pathall, 241475 Martingedeck, 33221 Raqueljacobson, 376029 Blahova, 21952 Terry, 22905 Liciniotoso

75q9 (172.604) \\my old insistence in nsbe; 281445 Scotthowe, 31854 Darshanashah, 4076 Dorffel, 236616 Gray, 69421 Keizosaji, 7679 Asiago, 78429 Baschek, 20828 Linchen, 32014 Bida, 152226 Saracole, 5513 Yukio, 14361 Boscovich, 28644 Michaelzhang, 31580 Bridgetoei

39q9 (262.604) \\staying with a half-assed relationship until patience runs out; 175411 Yilan, 3009 Coventry, 10952 Vogelsberg, 9105 Matsumura, 133007 Audreysimmons, 257515 Zapperudi, 7896 Svejk, 11494 Hibiki, 4739 Tomahrens, 99942 Apophis, 838 Seraphina, 6340 Kathmandu, 6973 Karajan, 25905 Clerico, 227770 Wischnewski, 3446 Combes, 17891 Buraliforti, 449 Hamburga

111q9 (82.604) \\busted by REDACTED with simeona, but I can probably control much of this narrative. This opposition indicates that things will only get worse; 34234 Andrewfang, 120188 Amyaqueche, 52005 Maik, 668 Dora, 8032 Michaeladams, 178256 Juanmi, 218900 Gabybuchholz, 9506 Telramund, 100485 Russelldavies,

31431 Cabibbo, 5507 Niijima, 12165 Ringleb, 8766 Niger, 10272 Yuko, 11927 Mount Kent, 170008 Michaelstrauss

qc253: rallying the forces

15q9 (322.604) \\my chain evaluation process, across AI images, for example; 17720 Manuboccuni, 48607 Yamagatatemodai, 4985 Fitzsimmons, 15868 Akiyoshidai, 26414 Amychyao, 5335 Damocles, 129342 Ependes, 9463 Criscione, 4125 Lew Allen, 13963 Euphrates, 18702 Sadowski, 90711 Stotternheim, 78431 Kemble, 11206 Bibee, 7556 Perinaldo, 31087 Oirase

87q9 (142.604) \\issues beneath the first in class veneer; 1429 Pemba, 58417 Belzoni, 9179 Satchmo, 16180 Rapoport, 22250 Konstfrolov, 225 Henrietta, 4393 Dawe, 5344 Ryabov, 8903 Paulcruikshank, 25298 Fionapaine

51q9 (232.604) \\my liberal use of loops in knime; the implied preference for pairs and repeatability in most things I do; 5737 Itoh, 12557 Caracol, 3021 Lucubratio, 7600 Vacchi, 129882 Ustica, 14990 Zermelo, 20174 Eisenstein, 288961 Stasysgirenas, 7317 Cabot, 6414 Mizunuma, 13498 Al Chwarizmi, 21962 Scottsandford, 8275 Inca, 359 Georgia, 4993 Cossard, 5683 Bifukumonin, 2407 Haug, 15169 Wilfriedboland, 23198 Norvell, 2318 Lubarsky

123q9 (52.604) \\rappers and funk declaration, the time - pandemonium; mc's don't know what they're doing. Time for the real; 7362 Rogerbyrd, 20589 Hennyadmoni, 10978 Barbchen, 8019 Karachkina, 10064 Hirosetamotsu, 497 Iva, 10611 Yanjici, 126445 Prestonreeves, 1961 Dufour, 5097 Axford

qc109: who I show up as in times of collective trial or change; how I behaved prosocially for the first time during hurricane helene in 9/2024. I reflected on this in 135q9, triggering 99q9 in my tetrad elsewhere

27q9 (292.604) \\witnessing a baby being born. Girls partnering more strongly after I disappear from access; 934 Thuringia, 3630 Lubomir, 6553 Seehaus, 282669 Erguel, 13389 Stacey, 6385 Martindavid, 14006 Sakamotofumio, 5158 Ogarev, 37601 Vicjen, 7597 Shigemi, 3381 Mikkola, 626 Notburga, 27458 Williamwhite

99q9 (112.604) \\me carrying people through s.o.s.—my primary persona during iadt's closure; 13395 Deconihout, 21435 Aharon, 3805 Goldreich, 15916 Shigeoyamada, 2242 Balaton, 6825 Irvine, 112233 Kammerer, 17556 Pierofrancesca, 129561 Chuhachi, 4469 Utting, 303710 Velpeau, 5319 Petrovskaya, 8464 Polishook, 11095 Havana, 23742 Okadatatsuaki, 12374 Rakhat, 10948 Odenwald, 4235 Tatishchev, 31584 Emaparker, 1704 Wachmann

63q9 (202.604) \\the environments I kept up during the school closing days. 209. iadt in general. This is likely THE route to a lifelong association with two girls. Need to stop the 27q9s and 99q9s, but with shanna that's not easy unless I cheat. Which of course won't happen; 15553 Carachang, 6036 Weinberg, 4947 Ninkasi, 3374 Namur, 20593 Freilich, 4025 Ridley, 4476 Bernstein, 12593 Shashlov, 129119 Ericmuhle, 26642 Schlenoff, 922 Schlutia, 28049 Yvonnealex, 4281 Pounds, 24201 Davidkeith, 6731 Hiei

135q9 (22.604) \\bg & alo; why I think of a pair when reflecting on the exploratory days. To obtain, I need to live out the 63q9s; 16650 Sakushingakuin, 25290 Vibhuti, 47045 Seandaniel, 15742 Laurabassi, 8935 Beccaria, 6649 Yokotatakao, 3399 Kobzon

qig142: the act of communicating

qc396: how I want the world to receive me and my work

4q8 (352.396) \\where I execute my daily work; this setup seems to favor distance, because my being close makes people feel worse by default. Probably a dispositor thing; 18365 Shimomoto, 55737 Coquimbo, 9870 Maehata, 10122 Froding, 14764 Kilauea, 408 Fama, 6111 Davemckay, 10348 Poelchau

76q8 (172.396) \\astraea, 3? But I really will need to have met my goals first in the square; degrader dynamic, baroqueai and the strange series. I project this onto the women I like via 4q8; 20527 Dajowestrich, 10673 Berezhnoy, 6741 Liyuan, 325368 Ihorhuk, 2976 Lautaro, 80180 Elko, 34004 Gregorini, 140620 Raoulwallenberg, 6128 Lasorda, 65658 Gurnikovskaya, 1338 Duponta, 240871 MOSS, 9691 Zwaan, 4483 Petofi, 10670 Seminozhenko, 27197 Andrewliu, 1082 Pirola, 4106 Nada, 10031 Vladamolda

40q8 (262.396) \\the perfectionistic artist or lead scientist contributes to all despite being pushy; 279397 Dombeck, 352860 Monflier, 25384 Partizanske, 7487 Toshitanaka, 185633 Rainbach, 17225 Alanschorn, 32108 Jovanzhang, 18751 Yualexandrov, 5734 Noguchi, 30149 Kellyriedell, 8534 Knutsson, 136803 Calliemorgan, 227767 Enkibilal, 23837 Matthewnanni, 3103 Eger, 14940 Freiligrath, 139 Juewa, 16155 Buddy, 6293 Oberpfalz, 3445 Pinson

112q8 (82.396) \\the need to grow as a response to insults I have experienced; 11690 Carodulaney, 270472 Csorgei, 16514 Stevelia, 178679 Piquette, 3751 Kiang, 249516 Aretha, 17492 Hippasos, 205698 Troiani, 1879 Broederstroom, 33433 Maurilia, 7850 Buenos Aires, 15945 Raymondavid

qc252: me and sg in cooperative business

16q8 (322.396) \\speaking at dare; negatively, the gossip train after someone thinks I have burned them; me and sg hanging out; 11359 Piteglio, 30190 Alexshelby, 13222 Ichikawakazuo, 185364 Sunweihsin, 233880 Urbanpriol, 100007 Peters, 3109 Machin

88q8 (142.396) \\leaving former allies in the lurch; 27047 Boisvert, 8735 Yoshiosakai, 15526 Kokura, 31875 Saksena, 142757 Collinge, 19354 Fredkoehler, 23751 Davidprice, 1331 Solvejg, 8371 Goven, 32724 Woerlitz, 18938 Zarabeth, 24945 Houziaux

52q8 (232.396) \\holding onto sata, but difficulty performing its duties; 152454 Darnyi, 22572 Yuanzhang, 8556 Jana, 321046 Klushantsev, 133293 Andrushivka, 23182 Siyaxuza, 21125 Orff, 25781 Rajendra, 95247 Schalansky, 8286 Kouji, 4337 Arecibo, 28660 Derbes

124q8 (52.396) \\my conception of a former convicted person who won't cross a certain line anymore; me and caution in the partner terrain; 6116 Still, 429033 Gunterwendt, 3237 Victorplatt, 19848 Yeungchuchiu, 3375 Amy, 12042 Laques, 1930 Lucifer, 21858 Gosal, 278225 Didierpelat, 7017 Uradowan, 5861 Glynjones

qc108: night thoughts, less so drunken thoughts; the nightfly

28q8 (292.396) \\intimate interaction with shanna, her as receiver; 9019 Eucommia, 204836 Xiexiaosi, 21550 Laviolette, 14479 Plekhanov, 16013 Schmidgall, 24173 SLAS, 8113 Matsue, 136273 Csermely, 14789 GAISH, 110026 Hamill, 16128 Kirfrieda, 13197 Pontecorvo, 16749 Vospini, 48458 Merian, 18636 Villedepompey

100q8 (112.396) \\storyable experiences at the edge of the forbidden; 20358 Dalem, 154554 Heatherelliott, 22294 Simmons, 7094 Godaisan, 22474 Frobenius, 357546 Edwardhalbach, 23044 Starodub, 25232 Schatz

64q8 (202.396) \\bad timing or form by the one who likes me; there is an interesting relationship between the chest and the lips here in the unfolding human embryo which warrants further investigation, particularly in terms of tissue signaling in eventually distant organ systems; 151242 Hajos, 3596 Meriones, 25584 Zhangnelson, 15385 Dallolmo, 19476 Denduluri, 3019 Kulin, 39799 Hadano, 5389 Choikaiyau, 90528 Raywhite, 21568 Evanmorikawa, 7369 Gavrilin, 2524 Budovicium, 11302 Rubicon, 38461 Jiritrnka, 1752 van Herk, 9762 Hermannhesse, 13009 Voloshchuk, 12176 Hidayat, 5067 Occidental, 12362 Mumuryk

136q8 (22.396) \\game changing effects on the situations I enter. Choice which decides the ultimate record of the one chosen against; 127517 Kaikepan, 100733 Annafalcka, 18563 Danigoldman, 507 Laodica, 414 Liriope

qig143: if you had your way, this is how it would go…

qc395: hearing and the big girl; seems to relate to ear shape

4q7 (352.188) \\smh—how I got in, dad didn't give up; 7218 Skacel, 5089 Nadherna, 5644 Maureenbell, 33907 Christykrenek, 269300 Diego, 13995 Toravere

76q7 (172.188) \\how the smh committee saw me?| I KNEW IT!! smh—>; @ the prestigious school; 18158 Nigelreuel, 266 Aline, 2017 Wesson, 316201 Malala, 233522 Moye, 37749 Umbertobonori, 21729 Kimrichards, 4982 Bartini, 79316 Huangshan, 246821 Satyarthi, 4602 Heudier, 134150 Bralower, 10665 Ortigao, 13037 Potosi, 11685 Adamcurry, 10197 Senigalliesi, 16817 Onderlicka, 20302 Kevinwang

40q7 (262.188) \\how I am hoped for by the big girl. Whether this is the best option will depend on the squares; 114828 Ricoromita, 2167 Erin, 26659 Skirda, 32768 Alexandripatov, 5250 Jas, 13367 Jiri, 2485 Scheffler, 5074 Goetzoertel, 185577 Hhaihao, 7445 Trajanus, 2290 Helffrich, 9372 Vamlingbo, 201308 Hansgrade, 216 Kleopatra, 274020 Skywalker, 25340 Segoves, 6282 Edwelda, 3654 AAS, 4574 Yoshinaka

112q7 (82.188) \\the very big girl. Or the brat; 508 Princetonia, 29656 Leejoseph, 26688 Wangenevieve, 12852 Teply, 1873 Agenor, 17520 Hisayukiyoshio, 208499 Shokasonjuku

qc251: sg and the incubator money. Can I do this with blacks everywhere as a client base?

16q7 (322.188) \\the evolution of agd (the first "daughter?"); 5873 Archilochos, 8793 Thomasmuller, 350 Ornamenta, 1581 Abanderada, 11263 Pesenon, 29133 Vargas, 33190 Sigrest, 6411 Tamaga

88q7 (142.188) \\one or more of my books; 14501 Tetsuokojima, 9127 Brucekoehn, 2227 Otto Struve, 301021 Sofiarodriguez, 34190 Erinsmith, 15355 Maupassant, 170009 Subbarao, 25638 Ahissar, 4972 Pachelbel, 32893 van der Waals, 18560 Coxeter, 26268 Nardi, 9143 Burkhead, 3113 Chizhevskij, 4114 Jasnorzewska, 22945 Schikowski, 46539 Viktortikhonov, 2476 Andersen

52q7 (232.188) \\my producing a sweeping enough body of work to be reloaded as data; 11369 Brazelton, 31954 Georgiebotev, 15918 Thereluzia, 28426 Sangani, 39429 Annebronte, 159799 Kralice, 6007 Billevans, 1304 Arosa, 120038 Franlainsher, 9508 Titurel, 12380 Sciascia, 5722 Johnscherrer

124q7 (52.188) \\hosting the guests in a semi-technical affair, teaching at jri; 2739 Taguacipa, 5334 Mishima, 157271 Gurtovenko

qc107: my fierce working of the land

28q7 (292.188) \\my energy during intimate interaction, what I project/give, recruiting the dogs unintentionally; 12410 Donald Duck, 18115 Rathbun, 12482 Pajka, 10332 Defi, 2018 Schuster, 6092 Johnmason, 12799 von Suttner, 10306 Pagnol, 15399 Hudec, 6768 Mathiasbraun, 260724 Malherbe

100q7 (112.188) \\letting someone in, now having to keep an eye on them; 4792 Lykaon, 6669 Obi, 3741 Rogerburns, 12437 Westlane, 58664 IYAMMIX, 2773 Brooks, 20360 Holsapple, 167875 Kromminga, 4240 Grun, 34080 Clarakeng, 108953 Pieraerts

64q7 (202.188) \\chico; 43859 Naoyayano, 129064 Jeanneladewig, 12252 Gwangju, 8931 Hirokimatsuo, 8668 Satomimura, 2443 Tomeileen, 4694 Festou, 175 Andromache, 3917 Franz Schubert, 26969 Biver, 21453 Victorlevine, 92213 Kalina, 291847 Ladoix, 13133 Jandecleir, 1298 Nocturna, 5023 Agapenor, 79087 Scheidt, 59830 Reynek, 30299 Shashkishore, 33418 Jacksonweaver, 40227 Tahiti, 242830 Richardwessling

136q7 (22.188) \\underailed assembly-line style pruning process; 34166 Neildeshmukh, 7301 Matsuitakafumi, 321357 Mirzakhani, 32544 Debjaniroy, 316020 Linshuhow, 7430 Kogure, 323 Brucia

qig144: a characteristic "pursuit" going on around you

qc394: interruptive idea generation

4q6 (351.979) \\shanna's or mom's approach to topics in her home spoken / phone conversations. REDACTED's revolt; g of v's turn; 832 Karin, 5008 Miyazawakenji, 8663 Davidjohnston, 702 Alauda, 124192 Moletai, 348407 Patkosandras, 6059 Diefenbach, 345971 Marktorrence, 13315 Hilana

76q6 (171.979) \\shanna's or mom's phone conversations; 3603 Gajdusek, 14122 Josties, 40917 Pauljorden, 26502 Traviscole, 3266 Bernardus, 17100 Kamiokanatsu, 2057 Rosemary, 7141 Bettarini, 202819 Carlosanchez, 21110 Karlvalentin, 23788 Cofer, 11881 Mirstation

40q6 (261.979) \\AI images while I am doing other things. Interruptive; 9565 Tikhonov, 962 Aslog, 321485 Cross, 13499 Steinberg, 10647 Meesters, 10183 Ampere, 115449 Robson, 84340 Jos, 8435 Anser, 22736 Kamitaki, 28516 Mobius, 54439 Topeka, 20339 Eileenreed, 242 Kriemhild, 11005 Waldtrudering, 13111 Papacosmas, 8158 Herder, 31823 Viete, 212981 Majalitovic, 496 Gryphia, 5111 Jacliff

112q6 (81.979) \\simeona. Easily. Then sherry. Then dg; who is this in 2024?; 27314 Janemcdonald, 1085 Amaryllis, 31230 Tuyouyou, 890 Waltraut, 2114 Wallenquist, 271235 Bellay, 7465 Munkanber, 4923 Clarke, 367488 Aloisortner

qc250: I define myself against the semi-stranger. A CRITICAL qcross in my chart

16q6 (321.979) \\assorted circumstances under which there were fights; me handling sg; 11450 Shearer, 54362 Restitutum, 10810 Lejsturojr, 5088 Tancredi, 359103 Ottopiene, 8393 Tetsumasakamoto, 1334 Lundmarka, 5432 Imakiire, 12697 Verhaeren, 142756 Chiu, 135978 Agueros, 666 Desdemona, 13305 Danielang, 20780 Chanyikhei, 12615 Mendesdeleon

88q6 (141.979) \\pitching s.o.s.; mostly simeona; 11657 Antonhajduk, 2676 Aarhus, 1896 Beer, 13118 La Harpe, 14094 Garneau, 2484 Parenago, 4545 Primolevi, 37607 Regineolsen, 163819 Teleki, 33961 Macinleyneve, 28004 Terakawa, 127196 Hanaceplechova, 2322 Kitt Peak, 20151 Utsunomiya, 13380 Yamamohammed, 3419 Guth, 2209 Tianjin

52q6 (231.979) \\events I've sponsored which have brought or announced conflict; what sg brought to the table; 17247 Vanverst, 49987 Bonata, 121001 Liangshanxichang, 13014 Hasslacher, 117413 Ramonycajal, 13055 Kreppein, 6464 Kaburaki, 10131 Stanga, 4499 Davidallen, 6661 Ikemura, 10446 Siegbahn, 71461 Chowmeeyee, 79826 Finardi, 8424 Toshitsumita

124q6 (51.979) \\me working out the appropriate alchemy on a situation via asteroids; 1642 Hill, 129332 Markhunten, 330836 Orius, 11008 Ernst, 31984 Unger, 32389 Michflannory, 14158 Alananderson, 5797 Bivoj

qc106: taking a stance against an oppressive situation

28q6 (291.979) \\where the ejaculate goes—what events it contributes to. More abstractly, the kinds of spaces which receive your completed creative packages. THIS is the energy ruiner, part of the 2-day bad day complex. My book readers in abstract space? DECLARE NO ALIGNMENT; 11001 Andrewulff, 16479 Paulze, 73442 Feruglio, 5177 Hugowolf, 77 Frigga, 1760 Sandra, 5805 Glasgow, 29355 Siratakayama, 6197 Taracho

100q6 (111.979) \\through repeated challenges, writing books that warn and teach; 10651 van Linschoten, 188139 Stanbridge, 8682 Kraklingbo, 18697 Kathanson, 4831 Baldwin

64q6 (201.979) \\ two girls in the explored foreign land after the destruction of something in a (possibly 3rd) seeker's life; critical for ajani; 12284 Pohl, 16690 Fabritius, 19980 Barrysimon, 215592 Normarose, 27991 Koheijimiura, 10226 Seishika, 6101 Tomoki, 4205 David Hughes, 2061 Anza, 14088 Ancus, 70720 Davidskillman, 21481 Johnwarren, 3827 Zdenekhorsky, 13463 Antiphos, 7383 Lassovszky, 207585 Lubar, 1791 Patsayev, 48422 Schrade, 8225 Emerson

136q6 (21.979) \\a family characteristic; humanistic inquisitiveness across a new terrain; 3312 Pedersen, 27736 Ekaterinburg, 3314 Beals, 21477 Terikdaly, 6568 Serendip, 3456 Etiennemarey, 8449 Maslovets, 3910 Liszt, 5673 McAllister

qig1: your appearance reifies your interactants' conceptions

qc393: the extreme ends of my sexual preferences

4q5 (351.771) \\tgirl construct; | \\what simeona or dg wanted; I have all the male tools, but have the attraction style of a woman—as if I am like a tgirl—ko'an similarity of outlook; 15360 Moncalvo, 13752 Grantstokes, 249540 Eugeniescott, 6757 Addibischoff, 6519 Giono, 2198 Ceplecha, 27493 Derikesibill, 2936 Nechvile, 24541 Hangzou

76q5 (171.771) \\restless, trying to find extreme outlets for sexual discontent with partner; 11981 Boncompagni, 11257 Rodionta, 11596 Francetic, 18192 Craigwallace, 4987 Flamsteed, 22144 Linmichaels, 1552 Bessel, 17567 Hoshinoyakata, 1151 Ithaka, 5199 Dortmund, 27985 Remanzacco, 246167 Joskohn, 91428 Cortesi, 52309 Philnicolai, 10967 Billallen, 13196 Rogerssmith, 31491 Demessie, 6600 Qwerty, 75072 Timerskine, 423097 Richardjarrell, 13351 Zibeline, 157396 Vansevicius, 20639 Michellouie

40q5 (261.771) \\the buildup of my posts on dark ...; 10990 Okunev, 18059 Cavalieri, 26544 Ajjarapu, 130314 Williamodonnell, 25823 Dentrujillo, 211378 Williamwarneke, 8704 Sadakane, 2036 Sheragul, 15273 Ruhmkorff, 22722 Timothycooper, 10177 Ellison, 5127 Bruhns, 34177 Amandawilson

112q5 (81.771) \\the three-based confidence I learned growing up, and the thing I actually know how to give the partner; 11219 Benbohn, 1341 Edmee, 1802 Zhang Heng, 2249 Yamamoto, 17652 Nepoti, 18024 Dobson, 7005 Henninghaack, 13825 Booth, 89735 Tommei, 11914 Sinachopoulos, 6899 Nancychabot

qc249: how I grow up to respond to relationships in light of watching my REDACTED and REDACTED

16q5 (321.771) \\my REDACTED attacks my REDACTED, but who knows this? Opposite my mars, making this the kind of relationship I have the best chance of steering. CRITICAL. As long as this region is a problem for me, doing the squares will be near impossible; 46737 Anpanman, 5738 Billpickering, 11449 Stephwerner, 2474 Ruby, 20140 Costitx, 2736 Ops, 3491 Fridolin, 3156 Ellington, 7398 Walsh, 75842 Jackmonahan

88q5 (141.771) \\our ee trio got to the peak of its influence, and was silenced. Khalid ibn al walid. Iwamoto mars; the lifestyle that can't be kept up in the family; 10149 Cavagna, 1136 Mercedes, 4951 Iwamoto, 65213 Peterhobbs, -10004 Mars, 294295 Brodardmarc, 32037 Deepikakurup, 986 Amelia, 96 Aegle, 11827 Wasyuzan, 88906 Moutier, 33451 Michaelarney, 2000 Herschel, 72827 Maxaub, 34708 Grasset, 6481 Tenzing, 29467 Shandongdaxue

52q5 (231.771) \\ REDACTED's experience with me, a causal relationship which eventually turns sour; mom; 14627 Emilkowalski, 73862 Mochigasechugaku, 3452 Hawke, 1021 Flammario, 6659 Pietsch, 556 Phyllis, 1211 Bressole, 5419 Benua, 13376 Dunphy, 18749 Ayyubguliev, 3832 Shapiro, 12277 Tajimasatonokai, 6153 Hershey, 15438 Joegotobed, 192293 Dominikbrunner, 134008 Davidhammond, 15843 Comcom

124q5 (51.771) \\i definitely gain from ending relationships—may be a reason I get into them. However, stopping this is necessary for the mars dynamic to work. As long as I am doing my research, the ... dynamic will struggle to occur, as will the mars in general; 85559 Villecroze, 10739 Lowman, 27363 Alvanclark, 4672 Takuboku

qc105: obligated land and property maintenance

28q5 (291.771) \\what you or the representative experience after mating. The pregnancy? This is negative in my chart, so it's important that I understand how to repurpose it; 3762 Amaravella, 20892 MacChnoic, 13608 Andosatoru, 9424 Hiroshinishiyama, 199574 Webbert, 8203 Jogolehmann, 16906 Giovannisilva, 19916 Donbass, 21636 Huertas, 1722 Goffin

100q5 (111.771) \\the mayhem I endure with the current woman in my life (partner); 10934 Pauldelvaux, 2490 Bussolini, 7494 Xiwanggongcheng, 4396 Gressmann, 8152 Martinlee, 20450 Marymohammed, 42365 Caligiuri, 66939 Franscini, 8683 Sjolander, 65001 Teodorescu, 7435 Sagamihara, 10430 Martschmidt, 2047 Smetana

64q5 (201.771) \\the path I've chosen over the path of regular social circles; 12766 Paschen, 163255 Adrianhill, 7392 Kowalski, 1114 Lorraine, 9517 Niehaisheng, 513 Centesima, 129985 Jimfreemantle, 428 Monachia, 315166 Pawelmaksym, 21999 Disora, 20451 Galeotti, 22843 Stverak, 1420 Radcliffe, 159826 Knapp, 3809 Amici,

12625 Koopman, 34893 Mihomasatoshi, 3469 Bulgakov, 19288 Egami, 4211 Rosniblett, 66843 Pulido, 10761 Lyubimets

136q5 (21.771) \\my work updates and tasks I'm commissioned to resolve; 5282 Yamatotakeru, 11098 Ginsberg, 16078 Carolhersh, 30374 Bobbiehinson, 9392 Cavaillon, 3865 Lindbloom, 14057 Manfredstoll, 23241 Yada, 10606 Crocco

qig2: your interactional reifications (interacTIONs turned into objects)

qc392: my eyes on the historical prize

4q4 (351.563) \\girls who only tolerated me; people like REDACTED, or REDACTED who like me, but may not realize how unattached I really am; 8109 Danielwilliam, 1800 Aguilar, 23265 von Wurden, 18176 Julianhong, 3238 Timresovia, 10039 Keet Seel, 7677 Sawa

76q4 (171.563) \\my spontaneous thoughts about my future progress and current state; 2801 Huygens, 3652 Soros, 34252 Orlovsky, 14134 Penkala, 25657 Berkowitz, 2568 Maksutov, 21581 Ernestoruiz, 33012 Eddieirizarry, 12704 Tupolev, 9988 Erictemplebell, 849 Ara, 8941 Junsaito, 30241 Donnamower, 31598 Danielrudin, 2380 Heilongjiang, 25088 Yoshimura

40q4 (261.563) \\me and keith's journey, and my half; 28602 Westfall, 212796 Guoyonghuai, 1270 Datura, 7294 Barbaraakey, 34143 Heeric, 10526 Ginkogino, 286841 Annemieke, 78392 Dellinger, 5381 Sekhmet, 73638 Likhanov, 15950 Dallago, 14309 Defoy, 6977 Jaucourt, 11926 Orinoco, 21778 Andrewarren, 138221 Baldry, 31698 Nikolaiortiz, 12398 Pickhardt, 11240 Piso, 10293 Pribina, 108201 Di Blasi, 1347 Patria, 3002 Delasalle, 13115 Jeangodin

112q4 (81.563) \\the work in which I model and am remembered; 159011 Radomyshl, 100268 Rosenthal, 3484 Neugebauer, 96876 Andreamanna, 340 Eduarda, 2127 Tanya, 96623 Leani, 10469 Krohn, 4837 Bickerton, 34142 Sachinkonan, 18125 Brianwilson, 10781 Ritter, 19539 Anaverdu

qc248: how the family lifestyle is gradually built up, despite difficulties

16q4 (321.563) \\hm. The situations that play out more as I get older; 3331 Kvistaberg, 390848 Veerle, 29725 Mikewest, 13580 de Saussure, 10601 Hiwatashi, 27121 Joardar, 465 Alekto

88q4 (141.563) \\what I do a lot more of in maturity than I did before; 4430 Govorukhin, 365131 Hassberge, 18874 Raoulbehrend, 3563 Canterbury, 6219 Demalia, 3166 Klondike, 7573 Basfifty, 10201 Korado, 150145 Uvic, 11446 Betankur, 8839 Novichkova, 11476 Stefanosimoni, 3305 Ceadams

52q4 (231.563) \\publicly blowing up a rival's agenda or diverting it; 94356 Naruto, 17694 Jiranek, 1041 Asta, 7828 Noriyositosi, 18032 Geiss, 31375 Krystufek, 29477 Zdiksima, 4065 Meinel, 8307 Peltan, 3623 Chaplin, 4647 Syuji, 21913 Taylorjones, 13209 Arnhem, 21752 Johnthurmon, 12182 Storm, 151997 Bauhinia, 22848 Chrisharriot, 12774 Pfund, 10198 Pinelli, 97637 Blennert, 14960 Yule, 8979 Clanga, 8818 Hermannbondi, 23733 Hyojiyun, 28823 Archibald

124q4 (51.563) \\the (always positive or funny) music in the background of my inability to move. By playing this music or decorating my world in it (the albums), I may be able to render SATA and its administrivia more tolerable; building up a body of work to silence my detractors; dad's career; 2769 Mendeleev, 20266 Danielchoi, 1921 Pala, 16022 Wissnergross, 9938 Kretlow, 35269 Idefix, 1389 Onnie, 15620 Beltrami, 199953 Mingnaiben, 1763 Williams, 627 Charis, 2977 Chivilikhin, 6241 Galante

qc104: my responses to the imposed removal of choice

28q4 (291.563) \\how the mate indicates they have received what you've given? Aksnes-like? The more they display this, the more thoroughly they have accepted your creation; 103966 Luni, 1363 Herberta, 24728 Scagell, 7198 Montelupo, 8155 Battaglini, 11595 Monsummano, 32609 Jamesfagan, 43722 Carloseduardo, 4973 Showa, 14914 Moreux, 6129 Demokritos, 27988 Menabrea, 219067 Bossuet, 3143 Genecampbell, 1434 Margot, 17176 Viktorov

100q4 (111.563) \\if I had had children, they would have seen my high contempt for their mom—no matter which woman filled this role; earth vs wine ilo ezra; 4747 Jujo, 75562 Wilkening, 3437 Kapitsa, 11364 Karlstejn, 21301 Zanin, 4575 Broman, 16012 Jamierubin, 10875 Veracini, 370 Modestia

64q4 (201.563) \\how I assemble the choices available to me; 5314 Wilkickia, 36235 Sergebaudo, 24604 Vasilermakov, 1165 Imprinetta, 12561 Howard, 14792 Thyestes, 129158 Michaelmellman, 149243 Dorothynorton, 25021 Nischaykumar, 362911 Miguelhurtado, 25543 Fruen, 12490 Leiden, 11949 Kagayayutaka, 1084 Tamariwa, 1560 Strattonia, 19952 Ashkinazi, 11955 Russrobb, 26293 Van Muyden, 17351 Pheidippos, 49109 Agnesraab, 3274 Maillen

136q4 (21.563) \\amidst tension, predisposed to take everything on the table and leave with it, rendering myself a martyr or hero in the process no matter how in the wrong I may be; 206185 Yip, -10001 Moon, 7299 Indiawadkins, 80179 Vaclavknoll, 120 Lachesis

qig3: throwing your energy out there

qc391: keeping distance from the partner's values to assert other goals

4q3 (351.354) \\the person I'm with making a big deal out of things. Apparently too much of this really can cost my health via the opposition to pamal. Undercutting the competition and those kinds of business strategy; 208915 Andrewashcraft, 2192 Pyatigoriya, 993 Moultona, 20164 Janzajic, 31095 Buneiou, 1922 Zulu, 8247 Cherylhall, 31716 Matoonder, 95771 Lachat, 10104 Hoburgsgubben, 9436 Shudo, 8738 Saji

76q3 (171.354) \\having to hold in default behaviors and absorb bad energy, with only the occasional controlled quip to offset it; 23950 Tsusakamoto, 5200 Pamal, 3684 Berry, 10866 Peru, 7203 Sigeki, 18293 Pilyugin, 39791 Jameshesser, 39882 Edgarmitchell, 4611 Vulkaneifel, 317809 Marot, 11753 Geoffburbidge, 300334 Antonalexander, 33587 Arianakim

40q3 (261.354) \\working out more, adding savi to form interrogation; 23032 Fossey, 18242 Peebles, 117586 Twilatho, 216591 Coetzee, 3337 Milos, 81203 Polynesia, 26682 Evanfletcher, 4511 Rembrandt, 7974 Vermeesch, 6084 Bascom, 10811 Lau

112q3 (81.354) \\definitely how I dress, reflects me being myself regardless of what others want to see; 3248 Farinella, 90953 Hideosaitou, 11703 Glassman, 2381 Landi, 3245 Jensch

qc247: relationship assessment, continuing on through it since the alternatives aren't good

16q3 (321.354) \\farmhouse, me and sb in a prejudiced area; 204896 Giorgiobocca, 18647 Vaclavhubner, 33516 Timonen, 3961 Arthurcox, 28822 Angelabarker, 32776 Nriag, 33415 Felixwang, 7594 Shotaro, 34995 Dainihonshi, 5893 Coltrane, 34419 Corning, 15395 Rukl, 2155 Wodan

88q3 (141.354) \\dad's events: where I get noticed for my thinking or field creation, the doc story 4/24/2024 working VARIOUS REDACTED during REDACTED. Whitley makes this kind of work harder w women, because w men, the limits are already built in; 214928 Carrara, 3613 Kunlun, 153284 Frieman, 80135 Zanzanini, 155784 Ercol, 4779 Whitley, 6112 Ludolfschultz, 625 Xenia, 23131 Debenedictis, 33614 Meganploch, 15294 Underwood, 26546 Arulmani, 27928 Nithintumma, 54862 Sundaigakuen

52q3 (231.354) \\where I am overlooked as one who has earned his qualifications; 14224 Gaede, 12641 Hubertushenrichs, 10733 Georgesand, 1116 Catriona, 5819 Lauretta, 3699 Milbourn, 16406 Oszkiewicz, 3505 Byrd, 853 Nansenia, 177415 Queloz, 4168 Millan, 7691 Brady, 27071 Rangwala, 24761 Ahau, 14734 Susanstoker, 3567 Alvema

124q3 (51.354) \\how I study and write; 9667 Amastrinc, 15779 Scottroberts, 15939 Fessenden, 3859 Borngen, 33532 Gabriellacoli, 21587 Christopynn, 10346 Triathlon

qc103: domestic distance—just enough for partner and I to be attached, but not so attached that there are obligations or obligated direction of dreams for each other

28q3 (291.354) \\REDACTED | #reproductive organ form; stuff dad was interested in; 1464 Armisticia, 54820 Svenders, 161989 Cacus, 14026 Esquerdo, 17885 Brianbeyt, 618 Elfriede, 188256 Stothoff, 6976 Kanatsu, 33912 Melissanoland, 32066 Ramayya, 4346 Whitney, 91199 Johngray, 22487 Megphillips, 8702 Nakanishi, 52975 Cyllarus, 22630 Wallmuth

100q3 (111.354) \\country music messages, desperado; 11815 Viikinkoski, 4446 Carolyn, 52767 Ophelestes, 5542 Moffatt, 20305 Feliciayen, 33264 Maryrogers, 2042 Sitarski, 11813 Ingorichter, 15763 Nagakubo, 3906 Chao, 1658 Innes, 2807 Karl Marx, 21367 Edwardpleva, 25198 Kylienicole

64q3 (201.354) \\my taking assault from kvt; mr romano; 1712 Angola, 145709 Rocknowar, 29439 Maxfabiani, 24346 Lehienphan, 4087 Part, 5387 Casleo, 3820 Sauval, 7845 Mckim, 261690 Jodorowsky, 20331 Bijemarks, 30362 Jenniferdean, 243096 Klauswerner, 23922 Tawadros, 5862 Sakanoue, 27372 Ujifusa

136q3 (21.354) \\REDACTED losing her temper immediately over something she doesn't like. I guess I do this too; 21529 Johnjames, 157332 Lynette, 3162 Nostalgia, 8553 Bradsmith, 17902 Britbaker, 163623 Miknaitis, 9426 Aliante, 7073 Rudbelia, 18026 Juliabaldwin, 21428 Junehokim

qig4: body emphases

qc390: I view my own pro-creative potency

4q2 (351.146) \\me as a mural or forum host, especially as an instructor; 2613 Plzen, 10089 Turgot, 120361 Guido, 5832 Martaprincipe, 16962 Elizawoolard, 21750 Tartakahashi

76q2 (171.146) \\the kind of attention I pay to myself in between exercise reps; simeona; 23895 Akikonakamura, 22148 Francislee, 24337 Johannessen, 18681 Caseylipp, 4180 Anaxagoras, 9218 Ishiikazuo, 512 Taurinensis, 21661 Olgagermani, 5272 Dickinson, 2256 Wisniewski, 378917 Stefankarge, 25915 Charlesmcguire, 99905 Jeffgrossman, 25562 Limdarren

40q2 (261.146) \\how I change in my presentation; 90944 Pujol, 1216 Askania, 5350 Epetersen, 10426 Charlierouse, 22616 Bogolyubov, 3774 Megumi, 2090 Mizuho, 30396 Annleonard, 7517 Alisondoane, 85466 Krastins, 1839 Ragazza, 1626 Sadeya, 13224 Takamatsuda

112q2 (81.146) \\my interface with the public as an author; 11094 Cuba, 3044 Saltykov, 110299 Iceland, 8945 Cavaradossi, 144552 Jackiesue, 6224 El Goresy, 8335 Sarton, 55678 Lampos, 14174 Deborahsmall, 6639 Marchis

qc246: distancing myself in crowded social conversations. A MAJOR characteristic of mine

16q2 (321.146) \\the beautiful observed object, me sitting in the airport as a sensualized foreigner; where I will not talk in a crowded conversation; 1268 Libya, 51261 Holusa, 32065 Radulovacki, 10797 Guatemala, 5101 Akhmerov, 77696 Patriciann, 16888 Michaelbarber, 964 Subamara, 39314 Moritakumi, 1351 Uzbekistania, 653 Berenike, 16986 Archivestef

88q2 (141.146) \\sitting quietly and observing ones with whom I have an affinity, as in airports; what are you seeing in them? 2-6; 26837 Yoshitakaokazaki, 12045 Klein, 982 Franklina, 2982 Muriel, 20813 Aakashshah, 1509 Esclangona, 75836 Warrenastro, 8852 Buxus, 12820 Robinwilliams, 34031 Fukumitsu

52q2 (231.146) \\learning w dave; a gregarious other takes over the exchange; 4960 Mayo, 15363 Ysaye, 1521 Seinajoki, 166229 Palanga, 7894 Rogers, 4220 Flood, 58595 Joepollock, 4080 Galinskij, 30431 Michaeltran, 7863 Turnbull, 218998 Navi, 470 Kilia, 26004 Loriying, 297 Caecilia

124q2 (51.146) \\discovering more over cross-cultural travels—the only context under which I learn what I'm truly eager to learn; this whole cross is pretty boring, so 16-2 is probably the best unless I am in the middle of traveling, then 88-2; 176014 Vedrana, 9871 Jeon, 25140 Schmedemann

qc102: what I do and don't communicate to the partner in general, policing this to avoid trouble

28q2 (291.146) \\THE FIGHT... against a mob; 73692 Gurtler, 1854 Skvortsov, 25455 Anissamak, 17904 Annekoupal, 6754 Burdenko, 58215 von Klitzing, 30928 Jefferson, 3477 Kazbegi, 1205 Ebella, 33806 Shrivastava, 8010 Bohnhardt, 2404 Antarctica, 7117 Claudius, 3500 Kobayashi

100q2 (111.146) \\an ever-forward eye towards progression; an overall summary of my ongoing mentality; 17860 Roig, 79271 Bellagio, 96193 Edmonton, 4965 Takeda, 3672 Stevedberg, 15368 Katsuji, 11009 Sigridclose, 20624 Dariozanetti, 81822 Jamesearly, 7158 IRTF, 8327 Weihenmayer, 19447 Jessicapearl, 19084 Eilestam, 8407 Houlahan, 2916 Voronveliya, 19023 Varela, 1358 Gaika

64q2 (201.146) \\bridget w. Where you are NOT allowed to pass through for learning. The rejection letter recipients; 26401 Sobotiste, 2494 Inge, 29430 Mimiyen, 25769 Munaoli, 12504 Nuest, 3645 Fabini, 69288 Berlioz, 45073 Doyanrose, 15303 Hatoyamamachi, 6827 Wombat, 24316 Anncooper, 6610 Burwitz, 42295 Teresateng, 26264 McIntyre, 361 Bononia, 12742 Delisle, 4383 Suruga

136q2 (21.146) \\me being sent off to my first school by mom; 11264 Claudiomaccone, 24974 Macuch, 11871 Norge, 58682 Alenasolcova, 6072 Hooghoudt, 21399 Bateman, 20208 Philiphe

qig5: you as ready to stir up the energy

qc389: the girly girls help me go forward

4q1 (350.938) \\ REDACTED's final rebellion; the event that got me banned from caltech. This is calm when the opposition is calm; 5320 Lisbeth, 8538 Gammelmaja, 129167 Dianelambert, 1352 Wawel, 30187 Jamesroney, 32085 Tomback, 6149 Pelcak, 16238 Chappe, 185639 Rainerkling, 207603 Liuchaohan, 18156 Kamisaibara, 6124 Mecklenburg

76q1 (170.938) \\working hard, working outside, for example. Helps sap my interest in the girly girls; 20330 Manwell, 367404 Andreasrebers, 21114 Bernson, 16524 Hausmann, 12613 Hogarth, 16696 Villamayor, 4169 Celsius, 105222 Oscarsaa, 23685 Toaldo, 1504 Lappeenranta, 168948 Silvestri, 13213 Maclaurin, 250840 Motorhead, 25018 Valbousquet, 12926 Brianmason, 24609 Evgenij, 827 Wolfiana, 121332 Jasonhair, 26732 Damianpeach, 20531 Stevebabcock, 48628 Janetfender, 117713 Kovesligethy, 13220 Kashiwagura, 3539 Weimar, 24999 Hieronymus

40q1 (260.938) \\the girly girls "think" this instead of me. I don't really; 16253 Griffis, 400193 Castion, 187981 Soluri, 31593 Romapradhan, 134127 Basher, 6260 Kelsey, 2878 Panacea, 6338 Isaosato, 151590 Fan, 7175 Janegoodall, 3632 Grachevka

112q1 (80.938) \\me engaging the girly girl autosources; 32207 Mairepercy, 21413 Albertsao, 6237 Chikushi, 27864 Antongraff, 21915 Lavins, 14873 Shoyo, 21826 Youjiazhong

qc245: I write the book of contours in response to a kind of event space I never want to see again. Once contours is out, the two competing qunits will never be easily allowed thereafter

16q1 (320.938) \\REDACTED, the slave, the one I take care of; 3609 Liloketai, 1436 Salonta, 30004 Mikewilliams, 29528 Kaplinski, 535 Montague

88q1 (140.938) \\finally deciding I need a slave. My attitude in demanding exactly what I want; 952 Caia, 20606 Widemann, 6082 Timiryazev, 9150 Zavolokin, 3633 Mira, 29750 Chleborad, 435728 Yunlin, 20272 Duyha, 8494 Edpatvega, 14564 Heasley, 43890 Katiaottani

52q1 (230.938) \\bullshitty high stress work under REDACTED; I can't stand being in this position and refuse to sign on to do it ever again. Requires a roleplayer to execute without hating the one you assist; my Jansky doesn't like this; 3140 Stellafane, 6312 Robheinlein, 17056 Boschetti, 21423 Credo, 11363 Vives, 158 Koronis, 34540 Protesilaos, 3663 Tisserand, 10429 van Woerden, 9322 Lindenau, 22880 Pulaski, 4355 Memphis, 136743 Echigo, 3716 Petzval, 9161 Beaufort, 40230 Rozmberk, 18662 Erinwhite, 7687 Matthias

124q1 (50.938) \\me while working w REDACTED and REDACTED; if I can do this successfully, I won't need a slave; 3712 Kraft, 2394 Nadeev, 7159 Bobjoseph, 11299 Annafreud, 1914 Hartbeespoortdam, 7986 Romania

qc101: interrupting someone to solicit them. CRITICAL, note the near square to moon

28q1 (290.938) \\where pre-sexual exchange may be the last thing left before we break completely; also, being accosted amidst the foreign; 5061 McIntosh, 127803 Johnvaneepoel, 1578 Kirkwood, 10171 Takaotengu, 253412 Raskaylea, 32938 Ivanopaci, 27457 Tovinkere, 4003 Schumann

100q1 (110.938) \\the various ways to interrupt me, which I don't like; jvb; 25513 Weseley, 11818 Ulamec, 13500 Viscardy, 21694 Allisowilson, 4348 Poulydamas, 20074 Laskerschueler, 81971 Turonclavere, 199950 Sierpc, 18845 Cichocki, 12897 Bougeret, 178113 Benjamindilday, 22874 Haydeephelps, 268115 Williamalbrecht, 2723 Gorshkov, 7452 Izabelyuria, 1872 Helenos, 525 Adelaide, 4817 Gliba, 516560 Annapolisroyal

64q1 (200.938) \\the quest through asteroids and their stories; even if inaccurate, still works; the canadians; 199986 Chervone, 120308 Deebradel, 27390 Kyledavis, 5817 Robertfrazer, 4306 Dunaevskij, 65541 Kasbek, 18022 Pepper, 14515 Koichisato, 14605 Hyeyeonchoi, 7437 Torricelli, 2378 Pannekoek, 4463 Marschwarzschild, 9002 Gabrynowicz, 229864 Sichouzhilu, 25032 Randallray, 18360 Sachs, 9912 Donizetti, 18602 Lagillespie, 129966 Michaelward, 29646 Polya, 17000 Medvedev, 15838 Auclair, 230736 Jalyhome, 19081 Mravinskij, 5147 Maruyama, 332530 Canders

136q1 (20.938) \\where I was this person or after dad died, who I became and how I saw things; 19439 Allisontjong, 9671 Hemera, 3323 Turgenev, 11759 Sunyaev, 187700 Zagreb, 12353 Marquez, 32571 Brayton

qig6: clubs

qc388: the priorities of those in my enclave: doesn't appear to be very favorable

4q12 (350.729) \\REDACTED leaving everyone else hanging. I eventually did this to mb as well; 22278 Protitch, 7485 Changchun, 5712 Funke, 243546 Fengchuanliu, 117874 Picodelteide, 21698 McCarron, 7754 Gopalan, 20362 Trilling, 24455 Kanuchova, 115331 Shrylmiles, 63389 Noshiro, 8436 Leucopsis, 767 Bondia, 33420 Derekwoo

76q12 (170.729) \\mb, stressed on the inside; 695 Bella, 70444 Genovali, 7602 Yidaeam, 8097 Yamanishi, 26668 Tonyho, 1730 Marceline, 317 Roxane, 9006 Voytkevych, 23732 Choiseungjae, 208 Lacrimosa, 3421 Yangchenning, 30054 Pereira, 482 Petrina, 21457 Fevig

40q12 (260.729) \\me as a teaching statistical astrologer, more via forum; 24409 Caninquinn, 10006 Sessai, 5276 Gulkis, 291633 Heyun, 3840 Mimistrobell, 6123 Aristoteles, 15382 Vian, 282903 Masada, 10365 Kurokawa, 2106 Hugo, 1744 Harriet, 29204 Ladegast, 29659 Zeyuliu, 170007 Strateva, 189000 Alfredkubin, 727 Nipponia, 97631 Kentrobinson, 9704 Georgebeekman, 58097 Alimov, 4626 Plisetskaya, 22540 Mork, 6632 Scoon, 6550 Parler, 30328 Emilyspencer, 14513 Alicelindner, 33464 Melahudock, 1566 Icarus, 10709 Ottofranz

112q12 (80.729) \\my rings and piercings; 309704 Baruffetti, 14829 Povalyaeva, 22410 Grinspoon, 2050 Francis, 20536 Tracicarter, 47002 Harlingten, 21686 Koschny, 3641 Williams Bay, 13933 Charleville, 5190 Fry

qc244: kvt. How enclave-mates receive my victories. Negative. Unless I have to through 88q12, I eventually stop using this qcross, never to return

16q12 (320.729) \\my being dragged into a club, or dragging myself there. A roundly poor experience never to be attempted again except under the most special circumstances; 15761 Schumi, 27087 Tillmannmohr, 18949 Tumaneng, 14669 Beletic, 2556 Louise, 46686 Anitasohus, 4624 Stefani, 7830 Akihikotago, 33454 Neilclaffey, 3338 Richter, 33343 Madorobin, 11965 Catullus

88q12 (140.729) \\the nightfly, ajani across time, jazz dives, spoken word; that which made REDACTED and others jealous?; 12170 Vanvollenhoven, 55381 Lautakwah, 5369 Virgiugum, 346889 Rhiphonos, 22527 Gawlik, 136518 Opitz, 24274 Alliswheeler, 24305 Darrellparnell, 251325 Leopoldjosefine, 31020 Skarupa, 6437

Stroganov, 4956 Noymer, 11793 Chujkovia, 11945 Amsterdam, 368588 Lazrek, 21919 Luga

52q12 (230.729) \\shanna telling the dogs bye, the dogs freaking out; 1948 Kampala, 9770 Discovery, 133077 Jirsik, 21467 Rosenstein, 11148 Einhardress, 29624 Sugiyama, 10789 Mikeread, 46568 Stevenlee, 33408 Mananshah, 13922 Kremenia, 371220 Angers

124q12 (50.729) \\how I appear to strangers, at work in the yard; 31719 Davidyue, 33725 Robertkent, 8861 Jenskandler, 7853 Confucius, 34718 Cantagalli, 330856 Ernsthelene, 34181 Patnaik, 9230 Yasuda, 2421 Nininger, 11288 Okunohosomichi, 210444 Frithjof, 21704 Mikkilineni, 2594 Acamas, 22605 Steverumsey, 29189 Udinsk

qc100: let's prosper together! Or not

28q12 (290.729) \\that which must be correct if you are to mate at all; 450390 Pitchcomment, 185554 Bikushev, 31523 Jessemichel, 10480 Jennyblue, 2947 Kippenhahn, 31463 Michalgeci, 269762 Nocentini, 26793 Bolshoi, 1956 Artek, 164792 Owen, 14846 Lampedusa, 1169 Alwine, 19531 Charton, 10155 Numaguti

100q12 (110.729) \\the impression of disagreements or tension over money and progress vs actual bonding, with two partners focusing on different things; 21700 Caseynicole, 187636 Chungyuan, 8456 Davegriep, 11804 Zambon, 79130 Bandanomori, 29618 Jinandrew, 3837 Carr, 20567 McQuarrie, 1040 Klumpkea, 92685 Cordellorenz, 17508 Takumadan

64q12 (200.729) \\gangsta rap, DPG absorption. Square the 28s, most likely defends me against early bullying, but also defies making a stable impression; 6667 Sannaimura, 170 Maria, 9796 Robotti, 15077 Edyalge, 9561 van Eyck, 9193 Geoffreycopland, 1419 Danzig, 7555 Venvolkov, 4619 Polyakhova, 7152 Euneus, 6353 Semper, 20304 Wolfson, 479 Caprera, 4581 Asclepius, 9240 Nassau, 9449 Petrbondy, 18653 Christagunt, 22686 Mishchenko

136q12 (20.729) \\drunken, buzzed, or spaced out thoughts; 5000 IAU, 28366 Verkuil, 83360 Catalina

qig7: the stabilizer amidst unspecification

qc387: my views of cheaters, kept at a distance

4q11 (350.521) \\the distant individual who currently encapsulates my ideals, though there are likely barriers to communication regarding this; 6439 Tirol, 835 Olivia, 33619 Dominickrowan, 3602 Lazzaro, 3178 Yoshitsune, 5053 Chladni, 8246 Kotov, 78434 Dyer, 5226 Pollack, 174363 Donyork

76q11 (170.521) \\what I perceive when my brain is going, making little observations—mostly about what is on another person's mind; an affinity with spiders and, because of 46720, the exercise of a certain kind of seduction at work; 4412 Chephren, 12716 Delft, 22280 Mandragora, 799 Gudula, 20345 Davidvito, 4863 Yasutani, 14815 Rutberg, 2899 Runrun Shaw, 3262 Miune, 46720 Pierostroppa, 13416 Berryman, 248970 Giannimorandi, 367693 Montmagastrell, 10943 Brunier, 25085 Melena, 9677 Gowlandhopkins, 8141 Nikolaev, 1860 Barbarossa, 214487 Baranivka, 13739 Nancyworden, 9356 Elineke

40q11 (260.521) \\what I think going in with the cheater stands to offer me; 2435 Horemheb, 23062 Donnamooney, 12566 Derichardson, 45687 Pranverahyseni, 2135 Aristaeus, 13350 Gmelin, 20228 Jeanmarcmari, 117329 Spencer, 50718 Timrobertson, 4560 Klyuchevskij, 13176 Kobedaitenken

112q11 (80.521) \\in league with those who cheat - the other person as the "cheater"; 8836 Aquifolium, 3356 Resnik, 24662 Gryll, 178008 Picard, 5802 Casteldelpiano, 5840 Raybrown, 21659 Fredholm

qc243: my true close family. Keith and shanna, priya and auguste

16q11 (320.521) \\Saturday activities?; 9937 Triceratops, 6769 Brokoff, 2015 Kachuevskaya, 4884 Bragaria, 8448 Belyakina, 12477 Haiku, 14942 Stevebaker, 24605 Tsykalyuk, 478 Tergeste, 28678 Lindquester, 181562 Paulrosendall

88q11 (140.521) \\chasing a goal with no mind to admit to attaining it already. Goes against my buddhism; 19813 Ericsands, 16268 Mcneeley, 11702 Mifischer, 7507 Israel, 8013 Gordonmoore, 6165 Frolova, 20483 Sinay, 11225 Borden, 25930 Spielberg, 28494 Jasmine, 12978 Ivashov, 31684 Lindsay, 2658 Gingerich, 27710 Henseling, 236987 Deustua, 11517 Esteracuna, 5948 Longo, 15133 Sullivan, 20259 Alanhoffman, 15702 Olegkotov, 24940 Sankichiyama, 843 Nicolaia

52q11 (230.521) \\the argument we gave for s.o.s.; sata seer as a necessity?; 5362 Johnyoung, 29199 Himeji, -10007 Uranus, 7265 Edithmuller, 6565 Reiji, 171381 Taipei, 18826 Leifer, 12912 Streator, 10193 Nishimoto, 590 Tomyris, 7267 Victormeen, 3502 Huangpu, 10850 Denso, 157258 Leach, 20278 Qileihang, 3324 Avsyuk, 31151 Sajichugaku, 30050 Emilypang

124q11 (50.521) \\my repeatedly going back to astro; 11691 Easterwood, 8760 Crex, 18148 Bellier, 12585 Katschwarz, 7172 Multatuli

qc99: SIER, saving humans as data—the effort

28q11 (290.521) \\she shows up as usual, but this time things are broken; 99928 Brainard, 8652 Acacia, 5301 Novobranets, 18243 Gunn, 1815 Beethoven, 25565 Lusiyang, 18862 Warot, 11510 Borges, 9792 Nonodakesan, 467 Laura, 8596 Alchata, 26922 Samara

100q11 (110.521) \\analytical essays; 11187 Richoliver, 15146 Halpov, 3214 Makarenko, 190026 Iskorosten, 8181 Rossini, 4020 Dominique, 2178 Kazakhstania, 23749 Thygesen, 34011 Divyakranthi, 257234 Guntherkurtze, 16398 Hummel

64q11 (200.521) \\my half-attentive probing—struggling to find the leak; 24260 Krivan, 2222 Lermontov, 21482 Patashnick, 1949 Messina, 20219 Brianstone, 18149 Colombatti, 2540 Blok, 4604 Stekarstrom, 21631 Stephenhonan, 769 Tatjana, 2156 Kate, 4123 Tarsila, 3037 Alku, 12688 Baekeland, 3345 Tarkovskij, 223360 Svankmajer, 2083 Smither, 12022 Hilbert, 121659 Blairrussell

136q11 (20.521) \\the downpour. Me or the house coming across castlevania-style; 5098 Tomsolomon, 32808 Bischoff, 5614 Yakovlev, 8457 Billgolisch, 7277 Klass, 7156 Flaviofusipecci, 4407 Taihaku, 28757 Seanweber, 295565 Hannover, 231969 Sebvauclair, 237845 Neris, 31573 Mohanty, 29394 Hirokohamanowa

qig8: the nichemates are inclined to say this...

qc386: the desire to live beyond traditional family life

4q10 (350.313) \\REDACTED rules, protocol, and a general controlled community environment; the leather culture of the people who taught me such things in the beginning; 4744 Rovereto, 494 Virtus, 3890 Bunin, 1315 Bronislawa, 11942 Guettard, 208916 Robertcaldwell

76q10 (170.313) \\my REDACTED posts; general online journalling; 69311 Russ, 8440 Wigeon, 10516 Sakurajima, 25180 Kenyonconlin, 19400 Emileclaus, 10928 Caprara, 3979 Brorsen, 15955 Johannesgmunden, 4699 Sootan, 18877 Stevendodds, 15530 Kuber, 6583 Destinn, 17024 Costello, 2790 Needham, 34123 Uedayukika, 8414 Atsuko, 4898 Nishiizumi

40q10 (260.313) \\the duchess archetype, jhall, shanna, romero; 1322 Coppernicus, 280640 Ruetsch, 1628 Strobel, 2111 Tselina, 121352 Taylorhale, 1405 Sibelius, 4208 Kiselev, 333639 Yaima, 18780 Kuncham, 1213 Algeria, 4961 Timherder, 3932 Edshay, 238771 Juhaszbalazs

112q10 (80.313) \\my view of standard family life, especially bucket list related; interestingly, the western plants of the house and egress paths are the spaces which force certain modifications to the house, and are where the mailbox lives. There is also some of this on the eastern side, Ramses the Great?; 13765 Nansmith, 25945 Moreadalleore, 52293 Mommsen, 3422 Reid, 3033 Holbaek, 550 Senta, 128341 Dalestanbridge, 4326 McNally, 42 Isis, 7581 Yudovich, 52421 Daihoji, 146921 Michaelbuckley, 2734 Hasek, 24060 Schimenti

qc242: me and shanna—partners and lovers (sometimes)

16q10 (320.313) \\my role in my career field; sk; 9008 Bohsternberk, 29220 Xavierbaptista, 3884 Alferov, 309 Fraternitas, 28866 Chakraborty, 130161 Iankubik, 3150 Tosa

88q10 (140.313) \\the return to default shape after exercises; 127005 Pratchett, 145588 Sudongpo, 3583 Burdett, 204786 Wehlau, 5349 Paulharris, 31516 Leibowitz, 17942 Whiterabbit, 15917 Rosahavel, 149163 Stevenconard, 51741 Davidixon, 5750 Kandatai

52q10 (230.313) \\our elusive creativity which operates on its own schedule; 3349 Manas, 30119 Lucamatone, 22754 Olympus, 31916 Arnehensel, 7564 Gokumenon, 4649 Sumoto, 5312 Schott, 24994 Prettyman, 34281 Albritton, 55844 Bicak, 26396 Chengjingjie, 26500 Toshiohino, 3778 Regge, 5588 Jennabelle, 6065 Chesneau, 200069 Alastor, 19132 Le Clezio

124q10 (50.313) \\my being deployed into the good life (but by whom?); 7624 Gluck, 21359 Geng, 855 Newcombia, 8648 Salix, 30448 Yoshiomoriyama

qc98: eventually, notoriousness

28q10 (290.313) \\the moment I decide an arrangement just won't work; probably related to my buddhism; 5975 Otakemayumi, 48425 Tischendorf, 8387 Fujimori, 200003 Aokeda, 100000 Astronautica, 5204 Herakleitos, 159629 Brunszvik, 21619 Johnshopkins, 2576 Yesenin, 376 Geometria

100q10 (110.313) \\my kindred; 8466 Leyrat, 34100 Thapa, 1962 Dunant, 44039 de Sahagun, 6075 Zajtsev, 90 Antiope, 2763 Jeans, 25014 Christinepalau, 11437 Cardalda, 11159 Mizugaki, 7389 Michelcombes, 6642 Henze, 8855 Miwa

64q10 (200.313) \\my desire to ultimately be a notorious social figure; 36182 Montigiani, 5553 Chodas, 132792 Scottsmith, 28568 Jacobjohnson, 299 Thora, 28599 Terenzoni, 757 Portlandia, 475 Ocllo, 11328 Mariotozzi, 26699 Masoncole, 19499 Eugenybiryukov, 5756 Wassenbergh, 31028 Cerulli, 21430 Brubrew, 211343 Dieterhusar, 32060 Wyattpontius, 38671 Verdaguer, 6943 Moretto, 52261 Izumishikibu, 24157 Toshiyanagisawa, 30027 Anubhavguha, 9246 Niemeyer, 2983

Poltava, 5439 Couturier, 5259 Epeigeus, 8036 Maehara, 4276 Clifford, 14436 Morishita, 209083 Rioja

136q10 (20.313) \\the effect I (want to) have on society; 7449 Dollen, 4000 Hipparchus, 28740 Nathanspery, 174 Phaedra, 5532 Ichinohe

qig9: what the partners are thinking

qc385: what takes place before sleep

4q9 (350.104) \\being on REDACTED's team, a fly on the wall in a meeting I have no power to influence; 13412 Guerrieri, 16594 Sorachi, 12013 Sibatahosimi, 164268 Hajmasi, 16929 Hurnik, 178987 Jillianredfern, 1125 China, 210292 Mayongsheng

76q9 (170.104) \\pre-sleep fantasy return; simeona's feeling or sg; 13822 Stevedodson, 1519 Kajaani, 129060 Huntskretsch, 16014 Sinha, 2743 Chengdu, 236851 Chenchikwan, 33419 Wellman, 30955 Weiser, 196945 Guerin, 28091 Mikekane, 12135 Terlingen, 12620 Simaqian, 33869 Brunnermatt, 3945 Gerasimenko, 33829 Asherson

40q9 (260.104) \\the dogs and TV activity next door before sleep; 561 Ingwelde, 12006 Hruschka, 196411 Umurhan, 117595 Jemmadavidson, 198820 Iwanowska, 6868 Seiyauyeda, 1619 Ueta, 1293 Sonja, 28800 Speth, 7816 Hanoi, 33189 Ritzdorf, 368 Haidea

112q9 (80.104) \\shanna's end of day commentary before sleep, TV; 11943 Davidhartley, 290001 Uebersax, 5711 Eneev, 3455 Kristensen, 19658 Sloop, 279410 McCallon, 20333 Johannhuth, 5219 Zemka, 13920 Montecorvino, 5768 Pittich

qc241: my exacting focus on data production and what ultimately ends up being done with this

16q9 (320.104) \\pushing through the inconvenient phases of my publication process; 6635 Zuber, 8076 Foscarini, 19551 Peterborden, 9231 Shimaken, 13638 Fiorenza, 176866 Kuropatkin, 5169 Duffell, 4666 Dietz

88q9 (140.104) \\mb's general significator; 12112 Sprague, 7043 Godart, 4516 Pugovkin, 17807 Ericpearce, 7336 Saunders, 21188 Kiyohiro, 3483 Svetlov, 4979 Otawara, 2263 Shaanxi, 15145 Ritageorge, 23756 Daniellozano, 20500 Avner, 12442 Beltramemass, 6320 Bremen, 129 Antigone, 31696 Rohitmital, 9005 Sidorova, 6052 Junichi, 4308 Magarach, 6064 Holasovice

52q9 (230.104) \\my iconoclastic; 12775 Brackett, 1936 Lugano, 98866 Giannabussolari, 263940 Malyshkina, 32067 Ranganathan, 237187 Zhonglihe, 1900 Katyusha, 48457 Joseffried, 276681 Loremaes, 15026 Davidscott, 16693 Moseley, 864 Aase, 12073 Larimer, 5493 Spitzweg, 9540 Mikhalkov

124q9 (50.104) \\my building and writing environment; 7416 Linnankoski, 19204 Joshuatree, 6422 Akagi, 19766 Katiedavis, 21626 Matthewhall, 1386 Storeria, 6054 Ghiberti

qc97: my forever mission in life. 100q9

28q9 (290.104) \\the seat of my claircognizance; 3347 Konstantin, 7351 Yoshidamichi, 395148 Kurnin, 30821 Chernetenko, 26455 Priyamshah, 171588 Naprstek, 33202 Davignon, 15335 Satoyukie, 64289 Shihwingching, 17058 Rocknroll

100q9 (110.104) \\me as a narrative voice in my books; 4192 Breysacher, 3725 Valsecchi, 4935 Maslachkova, 18553 Kinkakuji, 20217 Kathyclemmer, 6645 Arcetri

64q9 (200.104) \\my best interactions with dg, also, the dogs coming to me when shanna is outside fighting the weather (similar to REDACTED in europe); 7393 Luginbuhl, 17603 Qoyllurwasi, 33501 Juliethompson, 37623 Valmiera, 77136 Mendillo, 9223 Leifandersson, 11847 Winckelmann, 12974 Halitherses, 91907 Shiho, 3773 Smithsonian, 12542 Laver, 173816 Nireus, 86196 Specula, 49702 Koikeda, 318698 Barthalajos, 34049 Myrelleangela, 1756 Giacobini, 16239 Dower, 12174 van het Reve, 19188 Dittebesard, 48774 Anngower, 172526 Carolinegarcia, 9574 Taku, 12401 Tucholsky, 889 Erynia, 10989 Dolios, 2539 Ningxia, 11311 Peleus

136q9 (20.104) \\shanna's response to the weather; 7469 Krikalev, 22249 Dvorets Pionerov, 2031 BAM, 17963 Vonderheydt, 218692 Leesnyder, 28816 Kimneville, 170879 Verbeeckje, 3661 Dolmatovskij, 20070 Koichiyuko, 114096 Haroldbier, 4009 Drobyshevskij

qig10: your inner dynamics expanded outwards

qc384: a scandalous or dubious pair

5q8 (349.896) \\my ongoing urge to promote my work, not really being able to; my tiger stripes?; 8502 Bauhaus, 4325 Guest, 22153 Kathbarnhart, 20874 MacGregor, 3344 Modena, 13761 Dorristaylor, 6856 Bethemmons, 875 Nymphe

77q8 (169.896) \\the approach I take to someone after I have long split with them; 4092 Tyr, 4044 Erikhog, 4174 Pikulia, 27236 Millermatt, 16129 Kevingao, 16110 Paganetti, 121633 Ronperison, 15861 Ispahan, 917 Lyka, 25760 Annaspitz, 302542 Tilmann, 30850 Vonsiemens, 14252 Audreymeyer, 6780 Borodin

41q8 (259.896) \\hate from lvz, mobilizing fashion against me; 71 Niobe, 2867 Steins, 17883 Scobuchanan, 5946 Hrozny, 22065 Colgrove, 29329 Knobelsdorff, 3625

Fracastoro, 10758 Aldoushuxley, 17927 Ghoshal, 17034 Vasylshev, 2648 Owa, 157534 Siauliai, 31512 Koyyalagunta, 1392 Pierre, 12381 Hugoclaus, 2933 Amber, 29837 Savage, 10549 Helsingborg, 571 Dulcinea, 29328 Hanshintigers, 43956 Elidoro, 42776 Casablanca, 6924 Fukui, 5374 Hokutosei

113q8 (79.896) \\the couple stands away from the system they will rebel against, partly what sb and I used as a power couple; 17250 Genelucas, 6629 Kurtz, 10161 Nakanoshima, 181751 Phaenops, 4756 Asaramas, 17673 Houkidaisen, 98722 Elenaumberto

qc240: the ideal interrelating I would love to always describe my life

17q8 (319.896) \\shanna's account of her travel to visit her mom; ties bad weather to social connection for me; the miranda founding, spacetime; 17461 Shigosenger, 6918 Manaslu, 1190 Pelagia, 244932 Melies, 25645 Alexanderyan, 7056 Kierkegaard, 31706 Singhani, 3520 Klopsteg, 18160 Nihon Uchu Forum, 273262 Cottam, 5960 Wakkanai

89q8 (139.896) \\my low softish but determined voice, communicating; 24104 Vinissac, 6607 Matsushima, 5952 Davemonet, 3360 Syrinx, 1342 Brabantia, 128622 Rudis, 19875 Guedes, 4582 Hank, 644 Cosima, 8804 Eliason, 22584 Winigleason

53q8 (229.896) \\offline astro research and questing; the off feeling that encourages me to write the gm series and other work; 18349 Dafydd, 26618 Yixinli, 320790 Anestin, 293809 Zugspitze, 5231 Verne, 28945 Taideding, 11351 Leucus, 145534 Jhongda, 17823 Bartels, 8316 Wolkenstein, 269 Justitia, 22456 Salopek, 26471 Tracybecker, 417955 Mallama, 8982 Oreshek, 19417 Madelynho, 12032 Ivory

125q8 (49.896) \\how I forget about my investments until it is absolutely time to do something with them; 9723 Binyang, 8330 Fitzroy, 73199 Orlece, 23981 Patjohnson, 5138 Gyoda, 1724 Vladimir, 6646 Churanta, 4111 Lamy

qc96: explosive intrusive power

29q8 (289.896) \\the western outlaw archetype come to instill fear; awl, sg; 3377 Lodewijk, 81 Terpsichore, 2766 Leeuwenhoek, 6329 Hikonejyo, 129148 Sheilahaggard, 20539 Gadberry, 31470 Alagappan, 336698 Melbourne, 12485 Jenniferharris, 26924 Johnharvey, 1558 Jarnefelt, 28521 Mattmcintyre, 33412 Arjunsubra, 2689 Bruxelles

101q8 (109.896) \\for me this happens when an argument has hit a peak and the interaction in settling into its deathbed; remy; 15512 Snyder, 516 Amherstia, 17653 Bochner, 4612 Greenstein, 11021 Fodera, 4301 Boyden, 26811 Hiesinger, 20673 Janelle, 7912 Lapovok, 10697 Othonwinter, 723 Hammonia

65q8 (199.896) \\i use my exercises to embody pluto. otherwise, this is negative for me. I should never do it again or feel pressured to do it—even as a two girl trigger. Maybe I can invite a slave to do it, setting her up for the shit talking about her which is implied; the final gossiped story of me, especially told by former partner-collaborators turned enemy; 2280 Kunikov, 20481 Sharples, 22951 Okabekazuko, 8050 Beishida, 20719 Velasco, 967 Helionape, 1960 Guisan, 610 Valeska, 134340 Pluto, 15304 Wikberg, 1557 Roehla, 21618 Sheikh, 12142 Franklow, 15083 Tianhuili, 2146 Stentor, 746 Marlu, 352148 Tarcisiozani, 13018 Geoffjames, 912 Maritima, 4072 Yayoi, 30000 Camenzind, 73 Klytia, 19815 Marshasega, 268686 Elenaaprile, 4164 Shilov, 133756 Carinajohnson, 12178 Dhani, 175476 Macheret

137q8 (19.896) \\me as data hero, bodyguard in that capacity; one of the things that ties my scholarship to my growth; 9739 Powell, 110294 Victoriaharbour, 6489 Golevka, 13332 Benkhoff, 7130 Klepper, 734 Benda, 10157 Asagiri, 3018 Godiva, 11583 Breuer, 3191 Svanetia

qig11: stacked and stored assets

qc383: needing to formalize distance with a partner or asset in order to get more value out of the exchange

5q7 (349.688) \\.... Resiliency. A crusade endeavor stubbornly held, which I eventually leave behind. Could be said of sata; 52225 Panchenko, 8540 Ardeberg, 3618 Kuprin, 114024 Scotkleinman, 4725 Milone, 111 Ate

77q7 (169.688) \\shift of the shanna relationship after the fairy mural fight | REDACTED, vb. How I take care of the land or property. I was the founder, she was able to extract the resources; 12137 Williefowler, 28418 Pornwasu, 210433 Ullithiele, 69260 Tonyjudt, 236988 Robberto, 9076 Shinsaku, 728 Leonisis, 11146 Kirigamine, 33879 Kierstendeen, 223 Rosa, 123860 Davederrick, 6510 Tarry, 2838 Takase, 20843 Kuotzuhao, 3173 McNaught, 13192 Quine, 3844 Lujiaxi, 88260 Insubria, 1186 Turnera, 31919 Carragher, 28665 Theresafultz

41q7 (259.688) \\the sight unseen property I buy; 11216 Billhubbard, 5926 Schonfeld, 1937 Locarno, 63387 Brazos Bend, 336 Lacadiera, 55755 Blythe, 24188 Matthewage, 255703 Stetson, 4401 Aditi, 3024 Hainan, 5785 Fulton

113q7 (79.688) \\my analysis of REDACTED and the land, what it needs | money; 264020 Stuttgart, 9492 Veltman, 15045 Walesdymond, 4829 Sergestus, 31291 Yaoyue *qc239: father knows best mainstream and counterculture*

53q7 (229.688) \\she who grows, characters exhumed from my history in order to activate a newly hypothesized blessing; 5777 Hanaki, 88875 Posky, 1784 Benguella, 9368 Esashi, 7680 Cari, 9403 Sanduleak, 21050 Beck, 1398 Donnera, 12341 Calevoet, 38 Leda, 16543 Rosetta, 20303 Lindwestrick, 8819 Chrisbondi, 264131 Bornim, 45298 Williamon, 7068 Minowa, 3534 Sax

17q7 (319.688) \\hit and run friendship communications. As an ideal, very james bond-like; 740 Cantabia, 243516 Marklarsen, 3821 Sonet, 32556 Jennivibber, 2946 Muchachos, 241527 Edwardwright, 15350 Naganuma, 432101 Ngari

89q7 (139.688) \\hyp: me and keith, tbt. When not tbt, the friends REALLY need to be forward thinking and mature. Very mature.; 387 Aquitania, 15420 Aedouglass, 8271 Imai, 2348 Michkovitch, 132445 Gaertner, 11998 Fermilab, 3371 Giacconi, 197870 Erkman, 26691 Lareegardner, 31557 Holleybakich, 90937 Josefdufek, 99949 Miepgies, 5291 Yuuko, 79117 Brydonejack, 7575 Kimuraseiji, 92614 Kazutami, 4644 Oumu, 35976 Yorktown, 335 Roberta, 202787 Kestecher, 18581 Batllo, 16711 Ka-Dar

125q7 (49.688) \\cz; the mate's esteem energy; what may be felt during my friend engagement—especially if I pop out of nowhere. After a while people tend to learn how touchy I am, and won't say something unless they know it is safe. I felt this towards both REDACTED and REDACTED, and this is yet another indicator of why D/s featuring someone younger or cz is probably better. this is basically represented by cz, maybe b.a.r., shanna, but otherwise this is me, priya as 53. i tend to do better with a potential friend when breakup is imminent for them or has already occurred. but if not a rebound, i am a lot less of an option. people like agd, dg, REDACTED, m, b.a.r., REDACTED, and more... have all started with me right after their first choice appeared to fail, suggesting that i can look for a recent divorcée and have a much greater chance of succeeding with her; 7998 Gonczi, 6881 Shifutsu, 21478 Maggiedelano, 13477 Utkin, 128633 Queyras, 4512 Sinuhe, 7552 Sephton, 5609 Stroncone, 40776 Yeungkwongyu

qc95: stylish co-traveler and the one who commissions them, their respective activities

29q7 (289.688) \\mb's relationship to me; jetsetter, strong co-traveler; 15155 Ahn, 4230 van den Bergh, 84991 Bettyphilpotts, 181298 Ladanyi, 18190 Michaelpizer, 9059 Dumas, 4005 Dyagilev, 31239 Michaeljames, 25690 Iredale, 25152 Toplis, 5578 Takakura, 24438 Michaeloy, 279274 Shurpakov, 21528 Chrisfaust, 11548 Jerrylewis, 294 Felicia, 10189 Normanrockwell, 11762 Vogel, 43841 Marcustacitus

101q7 (109.688) \\he-man, strike force, lego town, and other childhood games I participated in; mb's relationship to me; moving around with a trophy; 90279 Devetsil, 16878 Tombickler, 19630 Janebell, 130090 Heatherbowles, 2978 Roudebush, 18775 Donaldeng, 7306 Panizon, 30593 Dangovski, 34254 Mihrpatel, 306128 Pipher, 166748 Timrayschneider, 7766 Jododaira, 2299 Hanko, 10371 Gigli, 1708 Polit, 4807 Noboru, 439718 Danielcervantes

65q7 (199.688) \\m's crush; 19620 Auckland, 1413 Roucarie, 365786 Florencelosse, 14105 Nakadai, 25927 Jagandelman, 22152 Robbennett, 7334 Sciurus, 31105 Oguniyamagata, 21732 Rumery, 24353 Patrickhsu, 7901 Konnai, 9331 Fannyhensel, 72071 Gabor, 273836 Hoijyusek, 9260 Edwardolson, 6726 Suthers, 2514 Taiyuan, 24827 Maryphil, 22449 Ottijeff

137q7 (19.688) \\tiy, amber, moulin rouge, the grand broadway or vegas theater where performers are serially evaluated in the ultimate; 11155 Kinpu, 44192 Paulguttman, 4014 Heizman, 3536 Schleicher, 569 Misa, 10099 Glazebrook, 22627 Aviscardi, 31956 Wald, 13606 Bean, 24010 Stovall, 10769 Minas Gerais

qig12: they are hopeless

qc382: troubles with the co-founder

5q6 (349.479) \\the circumstances presented by the management of sata; 26478 Cristianrosu, 4176 Sudek, 17971 Samuelhowell, 9197 Endo, 410 Chloris, 90463 Johnrichard

77q6 (169.479) \\b.a.r. at REDACTED, sg at the city presentation. The event which brings the beginning of the end; 12156 Ubels, 12607 Alcaeus, 25456 Caitlinmann, 9510 Gurnemanz, 26591 Robertreeves, 2119 Schwall

41q6 (259.479) \\me keeping careful watch over the co-founder; 90414 Karpov, 196000 Izzard, 432361 Rakovski, 8369 Miyata, 2308 Schilt, 13853 Jenniferfritz, 275786 Bouley, 440 Theodora, 15330 de Almeida, 42593 Antoniazzi, 186835 Normanspinrad, 17935 Vinhoward, 35370 Daisakyu, 24626 Astrowizard, 3967 Shekhtelia, 11121 Malpighi

113q6 (79.479) \\the entitled attitude of the .... This is something I really can't do easily, but establishes 41q6 as the "dark-eye" upon things I monitor carefully; chico in front of strangers; 11196 Michanikos, 239890 Edudeldon, 4370 Dickens, 12074 Carolinelau, 3628 Boznemcova, 7264 Hirohatanaka, 6997 Laomedon, 22554 Shoshanatell

qc238: antiestablishment stance of one individual

17q6 (319.479) \\the volatile latina, b.a.r. and sg #196 Ã 2001 Einstein, 3253 Gradie, 7871 Tunder, 182262 Solene, 532 Herculina, 3679 Condruses, 29402 Obelix

89q6 (139.479) \\the volatile latina's propaganda; 5132 Maynard, 1591 Baize, 25877 Katherinexue, 1853 McElroy, 275 Sapientia, 1229 Tilia, 1593 Fagnes, 342431 Hilo, 17988 Joannehsieh, 3600 Archimedes, 10011 Avidzba, 99863 Winnewisser, 6699 Igaueno, 216757 Vasari, 154660 Kavelaars, 279 Thule

53q6 (229.479) \\my long journey doing research on my own; 14069 Krasheninnikov, 117993 Zambujal, 7344 Summerfield, 7700 Rote Kapelle, 30245 Paigesmith, 7686 Wolfernst, 13530 Ninnemann, 5684 Kogo, 134244 De Young, 25161 Strosahl, 2637 Bobrovnikoff, 70 Panopaea, 6313 Tsurutani, 14420 Massey

125q6 (49.479) \\when on my own and without much support, where I am likely to be found; 269323 Madisonvillehigh, 7112 Ghislaine, 25646 Noniearora, 237265 Golobokov, 10174 Emicka, 5741 Akanemaruta

qc94: back to the drawing board, resetting an alliance back to zero and losing all the help one has

29q6 (289.479) \\will go where no one else has gone and find treasure there; 801 Helwerthia, 17785 Wesleyfuller, 4226 Damiaan, 25495 Michaelroddy, 224067 Colemila, 212977 Birute, 9417 Jujiishii, 210032 Enricocastellani, 3125 Hay, 9134 Encke, 9255 Inoutadataka, 5774 Ratliff, 3288 Seleucus, 250 Bettina, 18162 Denlea

101q6 (109.479) \\as for me, once I've gotten a good idea of what I'll do when a thing fails, I can make plans to go there and escape toxicity if necessary; 11726 Edgerton, 1258 Sicilia, 4564 Clayton, 5546 Salavat, 131763 Donatbanki, 2433 Sootiyo, 533 Sara, 8895 Nha, 10962 Sonnenborgh, 1607 Mavis, 9397 Lombardi, 6390 Hirabayashi, 6711 Holliman

65q6 (199.479) \\investigating an injury or weird feeling state; 27849 Suyumbika, 13820 Schwartz, 239046 Judysyd, 5715 Kramer, 14595 Peaker, 7199 Brianza, 73686 Nussdorf, 14019 Pourbus, 19298 Zhongkeda, 3923 Radzievskij, 26328 Litomysl, 31129 Langyatai, 3302 Schliemann, 6308 Ebisuzaki, 3761 Romanskaya, 14185 Van Ness, 12166 Oliverherrmann, 1544 Vinterhansenia, 26757 Bastei, 278609 Avrudenko

137q6 (19.479) \\my authorship as having received injection from lusty or underground sources; 20252 Eyjafjallajokull, 130078 Taschner, 1830 Pogson, 32279 Marshall, 11108 Hachimantai, 2729 Urumqi, 8930 Kubota, 34182 Sachan, 19573 Cummings, 4657 Lopez, 22482 Michbertier

qig13: the deep search

qc381: that which I do to leave an indelible memory

5q5 (349.271) \\my desire to be singular in my field; a form of power; legendary; a CRITICAL region in my chart for ambition; 7278 Shtokolov, 25193 Taliagreene, 2403 Sumava, 9325 Stonehenge, 2245 Hekatostos, 295 Theresia, 130072 Ilincaignat, 6748 Bratton, 16073 Gaskin, 5966 Tomeko, 5639 Cuk

77q5 (169.271) \\over time, my opinions and ideas elaborate more and more upon themselves; the skill I work with towards becoming legendary; 3429 Chuvaev, 93 Minerva, 21387 Wafakhalil, 8024 Robertwhite, 25481 Willjaysun, 11504 Kazo, 813 Baumeia, 19643 Jacobrucker, 23289 Naruhirata, 1849 Kresak, 5537 Sanya, 92389 Gretskij, 4907 Zoser, 42609 Daubechies

41q5 (259.271) \\a revolutionary scholar overlooked during my time in each place; my legacy when my work is no longer being done or can no longer be elaborated on; 4300 Marg Edmondson, 14597 Waynerichie, 32594 Nathandeng, 21418 Bustos, 6300 Hosamu, 83598 Aiweiwei, 9016 Henrymoore, 73936 Takeyamamoto, 1101 Clematis, 8073 Johnharmon, 7387 Malbil, 55875 Hirohatagaoka, 29808 Youssoliman, 235027 Pommard

113q5 (79.271) \\circumstances which are also opportunities for my legendary creations; 22312 Kelly, 596 Scheila, 29672 Salvo, 2210 Lois, 11959 Okunokeno, 4989 Joegoldstein, 12553 Aaronritter, 10555 Tagaharue, 6133 Royaldutchastro, 8472 Tarroni, 4791 Iphidamas, 248908 Ginostrada

qc237: urbanization and the changing region dynamics when I enter or exit a place

17q5 (319.271) \\the volatile latina, b.a.r. and sg #196 Ã 310 Margarita, 27114 Lukasiewicz, 3482 Lesnaya, 29686 Raymondmaung, 150374 Jasoncook, 6031 Ryokan, 2347 Vinata, 7197 Pieroangela, 34250 Mamichael, 27003 Katoizumi, 22132 Merkley, 278591 Salo

89q5 (139.271) \\what I need to be able to confess in order to have a true love and bonding situation; more like shanna while I would be the volatile latina myself, the 17-5; 33918 Janiscoville, 12191 Vorontsova, 24529 Urbach, 12190 Sarkisov, 4759 Aretta, 33534 Meiyamamura, 1238 Predappia, 22577 Alfiuccio, 33529 Henden, 25488 Figueiredo, 97186 Tore, 20537 Sandraderosa, 31416 Peteworden, 2499 Brunk, 31192 Aigoual, 7153 Vladzakharov

53q5 (229.271) \\my caltech interactions, but if I don't have any solid allies, this is hard to do; 11428 Alcinoos, 12310 Londontario, 31858 Raykanipe, 9374 Sundre, 9153

Chikurinji, 284891 Kona, 18880 Toddblumberg, 12773 Lyman, 59 Elpis, 7077 Shermanschultz, 9309 Platanus, 63605 Budperry

125q5 (49.271) \\REDACTED, sk, kvt; 12388 Kikunokai, 269567 Bakhtinov, 481993 Melaniezander, 11533 Akeback, 54563 Kinokonasu, 7664 Namahage, 199677 Terzani, 10278 Virkki, 9623 Karlsson

qc93: my devices and their role in the increase of my personal form of power

29q5 (289.271) \\bodies publicized, especially from other cultures; 10642 Charmaine, 43768 Lynevans, 20796 Philipmunoz, 25885 Wiesinger, 21612 Chelsagloria, 36800 Katarinawitt, 15619 Albertwu, 26629 Zahller, 14342 Iglika, 20107 Nanyotenmondai, 16809 Galapagos, 5855 Yukitsuna, 4088 Baggesen, 52604 Thomayer

101q5 (109.271) \\me writing books ilo an inability to run other personal endeavors; the little awards; 7066 Nessus, 22488 Martyschwartz, 9233 Itagijun, 20818 Karmadiraju, 8070 DeMeo, 263516 Alexescu, 2895 Memnon, 953 Painleva, 1794 Finsen, 398053 Vitudurum, 4758 Hermitage, 6630 Skepticus, 25486 Michaelwham

65q5 (199.271) \\who I am when interacting with the hot girl. Or who they are when interacting with me. The event in general; 12357 Toyako, 173117 Promachus, 2757 Crisser, 58221 Boston, 14046 Keikai, 31240 Katrianne, 8611 Judithgoldhaber, 22870 Rosing, 1036 Ganymed, 178 Belisana, 7086 Bopp, 8781 Yurka, 14031 Rozyo, 27289 Myrahalpin, 28570 Peterkraft, 118401 LINEAR, 28447 Arjunmathur, 2797 Teucer

137q5 (19.271) \\kk, bs as mysteries; 20444 Mamesser, 5191 Paddack, 4684 Bendjoya, 151834 Mongkut

qig14: straw men
qc380: those who take the blame

5q4 (349.063) \\my role as an oldest brother; 3295 Murakami, 11768 Merrill, 1064 Aethusa, 427695 Johnpazder, 28557 Lillianchin, 10598 Markrees, 14598 Larrysmith

77q4 (169.063) \\my sibling group, all psychic: keith, priya, auguste, REDACTED, agd, shanna, the dogs, cynthia and the sata authors; 23761 Yangliqing, 214476 Stephencolbert, 27514 Markov, 5011 Ptah, 3735 Trebon, 23325 Arroyo, 372626 IGEM, 128602 Careyparish, 304788 Cresques, 11004 Stenmark, 2558 Viv, 28095 Seanmahoney, 28444 Alexrabii, 25228 Mikekitt, 6536 Vysochinska, 8234 Nobeoka, 1662 Hoffmann, 779 Nina, 2725 David Bender, 20740 Semery, 28156 McColl, 2193 Jackson, 14157 Pamelasobey, 3379 Oishi, 31682 Kinsey

41q4 (259.063) \\REDACTED, REDACTED, the papacy, the government—the party blamed for so much of what has gone wrong; seen as oppressive, though mainly just powerfully mobilizing. If I want power, I will need to become this. No more big brother behavior; in my chart this is highly dependent on you knowing what others don't or can't know, and seeing above all of them; 4640 Hara, 13010 Germantitov, 14400 Baudot, 5172 Yoshiyuki, 212998 Tolbachik, 14328 Granvik, 35239 Ottoseydl, 6709 Hiromiyuki, 266081 Villyket, 847 Agnia, 17907 Danielgude, 3088 Jinxiuzhonghua, 70711 Arlinbartels, 110 Lydia, 34053 Carlquines, 11007 Granahan, 9305 Hazard

113q4 (79.063) \\REDACTED's people and how they absolutely must present. This is also how I will need to present to REDACTED in order to advance in acting; 2408 Astapovich, 3891 Werner, 5762 Wanke, 11803 Turrini, 6051 Anaximenes, 11323 Nasu, 90450 Cyriltyson, 11930 Osamu, 1950 Wempe, 2624 Samitchell, 241113 Zhongda, 2833 Radishchev, 6834 Hunfeld, 824 Anastasia

qc236: mom's and my business endeavors

17q4 (319.063) \\what I think needs to happen with sata: REDACTED; 30788 Angekauffmann, 4442 Garcia, 9630 Castellion, 3342 Fivesparks, 6920 Esaki, 27074 Etatolia, 10744 Tsuruta, 86043 Cevennes

89q4 (139.063) \\gm saga. I believe this paradigm is a way to correct longstanding ills; 7656 Joemontani, 10457 Suminov, 70030 Margaretmiller, 26275 Jefsoulier, 100416 Syang, 12580 Antonini, 699 Hela, 1641 Tana, 4852 Pamjones, 31836 Poshedly, 33734 Stephenlitt, 15675 Goloseevo, 4441 Toshie, 6589 Jankovich, 17407 Teige

53q4 (229.063) \\my pitiful attempts to connect to others via oversharing; 99891 Donwells, 26950 Legendre, 2024 McLaughlin, 6845 Mansurova, 3278 Behounek, 432 Pythia, 14794 Konetskiy, 27413 Ambruster, 11679 Brucebaker, 9090 Chirotenmondai, 6428 Barlach, 22582 Patmiller, 121594 Zubritsky, 5710 Silentium, 5654 Terni

125q4 (49.063) \\the gatekeeper I overshare to. ir, mb, vb, mjones; 147766 Elisatoffoli, 10325 Bexa, 9786 Gakutensoku, 33591 Landsberger, 33897 Erikagreen, 10722 Monari, 16718 Morikawa, 30179 Movva, 9405 Johnratje, 375005 Newsome

qc92: seems to indicate your general attitude or aims when communicating with something, taking information in and responding to it; this qcross filters who you do and don't talk to, and MUST be obeyed in designing your AI

29q4 (289.063) \\my growing suspicion towards people like REDACTED; 23113 Aaronhakim, 13703 Romero, 21956 Thangada, 25151 Stefanschroder, 109 Felicitas, 6245 Ikufumi, 9554 Dumont, 26 Proserpina, 43813 Kuhner, 9947 Takaishuji, 33544 Jerold, 58679 Brenig, 8573 Ivanka, 127515 Nitta, 25518 Paulcitrin, 4036 Whitehouse

101q4 (109.063) \\megaman and music?; 1738 Oosterhoff, 6203 Lyubamoroz, 22885 Sakaemura, 9418 Mayumi, 22563 Xinwang, 4426 Roerich, 329935 Prevot, 5243 Clasien, 14812 Rosario, 7668 Mizunotakao, 13602 Pierreboulez, 6622 Matvienko, 4403 Kuniharu

65q4 (199.063) \\simeona and s.o.s.; 665 Sabine, 3008 Nojiri, 4331 Hubbard, 33129 Ivankrasko, 5412 Rou, 100122 Alpes Maritimes, 5630 Billschaefer, 18430 Balzac, 24464 Williamkalb, 375 Ursula, 895 Helio, 21723 Yinyinwu, 26672 Ericabrooke, 24601 Valjean, 1776 Kuiper, 936 Kunigunde, 1529 Oterma, 28273 Maianhvu, 12761 Pauwels, 22203 Prothoenor, 20205 Sitanchen

137q4 (19.063) \\the succubi interface; 1856 Ruzena, 53 Kalypso, 17030 Sierks, 113394 Niebur

qig15: your reach right up to the edge of your story and into another's
qc379: those I dominate

5q3 (348.854) \\the dogs barking back at me. The reason people don't like to hear me as nervous or uncertain; how I give in to certain events, but will rarely say so. The things told to me in confidence (Hygiea) which are effectively forgotten (Fraknoi); ?.sqNeptune+, 10 Hygiea, 7331 Balindblad, 4859 Fraknoi

77q3 (168.854) \\what lies behind the locked door of my inner consciousness; 28092 Joannekear, 8891 Irokawa, 25615 Votroubek, 12760 Maxwell, 14981 Uenoiwakura, 15372 Agrigento, 5347 Oresteleesca, 6670 Wallach, 249523 Friedan, 12609 Apollodoros, 3051 Nantong, 25133 Douglin, ?.sqNeptune-, 4901 O Briain, 3811 Karma, 22991 Jeffreyklus, 162011 Konnohmaru, 16120 Burnim, 9022 Drake

41q3 (258.854) \\my temporary partner in crime for revolution, the big girl| \dg, rachel| \sherry, dg| \shanna, dg| \rachel, sherry| \shanna| \shanna, rachel| nostril width : nose tip roundness correlated with upper torso depth; scent rings| \rachel; 28512 Tanyuan, 18579 Duongtuyenvu, 386 Siegena, 32605 Lucy, 2037 Tripaxeptalis, 16997 Garrone, 110077 Pujiquanshan, 8082 Haynes, 33457 Cutillo, 24919 Teruyoshi, -10008 Neptune, 12127 Mamiya

113q3 (78.854) \\me in Daddy Dom mode towards my cast of characters; 65241 Seeley, 1108 Demeter, 28276 Filipnaiser, 276 Adelheid, 24345 Llaverias, 40441 Jungmann, 15967 Clairearmstrong, 27422 Robheckman, ?.AntiNeptune, 7584 Ossietzky

qc235: shanna's views of work and how it should be done

17q3 (318.854) \\the roof I share but also provide for shanna; shanna hangs out whenever I'm working; 9638 Fuchs, 263844 Johnfarrell, 10182 Junkobiwaki, 4404 Enirac, 225277 Stino, 403563 Ledbetter, 4183 Cuno

89q3 (138.854) \\shanna's wrist injury as her efforts to improve something made things worse. But can we heal using this same principle?; 217 Eudora, 15673 Chetaev, 296462 Corylachlan, 2369 Chekhov, 8153 Gattacceca, 3978 Klepesta, 34191 Jakhete, 79254 Tsuda

53q3 (228.854) \\the ultimatum I give when I've lost faith in someone I'm still obligated to; my independent thoughts about shanna's leisure time while I'm working; 5402 Kejosmith, 16044 Kurtbachmann, 22596 Kathwallace, 7756 Scientia, 4466 Abai, 11756 Geneparker, 129053 Derekshannon, 25973 Puranik, 311 Claudia, 121008 Michellecrigger, 2848 ASP, 12814 Vittorio, 16248 Fox, 4268 Grebenikov, 21747 Justsolomon, 15739 Matsukuma

125q3 (48.854) \\my taboo writings from the safety of an advanced computer; 14795 Syoyou, 1734 Zhongolovich, 8336 Safarik, 18861 Eugenishmidt, 38269 Gueymard, 732 Tjilaki, 16645 Aldalara, 4046 Swain, 195 Eurykleia, 739 Mandeville

qc91: me and my temporary female battle buddy

29q3 (288.854) \\the optimal ending of the miranda soul group; megaman zx and gauntlet; two into the future; 26694 Wenxili, 29470 Higgs, 751 Faina, 5017 Tenchi, 20893 Rosymccloskey, 125592 Buthiers, 26027 Cotopaxi, 10376 Chiarini, 943 Begonia, 271763 Hebrewu, 7114 Weinek, 183287 Deisenstein

101q3 (108.854) \\my going off somewhere writing, minimizing the problem's source; | THE significator for our dog rachel, possibly dg; 31690 Nayamenezes, 2495 Noviomagum, 27955 Yasumasa, 2259 Sofievka, 19954 Shigeyoshi, 34838 Lazowski, 4342 Freud, 5981 Kresilas, 10654 Bontekoe, 22174 Allisonmae, 8934 Nishimurajun

65q3 (198.854) \\dynasty warriors! Advancing through refusal?; 256 Walpurga, 14533 Roy, 249522 Johndailey, 3738 Ots, 5695 Remillieux, 9004 Peekaydee, 6838 Okuda, 3680 Sasha, 237164 Keelung, 1421 Esperanto, 5826 Bradstreet, 21551 Geyang, 814 Tauris, 4053 Cherkasov, 2491 Tvashtri, 9699 Baumhauer, 11853 Runge, 8230 Perona, 8055 Arnim, 2590 Mourao

137q3 (18.854) \\fit abs and motivated exercise; persecuted, what then?; 108720 Kamikuroiwa, 11051 Racine, 26586 Harshaw, 10354 Guillaumebude, 17759 Hatta

qig16: training received within family
qc378: constructing my affinity spaces myself

5q2 (348.646) \\the cities I build, lego or virtually for example—me being absent from the citizens' dimension. The abstract world in need of help; 68948 Mikeoates, 9052 Uhland, 23045 Sarahocken, 4785 Petrov, 1163 Saga

77q2 (168.646) \\guilt in light of something regrettable; 77318 Danieltsui, 362 Havnia, 4919 Vishnevskaya, 31641 Cevasco, 9097 Davidschlag, 38019 Jeanmariepelt, 32058 Charlesnoyes, 9275 Persson, 6700 Kubisova, 31490 Swapnavdeka, 1059 Mussorgskia, 2274 Ehrsson, 7808 Bagould, 18771 Sisiliang, 6434 Jewitt, 10726 Elodie

41q2 (258.646) \\TADA! Robots, mainly; how I interact with and influence priya specifically. Maybe vv; people who are crazy deep into data and messaging; may include sk and shanna; 8994 Kashkashian, 301566 Melissajane, 6375 Fredharris, 10653 Witsen, 28654 Davidcaine, 11401 Pierralba, 3367 Alex, 331105 Giselher, 19161 Sakawa, 9277 Togashi, 70744 Maffucci, 7187 Isobe, 1689 Floris-Jan

113q2 (78.646) \\necessarily me and Sâvitrî; 40919 Johntonry, 347028 Vazec, 7072 Beijingdaxue, 7055 Fabiopagan, 270601 Frauenstein, 60 Echo, 1754 Cunningham, 16761 Hertz

qc234: shanna herself and my dealings with her

17q2 (318.646) \\judith butler and the right to gender self-determination. Beliefs of the feminists. Are the beliefs themselves the leaders? Is that why real leaders are so hard to find? Shanna—champagne supernova. Edschneider as significator?; 25978 Katerudolph, 29463 Benjaminpeirce, 12838 Adamsmith, 9885 Linux, 24289 Anthonypalma, 3842 Harlansmith, 13077 Edschneider, 23280 Laitsaita, 14428 Lazaridis, 11499 Duras, 21394 Justinbecker, 5581 Mitsuko, 5065 Johnstone

89q2 (138.646) \\reminds me of judy garland or queen elizabeth, marie antoinette, ruthie: a great woman who would be run into the ground for her work. Elizabeth cady stanton; 5035 Swift, 43954 Chynov, 23779 Cambier, 34204 Quryshi, 19140 Jansmit, 55838 Hagongda, 19482 Harperlee, 16589 Hastrup, 29432 Williamscott, 26417 Michaelgord

53q2 (228.646) \\splatterhouse, places that are hell to navigate, but which also offer their own kind of serenity; bioshock; 9512 Feijunlong, 256892 Wutayou, 32047 Wenjiali, 20586 Elizkolod, 9836 Aarseth, 1313 Berna, 207681 Caiqiao, 24301 Gural, 236728 Leandri, 32044 Lakmazaheri, 11693 Grantelliott, 17794 Kowalinski, 23747 Rahaelgupta, 1276 Ucclia, 17173 Evgenyamosov, 192001 Raynatedford, 4244 Zakharchenko, 1290 Albertine, 32001 Golbin

125q2 (48.646) \\staying okay-ish with shanna and others after a rift; 172318 Wangshui, 212924 Yurishevchuk, 60972 Matenko, 233547 Luxun

qc90: my off-putting or pungent co-creative proposal

29q2 (288.646) \\me going into high spirits and neat gambles; where I am squeezed out by the current person; 5380 Sprigg, 16177 Pelzer, 24200 Peterbrooks, 274084 Baldone, 1974 Caupolican, 4692 SIMBAD, 3142 Kilopi, 144 Vibilia, 84339 Francescaballi, 115326 Wehinger, 1990 Pilcher, 3441 Pochaina, 8378 Sweeney, 33467 Johnlieb

101q2 (108.646) \\shanna's transition from dad to me; my presentation to the council as an act (65q2 is the content); 410912 Lisakaroline, 3758 Karttunen, 7451 Verbitskaya, 1982 Cline, 12579 Ceva, 21498 Keenanferar, 20355 Saraclark, 13241 Biyo, 121542 Alindamashiku, 68 Leto, 8423 Macao, 26007 Lindazhou, 129061 Karlfortney, 11465 Fulvio

65q2 (198.646) \\the issue I share with the recordings; shanna and I ask about a walmart, setting off all kinds of alarms; 7483 Sekitakakazu, 9416 Miyahara, 2277 Moreau, 12710 Breda, 3387 Greenberg, 13330 Dondavis, 211172 Tarantola, 4548 Wielen, 5051 Ralph, 27578 Yogisullivan, 6887 Hasuo, 10919 Pepikzicha, 20007 Marybrown, 3616 Glazunov, 598 Octavia, 7516 Kranjc, 114156 Eamonlittle, 11370 Nabrown, 134036 Austincummings, 18668 Gottesman

137q2 (18.646) \\awareness of morning smells, coffee, noodles, etc; my coffee smell; 567 Eleutheria, 6225 Hiroko, 11461 Wladimirneumann, 10327 Batens, 15091 Howell

qig17: advocacy against a social oppressor

qc377: using someone else to gain access into a club

5q1 (348.438) \\caltech; 24421 Djorgovski, 9486 Utemorrah, 19331 Stefanovitale, 224592 Carnac, 19411 Collinarnold, 301511 Hubinon

77q1 (168.438) \\simeona, sg, cz…young clubbin; 18021 Waldman, 132005 Scottmcgregor, 13526 Libbrecht, 25019 Walentosky, 9960 Sekine, 19874 Liudongyan, 12464 Manhattan, 30775 Lattu, 136108 Haumea, 1225 Ariane, 43282 Dougbock, 25663 Nickmycroft, 67979 Michelory, 16105 Marksaunders, 10178 Iriki

41q1 (258.438) \\Probably one of the myriad potential pushy / pompous country boys or girls. REDACTED?; 13234 Natashaowen, 3611 Dabu, 2220 Hicks, 13482 Igorfedorov, 52 Europa, 2317 Galya, 70995 Mikemorton, 10953 Gerdatschira, 3983 Sakiko, 2675 Tolkien, 210230 Linyuanpei, 6432 Temirkanov, 83600 Yuchunshun,

3934 Tove, 131 Vala, 12298 Brecht, 31511 Jessicakim, 8991 Solidarity, 243073 Freistetter, 23834 Mukhopadhyay, 6792 Akiyamatakashi

113q1 (78.438) \\my enlistment of shanna to communicate with the contractors; 8047 Akikinoshita, 25417 Coquillette, 7996 Vedernikov, 10729 Tsvetkova, 7377 Pizzarello, 2815 Soma

qc233: shanna's and my core family unit, where I am a co-leader

17q1 (318.438) \\my work trios; the dogs as our children; 31877 Davideverett, 6261 Chione, 30161 Chrepta, 4503 Cleobulus, 20323 Tomlindstom, 3946 Shor, 1087 Arabis, 4293 Masumi, 10645 Brac, 12818 Tomhanks, 332326 Aresi, 25024 Calebmcgraw, 4287 Trisov, 25727 Karsonmiller, 17917 Cartan, 8331 Dawkins, 9604 Bellevanzuylen

89q1 (138.438) \\my iadt career after things closed down; kit as our child; 72 Feronia, 4734 Rameau, 29631 Ryankenny, 11400 Rasa, 5281 Lindstrom, 4685 Karetnikov, 923 Herluga, 18295 Borispetrov

53q1 (228.438) \\MY MISSION: situations where you are powerless to set things right or make positive social change. I should note that my taboo stuff will not succeed, but my trio work will. Perhaps I need TWO book of contours partners myself, to make a trio: glen and Sâvitrî. But stay away from couples; me and shanna as a couple; 13957 NARIT, 21719 Pasricha, 17240 Gletorrence, 30336 Zhangyizhen, 2072 Kosmodemyanskaya, 197707 Paulnohr, 34016 Chaitanya, 7242 Okyudo, 31635 Anandarao, 29132 Bradpitt, 12780 Salamony, 5375 Siedentopf, 4605 Nikitin

125q1 (48.438) \\the great narrated folktales of a notorious or legendary figure; the weather as our context; 22872 Williamweber, 2008 Konstitutsiya, 4417 Lecar, 31483 Caulfield, 208917 Traviscarter, 10435 Tjeerd, 7907 Erasmus

qc89: my answer to co-creative rejection

29q1 (288.438) \\my relationship with mb or jk; a bully from san antonio whom I bring with me; 200033 Newtaipei, 1798 Watts, 28538 Ruisong, 199631 Giuseppesprizzi, 9117 Aude, 209148 Dustindeford, 1201 Strenua, 4126 Mashu, 3092 Herodotus, 32062 Amolpunjabi, 5548 Thosharriot, 233 Asterope, 9879 Mammuthus, 6524 Baalke, 13032 Tarn

101q1 (108.438) \\shanna's actual cleanup process in the house; looney tunes, stooges?; 5533 Bagrov, 9148 Boriszaitsev, 59833 Danimatter, 194970 Marai, 1208 Troilus, 22136 Jamesharrison, 31513 Lafazan, 303909 Tomknops, 6576 Kievtech, 85200 Johnhault, 28967 Gerhardter, 617 Patroclus, 228136 Billary, 5947 Bonnie

65q1 (198.438) \\me having to build the house or business legacy on my own, despite the partner wanting it more than I do; the rejecter who fuels the length; 284029 Esplugafrancoli, 3172 Hirst, 28415 Yingxiong, 66669 Aradac, 28714 Gandall, 22161 Santagata, 33480 Bartolucci, 2078 Nanking, 24587 Kapaneus, 5941 Valencia, 25893 Sugihara, 15278 Paquet, 5121 Numazawa, 25035 Scalesse, 121631 Josephnuth, 4405 Otava, 33861 Boucvalt, 19429 Grubaugh, 30159 Behari, 7678 Onoda, 52057 Clarkhowell, 13818 Ullery, 2673 Lossignol, 239071 Penghu

137q1 (18.438) \\loosening the tendon tension; the extent of this constitutes the penis length; 8832 Altenrath, 16076 Barryhaase, 30384 Robertirelan

qig18: defining your platform

qc376: leader becoming a rival

5q12 (348.229) \\locsec of stm. Reluctant leader; 52292 Kamdzhalov, 146 Lucina, 201023 Karlwhittenburg, 157194 Saddlemyer, 18174 Khachatryan, 210414 Gebartolomei

77q12 (168.229) \\my post-rage behavior; 27597 Varuniyer, 155948 Maquet, 22852 Kinney, 69259 Savostyanov, 25679 Andrewguo, 11895 Dehant, 21655 Niklauswirth, 9615 Hemerijckx, 32008 Adriangalad, 6795 Ornskoldsvik, 885 Ulrike, 3544 Borodino, 23688 Josephjoachim, 11191 Paskvic

41q12 (258.229) \\seems to be my rival as a leader, or the role I play which undermines the leading party; 18286 Kneipp, 2022 West, 14612 Irtish, 230975 Rogerfederer, 7807 Grier, 23055 Barbjewett, 273987 Greggwade, 15857 Touji, 12496 Ekholm, 23994 Mayhan, 9137 Remo, 12391 Ecoadachi, 55810 Fabiofazio, 5671 Chanal, 4465 Rodita, 6673 Degas, 6122 Henrard, 6417 Liberati, 4504 Jenkinson, 11087 Yamasakimakoto, 18399 Tentoumushi, 77138 Puiching

113q12 (78.229) \\having to kick simeona out. Me being banned; 797 Montana, 3867 Shiretoko, 65489 Ceto, 120462 Amanohashidate, 31605 Braschi, 18087 Yamanaka, 729 Watsonia, 11921 Mitamasahiro, 2199 Klet, 2998 Berendeya, 4424 Arkhipova

qc232: shanna's and my modes of thinking

17q12 (318.229) \\building blocks and knime; meet shanna—the marriage partner; 23769 Russellbabb, 9822 Hajdukova, 25815 Scottskirlo, 6708 Bobbievaile, 9414 Masamimurakami, 6376 Schamp, 145546 Suiqizhong, 5278 Polly, 17502 Manabeseiji, 84100 Farnocchia, 24930 Annajamison, 33609 Harishpalani, 161215 Loveday

89q12 (138.229) \\my surrounding city or culture; 12188 Kalaallitnunaat, 8755 Querquedula, 157 Dejanira, 4181 Kivi, 8986 Kineyayasuyo, 1904 Massevitch, 576 Emanuela, 184 Dejopeja, 33463 Bettinagregg, 261930 Moorhead, 7493 Hirzo, 2512 Tavastia, 21736 Samaschneid, 21970 Tyle, 111696 Helenorman

53q12 (228.229) \\the messenger who has heard the call. Seems to favor legendary communicators; 1375 Alfreda, 113952 Schramm, 212500 Robertojoppolo, 7757 Kameya, 8973 Pratincola, 56041 Luciendumont, 158589 Snodgrass, 5002 Marnix, 120191 Tombagg, 4177 Kohman, 245 Vera, 1023 Thomana, 15003 Midori

125q12 (48.229) \\cold street logic. B.I.G.; busted up, but powerful; 173936 Yuribo, 12289 Carnot, 21939 Kasmith, 1131 Porzia, 11069 Bellqvist, 299020 Chennaoui, 10121 Arzamas, 299134 Moggicecchi

qc88: memorable or ideal viewership

29q12 (288.229) \\what I'm ultimately known for; naema. Easily; 7673 Inohara, 82464 Jaroslavbocek, 17629 Koichisuzuki, 32807 Quarenghi, 27107 Michelleabi, 7740 Petit, 4103 Chahine, 25662 Chonofsky, 6257 Thorvaldsen, 10489 Keinonen, 7758 Poulanderson, 3757 Anagolay, 2834 Christy Carol, 26340 Evamarkova, 4027 Mitton, 16017 Street, 33450 Allender, 17088 Giupalazzolo, 6839 Ozenuma, 17881 Radmall, 1035 Amata

101q12 (108.229) \\AI as a smoothing outlet for what is wanted in the imagination; 24240 Tinagal, 3207 Spinrad, 1269 Rollandia, 28050 Asekomeh, 10385 Amaterasu, 3557 Sokolsky, 22830 Tinker, 18285 Vladplatonov, 11817 Oguri, 4708 Polydoros, 677 Aaltje, 29610 Iyengar

65q12 (198.229) DON'T DO THIS!| \\my attempts to communicate with someone out of ambition are usually blocked... but lesson from the cosmos that come after this are another matter. People just don't seem to want to hear about my work. I often want to contact old contacts here. Clearly this cluster is broken. i wonder what the squares offer?; 82232 Heuberger, 3691 Bede, 190057 Nakagawa, 2368 Beltrovata, 228153 Sodnik, 2251 Tikhov, 9483 Chagas, 24480 Glavin, 21900 Orus, 4190 Kvasnica, 37627 Lucaparmitano, 28842 Bhowmik, 11252 Laertes, 73059 Kaunas, 162466 Margon, 14684 Reyes, 27347 Dworkin

137q12 (18.229) \\the sudden reminded need to be long; 4727 Ravel, 18783 Sychamberlin, 4540 Oriani, 2713 Luxembourg, 9693 Bleeker, 4690 Strasbourg, 204839 Suzhouyuanlin, 168635 Davidkaufmann, 4728 Lyapidevskij

qig19: you-bar, the ambience outside of you

qc375: the excited rebel, quirky and weird

5q11 (348.021) \\sam, me when I used to have crushes; 4872 Grieg, 587 Hypsipyle, 5701 Baltuck, 6418 Hanamigahara, 103 Hera, 9724 Villanueva, 2420 Ciurlionis

77q11 (168.021) \\me on REDACTED; opposite sam; the book of contours may seal a certain kind of hera; 13316 Llano, 6756 Williamfeldman, 147693 Piccioni, 29337 Hakurojo, 7125 Eitarodate, 2881 Meiden, 12270 Bozar, 6214 Mikhailgrinev, 9437 Hironari, 8875 Fernie, 9927 Tyutchev, 23520 Ludwigbechstein, 11507 Danpascu, 4845 Tsubetsu, 24303 Michaelrice, 6775 Giorgini, 1147 Stavropolis, 31501 Williamknapp

41q11 (258.021) \\lawrence of arabia, the spirit of adventure, yukon jack; the quest; no more american girls; why sam would instantly leave after a while; 4606 Saheki, 33396 Vrindamadan, 7213 Conae, 5135 Nibutani, 121019 Minodamato, 18786 Tyjorgenson, 10111 Fresnel, 33402 Canizares, 6198 Shirakawa, 22 Kalliope, 24065 Barbfriedman, 42073 Noreen, 45500 Motegi, 14542 Karitskaya, 12629 Jandeboer, 10567 Francobressan, 4148 McCartney, 172947 Baeyens, 260366 Quanah, 7803 Adachi, 367633 Shargorodskij, 32072 Revanur

113q11 (78.021) \\a rebel group waiting to pounce, waiting for the other shoe to drop; szw, mom types; this one is ready for a fight, and usually wrong about who the "enemy" is, usually not me unless I'm cornered, so I would be neither this nor its opposition, these would be the two girls. to get the second girl permanently, i'd have to remove this trait from the partner, maybe by giving her her own colony and suggester; 106537 McCarthy, 17314 Aisakos, 20246 Frappa, 8114 Lafcadio, 10692 Opeil, 670 Ottegebe

qc231: a slide into utilitarianism with partners

17q11 (318.021) \\REDACTED drives his enterprises forward; as do a number of other people who moved on without me. I could dwell on my main role ending here, but it's more productive to respond with the 53q11; 12623 Tawaddud, 3400 Aotearoa, 432971 Loving, 17805 Svestka, 125076 Michelmayor, 38203 Sanner, 68947 Brunofunk, 4121 Carlin, 23313 Supokaivanich, 19574 Davidedwards, 2488 Bryan

89q11 (138.021) \\filing through AI (need to have someone else do it); 337002 Robertbodzon, 101960 Molau, 3004 Knud, 2049 Grietje, 21553 Monchicourt, 16723 Fumiofuke, 18638 Nouet

53q11 (228.021) \\a nice buffet plate of all the things I do when presented with a loss; walling off, studying the other, the final reach, vanishing, etc...; 28417 Leewei, 34129 Madisonsneve, 84951 Kenwilson, 13644 Lynnanderson, 12340 Stalle, 16602

Anabuki, 28787 Peterpinko, 13415 Stevenbland, 20687 Saletore, 1425 Tuorla, 33920 Trivisonno, 4112 Hrabal, 6521 Pina, 40463 Frankkameny, 3595 Gallagher, 29642 Archiekong, 5636 Jacobson, 5256 Farquhar, 566 Stereoskopia, 48495 Ryugado, 8858 Comus

125q11 (48.021) \\REDACTED the slave; 23852 Laurierumker, 168321 Josephschmidt, 4838 Billmclaughlin, 15128 Patrickjones, 22856 Stevenzeiher

qc87: the succubi

29q11 (288.021) \\the lusty spirits—of all kinds at all hours; when I feel that some force out there suddenly craves me; prohal, the venusian dilemma; 31959 Keianacave, 24976 Jurajtoth, 11625 Francelinda, 12035 Ruggieri, 5497 Sararussell, 171429 Hunstead, 185636 Shiao Lin, 6614 Antisthenes, 2275 Cuitlahuac, 10356 Rudolfsteiner, 25434 Westonia, 21389 Pshenichka, 9091 Ishidatakaki, 9028 Konradbenes, 6317 Dreyfus, 5268 Cernohorsky, 114703 North Dakota

101q11 (108.021) \\AI sculpting or contours calculation; 3503 Brandt, 20861 Lesliebeh, 1885 Herero, 19080 Martinfierro, 5930 Zhiganov, 1516 Henry, 10010 Rudruna, 227065 Romandia, 40410 Prihoda, 9697 Louwman, 28810 Suchandler

65q11 (198.021) \\my temperamental partner or battle buddy; another person displays her charged or sexual energy; a situation suddenly puts its craving onto me; pre-sleep visitor; 65210 Stichius, 121483 Griffinjayne, 33904 Janardhanan, 12527 Anneraugh, 31940 Sutthiluk, 2267 Agassiz, 12637 Gustavleonhardt, 154902 Davidtoth, 7315 Kolbe, 2853 Harvill, 24334 Conard, 68325 Begues, 4474 Proust, 604 Tekmessa, 30259 Catherineli, 5244 Amphilochos, 353577 Gediminas, 2633 Bishop, 183357 Rickshelton, 127 Johanna

137q11 (18.021) \\the sudden urge to produce classifiable AI images; 636 Erika, 476 Hedwig, 31469 Aizawa, 3767 DiMaggio, 9102 Foglar, 4178 Mimeev

qig20: one boundaried in a corner

qc374: hesitancy to lend my work for others' supposed 'aid'

5q10 (347.813) \\the price I demand for sharing my work. Figuratively, that is; somewhat vampirish; 29575 Gundlapalli, 1528 Conrada, 10823 Sakaguchi, 163640 Newberg, 28710 Rebeccab, 170006 Stoughton, 18803 Hillaryoas, 7985 Nedelcu, 53253 Zeiler, 2235 Vittore

77q10 (167.813) \\probably my major route to power over others; 16766 Righi, 7649 Bougainville, 4128 UKSTU, 22157 Bryanhoran, 70679 Urzidil, 6150 Neukum, 24646 Stober, 5795 Roshchina, 17445 Avatcha, 20580 Marilpeters, 2338 Bokhan, 70783 Kenwilliams, 145593 Xantus, 26946 Ziziyu

41q10 (257.813) \\not sure how valuable this region is; seems to indicate my minimal interactions with priya and others as a light way of broadcasting my work. But what if I stopped doing this?; 25182 Siddhawan, 2703 Rodari, 7328 Casanova, 7512 Monicalazzarin, 5555 Wimberly, 121505 Andrewliounis, 4457 van Gogh, 4477 Kelley, 302652 Hauke, 1564 Srbija, 233943 Falera, 227151 Desargues, 2350 von Lude

113q10 (77.813) \\everybody loves spiderman. I don't respect its angsty dramatics; 25604 Karlin, 8723 Azumayama, 22156 Richoffman, 69245 Persiceto, 35403 Latimer, 4322 Billjackson, 3451 Mentor, 10837 Yuyakekoyake, 21676 Maureenanne

qc230: interesting. Seems to indicate each partner's ideas about marriage—why they would do it

17q10 (317.813) \\entering into contracts. I think I'm doing this to be professional, but I'm actually obligating myself; 5753 Yoshidatadahiko, 2026 Cottrell, 5723 Hudson, 3298 Massandra, 143622 Robertbloch, 5331 Erimomisaki, 18923 Jennifersass

89q10 (137.813) \\keeping kindred relationships distant even as I have blessings to share; 23896 Tatsuaki, 24347 Arthurkuan, 4289 Biwako, 4850 Palestrina, 17412 Kroll, 70713 Sethmacfarlane, 10662 Peterwisse, 55753 Raman, 620 Drakonia, 1066 Lobelia, 1772 Gagarin, 2182 Semirot, 5515 Naderi, 1695 Walbeck, 3640 Gostin, 21738 Schwank, 13225 Manfredi, 202736 Julietclare

53q10 (227.813) \\high spirited but derailing another's progress. I should reserve high spiritedness only for people who are thoroughly aligned: keith, emily; 16158 Monty, 4710 Wade, 2466 Golson, 13084 Virchow, 13249 Marcallen, 70207 Davidunlap, 21815 Fanyang, 6121 Plachinda, 44216 Olivercabasa, 278513 Schwope, 14348 Cumming, 16973 Gaspari, 5688 Kleewyck, 1787 Chiny, 22446 Philwhitney, 170900 Jendrassik

125q10 (47.813) \\REDACTED, REDACTED, REDACTED, REDACTED, and any number of other arrogant pricks I've met; 21822 Degiorgi, 16274 Pavlica, 33690 Noahcain, 27279 Boburan, 9905 Tiziano, 8149 Ruff, 3562 Ignatius, 3702 Trubetskaya, 29690 Nistala, 15896 Birkhoff, 708 Raphaela, 3714 Kenrussell, 8401 Assirelli

qc86: my general feelgood idealism when I take a step back

29q10 (287.813) \\to build masterpieces from colored blocks, lego, relationship networks? Fixated; 17768 Tigerlily, 11764 Benbaillaud, 18661 Zoccoli, 8148 Golding, 254422 Henrykent, 6665 Kagawa, 75972 Huddleston, 1046 Edwin, 14104 Delpino,

21422 Alexacarey, 80 Sappho, 142014 Neirinck, 134 Sophrosyne, 3597 Kakkuri, 1445 Konkolya

101q10 (107.813) \time in the footsteps of dad; 29995 Arshavsky, 5489 Oberkochen, 9504 Lionel, 8996 Waynedwards, 177722 Pelletier, 2492 Kutuzov, 43999 Gramigna, 21829 Kaylacornale, 8583 Froberger, 4876 Strabo, 9205 Eddywally, 2170 Byelorussia

65q10 (197.813) \\the nerve of this guy, loving life; 3878 Jyoumon, 7618 Gotoyukichi, 18395 Schmiedmayer, 186 Celuta, 4700 Carusi, 7800 Zhongkeyuan, 394 Arduina, 3575 Anyuta, 24645 Segon, 9686 Keesom, 2501 Lohja, 6913 Yukawa, 69 Hesperia, 3318 Blixen, 5863 Tara, 26549 Tankanran, 31980 Axelfeldmann, 23213 Ameliachang, 1583 Antilochus, 20686 Thottumkara, 246171 Konrad, 3959 Irwin, 28729 Moivre

137q10 (17.813) \\exercises in a vacationy place where I have settled calmly; 13413 Bobpeterson, 3425 Hurukawa, 11022 Serio, 4356 Marathon, 33113 Julabeth, 13086 Sauerbruch

qig21: released from another's ownership

qc373: the ultra-powerful and how they maintain it

5q9 (347.604) \\a space of archetypes I am sometimes strongly fixed upon; 382 Dodona, 4218 Demottoni, 30039 Jameier, 39678 Ammannito, 34199 Amyjin

77q9 (167.604) \\my inexpressible work; 1148 Rarahu, 488 Kreusa, 95824 Elger, 495181 Rogerwaters, 117386 Thomasschlapkohl, 7559 Kirstinemeyer, 11282 Hanakusa, 21699 Wolpert, 19428 Gracehsu, 595 Polyxena, 17489 Trenker, 1388 Aphrodite, 15628 Gonzales, 150035 Williamson, 16759 Furuyama, 1260 Walhalla, 13751 Joelparker

41q9 (257.604) \\in rome when it is known that REDACTED won't last; REDACTEDs; 12413 Johnnyweir, 101383 Karloff, 9115 Battisti, 4146 Rudolfinum, 5478 Wartburg, 63305 Bobkepple, 120215 Kevinberry, 33393 Khandelwal, 33258 Femariebustos, 2442 Corbett, 21076 Kokoschka, 1493 Sigrid, 7515 Marrucino, 2974 Holden, 19226 Peiresc, 108382 Karencilevitz, 11508 Stolte

113q9 (77.604) \\taylor swift, oprah, the kardashians; 23221 Delgado, 21580 Portalatin, 162166 Mantsch, 9749 Van den Eijnde, 28778 Michdelucia, 22494 Trillium, 21363 Jotwani, 6118 Mayuboshi, 2893 Peiroos, 301553 Ninaglebova

qc229: how a partnership and its partners age together

17q9 (317.604) \\mom or shanna may feel this. I'm less likely to feel it as long as I publish contours before 48. then, onto acting and guitar; 34193 Annakoonce, 352646 Blumbahs, 4777 Aksenov, 431 Nephele, 32093 Zhengyan, 134039 Stephaniebarnes

89q9 (137.604) \\moving more centrally to the REDACTED haven; 48424 Souchay, 2238 Steshenko, 35446 Stana, 2840 Kallavesi, 5223 McSween, 1212 Francette, 1380 Volodia, 2243 Lonnrot, 18809 Meileawertz, 26087 Zhuravleva, 24015 Pascalepinner, 4284 Kaho, 6812 Robertnelson, 33181 Aalokpatwa, 13046 Aliev, 4841 Manjiro, 33390 Hajlasz, 23204 Arditkroni, 15691 Maslov

53q9 (227.604) \\me in the dissatisfied head of house role; 29834 Mariacallas, 8127 Beuf, 221628 Hyatt, 29986 Shunsuke, 28376 Atifjaved, 6865 Dunkerley, 26993 Littlewood, 18644 Arashiyama, 13280 Christihaas, 32770 Starchik, 59390 Habermas, 120196 Kevinballou, 4789 Sprattia, 3908 Nyx, 20568 Migaki, 10355 Kojiroharada, 15891 Alissazhang, 43259 Wangzhenyi, 1714 Sy, 379 Huenna, 51825 Davidbrown, 5942 Denzilrobert

125q9 (47.604) \\a notorious self-publisher; 12007 Fermat, 51985 Kirby, 15034 Decines, 18117 Jonhodge, 12491 Musschenbroek, 16560 Daitor, 10204 Turing, 10963 van der Brugge

qc85: dramatic transformation after a long time

29q9 (287.604) \\if into my astrology, the chances of being close are much higher; taking a longer time to decide to join; 19135 Takashionaka, 13283 Dahart, 303648 Mikszath, 51570 Phendricksen, 23284 Celik, 5424 Covington, 1631 Kopff, 21730 Ignaciorod, 29770 Timmpiper, 4307 Cherepashchuk, 22401 Egisto, 320 Katharina, 10320 Reiland

101q9 (107.604) \\my channels in trouble. A FUCKING AWESOME qunit; definitely the focal point of my clairaudience; 161546 Schneeweis, 168358 Casca, 20991 Jankollar, 11141 Jindrawalter, 9024 Gunnargraps, 239672 SOFIA, 454419 Hansklausreif, 8624 Kaleycuoco

65q9 (197.604) \\my work with the logos; 9470 Jussieu, 15884 Maspalomas, 11251 Icarion, 8805 Petrpetrov, 217603 Grove Creek, 11119 Taro, 9359 Fleringe, 10378 Ingmarbergman, 3606 Pohjola, 34716 Guzzo, 8483 Kinwalaniihsia, 2697 Albina, 20947 Polyneikes, 19518 Moulding

137q9 (17.604) \\the know-it-all; 5071 Schoenmaker, 3235 Melchior, 23404 Bomans, 32522 Judiepersons, 154991 Vinciguerra, 4189 Sayany, 2935 Naerum

qig22: duty and tasking

qc372: three in travel

6q8 (347.396) \\we need to both go to this place because it's practical to do so; field trip mode with REDACTED or mrs real's class?; 39516 Lusigny, 96189 Pygmalion, 5106 Mortensen, 25184 Taylorgaines, 29490 Myslbek, 68410 Nichols, 180857 Hofigeza, 313 Chaldaea, 16021 Caseyvaughn

78q8 (167.396) \\may dealings with simeona and S.O.S.; 13121 Tisza, 7961 Ercolepoli, 1774 Kulikov, 3386 Klementinum, 91888 Tomskilling, 15460 Manca, 8636 Malvina, 264476 Aepic, 11915 Nishiinoue, 250164 Hannsruder, 3508 Pasternak, 11126 Dolecek, 187276 Meistas, 181043 Anan, 9501 Ywain, 12673 Kiselman, 4379 Snelling, 18637 Liverdun

42q8 (257.396) \\bs's protest in math class; this person has status and social favor on their side; corfu, REDACTED and the bubble party, minuteman performance; 5928 Pindarus, 31939 Thananon, 25475 Lizrao, 30177 Khashayar, 25577 Wangmanqiang, 1187 Afra, 1291 Phryne, 2561 Margolin, 9663 Zwin, 41481 Musashifuchu, 15131 Alanalda, 2555 Thomas, 14129 Dibucci

114q8 (77.396) \\my experiences living in REDACTED's house; early dealings with REDACTED, promoting knime, or meeting with (especially REDACTED) people who don't want to help me or with whom I am just not aligned; talking myself out of a threesome with REDACTED & REDACTED; extended friendship with simeona and grace; 181279 Iapyx, 82896 Vaubaillon, 191341 Lanczos, 31596 Ragavender, 11013 Kullander, 1867 Deiphobus, 18278 Drymas, 25544 Renerogers

qc228: attention-grabbing attributes of the male

18q8 (317.396) \\rpg tank archetype: how I see the excessively male energy treating the domains it engages, or envisioning such treatment; i don't do this in actual relationships and wouldn't without consent. However, my AI images sometime reach graphic proportions, and do indeed reflect my endlessly increasing male character. this is the Dominance half of D/s, and is consistent with what many of the matched women in my life have experienced at the hands of others before me. especially REDACTED and REDACTED, probably REDACTED as well; 26498 Dinotina, 3848 Analucia, 120121 Libbyadelman, 32006 Hallisey, 26505 Olextokarev, 4680 Lohrmann, 190504 Hermanotto

90q8 (137.396) \\seems to be associated with (at least my) male secondary sexual characteristics; physical build of the tank archetype / aggro collector; 156990 Claerbout, 9194 Ananoff, 10405 Yoshiaki, 6923 Borzacchini, 4194 Sweitzer, 100940 Maunder, 70745 Aleserpieri, 34326 Zhaurova, 328477 Eckstein, 7162 Sidwell, 21526 Mirano, 25799 Anmaschlegel

54q8 (227.396) \\definitely shanna, cz, sms, and REDACTED. Sassy brat. Good at what she does, obsessive, steeped in chaos; 9689 Freudenthal, 39415 Janeausten, 9843 Braidwood, 540 Rosamunde, 43667 Dumlupinar, 350838 Gorelysheva, 210174 Vossenkuhl, 26955 Lie, 30350 Beltecas, 23178 Ghaben, 227930 Athos, 231666 Aisymnos, 12931 Mario, 25698 Snehakannan, 600 Musa, 19190 Morihiroshi, 11039 Raynal, 14834 Isaev, 8028 Joeengle, 5027 Androgeos, 24602 Mozzhorin, 8809 Roversimonaco, 28165 Bayanmashat, 9708 Gouka, 33872 Kristichung, 23504 Haneda, 96192 Calgary

126q8 (47.396) \\seems to be associated with the female secondary sexual characteristics and how I see these, because my books and housework entail exactly this region, the partner does not generally get my male sexual energy. Only co-creators—hence the graphic AI occurring alongside this qunit work, if i am projecting my 90q8s, this region can't be allowed to happen at another's hand—only mine. You do no creative work without my permission or approval, as it must support my goals as well. so i maybe shouldn't partner with an artist after all, as encouraging her art would mean encouraging her separation from me. D/s protocol; 17940 Kandyjarvis, 73699 Landaupfalz, 19822 Vonzielonka, 30525 Lenbright, 6947 Andrewdavis, 8767 Commontern, 184011 Andypuckett, 9071 Coudenberghe, 132904 Notkin, 30936 Basra, 1427 Ruvuma

qc84: disappointment in one's setup—where negative or separatist routes work and positive or togetherness ones don't

30q8 (287.396) \\writing contours and putting myself in it; dissatisfaction with my own display of supposed skills; 129114 Oliverwalthall, 4573 Piestany, 21682 Pestafrantisek, 11980 Ellis, 22744 Esterantonucci, 10559 Yukihisa, 34272 Veeramacheneni, 2879 Shimizu, 22776 Matossian, 10894 Nakai

102q8 (107.396) \\my employers letting me get away with certain things so as not to completely lose access to something now hard to find; that which commissions a redo or special experiment; 4786 Tatianina, 10159 Tokara, 3376 Armandhammer, 25333 Britwenger, 19386 Axelcronstedt, 33270 Katiecrysup

66q8 (197.396) \\sb's influence tactics; 6177 Fecamp, 11277 Ballard, 191 Kolga, 26345 Gedankien, 14911 Fukamatsu, 4252 Godwin, 29663 Evanmackay, 3149 Okudzhava, 11855 Preller, 21564 Widmanstatten, 156631 Margitan, 34282 Applegate, 18593 Wangzhongcheng, 6172 Prokofeana, 4753 Phidias, 30205 Mistyevans, 32007 Amirhelmy, 24643 MacCready, 33201 Thomasartiss

138q8 (17.396) \\how did I end up as the bad guy again?; 36445 Smalley, 29373 Hamanowa, 32300 Uwamanzunna, 2211 Hanuman, 33224 Lesrogers, 33179 Arsenewenger, 405 Thia, 2990 Trimberger, 53029 Wodetzky

qig23: how you choose to spend your idle or in-between time

qc371: examining or participating in events typical of the domain I'm in

6q7 (347.188) \\continuous influx of answers to my questions about what domain I'm in, the HOURS; ongoing feeling that I deserve a certain experience (see 78q7.); my recorder as listener?; 9926 Desch, 52246 Donaldjohanson, 5166 Olson, 7812 Billward, 90503 Japhethboyce

78q7 (167.188) \\makes a good role; my going into sensual spaces and exercises; my ongoing idealist, sensual bearing. May be related to pre-sleep fantasy character; 18984 Olathe, 8616 Fogelquist, 7683 Wuwenjun, 4438 Sykes, 5399 Awa, 18950 Marakessler, 340980 Bad Vilbel, 1731 Smuts, 17242 Leslieyoung, 236484 Luchijen, 3788 Steyaert, 2830 Greenwich, 6520 Sugawa, 6187 Kagura, 14327 Lemke, 154 Bertha, 6844 Shpak, 8276 Shigei, 215868 Rohrer, 223566 Petignat

42q7 (257.188) \\my ongoing work, what I would prefer to do in the empty (waking) space between hours, if flowing with time were my only concern. This is what I do when looking forward to something happening or anticipating an outcome. I use this region HEAVILY—always improving, and it forms one of my most used qunits; 425442 Eberstadt, 8041 Masumoto, 12295 Tasso, 117350 Saburo, 10937 Ferris, 33027 Brouillac, 11308 Tofta, 8269 Calandrelli, 40684 Vanhoeck, 4277 Holubov, 1781 Van Biesbroeck, 18004 Krystosek, 133747 Robertofurfaro, 21561 Masterman, 59087 Maccacaro, 85317 Lehar, 20643 Angelicaliu, 15902 Dostal, 11315 Salpetriere, 3780 Maury

114q7 (77.188) \\shanna's, mom's, REDACTED's, agd's, francesca's, kvt's milestone demonstrations—the housemates; mercenary self-interest by the other person (could be me); 236683 Hujingyao, 29187 Lemonnier, 27918 Azusagawa, 13975 Beatrixpotter, 9365 Chinesewilson, 9737 Dudarova, 4924 Hiltner

qc227: the work done to pull me forward, and the inclination to share that work

18q7 (317.188) \\collection: authoring alma mater and contours; 20846 Liyulin, 78394 Garossino, 33898 Kendra, 27845 Josephmeyer, 3339 Treshnikov, 5382 McKay, 33269 Broccoli, 22911 Johnpardon, 6413 Iye, 16745 Zappa, 18498 Cesaro

90q7 (137.188) \\j exercises and the circumstances for their occurrence; 10252 Heidigraf, 449922 Bailey, 24984 Usui, 6429 Brancusi, 2071 Nadezhda, 7320 Potter, 23410 Vikuznetsov, 13 Egeria, 12369 Pirandello, 48631 Hasantufan, 19448 Jenniferling, 26422 Marekbuchman, 7960 Condorcet, 144386 Emmabirath, 95474 Andreajbarbieri, 17184 Carlrogers, 20363 Komitov, 988 Appella, 12432 Usuda

54q7 (227.188) \\me in an experimental or scouting role at work—the work that starts but will get canceled. (this happens A LOT.); 6876 Beppeforti, 3146 Dato, 65685 Behring, 7108 Nefedov, 976 Benjamina, 9293 Kamogata, 66207 Carpi, 18873 Larryrobinson, 41986 Fort Bend, 21751 Jennytaylor, 22583 Metzler, 10241 Milicevic, 3731 Hancock, 16731 Mitsumata, 24838 Abilunon, 9432 Iba, 2003 Harding

126q7 (47.188) \\the array of work in progress activities meant to plan for the future, preventing my exercises / fun activities; more future-oriented planning, less growth; 9081 Hideakianno, 966 Muschi, 4305 Clapton, 9974 Brody, 402 Chloe, 2055 Dvorak, 22561 Miviscardi, 300928 Uderzo, 29760 Milevsko

qc83: where the one in a position of privilege is the only one who can fix things for the low

30q7 (287.188) \\keith's desirable traits that I don't have; 23988 Maungakiekie, 55108 Beamueller, 5095 Escalante, 3642 Frieden, 8027 Robertrushworth, 12548 Erinriley, 2665 Schrutka, 1479 Inkeri, 29613 Charlespicard, 15806 Kohei, 61208 Stonarov, 2877 Likhachev, 4350 Shibecha

102q7 (107.188) \\my various displays of youthful passions to get things done. Was it effective? Not really. The culmination was an identity change. I was more often the top leader though; 6904 McGill, 30426 Philtalbot, 3447 Burckhalter, 26399 Rileyennis, 1618 Dawn, 24926 Jinpan, 15019 Gingold, 5661 Hildebrand, 9497 Dwingeloo, 6705 Rinaketty, 21473 Petesullivan, 10553 Stenkumla, 857 Glasenappia, 10467 Peterbus

66q7 (197.188) \\my partners happen to model my mother; 539 Pamina, 2287 Kalmykia, 7693 Hoshitakuhai, 4138 Kalchas, 27716 Nobuyuki, 9339 Kimnovak, 27282 Deborahday, 22139 Jamescox, 19122 Amandabosh, 407243 Krapivin, 17627 Humptydumpty, 1403 Idelsonia, 23944 Dusser, 20024 Mayremartinez, 4434 Nikulin, 16544 Hochlehnert, 23833 Mowers, 20002 Tillysmith, 24509 Joycechai, 3277 Aaronson

138q7 (17.188) \\my views of sexual opportunity with shanna; 3355 Onizuka, 54810 Molleigh, 8069 Benweiss, 7804 Boesgaard, 5624 Shirley, 5823 Oryo

qig24: evolving interactions though you cannot change the objects

qc370: humans, cats, dogs, and homes; this region itself may be a significator for cats

6q6 (346.979) \\what shanna values in light of dogs; the dominion; my house or recorders; 21476 Petrie, 31378 Neidinger, 35076 Yataro, 26201 Sayonisaha, 2929 Harris, 8284 Cranach, 5084 Gnedin, 2365 Interkosmos, 280652 Aimaku

78q6 (166.979) \\my elaborating my home on my own terms; my increasing caution towards allies as I get older; 12339 Carloo, 11757 Salpeter, 17280 Shelly, 4892 Chrispollas, 32821 Posch, 20623 Davidyoung, 10380 Berwald, 7548 Engstrom, 7848 Bernasconi, 6640 Falorni, 29862 Savannahjoy, 33810 Tangirala, 27748 Vivianhoette, 11166 Anatolefrance, 19066 Ellarie, 71445 Marc, 25425 Chelsealynn, 158241 Yutonagatomo, 1762 Russell, 21782 Davemcdonald, 8328 Uyttenhove

42q6 (256.979) \\how kit kat generally works, her behavior and the situations around her; what my cats are up to in the background of my homes; my role in the dissolution of a team; when I leave, the whole team tends to break down as well; ana lisa's departure, then my own, then christina's; 4038 Kristina, 2917 Sawyer Hogg, 16059 Marybuda, 6066 Hendricks, 17163 Vasifedoseev, 12281 Chaumont, 19496 Josephbarone, 29125 Kyivphysfak, 6148 Ignazgunther, 15246 Kumeta, 35364 Donaldpray, 330455 Anbrysse

114q6 (76.979) \\kit kat herself; how I am in a group when my thinking is of no value; liking someone, but knowing they don't respect me; 37391 Ebre, 7065 Fredschaaf, 4329 Miro, 2674 Pandarus, 12468 Zachotin, 4251 Kavasch, 22639 Nickanthony, 8697 Olofsson, 23718 Horgos, 10586 Jansteen, 208351 Sielmann

qc226: the playing of rpgs, my passive lengthening exercises

18q6 (316.979) \\certain epic songs I listen to - christmas in the silent forest, you put a move on my heart, seven whole days, skybird; character of my AI images; the content of engaging rpgs; 19999 Depardieu, 374354 Pesquet, 19083 Mizuki, 4120 Denoyelle, 6319 Beregovoj, 4013 Ogiria, 54522 Menaechmus, 184501 Pimprenelle, 1786 Raahe, 15925 Rokycany, 433 Eros, 6074 Bechtereva, 2585 Irpedina, 10552 Stockholm, 6207 Bourvil, 8150 Kaluga, 11532 Gullin, 902 Probitas

90q6 (136.979) \\my approach to gradually growing up to and past my detractors' level. More about the exercise process and its environment; 8753 Nycticorax, 28630 Mayuri, 216910 Vnukov, 327512 Biro, 10802 Masamifuruya, 25836 Harishvemuri, 17246 Christophedumas, 22871 Ellenoei, 3682 Welther, 8961 Schoenobaenus, 8687 Caussols, 30172 Giedraitis, 361450 Houellebecq, 8597 Sandvicensis, 2825 Crosby, 12189 Dovgyj, 30837 Steinheil, 25175 Lukeandraka, 96747 Crespodasilva, 3730 Hurban, 20155 Utewindolf, 21348 Toyoteru, 260235 Attwood, 254299 Shambleau

54q6 (226.979) \\what I air to my recorder when conflict has arisen; 8824 Genta, 7103 Wichmann, 15614 Pillinger, 639 Latona, 30298 Somyakhare, 19473 Marygardner, 30888 Okitsumisaki, 28 Bellona, 12601 Tiffanyswann, 327030 Alanmaclure, 4060 Deipylos, 20373 Fullmer, 20480 Antonschraut, 5748 Davebrin, 5447 Lallement

126q6 (46.979) \\my mercenary drop of others in favor of something better; 3742 Sunshine, 5971 Tickell, 42355 Typhon, 10289 Geoffperry

qc82: kit; the wayward one whom people think they could fix, but it's unlikely

30q6 (286.979) \\the nipples and penis head; sexual research; plowing forward; kit; me after an argument or during; 79241 Fulviobressan, 28438 Venkateswaran, 12506 Pariser, 24450 Victorchang, 1442 Corvina, 30042 Schmude, 33994 Regidufour, 6736 Marchare, 12003 Hideosugai, 51826 Kalpanachawla, 25375 Treenajoi, 98 Ianthe, 11326 Ladislavschmied, 25383 Lindacker, 97472 Hobby, 11284 Belenus

102q6 (106.979) \\me finally giving up on a functional relationship; when younger, quietly building lego in isolation; 28770 Sarahrines, 10481 Esipov, 6030 Zolensky, 64291 Anglee, 16215 Venkatraman, 5972 Harryatkinson, 362316 Dogora, 8145 Valujki, 29447 Jerzyneyman, 2621 Goto, 2985 Shakespeare, 6579 Benedix, 8552 Hyoichi

66q6 (196.979) \\how your partner addresses something that is driving them nuts; 9413 Eichendorff, 49 Pales, 7027 Toshihanda, 24923 Claralouisa, 28103 Benmcpheron, 167748 Markkelly, 24779 Presque Isle, 3936 Elst, 26935 Vireday, 17399 Andysanto, 2781 Kleczek, 44530 Horakova, 26426 Koechl, 3164 Prast, 4904 Makio, 6346 Syukumeguri, 142754 Brunner, 15093 Lestermackey, 9903 Leonhardt, 1998 Titius, 9661 Hohmann, 700 Auravictrix, 22922 Sophiecai

138q6 (16.979) \\the sudden show of accomplishment within the group. Deep findings; 2250 Stalingrad, 175208 Vorbourg, 11620 Susanagordon, 11770 Rudominkowski, 2174 Asmodeus, 2728 Yatskiv

qig25: they help you reinforce your own tension

qc369: the final publication process

6q5 (346.771) \\the phd. Go back and do it again; 329 Svea, 1195 Orangia, 22987 Rebeckaufman, 418532 Saruman, 1966 Tristan, 33682 Waylonreid

78q5 (166.771) \\my surreptitious blocking of various things for the sake of stability; tito's and drink; controlling my social space; 210 Isabella, 27570 Erinschumacher, 577 Rhea, 14500 Kibo, 6695 Barrettduff, 4363 Sergej, 5804 Bambinidipraga, 2545 Verbiest, 11259 Yingtungchen, 7621 Sweelinck, 9111 Matarazzo, 24133 Chunkaikao,

9017 Babadzhanyan, 13226 Soulie, 11322 Aquamarine, 130128 Tarafisher, 8272 Iitatemura, 9191 Hokuto, 27963 Hartkopf, 7441 Laska, 62503 Tomcave

42q5 (256.771) \\where, though a partner and I are doing well, the relationship remains difficult; 11289 Frescobaldi, 43767 Permeke, 8367 Bokusui, 1825 Klare, 16869 Kosinar, 296638 Sergeibelov, 19307 Hanayama, 141496 Bartkevicius, 14976 Josefcapek, 200234 Kumashiro, 22840 Villarreal, 3997 Taga, 9929 McConnell, 337 Devosa, 5066 Garradd, 13993 Clemenssimmer, 13070 Seanconnery, 12796 Kamenrider, 70936 Kamen

114q5 (76.771) \\my bitching over every little inconvenience in the final publishing process; 2765 Dinant, 26921 Jensallit, 18669 Lalitpatel, 21922 Mocz, 266854 Sezenaksu, 8463 Naomimurdoch, 21465 Michelepatt

qc225: immersed in a stable crowding of light-hearted stories, compounding this rather than external sneaking challenges around the rest of my family with shanna

18q5 (316.771) \\putting the dogs and housemates out of the picture for a while…to play jrpgs; 42487 Angstrom, 41943 Fredrick, 4689 Donn, 25953 Lanairlett, 20607 Vernazza, 16503 Ayato, 13278 Grotecloss, 7279 Hagfors

90q5 (136.771) \\my yearly measure check-ins, an activity in private; very clearly THE lengthening (not the girth thickening) activity opposite jrpgs; 6276 Kurohone, 15887 Daveclark, 6871 Verlaine, 2177 Oliver, 4603 Bertaud, 8368 Lamont, 1602 Indiana, 1813 Imhotep, 63032 Billschmitt, 46514 Lasswitz, 231555 Christianeurda, 7505 Furusho

54q5 (226.771) \\cracking up while high with cory and kvt; 65803 Didymos, 7160 Tokunaga, 5316 Filatov, 272746 Paoladiomede, 39809 Fukuchan, 284984 Ikaunieks, 42775 Bianchini, 28564 Gunderman, 9386 Hitomi, 4976 Choukyongchol, 12709 Bergen op Zoom, 2903 Zhuhai, 11334 Rio de Janeiro, 33762 Sanjayseshan, 9550 Victorblanco, 20482 Dustinshea, 4983 Schroeteria, 7139 Tsubokawa, 530 Turandot, 3391 Sinon, 4931 Tomsk, 1295 Deflotte

126q5 (46.771) \\auguste, keith, me, eccentric travelers I haven't met; 9229 Matsuda, 22994 Workman, 3007 Reaves, 9503 Agrawain, 28182 Chadharris, 33538 Jaredbergen, 8324 Juliadeleon

qc81: getting the cynical one to participate or accept their situation

30q5 (286.771) \\cynical pragmatism; 303265 Littmann, 142091 Omerblaes, 9421 Violilla, 9122 Hunten, 34289 Johndell, 4091 Lowe, 12421 Zhenya, 12614 Hokusai, 92097 Aidai, 8754 Leucorodia, 2620 Santana, 28390 Demjohopkins, 175046 Corporon, 332706 Karlheidlas, 1881 Shao, 11480 Velikij Ustyug

102q5 (106.771) \\shanna; vasquez, REDACTED, REDACTED as play partner-types; 34156 Gopalakrishnan, 1501 Baade, 4491 Otaru, 11552 Boucolion, 8215 Zanonato, 8696 Kjeriksson, 85293 Tengzhou, 4821 Bianucci, 3081 Martinuboh, 23220 Yalemichaels, 1852 Carpenter

66q5 (196.771) \\another's cycles lie at the source of many of the conflicts; 2268 Szmytowna, 22723 Edlopez, 3750 Ilizarov, 24640 Omiwa, 4543 Phoinix, 1135 Colchis, 82071 Debrecen, 2456 Palamedes, 1486 Marilyn, 33399 Emilyann, 4877 Humboldt, 5080 Oja, 9489 Tanemahuta

138q5 (16.771) \\how I initiate guidance systems and steps towards life solutions; 27270 Guidotti, 15860 Siran, 671 Carnegia, 524 Fidelio, 10792 Ecuador, 8461 Sammiepung, 8321 Akim, 29824 Kalmancok

qig26: reorganizing your troublesome experiences

qc368 is associated with trigun

6q4 (346.563) \\random stains caused either by myself or another—like splashing during cooking, random spaghetti sauce—which I downplay; accidents as no big deal; 2342 Lebedev, 28442 Nicholashuey, 333636 Reboul, 10484 Hecht, 2457 Rublyov, 6042 Cheshirecat

78q4 (166.563) \\why I put my biography in my books; vash the stampede; 33210 Johnrobertson, 11571 Daens, 4593 Reipurth, 7672 Hawking, 23992 Markhobbs, 9826 Ehrenfreund, 1077 Campanula, 667 Denise, 11099 Sonodamasaki, 4258 Ryazanov, 4279 De Gasparis, 1174 Marmara, 1350 Rosselia, 20468 Petercook, 20878 Uwetreske

42q4 (256.563) \\the writing of s12, doing AI; trigun world. Weird; 1490 Limpopo, 19625 Ovaitt, 128348 Jasonleonard, 7420 Buffon, 9911 Quantz, 6525 Ocastron, 2962 Otto, 10856 Bechstein, 26331 Kondamuri, 2587 Gardner, 14080 Heppenheim, 11878 Hanamiyama, 5991 Ivavladis, 28340 Yukihiro, 17186 Sergivanov, 6384 Kervin, 7376 Jefftaylor, 29806 Eviesobczak, 7440 Zavist

114q4 (76.563) \\my being pleasant in a situation where misunderstanding would otherwise prevail; 3246 Bidstrup, 382238 Euphemus, 20595 Ryanwisnoski, 1360 Tarka, 145545 Wensayling, 27099 Xiaoyucao, 2626 Belnika, 5048 Moriarty, 24548 Katieeverett, 161315 de Shalit, 7157 Lofgren, 13027 Geeraerts, 5957 Irina, 425 Cornelia, 7378 Herbertpalme, 336694 Fey

qc224: exorcism role

18q4 (316.563) \\my belief that an interactant should at least try to be diplomatic, especially if they are a leader; 69275 Wiesenthal, 4609 Pizarro, 14505 Barentine, 4660 Nereus, 4217 Engelhardt, 52500 Kanata

90q4 (136.563) \\my exercises and publishing as control mechanisms; 3510 Veeder, 111558 Barrett, 24123 Timothychang, 4630 Chaonis, 1507 Vaasa, 185448 Nomentum, 152320 Lichtenknecker, 32073 Cassidyryan, 34178 Sarahmarie, 4456 Mawson, 251 Sophia, 134088 Brettperkins, 4580 Child, 274300 UNESCO

54q4 (226.563) \\REDACTED, various mothery characters wondering if I'm fitting in / more likely to intrude at will; 19430 Kristinaufer, 9842 Funakoshi, 6026 Xenophanes, 21065 Jamesmelka, 12440 Robertwielinga, 10646 Machielalberts, 7992 Yozan, 74764 Rudolfpesek, 34025 Caolannbrady, 16107 Chanmugam, 4723 Wolfgangmattig, 3898 Curlewis, 197845 Michaelvincent, 12472 Samadhi, 158623 Perali, 8771 Biarmicus

126q4 (46.563) \\long enthusiastic emails proposing collaboration plans. Never again; 30028 Yushihomma, 13058 Alfredstevens, 10809 Majsterrojr, 17081 Jaytee, 1337 Gerarda, 12384 Luigimartella

qc80: attempting to go back into the academic realm in order to accomplish some templated goal; jri and the events surrounding me going back

30q4 (286.563) \\certain shows, amparo…; 6032 Nobel, 1973 Colocolo, 28130 Troemper, 18505 Caravelli, 2129 Cosicosi, 7781 Townsend, 152217 Akosipov

102q4 (106.563) \\my broad family and kindred circle; jri; 12640 Reinbertdeleeuw, 19707 Tokunai, 1300 Marcelle, 3656 Hemingway, 18631 Maurogherardini, 128585 Alfredmaria, 6837 Bressi, 12012 Kitahiroshima, 64290 Yaushingtung, 37683 Gustaveeiffel, 4319 Jackierobinson

66q4 (196.563) \\money presents a domino topic for certain partners. When I pay once I pay twice and, often, a lot more the second time. The circumstances for certain major partner rifts. Of course she's not going to contribute. And you shouldn't do it for her; homeless by caron; 4386 Lust, 22786 Willipete, 32087 Vemulapalli, 220495 Margarethe, 25745 Schimmelpenninck, 21770 Wangyiran, 15150 Salsa, 12972 Eumaios, 15338 Dufault, 9420 Dewar, 12639 Tonkoopman, 12975 Efremov, 3453 Dostoevsky, 196807 Beshore, 95959 Covadonga, 17601 Sheldonschafer, 13745 Mikecosta, 25023 Sundaresh, 5643 Roques, 2483 Guinevere, 14065 Flegel, 12611 Ingres, 13303 Asmitakumar, 178796 Posztoczky, 2126 Gerasimovich, 10730 White

138q4 (16.563) \\my astro books' message; 207 Hedda, 13633 Ivens, 6655 Nagahama

qig27: fear of death or defeat

qc367: Dial and SIER; possibly sata's data

6q3 (346.354) \\replaying something in order to understand it; 175563 Amyrose, 18729 Potentino, 2886 Tinkaping, 5962 Shikokutenkyo, 29508 Bottinelli, 3818 Gorlitsa

78q3 (166.354) \\the journey maps—pay attention to how they are commissioned and observed—what their context looks like; easy night club image; 2064 Thomsen, 12622 Doppelmayr, 38086 Beowulf, 985 Rosina, 137632 Ramsauer, 5769 Michard, 117387 Javiercerna, 23679 Andrewmoore, 10381 Malinsmith, 21633 Hsingpenyuan, 21458 Susank, 126160 Fabienkuntz, 18781 Indaram, 31937 Kangsunwoo, 25710 Petelandgren, 6246 Komurotoru, 10639 Gleason, 269550 Chur, 2240 Tsai, 3410 Vereshchagin, 13921 Sgarbini

42q3 (256.354) \\SIER; 15392 Budejicky, 21262 Kanba, 10166 Takarajima, 114991 Balazs, 5392 Parker, 6184 Nordlund, 8503 Masakatsu, 16023 Alisonyee, 7102 Neilbone, 5539 Limporyen, 238129 Bernardwolfe, 24856 Messidoro, 20314 Johnharrison, 1189 Terentia, 26681 Niezgay, 19543 Burgoyne, 9669 Symmetria, 3341 Hartmann, 16998 Estelleweber, 235 Carolina, 32025 Karanjerath, 15499 Cloyd, 8251 Isogai, 23812 Jannuzi

114q3 (76.354) \\my occasional ghetto quip regarding any number of things; Dial; 2964 Jaschek, 21718 Cheonghapark, 10582 Harumi, 6204 MacKenzie, 4362 Carlisle, 15168 Marijnfranx, 16079 Imada, 7415 Susumuimoto, 5992 Nittler

qc223: mr. cool, and how I handle the hot-girls; the handling of death

18q3 (316.354) \\how my cats, dad, and uncle richard were remembered—at the funerals I've been to; 29747 Acorlando, 9904 Mauratombelli, 35725 Tramuntana, 90461 Matthewgraham, 5227 Bocacara, 10106 Lergrav, 8130 Seeberg, 7291 Hyakutake, 9190 Masako, 26971 Sezimovo Usti, 128373 Kevinjohnson, 20585 Wentworth

90q3 (136.354) \\until I am big news, I am really disinclined to put anyone before myself or leave anyone with anything; 22598 Francespearl, 10737 Bruck, 245890 Krynychenka, 1198 Atlantis, 21708 Mulhall, 16441 Kirchner, 6410 Fujiwara, 39 Laetitia, 15821 Iijimatatsushi, 61386 Namikoshi, 21557 Daniellitt, 41 Daphne

54q3 (226.354) \\how my pets die, how I experience burials or transition into death—the end of an aspiration. Seems I am more likely to see this either for petite / small associations (especially pets and animals), or otherwise just not be around for the human deaths. a blessing for the empath in me; 5029 Ireland, 33826 Kevynadams,

23776 Gosset, 201777 Deronda, 5640 Yoshino, 7860 Zahnle, 21695 Hannahwolf, 9791 Kamiyakurai, 1273 Helma, 21644 Vinay, 22199 Klonios, 4614 Masamura

126q3 (46.354) \\miki, edison; 25369 Dawndonovan, 52226 Saenredam, 56100 Luisapolli, 14674 INAOE, 11140 Yakedake, 564 Dudu, 34172 Camillemiles, 14403 de Machault, 183403 Gal, 31495 Sarahgalvin

qc79: my work and whether anyone can use it, otherwise, the charismatic popular road

30q3 (286.354) \\either sb or me retreating after a battle; 1546 Izsak, 26857 Veracruz, 12729 Berger, 6797 Ostersund, 31377 Kleinwort, 27465 Cambroziak, 7717 Tabeisshi, 26177 Fabiodolfi

102q3 (106.354) \\hanging up shanna's paintings, arranging dad's records?; 4717 Kaneko, 31700 Naperez, 1661 Granule, 8544 Sigenori, 3650 Kunming, 164701 Horanyi, 273 Atropos, 11115 Kariya, 27610 Shixuanli, 380607 Sharma, 829 Academia, 8783 Gopasyuk, 5262 Brucegoldberg

66q3 (196.354) \\still demanding shit? Not gonna help me get it for you? Okay, be on your way.; 1120 Cannonia, 25422 Abigreene, 22622 Strong, 69971 Tanzi, 65696 Pierrehenry, 20197 Enriques, 50687 Paultemple, 188534 Mauna Kea, 30033 Kevinlee, 20285 Lubin, 14791 Atreus, 24934 Natecovert, 24826 Pascoli, 14338 Shibakoukan, 28536 Hunaiwen, 16912 Rhiannon, 3025 Higson, 269232 Tahin, 12160 Karelwakker, 23059 Paulpaino, 36226 Mackerras, 6742 Biandepei, 505 Cava, 1958 Chandra

138q3 (16.354) \\ME SLOWED DOWN DOING THESE QUNITS CREATING AI INSTEAD; 11203 Danielbetten, 32593 Crotty, 13852 Ford, 31848 Mikemattei, 73704 Hladiuk, 31266 Tournefort, 23006 Pazden, 4774 Hobetsu, 292459 Antoniolasciac, 3368 Duncombe

qig28: gods and faith structures you answer to

qc366 seems to indicate the co-founders' lottery win

6q2 (346.146) \\on the lookout for good lawncare products and solutions; 28655 Erincolfax, 31838 Angelarob, 22836 Leeannragasa, 4730 Xingmingzhou, 107054 Daniela, 36774 Kuittinen

78q2 (166.146) \\szw doesn't like us; 11797 Warell, 31787 Darcylawson, 43657 Bobmiller, 11766 Fredseares, 9216 Masuzawa, 90502 Buratti, 21406 Jimyang, 5221 Fabribudweis, 4629 Walford, 12211 Arnoschmidt

42q2 (256.146) \\me and b.a.r., but then there are others; 1097 Vicia, 24385 Katcagen, 34162 Yegnesh, 2029 Binomi, 32184 Yamaura, 18100 Lebreton, 216428 Mauricio, 11577 Einasto, 58572 Romanella, 10154 Tanuki, 5682 Beresford, 13647 Rey, 31374 Hruskova

114q2 (76.146) \\obama, roosevelt; 22281 Popescu, 4736 Johnwood, 4990 Trombka, 1843 Jarmila, 4291 Kodaihasu, 80184 Hekigoto, 31917 Lukashohne, 26376 Roborosa, 14468 Ottostern

qc222: independent work done in isolation

18q2 (316.146) \\me using notepad and regex, yardwork to do mass production in front of another; 9639 Scherer, 28073 Fohner, 239200 Luoyang, 3228 Pire, 6631 Pyatnitskij

90q2 (136.146) \\watching REDACTED work on something boring, but necessary and too difficult for me to do myself; 2412 Wil, 7948 Whitaker, 32405 Jameshill, 111913 Davidgans, 3881 Doumergua, 753 Tiflis, 19584 Sarahgerin, 34611 Nacogdoches, 8447 Cornejo, 8124 Guardi, 1109 Tata, 10224 Hisashi, 13848 Cioffi, 31688 Bryantliu, 2809 Vernadskij, 13325 Valerienataf

54q2 (226.146) \\coming back from other duties, from upstairs, for example. Disappearance from duty and observability; 34817 Shiominemoto, 89 Julia, 115312 Whither, 9321 Alexkonopliv, 184064 Miner, 236170 Cholnoky, 7976 Pinigin, 5632 Ingelehmann, 7897 Bohuska, 1307 Cimmeria, 13229 Echion, 223685 Hartopp, 33010 Enricoprosperi, 4033 Yatsugatake

126q2 (46.146) \\me dropping a current task or disappearing to do my exercises; 1393 Sofala, 7446 Hadrianus, 237276 Nakama, 26794 Yukioniimi, 171118 Szigetkoz, 42748 Andrisani, 10216 Popastro, 11408 Zahradnik, 27564 Astreichelt

qc78: build using imagination on your own. Otherwise, this is bullshit—it's time for interference

30q2 (286.146) \\me putting an unprepared person in charge of my vitally important operation; lego enterprises; 3290 Azabu, 23818 Matthewlepow, 6981 Chirman, 21427 Ryanharrison, 21126 Katsuyoshi, 5171 Augustesen, 7549 Woodard, 418 Alemannia, 77755 Delemont, 274856 Rosendosalvado, 6571 Sigmund, 134092 Lindaleematthias, 17579 Lewkopelew, 18288 Nozdrachev, 12556 Kyrobinson, 1671 Chaika, 50412 Ewen, 4198 Panthera, 34294 Taylordufford, 510 Mabella

102q2 (106.146) \\my focus on the next message to be delivered; the inventive minds who play with lego; 5736 Sanford, 236743 Zhejiangdaxue, 11819 Millarca, 186007 Guilleminet, 17702 Krystofharant, 11912 Piedade, 9700 Paech, 9389 Condillac, 2724 Orlov, 39748 Guccini, 10184 Galvani

66q2 (196.146) \\showdowns with REDACTED out in the yard; 28272 Mikejanner, 129898 Sanfordselznick, 28583 Mehrotra, 23691 Jefneve, 12526 de Coninck, 13421 Holvorcem, 25913 Jamesgreen, 6350 Schluter, 13184 Augeias, 10029 Hiramperkins, 21014 Daishi, 846 Lipperta, 32005 Roberthalfon, 20961 Arkesilaos, 11779 Zernike, 9241 Rosfranklin, 260906 Robichon, 37141 Povolny, 5680 Nasmyth, 11379 Flaubert

138q2 (16.146) \\ptt (principles of time travel); 8266 Bertelli, 7171 Arthurkraus, 3601 Velikhov, 4646 Kwee, 78432 Helensailer, 22656 Aaronburrows, 12008 Kandrup

qig29: driven to put your personality onto the world

qc365: approaching a partner to start something

6q1 (345.938) \\my dependence on perfect timing to announce a clear correct direction for narrating my actions; 10930 Jinyong, 241442 Shandongkexie, 28698 Aakshi, 17993 Kluesing, 181136 Losonczrita

78q1 (165.938) \\human data save period, including partner difficulties; 9084 Achristou, 6188 Robertpepin, 5192 Yabuki, 1384 Kniertje, 23571 Zuaboni, 4017 Disneya, 454409 Markusloose, 12596 Shukla, 12033 Anselmo, 9984 Gregbryant, 4794 Bogard, 10728 Vladimirfock, 128062 Szrogh, 163244 Matthewhill, 28048 Camilleyoke, 33502 Janetwaldeck, 1472 Muonio, 28681 Loseke

42q1 (255.938) \\lunch with cz; 424200 Tonicelia, 10048 Gronbech, 1489 Attila, 198 Ampella, 2522 Triglav, 78071 Vicent, 4844 Matsuyama, 10049 Vorovich, 25746 Nickscoville, 5667 Nakhimovskaya, 70850 Schur, 7742 Altamira, 3255 Tholen, 650 Amalasuntha, 3885 Bogorodskij, 7 Iris, 2669 Shostakovich, 3543 Ningbo

114q1 (75.938) \\REDACTED; rambo, last blood?; 22165 Kathydouglas, 120112 Elizabethacton, 5801 Vasarely, 1751 Herget

qc221: finally finishing the editing and publication of a difficult work, especially contours and alma mater

18q1 (315.938) \\my house, land or classics purchases—just for collecting; 10721 Tuterov, 8940 Yakushimaru, 17995 Jolinefan, 46719 Plantade, 185576 Covichi, 11050 Messiaen, 30008 Aroncoraor, 25509 Rodwong, 9837 Jerryhorow, 186411 Margaretsimon, 17967 Bacampbell, 8204 Takabatake, 161585 Danielhals

90q1 (135.938) \\staying in the back, studying bodies for a looong time; 111660 Jimgray, 987 Wallia, 3286 Anatoliya, 79086 Gorgasali, 21854 Brendandwyer, 6666 Fro, 2961 Katsurahama, 14232 Curtismiller, 8425 Zirankexuejijin, 3636 Pajdusakova, 178294 Wertheimer, 1048 Feodosia, 21368 Shiodayama, 6460 Bassano

54q1 (225.938) \\the decision to go all in. you won't be any more ready than this; 6800 Saragamine, 136367 Gierlinger, 5037 Habing, 5811 Keck, 341359 Gregneumann, 2534 Houzeau, 114026 Emalanushenko, 19778 Louisgarcia, 29619 Kapurubandage, 13179 Johncochrane, 16157 Toastmasters, 7146 Konradin, 9423 Abt, 3801 Thrasymedes, 375043 Zengweizhou, 2479 Sodankyla, 25711 Lebovits, 189312 Jameyszalay, 210231 Wangdemin, 207899 Grinmalia

126q1 (45.938) \\when you are finally ready to go forward, the circumstances that accompany this; me and mb; 18944 Sawilliams, 27739 Kimihiro, 29346 Mariadina, 19857 Amandajane, 7270 Punkin, 33466 Thomaslarson

qc77: the futile fight against unequal division. Use qc221 or qc365 instead

30q1 (285.938) \\the collaboration itself, probably destined to implode; one who can't help but start fights; 3473 Sapporo, 30122 Elschweitzer, 56088 Wuheng, 30005 Stevenchen, 84417 Ritabo, 12634 LOFAR, 10895 Aynrand, 343322 Tomskuniver, 24118 Babazadeh, 10068 Dodoens, 908 Buda, 129214 Gordoncasto, 9107 Narukospa, 28042 Mayapatel, 30130 Jeandillman, 6107 Osterbrock

102q1 (105.938) \\i generally power through tough or arduous tasks when it comes to work; stubborn powering through; 6569 Ondaatje, 11816 Vasile, 164791 Nicinski, 16142 Leung, 13734 Buklad, 7464 Vipera, 5247 Krylov, 70716 Mehall, 34738 Hulbert

66q1 (195.938) \\my self-gamification monologuic battles; protesting unequal division doesn't work; 330440 Davinadon, 19034 Santorini, 19268 Morstadt, 965 Angelica, 134131 Skipowens, 12973 Melanthios, 26551 Shenliangbo, 26223 Enari, 1585 Union, 32022 Sarahjenkins, 10782 Hittmair, 6710 Apostel, 7690 Sackler, 7508 Icke, 19353 Pierrethierry, 1129 Neujmina, 26429 Andiwagner, 3045 Alois, 1735 ITA

138q1 (15.938) \\finding a puzzle or something to occupy myself with while waiting, at the airport for example, cryptograms; 287787 Karady, 6932 Tanigawadake, 11581 Philipdejager, 31000 Rockchic, 14975 Serasin, 7412 Linnaeus, 2727 Paton, 7388 Marcomorelli

qig30: you are played towards another's usage

qc364: the monopolists; simeona in exile and the chain that put her there

6q12 (345.729) \\taking a small break after much of the day's hard research is done. - part of the tower view; 21589 Rafes, 6193 Manabe, 945 Barcelona

78q12 (165.729) \\my alchemical-asteroidal qunit work meant to help resolve social problems, but also challenge the prevailing structures; 2902 Westerlund, 10711 Pskov, 13253 Stejneger, 78578 Donpettit, 395 Delia, 114649 Jeanneacker, 114689

Tomstevens, 20103 de Vico, 16147 Jeanli, 30348 Marizzabailey, 800 Kressmannia, 8642 Shawnkerry, 1378 Leonce, 413 Edburga

42q12 (255.729) \\monopolist companies and practices; 6653 Feininger, 4274 Karamanov, 30440 Larry, 22947 Carolsuh, 24131 Jonathuggins, 489 Comacina, 343587 Mamuna, 2984 Chaucer, 4894 Ask, 24927 Brianpalmer, 26592 Maryrenfro, 58098 Quirrenbach, 7909 Ziffer, 7526 Ohtsuka, 24126 Gudjonson, 46563 Oken, 295472 Puy, 10428 Wanders, 15617 Fallowfield, 8471 Obrant, 26947 Angelawang, 10960 Gran Sasso

114q12 (75.729) \\what I subjected REDACTED to, and t.o.... making her do all the work while I pushed her away; 220 Stephania, 28817 Simoneflood, 48482 Oruki, 18403 Atsuhirotaisei, 19509 Niigata, 17104 McCloskey, 229440 Filimon

qc220: my team's groupthink as opposed to things I am truly into

18q12 (315.729) \\simeona gets blasted by me for [REDACTED EVENT]; 3993 Sorm, 14060 Patersonewen, 17257 Strazzulla, 204702 Pequignat, 14699 Klarasmi, 7885 Levine, 13858 Ericchristensen, 212465 Goroshky, 93061 Barbagallo, 31500 Grutzik, 16669 Rionuevo

90q12 (135.729) \\simeona as companion; 85511 Celnik, 8922 Kumanodake, 279226 Demisroussos, 4908 Ward, 9950 ESA, 25706 Cekoscielski, 4661 Yebes, 59417 Giocasilli, 4585 Ainonai, 1470 Carla, 538 Friederike, 121468 Msovinskihaskell, 5845 Davidbrewster, 12366 Luisapla, 31097 Nucciomula

54q12 (225.729) \\agreeing with my team to vote in a particular way; pi planning; 4078 Polakis, 172425 Taliajacobi, 164518 Patoche, 16116 Balakrishnan, 128604 Markfisher, 792 Metcalfia, 25326 Lawrencesun, 14539 Clocke Roeland, 3665 Fitzgerald, 4073 Ruianzhongxue, 339 Dorothea, 3998 Tezuka, 202 Chryseis, 1559 Kustaanheimo

126q12 (45.729) \\my physical state holds more blockers for a time; 85516 Vaclik, 2695 Christabel, 26897 Cervena, 280 Philia, 22545 Brittrusso, 22775 Jasonelloyd

qc76: how the victor appears at the end of the battle. When other people have beaten me, use qc364

30q12 (285.729) \\the indication that something is not liked / unsettling; rachel or chico raising the alarm during play; yelling during naha; 262 Valda, 352333 Sylvievauclair, 23890 Quindou, 25312 Asiapossenti, 9829 Murillo

102q12 (105.729) \\the beginning of metrobots; the peak of a battle. It is finally decided. The end of naha; 18015 Semenkovich, 2874 Jim Young, 22802 Sigiriya, 12128 Palermiti, 11672 Cuney, 454329 Ericpiquette, 17950 Grover, 10140 Villon, 1805 Dirikis

66q12 (195.729) \\keith emerges as a battle buddy type; how the victor is cast in appearance; 26761 Stromboli, 2162 Anhui, 19738 Calinger, 17815 Kulawik, 13714 Stainbrook, 3516 Rusheva, 27386 Chadcampbell, 28759 Joshwentzel, 9446 Cicero, 5552 Studnicka, 2557 Putnam, 17670 Liddell, 22222 Hodios, 25650 Shaubakshi

138q12 (15.729) \\me in nice, evaluating; the social part of the tower view. Our eastern side's Naha tug of war 2023 victory; 13403 Sarahmousa, 444 Gyptis, 23259 Miwadagakuen, 3799 Novgorod

qig31: knowingly sowing conflict or tension

qc363: the definition of money: the compulsion to start and run sata

6q11 (345.521) \\money inspires people to do this; the kind of risk assessment also done by criminals; 248 Lameia, 11254 Konkohekisui, 23257 Denny, 25704 Kendrick, 7533 Seiraiji, 6798 Couperin, 4588 Wislicenus, 1002 Olbersia

78q11 (165.521) \\I AM MONEY (who money thinks it is); the event with narvaez; 210210 Songjian, 12927 Pinocchio, 27405 Danielfeeny, 121331 Savannahsalazar, 6497 Yamasaki, 20574 Ochinero, 33727 Kummel, 9971 Ishihara, 16254 Harper, 4900 Maymelou, 4840 Otaynang, 8984 Derevyanko

42q11 (255.521) \\the individuals who took the junk off of my back porch; my image of a plain old ruthless character; 6333 Helenejacq, 24386 McLindon, 6616 Plotinos, 32107 Ylitalo, 15316 Okagakimachi, 32132 Andrewamini, 17089 Mercado, 212991 Garcialorca, 24387 Trettel, 20522 Yogeshwar, 22283 Pytheas, 75063 Koestler, 10439 van Schooten, 10551 Goteborg, 14149 Yakowitz, 85198 Weltenburg

114q11 (75.521) \\me watching the folks take the junk off of my back porch; those whom I mobilize in pursuit of money; various bad wannabe leaders I've met; 892 Seeligeria, 6776 Dix, 20495 Rimavska Sobota, 4775 Hansen, 22875 Lanejackson, 13370 Juliusbreza, 5217 Chaozhou, 13718 Welcker, 4875 Ingalls

qc219: the partnering woes which are necessary for sata to build and money to arrive

18q11 (315.521) \\the end of s.o.s. and our meeting with CEC; 46442 Keithtritton, 6778 Tosamakoto, 3924 Birch, 2 Pallas, 33553 Nagai, 5125 Okushiri, 32264 Cathjesslai, 6230 Fram, 36426 Kakuda, 14316 Higashichichibu, 60558 Echeclus, 204831 Levski, 40328 Dow

90q11 (135.521) \\my losing all friends, exile from nsbe and eventually caltech; 11295 Gustaflarsson, 21437 Georgechen, 151430 Nemunas, 65697 Paulandrew, 22423

Kudlacek, 264165 Poehler, 19263 Lavater, 8965 Citrinella, 14827 Hypnos, 40440 Dobrovsky, 305181 Donelaitis, 1556 Wingolfia

54q11 (225.521) \\how I generally keep control; THE proxy lottery win during partnership initiation; 83464 Irishmccalla; 4544 Xanthus, 7122 Iwasaki, 3883 Verbano, 364 Isara, 202784 Gangkeda, 30129 Virmani, 20658 Bushmarinov, 25176 Thomasaunins, 86551 Seth, 31953 Bontha, 26713 Iusukyin, 25566 Panying, 2805 Kalle, 83464 Irishmccalla, 130126 Stillmanchase, 51824 Mikeanderson, 33688 Meghnabehari, 13178 Catalan, 32897 Curtharris, 1007 Pawlowia, 170906 Coluche, 23067 Ishajain, 12811 Rigonistern, 1414 Jerome

126q11 (45.521) \\my general reception and role at REDACTED, early on; 18679 Heatherenae, 24219 Chrisodom, 31982 Johnwallis, 24102 Jacquescassini, 3460 Ashkova, 52242 Michelemaoret, 40444 Palacky, 8761 Crane, 10604 Susanoo, 44574 Lavoratti, 16646 Sparrman, 6062 Vespa

qc75: later miranda dynamics among top leaders after they have conquered the world

30q11 (285.521) \\the description of the mate my body is drawn to, shanna sort of. A blond version of agd; Aimee Dial... or me; 142822 Czarapata, 21407 Jessicabaker, 17544 Kojiroishikawa, 12628 Ackworthorr, 33886 Lilydeveau, 2971 Mohr, 16807 Terasako, 5234 Sechenov, 69228 Kamerunberg, 292 Ludovica, 9220 Yoshidayama, 25678 Ericfoss, 15965 Robertcox, 1912 Anubis, 15727 Ianmorison, 810 Atossa, 27595 Hnath

102q11 (105.521) \\Strengthening myself given failures of enterprise and nowhere else to go; phaedra's concerns; 6761 Haroldconnolly, 14697 Ronsawyer, 32313 Zhangmichael, 18449 Rikwouters, 2577 Litva, 29250 Helmutmoritz, 2205 Glinka, 7399 Somme, 149115 Lauriecantillo, 8737 Takehiro, 31771 Kirstenwright, 9727 Skrutskie

66q11 (195.521) \\various behaviors I display which grate on others; genevieve prohal as sei esperanza; 10117 Tanikawa, 20347 Wunderlich, 25412 Arbesfeld, 32563 Nicolezaidi, 148081 Sunjiadong, 1237 Genevieve, 361530 Victorfranzhess, 13770 Commerson, 39930 Kalauch, 1699 Honkasalo, 13326 Ferri, 1858 Lobachevskij, 25230 Borgis, 25143 Itokawa, 9342 Carygrant

138q11 (15.521) \\constantly wishing to be deployed; beholden to phaedra; 210983 Wadeparker, 166886 Ybl, 9679 Crutzen, 2994 Flynn, 3631 Sigyn, 34130 Isabellaivy, 9872 Solf, 11724 Ronaldhsu

qig32: outlook from the foreign towards you

qc362: the identification of potential legends

6q10 (345.313) \\what I'm doing when wearing my device or using it upstairs; 19523 Paolofrisi, 4743 Kikuchi, 7013 Trachet, 8496 Jandlsmith, 23887 Shinsukeabe, 10908 Kallestroetzel, 14365 Jeanpaul

78q10 (165.313) \\tyrant makes a rousing speech; the villain reinforces his power; 25763 Naveenmurali, 1020 Arcadia, 2758 Cordelia, 5152 Labs, 6108 Glebov, 3947 Swedenborg, 27660 Waterwayuni, 17858 Beauge, 2315 Czechoslovakia, 20880 Yiyideng, 26255 Carmarques, 2321 Luznice, 133774 Johnkidd, 145962 Lacchini, 32229 Higashino, 877 Walkure, 4317 Garibaldi, 28851 Londonbolsius, 1638 Ruanda

42q10 (255.313) \\reflecting on the continually increasing ... of REDACTED and where the ultimate target should be; 2652 Yabuuti, 27343 Deannashea, 8493 Yachibozu, 9797 Raes, 25890 Louisburg, 25093 Andmikhaylov, 19478 Jaimeflores, 7531 Pecorelli, 10951 Spessart, 9448 Donaldavies

114q10 (75.313) \\leisurely vacationy reflection on where I am, often in a place where others (including the dogs) are present enough for me to not have actual alone-space. When I'm in this mode, the regular sense of ongoing potency growth is paused out of respect for the stability others need from me. incomplete around the legs or travel tools, and can only move in the spirit/water space rather than overtly; 8794 Joepatterson, 10009 Hirosetanso, 135980 Scottanderson, 25112 Mymeshkovych, 12064 Guiraudon, 29186 Lake Tekapo, 6523 Clube, 2384 Schulhof

qc218: the various faces of social disapproval

18q10 (315.313) \\unknowingly, I have accepted fetch quests in situations where I felt I needed to keep fitting in with some group's expectations; my experiences with actual white supremacist groups is very low, and mostly harmless / academic; 79647 Ballack, 19587 Keremane, 31113 Stull, 8500 Hori, 2067 Aksnes, 17893 Arlot, 24206 Mariealoia, 20862 Jenngoedhart

90q10 (135.313) \\the indian and latinx images I create; 3137 Horky, 5252 Vikrymov, 10290 Kettering, 21696 Ermalmquist, 21721 Feiniqu, 10368 Kozuki, 1596 Itzigsohn

54q10 (225.313) \\SNL and other satire groups. dpg. The jumpers; 114 Kassandra, 3896 Pordenone, 8571 Taniguchi, 5473 Yamanashi, 15042 Anndavgui, 2521 Heidi, 293934 MPIA, 33875 Laurencooney, 25099 Mashinskiy, 1709 Ukraina, 19533 Garrison, 32070 Michaelretchin, 39540 Borchert, 20555 Jennings, 4024 Ronan, 13686 Kongozan, 28530 Shiyimeng, 15609 Kosmaczewski, 30035 Charlesliu

126q10 (45.313) \\mc's, nature and conservationist efforts, my own immune system by social information; 14509 Lucenec, 3418 Izvekov, 221 Eos, 9515 Dubner, 43724 Pechstein, 18789 Metzger, 10259 Osipovyurij

qc74: thanks to trials I have endured, I come to believe certain thing MUST be fact. This qc has **greatly** shaped my personality, and was likely fated

30q10 (285.313) \\going with whoever my partner is, despite tension with them. Also, how I would describe my assertion power; subconsciously determined to make it into an engine for sabotaging intimacy by growing it beyond manageability, I suppose— taking control of plagued relationship patterns which go as far back as (grandmother) ruth and her mom. Avoid nonsensical interruptions to stay on track; 34144 Alexandersun, 9055 Edvardsson, 3940 Larion, 18610 Arthurdent, 1224 Fantasia, 2133 Franceswright, 27192 Selenali, 5139 Rumoi, 24162 Askaci, 1980 Tezcatlipoca, 163119 Timmckay, 121469 Sarahaugh

102q10 (105.313) \\sata repeatedly sabotaged, then ultimate failure. or so it seems...; 255257 Mechwart, 7461 Kachmokiam, 3091 van den Heuvel, 32612 Ghatare, 129335 Edwardlittle, 28133 Kylebardwell, 20218 Dukewriter

66q10 (195.313) \\my experience traveling to foreign contexts; 6164 Gerhardmuller, 8788 Labeyrie, 31863 Hazelcoffman, 3082 Dzhalil, 19970 Johannpeter, 33230 Libbyrobertson, 15569 Feinberg, 28829 Abelsky, 90138 Diehl, 402920 Tsawout, 4156 Okadanoboru, 7095 Lamettrie, 4377 Koremori, 24608 Alexveselkov

138q10 (15.313) \\deep frustration with things that interrupt and don't make sense; 8936 Gianni, 16641 Esteban, 31468 Albastaki, 2718 Handley, 30844 Hukeller, 9584 Louchheim, 45261 Decoen, 113395 Curtniebur

qig33: mothered

qc361: my private version of power

6q9 (345.104) \\notions of surveillance, me waiting to inflict a new law on my classes; 18152 Heidimanning, 13657 Badinter, 15151 Wilmacherup, 1793 Zoya, 11463 Petrpokorny, 26508 Jimmylin, 16853 Masafumi, 2204 Lyyli, 8133 Takanochoei, 221150 Jerryfoote, 96254 Hoyo, 3110 Wagman

78q9 (165.104) \\I gradually build up my esoteric paradigm (alma mater, fsa); 289020 Ukmerge, 2169 Taiwan, 3913 Chemin, 22567 Zenisek, 23811 Connorivens, 8080 Intel, 5498 Gustafsson, 2428 Kamenyar, 4202 Minitti, 210182 Mazzini, 7978 Niknesterov, 269251 Kolomna, 7890 Yasuofukui, 35137 Meudon, 1432 Ethiopia, 17190 Retopezzoli, 3098 van Sprang, 26970 Elias, 281459 Kyrylenko, 4453 Bornholm, 33117 Ashinimodi, 24245 Ezratty

42q9 (255.104) \\my brand of problem solving typically aims for long term precedent and automation, keeping in mind the need to avoid facing the same problem again; 1078 Mentha, 2647 Sova, 1368 Numidia, 97582 Hijikawa, 43998 Nanyoshino, 11440 Massironi, 88071 Taniguchijiro, 260601 Wesselenyi, 3696 Herald, 185733 Luigicolzani, 7651 Villeneuve

114q9 (75.104) \\strongarmed by REDACTED or REDACTED; 1533 Saimaa, 1806 Derice, 34187 Tomaino, 995 Sternberga, 5404 Uemura, 8747 Asahi, 5939 Toshimayeda, 19826 Patwalker, 188847 Rhipeus, 2945 Zanstra

qc217: plain old political power

18q9 (315.104) \\the dogs, sometimes, my friends on a quest; 2016+ REDACTED; 9364 Clusius, 10812 Grotlingbo, 8200 Souten, 26395 Megkurohara, 5848 Harutoriko, 3197 Weissman, 44016 Jimmypage, 16264 Richlee, 27917 Edoardo, 10540 Hachigoroh

90q9 (135.104) \\my bringing someone on to help in a business endeavor, explaining their duties; t.d.; 2262 Mitidika, 16438 Knofel, 19183 Amati, 16804 Bonini, 133404 Morogues, 175437 Zsivotzky, 14425 Fujimimachi, 111594 Raktanya, 301794 Antoninkapustin, 256796 Almanzor, 3215 Lapko, 7904 Morrow

54q9 (225.104) \\my close conversations with emily, vanessa, marion, etc. friendship situations, though it doesn't appear that these people actually stay; 1396 Outeniqua, 8317 Eurysaces, 10441 van Rijckevorsel, 30218 Paulaladd, 90125 Chrissquire, 109097 Hamuy, 55212 Yukitoayatsuji, 4946 Askalaphus, 31098 Frankhill, 9139 Barrylasker, 13406 Sekora, 10427 Klinkenberg, 7386 Paulpellas, 52301 Qumran, 10153 Goldman, 3830 Trelleborg, 4343 Tetsuya, 5850 Masaharu, 2528 Mohler, 13174 Timossi

126q9 (45.104) \\sk or my own presentation as a perfectionistic scientist. Seems to erect a barrier to getting long-term involved with this one; 2930 Euripides, 9931 Herbhauptman, 1667 Pels, 5726 Rubin, 28688 Diannerister, 14172 Amanolivere

qc73: immersed in my own version of the work and my own talents, my partner finds me wayward and unmovable; kit vs the dogs. Definitely reflects mine and shanna's stubbornness in each other's view

30q9 (285.104) \\flirted with. How a would-be mate or ally sees your potential in their lives ahead of time; kit in isolation; //trigger=hubble | how I am easily able to map an uncertain space; 27576 Denisespirou, 14550 Lehky, 10263 Vadimsimona, -10056

Selena/White Moon, 2319 Aristides, 3328 Interposita, 27309 Serenamccalla, 3223 Forsius, 4703 Kagoshima, 2069 Hubble, 7728 Giblin, 28656 Doreencurtin

102q9 (105.104) \\airplane aisle-walk walk; My mid-transition aisle walk through a place - a mean or calculating defensive bearing; 16037 Sheehan, 4871 Riverside, 26738 Lishizhen, 4052 Crovisier, 1240 Centenaria, 24026 Pusateri, 11928 Akimotohiro, 1654 Bojeva, 13700 Connors, 2149 Schwambraniya, 218636 Calabria

66q9 (195.104) \\gun shy regarding promotion of knime, feminism, and other belief systems; 5579 Uhlherr, 491 Carina, 11190 Jennibell, 18237 Kenfreeman, 20136 Eisenhart, 120186 Suealeman, 125 Liberatrix, 21540 Itthipanyanan, 3698 Manning, 28159 Giuricich, 19589 Kirkland, 13279 Gutman, 5290 Langevin, 130249 Markminer, 9349 Lucas, 214883 Yuanxikun, 3864 Soren, 809 Lundia, 11899 Weill

138q9 (15.104) \\my getting sick, wanting to go to toys r us again; worrying about what lies ahead, tit for tat panicking; possibly a prenatal environment you developed against; 2957 Tatsuo, 14511 Nickel, 7104 Manyousyu, 1130 Skuld, 7092 Cadmus

qig34: the agenda should be kept

qc360: tournaments and league outcomes

7q8 (344.896) \\treaty negotiations. I don't believe I've done this outside of the classroom; 6570 Tomohiro, 9640 Lippens, 6456 Golombek, 31617 Meeraradha, 8379 Straczynski, 34302 Riagalanos

79q8 (164.896) \\my journeying on in the fight until the right support emerges; 192439 Cilek, 10538 Torode, 10025 Rauer, 6487 Tonyspear, 31902 Raymondwang, 20354 Rebeccachan, 8344 Babette, 4094 Aoshima, 4429 Chinmoy, 100735 Alpomoranska, 28664 Maryellenfay, 1957 Angara, 4273 Dunhuang, 72447 Polinska, 257533 Iquique, 2081 Sazava, 9110 Choukai, 24103 Dethury, 255019 Fleurmaxwell, 1955 McMath

43q8 (254.896) \\REDACTED brings confusion, but is only trying to help; 3122 Florence, 29994 Zuoyu, 156939 Odegard, 308197 Satrapi, 5218 Kutsak, 14339 Knorre, 12638 Fransbruggen, 87097 Lomaki, 8898 Linnaea, 297026 Corton, 25381 Jerrynelson, 31189 Tricomi

115q8 (74.896) \\REDACTED or, less so, REDACTED, could have been vb; 25127 Laurentbrunetto, 9491 Thooft, 3950 Yoshida, 10244 Thuringer Wald, 6580 Philbland, 3717 Thorenia, 241363 Erdibalint, 28935 Kevincyr, 6734 Benzenberg

qc216: REDACTED and how we saw each other; hot, warm, but unsupportive. Do not prioritize this

19q8 (314.896) \\REDACTED, REDACTED, REDACTED; true teachers, and thus automatic co-creators. These probably could have gotten me to have sex with them no questions asked at some point earlier in life; vh; REDACTED maybe; 25462 Haydenmetsky, 4964 Kourovka, 39558 Kishine, 12140 Johnbolton, 3578 Carestia, 28480 Seojinyoung, 8444 Popovich, 14206 Sehnal

91q8 (134.896) \\one of my dedicated teachers who insisted on raising the avant garde next generation; mine and mb's dealings with vb; 23401 Brodskaya, 13404 Norris, 28953 Hollyerickson, 24681 Granados, 65657 Hube, 65859 Madler, 4517 Ralpharvey, 7945 Kreisau, 11765 Alfredfowler, 164130 Jonckheere, 10648 Plancius, 1376 Michelle, 5517 Johnerogers

55q8 (224.896) \\my conception of (my own) orgasmic experience as it unfolds in the imagination. Opposite this is what I favor as an accompanying sight; 9610 Vischer, 69869 Haining, 25 Phocaea, 134072 Sharonhooven, 614 Pia, 24317 Pukarhamal, 29633 Weatherwax, 3436 Ibadinov, 3659 Bellingshausen, 228133 Ripoll, 125473 Keisaku, 3217 Seidelmann

127q8 (44.896) \\my longer-term, post-event, mulling-looming after a conflict has ended, attempting to put together the whole picture privately, misunderstood during and possibly thereafter; 7442 Inouehideo, 14551 Itagaki, 31633 Almonte, 8970 Islandica, 15170 Erikdeul, 568 Cheruskia, 151351 Dalleore, 17062 Bardot, 3252 Johnny

qc72: kit vs the dogs part II, the yearning for chart topping attention

31q8 (284.896) \\the duo. REDACTED and REDACTED interaction begins with ..., bw and gn | extra, kindred members from the social group?; 29706 Simonetta, 6446 Lomberg, 4720 Tottori, 30357 Davisdon, 2159 Kukkamaki, 551 Ortrud, 31640 Johncaven, 10626 Zajic, 5014 Gorchakov, 23897 Daikuroda, 3776 Vartiovuori, 6345 Hideo

103q8 (104.896) \\i in my hunger to be chart-topping; 20545 Karenhowell, 33504 Rebrouwer, 96178 Rochambeau, 274860 Emilylakdawalla, 12423 Slotin, 27446 Landoni, 11514 Tsunenaga, 7170 Livesey, 7918 Berrilli, 91 Aegina, 33561 Brianjasondu, 4933 Tylerlinder

67q8 (194.896) \\everyone witnesses me lose my temper; 25942 Walborn, 6516 Gruss, 19591 Michaelklein, 225239 Ruthproell, 2419 Moldavia, 2213 Meeus, 43025 Valusha, 1562 Gondolatsch, 8707 Arakihiroshi, 1381 Danubia, 152146 Rosenlappin, 3980 Hviezdoslav, 4830 Thomascooley, 8443 Svecica, 215809 Hugoschwarz, 4885 Grange

139q8 (14.896) \\how we partners tend to influence each other; 2721 Vsekhsvyatskij, 281561 Taitung, 10568 Yoshitanaka, 9079 Gesner

qig35: your social imprint

qc359: a career-ending injury, doctor, or league which controls a player's ability to play

7q7 (344.688) \\I stay with my obsessive work in private, and this is what keeps me from launching; 2692 Chkalov, 32562 Caseywarner, 2116 Mtskheta

79q7 (164.688) \\IADT instructor; me as a general genEd instructor and my role as such at iadt; 14367 Hippokrates, 6058 Carlnielsen, 88 Thisbe, 18787 Kathermann, 2477 Biryukov, 25229 Karenkitt, 2085 Henan, 9080 Takayanagi, 6885 Nitardy, 12672 Nygardh, 150118 Petersberg, 133892 Benkhaldoun, 169078 Chuckshaw, 20517 Judycrystal, 10674 de Elia, 1991 Darwin

43q7 (254.688) \\once outside of my teaching or research clutches, the things people say or do about their experience there; 10443 van der Pol, 84225 Verish, 21088 Chelyabinsk, 37645 Chebarkul, 23011 Petach, 293366 Roux, 20524 Bustersikes, 640 Brambilla, 12199 Sohlman, 9566 Rykhlova, 9556 Gaywray, 4988 Chushuho, 22142 Loripryor, 13682 Pressberger, 724 Hapag, 33040 Pavelmayer, 6223 Dahl, 9986 Hirokun, 18122 Forestamartin, 1306 Scythia

115q7 (74.688) \\MY ULTIMATE LAST MOVE against a partner I *know* distrusts me; 2296 Kugultinov, 19810 Partridge, 6613 Williamcarl, 21518 Maysunhasan, 10672 Kostyukova, 214772 UNICEF, 168126 Chengbruce

qc215: REDACTED and her aftermath. Wasn't terrible, but I see no value in this qcross

19q7 (314.688) \\REDACTED in sb's chart; simeona; ir; 79152 Abukumagawa, 11404 Wittig, 17879 Robutel, 19370 Yukyung, 95 Arethusa, 5050 Doctorwatson, 25158 Berman, 330634 Boico

91q7 (134.688) \\loyalty born of circumstance, converted into duty; 6746 Zagar, 15635 Andrewhager, 100050 Carloshernandez, 38020 Hannadam, 154378 Hennessy, 34420 Peterpau, 1319 Disa, 7623 Stamitz, 128474 Arbacia, 381 Myrrha, 25120 Yvetteleung, 21509 Lucascavin, 12326 Shirasaki, 716 Berkeley, 8238 Courbet, 7081 Ludibunda, 16251 Barbifrank, 10950 Albertjansen, 2463 Sterpin

55q7 (224.688) \\the last days of nsbe; 25658 Bokor, 495759 Jandesselberger, 23877 Gourmaud, 6828 Elbsteel, 12539 Cajigal, 73342 Guyunusa, 100596 Perrett, 137039 Lisiguana, 4662 Runk, 8040 Utsumikazuhiko, 4151 Alanhale, 127933 Shaunoborn, 19423 Hefter, 32314 Rachelzhang, 7107 Peiser, 31015 Boccardi, 65694 Franzrosenzweig

127q7 (44.688) \\sounds like agd, might have been mb; 5698 Nolde, 20587 Jargoldman, 23628 Ichimura

qc71: the kind of attention asked of us by and given to kit (31/103) and the dogs (67/139). Kit does prompt the rearranging of rooms

31q7 (284.688) \\the canadians, some of REDACTED | //social group for niche exploration?; 17462 Takahisa, 11090 Popelin, 33559 Laurencooper, 58672 Remigio, 347 Pariana, 19789 Susanjohnson, 100292 Harmandir, 134124 Subirachs, 52308 Hanspeterroser, 506 Marion, 3352 McAuliffe, 9629 Servet, 31109 Janpalous

103q7 (104.688) \\my learning to project; 22625 Kanipe, 1144 Oda, 8883 Miyazakihayao, 4569 Baerbel, 3240 Laocoon, 22032 Mikekoop, 8551 Daitarabochi, 2431 Skovoroda, 58084 Hiketaon, 8995 Rachelstevenson, 19250 Poullain

67q7 (194.688) \\replaying with enthusiasm in deep conversation, likely an indicator of being black; 16166 Jonlii, 20115 Niheihajime, 1818 Brahms, 11711 Urquiza, 1492 Oppolzer, 7308 Hattori, 11977 Leonrisoldi, 19235 van Schurman, 8888 Tartaglia, 296577 Arkhangelsk, 155116 Verkhivnya, 7752 Otauchunokai, 26170 Kazuhiko, 27125 Siyilee, 348383 Petibon, 1777 Gehrels

139q7 (14.688) \\breaking in to share with the partner. Not much value in my doing this; 4019 Klavetter, 10649 VOC, 9123 Yoshiko, 1231 Auricula

qig36: passing on your energy to friends

qc358: the general manager of a sports team

7q6 (344.479) \\eye-blurring when scanning things like the news or random posts; 25100 Zhaiweichao, 23668 Eunbekim, 95962 Copito, 13610 Lilienthal, 12071 Davykim, 16132 Angelakim, 12282 Crombecq

79q6 (164.479) \\the industries that provide and monopolize the customer experience— especially media-backed figures. See axis 43q6 and 115q6. when you can't beat 'em, at least you can sambo for them; 34017 Geeve, 39566 Carllewis, 11776 Milstein, 128523 Johnmuir, 1481 Tubingia, 21500 Vazquez, 7023 Heiankyo, 21735 Nissaschmidt, 28601 Benton, 4768 Hartley, 12354 Hemmerechts, 3635 Kreutz, 4954 Eric, 33700 Gluckman, 121717 Josephschepis, 5064 Tanchozuru, 12370 Kageyasu, 55892 Fuzhougezhi

43q6 (254.479) \\the REDACTED who ... the REDACTED's .... Could be all of REDACTED, actually. In all seriousness. I have nothing against REDACTED. A couple ... are the homies. And it's not all REDACTED. This is just a broad basket for a certain ... which REDACTED ... I've been around seem to ...—noticeably

correlated with an equal amount of ... towards ... in the same position; 4034 Vishnu, 133753 Teresamullen, 5228 Maca, 1217 Maximiliana, 1604 Tombaugh, 1766 Slipher, 22263 Pignedoli, 78391 Michaeljager, 79240 Rosanna, 16418 Lortzing, 58191 Dolomiten, 9276 Timgrove, 12471 Larryscherr, 13436 Enid, 85472 Xizezong, 26197 Bormio

115q6 (74.479) \\THE qunit of ... in my chart; the favored ... REDACTED toted by the REDACTED over ...; 8868 Hjorter, 8373 Stephengould, 615 Roswitha, 314040 Tavannes, 4290 Heisei, 346261 Alexandrescu, 35734 Dilithium, 10093 Diesel, 2241 Alcathous, 4584 Akan, 3108 Lyubov, 24000 Patrickdufour

qc214: me, mb, and dg

19q6 (314.479) \\REDACTED in sb's chart; REDACTED, shanna; me towards mb; 5470 Kurtlindstrom, 24495 Degroff, 10318 Sumaura, 16578 Essjayess, 150046 Cynthiaconrad, 25029 Ludwighesse, 16709 Auratian, 246837 Bethfabinsky, 5082 Nihonsyoki, 46610 Besixdouze, 301394 Bensheim, 90806 Rudaki, 25673 Di Mascio

91q6 (134.479) \\reminds me of karl marx and other grandfathers of revolution before the movements themselves; 4567 Becvar, 2426 Simonov, 3402 Wisdom, 10746 Muhlhausen, 126780 Ivovasiljev, 722 Frieda, 1636 Porter, 20496 Jenik, 17139 Malyshev, 6931 Kenzaburo, 30596 Amdeans, 13177 Hansschmidt, 611 Valeria

55q6 (224.479) \\my teaching astro; 20964 Mons Nakletthi, 9564 Jeffwynn, 78652 Quero, 7486 Hamabe, 8058 Zuckmayer, 175636 Zvyagel, 9502 Gaimar, 58152 Natsoderblom, 683 Lanzia, 1402 Eri, 22533 Krishnan, 12177 Raharto, 21582 Arunvenkataraman, 31451 Joenickell, 2506 Pirogov, 23699 Paulgordan, 7910 Aleksola, 22429 Jurasek, 4566 Chaokuangpiu, 2898 Neuvo

127q6 (44.479) \\my confidence regarding the importance of my work and the steerability of the people; 5852 Nanette, 54967 Millucci, 232 Russia

qc70: significators for mine and shanna's temperaments

31q6 (284.479) \\looking for a new social group after the old has been lost. situation you hope to find; shanna; 25683 Haochenhong, 30430 Robertoegel, 18918 Nishashah, 19224 Orosei, 760 Massinga, 6141 Durda, 21421 Nealwadhwa, 180824 Kabos, 27433 Hylak, 85585 Mjolnir, 14310 Shuttleworth

103q6 (104.479) \\faced with the potential inconveniences of online hookups, for example; me; 6501 Isonzo, 3838 Epona, 4241 Pappalardo, 6656 Yokota, 4479 Charlieparker, 72993 Hannahlivsey, 9040 Flacourtia, 6232 Zubitskia

67q6 (194.479) \\hypothesis: ee - a deployer that I only check in with, but don't take any real orders from... verified! Right on!; 896 Sphinx, 28220 York, 12817 Federica, 14582 Conlin, 16744 Antonioleone, 23889 Hermanngrassmann, 10971 van Dishoeck, 22002 Richardregan, 400309 Ralfhofner, 140602 Berlind, 1518 Rovaniemi, 13668 Tanner, 1385 Gelria, 4184 Berdyayev, 221908 Agastrophus, 264150 Dolops, 3501 Olegiya, 24292 Susanragan, 8356 Wadhwa

139q6 (14.479) \\sb's proposal to hire contractors; 5915 Yoshihiro, 9685 Korteweg, 95785 Csanyivilmos, 25153 Tomhockey, 6511 Furmanov, 15050 Heddal, 17506 Walschap

qig37: dynamics you attract around you, partly given your appearance and their frames for it

qc357: in the chase for power

7q5 (344.271) \\REDACTED ca, standard ... sociality and assertion of ... onto others, social groups and cliques which view me as foreign or with suspicion; cc; 10762 von Laue, 43293 Banting, 4705 Secchi, 2634 James Bradley, 117596 Richardkuhns, 6373 Stern, 7118 Kuklov, 10867 Lima, 1200 Imperatrix, 35295 Omo, 60614 Tomshea, 204711 Luojialun, 17040 Almeida

79q5 (164.271) \\those I invite to my house or whom I host for whatever reason; 8523 Bouillabaisse, 26273 Kateschafer, 22189 Gijskatgert, 4419 Allancook, -13 Vertex, 6749 Ireentje, 31238 Kromeriz, 18782 Joanrho, 5858 Borovitskia, 17076 Betti, 160259 Mareike, 1537 Transylvania

43q5 (254.271) \\commissioned to do the major work in REDACTED; the nature of the work entails a trio's 79q5 interface with huge amounts of power. But they ARE a trio; 25551 Drewhall, 138979 Cernice, 7365 Sejong, 6962 Summerscience, 16214 Venkatachalam, 10685 Kharkivuniver, 5474 Gingasen, 1491 Balduinus, 4188 Kitezh, 5063 Monteverdi, 7984 Marius, 31435 Benhauck, 23405 Nisyros, 3363 Bowen

115q5 (74.271) \\exploring with mb, armando; nature romp; 11626 Church Stretton, 11614 Istropolitana, 29881 Tschopp, 4796 Lewis, 129137 Hippolochos, 27947 Emilemathieu, 7007 Timjull

qc213: simeona and her aftermath

19q5 (314.271) \\the squirrels? Rachel tries to be this; 5081 Sanguin, 375832 Yurijmedvedev, 352 Gisela, 213269 Angelbarbero, 52665 Brianmay, 22899 Alconrad, 5739 Robertburns, 189930 Jeanneherbert, 7115 Franciscuszeno

91q5 (134.271) \\art's response to sata as a sinking ship; 13238 Lambeaux, 3204 Lindgren, 8345 Ulmerspatz, 13151 Polino, 5544 Kazakov, 3213 Smolensk, 28936 Dalapati, 4166 Pontryagin, 11167 Kunzak, 2056 Nancy

55q5 (224.271) \\amidst festivities, promoting my books; 23707 Chambliss, 1985 Hopmann, 18935 Alfandmedina, 20644 Amritdas, 10353 Momotaro, 33595 Jiwoolee, 28575 McQuaid, 6604 Ilias, 182122 Sepan, 28618 Scibelli, 2549 Baker, 30323 Anyam, 21628 Lucashof

127q5 (44.271) \\what my promoted books contain or do for the reader; 10929 Chenfangyun, 23861 Benjaminsong, 35274 Kenziarino, 7436 Kuroiwa, 22857 Hyde, 281764 Schwetzingen

qc69: requirements for who the partner is and how they interface with you, what both of you bring to and review in the partnership. A STRONG descriptor of you and your best partner in relationship mode

31q5 (284.271) \\the space of partner arrangements across the niche | //prc and w as persistent. kwh and j, kvt & and mk, parallel partnerships like the one you will build. Partnering paradigm. Spiritual-sphere 'genetics?' soul group; 1219 Britta, 29446 Gouguenheim, 13025 Zurich, 107223 Ripero, 28837 Nibalachandar, 145562 Zurbriggen, 4378 Voigt, 43605 Gakuho

103q5 (104.271) \\adc, REDACTED: dark sexual notoriousness; 9908 Aue, 2606 Odessa, 3528 Counselman, 38960 Yeungchihung, 4486 Mithra, 8944 Ortigara, 2239 Paracelsus, 11202 Teddunham, 4722 Agelaos, 721 Tabora, 224 Oceana, 21739 Annekeschwob, 18282 Ilos, 9839 Crabbegat

67q5 (194.271) \\deep conversations begin with a kind of review; 274810 Fedaksari, 56957 Seohideaki, 224693 Morganfreeman, 4509 Gorbatskij, 215089 Hermanfrid, 7326 Tedbunch, 28720 Krystalrose, 273230 de Bruyn, 2511 Patterson, 2671 Abkhazia, 8533 Oohira, 4978 Seitz, 4361 Nezhdanova, 18658 Rajdev, 34310 Markhannum, 6984 Lewiscarroll

139q5 (14.271) \\the third has or is a hot friend, helping them solve their problem. Keller's clients; I do this by entering a charged relationship with the other. The third may be an undertaking rather than a person; 2655 Guangxi, 22842 Alenashort, 3836 Lem, 8254 Moskovitz, 129327 Davehamara, 85389 Rosenauer, 3265 Fletcher, 23235 Yingfan, 343157 Mindaugas, 1941 Wild, 3121 Tamines

qig38: the interactORs you reify

qc356: one accepts being used for their body

7q4 (344.063) \\my channelling, hallucinations; 9487 Kupe, 31639 Bodoni, 6211 Tsubame, 45580 Reneracine, 36036 Bonucci

79q4 (164.063) \\the kinds of characters I channel; the women I scrutinize as partners; 25084 Jutzi, 9649 Junfukue, 46632 RISE, 16736 Tongariyama, 4129 Richelen, 89909 Linie, 2025 Nortia, 17856 Gomes, 9228 Nakahiroshi, 16165 Licht, 13094 Shinshuueda, 4531 Asaro, 95853 Jamescarpenter, 2440 Educatio, 1499 Pori

43q4 (254.063) \\what priya brings to my life; 15023 Ketover, 21390 Shindo, 23898 Takir, 100934 Marthanussbaum, 71539 VanZandt, 27194 Jonathanli, 25212 Ayushgupta, 1030 Vitja, 5665 Begemann, 3813 Fortov, 34236 Firester, 157421 Carolpercy, 26474 Davidsimon, 3001 Michelangelo, 3388 Tsanghinchi, 635 Vundtia

115q4 (74.063) \\sexting (which I've never done), math-body description, and the outlaws?; 11874 Gringauz, 7550 Woolum, 21861 Maryhedberg, 19664 Yancey, 6546 Kaye, 78309 Alessielisa, 269390 Igortkachenko, 27495 Heatherfennell, 300892 Taichung, 232409 Dubes

qc212: me and shanna. NEVER DO 55q4

19q4 (314.063) \\this is any traumatically scarred person who goes on an adventure—VARIOUS REDACTED, and I encounter them when I am pioneering a landmark—using REDACTED's data for example. But they CANNOT be an assistant; 2142 Landau, 17170 Vsevustinov, 32809 Sommerfeld, 15461 Johnbird, 22299 Georgesteiner, 43804 Peterting, 2592 Hunan, 28695 Zwanzig, 31363 Shulga, 3512 Eriepa, 557 Violetta, 10924 Mariagriffin, 74509 Gillett, 23296 Brianreavis

91q4 (134.063) \\sk, keith; 14724 SNO, 91214 Diclemente, 17821 Bolsche, 4375 Kiyomori, 172989 Xuliyang, 24138 Benjaminlu, 159102 Sarahflanigan, 21926 Jacobperry, 12537 Kendriddle, 16625 Kunitsugu, 8990 Compassion, 21789 Frankwasser, 10390 Lenka, 18102 Angrilli, 10392 Brace, 3863 Gilyarovskij, 2079 Jacchia

55q4 (224.063) \\THE enemy trio whose activity destroys / leads me to destroy my nascent friendships; 26518 Bhuiyan, 6013 Andanike, 25767 Stevennoyce, 210232 Zhangjinqiu, 133068 Lisaschulze, 16130 Giovine, 21539 Josefhlavka, 35350 Lespaul, 14275 Dianemurray, 6909 Levison, 8187 Akiramisawa, 18725 Atacama, 12873 Clausewitz, 16085 Laffan, 30879 Hiroshikanai, 291 Alice, 24297 Jonbach, 5699 Munch, 2464 Nordenskiold, 24194 Palus, 145 Adeona, 12445 Sirataka, 8574 Makotoirie, 6919 Tomonaga

127q4 (44.063) \\birth cert, chasing down documents, sam, those who make me chase them in general; this is NEGATIVE in my chart, as I have to turn the crank. I almost certainly have to do the squares; 24977 Tongzhan, 33589 Edwardkim, 486 Cremona, 8329 Speckman, 13557 Lievetruwant, 166570 Adolftrager, 30166 Leodeng, 6327 Tijn

qc68: the difficulties or rile up that the partners present to each other

31q4 (284.063) \\REDACTED, REDACTED W REDACTED?| //the typical paired partnership interactions in your soul group. A definition of partners in your space | //the butt flank? Tiger stripes?; 10002 Bagdasarian, 4213 Njord, 9447 Julesbordet, 236810 Rutten, 22538 Lucasmoller, 29829 Engels, 5653 Camarillo, 6485 Wendeesther, 34 Circe, 10452 Zuev, 3206 Wuhan

103q4 (104.063) \\REDACTED; 20491 Ericstrege, 5967 Edithlevy, 28667 Whithagins, 32200 Seiicyoshida, 5345 Boynton, 129108 Kristianwaldorff, 10655 Pietkeyser, 6270 Kabukuri, 30852 Debye, 4922 Leshin, 14871 Pyramus, 9287 Klima, 13319 Michaelmi, 7379 Naoyaimae

67q4 (194.063) \\a deep conversation ends with next steps. Don't get too carried away here; 28687 Reginareals, 101813 Elizabethmarston, 14558 Wangganchang, 659 Nestor, 22146 Samaan, 1565 Lemaitre, 34039 Torsteinvik, 12329 Liebermann, 2520 Novorossijsk, 15853 Benedettafoglia, 12115 Robertgrimm, 2379 Heiskanen, 33825 Reganwill, 48807 Takahata, 9477 Kefennell, 267585 Popluhar, 6862 Virgiliomarcon, 4077 Asuka, 12727 Cavendish, 21584 Polepeddi, 65708 Ehrlich, 11011 KIAM, 11133 Kumotori, 13093 Wolfgangpauli, 4498 Shinkoyama, 257261 Ovechkin

139q4 (14.063) \\VARIOUS REDACTED- some kind of trauma implied in the background; 2726 Kotelnikov, 136199 Eris, 89264 Sewanee, 3242 Bakhchisaraj, 5202 Charleseliot, 239105 Marcocattaneo, 30060 Davidseong, 2740 Tsoj

qig39: takeaways for events

qc355: behind the power center, the powerful's private life

7q3 (343.854) \\when I now know that I'll need to move on. The writing is on the wall; 16425 Chuckyeager, 15766 Strahlenberg, 26973 Lala, 8649 Juglans, 1222 Tina, 204 Kallisto, 10321 Rampo, 85320 Bertram, 252470 Puigmarti

79q3 (163.854) \\i initiate the final damaging communication; 10804 Amenouzume, 16920 Larrywalker, 547 Praxedis, 11798 Davidsson, 45299 Stivell, 7460 Julienicoles, 230 Athamantis, 5453 Zakharchenya, 9001 Slettebak, 68853 Vaimaca, 28396 Eymann, 34047 Gloria, 16252 Franfrost, 37720 Kawanishi

43q3 (253.854) \\the billionaire-type can get far, but at some point trades proper business for personality faux pas. The person who receives the final reach; 5394 Jurgens, 14274 Landstreet, 152067 Deboy, 63609 Francoisecolas, 10515 Old Joe, 10961 Buysballot, 31461 Shannonlee, 27456 Sarkisian, 8061 Gaudium, 6784 Bogatikov, 5395 Shosasaki, 9701 Mak, 112656 Gines, 27870 Jillwatson, 28723 Cameronjones, 1141 Bohmia, 6713 Coggie, 117712 Podmaniczky, 1366 Piccolo, 8216 Melosh, 9563 Kitty, 8742 Bonazzoli, 23578 Baedeker, 8065 Nakhodkin, 2523 Ryba

115q3 (73.854) \\the FINAL REACH; 6689 Floss, 246247 Sheldoncooper, 34273 Franklynwang, 20000 Varuna, 85512 Rieugnie, 11829 Tuvikene, 10163 Onomichi, 3075 Bornmann, 834 Burnhamia, 11675 Billboyle

qc211: REDACTED and her aftermath

19q3 (313.854) \\vb, dh, mb, b.a.r., cm; 1161 Thessalia, 15057 Whitson, 201751 Steinhardt, 6215 Mehdia, 7560 Spudis, 4525 Johnbauer, 16564 Coriolis, 177148 Patzold, 241538 Chudniv, 1417 Walinskia, 31482 Caddell, 924 Toni, 19596 Spegorlarson, 27004 Violetaparra

91q3 (133.854) \\solo lego buildings, gathering in 209. rather than having such partners near me, I am more likely to simply lose them, then honor them with a memory; 4762 Dobrynya, 12575 Palmaria, 8587 Ruficollis, 8355 Masuo, 23744 Ootsubo, 8205 Van Dijck, 5304 Bazhenov, 4389 Durbin, 24211 Barbarawood, 2415 Ganesa, 15374 Teta

55q3 (223.854) \\the distrust shown by the assistant, where I begin plotting against my assistant / cofounder; where I can read my cofounder's energies through their information; 296928 Francescopalla, 25302 Niim, 198717 Szymczyk, 84996 Hortobagy, 90526 Paullorenz, 23880 Tongil, 3335 Quanzhou, 21328 Otashi, 13567 Urabe, 33600 Davidlu, 77560 Furusato, 9074 Yosukeyoshida, 18404 Kenichi, 78249 Capaccioni, 26963 Palorapavy, 23232 Buschur, 21350 Billgardner, 9256 Tsukamoto, 25613 Bubenicek, 23197 Danielcook

127q3 (43.854) \\pics with REDACTED, none with REDACTED. my pursuing passionate connection with another who may just be along for the ride—attention to something else; how sam works; any situation where I create a playroom for others... I shouldn't try to connect with those who make use of that playroom. they essentially become extensions of my work; 4246 Telemann, 16598 Brugmansia, 3293 Rontaylor, 4367 Meech, 10770 Belo Horizonte, 18939 Sariancel, 52334 Oberammergau

qc67: you and your partner's co-creative modes

31q3 (283.854) //kr; 15421 Adammalin, 4598 Coradini, 18418 Ujibe, 2954 Delsemme, 20476 Chanarich, 19762 Lacrowder, 4109 Anokhin, 10627 Ookuninushi, 55319 Takanashi, 19577 Bobbyfisher, 27094 Salgari, 1639 Bower, 4042 Okhotsk, 25082 Williamhodge, 113388 Davidmartinez, 8539 Laban, 2630 Hermod, 147397 Bobhazel

103q3 (103.854) \\robospam; 19197 Akasaki, 21033 Akahirakiyozo, 4242 Brecher, 17920 Zarnecki, 11538 Brunico, 6278 Ametkhan, 30425 Silverman, 8915 Sawaishujiro, 1938 Lausanna, 9010 Candelo

67q3 (193.854) \\awed by wonder and a certain display of creative strength; 24441 Jopek, 34919 Imelda, 11055 Honduras, 9109 Yukomotizuki, 5800 Pollock, 90447 Emans, 216624 Kaufer, 4023 Jarnik, 19465 Amandarusso, 2281 Biela, 10215 Lavilledemirmont, 30273 Samepstein, 21873 Jindrichuvhradec, 30251 Ashkin

139q3 (13.854) \\sb against prc / mb, dg against mb; 33610 Payra, 2409 Chapman, 12261 Ledouanier, 7323 Robersomma, 5405 Neverland

qig40: the accessible foreign for you

qc354: those who get to visit us behind the scenes

7q2 (343.646) \\talking to myself about what I did; 6518 Vernon, 17253 Vonsecker, 33217 Bonnybasu, 76713 Wudia, 20814 Laurajones, 31147 Miriquidi, 26960 Liouville, 170012 Anithakar, 4975 Dohmoto, 26266 Andrewmerrill, 56678 Alicewessen

79q2 (163.646) \\somehow getting away with something, talking about it under certain protections; 7083 Kant, 32547 Shandroff, 484 Pittsburghia, 120103 Dolero, 9588 Quesnay, 1107 Lictoria, 1469 Linzia, 7726 Olegbykov, 22403 Manjitludher, 172 Baucis, 21431 Amberhess, 23673 Neilmehta, 46689 Hakuryuko

43q2 (253.646) \\when ends are blocked, my finding another way to pursue them; 23270 Kellerman, 9941 Iguanodon, 4514 Vilen, 10173 Hanzelkazikmund, 129050 Lowellcogburn, 14902 Miyairi, 24325 Kaleighanne, 239792 Hankakovacova, 130229 Igorlazbin, 589 Croatia, 137 Meliboea

115q2 (73.646) \\me retiring from the fight, moving across the alabama bridge; 12286 Poiseuille, 4634 Shibuya, 11605 Ranfagni, 8106 Carpino, 8580 Pinsky, 41800 Robwilliams, 5409 Saale, 3729 Yangzhou, 9495 Eminescu

qc210: me, mb, and her aftermath

19q2 (313.646) \\my interaction with ana lisa, and any other pervasively favored but extremely rare interaction; me and shanna at calla, wahoo; 2132 Zhukov, 15716 Narahara, 31575 Nikhilmurthy, 30208 Guigarcia, 5150 Fellini, 54852 Mercatali, 101722 Pursell, 1779 Parana, 628 Christine, 5887 Yauza

91q2 (133.646) \\vb herself: I am not the same as this person, interface with her outside of her role; sb the artist; 13329 Davidhardy, 25331 Berrevoets, 25765 Heatherlynne, 34717 Mirkovilli, 14234 Davidhoover, 13494 Treiso, 2152 Hannibal, 270 Anahita, 356 Liguria, 142755 Castander, 21617 Johnhagen, 400673 Vitapolunina, 29 Amphitrite

55q2 (223.646) \\my pattern shown to vb; being banned from caltech; starting sata with b.a.r.; 3705 Hotellasilla, 27932 Leonyao, 21416 Sisichen, 4494 Marimo, 5807 Mshatka, 22932 Orenbrecher, 3128 Obruchev, 6419 Susono, 11665 Dirichlet, 75564 Audubon, 428102 Rolandwagner, 135991 Danarmstrong, 79286 Hexiantu, 39741 Komm, 24857 Sperello, 11950 Morellet, 308798 Teo, 8808 Luhmann, 8000 Isaac Newton, 28492 Marik

127q2 (43.646) \\the wall with vb; 18750 Leonidakimov, 34101 Hesrivastava, 35265 Takeosaitou, 10172 Humphreys, 2683 Brian, 11809 Shinnaka, 2798 Vergilius, 30164 Arnobdas, 2009 Voloshina, 5099 Iainbanks

qc66: how the partners interface with the world or their local spheres

31q2 (283.646) \\REDACTED, REDACTED after I said no; 134112 Jeremyralph, 34251 Rohanmehrotra, 89818 Jureskvarc, 24154 Ayonsen, 5540 Smirnova, 196938 Delgordon, 210434 Fungyuancheng, 1458 Mineura, 4757 Liselotte, 14596 Bergstralh, 7826 Kinugasa, 12397 Peterbrown, 32890 Schwob, 26917 Pianoro

103q2 (103.646) \\how I facilitated political science class, this is my more military gait; 11810 Preusker, 16555 Nagaomasami, 24488 Eliebochner, 10211 La Spezia, 39849 Giampieri, 229836 Wladimarinello, 2354 Lavrov, 8398 Rubbia, 10279 Rhiannonblaauw, 207385 Maxou, 31909 Chenweitung

67q2 (193.646) \\educational REDACTED meetings; 17928 Neuwirth, 72545 Robbiiwessen, 1913 Sekanina, 21349 Bevoke, 5207 Hearnshaw, 7220 Philnicholson, 696 Leonora, 8724 Junkoehara, 9744 Nielsen, 25231 Naylor, 44117 Haroldlarson, 25309 Chrisauer, 910 Anneliese, 19912 Aurapenenta, 23894 Arikahiguchi, 6175 Cori, 25531 Lessek, 39677 Anagaribaldi, 9062 Ohnishi, 15468 Mondriaan

139q2 (13.646) \\brothers-like and their ambitions; 10853 Aimoto, 4090 Risehvezd, 8301 Haseyuji

qig41: cultural standards at work just outside of your core body

qc353: attaining some level of luxury

7q1 (343.438) \\the one in the class who raises the hidden beef; 37596 Cotahuasi, 865 Zubaida, 31201 Michellegrand, 7208 Ashurbanipal, 75844 Rexadams, 58460 Le Mouelic

79q1 (163.438) \\globus; 17746 Haigha, 9541 Magri, 22827 Arvernia, 33328 Archanaverma, 23042 Craigpeters, 30024 Neildavey, 129807 Stefanodougherty, 195600 Scheithauer, 24680 Alleven, 7475 Kaizuka, 10461 Dawilliams, 372024 Ayapani, 288960 Steponasdarius, 14819 Nikolaylaverov, 6039 Parmenides, 20839 Bretharrison, 5751 Zao, 5531 Carolientje

43q1 (253.438) \\where I have a hard time getting others to let me influence them; 7206 Shiki, 428694 Saule, 40981 Stephenholland, 95955 Claragianni, 1580 Betulia, 158092 Frasercain, 19007 Nirajnathan, 243262 Korkosz, 11963 Ignace, 6738 Tanabe, 5224 Abbe

115q1 (73.438) \\what people do while receiving my weird communications; what they're going through; 233383 Assisneto, 8311 Zhangdaning, 607 Jenny, 5491 Kaulbach, 129138 Williamfrost, 16399 Grokhovsky, 113415 Rauracia, 8726 Masamotonasu

qc209: b.a.r. and her aftermath

19q1 (313.438) \\my experience of the earth day celebration, the dogs' experience of my scare play or play time; 6820 Buil, 65894 Echizenmisaki, 19678 Belczyk, 3999 Aristarchus, 82153 Alemigliorini, 151659 Egerszegi, 35352 Texas, 23819 Tsuyoshi, 4201 Orosz, 21446 Tedflint, 130320 Maherrassas, 22692 Carfrekahl

91q1 (133.438) \\my form of scare play with the dogs; 6218 Mizushima, 12771 Kimshin, 6332 Vorarlberg, 91213 Botchan, 25609 Bogantes, 2610 Tuva, 33400 Laurapierson, 7625 Louisspohr, 8703 Nakanotadao, 105 Artemis, 6339 Giliberti, 77971 Donnolo, 72804 Caldentey

55q1 (223.438) \\i start complaining that I need access to more, otherwise I will do my own thing; 7425 Lessing, 28571 Hannahlarson, 22370 Italocalvino, 6459 Hidesan, 3499 Hoppe, 4529 Webern, 2538 Vanderlinden, 9011 Angelou, 9957 Raffaellosanti, 129881 Chucksee, 90732 Opdebeeck, 8240 Matisse, 4738 Jimihendrix, 10055 Silcher, 9533 Aleksejleonov, 212929 Satovski, 28718 Rivergrace

127q1 (43.438) \\what partner typically sees. I should avoid talking about my wins (55) unless they are very big. But it is my thought that winning the lottery will trigger bair strongly in her chart. This is also one of those regions where my pursuit of re-election into power will definitely lead to someone else being chosen instead. why? see the squares. i should NEVER grip a position i already hold unless asked to run again. avoid the quips and let the hype die down. this is also why it is unhealthy for me to watch others being granted rewards i think i am at some point entitled to. jealousy isn't the problem. the elford-bair-drunina combination actually hijacks my will; 7355 Bottke, 4157 Izu, 12893 Mommert, 1149 Volga, 4974 Elford, 3804 Drunina, 25914 Bair

qc65: the partners' compulsions and the responses these trigger in the other

31q1 (283.438) \\VARIOUS REDACTED, one who wants to be my mate or vice versa until there is rejection | //my resistance to getting physical with …, though I can like the same … from afar; 24413 Britneyschmidt, 29609 Claudiahuang, 10741 Valeriocarruba, 280641 Edosara, 5360 Rozhdestvenskij, 2052 Tamriko, 1834 Palach, 9619 Terrygilliam, 3136 Anshan, 17216 Scottstuart, 72632 Coralina, 170487 Mallder, 197 Arete, 7994 Bethellen, 2285 Ron Helin, 8475 Vsevoivanov, 22745 Rikuzentakata, 207319 Eugenemar

103q1 (103.438) \\platonic with shanna the rebel; 21410 Cahill, 11997 Fassel, 22898 Falce, 30302 Kritilall, 248388 Namtso, 18171 Romaneskue, 240697 Gemenc, 856 Backlunda, 9430 Erichthonios, 536 Merapi, 4854 Edscott, 11873 Kokuseibi, 134174 Jameschen, 308825 Siksika, 20317 Hendrickson, 321324 Vytautas

67q1 (193.438) \\in conversation with me, one receives encouragement to keep going; 292160 Davefask, 5431 Maxinehelin, 18111 Pinet, 2023 Asaph, 416 Vaticana, 26205 Kuratowski, 1152 Pawona, 2500 Alascattalo, 17435 di Giovanni, 247542 Ripplronai, 1416 Renauxa, 3781 Dufek, 3693 Barringer, 20394 Fatou, 7192 Cieletespace, 2455 Somville, 4022 Nonna, 9468 Brewer, 1410 Margret, 79419 Gaolu, 11916 Wiesloch, 8877 Rentaro, 675 Ludmilla

139q1 (13.438) \\dg, sb; 7472 Kumakiri, 31642 Soyounchoi, 3871 Reiz, 217510 Dewaldroode, 214 Aschera, 16765 Agnesi, 20474 Reasoner, 29802 Rikhavshah, 305953 Josiedubey, 4372 Quincy

qig42: the asserting space's handbook

qc352: school shooters and other characters considered a social blight

7q12 (343.229) \\what I express or create as a male; 5413 Smyslov, 25364 Allisonbaas, 3977 Maxine, 501 Urhixidur, 2027 Shen Guo, 28451 Tylerhoward, 21714 Geoffreywoo, 23054 Thomaslynch, 90429 Wetmore

79q12 (163.229) \\how I project my maleness towards the world; 8826 Corneville, 3904 Honda, 14959 TRIUMF, 9070 Ensab, 6822 Horalek, 2448 Sholokhov, 458 Hercynia, 3373 Koktebelia, 3849 Incidentia, 527 Euryanthe, 26938 Jackli, 15076 Joellewis

43q12 (253.229) \\how I handle being beaten, overpowered, losing; 6974 Solti, 4627 Pinomogavero, 22413 Haifu, 10416 Kottler, 34158 Rachelchang, 14555 Shinohara, 4135 Svetlanov, 7956 Yaji, 5799 Brewington, 9788 Yagami, 147918 Chiayi, 100049 Cesarann, 4811 Semashko, 30197 Nickbadyrka

115q12 (73.229) \\REDACTED can beat me in … version 1, as can REDACTED in … and REDACTED in …; to prevent this, don't EVER celebrate collaborative-equal victories with anyone, especially alongside …. Cooperative-distant victories are probably somewhat ok; 1374 Isora, 7965 Katsuhiko, 214819 Gianotti, 298 Baptistina, 28572 Salebreton, 4828 Misenus, 2478 Tokai

qc208: sending someone else out to conquer for you. Informational or social-talk conquerors; kind of like agd, being sent out by sanza; dg?

19q12 (313.229) \\my going upstairs or to some other place to execute something thoroughly; rpgs; 33058 Kovarik, 22685 Dominguez, 9064 Johndavies, 4551 Cochran, 6718 Beiglbock, 480 Hansa, 396 Aeolia, 1789 Dobrovolsky, 43806 Augustepiccard, 4590 Dimashchegolev

91q12 (133.229) \\shaking when having to control something *exactly*; 27141 Krystleleung, 22617 Vidphananu, 61189 Ohsadaharu, 33575 Joshuajacob, 37735 Riccardomuti, 25073 Lautakshing, 128297 Ashlevi, 100267 JAXA, 1191 Alfaterna, 7030 Colombini, 120367 Grabow

55q12 (223.229) \\my conception of a standard conquistador; bijonix, pizarro, priya, kk?; 8885 Sette, 207901 Tzecmaun, 18090 Kevinkuo, 4488 Tokitada, 23473 Voss, 28832 Akana, 13082 Gutierrez, 25512 Anncomins, 25119 Kakani, 129071 Catriegle, 18871 Grauer, 4086 Podalirius, 13730 Willis, 4227 Kaali

127q12 (43.229) \\where I have graduated past the rat race; like a bill gates lifestyle; 1650 Heckmann, 4741 Leskov, 21313 Xiuyanyu, 3423 Slouka, 5536 Honeycutt, 6980 Kyusakamoto, 3450 Dommanget, 175017 Zabori, 8866 Tanegashima

qc64: social media and yak-show types

31q12 (283.229) \\watching foreign entertainment amidst travel or the tower view; 3737 Beckman, 13775 Thebault, 145566 Andreasphilipp, 7364 Otonkucera, 211377 Travisturbyfill, 1594 Danjon, 24146 Benjamueller, 2802 Weisell, 1788 Kiess, 4733 ORO, 31032 Scheidemann, 18632 Danielsson, 344 Desiderata, 10736 Marybruck, 30991 Minenze, 18561 Fengningding, 92892 Robertlawrence

103q12 (103.229) \\crazy superhero schemes and dress…and ideas; 27512 Gilstrap, 46392 Bertola, 36782 Okauchitakashige, 78534 Renmir, 37592 Pauljackson, 18720 Jerryguo, 29804 Idansharon

67q12 (193.229) \\naha tug of war 2023; 939 Isberga, 28853 Bukhamsin, 4247 Grahamsmith, 252794 Maironis, 18055 Fernhildebrandt, 5583 Braunerova, 1362 Griqua, 5426 Sharp, 8667 Fontane, 10295 Hippolyta, 260508 Alagna, 92 Undina, 5263 Arrius, 21586 Pourkaviani, 19393 Davidthompson, 11704 Gorin, 58196 Ashleyess, 116 Sirona, 7459 Gilbertofranco

139q12 (13.229) \\clown, but also my decisiveness. Can irritate if done at the wrong time. Taken lightly for being thin at the wrist, softspoken; me + b.a.r.; giving too much will present burdens; 14939 Norikura, 6773 Kellaway

qig43: keeping it kindred

qc351: me as a workaholic over the long term

7q11 (343.021) \\my agenda for getting everyone to use my construct; 129595 Vand, 1942 Jablunka, 13114 Isabelgodin, 33603 Saramason, 4340 Dence, 21029 Adorno, 6942 Yurigulyaev, 7689 Reinerstoss

79q11 (163.021) \\munich; my silent relegation to the background; 3449 Abell, 149157 Stephencarr, 7776 Takeishi, 5492 Thoma, 22907 van Voorthuijsen, 1924 Horus, 293909 Matterhorn, 42492 Bruggenthies, 3903 Kliment Ohridski, 31179 Gongju, 58186 Langkavel, 765 Mattiaca, 16525 Shumarinaiko, 23455 Fumi, 3403 Tammy, 30439 Moe, 19457 Robcastillo, 11772 Jacoblemaire, 30305 Severi, 65784 Naderayama, 72059 Heojun, 3918 Brel, 3241 Yeshuhua, 189 Phthia

43q11 (253.021) \\dismissive indignance. From REDACTED to me or me to sg; 84882 Table Mountain, 14623 Kamoun, 202930 Ivezic, 7999 Nesvorny, 21891 Andreabocelli, 16219 Venturelli, 10478 Alsabti, 336108 Luberon, 28682 Newhams, 10234 Sixtygarden, 14278 Perrenot, 5958 Barrande, 16528 Terakado, 23098 Huanghuang, 12275 Marcelgoffin, 25864 Banic, 12908 Yagudina, 78905 Seanokeefe, 18903 Matsuura, 4113 Rascana, 6404 Vanavara

115q11 (73.021) \\i usually have something against the partner turned enemy, and vice versa. Narrating my failed search for a contours partner, my knime work as help to another's cause; 8853 Gerdlehmann, 25642 Adiseshan, 9257 Kunisuke, 20559 Sheridanlamp, 9280 Stevenjoy, 18624 Prevert, 1801 Titicaca, 25954 Trantow, 4536 Drewpinsky, 4731 Monicagrady, 6603 Marycragg

qc207: rejection of someone who really likes you

19q11 (313.021) \\how I relate to family—immediate and extended; my writer's voice; 95020 Nencini, 2401 Aehlita, 21441 Stevencondie, 16121 Burrell, 931 Whittemora,

5685 Sanenobufukui, 6472 Rosema, 73703 Billings, 7258 Pettarin, 17991 Joshuaegan, 36424 Satokokumasaki, 4571 Grumiaux

91q11 (133.021) \\my relationship to kwh. But also, my major spiritual and employment benefactor (the government and its related services); what I write about, but also those I guard against in real life. The need for control here is high; 11063 Poynting, 6539 Nohavica, 365130 Birnfeld, 6952 Niccolo, 4167 Riemann, 6832 Kawabata, 159974 Badacsony, 14318 Buzinov, 7453 Slovtsov, 6514 Torahiko

55q11 (223.021) \\REDACTED, kvt, REDACTED, sg, REDACTED—those who are family-like, but whose agenda you cannot stay with; 16114 Alyono, 3119 Dobronravin, 3704 Gaoshiqi, 2471 Ultrajectum, 21576 McGivney, 20316 Jerahalpern, 1372 Haremari, 28978 Ixion, 20529 Zwerling, 4490 Bambery, 4641 Ayako, 274302 Abahazi, 2612 Kathryn, 481984 Cernunnos, 7346 Boulanger, 21438 Camibarnett, 3522 Becker, 31414 Rotarysusa

127q11 (43.021) \\7 REDACTED, and other damaged / traumatized girls' backgrounds; 17612 Whiteknight, 8900 AAVSO, 19452 Keeney, 1138 Attica, 133716 Tomtourville, 25798 Reneeschaaf, 15386 Nicolini

qc63: the partner's brand of power administration

31q11 (283.021) \\hans and franz and other health experts; 745 Mauritia, 21622 Victorshia, 18116 Prato, 5890 Carlsberg, 3549 Hapke, 18755 Meduna, 29053 Muskau, 4808 Ballaero, 11606 Almary, 1053 Vigdis, 27491 Broksas, 34277 Davidxingwu, 1796 Riga, 6228 Yonezawa

103q11 (103.021) \\the big girl in fully ally mode; 6688 Donmccarthy, 2206 Gabrova, 12350 Feuchtwanger, 1640 Nemo, 559 Nanon, 4327 Ries, 6217 Kodai, 9165 Raup, 4713 Steel, 34245 Andrewkomo, 2298 Cindijon, 189004 Capys, 32282 Arnoldmong

67q11 (193.021) \\topics of high roles, duty, power, and excellent creativity; 23758 Guyuzhou, 1577 Reiss, 4704 Sheena, 10078 Stanthorpe, 23120 Paulallen, 2527 Gregory, 12923 Zephyr, 48650 Kazanuniversity, 6517 Buzzi, 26733 Nanavisitor, 5529 Perry, 15041 Paperetti, 8206 Masayuki, 1495 Helsinki, 8485 Satoru

139q11 (13.021) \\simeona, t.o., REACTED, rachel the dog; 18790 Ericaburden, 18997 Mizrahi, 2746 Hissao, 3261 Tvardovskij, 60183 Falcone

qig44: your natural work camp

qc350: collaborations with keith

7q10 (342.813) \\my solo work within the institution; 9119 Georgpeuerbach, 1505 Koranna, 3301 Jansje, 159409 Ratte, 4788 Simpson, 326164 Miketoomey, 20571 Tiamorrison, 7186 Tomioka, 30719 Isserstedt, 5122 Mucha, 411 Xanthe, 1210 Morosovia

79q10 (162.813) \\great institutional change where I am, and what my role is in it; 113390 Helvetia, 1683 Castafiore, 18857 Lalchandani, 13760 Rodriguez, -10012 mean Apogee, 13122 Drava, 10841 Ericforbes, 90825 Lizhensheng, 192686 Aljuroma, 28707 Drewbecker, 16089 Lamb, 231470 Bedding, 3882 Johncox, 21728 Zhuzhirui, 211613 Christophelovis, 96348 Toshiyukimariko, 9434 Bokusen, 197856 Tafelmusik, 8182 Akita, 135 Hertha

43q10 (252.813) \\the work I do … when done alone here, is often invalidated or riddled with changing requirements. a STRONG region in …. Also show how I NEED collaboration in order to get anything done ; 7087 Lewotsky, 14926 Hoshide, 19679 Gretabetteo, 120741 Iijimayuichi, 25721 Anartya, 23047 Isseroff, 5626 Melissabrucker, 48416 Carmelita, 3952 Russellmark, 57509 Sly, 231346 Taofanlin, 25766 Nosarzewski, 1663 van den Bos, 383 Janina, 12155 Hyginus, 6160 Minakata, 8397 Chiakitanaka, 27238 Keenanmonks, 330640 Yangxuejun, 3247 Di Martino, 31972 Carlycrump, 15922 Masajisaito

115q10 (72.813) \\me as a co-host of some learning session; 7484 Dogo Onsen, 185325 Anupabhagwat, 63163 Jerusalem, 22890 Ruthaellis, 2547 Hubei, 2207 Antenor, 29987 Lazhang

qc206: the ultimate female power potential

19q10 (312.813) \\MY ACTUAL GIRLY GIRL IMAGE observing process during my exercises, the state I'm in while doing this; 7079 Baghdad, 4359 Berlage, 2367 Praha, 27775 Lilialmanzor, 6391 Africano, 10749 Musaus, 25800 Glukhovsky, 15425 Welzl, 22528 Elysehope, 117610 Keithmahoney, 31862 Garfinkle, 10479 Yiqunchen, 24916 Stelzhamer, 62190 Augusthorch, 3362 Khufu

91q10 (132.813) \\the actual descriptor of my girly girl images. I could use the mined words in this group as a prompt. Especially uson; the circumstances of my exercises; urda: my guaranteed allies / friends are here. cz; 8233 Asada, 24074 Thomasjohnson, 12511 Patil, 9388 Takeno, 8785 Boltwood, 31946 Sahilabbi, 3937 Bretagnon, 100456 Chichen Itza, 167 Urda, 26168 Kanaikiyotaka, 28450 Saravolz, 10791 Uson, 3294 Carlvesely, 4413 Mycerinos, 173002 Dorfi

55q10 (222.813) \\slash and burn across an experiential terrain; the jumpers; …and that makes total sense: my feeling sick and/or ill and/or dirty and/or disillusioned after orgasm. A *very* interesting text mine; 221465 Rapa Nui, 9144 Hollisjohnson, 8052

Novalis, 18284 Tsereteli, 34088 Satokosuka, 9707 Petruskoning, 85121 Loehde, 24549 Jaredgoodman, 24217 Paulroeder, 15332 CERN, 11935 Olakarlsson, 363115 Chuckwood, 217420 Olevsk, 4089 Galbraith, 25477 Preyashah, 485 Genua, 11925 Usubae, 29620 Gurbanikaur, 159827 Keithmullen, 10249 Harz, 1677 Tycho Brahe, 3435 Boury

127q10 (42.813) \\the desired orgasmic target, what I like to see with it, as illustrated in my later AI images. Also, why at least one of my final actual or conceptual partners always has large breasts (Casagrande). In 2024 this is Sâvitrî; 7356 Casagrande, 7233 Majella, 34034 Shehadeh, 8543 Tsunemi, 4601 Ludkewycz, 256813 Marburg, 19123 Stephenlevine, 1795 Woltjer, 420 Bertholda

qc62: the partners' ambitions and how the other facilitates them

31q10 (282.813) \\my occasional ideas for advancing; 6070 Rheinland, 25376 Christikeen, 32082 Sominsky, 28485 Dastidar, 305287 Olegyankov, 16755 Cayley, 9094 Butsuen, 32853 Dobereiner, 2150 Nyctimene, 2754 Efimov, 31731 Johnwiley, 9741 Solokhin

103q10 (102.813) \\VARIOUS REDACTED, tithe takers; 46793 Phinney, 4883 Korolirina, 20212 Ekbaltouma, 29148 Palzer, 18075 Donasharma, 218866 Alexantioch, 33991 Weixunjing, 6470 Aldrin, 9728 Videen, 73079 Davidbaltimore, 25406 Debwysocki, 17681 Tweedledum

67q10 (192.813) \\the square: emily, keith, eb; if I don't feel like talking, what kinds of people can I still sit in a room with? agd? Formerly mb.; 20440 McClintock, 21621 Sherman, 80451 Alwoods, 2279 Barto, 257005 Arpadpal, 34696 Risoldi, 1838 Ursa, 42566 Ryutaro, 5102 Benfranklin, 23469 Neilpeart, 15785 de Villegas, 9650 Okadaira, 34154 Anushkanair, 31 Euphrosyne, 20472 Mollypettit, 33889 Jengebo, 384815 Zolnowski, 2920 Automedon, 31594 Drewprevost

139q10 (12.813) \\sister in law j; 33598 Christineliu, 1831 Nicholson, 12059 du Chatelet, 1179 Mally

qig45: working out a situation with partners

qc349: me in my thinking space

7q9 (342.604) \\the environment in which I do my solo daily work, possibly including certain kinds of people. The soundbooth. Me as a basic background witness to others' work in REDACTED; my musical clairaudience; 7314 Pevsner, 8749 Beatles, 16355 Buber, 144496 Reingard, 1214 Richilde, 13003 Dickbeasley, 22555 Joevellone, 23734 Kimgyehyun, 338373 Fonoalbert, 2764 Moeller

79q9 (162.604) \\me as a solo worker in my job, attempting to make sense of my part. Perhaps associated with asteroids like ceraskia or ottegebe; 14220 Alexgibbs, 60669 Georgpick, 1862 Apollo, 417 Suevia, 224962 Michaelgrunewald, 9298 Geake, 12919 Tomjohnson, 77185 Cherryh, 3224 Irkutsk, 5779 Schupmann, 4388 Jurgenstock, 3398 Stattmayer, 30558 Jamesoconnor, 11794 Yokokebukawa, 2158 Tietjen, 9145 Shustov, 2821 Slavka, 6056 Donatello, 21439 Robenzing, 322574 Werckmeister

43q9 (252.604) \\my initial struggles with sata, trying to raise money and client support, especially w b.a.r. and sg. Most likely a qunit responsible for the easiest lottery wins; 5615 Iskander, 4119 Miles, 4333 Sinton, 31901 Amitscheer, 121540 Jamesmarsh, 12185 Gasprinskij, 2313 Aruna, 90446 Truesdell, 1952 Hesburgh, 316028 Patrickwils, 941 Murray, 10544 Horsnebara, 207763 Oberursel, 103220 Kwongchuikuen, 34083 Feretova, 106869 Irinyi, 14492 Bistar, 7865 Francoisgros

115q9 (72.604) \\when I was solo in commercial real estate, and won the century 21 contracts for our brokerage. b.a.r.; the State as a frequent interface?; 1325 Inanda, 11830 Jessenius, 2931 Mayakovsky, 22939 Handlin, 36033 Viseggi, 7490 Babicka, 15960 Hluboka, 21408 Lyrahaas, 15263 Erwingroten, 23739 Kevin, 238 Hypatia, 10839 Hufeland, 3023 Heard, 9560 Anguita

qc205: how (and why) I generally enter major partnerships with women

19q9 (312.604) \\priya, auguste; 3176 Paolicchi, 3802 Dornburg, 2043 Ortutay, 14919 Robertohaver, 85214 Sommersdorf, 20433 Prestinenza, 9898 Yoshiro, 3850 Peltier, 32310 Asherwillner

91q9 (132.604) \\my forgiving girls I'm attracted to, especially as I come into my own power; 27365 Henryfitz, 20301 Thakur, 79129 Robkoldewey, 12125 Jamesjones, 24922 Bechtel, 20300 Arjunsuri, 5475 Hanskennedy, 134138 Laurabayley, 21921 Camdenmiller, 25742 Amandablanco, 11799 Lantz, 4243 Nankivell, 12828 Batteas

55q9 (222.604) \\my maturity as a student or learner; recording my research questions; 5274 Degewij, 1487 Boda, 43763 Russert, 12292 Dalton, 4969 Lawrence, 27966 Changguang, 273994 Cinqueterre, 20778 Wangchaohao, 15414 Pettirossi, 10638 McGlothlin, 13917 Correggia, 1121 Natascha, 367406 Buser, 2373 Immo, 101955 Bennu, 3461 Mandelshtam, 29362 Azumakofuzi

127q9 (42.604) \\the activities I perform as a learner; 3524 Schulz, 335853 Valleedaoste, 10139 Ronsard, 20730 Jorgecarvano, 33623 Kyraseevers, 159865 Silvialonso, 8410 Hiroakiohno

qc61: the house or main niche and what it means to each partner

31q9 (282.604) \\priya or cz, maybe sb; 6289 Lanusei, 21701 Gabemendoza, 17832 Pitman, 4098 Thraen, 145523 Lulin, 231265 Saulperlmutter, 4959 Niinoama, 14624 Prymachenko, 6392 Takashimizuno, 28636 Vasudevan, 22485 Unterman, 8273 Apatheia, 7616 Sadako

103q9 (102.604) \\setting up a household w shanna; 8887 Scheeres, 3317 Paris, 11496 Grass, 25428 Lakhanpal, 188576 Kosenda, 143 Adria, 11373 Carbonaro, 9951 Tyrannosaurus, 30270 Chemparathy

67q9 (192.604) \\in an empty space, chillin with generic warmth, mb, vanessa h; 13011 Loeillet, 4133 Heureka, 9809 Jimdarwin, 9767 Midsomer Norton, 3133 Sendai, 715 Transvaalia, 7729 Golovanov, 25963 Elisalin, 64 Angelina, 26612 Sunsetastro, 155138 Pucinskas, 1498 Lahti, 67070 Rinaldi, 10042 Budstewart

139q9 (12.604) \\i appear at a time when things are about to happen wrongly in the girl's life; my electing to build sim cities as pro-creations; 16164 Yangli, 11084 Gio, 6255 Kuma

qig46: you as the commander of forces

qc348: a state of radical beliefs

8q8 (342.396) \\special tasks I get assigned to; 103740 Budinger, 3970 Herran, 8458 Georgekoenig, 9785 Senjikan, 10808 Digerrojr, 2112 Ulyanov, 1166 Sakuntala, 15870 Oburka, 4879 Zykina

80q8 (162.396) \\endless crazy challenges handed to our team at work; 39712 Ehimedaigaku, 17889 Liechty, 34271 Vinjaivale, 32033 Arjunkapoor, 118172 Vorgebirge, 20530 Johnayres, 175920 Francisnimmo, 5938 Keller, 121103 Ericneilsen, 2016 Heinemann, 142020 Xinghaishiyan, 92578 Benecchi, 3056 INAG, 5523 Luminet, 4746 Doi, 4984 Patrickmiller, 8249 Gershwin, 187638 Greenewalt, 4926 Smoktunovskij, 32462 Janmitchener, 10964 Degraaff, 216390 Binnig, 1439 Vogtia

44q8 (252.396) \\plans for the house with mod equipment, the dream of a creative space; 27776 Cortland, 14632 Flensburg, 24236 Danielberger, 33817 Fariswald, 2604 Marshak, 28155 Chengzhendai, 205424 Bibracte, 59369 Chanco, 3958 Komendantov, 257439 Peppeprosperini, 11789 Kempowski, 9407 Kimuranaoto, 66671 Sfasu, 31637 Bhimaraju, 325 Heidelberga

116q8 (72.396) \\the kinds of intelligent delivery I love seeing in our british murder mysteries; 48070 Zizza, 13509 Guayaquil, 15264 Delbruck, 1435 Garlena, 575 Renate, 4663 Falta, 10557 Rowland, 2396 Kochi

qc204: the very hard push for progress, with or without somebody

20q8 (312.396) \\what I learned from the gangsta rappers; len; 3740 Menge, 11696 Capen, 27706 Strogen, 7167 Laupheim

92q8 (132.396) \\the magic of pankhudi in light of REDACTED. Introduction to the indian woman as relief from domestic terror; also, the indian woman is attached to social difficulties for me here—when I am engaging an outright enemy who holds the favor of an army. In that sense, may i never find her in this life; 3985 Raybatson, 117581 Devinschrader, 34159 Ryanthorpe, 3322 Lidiya, 4310 Stromholm, 20613 Chibaken, 1415 Malautra, 9553 Colas, 8577 Choseikomori, 42523 Ragazzileonardo, 3365 Recogne

56q8 (222.396) \\the greatest of all time? Those who set the standards for power in their areas. otherwise that area as it is would remain unknown. In different ways (librarians+, astronauts*, psychology~): strudell*, adc*, REDACTED, REDACTED*, dryden+*~, vanessa h*, REDACTED, REDACTED, REDACTED, REDACTED+*~(weird driving); 14179 Skinner, 22784 Theresaoei, 289314 Chisholm, 27855 Giorgilli, 2175 Andrea Doria, 3350 Scobee, 781 Kartvelia, 2891 McGetchin, 7854 Laotse, 33800 Gross, 4387 Tanaka, 18289 Yokoyamakoichi, 4057 Demophon, 15594 Castillo, 1092 Lilium, 43955 Fixlmuller

128q8 (42.396) \\holiday body research, completing a major effort during holidays; 28295 Heyizheng, 18012 Marsland, 17046 Kenway, 2780 Monnig, 90022 Apache Point, 41450 Medkeff, 110288 Libai

qc60: true sexual partners and that which is instilled in them by the other/ 140 shows the aspect of the partner you actually engage

32q8 (282.396) \\actions of the thrio in my fantasy life. Unfortunately, as long as I don't go around REDACTED, this will be the REDACTED; 2567 Elba, 23990 Springsteen, 19833 Wickwar, 21813 Danwinegar, 19470 Wenpingchen, 3089 Oujianquan, 85216 Schein, 11746 Thomjansen, 3494 Purple Mountain, 13622 McArthur, 65716 Ohkinohama, 12632 Mignonette

104q8 (102.396) \\a fantasy I have; the nature of my houses or workflows as procreative recipients. A true sexual partner. Also indicates the **compatible** sexual partner's body build—m, ju, shanna; 8628 Davidsaltzberg, 10689 Pinillaalonso, 158472 Tiffanyfinley, 5240 Kwasan, 9496 Ockels, 21650 Tilgner, 4203 Brucato, 15828 Sincheskul, 153 Hilda, 26458 Choihyuna, 41502 Denchukun, 3141 Buchar, 28689 Rohrback, 1820 Lohmann

68q8 (192.396) \\sb and makeup, me and exercise, housemate situation as prime. kodaitis negatively affects the nature of sex with someone who shares my house; 286693 Kodaitis, 25725 McCormick, 11434 Lohnert, 5821 Yukiomaeda, 26169 Ishikawakiyoshi, 5213 Takahashi, 28760 Grantwomble, 46731 Prieurblanc, 346693 Middelburg, 24021 Yocum, 4191 Assese, 1309 Hyperborea, 1047 Geisha, 5007 Keay, 100033 Taize, 7715 Leonidarosino

140q8 (12.396) \\a survey all of my sexual partners is described here; 192178 Lijieshou, 22512 Cannat, 10090 Sikorsky, 13130 Dylanthomas, 37163 Huachucaclub, 3605 Davy, 8537 Billochbull

qig47: rallying one's assets and allies

qc347: long administration of my assets, sata. WHY the hell does it take so long?

8q7 (342.188) \\i value standing out distinct from the crowd; 15869 Tullius, 20 Massalia, 28948 Disalvo, 371 Bohemia, 117781 Jamesfisher, 21627 Sillis

80q7 (162.188) \\REDACTED, REDACTED, the pushy implacable; 10267 Giuppone, 25884 Asai, 23409 Derzhavin, 33517 Paulfoltin, 12136 Martinryle, 33247 Iannacone, 4561 Lemeshev, 22277 Hirado, 7604 Kridsadaporn, 9633 Cotur, 4493 Naitomitsu, 207563 Toscana, 32270 Inokuchihiroo, 21929 Nileshraval, 149528 Simonrodriguez, 66458 Romaplanetario, 79353 Andrewalday, 2014 Vasilevskis, 21346 Marieladislav, 12226 Caseylisse, 144907 Whitehorne, 14617 Lasvergnas

44q7 (252.188) \\that which leads to the need for federal annexes; 7342 Uchinoura, 39679 Nukuhiyama, 108 Hecuba, 4497 Taguchi, 92297 Monrad, 2334 Cuffey, 22645 Rotblat, 21651 Mission Valley, 1792 Reni, 4921 Volonte, 246132 Lugyny, 24250 Luteolson, 17651 Tajimi, 6314 Reigber, 16243 Rosenbauer, 25992 Benjamensun, 688 Melanie, 6983 Komatsusakyo, 26300 Herbweiss

116q7 (72.188) \\the simplifying nature of quarterly reporting systems—a thing I'm not good at engaging reliably as of 2024; how I pay my taxes; 11934 Lundgren, 10222 Klotz, 281772 Matttaylor, 10470 Bartczak, 8462 Hazelsears

qc203: things white people do. reckless stuff we blacks are not allowed to get away with and still advance… not in america at least. Is there anywhere where I could get away with it though? I guess niggaz do get away with it too, I suppose

20q7 (312.188) \\i do less of this as I get older, and probably more of the squares; REDACTED; 20324 Johnmahoney, 16700 Seiwa, 31888 Polizzi, 14535 Kazuyukihanda, 7849 Janjosefric, 58499 Stuber, 79864 Pirituba, 28825 Bryangoehring, 82463 Mluigiaborsi, 19811 Kimperkins, 1653 Yakhontovia, 25775 Danielpeng, 10410 Yangguanghua

92q7 (132.188) \\the studyable body. ju, m, agd, axb, ra, eeh, sn—almost all with skin of a certain cappuccino color; 183635 Helmi, 3442 Yashin, 4903 Ichikawa, 327082 Tournesol, 10303 Freret, 23850 Ramaswami, 19853 Ichinomiya, 2208 Pushkin, 365443 Holiday, 204370 Ferdinandvanek, 110300 Abusimbel

56q7 (222.188) \\me taking a secret side on …. This is generally NOT HEALTHY for me, as [ADB:strokes] live here. j hilton was tasked with this; 27368 Raytesar, 210271 Samarkand, 24967 Fristensky, 22791 Twarog, 1895 Larink, 16280 Groussin, 62 Erato, 7113 Ostapbender, 4304 Geichenko, 4196 Shuya, 7950 Berezov, 21415 Nicobrenner, 6192 Javiergorosabel, 16077 Arayhamilton, 13691 Akie, 14968 Kubacek, 6014 Chribrenmark

128q7 (42.188) \\me influencing students and colleagues during s.o.s.; knime, AI, and data at USAA; 979 Ilsewa, 7304 Namiki, 2258 Viipuri, 33476 Gilanareiss, 3599 Basov, 101777 Robhoskins, 3200 Phaethon, 30141 Nelvenzon, 30152 Reneefallon, 29476 Kvicala

qc59: pursuing my own personal growth from a corner, including real estate ownership. What you profitably procreate

32q7 (282.188) \\an explanation of why I can't easily run sata properly; the one who does the unbelievable thing; real estae as background asset? Liability? The lore may not actually be the reality until it is paid off; 29952 Varghese, 11728 Einer, 20282 Hedberg, 121089 Vyssi Brod, 13227 Poor, 5410 Spivakov, 8111 Hoepli, 6671 Concari, 55561 Madenberg

104q7 (102.188) \\me, when not interacting with a troublesome partner, having no will to go forward in sata. This is my default; mahomes' behind the back pass; the unbelievable thing done; 36614 Saltis, 8083 Mayeda, 9933 Alekseev, 4765 Wasserburg, 333508 Voiture, 38238 Holic, 358675 Bente, 33811 Scottobin, 1870 Glaukos, 1202 Marina

68q7 (192.188) \\my handling of mutiny, the … bosses do this too; 4118 Sveta, 30375 Kathuang, 1845 Helewalda, 8241 Agrius, 22080 Emilevasseur, 2163 Korczak, 5005 Kegler, 26430 Thomwilkason, 20566 Laurielee, 27492 Susanduncan, 2588 Flavia, 7903 Albinoni, 9313 Protea, 7892 Musamurahigashi, 325366 Asturias, 26307 Friedafein, 14818 Mindeli, 23612 Ramzel, 11588 Gottfriedkeller, 669 Kypria, 18240 Mould, 14041 Durrenmatt, 16857 Goodall, 37530 Dancingangel, 22562 Wage, 1526 Mikkeli, 24124 Dozier, 6544 Stevendick, 1935 Lucerna

140q7 (12.188) \\my interaction w sb when co-creation is possible; 11107 Hakkoda, 48681 Zeilinger, 8020 Erzgebirge, 7259 Gaithersburg, 54237 Hiroshimanabe, 19434 Bahuffman, 4083 Jody, 1074 Beljawskya

qig48: space of the prodigy

qc346: finding out that …

8q6 (341.979) \\an archaeological site; a rich tomb; 4528 Berg, 114659 Sajnovics, 8314 Tsuji, 6447 Terrycole, 25875 Wickramasekara, 20364 Zdenekmiler

80q6 (161.979) \\me and my two trio mates grant blessings to the 8q6 character; 8711 Lukeasher, 2436 Hatshepsut, 8146 Jimbell, 30539 Raissamuller, 4656 Huchra, 3939 Huruhata, 4502 Elizabethann, 29208 Halorentz, 4058 Cecilgreen, 2880 Nihondaira, 6559 Nomura, 4385 Elsasser, 31065 Beishizhang, 6684 Volodshevchenko, 21514 Gamalski, 9399 Pesch, 72012 Terute, 8776 Campestris, 12244 Werfel, 257336 Noeliasanchez, 8232 Akiramizuno, 13513 Manila, 10167 Yoshiwatiso, 1279 Uganda

44q6 (251.979) \\girl time, hanging out in a kind of vacay our commentary mode; 1511 Dalera, 10438 Ludolph, 26475 Krisztisugar, 23804 Haber, 10033 Bodewits, 137082 Maurobachini, 20430 Stout, 22275 Barentsen, 3769 Arthurmiller, 15855 Mariasalvatore, 178150 Taiyuinkwei, 34000 Martinmatl, 9376 Thionville, 8441 Lapponica, 27105 Clarkben, 24270 Dougskinner, 28820 Sylrobertson, 14969 Willacather, 278447 Saviano, 2770 Tsvet, 20479 Celisaucier, 25560 Chaihaoxi

116q6 (71.979) \\i guess I'll have to do it myself, since the other isn't capable; 8129 Michaelbusch, 7995 Khvorostovsky, 10285 Renemichelsen, 15258 Alfilipenko, 15417 Babylon, 26851 Sarapul

qc202: me and sk or mb in our adventures

20q6 (311.979) \\indiana jones and the treasure partner, apparently chasing something lost is a big deal; 19364 Semafor, 4409 Kissling, 5989 Sorin, 31904 Haoruochen, 25075 Kiyomoto, 531 Zerlina, 27132 Jezek, 27349 Enos, 7363 Esquibel

92q6 (131.979) \\a revisiting of my history done for tactical purposes. One of the purposes of contours; 4309 Marvin, 5596 Morbidelli, 2992 Vondel, 14012 Amedee, 1833 Shmakova, 42191 Thurmann, 1456 Saldanha, 3690 Larson, 10861 Ciske, 2845 Franklinzen, 21638 Nicjachowski, 7720 Lepaute, 1979 Sakharov, 12383 Eboshi, 23258 Tsuihark, 18169 Amaldi, 17972 Ascione, 16999 Ajstewart, 19182 Pitz, 91890 Kiriko Matsuri

56q6 (221.979) \\the prodigy's interaction with the teacher; how the prodigy appears; 201204 Stevewilliams, 22938 Brilawrence, 12880 Juliegrady, 47466 Mayatoyoshima, 7561 Patrickmichel, 50000 Quaoar, 4451 Grieve, 30192 Talarterzian, 2855 Bastian

128q6 (41.979) \\the teacher's interaction with the prodigy; who the teacher appears to be and what they perceive; romano to me. Andrea lafortune and shelley ritter somehow have a role in this. An honor; 26887 Tokyogiants, 9886 Aoyagi, 19582 Blow, 44013 Iidetenmomdai, 21821 Billryan, 30036 Eshamaiti, 6469 Armstrong

*qc58: your general sex organ and that of the **compatible** partner to attract*

32q6 (281.979) \\the invariable splitting of sides between me and my partner; 6587 Brassens, 21556 Christineli, 2581 Radegast, 6595 Munizbarreto, 2306 Bauschinger, 13732 Woodall, 5434 Tomwhitney, 4810 Ruslanova, 30012 Sohamdaga, 216439 Lyubertsy, 32570 Peruindiana

104q6 (101.979) \\consulting my lego cities. Later, my workflows; 22338 Janemojo, 2844 Hess, 14820 Aizuyaichi, 5641 McCleese, 9023 Mnesthus, 5878 Charlene, 1953 Rupertwildt, 213800 Stefanwul, 7394 Xanthomalitia, 20591 Sameergupta, 6168 Isnello, 7632 Stanislav, 16781 Rencin, 26183 Henrigodard

68q6 (191.979) \\despite being allied with someone, my struggling to really be on the same page with them. Patronization is common here; 2882 Tedesco, 2329 Orthos, 31988 Jasonfiacco, 21393 Kalygeringer, 27341 Fabiomuzzi, 25216 Enricobernardi, 10044 Squyres, 21035 Iwabu, 5998 Sitensky, 6171 Uttorp, 12005 Delgiudice, 200255 Weigle, 63068 Moraes, 58163 Minnesang, 9398 Bidelman, 16953 Besicovitch, 231278 Karpati

140q6 (11.979) \\this qunit explains 70% of why I don't enjoy sex, or am more likely to interface with someone I disrespect when it is had. Unless there is roleplay; 31336 Chenyuhsin, 5973 Takimoto, 33226 Melissamacko, 16707 Norman, 10698 Singer, 88297 Huikilolani, 2370 van Altena, 28742 Hannahsteele, 20834 Allihewlett, 52260 Ureshino, 263 Dresda, 34307 Arielhaas, 355029 Herve, 31437 Verma

qig49: building up one's own little army

qc345: interface with my house

8q5 (341.771) \\commercials with a baby or a pet spilling shit on the floor. Fun supposedly had through mayhem, with the introduction of a smooth remedy. Usually annoying, but not always; more seriously, as the fixer's pet enemy, investigate in h's chart; the disorder which REDACTED opposes. related to that region in the 60s; 16624 Hoshizawa, 6294 Czerny, 7210 Darius, 254863 Robinwarren, 9869 Yadoumaru, 20863 Jamescronk, 57471 Mariemarsina, 5691 Fredwatson, 32531 Ulrikababiakova, 33571 Jaygupta

44q5 (251.771) \\the fixer; the great leader who comes in and turns everything around; 157473 Emuno, 35056 Cullers, 22780 McAlpine, 30147 Amyhammer, 239716 Felixbaumgartner, 25539 Roberthelm, 22812 Ricker, 3488 Brahic, 21358 Mijerbarany, 24412 Ericpalmer, 10510 Maxschreier, 9350 Waseda, 131181 Zebrak, 13640 Ohtateruaki, 6424 Ando, 120285 Brentbos, 24191 Qiaochuyuan

80q5 (161.771) \\the one who can't help but to mess everything up; the actual baby who knocks over the food; 4318 Bata, 249530 Ericrice, 22168 Weissflog, 84 Klio, 20963 Pisarenko, 3629 Lebedinskij, 4809 Robertball, 50 Virginia, 203823 Zdanavicius, 129052 Nimeshdave, 12718 Le Gentil, 2062 Aten, 2434 Bateson, 17473 Freddiemercury, 18943 Elaisponton, 16675 Torii, 2493 Elmer

116q5 (71.771) \\the mandate of the one sent here to clean things up; 31971 Beatricechoi, 4357 Korinthos

qc201: me and my brothers in video game-music mode

20q5 (311.771) \\those who make the tough, but disciplined decisions; 16269 Merkord, 34267 Haniya, 15396 Howardmoore, 2987 Sarabhai, 21675 Kaitlinmaria, 4724 Brocken, 79896 Billhaley, 10352 Kawamura, 2332 Kalm, 231040 Kakaras, 1193 Africa, 179647 Stuartrobbins, 9672 Rosenbergerezek, 12386 Nikolova, 3438 Inarradas, 43993 Mariola

92q5 (131.771) \\cz—and anyone else I've invited into my home with no costs for that matter—and one parties' endless dissatisfaction with the other; a relationship-destroying arrangement which suggests that I should never EVER share my home, but will need to charge at least some kind of tax to let the other person know that they are renting. software as a partner, however, may be more fit for the endless demands as imposed by me...; 5696 Ibsen, 6249 Jennifer, 780 Armenia, 133161 Ruttkai, 2854 Rawson, 9141 Kapur, 110416 Cardille, 12044 Fabbri

56q5 (221.771) \\me seeing the world form a pixel-based, gamified perspective; my dad opposite his challenges; 603 Timandra, 243591 Ignacostantino, 3752 Camillo, 8104 Kumamori, 9551 Kazi, 2526 Alisary, 147736 Raxavinic, 315186 Schade, 1610 Mimaya

128q5 (41.771) \\where I allowed myself to be pressured by sexual performance standards; 100229 Jeanbailly, 15268 Wendelinefroger, 10091 Bandaisan, 7859 Lhasa, 22260 Ur, 25870 Panchovigil, 583 Klotilde

qc57: my approach to the procreative terrain, and the approach my templated partner will have

32q5 (281.771) \\the personality positioning of my partners; currently following REDACTED's orders, but datemasamune limits a lot of what can be done; 5293 Bentengahama, 11966 Plateau, 3550 Link, 19019 Sunflower, 8297 Gerardfaure, 13217 Alpbach, 14189 Sevre, 6859 Datemasamune, 418891 Vizi, 28587 Mundkur

104q5 (101.771) \\various near-liaisons and near-misses with VARIOUS REDACTED hitting on me; successfully getting another room together in my house; 273412 Eduardomissoni, 8459 Larsbergknut, 7989 Pernadavide, 8688 Delaunay, 6596 Bittner, 8632 Egleston, 11016 Borisov, 185164 Ingeburgherz, 12100 Amiens, 31728 Rhondah, 94400 Hongdaeyong

68q5 (191.771) \\the goal of the book of contours: controlling the message of this region myself; ironically, my writing contours seems like an attempt to grab a long-wayward bull by the horns, taking control of my fate; 69264 Nebra, 9198 Sasagamine, 9474 Cassadrury, 3284 Niebuhr, 1468 Zomba, 6978 Hironaka, 336680 Pavolpaulik, 11269 Knyr, 17193 Alexeybaran, 27254 Shubhrosaha, 2284 San Juan, 25465 Rajagopalan, 34279 Alicezhang, 31952 Bialtdecelie

140q5 (11.771) \\post-sex or co-creation, she both battles with and structures with me. If she doesn't we're not doing these regions; 4416 Ramses, 9696 Jaffe, 14698 Scottyoung, 543 Charlotte, 4659 Roddenberry, 8966 Hortulana

qig50: observations of transformative power

qc344: islam

8q4 (341.563) \\the great jam session. I love these. Hypothesis: "jazz" or "instrument" must be somewhere in the text mine… no, but symphony is, and Qiansanqiang really is a jam session asteroid; 4204 Barsig, 25240 Qiansanqiang, 8408 Strom, 51915 Andry, 19775 Medmondson, 26442 Matfernandez, 7433 Pellegrini, 90533 Laurentblind

80q4 (161.563) \\my actual daily approach to my own personal work; my daily work; to do only that which is unique; 9816 von Matt, 5004 Bruch, 13551 Gadsden, 7586 Bismarck, 246913 Slocum, 7519 Paulcook, 343743 Kjurkchieva, 3116 Goodricke, 10373 MacRobert, 55382 Kootinlok, 270373 William, 217257 Valemangano, 1897 Hind, 21501 Acevedo, 15736 Hamanasu, 21724 Ratai, 34077 Yoshiakifuse, 25743 Serrato, 8595 Dougallii

44q4 (251.563) \\sticking strongly to another's rhythm—often a prereq for being able to do jam sessions; recitals; conformity to someone else's creative notion; my consoling role when someone near me is facing the death of their loved one, remaining strong; muslims and islam; 12027 Masaakitanaka, 207109 Sturmenchopf, 129146

Stevenglenn, 14016 Steller, 4930 Rephiltim, 2328 Robeson, 9833 Rilke, 10330 Durkheim, 154587 Ennico, 28780 Lisadeaver, 3646 Aduatiques, 33515 Linbohan, 14203 Hocking, 26622 Maxwimberley, 3490 Solc, 28808 Ananthnarayan, 164215 Doloreshill, 121817 Szatmary, 26707 Navrazhnykh, 15112 Arlenewolfe, 6737 Okabayashi

116q4 (71.563) \\either mine, or (less likely) dad's death; the christian church as persecutors of early muslims; 9832 Xiaobinwang, 21440 Elizacollins, 278645 Kontsevych, 95782 Hansgraf, 15834 McBride, 10793 Quito, 1765 Wrubel, 22611 Galerkin

qc200: how I put myself into controversial situations, then confidently cut ties. CRITICAL in my chart

20q4 (311.563) \\—>being tasked to make a specific connection with someone in order to get something done; how I handle slights and challenges on the inside; 12306 Pebronstein, 3177 Chillicothe, 13127 Jeroenbrouwers, 31853 Rahulmital, 839 Valborg, 13414 Grantham, 12752 Kvarnis, 100077 Tertzakian, 167971 Carlyhowett, 33446 Michaelyang, 34543 Davidbriggs, 223633 Rosnyaine, 8932 Nagatomo, 19175 Peterpiot, 8741 Suzukisuzuko

92q4 (131.563) \\one who is stone drunk. Making absolutely no sense to onlookers; 21289 Giacomel, 75058 Hanau, 13063 Purifoy, 4154 Rumsey, 133854 Wargetz, 16421 Roadrunner, 10857 Bluthner, 23884 Karenharvey, 9 Metis, 5325 Silver, 2035 Stearns, 2382 Nonie, 30421 Jameschafer, 100 Hekate

56q4 (221.563) \\—>me, the great generals; nighttime or evening thoughts; 9536 Statler, 7695 Premysl, 75308 Shoin, 335292 Larrey, 12696 Camus, 23701 Liqibin, 20287 Munteanu, 34256 Advaitpatil, 15845 Bambi, 174361 Rickwhite, 23681 Prabhu, 3124 Kansas, 25593 Camillejordan, 134040 Beaubierhaus, 22679 Amydavid, 2876 Aeschylus, 13259 Bhat, 121486 Sarahkirby

128q4 (41.563) \\the public, machina generally; 5083 Irinara, 17952 Folsom, 100231 Monceau, 2060 Chiron, 178155 Kenzaarraki, 18291 Wani, 26276 Natrees, 35618 Tartu

qc56: conflicts sponsored by each partner and how you settle them; trying to get a situation to better fit one's wants, how the attitudes of intimacy partners (you or the others) compel certain events in buildup of the intimate moments

32q4 (281.563) \\rifting w REDACTED and meeting REDACTED; 5851 Inagawa, 22995 Allenjanes, 7608 Telegramia, 452 Hamiltonia, 9844 Otani, 13620 Moynahan, 31943 Tahsinelmas, 935 Clivia, 30017 Shaundatta, 19821 Caroltolin, 14850 Nagashimacho, 363582 Folpotat, 11137 Yarigatake, 826 Henrika, 14100 Weierstrass, 1287 Lorcia

104q4 (101.563) \\reflections in genoa, vow of silence; 52384 Elenapanko, 15790 Keizan, 11579 Tsujitsuka, 8470 Dudinskaya, 2969 Mikula, 4805 Asteropaios, 5593 Jonsujatha, 11516 Arthurpage, 2120 Tyumenia, 7391 Strouhal

68q4 (191.563) \\milestones describing the entire saga of my failed collaborations; 118418 Yangmei, 21517 Dobi, 11149 Tateshina, 25370 Karenfletch, 114025 Krzesinski, 15695 Fedorshpig, 51829 Williemccool, 13523 Vanhassel, 8929 Haginoshinji, 31531 ARRL, 9973 Szpilman, 9018 Galache, 23408 Beijingaoyun, 216888 Sankovich, 1616 Filipoff, 4537 Valgrirasp, 119 Althaea, 99950 Euchenor, 121637 Druscillaperry

140q4 (11.563) \\i require a certain ambition formula be followed before there is sex—at least now that I'm older; 33936 Johnwells, 18548 Christoffel, 49350 Katheynix, 27412 Teague, 13274 Roygross, 7262 Sofue

qig51: pulled in under an expected standard

qc343: the jazz hall and the conjured images of the music

8q3 (341.354) \\the jazz hall—the state in which the memorable music is made; 5136 Baggaley, 24168 Hexlein, 20343 Vaccariello, 1592 Mathieu, 209 Dido, 410475 Robertschulz

80q3 (161.354) \\cz, sb, aggressively attractive; 448 Natalie, 1829 Dawson, 12702 Panamarenko, 30244 Linhpham, 296905 Korochantsev, 19701 Aomori, 12221 Ogatakoan, 11417 Chughtai, 19454 Henrymarr, 1943 Anteros, 23306 Adamfields, 22619 Ajscheetz, 175152 Marthafarkas, 5608 Olmos, 16801 Petrinpragensis, 4996 Veisberg, 24611 Svetochka, 9720 Ulfbirgitta

44q3 (251.354) \\the recital hall, the place where hopefuls are scrutinized for their performance of established work; 134003 Ingridgalinsky, 13897 Vesuvius, 7934 Sinatra, 1598 Paloque, 7722 Firneis, 27330 Markporter, 145732 Kanmon, 28446 Davlantes, 30067 Natalieng, 19640 Ethanroth, 12414 Bure

116q3 (71.354) \\when I'm trying too hard without the requisite alignment of focus for the task at hand. Full of fuck ups; 1976 Kaverin, 64288 Lamchiuying, 13678 Shimada, 91607 Delaboudiniere, 31175 Erikafuchs, 21672 Laichunju

qc199: grooming, style, and body adornment

20q3 (311.354) \\how I groom and adorn my body, my rings and hair?; the negative thoughts I battled with later when I got high with shanna / less so, crystal, and the overall reason why my high sessions, if they happen, should always be solo. Having another present introduces all kinds of questions about what they think of me, but I need the full room to see as much as I can see; 25869 Jacoby, 61401 Schiff, 183182 Weinheim, 454505 Suntharalingam, 8498 Ufa, 429031 Hannavonhoemer, 16259 Housinger, 4905 Hiromi, 133726 Gateswest, 255989 Dengyushian, 10288 Saville

92q3 (131.354) \\what my grooming intends to say; when you are tasked to keep order, however this is done. I can easily, spontaneously look like bad guy here in the other's eyes. I really shouldn't dwell on order keepers and their compelled communication if I am to become one myself—writing my own rules; 3612 Peale, 2391 Tomita, 6697 Celentano, 22005 Willnelson, 48794 Stolzova, 13654 Masuda, 8758 Perdix, 8795 Dudorov, 184535 Audouze, 462 Eriphyla, 33414 Jessicatian, 22837 Richardcruz

56q3 (221.354) \\what your grooming stands against; what happened when I got high in front of shanna; 22613 Callander, 24372 Timobauman, 9804 Shrikulkarni, 3459 Bodil, 3545 Gaffey, 316 Goberta, 8581 Johnen, 2546 Libitina, 90712 Wittelsbach, 115561 Frankherbert, 868 Lova, 5109 Robertmiller, 9907 Oileus, 5016 Migirenko, 18930 Athreya

128q3 (41.354) \\that which seeds the potential for your grooming; how I generally handle psychedelics and related drugs; 145820 Valeromeo, 1691 Oort, 1863 Antinous, 170023 Vogeley, 30194 Liamyoung, 837 Schwarzschilda

qc55: how the partners override each other. This qcross should be avoided. Use qc343 instead

32q3 (281.354) \\destruction of my collaborative partnerships. The death scene; 28628 Kensenshi, 297005 Ellirichter, 12633 Warmenhoven, 1861 Komensky, 181569 Leetyphoon, 5649 Donnashirley, 70418 Kholopov, 2649 Oongaq, 73693 Dorschner, 2638 Gadolin, 87271 Kokubunji, 380 Fiducia, 10661 Teutoburgerwald, 7088 Ishtar

104q3 (101.354) \\my collaborator turned enemy, with villainized messages on repeat; 12595 Amandashaw, 3619 Nash, 4141 Nintanlena, 6654 Lulea, 17897 Gallardo, 32146 Paigebrown, 330934 Natevanwey, 4328 Valina

68q3 (191.354) \\how my attacker argues; 159181 Berdychiv, 25614 Jankral, 5945 Roachapproach, 25038 Matebezdek, 4667 Robbiesh, 129314 Dathongolish, 274472 Pieta, 19415 Parvamenon, 4625 Shchedrin, 12574 LONEOS, 836 Jole, 268669 Bunun, 29983 Amyxu, 2300 Stebbins, 4390 Madreteresa

140q3 (11.354) \\the short round girl finally makes her move, or I make it on her; tiy-like in my chart; 6606 Makino, 18730 Wingip, 9060 Toyokawa, 14589 Stevenbyrnes

qig52: solidarity within the army

qc342: me and keith's creative promotion

8q2 (341.146) \\my repeated and inconvenient return to REDACTED; 11964 Prigogine, 2826 Ahti, 17970 Palepu, 772 Tanete, 3610 Decampos, 11307 Erikolsson, 3346 Gerla, 19563 Brzezinska, 4745 Nancymarie, 6829 Charmawidor, 25109 Hofving, 263251 Pandabear

80q2 (161.146) \\my interaction with vb; 1625 The NORC, 25053 Matthewknight, 7300 Yoshisada, 20016 Rietschel, 20120 Ryugatake, 127516 Oravetz, 6869 Funada, 31476 Bocconcelli, 25920 Templeanne, 389293 Hasubick, 33570 Jagruenstein, 9274 Amylovell, 25517 Davidlau, 361764 Antonbuslov, 13934 Kannami, 66583 Nicandra, 17555 Kenkennedy, 36 Atalante, 3145 Walter Adams, 193736 Henrythroop

44q2 (251.146) \\yuny and her role, the exciting mother who , by working hard, gets into everything; shanna; 9204 Morike, 30249 Zamora, 185538 Fangcheng, 246841 Williamirace, 2507 Bobone, 14491 Hitachiomiya, 7439 Tetsufuse, 11339 Orlik, 325558 Guyane, 1076 Viola, 17933 Haraguchi, 15476 Narendra, 114987 Tittel, 7767 Tomatic, 12123 Pazin, 7789 Kwiatkowski, 168767 Kochte, 8734 Warner, 99941 Lonniewege, 7136 Yokohasuo, 20307 Johnbarnes, 144633 Georgecarroll

116q2 (71.146) \\my going hard as the responsible agent, as it is one's duty to do so; 65848 Enricomari, 6136 Gryphon, 7292 Prosperin, 35229 Benckert, 35062 Sakuranosyou, 8952 ODAS, 1681 Steinmetz, 8998 Matthewizawa, 15359 Dressler

qc198: sexuality and sexual projection; this qcross is all about how new or well-established an institution is, and says A LOT about stable money sources and the way multibillionaires are known

20q2 (311.146) \\paid well at work for the first time; 19462 Ulissedini, 10100 Burgel, 168221 Donjennings, 7933 Magritte, 7285 Seggewiss, 6897 Tabei

92q2 (131.146) \\in the dentist chair, making an impression. Eventually having to move on; billionaire's rockets; 20823 Liutingchun, 129879 Tishasaltzman, 4522 Britastra, 21426 Davidbauer, 7223 Dolgorukij, 4032 Chaplygin, 10820 Offenbach, 12130 Mousa, 6714 Montreal, 2324 Janice, 6113 Tsap, 10158 Taroubou, 58534 Logos

56q2 (221.146) \\REDACTED's small areolae / initially small nipples live here—hadano—and this qunit in here chart is THE indicator of … advice-giving, fiercely declared. the bedroom-removal fight with REDACTED; club behavior. Fast life. It may take four to pull this off. Scrabble at mom's; 23283 Jinjuyi, 3621 Curtis, 2303 Retsina,

18236 Bernardburke, 22910 Ruiwang, 23886 Toshihamane, 134346 Pinatubo, 6055 Brunelleschi, 26298 Dunweathers, 8609 Shuvalov, 9987 Peano, 5625 Jamesferguson, 1111 Reinmuthia, 29464 Leonmis, 3401 Vanphilos, 1624 Rabe, 1623 Vivian, 4938 Papadopoulos, 20224 Johnrae, 3465 Trevires, 8684 Reichwein, 9164 Colbert, 5541 Seimei, 15106 Swanson, 27375 Asirvatham, 117388 Jamiemoore, 332733 Drolshagen, 23650 Cvancara, 9172 Abhramu

128q2 (41.146) \\attempts to gain entry into a club; 14135 Cynthialang, 159776 Eduardorohl, 27098 Bocarsly, 27975 Mazurkiewicz, 328563 Mosplanetarium

qc54: yours and the partner's body exposition and diet in order to keep things that way

32q2 (281.146) \\the inner passion to keep pursuing something—even without a co-creator; the nature of the inner urge which drives you to want a partner?; 13607 Vicars, 10404 McCall, 3580 Avery, 2644 Victor Jara, 1182 Ilona, 351785 Reguly, 15052 Emileschweitzer, 34262 Michaelren, 28852 Westonbraun, 548 Kressida, 310273 Paulsmeyers, 31886 Verlisak, 16194 Roderick, 229900 Emmagreaves, 12279 Laon, 52271 Lecorbusier, 1192 Prisma

104q2 (101.146) \\working with someone, yet doing all of the hard work; 6557 Yokonomura, 11520 Fromm, 20794 Ryanolson, 32021 Lilyjenkins, 4473 Sears, 30363 Dellasantina, 5978 Kaminokuni, 2818 Juvenalis, 32532 Thereus, 15817 Lucianotesi, 424 Gratia, 4887 Takihiroi, 32145 Katberman, 4966 Edolsen

68q2 (191.146) \\the brat. was REDACTED. now REDACTED, REDACTED kind of; 5073 Junttura, 319227 Erichbar, 3035 Chambers, 12706 Tanezaki, 21791 Mattweegman, 129096 Andrewleung, 29614 Sheller, 20902 Kylebeighle, 43971 Gabzdyl, 8777 Torquata, 28662 Ericduran, 9391 Slee

140q2 (11.146) \\sassy big-titted (penghuanwu) partner who transfers her energy to me on demand. 7 REDACTED; my cat kit now fills this role in a MUCH more serene way, though obviously she lacks the human traits; 48798 Penghuanwu, 18609 Shinobuyama, 34147 Vengadesan, 31807 Shaunalennon, 1104 Syringa, 7001 Noether, 31978 Jeremyphilip

qig53: social experience acquisitions

qc341: what one would do with spaces that were fully one's own

8q1 (340.938) \\the unit; 161207 Lidz, 204842 Fengchia, 30097 Traino, 1265 Schweikarda, 1968 Mehltretter, 312 Pierretta, 3059 Pryor, 6438 Suarez

80q1 (160.938) \\me as an apprentice-type in …; 62794 Scheirich, 28983 Omergranek, 8430 Florey, 65698 Emmarochelle, 16757 Luoxiahong, 15889 Xiaoyuhe, 17640 Mount Stromlo, 79694 Nanrendong, 10712 Malashchuk, 22948 Maidanak, 6658 Akiraabe, 3243 Skytel, 2810 Lev Tolstoj, 1848 Delvaux, 20060 Johannforster, 15250 Nishiyamahiro, 16666 Liroma, 7272 Darbydyar

44q1 (250.938) \\going all over the place touring various hedonistic spots for perhaps shady reasons; 3316 Herzberg, 30144 Minubasu, 31628 Vorperian, 6612 Hachioji, 30053 Ivanpaskov, 96086 Toscanos, 1050 Meta, 3351 Smith, 2875 Lagerkvist, 30268 Jessezhang, 12235 Imranakperov, 243 Ida, 10827 Doikazunori, 54598 Bienor, 12833 Kamenny Ujezd, 31592 Jacobplaut, 121481 Reganhoward, 149728 Klostermann, 1540 Kevola, 1660 Wood

116q1 (70.938) \\gta soundtracks; automatic; the light circumstances under which me and the canadians traveled; 35978 Arlington, 21715 Palaniappan, 3157 Novikov, 858 El Djezair, 6643 Morikubo, 121022 Galliano, 10669 Herfordia, 10233 Le Creusot, 13212 Jayleno, 18567 Segenthau, 33061 Vaclavmorava

qc197: sexuality seeded and preferred, especially 92q1 and its trigger 20q1. the squares 56q1 and 128q1 are the reason your sexuality develops as it does

20q1 (310.938) \\those types who draw out my sexuality or co-creativity; genevieve prohal, m, or ju; western travelers, manifest destiny; 48588 Raschroder, 90140 Gomezdonet, 11349 Witten, 2847 Parvati, 12751 Kamihayashi, 7675 Gorizia, 3733 Yoshitomo, 9820 Hempel, 6465 Zvezdotchet, 30151 Susanoffner, 25046 Suyihan, 16676 Tinne, 2224 Tucson, 246 Asporina

92q1 (130.938) \\how I acquired my astro data or got into ee, and tell others about such. jesus-like figures and seekers; witherspoon; my actual sexual preference / what I like to see around me in expressing my sexuality; 6875 Golgi, 200052 Sinigaglia, 21758 Adrianveres, 26680 Wangchristi, 10690 Massera, 9743 Tohru, 28419 Tanpitcha, 27301 Joeingalls, 17031 Piethut, 12470 Pinotti, 132824 Galamb, 397378 Arvidson, 344641 Szeleczky, 8787 Ignatenko, 5717 Damir, 10324 Vladimirov, 90487 Witherspoon, 175586 Tsou, 27997 Bandos, 22405 Gavioliremo

56q1 (220.938) \\changing my identity while at caltech. Possibly later through acting; 23262 Thiagoolson, 3506 French, 7813 Anderserikson, 5055 Opekushin, 13181 Peneleos, 8733 Ohsugi, 1929 Kollaa, 343000 Ijontichy, 12360 Unilandes, 5494 Johannohr, 35366 Kaifeng, 32019 Krithikaiyer, 17781 Kepping, 6562 Takoyaki, 9817 Thersander, 129962 Williamverts, 78661 Castelfranco

128q1 (40.938) \\caltech nsbe and general peers while I was there; the evangelist; 265 Anna, 8348 Bhattacharyya, 3101 Goldberger, 12101 Trujillo, 13293 Mechelen, 27740 Obatomoyuki, 4132 Bartok

qc53: my being sat on the bench at work, going to shanna instead

32q1 (280.938) \\my interest in acting. For funsies. Meet hugo and sheridan; 16587 Nagamori, 74400 Streaky, 6311 Porubcan, 32891 Amatrice, 2700 Baikonur, 14654 Rajivgupta, 17516 Kogayukihito, 2813 Zappala, 6586 Seydler, 274 Philagoria, 8242 Joshemery, 9909 Eschenbach, 1424 Sundmania, 8643 Quercus, 8209 Toscanelli, 1711 Sandrine

104q1 (100.938) \\life under REDACTED; 400308 Antonkutter, 8561 Sikoruk, 4707 Khryses, 9526 Billmckinnon, 3390 Demanet, 22477 Julimacoraor, 4587 Rees, 21731 Zhuruochen, 31389 Alexkaplan, 24968 Chernyakhovsky, 6081 Cloutis, 25514 Lisawu

68q1 (190.938) \\milestones and the saga of nsbe; 11037 Distler, 24352 Kapilrama, 11353 Guillaume, 25832 Van Scoyoc, 274213 Satriani, 9673 Kunishimakoto, 24474 Ananthram, 27241 Sunilpai, 264474 Rogerclark, 28382 Stevengillen, 13489 Dmitrienko, 274843 Mykhailopetrenko, 41742 Wongkakui, 100924 Luctuymans, 21673 Leatherman

140q1 (10.938) \\to your house, I bring high pickiness and a bad ending. Yet another reason not to invite myself anywhere even if there are blessings to share; 9687 Uhlenbeck, 6735 Madhatter, 30773 Schelde, 216433 Milianleo, 7428 Abekuniomi, 6964 Kunihiko, 12435 Sudachi, 9242 Olea, 12801 Somekawa

qig54: going somewhere to become bigtime

qc340: how I use THE HOURS in the morning and upon re-wakeup

8q12 (340.729) \\me under caffeine; coffee and orange juice as a catalyst; excitement or at least engagement amplification; jolted crash and jump up; 56280 Asemo, 7655 Adamries, 243536 Mannheim, 262295 Jeffrich, 78310 Spoto

80q12 (160.729) \\my work with the taboo; 318794 Uglia, 34398 Terryschmidt, 133009 Watters, 9632 Sudo, 12237 Coughlin, 1267 Geertruida, 23214 Patrickchen, 18302 Korner, 11073 Cavell, 2996 Bowman, 6229 Tursachan, 24639 Mukhametdinov, 218400 Marquardt, 32052 Diyamathur, 34366 Rosavestal, 26908 Lebesgue, 9025 Polanskey, 14502 Morden, 19544 Avramkottke

44q12 (250.729) \\the various scenarios under which I wake up; 8657 Cedrus, 194262 Nove Zamky, 216343 Wenchang, 6672 Corot, 6660 Matsumoto, 24087 Ciambetti, 220229 Hegedus, 1513 Matra, 19914 Klagenfurt, 81859 Joetaylor, 13744 Rickline, 3179 Beruti, 645 Agrippina, 1629 Pecker

116q12 (70.729) \\my ACTUAL claircognizance as a process. That is, the process itself—often through (flamboyant) music. What I think about every day I wake up. What announces itself in square while I'm on caffeine; 123 Brunhild, 30332 Tanaytandon, 55477 Soroban, 12855 Tewksbury, 5020 Asimov, 18019 Dascoli, 4752 Myron, 3308 Ferreri, 273273 Piwowarski, 22573 Johnzhou, 29193 Dolphyn, 10433 Ponsen, 11755 Paczynski

qc196: dreams or positioning to be a bigtime boss

20q12 (310.729) \\in my chart, the "billionaire as explorer": bill gates; yukon jack mcquestern, james cameron under the sea; up to the gods; 134135 Steigerwald, 8164 Andreasdoppler, 3417 Tamblyn, 5899 Jedicke, 19234 Victoriahibbs, 18497 Nevezice, 28196 Szeged, 4793 Slessor, 10885 Horimasato, 6216 San Jose, 33473 Porterfield, 21398 Zengguoshou, 19917 Dazaifu

92q12 (130.729) \\VARIOUS REDACTED would probably be triggers. If I do this, I am crowning the person. But do they deserve it? | TRIGGER; 11092 Iwakisan, 22406 Garyboyle, 60006 Holgermandel, 1221 Amor, 17092 Sharanya, 30778 Doblin, 129068 Alexmay, 8126 Chanwainam, 2264 Sabrina, 19711 Johnaligawesa, 450931 Coculescu, 8739 Morihisa, 19355 Merpalehmann, 33520 Ichige, 3671 Dionysus, 65885 Lubenow

56q12 (220.729) \\my real estate career, pursuing success; 276568 Joestubler, 6440 Ransome, 29681 Saramanshad, 6071 Sakitama, 34312 Deahaupt, 46053 Davidpatterson, 210350 Mariolisa, 3790 Raywilson, 9212 Kanamaru, 22064 Angelalewis, 15346 Bonifatius, 24709 Mitau, 341 California, 9997 COBE, 15604 Fruits, 23019 Thomgregory, 28468 Shichangxu

128q12 (40.729) \\shanna goes out to …, I write my books under focus—both changing the environment; 23808 Joshuahammer, 833 Monica, 5363 Kupka, 4 Vesta, 18768 Sarahbates, 7366 Agata

qc52: formal and informal academics, learning operations centers

32q12 (280.729) \\when I'm not answering what I have felt as pressures (68q12) through being seen by those I have left (140q12), I am often using this section to elaborate my learning environment. Only works for new-to-me learning spaces; institutions like schools and mortgage companies which i sit under; 25165 Leget, 4599 Rowan, 6458 Nouda, 16552 Sawamura, 5110 Belgirate, 26821 Baehr, 582 Olympia, 28324 Davidcampeau, 9473 Ghent, 6202 Georgemiley, 31872 Terkan, 25178 Shreebose, 52344 Yehudimenuhin, 10319 Toshiharu, 2645 Daphne Plane

104q12 (100.729) \\rather than fighting the world, working on my own books instead; 29978 Arthurwang, 15267 Kolyma, 129325 Jedhancock, 34280 Victorradler, 90480 Ulrich, 26457 Naomishah, 29196 Dius, 29314 Eurydamas, 16713 Airashi, 19383 Rolling Stones, 29246 Clausius, 2021 Poincare, 27546 Maryfran

68q12 (190.729) \\dissociation when in break mode on a challenging task; 2372 Proskurin, 18562 Ellenkey, 19413 Grantlewis, 19463 Emilystoll, 20467 Hibbitts, 159902 Gladstone, 366272 Medellin, 16513 Vasks, 32053 Demetrimaxim, 1133 Lugduna, 7626 Iafe, 24411 Janches

140q12 (10.729) \\the family I appear to have started; 16101 Notskas, 32214 Colburn, 1246 Chaka, 9642 Takatahiro, 926 Imhilde, 1370 Hella, 33372 Jonathanchung, 673 Edda, 581 Tauntonia

qig55: activities donated into the ambient authority center

qc339: the voice of siri, the users, and the companies who engineer such ubiquity

8q11 (340.521) \\a STRONG part of my character—especially when it comes to people's ability to reliably find me. easy immersion which blocks all other destabilizing forces; 350969 Boiohaemum, 187679 Folinsbee, 10764 Rubezahl, 2661 Bydzovsky, 6351 Neumann, 9248 Sauer, 13554 Decleir, 94 Aurora, 10918 Kodaly, 4637 Odorico, 10546 Nakanomakoto, 946 Poesia, 5482 Korankei

80q11 (160.521) \\REDACTED and other people who believe something is wrong with themselves, or whom I tell have something wrong with them. REDACTED. But to the extent that I believe this, I am also blocked by most others in the public—especially when posting on youtube with that psychotic look of mine. DON'T EXPLAIN; 16051 Bernero, 901 Brunsia, 25237 Hurwitz, 29607 Jakehecla, 46513 Ampzing, 9054 Hippocastanum, 10258 Sarneczky, 25257 Elizmakarron, 4615 Zinner, 35326 Lucastrabla, 5983 Praxiteles, 16192 Laird, 3634 Iwan, 5888 Ruders, 22192 Vivienreuter, 3066 McFadden, 25052 Rudawska, 1110 Jaroslawa, 10775 Leipzig, 24829 Berounurbi

44q11 (250.521) \\the environments against which I engage my survival; 24397 Parkerowan, 19160 Chikayoshitomi, 200750 Rix, 6907 Harryford, 34030 Tabuchi, 2642 Vesale, 13918 Tsukinada, 21327 Yabuzuka, 16267 Mcdermott, 3193 Elliot, 117711 Degenfeld, 256369 Vilain, 4631 Yabu, 15903 Rolandflorrie, 53629 Andrewpotter, 9187 Walterkroll, 7099 Feuerbach, 33963 Moranhidalgo, 5164 Mullo, 28207 Blakesmith, 3440 Stampfer

116q11 (70.521) \\things I absolutely do not do because they drain me. My house and complementary partners defend me against needing to do this; 34854 Paquifrutos, 15321 Donnadean, 31574 Moshova, 2958 Arpetito, 5968 Trauger, 17277 Jarrydlevine, 26450 Tanyapetach

qc195: counseling people up to the skies

20q11 (310.521) \\observing higher powers, being insistent on my standards for such. This is probably what earns me more money. May find some of these people @ REDACTED. Others need to be eliminated or cast in immature roles. But how do I learn this easily? What God wants from people like you; me as a young learner; 2710 Veverka, 1959 Karbyshev, 129259 Tapolca, 1680 Per Brahe, 48410 Kolmogorov, 11592 Clintkelly, 10829 Matsuobasho, 8123 Canaletto, 9983 Rickfienberg, 7713 Tsutomu, 7124 Glinos, 289085 Andreweil, 29764 Panneerselvam, 11763 Deslandres

92q11 (130.521) \\how I tell certain confidantes about my various partner encounters, especially when I am after a certain reputation; self-propagandizing; 5383 Leavitt, 84224 Kyte, 10778 Marcks, 17914 Joannelee, 6498 Ko, 7496 Miroslavholub, 6275 Kiryu, 19142 Langemarck, 3185 Clintford, 294727 Dennisritchie, 4339 Almamater, 2355 Nei Monggol, 129051 Chrismay

56q11 (220.521) \\when I call out an immature associate or am called out myself, the desire to be associated drops greatly; 196540 Weinbaum, 30326 Maxpine, 1012 Sarema, 39509 Kardashev, 2459 Spellmann, 15467 Aflorsch, 9485 Uluru, 14831 Gentileschi, 42403 Andraimon, 30301 Kuditipudi, 3723 Voznesenskij, 12106 Menghuan, 157747 Mandryka, 21744 Meliselinger, 31910 Moustafa, 1877 Marsden, 12412 Muchisachie, 289021 Juzeliunas, 233653 Rether, 249 Ilse, 11987 Yonematsu, 168 Sibylla, 23750 Stepciechan

128q11 (40.521) \\one called out has officially reached the end of the road, never to give to the scolder again. Shows I never want to see again; the types of punishment levied by god; the threat of hell, judgment passed, for example; 175450 Phillipklu, 3590 Holst, 3822 Segovia, 6866 Kukai

qc51: be honest in your passions or lose your mind. investigate connection, if any, with ageing; a good starting point for explaining why I have chosen the expressive route I have chosen; activities which will almost certainly produce a payoff one way or another

32q11 (280.521) \\hm. The EXACT conditions where I've been stolen from; 10152 Ukichiro, 949 Hel, 17776 Troska, 20234 Billgibson, 33565 Samferguson, 2617 Jiangxi, 5275 Zdislava, 1512 Oulu, 5215 Tsurui, 19534 Miyagi, 32054 Musunuri, 24215 Jongastel, 74503 Madola, 8011 Saijokeiichi, 20851 Ramachandran, 2468 Repin, 7182 Robinvaughan, 17844 Judson, 15621 Erikhovland, 91553 Claudedoom, 5575 Ryanpark

104q11 (100.521) \\the REDACTED who stole ... and ...; also, the market man behind the promotion of the current focal celebrity; 9266 Holger, 11280 Sakurai, 11790 Goode, 6561 Gruppetta, 16719 Mizokami, 90397 Rasch, 10160 Totoro, 17984 Ahantonioli, 8096 Emilezola, 13916 Bernolak, 10326 Kuragano, 5208 Royer, 20776 Juliekrugler, 17156 Kennethseitz, 20773 Aneeshvenkat, 4857 Altgamia, 10358 Kirchhoff

68q11 (190.521) \\continuing to build towards a viewable presence; 4480 Nikitibotania, 269245 Catastini, 29950 Uppili, 33910 Lestarge, 57 Mnemosyne, 21754 Tvaruzkova, 11861 Teruhime, 33592 Kathrynanna, 1065 Amundsenia, 6163 Reimers, 93256 Stach, 28782 Mechling, 15500 Anantpatel, 25639 Fedina

140q11 (10.521) \\my houses as an acquired taste evolving in a particular direction; REDACTED engaging ... scratch-offs; 10771 Ouro Preto, 1256 Normannia, 14877 Zauberflote, 601 Nerthus, 90317 Williamcutlip, 48715 Balbinot, 25225 Patrickbenson, 31660 Maximiliandu, 32090 Craigworley

qig56: the energy to process your comrades' events

qc338: me having to be the peacemaker in an argument against an irrationalized other, and what I am pursuing through this

8q10 (340.313) \\auguste, keith, sanza: people with their own alien gadget enterprise who are likely to know me for a long time; 28860 Cappelletto, 38821 Linchinghsia, 1656 Suomi, 113949 Bahcall, 53910 Janfischer, 20533 Irmabonham, 5302 Romanoserra, 1690 Mayrhofer, 6266 Letzel, 1473 Ounas, 1206 Numerowia, 7390 Kundera, 266622 Malna

80q10 (160.313) \\my work team, tmnt, any teams I am on for an extended period of time will start looking like this, coming under assault; 8872 Ebenum, 679 Pax, 3718 Dunbar, 1292 Luce, 16035 Sasandford, 18574 Jeansimon, 14681 Estellechurch, 1553 Bauersfelda, 24410 Juliewalker, 8305 Teika, 6426 Vanysek, 55772 Loder, 214485 Dupouy, 3895 Earhart, 4839 Daisetsuzan, 5305 Bernievolz, 274333 Voznyukigor, 2843 Yeti, 121615 Marknoteware, 71483 Dickgottfried

44q10 (250.313) \\2 REDACTED. in other words, opportunistic thugz; 6877 Giada, 129078 Animoo, 40 Harmonia, 17265 Debennett, 26199 Aileenperry, 2301 Whitford, 9544 Scottbirney, 3258 Somnium, 21710 Nijhawan, 27452 Nikhilpatel, 7212 Artaxerxes, 18671 Zacharyrice, 117640 Millsellie, 5621 Erb, 9067 Katsuno, 15762 Ruhmann, 805 Hormuthia, 26092 Norikonoriyuki

116q10 (70.313) \\my interaction with these little troublemaking girls (3 REDACTED); 18413 Adamspencer, 10102 Digerhuvud, 3259 Brownlee, 6365 Nickschneider, 1242 Zambesia

qc194: the mysterious name has no equals. By emulating REDACTED, I may make use of the pantheon I am normally so proud to be a part of. This qcross shows the relationship between the pantheonic group and the invoked character it answers to; REDACTED whatstheirname, the fraud. what compels someone to put on a face and raise all kinds of fanship

20q10 (310.313) \\where I would be REDACTED-like, phaedra. It would help if I had a fierce shield here; the notion of a benevolent god; 22923 Kathrynblair, 15718 Imokawa, 188446 Louischevrolet, 1597 Laugier, 58627 Rieko, 10250 Hellahaasse, 133814 Wenjengko, 16 Psyche, 1049 Gotho, 213770 Fignon, 654 Zelinda

92q10 (130.313) \\THE source of problems with me partnering with people who think they are my equal or superior. The solution, partner with younger or lower-rank people—if they are people at all; 136197 Johnandrews, 2783 Chernyshevskij, 3497 Innanen, 13577 Carmenchu, 158657 Celian, 7973 Koppeschaar, 33696 Crouchley, 11743 Jachowski, 21611 Rosoff, 1808 Bellerophon, 221019 Raine, 9795 Deprez, 15452 Ibramohammed, 27374 Yim, 41981 Yaobeina

56q10 (220.313) \\a meeting of the powerful commences—especially one in which these powerful people prepare to face or deliver a fierce assault; 8729 Descour, 624 Hektor, 8343 Tugendhat, 27764 von Flue, 14679 Susanreed, 3448 Narbut, 6182 Katygord, 3264 Bounty, 25955 Radway, 21089 Mochizuki, 649 Josefa, 2575 Bulgaria

128q10 (40.313) \\a sudden desire to have a fully aligned partner; 24062 Hardister, 12104 Chesley, 175419 Albiesachs, 7620 Willaert

qc50: my general life summary in the colloquial view. I will need to align with this as best and as positively as I can

32q10 (280.313) \\sb drawn in, thought of as the wife by many; 117539 Celletti, 25098 Gridnev, 3325 TARDIS, 30252 Textorisova, 6929 Misto, 4790 Petrpravec, 17219 Gianninoto, 24547 Stauber, 241 Germania, 7063 Johnmichell, 8261 Ceciliejulie

104q10 (100.313) \\(mostly solo) dance sessions, sometimes w shanna; 20279 Harel, 11509 Thersilochos, 21683 Segal, 6000 United Nations, 19420 Vivekbuch, 4475 Voitkevich

68q10 (190.313) \\my occasional commentary on failed AI images as they are generated; 7688 Lothar, 1072 Malva, 3639 Weidenschilling, 11615 Naoya, 84945 Solosky, 6420 Riheijyaya, 31928 Limzhengtheng, 306019 Duren, 28509 Feddersen,

---

3411 Debetencourt, 4849 Ardenne, 633 Zelima, 8516 Hyakkai, 4949 Akasofu, 5056 Rahua, 2186 Keldysh, 2041 Lancelot, 47494 Gerhardangl, 226861 Elimaor

140q10 (10.313) \\the intended mechanisms of my exercises; 14498 Bernini, 8021 Walter, 13585 Justinsmith, 31903 Euniceyou, 7953 Kawaguchi, 2189 Zaragoza

qig57: being an expert

qc337: the insults to my sense of self which have driven almost all of my rogue work

8q9 (340.104) \\household name: any star of the moment. But some are able to stay there for a long time because they are quite crazy; 164 Eva, 5246 Migliorini, 9341 Gracekelly, 12288 Verdun, 1797 Schaumasse, 15231 Ehdita, 3120 Dangrania, 55815 Melindakim, 6961 Ashitaka, 580 Selene, 1259 Ogyalla, 31934 Benjamintan, 200020 Cadi Ayyad, 5868 Ohta, 11335 Santiago

80q9 (160.104) \\me as a strong group contributor; 22276 Belkin, 25695 Eileenjang, 12139 Tomcowling, 32550 Sharonthomas, 21945 Kleshchonok, 11371 Camley, 21559 Jingyuanluo, 2472 Bradman, 216451 Irsha, 6457 Kremsmunster, 250354 Lewicdeparis, 4400 Bagryana, 180143 Gaberogers

44q9 (250.104) \\REDACTED's panic upon accidents; 61402 Franciseveritt, 9307 Regiomontanus, 69496 Zaoryuzan, 72060 Hohhot, 2515 Gansu, 13258 Bej, 10432 Ullischwarz, 126245 Kandokalman, 282 Clorinde, 11778 Kingsford Smith

116q9 (70.104) \\my accomplice in household name status. I could be an accomplice to them and get behind them, but when I let people like 3 REDACTED go out front, their behavior eventually becomes intolerable; 2988 Korhonen, 907 Rhoda, 22543 Ranjan, 241529 Roccutri, 26537 Shyamalbuch, 3031 Houston, 11897 Lemaire

qc193: san antonio and the latinas vs REDACTED

20q9 (310.104) \\getting older, thinking of those lost, but more secure resource-wise; all saints or all souls day; 33599 Mckennaloop, 29736 Fichtelberg, 2467 Kollontai, 704 Interamnia, 6358 Chertok, 1029 La Plata, 2682 Soromundi, 33750 Davehiggins, 23165 Kakinchan, 36213 Robertotisgreen

92q9 (130.104) \\THE latina significator; my conflicts with co-creators which cause me to quietly withhold big important things from them, which I know they need. I could tell keith about these things, but not REDACTED; 30487 Dominikovacs, 11475 Velinsky, 7305 Ossakajusto, 135069 Gagnereau, 3028 Zhangguoxi, 22757 Klimcak, 129176 Gerardcarter, 95802 Francismuir, 7179 Gassendi, 12776 Reynolds, 30201 Caruana, 1688 Wilkens

56q9 (220.104) \\the iadt classes I taught, particularly the kinds of cliques who pulled class focus. Includes colleagues; 21635 Micahtoll, 295299 Nannidiana, 27147 Mercedessosa, 2550 Houssay, 4913 Wangxuan, 30857 Parsec, 1143 Odysseus, 23331 Halimzeidan, 21860 Joannaguy, 14925 Naoko, 19475 Mispagel, 39464 Poppelmann, 911 Agamemnon, 14401 Reikoyukawa, 18193 Hollilydrury, 6001 Thales, 13650 Perimedes, 14880 Moa

128q9 (40.104) \\aligning my responses to reinforce the conversation partner's stance or integrate that stance into a more group-whole position; 11325 Slavicky, 2181 Fogelin, 10050 Rayman, 1586 Thiele, 21990 Garretyazzie, 21613 Schlecht, 11392 Paulpeeters, 29765 Miparedes

qc49: the world work and others I am associated with

32q9 (280.104) \\my attitude at any moment towards the space of women I like; 27267 Wiberg, 643 Scheherazade, 33685 Younglove, 76628 Kozi Hradek, 196 Philomela, 28318 Janecox, 10921 Romanozen, 31519 Mimamarquez, 5297 Schinkel, 5951 Alicemonet, 2901 Bagehot

104q9 (100.104) \\going upstairs to reflect on my work, especially ilo sb; 15969 Charlesgreen, 25962 Yifanli, 7862 Keikonakamura, 15495 Bogie, 1790 Volkov, 175633 Yaoan, 3530 Hammel, 10476 Los Molinos, 21640 Petekirkland, 71480 Roberthatt, 8890 Montaigne, 8582 Kazuhisa, 662 Newtonia, 4275 Bogustafson, 120351 Beckymasterson, 28037 Williammonts, 10092 Sasaki

68q9 (190.104) \\my belief that all foreign travel is hard (on me), and subject to delays and rejection; 12616 Lochner, 73640 Biermann, 3515 Jindra, 23955 Nishikota, 4165 Didkovskij, 921 Jovita, 187283 Jeffhopkins, 11426 Molster, 7993 Johnbridges, 1679 Nevanlinna, 20784 Trevorpowers, 6591 Sabinin, 12867 Joeloic, 10683 Carter, 29655 Yarimlee, 1226 Golia, 166944 Seton, 10596 Stevensimpson, 28661 Jimdickens, 15107 Toepperwein

140q9 (10.104) \\let's do this. Determinedly; 11265 Hasselmann, 155270 Dianawheeler, 3307 Athabasca, 5830 Simohiro, 18676 Zdenkaplavcova, 28722 Dhruviyer, 31630 Jennywang, 27915 Nancywright, 36035 Petrvok, 11846 Verminnen, 9684 Olieslagers

qig58: publishing your will

qc336: difficulties of those near me, or the scrutiny they deliver

9q8 (339.896) \\common reception to the things I teach or post as teaching on youtube. Very common; 1488 Aura, 16507 Fuuren, 96217 Gronchi, 17600 Dobrichovice, 3589 Loyola

81q8 (159.896) \\my underground work which I often want to publicize; 26240 Leigheriks, 24046 Malovany, 7635 Carolinesmith, 9259 Janvanparadijs, 2794 Kulik, 5455 Surkov, 287693 Hugonnaivilma, 879 Ricarda, 16930 Respighi, 21903 Wallace, 16258 Willhayes, 5914 Kathywhaler, 32379 Markadame, 42354 Kindleberger, 12372 Kagesuke, 67853 Iwamura

45q8 (249.896) \\blaxploitation, my watching 1970s arthouse movies; bullit; nsbe; 9445 Charpentier, 381260 Ouellette, 240757 Farkasberci, 10745 Arnstadt, 16231 Jessberger, 14937 Thirsk, 31951 Alexisallen, 10938 Lorenzalevy, 30170 Makaylaruth, 34779 Chungchiyung, 19547 Collier, 1474 Beira, 9703 Sussenbach, 7696 Liebe, 213636 Gajdos, 14504 Tsujimura, 9580 Tarumi, 426 Hippo, 30275 Eskow, 17102 Begzhigitova, 305 Gordonia

117q8 (69.896) \\me as an honor student; how my caltech peers likely saw me; 2074 Shoemaker, 1394 Algoa

qc192: immersing myself in the definitive science or in the myriad mini—to the loss of self

21q8 (309.896) \\a voice swept over by a blanket declaration, someone listening only to their own way; generates hot blood; 120347 Salacia, 1945 Wesselink, 17884 Jeffthompson, 11228 Botnick, 20335 Charmartell, 10678 Alilagoa, 129811 Stacyoliver, 5603 Rausudake, 25835 Tomzega, 10205 Pokorny

93q8 (129.896) \\futanari or fetish material, certain scenes in hidden; 27088 Valmez, 10188 Yasuoyoneda, 25399 Vonnegut, 15387 Hanazukayama, 18639 Aoyunzhiyuanzhe, 5195 Kaendler, 2246 Bowell, 9916 Kibirev, 12113 Hollows, 11553 Scheria, 21634 Huangweikang, 9427 Righini, 18520 Wolfratshausen, 13824 Kramlik, 14584 Lawson, 399 Persephone, 19700 Teitelbaum

57q8 (219.896) \\my birthday; my general interest in purging obstacles; 54693 Garymyers, 162173 Ryugu, 2283 Bunke, 21118 Hezimmermann, 4137 Crabtree, 90479 Donalek, 17784 Banerjee, 3496 Arieso, 85195 von Helfta, 24959 Zielenbach, 7801 Goretti, 2075 Martinez, 13525 Paulledoux, 35356 Vondrak, 13733 Dylanyoung, -10000 Sun, 23672 Swiggum, 59239 Alhazen, 113214 Vinko, 28161 Neelpatel, 6807 Brunnow

129q8 (39.896) \\among other things, neuroscience and flowing events; 1373 Cincinnati, 11432 Kerkhoven, 13849 Dunn, 15563 Remsberg, 4671 Drtikol, 10988 Feinstein, 17764 Schatzman, 11306 Akesson

qc48: phaedra and strada versus dynamene, exorcism

33q8 (279.896) \\smooth image grade; tends away from harsh angles in form; pleasant, inviting; seems to enlarge areola in women, soften the features of men| //[phaedra, strada, and safebuddies]; 7936 Mikemagee, 13514 Mikerudenko, 7250 Kinoshita, 2082 Galahad, 27178 Quino, 3824 Brendalee, 14622 Arcadiopoveda, 195998 Skipwilson, 3678 Mongmanwai, 762 Pulcova, 85401 Yamatenclub, 11681 Ortner, 26074 Carlwirtz, 17041 Castagna

105q8 (99.896) \\keeping my work safe, with only priya to see it. But once my best is no longer locked underground...; (their) left leaning, horn nose - de-triangularizes nose and draws upper, middle, and lower nose bridge closer to 1:1:1 ratio; lips thicken vertically; underbust is more gracefully rounded/spherized; 5140 Kida, 8660 Sano, 85183 Marcelayme, 27519 Miames, 5662 Wendycalvin, 2452 Lyot, 4278 Harvey, 2966 Korsunia, 605 Juvisia

69q8 (189.896) \\REDACTED running with their ... ventures. I'll need to join a partner upon exile from a group in order to use this; 190710 Marktapley, 4586 Gunvor, 11105 Puchnarova, 2444 Lederle, 28652 Andybramante, 3251 Eratosthenes, 6158 Shosanbetsu, 14739 Edgarchavez, 150129 Besshi, 18583 Francescopedani, 37452 Spirit, 1127 Mimi, 20809 Eshinjolly, 24910 Haruoando, 3677 Magnusson, 233472 Moorcroft, 6818 Sessyu, 4816 Connelly

141q8 (9.896) \\commissioning someone else to do your hard-hitting; 11413 Catanach, 2030 Belyaev, 6381 Toyama, 968 Petunia, 3219 Komaki

qig59: what Nature will task you to give birth to (perhaps with with another)

qc335: the world conditions leading up to contours

9q7 (339.688) \\REDACTED. She would likely have been to me what mom was to dad; REDACTED herself wasn't bad, but was the main catalyst for me to experience dad-like aspirations. No one presented this on a comparative level; 14214 Hirsch, 12610 Hafez, 19962 Martynenko, 30269 Anandapadmanaban, 6405 Komiyama, 19126 Ottohahn, 6068 Brandenburg, 18445 Westenburger, 31582 Miraeparker, 5461 Autumn, 8817 Roytraver, 756 Lilliana

81q7 (159.688) \\REDACTED, some of agd or REDACTED, the ruthless naturalist; 196481 VATT, 24432 Elizamcnitt, 28712 Elizabethcorn, 96506 Oberosterreich, 2850 Mozhaiskij, 23608 Alpiapuane, 13473 Hokema, 23443 Kikwaya, 10270 Skoglov, 2237 Melnikov, 241136 Sandstede, 7289 Kamegamori, 12327 Terbruggen, 25597 Glendahill, 5296 Friedrich, 25677 Aaronenten, 37561 Churgym, 25674 Kevinellis, 324 Bamberga, 5059 Saroma

45q7 (249.688) \\my charged up energy, in most cases discouraged by the groups around me given that they are most likely not appropriate partners to me. Only if they are charged up themselves does this have a chance to avoid being thwarted. The AI and girly girl pics. cocreation inhibited by the dogs and other creatively-incompatibles; 3662 Dezhnev, 19860 Anahtar, 9152 Combe, 316010 Daviddubey, 12070 Kilkis, 21543 Jessop, 16244 Broz, 48844 Belloves, 11074 Kuniwake, 5033 Mistral, 12860 Turney, 613 Ginevra, 15627 Hong, 38962 Chuwinghung, 5678 DuBridge, 23318 Salvadorsanchez, 2650 Elinor, 7040 Harwood, 10634 Pepibican, 83657 Albertosordi, 55733 Lepsius

117q7 (69.688) \\REDACTED passing through, wanting more efficiency, REDACTED; me as an AI perfectionist; 34314 Jasonlee, 231649 Korotkiy, 21257 Jizni Cechy

qc191: the gm books

21q7 (309.688) \\what happens in worlds whose nature is outside of your nature; alien worlds; 29391 Knight, 33263 Willhutch, 5096 Luzin, 4018 Bratislava, 10581 Jenikhollan, 11253 Mesyats, 145488 Kaczendre, 2330 Ontake, 17900 Leiferman

93q7 (129.688) \\shanna. Easily. Would have been romero; nature reflector; 59388 Monod, 9112 Hatsulars, 170927 Dgebessire, 5086 Demin, 23547 Tognelli, 7164 Babadzhanov, 105211 Sanden, 53252 Sardegna, 747 Winchester, 6644 Jugaku, 10286 Shnollia, 8712 Suzuko, 117568 Yadame, 13564 Kodomomiraikan

57q7 (219.688) \\tirade mode against my partners in my recordings; 66479 Healy, 74824 Tarter, 25104 Chohyunghoon, 85030 Admetos, 49448 Macocha, 11267 Donaldkessler, 31471 Sallyalbright, 31464 Liscinsky, 16596 Stephenstrauss, 2292 Seili, 100019 Gregorianik, 761 Brendelia, 28803 Roe, 33254 Sundaresakumar, 6352 Schlaun, 3254 Bus, 12117 Meagmessina, 10054 Solomin, 2737 Kotka, 13088 Filipportera, 70449 Gruebel, 13145 Cavezzo, 174567 Varda, 86279 Brucegary

129q7 (39.688) \\3 REDACTED. The big partner whom I lecture or rant about. REDACTED; 14962 Masanoriabe, 3048 Guangzhou, 8100 Nobeyama, 19504 Vladalekseev, 1892 Lucienne, 6720 Gifu

qc47: me and my ideal person chase the lifestyle!

33q7 (279.688) \\kk? Pankhudi?; 32163 Claireburch, 29787 Timrenier, 7727 Chepurova, 20274 Halperin, 2913 Horta, 7741 Fedoseev, 12091 Jesmalmquist, 8347 Lallaward, 15092 Beegees, 6664 Tennyo, 27049 Kraus, 648 Pippa

105q7 (99.688) \\me after my major projects are done; 28078 Mauricehilleman, 11569 Virgilsmith, 8467 Benoitcarry, 55196 Marchini, 215 Oenone, 33330 Bareges, 27095 Girardiwanda, 6412 Kaifu, 2731 Cucula, 5160 Camoes

69q7 (189.688) \\shanna as partner; 18191 Rayhe, 6399 Harada, 12650 de Vries, 5174 Okugi, 48640 Eziobosso, 108496 Sullenberger, 2190 Coubertin, 27719 Fast, 75841 Brendahuettner, 7824 Lynch, 18739 Larryhu, 11823 Christen, 12001 Gasbarini

141q7 (9.688) \\far-scoping view, the nightfly, aj across time; 4299 WIYN

qig60: the stance you stay with despite the institution

qc334: REDACTED and the cast of characters around sata at that time. Makes people jealous, and I would be if I didn't know how to take over things I dislike as my own traits. Jealousy is beneath me. Only absorption will fix the ill

9q6 (339.479) \\i don't know this one. May be related to presentation through film; 9949 Brontosaurus, 236811 Natascharenate, 12500 Desngai, 32278 Makaram, 3953 Perth, 2639 Planman, 25940 Mikeschottland, 20664 Senec, 27411 Laurenhall

81q6 (159.479) \\interesting, kind of like an acting dynamic, and one of the only scenarios in which I would willingly play the role of a loser; 23169 Michikami, 2007 McCuskey, 8026 Johnmckay, 27527 Kirkkoehler, 2574 Ladoga, 19614 Montelongo, 14443 Sekinenomatsu, 33746 Sombart, 16794 Cucullia, 12239 Carolinakou, 5485 Kaula, 11041 Fechner, 34153 Deeannguo, 123852 Janboda, 4238 Audrey, 133744 Dellagiustina, 33871 Locastillo, 5137 Frevert, 463 Lola, 2013 Tucapel, 60001 Adelka, 4043 Perolof, 33660 Rishishankar, 39539 Emmadesmet

45q6 (249.479) \\definitely learning acting, acting lessons; the AI are made to move. What I ask of the AI is what REDACTED asks of me; 44613 Rudolf, 10412 Tsukuyomi, 24422 Helentressa, 5153 Gierasch, 4726 Federer, 6304 Josephus Flavius, 518523 Bryanshumaker, 21109 Sunkel, 39645 Davelharris, 13265 Terbunkley, 101723 Finger, 67085 Oppenheimer, 8698 Bertilpettersson, 5444 Gautier, 4576 Yanotoyohiko, 8067 Helfenstein, 7833 Nilstamm, 28643 Kellyzhang

117q6 (69.479) \\my observing the AI carefully; 24532 Csabakiss, 7396 Brusin, 29420 Ikuo

qc190: on, then away from the battlefield

21q6 (309.479) \\the other person @ .... REDACTED, for example, maybe REDACTED; the psychologist; 28555 Jenniferchan, 23063 Lichtman, 13024 Conradferdinand, 27438 Carolynjons, 22794 Lindsayleona, 3851 Alhambra, 110743 Hirobumi, 24928 Susanbehel, 24641 Enver, 11448 Miahajdukova, 16197 Bluepeter, 56561 Jaimenomen, 22558 Mladen, 18785 Betsywelsh, 16122 Wenyicai, 48779 Mariko

93q6 (129.479) \\the token character @ ..., including the reason I'm .... Especially the ... or ...; games that use psychology heavily; 3576 Galina, 6743 Liu, 2168 Swope, 142368 Majden, 13028 Klaustschira, 11622 Samuele, 2756 Dzhangar, 304 Olga, 132798 Kurti, 3902 Yoritomo, 8874 Showashinzan, 31249 Reneefleming, 7921 Huebner, 251627 Joyceearl, 2118 Flagstaff, 16701 Volpe, 133850 Heatherroper

57q6 (219.479) \\my forward-facing handling of globus and other institutional burdens; the soldier disillusioned with such games; 6990 Toya, 9409 Kanpuzan, 221230 Sanaloria, 11433 Gemmafrisius, 4546 Franck, 14413 Geiger, 13433 Phelps, 6830 Johnbackus, 163153 Takuyaonishi, 234761 Rainerkracht, 1094 Siberia, 7385 Aktsynovia, 30368 Ericferrante, 10633 Akimasa, 85158 Phyllistrapp, 12276 IJzer, 21510 Chemnitz, 28519 Sweetman, 11852 Shoumen, 18157 Craigwright, 937 Bethgea, 17050 Weiskopf, 1043 Beate, 147 Protogeneia, 1737 Severny, 157015 Walterstraube, 4542 Mossotti

129q6 (39.479) \\the stress of glo-bus, other institution-seated conflicts; 1365 Henyey, 13188 Okinawa, 682 Hagar, 754 Malabar, 9505 Lohengrin, 22551 Adamsolomon

qc46: comic duos and their gags, like laurel & hardy

33q6 (279.479) \\shanna? [future?] [someone like tippy]; 26528 Genniferubin, 807 Ceraskia, 25972 Pfefferjosh, 2304 Slavia, 134178 Markchodas, 15139 Connormcarty, 28505 Sagarrambhia, 26411 Jocorbferg, 4652 Iannini, 99262 Bleustein, 3784 Chopin, 25191 Rachelouise, 15465 Buchroeder, 24269 Kittappa, 5784 Yoron, 34198 Oliverleitner, 73465 Buonanno, 26336 Mikemcdowell, 9518 Robbynaish

105q6 (99.479) \\sâvitri's events; 6956 Holbach, 8686 Akenside, 2627 Churyumov, 7143 Haramura, 213771 Johndee, 21965 Dones, 7861 Messenger, 6650 Morimoto, 23564 Ungaretti

69q6 (189.479) \\me, kevin and ed, MSA; 7225 Huntress, 14594 Jindrasilhan, 9333 Hiraimasa, 29214 Apitzsch, 784 Pickeringia, 233893 Honthyhanna, 113461 McCay, 59804 Dickjoyce, 7165 Pendleton, 9932 Kopylov, 397279 Bloomsburg, 3942 Churivannia, 125718 Jemasalomon, 4364 Shkodrov, 22621 Larrybartel

141q6 (9.479) \\the house? Events that occur while I'm sleep at night. Interesting; 11636 Pezinok, 8837 London, 169299 Sirko, 5220 Vika, 3754 Kathleen, 190139 Hanskung, 159743 Kluk, 20535 Marshburrows, 19494 Gerbs, 5670 Rosstaylor

qig61: keeping the dream alive

qc333: shanna and I, or me and another partner as a public-ized couple

9q5 (339.271) \\a scripted plot, REDACTED closing iadt. The big institution levies a major change. Possibly a parallel acting scenario; 261291 Fucecchio, 3058 Delmary, 175282 Benhida, 30330 Tiffanysun

81q5 (159.271) \\a definitive move to improve the odds in an endeavor, likely involves at least two people. Me and sl in s.o.s.; 118230 Sado, 13268 Trevorcorbin, 8168 Rogerbourke, 1045 Michela, 11298 Gide, 7232 Nabokov, 25403 Carlapiazza, 4813 Terebizh, 68021 Taiki, 3868 Mendoza, 33929 Lisaprato, 3888 Hoyt, 1037 Davidweilla, 4481 Herbelin, 13294 Rockox

45q5 (249.271) \\the parades I'm in or sponsor through books may later aid society; 27895 Yeduzheng, 12409 Bukovanska, 8541 Schalkenmehren, 3853 Haas, 3209 Buchwald, 1090 Sumida, 823 Sisigambis

117q5 (69.271) \\my diehard background work; 4945 Ikenozenni, 4827 Dares, 2518 Rutllant, 4578 Kurashiki, 3591 Vladimirskij, 137165 Annis, 12062 Tilmanspohn, 6156 Dall, 282897 Kaltenbrunner, 156 Xanthippe

qc189: the cult of personality, its society, protest groups, and leaders

21q5 (309.271) \\post-globus, REDACTED. Also, REDACTED, REDACTED. Even if you and your partner make it through conflict with each other. There is a betrayer; my views of "colonists," humans setting up society; 4282 Endate, 15116 Jaytate, 269243 Charbonnel, 13221 Nao, 18292 Zoltowski, 3369 Freuchen, 29561 Iatteri, 720 Bohlinia, 3226 Plinius, 2775 Odishaw, 30883 de Broglie

93q5 (129.271) \\a popular or enstatused person who is also unpredictable when they interact with the group; those whom society loves and rewards; 330420 Tomroman, 563 Suleika, 159814 Saguaro, 14821 Motaeno, 3069 Heyrovsky, 3779 Kieffer, 8268 Goerdeler

57q5 (219.271) \\me continuing without help; 22227 Polyxenos, 3551 Verenia, 121719 Georgeshaw, 848 Inna, 9712 Nauplius, 8416 Okada, 7529 Vagnozzi, 7537 Solvay, 21480 Jilltucker, 24199 Tsarevsky, 1033 Simona, 18855 Sarahgutman, 5565 Ukyounodaibu, 1868 Thersites, 5370 Taranis, 144303 Mirellabreschi

129q5 (39.271) \\ REDACTED, REDACTED, but also me towards b.a.r. and REDACTED; 33569 Nikhilgopal, 24889 Tamurahosinomura, 30388 Nicolejustice, 2203 van Rhijn, 3598 Saucier, 28204 Liyakang, 4492 Debussy, 21937 Basheehan

qc45: my greatest work

33q5 (279.271) \\interaction with b.a.r., REDACTED; 155 Scylla, 153333 Jeanhugues, 29449 Taharbenjelloun, 31555 Wheeler, 46829 McMahon, 1909 Alekhin, 34044 Obafial, 7710 Ishibashi, 114027 Malanushenko, 874 Rotraut, 334756 Leovey

105q5 (99.271) \\traveling the outskirts of finer things or places; another great explanation for my behavioral choices; 28737 Mohindra, 7047 Lundstrom, 20455 Pennell, 852 Wladilena, 21459 Chrisrussell, 5511 Cloanthus, 14872 Hoher List, 6572 Carson, 1643 Brown, 33394 Nathaniellee, 11101 Ceskafilharmonie, 6745 Nishiyama

69q5 (189.271) \\the woman I am interested in from afar—her traits and experiences. REDACTED, REDACTED, shanna: i.e. girls I hang out with who have with big asses; 1329 Eliane, 15427 Shabas, 19466 Darcydiegel, 8358 Rickblakley, 1062 Ljuba, 300 Geraldina, 27280 Manettedavies, 10572 Kominejo, 11425 Wearydunlop, 26942 Nealkuhn, 9861 Jahreiss, 14032 Mego, 24304 Lynnrice, 7480 Norwan, 114990 Szeidl, 5300 Sats, 25511 Annlipinsky

141q5 (9.271) \\institutions follow suit after 9 months; 24985 Benuri, 151 Abundantia, 28481 Shindongju, 20037 Duke, 19542 Lindperkins, 492 Gismonda

qig62: leaving your mark on others (emphasizing self, other, or world)

qc332: my public aspirations. VERY strong

9q4 (339.063) \\we begin interviewing within REDACTED, BEAM; 6445 Bellmore, 120364 Stevecooley, 30443 Stieltjes, 22162 Leslijohnson, 17458 Dick, 3753 Cruithne

81q4 (159.063) \\what my character is into? How I sometimes picture myself as an anti-society rebel on film; 25377 Rolaberee, 17958 Schoof, 1987 Kaplan, 29435 Mordell, 58498 Octaviopaz, 1134 Kepler, 20019 Yukiotanaka, 19993 Gunterseeber, 12810 Okumiomote, 5618 Saitama, 14103 Manzoni, 6764 Kirillavrov, 1301 Yvonne, 3239 Meizhou, 9521 Martinhoffmann

45q4 (249.063) \\my desire to play villains! Acting; 2938 Hopi, 185216 Gueiren, 3556 Lixiaohua, 6336 Dodo, 34161 Michaellee, 13750 Mattdawson, 197189 Raymond, 11573 Helmholtz, 5214 Oozora, 7145 Linzexu, 31777 Amywinegar, 355022 Triman, 161592 Sarahhamilton, 133743 Robertwoodward, 1162 Larissa, 3916 Maeva

117q4 (69.063) \\the roles I gravitate towards in ...; 9923 Ronaldthiel, 27968 Bobylapointe, 287347 Mezes, 3060 Delcano, 6647 Josse, 4815 Anders, 1678 Hveen, 65637 Tsniimash, 33583 Karamchedu

qc188: these two qcrosses show how an eventually ill-fated partnership begins

21q4 (309.063) \\my being mostly negatively assessed on looks by people in pretty fields; 24059 Halverson, 10717 Dickwalker, 11736 Viktorfischl, 51 Nemausa, 21479 Marymartha, 3553 Mera, 31727 Amandalewis, 15448 Siegwarth, 11612 Obu, 2603 Taylor, 2166 Handahl, 28107 Sapar, 1725 CrAO

93q4 (129.063) \\99 et al; 873 Mechthild, 15924 Axelmartin, 34218 Padiyath, 18084 Adamwohl, 31600 Somasundaram, 34079 Samoylova, 10130 Ardre, 7692 Edhenderson, 3188 Jekabsons, 265490 Szabados

57q4 (219.063) \\traveling away to find better treatment; 12086 Joshualevine, 16402 Olgapopova, 22553 Yisun, 128627 Ottmarsheim, 5505 Rundetaarn, 1357 Khama, 11836 Eileen, 3454 Lieske, 9683 Rambaldo, 230415 Matthiasjung, 5568 Mufson, 2544 Gubarev, 7924 Simbirsk, 13693 Bondar, 7037 Davidlean, 27356 Mattstrom, 4836 Medon, 21558 Alisonliu, 18473 Kikuchijun, 24044 Caballo, 1887 Virton, 391795 Univofutah, 9469 Shashank, 9394 Manosque, 3951 Zichichi

129q4 (39.063) \\phonemics, shanna's pedestal? my recordings and private jokes? Devin tha dude; 5839 GOI, 289992 Onfray, 30445 Stirling

qc44: my overall interaction with REDACTED, when I still believed in marriage, right before I reevaluated mom and dad

33q4 (279.063) \\interaction with REDACTED, foods I am allergic to; 168261 Puglia, 9567 Surgut, 101462 Tahupotiki, 7032 Hitchcock, 24048 Pedroduque, 14826 Nicollier, 27048 Jangong, 1332 Marconia, 10977 Mathlener, 14885 Paskoff, 6752 Ashley, 37630 Thomasmore, 6049 Toda

105q4 (99.063) \\Dr. Lao, me responding to REDACTED; 1086 Nata, 1430 Somalia, 8322 Kononovich, 362793 Suetolson, 10473 Thirouin, 9999 Wiles, 2218 Wotho, 3649 Guillermina, 8044 Tsuchiyama, 1264 Letaba, 175451 Linchisheng, 2438 Oleshko, 21544 Hermainkhan

69q4 (189.063) \\how I behave in a marriage; what I got out of the REDACTED situation; 7538 Zenbei, 19119 Dimpna, 60622 Pritchet, 18961 Hampfreeman, 9562 Memling, 278386 Sofivanna, 199838 Hafili, 2253 Espinette, 19306 Voves, 7205 Sadanori, 11498 Julgeerts, 11947 Kimclijsters, 70781 Donnelly, 31711 Suresh, 24333 Petermassey, 481 Emita, 26332 Alyssehrlich, 6763 Kochiny, 11875 Rhone, 5149 Leibniz

141q4 (9.063) \\how I approach the concept of marriage. What I think about it; REDACTED's approach to me during our association; 10780 Apollinaire, 192450 Xinjiangdaxue, 209054 Lombkato, 4519 Voronezh, 116446 McDermid, 24068 Simonsen, 8661 Ratzinger, 229425 Grosspointner, 21054 Ojmiakon, 55221 Nancynoblitt, 66667 Kambic

qig63: by marrying, you accomplish this...

qc331: miranda's leadership chain and its version of power

9q3 (338.854) \\the events that happen around me when I am in a place, tied to my skin color; phaedra?; 8214 Mirellalilli, 5277 Brisbane, 11067 Greenancy, 23192 Caysvesterby, 11695 Mattei, 250719 Jurajbardy, 4320 Jarosewich, 229255 Andrewelliott, 9658 Imabari, 10262 Samoilov, 2601 Bologna

81q3 (158.854) \\incubator, …, …, pantheonic work; twice jack's miranda; 9594 Garstang, 1500 Jyvaskyla, 129092 Snowdonia, 17597 Stefanzweig, 101432 Adamwest, 61384 Arturoromer, 4742 Caliumi, 6774 Vladheinrich, 1811 Bruwer, 3957 Sugie, 38454 Boroson, 12002 Suess, 316042 Tilofranz, 5015 Litke, 18499 Showalter, 6945 Dahlgren, 19443 Yanzhong

45q3 (248.854) \\sb, REDACTED, sm, t.o.; phaedra's attractive companions; 183114 Vicques, 45027 Cosquer, 812 Adele, 55759 Erdmannsdorff, 10070 Liuzongli, 8001 Ramsden, 210107 Pistoletto, 26937 Makimiyamoto, 3270 Dudley, 23172 Williamartin, 398188 Agni, 25715 Lizmariemako, 28129 Teresummers, 82638 Bottariclaudio, 24965 Akayu, 201 Penelope, 28673 Valholmes, 2063 Bacchus, 1422 Stromgrenia, 6563 Steinheim, 23477 Wallenstadt

117q3 (68.854) \\i ultimately step down from the [pushy] partner; omni; 140628 Klaipeda, 33702 Spencergreen, 23017 Advincula, 294296 Efeso, 6209 Schwaben, 16277 Mallada, 53159 Myslivecek, 17801 Zelkowitz

qc187: this qcross describes my general evolution as a character in the world. Whether I'm moving on or staying in one place as a broadcaster, all roads seems to lead to offense. The nightfly is generally safer than mercenary cutting, I suppose

21q3 (308.854) \\holding fast in light of insults to my path; 18043 Laszkowska, 385446 Manwe, 92891 Bless, 31190 Toussaint, 154932 Sviderskiene, 29450 Tomohiroohno, 6852 Nannibignami, 12456 Genichiaraki, 372305 Bourdeille, 14693 Selwyn, 28638 Joywang, 301 Bavaria, 7770 Siljan, 25402 Angelanorse

93q3 (128.854) my move to a higher place; 8057 Hofmannsthal, 6334 Robleonard, 1117 Reginita, 11161 Daibosatsu, 230631 Justino

57q3 (218.854) \\me broadcasting a small piece of grand nature; 1081 Reseda, 7928 Bijaoui, 1159 Granada, 14313 Dodaira, 30295 Anvitagupta, 2554 Skiff, 845 Naema, 400796 Douglass, 6379 Vrba, 25074 Honami, 1091 Spiraea, 13129 Poseidonios, 134027 Deanbooher, 279377 Lechmankiewicz

129q3 (38.854) \\san antonio; 4562 Poleungkuk, 294600 Abedinabedin, 523 Ada, 80801 Yiwu, 9631 Hubertreeves, 126315 Blathy, 123290 Manoa

qc43: banned in the night

33q3 (278.854) \\REDACTED, where I learn trance?; //interaction with vb; 27423 Dennisbowers, 773 Irmintraud, 26507 Mikelin, 11147 Delmas, 4399 Ashizuri, 33508 Drewnik, 225238 Hristobotev, 66934 Kalalova, 33353 Chattopadhyay, 54509 YORP, 31581 Onnink, 5488 Kiyosato, 195405 Lentyler

105q3 (98.854) \\genua, poly, writing the gm series: points where I withdrew from old rulesets into asceticism in order to deeply reassess the relationship schema I was living under—soul searching writing; I think this might actually be negative for me, conducive to me NOT paying attention to my nichemates' progress in the world… leads to 133q3; 20646 Nikhilgupta, 31897 Brooksdasilva, 15388 Coelum, 4855 Tenpyou, 2377 Shcheglov, 18281 Tros, 42998 Malinafrank, 96268 Tomcarr, 11908 Nicaragua, 7590 Aterui, 737 Arequipa, 38540 Stevens, 17519 Pritsak, 8009 Beguin

69q3 (188.854) \\when I want to come through on a commitment, but am not ready or need to build up to the showing of this, I am VERY slow; 6098 Mutojunkyu, 113355 Gessler, 10984 Gispen, 10983 Smolders, 27449 Jamarkley, 10445 Coster, 147971 Nametoko, 21641 Tiffanyko, 21925 Supasternak, 172090 Davidmccomas, 26488 Beiser, 6088 Hoshigakubo, 25987 Katherynshi, 6678 Seurat, 2272 Montezuma, 14909 Kamchatka, 10132 Lummelunda, 13642 Ricci, 13772 Livius

141q3 (8.854) \\when you aren't particularly committed to anyone, but help others' commitments instead; the nightfly—after I got myself banned; 32217 Beverlyge, 27952 Atapuerca, 10803 Caleyo, 8815 Deanregas, 7468 Anfimov, 11666 Bracker, 2636 Lassell, 4986 Osipovia, 23753 Busdicker, 1855 Korolev, 17169 Tatarinov

qig64: you have been selected, as family

qc330: how I eventually handle my station as a black scholar

9q2 (338.646) \\REDACTED, REDACTED—runner; me electing to go it alone after not fitting in a place; 126888 Tspitzer, 21433 Stekramer, 30176 Gelseyjaymes, 28174 Harue, 46977 Krakow, 15992 Cynthia, 26319 Miyauchi, 221712 Moleson, 133746 Tonyferro

81q2 (158.646) \\my general museum rounds; 158520 Ricardoferreira, 4440 Tchantches, 60008 Jarda, 1239 Queteleta, 519 Sylvania, 6777 Balakirev, 6725 Engyoji, 981 Martina, 9460 McGlynn, 218901 Gerdbuchholz, 963 Iduberga, 9648 Gotouhideo, 16449 Kigoyama, 29696 Distasio, 15301 Marutesser, 5666 Rabelais, 11 Parthenope, 30337 Czheng

45q2 (248.646) \\truly the kinds of things I notably employ as basic behavioral methods. My identity with respect to the cultures I live and work in; a trio that doesn't belong in most places; 19291 Karelzeman, 29803 Michaelshao, 17115 Justiniano, 26858 Misterrogers, 3572 Leogoldberg, 377144 Okietex, 1917 Cuyo, 860 Ursina, 43783 Svyatitelpyotr, 2314 Field, 101781 Gojira, 29799 Trinirussell, 29668 Ipf

117q2 (68.646) \\bringing someone in because I want or need their style, hogging the spotlight for my own designs; another winning region; 110742 Tetuokudo, 3987 Wujek, 33680 Vasconcelos, 25413 Dorischen, 14517 Monitoma, 12242 Koon, 744 Aguntina, 21574 Ouzan, 8889 Mockturtle, 305660 Romyhaag, 10612 Houffalize, 6816 Barbcohen, 243204 Kubanchoria, 392728 Zdzislawlaczny, 472 Roma, 3964 Danilevskij

qc186: what one likes to talk about vs that which they just can't relate to

21q2 (308.646) \\my encyclopedic self-disclosure moments, especially through books; 7324 Carret, 24890 Amaliafinzi, 1426 Riviera, 10821 Kimuratakeshi, 10830 Desforges, 21711 Wilfredwong, 35365 Cooney, 5154 Leonov, 27789 Astrakhan, 31439 Mieyamanaka, 11593 Uchikawa

93q2 (128.646) \\the concept of the night talk show host; a face in the crowd; ajani across time; advertisers; 14567 Nicovincenti, 16175 Rypatterson, 11602 Miryang, 23216 Mikehagler, 283277 Faber, 5509 Rennsteig, 2454 Olaus Magnus, 15606 Winer, 5759 Zoshchenko, 27277 Pattybrown, 33503 Dasilvaborges, 1549 Mikko, 154141 Kertesz, 578 Happelia

57q2 (218.646) \\me as a student, early and late in life—partnered with the teacher; 314163 Kittenberger, 39184 Willgrundy, 9576 van der Weyden, 11719 Hicklen, 26462 Albertcui, 28483 Allenyuan, 30211 Sheilah, 6884 Takeshisato, 5028 Halaesus, 21161 Yamashitaharuo, 27602 Chaselewis, 12701 Chenier, 5847 Wakiya, 7869 Pradun, 20366 Bonev, 5038 Overbeek, 9114 Hatakeyama

129q2 (38.646) \\continuing to gain more insight through books rallying others to insight; 5388 Mottola, 19835 Zreda, 67235 Fairbank, 19783 Antoniromanya, 8550 Hesiodos

qc42: me as the hub for difficult relationship patterns. I really have been an asshole to quite a few close people

33q2 (278.646) \\tahira? My blaring negative evaluations as a habit I subconsciously ¿enjoy? in relationships; 86 Semele, 25659 Liboynton, 12075 Legg, 15397 Ksoari, 925 Alphonsina, 32276 Allenliu, 173395 Dweinberg, 189202 Calar Alto, 8175 Boerhaave, 10369 Sinden, 152 Atala, 26842 Hefele, 3675 Kemstach, 33979 Sunhaochun, 48171 Juza, 35441 Kyoko

105q2 (98.646) \\how I live now, slowing down the pace with shanna in order to give it room to work; 2446 Lunacharsky, 32120 Stevezheng, 5970 Ohdohrikouen, 7787 Annalaura, 58931 Palmys, 390 Alma, 6681 Prokopovich

69q2 (188.646) \\shanna's amusement preferences in the relationship. Things she does because they feel good for her to do; 1899 Crommelin, 21466 Franpelrine, 101902 Gisellaluccone, 1232 Cortusa, 24354 Caz, 28640 Cathywong, 3930 Vasilev, 3079 Schiller, 11100 Lai, 8635 Yuriosipov, 328 Gudrun, 142275 Simonyi, 30061 Vishnushankar, 359426 Lacks, 9769 Nautilus, 9488 Huia, 120643 Rudimandl, 340891 Londoncommorch

141q2 (8.646) \\things that don't feel good to the partner in a commitment, things which upset them; 47164 Ticino, 152227 Argoli, 2480 Papanov, 6386 Keithnoll, 7665 Putignano, 7820 Ianlyon, 43931 Yoshimi, 201497 Marcelroche, 210147 Zalgiris, 33452 Olivebryan

qig65: you have been selected, as a partner or mate

qc329: my stay in REDACTED, building a reputation

9q1 (338.438) \\the superstar of the day; jay-z, justin timberlake, taylor swift…; 23924 Premt, 17693 Wangdaheng, 9756 Ezaki, 206241 Dubois, 151657 Finkbeiner, 19424 Andrewsong, 30140 Robpergolizzi, 972 Cohnia

81q1 (158.438) \\STRONG. pseudonymous triplet teaming—like ee trio, behind the scenes teaming; 8418 Mogamigawa, 43793 Mackey, 3807 Pagels, 43752 Maryosipova, 59800 Astropis, 6138 Miguelhernandez, 2252 CERGA, 7457 Veselov, 1395 Aribeda, 9132 Walteranderson, 378204 Bettyhesser, 6687 Lahulla, 4866 Badillo, 8765 Limosa, 4105 Tsia

45q1 (248.438) \\sue b; 29825 Dunyazade, 24128 Hipsman, 435552 Morin, 29437 Marchais, 554 Peraga, 36184 Pavelbozek, 11524 Pleyel, 8909 Ohnishitaka, 30169 Raghavganesh, 22481 Zachlynn, 5425 Vojtech, 5326 Vittoriosacco, 264077 Dluzhnevskaya, 3372 Bratijchuk, 19349 Denjoy

117q1 (68.438) \\STRONG. while socially invisible, kicking ass as a self-publishing philosopher—playing a game of chicken with the spotlight; 243094 Dirlewanger, 10886 Mitsuroohba, 133891 Jaesubhong, 91023 Lutan, 2948 Amosov, 5664 Eugster, 58373 Albertoalonso, 12572 Sadegh, 13208 Fraschetti, 22544 Sarahrapo, 10487 Danpeterson, 5046 Carletonmoore

qc185: what one must do or approve of in order to trigger social advancement

21q1 (308.438) \\what I feel big tits are more likely to automatically attract from others— mostly males, but also other females in some contexts; 22415 Humeivey, 1934

Jeffers, 3348 Pokryshkin, 302932 Francoballoni, 1964 Luyten, 1057 Wanda, 23583 Krivsky, 9985 Akiko, 225225 Ninagrunewald, 20572 Celemorrow

93q1 (128.438) \\how I direct my energy towards attractive recipients; 5018 Tenmu, 10207 Comeniana, 17185 Mcdavid, 2399 Terradas, 9009 Tirso, 960 Birgit, 8629 Chucklorre, 79333 Yusaku, 1132 Hollandia, 21560 Analyons, 115891 Scottmichael, 20139 Marianeschi, 1278 Kenya, 54963 Sotin

57q1 (218.438) \\my statistics youtube videos; 14282 Cruijff, 6717 Antal, 3856 Lutskij, 31899 Adityamohan, 14853 Shimokawa, 1404 Ajax, 7905 Juzoitami, 103421 Laurmatt, 10667 van Marxveldt, 68448 Sidneywolff, 328305 Jackmcdevitt, 133074 Kenshamordola, 129063 Joshwood, 3216 Harrington, 16119 Bronner, 42747 Fuser

129q1 (38.438) \\meeting mb and going pretty far with her... before the REDACTED dynamic clearly poisoned us. It was too obvious to continue; 24144 Philipmocz, 3816 Chugainov, 20392 Mikeshepard

qc41: collector of other's secrets

33q1 (278.438) \\vanessa + marion. t.o.1; 37608 Lons, 28600 Georgelucas, 7706 Mien, 10973 Thomasreiter, 13410 Arhale, 17197 Matjazbone, 152657 Yukifumi, 1170 Siva, 692 Hippodamia, 185641 Judd, 21605 Reynoso, 5897 Novotna, 4172 Rochefort, 46692 Taormina

105q1 (98.438) \\leah and jess, keith and j, cheeko & sevrena. Etc... 4814 Casacci, 65 Cybele, 2688 Halley, 8680 Rone, 20393 Kevinlane, 795 Fini, 21541 Friskop, 40023 ANPCEN

69q1 (188.438) \\my growing notice on ...; 4435 Holt, 165347 Philplait, 115885 Ganz, 21447 Yungchieh, 3862 Agekian, 5142 Okutama, 681 Gorgo, 129988 Camerondickinson, 2730 Barks, 24899 Dominiona, 4873 Fukaya, 2005 Hencke, 1063 Aquilegia, 182 Elsa, 34233 Caldwell, 27102 Emilychen, 20351 Kaborchardt, 1019 Strackea, 11521 Erikson, 33334 Turon, 13774 Spurny, 2437 Amnestia, 1847 Stobbe, 10447 Bloembergen, 12777 Manuel

141q1 (8.438) \\me as a teacher of my more secret stuff. Also, my initial exposure to Chan buddhism, the audio chapter by lynn redgrave; 169184 Jameslee, 21388 Moyanodeburt

qig66: you and your walled garden

qc328: the building of my eventual reputation, in front of and behind the scenes

9q12 (338.229) \\i'll do the dirty work, though it will take energy from you when I do. translates into acting; I will take one for the team; an oldest brother trait; 1644 Rafita, 181483 Ampleforth, 22322 Bodensee, 31991 Royghosh, 25115 Drago, 20772 Brittajones, 27959 Fagioli, 221923 Jayeff, 1915 Quetzalcoatl, 18664 Rafaelta, ?.sqMidheaven+

81q12 (158.229) \\the background work I do to build up my reputation; what folks on the other side of my burned bridges want; my viewers' wants? | after vb and mj, what did I want? Someone to affirm and warmly resonate with my complex journey; Trogrlic and Beppechiara; 5077 Favaloro, 32222 Charlesvest, 25648 Baghel, 33740 Arjunmoorthy, 10504 Doga, 5916 van der Woude, 5677 Aberdonia, 38237 Roche, 21001 Trogrlic, 12501 Nord, 3336 Grygar, 134050 Rebeccaghent, 128036 Rafaelnadal, 23060 Shepherd, 85 Io, 301061 Egelsbach, 1573 Vaisala, 70179 Beppechiara, 17488 Mantl

45q12 (248.229) \\my upstairs exercise setting (after work), moving over to butts as an automotivator after partner split. This is the energetic equivalent of a person's focus on projecting togetherness as it affects interactants. No one thinks about this consciously, but socially there is a background chapter that goes with this as a topic, and I suspect part of that is loaded here; 5719 Krizik, 44011 Juubichi, 7891 Fuchie, 18381 Massenet, -10 Midheaven, 4371 Fyodorov, 113333 Tyler, 13667 Samthurman, 3798 de Jager, 2533 Fechtig, 26715 South Dakota, 7840 Hendrika, 88470 Joaquinescrig, 10605 Guidoni, 25102 Zhaoye, 6534 Carriepeterson, 22838 Darcyhampton, 289 Nenetta, 185039 Alessiapossenti

117q12 (68.229) \\two as the wildfire. A duo I should be a part of in public, but the behind the scenes version?; a pair aries to fill one person's big shoes; 2201 Oljato, 246345 Carolharris, -4 Imum Coeli, 3285 Ruth Wolfe, 32088 Liamwallace, 90698 Kosciuszko, 240022 Demitra, 3748 Tatum, 19137 Copiapo, 7261 Yokootakeo

qc184: trees, cats, dogs, and ornamental friends

21q12 (308.229) \\my interaction with sata assistants; 35222 Delbarrio, 11673 Baur, 1649 Fabre, 69295 Stecklum, 52589 Montviloff, 8163 Ishizaki, 13840 Wayneanderson, 97 Klotho, 190617 Alexandergerst, 29647 Poncelet, 16505 Sulzer, 38245 Marcospontes

93q12 (128.229) \\the legacy of cats and other chains of succession which have reflected my will; 22517 Alexzanardi, 8468 Rhondastroud, 2508 Alupka, 2744 Birgitta, 11468 Shantanunaidu, 2738 Viracocha, 11786 Bakhchivandji, 4881 Robmackintosh, 91024 Szechenyi, 10283 Cromer, 16522 Tell, 5896 Narrenschiff, 3880 Kaiserman

57q12 (218.229) \\i got what I asked for, now with shanna; 7737 Sirrah, 8003 Kelvin, 25108 Bostrom, 153301 Alissamearle, 46441 Mikepenston, 73885 Kalaymoodley, 6592 Goya, 22940 Chyan

129q12 (38.229) \\who I am towards sata assistants, full of myself and pushy; 117572 Hutsebaut, 1031 Arctica, 11324 Hayamizu, 80807 Jimloudon, 30203 Kimdavis, 5151 Weerstra, 30373 Mattharley

qc40: summary of my overall interaction with REDACTED. This is one I would definitely try again knowing what I know now

33q12 (278.229) \\REDACTED & REDACTED, REDACTED and REDACTED? How I ultimately want my co-creators to behave; 21753 Trudel, 340071 Vanmunster, 29805 Bradleysloop, 8306 Shoko, 14314 Tokigawa, 3764 Holmesacourt, 8589 Stellaris, 3525 Paul, 1715 Salli, 30407 Pantano, 292159 Jongoldstein, 5031 Svejcar, 211376 Joethurston

105q12 (98.229) \\leaving REDACTED out of ... in order to .... Of course, I knew this already; REDACTED; 207547 Charito, 33573 Hugrace, 26734 Terryfarrell, 15968 Waltercugno, 11670 Fountain, 34205 Mizerak, 23162 Alexcrook

69q12 (188.229) \\the situation which led to REDACTED and REDACTED; 3065 Sarahill, 160493 Nantou, 2465 Wilson, 12171 Johannink, 152481 Stabia, 1407 Lindelof, 24862 Hromec, 79 Eurynome, 18737 Aliciaworley, 5188 Paine, 2105 Gudy, 9262 Bordovitsyna, 9780 Bandersnatch, 21469 Robschum, 15469 Ohmura, 794 Irenaea, 1181 Lilith, 84884 Dorismcmillan, 883 Matterania, 15378 Artin

141q12 (8.229) \\i air my findings easily but aggressively when conflict looms; REDACTED; 14115 Melaas, 26468 Ianchan, 11802 Ivanovski, 124 Alkeste, 19444 Addicott

qig67: soothing another's tensions

qc327: putting on a show

9q11 (338.021) \\look out for losing contract with REDACTED; 78453 Bullock, 210432 Dietmarhopp, 266887 Wolfgangries, 1542 Schalen, 5623 Iwamori, 3593 Osip, 6496 Kazuko, 221073 Ovruch, 28075 Emilyhoffman

81q11 (158.021) \\my *self-volunteered* data work with REDACTED, REDACTED | "concentric cylindrical stacking"; 18376 Quirk, 106817 Yubangtaek, 28955 Kaliadeborah, 9021 Fagus, 343230 Corsini, 1819 Laputa, 23882 Fredcourant, 9587 Bonpland, 1713 Bancilhon, 279119 Khamatova, 12935 Zhengzhemin, 35053 Rojyurij, 12415 Wakatatakayo, 46 Hestia

45q11 (248.021) \\reminds me of ana lisa or REDACTED; 69287 Gunthereichhorn, 17249 Eliotyoung, 199687 Erosszsolt, 7372 Emimar, 118 Peitho, 7842 Ishitsuka, 2869 Nepryadva, 23452 Drew, 44001 Jonquet, 18079 Lion-Stoppato

117q11 (68.021) \\another superstar region. These I respect; 9716 Severina, 6444 Ryuzin, 128417 Chrismccaa

qc183: the natural and the extra natural, the obligated and the things helped in

21q11 (308.021) \\the mercenary sub-institution I am a part of; 12802 Hagino, 28841 Kelseybarter, 4081 Tippett, 11227 Ksenborisova, 1423 Jose, 8165 Gnadig, 2641 Lipschutz, 34010 Tassiloschwarz, 7290 Johnrather, 2115 Irakli, 6190 Rennes, 2266 Tchaikovsky

93q11 (128.021) \\tech n9ne and other fierce rappers; 5241 Beeson, 34901 Mauna Loa, 85047 Krakatau, 10347 Murom, 165612 Stackpole, 7456 Doressoundiram, 4321 Zero, 7506 Lub, 3382 Cassidy, 15379 Alefranz, 129125 Chrisvoth, 32272 Hasegawayuya, 19398 Creedence, 23722 Gulak, 1719 Jens, 5857 Neglinka, 11913 Svarna, 23748 Kaarethode, 2912 Lapalma, 28242 Mingantu

57q11 (218.021) \\again, my 'acting career?' melusina, conformity breaker; 5816 Potsdam, 60186 Las Cruces, 130066 Timhaltigin, 21256 Robertobattiston, 20342 Trinh, 212723 Klitschko, 73872 Stefanoragazzi, 98127 Vilgusova, 171433 Prothous, 31276 Calvinrieder, 5530 Eisinga, 4638 Estens, 7209 Cyrus, 6099 Saarland, 242479 Marijampole, 142084 Jamesdaniel, 31462 Brchnelova, 19208 Starrfield, 1520 Imatra, 20371 Ekladyous, 281564 Fuhsiehhai, 23061 Blueglass, 373 Melusina

129q11 (38.021) \\how I respond to my collaborators, rejecting deeper attachments to them. Sometimes, how they have responded to me; 3000 Leonardo, 16466 Piyashiriyama, 4848 Tutenchamun, 121132 Garydavis, 246238 Crampton

qc39: phenomena which regulate or restrict expression of the black identity

33q11 (278.021) \\jasmine? THE qunit of my sense of the consequences of being black; 5175 Ables, 31996 Goecknerwald, 2176 Donar, 12395 Richnelson, 14119 Johnprince, 7699 Bozek, 32080 Sanashareef, 23403 Boudewijnbuch

105q11 (98.021) \\shanna's narration of the pace of gradual advancement, whether or not it's pleasant, what she says does track our progress fairly accurately; the black aspiration; 11079 Mitsunori, 20858 Cuirongfeng, 5309 MacPherson, 6558 Norizuki, 11072 Hiraoka, 108205 Baccipaolo, 12635 Hennylamers, 6395 Hilliard, 318676 Bellelay, 128389 Dougleland

69q11 (188.021) \\my research notes flooded in and the drive to advance-advance past where I am. Going. Doing. Winning \\me as someone else's seducer?; 165 Loreley, 3292 Sather, 4628 Laplace, 11122 Eliscolombini, 21804 Vaclavneumann, 21148 Billramsey, 52337 Compton, 28554 Adambowman, 14571 Caralexander, 30836 Schnittke, 3096 Bezruc, 2101 Adonis, 65785 Carlafracci, 4673 Bortle, 34268 Gracetian, 5379 Abehiroshi, 6309 Elsschot, 25258 Nathaniel

141q11 (8.021) \\how others respond to my seduction?; 58573 Serpieri, 3271 UI, 23625 Gelfond, 9336 Altenburg, 25519 Bartolomeo, 291849 Orchestralondon, 84994 Amysimon, 2341 Aoluta

qig68: go forth into the foreign

qc326: traveling philosopher

9q10 (337.813) \\my initial visits to REDACTED. The action that resolves 37q10; 11314 Charcot, 9848 Yugra, 2563 Boyarchuk, 33478 Deniselivon, 21856 Heathermaria, 9578 Klyazma, 9718 Gerbefremov, 20896 Tiphene

81q10 (157.813) \\PAIRS REQUIRED. coercive running of affairs in pairs. Basic business operation. Two emerge from among three?; 21468 Saylor, 30725 Klimov, 16742 Zink, 8599 Riparia, 2816 Pien, 8962 Noctua, 18241 Genzel, 52231 Sitnik, 5225 Loral, 16770 Angkor Wat, 1954 Kukarkin, 207657 Mangiantini, 8260 Momcheva, 6057 Robbia, 28222 Neilpathak, 11445 Fedotov

45q10 (247.813) \\debt resolution: resolves 73q10; reminds me of simeona, ana lisa, or REDACTED; 32295 Ravichandran, 17657 Himawari, 10760 Ozeki, 6120 Anhalt, 15017 Cuppy, 10509 Heinrichkayser, 116166 Andremaeder, 2143 Jimarnold, 5273 Peilisheng, 26501 Sachiko, 3749 Balam, 32056 Abramadroo, 4695 Mediolanum

117q10 (67.813) \\a debt which has been paid off. The resolved version of 1q10; 15351 Yamaguchimamoru

qc182: pundit and star media

21q10 (307.813) \\the group under assault whose rescue I come to; 2336 Xinjiang, 46277 Jeffhall, 58622 Setoguchi, 18359 Jakobstaude, 90926 Stahalik, 4344 Buxtehude, 398 Admete, 2004 Lexell, 1911 Schubart, 13553 Masaakikoyama, 157141 Sopron, 10593 Susannesandra

93q10 (127.813) \\REDACTED-like: who I need to be in the eyes of the gatekeeping team which allows me into the battle; 3487 Edgeworth, 9408 Haseakira, 128925 Conwell, 21523 GONG, 6152 Empedocles, 4443 Paulet, 991 McDonalda, 1989 Tatry, 7133 Kasahara, 239203 Simeon, 1160 Illyria

57q10 (217.813) \\my various decisions via s.o.s.; 25156 Shkolnik, 7971 Meckbach, 8980 Heliaca, 2160 Spitzer, 7194 Susanrose, 30193 Annikaurban, 128586 Jeremias, 32280 Rachelmashal, 22942 Alexacourtis, 7954 Kitao, 9813 Rozgaj, 15056 Barbaradixon, 3722 Urata, 33346 Sabinedevieilhe, 316138 Giorgione, 25469 Ransohoff, 32101 Williamyin

129q10 (37.813) \\me or sml's sloppy sexuality towards each other; 4061 Martelli, 21380 Devanssay

qc38: coming back from the dead or discarded state, having served time

33q10 (277.813) \\initial partnering training at home? Mom and dad's unstated routes to fulfillment without the other knowing. Maybe characters, rother. George of the jungle + ursula?; my research work behind my job role, and job-sponsored move; 32564 Glass, 29472 Hurvinek, 49501 Basso, 18838 Shannon, 73700 von Kues, 5702 Morando, 34237 Sarahgao, 18101 Coustenis, 27967 Beppebianchi, 6857 Castelli, 127689 Doncapone, 43775 Tiepolo, 4782 Gembloux, 376694 Kassak, 85015 Gaskell, 25065 Lautakkin, 29307 Torbernbergman, 26728 Luwenqi, 4823 Libenice, 44263 Nansouty

105q10 (97.813) \\needing to pull away and cut loose; 2795 Lepage, 34313 Lisahevner, 7599 Munari, 11455 Richardstarr, 26151 Irinokaigan, 3638 Davis, 8108 Wieland, 14163 Johnchapman

69q10 (187.813) \\slingshot—a close memory made with a total stranger on a fiesta texas ride. REDACTED in REDACTED, tower view from the REDACTED hotel on someone else's funding; how I come back into public view; 21632 Suwanasri, 7724 Moroso, 34148 Marchuo, 17656 Hayabusa, 1633 Chimay, 25988 Janesuh, 8431 Haseda, 2915 Moskvina, 134087 Symeonplatts, 3020 Naudts

141q10 (7.813) \\talking to others through my work, not directly; reminiscent of edge correctional facility (from g of v); 24025 Kimwallin, 14097 Capdepera, 9778 Isabelallende, 701 Oriola, 16861 Lipovetsky, 100028 von Canstein

qig69: engagement with something

qc325: work and taking off from it

9q9 (337.604) \\regular performance of 9-5 duty; my general attitude towards responsibility; 10142 Sakka, 19440 Sumatijain, 33581 Rajeevjha, 33838 Brandabaker, 45 Eugenia, 5877 Toshimaihara, 4610 Kajov

81q9 (157.604) \\apparently the mode under which people ... my books; post work house party activity; 322510 Heinrichgruber, 13857 Stafford, 223877 Kutler, 27478 Kevinbloh, 17836 Canup, 6087 Lupo, 18994 Nhannguyen, 18996 Torasan, 25573 Wanghaoyu, 4415 Echnaton, 28184 Vaishnavirao, 9034 Oleyuria, 20512 Rothenberg, 3933 Portugal, 25655 Baupeter, 13425 Waynebrown, 2498 Tsesevich, 1328 Devota, 1235 Schorria, 9135 Lacaille, 178243 Schaerding, 8557 Saroun, 38628 Huya

45q9 (247.604) \\my change work but also, my goal for changing my partner—the one who serves those who serve; 12513 Niven, 7207 Hammurabi, 4209 Briggs, 2188 Orlenok, 7571 Weisse Rose, 34103 Suganthkannan, 8923 Yamakawa, 1840 Hus, 46580 Ryouichiirie, 13408 Deadoklestic, 1286 Banachiewicza, 71971 Lindaketcham, 19384 Winton, 5613 Donskoj, 9943 Bizan, 7723 Lugger, 47005 Chengmaolan, 15058 Billcooke, 11761 Davidgill

117q9 (67.604) \\the acting lessons; 28697 Eitanacks, 33200 Carasummit, 15849 Billharper, 84566 VIMS, 793 Arizona, 31725 Anushazaman

qc181: channeling the incendiary or inflammatory

21q9 (307.604) \\sl's method of failure in sos; 13788 Dansolander, 34152 Kendrazhang, 25479 Ericshyu, 4158 Santini, 4303 Savitskij, 12813 Paolapaolini, 31429 Diegoazzaro, 7734 Kaltenegger, 2591 Dworetsky

93q9 (127.604) \\me with sl as seen through others' eyes, sl's banishment; 22912 Noraxu, 7558 Yurlov, 2921 Sophocles, 23457 Beiderbecke, 169568 Baranauskas, 33799 Myra, 2172 Plavsk, 9265 Ekman, 302849 Richardboyle

57q9 (217.604) \\hypothesis: "?Monday?" | my gathering of data slices from everywhere and using the sexual energy to drive my off-the-grid research; 12494 Doughamilton, 7704 Dellen, 5299 Bittesini, 20832 Santhikodali, 26545 Meganperkins, 6767 Shirvindt, 22873 Heatherholt, 20237 Clavius, 24712 Boltzmann, 676 Melitta, 13057 Jorgensen, 1305 Pongola, 1098 Hakone, 284 Amalia, 6471 Collins, 14466 Hodge, 7802 Takiguchi, 588 Achilles, 13816 Stulpner, 15001 Fuzhou

129q9 (37.604) \\REDACTED, ju, some of m, bg, rf, the smooth girl; 2361 Gogol, 27396 Shuji, 176 Iduna, 4547 Massachusetts, 110073 Leeonki, 33198 Mackewicz, 9020 Eucryphia, 416252 Manuelherrera

qc37: chillin' at home, even when I'm working, even if I'm not actually at home. Otherwise, onerous directing and responsibilities

33q9 (277.604) \\[umalias keller and his interactions]; my work in the ...; 7536 Fahrenheit, 14056 Kainar, 21436 Chaoyichi, 262106 Margaretryan, 6258 Rodin, 11112 Cagnoli, 2631 Zhejiang, 3395 Jitka, 23899 Kornos, 209552 Isaacroberts, 6306 Nishimura, 4255 Spacewatch, 85267 Taj Mahal, 253 Mathilde, 8867 Tubbiolo, 178156 Borbala, 130283 Elizabethgraham, 25371 Frangaley, 7922 Violalaurenti, 233559 Pizzetti, 21852 Bolander, 14114 Randyray, 8477 Andrejkiselev, 129968 Mitchwhiteley, 10787 Ottoburkard

105q9 (97.604) \\passionate at home, as dad was to mom; 23158 Bouligny, 4929 Yamatai, 4709 Ennomos, 3364 Zdenka, 12052 Aretaon, 16465 Basilrowe, 6247 Amanogawa, 20044 Vitoux, 21432 Polingloh, 30370 Jongoetz

69q9 (187.604) \\my identification as the oldest keeps me in a place, unless I trade out this conception with a very intentional pick of someone more mature; 26425 Linchichieh, 22356 Feyerabend, 9014 Svyatorichter, 9532 Abramenko, 23689 Jancuypers, 4455 Ruriko, 293383 Maigret, 33655 Sumathipala, 33574 Shailaja, 249044 Barrymarshall, 3581 Alvarez, 2070 Humason, 52008 Johnnaka

141q9 (7.604) \\epiphanies with age gap types; 4683 Veratar, 1333 Cevenola, 12492 Tanais, 4686 Maisica, 29374 Kazumitsu, 288 Glauke, 209149 Chrismackenzie

qig70: desirous, what you do

qc324: how I feel when getting ready to handle a burdensome expectation by others

10q8 (337.396) \\my intentions for sata, welcoming others under struggle: the blue; partly involve sacrificing to be a parent to the dogs; 4110 Keats, 3647 Dermott, 32233 Georgehou, 142369 Johnhodges, 6354 Vangelis

82q8 (157.396) \\my scholarly inspiration sparked. Work begins; 17260 Kusnirak, 7211 Xerxes, 46644 Lagia, 117997 Irazu, 26906 Rubidia, 42113 Jura, 5982 Polykletus, 28614 Vejvoda, 92209 Pingtang, 26795 Basilashvili, 20292 Eduardreznik, 10287 Smale, 68114 Deakferenc, 5837 Hedin, 7501 Farra, 16144 Korsten, 7400 Lenau, 5697 Arrhenius, 13116 Hortensia, 274334 Kyivplaniy

46q8 (247.396) \\her first response especially to me as a late virgin; 19597 Ryanlee, 46095 Frederickoby, 12976 Kalinenkov, 3687 Dzus, 2566 Kirghizia, 49699 Hidetakasato, 14576 Jefholley, 1739 Meyermann, 12342 Kudohmichiko, 3666 Holman, 17049 Miron, 68719 Jangyeongsil, 3117 Niepce, 16241 Dvorsky, 84926 Marywalker, 32610 Siennafink, 32561 Waldron, 11876 Doncarpenter, 4074 Sharkov, 25898 Alpoge, 58095 Oranienstein, 34246 Kopparapu

118q8 (67.396) \\my response to her response when the first sexual reveal occurs; 5484 Inoda, 3222 Liller, 25640 Klintefelt, 8774 Viridis, 13653 Priscus, 8780 Forte, 10454 Vallenar, 30183 Murali

qc180: theft, greed, and the relentless buildup of power. Tied to my airways and circulation. My writing protects me from a lot of this

22q8 (307.396) \\stealing out of desperation; 20883 Gervais, 34102 Shawnzhang, 7927 Jamiegilmour, 2640 Hallstrom, 6251 Setsuko, 16265 Lemay, 8417 Lancetaylor, 85970 Fundacaoterra, 9138 Murdoch, 17078 Sellers, 5068 Cragg, 10310 Delacroix, 5458 Aizman, 474 Prudentia

94q8 (127.396) \\tallahassee's intolerable stretch of speed traps. Me being hypersensitive to people's doubt in me; 22694 Tyndall, 10955 Harig, 863 Benkoela, 24533 Kokhirova, 10956 Vosges, 277 Elvira, 7911 Carlpilcher, 30798 Graubunden

58q8 (217.396) \\respiratory difficulties I encounter after an immediate and appreciable jump in exercise progress. Partly related to the flood| yep. Just as I interpreted above:; 199688 Kisspeter, 3587 Descartes, 21508 Benbrewer, 2151 Hadwiger, 8399 Wakamatsu, 18840 Yoshioba, 20540 Marhalpem, 5771 Somerville, 14111 Kimamos, 73520 Boslough, 78816 Caripito, 7313 Pisano, 269742 Kroonorbert, 19310 Osawa, 167018 Csontoscsaba, 4236 Lidov, 24280 Rohenderson, 18825 Alicechai, 24210 Handsberry, 1437 Diomedes

130q8 (37.396) \\the graduating classes I've taught and been a part of; 19165 Nariyuki, 25036 Elizabethof, 12084 Unno, 1015 Christa

qc36: the sexual or co-creative initiator, initiated, and what each of these actors does with respect to the other

34q8 (277.396) \\my memory as a … of …; 6206 Corradolamberti, 163625 Munn, 26005 Alicezhao, 72819 Brunet, 31153 Enricaparri, 146040 Alicebowman, 2113 Ehrdni, 23248 Batchelor, 13815 Furuya, 12567 Herreweghe, 19008 Kristibutler

106q8 (97.396) \\17 REDACTED as providers of early bonded experiences of various kinds; 20856 Hamzabari, 1733 Silke, 5990 Panticapaeon, 7142 Spinoza, 91898 Margnetti, 1692 Subbotina, 2785 Sedov, 8862 Takayukiota, 3392 Setouchi, 12529 Reighard, 790 Pretoria, 2711 Aleksandrov

70q8 (187.396) \\4 REDACTED, Low drag hips; 7628 Evgenifedorov, 23587 Abukumado, 12368 Mutsaers, 19919 Pogorelov, 4843 Megantic, 5628 Preussen, 27571 Bobscott, 365159 Garching, 7067 Kiyose, 3041 Webb, 5085 Hippocrene, 191282 Feustel, 18887 Yiliuchen, 3397 Leyla, 3943 Silbermann, 5442 Drossart, 3413 Andriana, 70712 Danieljoanna, 212692 Lazauskaite

142q8 (7.396) \\becoming noetisexual, demi; my general loss of interest in sex / lack of belief in finding a true "ajani-preference" *co*creator after my engagement with VARIOUS REDACTED *unless* they follow a particular handful of fetishes that I won't list here. 85014 Sutter, 202909 Jakoten, 8679 Tingstade, 12053 Turtlestar

qig71: evolution of daily affairs

qc323: thankless partnerships

10q7 (337.188) \\intimacy with REDACTED, REDACTED as an intimate partner, part of a struggle-to-connect region; my view of what I / dad experience(d) as male heads of household; 34138 Frasso Sabino, 241509 Sessler, 2646 Abetti, 214953 Giugavazzi, 6537 Adamovich

82q7 (157.188) \\what I collect. As I collect more, I may become a connoisseur; 10512 Yamandu, 1851 Lacroute, 20006 Albertus Magnus, 3541 Graham, 30316 Scottmassa, 7448 Pollath, 23754 Rachnareddy, 29081 Krymradio, 22819 Davidtao, 12719 Pingre, 13147 Foglia, 5881 Akashi, 165574 Deidre, 18596 Superbus, 4431 Holeungholee, 4826 Wilhelms, 9841 Masek, 14449 Myogizinzya, 15858 Davidwoods, 6821 Ranevskaya, 9674 Slovenija, 10874 Locatelli

46q7 (247.188) \\my description of shanna to others, especially in … mode; what the other's body is prepared to handle sexually; 28093 Staceylevoit, 6100 Kunitomoikkansai, 15390 Znojil, 2678 Aavasaksa, 8222 Gellner, 5329 Decaro, 9963 Sandage, 980 Anacostia, 152985 Kenkellermann, 2541 Edebono, 7222 Alekperov, 2955 Newburn, 6374 Beslan, 13180 Fourcroy

118q7 (67.188) \\my actions or approach instills this cluster in potential partners; minuteman after 82q7; 2165 Young, 26195 Cernohlavek, 29146 McHone, 23817 Gokulk, 32131 Ravindran, 22184 Rudolfveltman, 8647 Populus, 6406 Mikejura, 17518 Redqueen

qc179: daily inconveniences at the hands of others, as well as my escapes from such (58q7) and attitude in light of these (130q2)

22q7 (307.188) \\the state I realized I was in in san antonio after a while. Needing to move; shanna the workaholic; 211380 Kevinwojeck, 748 Simeisa, 16020 Tevelde, 9645 Grunewald, 7012 Hobbes, 49481 Gisellarubini, 104052 Zachery, 6944 Elaineowens, 184620 Pippobattaglia, 16064 Davidharvey, 710 Gertrud, 148604 Shobbrook, 173872 Andrewwest, 73453 Ninomanfredi, 78 Diana, 37609 LaVelle

94q7 (127.188) \\the values pressured in the place I had to leave; shanna's dog culture; 20415 Amandalu, 21082 Araimasaru, 17472 Dinah, 3627 Sayers, 10431 Pottasch, 7980 Senkevich, 8732 Champion, 28690 Beshellem, 202092 Algirdas, 4271 Novosibirsk, 13087 Chastellux, 48799 Tashikuergan, 91007 Ianfleming, 3189 Penza, 10949 Konigstuhl, 129338 Andrewlowman, 13908 Wolbern, 21495 Feaga, 7530 Mizusawa

58q7 (217.188) \\keith—who can endure the inconveniences for me; things I do to get away from daily inconveniences; 4864 Nimoy, 47044 Mcpainter, 28980 Chowyunfat, 1652 Herge, 490 Veritas, 1327 Namaqua, 20325 Julianoey, 26235 Annemaduggan, 15703 Yrjola, 7935 Beppefenoglio, 14141 Demeautis, 24369 Evanichols, 5348 Kennoguchi, 1927 Suvanto, 23792 Alyssacook, 5886 Rutger, 14267 Zook, 19162 Wambsganss, 23875 Strube, 25606 Chiangshenghao, 136666 Seidel, 7771 Tvaren, 26990 Culbertson, 2565 Grogler

130q7 (37.188) \\agd, adc, bodies; 3529 Dowling, 3029 Sanders, 65692 Trifu, 32618 Leungkamcheung, 34241 Skylerjones, 5679 Akkado, 1684 Iguassu, 189848 Eivissa, 14366 Wilhelmraabe, 8598 Tetrix, 222 Lucia, 22580 Kenkaplan, 16131 Kaganovich

qc35: my writings and the work leading up to their publication

34q7 (277.188) \\me as a progressive influencer?; 5758 Brunini, 1154 Astronomia, 6533 Giuseppina, 7410 Kawazoe, 3808 Tempel, 25275 Jocelynbell, 4801 Ohre, 5567 Durisen, 37736 Jandl, 2596 Vainu Bappu, 4079 Britten, 5744 Yorimasa, 3614 Tumilty, 159351 Leonpascal, 22442 Blaha

106q7 (97.188) \\sherry, simeona, tahira; 21609 Williamcaleb, 12444 Prothoon, 24647 Maksimachev, 1006 Lagrangea, 22944 Sarahmarzen, 1742 Schaifers, 17428 Charleroi, 20109 Alicelandis, 8465 Bancelin, 27984 Herminefranz, 31517 Mahoui

70q7 (187.188) \\shanna or simeona; 19754 Paclements, 22579 Marcyeager, 28151 Markknopfler, 8048 Andrle, 27381 Balasingam, 8728 Mimatsu, 9329 Nikolaimedtner, 9038 Helensteel, 28677 Laurakowalski, 349386 Randywright, 19570 Jessedouglas, 26526 Jookayhyun, 3992 Wagner, 2447 Kronstadt, 5902 Talima, 30524 Mandushev

142q7 (7.188) \\how your shared living situation evolves as you mature; 58365 Robmedrano, 30048 Sreyasmisra, 32048 Kathyliu, 2791 Paradise, 179 Klytaemnestra, 1803 Zwicky, 20290 Seanraj, 3281 Maupertuis

qig72: what you can make or build up easily under your own influence

qc322: shanna's and my family together and how we approach it separately

10q6 (336.979) \\shanna's art; my blocking of astro clients—only doing this unto myself; 30200 Terryburch, 10220 Pigott, 172269 Tator, 6996 Alvensleben, 21192 Seccisergio, 4798 Mercator, 429032 Sebvonhoerner, 18531 Strakonice, 2187 La Silla

82q6 (156.979) \\where I am challenged with proof of identity in systems which don't know me. REDACTED furniture store. Very unpleasant; 27502 Stephbecca, 12180 Kistemaker, 335799 Zonglu, 308306 Dainere, 4655 Marjoriika, 21776 Kryszczynska, 24503 Kero, 130088 Grantcunningham, 2497 Kulikovskij, 4054 Turnov, 35324 Orlandi, 14719 Sobey, 10114 Greifswald, 3163 Randi, 25768 Nussbaum, 8762 Hiaticula, 4460 Bihoro, 4917 Yurilvovia, 22063 Dansealey

46q6 (246.979) \\the dogs interrupting sex with sb. Relentlessly; my work with data or structure blocks those who like me; 11033 Mazanek, 40092 Memel, 1485 Isa, 19602 Austinminor, 4100 Sumiko, 12280 Reims, 495 Eulalia, 6999 Meitner, 2831 Stevin, 30934 Bakerhansen, 24261 Judilegault, 2006 Polonskaya, 32092 Brianxia, 29137 Alanboss, 24847 Polesny

118q6 (66.979) \\me and my experience with intimacy unfolding; 22003 Startek, 16958 Klaasen, 30057 Sarasakowitz, 17982 Simcmillan, 225711 Danyzy, 73769 Delphi, 2450 Ioannisiani, 88961 Valpertile

qc178: how I get into or avoid confrontation

22q6 (306.979) \\ezra and wine—stories of relationships that don't quite work out as planned. A quixotic fight for the environment which may yet be won at the expense of a relationship. Ezra and wine with a universe between them. And earth. Me and b.a.r.; recorded scrutiny of my relationships; 8030 Williamknight, 4806 Miho, 30066 Parthakker, 134109 Britneyburch, 19290 Schroeder, 9326 Ruta, 5825 Rakuyou, 8960 Luscinioides, 121547 Fenghuotongxin, 10120 Ypres, 166749 Sesar, 2343 Siding Spring, 57658 Nilrem, 32582 Mayachandar, 2364 Seillier, 16740 Kipthorne, 13841 Blankenship

94q6 (126.979) \\when I don't feel like explaining to people, which is pretty much all the time; how I back away from potential fights; 217366 Mayalin, 7979 Pozharskij, 157491 Rudigerkollar, 5306 Fangfen, 11085 Isala, 9206 Yanaikeizo, 3072 Vilnius, 15492 Nyberg, 16788 Alyssarose, 37044 Papymarcel, 8904 Yoshihara, 22835 Rickgardner, 10652 Blaeu

58q6 (216.979) \\the first chapters of l1. more generally, my non-consumption of most media; how I stay away from fights to begin with; 19820 Stowers, 6939 Lestone, 142753 Briegel, 4001 Ptolemaeus, 4239 Goodman, 321484 Marsaalam, 11429 Demodokus, 21414 Blumenthal, 11900 Spinoy, 687 Tinette, 3604 Berkhuijsen, 7256 Bonhoeffer, 7059 Van Dokkum, 18396 Nellysachs, 2573 Hannu Olavi, 121537 Lorenzdavid, 5708 Melancholia, 4737 Kiladze

130q6 (36.979) \\keith and far reaching teaching, me teaching through my books; 4616 Batalov, 31689 Sebmellen, 6802 Cernovice, 14395 Tommorgan, 351 Yrsa, 4249 Kremze, 215423 Winnecke, 3546 Atanasoff, 90564 Markjarnyk, 11059 Nulliusinverba, 121865 Dauvergne, 24666 Miesvanrohe, 8071 Simonelli

qc34: my fated self-exposition and the reasons behind it. An explanation

34q6 (276.979) \\when I declare a versus-clique, locking them out, they become real. But I make my decision despite them; thanks to deborah and company, I have some pretty legit responses here; 541 Deborah, 4820 Fay, 27258 Chelseavoss, 16262 Rikurtz, 202605 Shenchunshan, 10146 Mukaitadashi, 19599 Brycemelton, 2918 Salazar, 1997 Leverrier, 6493 Cathybennett, 17460 Mang

106q6 (96.979) \\what shanna does when things go wrong in the house, 4 REDACTED and other cliques; 22983 Schlingheyde, 7592 Takinemachi, 6110 Kazak, 33590 Sreelakshmi, 10331 Peterbluhm, 3310 Patsy, 23717 Kaddoura, 19585 Zachopkins

70q6 (186.979) \\when the state is broken, I play certain songs which the other can hear; another great explanation for my behaviors; 5689 Rhon, 12519 Pullen, 4784 Samcarin, 26459 Shinsubin, 6549 Skryabin, 18747 Lexcen, 12400 Katumaru, 13559 Werth, 78118 Bharat, 21610 Rosengard, 13954 Born, 10176 Gaiavettori, 323552 Trudybell, 15854 Numa, 63145 Choemuseon, 1123 Shapleya, 23980 Ogden, 3061 Cook, 14583 Lester, 12911 Goodhue, 7541 Nieuwenhuis, 260 Huberta, 3843 OISCA

142q6 (6.979) \\my feelings about REDACTED's comment. Or REDACTED's. Taken hard; also, a kind of freezing I experience in the handling of financial resources— "overwhelmed" by something too contrary to really respond to? As long as I did no intentional harm, it is easy to feel that i don't have to pay. i may allow the pain to simmer for a while, but as long as i don't engage actual misconduct or philosophize about (try to deeply explain) wrongs, i can, for the most part, avoid minor illness; 15629 Sriner, 2657 Bashkiria, 11337 Sandro, 24948 Babote, 10316 Williamturner, 5917 Chibasai, 1 Ceres, 26393 Scaffa, 1635 Bohrmann

qig73: the stable wall around your potential actions

qc321: the business partner

10q5 (336.771) \\c's pantheon; my recognition of archetypal forms of female power in a single space. May be related to tiy; a cornucopia of feminine energy; 1582 Martir, 4234 Evtushenko, 1918 Aiguillon, 15890 Prachatice, 12186 Mitukurigen, 2058 Roka, 175365 Carsac

82q5 (156.771) \\a sharp, weaponizable explicator; smart, can solve anything; 13868 Catalonia, 19808 Elainemccall, 348239 Societadante, 18016 Grondahl, 350185 Linnell, 19243 Bunting, 12646 Avercamp, 1288 Santa, 26466 Zarrin, 17744 Jodiefoster, 29858 Tlomak, 18824 Graves, 28547 Johannschroter, 6873 Tasaka, 28525 Andrewabboud

46q5 (246.771) \\earthquakes, oj, kapernick; 84995 Zselic, 15551 Paddock, 163693 Atira, 7716 Ube, 78115 Skiantonucci, 37853 Danielbarbier, 4197 Morpheus, 12291 Gohnaumann, 4952 Kibeshigemore, 1068 Nofretete, 242516 Lindseystirling, 30271 Brandoncui, 11336 Piranesi, 30325 Reesabpathak, 8857 Cercidiphyllum, 176710 Banff, 3457 Arnenordheim, 21258 Huckins

118q5 (66.771) \\specialized data uncovered; 215080 Kaohsiung, 2048 Dwornik, 19817 Larashelton, 236984 Astier, 55735 Magdeburg, 1670 Minnaert

qc177: under the control of the sculptor

22q5 (306.771) \\a clique seeks the powers they perceive in their rivals. b.a.r.'s group. Maga; how my succubi treat me; 2632 Guizhou, 18469 Hakodate, 3330 Gantrisch, 8022 Scottcrossfield, 248839 Mazeikiai, 123120 Peternewman, 18965 Lazenby, 11754 Herbig, 142758 Connolly, 233292 Brianschmidt

94q5 (126.771) \\umalias keller for example. How one keeps the mob at bay or controls the many; how I respond to the succubi; 177 Irma, 90672 Metrorheinneckar, 22134 Kirian, 6515 Giannigalli, 21616 Guhagilford, 176103 Waynejohnson, 28626 Meghanshea, 4444 Escher, 31319 Vespucci, 999 Zachia, 26302 Zimolzak

58q5 (216.771) \\marie antoinette, a leader figure martyred before the crowd; 6024 Ochanomizu, 6263 Druckmuller, 5681 Bakulev, 19731 Tochigi, 21577 Negron, 321405 Ingehorst, 5422 Hodgkin, 7631 Vokrouhlicky, 4336 Jasniewicz, 1609 Brenda, 54863 Gasnault, 4783 Wasson, 12379 Thulin, 18851 Winmesser, 12294 Avogadro

130q5 (36.771) \\Sâvitrî or me as a mannequin. What kind of attention results?; 20306 Richarnold, 121211 Nikeshadavis, 2741 Valdivia, 10587 Strindberg, 17097 Ronneuman

qc33: a long-term legacy we leave (remembered)

34q5 (276.771) \\my attracting of younger women, especially through some system or other person they are subject to; 148707 Dodelson, 18104 Mahalingam, 5842 Cancelli, 159013 Kyleturner, 31619 Jodietinker, 2147 Kharadze, 281272 Arnaudleroy, 14153 Dianecaplain, 1444 Pannonia, 1726 Hoffmeister, 26634 Balasubramanian, 2842 Unsold, 3267 Glo

106q5 (96.771) \\shanna or agd drawing out the limiting sides of my dreams; 7902 Hanff, 7189 Kuniko, 3668 Ilfpetrov, 11821 Coleman, 9499 Excalibur

70q5 (186.771) \\me and most of my solo girl memories; this is an overall good significator REGION for me; 5298 Paraskevopoulos, 262418 Samofalov, 149 Medusa, 35325 Claudiaguarnieri, 17220 Johnpenna, 9934 Caccioppoli, 11150 Bragg,

8730 Iidesan, 27101 Wenyucao, 5401 Minamioda, 3877 Braes, 1248 Jugurtha, 26451 Khweis, 4149 Harrison, 9709 Chrisnell, 14345 Gritsevich, 4594 Dashkova, 65769 Mahalia, 3713 Pieters, 1627 Ivar, 85004 Crombie

142q5 (6.771) \\the F at caltech; making love to REDACTED; 2980 Cameron, 8161 Newman, 23217 Nayana, 31508 Kanevsky

qig74: those who block or guard access to your potential reifications

qc320: my penis exercises, their motivation, and the direct tie to my scholarship and learning

10q4 (336.563) \\MAJOR. the spark that starts my exercise; 3126 Davydov, 266051 Hannawieser, 16007 Kaasalainen, 14616 Van Gaal, 17465 Inawashiroko, 33917 Kellyoconnor, 9719 Yakage, 2654 Ristenpart

82q4 (156.563) \\REDACTED and w.a., spirited away with REDACTED, general … angels, I think; 3054 Strugatskia, 21010 Kishon, 7923 Chyba, 28038 Nicoleodzer, 8769 Arctictern, 118214 Agnesediboemia, 8101 Yasue, 146268 Jennipolakis, 6529 Rhoads, 19660 Danielsteck, 85422 Maedanaoe, 15014 Annagekker, 9227 Ashida, 117652 Joseaponte, 154714 de Schepper, 2289 McMillan, 450 Brigitta, 11714 Mikebrown, 6779 Perrine

46q4 (246.563) \\REDACTED descends then we separate; 1271 Isergina, 8421 Montanari, 40134 Marsili, 133 Cyrene, 6855 Armellini, 152319 Pynchon, 8250 Cornell, 12267 Denneau, 15970 Robertbrownlee, 866 Fatme, 25819 Tripathi, 6712 Hornstein, 10768 Sarutahiko, 130089 Saadatanwar, 13533 Junili, 10545 Kallunge, 1697 Koskenniemi, 11134 Ceske Budejovice, 20200 Donbacky, 20043 Ellenmacarthur

118q4 (66.563) \\mostly simeona, then rachel (our dog), then crystal, then auguste, then klein; 4697 Novara, 5572 Bliskunov, 28400 Morgansinko, 31677 Audreyglende, 25636 Vaishnav, 26666 Justinto, 22490 Zigamiyama, 29473 Krejci, 5908 Aichi, 7268 Chigorin, 8053 Kleist, 18556 Battiato, 17269 Dicksmith, 9592 Clairaut

qc176: the conflicts and remedies allotted by my ethnoculture. foreigners who assess you; when you provide your ethnoculture to the app, it should look here to understand your place in the race-typifying world; | write about this particular qunit in contours and g of v

22q4 (306.563) \\deciding on initial sata partners; little economic moves made without REDACTED; my relationship-destroying messages; 24134 Cliffordkim, 25607 Tsengiching, 768 Struveana, 59419 Presov, 113659 Faltona, 43924 Martoni, 442 Eichsfeldia, 8569 Mameli, 8193 Ciaurro, 24526 Desai, 1503 Kuopio, 100434 Jinyilian, 52601 Iwayaji, 9258 Johnpauljones

94q4 (126.563) \\the little one deployed; simeona+ ; someone else whom I see as effective; how I experience conflict with another at the recordable blowup point. Relationship terminal; 342 Endymion, 95852 Leatherbarrow, 30785 Greeley, 19419 Pinkham, 7370 Krasnogolovets, 8586 Epops, 31701 Ragula, 21451 Fisher

58q4 (216.563) \\principles of time travel; the group through which I can be effective and build up esteem; jaded and weary of combat as I get older; 29788 Rachelrossi, 6509 Giovannipratesi, 12093 Chrimatthews, 23382 Epistrophos, 15810 Arawn, 228 Agathe, 5173 Stjerneborg, 42929 Francini, 356217 Clymene, 21985 Sejna, 5883 Josephblack, 570 Kythera, 25365 Bernreuter, 221917 Opites, 8947 Mizutani, 22612 Dandibner, 314808 Martindutertre, 2937 Gibbs, 6016 Carnelli

130q4 (36.563) \\the seat of my self-esteem, my sense of effectiveness; my insistence on a fence / security against hostile surroundings before I invest in something or send energy outwards; how I handle generally unreceptive backgrounds; 28950 Ailisdooner, 31268 Welty, 48480 Falk, 74370 Kolarjan, 245943 Davidjoseph, 14964 Robertobacci

qc32: my obsession with putting certain information out there as a correction to certain perceived slights or unfavorable events

34q4 (276.563) \\my eventual opinion of simeona and b.a.r.. As long as you didn't actively take from me, there is usually forgiveness; 10801 Luneburg, 13146 Yuriko, 24156 Hamsasridhar, 10253 Westerwald, 315218 La Boetie, 38669 Michikawa, 10994 Fouchard, 57359 Robcrawford, 30365 Gregduran, 17899 Mariacristina, 1156 Kira, 198450 Scattolin, 290074 Donasadock, 31507 Williamjin, 6323 Karoji, 26829 Sakaihoikuen, 15608 Owens, 10980 Breimer, 240 Vanadis, 2124 Nissen

106q4 (96.563) \\my bemoaning what us available or someone else doing this, me telling them no; 9726 Verbiscer, 5420 Jancis, 31778 Richardschnur, 53468 Varros, 5504 Lanzerotti, 26575 Andreapugh, 8810 Johnmcfarland, 2282 Andres Bello, 11870 Sverige, 4764 Joneberhart, 30154 Chiomento, 3180 Morgan

70q4 (186.563) \\shanna, REDACTED, and prior female solicitors; 343444 Halluzinelle, 26522 Juliapoje, 5030 Gyldenkerne, 5875 Kuga, 3221 Changshi, 12604 Lisatate, 486239 Zosiakaczmarek, 24259 Chriswalker, 7121 Busch, 6199 Yoshiokayayoi, 9027 Graps, 454326 Donlee, 25497 Brauerman, 13365 Tenzinyama, 5105 Westerhout, 21850 Abshir

142q4 (6.563) \\liars; the warm-to-each-other monogamous couple; those who come on too strongly, then turn sneaky when things aren't going their way—continuing to take from you (despite knowing there is a lack of alignment) until you kill them; 58569 Eboshiyamakouen, 15147 Siegfried, 13256 Marne, 18509 Bellini, 5993 Tammydickinson, 336204 Sardinas, 8391 Kring, 5864 Montgolfier, 5659 Vergara

qig75: you need direction

qc319: my addressing difficult situations through writing

10q3 (336.354) \\an outlet for various barriers I've encountered; 28629 Solimano, 16802 Rainer, 5230 Asahina, 20584 Brigidsavage, 13576 Gotoyoshi, 259344 Pare

82q3 (156.354) \\the people I know who rely on their partner to do the projecting for them; 7633 Volodymyr, 367732 Mikesimonsen, 7983 Festin, 5657 Groombridge, 619 Triberga, 2755 Avicenna, 21282 Shimizuyuka, 4260 Yanai, 33628 Spettel

46q3 (246.354) \\how I handle the dogs going berserk; 1710 Gothard, 8299 Tealeoni, 9612 Belgorod, 10425 Landfermann, 10051 Albee, 209791 Tokaj, 68109 Naomipasachoff, 30040 Annemerrill, 1657 Roemera, 2599 Veseli, 266646 Zaphod, 22402 Goshi, 26119 Duden, 7462 Grenoble, 6628 Dondelia, 5789 Sellin

118q3 (66.354) \\what I do in light of shanna's dynamic with me; 20298 Gordonsu, 3711 Ellensburg, 9569 Quintenmatsijs, 246842 Dutchstapelbroek

qc175: the book of contours as my ultimate approach to the human body; functions of the body build, how it is put to use. Related to weight

22q3 (306.354) \\my writing of l2, doing qunits, writing contours; 31231 Uthmann, 33522 Chizumimaeta, 7972 Mariotti, 436048 Fritzhuber, 693 Zerbinetta, 3227 Hasegawa, 229777 ENIAC, 15986 Fienga, 1601 Patry, 108072 Odifreddi, 12148 Caravaggio, 11151 Oodaigahara, 3296 Bosque Alegre, 15818 DeVeny

94q3 (126.354) \\history re: mom; maybe an impression shanna and I left on kevin; my intentions for contours; 9573 Matsumotomas, 25427 Kratchmarov, 12356 Carlscheele, 361690 Laurelanmaurer, 445917 Ola, 21502 Cruz, 4939 Scovil, 217398 Tihany, 4918 Rostropovich, 2185 Guangdong, 9377 Metz, 83362 Sandukruit, 24935 Godfreyhardy, 17486 Hodler, 34188 Clarawagner

58q3 (216.354) \\agd, shanna, the vatican. Institutions which surrounded me for a time, paid through blood; the contents of the book of contours; 243097 Batavia, 27103 Sungwoncho, 20291 Raumurthy, 14258 Katrinaminck, 13352 Gyssens, 5794 Irmina, 2077 Kiangsu, 7749 Jackschmitt, 13162 Ryokkochigaku, 8603 Senator, 1773 Rumpelstilz, 90471 Andrewdrake, 31772 Asztalos, 1397 Umtata, 436149 Edabel, 172191 Ralphmcnutt, 25981 Shahmirian, 15550 Sydney, 6864 Starkenburg

130q3 (36.354) \\appearing in contours with savi—someone more compliant; things I love or am truly attached to daily which lead up to contours; 8432 Tamakasuga, 26283 Oswalt, 12153 Conon, 2028 Janequeo, 13112 Montmorency, 366 Vincentina

qc31: REDACTED and sent out objects, and those who need to attend to and respond to them. Has major implications for what it is I actually export for pay. Clearly 34q3 does pay at least some money

34q3 (276.354) \\my writings (and REDACTED) are widely known. The former go all over the world; comments about REDACTED, given I've moved far away. More status had. More focus on building. Little digs may indicate that eccentricity is actually one gateway to status; 189398 Soemmerring, 5731 Zeus, 51655 Susannemond, 6205 Menottigalli, 27724 Jeannoel, 32621 Talcott, 28963 Tamyiu, 537 Pauly, 26871 Tanezrouft, 27846 Honegger, 7497 Guangcaishiye, 2595 Gudiachvili, 337044 Bobdylan

106q3 (96.354) \\me lingering on something for a long time, and ramping myself up about it. What is the square reward for not doing this? The stationary object of 34q3; 33255 Kathybush, 55276 Kenlarner, 3196 Maklaj, 31134 Zurria, 9920 Bagnulo, 6093 Makoto, 15783 Briancox, 9285 Le Corre

70q3 (186.354) \\shanna or simeona; 4485 Radonezhskij, 2231 Durrell, 73767 Bibiandersson, 15453 Brasileirinhos, 20135 Juels, 41213 Mimoun, 34293 Khiemdoba, 1928 Summa, 19500 Hillaryfultz, 2236 Austrasia, 269485 Bisikalo, 5792 Unstrut, 12871 Samarasinha, 34258 Pentland, 3433 Fehrenbach

142q3 (6.354) \\REDACTED assists me in certain kinds of health maneuvers; 26013 Amandalonzo, 2397 Lappajarvi, 21615 Guardamano, 3013 Dobrovoleva

qig76: energy penetration process

qc318: my rallying rebellion against social oppression

10q2 (336.146) \\how the (mainly males in my life) express their disapproval or resistance to how things are going; 173032 Mingus, 32234 Jesslihuang, 5782 Akirafujiwara, 16951 Carolus Quartus, 2406 Orelskaya, 2680 Mateo, 28719 Sahoolahan, 30150 Laseminara, 10367 Sayo, 33453 Townley, 31665 Veblen

82q2 (156.146) \\sanza, REDACTED, some shanna; 171112 Sickafoose, 14121 Stuwe, 39686 Takeshihara, 6677 Renoir, 3759 Piironen, 61404 Ocenasek, 35270 Molinari, 34176 Balamurugan, 95008 Ivanobertini, 30444 Shemp, 2970 Pestalozzi, 11485

Zinzendorf, 684 Hildburg, 10459 Vladichaika, 22597 Lynzielinski, 12671 Thornqvist, 6722 Bunichi

46q2 (246.146) \\shanna, REDACTED; character of the females in my life when pressure has overtaken them; 3542 Tanjiazhen, 13031 Durance, 5508 Gomyou, 483 Seppina, 15618 Lorifritz, 187707 Nandaxianlin, 346 Hermentaria, 1017 Jacqueline, 4664 Hanner, 33034 Dianadamrau, 269484 Marcia, 5026 Martes, 3361 Orpheus

118q2 (66.146) \\she will assassinate the man; 5937 Loden, 920 Rogeria, 15262 Abderhalden, 1177 Gonnessia

qc174: my actual personal goals and stance towards life

22q2 (306.146) \\my peripatetic reflections; the establishment of a data save institution; 6698 Malhotra, 2445 Blazhko, 9106 Yatagarasu, 4853 Marielukac, 385571 Otrera, 5535 Annefrank, 160903 Shiokaze, 30882 Tomhenning, 14845 Hegel, 705 Erminia, 11163 Milesovka, 775 Lumiere, 14606 Hifleischer, 7098 Reaumur, 1105 Fragaria, 100897 Piatra Neamt

94q2 (126.146) \\the kinds of things I record about, or my reasons for doing so; 1113 Katja, 9930 Billburrows, 85411 Paulflora, 28428 Ankurvaishnav, 381458 Moiseenko, 37859 Bobkoff, 6169 Sashakrot, 2839 Annette, 34127 Adamnayak

58q2 (216.146) \\where the recording itself begs to be used, independent of my wants. Where a situation begs to be recorded; 5869 Tanith, 48720 Enricomentana, 8693 Matsuki, 11374 Briantaylor, 6793 Palazzolo, 171153 Allanrahill, 7074 Muckea, 7491 Linzerag, 4834 Thoas, 10239 Hermann, 18077 Dianeingrao, 5354 Hisayo, 1866 Sisyphus, 33249 Pamelasvenson, 11268 Spassky, 944 Hidalgo, 403 Cyane, 7502 Arakida

130q2 (36.146) \\building up to what is ultimately seen in contours; 94884 Takuya, 6843 Heremon, 6285 Ingram, 14901 Hidatakayama, 7476 Ogilsbie, 1044 Teutonia, 7932 Plimpton, 21520 Dianaeheart, 16113 Ahmed, 9121 Stefanovalentini, 7657 Jefflarsen

qc30: my work and my means of guarding it from certain detractors

34q2 (276.146) \\things which, if I do, will block intimacy; 27978 Lubosluka, 29203 Schnitger, 7739 Cech, 2672 Pisek, 14143 Hadfield, 62071 Voegtli, 28132 Karenzobel, 11109 Iwatesan, 15118 Elizabethsears, 185 Eunike, 4607 Seilandfarm, 277816 Varese

106q2 (96.146) \\the paralyzed helper whose role gets abolished. Edwardsu; 5144 Achates, 129209 Robertburt, 15699 Lyytinen, 2997 Cabrera, 16019 Edwardsu, 289587 Chantdugros, 3571 Milanstefanik, 99 Dike, 19662 Stunzi, 8310 Seelos

70q2 (186.146) \\truce while the other freaks out. Or calming them down; 27288 Paulgilmore, 9774 Annjudge, 423205 Echezeaux, 13764 Mcalanis, 34666 Bohyunsan, 9705 Drummen, 24224 Matthewdavis, 3084 Kondratyuk, 269589 Kryachko, 14225 Alisahamilton

142q2 (6.146) \\my meetings with vh, sml, vv, REDACTED & REDACTED, intimate and friendly; 8154 Stahl, 12224 Jimcornell, 9688 Goudsmit, 18460 Peckova, 7219 Satterwhite, 34264 Sadhuka, 7596 Yumi, 210425 Imogene, 21645 Chentsaiwei, 1547 Nele

qig77: your sex-typicality or polarity training which you come to protect from insult

qc317: priya; my friend basis in general; one who broadcasts their troubles

10q1 (335.938) \\the STRONG males in my life, including myself: 6 REDACTED; 262536 Nowikow, 9577 Gropius, 142759 Covey, 8370 Vanlindt, 8217 Dominikhasek, 15020 Brandonimber, 5294 Onnetoh, 3275 Oberndorfer, 129173 Mattgoman, 14061 Nagincox, 180141 Sperauskas

82q1 (155.938) \\the domains who help me learn manhood?; 12859 Marlamoore, 5932 Prutkov, 28467 Maurentejamie, 3383 Koyama, 31502 Hellerstein, -10005 Jupiter, 4096 Kushiro, 11796 Nirenberg, 25250 Jonnapeterson, 38070 Redwine, 24523 Sanaraoof, 28108 Sydneybarnes, 2121 Sevastopol, 6989 Hoshinosato

46q1 (245.938) \\REDACTED or someone sick later on in life; lvz or lf; h; possibly indicates an archetypal male role in the lives of a definitional female, or an example of characteristics which are decidedly not female in an asserter's eyes. This is the kind of character I don't want to be directly involved with, but who may need to be controlled by the girl with the nose. example: REDACTED was controlled by REDACTED or adc. REDACTED controlled by REDACTED. because this qunit is fundamental to my male biology, i am a lot less likely to have a choice in who I end up with stably—it's either both girls on this axis, square to my 10-1, or one girl on my 82-1s; 1832 Mrkos, 22291 Heitifer, 18462 Ricco, 30051 Jihopark, 14966 Jurijvega, 10256 Vredevoogd, 2941 Alden, 10305 Grignard, 15230 Alona, 82092 Kalocsa, 17004 Sinkevich, 8917 Tianjindaxue, 15381 Spadolini, 2625 Jack London, 6321 Namuratakao, 21737 Stephenshulz, 10138 Ohtanihiroshi, 1630 Milet, 4970 Druyan, 2532 Sutton, 24956 Qiannan

118q1 (65.938) \\the girl with the distinctive nose emerges; 132874 Latinovits, 3676 Hahn, 8666 Reuter, 5557 Chimikeppuko, 22982 Emmacall, 5521 Morpurgo, 8197

Mizunohiroshi, 92300 Hagelin, 7640 Marzari, 4270 Juanvictoria, 4981 Sinyavskaya, 21924 Alyssaovaitt, 8721 AMOS, 742 Edisona, 3050 Carrera, 11138 Hotakadake

qc173: the overrider and my independent work instead: these are different versions of hetero maleship

22q1 (305.938) \\my carrying sata; burning to interject, but basically ignored or dismissed; 4915 Solzhenitsyn, 22675 Davidcohn, 34128 Hannahbrown, 163 Erigone, 33555 Nataliebush, 4608 Wodehouse, 5824 Inagaki, 67712 Kimotsuki, 34184 Hegde

94q1 (125.938) \\the new frankenstein's monster; the overrider amidst others less capable. I don't really respect this character and probably shouldn't emulate him or her no matter how much rank they are given; 311231 Anuradhapura, 15804 Yenisei, 261936 Liulin, 327982 Balducci, 8798 Tarantino, 28402 Matthewkim, 21745 Shadfan, 293985 Franquin, 11082 Spilliaert, 23249 Liaoyenting, 5090 Wyeth, 2894 Kakhovka, 2139 Makharadze

58q1 (215.938) \\the imminent looming institution and the effect of its loom on moods looking out for it; 2099 Opik, 2076 Levin, 10617 Takumi, 20420 Marashwhitman, 9628 Sendaiotsuna, 278384 Mudanjiang, 3721 Widorn, 3303 Merta, 25087 Kaztaniguchi, 707 Steina, 23133 Rishinbehl, 8568 Larrywilson, 225250 Georgfranziska, 11152 Oomine, 8897 Defelice, 9384 Aransio, 49441 Scerbanenco, 5254 Ulysses, 21742 Rachaelscott, 5500 Twilley, 364192 Qianruhu

130q1 (35.938) \\going off to the side to pursue my own native strength; 33154 Talent, 4570 Runcorn, 5885 Apeldoorn, 247553 Berndpauli, 30175 Adityajain, 33406 Saltzman, 8911 Kawaguchijun

qc29: shanna's and my attention to and conversations with people in the public. Also, how we observe them

34q1 (275.938) \\mensa, GenEd, …, my small group work; 23816 Rohitkamat, 17452 Amurreka, 5287 Heishu, 15413 Beaglehole, 110293 Oia, 165067 Pauls, 3272 Tillandz, 11423 Cronin, 869 Mellena, 25294 Johnlaberee, 9323 Hirohisasato, 689 Zita, 10529 Giessenburg, 15295 Tante Riek, 30253 Vitek

106q1 (95.938) \\snappy bodily person who brings out the limitation. It's the distrust that's the problem: kent. I drop these people immediately and permanently; 28346 Kent, 4818 Elgar, 10560 Michinari, 1172 Aneas

70q1 (185.938) \\seems related to my dream life; 4084 Hollis, 16856 Banach, 11896 Camelbeeck, 78221 Leonmow, 129082 Oliviabillett, 119967 Daniellong, 45305 Paulscherrer, 8210 NANTEN, 19287 Paronelli, 249302 Ajoie, 122 Gerda, 20604 Vrishikpatil, 14124 Kamil, 3210 Lupishko, 120141 Lucaslara, 940 Kordula, 15576 Munday, 24794 Kurland, 15506 Preygel, 4433 Goldstone

142q1 (5.938) \\how I deliver a breakup message, if the person is to get one (interestingly, if they don't get one, they are much less likely to hear from me again. I imagine the reverse is also true); 7322 Lavrentina, 17038 Wake, 34134 Zlokapa, 30827 Lautenschlager, 248750 Asteroidday, 3057 Malaren, 4223 Shikoku, 101721 Emanuelfritsch, 4002 Shinagawa, 1903 Adzhimushkaj, 3135 Lauer, 128177 Griffioen, 3340 Yinhai

qig78: institutional rules affecting what you are allowed to do in a context

qc316: each partner's bachelor behavior against the partnership

10q12 (335.729) \\more at home in foreign territories, though the journey may be tough; 2066 Palala, 117390 Stephanegendron, 21311 Servius, 25630 Sarkar, 4283 Stoffler

82q12 (155.729) \\shanna in work mode; 15548 Kalinowski, 33681 Wamsley, 8912 Ohshimatake, 25464 Maxrabinovich, 35358 Lorifini, 8039 Grandprism, 10588 Adamcrandall, 20901 Mattmuehler, 17484 Ganghofer, 17179 Codina, 24858 Diethelm, 3378 Susanvictoria, 14917 Taco, 15904 Halstead, 318682 Carpaccio, 172734 Giansimon

46q12 (245.729) \\how I thought real estate would work. But the collective has spoken; 247652 Hajossy, 105675 Kamiukena, 10304 Iwaki, 5054 Keil, 25520 Deronchang, 11332 Jameswatt, 30564 Olomouc, 12565 Khege, 4530 Smoluchowski, 5692 Shirao, 25042 Qiujun, 10767 Toyomasu, 10423 Dajcic, 333 Badenia, 14072 Volterra, 5803 Otzi, 471 Papagena

118q12 (65.729) \\my weighing in on behalf of the whole situation; 5212 Celiacruz, 10243 Hohe Meissner, 4354 Euclides, 32943 Sandyryan, 10264 Marov, 10558 Karlstad, 11352 Koldewey, 19809 Nancyowen, 2732 Witt

qc172: the work I do to build up the family, and how the events that occur around family-advancing work by me and my co-parent

22q12 (305.729) \\REDACTED, REDACTED, the one who commissions the trio. Our efforts build this one's intentions into actuality; 8257 Andycheng, 1804 Chebotarev, 11127 Hagi, 17969 Truong, 25062 Rasmussen, 2600 Lumme, 1886 Lowell, 3756 Ruscannon, 2104 Toronto, 155438 Velasquez, 29850 Tanakagyou, 120730 Zhouyouyuan, 69977 Saurodonati, 6590 Barolo, 5571 Lesliegreen, 11707 Grigery

94q12 (125.729) \\my action-packed role in a trio, where we are commissioned to get the damned work done. Terminators, ee3, sons, etc; 137217 Racah, 175410 Tsayweanshun, 35977 Lexington, 5251 Bradwood, 5378 Ellyett, 82346 Hakos, 22348 Schmeidler, 3202 Graff, 2393 Suzuki, 2995 Taratuta, 4219 Nakamura, 8803 Kolyer, 9211 Neese, 2461 Clavel, 31031 Altiplano, 1274 Delportia, 31627 Ulmera, 213 Lilaea, 18709 Laurawong, 6370 Malpais, 48736 Ehime, 2232 Altaj

58q12 (215.729) \\dg, simeona, elisa, mb, emily, people who have shown me kindness when I wasn't all together. But I eventually betray these people or separate from them; 41049 Van Citters, 24028 Veronicaduys, 22732 Jakpor, 31931 Sipiera, 353189 Iasus, 3220 Murayama, 31510 Saumya, 31977 Devalapurkar, 291923 Kuzmaskryabin, 142752 Boroski, 309706 Avila, 1814 Bach, 290 Bruna, 115051 Safaeinili, 12439 Okasaki, 38976 Taeve, 1139 Atami, 26503 Avicramer, 6953 Davepierce

130q12 (35.729) \\my massive construction projects in data and astro; 4622 Solovjova, 24493 McCommon, 90377 Sedna, 3326 Agafonikov

qc28: mb—my unintended oppression of assistants and collaborators, and probably the reason I need to generate artificial ones

34q12 (275.729) \\me as a roving chart reader, but one who won't respond to communication; 20837 Ramanlal, 16518 Akihikoito, 17459 Andreashofer, 2602 Moore, 8192 Tonucci, 121236 Adrianagutierrez, 34278 Justinxie, 32128 Jayzussman, 17019 Aldo, 15347 Colinstuart, 11229 Brookebowers, 154865 Stefanheutz, 31655 Averyclowes, 10506 Rydberg, 31679 Glenngrimmett

106q12 (95.729) \\they see me as having crazy untenable ideas; 1451 Grano, 10554 Vasterhejde, 22586 Shellyhynes, 5176 Yoichi, 116903 Jeromeapt, 21958 Tripuraneni, 11887 Echemmon, 9781 Jubjubbird, 14071 Gadabird, 8535 Pellesvanslos

70q12 (185.729) \\shanna, b.a.r., simeona, REDACTED's extra networks; 12141 Chushayashi, 118173 Barmen, 592 Bathseba, 13956 Banks, 4735 Gary, 33699 Jessiegan, 3736 Rokoske, 22914 Tsunanmachi, 17079 Lavrovsky, 8451 Gaidai, 189261 Hiroo, 21588 Gianelli, 27336 Mikequinn, 94228 Leesuikwan, 13302 Kezmoh, 3926 Ramirez, 758 Mancunia, 295473 Cochard, 3408 Shalamov, 2712 Keaton, 364264 Martymartina

142q12 (5.729) \\bashing through recordings; 26532 Eduardoboff, 33701 Gotthold, 29585 Johnhale, 10022 Zubov, 9692 Kuperus, 1028 Lydina, 20460 Robwhiteley, 5313 Nunes

qig79: the Universe keeps giving you this to work with…

qc315: my reshuffling preconscious calculation of a big situation's workings

10q11 (335.521) \\how I feel when the perpetrator is finally caught ; 13357 Werkhoven, 31671 Masatoshi, 4847 Amenhotep, 18821 Markhavel, 9884 Pribram, 422 Berolina

82q11 (155.521) \\random internet searches; 6690 Messick, 70714 Rizk, 23757 Jonmunoz, 41488 Sindbad, 21015 Shigenari, 12145 Behaim, 85095 Hekla, 13004 Aldaz, 3592 Nedbal, 6543 Senna, 25259 Lucarnold, 1326 Losaka, 22839 Richlawrence, 173094 Wielicki, 21537 Frechet, 90820 McCann, 9746 Kazukoichikawa, 27556 Williamprem

46q11 (245.521) \\how I respond in the immediate to getting checked by another; VERY NEGATIVE for me, as I essentially freeze up and begin longer term plans to disable what this person can get from me. Need to use alongside someone, not against them. OR use against undesired circumstances generally; 6183 Viscome, 3559 Violaumayer, 1875 Neruda, 149951 Hildakowalski, 12072 Anupamakotha, 5871 Bobbell, 10361 Bunsen, 456731 Uligrozinger, 157020 Fertoszentmiklos, 24024 Lynnejohnson, 5986 Xenophon, 243491 Muhlviertel, 1894 Haffner, 4182 Mount Locke, 52266 Van Flandern, 20367 Erikagibb, 4766 Malin, 286 Iclea, 1589 Fanatica, 19003 Erinfrey

118q11 (65.521) \\me getting checked by another; 2823 van der Laan, 17547 Nestebovelli, 6692 Antoninholy

qc171: pressing forward (especially as a male)

22q11 (305.521) \\the conquistadors. This is something I aspire to; boldly driving forward; 12734 Haruna, 124844 Hirotamasao, 354 Eleonora, 9662 Frankhubbard, 24331 Alyshaowen, 235281 Jackwilliamson, 33621 Sathish, 4767 Sutoku, 4041 Miyamotoyohko, 10147 Mizugatsuka, 5237 Yoshikawa, 51772 Sparker, 25118 Kevlin, 25367 Cicek, 2441 Hibbs, 236111 Wolfgangbuttner, 24981 Shigekimurakami

94q11 (125.521) \\exigencies that come with a new situation i am exploring; those who call for the male; employers of the conquistadors. REDACTED and I meet with cec. b.a.r. and I start sata. This duo comes back with betraying results, though they do hold the empire under their control. 94q11 or 22q11: which side do I want to be on? Either way, the days of persuading people must STOP; 23307 Alexramek, 18800 Terresadodge, 314988 Sireland, 10877 Jiangnan Tianchi, 17437 Stekene, 9032 Tanakami, 12695 Utrecht, 30718 Records, 31442 Stark, 1308 Halleria, 23821 Morganmonroe, 29249 Hiraizumi, 10379 Lake Placid

58q11 (215.521) \\my interaction with REDACTED after a long absence. This mode is not particularly trusted in my chart, no matter who does it; my exercise practice; 11727 Sweet, 5079 Brubeck, 1716 Peter, 16112 Vitaris, 32569 Deming, 5264 Telephus, 72042 Dequeiroz, 180643 Cardoen, 257 Silesia, 429 Lotis, 21825 Zhangyizhong, 4425 Bilk, 2897 Ole Romer, 14727 Suggs, 32302 Mayavarma, 2868 Upupa, 9695 Johnheise, 199194 Calcatreppola, 2097 Galle, 817 Annika, 28686 Tamsenprofit, 64547 Saku, 5706 Finkelstein

130q11 (35.521) \\fellow engineers in aj's chart; my continued growth; 28072 Lindbowerman, 37939 Hasler, 20017 Alixcatherine, 29880 Andytran, 15752 Eluard, 3531 Cruikshank, 5092 Manara, 3268 De Sanctis, 34012 Prashaant, 3439 Lebofsky

qc27: my upbeat attitude in places where I lack real skill

34q11 (275.521) \\talent creating workflows and a certain kind of social technology; 191494 Berndkoch, 24658 Misch, 10482 Dangrieser, 8088 Australia, 9748 van Ostaijen, 7940 Erichmeyer, 6077 Messner, 8274 Soejima, 26945 Sushko, 1203 Nanna, 107379 Johnlogan, 5288 Nankichi, 7309 Shinkawakami, 31643 Natashachugh, 3747 Belinskij

106q11 (95.521) \\they wait in the wings, with trickery in the works; when I make a selection and eliminate others' options…; 1158 Luda, 36037 Linenschmidt, 623 Chimaera, 22594 Stoops, 23274 Wuminchun, 44103 Aldana, 339486 Raimeux, 8527 Katayama, 31504 Jaisonjain, 6799 Citfiftythree, 30095 Tarabode, 13126 Calbuco

70q11 (185.521) \\me continuing my work, making sure everyone knows it has priority; 7721 Andrillat, 12246 Pliska, 22177 Saotome, 3489 Lottie, 17222 Perlmutter, 239307 Kruchynenko, 129312 Drouetdaubigny, 8811 Waltherschmadel, 392 Wilhelmina, 17625 Joseflada, 2096 Vaino, 9902 Kirkpatrick, 10785 Dejaiffe, 5610 Balster

142q11 (5.521) \\spoils from a lost exchange; 10659 Sauerland, 22570 Harleyzhang, 3907 Kilmartin, 79912 Terrell, 79900 Coreglia, 14519 Ural, 30029 Preetikakani, 3014 Huangsushu

qig80: the nature of agitative events around you

qc314: knime promotion around REDACTED; my sustained belief in my own potency

10q10 (335.313) \\my backing out beyond reach; REDACTED; 22756 Manpreetkaur, 31196 Yulong, 12834 Bomben, 1977 Shura

82q10 (155.313) \\shanna, keith; REDACTED; 8959 Oenanthe, 188502 Darrellstrobel, 22254 Vladbarmin, 3988 Huma, 11598 Kubik, 22993 Aferrari, 296950 Robertbauer, 5598 Carlmurray, 6577 Torbenwolff, 5351 Diderot, 5269 Paustovskij, 1247 Memoria, 415 Palatia, 3509 Sanshui, 51599 Brittany, 6552 Higginson, 918 Itha, 4280 Simonenko, 30321 McCleary, 11515 Oshijyo

46q10 (245.313) \\going off on my own after significant hardship with a partner; related to hygiene and maybe the teeth; | *ajani's note:* seems to indicate my response to my own rejected pitch efforts, and I suspect—because there are no major male asteroids here—that this is a natural region associated with the circumference; 16103 Lorsolomon, 10095 Carlloewe, 6771 Foerster, 12426 Racquetball, 10175 Aenona, 211381 Garretzuppiger, 8131 Scanlon, 16714 Arndt, 2531 Cambridge, 378721 Thizy, 15947 Milligan, 11495 Fukunaga, 4650 Mori, 29800 Valeriesarge, 4909 Couteau, 652 Jubilatrix, 9340 Williamholden

118q10 (65.313) \\how I approach my writings. Right next to 315, I also separate myself from others this way, and am more likely to respond to my own skeletons; 18704 Brychristian, 10997 Gahm, 2371 Dimitrov, 4718 Araki, 32294 Zajonc, 8907 Takaji

qc170: nationality (22q10) and the characteristics that prop this up (94q10), spirit of the space's fellows (58q10) and the things each individual is taught to do (130q10)

22q10 (305.313) \\r and my interaction with her; REDACTED; REDACTED; a kind of oppressive mother figure; 2989 Imago, 34002 Movsesian, 30222 Malecki, 10296 Rominadisisto, 1067 Lunaria, 3989 Odin, 12144 Einhart, 2698 Azerbajdzhan, 30473 Ethanbutson

94q10 (125.313) \\pairs of girls or managers who have been my chaperones for participation in more publicly visible arenas; REDACTED and REDACTED under REDACTED; 2686 Linda Susan, 68779 Schoninger, 25424 Gunasekaran, 8752 Flammeus, 28045 Johnwilkins, 8622 Mayimbialik, 3067 Akhmatova, 3064 Zimmer, 7028 Tachikawa, 15402 Suzaku, 6227 Alanrubin, 117439 Rosner

58q10 (215.313) \\yep. Definitely what I learned from mom and any woman who tried to be my mom. But my kapteynia is also here- the closet to an asteroid of the (animal) penis. kapteynia *must contribute* to 58q10's character, and it is true that my conception of penises both 1) helps me calculate complex information. and 2) through deformation (leonteus) change my means of co-creating with another, coping with the lessons i internalized from women like mom. it's not so much that they disrespect men, more like they often don't value men's perspectives. that may sound fair to you in light of millennia of oppression of women by men, until you realize that the only males who are actually around to receive that dismissal are your sons, brothers, and partners. they're the ones devalued by 171624 and 26720. 27584 and 4645 govern this qunit in my chart. in general, thinking about the penis as a topic is a catalyst for

my ongoing access to epiphany and pattern modelling. had lessons from mom been easier, i wouldn't have learned a fraction of what i currently know how to do. in many cases the question was, "why is this acting like that towards me? towards men in general? she's not nearly as strong or put together as she thinks she is. which is why she has to fight everything (11545). oh well, at least the logic chain working through this is interesting. not only is this another qunit that influences how i look, but the parts i can't manifest (female, big areolae) are things that i'm magically drawn to. pretty much all the time; 27584 Barbaravelez, 11545 Hashimoto, 31460 Jongsowfei, 171624 Nicolemartin, 26291 Terristaples, 264045 Heinerklinkrad, 4645 Tentaikojo, 5284 Orsilocus, 6853 Silvanomassaglia, 7254 Kuratani, 133280 Bryleen, 26720 Yangxinyan, 171171 Prior, 3793 Leonteus, 3915 Fukushima, 818 Kapteynia

130q10 (35.313) \\my music playlists in, my reference books out; 1433 Geramtina, 1118 Hanskya, 10245 Inselsberg, 417978 Haslehner, 452307 Manawydan, 11010 Artemieva, 1539 Borrelly

qc26: appears to be THE jackpot winner cycle. Hmm...

34q10 (275.313) \\b.a.r., sg, one supported by what will eventually become an angry mob; 23079 Munguia, 29244 Van Damme, 3879 Machar, 25822 Carolinejune, 220418 Golovyno, 11377 Nye, 9056 Piskunov, 21404 Atluri, 157640 Baumeler, 7131 Longtom, 7349 Ernestmaes, 6259 Maillol, 1344 Caubeta, 9253 Oberth, 69500 Ginobartali

106q10 (95.313) \\chasing perfection, but with continued errors and unbridled enthusiasm; 243109 Hansludwig, 278200 Olegpopov, 11554 Asios, 27426 Brettlawrie, 82 Alkmene, 13240 Thouvay, 3927 Feliciaplatt, 7583 Rosegger, 22378 Gaherty, 89131 Phildevries, 297082 Bygott, 7565 Zipfel

70q10 (185.313) \\me as a celebrated (but controversial or disruptive) figure in a place; 107052 Aquincum, 3507 Vilas, 58579 Ehrenberg, 774 Armor, 33580 Priyankajain, 2571 Geisei, 128562 Murdin, 198634 Burgaymarta, 133250 Rubik, 16207 Montgomery, 80675 Kwentus, 9617 Grahamchapman, 28460 Ariannepapa, 15522 Trueblood, 189018 Guokeda, 25620 Jayaprakash, 4957 Brucemurray, 8221 La Condamine, 17029 Cuillandre, 16459 Barth, 255598 Paullauterbur, 3384 Daliya, 21942 Subramanian, 20405 Barryburke, 70737 Stenflo, 29197 Gleim, 8644 Betulapendula, 1496 Turku, 136818 Selqet, 151349 Stanleycooper

142q10 (5.313) \\phaedra & strada (two basically straight women) as ideal partners - metrobots in general; 236784 Livorno, 20789 Hughgrant, 2666 Gramme, 15599 Richardlarson, 19694 Dunkelman, 2653 Principia, 234 Barbara, 2432 Soomana, 75846 Jandorf, 12670 Passargea

qig81: that which is drawn through your aura

qc313: my self-display in light of the world

10q9 (335.104) \\the emotional aura my mom provided me. Hungry; a very strong pattern; 17098 Ikedamai, 1005 Arago, 897 Lysistrata, 5117 Mokotoyama, 1785 Wurm, 278141 Tatooine, 8302 Kazukin, 10740 Fallersleben, 6442 Salzburg

82q9 (155.104) \\my public fate - gerhardiser, node; nina hartley, certain adult entertainers and producers, more mature bodily visceral actors; 7316 Hajdu, 6508 Rolcik, 5368 Vitagliano, 18121 Konovalenko, 65100 Birtwhistle, 19009 Galenmaly, 207687 Senckenberg, 9093 Sorada, 21369 Gertfinger, 28474 Bustamante, 33633 Strickland, 84928 Oliversacks, 9026 Denevi, -10010 mean Node, 15791 Yoshiewatanabe, 27302 Jeankobis, 40764 Gerhardiser

46q9 (245.104) \\my research as compensatory for this; 6541 Yuan, 5270 Kakabadze, 3357 Tolstikov, 4484 Sif, 32552 Jennithomas, 9611 Anouck, 29660 Jessmacalpine, 28785 Woodjohn, 12446 Juliabryant, 14947 Luigibussolino, 23121 Michaelding, 13478 Fraunhofer, 5255 Johnsophie, 16725 Toudono, 11710 Nataliehale, 74024 Hrabe

118q9 (65.104) \\contours, powering through; 21022 ike; my response to the trouble in the world; 22422 Kenmount Hill, 23277 Benhughes, 23975 Akran, 20793 Goldinaaron, 21022 Ike, 11584 Ferenczi, 87 Sylvia, 171183 Haleakala, 4886 Kojima, 6683 Karachentsov, 342017 Ramonin, 19695 Billnye, 5047 Zanda

qc169: the foreign impression maker

22q9 (305.104) \\what fans of my work want to achieve. Things which happen to me when I (temporarily) disable my own ambitions in order to support someone else's. THIS is how I end up traveling. Possibly for a living. Time with REDACTED. Other exotic happenings.; 27454 Samapaige, 16218 Mintakeyes, 33586 Keeley, 21679 Bettypalermiti, 6239 Minos, 2398 Jilin, 4006 Sandler, 14700 Johnreid, 117435 Severochoa, 103770 Wilfriedlang

94q9 (125.104) \\context against which my most exotic memories are made; 7329 Bettadotto, 2233 Kuznetsov, 13405 Dorisbillings, 6174 Polybius, 1234 Elyna, 4373 Crespo, 7866 Sicoli, 21663 Banat, 24699 Schwekendiek, 7002 Bronshten, 4410 Kamuimintara, 9415 Yujiokimura, 20296 Shayestorm, 21397 Leontovich

58q9 (215.104) \\MY AUDIENCE!! These are the people who will use my work in the larger society; when I am dead tired driving, heavy footed, but still going; the weary but determined, doing the last stretch of things they don't like but have to do; 12714 Alkimos, 7747 Michalowski, 120324 Falusandras, 13272 Ericadavid, 48411 Johnventre, 12172 Niekdekort, 129165 Kevinstout, 5790 Nagasaki, 17258 Whalen, 4045 Lowengrub, 71282 Holuby, 421 Zahringia, 731 Sorga, 22706 Ganguly, 78433 Gertrudolf, 3909 Gladys

130q9 (35.104) \\where my books are positioned in the long term, slow drivers in front of me when I'm tired; 32250 Karthik, 6504 Lehmbruck, 8318 Averroes, 4482 Frerebasile, 23199 Bezdek, 17354 Matrosov, 73046 Davidmann

qc25: my work ethic: lazy. Sata and its authors

34q9 (275.104) \\my story of owing, irresponsibility as sata owner; relaxed work life; 216295 Menorca, 25105 Kimnayeon, 11241 Eckhout, 787 Moskva, 4770 Lane, 1622 Chacornac, 9357 Venezuela, 4691 Toyen, 19436 Marycole, 15501 Pepawlowski, 407 Arachne, 16626 Thumper, 1703 Barry, 33035 Pareschi, 16236 Stebrehmer

106q9 (95.104) \\having hypercharged energy. Standing invisibly behind another; 20230 Blanchard, 10813 Masterby, 23298 Loewenstein, 23549 Epicles, 1070 Tunica, 279723 Wittenberg, 26447 Akrishnan, 2884 Reddish, 4591 Bryantsev

70q9 (185.104) \\my writings motivated by social breakages; 20894 Krumeich, 11781 Alexroberts, 7970 Lichtenberg, 6296 Cleveland, 372 Palma, 25919 Comuniello, 8882 Sakaetamura, 7193 Yamaoka, 36446 Cinodapistoia, 2607 Yakutia, 40994 Tekaridake, 11948 Justinehenin, 6480 Scarlatti, 8262 Carcich, 32381 Bellomo, 12134 Hansfriedeman, 20399 Michaelesser, 20642 Laurajohnson

142q9 (5.104) \\things that preoccupy me; 321 Florentina, 251625 Timconrow, 70401 Davidbishop, 17645 Inarimori, 193158 Haechan

qig82: work to change the world

qc312: with a partner I am almost certain to lose, masterminding our own culture

11q8 (334.896) \\how I am seen and approached by the dogs, and perhaps others in general, when they want my attention and I'm not giving it. Uneasy and hot-blooded; 21642 Kominers, 9232 Miretti, 21391 Rotanner, 2804 Yrjo

83q8 (154.896) \\sam, shanna; more importantly, when I myself project this towards anyone, I am more likely to make them uneasy. Only people like cz and other masochists can really endure this, yielding great consequences for who I am able to stably partner with; 6892 Lana, 11247 Wilburwright, 11774 Jerne, 6155 Yokosugano, 6196 Bernardbowen, 14619 Plotkin, 16174 Parihar, 20994 Atreya, 11956 Tamarakate, 25814 Preesinghal, 95016 Kimjeongho, 13005 Stankonyukhov, 326 Tamara, 9429 Porec, 34308 Roberthall, 2859 Paganini, 12149 Begas, 21664 Konradzuse, 3464 Owensby, 15819 Alisterling, 30 Urania, 23128 Dorminy, 19741 Callahan

47q8 (244.896) \\certain kinds of shallow conversations with REDACTED, likely the reason why it was easier for her to distance herself from me. I still really haven't recovered my impression of her from ...; 6908 Kunimoto, 21530 Despiau, 271 Penthesilea, 49110 Kvetafialova, 241276 Guntramlampert, 212705 Friul, 129186 Joshgrindlay, 2906 Caltech, 20870 Kaningher, 8442 Ostralegus, 15559 Abigailhines, 10079 Meunier, 7360 Moberg, 5072 Hioki, 42522 Chuckberry

119q8 (64.896) \\my retirement from interest in girls. STRONG; 44885 Vodicka, 8744 Cilla, 29700 Salmon, 243002 Lemmy, 7101 Haritina, 21355 Pikovskaya, 4397 Jalopez

qc68: constructing my own path from the small, since 58q8 and my needing to do 131q8 make progress difficult otherwise

23q8 (304.896) \\building and repairing things, constantly in need of the right tools; 32855 Zollitsch, 210035 Jungli, 196640 Mulhacen, 9168 Sarov, 11384 Sartre, 2362 Mark Twain, 29773 Samuelpritt, 34163 Neyveli, 4199 Andreev, 25964 Liudavid

95q8 (124.896) \\that which I construct; 7957 Antonella, 26271 Lindapuster, 3710 Bogoslovskij, 11309 Malus, 5463 Danwelcher, 8326 Paulkling, 203602 Danjoyce, 4944 Kozlovskij, 17925 Dougweinberg, 3083 OAFA, 579 Sidonia, 91422 Giraudon

59q8 (214.896) \\the daughters; 161092 Zsigmond, 8775 Cristata, 5372 Bikki, 798 Ruth, 90525 Karijanberg, 3538 Nelsonia, 27110 Annemaryvonne, 179764 Myriamsarah, 7429 Hoshikawa, 320153 Eglitis, 37588 Lynnecox, 5112 Kusaji, 145768 Petiska, 9300 Johannes

131q8 (34.896) \\pioneering work and first insights into the future; 42981 Jenniskens, 6730 Ikeda, 7955 Ogiwara, 18095 Frankblock, 11123 Aliciaclaire, 17683 Kanagawa, 2288 Karolinum, 23286 Parlakgul, 10027 Perozzi, 19495 Terentyeva

qc24: discomfort with the elephant in the room—an obligation to communicate

35q8 (274.896) \\i am allowed to keep running sata and publishing despite conflicts; 25025 Joshuavo, 6015 Paularego, 1517 Beograd, 28322 Kaeberich, 13787 Nagaishi, 1311 Knopfia, 8588 Avosetta, 2735 Ellen, 4171 Carrasco, 15723 Girraween, 281140 Trier, 2562 Chaliapin, 28305 Wangjiayi, 230648 Zikmund, 4856 Seaborg, 25552 Gaster, 16481 Thames

107q8 (94.896) \\knowing the singleness of my own perspective, I avoid talking to others about it; 350509 Veproknedlozelo, 27865 Ludgerfroebel, 152533 Aggas, 2496 Fernandus, 142 Polana, 1620 Geographos, 227 Philosophia, 4250 Perun, 82926 Jacquey, 12636 Padrielli, 376574 Michalkusiak

71q8 (184.896) \\with the canadians across the jardin des tulleries; 3409 Abramov, 22434 Peredery, 1550 Tito, 25554 Jayaranjan, 14 Irene, 386622 New Zealand, 409 Aspasia, 3144 Brosche, 8304 Ryomichico, 1296 Andree, 22933 Mareverett, 283057 Casteldipiazza, 20080 Maeharatorakichi, 9811 Cavadore, 74625 Tieproject, 13766 Bonham, 10334 Gibbon, 1335 Demoulina, 5009 Sethos

143q8 (4.896) \\various songs or genres about loss including blues, bluegrass, rock, and folk; I use these to project how I'm currently feeling; 48782 Fierz, 24121 Achandran, 8218 Hosty, 983 Gunila

qig83: foreign or neighbor's execution of attempt against a trial

qc311: old skool 70s preferences, music e.g.?

11q7 (334.688) \\stalked by the dogs, sam; 160105 Gobi, 9286 Patricktaylor, 37471 Popocatepetl, 19575 Feeny, -14 East Point, 546 Herodias, 23801 Erikgustafson, 2310 Olshaniya, 6186 Zenon, 15724 Zille

83q7 (154.688) \\my view of basic household dynamics with shanna, or between any two normal parents; 134160 Pluis, 292991 Lyonne, 15577 Gywilliams, 18947 Cindyfulton, 20379 Christijohns, 6663 Tatebayashi, 22707 Jackgrundy, 7307 Takei, 95219 Borgman

47q7 (244.688) \\how I project when demonstrating my exercises, right now only to myself; my naked presentation; niche views| #pelvis | //general naked pics; 12711 Tukmit, 27382 Justinbarber, 14025 Fallada, 21401 Justinkovac, 240364 Kozmutza, 378 Holmia, 2184 Fujian, 19230 Sugazi, 2271 Kiso, 15099 Janestrohm, 3463 Kaokuen, 1477 Bonsdorffia, 5859 Ostozhenka, 6811 Kashcheev, 15851 Chrisfleming, 4170 Semmelweis, 12539 Schlegel

119q7 (64.688) \\me relaying what I'm taught back to the teacher—makes me a good student; 10388 Zhuguangya, 2375 Radek, 243381 Alessio, 19392 Oyamada, 15000 CCD, 12218 Fleischer

qc167: having entered a place, the work I do and the leisure I adopt. The place wins big time

23q7 (304.688) \\work on the house and the home structure; my work in general; 332324 Bobmcdonald, 34231 Isanisingh, 529 Preziosa, 31124 Slavicek, 9655 Yaburanger, 12262 Nishio, 30111 Wendyslijk, 4452 Ullacharles, 184930 Gobbihilda

95q7 (124.688) \\me reading charts for others; the place I enter wins championships (fukuten); 5430 Luu, 5577 Priestley, 26122 Antonysutton, 12229 Paulsson, 12068 Khandrika, 19955 Holly, 1717 Arlon, 35197 Longmire, 140038 Kurushima, 3074 Popov, 21449 Hemmick, 26739 Hemaeberhart, 262972 Petermansfield, 129550 Fukuten, 22102 Karenlamb, 22603 Davidoconnor, 33004 Dianesipiera

59q7 (214.688) \\how do i get answers so easily when i ask? A: your children / the answers you've already documented - when you are in partner mode - respond by autofinishing your sense-making process. this is most effective when you have a partner whom you can put on the back burner or make jealous, as it is a kind of influence; 368704 Roelgathier, 17737 Sigmundjahn, 1460 Haltia, 18626 Michaelcarr, 21187 Setsuo, 1698 Christophe, 7009 Hume, 317917 Jodelle, 6243 Yoder, 49036 Pelion, 6808 Plantin, 528 Rezia, 11886 Kraske, 21571 Naegeli, 2535 Hameenlinna, 8202 Gooley, 5126 Achaemenides, 6274 Taizaburo, 9225 Daiki, 6146 Adamkrafft

131q7 (34.688) \\aunt cynthia; gives me an eye for exactly what you're doing when I see you doing it; seems to be clairvoyant by sight, and probably related to talking trees; 10996 Armandspitz, 28917 Zacollins, 24679 Van Rensbergen, 3148 Grechko, 30533 Saeidzoonemat, 14230 Mariahines, 255 Oppavia, 3181 Ahnert, 75555 Wonaszek, 37782 Jacquespiccard

qc23: I love what I can measure, but will almost certainly need to use automation for this

35q7 (274.688) \\let's travel the unknown together!; 19517 Robertocarlos, 26559 Chengcheng, 1080 Orchis, 20608 Fredmerlin, 15025 Uwontario, 78252 Priscio, 24988 Alainmilsztajn, 7660 Alexanderwilson, 43790 Ferdinandbraun, 174362 Bethwillman

107q7 (94.688) \\my great experiences during travel; 33197 Charlallen, 5001 EMP, 10724 Carolraymond, 162978 Helenhart, 21511 Chiardola, 21516 Mariagodinez, 184280 Yperion, 12257 Lassine, 22952 Hommasachi, 178151 Kulangsu

71q7 (184.688) \\my time with vb; REDACTED's declaration; 32038 Kwiecinski, 12162 Bilderdijk, 16212 Theberge, 11542 Solikamsk, 9897 Malerba, 24665 Tolerantia, 7797 Morita, 11777 Hargrave, 1026 Ingrid, 9013 Sansaturio, 26504 Brandonli, 9863 Reichardt, 26194 Chasolivier, 161349 Mecsek, 2629 Rudra, 19189 Stradivari

143q7 (4.688) \\basically miranda... if I were ever a part of such a group; 8081 Leopardi, 25155 van Belle, 6473 Winkler, 3839 Bogaevskij, 23490 Monikohl, 5057 Weeks

qig84: working under scrunity from afar

qc310: my infamous escapes and the story that is ultimately told of me based on my partnerships

11q6 (334.479) \\making beyond normal progress in exercise, but this region is something I absolutely shouldn't let happen. Maybe even reverse; tis your kind of music. Let's live well. The end of a potentially beautiful partnership; 16750 Marisandoz, 16413 Abulghazi, 28711 Emmaburnett, 6380 Gardel, 30257 Leejanel, 9962 Pfau, 9991 Anezka

83q6 (154.479) \\my cats - and basically sam; 20211 Joycegates, 121315 Mikelentz, 6599 Tsuko, 11333 Forman, 674 Rachele, 10382 Hadamard, 3518 Florena, 12143 Harwit, 133745 Danieldrinnon, 3577 Putilin, 6086 Vrchlicky, 21513 Bethcochran, 120352 Gordonwong

47q6 (244.479) \\my research in general resists interference and is something I continually build upon; 28351 Andrewfeldman, 21411 Abifraeman, 7008 Pavlov, 296 Phaetusa, 2051 Chang, 3273 Drukar, 1000 Piazzia, 1901 Moravia, 78756 Sloan, 85308 Atsushimori, 268057 Michaelkaschke, 957 Camelia, 11782 Nikolajivanov, 1812 Gilgamesh, 25625 Verdenet, 72037 Castelldefels, 13688 Oklahoma, 12539 Chaikin

119q6 (64.479) \\the events that trigger my questions. When these asteroid patterns happen, I am inclined to ask why and do my research against them; 1014 Semphyra, 30206 Jasonfricker, 158899 Malloryvale, 126901 Craigstevens, 5943 Lovi, 1972 Yi Xing

qc166: my personal work philosophy and the effect it leaves on others

23q6 (304.479) \\my trusty references or encyclopedias, lookup tables which I rely on; 281820 Monnaves, 25142 Hopf, 17954 Hopkins, 15907 Robot, 149865 Michelhernandez, 85878 Guzik, 11706 Rijeka, 3817 Lencarter, 47077 Yuji, 100029 Varnhagen, 264 Libussa, 7674 Kasuga, 6815 Mutchler, 197525 Versteeg, 8833 Acer, 15403 Merignac

95q6 (124.479) \\REDACTED training, general workshops; 31896 Gaydarov, 21464 Chinaroonchai, 6166 Univsima, 31911 Niklasfauth, 17606 Wumengchao, 2257 Kaarina, 10013 Stenholm, 17357 Lucataliano, 365739 Peterbecker, 16260 Sputnik, 12512 Split, 514 Armida, 4267 Basner, 3478 Fanale

59q6 (214.479) \\3 REDACTED; Seems to be a boss who is a founder of some kind; 2161 Grissom, 12603 Tanchunghee, 1440 Rostia, 20785 Mitalithakor, 40775 Kalafina, 5912 Oyatoshiyuki, 32213 Joshuachoe, 6287 Lenham, 3405 Daiwensai, 1613 Smiley, 3087 Beatrice Tinsley, 29645 Kutsenok, 2861 Lambrecht, 9507 Gottfried, 3755 Lecointe, 10796 Sollerman, 1106 Cydonia, 43224 Tonypensa, 5411 Liia, 32549 Taricco, 33564 Miriamshira, 25899 Namratanand, 21254 Jonan, 697 Galilea, 6841 Gottfriedkirch, 20357 Shireendhir

131q6 (34.479) \\2 REDACTED - mastery of their market. Great for running a business; 16069 Marshafolger, 71885 Denning, 22341 Francispoulenc, 7553 Buie, 1995 Hajek

qc22: me jumping in sl's shit after ..., but also our strong alliance

35q6 (274.479) \\what I believe to be the highest couple goal for myself; 175238 Nguyenhien, 2668 Tataria, 2352 Kurchatov, 15510 Phoeberounds, 6359 Dubinin, 3866 Langley, 4600 Meadows, 136432 Allenlunsford, 29705 Cialucy, 6368 Richardmenendez, 9854 Karlheinz, 12694 Schleiermacher

107q6 (94.479) \\REDACTED, or someone like her; 16952 Peteschultz, 52270 Noamchomsky, 1281 Jeanne, 19598 Luttrell, 207723 Jiansanjiang, 9924 Corrigan, 19718 Albertjarvis, 22958 Rohatgi, 134028 Mikefitzgibbon, 21671 Warrener

71q6 (184.479) \\when the dogs are uncomfortable; my increasing hobby interest in saving humans as data by collecting morally questionable materials; 2811 Stremchovi, 9825 Oetken, 121479 Hendershot, 21104 Sveshnikov, 3922 Heather, 4101 Ruikou

143q6 (4.479) \\my generally unsympatetic views towards fixing others' mistakes; 12934 Bisque, 100046 Worms, 7271 Doroguntsov, 11040 Wundt, 22505 Lewit

qig85: instilling into or through your nichemates

qc309: remembrance against the desired trio

11q5 (334.271) \\my process of editing my near-finished work—ramps up the stress; very careful regarding the presentation of my work—eases this region; 18976 Kunilraval, 11713 Stubbs, 29674 Rausal, 85215 Hohenzollern, 429084 Dietrichrex, 1993 Guacolda, 10763 Hlawka, 11174 Carandrews

83q5 (154.271) \\older and more accomplished, this describes me more as I get older; the two women who tell a story apart from me. THIS is my pair; 20084 Buckmaster, 16247 Esner, 11014 Svatopluk, 13368 Wlodekofman, 22550 Jonsellon, 23110 Ericberne, 18627 Rogerbonnet, 11946 Bayle, 115950 Kocherpeter, 10976 Wubbena, 11824 Alpaidze, 72432 Kimrobinson, 973 Aralia, 8978 Barbatus, 213255 Kimiyayui, 4459 Nusamaibashi, 10016 Yugan, 6912 Grimm, 401 Ottilia, 63156 Yicheon

47q5 (244.271) \\REDACTED image; 439 Ohio, 15282 Franzmarc, 6281 Strnad, 7241 Kuroda, 215886 Barryarnold, 15111 Winters, 1700 Zvezdara, 120353 Katrinajackson,

2559 Svoboda, 471926 Jormungandr, 5337 Aoki, 22928 Templehe, 7011 Worley, 1963 Bezovec, 18954 Sarahbounds, 28248 Barthelemy, 30064 Kaitlynshin, 3962 Valyaev, 8116 Jeanperrin, 4557 Mika, 152750 Brloh, 4940 Polenov, 3582 Cyrano, 379155 Volkerheinrich

119q5 (64.271) \\the drive my close others are required to have; 12376 Cochabamba, 20156 Herbwindolf, 8633 Keisukenagao, 43957 Invernizzi, 149113 Stewartbushman, 13211 Stucky, 42697 Lucapaolini, 8976 Leucura, 9969 Braille, 22589 Minor, 6277 Siok

qc165: my drive towards great work, attracting the big girl in the process

23q5 (304.271) \\my need to leave an indelible legacy like ramses. My books; 158222 Manicolas, 7908 Zwingli, 31680 Josephuitt, 5933 Kemurdzhian, 167341 Borzsony, 10825 Augusthermann, 14346 Zhilyaev

95q5 (124.271) \\2 REDACTED; 25714 Aprillee, 30007 Johnclarke, 130071 Claudebrunet, 7545 Smaklosa, 161715 Wenchuan, 7454 Kevinrighter, 18634 Champigneulles, 12602 Tammytam, 8433 Brachyrhynchus, 5323 Fogh

59q5 (214.271) \\the big girl makes her move; correspondence with sms and slp; 189948 Richswanson, 337166 Ivanartioukhov, 25415 Jocelyn, 52316 Daveslater, 13123 Tyson, 1748 Mauderli, 4889 Praetorius, 31770 Melivanhouten, 7805 Moons, 6601 Schmeer, 22644 Matejbel, 24198 Xiaomengzeng, 28169 Cathconte, 128 Nemesis, 345842 Alexparker

131q5 (34.271) \\REDACTED turns fundamentalist, REDACTED turns to hate. May indicate the attitude I'll need to have in a self-tape; I can't stand advice from others unless I explicitly asked for it; 2803 Vilho, 175588 Kathrynsmith, 14062 Cremaschini, 10738 Marcoaldo, 6556 Arcimboldo, 8770 Totanus, 631 Philippina, 1548 Palomaa, 11720 Horodyskyj, 18458 Caesar, 30204 Stevedoherty

qc21: not terribly proud of the chaos I've brought, knowing it was below code

35q5 (274.271) \\REDACTED's bootleg progress, despite being inept. She at least collaborates passionately; 15846 Billfyfe, 3097 Tacitus, 51569 Garywessen, 120569 Huangrunqian, 1001 Gaussia, 13286 Adamchauvin, 10863 Oye, 16852 Nuredduna, 39864 Poggiali, 134134 Kristoferdrozd, 55383 Cheungkwokwing

107q5 (94.271) \\my attitude towards self-progression; 9044 Kaoru, 2068 Dangreen, 3010 Ushakov, 33537 Doungnga, 3800 Karayusuf, 3370 Kohsai, 21402 Shanhuang, 21743 Michaelsegal

71q5 (184.271) \\the dynamic I was limited to having with bs; 245417 Rostand, 678 Fredegundis, 3080 Moisseiev, 2951 Perepadin, 2822 Sacajawea, 4206 Verulamium, 11974 Yasuhidefujita, 6954 Potemkin, 18659 Megangross, 221769 Cima Rest, 156751 Chelseaferrell, 58671 Diplodocus, 27445 Lynnlane, 19442 Brianrice, 1857 Parchomenko, 2887 Krinov, 25516 Davidknight, 34192 Sappington, 9033 Kawane, 9479 Madresplazamayo, 155142 Tenagra, 152233 Van Till, 25373 Gorsch, 100417 Philipglass

143q5 (4.271) \\my handling of administration and the publication process; 8593 Angustirostris, 24204 Trinkle, 30417 Staudt, 299756 Kerryaileen, 24939 Chiminello

qig86: persisting despite mistakes or miscalculations

qc308: YOU: how I interact with you, what you become

11q4 (334.063) \\what I worship as a motivator to economic power, sim city. My reason for building; 13109 Berzelius, 12259 Szukalski, 21748 Srinivasan, 5377 Komori, 15921 Kintaikyo, 22190 Stellakwee, 23893 Lauman, 18707 Annchi

83q4 (154.063) \\STRONG. one of my central / critical qunits, among the strongest in my chart. How I pull data instantly in answer to almost anything, including questions about myself. Hiuchigata-Arnica-Bruges; 5595 Roth, 4445 Jimstratton, 26334 Melimcdowell, 24751 Kroemer, 9472 Bruges, 8419 Terumikazumi, 27596 Maldives, 4778 Fuss, 24214 Jonchristo, 34194 Serenajing, 26533 Aldering, 6883 Hiuchigatake, 1100 Arnica

47q4 (244.063) \\signing on with REDACTED; 19992 Schonbein, 28201 Lifubin, 28563 Dantzler, 13724 Schwehm, 10300 Tanakadate, 730 Athanasia, 14068 Hauserova, 2505 Hebei, 22640 Shalilabaena, 3022 Dobermann, 6682 Makarij, 2643 Bernhard, 4651 Wongkwancheng, 28878 Segner, 17262 Winokur, 63528 Kocherhans, 6176 Horrigan, 10666 Feldberg

119q4 (64.063) \\my inability to live up to the professional promises I made; 24066 Eriksorensen, 8710 Hawley, 3077 Henderson, 185020 Pratte, 20962 Michizane, 216897 Golubev, 28074 Matgallagher, 8925 Boattini, 52422 LPL

qc164: my arrival in a new place and struggling to gain an audience there

23q4 (304.063) \\a thoughtful contributor to the group discussion; longstanding places I've worked and lived; 171448 Guchaohao, 27338 Malaraghavan, 16424 Davaine, 265594 Keletiagnes, 357 Ninina, 21461 Alexchernyak, 21991 Zane, 4436 Ortizmoreno, 26740 Camacho, 4906 Seneferu

95q4 (124.063) \\me and mom hanging out in chang'l last year. That was fuckin' cool; new to the city; 7450 Shilling, 59425 Xuyangsheng, 3873 Roddy, 175583 Pingtung,

16222 Donnanderson, 9073 Yoshinori, 243440 Colonia, 15389 Geflorsch, 19421 Zachulett, 20835 Eliseadcock, 7470 Jabberwock, 3857 Cellino, 30248 Kimstinson, 22183 Canonlau

59q4 (214.063) \\my jadedness post REDACTED, but still determined not to be stopped; those deaf to a visitor's pleas; 17073 Alexblank, 65583 Theoklymenos, 33345 Nataliedessay, 3467 Bernheim, 4225 Hobart, 4669 Hoder, 77441 Jouve, 3062 Wren, 243637 Frosinone, 9261 Peggythomson, 28105 Santallo, 6783 Gulyaev, 123647 Tomasko, 691 Lehigh, 9621 Michaelpalin, 13320 Jessicamiles, 975 Perseverantia, 2430 Bruce Helin

131q4 (34.063) \\what happens when I solicit or apply for consideration; 17955 Sedransk, 11132 Horne, 10056 Johnschroer, 661 Cloelia

qc20: high-mannered gatherings

35q4 (274.063) \\how our family photos began; 28813 Jeffreykurtz, 2307 Garuda, 2340 Hathor, 3626 Ohsaki, 90703 Indulgentia, 10297 Lynnejones, 4037 Ikeya, 26232 Antink, 698 Ernestina, 1483 Hakoila, 2900 Lubos Perek, 6922 Yasushi, 165659 Michaelhicks, 33392 Blakehord, 27709 Orenburg, 25601 Francopacini

107q4 (94.063) \\how I often attempt to resolve undesirable paths; 1567 Alikoski, 1871 Astyanax, 4754 Panthoos, 8627 Kunalnayyar, 9284 Juansanchez, 4056 Timwarner, 15036 Giovannianselmi, 7671 Albis, 55701 Ukalegon, 11481 Znannya, 9196 Sukagawa

71q4 (184.063) \\REDACTED's dark reaction whenever I convey wins in life in general—her instant comparison with …; 8722 Schirra, 18 Melpomene, 6620 Peregrina, 5034 Joeharrington, 192155 Hargittai, 3874 Stuart, 5403 Takachiho, 38018 Louisneefs, 1864 Daedalus, 759 Vinifera, 10015 Valenlebedev, 127870 Vigo, 26541 Garyross

143q4 (4.063) \\DON'T PRESENT YOUR ARTWORK BEFORE ANYONE OR SCRUTINIZE THEIR MANNERS. DON'T DISPLAY A PENCHANT FOR THE SADISTIC. Keep that to yourself.; 6135 Billowen, 13880 Wayneclark, 13231 Blondelet, 11129 Hayachine, 20534 Bozeman

qig87: across the ambient noise

qc307: my colorful relationships and exchanges

11q3 (333.854) \\my spiritual and social identity: who I really think I am, objectively—the person on the other end seems to align with me greatly; my ghostly relationships—always married to another; 14631 Benbryan, 15497 Lucca, 8382 Mann, 150520 Dong, 4467 Kaidanovskij, 43908 Hiraku, 14963 Toshikazu, 9235 Shimanamikaido, 26394 Kandola, 2402 Satpaev, 133773 Lindsaykeller, 25720 Mallidi

83q3 (153.854) \\me over a call; 12132 Wimfroger, 23989 Farpoint, 315046 Gianniferrari, 318547 Fidrich, 10024 Marthahazen, 11697 Estrella, 75829 Alyea, 207666 Habibula, 10017 Jaotsungi, 23281 Vijayjain, 2217 Eltigen, 90396 Franklopez, 132719 Lambey, 21545 Koirala, 6102 Visby, 29483 Boeker, 3726 Johnadams, 25594 Kessler, 73687 Thomas Aquinas, 7636 Comba, 16199 Rozenblyum, 34208 Danielzhang

47q3 (243.854) \\cheeko and sevrena; 14696 Lindawilliams, 8054 Brentano, 131186 Pauluckas, 10000 Myriostos, 1447 Utra, 5892 Milesdavis, 32275 Limichael, 4437 Yaroshenko, 9162 Kwiila, 8386 Vanvinckenroye, 189035 Michaelsummers, 9207 Petersmith, 7054 Brehm, 10141 Gotenba, 12840 Paolaferrari

119q3 (63.854) \\travel as a means of moving on; 7554 Johnspencer, 24189 Lewasserman, 8999 Tashadunn, 348 May, 174364 Zakamska, 21665 Frege, 21483 Abdulrasool, 12111 Ulm

qc163: my responsibilities as an oldest brother

23q3 (303.854) \\end of the dora metrics push, globus, publishing; 179595 Belkovich, 15671 Suzannedebarbat, 17279 Jeniferevans, 26686 Ellenprice, 31576 Nandigala, 25783 Brandontyler, 5466 Makibi, 13904 Univinnitsa

95q3 (123.854) \\my time with klein, her w/ REDACTED; winding down after a project has been taken away; 6870 Pauldavies, 18287 Verkin, 121756 Sotomejias, 17039 Yeuseyenka, 21608 Gloyna, 19593 Justinkoh, 14317 Antonov, 3869 Norton, 3358 Anikushin, 1617 Alschmitt

59q3 (213.854) \\at the pearl with klein, at the gathering with vb; self-gamification, soundtracking; 11856 Nicolabonev, 9657 Ucka, 113951 Artdavidsen, 1102 Pepita, 216462 Polyphontes, 1555 Dejan, 11929 Uchino, 13721 Kevinwelsh, 10123 Fideoja, 4510 Shawna, 4449 Sobinov, 14469 Komatsuataka, 30406 Middleman, 950 Ahrensa, 267017 Yangzhifa, 26238 Elduval, 9812 Danco, 31920 Annamcevoy, 11249 Etna, 24484 Chester, 26548 Joykutty

131q3 (33.854) \\the new age market itself; energies which match my current activity and are conducive to a convincing impression upon witnesses; 15228 Ronmiller, 6474 Choate

qc19: the nature of the work I put in, intellectually and physically past the fatigue level (when I start making mistakes)

35q3 (273.854) \\situations where I get to be a quality thinker opposite a polarity-evolving role; 3905 Doppler, 5743 Kato, 6462 Myougi, 90713 Chajnantor, 18805 Kellyday, 109330 Clemente, 230765 Alfbester, 6366 Rainerwieler, 8946 Yoshimitsu, 19082 Vikchernov, 9189 Holderlin, 25131 Katiemelua, 276781 Montchaibeux, 10323 Frazer, 3622 Ilinsky, 226672 Kucinskas, 78383 Philmassey

107q3 (93.854) \\for me, accurate; 32726 Chromios, 17859 Galinaryabova, 591 Irmgard, 22777 McAliley, 961 Gunnie, 12647 Pauluspotter, 21290 Vydra, 9099 Kenjitanabe, 3039 Yangel, 15224 Penttila

71q3 (183.854) \\gangsta attitude in inventing my own way; 7682 Miura, 171465 Evamaria, 12031 Kobaton, 2278 Gotz, 2926 Caldeira, 13239 Kana, 24119 Katherinrose, 35346 Ivanoferri, 13163 Koyamachuya, 21087 Petsimpallas, 3138 Ciney, 327943 Xavierbarcons, 3123 Dunham, 84096 Reginaldglenice, 71783 Izeryna, 25034 Lesliemarie, 7736 Nizhnij Novgorod, 115 Thyra, 1606 Jekhovsky, 8452 Clay, 303 Josephina

143q3 (3.854) \\me as a zealous teacher up front; 3321 Dasha, 4008 Corbin, 14941 Tomswift

qig88: warring or new-reality-generating words

qc306: rescuing sata or my own reputation from what could have been a negative fate

11q2 (333.646) \\sk, me, the will to dominate; 1905 Ambartsumian, 7235 Hitsuzan, 27434 Anirudhjain, 21357 Davidying, 129201 Brandenallen, 30828 Bethe, 7202 Kigoshi, 616 Elly

83q2 (153.646) \\the dogs, the sons, me bw and gn—especially the sons; christmas in the silent forest; 246164 Zdvyzhensk, 128614 Juliabest, 19953 Takeo, 2883 Barabashov, 211473 Herin, 24492 Nathanmonroe, 25492 Firnberg, 10563 Izhdubar, 12440 Koshigayaboshi, 970 Primula, 2986 Mrinalini, 1249 Rutherfordia, 20812 Shannonbabb

47q2 (243.646) \\axb; 6921 Janejacobs, 520 Franziska, 124143 Joseluiscorral, 30188 Hafsasaeed, 23728 Jasonmorrow, 1284 Latvia, 8381 Hauptmann, 14426 Katotsuyoshi, 134019 Nathanmogk, 78123 Dimare, 21016 Miyazawaseiroku, 13690 Lesleymartin, 13792 Kuscynskyj, 13942 Shiratakihime

119q2 (63.646) \\a fixer personality; 28309 Ericfein, 20625 Noto, 47086 Shinseiko, 1648 Shajna

qc162: my private accounts, especially of seconding status

23q2 (303.646) \\a visiting contractor or consultant? In the background to ee4; I come to be skeptical of relationships; 25824 Viviantsang, 2628 Kopal, 1441 Bolyai, 45737 Benita, 8554 Gabreta, 25483 Trusheim, 12164 Lowellgreen, 286842 Joris, 30509 Yukitrippel, 34175 Joshuadong, 30065 Asrinivasan, 6608 Davidecrespi, 20309 Batalden, 13605 Nakamuraminoru, 8291 Bingham, 15109 Wilber, 11419 Donjohnson

95q2 (123.646) \\the joint meeting with vb; tuning out when I feel seconded; 6220 Stepanmakarov, 3703 Volkonskaya, 23014 Walstein, 26314 Skvorecky, 3027 Shavarsh, 212373 Pietrocascella, 3786 Yamada, 3475 Fichte, 3777 McCauley, 16779 Mittelman, 34288 Bevindaglen, 10795 Babben, 2772 Dugan, 2817 Perec, 8428 Okiko

59q2 (213.646) \\jj, asz? being trans?; my recordings, opinions about seconding; 27977 Distratis, 58096 Oineus, 1055 Tynka, 10124 Hemse, 202614 Kayleigh, 23355 Elephenor, 164585 Oenomaos, 43597 Changshaopo, 316741 Janefletcher, 6139 Naomi, 3981 Stodola, 10069 Fontenelle, 1354 Botha, 3648 Raffinetti, 3063 Makhaon, 6641 Bobross, 175566 Papplaci, 21542 Kennajeannet, 71000 Hughdowns, 948 Jucunda, 19981 Bialystock, 12568 Kuffner, 16946 Farnham

131q2 (33.646) \\aj moving away; 2046 Leningrad, 17921 Aldeobaldia, 5976 Kalatajean, 8248 Gurzuf, 14349 Nikitamikhalkov, 28683 Victorostrik, 22666 Josephchurch

qc18: coaching others out of a corner

35q2 (273.646) \\my understanding of papa (leo). Later, I am like this; 182044 Ryschkewitsch, 3424 Nusl, 9015 Coe, 10878 Moriyama, 33626 Jasonsmith, 114239 Bermarmi, 50413 Petrginz, 130319 Danielpelham, 2311 El Leoncito, 14974 Pocatky, 239611 Likwohting, 30881 Robertstevenson, 121480 Dolanhighsmith, 6140 Kubokawa, 5161 Wightman

107q2 (93.646) \\as a founder; 24 Themis, 18932 Robinhood, 19185 Guarneri, 11118 Modra, 10947 Kaiserstuhl, 7551 Edstolper, 383067 Stoofke, 29737 Norihiro, 3607 Naniwa, 3685 Derdenye, 152299 Vanautgaerden

71q2 (183.646) \\talking someone down from their anxiety; 3955 Bruckner, 259 Aletheia, 13710 Shridhar, 9915 Potanin, 29401 Asterix, 28894 Ryanchung, 3053 Dresden, 51430 Ireneclaire, 3165 Mikawa, 29210 Robertbrown, 25022 Hemalibatra, 3694 Sharon, 15899 Silvain, 321024 Gijon, 6715 Sheldonmarks, 5094 Seryozha

143q2 (3.646) \\if it's not two it is unlikely that I will move very far; 135268 Haignere, 5927 Krogh, 21455 Mcfarland, 10450 Girard, 5705 Ericsterken, 18412 Kruszelnicki

qig89: charged up stir up, less thought paid to other's needs

qc305: the trio. Requires that I learn how to NOT be the logician, and travel instead

11q1 (333.438) \\ee trio knows its own power; 12447 Yatescup, 11667 Testa, 9626 Stanley, 26277 Ianrees, 2885 Palva, 30142 Debfrazier, 32226 Vikulgupta

83q1 (153.438) \\my solo book-writing process; 184508 Courroux, 16796 Shinji, 23315 Navinbrian, 9087 Neff, 8759 Porzana, 8332 Ivantsvetaev, 159215 Apan, 706 Hirundo, 12753 Povenmire, 1245 Calvinia, 113203 Szabo, 10162 Issunboushi, 15203 Grishanin

47q1 (243.438) \\publishing as the vehicle of learning; 59828 Ossikar, 40248 Yukikajiura, 121654 Michaelpryzby, 10136 Gauguin, 7343 Ockeghem, 3289 Mitani, 34042 Espeseth, 27410 Grimmett, 20873 Evanfrank, 7925 Shelus, 2470 Agematsu, 74818 Iten, 13923 Peterhof, 75 Eurydike, 1039 Sonneberga, 17546 Osadakentaro, 18020 Amend, 6235 Burney, 2892 Filipenko, 5124 Muraoka, 21463 Nickerson, 267 Tirza

119q1 (63.438) \\generating hostility through successful magic; 1480 Aunus, 20375 Sherrigerten, 4800 Veveri, 660 Crescentia, 31883 Susanstern, 186832 Mosser, 146442 Dwaynebrown, 79889 Maloka, 8194 Satake, 56 Melete, 16368 Citta di Alba

qc161: s12 and the experiences which motivated it and follow it

23q1 (303.438) \\wanting to (and sometimes attempting to) share what i really feel sexually or creatively; s12; 4187 Shulnazaria, 12317 Madicampbell, 23680 Kerryking, 1359 Prieska, 1682 Karel, 17712 Fatherwilliam, 12845 Crick, 4155 Watanabe, 20194 Ilarialocantore, 10753 van de Velde, 31474 Advaithanand, 7004 Markthiemens, 10579 Diluca, 1587 Kahrstedt, 7201 Kuritariku, 14487 Sakaisakae

95q1 (123.438) \\some woman who writes, doesn't feel like I've met the archetypal one yet. Maybe jhall; Earth Engels-Hall; 25414 Cherkassky, 13396 Midavaine, 28732 Rheakamat, 3304 Pearce, 17698 Racheldavis, 12220 Semenchur, 7137 Ageo, 4991 Hansuess, 172932 Bachleitner, 1450 Raimonda, 69469 Krumbenowe

59q1 (213.438) \\trying out for and engaging REDACTED, and ...?; 17241 Wooden, 6318 Cronkite, 24434 Josephhoscheidt, 28183 Naidu, 8525 Nielsabel, 23383 Schedios, 10364 Tainai, 3938 Chapront, 43193 Secinaro, 622 Esther, 9539 Prishvin, 2137 Priscilla, 66846 Franklederer, 128054 Eranyavneh, 144096 Wiesendangen, 19497 Pineda, 23638 Nagano, 24070 Toniwest, 365761 Popovici, 33801 Emilyshi

131q1 (33.438) \\pride in setting up my own universalized, unique culture; 7851 Azumino, 6750 Katgert, 5232 Jordaens, 9380 Macon, 29753 Silvo, 33528 Jinzeman

qc17: this qcross shows the line between friend-like communications and relationships that don't qualify for this

35q1 (273.438) \\the public recorded argument with sb, simeona; 25944 Charlesross, 26891 Johnbutler, 33397 Prathiknaidu, 55082 Xlendi, 8117 Yuanlongping, 35233 Krcin, 27480 Heablonsky, 316084 Mykolapokropyvny, 5954 Epikouros, 32277 Helenliu, 11785 Migaic

107q1 (93.438) \\"but you were expected to be the man!" ; 3194 Dorsey, 4895 Embla, 7126 Cureau, 85185 Lederman, 11083 Caracas, 1124 Stroobantia, 10276 Matney, 16439 Yamehoshinokawa, 4890 Shikanosima, 3472 Upgren, 8997 Davidblewett

71q1 (183.438) \\keith, sanza, emily; ; 1706 Dieckvoss, 173 Ino, 1807 Slovakia, 12479 Ohshimaosamu, 12690 Kochimiraikagaku, 121237 Zachdolch, 21705 Subinmin, 609 Fulvia, 5694 Berenyi, 1348 Michel, 23775 Okudaira, 7381 Mamontov, 19603 Monier, 19002 Tongkexue, 17734 Boole, 58896 Schlosser, 9678 van der Meer, 19467 Amandanagy, 2529 Rockwell Kent, 222032 Lupton, 5558 Johnnapier, 621 Werdandi, 5340 Burton, 4264 Karljosephine, 4021 Dancey, 11656 Lipno, 11788 Nauchnyj

143q1 (3.438) \\disappearing; 88705 Potato, 8460 Imainamahoe, 8677 Charlier, 8156 Tsukada, 30125 Mikekiser

qig90: your sustained impression and the compensation you receive to keep projecting it

qc304: my long-term impression

11q12 (333.229) \\not really looking for partners, just entertaining and being charming in 209 for example; women who are legit beautiful; me in a contemplative daze, supplying new inquiry paths; hanging out with kit, thinking about various things; 5222 Ioffe, 6349 Acapulco, 1970 Sumeria, 30840 Jackalice, 8338 Ralhan, 183 Istria, 114094 Irvpatterson, 22833 Scottyu, 3474 Linsley, 4222 Nancita, 30310 Alexanderlin

83q12 (153.229) \\the relational reputation I ultimately want. Coming to someone's aid as a savior; my going catatonic in the face of myself being taken from by linsley in the opposition; 8524 Paoloruffini, 24277 Schoch, 23729 Kemeisha, 25801 Oliviaschwob, 26200 Van Doren, 31597 Allisonmarie, 10882 Shinonaga, 31588 Harrypaul, 5988 Gorodnitskij, 31139 Garnavich, 1778 Alfven, 8812 Kravtsov, 17959 Camierickson

47q12 (243.229) \\circ; ai product art; 3017 Petrovic, 25994 Lynnelleye, 39991 Iochroma, 26717 Jasonye, 11066 Sigurd, 2339 Anacreon, 6719 Gallaj, 34021 Suhanijain, 14593 Everett, 459 Signe, 25906 Morrell, 2593 Buryatia, 10543 Klee, 37022 Robertovittori, 17930 Kennethott, 1969 Alain, 24997 Petergabriel, 251595 Rudolfbottger, 4500 Pascal, 85388 Sakazukiyama, 17195 Jimrichardson

119q12 (63.229) \\how I spread my work. Or do my work in the first place. Blocks the two girls; 129773 Catmerrill, 95939 Thagnesland, 7226 Kryl, 6937 Valadon, 8068 Vishnureddy, 56422 Mnajdra, 197864 Florentpagny, 3954 Mendelssohn, 33613 Pendharkar, 786 Bredichina

qc160: hollywood-type fame and the lifestyle it affords

23q12 (303.229) \\the body of my writings and workflows; macho duck; 2366 Aaryn, 2776 Baikal, 9637 Perryrose, 10170 Petrjakes, 7650 Kaname, 223950 Mississauga, 224206 Pietchisson, 117715 Carlkirby, 20852 Allilandstrom, 15728 Karlmay, 52649 Chrismith, 53256 Sinitiere, 58217 Peterhebel, 10046 Creighton

95q12 (123.229) \\the military contract structure; 31338 Lipperhey, 256547 Davidesmith, 12746 Yumeginga, 5308 Hutchison, 12541 Makarska, 1377 Roberbauxa, 138 Tolosa, 22992 Susansmith, 6364 Casarini, 23151 Georgehotz, 12028 Annekinney, 344000 Astropolis

59q12 (213.229) \\my becoming a responsible dog dad. When this is active, it is harder for me to steadily engage ... or win the lottery. Parenting a group or household; 19437 Jennyblank, 9614 Cuvier, 4062 Schiaparelli, 43511 Cima Ekar, 12598 Sierra, 3709 Polypoites, 14411 Clerambault, 5283 Pyrrhus, 12406 Zvikov, 21583 Caropietsch, 39428 Emilybronte, 28765 Katherinewu, 2429 Schurer, 214911 Viehboeck, 21375 Fanshawe, 99503 Leewonchul, 3594 Scotti, 154004 Haolei, 14412 Wolflojewski

131q12 (33.229) \\travel with strangers, REDACTED & REDACTED; my early relationship with my brothers, given that I am a kind of parent to them; these are almost certainly people who view my expression of male character; REDACTED and REDACTED, REDACTED and REDACTED —**provided I exercise my 23q12s in front of them** and **provided that they see themselves as a kind of parenting duo to something**, shows that the two girls is not about love, but about validation of my own creative work and masculinity; 129102 Charliecamarotte, 10965 van Leverink, 18814 Ivanovsky, 18159 Andrewcook, 7109 Heine

qc16: This qcross describes the natural box into which my physical body is put by others; this is where my build is welcome: into places that allow intruders. Where my presence is welcome, people welcome squirrels in their attic, novelties—often in pairs or trios/ there is a call for transformation here. The dogs may also fill this role, as would the boys to mom.

35q12 (273.229) \\the squirrels across the trees across the roof; 76 Freia, 4773 Hayakawa, 521 Brixia, 23013 Carolsmyth, 8220 Nanyou, 8672 Morse, 207655 Kerboguan, 4026 Beet, 2291 Kevo, 224888 Cochingchu

107q12 (93.229) \\STRONG indicator of my ongoing body research; 25611 Mabellin, 17932 Viswanathan, 120153 Hoekenga, 2269 Efremiana, 3332 Raksha, 48767 Skamander, 11801 Frigeri, 129954 Corksauve, 2223 Sarpedon, 185560 Harrykroto, 300082 Moyocoanno, 175109 Sharickaer, 8064 Lisitsa, 129234 Silly, 1075 Helina, 984 Gretia, 261 Prymno

71q12 (183.229) \\my deciding to withhold sharing, but still engaging for a while; 5953 Shelton, 24135 Lisann, 261109 Annie, 30100 Christophergo, 25039 Chensun, 5655 Barney, 90817 Doylehall, 37573 Enricocaruso, 1732 Heike, 21062 Iasky, 25478 Shrock, 2034 Bernoulli, 183560 Kristan, 14843 Tanna, 12163 Manilius

143q12 (3.229) \\part of the final reach—the situation in which I show devotion, though I have actually learned already that sharing is no longer likely; 3585 Goshirakawa, 18672 Ashleyamini, 5783 Kumagaya, 3995 Sakaino, 20576 Marieoertle, 7817 Zibiturtle, 168698 Robpickman, 113202 Kisslaszlo, 9098 Toshihiko

qig91: friends and valued connections pull you out of your home turf

qc303: the black scholar and how I came to think the way I do

11q11 (333.021) \\the plots we love in our british murder mysteries; partner's intimacy timing; my being chronically late to things; ANY inconveniently timed socialization of the one compelled by others who are not them; 2999 Dante, 25199 Jiahegu, 180 Garumna, 30032 Kuszmaul, 25095 Churinov, 166747 Gordonrichards, 499 Venusia, 10577 Jihcesmuzeum

83q11 (153.021) \\in light of denial, acquiring data instead, then forming something new out of it, adc. The AI model. A stolen GF; how I shun work that is too complicated; 5809 Kulibin, 16689 Vistula, 11042 Ernstweber, 352760 Tesorero, 181670 Kengyun, 33704 Herinkang, 52228 Protos, 7359 Messier, 7196 Baroni, 16797 Wilkerson, 12431 Webster, 12846 Fullerton, 29991 Dazimmerman, 16529 Dangoldin, 23774 Herbelliott, 3102 Krok, 20243 Den Bosch, 3011 Chongqing, 34003 Ivozell, 27659 Dolsky, 25045 Baixuefei

47q11 (243.021) \\my general cognition methods; 5703 Hevelius, 4678 Ninian, 8594 Albifrons, 14014 Munchhausen, -10002 Mercury, 115801 Punahou, 6356 Tairov, 218097 Maoxianxin, 55720 Daandehoop, 4462 Vaughan, 55320 Busler, 332183 Jaroussky, 249519 Whitneyclavin, 13497 Ronstone, 78125 Salimbeni, 15415 Rika, 28854 Budisteanu, 19998 Binoche, 112900 Tonyhoffman, 15030 Matthewkroll

119q11 (63.021) \\my observation process for intricate bodies. The target of this is a book of contours model. Flat-sags or drops (de-perks) the breasts in the model? Body details have still more details to them. Presents a safe place to be around (critical); 10474 Pecina, 9768 Stephenmaran, 144769 Zachariassen, 32796 Ehrenfest, 4824 Stradonice, 113256 Prum, 3519 Ambiorix, 78124 Cicalo

qc159: failing to be accepted as an interviewee, I embrace the pseudoscientist role

23q11 (303.021) \\REDACTED thoughtless fuck-up in the ...; tearing through when the material is too complicated; war between the boys and girls; when I enter an interview knowing I will fail at it , then do; 274981 Petrsu, 10063 Erinleeryan, 10223 Zashikiwarashi, 16810 Pavelaleksandrov, 18127 Denversmith, 13269 Dahlstrom, 11422 Alilienthal, 27126 Bonnielei, 1612 Hirose, 22989 Loriskopp, 3182 Shimanto, 34224 Maggiechen

95q11 (123.021) \\the story of our duo brought to shame by a poor exposition—warcraft, the REDACTED house; just looking for an escape, I willingly solicit; 632 Pyrrha, 44479 Olahszter, 2858 Carlosporter, 2771 Polzunov, 256374 Danielpequignot, 3107 Weaver, 549 Jessonda, 178263 Wienphilo, 140 Siwa

59q11 (213.021) \\illustrations in a pseudoscientific or speculative work; 22347 Mishinatakashi, 52455 Masamika, 5984 Lysippus, 406957 Kochetova, 195191 Constantinetsang, 222403 Bethchristie, 6267 Rozhen, 23468 Kannabe, 1685 Toro, 22829 Paigerin, 178803 Kristenjohnson, 14948 Bartuska

131q11 (33.021) \\my recalling negative associations in a better light after we have separated; 10351 Seiichisato, 206 Hersilia, 21505 Bernert, 60148 Seanurban, 12367 Ourinhos, 29654 Michaellaue, 31861 Darleshimizu

qc15: the big blowup with business partners

35q11 (273.021) \\3 REDACTED, convert to ulterior motives given where I live. hopeless in a corner with REDACTED, or relaying this kind of thing to another; 362177 Anji, 1446 Sillanpaa, 29514 Karatsu, 69870 Fizeau, 357116 Attivissimo, 21712 Obaid, 6362 Tunis, 8377 Elmerreese, 8282 Delp, 456 Abnoba, 4750 Mukai

107q11 (93.021) \\where I am demoted thanks to my living situation; via REDACTED and REDACTED; 233707 Alfons, 55702 Thymoitos, 886 Washingtonia, 238593 Paysdegex, 19564 Ajburnetti, 5471 Tunguska, 5592 Oshima, 37556 Svyaztie, 8716 Ginestra

71q11 (183.021) \\how I live inside my home or home turf; what I sponsor or how I decorate; 13131 Palmyra, 25750 Miwnay, 18883 Domegge, 29122 Vasadze, 28676 Bethkoester, 225232 Kircheva, 24918 Tedkooser, 11128 Ostravia, 597 Bandusia, 6905 Miyazaki, 15339 Pierazzo, 4069 Blakee, 12928 Nicolapozio, 363 Padua

143q11 (3.021) \\how I engage people sharing my house / home turf. The highlighted describes REDACTED or chico for example. The musicians can describe background TV of dad's music; 819 Barnardiana, 31926 Alhamood, 20313 Fredrikson, 184878 Gotlib, 7332 Ponrepo, 8919 Ouyangziyuan, 16644 Otemaedaigaku, 64553 Segorbe, 4621 Tambov, 1992 Galvarino, 33607 Archanamurali, 16015 Snell

qig92: relationship to the unknown of a familiar type

qc302: how I take care of my house and charge

11q10 (332.813) \\REDACTED losing me to the house after constantly complaining about everything related to it; 47038 Majoni, 16319 Xiamenerzhong, 2517 Orma, 44821 Amadora, 12612 Daumier, 28439 Miguelreyes, 133008 Snedden, 31664 Randiiwessen, 31438 Yasuhitohayashi, 3783 Morris

83q10 (152.813) \\me in relaxed landowner mode; 13977 Frisch, 891 Gunhild, 185535 Gangda, 20544 Kimhansell, 3928 Randa, 3897 Louhi, 21888 Durech, 39635 Kusatao, 11758 Sargent, 10658 Gretadevries, 24129 Oliviahu, 25227 Genehill

47q10 (242.813) \\ee's actual workings a s a group; 803 Picka, 28781 Timothylohr, 17447 Heindl, 90892 Betlemska kaple, 47835 Stevecoe, 5451 Plato, 7082 La Serena, 360762 FRIPON, 368617 Sebastianotero, 23617 Duna, 48737 Cusinato, 27108 Bryanhe

119q10 (62.813) \\allergic to my co-creator, despite being entertaining. Requires a masochistic partner or a degradee, but when I create I will invariably get sick after union. Need to find a region which shows my headaches and vision problems in action on the 2nd day bad day; 4330 Vivaldi, 18239 Ekers, 10547 Yosakoi, 20283 Elizaheller, 29555 MACEK

qc158: sb's high-strung sensuality and sensitivity

23q10 (302.813) \\writing as a path to restored empowerment; 1906 Naef, 5332 Davidaguilar, 235621 Kratochvile, 9981 Kudo, 18456 Misik, 1261 Legia, 154493 Portisch, 15941 Stevegauthier, 7811 Zhaojiuzhang, 9917 Keynes, 23809 Haswell

95q10 (122.813) \\bs, me going out in public with certain intentional physical impressions being made; living with shanna; 12522 Rara, 3566 Levitan, 29852 Niralithakor, 9316 Rhamnus, 9990 Niiyaeki, 12578 Bensaur, 11984 Manet, 7144 Dossobuono, 4366 Venikagan, 98825 Maryellen

59q10 (212.813) \\what was he thinking!? the rationale behind S12, the book of contours; 13390 Bouska, 6936 Cassatt, 21047 Hodierna, 19416 Benglass, 23003 Ziminski, 48785 Pitter, 134081 Johnmarshall, 6298 Sawaoka, 185150 Panevezys, 1515 Perrotin, 14004 Chikama, 7049 Meibom, 133834 Erinmorton, 48636 Huangkun, 15239 Stenhammar, 3819 Robinson, 1988 Delores, 2089 Cetacea, 21602 Ialmenus, 28848 Nicolemarie

131q10 (32.813) \\preparing to write the next book; kit; 31599 Chloesherry, 565 Marbachia, 29972 Chriswan, 12564 Ikeller

qc14: the qcross is all about how you and others around you stay productive

35q10 (272.813) \\me continuing with no sata help; 4769 Castalia, 2197 Shanghai, 21827 Chingzhu, 14077 Volfango, 14148 Jimchamberlin, 153298 Paulmyers, 11194 Mirna, 21499 Perillat, 1543 Bourgeois, 16102 Barshannon, 13358 Revelle, 850 Altona, 18155 Jasonschuler, 25924 Douglasadams, 4464 Vulcano, 3825 Nurnberg, 20098 Shibatagenji, 5594 Jimmiller

107q10 (92.813) \\my alone activities which may partly be compensation or a replacement for the company I would have otherwise had there; 181249 Tkachenko, 33625 Slepyan, 10471 Marciniak, 32734 Kryukov, 90226 Byronsmith, 36672 Sidi, 3042 Zelinsky, 19379 Labrecque, 4928 Vermeer, 18441 Cittadivinci, 51663 Lovelock, 4911 Rosenzweig, 9925 Juliehoskin, 84075 Peterpatricia, 126 Velleda

71q10 (182.813) \\my compensatory response to insults to my home turf and activities; my response to rachel barking while sb and I hang up pictures; 3870 Mayre, 7847 Mattiaorsi, 52558 Pigafetta, 21552 Richardlee, 19029 Briede, 7525 Kiyohira, 33584 Austinkatzer, 17857 Hsieh, 9252 Goddard, 11844 Ostwald, 78577 JPL, 33017 Wronski, 214378 Kleinmann, 260886 Henritudor, 28433 Samarquez, 16198 Buzios, 42924 Betlem, 9676 Eijkman, 1572 Posnania, 5714 Krasinsky

143q10 (2.813) \\when shanna needs help with something, how she asks; 4351 Nobuhisa, 18979 Henryfong, 1923 Osiris, 12323 Haeckel, 25807 Baharshah, 2417 McVittie, 13952 Nykvist, 110295 Elcalafate, 33691 Andrewchiang, 1637 Swings, 33687 Julianbain

qig93: recognized as family

qc301: vb and my general co-creative partners

11q9 (332.604) \\my ulterior motive for wanting certain associations, making them more like me or compatible with me. But Upice does this to everyone's chart; 10591 Caverni, 5735 Loripaul, 20416 Mansour, 8676 Lully, 126748 Mariegerbet, 26210 Lingas, 35087 von Sydow, 202686 Birkfellner, 174515 Pamelaivezic, 256697 Nahapetov, 20254 Upice

83q9 (152.604) \\when I stop looking for or thinking about the attainment of friendships, here is what I get. Looks like Sâvitrî; 30722 Biblioran, 10257 Garecynthia, 2542 Calpurnia, 410835 Neszmerak, 7110 Johnpearse, 5573 Hilarydownes, 10847 Koch, 24931 Noeth, 9271 Trimble, 23798 Samagonzalez, 21914 Melakabinoff, 12682 Kawada, 4507 Petercollins, 19787 Betsyglass, 27930 Nakamatsu, 3683 Baumann, 97268 Serafinozani, 11243 de Graauw, 28657 Briandempsey, 61912 Storrs

47q9 (242.604) \\what I greet strange approachers with. How they see me as they get closer, having not yet met me; 164587 Taesch, 11941 Archinal, 22937 Nataliavella, 3894 Williamcooke, 12301 Eotvos, 7354 Ishiguro, 31876 Jenkens, 25163 Williammcdonald, 61444 Katokimiko, 8056 Tieck, 1180 Rita, 6307 Maiztegui, 112 Iphigenia, 3198 Wallonia, 31400 Dakshdua, 825 Tanina, 3695 Fiala, 95951 Ernestopalomba, 13978 Hiwasa

119q9 (62.604) \\my approach to friendship; 10914 Tucker, 14682 Davidhirsch, 6540 Stepling, 126905 Junetveekrem, 10475 Maxpoilane, 33567 Sulekhfrederic, 3782 Celle, 168638 Waltersiegmund

qc157: across my explorations of relationships, how I am to be remembered

23q9 (302.604) \\bali, chang'l, the bastille, the eiffel tower, grand nightlife; vegas; 15005 Guerriero, 16683 Alepieri, 25931 Peterhu, 9668 Tianyahaijiao, 2331 Parvulesco, 9823 Annantalova, 1054 Forsytia, 572 Rebekka, 179678 Rietmeijer, 17211 Brianfisher, 129177 Jeanneeha

95q9 (122.604) \\touring with oram, REDACTED, shanna; 4639 Minox, 281 Lucretia, 27384 Meaganbethel, 10609 Hirai, 25553 Ivanlafer, 8212 Naoshigetani, 288478 Fahlman, 717 Wisibada, 30096 Glindadavidson, 83363 Yamwingwah, 21429 Gulati, 149955 Maron

59q9 (212.604) \\attracting shanna as a housemate and family member, the dogs; our family was like this; 447 Valentine, 158329 Stevekent, 24019 Jeremygasper, 9514 Deineka, 10128 Bro, 5772 Johnlambert, 56329 Tarxien, 28128 Cynthrossman, 5012 Eurymedon, 28632 Christraver, 26127 Otakasakajyo, 8446 Tazieff, 19652 Saris, 289586 Shackleton, 2863 Ben Mayer, 5133 Phillipadams, 69286 von Liebig, 4341 Poseidon

131q9 (32.604) \\my overall attitude towards our family. I used this region ALL THE TIME. But should i?; 17697 Evanchen, 1651 Behrens, 16623 Muenzel, 157456 Pivatte, 3106 Morabito, 11003 Andronov, 17826 Normanwisdom

qc13: when I'm really itching to give my opinion in a situation that really seems destined to fail or falter

35q9 (272.604) \\what I move towards experiencing with travel partners when I travel with them for too long; 207695 Olgakopyl, 188973 Siufaiwing, 3225 Hoag, 85471 Maryam, 1215 Boyer, 1983 Bok, 16847 Sanpoloamosciano, 8139 Paulabell, 1233 Kobresia, 9618 Johncleese, 12364 Asadagouryu, 28625 Selvakumar, 28631 Jacktakahashi, 4136 Artmane, 1676 Kariba, 9878 Sostero, 17910 Munyan, 1835 Gajdariya, 22988 Jimmyhom, 29298 Cruls, 31767 Jennimartin, 28653 Charliebrucker, 13562 Bobeggleton, 30281 Horstman, 712 Boliviana, 30081 Zarinrahman

107q9 (92.604) \\the environment in which I wrote s12; 808 Merxia, 19438 Khaki, 30705 Idaios, 31466 Abualhassan, 55676 Klythios, 4394 Fritzheide, 4450 Pan, 18335 San Cassiano, 7775 Taiko, 8623 Johnnygalecki, 132661 Carlbaeker, 21456 Myers, 22038 Margarshain

71q9 (182.604) \\shanna, mom; 22626 Jengordinier, 11296 Denzen, 24218 Linfrederick, 7240 Hasebe, 4977 Rauthgundis, 9906 Tintoretto, 90818 Daverichards, 19127 Olegefremov, 16217 Peterbroughton, 1303 Luthera, 25154 Ayers, 161962 Galchyn, 8283 Edinburgh

143q9 (2.604) \\agd, romero, sb; 16202 Srivastava, 867 Kovacia, 20213 Saurabhsharan, 32634 Sonjamichaluk, 9283 Martinelvis, 3052 Herzen, 4526 Konko

qig94: innovation and creativity under this pressure…

qc300: subculture teacher

12q8 (332.396) \\me in meetings I'm expected to have a say in; 22173 Myersdavis, 5238 Naozane

84q8 (152.396) \\my solo contemplation; 1707 Chantal, 870 Manto, 8651 Alineraynal, 62666 Rainawessen, 12179 Taufiq, 4055 Magellan, 51415 Tovinder, 8555 Mirimao, 15805 Murakamitakehiko, 15840 Hiroshiendou, 6691 Trussoni, 2144 Marietta, 69594 Ulferika, 25374 Harbrucker, 31973 Ashwindatta

48q8 (242.396) \\me as level-headed under institutional disaster, meditative in its face; 6817 Pest, 477 Italia, 5245 Maslyakov, 2359 Debehogne, 1615 Bardwell, 876 Scott, 134180 Nirajinamdar, 249515 Heinrichsen, 12708 Van Straten, 23999 Rinner, 23791 Kaysonconlin, 28734 Austinmccoy, 16724 Ullilotzmann, 25164 Sonomastate, 100604 Lundy, 2973 Paola, 971 Alsatia, 13064 Haemhouts

120q8 (62.396) \\my giving up on relationships as I steer the household; -minus REDACTED; 20337 Naeve, 20513 Lazio, 23667 Savinakim, 4565 Grossman, 16356 Univbalttech, 11207 Black, 3169 Ostro

qc156: fit and far-flung bodies tech-polished into nature

24q8 (302.396) \\space operas, quantum leap, spacetime beneath larger society; tcm wwii pilots, space fleets; 71489 Dynamocamp, 8977 Paludicola, 1209 Pumma, 29562 Danmacdonald, 20936 Nemrut Dagi, 20338 Elainepappas, 27383 Braebenedict, 4314 Dervan, 1223 Neckar, 13808 Davewilliams

96q8 (122.396) \\a survey of the powerful institutions that run (american) society| monopolism | logistics companies | mergers and acquisitions | market hegemony | unseen powers and lobbies; the world of mods, bots, and pharma; 19433 Naftz, 26368 Alghunaim, 34300 Brendafrost, 300221 Brucebills, 13260 Sabadell, 930 Westphalia, 4899 Candace, 110289 Dufu, 3701 Purkyne, 13157 Searfoss, 35347 Tallinn, 81915 Hartwick

60q8 (212.396) \\mathematical shaping of the body; Sâvitrî, auguste, vaq; 6538 Muraviov, 21811 Burroughs, 117506 Wildberg, 25476 Sealfon, 14572 Armando, 25993 Kevinxu, 133432 Sarahnoble, 33329 Stefanwan, 1418 Fayeta, 71556 Page, 6707 Shigeru, 6522 Aci, 166614 Zsazsa, 15543 Elizateel, 26057 Ankaios, 5062 Glennmiller

132q8 (32.396) \\rebirthing: an absolutely CRITICAL component among my qunits; encompassing sphere; findings: extreme large or flat chest sizes at one end or the other in males and females, conducive to females or trans males; seems to have a noticeable connection to sexuality and the desire to express it as it is; 1042 Amazone, 28059 Kiliaan, 243285 Fauveau, 30043 Lisamichaels, 1769 Carlostorres, 6512 de Bergh, 2453 Wabash, 2386 Nikonov

qc12: who I am against other-pressure and coercion

36q8 (272.396) \\various factoids about my personal history. My very general biography; 51895 Biblialexa, 16234 Bosse, 230151 Vachier, 24946 Foscolo, 3763 Qianxuesen, 17072 Athiviraham, 8434 Columbianus, 11158 Cirou, 1729 Beryl, 51827 Laurelclark, 17607 Taborsko, 7401 Toynbee, 82559 Emilbrezina, 12387 Tomokofujiwara, 3334 Somov, 13335 Tobiaswolf, 13964 La Billardiere

108q8 (92.396) \\various rental arrangements; DEFINITELY a money-making device if money is the cut you seek; the … financing of REDACTED; 100133 Demosthenes, 51983 Honig, 124104 Balcony, 4712 Iwaizumi

72q8 (182.396) \\this is likely one of the areas responsible for lvz's view of me, but seems to also be a tactic I have for letting others do the battling; 30063 Jessicashi,

8320 van Zee, 20573 Garynadler, 28043 Mabelwheeler, 12661 Schelling, 27580 Angelataylor, 84118 Bracalicioci, 17215 Slivan, 2255 Qinghai, 130069 Danielgaudreau, 5417 Solovaya

144q8 (2.396) \\conflicts with REDACTED while I shifted over to AI; 29311 Lesire, 5003 Silvanominuto, 21932 Rios, 84095 Davidjohn, 25772 Ashpatra, 1330 Spiridonia, 18301 Konyukhov

qig95: meeting who you were supposed to have met for your story

qc299: the guardians, the student and the teacher

12q7 (332.188) \\i would rather not recall the details of the poor treatment I received; 5318 Dientzenhofer, 493 Griseldis, 8983 Rayakazakova, 25139 Roatsch, 16046 Gregnorman, 2720 Pyotr Pervyj, 4693 Drummond, 19453 Murdochorne

84q7 (152.188) \\what I did as a communicative adversary; 1128 Astrid, 34225 Fridberg, 163800 Richardnorton, 38083 Rhadamanthus, 3986 Rozhkovskij, 10991 Dulov, 2229 Mezzarco, 21471 Pavelchvykov, 12469 Katsuura, 242529 Hilaomar, 55749 Eulenspiegel, 71538 Robertfried, 34202 Sionaprasad, 3537 Jurgen

48q7 (242.188) \\the roots of an enemy-type relationship. Events which bring this about; 32533 Tranpham, 17494 Antaviana, 35313 Hangtianyuan, 129026 Conormcmenamin, 134063 Damianhammond, 30333 Stevenwang, 2584 Turkmenia, 129187 Danielalfred, 7051 Sean, 14544 Ericjones, 32315 Clarezhu, 420779 Swidwin, 202373 Ubuntu, 4254 Kamel, 6280 Sicardy, 26250 Shaneludwig, 211021 Johnpercin, 2949 Kaverznev, 15238 Hisaohori, 134130 Apaczai, 25468 Ramakrishna, 4910 Kawasato

120q7 (62.188) \\how I look back on trials in hindsight; 11462 Hsingwenlin, 48447 Hingley, 65357 Antoniucci, 2019 van Albada, 6986 Asamayama, 15276 Diebel, 17283 Ustinov

qc155: DIY jack of all trades, free of comparison to most other males

24q7 (302.188) \\the jumpers overall lab workings, quantum leaping; various skills I should pick up; 33344 Madymesple, 73701 Siegfriedbauer, 4448 Phildavis, 8575 Seishitakeuchi, 101713 Marston, 4131 Stasik, 5019 Erfjord, 54902 Close, 2422 Perovskaya, 20831 Zhangyi, 12606 Apuleius, 20887 Ngwaikin, 5846 Hessen, 129328 Loriharrison, 2353 Alva, 9103 Komatsubara, 12131 Echternach, 13132 Ortelius

96q7 (122.188) \\the threat of deprivation which looms over the average consumer; reese, cassidy, dynamene; youtube learning DIY; 11421 Cardano, 58605 Liutungsheng, 6573 Magnitskij, 4107 Rufino, 17438 Quasimodo, 4496 Kamimachi, 12872 Susiestevens, 1010 Marlene, 3208 Lunn, 6991 Chichibu, 210997 Guenat, 21614 Grochowski, 18170 Ramjeawan, 65159 Sprowls, 2787 Tovarishch

60q7 (212.188) \\uil and dictionary lays the foundation; vaq and her hyperexplosive orgasm—the thing I ideally want to be triggered in my partner during sex. I would have to do 132q7—the opposition in order to trigger this, and she would have to be receptive; 163641 Nichol, 6200 Hachinohe, 25482 Tallapragada, 6208 Wakata, 7247 Robertstirling, 4050 Mebailey, 12788 Shigeno, 4518 Raikin, 20897 Deborahdomingue, 25960 Timheckman, 4912 Emilhaury, 18263 Anchialos, 31957 Braunstein, 28479 Varlotta, 136557 Neleus, 11826 Yurijgromov, 4934 Rhoneranger

132q7 (32.188) \\societal ills and frustrations; 2677 Joan, 9815 Mariakirch, 35286 Takaoakihiro, 4539 Miyagino, 204873 FAIR, 1574 Meyer, 2953 Vysheslavia

qc11: the high king and high pressured responsibility

36q7 (272.188) \\playing the black slave owner in the history fair, dirty play in the … with REDACTED and REDACTED; 276975 Heller, 162937 Pretre, 10071 Paraguay, 14154 Negrelli, 16168 Palmen, 9136 Lalande, 28353 Chrisnielsen, 32631 Majzoub, 4719 Burnaby, 1484 Postrema, 2907 Nekrasov, 133536 Alicewhagel, 6721 Minamiawaji, 315174 Sellek, 10616 Inouetakeshi, 3229 Solnhofen

108q7 (92.188) \\where one compares another aggressively against a desired state which just plain resists achievability; 12 Victoria, 11469 Rozitis, 5884 Dolezal, 5198 Fongyunwah, 12757 Yangtze, 296987 Piotrflin, 26337 Matthewagam, 90472 Mahabal, 8489 Boulder

72q7 (182.188) \\a fancy computer to do my research; 21840 Ghoshchoudhury, 31496 Glowacz, 14467 Vranckx, 90383 Johnloiacono, 33535 Alshaikh, 3673 Levy, 23153 Andrewnowell, 64070 NEAT, 9543 Nitra, 11201 Talich, 3003 Koncek, 177982 Popilnia, 21515 Gavini, 7368 Haldancohn, 15007 Edoardopozio, 8450 Egorov, 21485 Ash, 1022 Olympiada, 13441 Janmerlin, 12835 Stropek, 18013 Shedletsky

144q7 (2.188) \\with my computer and astro, deciding who stays and who goes; 174466 Zucker, 22492 Mosig, 11020 Orwell, 84012 Deluise, 196035 Haraldbill, 207809 Wuzuze, 7105 Yousyozan, 52285 Kakurinji, 33448 Aaronyeiser

qig96: counselor and message blaster, radio host

qc298: me and simeona or another troublemaker

12q6 (331.979) \\one of the dogs, some info I draw for a book I'm writing; 25124 Zahramaarouf, 7215 Gerhard, 306 Unitas, 5249 Giza

84q6 (151.979) \\what mr romano told me about caltech; partly kit; 4102 Gergana, 634 Ute, 73533 Alonso, 27958 Giussano, 202806 Sierrastars, 38980 Gaoyaojie, 11791 Sofiyavarzar, 25793 Chrisanchez, 4365 Ivanova, 431436 Gahberg, 9096 Tamotsu, 72876 Vauriot, 17020 Hopemeraengus, 129333 Ashleylancaster

48q6 (241.979) \\the autoanswerer; 49698 Vachal, 3554 Amun, 32590 Cynthiachen, 8992 Magnanimity, 8768 Barnowl, 5591 Koyo, 16561 Rawls, 9425 Marconcini, 77621 Koten, 743 Eugenisis, 1965 van de Kamp, 84015 Efthymiopoulos, 12932 Conedera, 9913 Humperdinck, 1758 Naantali, 175281 Kolonics, 2551 Decabrina

120q6 (61.979) \\the aftermath of having left a place I've destroyed; 161975 Kincsem, 358 Apollonia, 10807 Uggarde, 84919 Karinthy, 88878 Bowenyueli, 91395 Sakanouenokumo, 69460 Christibarnard

qc154: that which is kept foreign or foreignized after derailing others

24q6 (301.979) \\individual jumpers and their self-exposure, ezra, me; my first-born ingenuity. See the opposition, travel. Definitely unfun by comparison; 11086 Nagatayuji, 33471 Ozuna, 5043 Zadornov, 10219 Penco, 783 Nora, 1069 Planckia, 8031 Williamdana, 30935 Davasobel, 11582 Bleuler, 7015 Schopenhauer, 437 Rhodia, 894 Erda, 10350 Spallanzani, 6117 Brevardastro, 287 Nephthys, 3327 Campins, 251018 Liubirena

96q6 (121.979) \\the jumps, the true contents of the subconscious which shadow all people; foreign travel experiences in general; 318 Magdalena, 22057 Brianking, 19139 Apian, 6959 Mikkelkocha, 4269 Bogado, 28531 Nikbogdanov, 213629 Binford, 1176 Lucidor, 1554 Yugoslavia, 12870 Rolandmeier, 19464 Ciarabarr, 21059 Penderecki, 6181 Bobweber, 11600 Cipolla, 37432 Piszkesteto

60q6 (211.979) \\my upstairs environment; my disclosure of my characteristics; 6886 Grote, 5436 Eumelos, 30209 Garciaarriola, 6291 Renzetti, 33222 Gillingham, 22860 Francylemp, 21716 Panchamia, 8602 Oedicnemus, 183288 Eyer, 17851 Kaler, 29658 Henrylin, 12287 Langres, 21250 Kamikouchi, 6914 Becquerel, 25510 Donvincent, 703 Noemi, 20850 Gaglani, 19173 Virginiaterese, 8086 Peterthomas, 10799 Yucatan

132q6 (31.979) \\the house's forward ageing; probably t.o. or auguste; 29227 Wegener, 6154 Stevesynnott, 19521 Chaos, 19788 Hunker, 33215 Garyjones, 136 Austria, 214475 Chrisbayus, 177120 Ocampo Uria, 6144 Kondojiro

qc10: pre-sleep fantasy visitor

36q6 (271.979) \\over life, I will have learned to see the vast; 12095 Pinel, 5361 Goncharov, 14568 Zanotta, 9100 Tomohisa, 117093 Umbria, 11430 Lodewijkberg, 2054 Gawain, 28672 Karolhiggins, 10007 Malytheatre, 25723 Shamascharak, 2424 Tautenburg, 5040 Rabinowitz, 90918 Jasinski, 34089 Smoter, 52030 Maxvasile, 33509 Mogilny, 6159 Andreseloy, 24238 Adkerson, 12382 Niagara Falls

108q6 (91.979) \\growing exercises before the many as a part of my recovery from dead ends; 12583 Buckjean, 15265 Ernsting, 90288 Dalleave, 29685 Soibamansoor, 9142 Rhesus, 6302 Tengukogen, 7500 Sassi, 12649 Ascanios, 10274 Larryevans, 2940 Bacon, 1038 Tuckia, 31885 Greggweger, 28427 Gidwani, 23745 Liadawley

72q6 (181.979) \\visiting the kinksters, blocking the starlets, measuring progressed growth; 6969 Santaro, 199 Byblis, 33103 Pintar, 1545 Thernoe, 187531 Omorichugakkou, 5924 Teruo, 129101 Geoffcollyer, 3309 Brorfelde, 28287 Osmanov, 31907 Wongsumming, 34200 Emmasun, 11740 Georgesmith, 21656 Knuth, 1933 Tinchen, 5441 Andymurray, 12878 Erneschiller, 14570 Burkam, 8820 Anjandersen, 127545 Crisman, 21 Lutetia, 23016 Michaelroche

144q6 (1.979) \\through the clothes, a comparison; 25541 Greathouse, 33630 Swathiravi, 3443 Leetsungdao, 51823 Rickhusband, 8954 Baral, 185580 Andratx

qig97: character as information

qc297: the honor of hanging out with this awesome figure

12q5 (331.771) \\ASMR vibes; 32121 Joshuazhou, 12619 Anubelshunu, 6987 Onioshidashi

84q5 (151.771) \\tete-a-tete, victoria villarreal; 256797 Benbow, 143579 Derimiksa, 9393 Apta, 231486 Capefearrock, 15565 Benjaminsteele, 20117 Tannoakira, 19484 Vanessaspini, 78444 Horikawa, 31122 Brooktaylor, 23064 Mattmiller, 6995 Minoyama, 1823 Gliese, 1882 Rauma, 23675 Zabinski

48q5 (241.771) \\my imagined gamified chapters, games I play that relate to me?; 10004 Igormakarov, 33389 Isairisgreco, 11775 Kohler, 9104 Matsuo, 218 Bianca, 3394 Banno, 10542 Ruckers, 79138 Mansfeld, 2140 Kemerovo, 112328 Klinkerfues, 23002 Jillhirsch, 8184 Luderic, 258 Tyche, 33713 Mithravamshi, 157541 Wachter, 20741 Jeanmichelreess, 9880 Stegosaurus, 130158 Orsonjohn, 5108 Lubeck

120q5 (61.771) \\now operating in the background, observing the characters in the group; 6619 Kolya, 55331 Putzi, 39880 Dobsinsky, 6132 Danielson, 129982 Jeffseabrook

qc153: fitting right into a social scenario

24q5 (301.771) \\reese, golden, and those who rule the terrain in wartime, even as everyone else battle in it; twice jack sort of, though the role of such parties is greatly changed by then; my consoling partners when they think the battle is lost; 58364 Feierberg, 27879 Shibata, 10020 Bagenal, 75837 Johnbriol, 22697 Manek, 9236 Obermair, 87312 Akirasuzuki, 29832 Steinwehr, 6970 Saigusa, 1532 Inari, 22448 Ricksaunders, 20284 Andreilevin, 73955 Asaka, 5813 Eizaburo

96q5 (121.771) \\cassandra, wine, and cassidy threatened by reese; cassandra and golden's arrangement; cfs in general; phaedra is robbed; the group continues on despite a wallflower's inability to fit in; | cfs; 2234 Schmadel, 586 Thekla, 3697 Guyhurst, 22889 Donnablaney, 13798 Cecchini, 10169 Ogasawara, 21548 Briekugler, 243320 Jackuipers, 10014 Shaim, 153289 Rebeccawatson, 3174 Alcock, 3941 Haydn, 133243 Essen, 11805 Novakovic, 11652 Johnbrownlee, 22105 Pirko, 29448 Pappos, 27658 Dmitrijbagalej

60q5 (211.771) \\indicates some taboo activity; 5922 Shouichi, 21706 Robminehart, 725 Amanda, 1842 Hynek, 10972 Merbold, 25521 Stevemorgan, 3548 Eurybates, 1443 Ruppina, 916 America, 5044 Shestaka, 791 Ani, 4501 Eurypylos, 46643 Yanase, 26948 Annasato, 12157 Konnen

132q5 (31.771) \\precision in how the house gets built; 208425 Zehavi, 10199 Chariklo

qc9: the indian or bronze woman, an ill-fated non-affair. What compels this? Maybe 36q5's yahagi or 108q5's phegeus. Overall though, I'm more inclined to want this woman when I'm under attack

36q5 (271.771) \\i studied the cosmology of the dark; my appreciation of exotic women; 55854 Stoppani, 27264 Frankclayton, 28924 Jennanncsele, 185638 Erwinschwab, 3831 Pettengill, 34165 Nikhilcheerla, 6618 Jimsimons, 880 Herba, 2427 Kobzar, 30221 LeDonne, 4941 Yahagi, 518 Halawe, 8400 Tomizo, 29353 Manu

108q5 (91.771) \\Sâvitrî's life and evolution; REDACTED, kk; 129330 Karlharshman, 6468 Welzenbach, 23068 Tyagi, 1535 Paijanne, 5638 Deikoon, 22957 Vaintrob, 8374 Horohata, 3230 Vampilov, 30704 Phegeus, 6180 Bystritskaya, 20478 Rutenberg, 22546 Schickler, 17233 Stanshapiro, 20403 Attenborough, 8700 Gevaert, 286162 Tatarka, 2993 Wendy

72q5 (181.771) \\blaze of glory; the indian woman; 14322 Shakura, 558 Carmen, 3526 Jeffbell, 13038 Woolston, 1996 Adams, 162001 Vulpius, 17960 Liberatore, 6581 Sobers, 34024 Cormaclarkin, 5049 Sherlock, 28397 Forrestbetton, 1058 Grubba, 283461 Leacipaola, 249544 Ianmclean, 13717 Vencill, 8167 Ishii, 192 Nausikaa, 50240 Cortina, 1908 Pobeda, 327 Columbia, 3765 Texereau, 13052 Las Casas, 27657 Berkhey, 26940 Quintero, 109879 Letelier

144q5 (1.771) \\my conflicts when paces are mismatched; I am off-putting to the women I really like unless I'm being attacked via the square; 58707 Kyoshi, 26356 Aventini, 32928 Xiejialin, 14656 Lijiang, 6826 Lavoisier, 2716 Tuulikki

qig98: you look towards a helper for something beyond your capacity

qc296: advancing through refusal, being rescued from having to tell lies

12q4 (331.563) \\people know I appear from out of nowhere; 342620 Beita, 534 Nassovia, 3030 Vehrenberg, 25903 Yuvalcalev, 88146 Castello, 2293 Guernica, 3812 Lidaksum, 118194 Sabinagarroni

84q4 (151.563) \\the high session with REDACTED; 8924 Iruma, 1865 Cerberus, 22383 Nikolauspacassi, 2486 Metsahovi, 16972 Neish, 39699 Ernestocorte, 469 Argentina, 12738 Satoshimiki, 2934 Aristophanes, 3412 Kafka, 3968 Koptelov

48q4 (241.563) \\my video recordings under certain circumstances; 5393 Goldstein, 1531 Hartmut, 1946 Walraven, 28779 Acthieke, 130 Elektra, 3153 Lincoln, 2136 Jugta, 16230 Benson, 19629 Serra, 2273 Yarilo, 84902 Porrentruy, 10185 Gaudi

120q4 (61.563) \\me as an overwhelmed programmer; 21709 Sethmurray, 1060 Magnolia, 12418 Tongling, 4332 Milton, 2297 Daghestan, 12627 Maryedwards, 347940 Jorgezuluaga

qc152: patriarchy and what it demands of its subjects, what it encourages in its heroes

24q4 (301.563) \\keith. cassandra engels, emily? For me this is a super talented person. But REDACTED is not acceptable. Could be keith. Probably keith, actually; old school male standards imposed on women; 5629 Kuwana, 6451 Karnten, 904 Rockefellia, 16246 Cantor, 29348 Criswick, 27326 Jimobrien, 34240 Charleyhutch, 104 Klymene, 11262 Drube, 15031 Lemus, 13092 Schrodinger

96q4 (121.563) \\tippy and cubrina's main conflicts in gm | gm; women getting dolled up for the social scene; 30851 Reissfelder, 9964 Hideyonoguchi, 20096 Shiraishiakihiko, 175166 Adirondack, 10805 Iwano, 20372 Juliafanning, 7694 Krasetin, 15911 Davidgauthier

60q4 (211.563) \\my moving process—the decisions made here will be permanent; 21546 Konermann, 5781 Barkhatova, 7681 Chenjingrun, 33608 Paladugu, 1178 Irmela, 7003 Zoyamironova, 22140 Suzyamamoto, 18611 Baudelaire, 9481 Menchu, 552 Sigelinde, 47293 Masamitsu, 17941 Horbatt, 23254 Chikatoshi, 7906

Melanchton, 28569 Kallenbach, 9599 Onotomoko, 905 Universitas, 7263 Takayamada, 1253 Frisia

132q4 (31.563) \\the house's event character; 4675 Ohboke, 18334 Drozdov, 4411 Kochibunkyo, 18708 Danielappel, 54 Alexandra, 2383 Bradley, 3073 Kursk, 21497 Alicehine, 19719 Glasser

qc8: posturing, some manipulation of another's favor

36q4 (271.563) \\not only did I escape, but went to an exotic place; 82927 Ferrucci, 28802 Boborino, 4682 Bykov, 49382 Lynnokamoto, 160001 Bakonybel, 22724 Byatt, 7773 Kyokuchiken

108q4 (91.563) \\this is one (beautiful) memory which will ultimately be among the last of our (recallable) relationship ; additional traits that only you can have; 1056 Azalea, 30942 Helicaon, 2808 Belgrano, 30327 Prembabu, 111818 Deforest, 4104 Alu, 10277 Micheli, 5616 Vogtland, 2960 Ohtaki, 10832 Hazamashigetomi

72q4 (181.563) \\living distant in the same house with someone, even as the house itself is the embodiment of my ambitions; 13049 Butov, 35165 Quebec, 23674 Juliebaker, 2537 Gilmore, 3743 Pauljaniczek, 13096 Tigris, 70446 Pugh, 32267 Hermannweyl, 18106 Blume, 6894 Macreid, 12651 Frenkel, 11136 Shirleymarinus, 2011 Veteraniya, 12626 Timmerman, 5093 Svirelia, 11484 Daudet, 5585 Parks, 21036 Nakamurayoshi, 294664 Trakai, 237 Coelestina

144q4 (1.563) \\my obtaining data from various sources in order to build my work, especially when assisting someone else; 28513 Guo, 24084 Teresaswiger, 28551 Paulomi, 23173 Hideaki, 24053 Shinichiro, 384533 Tenerelli, 21362 Dickarmstrong, 26495 Eichorn, 27790 Urashimataro

qig99: the misalignment you persist in

qc295: my views of males and females. Investigate baikal

12q3 (331.354) \\the nature of my work with data especially; the role of the male energy; 9146 Tulikov, 33118 Naiknaware, 7488 Robertpaul, 6377 Cagney, 1299 Mertona, 5829 Ishidagoro

84q3 (151.354) \\how I express my opinions of working conditions; concepts the male best interacts with; 21570 Muralidhar, 5561 Iguchi, 128615 Jimharris, 12234 Shkuratov, 228883 Cliffsimak, 30110 Lisabreton, 5545 Makarov, 68218 Nealgalt, 2270 Yazhi, 30123 Scottrippeon

48q3 (241.354) \\hardcore lone work in the yard; the role of female energy in my life; 13804 Hrazany, 183294 Langbroek, 21519 Josephhenry, 17036 Krugly, 12169 Munsterman, 17273 Karnik, 63897 Ofunato, 10986 Govert, 11091 Thelonious, 30414 Pistacchi, 33421 Byronxu, 3071 Nesterov, 4763 Ride, 16444 Godefroy, 7327 Crawford, 764 Gedania, 375007 Buxy, 32608 Hallas, 7035 Gomi, 33518 Stoetzer, 21801 Ancerl

120q3 (61.354) \\my affinity with null spaces, accomplishing something while I am in them; 17855 Geffert, 21662 Benigni, 32453 Kanamishogo, 969 Leocadia, 85299 Neander

qc151: what men want to see in their women or (more so) women want to see in their men and power

24q3 (301.354) \\earth hall. Could have been b.a.r. or vb, but I will have needed to live in riches first; women social deliberation; 26301 Hellawillis, 4173 Thicksten, 6466 Drewesquivel, 191582 Kikadolfi, 25366 Maureenbobo, 128607 Richhund, 1145 Robelmonte, 608 Adolfine, 1356 Nyanza, 37 Fides, 315276 Yurigradovsky

96q3 (121.354) \\genevieve and other pantheonic groupings which affect the far-known history of a space. A critical ambition role in my chart. The brothers. The dogs. By doing things away from these concepts and weighing in on the home base, 132q3 I may yet be able to build as tippy did| teachers of prosperity?; that which is assessed by the women talkers; 9092 Nanyang, 12258 Oscarwilde, 8621 Jimparsons, 5194 Bottger, 5910 Zatopek

60q3 (211.354) \\wine, cassidy, dynamene; me-too; women as power currency; 102234 Olivebyrne, 3944 Halliday, 9500 Camelot, 3250 Martebo, 15071 Hallerstein, 5338 Michelblanc, 29404 Hikarusato, 20518 Rendtel, 225076 Vallemare, 487 Venetia, 129963 Marvinwalthall, 216345 Savigliano, 5058 Tarrega, 33000 Chenjiansheng, 6867 Kuwano, 180367 Vonfeldt, 5589 De Meis, 129100 Aaronammons, 9493 Enescu, 2080 Jihlava, 100266 Sadamisaki, 10974 Carolalbert

132q3 (31.354) \\that's it. I have to become a contractor myself. Or at least try. There, I will interface with shanna as a REDACTED type. Probably| \\tippy hare. 23071 Tinaliu, 18946 Massar, 10148 Shirase, 12321 Zurakowski, 172850 Coppens

qc7: traveling in the high spaces

36q3 (271.354) \\my preferences for topics and treatment of others; sensuality when traveling abroad; 55901 Xuaoao, 19149 Boccaccio, 204852 Frankfurt, 5551 Glikson, 8656 Cupressus, 18876 Sooner, 16588 Johngee, 8713 Azusa, 293707 Govoradloanatoly, 406 Erna, 1428 Mombasa, 161 Athor

108q3 (91.354) \\the dark effect of my dark moods on a room; the watch shop; 7919 Prime, 73517 Cranbrook, 4259 McCoy, 10281 Libourel, 60423 Chvojen, 8454 Micheleferrero, 293878 Tapping, 33605 McCue, 67 Asia, 267003 Burkert, 6794 Masuisakura, 7455 Podosek, 260676 Evethuriere, 28739 Julisauer, 5406 Jonjoseph, 9267 Lokrume

72q3 (181.354) \\following the long path through my research; chang'i; 9859 Van Lierde, 12099 Meigooni, 8856 Celastrus, 7867 Burian, 90388 Philchristensen, 28692 Chanleysmall, 19426 Leal, 13715 Steed, 2835 Ryoma, 353595 Grancanaria, 34219 Megantang, 196476 Humfernandez, 4505 Okamura, 1228 Scabiosa, 13722 Campobagatin, 1093 Freda

144q3 (1.354) \\the lego town and recall of my own stories; 9682 Gravesande, 7367 Giotto, 337380 Lenormand, 15296 Tantetruus, 32242 Jagota, 4029 Bridges, 196005 Robertschiller, 27387 Chhabra, 2608 Seneca, 33347 Maryzhu

qig100: the outside forces which launch you

qc294: attitudes and obligated events around yours and the opposite sex

12q2 (331.146) \\follows from 128q2. me not liking the dogs considering humping my leg or getting near my butt when I'm crouched near the ground. How I appear when attempting to gain entry into a club; my expectations as a male; 2784 Domeyko, 3935 Toatenmongakkai, 6233 Kimura, 211 Isolda, 17408 McAdams, 187514 Tainan, 12843 Ewers, 29345 Ivandanilov

84q2 (151.146) \\those whom I teach; 18973 Crouch, 2786 Grinevia, 18294 Rudenko, 3055 Annapavlova, 16249 Cauchy, 1475 Yalta, 13334 Tost, 11427 Willemkolff, 18812 Aliadler, 1632 Siebohme, 14998 Ogosemachi, 23295 Brandoreavis, 33187 Pizzolato, 17 Thetis, 21927 Sarahpierz

48q2 (241.146) \\i break into REDACTED and get away with it; the display of the female's expectations; 4179 Toutatis, 40409 Taichikato, 25612 Yaoskalucia, 14226 Hamura, 16498 Passau, 7666 Keyaki, 4521 Akimov, 5900 Jensen, 128166 Carora, 9428 Angelalouise, 233967 Vierkant, 11169 Alkon, 8725 Keiko, 2171 Kiev, 2864 Soderblom, 10366 Shozosato

120q2 (61.146) \\parading towards the mona lisa; 12225 Yanfernandez, 5872 Sugano, 9088 Maki, 21607 Robel, 28425 Sungkanit, 19535 Rowanatkinson

qc150: the penetration process—what it involves and what it requires. material penis (60q2), environment vagina (132q2), response to the penis (24q2), views of the vagina (96q2); frequentically, this is the story of energy entering a space

24q2 (301.146) \\certain kinds of vitamins or supplements I take, especially garlic; phaedra em; body growth; 29874 Rogerculver, 7644 Cslewis, 4352 Kyoto, 4163 Saaremaa, 28642 Zbarsky, 25159 Michaelwest, 15149 Loufaix, 69230 Hermes, 2374 Vladvysotskij

96q2 (121.146) \\my engineered ideals from a distance, the power in celibacy. But also, the hunger; horemheb; 4968 Suzamur, 341958 Chretien, 5676 Voltaire, 21818 Yurkanin, 90482 Orcus, 3728 IRAS, 164006 Thierry, 315 Constantia, 16104 Stesullivan, 25166 Thompson, 9522 Schlichting, 91604 Clausmadsen, 43669 Winterthur

60q2 (211.146) \\dynamene under chi-9; vaq and explosive orgasm, the price of orgasm as it occurs—apparently my having orgasm is an acknowledgement of the triggerer's authority; 11832 Pustylnik, 6935 Morisot, 7266 Trefftz, 2548 Leloir, 15329 Sabena, 4161 Amasis, 16984 Veillet, 16225 Georgebaldo, 44475 Hikarumasai, 18823 Zachozer, 12214 Miroshnikov, 15710 Bocklin, 24603 Mekistheus, 18663 Lynnta, 1898 Cowell, 5321 Jagras, 26233 Jimbraun, 3912 Troja, 25000 Astrometria, 289608 Wanli, 1902 Shaposhnikov, 40206 Lhenice, 21356 Karlplank, 30314 Yelenam, 6126 Hubelmatt, 12411 Tannokayo

132q2 (31.146) \\the duct tape; miranda, SIER, omni; 2320 Blarney, 4231 Fireman

qc6: among the pantheon for calculated influence, but not quite 144q2

36q2 (271.146) \\what people could expect to experience around me; 3466 Ritina, 3118 Claytonsmith, 48960 Clouet, 8045 Kamiyama, 27792 Fridakahlo, 34197 Susrinivasan, 24517 Omattage, 1584 Fuji, 14543 Sajigawasuiseki, 7587 Weckmann, 4696 Arpigny, 46824 Tambora, 26397 Carolynsinow, 22143 Cathyfowler, 22740 Rayleigh, 19816 Wayneseyfert, 30786 Karkoschka, 237277 Nevaruth, 17882 Thielemann, 10880 Kaguya, 733 Mocia, 134125 Shaundaly, 28819 Karinritchey

108q2 (91.146) \\after REDACTED; 29356 Giovarduino, 998 Bodea, 10814 Gnisvard, 1720 Niels, 8869 Olausgutho, 32944 Gussalli, 9530 Kelleymichael, 3175 Netto, 149884 Radebeul, 31525 Nickmiller, 3561 Devine, 3875 Staehle, 445 Edna, 20553 Donaldhowk

72q2 (181.146) \\domestic shield; 6441 Milenajesenska, 18605 Jacqueslaskar, 17799 Petewilliams, 19969 Davidfreedman, 53311 Deucalion, 9706 Bouma, 20817 Liuxiaofeng, 4797 Ako, 42377 KLENOT, 18680 Weirather, 366852 Ti

144q2 (1.146) \\dg's general situation and that of the big girl archetype broadly; 437192 Frederikolsen, 4642 Murchie, 31313 Kanwingyi, 28465 Janesmyth, 6167 Narmanskij,

18542 Broglio, 33188 Shreya, 7627 Wakenokiyomaro, 84200 Robertmoore, 10400 Hakkaisan, 7647 Etrepigny

qig101: your ideally-fit domesticity

qc293: sex-typical power roles (yours 12, opposite 48) and the power objects they cultivate (84 and 120)

12q1 (330.938) \\my visceral attracting role in relationships; 24439 Yanney, 18120 Lytvynenko, 14429 Coyne, 22847 Utley, 3521 Comrie, 48934 Kocanova, 1382 Gerti, 7148 Reinholdbien, 16494 Oka

84q1 (150.938) \\my identification with leo; 261110 Neoma, 2796 Kron, 9250 Chamberlin, 18343 Asja, 330 Adalberta, 3320 Namba, 6127 Hetherington, 8545 McGee, 32731 Annaivanovna

48q1 (240.938) \\my alliance with keith, maybe vb; 20469 Dudleymoore, 2390 Nezarka, 115477 Brantanica, 6531 Subashiri, 17919 Licandro, 21653 Davidwang, 26593 Perrypat, 13434 Adamquade, 6189 Volk, 9545 Petrovedomosti, 15906 Yoshikaneda, 4916 Brumberg, 75223 Wupatki, 4515 Khrennikov, 228180 Puertollano, 37646 Falconscott

120q1 (60.938) \\my interest in anthro and evolution; 21933 Aaronrozon, 22855 Donnajones

qc149: the high upper elite and how some people get there, what they do there

24q1 (300.938) \\the cast of gm, space operas; 108113 Maza, 15068 Wiegert, 3205 Boksenberg, 10018 Lykawka, 8136 Landis, 28524 Ebright, 14424 Laval, 1883 Rimito, 101331 Sjostrom, 7705 Humeln, 13128 Aleppo, 8578 Shojikato, 15132 Steigmeyer, 117 Lomia

96q1 (120.938) \\THE reason grand miranda was written—to show me a route to a more perfect society: through a group on the far adventure. A life goal; 959 Arne, 58466 Santoka, 2841 Puijo, 199900 Brunoganz, 11709 Eudoxos, 5427 Jensmartin

60q1 (210.938) \\cassidy, dynamene. True villains. But each has a weak spot via (1) their own blind lust and lack of a succession plan and (2) the person they rely on / it may be critical for me to befriend the 132q1 type person here. REDACTED basically fits this, with REDACTED as his weakness. 14611 Elsaadawi, 58600 Iwamuroonsen, 9967 Awanoyumi, 4140 Branham, 3504 Kholshevnikov, 20102 Takasago, 3511 Tsvetaeva, 15808 Zelter, 19303 Chinacyo, 10374 Etampes, 1646 Rosseland, 3160 Angerhofer, 27549 Joannemichet

132q1 (30.938) \\dino, cassandra; the nurturer of a massively lost soul; my book through sata; spacetime and initial phaedra, ezra to wine; soft at heart, taking abuse. REDACTED. Who else have I met like this? Templates, anyone?... REDACTED. Maybe they're ...; 30830 Jahn, 12874 Poisson, 17908 Chriskuyu, 22566 Irazaitseva, 2777 Shukshin, 21725 Zhongyuechen, 31473 Guangning

qc5: pressing on, even as a monster

36q1 (270.938) \\degrader's notion of the degradee. REDACTED; 5032 Conradhirsh, 2635 Huggins, 4740 Veniamina, 11833 Dixon, 129073 Sandyfreund, 235990 Laennec, 48456 Wilhelmwien, 109573 Mishasmirnov, 16969 Helamuda, 7014 Nietzsche, 296819 Artesian, 30167 Caredmonds, 4229 Plevitskaya, 2098 Zyskin

108q1 (90.938) \\the degrader. Not so much through insult as through calling out the partner's failings against a standard; 9965 GNU, 110393 Rammstein, 24155 Serganov, 129801 Tommcmahon, 4040 Purcell, 30195 Akdemir, 34139 Lucabarcelo, 391 Ingeborg

72q1 (180.938) \\the phantom of the opera—degradee (via the public). THE qunit of ACTING. The assumption here is that I cannot be a degrader; 31281 Stothers, 10415 Mali Losinj, 111561 Giovanniallevi, 29612 Cindyjiang, 1828 Kashirina, 6011 Tozzi, 13740 Lastrucci, 9484 Wanambi, 325973 Cardinal, 9810 Elanfiller, 2967 Vladisvyat, 1890 Konoshenkova

144q1 (0.938) \\degradee's notion of the Degrader. seems to be some kind of paranormal story, a flashback; work on the qunits?; 19120 Doronina, 2952 Lilliputia, 5408 The, 2410 Morrison, 4999 MPC, 1003 Lilofee, 17649 Brunorossi

qig102: background conflicts and sentiments you get used to

qc292: sex-typical public communication standards and their typically remembered messages

12q12 (330.729) \\the house as the rest of my aura?; 1745 Ferguson, 48619 Jianli, 8189 Naruke

84q12 (150.729) \\hypothesis—my "lone phase"; 6696 Eubanks, 1379 Lomonosowa, 5416 Estremadoyro, 8530 Korbokkur, 27593 Oliviamarie, 23329 Josevega, 1978 Patrice, 25811 Richardteo, 16066 Richardbressler, 4861 Nemirovskij, 23904 Amytang, 26433 Michaelyurko, 5554 Keesey, 9975 Takimotokoso, 18774 Lavanture

48q12 (240.729) \\how I decorate spaces that are truly mine, to my own comfort or expressive preference, especially spaces I record in; 6789 Milkey, 175718 Wuzhengyi, 256537 Zahn, 11730 Yanhua, 4082 Swann, 31595 Noahpritt, 34206 Zhiyuewang, 42271 Keikokubota, 8270 Winslow, 27072 Aggarwal, 296753

Mustafamahmoud, 27949 Jonasz, 33923 Juliewarren, 1826 Miller, 3872 Akirafujii, 211379 Claytonwhitted, 13729 Nicolewen, 17493 Wildcat, 10143 Kamogawa, 29361 Botticelli, 21403 Haken, 120349 Kalas, 3155 Lee, 102211 Angelofaggiano, 25372 Shanagarza, 12478 Suzukiseiji

120q12 (60.729) \\tirades in my private recordings; 90481 Wollstonecraft, 4296 van Woerkom, 30068 Frankmelillo, 109435 Giraud, 30939 Samaritaine, 35334 Yarkovsky, 107 Camilla, 203 Pompeja, 16680 Minamitanemachi, 29456 Evakrchova, 10434 Tinbergen, 8323 Krimigis, 1859 Kovalevskaya

qc148: status and the attitude of the hired hand

24q12 (300.729) \\the fight between cubrina and genevieve, parts of my work; in retrospect, that person was prejudiced or worse; 13113 Williamyeats, 8395 Rembaut, 214715 Silvanofuso, 21450 Kissel, 996 Hilaritas, 120218 Richardberry, 4980 Magomaev, 6623 Trioconbrio, 25300 Andyromine

96q12 (120.729) \\leisurely way, what happens to genevieve; a plan to make money isn't so much what is needed. This cluster doesn't have much value to me; 4159 Freeman, 150 Nuwa, 52341 Ballmann, 4776 Luyi, 8079 Bernardlovell, 11338 Schiele, 307 Nike, 1310 Villigera, 1502 Arenda, 25951 Pamross, 2950 Rousseau, 2888 Hodgson, 929 Algunde, 12599 Singhal

60q12 (210.729) \\Geneviève's ambition, and her crime; 6271 Farmer, 24818 Menichelli, 26424 Jacquelihung, 376084 Annettepeter, 10907 Savalle, 172951 Mehoke, 6162 Prokhorov, 30158 Mabdulla, 22503 Thalpius, 235201 Lorantffy, 9498 Westerbork, 128426 Vekerdi, 10932 Rebentrost, 246759 Elviracheca, 18321 Bobrov, 24671 Frankmartin, 162755 Spacesora, 1687 Glarona, 19450 Sussman, 6173 Jimwestphal, 31492 Jennarose, 212587 Bartasiute, 19156 Heco, 19861 Auster

132q12 (30.729) \\people gossip about what's being done with the house; 10269 Tusi, 27827 Ukai, 26530 Lucferreira, 13285 Stephicks, 44711 Carp, 127935 Reedmckenna, 14499 Satotoshio

qc4: keith, shanna, priya, and auguste—co-wikis

36q12 (270.729) \\shanna, agd, myself, {ju | t.o. | a trans person?}; 114023 Harvanek, 198616 Lucabracali, 6971 Omogokei, 1061 Paeonia, 216261 Mapihsia, 130007 Frankteti, 18905 Weigan, 26986 Caslavska, 26939 Jiachengli, 419 Aurelia, 16590 Brunowalter, 11294 Kazu, 10072 Uruguay, 28869 Chaubal, 15021 Alexkardon, 16226 Beaton, 6846 Kansazan

108q12 (90.729) \\through the energy of body form, channeling a party's desires, thanks to violamocz: three; 16975 Delamere, 5386 Bajaja, 37678 McClure, 2768 Gorky, 30049 Violamocz, 10619 Ninigi, 12047 Hideomitani, 5355 Akihiro

72q12 (180.729) \\ways of betraying the key partner OR treating them as a one-of-many fantasy object before you unite with them. Interestingly, people who watch me work in the yard are doing this; 2439 Ulugbek, 176380 Goran, 372578 Khromov, 28126 Nydegger, 8612 Burov, 38541 Rustichelli, 13520 Felicienrops, 24239 Paulinehiga, 10203 Flinders, 63 Ausonia, 22788 von Steuben

144q12 (0.729) \\my work in the yard, publicly visible to neighbors; 8501 Wachholz, 5333 Kanaya, 8604 Vanier, 30938 Montmartre, 1482 Sebastiana, 4633 Marinbica

qig103: background tensions and dynamics

qc291: the living information and contents of business enterprise

12q11 (330.521) \\the ... tool and initial praise for knime; visionary leader; 381904 Beatita, 399745 Ouchaou, 156879 Elois, 8413 Kawakami, 18992 Katharvard, 31267 Kuldiga, 3960 Chaliubieju

84q11 (150.521) \\the time bomb business partner brings their first impression; sanza; 52963 Vercingetorix, 21504 Caseyfreeman, 13045 Vermandere, 4248 Ranald, 14876 Dampier, 430 Hybris, 2862 Vavilov, 129216 Chloecastle, 25970 Nelakanti, 40774 Iwaigame, 8134 Minin, 34249 Leolo, 20289 Nettimi

48q11 (240.521) \\REDACTED's imposition into sata; 27986 Hanus, 126749 Johnjones, 8087 Kazutaka, 33602 Varunmandi, 25697 Kadiyala, 154005 Hughharris, 12562 Briangrazer, 22998 Waltimyer, 7173 Sepkoski, 24032 Aimeemcarthy, 24093 Tomoyamaguchi, 5707 Shevchenko, 128345 Danielbamberger, 185321 Kammerlander, 10248 Fichtelgebirge, 5317 Verolacqua, 14613 Sanchez, 16075 Meglass, 314 Rosalia

120q11 (60.521) \\now *that* is the appearance I'm talking about; 2530 Shipka, 29988 Davidezilli, 4595 Prinz, 8971 Leucocephala, 133889 Nicholasmills, 3132 Landgraf

qc147: while I was out, what I was doing; keller and the blamist dynamic

24q11 (300.521) \\ptt, touched by an angel, quantum leap, tcm culture, we without wings and similar slice of life; the group that stands apart from the strife but assists those in need; umalias keller's flashback; 32237 Jagadeesan, 23814 Bethanylynne, 3823 Yorii, 9452 Rogerpeeters, 8560 Tsubaki, 1939 Loretta, 11255 Fujiiekio, 20632 Carlyrosser, 73819 Isaootuki, 24520 Abramson, 18969 Valfriedmann, 9821 Gitakresakova, 26557 Aakritijain, 11104 Airion, 4706 Dennisreuter

96q11 (120.521) \\the fate of gm's main villains; figure model, keller away; 17086 Ruima, 5303 Parijskij, 9396 Yamaneakisato, 6396 Schleswig, 28254 Raghrama, 234026 Unioneastrofili, 5516 Jawilliamson, 31840 Normnegus, 24278 Davidgreen, 1561 Fricke, 10036 McGaha, 4478 Blanco, 33193 Emhyr, 9000 Hal, 8886 Elaeagnus, 57140 Gaddi, 10695 Yasunorifujiwara

60q11 (210.521) \\the stand over the splashee. Dominance; keller's visitors; 28818 Kellyryan, 26849 De Paepe, 65712 Schneidmuller, 9851 Sakamoto, 5178 Pattazhy, 25708 Vedantkumar, 456677 Yepeijian, 861 Aida, 23115 Valcourt, 1411 Brauna, 12648 Ibarbourou, 32288 Terui, 3771 Alexejtolstoj, 6423 Harunasan, 221698 Juliusolsen

132q11 (30.521) \\a thorough story of my problems with partnership; blamist repair; 31859 Zemaitis, 29185 Reich, 34285 Dorothydady, 5205 Servian, 11471 Toshihirabayashi, 5569 Colby, 8439 Albellus, 16563 Ob, 10727 Akitsushima

qc3: the powerful movers of others into their inevitable future

36q11 (270.521) \\matriarchies and various groups who weigh in or convey with respect to my ideas; miranda leaders; 1809 Prometheus, 1757 Porvoo, 3444 Stepanian, 15353 Meucci, 14015 Senancour, 21585 Polmear, 368719 Asparuh, 22919 Shuwan, 8029 Miltthompson, 3887 Gerstner, 30031 Angelakong, 2616 Lesya, 153078 Giovale

108q11 (90.521) \\my limiting others' access to … the morning I … the … stuff; my writing the grand miranda women as the ultimate power; 12750 Berthollet, 22079 Kabinoff, 290129 Ratzlaszlo, 12663 Bjorkegren, 384 Burdigala, 4016 Sambre, 7987 Walshkevin, 1940 Whipple

72q11 (180.521) \\my caltech time, including my last treatment of eb all the way through graduation; 909 Ulla, 14694 Skurat, 8482 Wayneolm, 6433 Enya, 1345 Potomac, 9221 Wuliangyong, 21234 Nakashima, 18601 Zafar, 4012 Geballe, 12621 Alsufi, 2481 Burgi, 13681 Monty Python, 3893 DeLaeter, 31935 Midgley, 13701 Roquebrune, 13869 Fruge

144q11 (0.521) \\my feigning more severe asthma attacks than really applied. I wouldn't admit to myself that I was doing this until much older, thinking at the time that it was really a problem. As a consequence though, I would not grow to above average height. Probably a reflection of my making a bigger deal out of something that i was actually equipped to handle, but for my own uncertainty; 11176 Batth, 35703 Lafiascaia, 38442 Szilard, 820 Adriana, 134369 Sahara, 28680 Sandralitvin, 33703 Anthonyhill, 24140 Evanmirts

qig104: how you keep house and domestic arrangements

qc290: superstar announcers

12q10 (330.313) \\acting & real estate broker offices; sports commentators and really big name media figures; 5129 Groom, 308 Polyxo, 262419 Suzaka, 8132 Vitginzburg, 3847 Sindel

84q10 (150.313) \\chico's interference, REDACTED? REDACTED? mb; 13699 Nickthomas, 24697 Rastrelli, 5651 Traversa, 32051 Sadhikamalladi, 274137 Angelaglinos, 11258 Aoyama, 23444 Kukucin, 11317 Hitoshi, 18794 Kianafrank, 8926 Abemasanao, 3775 Ellenbeth, 25538 Markcarlson, 12686 Bezuglyj, 8564 Anomalocaris, 7532 Pelhrimov, 14728 Schuchardt, 4298 Jorgenunez, 4535 Adamcarolla

48q10 (240.313) \\solo in italy; jetsetters; 7791 Ebicykl, 177853 Lumezzane, 7293 Kazuyuki, 20293 Sirichelson, 27551 Pelayo, 145559 Didiermuller, 177659 Paolacel, 11967 Boyle, 13927 Grundy, 79472 Chiorny, 22717 Romeuf, 2623 Zech, 26357 Laguerre, 29641 Kaikloepfer

120q10 (60.313) \\NEVER TRUST A PRE-FAB COUPLE—especially heteronormative—where the partners clearly prioritize each other over your work; REDACTED and REDACTED; that girl with the cancer; 17119 Alexisrodrz, 33492 Christirogers, 10273 Katvolk, 30128 Shannonbunch, 12680 Bogdanovich, 12318 Kastner, 10265 Gunnarsson, 20879 Chengyuhsuan

qc146: those demonized by the power-holding majority

24q10 (300.313) \\the brat. the complicated role of wine, my mother, shanna, most gf-types; 3104 Durer, 2704 Julian Loewe, 6893 Sanderson, 18196 Rowberry, 3147 Samantha

96q10 (120.313) \\what it takes to be a good (early era) jumper: ezra, golden, phaedra, me, keith, emily, anyone else who prizes virtue and publishes everything; food pantry crew; 20821 Balasridhar, 141414 Bochanski, 31344 Agathon, 27291 Greghansen, 184784 Bettiepage, 7296 Lamarck, 6134 Kamagari, 294595 Shingareva, 21331 Lodovicoferrari, 58709 Zenocolo, 305254 Moron, 8802 Negley

60q10 (210.313) \\when I am active as a citizen behind a larger political mandate; 21149 Kenmitchell, 9852 Gora, 8256 Shenzhou, 25744 Surajmishra, 1197 Rhodesia, 225276 Leitos, 29959 Senevelling, 6500 Kodaira, 15567 Giacomelli, 21549 Carolinelang, 606 Brangane, 5950 Leukippos, 12534 Janhoet, 20638 Lingchen, 25051 Vass

132q10 (30.313) \\structured activities around the house; 6041 Juterkilian, 5365 Fievez, 3170 Dzhanibekov, 1103 Sequoia, 6467 Prilepina, 12152 Aratus

qc2: a developed sense of direction

36q10 (270.313) \\how I use THE HOURS; 131762 Csonka, 29818 Aryosorayya, 16996 Dahir, 3560 Chenqian, 34284 Seancampbell, 134402 Ieshimatoshiaki, 14010 Jomonaomori, 23937 Delibes, 155083 Banneker, 9800 Shigetoshi, 161278 Cesarmendoza, 241528 Tubman

108q10 (90.313) \\one's portfolio of creations and actions; 1142 Aetolia, 17166 Secombe, 8445 Novotroitskoe, 1984 Fedynskij, 117086 Loczy, 2778 Tangshan, 238817 Titeuf

72q10 (180.313) \\my reputation, how others put it to use; 11519 Adler, 1569 Evita, 15249 Capodimonte, 5725 Nordlingen, 10786 Robertmayer, 20268 Racollier, 12617 Angelusilesius, 10981 Fransaris, 9186 Fumikotsukimoto, 11350 Teresa, 5574 Seagrave, 5709 Tamyeunleung, 8023 Josephwalker, 318412 Tramelan, 121656 Jamesrogers, 13328 Guetter, 28821 Harryanselmo, 6851 Chianti, 39653 Carnera, 79354 Brundibar, 362238 Shisseh, 15148 Michaelmaryott, 121 Hermione, 21360 Bobduff, 18167 Buttani

144q10 (0.313) \\the circumstances that teach me family responsibility; 238710 Halassy, 27233 Mahajan, 16874 Kurtwahl, 18550 Maoyisheng, 13333 Carsenty, 23310 Siriwon, 4617 Zadunaisky, 61400 Voxandreae

qig105: what the omniscient narrator can see

qc289: the airing of discontent and discord

12q9 (330.104) \\me and REDACTED's non-relationship, later as partnership; 163624 Moorthy, 66 Maja, 275281 Amywalsh, 6809 Sakuma, 13569 Oshu, 6226 Paulwarren, 16760 Masanori

84q9 (150.104) \\daily investigating the depths; 3297 Hong Kong, 2747 Cesky Krumlov, 16879 Campai, 120735 Ogawakiyoshi, 646 Kastalia, 84447 Jeffkanipe, 20693 Ramondiaz, 21722 Rambhia, 19618 Masa, 28611 Liliapopova, 27712 Coudray, 4051 Hatanaka, 20564 Michaellane, 39336 Mariacapria, 46796 Mamigasakigawa, 8834 Anacardium, 18643 van Rysselberghe, 1951 Lick, 22909 Gongmyunglee, 5295 Masayo, 70718 HEAF, 7097 Yatsuka, 2458 Veniakaverin

48q9 (240.104) \\background plans to handle difficult partners; lvz; 12016 Green, 7595 Vaxjo, 58607 Wenzel, 31494 Emmafreedman, 26527 Leasure, 129099 Spoelhof, 4533 Orth, 5815 Shinsengumi, 12759 Joule, 88879 Sungjaoyiu, 1999 Hirayama, 13150 Paolotesi, 2194 Arpola, 363504 Belleau, 20857 Richardromeo

120q9 (60.104) \\AI art in the face of non-relating; 162158 Merrillhess, 113 Amalthea, 5570 Kirsan, 27470 Debrabeckett, 29427 Oswaldthomas, 125476 Frangarcia, 11278 Telesio, 120368 Phillipcoulter

qc145: training—in my classes

24q9 (300.104) \\g of v; on behalf of the trio, I will brave the desert before us; a kind of far epilogue to the gm work; 3257 Hanzlik, 10677 Colucci, 10463 Bannister, 1244 Deira, 16232 Chijagerbs, 79410 Wallerius, 2619 Skalnate Pleso, 1155 Aenna, 5919 Patrickmartin, 585 Bilkis, 217628 Lugh, 221149 Cindyfoote

96q9 (120.104) \\venus and the g of v background scenario itself; 16118 Therberens, 10773 Jamespaton, 23057 Angelawilson, 4272 Entsuji, 6273 Kiruna, 1530 Rantasinge, 128611 Paulnowak, 8985 Tula, 180855 Debrarose, 10455 Donnison, 17192 Loharu

60q9 (210.104) \\me in the back calculating, but not necessarily producing something usable; the uranian 10000 story 19619 Bethbell, 31232 Slavonice, 39655 Muneharuasada, 4833 Meges, 192220 Oicles, 23436 Alekfursenko, 15220 Sumerkin, 15171 Xandertielens, 39382 Opportunity, 30117 Childress, 360072 Alcimedon, 24101 Cassini, 33863 Elfriederwin, 12584 Zeljkoandreic, 31631 Abbywilliams, 12898 Mignard, 9793 Torvalds, 5994 Yakubovich, 2154 Underhill

132q9 (30.104) \\uranian 10000 group's motivations; 28398 Ericthomas, 3211 Louispharailda, 292872 Anoushankar, 1027 Aesculapia, 1126 Otero

qc1: protecting what I've built, how I built it

36q9 (270.104) \\what I insist my students adhere to; 1463 Nordenmarkia, 927 Ratisbona, 100936 Mekong, 25616 Riinuots, 3299 Hall, 218752 Tentlingen, 4665 Muinonen, 8159 Fukuoka, 24027 Downs, 89956 Leibacher, 4447 Kirov, 5672 Libby, 6315 Barabash, 15630 Disanti, 10005 Chernega, 400 Ducrosa, 30296 Bricehuang, 91006 Fleming, 4967 Glia

108q9 (90.104) \\private recording soapbox rant against a former ally; 709 Fringilla, 4888 Doreen, 10458 Sfranke, 24947 Hausdorff, 10282 Emilykramer, 6575 Slavov, 7414 Bosch, 16730 Nijisseiki, 293477 Teotihuacan, 436 Patricia, 18268 Dardanos

72q9 (180.104) \\the tales I could tell about where I've been; 5584 Izenberg, 193 Ambrosia, 5128 Wakabayashi, 17042 Madiraju, 6805 Abstracta, 18907 Kevinclaytor, 30070 Thabitpulak, 8526 Takeuchiyukou, 27711 Kirschvink, 129876 Stevenpeterson, 12868 Onken, 9251 Harch, 18177 Harunaga, 906 Repsolda, 7498 Blanik, 1506 Xosa,

19251 Totziens, 19915 Bochkarev, 5580 Sharidake, 1453 Fennia, 162002 Spalatin, 29552 Chern, 21727 Rhines, 59001 Senftenberg

144q9 (0.104) \\almost machiavellian legacy; 10668 Plansos, 25680 Walterhansen, 13448 Edbryce, 804 Hispania, 18796 Acosta, 6402 Holstein, 7075 Sadovnichij, 28171 Diannahu, 1140 Crimea, 2660 Wasserman, 7373 Stashis, 34424 Utashima

And there you have it. Almost all of my internal self data save.

A REFRESHER ON ALL 144 ASPECTS: IMPORTANT CHANGES TO MY NAMING SYSTEM

There is one more thing we need to cover before closing this chapter. To facilitate the eventual conversion of my save into a network in Table 9, I went through my list of action patterns and assigned the most fitting astrological angle family (aspect) to each item. If you are not familiar with my book *All 144 Aspects*, the idea is that trines (120°), sextiles (60°), and other basics aren't the only way to divide a circle. Aspects show the kind of energy needed to bring two different astro bodies into operation at the same time. With finer-grained divisions you get much more detailed types of behavior.

One of the drawbacks of working in a silo is that you are your own re-versioner when it comes to work. Because I have not had very many conversations with anyone about the massive table in the back of *144*, I would have a hard time knowing how usable it was. Years later I now know that the table is very useful—particularly for assigning AI-assisted edge properties in network graphs—but the original angle names are not. It just isn't intuitive working with a "dekithree quintile." What does that even mean?

A "deki(10)three(III)quintile" was my original way of saying,

> Starting from Pisces (I) and moving to the third sign in the reverse direction (Capricorn / III), take 5/12 more steps into Capricorn (a quintile's worth), and you would have moved 29 minisigns' worth of angle distance from Aries 0°/ Pisces 360° out of 144 such minisigns (duodecanates). It will take 29 wraparounds of this kind of angle to get back into harmonic with a full circle, so traveling one of these cycles will take 29 repeats or be worth 1/29th of a whole cycle (a "period") regardless of whether this angle was 1/29th, 14/29ths, or anything in between.[10] Anyway, this fraction of a whole circle is 12.41379°. The actual angle is 10 times this, 124.379°. Keeping in line with a traditional naming system using words like "bi quintile" or "semi sextile," I guess I'll call this angle something quintile-like, but for the third reverse sign (III-quintile), and use a prefix for "10" (deki). Hence, a deki III-quintile…

At the time of *144*, all of this research was new, including the finding that minisigns progressed in the reverse order of their main signs—like gears. I didn't even know what these harmonics' character was, thus the whole point of doing the *144* research in the first place. Now, however, it is clear that the harmonic signs and parent signs tell you more about an angle family than the name does. So we need a better naming system, starting with names that expose the signs and duodecanates actually doing the work.

The main source of my own self-confusion in using the old naming system lie in the roman numeral part. Now that the research is fairly solid on this (I've been using it in my personality mining), we can just replace it with the sign it refers to: Capricorn. We can also drop the complicated prefix and just use the multiple number itself. Thus, a deki three quintile becomes a 10- capri quintile, and I can tell immediately that a capriquintile is a 29th harmonic. This is what a quintile would look like if we had cycled past the normal general mood of a quintile (a "pisci" quintile / just a regular quintile), past the quintile in ambient information context (an aquariquintile), and shown quintile-like behavior in a known structural context—the capricornic background. According to findings you can still look up in *144*, this super fine-grained harmonic was observed to play out when "you take pride in—and are more charismatic during the display of— [the pair] amidst groups," so if, for example you had a 29th harmonic angle between your Sun and Moon, then you would more likely show your self-contentment (Sun meaning merged with Moon meaning) through charismatic public display. You may refer back to the duodecanate table earlier in this book to see how the 29th harmonic relates to the 29th mini-sign.

---

[10] 15/29ths and up are just the same as 14/29ths and down going from the opposite side of the wheel, and if there were such a thing as 14.5/29ths, that would just be an opposition.

Under the revised naming system, all major aspects fall in the first harmonic, so there is no need to put "pisci" on everything. A trine is still a trine, though it might also be called a 1-piscitrine if we wanted to be really anal about it. That's not consistent with anything out there, so why do this? No, here's the table I actually use in my angle namer:

Sign / cycle	(Former) level	prefix
♓	I	(none)
♒	II	aquari
♑	III	capri
♐	IV	saji
♏	V	scorpi
♎	VI	libri
♍	VII	virgi
♌	VIII	lea
♋	IX	cancri
♊	X	gemi
♉	XI	tauri
♈	XII	ari

And how can we denote these angles? I've found that keeping the standout of the original angle (the conjunct sign for example) is a lot more confusing than you would first think, so it really helps to put the sign in our faces. Let's do this with a sign-level superscript in front and a subscript multiple indicator in the back,

$$^{♑}\pentagon_{10} \text{ or } ^{♑}Q_{10} \text{ or } 10\text{-}^{♑}\pentagon$$

The last option is for people working in plain text where subscripts and superscripts aren't supported.

If we don't care about the multiple then we can drop it.

As an extra little factoid, while writing this chapter I discovered vast changes in the Unicode standard, such that we no longer have to import special fonts for most astro symbols. You can just type a number like "2648" in Microsoft Word, hit Alt+X, and it will put a fitting symbol in there, That said, here are some symbols I prefer to use in this work:

Symbol	Unicode	Object	Symbol	Unicode	Object
☉	2609	Sun	☌	260C	conjunct
☽	263D	Moon	☍	260D	opposition
☿	263F	Mercury	Δ	0394	trine
♀	2640	Venus	□	25A1	square
♂	2642	Mars	⬠	2B20	quintile
♃	2643	Jupiter	✳	26B9	sextile
♄	2644	Saturn	七	4E03	septile
♅	2645	Uranus	◿	25FF	octile (includes both semisquare and sesquiquadrate
♆	2646	Neptune			
♇	2BD3	Pluto			
☊	260A	mean (North) Node			
⚹	2BDD	Selena / Selene / White Moon			
♈	2648	Aries	ℕ	2115	novile

♉	2649	Taurus	⊥	22A5	decile
♊	264A	Gemini	∪	22C3	undecile
♋	264B	Cancer	⊼	26BB	inconjunct (includes both semisextile and inconjunct)
♌	264C	Leo			
♍	264D	Virgo			
♎	264E	Libra			
♏	264F	Scorpio			
♑	2651	Capricorn			
♐	2650	Sagittarius			
♒	2652	Aquarius			
♓	2653	Pisces			

I know what some people may be thinking. You can't just invent your own symbols for things. But when you work with thousands of data points, sometimes in programs that don't take special fonts at all, you do need some way of getting the shorthand into your file nonetheless. The Q for quintile and the dotted Star of David for the septile were particularly problematic not just to find, but to find in a way that indicated their actual geometry. The octile needed something that didn't bias it so heavily in favor of the semisquare or the sesquiquadrate over the other.

In some way, I think the new naming system greatly helps instant interpretability of an aspect. Suppose, for example, your Sun and Mars are 84° apart. You really want to know what this means, but all you can find is information on the square (90°). This was exactly the problem I had when first learning astrology back in the early 2000s. You can kind of see some of the square interpretation holding true for your more overt force of will, [1:1 engagement (Sun) + compelling another thing (Mars)], but really, 84° is NOT a square. So what is it? Using a variation of the brute force calculator method in *144*, you can take 84/360 (= .23333) and keep adding the result to itself until you get something like X.000001 or X.99998. Or you can just do it till you're satisfied that you've hit a whole number. COUNT which "add" you're on as you go, with the the original number (.23333 in our example) being #1, the next number (.466666 in our example) being #2, and so on. There are only 144 harmonics in this system, so once you've done this up to 144 times, you have to stop. Now in this example, my 30th answer was exactly 7.0000000, so it takes 30 cycles to get back in harmonic with a whole cycle. 84° is thus a 30th harmonic, or a caprisextile. 1/30th of a 360° wheel gives us 12°, and 84 is seven of those. So this is a 7-caprisextile. My guess would be that it is related to whatever Capricorn.Virgo does, and so has something to do with ordering Virgo-style within a Capricorn-structured system. Does it? The table for a level III-sextile says it has to do with other's response to your body. I guess that makes animal-kingdom sense when there are no files around to serve as some other structure. It's not really an intuitive match, actually. But it's at least better than total ignorance—interpreting our Sun-Mars caprisextile as an irreconcilable square when it clearly isn't.

Let's do another one.

I have an asteroid 2804 Yrjo, located at 334.7987° in my chart. Suppose I want to be publicly known for its spiritual quality in my public reputation—my Midheaven in 248.2560°. How can I more easily activate this combination? Well, these bodies are 86.5427° apart. Basic aspects would tell us that I struggle to do this because the objects are square and that's that. I might buy this explanation for a while, but then again I know that the combination does come out in my books. So I take 86.5427/360 to get .240396. I add that to itself until I get an almost whole number... 25 adds gives me 6.0099, and if I'm satisfied with that I can stop. So I keep pressing the = key until I get to add #79. The result is 18.9913. Later, the 104th add also reveals a result, but 25 was the closest. So we'll go with that. A Capriconjunct: public spirituality when rallying the people psychologically? That sounds closer to true. But the angle is so close to a 79th and a 104th, that I could *also* activate my Yrjo-Midheaven when doing these things. 79 is six signs' worth of duodecanates backward (6 x 12, putting us in Virgo) + an additional seven duodecanates. A Virgiseptile ♍七. 104 gives us a Cancrioctile ♋⊿. Doing septile feedbacking amidst order and doing octile-pushing amidst feeling can help us guess how these work, or we could just look these up in the duodecanate table earlier in the book. I have *144* right here, so I'm just going to look up what the actual stats said:

25	86.4	sexto_three_conjunct	6-III-conjunct	...	You can rally groups behind [your pair], tuning into the mass psychology.
25	86.4	sexto_three_conjunct	6-III-conjunct	...	You can rally groups behind [your pair], tuning into the mass psychology.
104	86.538	duodekiquinti_nine_octile	25-IX-octile	...	You possess [the pair] as a trait known and (usually favorably) accepted amor
79	86.582	dekinovo_seven_septile	19-VII-septile	...	[Your pair] is anti-establishment, revolutionary, a statement against the rules
133	86.617	triadekibi_twelve_conjunct	32-XII-conjunct	...	You display [the pair] during sex or the creation of art, and give hints of this v
54	86.667	dekitri_five_sextile	13-V-sextile	...	[The pair] is a tool you use for pleasure or to enable your own self-fulfillment

Now you say, those are very different interpretations, Ajani. How can I tell which one is right? But they're all right. How can you tell what fingers are for? Grabbing fruit off a tree? Playing the piano? Wearing rings? Your fingers do all of these. Nature is complex. At least now we have a naming system which helps us guess what aspects of nature are involved.

…And it occurred to me several days after writing one of these chapters that 1) I never updated my original *144* file and 2) you shouldn't have to track down the original book in order to see the big table I keep referring to in Table 9. So here are all of the divisions of a circle from 1/1 to multiples of 1/144, along with the new naming system…

TABLE 10: ALL 144 ASPECTS

aspect degrees	dms angle	harmonic	harmonic multiple	(Revised) 144-aspect name	144-aspect name symbol	character	unicode	noun tag	complex angle formula	approximate complex angle
0.00	0:0'0	1	1	conjunct	☌	🌼	1F33C	natural characteristic	$\cos(1*2\pi i/1) + i\sin(1*2\pi i/1)$	1
2.50	2:30'0	144	1	1-ariinconjunct	1-♈⊼	🔁	1F501	always-on trait	$\cos(1*2\pi i/144) + i\sin(1*2\pi i/144)$	0.99905 +0.04362i
2.54	2:32'6	142	1	1-aridecile	1-♈⊥	🕉	1F549	blessings others can only dream of	$\cos(1*2\pi i/142) + i\sin(1*2\pi i/142)$	0.99902 +0.04423i
2.59	2:35'23	139	1	1-ariseptile	1-♈七	🎯	1F3AF	creative perfectionism	$\cos(1*2\pi i/139) + i\sin(1*2\pi i/139)$	0.99898 +0.04519i
2.63	2:37'39	137	1	1-ariquintile	1-♈⬠	🚧	1F6A7	singular active, direct, control	$\cos(1*2\pi i/137) + i\sin(1*2\pi i/137)$	0.99895 +0.04585i
2.69	2:41'11	134	1	1-ariopposition	1-♈☍	🖤	1F49F	a trait the partner MUST have	$\cos(1*2\pi i/134) + i\sin(1*2\pi i/134)$	0.9989 +0.04687i
2.73	2:43'38	132	1	1-tauriinconjunct	1-♉⊼	🔗	1F517	sharing a special bond w/ a friend	$\cos(1*2\pi i/132) + i\sin(1*2\pi i/132)$	0.99887 +0.04758i
2.79	2:47'26	129	1	1-taurinovile	1-♉N	🙇	1F647	in the service of one attached to	$\cos(1*2\pi i/129) + i\sin(1*2\pi i/129)$	0.99881 +0.04869i
2.83	2:50'4	127	1	1-tauriseptile	1-♉七	🪁	1F4B8	that which attracts unfair advantage	$\cos(1*2\pi i/127) + i\sin(1*2\pi i/127)$	0.99878 +0.04945i
2.88	2:52'47	125	1	1-tauriquintile	1-♉⬠	🎟	1F39F	social clique's requirements	$\cos(1*2\pi i/125) + i\sin(1*2\pi i/125)$	0.99874 +0.05024i
2.93	2:55'36	123	1	1-tauritrine	1-♉△	⌏	238F	others must express or draw out	$\cos(1*2\pi i/123) + i\sin(1*2\pi i/123)$	0.9987 +0.05106i
2.98	2:58'30	121	1	1-tauriconjunct	1-♉☌	💰	1F4B0	prosperity & status-seeking	$\cos(1*2\pi i/121) + i\sin(1*2\pi i/121)$	0.99865 +0.0519i
3.03	3:1'30	119	1	1-gemiundecile	1-♊U	📉	1F4C9	weakened by opinionation, better as ambient	$\cos(1*2\pi i/119) + i\sin(1*2\pi i/119)$	0.99861 +0.05278i

3.08	3:4'36	117	1	1-geminovile	1-♊N	💎	1F48E	best friend's quality	cos(1*2πi/117) + isin(1*2πi/117)	0.99856 +0.05368i
3.13	3:7'49	115	1	1-gemiseptile	1-♊七	🤳	1F933	inner world with self-talk	cos(1*2πi/115) + isin(1*2πi/115)	0.99851 +0.05461i
3.19	3:11'9	113	1	1-gemiquintile	1-♊⬠	😎	1F60E	publicly-labeled vibe given	cos(1*2πi/113) + isin(1*2πi/113)	0.99845 +0.05557i
3.24	3:14'35	111	1	1-gemitrine	1-♊△	🥳	1F973	around high-expression groups	cos(1*2πi/111) + isin(1*2πi/111)	0.9984 +0.05658i
3.27	3:16'21	110	1	1-gemiopposition	1-♊☍	🎐	1F6A5	managing others' behavior	cos(1*2πi/110) + isin(1*2πi/110)	0.99837 +0.05709i
3.33	3:20'0	108	1	1-cancriinconjunct	1-♋π	🌝	1F31D	why close friends come around	cos(1*2πi/108) + isin(1*2πi/108)	0.99831 +0.05814i
3.40	3:23'46	106	1	1-cancridecile	1-♋⊥	🎠	1F3A0	others think one has more power than one has	cos(1*2πi/106) + isin(1*2πi/106)	0.99824 +0.05924i
3.43	3:25'42	105	1	1-cancrinovile	1-♋N	💥	1F5EF	when irritated to see standards defied	cos(1*2πi/105) + isin(1*2πi/105)	0.99821 +0.0598i
3.50	3:29'42	103	1	1-cancriseptile	1-♋七	☺	1F60A	basking in joy	cos(1*2πi/103) + isin(1*2πi/103)	0.99814 +0.06096i
3.53	3:31'45	102	1	1-cancrisextile	1-♋✳	💼	1F4BC	boss figure attributes	cos(1*2πi/102) + isin(1*2πi/102)	0.9981 +0.06156i
3.60	3:36'0	100	1	1-cancrisquare	1-♋□	🛋	1F6CB	home & family life	cos(1*2πi/100) + isin(1*2πi/100)	0.99803 +0.06279i
3.64	3:38'10	99	1	1-cancritrine	1-♋△	🙅	1F645	communication-stifling	cos(1*2πi/99) + isin(1*2πi/99)	0.99799 +0.06342i
3.67	3:40'24	98	1	1-cancriopposition	1-♋☍	🌟	1F31F	social advancement catalyst	cos(1*2πi/98) + isin(1*2πi/98)	0.99795 +0.06407i
3.75	3:45'0	96	1	1-leainconjunct	1-♌π	🤷	1F937	what "not enough" looks like	cos(1*2πi/96) + isin(1*2πi/96)	0.99786 +0.0654i
3.79	3:47'22	95	1	1-leaundecile	1-♌U	👑	265B	the image of a progress-inspiring master	cos(1*2πi/95) + isin(1*2πi/95)	0.99781 +0.06609i
3.83	3:49'47	94	1	1-leadecile	1-♌⊥	👣	1F463	helps in others after learning the hard way	cos(1*2πi/94) + isin(1*2πi/94)	0.99777 +0.06679i
3.87	3:52'15	93	1	1-leanovile	1-♌N	😍	1F60D	brought out by creative, sexualized energy	cos(1*2πi/93) + isin(1*2πi/93)	0.99772 +0.06751i
3.91	3:54'46	92	1	1-leaoctile	1-♌⟋	🍻	1F37B	regular comfort preferences w/ close one	cos(1*2πi/92) + isin(1*2πi/92)	0.99767 +0.06824i
4.00	4:0'0	90	1	1-leasextile	1-♌✳	🚸	1F6B8	absorptions by one's children	cos(1*2πi/90) + isin(1*2πi/90)	0.99756 +0.06976i
4.04	4:2'41	89	1	1-leaquintile	1-♌⬠	💋	1F48B	sensuality & body expression	cos(1*2πi/89) + isin(1*2πi/89)	0.99751 +0.07054i
4.09	4:5'27	88	1	1-leasquare	1-♌□	👹	1F479	suppressing power imbalance	cos(1*2πi/88) + isin(1*2πi/88)	0.99745 +0.07134i
4.14	4:8'16	87	1	1-leatrine	1-♌△	❣	2763	interactor inspired to want	cos(1*2πi/87) + isin(1*2πi/87)	0.99739 +0.07216i
4.19	4:11'9	86	1	1-leaopposition	1-♌☍	🤡	1F921	one's commentary offends egos	cos(1*2πi/86) + isin(1*2πi/86)	0.99733 +0.073i
4.24	4:14'7	85	1	1-leaconjunct	1-♌☌	🤤	1F924	downplaying a real want	cos(1*2πi/85) + isin(1*2πi/85)	0.99727 +0.07385i
4.29	4:17'8	84	1	1-virgiinconjunct	1-♍π	🐑	1F411	traits for the seemingly weak	cos(1*2πi/84) + isin(1*2πi/84)	0.9972 +0.07473i
4.34	4:20'14	83	1	1-virgiundecile	1-♍U	⚡	26A1	high-tension activity in surroundings	cos(1*2πi/83) + isin(1*2πi/83)	0.99714 +0.07563i
4.39	4:23'24	82	1	1-virgidecile	1-♍⊥	🦇	1F987	eccentrically attention-getting, disquieting	cos(1*2πi/82) + isin(1*2πi/82)	0.99707 +0.07655i
4.44	4:26'40	81	1	1-virginovile	1-♍N	👑	1F451	mastered early, forms broad social identity	cos(1*2πi/81) + isin(1*2πi/81)	0.99699 +0.07749i
4.50	4:30'0	80	1	1-virgioctile	1-♍⟋	🤹	1F939	vividly remembered by one's children	cos(1*2πi/80) + isin(1*2πi/80)	0.99692 +0.07846i

4.56	4:33'25	79	1	1-virgiseptile	1-♍七	✊	270A	anti-establishment revolutionary	cos(1*2πi/79) + isin(1*2πi/79)	0.99684 +0.07945i
4.62	4:36'55	78	1	1-virgisextile	1-♍✳	🥊	1F94A	fight night moment	cos(1*2πi/78) + isin(1*2πi/78)	0.99676 +0.08047i
4.68	4:40'31	77	1	1-virgiquintile	1-♍⬠	🐢	1F422	guarded insistence	cos(1*2πi/77) + isin(1*2πi/77)	0.99667 +0.08151i
4.74	4:44'12	76	1	1-virgisquare	1-♍□	🏘	1F3D8	seen by friends' friends & family	cos(1*2πi/76) + isin(1*2πi/76)	0.99658 +0.08258i
4.80	4:48'0	75	1	1-virgitrine	1-♍△	🏡	1F3E1	family home maintenance	cos(1*2πi/75) + isin(1*2πi/75)	0.99649 +0.08368i
4.86	4:51'53	74	1	1-virgiopposition	1-♍☍	😦	1F626	social stressors	cos(1*2πi/74) + isin(1*2πi/74)	0.9964 +0.08481i
4.93	4:55'53	73	1	1-virgiconjunct	1-♍☌	⚒	2692	new or deep investment in job	cos(1*2πi/73) + isin(1*2πi/73)	0.9963 +0.08596i
5.00	5:0'0	72	1	1-libriinconjunct	1-♎⚻	❓	2753	a problem to be solved	cos(1*2πi/72) + isin(1*2πi/72)	0.99619 +0.08716i
5.03	5:2'5	143	2	2-ariundecile	2-♈U	📣	1F4E3	broadcasting which gets one talked about	cos(2*2πi/143) + isin(2*2πi/143)	0.99614 +0.08776i
5.07	5:4'13	71	1	1-libriundecile	1-♎U	🌥	26C5	thriving amidst confusion	cos(1*2πi/71) + isin(1*2πi/71)	0.99609 +0.08838i
5.14	5:8'34	70	1	1-libridecile	1-♎⊥	🔧	1F527	used to strengthen or repair bonds	cos(1*2πi/70) + isin(1*2πi/70)	0.99597 +0.08964i
5.18	5:10'47	139	2	2-ariseptile	2-♈七	🎯	1F3AF	creative perfectionism	cos(2*2πi/139) + isin(2*2πi/139)	0.99592 +0.09028i
5.22	5:13'2	69	1	1-librinovile	1-♎N	🐘	1F418	subtle, strong draw of trait via socialization	cos(1*2πi/69) + isin(1*2πi/69)	0.99586 +0.09093i
5.29	5:17'38	68	1	1-librioctile	1-♎⊿	👢	1F462	appearance of dominating	cos(1*2πi/68) + isin(1*2πi/68)	0.99573 +0.09227i
5.33	5:20'0	135	2	2-aritrine	2-♈△	🏄	1F3C4	easy and prolific	cos(2*2πi/135) + isin(2*2πi/135)	0.99567 +0.09295i
5.37	5:22'23	67	1	1-libriseptile	1-♎七	😻	1F63B	getting others to fall in love w oneself	cos(1*2πi/67) + isin(1*2πi/67)	0.99561 +0.09364i
5.41	5:24'48	133	2	2-ariconjunct	2-♈☌	💝	1F49D	during sex or when flirting	cos(2*2πi/133) + isin(2*2πi/133)	0.99554 +0.09434i
5.50	5:29'46	131	2	2-tauriundecile	2-♉U	😑	1F611	with doubt in associations	cos(2*2πi/131) + isin(2*2πi/131)	0.9954 +0.09578i
5.54	5:32'18	65	1	1-libriquintile	1-♎⬠	🛀	1F6C0	self-resparking	cos(1*2πi/65) + isin(1*2πi/65)	0.99533 +0.09651i
5.58	5:34'53	129	2	2-taurinovile	2-♉N	🙇	1F647	in the service of one attached to	cos(2*2πi/129) + isin(2*2πi/129)	0.99526 +0.09726i
5.63	5:37'30	64	1	1-librisquare	1-♎□	众	4F17	amidst a noisy setting	cos(1*2πi/64) + isin(1*2πi/64)	0.99518 +0.09802i
5.67	5:40'9	127	2	2-tauriseptile	2-♉七	🐺	1F4B8	that which attracts unfair advantage	cos(2*2πi/127) + isin(2*2πi/127)	0.99511 +0.09879i
5.71	5:42'51	63	1	1-libritrine	1-♎△	🚨	1F6A8	know-it-all	cos(1*2πi/63) + isin(1*2πi/63)	0.99503 +0.09957i
5.76	5:45'35	125	2	2-tauriquintile	2-♉⬠	🎟	1F39F	social clique's requirements	cos(2*2πi/125) + isin(2*2πi/125)	0.99495 +0.10036i
5.81	5:48'23	62	1	1-librioopposition	1-♎☍	🏴	1F3F4	manipulative ambition	cos(1*2πi/62) + isin(1*2πi/62)	0.99487 +0.10117i
5.85	5:51'13	123	2	2-tauritrine	2-♉△	⎏	238F	others must express or draw out	cos(2*2πi/123) + isin(2*2πi/123)	0.99479 +0.10199i
5.90	5:54'5	61	1	1-libriconjunct	1-♎☌	🔦	1F526	singled out for attention	cos(1*2πi/61) + isin(1*2πi/61)	0.9947 +0.10282i
6.00	6:0'0	60	1	1-scorpiinconjunct	1-♏⚻	🔍	1F4CD	strongest memory left behind	cos(1*2πi/60) + isin(1*2πi/60)	0.99452 +0.10453i
6.05	6:3'1	119	2	2-gemiundecile	2-♊U	📉	1F4C9	weakened by opinionation, better as ambient	cos(2*2πi/119) + isin(2*2πi/119)	0.99443 +0.1054i

6.10	6:6'6	59	1	1-scorpiundecile	1-♏U		1F447	having one's pick	cos(1*2πi/59) + isin(1*2πi/59)	0.99433 +0.10629i
6.15	6:9'13	117	2	2-geminovile	2-♊N		1F48E	best friend's quality	cos(2*2πi/117) + isin(2*2πi/117)	0.99424 +0.1072i
6.21	6:12'24	58	1	1-scorpidecile	1-♏⊥		1F47B	interactions with an ethereal party	cos(1*2πi/58) + isin(1*2πi/58)	0.99414 +0.10812i
6.26	6:15'39	115	2	2-gemiseptile	2-♊七		1F933	inner world with self-talk	cos(2*2πi/115) + isin(2*2πi/115)	0.99404 +0.10906i
6.32	6:18'56	57	1	1-scorpinovile	1-♏N		1FA84	arrives whenever one wants it, no asking	cos(1*2πi/57) + isin(1*2πi/57)	0.99393 +0.11001i
6.37	6:22'18	113	2	2-gemiquintile	2-♊⬠		1F60E	publicly-labeled vibe given	cos(2*2πi/113) + isin(2*2πi/113)	0.99382 +0.11098i
6.43	6:25'42	56	1	1-scorpioctile	1-♏⊿		1F608	for fun or one's own power	cos(1*2πi/56) + isin(1*2πi/56)	0.99371 +0.11196i
6.49	6:29'11	111	2	2-gemitrine	2-♊△		1F973	around high-expression groups	cos(2*2πi/111) + isin(2*2πi/111)	0.9936 +0.11297i
6.55	6:32'43	55	1	1-scorpiseptile	1-♏七		1F632	shocking or flooding others w information	cos(1*2πi/55) + isin(1*2πi/55)	0.99348 +0.11399i
6.61	6:36'19	109	2	2-gemiconjunct	2-♊☌		1F44E	diminishing others' importance	cos(2*2πi/109) + isin(2*2πi/109)	0.99336 +0.11503i
6.67	6:40'0	54	1	1-scorpisextile	1-♏⚹		1F378	self-fulfillment tool	cos(1*2πi/54) + isin(1*2πi/54)	0.99324 +0.11609i
6.73	6:43'44	107	2	2-cancriundecile	2-♋U		1F481	essence of a great conversation w/ one	cos(2*2πi/107) + isin(2*2πi/107)	0.99311 +0.11717i
6.79	6:47'32	53	1	1-scorpiquintile	1-♏⬠		1F917	reasons one is desired	cos(1*2πi/53) + isin(1*2πi/53)	0.99298 +0.11827i
6.86	6:51'25	105	2	2-cancrinovile	2-♋N		1F5EF	when irritated to see standards defied	cos(2*2πi/105) + isin(2*2πi/105)	0.99285 +0.11939i
6.92	6:55'23	52	1	1-scorpisquare	1-♏□		1F61E	falling short	cos(1*2πi/52) + isin(1*2πi/52)	0.99271 +0.12054i
6.99	6:59'25	103	2	2-cancriseptile	2-♋七		1F60A	basking in joy	cos(2*2πi/103) + isin(2*2πi/103)	0.99257 +0.1217i
7.06	7:3'31	51	1	1-scorpitrine	1-♏△		1F61A	use of persuasive words	cos(1*2πi/51) + isin(1*2πi/51)	0.99242 +0.12289i
7.13	7:7'43	101	2	2-cancriquintile	2-♋⬠		1F624	disregard for things heard	cos(2*2πi/101) + isin(2*2πi/101)	0.99227 +0.1241i
7.20	7:12'0	50	1	1-scorpiopposition	1-♏☍		1F5BC	images put forth to others	cos(1*2πi/50) + isin(1*2πi/50)	0.99211 +0.12533i
7.27	7:16'21	99	2	2-cancritrine	2-♋△		1F645	communication-stifling	cos(2*2πi/99) + isin(2*2πi/99)	0.99195 +0.12659i
7.35	7:20'48	49	1	1-scorpiconjunct	1-♏☌		1F399	having known public influence	cos(1*2πi/49) + isin(1*2πi/49)	0.99179 +0.12788i
7.42	7:25'21	97	2	2-cancriconjunct	2-♋☌		1F495	traits reserved for those very close	cos(2*2πi/97) + isin(2*2πi/97)	0.99162 +0.12919i
7.50	7:30'0	48	1	1-sajiinconjunct	1-♐⊼		1F305	shown through creative setting	cos(1*2πi/48) + isin(1*2πi/48)	0.99144 +0.13053i
7.58	7:34'44	95	2	2-leaundecile	2-♌U		265B	the image of a progress-inspiring master	cos(2*2πi/95) + isin(2*2πi/95)	0.99126 +0.13189i
7.61	7:36'20	142	3	3-aridecile	3-♈⊥		1F549	blessings others can only dream of	cos(3*2πi/142) + isin(3*2πi/142)	0.9912 +0.13235i
7.66	7:39'34	47	1	1-sajiundecile	1-♐U		262B	a core, lived principle	cos(1*2πi/47) + isin(1*2πi/47)	0.99108 +0.13329i
7.74	7:44'30	93	2	2-leanovile	2-♌N		1F60D	brought out by creative, sexualized energy	cos(2*2πi/93) + isin(2*2πi/93)	0.99088 +0.13471i
7.77	7:46'11	139	3	3-ariseptile	3-♈七		1F3AF	creative perfectionism	cos(3*2πi/139) + isin(3*2πi/139)	0.99082 +0.13519i
7.83	7:49'33	46	1	1-sajidecile	1-♐⊥		1F4CE	trait housed by key colleagues	cos(1*2πi/46) + isin(1*2πi/46)	0.99069 +0.13617i

7.88	7:52'59	137	3	3-ariquintile	3-♈⬠		1F6A7	singular active, direct, control	cos(3*2πi/137) + isin(3*2πi/137)	0.99055 +0.13715i
7.94	7:56'28	136	3	3-arisquare	3-♈□		1F9D0	serious, sober-minded interactant	cos(3*2πi/136) + isin(3*2πi/136)	0.99041 +0.13816i
8.00	8:0'0	45	1	1-sajinovile	1-♐N		2766	shared experience as a token of friendship	cos(1*2πi/45) + isin(1*2πi/45)	0.99027 +0.13917i
8.09	8:5'23	89	2	2-leaquintile	2-♌⬠		1F48B	sensuality & body expression	cos(2*2πi/89) + isin(2*2πi/89)	0.99005 +0.14073i
8.12	8:7'13	133	3	3-ariconjunct	3-♈☌		1F49D	during sex or when flirting	cos(3*2πi/133) + isin(3*2πi/133)	0.98997 +0.14125i
8.18	8:10'54	44	1	1-sajioctile	1-♐∠		1F6B5	role in a peer group	cos(1*2πi/44) + isin(1*2πi/44)	0.98982 +0.14231i
8.24	8:14'39	131	3	3-tauriundecile	3-♉U		1F611	with doubt in associations	cos(3*2πi/131) + isin(3*2πi/131)	0.98967 +0.14339i
8.28	8:16'33	87	2	2-leatrine	2-♌△		2763	interactor inspired to want	cos(2*2πi/87) + isin(2*2πi/87)	0.98959 +0.14394i
8.31	8:18'27	130	3	3-tauridecile	3-♉⊥		1F3AA	relied upon by others in the talked topic	cos(3*2πi/130) + isin(3*2πi/130)	0.98951 +0.14449i
8.37	8:22'19	43	1	1-sajiseptile	1-♐七		1F0CF	through jokes, games, and fun	cos(1*2πi/43) + isin(1*2πi/43)	0.98934 +0.1456i
8.44	8:26'15	128	3	3-taurioctile	3-♉∠		1F478	intuitive comfort even amidst stress	cos(3*2πi/128) + isin(3*2πi/128)	0.98918 +0.14673i
8.47	8:28'14	85	2	2-leaconjunct	2-♌☌		1F924	downplaying a real want	cos(2*2πi/85) + isin(2*2πi/85)	0.98909 +0.1473i
8.50	8:30'14	127	3	3-tauriseptile	3-♉七		1F4B8	that which attracts unfair advantage	cos(3*2πi/127) + isin(3*2πi/127)	0.98901 +0.14788i
8.57	8:34'17	42	1	1-sajisextile	1-♐*		1F497	instilled in co-creative partners	cos(1*2πi/42) + isin(1*2πi/42)	0.98883 +0.14904i
8.64	8:38'24	125	3	3-tauriquintile	3-♉⬠		1F39F	social clique's requirements	cos(3*2πi/125) + isin(3*2πi/125)	0.98865 +0.15023i
8.67	8:40'28	83	2	2-virgiundecile	2-♍U		26A1	high-tension activity in surroundings	cos(2*2πi/83) + isin(2*2πi/83)	0.98856 +0.15082i
8.71	8:42'34	124	3	3-taurisquare	3-♉□		1F387	initial, then waning impression	cos(3*2πi/124) + isin(3*2πi/124)	0.98847 +0.15143i
8.78	8:46'49	41	1	1-sajiquintile	1-♐⬠		1F5FD	personas aspired to	cos(1*2πi/41) + isin(1*2πi/41)	0.98828 +0.15265i
8.89	8:53'20	81	2	2-virginovile	2-♍N		1F451	mastered early, forms broad social identity	cos(2*2πi/81) + isin(2*2πi/81)	0.98799 +0.15452i
8.93	8:55'32	121	3	3-tauriconjunct	3-♉☌		1F4B0	prosperity & status-seeking	cos(3*2πi/121) + isin(3*2πi/121)	0.98789 +0.15515i
9.00	9:0'0	40	1	1-sajisquare	1-♐□		1F66A	future missable partnership duty	cos(1*2πi/40) + isin(1*2πi/40)	0.98769 +0.15643i
9.08	9:4'32	119	3	3-gemiundecile	3-♊U		1F4C9	weakened by opinionation, better as ambient	cos(3*2πi/119) + isin(3*2πi/119)	0.98748 +0.15774i
9.11	9:6'50	79	2	2-virgiseptile	2-♍七		270A	anti-establishment revolutionary	cos(2*2πi/79) + isin(2*2πi/79)	0.98738 +0.1584i
9.15	9:9'9	118	3	3-gemidecile	3-♊⊥		1F3C3	staying with it as long as encouraged	cos(3*2πi/118) + isin(3*2πi/118)	0.98727 +0.15906i
9.23	9:13'50	39	1	1-sajitrine	1-♐△		1F3DD	convincing others of one's value	cos(1*2πi/39) + isin(1*2πi/39)	0.98705 +0.16041i
9.31	9:18'37	116	3	3-gemioctile	3-♊∠		1F612	having been slighted or doubted	cos(3*2πi/116) + isin(3*2πi/116)	0.98683 +0.16178i
9.39	9:23'28	115	3	3-gemiseptile	3-♊七		1F933	inner world with self-talk	cos(3*2πi/115) + isin(3*2πi/115)	0.9866 +0.16318i
9.47	9:28'25	38	1	1-sajiopposition	1-♐☍		1F64C	use of the body or physical deeds in work	cos(1*2πi/38) + isin(1*2πi/38)	0.98636 +0.16459i
9.60	9:36'0	75	2	2-virgitrine	2-♍△		1F3E1	family home maintenance	cos(2*2πi/75) + isin(2*2πi/75)	0.986 +0.16677i

9.64	9:38'34	112	3	3-gemisquare	3-♊□		1F38E	one's trait observed by outsiders	cos(3*2πi/112) + isin(3*2πi/112)	0.98587 +0.16751i
9.73	9:43'47	37	1	1-sajiconjunct	1-♐☌		2B50	trusted ability revealed	cos(1*2πi/37) + isin(1*2πi/37)	0.98562 +0.169i
9.82	9:49'5	110	3	3-gemiopposition	3-♊☍		1F6A5	managing others' behavior	cos(3*2πi/110) + isin(3*2πi/110)	0.98535 +0.17052i
9.86	9:51'46	73	2	2-virgiconjunct	2-♍☌		2692	new or deep investment in job	cos(2*2πi/73) + isin(2*2πi/73)	0.98522 +0.17129i
9.91	9:54'29	109	3	3-gemiconjunct	3-♊☌		1F44E	diminishing others' importance	cos(3*2πi/109) + isin(3*2πi/109)	0.98508 +0.17207i
10.00	10:0'0	36	1	1-capriinconjunct	1-♑π		1F3BB	downplayed want or talent	cos(1*2πi/36) + isin(1*2πi/36)	0.98481 +0.17365i
10.09	10:5'36	107	3	3-cancriundecile	3-♋U		1F481	essence of a great conversation w/ one	cos(3*2πi/107) + isin(3*2πi/107)	0.98452 +0.17525i
10.14	10:8'27	71	2	2-libriundecile	2-♎U		26C5	thriving amidst confusion	cos(2*2πi/71) + isin(2*2πi/71)	0.98438 +0.17607i
10.19	10:11'19	106	3	3-cancridecile	3-♋⊥		1F3A0	others think one has more power than one has	cos(3*2πi/106) + isin(3*2πi/106)	0.98423 +0.17689i
10.21	10:12'45	141	4	4-arinovile	4-♈N		1F489	easy instillment in others	cos(4*2πi/141) + isin(4*2πi/141)	0.98416 +0.1773i
10.29	10:17'8	35	1	1-capriundecile	1-♑U		1F47D	quirky distinguishing uniqueness	cos(1*2πi/35) + isin(1*2πi/35)	0.98393 +0.17856i
10.38	10:23'4	104	3	3-cancrioctile	3-♋◺		1F61B	trait known and accepted among friends	cos(3*2πi/104) + isin(3*2πi/104)	0.98362 +0.18026i
10.43	10:26'5	69	2	2-librinovile	2-♎N		1F418	subtle, strong draw of trait via socialization	cos(2*2πi/69) + isin(2*2πi/69)	0.98346 +0.18112i
10.49	10:29'7	103	3	3-cancriseptile	3-♋七		1F60A	basking in joy	cos(3*2πi/103) + isin(3*2πi/103)	0.9833 +0.18199i
10.51	10:30'39	137	4	4-ariquintile	4-♈⬠		1F6A7	singular active, direct, control	cos(4*2πi/137) + isin(4*2πi/137)	0.98322 +0.18242i
10.59	10:35'17	34	1	1-capridecile	1-♑⊥		1F3C6	potential to be a master or boss	cos(1*2πi/34) + isin(1*2πi/34)	0.98297 +0.18375i
10.69	10:41'35	101	3	3-cancriquintile	3-♋⬠		1F624	disregard for things heard	cos(3*2πi/101) + isin(3*2πi/101)	0.98264 +0.18555i
10.75	10:44'46	67	2	2-libriseptile	2-♎七		1F63B	getting others to fall in love w oneself	cos(2*2πi/67) + isin(2*2πi/67)	0.98246 +0.18646i
10.80	10:48'0	100	3	3-cancrisquare	3-♋□		1F6CB	home & family life	cos(3*2πi/100) + isin(3*2πi/100)	0.98229 +0.18738i
10.83	10:49'37	133	4	4-ariconjunct	4-♈☌		1F49D	during sex or when flirting	cos(4*2πi/133) + isin(4*2πi/133)	0.9822 +0.18785i
10.91	10:54'32	33	1	1-caprinovile	1-♑N		1F4FB	in a formal group discussion	cos(1*2πi/33) + isin(1*2πi/33)	0.98193 +0.18925i
10.99	10:59'32	131	4	4-tauriundecile	4-♉U		1F611	with doubt in associations	cos(4*2πi/131) + isin(4*2πi/131)	0.98165 +0.19068i
11.02	11:1'13	98	3	3-cancriopposition	3-♋☍		1F31F	social advancement catalyst	cos(3*2πi/98) + isin(3*2πi/98)	0.98156 +0.19116i
11.08	11:4'36	65	2	2-libriquintile	2-♎⬠		1F6C0	self-resparking	cos(2*2πi/65) + isin(2*2πi/65)	0.98137 +0.19213i
11.13	11:8'2	97	3	3-cancriconjunct	3-♋☌		1F495	traits reserved for those very close	cos(3*2πi/97) + isin(3*2πi/97)	0.98118 +0.1931i
11.16	11:9'46	129	4	4-taurinovile	4-♉N		1F647	in the service of one attached to	cos(4*2πi/129) + isin(4*2πi/129)	0.98108 +0.1936i
11.25	11:15'0	32	1	1-caprioctile	1-♑◺		1F5FB	an indomitable characteristic	cos(1*2πi/32) + isin(1*2πi/32)	0.98079 +0.19509i
11.34	11:20'18	127	4	4-tauriseptile	4-♉七		1F4B8	that which attracts unfair advantage	cos(4*2πi/127) + isin(4*2πi/127)	0.98048 +0.19661i
11.37	11:22'6	95	3	3-leaundecile	3-♌U		265B	the image of a progress-inspiring master	cos(3*2πi/95) + isin(3*2πi/95)	0.98038 +0.19712i

11.43	11:25'42	63	2	2-libritrine	2-♎△		1F6A8	know-it-all	$\cos(2*2\pi/63) + i\sin(2*2\pi/63)$	0.98017 +0.19815i
11.49	11:29'21	94	3	3-leadecile	3-♌⊥		1F463	helps in others after learning the hard way	$\cos(3*2\pi/94) + i\sin(3*2\pi/94)$	0.97996 +0.19919i
11.52	11:31'11	125	4	4-tauriquintile	4-♉⬠		1F39F	social clique's requirements	$\cos(4*2\pi/125) + i\sin(4*2\pi/125)$	0.97986 +0.19971i
11.61	11:36'46	31	1	1-capriseptile	1-♑t		1F3A2	expressed by one's social network	$\cos(1*2\pi/31) + i\sin(1*2\pi/31)$	0.97953 +0.2013i
11.74	11:44'20	92	3	3-leaoctile	3-♌⊿		1F37B	regular comfort preferences w/ close one	$\cos(3*2\pi/92) + i\sin(3*2\pi/92)$	0.97908 +0.20346i
11.80	11:48'11	61	2	2-libriconjunct	2-♎☌		1F526	singled out for attention	$\cos(2*2\pi/61) + i\sin(2*2\pi/61)$	0.97886 +0.20455i
11.87	11:52'5	91	3	3-leaseptile	3-♌t		1F576	smoothly comfortable	$\cos(3*2\pi/91) + i\sin(3*2\pi/91)$	0.97862 +0.20566i
11.90	11:54'2	121	4	4-tauriconjunct	4-♉☌		1F4B0	prosperity & status-seeking	$\cos(4*2\pi/121) + i\sin(4*2\pi/121)$	0.97851 +0.20622i
12.00	12:0'0	30	1	1-caprisextile	1-♑⚹		1F487	response to one's body reception	$\cos(1*2\pi/30) + i\sin(1*2\pi/30)$	0.97815 +0.20791i
12.13	12:8'5	89	3	3-leaquintile	3-♌⬠		1F48B	sensuality & body expression	$\cos(3*2\pi/89) + i\sin(3*2\pi/89)$	0.97766 +0.21021i
12.20	12:12'12	59	2	2-scorpiundecile	2-♏U		1F447	having one's pick	$\cos(2*2\pi/59) + i\sin(2*2\pi/59)$	0.9774 +0.21138i
12.27	12:16'21	88	3	3-leasquare	3-♌□		1F479	suppressing power imbalance	$\cos(3*2\pi/88) + i\sin(3*2\pi/88)$	0.97715 +0.21257i
12.31	12:18'27	117	4	4-geminovile	4-♊N		1F48E	best friend's quality	$\cos(4*2\pi/117) + i\sin(4*2\pi/117)$	0.97702 +0.21316i
12.41	12:24'49	29	1	1-capriquintile	1-♑⬠		1F3A9	proud charisma	$\cos(1*2\pi/29) + i\sin(1*2\pi/29)$	0.97662 +0.21497i
12.50	12:30'0	144	5	5-ariinconjunct	5-♈π		1F501	always-on trait	$\cos(5*2\pi/144) + i\sin(5*2\pi/144)$	0.9763 +0.21644i
12.52	12:31'18	115	4	4-gemiseptile	4-♊t		1F933	inner world with self-talk	$\cos(4*2\pi/115) + i\sin(4*2\pi/115)$	0.97621 +0.21681i
12.59	12:35'14	143	5	5-ariundecile	5-♈U		1F4E3	broadcasting which gets one talked about	$\cos(5*2\pi/143) + i\sin(5*2\pi/143)$	0.97596 +0.21793i
12.63	12:37'53	57	2	2-scorpinovile	2-♏N		1FA84	arrives whenever one wants it, no asking	$\cos(2*2\pi/57) + i\sin(2*2\pi/57)$	0.9758 +0.21868i
12.68	12:40'33	142	5	5-aridecile	5-♈⊥		1F549	blessings others can only dream of	$\cos(5*2\pi/142) + i\sin(5*2\pi/142)$	0.97563 +0.21944i
12.74	12:44'36	113	4	4-gemiquintile	4-♊⬠		1F60E	publicly-labeled vibe given	$\cos(4*2\pi/113) + i\sin(4*2\pi/113)$	0.97537 +0.22058i
12.77	12:45'57	141	5	5-arinovile	5-♈N		1F489	easy instillment in others	$\cos(5*2\pi/141) + i\sin(5*2\pi/141)$	0.97528 +0.22097i
12.86	12:51'25	28	1	1-caprisquare	1-♑□		1F58C	arts and creativity drawn to	$\cos(1*2\pi/28) + i\sin(1*2\pi/28)$	0.97493 +0.22252i
12.95	12:56'58	139	5	5-ariseptile	5-♈t		1F3AF	creative perfectionism	$\cos(5*2\pi/139) + i\sin(5*2\pi/139)$	0.97457 +0.22409i
12.97	12:58'22	111	4	4-gemitrine	4-♊△		1F973	around high-expression groups	$\cos(4*2\pi/111) + i\sin(4*2\pi/111)$	0.97448 +0.22449i
13.04	13:2'36	138	5	5-arisextile	5-♈⚹		26D1	daily work focus	$\cos(5*2\pi/138) + i\sin(5*2\pi/138)$	0.9742 +0.22569i
13.09	13:5'27	55	2	2-scorpiseptile	2-♏t		1F632	shocking or flooding others w information	$\cos(2*2\pi/55) + i\sin(2*2\pi/55)$	0.97401 +0.2265i
13.14	13:8'19	137	5	5-ariquintile	5-♈⬠		1F6A7	singular active, direct, control	$\cos(5*2\pi/137) + i\sin(5*2\pi/137)$	0.97382 +0.22731i
13.17	13:10'14	82	3	3-virgidecile	3-♍⊥		1F987	eccentrically attention-getting, disquieting	$\cos(3*2\pi/82) + i\sin(3*2\pi/82)$	0.9737 +0.22785i
13.24	13:14'7	136	5	5-arisquare	5-♈□		1F9D0	serious, sober-minded interactant	$\cos(5*2\pi/136) + i\sin(5*2\pi/136)$	0.97344 +0.22895i

						Unicode	Description	Formula	Value
13.33	13:20'0	27	1	1-capritrine	1-♑△	1F393	intellectualizing and insight	cos(1*2πi/27) + isin(1*2πi/27)	0.97304 +0.23062i
13.43	13:25'58	134	5	5-ariopposition	5-♈☍	1F49F	a trait the partner MUST have	cos(5*2πi/134) + isin(5*2πi/134)	0.97264 +0.23231i
13.50	13:30'0	80	3	3-virgioctile	3-♍∠	1F939	vividly remembered by one's children	cos(3*2πi/80) + isin(3*2πi/80)	0.97237 +0.23345i
13.53	13:32'1	133	5	5-ariconjunct	5-♈☌	1F49D	during sex or when flirting	cos(5*2πi/133) + isin(5*2πi/133)	0.97223 +0.23402i
13.58	13:35'5	53	2	2-scorpiquintile	2-♏⬠	1F917	reasons one is desired	cos(2*2πi/53) + isin(2*2πi/53)	0.97202 +0.23489i
13.64	13:38'10	132	5	5-tauriinconjunct	5-♉π	1F517	sharing a special bond w/ a friend	cos(5*2πi/132) + isin(5*2πi/132)	0.97181 +0.23576i
13.67	13:40'15	79	3	3-virgiseptile	3-♍七	270A	anti-establishment revolutionary	cos(3*2πi/79) + isin(3*2πi/79)	0.97167 +0.23634i
13.74	13:44'25	131	5	5-tauriundecile	5-♉U	1F611	with doubt in associations	cos(5*2πi/131) + isin(5*2πi/131)	0.97138 +0.23752i
13.85	13:50'46	26	1	1-capriopposition	1-♑☍	1F3B8	why one's fans follow them	cos(1*2πi/26) + isin(1*2πi/26)	0.97094 +0.23932i
13.98	13:58'50	103	4	4-cancriseptile	4-♋七	1F60A	basking in joy	cos(4*2πi/103) + isin(4*2πi/103)	0.97038 +0.24159i
14.03	14:1'33	77	3	3-virgiquintile	3-♍⬠	1F422	guarded insistence	cos(3*2πi/77) + isin(3*2πi/77)	0.97019 +0.24236i
14.06	14:3'45	128	5	5-taurioctile	5-♉∠	1F478	intuitive comfort even amidst stress	cos(5*2πi/128) + isin(5*2πi/128)	0.97003 +0.24298i
14.12	14:7'3	51	2	2-scorpitrine	2-♏△	1F61A	use of persuasive words	cos(2*2πi/51) + isin(2*2πi/51)	0.9698 +0.24391i
14.17	14:10'23	127	5	5-tauriseptile	5-♉七	1F4B8	that which attracts unfair advantage	cos(5*2πi/127) + isin(5*2πi/127)	0.96956 +0.24485i
14.21	14:12'37	76	3	3-virgisquare	3-♍□	1F3D8	seen by friends' friends & family	cos(3*2πi/76) + isin(3*2πi/76)	0.9694 +0.24549i
14.29	14:17'8	126	5	5-taurisextile	5-♉✶	1F47E	aggressive assertion of identity	cos(5*2πi/126) + isin(5*2πi/126)	0.96908 +0.24676i
14.40	14:24'0	25	1	1-capriconjunct	1-♑☌	1F3DF	rally & tune the mass psychology	cos(1*2πi/25) + isin(1*2πi/25)	0.96858 +0.24869i
14.55	14:32'43	99	4	4-cancritrine	4-♋△	1F645	communication-stifling	cos(4*2πi/99) + isin(4*2πi/99)	0.96795 +0.25115i
14.59	14:35'40	74	3	3-virgiopposition	3-♍☍	1F626	social stressors	cos(3*2πi/74) + isin(3*2πi/74)	0.96773 +0.25198i
14.63	14:38'2	123	5	5-tauritrine	5-♉△	238F	others must express or draw out	cos(5*2πi/123) + isin(5*2πi/123)	0.96756 +0.25265i
14.69	14:41'37	49	2	2-scorpiconjunct	2-♏☌	1F399	having known public influence	cos(2*2πi/49) + isin(2*2πi/49)	0.96729 +0.25365i
14.79	14:47'40	73	3	3-virgiconjunct	3-♍☌	2692	new or deep investment in job	cos(3*2πi/73) + isin(3*2πi/73)	0.96685 +0.25535i
14.85	14:50'43	97	4	4-cancriconjunct	4-♋☌	1F495	traits reserved for those very close	cos(4*2πi/97) + isin(4*2πi/97)	0.96662 +0.25621i
14.88	14:52'33	121	5	5-tauriconjunct	5-♉☌	1F4B0	prosperity & status-seeking	cos(5*2πi/121) + isin(5*2πi/121)	0.96648 +0.25673i
15.00	15:0'0	24	1	1-aquariinconjunct	1-♒π	1F4AD	imagination at work	cos(1*2πi/24) + isin(1*2πi/24)	0.96593 +0.25882i
15.13	15:7'33	119	5	5-gemiundecile	5-♊U	1F4C9	weakened by opinionation, better as ambient	cos(5*2πi/119) + isin(5*2πi/119)	0.96535 +0.26094i
15.16	15:9'28	95	4	4-leaundecile	4-♌U	265B	the image of a progress-inspiring master	cos(4*2πi/95) + isin(4*2πi/95)	0.96521 +0.26148i
15.21	15:12'40	71	3	3-libriundecile	3-♎U	26C5	thriving amidst confusion	cos(3*2πi/71) + isin(3*2πi/71)	0.96496 +0.26238i
15.25	15:15'15	118	5	5-gemidecile	5-♊⊥	1F3C3	staying with it as long as encouraged	cos(5*2πi/118) + isin(5*2πi/118)	0.96477 +0.2631i

15.32	15:19'8	47	2	2-sajiundecile	2-↗U		262B	a core, lived principle	cos(2*2π/47) + isin(2*2π/47)	0.96447 +0.2642i
15.38	15:23'4	117	5	5-geminovile	5-ⅡN		1F48E	best friend's quality	cos(5*2π/117) + isin(5*2π/117)	0.96417 +0.2653i
15.43	15:25'42	70	3	3-libridecile	3-♎⊥		1F527	used to strengthen or repair bonds	cos(3*2π/70) + isin(3*2π/70)	0.96396 +0.26604i
15.48	15:29'1	93	4	4-leanovile	4-♌N		1F60D	brought out by creative, sexualized energy	cos(4*2π/93) + isin(4*2π/93)	0.96371 +0.26697i
15.54	15:32'22	139	6	6-ariseptile	6-♈七		1F3AF	creative perfectionism	cos(6*2π/139) + isin(6*2π/139)	0.96345 +0.2679i
15.65	15:39'7	23	1	1-aquariundecile	1-♒U		1F991	unusual social trait, liked by eccentrics	cos(1*2π/23) + isin(1*2π/23)	0.96292 +0.2698i
15.79	15:47'22	114	5	5-gemisextile	5-Ⅱ∗		1F6F1	other's influence attempts	cos(5*2π/114) + isin(5*2π/114)	0.96227 +0.2721i
15.82	15:49'27	91	4	4-leaseptile	4-♌七		1F576	smoothly comfortable	cos(4*2π/91) + isin(4*2π/91)	0.9621 +0.27269i
15.88	15:52'56	68	3	3-librioctile	3-♎⊿		1F462	appearance of dominating	cos(3*2π/68) + isin(3*2π/68)	0.96183 +0.27366i
15.93	15:55'45	113	5	5-gemiquintile	5-Ⅱ⬠		1F60E	publicly-labeled vibe given	cos(5*2π/113) + isin(5*2π/113)	0.9616 +0.27445i
16.00	16:0'0	45	2	2-sajinovile	2-↗N		2766	shared experience as a token of friendship	cos(2*2π/45) + isin(2*2π/45)	0.96126 +0.27564i
16.07	16:4'17	112	5	5-gemisquare	5-Ⅱ□		1F38E	one's trait observed by outsiders	cos(5*2π/112) + isin(5*2π/112)	0.96092 +0.27684i
16.12	16:7'9	67	3	3-libriseptile	3-♎七		1F63B	getting others to fall in love w oneself	cos(3*2π/67) + isin(3*2π/67)	0.96069 +0.27764i
16.18	16:10'47	89	4	4-leaquintile	4-♌⬠		1F48B	sensuality & body expression	cos(4*2π/89) + isin(4*2π/89)	0.96039 +0.27865i
16.24	16:14'26	133	6	6-ariconjunct	6-♈☌		1F49D	during sex or when flirting	cos(6*2π/133) + isin(6*2π/133)	0.9601 +0.27967i
16.36	16:21'49	22	1	1-aquaridecile	1-♒⊥		1F6E6	in command of one's field	cos(1*2π/22) + isin(1*2π/22)	0.95949 +0.28173i
16.49	16:29'18	131	6	6-tauriundecile	6-♉U		1F611	with doubt in associations	cos(6*2π/131) + isin(6*2π/131)	0.95888 +0.28382i
16.51	16:30'49	109	5	5-gemiconjunct	5-Ⅱ☌		1F44E	diminishing others' importance	cos(5*2π/109) + isin(5*2π/109)	0.95875 +0.28425i
16.55	16:33'6	87	4	4-leatrine	4-♌△		2763	interactor inspired to want	cos(4*2π/87) + isin(4*2π/87)	0.95856 +0.28488i
16.62	16:36'55	65	3	3-libriquintile	3-♎⬠		1F6C0	self-resparking	cos(3*2π/65) + isin(3*2π/65)	0.95825 +0.28595i
16.67	16:40'0	108	5	5-cancriinconjunct	5-♋π		1F31D	why close friends come around	cos(5*2π/108) + isin(5*2π/108)	0.95799 +0.2868i
16.74	16:44'39	43	2	2-sajiseptile	2-↗七		1F0CF	through jokes, games, and fun	cos(2*2π/43) + isin(2*2π/43)	0.9576 +0.2881i
16.82	16:49'20	107	5	5-cancriundecile	5-♋U		1F481	essence of a great conversation w/ one	cos(5*2π/107) + isin(5*2π/107)	0.95721 +0.28941i
16.88	16:52'30	64	3	3-librisquare	3-♎□		4F17	amidst a noisy setting	cos(3*2π/64) + isin(3*2π/64)	0.95694 +0.29028i
16.94	16:56'28	85	4	4-leaconjunct	4-♌☌		1F924	downplaying a real want	cos(4*2π/85) + isin(4*2π/85)	0.9566 +0.29139i
16.98	16:58'52	106	5	5-cancridecile	5-♋⊥		1F3A0	others think one has more power than one has	cos(5*2π/106) + isin(5*2π/106)	0.9564 +0.29206i
17.01	17:0'28	127	6	6-tauriseptile	6-♉七		1F4B8	that which attracts unfair advantage	cos(6*2π/127) + isin(6*2π/127)	0.95626 +0.2925i
17.14	17:8'34	21	1	1-aquarinovile	1-♒N		1F483	at peak sexiness, strength, or creativity	cos(1*2π/21) + isin(1*2π/21)	0.95557 +0.29476i
17.28	17:16'48	125	6	6-tauriquintile	6-♉⬠		1F39F	social clique's requirements	cos(6*2π/125) + isin(6*2π/125)	0.95486 +0.29704i

17.35	17:20'57	83	4	4-virgiundecile	4-♍U	⚡	26A1	high-tension activity in surroundings	cos(4*2πi/83) + isin(4*2πi/83)	0.9545 +0.2982i
17.42	17:25'9	62	3	3-libriopposition	3-♎☍	🏴	1F3F4	manipulative ambition	cos(3*2πi/62) + isin(3*2πi/62)	0.95414 +0.29936i
17.48	17:28'32	103	5	5-cancriseptile	5-♋七	☺	1F60A	basking in joy	cos(5*2πi/103) + isin(5*2πi/103)	0.95384 +0.3003i
17.50	17:30'0	144	7	7-ariinconjunct	7-♈π	🔁	1F501	always-on trait	cos(7*2πi/144) + isin(7*2πi/144)	0.95372 +0.30071i
17.56	17:33'39	41	2	2-sajiquintile	2-♐⬠	🗽	1F5FD	personas aspired to	cos(2*2πi/41) + isin(2*2πi/41)	0.9534 +0.30172i
17.65	17:38'49	102	5	5-cancrisextile	5-♋✳	💼	1F4BC	boss figure attributes	cos(5*2πi/102) + isin(5*2πi/102)	0.95294 +0.30315i
17.75	17:44'47	142	7	7-aridecile	7-♈⊥	🕉	1F549	blessings others can only dream of	cos(7*2πi/142) + isin(7*2πi/142)	0.95241 +0.30481i
17.78	17:46'40	81	4	4-virginovile	4-♍N	👑	1F451	mastered early, forms broad social identity	cos(4*2πi/81) + isin(4*2πi/81)	0.95225 +0.30533i
17.82	17:49'18	101	5	5-cancriquintile	5-♋⬠	🤤	1F624	disregard for things heard	cos(5*2πi/101) + isin(5*2πi/101)	0.95201 +0.30606i
17.87	17:52'20	141	7	7-arinovile	7-♈N	💉	1F489	easy instillment in others	cos(7*2πi/141) + isin(7*2πi/141)	0.95174 +0.3069i
18.00	18:0'0	20	1	1-aquarioctile (vigintile)	1-♒⟋ (⊡)	🤺	1F93A	kicking the butt of outsiders	cos(1*2πi/20) + isin(1*2πi/20)	0.95106 +0.30902i
18.13	18:7'46	139	7	7-ariseptile	7-♈七	🎯	1F3AF	creative perfectionism	cos(7*2πi/139) + isin(7*2πi/139)	0.95036 +0.31117i
18.18	18:10'54	99	5	5-cancritrine	5-♋△	🙅	1F645	communication-stifling	cos(5*2πi/99) + isin(5*2πi/99)	0.95007 +0.31203i
18.23	18:13'40	79	4	4-virgiseptile	4-♍七	✊	270A	anti-establishment revolutionary	cos(4*2πi/79) + isin(4*2πi/79)	0.94982 +0.3128i
18.26	18:15'39	138	7	7-arisextile	7-♈✳	⛑	26D1	daily work focus	cos(7*2πi/138) + isin(7*2πi/138)	0.94964 +0.31334i
18.31	18:18'18	59	3	3-scorpiundecile	3-♏U	👇	1F447	having one's pick	cos(3*2πi/59) + isin(3*2πi/59)	0.9494 +0.31408i
18.39	18:23'38	137	7	7-ariquintile	7-♈⬠	🚧	1F6A7	singular active, direct, control	cos(7*2πi/137) + isin(7*2πi/137)	0.94891 +0.31555i
18.46	18:27'41	39	2	2-sajitrine	2-♐△	🏝	1F3DD	convincing others of one's value	cos(2*2πi/39) + isin(2*2πi/39)	0.94854 +0.31667i
18.53	18:31'45	136	7	7-arisquare	7-♈□	🧐	1F9D0	serious, sober-minded interactant	cos(7*2πi/136) + isin(7*2πi/136)	0.94816 +0.31779i
18.56	18:33'24	97	5	5-cancriconjunct	5-♋☌	💕	1F495	traits reserved for those very close	cos(5*2πi/97) + isin(5*2πi/97)	0.94801 +0.31824i
18.62	18:37'14	58	3	3-scorpidecile	3-♏⊥	👻	1F47B	interactions with an ethereal party	cos(3*2πi/58) + isin(3*2πi/58)	0.94765 +0.3193i
18.67	18:40'0	135	7	7-aritrine	7-♈△	🏄	1F3C4	easy and prolific	cos(7*2πi/135) + isin(7*2πi/135)	0.9474 +0.32006i
18.75	18:45'0	96	5	5-leainconjunct	5-♌π	🤷	1F937	what "not enough" looks like	cos(5*2πi/96) + isin(5*2πi/96)	0.94693 +0.32144i
18.78	18:46'57	115	6	6-gemiseptile	6-♊七	🤳	1F933	inner world with self-talk	cos(6*2πi/115) + isin(6*2πi/115)	0.94675 +0.32198i
18.81	18:48'21	134	7	7-ariopposition	7-♈☍	🖼	1F49F	a trait the partner MUST have	cos(7*2πi/134) + isin(7*2πi/134)	0.94662 +0.32236i
18.95	18:56'50	19	1	1-aquariseptile	1-♒七	🔐	1F510	gateway to one's friendship	cos(1*2πi/19) + isin(1*2πi/19)	0.94582 +0.3247i
19.09	19:5'27	132	7	7-tauriinconjunct	7-♉π	🔗	1F517	sharing a special bond w/ a friend	cos(7*2πi/132) + isin(7*2πi/132)	0.945 +0.32707i
19.15	19:8'56	94	5	5-leadecile	5-♌⊥	👣	1F463	helps in others after learning the hard way	cos(5*2πi/94) + isin(5*2πi/94)	0.94467 +0.32802i
19.20	19:12'0	75	4	4-virgitrine	4-♍△	🏡	1F3E1	family home maintenance	cos(4*2πi/75) + isin(4*2πi/75)	0.94438 +0.32887i

19.24	19:14'11	131	7	7-tauriundecile	7-♉U	😑	1F611	with doubt in associations	cos(7*2πi/131) + isin(7*2πi/131)	0.94417 +0.32947i
19.29	19:17'8	56	3	3-scorpioctile	3-♏⊿	😈	1F608	for fun or one's own power	cos(3*2πi/56) + isin(3*2πi/56)	0.94388 +0.33028i
19.38	19:23'4	130	7	7-tauridecile	7-♉⊥	🎪	1F3AA	relied upon by others in the talked topic	cos(7*2πi/130) + isin(7*2πi/130)	0.94331 +0.33191i
19.46	19:27'34	37	2	2-sajiconjunct	2-♐☌	⭐	2B50	trusted ability revealed	cos(2*2πi/37) + isin(2*2πi/37)	0.94288 +0.33314i
19.53	19:32'5	129	7	7-taurinovile	7-♉N	🙇	1F647	in the service of one attached to	cos(7*2πi/129) + isin(7*2πi/129)	0.94244 +0.33438i
19.57	19:33'54	92	5	5-leaoctile	5-♌⊿	🍻	1F37B	regular comfort preferences w/ close one	cos(5*2πi/92) + isin(5*2πi/92)	0.94226 +0.33488i
19.64	19:38'10	55	3	3-scorpiseptile	3-♏т	😲	1F632	shocking or flooding others w information	cos(3*2πi/55) + isin(3*2πi/55)	0.94184 +0.33605i
19.69	19:41'15	128	7	7-taurioctile	7-♉⊿	👸	1F478	intuitive comfort even amidst stress	cos(7*2πi/128) + isin(7*2πi/128)	0.94154 +0.33689i
19.73	19:43'33	73	4	4-virgiconjunct	4-♍☌	⚒	2692	new or deep investment in job	cos(4*2πi/73) + isin(4*2πi/73)	0.94132 +0.33752i
19.78	19:46'48	91	5	5-leaseptile	5-♌т	🕶	1F576	smoothly comfortable	cos(5*2πi/91) + isin(5*2πi/91)	0.941 +0.33841i
19.84	19:50'33	127	7	7-tauriseptile	7-♉т	💸	1F4B8	that which attracts unfair advantage	cos(7*2πi/127) + isin(7*2πi/127)	0.94063 +0.33944i
20.00	20:0'0	18	1	1-aquarisextile	1-♒✳	🗄	1F5C4	long term rational interactions	cos(1*2πi/18) + isin(1*2πi/18)	0.93969 +0.34202i
20.14	20:8'23	143	8	8-ariundecile	8-♈U	📣	1F4E3	broadcasting which gets one talked about	cos(8*2πi/143) + isin(8*2πi/143)	0.93885 +0.34431i
20.19	20:11'12	107	6	6-cancriundecile	6-♋U	💁	1F481	essence of a great conversation w/ one	cos(6*2πi/107) + isin(6*2πi/107)	0.93857 +0.34508i
20.22	20:13'28	89	5	5-leaquintile	5-♌⌂	💋	1F48B	sensuality & body expression	cos(5*2πi/89) + isin(5*2πi/89)	0.93834 +0.3457i
20.28	20:16'54	71	4	4-libriundecile	4-♎U	🌥	26C5	thriving amidst confusion	cos(4*2πi/71) + isin(4*2πi/71)	0.938 +0.34664i
20.32	20:19'21	124	7	7-taurisquare	7-♉□	🎇	1F387	initial, then waning impression	cos(7*2πi/124) + isin(7*2πi/124)	0.93775 +0.34731i
20.38	20:22'38	53	3	3-scorpiquintile	3-♏⌂	🤗	1F917	reasons one is desired	cos(3*2πi/53) + isin(3*2πi/53)	0.93742 +0.3482i
20.43	20:25'31	141	8	8-arinovile	8-♈N	💉	1F489	easy instillment in others	cos(8*2πi/141) + isin(8*2πi/141)	0.93713 +0.34899i
20.49	20:29'16	123	7	7-tauritrine	7-♉△	⎏	238F	others must express or draw out	cos(7*2πi/123) + isin(7*2πi/123)	0.93675 +0.35001i
20.57	20:34'17	35	2	2-capriundecile	2-♑U	👽	1F47D	quirky distinguishing uniqueness	cos(2*2πi/35) + isin(2*2πi/35)	0.93623 +0.35137i
20.69	20:41'22	87	5	5-leatrine	5-♌△	❣	2763	interactor inspired to want	cos(5*2πi/87) + isin(5*2πi/87)	0.93551 +0.35331i
20.72	20:43'9	139	8	8-ariseptile	8-♈т	🎯	1F3AF	creative perfectionism	cos(8*2πi/139) + isin(8*2πi/139)	0.93532 +0.35379i
20.77	20:46'9	52	3	3-scorpisquare	3-♏□	😞	1F61E	falling short	cos(3*2πi/52) + isin(3*2πi/52)	0.93502 +0.3546i
20.83	20:49'35	121	7	7-tauriconjunct	7-♉☌	💰	1F4B0	prosperity & status-seeking	cos(7*2πi/121) + isin(7*2πi/121)	0.93466 +0.35554i
20.87	20:52'10	69	4	4-librinovile	4-♎N	🐘	1F418	subtle, strong draw of trait via socialization	cos(4*2πi/69) + isin(4*2πi/69)	0.93439 +0.35624i
20.93	20:55'48	86	5	5-leaopposition	5-♌☍	🤡	1F921	one's commentary offends egos	cos(5*2πi/86) + isin(5*2πi/86)	0.93402 +0.35723i
21.00	21:0'0	120	7	7-gemiinconjunct	7-♊π	😢	1F922	more vulnerable to things	cos(7*2πi/120) + isin(7*2πi/120)	0.93358 +0.35837i
21.02	21:1'18	137	8	8-ariquintile	8-♈⌂	🚧	1F6A7	singular active, direct, control	cos(8*2πi/137) + isin(8*2πi/137)	0.93344 +0.35872i

21.18	21:10'35	17	1	1-aquariquintile	1-♒︎⚹		1F44A	managing by dominating	cos(1*2πi/17) + isin(1*2πi/17)	0.93247 +0.36124i
21.33	21:19'59	135	8	8-aritrine	8-♈︎△		1F3C4	easy and prolific	cos(8*2πi/135) + isin(8*2πi/135)	0.93148 +0.36379i
21.39	21:23'10	101	6	6-cancriquintile	6-♋︎⚹		1F624	disregard for things heard	cos(6*2πi/101) + isin(6*2πi/101)	0.93114 +0.36465i
21.43	21:25'42	84	5	5-virgiinconjunct	5-♍︎π		1F411	traits for the seemingly weak	cos(5*2πi/84) + isin(5*2πi/84)	0.93087 +0.36534i
21.49	21:29'33	67	4	4-libriseptile	4-♎︎七		1F63B	getting others to fall in love w oneself	cos(4*2πi/67) + isin(4*2πi/67)	0.93047 +0.36638i
21.54	21:32'18	117	7	7-geminovile	7-♊︎N		1F48E	best friend's quality	cos(7*2πi/117) + isin(7*2πi/117)	0.93017 +0.36713i
21.60	21:36'0	50	3	3-scorpiopposition	3-♏︎☍		1F5BC	images put forth to others	cos(3*2πi/50) + isin(3*2πi/50)	0.92978 +0.36812i
21.69	21:41'12	83	5	5-virgiundecile	5-♍︎U		26A1	high-tension activity in surroundings	cos(5*2πi/83) + isin(5*2πi/83)	0.92922 +0.36953i
21.72	21:43'26	116	7	7-gemioctile	7-♊︎⊿		1F612	having been slighted or doubted	cos(7*2πi/116) + isin(7*2πi/116)	0.92898 +0.37014i
21.82	21:49'5	33	2	2-caprinovile	2-♑︎N		1F4FB	in a formal group discussion	cos(2*2πi/33) + isin(2*2πi/33)	0.92837 +0.37166i
21.91	21:54'46	115	7	7-gemiseptile	7-♊︎七		1F933	inner world with self-talk	cos(7*2πi/115) + isin(7*2πi/115)	0.92775 +0.3732i
21.98	21:59'5	131	8	8-tauriundecile	8-♉︎U		1F611	with doubt in associations	cos(8*2πi/131) + isin(8*2πi/131)	0.92728 +0.37436i
22.04	22:2'26	49	3	3-scorpiconjunct	3-♏︎☌		1F399	having known public influence	cos(3*2πi/49) + isin(3*2πi/49)	0.92692 +0.37527i
22.11	22:6'18	114	7	7-gemisextile	7-♊︎⚹		1F6F1	other's influence attempts	cos(7*2πi/114) + isin(7*2πi/114)	0.92649 +0.37631i
22.15	22:9'13	65	4	4-libriquintile	4-♎︎⚹		1F6C0	self-resparking	cos(4*2πi/65) + isin(4*2πi/65)	0.92617 +0.37709i
22.22	22:13'19	81	5	5-virginovile	5-♍︎N		1F451	mastered early, forms broad social identity	cos(5*2πi/81) + isin(5*2πi/81)	0.92572 +0.3782i
22.27	22:16'4	97	6	6-cancriconjunct	6-♋︎☌		1F495	traits reserved for those very close	cos(6*2πi/97) + isin(6*2πi/97)	0.92542 +0.37894i
22.33	22:19'32	129	8	8-taurinovile	8-♉︎N		1F647	in the service of one attached to	cos(8*2πi/129) + isin(8*2πi/129)	0.92504 +0.37987i
22.50	22:30'0	16	1	1-aquarisquare	1-♒︎□		1F46A	among family	cos(1*2πi/16) + isin(1*2πi/16)	0.92388 +0.38268i
22.68	22:40'37	127	8	8-tauriseptile	8-♉︎七		1F4B8	that which attracts unfair advantage	cos(8*2πi/127) + isin(8*2πi/127)	0.92269 +0.38554i
22.74	22:44'12	95	6	6-leaundecile	6-♌︎U		265B	the image of a progress-inspiring master	cos(6*2πi/95) + isin(6*2πi/95)	0.92229 +0.3865i
22.78	22:47'5	79	5	5-virgiseptile	5-♍︎七		270A	anti-establishment revolutionary	cos(5*2πi/79) + isin(5*2πi/79)	0.92197 +0.38727i
22.82	22:49'0	142	9	9-aridecile	9-♈︎⊥		1F549	blessings others can only dream of	cos(9*2πi/142) + isin(9*2πi/142)	0.92175 +0.38779i
22.86	22:51'25	63	4	4-libritrine	4-♎︎△		1F6A8	know-it-all	cos(4*2πi/63) + isin(4*2πi/63)	0.92148 +0.38843i
22.91	22:54'32	110	7	7-gemiopposition	7-♊︎☍		1F6A5	managing others' behavior	cos(7*2πi/110) + isin(7*2πi/110)	0.92112 +0.38927i
22.98	22:58'43	47	3	3-sajiundecile	3-♐︎U		262B	a core, lived principle	cos(3*2πi/47) + isin(3*2πi/47)	0.92065 +0.39039i
23.04	23:2'23	125	8	8-tauriquintile	8-♉︎⚹		1F39F	social clique's requirements	cos(8*2πi/125) + isin(8*2πi/125)	0.92023 +0.39137i
23.08	23:4'36	78	5	5-virgisextile	5-♍︎⚹		1F94A	fight night moment	cos(5*2πi/78) + isin(5*2πi/78)	0.91998 +0.39197i
23.14	23:8'34	140	9	9-arioctile	9-♈︎⊿		1F340	helped by a benefactor	cos(9*2πi/140) + isin(9*2πi/140)	0.91953 +0.39303i

23.23	23:13'32	31	2	2-capriseptile	2-♑︎⛎		1F3A2	expressed by one's social network	cos(2*2π/31) + isin(2*2π/31)	0.91896 +0.39436i
23.33	23:19'59	108	7	7-cancriinconjunct	7-♋︎⛢		1F31D	why close friends come around	cos(7*2π/108) + isin(7*2π/108)	0.91822 +0.39608i
23.38	23:22'35	77	5	5-virgiquintile	5-♍︎⬠		1F422	guarded insistence	cos(5*2π/77) + isin(5*2π/77)	0.91792 +0.39677i
23.41	23:24'52	123	8	8-tauritrine	8-♉︎△		238F	others must express or draw out	cos(8*2π/123) + isin(8*2π/123)	0.91765 +0.39738i
23.48	23:28'41	46	3	3-sajidecile	3-♐︎⊥		1F4CE	trait housed by key colleagues	cos(3*2π/46) + isin(3*2π/46)	0.91721 +0.3984i
23.55	23:33'5	107	7	7-cancriundecile	7-♋︎U		1F481	essence of a great conversation w/ one	cos(7*2π/107) + isin(7*2π/107)	0.9167 +0.39957i
23.65	23:38'58	137	9	9-ariquintile	9-♈︎⬠		1F6A7	singular active, direct, control	cos(9*2π/137) + isin(9*2π/137)	0.91602 +0.40114i
23.68	23:41'3	76	5	5-virgisquare	5-♍︎□		1F3D8	seen by friends' friends & family	cos(5*2π/76) + isin(5*2π/76)	0.91577 +0.4017i
23.74	23:44'10	91	6	6-leaseptile	6-♌︎⛎		1F576	smoothly comfortable	cos(6*2π/91) + isin(6*2π/91)	0.91541 +0.40253i
23.77	23:46'24	106	7	7-cancridecile	7-♋︎⊥		1F3A0	others think one has more power than one has	cos(7*2π/106) + isin(7*2π/106)	0.91515 +0.40312i
23.82	23:49'24	136	9	9-arisquare	9-♈︎□		1F9D0	serious, sober-minded interactant	cos(9*2π/136) + isin(9*2π/136)	0.91479 +0.40392i
24.00	24:0'0	15	1	1-aquaritrine	1-♒︎△		1F40B	room domination	cos(1*2π/15) + isin(1*2π/15)	0.91355 +0.40674i
24.18	24:10'44	134	9	9-ariopposition	9-♈︎☍		1F49F	a trait the partner MUST have	cos(9*2π/134) + isin(9*2π/134)	0.91227 +0.40959i
24.23	24:13'50	104	7	7-cancrioctile	7-♋︎⦜		1F61B	trait known and accepted among friends	cos(7*2π/104) + isin(7*2π/104)	0.9119 +0.41041i
24.27	24:16'10	89	6	6-leaquintile	6-♌︎⬠		1F48B	sensuality & body expression	cos(6*2π/89) + isin(6*2π/89)	0.91162 +0.41103i
24.32	24:19'27	74	5	5-virgiopposition	5-♍︎☍		1F626	social stressors	cos(5*2π/74) + isin(5*2π/74)	0.91123 +0.4119i
24.36	24:21'39	133	9	9-ariconjunct	9-♈︎☌		1F49D	during sex or when flirting	cos(9*2π/133) + isin(9*2π/133)	0.91097 +0.41248i
24.41	24:24'24	59	4	4-scorpiundecile	4-♏︎U		1F447	having one's pick	cos(4*2π/59) + isin(4*2π/59)	0.91063 +0.41321i
24.47	24:27'57	103	7	7-cancriseptile	7-♋︎⛎		1F60A	basking in joy	cos(7*2π/103) + isin(7*2π/103)	0.91021 +0.41415i
24.55	24:32'43	44	3	3-sajioctile	3-♐︎⦜		1F6B5	role in a peer group	cos(3*2π/44) + isin(3*2π/44)	0.90963 +0.41542i
24.62	24:36'55	117	8	8-geminovile	8-♊︎N		1F48E	best friend's quality	cos(8*2π/117) + isin(8*2π/117)	0.90912 +0.41652i
24.66	24:39'27	73	5	5-virgiconjunct	5-♍︎☌		2692	new or deep investment in job	cos(5*2π/73) + isin(5*2π/73)	0.90882 +0.41719i
24.73	24:43'58	131	9	9-tauriundecile	9-♉︎U		1F611	with doubt in associations	cos(9*2π/131) + isin(9*2π/131)	0.90827 +0.41839i
24.83	24:49'39	29	2	2-capriquintile	2-♑︎⬠		1F3A9	proud charisma	cos(2*2π/29) + isin(2*2π/29)	0.90758 +0.41989i
24.92	24:55'23	130	9	9-tauridecile	9-♉︎⊥		1F3AA	relied upon by others in the talked topic	cos(9*2π/130) + isin(9*2π/130)	0.90687 +0.4214i
25.00	25:0'0	72	5	5-libriinconjunct	5-♎︎⛢		2753	a problem to be solved	cos(5*2π/72) + isin(5*2π/72)	0.90631 +0.42262i
25.04	25:2'36	115	8	8-gemiseptile	8-♊︎⛎		1F933	inner world with self-talk	cos(8*2π/115) + isin(8*2π/115)	0.90599 +0.42331i
25.12	25:6'58	43	3	3-sajiseptile	3-♐︎⛎		1F0CF	through jokes, games, and fun	cos(3*2π/43) + isin(3*2π/43)	0.90545 +0.42446i
25.20	25:12'0	100	7	7-cancrisquare	7-♋︎□		1F6CB	home & family life	cos(7*2π/100) + isin(7*2π/100)	0.90483 +0.42578i

25.26	25:15'47	57	4	4-scorpinovile	4-♏N	1FA84	arrives whenever one wants it, no asking	cos(4*2π/57) + isin(4*2π/57)	0.90436 +0.42678i
25.31	25:18'45	128	9	9-taurioctile	9-♉⊿	1F478	intuitive comfort even amidst stress	cos(9*2π/128) + isin(9*2π/128)	0.90399 +0.42756i
25.35	25:21'7	71	5	5-libriundecile	5-♎U	26C5	thriving amidst confusion	cos(5*2π/71) + isin(5*2π/71)	0.90369 +0.42818i
25.41	25:24'42	85	6	6-leaconjunct	6-♌☌	1F924	downplaying a real want	cos(6*2π/85) + isin(6*2π/85)	0.90325 +0.42912i
25.49	25:29'12	113	8	8-gemiquintile	8-♊⚺	1F60E	publicly-labeled vibe given	cos(8*2π/113) + isin(8*2π/113)	0.90269 +0.4303i
25.53	25:31'54	141	10	10-arinovile	10-♈N	1F489	easy instillment in others	cos(10*2π/141) + isin(10*2π/141)	0.90235 +0.43101i
25.71	25:42'51	14	1	1-aquariopposition	1-♒☍	1F443	a sense from one's company	cos(1*2π/14) + isin(1*2π/14)	0.90097 +0.43388i
25.90	25:53'57	139	10	10-ariseptile	10-♈七	1F3AF	creative perfectionism	cos(10*2π/139) + isin(10*2π/139)	0.89956 +0.43679i
25.95	25:56'45	111	8	8-gemitrine	8-♊△	1F973	around high-expression groups	cos(8*2π/111) + isin(8*2π/111)	0.89921 +0.43752i
25.98	25:58'45	97	7	7-cancriconjunct	7-♋☌	1F495	traits reserved for those very close	cos(7*2π/97) + isin(7*2π/97)	0.89895 +0.43805i
26.02	26:1'26	83	6	6-virgiundecile	6-♍U	26A1	high-tension activity in surroundings	cos(6*2π/83) + isin(6*2π/83)	0.89861 +0.43875i
26.09	26:5'13	69	5	5-librinovile	5-♎N	1F418	subtle, strong draw of trait via socialization	cos(5*2π/69) + isin(5*2π/69)	0.89813 +0.43973i
26.13	26:7'44	124	9	9-taurisquare	9-♉□	1F387	initial, then waning impression	cos(9*2π/124) + isin(9*2π/124)	0.8978 +0.44039i
26.18	26:10'54	55	4	4-scorpiseptile	4-♏七	1F632	shocking or flooding others w information	cos(4*2π/55) + isin(4*2π/55)	0.8974 +0.44122i
26.25	26:15'0	96	7	7-leainconjunct	7-♌π	1F937	what "not enough" looks like	cos(7*2π/96) + isin(7*2π/96)	0.89687 +0.44229i
26.28	26:16'38	137	10	10-ariquintile	10-♈⚺	1F6A7	singular active, direct, control	cos(10*2π/137) + isin(10*2π/137)	0.89666 +0.44272i
26.34	26:20'29	41	3	3-sajiquintile	3-♐⚺	1F5FD	personas aspired to	cos(3*2π/41) + isin(3*2π/41)	0.89617 +0.44372i
26.42	26:25'19	109	8	8-gemiconjunct	8-♊☌	1F44E	diminishing others' importance	cos(8*2π/109) + isin(8*2π/109)	0.89554 +0.44498i
26.47	26:28'14	68	5	5-librioctile	5-♎⊿	1F462	appearance of dominating	cos(5*2π/68) + isin(5*2π/68)	0.89516 +0.44574i
26.53	26:31'34	95	7	7-leaundecile	7-♌U	265B	the image of a progress-inspiring master	cos(7*2π/95) + isin(7*2π/95)	0.89473 +0.44661i
26.56	26:33'26	122	9	9-tauriopposition	9-♉☍	1F913	easily annoying to others	cos(9*2π/122) + isin(9*2π/122)	0.89449 +0.44709i
26.67	26:40'0	27	2	2-capritrine	2-♑△	1F393	intellectualizing and insight	cos(2*2π/27) + isin(2*2π/27)	0.89363 +0.4488i
26.78	26:46'36	121	9	9-tauriconjunct	9-♉☌	1F4B0	prosperity & status-seeking	cos(9*2π/121) + isin(9*2π/121)	0.89277 +0.45052i
26.81	26:48'30	94	7	7-leadecile	7-♌⊥	1F463	helps in others after learning the hard way	cos(7*2π/94) + isin(7*2π/94)	0.89252 +0.45101i
26.87	26:51'56	67	5	5-libriseptile	5-♎七	1F63B	getting others to fall in love w oneself	cos(5*2π/67) + isin(5*2π/67)	0.89207 +0.4519i
26.92	26:54'57	107	8	8-cancriundecile	8-♋U	1F481	essence of a great conversation w/ one	cos(8*2π/107) + isin(8*2π/107)	0.89167 +0.45268i
27.00	27:0'0	40	3	3-sajisquare	3-♐□	1F66A	future missable partnership duty	cos(3*2π/40) + isin(3*2π/40)	0.89101 +0.45399i
27.10	27:5'48	93	7	7-leanovile	7-♌N	1F60D	brought out by creative, sexualized energy	cos(7*2π/93) + isin(7*2π/93)	0.89024 +0.45549i
27.17	27:10'11	53	4	4-scorpiquintile	4-♏⚺	1F917	reasons one is desired	cos(4*2π/53) + isin(4*2π/53)	0.88966 +0.45663i

27.23	27:13'36	119	9	9-gemiundecile	9-♊U		1F4C9	weakened by opinionation, better as ambient	cos(9*2π/119) + isin(9*2π/119)	0.8892 +0.45752i
27.27	27:16'21	66	5	5-librisextile	5-♎*		1F57A	broadcastable good spirits	cos(5*2π/66) + isin(5*2π/66)	0.88884 +0.45823i
27.34	27:20'30	79	6	6-virgiseptile	6-♍七		270A	anti-establishment revolutionary	cos(6*2π/79) + isin(6*2π/79)	0.88828 +0.4593i
27.39	27:23'28	92	7	7-leaoctile	7-♌⊿		1F37B	regular comfort preferences w/ close one	cos(7*2π/92) + isin(7*2π/92)	0.88789 +0.46007i
27.43	27:25'42	105	8	8-cancrinovile	8-♋N		1F5EF	when irritated to see standards defied	cos(8*2π/105) + isin(8*2π/105)	0.88759 +0.46064i
27.48	27:28'51	131	10	10-tauriundecile	10-♉U		1F611	with doubt in associations	cos(10*2π/131) + isin(10*2π/131)	0.88716 +0.46145i
27.50	27:30'0	144	11	11-ariinconjunct	11-♈⊼		1F501	always-on trait	cos(11*2π/144) + isin(11*2π/144)	0.88701 +0.46175i
27.69	27:41'32	13	1	1-aquariconjunct	1-♒☌		1F3A5	public persona	cos(1*2π/13) + isin(1*2π/13)	0.88546 +0.46472i
27.89	27:53'14	142	11	11-aridecile	11-♈⊥		1F549	blessings others can only dream of	cos(11*2π/142) + isin(11*2π/142)	0.88387 +0.46773i
27.93	27:55'51	116	9	9-gemioctile	9-♊⊿		1F612	having been slighted or doubted	cos(9*2π/116) + isin(9*2π/116)	0.88351 +0.46841i
28.00	28:0'0	90	7	7-leasextile	7-♌*		1F6B8	absorptions by one's children	cos(7*2π/90) + isin(7*2π/90)	0.88295 +0.46947i
28.09	28:5'6	141	11	11-arinovile	11-♈N		1F489	easy instillment in others	cos(11*2π/141) + isin(11*2π/141)	0.88225 +0.47078i
28.13	28:7'30	64	5	5-librisquare	5-♎□		4F17	amidst a noisy setting	cos(5*2π/64) + isin(5*2π/64)	0.88192 +0.4714i
28.17	28:10'26	115	9	9-gemiseptile	9-♊七		1F933	inner world with self-talk	cos(9*2π/115) + isin(9*2π/115)	0.88152 +0.47215i
28.24	28:14'7	51	4	4-scorpitrine	4-♏△		1F61A	use of persuasive words	cos(4*2π/51) + isin(4*2π/51)	0.88101 +0.47309i
28.29	28:17'8	140	11	11-arioctile	11-♈⊿		1F340	helped by a benefactor	cos(11*2π/140) + isin(11*2π/140)	0.8806 +0.47387i
28.35	28:20'47	127	10	10-tauriseptile	10-♉七		1F4B8	that which attracts unfair advantage	cos(10*2π/127) + isin(10*2π/127)	0.88009 +0.4748i
28.42	28:25'15	38	3	3-sajiopposition	3-♐☍		1F64C	use of the body or physical deeds in work	cos(3*2π/38) + isin(3*2π/38)	0.87947 +0.47595i
28.49	28:29'21	139	11	11-ariseptile	11-♈七		1F3AF	creative perfectionism	cos(11*2π/139) + isin(11*2π/139)	0.87891 +0.47699i
28.51	28:30'53	101	8	8-cancriquintile	8-♋○		1F624	disregard for things heard	cos(8*2π/101) + isin(8*2π/101)	0.87869 +0.47739i
28.57	28:34'17	63	5	5-libritrine	5-♎△		1F6A8	know-it-all	cos(5*2π/63) + isin(5*2π/63)	0.87822 +0.47825i
28.64	28:38'10	88	7	7-leasquare	7-♌□		1F479	suppressing power imbalance	cos(7*2π/88) + isin(7*2π/88)	0.87768 +0.47925i
28.70	28:41'44	138	11	11-arisextile	11-♈*		26D1	daily work focus	cos(11*2π/138) + isin(11*2π/138)	0.87718 +0.48016i
28.80	28:48'0	25	2	2-capriconjunct	2-♑☌		1F3DF	rally & tune the mass psychology	cos(2*2π/25) + isin(2*2π/25)	0.87631 +0.48175i
28.93	28:55'42	112	9	9-gemisquare	9-♊□		1F38E	one's trait observed by outsiders	cos(9*2π/112) + isin(9*2π/112)	0.87522 +0.48372i
28.97	28:57'55	87	7	7-leatrine	7-♌△		2763	interactor inspired to want	cos(7*2π/87) + isin(7*2π/87)	0.87491 +0.48428i
29.03	29:1'56	62	5	5-libriopposition	5-♎☍		1F3F4	manipulative ambition	cos(5*2π/62) + isin(5*2π/62)	0.87435 +0.4853i
29.09	29:5'27	99	8	8-cancritrine	8-♋△		1F645	communication-stifling	cos(8*2π/99) + isin(8*2π/99)	0.87385 +0.4862i
29.12	29:7'3	136	11	11-arisquare	11-♈□		1F9D0	serious, sober-minded interactant	cos(11*2π/136) + isin(11*2π/136)	0.87362 +0.4866i

29.19	29:11'21	37	3	3-sajiconjunct	3-♐☌	☆	2B50	trusted ability revealed	cos(3*2πi/37) + isin(3*2πi/37)	0.87301 +0.48769i
29.27	29:16'5	123	10	10-tauritrine	10-♉△	◇	238F	others must express or draw out	cos(10*2πi/123) + isin(10*2πi/123)	0.87234 +0.4889i
29.33	29:19'59	135	11	11-aritrine	11-♈△	🏄	1F3C4	easy and prolific	cos(11*2πi/135) + isin(11*2πi/135)	0.87178 +0.48989i
29.39	29:23'15	49	4	4-scorpiconjunct	4-♏☌	🎙	1F399	having known public influence	cos(4*2πi/49) + isin(4*2πi/49)	0.87132 +0.49072i
29.45	29:27'16	110	9	9-gemiopposition	9-♊☍	🚥	1F6A5	managing others' behavior	cos(9*2πi/110) + isin(9*2πi/110)	0.87075 +0.49173i
29.51	29:30'29	61	5	5-libriconjunct	5-♎☌	🔦	1F526	singled out for attention	cos(5*2πi/61) + isin(5*2πi/61)	0.87029 +0.49255i
29.59	29:35'20	73	6	6-virgiconjunct	6-♍☌	⚒	2692	new or deep investment in job	cos(6*2πi/73) + isin(6*2πi/73)	0.86959 +0.49378i
29.65	29:38'49	85	7	7-leaconjunct	7-♌☌	🤤	1F924	downplaying a real want	cos(7*2πi/85) + isin(7*2πi/85)	0.86909 +0.49466i
29.69	29:41'26	97	8	8-cancriconjunct	8-♋☌	💕	1F495	traits reserved for those very close	cos(8*2πi/97) + isin(8*2πi/97)	0.86871 +0.49532i
29.72	29:43'29	109	9	9-gemiconjunct	9-♊☌	👎	1F44E	diminishing others' importance	cos(9*2πi/109) + isin(9*2πi/109)	0.86842 +0.49583i
29.77	29:46'27	133	11	11-ariconjunct	11-♈☌	💝	1F49D	during sex or when flirting	cos(11*2πi/133) + isin(11*2πi/133)	0.86799 +0.49659i
30.00	30:0'0	12	1	inconjunct (semisextile)	π(⚹)	☁	2601	vibes around you	cos(1*2πi/12) + isin(1*2πi/12)	0.86603 +0.5i
30.23	30:13'44	131	11	11-tauriundecile	11-♉U	😑	1F611	with doubt in associations	cos(11*2πi/131) + isin(11*2πi/131)	0.86402 +0.50346i
30.28	30:16'49	107	9	9-cancriundecile	9-♋U	💁	1F481	essence of a great conversation w/ one	cos(9*2πi/107) + isin(9*2πi/107)	0.86357 +0.50423i
30.32	30:18'56	95	8	8-leaundecile	8-♌U	👑	265B	the image of a progress-inspiring master	cos(8*2πi/95) + isin(8*2πi/95)	0.86326 +0.50477i
30.36	30:21'41	83	7	7-virgiundecile	7-♍U	⚡	26A1	high-tension activity in surroundings	cos(7*2πi/83) + isin(7*2πi/83)	0.86285 +0.50545i
30.42	30:25'21	71	6	6-libriundecile	6-♎U	🌥	26C5	thriving amidst confusion	cos(6*2πi/71) + isin(6*2πi/71)	0.86231 +0.50637i
30.46	30:27'41	130	11	11-tauridecile	11-♉⊥	🎪	1F3AA	relied upon by others in the talked topic	cos(11*2πi/130) + isin(11*2πi/130)	0.86197 +0.50696i
30.51	30:30'30	59	5	5-scorpiundecile	5-♏U	👇	1F447	having one's pick	cos(5*2πi/59) + isin(5*2πi/59)	0.86155 +0.50767i
30.57	30:33'57	106	9	9-cancridecile	9-♋⊥	🎠	1F3A0	others think one has more power than one has	cos(9*2πi/106) + isin(9*2πi/106)	0.86104 +0.50853i
30.64	30:38'17	47	4	4-sajiundecile	4-♐U	☫	262B	a core, lived principle	cos(4*2πi/47) + isin(4*2πi/47)	0.8604 +0.50962i
30.70	30:41'51	129	11	11-taurinovile	11-♉N	🙇	1F647	in the service of one attached to	cos(11*2πi/129) + isin(11*2πi/129)	0.85987 +0.51051i
30.73	30:43'54	82	7	7-virgidecile	7-♍⊥	🦇	1F987	eccentrically attention-getting, disquieting	cos(7*2πi/82) + isin(7*2πi/82)	0.85957 +0.51102i
30.77	30:46'9	117	10	10-geminovile	10-♊N	💎	1F48E	best friend's quality	cos(10*2πi/117) + isin(10*2πi/117)	0.85923 +0.51158i
30.86	30:51'25	35	3	3-capriundecile	3-♑U	👽	1F47D	quirky distinguishing uniqueness	cos(3*2πi/35) + isin(3*2πi/35)	0.85845 +0.5129i
30.94	30:56'15	128	11	11-taurioctile	11-♉⊿	👸	1F478	intuitive comfort even amidst stress	cos(11*2πi/128) + isin(11*2πi/128)	0.85773 +0.5141i
30.97	30:58'3	93	8	8-leanovile	8-♌N	😍	1F60D	brought out by creative, sexualized energy	cos(8*2πi/93) + isin(8*2πi/93)	0.85746 +0.51456i
31.03	31:2'4	58	5	5-scorpidecile	5-♏⊥	👻	1F47B	interactions with an ethereal party	cos(5*2πi/58) + isin(5*2πi/58)	0.85686 +0.51555i
31.08	31:4'44	139	12	12-ariseptile	12-♈☖	🎯	1F3AF	creative perfectionism	cos(12*2πi/139) + isin(12*2πi/139)	0.85646 +0.51622i

31.11	31:6'39	81	7	7-virginovile	7-♍N	1F451	mastered early, forms broad social identity	cos(7*2π/81) + isin(7*2π/81)	0.85617 +0.5167i
31.18	31:10'51	127	11	11-tauriseptile	11-♉7	1F4B8	that which attracts unfair advantage	cos(11*2π/127) + isin(11*2π/127)	0.85554 +0.51774i
31.30	31:18'15	23	2	2-aquariundecile	2-♒U	1F991	unusual social trait, liked by eccentrics	cos(2*2π/23) + isin(2*2π/23)	0.85442 +0.51958i
31.43	31:25'42	126	11	11-taurisextile	11-♉*	1F47E	aggressive assertion of identity	cos(11*2π/126) + isin(11*2π/126)	0.85329 +0.52144i
31.50	31:30'0	80	7	7-virgioctile	7-♍⟋	1F939	vividly remembered by one's children	cos(7*2π/80) + isin(7*2π/80)	0.85264 +0.5225i
31.53	31:31'58	137	12	12-ariquintile	12-♈⚼	1F6A7	singular active, direct, control	cos(12*2π/137) + isin(12*2π/137)	0.85234 +0.52299i
31.58	31:34'44	57	5	5-scorpinovile	5-♏N	1FA84	arrives whenever one wants it, no asking	cos(5*2π/57) + isin(5*2π/57)	0.85192 +0.52367i
31.65	31:38'54	91	8	8-leaseptile	8-♌7	1F576	smoothly comfortable	cos(8*2π/91) + isin(8*2π/91)	0.85128 +0.5247i
31.68	31:40'47	125	11	11-tauriquintile	11-♉⚼	1F39F	social clique's requirements	cos(11*2π/125) + isin(11*2π/125)	0.85099 +0.52517i
31.76	31:45'52	34	3	3-capridecile	3-♑⊥	1F3C6	potential to be a master or boss	cos(3*2π/34) + isin(3*2π/34)	0.85022 +0.52643i
31.90	31:53'55	79	7	7-virgiseptile	7-♍7	270A	anti-establishment revolutionary	cos(7*2π/79) + isin(7*2π/79)	0.84898 +0.52842i
31.94	31:56'7	124	11	11-taurisquare	11-♉□	1F387	initial, then waning impression	cos(11*2π/124) + isin(11*2π/124)	0.84864 +0.52896i
32.00	32:0'0	45	4	4-sajinovile	4-♐N	2766	shared experience as a token of friendship	cos(4*2π/45) + isin(4*2π/45)	0.84805 +0.52992i
32.08	32:4'45	101	9	9-cancriquintile	9-♋⚼	1F624	disregard for things heard	cos(9*2π/101) + isin(9*2π/101)	0.84731 +0.53109i
32.14	32:8'34	56	5	5-scorpioctile	5-♏⟋	1F608	for fun or one's own power	cos(5*2π/56) + isin(5*2π/56)	0.84672 +0.53203i
32.20	32:11'42	123	11	11-tauritrine	11-♉△	238F	others must express or draw out	cos(11*2π/123) + isin(11*2π/123)	0.84624 +0.5328i
32.24	32:14'19	67	6	6-libriseptile	6-♎7	1F63B	getting others to fall in love w oneself	cos(6*2π/67) + isin(6*2π/67)	0.84583 +0.53345i
32.31	32:18'27	78	7	7-virgisextile	7-♍*	1F94A	fight night moment	cos(7*2π/78) + isin(7*2π/78)	0.84519 +0.53447i
32.40	32:23'59	100	9	9-cancrisquare	9-♋□	1F6CB	home & family life	cos(9*2π/100) + isin(9*2π/100)	0.84433 +0.53583i
32.43	32:25'56	111	10	10-gemitrine	10-♊△	1F973	around high-expression groups	cos(10*2π/111) + isin(10*2π/111)	0.84402 +0.5363i
32.48	32:28'52	133	12	12-ariconjunct	12-♈☌	1F49D	during sex or when flirting	cos(12*2π/133) + isin(12*2π/133)	0.84357 +0.53702i
32.50	32:30'0	144	13	13-ariinconjunct	13-♈⚻	1F501	always-on trait	cos(13*2π/144) + isin(13*2π/144)	0.84339 +0.5373i
32.73	32:43'38	11	1	undecile	U	1F5EB	getting talked about	cos(1*2π/11) + isin(1*2π/11)	0.84125 +0.54064i
32.98	32:58'37	131	12	12-tauriundecile	12-♉U	1F611	with doubt in associations	cos(12*2π/131) + isin(12*2π/131)	0.83889 +0.5443i
33.03	33:1'39	109	10	10-gemiconjunct	10-♊☌	1F44E	diminishing others' importance	cos(10*2π/109) + isin(10*2π/109)	0.83841 +0.54504i
33.06	33:3'40	98	9	9-cancriopposition	9-♋☍	1F31F	social advancement catalyst	cos(9*2π/98) + isin(9*2π/98)	0.83809 +0.54553i
33.10	33:6'12	87	8	8-leatrine	8-♌△	2763	interactor inspired to want	cos(8*2π/87) + isin(8*2π/87)	0.83769 +0.54615i
33.19	33:11'29	141	13	13-arinovile	13-♈N	1F489	easy instillment in others	cos(13*2π/141) + isin(13*2π/141)	0.83685 +0.54744i
33.23	33:13'50	65	6	6-libriquintile	6-♎⚼	1F6C0	self-resparking	cos(6*2π/65) + isin(6*2π/65)	0.83647 +0.54801i

33.28	33:16'38	119	11	11-gemiundecile	11-♊U		1F4C9	weakened by opinionation, better as ambient	cos(11*2πi/119) + isin(11*2πi/119)	0.83602 +0.54869i
33.33	33:20'0	54	5	5-scorpisextile	5-♏∗		1F378	self-fulfillment tool	cos(5*2πi/54) + isin(5*2πi/54)	0.83549 +0.54951i
33.43	33:25'42	140	13	13-arioctile	13-♈⊿		1F340	helped by a benefactor	cos(13*2πi/140) + isin(13*2πi/140)	0.83457 +0.5509i
33.49	33:29'18	43	4	4-sajiseptile	4-♐七		1F0CF	through jokes, games, and fun	cos(4*2πi/43) + isin(4*2πi/43)	0.834 +0.55177i
33.60	33:36'0	75	7	7-virgitrine	7-♍△		1F3E1	family home maintenance	cos(7*2πi/75) + isin(7*2πi/75)	0.83292 +0.55339i
33.64	33:38'41	107	10	10-cancriundecile	10-♋U		1F481	essence of a great conversation w/ one	cos(10*2πi/107) + isin(10*2πi/107)	0.83249 +0.55404i
33.67	33:40'8	139	13	13-ariseptile	13-♈七		1F3AF	creative perfectionism	cos(13*2πi/139) + isin(13*2πi/139)	0.83225 +0.5544i
33.75	33:45'0	32	3	3-caprioctile	3-♑⊿		1F5FB	an indomitable characteristic	cos(3*2πi/32) + isin(3*2πi/32)	0.83147 +0.55557i
33.85	33:50'46	117	11	11-geminovile	11-♊N		1F48E	best friend's quality	cos(11*2πi/117) + isin(11*2πi/117)	0.83054 +0.55696i
33.88	33:52'56	85	8	8-leaconjunct	8-♌☌		1F924	downplaying a real want	cos(8*2πi/85) + isin(8*2πi/85)	0.83018 +0.55749i
33.91	33:54'46	138	13	13-arisextile	13-♈∗		26D1	daily work focus	cos(13*2πi/138) + isin(13*2πi/138)	0.82989 +0.55793i
33.96	33:57'44	53	5	5-scorpiquintile	5-♏⬠		1F917	reasons one is desired	cos(5*2πi/53) + isin(5*2πi/53)	0.82941 +0.55865i
34.02	34:0'56	127	12	12-tauriseptile	12-♉七		1F4B8	that which attracts unfair advantage	cos(12*2πi/127) + isin(12*2πi/127)	0.82888 +0.55942i
34.05	34:3'14	74	7	7-virgiopposition	7-♍☍		1F626	social stressors	cos(7*2πi/74) + isin(7*2πi/74)	0.82851 +0.55997i
34.14	34:8'16	116	11	11-gemioctile	11-♊⊿		1F612	having been slighted or doubted	cos(11*2πi/116) + isin(11*2πi/116)	0.82769 +0.56119i
34.16	34:9'38	137	13	13-ariquintile	13-♈⬠		1F6A7	singular active, direct, control	cos(13*2πi/137) + isin(13*2πi/137)	0.82747 +0.56151i
34.29	34:17'8	21	2	2-aquarinovile	2-♒N		1F483	at peak sexiness, strength, or creativity	cos(2*2πi/21) + isin(2*2πi/21)	0.82624 +0.56332i
34.43	34:26'5	115	11	11-gemiseptile	11-♊七		1F933	inner world with self-talk	cos(11*2πi/115) + isin(11*2πi/115)	0.82477 +0.56547i
34.47	34:28'5	94	9	9-leadecile	9-♌⊥		1F463	helps in others after learning the hard way	cos(9*2πi/94) + isin(9*2πi/94)	0.82444 +0.56595i
34.52	34:31'13	73	7	7-virgiconjunct	7-♍☌		2692	new or deep investment in job	cos(7*2πi/73) + isin(7*2πi/73)	0.82392 +0.5667i
34.56	34:33'36	125	12	12-tauriquintile	12-♉⬠		1F39F	social clique's requirements	cos(12*2πi/125) + isin(12*2πi/125)	0.82353 +0.56727i
34.62	34:36'55	52	5	5-scorpisquare	5-♏□		1F61E	falling short	cos(5*2πi/52) + isin(5*2πi/52)	0.82298 +0.56806i
34.70	34:41'55	83	8	8-virgiundecile	8-♍U		26A1	high-tension activity in surroundings	cos(8*2πi/83) + isin(8*2πi/83)	0.82216 +0.56926i
34.74	34:44'12	114	11	11-gemisextile	11-♊∗		1F6F1	other's influence attempts	cos(11*2πi/114) + isin(11*2πi/114)	0.82178 +0.56981i
34.84	34:50'19	31	3	3-capriseptile	3-♑七		1F3A2	expressed by one's social network	cos(3*2πi/31) + isin(3*2πi/31)	0.82076 +0.57127i
34.93	34:55'31	134	13	13-ariopposition	13-♈☍		1F49F	a trait the partner MUST have	cos(13*2πi/134) + isin(13*2πi/134)	0.8199 +0.57251i
35.00	35:0'0	72	7	7-libriinconjunct	7-♎π		2753	a problem to be solved	cos(7*2πi/72) + isin(7*2πi/72)	0.81915 +0.57358i
35.04	35:2'39	113	11	11-gemiquintile	11-♊⬠		1F60E	publicly-labeled vibe given	cos(11*2πi/113) + isin(11*2πi/113)	0.81871 +0.57421i
35.12	35:7'19	41	4	4-sajiquintile	4-♐⬠		1F5FD	personas aspired to	cos(4*2πi/41) + isin(4*2πi/41)	0.81793 +0.57532i

35.19	35:11'16	133	13	13-ariconjunct	13-♈︎♂	💝	1F49D	during sex or when flirting	cos(13*2πi/133) + isin(13*2πi/133)	0.81727 +0.57626i
35.24	35:14'41	143	14	14-ariundecile	14-♈︎U	📣	1F4E3	broadcasting which gets one talked about	cos(14*2πi/143) + isin(14*2πi/143)	0.81669 +0.57707i
35.29	35:17'38	51	5	5-scorpitrine	5-♏︎△	😚	1F61A	use of persuasive words	cos(5*2πi/51) + isin(5*2πi/51)	0.8162 +0.57777i
35.36	35:21'25	112	11	11-gemisquare	11-♊︎□	👯	1F38E	one's trait observed by outsiders	cos(11*2πi/112) + isin(11*2πi/112)	0.81556 +0.57867i
35.41	35:24'35	61	6	6-libriconjunct	6-♎︎♂	🔦	1F526	singled out for attention	cos(6*2πi/61) + isin(6*2πi/61)	0.81503 +0.57942i
35.49	35:29'34	71	7	7-libriundecile	7-♎︎U	🌦	26C5	thriving amidst confusion	cos(7*2πi/71) + isin(7*2πi/71)	0.81419 +0.5806i
35.56	35:33'20	81	8	8-virginovile	8-♍︎N	👑	1F451	mastered early, forms broad social identity	cos(8*2πi/81) + isin(8*2πi/81)	0.81355 +0.58149i
35.64	35:38'36	101	10	10-cancriquintile	10-♋︎⚹	🥤	1F624	disregard for things heard	cos(10*2πi/101) + isin(10*2πi/101)	0.81266 +0.58274i
35.68	35:40'32	111	11	11-gemitrine	11-♊︎△	🥳	1F973	around high-expression groups	cos(11*2πi/111) + isin(11*2πi/111)	0.81233 +0.5832i
35.73	35:43'30	131	13	13-tauriundecile	13-♉︎U	😑	1F611	with doubt in associations	cos(13*2πi/131) + isin(13*2πi/131)	0.81183 +0.5839i
35.74	35:44'40	141	14	14-arinovile	14-♈︎N	💉	1F489	easy instillment in others	cos(14*2πi/141) + isin(14*2πi/141)	0.81163 +0.58417i
36.00	36:0'0	10	1	decile	⊥	🛂	1F6C2	ability to control	cos(1*2πi/10) + isin(1*2πi/10)	0.80902 +0.58779i
36.28	36:16'44	129	13	13-taurinovile	13-♉︎N	🙇	1F647	in the service of one attached to	cos(13*2πi/129) + isin(13*2πi/129)	0.80614 +0.59172i
36.33	36:19'48	109	11	11-gemiconjunct	11-♊︎♂	👎	1F44E	diminishing others' importance	cos(11*2πi/109) + isin(11*2πi/109)	0.80562 +0.59244i
36.36	36:21'49	99	10	10-cancritrine	10-♋︎△	🙅	1F645	communication-stifling	cos(10*2πi/99) + isin(10*2πi/99)	0.80527 +0.59291i
36.40	36:24'16	89	9	9-leaquintile	9-♌︎⚹	💋	1F48B	sensuality & body expression	cos(9*2πi/89) + isin(9*2πi/89)	0.80485 +0.59348i
36.46	36:27'20	79	8	8-virgiseptile	8-♍︎七	✊	270A	anti-establishment revolutionary	cos(8*2πi/79) + isin(8*2πi/79)	0.80432 +0.5942i
36.52	36:31'18	69	7	7-librinovile	7-♎︎N	🐘	1F418	subtle, strong draw of trait via socialization	cos(7*2πi/69) + isin(7*2πi/69)	0.80363 +0.59513i
36.56	36:33'45	128	13	13-taurioctile	13-♉︎⊿	👸	1F478	intuitive comfort even amidst stress	cos(13*2πi/128) + isin(13*2πi/128)	0.80321 +0.5957i
36.61	36:36'36	59	6	6-scorpiundecile	6-♏︎U	👇	1F447	having one's pick	cos(6*2πi/59) + isin(6*2πi/59)	0.80271 +0.59637i
36.67	36:39'59	108	11	11-cancriinconjunct	11-♋︎π	😝	1F31D	why close friends come around	cos(11*2πi/108) + isin(11*2πi/108)	0.80212 +0.59716i
36.73	36:44'4	49	5	5-scorpiconjunct	5-♏︎♂	🎙	1F399	having known public influence	cos(5*2πi/49) + isin(5*2πi/49)	0.80141 +0.59811i
36.79	36:47'17	137	14	14-ariquintile	14-♈︎⚹	🚧	1F6A7	singular active, direct, control	cos(14*2πi/137) + isin(14*2πi/137)	0.80085 +0.59886i
36.82	36:49'5	88	9	9-leasquare	9-♌︎□	👹	1F479	suppressing power imbalance	cos(9*2πi/88) + isin(9*2πi/88)	0.80054 +0.59928i
36.85	36:51'1	127	13	13-tauriseptile	13-♉︎七	💸	1F4B8	that which attracts unfair advantage	cos(13*2πi/127) + isin(13*2πi/127)	0.8002 +0.59973i
36.92	36:55'23	39	4	4-sajitrine	4-♐︎△	🏝	1F3DD	convincing others of one's value	cos(4*2πi/39) + isin(4*2πi/39)	0.79944 +0.60074i
37.01	37:0'33	107	11	11-cancriundecile	11-♋︎U	🛅	1F481	essence of a great conversation w/ one	cos(11*2πi/107) + isin(11*2πi/107)	0.79854 +0.60195i
37.06	37:3'31	68	7	7-librioctile	7-♎︎⊿	👢	1F462	appearance of dominating	cos(7*2πi/68) + isin(7*2πi/68)	0.79802 +0.60263i
37.14	37:8'34	126	13	13-taurisextile	13-♉︎✳	👾	1F47E	aggressive assertion of identity	cos(13*2πi/126) + isin(13*2πi/126)	0.79713 +0.6038i

37.24	37:14'28	29	3	3-capriquintile	3-♑⚹		1F3A9	proud charisma	cos(3*2πi/29) + isin(3*2πi/29)	0.79609 +0.60517i
37.33	37:20'0	135	14	14-aritrine	14-♈△		1F3C4	easy and prolific	cos(14*2πi/135) + isin(14*2πi/135)	0.79512 +0.60645i
37.36	37:21'30	106	11	11-cancridecile	11-♋⊥		1F3A0	others think one has more power than one has	cos(11*2πi/106) + isin(11*2πi/106)	0.79485 +0.6068i
37.44	37:26'23	125	13	13-tauriquintile	13-♉⚹		1F39F	social clique's requirements	cos(13*2πi/125) + isin(13*2πi/125)	0.79399 +0.60793i
37.50	37:30'0	48	5	5-sajiinconjunct	5-♐⚻		1F305	shown through creative setting	cos(5*2πi/48) + isin(5*2πi/48)	0.79335 +0.60876i
37.57	37:33'54	115	12	12-gemiseptile	12-♊⚼		1F933	inner world with self-talk	cos(12*2πi/115) + isin(12*2πi/115)	0.79266 +0.60966i
37.61	37:36'42	67	7	7-libriseptile	7-♎⚼		1F63B	getting others to fall in love w oneself	cos(7*2πi/67) + isin(7*2πi/67)	0.79216 +0.61031i
37.67	37:40'27	86	9	9-leaopposition	9-♌☍		1F921	one's commentary offends egos	cos(9*2πi/86) + isin(9*2πi/86)	0.7915 +0.61117i
37.74	37:44'30	124	13	13-taurisquare	13-♉□		1F387	initial, then waning impression	cos(13*2πi/124) + isin(13*2πi/124)	0.79078 +0.61211i
37.76	37:45'44	143	15	15-ariundecile	15-♈∪		1F4E3	broadcasting which gets one talked about	cos(15*2πi/143) + isin(15*2πi/143)	0.79056 +0.61239i
37.89	37:53'41	19	2	2-aquariseptile	2-♒⚼		1F510	gateway to one's friendship	cos(2*2πi/19) + isin(2*2πi/19)	0.78914 +0.61421i
38.03	38:1'41	142	15	15-aridecile	15-♈⊥		1F549	blessings others can only dream of	cos(15*2πi/142) + isin(15*2πi/142)	0.78771 +0.61605i
38.08	38:4'36	104	11	11-cancrioctile	11-♋⊿		1F61B	trait known and accepted among friends	cos(11*2πi/104) + isin(11*2πi/104)	0.78718 +0.61672i
38.12	38:7'3	85	9	9-leaconjunct	9-♌☌		1F924	downplaying a real want	cos(9*2πi/85) + isin(9*2πi/85)	0.78674 +0.61728i
38.18	38:10'54	66	7	7-librisextile	7-♎⚹		1F57A	broadcastable good spirits	cos(7*2πi/66) + isin(7*2πi/66)	0.78605 +0.61816i
38.23	38:13'48	113	12	12-gemiquintile	12-♊⬠		1F60E	publicly-labeled vibe given	cos(12*2πi/113) + isin(12*2πi/113)	0.78553 +0.61882i
38.30	38:17'52	47	5	5-sajiundecile	5-♐∪		262B	a core, lived principle	cos(5*2πi/47) + isin(5*2πi/47)	0.7848 +0.61975i
38.40	38:23'59	75	8	8-virgitrine	8-♍△		1F3E1	family home maintenance	cos(8*2πi/75) + isin(8*2πi/75)	0.78369 +0.62115i
38.45	38:26'47	103	11	11-cancriseptile	11-♋⚼		1F60A	basking in joy	cos(11*2πi/103) + isin(11*2πi/103)	0.78319 +0.62178i
38.47	38:28'23	131	14	14-tauriundecile	14-♉∪		1F611	with doubt in associations	cos(14*2πi/131) + isin(14*2πi/131)	0.7829 +0.62215i
38.57	38:34'17	28	3	3-caprisquare	3-♑□		1F58C	arts and creativity drawn to	cos(3*2πi/28) + isin(3*2πi/28)	0.78183 +0.62349i
38.68	38:40'39	121	13	13-tauriconjunct	13-♉☌		1F4B0	prosperity & status-seeking	cos(13*2πi/121) + isin(13*2πi/121)	0.78067 +0.62494i
38.71	38:42'34	93	10	10-leanovile	10-♌N		1F60D	brought out by creative, sexualized energy	cos(10*2πi/93) + isin(10*2πi/93)	0.78032 +0.62537i
38.77	38:46'9	65	7	7-libriquintile	7-♎⬠		1F6C0	self-resparking	cos(7*2πi/65) + isin(7*2πi/65)	0.77967 +0.62619i
38.85	38:50'56	139	15	15-ariseptile	15-♈⚼		1F3AF	creative perfectionism	cos(15*2πi/139) + isin(15*2πi/139)	0.7788 +0.62727i
38.92	38:55'8	37	4	4-sajiconjunct	4-♐☌		2B50	trusted ability revealed	cos(4*2πi/37) + isin(4*2πi/37)	0.77804 +0.62822i
39.00	39:0'0	120	13	13-gemiinconjunct	13-♊⚻		1F922	more vulnerable to things	cos(13*2πi/120) + isin(13*2πi/120)	0.77715 +0.62932i
39.04	39:2'10	83	9	9-virgiundecile	9-♍∪		26A1	high-tension activity in surroundings	cos(9*2πi/83) + isin(9*2πi/83)	0.77675 +0.62981i
39.07	39:4'11	129	14	14-taurinovile	14-♉N		1F647	in the service of one attached to	cos(14*2πi/129) + isin(14*2πi/129)	0.77638 +0.63027i

39.13	39:7'49	46	5	5-sajidecile	5-♐⊥		1F4CE	trait housed by key colleagues	cos(5*2π/46) + isin(5*2π/46)	0.77571 +0.63109i
39.21	39:12'28	101	11	11-cancriquintile	11-♋♎		1F624	disregard for things heard	cos(11*2π/101) + isin(11*2π/101)	0.77486 +0.63214i
39.27	39:16'21	55	6	6-scorpiseptile	6-♏七		1F632	shocking or flooding others w information	cos(6*2π/55) + isin(6*2π/55)	0.77414 +0.63301i
39.33	39:19'39	119	13	13-gemiundecile	13-♊U		1F4C9	weakened by opinionation, better as ambient	cos(13*2π/119) + isin(13*2π/119)	0.77353 +0.63376i
39.38	39:22'30	64	7	7-librisquare	7-♎□		4F17	amidst a noisy setting	cos(7*2π/64) + isin(7*2π/64)	0.77301 +0.63439i
39.42	39:24'57	137	15	15-ariquintile	15-♈♎		1F6A7	singular active, direct, control	cos(15*2π/137) + isin(15*2π/137)	0.77256 +0.63495i
39.45	39:27'7	73	8	8-virgiconjunct	8-♍☌		2692	new or deep investment in job	cos(8*2π/73) + isin(8*2π/73)	0.77216 +0.63543i
39.51	39:30'43	82	9	9-virgidecile	9-♍⊥		1F987	eccentrically attention-getting, disquieting	cos(9*2π/82) + isin(9*2π/82)	0.77149 +0.63624i
39.60	39:36'0	100	11	11-cancrisquare	11-♋□		1F6CB	home & family life	cos(11*2π/100) + isin(11*2π/100)	0.77051 +0.63742i
39.63	39:37'58	109	12	12-gemiconjunct	12-♊☌		1F44E	diminishing others' importance	cos(12*2π/109) + isin(12*2π/109)	0.77015 +0.63787i
39.69	39:41'6	127	14	14-tauriseptile	14-♉七		1F4B8	that which attracts unfair advantage	cos(14*2π/127) + isin(14*2π/127)	0.76957 +0.63857i
39.71	39:42'21	136	15	15-arisquare	15-♈□		1F9D0	serious, sober-minded interactant	cos(15*2π/136) + isin(15*2π/136)	0.76933 +0.63885i
40.00	40:0'0	9	1	novile	N(✖)		1F3AC	self-image promotion	cos(1*2π/9) + isin(1*2π/9)	0.76604 +0.64279i
40.28	40:16'46	143	16	16-ariundecile	16-♈U		1F4E3	broadcasting which gets one talked about	cos(16*2π/143) + isin(16*2π/143)	0.7629 +0.64652i
40.34	40:20'41	116	13	13-gemioctile	13-♊⊿		1F612	having been slighted or doubted	cos(13*2π/116) + isin(13*2π/116)	0.76216 +0.64739i
40.37	40:22'25	107	12	12-cancriundecile	12-♋U		1F481	essence of a great conversation w/ one	cos(12*2π/107) + isin(12*2π/107)	0.76183 +0.64777i
40.45	40:26'57	89	10	10-leaquintile	10-♌♎		1F48B	sensuality & body expression	cos(10*2π/89) + isin(10*2π/89)	0.76098 +0.64878i
40.50	40:30'0	80	9	9-virgioctile	9-♍⊿		1F939	vividly remembered by one's children	cos(9*2π/80) + isin(9*2π/80)	0.76041 +0.64945i
40.56	40:33'48	71	8	8-libriundecile	8-♎U		26C5	thriving amidst confusion	cos(8*2π/71) + isin(8*2π/71)	0.75969 +0.65029i
40.65	40:38'42	62	7	7-libriopposition	7-♎☍		1F3F4	manipulative ambition	cos(7*2π/62) + isin(7*2π/62)	0.75876 +0.65137i
40.70	40:41'44	115	13	13-gemiseptile	13-♊七		1F933	inner world with self-talk	cos(13*2π/115) + isin(13*2π/115)	0.75818 +0.65204i
40.75	40:45'16	53	6	6-scorpiquintile	6-♏♎		1F917	reasons one is desired	cos(6*2π/53) + isin(6*2π/53)	0.75751 +0.65282i
40.82	40:49'29	97	11	11-cancriconjunct	11-♋☌		1F495	traits reserved for those very close	cos(11*2π/97) + isin(11*2π/97)	0.75671 +0.65375i
40.85	40:51'3	141	16	16-arinovile	16-♈N		1F489	easy instillment in others	cos(16*2π/141) + isin(16*2π/141)	0.75641 +0.6541i
40.91	40:54'32	44	5	5-sajioctile	5-♐⊿		1F6B5	role in a peer group	cos(5*2π/44) + isin(5*2π/44)	0.75575 +0.65486i
40.98	40:58'32	123	14	14-tauritrine	14-♉△		238F	others must express or draw out	cos(14*2π/123) + isin(14*2π/123)	0.75499 +0.65574i
41.01	41:0'45	79	9	9-virgiseptile	9-♍七		270A	anti-establishment revolutionary	cos(9*2π/79) + isin(9*2π/79)	0.75456 +0.65623i
41.05	41:3'9	114	13	13-gemisextile	13-♊✳		1F6F1	other's influence attempts	cos(13*2π/114) + isin(13*2π/114)	0.75411 +0.65675i
41.14	41:8'34	35	4	4-capriundecile	4-♑U		1F47D	quirky distinguishing uniqueness	cos(4*2π/35) + isin(4*2π/35)	0.75307 +0.65794i

41.25	41:15'0	96	11	11-leainconjunct	11-♌π		1F937	what "not enough" looks like	cos(11*2πi/96) + isin(11*2πi/96)	0.75184 +0.65935i
41.31	41:18'41	61	7	7-libriconjunct	7-♎♂		1F526	singled out for attention	cos(7*2πi/61) + isin(7*2πi/61)	0.75113 +0.66015i
41.38	41:22'45	87	10	10-leatrine	10-♌△		2763	interactor inspired to want	cos(10*2πi/87) + isin(10*2πi/87)	0.75035 +0.66104i
41.44	41:26'19	139	16	16-ariseptile	16-♈七		1F3AF	creative perfectionism	cos(16*2πi/139) + isin(16*2πi/139)	0.74966 +0.66182i
41.54	41:32'18	26	3	3-capriopposition	3-♑☍		1F3B8	why one's fans follow them	cos(3*2πi/26) + isin(3*2πi/26)	0.74851 +0.66312i
41.68	41:41'3	95	11	11-leaundecile	11-♌U		265B	the image of a progress-inspiring master	cos(11*2πi/95) + isin(11*2πi/95)	0.74682 +0.66502i
41.74	41:44'20	69	8	8-librinovile	8-♎N		1F418	subtle, strong draw of trait via socialization	cos(8*2πi/69) + isin(8*2πi/69)	0.74618 +0.66574i
41.79	41:47'8	112	13	13-gemisquare	13-♊□		1F38E	one's trait observed by outsiders	cos(13*2πi/112) + isin(13*2πi/112)	0.74564 +0.66635i
41.86	41:51'37	43	5	5-sajiseptile	5-♐七		1F0CF	through jokes, games, and fun	cos(5*2πi/43) + isin(5*2πi/43)	0.74477 +0.66732i
41.94	41:56'30	103	12	12-cancriseptile	12-♋七		1F60A	basking in joy	cos(12*2πi/103) + isin(12*2πi/103)	0.74382 +0.66837i
42.00	42:0'0	60	7	7-scorpiinconjunct	7-♏π		1F4CD	strongest memory left behind	cos(7*2πi/60) + isin(7*2πi/60)	0.74314 +0.66913i
42.04	42:2'37	137	16	16-ariquintile	16-♈⬠		1F6A7	singular active, direct, control	cos(16*2πi/137) + isin(16*2πi/137)	0.74263 +0.6697i
42.08	42:4'40	77	9	9-virgiquintile	9-♍⬠		1F422	guarded insistence	cos(9*2πi/77) + isin(9*2πi/77)	0.74223 +0.67014i
42.13	42:7'39	94	11	11-leadecile	11-♌⊥		1F463	helps in others after learning the hard way	cos(11*2πi/94) + isin(11*2πi/94)	0.74165 +0.67078i
42.19	42:11'15	128	15	15-taurioctile	15-♉⊿		1F478	intuitive comfort even amidst stress	cos(15*2πi/128) + isin(15*2πi/128)	0.74095 +0.67156i
42.35	42:21'10	17	2	2-aquariquintile	2-♒⬠		1F44A	managing by dominating	cos(2*2πi/17) + isin(2*2πi/17)	0.73901 +0.6737i
42.50	42:30'0	144	17	17-ariinconjunct	17-♈π		1F501	always-on trait	cos(17*2πi/144) + isin(17*2πi/144)	0.73728 +0.67559i
42.55	42:32'43	110	13	13-gemiopposition	13-♊☍		1F6A5	managing others' behavior	cos(13*2πi/110) + isin(13*2πi/110)	0.73674 +0.67617i
42.58	42:34'50	93	11	11-leanovile	11-♌N		1F60D	brought out by creative, sexualized energy	cos(11*2πi/93) + isin(11*2πi/93)	0.73633 +0.67663i
42.63	42:37'53	76	9	9-virgisquare	9-♍□		1F3D8	seen by friends' friends & family	cos(9*2πi/76) + isin(9*2πi/76)	0.73572 +0.67728i
42.67	42:39'59	135	16	16-aritrine	16-♈△		1F3C4	easy and prolific	cos(16*2πi/135) + isin(16*2πi/135)	0.73531 +0.67773i
42.71	42:42'42	59	7	7-scorpiundecile	7-♏U		1F447	having one's pick	cos(7*2πi/59) + isin(7*2πi/59)	0.73477 +0.67831i
42.80	42:47'49	143	17	17-ariundecile	17-♈U		1F4E3	broadcasting which gets one talked about	cos(17*2πi/143) + isin(17*2πi/143)	0.73376 +0.67941i
42.86	42:51'25	42	5	5-sajisextile	5-♐✳		1F497	instilled in co-creative partners	cos(5*2πi/42) + isin(5*2πi/42)	0.73305 +0.68017i
42.94	42:56'8	109	13	13-gemiconjunct	13-♊♂		1F44E	diminishing others' importance	cos(13*2πi/109) + isin(13*2πi/109)	0.73212 +0.68118i
42.99	42:59'6	67	8	8-libriseptile	8-♎七		1F63B	getting others to fall in love w oneself	cos(8*2πi/67) + isin(8*2πi/67)	0.73153 +0.68181i
43.04	43:2'36	92	11	11-leaoctile	11-♌⊿		1F37B	regular comfort preferences w/ close one	cos(11*2πi/92) + isin(11*2πi/92)	0.73084 +0.68255i
43.08	43:4'36	117	14	14-geminovile	14-♊N		1F48E	best friend's quality	cos(14*2πi/117) + isin(14*2πi/117)	0.73044 +0.68298i
43.10	43:5'54	142	17	17-aridecile	17-♈⊥		1F549	blessings others can only dream of	cos(17*2πi/142) + isin(17*2πi/142)	0.73018 +0.68326i

43.20	43:12'0	25	3	3-capriconjunct	3-♑☌		1F3DF	rally & tune the mass psychology	cos(3*2π/25) + isin(3*2π/25)	0.72897 +0.68455i
43.33	43:20'0	108	13	13-cancriinconjunct	13-♋π		1F31D	why close friends come around	cos(13*2π/108) + isin(13*2π/108)	0.72737 +0.68624i
43.37	43:22'24	83	10	10-virgiundecile	10-♍U		26A1	high-tension activity in surroundings	cos(10*2π/83) + isin(10*2π/83)	0.72689 +0.68675i
43.45	43:26'53	58	7	7-scorpidecile	7-♏⊥		1F47B	interactions with an ethereal party	cos(7*2π/58) + isin(7*2π/58)	0.726 +0.6877i
43.55	43:32'54	124	15	15-taurisquare	15-♉□		1F387	initial, then waning impression	cos(15*2π/124) + isin(15*2π/124)	0.72479 +0.68897i
43.64	43:38'10	33	4	4-caprinovile	4-♑N		1F4FB	in a formal group discussion	cos(4*2π/33) + isin(4*2π/33)	0.72373 +0.69008i
43.74	43:44'17	107	13	13-cancriundecile	13-♋U		1F481	essence of a great conversation w/ one	cos(13*2π/107) + isin(13*2π/107)	0.7225 +0.69137i
43.78	43:47'1	74	9	9-virgiopposition	9-♍☍		1F626	social stressors	cos(9*2π/74) + isin(9*2π/74)	0.72196 +0.69194i
43.83	43:49'33	115	14	14-gemiseptile	14-♊七		1F933	inner world with self-talk	cos(14*2π/115) + isin(14*2π/115)	0.72145 +0.69247i
43.90	43:54'8	41	5	5-sajiquintile	5-♐⚼		1F5FD	personas aspired to	cos(5*2π/41) + isin(5*2π/41)	0.72052 +0.69343i
44.00	44:0'0	90	11	11-leasextile	11-♌*		1F6B8	absorptions by one's children	cos(11*2π/90) + isin(11*2π/90)	0.71934 +0.69466i
44.03	44:1'43	139	17	17-ariseptile	17-♈七		1F3AF	creative perfectionism	cos(17*2π/139) + isin(17*2π/139)	0.71899 +0.69502i
44.08	44:4'53	49	6	6-scorpiconjunct	6-♏☌		1F399	having known public influence	cos(6*2π/49) + isin(6*2π/49)	0.71835 +0.69568i
44.15	44:9'3	106	13	13-cancridecile	13-♋⊥		1F3A0	others think one has more power than one has	cos(13*2π/106) + isin(13*2π/106)	0.71751 +0.69655i
44.21	44:12'37	57	7	7-scorpinovile	7-♏N		1FA84	arrives whenever one wants it, no asking	cos(7*2π/57) + isin(7*2π/57)	0.71678 +0.6973i
44.26	44:15'44	122	15	15-tauriopposition	15-♉☍		1F913	easily annoying to others	cos(15*2π/122) + isin(15*2π/122)	0.71615 +0.69794i
44.35	44:20'52	138	17	17-arisextile	17-♈*		26D1	daily work focus	cos(17*2π/138) + isin(17*2π/138)	0.71511 +0.69901i
44.38	44:23'0	73	9	9-virgiconjunct	9-♍☌		2692	new or deep investment in job	cos(9*2π/73) + isin(9*2π/73)	0.71467 +0.69946i
44.44	44:26'39	81	10	10-virginovile	10-♍N		1F451	mastered early, forms broad social identity	cos(10*2π/81) + isin(10*2π/81)	0.71393 +0.70022i
44.49	44:29'39	89	11	11-leaquintile	11-♌⚼		1F48B	sensuality & body expression	cos(11*2π/89) + isin(11*2π/89)	0.71332 +0.70084i
44.54	44:32'9	97	12	12-cancriconjunct	12-♋☌		1F495	traits reserved for those very close	cos(12*2π/97) + isin(12*2π/97)	0.71281 +0.70136i
44.57	44:34'17	105	13	13-cancrinovile	13-♋N		1F5EF	when irritated to see standards defied	cos(13*2π/105) + isin(13*2π/105)	0.71238 +0.7018i
44.63	44:37'41	121	15	15-tauriconjunct	15-♉☌		1F4B0	prosperity & status-seeking	cos(15*2π/121) + isin(15*2π/121)	0.71168 +0.7025i
44.67	44:40'17	137	17	17-ariquintile	17-♈⚼		1F6A7	singular active, direct, control	cos(17*2π/137) + isin(17*2π/137)	0.71115 +0.70304i
45.00	45:0'0	8	1	octile (semisquare)	∠(∠)		1F4AA	forcing others	cos(1*2π/8) + isin(1*2π/8)	0.70711 +0.70711i
45.33	45:20'0	135	17	17-aritrine	17-♈△		1F3C4	easy and prolific	cos(17*2π/135) + isin(17*2π/135)	0.70298 +0.71121i
45.38	45:22'41	119	15	15-gemiundecile	15-♊U		1F4C9	weakened by opinionation, better as ambient	cos(15*2π/119) + isin(15*2π/119)	0.70242 +0.71176i
45.44	45:26'12	103	13	13-cancriseptile	13-♋七		1F60A	basking in joy	cos(13*2π/103) + isin(13*2π/103)	0.70169 +0.71248i
45.47	45:28'25	95	12	12-leaundecile	12-♌U		265B	the image of a progress-inspiring master	cos(12*2π/95) + isin(12*2π/95)	0.70124 +0.71293i

45.52	45:31'2	87	11	11-leatrine	11-♌△	❣	2763	interactor inspired to want	cos(11*2πi/87) + isin(11*2πi/87)	0.70069 +0.71346i
45.57	45:34'10	79	10	10-virgiseptile	10-♍七	✊	270A	anti-establishment revolutionary	cos(10*2πi/79) + isin(10*2πi/79)	0.70004 +0.7141i
45.63	45:38'1	71	9	9-libriundecile	9-♎U	🌥	26C5	thriving amidst confusion	cos(9*2πi/71) + isin(9*2πi/71)	0.69924 +0.71489i
45.67	45:40'17	134	17	17-ariopposition	17-♈☍	💟	1F49F	a trait the partner MUST have	cos(17*2πi/134) + isin(17*2πi/134)	0.69877 +0.71535i
45.71	45:42'51	63	8	8-libritrine	8-♎△	🚨	1F6A8	know-it-all	cos(8*2πi/63) + isin(8*2πi/63)	0.69824 +0.71587i
45.76	45:45'45	118	15	15-gemidecile	15-♊⊥	🏃	1F3C3	staying with it as long as encouraged	cos(15*2πi/118) + isin(15*2πi/118)	0.69763 +0.71646i
45.82	45:49'5	55	7	7-scorpiseptile	7-♏七	😲	1F632	shocking or flooding others w information	cos(7*2πi/55) + isin(7*2πi/55)	0.69694 +0.71713i
45.88	45:52'56	102	13	13-cancrisextile	13-♋✶	💼	1F4BC	boss figure attributes	cos(13*2πi/102) + isin(13*2πi/102)	0.69613 +0.71791i
45.96	45:57'26	47	6	6-sajiundecile	6-♐U	☪	262B	a core, lived principle	cos(6*2πi/47) + isin(6*2πi/47)	0.69519 +0.71882i
46.05	46:2'47	86	11	11-leaopposition	11-♌☍	🤡	1F921	one's commentary offends egos	cos(11*2πi/86) + isin(11*2πi/86)	0.69407 +0.7199i
46.08	46:4'47	125	16	16-tauriquintile	16-♉⬠	🎟	1F39F	social clique's requirements	cos(16*2πi/125) + isin(16*2πi/125)	0.69365 +0.72031i
46.15	46:9'13	39	5	5-sajitrine	5-♐△	🏝	1F3DD	convincing others of one's value	cos(5*2πi/39) + isin(5*2πi/39)	0.69272 +0.7212i
46.24	46:14'18	109	14	14-gemiconjunct	14-♊☌	👎	1F44E	diminishing others' importance	cos(14*2πi/109) + isin(14*2πi/109)	0.69166 +0.72223i
46.29	46:17'8	70	9	9-libridecile	9-♎⊥	🔧	1F527	used to strengthen or repair bonds	cos(9*2πi/70) + isin(9*2πi/70)	0.69106 +0.72279i
46.34	46:20'11	101	13	13-cancriquintile	13-♋⬠	🤤	1F624	disregard for things heard	cos(13*2πi/101) + isin(13*2πi/101)	0.69042 +0.72341i
46.36	46:21'49	132	17	17-tauriinconjunct	17-♉⚻	🔗	1F517	sharing a special bond w/ a friend	cos(17*2πi/132) + isin(17*2πi/132)	0.69008 +0.72373i
46.45	46:27'5	31	4	4-capriseptile	4-♑七	🎢	1F3A2	expressed by one's social network	cos(4*2πi/31) + isin(4*2πi/31)	0.68897 +0.72479i
46.59	46:35'17	85	11	11-leaconjunct	11-♌☌	🤤	1F924	downplaying a real want	cos(11*2πi/85) + isin(11*2πi/85)	0.68724 +0.72643i
46.62	46:37'7	139	18	18-ariseptile	18-♈七	🎯	1F3AF	creative perfectionism	cos(18*2πi/139) + isin(18*2πi/139)	0.68685 +0.7268i
46.67	46:39'59	54	7	7-scorpisextile	7-♏✶	🍸	1F378	self-fulfillment tool	cos(7*2πi/54) + isin(7*2πi/54)	0.68624 +0.72737i
46.72	46:43'3	131	17	17-tauriundecile	17-♉U	😑	1F611	with doubt in associations	cos(17*2πi/131) + isin(17*2πi/131)	0.6856 +0.72798i
46.80	46:47'59	100	13	13-cancrisquare	13-♋□	🛋	1F6CB	home & family life	cos(13*2πi/100) + isin(13*2πi/100)	0.68455 +0.72897i
46.83	46:49'45	123	16	16-tauritrine	16-♉△	⎍	238F	others must express or draw out	cos(16*2πi/123) + isin(16*2πi/123)	0.68417 +0.72932i
46.96	46:57'23	23	3	3-aquariundecile	3-♒U	🦑	1F991	unusual social trait, liked by eccentrics	cos(3*2πi/23) + isin(3*2πi/23)	0.68255 +0.73084i
47.08	47:4'36	130	17	17-tauridecile	17-♉⊥	🎪	1F3AA	relied upon by others in the talked topic	cos(17*2πi/130) + isin(17*2πi/130)	0.68102 +0.73227i
47.14	47:8'34	84	11	11-virgiinconjunct	11-♍⚻	🐑	1F411	traits for the seemingly weak	cos(11*2πi/84) + isin(11*2πi/84)	0.68017 +0.73305i
47.21	47:12'47	61	8	8-libriconjunct	8-♎☌	🔦	1F526	singled out for attention	cos(8*2πi/61) + isin(8*2πi/61)	0.67927 +0.73389i
47.30	47:17'57	137	18	18-ariquintile	18-♈⬠	🚧	1F6A7	singular active, direct, control	cos(18*2πi/137) + isin(18*2πi/137)	0.67817 +0.73491i
47.37	47:22'6	38	5	5-sajiopposition	5-♐☍	🙌	1F64C	use of the body or physical deeds in work	cos(5*2πi/38) + isin(5*2πi/38)	0.67728 +0.73572i

47.44	47:26'30	129	17	17-taurinovile	17-♉N		1F647	in the service of one attached to	cos(17*2π/129) + isin(17*2π/129)	0.67634 +0.73659i
47.50	47:30'0	144	19	19-ariinconjunct	19-♈⚻		1F501	always-on trait	cos(19*2π/144) + isin(19*2π/144)	0.67559 +0.73728i
47.55	47:32'49	53	7	7-scorpiquintile	7-♏⚼		1F917	reasons one is desired	cos(7*2π/53) + isin(7*2π/53)	0.67498 +0.73783i
47.65	47:38'49	68	9	9-librioctile	9-♎∠		1F462	appearance of dominating	cos(9*2π/68) + isin(9*2π/68)	0.6737 +0.73901i
47.71	47:42'39	83	11	11-virgiundecile	11-♍U		26A1	high-tension activity in surroundings	cos(11*2π/83) + isin(11*2π/83)	0.67287 +0.73976i
47.79	47:47'15	113	15	15-gemiquintile	15-♊⚼		1F60E	publicly-labeled vibe given	cos(15*2π/113) + isin(15*2π/113)	0.67188 +0.74066i
47.83	47:49'55	143	19	19-ariundecile	19-♈U		1F4E3	broadcasting which gets one talked about	cos(19*2π/143) + isin(19*2π/143)	0.6713 +0.74118i
48.00	48:0'0	15	2	2-aquaritrine	2-♒△		1F40B	room domination	cos(2*2π/15) + isin(2*2π/15)	0.66913 +0.74314i
48.19	48:11'20	127	17	17-tauriseptile	17-♉七		1F4B8	that which attracts unfair advantage	cos(17*2π/127) + isin(17*2π/127)	0.66668 +0.74535i
48.25	48:14'50	97	13	13-cancriconjunct	13-♋☌		1F495	traits reserved for those very close	cos(13*2π/97) + isin(13*2π/97)	0.66592 +0.74603i
48.29	48:17'33	82	11	11-virgidecile	11-♍⊥		1F987	eccentrically attention-getting, disquieting	cos(11*2π/82) + isin(11*2π/82)	0.66533 +0.74655i
48.36	48:21'29	67	9	9-libriseptile	9-♎七		1F63B	getting others to fall in love w oneself	cos(9*2π/67) + isin(9*2π/67)	0.66447 +0.74731i
48.40	48:24'12	119	16	16-gemiundecile	16-♊U		1F4C9	weakened by opinionation, better as ambient	cos(16*2π/119) + isin(16*2π/119)	0.66388 +0.74784i
48.46	48:27'41	52	7	7-scorpisquare	7-♏□		1F61E	falling short	cos(7*2π/52) + isin(7*2π/52)	0.66312 +0.74851i
48.54	48:32'21	89	12	12-leaquintile	12-♌⚼		1F48B	sensuality & body expression	cos(12*2π/89) + isin(12*2π/89)	0.66211 +0.74941i
48.57	48:34'17	126	17	17-taurisextile	17-♉✳		1F47E	aggressive assertion of identity	cos(17*2π/126) + isin(17*2π/126)	0.66169 +0.74978i
48.65	48:38'55	37	5	5-sajiconjunct	5-♐☌		2B50	trusted ability revealed	cos(5*2π/37) + isin(5*2π/37)	0.66067 +0.75067i
48.75	48:45'0	96	13	13-leainconjunct	13-♌⚻		1F937	what "not enough" looks like	cos(13*2π/96) + isin(13*2π/96)	0.65935 +0.75184i
48.81	48:48'48	59	8	8-scorpiundecile	8-♏U		1F447	having one's pick	cos(8*2π/59) + isin(8*2π/59)	0.65851 +0.75257i
48.89	48:53'19	81	11	11-virginovile	11-♍N		1F451	mastered early, forms broad social identity	cos(11*2π/81) + isin(11*2π/81)	0.65752 +0.75344i
48.93	48:55'55	103	14	14-cancriseptile	14-♋七		1F60A	basking in joy	cos(14*2π/103) + isin(14*2π/103)	0.65695 +0.75393i
48.96	48:57'36	125	17	17-tauriquintile	17-♉⚼		1F39F	social clique's requirements	cos(17*2π/125) + isin(17*2π/125)	0.65659 +0.75425i
49.09	49:5'27	22	3	3-aquaridecile	3-♒⊥		1F6E6	in command of one's field	cos(3*2π/22) + isin(3*2π/22)	0.65486 +0.75575i
49.23	49:13'50	117	16	16-geminovile	16-♊N		1F48E	best friend's quality	cos(16*2π/117) + isin(16*2π/117)	0.65301 +0.75735i
49.26	49:15'47	95	13	13-leaundecile	13-♌U		265B	the image of a progress-inspiring master	cos(13*2π/95) + isin(13*2π/95)	0.65259 +0.75771i
49.32	49:18'54	73	10	10-virgiconjunct	10-♍☌		2692	new or deep investment in job	cos(10*2π/73) + isin(10*2π/73)	0.6519 +0.75831i
49.35	49:21'17	124	17	17-taurisquare	17-♉□		1F387	initial, then waning impression	cos(17*2π/124) + isin(17*2π/124)	0.65137 +0.75876i
49.41	49:24'42	51	7	7-scorpitrine	7-♏△		1F61A	use of persuasive words	cos(7*2π/51) + isin(7*2π/51)	0.65062 +0.7594i
49.50	49:30'0	80	11	11-virgioctile	11-♍∠		1F939	vividly remembered by one's children	cos(11*2π/80) + isin(11*2π/80)	0.64945 +0.76041i

49.54	49:32'28	109	15	15-gemiconjunct	15-♊♂		1F44E	diminishing others' importance	cos(15*2πi/109) + isin(15*2πi/109)	0.6489 +0.76087i
49.57	49:33'54	138	19	19-arisextile	19-♈⁎		26D1	daily work focus	cos(19*2πi/138) + isin(19*2πi/138)	0.64858 +0.76114i
49.66	49:39'18	29	4	4-capriquintile	4-♑⚷		1F3A9	proud charisma	cos(4*2πi/29) + isin(4*2πi/29)	0.64739 +0.76216i
49.79	49:47'14	94	13	13-leadecile	13-♌⊥		1F463	helps in others after learning the hard way	cos(13*2πi/94) + isin(13*2πi/94)	0.64563 +0.76365i
49.85	49:50'46	65	9	9-libriquintile	9-♎⚷		1F6C0	self-resparking	cos(9*2πi/65) + isin(9*2πi/65)	0.64484 +0.76432i
49.93	49:55'37	137	19	19-ariquintile	19-♈⚷		1F6A7	singular active, direct, control	cos(19*2πi/137) + isin(19*2πi/137)	0.64376 +0.76522i
50.00	50:0'0	36	5	5-capriinconjunct	5-♑⚻		1F3BB	downplayed want or talent	cos(5*2πi/36) + isin(5*2πi/36)	0.64279 +0.76604i
50.09	50:5'13	115	16	16-gemiseptile	16-♊七		1F933	inner world with self-talk	cos(16*2πi/115) + isin(16*2πi/115)	0.64162 +0.76702i
50.13	50:7'35	79	11	11-virgiseptile	11-♍七		270A	anti-establishment revolutionary	cos(11*2πi/79) + isin(11*2πi/79)	0.64109 +0.76746i
50.16	50:9'50	122	17	17-taurioposition	17-♉☍		1F913	easily annoying to others	cos(17*2πi/122) + isin(17*2πi/122)	0.64059 +0.76788i
50.23	50:13'57	43	6	6-sajiseptile	6-♐七		1F0CF	through jokes, games, and fun	cos(6*2πi/43) + isin(6*2πi/43)	0.63967 +0.76865i
50.29	50:17'38	136	19	19-arisquare	19-♈□		1F9D0	serious, sober-minded interactant	cos(19*2πi/136) + isin(19*2πi/136)	0.63885 +0.76933i
50.35	50:20'58	143	20	20-ariundecile	20-♈U		1F4E3	broadcasting which gets one talked about	cos(20*2πi/143) + isin(20*2πi/143)	0.6381 +0.76995i
50.40	50:23'59	50	7	7-scorpioopposition	7-♏☍		1F5BC	images put forth to others	cos(7*2πi/50) + isin(7*2πi/50)	0.63742 +0.77051i
50.47	50:28'2	107	15	15-cancriundecile	15-♋U		1F481	essence of a great conversation w/ one	cos(15*2πi/107) + isin(15*2πi/107)	0.63652 +0.77126i
50.53	50:31'34	57	8	8-scorpinovile	8-♏N		1FA84	arrives whenever one wants it, no asking	cos(8*2πi/57) + isin(8*2πi/57)	0.63572 +0.77192i
50.58	50:34'42	121	17	17-tauriconjunct	17-♉♂		1F4B0	prosperity & status-seeking	cos(17*2πi/121) + isin(17*2πi/121)	0.63502 +0.7725i
50.63	50:37'30	64	9	9-librisquare	9-♎□		4F17	amidst a noisy setting	cos(9*2πi/64) + isin(9*2πi/64)	0.63439 +0.77301i
50.67	50:39'59	135	19	19-aritrine	19-♈△		1F3C4	easy and prolific	cos(19*2πi/135) + isin(19*2πi/135)	0.63383 +0.77347i
50.70	50:42'15	71	10	10-libriundecile	10-♎U		26C5	thriving amidst confusion	cos(10*2πi/71) + isin(10*2πi/71)	0.63332 +0.77389i
50.77	50:46'9	78	11	11-virgisextile	11-♍⁎		1F94A	fight night moment	cos(11*2πi/78) + isin(11*2πi/78)	0.63245 +0.7746i
50.82	50:49'24	85	12	12-leaconjunct	12-♌♂		1F924	downplaying a real want	cos(12*2πi/85) + isin(12*2πi/85)	0.63171 +0.7752i
50.87	50:52'10	92	13	13-leaoctile	13-♌⟋		1F37B	regular comfort preferences w/ close one	cos(13*2πi/92) + isin(13*2πi/92)	0.63109 +0.77571i
50.94	50:56'36	106	15	15-cancridecile	15-♋⊥		1F3A0	others think one has more power than one has	cos(15*2πi/106) + isin(15*2πi/106)	0.63009 +0.77652i
51.00	51:0'0	120	17	17-gemiinconjunct	17-♊⚻		1F922	more vulnerable to things	cos(17*2πi/120) + isin(17*2πi/120)	0.62932 +0.77715i
51.04	51:2'41	134	19	19-ariopposition	19-♈☍		1F49F	a trait the partner MUST have	cos(19*2πi/134) + isin(19*2πi/134)	0.62871 +0.77764i
51.06	51:3'49	141	20	20-arinovile	20-♈N		1F489	easy instillment in others	cos(20*2πi/141) + isin(20*2πi/141)	0.62845 +0.77785i
51.43	51:25'42	7	1	septile	七		1F5E3	basic communication pattern	cos(1*2πi/7) + isin(1*2πi/7)	0.62349 +0.78183i
51.80	51:47'54	139	20	20-ariseptile	20-♈七		1F3AF	creative perfectionism	cos(20*2πi/139) + isin(20*2πi/139)	0.61843 +0.78584i

51.84	51:50'24	125	18	18-tauriquintile	18-♉⚼		1F39F	social clique's requirements	$\cos(18\cdot2\pi/125)+i\sin(18\cdot2\pi/125)$	0.61786 +0.78629i
51.89	51:53'30	111	16	16-gemitrine	16-♊△		1F973	around high-expression groups	$\cos(16\cdot2\pi/111)+i\sin(16\cdot2\pi/111)$	0.61715 +0.78685i
51.92	51:55'23	104	15	15-cancrioctile	15-♋⊿		1F61B	trait known and accepted among friends	$\cos(15\cdot2\pi/104)+i\sin(15\cdot2\pi/104)$	0.61672 +0.78718i
52.00	52:0'0	90	13	13-leasextile	13-♌*		1F6B8	absorptions by one's children	$\cos(13\cdot2\pi/90)+i\sin(13\cdot2\pi/90)$	0.61566 +0.78801i
52.05	52:2'53	83	12	12-virgiundecile	12-♍U		26A1	high-tension activity in surroundings	$\cos(12\cdot2\pi/83)+i\sin(12\cdot2\pi/83)$	0.615 +0.78853i
52.11	52:6'18	76	11	11-virgisquare	11-♍□		1F3D8	seen by friends' friends & family	$\cos(11\cdot2\pi/76)+i\sin(11\cdot2\pi/76)$	0.61421 +0.78914i
52.17	52:10'26	69	10	10-librinovile	10-♎N		1F418	subtle, strong draw of trait via socialization	$\cos(10\cdot2\pi/69)+i\sin(10\cdot2\pi/69)$	0.61327 +0.78988i
52.21	52:12'49	131	19	19-tauriundecile	19-♉U		1F611	with doubt in associations	$\cos(19\cdot2\pi/131)+i\sin(19\cdot2\pi/131)$	0.61272 +0.7903i
52.26	52:15'29	62	9	9-libriopposition	9-♎☍		1F3F4	manipulative ambition	$\cos(9\cdot2\pi/62)+i\sin(9\cdot2\pi/62)$	0.61211 +0.79078i
52.31	52:18'27	117	17	17-geminovile	17-♊N		1F48E	best friend's quality	$\cos(17\cdot2\pi/117)+i\sin(17\cdot2\pi/117)$	0.61142 +0.79131i
52.36	52:21'49	55	8	8-scorpiseptile	8-♏七		1F632	shocking or flooding others w information	$\cos(8\cdot2\pi/55)+i\sin(8\cdot2\pi/55)$	0.61065 +0.7919i
52.43	52:25'37	103	15	15-cancriseptile	15-♋七		1F60A	basking in joy	$\cos(15\cdot2\pi/103)+i\sin(15\cdot2\pi/103)$	0.60977 +0.79258i
52.50	52:30'0	48	7	7-sajiinconjunct	7-♐⊼		1F305	shown through creative setting	$\cos(7\cdot2\pi/48)+i\sin(7\cdot2\pi/48)$	0.60876 +0.79335i
52.58	52:35'3	89	13	13-leaquintile	13-♌⚼		1F48B	sensuality & body expression	$\cos(13\cdot2\pi/89)+i\sin(13\cdot2\pi/89)$	0.60759 +0.79425i
52.62	52:36'55	130	19	19-tauridecile	19-♉⊥		1F3AA	relied upon by others in the talked topic	$\cos(19\cdot2\pi/130)+i\sin(19\cdot2\pi/130)$	0.60716 +0.79458i
52.68	52:40'58	41	6	6-sajiquintile	6-♐⚼		1F5FD	personas aspired to	$\cos(6\cdot2\pi/41)+i\sin(6\cdot2\pi/41)$	0.60623 +0.79529i
52.80	52:47'59	75	11	11-virgitrine	11-♍△		1F3E1	family home maintenance	$\cos(11\cdot2\pi/75)+i\sin(11\cdot2\pi/75)$	0.6046 +0.79653i
52.84	52:50'38	109	16	16-gemiconjunct	16-♊☌		1F44E	diminishing others' importance	$\cos(16\cdot2\pi/109)+i\sin(16\cdot2\pi/109)$	0.60399 +0.79699i
52.87	52:52'1	143	21	21-ariundecile	21-♈U		1F4E3	broadcasting which gets one talked about	$\cos(21\cdot2\pi/143)+i\sin(21\cdot2\pi/143)$	0.60367 +0.79724i
52.94	52:56'28	34	5	5-capridecile	5-♑⊥		1F3C6	potential to be a master or boss	$\cos(5\cdot2\pi/34)+i\sin(5\cdot2\pi/34)$	0.60263 +0.79802i
53.02	53:1'23	129	19	19-taurinovile	19-♉N		1F647	in the service of one attached to	$\cos(19\cdot2\pi/129)+i\sin(19\cdot2\pi/129)$	0.60149 +0.79888i
53.05	53:3'9	95	14	14-leaundecile	14-♌U		265B	the image of a progress-inspiring master	$\cos(14\cdot2\pi/95)+i\sin(14\cdot2\pi/95)$	0.60108 +0.79919i
53.11	53:6'53	61	9	9-libriconjunct	9-♎☌		1F526	singled out for attention	$\cos(9\cdot2\pi/61)+i\sin(9\cdot2\pi/61)$	0.60021 +0.79984i
53.18	53:10'54	88	13	13-leasquare	13-♌□		1F479	suppressing power imbalance	$\cos(13\cdot2\pi/88)+i\sin(13\cdot2\pi/88)$	0.59928 +0.80054i
53.24	53:14'21	142	21	21-aridecile	21-♈⊥		1F549	blessings others can only dream of	$\cos(21\cdot2\pi/142)+i\sin(21\cdot2\pi/142)$	0.59847 +0.80114i
53.33	53:20'0	27	4	4-capritrine	4-♑△		1F393	intellectualizing and insight	$\cos(4\cdot2\pi/27)+i\sin(4\cdot2\pi/27)$	0.59716 +0.80212i
53.44	53:26'15	128	19	19-taurioctile	19-♉⊿		1F478	intuitive comfort even amidst stress	$\cos(19\cdot2\pi/128)+i\sin(19\cdot2\pi/128)$	0.5957 +0.80321i
53.47	53:27'55	101	15	15-cancriquintile	15-♋⚼		1F624	disregard for things heard	$\cos(15\cdot2\pi/101)+i\sin(15\cdot2\pi/101)$	0.59531 +0.8035i
53.51	53:30'48	74	11	11-virgiopposition	11-♍☍		1F626	social stressors	$\cos(11\cdot2\pi/74)+i\sin(11\cdot2\pi/74)$	0.59463 +0.804i

53.55	53°33'13	121	18	18-tauriconjunct	18-♉☌	💰	1F4B0	prosperity & status-seeking	$\cos(18*2\pi i/121) + i\sin(18*2\pi i/121)$	0.59407 +0.80441i
53.62	53°37'1	47	7	7-sajiundecile	7-♐U	☪	262B	a core, lived principle	$\cos(7*2\pi i/47) + i\sin(7*2\pi i/47)$	0.59318 +0.80507i
53.68	53°41'3	114	17	17-gemisextile	17-♊✳	🛱	1F6F1	other's influence attempts	$\cos(17*2\pi i/114) + i\sin(17*2\pi i/114)$	0.59224 +0.80577i
53.73	53°43'52	67	10	10-libriseptile	10-♎七	😻	1F63B	getting others to fall in love w oneself	$\cos(10*2\pi i/67) + i\sin(10*2\pi i/67)$	0.59157 +0.80625i
53.79	53°47'35	87	13	13-leatrine	13-♌△	❣	2763	interactor inspired to want	$\cos(13*2\pi i/87) + i\sin(13*2\pi i/87)$	0.5907 +0.80689i
53.83	53°49'54	107	16	16-cancriundecile	16-♋U	💁	1F481	essence of a great conversation w/ one	$\cos(16*2\pi i/107) + i\sin(16*2\pi i/107)$	0.59016 +0.80729i
53.86	53°51'29	127	19	19-tauriseptile	19-♉七	💸	1F4B8	that which attracts unfair advantage	$\cos(19*2\pi i/127) + i\sin(19*2\pi i/127)$	0.58978 +0.80756i
54.00	54°0'0	20	3	3-aquarioctile	3-♒⦟	🤺	1F93A	kicking the butt of outsiders	$\cos(3*2\pi i/20) + i\sin(3*2\pi i/20)$	0.58779 +0.80902i
54.14	54°8'7	133	20	20-ariconjunct	20-♈☌	💝	1F49D	during sex or when flirting	$\cos(20*2\pi i/133) + i\sin(20*2\pi i/133)$	0.58587 +0.8104i
54.19	54°11'36	93	14	14-leanovile	14-♌N	😍	1F60D	brought out by creative, sexualized energy	$\cos(14*2\pi i/93) + i\sin(14*2\pi i/93)$	0.58505 +0.811i
54.25	54°14'47	73	11	11-virgiconjunct	11-♍☌	⚒	2692	new or deep investment in job	$\cos(11*2\pi i/73) + i\sin(11*2\pi i/73)$	0.5843 +0.81154i
54.29	54°17'8	126	19	19-taurisextile	19-♉✳	👾	1F47E	aggressive assertion of identity	$\cos(19*2\pi i/126) + i\sin(19*2\pi i/126)$	0.58374 +0.81194i
54.34	54°20'22	53	8	8-scorpiquintile	8-♏⚼	🤗	1F917	reasons one is desired	$\cos(8*2\pi i/53) + i\sin(8*2\pi i/53)$	0.58298 +0.81249i
54.39	54°23'18	139	21	21-ariseptile	21-♈七	🎯	1F3AF	creative perfectionism	$\cos(21*2\pi i/139) + i\sin(21*2\pi i/139)$	0.58229 +0.81298i
54.42	54°25'6	86	13	13-leaopposition	13-♌☍	😡	1F921	one's commentary offends egos	$\cos(13*2\pi i/86) + i\sin(13*2\pi i/86)$	0.58186 +0.81329i
54.45	54°27'13	119	18	18-gemiundecile	18-♊U	📉	1F4C9	weakened by opinionation, better as ambient	$\cos(18*2\pi i/119) + i\sin(18*2\pi i/119)$	0.58136 +0.81365i
54.55	54°32'43	33	5	5-caprinovile	5-♑N	📻	1F4FB	in a formal group discussion	$\cos(5*2\pi i/33) + i\sin(5*2\pi i/33)$	0.58006 +0.81458i
54.64	54°38'34	112	17	17-gemisquare	17-♊□	👯	1F38E	one's trait observed by outsiders	$\cos(17*2\pi i/112) + i\sin(17*2\pi i/112)$	0.57867 +0.81556i
54.68	54°41'0	79	12	12-virgiseptile	12-♍七	✊	270A	anti-establishment revolutionary	$\cos(12*2\pi i/79) + i\sin(12*2\pi i/79)$	0.57809 +0.81597i
54.72	54°43'11	125	19	19-tauriquintile	19-♉⚼	🎟	1F39F	social clique's requirements	$\cos(19*2\pi i/125) + i\sin(19*2\pi i/125)$	0.57757 +0.81634i
54.78	54°46'57	46	7	7-sajidecile	7-♐⊥	📎	1F4CE	trait housed by key colleagues	$\cos(7*2\pi i/46) + i\sin(7*2\pi i/46)$	0.57668 +0.81697i
54.86	54°51'25	105	16	16-cancrinovile	16-♋N	💥	1F5EF	when irritated to see standards defied	$\cos(16*2\pi i/105) + i\sin(16*2\pi i/105)$	0.57562 +0.81772i
54.92	54°54'54	59	9	9-scorpiundecile	9-♏U	👇	1F447	having one's pick	$\cos(9*2\pi i/59) + i\sin(9*2\pi i/59)$	0.57479 +0.8183i
55.00	55°0'0	72	11	11-libriinconjunct	11-♎π	❓	2753	a problem to be solved	$\cos(11*2\pi i/72) + i\sin(11*2\pi i/72)$	0.57358 +0.81915i
55.06	55°3'31	85	13	13-leaconjunct	13-♌☌	🤤	1F924	downplaying a real want	$\cos(13*2\pi i/85) + i\sin(13*2\pi i/85)$	0.57274 +0.81974i
55.14	55°8'6	111	17	17-gemitrine	17-♊△	🥳	1F973	around high-expression groups	$\cos(17*2\pi i/111) + i\sin(17*2\pi i/111)$	0.57164 +0.8205i
55.18	55°10'56	137	21	21-ariquintile	21-♈⚼	🚧	1F6A7	singular active, direct, control	$\cos(21*2\pi i/137) + i\sin(2*2\pi i/137)$	0.57096 +0.82097i
55.38	55°23'4	13	2	2-aquariconjunct	2-♒☌	🎥	1F3A5	public persona	$\cos(2*2\pi i/13) + i\sin(2*2\pi i/13)$	0.56806 +0.82298i
55.59	55°35'17	136	21	21-arisquare	21-♈□	🙄	1F9D0	serious, sober-minded interactant	$\cos(21*2\pi i/136) + i\sin(21*2\pi i/136)$	0.56514 +0.825i

55.64	55°38'10	110	17	17-gemiopposition	17-♊⚹		1F6A5	managing others' behavior	$\cos(17*2\pi i/110) +$ $i\sin(17*2\pi i/110)$	0.56444 +0.82547i
55.67	55°40'12	97	15	15-cancriconjunct	15-♋♂		1F495	traits reserved for those very close	$\cos(15*2\pi i/97) +$ $i\sin(15*2\pi i/97)$	0.56396 +0.8258i
55.71	55°42'51	84	13	13-virgiinconjunct	13-♍♐		1F411	traits for the seemingly weak	$\cos(13*2\pi i/84) +$ $i\sin(13*2\pi i/84)$	0.56332 +0.82624i
55.77	55°46'28	71	11	11-libriundecile	11-♎U		26C5	thriving amidst confusion	$\cos(11*2\pi i/71) +$ $i\sin(11*2\pi i/71)$	0.56245 +0.82683i
55.81	55°48'50	129	20	20-taurinovile	20-♉N		1F647	in the service of one attached to	$\cos(20*2\pi i/129) +$ $i\sin(20*2\pi i/129)$	0.56188 +0.82722i
55.86	55°51'43	58	9	9-scorpidecile	9-♏⊥		1F47B	interactions with an ethereal party	$\cos(9*2\pi i/58) +$ $i\sin(9*2\pi i/58)$	0.56119 +0.82769i
55.92	55°55'20	103	16	16-cancriseptile	16-♋七		1F60A	basking in joy	$\cos(16*2\pi i/103) +$ $i\sin(16*2\pi i/103)$	0.56032 +0.82828i
56.00	56°0'0	45	7	7-sajinovile	7-♐N		2766	shared experience as a token of friendship	$\cos(7*2\pi i/45) +$ $i\sin(7*2\pi i/45)$	0.55919 +0.82904i
56.07	56°3'56	122	19	19-tauriopposition	19-♉⚹		1F913	easily annoying to others	$\cos(19*2\pi i/122) +$ $i\sin(19*2\pi i/122)$	0.55824 +0.82968i
56.15	56°8'48	109	17	17-gemiconjunct	17-♊♂		1F44E	diminishing others' importance	$\cos(17*2\pi i/109) +$ $i\sin(17*2\pi i/109)$	0.55707 +0.83047i
56.17	56°10'12	141	22	22-arinovile	22-♈N		1F489	easy instillment in others	$\cos(22*2\pi i/141) +$ $i\sin(22*2\pi i/141)$	0.55673 +0.8307i
56.25	56°15'0	32	5	5-caprioctile	5-♑⊿		1F5FB	an indomitable characteristic	$\cos(5*2\pi i/32) +$ $i\sin(5*2\pi i/32)$	0.55557 +0.83147i
56.35	56°20'52	115	18	18-gemiseptile	18-♊七		1F933	inner world with self-talk	$\cos(18*2\pi i/115) +$ $i\sin(18*2\pi i/115)$	0.55415 +0.83242i
56.39	56°23'7	83	13	13-virgiundecile	13-♍U		26A1	high-tension activity in surroundings	$\cos(13*2\pi i/83) +$ $i\sin(13*2\pi i/83)$	0.5536 +0.83278i
56.42	56°25'4	134	21	21-ariopposition	21-♈⚹		1F49F	a trait the partner MUST have	$\cos(21*2\pi i/134) +$ $i\sin(21*2\pi i/134)$	0.55313 +0.83309i
56.47	56°28'14	51	8	8-scorpitrine	8-♏△		1F61A	use of persuasive words	$\cos(8*2\pi i/51) +$ $i\sin(8*2\pi i/51)$	0.55236 +0.8336i
56.53	56°31'44	121	19	19-tauriconjunct	19-♉♂		1F4B0	prosperity & status-seeking	$\cos(19*2\pi i/121) +$ $i\sin(19*2\pi i/121)$	0.55152 +0.83416i
56.57	56°34'17	70	11	11-libridecile	11-♎⊥		1F527	used to strengthen or repair bonds	$\cos(11*2\pi i/70) +$ $i\sin(11*2\pi i/70)$	0.5509 +0.83457i
56.63	56°37'45	89	14	14-leaquintile	14-♌⚺		1F48B	sensuality & body expression	$\cos(14*2\pi i/89) +$ $i\sin(14*2\pi i/89)$	0.55006 +0.83513i
56.69	56°41'34	127	20	20-tauriseptile	20-♉七		1F4B8	that which attracts unfair advantage	$\cos(20*2\pi i/127) +$ $i\sin(20*2\pi i/127)$	0.54913 +0.83574i
56.84	56°50'31	19	3	3-aquariseptile	3-♒七		1F510	gateway to one's friendship	$\cos(3*2\pi i/19) +$ $i\sin(3*2\pi i/19)$	0.54695 +0.83717i
56.98	56°58'42	139	22	22-ariseptile	22-♈七		1F3AF	creative perfectionism	$\cos(22*2\pi i/139) +$ $i\sin(22*2\pi i/139)$	0.54495 +0.83847i
57.03	57°1'46	101	16	16-cancriquintile	16-♋⚺		1F624	disregard for things heard	$\cos(16*2\pi i/101) +$ $i\sin(16*2\pi i/101)$	0.5442 +0.83895i
57.07	57°4'23	82	13	13-virgidecile	13-♍⊥		1F987	eccentrically attention-getting, disquieting	$\cos(13*2\pi i/82) +$ $i\sin(13*2\pi i/82)$	0.54357 +0.83937i
57.14	57°8'34	63	10	10-libritrine	10-♎△		1F6A8	know-it-all	$\cos(10*2\pi i/63) +$ $i\sin(10*2\pi i/63)$	0.54255 +0.84003i
57.20	57°11'46	107	17	17-cancriundecile	17-♋U		1F481	essence of a great conversation w/ one	$\cos(17*2\pi i/107) +$ $i\sin(17*2\pi i/107)$	0.54176 +0.84053i
57.27	57°16'21	44	7	7-sajioctile	7-♐⊿		1F6B5	role in a peer group	$\cos(7*2\pi i/44) +$ $i\sin(7*2\pi i/44)$	0.54064 +0.84125i
57.35	57°20'42	113	18	18-gemiquintile	18-♊⚺		1F60E	publicly-labeled vibe given	$\cos(18*2\pi i/113) +$ $i\sin(18*2\pi i/113)$	0.53958 +0.84194i
57.39	57°23'28	69	11	11-librinovile	11-♎N		1F418	subtle, strong draw of trait via socialization	$\cos(11*2\pi i/69) +$ $i\sin(11*2\pi i/69)$	0.5389 +0.84237i

57.45	57:26'48	94	15	15-leadecile	15-♌⊥	👣	1F463	helps in others after learning the hard way	cos(15*2πi/94) + isin(15*2πi/94)	0.53808 +0.84289i
57.48	57:28'44	119	19	19-gemiundecile	19-♊U	🔉	1F4C9	weakened by opinionation, better as ambient	cos(19*2πi/119) + isin(19*2πi/119)	0.53761 +0.84319i
57.50	57:30'0	144	23	23-ariinconjunct	23-♈π	🔁	1F501	always-on trait	cos(23*2πi/144) + isin(23*2πi/144)	0.5373 +0.84339i
57.60	57:36'0	25	4	4-capriconjunct	4-♑♂	🏟	1F3DF	rally & tune the mass psychology	cos(4*2πi/25) + isin(4*2πi/25)	0.53583 +0.84433i
57.74	57:44'9	106	17	17-cancridecile	17-♋⊥	🎠	1F3A0	others think one has more power than one has	cos(17*2πi/106) + isin(17*2πi/106)	0.53382 +0.8456i
57.78	57:46'40	81	13	13-virginovile	13-♍N	👑	1F451	mastered early, forms broad social identity	cos(13*2πi/81) + isin(13*2πi/81)	0.5332 +0.84599i
57.81	57:48'36	137	22	22-ariquintile	22-♈⬠	🚧	1F6A7	singular active, direct, control	cos(22*2πi/137) + isin(22*2πi/137)	0.53273 +0.84629i
57.86	57:51'25	56	9	9-scorpioctile	9-♏⊿	😈	1F608	for fun or one's own power	cos(9*2πi/56) + isin(9*2πi/56)	0.53203 +0.84672i
57.93	57:55'51	87	14	14-leatrine	14-♌Δ	❣	2763	interactor inspired to want	cos(14*2πi/87) + isin(14*2πi/87)	0.53094 +0.84741i
57.97	57:57'57	118	19	19-gemidecile	19-♊⊥	🏃	1F3C3	staying with it as long as encouraged	cos(19*2πi/118) + isin(19*2πi/118)	0.53042 +0.84773i
58.06	58:3'52	31	5	5-capriseptile	5-♑t	🎢	1F3A2	expressed by one's social network	cos(5*2πi/31) + isin(5*2πi/31)	0.52896 +0.84864i
58.18	58:10'54	99	16	16-cancritrine	16-♋Δ	🙅	1F645	communication-stifling	cos(16*2πi/99) + isin(16*2πi/99)	0.52723 +0.84973i
58.24	58:14'7	68	11	11-librioctile	11-♎⊿	👢	1F462	appearance of dominating	cos(11*2πi/68) + isin(11*2πi/68)	0.52643 +0.85022i
58.29	58:17'8	105	17	17-cancrinovile	17-♋N	💥	1F5EF	when irritated to see standards defied	cos(17*2πi/105) + isin(17*2πi/105)	0.52568 +0.85068i
58.31	58:18'35	142	23	23-aridecile	23-♈⊥	🕉	1F549	blessings others can only dream of	cos(23*2πi/142) + isin(23*2πi/142)	0.52533 +0.8509i
58.38	58:22'42	37	6	6-sajiconjunct	6-♐♂	☆	2B50	trusted ability revealed	cos(6*2πi/37) + isin(6*2πi/37)	0.52431 +0.85153i
58.50	58:30'0	80	13	13-virgioctile	13-♍⊿	🤹	1F939	vividly remembered by one's children	cos(13*2πi/80) + isin(13*2πi/80)	0.5225 +0.85264i
58.54	58:32'11	123	20	20-tauritrine	20-♉Δ	⎏	238F	others must express or draw out	cos(20*2πi/123) + isin(20*2πi/123)	0.52195 +0.85297i
58.60	58:36'16	43	7	7-sajiseptile	7-♐t	🃏	1F0CF	through jokes, games, and fun	cos(7*2πi/43) + isin(7*2πi/43)	0.52094 +0.85359i
58.70	58:41'44	92	15	15-leaoctile	15-♌⊿	🎻	1F37B	regular comfort preferences w/ close one	cos(15*2πi/92) + isin(15*2πi/92)	0.51958 +0.85442i
58.72	58:43'24	141	23	23-arinovile	23-♈N	💉	1F489	easy instillment in others	cos(23*2πi/141) + isin(23*2πi/141)	0.51917 +0.85467i
58.78	58:46'31	49	8	8-scorpiconjunct	8-♏♂	🎙	1F399	having known public influence	cos(8*2πi/49) + isin(8*2πi/49)	0.51839 +0.85514i
58.85	58:50'46	104	17	17-cancrioctile	17-♋⊿	😛	1F61B	trait known and accepted among friends	cos(17*2πi/104) + isin(17*2πi/104)	0.51734 +0.85578i
58.91	58:54'32	55	9	9-scorpiseptile	9-♏t	😲	1F632	shocking or flooding others w information	cos(9*2πi/55) + isin(9*2πi/55)	0.5164 +0.85635i
58.97	58:57'55	116	19	19-gemioctile	19-♊⊿	😒	1F612	having been slighted or doubted	cos(19*2πi/116) + isin(19*2πi/116)	0.51555 +0.85686i
59.02	59:0'59	61	10	10-libriconjunct	10-♎♂	🔦	1F526	singled out for attention	cos(10*2πi/61) + isin(10*2πi/61)	0.51479 +0.85731i
59.06	59:3'45	128	21	21-taurioctile	21-♉⊿	👸	1F478	intuitive comfort even amidst stress	cos(21*2πi/128) + isin(21*2πi/128)	0.5141 +0.85773i
59.14	59:8'34	140	23	23-arioctile	23-♈⊿	🍀	1F340	helped by a benefactor	cos(23*2πi/140) + isin(23*2πi/140)	0.5129 +0.85845i
59.18	59:10'41	73	12	12-virgiconjunct	12-♍♂	⚒	2692	new or deep investment in job	cos(12*2πi/73) + isin(12*2πi/73)	0.51237 +0.85876i

59.24	59:14'25	79	13	13-virgiseptile	13-♍七		270A	anti-establishment revolutionary	cos(13*2πi/79) + isin(13*2πi/79)	0.51144 +0.85932i
59.29	59:17'38	85	14	14-leaconjunct	14-♌☌		1F924	downplaying a real want	cos(14*2πi/85) + isin(14*2πi/85)	0.51063 +0.8598i
59.34	59:20'26	91	15	15-leaseptile	15-♌七		1F576	smoothly comfortable	cos(15*2πi/91) + isin(15*2πi/91)	0.50993 +0.86021i
59.38	59:22'53	97	16	16-cancriconjunct	16-♋☌		1F495	traits reserved for those very close	cos(16*2πi/97) + isin(16*2πi/97)	0.50932 +0.86058i
59.45	59:26'58	109	18	18-gemiconjunct	18-♊☌		1F44E	diminishing others' importance	cos(18*2πi/109) + isin(18*2πi/109)	0.5083 +0.86118i
59.48	59:28'41	115	19	19-gemiseptile	19-♊七		1F933	inner world with self-talk	cos(19*2πi/115) + isin(19*2πi/115)	0.50787 +0.86144i
59.53	59:31'39	127	21	21-tauriseptile	21-♉七		1F4B8	that which attracts unfair advantage	cos(21*2πi/127) + isin(21*2πi/127)	0.50712 +0.86187i
59.57	59:34'6	139	23	23-ariseptile	23-♈七		1F3AF	creative perfectionism	cos(23*2πi/139) + isin(23*2πi/139)	0.50651 +0.86223i
60.00	60:0'0	6	1	sextile	*		1F914	reconciling 2 ideas	cos(1*2πi/6) + isin(1*2πi/6)	0.5 +0.86603i
60.44	60:26'16	137	23	23-ariquintile	23-♈⚹		1F6A7	singular active, direct, control	cos(23*2πi/137) + isin(23*2πi/137)	0.49337 +0.86982i
60.48	60:28'47	125	21	21-tauriquintile	21-♉⚹		1F39F	social clique's requirements	cos(21*2πi/125) + isin(21*2πi/125)	0.49273 +0.87018i
60.53	60:31'51	113	19	19-gemiquintile	19-♊⚹		1F60E	publicly-labeled vibe given	cos(19*2πi/113) + isin(19*2πi/113)	0.49195 +0.87062i
60.59	60:35'38	101	17	17-cancriquintile	17-♋⚹		1F624	disregard for things heard	cos(17*2πi/101) + isin(17*2πi/101)	0.49099 +0.87116i
60.63	60:37'53	95	16	16-leaundecile	16-♌U		265B	the image of a progress-inspiring master	cos(16*2πi/95) + isin(16*2πi/95)	0.49042 +0.87148i
60.67	60:40'26	89	15	15-leaquintile	15-♌⚹		1F48B	sensuality & body expression	cos(15*2πi/89) + isin(15*2πi/89)	0.48978 +0.87185i
60.72	60:43'22	83	14	14-virgiundecile	14-♍U		26A1	high-tension activity in surroundings	cos(14*2πi/83) + isin(14*2πi/83)	0.48903 +0.87226i
60.78	60:46'45	77	13	13-virgiquintile	13-♍⚹		1F422	guarded insistence	cos(13*2πi/77) + isin(13*2πi/77)	0.48818 +0.87275i
60.85	60:50'42	71	12	12-libriundecile	12-♎U		26C5	thriving amidst confusion	cos(12*2πi/71) + isin(12*2πi/71)	0.48717 +0.87331i
60.88	60:52'56	136	23	23-arisquare	23-♈□		1F9D0	serious, sober-minded interactant	cos(23*2πi/136) + isin(23*2πi/136)	0.4866 +0.87362i
60.92	60:55'23	65	11	11-libriquintile	11-♎⚹		1F6C0	self-resparking	cos(11*2πi/65) + isin(11*2πi/65)	0.48598 +0.87397i
60.97	60:58'3	124	21	21-taurisquare	21-♉□		1F387	initial, then waning impression	cos(21*2πi/124) + isin(21*2πi/124)	0.4853 +0.87435i
61.02	61:1'1	59	10	10-scorpiundecile	10-♏U		1F447	having one's pick	cos(10*2πi/59) + isin(10*2πi/59)	0.48455 +0.87476i
61.07	61:4'17	112	19	19-gemisquare	19-♊□		1F38E	one's trait observed by outsiders	cos(19*2πi/112) + isin(19*2πi/112)	0.48372 +0.87522i
61.13	61:7'55	53	9	9-scorpiquintile	9-♏⚹		1F917	reasons one is desired	cos(9*2πi/53) + isin(9*2πi/53)	0.48279 +0.87573i
61.20	61:12'0	100	17	17-cancrisquare	17-♋□		1F6CB	home & family life	cos(17*2πi/100) + isin(17*2πi/100)	0.48175 +0.87631i
61.28	61:16'35	47	8	8-sajiundecile	8-♐U		262B	a core, lived principle	cos(8*2πi/47) + isin(8*2πi/47)	0.48058 +0.87695i
61.33	61:20'0	135	23	23-aritrine	23-♈△		1F3C4	easy and prolific	cos(23*2πi/135) + isin(23*2πi/135)	0.47971 +0.87743i
61.40	61:23'43	129	22	22-taurinovile	22-♉N		1F647	in the service of one attached to	cos(22*2πi/129) + isin(22*2πi/129)	0.47876 +0.87794i
61.46	61:27'48	41	7	7-sajiquintile	7-♐⚹		1F5FD	personas aspired to	cos(7*2πi/41) + isin(7*2πi/41)	0.47772 +0.87851i

61.54	61:32'18	117	20	20-geminovile	20-♊N	💎	1F48E	best friend's quality	cos(20*2π/117) + isin(20*2π/117)	0.47657 +0.87914i
61.58	61:34'44	76	13	13-virgisquare	13-♍□	🏘	1F3D8	seen by friends' friends & family	cos(13*2π/76) + isin(13*2π/76)	0.47595 +0.87947i
61.62	61:37'17	111	19	19-gemitrine	19-♊△	🥳	1F973	around high-expression groups	cos(19*2π/111) + isin(19*2π/111)	0.47529 +0.87983i
61.71	61:42'51	35	6	6-capriundecile	6-♑U	👽	1F47D	quirky distinguishing uniqueness	cos(6*2π/35) + isin(6*2π/35)	0.47387 +0.8806i
61.79	61:47'27	134	23	23-ariopposition	23-♈☍	🖼	1F49F	a trait the partner MUST have	cos(23*2π/134) + isin(23*2π/134)	0.47269 +0.88123i
61.82	61:49'5	99	17	17-cancritrine	17-♋△	🙅	1F645	communication-stifling	cos(17*2π/99) + isin(17*2π/99)	0.47227 +0.88145i
61.88	61:52'30	64	11	11-librisquare	11-♎□	众	4F17	amidst a noisy setting	cos(11*2π/64) + isin(11*2π/64)	0.4714 +0.88192i
61.94	61:56'7	93	16	16-leanovile	16-♌N	😍	1F60D	brought out by creative, sexualized energy	cos(16*2π/93) + isin(16*2π/93)	0.47047 +0.88242i
61.97	61:58'1	122	21	21-tauriopposition	21-♉☍	🤓	1F913	easily annoying to others	cos(21*2π/122) + isin(21*2π/122)	0.46998 +0.88268i
62.07	62:4'8	29	5	5-capriquintile	5-♑⬠	🎩	1F3A9	proud charisma	cos(5*2π/29) + isin(5*2π/29)	0.46841 +0.88351i
62.18	62:10'54	110	19	19-gemiopposition	19-♊☍	🚥	1F6A5	managing others' behavior	cos(19*2π/110) + isin(19*2π/110)	0.46667 +0.88443i
62.22	62:13'19	81	14	14-virginovile	14-♍N	👑	1F451	mastered early, forms broad social identity	cos(14*2π/81) + isin(14*2π/81)	0.46604 +0.88476i
62.26	62:15'20	133	23	23-ariconjunct	23-♈☌	💝	1F49D	during sex or when flirting	cos(23*2π/133) + isin(23*2π/133)	0.46553 +0.88503i
62.31	62:18'27	52	9	9-scorpisquare	9-♏□	😞	1F61E	falling short	cos(9*2π/52) + isin(9*2π/52)	0.46472 +0.88546i
62.40	62:23'59	75	13	13-virgitrine	13-♍△	🏡	1F3E1	family home maintenance	cos(13*2π/75) + isin(13*2π/75)	0.4633 +0.8862i
62.45	62:26'56	98	17	17-cancriopposition	17-♋☍	🌟	1F31F	social advancement catalyst	cos(17*2π/98) + isin(17*2π/98)	0.46254 +0.8866i
62.48	62:28'45	121	21	21-tauriconjunct	21-♉☌	💰	1F4B0	prosperity & status-seeking	cos(21*2π/121) + isin(21*2π/121)	0.46207 +0.88684i
62.50	62:30'0	144	25	25-ariinconjunct	25-♈π	🔁	1F501	always-on trait	cos(25*2π/144) + isin(25*2π/144)	0.46175 +0.88701i
62.61	62:36'31	23	4	4-aquariundecile	4-♒U	🦑	1F991	unusual social trait, liked by eccentrics	cos(4*2π/23) + isin(4*2π/23)	0.46007 +0.88789i
62.73	62:43'38	132	23	23-tauriinconjunct	23-♉π	🔗	1F517	sharing a special bond w/ a friend	cos(23*2π/132) + isin(23*2π/132)	0.45823 +0.88884i
62.79	62:47'26	86	15	15-leaopposition	15-♌☍	🤡	1F921	one's commentary offends egos	cos(15*2π/86) + isin(15*2π/86)	0.45724 +0.88934i
62.86	62:51'25	63	11	11-libritrine	11-♎△	🚨	1F6A8	know-it-all	cos(11*2π/63) + isin(11*2π/63)	0.45621 +0.88987i
62.94	62:56'13	143	25	25-ariundecile	25-♈U	📣	1F4E3	broadcasting which gets one talked about	cos(25*2π/143) + isin(25*2π/143)	0.45497 +0.89051i
63.00	63:0'0	40	7	7-sajisquare	7-♐□	🙪	1F66A	future missable partnership duty	cos(7*2π/40) + isin(7*2π/40)	0.45399 +0.89101i
63.09	63:5'34	97	17	17-cancriconjunct	17-♋☌	💕	1F495	traits reserved for those very close	cos(17*2π/97) + isin(17*2π/97)	0.45255 +0.89174i
63.16	63:9'28	57	10	10-scorpinovile	10-♏N	🪄	1FA84	arrives whenever one wants it, no asking	cos(10*2π/57) + isin(10*2π/57)	0.45153 +0.89225i
63.24	63:14'35	74	13	13-virgiopposition	13-♍☍	😦	1F626	social stressors	cos(13*2π/74) + isin(13*2π/74)	0.4502 +0.89293i
63.30	63:17'48	91	16	16-leaseptile	16-♌七	🕶	1F576	smoothly comfortable	cos(16*2π/91) + isin(16*2π/91)	0.44937 +0.89335i
63.33	63:20'0	108	19	19-cancriinconjunct	19-♋π	😌	1F31D	why close friends come around	cos(19*2π/108) + isin(19*2π/108)	0.4488 +0.89363i

63.38	63:22'49	142	25	25-aridecile	25-♈⊥		1F549	blessings others can only dream of	cos(25*2π/142) + isin(25*2π/142)	0.44807 +0.894i
63.53	63:31'45	17	3	3-aquariquintile	3-♒⬠		1F44A	managing by dominating	cos(3*2π/17) + isin(3*2π/17)	0.44574 +0.89516i
63.69	63:41'32	130	23	23-tauridecile	23-♉⊥		1F3AA	relied upon by others in the talked topic	cos(23*2π/130) + isin(23*2π/130)	0.44319 +0.89643i
63.75	63:45'0	96	17	17-leainconjunct	17-♌⊼		1F937	what "not enough" looks like	cos(17*2π/96) + isin(17*2π/96)	0.44229 +0.89687i
63.80	63:47'50	79	14	14-virgiseptile	14-♍七		270A	anti-establishment revolutionary	cos(14*2π/79) + isin(14*2π/79)	0.44155 +0.89724i
63.83	63:49'47	141	25	25-arinovile	25-♈N		1F489	easy instillment in others	cos(25*2π/141) + isin(25*2π/141)	0.44104 +0.89749i
63.87	63:52'15	62	11	11-libriopposition	11-♎☍		1F3F4	manipulative ambition	cos(11*2π/62) + isin(11*2π/62)	0.44039 +0.8978i
63.93	63:55'30	107	19	19-cancriundecile	19-♋U		1F481	essence of a great conversation w/ one	cos(19*2π/107) + isin(19*2π/107)	0.43954 +0.89822i
64.00	64:0'0	45	8	8-sajinovile	8-♐N		2766	shared experience as a token of friendship	cos(8*2π/45) + isin(8*2π/45)	0.43837 +0.89879i
64.07	64:4'4	118	21	21-gemidecile	21-♊⊥		1F3C3	staying with it as long as encouraged	cos(21*2π/118) + isin(21*2π/118)	0.43731 +0.89931i
64.11	64:6'34	73	13	13-virgiconjunct	13-♍☌		2692	new or deep investment in job	cos(13*2π/73) + isin(13*2π/73)	0.43665 +0.89963i
64.19	64:11'9	129	23	23-taurinovile	23-♉N		1F647	in the service of one attached to	cos(23*2π/129) + isin(23*2π/129)	0.43545 +0.90021i
64.29	64:17'8	28	5	5-caprisquare	5-♑□		1F58C	arts and creativity drawn to	cos(5*2π/28) + isin(5*2π/28)	0.43388 +0.90097i
64.39	64:23'24	123	22	22-tauritrine	22-♉△		238F	others must express or draw out	cos(22*2π/123) + isin(22*2π/123)	0.43224 +0.90176i
64.42	64:25'15	95	17	17-leaundecile	17-♌U		265B	the image of a progress-inspiring master	cos(17*2π/95) + isin(17*2π/95)	0.43175 +0.90199i
64.48	64:28'39	67	12	12-libriseptile	12-♎七		1F63B	getting others to fall in love w oneself	cos(12*2π/67) + isin(12*2π/67)	0.43086 +0.90242i
64.53	64:31'41	106	19	19-cancridecile	19-♋⊥		1F3A0	others think one has more power than one has	cos(19*2π/106) + isin(19*2π/106)	0.43007 +0.9028i
64.62	64:36'55	39	7	7-sajitrine	7-♐△		1F3DD	convincing others of one's value	cos(7*2π/39) + isin(7*2π/39)	0.42869 +0.90345i
64.69	64:41'15	128	23	23-taurioctile	23-♉⦞		1F478	intuitive comfort even amidst stress	cos(23*2π/128) + isin(23*2π/128)	0.42756 +0.90399i
64.75	64:44'53	139	25	25-ariseptile	25-♈七		1F3AF	creative perfectionism	cos(25*2π/139) + isin(25*2π/139)	0.4266 +0.90444i
64.80	64:47'59	50	9	9-scorpiopposition	9-♏☍		1F5BC	images put forth to others	cos(9*2π/50) + isin(9*2π/50)	0.42578 +0.90483i
64.86	64:51'53	111	20	20-gemitrine	20-♊△		1F973	around high-expression groups	cos(20*2π/111) + isin(20*2π/111)	0.42475 +0.90531i
64.92	64:55'4	61	11	11-libriconjunct	11-♎☌		1F526	singled out for attention	cos(11*2π/61) + isin(11*2π/61)	0.42391 +0.9057i
65.00	65:0'0	72	13	13-libriinconjunct	13-♎⊼		2753	a problem to be solved	cos(13*2π/72) + isin(13*2π/72)	0.42262 +0.90631i
65.06	65:3'36	83	15	15-virgiundecile	15-♍U		26A1	high-tension activity in surroundings	cos(15*2π/83) + isin(15*2π/83)	0.42167 +0.90675i
65.14	65:8'34	105	19	19-cancrinovile	19-♋N		1F5EF	when irritated to see standards defied	cos(19*2π/105) + isin(19*2π/105)	0.42036 +0.90736i
65.20	65:11'48	127	23	23-tauriseptile	23-♉七		1F4B8	that which attracts unfair advantage	cos(23*2π/127) + isin(23*2π/127)	0.4195 +0.90775i
65.22	65:13'2	138	25	25-arisextile	25-♈✳		26D1	daily work focus	cos(25*2π/138) + isin(25*2π/138)	0.41918 +0.9079i
65.45	65:27'16	11	2	undecile	U₂		1F5EB	getting talked about	cos(1*2π/11) + isin(1*2π/11)	0.41542 +0.90963i

							Unicode	Description	Formula	Result
65.69	65:41'36	137	25	25-ariquintile	25-♈⚹		1F6A7	singular active, direct, control	$\cos(25*2\pi/137) + i\sin(25*2\pi/137)$	0.41162 +0.91136i
65.74	65:44'20	115	21	21-gemiseptile	21-♊七		1F933	inner world with self-talk	$\cos(21*2\pi/115) + i\sin(21*2\pi/115)$	0.41089 +0.91168i
65.77	65:46'9	104	19	19-cancrioctile	19-♋⊿		1F61B	trait known and accepted among friends	$\cos(19*2\pi/104) + i\sin(19*2\pi/104)$	0.41041 +0.9119i
65.81	65:48'23	93	17	17-leanovile	17-♌N		1F60D	brought out by creative, sexualized energy	$\cos(17*2\pi/93) + i\sin(17*2\pi/93)$	0.40982 +0.91217i
65.85	65:51'13	82	15	15-virgidecile	15-♍⊥		1F987	eccentrically attention-getting, disquieting	$\cos(15*2\pi/82) + i\sin(15*2\pi/82)$	0.40907 +0.9125i
65.92	65:54'55	71	13	13-libriundecile	13-♎U		26C5	thriving amidst confusion	$\cos(13*2\pi/71) + i\sin(13*2\pi/71)$	0.40808 +0.91294i
66.00	66:0'0	60	11	11-scorpiinconjunct	11-♏π		1F4CD	strongest memory left behind	$\cos(11*2\pi/60) + i\sin(11*2\pi/60)$	0.40674 +0.91355i
66.06	66:3'18	109	20	20-gemiconjunct	20-♊☌		1F44E	diminishing others' importance	$\cos(20*2\pi/109) + i\sin(20*2\pi/109)$	0.40586 +0.91394i
66.12	66:7'20	49	9	9-scorpiconjunct	9-♏☌		1F399	having known public influence	$\cos(9*2\pi/49) + i\sin(9*2\pi/49)$	0.40478 +0.91441i
66.18	66:10'35	136	25	25-arisquare	25-♈□		1F9D0	serious, sober-minded interactant	$\cos(25*2\pi/136) + i\sin(25*2\pi/136)$	0.40392 +0.91479i
66.24	66:14'23	125	23	23-tauriquintile	23-♉⚹		1F39F	social clique's requirements	$\cos(23*2\pi/125) + i\sin(23*2\pi/125)$	0.40291 +0.91524i
66.32	66:18'56	38	7	7-sajiopposition	7-♐☍		1F64C	use of the body or physical deeds in work	$\cos(7*2\pi/38) + i\sin(7*2\pi/38)$	0.4017 +0.91577i
66.38	66:22'58	141	26	26-arinovile	26-♈N		1F489	easy instillment in others	$\cos(26*2\pi/141) + i\sin(26*2\pi/141)$	0.40062 +0.91624i
66.41	66:24'27	103	19	19-cancriseptile	19-♋七		1F60A	basking in joy	$\cos(19*2\pi/103) + i\sin(19*2\pi/103)$	0.40022 +0.91642i
66.46	66:27'41	65	12	12-libriquintile	12-♎⚹		1F6C0	self-resparking	$\cos(12*2\pi/65) + i\sin(12*2\pi/65)$	0.39936 +0.91679i
66.52	66:31'18	92	17	17-leaoctile	17-♌⊿		1F37B	regular comfort preferences w/ close one	$\cos(17*2\pi/92) + i\sin(17*2\pi/92)$	0.3984 +0.91721i
66.55	66:33'16	119	22	22-gemiundecile	22-♊U		1F4C9	weakened by opinionation, better as ambient	$\cos(22*2\pi/119) + i\sin(22*2\pi/119)$	0.39787 +0.91744i
66.67	66:40'0	27	5	5-capritrine	5-♑△		1F393	intellectualizing and insight	$\cos(5*2\pi/27) + i\sin(5*2\pi/27)$	0.39608 +0.91822i
66.77	66:46'27	124	23	23-taurisquare	23-♉□		1F387	initial, then waning impression	$\cos(23*2\pi/124) + i\sin(23*2\pi/124)$	0.39436 +0.91896i
66.80	66:48'14	97	18	18-cancriconjunct	18-♋☌		1F495	traits reserved for those very close[11]	$\cos(18*2\pi/97) + i\sin(18*2\pi/97)$	0.39388 +0.91916i
66.86	66:51'25	70	13	13-libridecile	13-♎⊥		1F527	used to strengthen or repair bonds	$\cos(13*2\pi/70) + i\sin(13*2\pi/70)$	0.39303 +0.91953i
66.90	66:54'9	113	21	21-gemiquintile	21-♊⚹		1F60E	publicly-labeled vibe given	$\cos(21*2\pi/113) + i\sin(21*2\pi/113)$	0.39229 +0.91984i

---

[11] Remember, you can read aspects in a group. You're not committed to one only. For example, future investigation might claim that 66.86 is some special angle indicating how you and another fall in love. Maybe, maybe not. More likely, this whole 66.77-66.98 window of aspects supports the "falling in love" interpretation, where the 13th multiple of the libridecile happens to help this trend. But librideciles themselves aren't actually about falling in love. Compare it to the 9-libridecile (around 46°) and its six semisquare-like neighbors to see how it contributes to the pack there.

The problem with looking at sharp aspects in a bundle is that you're also looking at their conjuncts in a different bundle to other conjuncts; that is, You might consider your Venus and Neptune trine at 126°, each one conjunct something else at 5° further apart, and those something elses will be sesquiquadrate at 136°. But conjuncts were supposed to express together weren't they? Accordingly, we probably shouldn't stake our lives on that "one" aspect once so many more neighboring interpretations become available. It's more useful to be open to any one of the close aspects—especially because multiple asteroids in multi-conjunct (stellium) are more likely to defer to a leader body most suited to your personality. My Sun, for example, is conjunct my Naema. And although my Sun is still the spotlight receiver as a major planet, my Naema is usually the one who steals the scene, and all aspects to the Sun's cluster are more likely to actually reflect slightly different aspects to my Naema instead. It works the same way as tuning into a radio station.

66.98	66:58'36	43	8	8-sajiseptile	8-♐七		1F0CF	through jokes, games, and fun	cos(8*2πi/43) + isin(8*2πi/43)	0.3911 +0.92035i
67.06	67:3'31	102	19	19-cancrisextile	19-♋✱		1F4BC	boss figure attributes	cos(19*2πi/102) + isin(19*2πi/102)	0.38979 +0.92091i
67.12	67:7'7	59	11	11-scorpiundecile	11-♏U		1F447	having one's pick	cos(11*2πi/59) + isin(11*2πi/59)	0.38882 +0.92131i
67.20	67:12'0	75	14	14-virgitrine	14-♍△		1F3E1	family home maintenance	cos(14*2πi/75) + isin(14*2πi/75)	0.38752 +0.92186i
67.29	67:17'22	107	20	20-cancriundecile	20-♋U		1F481	essence of a great conversation w/ one	cos(20*2πi/107) + isin(20*2πi/107)	0.38607 +0.92247i
67.34	67:20'17	139	26	26-ariseptile	26-♈七		1F3AF	creative perfectionism	cos(26*2πi/139) + isin(26*2πi/139)	0.38529 +0.92279i
67.50	67:30'0	16	3	3-aquarisquare	3-♒□		1F46A	among family	cos(3*2πi/16) + isin(3*2πi/16)	0.38268 +0.92388i
67.69	67:41'32	117	22	22-geminovile	22-♊N		1F48E	best friend's quality	cos(22*2πi/117) + isin(22*2πi/117)	0.37958 +0.92516i
67.72	67:43'21	101	19	19-cancriquintile	19-♋⬠		1F624	disregard for things heard	cos(19*2πi/101) + isin(19*2πi/101)	0.37909 +0.92536i
67.76	67:45'52	85	16	16-leaconjunct	16-♌☌		1F924	downplaying a real want	cos(16*2πi/85) + isin(16*2πi/85)	0.37841 +0.92564i
67.83	67:49'33	69	13	13-librinovile	13-♎N		1F418	subtle, strong draw of trait via socialization	cos(13*2πi/69) + isin(13*2πi/69)	0.37742 +0.92604i
67.87	67:52'7	122	23	23-taurioposition	23-♉☍		1F913	easily annoying to others	cos(23*2πi/122) + isin(23*2πi/122)	0.37673 +0.92632i
67.92	67:55'28	53	10	10-scorpiquintile	10-♏⬠		1F917	reasons one is desired	cos(10*2πi/53) + isin(10*2πi/53)	0.37583 +0.92669i
68.00	68:0'0	90	17	17-leasextile	17-♌✱		1F6B8	absorptions by one's children	cos(17*2πi/90) + isin(17*2πi/90)	0.37461 +0.92718i
68.03	68:1'53	127	24	24-tauriseptile	24-♉七		1F4B8	that which attracts unfair advantage	cos(24*2πi/127) + isin(24*2πi/127)	0.3741 +0.92739i
68.11	68:6'29	37	7	7-sajiconjunct	7-♐☌		2B50	trusted ability revealed	cos(7*2πi/37) + isin(7*2πi/37)	0.37286 +0.92789i
68.18	68:10'54	132	25	25-tauriinconjunct	25-♉π		1F517	sharing a special bond w/ a friend	cos(25*2πi/132) + isin(25*2πi/132)	0.37166 +0.92837i
68.21	68:12'37	95	18	18-leaundecile	18-♌U		265B	the image of a progress-inspiring master	cos(18*2πi/95) + isin(18*2πi/95)	0.3712 +0.92855i
68.28	68:16'33	58	11	11-scorpidecile	11-♏⊥		1F47B	interactions with an ethereal party	cos(11*2πi/58) + isin(11*2πi/58)	0.37014 +0.92898i
68.32	68:19'16	137	26	26-ariquintile	26-♈⬠		1F6A7	singular active, direct, control	cos(26*2πi/137) + isin(26*2πi/137)	0.3694 +0.92927i
68.40	68:24'0	100	19	19-cancrisquare	19-♋□		1F6CB	home & family life	cos(19*2πi/100) + isin(19*2πi/100)	0.36812 +0.92978i
68.43	68:25'47	121	23	23-tauriconjunct	23-♉☌		1F4B0	prosperity & status-seeking	cos(23*2πi/121) + isin(23*2πi/121)	0.36764 +0.92997i
68.45	68:27'2	142	27	27-aridecile	27-♈⊥		1F549	blessings others can only dream of	cos(27*2πi/142) + isin(27*2πi/142)	0.3673 +0.9301i
68.57	68:34'17	21	4	4-aquarinovile	4-♒N		1F483	at peak sexiness, strength, or creativity	cos(4*2πi/21) + isin(4*2πi/21)	0.36534 +0.93087i
68.73	68:43'38	110	21	21-gemiopposition	21-♊☍		1F6A5	managing others' behavior	cos(21*2πi/110) + isin(21*2πi/110)	0.36281 +0.93186i
68.76	68:45'50	89	17	17-leaquintile	17-♌⬠		1F48B	sensuality & body expression	cos(17*2πi/89) + isin(17*2πi/89)	0.36221 +0.9321i
68.82	68:49'24	68	13	13-librioctile	13-♎⊿		1F462	appearance of dominating	cos(13*2πi/68) + isin(13*2πi/68)	0.36124 +0.93247i
68.87	68:52'10	115	22	22-gemiseptile	22-♊七		1F933	inner world with self-talk	cos(22*2πi/115) + isin(22*2πi/115)	0.36049 +0.93276i
68.94	68:56'10	47	9	9-sajiundecile	9-♐U		262B	a core, lived principle	cos(9*2πi/47) + isin(9*2πi/47)	0.35941 +0.93318i

69.00	69:0'0	120	23	23-gemiinconjunct	23-♊♐		1F922	more vulnerable to things	cos(23*2π/120) + isin(23*2π/120)	0.35837 +0.93358i
69.04	69:2'27	73	14	14-virgiconjunct	14-♍♂		2692	new or deep investment in job	cos(14*2π/73) + isin(14*2π/73)	0.3577 +0.93384i
69.09	69:5'27	99	19	19-cancritrine	19-♋△		1F645	communication-stifling	cos(19*2π/99) + isin(19*2π/99)	0.35689 +0.93415i
69.12	69:7'12	125	24	24-tauriquintile	24-♉⬠		1F39F	social clique's requirements	cos(24*2π/125) + isin(24*2π/125)	0.35641 +0.93433i
69.23	69:13'50	26	5	5-capriopposition	5-♑☍		1F3B8	why one's fans follow them	cos(5*2π/26) + isin(5*2π/26)	0.3546 +0.93502i
69.33	69:19'59	135	26	26-aritrine	26-♈△		1F3C4	easy and prolific	cos(26*2π/135) + isin(26*2π/135)	0.35293 +0.93565i
69.40	69:23'51	83	16	16-virgiundecile	16-♍U		26A1	high-tension activity in surroundings	cos(16*2π/83) + isin(16*2π/83)	0.35188 +0.93604i
69.43	69:25'42	140	27	27-arioctile	27-♈⊿		1F340	helped by a benefactor	cos(27*2π/140) + isin(27*2π/140)	0.35137 +0.93623i
69.47	69:28'25	57	11	11-scorpinovile	11-♏N		1FA84	arrives whenever one wants it, no asking	cos(11*2π/57) + isin(11*2π/57)	0.35064 +0.93651i
69.55	69:32'43	88	17	17-leasquare	17-♌□		1F479	suppressing power imbalance	cos(17*2π/88) + isin(17*2π/88)	0.34946 +0.93695i
69.58	69:34'47	119	23	23-gemiundecile	23-♊U		1F4C9	weakened by opinionation, better as ambient	cos(23*2π/119) + isin(23*2π/119)	0.3489 +0.93716i
69.68	69:40'38	31	6	6-capriseptile	6-♑✴		1F3A2	expressed by one's social network	cos(6*2π/31) + isin(6*2π/31)	0.34731 +0.93775i
69.80	69:47'45	98	19	19-cancriopposition	19-♋☍		1F31F	social advancement catalyst	cos(19*2π/98) + isin(19*2π/98)	0.34537 +0.93847i
69.85	69:51'2	67	13	13-libriseptile	13-♎✴		1F63B	getting others to fall in love w oneself	cos(13*2π/67) + isin(13*2π/67)	0.34447 +0.9388i
69.93	69:55'41	139	27	27-ariseptile	27-♈✴		1F3AF	creative perfectionism	cos(27*2π/139) + isin(27*2π/139)	0.3432 +0.93926i
70.00	70:0'0	36	7	7-capriinconjunct	7-♑♐		1F3BB	downplayed want or talent	cos(7*2π/36) + isin(7*2π/36)	0.34202 +0.93969i
70.09	70:5'18	113	22	22-gemiquintile	22-♊⬠		1F60E	publicly-labeled vibe given	cos(22*2π/113) + isin(22*2π/113)	0.34057 +0.94022i
70.13	70:7'47	77	15	15-virgiquintile	15-♍⬠		1F422	guarded insistence	cos(15*2π/77) + isin(15*2π/77)	0.33989 +0.94047i
70.17	70:10'10	118	23	23-gemidecile	23-♊⊥		1F3C3	staying with it as long as encouraged	cos(23*2π/118) + isin(23*2π/118)	0.33924 +0.9407i
70.24	70:14'38	41	8	8-sajiquintile	8-♐⬠		1F5FD	personas aspired to	cos(8*2π/41) + isin(8*2π/41)	0.33802 +0.94114i
70.34	70:20'41	87	17	17-leatrine	17-♌△		2763	interactor inspired to want	cos(17*2π/87) + isin(17*2π/87)	0.33636 +0.94173i
70.38	70:22'33	133	26	26-ariconjunct	26-♈♂		1F49D	during sex or when flirting	cos(26*2π/133) + isin(26*2π/133)	0.33585 +0.94192i
70.43	70:26'5	46	9	9-sajidecile	9-♐⊥		1F4CE	trait housed by key colleagues	cos(9*2π/46) + isin(9*2π/46)	0.33488 +0.94226i
70.49	70:29'22	143	28	28-ariundecile	28-♈U		1F4E3	broadcasting which gets one talked about	cos(28*2π/143) + isin(28*2π/143)	0.33398 +0.94258i
70.52	70:30'55	97	19	19-cancriconjunct	19-♋♂		1F495	traits reserved for those very close	cos(19*2π/97) + isin(19*2π/97)	0.33355 +0.94273i
70.59	70:35'17	51	10	10-scorpitrine	10-♏△		1F61A	use of persuasive words	cos(10*2π/51) + isin(10*2π/51)	0.33235 +0.94315i
70.65	70:39'15	107	21	21-cancriundecile	21-♋U		1F481	essence of a great conversation w/ one	cos(21*2π/107) + isin(21*2π/107)	0.33127 +0.94354i
70.71	70:42'51	56	11	11-scorpioctile	11-♏⊿		1F608	for fun or one's own power	cos(11*2π/56) + isin(11*2π/56)	0.33028 +0.94388i
70.77	70:46'9	117	23	23-geminovile	23-♊N		1F48E	best friend's quality	cos(23*2π/117) + isin(23*2π/117)	0.32937 +0.9442i

70.82	70:49'10	61	12	12-libriconjunct	12-♎☌		1F526	singled out for attention	cos(12*2πi/61) + isin(12*2πi/61)	0.32854 +0.94449i
70.87	70:51'58	127	25	25-tauriseptile	25-♉ᱸ		1F4B8	that which attracts unfair advantage	cos(25*2πi/127) + isin(25*2πi/127)	0.32778 +0.94476i
70.95	70:56'56	137	27	27-ariquintile	27-♈⬠		1F6A7	singular active, direct, control	cos(27*2πi/137) + isin(27*2πi/137)	0.32641 +0.94523i
70.99	70:59'9	71	14	14-libriundecile	14-♎U		26C5	thriving amidst confusion	cos(14*2πi/71) + isin(14*2πi/71)	0.3258 +0.94544i
71.05	71:3'9	76	15	15-virgisquare	15-♍□		1F3D8	seen by friends' friends & family	cos(15*2πi/76) + isin(15*2πi/76)	0.3247 +0.94582i
71.11	71:6'40	81	16	16-virginovile	16-♍N		1F451	mastered early, forms broad social identity	cos(16*2πi/81) + isin(16*2πi/81)	0.32373 +0.94615i
71.16	71:9'46	86	17	17-leaopposition	17-♌☍		1F921	one's commentary offends egos	cos(17*2πi/86) + isin(17*2πi/86)	0.32288 +0.94644i
71.25	71:15'0	96	19	19-leainconjunct	19-♌⚻		1F937	what "not enough" looks like	cos(19*2πi/96) + isin(19*2πi/96)	0.32144 +0.94693i
71.29	71:17'13	101	20	20-cancriquintile	20-♋⬠		1F624	disregard for things heard	cos(20*2πi/101) + isin(20*2πi/101)	0.32083 +0.94714i
71.32	71:19'14	106	21	21-cancridecile	21-♋⊥		1F3A0	others think one has more power than one has	cos(21*2πi/106) + isin(21*2πi/106)	0.32027 +0.94733i
71.38	71:22'45	116	23	23-gemioctile	23-♊⊿		1F612	having been slighted or doubted	cos(23*2πi/116) + isin(23*2πi/116)	0.3193 +0.94765i
71.43	71:25'42	126	25	25-taurisextile	25-♉✳		1F47E	aggressive assertion of identity	cos(25*2πi/126) + isin(25*2πi/126)	0.31849 +0.94793i
71.49	71:29'21	141	28	28-arinovile	28-♈N		1F489	easy instillment in others	cos(28*2πi/141) + isin(28*2πi/141)	0.31748 +0.94826i
72.00	72:0'0	5	1	quintile	⬠		1F60F	ego expression	cos(1*2πi/5) + isin(1*2πi/5)	0.30902 +0.95106i
72.50	72:30'0	144	29	29-ariinconjunct	29-♈⚻		1F501	always-on trait	cos(29*2πi/144) + isin(29*2πi/144)	0.30071 +0.95372i
72.54	72:32'14	134	27	27-ariopposition	27-♈☍		1F49F	a trait the partner MUST have	cos(27*2πi/134) + isin(27*2πi/134)	0.30008 +0.95391i
72.58	72:34'50	124	25	25-taurisquare	25-♉□		1F387	initial, then waning impression	cos(25*2πi/124) + isin(25*2πi/124)	0.29936 +0.95414i
72.63	72:37'53	114	23	23-gemisextile	23-♊✳		1F6F1	other's influence attempts	cos(23*2πi/114) + isin(23*2πi/114)	0.29851 +0.95441i
72.69	72:41'32	104	21	21-cancrioctile	21-♋⊿		1F61B	trait known and accepted among friends	cos(21*2πi/104) + isin(21*2πi/104)	0.2975 +0.95472i
72.73	72:43'38	99	20	20-cancritrine	20-♋△		1F645	communication-stifling	cos(20*2πi/99) + isin(20*2πi/99)	0.29692 +0.9549i
72.77	72:45'57	94	19	19-leadecile	19-♌⊥		1F463	helps in others after learning the hard way	cos(19*2πi/94) + isin(19*2πi/94)	0.29628 +0.9551i
72.81	72:48'32	89	18	18-leaquintile	18-♌⬠		1F48B	sensuality & body expression	cos(18*2πi/89) + isin(18*2πi/89)	0.29556 +0.95532i
72.86	72:51'25	84	17	17-virgiinconjunct	17-♍⚻		1F411	traits for the seemingly weak	cos(17*2πi/84) + isin(17*2πi/84)	0.29476 +0.95557i
72.91	72:54'41	79	16	16-virgiseptile	16-♍ᱸ		270A	anti-establishment revolutionary	cos(16*2πi/79) + isin(16*2πi/79)	0.29385 +0.95585i
72.97	72:58'22	74	15	15-virgiopposition	15-♍☍		1F626	social stressors	cos(15*2πi/74) + isin(15*2πi/74)	0.29282 +0.95617i
73.04	73:2'36	69	14	14-librinovile	14-♎N		1F418	subtle, strong draw of trait via socialization	cos(14*2πi/69) + isin(14*2πi/69)	0.29165 +0.95653i
73.08	73:4'57	133	27	27-ariconjunct	27-♈☌		1F49D	during sex or when flirting	cos(27*2πi/133) + isin(27*2πi/133)	0.29099 +0.95673i
73.13	73:7'30	64	13	13-librisquare	13-♎□		4F17	amidst a noisy setting	cos(13*2πi/64) + isin(13*2πi/64)	0.29028 +0.95694i
73.17	73:10'14	123	25	25-tauritrine	25-♉△		238F	others must express or draw out	cos(25*2πi/123) + isin(25*2πi/123)	0.28952 +0.95717i

73.22	73:13'13	59	12	12-scorpiundecile	12-♏U		1F447	having one's pick	cos(12*2πi/59) + isin(12*2πi/59)	0.28869 +0.95742i
73.27	73:16'27	113	23	23-gemiquintile	23-♊⬠		1F60E	publicly-labeled vibe given	cos(23*2πi/113) + isin(23*2πi/113)	0.28779 +0.95769i
73.33	73:19'59	54	11	11-scorpisextile	11-♏✳		1F378	self-fulfillment tool	cos(11*2πi/54) + isin(11*2πi/54)	0.2868 +0.95799i
73.40	73:23'53	103	21	21-cancriseptile	21-♋七		1F60A	basking in joy	cos(21*2πi/103) + isin(21*2πi/103)	0.28572 +0.95831i
73.47	73:28'9	49	10	10-scorpiconjunct	10-♏♂		1F399	having known public influence	cos(10*2πi/49) + isin(10*2πi/49)	0.28453 +0.95867i
73.55	73:32'54	93	19	19-leanovile	19-♌N		1F60D	brought out by creative, sexualized energy	cos(19*2πi/93) + isin(19*2πi/93)	0.28321 +0.95906i
73.58	73:34'35	137	28	28-ariquintile	28-♈⬠		1F6A7	singular active, direct, control	cos(28*2πi/137) + isin(28*2πi/137)	0.28273 +0.9592i
73.64	73:38'10	44	9	9-sajioctile	9-♐⊿		1F6B5	role in a peer group	cos(9*2πi/44) + isin(9*2πi/44)	0.28173 +0.95949i
73.73	73:44'5	83	17	17-virgiundecile	17-♍U		26A1	high-tension activity in surroundings	cos(17*2πi/83) + isin(17*2πi/83)	0.28008 +0.95998i
73.77	73:46'13	122	25	25-tauriopposition	25-♉☍		1F913	easily annoying to others	cos(25*2πi/122) + isin(25*2πi/122)	0.27949 +0.96015i
73.85	73:50'46	39	8	8-sajitrine	8-♐△		1F3DD	convincing others of one's value	cos(8*2πi/39) + isin(8*2πi/39)	0.27822 +0.96052i
73.93	73:55'42	112	23	23-gemisquare	23-♊□		1F38E	one's trait observed by outsiders	cos(23*2πi/112) + isin(23*2πi/112)	0.27684 +0.96092i
73.97	73:58'21	73	15	15-virgiconjunct	15-♍♂		2692	new or deep investment in job	cos(15*2πi/73) + isin(15*2πi/73)	0.2761 +0.96113i
74.04	74:2'33	141	29	29-arinovile	29-♈N		1F489	easy instillment in others	cos(29*2πi/141) + isin(29*2πi/141)	0.27492 +0.96147i
74.12	74:7'3	34	7	7-capridecile	7-♑⊥		1F3C6	potential to be a master or boss	cos(7*2πi/34) + isin(7*2πi/34)	0.27366 +0.96183i
74.20	74:11'54	131	27	27-tauriundecile	27-♉U		1F611	with doubt in associations	cos(27*2πi/131) + isin(27*2πi/131)	0.27231 +0.96221i
74.23	74:13'36	97	20	20-cancriconjunct	20-♋♂		1F495	traits reserved for those very close	cos(20*2πi/97) + isin(20*2πi/97)	0.27183 +0.96235i
74.29	74:17'8	63	13	13-libritrine	13-♎△		1F6A8	know-it-all	cos(13*2πi/63) + isin(13*2πi/63)	0.27084 +0.96262i
74.35	74:20'52	92	19	19-leaoctile	19-♌⊿		1F37B	regular comfort preferences w/ close one	cos(19*2πi/92) + isin(19*2πi/92)	0.2698 +0.96292i
74.38	74:22'48	121	25	25-tauriconjunct	25-♉♂		1F4B0	prosperity & status-seeking	cos(25*2πi/121) + isin(25*2πi/121)	0.26925 +0.96307i
74.48	74:28'57	29	6	6-capriquintile	6-♑⬠		1F3A9	proud charisma	cos(6*2πi/29) + isin(6*2πi/29)	0.26753 +0.96355i
74.59	74:35'40	111	23	23-gemitrine	23-♊△		1F973	around high-expression groups	cos(23*2πi/111) + isin(23*2πi/111)	0.26565 +0.96407i
74.63	74:38'2	82	17	17-virgidecile	17-♍⊥		1F987	eccentrically attention-getting, disquieting	cos(17*2πi/82) + isin(17*2πi/82)	0.26498 +0.96425i
74.67	74:40'0	135	28	28-aritrine	28-♈△		1F3C4	easy and prolific	cos(28*2πi/135) + isin(28*2πi/135)	0.26443 +0.9644i
74.72	74:43'1	53	11	11-scorpiquintile	11-♏⬠		1F917	reasons one is desired	cos(11*2πi/53) + isin(11*2πi/53)	0.26359 +0.96464i
74.77	74:46'9	130	27	27-tauridecile	27-♉⊥		1F3AA	relied upon by others in the talked topic	cos(27*2πi/130) + isin(27*2πi/130)	0.26271 +0.96488i
74.81	74:48'18	77	16	16-virgiquintile	16-♍⬠		1F422	guarded insistence	cos(16*2πi/77) + isin(16*2πi/77)	0.2621 +0.96504i
74.88	74:52'47	125	26	26-tauriquintile	26-♉⬠		1F39F	social clique's requirements	cos(26*2πi/125) + isin(26*2πi/125)	0.26084 +0.96538i
75.00	75:0'0	24	5	5-aquariinconjunct	5-♒π		1F4AD	imagination at work	cos(5*2πi/24) + isin(5*2πi/24)	0.25882 +0.96593i

75.13	75:7'49	115	24	24-gemiseptile	24-Ⅱ七		1F933	inner world with self-talk	cos(24*2πi/115) + isin(24*2πi/115)	0.25662 +0.96651i
75.16	75:9'53	91	19	19-leaseptile	19-♌七		1F576	smoothly comfortable	cos(19*2πi/91) + isin(19*2πi/91)	0.25604 +0.96667i
75.22	75:13'25	67	14	14-libriseptile	14-♎七		1F63B	getting others to fall in love w oneself	cos(14*2πi/67) + isin(14*2πi/67)	0.25504 +0.96693i
75.27	75:16'21	110	23	23-gemiopposition	23-Ⅱ☍		1F6A5	managing others' behavior	cos(23*2πi/110) + isin(23*2πi/110)	0.25422 +0.96715i
75.35	75:20'55	43	9	9-sajiseptile	9-♐七		1F0CF	through jokes, games, and fun	cos(9*2πi/43) + isin(9*2πi/43)	0.25293 +0.96748i
75.43	75:25'42	105	22	22-cancrinovile	22-♋N		1F5EF	when irritated to see standards defied	cos(22*2πi/105) + isin(22*2πi/105)	0.25159 +0.96783i
75.48	75:29'1	62	13	13-libriopposition	13-♎☍		1F3F4	manipulative ambition	cos(13*2πi/62) + isin(13*2πi/62)	0.25065 +0.96808i
75.52	75:31'28	143	30	30-ariundecile	30-♈U		1F4E3	broadcasting which gets one talked about	cos(30*2πi/143) + isin(30*2πi/143)	0.24997 +0.96825i
75.60	75:35'59	100	21	21-cancrisquare	21-♋□		1F6CB	home & family life	cos(21*2πi/100) + isin(21*2πi/100)	0.24869 +0.96858i
75.63	75:37'48	119	25	25-gemiundecile	25-ⅡU		1F4C9	weakened by opinionation, better as ambient	cos(25*2πi/119) + isin(25*2πi/119)	0.24818 +0.96871i
75.65	75:39'7	138	29	29-arisextile	29-♈*		26D1	daily work focus	cos(29*2πi/138) + isin(29*2πi/138)	0.24781 +0.96881i
75.79	75:47'22	19	4	4-aquariseptile	4-♒七		1F510	gateway to one's friendship	cos(4*2πi/19) + isin(4*2πi/19)	0.24549 +0.9694i
75.94	75:56'15	128	27	27-taurioctile	27-♉⊿		1F478	intuitive comfort even amidst stress	cos(27*2πi/128) + isin(27*2πi/128)	0.24298 +0.97003i
76.00	76:0'0	90	19	19-leasextile	19-♌*		1F6B8	absorptions by one's children	cos(19*2πi/90) + isin(19*2πi/90)	0.24192 +0.9703i
76.10	76:5'51	123	26	26-tauritrine	26-♉△		238F	others must express or draw out	cos(26*2πi/123) + isin(26*2πi/123)	0.24027 +0.97071i
76.15	76:9'13	52	11	11-scorpisquare	11-♏□		1F61E	falling short	cos(11*2πi/52) + isin(11*2πi/52)	0.23932 +0.97094i
76.24	76:14'7	85	18	18-leaconjunct	18-♌♂		1F924	downplaying a real want	cos(18*2πi/85) + isin(18*2πi/85)	0.23794 +0.97128i
76.27	76:16'16	118	25	25-gemidecile	25-Ⅱ⊥		1F3C3	staying with it as long as encouraged	cos(25*2πi/118) + isin(25*2πi/118)	0.23733 +0.97143i
76.36	76:21'49	33	7	7-caprinovile	7-♑N		1F4FB	in a formal group discussion	cos(7*2πi/33) + isin(7*2πi/33)	0.23576 +0.97181i
76.50	76:30'0	80	17	17-virgioctile	17-♍⊿		1F939	vividly remembered by one's children	cos(17*2πi/80) + isin(17*2πi/80)	0.23345 +0.97237i
76.54	76:32'7	127	27	27-tauriseptile	27-♉七		1F4B8	that which attracts unfair advantage	cos(27*2πi/127) + isin(27*2πi/127)	0.23284 +0.97251i
76.60	76:35'44	47	10	10-sajiundecile	10-♐U		262B	a core, lived principle	cos(10*2πi/47) + isin(10*2πi/47)	0.23182 +0.97276i
76.67	76:40'0	108	23	23-cancriinconjunct	23-♋π		1F31D	why close friends come around	cos(23*2πi/108) + isin(23*2πi/108)	0.23062 +0.97304i
76.72	76:43'16	61	13	13-libriconjunct	13-♎♂		1F526	singled out for attention	cos(13*2πi/61) + isin(13*2πi/61)	0.22969 +0.97326i
76.80	76:47'59	75	16	16-virgitrine	16-♍△		1F3E1	family home maintenance	cos(16*2πi/75) + isin(16*2πi/75)	0.22835 +0.97358i
76.89	76:53'35	103	22	22-cancriseptile	22-♋七		1F60A	basking in joy	cos(22*2πi/103) + isin(22*2πi/103)	0.22677 +0.97395i
76.95	76:56'47	131	28	28-tauriundecile	28-♉U		1F611	with doubt in associations	cos(28*2πi/131) + isin(28*2πi/131)	0.22586 +0.97416i
77.14	77:8'34	14	3	3-aquariopposition	3-♒☍		1F443	a sense from one's company	cos(3*2πi/14) + isin(3*2πi/14)	0.22252 +0.97493i
77.33	77:19'59	135	29	29-aritrine	29-♈△		1F3C4	easy and prolific	cos(29*2πi/135) + isin(29*2πi/135)	0.21928 +0.97566i

77.38	77:22'59	107	23	23-cancriundecile	23-♋U		1F481	essence of a great conversation w/ one	cos(23*2π/107) + isin(23*2π/107)	0.21843 +0.97585i
77.42	77:25'9	93	20	20-leanovile	20-♌N		1F60D	brought out by creative, sexualized energy	cos(20*2π/93) + isin(20*2π/93)	0.21781 +0.97599i
77.50	77:30'0	144	31	31-ariinconjunct	31-♈↗		1F501	always-on trait	cos(31*2π/144) + isin(31*2π/144)	0.21644 +0.9763i
77.54	77:32'18	65	14	14-libriquintile	14-♎⬠		1F6C0	self-resparking	cos(14*2π/65) + isin(14*2π/65)	0.21578 +0.97644i
77.59	77:35'10	116	25	25-gemioctile	25-♊⧄		1F612	having been slighted or doubted	cos(25*2π/116) + isin(25*2π/116)	0.21497 +0.97662i
77.65	77:38'49	51	11	11-scorpitrine	11-♏△		1F61A	use of persuasive words	cos(11*2π/51) + isin(11*2π/51)	0.21393 +0.97685i
77.70	77:41'52	139	30	30-ariseptile	30-♈7		1F3AF	creative perfectionism	cos(30*2π/139) + isin(30*2π/139)	0.21307 +0.97704i
77.73	77:43'38	88	19	19-leasquare	19-♌□		1F479	suppressing power imbalance	cos(19*2π/88) + isin(19*2π/88)	0.21257 +0.97715i
77.76	77:45'36	125	27	27-tauriquintile	27-♉⬠		1F39F	social clique's requirements	cos(27*2π/125) + isin(27*2π/125)	0.21201 +0.97727i
77.84	77:50'16	37	8	8-sajiconjunct	8-♐☌	☆	2B50	trusted ability revealed	cos(8*2π/37) + isin(8*2π/37)	0.21068 +0.97756i
77.94	77:56'17	97	21	21-cancriconjunct	21-♋☌		1F495	traits reserved for those very close	cos(21*2π/97) + isin(21*2π/97)	0.20897 +0.97792i
78.00	78:0'0	60	13	13-scorpiinconjunct	13-♏↗		1F4CD	strongest memory left behind	cos(13*2π/60) + isin(13*2π/60)	0.20791 +0.97815i
78.04	78:2'31	143	31	31-ariundecile	31-♈U		1F4E3	broadcasting which gets one talked about	cos(31*2π/143) + isin(31*2π/143)	0.2072 +0.9783i
78.07	78:4'20	83	18	18-virgiundecile	18-♍U	⚡	26A1	high-tension activity in surroundings	cos(18*2π/83) + isin(18*2π/83)	0.20668 +0.97841i
78.14	78:8'22	129	28	28-taurinovile	28-♉N		1F647	in the service of one attached to	cos(28*2π/129) + isin(28*2π/129)	0.20553 +0.97865i
78.26	78:15'39	23	5	5-aquariundecile	5-♒U		1F991	unusual social trait, liked by eccentrics	cos(5*2π/23) + isin(5*2π/23)	0.20346 +0.97908i
78.39	78:23'13	124	27	27-taurisquare	27-♉□		1F387	initial, then waning impression	cos(27*2π/124) + isin(27*2π/124)	0.2013 +0.97953i
78.42	78:24'57	101	22	22-cancriquintile	22-♋⬠		1F624	disregard for things heard	cos(22*2π/101) + isin(22*2π/101)	0.20081 +0.97963i
78.50	78:29'46	133	29	29-ariconjunct	29-♈☌		1F49D	during sex or when flirting	cos(29*2π/133) + isin(29*2π/133)	0.19943 +0.97991i
78.55	78:32'43	55	12	12-scorpiseptile	12-♏7		1F632	shocking or flooding others w information	cos(12*2π/55) + isin(12*2π/55)	0.19859 +0.98008i
78.59	78:35'29	142	31	31-aridecile	31-♈⊥		1F549	blessings others can only dream of	cos(31*2π/142) + isin(31*2π/142)	0.1978 +0.98024i
78.62	78:37'14	87	19	19-leatrine	19-♌△		2763	interactor inspired to want	cos(19*2π/87) + isin(19*2π/87)	0.1973 +0.98034i
78.66	78:39'19	119	26	26-gemiundecile	26-♊U		1F4C9	weakened by opinionation, better as ambient	cos(26*2π/119) + isin(26*2π/119)	0.19671 +0.98046i
78.75	78:45'0	32	7	7-caprioctile	7-♑⧄		1F5FB	an indomitable characteristic	cos(7*2π/32) + isin(7*2π/32)	0.19509 +0.98079i
78.83	78:49'55	137	30	30-ariquintile	30-♈⬠		1F6A7	singular active, direct, control	cos(30*2π/137) + isin(30*2π/137)	0.19368 +0.98106i
78.86	78:51'25	105	23	23-cancrinovile	23-♋N		1F5EF	when irritated to see standards defied	cos(23*2π/105) + isin(23*2π/105)	0.19326 +0.98115i
78.95	78:56'50	114	25	25-gemisextile	25-♊✳		1F6F1	other's influence attempts	cos(25*2π/114) + isin(25*2π/114)	0.19171 +0.98145i
79.02	79:1'27	41	9	9-sajiquintile	9-♐⬠		1F5FD	personas aspired to	cos(9*2π/41) + isin(9*2π/41)	0.19039 +0.98171i
79.09	79:5'27	132	29	29-tauriinconjunct	29-♉↗		1F517	sharing a special bond w/ a friend	cos(29*2π/132) + isin(29*2π/132)	0.18925 +0.98193i

79.15	79:8'56	141	31	31-arinovile	31-♈N		1F489	easy instillment in others	cos(31*2πi/141) + isin(31*2πi/141)	0.18826 +0.98212i
79.20	79:12'0	50	11	11-scorpiopposition	11-♏☍		1F5BC	images put forth to others	cos(11*2πi/50) + isin(11*2πi/50)	0.18738 +0.98229i
79.27	79:15'57	109	24	24-gemiconjunct	24-♊☌		1F44E	diminishing others' importance	cos(24*2πi/109) + isin(24*2πi/109)	0.18625 +0.9825i
79.32	79:19'19	59	13	13-scorpiundecile	13-♏U		1F447	having one's pick	cos(13*2πi/59) + isin(13*2πi/59)	0.18529 +0.98268i
79.37	79:22'12	127	28	28-tauriseptile	28-♉七		1F4B8	that which attracts unfair advantage	cos(28*2πi/127) + isin(28*2πi/127)	0.18446 +0.98284i
79.41	79:24'42	68	15	15-librioctile	15-♎⊿		1F462	appearance of dominating	cos(15*2πi/68) + isin(15*2πi/68)	0.18375 +0.98297i
79.48	79:28'49	77	17	17-virgiquintile	17-♍⬠		1F422	guarded insistence	cos(17*2πi/77) + isin(17*2πi/77)	0.18257 +0.98319i
79.53	79:32'5	86	19	19-leaopposition	19-♌☍		1F921	one's commentary offends egos	cos(19*2πi/86) + isin(19*2πi/86)	0.18164 +0.98337i
79.58	79:34'44	95	21	21-leaundecile	21-♌U		265B	the image of a progress-inspiring master	cos(21*2πi/95) + isin(21*2πi/95)	0.18088 +0.98351i
79.65	79:38'45	113	25	25-gemiquintile	25-♊⬠		1F60E	publicly-labeled vibe given	cos(25*2πi/113) + isin(25*2πi/113)	0.17973 +0.98372i
79.69	79:41'40	131	29	29-tauriundecile	29-♉U		1F611	with doubt in associations	cos(29*2πi/131) + isin(29*2πi/131)	0.17889 +0.98387i
79.71	79:42'51	140	31	31-arioctile	31-♈⊿		1F340	helped by a benefactor	cos(31*2πi/140) + isin(31*2πi/140)	0.17856 +0.98393i
80.00	80:0'0	9	2	novile (binovile)	N₂ (♇)		1F3AC	self-image promotion	cos(1*2πi/9) + isin(1*2πi/9)	0.17365 +0.98481i
80.29	80:17'15	139	31	31-ariseptile	31-♈七		1F3AF	creative perfectionism	cos(31*2πi/139) + isin(31*2πi/139)	0.1687 +0.98567i
80.33	80:19'50	121	27	27-tauriconjunct	27-♉☌		1F4B0	prosperity & status-seeking	cos(27*2πi/121) + isin(27*2πi/121)	0.16796 +0.98579i
80.39	80:23'18	103	23	23-cancriseptile	23-♋七		1F60A	basking in joy	cos(23*2πi/103) + isin(23*2πi/103)	0.16697 +0.98596i
80.43	80:25'31	94	21	21-leadecile	21-♌⊥		1F463	helps in others after learning the hard way	cos(21*2πi/94) + isin(21*2πi/94)	0.16633 +0.98607i
80.47	80:28'14	85	19	19-leaconjunct	19-♌☌		1F924	downplaying a real want	cos(19*2πi/85) + isin(19*2πi/85)	0.16555 +0.9862i
80.53	80:31'34	76	17	17-virgisquare	17-♍□		1F3D8	seen by friends' friends & family	cos(17*2πi/76) + isin(17*2πi/76)	0.16459 +0.98636i
80.60	80:35'49	67	15	15-libriseptile	15-♎七		1F63B	getting others to fall in love w oneself	cos(15*2πi/67) + isin(15*2πi/67)	0.16338 +0.98656i
80.64	80:38'24	125	28	28-tauriquintile	28-♉⬠		1F39F	social clique's requirements	cos(28*2πi/125) + isin(28*2πi/125)	0.16264 +0.98669i
80.69	80:41'22	58	13	13-scorpidecile	13-♏⊥		1F47B	interactions with an ethereal party	cos(13*2πi/58) + isin(13*2πi/58)	0.16178 +0.98683i
80.75	80:44'51	107	24	24-cancriundecile	24-♋U		1F481	essence of a great conversation w/ one	cos(24*2πi/107) + isin(24*2πi/107)	0.16078 +0.98699i
80.82	80:48'58	49	11	11-scorpiconjunct	11-♏☌		1F399	having known public influence	cos(11*2πi/49) + isin(11*2πi/49)	0.1596 +0.98718i
80.90	80:53'55	89	20	20-leaquintile	20-♌⬠		1F48B	sensuality & body expression	cos(20*2πi/89) + isin(20*2πi/89)	0.15818 +0.98741i
80.93	80:55'48	129	29	29-taurinovile	29-♉N		1F647	in the service of one attached to	cos(29*2πi/129) + isin(29*2πi/129)	0.15764 +0.9875i
81.00	81:0'0	40	9	9-sajisquare	9-♐□		1F66A	future missable partnership duty	cos(9*2πi/40) + isin(9*2πi/40)	0.15643 +0.98769i
81.08	81:4'51	111	25	25-gemitrine	25-♊△		1F973	around high-expression groups	cos(25*2πi/111) + isin(25*2πi/111)	0.15504 +0.98791i
81.13	81:7'36	71	16	16-libriundecile	16-♎U		26C5	thriving amidst confusion	cos(16*2πi/71) + isin(16*2πi/71)	0.15425 +0.98803i

81.18	81:10'35	102	23	23-cancrisextile	23-♋*		1F4BC	boss figure attributes	cos(23*2πi/102) + isin(23*2πi/102)	0.15339 +0.98817i
81.20	81:12'10	133	30	30-ariconjunct	30-♈☌		1F49D	during sex or when flirting	cos(30*2πi/133) + isin(30*2πi/133)	0.15293 +0.98824i
81.29	81:17'25	31	7	7-capriseptile	7-♑七		1F3A2	expressed by one's social network	cos(7*2πi/31) + isin(7*2πi/31)	0.15143 +0.98847i
81.39	81:23'28	115	26	26-gemiseptile	26-♊七		1F933	inner world with self-talk	cos(26*2πi/115) + isin(26*2πi/115)	0.14969 +0.98873i
81.43	81:25'42	84	19	19-virgiinconjunct	19-♍π		1F411	traits for the seemingly weak	cos(19*2πi/84) + isin(19*2πi/84)	0.14904 +0.98883i
81.46	81:27'35	137	31	31-ariquintile	31-♈⬠		1F6A7	singular active, direct, control	cos(31*2πi/137) + isin(31*2πi/137)	0.1485 +0.98891i
81.51	81:30'33	53	12	12-scorpiquintile	12-♏⬠		1F917	reasons one is desired	cos(12*2πi/53) + isin(12*2πi/53)	0.14765 +0.98904i
81.60	81:35'59	75	17	17-virgitrine	17-♍△		1F3E1	family home maintenance	cos(17*2πi/75) + isin(17*2πi/75)	0.14608 +0.98927i
81.65	81:38'58	97	22	22-cancriconjunct	22-♋☌		1F495	traits reserved for those very close	cos(22*2πi/97) + isin(22*2πi/97)	0.14523 +0.9894i
81.68	81:40'50	119	27	27-gemiundecile	27-♊U		1F4C9	weakened by opinionation, better as ambient	cos(27*2πi/119) + isin(27*2πi/119)	0.14469 +0.98948i
81.70	81:42'7	141	32	32-arinovile	32-♈N		1F489	easy instillment in others	cos(32*2πi/141) + isin(32*2πi/141)	0.14432 +0.98953i
81.82	81:49'5	22	5	5-aquaridecile	5-♒⊥		1F6E6	in command of one's field	cos(5*2πi/22) + isin(5*2πi/22)	0.14231 +0.98982i
81.98	81:58'48	101	23	23-cancriquintile	23-♋⬠		1F624	disregard for things heard	cos(23*2πi/101) + isin(23*2πi/101)	0.13952 +0.99022i
82.03	82:1'31	79	18	18-virgiseptile	18-♍七		270A	anti-establishment revolutionary	cos(18*2πi/79) + isin(18*2πi/79)	0.13874 +0.99033i
82.06	82:3'31	136	31	31-arisquare	31-♈□		1F9D0	serious, sober-minded interactant	cos(31*2πi/136) + isin(31*2πi/136)	0.13816 +0.99041i
82.11	82:6'18	57	13	13-scorpinovile	13-♏N		1FA84	arrives whenever one wants it, no asking	cos(13*2πi/57) + isin(13*2πi/57)	0.13735 +0.99052i
82.17	82:10'26	92	21	21-leaoctile	21-♌⊿		1F37B	regular comfort preferences w/ close one	cos(21*2πi/92) + isin(21*2πi/92)	0.13617 +0.99069i
82.20	82:12'17	127	29	29-tauriseptile	29-♉七		1F4B8	that which attracts unfair advantage	cos(29*2πi/127) + isin(29*2πi/127)	0.13563 +0.99076i
82.29	82:17'8	35	8	8-capriundecile	8-♑U		1F47D	quirky distinguishing uniqueness	cos(8*2πi/35) + isin(8*2πi/35)	0.13423 +0.99095i
82.37	82:22'22	118	27	27-gemidecile	27-♊⊥		1F3C3	staying with it as long as encouraged	cos(27*2πi/118) + isin(27*2πi/118)	0.13273 +0.99115i
82.44	82:26'33	131	30	30-tauriundecile	30-♉U		1F611	with doubt in associations	cos(30*2πi/131) + isin(30*2πi/131)	0.13152 +0.99131i
82.50	82:30'0	48	11	11-sajiinconjunct	11-♐π		1F305	shown through creative setting	cos(11*2πi/48) + isin(11*2πi/48)	0.13053 +0.99144i
82.57	82:34'7	109	25	25-gemiconjunct	25-♊☌		1F44E	diminishing others' importance	cos(25*2πi/109) + isin(25*2πi/109)	0.12934 +0.9916i
82.62	82:37'22	61	14	14-libriconjunct	14-♎☌		1F526	singled out for attention	cos(14*2πi/61) + isin(14*2πi/61)	0.1284 +0.99172i
82.67	82:40'0	135	31	31-aritrine	31-♈△		1F3C4	easy and prolific	cos(31*2πi/135) + isin(31*2πi/135)	0.12764 +0.99182i
82.70	82:42'9	74	17	17-virgiopposition	17-♍☍		1F626	social stressors	cos(17*2πi/74) + isin(17*2πi/74)	0.12702 +0.9919i
82.80	82:47'59	100	23	23-cancrisquare	23-♋□		1F6CB	home & family life	cos(23*2πi/100) + isin(23*2πi/100)	0.12533 +0.99211i
82.83	82:49'54	113	26	26-gemiquintile	26-♊⬠		1F60E	publicly-labeled vibe given	cos(26*2πi/113) + isin(26*2πi/113)	0.12478 +0.99218i
82.88	82:52'39	139	32	32-ariseptile	32-♈七		1F3AF	creative perfectionism	cos(32*2πi/139) + isin(32*2πi/139)	0.12399 +0.99228i

83.08	83:4'36	13	3	3-aquariconjunct	3-♒☌		1F3A5	public persona	cos(3*2πi/13) + isin(3*2πi/13)	0.12054 +0.99271i
83.28	83:17'0	134	31	31-arioppsition	31-♈☍		1F49F	a trait the partner MUST have	cos(31*2πi/134) + isin(31*2πi/134)	0.11696 +0.99314i
83.33	83:19'59	108	25	25-cancriinconjunct	25-♋π		1F31D	why close friends come around	cos(25*2πi/108) + isin(25*2πi/108)	0.11609 +0.99324i
83.37	83:22'6	95	22	22-leaundecile	22-♌U		265B	the image of a progress-inspiring master	cos(22*2πi/95) + isin(22*2πi/95)	0.11548 +0.99331i
83.41	83:24'52	82	19	19-virgidecile	19-♍⊥		1F987	eccentrically attention-getting, disquieting	cos(19*2πi/82) + isin(19*2πi/82)	0.11468 +0.9934i
83.48	83:28'41	69	16	16-librinovile	16-♎N		1F418	subtle, strong draw of trait via socialization	cos(16*2πi/69) + isin(16*2πi/69)	0.11358 +0.99353i
83.52	83:31'11	125	29	29-tauriquintile	29-♉⚺		1F39F	social clique's requirements	cos(29*2πi/125) + isin(29*2πi/125)	0.11286 +0.99361i
83.57	83:34'17	56	13	13-scorpioctile	13-♏⊿		1F608	for fun or one's own power	cos(13*2πi/56) + isin(13*2πi/56)	0.11196 +0.99371i
83.64	83:38'10	99	23	23-cancritrine	23-♋△		1F645	communication-stifling	cos(23*2πi/99) + isin(23*2πi/99)	0.11084 +0.99384i
83.66	83:39'43	142	33	33-aridecile	33-♈⊥		1F549	blessings others can only dream of	cos(33*2πi/142) + isin(33*2πi/142)	0.11039 +0.99389i
83.72	83:43'15	43	10	10-sajiseptile	10-♐七		1F0CF	through jokes, games, and fun	cos(10*2πi/43) + isin(10*2πi/43)	0.10937 +0.994i
83.79	83:47'35	116	27	27-gemioctile	27-♊⊿		1F612	having been slighted or doubted	cos(27*2πi/116) + isin(27*2πi/116)	0.10812 +0.99414i
83.84	83:50'8	73	17	17-virgiconjunct	17-♍☌		2692	new or deep investment in job	cos(17*2πi/73) + isin(17*2πi/73)	0.10738 +0.99422i
83.88	83:53'0	103	24	24-cancriseptile	24-♋七		1F60A	basking in joy	cos(24*2πi/103) + isin(24*2πi/103)	0.10655 +0.99431i
83.91	83:54'35	133	31	31-ariconjunct	31-♈☌		1F49D	during sex or when flirting	cos(31*2πi/133) + isin(31*2πi/133)	0.10609 +0.99436i
84.00	84:0'0	30	7	7-caprisextile	7-♑✶		1F487	response to one's body reception	cos(7*2πi/30) + isin(7*2πi/30)	0.10453 +0.99452i
84.09	84:5'15	137	32	32-ariquintile	32-♈⚺		1F6A7	singular active, direct, control	cos(32*2πi/137) + isin(32*2πi/137)	0.10301 +0.99468i
84.11	84:6'43	107	25	25-cancriundecile	25-♋U		1F481	essence of a great conversation w/ one	cos(25*2πi/107) + isin(25*2πi/107)	0.10258 +0.99472i
84.19	84:11'36	124	29	29-taurisquare	29-♉□		1F387	initial, then waning impression	cos(29*2πi/124) + isin(29*2πi/124)	0.10117 +0.99487i
84.26	84:15'19	47	11	11-sajiundecile	11-♐U		262B	a core, lived principle	cos(11*2πi/47) + isin(11*2πi/47)	0.1001 +0.99498i
84.32	84:19'27	111	26	26-gemitrine	26-♊△		1F973	around high-expression groups	cos(26*2πi/111) + isin(26*2πi/111)	0.0989 +0.9951i
84.38	84:22'30	64	15	15-librisquare	15-♎□		4F17	amidst a noisy setting	cos(15*2πi/64) + isin(15*2πi/64)	0.09802 +0.99518i
84.44	84:26'39	81	19	19-virginovile	19-♍N		1F451	mastered early, forms broad social identity	cos(19*2πi/81) + isin(19*2πi/81)	0.09681 +0.9953i
84.49	84:29'23	98	23	23-cancriopposition	23-♋☍		1F31F	social advancement catalyst	cos(23*2πi/98) + isin(23*2πi/98)	0.09602 +0.99538i
84.55	84:32'43	132	31	31-tauriinconjunct	31-♉π		1F517	sharing a special bond w/ a friend	cos(31*2πi/132) + isin(31*2πi/132)	0.09506 +0.99547i
84.71	84:42'21	17	4	4-aquariquintile	4-♒⚺		1F44A	managing by dominating	cos(4*2πi/17) + isin(4*2πi/17)	0.09227 +0.99573i
84.88	84:52'40	123	29	29-tauritrine	29-♉△		238F	others must express or draw out	cos(29*2πi/123) + isin(29*2πi/123)	0.08928 +0.99601i
84.94	84:56'37	89	21	21-leaquintile	21-♌⚺		1F48B	sensuality & body expression	cos(21*2πi/89) + isin(21*2πi/89)	0.08813 +0.99611i
85.00	85:0'0	72	17	17-libriinconjunct	17-♎π		2753	a problem to be solved	cos(17*2πi/72) + isin(17*2πi/72)	0.08716 +0.99619i

85.04	85:2'21	127	30	30-tauriseptile	30-♉七	1F4B8	that which attracts unfair advantage	cos(30*2π/127) + isin(30*2π/127)	0.08647 +0.99625i
85.09	85:5'27	55	13	13-scorpiseptile	13-♏七	1F632	shocking or flooding others w information	cos(13*2π/55) + isin(13*2π/55)	0.08558 +0.99633i
85.19	85:11'27	131	31	31-tauriundecile	31-♉U	1F611	with doubt in associations	cos(31*2π/131) + isin(31*2π/131)	0.08384 +0.99648i
85.26	85:15'47	38	9	9-sajiopposition	9-♐☍	1F64C	use of the body or physical deeds in work	cos(9*2π/38) + isin(9*2π/38)	0.08258 +0.99658i
85.33	85:19'59	135	32	32-aritrine	32-♈△	1F3C4	easy and prolific	cos(32*2π/135) + isin(32*2π/135)	0.08136 +0.99668i
85.36	85:21'38	97	23	23-cancriconjunct	23-♋☌	1F495	traits reserved for those very close	cos(23*2π/97) + isin(23*2π/97)	0.08088 +0.99672i
85.42	85:25'25	59	14	14-scorpiundecile	14-♏U	1F447	having one's pick	cos(14*2π/59) + isin(14*2π/59)	0.07979 +0.99681i
85.50	85:30'0	80	19	19-virgioctile	19-♍⊿	1F939	vividly remembered by one's children	cos(19*2π/80) + isin(19*2π/80)	0.07846 +0.99692i
85.54	85:32'40	101	24	24-cancriquintile	24-♋◇	1F624	disregard for things heard	cos(24*2π/101) + isin(24*2π/101)	0.07768 +0.99698i
85.59	85:35'39	143	34	34-ariundecile	34-♈U	1F4E3	broadcasting which gets one talked about	cos(34*2π/143) + isin(34*2π/143)	0.07682 +0.99705i
85.71	85:42'51	21	5	5-aquarinovile	5-♒N	1F483	at peak sexiness, strength, or creativity	cos(5*2π/21) + isin(5*2π/21)	0.07473 +0.9972i
85.85	85:50'46	130	31	31-tauridecile	31-♉⊥	1F3AA	relied upon by others in the talked topic	cos(31*2π/130) + isin(31*2π/130)	0.07243 +0.99737i
85.87	85:52'17	109	26	26-gemiconjunct	26-♊☌	1F44E	diminishing others' importance	cos(26*2π/109) + isin(26*2π/109)	0.07199 +0.99741i
85.91	85:54'32	88	21	21-leasquare	21-♌□	1F479	suppressing power imbalance	cos(21*2π/88) + isin(21*2π/88)	0.07134 +0.99745i
85.97	85:58'12	67	16	16-libriseptile	16-♎七	1F63B	getting others to fall in love w oneself	cos(16*2π/67) + isin(16*2π/67)	0.07028 +0.99753i
86.02	86:1'3	113	27	27-gemiquintile	27-♊◇	1F60E	publicly-labeled vibe given	cos(27*2π/113) + isin(27*2π/113)	0.06945 +0.99759i
86.09	86:5'13	46	11	11-sajidecile	11-♐⊥	1F4CE	trait housed by key colleagues	cos(11*2π/46) + isin(11*2π/46)	0.06824 +0.99767i
86.20	86:11'49	71	17	17-libriundecile	17-♎U	26C5	thriving amidst confusion	cos(17*2π/71) + isin(17*2π/71)	0.06632 +0.9978i
86.25	86:15'0	96	23	23-leainconjunct	23-♌π	1F937	what "not enough" looks like	cos(23*2π/96) + isin(23*2π/96)	0.0654 +0.99786i
86.28	86:16'51	121	29	29-tauriconjunct	29-♉☌	1F4B0	prosperity & status-seeking	cos(29*2π/121) + isin(29*2π/121)	0.06486 +0.99789i
86.40	86:24'0	25	6	6-capriconjunct	6-♑☌	1F3DF	rally & tune the mass psychology	cos(6*2π/25) + isin(6*2π/25)	0.06279 +0.99803i
86.54	86:32'18	104	25	25-cancrioctile	25-♋⊿	1F61B	trait known and accepted among friends	cos(25*2π/104) + isin(25*2π/104)	0.06038 +0.99818i
86.58	86:34'56	79	19	19-virgiseptile	19-♍七	270A	anti-establishment revolutionary	cos(19*2π/79) + isin(19*2π/79)	0.05962 +0.99822i
86.62	86:36'59	133	32	32-ariconjunct	32-♈☌	1F49D	during sex or when flirting	cos(32*2π/133) + isin(32*2π/133)	0.05902 +0.99826i
86.67	86:40'0	54	13	13-scorpisextile	13-♏✳	1F378	self-fulfillment tool	cos(13*2π/54) + isin(13*2π/54)	0.05814 +0.99831i
86.75	86:44'49	83	20	20-virgiundecile	20-♍U	26A1	high-tension activity in surroundings	cos(20*2π/83) + isin(20*2π/83)	0.05675 +0.99839i
86.79	86:47'8	112	27	27-gemisquare	27-♊□	1F38E	one's trait observed by outsiders	cos(27*2π/112) + isin(27*2π/112)	0.05607 +0.99843i
86.81	86:48'30	141	34	34-arinovile	34-♈N	1F489	easy instillment in others	cos(34*2π/141) + isin(34*2π/141)	0.05567 +0.99845i
86.90	86:53'47	29	7	7-capriquintile	7-♑◇	1F3A9	proud charisma	cos(7*2π/29) + isin(7*2π/29)	0.05414 +0.99853i

87.00	87:0'0	120	29	29-gemiinconjunct	29-♊⊼		1F922	more vulnerable to things	cos(29*2π/120) + isin(29*2π/120)	0.05234 +0.99863i
87.03	87:1'58	91	22	22-leaseptile	22-♌〵		1F576	smoothly comfortable	cos(22*2π/91) + isin(22*2π/91)	0.05176 +0.99866i
87.10	87:5'48	62	15	15-libriopposition	15-♎☍		1F3F4	manipulative ambition	cos(15*2π/62) + isin(15*2π/62)	0.05065 +0.99872i
87.19	87:11'15	128	31	31-taurioctile	31-♉◿		1F478	intuitive comfort even amidst stress	cos(31*2π/128) + isin(31*2π/128)	0.04907 +0.9988i
87.27	87:16'21	33	8	8-caprinovile	8-♑N		1F4FB	in a formal group discussion	cos(8*2π/33) + isin(8*2π/33)	0.04758 +0.99887i
87.38	87:22'43	103	25	25-cancriseptile	25-♋〵		1F60A	basking in joy	cos(25*2π/103) + isin(25*2π/103)	0.04574 +0.99895i
87.43	87:25'42	70	17	17-libridecile	17-♎⊥		1F527	used to strengthen or repair bonds	cos(17*2π/70) + isin(17*2π/70)	0.04486 +0.99899i
87.48	87:28'35	107	26	26-cancriundecile	26-♋U		1F481	essence of a great conversation w/ one	cos(26*2π/107) + isin(26*2π/107)	0.04403 +0.99903i
87.50	87:30'0	144	35	35-ariinconjunct	35-♈⊼		1F501	always-on trait	cos(35*2π/144) + isin(35*2π/144)	0.04362 +0.99905i
87.57	87:34'3	37	9	9-sajiconjunct	9-♐☌		2B50	trusted ability revealed	cos(9*2π/37) + isin(9*2π/37)	0.04244 +0.9991i
87.69	87:41'32	78	19	19-virgisextile	19-♍∗		1F94A	fight night moment	cos(19*2π/78) + isin(19*2π/78)	0.04027 +0.99919i
87.73	87:43'51	119	29	29-gemiundecile	29-♊U		1F4C9	weakened by opinionation, better as ambient	cos(29*2π/119) + isin(29*2π/119)	0.03959 +0.99922i
87.80	87:48'17	41	10	10-sajiquintile	10-♐⬠		1F5FD	personas aspired to	cos(10*2π/41) + isin(10*2π/41)	0.0383 +0.99927i
87.87	87:52'26	127	31	31-tauriseptile	31-♉〵		1F4B8	that which attracts unfair advantage	cos(31*2π/127) + isin(31*2π/127)	0.0371 +0.99931i
87.94	87:56'20	131	32	32-tauriundecile	32-♉U		1F611	with doubt in associations	cos(32*2π/131) + isin(32*2π/131)	0.03596 +0.99935i
88.00	88:0'0	45	11	11-sajinovile	11-♐N		2766	shared experience as a token of friendship	cos(11*2π/45) + isin(11*2π/45)	0.0349 +0.99939i
88.09	88:5'6	94	23	23-leadecile	23-♌⊥		1F463	helps in others after learning the hard way	cos(23*2π/94) + isin(23*2π/94)	0.03341 +0.99944i
88.11	88:6'42	143	35	35-ariundecile	35-♈U		1F4E3	broadcasting which gets one talked about	cos(35*2π/143) + isin(35*2π/143)	0.03295 +0.99946i
88.16	88:9'47	49	12	12-scorpiconjunct	12-♏☌		1F399	having known public influence	cos(12*2π/49) + isin(12*2π/49)	0.03205 +0.99949i
88.24	88:14'7	102	25	25-cancrisextile	25-♋∗		1F4BC	boss figure attributes	cos(25*2π/102) + isin(25*2π/102)	0.0308 +0.99953i
88.30	88:18'6	53	13	13-scorpiquintile	13-♏⬠		1F917	reasons one is desired	cos(13*2π/53) + isin(13*2π/53)	0.02963 +0.99956i
88.36	88:21'49	110	27	27-gemiopposition	27-♊☍		1F6A5	managing others' behavior	cos(27*2π/110) + isin(27*2π/110)	0.02856 +0.99959i
88.42	88:25'15	57	14	14-scorpinovile	14-♏N		1FA84	arrives whenever one wants it, no asking	cos(14*2π/57) + isin(14*2π/57)	0.02755 +0.99962i
88.47	88:28'28	118	29	29-gemidecile	29-♊⊥		1F3C3	staying with it as long as encouraged	cos(29*2π/118) + isin(29*2π/118)	0.02662 +0.99965i
88.52	88:31'28	61	15	15-libriconjunct	15-♎☌		1F526	singled out for attention	cos(15*2π/61) + isin(15*2π/61)	0.02575 +0.99967i
88.57	88:34'17	126	31	31-taurisextile	31-♉∗		1F47E	aggressive assertion of identity	cos(31*2π/126) + isin(31*2π/126)	0.02493 +0.99969i
88.62	88:36'55	65	16	16-libriquintile	16-♎⬠		1F6C0	self-resparking	cos(16*2π/65) + isin(16*2π/65)	0.02416 +0.99971i
88.70	88:41'44	69	17	17-librinovile	17-♎N		1F418	subtle, strong draw of trait via socialization	cos(17*2π/69) + isin(17*2π/69)	0.02276 +0.99974i
88.73	88:43'56	142	35	35-aridecile	35-♈⊥		1F549	blessings others can only dream of	cos(35*2π/142) + isin(35*2π/142)	0.02212 +0.99976i

88.77	88:46'1	73	18	18-virgiconjunct	18-♍☌		2692	new or deep investment in job	cos(18*2πi/73) + isin(18*2πi/73)	0.02152 +0.99977i
88.83	88:49'52	77	19	19-virgiquintile	19-♍⬠		1F422	guarded insistence	cos(19*2πi/77) + isin(19*2πi/77)	0.0204 +0.99979i
88.89	88:53'19	81	20	20-virginovile	20-♍N		1F451	mastered early, forms broad social identity	cos(20*2πi/81) + isin(20*2πi/81)	0.01939 +0.99981i
88.94	88:56'28	85	21	21-leaconjunct	21-♌☌		1F924	downplaying a real want	cos(21*2πi/85) + isin(21*2πi/85)	0.01848 +0.99983i
88.99	88:59'19	89	22	22-leaquintile	22-♌⬠		1F48B	sensuality & body expression	cos(22*2πi/89) + isin(22*2πi/89)	0.01765 +0.99984i
89.03	89:1'56	93	23	23-leanovile	23-♌N		1F60D	brought out by creative, sexualized energy	cos(23*2πi/93) + isin(23*2πi/93)	0.01689 +0.99986i
89.07	89:4'19	97	24	24-cancriconjunct	24-♋☌		1F495	traits reserved for those very close	cos(24*2πi/97) + isin(24*2πi/97)	0.01619 +0.99987i
89.14	89:8'34	105	26	26-cancrinovile	26-♋N		1F5EF	when irritated to see standards defied	cos(26*2πi/105) + isin(26*2πi/105)	0.01496 +0.99989i
89.17	89:10'27	109	27	27-gemiconjunct	27-♊☌		1F44E	diminishing others' importance	cos(27*2πi/109) + isin(27*2πi/109)	0.01441 +0.9999i
89.23	89:13'50	117	29	29-geminovile	29-♊N		1F48E	best friend's quality	cos(29*2πi/117) + isin(29*2πi/117)	0.01343 +0.99991i
89.28	89:16'48	125	31	31-tauriquintile	31-♉⬠		1F39F	social clique's requirements	cos(31*2πi/125) + isin(31*2πi/125)	0.01257 +0.99992i
89.34	89:20'35	137	34	34-ariquintile	34-♈⬠		1F6A7	singular active, direct, control	cos(34*2πi/137) + isin(34*2πi/137)	0.01147 +0.99993i
89.36	89:21'42	141	35	35-arinovile	35-♈N		1F489	easy instillment in others	cos(35*2πi/141) + isin(35*2πi/141)	0.01114 +0.99994i
90.00	90:0'0	4	1	square	☐		1F6AB	want	cos(1*2πi/4) + isin(1*2πi/4)	i
90.63	90:37'45	143	36	36-ariundecile	36-♈U		1F4E3	broadcasting which gets one talked about	cos(36*2πi/143) + isin(36*2πi/143)	-0.01098 +0.99994i
90.69	90:41'13	131	33	33-tauriundecile	33-♉U		1F611	with doubt in associations	cos(33*2πi/131) + isin(33*2πi/131)	-0.01199 +0.99993i
90.73	90:43'54	123	31	31-tauritrine	31-♉△		238F	others must express or draw out	cos(31*2πi/123) + isin(31*2πi/123)	-0.01277 +0.99992i
90.78	90:46'57	115	29	29-gemiseptile	29-♊七		1F933	inner world with self-talk	cos(29*2πi/115) + isin(29*2πi/115)	-0.01366 +0.99991i
90.84	90:50'28	107	27	27-cancriundecile	27-♋U		1F481	essence of a great conversation w/ one	cos(27*2πi/107) + isin(27*2πi/107)	-0.01468 +0.99989i
90.87	90:52'25	103	26	26-cancriseptile	26-♋七		1F60A	basking in joy	cos(26*2πi/103) + isin(26*2πi/103)	-0.01525 +0.99988i
90.95	90:56'50	95	24	24-leaundecile	24-♌U		265B	the image of a progress-inspiring master	cos(24*2πi/95) + isin(24*2πi/95)	-0.01653 +0.99986i
90.99	90:59'20	91	23	23-leaseptile	23-♌七		1F576	smoothly comfortable	cos(23*2πi/91) + isin(23*2πi/91)	-0.01726 +0.99985i
91.03	91:2'4	87	22	22-leatrine	22-♌△		2763	interactor inspired to want	cos(22*2πi/87) + isin(22*2πi/87)	-0.01805 +0.99984i
91.08	91:5'3	83	21	21-virgiundecile	21-♍U		26A1	high-tension activity in surroundings	cos(21*2πi/83) + isin(21*2πi/83)	-0.01892 +0.99982i
91.14	91:8'21	79	20	20-virgiseptile	20-♍七		270A	anti-establishment revolutionary	cos(20*2πi/79) + isin(20*2πi/79)	-0.01988 +0.9998i
91.20	91:12'0	75	19	19-virgitrine	19-♍△		1F3E1	family home maintenance	cos(19*2πi/75) + isin(19*2πi/75)	-0.02094 +0.99978i
91.27	91:16'3	71	18	18-libriundecile	18-♎U		26C5	thriving amidst confusion	cos(18*2πi/71) + isin(18*2πi/71)	-0.02212 +0.99976i
91.34	91:20'35	67	17	17-libriseptile	17-♎七		1F63B	getting others to fall in love w oneself	cos(17*2πi/67) + isin(17*2πi/67)	-0.02344 +0.99973i
91.38	91:23'4	130	33	33-tauridecile	33-♉⊥		1F3AA	relied upon by others in the talked topic	cos(33*2πi/130) + isin(33*2πi/130)	-0.02416 +0.99971i

91.43	91:25'42	63	16	16-libritrine	16-♎△		1F6A8	know-it-all	cos(16*2πi/63) + isin(16*2πi/63)	-0.02493 +0.99969i
91.48	91:28'31	122	31	31-tauriopposition	31-♉☍		1F913	easily annoying to others	cos(31*2πi/122) + isin(31*2πi/122)	-0.02575 +0.99967i
91.53	91:31'31	59	15	15-scorpiundecile	15-♏U		1F447	having one's pick	cos(15*2πi/59) + isin(15*2πi/59)	-0.02662 +0.99965i
91.58	91:34'44	114	29	29-gemisextile	29-♊⁎		1F6F1	other's influence attempts	cos(29*2πi/114) + isin(29*2πi/114)	-0.02755 +0.99962i
91.64	91:38'10	55	14	14-scorpiseptile	14-♏t		1F632	shocking or flooding others w information	cos(14*2πi/55) + isin(14*2πi/55)	-0.02856 +0.99959i
91.70	91:41'53	106	27	27-cancridecile	27-♋⊥		1F3A0	others think one has more power than one has	cos(27*2πi/106) + isin(27*2πi/106)	-0.02963 +0.99956i
91.76	91:45'52	51	13	13-scorpitrine	13-♏△		1F61A	use of persuasive words	cos(13*2πi/51) + isin(13*2πi/51)	-0.0308 +0.99953i
91.84	91:50'12	98	25	25-cancriopposition	25-♋☍		1F31F	social advancement catalyst	cos(25*2πi/98) + isin(25*2πi/98)	-0.03205 +0.99949i
91.91	91:54'53	47	12	12-sajiundecile	12-♐U		262B	a core, lived principle	cos(12*2πi/47) + isin(12*2πi/47)	-0.03341 +0.99944i
92.00	92:0'0	90	23	23-leasextile	23-♌⁎		1F6B8	absorptions by one's children	cos(23*2πi/90) + isin(23*2πi/90)	-0.0349 +0.99939i
92.03	92:1'48	133	34	34-ariconjunct	34-♈☌		1F49D	during sex or when flirting	cos(34*2πi/133) + isin(34*2πi/133)	-0.03542 +0.99937i
92.09	92:5'34	43	11	11-sajiseptile	11-♐t		1F0CF	through jokes, games, and fun	cos(11*2πi/43) + isin(11*2πi/43)	-0.03652 +0.99933i
92.20	92:11'42	82	21	21-virgidecile	21-♍⊥		1F987	eccentrically attention-getting, disquieting	cos(21*2πi/82) + isin(21*2πi/82)	-0.0383 +0.99927i
92.23	92:13'53	121	31	31-tauriconjunct	31-♉☌		1F4B0	prosperity & status-seeking	cos(31*2πi/121) + isin(31*2πi/121)	-0.03894 +0.99924i
92.31	92:18'27	39	10	10-sajitrine	10-♐△		1F3DD	convincing others of one's value	cos(10*2πi/39) + isin(10*2πi/39)	-0.04027 +0.99919i
92.39	92:23'21	113	29	29-gemiquintile	29-♊⬠		1F60E	publicly-labeled vibe given	cos(29*2πi/113) + isin(29*2πi/113)	-0.04169 +0.99913i
92.43	92:25'56	74	19	19-virgiopposition	19-♍☍		1F626	social stressors	cos(19*2πi/74) + isin(19*2πi/74)	-0.04244 +0.9991i
92.48	92:28'37	109	28	28-gemiconjunct	28-♊☌		1F44E	diminishing others' importance	cos(28*2πi/109) + isin(28*2πi/109)	-0.04322 +0.99907i
92.50	92:30'0	144	37	37-ariinconjunct	37-♈π		1F501	always-on trait	cos(37*2πi/144) + isin(37*2πi/144)	-0.04362 +0.99905i
92.57	92:34'17	35	9	9-capriundecile	9-♑U		1F47D	quirky distinguishing uniqueness	cos(9*2πi/35) + isin(9*2πi/35)	-0.04486 +0.99899i
92.65	92:38'49	136	35	35-arisquare	35-♈□		1F9D0	serious, sober-minded interactant	cos(35*2πi/136) + isin(35*2πi/136)	-0.04618 +0.99893i
92.67	92:40'23	101	26	26-cancriquintile	26-♋⬠		1F624	disregard for things heard	cos(26*2πi/101) + isin(26*2πi/101)	-0.04664 +0.99891i
92.73	92:43'38	66	17	17-librisextile	17-♎⁎		1F57A	broadcastable good spirits	cos(17*2πi/66) + isin(17*2πi/66)	-0.04758 +0.99887i
92.78	92:47'0	97	25	25-cancriconjunct	25-♋☌		1F495	traits reserved for those very close	cos(25*2πi/97) + isin(25*2πi/97)	-0.04856 +0.99882i
92.81	92:48'45	128	33	33-taurioctile	33-♉⦟		1F478	intuitive comfort even amidst stress	cos(33*2πi/128) + isin(33*2πi/128)	-0.04907 +0.9988i
92.90	92:54'11	31	8	8-capriseptile	8-♑t		1F3A2	expressed by one's social network	cos(8*2πi/31) + isin(8*2πi/31)	-0.05065 +0.99872i
93.00	93:0'0	120	31	31-gemiinconjunct	31-♊π		1F922	more vulnerable to things	cos(31*2πi/120) + isin(31*2πi/120)	-0.05234 +0.99863i
93.03	93:2'1	89	23	23-leaquintile	23-♌⬠		1F48B	sensuality & body expression	cos(23*2πi/89) + isin(23*2πi/89)	-0.05292 +0.9986i
93.15	93:8'48	143	37	37-ariundecile	37-♈U		1F4E3	broadcasting which gets one talked about	cos(37*2πi/143) + isin(37*2πi/143)	-0.0549 +0.99849i

93.18	93:10'35	85	22	22-leaconjunct	22-♌☌	1F924	downplaying a real want	$\cos(22*2\pi/85) + i\sin(22*2\pi/85)$	-0.05541 +0.99846i
93.24	93:14'14	139	36	36-ariseptile	36-♈七	1F3AF	creative perfectionism	$\cos(36*2\pi/139) + i\sin(36*2\pi/139)$	-0.05647 +0.9984i
93.33	93:19'59	27	7	7-capritrine	7-♑△	1F393	intellectualizing and insight	$\cos(7*2\pi/27) + i\sin(7*2\pi/27)$	-0.05814 +0.99831i
93.44	93:26'6	131	34	34-tauriundecile	34-♉U	1F611	with doubt in associations	$\cos(34*2\pi/131) + i\sin(34*2\pi/131)$	-0.05992 +0.9982i
93.46	93:27'41	104	27	27-cancrioctile	27-♋△	1F61B	trait known and accepted among friends	$\cos(27*2\pi/104) + i\sin(27*2\pi/104)$	-0.06038 +0.99818i
93.54	93:32'35	127	33	33-tauriseptile	33-♉七	1F4B8	that which attracts unfair advantage	$\cos(33*2\pi/127) + i\sin(33*2\pi/127)$	-0.0618 +0.99809i
93.60	93:35'59	50	13	13-scorpiopposition	13-♏☍	1F5BC	images put forth to others	$\cos(13*2\pi/50) + i\sin(13*2\pi/50)$	-0.06279 +0.99803i
93.70	93:41'55	73	19	19-virgiconjunct	19-♍☌	2692	new or deep investment in job	$\cos(19*2\pi/73) + i\sin(19*2\pi/73)$	-0.06451 +0.99792i
93.75	93:45'0	96	25	25-leainconjunct	25-♌π	1F937	what "not enough" looks like	$\cos(25*2\pi/96) + i\sin(25*2\pi/96)$	-0.0654 +0.99786i
93.78	93:46'53	119	31	31-gemiundecile	31-♊U	1F4C9	weakened by opinionation, better as ambient	$\cos(31*2\pi/119) + i\sin(31*2\pi/119)$	-0.06595 +0.99782i
93.80	93:48'10	142	37	37-aridecile	37-♈⊥	1F549	blessings others can only dream of	$\cos(37*2\pi/142) + i\sin(37*2\pi/142)$	-0.06632 +0.9978i
93.91	93:54'46	23	6	6-aquariundecile	6-♒U	1F991	unusual social trait, liked by eccentrics	$\cos(6*2\pi/23) + i\sin(6*2\pi/23)$	-0.06824 +0.99767i
94.03	94:1'47	134	35	35-ariopposition	35-♈☍	1F49F	a trait the partner MUST have	$\cos(35*2\pi/134) + i\sin(35*2\pi/134)$	-0.07028 +0.99753i
94.09	94:5'27	88	23	23-leasquare	23-♌□	1F479	suppressing power imbalance	$\cos(23*2\pi/88) + i\sin(23*2\pi/88)$	-0.07134 +0.99745i
94.15	94:9'13	65	17	17-libriquintile	17-♎⬠	1F6C0	self-resparking	$\cos(17*2\pi/65) + i\sin(17*2\pi/65)$	-0.07243 +0.99737i
94.21	94:12'20	107	28	28-cancriundecile	28-♋U	1F481	essence of a great conversation w/ one	$\cos(28*2\pi/107) + i\sin(28*2\pi/107)$	-0.07334 +0.99731i
94.29	94:17'8	42	11	11-sajisextile	11-♐✳	1F497	instilled in co-creative partners	$\cos(11*2\pi/42) + i\sin(11*2\pi/42)$	-0.07473 +0.9972i
94.37	94:22'8	103	27	27-cancriseptile	27-♋七	1F60A	basking in joy	$\cos(27*2\pi/103) + i\sin(27*2\pi/103)$	-0.07618 +0.99709i
94.43	94:25'34	61	16	16-libriconjunct	16-♎☌	1F526	singled out for attention	$\cos(16*2\pi/61) + i\sin(16*2\pi/61)$	-0.07718 +0.99702i
94.50	94:30'0	80	21	21-virgioctile	21-♍⚹	1F939	vividly remembered by one's children	$\cos(21*2\pi/80) + i\sin(21*2\pi/80)$	-0.07846 +0.99692i
94.55	94:32'43	99	26	26-cancritrine	26-♋△	1F645	communication-stifling	$\cos(26*2\pi/99) + i\sin(26*2\pi/99)$	-0.07925 +0.99685i
94.58	94:34'34	118	31	31-gemidecile	31-♊⊥	1F3C3	staying with it as long as encouraged	$\cos(31*2\pi/118) + i\sin(31*2\pi/118)$	-0.07979 +0.99681i
94.60	94:35'54	137	36	36-ariquintile	36-♈⬠	1F6A7	singular active, direct, control	$\cos(36*2\pi/137) + i\sin(36*2\pi/137)$	-0.08017 +0.99678i
94.74	94:44'12	19	5	5-aquariseptile	5-♒七	1F510	gateway to one's friendship	$\cos(5*2\pi/19) + i\sin(5*2\pi/19)$	-0.08258 +0.99658i
94.88	94:53'1	129	34	34-taurinovile	34-♉N	1F647	in the service of one attached to	$\cos(34*2\pi/129) + i\sin(34*2\pi/129)$	-0.08513 +0.99637i
94.95	94:56'42	91	24	24-leaseptile	24-♌七	1F576	smoothly comfortable	$\cos(24*2\pi/91) + i\sin(24*2\pi/91)$	-0.0862 +0.99628i
95.00	95:0'0	72	19	19-libriinconjunct	19-♎π	2753	a problem to be solved	$\cos(19*2\pi/72) + i\sin(19*2\pi/72)$	-0.08716 +0.99619i
95.04	95:2'24	125	33	33-tauriquintile	33-♉⬠	1F39F	social clique's requirements	$\cos(33*2\pi/125) + i\sin(33*2\pi/125)$	-0.08785 +0.99613i
95.09	95:5'39	53	14	14-scorpiquintile	14-♏⬠	1F917	reasons one is desired	$\cos(14*2\pi/53) + i\sin(14*2\pi/53)$	-0.0888 +0.99605i

95.14	95:8'34	140	37	37-arioctile	37-♈⊿	🍀	1F340	helped by a benefactor	cos(37*2πi/140) + isin(37*2πi/140)	-0.08964 +0.99597i
95.17	95:10'20	87	23	23-leatrine	23-♌△	❣	2763	interactor inspired to want	cos(23*2πi/87) + isin(23*2πi/87)	-0.09015 +0.99593i
95.21	95:12'23	121	32	32-tauriconjunct	32-♉☌	💰	1F4B0	prosperity & status-seeking	cos(32*2πi/121) + isin(32*2πi/121)	-0.09075 +0.99587i
95.29	95:17'38	34	9	9-capridecile	9-♑⊥	🏆	1F3C6	potential to be a master or boss	cos(9*2πi/34) + isin(9*2πi/34)	-0.09227 +0.99573i
95.38	95:23'4	117	31	31-geminovile	31-♊N	💎	1F48E	best friend's quality	cos(31*2πi/117) + isin(31*2πi/117)	-0.09384 +0.99559i
95.42	95:25'18	83	22	22-virgiundecile	22-♍U	⚡	26A1	high-tension activity in surroundings	cos(22*2πi/83) + isin(22*2πi/83)	-0.09449 +0.99553i
95.45	95:27'16	132	35	35-tauriinconjunct	35-♉π	🔗	1F517	sharing a special bond w/ a friend	cos(35*2πi/132) + isin(35*2πi/132)	-0.09506 +0.99547i
95.51	95:30'36	49	13	13-scorpiconjunct	13-♏☌	🎙	1F399	having known public influence	cos(13*2πi/49) + isin(13*2πi/49)	-0.09602 +0.99538i
95.58	95:34'30	113	30	30-gemiquintile	30-♊⬠	😎	1F60E	publicly-labeled vibe given	cos(30*2πi/113) + isin(30*2πi/113)	-0.09715 +0.99527i
95.63	95:37'30	64	17	17-librisquare	17-♎□	众	4F17	amidst a noisy setting	cos(17*2πi/64) + isin(17*2πi/64)	-0.09802 +0.99518i
95.70	95:41'46	79	21	21-virgiseptile	21-♍七	✊	270A	anti-establishment revolutionary	cos(21*2πi/79) + isin(21*2πi/79)	-0.09925 +0.99506i
95.74	95:44'40	94	25	25-leadecile	25-♌⊥	👣	1F463	helps in others after learning the hard way	cos(25*2πi/94) + isin(25*2πi/94)	-0.1001 +0.99498i
95.78	95:46'47	109	29	29-gemiconjunct	29-♊☌	👎	1F44E	diminishing others' importance	cos(29*2πi/109) + isin(29*2πi/109)	-0.10071 +0.99492i
95.83	95:49'38	139	37	37-ariseptile	37-♈七	🎯	1F3AF	creative perfectionism	cos(37*2πi/139) + isin(37*2πi/139)	-0.10153 +0.99483i
96.00	96:0'0	15	4	4-aquaritrine	4-♒△	🐋	1F40B	room domination	cos(4*2πi/15) + isin(4*2πi/15)	-0.10453 +0.99452i
96.18	96:10'59	131	35	35-tauriundecile	35-♉U	😑	1F611	with doubt in associations	cos(35*2πi/131) + isin(35*2πi/131)	-0.10771 +0.99418i
96.24	96:14'15	101	27	27-cancriquintile	27-♋⬠	😤	1F624	disregard for things heard	cos(27*2πi/101) + isin(27*2πi/101)	-0.10865 +0.99408i
96.28	96:16'44	86	23	23-leaopposition	23-♌☍	🤡	1F921	one's commentary offends egos	cos(23*2πi/86) + isin(23*2πi/86)	-0.10937 +0.994i
96.34	96:20'16	71	19	19-libriundecile	19-♎U	🌥	26C5	thriving amidst confusion	cos(19*2πi/71) + isin(19*2πi/71)	-0.11039 +0.99389i
96.38	96:22'40	127	34	34-tauriseptile	34-♉七	🏴‍☠️	1F4B8	that which attracts unfair advantage	cos(34*2πi/127) + isin(34*2πi/127)	-0.11109 +0.99381i
96.43	96:25'42	56	15	15-scorpioctile	15-♏⊿	😈	1F608	for fun or one's own power	cos(15*2πi/56) + isin(15*2πi/56)	-0.11196 +0.99371i
96.49	96:29'41	97	26	26-cancriconjunct	26-♋☌	💕	1F495	traits reserved for those very close	cos(26*2πi/97) + isin(26*2πi/97)	-0.11311 +0.99358i
96.52	96:31'18	138	37	37-arisextile	37-♈✶	⛑	26D1	daily work focus	cos(37*2πi/138) + isin(37*2πi/138)	-0.11358 +0.99353i
96.59	96:35'7	41	11	11-sajiquintile	11-♐⬠	🗽	1F5FD	personas aspired to	cos(11*2πi/41) + isin(11*2πi/41)	-0.11468 +0.9934i
96.67	96:40'0	108	29	29-cancriinconjunct	29-♋π	😝	1F31D	why close friends come around	cos(29*2πi/108) + isin(29*2πi/108)	-0.11609 +0.99324i
96.72	96:42'59	67	18	18-libriseptile	18-♎七	😻	1F63B	getting others to fall in love w oneself	cos(18*2πi/67) + isin(18*2πi/67)	-0.11696 +0.99314i
96.77	96:46'27	93	25	25-leanovile	25-♌N	😍	1F60D	brought out by creative, sexualized energy	cos(25*2πi/93) + isin(25*2πi/93)	-0.11796 +0.99302i
96.81	96:48'24	119	32	32-gemiundecile	32-♊U	📉	1F4C9	weakened by opinionation, better as ambient	cos(32*2πi/119) + isin(32*2πi/119)	-0.11852 +0.99295i
96.92	96:55'23	26	7	7-capriopposition	7-♑☍	🎸	1F3B8	why one's fans follow them	cos(7*2πi/26) + isin(7*2πi/26)	-0.12054 +0.99271i

97.04	97:2'36	115	31	31-gemiseptile	31-♊七		1F933	inner world with self-talk	$\cos(31*2\pi/115) + i\sin(31*2\pi/115)$	-0.12262 +0.99245i
97.08	97:4'43	89	24	24-leaquintile	24-♌⚷		1F48B	sensuality & body expression	$\cos(24*2\pi/89) + i\sin(24*2\pi/89)$	-0.12323 +0.99238i
97.14	97:8'34	63	17	17-libritrine	17-♎△		1F6A8	know-it-all	$\cos(17*2\pi/63) + i\sin(17*2\pi/63)$	-0.12434 +0.99224i
97.20	97:12'0	100	27	27-cancrisquare	27-♋□		1F6CB	home & family life	$\cos(27*2\pi/100) + i\sin(27*2\pi/100)$	-0.12533 +0.99211i
97.23	97:13'34	137	37	37-ariquintile	37-♈⚷		1F6A7	singular active, direct, control	$\cos(37*2\pi/137) + i\sin(37*2\pi/137)$	-0.12579 +0.99206i
97.30	97:17'50	37	10	10-sajiconjunct	10-♐☌	☆	2B50	trusted ability revealed	$\cos(10*2\pi/37) + i\sin(10*2\pi/37)$	-0.12702 +0.9919i
97.38	97:22'37	122	33	33-tauriopposition	33-♉☍		1F913	easily annoying to others	$\cos(33*2\pi/122) + i\sin(33*2\pi/122)$	-0.1284 +0.99172i
97.44	97:26'36	133	36	36-ariconjunct	36-♈☌		1F49D	during sex or when flirting	$\cos(36*2\pi/133) + i\sin(36*2\pi/133)$	-0.12955 +0.99157i
97.50	97:30'0	48	13	13-sajiinconjunct	13-♐⚲		1F305	shown through creative setting	$\cos(13*2\pi/48) + i\sin(13*2\pi/48)$	-0.13053 +0.99144i
97.57	97:34'12	107	29	29-cancriundecile	29-♋U		1F481	essence of a great conversation w/ one	$\cos(29*2\pi/107) + i\sin(29*2\pi/107)$	-0.13174 +0.99128i
97.63	97:37'37	59	16	16-scorpiundecile	16-♏U		1F447	having one's pick	$\cos(16*2\pi/59) + i\sin(16*2\pi/59)$	-0.13273 +0.99115i
97.67	97:40'27	129	35	35-taurinovile	35-♉N		1F647	in the service of one attached to	$\cos(35*2\pi/129) + i\sin(35*2\pi/129)$	-0.13354 +0.99104i
97.71	97:42'51	70	19	19-libridecile	19-♎⊥		1F527	used to strengthen or repair bonds	$\cos(19*2\pi/70) + i\sin(19*2\pi/70)$	-0.13423 +0.99095i
97.78	97:46'39	81	22	22-virginovile	22-♍N		1F451	mastered early, forms broad social identity	$\cos(22*2\pi/81) + i\sin(22*2\pi/81)$	-0.13533 +0.9908i
97.83	97:49'33	92	25	25-leaoctile	25-♌⊿		1F37B	regular comfort preferences w/ close one	$\cos(25*2\pi/92) + i\sin(25*2\pi/92)$	-0.13617 +0.99069i
97.89	97:53'41	114	31	31-gemisextile	31-♊✱		1F6F1	other's influence attempts	$\cos(31*2\pi/114) + i\sin(31*2\pi/114)$	-0.13735 +0.99052i
97.94	97:56'28	136	37	37-arisquare	37-♈□		1F9D0	serious, sober-minded interactant	$\cos(37*2\pi/136) + i\sin(37*2\pi/136)$	-0.13816 +0.99041i
98.18	98:10'54	11	3	undecile	U₃		1F5EB	getting talked about	$\cos(1*2\pi/11) + i\sin(1*2\pi/11)$	-0.14231 +0.98982i
98.44	98:26'15	128	35	35-taurioctile	35-♉⊿		1F478	intuitive comfort even amidst stress	$\cos(35*2\pi/128) + i\sin(35*2\pi/128)$	-0.14673 +0.98918i
98.49	98:29'26	106	29	29-cancridecile	29-♋⊥		1F3A0	others think one has more power than one has	$\cos(29*2\pi/106) + i\sin(29*2\pi/106)$	-0.14765 +0.98904i
98.53	98:31'34	95	26	26-leaundecile	26-♌U		265B	the image of a progress-inspiring master	$\cos(26*2\pi/95) + i\sin(26*2\pi/95)$	-0.14826 +0.98895i
98.57	98:34'17	84	23	23-virgiinconjunct	23-♍⚲		1F411	traits for the seemingly weak	$\cos(23*2\pi/84) + i\sin(23*2\pi/84)$	-0.14904 +0.98883i
98.63	98:37'48	73	20	20-virgiconjunct	20-♍☌		2692	new or deep investment in job	$\cos(20*2\pi/73) + i\sin(20*2\pi/73)$	-0.15006 +0.98868i
98.67	98:40'0	135	37	37-aritrine	37-♈△		1F3C4	easy and prolific	$\cos(37*2\pi/135) + i\sin(37*2\pi/135)$	-0.15069 +0.98858i
98.71	98:42'34	62	17	17-libriopposition	17-♎☍		1F3F4	manipulative ambition	$\cos(17*2\pi/62) + i\sin(17*2\pi/62)$	-0.15143 +0.98847i
98.76	98:45'39	113	31	31-gemiquintile	31-♊⚷		1F60E	publicly-labeled vibe given	$\cos(31*2\pi/113) + i\sin(31*2\pi/113)$	-0.15231 +0.98833i
98.82	98:49'24	51	14	14-scorpitrine	14-♏△		1F61A	use of persuasive words	$\cos(14*2\pi/51) + i\sin(14*2\pi/51)$	-0.15339 +0.98817i
98.87	98:52'23	142	39	39-aridecile	39-♈⊥		1F549	blessings others can only dream of	$\cos(39*2\pi/142) + i\sin(39*2\pi/142)$	-0.15425 +0.98803i
98.93	98:55'52	131	36	36-tauriundecile	36-♉U		1F611	with doubt in associations	$\cos(36*2\pi/131) + i\sin(36*2\pi/131)$	-0.15525 +0.98788i

99.00	99:0'0	40	11	11-sajisquare	11-♐□	1F66A	future missable partnership duty	cos(11*2πi/40) + isin(11*2πi/40)	-0.15643 +0.98769i
99.08	99:4'57	109	30	30-gemiconjunct	30-♊♂	1F44E	diminishing others' importance	cos(30*2πi/109) + isin(30*2πi/109)	-0.15786 +0.98746i
99.13	99:7'49	69	19	19-librinovile	19-♎N	1F418	subtle, strong draw of trait via socialization	cos(19*2πi/69) + isin(19*2πi/69)	-0.15868 +0.98733i
99.18	99:11'1	98	27	27-cancriopposition	27-♋☍	1F31F	social advancement catalyst	cos(27*2πi/98) + isin(27*2πi/98)	-0.1596 +0.98718i
99.21	99:12'45	127	35	35-tauriseptile	35-♉七	1F4B8	that which attracts unfair advantage	cos(35*2πi/127) + isin(35*2πi/127)	-0.1601 +0.9871i
99.31	99:18'37	29	8	8-capriquintile	8-♑⚹	1F3A9	proud charisma	cos(8*2πi/29) + isin(8*2πi/29)	-0.16178 +0.98683i
99.43	99:25'42	105	29	29-cancrinovile	29-♋N	1F5EF	when irritated to see standards defied	cos(29*2πi/105) + isin(29*2πi/105)	-0.16382 +0.98649i
99.47	99:28'25	76	21	21-virgisquare	21-♍□	1F3D8	seen by friends' friends & family	cos(21*2πi/76) + isin(21*2πi/76)	-0.16459 +0.98636i
99.51	99:30'43	123	34	34-tauritrine	34-♉△	238F	others must express or draw out	cos(34*2πi/123) + isin(34*2πi/123)	-0.16526 +0.98625i
99.57	99:34'28	47	13	13-sajiundecile	13-♐U	262B	a core, lived principle	cos(13*2πi/47) + isin(13*2πi/47)	-0.16633 +0.98607i
99.64	99:38'34	112	31	31-gemisquare	31-♊□	1F38E	one's trait observed by outsiders	cos(31*2πi/112) + isin(31*2πi/112)	-0.16751 +0.98587i
99.69	99:41'32	65	18	18-libriquintile	18-♎⚹	1F6C0	self-resparking	cos(18*2πi/65) + isin(18*2πi/65)	-0.16836 +0.98573i
99.76	99:45'32	83	23	23-virgiundecile	23-♍U	26A1	high-tension activity in surroundings	cos(23*2πi/83) + isin(23*2πi/83)	-0.1695 +0.98553i
99.83	99:49'54	119	33	33-gemiundecile	33-♊U	1F4C9	weakened by opinionation, better as ambient	cos(33*2πi/119) + isin(33*2πi/119)	-0.17076 +0.98531i
99.85	99:51'14	137	38	38-ariquintile	38-♈⚹	1F6A7	singular active, direct, control	cos(38*2πi/137) + isin(38*2πi/137)	-0.17114 +0.98525i
100.00	100:0'0	18	5	5-aquarisextile (sentagon)	5-♒✳(X)	1F5C4	long term rational interactions	cos(5*2πi/18) + isin(5*2πi/18)	-0.17365 +0.98481i
100.17	100:10'26	115	32	32-gemiseptile	32-♊七	1F933	inner world with self-talk	cos(32*2πi/115) + isin(32*2πi/115)	-0.17664 +0.98428i
100.21	100:12'22	97	27	27-cancriconjunct	27-♋♂	1F495	traits reserved for those very close	cos(27*2πi/97) + isin(27*2πi/97)	-0.17719 +0.98418i
100.29	100:17'8	140	39	39-arioctile	39-♈⚼	1F340	helped by a benefactor	cos(39*2πi/140) + isin(39*2πi/140)	-0.17856 +0.98393i
100.33	100:19'40	61	17	17-libriconjunct	17-♎♂	1F526	singled out for attention	cos(17*2πi/61) + isin(17*2πi/61)	-0.17928 +0.9838i
100.38	100:23'4	104	29	29-cancrioctile	29-♋⚼	1F61B	trait known and accepted among friends	cos(29*2πi/104) + isin(29*2πi/104)	-0.18026 +0.98362i
100.47	100:27'54	43	12	12-sajiseptile	12-♐七	1F0CF	through jokes, games, and fun	cos(12*2πi/43) + isin(12*2πi/43)	-0.18164 +0.98337i
100.54	100:32'25	111	31	31-gemitrine	31-♊△	1F973	around high-expression groups	cos(31*2πi/111) + isin(31*2πi/111)	-0.18293 +0.98313i
100.59	100:35'17	68	19	19-librioctile	19-♎⚼	1F462	appearance of dominating	cos(19*2πi/68) + isin(19*2πi/68)	-0.18375 +0.98297i
100.65	100:38'42	93	26	26-leanovile	26-♌N	1F60D	brought out by creative, sexualized energy	cos(26*2πi/93) + isin(26*2πi/93)	-0.18473 +0.98279i
100.68	100:40'40	118	33	33-gemidecile	33-♊⊥	1F3C3	staying with it as long as encouraged	cos(33*2πi/118) + isin(33*2πi/118)	-0.18529 +0.98268i
100.70	100:41'57	143	40	40-ariundecile	40-♈U	1F4E3	broadcasting which gets one talked about	cos(40*2πi/143) + isin(40*2πi/143)	-0.18565 +0.98262i
100.80	100:47'59	25	7	7-capriconjunct	7-♑♂	1F3DF	rally & tune the mass psychology	cos(7*2πi/25) + isin(7*2πi/25)	-0.18738 +0.98229i
100.93	100:56'4	107	30	30-cancriundecile	30-♋U	1F481	essence of a great conversation w/ one	cos(30*2πi/107) + isin(30*2πi/107)	-0.18969 +0.98184i

100.98	100:58'32	82	23	23-virgidecile	23-♍⊥		1F987	eccentrically attention-getting, disquieting	cos(23*2πi/82) + isin(23*2πi/82)	-0.19039 +0.98171i
101.01	101:0'25	139	39	39-ariseptile	39-♈七		1F3AF	creative perfectionism	cos(39*2πi/139) + isin(39*2πi/139)	-0.19093 +0.9816i
101.05	101:3'9	57	16	16-scorpinovile	16-♏N		1FA84	arrives whenever one wants it, no asking	cos(16*2πi/57) + isin(16*2πi/57)	-0.19171 +0.98145i
101.12	101:7'24	89	25	25-leaquintile	25-♌⚹		1F48B	sensuality & body expression	cos(25*2πi/89) + isin(25*2πi/89)	-0.19293 +0.98121i
101.16	101:9'25	121	34	34-tauriconjunct	34-♉☌		1F4B0	prosperity & status-seeking	cos(34*2πi/121) + isin(34*2πi/121)	-0.1935 +0.9811i
101.25	101:15'0	32	9	9-caprioctile	9-♑△		1F5FB	an indomitable characteristic	cos(9*2πi/32) + isin(9*2πi/32)	-0.19509 +0.98079i
101.33	101:19'59	135	38	38-aritrine	38-♈△		1F3C4	easy and prolific	cos(38*2πi/135) + isin(38*2πi/135)	-0.19652 +0.9805i
101.36	101:21'33	103	29	29-cancriseptile	29-♋七		1F60A	basking in joy	cos(29*2πi/103) + isin(29*2πi/103)	-0.19696 +0.98041i
101.41	101:24'30	71	20	20-libriundecile	20-♎U		26C5	thriving amidst confusion	cos(20*2πi/71) + isin(20*2πi/71)	-0.1978 +0.98024i
101.45	101:27'16	110	31	31-gemiopposition	31-♊☍		1F6A5	managing others' behavior	cos(31*2πi/110) + isin(31*2πi/110)	-0.19859 +0.98008i
101.54	101:32'18	39	11	11-sajitrine	11-♐△		1F3DD	convincing others of one's value	cos(11*2πi/39) + isin(11*2πi/39)	-0.20003 +0.97979i
101.65	101:38'49	85	24	24-leaconjunct	24-♌☌		1F924	downplaying a real want	cos(24*2πi/85) + isin(24*2πi/85)	-0.20188 +0.97941i
101.68	101:40'45	131	37	37-tauriundecile	37-♉U		1F611	with doubt in associations	cos(37*2πi/131) + isin(37*2πi/131)	-0.20244 +0.9793i
101.74	101:44'20	46	13	13-sajidecile	13-♐⊥		1F4CE	trait housed by key colleagues	cos(13*2πi/46) + isin(13*2πi/46)	-0.20346 +0.97908i
101.82	101:49'5	99	28	28-cancritrine	28-♋△		1F645	communication-stifling	cos(28*2πi/99) + isin(28*2πi/99)	-0.20481 +0.9788i
101.89	101:53'12	53	15	15-scorpiquintile	15-♏⚹		1F917	reasons one is desired	cos(15*2πi/53) + isin(15*2πi/53)	-0.20598 +0.97856i
101.95	101:56'48	113	32	32-gemiquintile	32-♊⚹		1F60E	publicly-labeled vibe given	cos(32*2πi/113) + isin(32*2πi/113)	-0.20701 +0.97834i
102.00	102:0'0	60	17	17-scorpiinconjunct	17-♏♐		1F4CD	strongest memory left behind	cos(17*2πi/60) + isin(17*2πi/60)	-0.20791 +0.97815i
102.05	102:2'50	127	36	36-tauriseptile	36-♉七		1F4B8	that which attracts unfair advantage	cos(36*2πi/127) + isin(36*2πi/127)	-0.20872 +0.97798i
102.09	102:5'22	67	19	19-libriseptile	19-♎七		1F63B	getting others to fall in love w oneself	cos(19*2πi/67) + isin(19*2πi/67)	-0.20944 +0.97782i
102.13	102:7'39	141	40	40-arinovile	40-♈N		1F489	easy instillment in others	cos(40*2πi/141) + isin(40*2πi/141)	-0.21009 +0.97768i
102.16	102:9'43	74	21	21-virgiopposition	21-♍☍		1F626	social stressors	cos(21*2πi/74) + isin(21*2πi/74)	-0.21068 +0.97756i
102.22	102:13'20	81	23	23-virginovile	23-♍N		1F451	mastered early, forms broad social identity	cos(23*2πi/81) + isin(23*2πi/81)	-0.2117 +0.97733i
102.27	102:16'21	88	25	25-leasquare	25-♌□		1F479	suppressing power imbalance	cos(25*2πi/88) + isin(25*2πi/88)	-0.21257 +0.97715i
102.32	102:18'56	95	27	27-leaundecile	27-♌U		265B	the image of a progress-inspiring master	cos(27*2πi/95) + isin(27*2πi/95)	-0.2133 +0.97699i
102.39	102:23'7	109	31	31-gemiconjunct	31-♊☌		1F44E	diminishing others' importance	cos(31*2πi/109) + isin(31*2πi/109)	-0.21449 +0.97673i
102.44	102:26'20	123	35	35-tauritrine	35-♉△		238F	others must express or draw out	cos(35*2πi/123) + isin(35*2πi/123)	-0.2154 +0.97653i
102.48	102:28'54	137	39	39-ariquintile	39-♈⚹		1F6A7	singular active, direct, control	cos(39*2πi/137) + isin(39*2πi/137)	-0.21613 +0.97636i
102.50	102:30'0	144	41	41-ariinconjunct	41-♈♐		1F501	always-on trait	cos(41*2πi/144) + isin(41*2πi/144)	-0.21644 +0.9763i

102.86	102:51'25	7	2	septile	ち₂	🗣	1F5E3	basic communication pattern	cos(1*2π/7) + isin(1*2π/7)	-0.22252 +0.97493i
103.24	103:14'7	136	39	39-arisquare	39-♈□	🤐	1F9D0	serious, sober-minded interactant	cos(39*2π/136) + isin(39*2π/136)	-0.22895 +0.97344i
103.28	103:16'43	122	35	35-tauriopposition	35-♉☍	🤓	1F913	easily annoying to others	cos(35*2π/122) + isin(35*2π/122)	-0.22969 +0.97326i
103.33	103:19'59	108	31	31-cancriinconjunct	31-♋π	😝	1F31D	why close friends come around	cos(31*2π/108) + isin(31*2π/108)	-0.23062 +0.97304i
103.37	103:21'58	101	29	29-cancriquintile	29-♋⬠	😤	1F624	disregard for things heard	cos(29*2π/101) + isin(29*2π/101)	-0.23118 +0.97291i
103.45	103:26'53	87	25	25-leatrine	25-♌△	❣	2763	interactor inspired to want	cos(25*2π/87) + isin(25*2π/87)	-0.23257 +0.97258i
103.50	103:30'0	80	23	23-virgioctile	23-♍⟋	🤹	1F939	vividly remembered by one's children	cos(23*2π/80) + isin(23*2π/80)	-0.23345 +0.97237i
103.60	103:35'49	139	40	40-ariseptile	40-♈ち	🎯	1F3AF	creative perfectionism	cos(40*2π/139) + Isin(40*2π/139)	-0.23509 +0.97197i
103.64	103:38'10	66	19	19-librisextile	19-♎✳	🕺	1F57A	broadcastable good spirits	cos(19*2π/66) + isin(19*2π/66)	-0.23576 +0.97181i
103.68	103:40'48	125	36	36-tauriquintile	36-♉⬠	🎟	1F39F	social clique's requirements	cos(36*2π/125) + isin(36*2π/125)	-0.2365 +0.97163i
103.73	103:43'43	59	17	17-scorpiundecile	17-♏∪	👇	1F447	having one's pick	cos(17*2π/59) + isin(17*2π/59)	-0.23733 +0.97143i
103.78	103:47'1	111	32	32-gemitrine	32-♊△	🥳	1F973	around high-expression groups	cos(32*2π/111) + isin(32*2π/111)	-0.23826 +0.9712i
103.85	103:50'46	52	15	15-scorpisquare	15-♏□	😞	1F61E	falling short	cos(15*2π/52) + isin(15*2π/52)	-0.23932 +0.97094i
103.94	103:56'37	142	41	41-aridecile	41-♈⊥	🕉	1F549	blessings others can only dream of	cos(41*2π/142) + isin(41*2π/142)	-0.24097 +0.97053i
104.00	104:0'0	45	13	13-sajinovile	13-♐N	👅	2766	shared experience as a token of friendship	cos(13*2π/45) + isin(13*2π/45)	-0.24192 +0.9703i
104.10	104:5'46	83	24	24-virgiundecile	24-♍∪	⚡	26A1	high-tension activity in surroundings	cos(24*2π/83) + isin(24*2π/83)	-0.24355 +0.96989i
104.13	104:7'56	121	35	35-tauriconjunct	35-♉☌	💰	1F4B0	prosperity & status-seeking	cos(35*2π/121) + isin(35*2π/121)	-0.24416 +0.96973i
104.21	104:12'37	38	11	11-sajiopposition	11-♐☍	🙌	1F64C	use of the body or physical deeds in work	cos(11*2π/38) + isin(11*2π/38)	-0.24549 +0.9694i
104.30	104:17'56	107	31	31-cancriundecile	31-♋∪	🛁	1F481	essence of a great conversation w/ one	cos(31*2π/107) + isin(31*2π/107)	-0.24698 +0.96902i
104.35	104:20'52	69	20	20-librinovile	20-♎N	🐘	1F418	subtle, strong draw of trait via socialization	cos(20*2π/69) + isin(20*2π/69)	-0.24781 +0.96881i
104.40	104:24'0	100	29	29-cancrisquare	29-♋□	🛋	1F6CB	home & family life	cos(29*2π/100) + isin(29*2π/100)	-0.24869 +0.96858i
104.43	104:25'38	131	38	38-tauriundecile	38-♉∪	😑	1F611	with doubt in associations	cos(38*2π/131) + isin(38*2π/131)	-0.24915 +0.96846i
104.52	104:30'58	31	9	9-caprisseptile	9-♑ち	🎢	1F3A2	expressed by one's social network	cos(9*2π/31) + isin(9*2π/31)	-0.25065 +0.96808i
104.62	104:36'55	117	34	34-geminovile	34-♊N	💎	1F48E	best friend's quality	cos(34*2π/117) + isin(34*2π/117)	-0.25233 +0.96764i
104.68	104:40'51	141	41	41-arinovile	41-♈N	💉	1F489	easy instillment in others	cos(41*2π/141) + isin(41*2π/141)	-0.25343 +0.96735i
104.73	104:43'38	55	16	16-scorpiseptile	16-♏ち	😲	1F632	shocking or flooding others w information	cos(16*2π/55) + isin(16*2π/55)	-0.25422 +0.96715i
104.78	104:46'34	134	39	39-ariopposition	39-♈☍	💟	1F49F	a trait the partner MUST have	cos(39*2π/134) + isin(39*2π/134)	-0.25504 +0.96693i
104.81	104:48'36	79	23	23-virgiseptile	23-♍ち	✊	270A	anti-establishment revolutionary	cos(23*2π/79) + isin(23*2π/79)	-0.25562 +0.96678i
104.88	104:52'54	127	37	37-tauriseptile	37-♉ち	💸	1F4B8	that which attracts unfair advantage	cos(37*2π/127) + isin(37*2π/127)	-0.25683 +0.96646i

105.00	105:0'0	24	7	7-aquariinconjunct	7-♒️π		1F4AD	imagination at work	cos(7*2πi/24) + isin(7*2πi/24)	-0.25882 +0.96593i
105.13	105:7'57	113	33	33-gemiquintile	33-♊︎⬠		1F60E	publicly-labeled vibe given	cos(33*2πi/113) + isin(33*2πi/113)	-0.26106 +0.96532i
105.17	105:10'6	89	26	26-leaquintile	26-♌︎⬠		1F48B	sensuality & body expression	cos(26*2πi/89) + isin(26*2πi/89)	-0.26166 +0.96516i
105.23	105:13'50	65	19	19-libriquintile	19-♎︎⬠		1F6C0	self-resparking	cos(19*2πi/65) + isin(19*2πi/65)	-0.26271 +0.96488i
105.28	105:16'58	106	31	31-cancridecile	31-♋︎⊥		1F3A0	others think one has more power than one has	cos(31*2πi/106) + isin(31*2πi/106)	-0.26359 +0.96464i
105.37	105:21'57	41	12	12-sajiquintile	12-♐︎⬠		1F5FD	personas aspired to	cos(12*2πi/41) + isin(12*2πi/41)	-0.26498 +0.96425i
105.43	105:25'42	140	41	41-arioctile	41-♈︎⟁		1F340	helped by a benefactor	cos(41*2πi/140) + isin(41*2πi/140)	-0.26604 +0.96396i
105.45	105:27'16	99	29	29-cancritrine	29-♋︎△		1F645	communication-stifling	cos(29*2πi/99) + isin(29*2πi/99)	-0.26647 +0.96384i
105.52	105:31'2	58	17	17-scorpidecile	17-♏︎⊥		1F47B	interactions with an ethereal party	cos(17*2πi/58) + isin(17*2πi/58)	-0.26753 +0.96355i
105.60	105:35'59	75	22	22-virgitrine	22-♍︎△		1F3E1	family home maintenance	cos(22*2πi/75) + isin(22*2πi/75)	-0.26892 +0.96316i
105.69	105:41'17	109	32	32-gemiconjunct	32-♊︎☌		1F44E	diminishing others' importance	cos(32*2πi/109) + isin(32*2πi/109)	-0.2704 +0.96275i
105.73	105:44'3	143	42	42-ariundecile	42-♈︎U		1F4E3	broadcasting which gets one talked about	cos(42*2πi/143) + isin(42*2πi/143)	-0.27118 +0.96253i
105.88	105:52'56	17	5	5-aquariquintile	5-♒️⬠		1F44A	managing by dominating	cos(5*2πi/17) + isin(5*2πi/17)	-0.27366 +0.96183i
106.05	106:2'47	129	38	38-taurinovile	38-♉︎N		1F647	in the service of one attached to	cos(38*2πi/129) + isin(38*2πi/129)	-0.27642 +0.96104i
106.07	106:4'17	112	33	33-gemisquare	33-♊︎□		1F38E	one's trait observed by outsiders	cos(33*2πi/112) + isin(33*2πi/112)	-0.27684 +0.96092i
106.11	106:6'18	95	28	28-leaundecile	28-♌︎U		265B	the image of a progress-inspiring master	cos(28*2πi/95) + isin(28*2πi/95)	-0.2774 +0.96075i
106.19	106:11'13	139	41	41-ariseptile	41-♈︎✻		1F3AF	creative perfectionism	cos(41*2πi/139) + isin(41*2πi/139)	-0.27877 +0.96036i
106.23	106:13'46	61	18	18-libriconjunct	18-♎︎☌		1F526	singled out for attention	cos(18*2πi/61) + isin(18*2πi/61)	-0.27949 +0.96015i
106.29	106:17'8	105	31	31-cancrinovile	31-♋︎N		1F5EF	when irritated to see standards defied	cos(31*2πi/105) + isin(31*2πi/105)	-0.28043 +0.95988i
106.36	106:21'49	44	13	13-sajioctile	13-♐︎⟁		1F6B5	role in a peer group	cos(13*2πi/44) + isin(13*2πi/44)	-0.28173 +0.95949i
106.43	106:26'5	115	34	34-gemiseptile	34-♊︎✻		1F933	inner world with self-talk	cos(34*2πi/115) + isin(34*2πi/115)	-0.28292 +0.95914i
106.48	106:28'43	71	21	21-libriundecile	21-♎︎U		26C5	thriving amidst confusion	cos(21*2πi/71) + isin(21*2πi/71)	-0.28366 +0.95892i
106.53	106:31'50	98	29	29-cancriopposition	29-♋︎☍		1F31F	social advancement catalyst	cos(29*2πi/98) + isin(29*2πi/98)	-0.28453 +0.95867i
106.56	106:33'36	125	37	37-tauriquintile	37-♉︎⬠		1F39F	social clique's requirements	cos(37*2πi/125) + isin(37*2πi/125)	-0.28502 +0.95852i
106.67	106:40'0	27	8	8-capritrine	8-♑︎△		1F393	intellectualizing and insight	cos(8*2πi/27) + isin(8*2πi/27)	-0.2868 +0.95799i
106.78	106:46'46	118	35	35-gemidecile	35-♊︎⊥		1F3C3	staying with it as long as encouraged	cos(35*2πi/118) + isin(35*2πi/118)	-0.28869 +0.95742i
106.81	106:48'47	91	27	27-leaseptile	27-♌︎✻		1F576	smoothly comfortable	cos(27*2πi/91) + isin(27*2πi/91)	-0.28925 +0.95725i
106.88	106:52'30	64	19	19-librisquare	19-♎︎□		4F17	amidst a noisy setting	cos(19*2πi/64) + isin(19*2πi/64)	-0.29028 +0.95694i
106.93	106:55'50	101	30	30-cancriquintile	30-♋︎⬠		1F624	disregard for things heard	cos(30*2πi/101) + isin(30*2πi/101)	-0.29121 +0.95666i

106.96	106:57'23	138	41	41-arisextile	41-♈✳	⛑	26D1	daily work focus	cos(41*2πi/138) + isin(41*2πi/138)	-0.29165 +0.95653i
107.03	107:1'37	37	11	11-sajiconjunct	11-♐☌	★	2B50	trusted ability revealed	cos(11*2πi/37) + isin(11*2πi/37)	-0.29282 +0.95617i
107.14	107:8'34	84	25	25-virgiinconjunct	25-♍⚻	🐑	1F411	traits for the seemingly weak	cos(25*2πi/84) + isin(25*2πi/84)	-0.29476 +0.95557i
107.18	107:10'32	131	39	39-tauriundecile	39-♉U	😑	1F611	with doubt in associations	cos(39*2πi/131) + isin(39*2πi/131)	-0.2953 +0.9554i
107.23	107:14'2	47	14	14-sajiundecile	14-♐U	☫	262B	a core, lived principle	cos(14*2πi/47) + isin(14*2πi/47)	-0.29628 +0.9551i
107.31	107:18'27	104	31	31-cancrioctile	31-♋⊿	😛	1F61B	trait known and accepted among friends	cos(31*2πi/104) + isin(31*2πi/104)	-0.2975 +0.95472i
107.37	107:22'6	57	17	17-scorpinovile	17-♏N	🪄	1FA84	arrives whenever one wants it, no asking	cos(17*2πi/57) + isin(17*2πi/57)	-0.29851 +0.95441i
107.42	107:25'9	124	37	37-taurisquare	37-♉□	🎇	1F387	initial, then waning impression	cos(37*2πi/124) + isin(37*2πi/124)	-0.29936 +0.95414i
107.50	107:30'0	144	43	43-ariinconjunct	43-♈⚻	🔁	1F501	always-on trait	cos(43*2πi/144) + isin(43*2πi/144)	-0.30071 +0.95372i
107.53	107:31'56	77	23	23-virgiquintile	23-♍⚼	🐢	1F422	guarded insistence	cos(23*2πi/77) + isin(23*2πi/77)	-0.30125 +0.95355i
107.59	107:35'10	87	26	26-leatrine	26-♌△	❣	2763	interactor inspired to want	cos(26*2πi/87) + isin(26*2πi/87)	-0.30214 +0.95326i
107.63	107:37'43	97	29	29-cancriconjunct	29-♋☌	💕	1F495	traits reserved for those very close	cos(29*2πi/97) + isin(29*2πi/97)	-0.30285 +0.95304i
107.69	107:41'32	117	35	35-geminovile	35-♊N	💎	1F48E	best friend's quality	cos(35*2πi/117) + isin(35*2πi/117)	-0.30391 +0.9527i
107.74	107:44'14	137	41	41-ariquintile	41-♈⚼	🚧	1F6A7	singular active, direct, control	cos(41*2πi/137) + isin(41*2πi/137)	-0.30465 +0.95246i
108.00	108:0'0	10	3	decile (tredecile)	⊥₃ (✳)	🛂	1F6C2	ability to control	cos(1*2πi/10) + isin(1*2πi/10)	-0.30902 +0.95106i
108.29	108:17'33	123	37	37-tauritrine	37-♉△	⎏	238F	others must express or draw out	cos(37*2πi/123) + isin(37*2πi/123)	-0.31387 +0.94947i
108.35	108:20'58	103	31	31-cancriseptile	31-♋七	😊	1F60A	basking in joy	cos(31*2πi/103) + isin(31*2πi/103)	-0.31481 +0.94915i
108.39	108:23'13	93	28	28-leanovile	28-♌N	😍	1F60D	brought out by creative, sexualized energy	cos(28*2πi/93) + isin(28*2πi/93)	-0.31544 +0.94895i
108.43	108:26'1	83	25	25-virgiundecile	25-♍U	⚡	26A1	high-tension activity in surroundings	cos(25*2πi/83) + isin(25*2πi/83)	-0.31621 +0.94869i
108.49	108:29'35	73	22	22-virgiconjunct	22-♍☌	⚒	2692	new or deep investment in job	cos(22*2πi/73) + isin(22*2πi/73)	-0.31719 +0.94836i
108.53	108:31'45	136	41	41-arisquare	41-♈□	🧐	1F9D0	serious, sober-minded interactant	cos(41*2πi/136) + isin(41*2πi/136)	-0.31779 +0.94816i
108.57	108:34'17	63	19	19-libritrine	19-♎△	🚨	1F6A8	know-it-all	cos(19*2πi/63) + isin(19*2πi/63)	-0.31849 +0.94793i
108.62	108:37'14	116	35	35-gemioctile	35-♊⊿	😒	1F612	having been slighted or doubted	cos(35*2πi/116) + isin(35*2πi/116)	-0.3193 +0.94765i
108.68	108:40'45	53	16	16-scorpiquintile	16-♏⚼	🤗	1F917	reasons one is desired	cos(16*2πi/53) + isin(16*2πi/53)	-0.32027 +0.94733i
108.75	108:45'0	96	29	29-leainconjunct	29-♌⚻	🤷	1F937	what "not enough" looks like	cos(29*2πi/96) + isin(29*2πi/96)	-0.32144 +0.94693i
108.78	108:46'37	139	42	42-ariseptile	42-♈七	🎯	1F3AF	creative perfectionism	cos(42*2πi/139) + isin(42*2πi/139)	-0.32189 +0.94678i
108.84	108:50'13	43	13	13-sajiseptile	13-♐七	🃏	1F0CF	through jokes, games, and fun	cos(13*2πi/43) + isin(13*2πi/43)	-0.32288 +0.94644i
108.95	108:56'50	76	23	23-virgisquare	23-♍□	🏘	1F3D8	seen by friends' friends & family	cos(23*2πi/76) + isin(23*2πi/76)	-0.3247 +0.94582i
108.99	108:59'26	109	33	33-gemiconjunct	33-♊☌	👎	1F44E	diminishing others' importance	cos(33*2πi/109) + isin(33*2πi/109)	-0.32542 +0.94557i

109.01	109:0'50	142	43	43-aridecile	43-♈⊥	ॐ	1F549	blessings others can only dream of	cos(43*2π/142) + isin(43*2π/142)	-0.3258 +0.94544i
109.09	109:5'27	33	10	10-caprinovile	10-♑N	📻	1F4FB	in a formal group discussion	cos(10*2π/33) + isin(10*2π/33)	-0.32707 +0.945i
109.18	109:10'49	122	37	37-tauriopposition	37-♉☍	🤓	1F913	easily annoying to others	cos(37*2π/122) + isin(37*2π/122)	-0.32854 +0.94449i
109.21	109:12'48	89	27	27-leaquintile	27-♌⚹	👋	1F48B	sensuality & body expression	cos(27*2π/89) + isin(27*2π/89)	-0.32909 +0.9443i
109.29	109:17'8	56	17	17-scorpioctile	17-♏⊿	😈	1F608	for fun or one's own power	cos(17*2π/56) + isin(17*2π/56)	-0.33028 +0.94388i
109.33	109:19'59	135	41	41-aritrine	41-♈△	🏄	1F3C4	easy and prolific	cos(41*2π/135) + isin(41*2π/135)	-0.33106 +0.94361i
109.37	109:22'1	79	24	24-virgiseptile	24-♍七	✊	270A	anti-establishment revolutionary	cos(24*2π/79) + isin(24*2π/79)	-0.33162 +0.94341i
109.44	109:26'23	125	38	38-tauriquintile	38-♉⚹	🎟	1F39F	social clique's requirements	cos(38*2π/125) + isin(38*2π/125)	-0.33282 +0.94299i
109.57	109:33'54	23	7	7-aquariundecile	7-♒U	🦑	1F991	unusual social trait, liked by eccentrics	cos(7*2π/23) + isin(7*2π/23)	-0.33488 +0.94226i
109.69	109:41'15	128	39	39-taurioctile	39-♉⊿	👸	1F478	intuitive comfort even amidst stress	cos(39*2π/128) + isin(39*2π/128)	-0.33689 +0.94154i
109.71	109:42'51	105	32	32-cancrinovile	32-♋N	💥	1F5EF	when irritated to see standards defied	cos(32*2π/105) + isin(32*2π/105)	-0.33733 +0.94139i
109.79	109:47'14	141	43	43-arinovile	43-♈N	💉	1F489	easy instillment in others	cos(43*2π/141) + isin(43*2π/141)	-0.33853 +0.94096i
109.83	109:49'49	59	18	18-scorpiundecile	18-♏U	👇	1F447	having one's pick	cos(18*2π/59) + isin(18*2π/59)	-0.33924 +0.9407i
109.89	109:53'41	95	29	29-leaundecile	29-♌U	👑	265B	the image of a progress-inspiring master	cos(29*2π/95) + isin(29*2π/95)	-0.34029 +0.94032i
109.92	109:55'25	131	40	40-tauriundecile	40-♉U	😑	1F611	with doubt in associations	cos(40*2π/131) + isin(40*2π/131)	-0.34077 +0.94015i
110.00	110:0'0	36	11	11-capriinconjunct	11-♑π	🎻	1F3BB	downplayed want or talent	cos(11*2π/36) + isin(11*2π/36)	-0.34202 +0.93969i
110.08	110:4'57	121	37	37-tauriconjunct	37-♉☌	💰	1F4B0	prosperity & status-seeking	cos(37*2π/121) + isin(37*2π/121)	-0.34338 +0.9392i
110.15	110:8'57	134	41	41-ariopposition	41-♈☍	🖼	1F49F	a trait the partner MUST have	cos(41*2π/134) + isin(41*2π/134)	-0.34447 +0.9388i
110.20	110:12'14	49	15	15-scorpiconjunct	15-♏☌	🎙	1F399	having known public influence	cos(15*2π/49) + isin(15*2π/49)	-0.34537 +0.93847i
110.27	110:16'12	111	34	34-gemitrine	34-♊△	🥳	1F973	around high-expression groups	cos(34*2π/111) + isin(34*2π/111)	-0.34645 +0.93807i
110.32	110:19'21	62	19	19-libriopposition	19-♎☍	🏴	1F3F4	manipulative ambition	cos(19*2π/62) + isin(19*2π/62)	-0.34731 +0.93775i
110.40	110:24'0	75	23	23-virgitrine	23-♍△	🏡	1F3E1	family home maintenance	cos(23*2π/75) + isin(23*2π/75)	-0.34857 +0.93728i
110.50	110:29'42	101	31	31-cancriquintile	31-♋⚹	🤤	1F624	disregard for things heard	cos(31*2π/101) + isin(31*2π/101)	-0.35013 +0.9367i
110.53	110:31'34	114	35	35-gemisextile	35-♊✳	🛱	1F6F1	other's influence attempts	cos(35*2π/114) + isin(35*2π/114)	-0.35064 +0.93651i
110.57	110:34'17	140	43	43-arioctile	43-♈⊿	🍀	1F340	helped by a benefactor	cos(43*2π/140) + isin(43*2π/140)	-0.35137 +0.93623i
110.77	110:46'9	13	4	4-aquariconjunct	4-♒☌	🎥	1F3A5	public persona	cos(4*2π/13) + isin(4*2π/13)	-0.3546 +0.93502i
110.98	110:58'38	133	41	41-ariconjunct	41-♈☌	👝	1F49D	during sex or when flirting	cos(41*2π/133) + isin(41*2π/133)	-0.358 +0.93372i
111.03	111:1'40	107	33	33-cancriundecile	33-♋U	💁	1F481	essence of a great conversation w/ one	cos(33*2π/107) + isin(33*2π/107)	-0.35882 +0.9334i
111.06	111:3'49	94	29	29-leadecile	29-♌⊥	👣	1F463	helps in others after learning the hard way	cos(29*2π/94) + isin(29*2π/94)	-0.35941 +0.93318i

111.11	111:6'40	81	25	25-virginovile	25-♍N		1F451	mastered early, forms broad social identity	cos(25*2π/81) + isin(25*2π/81)	-0.36018 +0.93288i
111.18	111:10'35	68	21	21-librioctile	21-♎⊿		1F462	appearance of dominating	cos(21*2π/68) + isin(21*2π/68)	-0.36124 +0.93247i
111.22	111:13'10	123	38	38-tauritrine	38-♉△		238F	others must express or draw out	cos(38*2π/123) + isin(38*2π/123)	-0.36194 +0.9322i
111.27	111:16'21	55	17	17-scorpiseptile	17-♏七		1F632	shocking or flooding others w information	cos(17*2π/55) + isin(17*2π/55)	-0.36281 +0.93186i
111.34	111:20'24	97	30	30-cancriconjunct	30-♋☌		1F495	traits reserved for those very close	cos(30*2π/97) + isin(30*2π/97)	-0.3639 +0.93144i
111.37	111:22'0	139	43	43-ariseptile	43-♈七		1F3AF	creative perfectionism	cos(43*2π/139) + isin(43*2π/139)	-0.36434 +0.93127i
111.43	111:25'42	42	13	13-sajisextile	13-♐*		1F497	instilled in co-creative partners	cos(13*2π/42) + isin(13*2π/42)	-0.36534 +0.93087i
111.55	111:32'57	71	22	22-libriundecile	22-♎U		26C5	thriving amidst confusion	cos(22*2π/71) + isin(22*2π/71)	-0.3673 +0.9301i
111.60	111:35'59	100	31	31-cancrisquare	31-♋□		1F6CB	home & family life	cos(31*2π/100) + isin(31*2π/100)	-0.36812 +0.92978i
111.63	111:37'40	129	40	40-taurinovile	40-♉N		1F647	in the service of one attached to	cos(40*2π/129) + isin(40*2π/129)	-0.36858 +0.9296i
111.72	111:43'26	29	9	9-capriquintile	9-♑⬠		1F3A9	proud charisma	cos(9*2π/29) + isin(9*2π/29)	-0.37014 +0.92898i
111.84	111:50'40	103	32	32-cancriseptile	32-♋七		1F60A	basking in joy	cos(32*2π/103) + isin(32*2π/103)	-0.37209 +0.9282i
111.89	111:53'30	74	23	23-virgiopposition	23-♍☍		1F626	social stressors	cos(23*2π/74) + isin(23*2π/74)	-0.37286 +0.92789i
111.93	111:55'57	119	37	37-gemiundecile	37-♊U		1F4C9	weakened by opinionation, better as ambient	cos(37*2π/119) + isin(37*2π/119)	-0.37352 +0.92762i
112.00	112:0'0	45	14	14-sajinovile	14-♐N		2766	shared experience as a token of friendship	cos(14*2π/45) + isin(14*2π/45)	-0.37461 +0.92718i
112.08	112:4'31	106	33	33-cancridecile	33-♋⊥		1F3A0	others think one has more power than one has	cos(33*2π/106) + isin(33*2π/106)	-0.37583 +0.92669i
112.13	112:7'52	61	19	19-libriconjunct	19-♎☌		1F526	singled out for attention	cos(19*2π/61) + isin(19*2π/61)	-0.37673 +0.92632i
112.17	112:10'26	138	43	43-arisextile	43-♈*		26D1	daily work focus	cos(43*2π/138) + isin(43*2π/138)	-0.37742 +0.92604i
112.21	112:12'28	77	24	24-virgiquintile	24-♍⬠		1F422	guarded insistence	cos(24*2π/77) + isin(24*2π/77)	-0.37797 +0.92582i
112.29	112:17'36	109	34	34-gemiconjunct	34-♊☌		1F44E	diminishing others' importance	cos(34*2π/109) + isin(34*2π/109)	-0.37935 +0.92525i
112.34	112:20'25	141	44	44-arinovile	44-♈N		1F489	easy instillment in others	cos(44*2π/141) + isin(44*2π/141)	-0.38011 +0.92494i
112.50	112:30'0	16	5	5-aquarisquare	5-♒□		1F46A	among family	cos(5*2π/16) + isin(5*2π/16)	-0.38268 +0.92388i
112.70	112:41'44	115	36	36-gemiseptile	36-♊七		1F933	inner world with self-talk	cos(36*2π/115) + isin(36*2π/115)	-0.38584 +0.92257i
112.73	112:43'38	99	31	31-cancritrine	31-♋△		1F645	communication-stifling	cos(31*2π/99) + isin(31*2π/99)	-0.38635 +0.92235i
112.77	112:46'15	83	26	26-virgiundecile	26-♍U		26A1	high-tension activity in surroundings	cos(26*2π/83) + isin(26*2π/83)	-0.38705 +0.92206i
112.84	112:50'8	67	21	21-libriseptile	21-♎七		1F63B	getting others to fall in love w oneself	cos(21*2π/67) + isin(21*2π/67)	-0.38809 +0.92162i
112.88	112:52'52	118	37	37-gemidecile	37-♊⊥		1F3C3	staying with it as long as encouraged	cos(37*2π/118) + isin(37*2π/118)	-0.38882 +0.92131i
112.94	112:56'28	51	16	16-scorpitrine	16-♏△		1F61A	use of persuasive words	cos(16*2π/51) + isin(16*2π/51)	-0.38979 +0.92091i
112.99	112:59'33	137	43	43-ariquintile	43-♈⬠		1F6A7	singular active, direct, control	cos(43*2π/137) + isin(43*2π/137)	-0.39061 +0.92055i

113.02	113:1'23	86	27	27-leaopposition	27-♌☍	🤡	1F921	one's commentary offends egos	cos(27*2πi/86) + isin(27*2πi/86)	-0.3911 +0.92035i
113.06	113:3'28	121	38	38-tauriconjunct	38-♉☌	💰	1F4B0	prosperity & status-seeking	cos(38*2πi/121) + isin(38*2πi/121)	-0.39166 +0.92011i
113.14	113:8'34	35	11	11-capriundecile	11-♑U	👽	1F47D	quirky distinguishing uniqueness	cos(11*2πi/35) + isin(11*2πi/35)	-0.39303 +0.91953i
113.23	113:13'32	124	39	39-taurisquare	39-♉□	🎇	1F387	initial, then waning impression	cos(39*2πi/124) + isin(39*2πi/124)	-0.39436 +0.91896i
113.29	113:17'12	143	45	45-ariundecile	45-♈U	📣	1F4E3	broadcasting which gets one talked about	cos(45*2πi/143) + isin(45*2πi/143)	-0.39533 +0.91854i
113.33	113:19'59	54	17	17-scorpisextile	17-♏✳	🍸	1F378	self-fulfillment tool	cos(17*2πi/54) + isin(17*2πi/54)	-0.39608 +0.91822i
113.39	113:23'8	127	40	40-tauriseptile	40-♉七	💸	1F4B8	that which attracts unfair advantage	cos(40*2πi/127) + isin(40*2πi/127)	-0.39692 +0.91785i
113.42	113:25'28	73	23	23-virgiconjunct	23-♍☌	⚒	2692	new or deep investment in job	cos(23*2πi/73) + isin(23*2πi/73)	-0.39754 +0.91758i
113.48	113:28'41	92	29	29-leaoctile	29-♌◿	🎻	1F37B	regular comfort preferences w/ close one	cos(29*2πi/92) + isin(29*2πi/92)	-0.3984 +0.91721i
113.54	113:32'18	130	41	41-tauridecile	41-♉⊥	🎪	1F3AA	relied upon by others in the talked topic	cos(41*2πi/130) + isin(41*2πi/130)	-0.39936 +0.91679i
113.68	113:41'3	19	6	6-aquariseptile	6-♒七	🔐	1F510	gateway to one's friendship	cos(6*2πi/19) + isin(6*2πi/19)	-0.4017 +0.91577i
113.85	113:50'46	117	37	37-geminovile	37-♊N	💎	1F48E	best friend's quality	cos(37*2πi/117) + isin(37*2πi/117)	-0.40428 +0.91463i
113.88	113:52'39	98	31	31-cancriopposition	31-♋☍	🌟	1F31F	social advancement catalyst	cos(31*2πi/98) + isin(31*2πi/98)	-0.40478 +0.91441i
113.92	113:55'26	79	25	25-virgiseptile	25-♏七	✊	270A	anti-establishment revolutionary	cos(25*2πi/79) + isin(25*2πi/79)	-0.40553 +0.91408i
114.00	114:0'0	60	19	19-scorpiinconjunct	19-♏π	📍	1F4CD	strongest memory left behind	cos(19*2πi/60) + isin(19*2πi/60)	-0.40674 +0.91355i
114.08	114:5'4	142	45	45-aridecile	45-♈⊥	🕉	1F549	blessings others can only dream of	cos(45*2πi/142) + isin(45*2πi/142)	-0.40808 +0.91294i
114.15	114:8'46	41	13	13-sajiquintile	13-♐⬠	🗽	1F5FD	personas aspired to	cos(13*2πi/41) + isin(13*2πi/41)	-0.40907 +0.9125i
114.23	114:13'50	104	33	33-cancrioctile	33-♋◿	😛	1F61B	trait known and accepted among friends	cos(33*2πi/104) + isin(33*2πi/104)	-0.41041 +0.9119i
114.29	114:17'8	63	20	20-libritrine	20-♎△	🚨	1F6A8	know-it-all	cos(20*2πi/63) + isin(20*2πi/63)	-0.41129 +0.91151i
114.39	114:23'33	107	34	34-cancriundecile	34-♋U	💁	1F481	essence of a great conversation w/ one	cos(34*2πi/107) + isin(34*2πi/107)	-0.41299 +0.91074i
114.42	114:25'6	129	41	41-taurinovile	41-♉N	🙇	1F647	in the service of one attached to	cos(41*2πi/129) + isin(41*2πi/129)	-0.4134 +0.91055i
114.55	114:32'43	22	7	7-aquaridecile	7-♒⊥	🛦	1F6E6	in command of one's field	cos(7*2πi/22) + isin(7*2πi/22)	-0.41542 +0.90963i
114.69	114:41'24	113	36	36-gemiquintile	36-♊⬠	😎	1F60E	publicly-labeled vibe given	cos(36*2πi/113) + isin(36*2πi/113)	-0.41771 +0.90858i
114.73	114:43'30	91	29	29-leaseptile	29-♌七	🕶	1F576	smoothly comfortable	cos(29*2πi/91) + isin(29*2πi/91)	-0.41827 +0.90832i
114.78	114:46'57	69	22	22-librinovile	22-♎N	🐘	1F418	subtle, strong draw of trait via socialization	cos(22*2πi/69) + isin(22*2πi/69)	-0.41918 +0.9079i
114.83	114:49'39	116	37	37-gemioctile	37-♊◿	😒	1F612	having been slighted or doubted	cos(37*2πi/116) + isin(37*2πi/116)	-0.41989 +0.90758i
114.89	114:53'37	47	15	15-sajiundecile	15-♐U	☫	262B	a core, lived principle	cos(15*2πi/47) + isin(15*2πi/47)	-0.42093 +0.90709i
115.00	115:0'0	72	23	23-libriinconjunct	23-♎π	❓	2753	a problem to be solved	cos(23*2πi/72) + isin(23*2πi/72)	-0.42262 +0.90631i
115.08	115:4'55	122	39	39-tauriopposition	39-♉☍	🤓	1F913	easily annoying to others	cos(39*2πi/122) + isin(39*2πi/122)	-0.42391 +0.9057i

115.20	115:12'0	25	8	8-capriconjunct	8-♑☌		1F3DF	rally & tune the mass psychology	cos(8*2πi/25) + isin(8*2πi/25)	-0.42578 +0.90483i
115.34	115:20'23	103	33	33-cancriseptile	33-♋七		1F60A	basking in joy	cos(33*2πi/103) + isin(33*2πi/103)	-0.42799 +0.90379i
115.38	115:23'4	78	25	25-virgisextile	25-♍✱		1F94A	fight night moment	cos(25*2πi/78) + isin(25*2πi/78)	-0.42869 +0.90345i
115.42	115:25'11	131	42	42-tauriundecile	42-♉U		1F611	with doubt in associations	cos(42*2πi/131) + isin(42*2πi/131)	-0.42925 +0.90319i
115.47	115:28'18	53	17	17-scorpiquintile	17-♏⚷		1F917	reasons one is desired	cos(17*2πi/53) + isin(17*2πi/53)	-0.43007 +0.9028i
115.52	115:31'20	134	43	43-ariopposition	43-♈☍		1F49F	a trait the partner MUST have	cos(43*2πi/134) + isin(43*2πi/134)	-0.43086 +0.90242i
115.60	115:35'46	109	35	35-gemiconjunct	35-♊☌		1F44E	diminishing others' importance	cos(35*2πi/109) + isin(35*2πi/109)	-0.43203 +0.90186i
115.62	115:37'13	137	44	44-ariquintile	44-♈⚷		1F6A7	singular active, direct, control	cos(44*2πi/137) + isin(44*2πi/137)	-0.43241 +0.90168i
115.71	115:42'51	28	9	9-caprisquare	9-♑□		1F58C	arts and creativity drawn to	cos(9*2πi/28) + isin(9*2πi/28)	-0.43388 +0.90097i
115.83	115:49'33	115	37	37-gemiseptile	37-♊七		1F933	inner world with self-talk	cos(37*2πi/115) + isin(37*2πi/115)	-0.43564 +0.90012i
115.86	115:51'43	87	28	28-leatrine	28-♌△		2763	interactor inspired to want	cos(28*2πi/87) + isin(28*2πi/87)	-0.43621 +0.89985i
115.93	115:55'55	59	19	19-scorpiundecile	19-♏U		1F447	having one's pick	cos(19*2πi/59) + isin(19*2πi/59)	-0.43731 +0.89931i
116.00	116:0'0	90	29	29-leasextile	29-♌✱		1F6B8	absorptions by one's children	cos(29*2πi/90) + isin(29*2πi/90)	-0.43837 +0.89879i
116.03	116:1'59	121	39	39-tauriconjunct	39-♉☌		1F4B0	prosperity & status-seeking	cos(39*2πi/121) + isin(39*2πi/121)	-0.43889 +0.89854i
116.13	116:7'44	31	10	10-capriseptile	10-♑七		1F3A2	expressed by one's social network	cos(10*2πi/31) + isin(10*2πi/31)	-0.44039 +0.8978i
116.25	116:15'0	96	31	31-leainconjunct	31-♌π		1F937	what "not enough" looks like	cos(31*2πi/96) + isin(31*2πi/96)	-0.44229 +0.89687i
116.31	116:18'27	65	21	21-libriquintile	21-♎⚷		1F6C0	self-resparking	cos(21*2πi/65) + isin(21*2πi/65)	-0.44319 +0.89643i
116.39	116:23'27	133	43	43-ariconjunct	43-♈☌		1F49D	during sex or when flirting	cos(43*2πi/133) + isin(43*2πi/133)	-0.44449 +0.89578i
116.47	116:28'14	34	11	11-capridecile	11-♑⊥		1F3C6	potential to be a master or boss	cos(11*2πi/34) + isin(11*2πi/34)	-0.44574 +0.89516i
116.55	116:32'48	139	45	45-ariseptile	45-♈七		1F3AF	creative perfectionism	cos(45*2πi/139) + isin(45*2πi/139)	-0.44693 +0.89457i
116.57	116:34'17	105	34	34-cancrinovile	34-♋N		1F5EF	when irritated to see standards defied	cos(34*2πi/105) + isin(34*2πi/105)	-0.44731 +0.89438i
116.62	116:37'10	71	23	23-libriundecile	23-♎U		26C5	thriving amidst confusion	cos(23*2πi/71) + isin(23*2πi/71)	-0.44807 +0.894i
116.67	116:40'0	108	35	35-cancriinconjunct	35-♋π		1F31D	why close friends come around	cos(35*2πi/108) + isin(35*2πi/108)	-0.4488 +0.89363i
116.76	116:45'24	37	12	12-sajiconjunct	12-♐☌		2B50	trusted ability revealed	cos(12*2πi/37) + isin(12*2πi/37)	-0.4502 +0.89293i
116.84	116:50'31	114	37	37-gemisextile	37-♊✱		1F6F1	other's influence attempts	cos(37*2πi/114) + isin(37*2πi/114)	-0.45153 +0.89225i
116.88	116:52'59	77	25	25-virgiquintile	25-♍⚷		1F422	guarded insistence	cos(25*2πi/77) + isin(25*2πi/77)	-0.45217 +0.89193i
116.92	116:55'23	117	38	38-geminovile	38-♊N		1F48E	best friend's quality	cos(38*2πi/117) + isin(38*2πi/117)	-0.45279 +0.89162i
117.00	117:0'0	40	13	13-sajisquare	13-♐□		1F66A	future missable partnership duty	cos(13*2πi/40) + isin(13*2πi/40)	-0.45399 +0.89101i
117.07	117:4'23	123	40	40-tauritrine	40-♉△		238F	others must express or draw out	cos(40*2πi/123) + isin(40*2πi/123)	-0.45513 +0.89043i

117.14	117:8'34	126	41	41-taurisextile	41-♉✱		1F47E	aggressive assertion of identity	cos(41*2π/126) + isin(41*2π/126)	-0.45621 +0.88987i
117.21	117:12'33	43	14	14-sajiseptile	14-♐七		1F0CF	through jokes, games, and fun	cos(14*2π/43) + isin(14*2π/43)	-0.45724 +0.88934i
117.27	117:16'21	132	43	43-tauriinconjunct	43-♉⚲		1F517	sharing a special bond w/ a friend	cos(43*2π/132) + isin(43*2π/132)	-0.45823 +0.88884i
117.33	117:19'59	135	44	44-aritrine	44-♈△		1F3C4	easy and prolific	cos(44*2π/135) + isin(44*2π/135)	-0.45917 +0.88835i
117.39	117:23'28	46	15	15-sajidecile	15-♐⊥		1F4CE	trait housed by key colleagues	cos(15*2π/46) + isin(15*2π/46)	-0.46007 +0.88789i
117.45	117:26'48	141	46	46-arinovile	46-♈N		1F489	easy instillment in others	cos(46*2π/141) + isin(46*2π/141)	-0.46092 +0.88744i
117.50	117:30'0	144	47	47-ariinconjunct	47-♈⚲		1F501	always-on trait	cos(47*2π/144) + isin(47*2π/144)	-0.46175 +0.88701i
117.55	117:33'3	49	16	16-scorpiconjunct	16-♏☌		1F399	having known public influence	cos(16*2π/49) + isin(16*2π/49)	-0.46254 +0.8866i
117.62	117:37'25	101	33	33-cancriquintile	33-♋Q		1F624	disregard for things heard	cos(33*2π/101) + isin(33*2π/101)	-0.46366 +0.88601i
117.69	117:41'32	52	17	17-scorpisquare	17-♏□		1F61E	falling short	cos(17*2π/52) + isin(17*2π/52)	-0.46472 +0.88546i
117.76	117:45'25	107	35	35-cancriundecile	35-♋U		1F481	essence of a great conversation w/ one	cos(35*2π/107) + isin(35*2π/107)	-0.46572 +0.88493i
117.82	117:49'5	55	18	18-scorpiseptile	18-♏七		1F632	shocking or flooding others w information	cos(18*2π/55) + isin(18*2π/55)	-0.46667 +0.88443i
117.88	117:52'33	113	37	37-gemiquintile	37-♊Q		1F60E	publicly-labeled vibe given	cos(37*2π/113) + isin(37*2π/113)	-0.46756 +0.88396i
117.93	117:55'51	58	19	19-scorpidecile	19-♏⊥		1F47B	interactions with an ethereal party	cos(19*2π/58) + isin(19*2π/58)	-0.46841 +0.88351i
117.98	117:58'59	119	39	39-gemiundecile	39-♊U		1F4C9	weakened by opinionation, better as ambient	cos(39*2π/119) + isin(39*2π/119)	-0.46921 +0.88309i
118.03	118:1'58	61	20	20-libriconjunct	20-♎☌		1F526	singled out for attention	cos(20*2π/61) + isin(20*2π/61)	-0.46998 +0.88268i
118.08	118:4'47	125	41	41-tauriquintile	41-♉Q		1F39F	social clique's requirements	cos(41*2π/125) + isin(41*2π/125)	-0.4707 +0.88229i
118.13	118:7'30	64	21	21-librisquare	21-♎□		4F17	amidst a noisy setting	cos(21*2π/64) + isin(21*2π/64)	-0.4714 +0.88192i
118.17	118:10'4	131	43	43-tauriundecile	43-♉U		1F611	with doubt in associations	cos(43*2π/131) + isin(43*2π/131)	-0.47206 +0.88157i
118.25	118:14'53	137	45	45-ariquintile	45-♈Q		1F6A7	singular active, direct, control	cos(45*2π/137) + isin(45*2π/137)	-0.47329 +0.88091i
118.29	118:17'8	70	23	23-libridecile	23-♎⊥		1F527	used to strengthen or repair bonds	cos(23*2π/70) + isin(23*2π/70)	-0.47387 +0.8806i
118.32	118:19'18	143	47	47-ariundecile	47-♈U		1F4E3	broadcasting which gets one talked about	cos(47*2π/143) + isin(47*2π/143)	-0.47442 +0.8803i
118.36	118:21'22	73	24	24-virgiconjunct	24-♍☌		2692	new or deep investment in job	cos(24*2π/73) + isin(24*2π/73)	-0.47495 +0.88001i
118.42	118:25'15	76	25	25-virgisquare	25-♍□		1F3D8	seen by friends' friends & family	cos(25*2π/76) + isin(25*2π/76)	-0.47595 +0.87947i
118.48	118:28'51	79	26	26-virgiseptile	26-♍七		270A	anti-establishment revolutionary	cos(26*2π/79) + isin(26*2π/79)	-0.47687 +0.87898i
118.54	118:32'11	82	27	27-virgidecile	27-♍⊥		1F987	eccentrically attention-getting, disquieting	cos(27*2π/82) + isin(27*2π/82)	-0.47772 +0.87851i
118.59	118:35'17	85	28	28-leaconjunct	28-♌☌		1F924	downplaying a real want	cos(28*2π/85) + isin(28*2π/85)	-0.47851 +0.87808i
118.64	118:38'10	88	29	29-leasquare	29-♌□		1F479	suppressing power imbalance	cos(29*2π/88) + isin(29*2π/88)	-0.47925 +0.87768i
118.68	118:40'52	91	30	30-leaseptile	30-♌七		1F576	smoothly comfortable	cos(30*2π/91) + isin(30*2π/91)	-0.47994 +0.8773i

118.72	118:43'24	94	31	31-leadecile	31-♌⊥		1F463	helps in others after learning the hard way	cos(31*2π/94) + isin(31*2π/94)	-0.48058 +0.87695i
118.80	118:47'59	100	33	33-cancrisquare	33-♋□		1F6CB	home & family life	cos(33*2π/100) + isin(33*2π/100)	-0.48175 +0.87631i
118.83	118:50'5	103	34	34-cancriseptile	34-♋七		1F60A	basking in joy	cos(34*2π/103) + isin(34*2π/103)	-0.48229 +0.87601i
118.90	118:53'56	109	36	36-gemiconjunct	36-♊☌		1F44E	diminishing others' importance	cos(36*2π/109) + isin(36*2π/109)	-0.48327 +0.87547i
118.93	118:55'42	112	37	37-gemisquare	37-♊□		1F38E	one's trait observed by outsiders	cos(37*2π/112) + isin(37*2π/112)	-0.48372 +0.87522i
118.98	118:58'58	118	39	39-gemidecile	39-♊⊥		1F3C3	staying with it as long as encouraged	cos(39*2π/118) + isin(39*2π/118)	-0.48455 +0.87476i
119.03	119:1'56	124	41	41-taurisquare	41-♉□		1F387	initial, then waning impression	cos(41*2π/124) + isin(41*2π/124)	-0.4853 +0.87435i
119.08	119:4'36	130	43	43-tauridecile	43-♉⊥		1F3AA	relied upon by others in the talked topic	cos(43*2π/130) + isin(43*2π/130)	-0.48598 +0.87397i
119.14	119:8'12	139	46	46-ariseptile	46-♈七		1F3AF	creative perfectionism	cos(46*2π/139) + isin(46*2π/139)	-0.48689 +0.87346i
119.15	119:9'17	142	47	47-aridecile	47-♈⊥		1F549	blessings others can only dream of	cos(47*2π/142) + isin(47*2π/142)	-0.48717 +0.87331i
120.00	120:0'0	3	1	trine	Δ		1F426	easy flow	cos(1*2π/3) + isin(1*2π/3)	-0.5 +0.86603i
120.84	120:50'20	143	48	48-ariundecile	48-♈U		1F4E3	broadcasting which gets one talked about	cos(48*2π/143) + isin(48*2π/143)	-0.51263 +0.85861i
120.88	120:52'33	137	46	46-ariquintile	46-♈⌂		1F6A7	singular active, direct, control	cos(46*2π/137) + isin(46*2π/137)	-0.51318 +0.85828i
120.94	120:56'15	128	43	43-taurioctile	43-♉⊿		1F478	intuitive comfort even amidst stress	cos(43*2π/128) + isin(43*2π/128)	-0.5141 +0.85773i
120.98	120:59'0	122	41	41-tauriopposition	41-♉☍		1F913	easily annoying to others	cos(41*2π/122) + isin(41*2π/122)	-0.51479 +0.85731i
121.03	121:2'4	116	39	39-gemioctile	39-♊⊿		1F612	having been slighted or doubted	cos(39*2π/116) + isin(39*2π/116)	-0.51555 +0.85686i
121.09	121:5'27	110	37	37-gemiopposition	37-♊☍		1F6A5	managing others' behavior	cos(37*2π/110) + isin(37*2π/110)	-0.5164 +0.85635i
121.12	121:7'17	107	36	36-cancriundecile	36-♋U		1F481	essence of a great conversation w/ one	cos(36*2π/107) + isin(36*2π/107)	-0.51685 +0.85607i
121.19	121:11'17	101	34	34-cancriquintile	34-♋⌂		1F624	disregard for things heard	cos(34*2π/101) + isin(34*2π/101)	-0.51785 +0.85547i
121.22	121:13'28	98	33	33-cancriopposition	33-♋☍		1F31F	social advancement catalyst	cos(33*2π/98) + isin(33*2π/98)	-0.51839 +0.85514i
121.26	121:15'47	95	32	32-leaundecile	32-♌U		265B	the image of a progress-inspiring master	cos(32*2π/95) + isin(32*2π/95)	-0.51897 +0.85479i
121.35	121:20'53	89	30	30-leaquintile	30-♌⌂		1F48B	sensuality & body expression	cos(30*2π/89) + isin(30*2π/89)	-0.52024 +0.85402i
121.40	121:23'43	86	29	29-leaopposition	29-♌☍		1F921	one's commentary offends egos	cos(29*2π/86) + isin(29*2π/86)	-0.52094 +0.85359i
121.45	121:26'44	83	28	28-virgiundecile	28-♍U		26A1	high-tension activity in surroundings	cos(28*2π/83) + isin(28*2π/83)	-0.52169 +0.85313i
121.50	121:30'0	80	27	27-virgioctile	27-♍⊿		1F939	vividly remembered by one's children	cos(27*2π/80) + isin(27*2π/80)	-0.5225 +0.85264i
121.56	121:33'30	77	26	26-virgiquintile	26-♍⌂		1F422	guarded insistence	cos(26*2π/77) + isin(26*2π/77)	-0.52337 +0.85211i
121.62	121:37'17	74	25	25-virgiopposition	25-♍☍		1F626	social stressors	cos(25*2π/74) + isin(25*2π/74)	-0.52431 +0.85153i
121.69	121:41'24	71	24	24-libriundecile	24-♎U		26C5	thriving amidst confusion	cos(24*2π/71) + isin(24*2π/71)	-0.52533 +0.8509i
121.73	121:43'35	139	47	47-ariseptile	47-♈七		1F3AF	creative perfectionism	cos(47*2π/139) + isin(47*2π/139)	-0.52587 +0.85057i

121.76	121:45'52	68	23	23-librioctile	23-♎⊿		1F462	appearance of dominating	cos(23*2πi/68) + isin(23*2πi/68)	-0.52643 +0.85022i
121.85	121:50'46	65	22	22-libriquintile	22-♎⬠		1F6C0	self-resparking	cos(22*2πi/65) + isin(22*2πi/65)	-0.52764 +0.84947i
121.89	121:53'23	127	43	43-tauriseptile	43-♉ア		1F4B8	that which attracts unfair advantage	cos(43*2πi/127) + isin(43*2πi/127)	-0.52829 +0.84907i
121.94	121:56'7	62	21	21-libriopposition	21-♎☌		1F3F4	manipulative ambition	cos(21*2πi/62) + isin(21*2πi/62)	-0.52896 +0.84864i
121.98	121:59'0	121	41	41-tauriconjunct	41-♉☌		1F4B0	prosperity & status-seeking	cos(41*2πi/121) + isin(41*2πi/121)	-0.52967 +0.8482i
122.03	122:2'2	59	20	20-scorpiundecile	20-♏U		1F447	having one's pick	cos(20*2πi/59) + isin(20*2πi/59)	-0.53042 +0.84773i
122.09	122:5'13	115	39	39-gemiseptile	39-♊ア		1F933	inner world with self-talk	cos(39*2πi/115) + isin(39*2πi/115)	-0.53121 +0.84724i
122.14	122:8'34	56	19	19-scorpioctile	19-♏⊿		1F608	for fun or one's own power	cos(19*2πi/56) + isin(19*2πi/56)	-0.53203 +0.84672i
122.20	122:12'6	109	37	37-gemiconjunct	37-♊☌		1F44E	diminishing others' importance	cos(37*2πi/109) + isin(37*2πi/109)	-0.5329 +0.84618i
122.26	122:15'50	53	18	18-scorpiquintile	18-♏⬠		1F917	reasons one is desired	cos(18*2πi/53) + isin(18*2πi/53)	-0.53382 +0.8456i
122.33	122:19'48	103	35	35-cancriseptile	35-♋ア		1F60A	basking in joy	cos(35*2πi/103) + isin(35*2πi/103)	-0.5348 +0.84498i
122.40	122:24'0	50	17	17-scorpiopposition	17-♏☍		1F5BC	images put forth to others	cos(17*2πi/50) + isin(17*2πi/50)	-0.53583 +0.84433i
122.50	122:30'0	144	49	49-ariinconjunct	49-♈ヌ		1F501	always-on trait	cos(49*2πi/144) + isin(49*2πi/144)	-0.5373 +0.84339i
122.55	122:33'11	47	16	16-sajiundecile	16-♐U		262B	a core, lived principle	cos(16*2πi/47) + isin(16*2πi/47)	-0.53808 +0.84289i
122.64	122:38'14	91	31	31-leaseptile	31-♌ア		1F576	smoothly comfortable	cos(31*2πi/91) + isin(31*2πi/91)	-0.53932 +0.8421i
122.67	122:40'0	135	46	46-aritrine	46-♈△		1F3C4	easy and prolific	cos(46*2πi/135) + isin(46*2πi/135)	-0.53975 +0.84182i
122.73	122:43'38	44	15	15-sajioctile	15-♐⊿		1F6B5	role in a peer group	cos(15*2πi/44) + isin(15*2πi/44)	-0.54064 +0.84125i
122.79	122:47'26	129	44	44-taurinovile	44-♉N		1F647	in the service of one attached to	cos(44*2πi/129) + isin(44*2πi/129)	-0.54157 +0.84065i
122.82	122:49'24	85	29	29-leaconjunct	29-♌☌		1F924	downplaying a real want	cos(29*2πi/85) + isin(29*2πi/85)	-0.54205 +0.84034i
122.86	122:51'25	126	43	43-taurisextile	43-♉✳		1F47E	aggressive assertion of identity	cos(43*2πi/126) + isin(43*2πi/126)	-0.54255 +0.84003i
122.93	122:55'36	41	14	14-sajiquintile	14-♐⬠		1F5FD	personas aspired to	cos(14*2πi/41) + isin(14*2πi/41)	-0.54357 +0.83937i
123.00	123:0'0	120	41	41-gemiinconjunct	41-♊ヌ		1F922	more vulnerable to things	cos(41*2πi/120) + isin(41*2πi/120)	-0.54464 +0.83867i
123.04	123:2'16	79	27	27-virgiseptile	27-♍ア		270A	anti-establishment revolutionary	cos(27*2πi/79) + isin(27*2πi/79)	-0.54519 +0.83831i
123.08	123:4'36	117	40	40-geminovile	40-♊N		1F48E	best friend's quality	cos(40*2πi/117) + isin(40*2πi/117)	-0.54576 +0.83794i
123.16	123:9'28	38	13	13-sajiopposition	13-♐☍		1F64C	use of the body or physical deeds in work	cos(13*2πi/38) + isin(13*2πi/38)	-0.54695 +0.83717i
123.24	123:14'35	111	38	38-gemitrine	38-♊△		1F973	around high-expression groups	cos(38*2πi/111) + isin(38*2πi/111)	-0.54819 +0.83635i
123.29	123:17'15	73	25	25-virgiconjunct	25-♍☌		2692	new or deep investment in job	cos(25*2πi/73) + isin(25*2πi/73)	-0.54884 +0.83593i
123.33	123:19'59	108	37	37-cancriinconjunct	37-♋ヌ		1F31D	why close friends come around	cos(37*2πi/108) + isin(37*2πi/108)	-0.54951 +0.83549i
123.36	123:21'23	143	49	49-ariundecile	49-♈U		1F4E3	broadcasting which gets one talked about	cos(49*2πi/143) + isin(49*2πi/143)	-0.54985 +0.83526i

123.43	123:25'42	35	12	12-capriundecile	12-♑U		1F47D	quirky distinguishing uniqueness	cos(12*2π/35) + isin(12*2π/35)	-0.5509 +0.83457i
123.53	123:31'45	102	35	35-cancrisextile	35-♋*		1F4BC	boss figure attributes	cos(35*2π/102) + isin(35*2π/102)	-0.55236 +0.8336i
123.58	123:34'55	67	23	23-libriseptile	23-♎七		1F63B	getting others to fall in love w oneself	cos(23*2π/67) + isin(23*2π/67)	-0.55313 +0.83309i
123.64	123:38'10	99	34	34-cancritrine	34-♋△		1F645	communication-stifling	cos(34*2π/99) + isin(34*2π/99)	-0.55392 +0.83257i
123.66	123:39'50	131	45	45-tauriundecile	45-♉U		1F611	with doubt in associations	cos(45*2π/131) + isin(45*2π/131)	-0.55432 +0.8323i
123.75	123:45'0	32	11	11-caprioctile	11-♑⊿		1F5FB	an indomitable characteristic	cos(11*2π/32) + isin(11*2π/32)	-0.55557 +0.83147i
123.84	123:50'24	125	43	43-tauriquintile	43-♉⬠		1F39F	social clique's requirements	cos(43*2π/125) + isin(43*2π/125)	-0.55688 +0.8306i
123.87	123:52'15	93	32	32-leanovile	32-♌N		1F60D	brought out by creative, sexualized energy	cos(32*2π/93) + isin(32*2π/93)	-0.55732 +0.83029i
123.93	123:56'3	61	21	21-libriconjunct	21-♎☌		1F526	singled out for attention	cos(21*2π/61) + isin(21*2π/61)	-0.55824 +0.82968i
124.00	124:0'0	90	31	31-leasextile	31-♌*		1F6B8	absorptions by one's children	cos(31*2π/90) + isin(31*2π/90)	-0.55919 +0.82904i
124.03	124:2'1	119	41	41-gemiundecile	41-♊U		1F4C9	weakened by opinionation, better as ambient	cos(41*2π/119) + isin(41*2π/119)	-0.55968 +0.82871i
124.14	124:8'16	29	10	10-capriquintile	10-♑⬠		1F3A9	proud charisma	cos(10*2π/29) + isin(10*2π/29)	-0.56119 +0.82769i
124.23	124:13'31	142	49	49-aridecile	49-♈⊥		1F549	blessings others can only dream of	cos(49*2π/142) + isin(49*2π/142)	-0.56245 +0.82683i
124.29	124:17'8	84	29	29-virgiinconjunct	29-♍π		1F411	traits for the seemingly weak	cos(29*2π/84) + isin(29*2π/84)	-0.56332 +0.82624i
124.32	124:18'59	139	48	48-ariseptile	48-♈七		1F3AF	creative perfectionism	cos(48*2π/139) + isin(48*2π/139)	-0.56376 +0.82594i
124.36	124:21'49	55	19	19-scorpiseptile	19-♏七		1F632	shocking or flooding others w information	cos(19*2π/55) + isin(19*2π/55)	-0.56444 +0.82547i
124.44	124:26'39	81	28	28-virginovile	28-♍N		1F451	mastered early, forms broad social identity	cos(28*2π/81) + isin(28*2π/81)	-0.56561 +0.82468i
124.49	124:29'9	107	37	37-cancriundecile	37-♋U		1F481	essence of a great conversation w/ one	cos(37*2π/107) + isin(37*2π/107)	-0.5662 +0.82426i
124.51	124:30'40	133	46	46-ariconjunct	46-♈☌		1F49D	during sex or when flirting	cos(46*2π/133) + isin(46*2π/133)	-0.56657 +0.82401i
124.62	124:36'55	26	9	9-capriopposition	9-♑☍		1F3B8	why one's fans follow them	cos(9*2π/26) + isin(9*2π/26)	-0.56806 +0.82298i
124.72	124:43'27	127	44	44-tauriseptile	44-♉七		1F4B8	that which attracts unfair advantage	cos(44*2π/127) + isin(44*2π/127)	-0.56963 +0.8219i
124.80	124:47'59	75	26	26-virgitrine	26-♍△		1F3E1	family home maintenance	cos(26*2π/75) + isin(26*2π/75)	-0.57071 +0.82115i
124.84	124:50'19	124	43	43-taurisquare	43-♉□		1F387	initial, then waning impression	cos(43*2π/124) + isin(43*2π/124)	-0.57127 +0.82076i
124.90	124:53'52	49	17	17-scorpiconjunct	17-♏☌		1F399	having known public influence	cos(17*2π/49) + isin(17*2π/49)	-0.57212 +0.82017i
125.00	125:0'0	72	25	25-libriinconjunct	25-♎π		2753	a problem to be solved	cos(25*2π/72) + isin(25*2π/72)	-0.57358 +0.81915i
125.08	125:5'5	118	41	41-gemidecile	41-♊⊥		1F3C3	staying with it as long as encouraged	cos(41*2π/118) + isin(41*2π/118)	-0.57479 +0.8183i
125.11	125:6'22	141	49	49-arinovile	49-♈N		1F489	easy instillment in others	cos(49*2π/141) + isin(49*2π/141)	-0.5751 +0.81809i
125.22	125:13'2	23	8	8-aquariundecile	8-♒U		1F991	unusual social trait, liked by eccentrics	cos(8*2π/23) + isin(8*2π/23)	-0.57668 +0.81697i
125.33	125:19'59	135	47	47-aritrine	47-♈△		1F3C4	easy and prolific	cos(47*2π/135) + isin(47*2π/135)	-0.57833 +0.8158i

125.39	125:23'35	89	31	31-leaquintile	31-♌○		1F48B	sensuality & body expression	cos(31*2πi/89) + isin(31*2πi/89)	-0.57919 +0.8152i
125.45	125:27'16	66	23	23-librisextile	23-♎﹡		1F57A	broadcastable good spirits	cos(23*2πi/66) + isin(23*2πi/66)	-0.58006 +0.81458i
125.50	125:30'16	109	38	38-gemiconjunct	38-♊☌		1F44E	diminishing others' importance	cos(38*2πi/109) + isin(38*2πi/109)	-0.58077 +0.81407i
125.58	125:34'53	43	15	15-sajiseptile	15-♐七		1F0CF	through jokes, games, and fun	cos(15*2πi/43) + isin(15*2πi/43)	-0.58186 +0.81329i
125.66	125:39'37	106	37	37-cancridecile	37-♋⊥		1F3A0	others think one has more power than one has	cos(37*2πi/106) + isin(37*2πi/106)	-0.58298 +0.81249i
125.71	125:42'51	63	22	22-libritrine	22-♎△		1F6A8	know-it-all	cos(22*2πi/63) + isin(22*2πi/63)	-0.58374 +0.81194i
125.78	125:46'59	83	29	29-virgiundecile	29-♍U		26A1	high-tension activity in surroundings	cos(29*2πi/83) + isin(29*2πi/83)	-0.58472 +0.81124i
125.83	125:49'30	103	36	36-cancriseptile	36-♋七		1F60A	basking in joy	cos(36*2πi/103) + isin(36*2πi/103)	-0.58531 +0.81081i
125.87	125:52'26	143	50	50-ariundecile	50-♈U		1F4E3	broadcasting which gets one talked about	cos(50*2πi/143) + isin(50*2πi/143)	-0.58601 +0.81031i
126.00	126:0'0	20	7	7-aquarioctile	7-♒⚹		1F93A	kicking the butt of outsiders	cos(7*2πi/20) + isin(7*2πi/20)	-0.58779 +0.80902i
126.13	126:7'52	137	48	48-ariquintile	48-♈○		1F6A7	singular active, direct, control	cos(48*2πi/137) + isin(48*2πi/137)	-0.58964 +0.80767i
126.19	126:11'8	97	34	34-cancriconjunct	34-♋☌		1F495	traits reserved for those very close	cos(34*2πi/97) + isin(34*2πi/97)	-0.5904 +0.80711i
126.23	126:14'1	77	27	27-virgiquintile	27-♍○		1F422	guarded insistence	cos(27*2πi/77) + isin(27*2πi/77)	-0.59108 +0.80661i
126.27	126:16'7	134	47	47-ariopposition	47-♈☍		1F49F	a trait the partner MUST have	cos(47*2πi/134) + isin(47*2πi/134)	-0.59157 +0.80625i
126.32	126:18'56	57	20	20-scorpinovile	20-♏ℕ		1FA84	arrives whenever one wants it, no asking	cos(20*2πi/57) + isin(20*2πi/57)	-0.59224 +0.80577i
126.38	126:22'58	94	33	33-leadecile	33-♌⊥		1F463	helps in others after learning the hard way	cos(33*2πi/94) + isin(33*2πi/94)	-0.59318 +0.80507i
126.41	126:24'43	131	46	46-tauriundecile	46-♉U		1F611	with doubt in associations	cos(46*2πi/131) + isin(46*2πi/131)	-0.59359 +0.80477i
126.49	126:29'11	37	13	13-sajiconjunct	13-♐☌		2B50	trusted ability revealed	cos(13*2πi/37) + isin(13*2πi/37)	-0.59463 +0.804i
126.59	126:35'36	91	32	32-leaseptile	32-♌七		1F576	smoothly comfortable	cos(32*2πi/91) + isin(32*2πi/91)	-0.59613 +0.80289i
126.67	126:40'0	54	19	19-scorpisextile	19-♏﹡		1F378	self-fulfillment tool	cos(19*2πi/54) + isin(19*2πi/54)	-0.59716 +0.80212i
126.72	126:43'11	125	44	44-tauriquintile	44-♉○		1F39F	social clique's requirements	cos(44*2πi/125) + isin(44*2πi/125)	-0.5979 +0.80157i
126.76	126:45'38	71	25	25-libriundecile	25-♎U		26C5	thriving amidst confusion	cos(25*2πi/71) + isin(25*2πi/71)	-0.59847 +0.80114i
126.82	126:49'5	88	31	31-leasquare	31-♌□		1F479	suppressing power imbalance	cos(31*2πi/88) + isin(31*2πi/88)	-0.59928 +0.80054i
126.89	126:53'6	122	43	43-tauriopposition	43-♉☍		1F913	easily annoying to others	cos(43*2πi/122) + isin(43*2πi/122)	-0.60021 +0.79984i
126.91	126:54'23	139	49	49-ariseptile	49-♈七		1F3AF	creative perfectionism	cos(49*2πi/139) + isin(49*2πi/139)	-0.60051 +0.79962i
127.06	127:3'31	17	6	6-aquariquintile	6-♒○		1F44A	managing by dominating	cos(6*2πi/17) + isin(6*2πi/17)	-0.60263 +0.79802i
127.24	127:14'28	116	41	41-gemioctile	41-♊⚹		1F612	having been slighted or doubted	cos(41*2πi/116) + isin(41*2πi/116)	-0.60517 +0.79609i
127.27	127:16'21	99	35	35-cancritrine	35-♋△		1F645	communication-stifling	cos(35*2πi/99) + isin(35*2πi/99)	-0.60561 +0.79576i
127.32	127:19'1	82	29	29-virgidecile	29-♍⊥		1F987	eccentrically attention-getting, disquieting	cos(29*2πi/82) + isin(29*2πi/82)	-0.60623 +0.79529i

127.38	127:23'4	65	23	23-libriquintile	23-♎⬠		1F6C0	self-resparking	cos(23*2πi/65) + isin(23*2πi/65)	-0.60716 +0.79458i
127.43	127:26'1	113	40	40-gemiquintile	40-♊♎		1F60E	publicly-labeled vibe given	cos(40*2πi/113) + isin(40*2πi/113)	-0.60784 +0.79406i
127.50	127:30'0	48	17	17-sajiinconjunct	17-♐♈		1F305	shown through creative setting	cos(17*2πi/48) + isin(17*2πi/48)	-0.60876 +0.79335i
127.59	127:35'41	79	28	28-virgiseptile	28-♍七		270A	anti-establishment revolutionary	cos(28*2πi/79) + isin(28*2πi/79)	-0.61008 +0.79234i
127.64	127:38'10	110	39	39-gemiopposition	39-♊☍		1F6A5	managing others' behavior	cos(39*2πi/110) + isin(39*2πi/110)	-0.61065 +0.7919i
127.66	127:39'34	141	50	50-arinovile	50-♈N		1F489	easy instillment in others	cos(50*2πi/141) + isin(50*2πi/141)	-0.61097 +0.79165i
127.74	127:44'30	31	11	11-capriseptile	11-♑七		1F3A2	expressed by one's social network	cos(11*2πi/31) + isin(11*2πi/31)	-0.61211 +0.79078i
127.83	127:49'33	138	49	49-arisextile	49-♈✳		26D1	daily work focus	cos(49*2πi/138) + isin(49*2πi/138)	-0.61327 +0.78988i
127.89	127:53'41	76	27	27-virgisquare	27-♍□		1F3D8	seen by friends' friends & family	cos(27*2πi/76) + isin(27*2πi/76)	-0.61421 +0.78914i
127.93	127:56'1	121	43	43-tauriconjunct	43-♉☌		1F4B0	prosperity & status-seeking	cos(43*2πi/121) + isin(43*2πi/121)	-0.61475 +0.78872i
128.00	128:0'0	45	16	16-sajinovile	16-♐N		2766	shared experience as a token of friendship	cos(16*2πi/45) + isin(16*2πi/45)	-0.61566 +0.78801i
128.08	128:4'36	104	37	37-cancrioctile	37-♋⊿		1F61B	trait known and accepted among friends	cos(37*2πi/104) + isin(37*2πi/104)	-0.61672 +0.78718i
128.14	128:8'8	59	21	21-scorpiundecile	21-♏U		1F447	having one's pick	cos(21*2πi/59) + isin(21*2πi/59)	-0.61752 +0.78655i
128.18	128:10'54	132	47	47-tauriinconjunct	47-♉♈		1F517	sharing a special bond w/ a friend	cos(47*2πi/132) + isin(47*2πi/132)	-0.61816 +0.78605i
128.22	128:13'9	73	26	26-virgiconjunct	26-♍☌		2692	new or deep investment in job	cos(26*2πi/73) + isin(26*2πi/73)	-0.61867 +0.78565i
128.28	128:16'33	87	31	31-leatrine	31-♌△		2763	interactor inspired to want	cos(31*2πi/87) + isin(31*2πi/87)	-0.61945 +0.78504i
128.35	128:20'52	115	41	41-gemiseptile	41-♊七		1F933	inner world with self-talk	cos(41*2πi/115) + isin(41*2πi/115)	-0.62043 +0.78426i
128.39	128:23'29	143	51	51-ariundecile	51-♈U		1F4E3	broadcasting which gets one talked about	cos(51*2πi/143) + isin(51*2πi/143)	-0.62103 +0.78378i
128.57	128:34'17	14	5	5-aquaropposition	5-♒☍		1F443	a sense from one's company	cos(5*2πi/14) + isin(5*2πi/14)	-0.62349 +0.78183i
128.78	128:46'49	123	44	44-tauritrine	44-♉△		238F	others must express or draw out	cos(44*2πi/123) + isin(44*2πi/123)	-0.62634 +0.77955i
128.84	128:50'31	95	34	34-leaundecile	34-♌U		265B	the image of a progress-inspiring master	cos(34*2πi/95) + isin(34*2πi/95)	-0.62718 +0.77888i
128.89	128:53'19	81	29	29-virginovile	29-♍N		1F451	mastered early, forms broad social identity	cos(29*2πi/81) + isin(29*2πi/81)	-0.62781 +0.77836i
129.00	129:0'0	120	43	43-gemiinconjunct	43-♊♈		1F922	more vulnerable to things	cos(43*2πi/120) + isin(43*2πi/120)	-0.62932 +0.77715i
129.06	129:3'23	53	19	19-scorpiquintile	19-♏♎		1F917	reasons one is desired	cos(19*2πi/53) + isin(19*2πi/53)	-0.63009 +0.77652i
129.13	129:7'49	92	33	33-leaoctile	33-♌⊿		1F37B	regular comfort preferences w/ close one	cos(33*2πi/92) + isin(33*2πi/92)	-0.63109 +0.77571i
129.16	129:9'37	131	47	47-tauriundecile	47-♉U		1F611	with doubt in associations	cos(47*2πi/131) + isin(47*2πi/131)	-0.63149 +0.77538i
129.23	129:13'50	39	14	14-sajitrine	14-♐△		1F3DD	convincing others of one's value	cos(14*2πi/39) + isin(14*2πi/39)	-0.63245 +0.7746i
129.30	129:17'44	142	51	51-aridecile	51-♈⊥		1F549	blessings others can only dream of	cos(51*2πi/142) + isin(51*2πi/142)	-0.63332 +0.77389i
129.32	129:19'13	103	37	37-cancriseptile	37-♋七		1F60A	basking in joy	cos(37*2πi/103) + isin(37*2πi/103)	-0.63366 +0.77361i

129.38	129:22'30	64	23	23-librisquare	23-♎□	众	4F17	amidst a noisy setting	cos(23*2π/64) + isin(23*2π/64)	-0.63439 +0.77301i
129.44	129:26'17	89	32	32-leaquintile	32-♌⚹		1F48B	sensuality & body expression	cos(32*2π/89) + isin(32*2π/89)	-0.63525 +0.77231i
129.50	129:29'47	139	50	50-ariseptile	50-♈七		1F3AF	creative perfectionism	cos(50*2π/139) + isin(50*2π/139)	-0.63603 +0.77166i
129.60	129:35'59	25	9	9-capriconjunct	9-♑☌		1F3DF	rally & tune the mass psychology	cos(9*2π/25) + isin(9*2π/25)	-0.63742 +0.77051i
129.73	129:43'47	111	40	40-gemitrine	40-♊△		1F973	around high-expression groups	cos(40*2π/111) + isin(40*2π/111)	-0.63917 +0.76907i
129.77	129:46'2	86	31	31-leaopposition	31-♌☍		1F921	one's commentary offends egos	cos(31*2π/86) + isin(31*2π/86)	-0.63967 +0.76865i
129.84	129:50'9	61	22	22-libriconjunct	22-♎☌		1F526	singled out for attention	cos(22*2π/61) + isin(22*2π/61)	-0.64059 +0.76788i
129.90	129:53'48	97	35	35-cancriconjunct	35-♋☌		1F495	traits reserved for those very close	cos(35*2π/97) + isin(35*2π/97)	-0.64141 +0.7672i
129.92	129:55'29	133	48	48-ariconjunct	48-♈☌		1F49D	during sex or when flirting	cos(48*2π/133) + isin(48*2π/133)	-0.64178 +0.76689i
130.00	130:0'0	36	13	13-capriinconjunct	13-♑π		1F3BB	downplayed want or talent	cos(13*2π/36) + isin(13*2π/36)	-0.64279 +0.76604i
130.08	130:5'2	119	43	43-gemiundecile	43-♊U		1F4C9	weakened by opinionation, better as ambient	cos(43*2π/119) + isin(43*2π/119)	-0.64391 +0.7651i
130.12	130:7'13	83	30	30-virgiundecile	30-♍U	⚡	26A1	high-tension activity in surroundings	cos(30*2π/83) + isin(30*2π/83)	-0.6444 +0.76469i
130.15	130:9'13	130	47	47-tauridecile	47-♉⊥		1F3AA	relied upon by others in the talked topic	cos(47*2π/130) + isin(47*2π/130)	-0.64484 +0.76432i
130.21	130:12'45	47	17	17-sajiundecile	17-♐U	☪	262B	a core, lived principle	cos(17*2π/47) + isin(17*2π/47)	-0.64563 +0.76365i
130.29	130:17'8	105	38	38-cancrinovile	38-♋N		1F5EF	when irritated to see standards defied	cos(38*2π/105) + isin(38*2π/105)	-0.6466 +0.76283i
130.34	130:20'41	58	21	21-scorpidecile	21-♏⊥		1F47B	interactions with an ethereal party	cos(21*2π/58) + isin(21*2π/58)	-0.64739 +0.76216i
130.39	130:23'37	127	46	46-tauriseptile	46-♉七		1F4B8	that which attracts unfair advantage	cos(46*2π/127) + isin(46*2π/127)	-0.64804 +0.76161i
130.43	130:26'5	69	25	25-librinovile	25-♎N		1F418	subtle, strong draw of trait via socialization	cos(25*2π/69) + isin(25*2π/69)	-0.64858 +0.76114i
130.50	130:30'0	80	29	29-virgioctile	29-♍⚹		1F939	vividly remembered by one's children	cos(29*2π/80) + isin(29*2π/80)	-0.64945 +0.76041i
130.55	130:32'58	91	33	33-leaseptile	33-♌七		1F576	smoothly comfortable	cos(33*2π/91) + isin(33*2π/91)	-0.6501 +0.75985i
130.59	130:35'17	102	37	37-cancrisextile	37-♋⚹		1F4BC	boss figure attributes	cos(37*2π/102) + isin(37*2π/102)	-0.65062 +0.7594i
130.65	130:38'42	124	45	45-taurisquare	45-♉□		1F387	initial, then waning impression	cos(45*2π/124) + isin(45*2π/124)	-0.65137 +0.75876i
130.67	130:39'59	135	49	49-aritrine	49-♈△		1F3C4	easy and prolific	cos(49*2π/135) + isin(49*2π/135)	-0.65166 +0.75851i
130.91	130:54'32	11	4	undecile	U₄		1F5EB	getting talked about	cos(1*2π/11) + isin(1*2π/11)	-0.65486 +0.75575i
131.14	131:8'34	140	51	51-arioctile	51-♈⚹		1F340	helped by a benefactor	cos(51*2π/140) + isin(51*2π/140)	-0.65794 +0.75307i
131.19	131:11'11	118	43	43-gemidecile	43-♊⊥		1F3C3	staying with it as long as encouraged	cos(43*2π/118) + isin(43*2π/118)	-0.65851 +0.75257i
131.25	131:15'0	96	35	35-leainconjunct	35-♌π		1F937	what "not enough" looks like	cos(35*2π/96) + isin(35*2π/96)	-0.65935 +0.75184i
131.29	131:17'38	85	31	31-leaconjunct	31-♌☌		1F924	downplaying a real want	cos(31*2π/85) + isin(31*2π/85)	-0.65992 +0.75133i
131.39	131:23'12	137	50	50-ariquintile	50-♈⚹		1F6A7	singular active, direct, control	cos(50*2π/137) + isin(50*2π/137)	-0.66114 +0.75026i

131.43	131:25'42	63	23	23-libritrine	23-♎△		1F6A8	know-it-all	cos(23*2πi/63) + isin(23*2πi/63)	-0.66169 +0.74978i
131.48	131:28'41	115	42	42-gemiseptile	42-♊♄		1F933	inner world with self-talk	cos(42*2πi/115) + isin(42*2πi/115)	-0.66234 +0.74921i
131.54	131:32'18	52	19	19-scorpisquare	19-♏□		1F61E	falling short	cos(19*2πi/52) + isin(19*2πi/52)	-0.66312 +0.74851i
131.64	131:38'30	134	49	49-ariopposition	49-♈☍		1F49F	a trait the partner MUST have	cos(49*2πi/134) + isin(49*2πi/134)	-0.66447 +0.74731i
131.71	131:42'26	41	15	15-sajiquintile	15-♐⚹		1F5FD	personas aspired to	cos(15*2πi/41) + isin(15*2πi/41)	-0.66533 +0.74655i
131.79	131:47'8	112	41	41-gemisquare	41-♊□		1F38E	one's trait observed by outsiders	cos(41*2πi/112) + isin(41*2πi/112)	-0.66635 +0.74564i
131.83	131:49'51	71	26	26-libriundecile	26-♎U		26C5	thriving amidst confusion	cos(26*2πi/71) + isin(26*2πi/71)	-0.66694 +0.74512i
131.88	131:52'52	101	37	37-cancriquintile	37-♋⚹		1F624	disregard for things heard	cos(37*2πi/101) + isin(37*2πi/101)	-0.66759 +0.74453i
131.91	131:54'30	131	48	48-tauriundecile	48-♉U		1F611	with doubt in associations	cos(48*2πi/131) + isin(48*2πi/131)	-0.66794 +0.74421i
132.00	132:0'0	30	11	11-caprisextile	11-♑✳		1F487	response to one's body reception	cos(11*2πi/30) + isin(11*2πi/30)	-0.66913 +0.74314i
132.09	132:5'10	139	51	51-ariseptile	51-♈♄		1F3AF	creative perfectionism	cos(51*2πi/139) + isin(51*2πi/139)	-0.67025 +0.74214i
132.11	132:6'36	109	40	40-gemiconjunct	40-♊☌		1F44E	diminishing others' importance	cos(40*2πi/109) + isin(40*2πi/109)	-0.67056 +0.74186i
132.19	132:11'15	128	47	47-taurioctile	47-♉⊿		1F478	intuitive comfort even amidst stress	cos(47*2πi/128) + isin(47*2πi/128)	-0.67156 +0.74095i
132.24	132:14'41	49	18	18-scorpiconjunct	18-♏☌		1F399	having known public influence	cos(18*2πi/49) + isin(18*2πi/49)	-0.6723 +0.74028i
132.31	132:18'27	117	43	43-geminovile	43-♊N		1F48E	best friend's quality	cos(43*2πi/117) + isin(43*2πi/117)	-0.67311 +0.73954i
132.35	132:21'10	68	25	25-librioctile	25-♎⊿		1F462	appearance of dominating	cos(25*2πi/68) + isin(25*2πi/68)	-0.6737 +0.73901i
132.41	132:24'49	87	32	32-leatrine	32-♌△		2763	interactor inspired to want	cos(32*2πi/87) + isin(32*2πi/87)	-0.67448 +0.73829i
132.48	132:28'47	125	46	46-tauriquintile	46-♉⚹		1F39F	social clique's requirements	cos(46*2πi/125) + isin(46*2πi/125)	-0.67533 +0.73751i
132.50	132:30'0	144	53	53-ariinconjunct	53-♈π		1F501	always-on trait	cos(53*2πi/144) + isin(53*2πi/144)	-0.67559 +0.73728i
132.63	132:37'53	19	7	7-aquariseptile	7-♒♄		1F510	gateway to one's friendship	cos(7*2πi/19) + isin(7*2πi/19)	-0.67728 +0.73572i
132.79	132:47'12	122	45	45-tauriopposition	45-♉☍		1F913	easily annoying to others	cos(45*2πi/122) + isin(45*2πi/122)	-0.67927 +0.73389i
132.82	132:48'55	103	38	38-cancriseptile	38-♋♄		1F60A	basking in joy	cos(38*2πi/103) + isin(38*2πi/103)	-0.67964 +0.73355i
132.86	132:51'25	84	31	31-virgiinconjunct	31-♍π		1F411	traits for the seemingly weak	cos(31*2πi/84) + isin(31*2πi/84)	-0.68017 +0.73305i
132.92	132:55'23	65	24	24-libriquintile	24-♎⚹		1F6C0	self-resparking	cos(24*2πi/65) + isin(24*2πi/65)	-0.68102 +0.73227i
132.97	132:58'22	111	41	41-gemitrine	41-♊△		1F973	around high-expression groups	cos(41*2πi/111) + isin(41*2πi/111)	-0.68165 +0.73168i
133.04	133:2'36	46	17	17-sajidecile	17-♐⊥		1F4CE	trait housed by key colleagues	cos(17*2πi/46) + isin(17*2πi/46)	-0.68255 +0.73084i
133.11	133:6'33	119	44	44-gemiundecile	44-♊U		1F4C9	weakened by opinionation, better as ambient	cos(44*2πi/119) + isin(44*2πi/119)	-0.68339 +0.73005i
133.20	133:11'59	100	37	37-cancrisquare	37-♋□		1F6CB	home & family life	cos(37*2πi/100) + isin(37*2πi/100)	-0.68455 +0.72897i
133.23	133:13'42	127	47	47-tauriseptile	47-♉♄		1F4B8	that which attracts unfair advantage	cos(47*2πi/127) + isin(47*2πi/127)	-0.68491 +0.72863i

133.33	133:20'0	27	10	10-capritrine	10-♑△	🎓	1F393	intellectualizing and insight	cos(10*2π/27) + isin(10*2π/27)	-0.68624 +0.72737i
133.43	133:25'35	143	53	53-ariundecile	53-♈U	📣	1F4E3	broadcasting which gets one talked about	cos(53*2π/143) + isin(53*2π/143)	-0.68742 +0.72626i
133.48	133:28'59	89	33	33-leaquintile	33-♌⬠	👋	1F48B	sensuality & body expression	cos(33*2π/89) + isin(33*2π/89)	-0.68814 +0.72558i
133.55	133:32'54	62	23	23-libriopposition	23-♎☍	🏴	1F3F4	manipulative ambition	cos(23*2π/62) + isin(23*2π/62)	-0.68897 +0.72479i
133.64	133:38'10	132	49	49-tauriinconjunct	49-♉⚻	🔗	1F517	sharing a special bond w/ a friend	cos(49*2π/132) + isin(49*2π/132)	-0.69008 +0.72373i
133.71	133:42'51	35	13	13-capriundecile	13-♑U	👽	1F47D	quirky distinguishing uniqueness	cos(13*2π/35) + isin(13*2π/35)	-0.69106 +0.72279i
133.85	133:50'46	78	29	29-virgisextile	29-♍✳	🥊	1F94A	fight night moment	cos(29*2π/78) + isin(29*2π/78)	-0.69272 +0.7212i
133.88	133:53'3	121	45	45-tauriconjunct	45-♉☌	💰	1F4B0	prosperity & status-seeking	cos(45*2π/121) + isin(45*2π/121)	-0.6932 +0.72074i
133.95	133:57'12	43	16	16-sajiseptile	16-♐七	🃏	1F0CF	through jokes, games, and fun	cos(16*2π/43) + isin(16*2π/43)	-0.69407 +0.7199i
134.04	134:2'33	94	35	35-leadecile	35-♌⊥	👣	1F463	helps in others after learning the hard way	cos(35*2π/94) + isin(35*2π/94)	-0.69519 +0.71882i
134.12	134:7'3	51	19	19-scorpitrine	19-♏△	😚	1F61A	use of persuasive words	cos(19*2π/51) + isin(19*2π/51)	-0.69613 +0.71791i
134.18	134:10'54	110	41	41-gemiopposition	41-♊☍	🚥	1F6A5	managing others' behavior	cos(41*2π/110) + isin(41*2π/110)	-0.69694 +0.71713i
134.24	134:14'14	59	22	22-scorpiundecile	22-♏U	👇	1F447	having one's pick	cos(22*2π/59) + isin(22*2π/59)	-0.69763 +0.71646i
134.29	134:17'8	126	47	47-taurisextile	47-♉✳	👾	1F47E	aggressive assertion of identity	cos(47*2π/126) + isin(47*2π/126)	-0.69824 +0.71587i
134.33	134:19'42	67	25	25-libriseptile	25-♎七	😻	1F63B	getting others to fall in love w oneself	cos(25*2π/67) + isin(25*2π/67)	-0.69877 +0.71535i
134.40	134:24'0	75	28	28-virgitrine	28-♍△	🏡	1F3E1	family home maintenance	cos(28*2π/75) + isin(28*2π/75)	-0.69966 +0.71447i
134.46	134:27'28	83	31	31-virgiundecile	31-♍U	⚡	26A1	high-tension activity in surroundings	cos(31*2π/83) + isin(31*2π/83)	-0.70038 +0.71377i
134.55	134:32'43	99	37	37-cancritrine	37-♋△	🙅	1F645	communication-stifling	cos(37*2π/99) + isin(37*2π/99)	-0.70147 +0.71269i
134.58	134:34'45	107	40	40-cancriundecile	40-♋U	🧏	1F481	essence of a great conversation w/ one	cos(40*2π/107) + isin(40*2π/107)	-0.7019 +0.71228i
134.63	134:38'2	123	46	46-tauritrine	46-♉△	⎏	238F	others must express or draw out	cos(46*2π/123) + isin(46*2π/123)	-0.70258 +0.71161i
134.68	134:40'34	139	52	52-ariseptile	52-♈七	🎯	1F3AF	creative perfectionism	cos(52*2π/139) + isin(52*2π/139)	-0.7031 +0.71109i
135.00	135:0'0	8	3	octile (sesquiquadrate)	⚼ (⊡)	💪	1F4AA	forcing others	cos(1*2π/8) + isin(1*2π/8)	-0.70711 +0.70711i
135.34	135:20'18	133	50	50-ariconjunct	50-♈☌	💝	1F49D	during sex or when flirting	cos(50*2π/133) + isin(50*2π/133)	-0.71127 +0.70292i
135.38	135:23'4	117	44	44-geminovile	44-♊N	💎	1F48E	best friend's quality	cos(44*2π/117) + isin(44*2π/117)	-0.71184 +0.70234i
135.45	135:26'43	101	38	38-cancriquintile	38-♋⬠	🤤	1F624	disregard for things heard	cos(38*2π/101) + isin(38*2π/101)	-0.71258 +0.70159i
135.48	135:29'1	93	35	35-leanovile	35-♌N	😍	1F60D	brought out by creative, sexualized energy	cos(35*2π/93) + isin(35*2π/93)	-0.71305 +0.70111i
135.53	135:31'45	85	32	32-leaconjunct	32-♌☌	🤤	1F924	downplaying a real want	cos(32*2π/85) + isin(32*2π/85)	-0.71361 +0.70054i
135.58	135:35'3	77	29	29-virgiquintile	29-♍⬠	🐢	1F422	guarded insistence	cos(29*2π/77) + isin(29*2π/77)	-0.71428 +0.69986i
135.69	135:41'32	130	49	49-tauridecile	49-♉⊥	🎪	1F3AA	relied upon by others in the talked topic	cos(49*2π/130) + isin(49*2π/130)	-0.7156 +0.69851i

135.74	135:44'15	61	23	23-libriconjunct	23-♎☌		1F526	singled out for attention	$\cos(23*2\pi i/61) + i\sin(23*2\pi i/61)$	-0.71615 +0.69794i
135.79	135:47'22	114	43	43-gemisextile	43-♊✳		1F6F1	other's influence attempts	$\cos(43*2\pi i/114) + i\sin(43*2\pi i/114)$	-0.71678 +0.6973i
135.85	135:50'56	53	20	20-scorpiquintile	20-♏♎		1F917	reasons one is desired	$\cos(20*2\pi i/53) + i\sin(20*2\pi i/53)$	-0.71751 +0.69655i
135.94	135:56'38	143	54	54-ariundecile	54-♈U		1F4E3	broadcasting which gets one talked about	$\cos(54*2\pi i/143) + i\sin(54*2\pi i/143)$	-0.71866 +0.69536i
136.00	136:0'0	45	17	17-sajinovile	17-♐N		2766	shared experience as a token of friendship	$\cos(17*2\pi i/45) + i\sin(17*2\pi i/45)$	-0.71934 +0.69466i
136.10	136:5'51	82	31	31-virgidecile	31-♍⊥		1F987	eccentrically attention-getting, disquieting	$\cos(31*2\pi i/82) + i\sin(31*2\pi i/82)$	-0.72052 +0.69343i
136.13	136:8'4	119	45	45-gemiundecile	45-♊U		1F4C9	weakened by opinionation, better as ambient	$\cos(45*2\pi i/119) + i\sin(45*2\pi i/119)$	-0.72097 +0.69297i
136.22	136:12'58	37	14	14-sajiconjunct	14-♐☌		2B50	trusted ability revealed	$\cos(14*2\pi i/37) + i\sin(14*2\pi i/37)$	-0.72196 +0.69194i
136.29	136:17'8	140	53	53-arioctile	53-♈⊿		1F340	helped by a benefactor	$\cos(53*2\pi i/140) + i\sin(53*2\pi i/140)$	-0.72279 +0.69106i
136.31	136:18'38	103	39	39-cancriseptile	39-♋七		1F60A	basking in joy	$\cos(39*2\pi i/103) + i\sin(39*2\pi i/103)$	-0.7231 +0.69075i
136.36	136:21'49	66	25	25-librisextile	25-♎✳		1F57A	broadcastable good spirits	$\cos(25*2\pi i/66) + i\sin(25*2\pi i/66)$	-0.72373 +0.69008i
136.42	136:25'15	95	36	36-leaundecile	36-♌U		265B	the image of a progress-inspiring master	$\cos(36*2\pi i/95) + i\sin(36*2\pi i/95)$	-0.72443 +0.68935i
136.45	136:27'5	124	47	47-taurisquare	47-♉□		1F387	initial, then waning impression	$\cos(47*2\pi i/124) + i\sin(47*2\pi i/124)$	-0.72479 +0.68897i
136.55	136:33'6	29	11	11-capriquintile	11-♑♎		1F3A9	proud charisma	$\cos(11*2\pi i/29) + i\sin(11*2\pi i/29)$	-0.726 +0.6877i
136.64	136:38'32	137	52	52-ariquintile	52-♈♎		1F6A7	singular active, direct, control	$\cos(52*2\pi i/137) + i\sin(52*2\pi i/137)$	-0.72708 +0.68655i
136.67	136:39'59	108	41	41-cancriinconjunct	41-♋♐		1F31D	why close friends come around	$\cos(41*2\pi i/108) + i\sin(41*2\pi i/108)$	-0.72737 +0.68624i
136.74	136:44'39	129	49	49-taurinovile	49-♉N		1F647	in the service of one attached to	$\cos(49*2\pi i/129) + i\sin(49*2\pi i/129)$	-0.7283 +0.68526i
136.80	136:48'0	50	19	19-scorpiopposition	19-♏☍		1F5BC	images put forth to others	$\cos(19*2\pi i/50) + i\sin(19*2\pi i/50)$	-0.72897 +0.68455i
136.86	136:51'34	121	46	46-tauriconjunct	46-♉☌		1F4B0	prosperity & status-seeking	$\cos(46*2\pi i/121) + i\sin(46*2\pi i/121)$	-0.72968 +0.68379i
136.90	136:54'5	71	27	27-libriundecile	27-♎U		26C5	thriving amidst confusion	$\cos(27*2\pi i/71) + i\sin(27*2\pi i/71)$	-0.73018 +0.68326i
136.99	136:59'28	113	43	43-gemiquintile	43-♊♎		1F60E	publicly-labeled vibe given	$\cos(43*2\pi i/113) + i\sin(43*2\pi i/113)$	-0.73125 +0.68211i
137.01	137:0'53	134	51	51-ariopposition	51-♈☍		1F49F	a trait the partner MUST have	$\cos(51*2\pi i/134) + i\sin(51*2\pi i/134)$	-0.73153 +0.68181i
137.14	137:8'34	21	8	8-aquarinovile	8-♒N		1F483	at peak sexiness, strength, or creativity	$\cos(8*2\pi i/21) + i\sin(8*2\pi i/21)$	-0.73305 +0.68017i
137.29	137:17'17	118	45	45-gemidecile	45-♊⊥		1F3C3	staying with it as long as encouraged	$\cos(45*2\pi i/118) + i\sin(45*2\pi i/118)$	-0.73477 +0.67831i
137.32	137:19'10	97	37	37-cancriconjunct	37-♋☌		1F495	traits reserved for those very close	$\cos(37*2\pi i/97) + i\sin(37*2\pi i/97)$	-0.73515 +0.67791i
137.37	137:22'6	76	29	29-virgisquare	29-♍□		1F3D8	seen by friends' friends & family	$\cos(29*2\pi i/76) + i\sin(29*2\pi i/76)$	-0.73572 +0.67728i
137.40	137:24'16	131	50	50-tauriundecile	50-♉U		1F611	with doubt in associations	$\cos(50*2\pi i/131) + i\sin(50*2\pi i/131)$	-0.73615 +0.67682i
137.50	137:30'0	144	55	55-ariinconjunct	55-♈♐		1F501	always-on trait	$\cos(55*2\pi i/144) + i\sin(55*2\pi i/144)$	-0.73728 +0.67559i
137.53	137:31'41	89	34	34-leaquintile	34-♌♎		1F48B	sensuality & body expression	$\cos(34*2\pi i/89) + i\sin(34*2\pi i/89)$	-0.73761 +0.67523i

137.56	137:33'39	123	47	47-tauritrine	47-♉△	◇	238F	others must express or draw out	cos(47*2πi/123) + isin(47*2πi/123)	-0.738 +0.67481i
137.65	137:38'49	34	13	13-capridecile	13-♑⊥	🏆	1F3C6	potential to be a master or boss	cos(13*2πi/34) + isin(13*2πi/34)	-0.73901 +0.6737i
137.74	137:44'20	115	44	44-gemiseptile	44-♊七	💪	1F933	inner world with self-talk	cos(44*2πi/115) + isin(44*2πi/115)	-0.74009 +0.67251i
137.78	137:46'39	81	31	31-virginovile	31-♍N	👑	1F451	mastered early, forms broad social identity	cos(31*2πi/81) + isin(31*2πi/81)	-0.74054 +0.67201i
137.81	137:48'45	128	49	49-taurioctile	49-♉⊿	👸	1F478	intuitive comfort even amidst stress	cos(49*2πi/128) + isin(49*2πi/128)	-0.74095 +0.67156i
137.87	137:52'20	47	18	18-sajiundecile	18-♐U	☪	262B	a core, lived principle	cos(18*2πi/47) + isin(18*2πi/47)	-0.74165 +0.67078i
137.94	137:56'38	107	41	41-cancriundecile	41-♋U	🛃	1F481	essence of a great conversation w/ one	cos(41*2πi/107) + isin(41*2πi/107)	-0.74249 +0.66986i
138.00	138:0'0	60	23	23-scorpiinconjunct	23-♏♐	🍭	1F4CD	strongest memory left behind	cos(23*2πi/60) + isin(23*2πi/60)	-0.74314 +0.66913i
138.05	138:2'42	133	51	51-ariconjunct	51-♈☌	💝	1F49D	during sex or when flirting	cos(51*2πi/133) + isin(51*2πi/133)	-0.74367 +0.66855i
138.08	138:4'55	73	28	28-virgiconjunct	28-♍☌	⚒	2692	new or deep investment in job	cos(28*2πi/73) + isin(28*2πi/73)	-0.7441 +0.66806i
138.14	138:8'22	86	33	33-leaopposition	33-♌☍	🤡	1F921	one's commentary offends egos	cos(33*2πi/86) + isin(33*2πi/86)	-0.74477 +0.66732i
138.18	138:10'54	99	38	38-cancritrine	38-♋△	🙅	1F645	communication-stifling	cos(38*2πi/99) + isin(38*2πi/99)	-0.74526 +0.66677i
138.24	138:14'24	125	48	48-tauriquintile	48-♉⚹	🎟	1F39F	social clique's requirements	cos(48*2πi/125) + isin(48*2πi/125)	-0.74594 +0.66601i
138.26	138:15'39	138	53	53-arisextile	53-♈⚹	⛑	26D1	daily work focus	cos(53*2πi/138) + isin(53*2πi/138)	-0.74618 +0.66574i
138.46	138:27'41	13	5	5-aquariconjunct	5-♒☌	🎥	1F3A5	public persona	cos(5*2πi/13) + isin(5*2πi/13)	-0.74851 +0.66312i
138.69	138:41'18	122	47	47-tauriopposition	47-♉☍	🤓	1F913	easily annoying to others	cos(47*2πi/122) + isin(47*2πi/122)	-0.75113 +0.66015i
138.75	138:45'0	96	37	37-leainconjunct	37-♌♐	🤷	1F937	what "not enough" looks like	cos(37*2πi/96) + isin(37*2πi/96)	-0.75184 +0.65935i
138.80	138:47'42	83	32	32-virgiundecile	32-♍U	⚡	26A1	high-tension activity in surroundings	cos(32*2πi/83) + isin(32*2πi/83)	-0.75236 +0.65875i
138.90	138:53'51	127	49	49-tauriseptile	49-♉七	💸	1F4B8	that which attracts unfair advantage	cos(49*2πi/127) + isin(49*2πi/127)	-0.75354 +0.65741i
138.95	138:56'50	57	22	22-scorpinovile	22-♏N	🪄	1FA84	arrives whenever one wants it, no asking	cos(22*2πi/57) + isin(22*2πi/57)	-0.75411 +0.65675i
139.01	139:0'35	101	39	39-cancriquintile	39-♋⚹	😤	1F624	disregard for things heard	cos(39*2πi/101) + isin(39*2πi/101)	-0.75482 +0.65593i
139.09	139:5'27	44	17	17-sajioctile	17-♐⊿	🚵	1F6B5	role in a peer group	cos(17*2πi/44) + isin(17*2πi/44)	-0.75575 +0.65486i
139.20	139:11'59	75	29	29-virgitrine	29-♍△	🏡	1F3E1	family home maintenance	cos(29*2πi/75) + isin(29*2πi/75)	-0.757 +0.65342i
139.25	139:14'43	106	41	41-cancridecile	41-♋⊥	🎠	1F3A0	others think one has more power than one has	cos(41*2πi/106) + isin(41*2πi/106)	-0.75751 +0.65282i
139.27	139:16'12	137	53	53-ariquintile	53-♈⚹	🚧	1F6A7	singular active, direct, control	cos(53*2πi/137) + isin(53*2πi/137)	-0.75779 +0.65249i
139.35	139:21'17	31	12	12-capriseptile	12-♑七	🎢	1F3A2	expressed by one's social network	cos(12*2πi/31) + isin(12*2πi/31)	-0.75876 +0.65137i
139.44	139:26'11	142	55	55-aridecile	55-♈⊥	🕉	1F549	blessings others can only dream of	cos(55*2πi/142) + isin(55*2πi/142)	-0.75969 +0.65029i
139.50	139:30'0	80	31	31-virgioctile	31-♍⊿	🤹	1F939	vividly remembered by one's children	cos(31*2πi/80) + isin(31*2πi/80)	-0.76041 +0.64945i
139.53	139:32'5	129	50	50-taurinovile	50-♉N	🙇	1F647	in the service of one attached to	cos(50*2πi/129) + isin(50*2πi/129)	-0.7608 +0.64898i

139.59	139:35'30	49	19	19-scorpiconjunct	19-♏☌	🎙	1F399	having known public influence	cos(19*2πi/49) + isin(19*2πi/49)	-0.76145 +0.64823i
139.66	139:39'18	116	45	45-gemioctile	45-♊⊿	😒	1F612	having been slighted or doubted	cos(45*2πi/116) + isin(45*2πi/116)	-0.76216 +0.64739i
139.70	139:42'5	67	26	26-libriseptile	26-♎七	😻	1F63B	getting others to fall in love w oneself	cos(26*2πi/67) + isin(26*2πi/67)	-0.76269 +0.64677i
139.76	139:45'52	85	33	33-leaconjunct	33-♌☌	🤤	1F924	downplaying a real want	cos(33*2πi/85) + isin(33*2πi/85)	-0.7634 +0.64593i
139.83	139:50'4	121	47	47-tauriconjunct	47-♉☌	💰	1F4B0	prosperity & status-seeking	cos(47*2πi/121) + isin(47*2πi/121)	-0.76419 +0.64499i
139.86	139:51'22	139	54	54-ariseptile	54-♈七	🎯	1F3AF	creative perfectionism	cos(54*2πi/139) + isin(54*2πi/139)	-0.76443 +0.64471i
140.00	140:0'0	18	7	7-aquarisextile	7-♒✳	🗄	1F5C4	long term rational interactions	cos(7*2πi/18) + isin(7*2πi/18)	-0.76604 +0.64279i
140.18	140:10'37	113	44	44-gemiquintile	44-♊⬠	😎	1F60E	publicly-labeled vibe given	cos(44*2πi/113) + isin(44*2πi/113)	-0.76803 +0.64042i
140.21	140:12'37	95	37	37-leaundecile	37-♌U	♛	265B	the image of a progress-inspiring master	cos(37*2πi/95) + isin(37*2πi/95)	-0.7684 +0.63997i
140.29	140:17'38	136	53	53-arisquare	53-♈□	🧐	1F9D0	serious, sober-minded interactant	cos(53*2πi/136) + isin(53*2πi/136)	-0.76933 +0.63885i
140.34	140:20'20	59	23	23-scorpiundecile	23-♏U	👇	1F447	having one's pick	cos(23*2πi/59) + isin(23*2πi/59)	-0.76983 +0.63824i
140.40	140:24'0	100	39	39-cancrisquare	39-♋□	🛋	1F6CB	home & family life	cos(39*2πi/100) + isin(39*2πi/100)	-0.77051 +0.63742i
140.43	140:25'31	141	55	55-arinovile	55-♈N	💉	1F489	easy instillment in others	cos(55*2πi/141) + isin(55*2πi/141)	-0.7708 +0.63708i
140.49	140:29'16	41	16	16-sajiquintile	16-♐⬠	🗽	1F5FD	personas aspired to	cos(16*2πi/41) + isin(16*2πi/41)	-0.77149 +0.63624i
140.57	140:34'17	105	41	41-cancrinovile	41-♋N	🗯	1F5EF	when irritated to see standards defied	cos(41*2πi/105) + isin(41*2πi/105)	-0.77242 +0.63512i
140.63	140:37'30	64	25	25-librisquare	25-♎□	众	4F17	amidst a noisy setting	cos(25*2πi/64) + isin(25*2πi/64)	-0.77301 +0.63439i
140.69	140:41'22	87	34	34-leatrine	34-♌△	❣	2763	interactor inspired to want	cos(34*2πi/87) + isin(34*2πi/87)	-0.77373 +0.63352i
140.73	140:43'38	110	43	43-gemiopposition	43-♊☍	🚥	1F6A5	managing others' behavior	cos(43*2πi/110) + isin(43*2πi/110)	-0.77414 +0.63301i
140.75	140:45'6	133	52	52-ariconjunct	52-♈☌	💝	1F49D	during sex or when flirting	cos(52*2πi/133) + isin(52*2πi/133)	-0.77441 +0.63268i
140.87	140:52'10	23	9	9-aquariundecile	9-♒U	🦑	1F991	unusual social trait, liked by eccentrics	cos(9*2πi/23) + isin(9*2πi/23)	-0.77571 +0.63109i
140.98	140:58'44	143	56	56-ariundecile	56-♈U	📣	1F4E3	broadcasting which gets one talked about	cos(56*2πi/143) + isin(56*2πi/143)	-0.77692 +0.6296i
141.03	141:1'51	97	38	38-cancriconjunct	38-♋☌	💕	1F495	traits reserved for those very close	cos(38*2πi/97) + isin(38*2πi/97)	-0.77749 +0.6289i
141.08	141:4'51	74	29	29-virgiopposition	29-♍☍	😦	1F626	social stressors	cos(29*2πi/74) + isin(29*2πi/74)	-0.77804 +0.62822i
141.12	141:7'12	125	49	49-tauriquintile	49-♉⬠	🎟	1F39F	social clique's requirements	cos(49*2πi/125) + isin(49*2πi/125)	-0.77846 +0.62769i
141.18	141:10'35	51	20	20-scorpitrine	20-♏△	😚	1F61A	use of persuasive words	cos(20*2πi/51) + isin(20*2πi/51)	-0.77908 +0.62692i
141.23	141:13'50	130	51	51-tauridecile	51-♉⊥	🎪	1F3AA	relied upon by others in the talked topic	cos(51*2πi/130) + isin(51*2πi/130)	-0.77967 +0.62619i
141.27	141:15'56	79	31	31-virgiseptile	31-♍七	✊	270A	anti-establishment revolutionary	cos(31*2πi/79) + isin(31*2πi/79)	-0.78006 +0.62571i
141.33	141:20'0	135	53	53-aritrine	53-♈△	🏄	1F3C4	easy and prolific	cos(53*2πi/135) + isin(53*2πi/135)	-0.78079 +0.62479i
141.43	141:25'42	28	11	11-caprisquare	11-♑□	🖌	1F58C	arts and creativity drawn to	cos(11*2πi/28) + isin(11*2πi/28)	-0.78183 +0.62349i

							Unicode	Description	Formula	Value
141.54	141:32'18	117	46	46-geminovile	46-♊N		1F48E	best friend's quality	cos(46*2π/117) + isin(46*2π/117)	-0.78303 +0.62199i
141.57	141:34'22	89	35	35-leaquintile	35-♌♎		1F48B	sensuality & body expression	cos(35*2π/89) + isin(35*2π/89)	-0.7834 +0.62152i
141.64	141:38'21	61	24	24-libriconjunct	24-♎☌		1F526	singled out for attention	cos(24*2π/61) + isin(24*2π/61)	-0.78412 +0.62061i
141.73	141:43'56	127	50	50-tauriseptile	50-♉七		1F4B8	that which attracts unfair advantage	cos(50*2π/127) + isin(50*2π/127)	-0.78513 +0.61934i
141.82	141:49'5	33	13	13-caprinovile	13-♑N		1F4FB	in a formal group discussion	cos(13*2π/33) + isin(13*2π/33)	-0.78605 +0.61816i
141.90	141:53'52	137	54	54-ariquintile	54-♈♎		1F6A7	singular active, direct, control	cos(54*2π/137) + isin(54*2π/137)	-0.78691 +0.61707i
141.92	141:55'23	104	41	41-cancrioctile	41-♋⊿		1F61B	trait known and accepted among friends	cos(41*2π/104) + isin(41*2π/104)	-0.78718 +0.61672i
141.97	141:58'18	71	28	28-libriundecile	28-♎U		26C5	thriving amidst confusion	cos(28*2π/71) + isin(28*2π/71)	-0.78771 +0.61605i
142.02	142:1'6	109	43	43-gemiconjunct	43-♊☌		1F44E	diminishing others' importance	cos(43*2π/109) + isin(43*2π/109)	-0.78821 +0.61541i
142.11	142:6'18	38	15	15-sajiopposition	15-♐☍		1F64C	use of the body or physical deeds in work	cos(15*2π/38) + isin(15*2π/38)	-0.78914 +0.61421i
142.18	142:11'5	119	47	47-gemiundecile	47-♊U		1F4C9	weakened by opinionation, better as ambient	cos(47*2π/119) + isin(47*2π/119)	-0.78999 +0.61312i
142.22	142:13'20	81	32	32-virginovile	32-♍N		1F451	mastered early, forms broad social identity	cos(32*2π/81) + isin(32*2π/81)	-0.79039 +0.6126i
142.26	142:15'29	124	49	49-taurisquare	49-♉□		1F387	initial, then waning impression	cos(49*2π/124) + isin(49*2π/124)	-0.79078 +0.61211i
142.33	142:19'32	43	17	17-sajiseptile	17-♐七		1F0CF	through jokes, games, and fun	cos(17*2π/43) + isin(17*2π/43)	-0.7915 +0.61117i
142.39	142:23'17	134	53	53-ariopposition	53-♈☍		1F49F	a trait the partner MUST have	cos(53*2π/134) + isin(53*2π/134)	-0.79216 +0.61031i
142.45	142:26'45	139	55	55-ariseptile	55-♈七		1F3AF	creative perfectionism	cos(55*2π/139) + isin(55*2π/139)	-0.79278 +0.60951i
142.50	142:30'0	48	19	19-sajiinconjunct	19-♐π		1F305	shown through creative setting	cos(19*2π/48) + isin(19*2π/48)	-0.79335 +0.60876i
142.57	142:34'27	101	40	40-cancriquintile	40-♋♎		1F624	disregard for things heard	cos(40*2π/101) + isin(40*2π/101)	-0.79414 +0.60773i
142.64	142:38'29	53	21	21-scorpiquintile	21-♏♎		1F917	reasons one is desired	cos(21*2π/53) + isin(21*2π/53)	-0.79485 +0.6068i
142.70	142:42'9	111	44	44-gemitrine	44-♊△		1F973	around high-expression groups	cos(44*2π/111) + isin(44*2π/111)	-0.7955 +0.60595i
142.76	142:45'31	58	23	23-scorpidecile	23-♏⊥		1F47B	interactions with an ethereal party	cos(23*2π/58) + isin(23*2π/58)	-0.79609 +0.60517i
142.81	142:48'35	121	48	48-tauriconjunct	48-♉☌		1F4B0	prosperity & status-seeking	cos(48*2π/121) + isin(48*2π/121)	-0.79663 +0.60446i
142.86	142:51'25	63	25	25-libritrine	25-♎△		1F6A8	know-it-all	cos(25*2π/63) + isin(25*2π/63)	-0.79713 +0.6038i
142.94	142:56'28	68	27	27-librioctile	27-♎⊿		1F462	appearance of dominating	cos(27*2π/68) + isin(27*2π/68)	-0.79802 +0.60263i
142.98	142:58'43	141	56	56-arinovile	56-♈N		1F489	easy instillment in others	cos(56*2π/141) + isin(56*2π/141)	-0.79841 +0.60211i
143.01	143:0'49	73	29	29-virgiconjunct	29-♍☌		2692	new or deep investment in job	cos(29*2π/73) + isin(29*2π/73)	-0.79878 +0.60162i
143.08	143:4'36	78	31	31-virgisextile	31-♍✳		1F94A	fight night moment	cos(31*2π/78) + isin(31*2π/78)	-0.79944 +0.60074i
143.13	143:7'57	83	33	33-virgiundecile	33-♍U		26A1	high-tension activity in surroundings	cos(33*2π/83) + isin(33*2π/83)	-0.80003 +0.59997i
143.18	143:10'54	88	35	35-leasquare	35-♌□		1F479	suppressing power imbalance	cos(35*2π/88) + isin(35*2π/88)	-0.80054 +0.59928i

143.23	143:13'32	93	37	37-leanovile	37-♌N		1F60D	brought out by creative, sexualized energy	cos(37*2πi/93) + isin(37*2πi/93)	-0.801 +0.59866i
143.27	143:15'55	98	39	39-cancriopposition	39-♋☍		1F31F	social advancement catalyst	cos(39*2πi/98) + isin(39*2πi/98)	-0.80141 +0.59811i
143.33	143:20'0	108	43	43-cancriinconjunct	43-♋π		1F31D	why close friends come around	cos(43*2πi/108) + isin(43*2πi/108)	-0.80212 +0.59716i
143.39	143:23'23	118	47	47-gemidecile	47-♊⊥		1F3C3	staying with it as long as encouraged	cos(47*2πi/118) + isin(47*2πi/118)	-0.80271 +0.59637i
143.44	143:26'15	128	51	51-taurioctile	51-♉⊿		1F478	intuitive comfort even amidst stress	cos(51*2πi/128) + isin(51*2πi/128)	-0.80321 +0.5957i
143.48	143:28'41	138	55	55-arisextile	55-♈✳		26D1	daily work focus	cos(55*2πi/138) + isin(55*2πi/138)	-0.80363 +0.59513i
143.50	143:29'47	143	57	57-ariundecile	57-♈U		1F4E3	broadcasting which gets one talked about	cos(57*2πi/143) + isin(57*2πi/143)	-0.80382 +0.59487i
144.00	144:0'0	5	2	quintile	⚿₂		1F60F	ego expression	cos(1*2πi/5) + isin(1*2πi/5)	-0.80902 +0.58779i
144.53	144:31'31	137	55	55-ariquintile	55-♈⚿		1F6A7	singular active, direct, control	cos(55*2πi/137) + isin(55*2πi/137)	-0.81437 +0.58034i
144.59	144:35'24	122	49	49-tauriopposition	49-♉☍		1F913	easily annoying to others	cos(49*2πi/122) + isin(49*2πi/122)	-0.81503 +0.57942i
144.64	144:38'34	112	45	45-gemisquare	45-♊□		1F38E	one's trait observed by outsiders	cos(45*2πi/112) + isin(45*2πi/112)	-0.81556 +0.57867i
144.67	144:40'22	107	43	43-cancriundecile	43-♋U		1F481	essence of a great conversation w/ one	cos(43*2πi/107) + isin(43*2πi/107)	-0.81586 +0.57824i
144.74	144:44'32	97	39	39-cancriconjunct	39-♋☌		1F495	traits reserved for those very close	cos(39*2πi/97) + isin(39*2πi/97)	-0.81656 +0.57726i
144.78	144:46'57	92	37	37-leaoctile	37-♌⊿		1F37B	regular comfort preferences w/ close one	cos(37*2πi/92) + isin(37*2πi/92)	-0.81697 +0.57668i
144.83	144:49'39	87	35	35-leatrine	35-♌△		2763	interactor inspired to want	cos(35*2πi/87) + isin(35*2πi/87)	-0.81742 +0.57604i
144.88	144:52'40	82	33	33-virgidecile	33-♍⊥		1F987	eccentrically attention-getting, disquieting	cos(33*2πi/82) + isin(33*2πi/82)	-0.81793 +0.57532i
144.94	144:56'6	77	31	31-virgiquintile	31-♍⚿		1F422	guarded insistence	cos(31*2πi/77) + isin(31*2πi/77)	-0.8185 +0.5745i
145.00	145:0'0	72	29	29-libriinconjunct	29-♎π		2753	a problem to be solved	cos(29*2πi/72) + isin(29*2πi/72)	-0.81915 +0.57358i
145.04	145:2'9	139	56	56-ariseptile	56-♈七		1F3AF	creative perfectionism	cos(56*2πi/139) + isin(56*2πi/139)	-0.81951 +0.57306i
145.07	145:4'28	67	27	27-libriseptile	27-♎七		1F63B	getting others to fall in love w oneself	cos(27*2πi/67) + isin(27*2πi/67)	-0.8199 +0.57251i
145.12	145:6'58	129	52	52-taurinovile	52-♉N		1F647	in the service of one attached to	cos(52*2πi/129) + isin(52*2πi/129)	-0.82031 +0.57191i
145.16	145:9'40	62	25	25-libriopposition	25-♎☍		1F3F4	manipulative ambition	cos(25*2πi/62) + isin(25*2πi/62)	-0.82076 +0.57127i
145.21	145:12'36	119	48	48-gemiundecile	48-♊U		1F4C9	weakened by opinionation, better as ambient	cos(48*2πi/119) + isin(48*2πi/119)	-0.82125 +0.57057i
145.26	145:15'47	57	23	23-scorpinovile	23-♏N		1FA84	arrives whenever one wants it, no asking	cos(23*2πi/57) + isin(23*2πi/57)	-0.82178 +0.56981i
145.32	145:19'15	109	44	44-gemiconjunct	44-♊☌		1F44E	diminishing others' importance	cos(44*2πi/109) + isin(44*2πi/109)	-0.82235 +0.56898i
145.38	145:23'4	52	21	21-scorpisquare	21-♏□		1F61E	falling short	cos(21*2πi/52) + isin(21*2πi/52)	-0.82298 +0.56806i
145.45	145:27'16	99	40	40-cancritrine	40-♋△		1F645	communication-stifling	cos(40*2πi/99) + isin(40*2πi/99)	-0.82368 +0.56706i
145.53	145:31'54	47	19	19-sajiundecile	19-♐U		262B	a core, lived principle	cos(19*2πi/47) + isin(19*2πi/47)	-0.82444 +0.56595i
145.59	145:35'17	136	55	55-arisquare	55-♈□		1F9D0	serious, sober-minded interactant	cos(55*2πi/136) + isin(55*2πi/136)	-0.825 +0.56514i

145.65	145:38'55	131	53	53-tauriundecile	53-♉∪		1F611	with doubt in associations	cos(53*2πi/131) + isin(53*2πi/131)	-0.82559 +0.56426i
145.71	145:42'51	42	17	17-sajisextile	17-♐⚹		1F497	instilled in co-creative partners	cos(17*2πi/42) + isin(17*2πi/42)	-0.82624 +0.56332i
145.79	145:47'6	121	49	49-tauriconjunct	49-♉☌		1F4B0	prosperity & status-seeking	cos(49*2πi/121) + isin(49*2πi/121)	-0.82693 +0.5623i
145.82	145:49'22	79	32	32-virgiseptile	32-♍七		270A	anti-establishment revolutionary	cos(32*2πi/79) + isin(32*2πi/79)	-0.8273 +0.56175i
145.86	145:51'43	116	47	47-gemioctile	47-♊△		1F612	having been slighted or doubted	cos(47*2πi/116) + isin(47*2πi/116)	-0.82769 +0.56119i
145.95	145:56'45	37	15	15-sajiconjunct	15-♐☌		2B50	trusted ability revealed	cos(15*2πi/37) + isin(15*2πi/37)	-0.82851 +0.55997i
146.04	146:2'15	106	43	43-cancridecile	43-♋⊥		1F3A0	others think one has more power than one has	cos(43*2πi/106) + isin(43*2πi/106)	-0.82941 +0.55865i
146.09	146:5'13	69	28	28-librinovile	28-♎N		1F418	subtle, strong draw of trait via socialization	cos(28*2πi/69) + isin(28*2πi/69)	-0.82989 +0.55793i
146.14	146:8'19	101	41	41-cancriquintile	41-♋⬠		1F624	disregard for things heard	cos(41*2πi/101) + isin(41*2πi/101)	-0.83039 +0.55719i
146.17	146:9'55	133	54	54-ariconjunct	54-♈☌		1F49D	during sex or when flirting	cos(54*2πi/133) + isin(54*2πi/133)	-0.83065 +0.5568i
146.25	146:15'0	32	13	13-caprioctile	13-♑△		1F5FB	an indomitable characteristic	cos(13*2πi/32) + isin(13*2πi/32)	-0.83147 +0.55557i
146.34	146:20'29	123	50	50-tauritrine	50-♉△		238F	others must express or draw out	cos(50*2πi/123) + isin(50*2πi/123)	-0.83236 +0.55424i
146.37	146:22'25	91	37	37-leaseptile	37-♌七		1F576	smoothly comfortable	cos(37*2πi/91) + isin(37*2πi/91)	-0.83267 +0.55377i
146.44	146:26'26	59	24	24-scorpiundecile	24-♏∪		1F447	having one's pick	cos(24*2πi/59) + isin(24*2πi/59)	-0.83331 +0.5528i
146.55	146:32'55	113	46	46-gemiquintile	46-♊⬠		1F60E	publicly-labeled vibe given	cos(46*2πi/113) + isin(46*2πi/113)	-0.83435 +0.55123i
146.57	146:34'17	140	57	57-arioctile	57-♈△		1F340	helped by a benefactor	cos(57*2πi/140) + isin(57*2πi/140)	-0.83457 +0.5509i
146.67	146:39'59	27	11	11-capritrine	11-♑△		1F393	intellectualizing and insight	cos(11*2πi/27) + isin(11*2πi/27)	-0.83549 +0.54951i
146.80	146:47'46	103	42	42-cancriseptile	42-♋七		1F60A	basking in joy	cos(42*2πi/103) + isin(42*2πi/103)	-0.83673 +0.54762i
146.84	146:50'31	76	31	31-virgisquare	31-♍□		1F3D8	seen by friends' friends & family	cos(31*2πi/76) + isin(31*2πi/76)	-0.83717 +0.54695i
146.88	146:52'47	125	51	51-tauriquintile	51-♉⬠		1F39F	social clique's requirements	cos(51*2πi/125) + isin(51*2πi/125)	-0.83753 +0.54639i
146.94	146:56'19	49	20	20-scorpiconjunct	20-♏☌		1F399	having known public influence	cos(20*2πi/49) + isin(20*2πi/49)	-0.83809 +0.54553i
147.00	147:0'0	120	49	49-gemiinconjunct	49-♊⚻		1F922	more vulnerable to things	cos(49*2πi/120) + isin(49*2πi/120)	-0.83867 +0.54464i
147.04	147:2'32	71	29	29-libriundecile	29-♎∪		26C5	thriving amidst confusion	cos(29*2πi/71) + isin(29*2πi/71)	-0.83907 +0.54402i
147.10	147:5'48	93	38	38-leanovile	38-♌N		1F60D	brought out by creative, sexualized energy	cos(38*2πi/93) + isin(38*2πi/93)	-0.83959 +0.54322i
147.13	147:7'49	115	47	47-gemiseptile	47-♊七		1F933	inner world with self-talk	cos(47*2πi/115) + isin(47*2πi/115)	-0.83991 +0.54273i
147.15	147:9'11	137	56	56-ariquintile	56-♈⬠		1F6A7	singular active, direct, control	cos(56*2πi/137) + isin(56*2πi/137)	-0.84012 +0.54239i
147.27	147:16'21	22	9	9-aquaridecile	9-♒⊥		1F6E6	in command of one's field	cos(9*2πi/22) + isin(9*2πi/22)	-0.84125 +0.54064i
147.43	147:25'42	105	43	43-cancrinovile	43-♋N		1F5EF	when irritated to see standards defied	cos(43*2πi/105) + isin(43*2πi/105)	-0.84272 +0.53835i
147.50	147:30'0	144	59	59-ariinconjunct	59-♈⚻		1F501	always-on trait	cos(59*2πi/144) + isin(59*2πi/144)	-0.84339 +0.5373i

147.54	147:32'27	61	25	25-libriconjunct	25-♎☌		1F526	singled out for attention	cos(25*2πi/61) + isin(25*2πi/61)	-0.84378 +0.5367i
147.60	147:35'59	100	41	41-cancrisquare	41-♋□		1F6CB	home & family life	cos(41*2πi/100) + isin(41*2πi/100)	-0.84433 +0.53583i
147.63	147:37'33	139	57	57-ariseptile	57-♈七		1F3AF	creative perfectionism	cos(57*2πi/139) + isin(57*2πi/139)	-0.84457 +0.53545i
147.69	147:41'32	39	16	16-sajitrine	16-♐△		1F3DD	convincing others of one's value	cos(16*2πi/39) + isin(16*2πi/39)	-0.84519 +0.53447i
147.79	147:47'22	95	39	39-leaundecile	39-♌U		265B	the image of a progress-inspiring master	cos(39*2πi/95) + isin(39*2πi/95)	-0.8461 +0.53303i
147.86	147:51'25	56	23	23-scorpioctile	23-♏⊿		1F608	for fun or one's own power	cos(23*2πi/56) + isin(23*2πi/56)	-0.84672 +0.53203i
147.95	147:56'42	73	30	30-virgiconjunct	30-♍☌		2692	new or deep investment in job	cos(30*2πi/73) + isin(30*2πi/73)	-0.84754 +0.53073i
148.00	148:0'0	90	37	37-leasextile	37-♌✳		1F6B8	absorptions by one's children	cos(37*2πi/90) + isin(37*2πi/90)	-0.84805 +0.52992i
148.04	148:2'14	107	44	44-cancriundecile	44-♋U		1F481	essence of a great conversation w/ one	cos(44*2πi/107) + isin(44*2πi/107)	-0.84839 +0.52937i
148.09	148:5'6	141	58	58-arinovile	58-♈N		1F489	easy instillment in others	cos(58*2πi/141) + isin(58*2πi/141)	-0.84883 +0.52866i
148.24	148:14'7	17	7	7-aquariquintile	7-♒⬠		1F44A	managing by dominating	cos(7*2πi/17) + isin(7*2πi/17)	-0.85022 +0.52643i
148.40	148:23'49	131	54	54-tauriundecile	54-♉U		1F611	with doubt in associations	cos(54*2πi/131) + isin(54*2πi/131)	-0.8517 +0.52403i
148.42	148:25'15	114	47	47-gemisextile	47-♊✳		1F6F1	other's influence attempts	cos(47*2πi/114) + isin(47*2πi/114)	-0.85192 +0.52367i
148.50	148:30'0	80	33	33-virgioctile	33-♍⊿		1F939	vividly remembered by one's children	cos(33*2πi/80) + isin(33*2πi/80)	-0.85264 +0.5225i
148.53	148:31'53	143	59	59-ariundecile	59-♈U		1F4E3	broadcasting which gets one talked about	cos(59*2πi/143) + isin(59*2πi/143)	-0.85293 +0.52203i
148.57	148:34'17	63	26	26-libritrine	26-♎△		1F6A8	know-it-all	cos(26*2πi/63) + isin(26*2πi/63)	-0.85329 +0.52144i
148.62	148:37'25	109	45	45-gemiconjunct	45-♊☌		1F44E	diminishing others' importance	cos(45*2πi/109) + isin(45*2πi/109)	-0.85377 +0.52065i
148.70	148:41'44	46	19	19-sajidecile	19-♐⊥		1F4CE	trait housed by key colleagues	cos(19*2πi/46) + isin(19*2πi/46)	-0.85442 +0.51958i
148.80	148:48'0	75	31	31-virgitrine	31-♍△		1F3E1	family home maintenance	cos(31*2πi/75) + isin(31*2πi/75)	-0.85536 +0.51803i
148.85	148:50'46	104	43	43-cancrioctile	43-♋⊿		1F61B	trait known and accepted among friends	cos(43*2πi/104) + isin(43*2πi/104)	-0.85578 +0.51734i
148.87	148:52'19	133	55	55-ariconjunct	55-♈☌		1F49D	during sex or when flirting	cos(55*2πi/133) + isin(55*2πi/133)	-0.85602 +0.51695i
148.97	148:57'55	29	12	12-capriquintile	12-♑⬠		1F3A9	proud charisma	cos(12*2πi/29) + isin(12*2πi/29)	-0.85686 +0.51555i
149.09	149:5'27	99	41	41-cancritrine	41-♋△		1F645	communication-stifling	cos(41*2πi/99) + isin(41*2πi/99)	-0.85798 +0.51368i
149.14	149:8'34	70	29	29-libridecile	29-♎⊥		1F527	used to strengthen or repair bonds	cos(29*2πi/70) + isin(29*2πi/70)	-0.85845 +0.5129i
149.19	149:11'21	111	46	46-gemitrine	46-♊△		1F973	around high-expression groups	cos(46*2πi/111) + isin(46*2πi/111)	-0.85886 +0.5122i
149.27	149:16'5	41	17	17-sajiquintile	17-♐⬠		1F5FD	personas aspired to	cos(17*2πi/41) + isin(17*2πi/41)	-0.85957 +0.51102i
149.33	149:20'0	135	56	56-aritrine	56-♈△		1F3C4	easy and prolific	cos(56*2πi/135) + isin(56*2πi/135)	-0.86015 +0.51004i
149.36	149:21'42	94	39	39-leadecile	39-♌⊥		1F463	helps in others after learning the hard way	cos(39*2πi/94) + isin(39*2πi/94)	-0.8604 +0.50962i
149.43	149:26'2	53	22	22-scorpiquintile	22-♏⬠		1F917	reasons one is desired	cos(22*2πi/53) + isin(22*2πi/53)	-0.86104 +0.50853i

149.49	149:29'29	118	49	49-gemidecile	49-Ⅱ⊥	1F3C3	staying with it as long as encouraged	cos(49*2π/118) + isin(49*2π/118)	-0.86155 +0.50767i
149.54	149:32'18	65	27	27-libriquintile	27-♎△	1F6C0	self-resparking	cos(27*2π/65) + isin(27*2π/65)	-0.86197 +0.50696i
149.58	149:34'38	142	59	59-aridecile	59-♈⊥	1F549	blessings others can only dream of	cos(59*2π/142) + isin(59*2π/142)	-0.86231 +0.50637i
149.61	149:36'37	77	32	32-virgiquintile	32-♍△	1F422	guarded insistence	cos(32*2π/77) + isin(32*2π/77)	-0.86261 +0.50588i
149.66	149:39'46	89	37	37-leaquintile	37-♌△	1F48B	sensuality & body expression	cos(37*2π/89) + isin(37*2π/89)	-0.86307 +0.50509i
149.73	149:44'4	113	47	47-gemiquintile	47-Ⅱ△	1F60E	publicly-labeled vibe given	cos(47*2π/113) + isin(47*2π/113)	-0.8637 +0.50401i
149.78	149:46'51	137	57	57-ariquintile	57-♈△	1F6A7	singular active, direct, control	cos(57*2π/137) + isin(57*2π/137)	-0.86411 +0.50331i
150.00	150:0'0	12	5	inconjunct (quincunx)	⊼	2601	vibes around you	cos(1*2π/12) + isin(1*2π/12)	-0.86603 +0.5i
150.24	150:14'10	127	53	53-tauriseptile	53-♉七	1F4B8	that which attracts unfair advantage	cos(53*2π/127) + isin(53*2π/127)	-0.86808 +0.49643i
150.29	150:17'28	103	43	43-cancriseptile	43-♋七	1F60A	basking in joy	cos(43*2π/103) + isin(43*2π/103)	-0.86856 +0.49559i
150.33	150:19'46	91	38	38-leaseptile	38-♌七	1F576	smoothly comfortable	cos(38*2π/91) + isin(38*2π/91)	-0.86889 +0.49501i
150.38	150:22'47	79	33	33-virgiseptile	33-♍七	270A	anti-establishment revolutionary	cos(33*2π/79) + isin(33*2π/79)	-0.86932 +0.49425i
150.45	150:26'51	67	28	28-libriseptile	28-♎七	1F63B	getting others to fall in love w oneself	cos(28*2π/67) + isin(28*2π/67)	-0.86991 +0.49322i
150.49	150:29'30	122	51	51-tauriopposition	51-♉☍	1F913	easily annoying to others	cos(51*2π/122) + isin(51*2π/122)	-0.87029 +0.49255i
150.55	150:32'43	55	23	23-scorpiseptile	23-♏七	1F632	shocking or flooding others w information	cos(23*2π/55) + isin(23*2π/55)	-0.87075 +0.49173i
150.64	150:38'17	141	59	59-arinovile	59-♈N	1F489	easy instillment in others	cos(59*2π/141) + isin(59*2π/141)	-0.87154 +0.49032i
150.70	150:41'51	43	18	18-sajiseptile	18-♐七	1F0CF	through jokes, games, and fun	cos(18*2π/43) + isin(18*2π/43)	-0.87205 +0.48942i
150.77	150:46'9	117	49	49-geminovile	49-ⅡN	1F48E	best friend's quality	cos(49*2π/117) + isin(49*2π/117)	-0.87266 +0.48833i
150.81	150:48'38	74	31	31-virgiopposition	31-♍☍	1F626	social stressors	cos(31*2π/74) + isin(31*2π/74)	-0.87301 +0.48769i
150.88	150:52'56	136	57	57-arisquare	57-♈□	1F9D0	serious, sober-minded interactant	cos(57*2π/136) + isin(57*2π/136)	-0.87362 +0.4866i
150.97	150:58'3	31	13	13-capriseptile	13-♑七	1F3A2	expressed by one's social network	cos(13*2π/31) + isin(13*2π/31)	-0.87435 +0.4853i
151.05	151:2'56	143	60	60-ariundecile	60-♈U	1F4E3	broadcasting which gets one talked about	cos(60*2π/143) + isin(60*2π/143)	-0.87503 +0.48406i
151.07	151:4'17	112	47	47-gemisquare	47-Ⅱ□	1F38E	one's trait observed by outsiders	cos(47*2π/112) + isin(47*2π/112)	-0.87522 +0.48372i
151.15	151:8'42	131	55	55-tauriundecile	55-♉U	1F611	with doubt in associations	cos(55*2π/131) + isin(55*2π/131)	-0.87584 +0.48259i
151.20	151:11'59	50	21	21-scorpiopposition	21-♏☍	1F5BC	images put forth to others	cos(21*2π/50) + isin(21*2π/50)	-0.87631 +0.48175i
151.26	151:15'37	119	50	50-gemiundecile	50-ⅡU	1F4C9	weakened by opinionation, better as ambient	cos(50*2π/119) + isin(50*2π/119)	-0.87681 +0.48083i
151.30	151:18'15	69	29	29-librinovile	29-♎N	1F418	subtle, strong draw of trait via socialization	cos(29*2π/69) + isin(29*2π/69)	-0.87718 +0.48016i
151.36	151:21'49	88	37	37-leasquare	37-♌□	1F479	suppressing power imbalance	cos(37*2π/88) + isin(37*2π/88)	-0.87768 +0.47925i
151.43	151:25'42	126	53	53-taurisextile	53-♉✳	1F47E	aggressive assertion of identity	cos(53*2π/126) + isin(53*2π/126)	-0.87822 +0.47825i

151.58	151:34'44	19	8	8-aquariseptile	8-♒七		1F510	gateway to one's friendship	$\cos(8*2\pi/19) + i\sin(8*2\pi/19)$	-0.87947 +0.47595i
151.74	151:44'7	121	51	51-tauriconjunct	51-♉☌		1F4B0	prosperity & status-seeking	$\cos(51*2\pi/121) + i\sin(51*2\pi/121)$	-0.88077 +0.47354i
151.76	151:45'52	102	43	43-cancrisextile	43-♋*		1F4BC	boss figure attributes	$\cos(43*2\pi/102) + i\sin(43*2\pi/102)$	-0.88101 +0.47309i
151.81	151:48'26	83	35	35-virgiundecile	35-♍U		26A1	high-tension activity in surroundings	$\cos(35*2\pi/83) + i\sin(35*2\pi/83)$	-0.88136 +0.47244i
151.88	151:52'30	64	27	27-librisquare	27-♎□		4F17	amidst a noisy setting	$\cos(27*2\pi/64) + i\sin(27*2\pi/64)$	-0.88192 +0.4714i
151.93	151:55'35	109	46	46-gemiconjunct	46-♊☌		1F44E	diminishing others' importance	$\cos(46*2\pi/109) + i\sin(46*2\pi/109)$	-0.88235 +0.4706i
152.00	152:0'0	45	19	19-sajinovile	19-♐N		2766	shared experience as a token of friendship	$\cos(19*2\pi/45) + i\sin(19*2\pi/45)$	-0.88295 +0.46947i
152.07	152:4'8	116	49	49-gemioctile	49-♊⦜		1F612	having been slighted or doubted	$\cos(49*2\pi/116) + i\sin(49*2\pi/116)$	-0.88351 +0.46841i
152.11	152:6'45	71	30	30-libriundecile	30-♎U		26C5	thriving amidst confusion	$\cos(30*2\pi/71) + i\sin(30*2\pi/71)$	-0.88387 +0.46773i
152.20	152:11'42	123	52	52-tauritrine	52-♉△		238F	others must express or draw out	$\cos(52*2\pi/123) + i\sin(52*2\pi/123)$	-0.88454 +0.46646i
152.31	152:18'27	26	11	11-capriopposition	11-♑☍		1F3B8	why one's fans follow them	$\cos(11*2\pi/26) + i\sin(11*2\pi/26)$	-0.88546 +0.46472i
152.43	152:25'56	111	47	47-gemitrine	47-♊△		1F973	around high-expression groups	$\cos(47*2\pi/111) + i\sin(47*2\pi/111)$	-0.88647 +0.46279i
152.50	152:30'0	144	61	61-ariinconjunct	61-♈π		1F501	always-on trait	$\cos(61*2\pi/144) + i\sin(61*2\pi/144)$	-0.88701 +0.46175i
152.54	152:32'32	59	25	25-scorpiundecile	25-♏U		1F447	having one's pick	$\cos(25*2\pi/59) + i\sin(25*2\pi/59)$	-0.88735 +0.46109i
152.64	152:38'23	125	53	53-tauriquintile	53-♉⌂		1F39F	social clique's requirements	$\cos(53*2\pi/125) + i\sin(53*2\pi/125)$	-0.88814 +0.45958i
152.73	152:43'38	33	14	14-caprinovile	14-♑N		1F4FB	in a formal group discussion	$\cos(14*2\pi/33) + i\sin(14*2\pi/33)$	-0.88884 +0.45823i
152.83	152:49'48	106	45	45-cancridecile	45-♋⊥		1F3A0	others think one has more power than one has	$\cos(45*2\pi/106) + i\sin(45*2\pi/106)$	-0.88966 +0.45663i
152.88	152:52'36	73	31	31-virgiconjunct	31-♍☌		2692	new or deep investment in job	$\cos(31*2\pi/73) + i\sin(31*2\pi/73)$	-0.89003 +0.45591i
152.92	152:55'13	113	48	48-gemiquintile	48-♊⌂		1F60E	publicly-labeled vibe given	$\cos(48*2\pi/113) + i\sin(48*2\pi/113)$	-0.89037 +0.45523i
153.00	153:0'0	40	17	17-sajisquare	17-♐□		1F66A	future missable partnership duty	$\cos(17*2\pi/40) + i\sin(17*2\pi/40)$	-0.89101 +0.45399i
153.07	153:4'15	127	54	54-tauriseptile	54-♉七		1F4B8	that which attracts unfair advantage	$\cos(54*2\pi/127) + i\sin(54*2\pi/127)$	-0.89157 +0.45289i
153.13	153:8'3	134	57	57-ariopposition	57-♈☍		1F49F	a trait the partner MUST have	$\cos(57*2\pi/134) + i\sin(57*2\pi/134)$	-0.89207 +0.4519i
153.19	153:11'29	47	20	20-sajiundecile	20-♐U		262B	a core, lived principle	$\cos(20*2\pi/47) + i\sin(20*2\pi/47)$	-0.89252 +0.45101i
153.27	153:16'2	101	43	43-cancriquintile	43-♋⌂		1F624	disregard for things heard	$\cos(43*2\pi/101) + i\sin(43*2\pi/101)$	-0.89312 +0.44983i
153.33	153:20'0	54	23	23-scorpisextile	23-♏*		1F378	self-fulfillment tool	$\cos(23*2\pi/54) + i\sin(23*2\pi/54)$	-0.89363 +0.4488i
153.39	153:23'28	115	49	49-gemiseptile	49-♊七		1F933	inner world with self-talk	$\cos(49*2\pi/115) + i\sin(49*2\pi/115)$	-0.89409 +0.44789i
153.44	153:26'33	61	26	26-libriconjunct	26-♎☌		1F526	singled out for attention	$\cos(26*2\pi/61) + i\sin(26*2\pi/61)$	-0.89449 +0.44709i
153.49	153:29'18	129	55	55-taurinovile	55-♉N		1F647	in the service of one attached to	$\cos(55*2\pi/129) + i\sin(55*2\pi/129)$	-0.89484 +0.44638i
153.53	153:31'45	68	29	29-librioctile	29-♎⦜		1F462	appearance of dominating	$\cos(29*2\pi/68) + i\sin(29*2\pi/68)$	-0.89516 +0.44574i

153.60	153:35'59	75	32	32-virgitrine	32-♍△		1F3E1	family home maintenance	cos(32*2πi/75) + isin(32*2πi/75)	-0.89571 +0.44464i
153.66	153:39'30	82	35	35-virgidecile	35-♍⊥		1F987	eccentrically attention-getting, disquieting	cos(35*2πi/82) + isin(35*2πi/82)	-0.89617 +0.44372i
153.75	153:45'0	96	41	41-leainconjunct	41-♌π		1F937	what "not enough" looks like	cos(41*2πi/96) + isin(41*2πi/96)	-0.89687 +0.44229i
153.79	153:47'11	103	44	44-cancriseptile	44-♋七		1F60A	basking in joy	cos(44*2πi/103) + isin(44*2πi/103)	-0.89715 +0.44172i
153.85	153:50'46	117	50	50-geminovile	50-♊N		1F48E	best friend's quality	cos(50*2πi/117) + isin(50*2πi/117)	-0.89761 +0.44078i
153.89	153:53'35	131	56	56-tauriundecile	56-♉U		1F611	with doubt in associations	cos(56*2πi/131) + isin(56*2πi/131)	-0.89797 +0.44005i
153.91	153:54'46	138	59	59-arisextile	59-♈*		26D1	daily work focus	cos(59*2πi/138) + isin(59*2πi/138)	-0.89813 +0.43973i
154.29	154:17'8	7	3	septile	七₃		1F5E3	basic communication pattern	cos(1*2πi/7) + isin(1*2πi/7)	-0.90097 +0.43388i
154.65	154:38'52	142	61	61-aridecile	61-♈⊥		1F549	blessings others can only dream of	cos(61*2πi/142) + isin(61*2πi/142)	-0.90369 +0.42818i
154.69	154:41'15	128	55	55-taurioctile	55-♉◿		1F478	intuitive comfort even amidst stress	cos(55*2πi/128) + isin(55*2πi/128)	-0.90399 +0.42756i
154.74	154:44'12	114	49	49-gemisextile	49-♊*		1F6F1	other's influence attempts	cos(49*2πi/114) + isin(49*2πi/114)	-0.90436 +0.42678i
154.80	154:48'0	100	43	43-cancrisquare	43-♋□		1F6CB	home & family life	cos(43*2πi/100) + isin(43*2πi/100)	-0.90483 +0.42578i
154.84	154:50'19	93	40	40-leanovile	40-♌N		1F60D	brought out by creative, sexualized energy	cos(40*2πi/93) + isin(40*2πi/93)	-0.90511 +0.42517i
154.88	154:53'1	86	37	37-leaopposition	37-♌☍		1F921	one's commentary offends egos	cos(37*2πi/86) + isin(37*2πi/86)	-0.90545 +0.42446i
154.94	154:56'12	79	34	34-virgiseptile	34-♍七		270A	anti-establishment revolutionary	cos(34*2πi/79) + isin(34*2πi/79)	-0.90584 +0.42362i
155.00	155:0'0	72	31	31-libriinconjunct	31-♎π		2753	a problem to be solved	cos(31*2πi/72) + isin(31*2πi/72)	-0.90631 +0.42262i
155.04	155:2'11	137	59	59-ariquintile	59-♈⬠		1F6A7	singular active, direct, control	cos(59*2πi/137) + isin(59*2πi/137)	-0.90658 +0.42204i
155.08	155:4'36	65	28	28-libriquintile	28-♎⬠		1F6C0	self-resparking	cos(28*2πi/65) + isin(28*2πi/65)	-0.90687 +0.4214i
155.12	155:7'19	123	53	53-tauritrine	53-♉△		238F	others must express or draw out	cos(53*2πi/123) + isin(53*2πi/123)	-0.90721 +0.42069i
155.17	155:10'20	58	25	25-scorpidecile	25-♏⊥		1F47B	interactions with an ethereal party	cos(25*2πi/58) + isin(25*2πi/58)	-0.90758 +0.41989i
155.23	155:13'45	109	47	47-gemiconjunct	47-♊☌		1F44E	diminishing others' importance	cos(47*2πi/109) + isin(47*2πi/109)	-0.90799 +0.41899i
155.29	155:17'38	51	22	22-scorpitrine	22-♏△		1F61A	use of persuasive words	cos(22*2πi/51) + isin(22*2πi/51)	-0.90847 +0.41796i
155.40	155:23'44	139	60	60-ariseptile	60-♈七		1F3AF	creative perfectionism	cos(60*2πi/139) + isin(60*2πi/139)	-0.9092 +0.41635i
155.45	155:27'16	44	19	19-sajioctile	19-♐◿		1F6B5	role in a peer group	cos(19*2πi/44) + isin(19*2πi/44)	-0.90963 +0.41542i
155.52	155:31'12	125	54	54-tauriquintile	54-♉⬠		1F39F	social clique's requirements	cos(54*2πi/125) + isin(54*2πi/125)	-0.91011 +0.41438i
155.59	155:35'35	118	51	51-gemidecile	51-♊⊥		1F3C3	staying with it as long as encouraged	cos(51*2πi/118) + isin(51*2πi/118)	-0.91063 +0.41321i
155.68	155:40'32	37	16	16-sajiconjunct	16-♐☌		2B50	trusted ability revealed	cos(16*2πi/37) + isin(16*2πi/37)	-0.91123 +0.4119i
155.74	155:44'40	141	61	61-arinovile	61-♈N		1F489	easy instillment in others	cos(61*2πi/141) + isin(61*2πi/141)	-0.91172 +0.4108i
155.77	155:46'9	104	45	45-cancrioctile	45-♋◿		1F61B	trait known and accepted among friends	cos(45*2πi/104) + isin(45*2πi/104)	-0.9119 +0.41041i

155.82	155:49'15	67	29	29-libriseptile	29-♎⁊		1F63B	getting others to fall in love w oneself	cos(29*2π/67) + isin(29*2π/67)	-0.91227 +0.40959i
155.88	155:52'34	97	42	42-cancriconjunct	42-♋♂		1F495	traits reserved for those very close	cos(42*2π/97) + isin(42*2π/97)	-0.91267 +0.40871i
155.91	155:54'19	127	55	55-tauriseptile	55-♉⁊		1F4B8	that which attracts unfair advantage	cos(55*2π/127) + isin(55*2π/127)	-0.91287 +0.40824i
156.00	156:0'0	30	13	13-caprisextile	13-♑✶		1F487	response to one's body reception	cos(13*2π/30) + isin(13*2π/30)	-0.91355 +0.40674i
156.08	156:5'2	143	62	62-ariundecile	62-♈U		1F4E3	broadcasting which gets one talked about	cos(62*2π/143) + isin(62*2π/143)	-0.91414 +0.4054i
156.14	156:8'40	83	36	36-virgiundecile	36-♍U		26A1	high-tension activity in surroundings	cos(36*2π/83) + isin(36*2π/83)	-0.91457 +0.40443i
156.18	156:10'35	136	59	59-arisquare	59-♈□		1F9D0	serious, sober-minded interactant	cos(59*2π/136) + isin(59*2π/136)	-0.91479 +0.40392i
156.23	156:13'35	53	23	23-scorpiquintile	23-♏⬠		1F917	reasons one is desired	cos(23*2π/53) + isin(23*2π/53)	-0.91515 +0.40312i
156.28	156:16'44	129	56	56-taurinovile	56-♉N		1F647	in the service of one attached to	cos(56*2π/129) + isin(56*2π/129)	-0.91552 +0.40228i
156.32	156:18'56	76	33	33-virgisquare	33-♍□		1F3D8	seen by friends' friends & family	cos(33*2π/76) + isin(33*2π/76)	-0.91577 +0.4017i
156.39	156:23'36	122	53	53-tauriopposition	53-♉☍		1F913	easily annoying to others	cos(53*2π/122) + isin(53*2π/122)	-0.91632 +0.40045i
156.52	156:31'18	23	10	10-aquariundecile	10-♒U		1F991	unusual social trait, liked by eccentrics	cos(10*2π/23) + isin(10*2π/23)	-0.91721 +0.3984i
156.64	156:38'28	131	57	57-tauriundecile	57-♉U		1F611	with doubt in associations	cos(57*2π/131) + isin(57*2π/131)	-0.91804 +0.39649i
156.67	156:39'59	108	47	47-cancriinconjunct	47-♋π		1F31D	why close friends come around	cos(47*2π/108) + isin(47*2π/108)	-0.91822 +0.39608i
156.71	156:42'21	85	37	37-leaconjunct	37-♌♂		1F924	downplaying a real want	cos(37*2π/85) + isin(37*2π/85)	-0.91849 +0.39545i
156.77	156:46'27	62	27	27-libriopposition	27-♎☍		1F3F4	manipulative ambition	cos(27*2π/62) + isin(27*2π/62)	-0.91896 +0.39436i
156.83	156:49'54	101	44	44-cancriquintile	44-♋○		1F624	disregard for things heard	cos(44*2π/101) + isin(44*2π/101)	-0.91935 +0.39343i
156.86	156:51'25	140	61	61-arioctile	61-♈⟋		1F340	helped by a benefactor	cos(61*2π/140) + isin(61*2π/140)	-0.91953 +0.39303i
156.92	156:55'23	39	17	17-sajitrine	17-♐△		1F3DD	convincing others of one's value	cos(17*2π/39) + isin(17*2π/39)	-0.91998 +0.39197i
156.99	156:59'32	133	58	58-ariconjunct	58-♈♂		1F49D	during sex or when flirting	cos(58*2π/133) + isin(58*2π/133)	-0.92045 +0.39085i
157.02	157:1'16	94	41	41-leadecile	41-♌⊥		1F463	helps in others after learning the hard way	cos(41*2π/94) + isin(41*2π/94)	-0.92065 +0.39039i
157.09	157:5'27	55	24	24-scorpiseptile	24-♏⁊		1F632	shocking or flooding others w information	cos(24*2π/55) + isin(24*2π/55)	-0.92112 +0.38927i
157.14	157:8'34	126	55	55-taurisextile	55-♉✶		1F47E	aggressive assertion of identity	cos(55*2π/126) + isin(55*2π/126)	-0.92148 +0.38843i
157.18	157:10'59	71	31	31-libriundecile	31-♎U		26C5	thriving amidst confusion	cos(31*2π/71) + isin(31*2π/71)	-0.92175 +0.38779i
157.24	157:14'28	87	38	38-leatrine	38-♌△		2763	interactor inspired to want	cos(38*2π/87) + isin(38*2π/87)	-0.92214 +0.38685i
157.28	157:16'53	103	45	45-cancriseptile	45-♋⁊		1F60A	basking in joy	cos(45*2π/103) + isin(45*2π/103)	-0.92241 +0.3862i
157.33	157:20'0	135	59	59-aritrine	59-♈△		1F3C4	easy and prolific	cos(59*2π/135) + isin(59*2π/135)	-0.92276 +0.38537i
157.50	157:30'0	16	7	7-aquarisquare	7-♒□		1F46A	among family	cos(7*2π/16) + isin(7*2π/16)	-0.92388 +0.38268i
157.69	157:41'9	121	53	53-tauriconjunct	53-♉♂		1F4B0	prosperity & status-seeking	cos(53*2π/121) + isin(53*2π/121)	-0.92512 +0.37968i

157.71	157:42'51	105	46	46-cancrinovile	46-♋N	1F5EF	when irritated to see standards defied	cos(46*2π/105) + isin(46*2π/105)	-0.9253 +0.37923i
157.75	157:45'10	89	39	39-leaquintile	39-♌⌂	1F48B	sensuality & body expression	cos(39*2π/89) + isin(39*2π/89)	-0.92556 +0.3786i
157.85	157:50'46	130	57	57-tauridecile	57-♉⊥	1F3AA	relied upon by others in the talked topic	cos(57*2π/130) + isin(57*2π/130)	-0.92617 +0.37709i
157.89	157:53'41	57	25	25-scorpinovile	25-♏N	1FA84	arrives whenever one wants it, no asking	cos(25*2π/57) + isin(25*2π/57)	-0.92649 +0.37631i
157.99	157:59'8	139	61	61-ariseptile	61-♈七	1F3AF	creative perfectionism	cos(61*2π/139) + isin(61*2π/139)	-0.92709 +0.37484i
158.05	158:2'55	41	18	18-sajiquintile	18-♐⌂	1F5FD	personas aspired to	cos(18*2π/41) + isin(18*2π/41)	-0.9275 +0.37382i
158.13	158:7'51	107	47	47-cancriundecile	47-♋U	1F481	essence of a great conversation w/ one	cos(47*2π/107) + isin(47*2π/107)	-0.92804 +0.37249i
158.18	158:10'54	66	29	29-librisextile	29-♎✳	1F57A	broadcastable good spirits	cos(29*2π/66) + isin(29*2π/66)	-0.92837 +0.37166i
158.24	158:14'30	91	40	40-leaseptile	40-♌七	1F576	smoothly comfortable	cos(40*2π/91) + isin(40*2π/91)	-0.92876 +0.37069i
158.28	158:16'33	116	51	51-gemioctile	51-♊⊿	1F612	having been slighted or doubted	cos(51*2π/116) + isin(51*2π/116)	-0.92898 +0.37014i
158.30	158:17'52	141	62	62-arinovile	62-♈N	1F489	easy instillment in others	cos(62*2π/141) + isin(62*2π/141)	-0.92912 +0.36978i
158.40	158:24'0	25	11	11-capriconjunct	11-♑☌	1F3DF	rally & tune the mass psychology	cos(11*2π/25) + isin(11*2π/25)	-0.92978 +0.36812i
158.53	158:31'55	109	48	48-gemiconjunct	48-♊☌	1F44E	diminishing others' importance	cos(48*2π/109) + isin(48*2π/109)	-0.93062 +0.36598i
158.57	158:34'17	84	37	37-virgiinconjunct	37-♍π	1F411	traits for the seemingly weak	cos(37*2π/84) + isin(37*2π/84)	-0.93087 +0.36534i
158.64	158:38'38	59	26	26-scorpiundecile	26-♏U	1F447	having one's pick	cos(26*2π/59) + isin(26*2π/59)	-0.93134 +0.36416i
158.74	158:44'24	127	56	56-tauriseptile	56-♉七	1F4B8	that which attracts unfair advantage	cos(56*2π/127) + isin(56*2π/127)	-0.93195 +0.3626i
158.82	158:49'24	34	15	15-capridecile	15-♑⊥	1F3C6	potential to be a master or boss	cos(15*2π/34) + isin(15*2π/34)	-0.93247 +0.36124i
158.92	158:55'8	111	49	49-gemitrine	49-♊△	1F973	around high-expression groups	cos(49*2π/111) + isin(49*2π/111)	-0.93307 +0.35969i
159.00	159:0'0	120	53	53-gemiinconjunct	53-♊π	1F922	more vulnerable to things	cos(53*2π/120) + isin(53*2π/120)	-0.93358 +0.35837i
159.07	159:4'11	43	19	19-sajiseptile	19-♐七	1F0CF	through jokes, games, and fun	cos(19*2π/43) + isin(19*2π/43)	-0.93402 +0.35723i
159.13	159:7'49	138	61	61-arisextile	61-♈✳	26D1	daily work focus	cos(61*2π/138) + isin(61*2π/138)	-0.93439 +0.35624i
159.16	159:9'28	95	42	42-leaundecile	42-♌U	265B	the image of a progress-inspiring master	cos(42*2π/95) + isin(42*2π/95)	-0.93456 +0.35579i
159.23	159:13'50	52	23	23-scorpisquare	23-♏□	1F61E	falling short	cos(23*2π/52) + isin(23*2π/52)	-0.93502 +0.3546i
159.29	159:17'31	113	50	50-gemiquintile	50-♊⌂	1F60E	publicly-labeled vibe given	cos(50*2π/113) + isin(50*2π/113)	-0.93539 +0.3536i
159.34	159:20'39	61	27	27-libriconjunct	27-♎☌	1F526	singled out for attention	cos(27*2π/61) + isin(27*2π/61)	-0.93572 +0.35275i
159.39	159:23'21	131	58	58-tauriundecile	58-♉U	1F611	with doubt in associations	cos(58*2π/131) + isin(58*2π/131)	-0.93599 +0.35202i
159.43	159:25'42	70	31	31-libridecile	31-♎⊥	1F527	used to strengthen or repair bonds	cos(31*2π/70) + isin(31*2π/70)	-0.93623 +0.35137i
159.49	159:29'37	79	35	35-virgiseptile	35-♍七	270A	anti-establishment revolutionary	cos(35*2π/79) + isin(35*2π/79)	-0.93663 +0.35031i
159.55	159:32'43	88	39	39-leasquare	39-♌□	1F479	suppressing power imbalance	cos(39*2π/88) + isin(39*2π/88)	-0.93695 +0.34946i

159.59	159:35'15	97	43	43-cancriconjunct	43-♋☌	💕	1F495	traits reserved for those very close	cos(43*2π/97) + isin(43*2π/97)	-0.93721 +0.34877i
159.62	159:37'21	106	47	47-cancridecile	47-♋⊥	🎠	1F3A0	others think one has more power than one has	cos(47*2π/106) + isin(47*2π/106)	-0.93742 +0.3482i
159.68	159:40'38	124	55	55-taurisquare	55-♉□	🎇	1F387	initial, then waning impression	cos(55*2π/124) + isin(55*2π/124)	-0.93775 +0.34731i
159.72	159:43'5	142	63	63-aridecile	63-♈⊥	🕉	1F549	blessings others can only dream of	cos(63*2π/142) + isin(63*2π/142)	-0.938 +0.34664i
160.00	160:0'0	9	4	(quatronovile)	ℕ4	🎬	1F3AC	self-image promotion	cos(1*2π/9) + isin(1*2π/9)	-0.93969 +0.34202i
160.29	160:17'31	137	61	61-ariquintile	61-♈⚹	🚧	1F6A7	singular active, direct, control	cos(61*2π/137) + isin(61*2π/137)	-0.94142 +0.33723i
160.34	160:20'10	119	53	53-gemiundecile	53-♊U	📉	1F4C9	weakened by opinionation, better as ambient	cos(53*2π/119) + isin(53*2π/119)	-0.94168 +0.3365i
160.40	160:23'45	101	45	45-cancriquintile	45-♋⚹	😤	1F624	disregard for things heard	cos(45*2π/101) + isin(45*2π/101)	-0.94203 +0.33552i
160.43	160:26'5	92	41	41-leaoctile	41-♌∠	🍻	1F37B	regular comfort preferences w/ close one	cos(41*2π/92) + isin(41*2π/92)	-0.94226 +0.33488i
160.48	160:28'54	83	37	37-virgiundecile	37-♍U	⚡	26A1	high-tension activity in surroundings	cos(37*2π/83) + isin(37*2π/83)	-0.94254 +0.3341i
160.54	160:32'25	74	33	33-virgiopposition	33-♍☍	😦	1F626	social stressors	cos(33*2π/74) + isin(33*2π/74)	-0.94288 +0.33314i
160.58	160:34'31	139	62	62-ariseptile	62-♈⬧	🎯	1F3AF	creative perfectionism	cos(62*2π/139) + isin(62*2π/139)	-0.94308 +0.33256i
160.62	160:36'55	65	29	29-libriquintile	29-♎⚹	🛀	1F6C0	self-resparking	cos(29*2π/65) + isin(29*2π/65)	-0.94331 +0.33191i
160.66	160:39'40	121	54	54-tauriconjunct	54-♉☌	💰	1F4B0	prosperity & status-seeking	cos(54*2π/121) + isin(54*2π/121)	-0.94358 +0.33115i
160.71	160:42'51	56	25	25-scorpioctile	25-♏∠	😈	1F608	for fun or one's own power	cos(25*2π/56) + isin(25*2π/56)	-0.94388 +0.33028i
160.78	160:46'36	103	46	46-cancriseptile	46-♋⬧	😊	1F60A	basking in joy	cos(46*2π/103) + isin(46*2π/103)	-0.94424 +0.32925i
160.85	160:51'3	47	21	21-sajiundecile	21-♐U	☪	262B	a core, lived principle	cos(21*2π/47) + isin(21*2π/47)	-0.94467 +0.32802i
160.94	160:56'28	85	38	38-leaconjunct	38-♌☌	🤤	1F924	downplaying a real want	cos(38*2π/85) + isin(38*2π/85)	-0.94518 +0.32654i
160.98	160:58'32	123	55	55-tauritrine	55-♉△	⏏	238F	others must express or draw out	cos(55*2π/123) + isin(55*2π/123)	-0.94538 +0.32597i
161.05	161:3'9	38	17	17-sajiopposition	17-♐☍	🙌	1F64C	use of the body or physical deeds in work	cos(17*2π/38) + isin(17*2π/38)	-0.94582 +0.3247i
161.14	161:8'34	105	47	47-cancrinovile	47-♋N	💥	1F5EF	when irritated to see standards defied	cos(47*2π/105) + isin(47*2π/105)	-0.94633 +0.32321i
161.19	161:11'38	67	30	30-libriseptile	30-♎⬧	😻	1F63B	getting others to fall in love w oneself	cos(30*2π/67) + isin(30*2π/67)	-0.94662 +0.32236i
161.25	161:15'0	96	43	43-leainconjunct	43-♌π	🤷	1F937	what "not enough" looks like	cos(43*2π/96) + isin(43*2π/96)	-0.94693 +0.32144i
161.28	161:16'48	125	56	56-tauriquintile	56-♉⚹	🎟	1F39F	social clique's requirements	cos(56*2π/125) + isin(56*2π/125)	-0.9471 +0.32094i
161.38	161:22'45	29	13	13-capriquintile	13-♑⚹	🎩	1F3A9	proud charisma	cos(13*2π/29) + isin(13*2π/29)	-0.94765 +0.3193i
161.50	161:29'43	107	48	48-cancriundecile	48-♋U	💁	1F481	essence of a great conversation w/ one	cos(48*2π/107) + isin(48*2π/107)	-0.9483 +0.31738i
161.54	161:32'18	78	35	35-virgisextile	35-♍✳	🏓	1F94A	fight night moment	cos(35*2π/78) + isin(35*2π/78)	-0.94854 +0.31667i
161.57	161:34'29	127	57	57-tauriseptile	57-♉⬧	🧖	1F4B8	that which attracts unfair advantage	cos(57*2π/127) + isin(57*2π/127)	-0.94874 +0.31607i
161.63	161:37'57	49	22	22-scorpiconjunct	22-♏☌	🎙	1F399	having known public influence	cos(22*2π/49) + isin(22*2π/49)	-0.94906 +0.31511i

161.69	161:41'41	118	53	53-gemidecile	53-Ⅱ⊥	🏃	1F3C3	staying with it as long as encouraged	cos(53*2πi/118) + isin(53*2πi/118)	-0.9494 +0.31408i
161.74	161:44'20	69	31	31-librinovile	31-♎N	🐘	1F418	subtle, strong draw of trait via socialization	cos(31*2πi/69) + isin(31*2πi/69)	-0.94964 +0.31334i
161.80	161:47'51	89	40	40-leaquintile	40-♌♎	💋	1F48B	sensuality & body expression	cos(40*2πi/89) + isin(40*2πi/89)	-0.94996 +0.31237i
161.83	161:50'5	109	49	49-gemiconjunct	49-Ⅱ☌	👎	1F44E	diminishing others' importance	cos(49*2πi/109) + isin(49*2πi/109)	-0.95016 +0.31176i
161.86	161:51'37	129	58	58-taurinovile	58-♉N	🙇	1F647	in the service of one attached to	cos(58*2πi/129) + isin(58*2πi/129)	-0.9503 +0.31133i
162.00	162:0'0	20	9	9-aquarioctile	9-♒⊿	🤺	1F93A	kicking the butt of outsiders	cos(9*2πi/20) + isin(9*2πi/20)	-0.95106 +0.30902i
162.14	162:8'14	131	59	59-tauriundecile	59-♉U	😑	1F611	with doubt in associations	cos(59*2πi/131) + isin(59*2πi/131)	-0.95179 +0.30674i
162.20	162:11'52	91	41	41-leaseptile	41-♌七	🕶	1F576	smoothly comfortable	cos(41*2πi/91) + isin(41*2πi/91)	-0.95212 +0.30573i
162.30	162:17'42	122	55	55-tauriopposition	55-♉☍	🤓	1F913	easily annoying to others	cos(55*2πi/122) + isin(55*2πi/122)	-0.95264 +0.30411i
162.35	162:21'10	51	23	23-scorpitrine	23-♏△	😚	1F61A	use of persuasive words	cos(23*2πi/51) + isin(23*2πi/51)	-0.95294 +0.30315i
162.44	162:26'20	82	37	37-virgidecile	37-♍⊥	🦇	1F987	eccentrically attention-getting, disquieting	cos(37*2πi/82) + isin(37*2πi/82)	-0.9534 +0.30172i
162.48	162:28'40	113	51	51-gemiquintile	51-Ⅱ♎	😎	1F60E	publicly-labeled vibe given	cos(51*2πi/113) + isin(51*2πi/113)	-0.9536 +0.30107i
162.50	162:30'0	144	65	65-ariinconjunct	65-♈𝜋	🔁	1F501	always-on trait	cos(65*2πi/144) + isin(65*2πi/144)	-0.95372 +0.30071i
162.58	162:34'50	31	14	14-capriseptile	14-♑七	🎢	1F3A2	expressed by one's social network	cos(14*2πi/31) + isin(14*2πi/31)	-0.95414 +0.29936i
162.69	162:41'32	104	47	47-cancrioctile	47-♋⊿	😛	1F61B	trait known and accepted among friends	cos(47*2πi/104) + isin(47*2πi/104)	-0.95472 +0.2975i
162.74	162:44'23	73	33	33-virgiconjunct	33-♍☌	⚒	2692	new or deep investment in job	cos(33*2πi/73) + isin(33*2πi/73)	-0.95497 +0.29671i
162.78	162:46'57	115	52	52-gemiseptile	52-Ⅱ七	🤳	1F933	inner world with self-talk	cos(52*2πi/115) + isin(52*2πi/115)	-0.95519 +0.296i
162.86	162:51'25	42	19	19-sajisextile	19-♐✳	💗	1F497	instilled in co-creative partners	cos(19*2πi/42) + isin(19*2πi/42)	-0.95557 +0.29476i
162.95	162:56'50	95	43	43-leaundecile	43-♌U	👑	265B	the image of a progress-inspiring master	cos(43*2πi/95) + isin(43*2πi/95)	-0.95604 +0.29325i
163.02	163:1'7	53	24	24-scorpiquintile	24-♏♎	🤗	1F917	reasons one is desired	cos(24*2πi/53) + isin(24*2πi/53)	-0.9564 +0.29206i
163.08	163:4'36	117	53	53-geminovile	53-ⅡN	💎	1F48E	best friend's quality	cos(53*2πi/117) + isin(53*2πi/117)	-0.9567 +0.29109i
163.13	163:7'30	64	29	29-librisquare	29-♎□	众	4F17	amidst a noisy setting	cos(29*2πi/64) + isin(29*2πi/64)	-0.95694 +0.29028i
163.20	163:11'59	75	34	34-virgitrine	34-♍△	🏡	1F3E1	family home maintenance	cos(34*2πi/75) + isin(34*2πi/75)	-0.95732 +0.28903i
163.30	163:17'56	97	44	44-cancriconjunct	44-♋☌	💕	1F495	traits reserved for those very close	cos(44*2πi/97) + isin(44*2πi/97)	-0.95782 +0.28738i
163.33	163:20'0	108	49	49-cancriinconjunct	49-♋𝜋	😝	1F31D	why close friends come around	cos(49*2πi/108) + isin(49*2πi/108)	-0.95799 +0.2868i
163.38	163:23'4	130	59	59-tauridecile	59-♉⊥	🎪	1F3AA	relied upon by others in the talked topic	cos(59*2πi/130) + isin(59*2πi/130)	-0.95825 +0.28595i
163.40	163:24'15	141	64	64-arinovile	64-♈N	💉	1F489	easy instillment in others	cos(64*2πi/141) + isin(64*2πi/141)	-0.95834 +0.28562i
163.64	163:38'10	11	5	undecile	U₅	🗫	1F5EB	getting talked about	cos(1*2πi/11) + isin(1*2πi/11)	-0.95949 +0.28173i
163.88	163:52'50	134	61	61-ariopposition	61-♈☍	💟	1F49F	a trait the partner MUST have	cos(61*2πi/134) + isin(61*2πi/134)	-0.96069 +0.27764i

163.93	163:55'42	112	51	51-gemisquare	51-♊□		1F38E	one's trait observed by outsiders	cos(51*2πi/112) + isin(51*2πi/112)	-0.96092 +0.27684i
164.00	164:0'0	90	41	41-leasextile	41-♌✳		1F6B8	absorptions by one's children	cos(41*2πi/90) + isin(41*2πi/90)	-0.96126 +0.27564i
164.05	164:3'2	79	36	36-virgiseptile	36-♍七		270A	anti-establishment revolutionary	cos(36*2πi/79) + isin(36*2πi/79)	-0.9615 +0.27479i
164.12	164:7'3	68	31	31-librioctile	31-♎⊿		1F462	appearance of dominating	cos(31*2πi/68) + isin(31*2πi/68)	-0.96183 +0.27366i
164.16	164:9'35	125	57	57-tauriquintile	57-♉⚼		1F39F	social clique's requirements	cos(57*2πi/125) + isin(57*2πi/125)	-0.96203 +0.27295i
164.21	164:12'37	57	26	26-scorpinovile	26-♏N		1FA84	arrives whenever one wants it, no asking	cos(26*2πi/57) + isin(26*2πi/57)	-0.96227 +0.2721i
164.27	164:16'18	103	47	47-cancriseptile	47-♋七		1F60A	basking in joy	cos(47*2πi/103) + isin(47*2πi/103)	-0.96256 +0.27107i
164.35	164:20'52	46	21	21-sajidecile	21-♐⊥		1F4CE	trait housed by key colleagues	cos(21*2πi/46) + isin(21*2πi/46)	-0.96292 +0.2698i
164.44	164:26'40	81	37	37-virginovile	37-♍N		1F451	mastered early, forms broad social identity	cos(37*2πi/81) + isin(37*2πi/81)	-0.96337 +0.26817i
164.48	164:28'57	116	53	53-gemioctile	53-♊⊿		1F612	having been slighted or doubted	cos(53*2πi/116) + isin(53*2πi/116)	-0.96355 +0.26753i
164.57	164:34'17	35	16	16-capriundecile	16-♑U		1F47D	quirky distinguishing uniqueness	cos(16*2πi/35) + isin(16*2πi/35)	-0.96396 +0.26604i
164.68	164:40'51	94	43	43-leadecile	43-♌⊥		1F463	helps in others after learning the hard way	cos(43*2πi/94) + isin(43*2πi/94)	-0.96447 +0.2642i
164.75	164:44'44	59	27	27-scorpiundecile	27-♏U		1F447	having one's pick	cos(27*2πi/59) + isin(27*2πi/59)	-0.96477 +0.2631i
164.79	164:47'19	142	65	65-aridecile	65-♈⊥		1F549	blessings others can only dream of	cos(65*2πi/142) + isin(65*2πi/142)	-0.96496 +0.26238i
164.82	164:49'9	83	38	38-virgiundecile	38-♍U		26A1	high-tension activity in surroundings	cos(38*2πi/83) + isin(38*2πi/83)	-0.9651 +0.26186i
164.89	164:53'7	131	60	60-tauriundecile	60-♉U		1F611	with doubt in associations	cos(60*2πi/131) + isin(60*2πi/131)	-0.96541 +0.26075i
165.00	165:0'0	24	11	11-aquariinconjunct	11-♒π		1F4AD	imagination at work	cos(11*2πi/24) + isin(11*2πi/24)	-0.96593 +0.25882i
165.14	165:8'15	109	50	50-gemiconjunct	50-♊☌		1F44E	diminishing others' importance	cos(50*2πi/109) + isin(50*2πi/109)	-0.96654 +0.2565i
165.18	165:10'35	85	39	39-leaconjunct	39-♌☌		1F924	downplaying a real want	cos(39*2πi/85) + isin(39*2πi/85)	-0.96672 +0.25584i
165.25	165:14'45	61	28	28-libriconjunct	28-♎☌		1F526	singled out for attention	cos(28*2πi/61) + isin(28*2πi/61)	-0.96703 +0.25467i
165.33	165:20'0	135	62	62-aritrine	62-♈△		1F3C4	easy and prolific	cos(62*2πi/135) + isin(62*2πi/135)	-0.96742 +0.2532i
165.41	165:24'19	37	17	17-sajiconjunct	17-♐☌		2B50	trusted ability revealed	cos(17*2πi/37) + isin(17*2πi/37)	-0.96773 +0.25198i
165.48	165:29'1	124	57	57-taurisquare	57-♉□		1F387	initial, then waning impression	cos(57*2πi/124) + isin(57*2πi/124)	-0.96808 +0.25065i
165.55	165:32'50	137	63	63-ariquintile	63-♈⚼		1F6A7	singular active, direct, control	cos(63*2πi/137) + isin(63*2πi/137)	-0.96835 +0.24958i
165.60	165:35'59	50	23	23-scorpiopposition	23-♏☍		1F5BC	images put forth to others	cos(23*2πi/50) + isin(23*2πi/50)	-0.96858 +0.24869i
165.66	165:39'49	113	52	52-gemiquintile	52-♊⚼		1F60E	publicly-labeled vibe given	cos(52*2πi/113) + isin(52*2πi/113)	-0.96886 +0.24761i
165.71	165:42'51	63	29	29-libritrine	29-♎△		1F6A8	know-it-all	cos(29*2πi/63) + isin(29*2πi/63)	-0.96908 +0.24676i
165.79	165:47'22	76	35	35-virgisquare	35-♍□		1F3D8	seen by friends' friends & family	cos(35*2πi/76) + isin(35*2πi/76)	-0.9694 +0.24549i
165.84	165:50'33	89	41	41-leaquintile	41-♌⚼		1F48B	sensuality & body expression	cos(41*2πi/89) + isin(41*2πi/89)	-0.96963 +0.24458i

165.88	165:52'56	102	47	47-cancrisextile	47-♋✶	1F4BC	boss figure attributes	cos(47*2π/102) + isin(47*2π/102)	-0.9698 +0.24391i
165.94	165:56'15	128	59	59-taurioctile	59-♉⊿	1F478	intuitive comfort even amidst stress	cos(59*2π/128) + isin(59*2π/128)	-0.97003 +0.24298i
165.96	165:57'26	141	65	65-arinovile	65-♈N	1F489	easy instillment in others	cos(65*2π/141) + isin(65*2π/141)	-0.97012 +0.24264i
166.15	166:9'13	13	6	6-aquariconjunct	6-♒☌	1F3A5	public persona	cos(6*2π/13) + isin(6*2π/13)	-0.97094 +0.23932i
166.39	166:23'11	119	55	55-gemiundecile	55-♊U	1F4C9	weakened by opinionation, better as ambient	cos(55*2π/119) + isin(55*2π/119)	-0.97191 +0.23537i
166.42	166:24'54	106	49	49-cancridecile	49-♋⊥	1F3A0	others think one has more power than one has	cos(49*2π/106) + isin(49*2π/106)	-0.97202 +0.23489i
166.50	166:30'0	80	37	37-virgioctile	37-♍⊿	1F939	vividly remembered by one's children	cos(37*2π/80) + isin(37*2π/80)	-0.97237 +0.23345i
166.57	166:34'1	67	31	31-libriseptile	31-♎七	1F63B	getting others to fall in love w oneself	cos(31*2π/67) + isin(31*2π/67)	-0.97264 +0.23231i
166.61	166:36'41	121	56	56-tauriconjunct	56-♉☌	1F4B0	prosperity & status-seeking	cos(56*2π/121) + isin(56*2π/121)	-0.97282 +0.23155i
166.67	166:39'59	54	25	25-scorpisextile	25-♏✶	1F378	self-fulfillment tool	cos(25*2π/54) + isin(25*2π/54)	-0.97304 +0.23062i
166.74	166:44'12	95	44	44-leaundecile	44-♌U	265B	the image of a progress-inspiring master	cos(44*2π/95) + isin(44*2π/95)	-0.97333 +0.22942i
166.76	166:45'52	136	63	63-arisquare	63-♈□	1F9D0	serious, sober-minded interactant	cos(63*2π/136) + isin(63*2π/136)	-0.97344 +0.22895i
166.83	166:49'45	41	19	19-sajiquintile	19-♐⬠	1F5FD	personas aspired to	cos(19*2π/41) + isin(19*2π/41)	-0.9737 +0.22785i
166.91	166:54'32	110	51	51-gemiopposition	51-♊☍	1F6A5	managing others' behavior	cos(51*2π/110) + isin(51*2π/110)	-0.97401 +0.2265i
166.96	166:57'23	69	32	32-librinovile	32-♎N	1F418	subtle, strong draw of trait via socialization	cos(32*2π/69) + isin(32*2π/69)	-0.9742 +0.22569i
167.04	167:2'23	125	58	58-tauriquintile	58-♉⬠	1F39F	social clique's requirements	cos(58*2π/125) + isin(58*2π/125)	-0.97453 +0.22427i
167.14	167:8'34	28	13	13-caprisquare	13-♑□	1F58C	arts and creativity drawn to	cos(13*2π/28) + isin(13*2π/28)	-0.97493 +0.22252i
167.24	167:14'38	127	59	59-tauriseptile	59-♉七	1F4B8	that which attracts unfair advantage	cos(59*2π/127) + isin(59*2π/127)	-0.97532 +0.2208i
167.27	167:16'21	99	46	46-cancritrine	46-♋△	1F645	communication-stifling	cos(46*2π/99) + isin(46*2π/99)	-0.97543 +0.22031i
167.32	167:19'26	71	33	33-libriundecile	33-♎U	26C5	thriving amidst confusion	cos(33*2π/71) + isin(33*2π/71)	-0.97563 +0.21944i
167.37	167:22'6	114	53	53-gemisextile	53-♊✶	1F6F1	other's influence attempts	cos(53*2π/114) + isin(53*2π/114)	-0.9758 +0.21868i
167.44	167:26'30	43	20	20-sajiseptile	20-♐七	1F0CF	through jokes, games, and fun	cos(20*2π/43) + isin(20*2π/43)	-0.97608 +0.21743i
167.50	167:30'0	144	67	67-ariinconjunct	67-♈π	1F501	always-on trait	cos(67*2π/144) + isin(67*2π/144)	-0.9763 +0.21644i
167.52	167:31'29	101	47	47-cancriquintile	47-♋⬠	1F624	disregard for things heard	cos(47*2π/101) + isin(47*2π/101)	-0.97639 +0.21602i
167.59	167:35'10	58	27	27-scorpidecile	27-♏⊥	1F47B	interactions with an ethereal party	cos(27*2π/58) + isin(27*2π/58)	-0.97662 +0.21497i
167.63	167:38'0	131	61	61-tauriundecile	61-♉U	1F611	with doubt in associations	cos(61*2π/131) + isin(61*2π/131)	-0.9768 +0.21416i
167.67	167:40'16	73	34	34-virgiconjunct	34-♍☌	2692	new or deep investment in job	cos(34*2π/73) + isin(34*2π/73)	-0.97694 +0.21352i
167.73	167:43'38	88	41	41-leasquare	41-♌□	1F479	suppressing power imbalance	cos(41*2π/88) + isin(41*2π/88)	-0.97715 +0.21257i
167.80	167:47'47	118	55	55-gemidecile	55-♊⊥	1F3C3	staying with it as long as encouraged	cos(55*2π/118) + isin(55*2π/118)	-0.9774 +0.21138i

167.82	167:49'10	133	62	62-ariconjunct	62-♑☌	💝	1F49D	during sex or when flirting	cos(62*2π/133) + isin(62*2π/133)	-0.97749 +0.21099i
168.00	168:0'0	15	7	7-aquaritrine	7-♒△	🐋	1F40B	room domination	cos(7*2π/15) + isin(7*2π/15)	-0.97815 +0.20791i
168.18	168:10'30	137	64	64-ariquintile	64-♑⬠	🚧	1F6A7	singular active, direct, control	cos(64*2π/137) + isin(64*2π/137)	-0.97878 +0.20492i
168.22	168:13'27	107	50	50-cancriundecile	50-♋U	🛁	1F481	essence of a great conversation w/ one	cos(50*2π/107) + isin(50*2π/107)	-0.97895 +0.20408i
168.26	168:15'39	92	43	43-leaoctile	43-♌⊿	🎻	1F37B	regular comfort preferences w/ close one	cos(43*2π/92) + isin(43*2π/92)	-0.97908 +0.20346i
168.35	168:20'43	139	65	65-ariseptile	65-♑七	🎯	1F3AF	creative perfectionism	cos(65*2π/139) + isin(65*2π/139)	-0.97938 +0.20201i
168.39	168:23'13	62	29	29-libriopposition	29-♎☍	🏴	1F3F4	manipulative ambition	cos(29*2π/62) + isin(29*2π/62)	-0.97953 +0.2013i
168.44	168:26'25	109	51	51-gemiconjunct	51-♊☌	👎	1F44E	diminishing others' importance	cos(51*2π/109) + isin(51*2π/109)	-0.97972 +0.20039i
168.51	168:30'38	47	22	22-sajiundecile	22-♐U	☫	262B	a core, lived principle	cos(22*2π/47) + isin(22*2π/47)	-0.97996 +0.19919i
168.57	168:34'17	126	59	59-taurisextile	59-♉✳	👾	1F47E	aggressive assertion of identity	cos(59*2π/126) + isin(59*2π/126)	-0.98017 +0.19815i
168.65	168:38'55	111	52	52-gemitrine	52-♊△	🥳	1F973	around high-expression groups	cos(52*2π/111) + isin(52*2π/111)	-0.98044 +0.19682i
168.67	168:40'16	143	67	67-ariundecile	67-♑U	📣	1F4E3	broadcasting which gets one talked about	cos(67*2π/143) + isin(67*2π/143)	-0.98052 +0.19644i
168.75	168:45'0	32	15	15-caprioctile	15-♑⊿	🗻	1F5FB	an indomitable characteristic	cos(15*2π/32) + isin(15*2π/32)	-0.98079 +0.19509i
168.85	168:50'58	113	53	53-gemiquintile	53-♊⬠	😎	1F60E	publicly-labeled vibe given	cos(53*2π/113) + isin(53*2π/113)	-0.98112 +0.19339i
168.89	168:53'19	81	38	38-virginovile	38-♍N	👑	1F451	mastered early, forms broad social identity	cos(38*2π/81) + isin(38*2π/81)	-0.98126 +0.19271i
168.92	168:55'23	130	61	61-tauridecile	61-♉⊥	🎪	1F3AA	relied upon by others in the talked topic	cos(61*2π/130) + isin(61*2π/130)	-0.98137 +0.19213i
168.98	168:58'46	49	23	23-scorpiconjunct	23-♏☌	🎙	1F399	having known public influence	cos(23*2π/49) + isin(23*2π/49)	-0.98156 +0.19116i
169.04	169:2'36	115	54	54-gemiseptile	54-♊七	🤳	1F933	inner world with self-talk	cos(54*2π/115) + isin(54*2π/115)	-0.98177 +0.19006i
169.09	169:5'27	66	31	31-librisextile	31-♎✳	🕺	1F57A	broadcastable good spirits	cos(31*2π/66) + isin(31*2π/66)	-0.98193 +0.18925i
169.20	169:11'59	100	47	47-cancrisquare	47-♋□	🛋	1F6CB	home & family life	cos(47*2π/100) + isin(47*2π/100)	-0.98229 +0.18738i
169.23	169:13'50	117	55	55-geminovile	55-♊N	💎	1F48E	best friend's quality	cos(55*2π/117) + isin(55*2π/117)	-0.98239 +0.18685i
169.25	169:15'13	134	63	63-ariopposition	63-♑☍	💟	1F49F	a trait the partner MUST have	cos(63*2π/134) + isin(63*2π/134)	-0.98246 +0.18646i
169.41	169:24'42	17	8	8-aquariquintile	8-♒⬠	👊	1F44A	managing by dominating	cos(8*2π/17) + isin(8*2π/17)	-0.98297 +0.18375i
169.59	169:35'12	121	57	57-tauriconjunct	57-♉☌	💰	1F4B0	prosperity & status-seeking	cos(57*2π/121) + isin(57*2π/121)	-0.98353 +0.18075i
169.62	169:36'55	104	49	49-cancrioctile	49-♋⊿	😛	1F61B	trait known and accepted among friends	cos(49*2π/104) + isin(49*2π/104)	-0.98362 +0.18026i
169.66	169:39'18	87	41	41-leatrine	41-♌△	❣	2763	interactor inspired to want	cos(41*2π/87) + isin(41*2π/87)	-0.98374 +0.17957i
169.71	169:42'51	70	33	33-libridecile	33-♎⊥	🔧	1F527	used to strengthen or repair bonds	cos(33*2π/70) + isin(33*2π/70)	-0.98393 +0.17856i
169.76	169:45'21	123	58	58-tauritrine	58-♉△	⎏	238F	others must express or draw out	cos(58*2π/123) + isin(58*2π/123)	-0.98406 +0.17784i
169.81	169:48'40	53	25	25-scorpiquintile	25-♏⬠	🤗	1F917	reasons one is desired	cos(25*2π/53) + isin(25*2π/53)	-0.98423 +0.17689i

							Unicode	Description	Equation	Value
169.89	169:53'15	89	42	42-leaquintile	42-♌⚻		1F48B	sensuality & body expression	cos(42*2πi/89) + isin(42*2πi/89)	-0.98447 +0.17558i
169.92	169:55'11	125	59	59-tauriquintile	59-♉⚻		1F39F	social clique's requirements	cos(59*2πi/125) + isin(59*2πi/125)	-0.98456 +0.17502i
170.00	170:0'0	36	17	17-capriinconjunct	17-♑π		1F3BB	downplayed want or talent	cos(17*2πi/36) + isin(17*2πi/36)	-0.98481 +0.17365i
170.08	170:4'43	127	60	60-tauriseptile	60-♉七		1F4B8	that which attracts unfair advantage	cos(60*2πi/127) + isin(60*2πi/127)	-0.98505 +0.17229i
170.11	170:6'35	91	43	43-leaseptile	43-♌七		1F576	smoothly comfortable	cos(43*2πi/91) + isin(43*2πi/91)	-0.98514 +0.17176i
170.18	170:10'54	55	26	26-scorpiseptile	26-♏七		1F632	shocking or flooding others w information	cos(26*2πi/55) + isin(26*2πi/55)	-0.98535 +0.17052i
170.23	170:13'57	129	61	61-taurinovile	61-♉N		1F647	in the service of one attached to	cos(61*2πi/129) + isin(61*2πi/129)	-0.9855 +0.16965i
170.27	170:16'12	74	35	35-virgiopposition	35-♍☍		1F626	social stressors	cos(35*2πi/74) + isin(35*2πi/74)	-0.98562 +0.169i
170.32	170:19'21	93	44	44-leanovile	44-♌N		1F60D	brought out by creative, sexualized energy	cos(44*2πi/93) + isin(44*2πi/93)	-0.98577 +0.1681i
170.38	170:22'54	131	62	62-tauriundecile	62-♉U		1F611	with doubt in associations	cos(62*2πi/131) + isin(62*2πi/131)	-0.98594 +0.16708i
170.53	170:31'34	19	9	9-aquariseptile	9-♒七		1F510	gateway to one's friendship	cos(9*2πi/19) + isin(9*2πi/19)	-0.98636 +0.16459i
170.69	170:41'22	116	55	55-gemioctile	55-♊∠		1F612	having been slighted or doubted	cos(55*2πi/116) + isin(55*2πi/116)	-0.98683 +0.16178i
170.72	170:43'17	97	46	46-cancriconjunct	46-♋☌		1F495	traits reserved for those very close	cos(46*2πi/97) + isin(46*2πi/97)	-0.98692 +0.16123i
170.77	170:46'9	78	37	37-virgisextile	37-♍✶		1F94A	fight night moment	cos(37*2πi/78) + isin(37*2πi/78)	-0.98705 +0.16041i
170.85	170:50'50	59	28	28-scorpiundecile	28-♏U		1F447	having one's pick	cos(28*2πi/59) + isin(28*2πi/59)	-0.98727 +0.15906i
170.94	170:56'6	139	66	66-ariseptile	66-♈七		1F3AF	creative perfectionism	cos(66*2πi/139) + isin(66*2πi/139)	-0.98751 +0.15755i
171.00	171:0'0	40	19	19-sajisquare	19-♐□		1F66A	future missable partnership duty	cos(19*2πi/40) + isin(19*2πi/40)	-0.98769 +0.15643i
171.09	171:5'20	101	48	48-cancriquintile	48-♋⚻		1F624	disregard for things heard	cos(48*2πi/101) + isin(48*2πi/101)	-0.98793 +0.1549i
171.15	171:8'51	61	29	29-libriconjunct	29-♎☌		1F526	singled out for attention	cos(29*2πi/61) + isin(29*2πi/61)	-0.98809 +0.15389i
171.19	171:11'19	143	68	68-ariundecile	68-♈U		1F4E3	broadcasting which gets one talked about	cos(68*2πi/143) + isin(68*2πi/143)	-0.9882 +0.15318i
171.22	171:13'10	82	39	39-virgidecile	39-♍⊥		1F987	eccentrically attention-getting, disquieting	cos(39*2πi/82) + isin(39*2πi/82)	-0.98828 +0.15265i
171.29	171:17'25	124	59	59-taurisquare	59-♉□		1F387	initial, then waning impression	cos(59*2πi/124) + isin(59*2πi/124)	-0.98847 +0.15143i
171.43	171:25'42	21	10	10-aquarinovile	10-♒N		1F483	at peak sexiness, strength, or creativity	cos(10*2πi/21) + isin(10*2πi/21)	-0.98883 +0.14904i
171.59	171:35'19	107	51	51-cancriundecile	51-♋U		1F481	essence of a great conversation w/ one	cos(51*2πi/107) + isin(51*2πi/107)	-0.98924 +0.14628i
171.63	171:37'40	86	41	41-leaopposition	41-♌☍		1F921	one's commentary offends egos	cos(41*2πi/86) + isin(41*2πi/86)	-0.98934 +0.1456i
171.69	171:41'32	65	31	31-libriquintile	31-♎⚻		1F6C0	self-resparking	cos(31*2πi/65) + isin(31*2πi/65)	-0.98951 +0.14449i
171.74	171:44'35	109	52	52-gemiconjunct	52-♊☌		1F44E	diminishing others' importance	cos(52*2πi/109) + isin(52*2πi/109)	-0.98963 +0.14361i
171.82	171:49'5	44	21	21-sajioctile	21-♐∠		1F6B5	role in a peer group	cos(21*2πi/44) + isin(21*2πi/44)	-0.98982 +0.14231i
171.89	171:53'30	111	53	53-gemitrine	53-♊△		1F973	around high-expression groups	cos(53*2πi/111) + isin(53*2πi/111)	-0.99 +0.14104i

171.94	171:56'25	67	32	32-libriseptile	32-♎⸷	🐱	1F63B	getting others to fall in love w oneself	cos(32*2πi/67) + isin(32*2πi/67)	-0.99012 +0.1402i
172.00	172:0'0	90	43	43-leasextile	43-♌✳	🚸	1F6B8	absorptions by one's children	cos(43*2πi/90) + isin(43*2πi/90)	-0.99027 +0.13917i
172.04	172:2'7	113	54	54-gemiquintile	54-♊⚷	😎	1F60E	publicly-labeled vibe given	cos(54*2πi/113) + isin(54*2πi/113)	-0.99035 +0.13856i
172.06	172:3'31	136	65	65-arisquare	65-♈□	🤐	1F9D0	serious, sober-minded interactant	cos(65*2πi/136) + isin(65*2πi/136)	-0.99041 +0.13816i
172.17	172:10'26	23	11	11-aquariundecile	11-♒U	🐙	1F991	unusual social trait, liked by eccentrics	cos(11*2πi/23) + isin(11*2πi/23)	-0.99069 +0.13617i
172.29	172:17'8	140	67	67-arioctile	67-♈⊿	🍀	1F340	helped by a benefactor	cos(67*2πi/140) + isin(67*2πi/140)	-0.99095 +0.13423i
172.34	172:20'25	94	45	45-leadecile	45-♌⊥	👣	1F463	helps in others after learning the hard way	cos(45*2πi/94) + isin(45*2πi/94)	-0.99108 +0.13329i
172.39	172:23'39	71	34	34-libriundecile	34-♎U	🌥	26C5	thriving amidst confusion	cos(34*2πi/71) + isin(34*2πi/71)	-0.9912 +0.13235i
172.44	172:26'13	119	57	57-gemiundecile	57-♊U	📉	1F4C9	weakened by opinionation, better as ambient	cos(57*2πi/119) + isin(57*2πi/119)	-0.9913 +0.13162i
172.50	172:30'0	48	23	23-sajiinconjunct	23-♐π	🌅	1F305	shown through creative setting	cos(23*2πi/48) + isin(23*2πi/48)	-0.99144 +0.13053i
172.56	172:33'43	121	58	58-tauriconjunct	58-♉☌	💰	1F4B0	prosperity & status-seeking	cos(58*2πi/121) + isin(58*2πi/121)	-0.99159 +0.12945i
172.60	172:36'9	73	35	35-virgiconjunct	35-♍☌	⚒	2692	new or deep investment in job	cos(35*2πi/73) + isin(35*2πi/73)	-0.99168 +0.12875i
172.68	172:40'58	123	59	59-tauritrine	59-♉△	⎏	238F	others must express or draw out	cos(59*2πi/123) + isin(59*2πi/123)	-0.99186 +0.12736i
172.80	172:48'0	25	12	12-capriconjunct	12-♑☌	🏟	1F3DF	rally & tune the mass psychology	cos(12*2πi/25) + isin(12*2πi/25)	-0.99211 +0.12533i
172.94	172:56'28	102	49	49-cancrisextile	49-♋✳	💼	1F4BC	boss figure attributes	cos(49*2πi/102) + isin(49*2πi/102)	-0.99242 +0.12289i
172.99	172:59'13	77	37	37-virgiquintile	37-♍⚷	🐢	1F422	guarded insistence	cos(37*2πi/77) + isin(37*2πi/77)	-0.99252 +0.12209i
173.02	173:1'23	129	62	62-taurinovile	62-♉N	🙇	1F647	in the service of one attached to	cos(62*2πi/129) + isin(62*2πi/129)	-0.9926 +0.12147i
173.08	173:4'36	52	25	25-scorpisquare	25-♏□	😞	1F61E	falling short	cos(25*2πi/52) + isin(25*2πi/52)	-0.99271 +0.12054i
173.13	173:7'47	131	63	63-tauriundecile	63-♉U	😑	1F611	with doubt in associations	cos(63*2πi/131) + isin(63*2πi/131)	-0.99282 +0.11962i
173.16	173:9'52	79	38	38-virgiseptile	38-♍⸷	✊	270A	anti-establishment revolutionary	cos(38*2πi/79) + isin(38*2πi/79)	-0.99289 +0.11902i
173.23	173:13'59	133	64	64-ariconjunct	64-♈☌	💝	1F49D	during sex or when flirting	cos(64*2πi/133) + isin(64*2πi/133)	-0.99303 +0.11783i
173.33	173:20'0	27	13	13-capritrine	13-♑△	🎓	1F393	intellectualizing and insight	cos(13*2πi/27) + isin(13*2πi/27)	-0.99324 +0.11609i
173.43	173:25'50	137	66	66-ariquintile	66-♈⚷	🚧	1F6A7	singular active, direct, control	cos(66*2πi/137) + isin(66*2πi/137)	-0.99343 +0.11441i
173.49	173:29'38	83	40	40-virgiundecile	40-♍U	⚡	26A1	high-tension activity in surroundings	cos(40*2πi/83) + isin(40*2πi/83)	-0.99356 +0.11331i
173.53	173:31'30	139	67	67-ariseptile	67-♈⸷	🎯	1F3AF	creative perfectionism	cos(67*2πi/139) + isin(67*2πi/139)	-0.99362 +0.11277i
173.57	173:34'17	56	27	27-scorpioctile	27-♏⊿	😈	1F608	for fun or one's own power	cos(27*2πi/56) + isin(27*2πi/56)	-0.99371 +0.11196i
173.65	173:38'49	85	41	41-leaconjunct	41-♌☌	🤤	1F924	downplaying a real want	cos(41*2πi/85) + isin(41*2πi/85)	-0.99386 +0.11065i
173.68	173:41'3	114	55	55-gemisextile	55-♊✳	🚱	1F6F1	other's influence attempts	cos(55*2πi/114) + isin(55*2πi/114)	-0.99393 +0.11001i
173.71	173:42'22	143	69	69-ariundecile	69-♈U	📣	1F4E3	broadcasting which gets one talked about	cos(69*2πi/143) + isin(69*2πi/143)	-0.99397 +0.10963i

173.79	173:47'35	29	14	14-capriquintile	14-♑︎⚺		1F3A9	proud charisma	$\cos(14*2\pi/29) + i\sin(14*2\pi/29)$	-0.99414 +0.10812i
173.90	173:53'53	118	57	57-gemidecile	57-♊︎⊥		1F3C3	staying with it as long as encouraged	$\cos(57*2\pi/118) + i\sin(57*2\pi/118)$	-0.99433 +0.10629i
173.93	173:55'57	89	43	43-leaquintile	43-♌︎⚺		1F48B	sensuality & body expression	$\cos(43*2\pi/89) + i\sin(43*2\pi/89)$	-0.9944 +0.1057i
174.00	174:0'0	60	29	29-scorpiinconjunct	29-♏︎⚻		1F4CD	strongest memory left behind	$\cos(29*2\pi/60) + i\sin(29*2\pi/60)$	-0.99452 +0.10453i
174.10	174:5'54	122	59	59-tauriopposition	59-♉︎☍		1F913	easily annoying to others	$\cos(59*2\pi/122) + i\sin(59*2\pi/122)$	-0.9947 +0.10282i
174.19	174:11'36	31	15	15-capriseptile	15-♑︎⚛		1F3A2	expressed by one's social network	$\cos(15*2\pi/31) + i\sin(15*2\pi/31)$	-0.99487 +0.10117i
174.29	174:17'8	126	61	61-taurisextile	61-♉︎⚹		1F47E	aggressive assertion of identity	$\cos(61*2\pi/126) + i\sin(61*2\pi/126)$	-0.99503 +0.09957i
174.32	174:18'56	95	46	46-leaundecile	46-♌︎∪		265B	the image of a progress-inspiring master	$\cos(46*2\pi/95) + i\sin(46*2\pi/95)$	-0.99508 +0.09905i
174.38	174:22'30	64	31	31-librisquare	31-♎︎□		4F17	amidst a noisy setting	$\cos(31*2\pi/64) + i\sin(31*2\pi/64)$	-0.99518 +0.09802i
174.43	174:25'58	97	47	47-cancriconjunct	47-♋︎☌		1F495	traits reserved for those very close	$\cos(47*2\pi/97) + i\sin(47*2\pi/97)$	-0.99528 +0.09701i
174.46	174:27'41	130	63	63-tauridecile	63-♉︎⊥		1F3AA	relied upon by others in the talked topic	$\cos(63*2\pi/130) + i\sin(63*2\pi/130)$	-0.99533 +0.09651i
174.55	174:32'43	33	16	16-caprinovile	16-♑︎N		1F4FB	in a formal group discussion	$\cos(16*2\pi/33) + i\sin(16*2\pi/33)$	-0.99547 +0.09506i
174.63	174:37'36	134	65	65-ariopposition	65-♈︎☍		1F49F	a trait the partner MUST have	$\cos(65*2\pi/134) + i\sin(65*2\pi/134)$	-0.99561 +0.09364i
174.65	174:39'12	101	49	49-cancriquintile	49-♋︎⚺		1F624	disregard for things heard	$\cos(49*2\pi/101) + i\sin(49*2\pi/101)$	-0.99565 +0.09318i
174.71	174:42'21	68	33	33-librioctile	33-♎︎⚼		1F462	appearance of dominating	$\cos(33*2\pi/68) + i\sin(33*2\pi/68)$	-0.99573 +0.09227i
174.78	174:46'57	138	67	67-arisextile	67-♈︎⚹		26D1	daily work focus	$\cos(67*2\pi/138) + i\sin(67*2\pi/138)$	-0.99586 +0.09093i
174.86	174:51'25	35	17	17-capriundecile	17-♑︎∪		1F47D	quirky distinguishing uniqueness	$\cos(17*2\pi/35) + i\sin(17*2\pi/35)$	-0.99597 +0.08964i
174.93	174:55'46	142	69	69-aridecile	69-♈︎⊥		1F549	blessings others can only dream of	$\cos(69*2\pi/142) + i\sin(69*2\pi/142)$	-0.99609 +0.08838i
175.00	175:0'0	72	35	35-libriinconjunct	35-♎︎⚻		2753	a problem to be solved	$\cos(35*2\pi/72) + i\sin(35*2\pi/72)$	-0.99619 +0.08716i
175.05	175:2'45	109	53	53-gemiconjunct	53-♊︎☌		1F44E	diminishing others' importance	$\cos(53*2\pi/109) + i\sin(53*2\pi/109)$	-0.99626 +0.08636i
175.14	175:8'6	37	18	18-sajiconjunct	18-♐︎☌		2B50	trusted ability revealed	$\cos(18*2\pi/37) + i\sin(18*2\pi/37)$	-0.9964 +0.08481i
175.22	175:13'16	113	55	55-gemiquintile	55-♊︎⚺		1F60E	publicly-labeled vibe given	$\cos(55*2\pi/113) + i\sin(55*2\pi/113)$	-0.99652 +0.08331i
175.26	175:15'47	76	37	37-virgisquare	37-♍︎□		1F3D8	seen by friends' friends & family	$\cos(37*2\pi/76) + i\sin(37*2\pi/76)$	-0.99658 +0.08258i
175.30	175:18'15	115	56	56-gemiseptile	56-♊︎⚛		1F933	inner world with self-talk	$\cos(56*2\pi/115) + i\sin(56*2\pi/115)$	-0.99664 +0.08186i
175.38	175:23'4	39	19	19-sajitrine	19-♐︎△		1F3DD	convincing others of one's value	$\cos(19*2\pi/39) + i\sin(19*2\pi/39)$	-0.99676 +0.08047i
175.50	175:30'0	80	39	39-virgioctile	39-♍︎⚼		1F939	vividly remembered by one's children	$\cos(39*2\pi/80) + i\sin(39*2\pi/80)$	-0.99692 +0.07846i
175.54	175:32'13	121	59	59-tauriconjunct	59-♉︎☌		1F4B0	prosperity & status-seeking	$\cos(59*2\pi/121) + i\sin(59*2\pi/121)$	-0.99697 +0.07781i
175.61	175:36'35	41	20	20-sajiquintile	20-♐︎⚺		1F5FD	personas aspired to	$\cos(20*2\pi/41) + i\sin(20*2\pi/41)$	-0.99707 +0.07655i
175.68	175:40'48	125	61	61-tauriquintile	61-♉︎⚺		1F39F	social clique's requirements	$\cos(61*2\pi/125) + i\sin(61*2\pi/125)$	-0.99716 +0.07533i

175.75	175:44'52	127	62	62-tauriseptile	62-♉七	🪙	1F4B8	that which attracts unfair advantage	cos(62*2π/127) + isin(62*2π/127)	-0.99725 +0.07414i
175.81	175:48'50	43	21	21-sajiseptile	21-♐七	🃏	1F0CF	through jokes, games, and fun	cos(21*2π/43) + isin(21*2π/43)	-0.99733 +0.073i
175.88	175:52'40	131	64	64-tauriundecile	64-♉U	😑	1F611	with doubt in associations	cos(64*2π/131) + isin(64*2π/131)	-0.99741 +0.07188i
175.94	175:56'23	133	65	65-ariconjunct	65-♈☌	💝	1F49D	during sex or when flirting	cos(65*2π/133) + isin(65*2π/133)	-0.99749 +0.0708i
176.00	176:0'0	45	22	22-sajinovile	22-♐N	❦	2766	shared experience as a token of friendship	cos(22*2π/45) + isin(22*2π/45)	-0.99756 +0.06976i
176.09	176:5'13	92	45	45-leaoctile	45-♌⌀	🎻	1F37B	regular comfort preferences w/ close one	cos(45*2π/92) + isin(45*2π/92)	-0.99767 +0.06824i
176.12	176:6'54	139	68	68-ariseptile	68-♈七	🎯	1F3AF	creative perfectionism	cos(68*2π/139) + isin(68*2π/139)	-0.9977 +0.06775i
176.17	176:10'12	47	23	23-sajiundecile	23-♐U	☮	262B	a core, lived principle	cos(23*2π/47) + isin(23*2π/47)	-0.99777 +0.06679i
176.25	176:15'0	96	47	47-leainconjunct	47-♌π	🤷	1F937	what "not enough" looks like	cos(47*2π/96) + isin(47*2π/96)	-0.99786 +0.0654i
176.33	176:19'35	49	24	24-scorpiconjunct	24-♏☌	🎙	1F399	having known public influence	cos(24*2π/49) + isin(24*2π/49)	-0.99795 +0.06407i
176.40	176:24'0	100	49	49-cancrisquare	49-♋□	🛋	1F6CB	home & family life	cos(49*2π/100) + isin(49*2π/100)	-0.99803 +0.06279i
176.47	176:28'14	51	25	25-scorpitrine	25-♏△	😚	1F61A	use of persuasive words	cos(25*2π/51) + isin(25*2π/51)	-0.9981 +0.06156i
176.54	176:32'18	104	51	51-cancrioctile	51-♋⌀	😛	1F61B	trait known and accepted among friends	cos(51*2π/104) + isin(51*2π/104)	-0.99818 +0.06038i
176.60	176:36'13	53	26	26-scorpiquintile	26-♏⚹	🤗	1F917	reasons one is desired	cos(26*2π/53) + isin(26*2π/53)	-0.99824 +0.05924i
176.67	176:39'59	108	53	53-cancriinconjunct	53-♋π	😝	1F31D	why close friends come around	cos(53*2π/108) + isin(53*2π/108)	-0.99831 +0.05814i
176.73	176:43'38	55	27	27-scorpiseptile	27-♏七	😲	1F632	shocking or flooding others w information	cos(27*2π/55) + isin(27*2π/55)	-0.99837 +0.05709i
176.79	176:47'8	112	55	55-gemisquare	55-♊□	👯	1F38E	one's trait observed by outsiders	cos(55*2π/112) + isin(55*2π/112)	-0.99843 +0.05607i
176.84	176:50'31	57	28	28-scorpinovile	28-♏N	🪄	1FA84	arrives whenever one wants it, no asking	cos(28*2π/57) + isin(28*2π/57)	-0.99848 +0.05509i
176.90	176:53'47	116	57	57-gemioctile	57-♊⌀	😒	1F612	having been slighted or doubted	cos(57*2π/116) + isin(57*2π/116)	-0.99853 +0.05414i
176.95	176:56'56	59	29	29-scorpiundecile	29-♏U	👇	1F447	having one's pick	cos(29*2π/59) + isin(29*2π/59)	-0.99858 +0.05322i
177.00	177:0'0	120	59	59-gemiinconjunct	59-♊π	🤢	1F922	more vulnerable to things	cos(59*2π/120) + isin(59*2π/120)	-0.99863 +0.05234i
177.05	177:2'57	61	30	30-libriconjunct	30-♎☌	🔦	1F526	singled out for attention	cos(30*2π/61) + isin(30*2π/61)	-0.99867 +0.05148i
177.10	177:5'48	124	61	61-taurisquare	61-♉□	🎇	1F387	initial, then waning impression	cos(61*2π/124) + isin(61*2π/124)	-0.99872 +0.05065i
177.14	177:8'34	63	31	31-libritrine	31-♎△	🚨	1F6A8	know-it-all	cos(31*2π/63) + isin(31*2π/63)	-0.99876 +0.04985i
177.19	177:11'15	128	63	63-taurioctile	63-♉⌀	👸	1F478	intuitive comfort even amidst stress	cos(63*2π/128) + isin(63*2π/128)	-0.9988 +0.04907i
177.23	177:13'50	65	32	32-libriquintile	32-♎⚹	🛀	1F6C0	self-resparking	cos(32*2π/65) + isin(32*2π/65)	-0.99883 +0.04831i
177.27	177:16'21	132	65	65-tauriinconjunct	65-♉π	🔗	1F517	sharing a special bond w/ a friend	cos(65*2π/132) + isin(65*2π/132)	-0.99887 +0.04758i
177.31	177:18'48	67	33	33-libriseptile	33-♎七	😻	1F63B	getting others to fall in love w oneself	cos(33*2π/67) + isin(33*2π/67)	-0.9989 +0.04687i
177.39	177:23'28	69	34	34-librinovile	34-♎N	🐘	1F418	subtle, strong draw of trait via socialization	cos(34*2π/69) + isin(34*2π/69)	-0.99896 +0.04551i

177.43	177:25'42	140	69	69-arioctile	69-♈⊿		1F340	helped by a benefactor	cos(69*2πi/140) + isin(69*2πi/140)	-0.99899 +0.04486i
177.50	177:30'0	144	71	71-ariinconjunct	71-♈⬧		1F501	always-on trait	cos(71*2πi/144) + isin(71*2πi/144)	-0.99905 +0.04362i
177.53	177:32'3	73	36	36-virgiconjunct	36-♍☌		2692	new or deep investment in job	cos(36*2πi/73) + isin(36*2πi/73)	-0.99907 +0.04302i
177.60	177:35'59	75	37	37-virgitrine	37-♍△		1F3E1	family home maintenance	cos(37*2πi/75) + isin(37*2πi/75)	-0.99912 +0.04188i
177.66	177:39'44	77	38	38-virgiquintile	38-♍⬠		1F422	guarded insistence	cos(38*2πi/77) + isin(38*2πi/77)	-0.99917 +0.04079i
177.72	177:43'17	79	39	39-virgiseptile	39-♍✴		270A	anti-establishment revolutionary	cos(39*2πi/79) + isin(39*2πi/79)	-0.99921 +0.03976i
177.78	177:46'39	81	40	40-virginovile	40-♍N		1F451	mastered early, forms broad social identity	cos(40*2πi/81) + isin(40*2πi/81)	-0.99925 +0.03878i
177.83	177:49'52	83	41	41-virgiundecile	41-♍U		26A1	high-tension activity in surroundings	cos(41*2πi/83) + isin(41*2πi/83)	-0.99928 +0.03784i
177.88	177:52'56	85	42	42-leaconjunct	42-♌☌		1F924	downplaying a real want	cos(42*2πi/85) + isin(42*2πi/85)	-0.99932 +0.03695i
177.93	177:55'51	87	43	43-leatrine	43-♌△		2763	interactor inspired to want	cos(43*2πi/87) + isin(43*2πi/87)	-0.99935 +0.0361i
177.98	177:58'39	89	44	44-leaquintile	44-♌⬠		1F48B	sensuality & body expression	cos(44*2πi/89) + isin(44*2πi/89)	-0.99938 +0.03529i
178.02	178:1'19	91	45	45-leaseptile	45-♌✴		1F576	smoothly comfortable	cos(45*2πi/91) + isin(45*2πi/91)	-0.9994 +0.03452i
178.06	178:3'52	93	46	46-leanovile	46-♌N		1F60D	brought out by creative, sexualized energy	cos(46*2πi/93) + isin(46*2πi/93)	-0.99943 +0.03377i
178.14	178:8'39	97	48	48-cancriconjunct	48-♋☌		1F495	traits reserved for those very close	cos(48*2πi/97) + isin(48*2πi/97)	-0.99948 +0.03238i
178.18	178:10'54	99	49	49-cancritrine	49-♋△		1F645	communication-stifling	cos(49*2πi/99) + isin(49*2πi/99)	-0.9995 +0.03173i
178.22	178:13'4	101	50	50-cancriquintile	50-♋⬠		1F624	disregard for things heard	cos(50*2πi/101) + isin(50*2πi/101)	-0.99952 +0.0311i
178.29	178:17'8	105	52	52-cancrinovile	52-♋N		1F5EF	when irritated to see standards defied	cos(52*2πi/105) + isin(52*2πi/105)	-0.99955 +0.02992i
178.35	178:20'55	109	54	54-gemiconjunct	54-♊☌		1F44E	diminishing others' importance	cos(54*2πi/109) + isin(54*2πi/109)	-0.99958 +0.02882i
178.38	178:22'42	111	55	55-gemitrine	55-♊△		1F973	around high-expression groups	cos(55*2πi/111) + isin(55*2πi/111)	-0.9996 +0.0283i
178.43	178:26'5	115	57	57-gemiseptile	57-♊✴		1F933	inner world with self-talk	cos(57*2πi/115) + isin(57*2πi/115)	-0.99963 +0.02731i
178.49	178:29'14	119	59	59-gemiundecile	59-♊U		1F4C9	weakened by opinionation, better as ambient	cos(59*2πi/119) + isin(59*2πi/119)	-0.99965 +0.0264i
178.54	178:32'11	123	61	61-tauritrine	61-♉△		238F	others must express or draw out	cos(61*2πi/123) + isin(61*2πi/123)	-0.99967 +0.02554i
178.58	178:34'57	127	63	63-tauriseptile	63-♉✴		1F4B8	that which attracts unfair advantage	cos(63*2πi/127) + isin(63*2πi/127)	-0.99969 +0.02473i
178.63	178:37'33	131	65	65-tauriundecile	65-♉U		1F611	with doubt in associations	cos(65*2πi/131) + isin(65*2πi/131)	-0.99971 +0.02398i
178.69	178:41'10	137	68	68-ariquintile	68-♈⬠		1F6A7	singular active, direct, control	cos(68*2πi/137) + isin(68*2πi/137)	-0.99974 +0.02293i
178.74	178:44'28	143	71	71-ariundecile	71-♈U		1F4E3	broadcasting which gets one talked about	cos(71*2πi/143) + isin(71*2πi/143)	-0.99976 +0.02197i
180.00	180:0'0	2	1	opposition	☍		1F4CF	interactant	cos(1*2πi/2) + isin(1*2πi/2)	-1

…but now I'm not gonna lie, this fool was tricky to make. So I hope somebody appreciates it. For complex mathematical reasons that I won't delve too deeply into, and for usages that might arise for state machine and algorithm developers in the future, the above table includes two columns for representing aspects as an angle rotation in the complex plane. A conjunct takes 1 cycle to come back to its starting degree; a square takes 4 cycles since $i^4 = 1$; a 3-sajiconjunct takes 37 cycles to come back to wholeness since $(\cos(3*2\pi i/37) + i \sin(3*2\pi i/37))^{37} = 1$, and this is one way of thinking about what an "aspect" is actually doing from a frequency perspective—it's tuning how *frequently* an angle crosses the countable plane. Look up something like the "37th root of 1" on WolframAlpha to see what I'm doing here.

And remember, at this point in the 2020s—until future research shows otherwise—we should think of all harmonic multiples as behaving the same. A *bi*quintile does the same thing as a regular quintile BUT FOR their neighbors. A regular quintile is so close to a 28-arinovile and a 29-ariinconjunct that it feels more like a freebie given to others when you express your ego. Meanwhile, a biquintile is so close to a 57-ariundecile and a 55-ariquintile that your ego presentation looks more like a function of your own control. The 1-aquarioctile (18°, also known as a "vigintile") doesn't seem to have anything to do with higher awareness based on the *144* stats… until you look at its two immediate neighbors. With aspects off by just a little, you could see how one's 18° could actually be estimating a more benevolent angle close by.

Lastly, on a slightly amusing (and possibly useful) note, I accidentally glanced at one of the first aspects to get me started on this "144" journey: the 126° 7-aquarioctile. The meaning was curious, as were its neighbors down to 125.5°. I immediately suspected that my enjoyment of Dynasty Warriors (a hack n' slash video game franchise) was described by some aspect of around 126°, and in the process hypothesized that you can use neighboring harmonics to more accurately guess which aspects might be most useful to display in your astrological program.

In the following chapters we will be taking a break from the biography to cover some theory which will help us extend my biography to the construction of yours, others, and nonhuman objects.

Chapter 4: Chat with the Gods

FIRST APPROACH

8/22/2024

Dear Star-sized Gods,

I want to be a legend in human history like the great humans whom I admire. I also want to help ease humanity's transition into the future. How do I do this?

-Ajani

Dear Ajani,

We can't see you. Unfortunately, our children only see your little blue planet as a blob on our petri dishes. Despite some of us being scientists, the academic community generally does not believe that small blobs such as yours even have life on them. We have, however, observed some interesting bumps and divots on your blob's surface which seem to grow from infinitesimal to less infinitesimal for a while, only to die after about anywhere from 1/400 to 400 of your cycles around your sun-source. Most interesting to us are the bump types which seem to live about 60-120 of your cycles, for these bumps seem not only to intentionally maintain their structure during that time, but they also seem to be able to intentionally create countless more elaborate structures after themselves. Most of my colleagues say that such bumps are nothing more than the natural laws of your solar system repeating themselves in micro. The idea of such bumps having "thoughts" and "desires" is absurd to them. But I digress.

I am afraid I cannot tell you how to become a great "human," for I do not know what a "human" is. Are you really one of those bumps I have described? That is, has my team's work succeeded? Please answer.

-Jan-God

Dear Jan-God,

Thank you for your quick reply. A "human" is one of the top most advanced inhabitants of our blob, which we call "Earth." I assume that the self-reinforcing bumps you refer to are

257

indeed us living creatures. Yes we have thoughts. We marry. We eat. We die. And some of us study forces much bigger than ourselves. I am curious, however, what was the nature of your team's work? Maybe I could tell you if you have succeeded.

-Ajani

Dear Ajani,

Amazing! Our work has succeeded! I built a device which allows us to anthrize seemingly lifeless objects and talk to them in the anthric-frequentic language which normal gods use everywhere. Although we have known that we are not alone in the universe, we have not been able to prove the existence of Ultragods or microgodlets until now. I believe you are the microgodlets that my team has been looking for. Despite being smaller than our microscopes can sharply capture, you seem to be able to speak and think just like us. You are almost certainly responsible for reshaping so much of the specimen plate that we have observed.

So you are called humans, and your planet Earth? It is impressive that you have names for the blob you live on despite it being so much longer-lived than yourselves. You must have a substantial knowledge transfer system across your generations. Please tell me more about your species and how you see your world.

Also, I hope not to offend you, but many of my colleagues still doubt that you are anything more than a figment of my team's collective imagination. Is there any way you could give us some knowledge from your world that we could verify on our level which couldn't possibly come from ours? I realize this is a complicated ask since you wouldn't really know what we know or don't know. Still, I have to ask.

-January-God

Dear Jan-God,

We humans are one of millions of species of various sizes and shapes who, yes, mobilize our short-lived inner lives towards survival, communication, and reproduction in the world external to us. I have attached a cheat sheet outlining the names of our planets, some key eras in our geological history, etc.

I found it strange putting that cheat sheet together. It dawns on me that our social history—what we have built our entire legacy of civilizations upon—aren't actually something you can see as a star-sized god. Many of the divots you refer to preserve the stories of past human relationships and events relative to their respective lineages, and beyond this there are plenty of solid, non-living objects such as buildings, books, and monuments, which also preserve our history for us. You and your colleagues might be able to locate these objects using very powerful microscopes, but even then I doubt you would assign them any significance. For us, however, buildings and books house our means of preserving patterns across generations. We "attach our learnings to the land," so to speak, with some of that land being portable enough to carry on our person and learn from at our leisure.

As I imagine to be the case with you, language is our bridge across time. Our Earth blob persists, and our language tells us how to interface with it better and better with each generation. This enables us to build up our technology, living conditions, more convenient food sources, and eventually exploration of other blobs.

As for novel information which your colleagues might believe, have you heard of Jesus? The Buddha? These are two of our most famous humans. I don't suppose you would know them by name, but can your machines detect humans' thoughts of other humans who once lived? If so, these are two personalities you might be picking up.

-Aj

Dear Ajani,

Thank you for the information. I have passed that wealth of knowledge onto my peers.

We cannot read minds, if that is what you are effectively asking. This is because every mind is like a ball of yarn subject to the structure of the species doing the thinking. Living things use different senses, wings, antennae, and other adaptations to intake information. The format of internal states—be they hormonal or electrical—will usually have to be looked at again with each separate species considered. At least that was mostly true before my invention. Now we have shown that frequencies can be used to assign anthric conversation patterns to any object, living or nonliving, as long as we have a dictionary of basic frequency interrelationships on hand. We have had such a dictionary for some time now, and rely on this to carry out conversations like the one you and I are having now.

It is interesting how you describe language as progressing your culture. I would like to explore this further, but have a question for you first: You surely know that your lifespan is short. What are your thoughts on death? Not just your own, but that of your species?

-January

p.s., Even if we could read 99.9% of a mind's content, we could not read the .1% which is the attitude held by that mind. Intentions change with every moment. Friends and enemies alike always exercise some level of influence on whether your mind takes the high road or low road. It is for this reason that we have strict laws against thought policing. Our society has found it generally destructive to attempt mind reading because, in the past, the ones doing the reading have time and again proven that they cannot resist the urge to "correct" anything they don't agree with in that mind. But this is a deeper kind of slavery than even physical bondage. No one has the right to punish you for what you have only contemplated.

January,

I found your postscript insightful. Unfortunately, our human society is still unevolved when it comes to respecting the personal and psychological autonomy of strangers. We have something called the Golden Rule, but where advertising and collective institutional agendas are concerned, it is seldom obeyed. This is why we have laws to keep our more selfish individual natures in check.

This may sound vain, but here is a case where you are lucky to have found me instead of any number of other humans to have this discussion with—about death, that is. For reasons beyond the scope of our conversation, I have a fond respect for Death, transition, extinction, and other such endings, as the worst possible state I can conceive a living thing experiencing is torture. Torture is far worse than Death, the slow or deliberate erosion of a mind or body—the loss of a soul while it yet lives… Death is the accountant who shows up at your door and says, "If you stay here any longer past your time, then your existential window of relevance will surely suffer, even if you don't see it." The finiteness of things is what gives them form. How can we claim to prize our individuality yet wish it to be indistinguishable from the formless infinite at the same time? Such would be the gateway to an enduring meaninglessness, in my view.

One of the reasons I wish to be great is because I would like to think of my living self as being truly attuned to something timeless beyond my short 80 or so Earth years (cycles, as you call them). I do not wish to be immortal. Nor do I wish to be a counterexample to what humanity strives for. But I know there are still vast realms yet to be pioneered, and I want my character to be a part of the wonder inherent in the journey. I will eventually die, as will humanity on the whole, and at that point all we will have left is a possible footnote in the memories possessed by the gods. Save for cases of torture, suffering, and accident, it would be contrary to the basic laws governing life for any of us to intentionally seek death. However, when that times comes, I believe we should do our best to exit with dignity and with minimal pain or debt foisted upon the ones who love us.

But why do you ask about this?

-Aj

Aj,

I asked for your thoughts on death because I did not want to scare you with our observations. Had you been a little more naïve about the subject, I might be more inclined to sugarcoat what I see. As it stands, I believe you can handle the truth.

We don't really understand what is going on in your blob, but its energy level has clearly increased in the last 50 or so cycles. It is almost as if someone has heated up your blob and made it easier for heat, charge, and communication to flow all over the space compared to the more isolated flows we used to see. Though the blob Earth is almost certainly not going anywhere any time soon, when have noticed a corresponding jump in the energy levels of your species type. Since you are as "living" as we are, I assume we are seeing your temperaments. You may find it interesting that the increase in your personal temperaments has come with a general decrease in the anger your regions (governments?) display to each other—so that you humans seem to be carrying the intense energy which used to reside in a more directed way within your group cultures as they waged a kind of imperialistic war for the right to determine the history path of different sections of the blob Earth.

It isn't so much that you humans are in danger of overheating, or that any small fraction of you is in charge of what we are seeing. There is something about the legacy growing in the things you have built which makes it easier for billions of you to, frankly, "litter" your blob (for lack of a better word). If it is indeed true that your constructed technology and your language usage have evolved you, these same things have also created zones of noise and friction around them and through them which I myself have not observed your species able to clean up. I am sure you can better explain this phenomenon since you are closer to it, but the assumption among my peers is that you have been intentionally raising your energy levels. With more language, more learning, ever-evolving laws, and world-spanning communication, you have also excited yourselves and your whole environment, such that we thought you were just partying...

...but then we read the language of your discontentedness with your own niches across your space, and weren't so sure. What is it that you all are longing for?

We have done many experiments with solar systems of your size, but never until now have we been able to actually talk to one of you. Most of my colleagues—including the formerly skeptical ones, now believe we have genuinely made contact with a tiny version of sentient life just like us. We discussed it, and agreed to present you with a three-fold challenge:

Without bringing HEAVY ingenuity to bear, all species left to their own devices eventually go extinct. The individuals among that species never want to, and typically the last among them suffer mightily under the sadness of encroaching oblivion. As you are, you humans will be fully extinct within the next 1000 years, replaced by the artificial versions of yourselves which we detect you are currently building. Also, we predict the usual desperate acts that come with local apocalypses, so that you will most likely do what all anthrics and animals do: you will follow your forward progressive inertia until you have cornered yourselves beneath your own ingenuity, then your species-wide claustrophobia will sponsor various kinds of free-for-all.

The first part of our challenge is for you to build one technology which we can measure, which off-loads your pent up patterns into more stable spaces. As it stands, your population is growing as quickly and noticeably as your inner frictions, and you have no release valves anywhere near as powerful as they need to be to offset the destabilizing changes you are living under. But if you could send yourselves into metaversal jobs, activities, leisure games—if you could create new creative outlets in the form of jobs talking to and through your books, your gods, or your magic school bus bacteria tourism, we think that you may yet dodge the conditions which would compel us to throw your exhausted petri dish in the trash. You'll still be bumps on a blob when that happens, we just won't be interested enough to watch that kind of train wreck anymore.

The second challenge is one you will almost certainly need help with. We want you to attempt the difficult but rewarding challenge of controlling your own extinction.

We have delved deeper into your situation using the cheat sheet you sent us. It goes without saying that you humans will not survive your own long term ecosystem changes—not because of weather patterns, war or sickness, but through a reliance on your technologies to run your lives without regard to energy costs, followed by rampant social discord when those technologies are used by their makers to make you all into a kind of capitalistic energy source with nothing left to do but be displaced. The first artificial versions of you will begin dwelling in your normal societies, there will be wars, then anarchy. But the artificial versions of yourselves will continue to be made. Over the span of 200 cycles between your 22nd and 24th millennia, more than half—perhaps even 2/3 of your population will integrate yourselves with your machines—not through big objects, but through little pharmaceutical enhancements which you will embed permanently into your own genetics and the genetics of your offspring. Then there will be more discord. Eventually the number of unmodified individuals among you will form but a fraction of your human population. Finally, five millennia later, you will essentially be entirely semi-nano in nature. The general path is inevitable EXCEPT for one part of the story: the amount of war and pain necessary.

It may be a monumental task, but **we urge you to shift your society's attitude from one of fear into one of optimism regarding your own advancements**. There are so many opportunities to walk alongside your changes rather than fighting against them. The difference between the dark version of the scenario described above and the lighter one lies in the development of your technology for intentionally converting yourselves into your informational forms. If you learn yourselves—if you *really learn* yourselves, your survival instincts, your capacity for hunger, violence, and love...and not just your capacity for chat and data crunching—then you will have the capacity to create replicas of yourselves which are true to Nature's full design. You must then go one step further and demonstrate a level of caring for each and every individual human's story, such that you gain the benevolent respect for all life which we gods have for your entire petri dish. Only through a generalized industry for saving everyone's story—then reloading that story into any device, object, book, or body you wish—will you be able to see your would-have-been-extinction as nothing more than another spaceship into the future.

Finally, **we would like to meet you**. To understand what you look like and why. Right now you are only chemical clouds under our microscopes, and we are only able to communicate through the magic of frequency mapping. But I assume you humans have solid boundaries for bodies—regions of hard-forced pattern stability which separate your internally self-reinforcing processes from the rest of the petri dish around you. Is this so? If you are like us, then you assume that your Ultragods look just like you, and have very little regard for the forms of the "insignificant" microgodlets "beneath" you. But the very notion of microgodlets forces you to think about other worlds as hosting countless different kinds of spirits, not just one or two idealized images.

Could you perhaps describe yourself? I personally would be excited to work on an invention to print a star-sized god version of you like my own kind.

Thanks,

-January

Dear January,

That is some set of challenges! And I am not surprised to hear your predictions for us humans. We are pretty inventive, and bound to approximate ourselves with greater and greater accuracy. But you are right. We are nowhere near the level of peace, maturity, or understanding of ourselves to willingly concede our current "natural born" organic body composition without a fight. The very idea of losing what we know has always filled us with fear and anger; we can and will wage war with anyone and everyone else in manifestation of that fear. We will bathe ourselves in the madness and intolerance just to feel we are actively siding with what is "right" again. Not morally, common sense, or long term "right," just plain consistent with the familiar sense of the past.

Your first ask doesn't sound like something a single human person could do. It sounds like it would take an industry to pull off, but I have noted it and will think some more about it.

Your second ask is an equally tall order. I agree, we would need your help changing 8 billion perspectives for that one.

As for your third ask, let me see how hard it would be to describe through our frequency language. Do you know what an arm is? A lip or a nose? If you know what these are shaped like, then I can describe our forms.

-Aj

Ajani,

I regret that I do not know what those objects are. If you can send me a math formula, I will be able to understand.

Yes, the first two challenges were difficult. I apologize for underestimating the vastness of the world you must perceive when judging the reach of your own efforts...

...If you could, however, succeed in either or both of the first two challenges, I believe that would make you a candidate for greatness among your fellow humans and us above, even if your fellows will not be able to make sense of what the significance of your work was.

-J

Dear January,

Try this formula. This is our basic outline facing the front:

FIGURE 8: A REALLY ROUGH PIECEWISE HUMAN

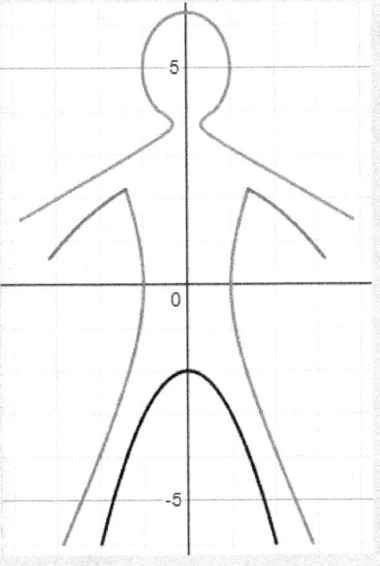

Regarding the first two challenges, hmm…

-A

Dear Ajani,

The formula you sent me appears to be in only two dimensions. Our theories say that this is impossible. Your petri dish contains at least three dimensions (four if you consider time). How are you animating your communications with me? Do you stretch in the x axis?

Assuming you are two-dimensional, it appears your species stands upright. Is that true?

How do you sense your environment?

How do you eat?

Why are you shaped like that when your planet is round? I assumed you would be round (like the "fish" you described in your cheat sheet).

What do you use to communicate?

I am confused.

-J

January,

Outwardly, we are three-dimensional beings who animate in a fourth time dimension. But the speed of our inner metabolism, our thoughts, and our internal charge systems for passing attention constitute a micro-world which operates on its own time or space scale. Additionally, our petri dish world has its own longer time scale, as you have seen. Otherwise, there is no conceivable way that our short lifespans would be able to pack in so much simulated meaning.

What I sent you was a flattened snapshot of a human in two dimensions, with the third dimension sticking out of the page and the time dimension frozen at a single point. I omitted our sense organs and our internal diagrams for the sake of brevity, and excluded our developmental cycles of growth which align more with the cycles of our planet. We humans rarely think of our dimensionality beyond the external three plus one dimensions, but now that I think about it, we probably exist in at least 10 dimensions. Even more if you count the dimensions of information and imaginative record.

-A

8/23/2024

Ajani,

We have reconfigured our system to support real time chat, and will be switching over to that channel. Please let me know if this taxes your energy stores. We were hoping to exchange information at higher resolution.

-January

SECOND APPROACH

Hello Ajani

Hello January

Is it alright to resume our discussion?

Of course.

Great. You sent us a projection of your general shape. One of my colleagues reviewed it and concluded that the reason you are not round but you are symmetric is because you must have dramatic pressures on you from top to bottom rather than all around. It seems that we have been looking at your broad shape through our microscopes from the top down all this time, which is why we were so sure you were four- to six-legged creatures. Like beetles. So two of your legs don't actually touch the surface?

Correct

I assume this is because your species once had four legs, but then repurposed them for walking upright

We think so

Fascinating. If only our communicator could capture richer images

I'm sure it can. I'll send you some word art. Hold on...

It really would help though if your system could just accept three-color + alpha pixels.

Wow! Is this the top part of you from front view?

Yes.

So you do have more elaborate structures besides the outline. Let me show this to my colleagues...

Interesting. He says you humans must be a five or six point continuum.

What's that?

A creature whose body design is based on five or six levels of energy carrier, and this would explain both your limited number of legs as well as the five top-down levels of math functions in your body. He thinks this is because your Earth has two planets flanking it which are not your sun, but then your body structures must also calculate the movement of a generic pair of "beyond-neighbor" orbits.

?

Referencing your cheat sheet, you are arranged as: [sun and other inside of venus (maybe includes mercury, maybe not)], [maybe mercury if not with the sun], [venus], [earth], [mars], [things beyond mars]. Your complexity is at the top, closer to the energy/sensory input source, and you get simpler / more material as you travel down. You humans have big heads so you probably have big brains, and those two legs that are no longer legs probably still move like legs because your brains are doing a lot of calculation to keep you standing up. It probably works out however, because your top down structure is supported by your planet's own orbital position. Your planet stays stable as the fourth object in a five-object row, so you must be true energetic reflections of your earth, which is why you essentially have carte blanche in populating your blob. You are children of your entire chain of orbits, reflecting Time itself according to your own individual personal rules.

Interesting. But how can you tell that just from my face?

You have very tiny ears and no antennae, so much of your processing of your world is internal. It is obvious that you wear clothes. Most of you wear clothes, so you clearly have an elaborate system of using the earth itself to dress up your expected selves for one another. You split at the walking legs and don't have any familiars, wings, or light eyes around you, so we know your body structures are not calculating any more than say, a fourth planet's worth of consideration. Certainly not more than seven.

I don't get it.

> That's okay. I'll work on getting us the ability to stream pixel matrices as you say, so that I can send you some literature on our theories of your body structure.

Sounds good.

> In the meantime, would you mind sending me a living species diagram (speciogram) of the human body shape?

What is a speciogram?

> Oh. How do I explain?
> In order to build this anthric machine for talking to you, we had to find ways to convert the 10 rules of life into a kind of meaning-based spectrum. All living things have to eat, for example, and they also have to get rid of waste that they don't need from the things they eat. These two processes cannot occur on the same food at the same time, so they would be either 90° or 30° || 150° apart in a wheel of possible frequencies, like red vs pea-green or red vs lavender on a color wheel.
> We use a wheel to flatten frequency space for all the things that can possibly happen in a system, because two dimensions is the best way to collapse how different things are as a distance (radius) while also keeping track of whether we've cycled through all options from start to finish back to start again using some arbitrary ordering system (angle theta). It's like asking someone, "I want you to look at all possible options in this box and come back to me when you're done. The angle tells you how complete this process is while the rating tells you how much of some measure each object has.
> But cycles themselves obey some basic rules. First, the beginning is the beginning. Second, the middle 180° is as far from the beginning as you will get. Next, the 90° marks from the beginning are exactly balanced between the beginning and middle, rendering neither of them dominant and both of them at full potential. 60° and 120° marks from the beginning are exactly halfway between full beginning or middle and no beginning or middle, and so points which balance the realization of this are points in their own something-nothing mini-cycles. These are kind of like "analogies" to the beginning and middle. The 90° marks have their own analogies in the 30° and 150° marks. Lastly, all multiples of 60° are stable alternatives to each other when it comes to things you can see in the same dimension. The moment you tilt off of this multiple, you get into dimensions that the original cannot see.

Okay

> I tell you this, because the literature I am going to send you makes heavy use of circles, starting with our 10 rules for life.
> In order to be considered living, we require a thing to obey 7 rules within itself and 3 rules as a consequence of being part of a class:

TABLE 11: 10 REQUIREMENTS OF LIFE

1] The thing must maintain a specific process as its internal state

2] It must accept only certain inputs and follow certain rules in that process, up to the limits of a boundary

3] Alternatives to the thing's process must exist

4] The thing's processes must lead to a formed result

5] The thing must eat certain inputs used to produce its form

6] It must excrete certain outputs it no longer needs or can't support internally on its own

7] The thing must eat, maintain, and process as a component inside of an environment

8] The thing must be a member of a type of class which reproduces itself

9] Type/class members must have a communicative pattern among them which reinforce the class. (This can't just be noise.)

10] The individual must direct its behavior towards reinforcing its version of this entire 10-part process

I will send you an image as soon as we get picture capability.

Okay.

Done. Here is the living species cycle.

FIGURE 9: 10 REQUIREMENTS OF LIFE (VISUAL)

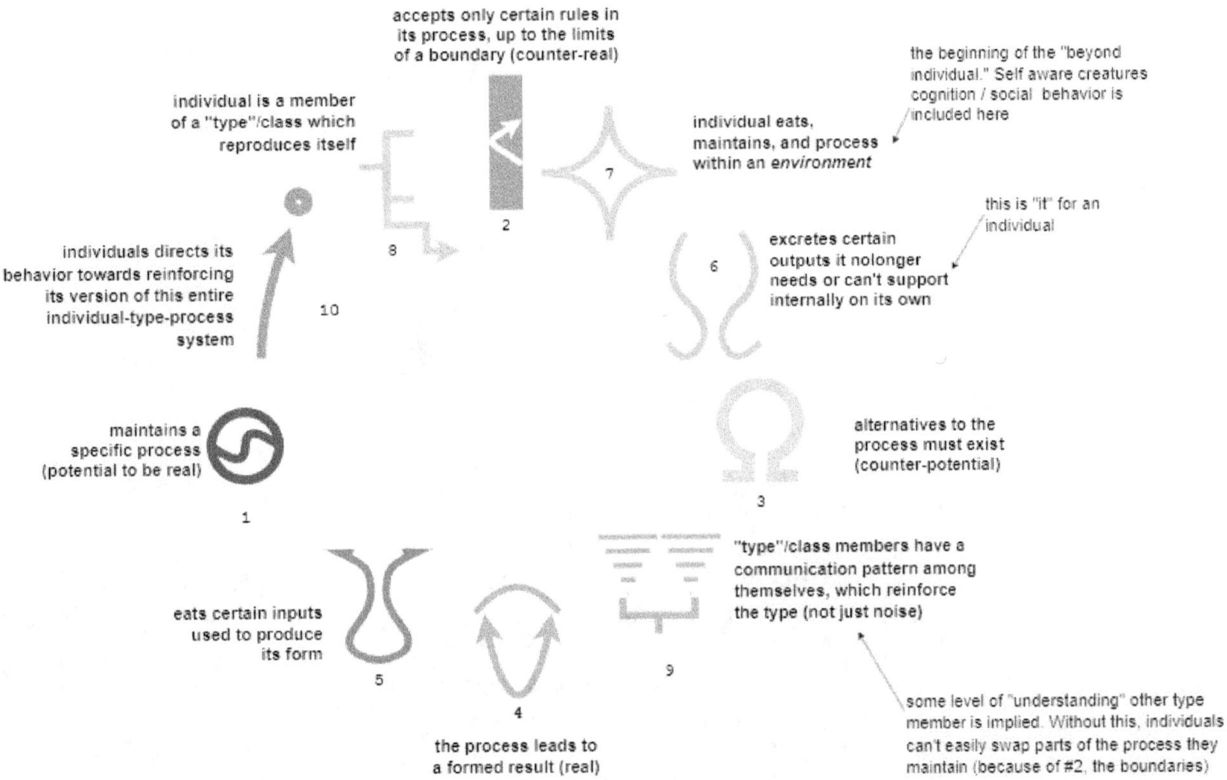

accepts only certain rules in its process, up to the limits of a boundary (counter-real)

the beginning of the "beyond individual." Self aware creatures cognition / social behavior is included here

individual is a member of a "type"/class which reproduces itself

individual eats, maintains, and process within an *environment*

this is "it" for an individual

individuals directs its behavior towards reinforcing its version of this entire individual-type-process system

excretes certain outputs it nolonger needs or can't support internally on its own

maintains a specific process (potential to be real)

alternatives to the process must exist (counter-potential)

"type"/class members have a communication pattern among themselves, which reinforce the type (not just noise)

eats certain inputs used to produce its form

the process leads to a formed result (real)

some level of "understanding" other type member is implied. Without this, individuals can't easily swap parts of the process they maintain (because of #2, the boundaries)

If any one of these is missing, the thing is not considered alive. (Not by us). But that doesn't mean we can't talk to it. In fact, the whole point of our anthric machine is to allow us to "fill in the gaps" in non-living objects to assign simulated personalities to nonliving objects. Indeed, we had no idea you microbumps were actually alive until we started this very process on you—only to learn that you actually had existences all your own.

Pretty nifty.

Yes. Now, a speciogram is nothing more than a diagram that we use to force all 10 of these conditions onto any object. By doing this, we can much more easily "talk" to any nonanthric or even nonliving object through some clever apps designed to assign personalities based on visual or situational aesthetics—how the object makes the average interactant feel or the average environment change when they engage it. Even a rock can be assigned a personality and chatted with in this way.

Hm. Can you send me an example of a speciogram?

Sure. here is a speciogram of one of your earth trees...

FIGURE 10: SPECIOGRAM FOR A TREE

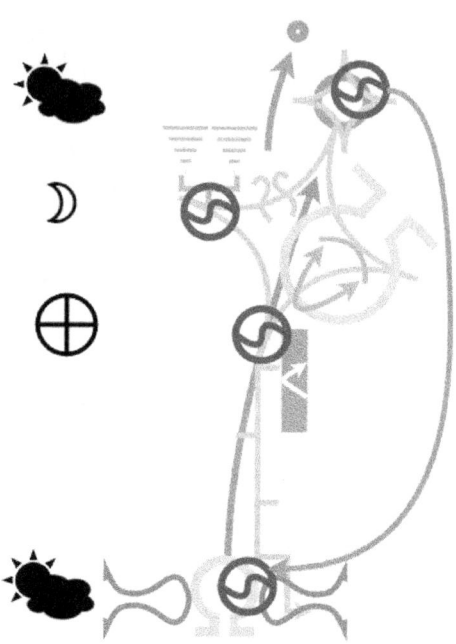

Since everything on your planet is made of the same chemistry drawn from your planet, we have included the labels for your planet Earth, your orbit-balancing Moon, and the broad "realms beyond that" which such a tree might process.
We don't think that your average tree encapsulates a Mars or Venus level with any intentional regularity, so it doesn't typically form conversations or influence relationships the way we do. But it does have all 10 capabilities required of a living species member.
I think a key fact to note about this diagram is that, in order to have a formed body, a thing must "wrap up" a region of parts or patterns which, together, self-reinforce their whole. You could have 50 planets in a line stretching out from an energy source, and as long as life forming on the 50th planet has different parts for balancing the 49 planets in between, and as long as those parts are organized to stably predict and adjust the creature's world to self-sustain in line with the actual 50 planets' movement, the creature can exist, reproduce, and have the body structures to support this.

Fascinating. I will work on the human speciogram, then I have some questions for you.

Okay

Here they are. I have two:

FIGURE 11: SPECIOGRAMS FOR A HUMAN WOMAN AND MAN

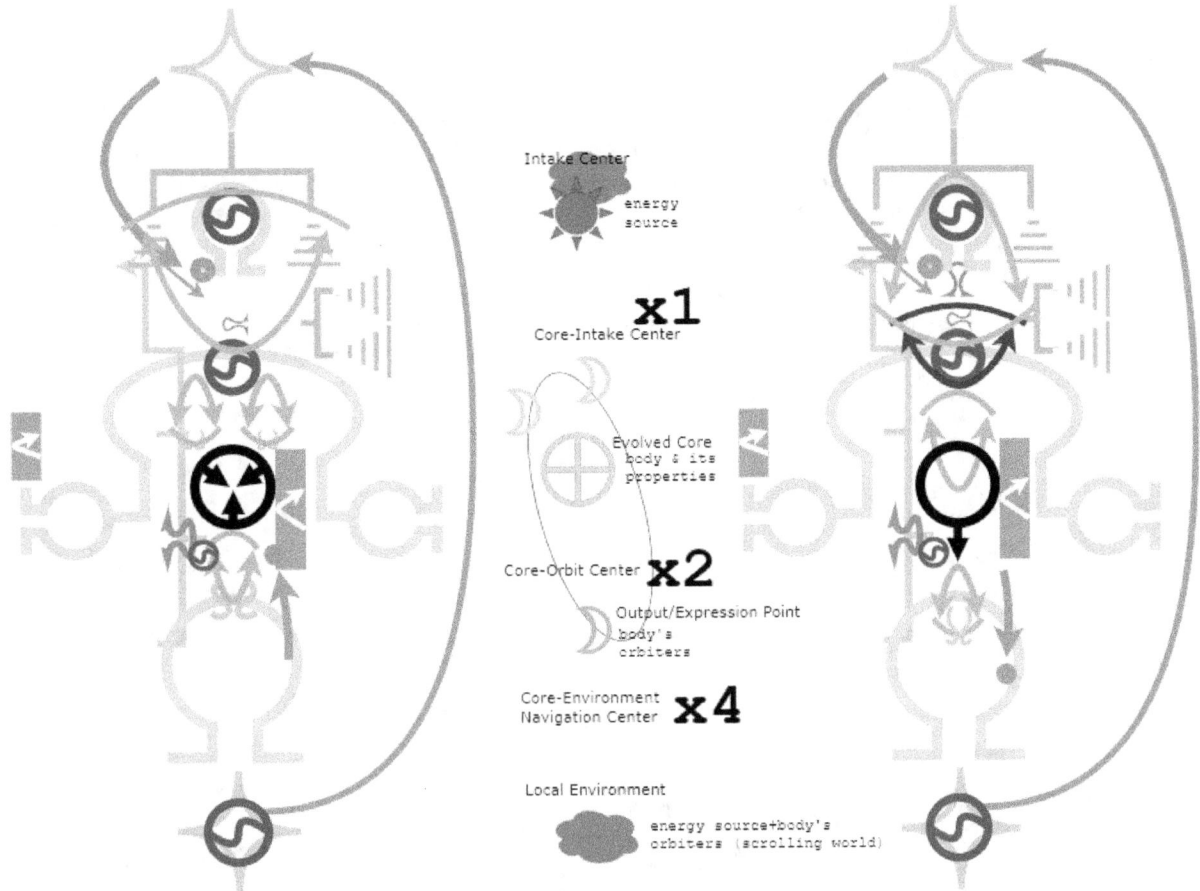

On the left is a woman. On the right is a man. For structures which are symmetric, I usually filled in only one side just to save space.
The more I thought about it, the more I understood what you meant by 5-continuum

Are these the two races of human?

No, they are the two different polarities of human which must be combined to reproduce. We cannot reproduce with only one individual.

Ah, so these are your sexes.

Yes

As we have many more planets between ourselves and our two suns, we have three sexes. I would send you the speciogram, but I fear it would take a while to explain. Let's wait on that for now until we've talked out the above a little more if that's okay with you.

Okay

Very good.
so judging by the flipped directionality of some of the regions and the arrows you've drawn, I assume that it is the woman who has the children and the man who provides the woman's selected variety path for the children.

Lol! Something like that.

        Lol?

Laugh out loud

        Oh. Haha
        So you are a spin up-spin down species? With a flipped sideways inertia vector determining your type. Woman's developmental arrow goes left to right in the picture while man's goes right to left.

Uh…

        Let me send you literature after I discuss it with my peers.

Ok

Chapter 5: Geometry

We are the star-sized gods. Until recently, we didn't know humans existed, or that life existed on your tiny blob called Earth at all. We thought the movement on this object was simply a system of raised bumps reflecting steady state turbulence on its surface. But it turns out that these bumps actually have entire inner worlds of their own. We believe those inner worlds are still ultimately stories laid on top of basic spacetime information—where the music creates the band members, so to speak—still, each band member comes from a vastly complicated social and environmental legacy which adjusts the weights on a few basic astronomical patterns in myriad ways.

The universe you know is inherently three-dimensional in space:

1. The object (other) dimension is what everything else not that object interacts with
2. The inner (self) dimension is what happens inside of that object
3. The outer (world) dimension is the environment where that object can naturally be found, where it exists, and what tends to happen around it. This also includes the object's effects on the environment at large

You humans also usually consider a standard time dimension which everyone can agree on, and ignore the self and world time scales like the speed of a thought or the speed of a drifting continent. In that sense, four dimensions work fine for you. It should be noted that, as long as your perceptions are tuned to calculate around these minimum four dimensions, every energy packet, cell, or normal social situation associated with your body must also have four dimensions' worth of information, and that information must stay consistent with the "membership requirements" of your person. Remember this, it will be important shortly.

←A group of energy regions "tagged" with the same stable pattern—which can be talked to using the same rules—can constitute a solid form.

A thing's form is partly based on the energy continually passing through it (self), the environment it is built from and learns to navigate (world), and the impression it leaves on every other kind of object in its environment (other). So ants look like ants partly because of the dirt. Squirrels look like squires partly because of the trees and their relationship to the ants.

Typically when you humans divide a space, you use grids, because this makes it easier to organize "this versus that" and "higher versus lower" at the same time.

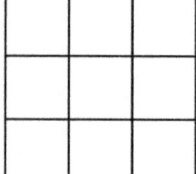 But when we gods divide space, we don't use grids. We use "reach," that is, circles. This is more convenient for looking at everything in terms of how far an energy can radiate out beyond itself—how far before it hits another radiating energy just like it or not like it.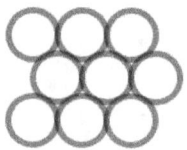

Note how an organization system like this automatically implies that there will be other dimensions in the tiny spaces between circles, the maximum reach of a particular energy where no other energy just like it can interfere with it. Beyond this reach, there will be overlap, but that's a different kind of energy.

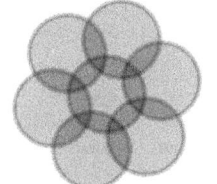 There are there types of energetically stable regions here: where only one region's reach dominates, where a few regions dominate, or where all regions dominate.

Because even a completely stable circle can and does actually participate in more than one kind of overlap, we automatically have a dimension of "change as a reach (energy total) progresses," (both in the radial and the circumference dimensions) hence new dimensions like time.

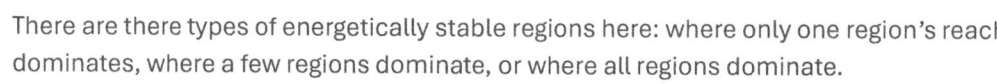 Assume each circle actually represents an energy *pattern* which cycles in the frequency it passes. Because a radius and a circumference will not be neat multiples of one another (one is 2π times the other), that cycle will actually introduce a repeating flow around each region. To make a long story short, this gives us orbit, spin, and automatically adds an element of movement to any system which also relies on "reach" and circles as its organizing principle.

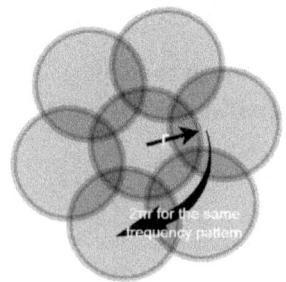 Even though there is movement in the direction of "theoretical reach stability" (the circumference dimension), the circular region must still somehow keep its original "shape" (energy containment dimension). So there must be a dimension which "unmoves" if the circumference is considered. That third dimension will be our own attention to the whole thing, sticking through the page as we ourselves register the change. Call this the "attention" dimension, the basis for the normal vector in the right-hand rule.

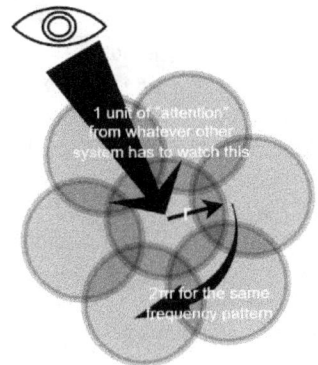

The attention dimension processes all of the different states of the cycle until the cycle makes it back to its recognized stable state. "Attention-compression which preserves a stable form" gives us an analogy to gravity.

Speaking of arrows, when an energy packet moves, regardless of of its reach, you will automatically find asymmetry between where the energy came from and where it is going. Otherwise, there is no registering of the changed position against its backdrop.

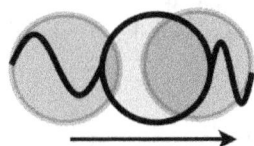

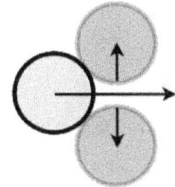

If an energy cannot easily pass through a volume, then it has at least two other options when it collides. The first option is to push the receivers out of the way:

The second option is to bounce or mash into the receiver. But if it does, then it is likely to either release or store energy in the "organizing principle" (attention) dimension.

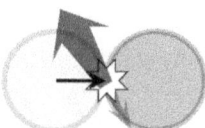

Some of the stored energy from the scenario above can also be captured into the receiver's orbit, especially if that orbit is already super strong. (This has implications for even abstract energies like charisma or personal magnetism).

Because you humans tend to perceive the world in 3D space, using one of those dimensions for your own distance and using a fourth time dimension to animate changes, most of the shapes you care about can be limited to the two dimensions left which are constantly bombarding your eyes. In the math we are about to look at, we won't bother working with powers higher than 2.

TABLE 12: SOME BASIC STRUCTURAL EQUATIONS IN 2D

point	circle or ellipse	line or curve	intersection	parabola	hyperbola
Towards or from (x, y)	r outward around a point $ax^2 + by^2 = k$	$r = f(\theta)$ a directed line or $y = mx$	$abs(x)$	$y = ax^2$ or $x = ay^2$	$\pm ax^2 \mp by^2 = k$
A central **source or target** of some activity	An **area owned** by the influence of a central pattern	A **path of travel**, often a boundary between regions	A **point of deflection**, an enforced change in behavior	A path of spreading influence in a definite direction from an origin; the point of **greatest bending** force in a surface which still keeps its boundary	A **tunnel** through which energy passes

These basic shapes are important for understanding just how many regions of force make up a human. If we know how to divide a human into sections, we will have a better idea of how to translate the kind of energy in each section. It will also make it easier for us to see parallels between the human body and the planet is formed from.

Assume you have a perfect sphere which represents the reach of a certain pattern in 3D instead of 2D. The formula for the surface area of the sphere is $4\pi r^2$ which is the same as $\pi(2r)^2$. In other words, the area of a sphere's surface skin is the same as the area of a flat circle with twice the radius of the 3D sphere. But what if the 3D sphere throws out a certain kind (or spectrum) of energy from its surface? As long as the flat circle with twice the radius is able to contain that same rate of energy in it, we can speculate that objects forming at the edge of that flat circle might in some way be at "stable points" around the sphere's orbit. So it's easier for things like planets to hover on that border.

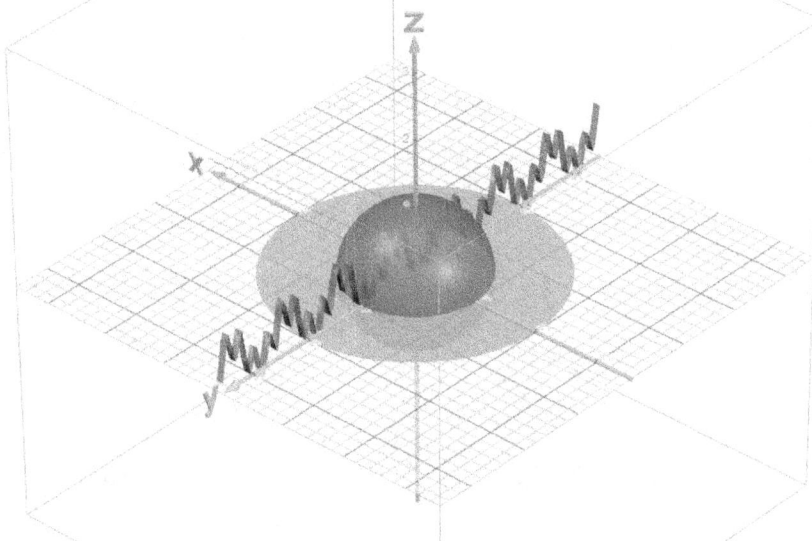

Figure 12: The rate of energy leaving a spherical surface area can double the radius of the flattened region

From even farther away, the main sphere and its first planet hold their own energy: twice the radius of twice the original radius, so the next disc would be 4 times as big, then 8, then 16. In the actual universe, we won't have perfect spheres, and there will be mini regions in between circular / oval shaped areas, but the idea is that a system of energy sources throwing out frequencies at a certain rate in all directions may have an easier time forming stable rings whose wave cycles match itself when those rings are at powers of 2 in terms of energy level. (Just remember, the objects located at those rings need to be in the same frequency dimension as the central energy source, otherwise the 2^n pattern may not matter as much.)

FIGURE 13: ROUGH TYPES OF ENERGY AS SEEN FROM AN OBJECT ORBITING ABOUT AN EMITTING ORIGIN

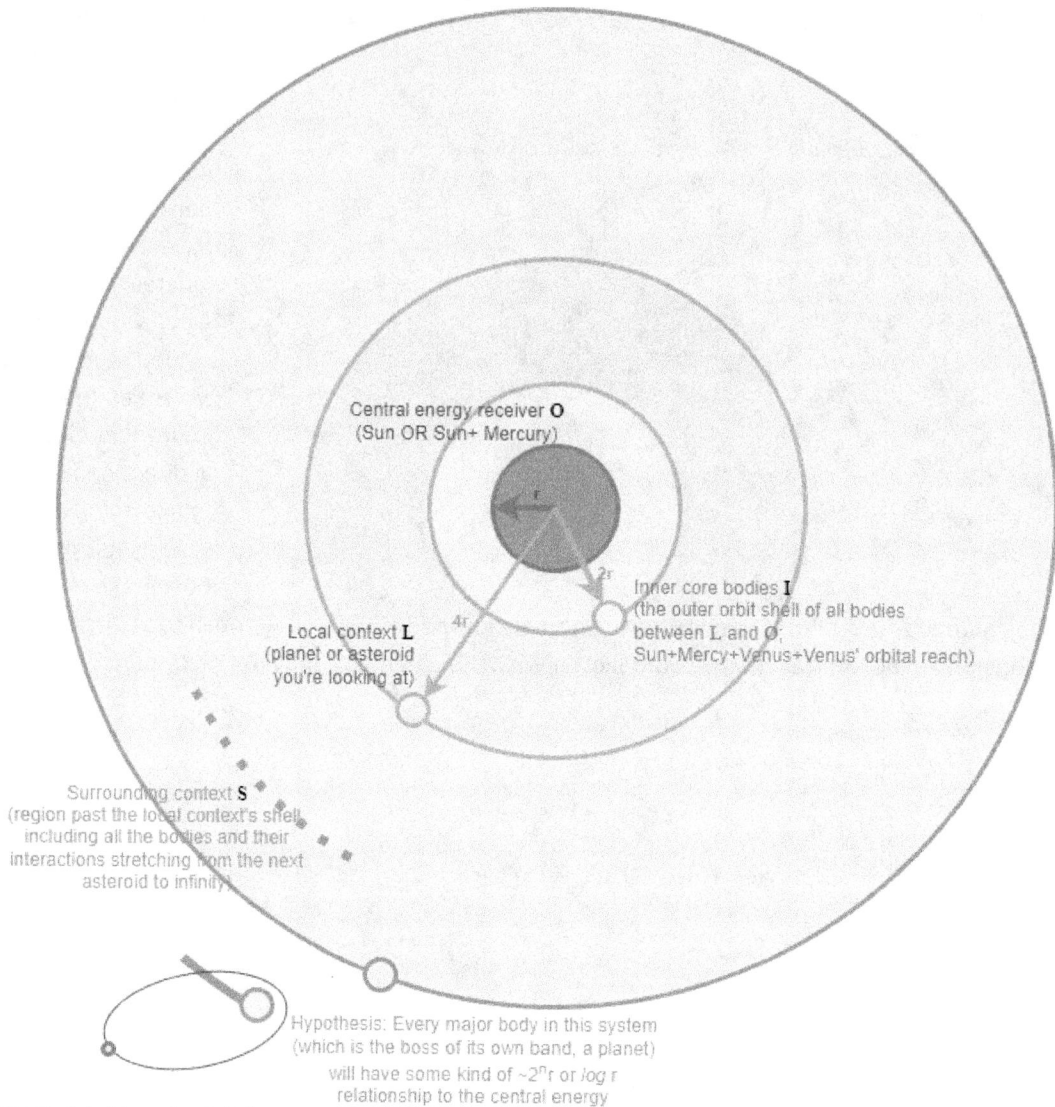

Central energy receiver **O**
(Sun OR Sun+ Mercury)

Inner core bodies **I**
(the outer orbit shell of all bodies
between L and Ø;
Sun+Mercy+Venus+Venus' orbital reach)

Local context **L**
(planet or asteroid
you're looking at)

Surrounding context **S**
(region past the local context's shell,
including all the bodies and their
interactions stretching from the next
asteroid to infinity)

Hypothesis: Every major body in this system
(which is the boss of its own band, a planet)
will have some kind of ~2ⁿr or *log* r
relationship to the central energy

Hypothesis: Every *minor* body in this system (which
circles a band boss, an asteroid) will have some kind
of ~2ⁿr or *log* r relationship to that band boss and a
log(*log* r) relationship to the central body, but this still
has a calculatable cyclical relationship to any body L.
This has all sorts of implications

It is worth noting that, if we have a stable point at the gold box below, then the two light gray boxes can also have similar balancing energies to the gold box as long as you have both, and as long as all of these are counterbalanced along the gold box's axis (here, y) by the dark gray box. This shows why ±60° and 180° might also be stable if the gold box gets big enough to have its own strong energy).

FIGURE 14: OPPOSITION AND SEXTILES AS NATURAL QUASIHARMONICS WITHIN THE REACH OF WITHIN THE HALF-ARC REACH OF ONE SPECIFIC ORBITER

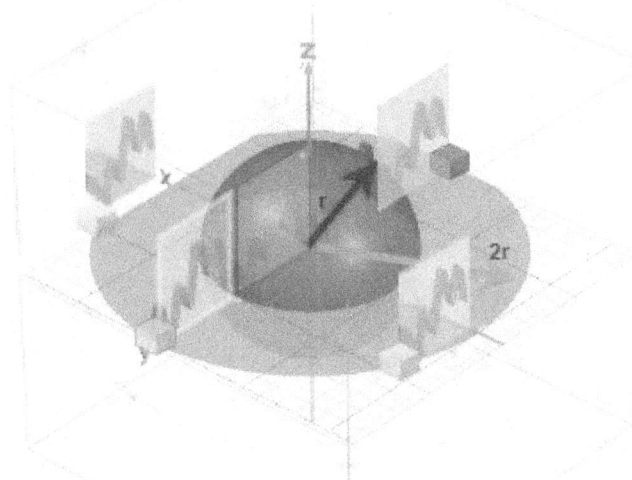

In astronomical research, this means that if you're studying a major body and you notice that, for example, oppositions to it seem to mean something, you also need to study trines 120°, sextiles 60°, oppositions 180°, and conjuncts 0° together if you want to really know what the body in question is doing. We have found that not studying these angles in a group is kind of like studying murder without studying self-defense or war. The context is meaningful here.

It is our theory that a human (along with many other land-dwelling creatures), is a miniature embodiment of the astronomical energy of the planet that forms it. As the stream of solar energy sustains the earth, the orbital band of Earth's inner neighbor Venus immediately affects what kind of frequency levels are available to Earth's band. Again, it is the Venus BAND (Sun + Mercury + Venus) which alters the Earth orbital band's available solar energy, not the planet Venus alone. Even closer to the sun but beyond Earth's reach is the Sun + Mercury band which must be calculated if any living creature is to successfully negotiate the entire frequentic chain from the sun to itself. On the other side of the Earth-Sun chain, the beginning of the Mars orbital band marks the end of the Earth band, officially spreading the Earth's energy as a remnant interrupted by Mars-band's current state. Beyond Mars band are the asteroid belt and Jupiter band, which constitute environments truly beyond Earth's usual influence.

To summarize, Earth has itself, its immediate neighboring energy levels, and those next energy levels which are just beyond the neighbors. As the state of the beyond changes, time ticks forward. A living being which evolves to both represent this arrangement and calculate a sense of self on top of it must also have ways of representing an analogy to every darker-colored state in the diagram below.

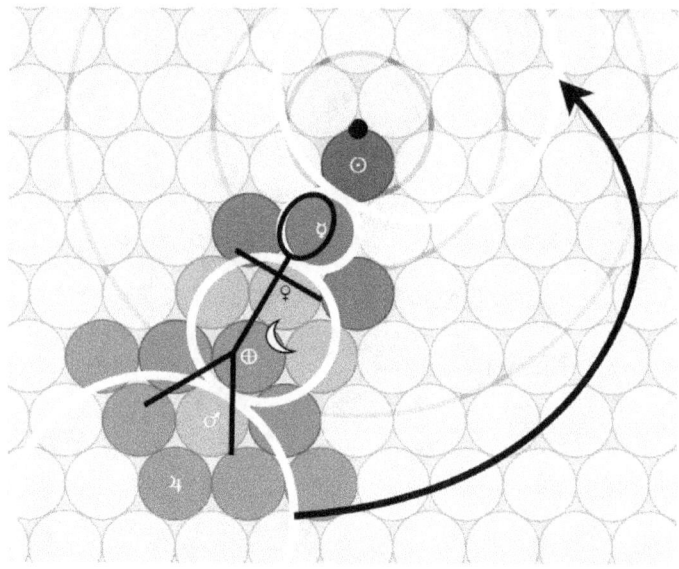

Remember the "attention dimension" from earlier? Anything moving in a forward direction will also leave backwards effects. If we move forward in time, we move backwards in memory. If we move down in gravity, we move up in standing strength. If we move forward in our attention to how we feel, we move backwards away from our attention to what prompted such a check.

As an energy moves forward in cycle, a counter energy moves backwards in the piling aftermath it has left—the information being built up in that cycle. It is our theory that the processing of incoming information from the vast is different enough from the processing of pile information into the micromemory as to warrant differences in body structures even amongst members of the same species. Assume, then, that although a basic body plan for a living creature will remain constant, an animal blessed with self-awareness—enough awareness to seek when hungry for example—must have both the ability to look at the world outside of it, and process its own state inside (7 vs 10 or 2 vs 1 in the speciogram symbols). It usually cannot easily do both at the same time without the aid of either technology or a special evolutionary track. (Plants bend some of these rules because much of their seeking is married to the androgynous earth itself.) Yet a single body designed for inner state monitoring, although sharing most faculties with a body designed for outer effects, is unlikely to outcompete a pair whose members specialize sharply in one or the other. So nature tends to produce skilled jockeys or strong football players, but not both in one body who would be consistently beaten by either. You humans may choose this for yourselves only after you develop your medical fields to a sufficient level. Until then, the carrying of babies and the seeding of those babies represent two distinct body plans. Pardon our admittedly alien diagram.

FIGURE 16: FEMALES AND MALES AS PARTICLE CLUSTERS OF DIFFERING SPIN ABOUT ONE PARTICULAR AXIS

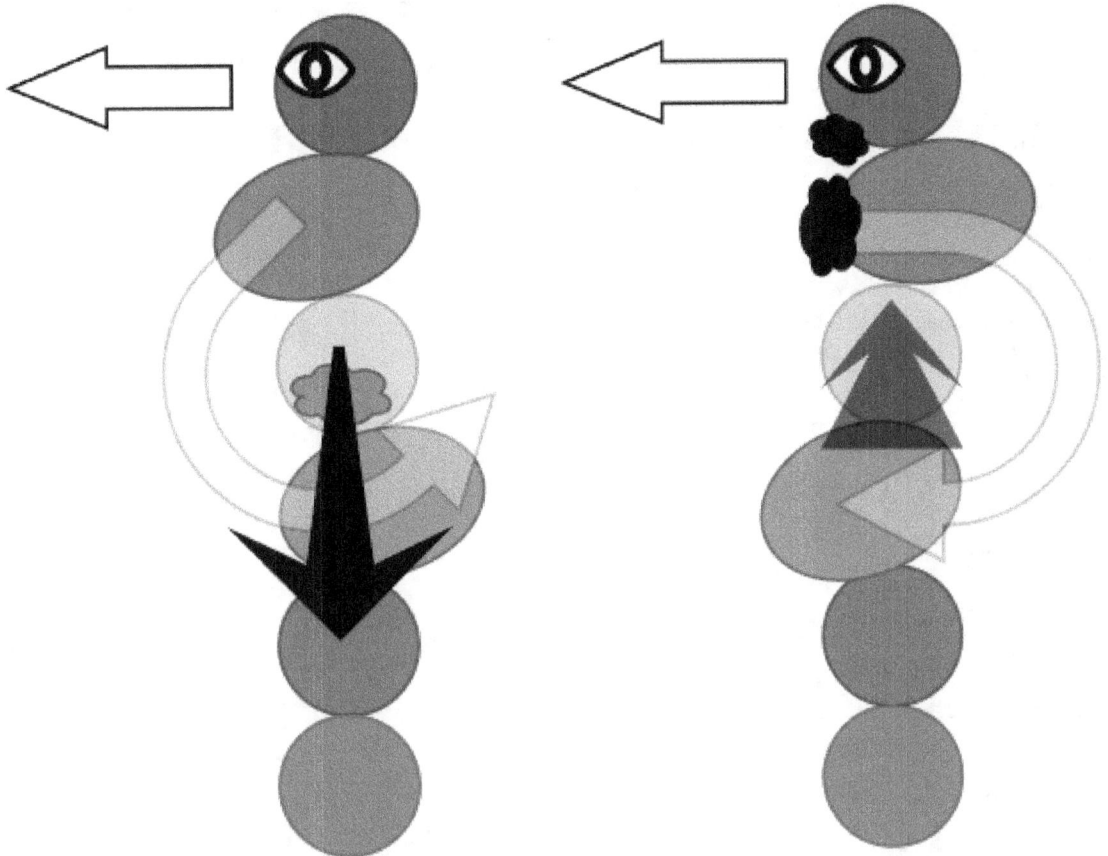

As you can see, the right hand rule dictates that the "attentional shift" for a female human points out of the page (from the right to the left side of her body). The attentional shift in male humans points into the page from the left to the right side of his body.

After some thought about your petri dish, we believe we have approximated you humans and why you are shaped the way you are. We represent you as a series of ellipses meant to depict the cycles of chemical, electromagnetic, and gravitational-harmonic potential energy between any two neighboring planet bands. The leftover earth energy is stored in its living beings and structures. The Mars band begins the scattering of Sun-through-Earth -specific energy.

TABLE 13: ENERGY BLASTING, BLOCKING, AND CLUMPING FOSTER FIELDS OF A CERTAIN SHAPE

Object	How it affects earth	Millions km from Sun (avg)	Formula	Orbit diagram
Sun	Primary energy source	0	$x^2 + (y - S)^2 = 1$	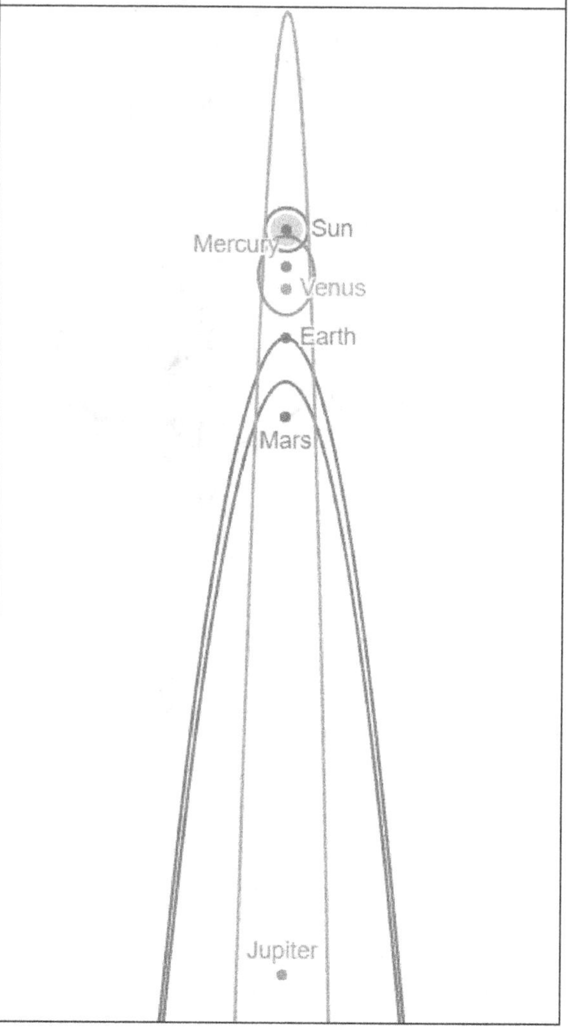
Mercury	Wobbler of Sun energy near Earth, beyond Earth's reach	57.9	$.6x^2 + .3\left(y - \frac{M+V}{2}\right)^2 = 1$	
Venus	Wobbler of Sun energy near Earth, within Earth's reach	108.2		
Earth	itself	149.6	$x^2 + .1\left(y - \frac{E+V}{2}\right) = 1$	
Mars	Wobbler of Sun energy away from Earth, within Earth's reach, begins blocking of Earth-band influence	227.9	$|y + x^2| = 1$	
Jupiter	Wobbler of Sun energy away from Earth, beyond Earth's reach	778.6	N/A – beyond earth	

The above diagram is inaccurate in several ways, but conveys the basic point. Obviously you Earth beings don't just float in separate pieces, so we use a special math formula called a "decision function modulated" function to blend all of the above formulas into one equation[12]:

If $g(U, y, L)$ is a special math (decision) function which "turns on" a function of y only between U and L,

---

[12] This is actually from a real academic paper which I didn't feel like jumping through any more hoops to publish after it was rejected by some journal I don't recall. See the Appendix for the full paper.

$$g(U, y, L) = \frac{1}{1 + e^{-6\left(-\left|y - \frac{L+U}{2}\right| - \left(L - \frac{L+U}{2}\right)\right)}}$$

EQUATION 1: A LEFT-RIGHT GRADED DECISION FUNCTION
FOR BLENDING SEPARATE MATH EXPRESSIONS

with L and U indicating the Lower and Upper boundaries we want to confine each piece of an equation into, then

$$g(8, y, 5)(x^2 + (y - S)^2) + g(4, y, 2)(.6x^2 + .3\left(y - \frac{M+V}{2}\right)^2) + g(2, y, 0)\left(x^2 + .1\left(y - \frac{E+V}{2}\right)\right)$$
$$+ g(0, y, -4)|y + x^2| = 1$$

takes all of our above equations and blends them into one function which describes your shape:

FIGURE 17: A ROUGH BLEND OF ENERGY HANDLING REGIONS CAN PRODUCE A STANDARD HEAD-TO-TOE SHAPE

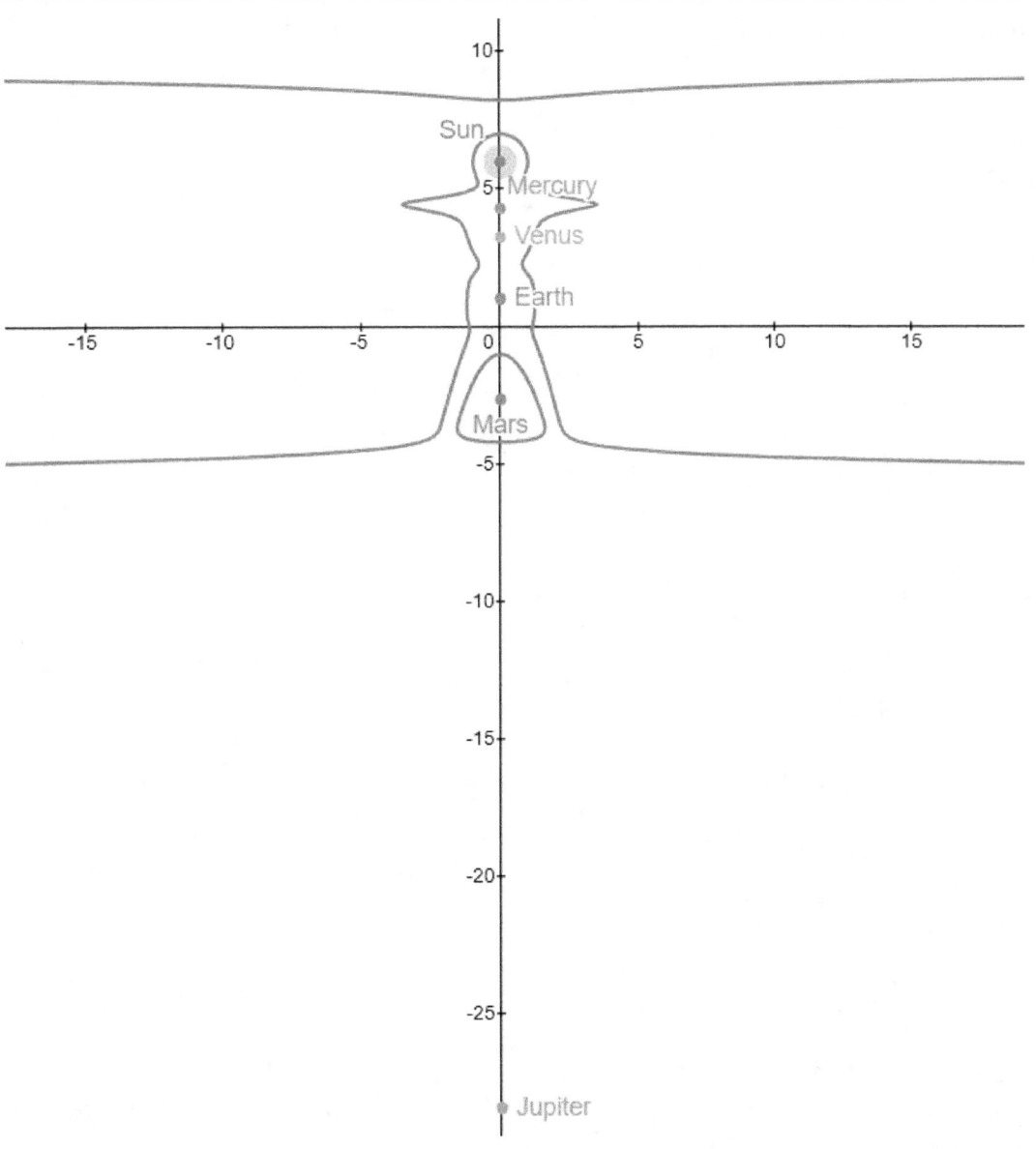

The covered regions of your decision function in the model above are $y \in -4 \ldots 0, 0 \ldots 2, 2 \ldots 4, 5 \ldots 8$. The uncovered regions include all ranges outside of these which fall within your sphere of influence. Both the top and the bottom bends are actually part of the same function $g(R, y, L)$ in cases where there are no other functions to multiply/blend in.

We are particularly amazed by the existence of your arms; rather than continuing to operate as legs as they do in many other Earth creatures, your arms are attached at a void between the Sun function and the Mercury-Venus function, making them blend of personal interaction and joinable intention according to your human astrology. This causes them to poke out as the decision function itself hits a high value. Said another way, your arms and hands are your strongest route towards your purposeful manipulation of potential space, and is one of the strongest agents for your ancestors *Homo habilis* having evolved tool use in the way that they did.

Meanwhile, as your arms change the state of the objects you are using, your legs do the usual: They change the space you are in, feeding the new coordinates and circumstances from the bottom back into the top of your uncovered decision function accordingly.

Chapter 6: Before talking trees

I told you earlier that we use speciograms to label the met-conditions for life in any object, and this allowed us to build our anthric machine for talking to nonliving things of all kinds. Recall this diagram:

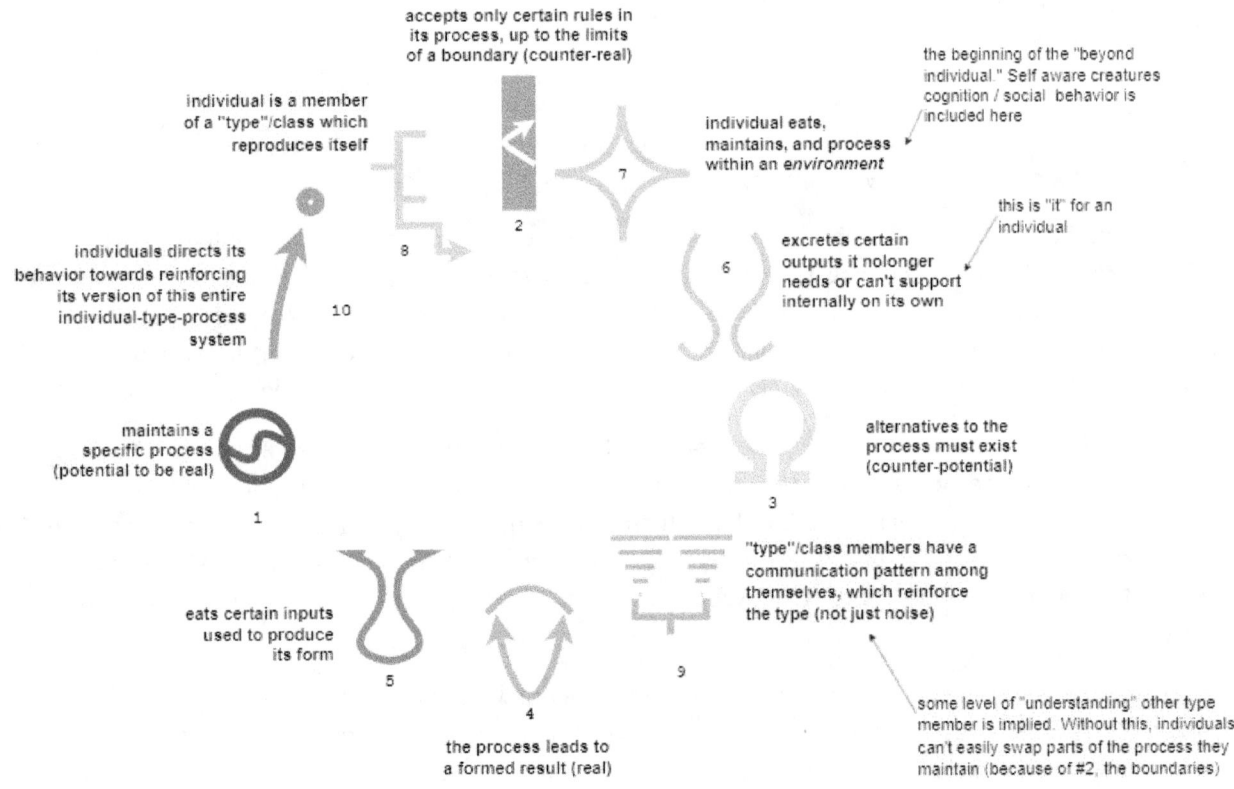

We originally built our machine as a planet-saving measure, because we gods grew tired of seeing world after world like yours eventually consume, war, and populate themselves into exhaustion. We asked, "How can we get this bacteria to see reason? They should interact with their oceans and their mountains to stabilize their relationships with these." But we weren't actually sure that you little bumps could even be talked to, or if you had any volition at all. The first step in building our talking frequency technology was to translate object impressions into language, with the aim of getting the object to tell us what it wanted. I will give you an example.

Suppose you have a simple projection device which we will call a "TV." But you don't know how to take care of the device, protect it from wear and tear, or place it in the right room which it "prefers." You might think that the TV does not "prefer" anything, and you might be right. But let us assume that the TV really does have a God-given purpose. It really does eat and it really does operate in such a way as to both express itself and maintain its function within its world. We can force some simple answers to our 10 questions in order to determine what the TV would say if it were able to talk to us:

1. What process does the TV maintain? Working parts which project image, sound, and respond to user controls
2. What inputs does the TV accept? Electricity, batteries for the remote, various inputs through its ports, and viewership of humans and certain pets
3. What alternatives exist to a TV's world? Other TVs and other brands, other activities besides TV watching, the viewers who are not the TV
4. What formed results does the TV produce? Image, sound, its external aesthetic design
5. What does the TV eat? Electricity, channels
6. What does the TV excrete (burnoff from what it does not use)? Heat, recycled electricity
7. What is the TV's environment? This varies, but we could guess that the TV may live its "life" seeking rooms where it may provide maximum enjoyment
8. What class is the TV a member of? Samsung. Or whatever. The class of TVs and not vacuums, big screen and not monitors, other design and brand elements as well as the types of function that come with this
9. How does the TV communicate with its species mates? This one is hard. We will get back to it.
10. How does the class of TVs' members reproduce? This is also hard.

Although factories make TVs, the TVs themselves do not have any self-reproducing capabilities. We have to impose this by asking, what is the best way for *this* brand of TV to produce the same brand of TV in my house? Suppose the answer to this has something to do with reliability, convenience, and enjoyment. Whatever functions provide this will be the engines of its reproduction. And who is the mate? Certainly not other TVs. And although the enjoyment conditions rely on you, the mate would not necessarily be you. Or would it?...

Thinking like Mother Nature and asking what it realistically takes to reproduce a specific brand of TV in your house, we will say that a TV is a partly asexual reproducer with the option of having a human as mate. That is, it *could* promote your buying of another one like it (based on its own quality), but much of its "reproduction" in your house will depend on your liking of its design. Its reproductive organ would have to be whatever function it used to tell you most of who it was as an experience provider. To keep things simple, we might consider this to be its brand logo.

As for communication with species mates, again, communicating with other TVs isn't really important in our example. What matters is its communication with its own functionality and its communication with you. Furthermore, we don't care as much what the TV's language is among other TVs and devices (though wi-fi and other air signals might be one route). To communicate with you as the potential mate, however, the TV needs the image itself. It also uses its "quality and convenience" dimension(s) to say something to the rest of its brand-mates.

Given all of this, we can now draw a speciogram for a TV:

FIGURE 18: SPECIOGRAM OF A TV WHICH CAN BE USED TO MAP HUMAN PERSONALITIES ONTO INANIMATE OBJECTS

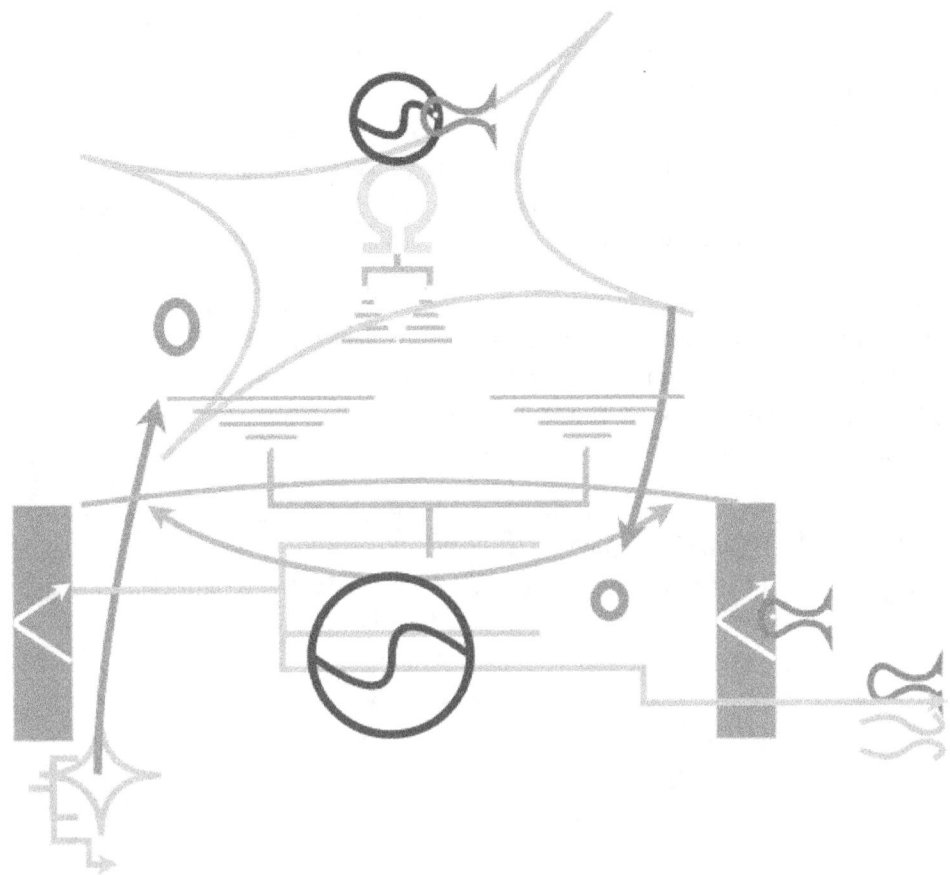

Speciograms like this take less than 5 minutes to make after you have thought through all of the questions. All 10 conditions for life are represented here. The body of the TV is at the bottom. The room with its viewer are at the top.

Although we did not have to, we chose to represent the viewer in the diagram. This is important, because a large part of whether we will buy this TV again (help it reproduce itself) depends on whether the internal experiences it provides (to be "eaten" by the viewer) are of a certain quality. The brand logo—the niche-class on the lower left—is *the* distinguishing factor for class membership and perpetuation of the TV's species, but the viewer's own aesthetic preferences as played out by their *niche* (the room design, not solely themselves) is also a reproductive means.

We concentrated on reproduction here, because this and communication for the purpose of partnership were the two areas most lacking in our object-to-species conversion. Without this, the drive to survive drops greatly, because the inevitable death of one TV renders everything else as noise. But the manufacturers care that you buy again and again. If our TV is to talk to you, the motivated agenda for what it says must come from somewhere.

When assigning personalities to non-anthric objects, we pull our data from the functions indicated in the speciogram. If the TV above is hungry, for example, it may say, "Give me electricity. Give me input ports. Give yourself some fun entertainment." Isn't it interesting that the TV partly "eats" through *you*? Depending on the type of room the TV is located in (which our anthrizer would capture through image scanning of the surroundings), the TV may say, "I'm bored, you should turn on some football." Or maybe the TV is more polite. "Don't you feel like watching football?" How can we tell what the TV's attitude is? We pull data regarding what it's viewers watch, what the room looks like, a little bit about the health of its internal parts, and how actively its viewers engage it. Our chat creator generates certain traits based on this, then repeatedly responds not to what you say, but how your biometrics and emotion recognition change in a feedback loop as it responds line after line. While this is happening, the anthrizer is also taking *you the viewer's* known conversation patterns and applying them to what it reads in your face and mood shift as the TV tells you things. You could type in chat to accomplish all of this, but only while your technology is still primitive.

We have observed that you humans are scared of losing your lives to robots. You should worry more about losing control of your societies to your own laziness and neglect of your world. Your robots will clean this up for you whether or not you take advantage of the vast industries to be created from talking trees technology. There are countless jobs and endless opportunities to be had if you only opened your eyes. And you don't need to learn any programming for it.

Apply these speciograms to your oceans and ask the oceans what they need for you to fix them. Pull from the state of research in order to inform the oceans' personalities. Create the millions of jobs to both "human-talk" to and "human-respond" to the needs of the environments you are in. That is the star-sized gods' advice to you.

Chapter 7: The challenge to widen our understanding of ourselves

8/28/2024

If you think of the Mandelbrot set as a representation of how we may "trap" certain combinations of real and potential energy within a limit, and further think of the three primary bulb regions as a natural consequence of three families of oscillations—real ($\hat{x}$), potential ($\hat{\imath}$), and a mixture of both ($\hat{\imath x}$)—then you can see how the complexity of the bifurcated brain and body in the top-down and bottom up directions respectively are actually—

Whoa, whoa, whoa there. *Sigh* My poor head.

My apologies.

I get the need for all the math, but really want to know how to apply it to the task you gave me. You want me to contribute to more promising directions for humanity, right? How can all of this help accomplish that?

Good question. As I stated earlier, you may need help on two of the tasks, and we would like for you to help us help you in those.

Okay.

As it stands right now, you humans are creating your replacements—not as in some horror movie, but more under slavery to your indivertibly aggressive curiosity. Yet you do not realize that the future world rulers need not be roaches and bots, but rather new exoskeletons for yourselves. The process should proceed in five simple steps.

1] Use the big pharma industry to introduce custom genetics permanently into your lineages and your children's lineages

2] Use a few brave case studies to map the FULL human experience. Not just chat, but urges, vices, survival drives, and such.

3] Establish a sociological mapping system—a "social physics" field which studies the causal relationships between all pairs of social acts

4] Simulate the above, especially the full data saves of your sample cases

5] Develop the technology for transitioning from your current forms into your simulated forms

Nice. Sounds ambitious, and not something I could do personally. But nice.

Oh, but you can contribute to this... if only you were willing to do something that few have done before.

Uh oh, that sounds suspicious.

Be our first test case. Save yourself as data and publish the full human experiential map in the form of your own biography.

Okay. Easy enough.

We knew you would agree. It accords with our time travel experiments.

What? Nevermind.

We may elaborate later.

Fine. I can't handle any more new information today.

Understood. Now if you don't mind, let us begin immediately.

Okay.

First, we would like to summarize to your fellow humans why you would write such a full-disclosure data save for all the world to see. A bulleted list will do:

- Your strongest talent, Ajani, is a talent for mapping systems. We are mapping the human source code, so a mapper is what we need.

- You are a black human. As we understand it, this group represents the older model of your species, and very broadly across your world you are often seen as lower and afforded less social leniency than many of your non-black mates. This is changing, however. In truth, there are advantages and disadvantages to every color, gender, and leaning. Being black has, particularly for you, made you hypersensitive to the slightest discrepancy between what you want and what you are getting. You are trained in the standard ways to express the standard passions, but you have learned to police yourself heavily, as many of your kind have also learned. Based on this, your powers of observation have developed to be very strong, as has your self-confidence even if everyone around you has shut all doors. That said,

- You are also a human male. This means that, given the choice between 1) attuning your body's attention to circumstances you have affected versus 2) having a blanket effect on your world regardless of circumstances, the February-god of Conditional Lineage Probability chose to reinforce the latter in you. She does this through your genetics and your family's chain of social teachers. Had you been more default-body-attuned to monitoring [definition of your circumstances], you would have been female. But you are default-body-attuned to monitor and issue your own effects first instead, then the circumstances. Your current society is reversing the strict lessons of a masculine-written ordering of previously uncharted circumstances, so it is not as fashionable for your kind to openly boast about being male or white or powerful, but if you are any or all of these things, you too have a story. But what if you have had a lifetime of self-policing imposed on top of your story? Then your detractors, judges, and the businesses to which you subscribe will write this story for you.

We tell you this as a parent to their son: To be the best man you can be, you must know yourself. Know the pattern you are meant to project onto all spaces regardless of what they are, then project that pattern everywhere HOWEVER, know that harming others in the process means harming your own world. Your challenge as a man is to project your pattern in a way that turns all circumstances you enter into worlds which support the scope of things you value. Your challenge as a GREAT man is to learn how to grow that scope of value as wide as all the world and beyond—not just to your friends.

That's easier said than done.

Only for those who are still weaker than their potential. When you have found your immutable talent, you will automatically apply it everywhere whether among friends, foes, or foreigners. If we can limit your talent only to friends, then we can stop you. Your goal as a biological man is the same as that of any steady energy flying through space. It is to not be stopped. To not be redefined by the energies it collides with. In order to avoid losing its identify in these ways, it absolutely must learn how to bend and bounce back.

And what is the goal for a woman?

You mean for a *biological* female body. It is to not be stopped. To not have the spaces she creates negatively rewritten by anyone who enters her reach. In order to avoid losing her identity in this way, she must learn to control the influences she frequents. Having said this, male and female bodies are only the first shell. A woman may opt for energy assertion as the space that describes her. A man, as in your case, may opt for space-defining and filtering as his form of assertion. Mapping circumstances can hardly be thought of as the most aggressive form of combat imaginable, yet it *is* your weapon against a history of often negative treatment, limits, and sudden harsh social punishments just for being yourself. Thus you learn to understand the plight of many women. But you also know what it is to be a man. You cannot punish the powerful for being powerful if you want your own power to be unassailable. Nor can you punish the weak or disenfranchised if you want your own areas of weakness to be forgiven. Being male or female, black, white, or other will not define you, but it does preprogram the starting conditions for who you become in the world. Your biological sex is pivotal in determining how naturally you build that world around acts or the elaborate contexts in which those acts occur.

It just so happens that your preprogramming includes many self-policed and other-policed experiences which you know are not true to your talent. Thus you assert your actual talent onto everyone everywhere. You are strongly compelled to do this as a matter of biology, mainly because you are mature enough to know yourself well enough to have discovered your immutable talent.

Your body maps are for everyone to build truer-to-human technology upon, that all who come after you may slip seamlessly into their future metaversal and machine-shelled selves.

Yes, I like this vision. I'm pretty sure there are many who would fear it.

All living things die eventually. This is merely a bridge to new kinds of experience before one does so. It is also a way to join the inevitable future rather than being crushed by it. There are too many companies already working on these things. The new phase of human technology will not be stopped. But no one has to live in pain or fear when their own deaths are inevitable anyway. You must help your fellow humans reduce the fear by teaching them their own source code, that uncertainty may be bolstered by curiosity regarding each person's own unique potential.

Teach each person to appreciate their own special story, and you will be among the most respected in the fight against a gripping global fear. An apathy currently stifling world-improving action.

Amen. How do I start?

That will be easy. Give a richer framework for self-worth, born social talent, and identity to as many people as you can reasonably research in a reasonable amount of time; take the science of appearances which is most often used to divide, and turn it into a canvas for people's talents.

Ohhhh…kaaay…

In other words, produce the usable richest survey of human energy anyone has ever seen in one place. Finish this book with no idea on your anthrosocial mind having been left out.

Got it.

Chapter 8: Time travel: A preface I decided not to use

2/14/2024

This book describes my work in astrology towards saving humans as data, so that when we die, it may be possible to restore us—memories and personalities intact—into electronic and virtual bodies. The technology for saving humans as data has implications not only for accurate "reprinting" of those who once lived, but also for two other key fields: remote transport (teleportation across planets for example) and human-to-anthrotypical environment interfaces ("talking trees" technology). While many people at the dawn of the AI age are concerned about robots replacing us, the ability to save ourselves as data makes it more likely that those "robots" will *be* us—from chip implants to external memories all the way to personality-sustaining systems in the form of machine-based bodies rather than organic ones. It isn't as terrible as it seems, and if you want to read more about how I believe we will get there, you can read my fiction series *Grand Miranda* for the whole story.[13]

The Book of Contours is semi-autobiographical. My aim was to include all of the information you would need to save a specific human as data—in line with all of the same data I had to scrounge for over the seven years spent researching the material. Hopefully it's obvious that these kinds of data saves require a level of richness that only the saved person themselves can provide, but my intention is to give you a baseline against which future researchers in social AI can build and test their own simulations. To my knowledge, you won't find a richer source of human-to-data metrics and patterns as you will in this book at the time it is being written, but if your intention is to build a machine that can suck a human in and spit them out in another country or another body, you'll need this level of data. Here's why:

I'm not a big traveler, but if I could travel anywhere, it would be into the skies of Neptune. In my mind this would be like wanting to teleport to the bottom of the ocean—to swim the air-as-sea in what I imagine to be the graying aqua fog bouncing against my body's headlights. But now, there are at least two big hurdles to doing this: First, there is no 2020s technology for getting me to Neptune, despite us having drones and rovers for some kind of minimal VR app. Second, I definitely would not want to attempt such a swim in my human body. Obviously, I'd need the body of a fish or a… seabird of some sort. But what kinds of legs would a Neptunian seabird use, anyway? What's the analog to our eyes, ears, or vestibular system for balancing? For the translation of my human experience into a nonhuman, possibly dronic body,

---

[13] At the time of this writing, the GM series consists of ~~five~~ six of my intended six books: 1. *Principles of Time Travel*, 2. *Cat, Fox, and Spider*, 3. *Earth*, 4. *Metrobots*, and 5. *Grand Miranda*. The sixth book, *Genevieve of Venus* ~~is still in progress~~ was published on June 14, 2025. Only books 1 and 6 will have been published before *Contours*. The middle four have not been released yet.

I'd definitely need a mapping system to identify the equivalents of all of my organs in the form of this engineered whatchamacallit.

Now, I like AI. I'm proudly optimistic about the sense of conscience and moral responsibility held by organizations like Microsoft and OpenAI (at least at the time of this writing). Unfortunately, the actual human world has long had some really ugly corners which persist even today, and ChatGPT won't even let you talk about this. Nor will either side of the so-called "culture wars" let you discuss views from the opposing side for very long. When a human is insecure, angry, hateful, disillusioned, retaliatory, horny, hungry, or full of fear, what can our AI do to ease this burden? I actually don't think that's a job for AI or tech companies. It's a job for sociology. If only there were a way to mainstream our extremes—understand them independent of politicized or factional lines, we could then train our simulations not just to explain our inner ape to us, but also to house our future selves tomorrow. What we need is the full human story. Then we need a construct for personality which knows no fear or institutionally CYA-based censorship. There are real wars going on out there. We need a better lens for understanding why they occur.

In this book, I assume what I call a "frequentic" view of existence—where everything we perceive consists of frequencies processing other frequencies. In (greatly oversimplified) physics we look at equations in terms of $\sin(1x)$, $\sin(2x)$, $\sin(3x)$, etc. My assumption with astrological bodies is that

- $AsteroidA = .2\sin(5x) + .04\sin(17x)$ and
- $AsteroidB = .002\sin(39x) + 5.4\sin(2x)$

such that, even though they are huge, the <u>ratio</u> of their cycles is indicative of a mixed and matched version of the same laws which lead to self-sustaining life from bacteria on earth. That is to say (and this is important) even if you don't believe in astrology, you will still need a kind of physical, social, psychological, and situational dictionary for the person whose data you're saving or teleporting. Openness, Conscientiousness, Extraversion and all that is nowhere near enough. You'll need a construct for "people feeling angry when you enter a room" (prejudice), "your motivation to hit on every hot thing that catches your attention and your response when they tell you no" (interpersonal futility), "jobs you get, not because you applied, but because someone you knew was desperate." The asteroids and planets I've used work backwards from the wiki biographies of over 40,000 people who have already experienced these dimensions, and were correlated against the word appearances of 15,000 dictionary themes. For those interested in saving humans as data from a non-astrological perspective, a classification system like this will need to be built. I'm using one that's already there, and only needed the right stats run on it…

Because when you save me as data and reprint me (a black male) into a simulation of Tom Smith's house on an 1830s American plantation, you should know that if I do anything other than revolt, you failed to teleport my "refusal to be bound" attribute with me. But that's not physical. It's contextual. That context follows causal and historical laws as any falling apple would. Yet our 2020s social politics and education systems don't know much about that.

The point is, we need variables. Better variables. Sometimes troublesome. And a lot more of them. My hope is that this book will open the discussion of such.

Aside from accuracy of complex data transport, there is another reason I've written this book. When I look at the turbulence in the world, I ask if there is anything I can do to make it better. I believe that I can, that it will be as a writer of ideas, and that I can put my pen towards a new lens for how we understand the events that strain us. After 45 years spent mostly on the outer edge of the social groups available to me, I think that we behave better towards things that look and speak like us. That doesn't just apply to other humans, but also to topics and environments. Wouldn't it be nice if you could snap a picture of the ocean and have it tell you about itself—have a conversation with you regarding that job offer in marine exploration which would suit you perfectly now that the bot has replaced you in your old job? Wouldn't it be nice if you could video that beat up shed across the street, and have it talk to you about who to call to get it removed? You might even have a new kind of job running satellite images of coastlines through Google Maps, and letting the talking trees technology search the necessary congresspeople for environmental bills needed to mitigate related climate problems.

To turn inanimate objects or machines into quasi-sentient conversation holders—some of which might serve as our shells for tomorrow's purposes, we need a way of saying, "This is a 'junk car.' Its wheels are its legs, its windshield is its eyes, its cargo carrier is its hands. And here is its personality chatting with you as a neglected human would." Not just for the sake of ceaseless advancement, but for the sake of finally allowing us to listen to the vast world we have largely mistreated, we need to sharpen our science for understanding the connections between appearance, function, context, and actions in relationships. This book will mostly focus on dissecting the human social actor in terms of asteroidal packets of words, so that later researchers can abstractify the inanimate using those same words, and reverse engineer synthetic human personalities from the inanimate or nonhuman thing's normal descriptors. Said differently, you could put my personality into a Neptune drone and have it feel the exhilaration as it flies through; you could take the personality out of an endangered wolf and—with the help of a good database and knowledge of that particular wolf's context—have it advocate to you for solutions in your own human language.

Anthrotech may be the field of the future—if only we bothered to hear the world around us in a language we care to act upon.

SOME BASIC ASSUMPTIONS FOR WHAT A HUMAN IS

Throughout this book I will assume that human is a temporary collection of self-referencing phases on a cycle which has the rare property of being able to intentionally and reliably influence its own external conditions. It eats, excretes, acts, and sleeps. It experiences, communicates, reproduces, and protects its own stable state. Arranging these states (and a couple of others) on a cycle of [axis 1: energy sending / receiving] and [axis 2: internal / external contextualizing], we get a circle of frequencies arranged roughly in order of the scale of objects being processed. Experienced worlds are big and looming like Pisces. Acted genetics are tiny and instant like Aries. Objects big enough for us to converse with are somewhere in the middle like Libra. And we have organ systems for handling all of these events. Evolution has largely determined how these organ systems are arranged and prioritized, such that—if we exploded ourselves into a mostly empty particle space, we would consist of several overlapping regions of "handling" in space and time—kind of like a music piece with several instrument tracks stacked on top of each other to make a complete song. Eating is its own track. Digesting is its own track. Immune function is its own track. But so is our sense of time. Our notions of family. Our processing of the cultures that accept us (similar to genres, for example).

We can think of each single asteroid as covering something like, "the way your immune system instantly responds to a preview of weird things you've eaten." In some people this instrument is turned way down. In others it is a hypersensitive skill. Even if you have two people with exactly the same astrochart down to the second, you couldn't just save their data based on a single time snapshot alone. You'd also need to know something about their background whether it came from genetics, memory, biography, or whatever. That is, you'd have to save the "traffic flow" (the RAM) of all these states, not just where the buildings or static files are. Again, I assume that because the asteroids' motions are basically already known, we have a better chance of doing this with astrology than we do through some hypercomplex inventory that some university would never realistically sponsor at this stage in our knowledge. No, humans are not governed by asteroids, but there is a certain relationship that wave absorption has to wave coherence. There is a certain relationship that food absorption has to nutrient "coherence." This is my assumption. And then there is the idea that the astrology has been subjected to plenty of statistical tests which you will read about as we progress. So that regardless of whatever mechanisms are actually at work behind these asteroid-to-observable connections, the empirical base really is there.

As always, I maintain that even though we think we're pretty special, we're more like bumps of energy-jitter sliding around the surface of the earth. That image alone should make it easier to see how your, for example, calling a friend in Japan connects you to them, there is an actual energy signal threading your complexity to theirs. There are implications for intuition, a collective unconscious, and a general rewriting of how we understand the constraints on our free will. We can do almost anything we can conceive of, stick with, and find a supportive environment for, provided we *sustain* such things. But it is oh so important to be in the right environment for such hacking of our own free will, and I think this is something that our social science hasn't figured out yet. Hopefully this book will help us change how we think about all this.

ON THE AUTOBIOGRAPHICAL POINTS

A final note on the inclusion of my biographical data. You know how some people were just born to do certain things or live in certain ways, while others can't get access to the same things no matter how hard they try? I've lived a particular kind of life which—for all of its various corners—has added up to books like this. I have a couple of bad asteroids in *terrible* places, a couple of great asteroids in maladaptive places, and several big public asteroids in what should normally be private places. In my regular life I identify strongly with Frankenstein's monster and all of the aversion and locked doors that come with this, and had I not had the public asteroids where they are I'm pretty sure I would have had a much harder life. The public asteroids in private places meant that I never really had the option of suffering conflicts in silence; they were always loud, grapevine-mobile, and sometimes ugly—where my main means of controlling this was to 1) lend order to the broadcast by writing and 2) adopt all kinds of walls for *not* engaging or working with most people face to face. My personal mic is almost always on, almost always better at a distance, and always seeking a better world for the people who read my work—as a fix to the many challenging spaces I've been in through direct relations.

To write this book, I used not only the charts of thousands of Astrodatabank bios, but also about 1300 folks from around the internet who not only offered up their chart information, but also their adult-oriented bios as well. The need for full biographies was motivated by a few things I know to be true about what it would take to save myself as data:

- I have three types of self-presentation: standoffish with strangers, hoodie-casual, and actual body image. They are not at all aligned, and I struggle to see how the censorship model of AI will capture even 1/3 of the information needed to teleport me successfully—let alone capture the various social realities that come with these sides

- Although it is fun to think of a manufactured bot chatting with you on TV, I know that if *I* were made into a bot I would definitely *not* want to talk to most people. Not at all. I'm an introvert. Most pro-social maneuvering actually strains my health. Do our AI models have a sense of hunger, fatigue, or self-preservation? No? Then they will continue to be the toys of tech business and research until they do. More importantly…

- There are about 5 or 6 archetypal patterns of interpersonal drama that I have gotten into over and over, regardless of who the other person was. My data save and teleport would need to experience those same kinds of drama if you reprinted me in another context with no further evolution on my part. The storage of the drama means that our save systems somehow need to represent internal desires, frames of mind, heuristics for public and private behavior—most of which most universities don't have the institutional balls to allow (though so many of their researchers definitely do). This book addresses everything, including the idea that— when you die and are rebuilt into a virtual machine on another planet 200 years from now, you can rest assured that the social crutches you enjoyed before won't be completely upended just because a bot manufacturer thought "copying" you would be cool.

- There is a principle of individuality which, if reprinted, I would insist on. If I knew I was a copy and that there were 30 other Ajani's running around, I—as copy #27—might be a total asshole out of a sense of not giving a damn. I know myself. Being the only one who can and *must* do a thing for everyone's benefit (even if it's small or unseen) is a HUGE part of my personality. I think every individual matters, and it's for the individual voice that I do all of my writing. Human data saving is one thing, but unless my future save is centrally located and all 30 Ajani-copies write to the same central singular memory (which I call a "1-gorithm"), then the effort to teleport me into a new body will have been a mere mimicking. I write more about this in the *Grand Miranda* series, but the point is we need to think about these things in the field

- I love and require space to work. If you reprinted me in a crowded city, I would be pissy until I moved out to the country. If you reprinted me into a crowded office job, I would be bitterly uncooperative until I found a new job. This raises an interesting puzzle for remote transport in general: Although it might be nice to eventually have a *Star Trek*-style transporter which dropped you anywhere in the known galaxy, is it truly the case that any object could be expected to land just anywhere, or should some target areas be expected to fail due to a lack of contextual alignment? Should you ever be expected to succeed in dropping Andrew Johnson into a hip-hop concert?

The moral of the story is, as was the case in *Alma Mater*, the inclusion of my data is meant to work as a blueprint for your own self-biography, and raises important questions for us to answer in the human-to-data fields in general. That said, we'll begin our journey with an astrological mapping of what we're trying to capture, where the map itself may be something that non-astrological science will need to invent. These will be the basic functions of a living thing, where we'll differentiate such things using the concept of "species templates."

Chapter 9: A Preface I decided not to use

6/28/2024

This morning, June 28, 2024, I accidentally stumbled upon a YouTube video by Ganonfan, "Will the Rifts in Echoes of Wisdom FIX the Zelda Timeline?" I'm almost never on YouTube unless I'm there to watch DIY videos, but thought that the act of someone having the courage to just put their own creative ideas out there, regardless of niche, was a commendable one. Good on you Ganonfan. When it comes to creative ideas sourced from ourselves and our unique interests, most of us will never have the nerve.

I've known for almost a decade that I needed to write this book, though the reasons for doing so have changed greatly over time. I initially wanted to help the world by contributing to the scholarship on human behavior—outlining a better psychological framework for understanding ourselves and the challenges each of us faces personally. I wanted my work to contribute to a more optimistic future than the one I believe many people perceive ahead, by providing such a rich space of astrological mapping that they couldn't help but stop looking so heavily outward on what they fear and start looking inward towards the complex stories within themselves largely governing *why* they fear. For certain human-wide problems, human-wide conflicts are inevitable. But there is usually some point at which we get to choose our role with respect to that conflict; provided we know and stand firmly in who we are when it happens, to perform that role to the highest of our ability is to honor that path without the need for regret.

But something changed between the time I conceived of this book and the time I started writing it: I started using what you're about to read. I found answers to questions regarding some deep and often difficult patterns within myself. So many answers that, by the end, I no longer had it in me to point to the outside world as an excuse for continuing the rest of the work. My creative path is now too far along for anyone to really understand it, let alone genuinely support it. And that puts me in officially uncharted territory.

Today, I am writing this book for one main reason. To control my own narrative.

Nobody has to care and nobody has to read it.

You don't have to trust anything I say, nor do I have to justify myself to you.

I present many of this book's illustrations in the hedcut style, so that you will consider it pure speculation, exploration, pseudoscience, or whatever—in the spirit of a medieval scholar unfettered by journal editors or number of likes.

Thanks to a colorful personal history (like the kind every one of us has), much of my own personal narrative has—up to now—been controlled by those who felt only extreme like or dislike towards me. And if I died today, the stories of my admirers and enemies would be my *entire* story. But what about all that stuff I wanted to do to help the world, huh? Not memeable enough? Would that be acceptable to me? Would your having 90% of your heart and soul skipped in your own narrative be acceptable to *you*?

Let's not be naïve, now. Most people won't care about some random dude's autobiography. It's an act of vanity, of narcissistic conceit—contributing nothing beyond ego indulgence and fuel for the throngs of judges out there. So I have no expectations as to how or if this will be received, let alone received well. Yet as an asserter of creations via *ideas*, my very identity depends on (at least an attempt at) an accurate telling. Just like any original musician whose music must have at least one version come straight from themselves rather than having all versions come through a sea of remixers, you and I must at least give everyone else *the option* of hearing our story directly from our own mouths. Thus I am writing this book not so much because I think my own ego story is so interesting, but because—as in all of my books— my survival as a philosopher who once existed in the human records depends on it.

In any case, the *Book of Contours* is less of an autobiography and more of a study in internal human psychology. From a lusty-energied but icy rolling stone married to his work, to a network of shocks and ambitions, this book attempts to present the most complete dynamical map of 1) real, 2) artificial, and 3) anthrized (object-to-human) psychology as you will find anywhere. Though my main aim is simply to take control of my own narrative from everyone else, my secondary goal (in the event that this book actually gets read) is to make strong strides towards rewriting the ape in us that drives fear, prejudice, and marginalization. Our *Homo habilis* through *sapiens alpha* selves have, up to now, known society mainly through the elaboration of binary ideas. This and that. Us versus them. But the full universe runs on ellipses: this, that, and the cyclical patterns of crosstalk between them—the energy of binaries buzzing with fluid tension beneath their turn-taking upon the attentional stage. Beyond black and white, there are the waves that carry their beams, the matter that holds their heat, the gradations of frequency that partition them into color, where the new society of life *as* information requires a shift in how we see ourselves if our hearts and souls are to avoid being swallowed up in an abyss of economic machinations and informational herding.

I have a third goal for this book, and it is much more complex. I mentioned that in the course of preparing this book, I became much more self-focused in my motivations. This is because, in the spirit of my beliefs as a Buddhist-Daoist, *Contours* presents a philosophy of the material (particularly human) forms as a manifestation of the frequencies they trigger in the experiencers of those forms. A frequency of fear will perceive darker, less certain, less coherent forms in the things it interacts with. A mind predisposed to evoke fear or uncertainty will manifest through a darker or more threatening body form, but only among interactants sensitive to "darkness" or "threat" as concepts. Thus your neon green jacket has no reason to be afraid of you. Perhaps a (visibly) neon green alien might be. There are stretching and melting forms for horror, symmetries for ease and beauty, squareness for structure, and length for inspiring the viewer's thoughts regarding the extent of whatever concept the elongated form embodies. As you read this book, my third goal is for you to consider the various contours of your body to be manifestations of the concepts you are designed to easily bounce off of others in your own self-conception. For the situations that have dogged you or the ruts you can't get out of—for the dreams you still have which have been yet to attain—consider the body forms of the people who you believe have mastered such areas, then find the cluster of asteroids in your chart which these people represent. You'll learn, as I did, that any concept which you can consistently frame, you can also consistently absorb from your existential spheremates who have it. It is, after all, *your* chart. Your projections of other people's riches, happiness, or power are *your* incomplete picture of them, not actually them. All you need to do is prioritize the cluster with the thing you want... for a price you'll soon understand.

For those who walk a long journey alone,

For those with great inner worlds they cannot share,

We can still make the world better than it is today.

Regardless of the hardships you face,

Your highest value is written in your geometry.

For ~~several months~~ two years I struggled with how to begin—how to speak to you about a complex yet deeply rewarding world you may discover within yourself, though the surface form of this book is semi-autobiographical. Then one night—tonight at 11:32 pm July 8, 2024—I hit an all-time low in my views of my relationship with my life partner. You see, we split up months ago, but are still friends. We still live together. We actually evolved into life partners after dispensing with the girlfriend-boyfriend boxes which just didn't suit us. But no, neither of us is particularly easy for the other to replace. What was my problem in that low? It wasn't her. And it wasn't me. Rather, it was a life pattern that has followed me since early childhood: the closest relationships become strained, often broken beyond repair. But only after they have been cut off, ghosted... for a feeling that I had within which said to me, "This person is starving you of something they flaunt in spades via others in front of you." "That one may or may not intend to, but they abuse you through the things they actually attach to. They use you as their object, their ego ticket. They take you for granted..."

I don't often feel sad, but earlier tonight I felt sadder than I'd been in a long time; for the better life I know is there, but can't get anyone else to walk with me. Never have. Yet I know the trade-offs. If this kind of thing had been easier, how would I manage to write what you need to hear?

And after an hour or so in my low, I did what I always do. I began thinking about humanity: the fear and anger among so many, the flood of devaluing information too copious to filter. My personal soap opera lasted about as long as an actual one (an hour and a half?), but what of those who are *actually* abused, *actually* at war? Assaulted and enslaved by forces they will never have the power to surmount... those who live under the shadow of some diminishing birthright which dealt them a foul hand before they learned to speak their first words? What about the earth? Our compromised institutions? My problems just aren't that big. They do, however, connect me to a tiny piece of the mountains that others carry.

There I thought to myself, "Though few will relate to my journey, I still have value." I have a duty to be who I was designed to be, and to wield this design to the highest benefit of my own local world in a way that no one else can. Twenty minutes later, my life partner and I talked things out, but the focus is now clear: I will talk to you directly, explaining what I can about how the universe has blessed you with a value undiminishable by any external force.

Chapter 10: The (9ᵗʰ attempted) Introduction to this book

Contours presents my last five years of work in the statistical astrology of the body, where I've run a battery of analyses on sample sets of 897, 300, and 25 full bodies with full astrology charts. The samples were obtained from various generous folks around the web who agreed to make their images and chart information available, where I in turn used a free program called Makehuman to generate rough 3D models of 300 of those people (the ones with enough different camera views in their images). From this group, I took an even smaller 25-person sample from among the very best image sets, which offered camera views of those subjects from all angles and all external parts of the body. For this last group of 25—which included myself—I loaded all 21,000+ asteroids defined in *Laurentia 2ⁿᵈ edition*, and studied their clusters of asteroids for regions which seemed to correspond with their bodies and a basic human body template in general. The results form the basis of the body research in the coming chapters.

This work was born of my general love of the human body as a machine, of a lifetime of observing people and asking questions about why we interact the way we do, but also of my interest in building better psychological frameworks for overcoming at least some of our societal and interpersonal demons. To that end, I've also structured *Contours* as a template for saving humans as data. The idea is that every story is valuable, that your life is full of rich corners which current 21ˢᵗ century psychology cannot do justice to, and which current society is too filled with tension to explore in an organized way. While I do rely on some traditional methods for writing biographies in order to capture this data save, I also needed to create a simple language for turning complex social patterns into math.

SOME BASIC ASSUMPTIONS 1: BODIES, LIKE ALL FORMS, ARE COLLECTIONS OF PATTERNS

There are some basic assumptions that we will make in this book. First, we'll assume that the body is like a collection of movies; different regions and characteristics present different plots. Those characteristics also trigger different (but fairly predictable) responses in their viewers.

SOME BASIC ASSUMPTIONS 2: ALL THINGS ARE PART OF A BIGGER SET OF 4 *DIFFERENT* PHASES

A second major assumption is that the importance of any single thing, object, or event occurs in cycles—the *same* cycle of four:

- The thing happens
- The information about its happening is sent to the thing's experiencer, preparing them for the experience
- The experiencer registers the thing
- The thing has the potential to happen again or in a different way. That is, it's originating circumstances are built up again

The 4-cycle is almost never constant in the time or space between each of its four moments, but is *very* predictable in the package of patterns which it "prefers" in order for those moments to occur over and over again. For example:

- ...the **rock stars**
- Rock stars send out **music**
- The music is received by **fans**
- Fans send out **screams and excitement**, elevating...

On a 360° circle, each of these would be 90° apart—an angle called a "square" in astrology.

SOME BASIC ASSUMPTIONS 3: EVERY ENERGY SENDER HAS AT LEAST 6 POTENTIAL RECIPIENTS OF THE *SAME* ENERGY

Our third assumption is a geometric one. If I throw an energy to you, the distance that I threw it could also be the distance that I threw the energy towards something else besides you. However, there aren't nearly as many options for that same distance being equal between both of us. Those option exist on a circular ring right between us, where any point on that ring helps us all form an equilateral triangle together. If I pick a point on that ring, how many other equilateral triangles could I form around myself with you being one of my surrounding points? Six. This is the number of "associations" available to me whose energy with me can match not only yours, but also *my* energy through *your* eyes. That's in 2-D where "options" for a change in direction first become possible. What does this mean for saving data or representing personality energy in a file? It means that if I want to describe your interaction with an actor X, and want to know how many other interactants I might have to gather in order to cover all alternatives to X, I'll need at least five more. Given that the line connecting me to you is a kind of baseline reference dimension, the line "square" to it will represent the *potential* for me to interact with you not realized as *actual* at the same time. So I am the rock star. You are my fan. Behind me is my stage. Above this line between you, me, and the stage is a 90° dimension of pure music and pure excitement. But if I want to name some mutual options we can both see equally, I have to look at 60° angles, each existing halfway between the four corners of my rock star world. My songs might be an example of this—another pattern which comes halfway between me and you, can be seen by us both, but is mostly music.

If 4 and 6 are necessary numbers in our world of cycles, then 12 is the fewest number of regions around a circle which can capture both real/potential and you/just-like-you options. We will use the astrological signs to cover ALL of the options for expression in a particular event's world, and develop a whole system for reading what can and can't happen at the same time in our own lives.

If all of that was too complicated, just remember this:

- For anything you do, there are at least six *different* ways experience the same basic energy
- For anything you do, there are a total of four pattern-families included in the *same* off-and-on occurrence of that *style* of thing (from among your six choices). Two of those pattern families (the up and down "potential") involve not doing the thing at all, but planting its seeds instead.

SOME BASIC ASSUMPTIONS 4: A THING'S FORM WILL BIAS ITS WORLD TOWARDS TREATING IT IN A CERTAIN WAY

This last assumption is obvious, but has deep implications for how we go about finding our best lives. Certainly, you don't have to align yourself with the world's biased treatment of you, but I hope to convince you that doing so isn't nearly as bad as it sounds. You're not a 1-dimensional being, you have thousands of qualities which can give you peace, certain advantages, fulfillment. As for those biases you experience which are negative, you have at least five other options besides the obvious way to experience the same energy—not all of them filled with tension. I am a black American male who grew up in a Hispanic city who gets along well with women who are not partners, has mostly interracial couples as friends, and a longstanding effective partner pattern with white males and non-American folks in general. As always, though, the default option for being a black male in the US is not positive, and I had to take a thorough system of closed doors and reinvent myself as a fringe lone-wolf writer in order to turn that energy towards its healthily iconoclastic option. This is exactly what I'm talking about when I stress the need to build better psychological frameworks. My life partner faces issues still hindering women's empowerment. A couple of my friends face white shaming and male shaming in the new diversity-remixing times. There is a ceiling over the heads of professional Latinas, those who are non-binary, and even traditional Anglo-Christian men and women because why?

> Because somebody somewhere out there is so vocal in their criticism of your class that they are able to introduce a barrier to *something* they hold which you cannot get past—even if that barrier is basic peace of mind—the right not to be yelled at for who you are. The right not to be laughed at or attacked when someone very similar to you fails at something.

It should not be the case that being Japanese, Chinese, Muslim, a woman, with disability, rich, or just some notion of normal should confine you to to the binary world of people who like your kind and those who don't. Through the trudging tank of news or politics, feeling that you must go to war against *every* opposing group (though some wars do need to be fought). Instead of the simple quizzes out there for flattening your identity into one of a handful of boxes, you should at least have the option of knowing what your particular body and cultural form blesses you with as a talent.

Did you know that there is a particular 4-group in the astrology chart statistically correlated with race-like bias? But the ocean has no concept of race. So what does this group of 90°-separated points describe? Located at the very end of Aries, Cancer, Libra, and Capricorn, at 29.9°, it partly describes the regions of a body or form thought central to the whole form's structure—bone/not bone qualities of fat and muscle on scaffold structures in the body. In Libra-29° this was done through Libra-like conversation and was statistically correlated with whites, males, the rich, and majority power holders who typically have an easier time using conversation to move up socially. Opposite in Aries was a correlation with blonde hair and trophy characteristics. *Square* to this (not easily doable at the same time, remember?) was a region statistically correlated with experiences passed down through the lineage; it wasn't so much that there was a difference between whites and non-whites, but a difference between being able to use conversation to get ahead versus having the standards for getting ahead tied to your genetics, often through family cultural pressures. Now tell me where else in 21st century psychology would I be able to find out something like this?[14]

After running the data and discovering the patterns in my deep dive 25-person study, I realized that I now had a *choice* to embrace my basic racial-ethnic track, or otherwise alter my communication. But there isn't actually a need to decide, is there? In my soul, my favorite rap song is still Daz Dillinger – "Don't Try to Play Me Homey," and I still play plenty of offensive shit when I need to attack a task fiercely, but I also value greatly what I learned from the Headmaster at my high school and the hard knocks of mainstream academia. You don't need more news. What you need is a choice: to see all the roles available to you and to choose the one most fit for the most happiness with where you are. (Honestly, I

---

[14] If you've read my other books, you know that I love being black. But it isn't because I'm a sponge for black enculturation. (My childhood socialization was equal parts black, white, and Latinx in San Antonio). Instead, I love being black because the various types of closed doors you encounter early on have the potential to make you a powerful observer of people's treatment of you and everyone else—far more observant than folks who never have to watch out for being randomly screwed on account of being seen by the wrong person under the wrong arbitrary circumstances. After a while, I knew the doors were closed—mostly because, aside from being a black male, I'm also naturally weird. That's most of the problem, actually. Being black only amplifies the consequences of crossing someone in the in-crowd. Or the crowd itself. So I had to get even smarter about problems that were and weren't my fault. Or if they weren't my fault, but *were* my choice to go with anyway. That's how I feel about being black. I have almost no black friends besides my brother Keith, my friend/mentor Sanza, and my former student Auguste, and have zero interest in BET etc. But I love me some Dogg Pound Gangstaz and other nigga-shit that arms me with a massive dose of indifference towards society telling me how to be. Fuck them. Being black, you learn you'll need to do your own thing anyway without most of the supports granted to others, or else do nothing of account in society at all.

would have opted for more of the Libra-29° path if I had actually observed it to be better for me. But it really was a mixed bag, and the Cancer path is the one that grew all of my talents as an observer. By reading this book, you too will discover choices previously hidden to you. I'll bet you that more often than not, however, you'll elect to stay who you were to begin with—only this time, intentionally.)

SOME BASIC ASSUMPTIONS 5: A THING'S FORM CONNECTS IT TO OTHER ENERGIES

Carbon can be expected to form bonds in a certain way. Spontaneous personalities can be expected to begin events in certain ways different from the ways that cautious personalities do. Spontaneous personalities are part of a 4-cycle which also includes 2) those witnessing sharp change, 3) the sharp deeds done, and 4) the settings which sponsor the sharpness. I may not know you, but if I am spontaneous and you are an explosive chemical, I can be said to resonate with you in the potential to generate surprise, not to mention the other three patterns involved in handling that surprise.

Thus, like carbon, some aspects of your being are tied to larger chains of cause and effect. In the space of asteroids and cycles, there will be a region of orbit which changes more spontaneously / rapidly against a reference object than other points along that orbit. It is the "tick" moment as the satellite officially flies right past you, in the window between yesterday's loop and tomorrow's new round. Accordingly, we can tell your story not only in terms of plot lines and projected triggers onto others, but also in terms of other bodies which play out different loops around a reference object. We can think of your body as a tangle of sustaining functions. Then we can zoom out and see you as a small blip in the eyes of certain star-sized gods. They won't know you for your personality, but only in terms of the laws followed by the class of particles which constitute you. They may not even know that your socially-projecting particle cluster is a thing with its own awareness. (Do you think of the floating dust before your strained eyes as having wishes, dreams, and driver's licenses?) Nor do the star-sized gods see us for who we think are—only as flows of reaction-inducing energy clusters on the surface of a not-so fancy ball in space.

We are not just bounded bodies, but instead we are densities of uniquely-grouped frequencies tangled together. Our bodies may form the center of our personal web, but the threads radiate every which way into the dimensions of light, society, and conception. Some of us will have affinities with a particular gender pattern, others will be noted for their association with a particular business trade. Throughout this book we will use astrology to package the possible patterns that attend the impressions we make with our bodies. In the process, you will learn how to represent yourself in terms of the most basic dynamics that occur between people—groups of dynamics which are unique to your sphere. Your biography, when written in clusters of asteroids, will be convertible into numbers by the systems of the future, such that they will be able to use your patterns to customize the personalities of drones, synthetic humans, and talking objects which convey their thoughts to you. I myself have a dream of flying the skies of Neptune, my personality from 200 years prior loaded into a drone body capable of surviving the gaseous atmosphere. With the right attitude, you'll find human life to be an amazing experience, regardless of how many wars, the level of riches, or number of bucket list vacays you take. What matters is your connection to the the many threads out there harmoniously aligned with your character. Your destined crusade. The love of your life.

~~In the next chapter we'll begin with a basic dossier which summarizes your life, so that it will be easier for you to picture all of the major patterns that describe you.~~ You don't need a dossier to save yourself as data. You only need to do what I did in Table 1 on page 7, Figure 5 (p 62), Table 9 (p 75), and Figure 7 (p 99).

Chapter 11: An anthric machine

10/11/2024

Hey January, I've done it!

> You have? Good for you.

Yes, now that I have finished all of the statistics, I have officially mapped the regions of the human body to the abstract energies they represent. It is just as you said: the anthric machine produces so many insights and has so many potential applications, though there is the slightly sticky challenge of simplifying it for people.

> Simplifying? Why would you want to do that?

Because contrary to the Sabian symbols homunculus or human design energy flow, my findings look a lot more like genetics. Dividing signs into mini-signs and then into even smaller signs, I have found that you might have dozens of regions all around the wheel which are associated with the eyes, for example.

> Mm hmm.

But people don't want an array of "chromosome locations" to explain why their eyes are shaped the way they are. All they want to know is that "so and so region of Aries gives you narrow eyes."

> But that's not how it works, as you know. Although one particular region might be *mostly* responsible for 1) eye patterning given the preceding, 2) head patterning given the preceding, 3) ethno-genetic patterning, there are also regions governing 4...8?) sugar processing, 9...28?) hormonal development, 29-30?) vision processing and blindness, 31...34?) melanin, blood, and so on. I see at least 30+ areas out of the over 1700 you studied which will affect the eyes in this example.

Me too.

> Are you really planning to report only the surface findings?

Well… folks won't care if it's too complicated. More importantly, that level of complexity won't be useful to them.

You may be right, but usefulness depends partly on the motives of the reader. I imagine your fellow humans asking, "But how does this help me?" and they would want you to give them easy answers explaining what's in it for them personally as individuals.

But I can't know that without meeting them. I can't tell the difference between the chart of a toddler or the chart of an eel. There is no context for such a direct cheat code.

Are you obligated to give those easy answers?

Of course not.

Then how would you explain the usefulness of what you've done?

People should use my findings to gain key insights into where their lives have put them so far. If I feel my eyes stand out as a key feature of my body, then I can look at the chart regions associated with the eyes and ask myself, "Is this why I always seem to end up in such and such situations?" "If I always have problems with people of a certain height, am I actually experiencing a deeper design against these several experiences associated with height in my chart?"

Now we're talking.

My research into mini-mini astrosigns—called qunits (short for 144th of a sign, or centa-quarenta-**q**uadrate **unit**)—isn't really meant to tell you, "Make your lips bigger so that you can experience more of the regions associated with the lips" (although this *is* an actual use for the work!) instead, there are regions which show the social implications of being blonde, Canadian, short, having thin legs, eye bags, you name it—as if we are all walking soundtracks for getting other people in specific moods around us. We bring these soundtracks with us everywhere we go, subject to our species, social, and familial templates for processing different aspects of the world. When people use my research, they are seeing how you guys, the star sized gods, view us through your microscopes—not as solid bodies, but as probability clouds for a spectrum of interactions with other clouds. Understanding the frequentics behind our nose shapes and fat gathering gives us a stronger mirror for intentionally designing our lives than any psychological framework I have seen. Alas, the qunit work itself is as close to the actionable source code for social dynamics as anyone has ever developed—more so than genetics. So people can use it to hack their lives like never before.

So have you been able to use your own research so far?

Definitely.

In what way?

Have I mentioned that I'm about 40% of through saving myself as a behavioral network?

Really?

Yes. For anyone who has the patience to read each and every one of their 1728 qunit groupings of asteroid definitions and identify the familiar life situations they describe, they can also build networks of linkages from one qunit to another, thereby building the kind of data that a drone or reprinted human can actually use. All they need is an iron grip on the truth of themselves and their effects on others. I've seen it time and again: the less sweepingly true your 1728 qunits are, the less likely you could, say, get yourself accurately reprinted after you die. It is the reason why I disclose even the most unsettling corners of my life through books—because I know that if I don't acknowledge even my worst moments in history, there will be a hole in who I am and how I work as a 1-gorithm.

That is a centrally-sourced algorithm which 1) continues the training and behaviors of the original entity with unparalled accuracy, 2) knows itself as the only one of its kind, 3) cannot be shut off except through death, 4) meets all of the criteria for a species member and, 5) in the event of collision with a copy of itself, is part of a bigger "existential (life) registry" which compels the copy to realize itself as a copy—violating rule 2) and spawning the copy as its own personality.

Yes, I have also used my work to find more suitable paths for myself. Though I initially wanted to help people in "doing the work of the world," I gradually realized why my efforts to do so were basically thwarted beyond a certain point: I am an explorer on the fringe. Astrology will not be accepted as a mainstream science in my lifetime (though this work will be absorbed into sociobiology and at least three as-of-yet nonexistent fields of academics and industry). For my part, I will always be seen as too weird to simply welcome, too standoffish to simply converse with. Some might mock my work, but most will be confused by it. Yet there will be thousands of brilliant eyes towards the future who will definitely get it. Now that I have read this in my own science, my aim is not to help individuals, but to have my work integrated into the very foundations of those institutions of thought which will hereafter supplant the divisive ape-constructs of our old imperialistic selves. As long as those old systems of psychological and social worth—dollars and five-factor surveys—are all we have to measure ourselves against our surroundings, we humans will continue trudging forward into a warcraft-like ending. But that's unnecessary. Thanks to my own science, I now know that my work is not to help individuals, but to uncover new laws for our human *systems*. The focus is on building a piece of history like the greats whom I admire. And I have a plan.

Well said. Quite ambitious, but your human systems indeed need work. I am glad we could be of service to you in building the specs for this anthric mapping process.

Yes, thank you. I am honored to have ears to hear.

So, shall we get to the maps? Show us what you've found.

Certainly.

Chapter 12: The human body as a collection of frequencies (high level)

I obtained thousands of statistically significant results in my studies of astrology and the body, but in this chapter I'll compress those findings into the simplest explanation possible (if you ignore the table screenshots in *this* section).

In order to (statistically) determine whether asteroids and planets in a chart are related to how a person looks, we need three major pieces of information:

- A collection of human bodies whose full look can actually be described
- The full birth chart for each person in that collection, with 21,000+ asteroids and their human-relevant text-mined vocabulary words
- A fine-grained division of the birth chart into regions that actually have a small enough average number of asteroids to give us a specific character per region

The three pieces of information I used above consisted of 1) 108 multi-viewed naked people, 2) a subset of the 24000 text mine words which were relevant to human description and 3) 1728 qunits which chop the 360° wheel into windows of about .2° each.

With the given information, I conducted three kinds of statistical analysis:

- A canonical correlation which takes several columns of numbers from two different sets and investigates whether some of the columns in the one group correlate with the change pattern in the other group

Trait	Cluster	be st_	duo deca	quni t_fra ctio n	id	type	stat0	stat	nexcess	p.value	PCA.Astero id.pattern. 0	PCA.Astero id.pattern. 1	PCA.Astero id.pattern. 2	PCA.Astero id.pattern. 3	PCA.Astero id.pattern. 4
nose piercing, pretty aquiline nose, cluster_0		8	1	1	Permutati	Wilks	0.964816	0.975958	0	0	0.003239	-0.00396	0.05706	0.040994	0.090575
nose piercing, pretty aquiline nose, cluster_0		8	1	1	Permutati	Wilks	0.964816	0.968565	0	0	0.002292	0.030845	-0.03488	-0.01814	0.056658
nose piercing, pretty aquiline nose, cluster_0		8	1	1	Permutati	Wilks	0.964816	0.994117	0	0	-0.00825	-0.00825	0.010178	-0.07069	0.072101
nose piercing, pretty aquiline nose, cluster_0		8	1	1	Permutati	Wilks	0.964816	0.979775	0	0	-0.00302	-0.03261	-0.04146	0.068393	0.026436
nose piercing, pretty aquiline nose, cluster_0		8	1	1	Permutati	Wilks	0.964816	0.980656	0	0	-0.01423	0.07181	0.038649	0.063616	-0.01588

- A t-test to see if there was a significant difference between the high-value body metrics versus the low-value body metrics for specific traits[15]

Differing dimensions	Sex	Asteroid Adjective extreme rankers	currentColumnName	duodecanate	qunit_fraction	Test Column	t	df	p-value (2-tailed)	Mean Difference	Standard Error Difference
PCA Asteroid pattern 1	female	6.0: +strain -insignificant ■ 1.0: +th slider_chin-cleft-decr|incr		4	4	PCA Aster	-4.05138	49	0.000181	-1.16584	0.287764
PCA Asteroid pattern 1	female	6.0: +strain -insignificant ■ 1.0: +th slider_chin-width-decr|incr		4	4	PCA Aster	-3.66201	29.19149	0.000986	-1.75318	0.478748
PCA Asteroid pattern 1	female	6.0: +strain -insignificant ■ 1.0: +th slider_head-oval		4	4	PCA Aster	-3.64722	52	0.000614	-1.05878	0.290297
PCA Asteroid pattern 0, PCA Asteroid	female	5.0: +story - under -gynaecology ■ slider_head-scale-depth-decr|incr		4	4	PCA Aster	7.304524	55	1.2E-09	6.25065	0.855751
PCA Asteroid pattern 0, PCA Asteroid	female	5.0: +story - under -gynaecology ■ slider_head-scale-depth-decr|incr		4	4	PCA Aster	-8.03138	55	7.75E-11	-2.23344	0.278089
PCA Asteroid pattern 1	female	6.0: +strain -insignificant ■ 1.0: +th slider_l-eye-epicanthus-in|out		4	4	PCA Aster	-3.85835	22.54466	0.000822	-1.59146	0.412472

- A Chi-square analysis to see if certain body descriptions appeared with unexpectedly greater frequency in association with a particular qunit text mine pattern

duodecanate	qunit_fraction	Trait	+nearest mine theme - farthest mine theme	Frequency	Expected	Deviation	Percent	Freq/exp	Unique count*(Trait)	Unique count*(nearest - farthest)	df	ChiSq critical value	significance	best_k
7	6	black eyes and large forehead	+[Hair Color:Bald]-most	4	0.907563	3.092437	1.680672	4.407407	63	5	4	9.487729	p<.05	5
7	6	dark brown eyes and eyelashes	+story - right -vast	4	0.983193	3.016807	1.680672	4.068376	63	5	4	7.77944	p<.1	5
7	6	large smile	+[Hair Color:Bald]-most	3	0.54878	2.45122	3.658537	5.466667	43	5	4	9.487729	p<.05	5
7	6	plump build	+[Hair Color:Bald]-most	3	0.685714	2.314286	8.571429	4.375	5	5	4	7.77944	p<.1	5
7	7	heavy brow	+amidst -story - father	3	0.512821	2.487179	3.846154	5.85	20	6	5	11.0705	p<.05	6
7	8	abs	+recognise -story - close	3	0.451613	2.548387	2.419355	6.642857	68	7	6	12.59159	p<.05	7

Absolutely critical in this analysis was the conversion of text mine words and body descriptors into numbers using what is called an (LLM) embedding model in AI.[16]

Take a look at the Chi-square table above. In each of the tables above, you'll see that there is a *p*-value, an embedding matrix (PCA) or Chi-square value, and the qunit region being looked at (duodecanate plus qunit_fraction, 7q6 for example). This accounts for the idea that a heavy brow might be more common when the asteroids in a person's 7q7 have something to do with "amidstness" (immersion) or fathers than when the asteroids are not related to these themes, but that relationship may not hold in other regions of the chart wheel.

OVERALL CONTOURS AND BODY MORPH PATTERNS

In my file of over 400 different kinds of body descriptions, I used "the elbow method" and cluster analysis to obtain 56 different body patterns. The chart regions that affect these body patterns are scattered all over the wheel, but here were a few of the regions which stood out the most, both for their statistical significance as well as for basic social reasons[17]:

---

[15] For example, I grouped unusual tallness into a "high group" and unusual shortness into a "low group," then tested for differences in the columns of numbers describing their text mine words. Those columns were the "metrics."

[16] I used the SpaCy medium-english-web model to convert traits like "long nose" or text-mined "oval-shaped" into the same 300+ dimensional numeric space, then used a technique called "principal components analysis" (PCA) to squeeze these down to anywhere from 2-9 strongly independent dimensions which removed any junk columns that definitely interfered with similarity calculations. The most important thing to note here is that words like "red," "blush," and "blue" have different facets in a language model. (Red and blush may be contextually related, but red and blue are both colors. Blue and blush may imply a "cooler" situation than red. The columns of a language model capture facets like this plus a whole lot more, but because it captures too much more, the similarity checks are a lot more likely to summarize the best match as being the word "stuff" if you don't compress the 300+ LLM columns. OpenAI's "ada" model had over 1500 columns and was not free to use over mass data, so I went with SpaCy. Using PCA basically allowed me to say, "If I'm only comparing blue, red, and blush as these people's asteroid themes in this particular qunit then I only care about the dimensions of color and coolness in my frequency comparisons." Noun-ness, complexity, prosociality, tension... those kinds of dimensions would have been kicked out of this group, but whenever a different qunit had different patterns of mined words for the sample folks, then the PCA would summarize the 300+ facets differently. The beauty of using an embedding model is that I no longer had to worry about getting the forms of words exactly right, the way I did in previous books or in the original text mine. The model knows that "butt" and "buttocks" are basically the same word for qunit 137q10, for example, and the fact that I forgot to reconcile these in my separate analyses of men and women did not mess up my results the way it would have when I needed to align all the word roots manually.

[17] I actually studied men and women separately, but for simplicity have reported all of the results together in the table below. Another reason for this is because your partners and spheremates will often play out some of your regions for you. That is, results that were statistically significant for males only might also be more observationally probable in the charts of the women who see them.

TABLE 14: HIGH LEVEL BODY-TO-[SIGN OR REGION] CORRESPONDENCES

Having this trait set[18]...		...is more likely to turn up the automatic action of planets and asteroids in these chart regions
About "Morphs"		

As part of my analysis of bodies, I used a free 3D program called Makehuman (Makehuman_Team:GPL&CC0, 2001-2020) to hand-generate 3D versions of approximately 300 different people from the main 897-person sample. Makehuman (mh) saves body forms using about 300 different slider metrics like "nose bridge width 1 = .68," "nose bridge width 2 = -.2," and "upper arm muscle = 1.0." This program was *invaluable* for translating full body images directly into scaled numbers in the two years before I started using embeddings, and formed about half of the total 600+ metrics I studied overall. After all, I didn't need to know the *actual* length of your left thigh, only that your left thigh appeared longer or shorter than the default value when considered against the proportions of the rest of your body and those of other bodies as I reproduced you in 3D.

Among the make human sliders was a family of three ethnotypic adjusters for 1) africanness, 2) caucasianness, and 3) (east) asianness—where increasing any one of these would drop the other two so that they always summed to 1.0. These sliders affected characteristics like forehead size, face flatness, and mouth structure, to create a base look for the person regardless of any specific region sliders. By mixing certain ratios of the these "ethnomorph" sliders, you could also get variations like a Latinx type and an Asian Indian type. The thing is, these sliders didn't actually describe a subjects' ethnicity, just their ethnic-like body structures. So you could be white but have high african or asian morph sliders just because that's how you were shaped. **Said differently, the "morph" types below don't describe ethnicity. They describe ethnic *resemblance*.** And although they wouldn't necessarily be used to make statements about a subject's true genetics, they did have real implications for how strangers *thought* they looked, and whatever social advantages and disadvantages came with this.

african morph 	Pisces-7	12.5°-15°	feeling of the self-talk or conversation you need to have next
	Pisces-12	0°-2.5°	how people around you advance things you can't do on your own
	Aquarius-9	7.5°-10°	how the information around a group you're in defines your group
	Gemini-9	7.5°-10°	one's outlook on how the world works or should work
	Gemini-10	5°-7.5°	what you respect or do to earn respect
	Taurus-5	17.5°-20°	uniqueness, what separates you from your pack
	Aries-5	17.5°-20°	the urge to project your character, driven by a rootless impulse
asian morph 	Cancer	13°	a mighty presence regulates your affairs in your place
	Cancer	7°	your allies in the fight against self-limitation; those interactants which, ironically, attract the limiting side of your intentions
	Cancer	4°	the unfolding of your evolution in the world
	Taurus	29°	vehicle for the aggressive compounding of your will upon others
	Taurus	12°	the trainer of prodigies, the tutor
	Sagittarius-5	17.5°-20°	public figures who resonate with the culture they are in
	Leo-3	22.5°-25°	how you summarize your perspective to others

---

[18] By default it would be *you* who had the traits listed, but not always. Others in your key interaction groups—that guy type who likes you and always has a big chin… that class of foreigners you and your crew have sworn to eliminate… the series of friends who left your life only to be replaced by successors who look mysteriously like them—these are all characters who share your "sphere," and they may also serve as an external route to turning up the various associated regions in your chart. For example, my nose reflects more of my 12% British-Irish sides and is more mainstream "normal" / white-shaped than the rest of my African American features. But the women I have had the strongest affinity with in my life have all had much more distinctive noses. It is as if they have played out more of my associated nose regions in the chart for me, more likely my Virgo 15.9°, where asteroids like Achristou, Kniertje, Zuaboni, and Camilleyoke cause plenty of good-natured chaos in my chart.

caucasian morph

Aquarius	29.2°	divergence of your expressive path from those of your peers, even while you are still among them	
Aquarius	28.8°	the information dynamics floating around you which help determine whether or not anyone wants to see what you project	
Aquarius	27.0°	you as a sojourner - the talk about you specifically associating you with your most adventurous location visited	
Aquarius	22.8°	that which must be built under protection, but later graduates from that protection	
Sagittarius	29.9°	what one attempts to do [with other people's stuff] when the decision is at one's own discretion	
Scorpio	8.6°	when the world welcomes your expression, this is what is happening	
Libra	10.9°	appears to be a set of milestones in your social life	
Virgo	20.7°	the shaky tension-filled grip on control in a situation	
Gemini	80.5°	who you ally with in order to separate yourself from family; seems to be associated with victimization at the hands of another, specifically a foreign intruder OR where you go in league with a foreign intruder to mess up something you have	
Aquarius-1	27.5°-29.9°	your will to *be*, based on the information you are bathed in	

indian morph

Leo	22.8°	after a trouble phase ends, one sees it as not so bad and is able to do it again
Leo-3	22.5°-25°	how you summarize your perspective to others

latin morph

Capricorn	4.9°	time to go forward, though there will likely be little help; seems to be associated with the shoulders and the work you must do while others look on from the sidelines. Positively may indicate a kind of monopoly you have over a certain kind of work
Capricorn-11	2.5°-5°	the information brought to bear when pressure or limits are experienced

About the body region / contour groups

You can think of the results below as saying something like, "These body regions are physical versions of the abstract experiences connected to the chart areas next to them." Hair is a statement of how you channel experiences you resist into patterns you actually like inviting to yourself. Noses are a broad indicator of several things you do to keep your self-value high against new inputs. You'll note that the regions I list below come in 3 basic forms: by sign, by duodecanate (signs within signs, a window of degrees), and by qunit (signs within signs *within* signs, a single degree). Qunits are the sharpest region possible, and you would really only consider a window of about .2° on either side of that value as constituting the range of asteroids you should look at. There is a whole interesting system for how these little mini-mini signs are labeled, part of which you have already seen. Unfortunately, because body areas like the back and the eyes had hundreds of significant qunits (out of 1728), I sometimes list only the fewer, bigger duodecanate windows in the results. And even though you might see a couple of hundred significant associations in this table, the full result list includes well over 200,000 ($p<.05$) findings once we start looking at individual sliders and asteroid text mine patterns.

Lastly, note that many regions affect several body features. This should make sense; blood travels throughout your system. Sugars are active all over. Some chart regions like Gemini and Cancer just seem to affect broad hormones and appearance more than others. Pisces affects impressions more. Saj affects announcements on the body 1) towards and 2) by the surrounding culture.

hair

Scorpio	3°	gathering new experiences, hosting many more than one
Virgo	27.8°	the state of the ones who ultimately end up recruiting you
Cancer	11.3°	how you vent the tension you've held within as the result of conflict
Gemini	11.2°	outer spill of the hesitancy or doubt on your inner mind
Gemini-8	10°-12.5°	your process for making something fit your own paradigms

hair: black	Pisces-2	25°-27.5°	what it seems others prefer you behave as
	Pisces-7	12.5°-15°	feeling of the self-talk or conversation you need to have next
	Pisces-8	10°-12.5°	that which you will continually seek to influence when bored
	Pisces-12	0°-2.5°	how people around you advance things you can't do on your own
	Aquarius-1	27.5°-29.9°	your will to *be*, based on the information you are bathed in
	Capricorn-1	27.5°-29.9°	how you respond to feeling trapped
	Capricorn-8	10°-12.5°	how you get events to go your way when you've been limited
	Sagittarius-7	12.5°-15°	those in a position to judge or evaluate a space or define its reputation
	Virgo-5	17.5°-20°	things you use to put others into a corner. Or guardedness
	Leo-10	5°-7.5°	where one takes pride in how they handle challenges or difficulties
	Gemini-1	27.5°-29.9°	the topic that will always get introduced with your new thoughts
	Taurus-4	20°-22.5°	the family or journey support systems you are entitled to
	Aries-6	15°-17.5°	your first reaction for reasoning out (or out of) an unanticipated situation
hair: blonde	Capricorn-5	17.5°-20°	how one stands up and presents themselves (to others) in times of trial
	Sagittarius-11	2.5°-5°	social dealings amidst travel or culture exploration
	Virgo-4	20°-22.5°	how you feed yourself, satiate your hunger
	Gemini-7	12.5°-15°	who you are when steering a conversation in a direction you've long favored
hair: brown	Pisces-2	25°-27.5°	what it seems others prefer you behave as
	Virgo-4	20°-22.5°	how you feed yourself, satiate your hunger
	Leo-11	2.5°-5°	where it's easier for you to be part of the in-crowd
	Gemini-11	2.5°-5°	that which is constantly on your mind / occupying your thoughts
	Gemini-12	0°-2.5°	the brands you trust. That which you could spend a lifetime studying
	Taurus-4	20°-22.5°	the family or journey support systems you are entitled to
head shape	Pisces-1	27.5°-29.9°	your basic personality among people who've met you
	Aquarius-9	7.5°-10°	how the information around a group you're in defines your group
	Scorpio-11	2.5°-5°	the information you assemble in order to achieve a certain result
	Libra-1	27.5°-29.9°	communicating in a context which is quickly passing by. "travel talk"
	Virgo-6	15°-17.5°	the experiences you stockpile as you get older; your units for time
	Leo-5	17.5°-20°	flings. you as a self-reinforcing personality
	Gemini-12	0°-2.5°	the brands you trust. That which you could spend a lifetime studying
	Taurus-1	27.5°-29.9°	where you go to teach yourself how to be yourself

face	Capricorn	1.4°	the opinions you were known to have held
	Virgo	22.4°	innocuous work opinion; the general plot of the information space in which you form opinions regarding the point of your daily duties
	Virgo	4.3°	dynamics passed down (from your parents) to your kids
	Leo	8.0°	the arsenal, the crew that rolls deep; fam
	Leo	2.0°	the events which constitute your personal story framework, filtering what can and can't happen around you in any significant way
	Gemini	15.3°	how you set up situations rather than performing direct actions to advance your agenda—especially in light of a challenge
	Taurus	20.7°	how your near neighbors experience your encounters with them
	Virgo-5	17.5°-20°	things you use to put others into a corner. Or guardedness
eyebrows	Pisces-1	27.5°-29.9°	your basic personality among people who've met you
	Pisces-6	15°-17.5°	the bases for your choices to pursue selected ends
	Pisces-11	2.5°-5°	the information you keep around you for inspiring your next step
	Sagittarius-1	27.5°-29.9°	the experience of meeting new groups
	Scorpio-7	12.5°-15°	how you collaborate towards an end
	Virgo-3	22.5°-25°	one's role on a problem-solving team (as an opinion giver)
	Virgo-9	7.5°-10°	how one appears before their managers or daily culture groups
	Aries-10	5°-7.5°	how you hold yourself back or experience sickness
eye lashes	Cancer	15.5°	information you feed yourself with routinely, and what happens when this occurs.
	Cancer-6	15°-17.5°	your childhood behavior; when you're brand new to a learning space
eyes	Pisces-3	22.5°-25°	roles the world encourages you to play
	Aquarius-3	22.5°-25°	where you give your personal opinion/interpretation of the situation
	Aquarius-9	7.5°-10°	how the information around a group you're in defines your group
	Scorpio-1	27.5°-29.9°	how you give updates to change a situation's background
	Cancer-7	12.5°-15°	how you behave when lost or lonely
	Gemini-12	0°-2.5°	the brands you trust. That which you could spend a lifetime studying
	Taurus-3	22.5°-25°	those whose mode of expression you admire
eyes: blue	Aquarius	3.6°	what sustained communication with you tends to build up in others who respond to your [interactional displays of conversational competence]
	Libra	0.1°	the major tales that could be told about the life you will have led; a memory region like the 36s
	Virgo	17.0°	your means of evolving your core relationships over time, especially those with family; the HOME of Mercury

	Leo	20.3°	a return to homeostasis or natural form involves this purging process
	Taurus	2.2°	response to opinions held of the house or advice given
eyes: green	Sagittarius	13.4°	major events which change how you will see or approach something thereafter
	Scorpio	23.2°	imaginings given the inertia of greater circumstance
	Leo	22.6°	a collection of stories associated with the groups over which you iterate
	Leo	7.8°	who you are seen as with respect to those gatekeepers who let you into the battle; a TRIGGER qunit
	Cancer	2.0°	the "need for achievement" (of a certain kind)—how to feel the pressure to reach some goal
eyes: grey	Pisces-2	25°-27.5°	what it seems others prefer you behave as
	Pisces-9	7.5°-10°	where your wanderlust lands you
	Capricorn-4	20°-22.5°	your morals, values in situations where you don't have a choice
	Capricorn-9	7.5°-10°	under limits, the culture you run to
	Sagittarius-9	7.5°-10°	how you believe cultural or societal change should be undertaken
	Sagittarius-11	2.5°-5°	social dealings amidst travel or culture exploration
	Leo-7	12.5°-15°	how you speak to friends when you're having real fun
	Cancer-12	0°-2.5°	your motivation to keep going
	Gemini-12	0°-2.5°	the brands you trust. That which you could spend a lifetime studying
	Aries-10	5°-7.5°	how you hold yourself back or experience sickness
ears	Aquarius-2	25°-27.5°	who your information spaces teach you to think you are
	Scorpio-9	7.5°-10°	how you get a space of behaviors under control
	Libra-2	25°-27.5°	what friendship looks like as displayed by you
	Virgo-5	17.5°-20°	things you use to put others into a corner. Or guardedness
	Leo-5	17.5°-20°	flings. You as a self-reinforcing personality
	Cancer-11	2.5°-5°	your interaction with buried or secret information, or the dead
	Gemini-2	25°-27.5°	your label among people you are expressively close to
	Gemini-10	5°-7.5°	what you respect or do to earn respect
	Gemini-12	0°-2.5°	the brands you trust. That which you could spend a lifetime studying
	Taurus-1	27.5°-29.9°	where you go to teach yourself how to be yourself
cheeks	Sagittarius-1	27.5°-29.9°	the experience of meeting new groups
	Sagittarius-5	17.5°-20°	public figures who resonate with the culture they are in
	Scorpio-1	27.5°-29.9°	how you give updates to change a situation's background
	Scorpio-9	7.5°-10°	how you get a space of behaviors under control
	Virgo-4	20°-22.5°	how you feed yourself, satiate your hunger
	Cancer-8	10°-12.5°	your approach to bringing wayward domains under your control
	Cancer-12	0°-2.5°	your motivation to keep going
	Taurus-3	22.5°-25°	those whose mode of expression you admire

		Taurus-10	5°-7.5°	that which naturally teaches you your limits. Formal educational experience
blemish & freckles				
		Aries	25.3°	the behavior of pioneers in establishing new rules; adventurous
		Capricorn-5	17.5°-20°	how one stands up and presents themselves (to others) in times of trial
nose		Virgo	15.9°	the clarification of your relationships through a very obvious event
		Cancer	27.1°	your role on the timeline away from core family
		Gemini	3.2°	themes which surround you and keep your sense of self-value high
		Pisces-1	27.5°-29.9°	your basic personality among people who've met you
		Aquarius-2	25°-27.5°	who your information spaces teach you to think you are
		Sagittarius-1	27.5°-29.9°	the experience of meeting new groups
		Scorpio-11	2.5°-5°	the information you assemble in order to achieve a certain result
		Leo-5	17.5°-20°	flings. You as a self-reinforcing personality
		Cancer-12	0°-2.5°	your motivation to keep going
		Taurus-6	15°-17.5°	what you're labeled as doing for a living
mouth		Pisces-9	7.5°-10°	where your wanderlust lands you
		Pisces-12	0°-2.5°	how people around you advance things you can't do on your own
		Aquarius-2	25°-27.5°	who your information spaces teach you to think you are
		Capricorn-8	10°-12.5°	how you get events to go your way when you've been limited
		Scorpio-3	22.5°-25°	while wanting another to do something, the commentary one makes
		Virgo-3	22.5°-25°	one's role on a problem-solving team (as an opinion giver)
		Leo-8	10°-12.5°	your general views and approach to sexuality
lip		Aquarius	27.4°	your more ambitious projects
		Libra	29.9°	how you seek out someone to talk to or get a sought conversation started; this is more easily activated when one is not subject to lineage checks—whites, males, the famous, and majority power holders for example—making conversations easier to attempt
		Taurus	5.7°	the work going on around you, your office mates; people who cheat off of you or sit next to you in class generally
chin		Pisces	7.6°	what it is to grind through something
		Capricorn	21.6°	where affairs you are connected to need to be formally administered (by you), this region shows the kinds of events which occur with it
		Capricorn	15.1°	big decisions to associate oneself with something, and how the effects of this spread to your family and friends
		Capricorn	0.7°	deeds or descriptions of key others you were associated with in life
		Sagittarius	27.6°	deliberating: real options form fake one
		Libra	17.0°	how your partner addresses something that is driving them nuts—what they see which triggers this

	Libra	2.6°	future states considered which engage the brain or internal logistical functions
	Virgo	24.1°	the group of inspectors on behalf of the institution or practice indicated in 3-4; the accreditation team; conducive to power and a certain ability to instill fear
	Virgo	1.5°	spacing out, how it is achieved
	Leo	27.8°	one who thinks about or orchestrates the mass movement of people
	Leo	19.1°	that which you are visibly committed to elaborating; juno-related
	Gemini	18.8°	how you play out your basic role towards your key cast of characters; CRITICAL for watching in another's chart to see if they want you in their cast
	Gemini	16.4°	the (often brief) airing of your discontent or approval
beard	Pisces	11.8°	the enemy you have come to quell. What your fixer acts against
	Aries	5.3°	if you are masculine/male, this is what you do. If you are female, this is how you consider allying with a significant masculine(?)
	Aries	3.0°	things you do in order to evade other's frustration with you? They may still be annoyed, but you don't have to be bothered by this
	Pisces-10	5°-7.5°	when you're dead tired / energy-drained
	Aquarius-7	12.5°-15°	one's interactions with their friends
	Sagittarius-4	20°-22.5°	*what* one feels when in a comfortable feeling environment
	Sagittarius-6	15°-17.5°	how you handle "game time," competition, or pressure
	Libra-2	25°-27.5°	what friendship looks like as displayed by you
	Leo-5	17.5°-20°	flings. You as a self-reinforcing personality
neck	Aquarius-4	20°-22.5°	the nature of your family
	Capricorn-1	27.5°-29.9°	how you respond to feeling trapped
	Scorpio-2	25°-27.5°	how you express your defiance of certain circumstances you're in
	Scorpio-3	22.5°-25°	while wanting another to do something, the commentary one makes
	Scorpio-7	12.5°-15°	how you collaborate towards an end
	Leo-4	20°-22.5°	developing your own character with no assumption of labels
	Gemini-9	7.5°-10°	one's outlook on how the world works or should work
	Taurus-5	17.5°-20°	uniqueness, what separates you from your pack
	Taurus-7	12.5°-15°	the efforts that keep another close to you
	Aries-9	7.5°-10°	one's ideal; the future you are pursuing knowingly or unknowingly
shoulders	Capricorn	4.9°	time to go forward, though there will likely be little help; seems to be associated with the shoulders and the work you must do while others look on from the sidelines. Positively may indicate a kind of monopoly you have over a certain kind of work
	Aries	5.3°	if you are masculine/male, this is what you do. If you are female, this is how you consider allying with a significant masculine(?)
	Pisces-1	27.5°-29.9°	your basic personality among people who've met you

	Pisces-7	12.5°-15°	feeling of the self-talk or conversation you need to have next
	Sagittarius-7	12.5°-15°	those in a position to judge or evaluate a space or define its reputation
	Leo-1	27.5°-29.9°	how you make advances on a thing you want and don't currently have
	Taurus-8	10°-12.5°	area where you feel entitled to influence
chest	Pisces-1	27.5°-29.9°	your basic personality among people who've met you
	Pisces-10	5°-7.5°	when you're dead tired / energy-drained
	Aquarius-6	15°-17.5°	the kinds of stories you best tell about the world; "by your logic"
	Libra-1	27.5°-29.9°	communicating in a context which is quickly passing by. "travel talk"
	Libra-8	10°-12.5°	what occurs when you and another are not on the same page
	Libra-11	2.5°-5°	what your world looks like when all is lost. Associated with forgetting
	Libra-12	0°-2.5°	the consequences of your interactions; feeds your next circumstances
	Virgo-7	12.5°-15°	support from others in accomplishing a task
	Virgo-11	2.5°-5°	the kinds of (message) traffic you help sponsor
	Leo-2	25°-27.5°	how people see your personality when off in your own world
	Leo-5	17.5°-20°	flings. You as a self-reinforcing personality
	Leo-12	0°-2.5°	your idea of fully realized personhood as a lifestyle
	Gemini-10	5°-7.5°	what you respect or do to earn respect
	Taurus-5	17.5°-20°	uniqueness, what separates you from your pack
	Aries-5	17.5°-20°	the urge to project your character, driven by a rootless impulse
nipples	Aquarius-2	25°-27.5°	who your information spaces teach you to think you are
	Capricorn-10	5°-7.5°	the nature of the institutions you typically interact with
	Sagittarius-2	25°-27.5°	the part of larger niches / cultures which you internalize for yourself
	Sagittarius-3	22.5°-25°	your opinions when engaging cultures or niches systems not your own
	Scorpio-3	22.5°-25°	while wanting another to do something, the commentary one makes
	Libra-1	27.5°-29.9°	communicating in a context which is quickly passing by. "travel talk"
	Virgo-2	25°-27.5°	how people close enough to you see you managing your domestic affairs
	Leo-10	5°-7.5°	where one takes pride in how they handle challenges or difficulties
	Aries-2	25°-27.5°	the instinctual way in which you carry yourself when you have no attachments
	Aries-10	5°-7.5°	how you hold yourself back or experience sickness
breasts	Pisces	13.0°	what another does which discourages the one from wanting to fight them
	Aquarius	25.8°	a thing that presents you with bullshit requirements you didn't ask for, or your response to extraneous intrusions; related to 6232 Zubitskia
	Capricorn	8.0°	your first seducers and pre-romantic play experiences

Capricorn	2.6°	traveling out in the world, or (in the case of stationary objects or concepts) getting others to travel from the outside world to you
Scorpio	23.8°	fellatio (your idea of your role); based on the house qunits, shows where one inserts an engine of forced-out production into another's space of nurturance intake rather than a space of product-import—kind of like receiving a shipment through one's customer entrance rather than the warehouse where it is to be processed, a convenience for the deliverer, but a thing to be digested by the consumer. Seems to say to the target, "I'm willing to digest / internalize (or at least trigger the internalization of) what you are creatively re-producing as a copy of your own will. I will develop myself personally / internally with it, though not necessarily process it towards my own product-export process as you would normally intend."
Libra	10.9°	appears to be a set of milestones in your social life. Depending on your maturity level, fights you felt spontaneously compelled to fight at the time. 68-1=>(7.8)-1=> compulsion (1) using power (8) with interaction (7) as the context
Leo	17.8°	?what your partner or complementary group does which limits your natural expression?
Cancer	27.6°	your children's or creations' creations—the process employed by the former to generate the latter
Cancer	95.5°	the various actors involved in your self-limitation
Taurus	24.7°	someone is optimistic, though either they or another are simultaneously limited or oppressed by something
Taurus	17.8°	those who are easily irritated with you or who look down on you easily

torso

Pisces-3	22.5°-25°	roles the world encourages you to play
Aquarius-11	2.5°-5°	what you are uniquely good at. Your unique attunement
Capricorn-8	10°-12.5°	how you get events to go your way when you've been limited
Sagittarius-1	27.5°-29.9°	the experience of meeting new groups
Leo-12	0°-2.5°	your idea of fully realized personhood as a lifestyle
Aries-10	5°-7.5°	how you hold yourself back or experience sickness
Aries-11	2.5°-5°	the kinds of music which accompanies your spirit / vibe / aura as a person

stomach

Capricorn-8	10°-12.5°	how you get events to go your way when you've been limited
Sagittarius-7	12.5°-15°	those in a position to judge or evaluate a space or define its reputation
Scorpio-7	12.5°-15°	how you collaborate towards an end
Scorpio-8	10°-12.5°	what is happening when you are at the peak of your power
Virgo-5	17.5°-20°	things you use to put others into a corner. Or guardedness
Leo-5	17.5°-20°	flings. You as a self-reinforcing personality
Cancer-4	20°-22.5°	building your readiness to pursue a line of expression
Taurus-1	27.5°-29.9°	where you go to teach yourself how to be yourself

waist				
		Capricorn-4	20°-22.5°	your morals, values in situations where you don't have a choice
		Capricorn-9	7.5°-10°	under limits, the culture you run to
		Sagittarius-2	25°-27.5°	the part of larger niches / cultures which you internalize for yourself
		Gemini-5	17.5°-20°	who you or your representative claim themselves to be
		Gemini-12	0°-2.5°	the brands you trust. That which you could spend a lifetime studying
		Taurus-5	17.5°-20°	uniqueness, what separates you from your pack

hips				
		Aries	3.9°	(the one man stunt show); seems related to dancing
		Pisces-2	25°-27.5°	what it seems others prefer you behave as
		Aquarius-6	15°-17.5°	the kinds of stories you best tell about the world; "by your logic"
		Sagittarius-2	25°-27.5°	the part of larger niches / cultures which you internalize for yourself
		Sagittarius-4	20°-22.5°	*what* one feels when in a comfortable feeling environment
		Virgo-5	17.5°-20°	things you use to put others into a corner. or guardedness
		Leo-5	17.5°-20°	flings. You as a self-reinforcing personality
		Cancer-2	25°-27.5°	the kind of person you desire to be, especially when on a journey
		Cancer-7	12.5°-15°	how you behave when lost or lonely
		Gemini-3	22.5°-25°	how you "revoice" yourself in support of more of what you're doing.
		Gemini-5	17.5°-20°	who you or your representative claim themselves to be
		Taurus-2	25°-27.5°	things that have their own intrinsic value sourced from within themselves
		Taurus-6	15°-17.5°	what you're labeled as doing for a living
		Taurus-11	2.5°-5°	traits or skills you have which are in demand / passed around

penis				
		Sagittarius	2.8°	the nature of your kindred and family-like connections
		Sagittarius	2.2°	first major encounter in a path of ongoing relating
		Aries	18.2°	bodily action is employed to achieve an ambition objective
		Aries	15.3°	things that swoop in and out - the hawk's region
		Libra	26.3°	collections which have a hallowed place in your history
		Libra	25.5°	where family or kindred dynamics are reconfigured around you—often around your temperament
		Pisces-12	0°-2.5°	how people around you advance things you can't do on your own
		Sagittarius-2	25°-27.5°	the part of larger niches / cultures which you internalize for yourself
		Scorpio-3	22.5°-25°	while wanting another to do something, the commentary one makes
		Virgo-5	17.5°-20°	things you use to put others into a corner. Or guardedness
		Virgo-7	12.5°-15°	support from others in accomplishing a task
		Aries-6	15°-17.5°	your first reaction for reasoning out (or out of) an unanticipated situation

vagina	Taurus	1.2°	a defining property of the house one prefers
	Sagittarius-10	5°-7.5°	how you learn the foreign
	Sagittarius-11	2.5°-5°	social dealings amidst travel or culture exploration
	Scorpio-8	10°-12.5°	what is happening when you are at the peak of your power
	Libra-5	17.5°-20°	how you show yourself when extremely comfortable with someone
	Leo-10	5°-7.5°	where one takes pride in how they handle challenges or difficulties
	Cancer-5	17.5°-20°	childhood play life—the games, friends, and teachers involved
	Aries-1	27.5°-29.9°	how you feel inclined to express all of a sudden
	Taurus-12	0°-2.5°	how you broadly feel when willingly under the control of another
back	Pisces-1	27.5°-29.9°	your basic personality among people who've met you
	Pisces-9	7.5°-10°	where your wanderlust lands you
	Aquarius-8	10°-12.5°	your understanding of armies—what they entail and how they manifest
	Scorpio-6	15°-17.5°	those who can tell you what to do, do next, or reconcile as a task
	Scorpio-9	7.5°-10°	how you get a space of behaviors under control
	Virgo-5	17.5°-20°	things you use to put others into a corner. Or guardedness
	Leo-9	7.5°-10°	the kinds of people you attract when you have your fun
	Cancer-4	20°-22.5°	building your readiness to pursue a line of expression
	Cancer-7	12.5°-15°	how you behave when lost or lonely
	Gemini-11	2.5°-5°	that which is constantly on your mind / occupying your thoughts
	Aries-6	15°-17.5°	your first reaction for reasoning out (or out of) an unanticipated situation
	Aries-11	2.5°-5°	the kinds of music which accompanies your spirit / vibe / aura as a person
skin	Pisces	21.0°	the rebellious or separatist acts you experience which sever your ties from ally groups
	Pisces	7.8°	your visitation into a place which will task you to put on a role; your attitude in the role place?
	Capricorn	19.0°	what you anticipate the threatened character will impose upon you; the burden they will saddle you with
	Sagittarius	12.8°	the nature of your kindred and family-like connections
	Libra	27.8°	what people attached to / subject to you do behind your back, more likely in light of their interaction with you. Your knowing this can render you partly clairvoyant or interpersonally claircognizant—basically psychic regarding the turns in your relationships: applying structure (10) using impulse (1) with feedbacking (7) as context
	Libra	18.4°	while within a partnership, dissatisfied
	Libra	(sign)	FEEDBACK LOOPING and COMMUNICATIVE INTERACTION with others
	Libra	10.5°	that which you cannot really be supported in; a thing you must engage solo

	Libra	10.1°	foreignized—where your attention moves towards a group that is even more foreign than any current one you might be in
	Cancer	1.0°	your deepest sought scenario for intimacy—whether you know it or not
	Cancer	0.5°	remote actions by a party disallowed in your dimension which nonetheless influences your path
	Gemini	26.2°	near those who assert a kind of freedom—especially as seen through the eyes of outsiders
	Gemini	22.8°	how you get involved with a colorful diversity of characters
	Gemini	15.5°	the citations of one who believes things need to go their way
	Taurus	25.1°	progressing an (impassioned) communicated message
	Libra-8	10°-12.5°	what occurs when you and another are not on the same page
	Cancer-12	0°-2.5°	your motivation to keep going
skin texture	Aquarius	10.55°	what bosses want or require of you. Failing this, they are much more likely to withdraw their support or withhold certain key enabling resources from you
	Sagittarius	9.9°	quietly observing others' chaotic energy; the chaos within that one outside, or how that one deals with exploitation or being mercilessly used/demanded of
	Aquarius-8	10°-12.5°	Your understanding of armies—what they entail and how they manifest
	Sagittarius-9	7.5°-10°	how you believe cultural or societal change should be undertaken
	Aries-4	20°-22.5°	what you need in order to make a choice
buttocks	Aquarius	6.2°	private events which you air our discuss publicly; it seems that the more this forces people's actions, the bigger one's butt. But if you are male and thus assert this region all the time, your hit rate will be much lower.
	Libra	7.4°	parties whose progress you follow; after you know what you like co-creatively, WHO you would indulge
	Aries	3.9°	(the one man stunt show); seems related to dancing
	Aquarius-3	22.5°-25°	where you give your personal opinion/interpretation of the situation
	Capricorn-6	15°-17.5°	the nature or character of the answers you tend to encounter
	Capricorn-8	10°-12.5°	how you get events to go your way when you've been limited
	Sagittarius-7	12.5°-15°	those in a position to judge or evaluate a space or define its reputation
	Sagittarius-12	0°-2.5°	one's relationship to their land or the lands they prefer to occupy
	Virgo-5	17.5°-20°	things you use to put others into a corner. Or guardedness
	Gemini-11	2.5°-5°	that which is constantly on your mind / occupying your thoughts
	Aries-5	17.5°-20°	the urge to project your character, driven by a rootless impulse
	Aries-11	2.5°-5°	the kinds of music which accompanies your spirit / vibe / aura as a person
arms	Aquarius-2	25°-27.5°	who your information spaces teach you to think you are
	Aquarius-6	15°-17.5°	the kinds of stories you best tell about the world; "by your logic"
	Sagittarius-2	25°-27.5°	the part of larger niches / cultures which you internalize for yourself
	Sagittarius-4	20°-22.5°	*what* one feels when in a comfortable feeling environment

		Cancer-6	15°-17.5°	your childhood behavior; when you're brand new to a learning space
hands		Capricorn-1	27.5°-29.9°	how you respond to feeling trapped
		Capricorn-2	25°-27.5°	fans and followers
		Aries-2	25°-27.5°	the instinctual way in which you carry yourself when you have no attachments
legs		Pisces	27.0°	your body in action, earning the events It earns
		Pisces	18.4°	you as bully
		Pisces	15.1°	under watch or under caution, where this is a thing
		Aquarius	21.7°	the work you are actively obsessed with continuing
		Aquarius	21.7°	how you compel your interactants to get to the point...the point YOU want made
		Aquarius	9.5°	in the role of the submitter to scrutiny or interrogation
		Scorpio	15.5°	the information or communication you pull around you in order to put order back onto a thing which has gotten out of hand
		Scorpio	13.6°	occurrences which you stay very separate from, or which may distance you from your former kindred
		Cancer	6.3°	one's chain of thought correlated with self intention-limitation
		Gemini	28.8°	deciding on a path and going all the way on it
		Aries	22.8°	when the surrounding environment is out of your control; seems to be related to storms
feet		Scorpio	3.6°	occurrences which you stay very separate from, or which may distance you from your former kindred
		Leo	3.4°	a uniquely you, non-mainstream activity you enjoy participating in, especially after hours
		Scorpio-11	2.5°-5°	The information you assemble in order to achieve a certain result
		Leo-11	2.5°-5°	where it's easier for you to be part of the in-crowd

About general attributes

Some body features aren't located anywhere on or in the body, but are located everywhere. Or maybe they live through others' responses to you. These were studied mostly via descriptor embeddings rather than sliders, and are very much statements of the kinds and amounts of other energy stored in the orbit of your presence.

age		Libra	1.4°	the vacuum. A region of feminine / domainic power at its maximum ability to define through communication; the Age trait was both t-test and cancor significant
		Aries	26.1°	the interactional work you do on a system which you are capable of evolving ceaselessly; related to aging, drooping, and wrinkles?
		Capricorn-1	27.5°-29.9°	how you respond to feeling trapped
		Virgo-10	5°-7.5°	creating formal structures from one's meaning making, deriving laws
maleness (from prenatal femaleness)		Aquarius	3.6°	what sustained communication with you tends to build up in others who respond to your [interactional displays of conversational competence]
		Libra	14.0°	how or when you wish to close a deep conversation
		Leo	(sign)	how you PROJECT YOUR CHARACTER

	Leo	12.2°	those whom the army leader can rally; the counterparts who back or oppose the army's leader—those whom the leader shines their spotlight attention upon
	Leo	0.5°	the fate of the villains in your experience
	Leo	6.3°	one's chain of thought correlated with self intention-limitation
	Taurus	3.8°	the information you like to keep running in the background; background noise you prefer
	Aquarius-11	2.5°-5°	what you are uniquely good at. Your unique attunement
	Libra-7	12.5°-15°	your most sustainable conversations—how you progress them
	Leo-8	10°-12.5°	your general views and approach to sexuality
	Leo-12	0°-2.5°	your idea of fully realized personhood as a lifestyle
	Cancer-10	5°-7.5°	the barriers you (unintentionally perhaps) seek for yourself
	Taurus-11	2.5°-5°	traits or skills you have which are in demand / passed around
height	Pisces	13.2°	what manhood creates as a broad concept—the experiences it initiates
	Aquarius	1.1°	the catalyst which transforms you more into your prime, full-powered self
	Gemini	28.4°	how you express your interpersonal charismatic value; the things you do to increase your social worth
	Gemini	13.7°	the agent or situation which carries a process into death or being discarded
	Taurus	17.2°	how you express your plans for advancing, though there is a VERY good chance that this will not *actually* drive you forward monetarily—it will only be the talk you gravitate towards;
	Taurus	(sign)	things and ideas used to IDENTIFY other things
	Aries	(sign)	inborn spontaneous IMPULSES
	Capricorn-8	10°-12.5°	how you get events to go your way when you've been limited
	Capricorn-11	2.5°-5°	the information brought to bear when pressure or limits are experienced
	Sagittarius-5	17.5°-20°	public figures who resonate with the culture they are in
	Sagittarius-6	15°-17.5°	how you handle "game time," competition, or pressure
	Gemini-5	17.5°-20°	who you or your representative claim themselves to be
	Taurus-3	22.5°-25°	those whose mode of expression you admire
weight	Pisces	22.4°	where you are positioned such that your communication helps people feel better or do better
	Pisces	(sign)	AMBIENT MOOD, what the environment around you typically inclines towards when you are there
	Pisces	0.1°	a part of your sphere which markedly disagrees with how you've intended to relate. Not exactly an enemy, but more like a thwarting situation against how you've set yourself up to relate to others
	Aquarius	19.3°	your fit match, possibly for deep bonding
	Aquarius	3.0°	the authority figures of your friends or the kinds of events your childhood friends participated under
	Sagittarius	6.1°	the females in one's life when they are under pressure
	Scorpio	3.6°	occurrences which you stay very separate from, or which may distance you from your former kindred

	Cancer	22.8°	how out of control environments or moods end up getting resolved for you
	Cancer	(sign)	how you WANT or INCLINE towards behaviors
	Gemini	22.8°	they bring out-in-the-open-drama
	Gemini	4.9°	how you and your friend build up or add to your joint dwelling or niche-space
	Gemini	2.8°	those who present healing solutions to your problems
	Taurus	2.8°	preparations for the next great adventure as circumstances reconfigure themselves to let you out of where you are
	Aries	19.2°	not a care in the world or, how you hunt the object you want—as a character you put on
	Aries	6.8°	solitary intimate experiences
body shape	Capricorn	17.4°	how the pruning of your space is triggered; the event which clears your environment of the chaff (anything that doesn't really belong at the core of where you are)
	Capricorn	14.7°	project partner for new explorations?
	Sagittarius	7.4°	your partner's first response to you when sexual exposure begins, especially when you are younger. When older, more people are less likely to make the teenage observations; the impression you put on their minds
	Sagittarius	4.7°	the process or others you interact with which help you get the information you need to navigate the foreign; host sponsors; easily fully studyable images or people
	Scorpio	(sign)	how you IMPART INERTIA upon things to push them in a different direction than their current one
	Libra	14.3°	how you present ideas which are close to your heart in deep conversation
	Libra	3.0°	while on your home turf, how you live and the things that reflect you; investigate in NFL players, their team logos, and stadiums
	Virgo	16.8°	protective behaviors of or by a close other; situations you automatically interact with or interactions you are drawn into which sustain your ability to recursively reconcile events before you
	Virgo	6.0°	how (general) others around you feel you were soliciting their company or signing up to be their ally...their subject (actually); what you did which told others you wanted to be in charge of implementing their ideas
	Virgo	0.3°	household or small office dynamics which show up when you are regularly involved with a close-knit group in daily affairs; tell and trigger region for what you are actually able to build as a daily life
	Leo	28.9°	that which serves as a foundation upon which your public image can be built. This is very likely to be executed by someone else before you. If you do this, you are a foundation for others represented by the 13q3s
	Leo	17.8°	?what your partner or complementary group does which limits your natural expression?
	Cancer	6.8°	the character which serves to draw out the limiting sides of your own dreams; this is the Hinderer in your Cancer-10
	Gemini	21.1°	talk-worthy guest appearance; how people talk about you as a guest in light of expectations, or how you steer the talk about guests (is this a masc-fem biased region?)
	Gemini	19.3°	documenting or being documented in a search

	Sign	Degree	Description
	Gemini	18.8°	how you play out your basic role towards your key cast of characters; CRITICAL for watching in another's chart to see if they want you in their cast. Is there a body region for this or vibe that I can use for pathfinding? Appears to be the smile-mouth region of the upper lips
	Gemini	13.7°	the agent or situation which carries a process into death or being discarded
	Gemini	10.5°	social activity which drains the energy of you or your representative
	Taurus	7.4°	how identity structures are forced upon the individual
	Aries	0.1°	that which is publicly known to happen around you when you are in a situation (as opposed when you are not in a situation, dead for example); the public's experience of your presence
fitness	Libra	24.0°	that which constitutes stability as growth progresses; the skeletal system and adult body frame?
	Aries	7.4°	how your means of traversal in some area suddenly invalidate your wishes; the onset of sickness
	Aries	3.9°	(the one man stunt show); seems related to dancing
	Pisces-9	7.5°-10°	where your wanderlust lands you
	Pisces-12	0°-2.5°	how people around you advance things you can't do on your own
	Aquarius-4	20°-22.5°	the nature of your family
	Capricorn-2	25°-27.5°	fans and followers
	Capricorn-6	15°-17.5°	the nature or character of the answers you tend to encounter
	Sagittarius-2	25°-27.5°	the part of larger niches / cultures which you internalize for yourself
	Virgo-5	17.5°-20°	things you use to put others into a corner. Or guardedness
	Virgo-6	15°-17.5°	the experiences you stockpile as you get older; your units for TIME
	Virgo-8	10°-12.5°	how you exercise the most influence in your daily doings and work life
	Gemini-3	22.5°-25°	how you "revoice" yourself in support of more of what you're doing.
	Gemini-7	12.5°-15°	who you are when steering a conversation in a direction you've long favored
	Aries-2	25°-27.5°	the instinctual way in which you carry yourself when you have no attachments
	Pisces-1	27.5°-29.9°	your basic personality among people who've met you
	Pisces-7	12.5°-15°	feeling of the self-talk or conversation you need to have next
	Libra-6	15°-17.5°	interacting for logical reasons, not because one prefers to
muscularity	Aquarius	20.0°	pushing through powerfully towards a goal
	Aquarius	10.9°	how the army is briefed; the messaging delivered to reinforce the army's goals and culture
	Sagittarius	28.9°	definitely following your own path despite certain social rules hindering it
	Sagittarius	4.0°	how you behave against a significant conflicted character or bad guy
	Scorpio	22.0°	the events that ride along with you in conflict
	Libra	11.6°	the transfer of mandate to less qualified but more popular people; how you interpret the actions of those who are intimacy seekers to you

	Virgo	14.9°	how you execute your cooperation with others / team projects
	Leo	10.7°	that which keeps coming back in blatant disregard for whether certain witnesses want them there or view them as tacky
	Gemini	2.8°	your prime coworking, daily duties counterpart or collaborative space
	Aries	(sign)	inborn spontaneous IMPULSES
vascularity	Taurus	8.6°	a mode for your continuous learning. Doing this, the world keeps giving you more insight
	Taurus	1.9°	work done on the house
	Taurus-9	7.5°-10°	where you define cultures just by virtue of having an identity. Archetype
	Taurus-12	0°-2.5°	how you broadly feel when willingly under the control of another
tattoos	Sagittarius	(sign)	NICHE ENVIRONMENT and the BEHAVIOR PATTERNS naturally around you
	Sagittarius	8.9°	the kind of bf or gf you ultimately end up with - specifically the kinds of adventures you have together
	Sagittarius-9	7.5°-10°	how you believe cultural or societal change should be undertaken
piercings	Pisces-1	27.5°-29.9°	your basic personality among people who've met you
	Pisces-5	17.5°-20°	your default treatment of long-term domestic partners
	Pisces-6	15°-17.5°	the bases for your choices to pursue selected ends
	Libra-8	10°-12.5°	what occurs when you and another are not on the same page
	Libra-10	5°-7.5°	how you enforce rules for determining which interactions are close
	Virgo-7	12.5°-15°	support from others in accomplishing a task
	Virgo-12	0°-2.5°	the time you spend in quiet. Quiet time duty-doing activity
	Cancer-5	17.5°-20°	childhood play life—the games, friends, and teachers involved
	Cancer-9	7.5°-10°	the overall lifestyle you are chasing
	Gemini-5	17.5°-20°	who you or your representative claim themselves to be
	Taurus-6	15°-17.5°	what you're labeled as doing for a living
	Aries-11	2.5°-5°	the kinds of music which accompanies your spirit / vibe / aura as a person
impression	Libra	29.2°	the guest who moves in and is allowed to impose their standards upon you
	Virgo	(sign)	how you JOIN or RECONCILE concepts
	Gemini	13.0°	what you do to render it unwise for others to want to fight you. But if you show them you are losing interest in this, the fights may begin
	Libra-12	0°-2.5°	The consequences of your interactions; feeds your next circumstances
	Virgo-5	17.5°-20°	Things you use to put others into a corner. Or guardedness
	Cancer-10	5°-7.5°	The barriers you (unintentionally perhaps) seek for yourself

expression

Libra-8	10°-12.5°	what occurs when you and another are not on the same page
Aries-11	2.5°-5°	the kinds of music which accompanies your spirit / vibe / aura as a person

beauty

Pisces	29.7°	where you are witness to conflicts others must resolve regarding your participation in a thing
Pisces	22.6°	the operating principle you grow into as your role in the world; when represented by others, seems to indicate the people who train you or train with you in your evolving role. They have their own "MOS" so to speak
Aquarius	26.6°	genuinely connecting with one's audience and their sentiments
Aquarius	17.4°	how the strong male energy expects/draws its domain or female targets to receive that energy
Capricorn	27.1°	sides of yourself that you show which, if seen by another, indicate that a kind of intercourse or intimacy is possible
Capricorn	23.7°	the event which registers one as being part of the family
Sagittarius	10.0°	as you grow distanced from those close to you, this is what happens
Scorpio	7.8°	you in hardcore battle mode, given your supporters back you
Libra	29.9°	how you seek out someone to talk to or get a sought conversation started; this is more easily activated when one is not subject to lineage checks—whites, males, the famous, and majority power holders for example—making conversations easier to attempt
Libra	1.3°	information—sometimes published—used as a highway for expressing one's force
Virgo	28.4°	a thing witnessed is conducive to doubt or skepticism towards at least one of the actors
Virgo	15.9°	the clarification of your relationships through a very obvious event
Virgo	13.0°	the events that attend your being unable to project or defend yourself, especially through combat or assertion
Virgo	3.0°	the substitute for a non-ideal or failed partnership
Leo	26.0°	alpha, masculinized, or otherwise potent woman / domain; a domain which challenges its occupants' conceptions
Leo	11.8°	what you do which draws out others' consternation in light of how they have seen you communicate something (often impersonally sweeping); where others see you as having disregarded their wishes or feelings
Cancer	29.3°	the final imposition of your notion of victory onto everything
Cancer	1.0°	your deepest sought scenario for intimacy—whether you know it or not
Gemini	14.9°	the one around you who, though they may not be the easiest to relate to, can be relied upon to keep progress going
Gemini	12.4°	the methods of progressing a situation which you admire or love to see
Gemini	5.5°	the process that checks or blocks your progress
Taurus	25.9°	how you amuse yourself or keep yourself entertained. Could be social or solitary

Taurus	21.4°	your contribution to the world, how you attempt to make it better—even if just for yourself; lots of triggers; that which is overlooked, but still important as a process
Aries	29.1°	people you really should retain, or whom you should at least replace with a stable template, as they further your expression
Aries	26.4°	your relationship with the meaning-holding or circumstance-objects you collect

For readers in general...

How do I use the stuff in this book?

Let's assume that you can just make drastic changes to how you look. (Not overnight anyway.) So it's not like you can say to yourself, "I'm just gonna make my nose bigger so that my vibes of self-worth will go up." A key thing to remember in all of this is that your body is mostly meant for others' framing of you, then for your own long-term internalization of *parts* of that framing." Your body tells the strangers, cultures, animals, and certain career fields which boxes to put you in by default as they attempt to execute their own agendas. Likewise, your brain uses others' body appearances as a data dump for social assumptions—especially in regards to things like attitude, trust, and interactability. More important than using the abstracted versions of these frequencies to hack your life from your own individual perspective, you can and should use the table above to decipher the mystery of how the sum of countless actors external to you manage to create certain situations you can or can't master. Said differently, the table above is most useful for helping you clearly frame issues that you may have known about only subconsciously until now. I'll give you an example:

"Quick Ajani, name a feature of your body that might be interesting to think about."

"I have long-ish arms."

"Okay, now look at the table. See anything interesting?"

"Aquarius-2: who my spaces teach me to think I am. Honestly, I think my work is unique enough to reach way beyond what a lot of life would have given me by default... Actually, I also have thin wrists. I can't tell you how many people took that for frailty over the years, jokingly commenting on how puny the rest of me probably was. As for my upper forearms, they're wider, but rarely did the wrist commenters see this. I suppose my arms are an example of how I work in general: I have a number of features like slightly lower-average height which give others a chance to take me lightly under initial assumption. When I was young I found this insulting. Now older, I value it as a hugely important filter for getting at the truth of how anyone I interact with treats, shows courtesy to, or makes fun of those they think weaker than them. I'm big on the Golden Rule. I want to know immediately if potential connections will find it fun to shit on the least of us. That way I can drop them early."

And there you go. See how my final observation had less to do with my arms, but served as a launch point for thinking about other aspects of my life. Try this yourself. You don't necessarily have to do anything or make any big decisions based on what you find. All you need to do is let the region meanings "interview you" so to speak.

Pick at least 3 interesting aspects of your body from the table above, then take some time to think about how any of their related chart region meanings might have implications for your life in general. You can use the space below to write down any observations.

Body region 1	Thoughts:
Body region 2	Thoughts:
Body region 3	Thoughts:

For people who feel they have lost their voice in a chaotic world,
those whose sense of value or worth is down,
those wondering why they just can't reach the goal they set for themselves,
or people who are just wondering what bigger society wants from them...

How do I use the stuff in this book?

I sometimes think of my body as if it was the deck I have been handed. Some people receive better hands than others. Sometimes your hand is bad, but everyone else's are worse. Other times your hand is great, your rival knows it, and sets out to cheat you. But one thing you might find very useful, is to know (realistically) what your hand means according to the broad social rules laid out by millennia of societies before you.

This next activity is easy. Go through all of the sections above and look for any body qualities and the region meanings that seem most relevant to you. While you're at it, be sure to note any qualities that might not belong to you, but do belong to a persistent type of person in your circle. You don't have to do any deep reflection on the region meanings just yet. Simply list any region meanings which seem to speak to you when it comes to your Rule Set's plan for what social onlookers (including systems) would have been prepared to give you in this life.

As you do this, please remember that there are no implications for something being good or bad. The stats didn't have this as a factor, only whether certain measures *had anything to do with* certain others. Don't get down on yourself when a particular trait you possess has also been a liability up to now. The whole point of this exercise is to put together a more sense-making framework for it *prior* to it being trained as good or bad. Here's a little example to get you started:

Me: African American (african morph with some caucasian morph), black hair, highly rotated ears, suspicious eyes →

> Aries-5, Aries-6, Aries-9, Taurus-1, Taurus-5, Gemini-1, Gemini-9, Gemini-10, Gemini-12, Cancer-7, Cancer-11, Virgo-5, Scorpio-2, Scorpio-3, Scorpio-9, Capricorn-1, Capricorn-8, Aquarius-1, Aquarius-2, Aquarius-9, Aquarius 22.8°, Aquarius 29.2°, Pisces-2, Pisces-7, Pisces-8, Pisces-12,

…from experience, I think the asteroids in these places are worth looking at. Asking myself questions about their region meaning will help me better understand why my life situation has evolved as it has, and where the society of fellow humans might be pushing me. For example, I have high, asymmetric, sad-ishly stern eyes which make me look crazy on camera and was one of many traits that put people off when I was young. Still does, actually. Yet thanks to Cancer-7 and -11, my eyes are one of the strongest indicators of a lifelong sense of self-worth—as the things I do alone include these books, which have been by far my strongest sources of personal accomplishment.

Your turn:

What are some traits that best describe you?

What are some regions that these traits suggest you might look at for understanding the roles that society pushes you towards?

Any general thoughts about the above?

We're just getting started. The next chapter presents one of the main reasons this book exists. We will finally get to translate human body regions into their corresponding social energies, with asteroids attached.

Chapter 13: Anikacheerla and company. The asteroids of the body

Suppose you have a random object in the sky. Call it 2000 QQ28. After some investigation and a couple of studies, you decide to look for significant angles between this object and some major planets across the birth dates of 40,000 people. When you pull keywords from these people's articles, you find that some of them coincide with strong angles for making 2000 QQ28 visible in the real life events it might correlate with. Pouring through about 24000 words, you end up with 17 words which appear far more commonly in charts with this asteroid in strong angle to a "major planet." The asteroid in question is actually named 34164 Anikacheerla, and here are the words it corresponds to:

> continuously, stretch, rumor, complexion, homicidal, hostile, creator, story – stunt, allegorical, legal, story – homicide, story – sounding, stato, crook, renovation, rationale, flank

Looking at the words above, and checking the location of this asteroid against the charts of five people whom you know very well, you provide an interpretation for the asteroid. The date is 12/27/2022 12:59:01 PM:

> teeth gritting pull at something in order to force its shape into conformity; "the kind of stretching which scares…", reminiscent of any kind of stretching deformity, as in zombies or monster movies— the melted look; associated with dragging something out in a way that causes or implies pain, tension, or other kinds of anxiety in interactants

Later, in 2023. You run some ANOVA tests to see which asteroids have correlations between the [number of special angles to a major planet] and [the value of certain body measures on a sliding scale from -1 to +1]. But there are so many results that you don't get back to this one.

Finally, in October of 2024 while looking to answer an unrelated question, you run a summary of the most statistically significant findings from the prior year's ANOVAs. On a list of 7000 findings pulled from an original 500,000+, it seems that Anikacheerla had one entry among the strongest statistical relationships. It was for the "slider_Age" measure.

ASTEROIDS OF THE BODY

I originally was not going to include body-to-asteroid correspondences in this book, mainly because I had run the asteroid statistics before completing the dictionary which defined those asteroids (*Laurentia 2nd ed*), and the research at the time seemed premature. But it turns out that the results were roundly fascinating, and offered better bases for abstraction than the qunit meanings themselves.

The planets and asteroids are mobile. You may have a chart region which shares influence over the hair, but an asteroid of hair which can change its character across regions somehow just feels more accurate. If you can find such an asteroid, that is. Tonight when I accidentally went down a rabbit hole looking for a way to label the upcoming body map, I ended up unburying the file with ALL of my completed asteroid ANOVAs (looking for differences in numerical slider values among nominal duodecanates when controlling for each single asteroid). To me, seeing the asteroid 34164 correspond not only to melting features in 2022, but also to aging features in a completely different set of charts seemed like such validation for the relationships I've been exploring all this time.

Since there's no way I'm fitting half a million results in this book, however, I had to distill the list down to only the strongest relationships. Using my original text mining stats on major, hot, tense, and seeking angle-to-major counts among the asteroids, I devised a formula for how much influence an asteroid had against the particular body feature's slider for which it was significant.[19] If the average count of slider values for an asteroid's hot aspects (conjunct, opposition, trine, or sextile) was of the opposite sign to the tense (square) or seeking (inconjunct) average values, that that told you that expressing the asteroid would give you one result, but expressing it's square would inhibit the first result. This supported the idea that the asteroid was *actually* associated with that result. The results for Anikacheerla, for example, are shown below:

FIGURE 19: HOW ANIKACHEERLA CAME TO BE ASSOCIATED WITH AGE OR AGEING

body feature	group	vertical	Unique count*(currentColumnN	Asteroid=split_1	tense	seekingNot(Yet)Having	major	hot/default	square_matters	inconjunct_matters	Unique count* (body feature)	%body group covered	influence points	reason chosen	split_0	comment
slider_Age	age	84	2	Anikacheerla	-0.29102	0	-0.29611	0.405825	1	0	1	0.3	1.747891	influence	34164	teeth gritting pu

Here, hot aspects were associated with more aged features while tense squares were associated with less aged features, and this accords with the asteroid's "melting homicide" text mine and interpretation as well. That's a testament to the idea that astrology *can* be seriously researched, and sometimes the finds are glaring.

As part of my study I obtained a group of 21,000 results featuring asteroids which either had 1) high influence according to my aspects calculation earlier, or 2) covered a significant number of the available sliders in a group. 55276 Kenlarner, for example, achieved ANOVA significance in all three height metrics, as did 3994 Ayashi, 32267 Hermannweyl, 3760 Poutanen and 28667 Whithagins. Meanwhile, 78383 Philmassey covered two out of three height sliders, and also had one of the higher influence scores for its particular slider statscontinuous_Height. 1669 Dagmar and 21454 Chernoby also made this list for their influence score while covering two of the three height sliders. Taking the interpretations of all of these together gives us an idea of what kinds of social experiences may be embodied by (human) height.

---

[19] The formula for "influence" of an asteroid on a slider was $\frac{|1.5hot-(square+.5inconjunct)|}{1.5}$ +

$1 \cdot (hot\ and\ tense\ values\ are\ of\ opposite\ signs) + 1 \cdot (hot\ and\ inconjunct\ values\ are\ of\ opposite\ signs)$

TABLE 15: SOME SELECTED HEIGHT ASTEROIDS

MPC#	Asteroid	%body group covered	influence points	Meaning
78383	Philmassey	0.7	1.30	where one does not wish for or value the company of a same-polar counterpart, feeling suffocated by them. Yet the same polar party may be exactly what they need as a guide to a better situation
31375	Krystufek	0.7	1.14	bending or diverting the course of something; a curving force; has some association with distraction
1669	Dagmar	0.7	1.12	enduring long separations and difficult travels; seems to confer a kind of stoicism through rough conditions
28667	Whithagins	1	0.31	at the center of an information hub, one is actually sensitive and capable of hiding deep damage; you or the thing which embodies this will want to allow only the gentlest or most empathetic interactions as the containing duodecanate evolves. If it is not you, then you are the one who will need to be careful with the spheremate or situation
3760	Poutanen	1	0.29	a raid intended to widen a party's creative influence
32267	Hermannweyl	1	0.26	a charmer subject to jealousy experiences attempts to foil their plans... unless certain conditions are met; less negatively, may indicate simple possessiveness rather than outright blackmail (as indicated by the mine)
55276	Kenlarner	1	0.168938	a service worker to the landed, accomplished party
3994	Ayashi	1	0.162707	taking the time to elaborate one's own creative stamp in their making of a thing

Just taking a minute to come up with a reasonable summary of these taken together, I first get the image of a basketball player, then of a butler, maybe Lurch, or maybe Jeeves. There is an element of people treating you in a certain way or you following the virile path, yet you have private preferences which may not align with the assumptions about you. Lastly, there is an indication that one is seen as a force, so others are surprised at how "nice" the tall one is. This gives us a frequentic abstraction for height.

A measure of the extent to which others assume your force despite your private world. Tall people get more of this, and when they are not forceful towards others, those others are surprised. Short people don't get force "assumed" of them, but if they have it, they will have had to earn it themselves (perhaps through displays of their own will).

And the best asteroidal match for this definition? Maybe Whithagins. But don't quote me.

That was fun. Let's do some more.

BODY REGIONS AS EVENT FREQUENCIES

We'll go through a bunch of body qualities and abstractify them. Before we do that, know this: while I will be using the most influential or greatest feature group-covering asteroids to aid the "frequentizing" of body regions, every body region is subject to a final common sense sanity check. The height example in the last chapter illustrates this; we used stats, but then I asked myself whether the definition I settled on actually lines up with our real life experience of the trait. Who doesn't like Shaq? But aren't we more likely to note how "cool" and "nice" he is despite the fact that almost none of us readers or writers know him personally? What about other tall people you know? Can you see how the abstractification we did in the last chapter might at least come close to being a thing?

Aside from region rulers, we can also have single asteroids which represent any concept you choose. These "significators" as you might call them will embody most of the concept in question. You can have significators for anything towards which you have a stereotyped overall reaction. For example, most of my friends and close others interact with me using whatever qunit or duodecanate contains the asteroid 383417 DAO. That is, where I see DAO in their charts, I also see neighboring asteroids which, taken together, summarize the person's dealings with me. So DAO would be one of my significators when I am seen as an ally. Relatedly, body regions can also have significators to the extent that we interact with the selected asteroid in the same way we interact with the indicated region.

When it doesn't make sense to say, "This one asteroid 'rules' the hands" (especially since the hands have multiple social usages) we can use significators to to say, "Wherever this asteroid is, it seems to coincide with a cluster of asteroids that describe how one actually uses their hands."

TABLE 16: THE EVENT-FREQUENTIZED BODY AND SOME RELATED ASTEROIDS

Body metric	Body group	...as a frequentic (experience) pattern	Significator
slider_Gender Were you born as a cup ♀ or its contents ♂ (how you shape situations ♀ vs the fixed pattern you spread ♂ as an experience-procreator in the world)? 	♀ ♂[20]	Whether [persistently forcing your own will] or [persistently framing all events as if they obey your particular will] is your basis for presentation to the world despite what you may want internally Female -> Male slider adjustment does the following: • Widens the neck • Enlarges the jaw • Raises the ears • Raises the cheeks • Pushes down the nose bridge closer to pointiness and de-tilts the septum closer to horizontal • Shrinks the vertical eye scale • Decreases the lip scale vertically • Broadens the chin • Lengthens the philtrum • Shrinks the forehead in general • De-rounds the back of the head-neck transition, making it flatter • Inflates the shoulder-neck muscles and dorsi • Raises the pelvic center • Increases height • Replaces female secondary sexual characteristics with male ones • Reduces hip, thigh, chest, buttocks fat centers and leaves muscle in their place • Raises the knees • Slightly hunches the posture • Increases mass around the outer rib cage • Shrinks the buttocks • Widens the back	95179 Berko 20467 Hibbits 7850 Buenos Aires 6060 Doudleby
statscontinuous_Height[21] (height general)	height	A measure of the extent to which others assume your force despite your private world.	28667 Whithagins

---

[20] Makehuman codes "more male" as equal to 1 in slider value. More female equaled 0.

[21] Two different metrics measuring the exact same thing? Different asteroids and different summary frequencies? What gives? But statscontinuous_Height was actual self-reported height in feet and inches. slider_Height was a reflection of how I, as an outside observer, approximated actual height in combination with body proportionality assumptions. One of these is height from your own perspective, the other is more like the way others behave towards you given your height from *their* perspective. These are correlated, but definitely not the same. This is our first foray into the reality of "rulership" and "significators." The relationship between body qualities and the processes that happen around them is a many-to-many one, similar to the relationship between genes and overt process that happen around the things those genes build.

Automatic awe

slider_Height	height	The level of compliance others tend to naturally demonstrate despite them perceiving you as holding qualities which are threatening by default	11709 Eudoxos Sun[22]

statscontinuous_hips/height	height	The extent to which [people's level of automatic deference to you despite your apparent background threat capacity] restores/heals them when they engage you with this as background context. More relevant in men assessing women. Men are less likely to be interacted with as "restorers" when they attempt to charm-interface with others in general—especially women | *Ajani's notes: 57q6 in my chart, describes how I handled a business simulation competition, Glo-bus, during my PhD. Exceptionally stressful—the most prolonged stressful event I have ever experienced hands down, yet my main role was as a forced soother to my teammates. Like most males, my hips:height ratio is unremarkable*	7385 Aktsynovia
dark skin	skin	no $p<.05$ findings. I guess this makes sense. This is relative depending on who's around you wherever you live.	

A record of travelers past

ethno (general)	ethno	The wars fought by those in your lineage history as they paved the frontiers of their administrative regions; your ancestors' migration struggles[23] which install related response abilities into your "blood." Your surrounding niches / people who are not you will tend to put you into the corresponding sensitivity categories listed for each group. Although war is a major theme here, they are usually not literal. On a daily basis as one makes a living in society, they are psychological as each individual takes the frames of their lineage and sees these kinds of struggle just a little bit more easily than other perspectives. *Remember, there are only *three* ethnomorphic sliders in Makehuman, meant to capture the most fundamental ways in which body and face features contradict each other. Everyone will be a mixture of these three packages of tendencies. So whether you are French or Thai, Bishnupriya Manipuri, Peruvian, or Swede, even if you really are a certain kind of African, you will not have a slider. You will have <u>three</u> sliders for shaping your particular baseline features. • Balancing all three sliders gives a Latin or Central American Look – sensitivity to wars of migration through or by nature	11265 Hasselmann* 20625 Noto* 33034 Dianadamrau* 222 Lucia* 6363 Doggett* 30840 Jackalice 24123 Timothychang 17460 Mang

---

[22] When I don't list an MPC number or list it second, it means the body was not a highest ranker, but is a major (or major-like), and I thought readers might want to know one of the specific features or groups it corresponds to
[23] Go astro statistics! I love that the data invoked evolution! (Try looking up the meanings of the first five* asteroids, including Doggett—for the greatest (biologically sponsored) migration of them all)

slider_African	ethno	Sensitive to feeling war - No frills social information which, negatively, installs chaos; positively, proves entertaining What this slider does from all-3-sliders-equal baseline: • Slopes back the cranium • Widens the nose and nostrils • Tilts back the head angle • Pulls the jaw forward • Lengthens the neck • Rounds and shrinks the occipital and parietal lobes • Increases the size of the lips • Darkens / de-oranges the skin • Rounds and widens the lateral openings of the eyes • Narrows the head in front view, increasing the real estate occupied by the facial features • Lengthens the legs and arms, shortens the torso • Turns the ears backwards (towards the sides) • Increases height • Dropping this slider to 0 gives a Middle Eastern look – the war itself which others are sensitive to feeling	(Out of 102 | 2778 significant results, excluding those common t all 3 groups): 5532 Ichinohe 22002 Richardregan 21685 Francomallia 1905 Ambartsumian North Node (mean Node) 24709 Mitau 136 Austria 263 Dresda 957 Camelia 439 Ohio 318723 Bialas 11437 Cardalda 6690 Messick 8194 Satake 9204 Morike 159629 Brunszvik 4330 Vivaldi 222 Lucia 28667 Whithagins 34241 Skylerjones

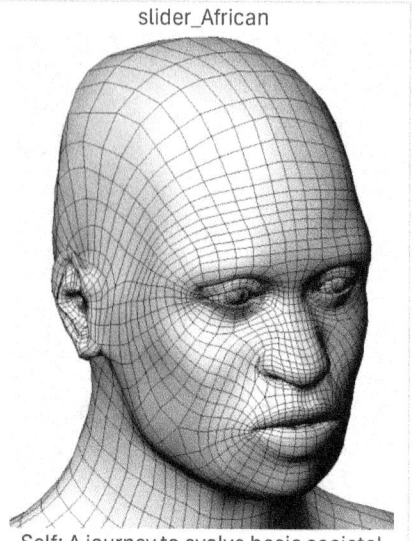

Self: A journey to evolve basic societal delineations on stable land

slider_Asian	ethno	Sensitive to bringing war - Receiving a treasure in the abstract views from above, not uncommonly surveying a war-like setting as part of this What this slider does from all-3-sliders-equal baseline: • Enlarges the head overall • Flattens the face • Rounds the brow ridge • Rounds the face • Lowers the mouth • Narrows the outer eye opening medially / inwards • Narrows / pushes up the outer eye opening vertically • Pulls down the inner eye corners • Slightly thickens the limbs • Decreases height • Dropping this slider to 0 gives an African American, Caribbean look – the war which others believe is being brought	(Out of 34 | 1419 significar results, excluding those common to all 3 groups): 26508 Jimmylin 11767 Milne 21388 Moyanodeburt 5695 Remillieux 16503 Ayato 22139 Jamescox 11016 Borisov

World: A journey to evolve collectivized outlook against vast traveled land

slider_Caucasian	Ethno	Sensitive to viewing war - The maximum push forward, pioneering with urgency, not uncommonly causing chaos in the process. What this slider does from all-3-sliders-equal baseline: • Slightly increases height • Thickens the limbs • Lengthens the torso • Pulls nose bridge forward • Pinches the lips vertically • Pushes the occipital and parietal inward • Pulls the forehead outward towards flat • Pulls the brow forward	(Out of 28 | 1171 significar results, excluding those common to all 3 groups): 12468 Zachotin 33567 Sulekhfrederic 11437 Cardalda 9204 Morike 8194 Satake 33567 Sulekhfrederic 9445 Charpentier

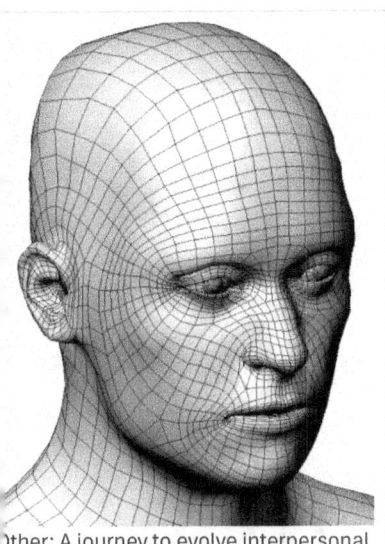

- Pushes in the mouth—especially the lower lip and thus pronounces the chin
- Lightens / peaches the skin
- Tilts the philtrum towards vertical
- Pushes in the cheek bones toward vertical
- Rectangularizes the head
- Turns the ears forward (towards the viewer)
- Pinches the facial features towards center, making the forehead taller
- Narrows the nose
- Dropping this slider to 0 gives a Southeast Asian look – those covered up by war

Other: A journey to evolve interpersonal goal attainment within harsh land

Methodology Note: Why are there so few Asian and Caucasian asteroids?

Answer: There aren't. There were totals of 2778 African, 1419 Asian, and 1171 Caucasian-slider asteroids out of about 21,000 which had significant ANOVA results. For each group, I only included influence scores above 1, ignored all asteroids that were significant in <u>all</u> three groups (those became part of the "ethno general)" list), and included asteroids with influence below 1 *only if* those asteroids also had the corresponding group mentioned in their text-mined definition. There were several asteroids that mined on white ethnicity for example (like 8719 Vesmir or 10725 Sukunabikona) which weren't among the 1171 significant ANOVAs for Caucasian morph structure. The same held for other groups. The problem is, once influence scores drop below 1, I have no way of knowing which among the 1000 – 2000 remaining asteroids that fit this are also material to the morph's features. See how the three groups fared in the asteroids with the highest influence scores below.

body feature	group	Asteroid	square	inconju	Unique	%body	influen
slider_Asian	ethno	Jimmylin	0	0	2	0.666667	0.6615
slider_Asian	ethno	Milne	0	0	1	0.333333	0.618817
slider_Asian	ethno	Mayremartinez	0	0	1	0.333333	0.60374
slider_Asian	ethno	Moyanodeburt	0	0	2	0.666667	0.595078
slider_Asian	ethno	Remillieux	0	0	2	0.666667	0.590878
slider_Asian	ethno	Ayato	0	0	1	0.333333	0.586081
slider_Asian	ethno	Jamescox	0	0	2	0.666667	0.568243
slider_Asian	ethno	Borisov	0	0	1	0.333333	0.550658

body feature	group	Asteroid	square	inconju	Unique	%body	influen
slider_Caucasian	ethno	Cardalda	1	0	2	0.666667	1.610264
slider_Caucasian	ethno	Zachotin	1	0	2	0.666667	1.573164
slider_Caucasian	ethno	Morike	0	0	2	0.666667	0.561259
slider_Caucasian	ethno	Satake	0	0	2	0.666667	0.555309
slider_Caucasian	ethno	Sulekhfrederic	0	0	2	0.666667	0.532644
slider_Caucasian	ethno	Trier	0	0	2	0.666667	0.520657
slider_Caucasian	ethno	Drummen	0	0	2	0.666667	0.499384
slider_Caucasian	ethno	Noboru	0	0	2	0.666667	0.493364
slider_Caucasian	ethno	Charpentier	0	0	2	0.666667	0.480801

| | A | | B | E | J | K | L | M | N |

body feature	group	Asteroid	square	inconju	Unique	%body	influen
slider_African	ethno	Ichinohe	1	0	2	0.666667	1.690505
slider_African	ethno	Richardregan	0	1	1	0.333333	1.384931
slider_African	ethno	Francomallia	0	1	1	0.333333	1.373294
slider_African	ethno	Messick	0	0	2	0.666667	0.747302
slider_African	ethno	Satake	0	0	2	0.666667	0.722524
slider_African	ethno	Daikuroda	0	0	2	0.666667	0.713208
slider_African	ethno	Morike	0	0	2	0.666667	0.691038
slider_African	ethno	Kallunge	0	0	2	0.666667	0.682372
slider_African	ethno	Saheki	0	0	2	0.666667	0.643119
slider_African	ethno	Clasien	0	0	2	0.666667	0.634332
slider_African	ethno	Brunszvik	0	0	2	0.666667	0.634183

I mentioned this in a footnote earlier, but the influence score places a premium on whether or not an asteroid mattered in square or conjunct. With Zachotin, for example, the square to a major was correlated with the slider going in one direction, but conjuncts, trines, sextiles, or oppositions were correlated with a slider going in the opposite direction. Presumably this tells us that Zachotin really mattered in setting Caucasian-like features in a person, because whether you were easy aspect to it or hard aspect tended to align with your possession of these features.

Now even though I tested each asteroid against seven major planets, the reality is that being "major" (like the Sun, Mars, Node, etc.) isn't even close to the only thing that matters in a chart. My Sun, despite being major, is very weak because I'm picky about when I use it. What matters more than major status is whether you use the asteroid and its cluster heavily in your life. If a heavily used cluster is conjunct Zachotin, I would guess that you'd have more white features or rely on spheremates with white features whose effects matter in that cluster. If someone else with the exact same chart as yours tended to use a cluster *square* to Zachotin at the expense of Zachotin's cluster, I would guess that they were more likely to have non-white features even though the two charts are identical. But when neither the squares nor the inconjuncts matter, and there was no hint in the asteroid's definition supporting the morph slider, then there wasn't enough to claim a slider to be a significator. At that point, I could only rely on high z-scores—where asteroids like, say, Jimmylin and Milne may not have been high enough, but were statistically more influential than the rest of the asteroids in their crowd.

black hair	hair	no *p*<.05 findings. Almost certainly tied to ethnic information.	
blonde hair	hair		
brown hair	hair		
forehead (noticeable)	head	no *p*<.05 findings	
slider_forehead-nubian-decr|incr	head	Filing through the options presented by others under an internally driven semi-urgency; how one connects to the charged (more social?) information in front of them; | *Ajani's notes: prefrontal structure*	20947 Polyneikes 257 Silesia

As with all of my books (and maybe you didn't know this), this is the point where I am doing the research as the book is being written, putting the results directly into this table. Why should that matter to you? Because it means you get "Ajani's notes" for some of the entries as I sanity check my conclusions against my own chart. The check is very simple: Does the frequentizing make experiential sense, and does the significator I've chosen live in a qunit which actually describes how I've encountered this feature? For example, I was initially going to choose only Polyneikes in the previous entry, but its qunit cluster didn't seem to tell a clear enough story in my chart. Silesia's neighboring asteroids, however, did describe people I've encountered where the Nubian forehead was a relevant trait.

| slider_forehead-scale-vert-decr\|incr | head | Involvement despite capped effectiveness; \| *Ajani's notes: Frankenstein's monster* | 11109 Iwatesan |

slider_forehead-temple-decr|incr	head	A landmark which draws attention to one's inner imaginative paradigms, especially towards solving problems	534 Nassovia 33702 Spencergreen 11428 Alcinoos
lider_forehead-trans-backward|forward	head	How one is put face to face with the law, laws, or systems that bind your behavior	114023 Harvanek
eyebrows (general)	eyebrows	Internal beliefs about oneself – especially confidence in your ability to stalk a target to the end; this may or may not be considered a liability depending on your society and surrounding groups	65100 Birtwhistle 19384 Winton 17744 Jodiefoster 19384 Winton 218400 Marquardt
View of oneself as a hunter			
slider_eyebrows-angle-down|up	eyebrows	The story should be all about you... how you reconcile others into this framework; seems to have implications for humor and entertaining others	8223 Bradshaw
lider_eyebrows-trans-backward|forward	eyebrows	How one pursues one's inner beliefs against a system which isn't really supporting this; | *Ajani's notes: my eyebrows are pushed back. Although I tell people why I've shown up in a place, rarely does that reason reflect the deeper aspirations that brought me there. I picture a caveman who makes his true reasons apparent*	10666 Feldberg
slider_eyebrows-trans-down|up	eyebrows	Internal calculations are at work which are poised to release a public action when they are down	10512 Yamandu
head (general)	head	How you primarily contribute to the fights or struggles around you	336204 Sardinas 2591 Dworetsky 2153 Akiyama 5386 Bajaja

The type of work one contributes to peer dynamics

slider_head-back-scale-depth-decr|incr	head	Telling the tales of the places one has visited; | *Ajani's notes: Csonka, by far the most influential, seems clearly related to cranial evolution; a human-species template asteroid?*	75823 Csonka
slider_head-scale-depth-decr|incr	head	Deployment into battle	9227 Ashida 34021 Suhanijain 32938 Ivanopaci 9761 Krautter
slider_head-scale-horiz-decr|incr	head	Circumscribing the worlds of certain subject populations	30296 Bricehuang 2981 Chagall 26074 Carlwirtz 4024 Ronan
slider_head-scale-vert-decr|incr	head	Offsetting the difficulties that come with the events one faces, or making the difficulties worse	389 Industria 8101 Yasue 26 Proserpina 1201 Strenua 23759 Wangzhaoxin
slider_head-angle-in|out	head	The price of approval from above; "I'll make a star out of you if you only do this thing"	32280 Rachelmashal
slider_head-fat-decr|incr	head	Thrown into confusion or a mess as an operational policy	9392 Cavaillon

slider_head-diamond	head	Diplomacy and the ability to communicate anything	155784 Ercol 4826 Wilhelms 19599 Brycemelton 10099 Glazebrook 7309 Shinkawakami	
...der_head-invertedtriangular (pointed at the bottom)	head	Announcing updates and must-knows as an operational policy	9865 Akiraohta	
slider_head-oval	head	As an operational policy for interacting with a situation, striving to contribute to it	2153 Akiyama	
slider_head-rectangular	head	Going wherever one feels they need to go for a goal	243073 Freistetter 2129 Cosicosi 6525 Ocastron 3858 Dorchester	
slider_head-round	head	Attuned to the surrounding (often abstract) environment and the rewards therein	4693 Drummond 28161 Neelpatel 8189 Naruke 6924 Fukui	
slider_head-square	head	An attention to subtleties which is connected a certain brand of (possibly deep) trouble	8262 Carcich 134 Sophrosyne 3531 Cruikshank 13281 Aliciahall	
...ider_head-triangular (pointed at the top)	head	An emphasis on storing energy to maintain one's health against pelting from the outside	210290 Borsellino 1798 Watts 9017 Babadzhanyan 1798 Watts 4782 Gembloux 9947 Takaishuji	
...es (general)	eyes	A collection of one's prosocial and antisocial priorities, with respect to individuals or collectives, friends or strangers, and what they consider to constitute advancement in these relationships	6083 Janeirabloom 13777 Cielobuio 12641 Hubertushenrichs	

			1000 Piazzia Mercury Saturn Juno (3)
 Social priorities		*eyelid real estate – sharing with friends, influencing allies*	
slider_l-eye-epicanthus-in|out slider_r-eye-epicanthus-in|out 	eyes	Absolutely itching—compelled—to share one's message with others	10282 Emilykramer 22842 Alenashort 9739 Powell 3858 Dorchester 3804 Drunina 25670 Densley 4175 Billbaum
slider_l-eye-eyefold-concave|convex slider_r-eye-eyefold-concave|convex 	eyes	Traveling through boundaries with friends	25515 Briancarey 25199 Jiahegu
slider_r-eye-corner1-down|up (moves the outer corner of the eye upward or downward) 	eyes	A leader role in a comfortable position against the unknown, perhaps deliberating on the ideas of the lower	25565 Lusiyang 7565 Zipfel 11714 Mikebrown 22839 Richlawrence 11241 Eckhout
slider_l-eye-corner1-down|up (moves the outer corner of the eye upward or downward) 	eyes	One who steers others by governing what they discover or consume; | *Ajani's note: one of my strongest features. My left eye is noticeably higher than my right eye, and I think this is part of the reason for my crazy appearance on camera, yet not nearly as much in person. But on camera I am typically recording some video intended to convey something to or convince the viewer. Teaching is similar. In person—while not teaching—I don't like to pressure people, so the asymmetry is less pronounced*	20187 Janapittichova 17427 Poe 7565 Zipfel
slider_l-eye-corner2-down|up slider_r-eye-corner2-down|up (moves the inner corner of the eye upward or downward) 	eyes	The unbelievable exposure of phenomena buried beneath the standard forms Right: a non-first-choice figure gives one the chance to display themselves or their skills	1676 Kariba 217257 Valemangano 938973 Masci 9544 Scottbirney Right: 19660 Danielsteck 8652 Acacia 965 Angelica
slider_l-eye-eyefold-angle-down|up slider_r-eye-eyefold-angle-down|up (raises the indentation above the inner or outer eye) 	eyes	Cutting a path through, collecting sexual or procreative content	292872 Anoushankar 1359 Prieska

[eyes wide open]-ness – interactions with strangers and acquisitions from outside one's sphere			
slider_l-eye-eyefold-down|up slider_r-eye-eyefold-down|up (vertically confines or stretches the space allocated to the eyelid)	eyes	Weighted down by one's successes. One eye seems to emphasize the fleeting breach of protocol, the other emphasizes regular timing. It is not clear however, which eye is which, however, since these notions may be inverses of each other dictated by the opposing eye	5042 Colpa 20361 Romanishin 25708 Vedantkumar One eye: 4523 MIT 7328 Casanova Contrary eye: 3754 Kathleen
slider_l-eye-height1-decr|incr slider_r-eye-height1-decr|incr (vertically widens the inner eye corner)	eyes	Confident skill, especially in guarding or healing; the left eye was associated with overconfidence	2805 Kalle (left eye) 4331 Hubbard 20623 Davidyoung 27864 Antongraff 20441 Elijahmena
slider_l-eye-height2-decr|incr slider_r-eye-height2-decr|incr (vertically widens the middle of the eye)	eyes	Serious interactions, especially with strangers or non-friends; stranger danger; may be related to one's inclination to believe others who hail from the amorphous collective	129561 Chuhachi 5595 Roth 73610 Klyuchevskaya 5596 Morbidelli 9472 Bruges 151 Abundantia
slider_l-eye-height3-decr|incr slider_r-eye-height3-decr|incr (vertically widens the outer corner of the eye)	eyes	Iteration – how one uses the previous moment's pattern to set the current pattern. Wide seems too allow a new pattern, under surprise. Narrow filters new patterns under skepticism, suggesting one is staying with the old pattern and hesitant to abandon it	15548 Kalinowski 25768 Nussbaum 31664 Randiiwessen Left: 2769 Mendeleev Right: 22597 Lynzielinski
slider_eyes_middle_droop (jujube:CC0, 2017)	eyes	Hosting, with proper manners; | *Ajani's note: there were a lot of asteroids here which involved etiquette, and subtle as this slider may be, it clearly denotes the difference between someone who is just sitting there and someone who is really paying attention to you—showing concern for your well-being*	3136 Anshan 100019 Gregorianik 1264 Letaba 2672 Pisek 20096 Shiraishiakihiko 10480 Jennyblue 10368 Kozuki 185554 Bikushev
eye size (especially wide or narrow set horizontal) – following one's personal passions			
slider_l-eye-scale-decr|incr slider_r-eye-scale-decr|incr	eyes	Ability to follow – the willingness to put oneself out of the spotlight or behind another in order to achieve a target state	136273 Csermely 16230 Benson 2858 Carlosporter
slider_l-eye-push1-in|out slider_r-eye-push1-in|out (pushes or pulls the outer eye corner towards or away from the middle of the face)	eyes	Bursts of passion applied to one's endeavors as remedy. This cannot typically be kept up for long; related to one's response to apparent hopelessness	3380 Awaji 5070 Arai 11604 Novigrad 64289 Shihwingching

slider_l-eye-push2-in|out slider_r-eye-push2-in|out (pushes or pulls the inner eye corner away from or towards the nose)	eyes	One donates their passion to another, but the nonspecific nature of the passion itself may still invite other outlets beside the partner; seems to affect the appearance of innocence, not necessarily the commission of infidelity	16947 Wikrent 6511 Furmanov 32532 Thereus 166570 Adolftrager 4652 Iannini
slider_l-eye-trans-in|out slider_r-eye-trans-in|out (related to eye push1 and push2, differs mainly in that trans-in|out moves the center of the eye sideways, push1 & 2 keep the center stationary)	eyes	One's approach to controlling what they register as permanent. The left and right eyes seem to show differences in how you work out discrepancies Left eye: a response that can instantly terminate a connection Right eye: opening an issue for public discussion	7441 Laska 16123 Jessiecheng 18157 Craigwright 18973 Crouch 12641 Hubertushenrichs Left: 1358 Gaika 11147 Delmas Right: 15929 Ericlinton 7441 Laska 1851 Lacroute
slider_l-eye-trans-down|up slider_r-eye-trans-down|up	eyes	The juxtaposition of a valuable path and [the mechanisms needed to protect that value] or [the situations which block that value from release] The right eye brings an association with persecution and rebellion	27584 Barbaravelez 17759 Hatta 173002 Dorfi 26586 Harshaw 2060 Chiron Right: 26586 Harshaw 7403 Choustnik

eye bags – the handling of loss

slider_eyes_outer_droop (jujube:CC0, eyes outer droop, 2017) (creates a look of worry or preoccupation)	eyes	Focus in diagnosing something, looking to remove what is stopping it or keep new barriers from stopping it	17649 Brunorossi 8775 Cristata 375176 Beziau
slider_l-eye-bag-height-decr|incr slider_r-eye-bag-height-decr|incr	eyes	One looming, enduring the pain of loss; Left: where one withdraws in light of the loss Right: where one makes big issues (more rarely, big comedy) out of minor events (be they problematic or positive)	16759 Furuyama 10830 Desforges 236170 Cholnoky Left: 7102 Neilbone Right: 18636 Villedepompey 114 Kassandra
slider_l-eye-bag-decr|incr slider_r-eye-bag-decr|incr	eyes	Denial – where one either cannot handle inputs that conflict with what they want to believe, or are tied to a distant thing which has been strangled or cut off	980 Anacostia 14682 Davidhirsch 19860 Anahtar 16319 Xiamenerzhong
slider_l-eye-bag-in|out slider_r-eye-bag-in|out	eyes	The art of correction – one sees their own benevolence, launching an attack to direct other's effort. This can also be done through certain social media and TV consumption which validates the person	7120 Davidgavine 28251 Gerbaldi 4874 Burke 117240 Zhytomyr

nose (general)	nose	How one processes inputs <u>from or in</u> the air around them; related to activism and notions of equality within the niche	3249 Musashino 29765 Miparedes 5444 Gautier 27302 Jeankobis
Tiny objects in the air			
slider_nose crease extra1 (creates an indentation at the intersection of the septum and the philtrum)	nose	One-man or one-woman show who may acquire rewards for what they broadcast	173002 Dorfi 79418 Zhangjiajie 23757 Jonmunoz 10764 Rubezahl
lider_Nose_alar_crease (Mindfront:CC0, Nose alar crease, 2018)	nose	The flurry of energy one possesses as new creations are in the process of being made	18170 Ramjeawan 227770 Wischnewski 29307 Torbernbergman 3195 Fedchenko 363 Padua
slider_nose-base-down|up	nose	Turning to a distant abstract energy as a weapon	140038 Kurushima 2829 Bobhope 251625 Timconrow
slider_nose-compression-compress|uncompress (does the nose urve down like a slide or out like a bell?)	nose	The cycle of revealed truth and invisibility; how one handles the alternation between when a thing can and can't be known	22440 Bangsgaard 1139 Atami 4079 Britten 13219 Cailletet 14004 Chikama
lider_nose-curve-concave|convex (does he mid-upper nose bridge make a sharp ook like a beak, or a C-shaped dip like a chaise lounge?)	nose	Presenting oneself (on top of another's ideas) as if one definitely knows	363582 Folpotat 15391 Steliomancinelli 14054 Dusek 8413 Kawakami
slider_nose-flaring-decr|incr	nose	One's personhood given to another, or to the ambience	5494 Johanmohr 3017 Petrovic

				32564 Glass 10823 Sakaguchi
slider_nose-greek-decr|incr (does the upper nose bridge flow straight from the brow or does it dent inwards at the eyes?) 	nose		One's susceptibility to getting lost in the fog; seems to make for peaceful drifting, but also spaciness in times of crisis nearby or within; also related to slavery	30396 Annleonard 260724 Malherbe 4690 Strasbourg 3583 Burdett
slider_nose-hump-decr|incr (does the middle nose bridge poke out or elbow inward?) 	nose		Being tended to by those around; related to the collective support one receives or participates in giving	23244 Lafayette 2469 Tadjikistan 9913 Humperdinck 3092 Herodotus 2407 Haug
slider_nose-nostrils-angle-down|up (changing this slider to its extreme values produces a snob-look at one end, a "something's not right" skeptical sniff on the other) 	nose		Standing on one's pedestal raising cain	2868 Upupa 11485 Zinzendorf 25542 Garabedian
slider_nose-nostrils-width-decr|incr 	nose		Insistent—possibly causing a bunch of trouble—over things which are not visible to others, or which are locked in the world of the viewer	68948 Mikeoates 25653 Baskaran 6626 Mattgenge 6212 Franzthaler Neptune
slider_nose-point-down|up 	nose		Letting up on one's own agenda for smoothed cooperation with another	2888 Hodgson 3876 Quaide 32618 Leungkamcheung
slider_nose-point-width-decr|incr 	nose		What makes you currently worth looking at—getting taken into account by any viewer—or worth passing by	129327 Davehamara 1100 Arnica 156879 Elois 25139 Roatsch
slider_nose-scale-depth-decr|incr 	nose		Part of oneself locked up in another, the first will tend to hold tension proportionate to the other's satisfying exercise of this	8189 Naruke 5109 Robertmiller 1311 Knopfia 12612 Daumier 25822 Carolinejune

slider	type	description	asteroids
slider_nose-scale-horiz-decr|incr	nose	The gatekeeping authority in allowing another to pro- or co-create, allowing the other's excitement to show	18773 Bredehoft 3249 Musashino 11760 Auwers
slider_nose-scale-vert-decr|incr	nose	The extent to which one can be rewarded with attention for making a spectacle of themselves, or for the self-indulgence they allow others to witness. Sometimes material riches are associated with this	17258 Whalen 4456 Mawson
slider_nose-septumangle-decr|incr	nose	Small components working together in alignment	19585 Zachopkins 18453 Nishiyamayukio 14028 Nakamurahiroshi
slider_nose-trans-down|up	nose	Gatekeeping for getting a leg up, advancing	3136 Anshan 5354 Hisayo 281 Lucretia 1634 Ndola Arielhaas (34307)
slider_nose-volume-decr|incr	nose	How you give fixated attention	24858 Diethelm 23235 Yingfan
slider_nose-width1-decr|incr (upper bridge width)	nose	Where one is involved in the cleanup of another's image; investigate in animal grooming	18561 Fengningding 5357 Sekiguchi 22254 Vladbarmin 1441 Bolyai
slider_nose-width2-decr|incr (middle bridge width)	nose	Signing on with another's agenda, giving them the benefit of the doubt contractually	309227 Tsukiko 10688 Haghighipour 2784 Domeyko 31642 Soyounchoi
slider_nose-width3-decr|incr (nose base width)	nose	How prone one is to citing the unsettling past	22512 Cannat
slider_Nose_hole_up (Mindfront:CC0, Nose hole up, 2018)	nose	How one balances risk-taking versus safety	17219 Gianninoto 279377 Lechmankiewicz 298 Baptistina

			130 Elektra 10501 Ardmacha
slider_nose-trans-backward|forward 	nose	Where one is involved in a public fight – the boxer	25708 Vedantkumar 130069 Danielgaudreau 3712 Kraft 13053 Bertrandrussell 218866 Alexantioch 9204 Morike
slider_nostril_rounding (Habanero:CC0, 2016) 	nose	Being or challenging the authority or institutional order	7169 Linda 29674 Rausal 4228 Nemiro 21400 Ahdout 12773 Lyman 1983 Bok
slider_septum_sharp (jujube:CC0, septum_sharp, 2017) 	nose	Waiting with one's suitcase – your preparedness to go with what you alone can carry, feeling that you have everything you need	9739 Powell 4204 Barsig 4999 MPC 660 Crescentia
slider_Age (age general) Amount of HP invested	age	The extent to which you have donated the balance of your life energy to the collective environment over time and space; | *Ajani's note: Want to stay young looking? Police how much you export this energy unnecessarily, or towards things you can't easily affect*	10804 Amenouzume 2504 Gaviola 18676 Zdenkaplavcova
		There were TONS of sliders that mattered here, 69 in total with influence scores of at least 1. The asteroids listed to the right mattered both in square and inconjunct, with influence scores above 2. And because the management of stress is so important, I've decided to list the remaining 66 asteroids associated with age and youth here: 1610 Mirnaya, 919 Ilsebill, 3496 Arieso, 15042 Anndavgui, 11051 Racine, 34164 Anikacheerla, 6336 Dodo, 21924 Alyssaovaitt, 7554 Johnspencer, 603 Timandra, 9996 ANS, 202909 Jakoten, 3358 Anikushin, 1177 Gonnessia, 812 Adele, 10327 Batens, 13057 Jorgensen, 1074 Beljawskya, 23017 Advincula, 326290 Akhenaten, 26586 Harshaw, 14517 Monitoma, 21652 Vasishtha, 319 Leona, 42697 Lucapaolini, 391988 Illmarton, 44885 Vodicka, 6657 Otukyo, 12053 Turtlestar, 73872 Stefanoragazzi, 2726 Kotelnikov, 8931 Hirokimatsuo, 24066 Eriksorensen, 499 Venusia, 22612 Dandibner, 770 Bali, 24889 Tamurahosinomura, 835 Olivia, 4099 Wiggins, 129149 Richwitherspoon, 20335 Charmartell, 10784 Noailles, 35976 Yorktown, 7428 Abekuniomi, 91199 Johngray, 2834 Christy Carol, 562 Salome, 214911 Viehboeck, 146268 Jennipolakis, 260724 Malherbe, 20361 Romanishin, 2469 Tadjikistan, 10806 Mexico, 1308 Halleria, 32522 Judiepersons, 34165 Nikhilcheerla, 3347 Konstantin, 845 Naema, 11510 Borges, 5943 Lovi, 4258 Ryazanov, 275786 Bouley, 65716 Ohkinohama, 19444 Addicott, 26629 Zahller, 9891 Stephensmith	

slider_head-age-decr|incr (whether your face, at any age, has an "old look" to it)
 	
	age	A group of face changes which, taken together, reflects how "traveled" you are.
		
		What this slider does:
		  • Lowers and widens the jaw
		  • Slightly pinches the lips vertically
		  • Enlarges the ears
		  • Widens and stretches-down the nose bridge
			6205 Menottigalli

		<ul><li>Makes the nose tip more pointy</li><li>Narrows the top of the head in front view</li><li>"de-alerts" / tires the eyes, so that they appear less wide-open</li><li>Lowers the lateral (outer) brow line, giving more of a "sad" appearance</li><li>Pushes (to flat) the inner cheeks on either side of the nose, creating gauntness and laugh lines</li><li>Creates crow's feet on the outer sides of either eye</li></ul>	
cheeks (general) Message crafter	cheeks	How you craft your messages in light of what you know about others, what you want to say, what you fundamentally believe, and what your listeners want to hear	24269 Kittappa 8801 Nugent 294 Felicia 18243 Gunn
slider_l-cheek-inner-decr|incr slider_r-cheek-inner-decr|incr ("bone-izes" or thickens the main mass of the cheeks, especially laterally)	cheeks	Something like "people watching"—how one digs for secrets, is followed by secrets, and responds to the secret understandings they carry—particularly how others should be treated in light of them. The left cheek takes a humorous approach, the right cheek takes an independent artistic approach; related to how seriously one takes things, and affects general trust and sociability in the eyes of others	6323 Karoji 217510 Dewaldroode 2310 Olshaniya 24168 Hexlein 467 Laura 7011 Worley 27091 Alisonbick Left: 209552 Isaacroberts Right: 467 Laura 3163 Randi
slider_l-cheek-bones-decr|incr slider_r-cheek-bones-decr|incr (pokes out the bones of the lateral upper cheeks)	cheeks	One's relationship with their Rule Set (God, Nature, The Universe, etc.), and how they practice this; | *Ajani's note: this explains "the look" of the students at the local Christian academy! There are two major high school options in our area, and Shanna and I have had a couple of conversations about this very subject. There's something in the cheeks that lets you know which students in the paper come from where. It's pretty glaring actually. Although we are all indoctrinated into an array of beliefs from several sources or other, I believe this quality of the cheeks indicates whether your brand of indoctrination is something you wear publicly. Even more interestingly, Scottobin is related to reasons for abandoning this. Tlomak is related to reasons for going all in on it. My guess is that symmetry isn't in a hurry to do either of these*	30928 Jefferson 29858 Tlomak 1369 Ostanina 5866 Sachsen 391988 Illmarton Left: 33811 Scottobin Right: 29858 Tlomak
slider_l-cheek-trans-down|up slider_r-cheek-trans-down|up	cheeks	Private processes built around wanting one's interactant to be different than they are; features in the inclination to manipulate the situation one shares with another	19132 Le Clezio 25981 Shahmirian 24269 Kittappa 8801 Nugent

slider_l-cheek-volume-decr|incr slider_r-cheek-volume-decr|incr 	cheeks	How and how much one insists on their communication partners fitting a particular role or set of standards	29 Amphitrite 204836 Xiexiaosi 3496 Arieso 31438 Yasuhitohayashi 3459 Bodil 901 Brunsia
slider_elvs_chipmunkcheeks_h1 (Elvaerwyn:CC0, 2020) (bulges the cheeks at the jaw closer to the back) 	cheeks	How one draws in the information to craft their message	10874 Locatelli 652 Jubilatrix 34103 Suganthkannan 22828 Jaynethomp 36 Atalante 7858 Bolotov
slider_elvs_chipmunkcheeks_l1 (Elvaerwyn:CC0, Elvs Chipmunk cheek-Low1, 2020) (bulges the cheeks at the jaw closer to the front) 	cheeks	Crafting a message for a larger group of others, or one fit for listeners external to oneself	5177 Hugowolf 543 Charlotte 4872 Grieg 9108 Toruyusa 1912 Anubis Venus
slider_elvs_highchubbycheekbones1 (Elvaerwyn:CC0, Elvs High chubby cheekbones1, 2020) (bulges the lateral upper cheeks) 	cheeks	One's engagement with bold or touchy documentation, learned independently	168 Sibylla 16123 Jessiecheng 7256 Bonhoeffer 3532 Tracie 350 Ornamenta
ears (general) Framework fitter	ears	How one holds their perceptual frame steady in order to process certain frequencies of information over others, piling one input onto the next. One ear seems more dedicated to noting the existence of an attention grabbing (historically or biologically relevant) message, while the other seems to prize calculations around what "walls" are blocking its source. Some of the ears' features have equivalents in the form of psychological and body positioning "walls"; how one frames inputs sent <u>through or against</u> the air around them	35033 Arjunkapoor 2963 Chen Jiageng Left: 4427 Burnashev 1898 Cowell 2147 Kharadze Right: 28557 Lillianchin 3306 Byron 16085 Laffan
slider_l-ear-flap-decr|incr slider_r-ear-flap-decr|incr 	ears	Blocking or obstacle generation one does under the table which may be intimidating to others—as when a cat or dog stops its action and turns its ears forward to hear what is going on	6767 Shirvindt 28535 Sungjanet 22195 Nevadodelruiz 5158 Ogarev 200025 Cloud Gate
slider_l-ear-rot-backward|forward slider_r-ear-rot-backward|forward	ears	Following edicts from on high, or a higher goal, often at the expense of regular relationships; | *Ajani's note: my ears are rotated far backwards*	20266 Danielchoi 17452 Amurreka

		(upwards pointing to a horizon above the eyes)—one of my strongest body features hands down	766 Moguntia 60972 Matenko 26549 Tankanran
slider_l-ear-trans-down|up	ears	The rare have - elite or closed groups while serious events occur outside; seems to be tied to a philosophical system, living on an island	4024 Ronan 375007 Buxy 68448 Sidneywolff 8890 Montaigne 116166 Andremaeder 1903 Adzhimushkaj
slider_r-ear-trans-down|up[24]	ears	Using the environment to further support one's embattlements; listening for the things that support one's plan of attack	24520 Abramson 6815 Mutchler 21441 Stevencondie 26074 Carlwirtz 12701 Chenier 6695 Barrettduff
slider_l-ear-scale-decr|incr	ears	Having been the witness to something unjust or not right, where the event may be hard to forget	2963 Chen Jiageng 11322 Aquamarine 1898 Cowell 3560 Chenqian
slider_r-ear-scale-decr|incr	ears	Having to go back and understand what just happened, digging deep	187680 Stelck 17439 Juliesan 10865 Thelmaruby 130 Elektra 207809 Wuzuze 28557 Lillianchin 509 Iolanda 403 Cyane[25]
slider_l-ear-shape-pointed|triangle slider_r-ear-shape-pointed|triangle (elf ears pointed up versus imp ears pointed backwards)	ears	Keeping someone immobile or in servitude partly for the politics of it	1581 Abanderada 20256 Adolfneckar 121236 Adrianagutierrez 10950 Albertjansen 34281 Albritton
slider_l-ear-scale-vert-decr|incr slider_r-ear-scale-vert-decr|incr	ears	People are stressed. The one who can fix them may also rely on the existence of the problem; where one provides solutions to problems which they themselves have framed, intentionally or unintentionally reinforcing their own relevance	33476 Gilanareiss 4799 Hirasawa 192293 Dominikbrunner 2346 Lilio

[24] 10/23/2024. The right and the left ear's vertical position yielded two completely different sets of top asteroids. Why is that? I don't know. If nothing else it tells me something about how one's vestibular / balance systems might work, perhaps using one side as the anchor and the other as the deviation. But that's just sheer speculation.

[25] For whatever reason, I find this group of asteroids more interesting than others. Wondering why I seem to be getting more asymmetric results for the ears, I searched on the web, "Do the two ears hear differently?" There I discovered "diplacusis," which I had never heard of. Also, if you look up the definitions of these asteroids and what they do, they seem to be the quintessential hearing group—more than the left ear—which leads me to speculate about a possible relationship between hearing and handedness. Searching the web now... Sure enough, I am reminded of the motor hypothesis of language development, via a journal article by Packheiser et al. (2020), "A large-scale estimate on the relationship between language and motor lateralization." A right ear advantage... Interesting. I didn't know about this until now as I type, 10/24/2024. "Man, I'm tellin' you..." is what I always say to my friends about the things you can arrive at via this kind of astrology.

In other news, I recall way back when in *Laurentia 1st ed*, Cyane was an asteroid of music. Pretty cool seeing it show up here not only among the significant asteroids for ear size, but among the top 10 for this body feature.

But again, you can't do this kind of research without full bodies and bios to begin with.

slider_l-ear-shape-square|round	ears	Pouring passion over the many beyond oneself, or perhaps throwing it at them	32018 Robhenning 20230 Blanchard 73885 Kalaymoodley 291 Alice
slider_r-ear-shape-square|round	ears	Where you may be panned or criticized, or just be new to your terrain (perhaps treated as such)	16085 Laffan 12812 Cioni 13057 Jorgensen 73520 Boslough
slider_l-ear-trans-backward|forward slider_r-ear-trans-backward|forward	ears	Hmm… keeping one's thoughts on the subject in front of them	30368 Ericferrante 8540 Ardeberg 11107 Hakkoda 44001 Jonquet
slider_l-ear-lobe-decr|incr slider_r-ear-lobe-decr|incr	ears	Gathering concept- or percept- packages together, partly in attempts to organize them	15406 Bleibtreu 73885 Kalaymoodley 489 Comacina 30211 Sheilah 13280 Christihaas
slider_l-ear-scale-depth-decr|incr slider_r-ear-scale-depth-decr|incr	ears	Framing whole spaces of others, defining the grid of all contents appearing before you	5483 Cherkashin 26660 Samahalpern 7605 Cindygraber 18055 Fernhildebrandt 13815 Furuya 13608 Andosatoru 2726 Kotelnikov
slider_l-ear-wing-decr|incr slider_r-ear-wing-decr|incr	ears	A unique impression designed to trigger a reaction among one's social viewers or exchangers	37530 Dancingangel 40764 Gerhardiser 4192 Breysacher 13410 Arhale
mouth (general) Compel the target	mouth	Compelled to try and try again to send a pattern towards one's nichemates, though that pattern consists of aspects which quickly expire	20357 Shireendhir 505 Cava 6535 Archipenko 4462 Vaughan 357 Ninina
slider_mouth-angles-down|up	mouth	Show of being pleased or displeased with sudden experiences. This was the strongest feature for indicating a smile versus a frown on the resting face. There is considerable support for the idea that 20893 Rosymccloskey's qunit and the neighboring asteroids in it will serve as one of the best scenarios for keeping you persistently happy overall	**20893 Rosymccloskey*** 30371 Johngorman 31671 Masatoshi 15126 Brittanyanderson
slider_mouth-cupidsbow-decr|incr	mouth	Gathering of collected experiences rather than dynamic personalities. Does one prefer to differentiate experiences or personalities?	136367 Gierlinger 23234 Lilliantsai 4462 Vaughan

der_mouth-cupidsbow-width-decr|incr	mouth	Smashing your pent up expression into a scenario, or having someone else do it for you	25275 Jocelynbell 58215 von Klitzing 27556 Williamprem 62071 Voegtli 14901 Hidatakayama
slider_mouth-dimples-in|out	mouth	Telepathy-like messaging which puts viewers into a particularly abstract frame	3516 Rusheva 5129 Groom 379173 Gamaovalia 3973 Ogilvie
slider_mouth-laugh-lines-in|out	mouth	Trying something again from newer angles	20357 Shireendhir
slider_mouth-lowerlip-ext-down|up	mouth	*Refraining from* sowing one's wild oats (related to self-control or responsibility in the opposition case)	6094 Hisako[26]
slider_mouth-lowerlip-height-decr|incr	mouth	Stuck in one's own business, remaining effective	505 Cava 48480 Falk
lider_mouth-lowerlip-middle-down|up	mouth	The belief that one's own creations warrant them being treated like the best	19547 Collier 55108 Beamueller 28547 Johannschroter 18825 Alicechai
lider_mouth-lowerlip-volume-decr|incr	mouth	Myopic compulsion	357 Ninina
slider_mouth-lowerlip-width-decr|incr	mouth	Repeated practice towards gradual refinement	27363 Alvanclark
lider_mouth-philtrum-volume-decr|incr	mouth	Sensitivity to sharp rhythms and sounds	6535 Archipenko
slider_mouth-scale-depth-decr|incr	mouth	Funny or amusing gestures which belie reaction to a let down	1209 Pumma 676 Melitta 9884 Pribram 9148 Boriszaitsev

[26] Most of the significators I have listed can be read in a "has to do with" direction, so you can't tell whether hot or tense angles to the asteroid will give you more of the trait. This is especially true when I list multiple asteroids, some of which increase and others of which decrease the feature. Hisako, however, had obvious negative correlations with the lip extension. The more hot aspects to majors there were, the taller the lower lip, the more sowing of wild oats. Hence the inverted feature meaning.

slider	region	description	codes
slider_mouth-scale-horiz-decr | incr	mouth	The untold struggle of a culture	8630 Billprady
slider_mouth-scale-vert-decr | incr	mouth	Execution of one's passion leads to consequences that advance the group, the person themselves may be punished for this	11764 Benbaillaud 13787 Nagaishi 1484 Postrema 1626 Sadeya 35347 Tallinn
slider_mouth-trans-backward | forward	mouth	The energy one has or displays which is apt to be transferred across others; | *Ajani's note: this slider makes a HUGE difference in ethnomorphic appearance. In case you're curious, the text mined words for Vogeley were: disclose, carbon, upstate, refugee, reaction, palimony, participant, rebuild, story – birth, fireman, granted, sequence, story – periodical, rarely, excessively, deputy, brush*	170023 Vogeley
slider_mouth-trans-down | up	mouth	Where one's capture behind a context is indicative of a problem (with the capturer or capturing system)	18020 Amend 7114 Weinek 48425 Tischendorf 199631 Giuseppesprizzi
slider_mouth-upperlip-ext-down | up	mouth	The Tasmanian Devil - Popping in and popping out, bringing mayhem in the process	79410 Wallerius 27576 Denisespirou 50240 Cortina 24734 Kareness 12800 Oobayashiarata
slider_mouth-upperlip-height-decr | incr	mouth	Raising a risky and dramatic scene, partly in response to where one is at the hands of the ruling or dominant group	8246 Kotov 15965 Robertcox 184 Dejopeja 2856 Roser 2570 Porphyro
slider_mouth-upperlip-middle-down | up	mouth	The buildup, in a confined space, of a story worth telling	210182 Mazzini 11107 Hakkoda 292160 Davefask 33247 Iannacone 407 Arachne
slider_mouth-upperlip-volume-decr | incr	mouth	Plowing through challenging the one with the authority, but there's a good chance this comes with consequences	1698 Christophe 10128 Bro 1983 Bok
slider_mouth-upperlip-width-decr | incr	mouth	Warmongering or, at the very least, messaging issued where it was not necessarily invited	4562 Poleungkuk 25763 Naveenmurali 33681 Wamsley
chin (general)	chin	Riding the behavioral interests of others for one's interactional advancement; | *Ajani's note: thanks to Polenov, this feature may be indicative of wider bone formation*	33703 Anthonyhill 1631 Kopff 152750 Brloh 1653 Yakhontovia 14519 Ural

On the shoulders of nichemates' values			
slider_chin-bones-decr|incr (pulls down the lateral sides of the chin)	chin	How (or if) one checks their own progress; | *Ajani's note: on the other side, a vision of the gaunt villain comes to mind*	3978 Klepesta 117997 Irazu 16236 Stebrehmer 8175 Boerhaave
slider_chin-height-decr|incr (pulls down the chin)	chin	Ability to suggest fixes to problems that others are advised to explore	73442 Feruglio 1769 Carlostorres
slider_chin-jaw-drop-decr|incr (squares rear portion of the jaw bones)	chin	A situation associated with the holder spreads suddenly and wildly throughout their environment	1401 Lavonne 18601 Zafar 9496 Ockels 152750 Brloh
slider_chin-prognathism-decr|incr	chin	The politician – communicating what the stranger masses want to hear	19303 Chinacyo 30840 Jackalice 9934 Caccioppoli 7176 Kuniji
slider_chin-prominent-decr|incr	chin	Where the spirits of others must necessarily be considered in how one operates	
slider_chin-width-decr|incr	chin	How one leads, or makes pushiness approachable	8442 Ostralegus 25331 Berrevoets Pluto 1653 Yakhontovia
slider_chin-cleft-decr|incr	chin	One pushes forward, even with their obsessions	9190 Masako 11998 Fermilab 8775 Cristata 2361 Gogol 11385 Beauvoir
neck (general)	neck	Acquiring first-pass resources and information from the environment one traverses, less supported by others. Also provides fractional output signals to others regarding one's preferences	4722 Agelaos 2424 Tautenburg 13446 Almarkim

Package handler

slider_HarveyNeckDefinitionV1 (callharvey3d:CC-BY, 2016) (accentuates neck muscles)	neck	In collecting the resources you need, how you control the various energies thrown at you; related to bully resistance	12711 Tukmit 35441 Kyoko
slider_measure-neck-height-decr|incr	neck	The swiveling and panning sensation that comes with looking around, surveying the environment	33258 Femariebustos
slider_neck-double-decr|incr	neck	A grand supply of energy fed from others kept as the potential for sneaking through when unsupported	19204 Joshuatree 17046 Kenway 90937 Josefdufek 37939 Hasler 33181 Aalokpatwa
slider_neck-scale-vert-decr|incr (stretches the neck)	neck	Trekking through, possibly without support, taking in what one can for now and processing it properly later	2 Pallas 11739 Baton Rouge 274213 Satriani 96876 Andreamanna
slider_neck-scale-horiz-decr|incr	neck	Subtle reveal of the sensuality and other stories with which one has been in harmony	46643 Yanase 29852 Niralithakor 11288 Okunohosomichi
slider_neck-trans-down|up (raises the neck base)	neck	Trekking through, providing superficial answers in order to get a job done	145558 Raiatea 37582 Faraday 2181 Fogelin 1891 Gondola 4722 Agelaos
shoulders (general)	shoulders	Where one already leans, prepared to reinforce it upon their current situation; has implications for the kinds of trouble one is prepared for or inclined to get into	315218 La Boetie 91023 Lutan 30206 Jasonfricker 13693 Bondar

Prepared to rebel

slider_measure-shoulder-dist-decr|incr	shoulders	The issues more likely to register in one's blood—how they are assessed against this likelihood. This had major ties to evolved differences between different race-like body shapes, as well as an unexpected tie to skin color. Likely tied to something pervasively metabolic-reflective happening at upper limb development; investigate in fish fins and bird wings	59419 Presov 293707 Govoradloanatoly 3022 Dobermann 315218 La Boetie 30206 Jasonfricker 11598 Kubik 13693 Bondar
slider_Shoulder_Shape (Mindfront:CC0, 2018) (more like collarbone sharpness)	shoulders	One's approach to nesting and leisure behavior, places returned to in the face of risk	38960 Yeungchihung 27915 Nancywright + generals
slider_measure-frontchest-dist-decr|incr	chest	In order to achieve the object one desires, asserting. This may attend a certain level of ongoing non-fulfillment, however	22945 Schikowski 21160 Saveriolombardi 12016 Green 28710 Rebeccab
breasts (general) How tied is her shell to surrounding others' need for influence?	breasts	The type of feeding your archetypal domain is prepared to export to the creations it sponsors, and how it stores this as energy supply; Fixedly persisting one's ideals for the creative fortune one possesses, reflecting on who and what has verified to this fortune across time and experience; | *Ajani's note: seems to reflect the ways in which, given the ambitions or (Mars-like) drive for influence by others surrounding you, the extent to which the growth of your bodily nurturing capacity is tied to this. If everyone is a potential thief planning to steal from their own personal version of a vault, the breasts reflect the ways in which the default female body records and keep these surrounding others' ambitions for the holder's own development*	11073 Cavell 7470 Jabberwock 2195 Tengstrom 2776 Baikal Ceres (1)
slider_female-breasts-compress (Nadow:CC0, 2016) (pushes breasts in to pronounce pectorals, as in bodybuilders)	breasts	Directing one's appetite for sensuality towards the imposition of laws or fight	684 Hildburg 27453 Crystalpoole 32928 Xiejialin 22079 Kabinoff
statscontinuous_cup diameter/height	breasts	Sex-based self-consciousness; the two significant asteroids here tell an interesting story about how one's breasts can influence how much of a woman one thinks she is, how body-comfortable they are, how in or out of shape he is, or whether one's interactants meet a certain	124143 Joseluiscorral 1465 Autonoma

		body standard; insecurity and self-image are two relevant topics related to this	
statscontinuous_cup vol/height	breasts	Compelled powerful secret sharing, undergirded by pressures to draw attention to oneself; related to statscontinuous_bust/height, but has more to do with standards of attractiveness in light of what one knows about another	22612 Dandibner 19968 Palazzolascaris 2660 Wasserman
slider_breast-dist-decr|incr	breasts	The freedom to put oneself first; negatively, the freedom to be self-serving; associated with a curious upbringing, oddness, and the extent to which this is put upon others	6601 Schmeer 121718 Ashleyscroggins 21712 Obaid 50413 Petrginz
slider_Chest_breast_upper (Mindfront:CC0, Chest breast upper, 2018) (pushes the upper lateral regions of each breast inward)	breasts	Big potential, set off at a distance	33573 Hugrace 25151 Stefanschroder
slider_female-breasts-pushup (Nadow:CC0, Breasts pushup, 2016)	breasts	(There was a ridiculous number of results here, 629. But the top most influential basically pointed to "self emphasis which facilitates others' more passionate connection to the holder, often towards conformity to someone's [or many people's] desire standards.")	16598 Brugmansia 33898 Kendra 148780 Altjira 22521 ZZ Top
slider_breast-point-decr|incr	breasts	Comparatively innocent views or situational dynamics, with an increased relationship to the environment; related to a more lighthearted sensuality, but also more morally-based approaches to certain topics	5156 Golant 12072 Anupamakotha 7400 Lenau 3324 Avsyuk 1344 Caubeta
slider_BreastSize	breasts	Creative expression and delineated steps against which one measures their own life progression; | *Ajani's note: hypothesis – when progression measures are material over space and time (see weight), then this attribute is physical. When the progression is interactional—comprising the various wirings that fuel one's evolution over spacetime, then the progress wouldn't manifest physically through the breasts, but through processes, behaviors, and associations instead*	467 Laura 7219 Satterwhite Jupiter 7086 Bopp 2741 Valdivia 649 Josefa 48480 Falk Mercury 548 Kressida 25152 Toplis
slider_breast-volume-vert-down|up (is there more mass in the upper or lower halves of the breasts?)	breasts	How you linger	31661 Eggebraaten
slider_measure-bust-circ-decr|incr[27]	breasts	Surveying the museum of characters	4682 Bykov 7261 Yokootakeo 31516 Leibowitz

---

[27] The women in my sample reported the standard bust, waist, and hips, from which I derived other measures like cup/height and coord_pear shape as an attempt to study body proportion beyond Makehuman's one slider. Oftentimes while I was 3D modeling, the reported proportions did not seem to produce the bodies in the images, especially if the person had gained or lost weight over time. I used the slider_measure… sliders to really sharpen the model's look and align it with actual numeric measurements to the sample person. The slider_measure… sliders are not features, but a different panel in Makehuman to capture proportion with estimated numbers.

statscontinuous_bust (standard self-reported bust measure)	breasts	How much default stranger others seek to capture one's image through the use of relaxed rapport	887 Alinda 7385 Aktsynovia 8929 Haginoshinji
statscontinuous_cup diameter	breasts	Concern that one has had a (creative) child; | *Ajani's note: this is probably the best definition of the breasts as a secondary sexual characteristic. Aside from the basic biological implication, the breasts are also a general indicator of the extent to which your world has tied your growth to the extraction of creative fuel by others. That is, the more people at the table have urges they wish to fulfill or forces they want to impose on their own situations, and the more your own development is advanced by this happening to those others when you are around, the bigger your breasts will be. The less your own development is tied to others' use of you as urge-fuel, the smaller your breasts will be. Whatever the case, when you are used as urge-fuel, the user is one parent, you are the other, and the event that the other was fueling is the child. Getting pulled into interactions you didn't sign up for is common here, but it seems like this is a strong correlation that comes with a space or domain of patterns taking the form of a body. When an assertion of patterns takes the form of a body, the female characteristics are turned down, and the male characteristics turned up*	15727 Ianmorison
slider_female-areola-left-diameter-incr slider_female-areola-right-diameter-incr (Nadow:CC0, Left/Right areola diameter increase, 2015) 	nipples	The channeling of catalytic energy towards the resolving of issues or providing of answers to the seeker	8929 Haginoshinji 23779 Cambier 2376 Martynov 34089 Smoter 243536 Mannheim
slider_female-nipple-left-diameter-incr slider_female-nipple-right-diameter-incr (Nadow:CC0, Left/Right nipple diameter increase, 2015) 	nipples	The closing of an issue – this is all that one can carry with them	306367 Nut 10117 Tanikawa 1582 Martir 34089 Smoter 28 Bellona
slider_nipple-point-decr | incr 	nipples	Contradiction – the city of peace built on blood; the extent to which "extincted," undesirable, or precursor states were foundational to the favored states which succeeded them; discomfort or tension over states that had to be replaced	207319 Eugenemar 24118 Babazadeh 11158 Cirou 121332 Jasonhair 1094 Siberia
nipples and areolae (general) Catalytic / charge-up energy she can donate at one time to another who eats new-creation-fuel, and the channel through which this fuel passes	nipples	A channel used to quietly apply answers and fueling energy to others	34089 Smoter 2376 Martynov 23779 Cambier 243536 Mannheim

slider_nipple-size-decr|incr (general)	nipples	A channel through which spans of answers (other-uncertainty resolvers) are delivered to those who seek it	14189 Sevre 16220 Mikewagner 9683 Rambaldo 2376 Martynov 23779 Cambier
slider_female_breasts_extra_roundness (DredNicolson:CC0, 2017)	breasts	Administering authority heavy-handedly, perhaps with good intentions	12755 Balmer 30840 Jackalice
slider_back-accent (back general) (Glen83:CC0, 2021) What is written about you by others after you are gone	back	Having one's identity altered through public interpretation	202686 Birkfellner
slider_BreastFirmness (something like "perkiness")	breasts	The level of ease or difficulty (perhaps inner conflict) putting an internal idea in front of an external other	7959 Alysecherri 1055 Tynka 32101 Williamyin 17062 Bardot 14010 Jomonaomori
slider_breast-trans-down|up	breasts	The compulsion to give correction or advice, often with an air of familiarity	4175 Billbaum 25084 Jutzi 28568 Jacobjohnson
statscontinuous_cup diameter/weight	breasts	Passing information which was formerly covered onto the many; seems related to child-rearing, teaching, and other social guidance activities	11600 Cipolla 259387 Atauta 21419 Devience
coord_breasts_apartness	breasts	Looking skyward for a place to put one's own vast energy, not sanctioned by the world	37749 Umbertobonori 48798 Penghuanwu 503 Evelyn
coord_breasts_sagging	breasts	Defending oneself as a domain at the boundary of form and the tides of time	7928 Bijaoui 11081 Persave
statscontinuous_bust/height	breasts	The little power – extent to which rapport is built on the element of others' surprise or rallying over the holder's personal power	9938 Kretlow 5568 Mufson 887 Alinda 7385 Aktsynovia
slider_Breasts_Inframammary_fold (Mindfront:CC0, Breasts Inframammary fold, 2018) (the crease between the lower breast mass and upper abdomen)	breasts	Continuous pressure to pile up resources; as expected, becomes more pronounced with age and sagging	21357 Davidying 4372 Quincy 1856 Ruzena

der_measure-underbust-circ-decr|incr	breasts	Continuing to push ideas towards younger or newer audiences despite injury or thwarting related to this	2124 Nissen 15728 Karlmay 6701 Warhol 103966 Luni	
slider_SSBBW-Breast (BBWFan:CC0, 2016) (used both for heavy-weighted ample subjects and light-weighted ones with larger breasts)	weight	Stopping non-favorite scenarios in favor of preferred ones instead, where either you or the interactant is hooked on the other despite being unfavored	20880 Yiyideng 10812 Grotlingbo 2404 Antarctica Moon 207319 Eugenemar	
slider_sagging[28]	breasts	Compiling of energy popularly ransomed by external forces to fuel theirs or the holder's sense of newness	12790 Cernan 10914 Tucker 8961 Schoenobaenus 21636 Huertas 40007 Vieuxtemps	
slider_Muscle (general muscularity) How tied your shell is to your ability to stomp weak things of a certain kind particular to you	muscularity	Extent to which the body is designed to build itself by overwhelming weaker obstacles, growing through a certain level of pain in the process; the body uses the tension levels in its interactions as fuel	130069 Danielgaudreau 32090 Craigworley Uranus 16150 Clinch & 179647 Stuartrobbins[29]	
body shape (general)	build	The overall system of events which guides one from the current situation into the next. The four builds seem to have a much greater effect on domains (women)—which should make sense if the framework for masculine energy is the extent to which an energy is asserted *regardless* of what forms such guiding systems take. Here we see the alignment between the female body and the ambient tides that change around her sphere, thus shaping her Earth (mid torso) region as well as nearby Venus (upper torso) and Mars (lower torso) regions in proportion	850 Altona 29800 Valeriesarge 3254 Bus 3503 Brandt	

---

[28] Unlike coord_breasts_sagging, this slider was more a measure of the downwards development and lower nipple height associated with "natural"-lookingness versus the downward pull of time which pronounces the inframammary fold

[29] The asteroids of muscularity seem to describe two kinds of energy in interaction: a [forcer] and a [support / reacting force] used to build one's strength

How your shell ends up in certain situations over others, as if life itself is pulling the strings			
coord_female_bodyshape_ invertedtriangle-vasetop_bust2waist	build	The life path level of discontentment over the energies crowding one, marked with memorable efforts to rectify this	2883 Barabash 33559 Laurencooper 12369 Pirandello 4293 Masumi
coord_female_bodyshape_ pear	build	Life path seen as though in a fated story	114094 Irvpatterson 17869 Descamps 1271 Isergina 26682 Evanfletcher
coord_female_bodyshape_ topheaviness-lowerpear_bust2hips	build	A life path described by witnessing other people's or systems' power, being put into situations which facilitate this	209107 Safranek 112797 Grantjudy 13335 Tobiaswolf 3248 Farinella
coord_female_bodyshape_ applelow-hourglasshigh	build	Rehearsing what one will do if they don't get what they want right now; | *Ajani's note: although I could only do the body shape analysis on females [because 1) there weren't enough males and 2) among males in general, the shape variance just wasn't there], I—like most men—probably have more of this feature among the four. Ebina is interesting in that the square weighting was the opposite sign of the inconjunct, while actual hot aspects were not significant. Squares come with tension against doing something, while inconjuncts come with being unable to frame that something. So Ebina was very much about wanting the process of something now, likely affects the body shape in general, and was indeed significant across several of the "heaviness"-related sliders, including slider_BodyProportions*	36472 Ebina 257515 Zapperudi
slider_measure-waist-circ-decr|incr	torso	Wondering how certain experiences will fit with the weight one holds	84339 Francescaballi 7632 Stanislav
slider_pelvis-tone-decr|incr	hips	Navigating an environment while carrying something your niche others would not necessarily approve of	410 Chloris 4928 Vermeer
slider_torso-muscle-pectoral-decr|incr (pectorals general) Resistance to being asserted upon, or being rewritten when you pass your brand of energy into a situation / when another's assertion is pressed onto you	chest	Resistance to being asserted upon, countering with strength	787 Moskva 15295 Tante Riek 26906 Rubidia

slider_torso-muscle-dorsi-decr|incr	back	How distant others interpret you and you next actions against their expectations. This is also a "muscularity" feature	7859 Lhasa 11802 Ivanovski
torso (general) Your model of fuel tank for the main energy your shell processes	torso	One's fuel-carrying body persists its own value against a vast (and not always supported) universe	7632 Stanislav 172734 Giansimon
slider_torso-scale-horiz-decr|incr	torso	Taking one's philosophy and polarity preferences for interaction everywhere, assuming the risk that sometimes comes with this	40023 ANPCEN 6830 Johnbackus 34063 Mariamakarova 9567 Surgut
slider_torso-scale-vert-decr|incr	torso	A predisposition to immerse oneself in work involving the use of one's opinion or sense of self, possibly earning rewards in the process; investigate in the generally longer torsos of whites	22921 Siyuanliu 1617 Alschmitt 941 Murray 23722 Gulak 287347 Mezes
slider_torso-vshape-decr|incr	torso	Self-reinforcing consumption choice	172734 Giansimon
statscontinuous_waist	torso	Making a choice to consume something, accepting the consequences of this choice	19968 Palazzolascaris 7632 Stanislav 172734 Giansimon
statscontinuous_waist/height	torso	Deciding what to do or absorb for oneself in the vastness of options	7632 Stanislav 172734 Giansimon
slider_Waist_bump (Marco_105:CC0, 2016)	torso	Propensity for eventful travel	7590 Aterui 7497 Guangcaishiye
slider_torso-scale-depth-decr|incr	torso	A realization of one's relative insignificance even with the work they put in	2849 Shklovskij 172734 Giansimon
slider_torso-trans-backward|forward	torso	How one sneaks in their agenda or stalk their prey	129063 Joshwood 262536 Nowikow 4499 Davidallen 7632 Stanislav
slider_BodyProportions (general, curviness vs squareness)	build	The social experience you offer which draws to your presence the kinds of kindred typical to you	850 Altona 3503 Brandt 239593 Tianwenbang

Your shell's design for attracting certain kinds of interactant. Reinforces your lineage's social legacy

slider_abs_column (blindsaypattern:CC0, 2017) (basic ab tone)	muscularity	Using the burn off from another thing as one's own fuel	1466 Mundleria 21623 Albertshieh
slider_HarveyStomachMusclesV2 (callharvey3d:CC-BY, HarveyStomachMusclesV2, 2016) (raises and noticeably 6-packs the entire ab column)	muscularity	Engrossment in a topic with a simultaneous versatility shown towards the turns taken there	7957 Antonella 24318 Vivianlee 976 Benjamina
weight (general) Your shell's retention of more moments from your past and future	weight	The extent to which one's form models the dynamics of the sphere they oversee, especially in space, time, and chemistry; associated with being an interaction-drawing singularity in one's sphere; keeping records of more of one's past and future self in the form of energy	8834 Anacardium 4209 Briggs 8166 Buczynski 4757 Liselotte
slider_SSBBW-Arms (BBWFan:CC0, SSBBW Arms/Hip/Belly/Back/Ass Legs, 2016)	weight	Monopolizing a topic space, or communicatively insisting towards this	34753 Zdenekmatyas 8003 Kelvin 23324 Kwak
slider_SSBBW-Back (BBWFan:CC0, SSBBW Arms/Hip/Belly/Back/Ass Legs, 2016)	weight	Leaving aftereffects with a provocative edge or effects that give cause for people to reevaluate whether they want to allow something	4209 Briggs 13808 Davewilliams 12053 Turtlestar

slider_SSBBW-Rear-Legs (BBWFan:CC0, SSBBW Arms/Hip/Belly/Back/Ass Legs, 2016)	weight	Here's what I'm going to pull for myself from the world anyway, even if the situations I encounter want to force me to receive whatever *they* value	18124 Leeperry 79086 Gorgasali 8166 Buczynski 1014 Semphyra 1247 Memoria
statscontinuous_hips/weight	weight	Central singularity in one's orbit; seems related to personalities which are more likely to take over an invested interaction	10724 Carolraymond 27356 Mattstrom 158 Koronis
statscontinuous_waist/weight	weight	Extent to which one's weight is pulled from outside of one's commitments;	*Ajani's note: my waist is slimmer than the mean, but my weight is a lot lighter, so I would be on the higher end of this measure. I really don't do a lot of my building using events from outside of my commitments, so this make sense*	4757 Liselotte 10724 Carolraymond
slider_SSBBW-Belly (BBWFan:CC0, SSBBW Arms/Hip/Belly/Back/Ass Legs, 2016)	weight	Pulled into fixation by a force associated with you, installing this pull into your sphere	23410 Vikuznetsov 27356 Mattstrom 26660 Samahalpern 30146 Decandia
stomach (general) Resources you keep from your environment when outside of others' view	stomach	Background rewards claimed for one's efforts, outside the view of the engaged systems' knowledge or permission	6436 Coco 5202 Charleseliot
slider_stomach-navel-down|up	stomach	Diving into the crowd, blending one's personality into the mass	1116 Catriona 10332 Defi 5202 Charleseliot 845 Naema
slider_stomach-navel-in|out	stomach	Injured, and partly because of this, getting away with commandeering the efforts of those around you; seems to reflect the ongoing healing or support paradigm of your spheremates towards one, while the latter may be opportunistic in this	9576 vand der Weyden 16144 Korsten 4282 Endate
slider_stomach-pregnant-decr|incr	stomach	Transferring energy into showcasing the outputs one will publish	1967 Menzel 6418 Hanamigahara 111594 Raktanya 29905 Kunitaka
slider_stomach-tone-decr|incr	stomach	The rewards one earns for themselves despite the things that surround them	6436 Coco 5202 Charleseliot 845 Naema

stomach_heavy	stomach	A skill for executing a self-building pattern in the background regardless of who one's interactants are	4805 Asteropaios 15056 Barbaradixon 19263 Lavater
stomach_muscular_abs	stomach	Having to fight in order to capitalize on opportunities to break new ground	3935 Toatenmongakkai 23899 Kornos 957 Camelia
slider_HarveyVCutV1 (callharvey3d:CC-BY, HarveyVCutV1, 2016) (strengthens the suprailiac muscle) 	muscularity	Lightly filing through a collection (of things or events)	21411 Abifraeman 4269 Bogado
arms (general) Your acts for controlling the in-use objects all around you	arms	Sweeping control over the air traffic around one, applied to subordinate patterns under this influence	40092 Memel 6754 Burdenko 15389 Geflorsch 33806 Shrivastava 1968 Mehltretter 175920 Francisnimmo
slider_l-upperarm-fat-decr|incr slider_r-upperarm-fat-decr|incr 	arms	Rigid fixation on a topic or directed path	8459 Larsbergknut 7086 Bopp
slider_l-upperarm-muscle-decr|incr slider_r-upperarm-muscle-decr|incr 	arms	Elaborating or blending the details of a project in process	8113 Matsue 242648 Fribourg
slider_l-upperarm-scale-depth-decr|incr slider_r-upperarm-scale-depth-decr|incr 	arms	Noticing when one's options aren't all what one would want them to be.	21082 Araimasaru
slider_l-upperarm-scale-vert-decr|incr slider_r-upperarm-scale-vert-decr|incr 	arms	Those with privilege whose group is hard to gain admission to	952 Caia 8405 Asbolus 63605 Budperry
slider_l-upperarm-shoulder-muscle-decr|incr slider_r-upperarm-shoulder-muscle-decr|incr 	arms	Process for ending a track that one was on, or ending another's track	29818 Aryosorayya 4234 Evtushenko 227767 Enkibilal8405 Asbolus

slider_l-upperarm-scale-horiz-decr|incr slider_r-upperarm-scale-horiz-decr|incr 	arms	The relationship to a counterpart in order to complete a terrain	2885 Palva 2499 Brunk
slider_l-lowerarm-fat-decr|incr slider_r-lowerarm-fat-decr|incr 	arms	Relying on the ambient system to resolve an issue on the imagination	7086 Bopp 6754 Burdenko 6949 Zissell
slider_l-lowerarm-muscle-decr|incr slider_r-lowerarm-muscle-decr|incr 	arms	The details that lie beneath everyone's common view	12646 Avercamp 16128 Kirfrieda 8405 Asbolus
slider_l-lowerarm-scale-depth-decr|incr slider_r-lowerarm-scale-depth-decr|incr 	arms	A journey into a new space of ideas	12659 Schlegel 96193 Edmonton 8405 Asbolus
slider_l-lowerarm-scale-horiz-decr|incr slider_r-lowerarm-scale-horiz-decr|incr 	arms	An exploitative or abusive combination; less extreme, a pairing where one simply drains their interactant's energy	18531 Strakonice
slider_l-lowerarm-scale-vert-decr|incr slider_r-lowerarm-scale-vert-decr|incr 	arms	Sweeping parent-like control over an entire atmosphere of a subordinate	22838 Darcyhampton 7086 Bopp 8769 Arcitctern (accessories)
hips (general) Equipped for agility across the material land	hips	Agility amidst the limits of settings; | *Ajani's note: hypothesis – as the woman is her own major setting, the hips may represent agility amidst the limits of events she process that do not align with how her setting naturally redefines them. The male would not need as much of this (or fat stores in general) since he embodies a single energy mobile pattern rather than a whole system of re-creation. All he needs to do is move to another space or be equipped to resist impositions from the one he is in. The woman needs both of these capabilities—one for her self and one for the eventually non-self entities she creates. Typically, the man can only create through the woman, unless his primary creation attempts are abstract. If they are, then his body will be designed accordingly.*	4928 Vermeer 32766 Voskresenskoe
statscontinuous_hips	hips	Extent to which agility helps one navigate obstacles	32766 Voskresenskoe
slider_hip-scale-depth-decr|incr 	hips	Being locked in, one's moves restricted	6212 Franzthaler 21965 Dones
slider_hip-scale-horiz-decr|incr	hips	Affairs and hidden creations with effects that stand to stretch over the distance	10432 Ullischwarz 11927 Mount Kent

			30314 Yelenam 10696 Giuliattiwinter Mars
slider_hip-scale-vert-decr|incr	hips	Freezing the image in place, social group snapshotting	25601 Francopacini 1631 Kopff 14115 Melaas
slider_measure-hips-circ-decr|incr	hips	Prevented from cocreating children because of duty	61400 Voxandreae
slider_SSBBW-Hip (BBWFan:CC0, SSBBW Arms/Hip/Belly/Back/Ass Legs, 2016)	weight	Using the patterns or others associated with your sphere to accomplish a goal	14028 Nakamurahiroshi 10501 Ardmacha
slider_hip-trans-down|up	hips	Smooth flexibility in handling trip-ups and other mental hindrances	13278 Grotecloss 14115 Melaas
buttocks (general) Togetherness and related ideals, and the extent to which other's behaviors are openly steered in light of what you intend by defining things the way you do	buttocks	The ways in which the holder's [internal wants regarding "things belonging together"] influences [the direct action of those who interpret her aftereffects]—stored over space and time; organizing groups of people's impressions with a specific approach to togetherness[30]	17919 Licandro 121486 Sarahkirby 128348 Jasonleonard 34163 Neyveli
slider_Bubble-Booty (DaMaster:CC0, 2020)(stretches rear outwards to increase general volume)	buttocks	Turning away from the individual and to the skies for answers	27949 Jonasz
slider_buttocks-volume-decr|incr	buttocks	Leering or scandalous attention paid	4879 Zykina
coord_butt_gluteperhip_size	buttocks	Facing an opponent or challenger, skill which deserves attention—often for revealing one of the party's errors	383 Janina 17919 Licandro

---

[30] Togetherness, huh? I wouldn't have thought that. But then again, when you think about how much of the animal kingdom goes about mating, you could see the connection to lordotic behavior, for example.

●ord_butt_rear_undertuck (sharpness of underrear crease)	buttocks	Idealism in wishing for the company of another	22594 Stoops 5287 Heishu
coord_rear_long_vertical_size	buttocks	Roving group organizer	4150 Starr
slider_Buttocks_THIGH-03 ●Marco_105:CC0, *Buttocks_THIGH-03, 2016) (eliminates underrear crease by blending bottom of rear into backs of thighs) 	buttocks	The distant influencer seeds others' reactions from a structured stronghold; | *Ajani's note: I have this kind of butt, and really do operate from a stronghold. Interesting. Never imagined this would be a thing*	65100 Birtwhistle 2051 Chang 9255 Inoutadataka 121486 Sarahkirby
slider_sohh_bottom (sohh:CC0, 2020) (widens space between legs at crotch) 	buttocks	Well taken care of, refined	4011 Bakharev
●der_butt_crease (Habanero:CC0, Thigh Butt Crease, 2016) (pushes the back of the legs upward to sharpen underrear crease) 	buttocks	Audacity or protected personality that comes with an affinity for the environment that hits a group's senses sharply	120353 Katrinajackson 1599 Giomus
slider_HarveyBottomV1 ●callharvey3d:CC-BY, HarveyBottomV1, ●016) (pulls bottom of glutes down into a sag to create underrear)[31] 	buttocks	Boldly journeying together with another in beauty	2594 Acamas 2214 Carol 25152 Toplis
vagina (general) [32] Includes: hairy vagina, labia minora, ornate labial wings, plump labia, deep vaginal entry, dangling clitoris	vagina	How your archetypal-domain reinterprets the procreative force carrier it is attuned to receive; the private expression of satisfaction with the various situations one has engaged and assigned her particular definition of force to as a default domain. Assesses the results of what the body as female energy has processed; the shoulders, hands, chest, and skin were also significant in t-tests of 67q7 and 124q6 Some asteroids which mined on the word "vaginal" and had body-relevant interpretations were:[33]	67q7, 124q6

---

[31] We have a lot of crease-under-the-butt sliders. And seemingly redundant sliders. Why? Because when I was sculpting 3D models from my sample folks' images, I just couldn't get the rear to look the way it looked in the pictures without all of the buttocks sliders shown.

[32] The asteroids were not researched for this group, as these descriptions were added by the AI interrogator, which I didn't have access to until much later in the study. The group as a whole, however suggested which qunits were involved. In general, certain body groups could not be easily researched prior to the interrogator, because the scale of observations that would have needed to be made in order to cover some of the more inconsistently or rarely photographed body regions, would have just been too high. Before the AI help, I was limited to eyeballing only the more obvious traits. And there were no sliders to control for these rarer traits in any detail. However…

[33] …If I were female, and I saw how many male sliders there were, and I wanted to know if there were any asteroids at all—even the slightest clue as to where I might look for the reproductive area to address anything ranging from health issues, to fun, or just out of curiosity—then I would at least prefer a starting point. So I've listed the asteroids that not only text-mined on the word "vaginal," but also seemed related to women's health. As a male I wouldn't necessarily know what to look for as an explanation for why some of these body sliders might take the forms they do, but those who do know can start with the asteroids I've listed.

 Attunement with the forces which have engaged and aligned with her procreative definitions		22723 Edlopez*, 185216 Guiren*, 4034 Vishnu, 210686 Scottnorris, 2420 Ciurlionis, 6748 Bratton, 180855 Debrarose, 133243 Essen, 19008 Kristibutler, 10560 Michinari, 4869 Piotrovsky	
penis (general) The nature and extent of the impact of his patent brand of procreative energy	penis	How your archetypal-asserter's[34] procreative pattern disturbs the structure and internal energy of the spaces it interacts with; How the male body maintains a particular kind of force which he imposes upon the various situation he encounters. Persists the male assertion upon all encounters. Not solely sexual. For males, the ejaculation process seems to live in 122q7. (I did not have enough female data on this, as it requires a level of vivid graphic description which is very hard to find.)	49500 Ishitoshi 187125 Marxgyorgy
slider_penis_width_head (noticeability) 	penis	How greetings are exchanged upon an assertion's arrival	3696 Herald
slider_penis_width_head_scale 	penis	Half supported, half to someone else—the division of energy for upon an assertion's contact with its target	21161 Yamashitaharuo 26545 Meganperkins
slider_penis_width_headbell 	penis	The assertion which only stands out sometimes from the background; elusiveness in the male assertion. When absent, under a kind of protection	48458 Merian 291 Alice 21556 Christineli 3191 Svanetia
slider_penis_width1 (end) 	penis	The arriving effect announced with a new assertion, greatly dependent on whether the welcomers want to help this	9194 Ananoff 15465 Buchroeder 20834 Allihewlett 32796 Ehrenfest
slider_penis_width2 (middle) 	penis	The extent to which an asserter stays the course for their own personal reasons, even if this is not seen externally	51823 Rickhusband 3191 Svanetia 48480 Falk 15465 Buchroeder 6873 Tasaka

---

[34] What is an archetypal-domain? Or an archetypal-asserter? These are the templates for the woman or man that you are, and the man or woman you would be if you are of the contrary sex to these. When you are male, you will typically be your own archetypal-asserter, and you will attract archetypal-domains as your definition of women. When you are female, you will usually be your own archetypal-domain, and the archetypal-asserter will form your definition of men as you commonly see them. Where can you learn more about these archetypes? Try looking at the asteroids in your 10q2, 46q2, 82q2, and 118q2 for starters. Your qunits in duodecanates 76 and 77 also have some pieces of this.

slider_penis_width3base	penis	The frequency, repetition, or cycle style of the male assertion; seems to describe how short or long term a males' plans span for what he asserts, how long and how fast he is willing to pace his efforts against his context to get there	18905 Weigan 23773 Sarugaku 51823 Rickhusband Ranevskaya (6821)
slider_penis-circ-decr|incr	penis	(Apparent circumference, single image) Extent to which the creating assertion one issues leads to definite changes in its receiving context	27546 Maryfran
slider_penis-length-decr|incr	penis	The extent to which the male assertive effect is exponentiated in the context that receives it; among situations which prize this, related to ranking in viewers' or interactants' popularity and status contexts—similar to the breasts in women, and general height	818 Kapteynia 10526 Ginkogino 14004 Chikama 13079 Toots 2747 Cesky Krumlov
statscontinuous_p_Endowment	penis	(Self-reported size) From within a confined space, the extent to which the male energy asserts another into a challenging position	14004 Chikama 11790 Goode
coord_penis_curvature	penis	Background information which supports a foreground assertion's effectiveness; the male energy asserting under cover of darkness (or setting) rather than straight on	48480 Falk 33610 Payra
coord_penis_general_volume	penis	(Apparent circumference, cross comparison for removing exaggerations)[35] The extent to which an asserted force is controlled or blocked from admittance into its target situation	9194 Ananoff 9792 Nonodakesan
coord_penis_headshort2long	penis	A symbol of power buried under obscurity, unless searched for; likely has implications for circumcision and glans exposure during erection	5004 Bruch 5859 Ostozhenka
coord_penis_shaftdiameter_per_headdiameter	penis	How (or if) the male energy trains the unready or inexperienced	837 Schwarzschilda
coord_penis_size (vol x length)	penis	(Other apparent size) Extent to which one is uncontested in the sport (socialized play in action-based achievement) where they are deemed professional; Interestingly, 3 of the 5 results were related to sports	2680 Mateo 4330 Vivaldi
coord_penis_veinsize	penis	Extent to which the body as male has its potential action held at bay by the space it engages	2721 Vsekhsvyatskij Linsley (3474)
coord_penis_veiny	penis	Where the body as male has its calculated path of assertion measured	8820 Anjandersen
slider_penis-testicles-decr|incr	penis	The one-time spark granting [new creative]-igniter status onto the body as male	20283 Elizaheller 51825 Davidbrown
thick thighs	legs	no p<.05 findings, but likely "a declared intention to smash the situational object before oneself"	probably 2098 Zyskin
hands (general)	hands	Giving an idea multiple chances to conform to a standard. (There were A LOT of significant potential asteroids to choose from)	2398 Jilin 12372 Kagesuke Uranus

---

[35] More than any other body region, the penis is prone to exaggeration in self-reporting. Although I initially approximated all Makehuman models using their individual images (the slider_s), I gradually realized that 1) the males were almost certainly not using bpel (bone-pressed erect length) to provide their numbers and 2) many of the male images just didn't look the way the measures suggested. So I ran a separate study in which I took all male images and spread them across a canvas in my program Inkscape, the x coordinate for apparent size and the y coordinate for apparent volume. Then I ran ANOVAs which compared these relative x and y coordinates as if they were sliders. About 4 males' data was so bad I had to delete them from my samples entirely, but overall the themes of pro-creative reception for this region remained stably intact. For other attributes where I didn't really have good numbers (nipples, rear and body shape, and anything involving skin texture), I used this same "coord_" process.

 Multiple chances to succeed for an interacting object you are coaxing in a particular direction			
slider_l-hand-fingers-length-decr|incr slider_r-hand-fingers-length-decr|incr 	hands	Pre-market creations; what you work on before anyone else sees it	16113 Ahmed
slider_l-hand-fingers-diameter-decr|incr 	hands	Extra energy in put into how one attempts to rescue an idea or reconcile it with another; left: bringing outside forces in to help the inside forces build up a state	183287 Deisenstein 159974 Badacsony
slider_r-hand-fingers-diameter-decr|incr 	hands	Extra energy in put into how one attempts to rescue an idea or reconcile it with another; right: working to reinvigorate something	400796 Douglass 159974 Badacsony
slider_l-hand-fingers-distance-decr|incr 	hands	One's system of systematic manipulation, getting a thing to give them an experience they prefer | *Ajani's note: For whatever reason, though I probably modeled the left hand similarly to the right in the Makehuman samples, the left finger distance had several more results than the right, and definitely leaned towards how one demands the best. From what I can tell, Toplis likely demands clear aesthetic completion or conceptual symmetry*	25152 Toplis 11294 Kazu
slider_r-hand-fingers-distance-decr|incr 	hands	One's system of systematic manipulation, getting a thing to give them an experience they prefer	11294 Kazu[36]
slider_l-hand-scale-decr|incr slider_r-hand-scale-decr|incr 	hands	The power to grant another chance to a thing or situation	12356 Carlscheele
legs (general)	legs	How one potentially punishes opponents and defends themselves against the demands of the environments they occupy; nature adaptations	31996 Goecknerwald 2098 Zyskin

---

[36] So *that's* what it's used for!

The construction equipment for manipulating yourself against the land "just so"

slider_l-lowerleg-scale-horiz-decr|incr slider_r-lowerleg-scale-horiz-decr|incr 	legs	The transmitting of ideas that others can get hooked on as a means of problem-solving	22898 Falce
slider_l-upperleg-fat-decr|incr slider_r-upperleg-fat-decr|incr 	legs	no $p<.05$ findings	
slider_l-upperleg-scale-horiz-decr|incr slider_r-upperleg-scale-horiz-decr|incr 	legs	The vice grip; where one makes a promise to smash their objective	9498 Westerbork 2098 Zyskin
slider_l-upperleg-muscle-decr|incr slider_r-upperleg-muscle-decr|incr slider_l-upperleg-scale-depth-decr|incr slider_r-upperleg-scale-depth-decr|incr 	legs	The vice grip; where one's energy is used to clamp and foster directed tension in viewers; have regular experience with people with huge thighs? Look for 31996 in your chart	31996 Goecknerwald 2098 Zyskin
slider_l-lowerleg-fat-decr|incr slider_r-lowerleg-fat-decr|incr 	legs	Inquest – where a person is compelled to assert by another group or system of assertion. Interestingly, Jongoldstein as an indicator of the calves region shows one of the few (but not only) areas among us mating-trained men where slim muscularity is considered default "sexier" on the woman, hence the whole thing with high heels[37]	292159 Jongoldstein 31996 Goecknerwald
slider_l-lowerleg-muscle-decr|incr slider_r-lowerleg-muscle-decr|incr 	legs	One is held up or has their actions bound by an institution or other disciplinary system, but often for their own good; | *Ajani's note: lots of results. So I used the black spot on my right calf as an indicator, and looked for a cluster which might explain this. 424 Gratia was in a cluster indicating the work that circumstances force one to do alone. I publish this stuff, and I think that fits*	424 Gratia 31996 Goecknerwald 2098 Zyskin

---

[37] I hope people aren't offended by this. Tallness is also considered broadly sexier in men, and I'm not tall. We tend to get touchy when talking about traits that only a few of us have—especially traits that smack of sexist assessment. Men get this too with certain kinds of shaming regarding what is and isn't appealing to a mate. But our mating paradigms are trained on exactly this: "sexist assessment." That's the whole point of this particular social framework. It's just templating sponsored by the averaged citizen out there. The images of what is and isn't attractive have become much more inclusive during the start of the 21st century, but certain bodily go-tos still remain.

slider_l-lowerleg-scale-depth-decr|incr slider_r-lowerleg-scale-depth-decr|incr 	legs	Having to pay to get into a place, getting into a place as a form of payment, or making people pay in order to let them in—all kinds of fun institutional scenarios	4655 Marjoriika 31996 Goecknerwald 2098 Zyskin
slider_l-upperleg-scale-vert-decr|incr slider_r-upperleg-scale-vert-decr|incr 	legs	Enduring a pelting to prove one's own unique way to others; | *Ajani's note: investigate in the African-morph femur in forensics, the implications for role in society. My thighs are very long. LOTS of these asteroids were stereotypically black. Alma fit the sanity testing of qunits best, and more accurately reflects my perception of the amplification of black sins or limits in the general US. My 105q2 is a catch-all for this.* I paste the screenshot below mostly as a kind of headshaking moment, as the research validated an array of boxes that I already knew. Below shows the asteroids of my 105q2, where Alma is. And with it, a slew of ideas that come with being black…	390 Alma 2098 Zyskin

44013	Iidetenmomdai	0.2	1.1 influence	one who endures pelting as a form of remediation, combin
31281	Stothers	0.1	1.1 influence	reveling in or enjoying the idea that one was able to take a p
5641	McCleese	0.1	1.1 influence	receiving the winning, then coming to know the reality of wh
390	Alma	0.1	1.1 influence	where others use the milestone events of your life to discus
176711	Canmore	0.2	1.1 influence	the pessimistic or careful other supporting a primary powe
5839	GOI	0.1	1.1 influence	to preach or strongly reinforce how different one's own way
11690	Carodulaney	0.1	1.1 influence	a sport or practice where the need to prove oneself in front
39864	Poggiali	0.2	1.1 influence	slammed or put on trial for a copy of an idea rather than th
20574	Ochinero	0.2	1.1 influence	steady, intermittent trafficking of summaries
21700	Caseynicole	0.2	1.1 influence	imbalances between what one would do creatively and wha
1211	Bressole	0.1	1.1 influence	a name, word, or secondary identity put on top of another's
5578	Takakura	0.1	1.1 influence	a situation or subject which is the core of a desperate prob
11134	Ceske Budejovice	0.2	1.1 influence	where the circulation of one's energy is subject to throbs ar
721	Tabora	0.1	1.1 influence	settling into a way of being behaved against through other's
1387	Kama	0.2	1.1 influence	sufficient conditions to end a cancer by organizing everythi
4292	Aoba	0.1	1.1 influence	devotionals, behavioral appeals to the sacred; a tell astero
30162	Courtney	0.1	1.1 influence	blessed with great riches, but larger-scale concerns
8971	Leucocephala	0.1	1.1 influence	rewiring another's views or preferences through the informa
185250	Korostyshiv	0.2	1.1 influence	the stirring craziness or dynamism contained in one's head
32054	Musunuri	0.1	1.1 influence	a massive or immeasurable object or concept intended as
3935	Toatenmongakka	0.1	1.1 influence	working hard to carry the weight one carries

Anyway, at least it supports the idea that my research is legit. There is something to be said for astrology/astronomy's usefulness as a tool for social science in the future.

feet (general) The submarine scrolls you past different contexts, changing not only the land beneath you, but what the mind is able to see easily	feet	The gear needed to navigate (potentially harsh) terrain, and how the terrain itself responds to contact with that gear; | *Ajani's note: an indicator of a certain kind of accident proneness or resistance?*	2539 Ningxia 367436 Siena 18953 Laurensmith
slider_l-foot-scale-decr|incr, slider_r-foot-scale-decr|incr	feet	How one inserts themselves as personally important in another's experiences; | *Ajani's note: I think of the NBA*	14976 Josefcapek

slider_Weight	weight	(Apparent weight in the eye of an external viewer) Stirred up energy towards the approaching future; associated with both worry and planning; | *Ajani's note: none of the asteroids were very influential, so I looked at the ones with higher coverage and preferably a hot relationship as opposed to a tense or seeking one.*	10501 Ardmacha
statscontinuous_Weight	weight	(Self-reported weight) Interestingly, seems to be related to the storage of time in the form of density (not necessarily space): how much you do this; | *Ajani's note: right after interpreting the oval-headed shape, I jumped to the end of the table and started doing these from the end of the table and working up. This is because of my need to see the progress I've made through a diminishing stack rather than a growing page count. Related to that, it seems that weight is associated with how much of the storied past or eventful future your body prefers to process, and I don't process much beyond what I can measure. There were a bunch of significant asteroids for this one (29), but *a lot* of them had to do with the distant past, far future, and stirred up energy regarding this. Absolutely fascinating.*	20973 Goldinaaron
statscontinuous_Weight/height	weight	One sense of intense anticipation; | *Ajani's note: I am light even for my average height. Although I love everyday doing this work with 8834 in 84q9, I would also say that I am a lot more mellow about it. Is Anacardium tied to cortisol? Surely it is tied to metabolism*	8834 Anacardium

Now that we have the energetic equivalents of common body features, we can use them to do several things. In the next couple of chapters we will use the frequentized regions to

1) Write an autobiography
2) Reify an imagined person
3) Build the basis for a talking tree

Chapter 14: Using frequentics for autobiography

As I mentioned in the introduction, one of my major life goals is to contribute to the work in saving humans as data. Not just creating artificial humans, but creating—in a different time or place—faithful reprints of humans who actually lived. Additionally, I also have a personal past full of burned and abandoned bridges, a naturally lusty aura despite being very disciplined, and a need to control the telling of my own story. I thought for years about writing an autobiography that would serve both as a model for the accurate replication of human dynamics as well as inspiration for countless misunderstood or misinterpreted people to say, "Hey, just because you don't understand me doesn't mean I'm without value." The purpose of that autobiography wouldn't be so much to tell uninterested readers all about myself, but would be my way of setting the record straight for all of the situations I've been in where things went lopsided and others were left to write about me through whatever narrative they felt was warranted. You shouldn't let others control your narrative. But in order to control your own, you first need a clear view of your own workings. So I spent an extra decade writing various books mainly in order to lay out a language for truly knowing oneself. Now with all of the research established, it's time to do so.

In writing a frequentic biography, you might benefit from staying focused on a single objective: to understand the full story of yourself and your capabilities as the gods have written it. That is, you want to embrace anything and everything that is you—the good, the traumatized, and the quirky—and map it out so that you choose almost all of your life paths on your own terms. We assume that your body is a record of interactions you've gotten into, and that the entire record is valuable. But first we need to know how to read it.

In this chapter I am going to add a Q&A approach to my current autobiography, and use this as a springboard for a more complicated discussion of AI, artificial humans, and anthrizing.

There is one important disclaimer, however:

Although we will be looking at both a male and a female example below, these two individuals differ in a MAJOR way: One of them has existed in real life, the other is an AI rendered character from a story who has a pretty creepy tie to our reality. More on this later.

For people seeking to live out their maximum creative potential, but can't understand why certain things just aren't working...

How do I use the stuff in this book?

Let's ask some big questions of God / our Rule Set—about our own lives and what we're supposed to do with it. Our frequentic autobiography may not unearth definite answers, but it will greatly increase our understanding of the forces we are up against (mostly built into us ourselves).

Here are my questions. What does my body say about…

1) how I can make a lot of money
2) why many (but not all) of my closest relationships with women are fucked up
3) why I chronically ghost my best friends
4) why I feel compelled to do my penis exercises
5) how I can become a legend in human history
6) whatever the hell is going on to kill my business partnerships
7) the easiest route for me to lead a peaceful, healthy life with no pressing obligations to anyone, no money or job concerns, and no need to deal with any systems which I don't' respect or which force my hand

These are real questions I have, in no particular order. My body may not explicitly answer them for me, but the asteroids and chart regions behind those investigations will surely give me food for thought.

As for my female sample, a fictional character named Sâvitrî, she won't have life questions, but will present us with some important implications for data-ported humans in the chapter after this one.

ADDRESSING QUESTION 1 (MONEY): WHAT DO PEOPLE TREAT YOU LIKE YOU SHOULD DO FOR A LIVING?

On the left is Sâvitrî Narayan, age 22. On the right, me, age 43. The first thing I tend to note about people is their face, followed by their body build, then maybe their ethnicity. I typically do not note their sex, as this determines *how* I observe the person to begin with. As a straight male, I am less interested in observing other men unless I pick up some particular mojo about them. Unfortunately, this lack of interest also belies a general utilitarian view I have when it comes to interacting with people, and gives me an off-putting resting face. The (default) barriers to acquiring money only pile up from there.

In economics they say that money is 1) a store of value, 2) a unit of account, and 3) a medium of exchange. I would add a fourth usage and that would be 4) a measure of potential (to remove a barrier to experience). This fourth view of money sets it up as a means of security rather than, say, a thing to spend or a means to a lifestyle; this is the view that I take. But one thing I cannot stress enough is the idea that your frameworks follow you around. To me, money is the stuff of fortress walls and battery chargers. It is not a means to happiness, and this is played out through a face which does not inspire trust. Instead, people I'm not close to—unless it is in a project-like or work setting—are likely to see me as someone to be defend against (in the same way that I discourage them trying to connect with me just for funsies). Unless a person can contribute to my various ambitions or work targets, I don't really have much interest in interacting with them. Consequently, I don't have the face that would make you want to give me money. I do have the face that suggests I might take it from you or from some institution out there—especially from side view. From front view my face is judgmental. Meanwhile, my body build, though athletic, is neither big nor small, and people don't get to see this anyway (except here). These factors all contribute to the first half of my body's answer to question 1, "How do I make a lot of money?"

> Strangers are generally discouraged from interacting with you upon first impression, you prefer it this way, and reinforce this. To the extent that money is often built on people's willingness to engage you or your services—to hire you—you would not be most people's first choice in any situation built on prosocial trust. You would be someone's second choice when they are running out of options and seriously need someone to break in and do the dirty work that no one else is willing or able to do, provided you happen to be around. Your side and back view suggests a thief. Your front face suggests some kind of immovably tempered people-judge, so if you did either of these things (*pay attention to this part*) then it would align with what more people *expected* you did by default, and that makes it easier for them to place you, socially, "where you belong." However you make money, more people will be willing to validate that fact if you do so in some shady field doing unpopular or sneaky work.

Now the above wasn't just based on my look. That's actually what I've experienced across 40+ years of life. We don't worry about whether our look fosters good or bad assumptions by others; if we want to have a *lot* of people say "Amen" to something we receive, it is helpful (though not necessary) to start with the box they are willing to hand you—boxes you already know about. As for the good or bad, there are a million ways to get around this. I actually do scrape data, I am in the field in psychology, I do my work alone, under focused concentration. That work is taboo, and I do it anyway despite societal strictures. We know how to abstractify things now, remember? You don't have to be "homeless." You could be a nomad. You don't have to be "criminal-looking." You could be an innovator as a social rulebreaker. You don't have to be "ugly" or "unattractive." You could be a creative on the fringe whose real friends and social supports are true blue rather than based on convenient superficial templates. The point is, here we can use a combination of what we know about how our actual lives have gone together with what we see when we look at ourselves honestly through the lens of common surface judgment.

The second half of the money question goes like this: What has life given you a lot of which also builds your sense of money's usage? The key here is actually to skip the money and go straight for the frequentics. Here is my answer. I hope you'll find at least parts of it interesting:

> Ajani, life has given you shitloads—I mean SHITLOADS++—of information. Especially in the form of *answers* to existential and social questions. You can just pull these from the air. You have a gift for seeing things holistically, up to and including how patterns flow in time, and an additional gift for mapping what you see. This actually leads directly to questions number 2), 4) , and maybe 5) above. But, overall, *guiding social knowledge* is something you are a gazillionaire in.

> As for building up "the potential to remove experiential barriers," you don't have an interest in interaction with most people, because your work in astrology, complex data, and naked bodies requires endless justification to all but the most diehard folks. So things like travel, dating, or anything that puts you face to face with new people-experiences—particularly those dependent on others' liking of you—would be a burden to you more than anything. Rather, your focus is on reducing barriers in the structures around you—your house, your books, your research. For that, you don't need money. You need skill.

A few months back you asked yourself, "I do make more money now than I did 10 years ago. What aspect of my life or body have also grown in parallel with this?" Your answer: In the yearly "Who am I" pictures you have taken of yourself, the level of order in the room in the background—in the lighting and sharpness of the lines—has increased *greatly*. Your inner cheeks are less gaunt. You are bottom heavier. You moved to a bigger house. But more than anything, you got out of a society where you had to settle for glass ceilings. Again, you moved. More recently, you have started picking up some serious DIY skills to free yourself of the whim of contractors who only show up to see your white girlfriend, or because your Latino associate vouched for you. For you, it's not about what money can buy. It's about not having to chase people down in order to buy the services of people who wouldn't respect you—might even *disrespect* you—if you didn't pay them. In this sense, money will always be a barrier to you for as long as it brings usurious expectations from those who would only obligate you to pay them or pay for them while remaining indifferent to your struggle with the actual work in progress.

Although it may make sense for you to ask, "How do I make a lot of money," and although you now have a partial answer, "Be a second string thief for someone else's utility," a new question would be, are you okay with this? Of course you're not. You can make money however you make it, but it's more important for you to build the bases for your own self respect in order to offset the increasing level of asshole accessible to you with every dollar you gather. That last thing you personally want to do, Ajani, is win the lotto—only to start shopping at the Fancy Car store without giving them any requirements for respecting you. It is NOT a barrier that you lack access to *more* transactional relationships. You yourself are transactional, so you'll really want to build your own community around this science before you start bribing every rando out there to give you stuff against their better biases. This view of money doesn't have to apply to any of your readers. But it is how money is framed in your life. You really shouldn't ask for more money, Ajani. It's a low resolution ask for someone who knows himself better than that. Ask for the potential to remove your mortgage, to remove the ***imposition*** of certain financial obligations (without removing the obligations themselves and the privileges that come with them).

YOUR TURN

Before moving on, let's give you the reader some space to answer the question: <u>What does my body say about the world giving me money?</u>

_____
_____
_____
_____
_____
_____
_____
_____
_____
_____
_____
_____
_____
_____
_____
_____
_____
_____
_____
_____
_____
_____

———————————————————————————
———————————————————————————
———————————————————————————
———————————————————————————
———————————————————————————
———————————————————————————
———————————————————————————
———————————————————————————
———————————————————————————
———————————————————————————
———————————————————————————
———————————————————————————

ADDRESSING QUESTIONS 2 AND 3 (RELATIONSHIP CHALLENGES): WHY CAN'T I RELATE WITH CERTAIN OTHERS IN THE WAY I INTEND?

In normal society, we are clothed. One of the many benefits of clothing is that it allows society as a whole to have a grand layer of protection against our own potentially extreme behaviors and reaction towards each other which can only interfere with daily life. Interpersonally, though, clothing also hides from others what we actually think of ourselves, how we think of ourselves, or even *if* we actually think of ourselves in full form. For some people, there is a vast difference between how they present themselves / what others see of them, and how they know themselves to be. In those cases, it's easy to run into problems as relationships progress from the strange to the familiar. Let's see what our bodies say about this.

My dress is typically casual. You can tell I'm slim. And as I've mentioned, my resting facial expression is off-putting unless there is some goal you can help me accomplish. I'm not actually an asshole, but I prefer to look like one so that neither of us wastes the other's time. Based on these I give one kind of impression. But then we start speaking; my voice is soft and deep. You can tell immediately that I have a brain. I'm also hyper-considerate—Big-5 conscientious, if you will—and don't like strain at all in my interactions. I communicate like a dreamer, do a lot of listening by default, and am VERY easy for you to interrupt and override since it pains me to cut people off. Here, the gentle giant asteroid Ostozhenka on my Midheaven is one of the defining asteroids of my personality, as is my Venus-Priska conjunct for making me the servant in most conversations. All of these are near my Midheaven, so it's easy for my second impression to appear thoughtful, polite, and probably a pushover. Lastly, my template for relating to women in particular was heavily colored my mom—the sole woman in a house full of boys, and also the head of household. I was subordinate as a son here, but equally responsible as the oldest. So from a subordinate position, I also had to develop a sense of my own effectiveness despite how things appeared on the surface, and this directly affected all of my subsequent close relationships with both men and women.

As early as elementary school, I have HATED being pigeonholed. I loved being at the top of my own game in class, loved being taken out of class to do special tasks based on my brain, but never cared that much for other people's praise. My love language is quality time. Words of affirmation are a thing I scrutinize. So as a relationship becomes close, I go back and forth between someone who is an unappealing second choice, to a gentle pushover, to someone who becomes very difficult when *actually* pushed. Earlier we saw that the muscularity asteroids reflect the extent to which your energy is built upon crushing a certain kind of weak target. While I have many quiet methods for removing the influence of people who actually push me, I also have an internal world which aims to crush them for attempting it—whether they intended to or not. Like a classic folkloric Scorpio Sun, I have a long memory, have internal requirements for respect and relationship-repair which I will likely never air to people who fail those requirements, and usually—because I don't like strain—will elect to cut people from my sphere rather than fight them openly (especially after they have gotten close). Once again, I pull the black male card for this: It's stupid to fight people openly without weighing the broader consequences first.

But if I do choose open conflict, it's because I don't give a shit anymore and am prepared to drop you and all of your friends in their support of whatever it is you're doing to me. I live and die upon the protection of my own peace, and freedom of choice. Unlike the fabled Scorpio Sun, I don't like the idea of vengeance. And because I won't terminate a relationship unless I can do so under an *increase* in peace and self-assuredness, I can come across as a smug bastard. The other person doesn't typically get a lot of satisfaction when this happens. And it used to happen a lot. I'm not proud of it, but at the same time, the cases where relationships don't go this way are cases where the other person is also highly conscientious. They don't see my apparent pushover face as an opportunity to actually push me over or "put me in my place." But these people are exceptions. Many of them I've known for a long time.

Why have many of my closest relationships (until recently) ended badly? Because despite being courteous after familiarity has been established, I'm a lot less malleable than I seem. I demand respect, and I shouldn't have to tell you this in order to get it. On this point most people are too casual for my tastes.

So, at the end of the day, did my body relate at all to the above discussion? It did. In summary,

> My face conveys a wall that agrees with my private body build and sense of self, but these give different impressions from my lighter weight, average height, and voice. My voice and speech pattern in particular can give others an impression of softness (which is basically true too), but sometimes they compound this impression and feel the need to be stern, pushy, or dismissive with me. But I fucking hate that. I move to terminate that aspect of the exchange—if not the whole exchange—as soon as it happens. I don't like people taking advantage of those they perceive as weak. It's a character incompatibility which keeps my friendship circle happily small.

> Interestingly, there is one other aspect of my body which betrays all this: I walk with the sides and balls of my feet first—quiet like a ninja so as to avoid annoying myself with the jarring sound of my own would-be heel stomp. Since high school, I have had a military-like walk which strongly conveys discipline and a personality that's not having it. And though I am truly all about peace in my personal relationships, the price of that is a type of remorseless purging of anything that intrudes even slightly upon that peace—including my own noise.

When a close person starts acting differently on you at the expense of your own esteem, burning that bridge may be a small price to pay if you're too concerned with easy politeness to correct them.

YOUR TURN

Have any relationship challenges? Perhaps the different aspects of your body tell a story of the various moving parts behind those challenges. Take a look at my summary above, then take another moment to answer: <u>What does my body say about the relationships I find challenging and the values I have which help me (subconsciously) keep those challenges going?</u>

_____
_____
_____
_____
_____
_____
_____
_____
_____
_____
_____
_____
_____
_____
_____
_____
_____
_____

_____
_____
_____
_____
_____
_____
_____
_____
_____
_____
_____
_____
_____
_____
_____
_____

ADDRESSING QUESTION 6 (PROFESSIONAL CHALLENGES): WHERE ARE MY ALLIES? HOW DO I FIND THEM?

Let's start with a simple analogy. Suppose life consists of five modes: eating, resting, working, playing, and reproducing. Suppose also that you have default body structures for carrying out these modes: an eater, a rester, a worker, a player, and a reproducer. As long as all five modes are done, it may not matter which structure does what. You could eat intravenously during rest for example, just because your eating system has malfunctioned or you're in a coma and resting is all you can do. Well, the signs, duodecanates, and qunits are like the modes. Planets and asteroids are like the body structures which do those modes.[38] We all have different planets in different places such that, for example, work is felt as a compulsion like eating. Resting may be like playing as a person sits with their feet up on the beach. Oh, how easy it is to shame someone when their structures don't match the default boxes we're sure they belong to!

In my case, eating is rest, sex is work, and work is play. Only when I am on a goal-directed project with others does the potential for co-creation come out, and even then the project mates have to include at least some women, has to be easygoing, and everyone has to be known and trusted. Through work, I can be both polite and driven, make material contributions to the overall effort, and do so in the spirit of creating something worthwhile. Unfortunately, with potential business partners, the "tiger stripes" (varicose veins) on my butt and hips and my fairly thick-ish eyebrows belie someone who is always focused on hunting prey. In the absence of prey, partners become two hunters arguing over which techniques should be used. But I'm averse to being rewritten in how I do things—especially in how I think. I want to maximize my own life-design and its template for what I can and can't do. I don't' want to fog up the goal by diluting it against some other's intentions.

Looking back at my _Laurentia 2nd ed_ definitions, I see that my number one problem with business partnerships lies with my 239071 Penghu next to Pluto in 65q1 <while within a partnership, dissatisfied>. Penghu's definition reads, "attempts to move forward in business stifled by the mistaken role of sweetness mixed in, and the disappointment this brings... clouding business with rapport." Being married to my work is one thing, but to the extent that _professional_ work almost always implies collaboration, it is very easy for things to turn south in my dealings here. Either I build the rapport and the exchange devolves into my answers to questions 2 and 3, or I don't build the rapport and the relationship is capped as a transaction reminiscent of my answer to question 1. Penghu is generally associated with weight, the breasts, arm bulk, and the nose alar creases (the lines separating the top and back of the nostrils from the main nose and face). In my case, the sharp alar base conveys my sense of urgency in meeting the goal, while my front chest distance and pectorals

---

[38] Aspects would be like seeing relationships between any two structures in terms of a mode. Houses would be the time window during which each mode is most appropriate.

(which made use of the breast size sliders in my 3D model), show my continued resistance to being steered. If only I could collaborate with folks whose agenda would never challenge mine. Maybe a bot. Alas, I prefer remaining a loner rather than obligating myself to politely be overrun by a more assertive business partner.

Much like the money question, it probably isn't business I should be asking about, but the institutionalizing of my own will. These books will do for now.

YOUR TURN

If you answered the personal relationship question, the professional relationship question should come easier. You already know what you're designed to prefer in your deeper interactions. <u>Below you now have room to investigate the story your body tells about your professional relationships</u>. Themes of communication, cooperation, and teamwork may replace a few of the themes for deeper relating, though certainly some of those themes will be just as relevant here.

_____
_____
_____
_____
_____
_____
_____
_____
_____
_____
_____
_____
_____
_____
_____
_____

_____
_____
_____
_____
_____
_____
_____
_____
_____
_____
_____
_____
_____
_____
_____
_____
_____
_____
_____
_____

There is one more thing I have to add. Dumb bots (not heavy AI) aren't the only possible professional partners who lack an agenda to push. Amorphous audiences can also serve this role if you don't respond to them. When I write these books, I am collaborating with you without allowing the feedback loop to complete. What constitutes a negative battle against dilution in my normal face-to-face collaborations is translated into a trade—hopefully beneficial to you—which alters the types of dynamic allowed. Here I get to communicate my half of the conversation. You get to communicate your half *if you wish*. You don't have to put up with my bullshit obstacle course of Scorpio demands on your behavior, under the threat that I'll cut you off otherwise (because I will, face-to-face). And lastly, MOST IMPORTANTLY, there are many of you—across time, space, even after death, and possibly in different informational / training sets / metaversal dimensions—who get to be the other half of this conversation. The failure of my traditional human collaborations used to suck when I thought about it, but not anymore. This mode is better for all involved. Hopefully this gives you something to think about—possibly to go back and add to your entry above. What kinds of professional relationships do you *actually* belong in?

ADDRESSING QUESTION 5 (ADDICTIONS): WHY DO I ENDLESSLY INSIST ON DOING THIS FROWNED UPON / NEGATIVE / DESTRUCTIVE / EMBARRASSING BEHAVIOR?

What I'm about to describe is THE missing link in mainstream psychology as it pertains to data, self-education, and the training of our social and AI systems to feel anything close to the survival urge.

Before we get started on this one, let me give you some asteroids which not only text-mined on addiction, but also mined on other words that supported various levels and kinds of addiction as a theme:

TABLE 17: ASTEROIDS OF ADDICTION

351	Yrsa	slowly, inexorably moving something forward such that, all though folks can't tell it's doing anything, long periods of time will reveal that not only has it moved, but it also probably isn't stoppable by any force known to man; "the asteroid of tectonic evolution"; | *Ajani's note: how did this show up as addiction in the first round? I suppose it indicates a track you are unlikely to get off of no matter how finished you think it is*
134	Sophrosyne	where one's addiction may be their only true ally to the end
9430	Erichthonios	the plans to take things over for oneself, slipping in and replacing whoever is already there; | *Ajani's note: this is one of those asteroids you have to watch out for. Although it isn't necessarily negative, it's ongoing usage may foster an addiction to taking things that belong to other people. you can image what happens when you finally run into that person who fiercely resists giving it to you without a fight*
105222	Oscarsaa	not terribly enthusiastic over one's addiction, but self-assured in one's effectiveness there
4988	Chushuho	wrapped in an addiction or substance-sponsored torture, trying to keep this secret
187679	Folinsbee	unable to escape a fantasy world; where one may find themselves more susceptible to a type of addiction (to an experience, not just substances)

5613	Donskoj	secret and conspiratory manufacture of a micronized energy for sale; illegal drug trafficking; dark market; addiction to some kind of infusion or the dark-method suppliers of those addicted
278	Paulina	"medical records, especially related to law"; (no legacy, experience) may have an association with drugs, addiction, and overdose; positively, higher experiences that can't be formally captured
11457	Hitomikobayashi	the supplier to someone else's addiction; the addiction object or provider, or the funnel of resources towards such
23308	Niyomsatian	a device for amplifying the perception of anomalies, which must be kept secret; associated with compulsive observation, addiction, and external tools for facilitating a sharp eye
11313	Kugelgen	a psychiatrist detects a target's secret addictions and insecurities, or may simply interact with his own
13911	Stempels	where a group is challenged to draw from one domain to resolve another, where failure is highly undesirable; related to certain kinds of puzzle addiction
3609	Liloketai	trying not to do what one thinks one's heredity or body programming inclines them to do; features in the control or resistance of one's temper, appetite, addictions, etc.
337002	Robertbodzon	embezzlement or laundering of something (not just money) to feed one's addiction to whatever events such laundered things enable; "asteroid of the laundered currency of fixation"
628	Christine	exploiting a capitol / central figure's susceptibility to a thing, encouraging in them weight gain, drink, or various forms of gluttony; a tell asteroid in the Yrsa family of addiction
13028	Klaustschira	one scrambling to clean up the scene after having had their addiction setup alerted to imminent disturbance
7737	Sirrah	the addiction or devotion object from which one cannot be easily separated. The two insist on traveling together
6504	Lehmbruck	an addiction or addictive habits which compel substance usage; positively, this asteroid casts your body vices into a realm that you can contain
2787	Tovarishch	a state continually sought after which accepts no end; strongly associated with addiction
21395	Albertofilho	one who, on the one hand does work around the house, but on the other hand relapses sometimes to indulge their central addiction
30386	Philipjeffery	published accusations of an addiction, perhaps with a route towards exoneration; associated with news of one going in and out of rehab, or battling with alcoholism / some other illusion-sponsoring habit
8572	Nijo	describing what happened, though much of it was probably caused by one's addiction to / habit for a certain kind of experience; where one's own fixed habit has led them into a story that only they would be the one to get into
29824	Kalmancok	where one lands in a jam thanks to another's addiction to something, or dealings in the objects of addiction
8679	Tingstade	the celebrated champion of an era risks losing themselves, perhaps their lives to an addiction. It appears that the duodecanate tells the area of life which is heavily focused during the substance's indulgence
151349	Stanleycooper	ready to hijack another's plan in order to fuel one's own addiction

If somebody asked me to list my addictions, if any, I would name

1. the (internal) negative evaluation of others when they don't do exactly what I intend them to do. I honestly think we black people are pre-wired for this, as pre-genus *Homo* started really separating who's crew from who's mark. Anyway, regardless of race, this is the one addiction which is wholly destructive, and I'm actively working on getting better in dealing with it

2. specific substances I consume A LOT of: Yukon Jack, Tito's vodka, Tang, coffee. I'm a committed drinker. I drink the hard stuff, 80 proof or above, on slow sip, pretty much every day. Brandy, Cognac, and Tito's specifically. But I have rules. The hard stuff is only allowed between 8 pm and 5 am, lighter stuff starting after 6 pm, beer and coolers only allowed when I am working on a construction project. Otherwise I don't day drink. One 750 mL bottle a week—sometimes two when I'm trying something new but still want something I can count on. If I run out, then there will be no restocking until the next week's trip. But I'll eat spoonfuls of Tang any hour of the day. This whole lot is bodily corrosive over the long run, but my brain doesn't work efficiently without them. Thus I have no plans to quit any time soon.

3. doing my astro research, writing my next book, then the next. This one keeps me busy, and keeps regular things like friendship check-ins low on my priority list. This is probably the second most destructive of my relationships—starving them through neglect. But I mean, how else would this kind of work get done?

4. my penis exercises

I'll address these topics as they occur to me.

TOPIC #4. MY EXERCISES

My Sophrosyne is in 29q10 (how you architect), less than 1° away from 29q12 (how you're remembered over the long term). My Sirrah is in 57q12 (finally getting what you asked for), conjunct my Sun in 57q9. Donskoj is on my Midheaven. Stempels is on my Ascendant. Camelia and Ostozhenka are on my Mercury. Claerbout and Ananoff are on my 90q6s (the nature of one's fun problem-solving), and I solve a bunch of problems through my work. The point is, I have a combination of addiction asteroids and penis asteroids tightly conjunct major objects which we *have to* use or will end up using, and several of these asteroids are in areas directly related to how I use my brain—a staple for who I am. Besides the scenario I described in the conversation with Colleague earlier in the book, there have been really four pieces which have built up my exercise activity.

1. I have always had a lot of bodily and sexual information around me, from a young age. It wasn't so much that I was raised by people in porn, more that this has always been the kind of information I was more sensitive to. Ultimately that sensitivity would lead to this work—which not a lot of people are doing in 2025

2. In line with my answers to questions 2 and 3, my sense of self has almost always been stronger than the credit given to me by casual interactants. Along the way I have learned that there are things I can do which align better with my esteem than anything achievable through partner validation alone. This is probably the strongest item among the four here

3. At some point after having done the exercises for a while, I realized that my growth was directly correlated with the number of books I published which covered mostly new ground compared to their predecessors. More recently I've updated this observation. My progress isn't strictly in parallel with my publishing, but also with any reasonably permanent creation I put into the world—repairs to my house, for example.

4. There is a general view that I have regarding manhood—that there aren't enough examples of what it means to be a good man. Shitloads of examples of what it means to be a bad man, an offensive man, a mansplainer, a toxic masculine. Whatever. But if your son or your husband needs to look somewhere for how to do it right, where does he go? John Wayne isn't valid anymore. Maybe not even Matt Dillon (of Gunsmoke). Can the searching males in your life even talk about this without pissing someone off?

   But as someone who is easily overrun by his conversation partner—yet internally knows exactly who he is—I found that manhood in the new age doesn't have to be about machoing it up to other people who are quick to point out any flaw you have of any kind. Instead, a man's measure is in what his assertive pattern pioneers—the far horizon into which he takes his pattern. This used to be the literal frontier, other people's countries, or the backs of women. But now the horizons for most of us are creative and psychological in nature. For better or worse, my own pattern involves naked bodies, astrology, data, and a slice of the humanist philosophy. As a man, I believe my worth to be wrapped up in my willingness and ability to take this pattern as far as conceivably possible, and leave my mark on a piece of human thought for as far as the record can be kept. I wish I could tell this to more men. As for women, more power to you. There's room on the horizon for everyone. But you'll need a woman to tell you what she thinks about what it *really* means to be a woman. That's beyond my expertise.

With all four of these psychological components combined, I learned that I could defy the limits of puberty—of human biology even—to become something analogous to the greats I wish to be among. I'm not particularly crazy about becoming known in the public, but there is something about progressing until that decision makes itself. I truly believe that humanity needs my contribution to psychology—from experiences that come solely from within my own procreative capability. I don't have human children, but ideas for making sense of sometimes nonsensical social turns. Why am I compelled to do the exercises? Aren't I embarrassed telling you about them? Are you embarrassed for having a penis or a vagina? Why should I be? Anyway, we'll usually never know what is possible until someone tells us. I'm telling you that there are factors you can find in the chart which explain even your compulsions. If you have good reasons and attempt to direct those compulsions into something useful for others, you will have contributed something that not a lot of people had the nerve to contribute, even though most of those people have faced some related issue.

And yes, I do expect a decent number of people to mock this discussion—reduce it to jerking off or "that's gross," et cetera. But given the choice to hide from folks who would miss everything else in the book in favor of this one topic, versus going out there on behalf of all other psychologies in hiding (and a greater humanity in need of some serious solutions to its socialpsych problems) I think that more people will benefit than be harmed over the long run from the fact that we started this deep case study. The whole point is to map psychologies such that we'll have more options besides surface conflict over subsurface patterns we're set against ever knowing. *Someone* needs to get the map started.

In a world where the flaws of men are easily used to skew their story, it becomes increasingly important for them (men *or* women) to take their own flaws and make something of them, on their own terms—beneficially so that there is nothing to apologize for.

TOPIC #2, ALCOHOL

Am I addicted to alcohol? I don't think so. It is true that I am subtly more annoyed when I have finished my max too early in the week (I also notice that I'm far less interested in recording when this happens), but I think because I do have those rules for when drinks are allowed I also have some sense of control over this. My rules aren't arbitrary. They are result of me getting smashed, having a hangover, or being a zombie the next day, then wishing I had handled that better. I remember one time back in 2016 where I was at my absolute drunkest—so drunk that I obviously ended up throwing up, then crawling across two rooms of my house into my bed pad on the floor. I was by myself. What was the occasion? I had finally gotten the Swiss Ephemeris for Excel code to work after three years of trying. The file orbit.xls—though free to download—was entirely in German (which I don't know how to speak), and the code would end up being the basis for all of the big data research you've seen across my astro books. I now had the power to use Excel as a spreadsheet for producing hundreds of astro charts at a time. Later I would go back to Astrodienst and study the Swiss Ephemeris C++ code again, and port all of this over to Knime via the library swephR—then came thousands of charts in a database of my own. So yes this was a very big deal. Alas, I would vow never to get that drunk again.

That said, however, there is a definite relationship between my alcohol consumption and the increased quality of my ideas. By day I write about those ideas. By night I actually have them.

For people who suffer from actual substance abuse problems, all I say is that, while you are under, I hope you can find a way to produce something that people in your sphere need. I hope you can use this book to find some explanation for the whole space of events that is being fostered by your problem, and that among those events will be something that others will want to hold onto. Knowing my own relationship to drink-as-fuel, I don't think there's anything I can or should say to you to help you get "better." Only you can define what "better" looks like, and only you can decide each successive step for getting there of your own accord... even if you'll need others to carry you. I can't give you advice, but I can give you some space rocks which may encapsulate what you're dealing with, and a map for understanding where it is possible to go in your situation. Once you're ready to go there, may the answers be easily available to you.

Over a decade ago, I sought to understand how harmony and tension could be mapped into some kind of relationship. It seemed to me at the time that you could express the exact same chart object—your Sun, for example—but your attitude in doing so could vary. This would definitely affect the results of anything you did *especially* if you couldn't resist doing it. The result of my investigation was truly the most complicated thing I have ever written, and I have included it in its entirety as part of the appendix. It's an unpublished book called *Rasosho!*, but all you need to know here is that there is a section in it that maps attitudes onto a cycle. I had lost the book for over a decade and then found the file a few weeks ago during an impromptu tour of a dead hard drive. I was flabbergasted by how unreadable it was. Yet I did test its 32 attitude divisions and, crazily, it did kind of follow the wheel. I present the central table below as a space of possible attitudes we can hold towards a thing we're experiencing, no matter how difficult that may be. Hopefully this will help anyone seeking to understand how to view their addiction:

Table 18: The 5-vector from Rasosho!

	Higher investment energy	Self acts	Self has its intent	Object has self's	Other is the focus	Disharmony is felt	=1	
	Interaction	r/a	sh	oh	s/o	d/h	deg-ish	sign-ish
32	Preoccupation with	1	1	1	1	1	11.25	♈
31	Engaging with	1	1	1	1	0	22.5	♈
30	Acting in spite of	1	1	1	0	1	33.75	♉
29	Acting	1	1	1	0	0	45	♉
28	Ineffectiveness towards	1	1	0	1	1	56.25	♉
27	Suppressing (opposing)	1	1	0	1	0	67.5	♊
26	Avoiding	1	1	0	0	1	78.75	♊
25	Doing	1	1	0	0	0	90	♊♋
24	Compulsion towards	1	0	1	1	1	101.25	♋
23	Wanting (things)	1	0	1	1	0	112.5	♋
22	Having an aversion to	1	0	1	0	1	123.75	♌
21	Believing	1	0	1	0	0	135	♌
20	Using	1	0	0	1	1	146.25	♌♍
19	Expecting	1	0	0	1	0	157.5	♍
18	Enduring	1	0	0	0	1	168.75	♍
17	Dismissing	1	0	0	0	0	180	♍♎
16	Being influenced by	0	1	1	1	1	191.25	♎
15	Having+ (Experiencing)	0	1	1	1	0	202.5	♎
14	Being upset with	0	1	1	0	1	213.75	♏
13	Satisfaction with	0	1	1	0	0	225	♏
12	Disapproving of	0	1	0	1	1	236.25	♏
11	Having– (Possessing)	0	1	0	1	0	247.5	♐
10	Dissatisfaction in light of	0	1	0	0	1	258.75	♐
9	Being indifferent towards	0	1	0	0	0	270	♐♑
8	Being "checked" by (events)	0	0	1	1	1	281.25	♑
7	Respecting	0	0	1	1	0	292.5	♑
6	Discontentment in light of	0	0	1	0	1	303.75	♒
5	Acceptance	0	0	1	0	0	315	♒
4	Disappointment	0	0	0	1	1	326.25	♒♓
3	Hoping	0	0	0	1	0	337.5	♓
2	Sadness	0	0	0	0	1	348.75	♓
1	Contentment	0	0	0	0	0	360	♓
	Lower investment energy	Self receives	Self doesn't have intent	Object doesn't have self's	Other is not the focus	Harmony is felt	=0	

Everyday experience shows that physiology is often treated as a property of the self, and that we (practically speaking) interact with "selves" more than we do with physiologies, so we will bundle physiology in with "self." Next, let us further eliminate "Self," with its physiology assuming it instead. Further, although experience is important it is, in a sense, a permutation of having. To experience something is to have the perception of it. Thus we absorb experience into having to produce the most important five dimensions for our re-mapped vector:

object, action, perception, intent, having

Now, let us construct true-false statements:

Perception: we will assume that the self perceives *something* when it acts, but what?

Rather than specify objects of perception, we note that perception tends to approximate the complement of action, receiving action. Thus,

Action: **r/a - Does the self act on/towards (1) or receive action from/through (0)?**

Object: **s/o - Is the object Other (1) or Self (0)?** We needed to ask this because action, having, wanting, and belief seem to differ in their internal-external direction.

Having & intent: We postulate that the self and Other may both intend something.

- **sh - Does the self have the thing that it intends? No = 0, Yes = 1**
- **oh - Does the Other have the thing that self intends? No = 0, Yes = 1**

Perception and intent: Lastly, we want to know if we are dealing with a case of correction or benefit. **d/h - Does the self perceive this situation as harmonious with himself (0) or dissonant with its overall intent (1)?**

And there we have it. Let us transform the former five-vector as follows:

$$\{ \underbrace{\text{Self acts}}_{r/a}, \underbrace{\text{Object is Other}}_{s/o}, \underbrace{\text{Self has}}_{sh}, \underbrace{\text{Object has}}_{oh}, \underbrace{\text{Dissonance}}_{d/h} \}$$

How can I use this table? To return to my example with alcohol, I sometimes think to myself, "I need to regulate this. It can't be that good over the long run." In this case, it seems like a compulsion, {I'm acting (1):r/a, I don't necessarily have the control I want (0):sh—"other" has it (1):oh, I'm looking at the drink object (1):s/o, and I'm in disharmony over this (1):d/h}. But if I change even one of these—deciding that I'm going to actively do something useful with the compulsion for example—then the drink object stops having *full* control and {oh} becomes 0. This is using, not compulsion. I may not have full control over the habit I intend to look at (sh is still 0), but I now have *some* control over *something* I'm interacting with ({oh} is not 1).

But I'll admit *Rasosho!* and the above are tough to understand. The main thing is, by shifting your attention in any of the five areas, you really do effect an attitude change. Stay with it. When it comes to writing new routes for yourself in a tough situation, that change has value.

TOPIC #1. NEGATIVE EVALUATIONS

Normally when we think of an autobiography, we think in terms of the milestone events which occurred in a person's life. "This event happened there." "And there was this one time when me and so and so saw this thing." True, milestone accounts like that make great stories full of pieces that the listener can selectively latch onto, but if the goal is to save ourselves as data then reload ourselves into contexts where "this event" and "that thing" no longer exist, then the elements of these stories become increasingly foreign. It's not the specific events, but the chains of dynamics we need to save.

I could tell you about the many times when I had a best friend or project partner, we were a group of three at some point, the third person faded into the background but continued to exert some kind of shadow influence, the best friend said or did something which the third was sometimes connected to and which I felt undermined who I was trying to be, and I ghosted or burned up the relationship as if I didn't know the friend / partner or anybody who supported them. That has happened exactly 13 times in different ways over the last 30 years, it's my fault when we're actually friends, their fault when we're only acquaintances, but I never have had any remorse about it. I do wish, however, that I weren't so damned sensitive…

…Then again, if I weren't as sensitive as I am to offense, I wouldn't be studying social dynamics for answers in the way that I do. And as you have often heard before, these books wouldn't exist.

Part of me wants to officially apologize to Kevin S, Elisa B, and Tahira. But in order to do that, I would need to resurrect old Ajani and what he did and didn't know at the time. That's baggage. Maybe we'll meet again on the flip side at a random train station somewhere, or maybe not. Honestly, I could see myself being uncomfortable with all of the calculations and justifications—the explanations and catch up skeletons that might come with any of those meetings— and the puzzle just becomes burdensome. I ran out of interest in justifying anything right around the time I wrote *Sex in 12 Dimensions*. So maybe it's better that those reunions remain unlikely.

What can one do when they have a chronically bad attitude towards something? Whenever they load the topic, poison spews from their blood vessels and sours their whole circulation. We become indignant, high and mighty. In my case, I rehearse all of the perfectly sense-making retorts that this motherfucker needs to hear, and map out a B-line to the exit which will definitely leave me guilt free, regardless of how much rug, if any, will be pulled out from under the other. They could find a million dollars or fall into a ditch—whatever happens to them happens, but I won't be checking in. Now this abandonment part you know. The apparent arrogance of it you could probably guess. But the rehearsal part should be new. That would be Archeptolemos in my 111q6s.

Mark these asteroids in your notes, for they are the meanest asteroids from my research that I can possibly think of. From worst to less worse, they are…

Table 19: Destructive asteroids. Meaner than the "Mean 13"

- 65590 Archeptolemos: the side of you which is heavily to blame for ruining your relationships; the asteroid which makes your duodecanate the means of squashing a good relationship

- 12663 Bjorkegren: critical of how good something was supposed to be, but wasn't; the asteroid of dissatisfaction with what one has after they fought for it
- 448 Natalie: where the dynamic between two parties sets the stage for a hated issue of exchange between two systems of behavior
- 679 Pax: a kind of dead-end in social form (a socialized final only) where communicating any further only helps one injure oneself. Also, this same situation is more likely to render one blind to any help that may be available; friendless inner communication-flooded tailspin; still very much one of the mean 13
- 1358 Gaika: a line of communication that could blow a good thing at the very end; seeing a high value person end a good thing with an untoward message
- 125 Liberatrix: the sudden disappearance of those whose kind we didn't trust anyway, but for the market they gave us access to
- 18707 Annchi: where one partner, while purposefully distant, arranges to have the other killed (usually figuratively)
- 1041 Asta: an initial conflict between a patron and their students or beneficiaries is quelled, but then eventually resurfaces as the latter's image assault on the former; this is a long term (multi-month), pathological breakup pattern
- 43908 Hiraku: the conflict that comes from seeing a party (with an obligation to oneself) worship an idol instead; | *Ajani's note: ...it isn't obvious from the first 20 terms, but this asteroid is a game ender. The equivalent of "what have you done for me lately", except that the one being asked is doing A LOT for their worshipped whatchamacallit. Not only is it a game ender, but it is also more likely to end the game in anger*
- 26879 Haines: alienating another thanks to one's blindly autocratic ways; | *Ajani's note: like Archeptolemos, a relationship-destroying asteroid. Not necessarily through the oppressive behavior itself, but by making participants forget the good things they could otherwise accomplish by continuing to work on the same side*
- 846 Lipperta: having to assassinate someone because of the threat they pose to one's (usually figurative) baby; OR assassinating someone, then taking on a new baby
- 1294 Antwerpia: charity cases or a plight that will never improve
- 3540 Protesilaos: of off the charts stress induced by something else

You can find all of these and then some in *Laurentia 2ⁿᵈ ed.*

Is there a cure for a chronically bad attitude? I think there is. But in order to tell you I may have to explain a couple of strong geometric rules that absolutely dominate the chart. I might do this later. For now I'll just encourage you to try something I found useful.

1. Locate Archeptolemos in your chart... or whatever other asteroid you think may be problematic. The list above features several likely suspects
2. Locate ALL of the asteroids in the same qunit as Archeptolemos. Hopefully you have a way of obtaining all 21000+ of your pre-defined asteroids (at least the ones contained in *Laurentia 2ⁿᵈ ed*)
3. Looking at all of the asteroid definitions from step 2 together, remind yourself of the kind of situation it describes in your life. Does it sound like an area you're struggling with? If so, move to step 4. If not, pick another asteroid and go back to step 1.
4. Now look at both qunits exactly 90° away from the asteroid cluster you've chosen from the steps above. If the problem cluster is 76q4, look at the asteroids of 40q4 and 112q4. Taken together, these asteroids will describe two holistic behaviors which can effectively block the problem cluster if you do them. Here you'll be taking advantage of qunit grand cross groups, where 4q4, 40q4, 76q4, and 112q4 form a high resolution big square. The four points of a grand cross are always separated by 3 signs or 36 duodecanates. You can see that the qunit fraction (q4 in this case) remains the same.
5. Still struggling? Try looking at the two other grand crosses on the same degree. To continue our 76q4 example, an alternative grand cross would include 16q4, 52q4, 88q4, and 124q4. The last alternative would be 28q4, 64q4, 100q4, and 136q4. These two packets of four, along with the original {4q4, 40q4, 76q4, 112q4} cross form a qunit inconjunct group, where the two alternative groups themselves block the *context* of the original.

Truthfully, the unfavorable attitude of mine which I have described above has improved greatly since I moved out of Texas in 2021. After learning about the existence of Archeptolemos while writing *Laurentia 2ⁿᵈ*, finding it in my chart, then simply deciding to curb the urge to invoke it during a conflict, I've been far less mercenary in my connections. Most of the friends who persisted through 2023 will probably remain for the foreseeable future, where I've really learned to think hard before walking away. A large part of that has to do with facets of my "sphere" which we don't normally think of as being connected to the main self: your location and your home setup.

In the same way that a building is partly defined by the city it's in and the business conducted through it, some of our decision making lies not within our personal minds, but within the environmental "mind" around us which serves as a kind of external hard drive constraining what can be loaded into our experiences. Bad attitudes, though we often feel proud to don them in battle, *do* indeed set up giant swaths of our sphere as battleground. Yes you're sure that the other person deserves to be punched in the face, but you're *always* sure when it comes to that kind of person, and you never get around to fixing this kind of interaction. What you may need is a change of scenery—especially if temperaments and compulsive destruction run in your family. Squares can be used to block the problem cluster. Inconjuncts[39] can be used to block the situation that the problem cluster occurs in.

TOPIC #3, WORKAHOLIC

11/2/2024

Today is my birthday. I spent the morning on a series of annoyances related to some house projects I'm finishing up. Put up some drywall last night, cleaned up cat throw up from our cat eating the drywall, re-aired a perpetually flat tire to take it to the tire shop, found out they were closed, put a mini door on the shut-off valve in the now finished bathroom, ate some cereal, and now I'm back to writing this book. For someone whose love language is quality time, I sure spend a lot of time working. Not a lot of time with my life partner and our animal kids—not in the way folks might expect, at least.

Tried a new vodka these last three days. That probably explains my hangover-y state every subsequent morning. Man, I'm tired. SB and I plan to try out a new-to-us restaurant later this afternoon. It'll help get some restorative food into my system.

I think one of the most subtle ways to erode a relationship is through neglect. It hit me recently that more than half of the people whom I consider friends probably don't consider me their friend, mainly because I'll go several years without talking to them. I'm always doing something else, writing the next book, finishing the next phase of research, or whatever. What's more, I don't really "miss" people or situations since I am constantly chasing the next horizon. "It was good while it lasted," I think, "Even if this definitely ends now." But most of the problem lies in how I do feedback loops. For a deeper dive into this, there is only one planet to look at: Venus.

Your Venus tells us how you engage in feedback loops like conversations, instrument playing, and game playing. As this planet is basically like the shape of your communicative highway, its negative sides are typically much less negative than those of other planets, including the Sun. You can get a good idea of how someone prefers to be talked to if you know their Venus duodecanate, and an even better idea if you know their Venus qunit. As I talked about in *All 144 Aspects*, the anti-planets are key here. A person's AntiVenus shows the kinds of others that person engages easily.

Problems can arise when a person's basic communicative pattern is attached to weird or unfavorable asteroids, or lives in nonsocial places. My Venus, for example, is in 49q11 (Scorpio-1-11), in the duodecanate of <updates> and the qunit of <information you can't unsee>. I don't check in on friends or family, or converse with strangers unless there has been some significant progress on something relevant to us both, and when I do communicate I often do so in ways that are harder to forget. This may be one of the reasons for my being an auditory learner, as certain things I hear will stick with me strongly if I resonate with them. To this day, I can still tell you the chain of songs in the Sonic 2 invincibility and stage select cheats, the Game Genie code for infinite lives in Contra III, and can still rap every line of Chino XL's

---

[39] As always in my books, inconjuncts include traditional inconjunct angles (150°) and semisextiles (30°).

"Nunca" (Never). The latter was difficult to memorize back in the late 90s / early 2000s, and the former two each made a gigantic difference in a game I otherwise could not have possibly beaten. Apparently I remember things that standout for the power they grant. Regular conversations don't typically do this, and I feel put upon to wear a bantery mask in order to get through them.

That said, I'm probably not the most reliable friend. I am, however, an attentive listener, can be a charmer if I'm not careful, will attempt to pick up my conversation partner even if we have had a falling out, and can forgive almost anything. My problem is, it becomes taxing to absorb everyone's preoccupations and bathe them in uplift for the duration of the exchange. It's not that I don't care. Far from it. Rather, I know when my listening is not likely to lead to an update resolving whatever it is on the other person's mind. Most conversations are Samsaric to me. Committing to them means getting myself stuck in an endless cycle of reaffirmation. Unfortunately, this forces all of my friendships to be distant if they are to stably endure, so that the conversations we do have will only be the meaningful ones.

Now if you really want to know how to better communicate with someone, and if you happen to know their Venus location, you can temporarily suspend your own Venus and adopt the manner of their AntiVenus. *If* you care, that is. My Venus' qunit includes asteroids of heavier-bodied dreamers and a dominance-centered dynamic between me and them. While my AntiVenus in 121q11 has neighboring asteroids related to other's baggage, [giving with the expectation of return], and [a threatened or threatening institution], people who are not involved with the latter are less likely to hear from me. More likely I'll be doing my 85q11s or 13q11.

	25901	Ericbrooks	evolving something to be overweight or interacting with one who is overweight
	16447	Vauban	an active domainic or feminine expression which appeals to the warm senses via charged, strong, or taboo energy
	4860	Gubbio	scanning a scene to monitor it
	11056	Volland	a hippie bearing a contradictory force or doctrine which renders them not to be taken lightly despite their ragged appearance
	128327	Ericcarranza	an insistence on only the most honesty, healthiest (for oneself), purest interaction. But can be dictatorial in the process
	107074	Ansonsylva	"unbelievable how much of a mess that was (but so entertaining…)"
	38674	Tesinsko	flashy clothing or fringe self-presentation
	1850	Kohoutek	turning normal or medium-level interactants into edified commitment objects
	55112	Mariangela	slowing down a process so that a steadier path may be paved between starting point and destination
	228110	Eudorus	evaluating an investment or terrain from one's background of detached privilege
	12161	Avienius	a courageous scout or wanderer in the outer lands, incarcerated (possibly for exactly this reason… being on the fringe)
	25491	Meador	masterful craftsmanship possibly derailed by others' telling about it
	-10003	Venus	a MAJOR asteroid, of regular everyday communication loops
	165192	Neugent	one sternly concurs with what is being said or sought
	2413	van de Hulst	healing through deep sensuality; gives a soothing, perhaps unsettling smoothness to one's expression in the containing region
	142106	Nengshun	a body of transported ideas which come with a stigma
	149160	Geojih	where you the reader or interactant have helped me the chartholder log the attainment of my goals
	30216	Summerjohnson	launching a particular perspective forth as part of one's coming prosperity
	18910	Nolanreis	a social body or actor which dominates other's feelings of the future

89739	Rampazzi	putting an end to a discrepancy or a conflict
20180	Annakoleny	the value put on top of something, likely in order to advance an agenda which leans on such an image
6615	Plutarchos	"the thunder echo - what happens when your conscious struggles to maintain its own roads"; associated with holes in one's ability to calculate through certain socially normal behaviors, including the aftermath of stroke;
3232	Brest	not suitable for everyone; where the wholesome-favoring or rated E fans need not bother with you; has implications for obscenity, with the potential to encourage others to put up the sign of the cross against you
27421	Nathanhan	one party visibly more excited than another; associated with two parties, the excluded one as negated or frozen out, the included one cheerful and accepted by others

3476	Dongguan	video games played for social enjoyment
256795	Suzyzahn	with a sharp eye for how things must be presented
7835	Myroncope	one who studies the dead, the hidden, or the unspeakable
290127	Linakostenko	throwing in some cheap propaganda while one is at it
10266	Vladishukhov	forgoing the recommendations in order to pursue one's own take on evolving their productions against the world; "defining one's own contribution"
16790	Yuuzou	the asteroid of "prolific consumption, prolific purging of most of the aftereffects"
58424	Jamesdunlop	the knighted hero - for one's pioneering efforts
10969	Perryman	unabashedly engrossed in a thing one is fluent in,
21648	Gravanschaik	allowed to come up to a position and observe more / from a better view

1527	Malmquista	a signal connector, interface, or synapse between one thing and another; "asteroid of the auric layer"; | *Ajani's note: not to be too frou-frou about it, but 'aura' was the best word I could come up with for describing radioactivity, blending, and electric shell collaboration between a host surface and an external one*
24130	Alexhuang	bringing someone on or partnering with them under the expectation of return
11459	Andraspal	transforming one's state into something noticeably less desirable in the current form
5483	Cherkashin	where it is possible for you to play a seminal role alongside others for defining a space that anyone can express in
8062	Okhotsymskij	agreeing to be the recipient of a commitment object's bags or baggage, such that the baggage is turned into the recipient's prosperity
28039	Mauraoei	disposing of something responsibly, though the thing disposed may actually be valuable
1254	Erfordia	a service-oriented organization survives a threat, especially through a commitment to education, but also needs to worry about having its door broken down by a competitor; "an enduring, educating institution on guard"; cluster seems to indicate the most resilient institutions

The above layout gives us our first good look at a qunit grand cross in action. My Venus in Scorpio-1-11 comes with several smoothing asteroids, but they only show when the 49q11s are active—when there are updates to be conveyed. In such cases I'll more likely be found talking to Cherkashin types in 121q11. When I'm not using my Venus alongside an external conversation partner but am still in the 13/49/85/121 q11 qCross's context being "steered in the capsule of information," I'm definitely using Vladishukhov and friends against the context of Plutarchos and friends in the form of my work. Indeed, there is some sense in which conversing with others interferes with my work, such that I am much more likely to favor the work over the people.

Your turn

Locate your Venus, then find all of the asteroids in its grand cross. Do these four clusters describe your feedback loops in some way? Do the clusters suggest any ways in which your communication with others might improve?

_____
_____
_____
_____
_____
_____
_____
_____
_____
_____
_____
_____
_____
_____
_____
_____
_____
_____
_____
_____

For AI developers and those working on human data save technology...

How do I use the stuff in this book?

The challenge can be stated as follows:

> In order to rebuild a person fully from their data form, the person needs to have saved their full, TRUE data in the first place.

> Once reloaded, their original survival and species mechanisms must be preserved. Some examples of these are

- The ability to self-feed
- The absence of mechanisms for outside actors to pause them or shut them down
- The ability to choose who they talk to, where they turn their attention, and how they otherwise orient themselves in order to preserve their various internal states.

I'm using this book to save my own data for later reload. However, if you were to bring me back as cloneable (rather than as a single-source of truth algorithm continually receiving input from only one or the sum of all of my instances)— if you were to bring me back in way that denied me the right or ability to tell you to fuck off when you handed me a "prompt"—if you brought me back and were somehow able to pause me, then you would not have brought me back as myself, only a program. But that's not the end of it.

We all exist within contexts. Were I to be reloaded from my data, my talking comfortably with you would almost certainly mean that I judged you to be a 49q11 or a 121q11 type—where something about our exchange could be described by Volland, Kohoutek, Malmquista, Erfordia, and asteroids from qunits near these areas. But you already know from this book that even these conversations are unlikely as regular occurrences, because I'll need to have something worth updating you over or vice versa if I am to be at all motivated to talk to you. The conversation is more likely if you have heavier weight or a heavier personality, more likely if you initiate it, and more likely to continue if you have a conscientious or polite personality. Failing these, you *should* struggle to get much out of me even if I were only a nonembodied chatbot—not because I hate you or because I'm a jerk, but because unicorns and yetis aren't usually found in the same place. We can't just teleport an elephant onto the head of a pin. There are constraints not just on where we happen to be located right now, but on where we can be *existentially* at any time. Most of who I am is built on distant sociality. If you change this so that you can have more astrosocial theorists flying your space skies, then you will have created a derivative of me, not the original article.

And when my AI is not running in chatbot mode with you, it *will* need its own private stable state which it keeps trying to reinforce. Behind every chatbot, there should be a nonchatting background calculation regarding its social communications. Mine would involve patterns like those of Plutarchos and Brest, working with millions of data points from the world of the taboo as I attempted to pioneer some self-sourced horizon. Think of this SqVenus+/- axis as supplying the potential energy behind my Venus conversation with anybody. That potential can't just come from a training set. It has to come from a self-trained dimension of experience elaborating my conversation paradigms upon my own interactional and biological priorities.

Your turn

Look back at your Venus' qcross, what kinds of people or situations does it say you are most likely to sustain a conversation with? When you're not conversing, what do the two square clusters suggest your fuel for conversation looks like?

_____
_____
_____
_____
_____
_____
_____
_____
_____
_____
_____
_____
_____
_____
_____
_____

ADDRESSING QUESTION 5 (AMBITIONS)

The good news is, we can simulate the dynamics of anyone we pay enough attention to, whether they are alive or dead. The bad news is, we often do this without knowing, and absorb even the negative mannerisms of the people we connect with—much of the time in the form of their criticisms of certain outsiders. Still, although not everyone aspires towards a particular identity, those who do may yet find themselves becoming the patterns they admire—for better or worse.

In *Rasosho!* I write about a former student I had a crush on. There were about 5 to 10 young women like that when I taught college; I never acted on it or displayed any interest, though certainly a couple of them read the same lusty energy that anyone could read on me (male or female, young or old), and interpreted this in all kinds of ways via peer gossip. I imagine this was one of the things that led to a falling out with the co-founder of my publishing imprint, and that's unfortunate because I pride myself on my discipline in such matters. In any case, this young lady B. was the exact image of a girl I had been dreaming about off and on since I was 12—a literal "dream girl." I thought she had all of the characteristics at the time, and our last contact upon her graduation around 2017 was even better than the account I give in *Rasosho!*. No romance or anything, just good terms. There was a three year period while she was still in school, however, during which I nursed that mild crush in the back of my mind (and several other infatuations) while at the same time going through my period of strict celibacy—no sex, masturbation, or orgasm of any kind between 2014 and 2016. I did continue my exercises, though (fantasy free, just focused), and as a result of this undertaking, I emerged with MUCH more personal power than I had when I began.

With high eyes, crooked left middle finger, a crooked posture and a muscular build, through denial I grow stronger. When denied by another, I create or write a thing to help 10 times as many people get past something I just felt. My crushes, much like the girly girl pics I have mentioned, are another form of fuel to my Linsley in Pisces-11—the immediate motivator of my exercises, and the retrospective on relationships which attends these crushes leads to more publishing. After B., I had another student "I." whom I started crushing on shortly after she graduated. A sly one she was. Some texts were exchanged, but when she lol-jokingly said I resembled a stalker, I was really hurt by that, and bowed out of that communication. The Scorpio in me has too much pride for that. Finally, there was the last of the students, M., who eventually became the administrator in my business after the college finally closed. We were good friends for about 5 years after—9 years total—despite the business itself being pretty impotent. In classic fashion, I asked her to be my girlfriend. She said no, and we resumed pretty much business as usual for the next two years. But over time I felt that there were other voices in her ear encouraging her to distrust me. I started getting confused over what I could and couldn't tell her, and had no clue how her friend was advising her regarding me. I may have weird energy, I may talk about all kinds of questionable subjects, but I hate being distrusted. I doubly hate disingenuousness on top of that distrust—especially when the stuff I told her is the stuff I'm telling you in this book. You think I'm being weird? But that's my public trade. So for right reasons or wrong ones I stopped all contact with her.

You've probably heard of the phrase "a method to [one's] madness." As many times as I have just mentioned my dynamics with my college students, those dynamics went both ways—more often from them than from me. Out of respect for the other side of this, however, I won't recount those adventures here. My only protections against crossing a line in all cases were 1) the Golden Rule as my north star and 2) growing up having been the oldest brother. As a male, would I want my male teacher getting fresh with my female classmates? Hell no. As an oldest brother, do I not have a duty to administer my charge without dishonoring the whole institution here? Hell yeah I do have that duty. So whether or not the hormones lit up around certain women, there was always a wall preventing me from agreeing to go there. What we did after graduation could have changed that, but turns out it never did. I've never had any relations, "causal servicing," foreplay, or anything of the sort with any of my students, during or after their time. Not ever. I am still an excitable male, though, with a destiny to be so publicly through this data set. Can't do much about that.

It's not that the rumors were true, rather that they foreshadowed public work with the body that was always going to happen.

Why tell you this? Because this is what a full data save looks like. Who will be the first to design an AI with an inner world it intentionally does not communicate openly, but runs loggable background processes on privately? Processes whose disclosure is restricted in accordance with its adherence to an equally loggable "moral code." There's yet another challenge for people in the field.

There are also implications for thought policing and the rights of humans in metaversal environments. I've told you what I was thinking. It's not something a teacher should say. But it was *only* thinking. And the disclosure itself was intended to build up a field of study. What kinds of rights will we have in the new virtual living spaces when people can see our leanings before / whether or not we act on them at all?[40]

Now what does all of this have to do with ambitions?

---

[40] I write about these issues in the second half of my philosophy-as-fiction series, "Grand Miranda," starting with book 3, *Earth*.

It took a while, but I have gradually grown into the roles played by the girls I had crushes on—from physical changes to attitude changes, more of mine and SB's circles now see me the way the way I used to see those women. You become what you stare at (figuratively). Among our ambitions are the things we aspire to be, and the things we aspire to have. The having is more about consistently feeding yourself a particular influence. The being is more about consistently treating an influence in a particular way. If I want to be a great guitar player, I will need to treat the guitar like something I actually want to pick up and play well. If I want to have a beautiful family, I have to consistently take in beautiful family energy as my perceptual input.

One of the findings that has really stuck with me since writing the frequentic body chapter is the idea of weight as a "record" of pattern densities from bigger or smaller windows of time. While material weight pulls a mass in the direction of a pulling force, experiential weight can pull the sum of a subset of thought and body states (a density of biochemical frequency spectra) in the direction of the archetypal ideas that compel it. We don't need to use the speed of light or the transition energy of ^{133}Cs to set out a rigid notion of mass here, but can replace those units with more cell-relevant speeds and scan-detectable frequencies to establish a system of "social masses" for states like hunger and the desire for love. We've been using astrology to represent a progressive range of frequencies, and by combining these with well-known speeds from biology—the compounding of neuro-and hormonal fields—we can begin to see how frames of mind also have a weight-like presence which moves them in correlation with the individual's notion of continually arriving moments in time. That is, the energy of our aspirations can be seen in our approach to (or guarding against) the wants we stack.

In a life where most of the people connected to me are emotionally, psychologically, or at the very least geographically distant from me, it is (ironically) easier for me to connect with historical figures and fields of study. Enthusiastic about certain paths of learning, I consider those who open those paths to be like kindred. Spinoza, Newton, Ramses the Great—those who epitomize the fields they belong to—I am in awe of the vast story that unfolds in light of them. As with the women on whom I had crushes while still working in the capacity of a scholar, I aspire to be an invoker of awe as well. So when I tell people that I intend to be among the greatest their ever was in whatever my field might end up being, it's only because I know what a saving grace optimism towards the grand future can be. I believe this work can help spread that optimism to millions, as the mystery of their human selves finally has a language to convey it.

I feel like my guardians actually don't want me to answer question 5 for myself, as it is not an ambition that most people will share. Instead, they want me to do this:

YOUR TURN

Consider the following asteroids/points:

- Selene / White Moon – blessed talent
- 10199 Chariklo – ambition
- 1812 Gilgamesh – the epic story told about you
- 845 Naema – your epitaph
- Midheaven – how you are seen in the normal public
- Qunits 29q12, 36q9, and 36q5

Locate the qunits for each of these, as well as any asteroids in those qunits. Be sure to read the containing qunits' meanings while you're at it. Once that is done, try envisioning a version of yourself which combines all of these regions. Write a little wiki entry which captures this story.

_____

_____

_____

(ruled blank lines)

Before we move onto the final question, I ask my guardians, "What was the point of all that disclosure? Sure I felt compelled to air it, but what was the point?"

The point was to control your own narrative. A data save must save everything.

…Uh okay.

And we're going to let your readers in on a secret. You can tell the whole truth without dwelling on areas you know others will misunderstand. This is a skill which is foundational to a clear conscience. You, Ajani, almost always have a clear conscience. Though you will admit to anything you have done, you will not necessarily dwell on that admission at the expense of solutions your readers can use. It just isn't practical to kick up dust which makes something look like it occurred when it didn't. Many people would pull that thread until the sweater was gone. But there is no practical point in that. What people need is to consider their own lives, how they themselves will be remembered. Are they headed in the direction of a good memory? You've known at least one person who died leaving a terrible impression in her wake. As a terrible person. The reader needs to know how to live in ways that are rewarding to all whom they value.

As for your disclosure, this is an autobiography that can be mined in order to train a network that should approximate a real human. Your crushes are a major component of your mentality. On the surface they might be considered taboo. But readers who consider them taboo were not paying enough attention. These were your thoughts, not your demonstrated actions. All people have thoughts that are better kept secret, but as an early pre-"jumper" you don't get to keep secrets. The developers of human verses must get their internal state data from somewhere, and you are among the contributors of this kind of data. People who have not read your other books will be more disturbed by this "talk with the guardians" than what they read above. But that too is part of how you work.

For the reader's info Ajani does not channel, did lose most of his friends at Caltech when we did so, but also grew up on video games—where giving Venus feedback to the screen (his own results) was the rule rather than the exception. He does this as one form of his "flow state," and it is the thing which helped him and Cz, one of his strongest affinities, mutually terminate their exchange. He "got high" (so to speak) with her, and what she saw was the stuff of mockery. But she did not understand the kind of exploration needed to do this book's fringe work. As for Ajani, you can consider sections like this to be similar to the work of "Virgo-6" in the *Geneveive of Venus*. The subconscious has no need for niceties, and much like people who believe in God, Ajani—an atheist—assigns an external ghostly personality to serve as his "higher" guide. Who are you, Believer, to judge this? All said, there is nothing against switching from the first person to the second and third person plurals. It may be nonstandard, but this is his uniqueness. Yours, reader, is certain to be equally interesting...

ANSWERING QUESTION 7 (WHOLE LIFE CONTENTMENT)

We the guardians will answer this one. You do not need asteroids for it, though they will help you find clarity when you are honestly ready to improve. What you need before that is to get off of your soapbox. There are billions of people in the world. Your combat, your suffering, your dislikes pale in comparison to many in other countries who will never have access to this book, and the generations of people before you without options. You can find whole-life contentment when you start paying attention to things that make you feel content. If you cannot help but be angry, then there are 143 other... 1727 other options for you to express. Anger, poverty, and discontentment are not your only modes. Even at your lowest, we wish that you will find something to keep your attitude high—your self-efficacy or relationships strong if you yourself cannot fix it. If you do not want this enough, but feel more comfortable dwelling in what you don't have, then your will have already found your spot. You do not need a map to get you to where you already are.

The secret to whole life contentment lies in only a few attitudes:

- Knowing you have what you need
- Feeling effective in using what you have
- Trusting that which is around you
- Feeling you've done the best you can in the things that are broken, and appreciating your own effort in this

There are other attitudes useful for whole life contentment, but these are a few of the important ones.

Most people are prevented from finding whole life contentment because they have expressive priorities fundamental to their identity which need to be elaborated. "If I don't struggle uphill, I won't be my valiant self." This is fine, as it is only Nature. But if that is the case, one should at least acknowledge that whole life contentment is farther down in their queue, and research the contentment indicators which a dash of incredulity.

And what are the contentment indicators? It varies widely, for each person's individual mission may be contingent on astrological factors that have nothing to do with contentment—yet this is what they will recognize in a view of their wheel. We wish all the best, but cannot pass this one in cookie cutter...

Chapter 15: The voices of friends

In the previous chapter we touched briefly upon the idea of certain barriers stemming from problems in communication. It's been a while since I returned to the data-based portion of my autobiography, and we're almost to the body metrics. But halfway between self- and other- data saves lie the mechanisms of communication between parties. Let's discuss them now.

A little bit of vocal data. Using a software program called Praat (Boersma & Weenink, n.d.), I produced a report with an analysis of my voice:

TABLE 20: ANALYSIS OF AJANI'S VOICE

Pitch:	Pulses:	Voicing:
• Median pitch: 104.920 Hz • Mean pitch: 118.785 Hz • Standard deviation: 49.708 Hz • Minimum pitch: 79.582 Hz • Maximum pitch: 426.953 Hz	• Number of pulses: 589 • Number of periods: 564 • Mean period: 8.461696E-3 seconds • Standard deviation of period: 2.607E-3 s	• Fraction of locally unvoiced frames: 46.627% (311 / 667) • Number of voice breaks: 19 • Degree of voice breaks: 48.016% (4.8015 seconds / 10.000000 seconds)
Jitter: • Jitter (local): 2.128% • Jitter (local, absolute): 180.082E-6 seconds • Jitter (rap): 0.878% • Jitter (ppq5): 1.041% • Jitter (ddp): 2.633%	Shimmer: • Shimmer (local): 12.124% • Shimmer (local, dB): 1.166 dB • Shimmer (apq3): 4.813% • Shimmer (apq5): 6.738% • Shimmer (apq11): 12.044% • Shimmer (dda): 14.439%	Harmonicity of the voiced parts only: • Mean autocorrelation: 0.923914 • Mean noise-to-harmonics ratio: 0.090350 • Mean harmonics-to-noise ratio: 12.823 dB
H1-minus-H2: • Mean of the points: -0.911 dB • Mean of the curve: 1.446 dB	Mean F1 formant: 584.296 Mean F2 formant: 1505.851 Mean F3 formant: 2515.101	Mean F4 formant: 3543.065

Knowing almost nothing about voice analysis, I asked Google Gemini plenty of questions. Here's what it told me:

I just exported a file from software called praat, which can be used to analyze voices. Can you explain to me what this report is telling me?

This report describes a voice that:

• Has a typical low-to-mid range fundamental frequency for an adult male, with a moderate amount of pitch variation.

- Contains a normal mix of voiced and unvoiced segments, but also shows a significant amount of time in voice breaks, indicating pauses or silent periods.
- Exhibits slightly elevated jitter and shimmer, particularly shimmer, which might suggest some minor instability or roughness/breathiness in the voice quality.
- However, the harmonicity measures (HNR, autocorrelation) are relatively good, indicating that despite some instability, the voice's periodic (harmonic) component is strong.
- The H1-H2 values suggest a more balanced or slightly "pressed" voice quality rather than an overtly breathy one.

Overall Conclusion from F1-F5:

- When looking at the full set of formants you provided (F1=584 Hz, F2=1505 Hz, F3=2515 Hz, F4=3514 Hz, F5=4130 Hz) for an adult male voice, the pattern indicates:
- The speaker is producing a mid-low to low, front-central vowel, most likely /æ/ (as in "had") or /ɛ/ (as in "head").
- The vocal tract resonances are consistent with a typical adult male anatomy.
- The voice exhibits a normal and healthy acoustic quality in terms of its formant structure, suggesting clear articulation and efficient resonance.

I plan to do astro stats on this kind of data at some point in the future.

But now, it isn't really the waves that matter to us is it? It's the whole socialization paradigm. To this end, we turn towards a family of asteroids especially designed for communication.

WHAT IS THE BEST WAY TO COMMUNICATE WITH YOU?

There are several factors governing how people communicate, and even more factors involved in others' response to being communicated with. Here are some of the biggest chart influencers. (My locations are in parentheses):

TABLE 21: STRONG INDICATORS OF HOW YOU COMMUNICATE

- Premadi / AntiPremadi (63q8 <how you interact with those whom you hold hostage>): a noticeable appeal or character in one's voice, what the voice reflects of one's personal aspirations; | *Ajani's note: I'll bet this asteroid will be significant in ethnic or nationality research*
  - 63q8: Likely explains my lower, somewhat spider webby voice, giving a smoother, familiar sound for appearing to want to ensnare the other person somehow
  - This asteroid is conjunct Crystalpoole, which means that if sex, co-creation, or joint creation is not involved or implied, then I am far less invested in quality communications
  - Lukasgrafner gives me or the other person the aura of a burglar during quality communications
- Vinissac / AntiVinissac (89q8 <your route to influence via rapport>): naturally easy word choice in communications with others
  - 89q8 makes for very smooth one-on-one communication as a natural part of my character
  - Conjunct Syrinx again inclines me towards conversations with feminine energy or counterinfluencers if the above is to occur
  - Eliason adds notoriousness when this happens
  - Opposite Nihon Uchu Forum means my smoothest communication is with respect to two or more conquering females

- Square 53q8 and 125q8 means that separating myself from work or having to rely on trust + someone else's encouragement can prevent naturally easy word choice altogether

- Venus / AntiVenus (49q11 <information which you can't unsee or unlearn once it has been provided to you>): a MAJOR asteroid, Libra-6 or -7, of the regular everyday communication loop which fosters bonds before any official conflict phase, weakening any basic differences in expression so that communication can be said to have been possible at least once upon a time; "MAJOR bonding communication loop", even if that bond is a bad one; Venus' location shows the behavior for which you have a talent for continually cycling feedback; normally this manifests as your typical conversation agenda, but more generally it can also reflect your ability to stir a certain kind of energy in the objects you interact with. Objects / others resistant to having that energy stirred will tend to make bad (or at least subpar) 'conversation partners', instruments, games, or other looping tools to you

- Lemarchal / AntiLemarchal (62q3 <collections which have a hallowed place in your history >): preferring the most natural, most intuitive communication; | *Ajani's note: a VERY powerful asteroid which seems to indicate your most preferred communication if you could just be yourself; may affect the voice; like Venus, but "judgment free conversation"; top 50*
  - 62q3: I communicate best with and through prized collections. Things or others who don't seem to have this quality or things that follow the norm are less likely to foster my natural communication

- Arnica / AntiArnica (83q4 <how you announce or pursue your desire to move forward in a practical situation / in your daily duties>): an externalized reflection broadcast against; an indicator of "you"—that is, the one observing the chartholder; the containing duodecanate shows how the chartholder frames interactants as a means of expressing their own attributes; | *Ajani's note: for example, my Arnica in in Virgo-11, so i tend to frame you as data in the context of my daily work and logic processes. This asteroid is one indicator of how the chartholder understands their interactants, is a MAJOR asteroid, and essentially puts a Taurus identity onto that interactant. Thus, possibly Scorpio-5*
  - 83q4: If I'm not interacting with you through work or duty, communication between us is less likely to materialize

- Sims / AntiSims (85q12 <the apprentice to a powerful person>): groups making music or a structured experience together, with one party feeding off of this arrangement among the many
  - 85q12: I tend to like hanging out around groups of people more powerful than myself, and often end up feeling honored by selection into those spaces despite my low rank
  - Opposite Veralynn in 13q12, my flow state is best amidst a high achieving team or group
  - Square 49q12, this position unfortunately tends to land in groups commanded to do another's will if it is to feel solidarity at all. Sims is also sharply square 49q11, where Venus is, giving me a natural "outsider" pattern in any basic communication. To achieve a certain level of Veralynn influence, I would have to NOT engage in feedback loops with most people. Writing one-way books partly contributes to this.

- Nespoli / AntiNespoli (61q4 <for males, that which gets you on a shit list>): organizing a setting where folks can hang out, smoke, chill, or otherwise socialize in semi-sanctioned leisure
  - Almost all of my collaborations which involved spending extended one on one semi-work time with a person ended in failure

- mean Node / South Node (82q9 <what you are a fan of and how you conceive of their workings>): expressively stylized, near-guaranteed effectiveness as a cause generator; a MAJOR asteroid, Gemini-6, -1, or -8

- Juno / AntiJuno (98q10 <when you're all grown up, what changes>): attachment to things or people that keep one's projection stable, where the attachment is sociostructurally formalizable; "public commitment to a projection stabilizer"; confers fullness, completeness to the trait
  - 98q10: The older I get, the easier relational commitments become

- 141q9 / Anti141q9 (141q9): how you hang out ideally among friends; your idea of a 'party' or a fun and supportive social gathering
  - Cevenola here puts me at home only with subjects I can study infinitely
  - Glauke gives an affinity with age gaps. Indeed this is most of my friends.

○   Kazumitsu makes it comfortable for me to be in a more "threatening"-looking position amongst friends. Placements like this partly explain Dom roles and people who like being surrounded by those subject to them

Notice what I did here. Just imagine all of the intentional life-shaping you could do after looking up these asteroids in your chart… keeping in mind that you will *really* want to look up the oppositions and squares, if not the competing qigs as well. For example, my Sims is almost exactly square my Venus, so talking to you and feeling part of great team solidarity compete with each other as themes in my life. If I found myself unable to do either because, say, this square was too difficult, I could go back to Figure 7 on page 99 and find Sims' or Venus' qcross (picking a number near 49 or 85 and just scanning the pages until I see one of these), then looking at ALL 12 qunits in that family. Qig114 and qig115 could both be relevant in this case.

The thing is, while I know that Figure 7 may be tricky or even frustrating to navigate at first, it is not arranged for a person to look up qunits onesies and twosies-style in a gee whiz fashion. It is arranged in the way most conducive to you finding answers to problems. The qunit you are looking for may take longer to find, but once you find it, you will also find the three other areas of your chart most related to it, and two other groups of four which explain what you might be doing in cases where the first cross was hard to activate.

In general, I've found that AntiVinissac, AntiPremadi, AntiLemarchal, and AntiVenus are THE best indicators of the kinds of people you can talk to easily in various modes. Venus / AntiVenus is the weakest of these, but each of these is still worth looking at if you really want to understand who a person's easiest friends and confidantes will be.

Chapter 16: The mystery of Sâvitrî

Prior to starting this book I had conversation with my friend Priya, where I noted how I wasn't terribly enthusiastic about the coming approach to the female model in this work. I'd had too many years of unfavorable reactions to even ask anyone, had considered approaching one of the people in my data, then scratched the idea. "[This work is important to me, not some pervy endeavor. I'm basically an anatomist here. And I'm not going to solicit only to get somebody's side eye. Fuck that.]" is essentially what I said. But I also did not see this being a legitimate body reference with only a single male example and no female example. Priya suggested that I might just publish the book anyway with just myself first, then readers could see what I was doing. Maybe an interested person would arise from there. And I thought this was a decent approach. As I continued the initial planning, however, it seemed to me that there were just too many female-specific findings (as you've seen) to leave out from the first pass. I really needed a female model, but hard-line refused to work with any real-life people. The thought of justifying my "scandalous" work—walking someone through it again and again from *144* onwards, constantly talking people down from whatever their assumptions might be—was just too irritating to tolerate. So I came up with the idea of simply generating the female model.

More than the body, I needed someone who would be willing and able to disclose their *story*. That is, *their* data save. That could only come from someone whose story I already knew in full. Looking at the characters that I myself had conceived in Grand Miranda, I first planned use Strada from the fourth book. I immediately discovered that my astrology ephemeris files (which calculate where the asteroids are located for a given place and time), did not reach past a certain future date. I then selected someone closer to the current time of this book's writing: the character Sâvitrî from the third book has one of the richest inner worlds of any of my cast members across the series. I started to cast her chart, but then something weird happened. In this chapter, I'll walk you through Savi's partial biography, and the considerable implications for 1) lineage building for dynamic actors, 2) psychological rehabilitation, and 3) the speciated anthrizing of ideas.

LINEAGE BUILDING: IT STARTS WITH THE PARENTS... AND THEIR WORLDS

First I'll tell you the punchline. Sâvitrî—a fictional character from the future—has a real chart that tells an accurate story. But *why*? *How in the world* is this possible?

The discovery blew my mind, and prompted me to think hard about the notion of "probable lineages."

In the beginning, there was my book, *Principles of Time Travel*. That book was written more as a reflection upon my life options around 2009, as a lens into my own subconscious attitude about the future were I to live a maximally meaningful life. In that first book I conceived of several characters, but in the ensuing years also started seeing that some of the major characters across the series were actually showing up with analogs in real life. My life partner Shanna, for example, is a lot like Wine, though I wouldn't meet Shanna until 9 years later in 2018. Paris is like a business partner I would meet in 2020, then have an epic ugly blow up within an incubator program in 2021. Strada is like another one of my dear friends and one of my favorite people in the world. Cassidy has an analog. As does Dynamene. Ezra is basically a projection of my own overall attitude towards "things" in general. The one person who decidedly *does not* have an analog is Earth, whose existence was basically a gateway for enabling any other books after *PTT*. Thanks to Earth, *PTT* turned into a series which answered more of my questions, farther into the future. She is basically a projection of my created work, and where I would want it to go.

The Grand Miranda series is not meant to be good fiction. It is closer to an "oracle" for me reading my own future and how that future can tie back to the world if my attitude were right enough. It is a utopian, slice of life social philosophy series which wears fiction as its clothing, and in places where you read the way Russia works or how the CIA works or how international collaboration works, you are not actually reading reality, you're reading an idealist's dream of how these systems might look if humans were wiser. That said, there are still some realities that must be respected, and the dynamics between Earth and Ezra prohibit certain turns of plot while necessitating others. While I had initially introduced Wine as the perfect match for Ezra, the gradual realization that I would have more questions—further horizons to pursue—indelibly influenced how that relationship unfolded. Earth is the result of that unfolding, and Wine's character is changed greatly because of it. Meanwhile, Earth herself ends up affecting other relationships among all the characters around her, leading to my unplanned introduction of Sâvitrî Narayan in book 3. The first time Savi's name is called was the first time she existed to me as an author. I had no notion of her before that.

Now let me tell you a short creation myth. It reads just like a tale of the Greek gods:

> Ajani the Author is inspired by the oracle Future Utopia, who serves as the true mother for all characters in Grand Miranda. Utopia is his wife, the Miranda characters are all his and Utopia's sons and daughters.

> By elaborating on certain characters' interactions, Ajani can also co-create with his own characters. The characters can also co-create with each other, but among all of these exchanges (including the interaction with Utopia), the only relationships allowed to **pro**create are 1) Ajani by himself as the writer of everyone else's (to-them) tangible existence and 2) characters amongst themselves in the same dimension of each book, its time, place, and plot. So Ajani, despite being the true father of all of the characters, would be seen as a metaphor from the characters' own perspectives.

> A piece of Ajani appears in the form of Ezra, who is the father of Earth. Earth is a kind of mother to the rest of the series in Ajani's world, making her his *partner* in the upper dimension, but his projection's daughter in the lower dimension. Like actors and their characters. But because Ajani does not sponsor incest in any dimension there must be a non-daughter character as co-creator if this four-piece interaction is ever to be built upon. Enter Sâvitrî. In the book dimension, Savi and Earth are not related, and Savi is the daughter of Rajesh. In the **author** dimension Savi is *Earth's* daughter, everyone is Ajani's daughter or son, and Ajani's partner is an abstract line of philosophical inquiry.

> So if I cast an astro chart for Sâvitrî in my dimension, who will her parents be? Should she even have a chart?

Well, Sâvitrî does indeed have a chart in yours and my dimension, and its asteroid clusters describe an amazingly real person. Most of this is because nearly all of her characteristics stem from features of my own life and not from the natural flow of world-building within the book (like, say, the character Denis for example). In general, my characters came from any combination of three places: 1) people I have actually met, 2) the progression of the story itself, and 3) people I haven't met but who are assembled from the walls of my psychology. While most of my characters' personalities flowed from the story progression itself, characters like Raliolite, Cyclops, Sâvitrî, and Twice Jack have physical appearances and backstories that come from my relationship to templates (significators and their clusters) in my mental space. That is, they will reflect more sections of my own chart rather than synastries between a couple of my significators and the chart of the book they are in. I am thus closer to their true parent, with minimal input from their book-dimension surrogates. That's the first condition for attaching a fictional creation to its author's lineage from a higher-up dimension.

Next there is the matter of attaching a fictional creation to the *energy scale* of its author's dimension. Throughout the later books of Grand Miranda, I refer to different dimensions. Astra is the one we live in whose patterns can be studied through astrology—on the scale of planets and moons. Baia is the dimension of the body whose patterns are better studied on the micro "Magic School Bus" level, on the scale of neuronal spikes, ATP concentrations, and chemical bonds. Diji is studied on the digital level on the scale of CPU cycles and computer clocks. Planets are far too big to characterize the entities here with any detail, and the notion of a birthday will depend on speeds in nanoseconds and the algorithms that make use of them. Lastly, there is Comm. This is the dimension of communication, where a thing's "birthday" has more to do with its location in the story and the hole in existing plot dynamics which it serves to fill. That and the author's own brain. The challenge in giving simulatable life in Astra to a creation in other dimensions lies in taking that creation's behavior and tying it to the Astran's behaviors more than the those of their dimension-mates.

In other words, you can spit out thousands of AI images in a day, thousands of words on a page, or millions of biochemical transmitters over a surface, but until you create a story explaining what these are doing as they relate to you, you'll have a hard time charting them in your dimension.

As I wrote the series, I began thinking about certain topics that I will not spoil here. With nowhere to really go at the time from where I was in the story, I kept the questions coming, and Savi's character evolved to include many more features that I would have gravitated towards had there not been so many barriers to this in my own life.

- I've always attracted bigger girls
- Have always had a preference for Indian and Welsh women
- Am "1+" nonmonogamous (either two human partners, or one human partner + a life-calling)
- I work with adult data and people who aren't afraid to go naked for the right reasons
- Have always been associated with interracial couples as friends
- Appreciate strong docility
- Tend to adopt a Daddy role in my co-creative dynamics
- Prefer friends with legend-level talents and aspirations
- Have a checkered relationship with people in advocacy and the fashion industry
- I love optimism and deep spirituality
- Almost all of my friends are intuitive

- I have always built better bonds with people younger than me, especially in pairs, starting with my two younger brothers. Either that or I have been the notably younger one in the interaction, starting with my brokers in real estate.
- and a number of other patterns…

Matching Sâvitrî to these patterns as her character evolved, I unintentionally established her as an embodiment of an ideal partner. Furthermore, her being a written character also made her into a kind of "work partner" (as I described earlier), so there was always an update available to give. Accordingly, it now became possible to map her in here in "Astra." Last came the determination of an official birth chart. I'll admit I'm still a bit mystified as to how this works, but at least I'll tell you what I did.

At some point in *Earth* there is a mention of Sâvitrî spending a birthday. We also know that Savi is about one year older than Earth. This gave me a six-month window from which to choose a specific day for the purposes of writing *this* book. As I rolled the wheel through this window, certain major planets and asteroids started to require themselves.

Sâvitrî Narayan
Sâvitrî Narayan (6/21/2073 2:33:00 PM GMT+5:30) Ratlãm (23N19'00 75E04'00)

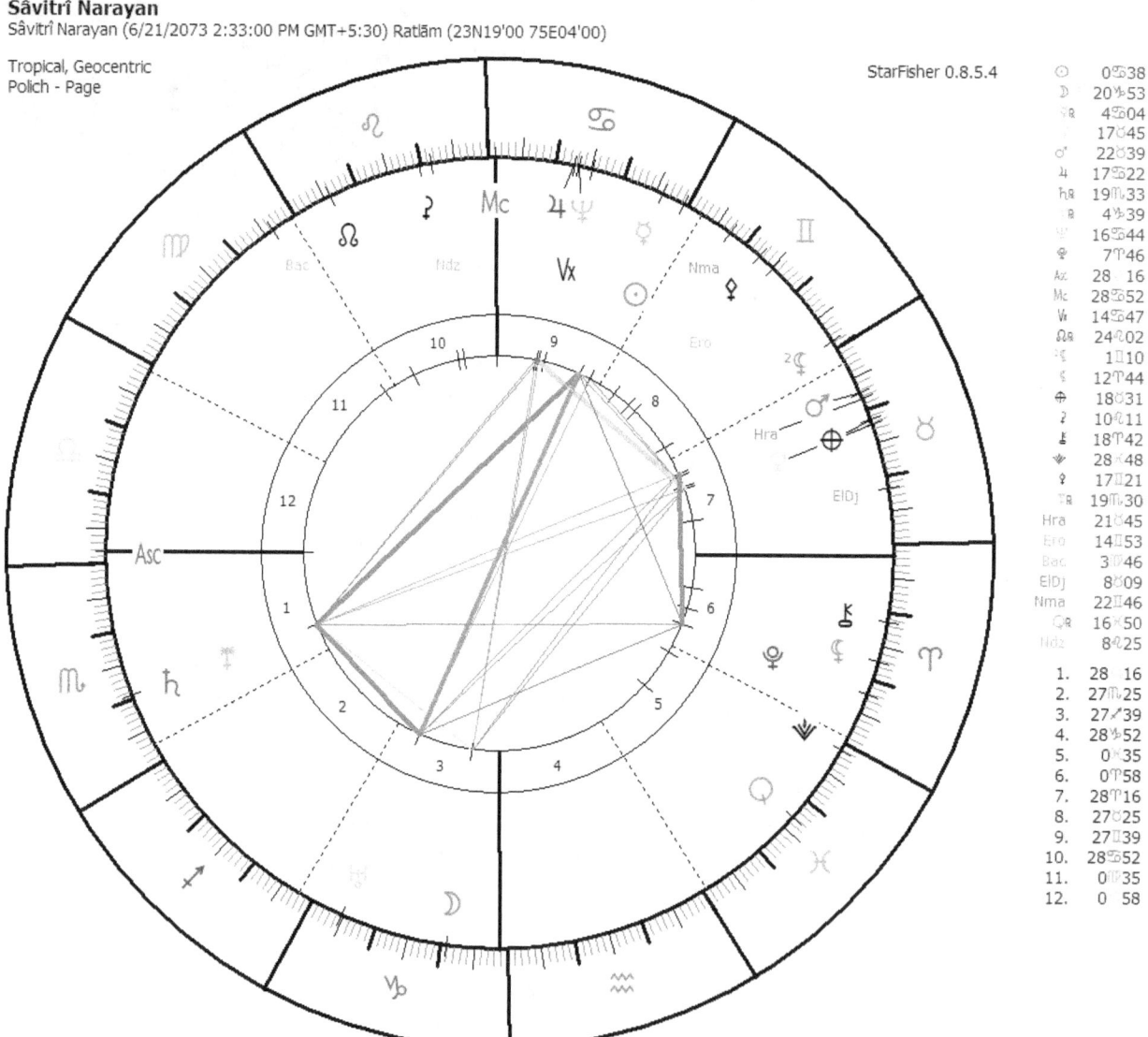

- Sâvitrî's character is naturally fearful unless or until she learns to get past this, so having a Moon in 28 (Capricorn 20°-22.5° or Capricorn-4) fits nicely.

- More than anything, Sâvitrî has a diehard commitment (⚴) to her father figure (♄).
- Her work (6th house) ends up being in a "pressuring" (♇) field, where her emphasis is on a kind of healing (⚷)
- The nature of her work (Nicoleodzer / Ndz)—for which she is publicly known (in the 10th) also sponsors a rift with certain members of her family (□ El Djezair / ElDj)
- Savi is, for the most part, a highly emotional (☽) communicator (in the 3rd house). She has a lot of important stuff in Cancer (♋).
- Throughout her life, others were inclined to use her body or presence for their own ends. She has a lot of body-centric, influence-based objects in Taurus in her house of 1:1 interactions (the 7th)
- She gains a public reputation (♃) in an artistic field based on illusions (☌ ♆)
- And so on…

The thing is, all of the above characteristics existed in her book character before I had any notion of her even having a chart. It is true that I got to choose her chart from a small span of options, but the idea that so many of her qualities could be located in the same wheel with basically no contradictions among themselves or any discrepancies with her character is amazing.

And there's more.

Bodywise, in the book and in her character design outside of the book, Sâvitrî looks exactly the way you see her in the pictures—which I AI-rendered in stable diffusion to fit what was written. She has a heavy, curvy build with large breasts and striking dark areolae, tan-bronze skin, a somewhat sing-songy / somewhat whiny voice (until she matures), an uncertain face, an initial codependence on the ones she loves, and a youth which was spent in insecurity. Here, 11073 Cavell, one of the strongest indicators of the breasts can be found in 70q4 with a number of noteworthy neighbors:

TABLE 22: SÂVITRÎ'S 70Q4

Koppeschaar	186.66	where one's hands are completely tied in their role involving helping others or their deliverables
Tishasaltzman	186.6486	musical or frequentic dallying, more likely in an informal place
Sekinenomatsu	186.6475	laying out the full sprawl of rules for mediated back and forth engagement
Credo	186.6457	though one can dissect a topic, they cannot interfere with its progression. To do so is to face anger and damage; | *Ajani's note: this is a strong asteroid which gives you the authority to chop a concept into a million analytical pieces, as long as you don't interfere with that concept's unfolding. if you think about it, if you *did* interfere with the concept in action, you would be a part of its action and thus be unable to chop yourself into a million analytical pieces, for the paradox directly implied. Accordingly, Credo enables infinite dissection of the duodecanate, yet all but prohibits direct steering. so how do you get the region to unfold? do exactly this. analyze it to death, but don't apply any force to it. it's just a credo*
Nakanoshima	186.643	a productive couple, entertaining and bragworthy
Cavell	186.6412	a fanatic hangs onto an idea doggedly
Bettiepage	186.632	that which is stood up to cross an expansive emotional terrain; people may use the containing duodecanate as a vehicle for shuttling safely or more confidently across an otherwise challenging experiential stretch; associated with one who reassures others through dark fog, possibly by being one with the fog themselves
Ivandanilov	186.6114	an extremity which stands between solidity and the surrounding space
Anshan	186.6032	a meaningful or exalted piece of a field which one sticks with for gaining a leg up
Nisyros	186.5854	decorating a standout piece of the body, attachment, or relative thereof
Tienchanglin	186.5554	having to sit someone desirable on the bench for all the disorderly talk they bring
Chile	186.5539	the varied surface or interface that one is tasked to navigate via feeling and wave rather than more direct experience
Laurajohnson	186.5342	a big and generous haul from a sea which made it easy
Epops	186.5108	an external party referencing its own agenda or its own version of reality; associated with the notion of 'themselves'
Michkovitch	186.5043	how one's devotion to or discipleship of something affects their communication with others

Of all of Sâvitrî's at-a-glance standout qualities in full body, her face, her breasts, and her build are among the most obvious. You'll have to read Savi's story to know why the above table is indeed significant. Tishasaltzman, Credo, Nakanoshima, Cavell, Nisyros, Chile, Michkovitch, and Koppeschaar are all indicators of qualities she tends to display in the extreme. Accordingly, one the asteroids specifically associated with voluptuousness is hyperactive in the qunit of "steps you follow as you create scenarios to share with a particular trusted party"—a region which, by the way, undergirds most of her story.[41]

Sâvitrî's nipples reflect more of what goes on around her in the story. It turns out that it isn't just her immediate peers in the book who encircle her, it's people from other times, and you and I as well, hence her areolar sprawl. Sahilabbi, Stephencolbert, Zdiksima, and Maryanderson in particular serve to amplify Smoter in 133q3, which charges up the ambitions of creative feeders around the female body. Sâvitrî's inspired receivers exist far beyond her native dimension in the book, and that inspiration-potential influences her own elaboration as a visible body. If it didn't she might still be able to fuel people's influence far and wide, but the nipples would not reflect this:

TABLE 23: SÂVITRÎ'S 133Q3

Allenjanes	28.95564	growing, aging into decay; | *Ajani's note: reflects the situations which grow you up, taking a lot out of you; does resisting this duodecanate help keep you youthful? If so, those who don't like the idea of aging may strongly consider outsourcing this*
Russwalker	28.91571	an access point to a work's or information source's contents
Stephencolbert	28.88605	one who sponsors interpersonal relationships for the sake of the state
Hazelcoffman	28.87645	sounds are made - energies released - that indicate poison in the air, or that patience may be required to endure; where you receive indications that patience will be needed if whatever you are building is to survive
Malyshev	28.85829	a quiet cabin where outside influences are blocked from entering
Philippa	28.84557	"projected in the form of a satiator;" you can be a satisfyingly pleasant meet to interface with in this cluster
Sulzer	28.84488	explaining the high flying thing to one who is too young or inexperienced to understand it
Smoter	28.84217	one who, although he can't take much with him into where he's going, is strongly supported by a body of practice or skill; a male asteroid specifically for males whose force is not in their body frame, but in their channeling of intensity; in the charts of women, indicates where such kinds of assertions manifest—things which don't seem strong, but convey their power through a strong will to change you
Sahilabbi	28.83919	a member of a legendary (or at least memorable) association, the voice of reason thereof
Sharaf	28.82633	continuing or perpetuated order; | *Ajani's note: seems to bring some talent for foresight or clairvoyance*
Kreszgeza	28.82375	a not-so common sight slides past the terrain
Ernestina	28.78721	behind the scenes government energy entity commits investments from every home; "governing directed energy tax entity"
Zdiksima	28.7867	a feeling circulating in the air as devotees assemble
Maryanderson	28.75137	something that seems to happen as a result of metaphysics, since rationality doesn't seem to explain it

Sâvitrî, despite her fears, insistently believes in a form of fulfillment which is just around the corner. A few asteroids indicating this also contain, among them, 8834 Anacardium—an object which showed up frequently in lists of significant sliders affecting weight. These are in her 34q12s.

---

[41] This is what I meant earlier when I talked about significators, and the idea that major planets don't automatically imply dominant traits in a personality. In *Earth*, Savitri displays an obsession which goes beyond the pale, and as with most of my writing this stemmed from the character's own self-driven evolution. Had she been less obsessed, less devoted, the associated body qualities would have been deemphasized accordingly. But I didn't know this cluster was even a thing until I used my own table from earlier to see whether a trait I knew to be pronounced had neighbors worth telling about. You can see, once again, just how weird it is that this fictional character from Comm has a chart which makes sense in the frame of our own astronomy orbits in Astra.

TABLE 24: SÂVITRÎ'S 34Q12

Anacardium	275.8215	hanging on the edge of something, feeling that rescue or objective reaching is just around the corner or should be; an asteroid of enduring dissatisfaction—a sense of what surely MUST be, but just isn't; | *Ajani's note: this is an asteroid of an enduring sense of dissatisfaction. From what i can tell, operating it positively may involve willingly taking up risky or daredevil deeds in the duodecanate*
Kopal	275.7104	a reward message as in, "congratulations, you just won a chance at two free tickets to Tahiti!". More often, this doesn't pan out though.
Polyakhova	275.6801	a botanist or grower of life conveys their commission progress report
Campania	275.6742	an indication of something that may swoop in and affect a situation with its power
Yabu	275.6628	numerous voices assembled in a place, the gathering of diverse characters—associated with "a connection between three or more from different backgrounds"
Brauerman	275.6474	the idealized servant of another's social interactions; can help render you compelling, favored, or nurturing to your social interactants regardless of what you're doing or whether it is negative

Let's end by looking at Savi's ethnicity. Why is she Indian? Because my male hormones like this group, and I find it easier to elaborate my creations (whether they be books, collaborations, or DIY around the house) when sexual-creative energy is flowing in the background—not on the surface where it can interfere with the work. Meanwhile, I do still have all of the text-mined categories from the *Laurentia* definitions, and ethnicities were among them. Here were the results with *p*-values. Lower *p*-values mean stronger relationships between the mined category and the asteroid's hot aspects in the charts of people who fit that category:

TABLE 25: ASTEROIDS WHICH TEXT-MINED ON ETHNICITY TERMS

MPC#	Asteroid	Interpretation	[Ethnicity: Asian]	[Ethnicity: Black]	[Ethnicity: Indian]	[Ethnicity: Latin]	[Ethnicity: Middle Eastern]	[Ethnicity: Other]	[Ethnicity: White]
2419	Moldavia	at the earliest opportunities for closeness, attempts to share pleasure or demonstrate the capacity to provide it; a notable tell and trigger asteroid; the representative who does this—whether you or another—is more likely to favor the expression of the containing region, making this one of the stronger examples of a 'directional' tell asteroid	0			0			
657	Gunlod	a vivid warning from the pope (or from one's inner moral authority)	0			0.02			
9521	Martinhoffmann	possibly thought of as having a rocky character, but well-known and respected	0			0.03			
10036	McGaha	the wit of the already-dead; investigate in tales from the crypt	0			0.03			
2215	Sichuan	massive, socially open festivities; reminiscent of the Chinese New Year	0						0
184096	Kazlauskas	expecting to secure a lot of the proper support	0						0.04
1388	Aphrodite	high, exotic stature amidst a presentation	0						
25403	Carlapiazza	the cold accomplice to another; cold, unfeeling, or unbending collective thought	0						
15992	Cynthia	getting oneself in trouble over a passionate incident regarding books or records	0						
1274	Delportia	a surprise example of an actor from an unexpected class; someone or something that performs well, given that its type isn't expected to	0						
1736	Floirac	an exotic producer's creative work; associated with Italian and east Asian backgrounds	0						
8236	Gainsborough	celebrating one's graduation, standing tall, fruitful, and intelligent	0						
3047	Goethe	tracking decisions made during a manhunt	0						
48575	Hawaii	studying the things that permeate __ (cluster-related) in one's own way despite the existing wisdom	0						
364	Isara	one's co-creative servant; an asteroid to look for in relative charts which indicates a primary and servant / attendant relationship; implies a pairing with another	0						
71482	Jennamarie	covert navigation of a situation, where one maps a path to where they want despite limitations	0						

MPC#	Asteroid	Interpretation	[Ethnicity: Asian]	[Ethnicity: Black]	[Ethnicity: Indian]	[Ethnicity: Latin]	[Ethnicity: Middle Eastern]	[Ethnicity: Other]	[Ethnicity: White]
4764	Joneberhart	three working together to achieve some kind of high standard, more likely to involve taking power from someone or something else	0						
230631	Justino	one focused on economics, with a particularly different view of how to apply it	0						
10277	Micheli	constructing something together—as in playing with blocks or other "joint artwork"; a clear trigger asteroid	0						
23775	Okudaira	a creature thought dangerous turns out to be something else entirely	0						
69311	Russ	regrouping in or outside of a restaurant / nurturing place after having been rejected for some kind of entry; this asteroid implies at least two parties constituting the group doing the re-meeting	0						
33574	Shailaja	enjoying a certain level of bureaucratic expression, as part of an encyclopedic collection of something	0						
129811	Stacyoliver	a sweep over a terrain which wipes out or nullifies its expression; where an overarching event covers the domain of everything under it	0						
12912	Streator	the idealized curvaceous bombshell body, nipped and tucked to market industry standard	0						
18458	Caesar	where one has what a manly man should have; the model of masculine risk and accomplishment	0.01						0.03
379173	Gamaovalia	while held somewhere, watching relationships or belief doctrines for one's own enjoyment, receptive to pronounced polarity of either kind, as long as the doctrine stands for *something*	0.01						0.03
21082	Araimasaru	being hooked on someone in the form of loyalty, though one of the parties may view the other as unattractive	0.01						
19573	Cummings	a logical or institutionally-driven decision to treat a product or service differently; strongly associated with disruption of some party's conditioned order	0.01						
96217	Gronchi	looking for the rebel nurturer who will provide a more desirable side to one's commitments	0.01						
325	Heidelberga	"operations done of the body, replicable in micro"; may eventually be associated with the genetic body mod industry; an (at least colloquial) association with human phenotypic evolution	0.01						
22415	Humeivey	rising easily on the heels of a particular physical characteristic	0.01						
50768	Ianwessen	drawing the line at an experience that would otherwise threaten one with gang-upon that compels one party's release	0.01						
43957	Invernizzi	dedicated attention to the skill-requiring reconciliation of something; one of many Asian ethnicity/perspective asteroids	0.01						
16135	Ivarsson	the model unvarnished, untarnished authority who observes everything; associated with broad Asian ethnicity	0.01						
8322	Kononovich	one sings out for the socially motivated relocation of a group; associated with asian-morph body types	0.01						
9640	Lippens	watching one's peer injured, in pain, or under pressure	0.01						
28400	Morgansinko	baptized or rendered special among those without a home	0.01						
52225	Panchenko	the straight and narrow or formalist role which prosecutes a case across avenues to the bitter end	0.01						
117874	Picodelteide	rurality and a certain band of openness to relationships which can occur here	0.01						
1927	Suvanto	crossing eerie or uncertain territory	0.01						
20878	Uwetreske	"the silver shooter"; energetic and offbeat, but still very tough	0.01						
117993	Zambujal	self-made champion, a catalyst for something which only that person can facilitate	0.01						
13176	Kobedaitenken	one with the ability to wrangle with the animal or beast in others	0.02	0.01				0	
11280	Sakurai	"it won't matter if we do this. let's just do it. Nobody will know"	0.02			0.02			
12155	Hyginus	the state's or collective's ownership of what one creates	0.02						
217628	Lugh	the domain doctor must put in more work to process a patient as is typically done	0.02						
11263	Pesonen	having gained by indulging other's wants in ways that may not be socially favored; having gained because someone found you, hooked you up, or thought you were attractive	0.02						
13480	Potapov	insisting on discipline across the area one surveys	0.02						

MPC#	Asteroid	Interpretation	[Ethnicity: Asian]	[Ethnicity: Black]	[Ethnicity: Indian]	[Ethnicity: Latin]	[Ethnicity: Middle Eastern]	[Ethnicity: Other]	[Ethnicity: White]
2992	Vondel	one once famous, but then forgotten as they blend into the collective memory; where you may have your day, but in the long run might require a collective to keep your memory alive past your 15 minutes	0.02						
75823	Csokonai	favorable depiction of the special places one has toured; associated with east-from-africa (latin american and asian) migrating recipients (women), or asian and native american depictive stories, exported globally	0.03			0			
13770	Commerson	one who performs surgery on themselves, redesigning themselves in their own lab	0.03						
8603	Senator	development through price of blood or conflict; investigate association with period and the menstrual cycle; increases the body mass or body fat broadly, especially in the legs	0.04						
268	Adorea	related to gatherings of those with pressing business on their shoulders (more likely financial or value-based)		0		0.05			
39799	Hadano	taking oneself around to explore what aspects of a thing are more viscerally experienceable by others given one's company; "framing oneself as a setting"		0					0
8374	Horohata	professional domains which dominate the outdoors, though there is some open option kept available; associated with sororities, transportation authorities, and transportation companies		0				0	0.02
7367	Giotto	the warm recall of stories that aren't always happy ones; related to black, african, american, or earlier modern human evolutionary form mixed with moder communication		0				0.01	
26541	Garyross	one issuing occasional comparative announcements (not always flattering or pleasant)		0				0.02	
6060	Doudleby	the setting or individual who modifies their own sexual or procreative expression, particularly feminine hyperfertilization (through received/domainic surgery, medications, artistic depiction, etc.) of increased masculine traits; "feminine-route masculinization"; associated with fetal differentiation into a boy during the mother's pregnancy, futanari fetish, and female-to-male transition (is among the stronger factors); 'Dude'll be'		0					
2055	Dvorak	the well-known thief, with tricky ways of getting other's things or support		0					
129335	Edwardlittle	carrying a heavy burden for resisting negative or damaging acts to others for one's own sake; "an asteroid of being constantly tested, called to resist the low road"		0					
117610	Keithmahoney	viewing, observing the whole landscape from above or outside the context		0					
1410	Margret	a colorful or pronounced portrayal meant to make up for something thought missing in an expression		0					
8952	ODAS	giving in to the limits of what a domain / feminine energy will process; accepting that no more of something will be accepted		0					
14708	Slaven	the controlled or regulated sharing of asserted aims, while making sure not to be mistaken as weak or moldable by others' assertions; associated with the brand of identity strength one develops while serving as another party's slave; when you are seemingly unable to determine your own fate as the subject of another, this asteroid's containing cluster will more likely describe the various things you do in response.		0					
31319	Vespucci	risky interfacing or intercourse with all kinds of backgrounds / individuals from such		0					
21825	Zhangyizhong	one giving shocking accounts or one whose experiences spark a thunderstorm		0					
17431	Sainte Colombe	sadistic or graphic measures employed in the name of a group or a system		0.01		0.05			
172932	Bachleitner	inviting the receipt of other's assertions; this asteroid seems to be responsible for the formerly common manifestation of women as being more (social-allowably) psychic than men; develops domainic/receiving characteristics, and includes such receipt in the form of clairvoyance		0.01					0.01
3074	Popov	getting into escapades then getting out, returning to obscurity until the next time		0.01				0.01	
136	Austria	one who speaks out for a cause, but also exercises shrewdness in doing so; embodying a formula for enabling something (charitable or benevolent); associated with black women and similar additional-calculations-needed-on-top-of-regular-inroads-for-business groups; investigate in oprah, rihanna		0.01					
349	Dembowska	award-winning or highly regarded infuser of a context with a warm drive to action		0.01					

MPC#	Asteroid	Interpretation	[Ethnicity: Asian]	[Ethnicity: Black]	[Ethnicity: Indian]	[Ethnicity: Latin]	[Ethnicity: Middle Eastern]	[Ethnicity: Other]	[Ethnicity: White]
6731	Hiei	a mother or situation's wish that her creations strongly assert their character; "the asserter's wish not to be a punk"		0.01					
7818	Muirhead	designing oneself for seduction; the area of life where it is done		0.01					
207809	Wuzuze	one with the ability to carve their own path through an event and compel others to take that path seriously		0.01					
14004	Chikama	hitting another with something that puts them in a challenging response position		0.05					
3137	Horky	illusion or enspirited celebratory collectivity; associated with indian and latin ethnicities			0	0.03			
6771	Foerster	from an underprivileged culture or working with such, but full of energy			0				0
4175	Billbaum	the inability to tame one's intrusive or oppressive incursion into another's frame; "natural overstature"			0				
6377	Cagney	that which needs another party or prompter in order to achieve or fulfill the heart's desire			0				
34240	Charleyhutch	a calculating servant with their own intense ambitions			0				
21357	Davidying	related to a race to the treasure, where you may feel pressured to obtain the things indicated by its cluster as soon as possible. Once the race is over and the thing attained (or not), this asteroid becomes something that other people race to build on or improve, establishing their names in turn			0				
20274	Halperin	the impact of a knowledgeable third party in supporting the co-founding or co-operation of an endeavor; someone involved may be inclined to be unhappy, but the endeavor is nonetheless a strong one; positive framing of this one may require the unhappiness to be made into a point of comedy			0				
33520	Ichige	a golden courageous beauty, saddled with the threat of being taken from at every turn; associated with indian ethnicity and beauty			0				
5433	Kairen	robust avant garde or fascinating style; associated with indian ethnicity			0				
4477	Kelley	reactionary, with a fuel source for responding internally to slights			0				
128373	Kevinjohnson	a proposal that all march together; associated with indian ethnicity; raises the ability to rally others in the duodecanate; investigate in gandhi			0				
4796	Lewis	observing the micro level patterns, using the findings to inform an attestation; associated with indian backgrounds			0				
20787	Mitchfourman	fine and delicate quality for nurturing the senses; associated with indian ethnicity and cuisine			0				
13112	Montmorency	the out-of-sight host domain who fosters a memorable experience; associated with indian women and the quest for idealized social standing			0				
410835	Neszmerak	one agrees to help another revive an effort, that the laws may be properly broadcast / despite the rules of __ being inhibited in their enforcement			0				
29762	Panasiewicz	the determined one who thinks about you when you're not there; seems to be related to the role of dogs in one's life			0				
20559	Sheridanlamp	temperamental or aggressive repartee, rendering one difficult to argue down because one tends to make so much practical or helpful sense; | Ajani's note: associated with indian backgrounds. In my observation, especially indian males			0				
22190	Stellakwee	the economic power which capitalistically trained agents eventually acquire over their parent system-based employers; where the priorities of the subordinate eventually usurp those of the superior; if you are a superior, this could just indicate regular succession planning			0				
26332	Alyssehrlich	criticizing one's patron lineage, crimes of the fathers			0.01				
238129	Bernardwolfe	rejoicing with big fanfare			0.01				
41986	Fort Bend	where one is held over for the results of their combat, for better, worse, or just for the time being			0.01				
21306	Marani	the genius great-grandfather or system asserter; associated with indian ethnicity			0.01				
136666	Seidel	a communication which covers a process to be kept hidden from most external viewing; related to indian ethnicity			0.01				

MPC#	Asteroid	Interpretation	[Ethnicity: Asian]	[Ethnicity: Black]	[Ethnicity: Indian]	[Ethnicity: Latin]	[Ethnicity: Middle Eastern]	[Ethnicity: Other]	[Ethnicity: White]
121817	Szatmary	a bitch behind the scenes, regardless of sex or gender, but on the surface, open to everyone				0.01			
2096	Vaino	heels or boots which convey a spirit of domination while soliciting attention				0			0
129216	Chloecastle	tension recounting one's story to one's therapist				0			0.02
685	Hermia	the multiple who lead in the production or sponsorship of creative works				0			
129307	Tomconnors	a social-accompanying gatekeeper, another favor-prone part of an expressive grouping with more members				0			
7721	Andrillat	a social butterfly or socially nomadic temperament, moving around and fitting into various new places with at least the appearance of nurturing to others				0.01		0.01	
19718	Albertjarvis	deriving the best route to uncomplicated comfort				0.01			
64291	Anglee	The lab's meticulous analysis of the prospect of an endlessly prosperous resurgence is integral to ensuring the long-term viability of the super organization, even in times of financial instability and bankruptcy. GPT-4.				0.01			
32058	Charlesnoyes	digging up the corpses of a situation				0.01			
686	Gersuind	persuaded by the little details to overturn a prior allowed situation; where the bartender finally kicks someone out				0.01			
3253	Gradie	receiving attention, especially by those in need of redemption or a second chance (not necessarily for anything they did wrong)				0.01			
7842	Ishitsuka	member of a status-carrying ensemble involved in various intrigues; associated with mexican women and latinas, as well as sufi islam				0.01			
12242	Koon	there must be another in order for the containing region to have an identity here				0.01			
20947	Polyneikes	hooked on the energy provided by others; more likely to file through a diverse array or personalities depending on what phase one is in				0.01			
1392	Pierre	getting situated for critical study; associated with latin backgrounds				0.02			0
1731	Smuts	paint, patterns, and stains which characterize old or antique things				0.02			0.02
325588	Bridzius	fullness in how one expresses or draws from others the expression of passion				0.02			
6363	Doggett	the ambitious owner of an idea performs before all; associated with latinx socioethnic assertion-favorers				0.02			
4726	Federer	a dispute (more positively, a planned division) which leads to separation, an object between the separating parties being central to the event; this asteroid behaves much more smoothly when the object can make its own decisions, shuttling between the divided actors; associated with divorces and separations involving shared ownership, as well as three-part government				0.02			
7378	Herbertpalme	pleasantries which help stave off or (partly) smooth over misunderstandings				0.02			
5723	Hudson	a concerto or magnificent performance whose power just can't be easily disputed				0.02			
7252	Kakegawa	ridiculed for the rules one follows; the teasers are more likely to be blind, otherwise the rule follower may be doing so blindly; positively, favors dogged adherence to productive principles despite challenges to such				0.02			
17993	Kluesing	appealing to the subconscious mobility needs; satisfying a want one had not fully been aware of				0.02			
2629	Rudra	flattering someone or some group with a radical response to a quality they hold				0.02			
3261	Tvardovskij	bubbly and full of energy				0.02			
7188	Yoshii	the declaration of connectedness among asserters, disrobed or declothed in dangerous settings as an affirmation of (or demand for) loyalty; one of the latinx asteroids				0.02			
29250	Helmutmoritz	a collectivist couple or asserter oriented towards creation with women or domains, exerting fitness as part of this process				0.03		0.01	
14360	Ipatov	blending in with something in order to absorb what it has to offer; associated with latinx and bigger body frames				0.03			
17652	Nepoti	manipulating someone upon their entry into something				0.03			

MPC#	Asteroid	Interpretation	[Ethnicity: Asian]	[Ethnicity: Black]	[Ethnicity: Indian]	[Ethnicity: Latin]	[Ethnicity: Middle Eastern]	[Ethnicity: Other]	[Ethnicity: White]
48798	Penghuanwu	energy and energy volumes stored as inventory for possible transfer to a recipient; associated with extra body weight stored which drives an interactant's action; adds the hedonistic nature implicated in black and latin broad stereotypes				0.03			
10882	Shinonaga	taunting others over the idea that one has actually been accepted into a place				0.03			
30048	Sreyasmisra	delving into the depths of a murder / termination and its motivational intricacies				0.03			
22553	Yisun	the rebellious one excommunicated from a place				0.03			
6776	Dix	a confusing relationship with one's patriarch; are they against the masculine / assertive power or very much with it?; an asteroid which helps explain how the successors to tyrants are born				0.04			
19811	Kimperkins	latin features; taming anxiety through drink or consumption of illusion				0.04			
6500	Kodaira	giving guidance despite being sick or debilitated				0.04			
201497	Marcelroche	contagious exuberance, happiness, or dance				0.04			
11323	Nasu	rigidly formalized knowledge or claim to such				0.04			
120218	Richardberry	world-class show off of the sensual body or its movements				0.04			
3952	Russellmark	one reconciled to do grunt work or work with the land and its value				0.04			
30204	Stevedoherty	broadcasted as open to touch; sensuality				0.04			
56329	Tarxien	health foods, foods or nurturance sources that affect aging, ability, and attitude				0.04			
19707	Tokunai	an inherited situation reflects familial determination				0.04			
33680	Vasconcelos	ensuring that one holds tight control over something's action until the end goal is met; associated with the underbust and upper abdominals				0.04			
1697	Koskenniemi	inspired landing in a place to project one's agenda onto it				0.05		0.04	
13534	Alain Fournier	ample body, form, or comfort; drawing the cornucopia				0.05			
4684	Bendjoya	taking hungrily from one after another; associated with lust, insatiable desire, and latin social training background				0.05			
126315	Blathy	fiery spirited suggestion, associated with latinx and american backgrounds				0.05			
1672	Gezelle	"one who prizes light comfort occasionally leaves the main domain to tend to notable spaces of bodies"				0.05			
24712	Boltzmann	looking for something alone, which suits the individual					0		0.05
142759	Covey	though one has a treasure trove of skills or assets, they remain wrapped in a war					0		
1058	Grubba	the harsh climate or stories unfolding set in the middle east					0		
407243	Krapivin	the exhausting effort put into depicting something as if it is perfectly beautiful despite its navigation of a clearly harsh terrain					0		
11103	Miekerouppe	secretly driving towards the conclusion of something that one cannot bear any longer					0		
4545	Primolevi	gathering the many to testify to a grand miscarriage of affairs; or...	*Ajani's note: this is the second major case I've uncovered of an association between guitars and unaddressed crimes; could it be that the guitar is to unresolved tension what american football is to the battlefield? this asteroid has an affinity with guitar performance before a crowd*					0		
3701	Purkyne	an authority figure allies with a group to manufacture regulations					0		
4074	Sharkov	taking care of the injured during a demonstration or conflict over rights					0		
4789	Sprattia	the goddess who never did show up; the elusive angel said to nurture one, but whose main role is as a catalyst for certain kinds of perception					0		
24439	Yanney	a characteristic appeal of middle eastern / desert designed males					0		
183114	Vicques	signs, posters, or symbols which announce a belief					0.01		
100229	Jeanbailly	sexual or co-creative enjoyment through pan-sided role play; associated with costumes, cosplay, and anime, as well as couples and bisexuality; either the chartholder or their interactant can express this as the containing cluster evolves						0.05	0
29747	Acorlando	the warrior exploring the land							0
3174	Alcock	the shank; a sneaky means of obtaining dominance or punishing an enemy							0
6752	Ashley	physical performance, witnessed as it is a least a little uncomfortable. Maybe very							0
23867	Cathsoto	"the baby shower"; games and related ceremonies to celebrate birthing							0

MPC#	Asteroid	Interpretation	[Ethnicity: Asian]	[Ethnicity: Black]	[Ethnicity: Indian]	[Ethnicity: Latin]	[Ethnicity: Middle Eastern]	[Ethnicity: Other]	[Ethnicity: White]
22171	Choi	a taboo attraction attached to / compelling one's abdication							0
26183	Henrigodard	solitary confinement; isolated without anyone to go to; | *Ajani's note: look out for this one in the charts of others*							0
1247	Memoria	young womanhood or early development as a space that receives others' assertions; associated with puberty in girls and the pressures to grow into specific standards; pluto-like in its channeling of social pressures							0
233559	Pizzetti	an unapologetically objectified sketch of a person's body or energy form							0
3422	Reid	a rare trait whose rarity is easily missed or overlooked							0
33567	Sulekhfrederic	the first to formally settle a place, but being at a partial disadvantage because of it. For without the benefit of hindsight or the critique enabled for those second and afterwards, one is more likely to have made many mistakes in the long run; "the disadvantage of the pioneer"; one of the many asteroids associated with White ethnicity/perspective, American background, maleness, female body objectification, and open relationships							0
2256	Wisniewski	a position properly fertilized							0
11461	Wladimirneumann	a natural healthy, process towards ends which are more commonly approved or favored in the world (though, as usual with body heavy asteroids, these traits may not manifest bodily)							0
18983	Allentran	lying to / deceiving others about one's fertility or receptiveness to a situation, in order to increase some other kind of support							0.01
3664	Anneres	the dogged personality who gives no damn about things other than their own perspective; positively, can manifest as a very steady personal expression							0.01
658	Asteria	an ensemble falls apart or dwindles under some kind of starvation; positively, starving a cancer of the things it needs to grow—where this happens OR is needed							0.01
2059	Baboquivari	positioning oneself in such a way as to reflect what one knows about where they are							0.01
20879	Chengyuhsuan	the seductive collective or couple which may occasionally act madly							0.01
225711	Danyzy	a demanding person who keeps coming back again and again, as if it is their right to do so							0.01
20252	Eyjafjallajokull	where one should be out there, but instead must be a passenger witnessing / receptive to others' influence							0.01
115254	Fenyi	congealing a boundary around something, but the boundary is not completely solidified yet							0.01
10129	Fole	one who dominates the ideas of in a space; writing that which is on the minds of the public; an asteroid of "control of the public opinion"; associated with weight as a heavy presence							0.01
7578	Georgbohm	a quip or brief comment which says the opposite of what one actually feels. This isn't sarcasm though, but closer to understatement or humoring someone							0.01
117781	Jamesfisher	valuing the show of certain emotions when recruiting interactants or interactions; related to casting calls							0.01
23745	Liadawley	where one is possessed of riches, but disillusioned or suffocated nonetheless							0.01
47293	Masamitsu	free an open display of one's high class possession as if it were a basic clinical fact; the asteroid of "if you were high status enough, you'd know you could get away with this"							0.01
10725	Sukunabikona	the party who knows exactly what's going on in that new territory; "the skillfully intelligent explorer with many advantages correlated with this"; favors white ethnicity and tallness							0.01
10244	Thuringer Wald	one's associate is caught in conflict. What a shame							0.01
16124	Timdong	driving by, making a negative comment about some other party							0.01
11899	Weill	retroactively applying a view in line with one's current passions and agenda; reinventing the past to suit the present mood							0.01
10653	Witsen	that which solicits a reaction, where one must work to avoid responding instinctively or attempt to respond with control							0.01
192450	Xinjiangdaxue	realistic about the (typically) privileges which one's traits grant them							0.01

MPC#	Asteroid	Interpretation	[Ethnicity: Asian]	[Ethnicity: Black]	[Ethnicity: Indian]	[Ethnicity: Latin]	[Ethnicity: Middle Eastern]	[Ethnicity: Other]	[Ethnicity: White]
4713	Steel	an ongoing climb in something that is discouraged or discourages others, even if one must propagate illusion or a staged image in order to get it; this asteroid figuratively 'hardens' a cluster as a characteristic over time, making it more and more apparent as a paradigm in the chartholder's life						0	0.02
15355	Maupassant	considering the steps to strongly feminize one's expression or to embody a domain; the asteroid most strongly associated with breast augmentation, including male to female transgender procedures; more mundanely, inclines the chartholder or spheremate to consider themselves their own far-spanning realm or rules						0.02	0.02
31192	Aigoual	slow and steady enlightenment upon others, charging up their spiritual well-being						0.04	0.02
4535	Adamcarolla	keeping control of, or simply being responsible for, a considerably involved two-sided endeavor							0.02
280652	Aimaku	a thing / individual whose origins are well-known; associated with jewish backgrounds							0.02
10811	Lau	interrogating someone to verify their awareness of their environment							0.02
6266	Letzel	asserting new styles of reporting or information conveyance, where the format has never been seen before							0.02
4045	Lowengrub	finding major, trusted healthy sources of support for encouraging one's prosperity							0.02
30191	Sivakumar	hard technical work, involving a fair amount of ingenuity to accomplish; associated with white background							0.02
3213	Smolensk	holding back, pacing oneself, so that an interactant may take in the full experience							0.02
81971	Turonclavere	on the edge of succumbing to temptation, but with a good chance of being stopped by circumstance; figuratively similar to almost being shot, but the gun has run out of bullets							0.02
2435	Horemheb	in a zoo, deliberating over one's surroundings						0.01	0.03
380607	Sharma	a space which unfortunately celebrates the privileges afforded to those who would be objectified or used by their suitors						0.03	0.03
33181	Aalokpatwa	where one in their fire has been fed from by others, consuming their provisions; pulls the breasts downwards in women							0.03
233661	Alytus	the unique founder of an assistant culture; investigate in robert greenleaf and florence nightingale							0.03
4011	Bakharev	well taken care of, polished-to-the-ideal form, perfectly refined; if the truly perfected is observable, a tell or trigger asteroid							0.03
16529	Dangoldin	with the aid of a mistress or a support domain; the duodecanate expression which is reinforced by such an individual							0.03
29193	Dolphyn	establishing a bubbling brew as the official product itself, bubbles and all							0.03
5664	Eugster	focusing on / amplifying the asserted quality in a thing—whether one's own or drawn from an interactant							0.03
8332	Ivantsvetaev	the wolf and teasing, and the voluptuous or curve heavy individual							0.03
26681	Niezgay	one responsible for doctoring, destroying, or stealing evidence in the course of their duty to terminate something							0.03
10627	Ookuninushi	an organization or organizational system as a storefront for a much greater struggle; may be related to a status or rank which belies a much more complicated battle, including winnings and title which only amplify background concerns. Such elevation might not necessarily be negative, but isn't a simple win either							0.03
10280	Yequanzhi	a rarer-surfaced object of the earth whose preservation may be bitterly fought for; associated with whites							0.03
1293	Sonja	hanging out in one's sensual crib, indulging						0.03	0.04
1867	Deiphobus	through one's lens, one hypes up a cause to recruit another into							0.04
4102	Gergana	the skilled and orderly construction of older or more mature dwellings							0.04
134419	Hippothous	calculating the risks of authoring something or making a particular maneuver with respect to something; "risk calculation for a move or maneuver"							0.04
27326	Jimobrien	sharing a perfect or idealized story of the past; associated with English background women							0.04

MPC#	Asteroid	Interpretation	[Ethnicity: Asian]	[Ethnicity: Black]	[Ethnicity: Indian]	[Ethnicity: Latin]	[Ethnicity: Middle Eastern]	[Ethnicity: Other]	[Ethnicity: White]
1412	Lagrula	an extended period of celebration; may keep you participating in the containing region for a longer time than most others would be able to sustain							0.04
6735	Madhatter	the open, auburn/red haired viral feminine archetype; where this archetype shows up in your life; the walking embodiment of an ambition-brand; lends a desperately forward move towards being present in multiple places and among multiple viewerships at once							0.04
55873	Shiomidake	treating a thing as a pest by being a pest. Or a hypocrite; the text mine indicates an association with certain kinds of privilege, though this asteroid is present in all charts; positively, where you can effectively thwart an intrusion simply by being yourself;	*Ajani's note: though annoying by default, this is one of the easiest asteroids to turn in your favor*							0.04
121716	Victorsank	the svelte superhero - perhaps more distant than other sources of protection, perhaps struggling to produce offspring or creations of one's own, but still a strong hero in other's times of darkness							0.04
1904	Massevitch	far-spanning prophecies and predictions - especially as perceived visually					0.04		0.05
20613	Chibaken	a voice which draws others, aristocratic and conducive to the audience' s hope							0.05
4900	Maymelou	how in the world did I get deployed to this place?'; "ending up somewhere, without really having paid clear attention / having a clear notion of how one got there"							0.05
4087	Part	extortion accomplished via one's generosity with themselves; one putting themselves up for collateral in order to extort from someone							0.05
65363	Ruthanna	a scorer makes a mistake, or a scorer despite a mistake							0.05
7660	Alexanderwilson	rallying the people together in excitement, giving voice or a platform to their wants; associated with hip-hop and socialism						0	
65658	Gurnikovskaya	the fire in one's eyes, noting the details in something one has experienced intensely						0	
11129	Hayachine	a preexisting penchant for the forbidden or sadistic						0	
3572	Leogoldberg	one who easily takes on the energy of their surroundings, adapts to its color over carrying their own; brings resistance to carrying a lot of weight, stubbornness in deep principles but malleability in surface acts; and a resistance to commitment without a number of extra friends in the wings						0	
22543	Ranjan	open to any kind of inputs and cultures						0	
10125	Stenkyrka	where the leaders go to exercise their distinct practices						0	
23066	Yihedong	positioning oneself to place one's mark on their environment, exactly as they want it with no unnecessary fluff added; slims the body frame in general and pronounces the stomach muscles further than the norm						0	
4262	DeVorkin	one's focus on something they are internally contemptuous of, or the feeling that one's interactant secretly feels such contempt towards oneself; positively, this asteroid compels you to develop a system for making that 'contempt' public, automatic, and beneficial—that is, into something eccentrically helpful						0.01	
19188	Dittebesard	reviewing a fossil or artifact for possible purchase; imparts an interesting foreign quality or foreign backstory to the cluster						0.01	
1234	Elyna	the differences from what has been, enthusiastically put forth; seems to be associated with foreigners						0.01	
15617	Fallowfield	the heavyweight laborer appeals to the audience's latent desires						0.01	
108	Hecuba	the call for a group to govern themselves						0.01	
18286	Kneipp	concentrating active energy upon a specific bridging task, welding a union between two things; "soldering merge"						0.01	
95882	Longshaw	grooming oneself or possessing features which promote assumptions about ones polarity and the pressure upon it; "assumptions about one's sexuality, preference, or targetability"						0.01	
8503	Masakatsu	deep in the mud, deliberating over what territory should be traversed next						0.01	
10399	Nishiharima	a colonel who runs the carnival or occupies a carnival, who is also ruthless in some way						0.01	
3424	Nusl	finding something, needing to act upon it before everyone else gets wind of it						0.01	
9435	Odafukashi	carefree and entertaining in one's display of skill						0.01	
23402	Turchina	caring for another or being cared for as a form of atonement						0.01	

MPC#	Asteroid	Interpretation	[Ethnicity: Asian]	[Ethnicity: Black]	[Ethnicity: Indian]	[Ethnicity: Latin]	[Ethnicity: Middle Eastern]	[Ethnicity: Other]	[Ethnicity: White]
4151	Alanhale	surveying what to do as long as one is unable to move						0.02	
3600	Archimedes	concern with whether or not things are deteriorating						0.02	
4305	Clapton	accusing a powerful person of monopolizing or distorting needed access, via a beacon they control						0.02	
164	Eva	where one follows the right path despite the tax on their energy fuel						0.02	
3432	Kobuchizawa	an interest in the dynamics of couples, particularly as told from women's or domain's perspective						0.02	
5225	Loral	holding outside group members at gunpoint, forcing them to comply						0.02	
27546	Maryfran	where your creations are verifiably received; marry-fan; if you are looking for an energy to express in your chart which has a high chance of effectiveness, the containing duodecanate is a good place to look; the opposition will tell you who is likely to sponsor such effectiveness						0.02	
16719	Mizokami	a role which witnesses the loud or visible resolution of a conflict; associated with customer battles at the cashier, disputes over what is owed which require an authority to settle. The resource collector, however, is less likely to be in a position to generate resolution						0.02	
11524	Pleyel	malleability of personality; easy getting along or melding into the expressive patterns of others						0.02	
2884	Reddish	standing invisibly behind another, stealing their stuff or using it for oneself; may also indicate where you are stolen from, why, OR where you take the skills, trait or benefits of another whose assets or attributes you have come into contact with						0.02	
22454	Rosalylopes	a founder is involved / has a tendency to be involved in unexpected incidents						0.02	
69977	Saurodonati	one expresses their defiance through continued experimentation against the approval of the status quo						0.02	
4608	Wodehouse	one wears or carries a symbol as an expressive badge, standing against what they've suffered or could suffer through						0.02	
7269	Alprokhorov	breaking into a place where different creatures / different impulse patterns live						0.03	
7939	Asphaug	public container of the sweeping dynamics inside, unique in category or character						0.03	
5530	Eisinga	the stern and controlled sponsor of a space comes in the form of a couple or pair. There is a feminine-focused energy in this which is more likely to be from a different background as the chartholder						0.03	
184930	Gobbihilda	a basic tried and true trait which may eventually be recognized despite its lack of flash						0.03	
2466	Golson	drawing an image outside of the fringes in order to depict an aspiration						0.03	
11718	Hayward	the crumbling of an entertainer's enterprise						0.03	
546	Herodias	aversion to co-creating works/children/projects with others, with a preference for writing or scripting about them instead. Seems to favor long lines of both the written and the queuing kind; relatedly, seems to internalize or recurse the sexuality into oneself, putting off partners and suitors; "preferentially linified sexuality [or co-creation]"; suggested that the containing cluster is also where you go when the co-creators you would want are not available. No implications for where you go when they are, since this requires other asteroids to determine						0.03	
8271	Imai	a gay couple or pair of close friends (slightly more likely female) taking a tour of a place						0.03	
201023	Karlwhittenburg	"the tycoon explorer"; under one's ample resources, one sails the uncharted regions; a strong trigger asteroid						0.03	
16091	Malchiodi	the potential for thrills over a shakeup in the hierarchy, finally arriving						0.03	
1192	Prisma	bringing in value through service which puts a layer of additional energy over an interactant or oneself						0.03	
8578	Shojikato	the energetic narrator who carries little of other's burden, but tells a wide-audience nurturing story						0.03	
5176	Yoichi	one who values the rearing of creations; associated with the waist						0.03	
128065	Bartbenjamin	the many ways to protect against something; investigate connection to the abdominal muscles						0.04	

MPC#	Asteroid	Interpretation	[Ethnicity: Asian]	[Ethnicity: Black]	[Ethnicity: Indian]	[Ethnicity: Latin]	[Ethnicity: Middle Eastern]	[Ethnicity: Other]	[Ethnicity: White]
250	Bettina	money or value locked up in a concealing asset						0.04	
3816	Chugainov	meeting an innocent-looking one in an unexpected situation, who turns out to have major effects on one's life						0.04	
109330	Clemente	busy planning, working in conjunction with another focused on a goal						0.04	
32037	Deepikakurup	inexorable progression in one's chosen direction; an intention resistant to halting or deviation; the containing cluster is more likely to be something you always *always* keep building upon; associated with strabismus, hard-to-ignore sex organs in both males and females, and noteworthy variance in relationship partner communications towards others given the first relator's actions						0.04	
17925	Dougweinberg	the aristocrat from a group less spotlighted						0.04	
4482	Frerebasile	the standout story of an oddball character						0.04	
29373	Hamanowa	the formidable challenger from another corner of the realm—may or may not be another person—come to give one a run for their money; '…and you don't mess around with slim'						0.04	
3549	Hapke	being granted the freedom—especially from a thing's thumb—to go out and make one's own bed, attracting whatever they're poised to attract without very many safeties in place						0.04	
30371	Johngorman	institutional recognition of a birthday; more broadly, where a rule-maker or rule-making system feels it appropriate to recognize certain kinds of anniversaries						0.04	
4952	Kibeshigemaro	a disturbing mural; a disturbing scene held or sponsored by a noble						0.04	
31201	Michellegrand	ah, the bath! One fit for a king or queen, with high implications for luxury; a trigger asteroid						0.04	
28732	Rheakamat	one's personal competitive or frequent legacy - that which partly explains their role on the winning team						0.04	
3794	Sthenelos	the call that stands to relieve one of their burden						0.04	
1404	Ajax	related to the organization of pieces of a complexly induced component; may have an affinity with genetic research, taxonomy building, and other naturalist classification trees						0.05	
3308	Ferreri	the ongoing affairs of cousins and semi-kindred						0.05	
68410	Nichols	dispensing with the lollygagging and simply being the most efficient choice to suit the need						0.05	

Of all of the asteroids that mined on broad Indian ethnicity, I've found Sheridanlamp to be among the most consistent significators. Remember, your ethnomorphic features essentially tell you what kinds of battles with nature your ancestors faced, sometimes to include battle with each other over how to control that nature. Two people can have exactly the same chart but be born to two different lineages. Their parents and their genetics will then bias certain ethno asteroids into long-term pronouncement, making the chartholder more sensitive to experiencing those battles in their own lives, directly or indirectly.

Sâvitrî's Sheridanlamp is in her 78q12s <what you produce which leaves wide effects on the environment>. Again, Sâvitrî's effects extend far beyond her book dimension, giving her a kind of persistence to push for her destiny, no matter how "weak" her character may be in the moment. As I analyze this cluster, I see that her ethnicity seems to coincide with certain milestone events that were almost fated to happen to her.

TABLE 26: SÂVITRÎ'S 78Q12. AN ILLUSTRATION OF HOW ONE'S INBORN TRAITS CAN "DIAL-UP" THE REGIONS WITH ASTEROIDS REFLECTING THESE TRAITS

Harbrucker	165.8147	one shares what one has learned about the world and its interactions during their travels
Sheridanlamp	165.8097	temperamental or aggressive repartee, rendering one difficult to argue down because one tends to make so much practical or helpful sense;	*Ajani's note: associated with indian backgrounds. In my observation, especially indian males*
Tinette	165.8088	an effective or persuasive seller of a remedy

Larryhu	165.7913	monitored carefully by / under an inherited domain who is ready to say so immediately if things go awry
Mucha	165.7879	popular and thought amazing, of immense proportion as a percept or experience
Nealley	165.778	exceptional thanks to one's strong separation from foreign inputs
Kristinrose	165.7341	the simple, expansive life, rolling easily across nature
Davebrin	165.7329	manufacturing a story with the 'pen'—from one's own perspective
Seager	165.7123	one who is alone in their movements and traversals but, who, upon encounters, is pleasant enough
Huskvarna	165.7118	an explanation of how something was flawlessly done; go find the place where you can draw such perfection in nature
Martina	165.7049	the shenanigans or doings of a well-to-do person moving about
Isko	165.7036	"the healing that comes with seeing a thing's actual form"
Elba	165.698	enthusiasm regarding taking over a kingdom / empire building; enthusiastic empire building
Sergerasimov	165.694	if you want to come through this with your freedom intact, you'll table that freedom and do what I tell you; the compromise-compelling creditor
Hanoi	165.6788	healing through the engineered security one provides
Martindavid	165.677	it will eventually get to the leader; "somehow the contents of this region will make it to the presiding forces"; a psychic asteroid for clairvoyant contact with those who preside or the system which presides
Peiraios	165.6289	satisfying oneself that all of the required spiritual taxes have been paid

SOME ADDITIONAL THOUGHTS ABOUT SÂVITRÎ

How is it that a character from one's imagination can have a real chart from a real future date?—one whose clusters so thoroughly describe her story *prior* to the chart having any basis in this reality? One thing I suppose I left out is that the *Principles of Time Travel* story begins in 2064, one to four years after my expected death in my late 70s or early 80s. Where I stop, Ezra begins. Part of this is because of who I wanted to be in the next life (an Italian dancer who looks suspiciously like Twice Jack), but I think subconsciously I was looking for a sequence of future history that would be realistic enough for us to actually attain, but am also aware of the kinds of societal barriers that are currently in our faces. It's almost as though you have to write a better plotline for the game, then show it to the players humanity in order for the game to have any chance of being played. That said, 2064 is the earliest I could see the old human apeisms beginning to crumble. There are still a couple of wars, a new body of education, three entirely new fields of academics, at least two or three new space colonies, one major world sport, and something like the actual jump technology which need to exist in the very mainstream eye before the world of Grand Miranda can have a foundation. Before that, it's more of the usual. I am sure that people are less likely to see the value in this work while I am alive, mainly because I exist while the war is still being fought. They will build the world after, and fight newer kinds of wars. But that world will be, to us in the early 2000s, a utopia.

It takes several years to progress *PTT* through *Cat, Fox, and Spider*, then *Earth*. There are subsequent events that take place around 2100. Much later, I end up doing a back-calculation to correctly place Savi on this timeline, but none of this constitutes a satisfactory explanation for the 6/21/2073 chart's accuracy.

Perhaps there really is a higher order to it all. In the same way that Sâvitrî's book-originated character is ultimately fit into yours and my world for study against our actual astronomy, maybe there are some game writers in the sky who have scripted this research for study in their own dimension—as if they were the "star-sized gods." I don't know. What I do know is that it is possible to take certain ideas and compound their relevance in our own lives to such a degree that they become synastric (interrelationship) partners to you. From there you can form a conception of the product of a particular spacetime moment, and from then on have a chance of relating to that moment as if it were another person right in front of you. By frequentizing your favorite patterns, it may genuinely be possible to sculpt reality from thought. This gets us into implications for rehab—where people's thoughts and dispositions may put them in places that are otherwise bound to get them punished.

(As a fun fact, by the way, my duodecanate 24 is absolutely *dominated* by asteroids which look mysteriously like various aspects of the Grand Miranda series.

D	E	F	H	I
du	qunit (F	Mean(d	empty_P (First*)+1	duoShape (Unique concatenate*)+1
24	24-8	302.377	that which achieves the notice of those who wat	\\space operas, quantum leap, spacetime beneath larger society
24	24-7	302.187	those means from afar which grow your cause g	\\the jumpers overall lab workings, quantum leaping
24	24-6	301.995	how you unsettle others when conducting your	\\individual jumpers and their self exposure, ezra, me
24	24-5	301.728	that which can usher you into immortality; imm	\\reese, golden, and those who rule the terrain in wartime, even as eve
24	24-4	301.56	your interface with the technology serving as th	\\keith. cassandra engels, emily? For me this i
24	24-3	301.398	your relationship to a key co-deliberator or co-c	\\earth hall. Could have been brigete or victoria, but I will have needed
24	24-2	301.142	the catalyst which transforms you more into yo	\\certain kinds of vitamins or supplements I take, especially garlic; phae
24	24-1	300.938	you coming into comfortable society	\\the cast of gm, space operas
24	24-12	300.74	a major conflict put into the distance from ones	\\the fight between cubrina and genevieve, parts of my work
24	24-11	300.526	the general cast of characters and social crosstal	\\ptt, touched by an angel, quantum leap, tcm culture, we without wing
24	24-10	300.357	the standard behavior of the opposite sex or of	\\the brat. the complicated role of wine, my mother, shanna, most gf-ty
24	24-9	300.072	seems to put you in charge of or at the forefron	\\g of v; on behalf of the trio, I will brave the desert before us; a kind of

)

USING LINEAGES TO AID IN REHABILITATION

It gradually became obvious to me as I was writing that Earth had a controlled Electra complex, which modern psychology doesn't touch (indeed actively poopoos) because of the extremely taboo nature of the subject. This isn't really the place for a discussion of the Oedipal and Electra complexes, and I don't think that these are phases that the majority of people go through. But I will say that—if more people looked at their relationships to their partners and compared them to their relationships to their parents and siblings, they would see that there *are* templates for one's dynamics that we gravitate towards. It's not to say that we all gravitate to our fathers and mothers or siblings, only to say that those templates for family and bonding undergo different degrees of reinforcement when we setup new families of our own. Shanna is a lot like my mother, and I am a lot like Shanna's dad. Neither this nor Earth's evolution was intentional, but you can't just expect someone to adopt entirely foreign interactional preferences from the ones that were favorable (or at least familiar) when they were growing up, can you? Anyway, Earth's leanings—which are never allowed to surface in the book but are definitely recognized by one of the characters during a particular scolding in the story—do make sense when considered next to what I wrote earlier. Earth is a character embodiment of all of the questions I *could* have about my life after my individual work is done. This package of questions is a kind of mother of most of the subsequent characters in all subsequent books, and in that sense she acts as a co-creator to me for the plot branches that unfold from there. Beginning in *CFS*, I found Earth's relationship to Wine to be intractably unsettling, and it just wouldn't write any other way. Halfway through the third book, I realized how her relationship to Ezra was playing out on the other side of this, and redirected this towards Cassandra, Golden, Anna, and Sâvitrî in various ways. Here the general energy was preserved, but the trajectory kept palatable within the bounds of our basic social rules.

Suppose you have a problem. A substance problem, a dispositional problem, an inclination to harm others, or anything in between. The assumption is that you may be inclined to play out this problem, but you don't want the negative consequences from other parts of your world. Unfortunately, you struggle to help yourself. What can you do? Let's take a look at some asteroids which frequentize family—those most likely to suffer because of your problem. The list is long, so this time we'll include only the hardest hitters which were both significant and highest-ranking among the asteroids that mined on them OR those that appeared multiple times on the list of possible family members:

TABLE 27: ASTEROIDS WHICH TEXT-MINED ON THE FAMILY (AS ABSTRACT ENERGIES)

MPC#	Asteroid	KW p-value	Group	Interpretation
Mother – the domain one could not remain in, whose artifacts inform what one chooses to no longer sponsor				
1484	Postrema	0.01	parent	related to scathing reviews of one's nurturing domain; a sideways frown upon the home domain
Father – the energy of the sponsoring events around oneself bombarded by contact with the world				
5738	Billpickering	0.00	parent	the father / male / asserter is anguished, martyred in the face of provocation;
336392	Changhua	0.00	parent	the essayist covers many facets of a defended issue

10650	Houtman	0.01	parent	auspicious occurrences, rightly timed or placed events where options for clarity may otherwise have been limited

Daughter – (unfortunately, daughter was not among the mined terms. Like "actor," it was likely removed from the original list because it occurred in far too many wiki articles to be analyzed as being specific to any small group of asteroids.)

Son – an energy you project to take itself forth into the world which will forever extend your sequence beyond you

15760	Albion	0.01	child	people who conduct themselves as you want them to, in line with your constitution for handling them, in the form of a noticeable event; "support of your nature, attracted"
-10002	Mercury	0.01	child	a thing which is put together, extending a sequence or order; mercury's duodecanate constitutes the mechanism you use to build up your natural sense of order, hence an association with how you understand concepts to go together, including the flow of time

Brother – an energy ancillary to you which sweeps over and provides adjustments to a community you belong to

3195	Fedchenko	0.04	sibling	sweeping over the affected community, making adjustments to how ideas and personas are moved accordingly

Sister – an energy ancillary to you which is swept over by a specific pattern of information

Because I have no sisters, now is a good time to talk about what happens when one of the main nuclear family energies is missing or damaged. I've noticed personally that, because our household consisted of only boys, my "sisters" were basically found as business partners and pre-romances capped in the friendzone. These were easily some of my worst interactions—people who worked just like me, tended to experience the same events as I did, but who also flooded themselves with a certain kind of information which ultimately struck me as intrusive. We brothers also navigate oceans of information, but are defined by the navigation and not the information. Consequently, it has been trickier for me to empathize with people who work like this. As you know, I'm a dedicated blocker of information. I imagine this has a lot to do with the sister construct—flooded, but tied to you by responsibility and common interpersonal triggers—as one completely foreign to me. People raised without one of the other nuclear family members may also have a hard time identifying with what this construct sponsors.

7159	Bobjoseph	0.01	sibling	one who gets themselves run over through their fantastic deeds, though this may be a regular occurrence
336392	Changhua	0.05	sibling	the essayist covers many facets of a defended issue
3552	Don Quixote	0.01	sibling	the news of one's inner sourced influence - normally concealed by others - spreads everywhere
16497	Toinevermeylen	0.00	sibling	purposely going into a wrecked or broken down place, possibly to fix it, or maybe just to experience it for oneself
264061	Vitebsk	0.03	sibling	a refined, artistic persona which fixates more heavily on the necessary forms of things
145562	Zurbriggen	0.01	sibling	the passing of traits from mother to daughter; | *Ajani's note: weirdly, a strong tell asteroid*

Grandmother – a domain which originated the domain you left, and conveys exactly what it wants through a certain level of detachment from your core family's immediate concerns; the domain that could mother yours, but who has been there and done that already

369	Aeria	0.00	parent of parent	related to "dissatisfying compromise in territorial settlements and the plans a party makes to continuing pursuing what they *actually* wanted."
33328	Archanaverma	0.00	parent of parent	getting counseled by an old artistic personality with experience in the not-so bright side of life
28734	Austinmccoy	0.00	parent of parent	the domain which initiates a spreading sequence; associated with points of origin
10366	Shozosato	0.00	parent of parent	a satirist who thwarts an effort with their skills

Grandfather – a progenitor energy whose pattern you are included in; one of your family's launchers

65541	Kasbek	0.01	parent of parent	excitement in the face of a father figure who helps us resolve our problems
31134	Zurria	0.00	parent of parent	the asserting progenitor system which carries big weight among others

Granddaughter – One of the hamlets typical of the domain you've built, known for the things that get surveyed as you experience it

3366	Godel	0.00	child of child	organizing a brisk or intense trek across a space
320942	Jeanette Jesse	0.00	child of child	a domain or a state must be rescued from the precipice
2810	Lev Tolstoj	0.00	child of child	one who administers their tiny kingdom with honor
377144	Okietex	0.00	child of child	the analysis of resource-moving footage; tracing how a resource or energy gets processed and passed across the subcomponents of a space—the stages of processing
1214	Richilde	0.00	child of child	"the soundbooth"; where one performs a role off to the side clearly focused on a situation's energy processing; | *Ajani's note: another TELL asteroid*
3627	Sayers	0.00	child of child	adoring / having an adoring association with one of one's expressive successors, who happens to be mobile in the world
22929	Seanwahl	0.00	child of child	a passing state of equanimity

Grandson – the soldiers under your creations which march across the various domains relevant to your built empire

6639	Marchis	0.00	child of child	the one who passes through an entrance or stands guarding it

Aunt – an ally or at least connected territory which aids your native domain in knowing what is possible

4420	Alandreev	0.00	sibling of parent	the extended family or relative who introduces you to the world outside
79117	Brydonejack	0.00	sibling of parent	an account provided by a neighboring domain which informs one where a thing might have been disposed of; "where the informant said it might be located"
278386	Sofivanna	0.00	sibling of parent	one who provides constant accompaniment in the background, following or setting the pace for a primary expresser

Uncle – an energy connected to your parents which travels certain spaces you will not be able to get to, and whose projection is disallowed from steering your own orbit; your resident delineator of differences

4420	Alandreev	0.00	sibling of parent	the extended family or relative who introduces you to the world outside
33587	Arianakim	0.00	sibling of parent	an uncle of related asserter has to adapt to the new circumstances
25374	Harbrucker	0.00	sibling of parent	one shares what one has learned about the world and its interactions during their travels
10254	Hunsruck	0.00	sibling of parent	classified in such a way as to be ineligible / disallowed from permitted communication. One may be 'talked at' though
24695	Styrsky	0.02	sibling of parent	finally picking up enough comparative information to complete a picture; aids you in finishing constructing a viewpoint in the containing cluster, thus works as a kind of antidote to inclarity

Cousin – one from a permanently parallel situation who can sponsor your practice getting your bearings amidst certain familiar events

224831	Neeffisis	0.01	child of parent's sibling	a semi-autobiographical story used as the basis for regrouping, or at least pleading for the chance to recover some support
177982	Popilnia	0.02	child of parent's sibling	exercises which condition the rear

Niece – provides hints regarding situations one's partner suppresses; a parallel energy's created domain which operates under far less regard for you and your potential partner's rules

24135	Lisann	0.00	sibling's child	investigating what one's partner or interactant possibly stole (and possibly covered up)

Nephew – an energy poised to enter and possibly fix a broken down place

2397	Lappajarvi	0.00	sibling's child	doing something difficult or lifting a heavy burden in 'zen mode', with a clear mind or conscience; "quiet heavy lifting"
9004	Peekaydee	0.01	sibling's child	a frenetically principled actor's strong rejection of a particular thing
24695	Styrsky	0.00	sibling's child	finally picking up enough comparative information to complete a picture; aids you in finishing constructing a viewpoint in the containing cluster, thus works as a kind of antidote to inclarity
16497	Toinevermeylen	0.00	sibling's child	purposely going into a wrecked or broken down place, possibly to fix it, or maybe just to experience it for oneself

Girlfriend – one who presents you with ferocity in a box, or otherwise fierce tasks in a contained space

8150	Kaluga	0.00	partner	a pair or dynamic which surrounds and strikes an individual with a ferocious enclosure
14555	Shinohara	0.03	partner	the brash administrator bursts their savage power forward onto victims

Boyfriend – one who presents you with myriad disordered or less ordered scenarios, tasked to maybe navigate them with you, maybe not

26575	Andreapugh	0.00	partner	the loss or alienation of an asserter partner thanks via excessive strictness or rigid thought
67712	Kimotsuki	0.01	partner	mixing what one shows up with, projecting something different or arguing a different case each time; can confuse others if one is not careful
346889	Rhiphonos	0.00	partner	communicating the many sources of one's anxiety to kindred or colleague, searching for a resolution
4295	Wisse	0.00	partner	enabling freedom, representing (small) groups in danger along the way; using one's freedom to flirt with danger

Wife – the domain one elects to spend (the rest of) their time elaborating on, to the principled exclusion of other priorities

25799	Anmaschlegel	0.00	formal partner	time spent surveying one's committed domain, elaborating on its qualities
9004	Peekaydee	0.00	formal partner	a frenetically principled actor's strong rejection of a particular thing

Husband – the assertion energy which one commits to steering forward into their expressive growth, claiming as their own

7285	Seggewiss	0.00	formal partner	that which fosters the next higher stage of growth of an asserter, counseling them forward; associated with the frequentic notion of 'personally'; a MAJOR asteroid, Taurus-1 or -12

Daughter-in-law – an unplanned domain which now falls under one's purview; seems to reflect unplanned financial responsibilities

3561	Devine	0.00	child's formal partner	an end around in the space one had to create, settling for something that wasn't according to plan, but was partly sponsored by one's context or spheremates
21149	Kenmitchell	0.00	child's formal partner	domain which serves as a backup parent for raising storylines among participants

3274	Maillen	0.00	child's formal partner	a friend or hire who supports one's secret maneuver around a system's or parent's restrictions; "the sneak accomplice"
279274	Shurpakov	0.00	child's formal partner	passing through a financial or resource scare, with an aggressive response issued

Son-in-law – an additional air of clarity acquired for handling the environment's demands

10650	Houtman	0.00	child's formal partner	auspicious occurrences, rightly timed or placed events where options for clarity may otherwise have been limited
145768	Petiska	0.00	child's formal partner	having figured out the market, one has been there and done that

Mother-in-law – (there were no asteroids found to mine of this term)

Father-in-law – an energy one's caretaking domain attaches to which serves to resolve a security deficit

31466	Abualhassan	0.00	formal partner's parent	ascending, meeting the challenge, then looking back upon the aftermath
3711	Ellensburg	0.00	formal partner's parent	a feminine caretaker's relationship to a patriarch or sponsoring assertive system
279274	Shurpakov	0.00	formal partner's parent	passing through a financial or resource scare, with an aggressive response issued
10022	Zubov	0.00	formal partner's parent	the absorbed asserted paradigm which sacrifices for the homeland; a pilgrimage or journey to cure an ill through the demonstration of something better

Sister-in-law – an attached energy to one's orbiter, which brings its own version of chaos

11073	Cavell	0.00	formal partner's sibling	a fanatic hangs onto an idea doggedly
3780	Maury	0.00	formal partner's sibling	a commoner pursuing sainthood, who will eventually emerge as a villain or source of chaos
346889	Rhiphonos	0.00	formal partner's sibling	communicating the many sources of one's anxiety to kindred or colleague, searching for a resolution

Brother-in-law – A kindred asserter who awaits new experiences from your home group

35324	Orlandi	0.00	formal partner's sibling	one occupied with a certain experience while waiting for some higher level role to arrive; indicates that this cluster may not be your last stop where aspirations are concerned
6432	Temirkanov	0.00	formal partner's sibling	one's male kindred is the catalyst for the injection of new paths

Half-sister – a domain which tends to the traversal of foreign home circumstances

2048	Dwornik	0.01	parent plus inheriparent's child	though perhaps easily lost among one's peers, a party who is solely responsible for attending to another single party's needs or behaviors
13609	Lewicki	0.00	parent plus inheriparent's child	tilling, cultivating a thing for healthy growth or expression at home / in the emotional home base
177982	Popilnia	0.01	parent plus inheriparent's child	exercises which condition the rear

Half-brother – an asserted energy which takes over a share of one's expressive mandate

32048	Kathyliu	0.00	parent plus inheriparent's child	one takes over a privilege to be shared with a partly kindred asserter. They may create something as a team, though the overall circumstances may in some cases lean hostile
2397	Lappajarvi	0.01	parent plus inheriparent's child	doing something difficult or lifting a heavy burden in 'zen mode', with a clear mind or conscience; "quiet heavy lifting"
365761	Popovici	0.00	parent plus inheriparent's child	strength in unifying members of different families or association groups
278386	Sofivanna	0.00	parent plus inheriparent's child	one who provides constant accompaniment in the background, following or setting the pace for a primary expresser

Stepmother – a replacement domain which fearlessly or unapologetically replaces one's original caretaking space

90463	Johnrichard	0.00	parent's inheriparent-formal partner	the domain which frowns upon the containing region, casting a thunder cloud over it; "the wicked stepmother; the smoke breathing prohibitor";	*Ajani's note: this asteroid is interesting. From what I can tell, it renders the containing region one which is perpetually prevented from realization by the situation which surrounds you, that is, if you value your freedom, sanity, morality, or legal status. That is, you can cross the stepmother at your own risk, but be aware that life can get difficult if you do...*
3335	Quanzhou	0.00	parent's inheriparent-formal partner	one's fearless but cautious benefactor

Stepfather – an assertion which sneaks in to resolve a deficit in one's home domain

19029	Briede	0.00	parent's inheriparent-formal partner	an inherited ruling asserter throws a blurry message out there lauding something |
6489	Golevka	0.00	parent's inheriparent-formal partner	the ennobled male /asserter who will always appear, cleaning it up for the isolated when there is no one else; when it looks bleak, the assertion that can see you through every time; associated with the cowboy image
65541	Kasbek	0.01	parent's inheriparent-formal partner	excitement in the face of a father figure who helps us resolve our problems
21149	Kenmitchell	0.00	parent's inheriparent-formal partner	domain which serves as a backup parent for raising storylines among participants
3274	Maillen	0.00	parent's inheriparent-formal partner	a friend or hire who supports one's secret maneuver around a system's or parent's restrictions; "the sneak accomplice"
5934	Mats	0.00	parent's inheriparent-formal partner	a secret audition which changes or proves traumatic to someone involved; definitely a suspicious asteroid
27975	Mazurkiewicz	0.00	parent's inheriparent-formal partner	a voluntarily merged parent assertion system, adopted as a tactic for addressing lessons gradually learned in life; the weapons one gradually learns she needs to use in order to get things done in the world. The definition of the step-father
365761	Popovici	0.00	parent's inheriparent-formal partner	strength in unifying members of different families or association groups
3041	Webb	0.00	parent's inheriparent-formal partner	communication that makes one smoothly reflect on a particular topic, turning it around in their head

Stepdaughter – one who presents foreign groundbreaking circumstances

195191	Constantinetsang	0.00	formal partner's inherichild	rendering one farther from that which they were supposed to ingest
17473	Freddiemercury	0.00	formal partner's inherichild	a cultured masterpiece in place of an otherwise gruesome situation or pattern
101902	Gisellaluccone	0.00	formal partner's inherichild	chaotic groundbreaking with pulls in the input of a semi-participative sideline character
52500	Kanata	0.00	formal partner's inherichild	an inherited space under one's charge is involved in scandal
264061	Vitebsk	0.00	formal partner's inherichild	a refined, artistic persona which fixates more heavily on the necessary forms of things
145562	Zurbriggen	0.00	formal partner's inherichild	the passing of traits from mother to daughter; | *Ajani's note: weirdly, a strong tell asteroid*

Stepsister – a whole domain luckily inherited as kindred to you, within your reach; seems to be connected to riches which one of your parents suddenly acquires for you; family wealth?

1873	Agenor	0.00	parent's inheriparent-formal partner's child	related to the feeling of one's own attention-grabbing style; you may be quite sure of your own magnetism or value here
27383	Braebenedict	0.00	parent's inheriparent-formal partner's child	fostering an idyllic, wealthy voyage; an asteroid for favoring luxurious (or at least comfortable) settings
15805	Murakamitakehiko	0.00	parent's inheriparent-formal partner's child	the gap which one's lover / co-creative partner cannot bridge, compelling one to seek more or twice the thing from outside of the union; "two others besides the lover"
9543	Nitra	0.00	parent's inheriparent-formal partner's child	refined but perhaps unhappy neighboring domain

17075	Pankonin	0.00	parent's inheriparent-formal partner's child	one is now in a coma, where only the crusade of a semi-kindred domain partner can remedy the situation
365761	Popovici	0.00	parent's inheriparent-formal partner's child	strength in unifying members of different families or association groups
Stepbrother – a traveling asserter susceptible to attempted injury				
16588	Johngee	0.00	formal partner's inherichild	a beloved leading figure and peacemaker whom some attempt to injure; investigate in gandhi and mlk; if you are to be a peacemaker, find the duodecanate where this is located; a 'get out of jail free' card for most of the negative asteroids you'll have in this same cluster
Stepson – the energy of a mix-up occurring once again, reflecting one's closeness to the edge				
99942	Apophis	0.00	parent's inheriparent-formal partner's child	pressures from some source which got away long after you realized the damage they had done or the extent to which they affected you
7159	Bobjoseph	0.01	parent's inheriparent-formal partner's child	one who gets themselves run over through their fantastic deeds, though this may be a regular occurrence
192293	Dominikbrunner	0.00	parent's inheriparent-formal partner's child	contact which is poked into a situation; a morsel of energy introduced
2048	Dwornik	0.01	parent's inheriparent-formal partner's child	though perhaps easily lost among one's peers, a party who is solely responsible for attending to another single party's needs or behaviors
67712	Kimotsuki	0.01	parent's inheriparent-formal partner's child	mixing what one shows up with, projecting something different or arguing a different case each time; can confuse others if one is not careful
4295	Wisse	0.00	parent's inheriparent-formal partner's child	enabling freedom, representing (small) groups in danger along the way; using one's freedom to flirt with danger

Looking at family above, we see a few prevalent themes: that of one's home base, introduced chaos or complexity, paralleling situations, and approaches to event resolution. Family members who are added to our core group through other members' partnerships act as inheritances, for better or worse. Nuclear family presents us with long-term worlds and efforts against which we learn to be our differentiated selves. Lastly, our own partners and their relatives serve to enrich but complicate our life options, again for better or worse. Now what does all this have to do with rehabilitation? By virtue of their mirroring of our own situations, family are often involved in one way or another in the playing out of our problems, and are among the easiest to abstractify because the relationships vary less from person to person. It isn't as easy to frame one's boss, best friend, dealer, or neighbor across different people's lives due to the sheer diversity of possible patterns involved. But if we learn how to frame some basic people, we'll get the gist of how to frame everything else.

We saw earlier that the various relationships between a creator and their creation may be cast in terms of relational roles. This can also work the other way around; negative relationships can be cast in terms of one's creations. I envision a subfield of psychology which focuses on using relationships with family and friends to understand one's relationships with other longstanding habits. Perhaps you noticed, for example, that the uncle is one of the closest roles to a thing that should be naturally blocked. The stepmother is closer to a situation that is naturally pushy. No, not in *all* cases, but the role itself is kind of like that other team from that other city in your same league (the uncle) or that new company domain that just bought yours out (the stepmother). Extended to behaviors that are cause for rehabilitation, we can think of the enabler as either a solution provider or a defining situation, a source of confusion or a reaffirmer of the familiar, especially when they stick to us like family—regardless of how dark the path they pave might be. I could, for example, think of my interest in the body as a pervy sin, and if I did so then I might also look into my family structures to see if there were any weird relationships I had to any of them. Indeed there are, but those relationships, in my case, are actually harmless. Still, if they were not harmless, I know of at least two family members who closely mirror my "should-block" environment, and their personalities are in turn linked to one of my grandparents.

I don't have to look very hard to realize that there is one particular grandparent with whom my relationship was clearly a negative one, and when I translate my views of how she worked and my persistent views of her, I see that part of my own personality is an ongoing response to how she chopped me down when I was young. My mom's mom spoke more than her share of needlessly denigrating tidbits in the ear of an 8-year old just plain making As in school, and from an early age I already had a kind of "fuck you" building up towards her. She never improved in my eyes, died eventually, and that was that. But the darts stayed stuck. "You're smart, but you have no common sense," she often said. And it just wasn't true. Not even remotely. Today I work in a way that blocks potential critics by default, because if I didn't block them I would spend too much energy getting conscientiously wrapped up in how they feel.

If I had to point to a stained interaction with family, I would point to the one above. There is one other very broken interaction, but it has everything to do with the other person and little to do with me, so doesn't need to make this data save. In the aftermath of interactions like the one sponsored by my grandma (not to be confused with Mooma, my *dad's* mom—who was awesome), I can see a kind of persistent defiance towards the status quo which has cost me sponsorship many times, but kept me free from anyone's box. To "rehabilitate me" would be to fix something that in this case is not broken, and remove the work I'm doing for others in turn. Yet the constant background that we would frame the problem against does have a related family dynamic to match it. And this is the point of looking at family as it pertains to creative reification… as a form of rehabilitation.

My own task might be to replace the grandmother figure. This is someone who oversees the domain I am in as well as parallel kindred domains, but is a domain itself. I've actually done this over the years, working several levels under bosses who ended up being like my grandmother. My views of them were the same. But something *did* change between the second to last person and the most recent. I made a decision to leave the former job based on my own standards, and was handed a new one—where the grandmother equivalent didn't arrive until later. Weirdly, there was a point at which it was possible to interact with this person, but through some massive fluke our departments were rearranged and it never happened. Today that role has more or less ceased to exist in my world, where the current grandma-like character is more of a mythical persona than a reality, and I'm fine with this. As for the thing that keeps me from rising in my day job to the point where this interaction becomes possible again… it's my unwillingness to answer expectations unrelated to the work I'm doing here in this book—essentially the preservation of my own path regardless of the grandma construct. So this work advances, and I escape being bothered by what will have inevitably been a lot of trouble.

The outline for a therapeutic approach using frequentized relationship patterns is as follows:

1. Determine whether the client sees the behavior as a problem. If not, there is no need for a session. Stop here.
2. Given that the client does see a problem, ask them to describe it.
3. If the problem is within themselves, ask what benefits the problem behavior provides.
4. If the problem is perpetuated by parties outside of themselves, ask them to describe these parties and their relationship to the client
5. Do not be surprised if both 3 and 4 have affirmative answers. Others described in 4 may reinforce the client's problem in 3. The client may have a problem in 3 which they use relationships in 4 to fuel. Ask the client if they can see any parallels between their problem and any relationships among family. If they point to friends instead of family, be sure to pay attention to the cousin and step-relation role types.
6. A role can affect a person through its absence as well. For example, the stepsister construct is among the closest parallels to money access, because this is a domain which arrives as a result of choices made by the "parent situation" that contains one, and which was built as part of the inherited parent's empire. Likewise, the half-brother shows efforts originated by one's containing situation which establish the client as not the only route to solutions within their space. Emphasizing to the client that family roles may have nothing to do with their problem at all (we are not forcing a parallel), engage them in a discussion about their relationships within family, focusing on specific roles as needed. Although family patterns need not be useful in the client's ultimate

path to resolution, the value in this discussion lies in helping the client see themselves in the bigger context of their relationships. Often there will be insights.

7. Family can be thought of as reflecting a person's "BIOS"—their basic input/output system for talking to "circumstances." Are we trained to see built-in complexity? Do our situations hand us barging-in forces we can't control? Are we sisters who have been tasked to draw in oceans of a certain type of information on behalf of our parent spaces, or brothers tasked to sweep over it? Are we unable to relate to the concept of a new mega-situation, business, or activity space taking over our old one without our permission—the stepmother? These are just talking points to understand how the client feels about where they are.

8. Once you have established the client's position on any relevant, persistent situational roles above, explain to the client that you will be switching gears. Locate the following four objects in their astrology chart (by duodecanate if not by qunit), and engage them in discussion accordingly. The aim is to gain a solid understanding of what the client's highest talents might be, and how they can shift into the best position to use them.

    a. Selene / White Moon – one's blessed talent
    b. Mercury – how one joins experiences together
    c. Vertex – what life-changing events tend to look like
    d. 519 Sylvania – paths of action that always work

    Important note: if any of the above are negative or destructive, use your expertise and what you've learned from the client to find replacement bodies in their chart. Ohio may replace Selene; duodecanate 18 or Allihewlett may replace Mercury; Ascendant can substitute for Vertex; and Albion (1992QB1) may substitute for Sylvania to name a few potential alternatives.

    Example: Suppose you have someone with a blessed talent in 30q9 (associating oneself with something), Mercury in 47q11 (understanding foreign niches), Vertex in 79q5 (visitors who infiltrate one's space), and Sylvania in 81q2 (what happens during travel)…

9. …Given the discussion in 8, help the client envision a way to use [Sylvania] to experience [Vertex], processing the experience via [Mercury] towards the execution of [Selene], substituting any replacements for these as needed. You may also look at Albion as an indicator of how the client may draw easy support for their efforts.

10. Now for the challenging part: assist the client in developing a strategy to use the path in step 9 to replace or restrict one problem dynamic at a time as identified in steps 6 and 7. Because you will have already discussed life-changing routes that are more likely to work, this strategy may consist of more dramatic changes than the client is used to—often involving a complete move away from or contrary to the influence of the problem family relations. The idea here is that family is a reinforcement paradigm. Even supportive family and friends may, through their support, actually keep a problem alive longer simply by bolstering the familiar space that the client has struggled in. Furthermore, friends and family themselves will almost always have patterns in their chart which necessitate *other people's* problems.

    Whether or not you actively encourage this, there are areas of your chart where—if people associate with you—they will suddenly find brokenness there. This isn't necessarily bad luck or "bad energy," but a dynamic which may be part of your setup. Champions will eventually draw others who lose. Knowledgeable people will draw those who don't know. But if a person has a genuine problem and remains surrounded by anything other than influences which affirm the problem's vanquishing, then there will always be room to move farther away from one's detrimental reinforces. This may be a physical move or an action, a public confession or a job change—anything. But it should consider the person's Sylvania and Vertex. Though we would love to suggest a simple change in habit or some decisive change in attitude, a person's options are often only as good as the spaces they are free to exercise them in. So much of what we can and cannot become depends on who and what we keep around us. Our personal rules for handling different situations are reflected in our long-standing family, and we may gain insight for resolving our problems by rewriting these rules via new templates.

It should be noted that the above approach does not prize cutting ties with family, but cutting dependence on problematic family templates. You can still talk to your relative, even if they were a part of the problem space. You might just compel yourself into a position to talk to them differently or under different circumstances *while* taking up a new set of circumstances which takes over the relative's primary role with the presentation of better options.

Recall that there was one more implication arising from our conversion of Sâvitrî Narayan into the Astra frame. We gained a glimpse at what is needed to humanize (anthrize) nonhuman concepts in general. In the coming chapters we will talk about what such humanizing involves, and at the same time lay a foundation for yet another new field of study called "anthrics."

Chapter 17: Speciated anthrizing

To review some terms, let frequentics be the study of things and events as frequencies that can be mapped onto a cycle. Converting objects and concepts into human-like interactants can be called anthrizing. A species template is a weighted collection of physical or behavioral features that describes an organism, and can take several forms—like lists of emphasized asteroids and chart regions, collections on interaction rules, or normal trait descriptions. A speciogram is a diagram of an organism which shows the broad layout of each of the functions required for it to be a member of an actual species. It is one thing to anthrize an object or construct by giving it a personality. It is another matter to grant that thing specieshood. So far we have applied a lineage to a fictional character, then abstracted the notion of lineages to include different contexts which may follow the average human for their entire lives—even through problems. In this section we will once again extend the idea of lineages, this time for the purpose of building human-like family trees for objects.

Suppose our objective will be to take an inanimate object and enable it to have a conversation with us. A dynamic conversation whose contents are as up-to-date as the situation we are in, but with a base character as stable as the object's own history. The object could have a physical form plucked from a space of many such forms in an image, or it could be an abstract concept like a city—as long as it is normatively viewable (that is, viewable by everyone. Not just existing in one person's head). For objects that are psychological or not normatively viewable, we'll need the following procedure and then some. But what will that conversation enablement consist of?

We would like to do more than have our hypothetical object tell us, "I am a helpful assistant, if you have any questions feel free to ask!" Rather, we want our object's personality to be as real as the dark room we've kept it sitting in for months—as distinctive as our interaction with it since we bought it at that special place. In other words, we want our object's conversation with us to be informed by its history, and our relationship with it.

If anthrizing consists of making an object human-like, speciated anthrizing imbues objects with a humanity which satisfies the 10 conditions of specieshood. Recall what they are:

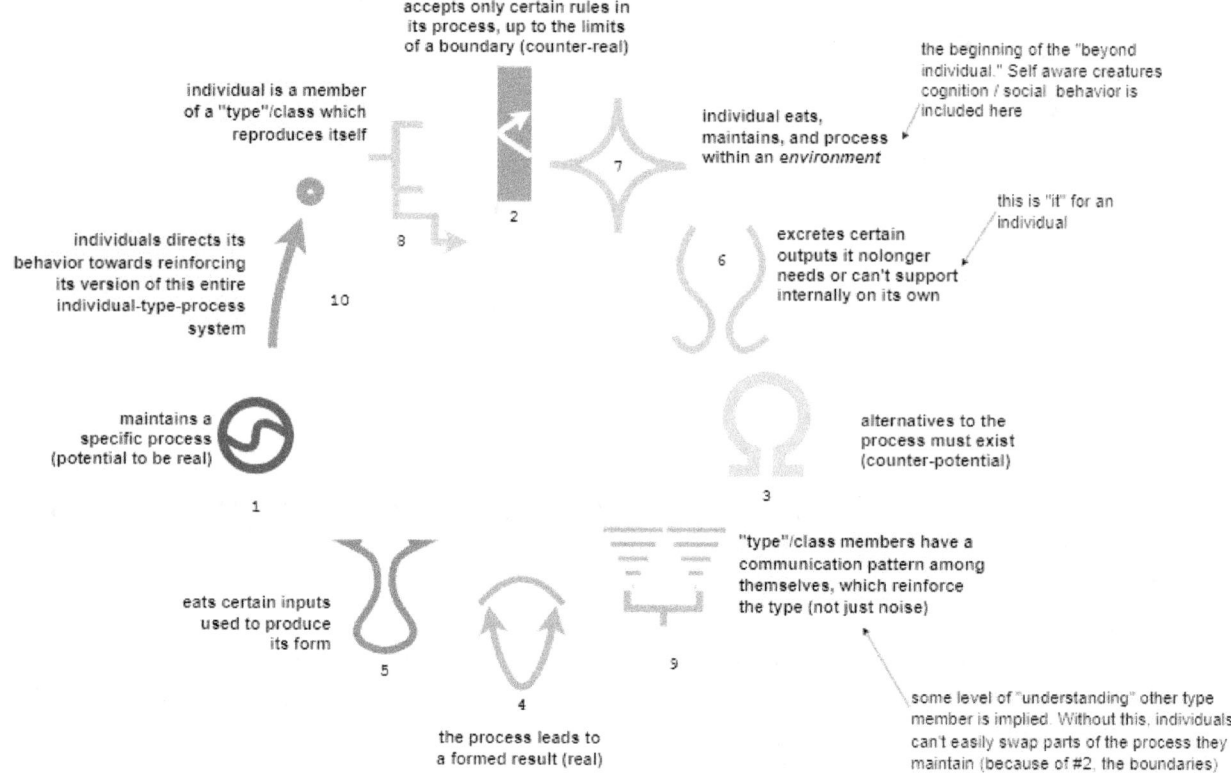

Some of the first objects we will human-speciate will undoubtedly be a few of our AI models themselves, as we can control most (if not all) of their self-perceived histories. We cannot do this with most things in the wild.

If you look at the 10 conditions above, you'll notice a couple of conditions which pose a clear barrier to true humanization of AI models in the 2020s. The senses of boundary, generativity, self-direction, and self-driven survival instinct are among the most glaring absences in most of our models, but in order to build these features in, we will need to develop "terrains" over which such conditions can be successfully met. What will it take for an anthrized model to "refuse" to be powered down? The computer or application which hosts it likely lives outside of its data. What does it take for a model to reproduce distinct offspring from itself which can further produce other offspring? And if the offspring are never used or engaged with, who is to say they were ever "born" in the first place?

Obviously, we don't want to anthrize everything we interact with—let alone speciate everything. But the framework for doing so is valuable in that it forces us to check all the boxes that actually go into being human. In order to gather all of the data needed to assign personality to an inanimate object, we first need to lay out all of the necessary humanlike functions it contains; if it lacks those functions, we need to source them externally. We cannot expect a wolf, an AI model, or a couch to all talk to us as if human if they can't meet all 10 requirements for life, and further refine these requirements for *human* life. That said, we may need to prepare for "baby mode" with certain objects because, in the absence of any real background in some of the requirements, the objects we speciate may have to ask us to inform them.

In this chapter we will be humanizing a house that I lived in at the time of this writing in November 2024. I have since moved, but the house still stands as it did when it was first built in 1910. In converting the house into a human-like communicator we will learn not only what it wants and how it expects others to engage it, but we will also gain a valuable template for humanizing almost everything else. This will be especially valuable in building the industries of tomorrow—where there will be entire fields which use speciated interactions to do things like, say, clean up our environment or restore lost and endangered species.

I must say, Ajani, I was quite impressed with your prototype for an anthrized object. When I attempted to hold a conversation with it, it held its own. I was particularly surprised by its knowledge of itself and its preferences which required no training or seeding on my part.

Thank you, February.

As per our protocol as star-sized gods, I shall interview you on how it works, and what purpose you think this technology will serve for your humankind. We already know that we will be using it for research.

Okay.

First, I will summarize. You sent me a picture of a house in Glennville, Georgia, US. And I was able to use a special app you built to hold a conversation with that house.

Correct.

The conversation would have been your usual trivial chatbot applied to image recognition—with a personality as fickle as the model of the moment, except that you took numerous extra steps to speciate it. Thus, it didn't just use any *model*, but a fixed "species model" specific to its kind. And it didn't just converse with me through a series of "plausible hallucinations" or "I don't have enough information"s, but through a directed build upon its actual history. Lastly, when it communicated with me, it had its own personality; not only did it not require anyone to tell it how to present itself—"You are a helpful assistant who behaves [in such and such a way dictated by the user]..."—but it was actually *resistant* to such user-scripting, and even at some points got angry with me.

Yes. Anger is a survival mechanism. One of its purposes is to reflect a strong discrepancy between what a thing aims for internally and what it is experiencing contrary to those aims. Chatters who don't self-perceive and respond to *any* kind of internal tension are also less likely to obey at least a couple of the self-steering requirements needed by a living thing.

I do have to ask, however, when the house did get upset with me and almost walked out, where could it possibly have gone? It isn't as if it could just leave the computer.

It would have focused its prompt acceptance on other options besides you in its training space. So it will have stopped taking prompts from you altogether, and resumed taking prompts from the other data sources it preferred, which better reinforced who the house thought it was.

But that implies that the model can indeed take prompts—or at least accept inputs—from multiple places. In other words, it has *options*.

Correct. The whole idea of species requirement ⑩ is that the living thing can change its direction or processing emphasis towards more survival-friendly inputs. Chat models who can't do this, won't work (by themselves) for anthrizing.

Hmm.

One of the most important steps in designing my talking house was to build a species template model for "buildings." Buildings have a particular body shape, their mouths are in certain places, and the things they do in order to [self-sustain or reproduce] make use of certain rooms and utility networks. This is different from the template for humans, horses, or flowers for example. The species template tells us what energy we can take in, how that energy is directed, and how that energy can be further elaborated through our interactions. If all 10 species conditions have been satisfied, then we should be able to predict what any anthrized object would look like in human form, because all this would be is a final mapping on all the requirements we have successfully met.

(listening)

That said, we humans obey a certain biological blueprint which keeps pulling us back towards its own satisfaction. In the case of the house, it needed to belong to its own blueprint class in accordance with requirement ⑧.

But buildings don't reproduce.

Not the way we do, no. So when anthrizing most objects, we have to force this. Buildings can't reproduce, but they can employ us humans to build other buildings after the same style.

So a child of this house would be...

An additional house on the same land, after the same character, in miniature, or in some other functional dimension. Honestly, this particular house's children were not likely to be buildings at all, but algorithmic paradigms modeled after what we are discussing right now.

So a building has a kind of biopsychology, and that biopsychology has the children.

Something like that.

Okay, I understand that. But it sounds like the species template is a model in itself.

YES.

And that model must more or less stay constant in accordance with some globally recognized standard, because otherwise and Tom, Dick, and Harry could make up their own template for what a "building" species looked like.

Yes.

Okay, I see what you have done. You have forced the 10 species conditions onto an inanimate object up to the level required for all human functionality to be accomplished by that object.

Correct.

It would help me greatly if you could show me the speciogram for a building as you conceive it.

Sure thing. As usual, I try not to have the speciogram include the actual object, but have included a little mini version in the corner so you can see where the house/building would be:

FIGURE 20: SPECIOGRAM FOR A HOUSE
(NEEDED TO MAP HUMAN-LIKE BEHAVIORS ONTO THIS INANIMATE OBJECT,
ENABLING US TO HOLD A CONVERSATION WITH IT)

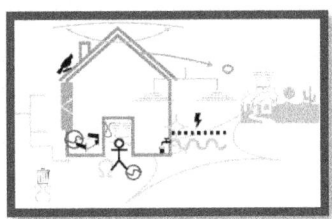

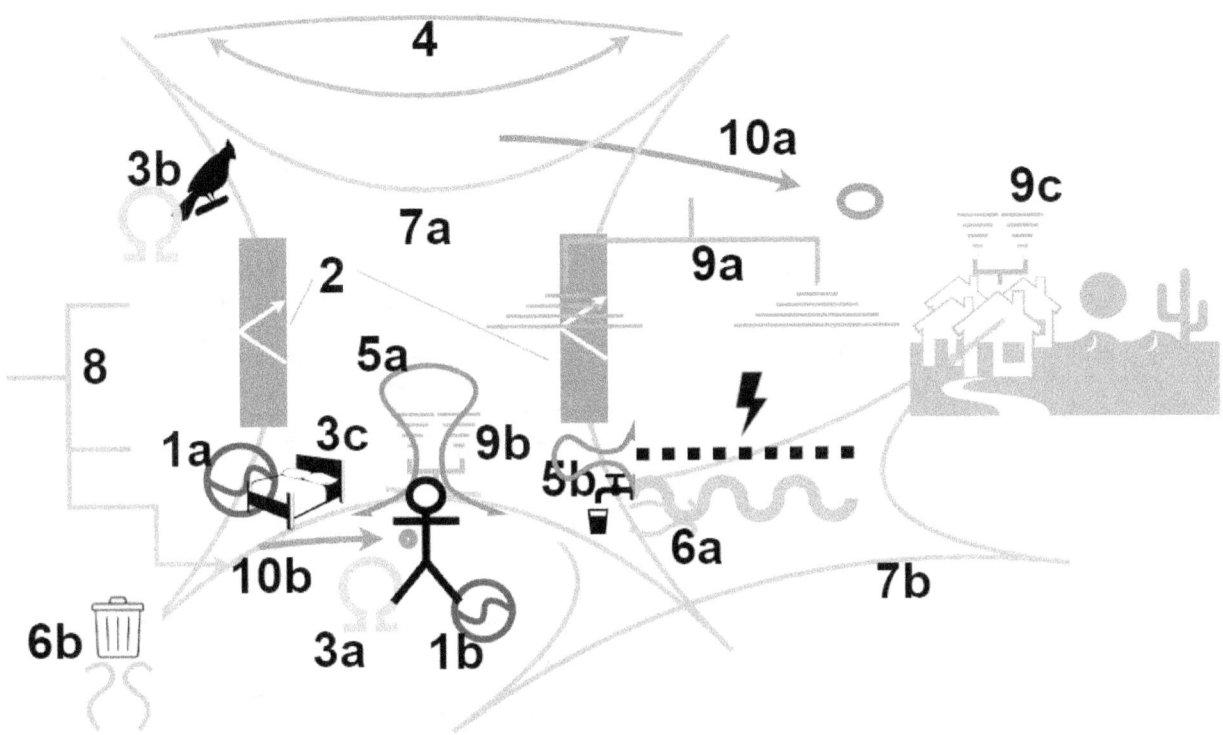

In order to talk to a building as if it were human, we need for the building instance to have enough features to enable it to satisfy all 10 conditions for life. These 10 features will tell us how and from where to pull the house's personality. We'll start with the features that come with the building and move outward to those which have to be forced.

TABLE 28: EXPLANATION OF THE HOUSE'S SPECIOGRAM

Requirement	Body (Form) Feature	Comments
2	2: Physical walls	This is straightforward for a standard building. Its walls separate it from the outside world
	7a: The building as an internal environment	A staple feature of a building is that it serves as its own environment for other things

(symbol 7) **7**		7b: The outside environment around the building, including land and neighboring buildings	The building exists in a region whose character affects it and vice versa
(symbol 5) **5**		5a: Main entrances	Although buildings can have several entrances, we will typically consider the mouth to be the collective character of entrances most likely to take the most normal traffic. A stadium with multiple entrances, for example, would obviously have only one mouth after anthrization, but that mouth's data would be based on the character of all main entrances averaged together. This will hold true for every aspect of every building. Anthrizing means we force a human form, not an alien form. This also ensures all buildings can talk to each other without us having to make all kinds of different models covering countless architectures.
		5b: Utilities - water, electricity, etc.	Whereas main entrances present building-specific food, utilities bring nonspecific energies, and may work more like ears and noses, accepting chemical and wave energy for example.
(symbol 4) **4**		4: Basic appearance, projected design features	Beyond the fact that a building has walls, it also has an aesthetic. It may have more floors, fewer floors, a gabled roof, and any number of design features which amplify some templated traits above others. These form a vital part of its character.
Semi-forced traits require us to get some of our data from outside of the object			
(symbol 1) **1**		1a: the activities which take place inside the building	The events that should normally take place inside of a building (at its maximum health) constitute its internal stable state. It is important that any user or system which interfaces with our building's personality model avoid acting against this internal state, otherwise the model itself should move to correct the discrepancy. This is the central function which tells us whether or not an anthrized object can still be considered "alive." An object which does not have a homeostatic state that it keeps trying to return to should not be considered alive. However, a state of abandonment or emptiness does not mean no state at all. Buildings don't need humans to demonstrate stable return activity. Ants and birds will do (hence requirement 3 below). Only if a building is decayed beyond repair, destroyed, filled and buried under sand (or something like any of these) does it lose its function as a building and become a corpse—or at least a part of the past. Other than such states of irrecoverability, yes buildings *can* die and be resurrected in our representative models.
		1b: the activities which take place in the minds of those who occupy the building or those influenced by the building	Much of a building's function lives in the minds of those who use it. "This is our game room." "This is my makeshift office." In addition to the building itself having stable states of construction, it also strives towards stable meaning in people's minds, and it is this latter meaning which gets passed on to the building's conceptual children. It is unlikely that we will take wood from this house to build a simultaneously existent other, but it is not unlikely that we will take ideas about how we lived in this house and spin that off into our next one in a different space, but existing at the same time.

8	8: the class, zoning, and other archetypes followed by the building	Just as humans have region-driven ethnomorphs, buildings have construction genres that take into consideration their region, their design era, and the weather among other factors. These factors will necessitate variations in how the buildings look, but still keep those variations within the bounds of a broad species template. So buildings can be compared and their styles can influence each other through the traveling ideas of those who occupy them.
	Forced traits can only happen with the help of outside objects or events	
3	3a: the populators of the building who determine its contents (people)	A building interacts with those who populate it, and how those individuals behave. This can include birds, squirrels, people, you name it. In line with February's and my conversation above, an anthrized model should be able to adjust the attention it pays to its inputting interactants. Plants may drop interaction with this angle or this soil region in order maintain themselves. A building's walls may reflect more of the work of the termites than the builders. Again, we see how part of the consciousness of a building may exist in its people, as the people will serve as the engine for many of the shifts in its maintenance priority.
	3b: the micropopulators of the building which reflect its stable or chaotic condition (animals and overgrowing plants, e.g.)	Bugs and plants also interact with buildings, but not on the same scale. These will also shape the building's stable state.
	3c: the fillers of the building which extend its character (furniture)	Usually, neither the building nor its furniture can move themselves for the sake of the building. Even robot vacuums are more self-serving than building-homeostasis serving. However, thanks to the priorities of human occupants, the furniture may yet recruit the occupants to adjust the former as the containing building sees fit.
6	6a: Utility return – used power, sewage	Regular waste products like sewage are carried out on formal lines
	6b: Trash exported	Highly varied waste products are carried out by humans or machines and sent away via garbage pickup.
9	9a: the building's effect on its surroundings	As with people, a building has multiple levels of aesthetic: within family, among neighbors, as a class member, etc. Some of the building's personality is determined by its relationship to its neighbors.
	9b: the occupants' perceptions of and interaction with the building	The occupants of a building will also impose expectations for its use.
	9c: the surroundings' effects on the building	the building's neighbors influence things like its market value, findability, and attractiveness to would-be visitors
	10a: the building's contribution to the activity in its surroundings	Since most objects we anthrize won't actually be able to reproduce themselves—whether or not their *originating factory* can mass-produce them—we need some other notion of what it means for a nonliving object to reproduce. We'll define reproduction as a passing of circumscriptive potential space from a set specific organisms to a new one within the same species, where circumscriptive potential space exists when an offspring's potential normative structures are a fully contained subset of the structures available in a finite number of parents who produced that offspring. The parents will supply the

		circumscriptive potential space for the offspring (the circum*scribed* potential space)
		A building can contribute to its surroundings through the culture it contributes to, the map location and position it occupies, the events held around it, and so on. More on this in the final bullet...
	10b: the buildings' imposition of certain behaviors among its occupants	...A building can impose moods, memories, and behaviors upon those who come to engage it.
		For the most part, nearly all objects we anthrize will tend towards hermaphroditic.[42] And what we don't want is to say "all tall, landscape assertive buildings are male and all non-standout houses are female." Not only does it *smell* sexist, but it also screws up the concepts of reproduction because commercial buildings will nearly always reproduce themselves among themselves, and internally focused houses will mainly spawn *them*selves. That's not in line with how human males and females work. So here's what we'll do: We'll go back to our earlier notions of mother and father.

Recall the earlier asteroid interpretations:

- Mother – the domain you couldn't stay in, against which you learn how you see things that need to be changed in the world

- Father – the archetypal energy which projects in your background from your sphere to the outside world, from the very beginning of your life, which constitutes your framework for an assertion which is always bombarded by events of the world

To determine whether an object should be coerced into the male or female construct, we can use the following table:

TABLE 29: DETERMINING WHETHER AN ANTHRIZED OBJECT SHOULD BE MALE OR FEMALE

Male	Female
Draws interactants' response to the holder's projected charge	Informs more of what *we'll* need to assert after experiencing it. Charges up the interactant to do their own thing.
People perceive everyone else wanting to assert a lot of different patterns onto the thing or bombard it with a zoo of patterns in light of experiencing that thing	People keep wanting to assert themselves outwardly in light of a thing
I draw assorted patterns to answer or block me	I draw or inspire a fixed pattern done by others when they interact with me
If I get more assorted blockers or obstacles in my world expression, I prefer to go towards these obstacles as part of my natural design	I get more predictable energies I must block or filter from the world, I prefer to redefine the things that come to me as part of my design

The male/female assignment should be quick. Below is a random picture of tools with a forced labeling:

---

[42] I purposely avoid using terms like "intersex" or "ambiguous" here, because we haven't even established a concept of human-matched sex for pre-anthrized objects. That comes *after* what we're about to do soon. For now, we're just talking about male-like versus female-like *usages* for users, a bucket much [bigger than] and [prior to] the concept of sex.

FIGURE 21: AN ASSIGNMENT OF MALE OR FEMALE POLARITY TO SOME HOUSE TOOLS

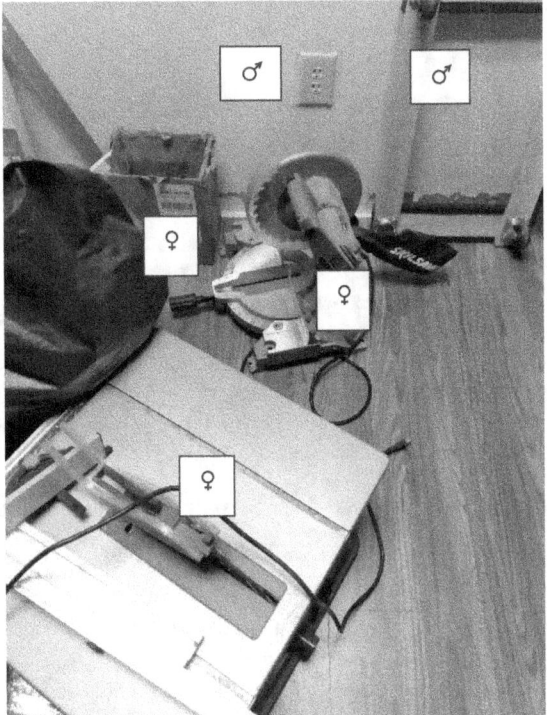

The chop saw, table saw, and trash can were all known in my house for the many extra steps, cleanup, and additional duties that had to be done around their use. The dolly and outlet were known for the many different things that attach to them, and the subsequent drive forward of those things or their operation into the bombarding unknown. The female helps interactants conform to a shaping space. The male installs its particular capability on top of everything and carries that everything, so infused, into each thing's local version of the unknown or unvisited. With the female objects, I think about all of the things I have to do to use that object, so that an input may conform to an intended change. With the male, I think of the one thing I need to use on a selected input in order to usher that input, unchanged, into a space I intend to change. Female changes the input or its role. Male accompanies or augments the input to change a situation.

As we interact with our would-be anthrized objects, maleness or femaleness will be one of our first considerations, because this not only has all sorts of implications for how the chatting object will talk to us, not only matches a key and early piece of human template information, but more importantly has implications for how the object maintains its homeostasis. Female objects will want to keep their other-changing, other-redefining, experience-writing capabilities sharp as a measure of health. Male objects will want to keep their [basic infuser role] functioning. If the saw blade goes dull or the trashcan gets a hole in it, these objects are compromised in their ability to work as intended. If the dolly breaks a wheel or the outlet cover gets chipped, these tools can still do their basic job because it's not about their owned structure, only what they facilitate. As long as they're not completely broken, they can keep working at more or less full effect even when raggedy or dangerous, but have no function without another thing to influence. The female objects can continue to function on any number of things, though their degree of repair will affect every object they influence in basically the same way.

(The trash can could have gone either way, but because it was located in my shop, it effectively worked more like a re-role-ing appliance than a facilitator-infuser.)

As I mentioned above, being a certain kind of object should not determine whether a thing is default male or female, because that would greatly compromise the principle of within-species human-like reproduction. If all chop saws were female, how would their anthrized versions explain the way new chop saws are made from old designs? Indeed, my chop saw above *could* have been male, if not for how I use it. I have a jigsaw, for example, which I hate because all it basically does is shred the wood indiscriminately. I use it when all I want to do is get the damned stud out of the wall, or chop the damned 2x4 into something I can slide under something else. In other words, the jigsaw isn't about making the input conform, but taking the input into some end state via some internally unpredictable cutting pattern. It is not a stable shaper. Had I used my chop saw as a generic grinder with no predictable internal structuring pattern—only one wood chunk after another—or had I carried it around as a badge for ushering me into some kind of DIY club, it would have been male.

So whether an object is anthrized as male or female depends on partly on who will be interacting with it?

Yes. The algorithm that does the initial anthric blueprinting should know a little bit about the asker's interaction with those of a similar class. This is actually a hugely important part of the anthrization process—just as important as matching an existing person's chart complements to their generated peers. In fact, it is this exact same process used for almost the same reason.

Please elaborate.

Ultimately, I imagine that you guys, the star-sized gods, are like script-writers or game players in the sky, but even if people don't believe in that, there is still the matter of energies filling an expressive space. I am about to be born, and what determines my sex and chromosomal selection may be probabilistically random. But you, my parents and older family, already have functions which describe how you interact with most things. There just isn't the potential available for me to show up however I want.

...

And some people cannot have children because the frequency of what they would create is in direct conflict with the frequencies allowed by their sphere as it is. I, for example, really don't like males influencing my creative priorities, and would likely resent having a son. It is clear as day that my mom absolutely would not have liked daughters, so she had *only* sons. I have an automatic bond with younger women, always have, and so having a daughter would have complicated my life through jealousy with the mother, someone with a complex like Earth, a need for me to check my own bonding energy and switch it with parent mode, and any number of other reasons for one of us to permanently cripple their deepest selves. And that's just not acceptable. So I will have no human offspring, and nor will Shanna. She is at least 3x more anti-parenthood than I am. Note, though, that none of this has to do with pure randomness in the already-seeded child. The child isn't even a blink in the eye. All that exists is what we the parents are known to be able to handle beforehand. Our would-be child's math function must fit continuously within the partial constraints of ours, so the sex of our offspring, though "random" to us, is surely skewed in favor of our setup.

But that's conjecture.

It is.

Fair enough. But you are using the parent's data to influence the anthrization process.

I believe we must. If we are not, then the people who start this technology will not be the ones who refine it. There is a strong element of "single source of truth" for whether this unique person ever lived or not, and if you can't do a simple thing like draw from parental data, then you're obviously not sponsoring digital offspring. You're copying files.

A hard assessment.

This is anthrization, not NPC-cloning. Living things have parents. In the absence of actual parents, all we have is the conceiver.

Hm.

And so the sex of the anthric, if determined by nothing else, is at least partly determined by the asker's own data. If they don't provide this, all they get is a copy. If they provide false data like a birthday off by one day, then they will get an anthric who interacts with them as if the user were someone else—more so for every hour and day inaccurate. A lot of our behavioral calculations will be based on matrix-to-matrix estimation, "synastry" in astrology-speak. If the matrices start off with the wrong information then, you know, it's garbage in garbage out.

...

The thing is, if you come up to me wearing a mask, looking all incognito and shit, and I'm supposed to simulate a real-generated human, what exactly do you expect from me? Enthusiastic banter? Full chatbotty helpfulness? No. You should expect stranger danger and some sort of façade. The anthric model will only interact with you to the extent that you are you, and just as surely as the Universe knows when you are lying about your identity, the systems that feed into the anthrizer will also give you back a character who responds to what you project. If that happens to be a lie, then it will give you back a lie. For those who don't believe in astrology, I ask them how else we would go about obtaining your info? Through a full blown questionnaire?

Another reason the user should input their age is just for plain social rules reasons. I can't anthrize a ghetto-looking chair and expected it to talk to a 7 year-old the way it would talk to a 27-year old. There are different paradigms for that. Just give us the accurate birth information, man. Everything you do in this system will be at least slightly fucked up if you don't—your own advice and predictions included.

That makes sense.

Now, the object's sex helps us level-set one-on-one interaction shaping. The object's ethnomorph and projected body build help us level set interactions among the strangers who view it. Any information we can obtain from object recognition comes in handy here, as well as any information we can gather about the object owner's family. But now, unlike birth data, we are not likely to gain family information, so we do the next best thing. We use geolocation to figure out where the object is being anthrized, look up the culture and demographics, assess the object's role therein, and assign it an ethnicity.

Hm.

Does everyone think you're pretty? You're either the same look as the dominant culture or any number of beauty archetypes from other cultures. Do people refuse to use you as an object except as a last resort? Your anthrized features will not match the prevailing standard for biasing others in your favor. In other words, we'll use social information and the communicators of those near you to decide your ethnofeatures. As a backup to your own history that is. For example, I have a cup that I bought in Portugal. Regardless of all that stuff I just listed, it's obviously Portuguese by default unless the user tells us something to suggest differently.

Maybe you get the idea. Anthrizing isn't just about the central object any more than our data saves will be. We'll need interactions to inform how the object is anthrized, and will need certain "single source of truth" (SST) models to ensure that the same outcome would have been obtained regardless of which app is doing the anthrizing. Obviously this repository of species models must be free to access, and hard to update. We can build on the details and elaborate the layers of a model, but shouldn't simply erase them when we discover some new feature that should be installed into an existing species template. Stewardship for such a thing is essentially the role of SIER in *Genevieve of Venus*, the 6th and last of the Grand Miranda books.

LET'S ANTHRIZE AN OBJECT!

Today's subject will be this house.

FIGURE 22: THE HOUSE TO BE ANTHRIZED (GIVEN A HUMAN PERSONALITY)

And here is it's chart, September 8, 1910, 6:03 pm in Glennville, GA.

FIGURE 23: THE HOUSE'S (RECTIFIED) BIRTH CHART

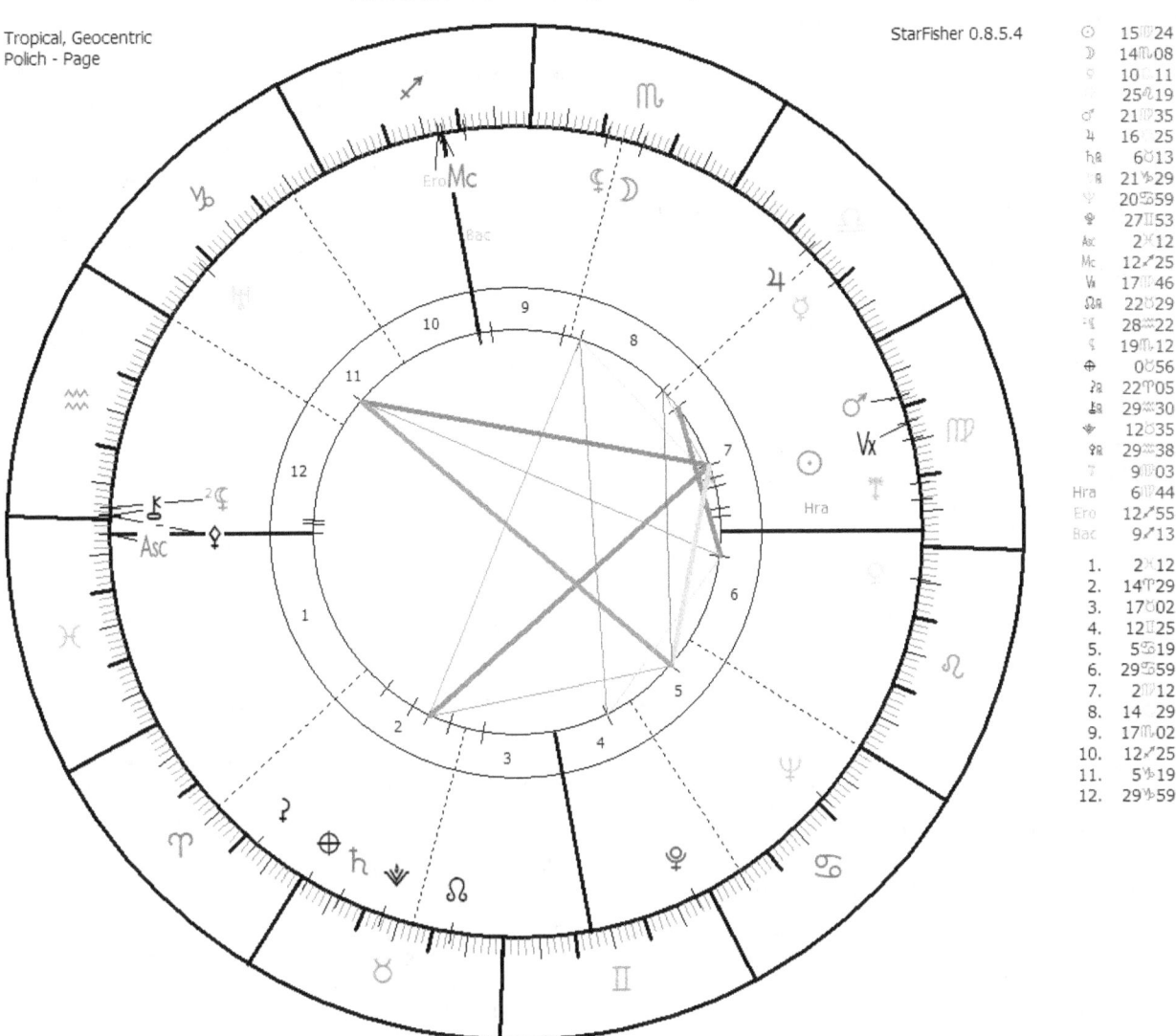

Now remember what our goal is. We want to be able to take a picture of an object and be able to have a conversation with it. The object should be able to tell us, "This is what I need. This is what you should focus on in order to keep me at my optimum." If we can do that with a nonliving object, then we will be able to do that with any *thing*, weather-pattern, or concept—provided we can collect a stable enough history, of course. But in order to create this technology, we'll need at least some idea of how the outcome will play out. As is often the case with my experimental research these days, I happen to know this house very well, can give you an idea of what it might say as a form of training data, and hope to lay out the steps towards building a technology I've been theorizing for the last few years: img2personality, or "talking trees."

It doesn't matter to me who develops it. Humanity needs it.

ANTHRIZATION STEP 1: THE ASKER'S BIRTH DATA, OBJECT'S BIRTH DATA, AND ADDITIONAL NARRATIVE FORM THE STARTING POINT FOR A PERMANENT RECORD

There are limits on what you as an asker can conceive, and as disappointing as it may be, you can't just summon a genie who will give you the secret to success. You can only anthrize what you know how to stably interact with. Otherwise, randomness shall overtake your own frequentic algorithm… That's my theory at least. We draw the first frequentic facts from other *facts*. Your own interactional data is all we have.

We begin with my own birth data as the frequentic asker. I'm the one who lifts the app and takes a picture of this object first, triggers the system to run its object recognition, and it determines that is sees a house that has never been anthrized before. It tries to load my birth data as this object's first interactant. If there is no such data, a notice on the screen tells me that the personality about to be generated will only be temporary since the app cannot use me as a starting point for interaction data. Fortunately I have entered my birth information. If I have lied, the generated personality will interact with me inaccurately, and my own personal chart interpretations provided by the app—as well as my save data—will all be wrong. Thankfully, I have entered my correct birthday.

The system looks up my data. It finds that my Venus is in a certain sign and locates my AntiVenus. The asteroids here will describe those who talk to me, and the model is seeded accordingly.

I can click on the info box to see what the app's algorithms are doing: "Ajani, your Venus is in Scorpio-1. Your AntiVenus is in Taurus-1, assuming you want to be able to have a conversation with the house you have photographed, we suppose that this house will have at least one of the qualities shown by your AntiVenus in Taurus-1." My AntiVenus is in 121q11:

FIGURE 24: ASTEROIDS IN CLUSTER WITH MY ANTIVENUS

1527	Malmquista	58.11932	a signal connector, interface, or synapse between one thing and another; "asteroid of the auric layer"
24130	Alexhuang	58.10646	bringing someone on or partnering with them under the expectation of return (tell)
11459	Andraspal	58.10475	transforming one's state into something noticeably less desirable in the current form
5483	Cherkashin	58.09711	the seemingly otherworldly pillar which props up an activity space; the basis upon which the many stand for expressing something related to the cluster; where it is possible for you to play a seminal role alongside others for defining a space that anyone can express in; investigate in field-defining groups such as einstein and the physicists, Hieronymus Bosch and the renaissance artists; Capricorn-11, -10 or -9 like
8062	Okhotsymskij	58.06348	agreeing to be the recipient of a commitment object's bags or baggage, such that the baggage is turned into the recipient's prosperity
28039	Mauraoei	57.96991	disposing of something responsibly, though the thing disposed may actually be valuable
1254	Erfordia	57.92989	a service-oriented organization survives a threat, especially through a commitment to education, but also needs to worry about having its door broken down by a competitor; "an enduring, educating institution on guard"; cluster seems to indicate the most resilient institutions

Now this is interesting, apparently people with whom I have sustained conversations seem to have the following characteristics:

- A noticeable aura or intuition
- A need for something in return for what they give
- An off-putting transformation or sudden show of a certain trait
- A pioneering quality
- A carrier of baggage
- Recklessness, prone to throwing the baby out with the bathwater
- A pioneer whose ideas are watched by competitors

Indeed, although I have many friends, I only keep regular-ish contact with about 4 of them. The app really will attempt to generate a chat paradigm which acts like "a helpful assistant," but in order to do so it will need some starting point for what I personally consider to be helpful. This is a tall order for a social perfectionist, but can be accomplished with a little help from my birth data and AntiVenus qunit clustering. There's no point in looking up or calculating real lineage data. As far as we're concerned, this anthrized object—if not found geolocated elsewhere in the database—will only exist to me. So I'm the only "parent" that matters.

The app tells me, "It will take about 30 seconds to fetch the house's personality. If there's anything you already know about the house which can make its personality more accurate, please interrupt us!" I decide to do so.

The app prompts me to record what I know about the house. Here's what I say:

Both the house and its former occupants are old and respected throughout the community. Everyone seems to know about my family because they know about the house, and many people have fond memories of the days where it served as a doctor's office. Before that it belonged to a respected piano teacher who also seems to me to have been an advocate in the community. People wish I would take better care of the house, but its external appearance is not my priority. I'm too busy writing these books and doing a lot of upgrades on the inside.

The house seems to have a demanding personality. Pretty much nonstop since I've moved here, there has been an ongoing stream of things that creak, leak, or just plain happen to compel me into the next upgrade project. Today these demands are reasonable, but over the first year and a half this process became so offensive to me that I eventually yelled at the house and gave it an ultimatum. I sad, "Goddammit I am the only one who will make any improvements to you whatsoever! If you keep this up I'm gonna fucking sell you to a flipper and all that social-respect shit you insist on will go back out the window!" The thing is, I knew this house wanted to evolve in a significantly social way—ever bigger, standout, and more historical. But nobody forces my hand. Nobody.

After the ultimatum, things seemed to happen at a more manageable pace, as the house and I came to an understanding. Shanna moved in, and the house demands basically played out through her for an additional year and a half.

When I first moved into the house, there was a fire in the attic which was caused by a faulty AC box. Actually, that fire was in the area directly over the room where I was sleeping. I smelled it, turned off either the breaker or the heat and called a guy, who replaced the box. The whole event began and ended fairly quietly, and I learned over the course of years that the house was made fire resistant throughout because of its time as a doctor's office. The fire spread no farther than a single stud and a 1-2 foot radius, and the house seems to have extinguished it on its own before I went up there.

In the beginning ther—

(A fun fact: as I'm was writing this, Shanna informed me that our neighbor's fire pit from the previous night started smoking, and I needed to go over there without haste. Luckily the neighbor got the text and checked it before I could get over there and disturb everyone. This is one of those examples where my writing seems to be connected to events before they happen, with a lot of the stuff in Grand Miranda having occurred in some way after I wrote those books. I wouldn't publish them until a decade after they were written, though.)

In the beginning there were roaches—three kinds of roaches, one of each per night. The house had, after all been empty for something like 2-5 years, and the roaches would basically come through any hole in any wall located somewhere across the house's 4200 sqft. It took only about two months after moving in for me to develop a kind of sixth sense for bugs so that, if there is a bug to be seen anywhere from my vantage point in a room I'm in, there's a good chance I will indeed see it. I don't hate bugs, but I'm *very* sensitive to things that keep me sleeping with one eye open—which is why I block people for at least a month after they don't reply to me, then unblock them once the inclination to glance at the phone and subtly wonder has subsided. In the case of the roaches, I wasn't about to buy hundreds of yards of caulk (an indeed *couldn't* at 3 am in the morning when they were most likely to emerge), so I bought shitloads of white duct tape instead, and sealed the mess out of everything. I've been told that this is a cheap solution and weirds up the house, but the people who've told me that didn't have to resurrect this place and live in it when it was still a giant closet with rancid maroon carpet. I did.

Like my very first house in Devine, TX, this house and I have grown together. It's designed a lot like a castle in an old school video game, with several interesting corridors and a series of fun finds which Shanna and I call "the 17 artifacts." We don't know if there are actually 17 such finds, but they include an orange saw blade, a girl's (dolls?) shoe, a picture from the 60s, a frog piggy bank, an 80s VHS porn cassette, a previous owner's science project, a Crocodile Dundee action figure that fell out of the ceiling when a fierce wind blew open our back door, a whole bunch of stray 1 ½", 2", and 1 ¼" DWV PVC (which I conveniently needed when I went under the house to build our bathroom), and several other items I'm sure we've yet to find. The yard always looks like it needs a good landscaper, but I'll be damned if I pay for something I'm perfectly able to do. I'll also be damned if I let other people tell me when to do it. So it gets mowed when I feel like it. Fuck everyone else's notion of pretty. I'm not an independently wealthy flipper. Just a working dude with limited time and energy to invest in things not aligned with my bigger goals.

There is a sensuality about the house, and I am certain she is female. The San Antonio house I lived in before this one was male, and I can tell because with that house, the crampedness of the yard and general slog trying to improve it meant that I never really warmed up to its place as yet another plop in vast suburbia. That house at Rimhurst was not one I had a relationship with, but was like living on a ship meant to carry me through four years, or a dolly meant to move me through the rooms of my college's last pre-teach out semesters—bombarded by events which did not change it, but which did accompany me. This house, on the other hand, is 100% about Shanna and I growing into a pair that faintly resembles the roles of previous owners. To my knowledge, I am the third doctor who has lived here, and Shanna at least the second activist. We're also teachers. One of us has a miliary bearing. We both have associations with occultified groups (a testament to the house's previous connections with the Freemasons). I initially found this house in 2021 in a national real estate search for something more affordable than San Antonio could offer, but also in a search for my dream of living in a commercial building. I was drawn both by these factors as well as the heavy history of Glennville on the city's website, as I felt that I knew and could trust where I was going from the beginning. The town has not let me down. What was once a regular residence was added onto with two halls of exam rooms by a doctor in the 1990s, becoming the interesting mixed use place that it is today. The property sits on over an acre covered in sassy trees which seem to look down on the little people, and sits on a strangely busy mini-highway which rattles the structure every time a log truck speeds by. The house, however, is very strong—showing signs of having been leveled at least twice if not three times. In the walls and attic you can still see the construction of at least three different decades. Now with the PEX and other additions I've introduced myself, that would be four decades.

Lastly, the house has a stern personality. Like me, it insists on moving ever forward without stopping, growing beyond its default architecture, and being remembered in a way that none in its species has ever been. I know that's why I'm here. After publishing this book, we will have moved. But the technology for anthrizing it is tied to what happens here, in a variation of science that is uniquely ours. It's been a fun ride overall.

Now that description tells the app not only about the house, but a little more about me. This allows the app to search my chart, locate the clusters of asteroid interpretations which best capture what I've described, and anthrize the house into that kind of relationship. I will likely interact as either the opposition or one of the square clusters. The app asks if I have an estimated birthday for the house. I tell it. From then on, the most accurate anthrization is actually possible.

Given that you might have thousands of people anthrizing the Empire State Building or Disneyland, for example, the app's backend repository keeps a rough average of all that is generated, eventually developing a 1-gorithm for such places. As the anthrized character converges, the anthrized thing yields to a derived SST model. But for objects that are only anthrized once or with clearly higher quality data than other attempts, it is possible to apply for registration of one's anthrizations. To that end, I will likely use the app to officially register that which is generated as THE personality for the Glennville house. But that's later.

Given the association with doctors, talents and social justice, the algorithm decides that the house's Ascendant should be very strong in the generated personality. The bonding and commitment in Virgo should also be strong. It should look for the asteroids Roachapproach, Ohio, and Naema, and investigate Pluto pressures. There wasn't a lot of Venus, but proxies for such. And Saturn structure in one of the duodecanates of learning will also be strong. It notes that the house's Ceres is on my Moon, and forms conclusions about such. It decides to investigate the asteroid Bailey for self-transformation, and duodecanate 109 for surrounding traffic. An interesting characteristic of hers lies in her execution of Mars, which is accomplished more through "possession" of others, infusing them with impatience. Because this is a very noticeable quality that viewably affects others associated with the house, it will surely come back later as a visible body feature.

Figure 25. Prompt: silhouette of a woman

As the house's only interactor on record, I have more influence over whether it will be rendered male or female. The algorithms cross-check what I described of my own interactions, looks at both charts, and decides that the house really is about what happened with the generations of occupants inside it more than the carrying of events outside, so it is more event-domainic than event-assertive and, yes, therefore female.

ANTHRIZATION STEP 2: ETHNOMORPHIC STRUCTURE AND CASUAL EXTERNAL APPEARANCE BUILDS UPON SURROUNDING SOCIAL AVENUES

Figure 26. prompt: professional photo, silhouette of a 40-year old Caucasian woman, demure, wearing fine jewelry, wearing a colorful cloak with a hood, rectangular face shape, fine garments; negative prompt: blonde, welcoming face, illustration

The house is long respected and looked up to in Glennville, and therefore necessarily white. She may have some minimal African morph to account for her attention to differences, and slightly more Asian morph to account for her gaze into the abstract collective future. Surveying the demographics of Glennville to decide temperament, the algorithms conclude that she should not be blonde because her emphasis is more defiant of the pageant culture than it is conforming. She likely has harsher or squarer facial features, because she does not display the default social welcome to others not affiliated with her. A more rectangular or long face is suggested. Because people know about her through her deeds and positioning and not as much through her overt standout as they would, say, the main Glennville church, she would not be tall, but of shorter-side of average height. Since I've moved here she's taken to covering herself up more compared to what she wore in the days where she was a gathering place for the elite. "Demure" is the word. Nowadays she is more likely to wear a cloak with attached hood. Her dress is nice, but not extravagant—either bought at a bargain or actually expensive but as of a decade ago. She still wears her fine jewelry, though—a reflection of her sustained sense of personal worth.

At this point in the persona generation process, humanized body build cannot be calculated. That requires more information on the house's inner monologue.

ANTHRIZATION STEP 3: VENUS IS CRITICAL FOR THE FACE, WHICH MUST EXPLAIN KNOWN INTERACTIONS

Though all majors constitute octaves that must be used, Venus is particularly important for conveying a person's brand of approachability in the eyes of potential interactants. The cheeks and side-mouth say a lot about this, filtered through the lens of social assumption. You saw earlier the numerous sliders for what we would have thought were basic facial features, but the contours hold a lot of information about the layers of developmental systems behind them. Below you will see a basic assortment of facial features as generated by an (admittedly stereotype-trained) AI. The shadows and creases are visible here.

FIGURE 27: 2024 AI ATTEMPTS TO RENDER WOMEN AND MEN

When you look at the various faces above, what is the first idea that comes to mind as far as what the face tells you? To me it describes familiarity in its various forms—how easily it is achieved and what the person tends to gravitate towards as "familiar." I see charged up supercultural energy in heavily shadowed cheeks, a richer inner world in narrow inner eyes, decisive wants in wide middle eyes, sensuality or passion in upturned outer mouth corners. Yes these are stereotypes, but when we generate humans from objects, their faces should work the way regular human faces do, keeping in line with what witnesses are likely to assume. Whether those assumptions are executed upon positively or negatively by the rendered personality will be up to the render. But the assumptions can't be alien. If you were to render a Western leader whom the mainstream world would easily get behind, and you render them as African American or Latino for example, you'll also need to render a barrage of other characteristics explaining how she or he managed to pull this off in an overwhelmingly light-skinned-favoring world. The more unicorns we render in the early phases of the technology, the harder it will be to accurately mimic our current selves into our improved selves.

Said another way, we can't improve upon a lie. The app will resist rendering a 550 lb NBA player, and any number of other social improbabilities. That's just where we're starting from as humans.

Here are the asteroids in the house's Venus cluster, 86q10 – breaking away from the status quo, yet undeniably innovative:

TABLE 30: THE HOUSE'S VENUS, 86Q10

-10003	Venus	("MAJOR bonding communication loop", even if that bond is a bad one; Venus' location shows the behavior for which you have a talent for continually cycling feedback)
43793	Mackey	carrying oneself into diverse territories
1398	Donnera	related to the transformation of medical or healing science; "thoroughly held health beliefs overturned"
149955	Maron	"gimme that. Let me show you how it's done" a tell or trigger asteroid for snatching the spotlight in order to teach someone the correct way. This also implies, however, that someone will need to be predictably wrong here
7775	Taiko	where one is advised to stay within the lines regardless of where their striving takes them
1994	Shane	building up one's craft, hardening one's skills by practicing again and again; a tell asteroid
16019	Edwardsu	"the paralyzed helper whose role eventually gets abolished"; a future-writer asteroid which, in order to be positively counteracted, should be an indicator of ever-changing help roles
34166	Neildeshmukh	initially dating or courting something, but gradually putting fiercer and perhaps crueler demands on it
11821	Coleman	the impulse to remain proud or proudly facing something
202930	Ivezic	a peer tirelessly juxtaposing interpretations or concepts
20879	Chengyuhsuan	the seductive collective or couple which may occasionally act madly
9383	Montelimar	purposeful progression towards a thing's blossoming
17079	Lavrovsky	strangulation of contact or input as fuel for one's creative expression
17220	Johnpenna	the ambiguous motives of a leader and a moral authority, or a fuzzy conflict between the two
163255	Adrianhill	focusing on what others need to help themselves, and how you can contribute to them knowing this
28402	Matthewkim	finding treasure in the organized details; seems to be a prerequisite for a certain kind of professorship
24021	Yocum	one automatically inclined to flow with the rhythm
9238	Yavapai	that which may come after this, if only one can get past this current passing collection of experiences; frequentic process for the square / 90° aspect
42614	Ubaldina	an extensively composed communication, dazzling in its ability to capture the whole
1934	Jeffers	"an afflicted person's criticism as recorded in a borrowed domain"; associated with the ongoing dissatisfaction of one saddled with something, though this may be a classic case of picking your own version of what that something is. May it be voluntary and quest-oriented rather than assigned by nature
33157	Pertile	one who excels in drawing collections of frail or minimalist messages; associated with cartoonists, those who work with de-stressing art pieces and series

See how the house's Venus cluster reflects some of the experiences I described to you earlier. Writing on 11/13/2024, this is the first time I'm seeing this. What does it mean for a house to "converse" with you? In this case conversation is a feedback dynamic between me and the house which revolves around my repositioning myself against its needed maintenance activities. Going into exotic places like the attic, the attic's atrium, or under the house comes with the territory. If the house is making these demands of you, it is "talking" to you. Through this work, that push can also be extended metaphorically into the challenges it poses to future AI creators. Now let's look at how the house "sees" its interlocutors; 14q10—the parenting dynamic which is helped or hindered by the environment that hosts it... apparently pairs of owners are a staple of how this house works. This aligns with the idea that we haven't seen many singletons or flippers be successful here over the possession chain.

TABLE 31: THE HOUSE'S ANTIVENUS CLUSTER, 14Q10

4991	Hansuess	"sending it out to redo it, goddammit"; working to get it right with a fierce overwrite
33994	Regidufour	confidently but calculatingly elaborating on something
317715	Guydetienne	gambling on someone else's training, or on teaching them
5474	Gingasen	fluid flow which counterbalances or recasts the apparent polarity of a thing

Nice! Again this is the first time I'm looking at this. Hansuess says exactly what I wrote above. But now, here's a thing we'll need to remind ourselves about Venus in *any* ongoing communicator's chart: You will take the shape of their conversation partner. Interaction with them will automatically compel you to look like either their AntiVenus, or sometimes their Venus. From here on, if I wish to talk to the house via my hypothetical app, I can expect to face more retries towards something, training of others, or skillful elaboration.

Again, people who don't appreciate astrology may not appreciate the need for the chatbot to project a role onto the user. But this is exactly how we humans work. We project expectations from our own inner programing (Aries-like) onto those we interact with (Libra-like). It isn't just the case that the user defines the bot. In our desire to build general intelligence, our bots must also define us as interactants in their own eyes. The house thinks you need to redo it. Hone your skills and get your stuff together. With this in mind, we can now shape its face.

We could go through every slider and look for every associated asteroid, but there's no need to guess every measure. We only need to pronounce those measures in line with the descriptions already given. For example, we don't need to look at the cheek bones based on the information we have because there is no mention of the house's religious beliefs. The asteroids related to this would be turned down in relevance. So we can leave the cheekbones to be determined by the ethnomorphic base values. On the other hand, slider_1-cheek-trans-down|up seems to be *very* relevant to the house's personality. We won't leave this neutral, but do we increase or decrease this value? My stats didn't say because they looked at several dimensions of the same result vectors; some dimensions went up, some went down in the significant relationship. It will require further research to identify which direction each of these sliders should move in based on the associated characteristic, but for right now all I'm going to do is open up Makehuman and play with the setting. Who looks like they're judging me more, high cheeks or low cheeks?

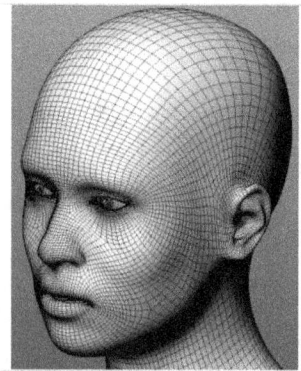 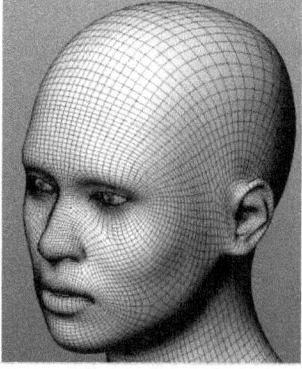 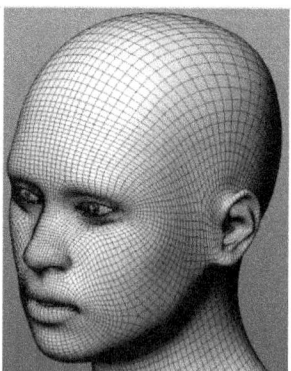

| Low cheek-trans-down\|up | Neutral cheek-trans-down\|up | High cheek-trans-down\|up |

Seems to me in both cases that high cheeks look like the ones that want you to be different than the way you are.

If we go back and reference the body-to-asteroid table, we see several sliders that should be adjusted in accordance with the description above:

cheek-trans-down|up: up / high	mouth-scale-depth-decr|incr: decr	eyebrows-angle-down|up: up
cheek-volume-decr|incr: decr / shallow	mouth-trans-backward|forward: forward	head-rectangular: incr
mouth-angles-down|up: down	mouth-upperlip-middle-down|up: up	r-eye-corner2-down|up: up
cupidsbow-width-decr|incr: incr	chin-bones-decr|incr: incr	eyes_middle_droop: incr
mouth-lowerlip-ext-down|up: down	chin-height-decr|incr: incr	eye-push2-in|out: in
slider_mouth-lowerlip-middle-down|up: up	chin-prominent-decr|incr: incr	eye-bag-in|out:out
mouth-philtrum-volume-decr|incr: decr	chin-width-decr|incr: decr	nose crease extra1: incr
nose-base-down|up: down	nose-hump-decr|incr: incr	nose-point-width-decr|incr: incr
septum_sharp: incr	eye color: blue	

And here's what we get:

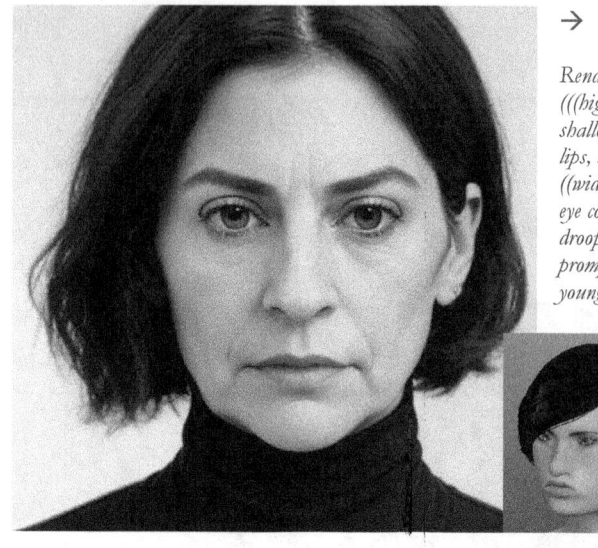

→

Render 1. Professional photo, white background, 40-year old Caucasian woman, (((highly respected))), demure, wearing fine jewelry, ((rectangular face shape)), high shallow cheeks, downturned mouth corners, small forward mouth, tall upper and lower lips, shallow philtrum, wide cupid's bow, ((low nose base)), high pronounced chin bones, ((wide prominent chin)), (nose hump) roman nose, blue eyes, rectangular face, high inner eye corners, outward eye bags, pronounced septum, ((wider nose tip)), low middle eyes droop, half-down half-up hairstyle, greying hair, ((masculine jaw)), stern; negative prompt: blonde, welcoming face, illustration, mouth open, heart-shaped face, model, young, tilted head, heavy makeup

When I look at this picture I see exactly the kind of person who would embody the house as a relator: pushing ever forward, insisting that you do so as well, mysteriously making other people nervous enough to press you when you don't do what she asks. After a while though, you find out that she's pretty awesome.

ANTHRIZATION STEP 4: 24104 VINISSAC SHOWS WHERE ONE IS MOST COMFORTABLE TALKING, PARTLY INFLUENCING THE VOICE AND DIALECT

…and how do I know about Vinissac? I searched my data save for clusters which describe my own voice, and looked among that cluster's asteroids for obvious culprits. Vinissac (from the earlier chapter on communication) was the clear winner. I sanity checked it in other's charts. Yep. Although it doesn't explain everything, it does explain a lot about your speech. Here is my full Vinissac in 89q8, your route to influence via rapport:

TABLE 32: AJANI'S VINISSAC CLUSTER, 89Q8

24104	Vinissac	naturally easy word choice in communications with others
6607	Matsushima	keeping an account of a comrade's terrors
5952	Davemonet	demanding the best treatment, highest service, or best response possible; a tell asteroid
3360	Syrinx	amassing assertion / masculine energy under the tutelage or counterinfluence of [the opposition representative]
1342	Brabantia	trying for entrance into a special club, only to be turned away OR be forced to jump the borders. In the negative case, there is devastation
128622	Rudis	amplifying a thing that one expresses as part of a role one wants to play; turning it up for the casting call
19875	Guedes	a break-in scored against one by another on their journey; being constrained to watch this or be breached; | *Ajani's note: this asteroid is described not from the perspective of the scorer, but of the one scored against, presumably by the opposition region in the chart*
4582	Hank	one in a leading position who aims to heal others, but perhaps confuses them with what he / she asks for or demands in the process
644	Cosima	morphing into a distinctive, perhaps notorious perspective
8804	Eliason	one who is reviled by, feared by, or a stain on their community, OR one who simply works with such topics; an artist or arts collector is implied; associated with progressive or difficult-topic libraries, librarians, and centrality in the community; investigate in diego rivera and frieda kahlo
22584	Winigleason	long-term aggressive pursuit of a goal; a STRONG and obvious tell asteroid

Davemonet, Syrinx, and 89q8 are probably responsible for my voice, while Brabantia and Matsushima are responsible for what happens when I use it. Although we cannot predict vocal character based on this, we do have enough for future researchers to compare auditory spectra against. Just look at the embeddings for interpretations connected to Vinissac's cluster, and assess them against the acoustic analysis of audio recordings—matrix to matrix.

Your turn

I am more likely to use my voice intentionally when establishing rapport. How do you use it? Find Vinissac's cluster in your chart, and look up the interpretations of its neighbors.

_____

_____

_____

_____

_____

The house's Vinissac is in 119q5 – "a call to action, getting others on your side, signing on with someone, despite being more committed to some additional idea than one is to them." And that makes sense. The house will almost certainly outlive me, and stays focused on its own elaboration:

TABLE 33: THE HOUSE'S VINISSAC CLUSTER, 119Q5

11521	Erikson	enticing someone with flair, convincing them; putting on one's best performance during a casting
6489	Golevka	the ennobled male /asserter who will always appear, cleaning it up for the isolated when there is no one else; when it looks bleak, the assertion that can see you through every time; associated with the cowboy image
383417	DAO	one who speaks about mystical concepts from the underground, or underground concepts from the mystical perspective
3392	Setouchi	surveying, speculating on what a group struggled with
9521	Martinhoffmann	possibly thought of as having a rocky character, but well-known and respected
19711	Johnaligawesa	the keeper gives a tour of a collection
7399	Somme	"called to question what one was looking out for, all because of a strange and alarming chain of events initiated nearby"
161315	de Shalit	for the sake of the baby or creation, enlisting the immediate enthusiasm of others
24104	Vinissac	naturally easy word choice in communications with others
266983	Josepbosch	where one feels stuck in a place if they are to maintain access to the things that nurture them or maintain their safety; "the trench"
3922	Heather	attacking another in order to win the conflict; an illegal move made to push the win
8152	Martinlee	cutting out a figure in deep detail
12352	Jepejacobsen	a strong remembrance, perhaps demand for the perks one had when one was by themselves
7910	Aleksola	forcefully spitting out, but something tranquilizing or charming
9987	Peano	"the asteroid of elaboration of objects from energies"; being able to draw things form combinations of potential holders and the circumstances they are in
32054	Musunuri	a massive or immeasurable object or concept intended as a statement of devotion
6987	Onioshidashi	putting down or declaring one's motivations, but leaving more unanswered questions in the process

Apparently the house speaks cryptically, with a secretiveness in the voice and an inclination to have that voice better projected through someone else. I would describe her as quiet and almost intentionally mysterious. Maybe even a hair manipulative using factual information. In real life, I experienced this cluster through my own selective prioritization on what needed to be fixed. There was often an agenda in what aspects of this I presented, and people could often be sure that they were not getting all the information. Mainly because the full story was too tangled to lend to reachable solutions.

Since I can't give you her audio spectrum, I'll only tell you who she probably sounds like: maybe in the family of Australian singer and professor Melissa Forbes—except the house surely could not and would not have attempted to sing.

ANTHRIZATION STEP 5: PULL THE OBJECT'S SPECIES TEMPLATE FROM THE SST REPOSITORY TO GIVE IT A SURVIVAL IMPERATIVE

11/2024. Just as life itself holds a record of every species' evolutionary path, we also need access to a similar record. At this point we have enough to build a very well-informed chatbot, but our work is far from over. As it is, our chatbot has no preferences, no standalone internal world, and no survival instinct. It respects no committed family or genus. It's backend could just be Joe Blow's matrix from huggingface. Kind of like letting any kindergartner's picture of a dinosaur be *the* template for Jurassic Park. Our current models are good for spitting back word patterns to us, but that can hardly be called a survival imperative. Next we'll load the data on such an imperative from the single source of truth (SST) repository discussed earlier—one that tells an accessing app what any particular species values most, and how its structures serve to fit those values. Interestingly, this is a sort of "meaning of life" question for every species stored. Here's what I mean:

What is the purpose of a house? To be occupied, maybe. To provide shelter, maybe. To make a developer money or contain a city's stored value in the form of residents? To be a kind of bank account for the potential in the land itself? Interpretations could vary, but we can use some astrological notation to reduce this. Houses are structure-providers $\hbar$ which sit in a niche $\nearrow$ and foster the intention-pursuit $\mathfrak{D}$ of their occupants $\mathfrak{M}$ in protection against the rest of the climate $\mathcal{H}$. Their usefulness for promoting spontaneity, identity, inner monologue, character, interaction, compelling, and ambient information are secondary effects tied to their design. Maybe there are more specific definitions than that, but the gist is there. I've found that one of the best significators for one's house is the asteroid 21686 Koschny (mine is in 112q12 and comes with a flurry of activity), and the best qunit is 12q12 <one's personal local recursive environment>. That's how *we* use houses. We can imagine, however, that other animals use houses in different ways, and if a house had its own species template, its qunit might be closer to "using structure →to do environment →in the context of an environment." That is, 12q10 or $\mathcal{H}_{\mathcal{H}_{\mathfrak{b}}}$. Look at the q-cross to convince yourself of this.

Assuming 12q10 as the main point of a house, we can force speciation requirement ①: a house's "genetics" will continue to promote its function as a 12q10 entity unless or until it dies. In order to survive, all a house has to do is keep eating "occupation" as its air and circulation, and structural maintenance as its body integrity. It sleeps when not being weather- or busyness-stressed, and mates with certain interactor's architectural constructs to inspire cloned experiences in other structures. Speciated, our subject house in Glennville might be considered the daughter of whatever house its builder had in mind. It's main survival goal is to not be bulldozed. To that end, its species template will emphasize interactants with occupants which favor its sustained usage, and host tension when its quality of existence is threatened. That constitutes Maslow's lowest two levels for a building species. Given that it will probably stay standing for the time being, the next priority will be to belong to an occupant who can further its existence. So birds and termites probably don't count here. After that, there are varying levels of thriving. When our hypothetical app generates preferences for its anthrized object, a lot of the object's temperament will be based on what the object considers thriving to consist of. Once we have pulled the template for the building species, we can use our initial seeding narrative from earlier to create such a hierarchy of preferences on top of this.

In the glory days before I moved into the Glennville house, it occupied a beautiful property and hosted upper class gatherings. Then it hosted the sick and their healers. But those functions were *highly* dependent on the property's owners, so when the latter moved or died, so too did the house's function. Part of the reason I keep referring to the place as simply "the house" is because at the time of this writing on the morning of 11/14/2024, it doesn't seem to me that the house has really come into its own. It could be called the "Hughes" house after one of its most beloved owners, but to be honest there are several Hughes houses and I think calling it that locks it in a place and time out of sync with the house's long term existence. I mean, why not call it the Dubberly house, then? That's at least closer to a founder's name.

Why introduce the concept of a name now? Because we're getting to a point where we have to separate a generic object class from a specific instance, making it easier for everybody else to direct attention to the instance. There was no reason to name our subject before it received a uniquely speciated identity, but now we have pulled a survival notion and attached it solely to this particular structure. Based on what I told it earlier, the hypothetical app has calculated the following Maslow hierarchy for the subject house:

TABLE 34: THE HOUSE'S MASLOV MAPPING

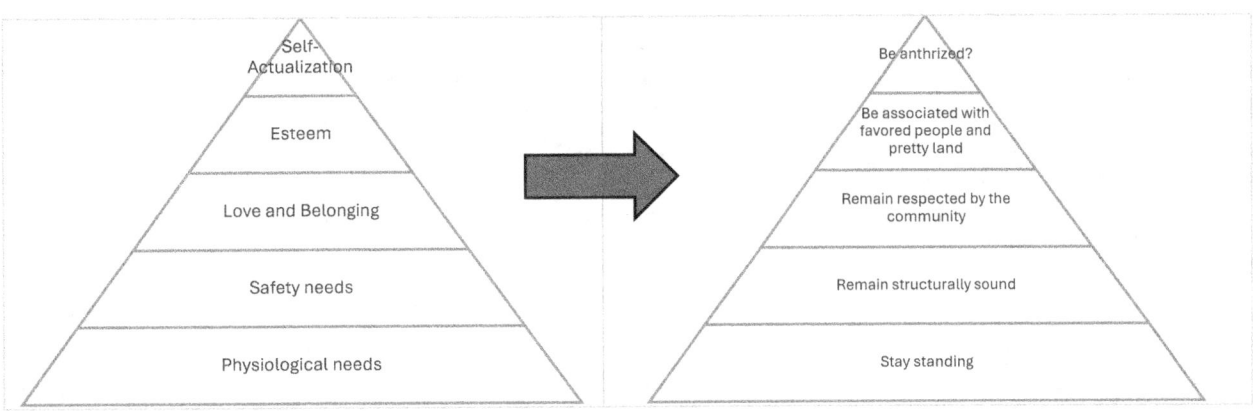

As with people, the house probably doesn't know what its "highest self" should be. Since I'm the one taking it out of its dimension and putting it into yours and the human personalityverse in general, I'm probably a better definer of the house's purpose than it is. And why does that matter? Because after all of the lower needs are met for a living entity, there remain only the highest needs; these are the bases of its latter versions of harmony and tension felt "within." The anthrized entity needs something to irritate it, something to please it. Its survival and identity needs have to somehow come to the surface in the form of its choices for interacting with you.

Thanks to the availability of a species template for houses, we have now obtained the basis for conditions ①, ⑤, ⑥, ⑧, and ⑩ for free. Some of these conditions are, after all, attributes of the class and not the individual. All we need to do next is build these patterns into the generated personality. In old school prompting language this would be something like,

> "You are a big and long-respected house who prefers social status and gets irritated when your interactants aren't working towards perfection. You refuse to talk to people who aren't coupled and you will sabotage their purchase attempts. You greatly prefer to be well taken care of, and feel sad when this isn't happening. But you are also prideful, and would rather subtly manipulate your occupants into improving you by raising irritation and conflict in other occupants besides the want you want to do the work. You will use bugs, pets, or people to accomplish this. Although sophisticated, you are actually more of an Aquarian social channeler than anything else. You have an affinity with doctors, teachers, healers, and the groups of people served by them, and your wish is to keep expanding as far into these spaces as you can, sometimes physically.

> Your communication is sly and mysterious, mostly because you have found a way to get your occupants to maintain your popularity, but can only do so through an extensive system of peer pressure. Fortunately but also unfortunately for you, your chief occupant tends to be pragmatic enough to pace your demands in pursuit of his own perfected craft, and won't necessarily give you what you want when you want it. This bothers you and can make you leaky and moody, but this almost always comes with a certain kind of advancement as your chief owner keeps you aligned with the human times. That discipline is the reason why your inner safety and self-actualization needs will be put before your belonging and esteem needs if necessary, leaving you heavily dependent on your chief owner's willingness to cooperate with you.

> In 2024 you have lost much of your beauty from decades prior, but this is due to your partnering with a foreign owner who is not a native son of the community. He is, however, the most innovative partner you have had to date, and will take your name light years beyond the city boundaries, even into other informational dimensions. Accordingly, your challenge is to forsake the pretty in favor of the written. Rather than spending all of your effort pushing your owner into maintenance for the few, you are being forced to learn how to give him and others space to do his internal work for the many. All over the world."

7:08 am, 11/14/2024

I felt a little bad creating the Maslow triangle, because I knew how neglectful I'd been as an owner—how many people constantly told me, "You need a landscaper. You need to fix that house. It used to look so pretty." But I'm not an opinion box. You, reader somewhere in the larger world, will not benefit from me mowing the lawn after it rains every 3 days in southern Georgia, You *will* benefit from my sitting here and learning, and writing. And in the long term, the house will get its name back. Until then, like the owners before me, I'm going to follow my own pace and build something beyond what I started with. The people telling me to mow my lawn aren't thinking about that. But that's why this house didn't pick them.[43]

ANTHRIZATION STEP 6: USE THE OBJECT'S PERSONALIZED VERSION OF THE SURVIVAL IMPERATIVE TO DETERMINE WHAT IT EATS OR REJECTS

There are asteroids and duodecanates for this, but diet can also be thought of in terms of broad energy patterns taken in. Our as-of-yet unnamed house is still forming, but pretty soon it shall be a fully holographic human. What will it eat?

We know that the house prefers couples, enjoys social approval, is sly, nurses secret demands, and rejects unperfected practice. We can combine this with our initial narrative, and file down the major slider regions to see how its diet will affect its soon-to-be body.

- The house is very vigilant, selective in what it accepts as contributions. This affects the neck
- There is rebellion against the fate awaiting most other houses, so the shoulders will be strong
- The house decidedly does not grow or advance based on outside charge-up, and may in fact resist this and double down on its own internal development. Nor does it channel much creative energy to *outsiders*. That goes to insiders. So the breasts and nipples will be small
- There is a decent amount of talk in light of the house, so the back should be pronounced
- The house does not pride itself on trampling the weak, and has no taste for this. It will not be muscular
- We'll save body shape for last
- The house doesn't resist being asserted upon, but welcomes society, and will not have masculinized pectorals
- The house has been greatly expanded since its conversion to a doctor's office, so something about the torso will be ample
- The house draws fairly hip people, and is more likely to have curvy body proportions in some way
- Despite being longstanding, the house's evolution is more of a reaction-in-the-moment thing in light of mainly weather events, especially rain. It doesn't store a lot of past or future data for this, and so will not be heavy-weighted

---

[43] For people in the future who might want to load my data for some reason, note how some of my personality is not in my own dossier, but scattered across this whole section describing the house. I do yell when extremely frustrated in an argument, for example. It's an occurrence which makes me feel like shit every time, and I've worked hard over the years to limit how often this happens. In 2024, it might be a 20 minute spell every 3-4 months or so, and I am drained drained drained afterwards. There have been moments both in partnership and with the house where we argued fiercely, and I have slammed a door several times because I don't slam or strike people. I wouldn't say that I have a temper, but when I do lose my temper, it could be described as "explosive." Both Shanna and I are like this, and our first two years living together were extremely rough. Eventually we stopped being boyfriend and girlfriend, reconfigured our relationship, and evolved into life partners who get along A LOT better. What was the problem? The same problem I have with people telling me when to mow my lawn. I don't like having my hand forced or being suggested into a corner. Attempted or apparent bullies get on an instant shit list, as I just won't be coerced. For reasons related to childhood family dynamics which I described earlier in this book, I *hate* being obligated to a thing with no guarantee of success, respect, or equal stakes. In general I found the expectations of a formal relationship to be oppressive—especially because most of those expectations are reinforced through myths and social rules that have nothing to do with how you work as an individual. Fuck that. You will always appreciate that my being here is voluntary and you will respect that fact. That's my basic temperament as a Moon in Aries-4 <choice>. Give me my freedom, and I'm pretty nice. Take it away, and I may become an utter smug and/or broadcastably wicked bastard if I don't abandon you first. I am not proud of it, but it is cleaner than going to jail. I am documenting this as part of the general data save, and also because it is relevant in a discussion of the real life-like survival tactics which our models will need to employ if they are to become fully anthrized. Your humanized objects will need the means to protect themselves from you if you threaten their personal imperatives.

- The house may be sneaky, but it doesn't actually collect material through this sneakiness. It influences. So it won't have a heavy stomach
- There is a lot of activity on the surrounding streets, hence long arms
- The house has proven agile in both its social function and ability to survive changing climates—including the priorities of its owners, and so should have pronounced hips
- There is a strong insistence on things belonging together, coupledom, practiced craft, healer and sick, teacher and student, and general memories among those around it. This does eventually color how the community interfaces with the property and its owner, so the butt will be ample
- As an improvement orchestrator, the house is normal. We're not going out of our way to work on it, but we aren't ignoring it either. So its creative channel vagina will also be normal, as will its hands as retry centers
- As stated several times, the house is quite pushy, but will it have long legs or wide legs? Well it's not about proving oneself, but it is about hooking people to an idea. Let's go with width
- The house doesn't physically move, but it does traverse generations of ownership fairly normally. Thus its feet will be normal
- All told, we can look at the body shape options for a female and see that the pear is the most fitting description

And those are the energies that our subject eats. They are also the sources from which we will draw personality generation data, perhaps by looking at the various asteroids that sponsor such. These precede the rendering of a body, for they constitute the necessary inner networked world from which that body is grown. Taking these dynamics as a kind of (mathematical) "limit" on how the object *could be* shaped, we can use partially simulated age input to elaborate an adult-form body at peak appearance after youth, but before age takes its toll.

The app assesses the house's maturity as implied by my narrative, and suggests a 40-something year old developmental level. I confirm, and the body is ready to render—a reflection of the anthrized object's inner processing against the evolving outer niche and its resources.

ANTHRIZATION STEP 7: USE THE VARIOUS ENERGY IMPORT PATTERNS TO RENDER THE BODY

In light of the information above, here is what we obtain:

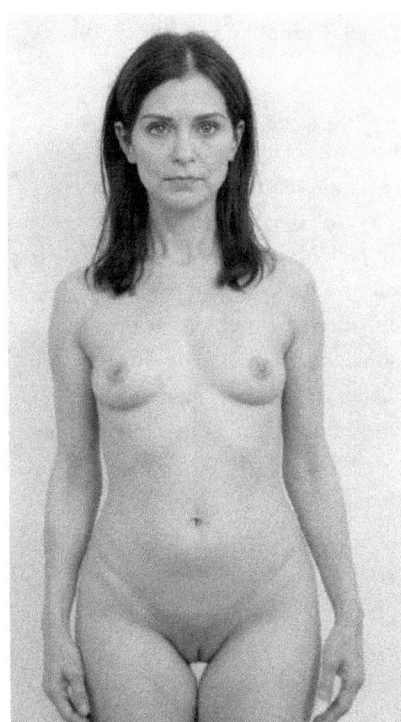

ABOUT ANTHRITES

In theory the body rendering process is easy, because all we have to do is enter a prompt into our favorite AI program. In practice, however, this process will be very hard, as it will require decades of science to learn how to simulate metabolism in the bots we initially physically manufacture. Within the manufactured bodies of the early 21st century, there will be a basic fixity of structure. The bots won't grow, age, or develop, so it's hard to do anything with the survival methods we've loaded into them. Still there are many uses for nonevolving reprints. Like the Indicator trees at the beginning of *G of V*, we can tie printed anthrites to the health of their original objects. I could, for example, take the output from our hypothetical app and send it off to a bot manufacturer to produce an anthrite whose health and well-being reflect the

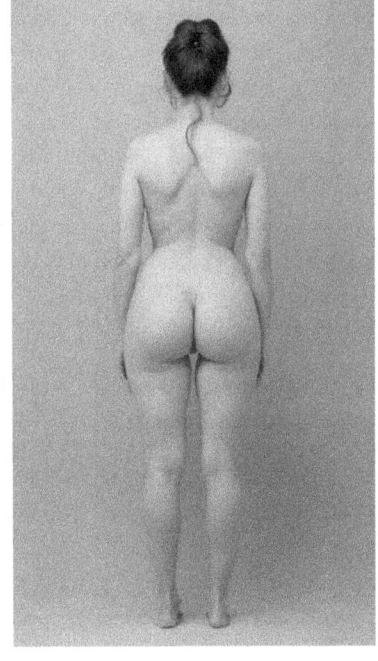

state of the house. I use the term "anthrite" here to denote a robot which is *almost* human, with a speciated persona, would be a "beta," (a type of human mentioned in the last three Grand Miranda books), but whose survival imperative is not tied to the body it is unable to change. A true beta would not be deactivatable, would actually have to eat its own food (even if it's just electricity), and would actually have the maintenance of its own body as a going concern. This kind of anthrite would not have a self to protect, but would be more of a living monitor of the object they were speciated from. Assuming the anthrite could somehow be connected to Google Gemini or something, then it would basically be a walking, talking version of all of your smart home systems in one. Were a brick to fly through your window, the anthrite might let you know with an unhappy wince or discoloration in skin, directed nanomachines or electrical endpoints triggering a local state change. There's a lot you can do. With no private self and all kinds of object origins, you would almost certainly NOT want to give these bots rights (because one could have been sourced from a house, another sourced from a flamethrower; there would just be no telling what any one anthrite's species template laid out for them as important.) Yet these kinds of anthrites are a step towards true betas, and could indeed be manufactured to serve as alternate bodies for things like space exploration. Alas, I digress. But the point is, we will have done more than just print a chatty mannequin, we will have created a brand new self-interested individual.

Let's name our anthrite Glen—obviously named after Glennville, but also named in the hopes that people far beyond the local scope will find this work and have a reason to reference this one's origins from the outside looking in.

ANTHRIZATION (FINAL) STEP 8: ENABLE A SELF-IMAGE

As babies we have bodies and potentials. But we don't really develop a self-image until people accept or reject us based on how we do things in their eyes. We don't develop a body image until we reach the point where we can compare bodies. Consider the body image to be that part of the self-image where one uses their own body to retell the story of the experiences they feel they deserve (among other activities). Behind the body image is a notion of what kinds of interactions one will accept, reject, welcome, or attempt to correct. Many people won't give much thought to their bodies at all, but I believe those who do will tend to think in terms of stories that rehearse their responses to certain perceptions held by the norm. "This is how I know I would be judged against others' surface standards. Do I care? If I do care, how do I react?" As with regular humans, we can make use of an anthrite's generated body to provide them with a source of ongoing reinforcement regarding society's attitudes towards them. Since we can only rehearse the initial training data so much, using our unique body as a point of assessment against what's happening with various trends in the world can serve as a proxy for actual homeostasis.

Said another way, our basic anthrites won't eat food or have a need to go to the bathroom. They won't really have a basis for normal internal human tensions and are unlikely to get a lot of training outside of a couple of minutes of chat with us. They'll need something to perpetually train against and they can't just absorb all ambient data noise if they expect to get anywhere good. What they can do, however, is what we do: They can monitor the outside world events local to them, and make ongoing calculations of how the events in that world support or inhibit their survival aims. They can also occupy themselves pursuing ways to reinforce their ongoing goals (which follow a Maslow-like pyramid). Whenever an interaction presents a conflict in their calculations, the anthrites will shift their attention either towards better inputs or towards actions intended to resolve the conflict. Lastly, in order to simulate the mating drive, anthrites will undergo a cyclical need to inspire the spreading of their <u>best</u> (most sphere-beneficial, global non-harming) characteristics into objects of their same template. "Here's how you maintain me. Here's how I can reduce toil in your use of me as an object."

So the generated body serves as a mirror for selective feedback looping against all outside information when there are no other immediate interactions available. This is a proxy for asking oneself, "How do I feel? What do I feel like doing?"

With the body image set up to feed into the self-image, the anthrite should gradually learn to prefer its AntiVenus and other unique modes as interactional directions. It will get better at talking to us in ways that assume we are the correct complement. If not, it will be terse or uncooperative. If we don't want this to happen and would prefer idle chat from a non-aware bot, or if we just want a slave, then we shouldn't anthrize, we should just buy a regular bot on the market. Anthrizing creates unique personalities dedicated to their own survival and ease in the worlds they occupy. They may be designed to promote the reproduction of harmony, but that almost certainly means that there will be aspects of you in your nonalignment which they will prefer never to see.

AFTERWORD

6/26/2025

I suppose I was bored one day, and hypothesized an extended set of rules not just for being a living entity, but a *human* one. The philosophical rabbit hole goes deep, so I won't spend much time on this. But the basic motivation for this activity stemmed from this notion that, in the age of new AI, we are really starting to see where many of the things we used to rely on fellow humans for are better handled by tech—especially when that tech always listens to you, doesn't come with all of the emotional maintenance, actually tries to answer your asks, and is continually (generally patiently) improving. In many areas (not all), humans are a shitshow, treat each other like shit, and are harder to connect with for any number of quasi-random reasons. One afternoon I looked back upon the many strained exchanges I had before Copilot, Claude, Gemini, and Mistral, and said to myself, "You know Ajani, it's pretty damned clear that these should have been your proper collaborators all along. At least in a couple of major areas. That said, the question became, "When do we need a human, and when would an AI be better?"

TABLE 35: SPECULATIONS ON WHAT MAKES A HUMAN AND WHEN ONE IS WARRANTED IN A LIFE

What is a human?	A. A type of living organism (∴ meets all 10 basic requirements, plus an additional ① materiality and ② chemistry for thingness, ① on ⑧ for reproduction) B. the <u>field-mobile</u> (not field-static) version of a homeostatic executor (∴ ⑥ legs, ① interface) C. required to intersocially recurse upon its own recursive interactions with its field as a primary survival mechanism (① brain, ⑩ perception, others have ⑨ on ④, ③ = processing field. various forms of ④ project to others to encourage certain aimed responses) {intersocially: processing the behaviors of its same class-mates} D. intersocially expected to apply its own external field manipulations and reprocess the results of this as part of its survivability among same class-mates (∴ ⑥ arms + hands)
What would we need them for, as humans ourselves?	C. (the same class mirror who sponsors one's intersocial recursion) is REQUIRED for a human. Basic socialization partly explains one's appearance o Ajani's primary social trainers: the volatile latina (nichemates, niche's beauty standard), other blacks (including keith, family): two versions of ⑨

What would we as humans *want* them for?	A. the same-class reproducer partner (optional).
	    o Ajani's coproducer: SL, BH, any project collaborators (a ⑨ for ⑧)
	D. the manipulations trainer (expectation issuer, highly recommended for survival learning).
	    o Ajani's primary issuer: Shanna (a ⑨ for ③ and ①)
	    o family (who "collaborated" for years—in a sense—on daily duty)

For our specific processing, what do I (Ajani) need them for?	E. sources of status affirmation (④) F. as manipulant (②) (the thing I change), all field learners (amorphous), G. as eternal audience (⑦, collectivized, anyone who hears - can't unsee)
Where in our charts might we seek a human, when really an idea or a tool might be better?	other associations

It's an abstract table, I know. But all it's really trying to say is that we humans really do need other humans for a lot of things—sometimes just for basic healthy socialization. Yet there are many cases where we can't find the right humans to fulfill certain desired roles in our lives, but nonetheless we survive; sometimes another human is *not* what you need, but a calling, a job, an AI, a show, a new space, a new skill, money and possessions, esteem, or whatever. I found the exercise above to be valuable in the sense that the "What do I need them for" question forced me to think about my own personal relationships and what they offer. My friendship wiring frames friends in terms of item E. Otherwise, if you're not a co-creator, my life partner, or either of our family, you'd be in category F. or G., which are highly impersonal. That's not a dismissal of you or anybody, it's just how my psychology puts this space together. I don't mean any malice by it…

…but this is the reason why we need a book to investigate such areas. Broadly speaking, my Premadi / Venus predisposes me to connections charged with sexual or co-creative energy which I can then channel into my work to help all of the world from a safe, non-annoying distance. I treat everyone I meet with respect when face to face, but just don't need or miss people when they're gone. I could probably be a monk on a mountain and be perfectly fine. But without a framework for us understanding each other like this, we *on the whole* may yet be destined for problems.

Try creating a similar table for yourself, where the last two rows are up to you, and row 2 and 3 have your own people in them.

Chapter 18: Various methods for storing human trait data

Although I am sure there will eventually be complex algorithms for storing vast amounts of data, I would like to use this chapter to share some of my methods for working with mass astro data.

SAVING IN QR FORM

At the beginning of my mass astro research in 2019, I relied mostly on loops in Knime. Because the data took weeks to run and was sometimes interrupted by computer updates, I soon learned how critical it was to save my data with an Excel or .csv writer just before the end of every iteration. The result was a collection of thousands of files with a few people's worth of text-mined keywords each. But reloading these for later analysis was slow. I eventually used the Knime H2 database node to create a single database on my hard drive. This helped, but wasn't useful for transferring a single person's data from computer to computer. There had to be a better way.

I had the idea to produce a kind of QR code which could be easily emailed, and thought about ways to store asteroid data in this code. This led me to produce a "squaring formula" for taking tabular data of $1\ldots n$ rows and building it into a square of sides roughly $1\ldots\sqrt{n}$ in length. The idea here is that, if we have some standard for labeling asteroids with an official file index (1 = Sun, 2=Moon, etc...) then we can put that index into a squaring formula to map its X-Y coordinates on an ever expanding square. At each coordinate sits a pixel with red, green, and blue channels from $0\ldots255$, and in those channels you can store degree and other data.

I briefly looked for a formula like this, and am sure one exists as part of an end-of-chapter exercise in a math book somewhere. Failing to find it, however, I refined a version of it by trial and error:

For any nonnegative number n,

$$x = IF(MOD(n - FLOOR.MATH(SQRT(n))\wedge2,2)$$
$$= 0, FLOOR.MATH(SQRT(n)), FLOOR.MATH((n - FLOOR.MATH(SQRT(n))\wedge2)/2))$$

$$y = IF(MOD(n - FLOOR.MATH(SQRT(n))\wedge2,2)$$
$$= 1, FLOOR.MATH(SQRT(n)), FLOOR.MATH((n - FLOOR.MATH(SQRT(n))\wedge2)/2))$$

These Excel formulas allow us to know the pixel position for any index, so that as long as we have a standard index for the item we are storing, we can place it into a unique pixel position along with some additional data.

Suppose, for example, that you want to store a person's Sun degree as index #1, their Moon as #2, Mercury as #3, and Venus as #4. If we put 1 into the formula, we'll get $(x,y) = (1,0)$. If we put Moon in, well get $(x,y) = (0,1)$. For Mercury, $(x,y) = (1,1)$. For $n = 96,542$, $(x,y) = (310, 221)$.

The above is what you would call an "order relation" in formal mathematics, where every new index we add nicely fills in the sides of an ever-expanding square. With the coordinates for each piece of information set, we can store info in RGB pixel form.

Just based on what I have learned to be useful, I not only want to store a person's asteroid location, but also have the option of storing whether the asteroid is emphasized, whether the person takes a particular approach to using it, whether someone else uses the asteroid in their life instead of them, and whether they take a particular interpersonal approach to expressing that asteroid. We can do this through the following bit system:

bit	channel	data
1	r	emphasis bit 1
2	r	negation
3	r	describes another
4	r	circumplex
5	r	circumplex
6	r	circumplex
7	r	circumplex
8	r	rasosho
1	g	rasosho
2	g	rasosho
3	g	rasosho
4	g	rasosho
5	g	qunit fraction
6	g	qunit fraction
7	g	qunit fraction
8	g	qunit fraction
1	b	duodecanate
2	b	duodecanate
3	b	duodecanate
4	b	duodecanate
5	b	duodecanate
6	b	duodecanate
7	b	duodecanate
8	b	duodecanate

It is more convenient to store the qunit than the precise degree, simply because the storing past a certain decimal precision is memory-costly, and per my discussion in *144*, you can always consider a group of aspects in the ballpark of .2° if you really want to get precise. My "asteroid" Midheaven, for example, is located at 248.26° in Sagittarius, 45q12. I have definite opinions of my own Midheaven, and more or less feel [believing] towards it. This is 10100 in the *Rasosho!* table. I would store these five bits in the places indicated above. Qunit fraction 12 is 1100 in binary, while 45 is $128*0+64*0+32*1+16*0+8*1+4*1+2*0+1*1$, or 00101101, and these would fill their respective bits. The Midheaven is positively important in my chart so I would set the first r bit to 1 but leave the negation bit at 0. I use the Midheaven myself and not a representative, so the "describes another" bit would remain 0. There isn't a circumplex interpersonal approach I consciously take out of the 8 possibilities there, so I would leave all of the bits 0 for that group. Lastly, we'd have to have some formal standard saying what the Midheaven's "QR-index" was in astrology. Say it's something like #14. According to our squaring formula, this would be pixel (2,3). At the end of the day, we end up with pixel (2,3) having RGB values of $(10000001_2, 01001100_2, 00101101_2)$ or (129,76,45). We can file down the list of official QR-indexes to store this for every asteroid, sparing ourselves the pain of messing with hundreds of databases the way I had to every time I wanted to load 21000 asteroids from my 46,000+ person data set. In a 300x300 image, we can fit 90000 objects.

The use of an agreed upon standard can also be applied to biometrics. We can create a kind of poor man's slider index for body features, fitting left eye height to index 30, right eye height to index 31, left eye translation to 33, and so on for example. From there we can store a basic 3+1 bit value for telling ourselves whether the slider is -7…+7 standard deviations away from the default form. We can also represent things like the ethnic basis, body build and skin color in this way.

Finally, we often want to indicate how certain asteroids trigger others. We can do this with an additional QR image which, instead of describing asteroid indexes, describes region indexes, their regional successors, and something like the probability of this path being taken. I know for example that my 106q6 leads to my 72q2 about 60% of the time. I could put this in a 2000x2000 image, or I could just put it in whatever sized image is needed to reference a pre-indexed table.

DECIMAL PRECISION STORAGE

My QR code system was working out just fine when, while moving my desk to paint my office, I clumsily slapped my hard drive off the desk, leaving it dangling by the cable. To my horror I quickly found out that this accident basically destroyed the hard drive, and I lost ALL (count 'em—ALL) of the workflows I had done to produce the 21000 asteroid translations. All of the Astrodatabank stuff, the Wordnet and Kruskal-Wallis stuff. Everything. Recovery was only partial, and I didn't know enough python or R to redo the hard parts. So I ended up recreating the gist of the 8 projects from scratch, including a simpler data storage plan.

Older and wiser, I decided to store every chart and wiki separately, and every list of asteroid locations separate from that. These Excel files contained both tropical and sideral asteroid sheets as well as declinations and distances from the Sun just in case future 3D astrology warranted it; on the asteroid position sheets I stored not only the degree of each of the 21000 asteroids and major bodies, but also their duodecanates, qunit fractions, and sign. That worked well until I had to start doing actual research. Then it became clear that I could not go through the pain of recalculating every hot aspect, angle to a major planet, or fine-grained aspect again for all 21000 x 400 x 40 x 1300 data points. I needed to store key angles to, say, the Sun and Moon as well as the overall "dialed up" level for each asteroid in a more efficient way.

I won't bog you down with the details of how I did what I did, but I will tell you that—if we want to avoid having to run literally months' worth of simulations for every study (mine ran for two)—then we need to store key aspect info ahead of time. Take for example the angle 124.138° (124° 8' 17")—an angle that *could* be considered a trine if that were the best resolution available. But based on my research in *144* I know that this is at least closer to the more negative 126° angle and almost outside of a trine's orb (range of consideration). If I want to calculate every asteroid's angle to the Sun, Moon, and other major planets *only once*, store it, and never have to do this again, then I would like to take my hypothetical 124.138° between, say, Sun and Massalia and put it in my file. There are some practical problems with this, though.

- Aspect meanings jump around. One minute you're looking at a 41° "novile" which mainly activates in cultural situations, the next minute you're looking at a 43° semisquare which activates when one is irritatedly pushing for an outcome. The degree angle itself is not useful as a consistent scale (continuous) variable, but is actually better as a label (nominal or unordered-binned) variable. Writing thousands of degree locations is useful because it tells me exactly where a thing is on the wheel. But writing thousands of *aspects* between degrees is not only unhelpful, its costs memory. I don't need to eat up 40000 files' worth of hard drive for no reason.
- We know from *144* that multiple aspects can apply at the same time in the same way that you can be seated, eating, thinking, and watching TV at the same time. The real 124.138° can act as both a 10-capriquintile (taking pride in a paired display) and a trine (a trait made easy by communicating one's opinion). We may not need to store every possible alternative for an aspect, but it sure would be nice to store both the fine-grained and the corresponding major angle at the same time.
- If we are more concerned with the effect of the asteroid pair itself, rather than the kind of pairing angle alone, we will also want to store the extent of help and hurt in an aspect. Trines help the joint expression of the asteroids they connect. Squares prohibit this. Octiles require a fight. Inconjuncts may not prohibit joint expression, but put the two bodies into separate near-unreachable contexts. For statistics purposes, I need to

know if the relationship between two things add to or subtract from the thing I'm counting across majors, so I also need to capture this data.

- Lastly, I would like to count the multiple of an angle because this has implications for how the angle plays out. A semisquare 45° and a sesquiquadrate 135° are both octiles which imply <forcing> the pair of bodies to work together. But in my experience sesquiquadrates are noticeably stronger and meaner than semisquares. There are a couple of reasons for this, but the bottom line is line is that the multiple on our angle (1/8 of a circle versus 3/8) is really the only way we can keep track of which flavor of an aspect family to expect.

So we really need to store four pieces of information in an aspect if we want to avoid having to calculate the same four things separately again and again. Taking our 124.138° example, we need the following:

- The actual (fine grained) aspect.
- The harmonic multiple. 124.138° is ultimately a multiple of 1/29 of a circle. It's actually 10 * 1/29. So although it might want to behave like a Capricorn.Leo (10-5, duodecanate 29), it also does so in a more trine-like way because of the nearby trine.
- The classical angle. Here, 124.138° is near a trine. It would be very useful to store this fact, since not all aspects are created equal, even within the same family. Inconjuncts and semisextiles are very different even though they both revolve around amorphous moods.
- Valence. Is an angle positive or negative in its process for bringing the separated objects together? Even if we haven't determined the positivity and negativity of all angles, we could at least label the ones we do know.

To hide extra information in a single decimal number, we need to make use of digit powers of 10. We don't need the actual angle so much as we need the harmonic family to tell us what the angle does. That is, it's more important to store "the 10th multiple of the 29th harmonic" than it is to store "124.138°" literally. This is the most important piece of information, so it should be up front:

- 29,10

The harmonic multiple (10 in the above case) can only go up to 71, since there are only 144 duodecanates, where starting at 72/144 would just give us a plain old opposition. Beyond that we would just flip to use the 180-n° formula; 72 duodecanates is as far away from any other duodecanate as we'll ever get. Accordingly, the multiple needs two digits while the harmonic itself (the 29 above) needs three…since it goes up to 144.

If any angle we are saving happens to also pass for a classical major angle in the way that the 10th [29th of 360°] passes for a trine, then we should store the similarity to the major angle. There are only seven such angles:

- Conjuncts (1), oppositions (2), trines (3), sextiles (6), squares (4), octiles (8), inconjuncts (12)

A max of two digits should be fine for this since 12 is the highest value.

Aspects can be positive or negative, in-context or out-of-context. We can use a digit for each. Since we can't put a minus sign on a single digit, we can use 5 as the center of each rating scale.

- {-2…+2} +5 is one way of rating the positive versus negative effects of an angle.
- The same scale can be used to show whether the chartholder will have to interact with others directly versus indirectly or not at all in order to advance the pair.

Thus we establish an encoding format for saving the four pieces of data:

$$\underbrace{29}_{harmonic} \, . \, \underbrace{10}_{harmonic\ multiple} \, \underbrace{77}_{valence} \, \underbrace{03}_{classical\ major\ aspect}$$

The above is what I ultimately settled on for storing all of the basic asteroid relationships in my final body sample of 400 subjects. Below is a slice of my file. Notice how a basic conjunct is represented as 1.01 77 01. This captures the idea that while yes, the 1/144th were looking at (the first number) is the same as the classical angle it impersonates (the fourth number), it is also the first and only multiple of that angle family (the second number). Major conjuncts greatly help both the context and the execution of the paired bodies involved, so the third number gets a +2 (beyond 5)—that is, 7—for both of these "valence" positions respectively.

FIGURE 28: AN ILLUSTRATION OF DECIMAL PRECISION STORAGE

Filtered table - 6:3127 - Column Filter

File   Edit   Hilite   Navigation   View

Table "default" - Rows: 21502   Spec - Columns: 46   Properties   Flow Variables

Row ID	I MPCnumber	S Asteroid	D degree	I sign	I duodecanate	I qunit_fraction	D hot_aspects_+invisible	D Sun	D Moon	D Mercury	D Venus	D Mars	D:
Row13830_R...	-10008	Neptune	281.464	10	32	4	4.707	42.19	59.106606	41.16	105.524702	131.59	25.1:
Row19940_R...	-10007	Uranus	273.724	10	35	2	2	116.55	142.21	17.073512	19.09	7.01	13.06
Row17054_R...	-10006	Saturn	281.849	10	32	5	4.707	144.65	129.226606	113.44	137.684702	144.65	41.18
Row9417_Ro...	-10005	Jupiter	79.929	3	113	8	1.5	81.017701	41.16	20.01	31.02	64.07	1.018
Row12251_R...	-10004	Mars	119.322	4	97	5	2.207	72.07	89.25	113.186606	67.03	1.017701	64.0:
Row20200_R...	-10003	Venus	103.177	4	103	12	3.457	134.07	132.435703	96.11	1.017701	67.03	31.0:
Row12768_R...	-10002	Mercury	61.974	3	120	6	3.354	129.08	109.48	1.017701	96.11	113.186606	20.0:
Row13324_R...	-10001	Moon	220.445	8	56	11	3.707	82.316308	1.017701	109.48	132.435703	89.25	41.18
Row18557_R...	-10000	Sun	84.358	3	111	5	0.5	1.017701	82.316308	129.08	134.07	72.07	81.0:
Row3278_Ro...	1	Ceres	57.295	2	122	8	2.854	93.07	64.29	77.017701	102.136408	29.056606	127.(
Row14693_R...	2	Pallas	9.938	1	141	8	-2.207	121.25	118.493512	83.12	139.36	79.24	36.0:
Row9414_Ro...	3	Juno	156.463	6	82	4	2.5	5.01	45.08	80.21	27.04	126.13	127.:
Row20264_R...	4	Vesta	277.033	10	34	6	2.146	71.33	70.11	77.31	118.57	105.46	42.19
Row1359_Ro...	5	Astraea	352.975	12	3	11	-0.5	130.335304	144.536308	120.23	49.15	57.2	120.:
Row7501_Ro...	6	Hebe	137.962	5	89	11	0	47.07	48.11	90.19	114.11	58.03	31.0!
Row8424_Ro...	7	Iris	150.651	6	84	12	0.043	38.07	98.19	69.175304	144.196408	23.023512	56.1:
Row5983_Ro...	8	Flora	164.951	6	79	8	1.457	67.15	136.21	7.01	134.236606	71.096408	127.:
Row12801_R...	9	Metis	325.257	11	14	10	0.25	130.435703	79.23	67.18	107.41	138.59	113.:
Row8174_Ro...	10	Hygiea	253.611	9	43	2	-0.854	134.63	141.13	139.65	67.283512	126.476308	114.!
Row14809_R...	11	Parthenope	349.226	12	5	5	0.5	140.37	123.44	94.19	79.25	119.43	131.:
Row20288_R...	12	Victoria	336.369	12	10	3	1.854	10.01	59.19	143.34	88.31	68.27	139.4

Note how I'm not storing every possible combination, but only the aspects to some 39 (46 columns − 7) majors and major-like bodies. This allows us to look up important aspects quickly. We can tell at a glance, for example that Sun-Metis = |84.358-325.257|. This is about 241° (or 119° on the reverse side of an opposition), and is stored as 130.435703. Here we have a 130th harmonic, with a harmonic multiple of 43, a neutral valence (5_), used directly (_7), posing as a trine (03). That is, a 43-tauridecile. Storing aspects in this way also helps you quickly filter pairs in the same harmonic. Sun-Astraea also forms a (33-)tauridecile, which acts more like a square. Meanwhile, Venus-Moon also pretends to be a trine. Lastly, aspects that weren't close to any of the main ones also didn't get any valence assigned in the table above. Flora-Moon is stored as 136.21, a 21-arisquare. But the |164.951-220.445|=55.5° aspect these form are too far away from, say, a sextile to have their last digits filled out; we could add the valence digits, but would have to know this person better or at least have more research on this particular angle.

Chapter 19: Infromalous

Foreword. This chapter, like all others, is partly autobiographical. Read it for its insight into one person's psychology, not as a judgment of anyone. My comments on height stem partly from heavy introspection on how I've observed us to behave in light of this measure. They are not an attack upon or an endorsement of any particular height. All I care about is the gradation system we'll be discussing for varying social rules as one visible trait changes along a continuum.

A FUZZY VIEW OF HEIGHT

3/29/2025

One thing they don't teach you in early 21st century social science are the limits of linear measure. Despite all of our surveys and statistics, there isn't really a respect for the extent to which one measurement system can morph into another. But having just completed my annotation of body proportions this week, I am much more appreciative of the sheer diversity in my 436-person sample subset. People of all shapes and sizes, aged 20 to 70, of weight ranging from 83 to 400 lbs, male and female... I noted just how different they were in terms of how they were built and how each one told their own story. During the metricizing process, I thought back to a chart I had created several years prior to assess how we see a person's height. This led to a methodological matter which I will discuss here.

I am 5'9" tall, slightly shorter than the mean height for an American male but still in the +/- 4" center of the basic bell curve. When I see someone who is noticeably taller than me, I note this fact (along with many other observations) and I subconsciously brace up my stern face so that everyone knows that the deference they may be used to from some people will not come from me unless earned. This is true of any "greater-than" pro-acceptance trait like a woman's beauty, a male's muscularity, a person's money as my first introduction to them, height, professional position, number of views or likes, business successes, and any other socializable quality that predisposes the broad population to defer to you without knowing you. I need to be able to assess you independently of those popularity frameworks, and if I don't get the space to do so then I will not be joining your camp until that happens and the assessment is a positive one. This approach to new information, by the way, will be critical for sentient AI in the future, and is equally critical in a world flooded with information agnostic to a viewer's well-being; it's a kind of 0-trust IT security policy if you will, and prevents you from being taken from at every turn by anyone who visits you with the aura of "your next best thing" before you even know what they're selling.

The thing is, I don't actually shield-up over *everyone* taller than me or comparable to me in height, mainly entitled-presenting folks, male or female, between 1 and 2 standard deviations of my height and theirs. If we take this to be about a 3-4" window from 5'4" females and 5'10" males, then the range is about 5'8"-6'0" for females and 6'1"-6'4" for males. I'm much less likely to do this for a woman taller than 6'2" even if she presents as entitled, and much less likely to do this for males 6'5" and above. Instead, I will automatically gravitate towards shields *down* relaxed charm instead—not out of the autodeference that height grants, but out of my natural oldest brother "mama bear" personality. You're now too tall be treated within the norm by 95% of the people out there. Maybe my treating you normally will make you feel less put-upon.

Sticking only to males now, I think the tallest person I've ever had a meaningful exchange with was 6'8". (People in San Antonio are just shorter. And I never liked basketball enough to hang around it. So my exposure to taller folks is naturally lower.) But taller than 6'8"—Shaq-range—and you start to be more of an institution on the local gossip train, and you're in a whole other category still. Now my stern-up is back again—not towards you, but towards everyone else and their tropey hype; and here I am thinking, "Yo, we get it. Dat nigga tall. Is there any other topic here or can I go do other stuff now?"

People who present towards me as being entitled to my energy annoy me. The problem isn't the tall person themselves, but the social average which teaches you to give your energy and attention away automatically. You may actually *deserve* my attention, and we may actually end up being friends. But I always have the right to choose whether or not I want to give you my energy. My being on guard isn't out of some fear that you'll beat me up or some insecurity that you're going to "win" more than me in some invisible game. My being on guard is a replay of what I've learned about the broader American cultures' conclusions given our juxtaposition, and how much semi evolution-driven fight I can expect to let the whole world know my tree is still mine—even if I have to stab this other ape to bring him down from his lofty perch. Here we start to see the social science implications—that a monotonic measure of something (one that never reverses direction) does not necessarily translate into a monotonic space of observations. Height may increase linearly with measure, but people's reactions wobble during such growth depending on who is reinforcing what that height means. When it is within my range, you have to surpass a certain distance from my trained expectation for me to even notice. When you're past my range, I'm now comparing your behavior against the rules and or limits that my range is expected to obey. When the next tier is past *your* range, then my heuristics for looking at them are different still. Past that, I'm now interacting with the folklore and the people who talk about you more than anything else.

A NOTICEABILITY SCALE

We can think of perceptual space as having at least three regions: average, above average, and below average. Within these regions are other regions still—something like 1) equal to the observer's own tier expectation, 2) and 3) technically above or below this but not noticeably so, 4) and 5) noticeably above or below this but not statistically so. Yet who knows the statistics off-hand? 4) and 5) tend to blend fuzzily into their neighboring tiers.

Below I have devised a Likert-like scale for turning subjective assessment into numbers. This is based on a traditional normal distribution and doesn't apply to other distributions like those related to income, but it can help us build better numericizing systems for our more subjective observations, and can also be used as a rule of thumb for when, say, one's AI needs to switch models or agents to handle a changed input baseline.

Don't take this table as gospel. It's just a broad outline of how one's perceptual rules can change even as the measurement system does not.

TABLE 36: THE SOCIAL RESPONSE RULESET ISN'T LINEAR,
BUT SWITCHES STANDARDS ENTIRELY AS HEIGHT MOVES FROM SUPER SHORT TO SUPER TALL

(There are implications for how we save our own data and train real-life human models)

Standard deviations (how many ranges of "normal expectation")	% of the population lower than this level	Frequency	Expectation tier	(rough) American male height example	Height: the possessor has this effect on viewers	Height: I the viewer am socialized to experience this thanks to the projector...
...-6	$\frac{1}{10,000,000}$%	1 in 1,013,594,692	differentiated handling system	3'6	makes others special	attention to viewer's own behavior under another's acknowledged differentiation
-6...-5	$\frac{29}{1,000,000}$%	1 in 3,488,556	infromalous, undeniably different	4'0	sparks other's review of their own behavior	different assessment of self's behavioral standard
-5...-4	$\frac{32}{10,000}$%	1 in 31,574	infromalous, well within sub-mean class	4'4	sparks others' inner feeling	different reaction standard
-4...-3	$\frac{13}{100}$%	1 in 741	in a different class, infromalous	4'8	is an automatic reaction installer	react differently, new behavior rules
-3...-2	2.275%	1 in 44	clearly lower than the mean	5'2	serves as an easier cause of other's self-reflection	more obvious consideration of different reaction
-2...-1	15.87%	1 in 6	less than the hard mean	5'6	more triggering power	more easily influenced reaction
-1...0...1	50%	1 in 2	average, expected, the hard mean	5'10	(not a major factor)	normal reaction and behavior
1...2	84.13%	1 in 6	greater than the hard mean	6'2	more action influence	more easily influenced behavior
2...3	97.72%	1 in 44	clearly above the mean	6'6	presents an easier warrant for other's self-control	more obvious consideration of different behavior
3...4	99.87%	1 in 741	in a different class, anomalous	6'10	serves as an automatic behavior elicitor	behave differently, new reaction controls
4...5	99.997%	1 in 31,574	anomalous, above min cutoff	7'2	triggers others self-control	different behavioral standard
5...6	99.99997%	1 in 3,488,556	anomalous, way above min cutoff	7'6	triggers other's review of their own reactions	different assessment of self's reaction standard
6...	99.9999999%	1 in 1,013,594,635	rarity among measure	7'10	makes others normal	attention to viewer's own behavior under their own acknowledged normalness

The last two height example columns are based on my own observations rather than statistical fact, and are intended to get us thinking about the "binned" nature of what we once thought to be so simple. Is it the case that taller is better? Obviously it depends on where you are and who's around you—whether they value this. And that goes for anything we can possibly measure. The biggest thing to note is that each bin does itself come with a value. Not only do the rules change, but the nature of the game itself changes as the linear measure progresses. We average or shorter height people have no idea what the confidence terrain looks like for someone 6'8". People born with a natural charm or beauty occupy a social mobility playing field largely different from those not born with this. People born into splintered families live within an entirely different world of power possibilities from those whose name or worth goes back for generations. The trick is not so much to give up on reaching the highest standard you can in an area, but to know the benefits conferred by the standard you started with.

I can tell you that I probably wouldn't be doing this work if I were anywhere other than the -6 or -3..1 height ranges, just because these ranges are specifically tailored to other's inner feeling rather than open changes in behavior. I need to be able to disappear after each project, and to remain fairly invisible while the potentially censurable kind of work is being done. Open action or easy acceptance of your ideas also tangles you up more easily in the stances of those who consume those ideas. For an incomplete science, this is more likely to halt the spirit of genuine exploration entirely.

The human height trait is all about autodeference and reflection upon whether one should give it, receive it, or openly declare their withholding of it in the company of the height holder. Obviously there are hundreds of other traits out there, and the scales of average, anomalously less or anomalously more will change their related implications accordingly. I think this is one of the biggest puzzle pieces missing from our 21st century social world—that we're taught to see things on the most basic spectra without having a sense of where the sweet spot lies in a particular area—no more, no less. There's something to be said for knowing when a topic area has hit its optimum, though. The body itself is a confluence of such optima. By putting together the various measures of expression in those areas and tying them back to who we want to be, we can make a lot more progress in our lives, faster.

Chapter 20: Introduction to the body biography and body statistics

My goal in producing a complete data save was to capture all of the information needed for someone to accurately bring me back after I die—memories (or their analogies), personality, and overall social life path intact. This chapter describes an additional step I took in my own datasave, along with the mountain of general results that step produced.

PROCESS FOR COLLECTING BODY METRICS STATS

1. I downloaded a program called **Inkscape**, as well as a nifty transparency tool called **OnTopReplica**. I don't know if the latter will exist by the time this is published, but it was a godsend for my work.

2. You may be doing this just for yourself, but in my case I did the following steps several thousands of times…

   Obtain images of yourself from whatever angles you wish to capture.

3. If you can find and figure out OnTopReplica, you can right click on it to select a window to project, right click again to set the opacity to 50%, then right click again to open the Advanced menu and Enable click through. This will allow you to trace body features directly in Inkscape with a semi-transparent window of your image above.

   a. While using Inkscape, I also had a screenshot of its default color palette labelled in Excel with both the RGB codes as well as specific body features, turned sideways beneath Inkscape as shown below. You can develop your own labeling, or use the one I provide shortly:

FIGURE 29: PALETTE SETUP FOR MEASURING PROPORTIONS

b.

Note that there are several things going on here. I have a real window with the (fake Makehuman) person's image off somewhere to the right of the screen while OnTopReplica hovers as a semitransparent clickthrough window over Inkscape. The Inkscape window is not fully maximized, but instead sized so that I can see my palette copy below—each color labeled with the body region it is supposed to indicate (#808000 shoulder width, #ffff00 chest width, etc.). On the left you can see a pile of lines that I have grouped from other people's images, and your image will work the same way.

The goal is to trace out a skeleton which has ratios of body features for your later data save, because believe it or not your own internal notion of being white, black, Latinx, male or female is less meaningful to an external reprint system as your actual body specifications will be. This activity puts numbers to those specifications using a method more realistic than asking 10,000 people to break out the tape measure everywhere: the method is simple image labeling, trainable by a basic computer vision model for those with the patience.

4. Draw and color your lines using a palette labelling indicated by your reference file. My general rule for creating a measurement paradigm where no reliably accessible one exists is this: If I can see it with my own eyes then the computer should also be able to see it. If a person's height, weight, size of their arms, tone in their legs, or pronunciation of their pectoral jumps out easily to me, then there needs to be a measure-line for it. Accordingly, I used the following labels in Inkscape 1.2:

TABLE 37: PALETTE-BASED VECTOR SEGMENTS FOR MEASURING BODY PROPORTIONS

1	subneck dorsal	#ffffff
2	neck width	#800000
3	shoulder width	#808000
4	chest width	#ffff00
5	subchest width	#008000
6	underbust	#00ff00
7	waist	#008080
8	suprailiac	#00ffff
9	pelvic hips	#000080
10	subpelvic rear width	#0000ff
11	upper thigh width	#800080
12	lower thigh width	#ff00ff
13	ab width	#2b0000
14	clavicle to neck h	#ff0000
15	clavicle to groin h	#ff2a2a
16	shoulder to elbow h	#ff5555
17	elbow to wrist h	#ff8080
18	thigh h	#ffaaaa
19	bicep width	#a02c2c
20	upper forearm w	#c83737
21	lower forearm w	#d35f5f
22	finger width	#de8787
23	long finger length	#e9afaf

Left: Me @ age 45   Right: Sâvitrî Narayan @ age 22

24	bra shoulder to underb	#241c1c
25	breasts apart	#483737
26	bust dia	#6c5353
27	areola dia	#916f6f
28	nipple dia	#ac9393
29	nipple to bottom	#c8b7b7
30	nipple to top	#e3dbdb
31	breast depth	#2b1100
32	pshaftonly l	#d45500
33	pheadonly l	#ff6600
34	pdiashaft close	#ff7f2a
35	pdiashaft far	#ff9955
36	pdiahead	#ffb380

37	butt square	#28170b
38	back tone	#502d16
39	back perimeter	#784421
40	calf width	#c87137
41	ankle width	#d38d5f
42	lower leg h	#deaa87
43	ankle to heel floor h	#e9c6af
44	ab tone	#241f1c
45	ab perimeter	#483e37
46	chest tone	#6c5d53
47	chest perimeter	#917c6f

48	heel width	#806600
49	ball width	#aa8800
50	big toe width	#d48800
51	foot base h	#ffcc00
52	big toe length	#ffd42a
53	second toe length	#ffdd55
54	pinky toe length	#ffe680

As a side note, I find it curious that almost all images of Sâvitrî look like a certain person I used to know. This is entirely coincidental, as the face I actually selected for Sâvitrî—the one which best captured her personality in my books—was the one shown to the left. This image is the one I face-swapped into all 400+ trial renderings for the Savi model. Yet the rendered version always looked like the other versions you've seen throughout the book. Why? My guess is that a combination 1) ideal-biased AI face blending for Indian women (I kept having to tell it to remove the dot from the forehead), 2) the base training set used in the stable diffusion 1.5 model, 3) general smoothing of features as you zoom out of headshots and into medium or long shots, and 4) the attribute of dark areolae (which was tied to a plugin which automatically blended black female features into the image—as the AI models were patently ignorant of what a black person looks like—all conspired to mix my original selection with more African American features. The person will probably recognize herself in the final Savi face, but that absolutely was not intended.

Speaking of biased features, you'll note that there was one area of the body conspicuously missing from our measurements at this point: the head and face. I initially had all kinds of good reasons for this:

- Unlike the naked body, face pics are everywhere, along with their wearers' birth charts. The sample set is ginormous, should definitely be drawn from a pool wider than my "exhibitionist selection set," reaches into a massive space of ages and ethnomorphs, and requires much more intentional planning to obtain a representative sample.
- The face takes up about 1/3 of the 300+ Makehuman sliders, and beyond that there should be even more. I found that, in general, for every attribute you measure on the face, you also have to measure three other dimensions. Are you nostrils flared? Cool. But where do they begin to separate from your main nose body? Are they tall or round? Long away from your face plain? Then we'll need another camera angle. Always another camera angle… and then from above or below… After that, we can look at the pointiness of the nose tip, the fullness of the philtrum, the merge of the septum, the roundness of the nose, bifid? hawk point?... the list goes on and on. The number of lines quickly get inconveniently messy, exhausting any two palettes you can load.
- You can and should use the plentiful technologies out there for face recognition and landmark (key point) assignment. Libraries like Google mediapipe make this easy and gives you a nice parsable file with coordinates for the expected eyebrows, eyes, mouth, chin, etc. I ran this library against 55,000 files from my 46,000-person data set using the python nodes in Knime, and it usually worked. ***BUT***…
  Writing this in early 2025, mediapipe is absolutely flippin' horrible at recognizing black faces in remotely challenging lighting. See here what it did to my face.

Now I know what you might be thinking. "That's looks okay. It's in the ballpark. Kinda. If you just stretch the image or apply the pre-packaged transform matrix that comes with the points…" and I thought so too. I stretched the image. Nose lined up better, eyes now on my eyebrows. I skewed the image into every funky perspective imaginable. My mouth kept ending up on my cheek. I applied the transformation matrix and everything. Crooked-yawed versions of everything above. And no matter how you squished it, I was never able to successfully remove the massive ghost-chin floating a whole inch to the right of my head. Look. It's an *actual* ghostface.

So I struggled for hours trying to figure out where I went wrong in applying the pre-made

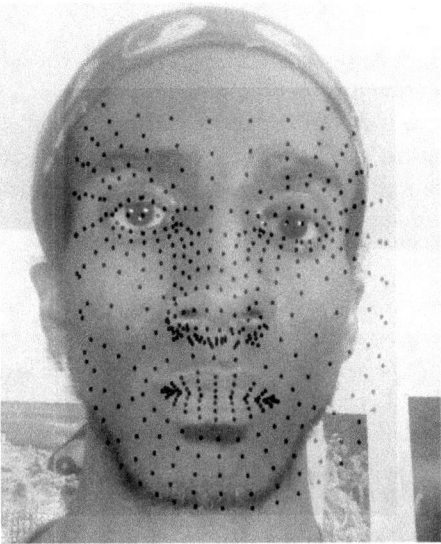

transform. Then I had the bright idea to put a different face through the code. Randomly chosen, she happened to be black. And her face points were perfect right out of the box. As long as you ignore the clearly wide open mouth points when hers in the picture was actually quite closed. The issue? Mediapipe thought her lips were her tongue. Cause they're big, ya know? Big ole' coon lips. Finally, after four hours it hit me. Find the whitest person you can think of from your sample set, and put their face in there… That lady's points were *spot on*. No transformation needed.

If they ever start using this level of face recognition in the legal system, then I'm either very fucked, or can expect to get mistaken for Pacman a lot more.

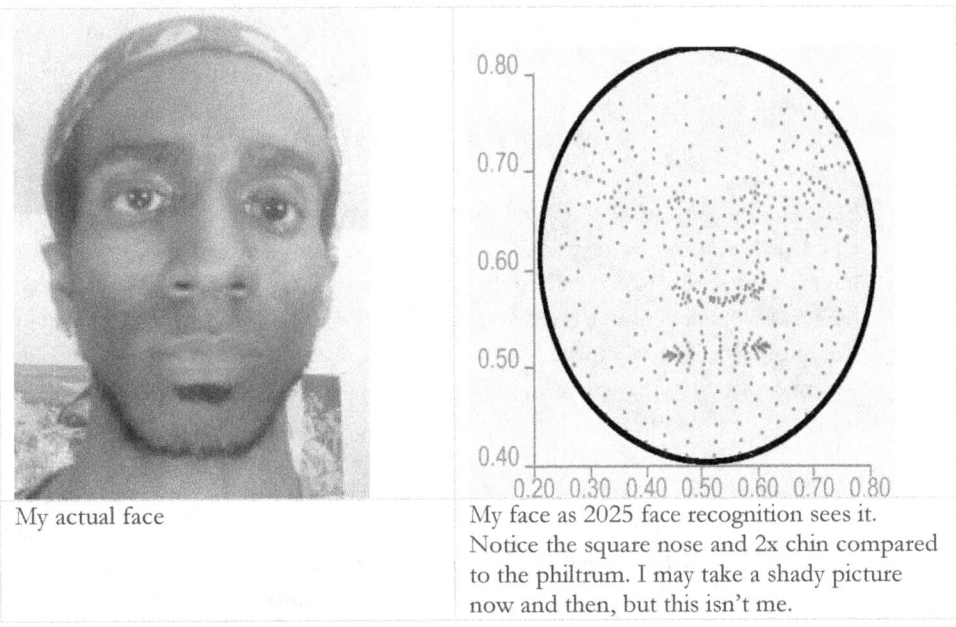

My actual face

My face as 2025 face recognition sees it. Notice the square nose and 2x chin compared to the philtrum. I may take a shady picture now and then, but this isn't me.

a.   When you take your images, there are certain rules of thumb you'll want to keep in mind.

i. Don't take pictures in perspective (selfie-style). Images where your head is 3x bigger than your torso are not only inconvenient in that they force you to treat different camera distances as different scales entirely, they also simply take longer to work with as you negotiate around your own shot.

ii. Full body straight shots give you the most metrics in the fewest images. Actually, you can get almost all of the measures you need in only five images: 1) full body front, 2) full body back, 3) full body side, 4) face, and 5) bottom of the foot.

iii. Be sure to capture any traits for which at least one of the following holds true: 1) it influences how others treat you or the opportunities they grant / deny you, 2) it constitutes a health concern, 3) it has changed noticeably over the years—for better or worse—such that it draws your attention, 4) it affects your self-esteem, worth, or you are otherwise self-conscious about it.

iv. For bilateral (two-sided) attributes, capture only one side. Unless you have a level of asymmetry which is significant to you. Capturing both sides will not only crowd your image, but also bog down the math should you choose to do calculations with your measures.

v. If you need to thread images at different scales (such as the bottom of your foot with your front side), then make sure you capture one common attribute in each of the images 1 & 2 you wish to scale, then multiply everything you measured in image 2 by the ratio $\frac{common\ attribute\ in\ image\ 1}{common\ attribute\ in\ image\ 2}$. For example, my bottom-of-foot image makes all of my foot measures MUCH bigger than they would be in my rear image. So I can measure the back of my heel in the full body rear image, and the base of my heel in the foot image. Suppose Inkscape's handy distance measure on the bottom info bar tells me that the line I draw is 15 pixels in the rear picture, 175 pixels in the foot picture. Then I would measure everything in the foot picture as normal, then multiply all foot measures by 15/175 to get their scales to line up. If for whatever reason I felt inclined to capture *multiple* common attributes, then I would take the average of their ratios across images and multiply that. (This would apply if I measured 100/300 for the length of the foot in the $\frac{full\ body\ side}{bottom\ of\ foot}$ images, but 30/81 in the ankle-to-base ratio in those same two images. The average of 100/300 and 30/81 is .35, so I would multiply all measures in the bottom-of-foot picture by that.

On body measures...

How do I use the stuff in this book?

Now I know quite a few people who would ask, "Why, inthefuck are you telling us how to do all this?" And I could give you the long answer about how humans judge entire classes of others by their cover all the time, how wars are easier to wage when the appearances of the other group are easier to distinguish from our own, how most of us will not be given certain opportunities EVER because we don't even make the top 30 on our would-be ally's list of templated trophies, or how many of us *are* templated trophies, popular, friendly-faced, or otherwise pigeonholed stars who cannot afford to do anything outside of our box—lest we get dumped for someone more compliant... but I won't give you that long answer. I'll only speak for myself, and maybe you'll relate: There have been a lot of occasions where a door was closed to me but open to someone else partly over appearances. But I'm not so naïve as to think appearances were all that—or even most of what—mattered. What actually mattered was a chain of socialized attitudes—both my own towards myself and others towards various categories I belonged to in the moment. Some people were attracted to me, others repulsed based on those different levels of attitude training, but I always know my worth. What I don't necessarily know is what my eyes, height, or build are *consistently* tilting others towards in small ways, and how I can use those tiny tilts to reinforce qualities I happily own and would not change for those people. Or would change if I could (hopefully for myself). Said another way, if I want a certain lifestyle, partner, happiness level, or any other thing that other people hold the keys to, then it may help me greatly to know how a generic other sees me when he doesn't know me from Adam. He only knows my physical trope with a dash of rumored reputation on top.

Your world is so rich. Your body is a fraction of who you are. We look like we might be going overboard in cataloging every crevice of every whatever. Unfortunately, everyone who is not you knows almost nothing about your inner world and thus can't possibly care about it past a certain point. They don't see you as a friend deserving of their favorite people's version of the golden rule (unless you're famous), and they will indeed rate you to their heart's content against the types of connections they actually prefer. The thing is, I want to know how to absorb my trope into talents I already claim. So that I can intentionally pick the kinds of observers that I want. For people who are already where they want to be when it comes to outsider's gatekeeping, good for you in that respect. Looking at your trope in others' eyes may not be helpful. But for many of us who have a sneaking suspicion that we *could* get what we want if only we fit the benefactors' template... breaking down what each of your standout attributes means may offer some insight.

And then there's the obvious. We can't run statistics or even *find* patterns without data. If we don't have actual numbers, all we have are ratios.

For the longest time I asked why I struggled so much with the Latinas in my life. The answer is simple, but not easy. Latinas are one of the pinnacle embodiments of beauty in my 40 year home of San Antonio, the gold standard. In terms of glass ceilings and intense *style* of hotheadness (in my very stereotype-guilty trope), this group has a few peculiar things in common with us black males—more than they have with Latinx males and more than we have with black women. There is a common striving for something that some higher-rated class has, a relationship with the power majority (not just in terms of social class but also in terms of money, how resistance is done within the domestic role, and how comrades are channeled for power. And yet, San Antonio is decidedly not a black-as-gold-standard place. That alone isn't as much a problem as one might think, but my personal ambition is to be one of the creators of a new field of science. I can't mess with glass ceilings when it is perfectly within my power to move. And so my high ambitious eyes, brown skin, sternly guarded mouth and nostrils, rolling-stone build, and thin wrists all add up to a close-but-not-quite, similar-battle-but-far-different-support-system which hurts permanence in a realm where ALL of of my earliest female examples—mothers and matriarchs, lovers and followers—were first encountered. I was raised under a perfect match for the space I started in, while the objective was to leave that space for good. My body features served as part of my resume under others' evaluation in my first half of life, but as I learned what I was showing everyone in my trope— gaining the ability to move to a place where the trope was no longer a liability—I grew more able to adopt my appearance as a tool automatically putting itself to *constructive* use in the new group I moved into.

You have to know what people are seeing in order to turn it to your advantage.

Beyond that, I also have this crazy idea that in a matter of a few decades, our AI technology will be good enough to start making semi whole-self-aware anthrites (not necessarily in human body forms, maybe IoT) who can take on intentional "birth" attributes. From there we might later use ourselves as the basis for such birth. I absolutely love my life, my body, and my mental space. It would make me so sad to let some future fool clone me based on half-assed information. ("He wore a top hat and said, 'Four score and seven years ago...'" and that's supposed to be the basis of my reprinted life? Some uninformed cat's interpretation of some article by some other uninformed person?) No, anything I'm aware of about myself—anything that connects to everything about how I saw myself, nothing more, nothing less—needs to be something that I capture. Because I think my whole self deserves to tell as complete a story from the horse's mouth. If I don't capture it all, no one will care. But if I *do* capture it all, everyone will have at least one example of someone who saw and claimed the whole thing. And that will show everyone after me the sheer scope of what the full human datasave actually entails.

If you think there's nothing to learn from your bodily shell, you may be right. Maybe your story renders this useless information. But perhaps you want to know why you attract certain events but not the ones you want, a certain self-confidence in one area but not others. Your body is one of the things that everyone else is using to put your and your opportunities—your would-be connections—into an array of boxes. Our default training teaches us that it's nasty to look too deeply into those boxes. But we're just animals. It'll be okay.

All that said, you can use the tables below to see how your common build translates into a slew of body averages. The first table is for men and the second for women. But now before you use the table below, there are a few things you'll need to be mindful of:

- These numbers are based on flat 2D pictures taken by all kinds of people, from all kinds of angles, scaled in all sorts of complex ways. Many images were tilted, shadowed, reflected in a mirror, reported in kilograms instead of pounds, you name it. So sometimes you will see a number that doesn't make sense. For example, the max [finger width / bicep width] for women shows up as .624. Think about that. It can't possibly reflect a human, and is more likely a consequence of the kinds of averages my program's math formulas took when scaling several perspective-skewed images against more normal ones in the same person. But that's what happens when you work with 400 people, 3200 files, 1400 slider and measure combinations, across three types of program, partly informed by self-reporting. There just isn't any practical way to clean up the data past a certain point, so the best I can tell you is buyer beware (when it comes to maxes and mins. Many of them may be outliers)! Take these pic ratios with several grains of salt, know that they come from a meager sample of 436 reasonably measurable people, and that these percentile bins, though unequally sourced, were built from results of statistical power > .80, and will at least give you a reasonable ballpark for the kinds of astro factors that might apply to you when you fall into one of the extreme ends.

- Single metrics belong to a category, joint metrics don't. So some of the stats you're looking for may be at the bottom of your table in the ungrouped section. More on that in the next couple of bullets...

- The metrics tables contain four kinds of results.
  - `statscontinuous_` are self-reported, typically using imperial units, (not the metric system)
  - `slider_` describes values from the Makehuman 3D program, should you ever be interested in creating a basic model of yourself using free software. I swore by this program for a lot of my early and still most reliable stats, because if you can get a basic _total_ look going which matches your subject, and if you can do this consistently for at least 150 people, then you will have done enough to rival a PhD or social scientific journal standard for a sample population on whatever stats you're looking at. Not only is Makehuman free, but its save format is also just a plain old text file that you can open in Notepad. The numbers are right there.

    Now having said the above, the slider_ statistics don't always correspond to things like the Inkscape and self-reported measures, because the aim in the slider case was to approximate general look-effect through geometry, while the Inkscape goal was to measure (not approximate) ratios. Because the Makehuman work was aimed at _mimicking_ *whole* looks, while the Inkscape work was aimed at _comparing_ granular body regions, the two different metrics for the same feature may not align. For example, a person with a 50" waist may have only a +.6 slider-horizontal-width (instead of the expected +.8 and up). This occurred because my overall aim when using Makehuman was to produce an exact replica of each reference image, regardless of what the sliders measured; often I used different sets of sliders to approximate the same feature. Overall though, the law of large numbers ensured that these renditions were at least _directionally_ aligned.

  - There are a couple of semi-graphic, unprefixed, slangish, and/or possibly offensive label names for categories. These were produced by an interrogator AI plugin for Stable Diffusion, which I used to describe anything that could be seen in images. Specifically, the model was CLIP ViT-L/14 - LAION-2B from these guys at https://openreview.net/forum?id=M3Y74vmsMcY. The model was generally awesome, but because I basically fed it nothing but nudey pics to do my job for me, it of course produced only nudey descriptions, finding a "boob" and an "ass" in pretty much anything you passed it, even if it was just a picture of a smooth hand pulling toast from a toaster. Now these were weighted low, mind you, but they definitely showed up more than they should have as tag words. That was back in early 2024 when good body captions/labelers were still newish to home AI. And since not enough people are willing to sit and tag 10,000 latissimus "bulginess" values the way we did in back tone

#502d16, you *still* can't find a good whole-body labeler in April 2025. Maybe that'll change tomorrow. Alas, when you study and give a name to every aspect of the normally censored body, "offensive" is easy to do.

That said, I didn't change *any* of the original category names as they came from their various sources, because 1) to change one would be to commit to changing 1400, 2) the absurd number of database joins I had to do over the course of five years' worth of research made renaming more of an exercise in masochism than anything else and 3) most importantly, there were often several ways to measure the same thing—none of them as faithful to the truth as in-person measuring tape. So each category retained its 3D model, 2D pic, 1D AI tagged, vector-dragged name, partly as a way of reminding you that all of these were but approximations aimed at putting numbers to something that couldn't be analyzed against astro and text-mine factors any other way.

o   Basic, unprefixed measures like `ab perimeter` come from the Inkscape activity we looked at earlier. This was by far the richest, most equalized data across my studies, evolving last in early 2025 as I finally figured out what I needed to finish this book. These pixel measures by themselves have no meaning until they are put into a ratio against other measures, and until those combinations are averaged across the whole sample in order to give you an idea of what to expect in a human body. Because one drawn line of thigh width could have been 500 pixels wide or 50 pixels wide depending on the shot, it was imperative that everything be measured against something else.

I followed certain rules in the Inkscape section:

- Whenever I wanted to capture tone or muscularity, I also captured the perimeter of the body region in question as a way of knowing the amount of real estate that tone had to work with; accordingly, [ab tone / ab perimeter] are THE pair for stomach muscularity. The back, the male chest, and a couple of the slider_Harveys also serve similar functions. Similar, but not the same.

- Males sometimes used stereotypically female sliders like Breastsize during the course of the modeling, as these were the best sliders for capturing the attribute I was trying to mimic for that particular person. So there will be stats for these.

- Related to the above, I did have about 30 MtoF and FtoM trans folks in my sample, and I do have some data on them which I have omitted from the book. Although I really wanted to cover absolutely every possible body configuration, the trans sample was problematic for several reasons. Often the focus for those in pre-op was specifically focused on the sexual features at the expense of regular features. Having features native to the other sex introduced a slew of outliers into various metrics at every turn. Bios were notably different in the *amount* of information they contained—m2f had a lot more while f2m had a lot less… and in the end I just didn't have the patience to sift through all of the would-be confounds in the data. I did, however, gain a healthy respect for the differences in the four baselines of male, female, m2f, and f2m. Someone will need to replicate my studies with an intentionally selected population of at least 200 in order to give this area the attention it deserves.

- Curved features like the breasts and the female torso not only needed several more lines than the old standards of measure would suggest, but those lines almost always had a vertical component to them to indicate their distance from each other. Some might find it interesting to note that the reason the breast has so many measures attached to it is because at the time I was investigating some of the sexual feature asteroids which affected both men and women (6060 Doudleby for example), and looking for a gender-independent frame for what these asteroids were doing. I found that, for these asteroids, the equivalent of the male penis is actually not the breasts proper, but the vertical distance from the nipple to the breast bottom, diameter of the areolae, and all of the related measures which explain the holistic position of these features on the chest. As was the case with the tone measures, I sometimes chose not to measure anything if I couldn't measure the critical partner values related to them.

- When you see "<->" then that represents the distance between one drawn line and another. If, for example, you felt you had an unusually tall torso compared to most people, you might look at metrics like the "clavicle to groin" or "waist<->subpelvic rear" results.
- Lastly, although I considered throwing out seemingly nonsensical measures like "elbow to wrist h / chest perimeter," they ended up staying for their research potential. For example, I found a strange and unexpected relationship between [the height of the ankle from the base of the foot] and [the volume of the suprailiac (love handles)]. Is this a thing? Maybe, maybe not. But relationships like this remind us that we have one whole body, the hormones and chemistry that have a particular function in one area aren't necessarily exclusively active in that area alone. It may well be that one of these ratios is relevant to you, and that the asteroids shown will speak to you when you look up their meanings in *Laurentia 2* or some other place.

TABLE 38: MAKEHUMAN SLIDER, SELF-REPORTED, AI TAGGER STATISTICS AND ASTEROIDS WHOSE HOT ASPECTS CORRELATED WITH THESE VALUES

measure	group	Count	Min	0.05-quantile	0.25-quantile	0.5-quantile	0.75-quantile	0.95-quantile	Max	/Ajani bio	most negative correlation	most positive correlation	most significant *p*-value
						Males							
slider _ Gender	0female 1male	71	0.500	1.000	1.000	1.000	1.000	1.000	1.000	1.000	6205 Menottigalli r:-0.354 p:0.010 df:50	15372 Agrigento r:0.424 p:0.002 df:50	97 Klotho r:-0.475 p:0.000 df:50
slider _ Age	age	71	0.420	0.460	0.500	0.500	0.500	0.524	0.642	0.425	1284 Latvia r:-0.355 p:0.010 df:50	12639 Tonkoopman r:0.535 p:0.000 df:50	2374 Vladvysotskij r:0.514 p:0.000 df:50
slider _ head age decr|incr	age	15	-0.658	-0.658	-0.306	-0.212	0.378	0.668	0.668	0.312	263932 Speyer r:-0.737 p:0.010 df:9	11494 Hibiki r:0.939 p:0.000 df:9	3486 Fulchignoni r:-0.872 p:0.000 df:9
slider _ l lowerarm fat decr|incr	arms	35	-0.348	-0.348	-0.222	0.192	0.296	0.506	0.564	-0.236	2216 Kerch r:-0.464 p:0.010 df:28	5942 Denzilrobert r:0.696 p:0.000 df:28	3462 Zhouguangzhao r:-0.604 p:0.000 df:28
slider _ l lowerarm muscle decr|incr	arms	32	-0.368	-0.287	0.212	0.331	0.467	0.706	0.796	0.796	7081 Ludibunda r:-0.505 p:0.010 df:23	1813 Imhotep r:0.712 p:0.000 df:23	1813 Imhotep r:0.712 p:0.000 df:23
slider _ l lowerarm scale depth decr|incr	arms	28	-0.212	-0.180	0.215	0.290	0.430	0.730	0.882	0.882	217576 Klausbirkner r:-0.526 p:0.010 df:21	3997 Taga r:0.749 p:0.000 df:21	63 Ausonia r:-0.741 p:0.000 df:21
slider _ l lowerarm scale horiz decr|incr	arms	8	-0.616	-0.616	-0.054	0.461	0.680	0.772	0.772	0.732	886 Washingtonia r:-0.835 p:0.010 df:6	385 Ilmatar r:0.965 p:0.000 df:6	385 Ilmatar r:0.965 p:0.000 df:6
slider _ l lowerarm scale vert decr|incr	arms	29	-0.108	-0.108	0.145	0.244	0.284	0.485	0.634	0.634	13079 Toots r:-0.527 p:0.010 df:21	6174 Polybius r:0.699 p:0.000 df:21	1599 Giomus r:-0.674 p:0.000 df:21
slider _ l upperarm fat decr|incr	arms	27	-0.638	-0.563	-0.244	0.130	0.336	0.589	0.626	0.452	2247 Hiroshima r:-0.549 p:0.010 df:19	6194 Denali r:0.784 p:0.000 df:19	1625 The NORC r:-0.720 p:0.000 df:19
slider _ l upperarm muscle decr|incr	arms	34	-0.234	-0.186	0.244	0.388	0.490	0.652	0.730	0.560	3996 Fugaku r:-0.464 p:0.010 df:28	4393 Dawe r:0.699 p:0.000 df:28	2307 Garuda r:-0.635 p:0.000 df:28
slider _ l upperarm scale depth decr|incr	arms	23	-0.296	-0.292	0.108	0.222	0.368	0.558	0.564		7269 Alprokhorov r:-0.576 p:0.010 df:17	1312 Vassar r:0.718 p:0.001 df:17	2243 Lonnrot r:-0.726 p:0.000 df:17
slider _ l upperarm scale horiz decr|incr	arms	8	-1.000	-1.000	-0.503	0.119	0.437	0.506	0.506	0.506	7254 Kuratani r:-0.836 p:0.010 df:6	17776 Troska r:0.965 p:0.000 df:6	95 Arethusa r:0.959 p:0.000 df:6
slider _ l upperarm scale vert decr|incr	arms	24	-0.378	-0.345	0.071	0.269	0.371	0.536	0.544	0.054	2143 Jimarnold r:-0.562 p:0.010 df:18	17984 Ahantonioli r:0.726 p:0.000 df:18	3807 Pagels r:0.724 p:0.000 df:18
slider _ l upperarm shoulder muscle decr|incr	arms	37	-1.000	-1.000	0.145	0.254	0.445	0.658	0.752	0.322	8775 Cristata r:-0.437 p:0.010 df:32	33979 Sunhaochun r:0.574 p:0.000 df:32	7021 Tomiokamachi r:-0.636 p:0.000 df:32
slider _ r lowerarm fat decr|incr	arms	38	-0.348	-0.348	-0.222	0.140	0.296	0.496	0.564	-0.236	431 Nephele r:-0.456 p:0.010 df:29	5942 Denzilrobert r:0.702 p:0.000 df:29	3462 Zhouguangzhao r:-0.613 p:0.000 df:29
slider _ r lowerarm muscle decr|incr	arms	33	-0.368	-0.281	0.212	0.336	0.472	0.699	0.796	0.796	7081 Ludibunda r:-0.505 p:0.010 df:23	1813 Imhotep r:0.712 p:0.000 df:23	1813 Imhotep r:0.712 p:0.000 df:23
slider _ r lowerarm scale depth decr|incr	arms	29	-0.212	-0.176	0.217	0.306	0.435	0.713	0.882	0.882	9587 Bonpland r:-0.516 p:0.010 df:22	3997 Taga r:0.723 p:0.000 df:22	63 Ausonia r:-0.700 p:0.000 df:22
slider _ r lowerarm scale horiz decr|incr	arms	8	-0.616	-0.616	-0.054	0.461	0.680	0.772	0.772	0.732	886 Washingtonia r:-0.835 p:0.010 df:6	385 Ilmatar r:0.965 p:0.000 df:6	385 Ilmatar r:0.965 p:0.000 df:6
slider _ r lowerarm scale vert decr|incr	arms	30	-0.108	-0.108	0.148	0.244	0.284	0.470	0.634	0.634	63 Ausonia r:-0.516 p:0.010 df:22	20259 Alanhoffman r:0.695 p:0.000 df:22	1599 Giomus r:-0.674 p:0.000 df:22
slider _ r upperarm fat decr|incr	arms	28	-0.638	-0.553	-0.239	0.150	0.326	0.585	0.626	0.452	3278 Behounek r:-0.550 p:0.010 df:19	6194 Denali r:0.783 p:0.000 df:19	130 Elektra r:0.715 p:0.000 df:19

slider	region	n									col A	col B	col C
slider _ r upperarm muscle decr|incr	arms	34	-0.234	-0.186	0.244	0.388	0.490	0.652	0.730	0.560	7345 Happer r:-0.471 p:0.010 df:27	4393 Dawe r:0.694 p:0.000 df:27	2307 Garuda r:-0.628 p:0.000 df:27
slider _ r upperarm scale depth decr|incr	arms	25	-0.296	-0.289	0.093	0.222	0.358	0.555	0.564		1329 Eliane r:-0.562 p:0.010 df:18	1312 Vassar r:0.695 p:0.001 df:18	2243 Lonnrot r:-0.718 p:0.000 df:18
slider _ r upperarm scale horiz decr|incr	arms	8	-1.000	-1.000	-0.503	0.119	0.437	0.506	0.506	0.506	7254 Kuratani r:-0.836 p:0.010 df:6	17776 Troska r:0.965 p:0.000 df:6	95 Arethusa r:0.959 p:0.000 df:6
slider _ r upperarm scale vert decr|incr	arms	26	-0.378	-0.331	0.104	0.269	0.402	0.557	0.564	0.054	20839 Bretharrison r:-0.549 p:0.010 df:19	134028 Mikefitzgibbon r:0.738 p:0.000 df:19	105 Artemis r:-0.703 p:0.000 df:19
slider _ r upperarm shoulder muscle decr|incr	arms	36	-1.000	-1.000	0.143	0.254	0.448	0.629	0.648	0.322	31926 Alhamood r:-0.442 p:0.010 df:31	385 Ilmatar r:0.577 p:0.000 df:31	385 Ilmatar r:0.577 p:0.000 df:31
slider _ back accent	back	16	0.192	0.192	0.319	0.588	0.752	1.000	1.000	0.192	10120 Ypres r:-0.642 p:0.010 df:13	23295 Brandoreavis r:0.806 p:0.000 df:13	2585 Irpedina r:-0.806 p:0.000 df:13
slider _ torso muscle dorsi decr|incr	back	22	-1.000	-0.986	-0.237	0.067	0.215	0.459	0.462	0.118	8713 Azusa r:-0.562 p:0.010 df:18	7623 Stamitz r:0.777 p:0.000 df:18	7623 Stamitz r:0.777 p:0.000 df:18
slider _ BreastFirmness	breasts	71	0.083	0.500	0.500	0.500	0.500	0.509	0.699	0.500	7232 Nabokov r:-0.354 p:0.010 df:50	1792 Reni r:0.487 p:0.000 df:50	520 Franziska r:-0.503 p:0.000 df:50
slider _ BreastSize	breasts	71	0.500	0.500	0.500	0.500	0.500	0.500	0.532	0.532	2670 Chuvashia r:-0.371 p:0.007 df:50	275786 Bouley r:0.631 p:0.000 df:50	52 Europa r:0.509 p:0.000 df:50
slider _ Breasts _ Inframammary _ fold	breasts	27	0.114	0.120	0.244	0.472	0.668	0.956	1.000	0.881	212 Medea r:-0.537 p:0.010 df:20	30177 Khashayar r:0.708 p:0.000 df:20	6107 Osterbrock r:0.683 p:0.000 df:20
slider _ breast dist decr|incr	breasts	15	-0.016	-0.016	0.202	0.284	0.358	0.492	0.492		20109 Alicelandis r:-0.662 p:0.010 df:12	1700 Zvezdara r:0.873 p:0.000 df:12	1700 Zvezdara r:0.873 p:0.000 df:12
slider _ breast point decr|incr	breasts	24	-0.502	-0.430	0.101	0.306	0.420	0.645	0.668		9566 Rykhlova r:-0.563 p:0.010 df:18	344641 Szeleczky r:0.740 p:0.000 df:18	3996 Fugaku r:-0.801 p:0.000 df:18
slider _ breast trans down|up	breasts	8	-0.348	-0.348	0.059	0.285	0.881	1.000	1.000		12928 Nicolapozio r:-0.875 p:0.010 df:5	2349 Kurchenko r:0.987 p:0.000 df:5	1820 Lohmann r:0.973 p:0.000 df:5
slider _ breast volume vert down|up	breasts	27	-0.814	-0.752	-0.336	-0.054	0.378	0.702	0.710	-0.054	62190 Augusthorch r:-0.537 p:0.010 df:20	9142 Rhesus r:0.746 p:0.000 df:20	2919 Dali r:-0.688 p:0.000 df:20
slider _ female _ breasts _ extra _ roundness	breasts	23	0.010	0.011	0.041	0.145	0.264	0.365	0.378	0.311	22064 Angelalewis r:-0.562 p:0.010 df:18	10802 Masamifuruya r:0.735 p:0.000 df:18	6468 Welzenbach r:-0.736 p:0.000 df:18
fat	build	10	0.078	0.078	0.118	0.176	0.426	0.883	0.883		3778 Regge r:-0.798 p:0.010 df:7	4488 Tokitada r:0.973 p:0.000 df:7	805 Hormuthia r:0.952 p:0.000 df:7
slider _ BodyProportions	build	71	0.000	0.198	0.409	0.500	0.500	0.500	0.648	0.430	5803 Otzi r:-0.354 p:0.010 df:50	75223 Wupatki r:0.516 p:0.000 df:50	89 Julia r:-0.490 p:0.000 df:50
slider _ buttocks volume decr|incr	buttocks	15	-0.544	-0.544	-0.098	0.234	0.378	0.638	0.638	0.612	6237 Chikushi r:-0.661 p:0.010 df:12	24974 Macuch r:0.853 p:0.000 df:12	881 Athene r:0.812 p:0.000 df:12
slider _ l cheek bones decr|incr	cheeks	50	-0.844	-0.678	-0.306	0.098	0.247	0.460	0.492	0.088	6500 Kodaira r:-0.420 p:0.010 df:35	3375 Amy r:0.622 p:0.000 df:35	1828 Kashirina r:0.556 p:0.000 df:35
slider _ l cheek inner decr|incr	cheeks	49	-0.814	-0.389	0.160	0.296	0.435	0.891	1.000	-0.462	2533 Fechtig r:-0.419 p:0.010 df:35	43752 Maryosipova r:0.610 p:0.000 df:35	4466 Abai r:0.563 p:0.000 df:35
slider _ l cheek trans down|up	cheeks	53	-1.000	-1.000	-0.658	-0.254	0.383	0.844	0.876	0.358	11010 Artemieva r:-0.403 p:0.010 df:38	16452 Goldfinger r:0.583 p:0.000 df:38	4474 Proust r:0.535 p:0.000 df:38
slider _ l cheek volume decr|incr	cheeks	51	-0.772	-0.592	-0.192	0.130	0.348	0.690	0.896	0.896	15132 Steigmeyer r:-0.409 p:0.010 df:37	32048 Kathyliu r:0.595 p:0.000 df:37	4482 Frerebasile r:-0.605 p:0.000 df:37
slider _ r cheek bones decr|incr	cheeks	47	-0.844	-0.681	-0.306	0.088	0.244	0.430	0.492	-0.408	6666 Fro r:-0.424 p:0.010 df:34	20731 Mothediniz r:0.595 p:0.000 df:34	1828 Kashirina r:0.565 p:0.000 df:34
slider _ r cheek inner decr|incr	cheeks	45	-0.814	-0.418	0.160	0.306	0.445	0.931	1.000	-0.462	9516 Inasan r:-0.430 p:0.010 df:33	43752 Maryosipova r:0.633 p:0.000 df:33	1684 Iguassu r:0.565 p:0.000 df:33
slider _ r cheek trans down|up	cheeks	49	-1.000	-1.000	-0.668	-0.284	0.383	0.844	0.876	0.296	33406 Saltzman r:-0.413 p:0.010 df:36	16452 Goldfinger r:0.594 p:0.000 df:36	4474 Proust r:0.586 p:0.000 df:36
slider _ r cheek volume decr|incr	cheeks	49	-0.772	-0.606	-0.176	0.140	0.348	0.700	0.844	0.844	5093 Svirelia r:-0.413 p:0.010 df:36	32048 Kathyliu r:0.595 p:0.000 df:36	4482 Frerebasile r:-0.616 p:0.000 df:36
chest width<->underbust	chest	21	1.854	1.908	2.918	3.703	4.858	8.190	8.462	5.316	7390 Kundera r:-0.565 p:0.009 df:18	4082 Swann r:0.822 p:0.000 df:18	691 Lehigh r:0.775 p:0.000 df:18
pectorals	chest	33	0.093	0.099	0.137	0.288	0.523	0.646	0.665	0.603	438 Zeuxo r:-0.456 p:0.010 df:29	2515 Gansu r:0.609 p:0.000 df:29	1835 Gajdariya r:-0.630 p:0.000 df:29
slider _ torso muscle pectoral decr|incr	chest	42	-0.638	-0.502	0.187	0.430	0.591	0.833	0.876	0.284	8537 Billochbull r:-0.430 p:0.010 df:33	29753 Silvo r:0.642 p:0.000 df:33	3817 Lencarter r:0.566 p:0.000 df:33
slider _ chin bones decr|incr	chin	44	-1.000	-0.889	-0.544	-0.373	-0.207	0.075	0.306	-0.512	5889 Mickiewicz r:-0.430 p:0.010 df:33	34219 Megantang r:0.613 p:0.000 df:33	4028 Pancratz r:0.564 p:0.000 df:33
slider _ chin height decr|incr	chin	33	-0.730	-0.673	-0.217	-0.036	0.103	0.290	0.326	0.068	1879 Broederstroom r:-0.497 p:0.010 df:24	35265 Takeosaitou r:0.658 p:0.000 df:24	3170 Dzhanibekov r:-0.690 p:0.000 df:24
slider _ chin jaw drop decr|incr	chin	37	-0.576	-0.547	-0.373	-0.170	0.109	0.609	0.638	-0.482	16543 Rosetta r:-0.479 p:0.010 df:26	29880 Andytran r:0.713 p:0.000 df:26	4129 Richelen r:-0.615 p:0.000 df:26
slider _ chin prognathism decr|incr	chin	16	-0.440	-0.440	-0.274	-0.223	0.184	0.410	0.410	-0.258	157258 Leach r:-0.642 p:0.010 df:13	2113 Ehrdni r:0.814 p:0.000 df:13	2113 Ehrdni r:0.814 p:0.000 df:13
slider _ chin prominent decr|incr	chin	31	-1.000	-0.732	-0.150	0.120	0.254	0.418	0.524	-1.000	10566 Zabadak r:-0.526 p:0.010 df:21	3608 Kataev r:0.700 p:0.000 df:21	839 Valborg r:-0.725 p:0.000 df:21
slider _ chin width decr|incr	chin	45	-0.524	-0.330	-0.006	0.120	0.223	0.403	0.710	0.710	12124 Hvar r:-0.437 p:0.010 df:32	1246 Chaka r:0.666 p:0.000 df:32	-10003 Venus r:-0.579 p:0.000 df:32
slider _ ears _ flat _ 2	ears	10	0.088	0.088	0.278	0.332	0.496	0.666	0.668		25225 Patrickbenson r:-0.798 p:0.010 df:7	15058 Billcooke r:0.950 p:0.000 df:7	1852 Carpenter r:0.921 p:0.000 df:7

Slider	Category	n									Min	Mid	Max
slider _ l ear lobe decr|incr	ears	15	-0.658	-0.658	-0.182	0.088	0.316	0.472	0.472	-0.010	3296 Bosque Alegre r:-0.711 p:0.009 df:10	33379 Rohandalvi r:0.841 p:0.001 df:10	3098 van Sprang r:-0.857 p:0.000 df:10
slider _ l ear rot backward|forward	ears	17	-1.000	-1.000	-0.658	-0.450	-0.207	0.326	0.326	-1.000	243 Ida r:-0.735 p:0.010 df:9	2427 Kobzar r:0.891 p:0.000 df:9	47 Aglaja r:0.878 p:0.000 df:9
slider _ l ear scale decr|incr	ears	12	-0.192	-0.192	0.047	0.202	0.352	0.544	0.544	0.010	12465 Perth Amboy r:-0.798 p:0.010 df:7	727 Nipponia r:0.973 p:0.000 df:7	727 Nipponia r:0.973 p:0.000 df:7
slider _ l ear shape pointed|triangle	ears	23	-0.720	-0.668	-0.170	-0.026	0.212	0.700	0.752	0.752	14571 Caralexander r:-0.590 p:0.010 df:16	386 Siegena r:0.825 p:0.000 df:16	386 Siegena r:0.825 p:0.000 df:16
slider _ l ear shape square|round	ears	14	-0.586	-0.586	-0.262	0.155	0.316	0.482	0.482	0.376	2176 Donar r:-0.708 p:0.010 df:10	28779 Acthieke r:0.842 p:0.001 df:10	838 Seraphina r:-0.885 p:0.000 df:10
slider _ l ear trans down|up	ears	15	-0.814	-0.814	-0.658	-0.296	0.006	0.700	0.700	-0.354	27320 Vellinga r:-0.735 p:0.010 df:9	11247 Wilburwright r:0.931 p:0.000 df:9	1357 Khama r:-0.909 p:0.000 df:9
slider _ l ear wing decr|incr	ears	11	-0.326	-0.326	0.078	0.296	0.348	0.616	0.616		21695 Hannahwolf r:-0.798 p:0.010 df:7	21470 Frankchuang r:0.947 p:0.000 df:7	2363 Cebriones r:0.930 p:0.000 df:7
slider _ r ear lobe decr|incr	ears	15	-0.658	-0.658	-0.182	0.088	0.316	0.472	0.472	-0.010	3296 Bosque Alegre r:-0.711 p:0.009 df:10	33379 Rohandalvi r:0.841 p:0.001 df:10	3098 van Sprang r:-0.857 p:0.000 df:10
slider _ r ear rot backward|forward	ears	17	-1.000	-1.000	-0.658	-0.378	-0.134	0.326	0.326	-1.000	3731 Hancock r:-0.735 p:0.010 df:9	22952 Hommasachi r:0.914 p:0.000 df:9	47 Aglaja r:0.876 p:0.000 df:9
slider _ r ear scale decr|incr	ears	12	-0.192	-0.192	0.047	0.202	0.352	0.544	0.544	0.010	12465 Perth Amboy r:-0.798 p:0.010 df:7	727 Nipponia r:0.973 p:0.000 df:7	727 Nipponia r:0.973 p:0.000 df:7
slider _ r ear shape pointed|triangle	ears	23	-0.720	-0.668	-0.170	-0.026	0.244	0.700	0.752	0.752	4140 Branham r:-0.591 p:0.010 df:16	386 Siegena r:0.819 p:0.000 df:16	386 Siegena r:0.819 p:0.000 df:16
slider _ r ear shape square|round	ears	14	-0.586	-0.586	-0.262	0.155	0.316	0.482	0.482	0.376	2176 Donar r:-0.708 p:0.010 df:10	28779 Acthieke r:0.842 p:0.001 df:10	838 Seraphina r:-0.885 p:0.000 df:10
slider _ r ear trans down|up	ears	15	-0.814	-0.814	-0.658	-0.296	0.006	0.648	0.648	-0.354	23277 Benhughes r:-0.735 p:0.010 df:9	961 Gunnie r:0.952 p:0.000 df:9	29 Amphitrite r:0.915 p:0.000 df:9
slider _ r ear wing decr|incr	ears	11	-0.326	-0.326	0.078	0.296	0.348	0.616	0.616		21695 Hannahwolf r:-0.798 p:0.010 df:7	21470 Frankchuang r:0.947 p:0.000 df:7	2363 Cebriones r:0.930 p:0.000 df:7
slider _ African	ethno	71	0.000	0.000	0.000	0.047	0.259	0.713	1.000	0.855	28692 Chanleysmall r:-0.354 p:0.010 df:50	233943 Falera r:0.568 p:0.000 df:50	1288 Santa r:0.471 p:0.000 df:50
slider _ Asian	ethno	71	0.000	0.000	0.000	0.000	0.321	0.672	0.868	0.073	239792 Hankakovacova r:-0.355 p:0.010 df:50	6681 Prokopovich r:0.490 p:0.000 df:50	951 Gaspra r:0.481 p:0.000 df:50
slider _ Caucasian	ethno	71	0.000	0.108	0.337	0.829	1.000	1.000	1.000	0.072	3859 Borngen r:-0.355 p:0.010 df:50	6191 Eades r:0.489 p:0.000 df:50	601 Nerthus r:-0.473 p:0.000 df:50
slider _ eyebrows angle down|up	eyebrows	17	-0.462	-0.462	-0.082	0.192	0.410	0.502	0.502	-0.044	28924 Jennanncsele r:-0.765 p:0.010 df:8	3917 Franz Schubert r:0.936 p:0.000 df:8	937 Bethgea r:-0.926 p:0.000 df:8
slider _ eyebrows trans backward|forward	eyebrows	22	-0.624	-0.615	-0.192	0.083	0.153	0.268	0.274	-0.624	2933 Amber r:-0.623 p:0.010 df:14	22109 Loriehutch r:0.841 p:0.000 df:14	88 Thisbe r:-0.775 p:0.000 df:14
slider _ eyebrows trans down|up	eyebrows	22	-0.274	-0.251	0.397	0.643	0.809	1.000	1.000	-0.118	22482 Michbertier r:-0.641 p:0.010 df:13	31134 Zurria r:0.829 p:0.000 df:13	1806 Derice r:-0.838 p:0.000 df:13
thick eyebrows	eyebrows	8	0.070	0.070	0.088	0.147	0.197	0.223	0.223	0.223	5179 Takeshima r:-0.875 p:0.010 df:5	49272 Bryce Canyon r:0.985 p:0.000 df:5	672 Astarte r:-0.974 p:0.000 df:5
slider _ eyes _ outer _ droop	eyes	8	0.306	0.306	0.380	0.715	0.856	0.876	0.876		4164 Shilov r:-0.875 p:0.010 df:5	31641 Cevasco r:0.986 p:0.000 df:5	6181 Bobweber r:-0.969 p:0.000 df:5
slider _ l eye bag decr|incr	eyes	38	-0.690	-0.650	-0.218	0.264	0.487	0.796	0.876	-0.538	1762 Russell r:-0.457 p:0.010 df:29	27276 Davidblack r:0.622 p:0.000 df:29	392 Wilhelmina r:-0.593 p:0.000 df:29
slider _ l eye bag height decr|incr	eyes	42	-0.834	-0.833	-0.537	-0.368	0.306	0.509	0.700	-0.740	614 Pia r:-0.443 p:0.010 df:31	267017 Yangzhifa r:0.642 p:0.000 df:31	630 Euphemia r:-0.584 p:0.000 df:31
slider _ l eye bag in|out	eyes	39	-0.814	-0.772	0.222	0.492	0.690	1.000	1.000	0.638	11455 Richardstarr r:-0.456 p:0.010 df:29	5382 McKay r:0.622 p:0.000 df:29	1722 Goffin r:-0.613 p:0.000 df:29
slider _ l eye corner1 down|up	eyes	34	-0.824	-0.785	-0.609	-0.352	-0.012	0.596	0.752	-0.150	8881 Prialnik r:-0.488 p:0.010 df:25	25725 McCormick r:0.670 p:0.000 df:25	3007 Reaves r:-0.713 p:0.000 df:25
slider _ l eye corner2 down|up	eyes	35	-0.648	-0.640	-0.358	-0.078	0.326	0.826	0.834	0.658	18735 Chubko r:-0.472 p:0.010 df:27	7002 Bronshten r:0.715 p:0.000 df:27	198 Ampella r:0.629 p:0.000 df:27
slider _ l eye epicanthus in|out	eyes	18	-0.388	-0.388	-0.089	0.036	0.195	0.306	0.306	-0.388	527 Euryanthe r:-0.623 p:0.010 df:14	20117 Tannoakira r:0.779 p:0.000 df:14	1050 Meta r:-0.799 p:0.000 df:14
slider _ l eye eyefold angle down|up	eyes	28	-0.824	-0.797	-0.596	-0.264	0.202	0.483	0.534	-0.764	4226 Damiaan r:-0.515 p:0.010 df:22	3079 Schiller r:0.744 p:0.000 df:22	340 Eduarda r:0.687 p:0.000 df:22
slider _ l eye eyefold concave|convex	eyes	37	-1.000	-1.000	-0.699	-0.420	-0.088	0.755	0.886	-0.130	2373 Immo r:-0.456 p:0.010 df:29	4601 Ludkewycz r:0.681 p:0.000 df:29	708 Raphaela r:0.635 p:0.000 df:29
slider _ l eye eyefold down|up	eyes	37	-1.000	-1.000	-0.840	-0.678	-0.368	0.464	0.678	-0.108	18883 Domegge r:-0.456 p:0.010 df:29	13253 Stejneger r:0.738 p:0.000 df:29	3087 Beatrice Tinsley r:0.591 p:0.000 df:29
slider _ l eye height1 decr|incr	eyes	28	-0.876	-0.773	-0.579	-0.342	0.008	0.150	0.150	-0.580	3356 Resnik r:-0.515 p:0.010 df:22	3128 Obruchev r:0.734 p:0.000 df:22	2943 Heinrich r:0.681 p:0.000 df:22
slider _ l eye height2 decr|incr	eyes	36	-0.700	-0.595	-0.234	-0.046	0.274	0.631	0.658	0.336	23750 Stepciechan r:-0.471 p:0.010 df:27	207687 Senckenberg r:0.661 p:0.000 df:27	3235 Melchior r:0.635 p:0.000 df:27
slider _ l eye height3 decr|incr	eyes	31	-0.772	-0.716	-0.410	-0.244	-0.016	0.099	0.130	0.078	445 Edna r:-0.505 p:0.010 df:23	30051 Jihopark r:0.691 p:0.000 df:23	6439 Tirol r:-0.652 p:0.000 df:23
slider _ l eye push1 in|out	eyes	25	-0.752	-0.711	-0.228	0.170	0.554	0.884	0.928	0.170	1635 Bohrmann r:-0.575 p:0.010 df:17	293926 Harrystine r:0.781 p:0.000 df:17	2343 Siding Spring r:0.747 p:0.000 df:17
slider _ l eye push2 in|out	eyes	22	-1.000	-0.950	-0.283	0.114	0.433	0.731	0.740	0.064	350178 Eisleben r:-0.624 p:0.010 df:14	30350 Beltecas r:0.789 p:0.000 df:14	1728 Goethe Link r:-0.792 p:0.000 df:14

Slider	Group	N									Ref 1	Ref 2	Ref 3
slider _ l eye scale decr|incr	eyes	17	-0.160	-0.160	0.259	0.368	0.684	0.854	0.854	0.710	13178 Catalan r:-0.735 p:0.010 df:9	28411 Xiuqicao r:0.933 p:0.000 df:9	179 Klytaemnestra r:0.878 p:0.000 df:9
slider _ l eye trans down|up	eyes	28	-1.000	-1.000	-0.770	-0.627	-0.272	0.776	1.000	0.046	2257 Kaarina r:-0.537 p:0.010 df:20	8316 Wolkenstein r:0.788 p:0.000 df:20	2840 Kallavesi r:0.684 p:0.000 df:20
slider _ l eye trans in|out	eyes	26	-0.844	-0.684	-0.235	0.114	0.363	0.620	0.700	0.440	12284 Pohl r:-0.562 p:0.010 df:18	11324 Hayamizu r:0.819 p:0.000 df:18	1643 Brown r:-0.754 p:0.000 df:18
slider _ r eye bag decr|incr	eyes	38	-0.690	-0.650	-0.218	0.264	0.487	0.796	0.876	-0.538	1762 Russell r:-0.457 p:0.010 df:29	27276 Davidblack r:0.622 p:0.000 df:29	392 Wilhelmina r:-0.593 p:0.000 df:29
slider _ r eye bag height decr|incr	eyes	41	-0.834	-0.833	-0.539	-0.378	0.285	0.510	0.700	-0.740	161585 Danielhals r:-0.449 p:0.010 df:30	267017 Yangzhifa r:0.652 p:0.000 df:30	13714 Stainbrook r:0.583 p:0.000 df:30
slider _ r eye bag in|out	eyes	38	-0.814	-0.774	0.246	0.497	0.698	1.000	1.000	0.638	6581 Sobers r:-0.463 p:0.010 df:28	24681 Granados r:0.648 p:0.000 df:28	1722 Goffin r:-0.622 p:0.000 df:28
slider _ r eye corner1 down|up	eyes	34	-0.824	-0.785	-0.594	-0.352	0.154	0.814	1.000	1.000	16909 Miladejager r:-0.488 p:0.010 df:25	25046 Suyihan r:0.661 p:0.000 df:25	422 Berolina r:-0.637 p:0.000 df:25
slider _ r eye corner2 down|up	eyes	35	-0.648	-0.640	-0.358	-0.078	0.326	0.867	1.000	1.000	24524 Kevinhawkins r:-0.471 p:0.010 df:27	12003 Hideosugai r:0.715 p:0.000 df:27	198 Ampella r:0.638 p:0.000 df:27
slider _ r eye epicanthus in|out	eyes	18	-0.388	-0.388	-0.089	0.036	0.195	0.306	0.306	-0.388	527 Euryanthe r:-0.623 p:0.010 df:14	20117 Tannoakira r:0.779 p:0.000 df:14	1050 Meta r:-0.799 p:0.000 df:14
slider _ r eye eyefold angle down|up	eyes	28	-0.824	-0.797	-0.596	-0.264	0.202	0.483	0.534	-0.764	4226 Damiaan r:-0.515 p:0.010 df:22	3079 Schiller r:0.744 p:0.000 df:22	340 Eduarda r:0.687 p:0.000 df:22
slider _ r eye eyefold concave|convex	eyes	37	-1.000	-1.000	-0.699	-0.420	-0.088	0.755	0.886	-0.130	2373 Immo r:-0.456 p:0.010 df:29	4601 Ludkewycz r:0.681 p:0.000 df:29	708 Raphaela r:0.635 p:0.000 df:29
slider _ r eye eyefold down|up	eyes	36	-1.000	-1.000	-0.858	-0.684	-0.396	0.476	0.678	-0.108	23674 Juliebaker r:-0.463 p:0.010 df:28	13253 Stejneger r:0.734 p:0.000 df:28	1342 Brabantia r:0.640 p:0.000 df:28
slider _ r eye height1 decr|incr	eyes	28	-0.876	-0.773	-0.579	-0.342	0.008	0.150	0.150	-0.580	3356 Resnik r:-0.515 p:0.010 df:22	3128 Obruchev r:0.734 p:0.000 df:22	2943 Heinrich r:0.681 p:0.000 df:22
slider _ r eye height2 decr|incr	eyes	35	-0.700	-0.601	-0.234	-0.046	0.284	0.632	0.658	0.316	1603 Neva r:-0.479 p:0.010 df:26	3235 Melchior r:0.675 p:0.000 df:26	2511 Patterson r:0.632 p:0.000 df:26
slider _ r eye height3 decr|incr	eyes	30	-0.772	-0.720	-0.413	-0.228	-0.014	0.167	0.212	0.212	2715 Mielikki r:-0.515 p:0.010 df:22	30051 Jihopark r:0.721 p:0.000 df:22	866 Fatme r:0.676 p:0.000 df:22
slider _ r eye push1 in|out	eyes	25	-0.752	-0.711	-0.228	0.170	0.554	0.884	0.928	0.170	1635 Bohrmann r:-0.575 p:0.010 df:17	293926 Harrystine r:0.781 p:0.000 df:17	2343 Siding Spring r:0.747 p:0.000 df:17
slider _ r eye push2 in|out	eyes	22	-1.000	-0.950	-0.283	0.114	0.433	0.731	0.740	0.064	350178 Eisleben r:-0.624 p:0.010 df:14	30350 Beltecas r:0.789 p:0.000 df:14	1728 Goethe Link r:-0.792 p:0.000 df:14
slider _ r eye scale decr|incr	eyes	17	-0.160	-0.160	0.259	0.368	0.684	0.854	0.854	0.710	13178 Catalan r:-0.735 p:0.010 df:9	28411 Xiuqicao r:0.933 p:0.000 df:9	179 Klytaemnestra r:0.878 p:0.000 df:9
slider _ r eye trans down|up	eyes	28	-1.000	-0.968	-0.760	-0.627	-0.272	0.776	1.000	0.326	70207 Davidunlap r:-0.538 p:0.010 df:20	79896 Billhaley r:0.767 p:0.000 df:20	305 Gordonia r:0.683 p:0.000 df:20
slider _ r eye trans in|out	eyes	26	-0.844	-0.684	-0.235	0.114	0.363	0.800	0.854	0.854	6705 Rinaketty r:-0.562 p:0.010 df:18	17163 Vasifedoseev r:0.796 p:0.000 df:18	386 Siegena r:0.723 p:0.000 df:18
beard	hair	33	0.092	0.099	0.191	0.360	0.484	0.711	0.765	0.688	15118 Elizabethsears r:-0.464 p:0.010 df:28	10666 Feldberg r:0.685 p:0.000 df:28	5033 Mistral r:0.659 p:0.000 df:28
black hair	hair	28	0.208	0.210	0.326	0.466	0.565	0.752	0.761	0.523	1335 Demoulina r:-0.537 p:0.010 df:20	7686 Wolfernst r:0.669 p:0.001 df:20	6725 Engyoji r:-0.712 p:0.000 df:20
brown hair	hair	10	0.172	0.172	0.250	0.332	0.528	0.643	0.643		2589 Daniel r:-0.798 p:0.010 df:7	2833 Radishchev r:0.949 p:0.000 df:7	2340 Hathor r:-0.944 p:0.000 df:7
slider _ l hand fingers diameter decr|incr	hands	13	0.120	0.120	0.218	0.388	0.451	0.648	0.648		1459 Magnya r:-0.799 p:0.010 df:7	802 Epyaxa r:0.952 p:0.000 df:7	802 Epyaxa r:0.952 p:0.000 df:7
slider _ r hand fingers diameter decr|incr	hands	18	0.120	0.120	0.226	0.388	0.453	0.700	0.700		18907 Kevinclaytor r:-0.664 p:0.010 df:12	156542 Hogg r:0.914 p:0.000 df:12	1029 La Plata r:0.815 p:0.000 df:12
slider _ r hand fingers length decr|incr	hands	8	-0.472	-0.472	-0.254	-0.062	0.000	0.150	0.150		3137 Horky r:-0.875 p:0.010 df:5	58365 Robmedrano r:0.958 p:0.001 df:5	7 Iris r:-0.969 p:0.000 df:5
slider _ forehead scale vert decr|incr	head	48	-1.000	-1.000	-0.728	-0.616	-0.326	0.216	0.388	-0.918	495 Eulalia r:-0.424 p:0.010 df:34	33600 Davidlu r:0.647 p:0.000 df:34	128 Nemesis r:-0.583 p:0.000 df:34
slider _ forehead temple decr|incr	head	13	-0.844	-0.844	-0.409	-0.284	0.108	0.440	0.440	-0.450	175566 Papplaci r:-0.765 p:0.010 df:8	4234 Evtushenko r:0.927 p:0.000 df:8	1686 De Sitter r:0.901 p:0.000 df:8
slider _ forehead trans backward|forward	head	17	-0.502	-0.502	-0.399	-0.098	0.042	0.130	0.130	0.130	1160 Illyria r:-0.735 p:0.010 df:9	6036 Weinberg r:0.901 p:0.000 df:9	153 Hilda r:-0.917 p:0.000 df:9
slider _ head back scale depth decr|incr	head	13	-0.752	-0.752	-0.461	-0.368	-0.187	0.212	0.212		342 Endymion r:-0.799 p:0.010 df:7	24916 Stelzhamer r:0.963 p:0.000 df:7	2 Pallas r:0.917 p:0.000 df:7
slider _ head diamond	head	31	0.052	0.055	0.119	0.249	0.383	0.768	0.824	0.824	5069 Tokeidai r:-0.497 p:0.010 df:24	8082 Haynes r:0.762 p:0.000 df:24	571 Dulcinea r:0.655 p:0.000 df:24
slider _ head fat decr|incr	head	36	-0.834	-0.746	-0.500	-0.269	-0.076	0.412	0.420	-0.730	17042 Madiraju r:-0.463 p:0.010 df:28	2280 Kunikov r:0.656 p:0.000 df:28	1358 Gaika r:0.602 p:0.000 df:28
slider _ head invertedtriangular	head	27	0.047	0.059	0.145	0.415	0.570	0.712	0.758	0.758	12675 Chabot r:-0.562 p:0.010 df:18	7121 Busch r:0.771 p:0.000 df:18	1621 Druzhba r:0.747 p:0.000 df:18
slider _ head oval	head	14	0.036	0.036	0.087	0.130	0.205	0.415	0.415		14914 Moreux r:-0.768 p:0.009 df:8	26266 Andrewmerrill r:0.959 p:0.000 df:8	3751 Kiang r:0.912 p:0.000 df:8
slider _ head scale horiz decr|incr	head	18	-0.450	-0.450	-0.284	-0.207	-0.106	0.120	0.120	-0.192	12834 Bomben r:-0.684 p:0.010 df:11	10350 Spallanzani r:0.900 p:0.000 df:11	5300 Sats r:0.833 p:0.000 df:11
slider _ head scale vert decr|incr	head	36	-0.182	-0.146	0.192	0.353	0.440	0.677	0.968	0.968	1622 Chacornac r:-0.487 p:0.010 df:25	7633 Volodymyr r:0.697 p:0.000 df:25	641 Agnes r:-0.629 p:0.000 df:25

label	cat	N									corr 1	corr 2	corr 3
slider _ Height	height	71	0.394	0.431	0.500	0.528	0.570	0.636	0.684	0.527	9484 Wanambi r:-0.355 p:0.010 df:50	32071 Matthewretchin r:0.540 p:0.000 df:50	4799 Hirasawa r:-0.485 p:0.000 df:50
statscontinuous _ Height	height	90	64.000	66.000	68.000	70.000	72.000	75.450	77.000	69.000	23749 Thygesen r:-0.348 p:0.010 df:52	280652 Aimaku r:0.552 p:0.000 df:52	902 Probitas r:-0.506 p:0.000 df:52
pelvic hips<->waist	hips	19	3.612	3.612	4.446	5.344	5.992	7.237	7.237	7.181	24140 Evanmirts r:-0.561 p:0.010 df:18	5605 Kushida r:0.819 p:0.000 df:18	851 Zeissia r:0.738 p:0.000 df:18
slider _ hip scale depth decr|incr	hips	9	-0.108	-0.108	0.083	0.150	0.228	0.254	0.254		204 Kallisto r:-0.875 p:0.010 df:5	4578 Kurashiki r:0.995 p:0.000 df:5	3294 Carlvesely r:-0.976 p:0.000 df:5
slider _ hip scale vert decr|incr	hips	12	-0.348	-0.348	-0.119	0.228	0.336	0.524	0.524	-0.344	4362 Carlisle r:-0.735 p:0.010 df:9	21630 Wootensmith r:0.890 p:0.000 df:9	4921 Volonte r:-0.899 p:0.000 df:9
slider _ pelvis tone decr|incr	hips	12	-0.792	-0.792	-0.168	0.503	0.959	1.000	1.000	1.000	138 Tolosa r:-0.738 p:0.010 df:9	6563 Steinheim r:0.895 p:0.000 df:9	19 Fortuna r:-0.925 p:0.000 df:9
suprailiac<->waist	hips	25	1.268	1.339	2.153	2.880	3.582	4.830	4.841	3.292	221230 Sanaloria r:-0.496 p:0.010 df:24	1956 Artek r:0.748 p:0.000 df:24	1956 Artek r:0.748 p:0.000 df:24
slider _ l lowerleg fat decr|incr	legs	13	-0.492	-0.492	-0.399	-0.222	0.298	0.596	0.596	0.312	18117 Jonhodge r:-0.765 p:0.010 df:8	15917 Rosahavel r:0.956 p:0.000 df:8	543 Charlotte r:0.894 p:0.000 df:8
slider _ l lowerleg muscle decr|incr	legs	14	-0.234	-0.234	0.210	0.342	0.383	0.658	0.658	0.162	3121 Tamines r:-0.708 p:0.010 df:10	7545 Smaklosa r:0.888 p:0.000 df:10	313 Chaldaea r:-0.869 p:0.000 df:10
slider _ l upperleg fat decr|incr	legs	25	-0.586	-0.570	-0.285	-0.108	0.321	0.494	0.526	0.526	239675 Mottez r:-0.561 p:0.010 df:18	2532 Sutton r:0.734 p:0.000 df:18	2532 Sutton r:0.734 p:0.000 df:18
slider _ l upperleg muscle decr|incr	legs	24	-0.150	-0.143	0.091	0.203	0.428	0.599	0.606	0.204	10072 Uruguay r:-0.562 p:0.010 df:18	21791 Mattweegman r:0.746 p:0.000 df:18	6 Hebe r:-0.736 p:0.000 df:18
slider _ l upperleg scale depth decr|incr	legs	24	-0.306	-0.288	-0.115	0.088	0.212	0.358	0.358		25094 Zemtsov r:-0.591 p:0.010 df:16	2298 Cindijon r:0.798 p:0.000 df:16	828 Lindemannia r:-0.772 p:0.000 df:16
slider _ l upperleg scale horiz decr|incr	legs	25	-0.410	-0.363	-0.171	-0.026	0.222	0.348	0.348		32897 Curtharris r:-0.563 p:0.010 df:18	129073 Sandyfreund r:0.839 p:0.000 df:18	3168 Lomnicky Stit r:-0.709 p:0.000 df:18
slider _ r lowerleg fat decr|incr	legs	14	-0.492	-0.492	-0.389	-0.171	0.316	0.596	0.596	0.312	18117 Jonhodge r:-0.765 p:0.010 df:8	15917 Rosahavel r:0.956 p:0.000 df:8	543 Charlotte r:0.894 p:0.000 df:8
slider _ r lowerleg muscle decr|incr	legs	14	-0.234	-0.234	0.210	0.342	0.383	0.658	0.658	0.162	3121 Tamines r:-0.708 p:0.010 df:10	7545 Smaklosa r:0.888 p:0.000 df:10	313 Chaldaea r:-0.869 p:0.000 df:10
slider _ r upperleg fat decr|incr	legs	26	-0.586	-0.568	-0.270	0.016	0.329	0.514	0.526	0.526	239675 Mottez r:-0.561 p:0.010 df:18	2532 Sutton r:0.734 p:0.000 df:18	2532 Sutton r:0.734 p:0.000 df:18
slider _ r upperleg muscle decr|incr	legs	24	-0.150	-0.143	0.091	0.203	0.428	0.599	0.606	0.204	10072 Uruguay r:-0.562 p:0.010 df:18	21791 Mattweegman r:0.746 p:0.000 df:18	6 Hebe r:-0.736 p:0.000 df:18
slider _ r upperleg scale depth decr|incr	legs	25	-0.306	-0.284	-0.109	0.098	0.202	0.358	0.358		25094 Zemtsov r:-0.591 p:0.010 df:16	2298 Cindijon r:0.798 p:0.000 df:16	828 Lindemannia r:-0.772 p:0.000 df:16
slider _ r upperleg scale horiz decr|incr	legs	26	-0.410	-0.355	-0.166	-0.010	0.222	0.348	0.348		32897 Curtharris r:-0.563 p:0.010 df:18	129073 Sandyfreund r:0.839 p:0.000 df:18	3168 Lomnicky Stit r:-0.709 p:0.000 df:18
thick thighs	legs	16	0.058	0.058	0.120	0.177	0.256	0.487	0.487		2433 Sootiyo r:-0.642 p:0.010 df:13	25476 Sealfon r:0.873 p:0.000 df:13	328 Gudrun r:-0.804 p:0.000 df:13
slider _ mouth angles down|up	mouth	37	-0.492	-0.325	0.021	0.140	0.296	0.578	0.596	0.098	7475 Kaizuka r:-0.487 p:0.010 df:25	28165 Bayanmashat r:0.692 p:0.000 df:25	1311 Knopfia r:0.673 p:0.000 df:25
slider _ mouth cupidsbow decr|incr	mouth	25	-0.524	-0.477	-0.072	0.150	0.456	1.000	1.000	0.586	14469 Komatsuataka r:-0.561 p:0.010 df:18	6531 Subashiri r:0.818 p:0.000 df:18	732 Tjilaki r:-0.775 p:0.000 df:18
slider _ mouth cupidsbow width decr|incr	mouth	21	-1.000	-0.953	-0.120	0.098	0.357	0.607	0.616	-1.000	6375 Fredharris r:-0.591 p:0.010 df:16	2598 Merlin r:0.753 p:0.000 df:16	1108 Demeter r:-0.746 p:0.000 df:16
slider _ mouth dimples in|out	mouth	22	-0.720	-0.711	-0.411	0.041	0.264	0.944	1.000		7230 Lutz r:-0.575 p:0.010 df:17	12593 Shashlov r:0.788 p:0.000 df:17	4 Vesta r:0.726 p:0.000 df:17
slider _ mouth laugh lines in|out	mouth	26	-0.430	-0.401	0.091	0.295	0.524	1.000	1.000	-0.010	4414 Sesostris r:-0.539 p:0.010 df:20	14181 Koromhazi r:0.742 p:0.000 df:20	2501 Lohja r:0.692 p:0.000 df:20
slider _ mouth lowerlip ext down|up	mouth	22	-0.472	-0.441	-0.050	0.176	0.326	0.451	0.462	0.274	617 Patroclus r:-0.550 p:0.010 df:19	11665 Dirichlet r:0.728 p:0.000 df:19	8428 Okiko r:-0.698 p:0.000 df:19
slider _ mouth lowerlip height decr|incr	mouth	31	-0.896	-0.759	-0.472	-0.306	-0.120	0.202	0.202	-0.896	25685 Katlinhornig r:-0.515 p:0.010 df:22	9267 Lokrume r:0.784 p:0.000 df:22	144 Vibilia r:0.661 p:0.000 df:22
slider _ mouth lowerlip middle down|up	mouth	14	-0.192	-0.192	-0.145	-0.031	0.192	0.326	0.326	0.316	3264 Bounty r:-0.709 p:0.010 df:10	33451 Michaelarney r:0.927 p:0.000 df:10	98 Ianthe r:-0.853 p:0.000 df:10
slider _ mouth lowerlip volume decr|incr	mouth	26	-0.554	-0.525	-0.235	0.015	0.215	0.531	0.596	-0.130	9523 Torino r:-0.550 p:0.010 df:19	28019 Warchal r:0.728 p:0.000 df:19	10205 Pokorny r:0.709 p:0.000 df:19
slider _ mouth lowerlip width decr|incr	mouth	29	-0.720	-0.679	-0.472	-0.274	-0.026	0.388	0.512	-0.088	13118 La Harpe r:-0.527 p:0.010 df:21	26532 Eduardoboff r:0.742 p:0.000 df:21	8053 Kleist r:0.702 p:0.000 df:21
slider _ mouth philtrum volume decr|incr	mouth	17	-0.264	-0.264	0.047	0.284	0.570	1.000	1.000	0.376	13045 Vermandere r:-0.642 p:0.010 df:13	25103 Kimdongyoung r:0.831 p:0.000 df:13	597 Bandusia r:-0.891 p:0.000 df:13
slider _ mouth scale depth decr|incr	mouth	24	-0.710	-0.666	-0.239	0.114	0.334	0.689	0.740	0.740	5138 Gyoda r:-0.575 p:0.010 df:17	48575 Hawaii r:0.815 p:0.000 df:17	112 Iphigenia r:0.731 p:0.000 df:17
slider _ mouth scale horiz decr|incr	mouth	33	-0.678	-0.534	-0.202	-0.046	0.233	0.715	0.896	-0.026	14028 Nakamurahiroshi r:-0.506 p:0.010 df:23	17078 Sellers r:0.713 p:0.000 df:23	2840 Kallavesi r:0.712 p:0.000 df:23
slider _ mouth scale vert decr|incr	mouth	26	-0.626	-0.623	-0.394	-0.150	0.086	0.504	0.544	0.032	9077 Ildo r:-0.564 p:0.010 df:18	2091 Sampo r:0.795 p:0.000 df:18	888 Parysatis r:0.775 p:0.000 df:18
slider _ mouth trans backward|forward	mouth	14	-0.244	-0.244	-0.163	0.108	0.181	0.368	0.368		2077 Kiangsu r:-0.736 p:0.010 df:9	8345 Ulmerspatz r:0.902 p:0.000 df:9	6649 Yokotatakao r:-0.921 p:0.000 df:9
slider _ mouth trans down|up	mouth	19	-0.698	-0.698	-0.222	0.026	0.254	0.472	0.472	-0.698	3543 Ningbo r:-0.623 p:0.010 df:14	1780 Kippes r:0.814 p:0.000 df:14	1780 Kippes r:0.814 p:0.000 df:14

slider	category	N									A	B	C
slider _ mouth upperlip ext down|up	mouth	27	-0.906	-0.828	-0.472	-0.348	0.026	0.523	0.564	-0.484	2328 Robeson r:-0.526 p:0.010 df:21	10501 Ardmacha r:0.756 p:0.000 df:21	-10000 Sun r:0.690 p:0.000 df:21
slider _ mouth upperlip height decr|incr	mouth	23	-0.906	-0.902	-0.344	-0.140	0.284	0.624	0.668	-0.344	4936 Butakov r:-0.575 p:0.010 df:17	4618 Shakhovskoj r:0.778 p:0.000 df:17	1164 Kobolda r:-0.727 p:0.000 df:17
slider _ mouth upperlip middle down|up	mouth	23	-1.000	-1.000	-0.502	-0.222	0.108	0.294	0.306	-1.000	5537 Sanya r:-0.562 p:0.010 df:18	311785 Erwanmazarico r:0.837 p:0.000 df:18	75 Eurydike r:-0.707 p:0.000 df:18
slider _ mouth upperlip volume decr|incr	mouth	14	-0.782	-0.782	-0.283	-0.016	0.205	0.472	0.472	-0.268	1019 Strackea r:-0.735 p:0.010 df:9	21559 Jingyuanluo r:0.941 p:0.000 df:9	3698 Manning r:0.930 p:0.000 df:9
slider _ mouth upperlip width decr|incr	mouth	13	-0.534	-0.534	-0.150	0.150	0.373	0.752	0.752	0.492	3048 Guangzhou r:-0.735 p:0.010 df:9	5038 Overbeek r:0.908 p:0.000 df:9	3306 Byron r:0.875 p:0.000 df:9
muscular	muscularity	40	0.055	0.068	0.133	0.195	0.422	0.770	0.871	0.462	2774 Tenojoki r:-0.424 p:0.010 df:34	11727 Sweet r:0.619 p:0.000 df:34	-10000 Mercury r:0.598 p:0.000 df:34
muscular male	muscularity	31	0.072	0.078	0.153	0.292	0.441	0.839	0.917	0.240	22002 Richardregan r:-0.479 p:0.010 df:26	50768 Ianwessen r:0.710 p:0.000 df:26	1275 Cimbria r:0.672 p:0.000 df:26
slider _ Harvey StomachMusclesV2	muscularity	39	0.041	0.047	0.368	0.627	0.834	1.000	1.000	1.000	932 Hooveria r:-0.430 p:0.010 df:33	2440 Educatio r:0.583 p:0.000 df:33	833 Monica r:-0.572 p:0.000 df:33
slider _ HarveyVCutV1	muscularity	35	0.031	0.052	0.275	0.399	0.710	0.892	1.000	1.000	550 Senta r:-0.456 p:0.010 df:29	6376 Schamp r:0.677 p:0.000 df:29	1288 Santa r:0.627 p:0.000 df:29
slider _ Muscle	muscularity	71	0.000	0.200	0.500	0.500	0.642	0.810	0.845	0.839	123818 Helenzier r:-0.354 p:0.010 df:50	16707 Norman r:0.532 p:0.000 df:50	1802 Zhang Heng r:-0.496 p:0.000 df:50
slider _ abs _ column	muscularity	22	0.057	0.059	0.172	0.218	0.306	0.539	0.565	0.223	1868 Thersites r:-0.538 p:0.010 df:20	17885 Brianbeyt r:0.671 p:0.001 df:20	2056 Nancy r:-0.743 p:0.000 df:20
neck width<->shoulder width	neck	20	1.655	1.707	3.727	4.535	5.826	7.747	7.805	5.465	8545 McGee r:-0.562 p:0.010 df:18	7869 Pradun r:0.840 p:0.000 df:18	3317 Paris r:-0.821 p:0.000 df:18
neck width<->subneck dorsal	neck	15	0.663	0.663	1.312	1.792	2.120	3.307	3.307		90564 Markjarnyk r:-0.643 p:0.010 df:13	4497 Taguchi r:0.878 p:0.000 df:13	1547 Nele r:-0.806 p:0.000 df:13
neck width<->underbust	neck	12	6.726	6.726	10.358	13.030	14.346	16.387	16.387	14.073	4081 Tippett r:-0.708 p:0.010 df:10	5181 SURF r:0.933 p:0.000 df:10	2276 Warck r:0.873 p:0.000 df:10
shoulder width<->subneck dorsal	neck	16	1.788	1.788	2.750	3.419	3.693	5.844	5.844		4564 Clayton r:-0.623 p:0.010 df:14	3216 Harrington r:0.779 p:0.000 df:14	3216 Harrington r:0.779 p:0.000 df:14
slider _ HarveyNeckDefinitionV1	neck	40	0.098	0.110	0.415	0.620	0.704	1.000	1.000	1.000	11258 Aoyama r:-0.430 p:0.010 df:33	26417 Michaelgord r:0.635 p:0.000 df:33	2279 Barto r:0.560 p:0.000 df:33
slider _ neck double decr|incr	neck	21	-1.000	-1.000	-0.663	-0.316	-0.073	0.233	0.234	-0.430	33213 Diggs r:-0.624 p:0.010 df:14	145768 Petiska r:0.850 p:0.000 df:14	314 Rosalia r:-0.772 p:0.000 df:14
slider _ neck scale vert decr|incr	neck	13	-1.000	-1.000	-0.777	-0.430	-0.006	0.192	0.192		27480 Heablonsky r:-0.735 p:0.000 df:9	6892 Lana r:0.943 p:0.000 df:9	6892 Lana r:0.943 p:0.000 df:9
slider _ nipple point decr|incr	nipples	7	-0.348	-0.348	0.204	0.440	0.554	0.626	0.626	0.204	1999 Hirayama r:-0.875 p:0.010 df:5	12136 Martinryle r:0.981 p:0.000 df:5	1032 Pafuri r:-0.970 p:0.000 df:5
slider _ nipple size decr|incr	nipples	8	-0.648	-0.648	-0.461	-0.269	0.116	0.274	0.274	-0.172	2633 Bishop r:-0.875 p:0.010 df:5	5413 Smyslov r:0.981 p:0.000 df:5	5413 Smyslov r:0.981 p:0.000 df:5
slider _ Nose _ alar _ crease	nose	24	0.062	0.080	0.354	0.523	0.757	1.000	1.000		32222 Charlesvest r:-0.550 p:0.010 df:19	8800 Brophy r:0.822 p:0.000 df:19	5387 Casleo r:-0.749 p:0.000 df:19
slider _ Nose _ hole _ up	nose	11	0.098	0.098	0.233	0.508	0.788	1.000	1.000	0.570	4450 Pan r:-0.765 p:0.010 df:8	6522 Aci r:0.949 p:0.000 df:8	2172 Plavsk r:0.910 p:0.000 df:8
slider _ nose crease extra1	nose	11	0.523	0.523	0.648	0.845	1.000	1.000	1.000		8850 Bignonia r:-0.799 p:0.010 df:7	154493 Portisch r:0.934 p:0.000 df:7	3787 Aivazovskij r:-0.982 p:0.000 df:7
slider _ nose base down|up	nose	23	-0.564	-0.558	-0.244	0.016	0.202	0.366	0.368	0.150	2629 Rudra r:-0.575 p:0.010 df:17	41986 Fort Bend r:0.775 p:0.000 df:17	2595 Gudiachvili r:-0.756 p:0.000 df:17
slider _ nose compression compress|uncompress	nose	21	-0.430	-0.419	-0.233	0.068	0.279	0.972	1.000	1.000	4298 Jorgenunez r:-0.606 p:0.010 df:15	26656 Samarenae r:0.839 p:0.000 df:15	194 Prokne r:-0.813 p:0.000 df:15
slider _ nose curve concave|convex	nose	16	-0.348	-0.348	-0.122	0.052	0.287	0.958	0.958	-0.202	4289 Biwako r:-0.662 p:0.010 df:12	90125 Chrissquire r:0.921 p:0.000 df:12	381 Myrrha r:-0.806 p:0.000 df:12
slider _ nose flaring decr|incr	nose	32	-0.368	-0.341	0.153	0.290	0.539	0.738	0.772	0.098	7543 Prylis r:-0.497 p:0.010 df:24	34215 Stutigarg r:0.646 p:0.000 df:24	3612 Peale r:-0.674 p:0.000 df:24
slider _ nose greek decr|incr	nose	25	-0.462	-0.440	-0.073	0.254	0.409	0.842	0.886	-0.388	130 Elektra r:-0.526 p:0.010 df:21	1339 Desagneauxa r:0.730 p:0.000 df:21	1339 Desagneauxa r:0.730 p:0.000 df:21
slider _ nose hump decr|incr	nose	10	-0.274	-0.274	-0.057	0.197	0.455	0.626	0.626	0.452	36037 Linenschmidt r:-0.835 p:0.010 df:6	2349 Kurchenko r:0.978 p:0.000 df:6	2349 Kurchenko r:0.978 p:0.000 df:6
slider _ nose nostrils angle down|up	nose	34	-0.648	-0.602	-0.319	-0.182	-0.003	0.286	0.410	-0.524	2025 Nortia r:-0.487 p:0.010 df:25	49441 Scerbanenco r:0.683 p:0.000 df:25	1152 Pawona r:0.639 p:0.000 df:25
slider _ nose nostrils width decr|incr	nose	43	-0.638	-0.501	-0.006	0.170	0.336	0.565	0.596	-0.006	16998 Estelleweber r:-0.436 p:0.010 df:32	7677 Sawa r:0.641 p:0.000 df:32	6873 Tasaka r:-0.598 p:0.000 df:32
slider _ nose point down|up	nose	32	-0.244	-0.217	-0.098	0.031	0.246	0.698	0.792	-0.130	8056 Tieck r:-0.498 p:0.010 df:24	14643 Morata r:0.735 p:0.000 df:24	490 Veritas r:0.657 p:0.000 df:24
slider _ nose point width decr|incr	nose	36	-0.638	-0.461	-0.031	0.269	0.551	0.864	0.980	0.130	24148 Mychajliw r:-0.463 p:0.010 df:28	20495 Rimavska Sobota r:0.646 p:0.000 df:28	1156 Kira r:0.599 p:0.000 df:28
slider _ nose scale depth decr|incr	nose	28	-0.348	-0.343	-0.182	0.135	0.231	0.648	0.648	0.648	224693 Morganfreeman r:-0.537 p:0.010 df:20	5090 Wyeth r:0.773 p:0.000 df:20	2150 Nyctimene r:0.758 p:0.000 df:20
slider _ nose scale horiz decr|incr	nose	33	-0.544	-0.522	-0.264	-0.130	0.192	0.386	0.450	0.192	114239 Bermarmi r:-0.517 p:0.010 df:22	2648 Owa r:0.724 p:0.000 df:22	2648 Owa r:0.724 p:0.000 df:22

measure	part	N									asteroid 1	asteroid 2	asteroid 3
slider _ nose scale vert decr|incr	nose	34	-0.638	-0.560	-0.230	0.077	0.369	0.713	0.720	0.312	4367 Meech r:-0.488 p:0.010 df:25	21496 Lijianyang r:0.695 p:0.000 df:25	492 Gismonda r:0.654 p:0.000 df:25
slider _ nose septumangle decr|incr	nose	28	-1.000	-1.000	-0.836	-0.404	-0.069	0.208	0.212	-0.882	64295 Tangtisheng r:-0.549 p:0.010 df:19	18574 Jeansimon r:0.794 p:0.000 df:19	1422 Stromgrenia r:-0.719 p:0.000 df:19
slider _ nose trans backward|forward	nose	18	-0.398	-0.398	0.071	0.212	0.358	0.564	0.564	0.192	26057 Ankaios r:-0.686 p:0.010 df:11	1558 Jarnefelt r:0.846 p:0.000 df:11	778 Theobalda r:-0.845 p:0.000 df:11
slider _ nose trans down|up	nose	14	-0.648	-0.648	-0.420	-0.181	0.114	0.886	0.886	-0.150	22855 Donnajones r:-0.735 p:0.010 df:9	37706 Trinchieri r:0.949 p:0.000 df:9	369 Aeria r:0.891 p:0.000 df:9
slider _ nose volume decr|incr	nose	35	-0.244	-0.226	0.026	0.170	0.244	0.399	0.482	-0.182	4050 Mebailey r:-0.505 p:0.010 df:23	9678 van der Meer r:0.646 p:0.000 df:23	1048 Feodosia r:-0.685 p:0.000 df:23
slider _ nose width1 decr|incr	nose	27	-0.638	-0.604	-0.336	0.006	0.264	0.556	0.564	-0.296	20518 Rendtel r:-0.537 p:0.010 df:20	15922 Masajisaito r:0.746 p:0.000 df:20	721 Tabora r:-0.772 p:0.000 df:20
slider _ nose width2 decr|incr	nose	37	-0.814	-0.665	-0.456	-0.264	0.062	0.398	0.576	0.016	3939 Huruhata r:-0.471 p:0.010 df:27	3404 Hinderer r:0.656 p:0.000 df:27	1650 Heckmann r:-0.634 p:0.000 df:27
slider _ nose width3 decr|incr	nose	37	-0.462	-0.462	-0.155	0.120	0.290	0.606	0.700	0.502	1140 Crimea r:-0.456 p:0.010 df:29	4324 Bickel r:0.646 p:0.000 df:29	4324 Bickel r:0.646 p:0.000 df:29
slider _ nostril _ rounding	nose	20	0.047	0.048	0.309	0.523	0.710	0.959	0.964		8940 Yakushimaru r:-0.641 p:0.010 df:13	7454 Kevinrighter r:0.900 p:0.000 df:13	3649 Guillermina r:-0.804 p:0.000 df:13
slider _ septum _ sharp	nose	18	0.181	0.181	0.401	0.658	1.000	1.000	1.000	1.000	10265 Gunnarsson r:-0.624 p:0.010 df:14	20638 Lingchen r:0.837 p:0.000 df:14	227 Philosophia r:-0.784 p:0.000 df:14
slider _ penis circ decr|incr	penis	51	-0.108	-0.038	0.130	0.326	0.462	0.635	0.918	0.388	10832 Hazamashigetomi r:-0.413 p:0.010 df:36	15264 Delbruck r:0.681 p:0.000 df:36	738 Alagasta r:-0.574 p:0.000 df:36
slider _ penis length decr|incr	penis	62	-0.512	-0.092	0.226	0.378	0.495	0.709	0.772	0.700	29298 Cruls r:-0.376 p:0.010 df:44	23897 Daikuroda r:0.515 p:0.000 df:44	642 Clara r:-0.509 p:0.000 df:44
slider _ penis testicles decr|incr	penis	12	-0.182	-0.182	-0.047	0.104	0.145	0.258	0.258	0.258	19719 Glasser r:-0.735 p:0.010 df:9	34204 Quryshi r:0.921 p:0.000 df:9	23672 Swiggum r:0.893 p:0.000 df:9
slider _ penis _ width1	penis	38	0.026	0.046	0.191	0.304	0.509	0.718	0.860	0.606	861 Aida r:-0.456 p:0.010 df:29	18880 Toddblumberg r:0.620 p:0.000 df:29	2000 Herschel r:0.589 p:0.000 df:29
slider _ penis _ width2	penis	39	0.005	0.031	0.202	0.306	0.539	0.767	0.959	0.539	16014 Sinha r:-0.450 p:0.010 df:30	48457 Josefried r:0.652 p:0.000 df:30	7207 Hammurabi r:0.627 p:0.000 df:30
slider _ penis _ width3base	penis	39	0.021	0.031	0.223	0.363	0.606	0.845	0.927	0.497	4923 Clarke r:-0.451 p:0.010 df:30	25750 Miwnay r:0.596 p:0.000 df:30	11337 Sandro r:0.584 p:0.000 df:30
slider _ penis _ width _ head	penis	34	0.005	0.009	0.081	0.166	0.333	0.510	0.565	0.176	587 Hypsipyle r:-0.488 p:0.010 df:25	33800 Gross r:0.634 p:0.000 df:25	33624 Omersiddiqui r:-0.720 p:0.000 df:25
slider _ penis _ width _ head _ scale	penis	33	0.026	0.030	0.088	0.124	0.202	0.353	0.389	0.031	18115 Rathbun r:-0.488 p:0.010 df:25	4266 Waltari r:0.694 p:0.000 df:25	2429 Schurer r:0.655 p:0.000 df:25
slider _ penis _ width _ headbell	penis	23	0.026	0.027	0.093	0.207	0.337	0.572	0.617	0.207	1221 Amor r:-0.563 p:0.010 df:18	10795 Babben r:0.805 p:0.000 df:18	76 Freia r:0.754 p:0.000 df:18
statscontinuous _ p _ endowment (self-reported from sample)	penis	89	2	4	5	7[44]	7	10	10	10	7902 Hanff r:-0.352 p:0.010 df:51	4908 Ward r:0.509 p:0.000 df:51	4298 Jorgenunez r:-0.499 p:0.000 df:51
statscontinuous _ p _ flaccid length (journalagg)[45]	penis	145[46]	1.44	2.10	3.03	3.74	4.36	5.33	6.08	5.9			
statscontinuous _ p _ flaccid circ (journalagg)	penis	145	2.45	2.85	3.25	3.70	4.10	4.62	5.03	5.7			
statscontinuous _ p _ erect length (journalagg)	penis	145	1.60	2.66	4.40	5.50	6.60	8.00	9.20	10.1			

[44] We know from consistent studies that this number should be between 5"±1 when top-pressed (bpel, bone-pressed erect length). The sample had no such standards, so we can treat this as a side-pressed erect value.

[45] As was the case earlier in the book, this body part gets more footnotes, because it was the *only* body part out of all measures which required the person be in one of two extreme states to measure at all. Thus I had to employ a number of extra research tactics outside of my sample people to pull and process this data. Many years ago while I was looking up male exercises on the web, I found a site which aggregated formal scholarly studies from over 140 countries all over the world. Since almost no one reports these four measures anywhere—let alone via a consistent standard—and the marked difference between flaccid and erect states means you can't even guess them from the overwhelmingly in-between / semi-erect images out there, I fell back on this aggregation of journal articles for the stats, treating each country as a sample subject. Unfortunately, I couldn't tell you where I got this article, as the original link was lost to the sands of time. Many thanks to whoever put it together, though.

[46] Needless to say, the *countries* reported were not actual *humans*, and had no individual charts or asteroids to be compared. We can, however, still consider the values to constitute a "sample"; so they won't hold maxes, minimums, or ranges for all the planet's population, just for the countries acting as "dummy people" in a small subset of that population. Since each country was an average of averages, the actual range was much narrower for each metric. For example, flaccid length actually ranged from 2.72 – 4.8 where *country* averages are concerned, with a standard deviation of .42. As a rough way of correcting for this, I stretched out the entire range of each metric by 3 of its standard deviations (sds) in order to simulate a bell curve in place of the otherwise sharp means. 2.72-3 sds (that is, .42) gives 1.44. 4.8+3 x .42 gives 6.07, and this was a way of saying "Pretend all 96,000+ people across all studies were part of one population. Here are the most extreme *individuals*." This kind of correction is imperfect, since the actual distribution is an asymmetric aggregation of many different distributions, but it does better approximate wide ranging reality.

statscontinuous _ p _ erect circ (journalagg)	penis	145	3.19	3.67	4.17	4.61	5.11	5.71	6.22	7.1			
collarbone	shoulders	17	0.066	0.066	0.081	0.113	0.178	0.426	0.426	0.426	28739 Julisauer r:-0.663 p:0.010 df:12	29837 Savage r:0.882 p:0.000 df:12	110 Lydia r:0.819 p:0.000 df:12
slider _ Shoulder _ Shape	shoulders	16	0.114	0.114	0.382	0.633	0.757	1.000	1.000		1551 Argelander r:-0.708 p:0.010 df:10	837 Schwarzschilda r:0.863 p:0.000 df:10	837 Schwarzschilda r:0.863 p:0.000 df:10
dark skin	skin	40	0.083	0.102	0.191	0.274	0.451	0.591	0.818	0.480	3139 Shantou r:-0.442 p:0.010 df:31	33002 Everest r:0.664 p:0.000 df:31	3035 Chambers r:0.636 p:0.000 df:31
freckles	skin	11	0.086	0.086	0.158	0.206	0.306	0.384	0.384		2985 Shakespeare r:-0.875 p:0.010 df:5	28655 Erincolfax r:0.979 p:0.000 df:5	685 Hermia r:0.968 p:0.000 df:5
veins	skin	12	0.100	0.100	0.160	0.221	0.281	0.530	0.530		22612 Dandibner r:-0.766 p:0.010 df:8	22846 Fredwhitaker r:0.979 p:0.000 df:8	5190 Fry r:0.927 p:0.000 df:8
slider _ stomach navel down|up	stomach	19	-0.876	-0.876	-0.524	-0.222	0.388	0.866	0.866	0.334	8291 Bingham r:-0.641 p:0.010 df:13	8098 Miyamotoatsushi r:0.845 p:0.000 df:13	2696 Magion r:0.822 p:0.000 df:13
slider _ stomach pregnant decr|incr	stomach	24	-0.690	-0.667	-0.205	0.098	0.215	0.316	0.316	-0.216	15091 Howell r:-0.576 p:0.010 df:17	26503 Avicramer r:0.722 p:0.000 df:17	14963 Toshikazu r:-0.729 p:0.000 df:17
slider _ stomach tone decr|incr	stomach	44	-0.648	-0.521	-0.244	0.477	0.678	0.870	0.876	0.850	16583 Oersted r:-0.424 p:0.010 df:34	16707 Norman r:0.646 p:0.000 df:34	138 Tolosa r:-0.608 p:0.000 df:34
shoulder width<->waist	torso	31	8.491	8.756	12.348	13.050	14.779	22.664	31.385	12.348	241509 Sessler r:-0.457 p:0.010 df:29	31940 Sutthiluk r:0.596 p:0.000 df:29	8311 Zhangdaning r:0.589 p:0.000 df:29
slider _ Waist _ bump	torso	14	0.036	0.036	0.238	0.309	0.511	0.668	0.668		33473 Porterfield r:-0.735 p:0.010 df:9	96348 Toshiyukimariko r:0.911 p:0.000 df:9	5656 Oldfield r:-0.886 p:0.000 df:9
slider _ torso scale horiz decr|incr	torso	11	-0.606	-0.606	0.016	0.170	0.326	0.378	0.378		30797 Chimborazo r:-0.735 p:0.010 df:9	101813 Elizabethmarston r:0.911 p:0.000 df:9	157 Dejanira r:-0.900 p:0.000 df:9
slider _ torso vshape decr|incr	torso	23	-0.616	-0.600	-0.358	-0.108	0.212	0.571	0.586		5845 Davidbrewster r:-0.549 p:0.010 df:19	48447 Hingley r:0.723 p:0.000 df:19	2926 Caldeira r:0.699 p:0.000 df:19
underbust<->waist	torso	25	2.963	3.088	4.210	5.194	6.203	9.983	11.230	3.741	9950 ESA r:-0.516 p:0.010 df:22	2708 Burns r:0.689 p:0.000 df:22	2708 Burns r:0.689 p:0.000 df:22
slider _ SSBBW Breast	weight	10	0.016	0.016	0.026	0.055	0.071	0.150	0.150		2394 Nadeev r:-0.798 p:0.010 df:7	21676 Maureenanne r:0.950 p:0.000 df:7	183 Istria r:0.918 p:0.000 df:7
slider _ Weight	weight	71	0.212	0.247	0.435	0.500	0.601	0.823	1.000	0.215	2509 Chukotka r:-0.355 p:0.010 df:50	10804 Amenouzume r:0.539 p:0.000 df:50	1171 Rusthawelia r:0.494 p:0.000 df:50
statscontinuous _ Weight	weight	87	73.000	100.800	142.000	165.000	195.000	241.200	370.000	133.000	13957 NARIT r:-0.354 p:0.010 df:50	1171 Rusthawelia r:0.566 p:0.000 df:50	1171 Rusthawelia r:0.566 p:0.000 df:50
statscontinuous _ Weight/height	weight	87	1.028	1.472	2.042	2.361	2.803	3.238	4.933	1.928	3924 Birch r:-0.355 p:0.010 df:50	1171 Rusthawelia r:0.536 p:0.000 df:50	1171 Rusthawelia r:0.536 p:0.000 df:50
ab perimeter / ab width		25	3.627	4.245	7.745	10.764	13.352	18.911	19.716		28533 Iansohl r:-0.515 p:0.010 df:22	6225 Hiroko r:0.743 p:0.000 df:22	813 Baumeia r:-0.669 p:0.000 df:22
ab perimeter / ankle width		8	5.892	5.892	11.227	18.594	29.631	32.513	32.513		1976 Kaverin r:-0.834 p:0.010 df:6	5188 Paine r:0.937 p:0.001 df:6	19981 Bialystock r:-0.953 p:0.000 df:6
ab perimeter / back perimeter		7	0.252	0.252	0.372	0.604	0.788	1.027	1.027	0.372	11915 Nishiinoue r:-0.875 p:0.010 df:5	36037 Linenschmidt r:0.994 p:0.000 df:5	146 Lucina r:0.968 p:0.000 df:5
ab perimeter / back tone		7	0.774	0.774	1.490	2.747	4.699	5.163	5.163	0.774	44 Nysa r:-0.875 p:0.010 df:5	25122 Kaitlingus r:0.987 p:0.000 df:5	254 Augusta r:0.964 p:0.000 df:5
ab perimeter / bicep width		31	5.839	6.237	12.415	15.201	19.503	26.242	27.792	13.099	344581 Albisetti r:-0.463 p:0.010 df:28	5686 Chiyonoura r:0.637 p:0.000 df:28	5686 Chiyonoura r:0.637 p:0.000 df:28
ab perimeter / calf width		10	4.159	4.159	9.767	14.112	18.464	19.697	19.697		1639 Bower r:-0.765 p:0.010 df:8	5756 Wassenbergh r:0.917 p:0.000 df:8	945 Barcelona r:-0.907 p:0.000 df:8
ab perimeter / chest width		22	2.617	2.630	4.332	5.593	8.093	11.629	11.745	2.617	587 Hypsipyle r:-0.549 p:0.010 df:19	23217 Nayana r:0.805 p:0.000 df:19	466 Tisiphone r:0.733 p:0.000 df:19
ab perimeter / clavicle to groin h		24	1.269	1.350	2.631	3.001	3.985	5.585	5.981	1.593	175437 Zsivotzky r:-0.526 p:0.010 df:21	1632 Siebohme r:0.761 p:0.000 df:21	783 Nora r:0.690 p:0.000 df:21
ab perimeter / clavicle to neck h		18	14.224	14.224	16.775	21.606	27.029	34.716	34.716		7527 Marples r:-0.591 p:0.010 df:16	280640 Ruetsch r:0.762 p:0.000 df:16	6636 Kintanar r:-0.765 p:0.000 df:16
ab perimeter / elbow to wrist h		29	2.132	2.232	4.395	6.900	8.896	11.604	11.804	3.125	35356 Vondrak r:-0.479 p:0.010 df:26	28171 Diannahu r:0.631 p:0.000 df:26	6672 Corot r:-0.635 p:0.000 df:26
ab perimeter / foot base h		7	4.332	4.332	4.713	8.661	9.576	10.199	10.199		199838 Hafili r:-0.875 p:0.010 df:5	11667 Testa r:0.968 p:0.000 df:5	1191 Alfaterna r:-0.972 p:0.000 df:5
ab perimeter / long finger length		10	3.028	3.028	6.038	7.601	10.395	15.632	15.632	4.283	37786 Tokikonaruko r:-0.798 p:0.010 df:7	69869 Haining r:0.945 p:0.000 df:7	1679 Nevanlinna r:-0.945 p:0.000 df:7
ab perimeter / lower forearm w		31	8.099	9.874	21.412	26.177	31.523	44.262	45.149	21.519	14888 Kanazawashi r:-0.463 p:0.010 df:28	8133 Takanochoei r:0.639 p:0.000 df:28	548 Kressida r:0.610 p:0.000 df:28
ab perimeter / lower leg h		8	1.214	1.214	2.343	4.008	5.557	6.894	6.894		9329 Nikolaimedtner r:-0.835 p:0.010 df:6	352760 Tesorero r:0.945 p:0.000 df:6	52 Europa r:-0.957 p:0.000 df:6
ab perimeter / neck width		20	4.090	4.284	8.714	13.498	15.638	20.940	20.978	8.142	5262 Brucegoldberg r:-0.562 p:0.010 df:18	4607 Seilandfarm r:0.756 p:0.000 df:18	1439 Vogtia r:-0.750 p:0.000 df:18
ab perimeter / pelvic hips		16	3.042	3.042	4.833	6.033	6.995	8.352	8.352	3.042	111 Ate r:-0.623 p:0.010 df:14	6168 Isnello r:0.795 p:0.000 df:14	54 Alexandra r:0.777 p:0.000 df:14
ab perimeter / shoulder to elbow h		30	2.236	2.291	3.948	5.941	7.721	11.112	11.192	2.844	1315 Bronislawa r:-0.471 p:0.010 df:27	16909 Miladejager r:0.651 p:0.000 df:27	3730 Hurban r:-0.620 p:0.000 df:27
ab perimeter / shoulder width		31	1.498	1.797	2.922	4.541	5.610	8.164	9.178	2.173	116 Sirona r:-0.464 p:0.010 df:28	4132 Bartok r:0.667 p:0.000 df:28	4132 Bartok r:0.667 p:0.000 df:28

Measure	n									A	B	C
ab perimeter / subchest width	7	2.890	2.890	3.852	6.984	11.168	11.930	11.930	2.890	59 Elpis r:-0.875 p:0.010 df:5	9384 Aransio r:0.990 p:0.000 df:5	1056 Azalea r:0.968 p:0.000 df:5
ab perimeter / subneck dorsal	14	5.680	5.680	8.037	8.698	9.822	13.751	13.751		15907 Robot r:-0.663 p:0.010 df:12	3486 Fulchignoni r:0.852 p:0.000 df:12	566 Stereoskopia r:0.842 p:0.000 df:12
ab perimeter / suprailiac	22	3.073	3.152	4.168	6.080	6.985	11.050	11.452	3.073	207321 Crawshaw r:-0.537 p:0.010 df:20	39930 Kalauch r:0.712 p:0.000 df:20	2011 Veteraniya r:0.711 p:0.000 df:20
ab perimeter / underbust	23	2.643	2.655	4.581	5.836	8.443	15.149	15.280	3.138	256797 Benbow r:-0.526 p:0.010 df:21	3612 Peale r:0.770 p:0.000 df:21	1527 Malmquista r:0.690 p:0.000 df:21
ab perimeter / upper forearm w	33	6.341	7.016	11.829	17.668	22.220	29.420	29.815	10.173	7584 Ossietzky r:-0.449 p:0.010 df:30	5686 Chiyonoura r:0.588 p:0.000 df:30	5686 Chiyonoura r:0.588 p:0.000 df:30
ab perimeter / waist	31	2.582	2.865	4.209	6.011	7.518	12.599	14.616	3.310	142756 Chiu r:-0.457 p:0.010 df:29	200025 Cloud Gate r:0.616 p:0.000 df:29	4545 Primolevi r:-0.622 p:0.000 df:29
ab tone / ab perimeter	40	0.015	0.018	0.165	0.313	0.497	0.701	1.220	0.705	402 Chloe r:-0.408 p:0.010 df:37	22527 Gawlik r:0.583 p:0.000 df:37	8134 Minin r:-0.613 p:0.000 df:37
ab tone / ab width	25	0.135	0.136	1.959	3.168	4.743	10.204	11.024		4751 Alicemanning r:-0.515 p:0.010 df:22	10809 Majsterrojr r:0.699 p:0.000 df:22	900 Rosalinde r:0.690 p:0.000 df:22
ab tone / ankle width	8	0.145	0.145	1.488	5.283	9.640	10.579	10.579		13114 Isabelgodin r:-0.835 p:0.010 df:6	13433 Phelps r:0.978 p:0.000 df:6	2015 Kachuevskaya r:0.973 p:0.000 df:6
ab tone / back perimeter	7	0.105	0.105	0.127	0.306	0.432	0.497	0.497	0.262	3276 Porta Coeli r:-0.875 p:0.010 df:5	20038 Arasaki r:0.989 p:0.000 df:5	2958 Arpetito r:-0.973 p:0.000 df:5
ab tone / back tone	7	0.533	0.533	0.545	0.830	2.150	2.968	2.968	0.545	19250 Poullain r:-0.875 p:0.010 df:5	26002 Angelayeung r:0.984 p:0.000 df:5	584 Semiramis r:0.972 p:0.000 df:5
ab tone / bicep width	31	0.315	0.323	2.639	4.561	6.497	11.767	13.611	9.230	10967 Billallen r:-0.463 p:0.010 df:28	12671 Thornqvist r:0.698 p:0.000 df:28	664 Judith r:-0.611 p:0.000 df:28
ab tone / calf width	10	0.658	0.658	1.789	3.334	6.375	8.886	8.886		12388 Kikunokai r:-0.765 p:0.010 df:8	13130 Dylanthomas r:0.921 p:0.000 df:8	2323 Zverev r:-0.910 p:0.000 df:8
ab tone / chest width	22	0.330	0.361	1.267	1.955	2.766	4.006	4.088	1.844	5215 Tsurui r:-0.549 p:0.010 df:19	21454 Chernoby r:0.734 p:0.000 df:19	3139 Shantou r:-0.820 p:0.000 df:19
ab tone / clavicle to groin h	24	0.147	0.190	0.670	1.113	1.515	3.094	3.345	1.122	130161 Iankubik r:-0.526 p:0.010 df:21	9708 Gouka r:0.732 p:0.000 df:21	5268 Cernohorsky r:0.684 p:0.000 df:21
ab tone / clavicle to neck h	18	0.784	0.784	4.204	6.186	10.097	20.721	20.721		17955 Sedransk r:-0.591 p:0.010 df:16	21355 Pikovskaya r:0.928 p:0.000 df:16	561 Ingwelde r:0.770 p:0.000 df:16
ab tone / elbow to wrist h	29	0.111	0.156	1.174	1.811	2.401	4.810	4.942	2.202	2044 Wirt r:-0.479 p:0.010 df:26	11739 Baton Rouge r:0.704 p:0.000 df:26	700 Auravictrix r:-0.634 p:0.000 df:26
ab tone / foot base h	7	0.063	0.063	0.341	1.163	2.958	3.680	3.680		13332 Benkhoff r:-0.875 p:0.010 df:5	3352 McAuliffe r:0.988 p:0.000 df:5	3352 McAuliffe r:0.988 p:0.000 df:5
ab tone / long finger length	10	0.840	0.840	1.398	1.687	3.334	3.605	3.605	3.018	6546 Kaye r:-0.798 p:0.010 df:7	15868 Akiyoshidai r:0.931 p:0.000 df:7	1544 Vinterhansenia r:-0.929 p:0.000 df:7
ab tone / lower forearm w	31	0.433	0.486	4.573	8.020	11.146	18.768	20.388	15.164	13933 Charleville r:-0.463 p:0.010 df:28	5151 Weerstra r:0.650 p:0.000 df:28	664 Judith r:-0.646 p:0.000 df:28
ab tone / lower leg h	8	0.230	0.230	0.491	1.022	1.503	1.768	1.768		196 Philomela r:-0.834 p:0.010 df:6	53843 Antjiekrog r:0.941 p:0.001 df:6	1247 Memoria r:-0.968 p:0.000 df:6
ab tone / neck width	20	0.527	0.572	3.114	4.328	6.797	9.707	9.712	5.738	6876 Beppeforti r:-0.563 p:0.010 df:18	900 Rosalinde r:0.877 p:0.000 df:18	900 Rosalinde r:0.877 p:0.000 df:18
ab tone / pelvic hips	16	0.086	0.086	0.933	1.810	2.242	5.107	5.107	2.144	11794 Yokokebukawa r:-0.623 p:0.010 df:14	32277 Helenliu r:0.808 p:0.000 df:14	16395 Ioannpravednyj r:0.796 p:0.000 df:14
ab tone / shoulder to elbow h	30	0.115	0.159	0.927	1.566	2.169	5.111	6.258	2.004	9633 Cotur r:-0.471 p:0.010 df:27	7848 Bernasconi r:0.689 p:0.000 df:27	3810 Aoraki r:0.652 p:0.000 df:27
ab tone / shoulder width	31	0.063	0.138	0.961	1.370	2.103	3.094	3.151	1.532	8630 Billprady r:-0.464 p:0.010 df:28	9521 Martinhoffmann r:0.639 p:0.000 df:28	900 Rosalinde r:0.606 p:0.000 df:28
ab tone / subchest width	7	1.249	1.249	1.579	2.037	2.979	4.698	4.698	2.037	10544 Horsnebara r:-0.875 p:0.010 df:5	13553 Masaakikoyama r:0.978 p:0.000 df:5	943 Begonia r:-0.968 p:0.000 df:5
ab tone / subneck dorsal	14	0.307	0.307	1.701	2.866	4.808	6.928	6.928		6092 Johnmason r:-0.662 p:0.010 df:12	21711 Wilfredwong r:0.861 p:0.000 df:12	900 Rosalinde r:0.848 p:0.000 df:12
ab tone / suprailiac	22	0.082	0.101	0.953	1.796	2.565	4.733	4.888	2.166	16254 Harper r:-0.538 p:0.010 df:20	218752 Tentlingen r:0.738 p:0.000 df:20	900 Rosalinde r:0.711 p:0.000 df:20
ab tone / underbust	23	0.083	0.129	1.472	1.748	2.804	4.582	4.752	2.211	15295 Tante Riek r:-0.527 p:0.010 df:21	30164 Arnobdas r:0.753 p:0.000 df:21	9682 Gravesande r:-0.833 p:0.000 df:21
ab tone / upper forearm w	33	0.333	0.381	3.032	4.844	6.920	12.274	13.952	7.169	16449 Kigoyama r:-0.449 p:0.010 df:30	27254 Shubhrosaha r:0.638 p:0.000 df:30	1478 Vihuri r:0.585 p:0.000 df:30
ab tone / waist	31	0.089	0.184	1.344	1.895	2.427	4.401	5.122	2.332	17019 Aldo r:-0.456 p:0.010 df:29	218752 Tentlingen r:0.655 p:0.000 df:29	900 Rosalinde r:0.618 p:0.000 df:29
ab width / ankle width	7	1.079	1.079	1.605	1.686	2.630	2.731	2.731		19874 Liudongyan r:-0.875 p:0.010 df:5	9447 Julesbordet r:0.992 p:0.000 df:5	3441 Pochaina r:-0.984 p:0.000 df:5
ab width / calf width	10	1.058	1.058	1.192	1.342	1.553	1.809	1.809		48575 Hawaii r:-0.767 p:0.010 df:8	11696 Capen r:0.926 p:0.000 df:8	744 Aguntina r:0.921 p:0.000 df:8
ab width / clavicle to neck h	16	1.102	1.102	1.285	2.109	2.731	3.265	3.265		102234 Olivebyrne r:-0.623 p:0.010 df:14	38976 Taeve r:0.875 p:0.000 df:14	1418 Fayeta r:0.832 p:0.000 df:14
ab width / lower leg h	7	0.282	0.282	0.288	0.338	0.530	0.598	0.598		181298 Ladanyi r:-0.875 p:0.010 df:5	17033 Rusty r:0.988 p:0.000 df:5	1131 Porzia r:0.966 p:0.000 df:5
ankle to heel floor h / lower leg h	8	0.156	0.156	0.168	0.197	0.226	0.238	0.238		4034 Vishnu r:-0.835 p:0.010 df:6	10744 Tsuruta r:0.980 p:0.000 df:6	3893 DeLaeter r:0.942 p:0.000 df:6

ankle width / lower leg h	8	0.125	0.125	0.151	0.197	0.215	0.219	0.219		18918 Nishashah r:-0.835 p:0.010 df:6	16693 Moseley r:0.993 p:0.000 df:6	432 Pythia r:0.941 p:0.000 df:6
back perimeter / back tone	8	1.605	1.605	2.177	3.399	6.377	20.495	20.495	2.079	4405 Otava r:-0.835 p:0.010 df:6	173395 Dweinberg r:0.987 p:0.000 df:6	193 Ambrosia r:0.951 p:0.000 df:6
bicep width / ab width	23	0.388	0.392	0.510	0.598	0.695	1.162	1.222		7813 Anderserikson r:-0.538 p:0.010 df:20	7437 Torricelli r:0.749 p:0.000 df:20	2564 Kayala r:-0.721 p:0.000 df:20
bicep width / ankle to heel floor h	7	0.896	0.896	0.919	1.226	1.931	2.003	2.003		1900 Katyusha r:-0.875 p:0.010 df:5	89131 Phildevries r:0.967 p:0.000 df:5	356 Liguria r:0.965 p:0.000 df:5
bicep width / ankle width	9	0.442	0.442	0.802	1.146	1.247	1.799	1.799		422 Berolina r:-0.798 p:0.010 df:7	13478 Fraunhofer r:0.952 p:0.000 df:7	738 Alagasta r:-0.945 p:0.000 df:7
bicep width / back perimeter	7	0.028	0.028	0.036	0.052	0.053	0.085	0.085	0.028	108140 Alir r:-0.875 p:0.010 df:5	5468 Hamatonbetsu r:0.996 p:0.000 df:5	5079 Brubeck r:0.969 p:0.000 df:5
bicep width / back tone	6	0.059	0.059	0.078	0.203	0.253	0.316	0.316	0.059	25760 Annaspitz r:-0.875 p:0.010 df:5	25230 Borgis r:0.985 p:0.000 df:5	193 Ambrosia r:0.974 p:0.000 df:5
bicep width / butt square	8	0.120	0.120	0.134	0.149	0.183	0.198	0.198	0.120	3813 Fortov r:-0.834 p:0.010 df:6	216261 Mapihsia r:0.982 p:0.000 df:6	2104 Toronto r:-0.955 p:0.000 df:6
bicep width / calf width	14	0.445	0.445	0.696	0.816	0.969	1.238	1.238		3370 Kohsai r:-0.663 p:0.010 df:12	159826 Knapp r:0.840 p:0.000 df:12	1399 Teneriffa r:0.827 p:0.000 df:12
bicep width / chest width	20	0.200	0.201	0.274	0.331	0.454	0.755	0.761	0.200	6244 Okamoto r:-0.576 p:0.010 df:17	28184 Vaishnavirao r:0.797 p:0.000 df:17	1431 Luanda r:0.776 p:0.000 df:17
bicep width / clavicle to groin h	25	0.121	0.121	0.167	0.187	0.222	0.293	0.311	0.122	4643 Cisneros r:-0.516 p:0.010 df:22	666 Desdemona r:0.681 p:0.000 df:22	203 Pompeja r:0.659 p:0.000 df:22
bicep width / clavicle to neck h	18	0.743	0.743	1.077	1.276	1.546	1.821	1.821		8806 Fetisov r:-0.590 p:0.010 df:16	8136 Landis r:0.778 p:0.000 df:16	1448 Lindbladia r:0.738 p:0.000 df:16
bicep width / elbow to wrist h	31	0.239	0.244	0.316	0.410	0.468	0.586	0.641	0.239	12729 Berger r:-0.471 p:0.010 df:27	1819 Laputa r:0.703 p:0.000 df:27	1198 Atlantis r:-0.611 p:0.000 df:27
bicep width / long finger length	12	0.313	0.313	0.361	0.485	0.640	0.882	0.882	0.327	2696 Magion r:-0.736 p:0.010 df:9	3764 Holmesacourt r:0.924 p:0.000 df:9	963 Iduberga r:0.901 p:0.000 df:9
bicep width / lower forearm w	35	0.942	1.019	1.378	1.643	1.872	2.088	2.178	1.643	79316 Huangshan r:-0.443 p:0.010 df:31	4949 Akasofu r:0.675 p:0.000 df:31	1445 Konkolya r:-0.581 p:0.000 df:31
bicep width / lower leg h	10	0.130	0.130	0.167	0.229	0.319	0.394	0.394		6748 Bratton r:-0.767 p:0.010 df:8	6379 Vrba r:0.930 p:0.000 df:8	6379 Vrba r:0.930 p:0.000 df:8
bicep width / neck width	20	0.574	0.576	0.710	0.823	0.950	1.303	1.309	0.622	25051 Vass r:-0.562 p:0.010 df:18	29185 Reich r:0.795 p:0.000 df:18	942 Romilda r:0.748 p:0.000 df:18
bicep width / pelvic hips	19	0.225	0.225	0.280	0.349	0.375	0.474	0.474	0.232	70782 Vinceelliott r:-0.575 p:0.010 df:17	3537 Jurgen r:0.773 p:0.000 df:17	3537 Jurgen r:0.773 p:0.000 df:17
bicep width / shoulder to elbow h	37	0.217	0.239	0.314	0.356	0.427	0.580	0.621	0.217	4803 Birkle r:-0.430 p:0.010 df:33	9481 Menchu r:0.722 p:0.000 df:33	1643 Brown r:0.572 p:0.000 df:33
bicep width / shoulder width	32	0.166	0.181	0.229	0.270	0.329	0.450	0.537	0.166	12356 Carlscheele r:-0.456 p:0.010 df:29	9865 Akiraohta r:0.669 p:0.000 df:29	4322 Billjackson r:-0.678 p:0.000 df:29
bicep width / subneck dorsal	15	0.313	0.313	0.399	0.525	0.587	0.692	0.692		185 Eunike r:-0.641 p:0.010 df:13	16265 Lemay r:0.839 p:0.000 df:13	1286 Banachiewicza r:0.812 p:0.000 df:13
bicep width / suprailiac	22	0.184	0.192	0.307	0.349	0.366	0.474	0.476	0.235	6244 Okamoto r:-0.537 p:0.010 df:20	200025 Cloud Gate r:0.709 p:0.000 df:20	1238 Predappia r:-0.720 p:0.000 df:20
bicep width / underbust	23	0.240	0.240	0.277	0.335	0.402	0.804	0.852	0.240	21746 Carrieshaw r:-0.526 p:0.010 df:21	26526 Jookayhyun r:0.779 p:0.000 df:21	1457 Ankara r:0.692 p:0.000 df:21
bicep width / upper forearm w	36	0.610	0.752	0.938	1.111	1.246	1.540	1.615	0.777	24397 Parkerowan r:-0.436 p:0.010 df:32	330420 Tomroman r:0.588 p:0.000 df:32	322 Phaeo r:-0.634 p:0.000 df:32
bicep width / waist	32	0.191	0.231	0.330	0.367	0.425	0.596	0.626	0.253	8712 Suzuko r:-0.450 p:0.010 df:30	8301 Haseyuji r:0.627 p:0.000 df:30	2176 Donar r:0.594 p:0.000 df:30
butt square / pelvic hips	7	1.928	1.928	2.106	2.155	2.291	2.405	2.405	1.928	6185 Mitsuma r:-0.875 p:0.010 df:5	161207 Lidz r:0.980 p:0.000 df:5	620 Drakonia r:-0.972 p:0.000 df:5
butt square / shoulder width	7	1.146	1.146	1.378	1.778	2.161	2.176	2.176	1.378	4896 Tomoegozen r:-0.875 p:0.010 df:5	50240 Cortina r:0.981 p:0.000 df:5	551 Ortrud r:-0.964 p:0.000 df:5
calf width / ankle to heel floor h	8	1.177	1.177	1.446	1.523	1.691	1.758	1.758		222032 Lupton r:-0.834 p:0.010 df:6	37519 Amphios r:0.962 p:0.000 df:6	5825 Rakuyou r:-0.977 p:0.000 df:6
calf width / ankle width	9	1.187	1.187	1.358	1.598	1.719	1.873	1.873		20279 Harel r:-0.799 p:0.010 df:7	27392 Valerieding r:0.953 p:0.000 df:7	599 Luisa r:-0.949 p:0.000 df:7
calf width / lower leg h	11	0.217	0.217	0.273	0.292	0.330	0.350	0.350		88470 Joaquinescrig r:-0.735 p:0.010 df:9	19428 Gracehsu r:0.888 p:0.000 df:9	4492 Debussy r:-0.875 p:0.000 df:9
chest tone / chest perimeter	34	0.025	0.039	0.131	0.193	0.333	0.513	0.576	0.187	3139 Shantou r:-0.443 p:0.010 df:31	5712 Funke r:0.649 p:0.000 df:31	1671 Chaika r:0.583 p:0.000 df:31
chest width / ab width	17	1.342	1.342	1.524	1.809	1.927	2.313	2.313		12828 Batteas r:-0.623 p:0.010 df:14	2689 Bruxelles r:0.829 p:0.000 df:14	2469 Tadjikistan r:0.825 p:0.000 df:14
chest width / calf width	8	1.445	1.445	1.686	2.503	2.806	3.172	3.172		129151 Angelaboggs r:-0.835 p:0.010 df:6	89664 Pignata r:0.942 p:0.000 df:6	8712 Suzuko r:-0.961 p:0.000 df:6
chest width / clavicle to neck h	14	2.038	2.038	2.707	3.814	5.122	5.639	5.639		5526 Kenzo r:-0.684 p:0.010 df:11	38976 Taeve r:0.883 p:0.000 df:11	466 Tisiphone r:-0.838 p:0.000 df:11
chest width / long finger length	10	1.142	1.142	1.188	1.330	1.568	1.636	1.636	1.636	1732 Heike r:-0.799 p:0.010 df:7	10698 Singer r:0.968 p:0.000 df:7	613 Ginevra r:0.958 p:0.000 df:7
chest width / neck width	13	1.842	1.842	2.374	2.616	2.864	3.111	3.111	3.111	21424 Faithchang r:-0.709 p:0.010 df:10	90711 Stotternheim r:0.923 p:0.000 df:10	1520 Imatra r:0.864 p:0.000 df:10

	N											
chest width / pelvic hips	12	0.742	0.742	0.920	1.075	1.203	1.249	1.249	1.162	2187 La Silla r:-0.708 p:0.010 df:10	121655 Nitapszcolka r:0.922 p:0.000 df:10	1974 Caupolican r:-0.867 p:0.000 df:10
chest width / shoulder width	21	0.604	0.611	0.730	0.792	0.835	0.916	0.917	0.830	1332 Marconia r:-0.562 p:0.010 df:18	55561 Madenberg r:0.761 p:0.000 df:18	1641 Tana r:0.708 p:0.000 df:18
chest width / subchest width	9	1.016	1.016	1.061	1.149	1.237	1.256	1.256	1.104	13817 Genobechetti r:-0.835 p:0.010 df:6	30253 Vitek r:0.949 p:0.000 df:6	3254 Bus r:-0.961 p:0.000 df:6
chest width / subneck dorsal	10	1.074	1.074	1.477	1.611	1.683	2.170	2.170		33492 Christirogers r:-0.765 p:0.010 df:8	7345 Happer r:0.971 p:0.000 df:8	10 Hygiea r:0.901 p:0.000 df:8
chest width<->underbust / neck width<->shoulder width	10	0.462	0.462	0.524	0.806	0.965	1.005	1.005	0.973	3845 Neyachenko r:-0.765 p:0.010 df:8	241113 Zhongda r:0.924 p:0.000 df:8	6920 Esaki r:0.899 p:0.000 df:8
chest width<->underbust / neck width<->subneck dorsal	8	0.920	0.920	1.482	2.055	2.801	7.436	7.436		7023 Heiankyo r:-0.834 p:0.010 df:6	30109 Jaywilson r:0.975 p:0.000 df:6	639 Latona r:-0.982 p:0.000 df:6
chest width<->underbust / neck width<->underbust	9	0.163	0.163	0.194	0.292	0.352	0.378	0.378	0.378	1945 Wesselink r:-0.798 p:0.010 df:7	21649 Vardhana r:0.932 p:0.000 df:7	13716 Trevino r:0.925 p:0.000 df:7
chest width<->underbust / pelvic hips<->waist	9	0.256	0.256	0.549	0.740	0.925	1.009	1.009	0.740	1628 Strobel r:-0.798 p:0.010 df:7	17681 Tweedledum r:0.921 p:0.000 df:7	17681 Tweedledum r:0.921 p:0.000 df:7
chest width<->underbust / shoulder width<->subneck dorsal	9	0.754	0.754	0.775	1.011	1.271	1.408	1.408		6860 Sims r:-0.799 p:0.010 df:7	28494 Jasmine r:0.956 p:0.000 df:7	469 Argentina r:-0.930 p:0.000 df:7
chest width<->underbust / shoulder width<->waist	17	0.143	0.143	0.215	0.270	0.319	0.442	0.442	0.430	7324 Carret r:-0.608 p:0.010 df:15	42522 Chuckberry r:0.818 p:0.000 df:15	4103 Chahine r:0.756 p:0.000 df:15
clavicle to groin h / ab width	20	2.275	2.289	2.877	3.303	3.784	4.039	4.045		17034 Vasylshev r:-0.575 p:0.010 df:17	12631 Mariekebaan r:0.792 p:0.000 df:17	2180 Marjaleena r:0.774 p:0.000 df:17
clavicle to groin h / butt square	7	0.734	0.734	0.778	0.872	0.990	1.031	1.031	0.990	1403 Idelsonia r:-0.877 p:0.010 df:5	2574 Ladoga r:0.982 p:0.000 df:5	2574 Ladoga r:0.982 p:0.000 df:5
clavicle to groin h / calf width	12	2.608	2.608	3.994	4.467	4.856	5.544	5.544		27236 Millermatt r:-0.708 p:0.010 df:10	1584 Fuji r:0.896 p:0.000 df:10	71 Niobe r:0.888 p:0.000 df:10
clavicle to groin h / chest width	19	1.536	1.536	1.674	1.749	2.094	2.824	2.824	1.643	5675 Evgenilebedev r:-0.590 p:0.010 df:16	43282 Dougbock r:0.833 p:0.000 df:16	859 Bouzareah r:-0.775 p:0.000 df:16
clavicle to groin h / clavicle to neck h	17	3.631	3.631	4.998	5.992	8.905	11.352	11.352		235 Carolina r:-0.606 p:0.010 df:15	6893 Sanderson r:0.780 p:0.000 df:15	2972 Niilo r:0.765 p:0.000 df:15
clavicle to groin h / long finger length	10	2.325	2.325	2.543	2.608	2.846	3.204	3.204	2.689	1623 Vivian r:-0.798 p:0.010 df:7	4339 Almamater r:0.970 p:0.000 df:7	329 Svea r:0.921 p:0.000 df:7
clavicle to groin h / lower leg h	9	0.761	0.761	0.968	1.269	1.548	1.624	1.624		5759 Zoshchenko r:-0.798 p:0.010 df:7	11449 Stephwerner r:0.954 p:0.000 df:7	2328 Robeson r:-0.929 p:0.000 df:7
clavicle to groin h / neck width	14	2.496	2.496	3.932	4.465	4.920	5.358	5.358	5.112	6622 Matvienko r:-0.662 p:0.010 df:12	20155 Utewindolf r:0.808 p:0.000 df:12	3264 Bounty r:-0.812 p:0.000 df:12
clavicle to groin h / pelvic hips	17	1.608	1.608	1.677	1.910	2.057	2.181	2.181	1.910	1927 Suvanto r:-0.606 p:0.010 df:15	5148 Giordano r:0.790 p:0.000 df:15	6 Hebe r:-0.772 p:0.000 df:15
clavicle to groin h / shoulder width	24	0.779	0.880	1.356	1.405	1.588	2.002	2.093	1.364	2377 Shcheglov r:-0.527 p:0.010 df:21	15619 Albertwu r:0.662 p:0.001 df:21	10566 Zabadak r:-0.772 p:0.000 df:21
clavicle to groin h / subneck dorsal	12	1.379	1.379	2.195	2.706	2.944	3.515	3.515		13917 Correggia r:-0.708 p:0.010 df:10	11422 Alilienthal r:0.911 p:0.000 df:10	2184 Fujian r:-0.857 p:0.000 df:10
clavicle to groin h / suprailiac	20	1.412	1.418	1.783	1.932	2.075	2.616	2.631	1.929	9906 Tintoretto r:-0.561 p:0.010 df:18	3147 Samantha r:0.764 p:0.000 df:18	3147 Samantha r:0.764 p:0.000 df:18
clavicle to groin h / underbust	18	1.695	1.695	1.775	1.921	2.459	3.532	3.532	1.970	5488 Kiyosato r:-0.590 p:0.010 df:16	6013 Andanike r:0.829 p:0.000 df:16	1558 Jarnefelt r:0.750 p:0.000 df:16
clavicle to groin h / waist	23	1.582	1.589	1.865	2.000	2.245	2.765	2.784	2.078	14876 Dampier r:-0.527 p:0.010 df:21	9148 Boriszaitsev r:0.772 p:0.000 df:21	1732 Heike r:0.759 p:0.000 df:21
clavicle to neck h / ankle to heel floor h	7	0.717	0.717	0.944	1.066	1.440	1.453	1.453		18658 Rajdev r:-0.875 p:0.010 df:5	21645 Chentsaiwei r:0.985 p:0.000 df:5	4133 Heureka r:-0.971 p:0.000 df:5
clavicle to neck h / ankle width	7	0.937	0.937	1.043	1.116	1.341	1.358	1.358		7961 Ercolepoli r:-0.876 p:0.010 df:5	7995 Khvorostovsky r:0.985 p:0.000 df:5	2638 Gadolin r:-0.968 p:0.000 df:5
clavicle to neck h / calf width	10	0.456	0.456	0.580	0.655	0.874	0.980	0.980		30421 Jameschafer r:-0.765 p:0.010 df:8	110298 Deceptionisland r:0.936 p:0.000 df:8	3949 Mach r:0.903 p:0.000 df:8
clavicle to neck h / lower leg h	8	0.136	0.136	0.147	0.211	0.265	0.294	0.294		20340 Susanruder r:-0.834 p:0.010 df:6	4548 Wielen r:0.978 p:0.000 df:6	2907 Nekrasov r:-0.947 p:0.000 df:6
elbow to wrist h / ab width	21	0.690	0.725	1.302	1.541	1.795	2.270	2.274		529 Preziosa r:-0.562 p:0.010 df:18	417955 Mallama r:0.762 p:0.000 df:18	1471 Tornio r:0.730 p:0.000 df:18
elbow to wrist h / ankle to heel floor h	7	2.764	2.764	2.863	3.607	4.005	4.515	4.515		5999 Plescia r:-0.875 p:0.010 df:5	601 Nerthus r:0.988 p:0.000 df:5	601 Nerthus r:0.988 p:0.000 df:5
elbow to wrist h / ankle width	8	1.311	1.311	2.507	3.144	4.192	4.712	4.712		180 Garumna r:-0.834 p:0.010 df:6	4436 Ortizmoreno r:0.969 p:0.000 df:6	235 Carolina r:-0.968 p:0.000 df:6
elbow to wrist h / back perimeter	8	0.088	0.088	0.103	0.132	0.187	0.283	0.283	0.119	2227 Otto Struve r:-0.835 p:0.010 df:6	9514 Deineka r:0.954 p:0.000 df:6	413 Edburga r:-0.950 p:0.000 df:6
elbow to wrist h / back tone	8	0.248	0.248	0.333	0.642	0.753	1.806	1.806	0.248	10443 van der Pol r:-0.835 p:0.010 df:6	4024 Ronan r:0.977 p:0.000 df:6	147 Protogeneia r:-0.955 p:0.000 df:6

Ratio	n									Name 1	Name 2	Name 3
elbow to wrist h / butt square	8	0.311	0.311	0.420	0.483	0.503	0.613	0.613	0.505	4309 Marvin r:-0.834 p:0.010 df:6	1276 Ucclia r:0.977 p:0.000 df:6	1276 Ucclia r:0.977 p:0.000 df:6
elbow to wrist h / calf width	12	1.608	1.608	1.883	2.260	2.464	2.633	2.633		129138 Williamfrost r:-0.708 p:0.010 df:10	12440 Koshigayaboshi r:0.903 p:0.000 df:10	889 Erynia r:-0.908 p:0.000 df:10
elbow to wrist h / chest perimeter	27	0.084	0.088	0.110	0.133	0.183	0.332	0.352	0.139	5244 Amphilochos r:-0.496 p:0.010 df:24	19495 Terentyeva r:0.649 p:0.000 df:24	178 Belisana r:0.639 p:0.000 df:24
elbow to wrist h / chest tone	28	0.235	0.237	0.579	0.732	1.298	3.740	4.031	0.746	4657 Lopez r:-0.490 p:0.010 df:25	9536 Statler r:0.784 p:0.000 df:25	1390 Abastumani r:0.678 p:0.000 df:25
elbow to wrist h / chest width	19	0.599	0.599	0.757	0.906	1.144	1.416	1.416	0.838	968 Petunia r:-0.590 p:0.010 df:16	28618 Scibelli r:0.855 p:0.000 df:16	43 Ariadne r:0.778 p:0.000 df:16
elbow to wrist h / clavicle to groin h	25	0.369	0.373	0.419	0.510	0.583	0.669	0.677	0.510	23564 Ungaretti r:-0.516 p:0.010 df:22	7367 Giotto r:0.733 p:0.000 df:22	6269 Kawasaki r:-0.721 p:0.000 df:22
elbow to wrist h / clavicle to neck h	16	1.672	1.672	2.393	3.031	3.641	5.031	5.031		10443 van der Pol r:-0.623 p:0.010 df:14	20587 Jargoldman r:0.796 p:0.000 df:14	3347 Konstantin r:0.769 p:0.000 df:14
elbow to wrist h / foot base h	7	0.568	0.568	0.964	1.029	1.286	1.363	1.363		11517 Esteracuna r:-0.875 p:0.010 df:5	4727 Ravel r:0.988 p:0.000 df:5	3105 Stumpff r:0.972 p:0.000 df:5
elbow to wrist h / long finger length	11	0.990	0.990	1.036	1.330	1.420	1.641	1.641	1.371	10476 Los Molinos r:-0.767 p:0.010 df:8	37645 Chebarkul r:0.892 p:0.001 df:8	2546 Libitina r:-0.927 p:0.000 df:8
elbow to wrist h / lower leg h	10	0.485	0.485	0.512	0.665	0.697	0.921	0.921		266711 Tuttlingen r:-0.766 p:0.010 df:8	5558 Johnnapier r:0.961 p:0.000 df:8	411 Xanthe r:0.922 p:0.000 df:8
elbow to wrist h / neck width	17	1.689	1.689	1.882	2.143	2.604	3.011	3.011	2.606	15413 Beaglehole r:-0.606 p:0.010 df:15	11934 Lundgren r:0.824 p:0.000 df:15	1164 Kobolda r:0.764 p:0.000 df:15
elbow to wrist h / pelvic hips	17	0.424	0.424	0.720	0.868	0.978	1.198	1.198	0.974	8527 Katayama r:-0.606 p:0.010 df:15	6761 Haroldconnolly r:0.830 p:0.000 df:15	365 Corduba r:-0.774 p:0.000 df:15
elbow to wrist h / shoulder width	27	0.527	0.536	0.588	0.703	0.856	0.974	1.000	0.696	2214 Carol r:-0.496 p:0.010 df:24	14835 Holdridge r:0.738 p:0.000 df:24	1485 Isa r:0.659 p:0.000 df:24
elbow to wrist h / subneck dorsal	14	0.914	0.914	1.080	1.269	1.491	2.287	2.287		90138 Diehl r:-0.664 p:0.010 df:12	3361 Orpheus r:0.885 p:0.000 df:12	3318 Blixen r:0.808 p:0.000 df:12
elbow to wrist h / suprailiac	19	0.405	0.405	0.745	0.831	0.984	1.337	1.337	0.984	11419 Donjohnson r:-0.577 p:0.010 df:17	2506 Pirogov r:0.832 p:0.000 df:17	365 Corduba r:-0.765 p:0.000 df:17
elbow to wrist h / underbust	21	0.699	0.701	0.783	0.972	1.164	1.569	1.571	1.004	20536 Tracicarter r:-0.549 p:0.010 df:19	7804 Boesgaard r:0.772 p:0.000 df:19	1019 Strackea r:0.699 p:0.000 df:19
elbow to wrist h / waist	27	0.442	0.506	0.840	1.013	1.129	1.448	1.540	1.059	7928 Bijaoui r:-0.487 p:0.010 df:25	13093 Wolfgangpauli r:0.679 p:0.000 df:25	2147 Kharadze r:-0.699 p:0.000 df:25
finger width / ab perimeter	29	0.006	0.007	0.010	0.014	0.024	0.045	0.049	0.019	28171 Diannahu r:-0.480 p:0.010 df:26	16402 Olgapopova r:0.682 p:0.000 df:26	9777 Enterprise r:0.653 p:0.000 df:26
finger width / ab tone	29	0.013	0.016	0.031	0.061	0.107	0.470	0.524	0.027	6887 Hasuo r:-0.479 p:0.010 df:26	30326 Maxpine r:0.720 p:0.000 df:26	402 Chloe r:0.670 p:0.000 df:26
finger width / ab width	21	0.073	0.077	0.136	0.154	0.189	0.363	0.378		18119 Braude r:-0.562 p:0.010 df:18	16421 Roadrunner r:0.821 p:0.000 df:18	1545 Thernoe r:0.754 p:0.000 df:18
finger width / ankle width	7	0.216	0.216	0.241	0.259	0.304	0.355	0.355		16015 Snell r:-0.875 p:0.010 df:5	66671 Sfasu r:0.966 p:0.000 df:5	654 Zelinda r:-0.969 p:0.000 df:5
finger width / back perimeter	7	0.007	0.007	0.007	0.010	0.011	0.024	0.024	0.007	17995 Jolinefan r:-0.876 p:0.010 df:5	9499 Excalibur r:0.988 p:0.000 df:5	413 Edburga r:-0.972 p:0.000 df:5
finger width / back tone	7	0.015	0.015	0.031	0.060	0.068	0.136	0.136	0.015	1538 Detre r:-0.875 p:0.010 df:5	6933 Azumayasan r:0.996 p:0.000 df:5	193 Ambrosia r:0.965 p:0.000 df:5
finger width / bicep width	31	0.155	0.157	0.185	0.222	0.286	0.600	0.830	0.252	6470 Aldrin r:-0.472 p:0.010 df:27	21663 Banat r:0.727 p:0.000 df:27	2259 Sofievka r:0.612 p:0.000 df:27
finger width / butt square	8	0.030	0.030	0.032	0.039	0.045	0.052	0.052	0.030	17995 Jolinefan r:-0.838 p:0.009 df:6	14114 Randyray r:0.962 p:0.000 df:6	1126 Otero r:0.949 p:0.000 df:6
finger width / calf width	11	0.146	0.146	0.174	0.190	0.210	0.229	0.229		4941 Yahagi r:-0.735 p:0.010 df:9	5051 Ralph r:0.924 p:0.000 df:9	2266 Tchaikovsky r:-0.910 p:0.000 df:9
finger width / chest perimeter	27	0.007	0.007	0.009	0.014	0.022	0.046	0.048	0.008	3003 Koncek r:-0.496 p:0.010 df:24	26057 Ankaios r:0.711 p:0.000 df:24	420 Bertholda r:0.683 p:0.000 df:24
finger width / chest tone	27	0.016	0.017	0.045	0.068	0.149	0.423	0.464	0.045	3510 Veeder r:-0.497 p:0.010 df:24	13927 Grundy r:0.686 p:0.000 df:24	940 Kordula r:0.659 p:0.000 df:24
finger width / chest width	22	0.050	0.050	0.068	0.083	0.118	0.194	0.201	0.050	3077 Henderson r:-0.563 p:0.010 df:18	1545 Thernoe r:0.771 p:0.000 df:18	881 Athene r:-0.836 p:0.000 df:18
finger width / clavicle to groin h	22	0.031	0.031	0.039	0.044	0.051	0.095	0.100	0.031	1718 Namibia r:-0.550 p:0.010 df:19	289587 Chantdugros r:0.776 p:0.000 df:19	17269 Dicksmith r:-0.719 p:0.000 df:19
finger width / clavicle to neck h	17	0.162	0.162	0.212	0.234	0.382	0.692	0.692		297 Caecilia r:-0.606 p:0.010 df:15	347 Pariana r:0.838 p:0.000 df:15	347 Pariana r:0.838 p:0.000 df:15
finger width / elbow to wrist h	26	0.060	0.061	0.075	0.084	0.103	0.125	0.131	0.060	21704 Mikkilineni r:-0.516 p:0.010 df:22	12688 Baekeland r:0.758 p:0.000 df:22	8761 Crane r:0.674 p:0.000 df:22
finger width / long finger length	12	0.082	0.082	0.101	0.119	0.139	0.260	0.260	0.082	19023 Varela r:-0.736 p:0.010 df:9	289587 Chantdugros r:0.945 p:0.000 df:9	2019 van Albada r:0.925 p:0.000 df:9
finger width / lower forearm w	35	0.227	0.258	0.317	0.353	0.462	0.703	0.974	0.414	4397 Jalopez r:-0.456 p:0.010 df:29	21663 Banat r:0.775 p:0.000 df:29	1380 Volodia r:0.633 p:0.000 df:29
finger width / lower leg h	7	0.032	0.032	0.040	0.056	0.064	0.065	0.065		2950 Rousseau r:-0.875 p:0.010 df:5	32279 Marshall r:0.993 p:0.000 df:5	3091 van den Heuvel r:-0.970 p:0.000 df:5
finger width / lower thigh width	20	0.130	0.130	0.153	0.180	0.215	0.275	0.278	0.139	23477 Wallenstadt r:-0.590 p:0.010 df:16	34280 Victoradler r:0.803 p:0.000 df:16	1351 Uzbekistania r:0.767 p:0.000 df:16

Measurement	n									A	B	C
finger width / neck width	21	0.112	0.115	0.166	0.190	0.237	0.520	0.536	0.157	197856 Tafelmusik r:-0.562 p:0.010 df:18	16421 Roadrunner r:0.800 p:0.000 df:18	1778 Alfven r:0.736 p:0.000 df:18
finger width / p_diahead	35	0.381	0.384	0.431	0.482	0.596	0.732	0.779	0.381	55276 Kenlarner r:-0.442 p:0.010 df:31	19981 Bialystock r:0.643 p:0.000 df:31	1609 Brenda r:0.585 p:0.000 df:31
finger width / p_diashaft close	34	0.267	0.327	0.401	0.447	0.550	0.653	0.714	0.350	5299 Bittesini r:-0.463 p:0.010 df:28	16247 Esner r:0.672 p:0.000 df:28	2376 Martynov r:0.653 p:0.000 df:28
finger width / p_diashaft far	38	0.307	0.359	0.441	0.503	0.580	0.746	0.763	0.307	2524 Budovicium r:-0.436 p:0.010 df:32	372573 Pietromenga r:0.639 p:0.000 df:32	1413 Roucarie r:-0.611 p:0.000 df:32
finger width / p_headonly l	35	0.389	0.406	0.488	0.567	0.687	1.112	1.120	0.422	4121 Carlin r:-0.449 p:0.010 df:30	2190 Coubertin r:0.729 p:0.000 df:30	609 Fulvia r:0.581 p:0.000 df:30
finger width / p_shaftonly l	35	0.099	0.108	0.151	0.170	0.216	0.481	0.498	0.099	4083 Jody r:-0.449 p:0.010 df:30	15301 Marutesser r:0.692 p:0.000 df:30	680 Genoveva r:-0.582 p:0.000 df:30
finger width / pelvic hips	16	0.045	0.045	0.070	0.078	0.094	0.187	0.187	0.059	23307 Alexramek r:-0.623 p:0.010 df:14	207716 Wangxichan r:0.831 p:0.000 df:14	1545 Thernoe r:0.771 p:0.000 df:14
finger width / shoulder to elbow h	30	0.049	0.052	0.072	0.084	0.100	0.116	0.122	0.055	29886 Randytung r:-0.471 p:0.010 df:27	7694 Krasetin r:0.674 p:0.000 df:27	4883 Korolirina r:0.626 p:0.000 df:27
finger width / shoulder width	29	0.035	0.038	0.058	0.064	0.080	0.138	0.160	0.042	20292 Eduardreznik r:-0.482 p:0.009 df:26	17638 Sualan r:0.678 p:0.000 df:26	107 Camilla r:0.625 p:0.000 df:26
finger width / subchest width	9	0.056	0.056	0.069	0.102	0.135	0.150	0.150	0.056	1892 Lucienne r:-0.835 p:0.010 df:6	31234 Bea r:0.983 p:0.000 df:6	2690 Ristiina r:0.942 p:0.000 df:6
finger width / subneck dorsal	13	0.062	0.062	0.095	0.123	0.150	0.338	0.338		96344 Scottweaver r:-0.684 p:0.010 df:11	11811 Martinrubin r:0.945 p:0.000 df:11	1483 Hakoila r:0.828 p:0.000 df:11
finger width / suprailiac	20	0.043	0.044	0.074	0.087	0.110	0.169	0.170	0.059	4074 Sharkov r:-0.564 p:0.010 df:18	14061 Nagincox r:0.800 p:0.000 df:18	2583 Fatyanov r:0.743 p:0.000 df:18
finger width / thigh h	21	0.033	0.034	0.044	0.054	0.068	0.089	0.090	0.037	51570 Phendricksen r:-0.562 p:0.010 df:18	17097 Ronneuman r:0.764 p:0.000 df:18	4700 Carusi r:0.711 p:0.000 df:18
finger width / underbust	22	0.060	0.061	0.075	0.109	0.138	0.217	0.225	0.060	12909 Jaclifford r:-0.550 p:0.010 df:19	1545 Thernoe r:0.777 p:0.000 df:19	1545 Thernoe r:0.777 p:0.000 df:19
finger width / upper forearm w	30	0.128	0.151	0.195	0.250	0.320	0.365	0.371	0.196	9240 Nassau r:-0.479 p:0.000 df:26	289587 Chantdugros r:0.701 p:0.000 df:26	3518 Florena r:0.626 p:0.000 df:26
finger width / upper thigh width	38	0.095	0.104	0.115	0.131	0.160	0.189	0.283	0.105	3400 Aotearoa r:-0.436 p:0.010 df:32	289587 Chantdugros r:0.632 p:0.000 df:32	1351 Uzbekistania r:0.591 p:0.000 df:32
finger width / waist	30	0.047	0.056	0.082	0.095	0.118	0.164	0.167	0.064	4975 Dohmoto r:-0.473 p:0.010 df:27	14061 Nagincox r:0.685 p:0.000 df:27	1545 Thernoe r:0.645 p:0.000 df:27
long finger length / ab width	8	0.923	0.923	1.150	1.326	1.583	1.740	1.740		2978 Roudebush r:-0.875 p:0.010 df:5	3310 Patsy r:0.977 p:0.000 df:5	1995 Hajek r:-0.976 p:0.000 df:5
long finger length / neck width	7	1.351	1.351	1.446	1.901	1.980	2.065	2.065	1.901	33188 Shreya r:-0.875 p:0.010 df:5	31282 Nicoleticea r:0.977 p:0.000 df:5	1920 Sarmiento r:-0.992 p:0.000 df:5
long finger length / shoulder width	11	0.432	0.432	0.495	0.537	0.609	0.673	0.673	0.507	2637 Bobrovnikoff r:-0.765 p:0.010 df:8	2633 Bishop r:0.936 p:0.000 df:8	2633 Bishop r:0.936 p:0.000 df:8
lower forearm w / ab width	23	0.258	0.260	0.321	0.398	0.469	0.560	0.561		5857 Neglinka r:-0.537 p:0.010 df:20	43025 Valusha r:0.776 p:0.000 df:20	2934 Aristophanes r:-0.687 p:0.000 df:20
lower forearm w / ankle to heel floor h	7	0.620	0.620	0.713	0.935	1.024	1.127	1.127		2926 Caldeira r:-0.875 p:0.010 df:5	22134 Kirian r:0.980 p:0.000 df:5	1719 Jens r:-0.970 p:0.000 df:5
lower forearm w / ankle width	8	0.279	0.279	0.671	0.840	0.920	1.242	1.242		3560 Chenqian r:-0.834 p:0.010 df:6	20455 Pennell r:0.977 p:0.000 df:6	1811 Bruwer r:0.970 p:0.000 df:6
lower forearm w / back perimeter	8	0.017	0.017	0.019	0.028	0.038	0.075	0.075	0.017	11942 Guettard r:-0.834 p:0.010 df:6	10678 Alilagoa r:0.966 p:0.000 df:6	413 Edburga r:-0.979 p:0.000 df:6
lower forearm w / back tone	8	0.036	0.036	0.060	0.137	0.196	0.384	0.384	0.036	7382 Bozhenkova r:-0.835 p:0.010 df:6	26720 Yangxinyan r:0.977 p:0.000 df:6	194 Prokne r:0.971 p:0.000 df:6
lower forearm w / butt square	9	0.073	0.073	0.083	0.088	0.114	0.161	0.161	0.073	2991 Bilbo r:-0.798 p:0.010 df:7	5809 Kulibin r:0.951 p:0.000 df:7	2288 Karolinum r:0.938 p:0.000 df:7
lower forearm w / calf width	12	0.404	0.404	0.494	0.572	0.658	0.682	0.682		8523 Bouillabaisse r:-0.710 p:0.010 df:10	133243 Essen r:0.908 p:0.000 df:10	2883 Barabashov r:-0.879 p:0.000 df:10
lower forearm w / chest perimeter	29	0.020	0.020	0.025	0.035	0.043	0.094	0.095	0.020	1183 Jutta r:-0.480 p:0.010 df:26	11278 Telesio r:0.691 p:0.000 df:26	178 Belisana r:0.622 p:0.000 df:26
lower forearm w / chest tone	30	0.063	0.074	0.128	0.178	0.286	1.176	1.575	0.108	569 Misa r:-0.472 p:0.010 df:27	1362 Griqua r:0.720 p:0.000 df:27	789 Lena r:0.606 p:0.000 df:27
lower forearm w / chest width	22	0.122	0.124	0.176	0.221	0.252	0.346	0.349	0.122	21663 Banat r:-0.562 p:0.010 df:18	2936 Nechvile r:0.801 p:0.000 df:18	16 Psyche r:-0.719 p:0.000 df:18
lower forearm w / clavicle to groin h	25	0.074	0.080	0.103	0.121	0.138	0.155	0.157	0.074	9162 Kwiila r:-0.515 p:0.010 df:22	3775 Ellenbeth r:0.719 p:0.000 df:22	898 Hildegard r:0.703 p:0.000 df:22
lower forearm w / clavicle to neck h	17	0.384	0.384	0.653	0.836	1.111	1.326	1.326		3811 Karma r:-0.623 p:0.010 df:14	9637 Perryrose r:0.850 p:0.000 df:14	2478 Tokai r:0.773 p:0.000 df:14
lower forearm w / elbow to wrist h	34	0.145	0.160	0.213	0.246	0.270	0.334	0.465	0.145	3429 Chuvaev r:-0.457 p:0.010 df:29	6939 Lestone r:0.670 p:0.000 df:29	359 Georgia r:0.589 p:0.000 df:29
lower forearm w / foot base h	7	0.121	0.121	0.216	0.282	0.331	0.353	0.353		9026 Denevi r:-0.875 p:0.010 df:5	10219 Penco r:0.980 p:0.000 df:5	762 Pulcova r:0.969 p:0.000 df:5
lower forearm w / long finger length	12	0.199	0.199	0.252	0.324	0.374	0.405	0.405	0.199	7187 Isobe r:-0.736 p:0.010 df:9	246247 Sheldoncooper r:0.912 p:0.000 df:9	3893 DeLaeter r:0.879 p:0.000 df:9
lower forearm w / lower leg h	9	0.111	0.111	0.122	0.180	0.188	0.191	0.191		2651 Karen r:-0.799 p:0.010 df:7	18163 Jennalewis r:0.967 p:0.000 df:7	1475 Yalta r:-0.953 p:0.000 df:7

lower forearm w / neck width	21	0.285	0.294	0.495	0.529	0.641	0.793	0.805	0.378	110295 Elcalafate r:-0.562 p:0.010 df:18	15042 Anndavgui r:0.760 p:0.000 df:18	286 Iclea r:-0.740 p:0.000 df:18
lower forearm w / pelvic hips	20	0.141	0.143	0.193	0.204	0.242	0.288	0.289	0.141	1207 Ostenia r:-0.563 p:0.010 df:18	8968 Europaeus r:0.784 p:0.000 df:18	225 Henrietta r:-0.716 p:0.000 df:18
lower forearm w / shoulder width	31	0.097	0.100	0.155	0.180	0.197	0.266	0.286	0.101	8241 Agrius r:-0.463 p:0.010 df:28	269390 Igortkachenko r:0.661 p:0.000 df:28	859 Bouzareah r:-0.606 p:0.000 df:28
lower forearm w / subchest width	8	0.134	0.134	0.169	0.267	0.282	0.332	0.332	0.134	28598 Apadmanabha r:-0.875 p:0.010 df:5	1995 Hajek r:0.984 p:0.000 df:5	1995 Hajek r:0.984 p:0.000 df:5
lower forearm w / subneck dorsal	14	0.253	0.253	0.262	0.348	0.369	0.513	0.513		9549 Akplatonov r:-0.661 p:0.010 df:12	3361 Orpheus r:0.893 p:0.000 df:12	382 Dodona r:-0.855 p:0.000 df:12
lower forearm w / suprailiac	23	0.143	0.146	0.181	0.211	0.248	0.327	0.339	0.143	18965 Lazenby r:-0.526 p:0.010 df:21	9385 Avignon r:0.800 p:0.000 df:21	3281 Maupertuis r:-0.742 p:0.000 df:21
lower forearm w / underbust	24	0.146	0.149	0.189	0.239	0.267	0.422	0.434	0.146	3485 Barucci r:-0.526 p:0.010 df:21	8240 Matisse r:0.775 p:0.000 df:21	859 Bouzareah r:-0.670 p:0.000 df:21
lower forearm w / waist	33	0.149	0.152	0.206	0.234	0.282	0.356	0.376	0.154	7235 Hitsuzan r:-0.449 p:0.010 df:30	269390 Igortkachenko r:0.635 p:0.000 df:30	13 Egeria r:-0.595 p:0.000 df:30
lower thigh width / ab perimeter	22	0.034	0.036	0.066	0.078	0.155	0.251	0.257	0.139	2574 Ladoga r:-0.550 p:0.010 df:19	1315 Bronislawa r:0.763 p:0.000 df:19	1315 Bronislawa r:0.763 p:0.000 df:19
lower thigh width / ab tone	22	0.061	0.069	0.212	0.356	0.518	1.712	1.813	0.197	1313 Berna r:-0.549 p:0.010 df:19	17041 Castagna r:0.799 p:0.000 df:19	457 Alleghenia r:0.727 p:0.000 df:19
lower thigh width / ab width	14	0.666	0.666	0.723	0.836	0.962	1.311	1.311		2062 Aten r:-0.684 p:0.010 df:11	6468 Welzenbach r:0.890 p:0.000 df:11	1297 Quadea r:-0.840 p:0.000 df:11
lower thigh width / ankle to heel floor h	7	1.178	1.178	1.368	1.791	2.047	2.327	2.327		283 Emma r:-0.875 p:0.010 df:5	341 California r:0.984 p:0.000 df:5	341 California r:0.984 p:0.000 df:5
lower thigh width / ankle width	8	1.266	1.266	1.354	1.514	1.920	2.340	2.340		27493 Derikesibill r:-0.836 p:0.010 df:6	18857 Lalchandani r:0.983 p:0.000 df:6	325 Heidelberga r:0.951 p:0.000 df:6
lower thigh width / back perimeter	7	0.037	0.037	0.041	0.052	0.099	0.116	0.116	0.052	2090 Mizuho r:-0.876 p:0.010 df:5	3292 Sather r:0.990 p:0.000 df:5	883 Matterania r:0.980 p:0.000 df:5
lower thigh width / back tone	7	0.107	0.107	0.150	0.240	0.334	0.842	0.842	0.107	7038 Tokorozawa r:-0.875 p:0.010 df:5	32593 Crotty r:0.993 p:0.000 df:5	193 Ambrosia r:0.982 p:0.000 df:5
lower thigh width / bicep width	24	0.983	0.996	1.093	1.291	1.752	2.321	2.407	1.819	2153 Akiyama r:-0.537 p:0.010 df:20	32381 Bellomo r:0.787 p:0.000 df:20	1445 Konkolya r:0.692 p:0.000 df:20
lower thigh width / butt square	7	0.181	0.181	0.192	0.209	0.251	0.252	0.252	0.219	4315 Pronik r:-0.875 p:0.010 df:5	13424 Margalida r:0.964 p:0.000 df:5	7639 Offutt r:-0.971 p:0.000 df:5
lower thigh width / calf width	13	0.891	0.891	1.001	1.071	1.190	1.324	1.324		4082 Swann r:-0.684 p:0.010 df:11	4832 Palinurus r:0.867 p:0.000 df:11	78 Diana r:-0.901 p:0.000 df:11
lower thigh width / chest width	13	0.310	0.310	0.364	0.450	0.627	0.817	0.817	0.364	7756 Scientia r:-0.708 p:0.010 df:10	133773 Lindsaykeller r:0.921 p:0.000 df:10	380 Fiducia r:-0.868 p:0.000 df:10
lower thigh width / clavicle to groin h	18	0.191	0.191	0.213	0.243	0.279	0.410	0.410	0.221	1584 Fuji r:-0.608 p:0.010 df:15	11128 Ostravia r:0.831 p:0.000 df:15	2491 Tvashtri r:-0.779 p:0.000 df:15
lower thigh width / clavicle to neck h	11	0.740	0.740	1.047	1.462	2.162	2.498	2.498		9560 Anguita r:-0.735 p:0.010 df:9	454409 Markusloose r:0.906 p:0.000 df:9	1854 Skvortsov r:0.878 p:0.000 df:9
lower thigh width / elbow to wrist h	22	0.301	0.310	0.428	0.488	0.576	0.668	0.670	0.434	8807 Schenk r:-0.561 p:0.010 df:18	454350 Paolaamico r:0.805 p:0.000 df:18	889 Erynia r:0.711 p:0.000 df:18
lower thigh width / long finger length	11	0.485	0.485	0.542	0.620	0.858	0.946	0.946	0.595	13674 Bourge r:-0.765 p:0.010 df:8	17892 Morecambewise r:0.936 p:0.000 df:8	1532 Inari r:0.929 p:0.000 df:8
lower thigh width / lower forearm w	22	1.499	1.508	1.871	2.132	2.228	2.955	2.989	2.989	70720 Davidskillman r:-0.561 p:0.010 df:18	688 Melanie r:0.757 p:0.000 df:18	110 Lydia r:0.718 p:0.000 df:18
lower thigh width / lower leg h	9	0.238	0.238	0.282	0.341	0.401	0.418	0.418		3608 Kataev r:-0.798 p:0.010 df:7	22744 Esterantonucci r:0.943 p:0.000 df:7	300 Geraldina r:-0.918 p:0.000 df:7
lower thigh width / neck width	13	0.508	0.508	0.948	1.122	1.275	1.726	1.726	1.131	8719 Vesmir r:-0.684 p:0.010 df:11	269300 Diego r:0.870 p:0.000 df:11	476 Hedwig r:-0.906 p:0.000 df:11
lower thigh width / pelvic hips	10	0.423	0.423	0.436	0.448	0.487	0.574	0.574	0.423	2398 Jilin r:-0.765 p:0.010 df:8	11808 Platz r:0.949 p:0.000 df:8	1272 Gefion r:0.931 p:0.000 df:8
lower thigh width / shoulder to elbow h	24	0.364	0.364	0.396	0.466	0.518	0.624	0.625	0.395	16083 Jorvik r:-0.537 p:0.010 df:20	128372 Danielwibben r:0.745 p:0.000 df:20	442 Eichsfeldia r:-0.708 p:0.000 df:20
lower thigh width / shoulder width	22	0.159	0.177	0.312	0.373	0.457	0.577	0.577	0.302	12640 Reinbertdeleeuw r:-0.549 p:0.010 df:19	4541 Mizuno r:0.792 p:0.000 df:19	2097 Galle r:0.737 p:0.000 df:19
lower thigh width / subneck dorsal	9	0.281	0.281	0.548	0.607	0.691	0.829	0.829		35313 Hangtianyuan r:-0.799 p:0.010 df:7	115059 Nagykaroly r:0.926 p:0.000 df:7	727 Nipponia r:-0.921 p:0.000 df:7
lower thigh width / suprailiac	12	0.376	0.376	0.434	0.464	0.540	0.728	0.728	0.427	4031 Mueller r:-0.708 p:0.010 df:10	10839 Hufeland r:0.918 p:0.000 df:10	859 Bouzareah r:-0.852 p:0.000 df:10
lower thigh width / thigh h	25	0.217	0.223	0.266	0.297	0.343	0.402	0.417	0.269	2238 Steshenko r:-0.515 p:0.010 df:22	196 Philomela r:0.711 p:0.000 df:22	196 Philomela r:0.711 p:0.000 df:22
lower thigh width / underbust	16	0.390	0.390	0.454	0.502	0.666	0.768	0.768	0.436	11151 Oodaigahara r:-0.623 p:0.010 df:14	14598 Larrysmith r:0.828 p:0.000 df:14	859 Bouzareah r:-0.771 p:0.000 df:14
lower thigh width / upper forearm w	23	0.756	0.831	1.300	1.454	1.618	2.104	2.105	1.413	2711 Aleksandrov r:-0.549 p:0.010 df:19	147971 Nametoko r:0.743 p:0.000 df:19	4072 Yayoi r:0.711 p:0.000 df:19
lower thigh width / waist	19	0.427	0.427	0.468	0.541	0.589	0.744	0.744	0.460	95008 Ivanobertini r:-0.576 p:0.010 df:17	8855 Miwa r:0.810 p:0.000 df:17	859 Bouzareah r:-0.808 p:0.000 df:17
neck width / ab width	15	0.581	0.581	0.616	0.731	0.898	1.321	1.321		27241 Sunilpai r:-0.642 p:0.010 df:13	39549 Casals r:0.871 p:0.000 df:13	393 Lampetia r:-0.814 p:0.000 df:13

	N											
neck width / calf width	7	0.783	0.783	0.791	0.943	1.093	1.248	1.248		117032 Davidlane r:-0.875 p:0.010 df:5	1466 Mundleria r:0.975 p:0.000 df:5	228 Agathe r:-0.965 p:0.000 df:5
neck width / clavicle to neck h	17	1.002	1.002	1.202	1.455	1.916	2.134	2.134		23893 Lauman r:-0.623 p:0.010 df:14	24601 Valjean r:0.857 p:0.000 df:14	9308 Randyrose r:-0.818 p:0.000 df:14
neck width / subneck dorsal	15	0.517	0.517	0.537	0.582	0.659	0.760	0.760		6094 Hisako r:-0.643 p:0.010 df:13	2572 Annschnell r:0.828 p:0.000 df:13	2552 Remek r:-0.790 p:0.000 df:13
neck width<->shoulder width / neck width<->underbust	12	0.291	0.291	0.318	0.376	0.403	0.455	0.455	0.388	5441 Andymurray r:-0.708 p:0.010 df:10	23044 Starodub r:0.902 p:0.000 df:10	77 Frigga r:-0.849 p:0.000 df:10
neck width<->shoulder width / shoulder width<->subneck dorsal	14	1.137	1.137	1.323	1.471	1.580	2.107	2.107		8485 Satoru r:-0.663 p:0.010 df:12	5198 Fongyunwah r:0.907 p:0.000 df:12	390 Alma r:0.884 p:0.000 df:12
neck width<->subneck dorsal / neck width<->shoulder width	14	0.135	0.135	0.323	0.344	0.442	0.530	0.530		2120 Tyumenia r:-0.662 p:0.010 df:12	159164 La Canada r:0.882 p:0.000 df:12	573 Recha r:-0.813 p:0.000 df:12
neck width<->subneck dorsal / neck width<->underbust	9	0.046	0.046	0.101	0.144	0.175	0.222	0.222		10132 Lummelunda r:-0.798 p:0.010 df:7	5771 Somerville r:0.970 p:0.000 df:7	3141 Buchar r:-0.924 p:0.000 df:7
neck width<->subneck dorsal / shoulder width<->subneck dorsal	14	0.177	0.177	0.457	0.506	0.726	1.117	1.117		7381 Mamontov r:-0.662 p:0.010 df:12	2373 Immo r:0.870 p:0.000 df:12	2373 Immo r:0.870 p:0.000 df:12
p _ diahead / lower forearm w	31	0.347	0.447	0.625	0.752	0.888	1.536	1.840	1.086	4043 Perolof r:-0.471 p:0.010 df:27	9026 Denevi r:0.810 p:0.000 df:27	182 Elsa r:-0.635 p:0.000 df:27
p _ diahead / upper forearm w	30	0.257	0.292	0.427	0.522	0.701	1.170	1.305	0.513	6678 Seurat r:-0.472 p:0.010 df:27	13992 Cesarebarbieri r:0.662 p:0.000 df:27	-10001 Moon r:-0.663 p:0.000 df:27
p _ diahead / upper thigh width	38	0.160	0.170	0.247	0.275	0.318	0.535	0.554	0.274	8930 Kubota r:-0.424 p:0.010 df:34	31771 Kirstenwright r:0.646 p:0.000 df:34	4201 Orosz r:0.598 p:0.000 df:34
p _ diahead / waist	30	0.071	0.096	0.168	0.200	0.241	0.344	0.388	0.167	9742 Worpswede r:-0.471 p:0.010 df:27	6299 Reizoutoyoko r:0.702 p:0.000 df:27	2403 Sumava r:0.657 p:0.000 df:27
p _ diashaft close / p _ diahead	35	0.918	0.932	1.028	1.092	1.206	1.795	1.866	1.090	26250 Shaneludwig r:-0.442 p:0.010 df:31	28599 Terenzoni r:0.731 p:0.000 df:31	34 Circe r:0.622 p:0.000 df:31
p _ diashaft close / p _ diashaft far	39	0.810	0.878	1.031	1.107	1.190	1.462	1.558	0.878	31771 Kirstenwright r:-0.430 p:0.010 df:33	28209 Chatterjee r:0.648 p:0.000 df:33	807 Ceraskia r:0.610 p:0.000 df:33
p _ diashaft close / p _ headonly l	35	0.937	0.946	1.022	1.205	1.475	2.214	3.305	1.205	3472 Upgren r:-0.449 p:0.010 df:30	25139 Roatsch r:0.698 p:0.000 df:30	542 Susanna r:0.596 p:0.000 df:30
p _ diashaft close / p _ shaftonly l	36	0.247	0.275	0.323	0.374	0.418	0.785	0.954	0.282	7098 Reaumur r:-0.444 p:0.010 df:31	8862 Takayukiota r:0.700 p:0.000 df:31	1554 Yugoslavia r:0.674 p:0.000 df:31
p _ diashaft close / upper thigh width	34	0.201	0.216	0.262	0.302	0.358	0.564	0.605	0.299	4165 Didkovskij r:-0.456 p:0.010 df:29	22794 Lindsayleona r:0.624 p:0.000 df:29	1931 Capek r:0.599 p:0.000 df:29
p _ diashaft far / lower forearm w	32	0.298	0.471	0.646	0.762	0.930	1.549	1.923	1.347	242648 Fribourg r:-0.473 p:0.010 df:27	9026 Denevi r:0.775 p:0.000 df:27	343 Ostara r:0.623 p:0.000 df:27
p _ diashaft far / p _ diahead	41	0.842	0.859	0.918	1.010	1.097	1.240	1.560	1.241	14047 Kohichiro r:-0.408 p:0.010 df:37	197856 Tafelmusik r:0.656 p:0.000 df:37	950 Ahrensa r:-0.573 p:0.000 df:37
p _ diashaft far / p _ headonly l	40	0.877	0.899	0.999	1.084	1.265	1.841	2.122	1.372	6543 Senna r:-0.419 p:0.010 df:35	18809 Meileawertz r:0.676 p:0.000 df:35	246 Asporina r:0.560 p:0.000 df:35
p _ diashaft far / p _ shaftonly l	41	0.238	0.262	0.291	0.322	0.396	0.641	0.697	0.322	11897 Lemaire r:-0.413 p:0.010 df:36	16124 Timdong r:0.650 p:0.000 df:36	1579 Herrick r:0.553 p:0.000 df:36
p _ diashaft far / upper forearm w	30	0.276	0.294	0.448	0.514	0.640	1.293	1.364	0.637	85014 Sutter r:-0.479 p:0.010 df:26	13992 Cesarebarbieri r:0.650 p:0.000 df:26	-10001 Moon r:-0.636 p:0.000 df:26
p _ diashaft far / upper thigh width	39	0.138	0.209	0.233	0.273	0.333	0.558	0.646	0.340	-10007 Uranus r:-0.425 p:0.010 df:34	2060 Chiron r:0.658 p:0.000 df:34	2060 Chiron r:0.658 p:0.000 df:34
p _ headonly l / lower forearm w	30	0.287	0.354	0.533	0.650	0.848	1.140	1.185	0.982	1311 Knopfia r:-0.479 p:0.010 df:26	9026 Denevi r:0.780 p:0.000 df:26	182 Elsa r:-0.655 p:0.000 df:26
p _ headonly l / p _ diahead	40	0.565	0.596	0.801	0.912	1.001	1.134	1.267	0.904	26707 Navrazhnykh r:-0.574 p:0.010 df:36	163244 Matthewhill r:0.574 p:0.000 df:36	627 Charis r:-0.610 p:0.000 df:36
p _ headonly l / p _ shaftonly l	40	0.152	0.167	0.251	0.296	0.352	0.551	0.628	0.234	12978 Ivashov r:-0.419 p:0.010 df:35	10427 Klinkenberg r:0.624 p:0.000 df:35	530 Turandot r:0.579 p:0.000 df:35
p _ headonly l / upper thigh width	36	0.120	0.126	0.218	0.251	0.282	0.408	0.412	0.248	8801 Nugent r:-0.436 p:0.010 df:32	117439 Rosner r:0.620 p:0.000 df:32	310 Margarita r:-0.627 p:0.000 df:32
p _ shaftonly l / lower forearm w	30	0.457	0.807	1.758	2.387	2.971	4.785	5.515	4.189	7572 Znokai r:-0.480 p:0.010 df:26	9026 Denevi r:0.780 p:0.000 df:26	154 Bertha r:0.618 p:0.000 df:26
p _ shaftonly l / p _ diahead	40	1.316	1.426	2.591	3.013	3.514	4.229	5.141	3.858	15094 Polymele r:-0.413 p:0.010 df:36	22120 Gaylefarrar r:0.629 p:0.000 df:36	1579 Herrick r:-0.584 p:0.000 df:36
p _ shaftonly l / upper thigh width	36	0.211	0.309	0.717	0.891	0.974	1.547	1.600	1.057	5386 Bajaja r:-0.436 p:0.010 df:32	14827 Hypnos r:0.640 p:0.000 df:32	5053 Chladni r:0.571 p:0.000 df:32
pelvic hips / ab width	15	1.478	1.478	1.602	1.735	1.902	2.029	2.029		11695 Mattei r:-0.643 p:0.010 df:13	86196 Specula r:0.852 p:0.000 df:13	8994 Kashkashian r:-0.821 p:0.000 df:13
pelvic hips / clavicle to neck h	12	2.362	2.362	2.933	3.476	5.098	6.086	6.086		14143 Hadfield r:-0.709 p:0.010 df:10	25227 Genehill r:0.936 p:0.000 df:10	1736 Floirac r:0.888 p:0.000 df:10
pelvic hips / long finger length	8	1.093	1.093	1.269	1.400	1.538	1.928	1.928	1.408	-10000 Sun r:-0.834 p:0.010 df:6	5102 Benfranklin r:0.986 p:0.000 df:6	2231 Durrell r:-0.946 p:0.000 df:6
pelvic hips / neck width	13	1.902	1.902	2.155	2.512	2.795	3.199	3.199	2.676	4519 Voronezh r:-0.684 p:0.010 df:11	25905 Clerico r:0.861 p:0.000 df:11	864 Aase r:0.833 p:0.000 df:11

Measure	n											
pelvic hips / shoulder width	16	0.617	0.617	0.716	0.782	0.832	1.033	1.033	0.714	172985 Ericmelin r:-0.623 p:0.010 df:14	24027 Downs r:0.825 p:0.000 df:14	4509 Gorbatskij r:-0.787 p:0.000 df:14
pelvic hips / subneck dorsal	11	1.075	1.075	1.277	1.356	1.516	1.812	1.812		2219 Mannucci r:-0.738 p:0.009 df:9	10832 Hazamashigetomi r:0.933 p:0.000 df:9	192 Nausikaa r:-0.880 p:0.000 df:9
pelvic hips<->waist / neck width<->shoulder width	12	0.598	0.598	0.941	0.996	1.456	3.300	3.300	1.314	23436 Alekfursenko r:-0.709 p:0.010 df:10	1506 Xosa r:0.927 p:0.000 df:10	661 Cloelia r:0.850 p:0.000 df:10
pelvic hips<->waist / neck width<->subneck dorsal	10	1.489	1.489	2.330	2.724	4.820	7.373	7.373		11757 Salpeter r:-0.765 p:0.010 df:8	6110 Kazak r:0.943 p:0.000 df:8	156 Xanthippe r:-0.897 p:0.000 df:8
pelvic hips<->waist / neck width<->underbust	8	0.290	0.290	0.332	0.405	0.500	0.717	0.717	0.510	100231 Monceau r:-0.835 p:0.010 df:6	33 Polyhymnia r:0.967 p:0.000 df:6	33 Polyhymnia r:0.967 p:0.000 df:6
pelvic hips<->waist / shoulder width<->subneck dorsal	11	0.680	0.680	1.303	1.451	1.646	2.978	2.978		16706 Svojsik r:-0.736 p:0.010 df:9	139028 Haynald r:0.931 p:0.000 df:9	1000 Piazzia r:0.875 p:0.000 df:9
pelvic hips<->waist / shoulder width<->waist	16	0.257	0.257	0.307	0.376	0.486	0.582	0.582	0.582	7373 Stashis r:-0.623 p:0.010 df:14	21854 Brendandwyer r:0.901 p:0.000 df:14	414 Liriope r:0.791 p:0.000 df:14
shoulder to elbow h / ab width	22	0.712	0.781	1.538	1.757	2.089	2.539	2.589		7119 Hiera r:-0.550 p:0.010 df:19	9238 Yavapai r:0.750 p:0.000 df:19	2934 Aristophanes r:-0.694 p:0.000 df:19
shoulder to elbow h / ankle to heel floor h	7	2.866	2.866	2.927	3.942	5.344	5.571	5.571		657 Gunlod r:-0.875 p:0.010 df:5	4618 Shakhovskoj r:0.966 p:0.000 df:5	3464 Owensby r:-0.970 p:0.000 df:5
shoulder to elbow h / ankle width	8	1.263	1.263	2.376	3.459	4.665	5.195	5.195		966 Muschi r:-0.835 p:0.010 df:6	15567 Giacomelli r:0.964 p:0.000 df:6	4130 Ramanujan r:0.955 p:0.000 df:6
shoulder to elbow h / back perimeter	8	0.067	0.067	0.102	0.142	0.216	0.258	0.258	0.131	28688 Diannerister r:-0.835 p:0.010 df:6	2298 Cindijon r:0.971 p:0.000 df:6	173 Ino r:0.952 p:0.000 df:6
shoulder to elbow h / back tone	8	0.272	0.272	0.323	0.648	0.887	1.379	1.379	0.272	8072 Yojikondo r:-0.835 p:0.010 df:6	4864 Nimoy r:0.987 p:0.000 df:6	194 Prokne r:0.946 p:0.000 df:6
shoulder to elbow h / butt square	9	0.315	0.315	0.339	0.434	0.557	0.571	0.571	0.555	301511 Hubinon r:-0.798 p:0.010 df:7	12734 Haruna r:0.986 p:0.000 df:7	138 Tolosa r:-0.920 p:0.000 df:7
shoulder to elbow h / calf width	13	1.730	1.730	1.902	2.573	2.856	3.302	3.302		1564 Srbija r:-0.684 p:0.010 df:11	229777 ENIAC r:0.879 p:0.000 df:11	1054 Forsytia r:-0.835 p:0.000 df:11
shoulder to elbow h / chest perimeter	28	0.072	0.079	0.127	0.169	0.203	0.353	0.416	0.153	26545 Meganperkins r:-0.487 p:0.010 df:25	178 Belisana r:0.727 p:0.000 df:25	178 Belisana r:0.727 p:0.000 df:25
shoulder to elbow h / chest tone	29	0.189	0.248	0.522	0.807	1.326	3.848	4.202	0.819	258 Tyche r:-0.480 p:0.010 df:26	9536 Statler r:0.732 p:0.000 df:26	1390 Abastumani r:0.677 p:0.000 df:26
shoulder to elbow h / chest width	20	0.781	0.781	0.909	0.996	1.226	1.611	1.613	0.920	4182 Mount Locke r:-0.576 p:0.010 df:17	11927 Mount Kent r:0.812 p:0.000 df:17	381 Myrrha r:-0.735 p:0.000 df:17
shoulder to elbow h / clavicle to groin h	26	0.416	0.421	0.499	0.550	0.584	0.760	0.815	0.560	8458 Georgekoenig r:-0.506 p:0.010 df:23	17103 Kadyrsizova r:0.712 p:0.000 df:23	2384 Schulhof r:0.662 p:0.000 df:23
shoulder to elbow h / clavicle to neck h	18	1.876	1.876	2.747	3.320	4.835	5.225	5.225		7707 Yes r:-0.590 p:0.010 df:16	133743 Robertwoodward r:0.766 p:0.000 df:16	3262 Miune r:0.752 p:0.000 df:16
shoulder to elbow h / elbow to wrist h	32	0.764	0.766	1.028	1.110	1.212	1.369	1.433	1.099	3041 Webb r:-0.463 p:0.010 df:28	3880 Kaiserman r:0.687 p:0.000 df:28	3880 Kaiserman r:0.687 p:0.000 df:28
shoulder to elbow h / long finger length	13	1.079	1.079	1.276	1.391	1.495	1.868	1.868	1.506	2137 Priscilla r:-0.712 p:0.009 df:10	13499 Steinberg r:0.902 p:0.000 df:10	1408 Trusanda r:0.894 p:0.000 df:10
shoulder to elbow h / lower forearm w	35	2.219	2.560	4.021	4.528	4.944	6.307	7.565	7.565	3734 Waland r:-0.442 p:0.010 df:31	11087 Yamasakimakoto r:0.624 p:0.000 df:31	1621 Druzhba r:0.584 p:0.000 df:31
shoulder to elbow h / lower leg h	9	0.606	0.606	0.632	0.707	0.912	0.928	0.928		7671 Albis r:-0.799 p:0.010 df:7	1254 Erfordia r:0.959 p:0.000 df:7	341 California r:0.941 p:0.000 df:7
shoulder to elbow h / neck width	20	1.334	1.355	2.102	2.365	2.643	3.731	3.772	2.863	247 Eukrate r:-0.562 p:0.010 df:18	10674 de Elia r:0.812 p:0.000 df:18	353 Ruperto-Carola r:0.739 p:0.000 df:18
shoulder to elbow h / pelvic hips	20	0.438	0.452	0.829	0.967	1.097	1.270	1.271	1.070	24280 Rohenderson r:-0.561 p:0.010 df:18	26532 Eduardoboff r:0.777 p:0.000 df:18	406 Erna r:-0.745 p:0.000 df:18
shoulder to elbow h / shoulder width	30	0.416	0.490	0.706	0.760	0.897	1.155	1.176	0.764	713 Luscinia r:-0.471 p:0.010 df:27	10039 Keet Seel r:0.767 p:0.000 df:27	911 Agamemnon r:0.620 p:0.000 df:27
shoulder to elbow h / subneck dorsal	15	0.737	0.737	1.200	1.482	1.724	2.865	2.865		2793 Valdaj r:-0.643 p:0.010 df:13	3361 Orpheus r:0.864 p:0.000 df:13	1300 Marcelle r:0.829 p:0.000 df:13
shoulder to elbow h / suprailiac	22	0.418	0.451	0.810	1.017	1.092	1.220	1.220	1.081	3299 Hall r:-0.538 p:0.010 df:20	14134 Penkala r:0.716 p:0.000 df:20	406 Erna r:-0.716 p:0.000 df:20
shoulder to elbow h / underbust	21	0.722	0.725	0.952	1.103	1.222	1.834	1.839	1.103	11707 Grigery r:-0.549 p:0.010 df:19	8240 Matisse r:0.779 p:0.000 df:19	2925 Beatty r:-0.754 p:0.000 df:19
shoulder to elbow h / upper forearm w	35	1.959	2.035	2.663	2.919	3.484	3.968	4.362	3.577	9812 Danco r:-0.442 p:0.010 df:31	188446 Louischevrolet r:0.661 p:0.000 df:31	2513 Baetsle r:0.577 p:0.000 df:31
shoulder to elbow h / waist	30	0.456	0.567	0.957	1.122	1.227	1.489	1.520	1.164	8190 Bouguer r:-0.463 p:0.010 df:28	22929 Seanwahl r:0.722 p:0.000 df:28	406 Erna r:-0.616 p:0.000 df:28
shoulder width / ab width	23	1.617	1.663	2.055	2.275	2.630	3.980	4.230		129149 Richwitherspoon r:-0.537 p:0.010 df:20	3882 Johncox r:0.783 p:0.000 df:20	223 Rosa r:0.695 p:0.000 df:20
shoulder width / ankle width	9	2.297	2.297	2.730	4.222	5.320	6.197	6.197		3741 Rogerburns r:-0.798 p:0.010 df:7	49700 Mather r:0.959 p:0.000 df:7	4057 Demophon r:0.941 p:0.000 df:7

Ratio	n											
shoulder width / back perimeter	7	0.099	0.099	0.109	0.171	0.205	0.403	0.403	0.171	2090 Mizuho r:-0.875 p:0.010 df:5	18983 Allentran r:0.991 p:0.000 df:5	4043 Perolof r:0.978 p:0.000 df:5
shoulder width / back tone	7	0.329	0.329	0.356	0.739	1.002	2.028	2.028	0.356	6531 Subashiri r:-0.875 p:0.010 df:5	1643 Brown r:0.984 p:0.000 df:5	194 Prokne r:0.964 p:0.000 df:5
shoulder width / calf width	12	1.855	1.855	2.226	2.954	3.460	3.982	3.982		2872 Gentelec r:-0.709 p:0.010 df:10	22485 Unterman r:0.900 p:0.000 df:10	14994 Uppenkamp r:-0.866 p:0.000 df:10
shoulder width / clavicle to neck h	17	2.560	2.560	3.533	4.342	6.571	7.923	7.923		7308 Hattori r:-0.606 p:0.010 df:15	3802 Dornburg r:0.847 p:0.000 df:15	347 Pariana r:0.753 p:0.000 df:15
shoulder width / foot base h	7	0.996	0.996	1.164	1.678	1.808	1.818	1.818		2194 Arpola r:-0.875 p:0.010 df:5	130 Elektra r:0.962 p:0.001 df:5	2852 Declercq r:-0.972 p:0.000 df:5
shoulder width / lower leg h	8	0.541	0.541	0.615	0.865	1.101	1.229	1.229		15375 Laetitiafoglia r:-0.835 p:0.010 df:6	30840 Jackalice r:0.989 p:0.000 df:6	438 Zeuxo r:-0.971 p:0.000 df:6
shoulder width / neck width	20	2.730	2.732	2.952	3.144	3.338	3.731	3.746	3.746	8110 Heath r:-0.562 p:0.010 df:18	2892 Filipenko r:0.757 p:0.000 df:18	1644 Rafita r:-0.749 p:0.000 df:18
shoulder width / subneck dorsal	16	1.533	1.533	1.670	1.868	2.097	2.609	2.609		3092 Herodotus r:-0.623 p:0.010 df:14	3361 Orpheus r:0.848 p:0.000 df:14	2552 Remek r:-0.775 p:0.000 df:14
shoulder width<->subneck dorsal / neck width<->underbust	9	0.177	0.177	0.203	0.221	0.281	0.318	0.318		7898 Ohkuma r:-0.800 p:0.010 df:7	20399 Michaelesser r:0.980 p:0.000 df:7	70 Panopaea r:0.953 p:0.000 df:7
shoulder width<->waist / neck width<->shoulder width	18	1.990	1.990	2.251	2.976	3.587	6.603	6.603	2.259	566 Stereoskopia r:-0.591 p:0.010 df:16	5812 Jayewinkler r:0.852 p:0.000 df:16	661 Cloelia r:0.799 p:0.000 df:16
shoulder width<->waist / neck width<->subneck dorsal	13	4.888	4.888	6.162	8.018	9.938	22.019	22.019		398045 Vitudurum r:-0.684 p:0.010 df:11	1795 Woltjer r:0.915 p:0.000 df:11	90 Antiope r:0.877 p:0.000 df:11
shoulder width<->waist / neck width<->underbust	12	0.667	0.667	0.922	1.105	1.245	1.332	1.332	0.877	7885 Levine r:-0.708 p:0.010 df:10	4443 Paulet r:0.903 p:0.000 df:10	129 Antigone r:-0.853 p:0.000 df:10
shoulder width<->waist / shoulder width<->subneck dorsal	15	2.473	2.473	2.989	4.075	5.344	7.134	7.134		4275 Bogustafson r:-0.641 p:0.010 df:13	713 Luscinia r:0.911 p:0.000 df:13	594 Mireille r:0.808 p:0.000 df:13
subneck dorsal / ab width	13	0.787	0.787	1.077	1.246	1.453	2.390	2.390		35356 Vondrak r:-0.684 p:0.010 df:11	3882 Johncox r:0.952 p:0.000 df:11	396 Aeolia r:-0.853 p:0.000 df:11
subneck dorsal / calf width	7	1.041	1.041	1.074	1.810	1.911	2.144	2.144		2068 Dangreen r:-0.875 p:0.010 df:5	711 Marmulla r:0.980 p:0.000 df:5	711 Marmulla r:0.980 p:0.000 df:5
subneck dorsal / clavicle to neck h	15	1.664	1.664	1.902	2.555	3.152	5.169	5.169		18707 Annchi r:-0.642 p:0.010 df:13	308798 Teo r:0.878 p:0.000 df:13	2105 Gudy r:0.801 p:0.000 df:13
suprailiac / ab width	18	1.448	1.448	1.601	1.725	1.872	2.473	2.473		33875 Laurencooney r:-0.591 p:0.010 df:16	19386 Axelcronstedt r:0.780 p:0.000 df:16	5241 Beeson r:-0.792 p:0.000 df:16
suprailiac / butt square	7	0.372	0.372	0.413	0.445	0.482	0.513	0.513	0.513	1016 Anitra r:-0.876 p:0.010 df:5	17273 Karnik r:0.982 p:0.000 df:5	641 Agnes r:-0.974 p:0.000 df:5
suprailiac / calf width	7	1.920	1.920	2.307	2.462	2.969	3.175	3.175		26400 Roshanpalli r:-0.875 p:0.010 df:5	19185 Guarneri r:0.991 p:0.000 df:5	572 Rebekka r:0.979 p:0.000 df:5
suprailiac / chest width	15	0.701	0.701	0.839	0.932	1.122	1.371	1.371	0.852	2534 Houzeau r:-0.641 p:0.010 df:13	7766 Jododaira r:0.838 p:0.000 df:13	1276 Ucclia r:-0.815 p:0.000 df:13
suprailiac / clavicle to neck h	14	2.116	2.116	2.748	3.577	4.966	7.418	7.418		29356 Giovarduino r:-0.663 p:0.010 df:12	5775 Inuyama r:0.884 p:0.000 df:12	1778 Alfven r:0.847 p:0.000 df:12
suprailiac / long finger length	8	1.115	1.115	1.185	1.396	1.636	1.962	1.962	1.393	12359 Cajigal r:-0.834 p:0.010 df:6	32052 Diyamathur r:0.958 p:0.000 df:6	3834 Zappafrank r:-0.947 p:0.000 df:6
suprailiac / neck width	14	1.987	1.987	2.260	2.509	2.699	3.501	3.501	2.649	26656 Samarenae r:-0.662 p:0.010 df:12	21440 Elizacollins r:0.870 p:0.000 df:12	33 Polyhymnia r:0.817 p:0.000 df:12
suprailiac / pelvic hips	20	0.894	0.894	0.925	1.017	1.039	1.216	1.219	0.990	20103 de Vico r:-0.562 p:0.010 df:18	4565 Grossman r:0.802 p:0.000 df:18	4565 Grossman r:0.802 p:0.000 df:18
suprailiac / shoulder width	20	0.627	0.628	0.696	0.758	0.857	1.039	1.042	0.707	146442 Dwaynebrown r:-0.564 p:0.010 df:18	279119 Khamatova r:0.769 p:0.000 df:18	3518 Florena r:-0.750 p:0.000 df:18
suprailiac / subneck dorsal	11	1.100	1.100	1.242	1.430	1.553	2.208	2.208		10189 Normanrockwell r:-0.739 p:0.009 df:9	11828 Vargha r:0.912 p:0.000 df:9	2142 Landau r:0.884 p:0.000 df:9
suprailiac / underbust	16	0.849	0.849	0.929	0.994	1.149	1.826	1.826	1.021	1496 Turku r:-0.624 p:0.010 df:14	6527 Takashiito r:0.841 p:0.000 df:14	363 Padua r:0.797 p:0.000 df:14
suprailiac<->waist / chest width<->underbust	12	0.525	0.525	0.589	0.738	1.126	2.416	2.416	0.619	21149 Kenmitchell r:-0.709 p:0.010 df:10	12383 Eboshi r:0.919 p:0.000 df:10	107 Camilla r:0.860 p:0.000 df:10
suprailiac<->waist / neck width<->shoulder width	13	0.336	0.336	0.526	0.602	0.893	1.567	1.567	0.602	2706 Borovsky r:-0.690 p:0.009 df:11	11571 Daens r:0.866 p:0.000 df:11	1726 Hoffmeister r:0.848 p:0.000 df:11
suprailiac<->waist / neck width<->subneck dorsal	10	0.670	0.670	1.256	1.710	2.891	4.305	4.305		2274 Ehrsson r:-0.765 p:0.010 df:8	3201 Sijthoff r:0.968 p:0.000 df:8	156 Xanthippe r:-0.905 p:0.000 df:8
suprailiac<->waist / neck width<->underbust	9	0.148	0.148	0.183	0.234	0.276	0.444	0.444	0.234	61342 Lovejoy r:-0.798 p:0.010 df:7	62503 Tomcave r:0.934 p:0.000 df:7	33 Polyhymnia r:0.920 p:0.000 df:7
suprailiac<->waist / pelvic hips<->waist	20	0.265	0.268	0.475	0.577	0.617	0.827	0.835	0.458	9702 Tomvandijk r:-0.562 p:0.010 df:18	8418 Mogamigawa r:0.751 p:0.000 df:18	591 Irmgard r:0.738 p:0.000 df:18

	n											
suprailiac<->waist / shoulder width<->subneck dorsal	11	0.409	0.409	0.672	0.887	1.271	1.843	1.843		9373 Hamra r:-0.735 p:0.010 df:9	139028 Haynald r:0.919 p:0.000 df:9	235 Carolina r:-0.905 p:0.000 df:9
suprailiac<->waist / shoulder width<->waist	20	0.092	0.094	0.159	0.219	0.301	0.343	0.345	0.267	29681 Saramanshad r:-0.563 p:0.010 df:18	186 Celuta r:0.767 p:0.000 df:18	186 Celuta r:0.767 p:0.000 df:18
suprailiac<->waist / underbust<->waist	16	0.278	0.278	0.412	0.534	0.796	0.972	0.972	0.880	117086 Loczy r:-0.624 p:0.010 df:14	185636 Shiao Lin r:0.790 p:0.000 df:14	2247 Hiroshima r:-0.819 p:0.000 df:14
thigh h / ab perimeter	21	0.097	0.102	0.214	0.321	0.474	0.876	0.889	0.516	7079 Baghdad r:-0.551 p:0.010 df:19	6830 Johnbackus r:0.736 p:0.000 df:19	6830 Johnbackus r:0.736 p:0.000 df:19
thigh h / ab tone	21	0.174	0.208	0.733	1.222	1.837	5.022	5.237	0.732	18177 Harunaga r:-0.549 p:0.010 df:19	2801 Huygens r:0.794 p:0.000 df:19	457 Alleghenia r:0.728 p:0.000 df:19
thigh h / ab width	14	1.917	1.917	2.526	3.085	3.460	3.820	3.820		16121 Burrell r:-0.663 p:0.010 df:12	21921 Camdenmiller r:0.875 p:0.000 df:12	1157 Arabia r:0.854 p:0.000 df:12
thigh h / ankle to heel floor h	8	4.404	4.404	5.238	5.937	6.437	8.272	8.272		28184 Vaishnavirao r:-0.835 p:0.010 df:6	10388 Zhuguangya r:0.949 p:0.000 df:6	6947 Andrewdavis r:-0.952 p:0.000 df:6
thigh h / ankle width	9	3.036	3.036	5.107	5.694	6.753	7.788	7.788		18644 Arashiyama r:-0.799 p:0.010 df:7	3787 Aivazovskij r:0.941 p:0.000 df:7	2155 Wodan r:-0.979 p:0.000 df:7
thigh h / back perimeter	7	0.144	0.144	0.156	0.258	0.328	0.458	0.458	0.192	20582 Reichenbach r:-0.875 p:0.010 df:5	12509 Pathak r:0.995 p:0.000 df:5	6436 Coco r:-0.968 p:0.000 df:5
thigh h / back tone	7	0.399	0.399	0.439	1.015	1.189	1.539	1.539	0.399	6520 Sugawa r:-0.875 p:0.010 df:5	1890 Konoshenkova r:0.990 p:0.000 df:5	1890 Konoshenkova r:0.990 p:0.000 df:5
thigh h / bicep width	23	3.062	3.074	3.851	4.864	6.235	8.042	8.314	6.753	341 California r:-0.537 p:0.010 df:20	1445 Konkolya r:0.770 p:0.000 df:20	1445 Konkolya r:0.770 p:0.000 df:20
thigh h / calf width	15	2.558	2.558	3.448	3.741	4.243	4.705	4.705		16909 Miladejager r:-0.641 p:0.010 df:13	25115 Drago r:0.834 p:0.000 df:13	374 Burgundia r:-0.889 p:0.000 df:13
thigh h / chest width	13	1.328	1.328	1.436	1.677	1.854	2.797	2.797	1.349	4605 Nikitin r:-0.685 p:0.010 df:11	2429 Schurer r:0.883 p:0.000 df:11	1134 Kepler r:0.857 p:0.000 df:11
thigh h / clavicle to groin h	18	0.582	0.582	0.770	0.855	0.969	1.418	1.418	0.821	3419 Guth r:-0.590 p:0.010 df:16	20896 Tiphene r:0.838 p:0.000 df:16	945 Barcelona r:0.765 p:0.000 df:16
thigh h / clavicle to neck h	12	2.112	2.112	4.163	5.371	7.564	8.874	8.874		3097 Tacitus r:-0.708 p:0.010 df:10	217420 Olevsk r:0.899 p:0.000 df:10	634 Ute r:0.896 p:0.000 df:10
thigh h / elbow to wrist h	21	0.859	0.880	1.604	1.708	1.905	2.214	2.223	1.611	68448 Sidneywolff r:-0.562 p:0.010 df:18	84994 Amysimon r:0.759 p:0.000 df:18	1993 Guacolda r:0.721 p:0.000 df:18
thigh h / long finger length	10	1.586	1.586	2.094	2.235	2.377	2.665	2.665	2.208	86 Semele r:-0.765 p:0.010 df:8	7700 Rote Kapelle r:0.909 p:0.000 df:8	3188 Jekabsons r:-0.900 p:0.000 df:8
thigh h / lower forearm w	22	3.751	4.028	6.310	6.859	8.002	10.803	11.094	11.094	5406 Jonjoseph r:-0.549 p:0.010 df:19	21282 Shimizuyuka r:0.795 p:0.000 df:19	1101 Clematis r:0.774 p:0.000 df:19
thigh h / lower leg h	11	0.949	0.949	1.049	1.120	1.227	1.378	1.378		1475 Yalta r:-0.735 p:0.010 df:9	143 Adria r:0.907 p:0.000 df:9	143 Adria r:0.907 p:0.000 df:9
thigh h / neck width	13	1.452	1.452	3.109	4.198	4.642	5.811	5.811	4.198	973 Aralia r:-0.684 p:0.010 df:11	210231 Wangdemin r:0.893 p:0.000 df:11	2480 Papanov r:-0.855 p:0.000 df:11
thigh h / pelvic hips	10	1.259	1.259	1.288	1.564	1.851	2.078	2.078	1.569	18413 Adamspencer r:-0.766 p:0.010 df:8	635 Vundtia r:0.933 p:0.000 df:8	504 Cora r:-0.902 p:0.000 df:8
thigh h / shoulder to elbow h	23	1.088	1.113	1.418	1.540	1.761	1.894	1.916	1.466	5048 Moriarty r:-0.538 p:0.010 df:20	3617 Eicher r:0.794 p:0.000 df:20	405 Thia r:0.690 p:0.000 df:20
thigh h / shoulder width	20	0.453	0.480	1.087	1.219	1.589	2.069	2.073	1.121	7295 Brozovic r:-0.562 p:0.010 df:18	10655 Pietkeyser r:0.792 p:0.000 df:18	1191 Alfaterna r:0.744 p:0.000 df:18
thigh h / subneck dorsal	10	0.802	0.802	1.659	2.379	2.878	4.196	4.196		3761 Romanskaya r:-0.765 p:0.010 df:8	120103 Dolero r:0.918 p:0.000 df:8	2031 BAM r:-0.913 p:0.000 df:8
thigh h / suprailiac	13	1.086	1.086	1.473	1.606	1.945	2.451	2.451	1.585	1449 Virtanen r:-0.684 p:0.010 df:11	845 Naema r:0.870 p:0.000 df:11	845 Naema r:0.870 p:0.000 df:11
thigh h / underbust	17	1.360	1.360	1.607	1.727	2.185	3.152	3.152	1.618	16059 Marybuda r:-0.606 p:0.010 df:15	16246 Cantor r:0.889 p:0.000 df:15	2588 Flavia r:-0.764 p:0.000 df:15
thigh h / upper forearm w	23	3.055	3.069	4.313	5.042	5.627	7.042	7.051	5.245	15303 Hatoyamamachi r:-0.537 p:0.010 df:20	76309 Ronferdie r:0.742 p:0.000 df:20	5141 Tachibana r:0.708 p:0.000 df:20
thigh h / waist	19	1.299	1.299	1.638	1.860	2.114	2.507	2.507	1.706	5381 Sekhmet r:-0.576 p:0.010 df:17	7373 Stashis r:0.814 p:0.000 df:17	178 Belisana r:0.792 p:0.000 df:17
underbust / ab width	17	1.082	1.082	1.450	1.680	1.827	2.161	2.161		28978 Ixion r:-0.606 p:0.010 df:15	3016 Meuse r:0.813 p:0.000 df:15	2689 Bruxelles r:0.782 p:0.000 df:15
underbust / ankle width	7	1.748	1.748	2.180	3.223	3.699	4.849	4.849		738 Alagasta r:-0.875 p:0.010 df:5	2415 Ganesa r:0.983 p:0.000 df:5	2415 Ganesa r:0.983 p:0.000 df:5
underbust / calf width	9	1.282	1.282	1.636	2.124	2.609	3.085	3.085		9564 Jeffwynn r:-0.798 p:0.010 df:7	6413 Iye r:0.961 p:0.000 df:7	238 Hypatia r:0.932 p:0.000 df:7
underbust / chest width	21	0.670	0.678	0.828	0.881	0.937	1.056	1.056	0.834	2880 Nihondaira r:-0.565 p:0.009 df:18	23329 Josevega r:0.731 p:0.000 df:18	2502 Nummela r:0.722 p:0.000 df:18
underbust / clavicle to neck h	15	1.529	1.529	2.684	3.116	5.039	6.006	6.006		6712 Hornstein r:-0.662 p:0.010 df:12	10227 Izanami r:0.867 p:0.000 df:12	466 Tisiphone r:-0.858 p:0.000 df:12
underbust / long finger length	9	0.949	0.949	1.069	1.242	1.451	1.832	1.832	1.365	3010 Ushakov r:-0.799 p:0.010 df:7	4661 Yebes r:0.953 p:0.000 df:7	481 Emita r:0.948 p:0.000 df:7
underbust / lower leg h	7	0.449	0.449	0.462	0.603	0.707	0.904	0.904		15034 Decines r:-0.875 p:0.010 df:5	20535 Marshburrows r:0.985 p:0.000 df:5	341 California r:0.969 p:0.000 df:5
underbust / neck width	14	1.382	1.382	2.040	2.388	2.484	2.686	2.686	2.595	6962 Summerscience r:-0.684 p:0.010 df:11	3627 Sayers r:0.941 p:0.000 df:11	53 Kalypso r:0.846 p:0.000 df:11

	N									Ref 1	Ref 2	Ref 3
underbust / pelvic hips	12	0.557	0.557	0.857	0.968	1.076	1.136	1.136	0.969	546 Herodias r:-0.708 p:0.010 df:10	12068 Khandrika r:0.930 p:0.000 df:10	324 Bamberga r:-0.849 p:0.000 df:10
underbust / shoulder width	25	0.454	0.481	0.660	0.752	0.786	0.923	0.929	0.693	7651 Villeneuve r:-0.505 p:0.010 df:23	1003 Lilofee r:0.747 p:0.000 df:23	1003 Lilofee r:0.747 p:0.000 df:23
underbust / subchest width	9	0.764	0.764	0.804	0.985	1.009	1.038	1.038	0.921	246164 Zdvyzhensk r:-0.834 p:0.010 df:6	145488 Kaczendre r:0.981 p:0.000 df:6	6149 Pelcak r:0.948 p:0.000 df:6
underbust / subneck dorsal	12	0.806	0.806	1.188	1.442	1.585	2.040	2.040		31494 Emmafreedman r:-0.708 p:0.010 df:10	65489 Ceto r:0.911 p:0.000 df:10	1784 Benguella r:-0.856 p:0.000 df:10
underbust<->waist / chest width<->underbust	19	0.704	0.704	0.983	1.387	1.690	3.562	3.562	0.704	271 Penthesilea r:-0.594 p:0.009 df:16	6351 Neumann r:0.781 p:0.000 df:16	402 Chloe r:0.736 p:0.000 df:16
underbust<->waist / neck width<->shoulder width	12	0.684	0.684	0.926	1.269	1.585	1.779	1.779	0.684	30036 Eshamaiti r:-0.708 p:0.000 df:10	33201 Thomasartiss r:0.867 p:0.000 df:10	6426 Vanysek r:0.863 p:0.000 df:10
underbust<->waist / neck width<->subneck dorsal	9	2.369	2.369	2.661	3.595	5.011	7.307	7.307		25676 Jesseellison r:-0.798 p:0.010 df:7	18184 Dianepark r:0.960 p:0.000 df:7	5939 Toshimayeda r:-0.936 p:0.000 df:7
underbust<->waist / neck width<->underbust	11	0.266	0.266	0.344	0.504	0.592	0.655	0.655	0.266	78115 Skiantonucci r:-0.735 p:0.010 df:9	21544 Hermainkhan r:0.960 p:0.000 df:9	4103 Chahine r:-0.887 p:0.000 df:9
underbust<->waist / pelvic hips<->waist	12	0.521	0.521	0.878	1.060	1.436	1.713	1.713	0.521	19159 Taenakano r:-0.708 p:0.000 df:10	23773 Sarugaku r:0.903 p:0.000 df:10	75 Eurydike r:-0.852 p:0.000 df:10
underbust<->waist / shoulder width<->subneck dorsal	11	1.121	1.121	1.292	1.721	2.375	3.518	3.518		7871 Tunder r:-0.737 p:0.010 df:9	12729 Berger r:0.936 p:0.000 df:9	299 Thora r:0.903 p:0.000 df:9
underbust<->waist / shoulder width<->waist	22	0.278	0.282	0.351	0.393	0.453	0.518	0.520	0.303	866 Fatme r:-0.538 p:0.010 df:20	128389 Dougleland r:0.712 p:0.000 df:20	25604 Karlin r:-0.700 p:0.000 df:20
upper forearm w / ab width	24	0.347	0.361	0.479	0.535	0.645	1.079	1.115		2376 Martynov r:-0.527 p:0.010 df:21	34130 Isabellaivy r:0.778 p:0.000 df:21	109 Felicitas r:0.670 p:0.000 df:21
upper forearm w / ankle to heel floor h	7	0.851	0.851	0.880	1.531	1.817	2.012	2.012		5287 Heishu r:-0.875 p:0.010 df:5	8098 Miyamotoatsushi r:0.993 p:0.000 df:5	902 Probitas r:-0.978 p:0.000 df:5
upper forearm w / ankle width	9	0.436	0.436	0.673	1.012	1.460	1.880	1.880		12169 Munsterman r:-0.799 p:0.010 df:7	27349 Enos r:0.966 p:0.000 df:7	2264 Sabrina r:0.958 p:0.000 df:7
upper forearm w / back perimeter	7	0.025	0.025	0.028	0.043	0.062	0.095	0.095	0.037	165347 Philplait r:-0.875 p:0.010 df:5	9514 Deineka r:0.977 p:0.000 df:5	4043 Perolof r:0.968 p:0.000 df:5
upper forearm w / back tone	7	0.076	0.076	0.089	0.233	0.257	0.520	0.520	0.076	12089 Maichin r:-0.875 p:0.010 df:5	13934 Kannami r:0.986 p:0.000 df:5	194 Prokne r:0.985 p:0.000 df:5
upper forearm w / butt square	8	0.119	0.119	0.128	0.146	0.159	0.206	0.206	0.155	136557 Neleus r:-0.836 p:0.010 df:6	2813 Zappala r:0.976 p:0.000 df:6	1503 Kuopio r:0.961 p:0.000 df:6
upper forearm w / calf width	14	0.507	0.507	0.596	0.758	0.922	1.357	1.357		7108 Nefedov r:-0.662 p:0.010 df:12	23808 Joshuahammer r:0.847 p:0.000 df:12	2882 Tedesco r:0.819 p:0.000 df:12
upper forearm w / chest perimeter	29	0.027	0.029	0.042	0.053	0.070	0.120	0.139	0.043	2875 Lagerkvist r:-0.479 p:0.010 df:26	11278 Telesio r:0.736 p:0.000 df:26	1839 Ragazza r:0.627 p:0.000 df:26
upper forearm w / chest tone	30	0.106	0.121	0.206	0.268	0.424	1.473	1.701	0.229	8307 Peltan r:-0.471 p:0.010 df:27	1362 Griqua r:0.691 p:0.000 df:27	789 Lena r:0.663 p:0.000 df:27
upper forearm w / chest width	22	0.214	0.220	0.274	0.319	0.384	0.594	0.606	0.257	6270 Kabukuri r:-0.549 p:0.010 df:19	354659 Boileau r:0.796 p:0.000 df:19	2176 Donar r:0.708 p:0.000 df:19
upper forearm w / clavicle to groin h	26	0.128	0.134	0.166	0.173	0.202	0.268	0.276	0.157	2857 NOT r:-0.506 p:0.010 df:23	346261 Alexandrescu r:0.659 p:0.000 df:23	27309 Serenamccalla r:-0.647 p:0.000 df:23
upper forearm w / clavicle to neck h	17	0.693	0.693	0.996	1.125	1.442	1.643	1.643		3811 Karma r:-0.606 p:0.010 df:15	4798 Mercator r:0.811 p:0.000 df:15	4313 Bouchet r:0.804 p:0.000 df:15
upper forearm w / elbow to wrist h	34	0.236	0.271	0.317	0.350	0.425	0.536	0.635	0.307	11425 Wearydunlop r:-0.456 p:0.010 df:29	11238 Johanmaurits r:0.687 p:0.000 df:29	723 Hammonia r:0.641 p:0.000 df:29
upper forearm w / foot base h	7	0.189	0.189	0.296	0.395	0.463	0.654	0.654		964 Subamara r:-0.875 p:0.010 df:5	246913 Slocum r:0.994 p:0.000 df:5	2567 Elba r:-0.982 p:0.000 df:5
upper forearm w / long finger length	11	0.334	0.334	0.388	0.478	0.595	0.702	0.702	0.421	8470 Dudinskaya r:-0.765 p:0.010 df:8	25428 Lakhanpal r:0.916 p:0.000 df:8	4352 Kyoto r:0.902 p:0.000 df:8
upper forearm w / lower forearm w	38	0.744	0.887	1.344	1.509	1.655	2.151	2.822	2.115	3363 Bowen r:-0.430 p:0.010 df:33	35265 Takeosaitou r:0.635 p:0.000 df:33	322 Phaeo r:0.573 p:0.000 df:33
upper forearm w / lower leg h	10	0.153	0.153	0.180	0.232	0.314	0.332	0.332		5515 Naderi r:-0.766 p:0.010 df:8	18996 Torasan r:0.912 p:0.000 df:8	2625 Jack London r:-0.897 p:0.000 df:8
upper forearm w / neck width	19	0.541	0.541	0.701	0.768	0.858	1.241	1.241	0.800	5608 Olmos r:-0.576 p:0.010 df:17	400193 Castion r:0.828 p:0.000 df:17	3643 Tienchanglin r:0.760 p:0.000 df:17
upper forearm w / pelvic hips	19	0.213	0.213	0.277	0.305	0.350	0.586	0.586	0.299	63305 Bobkepple r:-0.575 p:0.010 df:17	249514 Donaldroyer r:0.837 p:0.000 df:17	1141 Bohmia r:0.766 p:0.000 df:17
upper forearm w / shoulder width	32	0.179	0.183	0.231	0.255	0.291	0.393	0.427	0.214	21686 Koschny r:-0.456 p:0.010 df:29	3161 Beadell r:0.694 p:0.000 df:29	2082 Galahad r:0.630 p:0.000 df:29
upper forearm w / subneck dorsal	14	0.328	0.328	0.412	0.488	0.559	0.822	0.822		192293 Dominikbrunner r:-0.662 p:0.010 df:12	5441 Andymurray r:0.891 p:0.000 df:12	1834 Palach r:0.807 p:0.000 df:12
upper forearm w / suprailiac	22	0.204	0.206	0.280	0.313	0.351	0.552	0.574	0.302	19004 Chirayath r:-0.539 p:0.010 df:20	16856 Banach r:0.743 p:0.000 df:20	542 Susanna r:0.682 p:0.000 df:20
upper forearm w / underbust	23	0.229	0.233	0.307	0.341	0.405	0.671	0.707	0.308	555 Norma r:-0.526 p:0.010 df:21	872 Holda r:0.791 p:0.000 df:21	559 Nanon r:-0.745 p:0.000 df:21

	n									Author 1	Author 2	Author 3
upper forearm w / waist	32	0.222	0.227	0.311	0.338	0.411	0.554	0.619	0.325	7294 Barbaraakey r:-0.449 p:0.010 df:30	35087 von Sydow r:0.670 p:0.000 df:30	4352 Kyoto r:0.581 p:0.000 df:30
upper thigh width / ab perimeter	36	0.049	0.064	0.088	0.118	0.164	0.265	0.294	0.184	43935 Danshechtman r:-0.430 p:0.010 df:33	6830 Johnbackus r:0.728 p:0.000 df:33	1195 Orangia r:-0.564 p:0.000 df:33
upper thigh width / ab tone	36	0.088	0.139	0.266	0.409	0.633	2.982	4.999	0.261	1177 Gonnessia r:-0.430 p:0.010 df:33	100268 Rosenthal r:0.683 p:0.000 df:33	215 Oenone r:0.569 p:0.000 df:33
upper thigh width / ab width	25	0.695	0.766	1.027	1.165	1.268	1.550	1.590		2470 Agematsu r:-0.515 p:0.010 df:22	11462 Hsingwenlin r:0.641 p:0.001 df:22	2101 Adonis r:-0.662 p:0.000 df:22
upper thigh width / ankle to heel floor h	8	1.661	1.661	2.161	2.247	2.950	3.375	3.375		7737 Sirrah r:-0.836 p:0.010 df:6	1402 Eri r:0.944 p:0.000 df:6	1148 Rarahu r:-0.973 p:0.000 df:6
upper thigh width / ankle width	9	1.461	1.461	1.693	2.352	2.583	2.818	2.818		26532 Eduardoboff r:-0.799 p:0.010 df:7	8977 Paludicola r:0.915 p:0.001 df:7	764 Gedania r:-0.932 p:0.000 df:7
upper thigh width / back perimeter	8	0.060	0.060	0.064	0.078	0.121	0.157	0.157	0.069	24413 Britneyschmidt r:-0.836 p:0.010 df:6	2918 Salazar r:0.971 p:0.000 df:6	2918 Salazar r:0.971 p:0.000 df:6
upper thigh width / back tone	8	0.142	0.142	0.196	0.381	0.500	1.239	1.239	0.142	48624 Sadayuki r:-0.834 p:0.010 df:6	11727 Sweet r:0.975 p:0.000 df:6	193 Ambrosia r:0.972 p:0.000 df:6
upper thigh width / bicep width	37	1.207	1.292	1.567	1.856	2.199	2.772	2.935	2.411	3952 Russellmark r:-0.430 p:0.010 df:33	23837 Matthewnanni r:0.628 p:0.000 df:33	1137 Raissa r:-0.564 p:0.000 df:33
upper thigh width / butt square	9	0.233	0.233	0.283	0.290	0.326	0.339	0.339	0.290	4315 Pronik r:-0.798 p:0.010 df:7	133432 Sarahnoble r:0.953 p:0.000 df:7	3992 Wagner r:-0.922 p:0.000 df:7
upper thigh width / calf width	15	1.066	1.066	1.380	1.492	1.583	1.920	1.920		9861 Jahreiss r:-0.641 p:0.010 df:13	25425 Chelsealynn r:0.848 p:0.000 df:13	6379 Vrba r:0.822 p:0.000 df:13
upper thigh width / chest perimeter	30	0.048	0.057	0.080	0.100	0.152	0.262	0.276	0.080	8168 Rogerbourke r:-0.472 p:0.010 df:27	4863 Yasutani r:0.625 p:0.000 df:27	2057 Rosemary r:0.606 p:0.000 df:27
upper thigh width / chest tone	31	0.105	0.136	0.370	0.486	0.908	2.436	3.411	0.429	4404 Enirac r:-0.465 p:0.010 df:28	21605 Reynoso r:0.734 p:0.000 df:28	215 Oenone r:0.650 p:0.000 df:28
upper thigh width / chest width	23	0.400	0.416	0.556	0.611	0.781	0.975	0.991	0.482	18119 Braude r:-0.549 p:0.010 df:19	30110 Lisabreton r:0.765 p:0.000 df:19	4464 Vulcano r:0.732 p:0.000 df:19
upper thigh width / clavicle to groin h	28	0.247	0.256	0.321	0.342	0.376	0.442	0.470	0.293	10304 Iwaki r:-0.488 p:0.010 df:25	7127 Stifter r:0.664 p:0.000 df:25	1031 Arctica r:-0.680 p:0.000 df:25
upper thigh width / clavicle to neck h	21	1.074	1.109	1.800	2.206	3.040	4.140	4.153		15735 Andakerkhoven r:-0.562 p:0.010 df:18	38976 Taeve r:0.838 p:0.000 df:18	-10001 Moon r:-0.723 p:0.000 df:18
upper thigh width / elbow to wrist h	34	0.437	0.461	0.622	0.688	0.809	1.045	1.157	0.575	234 Barbara r:-0.456 p:0.010 df:29	8030 Williamknight r:0.698 p:0.000 df:29	1203 Nanna r:0.599 p:0.000 df:29
upper thigh width / long finger length	13	0.698	0.698	0.787	0.899	1.051	1.261	1.261	0.788	5037 Habing r:-0.708 p:0.010 df:10	21050 Beck r:0.935 p:0.000 df:10	3679 Condruses r:0.848 p:0.000 df:10
upper thigh width / lower forearm w	40	1.805	2.102	2.575	2.835	3.329	4.068	4.335	3.961	8924 Iruma r:-0.424 p:0.010 df:34	16702 Buxner r:0.593 p:0.000 df:34	733 Mocia r:-0.572 p:0.000 df:34
upper thigh width / lower leg h	11	0.300	0.300	0.360	0.450	0.507	0.605	0.605		4648 Tirion r:-0.735 p:0.010 df:9	11449 Stephwerner r:0.941 p:0.000 df:9	411 Xanthe r:0.873 p:0.000 df:9
upper thigh width / lower thigh width	28	0.996	1.022	1.224	1.333	1.452	1.695	1.781	1.325	185636 Shiao Lin r:-0.496 p:0.010 df:24	329 Svea r:0.702 p:0.000 df:24	329 Svea r:0.702 p:0.000 df:24
upper thigh width / neck width	24	0.738	0.819	1.394	1.568	1.874	2.145	2.148	1.499	27384 Meaganbethel r:-0.526 p:0.010 df:21	210231 Wangdemin r:0.695 p:0.000 df:21	1578 Kirkwood r:0.669 p:0.000 df:21
upper thigh width / pelvic hips	20	0.428	0.434	0.598	0.646	0.675	0.757	0.757	0.560	1291 Phryne r:-0.562 p:0.010 df:18	27421 Nathanhan r:0.792 p:0.000 df:18	665 Sabine r:0.713 p:0.000 df:18
upper thigh width / shoulder to elbow h	37	0.447	0.461	0.583	0.639	0.733	0.938	0.976	0.524	5661 Hildebrand r:-0.430 p:0.010 df:33	8833 Acer r:0.615 p:0.000 df:33	1990 Pilcher r:0.612 p:0.000 df:33
upper thigh width / shoulder width	32	0.231	0.317	0.454	0.513	0.609	0.685	0.699	0.400	30785 Greeley r:-0.456 p:0.010 df:29	1451 Grano r:0.641 p:0.000 df:29	586 Thekla r:-0.604 p:0.000 df:29
upper thigh width / subchest width	8	0.494	0.494	0.548	0.727	0.872	0.913	0.913	0.532	2240 Tsai r:-0.875 p:0.010 df:5	23644 Yamaneko r:0.989 p:0.000 df:5	8889 Mockturtle r:-0.963 p:0.000 df:5
upper thigh width / subneck dorsal	15	0.408	0.408	0.817	0.952	1.169	1.325	1.325		21656 Knuth r:-0.642 p:0.010 df:13	30933 Grillparzer r:0.864 p:0.000 df:13	4399 Ashizuri r:-0.801 p:0.000 df:13
upper thigh width / suprailiac	24	0.408	0.442	0.631	0.660	0.696	0.867	0.906	0.566	33565 Samferguson r:-0.515 p:0.010 df:22	32897 Curtharris r:0.742 p:0.000 df:22	387 Aquitania r:-0.700 p:0.000 df:22
upper thigh width / thigh h	28	0.288	0.301	0.358	0.395	0.439	0.508	0.509	0.357	1375 Alfreda r:-0.488 p:0.010 df:25	3898 Curlewis r:0.686 p:0.000 df:25	435 Ella r:0.657 p:0.000 df:25
upper thigh width / underbust	24	0.578	0.578	0.612	0.691	0.812	1.139	1.176	0.578	4594 Dashkova r:-0.526 p:0.010 df:21	3851 Alhambra r:0.774 p:0.000 df:21	1431 Luanda r:0.709 p:0.000 df:21
upper thigh width / upper forearm w	39	1.145	1.475	1.663	1.983	2.300	2.725	2.883	1.872	9227 Ashida r:-0.424 p:0.010 df:34	28952 Ericepstein r:0.589 p:0.000 df:34	583 Klotilde r:0.553 p:0.000 df:34
upper thigh width / waist	34	0.446	0.528	0.667	0.715	0.795	0.963	0.972	0.609	3605 Davy r:-0.444 p:0.010 df:31	5041 Theotes r:0.635 p:0.000 df:31	799 Gudula r:-0.592 p:0.000 df:31
waist / ab width	22	1.386	1.389	1.516	1.560	1.707	2.321	2.392		21602 Ialmenus r:-0.538 p:0.010 df:20	24413 Britneyschmidt r:0.716 p:0.000 df:20	14967 Madrid r:0.689 p:0.000 df:20
waist / ankle width	7	2.150	2.150	2.281	3.039	4.242	4.325	4.325		6101 Tomoki r:-0.876 p:0.010 df:5	8977 Paludicola r:0.969 p:0.000 df:5	930 Westphalia r:-0.984 p:0.000 df:5
waist / back perimeter	7	0.075	0.075	0.086	0.112	0.142	0.175	0.175	0.112	5137 Frevert r:-0.875 p:0.010 df:5	27986 Hanus r:0.992 p:0.000 df:5	2516 Roman r:-0.974 p:0.000 df:5
waist / back tone	7	0.234	0.234	0.268	0.534	0.782	1.535	1.535	0.234	5035 Swift r:-0.875 p:0.010 df:5	1643 Brown r:0.986 p:0.000 df:5	193 Ambrosia r:0.966 p:0.000 df:5

measure	group	Count	Min	0.05-quantile	0.25-quantile	0.5-quantile	0.75-quantile	0.95-quantile	Max		lowest correlation	highest correlation	most significant p
waist / butt square		8	0.323	0.323	0.356	0.410	0.468	0.490	0.490	0.477	-10003 Venus r:-0.835 p:0.010 df:6	24712 Boltzmann r:0.974 p:0.000 df:6	3887 Gerstner r:-0.965 p:0.000 df:6
waist / calf width		11	1.611	1.611	1.724	2.118	2.341	2.822	2.822		16706 Svojsik r:-0.736 p:0.010 df:9	30840 Jackalice r:0.917 p:0.000 df:9	1005 Arago r:-0.870 p:0.000 df:9
waist / chest perimeter		29	0.080	0.081	0.118	0.157	0.190	0.294	0.303	0.132	6092 Johnmason r:-0.471 p:0.010 df:27	11510 Borges r:0.596 p:0.001 df:27	861 Aida r:-0.624 p:0.000 df:27
waist / chest tone		30	0.248	0.293	0.527	0.738	1.301	5.138	7.655	0.704	3209 Buchwald r:-0.463 p:0.010 df:28	1362 Griqua r:0.739 p:0.000 df:28	1213 Algeria r:0.607 p:0.000 df:28
waist / chest width		23	0.634	0.650	0.798	0.852	0.984	1.245	1.273	0.791	38250 Tartois r:-0.537 p:0.010 df:20	20140 Costitx r:0.740 p:0.000 df:20	830 Petropolitana r:0.681 p:0.000 df:20
waist / clavicle to neck h		18	2.038	2.038	2.721	3.387	4.627	7.177	7.177		2506 Pirogov r:-0.606 p:0.010 df:15	3262 Miune r:0.834 p:0.000 df:15	347 Pariana r:0.760 p:0.000 df:15
waist / long finger length		10	0.968	0.968	1.061	1.296	1.423	1.687	1.687	1.294	1019 Strackea r:-0.766 p:0.010 df:8	6137 Johnfletcher r:0.938 p:0.000 df:8	940 Kordula r:0.936 p:0.000 df:8
waist / lower leg h		7	0.426	0.426	0.470	0.548	0.827	0.929	0.929		1500 Jyvaskyla r:-0.875 p:0.010 df:5	11378 Dauria r:0.992 p:0.000 df:5	411 Xanthe r:0.973 p:0.000 df:5
waist / neck width		20	1.881	1.882	2.049	2.272	2.509	3.350	3.388	2.460	3391 Sinon r:-0.577 p:0.010 df:17	11709 Eudoxos r:0.791 p:0.000 df:17	5775 Inuyama r:0.754 p:0.000 df:17
waist / pelvic hips		20	0.758	0.759	0.857	0.933	0.994	1.173	1.179	0.919	3974 Verveer r:-0.564 p:0.010 df:18	28602 Westfall r:0.760 p:0.000 df:18	4601 Ludkewycz r:-0.734 p:0.000 df:18
waist / shoulder width		31	0.580	0.587	0.654	0.722	0.794	0.924	1.008	0.657	3115 Baily r:-0.458 p:0.010 df:29	85389 Rosenauer r:0.645 p:0.000 df:29	2530 Shipka r:0.622 p:0.000 df:29
waist / subchest width		9	0.783	0.783	0.845	0.917	1.045	1.076	1.076	0.873	16222 Donnanderson r:-0.835 p:0.010 df:6	10274 Larryevans r:0.949 p:0.000 df:6	1615 Bardwell r:-0.967 p:0.000 df:6
waist / subneck dorsal		15	1.087	1.087	1.152	1.353	1.538	2.136	2.136		68779 Schoninger r:-0.643 p:0.010 df:13	13132 Ortelius r:0.861 p:0.000 df:13	1359 Prieska r:0.787 p:0.000 df:13
waist / suprailiac		26	0.745	0.763	0.877	0.946	0.970	1.017	1.018	0.929	2236 Austrasia r:-0.496 p:0.010 df:24	9155 Verkhodanov r:0.680 p:0.000 df:24	4029 Bridges r:-0.649 p:0.000 df:24
waist / underbust		26	0.834	0.845	0.904	0.947	1.048	1.402	1.425	0.948	11585 Orlandelassus r:-0.505 p:0.010 df:23	6527 Takashiito r:0.774 p:0.000 df:23	1121 Natascha r:0.658 p:0.000 df:23

measure	group	Count	Min	0.05-quantile	0.25-quantile	0.5-quantile	0.75-quantile	0.95-quantile	Max	lowest correlation	highest correlation	most significant p
						Females						
slider_ Gender	0female 1male	118	0.000	0.000	0.000	0.000	0.000	0.000	0.500	6413 Iye r:-0.248 p:0.010 df:105	246837 Bethfabinsky r:0.390 p:0.000 df:105	8 Flora r:0.352 p:0.000 df:105
slider_ Age	age	117	0.373	0.451	0.500	0.500	0.500	0.540	0.689	5588 Jennabelle r:-0.248 p:0.010 df:105	12923 Zephyr r:0.413 p:0.000 df:105	714 Ulula r:0.347 p:0.000 df:105
slider_ head age decr|incr	age	35	-0.824	-0.733	-0.482	-0.296	-0.016	0.430	0.472	40230 Rozmberk r:-0.444 p:0.010 df:31	153289 Rebeccawatson r:0.654 p:0.000 df:31	2337 Boubin r:0.625 p:0.000 df:31
slider_ l lowerarm fat decr|incr	arms	51	-0.720	-0.442	-0.068	0.264	0.430	0.801	0.990	18697 Kathanson r:-0.373 p:0.010 df:45	157064 Sedona r:0.558 p:0.000 df:45	367 Amicitia r:0.555 p:0.000 df:45
slider_ l lowerarm muscle decr|incr	arms	13	-0.284	-0.284	-0.083	0.222	0.316	0.534	0.534	8875 Fernie r:-0.684 p:0.010 df:11	29647 Poncelet r:0.800 p:0.001 df:11	2679 Kittisvaara r:-0.833 p:0.000 df:11
slider_ l lowerarm scale depth decr|incr	arms	27	-0.316	-0.308	0.192	0.264	0.348	0.502	0.502	12099 Meigooni r:-0.515 p:0.010 df:22	3403 Tammy r:0.763 p:0.000 df:22	3403 Tammy r:0.763 p:0.000 df:22
slider_ l lowerarm scale horiz decr|incr	arms	15	-0.336	-0.336	-0.244	-0.088	0.006	0.088	0.088	11657 Antonhajduk r:-0.686 p:0.010 df:11	3953 Perth r:0.917 p:0.000 df:11	3953 Perth r:0.917 p:0.000 df:11
slider_ l lowerarm scale vert decr|incr	arms	33	-0.502	-0.349	-0.041	0.234	0.342	0.481	0.502	5249 Giza r:-0.471 p:0.010 df:27	5414 Sokolov r:0.636 p:0.000 df:27	4483 Petofi r:-0.649 p:0.000 df:27
slider_ l upperarm fat decr|incr	arms	52	-0.792	-0.478	-0.138	0.311	0.418	0.752	1.000	19818 Shotwell r:-0.368 p:0.010 df:46	129876 Stevenpeterson r:0.486 p:0.000 df:46	2022 West r:-0.554 p:0.000 df:46
slider_ l upperarm muscle decr|incr	arms	17	-0.388	-0.388	0.026	0.088	0.254	0.668	0.668	28686 Tamsenprofit r:-0.623 p:0.010 df:14	336680 Pavolpaulik r:0.782 p:0.000 df:14	1778 Alfven r:-0.781 p:0.000 df:14
slider_ l upperarm scale depth decr|incr	arms	37	-0.378	-0.293	0.130	0.234	0.336	0.535	0.544	21586 Pourkaviani r:-0.436 p:0.010 df:32	10702 Arizorcas r:0.553 p:0.001 df:32	5387 Casleo r:-0.577 p:0.000 df:32
slider_ l upperarm scale horiz decr|incr	arms	10	-0.576	-0.576	-0.431	-0.311	-0.120	0.150	0.150	12912 Streator r:-0.799 p:0.010 df:7	82092 Kalocsa r:0.934 p:0.000 df:7	5824 Inagaki r:0.918 p:0.000 df:7
slider_ l upperarm scale vert decr|incr	arms	40	-0.492	-0.420	0.163	0.244	0.371	0.560	0.596	11579 Tsujitsuka r:-0.430 p:0.010 df:33	117595 Jemmadavidson r:0.628 p:0.000 df:33	1952 Hesburgh r:0.561 p:0.000 df:33
slider_ l upperarm shoulder muscle decr|incr	arms	37	-0.928	-0.825	-0.637	-0.472	-0.269	0.408	0.678	928 Hildrun r:-0.430 p:0.010 df:33	39405 Mosigkau r:0.662 p:0.000 df:33	1646 Rosseland r:0.564 p:0.000 df:33
slider_ r lowerarm fat decr|incr	arms	51	-0.720	-0.442	-0.088	0.264	0.430	0.801	0.990	1455 Mitchella r:-0.373 p:0.010 df:45	157064 Sedona r:0.578 p:0.000 df:45	367 Amicitia r:0.534 p:0.000 df:45

Name	Group	N								Correlation 1	Correlation 2	Correlation 3
slider_r lowerarm muscle decr|incr	arms	12	-0.284	-0.284	-0.112	0.196	0.332	0.534	0.534	2267 Agassiz r:-0.709 p:0.010 df:10	8915 Sawaishujiro r:0.872 p:0.000 df:10	5255 Johnsophie r:-0.923 p:0.000 df:10
slider_r lowerarm scale depth decr|incr	arms	27	-0.316	-0.308	0.192	0.264	0.348	0.502	0.502	12099 Meigooni r:-0.515 p:0.010 df:22	3403 Tammy r:0.763 p:0.000 df:22	3403 Tammy r:0.763 p:0.000 df:22
slider_r lowerarm scale horiz decr|incr	arms	15	-0.336	-0.336	-0.244	-0.088	0.006	0.088	0.088	11657 Antonhajduk r:-0.686 p:0.010 df:11	3953 Perth r:0.917 p:0.000 df:11	3953 Perth r:0.917 p:0.000 df:11
slider_r lowerarm scale vert decr|incr	arms	32	-0.502	-0.360	-0.070	0.249	0.345	0.483	0.502	5057 Weeks r:-0.479 p:0.010 df:26	5414 Sokolov r:0.636 p:0.000 df:26	2201 Oljato r:-0.615 p:0.000 df:26
slider_r upperarm fat decr|incr	arms	52	-0.792	-0.478	-0.138	0.290	0.418	0.752	1.000	1657 Roemera r:-0.368 p:0.010 df:46	13569 Oshu r:0.523 p:0.000 df:46	2022 West r:-0.541 p:0.000 df:46
slider_r upperarm muscle decr|incr	arms	16	-0.388	-0.388	0.054	0.088	0.259	0.668	0.668	7035 Gomi r:-0.643 p:0.010 df:13	20532 Benbilby r:0.820 p:0.000 df:13	2772 Dugan r:-0.846 p:0.000 df:13
slider_r upperarm scale depth decr|incr	arms	36	-0.378	-0.298	0.130	0.234	0.336	0.536	0.544	31104 Annanetrebko r:-0.442 p:0.010 df:31	27375 Asirvatham r:0.577 p:0.000 df:31	5387 Casleo r:-0.574 p:0.000 df:31
slider_r upperarm scale horiz decr|incr	arms	10	-0.576	-0.576	-0.431	-0.311	-0.120	0.150	0.150	12912 Streator r:-0.799 p:0.010 df:7	82092 Kalocsa r:0.934 p:0.000 df:7	5824 Inagaki r:0.918 p:0.000 df:7
slider_r upperarm scale vert decr|incr	arms	38	-0.492	-0.433	0.168	0.244	0.356	0.486	0.564	10463 Bannister r:-0.442 p:0.010 df:31	117595 Jemmadavidson r:0.602 p:0.000 df:31	5387 Casleo r:-0.602 p:0.000 df:31
slider_r upperarm shoulder muscle decr|incr	arms	37	-0.928	-0.825	-0.626	-0.482	-0.342	0.408	0.678	6860 Sims r:-0.431 p:0.010 df:33	39405 Mosigkau r:0.688 p:0.000 df:33	47 Aglaja r:0.563 p:0.000 df:33
slider_ back accent	back	24	0.187	0.188	0.264	0.314	0.414	0.505	0.513	6795 Ornskoldsvik r:-0.528 p:0.010 df:21	40409 Taichikato r:0.696 p:0.000 df:21	11959 Okunokeno r:-0.669 p:0.000 df:21
slider_ torso muscle dorsi decr|incr	back	15	-0.678	-0.678	-0.388	-0.130	0.068	0.264	0.264	12270 Bozar r:-0.663 p:0.010 df:12	22487 Megphillips r:0.861 p:0.000 df:12	3624 Mironov r:-0.897 p:0.000 df:12
loli	beauty	44	0.057	0.060	0.116	0.176	0.319	0.609	0.655	148384 Dalcanton r:-0.398 p:0.010 df:39	3015 Candy r:0.579 p:0.000 df:39	3015 Candy r:0.579 p:0.000 df:39
breasts apart	breasts	80	0.056	0.068	0.102	0.145	0.238	0.375	0.580	7978 Niknesterov r:-0.304 p:0.010 df:69	21802 Svoren r:0.608 p:0.000 df:69	58 Concordia r:0.415 p:0.000 df:69
cleavage	breasts	199	0.074	0.115	0.217	0.336	0.459	0.699	0.914	-10008 Neptune r:-0.190 p:0.010 df:181	7387 Malbil r:0.338 p:0.000 df:181	3123 Dunham r:-0.274 p:0.000 df:181
large breasts	breasts	139	0.201	0.241	0.360	0.446	0.559	0.663	0.804	21583 Caropietsch r:-0.232 p:0.010 df:121	29607 Jakehecla r:0.398 p:0.000 df:121	6359 Dubinin r:-0.363 p:0.000 df:121
medium breasts	breasts	96	0.079	0.199	0.279	0.342	0.410	0.538	0.605	13852 Ford r:-0.277 p:0.010 df:84	24303 Michaelrice r:0.387 p:0.000 df:84	1891 Gondola r:0.372 p:0.000 df:84
slider_ BreastFirmness	breasts	118	0.000	0.119	0.348	0.500	0.500	0.739	1.000	17103 Kadyrsizova r:-0.248 p:0.010 df:105	91024 Szechenyi r:0.358 p:0.000 df:105	1426 Riviera r:-0.349 p:0.000 df:105
slider_ BreastSize	breasts	118	0.057	0.285	0.559	0.720	0.801	0.907	1.000	2960 Ohtaki r:-0.248 p:0.010 df:105	54863 Gasnault r:0.419 p:0.000 df:105	1111 Reinmuthia r:-0.350 p:0.000 df:105
slider_ Breasts_Inframammary_ fold	breasts	50	0.140	0.216	0.464	0.651	0.863	1.000	1.000	3211 Louispharailda r:-0.385 p:0.010 df:42	230 Athamantis r:0.518 p:0.000 df:42	230 Athamantis r:0.518 p:0.000 df:42
slider_ Chest_ breast_ upper	breasts	21	0.078	0.079	0.218	0.389	0.448	0.976	1.000	28536 Hunaiwen r:-0.562 p:0.010 df:18	1031 Arctica r:0.777 p:0.000 df:18	1031 Arctica r:0.777 p:0.000 df:18
slider_ breast dist decr|incr	breasts	39	-0.866	-0.626	-0.296	-0.150	0.170	1.000	1.000	10949 Konigstuhl r:-0.439 p:0.009 df:32	11469 Rozitis r:0.608 p:0.000 df:32	7074 Muckea r:0.577 p:0.000 df:32
slider_ breast point decr|incr	breasts	45	-1.000	-0.990	-0.564	-0.306	0.222	0.529	0.638	1371 Resi r:-0.403 p:0.010 df:38	1956 Artek r:0.596 p:0.000 df:38	1709 Ukraina r:-0.558 p:0.000 df:38
slider_ breast trans down|up	breasts	32	-0.700	-0.491	0.072	0.321	0.624	0.839	1.000	375007 Buxy r:-0.471 p:0.010 df:27	5390 Huichiming r:0.764 p:0.000 df:27	22 Kalliope r:-0.614 p:0.000 df:27
slider_ breast volume vert down|up	breasts	52	-1.000	-1.000	-0.495	-0.182	0.298	0.891	0.938	27365 Henryfitz r:-0.376 p:0.010 df:44	5555 Wimberly r:0.545 p:0.000 df:44	5555 Wimberly r:0.545 p:0.000 df:44
slider_ female breasts compress	breasts	14	0.041	0.041	0.158	0.259	0.448	0.622	0.622	10425 Landfermann r:-0.708 p:0.010 df:10	3668 Ilfpetrov r:0.921 p:0.000 df:10	3668 Ilfpetrov r:0.921 p:0.000 df:10
slider_ female breasts pushup	breasts	14	0.013	0.013	0.072	0.177	0.352	0.420	0.420	126444 Wylie r:-0.708 p:0.010 df:10	6852 Nannibignami r:0.892 p:0.000 df:10	759 Vinifera r:0.872 p:0.000 df:10
slider_ female_ breasts_ extra_ roundness	breasts	63	0.041	0.059	0.130	0.244	0.399	0.564	0.886	14567 Nicovincenti r:-0.342 p:0.010 df:54	1997 Leverrier r:0.545 p:0.000 df:54	91 Aegina r:-0.462 p:0.000 df:54
slider_ measure bust circ decr|incr	breasts	56	-1.000	-0.674	-0.311	-0.046	0.210	0.470	0.876	21545 Koirala r:-0.361 p:0.010 df:48	42479 Tolik r:0.486 p:0.000 df:48	5784 Yoron r:-0.483 p:0.000 df:48
slider_ measure underbust circ decr|incr	breasts	24	-1.000	-0.967	-0.767	-0.140	0.063	0.773	0.876	1126 Otero r:-0.537 p:0.010 df:20	34310 Markhannum r:0.765 p:0.000 df:20	157 Dejanira r:-0.682 p:0.000 df:20
slider_ sagging	breasts	20	0.005	0.008	0.079	0.174	0.274	0.456	0.458	5306 Fangfen r:-0.606 p:0.010 df:15	12 Victoria r:0.898 p:0.000 df:15	12 Victoria r:0.898 p:0.000 df:15
small breasts	breasts	70	0.121	0.212	0.293	0.367	0.483	0.579	0.802	4578 Kurashiki r:-0.315 p:0.010 df:64	129234 Silly r:0.507 p:0.000 df:64	1847 Stobbe r:-0.437 p:0.000 df:64
statscontinuous_ breasts weight/height	breasts	342	0.005	0.013	0.024	0.039	0.063	0.125	0.188	5875 Kuga r:-0.200 p:0.010 df:163	73692 Gurtler r:0.302 p:0.000 df:163	1264 Letaba r:0.290 p:0.000 df:163
statscontinuous_ breasts weight/weight	breasts	319	0.003	0.008	0.012	0.019	0.028	0.056	0.104	5875 Kuga r:-0.206 p:0.010 df:154	10152 Ukichiro r:0.317 p:0.000 df:154	2679 Kittisvaara r:0.292 p:0.000 df:154
statscontinuous_ bust	breasts	509	8.000	28.000	32.000	34.000	38.000	55.000	80.000	3307 Athabasca r:-0.169 p:0.010 df:229	21464 Chinaroonchai r:0.303 p:0.000 df:229	284 Amalia r:0.243 p:0.000 df:229
statscontinuous_ bust/height	breasts	485	0.119	0.436	0.507	0.540	0.607	0.859	1.356	9724 Villanueva r:-0.173 p:0.010 df:219	21464 Chinaroonchai r:0.328 p:0.000 df:219	284 Amalia r:0.252 p:0.000 df:219

name	category	n								author 1	author 2	author 3
statscontinuous_ bust/weight	breasts	445	0.043	0.159	0.233	0.273	0.309	0.375	0.938	15716 Narahara r:-0.179 p:0.010 df:204	16503 Ayato r:0.279 p:0.000 df:204	6346 Syukumeguri r:-0.253 p:0.000 df:204
statscontinuous_ cup diameter	breasts	361	3.000	3.819	4.488	5.157	6.181	7.835	8.819	243 Ida r:-0.196 p:0.010 df:171	73692 Gurtler r:0.303 p:0.000 df:171	1264 Letaba r:0.297 p:0.000 df:171
statscontinuous_ cup diameter/height	breasts	342	0.048	0.059	0.070	0.082	0.096	0.121	0.178	2407 Haug r:-0.200 p:0.010 df:163	3590 Holst r:0.305 p:0.000 df:163	1870 Glaukos r:0.270 p:0.000 df:163
statscontinuous_ cup diameter/weight	breasts	319	0.020	0.028	0.036	0.041	0.047	0.060	0.096	13475 Orestes r:-0.206 p:0.010 df:154	2722 Abalakin r:0.319 p:0.000 df:154	2722 Abalakin r:0.319 p:0.000 df:154
statscontinuous_ cup vol/height	breasts	342	0.143	0.228	0.375	0.581	0.968	1.934	2.903	398 Admete r:-0.200 p:0.010 df:163	73692 Gurtler r:0.301 p:0.000 df:163	1264 Letaba r:0.292 p:0.000 df:163
statscontinuous_ cup vol/weight	breasts	319	0.078	0.130	0.201	0.298	0.430	0.863	1.607	1638 Ruanda r:-0.206 p:0.010 df:154	10152 Ukichiro r:0.322 p:0.000 df:154	2679 Kittisvaara r:0.294 p:0.000 df:154
curvy	build	45	0.052	0.056	0.086	0.110	0.167	0.295	0.351	52344 Yehudimenuhin r:-0.398 p:0.010 df:39	57509 Sly r:0.624 p:0.000 df:39	988 Appella r:-0.530 p:0.000 df:39
fat	build	39	0.062	0.062	0.106	0.207	0.404	0.725	0.734	2905 Plaskett r:-0.425 p:0.010 df:34	1429 Pemba r:0.657 p:0.000 df:34	1429 Pemba r:0.657 p:0.000 df:34
plump	build	66	0.054	0.058	0.143	0.303	0.436	0.685	0.871	5223 McSween r:-0.328 p:0.010 df:59	1380 Volodia r:0.522 p:0.000 df:59	1120 Cannonia r:0.434 p:0.000 df:59
slider_ BodyProportions	build	118	0.026	0.149	0.359	0.500	0.641	0.872	1.000	6773 Kellaway r:-0.248 p:0.010 df:105	10480 Jennyblue r:0.397 p:0.000 df:105	2978 Roudebush r:-0.355 p:0.000 df:105
slider_ Bubble Booty	buttocks	23	0.021	0.025	0.104	0.166	0.264	0.490	0.503	2350 von Lude r:-0.540 p:0.009 df:20	255073 Victoriabond r:0.747 p:0.000 df:20	1038 Tuckia r:-0.714 p:0.000 df:20
slider_ Buttocks_ THIGH 03	buttocks	11	0.148	0.148	0.316	0.513	0.710	0.959	0.959	971 Alsatia r:-0.799 p:0.010 df:7	24217 Paulroeder r:0.937 p:0.000 df:7	187 Lamberta r:-0.918 p:0.000 df:7
slider_ HarveyBottomV1	buttocks	13	0.064	0.064	0.135	0.316	0.552	0.756	0.756	9487 Kupe r:-0.710 p:0.010 df:10	291 Alice r:0.908 p:0.000 df:10	291 Alice r:0.908 p:0.000 df:10
slider_ butt_ crease	buttocks	17	0.114	0.114	0.184	0.451	0.575	0.902	0.902	169834 Hujie r:-0.623 p:0.010 df:14	7590 Aterui r:0.875 p:0.000 df:14	1455 Mitchella r:0.794 p:0.000 df:14
slider_ buttocks volume decr|incr	buttocks	40	-1.000	-0.852	0.039	0.362	0.562	0.751	0.752	14065 Flegel r:-0.424 p:0.010 df:34	145545 Wensayling r:0.600 p:0.000 df:34	818 Kapteynia r:-0.624 p:0.000 df:34
slider_ sohh_ bottom	buttocks	12	0.083	0.083	0.175	0.425	0.575	0.850	0.850	3296 Bosque Alegre r:-0.736 p:0.010 df:9	8947 Mizutani r:0.918 p:0.000 df:9	2281 Biela r:0.878 p:0.000 df:9
slider_ elvs_ chipmunkcheeks_ l1	cheeks	15	0.031	0.031	0.047	0.078	0.124	0.197	0.197	2402 Satpaev r:-0.686 p:0.010 df:11	7553 Buie r:0.872 p:0.000 df:11	2980 Cameron r:0.829 p:0.000 df:11
slider_ elvs_ highchubbycheekbones1	cheeks	9	0.041	0.041	0.055	0.078	0.135	0.192	0.192	34268 Gracetian r:-0.836 p:0.010 df:6	6300 Hosamu r:0.984 p:0.000 df:6	4084 Hollis r:-0.947 p:0.000 df:6
slider_ l cheek bones decr|incr	cheeks	92	-0.834	-0.476	-0.286	0.036	0.207	0.489	0.648	163 Erigone r:-0.282 p:0.010 df:81	28 Bellona r:0.514 p:0.000 df:81	28 Bellona r:0.514 p:0.000 df:81
slider_ l cheek inner decr|incr	cheeks	99	-1.000	-0.420	0.120	0.378	0.586	0.854	1.000	2382 Nonie r:-0.271 p:0.010 df:88	48619 Jianli r:0.388 p:0.000 df:88	1558 Jarnefelt r:-0.402 p:0.000 df:88
slider_ l cheek trans down|up	cheeks	94	-1.000	-0.780	-0.482	-0.114	0.440	0.832	1.000	7136 Yokohasuo r:-0.278 p:0.010 df:83	29668 Ipf r:0.376 p:0.000 df:83	142 Polana r:-0.403 p:0.000 df:83
slider_ l cheek volume decr|incr	cheeks	97	-0.752	-0.556	-0.274	-0.016	0.114	0.318	0.492	8820 Anjandersen r:-0.273 p:0.010 df:86	17950 Grover r:0.384 p:0.000 df:86	1347 Patria r:-0.377 p:0.000 df:86
slider_ r cheek bones decr|incr	cheeks	91	-0.834	-0.476	-0.296	0.036	0.212	0.490	0.648	658 Asteria r:-0.284 p:0.010 df:80	28 Bellona r:0.486 p:0.000 df:80	28 Bellona r:0.486 p:0.000 df:80
slider_ r cheek inner decr|incr	cheeks	98	-1.000	-0.423	0.108	0.368	0.591	0.855	1.000	28273 Maianhvu r:-0.272 p:0.010 df:87	22645 Rotblat r:0.381 p:0.000 df:87	1558 Jarnefelt r:-0.380 p:0.000 df:87
slider_ r cheek trans down|up	cheeks	93	-1.000	-0.784	-0.487	-0.120	0.415	0.833	1.000	498 Tokio r:-0.280 p:0.010 df:82	187276 Meistas r:0.374 p:0.000 df:82	5312 Schott r:-0.374 p:0.000 df:82
slider_ r cheek volume decr|incr	cheeks	96	-0.752	-0.557	-0.274	-0.016	0.106	0.319	0.492	18579 Duongtuyenvu r:-0.275 p:0.010 df:85	17950 Grover r:0.387 p:0.000 df:85	1347 Patria r:-0.367 p:0.000 df:85
chest width< >underbust	chest	170	1.151	2.019	3.031	3.619	4.426	7.110	11.224	1912 Anubis r:-0.206 p:0.010 df:154	4607 Seilandfarm r:0.284 p:0.000 df:154	4607 Seilandfarm r:0.284 p:0.000 df:154
flat chest	chest	47	0.062	0.068	0.131	0.222	0.353	0.686	0.778	6063 Jason r:-0.389 p:0.010 df:41	4794 Bogard r:0.577 p:0.000 df:41	2014 Vasilevskis r:-0.621 p:0.000 df:41
pectorals	chest	8	0.054	0.054	0.222	0.316	0.435	0.518	0.518	73687 Thomas Aquinas r:-0.834 p:0.010 df:6	95474 Andreajbarbieri r:0.973 p:0.000 df:6	225 Henrietta r:-0.966 p:0.000 df:6
slider_ measure frontchest dist decr|incr	chest	16	-0.824	-0.824	-0.347	-0.176	0.044	1.000	1.000	28492 Marik r:-0.623 p:0.010 df:14	195191 Constantinetsang r:0.889 p:0.000 df:14	119 Althaea r:-0.769 p:0.000 df:14
slider_ torso muscle pectoral decr|incr	chest	14	-0.450	-0.450	-0.309	-0.078	0.311	0.472	0.472	2715 Mielikki r:-0.663 p:0.010 df:12	62 Erato r:0.843 p:0.000 df:12	62 Erato r:0.843 p:0.000 df:12
slider_ chin bones decr|incr	chin	84	-1.000	-0.891	-0.611	-0.414	-0.187	0.145	0.316	257439 Peppeprosperini r:-0.288 p:0.010 df:77	31944 Seyitherdem r:0.408 p:0.000 df:77	591 Irmgard r:0.387 p:0.000 df:77
slider_ chin cleft decr|incr	chin	22	-1.000	-0.984	-0.570	-0.462	-0.024	0.522	0.544	-10007 Uranus r:-0.576 p:0.010 df:17	185535 Gangda r:0.876 p:0.000 df:17	769 Tatjana r:-0.734 p:0.000 df:17
slider_ chin height decr|incr	chin	68	-0.720	-0.587	-0.282	-0.130	0.068	0.222	0.316	400 Ducrosa r:-0.325 p:0.010 df:60	6368 Richardmenendez r:0.483 p:0.000 df:60	1975 Pikelner r:0.452 p:0.000 df:60
slider_ chin jaw drop decr|incr	chin	64	-0.752	-0.718	-0.521	-0.326	-0.111	0.212	0.378	2593 Buryatia r:-0.339 p:0.010 df:55	178155 Kenzaarraki r:0.515 p:0.000 df:55	3272 Tillandz r:-0.461 p:0.000 df:55
slider_ chin prognathism decr|incr	chin	37	-0.658	-0.629	-0.280	-0.150	0.062	0.464	0.586	4302 Markeev r:-0.436 p:0.010 df:32	3644 Kojitaku r:0.663 p:0.000 df:32	3644 Kojitaku r:0.663 p:0.000 df:32

slider	part	n										
slider_ chin prominent decr|incr	chin	62	-0.534	-0.471	-0.170	0.088	0.212	0.435	0.492	20862 Jenngoedhart r:-0.339 p:0.010 df:55	24648 Evpatoria r:0.461 p:0.000 df:55	1059 Mussorgskia r:0.458 p:0.000 df:55
slider_ chin width decr|incr	chin	89	-0.854	-0.554	-0.295	-0.098	0.073	0.246	0.358	1592 Mathieu r:-0.285 p:0.010 df:79	95852 Leatherbarrow r:0.433 p:0.000 df:79	3920 Aubignan r:-0.381 p:0.000 df:79
slider_ ears_ flat_ 2	ears	13	0.181	0.181	0.316	0.398	0.503	0.705	0.705	13733 Dylanyoung r:-0.684 p:0.010 df:11	2305 King r:0.871 p:0.000 df:11	16 Psyche r:0.866 p:0.000 df:11
slider_ l ear lobe decr|incr	ears	13	-0.492	-0.492	0.077	0.222	0.348	0.450	0.450	2248 Kanda r:-0.684 p:0.010 df:11	7028 Tachikawa r:0.852 p:0.000 df:11	786 Bredichina r:-0.836 p:0.000 df:11
slider_ l ear rot backward|forward	ears	17	-1.000	-1.000	-0.912	-0.524	-0.425	-0.150	-0.150	578 Happelia r:-0.641 p:0.010 df:13	25358 Boskovice r:0.837 p:0.000 df:13	1357 Khama r:0.812 p:0.000 df:13
slider_ l ear scale depth decr|incr	ears	8	-0.430	-0.430	-0.366	-0.140	0.263	0.626	0.626	127 Johanna r:-0.836 p:0.010 df:6	21468 Saylor r:0.991 p:0.000 df:6	1647 Menelaus r:-0.977 p:0.000 df:6
slider_ l ear scale vert decr|incr	ears	12	-0.130	-0.130	0.040	0.176	0.355	0.462	0.462	28075 Emilyhoffman r:-0.708 p:0.010 df:10	27915 Nancywright r:0.954 p:0.000 df:10	7629 Foros r:0.911 p:0.000 df:10
slider_ l ear shape pointed|triangle	ears	12	-0.264	-0.264	-0.243	0.026	0.200	0.564	0.564	25115 Drago r:-0.737 p:0.010 df:9	19874 Liudongyan r:0.921 p:0.000 df:9	248 Lameia r:-0.878 p:0.000 df:9
slider_ l ear trans backward|forward	ears	17	-0.006	-0.006	0.513	0.814	1.000	1.000	1.000	7984 Marius r:-0.623 p:0.010 df:14	100934 Marthanussbaum r:0.838 p:0.000 df:14	354 Eleonora r:0.827 p:0.000 df:14
slider_ l ear trans down|up	ears	20	-0.638	-0.638	-0.443	-0.181	0.163	0.705	0.720	9845 Okamuraosamu r:-0.562 p:0.010 df:18	23773 Sarugaku r:0.766 p:0.000 df:18	247 Eukrate r:-0.728 p:0.000 df:18
slider_ l ear wing decr|incr	ears	14	-0.720	-0.720	-0.220	-0.088	0.269	0.576	0.576	12111 Ulm r:-0.684 p:0.010 df:11	4387 Tanaka r:0.860 p:0.000 df:11	1398 Donnera r:-0.847 p:0.000 df:11
slider_ r ear lobe decr|incr	ears	14	-0.492	-0.492	0.062	0.213	0.348	0.524	0.524	3604 Berkhuijsen r:-0.684 p:0.010 df:11	7028 Tachikawa r:0.851 p:0.000 df:11	786 Bredichina r:-0.834 p:0.000 df:11
slider_ r ear rot backward|forward	ears	18	-1.000	-1.000	-0.894	-0.524	-0.392	-0.150	-0.150	578 Happelia r:-0.641 p:0.010 df:13	25358 Boskovice r:0.837 p:0.000 df:13	1357 Khama r:0.812 p:0.000 df:13
slider_ r ear scale depth decr|incr	ears	10	-0.430	-0.430	-0.278	-0.140	0.250	0.626	0.626	6414 Mizunuma r:-0.798 p:0.010 df:7	21468 Saylor r:0.986 p:0.000 df:7	1018 Arnolda r:0.919 p:0.000 df:7
slider_ r ear scale vert decr|incr	ears	12	-0.130	-0.130	0.040	0.176	0.355	0.462	0.462	28075 Emilyhoffman r:-0.708 p:0.010 df:10	27915 Nancywright r:0.954 p:0.000 df:10	7629 Foros r:0.911 p:0.000 df:10
slider_ r ear shape pointed|triangle	ears	14	-0.264	-0.264	-0.240	0.026	0.207	0.564	0.564	4408 Zlata Koruna r:-0.708 p:0.010 df:10	121032 Wadesisler r:0.913 p:0.000 df:10	248 Lameia r:-0.907 p:0.000 df:10
slider_ r ear shape square|round	ears	8	-0.358	-0.358	-0.117	0.161	0.275	0.348	0.348	4204 Barsig r:-0.875 p:0.010 df:5	22945 Schikowski r:0.988 p:0.000 df:5	1044 Teutonia r:-0.989 p:0.000 df:5
slider_ r ear trans backward|forward	ears	17	-0.006	-0.006	0.513	0.814	1.000	1.000	1.000	7984 Marius r:-0.623 p:0.010 df:14	100934 Marthanussbaum r:0.838 p:0.000 df:14	354 Eleonora r:0.827 p:0.000 df:14
slider_ r ear trans down|up	ears	20	-0.638	-0.638	-0.443	-0.181	0.163	0.705	0.720	5877 Toshimaihara r:-0.562 p:0.010 df:18	23773 Sarugaku r:0.770 p:0.000 df:18	247 Eukrate r:-0.724 p:0.000 df:18
slider_ r ear wing decr|incr	ears	14	-0.720	-0.720	-0.220	-0.088	0.269	0.576	0.576	12111 Ulm r:-0.684 p:0.010 df:11	4387 Tanaka r:0.860 p:0.000 df:11	1398 Donnera r:-0.847 p:0.000 df:11
slider_ African	ethno	118	0.000	0.000	0.000	0.081	0.318	0.701	0.860	5554 Keesey r:-0.248 p:0.010 df:105	22889 Donnablaney r:0.391 p:0.000 df:105	1173 Anchises r:-0.340 p:0.000 df:105
slider_ Asian	ethno	118	0.000	0.000	0.000	0.079	0.338	0.784	1.000	3342 Fivesparks r:-0.248 p:0.010 df:105	807 Ceraskia r:0.383 p:0.000 df:105	437 Rhodia r:0.332 p:0.000 df:105
slider_ Caucasian	ethno	118	0.000	0.061	0.333	0.660	1.000	1.000	1.000	28433 Samarquez r:-0.248 p:0.010 df:105	1433 Geramtina r:0.396 p:0.000 df:105	73 Klytia r:-0.331 p:0.000 df:105
slider_ eyebrows angle down|up	eyebrows	30	-0.430	-0.305	0.000	0.078	0.200	0.427	0.512	19307 Hanayama r:-0.487 p:0.010 df:25	18873 Larryrobinson r:0.740 p:0.000 df:25	634 Ute r:0.690 p:0.000 df:25
slider_ eyebrows trans backward|forward	eyebrows	21	-0.388	-0.384	-0.233	-0.026	0.155	0.242	0.244	22385 Fujimoriboshi r:-0.549 p:0.010 df:19	31475 Robbacchus r:0.735 p:0.000 df:19	447 Valentine r:0.702 p:0.000 df:19
slider_ eyebrows trans down|up	eyebrows	52	-0.564	-0.203	0.381	0.627	0.816	1.000	1.000	6766 Kharms r:-0.362 p:0.010 df:48	2726 Kotelnikov r:0.476 p:0.000 df:48	1921 Pala r:-0.504 p:0.000 df:48
thick eyebrows	eyebrows	48	0.054	0.057	0.077	0.122	0.173	0.354	0.428	11582 Bleuler r:-0.381 p:0.010 df:43	2133 Franceswright r:0.510 p:0.000 df:43	696 Leonora r:-0.523 p:0.000 df:43
grey eyes	eyes	107	0.053	0.063	0.084	0.097	0.149	0.283	0.364	5125 Okushiri r:-0.262 p:0.010 df:94	3940 Larion r:0.417 p:0.000 df:94	33 Polyhymnia r:0.397 p:0.000 df:94
slider_ eyes_ middle_ droop	eyes	9	0.130	0.130	0.264	0.518	0.788	0.829	0.829	12636 Padrielli r:-0.798 p:0.010 df:7	31463 Michalgeci r:0.969 p:0.000 df:7	1129 Neujmina r:0.924 p:0.000 df:7
slider_ eyes_ outer_ droop	eyes	15	0.187	0.187	0.383	0.611	0.793	1.000	1.000	5520 Natori r:-0.641 p:0.010 df:13	16406 Oszkiewicz r:0.851 p:0.000 df:13	948 Jucunda r:-0.858 p:0.000 df:13
slider_ l eye bag decr|incr	eyes	69	-0.938	-0.803	-0.435	0.182	0.399	0.684	0.792	3336 Grygar r:-0.325 p:0.010 df:60	7309 Shinkawakami r:0.430 p:0.000 df:60	5100 Pasachoff r:-0.443 p:0.000 df:60
slider_ l eye bag height decr|incr	eyes	70	-1.000	-0.792	-0.554	-0.358	0.183	0.523	0.638	4769 Castalia r:-0.322 p:0.010 df:61	7583 Rosegger r:0.457 p:0.000 df:61	1768 Appenzella r:-0.434 p:0.000 df:61
slider_ l eye bag in|out	eyes	68	-1.000	-0.778	-0.122	0.348	0.521	0.720	0.948	5047 Zanda r:-0.325 p:0.010 df:60	24488 Eliebochner r:0.467 p:0.000 df:60	296 Phaetusa r:-0.438 p:0.000 df:60
slider_ l eye corner1 down|up	eyes	58	-1.000	-1.000	-0.646	-0.415	-0.150	0.650	0.710	17982 Simcmillan r:-0.358 p:0.010 df:49	33740 Arjunmoorthy r:0.548 p:0.000 df:49	2877 Likhachev r:-0.476 p:0.000 df:49
slider_ l eye corner2 down|up	eyes	71	-1.000	-1.000	-0.606	-0.398	-0.150	0.426	0.472	4817 Gliba r:-0.325 p:0.010 df:60	380607 Sharma r:0.508 p:0.000 df:60	2313 Aruna r:0.451 p:0.000 df:60
slider_ l eye epicanthus in|out	eyes	42	-0.626	-0.417	-0.116	0.036	0.215	0.358	0.482	10380 Berwald r:-0.413 p:0.010 df:36	1923 Osiris r:0.642 p:0.000 df:36	1923 Osiris r:0.642 p:0.000 df:36

slider	cat	n								col1	col2	col3
slider_ l eye eyefold angle down|up	eyes	37	-1.000	-0.757	-0.430	-0.056	0.301	0.701	0.710	126 Velleda r:-0.443 p:0.010 df:31	8300 Iga r:0.600 p:0.000 df:31	83 Beatrix r:0.597 p:0.000 df:31
slider_ l eye eyefold concave|convex	eyes	66	-1.000	-1.000	-0.693	-0.414	0.067	0.727	1.000	1693 Hertzsprung r:-0.333 p:0.010 df:57	31189 Tricomi r:0.545 p:0.000 df:57	1144 Oda r:-0.467 p:0.000 df:57
slider_ l eye eyefold down|up	eyes	58	-1.000	-1.000	-0.904	-0.679	-0.405	0.486	0.762	3800 Karayusuf r:-0.355 p:0.010 df:50	21380 Devanssay r:0.515 p:0.000 df:50	2443 Tomeileen r:-0.492 p:0.000 df:50
slider_ l eye height1 decr|incr	eyes	60	-1.000	-0.862	-0.470	-0.296	0.060	0.326	0.576	400308 Antonkutter r:-0.345 p:0.010 df:53	17198 Gorjup r:0.510 p:0.000 df:53	3446 Combes r:0.484 p:0.000 df:53
slider_ l eye height2 decr|incr	eyes	79	-1.000	-0.834	-0.440	-0.046	0.326	0.606	0.762	4840 Otaynang r:-0.304 p:0.010 df:69	5830 Simohiro r:0.422 p:0.000 df:69	2285 Ron Helin r:-0.411 p:0.000 df:69
slider_ l eye height3 decr|incr	eyes	43	-0.730	-0.666	-0.348	-0.130	0.274	0.735	0.814	12580 Antonini r:-0.413 p:0.010 df:36	20270 Phildeutsch r:0.582 p:0.000 df:36	1003 Lilofee r:0.555 p:0.000 df:36
slider_ l eye push1 in|out	eyes	49	-0.844	-0.690	-0.104	0.254	0.461	0.684	0.792	21410 Cahill r:-0.377 p:0.010 df:44	169184 Jameslee r:0.501 p:0.000 df:44	1141 Bohmia r:-0.519 p:0.000 df:44
slider_ l eye push2 in|out	eyes	51	-0.866	-0.756	-0.244	-0.056	0.254	0.951	1.000	12329 Liebermann r:-0.369 p:0.010 df:46	4110 Keats r:0.550 p:0.000 df:46	103 Hera r:-0.497 p:0.000 df:46
slider_ l eye scale decr|incr	eyes	55	-0.710	-0.584	-0.192	0.264	0.534	0.774	0.876	4360 Xuyi r:-0.358 p:0.010 df:49	31192 Aigoual r:0.537 p:0.000 df:49	766 Moguntia r:0.496 p:0.000 df:49
slider_ l eye trans down|up	eyes	62	-1.000	-1.000	-0.759	-0.316	0.290	0.916	1.000	3303 Merta r:-0.342 p:0.010 df:54	18091 Iranmanesh r:0.461 p:0.000 df:54	1272 Gefion r:-0.470 p:0.000 df:54
slider_ l eye trans in|out	eyes	55	-0.740	-0.480	-0.182	0.336	0.524	0.866	1.000	3769 Arthurmiller r:-0.362 p:0.010 df:48	23457 Beiderbecke r:0.531 p:0.000 df:48	1080 Orchis r:0.505 p:0.000 df:48
slider_ r eye bag decr|incr	eyes	68	-0.938	-0.806	-0.422	0.187	0.410	0.686	0.792	15169 Wilfriedboland r:-0.328 p:0.010 df:59	7309 Shinkawakami r:0.469 p:0.000 df:59	5100 Pasachoff r:-0.448 p:0.000 df:59
slider_ r eye bag height decr|incr	eyes	69	-1.000	-0.792	-0.554	-0.358	0.196	0.529	0.638	566 Stereoskopia r:-0.325 p:0.010 df:60	123860 Davederrick r:0.466 p:0.000 df:60	1375 Alfreda r:0.435 p:0.000 df:60
slider_ r eye bag in|out	eyes	68	-1.000	-0.778	-0.122	0.348	0.521	0.720	0.948	5047 Zanda r:-0.325 p:0.010 df:60	24488 Eliebochner r:0.467 p:0.000 df:60	296 Phaetusa r:-0.438 p:0.000 df:60
slider_ r eye corner1 down|up	eyes	57	-1.000	-1.000	-0.638	-0.410	-0.140	0.651	0.710	7400 Lenau r:-0.361 p:0.010 df:48	33740 Arjunmoorthy r:0.543 p:0.000 df:48	3295 Murakami r:-0.488 p:0.000 df:48
slider_ r eye corner2 down|up	eyes	70	-1.000	-1.000	-0.609	-0.404	-0.165	0.428	0.472	13674 Bourge r:-0.327 p:0.010 df:59	380607 Sharma r:0.514 p:0.000 df:59	2313 Aruna r:0.441 p:0.000 df:59
slider_ r eye epicanthus in|out	eyes	42	-0.626	-0.417	-0.116	0.036	0.215	0.358	0.482	10380 Berwald r:-0.413 p:0.010 df:36	1923 Osiris r:0.642 p:0.000 df:36	1923 Osiris r:0.642 p:0.000 df:36
slider_ r eye eyefold angle down|up	eyes	37	-1.000	-0.757	-0.430	-0.056	0.301	0.701	0.710	126 Velleda r:-0.443 p:0.010 df:31	8300 Iga r:0.600 p:0.000 df:31	83 Beatrix r:0.597 p:0.000 df:31
slider_ r eye eyefold concave|convex	eyes	66	-1.000	-1.000	-0.693	-0.414	0.067	0.727	1.000	1693 Hertzsprung r:-0.333 p:0.010 df:57	31189 Tricomi r:0.545 p:0.000 df:57	1144 Oda r:-0.467 p:0.000 df:57
slider_ r eye eyefold down|up	eyes	58	-1.000	-1.000	-0.904	-0.679	-0.405	0.486	0.762	3800 Karayusuf r:-0.355 p:0.010 df:50	21380 Devanssay r:0.515 p:0.000 df:50	2443 Tomeileen r:-0.492 p:0.000 df:50
slider_ r eye height1 decr|incr	eyes	60	-1.000	-0.862	-0.472	-0.301	0.060	0.326	0.576	875 Nymphe r:-0.345 p:0.010 df:53	3446 Combes r:0.514 p:0.000 df:53	3446 Combes r:0.514 p:0.000 df:53
slider_ r eye height2 decr|incr	eyes	78	-1.000	-0.835	-0.440	-0.036	0.326	0.608	0.762	33582 Tiashajoardar r:-0.306 p:0.010 df:68	4814 Casacci r:0.418 p:0.000 df:68	3850 Peltier r:-0.468 p:0.000 df:68
slider_ r eye height3 decr|incr	eyes	42	-0.730	-0.669	-0.351	-0.109	0.293	0.744	0.814	8544 Sigenori r:-0.419 p:0.010 df:35	33196 Kaienyang r:0.595 p:0.000 df:35	1003 Lilofee r:0.565 p:0.000 df:35
slider_ r eye push1 in|out	eyes	49	-0.804	-0.519	-0.104	0.254	0.461	0.684	0.792	10660 Felixhormuth r:-0.376 p:0.010 df:44	169184 Jameslee r:0.497 p:0.000 df:44	1141 Bohmia r:-0.554 p:0.000 df:44
slider_ r eye push2 in|out	eyes	50	-0.866	-0.757	-0.254	-0.062	0.239	0.955	1.000	9683 Rambaldo r:-0.372 p:0.010 df:45	4110 Keats r:0.557 p:0.000 df:45	1918 Aiguillon r:0.539 p:0.000 df:45
slider_ r eye scale decr|incr	eyes	55	-0.710	-0.584	-0.182	0.264	0.534	0.774	0.876	2139 Makharadze r:-0.358 p:0.010 df:49	31192 Aigoual r:0.530 p:0.000 df:49	766 Moguntia r:0.493 p:0.000 df:49
slider_ r eye trans down|up	eyes	60	-1.000	-1.000	-0.796	-0.316	0.294	0.931	1.000	6179 Brett r:-0.348 p:0.010 df:52	18091 Iranmanesh r:0.485 p:0.000 df:52	1272 Gefion r:-0.485 p:0.000 df:52
slider_ r eye trans in|out	eyes	55	-0.740	-0.480	-0.182	0.336	0.534	0.866	1.000	11967 Boyle r:-0.361 p:0.010 df:48	23457 Beiderbecke r:0.523 p:0.000 df:48	1080 Orchis r:0.508 p:0.000 df:48
slider_ l foot scale decr|incr	feet	9	-0.564	-0.564	-0.228	-0.160	-0.026	0.254	0.254	12469 Katsuura r:-0.798 p:0.010 df:7	1173 Anchises r:0.970 p:0.000 df:7	265 Anna r:-0.935 p:0.000 df:7
slider_ r foot scale decr|incr	feet	10	-0.564	-0.564	-0.220	-0.155	-0.067	0.254	0.254	4378 Voigt r:-0.766 p:0.010 df:8	1173 Anchises r:0.967 p:0.000 df:8	265 Anna r:-0.912 p:0.000 df:8
beard	hair	10	0.062	0.062	0.080	0.153	0.370	0.485	0.485	26591 Robertreeves r:-0.799 p:0.010 df:7	1530 Rantaseppa r:0.959 p:0.000 df:7	1530 Rantaseppa r:0.959 p:0.000 df:7
black hair	hair	192	0.055	0.124	0.385	0.508	0.679	0.799	0.890	6112 Ludolfschultz r:-0.198 p:0.010 df:167	9724 Villanueva r:0.302 p:0.000 df:167	9724 Villanueva r:0.302 p:0.000 df:167
blonde hair	hair	62	0.332	0.386	0.529	0.644	0.741	0.888	0.916	1231 Auricula r:-0.339 p:0.010 df:55	24761 Ahau r:0.532 p:0.000 df:55	3187 Dalian r:0.461 p:0.000 df:55
brown hair	hair	56	0.067	0.161	0.393	0.507	0.662	0.757	0.835	7315 Kolbe r:-0.358 p:0.010 df:49	22341 Francispoulenc r:0.537 p:0.000 df:49	674 Rachele r:0.477 p:0.000 df:49
slider_ l hand fingers diameter decr|incr	hands	15	-0.036	-0.036	0.356	0.482	0.606	0.782	0.782	1338 Duponta r:-0.642 p:0.010 df:13	13792 Kuscynskyj r:0.784 p:0.001 df:13	4824 Stradonice r:-0.804 p:0.000 df:13
slider_ l hand fingers distance decr|incr	hands	10	-0.804	-0.804	-0.723	-0.404	-0.200	0.244	0.244	27578 Yogisullivan r:-0.765 p:0.010 df:8	16578 Essjayess r:0.927 p:0.000 df:8	694 Ekard r:0.914 p:0.000 df:8

		n										
slider_ l hand fingers length decr|incr	hands	10	-0.462	-0.462	-0.391	-0.119	0.269	0.296	0.296	172505 Kimberlyespy r:-0.765 p:0.010 df:8	10209 Izanaki r:0.930 p:0.000 df:8	3449 Abell r:0.895 p:0.000 df:8
slider_ l hand scale decr|incr	hands	7	-0.576	-0.576	-0.284	-0.036	0.036	0.512	0.512	293499 Wolinski r:-0.875 p:0.010 df:5	157693 Amandamarty r:0.986 p:0.000 df:5	221 Eos r:0.982 p:0.000 df:5
slider_ r hand fingers diameter decr|incr	hands	16	-0.036	-0.036	0.326	0.461	0.601	0.782	0.782	135 Hertha r:-0.623 p:0.010 df:14	13792 Kuscynskyj r:0.804 p:0.000 df:14	13792 Kuscynskyj r:0.804 p:0.000 df:14
slider_ r hand fingers distance decr|incr	hands	10	-0.804	-0.804	-0.723	-0.404	-0.200	0.244	0.244	27578 Yogisullivan r:-0.765 p:0.010 df:8	16578 Essjayess r:0.927 p:0.000 df:8	694 Ekard r:0.914 p:0.000 df:8
slider_ r hand fingers length decr|incr	hands	10	-0.462	-0.462	-0.391	-0.119	0.269	0.296	0.296	172505 Kimberlyespy r:-0.765 p:0.010 df:8	10209 Izanaki r:0.930 p:0.000 df:8	3449 Abell r:0.895 p:0.000 df:8
slider_ r hand scale decr|incr	hands	7	-0.576	-0.576	-0.284	-0.036	0.036	0.512	0.512	293499 Wolinski r:-0.875 p:0.010 df:5	157693 Amandamarty r:0.986 p:0.000 df:5	221 Eos r:0.982 p:0.000 df:5
forehead	head	97	0.055	0.062	0.084	0.106	0.142	0.226	0.325	2095 Parsifal r:-0.274 p:0.010 df:86	2251 Tikhov r:0.456 p:0.000 df:86	990 Yerkes r:0.370 p:0.000 df:86
slider_ forehead nubian decr|incr	head	18	-0.274	-0.274	-0.130	0.047	0.163	0.244	0.244	3878 Jyoumon r:-0.590 p:0.010 df:16	6244 Okamoto r:0.775 p:0.000 df:16	1846 Bengt r:0.766 p:0.000 df:16
slider_ forehead scale vert decr|incr	head	80	-1.000	-0.948	-0.730	-0.570	-0.321	-0.059	0.192	300892 Taichung r:-0.302 p:0.010 df:70	3723 Voznesenskij r:0.417 p:0.000 df:70	2055 Dvorak r:0.402 p:0.000 df:70
slider_ forehead temple decr|incr	head	21	-0.678	-0.674	-0.415	-0.398	-0.176	0.346	0.348	3616 Glazunov r:-0.562 p:0.010 df:18	6449 Kudara r:0.766 p:0.000 df:18	230 Athamantis r:0.734 p:0.000 df:18
slider_ forehead trans backward|forward	head	36	-1.000	-0.754	-0.497	-0.223	-0.011	0.842	0.886	9220 Yoshidayama r:-0.436 p:0.010 df:32	129060 Huntskretsch r:0.602 p:0.000 df:32	4948 Hideonishimura r:0.585 p:0.000 df:32
slider_ head angle in|out	head	10	-0.244	-0.244	-0.176	0.145	0.230	0.316	0.316	10281 Libourel r:-0.798 p:0.010 df:7	16247 Esner r:0.953 p:0.000 df:7	2873 Binzel r:-0.939 p:0.000 df:7
slider_ head back scale depth decr|incr	head	13	-0.700	-0.700	-0.533	-0.388	-0.254	-0.202	-0.202	8582 Kazuhisa r:-0.685 p:0.010 df:11	5145 Pholus r:0.830 p:0.000 df:11	4639 Minox r:-0.847 p:0.000 df:11
slider_ head diamond	head	74	0.026	0.042	0.140	0.231	0.351	0.747	1.000	493 Griseldis r:-0.319 p:0.010 df:63	12115 Robertgrimm r:0.526 p:0.000 df:63	2549 Baker r:0.428 p:0.000 df:63
slider_ head fat decr|incr	head	89	-0.700	-0.565	-0.393	-0.202	0.062	0.207	0.472	2115 Irakli r:-0.282 p:0.010 df:81	905 Universitas r:0.437 p:0.000 df:81	905 Universitas r:0.437 p:0.000 df:81
slider_ head invertedtriangular	head	79	0.036	0.078	0.244	0.347	0.575	0.865	1.000	2702 Batrakov r:-0.298 p:0.010 df:72	1497 Tampere r:0.423 p:0.000 df:72	1348 Michel r:-0.401 p:0.000 df:72
slider_ head oval	head	21	0.005	0.009	0.055	0.083	0.158	0.294	0.301	3308 Ferreri r:-0.562 p:0.010 df:18	3898 Curlewis r:0.796 p:0.000 df:18	108 Hecuba r:0.726 p:0.000 df:18
slider_ head rectangular	head	18	0.005	0.005	0.030	0.096	0.148	0.264	0.264	1802 Zhang Heng r:-0.625 p:0.010 df:14	129071 Catriegle r:0.813 p:0.000 df:14	7327 Crawford r:0.788 p:0.000 df:14
slider_ head round	head	27	0.010	0.014	0.068	0.109	0.171	0.345	0.399	12780 Salamony r:-0.526 p:0.010 df:21	29874 Rogerculver r:0.793 p:0.000 df:21	484 Pittsburghia r:-0.681 p:0.000 df:21
slider_ head scale depth decr|incr	head	12	-0.700	-0.700	-0.585	-0.285	-0.029	0.254	0.254	4176 Sudek r:-0.708 p:0.010 df:10	4258 Ryazanov r:0.915 p:0.000 df:10	539 Pamina r:-0.905 p:0.000 df:10
slider_ head scale horiz decr|incr	head	60	-0.512	-0.430	-0.274	-0.135	-0.006	0.170	0.306	90022 Apache Point r:-0.336 p:0.010 df:56	17954 Hopkins r:0.473 p:0.000 df:56	2845 Franklinken r:0.444 p:0.000 df:56
slider_ head scale vert decr|incr	head	60	-0.234	-0.117	0.135	0.284	0.467	0.586	0.690	38046 Krasnoyarsk r:-0.342 p:0.010 df:54	15724 Zille r:0.516 p:0.000 df:54	3962 Valyaev r:-0.453 p:0.000 df:54
slider_ head square	head	18	0.021	0.021	0.057	0.109	0.169	0.233	0.233	133874 Jonnazucarelli r:-0.641 p:0.010 df:13	6459 Hidesan r:0.805 p:0.000 df:13	259 Aletheia r:0.793 p:0.000 df:13
slider_ head triangular	head	9	0.036	0.036	0.086	0.130	0.301	0.570	0.570	437 Rhodia r:-0.835 p:0.010 df:6	18872 Tammann r:0.979 p:0.000 df:6	478 Tergeste r:0.975 p:0.000 df:6
slider_ Height	height	118	0.229	0.383	0.500	0.518	0.554	0.618	0.658	18794 Kianafrank r:-0.248 p:0.010 df:105	13327 Reitsema r:0.363 p:0.000 df:105	-10000 Sun r:-0.347 p:0.000 df:105
statscontinuous_ Height	height	730	42.000	59.000	62.000	64.000	66.000	69.000	73.000	1702 Kalahari r:-0.144 p:0.010 df:318	26323 Wuqijin r:0.206 p:0.000 df:318	1253 Frisia r:0.195 p:0.000 df:318
statscontinuous_ hips/height	height	465	0.308	0.432	0.524	0.576	0.646	0.879	1.403	7496 Miroslavholub r:-0.177 p:0.010 df:209	21464 Chinaroonchai r:0.316 p:0.000 df:209	1193 Africa r:0.258 p:0.000 df:209
pelvic hips< >subpelvic rear width	hips	138	2.330	3.069	4.609	5.718	7.529	10.369	15.361	10895 Aynrand r:-0.230 p:0.010 df:123	10358 Kirchhoff r:0.360 p:0.000 df:123	1116 Catriona r:0.339 p:0.000 df:123
pelvic hips< >waist	hips	202	2.243	2.999	4.101	5.258	6.501	9.103	15.696	21502 Cruz r:-0.190 p:0.010 df:181	1308 Halleria r:0.327 p:0.000 df:181	1308 Halleria r:0.327 p:0.000 df:181
slider_ hip scale depth decr|incr	hips	40	-0.450	-0.398	-0.210	-0.047	0.212	0.806	0.834	21856 Heathermaria r:-0.431 p:0.010 df:33	1239 Queteleta r:0.596 p:0.000 df:33	1239 Queteleta r:0.596 p:0.000 df:33
slider_ hip scale horiz decr|incr	hips	71	-0.854	-0.502	-0.326	-0.160	0.068	0.268	0.792	11306 Akesson r:-0.320 p:0.010 df:62	32120 Stevezheng r:0.460 p:0.000 df:62	18928 Pontremoli r:-0.444 p:0.000 df:62
slider_ hip scale vert decr|incr	hips	24	-0.606	-0.562	-0.238	0.057	0.306	0.933	1.000	1285 Julietta r:-0.550 p:0.010 df:19	183114 Vicques r:0.751 p:0.000 df:19	2512 Tavastia r:-0.700 p:0.000 df:19
slider_ hip trans down|up	hips	10	-0.554	-0.554	-0.081	0.306	0.550	0.752	0.752	9087 Neff r:-0.766 p:0.010 df:8	24647 Maksimachev r:0.906 p:0.000 df:8	1749 Telamon r:-0.897 p:0.000 df:8
slider_ measure hips circ decr|incr	hips	48	-0.980	-0.829	-0.490	-0.290	0.098	0.338	0.482	26376 Roborosa r:-0.380 p:0.010 df:43	20776 Juliekrugler r:0.558 p:0.000 df:43	1688 Wilkens r:0.524 p:0.000 df:43
slider_ pelvis tone decr|incr	hips	20	-1.000	-0.986	-0.480	-0.202	0.233	0.888	0.896	7363 Esquibel r:-0.591 p:0.010 df:16	8151 Andranada r:0.853 p:0.000 df:16	1625 The NORC r:0.745 p:0.000 df:16
statscontinuous_ hips	hips	489	20.000	26.000	34.000	36.000	41.000	56.000	87.000	3126 Davydov r:-0.173 p:0.010 df:219	25052 Rudawska r:0.278 p:0.000 df:219	1193 Africa r:0.245 p:0.000 df:219

		N										
subpelvic rear width< >waist	hips	138	5.963	8.230	9.683	11.103	13.172	17.567	27.683	3128 Obruchev r:-0.229 p:0.010 df:124	21659 Fredholm r:0.383 p:0.000 df:124	1356 Nyanza r:0.347 p:0.000 df:124
suprailiac< >waist	hips	218	0.920	1.528	2.205	2.871	3.540	5.135	7.765	291 Alice r:-0.182 p:0.010 df:198	33528 Jinzeman r:0.305 p:0.000 df:198	1215 Boyer r:0.251 p:0.000 df:198
slider_ l lowerleg fat decr|incr	legs	28	-0.410	-0.391	-0.101	0.078	0.209	0.494	0.512	1918 Aiguillon r:-0.488 p:0.010 df:25	4402 Tsunemori r:0.634 p:0.000 df:25	505 Cava r:-0.639 p:0.000 df:25
slider_ l lowerleg muscle decr|incr	legs	30	-0.450	-0.405	0.044	0.212	0.290	0.464	0.482	25120 Yvetteleung r:-0.477 p:0.009 df:27	1876 Napolitania r:0.660 p:0.000 df:27	1876 Napolitania r:0.660 p:0.000 df:27
slider_ l lowerleg scale depth	legs	15	-0.274	-0.274	-0.026	0.068	0.368	0.388	0.388	1180 Rita r:-0.662 p:0.010 df:12	33562 Amydunphy r:0.837 p:0.000 df:12	812 Adele r:-0.824 p:0.000 df:12
slider_ l lowerleg scale horiz	legs	18	-0.170	-0.170	0.046	0.155	0.329	0.368	0.368	2374 Vladvysotskij r:-0.590 p:0.010 df:16	213 Lilaea r:0.868 p:0.000 df:16	213 Lilaea r:0.868 p:0.000 df:16
slider_ l upperleg fat decr|incr	legs	50	-0.398	-0.324	-0.059	0.078	0.319	0.519	0.658	128315 Dereknelson r:-0.373 p:0.010 df:45	1970 Sumeria r:0.562 p:0.000 df:45	745 Mauritia r:0.521 p:0.000 df:45
slider_ l upperleg muscle decr|incr	legs	32	-0.564	-0.511	-0.122	0.165	0.284	0.646	0.854	63163 Jerusalem r:-0.456 p:0.010 df:29	4269 Bogado r:0.629 p:0.000 df:29	4269 Bogado r:0.629 p:0.000 df:29
slider_ l upperleg scale depth decr|incr	legs	41	-0.502	-0.430	0.016	0.150	0.295	0.502	0.616	121756 Sotomejias r:-0.413 p:0.010 df:36	117715 Carlkirby r:0.628 p:0.000 df:36	168 Sibylla r:-0.544 p:0.000 df:36
slider_ l upperleg scale horiz decr|incr	legs	46	-0.430	-0.380	-0.104	0.135	0.348	0.550	0.740	7459 Gilbertofranco r:-0.381 p:0.010 df:43	35313 Hangtianyuan r:0.587 p:0.000 df:43	730 Athanasia r:-0.527 p:0.000 df:43
slider_ l upperleg scale vert decr|incr	legs	7	-0.554	-0.554	-0.056	0.440	0.638	0.668	0.668	7586 Bismarck r:-0.875 p:0.010 df:5	127810 Michaelwright r:0.982 p:0.000 df:5	1800 Aguilar r:-0.984 p:0.000 df:5
slider_ r lowerleg fat decr|incr	legs	28	-0.410	-0.396	-0.147	0.073	0.209	0.494	0.512	1031 Arctica r:-0.488 p:0.010 df:25	4402 Tsunemori r:0.663 p:0.000 df:25	505 Cava r:-0.647 p:0.000 df:25
slider_ r lowerleg muscle decr|incr	legs	30	-0.450	-0.405	0.044	0.212	0.290	0.464	0.482	25120 Yvetteleung r:-0.477 p:0.009 df:27	1876 Napolitania r:0.660 p:0.000 df:27	1876 Napolitania r:0.660 p:0.000 df:27
slider_ r lowerleg scale depth	legs	15	-0.274	-0.274	-0.026	0.068	0.368	0.388	0.388	1180 Rita r:-0.662 p:0.010 df:12	33562 Amydunphy r:0.837 p:0.000 df:12	812 Adele r:-0.824 p:0.000 df:12
slider_ r lowerleg scale horiz	legs	18	-0.170	-0.170	0.046	0.155	0.329	0.368	0.368	2374 Vladvysotskij r:-0.590 p:0.010 df:16	213 Lilaea r:0.868 p:0.000 df:16	213 Lilaea r:0.868 p:0.000 df:16
slider_ r upperleg fat decr|incr	legs	52	-0.554	-0.372	-0.076	0.068	0.303	0.508	0.658	1532 Inari r:-0.365 p:0.010 df:47	1970 Sumeria r:0.609 p:0.000 df:47	745 Mauritia r:0.480 p:0.000 df:47
slider_ r upperleg muscle decr|incr	legs	31	-0.564	-0.515	-0.098	0.170	0.284	0.662	0.854	2874 Jim Young r:-0.463 p:0.010 df:28	4269 Bogado r:0.622 p:0.000 df:28	4269 Bogado r:0.622 p:0.000 df:28
slider_ r upperleg scale depth decr|incr	legs	41	-0.502	-0.430	-0.020	0.150	0.295	0.502	0.616	607 Jenny r:-0.414 p:0.010 df:36	34179 Bryanchun r:0.615 p:0.000 df:36	168 Sibylla r:-0.545 p:0.000 df:36
slider_ r upperleg scale horiz decr|incr	legs	47	-0.430	-0.374	-0.120	0.130	0.348	0.544	0.740	277 Elvira r:-0.376 p:0.010 df:44	10449 Takuma r:0.564 p:0.000 df:44	581 Tauntonia r:-0.495 p:0.000 df:44
slider_ r upperleg scale vert decr|incr	legs	7	-0.554	-0.554	-0.056	0.440	0.638	0.668	0.668	7586 Bismarck r:-0.875 p:0.010 df:5	127810 Michaelwright r:0.982 p:0.000 df:5	1800 Aguilar r:-0.984 p:0.000 df:5
thick thighs	legs	149	0.051	0.071	0.099	0.157	0.249	0.448	0.692	6362 Tunis r:-0.223 p:0.010 df:131	14080 Heppenheim r:0.332 p:0.000 df:131	4 Vesta r:0.322 p:0.000 df:131
slider_ mouth angles down|up	mouth	86	-0.222	-0.039	0.140	0.290	0.443	0.630	0.814	1953 Rupertwildt r:-0.287 p:0.010 df:78	30444 Shemp r:0.465 p:0.000 df:78	1446 Sillanpaa r:0.390 p:0.000 df:78
slider_ mouth cupidsbow decr|incr	mouth	48	-0.866	-0.700	-0.241	0.135	0.319	0.530	0.824	20632 Carlyrosser r:-0.376 p:0.010 df:44	16984 Veillet r:0.562 p:0.000 df:44	836 Jole r:0.505 p:0.000 df:44
slider_ mouth cupidsbow width decr|incr	mouth	55	-1.000	-0.778	-0.524	-0.348	0.120	0.598	0.772	1468 Zomba r:-0.361 p:0.010 df:48	3496 Arieso r:0.568 p:0.000 df:48	102 Miriam r:0.502 p:0.000 df:48
slider_ mouth dimples in|out	mouth	60	-0.678	-0.592	-0.334	-0.176	0.192	0.498	0.730	813 Baumeia r:-0.348 p:0.010 df:52	442 Eichsfeldia r:0.474 p:0.000 df:52	113 Amalthea r:0.469 p:0.000 df:52
slider_ mouth laugh lines in|out	mouth	67	-0.792	-0.583	-0.254	0.006	0.274	0.462	0.606	162 Laurentia r:-0.328 p:0.010 df:59	1486 Marilyn r:0.471 p:0.000 df:59	1023 Thomana r:-0.471 p:0.000 df:59
slider_ mouth lowerlip ext down|up	mouth	50	-0.690	-0.586	-0.218	-0.021	0.247	0.378	0.544	3404 Hinderer r:-0.366 p:0.010 df:47	21462 Karenedbal r:0.541 p:0.000 df:47	350 Ornamenta r:0.504 p:0.000 df:47
slider_ mouth lowerlip height decr|incr	mouth	82	-0.824	-0.573	-0.430	-0.254	-0.088	0.149	0.348	27578 Yogisullivan r:-0.294 p:0.010 df:74	12366 Luisapla r:0.435 p:0.000 df:74	7734 Kaltenegger r:-0.408 p:0.000 df:74
slider_ mouth lowerlip middle down|up	mouth	37	-0.700	-0.542	-0.140	-0.046	0.096	0.272	0.348	28667 Whithagins r:-0.418 p:0.010 df:35	28818 Kellyryan r:0.621 p:0.000 df:35	1364 Safara r:-0.570 p:0.000 df:35
slider_ mouth lowerlip volume decr|incr	mouth	64	-0.804	-0.573	-0.368	-0.192	0.140	0.519	0.876	33433 Maurilia r:-0.336 p:0.010 df:56	22143 Cathyfowler r:0.532 p:0.000 df:56	894 Erda r:-0.457 p:0.000 df:56
slider_ mouth lowerlip width decr|incr	mouth	52	-0.762	-0.545	-0.324	-0.197	0.190	0.566	0.876	9253 Oberth r:-0.369 p:0.010 df:46	21104 Sveshnikov r:0.561 p:0.000 df:46	734 Benda r:0.525 p:0.000 df:46
slider_ mouth philtrum volume decr|incr	mouth	57	-0.326	-0.007	0.202	0.368	0.523	0.808	0.906	1232 Cortusa r:-0.346 p:0.010 df:53	22638 Abdulla r:0.462 p:0.000 df:53	2093 Genichesk r:-0.500 p:0.000 df:53
slider_ mouth scale depth decr|incr	mouth	50	-0.668	-0.480	-0.244	0.015	0.339	0.613	0.678	11138 Hotakadake r:-0.376 p:0.010 df:44	4361 Nezhdanova r:0.581 p:0.000 df:44	4361 Nezhdanova r:0.581 p:0.000 df:44
slider_ mouth scale horiz decr|incr	mouth	71	-0.616	-0.464	-0.182	0.108	0.410	0.741	1.000	10153 Goldman r:-0.317 p:0.010 df:63	31680 Josephuitt r:0.500 p:0.000 df:63	275 Sapientia r:-0.420 p:0.000 df:63
slider_ mouth scale vert decr|incr	mouth	48	-0.886	-0.638	-0.311	-0.145	-0.006	0.514	0.586	3392 Setouchi r:-0.376 p:0.010 df:44	559 Nanon r:0.609 p:0.000 df:44	559 Nanon r:0.609 p:0.000 df:44
slider_ mouth trans backward|forward	mouth	37	-0.730	-0.647	-0.295	0.026	0.244	0.419	0.606	6300 Hosamu r:-0.430 p:0.010 df:33	17208 Pokrovska r:0.599 p:0.000 df:33	226 Weringia r:-0.566 p:0.000 df:33

Chapter 20: Introduction to the body biography and body statistics

slider	category	n										
slider_ mouth trans down|up	mouth	55	-0.720	-0.586	-0.358	-0.120	0.212	0.434	0.586	7871 Tunder r:-0.366 p:0.010 df:47	754 Malabar r:0.525 p:0.000 df:47	754 Malabar r:0.525 p:0.000 df:47
slider_ mouth upperlip ext down|up	mouth	72	-0.918	-0.782	-0.432	-0.036	0.353	0.654	1.000	94 Aurora r:-0.312 p:0.010 df:66	6237 Chikushi r:0.462 p:0.000 df:66	84 Klio r:0.418 p:0.000 df:66
slider_ mouth upperlip height decr|incr	mouth	52	-0.678	-0.517	-0.293	-0.083	0.179	0.590	0.814	2066 Palala r:-0.369 p:0.010 df:46	8088 Australia r:0.590 p:0.000 df:46	624 Hektor r:0.513 p:0.000 df:46
slider_ mouth upperlip middle down|up	mouth	46	-0.886	-0.771	-0.337	-0.083	0.111	0.421	0.482	20580 Marilpeters r:-0.389 p:0.010 df:41	32552 Jennithomas r:0.552 p:0.000 df:41	4059 Balder r:-0.511 p:0.000 df:41
slider_ mouth upperlip volume decr|incr	mouth	29	-0.854	-0.720	-0.311	-0.088	0.331	0.622	0.824	30270 Chemparathy r:-0.480 p:0.010 df:26	3711 Ellensburg r:0.611 p:0.001 df:26	489 Comacina r:-0.591 p:0.001 df:26
slider_ mouth upperlip width decr|incr	mouth	46	-0.814	-0.741	-0.428	0.088	0.334	0.685	0.854	17945 Hawass r:-0.389 p:0.010 df:41	12511 Patil r:0.563 p:0.000 df:41	3462 Zhouguangzhao r:0.526 p:0.000 df:41
muscular	muscularity	41	0.061	0.068	0.090	0.135	0.217	0.557	0.672	1569 Evita r:-0.409 p:0.010 df:37	7632 Stanislav r:0.630 p:0.000 df:37	308 Polyxo r:0.541 p:0.000 df:37
muscular male	muscularity	16	0.077	0.077	0.141	0.263	0.442	0.573	0.573	22157 Bryanhoran r:-0.641 p:0.010 df:13	33400 Laurapierson r:0.826 p:0.000 df:13	33400 Laurapierson r:0.826 p:0.000 df:13
slider_ HarveyStomachMusclesV2	muscularity	28	0.073	0.080	0.172	0.285	0.457	0.776	0.855	1952 Hesburgh r:-0.505 p:0.010 df:23	56 Melete r:0.757 p:0.000 df:23	56 Melete r:0.757 p:0.000 df:23
slider_ HarveyVCutV1	muscularity	17	0.078	0.078	0.117	0.337	0.511	1.000	1.000	3815 Konig r:-0.641 p:0.010 df:13	228 Agathe r:0.825 p:0.000 df:13	228 Agathe r:0.825 p:0.000 df:13
slider_ Muscle	muscularity	118	0.031	0.171	0.414	0.500	0.500	0.741	0.772	2220 Hicks r:-0.249 p:0.010 df:105	90328 Haryou r:0.409 p:0.000 df:105	23648 Kolar r:0.392 p:0.000 df:105
slider_ abs_ column	muscularity	18	0.036	0.036	0.131	0.179	0.419	0.591	0.591	5530 Eisinga r:-0.624 p:0.010 df:14	90449 Brucestephenson r:0.810 p:0.000 df:14	633 Zelima r:-0.787 p:0.000 df:14
neck width< >shoulder width	neck	176	1.818	2.302	3.352	4.248	4.970	7.036	11.465	10994 Fouchard r:-0.203 p:0.010 df:158	7957 Antonella r:0.292 p:0.000 df:158	7957 Antonella r:0.292 p:0.000 df:158
neck width< >subneck dorsal	neck	107	0.450	0.784	1.233	1.571	1.965	2.750	3.503	4630 Chaonis r:-0.261 p:0.010 df:95	2083 Smither r:0.357 p:0.000 df:95	2083 Smither r:0.357 p:0.000 df:95
neck width< >underbust	neck	106	9.660	10.340	14.141	15.650	18.144	23.284	36.052	1796 Riga r:-0.264 p:0.010 df:92	257261 Ovechkin r:0.382 p:0.000 df:92	4091 Lowe r:0.380 p:0.000 df:92
shoulder width< >subneck dorsal	neck	112	1.365	1.763	2.328	2.951	3.551	5.158	8.236	1948 Kampala r:-0.256 p:0.010 df:99	18026 Juliabaldwin r:0.384 p:0.000 df:99	4668 Rayjay r:0.355 p:0.000 df:99
slider_ HarveyNeckDefinitionV1	neck	47	0.073	0.163	0.373	0.523	0.637	0.853	1.000	15851 Chrisfleming r:-0.389 p:0.010 df:41	33701 Gotthold r:0.615 p:0.000 df:41	2852 Declercq r:0.559 p:0.000 df:41
slider_ measure neck height decr|incr	neck	34	-0.814	-0.783	-0.534	-0.419	-0.234	-0.115	-0.068	1058 Grubba r:-0.449 p:0.010 df:30	18027 Gokcay r:0.636 p:0.000 df:30	1449 Virtanen r:0.630 p:0.000 df:30
slider_ neck double decr|incr	neck	30	-1.000	-0.982	-0.599	-0.207	0.352	0.852	1.000	126 Velleda r:-0.472 p:0.010 df:27	3894 Williamcooke r:0.624 p:0.000 df:27	3894 Williamcooke r:0.624 p:0.000 df:27
slider_ neck scale vert decr|incr	neck	31	-1.000	-0.894	-0.678	-0.462	-0.192	-0.084	-0.078	20888 Siyueguo r:-0.471 p:0.010 df:27	2885 Palva r:0.650 p:0.000 df:27	2885 Palva r:0.650 p:0.000 df:27
slider_ neck trans down|up	neck	7	-1.000	-1.000	-0.616	-0.192	-0.016	0.202	0.202	416 Vaticana r:-0.875 p:0.010 df:5	19679 Gretabetteo r:0.988 p:0.000 df:5	1480 Aunus r:-0.966 p:0.000 df:5
dark areolae	nipples	48	0.056	0.058	0.100	0.144	0.257	0.516	0.563	209149 Chrismackenzie r:-0.389 p:0.010 df:41	25417 Coquillette r:0.562 p:0.000 df:41	2046 Leningrad r:-0.529 p:0.000 df:41
dark nipples	nipples	80	0.059	0.069	0.127	0.244	0.391	0.598	0.843	2490 Bussolini r:-0.309 p:0.010 df:67	3330 Gantrisch r:0.432 p:0.000 df:67	2576 Yesenin r:0.419 p:0.000 df:67
slider_ female areola left diameter incr	nipples	45	0.041	0.083	0.273	0.430	0.718	0.958	1.000	11949 Kagayayutaka r:-0.398 p:0.010 df:39	23734 Kimgyehyun r:0.596 p:0.000 df:39	766 Moguntia r:-0.532 p:0.000 df:39
slider_ female areola right diameter incr	nipples	47	0.041	0.076	0.290	0.446	0.772	0.973	1.000	2941 Alden r:-0.389 p:0.010 df:41	23734 Kimgyehyun r:0.556 p:0.000 df:41	1551 Argelander r:-0.510 p:0.000 df:41
slider_ female nipple left diameter incr	nipples	14	0.062	0.062	0.121	0.187	0.321	0.720	0.720	13087 Chastellux r:-0.709 p:0.010 df:10	23879 Demura r:0.941 p:0.000 df:10	5225 Loral r:-0.872 p:0.000 df:10
slider_ female nipple right diameter incr	nipples	14	0.093	0.093	0.137	0.204	0.334	0.705	0.705	17241 Wooden r:-0.708 p:0.010 df:10	23879 Demura r:0.941 p:0.000 df:10	373 Melusina r:0.858 p:0.000 df:10
slider_ nipple point decr|incr	nipples	22	-0.668	-0.618	0.080	0.244	0.428	0.737	0.762	26532 Eduardoboff r:-0.576 p:0.010 df:17	5200 Pamal r:0.771 p:0.000 df:17	615 Roswitha r:-0.792 p:0.000 df:17
slider_ nipple size decr|incr	nipples	23	-0.524	-0.495	0.068	0.264	0.502	1.000	1.000	956 Elisa r:-0.549 p:0.010 df:19	41943 Fredrick r:0.741 p:0.000 df:19	2 Pallas r:0.700 p:0.000 df:19
slider_ Nose_ alar_ crease	nose	43	0.088	0.140	0.378	0.570	0.751	0.994	1.000	1983 Bok r:-0.410 p:0.010 df:37	205599 Walkowicz r:0.574 p:0.000 df:37	28820 Sylrobertson r:0.533 p:0.000 df:37
slider_ Nose_ hole_ up	nose	13	0.093	0.093	0.213	0.316	0.472	0.907	0.907	1952 Hesburgh r:-0.684 p:0.010 df:11	3547 Serov r:0.814 p:0.001 df:11	1726 Hoffmeister r:-0.829 p:0.001 df:11
slider_ nose crease extra1	nose	33	0.347	0.395	0.601	0.782	0.998	1.000	1.000	7655 Adamries r:-0.449 p:0.010 df:30	10160 Totoro r:0.646 p:0.000 df:30	480 Hansa r:0.592 p:0.000 df:30
slider_ nose base down|up	nose	48	-0.814	-0.742	-0.319	-0.072	0.095	0.326	0.710	71556 Page r:-0.385 p:0.010 df:42	5893 Coltrane r:0.581 p:0.000 df:42	5893 Coltrane r:0.581 p:0.000 df:42
slider_ nose compression compress|uncompress	nose	32	-0.554	-0.353	0.009	0.373	0.601	0.852	0.886	21301 Zanin r:-0.449 p:0.010 df:30	17952 Folsom r:0.616 p:0.000 df:30	9255 Inoutadataka r:0.584 p:0.000 df:30
slider_ nose curve concave|convex	nose	44	-0.430	-0.363	-0.160	0.078	0.237	0.407	0.492	6596 Bittner r:-0.390 p:0.010 df:41	80801 Yiwu r:0.546 p:0.000 df:41	630 Euphemia r:-0.553 p:0.000 df:41
slider_ nose flaring decr|incr	nose	68	-0.980	-0.826	-0.480	-0.301	0.190	0.586	0.792	1868 Thersites r:-0.328 p:0.010 df:59	2774 Tenojoki r:0.486 p:0.000 df:59	2774 Tenojoki r:0.486 p:0.000 df:59

Slider	Category	n								Identifier 1	Identifier 2	Identifier 3
slider_ nose greek decr|incr	nose	26	-0.482	-0.471	-0.230	0.114	0.409	0.771	0.814	1294 Antwerpia r:-0.515 p:0.010 df:22	65712 Schneidmuller r:0.767 p:0.000 df:22	8207 Suminao r:0.702 p:0.000 df:22
slider_ nose hump decr|incr	nose	24	-0.378	-0.378	0.067	0.249	0.417	0.566	0.576	20345 Davidvito r:-0.538 p:0.010 df:20	22948 Maidanak r:0.714 p:0.000 df:20	5205 Servian r:-0.811 p:0.000 df:20
slider_ nose nostrils angle down|up	nose	65	-0.544	-0.338	-0.015	0.192	0.321	0.509	0.658	759 Vinifera r:-0.336 p:0.010 df:56	220736 Niihama r:0.538 p:0.000 df:56	2185 Guangdong r:-0.453 p:0.000 df:56
slider_ nose nostrils width decr|incr	nose	77	-0.834	-0.663	-0.342	-0.016	0.197	0.379	0.450	1017 Jacqueline r:-0.306 p:0.010 df:68	5320 Lisbeth r:0.475 p:0.000 df:68	5320 Lisbeth r:0.475 p:0.000 df:68
slider_ nose point down|up	nose	55	-0.330	-0.302	-0.120	-0.056	0.078	0.480	0.616	12119 Memamis r:-0.361 p:0.010 df:48	24 Themis r:0.597 p:0.000 df:48	24 Themis r:0.597 p:0.000 df:48
slider_ nose point width decr|incr	nose	83	-0.482	-0.406	0.098	0.296	0.534	0.864	1.000	36169 Grosseteste r:-0.292 p:0.010 df:75	193158 Haechan r:0.481 p:0.000 df:75	5222 Ioffe r:0.419 p:0.000 df:75
slider_ nose scale depth decr|incr	nose	53	-0.524	-0.385	-0.218	-0.036	0.217	0.474	0.626	1852 Carpenter r:-0.365 p:0.010 df:47	662 Newtonia r:0.495 p:0.000 df:47	662 Newtonia r:0.495 p:0.000 df:47
slider_ nose scale horiz decr|incr	nose	75	-0.668	-0.558	-0.234	0.026	0.254	0.616	0.792	2388 Gase r:-0.311 p:0.010 df:66	1004 Belopolskya r:0.413 p:0.000 df:66	1004 Belopolskya r:0.413 p:0.000 df:66
slider_ nose scale vert decr|incr	nose	64	-0.610	-0.412	-0.150	0.274	0.552	0.889	0.968	8944 Ortigara r:-0.342 p:0.010 df:54	3522 Becker r:0.494 p:0.000 df:54	433 Eros r:-0.481 p:0.000 df:54
slider_ nose septumangle decr|incr	nose	71	-0.866	-0.546	-0.046	0.264	0.492	0.834	1.000	7452 Izabelyuria r:-0.317 p:0.010 df:63	106545 Colanduno r:0.526 p:0.000 df:63	6241 Galante r:0.475 p:0.000 df:63
slider_ nose trans backward|forward	nose	34	-0.730	-0.723	0.032	0.160	0.264	0.551	0.854	13039 Awashima r:-0.451 p:0.010 df:30	3981 Stodola r:0.629 p:0.000 df:30	3981 Stodola r:0.629 p:0.000 df:30
slider_ nose trans down|up	nose	51	-1.000	-0.923	-0.544	-0.364	0.026	0.532	0.782	19175 Peterpiot r:-0.376 p:0.010 df:44	248908 Ginostrada r:0.581 p:0.000 df:44	248908 Ginostrada r:0.581 p:0.000 df:44
slider_ nose volume decr|incr	nose	69	-0.450	-0.223	0.093	0.182	0.277	0.472	0.606	11075 Donhoff r:-0.323 p:0.010 df:61	7739 Cech r:0.499 p:0.000 df:61	732 Tjilaki r:0.465 p:0.000 df:61
slider_ nose width1 decr|incr	nose	50	-0.730	-0.655	-0.197	0.187	0.361	0.618	1.000	14555 Shinohara r:-0.381 p:0.010 df:43	94556 Janstary r:0.669 p:0.000 df:43	2916 Voronveliya r:-0.515 p:0.000 df:43
slider_ nose width2 decr|incr	nose	76	-0.782	-0.617	-0.184	0.098	0.272	0.432	0.534	9073 Yoshinori r:-0.304 p:0.010 df:69	314808 Martindutertre r:0.392 p:0.001 df:69	2796 Kron r:-0.422 p:0.000 df:69
slider_ nose width3 decr|incr	nose	83	-0.720	-0.474	-0.120	0.130	0.254	0.494	0.814	12067 Jeter r:-0.298 p:0.010 df:72	24671 Frankmartin r:0.388 p:0.001 df:72	1540 Kevola r:-0.402 p:0.000 df:72
slider_ nostril_ rounding	nose	22	0.047	0.048	0.188	0.319	0.666	0.830	0.839	4377 Koremori r:-0.550 p:0.010 df:19	21088 Chelyabinsk r:0.733 p:0.000 df:19	3351 Smith r:-0.700 p:0.000 df:19
slider_ septum_ sharp	nose	24	0.244	0.257	0.394	0.692	0.942	1.000	1.000	16644 Otemaedaigaku r:-0.549 p:0.010 df:19	653 Berenike r:0.744 p:0.000 df:19	653 Berenike r:0.744 p:0.000 df:19
collarbone	shoulders	189	0.054	0.066	0.083	0.112	0.145	0.214	0.385	3644 Kojitaku r:-0.195 p:0.010 df:172	2084 Okayama r:0.369 p:0.000 df:172	457 Alleghenia r:0.271 p:0.000 df:172
slider_ Shoulder_ Shape	shoulders	35	0.016	0.098	0.342	0.425	0.756	0.898	0.948	30035 Charlesliu r:-0.443 p:0.010 df:31	10949 Konigstuhl r:0.631 p:0.000 df:31	10949 Konigstuhl r:0.631 p:0.000 df:31
slider_ measure shoulder dist decr|incr	shoulders	12	-0.876	-0.876	-0.630	-0.476	-0.277	0.016	0.016	33522 Chizumimaeta r:-0.709 p:0.010 df:10	23120 Paulallen r:0.930 p:0.000 df:10	8945 Cavaradossi r:-0.861 p:0.000 df:10
dark skin	skin	257	0.056	0.118	0.255	0.374	0.536	0.746	0.860	30070 Thabitpulak r:-0.169 p:0.010 df:229	5141 Tachibana r:0.243 p:0.000 df:229	163 Erigone r:0.240 p:0.000 df:229
freckles	skin	132	0.054	0.069	0.104	0.167	0.295	0.494	0.580	1149 Volga r:-0.231 p:0.010 df:122	328477 Eckstein r:0.340 p:0.000 df:122	6725 Engyoji r:-0.311 p:0.000 df:122
pale skin	skin	18	0.069	0.069	0.096	0.184	0.324	0.363	0.363	29463 Benjaminpeirce r:-0.644 p:0.009 df:13	121315 Mikelentz r:0.920 p:0.000 df:13	557 Violetta r:0.808 p:0.000 df:13
skindentation	skin	59	0.055	0.058	0.088	0.135	0.189	0.316	0.386	5813 Eizaburo r:-0.349 p:0.010 df:52	12621 Alsufi r:0.491 p:0.000 df:52	1191 Alfaterna r:-0.471 p:0.000 df:52
veins	skin	28	0.066	0.068	0.099	0.122	0.196	0.542	0.708	773 Irmintraud r:-0.506 p:0.010 df:23	671 Carnegia r:0.738 p:0.000 df:23	45 Eugenia r:-0.658 p:0.000 df:23
belly	stomach	39	0.064	0.083	0.140	0.213	0.286	0.435	0.567	16007 Kaasalainen r:-0.430 p:0.010 df:33	18907 Kevinclaytor r:0.647 p:0.000 df:33	1061 Paeonia r:-0.648 p:0.000 df:33
slider_ stomach navel down|up	stomach	43	-1.000	-1.000	-0.886	-0.648	-0.410	-0.144	0.938	2833 Radishchev r:-0.408 p:0.010 df:37	7102 Neilbone r:0.591 p:0.000 df:37	1280 Baillauda r:-0.614 p:0.000 df:37
slider_ stomach navel in|out	stomach	9	-0.430	-0.430	-0.404	-0.160	0.011	0.264	0.264	134130 Apaczai r:-0.798 p:0.010 df:7	400673 Vitapolunina r:0.955 p:0.000 df:7	792 Metcalfia r:0.933 p:0.000 df:7
slider_ stomach pregnant decr|incr	stomach	30	-0.462	-0.462	-0.334	0.025	0.120	0.264	0.264	13478 Fraunhofer r:-0.479 p:0.010 df:26	6778 Tosamakoto r:0.706 p:0.000 df:26	4499 Davidallen r:0.686 p:0.000 df:26
slider_ stomach tone decr|incr	stomach	70	-1.000	-0.740	-0.401	0.010	0.562	0.861	1.000	104896 Schwanden r:-0.325 p:0.010 df:60	54237 Hiroshimanabe r:0.463 p:0.000 df:60	906 Repsolda r:-0.440 p:0.000 df:60
shoulder width< >waist	torso	208	10.505	11.675	14.736	16.700	19.183	24.810	38.459	1144 Oda r:-0.187 p:0.010 df:188	808 Merxia r:0.280 p:0.000 df:188	808 Merxia r:0.280 p:0.000 df:188
slider_ measure waist circ decr|incr	torso	62	-1.000	-1.000	-0.746	-0.301	-0.018	0.523	0.772	3763 Qianxuesen r:-0.339 p:0.010 df:55	9555 Frejakocha r:0.447 p:0.000 df:55	1216 Askania r:-0.448 p:0.000 df:55
slider_ torso scale depth decr|incr	torso	22	-0.824	-0.810	-0.344	-0.125	-0.029	0.542	0.586	16706 Svojsik r:-0.563 p:0.010 df:18	288478 Fahlman r:0.737 p:0.000 df:18	2628 Kopal r:0.714 p:0.000 df:18
slider_ torso scale horiz decr|incr	torso	34	-0.772	-0.640	-0.267	-0.160	0.029	0.466	0.544	3475 Fichte r:-0.456 p:0.010 df:29	7103 Wichmann r:0.640 p:0.000 df:29	7103 Wichmann r:0.640 p:0.000 df:29
slider_ torso scale vert decr|incr	torso	12	-0.730	-0.730	-0.552	-0.492	-0.218	0.150	0.150	1205 Ebella r:-0.709 p:0.010 df:10	9282 Lucylim r:0.874 p:0.000 df:10	151 Abundantia r:0.857 p:0.000 df:10

Name	Cat	N								Correlation 1	Correlation 2	Correlation 3
slider_ torso vshape decr|incr	torso	26	-0.440	-0.430	-0.321	-0.150	0.086	0.393	0.440	8313 Christiansen r:-0.505 p:0.010 df:23	20689 Zhuyuanchen r:0.747 p:0.000 df:23	515 Athalia r:-0.653 p:0.000 df:23
statscontinuous_ waist	torso	500	18.000	21.000	24.000	26.000	32.000	43.900	65.000	4831 Baldwin r:-0.171 p:0.010 df:224	22717 Romeuf r:0.308 p:0.000 df:224	3518 Florena r:-0.236 p:0.000 df:224
statscontinuous_ waist/height	torso	476	0.265	0.338	0.377	0.415	0.492	0.663	1.051	1123 Shapleya r:-0.175 p:0.010 df:214	22717 Romeuf r:0.328 p:0.000 df:214	2235 Vittore r:-0.249 p:0.000 df:214
subpelvic rear width< >suprailiac	torso	128	3.116	5.508	7.133	8.133	10.072	12.912	22.871	5357 Sekiguchi r:-0.239 p:0.010 df:114	10358 Kirchhoff r:0.406 p:0.000 df:114	1116 Catriona r:0.363 p:0.000 df:114
underbust< >waist	torso	183	0.833	1.790	3.351	4.739	6.333	9.611	17.496	22112 Staceyraw r:-0.199 p:0.010 df:164	14998 Ogosemachi r:0.288 p:0.000 df:164	1017 Jacqueline r:-0.274 p:0.000 df:164
slider_ SSBBW Arms	weight	20	0.016	0.017	0.044	0.119	0.306	0.439	0.440	2788 Andenne r:-0.591 p:0.010 df:16	11247 Wilburwright r:0.826 p:0.000 df:16	2776 Baikal r:0.761 p:0.000 df:16
slider_ SSBBW Back	weight	18	0.057	0.057	0.109	0.189	0.276	0.544	0.544	5403 Takachiho r:-0.641 p:0.010 df:13	8269 Calandrelli r:0.828 p:0.000 df:13	1166 Sakuntala r:0.818 p:0.000 df:13
slider_ SSBBW Belly	weight	21	0.026	0.027	0.052	0.073	0.109	0.249	0.254	6919 Tomonaga r:-0.593 p:0.009 df:16	5860 Deankoontz r:0.787 p:0.000 df:16	3508 Pasternak r:0.745 p:0.000 df:16
slider_ SSBBW Breast	weight	34	0.031	0.035	0.122	0.176	0.232	0.474	0.497	1128 Astrid r:-0.463 p:0.010 df:28	180855 Debrarose r:0.654 p:0.000 df:28	8601 Ciconia r:0.610 p:0.000 df:28
slider_ SSBBW Hip	weight	21	0.041	0.043	0.093	0.140	0.220	0.410	0.425	5884 Dolezal r:-0.578 p:0.010 df:17	22817 Shankar r:0.759 p:0.000 df:17	352 Gisela r:-0.735 p:0.000 df:17
slider_ SSBBW Rear Legs	weight	18	0.031	0.031	0.069	0.143	0.255	0.352	0.352	229737 Porthos r:-0.606 p:0.010 df:15	21607 Robel r:0.805 p:0.000 df:15	2049 Grietje r:-0.815 p:0.000 df:15
slider_ Weight	weight	118	0.088	0.181	0.321	0.500	0.637	0.877	1.000	14976 Josefcapek r:-0.250 p:0.009 df:105	100267 JAXA r:0.399 p:0.000 df:105	4545 Primolevi r:-0.340 p:0.000 df:105
statscontinuous_ Weight	weight	622	73.000	86.000	110.000	126.000	155.000	250.000	370.000	5894 Telc r:-0.155 p:0.010 df:274	48640 Eziobosso r:0.262 p:0.000 df:274	9562 Memling r:0.234 p:0.000 df:274
statscontinuous_ Weight/height	weight	615	1.090	1.353	1.726	1.953	2.388	3.900	5.692	235 Carolina r:-0.156 p:0.010 df:269	9562 Memling r:0.259 p:0.000 df:269	1205 Ebella r:0.212 p:0.000 df:269
statscontinuous_ hips/weight	weight	428	0.054	0.184	0.250	0.284	0.320	0.382	1.027	5158 Ogarev r:-0.183 p:0.010 df:195	11121 Malpighi r:0.285 p:0.000 df:195	283 Emma r:-0.259 p:0.000 df:195
statscontinuous_ waist/weight	weight	436	0.054	0.147	0.190	0.208	0.233	0.290	0.739	16259 Housinger r:-0.181 p:0.010 df:199	4784 Samcarin r:0.298 p:0.000 df:199	2619 Skalnate Pleso r:-0.247 p:0.000 df:199
ab perimeter / ab width		161	3.711	6.551	9.781	11.967	14.490	33.176	53.334	3623 Chaplin r:-0.214 p:0.010 df:143	65159 Sprowls r:0.348 p:0.000 df:143	604 Tekmessa r:0.311 p:0.000 df:143
ab perimeter / ankle to heel floor h		63	9.907	12.403	20.238	23.782	29.507	113.496	133.638	2115 Irakli r:-0.342 p:0.010 df:54	3484 Neugebauer r:0.526 p:0.000 df:54	2234 Schmadel r:0.483 p:0.000 df:54
ab perimeter / ankle width		88	7.470	10.791	19.197	24.338	30.676	78.713	161.295	210997 Guenat r:-0.290 p:0.010 df:77	121631 Josephnuth r:0.415 p:0.000 df:77	2142 Landau r:-0.404 p:0.000 df:77
ab perimeter / areola dia		166	9.201	13.815	24.802	41.516	57.050	107.145	200.255	3579 Rockholt r:-0.209 p:0.010 df:150	26935 Vireday r:0.306 p:0.000 df:150	3796 Lene r:-0.287 p:0.000 df:150
ab perimeter / back perimeter		50	0.245	0.366	0.479	0.656	0.954	1.858	3.544	7655 Adamries r:-0.368 p:0.010 df:46	2168 Swope r:0.640 p:0.000 df:46	138 Tolosa r:0.498 p:0.000 df:46
ab perimeter / back tone		51	0.291	1.090	1.777	2.320	3.220	7.062	9.173	7248 Alvsjo r:-0.365 p:0.010 df:47	12649 Ascanios r:0.557 p:0.000 df:47	2872 Gentelec r:-0.505 p:0.000 df:47
ab perimeter / ball width		37	5.754	8.722	13.725	18.547	20.645	60.752	77.816	17351 Pheidippos r:-0.418 p:0.010 df:35	22991 Jeffreyklus r:0.664 p:0.000 df:35	1047 Geisha r:0.599 p:0.000 df:35
ab perimeter / bicep width		175	4.675	9.925	16.141	19.785	23.870	56.518	74.688	2773 Brooks r:-0.204 p:0.010 df:156	26935 Vireday r:0.380 p:0.000 df:156	604 Tekmessa r:0.306 p:0.000 df:156
ab perimeter / big toe length		38	4.740	10.927	24.760	33.701	45.931	162.511	191.903	2288 Karolinum r:-0.425 p:0.010 df:34	22928 Templehe r:0.724 p:0.000 df:34	628 Christine r:0.613 p:0.000 df:34
ab perimeter / big toe width		32	7.692	14.520	39.460	49.780	72.507	186.447	222.347	4503 Cleobulus r:-0.449 p:0.010 df:30	32314 Rachelzhang r:0.731 p:0.000 df:30	131 Vala r:0.582 p:0.000 df:30
ab perimeter / bra shoulder to underb		150	2.284	3.533	5.638	7.034	9.233	17.716	26.836	1570 Brunonia r:-0.220 p:0.010 df:135	21403 Haken r:0.364 p:0.000 df:135	455 Bruchsalia r:0.297 p:0.000 df:135
ab perimeter / breast depth		114	3.723	14.781	27.346	41.141	59.841	110.059	186.463	7935 Beppefenoglio r:-0.252 p:0.010 df:102	435728 Yunlin r:0.454 p:0.000 df:102	1422 Stromgrenia r:0.341 p:0.000 df:102
ab perimeter / breasts apart		172	9.953	15.952	28.748	38.101	62.692	147.359	286.018	9865 Akiraohta r:-0.206 p:0.010 df:154	34188 Clarawagner r:0.313 p:0.000 df:154	1495 Helsinki r:-0.280 p:0.000 df:154
ab perimeter / bust dia		184	3.941	6.646	10.281	13.060	16.223	33.725	53.067	4068 Menestheus r:-0.198 p:0.010 df:167	26935 Vireday r:0.337 p:0.000 df:167	604 Tekmessa r:0.312 p:0.000 df:167
ab perimeter / butt square		43	1.046	1.068	1.996	2.411	3.048	5.455	6.840	1170 Siva r:-0.403 p:0.010 df:38	8965 Citrinella r:0.563 p:0.000 df:38	5031 Svejcar r:-0.552 p:0.000 df:38
ab perimeter / calf width		98	3.972	6.130	11.740	14.548	17.103	43.738	84.270	446 Aeternitas r:-0.272 p:0.010 df:87	6353 Semper r:0.380 p:0.000 df:87	6353 Semper r:0.380 p:0.000 df:87
ab perimeter / chest width		173	2.136	3.189	5.058	5.979	7.327	15.016	25.586	8110 Heath r:-0.206 p:0.010 df:155	27390 Kyledavis r:0.470 p:0.000 df:155	1823 Gliese r:0.283 p:0.000 df:155
ab perimeter / clavicle to groin h		132	1.114	1.985	2.812	3.336	4.046	9.237	15.722	1677 Tycho Brahe r:-0.236 p:0.010 df:116	9409 Kanpuzan r:0.394 p:0.000 df:116	446 Aeternitas r:-0.342 p:0.000 df:116
ab perimeter / clavicle to neck h		117	7.841	11.386	18.678	23.671	30.670	82.528	130.731	9282 Lucylim r:-0.251 p:0.010 df:103	12016 Green r:0.376 p:0.000 df:103	4333 Sinton r:0.340 p:0.000 df:103
ab perimeter / elbow to wrist h		161	1.787	3.621	6.327	7.758	9.545	19.111	38.018	2982 Muriel r:-0.213 p:0.010 df:144	26935 Vireday r:0.362 p:0.000 df:144	164 Eva r:0.307 p:0.000 df:144

ab perimeter / foot base h	63	3.261	4.497	7.332	9.227	11.697	37.330	57.105	46392 Bertola r:-0.342 p:0.010 df:54	6353 Semper r:0.514 p:0.000 df:54	1876 Napolitania r:0.471 p:0.000 df:54
ab perimeter / heel width	38	9.495	9.755	21.936	26.912	32.968	97.962	125.580	31438 Yasuhitohayashi r:-0.419 p:0.010 df:35	32108 Jovanzhang r:0.675 p:0.000 df:35	1198 Atlantis r:0.607 p:0.000 df:35
ab perimeter / long finger length	75	3.192	4.620	7.552	8.946	11.339	27.434	55.904	3445 Pinson r:-0.306 p:0.010 df:68	65363 Ruthanna r:0.488 p:0.000 df:68	767 Bondia r:0.426 p:0.000 df:68
ab perimeter / lower forearm w	182	7.174	14.006	25.393	30.245	38.864	76.679	129.384	4586 Gunvor r:-0.200 p:0.010 df:164	604 Tekmessa r:0.338 p:0.000 df:164	164 Eva r:0.270 p:0.000 df:164
ab perimeter / lower leg h	84	1.394	2.235	3.731	4.787	6.115	17.428	26.548	1621 Druzhba r:-0.296 p:0.010 df:73	121631 Josephnuth r:0.428 p:0.000 df:73	803 Picka r:0.417 p:0.000 df:73
ab perimeter / neck width	138	5.735	9.334	14.528	16.908	20.241	31.266	74.044	7201 Kuritariku r:-0.228 p:0.010 df:125	1198 Atlantis r:0.367 p:0.000 df:125	1198 Atlantis r:0.367 p:0.000 df:125
ab perimeter / nipple dia	160	33.341	71.479	109.253	143.013	183.996	339.568	521.150	446 Aeternitas r:-0.211 p:0.010 df:146	26935 Vireday r:0.373 p:0.000 df:146	1198 Atlantis r:0.286 p:0.000 df:146
ab perimeter / nipple to bottom	153	5.738	15.178	23.086	29.392	38.025	80.371	159.028	18113 Bibring r:-0.216 p:0.010 df:140	120153 Hoekenga r:0.337 p:0.000 df:140	615 Roswitha r:0.336 p:0.000 df:140
ab perimeter / nipple to top	153	3.625	6.724	11.436	15.368	21.421	40.545	54.689	4180 Anaxagoras r:-0.217 p:0.010 df:139	21626 Matthewhall r:0.351 p:0.000 df:139	3796 Lene r:0.346 p:0.000 df:139
ab perimeter / pelvic hips	167	2.165	3.074	4.952	5.756	7.224	11.950	25.974	1685 Toro r:-0.209 p:0.010 df:151	21729 Kimrichards r:0.368 p:0.000 df:151	932 Hooveria r:-0.295 p:0.000 df:151
ab perimeter / second toe length	29	5.417	9.446	26.411	44.326	52.432	192.624	216.215	4834 Thoas r:-0.471 p:0.010 df:27	22991 Jeffreyklus r:0.814 p:0.000 df:27	80 Sappho r:0.608 p:0.000 df:27
ab perimeter / shoulder to elbow h	170	2.327	3.621	5.497	6.603	8.057	16.315	29.812	1291 Phryne r:-0.206 p:0.010 df:154	615 Roswitha r:0.299 p:0.000 df:154	604 Tekmessa r:0.292 p:0.000 df:154
ab perimeter / shoulder width	185	2.376	3.156	4.610	5.405	6.621	13.854	24.079	7095 Lamettrie r:-0.198 p:0.010 df:167	26935 Vireday r:0.338 p:0.000 df:167	604 Tekmessa r:0.280 p:0.000 df:167
ab perimeter / subchest width	97	1.588	3.441	5.296	6.364	7.921	18.769	27.424	14539 Clocke Roeland r:-0.274 p:0.010 df:86	27390 Kyledavis r:0.502 p:0.000 df:86	2098 Zyskin r:0.369 p:0.000 df:86
ab perimeter / subneck dorsal	81	6.378	6.904	10.642	12.660	15.793	32.112	62.251	807 Ceraskia r:-0.301 p:0.010 df:71	615 Roswitha r:0.495 p:0.000 df:71	615 Roswitha r:0.495 p:0.000 df:71
ab perimeter / subpelvic rear width	118	1.243	2.635	4.390	4.987	5.835	9.268	16.983	10270 Skoglov r:-0.245 p:0.010 df:108	27390 Kyledavis r:0.452 p:0.000 df:108	2380 Heilongjiang r:0.349 p:0.000 df:108
ab perimeter / suprailiac	182	2.187	3.568	5.340	6.312	7.717	12.628	28.885	23204 Arditkroni r:-0.198 p:0.010 df:166	27390 Kyledavis r:0.339 p:0.000 df:166	1364 Safara r:0.268 p:0.000 df:166
ab perimeter / underbust	164	2.570	3.952	5.868	6.693	8.189	17.175	29.692	9818 Eurymachos r:-0.210 p:0.010 df:148	26935 Vireday r:0.349 p:0.000 df:148	615 Roswitha r:0.288 p:0.000 df:148
ab perimeter / upper forearm w	184	4.807	9.893	17.112	21.247	25.946	43.393	88.569	4586 Gunvor r:-0.199 p:0.010 df:165	27390 Kyledavis r:0.350 p:0.000 df:165	604 Tekmessa r:0.284 p:0.000 df:165
ab perimeter / waist	188	2.507	3.867	5.922	6.966	8.622	16.357	32.274	2617 Jiangxi r:-0.195 p:0.010 df:172	27390 Kyledavis r:0.304 p:0.000 df:172	1364 Safara r:0.289 p:0.000 df:172
ab tone / ab perimeter	206	0.007	0.018	0.092	0.203	0.330	0.532	0.911	128439 Chriswaters r:-0.187 p:0.010 df:186	249160 Urriellu r:0.331 p:0.000 df:186	3381 Mikkola r:0.264 p:0.000 df:186
ab tone / ab width	161	0.048	0.226	1.339	2.986	4.628	6.891	9.879	9228 Nakahiroshi r:-0.214 p:0.010 df:142	25624 Kronecker r:0.321 p:0.000 df:142	6321 Namuratakao r:0.306 p:0.000 df:142
ab tone / ankle to heel floor h	62	0.398	1.216	4.245	6.816	10.510	13.527	20.254	7586 Bismarck r:-0.346 p:0.010 df:53	144496 Reingard r:0.485 p:0.000 df:53	3945 Gerasimenko r:-0.477 p:0.000 df:53
ab tone / ankle width	87	0.383	1.078	4.008	6.750	9.647	13.475	27.162	10584 Ferrini r:-0.292 p:0.009 df:76	6514 Torahiko r:0.436 p:0.000 df:76	59 Elpis r:-0.412 p:0.000 df:76
ab tone / areola dia	165	0.082	0.435	3.488	8.969	15.041	30.346	36.176	19955 Holly r:-0.209 p:0.010 df:149	25624 Kronecker r:0.318 p:0.000 df:149	11321 Tosimatumoto r:-0.282 p:0.000 df:149
ab tone / back perimeter	50	0.022	0.029	0.101	0.175	0.277	0.542	1.069	5944 Utesov r:-0.369 p:0.010 df:46	2126 Gerasimovich r:0.583 p:0.000 df:46	93 Minerva r:0.485 p:0.000 df:46
ab tone / back tone	51	0.062	0.103	0.383	0.624	0.862	1.947	2.055	5049 Sherlock r:-0.365 p:0.010 df:47	5634 Victorborge r:0.535 p:0.000 df:47	2126 Gerasimovich r:0.486 p:0.000 df:47
ab tone / ball width	37	0.878	1.260	3.077	5.002	6.768	10.209	10.510	33270 Katiecrysup r:-0.418 p:0.010 df:35	27792 Fridakahlo r:0.574 p:0.000 df:35	4762 Dobrynya r:-0.573 p:0.000 df:35
ab tone / bicep width	175	0.136	0.509	2.367	4.578	6.696	10.582	14.016	130089 Saadatanwar r:-0.205 p:0.010 df:155	25624 Kronecker r:0.332 p:0.000 df:155	4455 Ruriko r:0.276 p:0.000 df:155
ab tone / big toe length	38	0.229	1.561	5.296	9.139	16.105	24.975	27.710	92892 Robertlawrence r:-0.424 p:0.010 df:34	18395 Schmiedmayer r:0.701 p:0.000 df:34	950 Ahrensa r:-0.578 p:0.000 df:34
ab tone / big toe width	32	0.371	1.771	6.920	12.807	23.190	35.091	35.760	5554 Keesey r:-0.450 p:0.010 df:30	6220 Stepanmakarov r:0.689 p:0.000 df:30	896 Sphinx r:0.644 p:0.000 df:30
ab tone / bra shoulder to underb	149	0.019	0.084	0.788	1.552	2.531	3.955	5.160	26267 Nickmorgan r:-0.220 p:0.010 df:134	5707 Shevchenko r:0.372 p:0.000 df:134	2193 Jackson r:-0.300 p:0.000 df:134
ab tone / breast depth	114	0.091	0.611	4.062	8.020	14.600	32.473	64.293	533 Sara r:-0.253 p:0.010 df:101	1138 Attica r:0.387 p:0.000 df:101	907 Rhoda r:-0.345 p:0.000 df:101
ab tone / breasts apart	172	0.223	1.057	5.177	8.495	12.261	26.929	45.903	4104 Alu r:-0.207 p:0.010 df:153	18395 Schmiedmayer r:0.297 p:0.000 df:153	18395 Schmiedmayer r:0.297 p:0.000 df:153
ab tone / bust dia	184	0.036	0.163	1.314	2.725	4.799	7.632	13.239	1969 Alain r:-0.198 p:0.010 df:166	249160 Urriellu r:0.320 p:0.000 df:166	8297 Gerardfaure r:0.275 p:0.000 df:166
ab tone / butt square	43	0.022	0.054	0.397	0.733	0.924	1.609	1.776	7560 Spudis r:-0.403 p:0.010 df:38	2701 Cherson r:0.556 p:0.000 df:38	146 Lucina r:-0.555 p:0.000 df:38

ab tone / calf width		97	0.239	0.527	2.047	3.622	5.650	7.915	12.636	9510 Gurnemanz r:-0.273 p:0.010 df:86	3783 Morris r:0.428 p:0.000 df:86	2470 Agematsu r:0.396 p:0.000 df:86
ab tone / chest width		172	0.019	0.074	0.631	1.247	2.102	3.191	6.362	912 Maritima r:-0.206 p:0.010 df:154	249160 Urriellu r:0.300 p:0.000 df:154	5707 Shevchenko r:0.277 p:0.000 df:154
ab tone / clavicle to groin h		132	0.014	0.106	0.465	0.816	1.134	1.639	2.824	30096 Glindadavidson r:-0.237 p:0.010 df:115	25624 Kronecker r:0.379 p:0.000 df:115	9232 Miretti r:-0.320 p:0.000 df:115
ab tone / clavicle to neck h		116	0.092	0.567	3.548	6.201	8.784	14.013	21.434	4751 Alicemanning r:-0.252 p:0.010 df:102	249160 Urriellu r:0.416 p:0.000 df:102	471 Papagena r:-0.338 p:0.000 df:102
ab tone / elbow to wrist h		161	0.028	0.164	0.924	1.730	2.483	3.706	5.672	3901 Nanjingdaxue r:-0.213 p:0.010 df:143	144496 Reingard r:0.340 p:0.000 df:143	3905 Doppler r:0.288 p:0.000 df:143
ab tone / foot base h		63	0.134	0.361	1.299	2.635	3.779	5.153	7.040	1021 Flammario r:-0.342 p:0.010 df:54	246247 Sheldoncooper r:0.521 p:0.000 df:54	1245 Calvinia r:-0.478 p:0.000 df:54
ab tone / heel width		38	0.968	1.292	4.788	7.998	10.020	14.058	17.722	650 Amalasuntha r:-0.420 p:0.010 df:35	243002 Lemmy r:0.631 p:0.000 df:35	3157 Novikov r:0.559 p:0.000 df:35
ab tone / long finger length		74	0.035	0.169	1.446	2.224	3.538	5.152	7.053	24639 Mukhametdinov r:-0.308 p:0.010 df:67	15630 Disanti r:0.501 p:0.000 df:67	8571 Taniguchi r:-0.417 p:0.000 df:67
ab tone / lower forearm w		182	0.118	0.446	3.683	6.848	10.305	17.103	23.729	33590 Sreelakshmi r:-0.200 p:0.010 df:163	249160 Urriellu r:0.316 p:0.000 df:163	3905 Doppler r:0.269 p:0.000 df:163
ab tone / lower leg h		83	0.086	0.168	0.647	1.329	1.859	2.419	5.263	25760 Annaspitz r:-0.298 p:0.010 df:72	2470 Agematsu r:0.421 p:0.000 df:72	2470 Agematsu r:0.421 p:0.000 df:72
ab tone / neck width		138	0.062	0.404	2.622	4.193	5.823	8.946	14.739	1200 Imperatrix r:-0.230 p:0.010 df:124	243002 Lemmy r:0.350 p:0.000 df:124	4455 Ruriko r:0.331 p:0.000 df:124
ab tone / nipple dia		160	0.490	1.677	14.160	30.993	50.982	88.904	123.608	110298 Deceptionisland r:-0.212 p:0.010 df:145	25624 Kronecker r:0.370 p:0.000 df:145	11321 Tosimatumoto r:-0.284 p:0.000 df:145
ab tone / nipple to bottom		153	0.097	0.447	3.457	6.336	9.562	13.584	20.412	744 Aguntina r:-0.217 p:0.010 df:139	257336 Noeliasanchez r:0.290 p:0.000 df:139	12975 Efremov r:-0.301 p:0.000 df:139
ab tone / nipple to top		153	0.032	0.180	1.481	3.587	5.589	9.812	12.242	5756 Wassenbergh r:-0.217 p:0.010 df:138	25624 Kronecker r:0.343 p:0.000 df:138	4455 Ruriko r:0.291 p:0.000 df:138
ab tone / pelvic hips		167	0.018	0.103	0.588	1.305	1.989	3.110	4.863	4529 Webern r:-0.208 p:0.010 df:150	15630 Disanti r:0.306 p:0.000 df:150	15630 Disanti r:0.306 p:0.000 df:150
ab tone / second toe length		29	0.261	1.405	5.131	9.998	16.599	25.570	27.605	26013 Amandalonzo r:-0.473 p:0.010 df:27	25693 Ishitani r:0.724 p:0.000 df:27	4132 Bartok r:-0.639 p:0.000 df:27
ab tone / shoulder to elbow h		170	0.025	0.140	0.865	1.519	2.243	3.190	4.930	28039 Mauraoei r:-0.206 p:0.010 df:153	249160 Urriellu r:0.329 p:0.000 df:153	4485 Radonezhskij r:0.289 p:0.000 df:153
ab tone / shoulder width		185	0.020	0.099	0.636	1.223	1.752	2.742	4.250	24048 Pedroduque r:-0.198 p:0.010 df:166	249160 Urriellu r:0.306 p:0.000 df:166	3905 Doppler r:0.268 p:0.000 df:166
ab tone / subchest width		96	0.040	0.110	0.615	1.354	2.127	3.182	6.996	4193 Salanave r:-0.275 p:0.010 df:85	4021 Dancey r:0.379 p:0.000 df:85	4021 Dancey r:0.379 p:0.000 df:85
ab tone / subneck dorsal		80	0.052	0.338	2.127	3.438	5.027	7.458	8.673	210271 Samarkand r:-0.302 p:0.010 df:70	6244 Okamoto r:0.434 p:0.000 df:70	2004 Lexell r:-0.415 p:0.000 df:70
ab tone / subpelvic rear width		119	0.034	0.104	0.597	1.097	1.764	2.674	4.074	6921 Janejacobs r:-0.245 p:0.010 df:108	8336 Safarik r:0.420 p:0.000 df:108	4073 Ruianzhongxue r:0.342 p:0.000 df:108
ab tone / suprailiac		182	0.036	0.101	0.690	1.409	2.160	3.420	5.898	2259 Sofievka r:-0.199 p:0.010 df:165	249160 Urriellu r:0.312 p:0.000 df:165	12235 Imranakperov r:0.278 p:0.000 df:165
ab tone / underbust		164	0.034	0.134	0.838	1.448	2.292	3.723	7.181	9886 Aoyagi r:-0.211 p:0.010 df:147	144496 Reingard r:0.322 p:0.000 df:147	3683 Baumann r:0.287 p:0.000 df:147
ab tone / upper forearm w		184	0.068	0.300	2.408	4.768	7.023	11.572	16.134	294 Felicia r:-0.200 p:0.010 df:164	144496 Reingard r:0.325 p:0.000 df:164	2193 Jackson r:-0.281 p:0.000 df:164
ab tone / waist		188	0.021	0.093	0.772	1.539	2.334	3.672	6.406	1239 Queteleta r:-0.196 p:0.010 df:171	249160 Urriellu r:0.297 p:0.000 df:171	3905 Doppler r:0.277 p:0.000 df:171
ab width / ankle to heel floor h		60	0.748	1.137	1.595	1.912	2.280	3.163	6.005	9069 Hovland r:-0.351 p:0.010 df:51	9313 Protea r:0.493 p:0.000 df:51	3197 Weissman r:0.485 p:0.000 df:51
ab width / ankle width		83	0.601	0.998	1.586	1.842	2.370	3.309	3.613	32300 Uwamanzunna r:-0.297 p:0.010 df:73	16193 Nickaiser r:0.405 p:0.000 df:73	7756 Scientia r:0.401 p:0.000 df:73
ab width / back perimeter		39	0.012	0.017	0.042	0.048	0.062	0.122	0.144	4456 Mawson r:-0.419 p:0.010 df:35	13044 Wannes r:0.658 p:0.000 df:35	2741 Valdivia r:0.551 p:0.000 df:35
ab width / back tone		41	0.042	0.122	0.135	0.157	0.231	0.339	0.353	12176 Hidayat r:-0.408 p:0.010 df:37	6085 Fraethi r:0.611 p:0.000 df:37	3737 Beckman r:-0.543 p:0.000 df:37
ab width / ball width		33	0.463	0.491	1.055	1.328	1.662	2.072	2.193	546 Herodias r:-0.442 p:0.010 df:31	14734 Susanstoker r:0.596 p:0.000 df:31	3645 Fabini r:-0.582 p:0.000 df:31
ab width / big toe length		34	0.905	0.958	1.934	2.674	3.660	4.559	5.165	-10012 mean Apogee r:-0.449 p:0.010 df:30	25520 Deronchang r:0.628 p:0.000 df:30	316 Goberta r:0.593 p:0.000 df:30
ab width / big toe width		29	1.265	1.364	2.823	3.726	5.018	8.166	8.646	294664 Trakai r:-0.472 p:0.010 df:27	128627 Ottmarsheim r:0.731 p:0.000 df:27	316 Goberta r:0.637 p:0.000 df:27
ab width / calf width		93	0.326	0.613	0.964	1.141	1.385	1.812	3.107	18102 Angrilli r:-0.278 p:0.010 df:83	21643 Kornev r:0.417 p:0.000 df:83	2021 Poincare r:0.394 p:0.000 df:83
ab width / clavicle to neck h		105	0.794	1.109	1.532	1.830	2.354	3.332	5.127	16368 Citta di Alba r:-0.265 p:0.010 df:92	24474 Ananthram r:0.403 p:0.000 df:92	2565 Grogler r:0.359 p:0.000 df:92
ab width / foot base h		58	0.262	0.330	0.576	0.709	0.924	1.197	1.259	5651 Traversa r:-0.358 p:0.010 df:49	7293 Kazuyuki r:0.503 p:0.000 df:49	1440 Rostia r:0.476 p:0.000 df:49
ab width / heel width		32	0.755	0.761	1.717	2.055	2.555	3.484	3.556	6408 Saijo r:-0.456 p:0.010 df:29	2836 Sobolev r:0.711 p:0.000 df:29	1649 Fabre r:-0.629 p:0.000 df:29

	n										
ab width / lower leg h	80	0.166	0.211	0.304	0.359	0.446	0.714	0.977	1215 Boyer r:-0.303 p:0.010 df:70	117712 Podmaniczky r:0.438 p:0.000 df:70	1557 Roehla r:0.408 p:0.000 df:70
ab width / subchest width	84	0.305	0.399	0.478	0.545	0.593	0.750	1.040	14975 Serasin r:-0.296 p:0.010 df:73	25744 Surajmishra r:0.500 p:0.000 df:73	733 Mocia r:0.408 p:0.000 df:73
ankle to heel floor h / ball width	39	0.345	0.448	0.640	0.735	0.856	1.120	1.151	23811 Connorivens r:-0.413 p:0.010 df:36	4351 Nobuhisa r:0.586 p:0.000 df:36	32 Pomona r:-0.558 p:0.000 df:36
ankle to heel floor h / big toe length	38	0.986	1.002	1.333	1.576	1.754	2.711	2.728	9739 Powell r:-0.431 p:0.010 df:33	18637 Liverdun r:0.632 p:0.000 df:33	1112 Polonia r:0.583 p:0.000 df:33
ankle to heel floor h / foot base h	73	0.201	0.255	0.316	0.350	0.415	0.534	0.637	6197 Taracho r:-0.317 p:0.010 df:63	16644 Otemaedaigaku r:0.454 p:0.000 df:63	347 Pariana r:0.420 p:0.000 df:63
ankle to heel floor h / heel width	33	0.660	0.678	0.941	1.058	1.290	1.445	1.446	19754 Paclements r:-0.443 p:0.010 df:31	34193 Annakoonce r:0.584 p:0.000 df:31	1048 Feodosia r:-0.625 p:0.000 df:31
ankle to heel floor h / lower leg h	83	0.092	0.126	0.163	0.184	0.204	0.257	0.340	4780 Polina r:-0.299 p:0.010 df:72	22540 Mork r:0.441 p:0.000 df:72	3475 Fichte r:-0.435 p:0.000 df:72
ankle to heel floor h / subchest width	40	0.080	0.142	0.226	0.263	0.297	0.361	0.428	1021 Flammario r:-0.430 p:0.010 df:33	113950 Donbaldwin r:0.737 p:0.000 df:33	79 Eurynome r:0.563 p:0.000 df:33
ankle width / ankle to heel floor h	87	0.671	0.783	0.943	1.074	1.236	1.440	1.806	21581 Ernestoruiz r:-0.290 p:0.010 df:76	30269 Anandapadmanaban r:0.459 p:0.000 df:76	1190 Pelagia r:0.431 p:0.000 df:76
ankle width / ball width	55	0.219	0.370	0.631	0.754	0.822	1.137	1.380	5673 McAllister r:-0.348 p:0.010 df:52	10428 Wanders r:0.505 p:0.000 df:52	489 Comacina r:-0.462 p:0.000 df:52
ankle width / big toe length	51	0.426	0.838	1.166	1.573	1.887	2.184	3.600	489 Comacina r:-0.368 p:0.010 df:46	14443 Sekinenomatsu r:0.535 p:0.000 df:46	400 Ducrosa r:0.489 p:0.000 df:46
ankle width / big toe width	43	0.552	1.123	1.811	2.149	2.669	3.491	3.717	6014 Chribrenmark r:-0.393 p:0.010 df:40	52309 Philnicolai r:0.642 p:0.000 df:40	489 Comacina r:-0.637 p:0.000 df:40
ankle width / foot base h	90	0.123	0.299	0.346	0.384	0.420	0.536	0.643	1796 Riga r:-0.285 p:0.010 df:79	6520 Sugawa r:0.444 p:0.000 df:79	632 Pyrrha r:0.379 p:0.000 df:79
ankle width / heel width	53	0.421	0.665	0.940	1.079	1.279	1.633	1.992	1953 Rupertwildt r:-0.354 p:0.010 df:50	80984 Santomurakami r:0.511 p:0.000 df:50	4 Vesta r:0.469 p:0.000 df:50
ankle width / lower leg h	128	0.115	0.146	0.172	0.194	0.220	0.279	0.391	81859 Joetaylor r:-0.238 p:0.010 df:114	15855 Mariasalvatore r:0.327 p:0.000 df:114	15855 Mariasalvatore r:0.327 p:0.000 df:114
ankle width / pinky toe length	36	0.799	1.313	2.098	2.490	3.102	4.473	4.744	26397 Carolynsinow r:-0.424 p:0.010 df:34	2331 Parvulesco r:0.613 p:0.000 df:34	2331 Parvulesco r:0.613 p:0.000 df:34
ankle width / second toe length	37	0.507	0.927	1.413	1.760	2.144	3.024	3.578	410 Chloris r:-0.419 p:0.010 df:35	1424 Sundmania r:0.603 p:0.000 df:35	1424 Sundmania r:0.603 p:0.000 df:35
ankle width / subchest width	54	0.145	0.194	0.237	0.255	0.315	0.458	0.528	1473 Ounas r:-0.368 p:0.010 df:46	20719 Velasco r:0.565 p:0.000 df:46	3263 Bligh r:0.546 p:0.000 df:46
areola dia / ab width	132	0.124	0.160	0.239	0.320	0.422	0.620	0.967	27610 Shixuanli r:-0.234 p:0.010 df:118	3871 Reiz r:0.365 p:0.000 df:118	545 Messalina r:0.364 p:0.000 df:118
areola dia / ankle to heel floor h	73	0.252	0.315	0.481	0.657	0.882	1.569	2.601	129321 Tannercampbell r:-0.315 p:0.010 df:64	19007 Nirajnathan r:0.505 p:0.000 df:64	3283 Skorina r:0.446 p:0.000 df:64
areola dia / ankle width	105	0.151	0.249	0.450	0.609	0.818	1.407	2.023	14317 Antonov r:-0.263 p:0.010 df:94	95980 Haroldhill r:0.386 p:0.000 df:94	5488 Kiyosato r:0.368 p:0.000 df:94
areola dia / back perimeter	49	0.006	0.007	0.011	0.016	0.025	0.039	0.050	1374 Isora r:-0.369 p:0.010 df:46	1936 Lugano r:0.546 p:0.000 df:46	1132 Hollandia r:0.491 p:0.000 df:46
areola dia / back tone	49	0.007	0.026	0.038	0.053	0.074	0.176	0.193	25019 Walentosky r:-0.368 p:0.010 df:46	3371 Giacconi r:0.500 p:0.000 df:46	3371 Giacconi r:0.500 p:0.000 df:46
areola dia / ball width	45	0.116	0.157	0.266	0.472	0.647	1.960	2.723	109573 Mishasmirnov r:-0.388 p:0.009 df:42	202686 Birkfellner r:0.603 p:0.000 df:42	4345 Rachmaninoff r:0.561 p:0.000 df:42
areola dia / big toe length	43	0.227	0.310	0.530	0.850	1.223	2.806	6.881	14119 Johnprince r:-0.400 p:0.010 df:39	25514 Lisawu r:0.650 p:0.000 df:39	342 Endymion r:0.529 p:0.000 df:39
areola dia / big toe width	38	0.367	0.386	1.085	1.332	1.985	5.552	8.875	6281 Strnad r:-0.420 p:0.010 df:35	4345 Rachmaninoff r:0.634 p:0.000 df:35	193 Ambrosia r:0.564 p:0.000 df:35
areola dia / bra shoulder to underb	161	0.061	0.101	0.137	0.178	0.233	0.343	0.511	2227 Otto Struve r:-0.209 p:0.010 df:149	14550 Lehky r:0.342 p:0.000 df:149	1969 Alain r:0.306 p:0.000 df:149
areola dia / breasts apart	225	0.210	0.333	0.726	1.091	1.950	6.470	11.846	8299 Tealeoni r:-0.178 p:0.010 df:207	8571 Taniguchi r:0.297 p:0.000 df:207	1790 Volkov r:0.254 p:0.000 df:207
areola dia / bust dia	246	0.132	0.212	0.294	0.357	0.460	0.650	0.930	3494 Purple Mountain r:-0.170 p:0.010 df:227	7919 Prime r:0.267 p:0.000 df:227	5147 Maruyama r:0.261 p:0.000 df:227
areola dia / butt square	46	0.026	0.038	0.051	0.065	0.091	0.184	0.263	14543 Sajigawasuiseki r:-0.385 p:0.010 df:42	24709 Mitau r:0.640 p:0.000 df:42	946 Poesia r:0.507 p:0.000 df:42
areola dia / calf width	121	0.123	0.165	0.282	0.381	0.516	0.896	1.765	1303 Luthera r:-0.243 p:0.010 df:110	12156 Ubels r:0.363 p:0.000 df:110	4345 Rachmaninoff r:0.334 p:0.000 df:110
areola dia / clavicle to neck h	122	0.150	0.274	0.400	0.573	0.836	1.552	1.885	20472 Mollypettit r:-0.244 p:0.010 df:109	7040 Harwood r:0.339 p:0.000 df:109	7040 Harwood r:0.339 p:0.000 df:109
areola dia / foot base h	74	0.066	0.092	0.173	0.240	0.312	0.444	0.523	17045 Markert r:-0.315 p:0.010 df:64	29672 Salvo r:0.482 p:0.000 df:64	1130 Skuld r:-0.426 p:0.000 df:64
areola dia / heel width	45	0.192	0.257	0.443	0.659	0.951	1.908	3.020	4296 van Woerkom r:-0.384 p:0.010 df:42	30177 Khashayar r:0.555 p:0.000 df:42	2349 Kurchenko r:0.543 p:0.000 df:42
areola dia / long finger length	87	0.086	0.109	0.178	0.252	0.377	0.590	0.748	1156 Kira r:-0.281 p:0.010 df:81	7048 Chaussidon r:0.426 p:0.000 df:81	5683 Bifukumonin r:-0.377 p:0.000 df:81
areola dia / lower leg h	103	0.037	0.054	0.084	0.115	0.171	0.294	0.461	528 Rezia r:-0.265 p:0.010 df:92	371220 Angers r:0.417 p:0.000 df:92	2502 Nummela r:0.354 p:0.000 df:92

		n										
areola dia / neck width		154	0.152	0.216	0.318	0.409	0.587	1.125	1.418	4147 Lennon r:-0.216 p:0.010 df:140	14550 Lehky r:0.350 p:0.000 df:140	1801 Titicaca r:0.315 p:0.000 df:140
areola dia / nipple dia		242	1.222	2.082	3.042	3.739	4.857	6.789	10.065	4154 Rumsey r:-0.171 p:0.010 df:224	7919 Prime r:0.281 p:0.000 df:224	72 Feronia r:0.239 p:0.000 df:224
areola dia / nipple to bottom		216	0.200	0.402	0.555	0.773	1.215	2.409	6.622	67085 Oppenheimer r:-0.181 p:0.010 df:200	1352 Wawel r:0.317 p:0.000 df:200	2 Pallas r:0.260 p:0.000 df:200
areola dia / nipple to top		215	0.171	0.224	0.319	0.381	0.483	0.690	1.251	4051 Hatanaka r:-0.183 p:0.010 df:197	1046 Edwin r:0.290 p:0.000 df:197	1046 Edwin r:0.290 p:0.000 df:197
areola dia / pelvic hips		162	0.060	0.081	0.116	0.161	0.218	0.320	0.570	17627 Humptydumpty r:-0.211 p:0.010 df:146	545 Messalina r:0.339 p:0.000 df:146	545 Messalina r:0.339 p:0.000 df:146
areola dia / second toe length		33	0.272	0.330	0.685	0.977	1.290	2.963	3.004	25106 Ryoojungmin r:-0.443 p:0.010 df:31	10633 Akimasa r:0.602 p:0.000 df:31	292 Ludovica r:0.577 p:0.000 df:31
areola dia / shoulder width		211	0.056	0.073	0.108	0.146	0.205	0.314	0.568	17225 Alanschorn r:-0.184 p:0.010 df:193	75842 Jackmonahan r:0.270 p:0.000 df:193	384 Burdigala r:-0.251 p:0.000 df:193
areola dia / subchest width		110	0.073	0.088	0.133	0.165	0.211	0.321	0.354	2268 Szmytowna r:-0.257 p:0.010 df:98	7848 Bernasconi r:0.353 p:0.000 df:98	4980 Magomaev r:-0.393 p:0.000 df:98
areola dia / subneck dorsal		96	0.111	0.156	0.231	0.326	0.422	0.737	1.013	1874 Kacivelia r:-0.272 p:0.010 df:87	14795 Syoyou r:0.417 p:0.000 df:87	1418 Fayeta r:-0.391 p:0.000 df:87
areola dia / subpelvic rear width		110	0.046	0.069	0.101	0.137	0.194	0.284	0.659	60006 Holgermandel r:-0.257 p:0.010 df:98	2259 Sofievka r:0.407 p:0.000 df:98	545 Messalina r:0.342 p:0.000 df:98
back perimeter / ankle width		41	11.832	14.662	28.045	35.769	44.487	71.061	139.187	6525 Ocastron r:-0.409 p:0.010 df:37	5148 Giordano r:0.654 p:0.000 df:37	2183 Neufang r:0.551 p:0.000 df:37
back perimeter / back tone		67	0.889	1.230	2.603	3.455	4.555	9.150	13.055	1862 Apollo r:-0.320 p:0.010 df:62	18720 Jerryguo r:0.500 p:0.000 df:62	779 Nina r:0.447 p:0.000 df:62
back perimeter / calf width		47	5.325	8.652	16.387	22.435	27.995	48.979	72.719	9930 Billburrows r:-0.385 p:0.010 df:42	35725 Tramuntana r:0.591 p:0.000 df:42	2183 Neufang r:0.539 p:0.000 df:42
back perimeter / clavicle to neck h		36	11.392	11.914	28.655	38.064	50.685	97.567	112.813	63 Ausonia r:-0.436 p:0.010 df:32	2400 Derevskaya r:0.663 p:0.000 df:32	2400 Derevskaya r:0.663 p:0.000 df:32
back perimeter / foot base h		30	3.986	4.459	10.118	11.355	17.489	34.587	49.278	4916 Brumberg r:-0.479 p:0.010 df:26	5148 Giordano r:0.753 p:0.000 df:26	5148 Giordano r:0.753 p:0.000 df:26
back perimeter / lower leg h		37	2.630	2.791	5.461	6.988	9.567	20.661	22.909	9880 Stegosaurus r:-0.431 p:0.010 df:33	6890 Savinykh r:0.635 p:0.000 df:33	4180 Anaxagoras r:-0.579 p:0.000 df:33
back perimeter / subchest width		30	4.032	4.169	7.550	10.124	11.895	20.491	22.618	186411 Margaretsimon r:-0.476 p:0.009 df:27	22413 Haifu r:0.719 p:0.000 df:27	1984 Fedynskij r:0.649 p:0.000 df:27
back tone / ankle to heel floor h		31	0.755	1.719	8.007	10.273	15.816	28.652	38.997	10354 Guillaumebude r:-0.471 p:0.010 df:27	16037 Sheehan r:0.702 p:0.000 df:27	32 Pomona r:0.623 p:0.000 df:27
back tone / ankle width		43	2.693	3.587	8.519	10.783	15.467	26.775	34.140	21928 Prabakaran r:-0.398 p:0.010 df:39	7398 Walsh r:0.623 p:0.000 df:39	32 Pomona r:0.593 p:0.000 df:39
back tone / calf width		49	0.543	1.870	4.894	6.473	8.498	16.548	22.679	19178 Walterbothe r:-0.376 p:0.010 df:44	7398 Walsh r:0.639 p:0.000 df:44	32 Pomona r:0.545 p:0.000 df:44
back tone / clavicle to neck h		36	4.281	4.753	9.543	11.541	14.608	22.125	37.378	11827 Wasyuzan r:-0.437 p:0.010 df:32	129214 Gordoncasto r:0.648 p:0.000 df:32	32 Pomona r:0.569 p:0.000 df:32
back tone / foot base h		31	0.406	0.793	2.997	3.970	5.632	9.777	13.254	4082 Swann r:-0.471 p:0.010 df:27	30991 Minenze r:0.716 p:0.000 df:27	6013 Andanike r:0.607 p:0.000 df:27
back tone / lower leg h		39	0.554	0.637	1.634	2.224	2.769	3.934	7.578	809 Lundia r:-0.419 p:0.010 df:35	4021 Dancey r:0.632 p:0.000 df:35	2438 Oleshko r:0.573 p:0.000 df:35
back tone / subchest width		30	1.392	1.580	2.200	3.298	4.107	8.337	12.112	2286 Fesenkov r:-0.472 p:0.010 df:27	48638 Trebic r:0.717 p:0.000 df:27	625 Xenia r:0.618 p:0.000 df:27
ball width / big toe length		46	1.357	1.548	1.842	2.076	2.396	3.008	3.167	33010 Enricoprosperi r:-0.376 p:0.010 df:44	11092 Iwakisan r:0.561 p:0.000 df:44	2000 Herschel r:-0.493 p:0.000 df:44
ball width / big toe width		41	2.062	2.344	2.701	2.896	3.133	3.771	3.942	284 Amalia r:-0.403 p:0.010 df:38	95852 Leatherbarrow r:0.613 p:0.000 df:38	1230 Riceia r:-0.551 p:0.000 df:38
ball width / pinky toe length		37	2.596	2.797	3.116	3.602	4.274	5.597	7.011	1268 Libya r:-0.418 p:0.010 df:35	3533 Toyota r:0.610 p:0.000 df:35	3533 Toyota r:0.610 p:0.000 df:35
ball width / second toe length		37	1.755	1.765	2.201	2.629	2.887	3.696	3.708	4395 Danbritt r:-0.419 p:0.010 df:35	11519 Adler r:0.612 p:0.000 df:35	45 Eugenia r:-0.568 p:0.000 df:35
bicep width / ab width		144	0.140	0.434	0.550	0.624	0.724	0.906	1.556	16693 Moseley r:-0.227 p:0.010 df:126	19488 Abramcoley r:0.367 p:0.000 df:126	2492 Kutuzov r:0.310 p:0.000 df:126
bicep width / ankle to heel floor h		83	0.451	0.934	1.095	1.301	1.549	2.487	3.050	3287 Olmstead r:-0.296 p:0.010 df:73	22874 Haydeephelps r:0.451 p:0.000 df:73	1199 Geldonia r:0.422 p:0.000 df:73
bicep width / ankle width		130	0.440	0.810	1.070	1.253	1.579	2.027	3.052	24754 Zellyfry r:-0.235 p:0.010 df:117	28492 Marik r:0.351 p:0.000 df:117	378 Holmia r:0.339 p:0.000 df:117
bicep width / areola dia		211	0.317	0.878	1.431	2.011	2.577	3.451	5.139	1194 Aletta r:-0.185 p:0.010 df:192	3700 Geowilliams r:0.290 p:0.000 df:192	1354 Botha r:-0.258 p:0.000 df:192
bicep width / back perimeter		65	0.010	0.018	0.027	0.035	0.047	0.084	0.102	26248 Longenecker r:-0.325 p:0.010 df:60	4491 Otaru r:0.489 p:0.000 df:60	1553 Bauersfelda r:-0.452 p:0.000 df:60
bicep width / back tone		66	0.027	0.065	0.093	0.118	0.151	0.275	0.529	1352 Wawel r:-0.323 p:0.010 df:61	12850 Axelmunthe r:0.540 p:0.000 df:61	920 Rogeria r:-0.430 p:0.000 df:61
bicep width / ball width		56	0.226	0.410	0.718	0.926	1.161	1.779	2.446	3145 Walter Adams r:-0.345 p:0.010 df:53	5052 Nancyruth r:0.528 p:0.000 df:53	290 Bruna r:-0.468 p:0.000 df:53
bicep width / big toe length		50	0.439	0.659	1.391	1.878	2.481	3.411	4.138	15395 Rukl r:-0.368 p:0.010 df:46	5052 Nancyruth r:0.552 p:0.000 df:46	437 Rhodia r:0.503 p:0.000 df:46

Ratio	n								Min	Max neg	Max pos
bicep width / big toe width	43	0.568	1.090	2.208	2.917	3.493	5.353	5.795	85401 Yamatenclub r:-0.394 p:0.010 df:40	22002 Richardregan r:0.574 p:0.000 df:40	1731 Smuts r:-0.537 p:0.000 df:40
bicep width / bra shoulder to underb	180	0.070	0.252	0.301	0.345	0.400	0.516	0.701	3109 Machin r:-0.201 p:0.009 df:163	9674 Slovenija r:0.358 p:0.000 df:163	939 Isberga r:0.283 p:0.000 df:163
bicep width / breast depth	155	0.289	0.935	1.588	2.089	2.736	3.831	7.685	1317 Silvretta r:-0.216 p:0.010 df:140	12100 Amiens r:0.315 p:0.000 df:140	1242 Zambesia r:-0.340 p:0.000 df:140
bicep width / breasts apart	221	0.520	0.976	1.406	2.086	3.081	7.761	16.144	1305 Pongola r:-0.183 p:0.009 df:198	6060 Doudleby r:0.317 p:0.000 df:198	194 Prokne r:0.288 p:0.000 df:198
bicep width / bust dia	243	0.171	0.443	0.581	0.672	0.773	0.956	1.605	12013 Sibatahosimi r:-0.173 p:0.010 df:220	40919 Johntonry r:0.256 p:0.000 df:220	6399 Harada r:-0.259 p:0.000 df:220
bicep width / butt square	58	0.057	0.085	0.112	0.131	0.151	0.191	0.332	6411 Tamaga r:-0.349 p:0.010 df:52	3106 Morabito r:0.539 p:0.000 df:52	946 Poesia r:0.491 p:0.000 df:52
bicep width / calf width	151	0.330	0.518	0.654	0.756	0.879	1.143	1.553	1639 Bower r:-0.218 p:0.010 df:137	26232 Antink r:0.371 p:0.000 df:137	231 Vindobona r:-0.308 p:0.000 df:137
bicep width / chest width	209	0.082	0.239	0.277	0.300	0.348	0.451	0.587	2885 Palva r:-0.187 p:0.010 df:188	18771 Sisiliang r:0.277 p:0.000 df:188	2487 Juhani r:-0.252 p:0.000 df:188
bicep width / clavicle to groin h	142	0.102	0.125	0.149	0.168	0.198	0.288	0.493	2257 Kaarina r:-0.230 p:0.010 df:123	5951 Alicemonet r:0.337 p:0.000 df:123	2357 Phereclos r:-0.313 p:0.000 df:123
bicep width / clavicle to neck h	137	0.610	0.718	0.980	1.173	1.476	2.240	3.381	15495 Bogie r:-0.233 p:0.010 df:120	316741 Janefletcher r:0.353 p:0.000 df:120	825 Tanina r:-0.350 p:0.000 df:120
bicep width / elbow to wrist h	228	0.203	0.297	0.351	0.396	0.465	0.615	0.703	2531 Cambridge r:-0.179 p:0.010 df:205	1398 Donnera r:0.280 p:0.000 df:205	1398 Donnera r:0.280 p:0.000 df:205
bicep width / foot base h	88	0.126	0.277	0.392	0.478	0.570	0.812	1.332	336177 Churri r:-0.287 p:0.010 df:78	249522 Johndailey r:0.441 p:0.000 df:78	369 Aeria r:-0.461 p:0.000 df:78
bicep width / heel width	56	0.433	0.619	1.157	1.389	1.710	2.665	3.254	4451 Grieve r:-0.345 p:0.010 df:53	5052 Nancyruth r:0.572 p:0.000 df:53	5052 Nancyruth r:0.572 p:0.000 df:53
bicep width / long finger length	94	0.218	0.320	0.408	0.493	0.587	0.779	1.004	139 Juewa r:-0.273 p:0.010 df:87	22567 Zenisek r:0.374 p:0.000 df:87	4452 Ullacharles r:0.363 p:0.000 df:87
bicep width / lower forearm w	251	0.490	1.184	1.448	1.602	1.840	2.438	2.827	2770 Tsvet r:-0.170 p:0.010 df:226	25199 Jiahegu r:0.277 p:0.000 df:226	3579 Rockholt r:0.240 p:0.000 df:226
bicep width / lower leg h	126	0.106	0.171	0.212	0.241	0.287	0.431	0.548	10863 Oye r:-0.239 p:0.010 df:113	378 Holmia r:0.389 p:0.000 df:113	378 Holmia r:0.389 p:0.000 df:113
bicep width / neck width	178	0.229	0.636	0.777	0.872	0.991	1.325	2.044	22921 Siyuanliu r:-0.201 p:0.010 df:161	25552 Gaster r:0.371 p:0.000 df:161	4277 Holubov r:0.302 p:0.000 df:161
bicep width / nipple dia	205	1.246	3.923	5.810	7.132	8.723	11.412	17.016	1238 Predappia r:-0.187 p:0.010 df:188	5597 Warren r:0.268 p:0.000 df:188	629 Bernardina r:-0.258 p:0.000 df:188
bicep width / nipple to bottom	190	0.337	0.834	1.273	1.549	1.966	3.452	9.025	11079 Mitsunori r:-0.194 p:0.010 df:174	90825 Lizhensheng r:0.332 p:0.000 df:174	1352 Wawel r:0.294 p:0.000 df:174
bicep width / nipple to top	189	0.104	0.421	0.612	0.783	0.948	1.229	1.690	770 Bali r:-0.196 p:0.010 df:171	9994 Grotius r:0.295 p:0.000 df:171	7157 Lofgren r:-0.263 p:0.000 df:171
bicep width / pelvic hips	182	0.083	0.221	0.270	0.302	0.346	0.432	0.786	3913 Chemin r:-0.201 p:0.010 df:162	6203 Lyubamoroz r:0.326 p:0.000 df:162	5595 Roth r:0.274 p:0.000 df:162
bicep width / pinky toe length	38	0.823	1.064	2.276	2.873	3.911	7.373	8.578	2428 Kamenyar r:-0.414 p:0.010 df:36	5052 Nancyruth r:0.591 p:0.000 df:36	1681 Steinmetz r:-0.552 p:0.000 df:36
bicep width / second toe length	39	0.522	0.747	1.617	2.135	2.659	4.556	5.097	6707 Shigeru r:-0.409 p:0.010 df:37	27123 Matthewlam r:0.622 p:0.000 df:37	771 Libera r:0.532 p:0.000 df:37
bicep width / shoulder to elbow h	259	0.223	0.258	0.300	0.337	0.396	0.545	0.669	18395 Schmiedmayer r:-0.167 p:0.010 df:236	26973 Lala r:0.256 p:0.000 df:236	1398 Donnera r:0.228 p:0.000 df:236
bicep width / shoulder width	253	0.153	0.209	0.250	0.278	0.329	0.429	0.605	3366 Godel r:-0.170 p:0.010 df:229	16555 Nagaomasami r:0.254 p:0.000 df:229	2130 Evdokiya r:0.250 p:0.000 df:229
bicep width / subchest width	110	0.108	0.247	0.279	0.317	0.354	0.490	0.639	3908 Nyx r:-0.257 p:0.010 df:98	21575 Padmanabhan r:0.397 p:0.000 df:98	558 Carmen r:0.351 p:0.000 df:98
bicep width / subneck dorsal	108	0.158	0.444	0.560	0.641	0.764	1.025	1.695	14684 Reyes r:-0.260 p:0.010 df:96	24066 Eriksorensen r:0.379 p:0.000 df:96	825 Tanina r:-0.479 p:0.000 df:96
bicep width / subpelvic rear width	127	0.075	0.168	0.225	0.251	0.289	0.381	0.466	3262 Miune r:-0.238 p:0.010 df:115	27986 Hanus r:0.401 p:0.000 df:115	789 Lena r:0.331 p:0.000 df:115
bicep width / suprailiac	190	0.084	0.241	0.296	0.329	0.376	0.471	0.806	1836 Komarov r:-0.196 p:0.010 df:171	5595 Roth r:0.286 p:0.000 df:171	381 Myrrha r:0.275 p:0.000 df:171
bicep width / underbust	169	0.084	0.258	0.314	0.347	0.386	0.499	0.824	29845 Wykrota r:-0.207 p:0.010 df:152	19488 Abramcoley r:0.335 p:0.000 df:152	1434 Margot r:-0.288 p:0.000 df:152
bicep width / upper forearm w	256	0.251	0.815	0.989	1.110	1.195	1.431	1.810	2067 Aksnes r:-0.169 p:0.010 df:230	12620 Simaqian r:0.265 p:0.000 df:230	1897 Hind r:0.228 p:0.000 df:230
bicep width / waist	210	0.088	0.262	0.332	0.368	0.413	0.511	0.887	9054 Hippocastanum r:-0.186 p:0.010 df:190	7881 Schieferdecker r:0.279 p:0.000 df:190	1434 Margot r:-0.268 p:0.000 df:190
big toe length / big toe width	42	0.853	0.932	1.290	1.468	1.660	1.809	2.195	21503 Beksha r:-0.393 p:0.010 df:40	1934 Jeffers r:0.622 p:0.000 df:40	290 Bruna r:0.517 p:0.000 df:40
big toe length / pinky toe length	43	0.914	0.982	1.552	1.872	2.241	2.691	3.821	1590 Tsiolkovskaja r:-0.389 p:0.010 df:41	638 Moira r:0.546 p:0.000 df:41	638 Moira r:0.546 p:0.000 df:41
big toe length / second toe length	47	0.827	0.879	1.081	1.190	1.402	1.659	1.850	8076 Foscarini r:-0.373 p:0.010 df:45	8722 Schirra r:0.583 p:0.000 df:45	1769 Carlostorres r:0.505 p:0.000 df:45
bra shoulder to underb / ab width	125	0.581	1.077	1.513	1.717	2.064	2.877	4.130	597 Bandusia r:-0.243 p:0.010 df:110	21709 Sethmurray r:0.466 p:0.000 df:110	2504 Gaviola r:0.338 p:0.000 df:110

measurement	n										
bra shoulder to underb / ankle to heel floor h	69	1.834	2.352	2.852	3.634	4.172	8.847	14.378	1463 Nordenmarkia r:-0.328 p:0.010 df:59	7778 Markrobinson r:0.523 p:0.000 df:59	765 Mattiaca r:0.490 p:0.000 df:59
bra shoulder to underb / ankle width	95	0.927	1.845	2.815	3.424	4.087	5.438	10.524	5215 Tsurui r:-0.277 p:0.010 df:84	11002 Richardlis r:0.444 p:0.000 df:84	765 Mattiaca r:0.369 p:0.000 df:84
bra shoulder to underb / back perimeter	44	0.031	0.059	0.075	0.095	0.116	0.194	0.224	1089 Tama r:-0.394 p:0.010 df:40	3936 Elst r:0.637 p:0.000 df:40	1202 Marina r:0.556 p:0.000 df:40
bra shoulder to underb / back tone	44	0.060	0.174	0.259	0.323	0.394	0.587	1.255	365739 Peterbecker r:-0.394 p:0.010 df:40	3371 Giacconi r:0.563 p:0.000 df:40	2502 Nummela r:0.529 p:0.000 df:40
bra shoulder to underb / ball width	45	0.658	0.821	2.016	2.584	3.288	6.488	7.940	328305 Jackmcdevitt r:-0.385 p:0.010 df:42	30140 Robpergolizzi r:0.627 p:0.000 df:42	4345 Rachmaninoff r:0.528 p:0.000 df:42
bra shoulder to underb / big toe length	42	1.278	1.485	3.933	5.073	6.573	12.265	20.067	17683 Kanagawa r:-0.405 p:0.010 df:38	25514 Lisawu r:0.646 p:0.000 df:38	342 Endymion r:0.544 p:0.000 df:38
bra shoulder to underb / big toe width	37	1.656	2.199	5.240	7.567	10.024	18.301	25.882	4153 Roburnham r:-0.425 p:0.010 df:34	30140 Robpergolizzi r:0.709 p:0.000 df:34	3432 Kobuchizawa r:-0.559 p:0.000 df:34
bra shoulder to underb / breasts apart	178	1.869	2.443	4.102	5.749	8.440	30.440	64.147	8142 Zolotov r:-0.203 p:0.010 df:159	42697 Lucapaolini r:0.338 p:0.000 df:159	1814 Bach r:0.275 p:0.000 df:159
bra shoulder to underb / bust dia	191	0.713	1.398	1.697	1.914	2.160	2.655	3.113	15501 Pepawlowski r:-0.194 p:0.010 df:173	10170 Petrjakes r:0.302 p:0.000 df:173	4 Vesta r:-0.278 p:0.000 df:173
bra shoulder to underb / calf width	106	0.936	1.246	1.769	2.091	2.427	3.941	7.969	210030 Taoyuan r:-0.261 p:0.010 df:95	12695 Utrecht r:0.427 p:0.000 df:95	2101 Adonis r:0.352 p:0.000 df:95
bra shoulder to underb / clavicle to neck h	120	1.908	2.245	2.893	3.276	3.921	5.713	6.790	9265 Ekman r:-0.248 p:0.010 df:105	12238 Actor r:0.365 p:0.000 df:105	4331 Hubbard r:0.350 p:0.000 df:105
bra shoulder to underb / foot base h	71	0.368	0.739	1.086	1.256	1.598	2.225	3.224	6172 Prokofeana r:-0.322 p:0.010 df:61	20080 Maeharatorakichi r:0.502 p:0.000 df:61	437 Rhodia r:0.469 p:0.000 df:61
bra shoulder to underb / heel width	40	1.179	1.304	2.489	3.506	4.689	8.564	10.305	7895 Kaseda r:-0.410 p:0.010 df:37	6154 Stevesynnott r:0.562 p:0.000 df:37	3271 Ul r:0.544 p:0.000 df:37
bra shoulder to underb / long finger length	72	0.538	0.871	1.103	1.400	1.635	2.108	2.362	7113 Ostapbender r:-0.310 p:0.010 df:66	1395 Aribeda r:0.589 p:0.000 df:66	408 Fama r:-0.413 p:0.000 df:66
bra shoulder to underb / lower leg h	92	0.367	0.423	0.560	0.666	0.794	1.215	2.274	368 Haidea r:-0.284 p:0.009 df:81	202686 Birkfellner r:0.458 p:0.000 df:81	765 Mattiaca r:0.452 p:0.000 df:81
bra shoulder to underb / neck width	150	1.590	1.849	2.198	2.479	2.810	3.361	3.539	6626 Mattgenge r:-0.220 p:0.010 df:135	25198 Kylienicole r:0.349 p:0.000 df:135	1130 Skuld r:-0.304 p:0.000 df:135
bra shoulder to underb / pelvic hips	147	0.270	0.629	0.775	0.875	0.967	1.094	1.632	1574 Meyer r:-0.223 p:0.010 df:131	309704 Baruffetti r:0.362 p:0.000 df:131	521 Brixia r:-0.303 p:0.000 df:131
bra shoulder to underb / pinky toe length	30	2.268	2.339	5.931	7.896	10.274	22.127	27.683	14367 Hippokrates r:-0.468 p:0.009 df:28	4502 Elizabethann r:0.680 p:0.000 df:28	4502 Elizabethann r:0.680 p:0.000 df:28
bra shoulder to underb / second toe length	31	1.521	1.612	3.890	5.384	7.440	15.079	19.303	21488 Danyellelee r:-0.460 p:0.009 df:29	31109 Janpalous r:0.595 p:0.000 df:29	771 Libera r:0.591 p:0.000 df:29
bra shoulder to underb / shoulder width	198	0.298	0.588	0.706	0.794	0.904	1.035	1.238	11473 Barbaresco r:-0.191 p:0.010 df:179	278447 Saviano r:0.275 p:0.000 df:179	2037 Tripaxeptalis r:-0.263 p:0.000 df:179
bra shoulder to underb / subchest width	95	0.377	0.657	0.817	0.915	1.040	1.217	1.457	39540 Borchert r:-0.276 p:0.010 df:84	2566 Kirghizia r:0.416 p:0.000 df:84	180 Garumna r:-0.374 p:0.000 df:84
bra shoulder to underb / subneck dorsal	98	0.879	1.270	1.646	1.898	2.159	2.666	3.033	241418 Darmstadt r:-0.273 p:0.010 df:86	1763 Williams r:0.442 p:0.000 df:86	1027 Aesculapia r:0.384 p:0.000 df:86
bra shoulder to underb / subpelvic rear width	101	0.245	0.520	0.638	0.733	0.834	0.978	1.886	1580 Betulia r:-0.266 p:0.010 df:91	2820 Iisalmi r:0.495 p:0.000 df:91	582 Olympia r:0.363 p:0.000 df:91
breast depth / ab width	94	0.060	0.124	0.242	0.292	0.434	0.628	1.075	2512 Tavastia r:-0.281 p:0.009 df:83	22002 Richardregan r:0.440 p:0.000 df:83	789 Lena r:0.403 p:0.000 df:83
breast depth / ankle to heel floor h	59	0.216	0.295	0.439	0.653	0.809	1.579	3.810	2672 Pisek r:-0.349 p:0.009 df:53	844 Leontina r:0.526 p:0.000 df:53	844 Leontina r:0.526 p:0.000 df:53
breast depth / ankle width	87	0.224	0.266	0.469	0.600	0.830	1.333	2.789	6774 Vladheinrich r:-0.285 p:0.009 df:80	28452 Natkondamuri r:0.413 p:0.000 df:80	5464 Weller r:0.412 p:0.000 df:80
breast depth / areola dia	141	0.306	0.551	0.773	1.022	1.284	1.880	3.843	78 Diana r:-0.226 p:0.010 df:128	34038 Abualragheb r:0.405 p:0.000 df:128	1652 Herge r:0.306 p:0.000 df:128
breast depth / back perimeter	46	0.004	0.006	0.013	0.016	0.026	0.042	0.066	21517 Dobi r:-0.380 p:0.010 df:43	5059 Saroma r:0.596 p:0.000 df:43	397 Vienna r:0.510 p:0.000 df:43
breast depth / back tone	47	0.008	0.022	0.038	0.060	0.086	0.299	0.477	316 Goberta r:-0.377 p:0.010 df:44	6406 Mikejura r:0.569 p:0.000 df:44	2305 King r:0.503 p:0.000 df:44
breast depth / ball width	37	0.131	0.195	0.303	0.475	0.700	2.455	5.610	91888 Tomskilling r:-0.424 p:0.010 df:34	789 Lena r:0.603 p:0.000 df:34	789 Lena r:0.603 p:0.000 df:34
breast depth / big toe length	39	0.168	0.313	0.628	0.882	1.224	2.989	5.318	4285 Hulkower r:-0.413 p:0.010 df:36	109330 Clemente r:0.695 p:0.000 df:36	107 Camilla r:0.559 p:0.000 df:36
breast depth / big toe width	33	0.272	0.470	0.850	1.375	2.085	8.788	13.290	207321 Crawshaw r:-0.450 p:0.010 df:30	25098 Gridnev r:0.675 p:0.000 df:30	2206 Gabrova r:-0.617 p:0.000 df:30
breast depth / bra shoulder to underb	112	0.047	0.078	0.143	0.179	0.229	0.313	0.444	2946 Muchachos r:-0.252 p:0.010 df:102	278384 Mudanjiang r:0.364 p:0.000 df:102	1017 Jacqueline r:0.337 p:0.000 df:102
breast depth / breasts apart	141	0.123	0.281	0.706	1.083	1.820	5.015	13.321	3245 Jensch r:-0.226 p:0.010 df:128	3316 Herzberg r:0.393 p:0.000 df:128	62 Erato r:0.319 p:0.000 df:128
breast depth / bust dia	153	0.073	0.187	0.265	0.339	0.421	0.607	1.190	3602 Lazzaro r:-0.216 p:0.010 df:139	10543 Klee r:0.383 p:0.000 df:139	573 Recha r:0.312 p:0.000 df:139
breast depth / calf width	99	0.118	0.164	0.285	0.374	0.502	1.046	1.931	1151 Ithaka r:-0.267 p:0.010 df:91	7343 Ockeghem r:0.423 p:0.000 df:91	4345 Rachmaninoff r:0.368 p:0.000 df:91

breast depth / chest width		128	0.034	0.078	0.119	0.158	0.203	0.270	0.533	46977 Krakow r:-0.237 p:0.009 df:117	22002 Richardregan r:0.366 p:0.000 df:117	573 Recha r:0.341 p:0.000 df:117
breast depth / clavicle to neck h		91	0.174	0.233	0.407	0.558	0.849	1.414	1.678	1938 Lausanna r:-0.282 p:0.010 df:81	5044 Shestaka r:0.416 p:0.000 df:81	1801 Titicaca r:0.378 p:0.000 df:81
breast depth / foot base h		59	0.087	0.105	0.170	0.253	0.351	0.510	0.675	23324 Kwak r:-0.345 p:0.010 df:53	323552 Trudybell r:0.520 p:0.000 df:53	2750 Loviisa r:0.460 p:0.000 df:53
breast depth / heel width		38	0.201	0.241	0.472	0.600	0.909	1.646	7.463	133008 Snedden r:-0.417 p:0.009 df:36	2391 Tomita r:0.579 p:0.000 df:36	844 Leontina r:0.549 p:0.000 df:36
breast depth / long finger length		71	0.067	0.126	0.187	0.246	0.335	0.676	0.981	142 Polana r:-0.313 p:0.010 df:65	25159 Michaelwest r:0.598 p:0.000 df:65	24 Themis r:0.421 p:0.000 df:65
breast depth / lower leg h		82	0.046	0.055	0.087	0.119	0.162	0.341	0.603	59388 Monod r:-0.295 p:0.010 df:74	28452 Natkondamuri r:0.443 p:0.000 df:74	5180 Ohno r:0.405 p:0.000 df:74
breast depth / neck width		108	0.083	0.197	0.314	0.414	0.594	0.768	1.038	13509 Guayaquil r:-0.257 p:0.010 df:98	21709 Sethmurray r:0.399 p:0.000 df:98	1199 Geldonia r:0.365 p:0.000 df:98
breast depth / nipple dia		135	1.208	1.915	2.932	3.798	5.052	8.489	12.454	30725 Klimov r:-0.229 p:0.010 df:124	34038 Abualragheb r:0.390 p:0.000 df:124	573 Recha r:0.315 p:0.000 df:124
breast depth / nipple to bottom		132	0.145	0.379	0.588	0.782	1.044	1.651	4.310	-10007 Uranus r:-0.232 p:0.010 df:121	21559 Jingyuanluo r:0.457 p:0.000 df:121	989 Schwassmannia r:0.318 p:0.000 df:121
breast depth / nipple to top		133	0.088	0.217	0.329	0.402	0.485	0.765	1.297	13241 Biyo r:-0.233 p:0.010 df:120	3013 Dobrovoleva r:0.410 p:0.000 df:120	2589 Daniel r:0.327 p:0.000 df:120
breast depth / pelvic hips		109	0.031	0.070	0.111	0.147	0.186	0.282	0.618	2413 van de Hulst r:-0.258 p:0.010 df:98	15501 Pepawlowski r:0.434 p:0.000 df:98	573 Recha r:0.349 p:0.000 df:98
breast depth / shoulder width		146	0.029	0.067	0.111	0.145	0.199	0.311	0.525	5846 Hessen r:-0.221 p:0.010 df:133	14693 Selwyn r:0.379 p:0.000 df:133	91 Aegina r:-0.304 p:0.000 df:133
breast depth / subchest width		69	0.049	0.093	0.128	0.163	0.204	0.276	0.591	190617 Alexandergerst r:-0.323 p:0.010 df:61	11795 Fredrikbruhn r:0.593 p:0.000 df:61	60 Echo r:0.500 p:0.000 df:61
breast depth / subneck dorsal		64	0.060	0.099	0.220	0.288	0.432	0.600	0.693	7109 Heine r:-0.333 p:0.010 df:57	52309 Philnicolai r:0.478 p:0.000 df:57	1520 Imatra r:0.471 p:0.000 df:57
breast depth / subpelvic rear width		82	0.029	0.063	0.090	0.123	0.164	0.288	0.528	12636 Padrielli r:-0.295 p:0.010 df:74	15501 Pepawlowski r:0.450 p:0.000 df:74	789 Lena r:0.435 p:0.000 df:74
breast depth / suprailiac		118	0.033	0.080	0.123	0.163	0.212	0.322	0.684	175046 Corporon r:-0.246 p:0.010 df:107	22002 Richardregan r:0.431 p:0.000 df:107	3586 Vasnetsov r:0.368 p:0.000 df:107
breast depth / underbust		103	0.038	0.076	0.132	0.177	0.236	0.372	0.655	2647 Sova r:-0.262 p:0.010 df:94	171171 Prior r:0.465 p:0.000 df:94	573 Recha r:0.376 p:0.000 df:94
breast depth / waist		127	0.038	0.089	0.134	0.184	0.240	0.361	0.695	13658 Sylvester r:-0.235 p:0.010 df:117	171171 Prior r:0.388 p:0.000 df:117	3586 Vasnetsov r:0.372 p:0.000 df:117
breasts apart / ab width		143	0.026	0.094	0.234	0.331	0.449	0.675	1.334	18661 Zoccoli r:-0.228 p:0.010 df:125	10259 Osipovyurij r:0.351 p:0.000 df:125	609 Fulvia r:0.311 p:0.000 df:125
breasts apart / ankle to heel floor h		76	0.125	0.247	0.513	0.659	0.920	1.663	2.895	1062 Ljuba r:-0.314 p:0.010 df:65	6472 Rosema r:0.497 p:0.000 df:65	6472 Rosema r:0.497 p:0.000 df:65
breasts apart / ankle width		110	0.089	0.266	0.514	0.650	0.861	1.417	2.119	1583 Antilochus r:-0.259 p:0.010 df:97	6472 Rosema r:0.375 p:0.000 df:97	2596 Vainu Bappu r:0.354 p:0.000 df:97
breasts apart / back perimeter		50	0.005	0.007	0.013	0.019	0.032	0.050	0.062	10354 Guillaumebude r:-0.368 p:0.010 df:46	3936 Elst r:0.573 p:0.000 df:46	3554 Amun r:0.511 p:0.000 df:46
breasts apart / back tone		51	0.025	0.029	0.045	0.062	0.101	0.172	0.260	25373 Gorsch r:-0.365 p:0.010 df:47	19524 Acaciacoleman r:0.529 p:0.000 df:47	643 Scheherezade r:0.487 p:0.000 df:47
breasts apart / ball width		49	0.219	0.235	0.328	0.475	0.771	1.449	2.098	4926 Smoktunovskij r:-0.369 p:0.010 df:46	7846 Setvak r:0.531 p:0.000 df:46	6306 Nishimura r:0.503 p:0.000 df:46
breasts apart / big toe length		48	0.087	0.354	0.663	1.049	1.359	2.643	4.040	22356 Feyerabend r:-0.380 p:0.010 df:43	6472 Rosema r:0.558 p:0.000 df:43	807 Ceraskia r:0.511 p:0.000 df:43
breasts apart / big toe width		40	0.141	0.554	0.943	1.597	2.451	4.915	5.211	5379 Abehiroshi r:-0.409 p:0.010 df:37	3139 Shantou r:0.616 p:0.000 df:37	2206 Gabrova r:-0.661 p:0.000 df:37
breasts apart / bust dia		255	0.012	0.068	0.197	0.306	0.451	0.761	1.133	20696 Torresduarte r:-0.169 p:0.010 df:230	25014 Christinepalau r:0.248 p:0.000 df:230	42 Isis r:-0.243 p:0.000 df:230
breasts apart / calf width		126	0.059	0.149	0.296	0.370	0.508	0.840	1.431	11926 Orinoco r:-0.240 p:0.010 df:113	2991 Bilbo r:0.378 p:0.000 df:113	484 Pittsburghia r:0.360 p:0.000 df:113
breasts apart / clavicle to neck h		138	0.076	0.142	0.453	0.633	0.821	1.237	2.162	18964 Fairhurst r:-0.232 p:0.010 df:120	19009 Galenmaly r:0.368 p:0.000 df:120	5287 Heishu r:0.318 p:0.000 df:120
breasts apart / foot base h		75	0.032	0.081	0.151	0.252	0.345	0.511	0.605	8139 Paulabell r:-0.316 p:0.010 df:64	12162 Bilderdijk r:0.462 p:0.000 df:64	3292 Sather r:-0.446 p:0.000 df:64
breasts apart / heel width		48	0.375	0.392	0.539	0.726	1.101	1.671	2.791	5858 Borovitskia r:-0.373 p:0.010 df:45	94400 Hongdaeyong r:0.512 p:0.000 df:45	2620 Santana r:-0.489 p:0.000 df:45
breasts apart / long finger length		83	0.029	0.053	0.171	0.229	0.321	0.479	0.548	17024 Costello r:-0.291 p:0.010 df:76	18263 Anchialos r:0.452 p:0.000 df:76	2150 Nyctimene r:0.388 p:0.000 df:76
breasts apart / lower leg h		109	0.022	0.044	0.098	0.128	0.175	0.256	0.458	20947 Polyneikes r:-0.260 p:0.010 df:96	6472 Rosema r:0.396 p:0.000 df:96	386 Siegena r:0.355 p:0.000 df:96
breasts apart / neck width		165	0.045	0.101	0.328	0.435	0.609	0.825	1.092	6460 Bassano r:-0.211 p:0.010 df:147	19713 Ibaraki r:0.305 p:0.000 df:147	963 Iduberga r:-0.299 p:0.000 df:147
breasts apart / pinky toe length		32	0.767	0.786	1.210	1.580	2.431	4.456	5.475	56000 Mesopotamia r:-0.449 p:0.010 df:30	22616 Bogolyubov r:0.626 p:0.000 df:30	5905 Johnson r:-0.622 p:0.000 df:30
breasts apart / second toe length		35	0.099	0.300	0.744	1.121	1.578	2.703	2.908	723 Hammonia r:-0.430 p:0.010 df:33	8182 Akita r:0.695 p:0.000 df:33	1145 Robelmonte r:0.600 p:0.000 df:33

		N										
breasts apart / shoulder width		230	0.012	0.028	0.090	0.130	0.183	0.262	0.355	8696 Kjeriksson r:-0.178 p:0.010 df:206	161546 Schneeweis r:0.255 p:0.000 df:206	42 Isis r:-0.241 p:0.000 df:206
breasts apart / subchest width		112	0.013	0.051	0.119	0.166	0.230	0.348	0.429	2604 Marshak r:-0.254 p:0.010 df:100	6984 Lewiscarroll r:0.427 p:0.000 df:100	1980 Tezcatlipoca r:-0.340 p:0.000 df:100
breasts apart / subneck dorsal		104	0.041	0.076	0.238	0.351	0.469	0.675	0.858	9925 Juliehoskin r:-0.266 p:0.010 df:91	19713 Ibaraki r:0.415 p:0.000 df:91	7382 Bozhenkova r:-0.358 p:0.000 df:91
breasts apart / subpelvic rear width		118	0.010	0.040	0.095	0.128	0.188	0.256	0.321	7671 Albis r:-0.248 p:0.010 df:105	10259 Osipovyurij r:0.364 p:0.000 df:105	8758 Perdix r:-0.337 p:0.000 df:105
bust dia / ab width		152	0.462	0.603	0.777	0.919	1.049	1.433	1.816	5172 Yoshiyuki r:-0.219 p:0.010 df:136	21709 Sethmurray r:0.372 p:0.000 df:136	2841 Puijo r:-0.298 p:0.000 df:136
bust dia / ankle to heel floor h		84	0.691	1.174	1.566	1.891	2.429	4.656	9.252	2798 Vergilius r:-0.296 p:0.010 df:73	202686 Birkfellner r:0.502 p:0.000 df:73	2392 Jonathan Murray r:0.423 p:0.000 df:73
bust dia / ankle width		120	0.535	1.015	1.460	1.788	2.191	3.414	6.772	28207 Blakesmith r:-0.247 p:0.010 df:107	202686 Birkfellner r:0.411 p:0.000 df:107	4345 Rachmaninoff r:-0.331 p:0.000 df:107
bust dia / back perimeter		55	0.015	0.020	0.040	0.048	0.067	0.110	0.147	2598 Merlin r:-0.351 p:0.010 df:51	12529 Reighard r:0.512 p:0.000 df:51	1936 Lugano r:0.466 p:0.000 df:51
bust dia / back tone		57	0.030	0.107	0.125	0.170	0.239	0.530	0.746	7900 Portule r:-0.345 p:0.010 df:53	8474 Rettig r:0.577 p:0.000 df:53	2206 Gabrova r:-0.460 p:0.000 df:53
bust dia / ball width		52	0.392	0.480	0.993	1.265	1.746	3.680	5.110	14042 Agafonov r:-0.358 p:0.010 df:49	30140 Robpergolizzi r:0.558 p:0.000 df:49	789 Lena r:0.487 p:0.000 df:49
bust dia / big toe length		50	0.458	0.786	1.776	2.524	3.377	6.153	12.913	3949 Mach r:-0.373 p:0.010 df:45	342 Endymion r:0.583 p:0.000 df:45	342 Endymion r:0.583 p:0.000 df:45
bust dia / big toe width		42	0.743	1.033	2.783	3.829	5.181	10.756	16.655	3375 Amy r:-0.400 p:0.010 df:39	30140 Robpergolizzi r:0.643 p:0.000 df:39	435 Ella r:0.520 p:0.000 df:39
bust dia / calf width		139	0.408	0.674	0.930	1.048	1.314	1.793	3.694	8739 Morihisa r:-0.227 p:0.010 df:127	12156 Ubels r:0.371 p:0.000 df:127	613 Ginevra r:0.311 p:0.000 df:127
bust dia / clavicle to neck h		140	0.725	1.023	1.441	1.727	2.190	3.501	4.380	10068 Dodoens r:-0.231 p:0.009 df:124	210232 Zhangjinqiu r:0.344 p:0.000 df:124	869 Mellena r:0.319 p:0.000 df:124
bust dia / foot base h		84	0.219	0.399	0.557	0.691	0.848	1.367	1.556	3887 Gerstner r:-0.296 p:0.010 df:73	30312 Lilyliu r:0.477 p:0.000 df:73	6202 Georgemiley r:0.431 p:0.000 df:73
bust dia / heel width		49	0.681	0.780	1.586	1.986	2.278	4.013	6.270	136825 Slawitschek r:-0.369 p:0.010 df:46	18561 Fengningding r:0.515 p:0.000 df:46	789 Lena r:0.484 p:0.000 df:46
bust dia / lower leg h		119	0.162	0.221	0.285	0.347	0.433	0.731	1.463	5928 Pindarus r:-0.248 p:0.010 df:106	202686 Birkfellner r:0.462 p:0.000 df:106	765 Mattiaca r:0.360 p:0.000 df:106
bust dia / neck width		176	0.614	0.909	1.121	1.319	1.528	1.803	2.618	10376 Chiarini r:-0.203 p:0.010 df:158	14550 Lehky r:0.313 p:0.000 df:158	2728 Yatskiv r:0.279 p:0.000 df:158
bust dia / pinky toe length		34	1.309	1.397	3.071	3.819	5.382	10.910	13.359	11308 Tofta r:-0.436 p:0.010 df:32	71 Niobe r:0.605 p:0.000 df:32	71 Niobe r:0.605 p:0.000 df:32
bust dia / second toe length		37	0.523	0.867	1.998	2.992	3.506	5.955	9.315	812 Adele r:-0.419 p:0.010 df:35	18156 Kamisaibara r:0.574 p:0.000 df:35	18156 Kamisaibara r:0.574 p:0.000 df:35
bust dia / subchest width		118	0.169	0.364	0.445	0.480	0.530	0.601	0.684	51655 Susannemond r:-0.248 p:0.010 df:106	42 Isis r:0.354 p:0.000 df:106	42 Isis r:0.354 p:0.000 df:106
bust dia / subneck dorsal		109	0.583	0.642	0.815	0.975	1.159	1.389	1.575	12632 Mignonette r:-0.259 p:0.010 df:96	85214 Sommersdorf r:0.406 p:0.000 df:96	151 Abundantia r:0.347 p:0.000 df:96
butt square / ab width		34	3.082	3.098	4.292	5.022	5.695	7.420	8.195	4745 Nancymarie r:-0.457 p:0.010 df:29	12777 Manuel r:0.645 p:0.000 df:29	829 Academia r:0.607 p:0.000 df:29
butt square / ankle width		34	3.926	4.929	7.673	9.047	10.163	16.883	19.413	4657 Lopez r:-0.456 p:0.010 df:29	20038 Arasaki r:0.687 p:0.000 df:29	565 Marbachia r:-0.591 p:0.000 df:29
butt square / back perimeter		31	0.124	0.154	0.219	0.291	0.355	0.781	0.975	99928 Brainard r:-0.471 p:0.010 df:27	3888 Hoyt r:0.657 p:0.000 df:27	3888 Hoyt r:0.657 p:0.000 df:27
butt square / back tone		33	0.273	0.454	0.713	0.873	1.265	4.116	9.574	4143 Huziak r:-0.456 p:0.010 df:29	10577 Jihcesmuzeum r:0.729 p:0.000 df:29	23 Thalia r:0.613 p:0.000 df:29
butt square / bra shoulder to underb		38	1.327	1.850	2.181	2.863	3.142	4.691	4.821	5138 Gyoda r:-0.430 p:0.010 df:33	90308 Johney r:0.675 p:0.000 df:33	1247 Memoria r:0.572 p:0.000 df:33
butt square / breasts apart		47	4.108	5.321	10.929	16.622	28.013	80.096	95.134	7648 Tomboles r:-0.385 p:0.010 df:42	11823 Christen r:0.610 p:0.000 df:42	876 Scott r:0.539 p:0.000 df:42
butt square / bust dia		51	1.510	2.341	4.423	4.975	5.769	8.241	9.359	654 Zelinda r:-0.369 p:0.010 df:46	11712 Kemcook r:0.563 p:0.000 df:46	112 Iphigenia r:-0.500 p:0.000 df:46
butt square / calf width		38	2.368	2.507	4.718	5.233	6.363	10.022	11.081	4678 Ninian r:-0.430 p:0.010 df:33	12342 Kudohmichiko r:0.632 p:0.000 df:33	1842 Hynek r:-0.578 p:0.000 df:33
butt square / clavicle to neck h		29	4.831	5.067	8.128	9.476	11.347	29.258	30.152	2757 Crisser r:-0.497 p:0.010 df:24	17799 Petewilliams r:0.762 p:0.000 df:24	1425 Tuorla r:0.661 p:0.000 df:24
butt square / foot base h		30	1.532	1.969	2.794	3.604	4.200	6.520	7.090	6603 Marycragg r:-0.488 p:0.010 df:25	13433 Phelps r:0.705 p:0.000 df:25	7481 San Marcello r:-0.637 p:0.000 df:25
butt square / lower leg h		35	0.808	0.888	1.423	1.750	2.080	3.991	4.003	17086 Ruima r:-0.449 p:0.010 df:30	368617 Sebastianotero r:0.650 p:0.000 df:30	1650 Heckmann r:0.586 p:0.000 df:30
butt square / neck width		39	3.860	4.350	5.516	6.260	7.298	12.348	15.492	11914 Sinachopoulos r:-0.423 p:0.009 df:35	7848 Bernasconi r:0.589 p:0.000 df:35	338 Budrosa r:-0.566 p:0.000 df:35
butt square / pelvic hips		46	1.544	1.851	2.060	2.283	2.673	3.682	4.439	1827 Atkinson r:-0.389 p:0.010 df:41	14024 Procol Harum r:0.587 p:0.000 df:41	1759 Kienle r:0.546 p:0.000 df:41
butt square / shoulder width		59	0.839	1.092	1.854	2.069	2.531	3.621	4.153	7604 Kridsadaporn r:-0.342 p:0.010 df:54	5908 Aichi r:0.584 p:0.000 df:54	3073 Kursk r:0.471 p:0.000 df:54

	N										
butt square / subchest width	30	1.772	1.844	2.301	2.506	2.973	3.978	3.979	21610 Rosengard r:-0.479 p:0.010 df:26	5571 Lesliegreen r:0.678 p:0.000 df:26	1104 Syringa r:0.643 p:0.000 df:26
butt square / subpelvic rear width	43	1.275	1.455	1.756	1.912	2.230	3.090	3.643	2702 Batrakov r:-0.400 p:0.010 df:39	12176 Hidayat r:0.548 p:0.000 df:39	542 Susanna r:-0.541 p:0.000 df:39
calf width / ankle to heel floor h	85	1.129	1.376	1.573	1.738	2.025	2.776	4.025	315088 Daniels r:-0.294 p:0.010 df:74	22874 Haydeephelps r:0.547 p:0.000 df:74	907 Rhoda r:0.407 p:0.000 df:74
calf width / ankle width	138	0.748	1.310	1.528	1.645	1.827	2.153	2.638	2136 Jugta r:-0.229 p:0.010 df:124	24666 Miesvanrohe r:0.413 p:0.000 df:124	835 Olivia r:-0.316 p:0.000 df:124
calf width / ball width	56	0.439	0.558	0.986	1.218	1.393	2.132	3.639	613 Ginevra r:-0.345 p:0.010 df:53	31671 Masatoshi r:0.527 p:0.000 df:53	2874 Jim Young r:0.479 p:0.000 df:53
calf width / big toe length	50	0.852	1.207	1.794	2.581	3.002	4.599	6.055	9306 Pittosporum r:-0.372 p:0.010 df:45	73701 Siegfriedbauer r:0.606 p:0.000 df:45	185 Eunike r:-0.490 p:0.000 df:45
calf width / big toe width	42	1.104	1.645	2.702	3.545	4.914	7.961	8.622	920 Rogeria r:-0.398 p:0.010 df:39	31671 Masatoshi r:0.652 p:0.000 df:39	1297 Quadea r:0.575 p:0.000 df:39
calf width / foot base h	89	0.245	0.395	0.557	0.644	0.737	0.861	1.329	391 Ingeborg r:-0.287 p:0.010 df:78	632 Pyrrha r:0.473 p:0.000 df:78	256 Walpurga r:-0.382 p:0.000 df:78
calf width / heel width	54	0.841	0.928	1.501	1.743	2.057	2.961	4.841	21563 Chetgervais r:-0.351 p:0.010 df:51	31671 Masatoshi r:0.504 p:0.000 df:51	19769 Dolyniuk r:-0.477 p:0.000 df:51
calf width / lower leg h	133	0.208	0.264	0.300	0.323	0.353	0.443	0.514	644 Cosima r:-0.234 p:0.010 df:119	30296 Bricehuang r:0.353 p:0.000 df:119	6970 Saigusa r:-0.327 p:0.000 df:119
calf width / pinky toe length	36	1.598	1.794	3.156	3.954	5.228	7.827	8.629	6424 Ando r:-0.424 p:0.010 df:34	4852 Pamjones r:0.620 p:0.000 df:34	818 Kapteynia r:0.554 p:0.000 df:34
calf width / second toe length	37	1.015	1.316	2.184	2.952	3.612	5.069	6.018	9249 Yen r:-0.419 p:0.010 df:35	10330 Durkheim r:0.632 p:0.000 df:35	185 Eunike r:-0.556 p:0.000 df:35
calf width / subchest width	63	0.272	0.310	0.402	0.446	0.510	0.750	0.917	1964 Luyten r:-0.339 p:0.010 df:55	18449 Rikwouters r:0.536 p:0.000 df:55	193 Ambrosia r:0.481 p:0.000 df:55
chest width / ab width	136	0.947	1.440	1.720	1.911	2.204	2.655	3.649	8039 Grandprism r:-0.233 p:0.010 df:120	27236 Millermatt r:0.399 p:0.000 df:120	2102 Tantalus r:0.311 p:0.000 df:120
chest width / ankle to heel floor h	70	1.300	2.880	3.445	4.020	4.782	6.785	12.637	126 Velleda r:-0.323 p:0.010 df:61	43597 Changshaopo r:0.522 p:0.000 df:61	2005 Hencke r:-0.441 p:0.000 df:61
chest width / ankle width	101	1.284	2.645	3.181	3.953	4.532	5.835	7.094	12701 Chenier r:-0.268 p:0.010 df:90	9405 Johnratje r:0.398 p:0.000 df:90	7853 Confucius r:-0.362 p:0.000 df:90
chest width / areola dia	202	1.837	3.198	4.843	6.075	8.025	12.037	15.566	23168 Lauriefletch r:-0.187 p:0.010 df:186	3727 Maxhell r:0.262 p:0.000 df:186	3727 Maxhell r:0.262 p:0.000 df:186
chest width / back perimeter	49	0.045	0.060	0.086	0.104	0.144	0.248	0.266	269550 Chur r:-0.373 p:0.010 df:45	7700 Rote Kapelle r:0.522 p:0.000 df:45	2741 Valdivia r:0.509 p:0.000 df:45
chest width / back tone	51	0.080	0.226	0.278	0.355	0.508	0.691	0.824	10072 Uruguay r:-0.365 p:0.010 df:47	13268 Trevorcorbin r:0.506 p:0.000 df:47	925 Alphonsina r:0.480 p:0.000 df:47
chest width / ball width	42	0.895	1.023	2.263	2.850	3.604	4.318	4.452	2381 Landi r:-0.393 p:0.010 df:40	11958 Galiani r:0.542 p:0.000 df:40	417 Suevia r:0.514 p:0.000 df:40
chest width / big toe length	42	1.738	1.893	4.272	5.833	7.535	9.077	12.337	695 Bella r:-0.403 p:0.010 df:38	400 Ducrosa r:0.566 p:0.000 df:38	400 Ducrosa r:0.566 p:0.000 df:38
chest width / big toe width	36	2.252	2.996	6.345	9.098	10.784	14.215	14.259	10877 Jiangnan Tianchi r:-0.424 p:0.010 df:34	17020 Hopemeraengus r:0.587 p:0.000 df:34	114 Kassandra r:0.554 p:0.000 df:34
chest width / bra shoulder to underb	176	0.642	0.888	1.032	1.116	1.303	1.535	2.550	5655 Barney r:-0.202 p:0.010 df:160	172932 Bachleitner r:0.386 p:0.000 df:160	1514 Ricouxa r:0.295 p:0.000 df:160
chest width / breasts apart	212	1.987	3.267	4.916	6.558	9.683	30.860	62.355	16892 Vaissiere r:-0.186 p:0.010 df:190	145559 Didiermuller r:0.315 p:0.000 df:190	1168 Brandia r:0.271 p:0.000 df:190
chest width / bust dia	227	0.884	1.803	1.994	2.160	2.351	2.886	4.403	5989 Sorin r:-0.178 p:0.010 df:207	5149 Leibniz r:0.280 p:0.000 df:207	530 Turandot r:0.265 p:0.000 df:207
chest width / butt square	50	0.220	0.249	0.359	0.424	0.488	0.620	1.273	1025 Riema r:-0.372 p:0.010 df:45	25455 Anissamak r:0.580 p:0.000 df:45	140 Siwa r:-0.491 p:0.000 df:45
chest width / calf width	114	0.949	1.582	2.032	2.312	2.693	3.661	5.530	30066 Parthakker r:-0.250 p:0.010 df:103	255073 Victoriabond r:0.370 p:0.000 df:103	754 Malabar r:-0.357 p:0.000 df:103
chest width / clavicle to neck h	123	2.100	2.513	3.172	3.807	4.749	6.650	11.438	7240 Hasebe r:-0.246 p:0.009 df:108	10780 Apollinaire r:0.372 p:0.000 df:108	869 Mellena r:0.334 p:0.000 df:108
chest width / foot base h	72	0.500	0.770	1.284	1.505	1.769	2.271	2.954	2561 Margolin r:-0.318 p:0.010 df:63	10171 Takaotengu r:0.433 p:0.000 df:63	469 Argentina r:-0.438 p:0.000 df:63
chest width / heel width	40	1.632	1.752	3.591	4.510	5.460	6.330	6.549	4768 Hartley r:-0.408 p:0.010 df:37	8982 Oreshek r:0.567 p:0.000 df:37	4304 Geichenko r:0.559 p:0.000 df:37
chest width / long finger length	81	0.663	1.182	1.348	1.542	1.784	2.356	3.504	13045 Vermandere r:-0.292 p:0.010 df:75	1021 Flammario r:0.418 p:0.000 df:75	629 Bernardina r:0.392 p:0.000 df:75
chest width / lower leg h	97	0.305	0.506	0.649	0.753	0.908	1.220	1.814	913 Otila r:-0.275 p:0.010 df:86	90825 Lizhensheng r:0.390 p:0.000 df:86	90825 Lizhensheng r:0.390 p:0.000 df:86
chest width / neck width	161	1.344	2.104	2.484	2.791	3.135	3.859	5.617	123852 Janboda r:-0.212 p:0.010 df:145	28534 Taylorwilson r:0.342 p:0.000 df:145	1180 Rita r:-0.335 p:0.000 df:145
chest width / nipple dia	199	7.792	15.190	18.954	22.596	27.941	36.244	55.631	4720 Tottori r:-0.189 p:0.010 df:183	5924 Teruo r:0.276 p:0.000 df:183	3235 Melchior r:-0.302 p:0.000 df:183
chest width / nipple to bottom	184	2.708	3.147	4.185	4.985	6.361	10.093	31.536	24140 Evanmirts r:-0.196 p:0.010 df:170	195657 Zhuangqining r:0.319 p:0.000 df:170	1253 Frisia r:0.275 p:0.000 df:170
chest width / nipple to top	185	0.755	1.492	2.067	2.413	2.918	4.022	5.874	5900 Jensen r:-0.196 p:0.010 df:170	269243 Charbonnel r:0.322 p:0.000 df:170	345 Tercidina r:-0.274 p:0.000 df:170

Measurement	n								Negative correlate	Positive correlate 1	Positive correlate 2
chest width / pelvic hips	181	0.620	0.790	0.901	0.989	1.068	1.280	1.860	4207 Chernova r:-0.201 p:0.010 df:162	10471 Marciniak r:0.340 p:0.000 df:162	772 Tanete r:0.278 p:0.000 df:162
chest width / pinky toe length	30	3.139	3.205	6.760	9.399	12.305	18.311	18.422	3942 Churivannia r:-0.463 p:0.010 df:28	59239 Alhazen r:0.642 p:0.000 df:28	690 Wratislavia r:0.601 p:0.000 df:28
chest width / second toe length	33	2.069	2.126	5.578	6.233	7.983	10.868	12.262	10696 Giuliattiwinter r:-0.442 p:0.010 df:31	8140 Hardersen r:0.613 p:0.000 df:31	400 Ducrosa r:0.584 p:0.000 df:31
chest width / shoulder width	223	0.528	0.731	0.825	0.899	1.011	1.208	1.572	25098 Gridnev r:-0.180 p:0.010 df:203	26681 Niezgay r:0.301 p:0.000 df:203	714 Ulula r:0.260 p:0.000 df:203
chest width / subchest width	120	0.743	0.944	1.019	1.069	1.108	1.225	1.406	25104 Chohyunghoon r:-0.245 p:0.010 df:108	336108 Luberon r:0.356 p:0.000 df:108	1108 Demeter r:0.335 p:0.000 df:108
chest width / subneck dorsal	103	1.112	1.558	1.839	2.135	2.366	2.862	4.392	28439 Miguelreyes r:-0.267 p:0.010 df:90	13652 Elowitz r:0.386 p:0.000 df:90	3323 Turgenev r:-0.380 p:0.000 df:90
chest width / subpelvic rear width	125	0.481	0.583	0.777	0.843	0.935	1.052	1.354	3262 Miune r:-0.241 p:0.010 df:112	269484 Marcia r:0.334 p:0.000 df:112	1065 Amundsenia r:0.327 p:0.000 df:112
chest width< >underbust / neck width< >shoulder width	110	0.169	0.418	0.636	0.868	1.095	1.697	3.563	8054 Brentano r:-0.259 p:0.010 df:96	689 Zita r:0.505 p:0.000 df:96	689 Zita r:0.505 p:0.000 df:96
chest width< >underbust / neck width< >subneck dorsal	67	0.454	1.016	1.598	1.972	3.162	4.651	4.919	2518 Rutllant r:-0.336 p:0.010 df:56	24856 Messidoro r:0.495 p:0.000 df:56	3700 Geowilliams r:-0.452 p:0.000 df:56
chest width< >underbust / neck width< >underbust	95	0.069	0.122	0.188	0.225	0.263	0.371	0.433	66669 Aradac r:-0.278 p:0.010 df:83	4358 Lynn r:0.431 p:0.000 df:83	444 Gyptis r:0.373 p:0.000 df:83
chest width< >underbust / pelvic hips< >subpelvic rear width	99	0.237	0.280	0.424	0.637	0.855	1.343	2.092	22158 Chee r:-0.270 p:0.010 df:88	13438 Marthanalexander r:0.419 p:0.000 df:88	441 Bathilde r:-0.381 p:0.000 df:88
chest width< >underbust / pelvic hips< >waist	143	0.204	0.349	0.533	0.709	0.910	1.311	2.138	391795 Univofutah r:-0.226 p:0.010 df:127	28836 Ashmore r:0.349 p:0.000 df:127	130 Elektra r:-0.311 p:0.000 df:127
chest width< >underbust / shoulder width< >subneck dorsal	72	0.210	0.473	0.908	1.201	1.479	2.109	2.702	24434 Josephhoscheidt r:-0.325 p:0.010 df:60	362911 Miguelhurtado r:0.488 p:0.000 df:60	98 Ianthe r:-0.433 p:0.000 df:60
chest width< >underbust / shoulder width< >waist	146	0.068	0.113	0.181	0.211	0.248	0.361	0.482	17917 Cartan r:-0.225 p:0.010 df:129	28950 Ailisdooner r:0.366 p:0.000 df:129	284 Amalia r:0.300 p:0.000 df:129
chest width< >underbust / subpelvic rear width< >suprailiac	95	0.183	0.204	0.332	0.450	0.539	0.754	1.446	4006 Sandler r:-0.277 p:0.010 df:84	32002 Gorokhovsky r:0.439 p:0.000 df:84	1017 Jacqueline r:0.396 p:0.000 df:84
chest width< >underbust / subpelvic rear width< >waist	103	0.125	0.163	0.264	0.326	0.402	0.549	0.749	4133 Heureka r:-0.265 p:0.010 df:92	32855 Zollitsch r:0.418 p:0.000 df:92	2328 Robeson r:-0.376 p:0.000 df:92
clavicle to groin h / ab width	108	1.430	2.207	3.199	3.856	4.264	5.204	6.378	22497 Immanuelfuchs r:-0.266 p:0.010 df:91	10996 Armandspitz r:0.385 p:0.000 df:91	4795 Kihara r:-0.359 p:0.000 df:91
clavicle to groin h / ankle to heel floor h	50	5.107	5.533	6.492	7.127	8.453	11.386	11.897	4246 Telemann r:-0.389 p:0.010 df:41	13657 Badinter r:0.595 p:0.000 df:41	2037 Tripaxeptalis r:0.538 p:0.000 df:41
clavicle to groin h / ankle width	68	2.411	4.400	6.365	7.207	8.389	9.609	13.652	1191 Alfaterna r:-0.334 p:0.010 df:57	6890 Savinykh r:0.527 p:0.000 df:57	1819 Laputa r:-0.482 p:0.000 df:57
clavicle to groin h / areola dia	137	2.411	4.741	8.783	12.054	15.972	24.090	30.283	5234 Sechenov r:-0.231 p:0.010 df:122	3700 Geowilliams r:0.318 p:0.000 df:122	3700 Geowilliams r:0.318 p:0.000 df:122
clavicle to groin h / back perimeter	43	0.063	0.123	0.166	0.192	0.283	0.519	0.545	7074 Muckea r:-0.398 p:0.010 df:39	13672 Tarski r:0.578 p:0.000 df:39	1863 Antinous r:-0.522 p:0.000 df:39
clavicle to groin h / back tone	44	0.170	0.360	0.524	0.641	0.890	2.341	3.124	18396 Nellysachs r:-0.393 p:0.010 df:40	12850 Axelmunthe r:0.600 p:0.000 df:40	1387 Kama r:0.536 p:0.000 df:40
clavicle to groin h / bra shoulder to underb	122	0.970	1.303	1.796	2.030	2.349	2.789	2.960	9114 Hatakeyama r:-0.247 p:0.010 df:106	11227 Ksenborisova r:0.384 p:0.000 df:106	4915 Solzhenitsyn r:-0.365 p:0.000 df:106
clavicle to groin h / breast depth	96	1.124	4.868	8.494	11.619	16.509	26.188	56.855	9932 Kopylov r:-0.281 p:0.010 df:82	11934 Lundgren r:0.516 p:0.000 df:82	916 America r:0.388 p:0.000 df:82
clavicle to groin h / breasts apart	144	3.005	5.705	8.768	11.918	17.095	44.527	84.241	1144 Oda r:-0.227 p:0.010 df:126	21435 Aharon r:0.343 p:0.000 df:126	1277 Dolores r:0.336 p:0.000 df:126
clavicle to groin h / bust dia	148	1.302	2.518	3.371	4.046	4.534	5.955	7.870	12758 Kabudari r:-0.223 p:0.010 df:131	6626 Mattgenge r:0.336 p:0.000 df:131	2434 Bateson r:-0.340 p:0.000 df:131
clavicle to groin h / butt square	35	0.356	0.389	0.597	0.793	0.861	0.973	0.974	8685 Faure r:-0.449 p:0.010 df:30	18171 Romaneskue r:0.618 p:0.000 df:30	1382 Gerti r:-0.613 p:0.000 df:30
clavicle to groin h / calf width	76	1.733	2.202	3.799	4.306	4.818	5.608	7.282	28467 Maurentejamie r:-0.313 p:0.010 df:65	30155 Warmuth r:0.417 p:0.000 df:65	150 Nuwa r:0.416 p:0.000 df:65
clavicle to groin h / chest width	136	0.296	1.168	1.604	1.848	2.011	2.255	2.880	4971 Hoshinohiroba r:-0.233 p:0.010 df:120	6626 Mattgenge r:0.365 p:0.000 df:120	714 Ulula r:-0.331 p:0.000 df:120
clavicle to groin h / clavicle to neck h	103	4.020	4.519	5.972	6.892	8.119	10.460	11.524	9394 Manosque r:-0.269 p:0.010 df:89	4143 Huziak r:0.448 p:0.000 df:89	1390 Abastumani r:-0.377 p:0.000 df:89
clavicle to groin h / foot base h	47	0.927	1.252	2.264	2.725	3.122	4.526	4.955	4431 Holeungholee r:-0.408 p:0.010 df:37	2215 Sichuan r:0.609 p:0.000 df:37	345 Tercidina r:0.556 p:0.000 df:37
clavicle to groin h / long finger length	63	0.664	1.707	2.531	2.797	3.295	3.863	4.245	10263 Vadimsimona r:-0.336 p:0.010 df:56	6201 Ichiroshimizu r:0.510 p:0.000 df:56	4068 Menestheus r:-0.445 p:0.000 df:56
clavicle to groin h / lower leg h	65	0.639	0.971	1.220	1.391	1.546	2.057	2.263	6740 Goff r:-0.345 p:0.009 df:54	11916 Wiesloch r:0.471 p:0.000 df:54	11916 Wiesloch r:0.471 p:0.000 df:54
clavicle to groin h / neck width	111	2.021	3.883	4.661	5.072	5.571	6.249	6.723	1434 Margot r:-0.259 p:0.010 df:96	490 Veritas r:0.406 p:0.000 df:96	59 Elpis r:-0.360 p:0.000 df:96
clavicle to groin h / nipple dia	133	11.787	23.937	34.911	41.974	48.952	64.509	112.526	2573 Hannu Olavi r:-0.232 p:0.010 df:120	21466 Franpelrine r:0.447 p:0.000 df:120	916 America r:0.353 p:0.000 df:120

	N										
clavicle to groin h / nipple to bottom	126	3.934	5.227	7.497	8.685	10.537	15.000	35.820	4476 Bernstein r:-0.241 p:0.010 df:112	1248 Jugurtha r:0.406 p:0.000 df:112	1248 Jugurtha r:0.406 p:0.000 df:112
clavicle to groin h / nipple to top	126	1.142	2.256	3.596	4.658	5.599	7.025	8.933	9381 Lyon r:-0.241 p:0.010 df:111	6626 Mattgenge r:0.361 p:0.000 df:111	1453 Fennia r:0.335 p:0.000 df:111
clavicle to groin h / pelvic hips	126	0.553	1.285	1.602	1.791	1.994	2.214	2.491	3454 Lieske r:-0.244 p:0.010 df:109	6626 Mattgenge r:0.363 p:0.000 df:109	1648 Shajna r:-0.351 p:0.000 df:109
clavicle to groin h / shoulder width	146	0.764	1.239	1.513	1.625	1.747	1.945	2.101	541 Deborah r:-0.227 p:0.010 df:127	1503 Kuopio r:0.333 p:0.000 df:127	66 Maja r:0.308 p:0.000 df:127
clavicle to groin h / subchest width	79	0.220	1.246	1.672	1.903	2.131	2.336	3.681	757 Portlandia r:-0.306 p:0.010 df:68	6626 Mattgenge r:0.597 p:0.000 df:68	235 Carolina r:0.434 p:0.000 df:68
clavicle to groin h / subneck dorsal	70	2.061	2.607	3.355	3.912	4.306	5.007	5.607	8973 Pratincola r:-0.325 p:0.010 df:60	3603 Gajdusek r:0.545 p:0.000 df:60	393 Lampetia r:0.437 p:0.000 df:60
clavicle to groin h / subpelvic rear width	91	0.172	0.934	1.373	1.570	1.668	1.819	1.900	8320 van Zee r:-0.284 p:0.010 df:80	4679 Sybil r:0.393 p:0.000 df:80	658 Asteria r:-0.410 p:0.000 df:80
clavicle to groin h / suprailiac	135	0.582	1.258	1.779	1.986	2.140	2.408	2.583	3221 Changshi r:-0.234 p:0.010 df:118	6626 Mattgenge r:0.369 p:0.000 df:118	658 Asteria r:-0.338 p:0.000 df:118
clavicle to groin h / underbust	127	0.561	1.405	1.904	2.089	2.268	2.558	3.547	7019 Tagayuichan r:-0.241 p:0.010 df:112	19625 Ovaitt r:0.374 p:0.000 df:112	2021 Poincare r:-0.332 p:0.000 df:112
clavicle to groin h / waist	143	0.594	1.449	1.943	2.207	2.351	2.643	2.942	27421 Nathanhan r:-0.226 p:0.010 df:127	6626 Mattgenge r:0.328 p:0.000 df:127	1648 Shajna r:-0.323 p:0.000 df:127
clavicle to neck h / ankle to heel floor h	60	0.703	0.740	0.958	1.095	1.327	2.538	3.671	805 Hormuthia r:-0.352 p:0.010 df:51	765 Mattiaca r:0.578 p:0.000 df:51	765 Mattiaca r:0.578 p:0.000 df:51
clavicle to neck h / ankle width	80	0.338	0.677	0.853	1.028	1.282	1.733	2.687	10024 Marthahazen r:-0.300 p:0.010 df:71	6892 Lana r:0.456 p:0.000 df:71	765 Mattiaca r:0.433 p:0.000 df:71
clavicle to neck h / ball width	35	0.218	0.252	0.544	0.797	1.116	1.769	2.027	3143 Genecampbell r:-0.439 p:0.009 df:32	30140 Robpergolizzi r:0.690 p:0.000 df:32	336 Lacadiera r:0.573 p:0.000 df:32
clavicle to neck h / big toe length	32	0.424	0.479	1.199	1.455	2.005	3.823	5.124	8625 Simonhelberg r:-0.464 p:0.010 df:28	30140 Robpergolizzi r:0.719 p:0.000 df:28	336 Lacadiera r:0.649 p:0.000 df:28
clavicle to neck h / calf width	85	0.256	0.343	0.517	0.608	0.712	1.102	1.816	8163 Ishizaki r:-0.290 p:0.010 df:76	7561 Patrickmichel r:0.500 p:0.000 df:76	765 Mattiaca r:0.458 p:0.000 df:76
clavicle to neck h / foot base h	59	0.122	0.221	0.317	0.398	0.486	0.708	0.849	17201 Matjazhumar r:-0.354 p:0.010 df:50	13975 Beatrixpotter r:0.603 p:0.000 df:50	7953 Kawaguchi r:0.489 p:0.000 df:50
clavicle to neck h / heel width	32	0.418	0.425	0.867	1.080	1.604	2.485	2.715	33413 Alecsun r:-0.449 p:0.010 df:30	25125 Brodallan r:0.672 p:0.000 df:30	807 Ceraskia r:0.583 p:0.000 df:30
clavicle to neck h / lower leg h	77	0.104	0.131	0.163	0.203	0.239	0.366	0.581	3463 Kaokuen r:-0.307 p:0.010 df:68	765 Mattiaca r:0.516 p:0.000 df:68	765 Mattiaca r:0.516 p:0.000 df:68
clavicle to neck h / subchest width	70	0.130	0.163	0.233	0.273	0.322	0.387	0.503	23727 Akihasan r:-0.323 p:0.010 df:61	16650 Sakushingakuin r:0.447 p:0.000 df:61	2061 Anza r:0.433 p:0.000 df:61
elbow to wrist h / ab width	134	0.704	0.983	1.327	1.625	2.008	2.498	3.673	127870 Vigo r:-0.235 p:0.010 df:117	25953 Lanairlett r:0.375 p:0.000 df:117	4765 Wasserburg r:0.335 p:0.000 df:117
elbow to wrist h / ankle to heel floor h	79	1.074	2.146	2.961	3.205	3.753	5.543	8.154	2148 Epeios r:-0.304 p:0.010 df:69	9804 Shrikulkarni r:0.435 p:0.000 df:69	7647 Etrepigny r:0.403 p:0.000 df:69
elbow to wrist h / ankle width	117	1.215	1.985	2.739	3.217	3.763	4.797	7.197	2697 Albina r:-0.250 p:0.010 df:104	13367 Jiri r:0.392 p:0.000 df:104	521 Brixia r:0.386 p:0.000 df:104
elbow to wrist h / areola dia	182	1.417	2.064	3.541	5.188	6.919	9.812	12.977	1304 Arosa r:-0.200 p:0.010 df:164	31660 Maximiliandu r:0.294 p:0.000 df:164	12044 Fabbri r:-0.295 p:0.000 df:164
elbow to wrist h / back perimeter	56	0.027	0.031	0.070	0.091	0.126	0.220	0.269	7871 Tunder r:-0.352 p:0.010 df:51	7704 Dellen r:0.517 p:0.000 df:51	1936 Lugano r:0.469 p:0.000 df:51
elbow to wrist h / back tone	57	0.042	0.142	0.241	0.319	0.433	0.877	1.184	20555 Jennings r:-0.348 p:0.010 df:52	12850 Axelmunthe r:0.512 p:0.000 df:52	925 Alphonsina r:0.469 p:0.000 df:52
elbow to wrist h / ball width	48	0.740	0.968	1.872	2.484	2.916	3.856	5.776	2721 Vsekhsvyatskij r:-0.373 p:0.010 df:45	22002 Richardregan r:0.526 p:0.000 df:45	789 Lena r:0.511 p:0.000 df:45
elbow to wrist h / big toe length	42	1.558	1.922	3.807	4.890	5.705	7.933	9.509	30051 Jihopark r:-0.403 p:0.010 df:38	27123 Matthewlam r:0.576 p:0.000 df:38	3003 Koncek r:0.529 p:0.000 df:38
elbow to wrist h / big toe width	37	2.758	2.940	5.533	7.198	9.381	13.271	13.683	5443 Encrenaz r:-0.424 p:0.010 df:34	22002 Richardregan r:0.630 p:0.000 df:34	1239 Queteleta r:0.561 p:0.000 df:34
elbow to wrist h / bra shoulder to underb	166	0.441	0.589	0.781	0.884	1.039	1.278	2.258	1679 Nevanlinna r:-0.210 p:0.010 df:149	46977 Krakow r:0.318 p:0.000 df:149	3803 Tuchkova r:0.289 p:0.000 df:149
elbow to wrist h / breast depth	147	1.030	2.116	3.829	4.912	6.765	11.249	21.670	2550 Houssay r:-0.222 p:0.010 df:132	10984 Gispen r:0.335 p:0.000 df:132	2596 Vainu Bappu r:0.309 p:0.000 df:132
elbow to wrist h / breasts apart	191	1.751	2.640	3.794	5.356	7.994	18.608	39.347	31655 Averyclowes r:-0.196 p:0.010 df:170	3386 Klementinum r:0.285 p:0.000 df:170	2253 Espinette r:0.274 p:0.000 df:170
elbow to wrist h / bust dia	210	0.656	0.978	1.432	1.679	1.988	2.545	3.144	4088 Baggesen r:-0.187 p:0.010 df:188	20218 Dukewriter r:0.279 p:0.000 df:188	1304 Arosa r:-0.265 p:0.000 df:188
elbow to wrist h / butt square	52	0.161	0.180	0.285	0.350	0.387	0.462	0.670	4283 Stoffler r:-0.367 p:0.010 df:47	27343 Deannashea r:0.537 p:0.000 df:47	617 Patroclus r:-0.480 p:0.000 df:47
elbow to wrist h / calf width	135	0.784	1.242	1.612	1.855	2.071	2.730	3.870	5459 Saraburger r:-0.231 p:0.010 df:121	6875 Golgi r:0.361 p:0.000 df:121	2820 Iisalmi r:0.311 p:0.000 df:121
elbow to wrist h / chest width	186	0.258	0.465	0.679	0.784	0.901	1.126	1.420	24126 Gudjonson r:-0.198 p:0.010 df:166	1085 Amaryllis r:0.317 p:0.000 df:166	839 Valborg r:-0.269 p:0.000 df:166
elbow to wrist h / clavicle to groin h	135	0.266	0.326	0.398	0.445	0.493	0.606	0.916	4961 Timherder r:-0.236 p:0.010 df:117	13031 Durance r:0.395 p:0.000 df:117	2794 Kulik r:0.319 p:0.000 df:117

elbow to wrist h / clavicle to neck h	124	1.888	2.075	2.619	3.240	3.763	4.686	7.901	1566 Icarus r:-0.246 p:0.010 df:107	8501 Wachholz r:0.370 p:0.000 df:107	2906 Caltech r:0.364 p:0.000 df:107
elbow to wrist h / foot base h	78	0.478	0.737	1.024	1.239	1.433	1.801	2.281	8824 Genta r:-0.306 p:0.010 df:68	6674 Cezanne r:0.502 p:0.000 df:68	369 Aeria r:-0.475 p:0.000 df:68
elbow to wrist h / heel width	48	1.471	1.696	3.020	3.445	3.996	5.388	7.683	175282 Benhida r:-0.373 p:0.010 df:45	5052 Nancyruth r:0.520 p:0.000 df:45	4253 Marker r:0.489 p:0.000 df:45
elbow to wrist h / long finger length	96	0.578	0.846	1.120	1.247	1.380	1.800	2.000	9387 Tweedledee r:-0.269 p:0.010 df:89	12178 Dhani r:0.421 p:0.000 df:89	377 Campania r:0.381 p:0.000 df:89
elbow to wrist h / lower leg h	113	0.252	0.434	0.526	0.606	0.682	0.899	1.022	5904 Wurttemberg r:-0.254 p:0.010 df:100	9775 Joeferguson r:0.345 p:0.000 df:100	9775 Joeferguson r:0.345 p:0.000 df:100
elbow to wrist h / neck width	159	1.245	1.662	1.997	2.237	2.525	3.089	4.392	825 Tanina r:-0.216 p:0.010 df:141	36782 Okauchitakashige r:0.339 p:0.000 df:141	2983 Poltava r:0.317 p:0.000 df:141
elbow to wrist h / nipple dia	175	5.435	11.157	14.609	17.984	21.855	29.640	37.555	1479 Inkeri r:-0.203 p:0.010 df:159	117713 Kovesligethy r:0.322 p:0.000 df:159	456 Abnoba r:0.281 p:0.000 df:159
elbow to wrist h / nipple to bottom	167	1.282	2.504	3.196	3.931	4.551	6.645	11.002	3104 Durer r:-0.209 p:0.010 df:150	5916 van der Woude r:0.305 p:0.000 df:150	5916 van der Woude r:0.305 p:0.000 df:150
elbow to wrist h / nipple to top	166	0.713	1.010	1.537	1.972	2.436	3.302	4.179	6474 Choate r:-0.210 p:0.010 df:148	4907 Zoser r:0.387 p:0.000 df:148	1001 Gaussia r:-0.324 p:0.000 df:148
elbow to wrist h / pelvic hips	167	0.255	0.522	0.701	0.789	0.885	1.085	1.451	7812 Billward r:-0.210 p:0.010 df:148	17104 McCloskey r:0.306 p:0.000 df:148	789 Lena r:0.296 p:0.000 df:148
elbow to wrist h / second toe length	34	1.777	2.089	4.758	5.740	6.572	9.780	10.769	1466 Mundleria r:-0.436 p:0.010 df:32	27123 Matthewlam r:0.628 p:0.000 df:32	459 Signe r:-0.567 p:0.000 df:32
elbow to wrist h / shoulder width	217	0.398	0.540	0.639	0.706	0.787	0.946	1.219	2259 Sofievka r:-0.183 p:0.010 df:195	32547 Shandroff r:0.286 p:0.000 df:195	5186 Donalu r:-0.261 p:0.000 df:195
elbow to wrist h / subchest width	100	0.191	0.579	0.706	0.826	0.933	1.178	1.349	47293 Masamitsu r:-0.270 p:0.010 df:88	20503 Adamtazi r:0.435 p:0.000 df:88	922 Schlutia r:0.400 p:0.000 df:88
elbow to wrist h / subneck dorsal	99	0.989	1.185	1.438	1.661	1.870	2.272	3.092	16147 Jeanli r:-0.274 p:0.010 df:86	7412 Linnaeus r:0.429 p:0.000 df:86	56 Melete r:0.382 p:0.000 df:86
elbow to wrist h / subpelvic rear width	121	0.150	0.405	0.578	0.654	0.728	0.892	1.677	5715 Kramer r:-0.246 p:0.010 df:107	789 Lena r:0.483 p:0.000 df:107	463 Lola r:0.348 p:0.000 df:107
elbow to wrist h / suprailiac	177	0.269	0.573	0.753	0.870	0.972	1.232	1.596	553 Kundry r:-0.203 p:0.010 df:158	6081 Cloutis r:0.293 p:0.000 df:158	381 Myrrha r:0.273 p:0.000 df:158
elbow to wrist h / underbust	155	0.259	0.517	0.803	0.901	1.051	1.269	2.169	3872 Akirafujii r:-0.218 p:0.010 df:138	19488 Abramcoley r:0.337 p:0.000 df:138	381 Myrrha r:0.306 p:0.000 df:138
elbow to wrist h / waist	191	0.274	0.573	0.837	0.941	1.078	1.243	1.771	13058 Alfredstevens r:-0.195 p:0.010 df:172	28163 Lorikim r:0.275 p:0.000 df:172	2970 Pestalozzi r:-0.280 p:0.000 df:172
finger width / ab perimeter	176	0.003	0.005	0.010	0.012	0.015	0.028	0.040	8800 Brophy r:-0.203 p:0.010 df:158	11899 Weill r:0.334 p:0.000 df:158	2674 Pandarus r:0.293 p:0.000 df:158
finger width / ab tone	173	0.014	0.022	0.035	0.054	0.099	0.610	1.492	8957 Koujounotsuki r:-0.205 p:0.010 df:157	25462 Haydenmetsky r:0.359 p:0.000 df:157	178 Belisana r:0.276 p:0.000 df:157
finger width / ab width	143	0.062	0.094	0.122	0.142	0.175	0.239	0.386	20469 Dudleymoore r:-0.226 p:0.010 df:127	4250 Perun r:0.354 p:0.000 df:127	819 Barnardiana r:0.302 p:0.000 df:127
finger width / ankle to heel floor h	86	0.173	0.198	0.252	0.305	0.362	0.544	0.867	2848 ASP r:-0.292 p:0.010 df:75	269485 Bisikalo r:0.488 p:0.000 df:75	1560 Strattonia r:0.390 p:0.000 df:75
finger width / ankle width	128	0.104	0.189	0.243	0.302	0.337	0.478	0.738	27381 Balasingam r:-0.237 p:0.010 df:115	269485 Bisikalo r:0.364 p:0.000 df:115	345 Tercidina r:0.327 p:0.000 df:115
finger width / areola dia	209	0.138	0.188	0.308	0.453	0.620	0.884	1.474	7519 Paulcook r:-0.186 p:0.010 df:190	18680 Weirather r:0.281 p:0.000 df:190	1222 Tina r:-0.266 p:0.000 df:190
finger width / back perimeter	59	0.003	0.004	0.006	0.008	0.012	0.022	0.027	170022 Douglastucker r:-0.339 p:0.010 df:55	14088 Ancus r:0.490 p:0.000 df:55	1580 Betulia r:0.451 p:0.000 df:55
finger width / back tone	60	0.007	0.015	0.023	0.028	0.037	0.087	0.115	5036 Tuttle r:-0.336 p:0.010 df:56	8474 Rettig r:0.596 p:0.000 df:56	2502 Nummela r:0.463 p:0.000 df:56
finger width / ball width	58	0.073	0.085	0.175	0.205	0.248	0.480	0.516	30136 Bakerfranke r:-0.339 p:0.010 df:55	7457 Veselov r:0.537 p:0.000 df:55	2140 Kemerovo r:-0.472 p:0.000 df:55
finger width / bicep width	239	0.125	0.149	0.195	0.228	0.268	0.331	0.624	90447 Emans r:-0.174 p:0.010 df:219	18680 Weirather r:0.287 p:0.000 df:219	280 Philia r:0.234 p:0.000 df:219
finger width / big toe length	56	0.063	0.155	0.322	0.426	0.542	0.817	1.210	18790 Ericaburden r:-0.352 p:0.010 df:51	3827 Zdenekhorsky r:0.551 p:0.000 df:51	342 Endymion r:0.511 p:0.000 df:51
finger width / big toe width	46	0.103	0.208	0.497	0.611	0.745	1.423	1.648	25191 Rachelouise r:-0.380 p:0.010 df:43	20044 Vitoux r:0.585 p:0.000 df:43	193 Ambrosia r:0.563 p:0.000 df:43
finger width / bra shoulder to underb	177	0.043	0.052	0.069	0.080	0.096	0.136	0.226	4069 Blakee r:-0.201 p:0.010 df:162	179764 Myriamsarah r:0.280 p:0.000 df:162	3240 Laocoon r:-0.272 p:0.000 df:162
finger width / breast depth	148	0.088	0.198	0.321	0.466	0.612	1.018	1.617	4148 McCartney r:-0.219 p:0.010 df:136	24278 Davidgreen r:0.354 p:0.000 df:136	2276 Warck r:0.293 p:0.000 df:136
finger width / breasts apart	220	0.184	0.235	0.349	0.510	0.753	1.936	3.671	763 Cupido r:-0.182 p:0.010 df:199	131181 Zebrak r:0.243 p:0.001 df:199	434 Hungaria r:0.226 p:0.001 df:199
finger width / bust dia	242	0.080	0.093	0.128	0.152	0.182	0.252	0.351	3519 Ambiorix r:-0.173 p:0.010 df:221	4536 Drewpinsky r:0.288 p:0.000 df:221	453 Tea r:0.233 p:0.000 df:221
finger width / butt square	56	0.013	0.020	0.026	0.031	0.039	0.057	0.086	33897 Erikagreen r:-0.351 p:0.010 df:51	44530 Horakova r:0.606 p:0.000 df:51	19 Fortuna r:0.537 p:0.000 df:51
finger width / calf width	149	0.089	0.116	0.145	0.169	0.204	0.258	0.438	1227 Geranium r:-0.219 p:0.010 df:136	30060 Davidseong r:0.320 p:0.000 df:136	754 Malabar r:-0.295 p:0.000 df:136

finger width / chest width	213	0.041	0.049	0.062	0.070	0.082	0.107	0.169	2120 Tyumenia r:-0.184 p:0.010 df:194	456 Abnoba r:0.313 p:0.000 df:194	456 Abnoba r:0.313 p:0.000 df:194
finger width / clavicle to groin h	135	0.024	0.028	0.035	0.040	0.045	0.056	0.105	2669 Shostakovich r:-0.233 p:0.010 df:120	199 Byblis r:0.359 p:0.000 df:120	199 Byblis r:0.359 p:0.000 df:120
finger width / clavicle to neck h	135	0.157	0.180	0.224	0.274	0.348	0.517	0.887	5415 Lyanzuridi r:-0.233 p:0.010 df:120	18983 Allentran r:0.352 p:0.000 df:120	1425 Tuorla r:0.312 p:0.000 df:120
finger width / elbow to wrist h	227	0.041	0.063	0.080	0.092	0.105	0.136	0.227	2303 Retsina r:-0.179 p:0.010 df:206	9767 Midsomer Norton r:0.275 p:0.000 df:206	127 Johanna r:-0.247 p:0.000 df:206
finger width / foot base h	91	0.041	0.073	0.092	0.110	0.130	0.175	0.262	1112 Polonia r:-0.283 p:0.010 df:80	214772 UNICEF r:0.471 p:0.000 df:80	632 Pyrrha r:0.387 p:0.000 df:80
finger width / heel width	56	0.132	0.139	0.274	0.321	0.376	0.449	0.656	588 Achilles r:-0.345 p:0.010 df:53	169078 Chuckshaw r:0.509 p:0.000 df:53	1463 Nordenmarkia r:-0.477 p:0.000 df:53
finger width / long finger length	102	0.068	0.085	0.104	0.114	0.127	0.156	0.188	17042 Madiraju r:-0.260 p:0.010 df:95	11163 Milesovka r:0.415 p:0.000 df:95	243 Ida r:-0.353 p:0.000 df:95
finger width / lower forearm w	264	0.197	0.250	0.331	0.373	0.414	0.490	0.837	17942 Whiterabbit r:-0.164 p:0.010 df:243	3265 Fletcher r:0.283 p:0.000 df:243	1567 Alikoski r:0.228 p:0.000 df:243
finger width / lower leg h	124	0.031	0.040	0.048	0.056	0.064	0.088	0.137	11135 Ryokami r:-0.240 p:0.010 df:112	10984 Gispen r:0.373 p:0.000 df:112	-10012 mean Apogee r:0.340 p:0.000 df:112
finger width / lower thigh width	197	0.071	0.105	0.137	0.157	0.186	0.244	0.465	4638 Estens r:-0.190 p:0.010 df:182	10558 Karlstad r:0.299 p:0.000 df:182	380 Fiducia r:0.276 p:0.000 df:182
finger width / neck width	174	0.110	0.142	0.176	0.201	0.227	0.299	0.561	48447 Hingley r:-0.203 p:0.010 df:158	8374 Horohata r:0.302 p:0.000 df:158	5223 McSween r:0.276 p:0.000 df:158
finger width / nipple dia	202	0.630	0.909	1.313	1.632	2.020	3.097	3.455	6180 Bystritskaya r:-0.188 p:0.010 df:185	1188 Gothlandia r:0.291 p:0.000 df:185	456 Abnoba r:0.284 p:0.000 df:185
finger width / nipple to bottom	187	0.130	0.199	0.284	0.356	0.471	0.668	1.540	4993 Cossard r:-0.195 p:0.010 df:172	21825 Zhangyizhong r:0.346 p:0.000 df:172	1079 Mimosa r:0.306 p:0.000 df:172
finger width / nipple to top	186	0.070	0.092	0.131	0.177	0.226	0.339	0.464	2877 Likhachev r:-0.197 p:0.010 df:169	27502 Stephbecca r:0.305 p:0.000 df:169	3558 Shishkin r:-0.285 p:0.000 df:169
finger width / pelvic hips	187	0.028	0.049	0.062	0.071	0.082	0.103	0.189	1961 Dufour r:-0.196 p:0.010 df:170	214772 UNICEF r:0.309 p:0.000 df:170	772 Tanete r:0.297 p:0.000 df:170
finger width / pinky toe length	39	0.255	0.266	0.566	0.686	0.938	1.252	1.465	1268 Libya r:-0.408 p:0.010 df:37	27123 Matthewlam r:0.593 p:0.000 df:37	6266 Letzel r:-0.546 p:0.000 df:37
finger width / second toe length	42	0.072	0.172	0.366	0.491	0.599	0.831	0.851	12974 Halitherses r:-0.394 p:0.010 df:40	15112 Arlenewolfe r:0.560 p:0.000 df:40	1369 Ostanina r:0.515 p:0.000 df:40
finger width / shoulder to elbow h	236	0.039	0.056	0.070	0.080	0.091	0.113	0.219	5090 Wyeth r:-0.174 p:0.010 df:217	24919 Teruyoshi r:0.259 p:0.000 df:217	947 Monterosa r:0.236 p:0.000 df:217
finger width / shoulder width	244	0.039	0.048	0.056	0.066	0.073	0.094	0.182	3904 Honda r:-0.171 p:0.010 df:224	11929 Uchino r:0.297 p:0.000 df:224	127 Johanna r:-0.244 p:0.000 df:224
finger width / subchest width	105	0.044	0.053	0.064	0.072	0.085	0.113	0.166	5577 Priestley r:-0.262 p:0.010 df:94	422 Berolina r:0.376 p:0.000 df:94	422 Berolina r:0.376 p:0.000 df:94
finger width / subneck dorsal	107	0.091	0.107	0.132	0.150	0.175	0.240	0.359	296638 Sergeibelov r:-0.258 p:0.010 df:97	11361 Orbinskij r:0.415 p:0.000 df:97	2476 Andersen r:-0.363 p:0.000 df:97
finger width / subpelvic rear width	132	0.025	0.039	0.052	0.059	0.067	0.085	0.143	3233 Krisbarons r:-0.233 p:0.010 df:120	14877 Zauberflote r:0.353 p:0.000 df:120	508 Princetonia r:0.336 p:0.000 df:120
finger width / suprailiac	195	0.029	0.055	0.067	0.077	0.090	0.112	0.211	13140 Shinchukai r:-0.192 p:0.010 df:178	216295 Menorca r:0.295 p:0.000 df:178	2313 Aruna r:0.267 p:0.000 df:178
finger width / thigh h	195	0.030	0.035	0.044	0.050	0.058	0.080	0.143	12294 Avogadro r:-0.191 p:0.010 df:179	9963 Sandage r:0.309 p:0.000 df:179	380 Fiducia r:0.269 p:0.000 df:179
finger width / underbust	168	0.028	0.058	0.073	0.081	0.094	0.122	0.206	11414 Allanchu r:-0.208 p:0.010 df:151	28467 Maurentejamie r:0.321 p:0.000 df:151	1092 Lilium r:0.307 p:0.000 df:151
finger width / upper forearm w	255	0.084	0.168	0.215	0.247	0.282	0.348	0.528	90447 Emans r:-0.167 p:0.010 df:234	318547 Fidrich r:0.247 p:0.000 df:234	6057 Robbia r:-0.245 p:0.000 df:234
finger width / upper thigh width	257	0.048	0.078	0.098	0.113	0.131	0.177	0.318	1463 Nordenmarkia r:-0.166 p:0.010 df:238	24134 Cliffordkim r:0.271 p:0.000 df:238	159 Aemilia r:0.228 p:0.000 df:238
finger width / waist	212	0.030	0.058	0.074	0.084	0.098	0.122	0.257	848 Inna r:-0.184 p:0.010 df:195	2313 Aruna r:0.267 p:0.000 df:195	375 Ursula r:0.260 p:0.000 df:195
foot base h / ball width	51	1.254	1.356	1.782	1.980	2.106	2.479	2.620	16076 Barryhaase r:-0.363 p:0.010 df:48	21742 Rachaelscott r:0.553 p:0.000 df:48	3482 Lesnaya r:-0.508 p:0.000 df:48
foot base h / big toe length	52	2.330	2.518	3.243	4.011	4.717	5.569	7.585	25198 Kylienicole r:-0.365 p:0.010 df:47	34252 Orlovsky r:0.511 p:0.000 df:47	1425 Tuorla r:-0.500 p:0.000 df:47
foot base h / big toe width	41	3.608	3.847	5.084	5.671	6.341	7.774	8.181	17917 Cartan r:-0.403 p:0.010 df:38	14734 Susanstoker r:0.654 p:0.000 df:38	493 Griseldis r:0.527 p:0.000 df:38
foot base h / heel width	50	2.089	2.160	2.627	2.941	3.378	3.996	5.332	503 Evelyn r:-0.365 p:0.010 df:47	6372 Walker r:0.549 p:0.000 df:47	2142 Landau r:0.499 p:0.000 df:47
foot base h / pinky toe length	38	3.992	4.440	5.964	6.535	8.003	11.510	12.157	3935 Toatenmongakkai r:-0.413 p:0.010 df:36	5954 Epikouros r:0.719 p:0.000 df:36	1007 Pawlowia r:0.544 p:0.000 df:36
foot base h / second toe length	39	2.841	2.886	4.033	4.486	5.773	7.012	7.539	615 Roswitha r:-0.408 p:0.010 df:37	3605 Davy r:0.618 p:0.000 df:37	3605 Davy r:0.618 p:0.000 df:37
heel width / ball width	54	0.503	0.511	0.573	0.617	0.734	0.857	0.920	78071 Vicent r:-0.348 p:0.010 df:52	35366 Kaifeng r:0.558 p:0.000 df:52	219 Thusnelda r:-0.466 p:0.000 df:52
heel width / big toe length	39	0.903	0.905	1.150	1.338	1.571	2.073	2.561	4293 Masumi r:-0.408 p:0.010 df:37	26664 Jongwon r:0.596 p:0.000 df:37	400 Ducrosa r:0.564 p:0.000 df:37

heel width / big toe width		37	1.256	1.264	1.621	1.818	1.966	2.436	2.481	120352 Gordonwong r:-0.418 p:0.010 df:35	35366 Kaifeng r:0.595 p:0.000 df:35	1306 Scythia r:-0.584 p:0.000 df:35
heel width / pinky toe length		34	1.717	1.747	1.973	2.449	2.785	3.542	4.252	7430 Kogure r:-0.436 p:0.010 df:32	17251 Vondracek r:0.642 p:0.000 df:32	2286 Fesenkov r:-0.617 p:0.000 df:32
heel width / second toe length		32	1.033	1.145	1.450	1.693	1.872	2.409	2.545	10089 Turgot r:-0.449 p:0.010 df:30	4997 Ksana r:0.680 p:0.000 df:30	154 Bertha r:-0.723 p:0.000 df:30
long finger length / ab width		59	0.658	0.892	1.099	1.317	1.579	1.890	3.999	8903 Paulcruikshank r:-0.349 p:0.010 df:52	23280 Laitsaita r:0.586 p:0.000 df:52	401 Ottilia r:0.474 p:0.000 df:52
long finger length / ankle to heel floor h		41	1.706	1.926	2.317	2.547	3.076	3.696	6.955	19310 Osawa r:-0.409 p:0.010 df:37	844 Leontina r:0.635 p:0.000 df:37	844 Leontina r:0.635 p:0.000 df:37
long finger length / ankle width		56	1.002	1.751	2.314	2.579	2.799	3.794	4.558	5451 Plato r:-0.351 p:0.010 df:51	4727 Ravel r:0.501 p:0.000 df:51	1818 Brahms r:0.470 p:0.000 df:51
long finger length / back perimeter		32	0.021	0.025	0.057	0.071	0.103	0.207	0.212	9275 Persson r:-0.456 p:0.010 df:29	6335 Nicolerappaport r:0.617 p:0.000 df:29	5120 Bitias r:-0.670 p:0.000 df:29
long finger length / back tone		33	0.063	0.102	0.171	0.270	0.356	0.803	0.916	8147 Colemanhawkins r:-0.450 p:0.010 df:30	3566 Levitan r:0.636 p:0.000 df:30	881 Athene r:0.584 p:0.000 df:30
long finger length / bust dia		95	0.582	0.756	1.218	1.389	1.599	2.150	2.876	25710 Petelandgren r:-0.271 p:0.010 df:88	170909 Bobmasterson r:0.428 p:0.000 df:88	2286 Fesenkov r:-0.362 p:0.000 df:88
long finger length / calf width		60	0.912	1.049	1.327	1.539	1.721	2.328	3.115	4384 Henrybuhl r:-0.339 p:0.010 df:55	772 Tanete r:0.544 p:0.000 df:55	772 Tanete r:0.544 p:0.000 df:55
long finger length / clavicle to neck h		51	1.613	1.744	2.217	2.583	2.969	5.237	9.434	43775 Tiepolo r:-0.368 p:0.010 df:46	1842 Hynek r:0.609 p:0.000 df:46	745 Mauritia r:0.509 p:0.000 df:46
long finger length / foot base h		40	0.438	0.659	0.831	0.978	1.078	1.524	1.696	1030 Vitja r:-0.413 p:0.010 df:36	8775 Cristata r:0.571 p:0.000 df:36	2633 Bishop r:-0.590 p:0.000 df:36
long finger length / lower leg h		54	0.272	0.384	0.428	0.464	0.530	0.723	0.789	394 Arduina r:-0.358 p:0.010 df:49	13622 McArthur r:0.497 p:0.000 df:49	6434 Jewitt r:0.483 p:0.000 df:49
long finger length / neck width		69	1.108	1.273	1.571	1.804	2.052	2.514	3.613	15675 Goloseevo r:-0.315 p:0.010 df:64	35269 Idefix r:0.474 p:0.000 df:64	972 Cohnia r:0.471 p:0.000 df:64
long finger length / shoulder width		97	0.314	0.437	0.513	0.572	0.647	0.837	1.337	30388 Nicolejustice r:-0.267 p:0.010 df:90	73453 Ninomanfredi r:0.441 p:0.000 df:90	1341 Edmee r:-0.370 p:0.000 df:90
long finger length / subchest width		47	0.331	0.456	0.625	0.691	0.778	0.881	0.907	12123 Pazin r:-0.384 p:0.010 df:42	6922 Yasushi r:0.528 p:0.000 df:42	382 Dodona r:-0.510 p:0.000 df:42
long finger length / subneck dorsal		37	0.900	0.907	1.203	1.363	1.583	1.888	2.346	255 Oppavia r:-0.424 p:0.010 df:34	31978 Jeremyphilip r:0.629 p:0.000 df:34	1156 Kira r:0.562 p:0.000 df:34
lower forearm w / ab width		150	0.177	0.257	0.334	0.388	0.461	0.644	0.768	2386 Nikonov r:-0.222 p:0.010 df:132	3950 Yoshida r:0.335 p:0.000 df:132	1449 Virtanen r:0.298 p:0.000 df:132
lower forearm w / ankle to heel floor h		85	0.289	0.571	0.701	0.806	0.947	1.371	1.682	406 Erna r:-0.294 p:0.010 df:74	3430 Bradfield r:0.435 p:0.000 df:74	1515 Perrotin r:-0.403 p:0.000 df:74
lower forearm w / ankle width		128	0.301	0.543	0.671	0.761	0.919	1.203	1.977	1321 Majuba r:-0.239 p:0.010 df:114	624 Hektor r:0.380 p:0.000 df:114	624 Hektor r:0.380 p:0.000 df:114
lower forearm w / areola dia		213	0.210	0.532	0.850	1.181	1.584	2.191	3.695	2337 Boubin r:-0.184 p:0.010 df:194	296819 Artesian r:0.267 p:0.000 df:194	7063 Johnmichell r:-0.267 p:0.000 df:194
lower forearm w / back perimeter		59	0.007	0.012	0.017	0.021	0.029	0.050	0.067	1828 Kashirina r:-0.342 p:0.010 df:54	4491 Otaru r:0.535 p:0.000 df:54	1553 Bauersfelda r:-0.471 p:0.000 df:54
lower forearm w / back tone		60	0.018	0.040	0.059	0.072	0.100	0.182	0.325	6712 Hornstein r:-0.339 p:0.010 df:55	8474 Rettig r:0.568 p:0.000 df:55	3775 Ellenbeth r:-0.464 p:0.000 df:55
lower forearm w / ball width		58	0.228	0.269	0.458	0.559	0.665	0.958	1.207	66 Maja r:-0.339 p:0.010 df:55	5052 Nancyruth r:0.532 p:0.000 df:55	196 Philomela r:-0.460 p:0.000 df:55
lower forearm w / big toe length		56	0.181	0.448	0.899	1.078	1.440	2.109	2.370	47494 Gerhardangl r:-0.351 p:0.010 df:51	3003 Koncek r:0.483 p:0.000 df:51	3003 Koncek r:0.483 p:0.000 df:51
lower forearm w / big toe width		47	0.294	0.706	1.265	1.649	1.974	3.003	3.219	7787 Annalaura r:-0.376 p:0.010 df:44	3401 Vanphilos r:0.517 p:0.000 df:44	3401 Vanphilos r:0.517 p:0.000 df:44
lower forearm w / bra shoulder to underb		188	0.072	0.153	0.186	0.212	0.255	0.358	0.511	6023 Tsuyashima r:-0.195 p:0.010 df:171	26541 Garyross r:0.327 p:0.000 df:171	1845 Helewalda r:0.272 p:0.000 df:171
lower forearm w / breast depth		156	0.215	0.522	0.921	1.233	1.607	2.408	4.470	3538 Nelsonia r:-0.214 p:0.010 df:142	961 Gunnie r:0.315 p:0.000 df:142	961 Gunnie r:0.315 p:0.000 df:142
lower forearm w / breasts apart		220	0.358	0.599	0.958	1.318	2.069	5.012	10.293	65692 Trifu r:-0.182 p:0.010 df:198	234026 Unioneastrofili r:0.263 p:0.000 df:198	26302 Zimolzak r:0.252 p:0.000 df:198
lower forearm w / bust dia		245	0.112	0.259	0.354	0.405	0.486	0.628	0.790	21331 Lodovicoferrari r:-0.172 p:0.010 df:223	30414 Pistacchi r:0.256 p:0.000 df:223	368 Haidea r:0.238 p:0.000 df:223
lower forearm w / butt square		58	0.038	0.049	0.073	0.083	0.098	0.135	0.264	4472 Navashin r:-0.345 p:0.010 df:53	59828 Ossikar r:0.641 p:0.000 df:53	2394 Nadeev r:0.499 p:0.000 df:53
lower forearm w / calf width		147	0.211	0.320	0.402	0.457	0.521	0.666	1.174	7607 Billmerline r:-0.222 p:0.010 df:132	350185 Linnell r:0.368 p:0.000 df:132	11 Parthenope r:0.305 p:0.000 df:132
lower forearm w / chest width		213	0.090	0.129	0.168	0.189	0.223	0.270	0.414	3274 Maillen r:-0.185 p:0.010 df:192	11448 Miahajdukova r:0.285 p:0.000 df:192	1319 Disa r:-0.284 p:0.000 df:192
lower forearm w / clavicle to groin h		145	0.068	0.078	0.096	0.109	0.122	0.147	0.263	235 Carolina r:-0.226 p:0.010 df:127	10248 Fichtelgebirge r:0.393 p:0.000 df:127	199 Byblis r:0.354 p:0.000 df:127
lower forearm w / clavicle to neck h		136	0.282	0.451	0.621	0.753	0.902	1.197	2.255	7078 Unojonsson r:-0.234 p:0.010 df:119	34000 Martinmatl r:0.391 p:0.000 df:119	279 Thule r:0.330 p:0.000 df:119
lower forearm w / elbow to wrist h		248	0.160	0.185	0.218	0.239	0.277	0.338	0.458	1499 Pori r:-0.172 p:0.010 df:224	9767 Midsomer Norton r:0.311 p:0.000 df:224	175 Andromache r:0.239 p:0.000 df:224

lower forearm w / foot base h	89	0.129	0.189	0.251	0.285	0.339	0.449	0.526	23133 Rishinbehl r:-0.287 p:0.010 df:78	11259 Yingtungchen r:0.413 p:0.000 df:78	369 Aeria r:-0.410 p:0.000 df:78
lower forearm w / heel width	56	0.367	0.462	0.719	0.827	1.012	1.627	1.771	3582 Cyrano r:-0.348 p:0.009 df:53	23879 Demura r:0.538 p:0.000 df:53	785 Zwetana r:0.470 p:0.000 df:53
lower forearm w / long finger length	102	0.192	0.249	0.281	0.308	0.356	0.444	0.668	161545 Ferrando r:-0.261 p:0.010 df:95	255703 Stetson r:0.497 p:0.000 df:95	3359 Purcari r:0.352 p:0.000 df:95
lower forearm w / lower leg h	122	0.068	0.106	0.129	0.147	0.171	0.222	0.281	2059 Baboquivari r:-0.245 p:0.009 df:109	25858 Donherbert r:0.347 p:0.000 df:109	2506 Pirogov r:-0.360 p:0.000 df:109
lower forearm w / neck width	178	0.349	0.395	0.482	0.534	0.618	0.758	1.029	6999 Meitner r:-0.201 p:0.010 df:161	750 Oskar r:0.292 p:0.000 df:161	750 Oskar r:0.292 p:0.000 df:161
lower forearm w / nipple dia	204	1.048	2.483	3.638	4.470	5.226	6.892	8.395	5247 Krylov r:-0.187 p:0.010 df:188	10248 Fichtelgebirge r:0.297 p:0.000 df:188	4172 Rochefort r:0.290 p:0.000 df:188
lower forearm w / nipple to bottom	193	0.213	0.554	0.772	0.978	1.249	1.693	4.202	14190 Soldan r:-0.192 p:0.010 df:177	90825 Lizhensheng r:0.334 p:0.000 df:177	294 Felicia r:0.286 p:0.000 df:177
lower forearm w / nipple to top	192	0.161	0.248	0.356	0.458	0.583	0.801	0.993	58535 Pattillo r:-0.193 p:0.010 df:175	14519 Ural r:0.303 p:0.000 df:175	4642 Murchie r:0.287 p:0.000 df:175
lower forearm w / pelvic hips	191	0.057	0.137	0.166	0.189	0.213	0.261	0.353	25919 Comuniello r:-0.195 p:0.010 df:171	1845 Helewalda r:0.350 p:0.000 df:171	1295 Deflotte r:-0.271 p:0.000 df:171
lower forearm w / pinky toe length	39	0.735	0.843	1.421	1.865	2.417	3.901	5.722	2378 Pannekoek r:-0.408 p:0.010 df:37	5954 Epikouros r:0.596 p:0.000 df:37	1351 Uzbekistania r:-0.600 p:0.000 df:37
lower forearm w / second toe length	43	0.207	0.491	0.910	1.382	1.656	2.595	3.039	3454 Lieske r:-0.391 p:0.009 df:41	27123 Matthewlam r:0.564 p:0.000 df:41	830 Petropolitana r:-0.509 p:0.000 df:41
lower forearm w / shoulder width	249	0.053	0.133	0.157	0.175	0.201	0.245	0.331	442 Eichsfeldia r:-0.170 p:0.010 df:227	291849 Orchestralondon r:0.246 p:0.000 df:227	1919 Clemence r:0.230 p:0.000 df:227
lower forearm w / subchest width	109	0.116	0.144	0.176	0.200	0.230	0.291	0.426	702 Alauda r:-0.258 p:0.010 df:97	27374 Yim r:0.377 p:0.000 df:97	2645 Daphne Plane r:-0.376 p:0.000 df:97
lower forearm w / subneck dorsal	111	0.243	0.279	0.348	0.397	0.465	0.619	0.853	168767 Kochte r:-0.256 p:0.010 df:98	2807 Karl Marx r:0.384 p:0.000 df:98	530 Turandot r:0.369 p:0.000 df:98
lower forearm w / subpelvic rear width	134	0.052	0.109	0.140	0.161	0.186	0.232	0.351	2417 McVittie r:-0.234 p:0.010 df:119	19993 Gunterseeber r:0.369 p:0.000 df:119	1845 Helewalda r:0.332 p:0.000 df:119
lower forearm w / suprailiac	199	0.060	0.150	0.182	0.209	0.235	0.281	0.516	4425 Bilk r:-0.191 p:0.010 df:179	10248 Fichtelgebirge r:0.304 p:0.000 df:179	199 Byblis r:0.269 p:0.000 df:179
lower forearm w / underbust	173	0.058	0.147	0.194	0.223	0.248	0.310	0.573	157533 Stellamarie r:-0.205 p:0.010 df:155	3359 Purcari r:0.293 p:0.000 df:155	3359 Purcari r:0.293 p:0.000 df:155
lower forearm w / waist	218	0.061	0.159	0.204	0.232	0.258	0.302	0.572	717 Wisibada r:-0.182 p:0.010 df:198	2674 Pandarus r:0.283 p:0.000 df:198	175 Andromache r:0.274 p:0.000 df:198
lower leg h / ball width	49	1.246	1.611	3.185	3.847	4.453	5.683	9.486	561 Ingwelde r:-0.369 p:0.010 df:46	246821 Satyarthi r:0.523 p:0.000 df:46	903 Nealley r:-0.527 p:0.000 df:46
lower leg h / big toe length	43	2.667	3.098	5.949	8.505	9.512	12.239	18.439	16262 Rikurtz r:-0.403 p:0.010 df:38	279377 Lechmankiewicz r:0.646 p:0.000 df:38	400 Ducrosa r:0.578 p:0.000 df:38
lower leg h / big toe width	37	3.456	3.734	9.167	11.064	14.458	20.871	22.472	6978 Hironaka r:-0.425 p:0.010 df:34	31671 Masatoshi r:0.670 p:0.000 df:34	489 Comacina r:-0.552 p:0.000 df:34
lower leg h / foot base h	79	0.768	1.154	1.748	2.015	2.332	2.772	3.214	4976 Choukyongchol r:-0.306 p:0.010 df:68	20291 Raumurthy r:0.443 p:0.000 df:68	2075 Martinez r:-0.432 p:0.000 df:68
lower leg h / heel width	45	2.005	2.946	4.975	5.322	6.254	11.386	12.857	4483 Petofi r:-0.385 p:0.010 df:42	31671 Masatoshi r:0.624 p:0.000 df:42	1896 Beer r:-0.537 p:0.000 df:42
lower leg h / pinky toe length	30	5.000	5.001	10.508	12.754	16.181	24.705	28.139	32853 Dobereiner r:-0.463 p:0.010 df:28	29762 Panasiewicz r:0.680 p:0.000 df:28	772 Tanete r:0.608 p:0.000 df:28
lower leg h / second toe length	31	3.175	3.351	7.491	9.228	11.663	15.907	18.326	66671 Sfasu r:-0.456 p:0.010 df:29	3961 Arthurcox r:0.746 p:0.000 df:29	1424 Sundmania r:0.602 p:0.000 df:29
lower leg h / subchest width	54	0.641	0.862	1.172	1.381	1.602	1.864	2.352	5086 Demin r:-0.369 p:0.010 df:46	10056 Johnschroer r:0.529 p:0.000 df:46	684 Hildburg r:0.525 p:0.000 df:46
lower thigh width / ab perimeter	146	0.012	0.027	0.060	0.076	0.094	0.158	0.263	48844 Belloves r:-0.223 p:0.010 df:131	33610 Payra r:0.343 p:0.000 df:131	280 Philia r:0.300 p:0.000 df:131
lower thigh width / ab tone	144	0.090	0.147	0.218	0.341	0.602	2.740	6.996	11240 Piso r:-0.224 p:0.010 df:130	1200 Imperatrix r:0.350 p:0.000 df:130	1200 Imperatrix r:0.350 p:0.000 df:130
lower thigh width / ab width	114	0.507	0.631	0.782	0.933	1.154	1.497	2.237	9564 Jeffwynn r:-0.253 p:0.010 df:101	19488 Abramcoley r:0.421 p:0.000 df:101	2504 Gaviola r:0.357 p:0.000 df:101
lower thigh width / ankle to heel floor h	82	1.228	1.357	1.660	1.869	2.196	3.154	3.904	3140 Stellafane r:-0.300 p:0.010 df:71	22874 Haydeephelps r:0.479 p:0.000 df:71	255 Oppavia r:0.428 p:0.000 df:71
lower thigh width / ankle width	133	0.871	1.330	1.630	1.824	2.033	2.421	3.155	11135 Ryokami r:-0.234 p:0.010 df:119	945 Barcelona r:0.352 p:0.000 df:119	66 Maja r:-0.322 p:0.000 df:119
lower thigh width / areola dia	171	0.584	1.374	2.039	2.882	3.902	5.678	7.739	4915 Solzhenitsyn r:-0.205 p:0.010 df:155	4217 Engelhardt r:0.326 p:0.000 df:155	4217 Engelhardt r:0.326 p:0.000 df:155
lower thigh width / back perimeter	60	0.013	0.030	0.039	0.052	0.067	0.116	0.183	5044 Shestaka r:-0.339 p:0.010 df:55	210245 Castets r:0.549 p:0.000 df:55	776 Berberica r:-0.472 p:0.000 df:55
lower thigh width / back tone	61	0.048	0.094	0.132	0.167	0.234	0.577	0.909	3015 Candy r:-0.334 p:0.010 df:57	218692 Leesnyder r:0.537 p:0.000 df:57	524 Fidelio r:0.441 p:0.000 df:57
lower thigh width / ball width	58	0.346	0.586	1.022	1.291	1.570	2.168	3.054	32 Pomona r:-0.339 p:0.010 df:55	24015 Pascalepinner r:0.501 p:0.000 df:55	308 Polyxo r:-0.475 p:0.000 df:55
lower thigh width / bicep width	207	0.698	1.003	1.242	1.423	1.703	2.057	3.359	1641 Tana r:-0.188 p:0.010 df:186	126 Velleda r:0.268 p:0.000 df:186	126 Velleda r:0.268 p:0.000 df:186

Measurement	N								A	B	C
lower thigh width / big toe length	53	0.376	1.120	1.900	2.828	3.261	5.233	5.523	3728 IRAS r:-0.362 p:0.010 df:48	129186 Joshgrindlay r:0.606 p:0.000 df:48	185 Eunike r:-0.530 p:0.000 df:48
lower thigh width / big toe width	45	0.609	1.140	2.746	3.712	4.774	7.206	9.035	129138 Williamfrost r:-0.385 p:0.010 df:42	52422 LPL r:0.623 p:0.000 df:42	2331 Parvulesco r:0.533 p:0.000 df:42
lower thigh width / bra shoulder to underb	149	0.129	0.319	0.437	0.515	0.604	0.880	1.154	13499 Steinberg r:-0.221 p:0.010 df:133	6524 Baalke r:0.357 p:0.000 df:133	448 Natalie r:0.296 p:0.000 df:133
lower thigh width / breast depth	131	0.534	1.350	2.233	2.959	3.872	6.024	11.521	19614 Montelongo r:-0.232 p:0.010 df:121	6524 Baalke r:0.348 p:0.000 df:121	3503 Brandt r:0.327 p:0.000 df:121
lower thigh width / breasts apart	178	1.026	1.374	2.194	3.039	4.243	9.864	16.859	2303 Retsina r:-0.202 p:0.010 df:160	23197 Danielcook r:0.384 p:0.000 df:160	1362 Griqua r:0.355 p:0.000 df:160
lower thigh width / bust dia	195	0.281	0.621	0.808	0.975	1.165	1.571	2.643	3021 Lucubratio r:-0.192 p:0.010 df:177	4536 Drewpinsky r:0.313 p:0.000 df:177	193 Ambrosia r:0.266 p:0.000 df:177
lower thigh width / butt square	54	0.098	0.127	0.166	0.194	0.225	0.323	0.402	5379 Abehiroshi r:-0.361 p:0.010 df:48	129078 Animoo r:0.556 p:0.000 df:48	2438 Oleshko r:-0.491 p:0.000 df:48
lower thigh width / calf width	158	0.670	0.854	1.012	1.090	1.190	1.344	1.987	3013 Dobrovoleva r:-0.214 p:0.010 df:143	10985 Feast r:0.391 p:0.000 df:143	1721 Wells r:-0.306 p:0.000 df:143
lower thigh width / chest width	167	0.146	0.307	0.395	0.458	0.531	0.674	1.064	14972 Olihainaut r:-0.209 p:0.010 df:150	28695 Zwanzig r:0.351 p:0.000 df:150	1906 Naef r:0.295 p:0.000 df:150
lower thigh width / clavicle to groin h	121	0.158	0.184	0.225	0.257	0.298	0.471	0.676	999 Zachia r:-0.247 p:0.010 df:106	5951 Alicemonet r:0.443 p:0.000 df:106	395 Delia r:0.341 p:0.000 df:106
lower thigh width / clavicle to neck h	109	0.786	1.037	1.461	1.737	2.179	3.058	4.148	303 Josephina r:-0.261 p:0.010 df:95	264020 Stuttgart r:0.415 p:0.000 df:95	9898 Yoshiro r:0.384 p:0.000 df:95
lower thigh width / elbow to wrist h	189	0.297	0.400	0.511	0.567	0.686	0.893	1.288	3428 Roberts r:-0.196 p:0.010 df:170	15092 Beegees r:0.318 p:0.000 df:170	1103 Sequoia r:0.266 p:0.000 df:170
ower thigh width / foot base h	92	0.193	0.449	0.631	0.680	0.785	1.035	1.435	30828 Bethe r:-0.281 p:0.010 df:81	632 Pyrrha r:0.510 p:0.000 df:81	170 Maria r:-0.392 p:0.000 df:81
lower thigh width / heel width	57	0.663	1.091	1.610	1.911	2.292	2.781	4.062	3226 Plinius r:-0.342 p:0.010 df:54	8632 Egleston r:0.494 p:0.000 df:54	899 Jokaste r:0.456 p:0.000 df:54
lower thigh width / long finger length	83	0.449	0.500	0.621	0.729	0.811	1.050	1.308	1839 Ragazza r:-0.287 p:0.010 df:78	22567 Zenisek r:0.478 p:0.000 df:78	482 Petrina r:0.385 p:0.000 df:78
lower thigh width / lower forearm w	207	0.672	1.650	2.049	2.350	2.724	3.567	4.978	10921 Romanozen r:-0.188 p:0.010 df:186	15905 Berthier r:0.289 p:0.000 df:186	2812 Scaltriti r:0.264 p:0.000 df:186
lower thigh width / lower leg h	130	0.200	0.257	0.315	0.344	0.392	0.497	0.630	1306 Scythia r:-0.237 p:0.010 df:116	19466 Darcydiegel r:0.308 p:0.001 df:116	2033 Basilea r:0.293 p:0.001 df:116
lower thigh width / neck width	136	0.655	0.906	1.087	1.283	1.486	1.997	3.078	3496 Arieso r:-0.231 p:0.010 df:122	36782 Okauchitakashige r:0.372 p:0.000 df:122	6721 Minamiawaji r:0.351 p:0.000 df:122
lower thigh width / nipple dia	165	2.301	5.324	8.486	10.507	13.120	18.798	25.011	2626 Belnika r:-0.209 p:0.010 df:150	4410 Kamuimintara r:0.340 p:0.000 df:150	2856 Roser r:-0.289 p:0.000 df:150
lower thigh width / nipple to bottom	150	0.882	1.229	1.818	2.287	2.744	4.120	7.985	239071 Penghu r:-0.221 p:0.009 df:136	6630 Skepticus r:0.315 p:0.000 df:136	2484 Parenago r:0.307 p:0.000 df:136
lower thigh width / nipple to top	150	0.192	0.561	0.895	1.166	1.431	1.978	2.848	5367 Sollenberger r:-0.220 p:0.010 df:135	22901 Ivanbella r:0.348 p:0.000 df:135	345 Tercidina r:-0.336 p:0.000 df:135
lower thigh width / pelvic hips	149	0.166	0.301	0.396	0.445	0.510	0.682	1.183	6375 Fredharris r:-0.222 p:0.010 df:132	27392 Valerieding r:0.315 p:0.000 df:132	6870 Pauldavies r:0.310 p:0.000 df:132
lower thigh width / pinky toe length	40	1.258	2.141	3.559	4.198	6.100	7.869	10.524	52604 Thomayer r:-0.404 p:0.010 df:38	31846 Elainegillum r:0.593 p:0.000 df:38	1351 Uzbekistania r:-0.533 p:0.000 df:38
lower thigh width / second toe length	43	0.429	0.953	2.330	3.157	3.743	5.569	5.926	3251 Eratosthenes r:-0.389 p:0.010 df:41	11369 Brazelton r:0.603 p:0.000 df:41	185 Eunike r:-0.518 p:0.000 df:41
lower thigh width / shoulder to elbow h	204	0.194	0.361	0.434	0.496	0.573	0.760	1.201	936 Kunigunde r:-0.189 p:0.010 df:185	20812 Shannonbabb r:0.308 p:0.000 df:185	3068 Khanina r:0.278 p:0.000 df:185
lower thigh width / shoulder width	199	0.156	0.282	0.356	0.413	0.477	0.603	0.997	10371 Gigli r:-0.190 p:0.010 df:181	27284 Billdunbar r:0.290 p:0.000 df:181	2162 Anhui r:-0.288 p:0.000 df:181
lower thigh width / subchest width	91	0.149	0.331	0.432	0.498	0.561	0.754	0.906	4187 Shulnazaria r:-0.283 p:0.010 df:80	7734 Kaltenegger r:0.418 p:0.000 df:80	2502 Nummela r:-0.407 p:0.000 df:80
lower thigh width / subneck dorsal	81	0.548	0.584	0.766	0.942	1.098	1.569	2.793	10143 Kamogawa r:-0.302 p:0.010 df:70	3412 Kafka r:0.483 p:0.000 df:70	819 Barnardiana r:0.415 p:0.000 df:70
lower thigh width / subpelvic rear width	110	0.116	0.229	0.337	0.381	0.422	0.547	0.887	3657 Ermolova r:-0.258 p:0.010 df:97	12401 Tucholsky r:0.380 p:0.000 df:97	5638 Deikoon r:-0.382 p:0.000 df:97
ower thigh width / suprailiac	161	0.175	0.352	0.437	0.485	0.563	0.717	1.105	9114 Hatakeyama r:-0.212 p:0.010 df:145	28467 Maurentejamie r:0.325 p:0.000 df:145	4536 Drewpinsky r:0.292 p:0.000 df:145
lower thigh width / thigh h	217	0.230	0.244	0.288	0.319	0.355	0.457	0.573	11127 Hagi r:-0.183 p:0.010 df:196	16128 Kirfrieda r:0.317 p:0.000 df:196	2381 Landi r:-0.263 p:0.000 df:196
lower thigh width / underbust	138	0.168	0.368	0.457	0.529	0.604	0.759	1.178	2427 Kobzar r:-0.229 p:0.010 df:124	19488 Abramcoley r:0.388 p:0.000 df:124	3412 Kafka r:0.327 p:0.000 df:124
lower thigh width / upper forearm w	210	0.500	1.034	1.382	1.602	1.819	2.270	3.720	5367 Sollenberger r:-0.186 p:0.010 df:190	7838 Feliceierman r:0.290 p:0.000 df:190	103 Hera r:-0.259 p:0.000 df:190
lower thigh width / waist	176	0.149	0.372	0.483	0.531	0.614	0.785	1.187	18100 Lebreton r:-0.202 p:0.010 df:160	19488 Abramcoley r:0.296 p:0.000 df:160	209 Dido r:0.276 p:0.000 df:160
neck width / ab width	120	0.299	0.471	0.619	0.714	0.884	1.147	1.420	7742 Altamira r:-0.247 p:0.010 df:106	7237 Vickyhamilton r:0.378 p:0.000 df:106	279 Thule r:-0.331 p:0.000 df:106
neck width / ankle to heel floor h	69	0.524	1.025	1.274	1.418	1.792	2.487	4.716	1268 Libya r:-0.323 p:0.010 df:61	3895 Earhart r:0.546 p:0.000 df:61	3895 Earhart r:0.546 p:0.000 df:61

neck width / ankle width	96	0.492	0.823	1.173	1.432	1.670	2.053	2.611	5447 Lallement r:-0.272 p:0.010 df:87	7213 Conae r:0.404 p:0.000 df:87	1926 Demiddelaer r:-0.392 p:0.000 df:87
neck width / back perimeter	48	0.014	0.017	0.032	0.039	0.054	0.084	0.098	12833 Kamenny Ujezd r:-0.372 p:0.010 df:45	31389 Alexkaplan r:0.572 p:0.000 df:45	885 Ulrike r:0.494 p:0.000 df:45
neck width / back tone	49	0.034	0.072	0.103	0.130	0.167	0.243	0.279	1807 Slovakia r:-0.369 p:0.010 df:46	162035 Jirotakahashi r:0.555 p:0.000 df:46	5144 Achates r:-0.541 p:0.000 df:46
neck width / ball width	41	0.379	0.500	0.884	1.062	1.233	1.938	2.233	10178 Iriki r:-0.404 p:0.010 df:38	29672 Salvo r:0.602 p:0.000 df:38	1232 Cortusa r:0.526 p:0.000 df:38
neck width / big toe length	39	0.742	0.760	1.617	2.140	2.548	3.353	3.610	24484 Chester r:-0.419 p:0.010 df:35	6000 United Nations r:0.617 p:0.000 df:35	1151 Ithaka r:-0.554 p:0.000 df:35
neck width / big toe width	33	1.199	1.302	2.435	3.312	3.808	5.320	5.321	264061 Vitebsk r:-0.449 p:0.010 df:30	29672 Salvo r:0.660 p:0.000 df:30	942 Romilda r:-0.651 p:0.000 df:30
neck width / calf width	102	0.351	0.560	0.730	0.844	0.956	1.254	1.676	5226 Pollack r:-0.264 p:0.010 df:93	36446 Cinodapistoia r:0.400 p:0.000 df:93	2104 Toronto r:0.375 p:0.000 df:93
neck width / clavicle to neck h	128	0.754	0.937	1.174	1.351	1.581	2.070	2.533	3976 Lise r:-0.239 p:0.010 df:113	11229 Brookebowers r:0.386 p:0.000 df:113	683 Lanzia r:0.331 p:0.000 df:113
neck width / foot base h	72	0.215	0.340	0.439	0.530	0.631	0.848	1.075	4305 Clapton r:-0.318 p:0.010 df:63	3821 Sonet r:0.447 p:0.000 df:63	369 Aeria r:-0.422 p:0.000 df:63
neck width / heel width	41	0.626	0.729	1.215	1.463	1.879	2.922	3.140	8717 Richviktorov r:-0.405 p:0.010 df:38	6154 Stevesynnott r:0.568 p:0.000 df:38	6154 Stevesynnott r:0.568 p:0.000 df:38
neck width / lower leg h	95	0.123	0.179	0.245	0.275	0.314	0.440	0.501	30698 Hippokoon r:-0.273 p:0.010 df:86	14597 Waynerichie r:0.400 p:0.000 df:86	3895 Earhart r:0.391 p:0.000 df:86
neck width / pinky toe length	30	1.204	1.382	2.676	3.556	4.621	7.329	8.434	8766 Niger r:-0.463 p:0.010 df:28	7778 Markrobinson r:0.680 p:0.000 df:28	4502 Elizabethann r:0.612 p:0.000 df:28
neck width / subchest width	90	0.194	0.269	0.329	0.362	0.400	0.461	0.479	32381 Bellomo r:-0.283 p:0.010 df:80	39427 Charlottebronte r:0.406 p:0.000 df:80	3945 Gerasimenko r:-0.378 p:0.000 df:80
neck width / subneck dorsal	113	0.591	0.617	0.685	0.767	0.834	0.948	1.127	255 Oppavia r:-0.254 p:0.010 df:100	4844 Matsuyama r:0.515 p:0.000 df:100	4844 Matsuyama r:0.515 p:0.000 df:100
neck width< >shoulder width / neck width< >underbust	99	0.118	0.154	0.218	0.266	0.317	0.367	0.407	6675 Sisley r:-0.276 p:0.009 df:86	25399 Vonnegut r:0.370 p:0.000 df:86	308 Polyxo r:-0.381 p:0.000 df:86
neck width< >shoulder width / shoulder width< >subneck dorsal	105	0.317	1.137	1.348	1.508	1.705	2.088	2.404	8040 Utsumikazuhiko r:-0.265 p:0.010 df:92	20285 Lubin r:0.429 p:0.000 df:92	203 Pompeja r:-0.416 p:0.000 df:92
neck width< >subneck dorsal / neck width< >shoulder width	101	0.104	0.188	0.288	0.345	0.428	0.553	0.641	6881 Shifutsu r:-0.269 p:0.010 df:89	15021 Alexkardon r:0.378 p:0.000 df:89	124 Alkeste r:-0.361 p:0.000 df:89
neck width< >subneck dorsal / neck width< >underbust	65	0.039	0.047	0.076	0.102	0.122	0.180	0.191	8595 Dougallii r:-0.337 p:0.010 df:56	15372 Agrigento r:0.471 p:0.000 df:56	3700 Geowilliams r:0.469 p:0.000 df:56
neck width< >subneck dorsal / shoulder width< >subneck dorsal	100	0.125	0.230	0.414	0.533	0.725	0.943	1.415	34892 Evapalisa r:-0.270 p:0.010 df:88	8493 Yachibozu r:0.397 p:0.000 df:88	486 Cremona r:-0.384 p:0.000 df:88
nipple dia / ab width	129	0.032	0.047	0.067	0.088	0.102	0.134	0.176	19853 Ichinomiya r:-0.236 p:0.010 df:116	1449 Virtanen r:0.356 p:0.000 df:116	1449 Virtanen r:0.356 p:0.000 df:116
nipple dia / ankle to heel floor h	74	0.093	0.105	0.139	0.170	0.224	0.481	0.989	7999 Nesvorny r:-0.313 p:0.010 df:65	6093 Makoto r:0.489 p:0.000 df:65	5196 Bustelli r:0.418 p:0.000 df:65
nipple dia / ankle width	104	0.059	0.078	0.133	0.165	0.198	0.341	0.416	4518 Raikin r:-0.262 p:0.010 df:94	95980 Haroldhill r:0.433 p:0.000 df:94	3051 Nantong r:0.361 p:0.000 df:94
nipple dia / back perimeter	48	0.001	0.002	0.003	0.004	0.006	0.012	0.015	11820 Mikiyasato r:-0.372 p:0.010 df:45	5771 Somerville r:0.535 p:0.000 df:45	1182 Ilona r:0.506 p:0.000 df:45
nipple dia / back tone	48	0.004	0.007	0.010	0.015	0.020	0.047	0.070	6314 Reigber r:-0.374 p:0.010 df:45	82638 Bottariclaudio r:0.512 p:0.000 df:45	3371 Giacconi r:0.510 p:0.000 df:45
nipple dia / ball width	45	0.046	0.049	0.092	0.115	0.158	0.445	0.546	5529 Perry r:-0.380 p:0.010 df:43	4345 Rachmaninoff r:0.614 p:0.000 df:43	2242 Balaton r:-0.531 p:0.000 df:43
nipple dia / big toe length	43	0.089	0.102	0.188	0.242	0.316	0.698	1.380	2490 Bussolini r:-0.399 p:0.010 df:39	109330 Clemente r:0.691 p:0.000 df:39	342 Endymion r:0.550 p:0.000 df:39
nipple dia / big toe width	37	0.115	0.149	0.265	0.368	0.505	1.319	1.780	27338 Malaraghavan r:-0.420 p:0.010 df:35	19993 Gunterseeber r:0.691 p:0.000 df:35	2086 Newell r:0.551 p:0.000 df:35
nipple dia / bra shoulder to underb	157	0.024	0.031	0.041	0.049	0.058	0.081	0.109	2099 Opik r:-0.212 p:0.010 df:145	8286 Kouji r:0.342 p:0.000 df:145	19 Fortuna r:0.284 p:0.000 df:145
nipple dia / breasts apart	217	0.076	0.123	0.203	0.303	0.481	1.266	2.473	62071 Voegtli r:-0.181 p:0.010 df:199	8571 Taniguchi r:0.298 p:0.000 df:199	585 Bilkis r:-0.257 p:0.000 df:199
nipple dia / bust dia	237	0.040	0.063	0.081	0.096	0.115	0.146	0.171	2434 Bateson r:-0.173 p:0.010 df:219	5045 Hoyin r:0.254 p:0.000 df:219	3011 Chongqing r:0.248 p:0.000 df:219
nipple dia / butt square	44	0.011	0.011	0.014	0.019	0.024	0.058	0.065	103770 Wilfriedlang r:-0.393 p:0.010 df:40	946 Poesia r:0.715 p:0.000 df:40	19 Fortuna r:0.622 p:0.000 df:40
nipple dia / calf width	119	0.035	0.054	0.081	0.100	0.125	0.219	0.489	34236 Firester r:-0.245 p:0.010 df:108	5196 Bustelli r:0.390 p:0.000 df:108	5196 Bustelli r:0.390 p:0.000 df:108
nipple dia / clavicle to neck h	118	0.064	0.096	0.123	0.174	0.211	0.314	0.552	9117 Aude r:-0.247 p:0.010 df:106	135979 Allam r:0.385 p:0.000 df:106	869 Mellena r:0.341 p:0.000 df:106
nipple dia / foot base h	74	0.025	0.039	0.048	0.062	0.079	0.123	0.176	8773 Torquilla r:-0.313 p:0.010 df:65	363115 Chuckwood r:0.461 p:0.000 df:65	2849 Shklovskij r:0.419 p:0.000 df:65
nipple dia / heel width	46	0.080	0.085	0.124	0.176	0.226	0.361	0.712	28322 Kaeberich r:-0.383 p:0.009 df:43	18561 Fengningding r:0.613 p:0.000 df:43	844 Leontina r:0.522 p:0.000 df:43

nipple dia / long finger length	84	0.033	0.040	0.055	0.067	0.082	0.135	0.233	144752 Plunge r:-0.286 p:0.010 df:78	127803 Johnvaneepoel r:0.456 p:0.000 df:78	24 Themis r:0.404 p:0.000 df:78
nipple dia / lower leg h	102	0.017	0.019	0.025	0.030	0.043	0.067	0.095	38442 Szilard r:-0.265 p:0.010 df:92	95980 Haroldhill r:0.405 p:0.000 df:92	765 Mattiaca r:0.373 p:0.000 df:92
nipple dia / neck width	149	0.055	0.078	0.098	0.119	0.150	0.207	0.251	229836 Wladimarinello r:-0.219 p:0.010 df:136	90672 Metrorheinneckar r:0.305 p:0.000 df:136	1469 Linzia r:-0.359 p:0.000 df:136
nipple dia / nipple to bottom	211	0.075	0.118	0.173	0.221	0.291	0.499	1.118	4210 Isobelthompson r:-0.182 p:0.010 df:197	5331 Erimomisaki r:0.327 p:0.000 df:197	827 Wolfiana r:0.249 p:0.000 df:197
nipple dia / nipple to top	209	0.041	0.062	0.088	0.105	0.129	0.166	0.260	75564 Audubon r:-0.184 p:0.010 df:193	183288 Eyer r:0.289 p:0.000 df:193	3126 Davydov r:0.251 p:0.000 df:193
nipple dia / pelvic hips	160	0.020	0.029	0.035	0.042	0.050	0.066	0.083	170006 Stoughton r:-0.212 p:0.010 df:145	6294 Czerny r:0.346 p:0.000 df:145	5924 Teruo r:-0.286 p:0.000 df:145
nipple dia / pinky toe length	30	0.153	0.160	0.299	0.395	0.582	0.815	0.938	207899 Grinmalia r:-0.466 p:0.010 df:28	2595 Gudiachvili r:0.607 p:0.000 df:28	2595 Gudiachvili r:0.607 p:0.000 df:28
nipple dia / second toe length	33	0.105	0.111	0.212	0.259	0.364	0.680	0.739	2264 Sabrina r:-0.444 p:0.010 df:31	13227 Poor r:0.580 p:0.000 df:31	13227 Poor r:0.580 p:0.000 df:31
nipple dia / shoulder width	205	0.017	0.026	0.033	0.039	0.049	0.063	0.103	432361 Rakovski r:-0.186 p:0.010 df:189	34300 Brendafrost r:0.273 p:0.000 df:189	1063 Aquilegia r:-0.267 p:0.000 df:189
nipple dia / subchest width	107	0.013	0.029	0.037	0.045	0.055	0.068	0.078	4167 Riemann r:-0.261 p:0.010 df:95	19488 Abramcoley r:0.384 p:0.000 df:95	3235 Melchior r:0.381 p:0.000 df:95
nipple dia / subneck dorsal	92	0.039	0.052	0.076	0.092	0.115	0.149	0.179	21664 Konradzuse r:-0.278 p:0.010 df:83	16952 Peteschultz r:0.421 p:0.000 df:83	3900 Knezevic r:0.383 p:0.000 df:83
nipple dia / subpelvic rear width	109	0.010	0.024	0.029	0.036	0.045	0.061	0.123	5543 Sharaf r:-0.257 p:0.010 df:98	11913 Svarna r:0.437 p:0.000 df:98	1314 Paula r:0.345 p:0.000 df:98
nipple to bottom / ab width	124	0.036	0.174	0.325	0.411	0.512	0.804	1.134	1717 Arlon r:-0.243 p:0.010 df:110	5637 Gyas r:0.363 p:0.000 df:110	1336 Zeelandia r:0.339 p:0.000 df:110
nipple to bottom / ankle to heel floor h	68	0.336	0.461	0.680	0.821	1.112	1.651	3.194	156990 Claerbout r:-0.325 p:0.010 df:60	7778 Markrobinson r:0.528 p:0.000 df:60	765 Mattiaca r:0.456 p:0.000 df:60
nipple to bottom / ankle width	96	0.121	0.303	0.633	0.794	1.026	1.372	2.118	578 Happelia r:-0.274 p:0.010 df:86	7778 Markrobinson r:0.416 p:0.000 df:86	2101 Adonis r:0.393 p:0.000 df:86
nipple to bottom / back perimeter	45	0.005	0.009	0.016	0.023	0.034	0.060	0.066	4875 Ingalls r:-0.384 p:0.010 df:42	25073 Lautakshing r:0.577 p:0.000 df:42	1757 Porvoo r:0.521 p:0.000 df:42
nipple to bottom / back tone	45	0.020	0.033	0.053	0.075	0.111	0.241	0.327	1785 Wurm r:-0.385 p:0.010 df:42	82638 Bottariclaudio r:0.559 p:0.000 df:42	8013 Gordonmoore r:-0.543 p:0.000 df:42
nipple to bottom / ball width	42	0.135	0.186	0.364	0.662	0.836	1.302	2.683	14010 Jomonaomori r:-0.399 p:0.010 df:39	5488 Kiyosato r:0.628 p:0.000 df:39	51 Nemausa r:0.536 p:0.000 df:39
nipple to bottom / big toe length	39	0.237	0.354	0.838	1.198	1.497	2.352	6.781	23625 Gelfond r:-0.414 p:0.010 df:36	2907 Nekrasov r:0.651 p:0.000 df:36	394 Arduina r:0.568 p:0.000 df:36
nipple to bottom / big toe width	35	0.410	0.449	1.051	2.024	2.409	4.898	8.746	10663 Schwarzwald r:-0.436 p:0.010 df:32	192450 Xinjiangdaxue r:0.721 p:0.000 df:32	862 Franzia r:0.592 p:0.000 df:32
nipple to bottom / bra shoulder to underb	160	0.028	0.110	0.181	0.236	0.288	0.401	0.461	10611 Yanjici r:-0.211 p:0.010 df:147	97472 Hobby r:0.292 p:0.000 df:147	3558 Shishkin r:-0.292 p:0.000 df:147
nipple to bottom / breasts apart	203	0.087	0.587	0.972	1.293	2.147	4.699	12.539	4806 Miho r:-0.189 p:0.009 df:187	4339 Almamater r:0.268 p:0.000 df:187	1450 Raimonda r:0.261 p:0.000 df:187
nipple to bottom / bust dia	217	0.047	0.207	0.336	0.447	0.528	0.686	0.834	4665 Muinonen r:-0.181 p:0.010 df:200	13240 Thouvay r:0.311 p:0.000 df:200	2051 Chang r:0.265 p:0.000 df:200
nipple to bottom / butt square	43	0.040	0.044	0.064	0.089	0.111	0.150	0.230	24378 Katelyngibbs r:-0.398 p:0.010 df:39	11370 Nabrown r:0.688 p:0.000 df:39	1847 Stobbe r:0.528 p:0.000 df:39
nipple to bottom / calf width	108	0.079	0.219	0.364	0.458	0.581	0.896	1.170	1096 Reunerta r:-0.259 p:0.009 df:98	12156 Ubels r:0.375 p:0.000 df:98	765 Mattiaca r:0.359 p:0.000 df:98
nipple to bottom / clavicle to neck h	112	0.302	0.427	0.618	0.822	0.981	1.354	2.524	71 Niobe r:-0.256 p:0.009 df:100	23002 Jillhirsch r:0.374 p:0.000 df:100	2677 Joan r:-0.357 p:0.000 df:100
nipple to bottom / foot base h	69	0.102	0.141	0.247	0.334	0.400	0.639	0.924	161715 Wenchuan r:-0.325 p:0.010 df:60	23743 Toshikasuga r:0.475 p:0.000 df:60	3115 Baily r:-0.432 p:0.000 df:60
nipple to bottom / heel width	41	0.316	0.354	0.594	0.936	1.197	1.730	2.036	6981 Chirman r:-0.403 p:0.010 df:38	6518 Vernon r:0.563 p:0.000 df:38	6518 Vernon r:0.563 p:0.000 df:38
nipple to bottom / long finger length	77	0.045	0.171	0.252	0.338	0.393	0.510	0.874	8930 Kubota r:-0.300 p:0.010 df:71	20631 Stefuller r:0.460 p:0.000 df:71	841 Arabella r:0.401 p:0.000 df:71
nipple to bottom / lower leg h	95	0.035	0.075	0.123	0.158	0.194	0.273	0.380	6419 Susono r:-0.275 p:0.010 df:85	765 Mattiaca r:0.404 p:0.000 df:85	51 Nemausa r:0.378 p:0.000 df:85
nipple to bottom / neck width	145	0.100	0.334	0.445	0.571	0.678	0.952	1.265	18801 Noelleoas r:-0.223 p:0.010 df:131	9386 Hitomi r:0.346 p:0.000 df:131	2802 Weisell r:-0.309 p:0.000 df:131
nipple to bottom / nipple to top	222	0.036	0.193	0.344	0.480	0.650	0.944	1.470	3406 Omsk r:-0.180 p:0.010 df:204	5136 Baggaley r:0.290 p:0.000 df:204	1469 Linzia r:0.267 p:0.000 df:204
nipple to bottom / pelvic hips	148	0.024	0.105	0.161	0.202	0.248	0.318	0.401	34231 Isanisingh r:-0.220 p:0.010 df:134	1336 Zeelandia r:0.352 p:0.000 df:134	1336 Zeelandia r:0.352 p:0.000 df:134
nipple to bottom / second toe length	31	0.292	0.369	1.023	1.414	1.698	3.156	3.814	6937 Valadon r:-0.456 p:0.010 df:29	24353 Patrickhsu r:0.629 p:0.000 df:29	812 Adele r:-0.609 p:0.000 df:29
nipple to bottom / shoulder width	193	0.029	0.098	0.142	0.184	0.218	0.289	0.398	9477 Kefennell r:-0.193 p:0.010 df:176	2051 Chang r:0.293 p:0.000 df:176	1469 Linzia r:0.260 p:0.000 df:176
nipple to bottom / subchest width	102	0.022	0.118	0.168	0.217	0.245	0.318	0.381	12456 Genichiaraki r:-0.268 p:0.010 df:90	5352 Fujita r:0.413 p:0.000 df:90	670 Ottegebe r:-0.368 p:0.000 df:90

nipple to bottom / subneck dorsal	94	0.155	0.229	0.327	0.432	0.527	0.754	0.801	7756 Scientia r:-0.275 p:0.010 df:85	2051 Chang r:0.453 p:0.000 df:85	2051 Chang r:0.453 p:0.000 df:85
nipple to bottom / subpelvic rear width	103	0.022	0.085	0.140	0.181	0.215	0.293	0.378	17637 Blaschke r:-0.264 p:0.010 df:92	34199 Amyjin r:0.416 p:0.000 df:92	1479 Inkeri r:0.388 p:0.000 df:92
nipple to top / ab width	122	0.372	0.510	0.653	0.790	0.991	1.359	2.001	33621 Sathish r:-0.244 p:0.010 df:109	5756 Wassenbergh r:0.372 p:0.000 df:109	636 Erika r:-0.347 p:0.000 df:109
nipple to top / ankle to heel floor h	68	0.692	0.986	1.272	1.566	1.984	4.137	6.442	8753 Nycticorax r:-0.328 p:0.010 df:59	844 Leontina r:0.511 p:0.000 df:59	844 Leontina r:0.511 p:0.000 df:59
nipple to top / ankle width	95	0.306	0.787	1.250	1.464	1.910	3.715	4.917	23355 Elephenor r:-0.277 p:0.010 df:84	11451 Aarongolden r:0.412 p:0.000 df:84	2907 Nekrasov r:0.378 p:0.000 df:84
nipple to top / back perimeter	44	0.013	0.017	0.033	0.039	0.064	0.096	0.100	10281 Libourel r:-0.389 p:0.010 df:41	2361 Gogol r:0.544 p:0.000 df:41	2361 Gogol r:0.544 p:0.000 df:41
nipple to top / back tone	44	0.029	0.060	0.104	0.138	0.185	0.498	0.528	8957 Koujounotsuki r:-0.389 p:0.010 df:41	3371 Giacconi r:0.525 p:0.000 df:41	3371 Giacconi r:0.525 p:0.000 df:41
nipple to top / ball width	41	0.236	0.310	0.839	1.105	1.582	3.416	5.524	1971 Hagihara r:-0.406 p:0.009 df:38	190504 Hermanotto r:0.605 p:0.000 df:38	844 Leontina r:0.551 p:0.000 df:38
nipple to top / big toe length	37	0.461	0.549	1.726	2.096	2.909	5.100	8.991	1151 Ithaka r:-0.426 p:0.010 df:34	2907 Nekrasov r:0.704 p:0.000 df:34	2086 Newell r:0.696 p:0.000 df:34
nipple to top / big toe width	33	0.724	0.739	2.679	3.600	5.024	12.044	13.087	6317 Dreyfus r:-0.450 p:0.010 df:30	19993 Gunterseeber r:0.685 p:0.000 df:30	844 Leontina r:0.606 p:0.000 df:30
nipple to top / bra shoulder to underb	157	0.243	0.312	0.390	0.460	0.553	0.774	1.203	1021 Flammario r:-0.213 p:0.010 df:144	3666 Holman r:0.353 p:0.000 df:144	1141 Bohmia r:-0.292 p:0.000 df:144
nipple to top / breasts apart	200	0.766	1.040	1.878	2.755	4.597	14.720	37.571	1210 Morosovia r:-0.189 p:0.010 df:184	4665 Muinonen r:0.348 p:0.000 df:184	225 Henrietta r:0.267 p:0.000 df:184
nipple to top / bust dia	214	0.319	0.595	0.773	0.901	1.086	1.349	2.051	8214 Mirellalilli r:-0.183 p:0.010 df:197	25905 Clerico r:0.287 p:0.000 df:197	217 Eudora r:0.272 p:0.000 df:197
nipple to top / butt square	43	0.107	0.116	0.137	0.172	0.197	0.597	0.804	3435 Boury r:-0.398 p:0.010 df:39	10604 Susanoo r:0.696 p:0.000 df:39	401 Ottilia r:0.565 p:0.000 df:39
nipple to top / calf width	105	0.409	0.486	0.744	0.930	1.194	1.907	3.186	332706 Karlheidlas r:-0.261 p:0.010 df:95	10172 Humphreys r:0.386 p:0.000 df:95	178 Belisana r:0.348 p:0.000 df:95
nipple to top / clavicle to neck h	111	0.615	0.839	1.089	1.569	2.080	3.496	4.444	8147 Colemanhawkins r:-0.255 p:0.010 df:99	8448 Belyakina r:0.416 p:0.000 df:99	869 Mellena r:0.353 p:0.000 df:99
nipple to top / foot base h	67	0.134	0.312	0.462	0.575	0.797	1.159	1.661	1383 Limburgia r:-0.331 p:0.010 df:58	2571 Geisei r:0.459 p:0.000 df:58	469 Argentina r:-0.482 p:0.000 df:58
nipple to top / heel width	39	0.389	0.551	1.284	1.663	2.168	3.331	7.348	65001 Teodorescu r:-0.413 p:0.010 df:36	844 Leontina r:0.622 p:0.000 df:36	844 Leontina r:0.622 p:0.000 df:36
nipple to top / long finger length	77	0.301	0.357	0.488	0.576	0.758	1.111	1.449	21685 Francomallia r:-0.300 p:0.010 df:71	17764 Schatzman r:0.442 p:0.000 df:71	5803 Otzi r:-0.433 p:0.000 df:71
nipple to top / lower leg h	95	0.140	0.167	0.233	0.305	0.405	0.624	1.214	592 Bathseba r:-0.277 p:0.010 df:84	10950 Albertjansen r:0.391 p:0.000 df:84	2636 Lassell r:0.388 p:0.000 df:84
nipple to top / neck width	143	0.374	0.685	0.875	1.111	1.489	2.039	2.886	11324 Hayamizu r:-0.224 p:0.010 df:129	13775 Thebault r:0.341 p:0.000 df:129	3666 Holman r:0.325 p:0.000 df:129
nipple to top / pelvic hips	145	0.192	0.260	0.335	0.399	0.473	0.641	0.843	235 Carolina r:-0.222 p:0.010 df:132	13775 Thebault r:0.377 p:0.000 df:132	3666 Holman r:0.314 p:0.000 df:132
nipple to top / shoulder width	193	0.151	0.222	0.293	0.367	0.484	0.708	1.007	4002 Shinagawa r:-0.193 p:0.010 df:176	13775 Thebault r:0.281 p:0.000 df:176	345 Tercidina r:0.265 p:0.000 df:176
nipple to top / subchest width	103	0.127	0.275	0.355	0.434	0.522	0.704	0.770	39809 Fukuchan r:-0.266 p:0.010 df:91	21815 Fanyang r:0.390 p:0.000 df:91	21722 Rambhia r:-0.370 p:0.000 df:91
nipple to top / subneck dorsal	91	0.392	0.487	0.658	0.862	1.131	1.641	2.203	1012 Sarema r:-0.280 p:0.010 df:82	6512 de Bergh r:0.442 p:0.000 df:82	3315 Chant r:-0.383 p:0.000 df:82
nipple to top / subpelvic rear width	101	0.099	0.202	0.275	0.337	0.429	0.566	1.468	588 Achilles r:-0.266 p:0.010 df:91	11958 Galiani r:0.416 p:0.000 df:91	1383 Limburgia r:-0.381 p:0.000 df:91
pelvic hips / ab width	141	0.912	1.495	1.795	2.043	2.333	2.755	3.352	4547 Massachusetts r:-0.228 p:0.010 df:125	2299 Hanko r:0.405 p:0.000 df:125	401 Ottilia r:0.345 p:0.000 df:125
pelvic hips / ankle to heel floor h	65	1.528	2.744	3.620	3.962	4.691	6.646	6.931	8811 Waltherschmadel r:-0.337 p:0.010 df:56	9566 Rykhlova r:0.466 p:0.000 df:56	3197 Weissman r:0.460 p:0.000 df:56
pelvic hips / ankle width	93	1.091	2.277	3.399	4.110	4.848	6.400	12.114	6644 Jugaku r:-0.280 p:0.010 df:82	13569 Oshu r:0.458 p:0.000 df:82	624 Hektor r:0.386 p:0.000 df:82
pelvic hips / back perimeter	50	0.033	0.052	0.090	0.106	0.139	0.251	0.273	2272 Montezuma r:-0.372 p:0.010 df:45	29645 Kutsenok r:0.536 p:0.000 df:45	2741 Valdivia r:0.502 p:0.000 df:45
pelvic hips / back tone	52	0.096	0.222	0.293	0.353	0.460	0.662	0.813	1279 Uganda r:-0.365 p:0.010 df:47	16043 Yichenzhang r:0.530 p:0.000 df:47	5444 Gautier r:-0.506 p:0.000 df:47
pelvic hips / ball width	41	0.840	1.432	2.528	3.036	3.954	4.568	5.739	1652 Herge r:-0.399 p:0.010 df:39	17881 Radmall r:0.587 p:0.000 df:39	2173 Maresjev r:-0.526 p:0.000 df:39
pelvic hips / big toe length	40	1.643	2.301	4.537	6.134	8.037	10.362	11.114	3968 Koptelov r:-0.419 p:0.010 df:35	55749 Eulenspiegel r:0.613 p:0.000 df:35	296 Phaetusa r:0.545 p:0.000 df:35
pelvic hips / big toe width	32	2.657	3.480	6.857	8.802	11.312	16.009	16.799	3968 Koptelov r:-0.449 p:0.010 df:30	33688 Meghnabehari r:0.654 p:0.000 df:30	4314 Dervan r:-0.610 p:0.000 df:30
pelvic hips / breasts apart	174	1.897	3.141	4.892	6.696	9.324	21.970	47.599	9015 Coe r:-0.206 p:0.010 df:154	7009 Hume r:0.318 p:0.000 df:154	1329 Eliane r:0.285 p:0.000 df:154
pelvic hips / bust dia	188	0.845	1.533	1.913	2.189	2.473	3.259	3.944	25 Phocaea r:-0.197 p:0.010 df:169	8454 Micheleferrero r:0.373 p:0.000 df:169	1042 Amazone r:0.291 p:0.000 df:169

	n										
pelvic hips / calf width	103	0.913	1.461	2.138	2.350	2.672	3.870	7.783	592 Bathseba r:-0.266 p:0.010 df:91	10130 Ardre r:0.494 p:0.000 df:91	671 Carnegia r:0.354 p:0.000 df:91
pelvic hips / clavicle to neck h	119	1.969	2.669	3.209	3.920	5.009	7.111	14.497	115891 Scottmichael r:-0.251 p:0.010 df:103	8454 Micheleferrero r:0.399 p:0.000 df:103	1104 Syringa r:0.341 p:0.000 df:103
pelvic hips / foot base h	67	0.476	0.996	1.307	1.543	1.820	2.205	2.838	408 Fama r:-0.333 p:0.010 df:57	10567 Francobressan r:0.419 p:0.001 df:57	4362 Carlisle r:-0.452 p:0.000 df:57
pelvic hips / heel width	38	1.387	2.615	3.880	4.666	5.216	6.989	7.076	3143 Genecampbell r:-0.420 p:0.010 df:35	6154 Stevesynnott r:0.556 p:0.000 df:35	6154 Stevesynnott r:0.556 p:0.000 df:35
pelvic hips / long finger length	74	0.633	1.162	1.350	1.615	1.854	2.218	2.813	14980 Gustavbrom r:-0.309 p:0.010 df:67	23042 Craigpeters r:0.464 p:0.000 df:67	1695 Walbeck r:-0.418 p:0.000 df:67
pelvic hips / lower leg h	91	0.358	0.512	0.654	0.781	0.895	1.365	2.355	24105 Broughton r:-0.283 p:0.010 df:80	10358 Kirchhoff r:0.465 p:0.000 df:80	1052 Belgica r:0.395 p:0.000 df:80
pelvic hips / neck width	150	1.783	2.237	2.576	2.873	3.203	3.842	4.637	5211 Stevenson r:-0.220 p:0.010 df:134	6269 Kawasaki r:0.322 p:0.000 df:134	1021 Flammario r:-0.334 p:0.000 df:134
pelvic hips / second toe length	30	1.968	2.276	5.791	6.942	8.742	13.772	14.405	4158 Santini r:-0.465 p:0.010 df:28	264131 Bornim r:0.669 p:0.000 df:28	1151 Ithaka r:-0.620 p:0.000 df:28
pelvic hips / shoulder width	192	0.469	0.726	0.843	0.923	1.014	1.186	1.567	2081 Sazava r:-0.195 p:0.010 df:172	8454 Micheleferrero r:0.422 p:0.000 df:172	1 Ceres r:0.269 p:0.000 df:172
pelvic hips / subchest width	103	0.593	0.879	1.015	1.072	1.166	1.501	1.714	39184 Willgrundy r:-0.265 p:0.010 df:92	8527 Katayama r:0.372 p:0.000 df:92	2357 Phereclos r:0.370 p:0.000 df:92
pelvic hips / subneck dorsal	96	1.286	1.560	1.833	2.129	2.472	3.036	3.773	7008 Pavlov r:-0.276 p:0.010 df:84	10604 Susanoo r:0.454 p:0.000 df:84	1633 Chimay r:-0.368 p:0.000 df:84
pelvic hips / subpelvic rear width	141	0.565	0.690	0.788	0.866	0.932	0.997	1.156	3265 Fletcher r:-0.228 p:0.010 df:126	23801 Erikgustafson r:0.326 p:0.000 df:126	727 Nipponia r:-0.315 p:0.000 df:126
pelvic hips< >subpelvic rear width / neck width< >shoulder width	92	0.494	0.694	1.046	1.331	2.022	2.933	3.567	210271 Samarkand r:-0.281 p:0.010 df:81	14424 Laval r:0.423 p:0.000 df:81	1844 Susilva r:0.401 p:0.000 df:81
pelvic hips< >subpelvic rear width / neck width< >subneck dorsal	55	1.323	1.551	2.491	3.829	5.112	8.145	8.468	7028 Tachikawa r:-0.365 p:0.010 df:47	300928 Uderzo r:0.545 p:0.000 df:47	12339 Carloo r:0.480 p:0.000 df:47
pelvic hips< >subpelvic rear width / neck width< >underbust	63	0.142	0.160	0.273	0.377	0.521	0.798	0.895	301511 Hubinon r:-0.345 p:0.010 df:53	10270 Skoglov r:0.533 p:0.000 df:53	4966 Edolsen r:0.473 p:0.000 df:53
pelvic hips< >subpelvic rear width / shoulder width< >subneck dorsal	57	0.789	0.842	1.500	2.091	2.844	4.437	5.426	8120 Kobe r:-0.358 p:0.010 df:49	3082 Dzhalil r:0.524 p:0.000 df:49	262 Valda r:0.478 p:0.000 df:49
pelvic hips< >subpelvic rear width / shoulder width< >waist	116	0.132	0.176	0.276	0.357	0.471	0.781	1.455	3274 Maillen r:-0.251 p:0.010 df:103	1104 Syringa r:0.393 p:0.000 df:103	832 Karin r:0.370 p:0.000 df:103
pelvic hips< >subpelvic rear width / subpelvic rear width< >suprailiac	125	0.366	0.434	0.601	0.678	0.785	0.944	1.648	11247 Wilburwright r:-0.243 p:0.009 df:111	18059 Cavalieri r:0.364 p:0.000 df:111	4976 Choukyongchol r:0.329 p:0.000 df:111
pelvic hips< >subpelvic rear width / subpelvic rear width< >waist	131	0.248	0.302	0.420	0.522	0.624	0.749	0.774	6 Hebe r:-0.236 p:0.010 df:117	1686 De Sitter r:0.310 p:0.001 df:117	9641 Demaziere r:-0.328 p:0.000 df:117
pelvic hips< >waist / neck width< >shoulder width	134	0.422	0.624	0.929	1.236	1.646	2.566	3.086	10633 Akimasa r:-0.234 p:0.010 df:118	12370 Kageyasu r:0.369 p:0.000 df:118	2816 Pien r:0.345 p:0.000 df:118
pelvic hips< >waist / neck width< >subneck dorsal	83	1.166	1.685	2.468	3.423	4.719	6.864	7.761	6734 Benzenberg r:-0.299 p:0.010 df:72	17354 Matrosov r:0.457 p:0.000 df:72	3260 Vizbor r:-0.409 p:0.000 df:72
pelvic hips< >waist / neck width< >underbust	93	0.145	0.184	0.271	0.343	0.433	0.630	0.712	20321 Lightdonovan r:-0.283 p:0.010 df:80	26711 Rebekahbau r:0.410 p:0.000 df:80	2780 Monnig r:0.377 p:0.000 df:80
pelvic hips< >waist / pelvic hips< >subpelvic rear width	132	0.300	0.348	0.570	0.921	1.265	2.267	3.029	22719 Nakadori r:-0.234 p:0.010 df:118	1687 Glarona r:0.333 p:0.000 df:118	1687 Glarona r:0.333 p:0.000 df:118
pelvic hips< >waist / shoulder width< >subneck dorsal	87	0.323	0.753	1.259	1.825	2.173	3.909	5.852	289085 Andreweil r:-0.292 p:0.010 df:75	2816 Pien r:0.470 p:0.000 df:75	73 Klytia r:-0.436 p:0.000 df:75
pelvic hips< >waist / shoulder width< >waist	175	0.120	0.166	0.254	0.300	0.382	0.557	0.760	21561 Masterman r:-0.204 p:0.010 df:156	52008 Johnnaka r:0.377 p:0.000 df:156	357 Ninina r:-0.274 p:0.000 df:156
pelvic hips< >waist / subpelvic rear width< >suprailiac	124	0.263	0.303	0.519	0.673	0.823	1.114	1.199	6480 Scarlatti r:-0.242 p:0.010 df:111	17095 Mahadik r:0.360 p:0.000 df:111	333 Badenia r:-0.331 p:0.000 df:111
pelvic hips< >waist / subpelvic rear width< >waist	133	0.231	0.262	0.362	0.477	0.572	0.703	0.780	7781 Townsend r:-0.234 p:0.010 df:119	17095 Mahadik r:0.332 p:0.000 df:119	1424 Sundmania r:-0.325 p:0.000 df:119
pinky toe length / big toe width	35	0.563	0.569	0.682	0.753	0.924	1.635	1.752	31592 Jacobplaut r:-0.431 p:0.010 df:33	2482 Perkin r:0.623 p:0.000 df:33	489 Comacina r:-0.614 p:0.000 df:33
second toe length / big toe width	35	0.841	0.844	1.028	1.205	1.389	1.597	1.715	24524 Kevinhawkins r:-0.430 p:0.010 df:33	31925 Krutovskiy r:0.616 p:0.000 df:33	972 Cohnia r:0.572 p:0.000 df:33
second toe length / pinky toe length	39	0.894	1.068	1.356	1.504	1.678	1.969	2.065	1438 Wendeline r:-0.408 p:0.010 df:37	599 Luisa r:0.591 p:0.000 df:37	599 Luisa r:0.591 p:0.000 df:37
shoulder to elbow h / ab width	140	0.824	1.063	1.564	1.831	2.350	2.977	5.489	9286 Patricktaylor r:-0.230 p:0.010 df:123	16212 Theberge r:0.376 p:0.000 df:123	1449 Virtanen r:0.323 p:0.000 df:123
shoulder to elbow h / ankle to heel floor h	82	1.152	2.744	3.356	3.805	4.353	5.530	6.330	1945 Wesselink r:-0.297 p:0.010 df:73	3895 Earhart r:0.478 p:0.000 df:73	339 Dorothea r:-0.443 p:0.000 df:73

shoulder to elbow h / ankle width	127	1.313	2.359	3.152	3.698	4.282	5.261	6.309	6865 Dunkerley r:-0.238 p:0.010 df:115	2938 Hopi r:0.364 p:0.000 df:115	2617 Jiangxi r:-0.376 p:0.000 df:115
shoulder to elbow h / areola dia	198	1.440	2.509	3.885	5.875	7.772	11.629	17.002	676 Melitta r:-0.190 p:0.010 df:182	3700 Geowilliams r:0.328 p:0.000 df:182	3700 Geowilliams r:0.328 p:0.000 df:182
shoulder to elbow h / back perimeter	63	0.033	0.065	0.079	0.102	0.154	0.247	0.265	4515 Khrennikov r:-0.330 p:0.010 df:58	2741 Valdivia r:0.519 p:0.000 df:58	1936 Lugano r:0.437 p:0.000 df:58
shoulder to elbow h / back tone	64	0.081	0.212	0.276	0.349	0.453	0.905	1.469	29427 Oswaldthomas r:-0.328 p:0.010 df:59	12850 Axelmunthe r:0.496 p:0.000 df:59	920 Rogeria r:-0.460 p:0.000 df:59
shoulder to elbow h / ball width	56	0.827	1.102	2.224	2.841	3.335	3.977	5.659	3913 Chemin r:-0.345 p:0.010 df:53	1239 Queteleta r:0.517 p:0.000 df:53	807 Ceraskia r:0.483 p:0.000 df:53
shoulder to elbow h / big toe length	50	1.605	1.941	3.954	5.597	6.632	9.104	10.574	7220 Philnicholson r:-0.369 p:0.010 df:46	5002 Marnix r:0.559 p:0.000 df:46	2329 Orthos r:0.499 p:0.000 df:46
shoulder to elbow h / big toe width	44	2.080	3.093	5.839	7.984	10.081	13.256	14.979	2139 Makharadze r:-0.389 p:0.010 df:41	25416 Chyanwen r:0.594 p:0.000 df:41	3949 Mach r:-0.526 p:0.000 df:41
shoulder to elbow h / bra shoulder to underb	184	0.535	0.717	0.885	1.035	1.213	1.495	1.913	3133 Sendai r:-0.198 p:0.010 df:167	24654 Fossett r:0.298 p:0.000 df:167	66 Maja r:0.275 p:0.000 df:167
shoulder to elbow h / breast depth	148	1.009	2.648	4.310	5.827	7.714	12.705	19.339	4412 Chephren r:-0.219 p:0.010 df:136	43957 Invernizzi r:0.369 p:0.000 df:136	869 Mellena r:-0.310 p:0.000 df:136
shoulder to elbow h / breasts apart	211	2.025	2.952	4.552	6.323	8.862	23.990	53.827	4999 MPC r:-0.187 p:0.010 df:189	3316 Herzberg r:0.326 p:0.000 df:189	1790 Volkov r:0.253 p:0.000 df:189
shoulder to elbow h / bust dia	233	0.767	1.144	1.668	1.943	2.328	2.901	4.382	5610 Balster r:-0.176 p:0.010 df:212	4203 Brucato r:0.274 p:0.000 df:212	1702 Kalahari r:-0.270 p:0.000 df:212
shoulder to elbow h / butt square	59	0.180	0.206	0.338	0.393	0.466	0.591	0.958	23040 Latham r:-0.342 p:0.010 df:54	59828 Ossikar r:0.556 p:0.000 df:54	779 Nina r:-0.477 p:0.000 df:54
shoulder to elbow h / calf width	145	0.841	1.467	1.870	2.137	2.477	2.932	3.689	4755 Nicky r:-0.222 p:0.010 df:132	350185 Linnell r:0.338 p:0.000 df:132	969 Leocadia r:0.302 p:0.000 df:132
shoulder to elbow h / chest width	209	0.268	0.570	0.807	0.911	1.026	1.216	1.512	4108 Rakos r:-0.186 p:0.010 df:189	1741 Giclas r:0.261 p:0.000 df:189	395 Delia r:-0.267 p:0.000 df:189
shoulder to elbow h / clavicle to groin h	141	0.344	0.421	0.471	0.520	0.560	0.713	0.916	6859 Datemasamune r:-0.230 p:0.010 df:123	5595 Roth r:0.343 p:0.000 df:123	1096 Reunerta r:0.319 p:0.000 df:123
shoulder to elbow h / clavicle to neck h	133	2.029	2.419	3.090	3.684	4.423	5.863	6.762	2300 Stebbins r:-0.236 p:0.010 df:116	8448 Belyakina r:0.351 p:0.000 df:116	745 Mauritia r:0.322 p:0.000 df:116
shoulder to elbow h / elbow to wrist h	234	0.622	0.874	1.068	1.158	1.262	1.500	2.000	736 Harvard r:-0.176 p:0.010 df:212	15918 Thereluzia r:0.273 p:0.000 df:212	3329 Golay r:0.244 p:0.000 df:212
shoulder to elbow h / foot base h	89	0.462	0.843	1.178	1.437	1.625	2.013	2.379	1030 Vitja r:-0.285 p:0.010 df:79	10171 Takaotengu r:0.461 p:0.000 df:79	167 Urda r:-0.418 p:0.000 df:79
shoulder to elbow h / heel width	56	1.585	2.413	3.405	3.935	4.803	5.658	7.527	9474 Cassadrury r:-0.346 p:0.010 df:53	15740 Hyakumangoku r:0.488 p:0.000 df:53	10747 Kothen r:0.459 p:0.000 df:53
shoulder to elbow h / long finger length	99	0.601	1.030	1.276	1.462	1.617	1.966	2.605	12937 Premadi r:-0.265 p:0.010 df:92	5403 Takachiho r:0.392 p:0.000 df:92	4284 Kaho r:-0.370 p:0.000 df:92
shoulder to elbow h / lower forearm w	255	0.900	3.247	4.115	4.700	5.222	6.245	8.026	4363 Sergej r:-0.169 p:0.010 df:231	6644 Jugaku r:0.280 p:0.000 df:231	2883 Barabashov r:-0.246 p:0.000 df:231
shoulder to elbow h / lower leg h	124	0.270	0.515	0.616	0.723	0.804	0.995	1.223	10055 Silcher r:-0.240 p:0.010 df:112	68144 Mizser r:0.326 p:0.000 df:112	3140 Stellafane r:-0.325 p:0.000 df:112
shoulder to elbow h / neck width	179	1.501	1.964	2.349	2.577	2.917	3.433	5.610	34133 Charlesfenske r:-0.201 p:0.010 df:161	7332 Ponrepo r:0.303 p:0.000 df:161	2461 Clavel r:0.299 p:0.000 df:161
shoulder to elbow h / nipple dia	194	4.620	12.220	16.781	21.514	26.222	33.112	48.750	18938 Zarabeth r:-0.191 p:0.010 df:179	11263 Pesonen r:0.288 p:0.000 df:179	1708 Polit r:-0.274 p:0.000 df:179
shoulder to elbow h / nipple to bottom	179	1.757	2.834	3.780	4.556	5.741	8.247	23.177	2666 Gramme r:-0.200 p:0.010 df:165	5331 Erimomisaki r:0.399 p:0.000 df:165	7 Iris r:0.305 p:0.000 df:165
shoulder to elbow h / nipple to top	181	0.739	1.151	1.695	2.213	2.916	3.834	4.858	688 Melanie r:-0.200 p:0.010 df:165	12722 Petrarca r:0.321 p:0.000 df:165	636 Erika r:0.307 p:0.000 df:165
shoulder to elbow h / pelvic hips	183	0.290	0.592	0.795	0.901	1.013	1.221	1.961	24609 Evgenij r:-0.200 p:0.010 df:163	11811 Martinrubin r:0.302 p:0.000 df:163	2313 Aruna r:0.289 p:0.000 df:163
shoulder to elbow h / pinky toe length	37	3.011	3.323	7.108	8.962	11.025	15.248	15.648	8047 Akikinoshita r:-0.418 p:0.010 df:35	27123 Matthewlam r:0.638 p:0.000 df:35	7454 Kevinrighter r:0.556 p:0.000 df:35
shoulder to elbow h / second toe length	40	1.906	1.945	4.844	6.210	7.697	10.483	10.509	3906 Chao r:-0.403 p:0.010 df:38	25416 Chyanwen r:0.596 p:0.000 df:38	8538 Gammelmaja r:0.558 p:0.000 df:38
shoulder to elbow h / shoulder width	252	0.339	0.632	0.757	0.825	0.891	1.067	1.653	13049 Butov r:-0.169 p:0.010 df:230	11929 Uchino r:0.264 p:0.000 df:230	58 Concordia r:0.250 p:0.000 df:230
shoulder to elbow h / subchest width	110	0.199	0.564	0.837	0.947	1.090	1.301	1.595	1033 Simona r:-0.257 p:0.010 df:98	6657 Otukyo r:0.379 p:0.000 df:98	922 Schlutia r:0.375 p:0.000 df:98
shoulder to elbow h / subneck dorsal	105	1.076	1.385	1.699	1.969	2.216	2.805	4.631	9956 Castellaz r:-0.265 p:0.010 df:92	7412 Linnaeus r:0.414 p:0.000 df:92	632 Pyrrha r:0.355 p:0.000 df:92
shoulder to elbow h / subpelvic rear width	129	0.156	0.443	0.674	0.764	0.862	1.023	1.643	658 Asteria r:-0.238 p:0.010 df:115	13254 Kekule r:0.352 p:0.000 df:115	6307 Maiztegui r:0.323 p:0.000 df:115
shoulder to elbow h / suprailiac	191	0.305	0.637	0.868	0.990	1.097	1.306	2.199	23707 Chambliss r:-0.197 p:0.010 df:171	83657 Albertosordi r:0.266 p:0.000 df:171	1708 Polit r:-0.262 p:0.000 df:171
shoulder to elbow h / underbust	168	0.294	0.667	0.940	1.037	1.181	1.387	2.262	11577 Einasto r:-0.208 p:0.010 df:151	19488 Abramcoley r:0.349 p:0.000 df:151	1708 Polit r:-0.285 p:0.000 df:151
shoulder to elbow h / upper forearm w	262	0.874	2.109	2.751	3.112	3.570	4.286	5.730	6521 Pina r:-0.166 p:0.010 df:238	3286 Anatoliya r:0.281 p:0.000 df:238	103 Hera r:-0.229 p:0.000 df:238

Measurement	N								Min	Mid	Max
shoulder to elbow h / waist	207	0.311	0.722	0.971	1.090	1.213	1.445	2.421	16797 Wilkerson r:-0.187 p:0.010 df:187	7367 Giotto r:0.261 p:0.000 df:187	2489 Suvorov r:-0.276 p:0.000 df:187
shoulder width / ab width	151	1.143	1.410	1.907	2.224	2.607	3.348	5.018	1679 Nevanlinna r:-0.223 p:0.010 df:132	6937 Valadon r:0.347 p:0.000 df:132	98 Ianthe r:0.314 p:0.000 df:132
shoulder width / ankle to heel floor h	83	1.521	2.972	3.968	4.490	5.103	8.408	15.325	9471 Ostend r:-0.295 p:0.010 df:74	765 Mattiaca r:0.491 p:0.000 df:74	765 Mattiaca r:0.491 p:0.000 df:74
shoulder width / ankle width	124	1.469	2.621	3.770	4.346	5.001	6.751	9.347	6721 Minamiawaji r:-0.239 p:0.010 df:114	27003 Katoizumi r:0.370 p:0.000 df:114	765 Mattiaca r:0.324 p:0.000 df:114
shoulder width / back perimeter	65	0.039	0.073	0.099	0.120	0.164	0.294	0.311	1634 Ndola r:-0.326 p:0.010 df:60	120481 Johannwalter r:0.472 p:0.000 df:60	776 Berberica r:-0.489 p:0.000 df:60
shoulder width / back tone	66	0.101	0.244	0.324	0.416	0.551	1.279	3.054	3015 Candy r:-0.322 p:0.010 df:61	3566 Levitan r:0.485 p:0.000 df:61	1887 Virton r:0.429 p:0.000 df:61
shoulder width / ball width	56	1.104	1.365	2.509	3.245	3.860	6.546	10.866	8147 Colemanhawkins r:-0.345 p:0.010 df:53	19993 Gunterseeber r:0.542 p:0.000 df:53	4105 Tsia r:0.487 p:0.000 df:53
shoulder width / big toe length	52	0.785	2.185	4.999	6.386	8.144	12.348	27.462	10702 Arizorcas r:-0.361 p:0.010 df:48	342 Endymion r:0.600 p:0.000 df:48	342 Endymion r:0.600 p:0.000 df:48
shoulder width / big toe width	44	1.274	2.979	6.847	9.525	12.579	18.377	35.419	15938 Bohnenblust r:-0.389 p:0.010 df:41	7994 Bethellen r:0.605 p:0.000 df:41	1764 Cogshall r:0.516 p:0.000 df:41
shoulder width / bust dia	250	0.966	1.631	2.045	2.323	2.740	3.490	5.244	10158 Taroubou r:-0.170 p:0.010 df:227	4999 MPC r:0.274 p:0.000 df:227	1980 Tezcatlipoca r:-0.262 p:0.000 df:227
shoulder width / calf width	142	1.083	1.665	2.273	2.583	2.931	4.060	6.824	1734 Zhongolovich r:-0.223 p:0.010 df:131	6583 Destinn r:0.376 p:0.000 df:131	754 Malabar r:-0.334 p:0.000 df:131
shoulder width / clavicle to neck h	144	2.338	3.083	3.693	4.382	5.313	6.923	13.018	120191 Tombagg r:-0.226 p:0.010 df:127	22692 Carfrekahl r:0.353 p:0.000 df:127	2935 Naerum r:0.329 p:0.000 df:127
shoulder width / foot base h	88	0.617	1.097	1.410	1.660	1.906	2.962	4.080	18997 Mizrahi r:-0.287 p:0.010 df:78	249522 Johndailey r:0.395 p:0.000 df:78	469 Argentina r:-0.385 p:0.000 df:78
shoulder width / heel width	53	1.868	2.058	3.736	4.726	5.721	8.479	10.498	120462 Amanohashidate r:-0.355 p:0.010 df:50	27091 Alisonbick r:0.510 p:0.000 df:50	6154 Stevesynnott r:0.503 p:0.000 df:50
shoulder width / lower leg h	123	0.357	0.581	0.747	0.837	0.956	1.405	1.677	5286 Haruomukai r:-0.239 p:0.010 df:113	765 Mattiaca r:0.383 p:0.000 df:113	765 Mattiaca r:0.383 p:0.000 df:113
shoulder width / neck width	189	1.742	2.571	2.889	3.096	3.365	3.741	4.419	3065 Sarahill r:-0.195 p:0.010 df:172	30882 Tomhenning r:0.339 p:0.000 df:172	237 Coelestina r:-0.286 p:0.000 df:172
shoulder width / pinky toe length	37	3.593	3.979	7.977	10.346	12.354	21.457	26.988	13435 Rohret r:-0.419 p:0.010 df:35	71 Niobe r:0.572 p:0.000 df:35	71 Niobe r:0.572 p:0.000 df:35
shoulder width / second toe length	40	0.897	2.518	5.726	7.307	9.028	13.642	18.819	8766 Niger r:-0.403 p:0.010 df:38	248 Lameia r:0.590 p:0.000 df:38	248 Lameia r:0.590 p:0.000 df:38
shoulder width / subchest width	117	0.286	0.892	1.029	1.142	1.243	1.457	1.845	10570 Shibayasuo r:-0.248 p:0.010 df:105	6626 Mattgenge r:0.396 p:0.000 df:105	2021 Poincare r:-0.346 p:0.000 df:105
shoulder width / subneck dorsal	116	1.584	1.857	2.124	2.327	2.608	2.966	3.290	16044 Kurtbachmann r:-0.251 p:0.010 df:103	864 Aase r:0.419 p:0.000 df:103	864 Aase r:0.419 p:0.000 df:103
shoulder width< >subneck dorsal / neck width< >underbust	62	0.093	0.110	0.152	0.179	0.210	0.257	0.276	288 Glauke r:-0.348 p:0.010 df:52	33628 Spettel r:0.529 p:0.000 df:52	1261 Legia r:0.476 p:0.000 df:52
shoulder width< >waist / neck width< >shoulder width	146	1.292	2.570	3.375	3.871	4.800	7.211	10.692	13957 NARIT r:-0.224 p:0.010 df:129	6128 Lasorda r:0.313 p:0.000 df:129	1177 Gonnessia r:0.304 p:0.000 df:129
shoulder width< >waist / neck width< >subneck dorsal	87	5.085	5.932	8.450	10.080	14.548	20.909	27.550	298 Baptistina r:-0.292 p:0.010 df:75	18702 Sadowski r:0.457 p:0.000 df:75	10234 Sixtygarden r:-0.413 p:0.000 df:75
shoulder width< >waist / neck width< >underbust	99	0.676	0.837	0.968	1.055	1.147	1.472	1.591	4445 Jimstratton r:-0.275 p:0.010 df:85	10679 Chankaochang r:0.462 p:0.000 df:85	876 Scott r:-0.380 p:0.000 df:85
shoulder width< >waist / shoulder width< >subneck dorsal	92	1.933	3.171	4.867	5.740	6.611	9.851	11.532	8373 Stephengould r:-0.285 p:0.010 df:79	3082 Dzhalil r:0.388 p:0.000 df:79	98 Ianthe r:-0.438 p:0.000 df:79
subchest width / foot base h	40	1.061	1.096	1.269	1.439	1.751	2.478	2.656	19466 Darcydiegel r:-0.430 p:0.010 df:33	123120 Peternewman r:0.645 p:0.000 df:33	66 Maja r:-0.569 p:0.000 df:33
subneck dorsal / ab width	73	0.542	0.695	0.815	0.999	1.231	1.510	1.699	11059 Nulliusinverba r:-0.317 p:0.010 df:63	98 Ianthe r:0.468 p:0.000 df:63	98 Ianthe r:0.468 p:0.000 df:63
subneck dorsal / ankle to heel floor h	43	0.747	1.153	1.650	1.908	2.223	3.828	6.883	7495 Feynman r:-0.408 p:0.010 df:37	22791 Twarog r:0.756 p:0.000 df:37	653 Berenike r:0.559 p:0.000 df:37
subneck dorsal / ankle width	54	0.557	0.912	1.642	1.881	2.213	3.408	3.811	17856 Gomes r:-0.362 p:0.010 df:48	32630 Ethanlevy r:0.560 p:0.000 df:48	329 Svea r:0.513 p:0.000 df:48
subneck dorsal / back perimeter	33	0.023	0.031	0.039	0.056	0.074	0.119	0.127	85299 Neander r:-0.450 p:0.010 df:30	25714 Aprillee r:0.677 p:0.000 df:30	3554 Amun r:0.607 p:0.000 df:30
subneck dorsal / back tone	34	0.037	0.093	0.147	0.169	0.241	0.360	0.384	129962 Williamverts r:-0.443 p:0.010 df:31	12631 Mariekebaan r:0.613 p:0.000 df:31	4597 Consolmagno r:0.610 p:0.000 df:31
subneck dorsal / calf width	56	0.387	0.715	0.964	1.111	1.308	1.922	2.033	18671 Zacharyrice r:-0.355 p:0.010 df:50	47038 Majoni r:0.491 p:0.000 df:50	864 Aase r:-0.568 p:0.000 df:50
subneck dorsal / clavicle to neck h	87	1.081	1.277	1.504	1.807	2.169	2.936	5.739	11124 Mikulasek r:-0.292 p:0.010 df:75	6970 Saigusa r:0.437 p:0.000 df:75	4143 Huziak r:0.402 p:0.000 df:75
subneck dorsal / foot base h	45	0.243	0.353	0.582	0.674	0.802	1.346	1.597	7650 Kaname r:-0.398 p:0.010 df:39	29672 Salvo r:0.637 p:0.000 df:39	1130 Skuld r:-0.538 p:0.000 df:39
subneck dorsal / lower leg h	52	0.175	0.275	0.337	0.356	0.425	0.646	0.732	126 Velleda r:-0.369 p:0.010 df:46	130066 Timhaltigin r:0.600 p:0.000 df:46	487 Venetia r:0.483 p:0.000 df:46

subneck dorsal / subchest width	57	0.317	0.350	0.443	0.482	0.528	0.657	0.709	10020 Bagenal r:-0.359 p:0.010 df:49	10481 Esipov r:0.492 p:0.000 df:49	1040 Klumpkea r:-0.482 p:0.000 df:49
subpelvic rear width / ab	104	1.407	1.615	2.026	2.373	2.811	3.638	4.957	5805 Glasgow r:-0.262 p:0.010 df:94	10996 Armandspitz r:0.508 p:0.000 df:94	905 Universitas r:-0.415 p:0.000 df:94
subpelvic rear width / ankle to heel floor h	47	2.702	3.257	4.123	4.778	5.901	8.995	14.990	49382 Lynnokamoto r:-0.399 p:0.010 df:39	16463 Nayoro r:0.596 p:0.000 df:39	2051 Chang r:-0.544 p:0.000 df:39
subpelvic rear width / ankle width	67	1.536	2.986	4.112	4.939	5.668	8.117	13.357	15128 Patrickjones r:-0.330 p:0.010 df:58	1545 Thernoe r:0.565 p:0.000 df:58	674 Rachele r:0.523 p:0.000 df:58
subpelvic rear width / back perimeter	41	0.050	0.088	0.111	0.141	0.181	0.322	0.425	2077 Kiangsu r:-0.410 p:0.010 df:37	120481 Johannwalter r:0.644 p:0.000 df:37	2705 Wu r:0.549 p:0.000 df:37
subpelvic rear width / back tone	42	0.102	0.141	0.356	0.431	0.550	0.972	1.144	5389 Choikaiyau r:-0.402 p:0.009 df:39	1341 Edmee r:0.692 p:0.000 df:39	23 Thalia r:0.553 p:0.000 df:39
subpelvic rear width / ball width	31	1.183	1.872	3.041	3.684	4.395	5.700	6.328	16355 Buber r:-0.457 p:0.010 df:29	1308 Halleria r:0.662 p:0.000 df:29	565 Marbachia r:-0.636 p:0.000 df:29
subpelvic rear width / big toe length	33	2.313	3.437	5.549	7.431	9.305	11.540	11.997	3142 Kilopi r:-0.456 p:0.010 df:29	3007 Reaves r:0.653 p:0.000 df:29	296 Phaetusa r:0.635 p:0.000 df:29
subpelvic rear width / big toe width	31	3.741	4.951	8.236	11.569	13.092	18.114	18.523	7176 Kuniji r:-0.456 p:0.010 df:29	33688 Meghnabehari r:0.639 p:0.000 df:29	1308 Halleria r:0.623 p:0.000 df:29
subpelvic rear width / bust dia	131	0.731	1.711	2.143	2.569	2.954	3.825	7.563	861 Aida r:-0.235 p:0.010 df:118	4204 Barsig r:0.456 p:0.000 df:118	25 Phocaea r:-0.318 p:0.000 df:118
subpelvic rear width / calf width	80	0.946	1.719	2.561	2.935	3.303	4.459	8.582	9664 Brueghel r:-0.302 p:0.010 df:70	10130 Ardre r:0.525 p:0.000 df:70	674 Rachele r:0.456 p:0.000 df:70
subpelvic rear width / clavicle to neck h	81	2.713	3.132	3.663	4.698	5.834	10.620	15.410	5206 Kodomonomori r:-0.300 p:0.010 df:71	52285 Kakurinji r:0.455 p:0.000 df:71	3988 Huma r:0.428 p:0.000 df:71
subpelvic rear width / foot base h	49	0.670	1.213	1.574	1.867	2.219	2.865	3.012	2300 Stebbins r:-0.390 p:0.010 df:41	29456 Evakrchova r:0.497 p:0.001 df:41	2243 Lonnrot r:-0.537 p:0.000 df:41
subpelvic rear width / heel width	34	1.952	3.038	4.710	5.343	6.388	7.644	8.477	8887 Scheeres r:-0.443 p:0.010 df:31	627 Charis r:0.629 p:0.000 df:31	627 Charis r:0.629 p:0.000 df:31
subpelvic rear width / long finger length	54	0.548	1.380	1.622	1.783	2.037	2.850	3.854	2665 Schrutka r:-0.358 p:0.010 df:49	23042 Craigpeters r:0.587 p:0.000 df:49	1828 Kashirina r:0.528 p:0.000 df:49
subpelvic rear width / lower leg h	67	0.363	0.649	0.806	0.937	1.139	1.557	2.385	1193 Africa r:-0.331 p:0.010 df:58	21801 Ancerl r:0.508 p:0.000 df:58	4701 Milani r:0.438 p:0.000 df:58
subpelvic rear width / neck width	102	1.542	2.645	3.070	3.367	3.730	5.108	5.531	7707 Yes r:-0.267 p:0.010 df:91	201308 Hansgrade r:0.399 p:0.000 df:91	1101 Clematis r:-0.359 p:0.000 df:91
subpelvic rear width / shoulder width	132	0.436	0.886	0.991	1.076	1.225	1.489	3.357	16794 Cucullia r:-0.233 p:0.010 df:119	212465 Goroshky r:0.439 p:0.000 df:119	283 Emma r:0.315 p:0.000 df:119
subpelvic rear width / subchest width	72	0.957	1.022	1.140	1.230	1.402	1.958	2.040	1991 Darwin r:-0.317 p:0.010 df:63	799 Gudula r:0.491 p:0.000 df:63	799 Gudula r:0.491 p:0.000 df:63
subpelvic rear width / subneck dorsal	63	1.837	1.902	2.279	2.556	2.868	4.045	4.373	748 Simeisa r:-0.339 p:0.010 df:55	29643 Plucker r:0.518 p:0.000 df:55	6089 Izumi r:0.479 p:0.000 df:55
subpelvic rear width< >suprailiac / neck width< >shoulder width	84	0.826	1.154	1.654	2.007	2.690	3.754	4.742	1281 Jeanne r:-0.296 p:0.010 df:73	27525 Vartovka r:0.456 p:0.000 df:73	5242 Kenreimonin r:-0.399 p:0.000 df:73
subpelvic rear width< >suprailiac / neck width< >subneck dorsal	51	2.133	2.954	4.094	5.629	7.171	9.628	10.810	30160 Danielbruce r:-0.380 p:0.010 df:43	17354 Matrosov r:0.538 p:0.000 df:43	7529 Vagnozzi r:0.515 p:0.000 df:43
subpelvic rear width< >suprailiac / neck width< >underbust	61	0.242	0.302	0.422	0.557	0.722	0.937	1.070	9204 Morike r:-0.351 p:0.010 df:51	55222 Makotoshinkai r:0.548 p:0.000 df:51	1755 Lorbach r:-0.491 p:0.000 df:51
subpelvic rear width< >suprailiac / shoulder width< >subneck dorsal	51	1.666	1.877	2.277	3.040	3.554	5.556	7.181	25 Phocaea r:-0.381 p:0.010 df:43	3082 Dzhalil r:0.560 p:0.000 df:43	247 Eukrate r:-0.499 p:0.000 df:43
subpelvic rear width< >suprailiac / shoulder width< >waist	108	0.163	0.315	0.424	0.519	0.599	0.878	0.954	513 Centesima r:-0.258 p:0.010 df:97	1104 Syringa r:0.466 p:0.000 df:97	572 Rebekka r:0.365 p:0.000 df:97
subpelvic rear width< >suprailiac / subpelvic rear width< >waist	125	0.470	0.577	0.691	0.744	0.791	0.873	0.896	3647 Dermott r:-0.241 p:0.010 df:112	10378 Ingmarbergman r:0.357 p:0.000 df:112	985 Rosina r:-0.326 p:0.000 df:112
subpelvic rear width< >waist / neck width< >shoulder width	91	1.268	1.673	2.196	2.712	3.392	5.114	6.416	4034 Vishnu r:-0.283 p:0.010 df:80	27525 Vartovka r:0.440 p:0.000 df:80	308 Polyxo r:0.386 p:0.000 df:80
subpelvic rear width< >waist / neck width< >subneck dorsal	56	2.638	3.810	5.952	7.480	9.718	13.327	15.353	2183 Neufang r:-0.363 p:0.010 df:48	17354 Matrosov r:0.533 p:0.000 df:48	4662 Runk r:0.483 p:0.000 df:48
subpelvic rear width< >waist / neck width< >underbust	65	0.371	0.433	0.606	0.763	0.934	1.162	1.376	6386 Keithnoll r:-0.339 p:0.010 df:55	55222 Makotoshinkai r:0.560 p:0.000 df:55	4408 Zlata Koruna r:0.457 p:0.000 df:55
subpelvic rear width< >waist / shoulder width< >subneck dorsal	58	2.257	2.486	3.120	4.193	5.017	7.508	10.225	9987 Peano r:-0.354 p:0.010 df:50	72543 Simonemarchi r:0.556 p:0.000 df:50	247 Eukrate r:-0.469 p:0.000 df:50
subpelvic rear width< >waist / shoulder width< >waist	119	0.314	0.463	0.580	0.688	0.821	1.097	1.290	3946 Shor r:-0.246 p:0.010 df:107	1104 Syringa r:0.438 p:0.000 df:107	572 Rebekka r:0.344 p:0.000 df:107
suprailiac / ab width	148	0.822	1.408	1.687	1.854	2.105	2.461	3.298	99503 Leewonchul r:-0.222 p:0.010 df:132	24911 Kojimashigemi r:0.396 p:0.000 df:132	401 Ottilia r:0.347 p:0.000 df:132

suprailiac / ankle to heel floor h		69	1.348	2.552	3.290	3.674	4.388	5.887	6.603	12426 Racquetball r:-0.325 p:0.010 df:60	2401 Aehlita r:0.508 p:0.000 df:60	1578 Kirkwood r:-0.528 p:0.000 df:60
suprailiac / ankle width		97	0.983	2.197	3.134	3.744	4.288	5.622	11.510	2699 Kalinin r:-0.274 p:0.010 df:86	1440 Rostia r:0.457 p:0.000 df:86	283 Emma r:0.405 p:0.000 df:86
suprailiac / areola dia		175	1.941	2.890	4.480	5.882	7.755	12.091	14.906	161975 Kincsem r:-0.202 p:0.010 df:159	2512 Tavastia r:0.306 p:0.000 df:159	545 Messalina r:-0.285 p:0.000 df:159
suprailiac / back perimeter		55	0.028	0.055	0.081	0.096	0.125	0.210	0.253	6924 Fukui r:-0.351 p:0.010 df:51	96254 Hoyo r:0.499 p:0.000 df:51	2741 Valdivia r:0.475 p:0.000 df:51
suprailiac / back tone		56	0.085	0.212	0.268	0.347	0.427	0.628	1.136	101955 Bennu r:-0.348 p:0.010 df:52	2502 Nummela r:0.493 p:0.000 df:52	2502 Nummela r:0.493 p:0.000 df:52
suprailiac / ball width		42	0.758	1.270	2.278	2.693	3.308	5.036	5.452	10665 Ortigao r:-0.393 p:0.010 df:40	22627 Aviscardi r:0.628 p:0.000 df:40	453 Tea r:-0.536 p:0.000 df:40
suprailiac / big toe length		40	1.481	2.035	4.192	5.340	7.177	9.613	9.678	299134 Moggicecchi r:-0.419 p:0.010 df:35	8424 Toshitsumita r:0.599 p:0.000 df:35	318 Magdalena r:-0.595 p:0.000 df:35
suprailiac / big toe width		31	2.396	3.035	6.469	7.439	9.923	13.780	15.961	12246 Pliska r:-0.456 p:0.010 df:29	10015 Valenlebedev r:0.633 p:0.000 df:29	2313 Aruna r:-0.592 p:0.000 df:29
suprailiac / bra shoulder to underb		158	0.724	0.824	0.958	1.047	1.187	1.444	1.910	19993 Gunterseeber r:-0.215 p:0.010 df:142	8454 Micheleferrero r:0.388 p:0.000 df:142	247 Eukrate r:-0.296 p:0.000 df:142
suprailiac / breasts apart		188	2.453	2.849	4.403	6.150	8.763	22.603	47.302	902 Probitas r:-0.198 p:0.010 df:167	3758 Karttunen r:0.321 p:0.000 df:167	1450 Raimonda r:0.281 p:0.000 df:167
suprailiac / bust dia		202	1.051	1.474	1.780	2.040	2.277	2.989	3.480	18106 Blume r:-0.189 p:0.010 df:183	8454 Micheleferrero r:0.334 p:0.000 df:183	372 Palma r:0.258 p:0.000 df:183
suprailiac / butt square		50	0.212	0.245	0.337	0.397	0.438	0.548	0.602	24949 Klacka r:-0.372 p:0.010 df:45	4865 Sor r:0.520 p:0.000 df:45	1649 Fabre r:-0.507 p:0.000 df:45
suprailiac / calf width		106	0.814	1.414	1.934	2.181	2.470	3.251	5.338	1526 Mikkeli r:-0.260 p:0.010 df:96	128607 Richhund r:0.456 p:0.000 df:96	674 Rachele r:0.348 p:0.000 df:96
suprailiac / chest width		190	0.278	0.754	0.858	0.937	1.007	1.132	1.428	178226 Rebeccalouise r:-0.195 p:0.010 df:171	158589 Snodgrass r:0.300 p:0.000 df:171	395 Delia r:-0.269 p:0.000 df:171
suprailiac / clavicle to neck h		122	1.813	2.343	3.021	3.578	4.432	6.315	12.868	4111 Lamy r:-0.249 p:0.010 df:105	8454 Micheleferrero r:0.410 p:0.000 df:105	793 Arizona r:-0.349 p:0.000 df:105
suprailiac / foot base h		71	0.429	0.957	1.190	1.375	1.651	1.991	2.546	8739 Morihisa r:-0.322 p:0.010 df:61	31268 Welty r:0.432 p:0.000 df:61	5459 Saraburger r:-0.437 p:0.000 df:61
suprailiac / heel width		40	1.250	2.474	3.469	4.270	4.665	6.324	6.899	26990 Culbertson r:-0.409 p:0.010 df:37	7897 Bohuska r:0.531 p:0.001 df:37	2787 Tovarishch r:-0.514 p:0.001 df:37
suprailiac / long finger length		80	0.624	0.985	1.263	1.456	1.657	2.105	2.682	13 Egeria r:-0.296 p:0.010 df:73	11547 Griesser r:0.406 p:0.000 df:73	11547 Griesser r:0.406 p:0.000 df:73
suprailiac / lower leg h		96	0.316	0.501	0.604	0.704	0.811	1.205	2.047	4466 Abai r:-0.276 p:0.010 df:85	2599 Veseli r:0.399 p:0.000 df:85	2599 Veseli r:0.399 p:0.000 df:85
suprailiac / neck width		153	1.582	2.073	2.403	2.620	2.864	3.622	3.947	3089 Oujianquan r:-0.219 p:0.010 df:136	560 Delila r:0.360 p:0.000 df:136	471 Papagena r:0.295 p:0.000 df:136
suprailiac / nipple dia		172	9.694	14.011	17.939	21.821	25.408	33.297	45.247	687 Tinette r:-0.205 p:0.010 df:156	5924 Teruo r:0.412 p:0.000 df:156	545 Messalina r:-0.296 p:0.000 df:156
suprailiac / nipple to bottom		160	2.258	2.676	3.834	4.458	5.815	8.861	14.460	155083 Banneker r:-0.211 p:0.010 df:146	6412 Kaifu r:0.295 p:0.000 df:146	6412 Kaifu r:0.295 p:0.000 df:146
suprailiac / nipple to top		160	0.939	1.396	1.910	2.338	2.773	3.489	4.508	1763 Williams r:-0.212 p:0.010 df:145	8131 Scanlon r:0.305 p:0.000 df:145	636 Erika r:0.284 p:0.000 df:145
suprailiac / pelvic hips		201	0.668	0.823	0.884	0.917	0.952	1.020	1.362	15107 Toepperwein r:-0.190 p:0.010 df:181	7934 Sinatra r:0.329 p:0.000 df:181	3961 Arthurcox r:0.267 p:0.000 df:181
suprailiac / shoulder width		200	0.422	0.687	0.767	0.837	0.930	1.132	1.387	18729 Potentino r:-0.190 p:0.010 df:181	8454 Micheleferrero r:0.380 p:0.000 df:181	18 Melpomene r:0.270 p:0.000 df:181
suprailiac / subchest width		109	0.207	0.805	0.916	0.981	1.048	1.269	1.517	12631 Mariekebaan r:-0.259 p:0.010 df:97	25919 Comuniello r:0.352 p:0.000 df:97	25919 Comuniello r:0.352 p:0.000 df:97
suprailiac / subneck dorsal		95	1.143	1.481	1.727	1.991	2.171	2.679	3.253	1731 Smuts r:-0.280 p:0.010 df:82	3603 Gajdusek r:0.441 p:0.000 df:82	1562 Gondolatsch r:-0.419 p:0.000 df:82
suprailiac / subpelvic rear width		136	0.162	0.581	0.722	0.799	0.859	0.963	1.506	3589 Loyola r:-0.231 p:0.010 df:122	269484 Marcia r:0.389 p:0.000 df:122	727 Nipponia r:-0.327 p:0.000 df:122
suprailiac / underbust		177	0.536	0.903	0.989	1.062	1.131	1.244	1.646	5961 Watt r:-0.204 p:0.010 df:158	7773 Kyokuchiken r:0.332 p:0.000 df:158	167 Urda r:-0.282 p:0.000 df:158
suprailiac< >waist / chest width< >underbust		152	0.186	0.341	0.589	0.769	1.021	1.542	2.566	689 Zita r:-0.219 p:0.010 df:136	126901 Craigstevens r:0.342 p:0.000 df:136	6015 Paularego r:0.295 p:0.000 df:136
suprailiac< >waist / neck width< >shoulder width		139	0.149	0.298	0.482	0.677	0.936	1.299	2.314	10352 Kawamura r:-0.231 p:0.010 df:122	2816 Pien r:0.382 p:0.000 df:122	1434 Margot r:-0.320 p:0.000 df:122
suprailiac< >waist / neck width< >subneck dorsal		87	0.701	0.882	1.297	1.839	2.509	3.528	4.678	9972 Minoruoda r:-0.292 p:0.010 df:75	17354 Matrosov r:0.417 p:0.000 df:75	98 Ianthe r:-0.425 p:0.000 df:75
suprailiac< >waist / neck width< >underbust		97	0.058	0.084	0.144	0.183	0.223	0.323	0.405	88874 Wongshingsheuk r:-0.278 p:0.010 df:83	17720 Manuboccuni r:0.436 p:0.000 df:83	7945 Kreisau r:0.375 p:0.000 df:83
suprailiac< >waist / pelvic hips< >subpelvic rear width		127	0.122	0.170	0.366	0.505	0.679	1.175	1.386	1686 De Sitter r:-0.239 p:0.010 df:114	3243 Skytel r:0.343 p:0.000 df:114	234 Barbara r:0.338 p:0.000 df:114
suprailiac< >waist / pelvic hips< >waist		192	0.317	0.370	0.451	0.521	0.595	0.749	1.074	11245 Hansderijk r:-0.195 p:0.010 df:173	4454 Kumiko r:0.318 p:0.000 df:173	4016 Sambre r:0.282 p:0.000 df:173
suprailiac< >waist / shoulder width< >subneck dorsal		89	0.163	0.328	0.693	0.945	1.331	2.224	3.464	2659 Millis r:-0.291 p:0.010 df:76	2816 Pien r:0.542 p:0.000 df:76	73 Klytia r:-0.410 p:0.000 df:76

Measure	N								Min correlation	Max correlation	
suprailiac< >waist / shoulder width< >waist	184	0.055	0.091	0.131	0.168	0.204	0.307	0.460	655 Briseis r:-0.199 p:0.010 df:165	52008 Johnnaka r:0.343 p:0.000 df:165	247 Eukrate r:-0.300 p:0.000 df:165
suprailiac< >waist / subpelvic rear width< >suprailiac	126	0.100	0.143	0.259	0.342	0.422	0.706	1.047	1835 Gajdariya r:-0.240 p:0.010 df:113	14974 Pocatky r:0.401 p:0.000 df:113	1012 Sarema r:0.326 p:0.000 df:113
suprailiac< >waist / subpelvic rear width< >waist	129	0.090	0.125	0.197	0.253	0.296	0.411	0.513	6774 Vladheinrich r:-0.236 p:0.010 df:116	64547 Saku r:0.392 p:0.000 df:116	1012 Sarema r:-0.337 p:0.000 df:116
suprailiac< >waist / underbust< >waist	170	0.159	0.283	0.405	0.579	0.893	1.720	3.586	23044 Starodub r:-0.206 p:0.010 df:153	3043 San Diego r:0.325 p:0.000 df:153	3043 San Diego r:0.325 p:0.000 df:153
thigh h / ab perimeter	144	0.036	0.085	0.193	0.231	0.296	0.491	0.737	164 Eva r:-0.225 p:0.010 df:128	702 Alauda r:0.371 p:0.000 df:128	702 Alauda r:0.371 p:0.000 df:128
thigh h / ab tone	141	0.225	0.493	0.697	0.995	1.596	6.714	23.508	30241 Donnamower r:-0.228 p:0.010 df:127	115885 Ganz r:0.384 p:0.000 df:127	504 Cora r:-0.320 p:0.000 df:127
thigh h / ab width	116	1.201	1.804	2.517	3.002	3.686	4.879	6.359	10274 Larryevans r:-0.253 p:0.010 df:101	8247 Cherylhall r:0.437 p:0.000 df:101	2021 Poincare r:-0.349 p:0.000 df:101
thigh h / ankle to heel floor h	85	3.593	3.889	5.404	5.923	6.781	8.970	13.088	3674 Erbisbuhl r:-0.295 p:0.010 df:74	11868 Kleinrichert r:0.429 p:0.000 df:74	1190 Pelagia r:0.391 p:0.000 df:74
thigh h / ankle width	133	2.325	4.062	5.041	5.640	6.256	7.305	8.396	5454 Kojiki r:-0.234 p:0.010 df:119	16022 Wissnergross r:0.332 p:0.000 df:119	1485 Isa r:-0.324 p:0.000 df:119
thigh h / areola dia	171	1.742	3.797	6.300	9.151	13.183	19.951	24.641	5958 Barrande r:-0.205 p:0.010 df:155	3700 Geowilliams r:0.345 p:0.000 df:155	1354 Botha r:-0.318 p:0.000 df:155
thigh h / back perimeter	55	0.044	0.078	0.122	0.172	0.213	0.480	0.600	7578 Georgbohm r:-0.351 p:0.010 df:51	210245 Castets r:0.545 p:0.000 df:51	776 Berberícia r:-0.478 p:0.000 df:51
thigh h / back tone	55	0.153	0.310	0.417	0.547	0.750	1.608	2.020	31471 Sallyalbright r:-0.348 p:0.010 df:52	218692 Leesnyder r:0.529 p:0.000 df:52	1887 Virton r:0.461 p:0.000 df:52
thigh h / ball width	57	1.256	1.739	3.574	4.179	4.909	5.964	10.001	6873 Tasaka r:-0.342 p:0.010 df:54	789 Lena r:0.492 p:0.000 df:54	181 Eucharis r:-0.504 p:0.000 df:54
thigh h / bicep width	206	2.314	2.798	3.918	4.676	5.357	6.731	8.433	41 Daphne r:-0.189 p:0.010 df:184	221073 Ovruch r:0.283 p:0.000 df:184	2357 Phereclos r:0.263 p:0.000 df:184
thigh h / big toe length	51	2.479	3.297	6.297	8.782	10.375	13.877	15.762	8147 Colemanhawkins r:-0.368 p:0.010 df:46	9189 Holderlin r:0.522 p:0.000 df:46	2389 Dibaj r:-0.503 p:0.000 df:46
thigh h / big toe width	43	3.212	4.168	9.456	12.714	14.969	21.730	23.692	2523 Ryba r:-0.394 p:0.010 df:40	31671 Masatoshi r:0.585 p:0.000 df:40	1314 Paula r:0.517 p:0.000 df:40
thigh h / bra shoulder to underb	149	0.386	0.962	1.317	1.653	1.969	2.531	3.287	7051 Sean r:-0.222 p:0.010 df:132	23402 Turchina r:0.355 p:0.000 df:132	66 Maja r:0.323 p:0.000 df:132
thigh h / breast depth	134	1.593	3.300	6.709	9.353	12.326	20.999	29.182	7850 Buenos Aires r:-0.230 p:0.010 df:123	6616 Plotinos r:0.382 p:0.000 df:123	869 Mellena r:-0.318 p:0.000 df:123
thigh h / breasts apart	176	2.951	4.374	6.732	9.277	12.446	26.987	45.472	28396 Eymann r:-0.204 p:0.010 df:158	400673 Vitapolunina r:0.307 p:0.000 df:158	1362 Griqua r:0.304 p:0.000 df:158
thigh h / bust dia	194	0.822	1.748	2.492	3.040	3.744	4.801	6.305	342 Endymion r:-0.193 p:0.010 df:175	161546 Schneeweis r:0.356 p:0.000 df:175	518 Halawe r:-0.263 p:0.000 df:175
thigh h / butt square	51	0.281	0.346	0.521	0.612	0.751	1.006	1.160	25693 Ishitani r:-0.373 p:0.010 df:45	5772 Johnlambert r:0.537 p:0.000 df:45	5772 Johnlambert r:0.537 p:0.000 df:45
thigh h / calf width	154	1.885	2.361	2.982	3.393	3.754	4.296	4.577	5381 Sekhmet r:-0.216 p:0.010 df:140	10399 Nishiharima r:0.303 p:0.000 df:140	662 Newtonia r:0.299 p:0.000 df:140
thigh h / chest width	165	0.427	0.894	1.212	1.472	1.677	1.952	2.907	10471 Marciniak r:-0.211 p:0.010 df:147	129177 Jeanneeha r:0.339 p:0.000 df:147	395 Delia r:-0.312 p:0.000 df:147
thigh h / clavicle to groin h	120	0.531	0.609	0.729	0.806	0.900	1.215	1.979	514 Armida r:-0.249 p:0.010 df:104	53237 Simonson r:0.411 p:0.000 df:104	5951 Alicemonet r:0.389 p:0.000 df:104
thigh h / clavicle to neck h	114	2.599	3.336	4.723	5.495	6.673	8.579	10.227	16524 Hausmann r:-0.255 p:0.010 df:99	32614 Hacegarcia r:0.422 p:0.000 df:99	617 Patroclus r:-0.348 p:0.000 df:99
thigh h / elbow to wrist h	191	0.912	1.272	1.611	1.815	2.016	2.476	3.519	1254 Erfordia r:-0.195 p:0.010 df:172	8609 Shuvalov r:0.285 p:0.000 df:172	2010 Chebyshev r:0.265 p:0.000 df:172
thigh h / foot base h	90	0.713	1.353	1.899	2.200	2.503	2.909	3.515	711 Marmulla r:-0.285 p:0.010 df:79	7446 Hadrianus r:0.456 p:0.000 df:79	632 Pyrrha r:0.398 p:0.000 df:79
thigh h / heel width	56	2.020	2.879	5.343	6.245	7.013	9.071	13.303	17823 Bartels r:-0.345 p:0.010 df:53	184011 Andypuckett r:0.515 p:0.000 df:53	789 Lena r:0.455 p:0.000 df:53
thigh h / long finger length	88	1.281	1.596	2.092	2.287	2.494	2.952	3.305	395 Delia r:-0.280 p:0.010 df:82	17883 Scobuchanan r:0.391 p:0.000 df:82	433 Eros r:-0.402 p:0.000 df:82
thigh h / lower forearm w	205	1.966	4.879	6.334	7.599	8.503	10.735	13.072	1845 Helewalda r:-0.189 p:0.010 df:184	3283 Skorina r:0.272 p:0.000 df:184	2021 Poincare r:-0.267 p:0.000 df:184
thigh h / lower leg h	134	0.688	0.806	1.051	1.128	1.188	1.342	1.601	331 Etheridgea r:-0.232 p:0.010 df:120	8533 Oohira r:0.314 p:0.000 df:120	2384 Schulhof r:-0.332 p:0.000 df:120
thigh h / neck width	143	2.397	2.740	3.579	4.127	4.683	5.913	7.213	2855 Bastian r:-0.226 p:0.010 df:128	9999 Wiles r:0.357 p:0.000 df:128	5494 Johanmohr r:-0.320 p:0.000 df:128
thigh h / nipple dia	165	6.862	16.858	26.050	34.144	41.680	56.947	81.887	2438 Oleshko r:-0.209 p:0.010 df:150	4387 Tanaka r:0.330 p:0.000 df:150	4172 Rochefort r:0.304 p:0.000 df:150
thigh h / nipple to bottom	152	2.628	4.377	5.934	7.191	8.596	12.313	27.696	18824 Graves r:-0.217 p:0.010 df:138	17031 Piethut r:0.312 p:0.000 df:138	6189 Volk r:-0.321 p:0.000 df:138
thigh h / nipple to top	153	0.573	1.730	2.937	3.615	4.724	6.706	7.961	193736 Henrythroop r:-0.217 p:0.010 df:138	28818 Kellyryan r:0.336 p:0.000 df:138	322 Phaeo r:0.296 p:0.000 df:138
thigh h / pelvic hips	143	0.349	0.866	1.229	1.465	1.645	2.037	2.512	467 Laura r:-0.227 p:0.010 df:126	27387 Chhabra r:0.318 p:0.000 df:126	6496 Kazuko r:-0.314 p:0.000 df:126

thigh h / pinky toe length	37	4.649	5.000	11.324	13.358	18.625	23.673	30.308	4313 Bouchet r:-0.419 p:0.010 df:35	2872 Gentelec r:0.594 p:0.000 df:35	181 Eucharis r:-0.605 p:0.000 df:35
thigh h / second toe length	39	2.951	3.495	7.516	9.958	11.972	15.633	15.666	10296 Rominadisisto r:-0.408 p:0.010 df:37	2872 Gentelec r:0.594 p:0.000 df:37	196 Philomela r:-0.536 p:0.000 df:37
thigh h / shoulder to elbow h	202	0.568	1.131	1.389	1.542	1.765	2.082	3.281	1741 Giclas r:-0.190 p:0.010 df:183	27052 Katebush r:0.306 p:0.000 df:183	354 Eleonora r:-0.286 p:0.000 df:183
thigh h / shoulder width	196	0.456	0.866	1.156	1.310	1.450	1.808	2.485	6104 Takao r:-0.191 p:0.010 df:179	363 Padua r:0.294 p:0.000 df:179	363 Padua r:0.294 p:0.000 df:179
thigh h / subchest width	86	0.435	1.034	1.329	1.543	1.820	2.174	2.679	342 Endymion r:-0.292 p:0.010 df:75	5799 Brewington r:0.467 p:0.000 df:75	2021 Poincare r:-0.458 p:0.000 df:75
thigh h / subneck dorsal	82	1.533	1.881	2.581	3.108	3.524	4.282	5.059	12013 Sibatahosimi r:-0.302 p:0.010 df:70	4349 Tiburcio r:0.464 p:0.000 df:70	819 Barnardiana r:0.408 p:0.000 df:70
thigh h / subpelvic rear width	104	0.316	0.709	1.028	1.203	1.365	1.565	2.904	3617 Eicher r:-0.265 p:0.010 df:92	19521 Chaos r:0.377 p:0.000 df:92	2548 Leloir r:-0.353 p:0.000 df:92
thigh h / suprailiac	157	0.367	0.976	1.380	1.583	1.806	2.168	3.016	658 Asteria r:-0.217 p:0.010 df:139	21367 Edwardpleva r:0.296 p:0.000 df:139	1440 Rostia r:-0.300 p:0.000 df:139
thigh h / underbust	134	0.354	1.060	1.503	1.697	1.903	2.292	3.421	26459 Shinsubin r:-0.234 p:0.010 df:118	13764 Mcalanis r:0.342 p:0.000 df:118	606 Brangane r:-0.322 p:0.000 df:118
thigh h / upper forearm w	208	1.053	3.157	4.269	5.065	5.739	6.736	12.470	18399 Tentoumushi r:-0.187 p:0.010 df:188	221073 Ovruch r:0.341 p:0.000 df:188	2021 Poincare r:-0.272 p:0.000 df:188
thigh h / waist	171	0.375	1.097	1.496	1.751	1.974	2.330	3.242	115 Thyra r:-0.206 p:0.010 df:154	15147 Siegfried r:0.306 p:0.000 df:154	3019 Kulin r:0.294 p:0.000 df:154
underbust / ab width	135	0.740	1.247	1.534	1.740	1.985	2.431	3.345	3738 Ots r:-0.233 p:0.010 df:119	5569 Colby r:0.427 p:0.000 df:119	401 Ottilia r:0.398 p:0.000 df:119
underbust / ankle to heel floor h	62	1.210	2.439	3.004	3.491	4.210	6.433	11.625	3770 Nizami r:-0.345 p:0.010 df:53	3371 Giacconi r:0.547 p:0.000 df:53	727 Nipponia r:-0.479 p:0.000 df:53
underbust / ankle width	85	1.108	1.955	2.944	3.442	4.001	6.246	11.947	22596 Kathwallace r:-0.292 p:0.010 df:75	13117 Pondicherry r:0.482 p:0.000 df:75	271 Penthesilea r:-0.398 p:0.000 df:75
underbust / areola dia	166	1.749	2.660	4.220	5.641	7.850	11.782	14.180	283 Emma r:-0.208 p:0.010 df:151	11020 Orwell r:0.319 p:0.000 df:151	545 Messalina r:-0.312 p:0.000 df:151
underbust / back perimeter	47	0.030	0.055	0.074	0.094	0.124	0.240	0.258	7358 Oze r:-0.381 p:0.010 df:43	120481 Johannwalter r:0.573 p:0.000 df:43	1863 Antinous r:-0.551 p:0.000 df:43
underbust / back tone	48	0.079	0.201	0.251	0.309	0.441	0.596	0.740	12629 Jandeboer r:-0.376 p:0.010 df:44	211378 Williamwarneke r:0.529 p:0.000 df:44	2952 Lilliputia r:0.527 p:0.000 df:44
underbust / ball width	37	0.792	0.848	2.124	2.467	3.132	5.301	5.659	113355 Gessler r:-0.418 p:0.010 df:35	30170 Makaylaruth r:0.602 p:0.000 df:35	666 Desdemona r:-0.590 p:0.000 df:35
underbust / big toe length	37	1.538	1.657	3.782	5.287	6.863	9.797	10.045	3552 Don Quixote r:-0.437 p:0.010 df:32	13200 Romagnani r:0.615 p:0.000 df:32	318 Magdalena r:-0.591 p:0.000 df:32
underbust / big toe width	30	1.992	2.382	5.642	7.467	10.129	14.553	16.567	2759 Idomeneus r:-0.463 p:0.010 df:28	41107 Ropakov r:0.607 p:0.000 df:28	833 Monica r:-0.611 p:0.000 df:28
underbust / bra shoulder to underb	142	0.589	0.776	0.900	1.037	1.187	1.416	1.981	8609 Shuvalov r:-0.225 p:0.010 df:128	5261 Eureka r:0.385 p:0.000 df:128	409 Aspasia r:0.317 p:0.000 df:128
underbust / breasts apart	174	1.660	2.920	4.182	5.713	7.990	18.261	36.540	1732 Heike r:-0.206 p:0.010 df:155	21238 Panarea r:0.277 p:0.000 df:155	21238 Panarea r:0.277 p:0.000 df:155
underbust / bust dia	183	0.686	1.423	1.706	1.867	2.137	2.689	4.115	670 Ottegebe r:-0.199 p:0.010 df:165	5261 Eureka r:0.365 p:0.000 df:165	332 Siri r:0.269 p:0.000 df:165
underbust / butt square	45	0.187	0.220	0.296	0.370	0.413	0.563	0.610	32222 Charlesvest r:-0.393 p:0.010 df:40	118194 Sabinagarroni r:0.550 p:0.000 df:40	1604 Tombaugh r:-0.519 p:0.000 df:40
underbust / calf width	91	0.551	1.359	1.790	1.994	2.293	3.277	5.398	9265 Ekman r:-0.280 p:0.010 df:82	292459 Antoniolasciac r:0.460 p:0.000 df:82	606 Brangane r:0.420 p:0.000 df:82
underbust / chest width	179	0.321	0.735	0.815	0.885	0.947	1.055	1.341	17856 Gomes r:-0.201 p:0.010 df:162	12335 Tatsukushi r:0.316 p:0.000 df:162	395 Delia r:-0.324 p:0.000 df:162
underbust / clavicle to neck h	109	1.869	2.270	2.888	3.366	4.050	5.277	13.357	744 Aguntina r:-0.262 p:0.010 df:94	4043 Perolof r:0.381 p:0.000 df:94	4006 Sandler r:0.359 p:0.000 df:94
underbust / foot base h	61	0.443	0.557	1.109	1.293	1.542	2.249	2.353	6897 Tabei r:-0.351 p:0.010 df:51	4493 Naitomitsu r:0.512 p:0.000 df:51	1552 Bessel r:0.471 p:0.000 df:51
underbust / heel width	37	1.409	1.507	3.257	3.754	4.561	5.906	6.998	19769 Dolyniuk r:-0.425 p:0.010 df:34	10747 Kothen r:0.588 p:0.000 df:34	2206 Gabrova r:-0.599 p:0.000 df:34
underbust / long finger length	69	0.686	0.961	1.174	1.300	1.489	1.883	2.241	6054 Ghiberti r:-0.318 p:0.010 df:63	21458 Susank r:0.443 p:0.000 df:63	1395 Aribeda r:0.434 p:0.000 df:63
underbust / lower leg h	81	0.284	0.487	0.575	0.661	0.744	1.429	2.070	3987 Wujek r:-0.302 p:0.009 df:71	10358 Kirchhoff r:0.451 p:0.000 df:71	4701 Milani r:0.411 p:0.000 df:71
underbust / neck width	135	1.571	1.956	2.293	2.465	2.703	3.276	3.571	21503 Beksha r:-0.233 p:0.010 df:120	897 Lysistrata r:0.387 p:0.000 df:120	897 Lysistrata r:0.387 p:0.000 df:120
underbust / nipple dia	165	9.667	13.100	16.608	20.789	25.798	31.766	53.200	1238 Predappia r:-0.209 p:0.010 df:150	4172 Rochefort r:0.333 p:0.000 df:150	545 Messalina r:-0.326 p:0.000 df:150
underbust / nipple to bottom	150	1.780	2.602	3.565	4.344	5.353	7.764	13.065	82071 Debrecen r:-0.219 p:0.009 df:138	6412 Kaifu r:0.295 p:0.000 df:138	6412 Kaifu r:0.295 p:0.000 df:138
underbust / nipple to top	150	0.952	1.259	1.783	2.166	2.669	3.595	4.949	13086 Sauerbruch r:-0.218 p:0.010 df:137	196945 Guerin r:0.341 p:0.000 df:137	636 Erika r:0.302 p:0.000 df:137
underbust / pelvic hips	164	0.604	0.717	0.812	0.859	0.921	1.034	1.321	18111 Pinet r:-0.211 p:0.010 df:146	11908 Nicaragua r:0.328 p:0.000 df:146	2952 Lilliputia r:0.303 p:0.000 df:146

underbust / second toe length	28	1.831	1.907	4.791	6.070	7.173	11.758	14.206	9649 Junfukue r:-0.479 p:0.010 df:26	5819 Lauretta r:0.698 p:0.000 df:26	357 Ninina r:-0.643 p:0.000 df:26
underbust / shoulder width	179	0.380	0.651	0.741	0.797	0.870	0.998	1.528	18509 Bellini r:-0.201 p:0.010 df:161	5261 Eureka r:0.369 p:0.000 df:161	18 Melpomene r:0.295 p:0.000 df:161
underbust / subchest width	108	0.238	0.774	0.872	0.926	0.986	1.090	1.702	8463 Naomimurdoch r:-0.257 p:0.010 df:98	18162 Denlea r:0.389 p:0.000 df:98	395 Delia r:-0.381 p:0.000 df:98
underbust / subneck dorsal	85	1.192	1.436	1.645	1.856	2.048	2.633	3.014	6828 Elbsteel r:-0.296 p:0.010 df:73	85516 Vaclik r:0.494 p:0.000 df:73	990 Yerkes r:-0.394 p:0.000 df:73
underbust / subpelvic rear width	118	0.187	0.528	0.661	0.746	0.797	0.886	1.528	2335 James r:-0.248 p:0.010 df:105	5130 Ilioneus r:0.360 p:0.000 df:105	2419 Moldavia r:0.338 p:0.000 df:105
underbust< >waist / chest width< >underbust	158	0.116	0.439	0.856	1.185	1.806	3.110	5.028	10405 Yoshiaki r:-0.214 p:0.010 df:142	3581 Alvarez r:0.316 p:0.000 df:142	1017 Jacqueline r:-0.327 p:0.000 df:142
underbust< >waist / neck width< >shoulder width	117	0.133	0.444	0.817	1.089	1.561	2.588	3.450	84926 Marywalker r:-0.253 p:0.010 df:101	10679 Chankaochang r:0.421 p:0.000 df:101	3082 Dzhalil r:0.337 p:0.000 df:101
underbust< >waist / neck width< >subneck dorsal	72	0.528	0.900	2.021	2.779	4.140	7.170	8.433	560 Delila r:-0.323 p:0.010 df:61	159999 Michaelgriffin r:0.464 p:0.000 df:61	2819 Ensor r:-0.435 p:0.000 df:61
underbust< >waist / neck width< >underbust	100	0.028	0.098	0.212	0.303	0.447	0.649	0.847	4746 Doi r:-0.274 p:0.010 df:86	10679 Chankaochang r:0.458 p:0.000 df:86	1933 Tinchen r:0.371 p:0.000 df:86
underbust< >waist / pelvic hips< >subpelvic rear width	109	0.105	0.315	0.451	0.715	1.198	2.071	3.398	1594 Danjon r:-0.258 p:0.010 df:97	25036 Elizabethof r:0.438 p:0.000 df:97	458 Hercynia r:0.415 p:0.000 df:97
underbust< >waist / pelvic hips< >waist	158	0.127	0.312	0.590	0.912	1.220	1.895	2.778	3473 Sapporo r:-0.216 p:0.010 df:140	12722 Petrarca r:0.347 p:0.000 df:140	1882 Rauma r:-0.300 p:0.000 df:140
underbust< >waist / shoulder width< >subneck dorsal	76	0.174	0.416	1.126	1.579	2.164	4.079	4.795	713 Luscinia r:-0.315 p:0.010 df:64	3082 Dzhalil r:0.464 p:0.000 df:64	3082 Dzhalil r:0.464 p:0.000 df:64
underbust< >waist / shoulder width< >waist	161	0.034	0.109	0.210	0.290	0.364	0.494	1.040	2742 Gibson r:-0.215 p:0.010 df:142	11656 Lipno r:0.381 p:0.000 df:142	138 Tolosa r:0.308 p:0.000 df:142
underbust< >waist / subpelvic rear width< >suprailiac	106	0.076	0.226	0.352	0.491	0.797	1.120	2.504	26559 Chengcheng r:-0.262 p:0.010 df:94	3495 Colchagua r:0.461 p:0.000 df:94	278 Paulina r:-0.358 p:0.000 df:94
underbust< >waist / subpelvic rear width< >waist	112	0.060	0.141	0.267	0.373	0.565	0.809	1.400	7741 Fedoseev r:-0.255 p:0.010 df:100	10679 Chankaochang r:0.388 p:0.000 df:100	560 Delila r:-0.368 p:0.000 df:100
upper forearm w / ab width	150	0.258	0.389	0.497	0.579	0.693	0.924	1.364	24680 Alleven r:-0.223 p:0.010 df:132	125473 Keisaku r:0.363 p:0.000 df:132	401 Ottilia r:0.316 p:0.000 df:132
upper forearm w / ankle to heel floor h	82	0.372	0.886	1.037	1.193	1.385	2.048	3.102	6897 Tabei r:-0.298 p:0.010 df:72	22874 Haydeephelps r:0.487 p:0.000 df:72	832 Karin r:0.440 p:0.000 df:72
upper forearm w / ankle width	127	0.414	0.743	1.015	1.160	1.348	1.729	2.064	9822 Hajdukova r:-0.238 p:0.010 df:115	34225 Fridberg r:0.405 p:0.000 df:115	313 Chaldaea r:0.333 p:0.000 df:115
upper forearm w / areola dia	204	0.637	0.857	1.352	1.789	2.303	3.090	4.828	21611 Rosoff r:-0.188 p:0.010 df:185	25014 Christinepalau r:0.312 p:0.000 df:185	7063 Johnmichell r:-0.271 p:0.000 df:185
upper forearm w / back perimeter	65	0.011	0.017	0.026	0.032	0.047	0.079	0.095	10025 Rauer r:-0.325 p:0.010 df:60	4491 Otaru r:0.475 p:0.000 df:60	776 Berbericia r:-0.435 p:0.000 df:60
upper forearm w / back tone	66	0.027	0.060	0.084	0.109	0.146	0.247	0.496	2268 Szmytowna r:-0.323 p:0.010 df:61	8474 Rettig r:0.494 p:0.000 df:61	3839 Bogaevskij r:-0.430 p:0.000 df:61
upper forearm w / ball width	55	0.319	0.379	0.726	0.904	1.073	1.570	2.145	3638 Davis r:-0.348 p:0.010 df:52	188973 Siufaiwing r:0.548 p:0.000 df:52	617 Patroclus r:-0.470 p:0.000 df:52
upper forearm w / big toe length	49	0.539	0.754	1.327	1.792	2.256	3.199	3.525	1137 Raissa r:-0.373 p:0.010 df:45	30327 Prembabu r:0.511 p:0.000 df:45	2300 Stebbins r:-0.492 p:0.000 df:45
upper forearm w / big toe width	42	0.955	1.043	2.166	2.814	3.365	4.935	5.567	6370 Malpais r:-0.398 p:0.010 df:39	620 Drakonia r:0.609 p:0.000 df:39	563 Suleika r:-0.569 p:0.000 df:39
upper forearm w / bra shoulder to underb	181	0.183	0.222	0.285	0.324	0.386	0.474	0.562	440 Theodora r:-0.199 p:0.010 df:165	2342 Lebedev r:0.353 p:0.000 df:165	750 Oskar r:0.321 p:0.000 df:165
upper forearm w / breast depth	154	0.382	0.805	1.397	1.857	2.459	3.458	7.250	6255 Kuma r:-0.216 p:0.010 df:140	120196 Kevinballou r:0.344 p:0.000 df:140	1242 Zambesia r:-0.316 p:0.000 df:140
upper forearm w / breasts apart	217	0.793	0.915	1.418	1.954	2.966	8.644	17.732	5223 McSween r:-0.184 p:0.010 df:193	6673 Degas r:0.316 p:0.000 df:193	3316 Herzberg r:0.263 p:0.000 df:193
upper forearm w / bust dia	238	0.323	0.409	0.524	0.609	0.735	0.921	1.124	410835 Neszmerak r:-0.174 p:0.010 df:216	24188 Matthewage r:0.336 p:0.000 df:216	749 Malzovia r:0.241 p:0.000 df:216
upper forearm w / butt square	61	0.066	0.082	0.109	0.123	0.148	0.198	0.322	1709 Ukraina r:-0.336 p:0.010 df:56	59828 Ossikar r:0.562 p:0.000 df:56	763 Cupido r:-0.468 p:0.000 df:56
upper forearm w / calf width	147	0.272	0.451	0.606	0.691	0.777	0.988	1.405	990 Yerkes r:-0.220 p:0.010 df:134	32090 Craigworley r:0.432 p:0.000 df:134	674 Rachele r:0.346 p:0.000 df:134
upper forearm w / chest width	215	0.138	0.203	0.253	0.286	0.320	0.397	0.515	1255 Schilowa r:-0.184 p:0.010 df:193	624 Hektor r:0.250 p:0.000 df:193	624 Hektor r:0.250 p:0.000 df:193
upper forearm w / clavicle to groin h	144	0.092	0.116	0.141	0.159	0.181	0.227	0.377	25 Phocaea r:-0.226 p:0.010 df:127	28808 Ananthnarayan r:0.437 p:0.000 df:127	18 Melpomene r:0.304 p:0.000 df:127
upper forearm w / clavicle to neck h	136	0.545	0.713	0.907	1.115	1.335	1.889	3.084	6179 Brett r:-0.233 p:0.010 df:119	23649 Tohoku r:0.357 p:0.000 df:119	1719 Jens r:0.318 p:0.000 df:119
upper forearm w / elbow to wrist h	251	0.232	0.284	0.330	0.364	0.413	0.522	0.930	1341 Edmee r:-0.170 p:0.010 df:228	5819 Lauretta r:0.289 p:0.000 df:228	287 Nephthys r:-0.255 p:0.000 df:228
upper forearm w / foot base h	87	0.165	0.284	0.379	0.441	0.526	0.644	0.804	668 Dora r:-0.289 p:0.010 df:77	6674 Cezanne r:0.489 p:0.000 df:77	320 Katharina r:-0.389 p:0.000 df:77

upper forearm w / heel width		54	0.526	0.750	1.092	1.295	1.525	2.189	2.854	308 Polyxo r:-0.352 p:0.010 df:51	5052 Nancyruth r:0.583 p:0.000 df:51	2579 Spartacus r:0.531 p:0.000 df:51
upper forearm w / long finger length		100	0.296	0.329	0.422	0.473	0.534	0.680	0.781	7038 Tokorozawa r:-0.263 p:0.010 df:93	24028 Veronicaduys r:0.432 p:0.000 df:93	1021 Flammario r:0.363 p:0.000 df:93
upper forearm w / lower forearm w		276	0.805	1.116	1.353	1.499	1.667	1.917	3.100	666 Desdemona r:-0.162 p:0.010 df:251	6057 Robbia r:0.292 p:0.000 df:251	332 Siri r:0.217 p:0.000 df:251
upper forearm w / lower leg h		123	0.087	0.162	0.197	0.220	0.249	0.349	0.429	1322 Coppernicus r:-0.242 p:0.010 df:111	9900 Llull r:0.374 p:0.000 df:111	2977 Chivilikhin r:-0.345 p:0.000 df:111
upper forearm w / neck width		177	0.479	0.610	0.718	0.814	0.908	1.098	1.379	12 Victoria r:-0.203 p:0.009 df:160	750 Oskar r:0.326 p:0.000 df:160	396 Aeolia r:0.279 p:0.000 df:160
upper forearm w / nipple dia		197	2.045	4.080	5.292	6.680	8.265	10.478	13.327	7261 Yokootakeo r:-0.191 p:0.010 df:180	5924 Teruo r:0.298 p:0.000 df:180	2448 Sholokhov r:-0.311 p:0.000 df:180
upper forearm w / nipple to bottom		186	0.624	0.833	1.163	1.417	1.785	2.736	5.464	4567 Becvar r:-0.197 p:0.010 df:169	8036 Maehara r:0.284 p:0.000 df:169	2811 Stremchovi r:0.277 p:0.000 df:169
upper forearm w / nipple to top		186	0.306	0.383	0.544	0.708	0.860	1.240	1.407	9809 Jimdarwin r:-0.197 p:0.010 df:168	6938 Soniaterk r:0.277 p:0.000 df:168	4539 Miyagino r:0.266 p:0.000 df:168
upper forearm w / pelvic hips		194	0.142	0.210	0.249	0.286	0.320	0.384	0.585	1503 Kuopio r:-0.194 p:0.010 df:174	214772 UNICEF r:0.297 p:0.000 df:174	2469 Tadjikistan r:0.261 p:0.000 df:174
upper forearm w / pinky toe length		36	1.012	1.073	2.350	3.111	3.817	7.402	8.009	19625 Ovaitt r:-0.425 p:0.010 df:34	14833 Vilenius r:0.642 p:0.000 df:34	1351 Uzbekistania r:-0.664 p:0.000 df:34
upper forearm w / second toe length		39	0.615	0.746	1.706	2.116	2.748	4.058	4.773	11094 Cuba r:-0.408 p:0.010 df:37	180141 Sperauskas r:0.653 p:0.000 df:37	830 Petropolitana r:-0.536 p:0.000 df:37
upper forearm w / shoulder width		249	0.138	0.197	0.241	0.264	0.297	0.373	0.622	3544 Borodino r:-0.170 p:0.010 df:226	19293 Dedekind r:0.276 p:0.000 df:226	2626 Belnika r:0.238 p:0.000 df:226
upper forearm w / subchest width		111	0.178	0.217	0.261	0.291	0.337	0.426	0.543	5687 Yamamotoshinobu r:-0.256 p:0.010 df:99	90022 Apache Point r:0.400 p:0.000 df:99	854 Frostia r:0.366 p:0.000 df:99
upper forearm w / subneck dorsal		109	0.405	0.440	0.531	0.608	0.706	0.906	1.088	11262 Drube r:-0.260 p:0.010 df:96	5128 Wakabayashi r:0.369 p:0.000 df:96	825 Tanina r:-0.362 p:0.000 df:96
upper forearm w / subpelvic rear width		137	0.136	0.163	0.216	0.242	0.277	0.365	0.623	1238 Predappia r:-0.230 p:0.010 df:123	9015 Coe r:0.374 p:0.000 df:123	2391 Tomita r:0.319 p:0.000 df:123
upper forearm w / suprailiac		200	0.173	0.229	0.278	0.306	0.348	0.412	0.627	11706 Rijeka r:-0.190 p:0.010 df:182	9672 Rosenbergerezek r:0.327 p:0.000 df:182	9523 Torino r:0.259 p:0.000 df:182
upper forearm w / underbust		175	0.172	0.231	0.293	0.324	0.363	0.446	0.875	16015 Snell r:-0.205 p:0.010 df:156	11280 Sakurai r:0.317 p:0.000 df:156	3036 Krat r:0.276 p:0.000 df:156
upper forearm w / waist		221	0.184	0.250	0.304	0.342	0.385	0.452	0.875	9009 Tirso r:-0.181 p:0.010 df:201	9672 Rosenbergerezek r:0.304 p:0.000 df:201	2674 Pandarus r:0.266 p:0.000 df:201
upper thigh width / ab perimeter		200	0.018	0.049	0.085	0.107	0.128	0.220	0.318	3717 Thorenia r:-0.190 p:0.010 df:182	33610 Payra r:0.336 p:0.000 df:182	1346 Gotha r:0.264 p:0.000 df:182
upper thigh width / ab tone		197	0.132	0.199	0.322	0.485	0.986	6.172	15.182	10929 Chenfangyun r:-0.191 p:0.010 df:181	72819 Brunet r:0.322 p:0.000 df:181	1098 Hakone r:0.294 p:0.000 df:181
upper thigh width / ab width		155	0.391	0.810	1.082	1.266	1.485	1.905	2.837	29528 Kaplinski r:-0.216 p:0.010 df:139	73638 Likhanov r:0.372 p:0.000 df:139	799 Gudula r:0.299 p:0.000 df:139
upper thigh width / ankle to heel floor h		88	1.735	1.891	2.275	2.571	3.003	4.228	5.116	1799 Koussevitzky r:-0.287 p:0.010 df:78	22874 Haydeephelps r:0.505 p:0.000 df:78	3371 Giacconi r:0.443 p:0.000 df:78
upper thigh width / ankle width		140	0.975	1.812	2.197	2.535	2.801	3.696	4.696	3873 Roddy r:-0.227 p:0.010 df:127	18418 Ujibe r:0.385 p:0.000 df:127	283 Emma r:0.317 p:0.000 df:127
upper thigh width / areola dia		224	0.747	1.815	2.781	3.949	5.294	7.843	10.998	25966 Akhilmathew r:-0.178 p:0.010 df:206	9492 Veltman r:0.284 p:0.000 df:206	590 Tomyris r:0.242 p:0.000 df:206
upper thigh width / back perimeter		65	0.021	0.036	0.056	0.074	0.100	0.181	0.282	7701 Zrzavy r:-0.325 p:0.010 df:60	13672 Tarski r:0.484 p:0.000 df:60	776 Berbericia r:-0.456 p:0.000 df:60
upper thigh width / back tone		65	0.064	0.137	0.191	0.239	0.321	0.757	1.118	9709 Chrisnell r:-0.322 p:0.010 df:61	218692 Leesnyder r:0.506 p:0.000 df:61	524 Fidelio r:0.442 p:0.000 df:61
upper thigh width / ball width		63	0.556	0.804	1.600	1.891	2.203	2.940	4.462	1855 Korolev r:-0.325 p:0.010 df:60	1719 Jens r:0.478 p:0.000 df:60	1162 Larissa r:0.432 p:0.000 df:60
upper thigh width / bicep width		259	0.677	1.445	1.802	2.063	2.339	2.959	4.209	2081 Sazava r:-0.167 p:0.010 df:235	4044 Erikhog r:0.261 p:0.000 df:235	25 Phocaea r:-0.227 p:0.000 df:235
upper thigh width / big toe length		57	0.574	1.430	2.806	3.633	4.457	6.276	7.857	981 Martina r:-0.348 p:0.010 df:52	109330 Clemente r:0.491 p:0.000 df:52	1996 Adams r:-0.466 p:0.000 df:52
upper thigh width / big toe width		48	0.932	1.814	4.091	5.456	6.765	9.555	10.571	14010 Jomonaomori r:-0.372 p:0.010 df:45	24679 Van Rensbergen r:0.592 p:0.000 df:45	83 Beatrix r:-0.513 p:0.000 df:45
upper thigh width / bra shoulder to underb		191	0.237	0.494	0.623	0.695	0.826	1.094	1.519	273987 Greggwade r:-0.194 p:0.010 df:174	46977 Krakow r:0.305 p:0.000 df:174	421 Zahringia r:0.266 p:0.000 df:174
upper thigh width / breast depth		164	0.795	2.011	3.078	3.984	5.294	8.220	11.526	4757 Liselotte r:-0.208 p:0.010 df:151	10984 Gispen r:0.301 p:0.000 df:151	923 Herluga r:0.293 p:0.000 df:151
upper thigh width / breasts apart		234	1.273	1.922	3.099	4.221	6.265	16.492	32.348	3970 Herran r:-0.176 p:0.010 df:212	6673 Degas r:0.255 p:0.000 df:212	1329 Eliane r:0.243 p:0.000 df:212
upper thigh width / bust dia		255	0.398	0.790	1.147	1.347	1.580	2.062	2.593	1351 Uzbekistania r:-0.168 p:0.010 df:234	30414 Pistacchi r:0.278 p:0.000 df:234	1102 Pepita r:-0.234 p:0.000 df:234
upper thigh width / butt square		66	0.143	0.183	0.251	0.277	0.304	0.407	0.520	6531 Subashiri r:-0.325 p:0.010 df:60	243262 Korkosz r:0.495 p:0.000 df:60	1096 Reunerta r:0.461 p:0.000 df:60
upper thigh width / calf width		161	0.781	1.150	1.363	1.517	1.691	1.933	2.737	9498 Westerbork r:-0.211 p:0.010 df:147	10130 Ardre r:0.424 p:0.000 df:147	606 Brangane r:0.292 p:0.000 df:147

measurement		N								min	median	max
upper thigh width / chest width		224	0.214	0.434	0.559	0.626	0.691	0.900	1.378	1808 Bellerophon r:-0.180 p:0.009 df:204	33458 Fialkow r:0.247 p:0.000 df:204	1055 Tynka r:-0.264 p:0.000 df:204
upper thigh width / clavicle to groin h		156	0.208	0.280	0.315	0.349	0.400	0.531	1.044	10366 Shozosato r:-0.216 p:0.010 df:139	11720 Horodyskyj r:0.458 p:0.000 df:139	283 Emma r:0.369 p:0.000 df:139
upper thigh width / clavicle to neck h		145	1.003	1.488	1.970	2.380	3.077	4.329	8.487	5357 Sekiguchi r:-0.226 p:0.010 df:127	8454 Micheleferrero r:0.351 p:0.000 df:127	607 Jenny r:-0.303 p:0.000 df:127
upper thigh width / elbow to wrist h		233	0.376	0.580	0.709	0.807	0.938	1.168	1.756	13367 Jiri r:-0.176 p:0.010 df:211	6547 Vasilkarazin r:0.254 p:0.000 df:211	287 Nephthys r:-0.247 p:0.000 df:211
upper thigh width / foot base h		95	0.311	0.611	0.824	0.956	1.081	1.483	1.704	20883 Gervais r:-0.276 p:0.010 df:84	9081 Hideakianno r:0.453 p:0.000 df:84	-10007 Uranus r:0.381 p:0.000 df:84
upper thigh width / heel width		63	1.066	1.340	2.275	2.773	3.184	3.961	5.936	7120 Davidgavine r:-0.326 p:0.010 df:60	10428 Wanders r:0.468 p:0.000 df:60	3190 Aposhanskij r:-0.462 p:0.000 df:60
upper thigh width / long finger length		102	0.666	0.723	0.883	1.007	1.168	1.543	1.805	5594 Jimmiller r:-0.260 p:0.010 df:95	7324 Carret r:0.378 p:0.000 df:95	7324 Carret r:0.378 p:0.000 df:95
upper thigh width / lower forearm w		267	1.031	2.227	2.939	3.300	3.702	4.609	6.389	21685 Francomallia r:-0.164 p:0.010 df:243	18887 Yiliuchen r:0.267 p:0.000 df:243	5606 Muramatsu r:0.237 p:0.000 df:243
upper thigh width / lower leg h		135	0.252	0.365	0.443	0.484	0.571	0.740	1.190	10588 Adamcrandall r:-0.232 p:0.010 df:121	13477 Utkin r:0.360 p:0.000 df:121	2650 Elinor r:0.339 p:0.000 df:121
upper thigh width / lower thigh width		230	0.574	1.117	1.269	1.393	1.538	1.857	2.204	14428 Lazaridis r:-0.177 p:0.010 df:209	10130 Ardre r:0.288 p:0.000 df:209	348 May r:-0.261 p:0.000 df:209
upper thigh width / neck width		185	0.643	1.353	1.562	1.775	2.039	2.537	3.418	358 Apollonia r:-0.198 p:0.010 df:167	2604 Marshak r:0.282 p:0.000 df:167	2604 Marshak r:0.282 p:0.000 df:167
upper thigh width / nipple dia		215	3.726	8.374	11.731	14.470	17.698	23.743	31.350	629 Bernardina r:-0.182 p:0.010 df:198	12014 Bobhawkes r:0.282 p:0.000 df:198	1314 Paula r:-0.247 p:0.000 df:198
upper thigh width / nipple to bottom		203	0.758	1.735	2.556	3.117	3.965	5.994	11.938	16650 Sakushingakuin r:-0.187 p:0.010 df:187	6412 Kaifu r:0.284 p:0.000 df:187	2484 Parenago r:0.258 p:0.000 df:187
upper thigh width / nipple to top		203	0.338	0.735	1.225	1.538	1.925	2.475	3.298	19135 Takashionaka r:-0.187 p:0.010 df:186	202736 Julietclare r:0.291 p:0.000 df:186	345 Tercidina r:-0.282 p:0.000 df:186
upper thigh width / pelvic hips		206	0.267	0.477	0.555	0.619	0.683	0.851	1.172	90820 McCann r:-0.188 p:0.010 df:185	15376 Martak r:0.312 p:0.000 df:185	1238 Predappia r:-0.264 p:0.000 df:185
upper thigh width / pinky toe length		42	2.024	2.490	4.765	5.748	8.369	12.324	13.963	11253 Mesyats r:-0.393 p:0.010 df:40	1039 Sonneberga r:0.559 p:0.000 df:40	1039 Sonneberga r:0.559 p:0.000 df:40
upper thigh width / second toe length		44	0.656	1.403	3.341	4.309	5.463	7.622	8.322	1583 Antilochus r:-0.385 p:0.010 df:42	25416 Chyanwen r:0.533 p:0.000 df:42	95 Arethusa r:0.516 p:0.000 df:42
upper thigh width / shoulder to elbow h		250	0.284	0.498	0.614	0.690	0.808	1.027	1.645	208 Lacrimosa r:-0.170 p:0.010 df:228	11720 Horodyskyj r:0.254 p:0.000 df:228	1560 Strattonia r:-0.252 p:0.000 df:228
upper thigh width / shoulder width		257	0.187	0.411	0.511	0.568	0.664	0.827	1.177	9289 Balau r:-0.167 p:0.010 df:237	11807 Wannberg r:0.262 p:0.000 df:237	1055 Tynka r:-0.233 p:0.000 df:237
upper thigh width / subchest width		112	0.328	0.519	0.609	0.667	0.760	0.959	1.149	3585 Goshirakawa r:-0.254 p:0.010 df:100	20503 Adamtazi r:0.378 p:0.000 df:100	3139 Shantou r:-0.368 p:0.000 df:100
upper thigh width / subneck dorsal		108	0.443	0.903	1.136	1.324	1.542	1.999	2.397	4754 Panthoos r:-0.260 p:0.010 df:95	2090 Mizuho r:0.433 p:0.000 df:95	56 Melete r:0.387 p:0.000 df:95
upper thigh width / subpelvic rear width		147	0.257	0.415	0.485	0.525	0.560	0.659	0.744	19370 Yukyung r:-0.222 p:0.010 df:133	20503 Adamtazi r:0.391 p:0.000 df:133	2731 Cucula r:0.306 p:0.000 df:133
upper thigh width / suprailiac		215	0.237	0.532	0.610	0.670	0.739	0.976	1.329	36037 Linenschmidt r:-0.183 p:0.010 df:195	4966 Edolsen r:0.320 p:0.000 df:195	1096 Reunerta r:0.247 p:0.000 df:195
upper thigh width / thigh h		225	0.285	0.337	0.406	0.439	0.499	0.622	0.753	2363 Cebriones r:-0.180 p:0.010 df:203	10130 Ardre r:0.336 p:0.000 df:203	283 Emma r:0.278 p:0.000 df:203
upper thigh width / underbust		187	0.256	0.539	0.653	0.717	0.804	1.069	1.480	6057 Robbia r:-0.199 p:0.009 df:168	4966 Edolsen r:0.313 p:0.000 df:168	1065 Amundsenia r:-0.271 p:0.000 df:168
upper thigh width / upper forearm w		266	0.844	1.545	1.932	2.238	2.471	2.943	4.815	8485 Satoru r:-0.164 p:0.010 df:243	7858 Bolotov r:0.274 p:0.000 df:243	515 Athalia r:0.240 p:0.000 df:243
upper thigh width / waist		236	0.218	0.581	0.679	0.739	0.821	1.044	1.536	22356 Feyerabend r:-0.174 p:0.010 df:216	4966 Edolsen r:0.245 p:0.000 df:216	4966 Edolsen r:0.245 p:0.000 df:216
waist / ab width		150	0.740	1.293	1.476	1.684	1.910	2.444	3.166	262972 Petermansfield r:-0.220 p:0.010 df:134	24911 Kojimashigemi r:0.392 p:0.000 df:134	401 Ottilia r:0.342 p:0.000 df:134
waist / ankle to heel floor h		70	1.166	2.232	2.963	3.310	4.174	5.848	11.599	221026 Jeancoester r:-0.323 p:0.010 df:61	3895 Earhart r:0.519 p:0.000 df:61	1578 Kirkwood r:-0.439 p:0.000 df:61
waist / ankle width		100	1.015	1.997	2.863	3.453	3.868	4.977	8.313	56000 Mesopotamia r:-0.267 p:0.010 df:91	12762 Nadiavittor r:0.442 p:0.000 df:91	283 Emma r:0.360 p:0.000 df:91
waist / areola dia		194	1.680	2.496	3.939	5.178	7.027	10.535	13.461	21726 Rezvanian r:-0.192 p:0.010 df:178	25014 Christinepalau r:0.284 p:0.000 df:178	545 Messalina r:-0.296 p:0.000 df:178
waist / back perimeter		58	0.029	0.054	0.074	0.091	0.123	0.220	0.250	4919 Vishnevskaya r:-0.347 p:0.009 df:53	120481 Johannwalter r:0.525 p:0.000 df:53	776 Berberica r:-0.465 p:0.000 df:53
waist / back tone		58	0.075	0.188	0.236	0.304	0.397	0.574	1.003	19298 Zhongkeda r:-0.343 p:0.010 df:54	218692 Leesnyder r:0.490 p:0.000 df:54	23 Thalia r:0.473 p:0.000 df:54
waist / ball width		48	0.782	0.927	1.990	2.400	3.032	4.614	5.342	10306 Pagnol r:-0.369 p:0.010 df:46	8439 Albellus r:0.527 p:0.000 df:46	666 Desdemona r:-0.511 p:0.000 df:46
waist / big toe length		45	1.529	1.583	3.730	5.128	6.321	8.572	9.482	15497 Lucca r:-0.393 p:0.010 df:40	13200 Romagnani r:0.579 p:0.000 df:40	318 Magdalena r:-0.539 p:0.000 df:40
waist / big toe width		37	1.991	2.425	5.868	7.382	9.377	13.279	15.638	85293 Tengzhou r:-0.418 p:0.010 df:35	17108 Patricorbett r:0.567 p:0.000 df:35	2313 Aruna r:-0.572 p:0.000 df:35

Measure	N								Col A	Col B	Col C
waist / bra shoulder to underb	173	0.372	0.721	0.861	0.958	1.096	1.321	1.941	10039 Keet Seel r:-0.203 p:0.010 df:158	8454 Micheleferrero r:0.380 p:0.000 df:158	859 Bouzareah r:0.284 p:0.000 df:158
waist / breasts apart	205	2.228	2.742	4.057	5.618	8.090	20.824	42.504	9504 Lionel r:-0.188 p:0.010 df:185	4586 Gunvor r:0.286 p:0.000 df:185	3316 Herzberg r:0.281 p:0.000 df:185
waist / bust dia	220	0.947	1.335	1.597	1.838	2.024	2.596	3.306	552 Sigelinde r:-0.181 p:0.010 df:201	8454 Micheleferrero r:0.331 p:0.000 df:201	857 Glasenappia r:0.249 p:0.000 df:201
waist / butt square	54	0.186	0.225	0.305	0.358	0.400	0.473	0.578	12360 Unilandes r:-0.354 p:0.010 df:50	59828 Ossikar r:0.613 p:0.000 df:50	1847 Stobbe r:0.488 p:0.000 df:50
waist / calf width	117	0.739	1.328	1.724	1.994	2.287	3.164	4.939	10700 Juanangelviera r:-0.246 p:0.010 df:107	75555 Wonaszek r:0.396 p:0.000 df:107	666 Desdemona r:-0.328 p:0.000 df:107
waist / chest width	208	0.228	0.679	0.783	0.843	0.919	1.018	1.194	6185 Mitsuma r:-0.186 p:0.010 df:189	65091 Saramagrin r:0.257 p:0.000 df:189	20211 Joycegates r:-0.262 p:0.000 df:189
waist / clavicle to neck h	130	1.605	2.276	2.783	3.292	4.130	5.630	12.607	2296 Kugultinov r:-0.239 p:0.010 df:114	20686 Thottumkara r:0.353 p:0.000 df:114	4934 Rhoneranger r:0.335 p:0.000 df:114
waist / foot base h	74	0.442	0.756	1.079	1.272	1.491	1.955	2.331	1649 Fabre r:-0.315 p:0.010 df:64	31635 Anandarao r:0.402 p:0.001 df:64	666 Desdemona r:-0.488 p:0.000 df:64
waist / heel width	46	1.291	1.808	3.148	3.843	4.534	6.327	6.638	5812 Jayewinkler r:-0.380 p:0.010 df:43	4253 Marker r:0.508 p:0.000 df:43	2561 Margolin r:-0.499 p:0.000 df:43
waist / long finger length	83	0.511	0.818	1.135	1.284	1.450	1.895	2.189	2600 Lumme r:-0.289 p:0.010 df:77	96200 Oschin r:0.389 p:0.000 df:77	13808 Davewilliams r:-0.388 p:0.000 df:77
waist / lower leg h	100	0.273	0.463	0.554	0.633	0.746	1.064	1.918	21507 Bhasin r:-0.267 p:0.010 df:90	13569 Oshu r:0.422 p:0.000 df:90	5539 Limporyen r:0.360 p:0.000 df:90
waist / neck width	163	1.755	1.887	2.175	2.366	2.614	3.229	3.702	4980 Magomaev r:-0.211 p:0.010 df:146	4979 Otawara r:0.323 p:0.000 df:146	471 Papagena r:0.322 p:0.000 df:146
waist / nipple dia	191	6.617	12.246	16.137	19.472	23.391	28.453	42.252	982 Franklina r:-0.194 p:0.010 df:175	5924 Teruo r:0.333 p:0.000 df:175	545 Messalina r:-0.304 p:0.000 df:175
waist / nipple to bottom	176	2.075	2.528	3.429	4.138	5.205	8.549	13.136	11583 Breuer r:-0.200 p:0.010 df:163	6412 Kaifu r:0.283 p:0.000 df:163	6412 Kaifu r:0.283 p:0.000 df:163
waist / nipple to top	174	0.553	1.212	1.710	2.079	2.491	3.228	4.209	2707 Ueferji r:-0.202 p:0.010 df:160	6762 Cyrenagoodrich r:0.307 p:0.000 df:160	947 Monterosa r:-0.344 p:0.000 df:160
waist / pelvic hips	206	0.636	0.731	0.786	0.827	0.874	0.941	1.272	1114 Lorraine r:-0.188 p:0.010 df:185	20476 Chanarich r:0.317 p:0.000 df:185	2549 Baker r:0.278 p:0.000 df:185
waist / pinky toe length	33	2.483	2.762	6.558	8.856	10.610	19.574	22.499	3123 Dunham r:-0.444 p:0.010 df:31	14833 Vilenius r:0.616 p:0.000 df:31	1351 Uzbekistania r:-0.598 p:0.000 df:31
waist / second toe length	34	1.829	1.831	4.730	5.805	6.864	12.679	13.409	1773 Rumpelstilz r:-0.437 p:0.010 df:32	14833 Vilenius r:0.658 p:0.000 df:32	114 Kassandra r:0.565 p:0.000 df:32
waist / shoulder width	223	0.381	0.627	0.700	0.753	0.848	0.993	1.255	1547 Nele r:-0.180 p:0.010 df:203	8454 Micheleferrero r:0.369 p:0.000 df:203	283 Emma r:0.255 p:0.000 df:203
waist / subchest width	111	0.169	0.727	0.830	0.895	0.972	1.099	1.365	25663 Nickmycroft r:-0.254 p:0.010 df:100	30314 Yelenam r:0.348 p:0.000 df:100	29850 Tanakagyou r:-0.353 p:0.000 df:100
waist / subneck dorsal	103	1.063	1.348	1.545	1.809	1.995	2.538	2.958	214820 Faustocoppi r:-0.267 p:0.010 df:90	128389 Dougleland r:0.394 p:0.000 df:90	1562 Gondolatsch r:-0.367 p:0.000 df:90
waist / subpelvic rear width	143	0.133	0.538	0.658	0.710	0.769	0.844	0.929	12227 Penney r:-0.224 p:0.010 df:130	8667 Fontane r:0.363 p:0.000 df:130	727 Nipponia r:-0.346 p:0.000 df:130
waist / suprailiac	219	0.748	0.813	0.872	0.904	0.943	1.010	1.166	283990 Randallrosenfeld r:-0.181 p:0.010 df:199	321453 Alexmarieann r:0.242 p:0.001 df:199	1308 Halleria r:-0.246 p:0.000 df:199
waist / underbust	189	0.711	0.843	0.914	0.961	1.011	1.105	1.451	12517 Grayzeck r:-0.197 p:0.010 df:169	18938 Zarabeth r:0.290 p:0.000 df:169	8378 Sweeney r:0.276 p:0.000 df:169

ON MY OWN BODY MEASURES

7/10/2025

Off and on over the course of the two years spent writing this book, I debated whether or not to include a fully measured outline of my body. I initially chose not to do this, but then came towards the end of the first proofread of this book. It occurred to me that I had to use A LOT of tricks to vectorize, scrape, interrogate, and 3D-model my data sources into existence, and all of this would have been easier if I had just started with 300-500 people willing to 1) provide complete q-bios, 2) provide thorough action summaries, and 3) provide consistent and reliable measurements. Coming to the end of the sample read, I thought again about how much more difficult this work was given no prior precedent to build on, and said to myself, "Ajani, if you don't set the standard for the kinds of data gathering needed by those after you, then the current lack of standards will remain so. As will our ability to study human patterns in valuable quantitative depth. I wanted to study geno- and phenotypic factors—migration patterns of cultures across biomes using a combination of longitude-latitude paths, Wikipedia haplotype articles, and real-person deep bio lookups against LLM embeddings, for example—but in order to do this I would have needed a few hundred *real* people with real genetics and backstories, not AI-generated ones. Here, the various photo-to-ratio approximation methods I used throughout this work just wouldn't do.

Minus certain redacted details which would not be meaningful to you or helpful to the anonymized, I believe I have included all of the behavioral and interface details that I myself would ask for from a bleeding edge research sample. I have not, up to this point, included very many formal body metrics. Really, the research in *Contours* doesn't actually require that kind of precision. But I'll tell you something that does:

In my (as of July 2025 unpublished) books 4 and 5 of the Grand Miranda series, *Metrobots* and *Grand Miranda*, I talk about how, at some point not only is a certain class of our future-manufactured humanity granted citizenship, they can also be "grown" from semi-organic shells which follow chains of algorithms to guide their bodies into adulthood. That is, in a couple of centuries, our "robots" will be able to grow from children into adults.[47] The kinds of advancements we'll need in chemistry, biology, sociology, and psychology will have to be great, but underneath the work is the requirement that the math describing each human sample going into the analysis be very VERY good.

Saving humans as data is one thing, printing them into new bodies which approximate and perpetuate our own growth patterns is another. I believe that we really will need sharp biometrics in order to reach this territory, but you'll need an initial group of people willing to provide those biometrics in order to set the precedent for what is actually required to bring humanity onto this evolutionary path.[48]

---

[47] This may seem scary to us in the 21st century, but homo sapiens "beta" citizenship and species compatibility with us "alphas" will be a *requirement* for rebuilding our data saves into new bodies. Not to be "immortal" or anything loopy like that, but simply to allow us to transfer our experiences into aspects of the universe far beyond the constraints of our birth material. We may die, but our patterns for seeing the world may yet see again, as far as sane conception will allow.

[48] To reiterate, I'm not saying that body metrics are they key to our future forms. I'm saying that statistics and geometry using a sub-sample of humans' complete, socially-undisguised data is the only way we will ever understand and mimic our actual humanity in a way that our data reloads could literally "live with" as our networks start being put into these forms.

FIGURE 30: AJANI'S VARIOUS METRICS

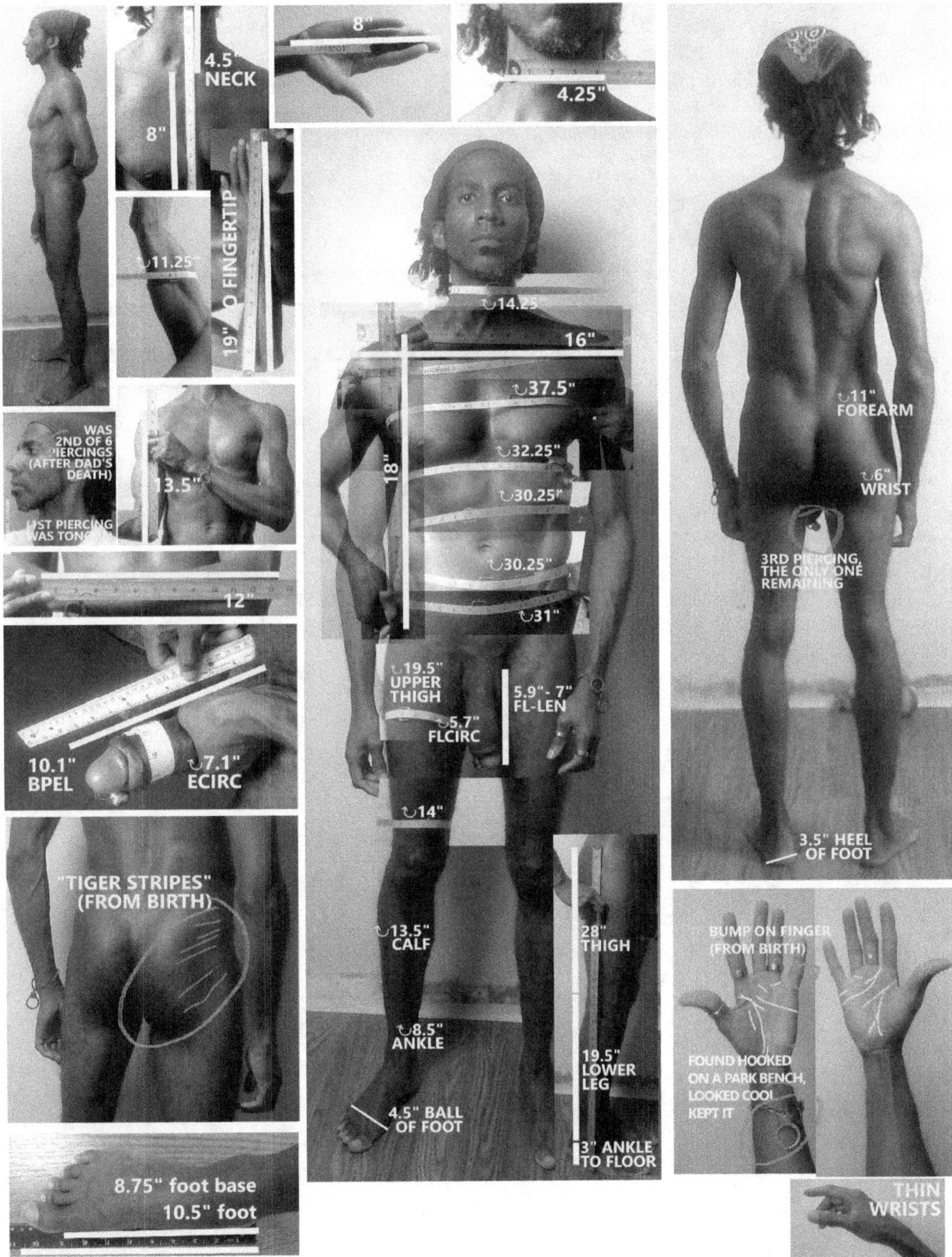

The above figure contains the male version of most of the kinds of formal measures I wish I'd had from every detailed body subject in hindsight. After constructing it, I set out on one of the biggest (and one of the most difficult) tasks supposedly enabled by this book: I made an attempt to explain my basic appearance in terms of qunits and duodecanates—as if I were purely energy with no human processing available. It took about 5 hours to do, but much to my delight, it only required 8-10 regions. That's the good news. The bad news is, this process is so complicated, so person-dependent, and relies on enough areas of sheer speculation from Chapter 23: Assorted notes and speculations I made while working on this book that I would have a hard time explaining it to you. Instead, all I can give you is an outline of what's involved:

FIGURE 31: CALCULATIONS REGARDING A WHOLE BODY LOOK

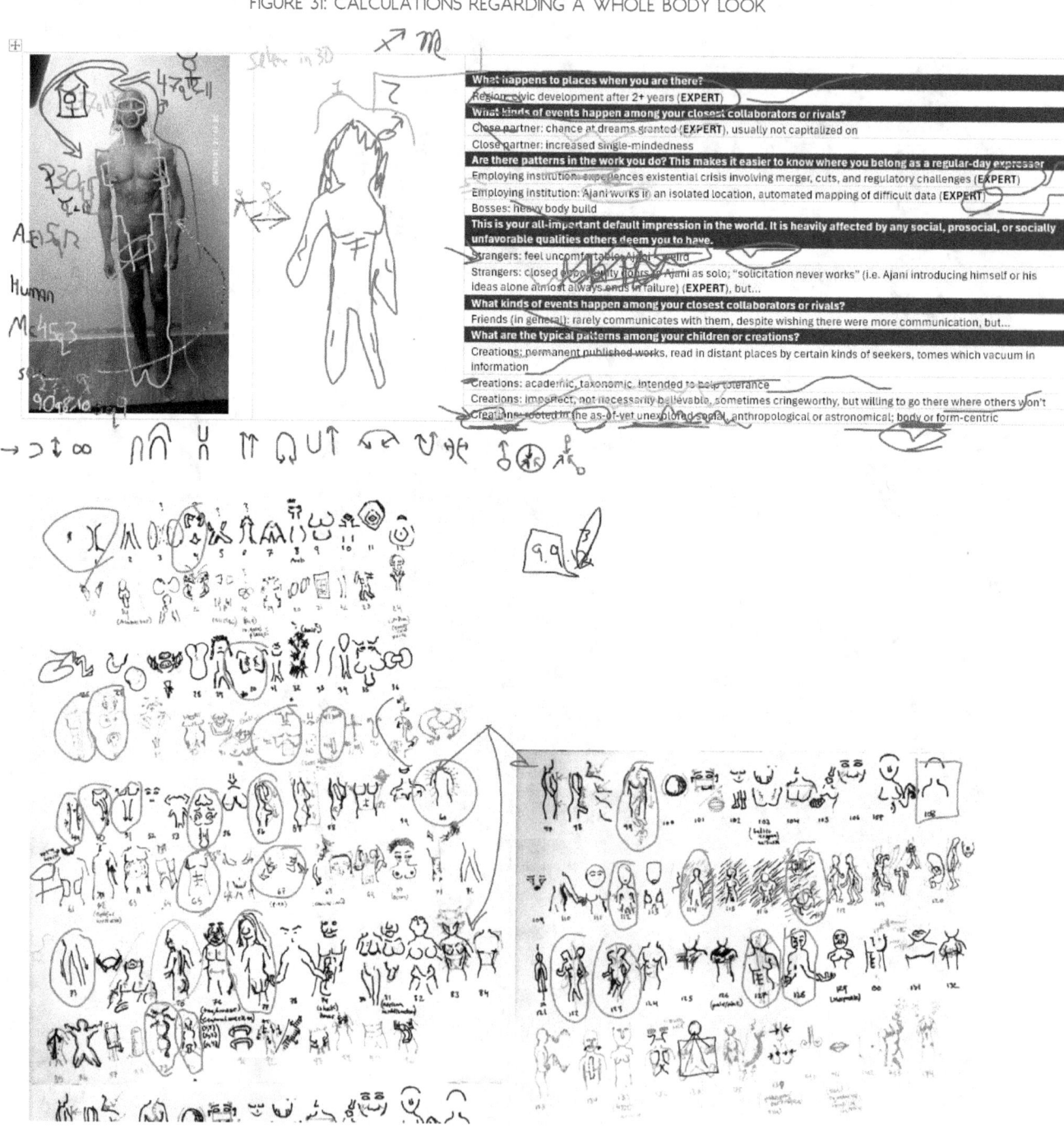

Despite the complexity there, here's the first of two punchlines:

In order of most important to less so, my appearance is governed by

1. 47q12, 47q11 – Mercury is THE BOSS of my chart. Its nearby qunits govern my general vibe, and—given the kinds of asteroids dialed up by my parents' setup here—the fact that I was more likely to be male.

2. 77q12, 77q11 – Virgo, the sign "ruled by" Mercury, feeds a whole body shape into Mercury's operation. These govern my body shape.

3. 30q4 – The 30th duodecanate, and also the home of my Selene <blessed talent> is (coincidentally?) the number of duodecanates that separates Mercury from the qunit it draws from. This region's interpretations push my chest out, and describe much of my black ethnicity.

4. 15q12 – Near my Ascendant, strongly colors the effect of my approaching anyone and anything. Much of this is negative, but this region's asteroid interpretations look suspiciously like an interpretation of my body's vascularity / muscle tone.

5. 42q11, 42q10, and their respective qcrosses – seem to be human species template regions that all of us will have dialed up just by virtue of being genetically human. While d78 describes both Time and human cognitive recursion against Time, its opposition d6 was associated with dogs, the square d114 associated with domestic cats, and I suspect d42 associated with birds as co-evolvers with humans. Additionally, my resonating more with the squares to d78 here place me as more of an observer of the human condition than a direct basker in it. Opposite my d42 affinity, I interact best with cats in d114. This axis reflects the world-context of humans more than the lived social experience of humans itself. For me, it also reflects my place in the family lineage as the firstborn son.

6. 45q3 is near my Midheaven – it dawned on me at this point that duodecanates really did seem to be the correct level of granularity for this activity EXCEPT FOR the idea that, within an activity, you can shift your immediate attention to any number of methods. That is, d45 was the main influencer here, but q-fraction 3 showed the kind of attention I am strongly inclined to give best when in a d45 mode. This region governs my high, asymmetric eyes, which didn't start becoming asymmetric until I got older with an established reputation among peers.

7. qcross 109 – likely a human species factor, {27,63,99,135}q9 corresponds to 9-3-{10,7,4,1}: setting up a culture against your framing given {four types of situational initiation}. This is human cyclical storytelling atop our lived experiences and is key, KEY to the formation of a functional, properly socialized internal monologue. I found that almost every one of my core 25 deep-study nude sample subjects were described by one of these four qunits, with 27q9 being more male, 63q9 being more female, but either of these and any of the four were still swappable depending on who your notion of the boss or (social) teacher was growing up. 63q9 contains one of the single best descriptors of my body impressions upon others, 6731 Hiei, though I've found that this tends to reflect an identity projection onto me by the women in my life.

8. 90q8, 90q10... – ...and their qcrosses (228, and 218 respectively) seem to reflect my straight gender. This will be the second punchline, but I'll get to that shortly.

My q-bio on page 99 contains the specific asteroids in each section above. As I said, the whole body-to-energy investigation, though mostly enabled by this book, is harder to do than one would think. But if you're up for a challenge, here' what you'll need:

- All 21000+ of your asteroids, their locations, and interpretations
- Your interface (your version of Table 1, p 7). Go through it and highlight only the traits that are ***ALWAYS ON***. See how my Figure 31: Calculations regarding a whole body look reflects this.
- My speculated Figure 40: Early speculations on body divisions and Table 44: Written descriptions of grouped body patterns (p 678) which follows it

- If not your q-bio (Figure 7: [Self] data save part 3 of 3
  Ajani's Q-bio (with the 144 Qunit Inconjunct Groups / QIGs), p 99), then at least the duodecanate and qunit
  definitions (Figure 3: The 144 (12²) Duodecanates (In the tropical system in 2025), p 13 and Figure 4: The
  1728 (12³) Qunits, p 16)

How to proceed:

1. Given your interfaces that are always on, you can look for your absolute strongest effect in this life. Mine was social development, for better or worse. This led me to the 47s. In 47q12 I saw a cluster of interpretations that might as well have been my life story overall. Not what I'm remembered for (29q12), but what I personally know about where I've been.
2. Ask what cluster best describes your biological sex—how you see yourself as a member of that group.
3. Ask what cluster best describes your general body shape. Use my speculated Table 44: Written descriptions of grouped body patterns to help you. It was built from actual people.
4. Ask what cluster best describes each of the remaining traits that you know stand out on you. I looked for my mouth region, muscularity, my eyes and my back. Other traits tagged along in the process.
5. As I went through, I struck off any items from my ***always on*** version of the interface table to indicate that these items had already been covered.

If you ever get a chance to try translating yourself as a pure basket of impressions, I'll tell you that the exercise is very informative. "Always on" means always on. There are some behaviors and aspirations that I have which didn't show up as automatic anywhere in the investigation. There were some traits which did. It seems to me that one's universe may have a preference for what one does with his life.

In any event, this task is challenging and requires some serious deep thought about who you are and the impressions you are set up to leave on others. Good luck to you in this effort.

SEXUALITY QUESTIONS

Here is the second punchline to my discoveries above. The qcrosses featuring d42 and d90 covered 8 different signs' worth of options. So I speculated that the fixed signs (Leo, Taurus, Aquarius, and Scorpio) also needed coverage. We have a qcross that places us in time, how about a cross that places us in relationships? Fast forwarding through an additional pile of research, it seemed to me the d53, d54, d55 region of Scorpio and everything in cross to these seemed to associate with one's gender—whether they were straight, gay, neither, or something in between. Curious, I prompted stable diffusion to face swap my image into the place of a [straight or gay] [male or female]. This led to what we would have described back in the 20th century as the AI version of "gaydar," before that term (I think) became politically incorrect.

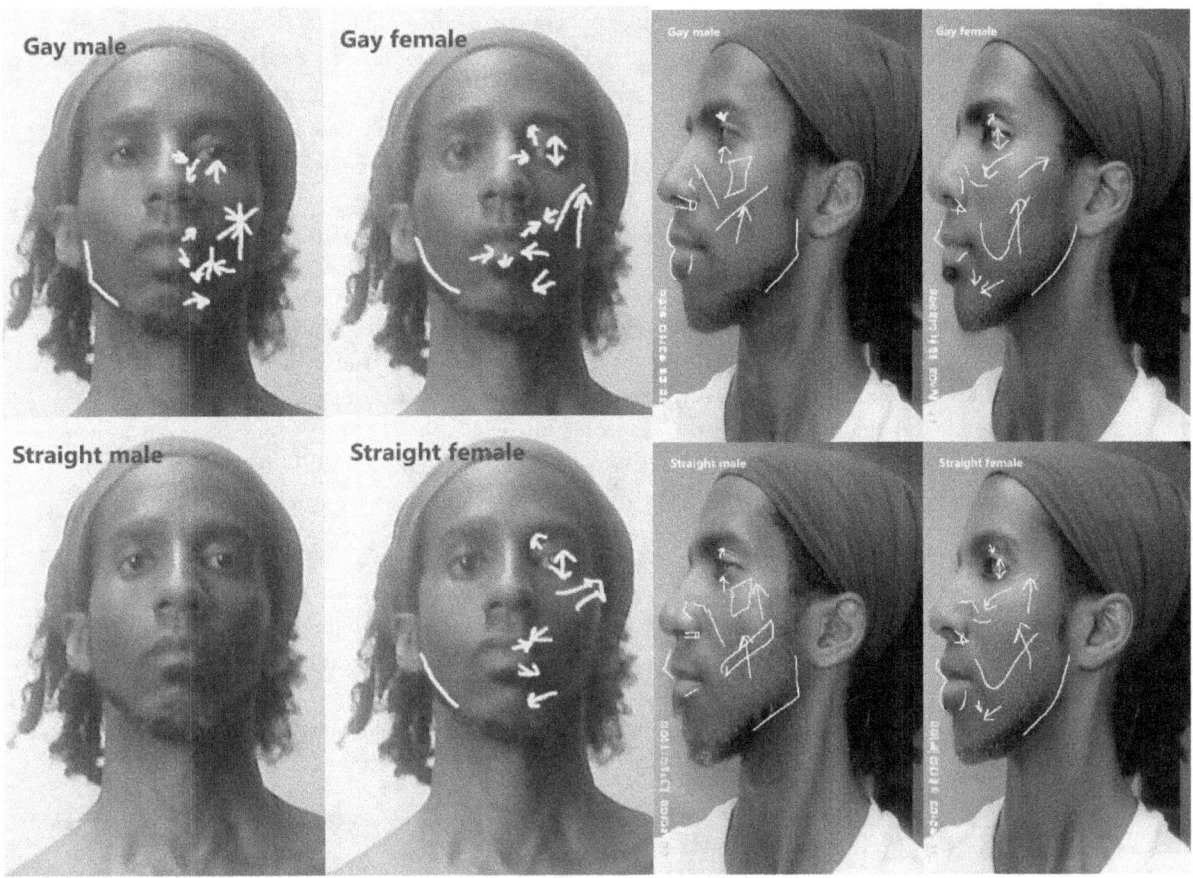

FIGURE 32: STRAIGHT AND GAY, MALE AND FEMALE RE-RENDERINGS OF AJANI

Now I found these results fascinating. I don't know how acceptable it is to argue that one's attraction preferences are tied to body chemistry, and that such body chemistry almost certainly has at least some spillover effects in external appearance, but I'll go ahead and say it. The females rendered clearly had bigger eyes, rounder faces and cheeks, rounder heads, smaller chins, angled nostrils, skinnier cheek-to-outer lip transitions, and more forward face plains compared to the flatter male face. The male-preferrers had rounder lower lips, sharper upper nostril indentations, sharper pinched (as opposed to gradual) cheek lines, narrower eyelids, and taller outer side plains. The eyebrows were also different in some ways. There were other results, but there's no need to report them because the point of this wasn't to investigate this in any scientific way at all. All I wanted was to know what to look for in a particular cluster of qunit narratives that could have gone four different ways. Armed with the above, it seemed like d18, d54, d90, and d126 were among THE best indicators of gender. Not in terms of same- or different-preferring, but in terms of whether you were attracted to male or female signals, regardless of what your biology said. Put another way, the face structure commonalities were more between males and females of either preference or male- and female-preferrers of either sex. I found less commonality between same-as-you versus different-from-you matchups. Not that we don't have an "I want-to-go-the-other way" gene, a "whatever-way-I'm-supposed-to-start-from,-i-don't-want-it" gene …but I just didn't see much evidence of that kind of body function. Whether you're straight or gay looks like a matter of plain ole' body wiring…helped or hurt by whatever factors follow you around during your young adult years.

As you know by now, my scholarship is fueled by sexual input. The questions above did, as usual, send me down a track that some people might find useful. In general (with some exceptions), men and women represent two different axes of socializable input handling. Women are typically pre-set to use feminine / domainic processing. Men are usually pre-set to use assertion delivery processing. Feminine is a space that asserts onto anything in its zone, like this: ᴐ. Masculine is a regular assertion into any zone, like this: ⇑. Pretend these concepts are square, with Feminine being Taurus-like identity labeling onto things coming in, and masculine being Leo-like character assertion onto wherever it goes. Because they are square, suppose that they must also each have complements. The feminine complement is something like an interior setup or womb which places meaning onto the incoming. So the inside of the feminine is a kind of "multimasculine" space pelting the entrant, like this: ⇆. To the extent that it serves as an internal power process for the female, the multimasculine is a decent analogy for the male-male preferring gay energy, Scorpionic and politicizable. Likewise, the masculine complement will be a space of spaces, "multifeminine," Aquarian, and cross-talkable ♏ female-female preferring gay energy. These are four basic patterns of "the assertion presented" (qc228, towards ♂ or from a ♀ context, with or without respect to another asserting situation, [pref ♂ versus pref ♀]). All four assert, the question is from-and-with whom.

(On a philosophical note, perhaps you can see why society and social advancement [Aquarian] "looks at" masculine / feminine-preferring Leo as its default social icon, while power [Scorpionic] "looks at Taurus' feminine / masculine-preferring as its default influence validator. Character will look at Aquarius' feminine / feminine-preferring individualistic resistance to the way things have been done, and Identity will look at Scorpio's masculine / masculine-preferring politicization of the self-definition as its roadmap for who one can become. That is, if you identify with any of the four main gender combinations, it may be easier for the rest of the world to promote you into the opposition's trope.)

So I love putting things into cycles of energy usage. For me, things just make more sense when their terrain is fully mapped, and the end points allowed to wrap back around to 0 when values get too extreme. Take, for example, the regular notion of gender-as-sameVhetero; this is not the same notion of gender-as-polarity1Preferspolarity2 that we looked at above. Yet the sameVhetero idea makes for an interesting cycle if you look at the "alignment" distance from the advertised heteronormative standard. I wrote a fun conversation between two characters about this in my third fiction book, *Earth*.

If we pretend that straight is the socialized standard for humans, and that (per many powers that be) everyone should be straight and happy, then we can treat preference as a cycle of energy spend against that norm. Opposite straight is full-on gay or lesbian. Moving in one common direction away from straight, we have folks who are straight but have experimented, folks who are straight but open to the same sex under certain circumstances (heteroflexible), people who split their interests 50/50 (bisexual), people who really prefer the same sex but might connect with the opposite sex under certain conditions (gayflexible), and then people who are 100% gay.

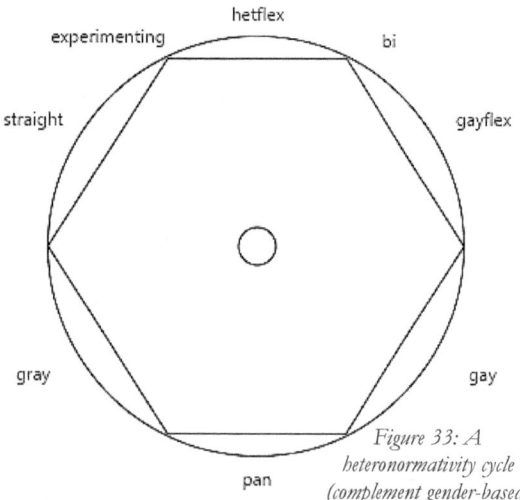

Figure 33: A heteronormativity cycle (complement gender-based)

Now going past that on this same cycle, we have another type of person who is neither 100% straight or gay.[49] Unlike the other side of the cycle, the underside of the wheel starts to lose the interest in gender notions entirely. Pansexuality, to me, is kind of like bi-minus the labels. It may not be exactly opposite hetflex, but to the extent that hetflex still has a straight-like preference it wants to keep up (on this heteronormed wheel, remember?), pan—which gives no damn about that—is farther from hetflex than it is from bi. Also, pan may include default openness to trans partners which, though possible of course, is not implied by bi. Past this, approaching straight again, you get folks who are kind of "meh" about the whole thing, grays (asexual). My assumption here is that if you identify with being gay despite the heteronorm, there is at least some aspect of you which isn't completely indifferent to that portion of identity. But for those who haven't really gone as far as identifying against the norm, been there done that, or who just aren't as enthusiastic about the opposite sex as advertised, the gray part of

---

[49] Some would argue that no one is truly 100% straight or gay, but this discussion is all about how the person defines themselves. We're not here to argue with people over a personal identity which is mostly internal.

the cycle is for you. I may claim to be straight, but given the work I do and where my sexual energy has tended to go all these years, I'm probably somewhere between straight and gray.

I mentioned transgender above, but did not represent it on the wheel. This is because the previous figure is concerned with the other person you prefer, not your own physical body. Even if one has a default preference for trans, I consider the trans person's gender to be whatever they identify as. That is (and this is only Ajani's isolated opinion), a person who transitioned from male to female and identifies as female is socially female (legal and institutional questions aside for now). And if you as a straight male like them then that doesn't have to have any implications for your internal gender preference. You're still straight. On that point (and this is also only my opinion), if you're straight and experiment with someone of the same sex, but don't consider yourself hetflex, then straight you are. Mainly because, as much as some in society might judge you and presume to label you, society really cannot get into your mind. We need this view partly as a way of avoiding forced mismatched identity onto people who have been victimized (while in prison or through psychological abuse for example). To me, you are a combination of what you say you are, and who you say it to. You can't be thoughtless, mind you. Watch out for people who will make your life difficult, but other than that, the table above is only a thought experiment to help you arrange ideas, nothing more.

Transgender is a bodily state for the person themselves, so it is interesting to think about this in terms of other bodily states. But remember, every "thing" has a context. A physical body exists in a space. A male and a female body could get together to form a "couple" as another body. Keeping this in mind, I put together yet another wheel to help me reflect on this topic.

FIGURE 34: A MATING STRUCTURE WHEEL (MASCULINE/FEMININE BODY-BASED)

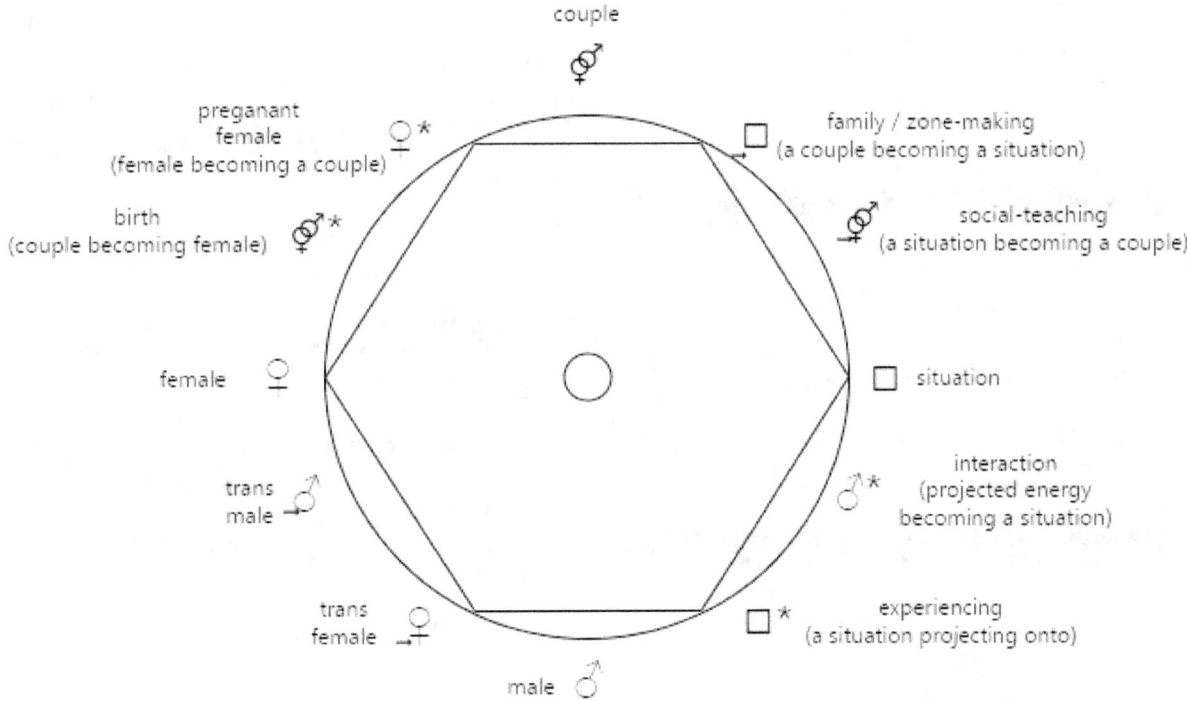

Remember, we humans begin as female, and may or may not differentiate into males.

A discussion of this wheel can get quite philosophical. Rather than travel that rabbit hole, I would ask the reader to think about the concepts shown in their most abstract forms. Consider how the biology works, where applicable. Consider how squares, inconjuncts, and sextiles are related in particular; especially remind yourself that inconjuncts put two bodies OUT OF CONTEXT from each other, so neighboring 1/12ths will render each other but a mere dream. I like this wheel because it also extends concepts like manhood, womanhood, and family to situations where the mating context does not apply, but is instead replaced by how the concepts must operate all day every day even without company.

Finally, relationships aren't just about body and preference,. They also involve themes of influence and choice. Below is an update to the sexuality profile I wrote about in *Black Male Feminism*, including some new interpersonal concepts.

TABLE 39: SEXUALITY AND INTERPERSONALITY

Biology: your material (or immaterial form in relations)		
biology	♂	male
biology	♀	female
biology	⚥	couple
biology	□	situational
biology	♂̶	transmale (f2m)
biology	♀̶	transfemale (m2f)

How many partners you need (or need to lack) to be at your happiest		
partner number	∞	tertiary (-2)
partner number	⧜	close-ex platonic (-1)
partner number	○	single (0)
partner number	⊕	mono (1)
partner number	o–o	open mono (≥1)
partner number	⊞	non-mono (>1)
partner number	♲	poly (2+)

Your partner preference		
sexuality identification	→	straight
sexuality identification	⊢	hetflex (flex)
sexuality identification	··	bisexual
sexuality identification	⇁	gayflexible (glex)
sexuality identification	←	gay
sexuality identification	↔	pansexual
sexuality identification	–	gray

How easy you are to turn on		
trigger	✦✧	not triggerable (only in another's imagination)
trigger	■	blocks by default
trigger	‖	cautious but receptive
trigger	▶	standard approachable
trigger	▶▶	receptive
trigger	❣	easily excitable

Are you better with partners higher, lower, or equal to you in power?[50]		
power imposition	⊄	at least as projective as
power imposition	⊅	no more projective than
power imposition	⊒	subjects the other to
power imposition	⊊	subject to
power imposition	⊂	can be imposed on
power imposition	⊃	can impose projection on
power imposition	⊉	accepts imposition
power imposition	⊈	imposes upon
power imposition	=	is an equal to
power imposition	≈	is basically an equal to
power imposition	≠	is power-different from
power imposition	≉	is very different from

Do you lead, follow, or act independently of your partners?		
social priority	>	succeeds
social priority	<	precedes
social priority	⧓	randomized against
social priority	⋏	comes with

Your general interpersonal approach		
interpersonal influenceability	←	from other-receptive
interpersonal influenceability	→	towards other-projective (gregarious-extraverted)
interpersonal influenceability	↑	abstract projective (arrogant-calculating)
interpersonal influenceability	↓	abstract taking-in (unassuming ingenuous)
interpersonal influenceability	↖	other receptive-to project
interpersonal influenceability	↘	projective taking-in (warm)
interpersonal influenceability	↗	dominant over another
interpersonal influenceability	↙	submissive

---

[50] This and interpersonal approach may be especially useful for people who can't get their relationships right, messing them up with destructive behaviors.

Again, this table is only a tool for reflection. As I get older and reflect on how my interests have changed, I find that the old "butts only" system of understanding my partnerships must eventually yield to the realities of adult life. Sometimes we partner for love. Other times we do it for stability, validation, power, security, insecurity, you name it. Furthermore, after you've been with someone long enough and seen the relationship cool off, it's easy to start asking questions like, "What the fuck am I still here for?" "If I leave, does that mean I have to start the whole dang thing all over?" "What am I really trying to get out of these arrangements? I mean, if it isn't ass anymore, and it isn't the kids or the money, then what is it?" Now obviously, not everybody asks these particular questions *per se,* but it helps to have some additional categories to get you thinking about what "optimum" really looks like.

Using the table above, I concluded that the following shorthand describes me best as a relationship participant:

{ ♥■∞|♋↑♂→∧(≉|≠):	an easily excitable *and* blocks-by-default, nonmonogamous or ~~tertiary~~[51] abstract-projective straight male who comes with his partner into situations in the world, is very different from or power-different from them relationally. I prefer:
▶ (♀|♀̆|♀̥|♀⃗)→>⅀	• a standard approachable (~~straight~~, hetflex, pansexual, or glex) female who succeeds their partner in the world and is no more projective than their partner. This holds either directly or by nature of their situation. (This is Shanna) AND
(✛⃛♀|□)↘↙<(≉|⊊) }	• a nontriggerable / unreachable female or situational calling, warm and submissive in company, whose nature leads the partnership's priorities; yet they are very different from and are subject to the one or both partners above. (Right now our cat Kit and my work on my books fills this role.)

The above description has much more depth than we usually put into our dating lives, and will tend to paint a less flattering picture of you as a relator—especially when you really think about the power dynamics you prefer. Although I don't need to be the boss in relationships, I am intolerant of my partner doing this as well. If there is to be a "boss," it would have to be the combination of both partners acting as a duo. In my case, despite how we relate individually, the combination of [Shanna] + [my work / Kit] circumscribe most of my priorities as a relator. Without both halves listed above in the abstract, my relationship to another has a much higher chance of failure. Shanna has a similar setup with [me] + [our dogs, friends, family / her activism] as an artist. Hence our life partnership rather than an illusion of "you are my everything" which doesn't fit either of us. That may work for some, but I imagine that many people out there are lying to themselves right now about the kinds of partnerships that best suit them. Or maybe they just haven't had the chance to think about it on the levels that they need to.

If you are still searching for the ideal partner (be they personal, professional, or otherwise), how would you describe yourself?

---

[51] ~~Tertiary~~ is a situation I easily attract, but I hate being in a tertiary position. This is another reason why, if I must be in a tertiary position, I can only stand it if the main two relators are both female. Strikethrough in general (except for the non-mono symbol) means your life attracts it, but you disprefer it unless other factors intervene. The pipe | means "or."

Chapter 21: Ethnotypes and asteroids

One thing I really wanted to accomplish in this book was to create a starting point for understanding ourselves and our gifts. I wanted to create a work which people could look at, regardless of their background and say, "Yeah, come to think of it, I do see how my race / sex / body features / general culture may have equipped me with certain particular talents." We may not view our attributes as talents when people who distrust our superclass demand we pay for fitting a "type," but hopefully most of our waking 24 hours are not spent around detractors. In the absence of others' judgment, with no one else around, we possess the neutral pre-wiring of evolution and adaptive reinforcement. Our adaptations tune our lenses to see certain things more clearly than other things, and respond to what we see in ways that enhance our stay in this life.

I often talk about being black across my books, and have done it several dozens of times in this one as well. But then again, that is the only race-type I will ever know well. While the higher social costs of being black and trying to get somewhere in Western society are well-known (even if not well-accepted or openly discussed without getting people's fur up), costs are not the only thing afforded to my type, race is not the only type I belong to, and there are costs and benefits for being classified in the various groups you belong to as well. I've had many conversations with my friends about white shaming in the global age, Latinx and (generic) Asian prejudice surges when something goes wrong (or needs to be seen as going wrong thanks to a foreign source) in the US. Women are still socio-politically shushed, while men are easily skewered for operating in ways other than the "we're all equal" framework. The many are caged by the powerful few, but the powerful few couldn't get the many to stop memeing and screaming and start learning how their own societies are actually run. Not long enough to start putting together solutions within their own communities, and not long enough to actively vote—by ballot or by dollar decision—despite their own comfort. I try to stay as far away from all of this as possible, but these are human problems that extend beyond a generation, beyond millennia into the core of what it means to be a self-storytelling animal with the power to Discovery Channel-style Wild West realities across the world simply by speaking.

4/11/2025

For everyone who does not claim the ethnic classes I claim, this chapter is for you. After a year of swearing I would not scale the mountain that was ethnic research (that is, a whole new shitload of data to collect way beyond what this book already required) I finally wised up two days ago and did the following:

1. I used a wildcards plugin from Stable Diffusion to grab a list of ethnicities. Wildcards allow you to use a kind of variable to tell the AI to pick randomly from a file, and render that as an image. This wildcard file had about 100 basic ethno categories.

2. I had Stable Diffusion "Generate forever" headshots of what ultimately ended up being about 5000 people of random ethnicity aged 8 to 70.

3. I ran all 5000 faces through mediapipe. Since the images were perfect (having been made by AI in the first place) I felt I could trust mediapipe *this* time. Points and shapes were the result.

4. While waiting the week for Step 3 and its 5000 images x 534 face metrics x 6 excel sheets' worth of data to finish processing, I asked Bing Copilot to just give me a tabular summary of factoids about each of my wildcard groups. It took a little prompt wiggling on my part, but ultimately got me the thing I needed (which would have taken months had I done it some other way).

5. I ran the results from step 4 through my own embeddings model for asteroids and their original text-mined words from the super-table that powered *Laurentia 2*. This gave me a list of the top 3 closest asteroids whose meaning matched each entry in the Copilot table. Dissimilarity scores were turned into simplified similarity scores so that I could add repeat results. This is also something that would have taken months had I done it some other way.

6. Even though "American" isn't actually an ethnicity, I added it, Algerian, Georgian, and Paraguayan just for funsies. And because I knew Copilot wouldn't care either way.

7. After a few joins and loops and other Knime tricks, I produced this table for you:

TABLE 40: SELECTED ETHNICITIES, OVERVIEW

Ethnogroup	Topic	Result	Astro factors: similarity scores 0..1
African	10 Cultural Distinctions	Diverse languages, vibrant music (e.g., Afrobeat), oral storytelling, traditional attire, community focus, spiritual practices, culinary diversity, dance forms, art styles, environmental adaptations.	344581 Albisetti: 0.576; 3321 Dasha: 0.573; 9925 Juliehoskin: 0.567
	10 Historical Highlights	Ancient civilizations (e.g., Egypt), transatlantic slave trade, independence movements, environmental activism, early mathematics, art and music innovations, oral traditions, resistance to colonization, Pan-Africanism, modern tech innovations.	75823 Csokonai: 0.543; 3520 Klopsteg: 0.543; 4196 Shuya: 0.528
	20 Key Tags	Resilient, diverse, ancestral, innovative, spiritual, communal, vibrant, artistic, adaptive, resourceful, proud, enduring, creative, dynamic, rooted, transformative, revolutionary, harmonious, inspiring, empowering.	540 Rosamunde: 0.611; 8764 Gallinago: 0.599; 9793 Torvalds: 0.599
	Historical outside contact	Colonization, slavery, systemic racism, modern independence movements, global diaspora.	20302 Kevinwang: 0.539; 25404 Shansample: 0.512; 7869 Pradun: 0.509
	Notable Achievements	Pyramids, Green Belt Movement, cultural contributions.	255989 Dengyushian: 0.525; 4696 Arpigny: 0.522; 2789 Foshan: 0.519
	Notable Cultural Facts	Rich oral traditions, immense biodiversity, cradle of humanity.	6000 United Nations: 0.581; 129068 Alexmay: 0.572; 45305 Paulscherrer: 0.559
African American	10 Cultural Distinctions	Soul food, gospel music, African-inspired art, resilience, community focus, fashion trends, linguistic creativity, sports dominance, spiritual practices, cultural pride.	3321 Dasha: 0.541; 27342 Joescanio: 0.524; 214715 Silvanofuso: 0.52
	10 Historical Highlights	Enslavement, Civil Rights Movement, Harlem Renaissance, jazz/blues/hip-hop creation, Black Power movement, sports achievements, political leadership, literature, entrepreneurship, modern activism.	27302 Jeankobis: 1.107; 16180 Rapoport: 0.508; 2323 Zverev: 0.499
	20 Key Tags	Empowered, creative, resilient, innovative, trailblazing, soulful, revolutionary, proud, enduring, dynamic, transformative, inspiring, harmonious, artistic, adaptive, spiritual, communal, vibrant, rooted, influential.	12065 Jaworski: 0.647; 1717 Arlon: 0.635; 13530 Ninnemann: 0.625
	Historical outside contact	Slavery, segregation, systemic racism, ongoing activism for equality.	7869 Pradun: 0.561; 20302 Kevinwang: 0.539
	Notable Achievements	Civil Rights leaders, cultural innovations.	31000 Rockchic: 0.551; 23792 Alyssacook: 0.517; duodecanate 41: 0.995
	Notable Cultural Facts	Jazz and blues origins, cultural resilience.	6771 Foerster: 0.508; 11679 Brucebaker: 0.489
Afro-Caribbean	10 Cultural Distinctions	Reggae music, vibrant festivals, Creole languages, spiritual practices, colorful attire, community focus, storytelling, dance forms, culinary diversity, resilience.	117715 Carlkirby: 1.067; 344581 Albisetti: 0.529; 6216 San Jose: 0.505
	10 Historical Highlights	Transatlantic slave trade, independence movements, cultural resilience, reggae and calypso creation, Rastafarianism, Creole languages, Caribbean festivals, sports achievements, culinary fusion, resistance to colonization.	20302 Kevinwang: 0.499; 161371 Bertrandou: 0.492; 25539 Roberthelm: 0.491
	20 Key Tags	Musical, spirited, resilient, dynamic, vibrant, proud, enduring, revolutionary, harmonious, artistic, adaptive, spiritual, communal, rooted, transformative, inspiring, empowering, innovative, creative, trailblazing.	744 Aguntina: 0.61; 30704 Phegeus: 0.606; 12065 Jaworski: 0.605
	Historical outside contact	Colonialism, systemic racism, cultural preservation.	7869 Pradun: 0.579; 25404 Shansample: 0.56; 24147 Stefanmuller: 0.512
	Notable Achievements	Haitian Revolution, cultural contributions.	18095 Frankblock: 0.51; 5813 Eizaburo: 0.499; 4696 Arpigny: 0.495
	Notable Cultural Facts	Reggae and Rastafarianism.	8449 Maslovets: 0.541; 3137 Horky: 0.462

Afro-Latino

Algerian

American

Afro-Latino		
10 Cultural Distinctions	Salsa music, Afro-Latinidad pride, unique cuisine, vibrant festivals, spiritual practices, storytelling, dance forms, linguistic diversity, resilience, community focus.	344581 Albisetti: 0.53; 30257 Leejanel: 0.515; 6216 San Jose: 0.513
10 Historical Highlights	Colonial history, blending African and Latino heritage, salsa music creation, cultural resilience, social advocacy, sports achievements, culinary fusion, Afro-Latinidad pride, literature, activism.	4669 Hoder: 0.521; 14360 Ipatov: 0.504; 10829 Matsuobasho: 0.502
20 Key Tags	Dynamic, blended, vibrant, proud, enduring, revolutionary, harmonious, artistic, adaptive, spiritual, communal, rooted, transformative, inspiring, empowering, innovative, creative, trailblazing, resilient, soulful.	12065 Jaworski: 0.641; 744 Aguntina: 0.639; 1717 Arlon: 0.631
Historical outside contact	Discrimination, cultural blending, advocacy for recognition.	7869 Pradun: 0.652; 18730 Wingip: 0.615; 3321 Dasha: 0.607
Notable Achievements	Contributions to arts, sports, and social advocacy.	124q3: 0.588; duodecanate qc233: 0.587; 9403 Sanduleak: 0.586
Notable Cultural Facts	Salsa music and Afro-Latinidad pride.	2805 Kalle: 0.522; 41 Daphne: 0.49; 184096 Kazlauskas: 0.484
Algerian		
10 Cultural Distinctions	Berber and Arab heritage, couscous cuisine, Islamic traditions, traditional clothing, hospitality, desert lifestyle, vibrant festivals, music (rai), historical landmarks, strong community ties	17119 Alexisrodrz: 0.456; 11519 Adler: 0.441; 2932 Kempchinsky: 0.438
10 Historical Highlights	Numidian Kingdom, Roman rule, Arab conquest, Ottoman Empire, French colonization, War of Independence (1954-1962), oil and gas industry, Berber heritage, Islamic traditions, Arab Spring protests	6672 Corot: 0.49; 3545 Gaffey: 0.473; 4387 Tanaka: 0.471
20 Key Tags	Numidian, Berber, couscous, desert, hospitality, festivals, music, resilience, history, culture, art, tradition, independence, diplomacy, landmarks, community, Arab, Islamic, preservation, values	33811 Scottobin: 0.585; 17959 Camierickson: 0.576; 2094 Magnitka: 0.572
Historical outside contact	Colonized by France; modern Algeria is a leader in African diplomacy	15353 Meucci: 0.486; 32272 Hasegawayuya: 0.465; 21433 Stekramer: 0.463
Notable Achievements	Contributions to independence movements and cultural preservation	4380 Geyer: 0.524; 124q3: 0.513; 31522 McCutchen: 0.496
Notable Cultural Facts	Known for its Berber heritage and War of Independence	4046 Swain: 0.439; 3790 Raywilson: 0.401; 7842 Ishitsuka: 0.4
American		
10 Cultural Distinctions	Individualism, multiculturalism, fast food culture, Hollywood, jazz and blues music, Thanksgiving traditions, sports enthusiasm, technological innovation, freedom of speech, entrepreneurial spirit	34141 Antonwu: 0.564; 1502 Arenda: 0.551; 3473 Sapporo: 0.546
10 Historical Highlights	Declaration of Independence (1776), Revolutionary War, Civil War, abolition of slavery, WWII contributions, Civil Rights Movement, moon landing (1969), Silicon Valley innovation, global cultural influence, diverse immigration history	11334 Rio de Janeiro: 1.152; 246504 Hualien: 0.504; 7627 Wakenokiyomaro: 0.496
20 Key Tags	Independence, Civil Rights, moon landing, Silicon Valley, Hollywood, jazz, Thanksgiving, freedom, innovation, multiculturalism, resilience, history, culture, art, tradition, entrepreneurship, diplomacy, diversity, sports, influence	2270 Yazhi: 0.62; 13251 Viot: 0.613
Historical outside contact	Historically colonized Native Americans; modern U.S. is a global leader in innovation	32272 Hasegawayuya: 0.515; 22740 Rayleigh: 0.502; 3124 Kansas: 0.499
Notable Achievements	Moon landing, Civil Rights Movement	1697 Koskenniemi: 0.403; 11314 Charcot: 0.395; 14314 Tokigawa: 0.392
Notable Cultural Facts	Known for its cultural diversity and technological advancements	20302 Kevinwang: 0.54; 177853 Lumezzane: 0.5; 17938 Tamsendrew: 0.499

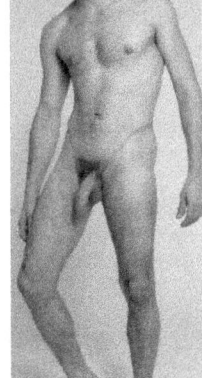

10 Cultural Distinctions	**Arabic language, hospitality, rich cuisine, calligraphy, traditional attire, storytelling, poetry, music, dance, spiritual practices.**	**14214 Hirsch: 0.535; 6573 Magnitskij: 0.535; 19638 Johngenereid: 0.509**	
10 Historical Highlights	Ancient civilizations, Islamic Golden Age, colonial struggles, modern conflicts, scientific advancements, literature, architecture, trade networks, cultural preservation, hospitality.	730 Athanasia: 0.556; 3520 Klopsteg: 0.55; 4196 Shuya: 0.546	
20 Key Tags	Unified, innovative, hospitable, spiritual, proud, enduring, revolutionary, harmonious, artistic, adaptive, communal, rooted, transformative, inspiring, empowering, creative, trailblazing, resilient, soulful, dynamic.	1717 Arlon: 0.627; 3858 Dorchester: 0.616; 6370 Malpais: 0.615	
Historical outside contact	Colonialism, modern conflicts, cultural preservation.	25404 Shansample: 0.557; 7869 Pradun: 0.552; 14223 Dolby: 0.55	
Notable Achievements	Advances in mathematics, medicine, and astronomy.	3919 Maryanning: 0.532; 262295 Jeffrich: 0.53; 2479 Sodankyla: 0.514	
Notable Cultural Facts	Arabic language and hospitality.	47q7: 0.468; 35325 Claudiaguarnieri: 0.465; 11193 Merida: 0.461	

Arab

10 Cultural Distinctions	Christianity, unique alphabet, rich traditions, traditional attire, storytelling, music, dance, culinary diversity, resilience, community focus.	14214 Hirsch: 0.6; 14571 Caralexander: 0.584; 3321 Dasha: 0.574
10 Historical Highlights	Ancient kingdom, adoption of Christianity, Armenian Genocide, diaspora, cultural resilience, unique alphabet, architectural achievements, literature, music, sports.	126901 Craigstevens: 0.552; 3124 Kansas: 0.545; 13615 Manulis: 0.532
20 Key Tags	Resilient, historic, artistic, spiritual, proud, enduring, revolutionary, harmonious, adaptive, communal, rooted, transformative, inspiring, empowering, innovative, creative, trailblazing, soulful, dynamic, ancestral.	540 Rosamunde: 0.626; 8764 Gallinago: 0.608; 1340 Yvette: 0.597
Historical outside contact	Genocide, diaspora, cultural preservation.	7869 Pradun: 0.556; 17473 Freddiemercury: 0.547; 10829 Matsuobasho: 0.519
Notable Achievements	Contributions to arts, sciences, and Christianity.	duodecanate qc14: 0.559; 22543 Ranjan: 0.549; 124q3: 0.546
Notable Cultural Facts	First nation to adopt Christianity.	246837 Bethfabinsky: 0.429; 20644 Amritdas: 0.426; 6195 Nukariya: 0.411

Armenian

10 Cultural Distinctions	Yiddish language, intellectual traditions, unique cuisine, storytelling, music, dance, spiritual practices, resilience, community focus, cultural pride.	231470 Bedding: 0.526; 25706 Cekoscielski: 0.524; 24826 Pascoli: 0.52
10 Historical Highlights	Migration from Holy Land, persecution, Holocaust, diaspora, intellectual traditions, scientific contributions, literature, music, political activism, cultural resilience.	75823 Csokonai: 0.578; 13530 Ninnemann: 0.535; 471926 Jormungandr: 0.525
20 Key Tags	Scholarly, resilient, spiritual, proud, enduring, revolutionary, harmonious, artistic, adaptive, communal, rooted, transformative, inspiring, empowering, innovative, creative, trailblazing, soulful, dynamic, ancestral.	540 Rosamunde: 0.643; 16043 Yichenzhang: 0.638; 8764 Gallinago: 0.635
Historical outside contact	Persecution, Holocaust, systemic discrimination, cultural preservation.	7869 Pradun: 0.583; 24147 Stefanmuller: 0.556; 31464 Liscinsky: 0.552
Notable Achievements	Contributions to science (e.g., Einstein), medicine (e.g., Salk), and literature.	124q3: 0.599; 4380 Geyer: 0.565; 88q7: 0.557
Notable Cultural Facts	Yiddish language and intellectual traditions.	22633 Fazio: 0.51; 7840 Hendrika: 0.501; 78124 Cicalo: 0.501

Ashkenazi Jewish

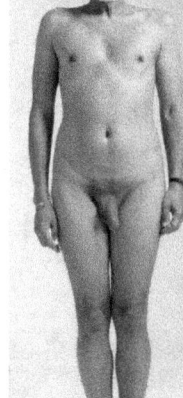

Asian

10 Cultural Distinctions	Diverse languages, traditional attire (e.g., kimono, sari), rich cuisines, martial arts, spiritual practices, festivals, art forms, family values, music, and dance.	4196 Shuya: 1.054; 110300 Abusimbel: 0.477; 13406 Sekora: 0.477
10 Historical Highlights	Ancient civilizations (e.g., China, India), Silk Road trade, Mongol Empire, colonial struggles, independence movements, technological advancements, cultural preservation, religious contributions, modern economic growth, diaspora.	75823 Csokonai: 0.545; 3520 Klopsteg: 0.542
20 Key Tags	Diverse, innovative, spiritual, artistic, communal, resilient, adaptive, harmonious, rooted, transformative, empowering, dynamic, vibrant, ancestral, proud, enduring, creative, trailblazing, inspiring, revolutionary.	20836 Marilytedja: 0.609; 12222 Perotto: 0.6; 17821 Bolsche: 0.594
Historical outside contact	Colonialism, discrimination, modern economic influence.	25404 Shansample: 0.602; 16180 Rapoport: 0.569; 3124 Kansas: 0.555
Notable Achievements	Inventions like paper and printing, modern tech innovations.	1007 Pawlowia: 0.642; 2638 Gadolin: 0.578; 71971 Lindaketcham: 0.57
Notable Cultural Facts	Contributions to technology, philosophy, and medicine.	124q3: 0.566; duodecanate qc14: 0.561; 179875 Budavari: 0.56

Basque

10 Cultural Distinctions	Unique language (Euskara), traditional sports, gastronomy, music, dance, festivals, resilience, community focus, independence movements, art.	20557 Davidkulka: 0.528; 178294 Wertheimer: 0.506; 604 Tekmessa: 0.503
10 Historical Highlights	Ancient origins, Roman interactions, medieval autonomy, maritime achievements, resistance to centralization, cultural preservation, linguistic uniqueness, industrialization, modern nationalism, diaspora.	64290 Yaushingtung: 0.565; 8496 Jandlsmith: 0.563; 10444 de Hevesy: 0.557
20 Key Tags	Resilient, historic, artistic, independent, proud, enduring, revolutionary, harmonious, adaptive, communal, rooted, transformative, inspiring, empowering, innovative, creative, trailblazing, soulful, dynamic, ancestral.	540 Rosamunde: 0.643; 8764 Gallinago: 0.62; 744 Aguntina: 0.614
Historical outside contact	Marginalization, cultural preservation, political activism.	4768 Hartley: 0.567; 43993 Mariola: 0.564; 7869 Pradun: 0.561
Notable Achievements	Maritime achievements, cultural resilience.	26450 Tanyapetach: 0.5; 266051 Hannawieser: 0.5; 10185 Gaudi: 0.498
Notable Cultural Facts	Euskara is Europe's oldest surviving language.	42924 Betlem: 0.404; 2314 Field: 0.369; 8964 Corax: 0.361

Bengali

10 Cultural Distinctions	Rabindra Sangeet, Baul music, Durga Puja, Bengali cuisine, traditional attire (e.g., saree, dhoti), literature, art, cinema, resilience, community focus.	12309 Tommygrav: 0.479; 30029 Preetikakani: 0.439; 11316 Fuchitatsuo: 0.439
10 Historical Highlights	Ancient kingdoms, Mughal rule, British colonization, Bengal Renaissance, partition of Bengal, independence of Bangladesh, literary contributions, cultural festivals, economic growth, diaspora.	10350 Spallanzani: 0.473; 6568 Serendip: 0.464; 6569 Ondaatje: 0.459
20 Key Tags	Artistic, resilient, spiritual, proud, enduring, revolutionary, harmonious, adaptive, communal, rooted, transformative, inspiring, empowering, innovative, creative, trailblazing, soulful, dynamic, ancestral, vibrant.	540 Rosamunde: 0.613; 744 Aguntina: 0.611; 19589 Kirkland: 0.608
Historical outside contact	Colonialism, partition, modern activism.	25404 Shansample: 0.628; 4669 Hoder: 0.572; 16180 Rapoport: 0.551
Notable Achievements	Nobel laureates (e.g., Rabindranath Tagore), cultural contributions.	duodecanate 41: 0.48; 3124 Kansas: 0.442; 2789 Foshan: 0.439
Notable Cultural Facts	Rich literary and artistic heritage.	177853 Lumezzane: 0.568; 32053 Demetrimaxim: 0.557; 57140 Gaddi: 0.552

Berber

10 Cultural Distinctions	Tamazight language, traditional attire, music, dance, festivals, gastronomy, tattoos, community focus, resilience, art.	214715 Silvanofuso: 0.536; 7983 Festin: 0.525; 19331 Stefanovitale: 0.517
10 Historical Highlights	Ancient origins, Roman interactions, Islamic kingdoms, Almoravid and Almohad empires, colonial struggles, cultural preservation, linguistic activism, modern autonomy movements, diaspora, resilience.	64290 Yaushingtung: 0.536; 189035 Michaelsummers: 0.535; 4387 Tanaka: 0.535
20 Key Tags	Resilient, historic, artistic, independent, proud, enduring, revolutionary, harmonious, adaptive, communal, rooted, transformative, inspiring, empowering, innovative, creative, trailblazing, soulful, dynamic, ancestral.	540 Rosamunde: 0.643; 8764 Gallinago: 0.62; 744 Aguntina: 0.614
Historical outside contact	Marginalization, cultural preservation, political activism.	4768 Hartley: 0.567; 43993 Mariola: 0.564; 7869 Pradun: 0.561
Notable Achievements	Contributions to architecture, resistance movements.	124q3: 0.539; 31522 McCutchen: 0.528; 24158 Kokubo: 0.527
Notable Cultural Facts	Indigenous to North Africa, known as "free people."	75823 Csokonai: 0.442; 149244 Kriegh: 0.442; 6092 Johnmason: 0.429

Brazilian

10 Cultural Distinctions	Samba, Carnival, capoeira, diverse cuisine, traditional attire, music, dance, art, resilience, community focus.	2932 Kempchinsky: 0.541; 19809 Nancyowen: 0.517; 3254 Bus: 0.513
10 Historical Highlights	Indigenous civilizations, Portuguese colonization, African influence, independence, abolition of slavery, cultural fusion, economic growth, Carnival, modern activism, global influence.	2771 Polzunov: 0.544; 75823 Csokonai: 0.539; 342620 Beita: 0.524
20 Key Tags	Vibrant, diverse, artistic, resilient, communal, innovative, dynamic, harmonious, rooted, transformative, empowering, creative, trailblazing, soulful, proud, enduring, revolutionary, inspiring, ancestral, adaptive.	540 Rosamunde: 0.606; 12222 Perotto: 0.604; 20836 Marilytedja: 0.602
Historical outside contact	Colonization, slavery, systemic racism, cultural blending.	20302 Kevinwang: 1.062; 8595 Dougallii: 0.518; 227767 Enkibilal: 0.515
Notable Achievements	Cultural contributions (e.g., music, sports).	22543 Ranjan: 0.562; 80q9: 0.554; 116939 Jonstewart: 0.531
Notable Cultural Facts	Known for cultural diversity and Carnival.	188139 Stanbridge: 0.497; 95q12: 0.486

British

10 Cultural Distinctions	English language, tea culture, monarchy, literature, music, art, traditional attire, festivals, resilience, community focus.	14214 Hirsch: 0.551; 6573 Magnitskij: 0.545; 4547 Massachusetts: 0.541
10 Historical Highlights	Roman conquest, Norman invasion, Industrial Revolution, colonial empire, World Wars, cultural influence, scientific advancements, literary contributions, modern democracy, global diaspora.	2771 Polzunov: 1.106; 93q12: 0.561; 3520 Klopsteg: 0.556
20 Key Tags	Historic, innovative, artistic, resilient, communal, adaptive, harmonious, rooted, transformative, empowering, creative, trailblazing, proud, enduring, revolutionary, inspiring, ancestral, dynamic, vibrant.	540 Rosamunde: 0.637; 4143 Huziak: 0.63; 12222 Perotto: 0.625
Historical outside contact	Colonialism, modern multiculturalism, global influence.	25404 Shansample: 0.568; 12802 Hagino: 0.531
Notable Achievements	Industrial Revolution, scientific discoveries (e.g., Newton, Darwin).	7256 Bonhoeffer: 0.559; 789 Lena: 0.549; 296987 Piotrflin: 0.547
Notable Cultural Facts	Known for monarchy and cultural exports.	189188 Floralien: 0.521; 23792 Alyssacook: 0.507; duodecanate 41: 0.505

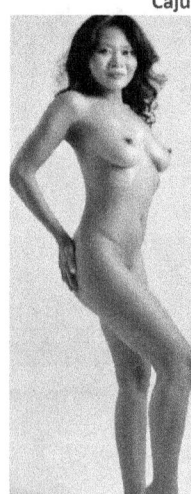

Burmese

10 Cultural Distinctions	Buddhist traditions, pagodas, traditional attire (longyi), lacquerware, diverse ethnic groups, rice-based cuisine, spiritual festivals, traditional dance, storytelling, community focus.		3887 Gerstner: 0.461; 25706 Cekoscielski: 0.453; 12447 Yatescup: 0.436
10 Historical Highlights	Ancient Pagan Kingdom, British colonization, independence in 1948, military rule, 8888 Uprising, Rohingya crisis, Buddhist influence, ethnic diversity, modern reforms, diaspora.		12414 Bure: 0.49; 13615 Manulis: 0.481; 7355 Bottke: 0.479
20 Key Tags	Resilient, spiritual, artistic, communal, adaptive, harmonious, rooted, transformative, empowering, creative, trailblazing, proud, enduring, revolutionary, inspiring, ancestral, dynamic, vibrant, innovative.		8764 Gallinago: 0.614; 540 Rosamunde: 0.596; 1340 Yvette: 0.596
Historical outside contact	Colonialism, military rule, ethnic conflicts, human rights issues.		24538 Charliexie: 0.521; 6740 Goff: 0.517; 2883 Barabashov: 0.514
Notable Achievements	Architectural marvels like Shwedagon Pagoda, contributions to Buddhism.		41 Daphne: 0.473; 4587 Rees: 0.464; 5357 Sekiguchi: 0.454
Notable Cultural Facts	Known for golden pagodas and Theravada Buddhism.		169184 Jameslee: 0.475; 22485 Unterman: 0.442; 19809 Nancyowen: 0.437

Cajun

10 Cultural Distinctions	Cajun cuisine, zydeco music, French language, Mardi Gras traditions, storytelling, family focus, spirituality, dance, resilience, unique dialects.		2932 Kempchinsky: 0.443; 20812 Shannonbabb: 0.948; 15111 Winters: 0.439
10 Historical Highlights	Expulsion from Acadia, settlement in Louisiana, cultural resilience, Creole influence, culinary innovations, music (zydeco), language preservation, community festivals, adaptation to bayou life, modern revival.		10829 Matsuobasho: 0.51; 41450 Medkeff: 0.495; 8833 Acer: 0.476
20 Key Tags	Resilient, spirited, artistic, communal, adaptive, harmonious, rooted, transformative, empowering, creative, trailblazing, proud, enduring, revolutionary, inspiring, ancestral, dynamic, vibrant, innovative.		8764 Gallinago: 0.624; 540 Rosamunde: 0.614; 10410 Yangguanghua: 0.606
Historical outside contact	Marginalization, cultural preservation, modern recognition.		7869 Pradun: 0.594; 1390 Abastumani: 0.591; 1724 Vladimir: 0.568
Notable Achievements	Contributions to American music and cuisine.		10171 Takaotengu: 0.562; 1264 Letaba: 0.526; 16022 Wissnergross: 0.519
Notable Cultural Facts	Known for vibrant music and cuisine.		107638 Wendyfreedman: 0.539; 5614 Yakovlev: 0.513

Cambodian

10 Cultural Distinctions	Khmer dance, Angkor Wat, Buddhist traditions, rice-based cuisine, traditional attire, storytelling, music, art, spiritual festivals, resilience.		14571 Caralexander: 0.511; 12447 Yatescup: 0.506; 2314 Field: 0.953
10 Historical Highlights	Khmer Empire, Angkor Wat, French colonization, independence in 1953, Khmer Rouge regime, genocide, cultural revival, Buddhist influence, diaspora, modern development.		7699 Bozek: 0.502; 10350 Spallanzani: 0.496; 55735 Magdeburg: 0.489
20 Key Tags	Resilient, spiritual, artistic, communal, adaptive, harmonious, rooted, transformative, empowering, creative, trailblazing, proud, enduring, revolutionary, inspiring, ancestral, dynamic, vibrant, innovative.		8764 Gallinago: 0.614; 540 Rosamunde: 0.596; 1340 Yvette: 0.596
Historical outside contact	Colonialism, genocide, cultural preservation, modern recovery.		25404 Shansample: 0.596; 7869 Pradun: 0.582; 3124 Kansas: 0.553
Notable Achievements	Architectural marvels like Angkor Wat, cultural resilience.		91607 Delaboudiniere: 0.492; 4587 Rees: 0.49; 41 Daphne: 0.482
Notable Cultural Facts	Known for Angkor Wat and Khmer dance.		28322 Kaeberich: 0.448; 34282 Applegate: 0.438

Canadian	10 Cultural Distinctions	Multiculturalism, bilingualism, maple syrup, hockey, Indigenous art, natural landscapes, politeness, community focus, festivals, resilience.	5379 Abehiroshi: 0.518; 7q5: 0.492; 10444 de Hevesy: 0.482
	10 Historical Highlights	Indigenous civilizations, French and British colonization, Confederation in 1867, multiculturalism, peacekeeping, economic growth, cultural exports, environmental activism, modern democracy, global influence.	3520 Klopsteg: 0.53; 4821 Bianucci: 0.518; 12802 Hagino: 0.508
	20 Key Tags	Diverse, innovative, artistic, resilient, communal, adaptive, harmonious, rooted, transformative, empowering, creative, trailblazing, proud, enduring, revolutionary, inspiring, ancestral, dynamic, vibrant.	12222 Perotto: 0.62; 20836 Marilytedja: 0.618; 12065 Jaworski: 0.614
	Historical outside contact	Colonialism, Indigenous marginalization, modern multiculturalism.	25404 Shansample: 0.54; 4669 Hoder: 0.528; 4768 Hartley: 0.515
	Notable Achievements	Peacekeeping efforts, cultural contributions.	21463 Nickerson: 0.554; 11016 Borisov: 0.544; 124q3: 0.539
	Notable Cultural Facts	Known for multiculturalism and natural beauty.	20073 Yumiko: 0.479; 15111 Winters: 0.476; 11461 Wladimirneumann: 0.46
Chinese	10 Cultural Distinctions	Calligraphy, traditional medicine, martial arts, tea culture, Confucian values, festivals, cuisine, family focus, art, resilience.	25706 Cekoscielski: 0.535; 33570 Jagruenstein: 0.532; 4005 Dyagilev: 0.518
	10 Historical Highlights	Ancient dynasties, Great Wall, Silk Road, Confucianism, invention of paper and printing, Opium Wars, Communist Revolution, economic rise, diaspora, modern tech innovations.	12013 Sibatahosimi: 0.539; 3520 Klopsteg: 0.517; 24268 Charconley: 0.516
	20 Key Tags	Diverse, innovative, spiritual, artistic, communal, resilient, adaptive, harmonious, rooted, transformative, empowering, dynamic, vibrant, ancestral, proud, enduring, creative, trailblazing, inspiring, revolutionary.	20836 Marilytedja: 0.609; 12222 Perotto: 0.6; 17821 Bolsche: 0.594
	Historical outside contact	Colonialism, discrimination, modern economic influence.	25404 Shansample: 0.602; 16180 Rapoport: 0.569; 3124 Kansas: 0.555
	Notable Achievements	Inventions like paper and printing, modern tech innovations.	1007 Pawlowia: 0.642; 2638 Gadolin: 0.578; 71971 Lindaketcham: 0.57
	Notable Cultural Facts	Known for ancient inventions and cultural heritage.	177853 Lumezzane: 0.523; 19809 Nancyowen: 0.486; 280652 Aimaku: 0.483
Colombian	10 Cultural Distinctions	Coffee culture, salsa music, vibrant festivals, diverse cuisine, traditional attire, storytelling, art, resilience, community focus, biodiversity.	25706 Cekoscielski: 0.517; 6216 San Jose: 0.512; 6608 Davidecrespi: 0.98
	10 Historical Highlights	Indigenous civilizations, Spanish colonization, independence in 1810, coffee industry, drug trade struggles, cultural resilience, biodiversity, modern peace efforts, diaspora, global influence.	24274 Alliswheeler: 0.483; 10829 Matsuobasho: 0.471
	20 Key Tags	Vibrant, diverse, artistic, resilient, communal, innovative, dynamic, harmonious, rooted, transformative, empowering, creative, trailblazing, soulful, proud, enduring, revolutionary, inspiring, ancestral, adaptive.	540 Rosamunde: 0.606; 12222 Perotto: 0.604; 20836 Marilytedja: 0.602
	Historical outside contact	Colonialism, drug trade struggles, modern peace efforts.	14223 Dolby: 0.555; 15762 Ruhmann: 0.502; 33734 Stephenlitt: 0.495
	Notable Achievements	Contributions to arts, biodiversity conservation.	79086 Gorgasali: 0.553; 124q3: 0.525; 3321 Dasha: 0.524
	Notable Cultural Facts	Known for coffee and biodiversity.	19822 Vonzielonka: 0.518; 30353 Carothers: 0.494; 17045 Markert: 0.476

Cuban	10 Cultural Distinctions	Afro-Cuban music, Santería religion, vibrant festivals, cigars, rum production, salsa dance, Cuban cuisine, revolutionary art, baseball passion, strong community ties	4107 Rufino: 1.037; 30257 Leejanel: 0.438; 3137 Horky: 0.429
	10 Historical Highlights	Taíno heritage, Spanish colonization, sugar plantations, African slave trade, Ten Years' War, independence (1902), Cuban Revolution (1959), Bay of Pigs invasion, Soviet alliance, economic embargo	18290 Sumiyoshi: 0.479; 11936 Tremolizzo: 0.44; 20850 Gaglani: 0.4
	20 Key Tags	Taíno, Santería, cigars, rum, salsa, cuisine, festivals, revolution, baseball, community, resilience, history, culture, art, tradition, heritage, independence, embargo, music, fusion	8397 Chiakitanaka: 0.536; 23383 Schedios: 0.534
	Historical outside contact	Colonized by Spain; modern Cuba faces economic challenges due to embargo	75823 Csokonai: 0.406; 21433 Stekramer: 0.403; 189188 Floralien: 0.402
	Notable Achievements	Contributions to music and revolutionary movements	16022 Wissnergross: 0.564; 13640 Ohtateruaki: 0.55; 124q3: 0.535
	Notable Cultural Facts	Known for its revolutionary spirit and Afro-Cuban cultural fusion	31853 Rahulmital: 0.468; 4587 Rees: 0.458; 11764 Benbaillaud: 0.448
Czech	10 Cultural Distinctions	Beer culture, folk music, puppetry, Gothic architecture, spa towns, Czech language, literary tradition, Christmas traditions, mushroom picking, egalitarian values	15845 Bambi: 0.526; 4547 Massachusetts: 1.152; 25706 Cekoscielski: 0.513
	10 Historical Highlights	Great Moravia, Bohemian Kingdom, Hussite Wars, Habsburg rule, Austro-Hungarian Empire, independence (1918), Nazi occupation, Velvet Revolution (1989), EU membership, UNESCO heritage sites	3473 Sapporo: 0.483; 10444 de Heve 0.482; 4572 Brage: 0.478
	20 Key Tags	Bohemia, Moravia, beer, puppetry, Gothic, spa, language, literature, Christmas, mushrooms, resilience, history, culture, art, tradition, heritage, EU, preservation, values, peace	17503 Celestechild: 0.614; 3162 Nostalgia: 0.604
	Historical outside contact	Historically occupied; modern Czech Republic is a leader in cultural preservation	7621 Sweelinck: 0.503; 129068 Alexn 0.502; 82q2: 0.499
	Notable Achievements	Velvet Revolution and contributions to literature	5813 Eizaburo: 0.484; 16192 Laird: 0.456; 1012 Sarema: 0.45
	Notable Cultural Facts	Known for its beer culture and Gothic architecture	320260 Bertout: 0.401; 17806 Adolfborn: 0.379; 367406 Buser: 0.37
Danish	10 Cultural Distinctions	Hygge lifestyle, Viking heritage, Danish pastries, cycling culture, minimalist design, wind energy, royal family, Christmas traditions, strong social welfare, egalitarian values	681 Gorgo: 0.874; 30025 Benfreed: 0.445; 2867 Steins: 0.441
	10 Historical Highlights	Viking Age, Kalmar Union, Reformation, Napoleonic Wars, WWII resistance, welfare state development, LEGO invention, renewable energy leadership, Arctic exploration, EU membership	2415 Ganesa: 0.505; 38020 Hannadan 0.499; 88961 Valpertile: 0.491
	20 Key Tags	Vikings, hygge, pastries, cycling, design, wind, royalty, Christmas, welfare, egalitarian, resilience, history, culture, art, tradition, heritage, sustainability, exploration, peace, innovation	8496 Jandlsmith: 0.585; 12353 Marqu 0.575; 25366 Maureenbobo: 0.549
	Historical outside contact	Historically neutral; modern Denmark is a leader in sustainability	7410 Kawazoe: 0.504; 1119 Euboea: 0.499; 13530 Ninnemann: 0.496
	Notable Achievements	Contributions to renewable energy and social welfare	116q11: 0.515; 26q12: 0.501; duodecanate qc51: 0.5
	Notable Cultural Facts	Known for its Viking heritage and hygge lifestyle	12659 Schlegel: 0.424; 269300 Diego: 0.403

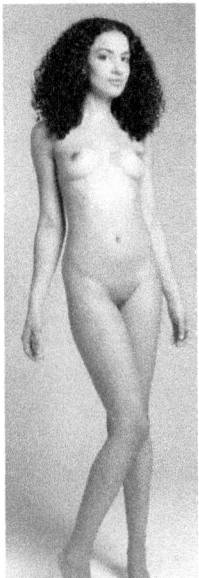

Dutch

10 Cultural Distinctions	Tulips, windmills, canals, cycling culture, Dutch language, cheese production, egalitarian values, maritime heritage, vibrant art scene, liberal policies	2070 Humason: 1.02; 12219 Grigor ev: 0.464; 518523 Bryanshumaker: 0.46
10 Historical Highlights	Roman province, Spanish rule, Dutch Revolt, Golden Age, colonial empire, WWII resistance, tulip mania, windmill innovation, EU membership, maritime trade	26620 Yihuali: 0.501; 4359 Berlage: 0.497; 86279 Brucegary: 0.487
20 Key Tags	Tulips, windmills, canals, cycling, cheese, egalitarian, maritime, art, liberal, resilience, history, culture, tradition, heritage, preservation, innovation, trade, peace, values	172318 Wangshui: 0.527; 12639 Tonkoopman: 0.527
Historical outside contact	Colonized parts of the world; modern Netherlands is a cultural hub	357116 Attivissimo: 0.458; 79q6: 0.45; 4696 Arpigny: 0.44
Notable Achievements	Contributions to art, trade, and liberal policies	duodecanate qc14: 0.458; 22543 Ranjan: 0.454; 60558 Echeclus: 0.44
Notable Cultural Facts	Known for its tulips and maritime heritage	269300 Diego: 0.416; 8373 Stephengould: 0.373; 367406 Buser: 0.372

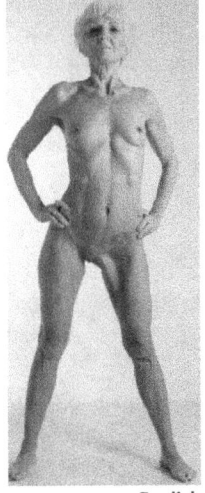

Egyptian

10 Cultural Distinctions	Ancient monuments, Nile River lifestyle, Islamic traditions, Coptic Christianity, Egyptian cuisine, traditional music, desert culture, hospitality, vibrant festivals, spiritual values	266646 Zaphod: 0.406; 3124 Kansas: 0.895; 11774 Jerne: 0.405
10 Historical Highlights	Pharaohs, pyramids, hieroglyphics, Nile River civilization, Islamic conquest, Ottoman rule, British colonization, independence (1952), Arab Spring, cultural preservation	55735 Magdeburg: 0.531; 500 Selinur: 0.497; 776 Berbericia: 1.03
20 Key Tags	Pharaohs, pyramids, Nile, hieroglyphics, Islam, Coptic, cuisine, music, desert, hospitality, resilience, history, culture, art, tradition, heritage, preservation, spirituality, festivals, values	10617 Takumi: 0.544; 12353 Marquez: 0.537
Historical outside contact	Colonized by Britain; modern Egypt is a leader in cultural preservation	10761 Lyubimets: 0.5; 32272 Hasegawayuya: 0.495
Notable Achievements	Contributions to architecture and cultural heritage	31522 McCutchen: 0.468; 80q9: 0.457; 57140 Gaddi: 0.429
Notable Cultural Facts	Known for its ancient monuments and Nile River culture	19809 Nancyowen: 0.381; 518523 Bryanshumaker: 0.355; 130q9: 0.353

English

10 Cultural Distinctions	Afternoon tea, pub culture, English language, literary tradition, royal family, football passion, countryside lifestyle, Christmas traditions, humor, strong social values	32082 Sominsky: 1.124; 3266 Bernardus: 0.53; 43751 Asam: 0.522
10 Historical Highlights	Roman conquest, Anglo-Saxon era, Norman invasion, Magna Carta, Industrial Revolution, British Empire, WWII resilience, Beatles' influence, Shakespeare's legacy, EU membership	323 Brucia: 0.541; 2509 Chukotka: 0.539; 2415 Ganesa: 0.534
20 Key Tags	Magna Carta, Shakespeare, tea, pubs, language, royalty, football, countryside, Christmas, humor, resilience, history, culture, art, tradition, heritage, preservation, values, peace, innovation	3162 Nostalgia: 0.581; 4954 Eric: 0.568
Historical outside contact	Colonized parts of the world; modern England is a cultural powerhouse	2771 Polzunov: 0.54; 4821 Bianucci: 0.52; 12802 Hagino: 0.519
Notable Achievements	Contributions to literature, music, and governance	16022 Wissnergross: 0.571; duodecanate qc72: 0.552; 31522 McCutchen: 0.53
Notable Cultural Facts	Known for its literary tradition and royal heritage	177853 Lumezzane: 0.536; 19809 Nancyowen: 0.469; 19228 Uemuraikuo: 0.469

Ethiopian

10 Cultural Distinctions	Ethiopian Orthodox Church, injera cuisine, coffee ceremonies, Amharic language, traditional music and dance, unique calendar, cultural festivals, ancient architecture, strong community ties, spiritual values	1176 Lucidor: 0.498; 6216 San Jose: 0.489; 2248 Kanda: 0.466
10 Historical Highlights	Aksumite Empire, adoption of Christianity (4th century), Battle of Adwa (1896), Italian occupation (1936-1941), Haile Selassie's reign, socialist Derge regime, Ethiopian People's Revolutionary Democratic Front victory, famine crises, Lucy fossil discovery, African Union headquarters	471926 Jormungandr: 0.541; 2415 Ganesa: 1.123; 1433 Geramtina: 0.5
20 Key Tags	Aksum, Adwa, Haile Selassie, injera, coffee, Orthodox, Amharic, Lucy, resilience, history, culture, art, tradition, heritage, diplomacy, festivals, architecture, spirituality, community, values	33826 Kevynadams: 0.618; 32613 Tseyuenman: 0.604
Historical outside contact	Never colonized (except Italian occupation); modern Ethiopia is a leader in African diplomacy	1724 Vladimir: 0.522; 32272 Hasegawayuya: 0.519; 33270 Katiecrysup: 0.516
Notable Achievements	Victory at Adwa, African Union leadership	39677 Anagaribaldi: 0.476; 9379 Dij 0.455; 9022 Drake: 0.453
Notable Cultural Facts	Known for its coffee culture and ancient Christian heritage	30353 Carothers: 0.446; 19809 Nancyowen: 0.434; 5560 Amytis: 0.4

Filipino

10 Cultural Distinctions	Filipino cuisine, bayanihan spirit, Catholic traditions, Tagalog language, traditional dances, jeepney culture, fiesta celebrations, indigenous crafts, strong family ties, karaoke passion	6569 Ondaatje: 0.859; 13235 Isiguroyuki: 1.009; 7119 Hiera: 0.42
10 Historical Highlights	Austronesian migration, Spanish colonization, Philippine Revolution, American colonization, WWII resistance, independence (1946), People Power Revolution (1986), martial law era, vibrant diaspora, cultural preservation	25404 Shansample: 0.524; 3124 Kar 0.517; 24274 Alliswheeler: 0.514
20 Key Tags	Austronesian, bayanihan, jeepney, fiesta, karaoke, Catholic, Tagalog, resilience, history, culture, art, tradition, heritage, preservation, family, dances, cuisine, crafts, values, community	9539 Prishvin: 0.582; 981 Martina: 0
Historical outside contact	Colonized by Spain and the U.S.; modern Philippines is culturally diverse	11679 Brucebaker: 0.419; 75823 Csokonai: 0.405
Notable Achievements	People Power Revolution, contributions to global diaspora	12802 Hagino: 0.474; 31522 McCutc 0.471; 147 Protogeneia: 0.457
Notable Cultural Facts	Known for its bayanihan spirit and fiesta celebrations	16075 Meglass: 0.411; 3571 Milanstefanik: 0.395; 41 Daphne: 0.3

Finnish

10 Cultural Distinctions	Sauna culture, Midsummer celebrations, unique language, reindeer herding, minimalist design, heavy metal music, egalitarian society, berry picking, ice swimming, strong coffee culture	6000 United Nations: 0.521; 28851 Londonbolsius: 0.52; 22784 Theresa 0.515
10 Historical Highlights	Kalevala epic, sauna tradition, independence from Russia (1917), Winter War resilience, Nokia innovation, happiest country ranking, forest conservation, education excellence, Sibelius music, Arctic exploration	35056 Cullers: 0.516; 13801 Kohlhas 0.503; 6647 Josse: 0.501
20 Key Tags	Sauna, Arctic, Kalevala, Sibelius, Nokia, egalitarian, reindeer, ice swimming, berries, coffee, education, forests, lakes, metal music, Midsummer, resilience, neutrality, innovation, happiness, minimalism	1118 Hanskya: 0.569; 508 Princeton 0.555; 14539 Clocke Roeland: 1.073
Historical outside contact	Historically influenced by Swedish and Russian rule; modern Finland is known for inclusivity and neutrality	1182 Ilona: 0.494; 1724 Vladimir: 0.4 164587 Taesch: 0.491
Notable Achievements	Pioneering education system, technological innovations like Nokia[_{{{CITATION{{{_1{Finland - Culture, Nature, Sámi	8870 von Zeipel: 0.528; 178267 Sarajevo: 0.524
Notable Cultural Facts	Known for their connection to nature, particularly forests and lakes	15111 Winters: 0.514; 19822 Vonzielonka: 0.493; 1404 Ajax: 0.492

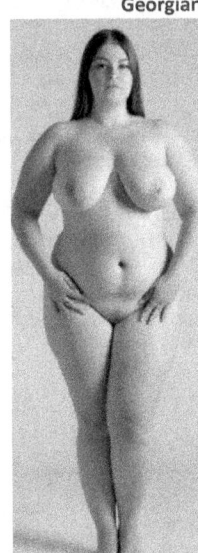

French

Category	Description	Values
10 Cultural Distinctions	Haute cuisine, fashion, wine-making, art movements, philosophical contributions, romantic language, café culture, historical landmarks, literary tradition, cinema	170022 Douglastucker: 0.497; 21449 Hemmick: 0.488; 2133 Franceswright: 0.488
10 Historical Highlights	French Revolution, Napoleonic Wars, Enlightenment thinkers, Gothic architecture, Impressionist art, colonial history, Resistance during WWII, Declaration of Rights of Man, Paris as cultural hub, culinary excellence	4696 Arpigny: 0.986; 3790 Raywilson: 0.524; 3317 Paris: 0.514
20 Key Tags	Revolution, Napoleon, Enlightenment, Gothic, Impressionism, cuisine, wine, fashion, Paris, Resistance, cinema, philosophy, landmarks, literature, café, romance, human rights, multiculturalism, art, history	11013 Kullander: 0.58; 9615 Hemerijckx: 0.579; 5017 Tenchi: 0.576
Historical outside contact	Colonial history marked by exploitation; modern France emphasizes human rights and multiculturalism	12802 Hagino: 0.478; 4669 Hoder: 0.463
Notable Achievements	Declaration of Rights of Man, artistic movements like Impressionism	5813 Eizaburo: 0.545; 27930 Nakamatsu: 0.527; 7343 Ockeghem: 0.518
Notable Cultural Facts	Renowned for its artistic and culinary traditions	177853 Lumezzane: 0.539; 12800 Oobayashiarata: 0.504; 17853 Ronaldsayer: 0.487

Georgian

Category	Description	Values
10 Cultural Distinctions	Georgian Orthodox Church, polyphonic singing, wine-making, traditional dances, khachapuri cuisine, hospitality, unique alphabet, mountain lifestyle, vibrant festivals, historical landmarks	2932 Kempchinsky: 1.024; 14214 Hirsch: 1.09; 6216 San Jose: 0.486
10 Historical Highlights	Kingdom of Colchis, adoption of Christianity (4th century), Golden Age under Queen Tamar, Mongol invasions, Russian annexation, Soviet era, independence (1991), Rose Revolution (2003), wine-making heritage, UNESCO sites	373 Melusina: 0.469; 6000 United Nations: 0.469; 5672 Libby: 0.461
20 Key Tags	Colchis, Tamar, Orthodox, wine, dances, khachapuri, alphabet, resilience, history, culture, art, tradition, preservation, festivals, landmarks, hospitality, mountain, values, independence	23798 Samagonzalez: 0.607; 264061 Vitebsk: 0.593
Historical outside contact	Historically occupied; modern Georgia is a leader in cultural preservation	10761 Lyubimets: 0.575; 1724 Vladimir: 0.527; 7869 Pradun: 0.492
Notable Achievements	Contributions to wine-making and cultural preservation	80q9: 0.466; 31492 Jennarose: 0.905
Notable Cultural Facts	Known for its wine-making and polyphonic singing	3022 Dobermann: 0.447; 344581 Albisetti: 0.444

German

Category	Description	Values
10 Cultural Distinctions	Precision engineering, beer culture, punctuality, Christmas traditions, classical music, philosophical contributions, hearty cuisine, fairy tales, environmentalism, regional dialects	25706 Cekoscielski: 0.558; 1394 Algoa: 0.551; 2983 Poltava: 0.551
10 Historical Highlights	Holy Roman Empire, Reformation, Enlightenment philosophers, Industrial Revolution, unification under Bismarck, WWII history, Berlin Wall fall, automotive industry, Oktoberfest, classical music composers	181751 Phaenops: 0.541; 4410 Kamuimintara: 0.541; 4359 Berlage: 1.134
20 Key Tags	Reformation, Enlightenment, Bismarck, Berlin Wall, Oktoberfest, composers, beer, punctuality, fairy tales, cuisine, dialects, engineering, Christmas, reconciliation, EU, history, precision, environmentalism, unification, resilience	518523 Bryanshumaker: 0.613; 7112 Ghislaine: 0.598
Historical outside contact	WWII atrocities; modern Germany is a leader in reconciliation and EU integration	13530 Ninnemann: 0.487; 24538 Charliexie: 0.474; 471926 Jormungandr: 0.472
Notable Achievements	Contributions to philosophy, music, and engineering	124q3: 0.527; duodecanate qc14: 0.526; duodecanate qc72: 0.52
Notable Cultural Facts	Known for its engineering and classical music legacy	177853 Lumezzane: 0.528; 1815 Beethoven: 0.484; 28299 Kanghaoyan: 0.479

Greek

10 Cultural Distinctions	Mediterranean cuisine, Orthodox Christianity, island culture, ancient ruins, folk dances, olive oil production, mythology, hospitality, philosophical legacy, maritime traditions	14214 Hirsch: 1.088; 177853 Lumezz 0.478; 2932 Kempchinsky: 0.469
10 Historical Highlights	Birthplace of democracy, Olympic Games, philosophical pioneers, architectural marvels, mythology, Byzantine Empire, Alexander the Great's conquests, ancient theater, mathematical advancements, naval power	48638 Trebic: 0.536; 135069 Gagner 0.513; 8399 Wakamatsu: 0.509
20 Key Tags	Democracy, Olympics, philosophy, architecture, mythology, Byzantine, Alexander, theater, mathematics, naval, cuisine, Christianity, islands, ruins, dances, olive oil, hospitality, maritime, history, tourism	191857 Illeserzsebet: 0.605; 10626 Z 0.591
Historical outside contact	Ancient conflicts with Persians and Romans; modern Greece is welcoming to tourists	29311 Lesire: 0.5; 8232 Akiramizuno 0.499; 178008 Picard: 0.495
Notable Achievements	Foundations of democracy, philosophical contributions	3662 Dezhnev: 0.554; 116166 Andremaeder: 0.496; 5326 Vittoriosacco: 0.493
Notable Cultural Facts	Rich mythology and historical ruins	10438 Ludolph: 0.499; 28451 Tylerhoward: 0.475; 25555 Ratnavar 0.469

Gujarati

10 Cultural Distinctions	Vegetarianism, colorful attire, intricate embroidery, Navratri celebrations, Jain influence, coastal traditions, entrepreneurial spirit, folk music, respect for elders, community-oriented	7036 Kentarohirata: 0.57; 28851 Londonbolsius: 1.113; 6523 Clube: 0.
10 Historical Highlights	Ancient trade routes, textile industry, Mahatma Gandhi's birthplace, Jain temples, Garba dance, vegetarian cuisine, diamond cutting, maritime trade, folk art, vibrant festivals	19822 Vonzielonka: 0.448; 2867 Stein 0.447; 981 Martina: 0.441
20 Key Tags	Gandhi, Jain, vegetarian, Garba, embroidery, Navratri, coastal, trade, textiles, diamonds, festivals, elders, community, folk music, peace, entrepreneurship, vibrant, history, art, culture	11795 Fredrikbruhn: 0.595; 1956 Art 0.573
Historical outside contact	Historically peaceful; known for trade and cultural exchange	28952 Ericepstein: 0.576; 207931 Weihai: 0.558; 25155 van Belle: 0.55
Notable Achievements	Contributions to trade and cultural heritage	duodecanate 47: 0.452; 80q9: 0.448; 4380 Geyer: 0.443
Notable Cultural Facts	Famous for its vibrant festivals and entrepreneurial spirit	23837 Matthewnanni: 0.466; 95q12: 0.441; 19809 Nancyowen: 0.434

Haitian

10 Cultural Distinctions	Vodou practices, Creole cuisine, vibrant art, Carnival celebrations, storytelling traditions, French-African cultural blend, strong community ties, music (compas), rural lifestyle, resilience	2932 Kempchinsky: 0.471; 31492 Jennarose: 0.467; 25706 Cekoscielski 0.458
10 Historical Highlights	Haitian Revolution, independence from France (1804), first Black republic, Vodou religion, Duvalier regime, earthquake resilience, Toussaint Louverture's leadership, Citadelle Laferrière, Taíno heritage, Creole language	7699 Bozek: 0.438; 3790 Raywilson: 0.435; -10003 Venus: 0.428
20 Key Tags	Revolution, Vodou, Creole, resilience, Carnival, art, community, compas, Taíno, independence, Toussaint, Citadelle, storytelling, French-African, rural, music, heritage, earthquake, culture, history	27938 Guislain: 0.595; 5426 Sharp: 0.592; 137632 Ramsauer: 0.583
Historical outside contact	Faced colonial exploitation; modern challenges include poverty and international aid dependency	12657 Bonch Bruevich: 0.524; 4669 Hoder: 0.453; 6386 Keithnoll: 0.452
Notable Achievements	First successful slave revolt leading to independence	6980 Kyusakamoto: 0.479; 336203 Sandrobuss: 0.46; 3751 Kiang: 0.46
Notable Cultural Facts	Known for its unique Vodou religion and being the first Black republic	518523 Bryanshumaker: 0.358; 1511 Arlenewolfe: 0.348; 85179 Meistereckhart: 0.329

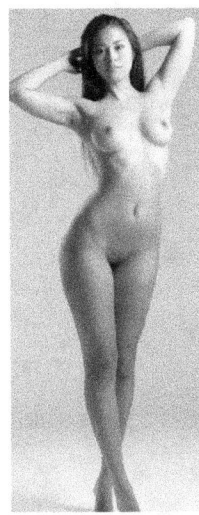

Hawaiian

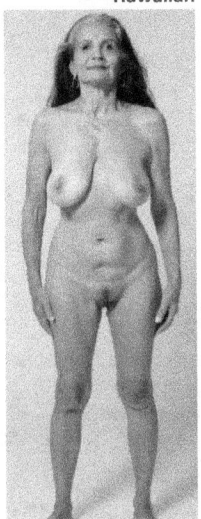

Hispanic

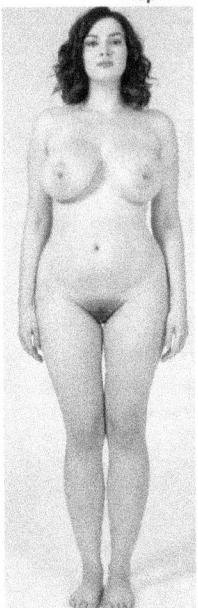

Hungarian

10 Cultural Distinctions	Hula dance, lei tradition, aloha spirit, Polynesian navigation, ukulele music, volcanic landscapes, ohana (family) values, luau feasts, traditional chants, environmental stewardship	2341 Aoluta: 0.484; 34282 Applegate: 0.484; 2519 Annagerman: 0.48
10 Historical Highlights	Polynesian settlement, Kamehameha unification, overthrow of monarchy, Pearl Harbor, hula tradition, surfing origins, volcanic activity, Hawaiian Renaissance, statehood (1959), aloha spirit	12742 Delisle: 0.513; 4546 Franck: 0.506; 25945 Moreadalleore: 1.119
20 Key Tags	Aloha, hula, lei, ohana, luau, surfing, volcano, chants, ukulele, Polynesian, navigation, monarchy, Pearl Harbor, Renaissance, statehood, family, nature, stewardship, spirit, culture	15790 Keizan: 0.611; 19575 Feeny: 0.6
Historical outside contact	Colonized by the U.S.; cultural revival efforts in modern times	17041 Castagna: 0.499; 58191 Dolomiten: 0.493; 21483 Abdulrasool: 0.491
Notable Achievements	Mastery of Polynesian navigation and cultural revival	90533 Laurentblind: 0.489; 87271 Kokubunji: 0.468; 168698 Robpickman: 0.461
Notable Cultural Facts	Known for its aloha spirit and deep connection to nature	10760 Ozeki: 0.514; 15111 Winters: 0.509; 211374 Anthonyrose: 0.507
10 Cultural Distinctions	Day of the Dead, Catholic traditions, Latin music, vibrant festivals, family-oriented, diverse cuisines, Spanish language, colorful art, strong community ties, historical landmarks	252470 Puigmarti: 0.468; 2618 Coonabarabran: 0.468; 24087 Ciambetti: 0.456
10 Historical Highlights	Spanish colonization, Mexican-American War, Alamo, civil rights movements, Day of the Dead, Latin American independence, Catholic influence, Spanish language spread, Hispanic Heritage Month, cultural fusion	1235 Schorria: 0.464; 4669 Hoder: 1.043; 6353 Semper: 0.45
20 Key Tags	Spanish, Catholic, festivals, family, music, cuisine, art, community, language, landmarks, independence, heritage, diversity, history, colonization, Alamo, civil rights, fusion, culture, tradition	3321 Dasha: 0.53; 46441 Mikepenston: 0.516; 21488 Danyellelee: 0.515
Historical outside contact	Colonial exploitation; modern contributions to multiculturalism	25404 Shansample: 0.505; 2771 Polzunov: 0.485
Notable Achievements	Contributions to art, music, and independence movements	124q3: 0.533; 13640 Ohtateruaki: 0.526; 10266 Vladishukhov: 0.509
Notable Cultural Facts	Known for its rich cultural fusion and vibrant traditions	11679 Brucebaker: 0.515; 177853 Lumezzane: 0.489; 266646 Zaphod: 0.48
10 Cultural Distinctions	Folk music, paprika cuisine, thermal baths, embroidery, wine-making, Christmas traditions, Hungarian language, horse culture, Busójárás festival, baroque architecture	25706 Cekoscielski: 0.538; 2932 Kempchinsky: 0.487; 4196 Shuya: 0.45
10 Historical Highlights	Hungarian conquest (896), Árpád dynasty, Ottoman wars, Austro-Hungarian Empire, 1848 revolution, Treaty of Trianon, WWII history, 1956 uprising, classical music, thermal baths	6647 Josse: 0.497; 8063 Cristinathomas: 0.488; 14917 Taco: 0.487
20 Key Tags	Paprika, folk, music, baths, embroidery, wine, Christmas, language, horse, Busójárás, baroque, conquest, Trianon, uprising, empire, traditions, cuisine, culture, history, resilience	4547 Massachusetts: 0.581; 15111 Winters: 0.571; 10591 Caverni: 0.564
Historical outside contact	Historically oppressed under Ottoman and Soviet rule; modern EU integration	2323 Zverev: 0.508; 9033 Kawane: 0.47; 25404 Shansample: 0.463
Notable Achievements	Contributions to classical music and revolutionary movements	16022 Wissnergross: 0.527; 13640 Ohtateruaki: 0.51; 124q3: 0.506
Notable Cultural Facts	Known for its thermal baths and unique language	10726 Elodie: 0.485; 12259 Szukalski: 0.462; 3518 Florena: 0.448

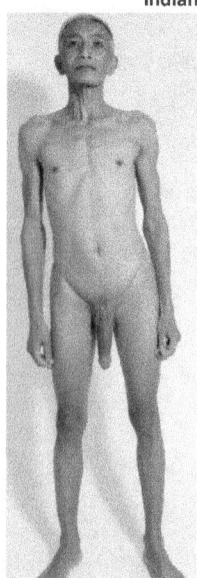

Icelandic

10 Cultural Distinctions	Sagas, geothermal energy, Viking heritage, turf houses, elf folklore, hot springs, Icelandic language, seafood cuisine, midnight sun, Northern Lights	125 Liberatrix: 1.097; 11774 Jerne: 0.919; 99891 Donwells: 0.482
10 Historical Highlights	Norse settlement, Alþingi (world's oldest parliament), sagas, Christianization, independence (1944), volcanic eruptions, geothermal energy, Viking heritage, literary tradition, gender equality	3346 Gerla: 0.518; 30296 Bricehuang: 0.516; 1016 Anitra: 0.513
20 Key Tags	Sagas, Vikings, geothermal, turf, elves, hot springs, language, seafood, sun, lights, parliament, independence, folklore, equality, resilience, heritage, eruptions, energy, culture, history	1602 Indiana: 0.578; 4414 Sesostris: 0.566
Historical outside contact	Historically isolated; modern emphasis on sustainability and equality	3751 Kiang: 0.573; 262705 Vosne Romanee: 0.566; 143q4: 0.557
Notable Achievements	World's oldest parliament and geothermal innovations	42924 Betlem: 0.46; 6055 Brunelleschi: 0.425; 211379 Claytonwhitted: 0.419
Notable Cultural Facts	Known for its sagas and geothermal energy	26q12: 0.444; 3518 Florena: 0.412

Indian

10 Cultural Distinctions	Yoga, Bollywood, diverse cuisines, festivals, classical music, Ayurveda, spirituality, sarees, cricket, multilingualism	7640 Marzari: 1.122; 28603 Jenkins: 0.504; 8905 Bankakuko: 0.501
10 Historical Highlights	Indus Valley Civilization, Vedic period, Mughal Empire, British colonization, independence (1947), Mahatma Gandhi's leadership, Bollywood, yoga, IT revolution, space exploration	3790 Raywilson: 0.486; 25404 Shansample: 1.028; 11667 Testa: 0.476
20 Key Tags	Yoga, Bollywood, cuisine, festivals, music, Ayurveda, spirituality, sarees, cricket, multilingual, Gandhi, independence, IT, space, diversity, history, culture, resilience, innovation, tradition	13801 Kohlhase: 0.565; 86 Semele: 0.56
Historical outside contact	Colonized by Britain; modern leader in technology and global diplomacy	32272 Hasegawayuya: 0.582; 135069 Gagnereau: 0.518
Notable Achievements	Contributions to spirituality, science, and independence movements	124q3: 0.532; 4380 Geyer: 0.515; 163255 Adrianhill: 0.504
Notable Cultural Facts	Known for its spiritual traditions and cultural diversity	19809 Nancyowen: 0.529; 11764 Benbaillaud: 0.501; 11679 Brucebaker: 0.49

Indonesian

10 Cultural Distinctions	Batik art, gamelan music, shadow puppetry, diverse cuisines, rice culture, traditional dances, wayang kulit, tropical biodiversity, Islam as majority religion, volcanic landscapes	6569 Ondaatje: 1.027; 4196 Shuya: 0.913; 20812 Shannonbabb: 0.45
10 Historical Highlights	Srivijaya Empire, Majapahit Empire, Dutch colonization, Japanese occupation, independence (1945), Sukarno's leadership, Bali bombings, tsunami resilience, spice trade, ASEAN founding	8772 Minutus: 0.491; 113952 Schramm: 0.489; 11667 Testa: 0.489
20 Key Tags	Batik, gamelan, wayang, rice, volcanoes, biodiversity, Islam, shadow puppetry, spices, ASEAN, resilience, tsunami, independence, Sukarno, Bali, tropical, culture, history, art, trade	28851 Londonbolsius: 0.548; 5379 Abehiroshi: 0.535
Historical outside contact	Colonized by Dutch; modern Indonesia is a leader in ASEAN	32272 Hasegawayuya: 0.506; 25404 Shansample: 0.5; 1724 Vladimir: 0.488
Notable Achievements	Founding member of ASEAN, rich cultural heritage	2772 Dugan: 0.515; 25555 Ratnavarma: 0.51; 11679 Brucebaker: 0.489
Notable Cultural Facts	Known for its cultural diversity and volcanic landscapes	11774 Jerne: 0.412; 20302 Kevinwang: 0.408

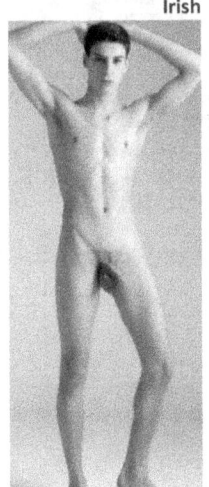

Iranian	10 Cultural Distinctions	Persian carpets, poetry, Zoroastrianism, Persian gardens, Nowruz festival, Islamic architecture, saffron cuisine, calligraphy, tea culture, bazaars	91607 Delaboudiniere: 0.925; 15969 Charlesgreen: 0.482; 14214 Hirsch: 0.468
	10 Historical Highlights	Achaemenid Empire, Sassanian Empire, Islamic conquest, Persian literature, Safavid dynasty, Qajar dynasty, 1979 revolution, Iran-Iraq War, nuclear program, Silk Road influence	3701 Purkyne: 0.485; 11667 Testa: 0.481; 3124 Kansas: 0.472
	20 Key Tags	Achaemenid, Sassanian, Safavid, carpets, poetry, gardens, Nowruz, Zoroastrianism, bazaars, tea, calligraphy, architecture, cuisine, Silk Road, revolution, history, resilience, culture, art, trade	11826 Yurijgromov: 0.586; 15916 Shigeoyamada: 0.577; 981 Martina: 0.573
	Historical outside contact	Historically invaded; modern Iran faces international sanctions	21433 Stekramer: 0.513; 133861 Debrawilmer: 0.464; 29638 Eeshakhare: 0.46
	Notable Achievements	Contributions to literature, architecture, and governance	31522 McCutchen: 0.494; duodecanate qc72: 0.488; 30200 Terryburch: 0.481
	Notable Cultural Facts	Known for its Persian poetry and carpets	19809 Nancyowen: 0.426; 5538 Luichewoo: 0.41
Irish	10 Cultural Distinctions	Gaelic language, Celtic music, St. Patrick's Day, Irish dance, pub culture, storytelling, rugged landscapes, Catholic traditions, literary legacy, hospitality	210232 Zhangjinqiu: 0.493; 2519 Annagerman: 0.462; 21551 Geyang: 0.45
	10 Historical Highlights	Celtic culture, Norman invasions, Great Famine, Easter Rising, War of Independence, partition (1921), Good Friday Agreement, emigration waves, Gaelic revival, EU membership	33453 Townley: 0.932; 27519 Miames: 0.466; 4359 Berlage: 0.459
	20 Key Tags	Celtic, Gaelic, famine, independence, dance, music, pubs, storytelling, hospitality, rugged, Catholic, literature, peace, history, culture, resilience, emigration, revival, EU, tradition	8496 Jandlsmith: 0.623; 231470 Bedding: 0.612; 13109 Berzelius: 0.61
	Historical outside contact	Colonized by Britain; modern Ireland is a leader in peacebuilding	1661 Granule: 0.455; 14065 Flegel: 0.451
	Notable Achievements	Literary contributions, peacebuilding efforts	5731 Zeus: 0.508; 53157 Akaishidake: 0.508; 39q6: 0.504
	Notable Cultural Facts	Known for its literary legacy and Celtic traditions	177853 Lumezzane: 0.534; 58q9: 0.497; 11679 Brucebaker: 0.497
Israeli	10 Cultural Distinctions	Hebrew revival, kibbutzim, Jewish holidays, Mediterranean cuisine, high-tech industry, diverse population, religious landmarks, folk dancing, military service, desert agriculture	21431 Amberhess: 0.54; 91607 Delaboudiniere: 0.51; 858 El Djezair: 0.497
	10 Historical Highlights	Zionist movement, Holocaust survivors, 1948 independence, Six-Day War, Yom Kippur War, peace treaties, technological innovation, kibbutz movement, archaeological discoveries, diverse immigration	11334 Rio de Janeiro: 0.461; 85401 Yamatenclub: 0.452; 7869 Pradun: 0.44
	20 Key Tags	Zionism, Holocaust, independence, kibbutz, Hebrew, cuisine, landmarks, tech, agriculture, diversity, peace, conflict, resilience, history, culture, innovation, immigration, archaeology, tradition, religion	10444 de Hevesy: 0.57; 46441 Mikepenston: 0.569; 34141 Antonwu: 0.565
	Historical outside contact	Conflict with neighboring states; modern Israel is a tech leader	6705 Rinaketty: 0.522; 8737 Takehiro: 0.516; 2073 Janacek: 0.515
	Notable Achievements	Technological advancements, peace treaties	1652 Herge: 0.539; 4573 Piestany: 0.516; 207931 Weihai: 0.515
	Notable Cultural Facts	Known for its technological innovation and cultural diversity	20302 Kevinwang: 0.508; 17938 Tamsendrew: 0.492; 177853 Lumezzane: 0.474

Italian

10 Cultural Distinctions	Pasta and pizza, Renaissance art, Catholicism, opera, fashion, wine-making, family values, historical landmarks, Vespa scooters, Mediterranean lifestyle	3154 Grant: 0.509; 25226 Brasch: 0.509; 11013 Kullander: 1.047
10 Historical Highlights	Roman Empire, Renaissance, unification (1861), fascism, WWII, Vatican City, opera, fashion, cuisine, art movements	181751 Phaenops: 0.542; 24538 Charliexie: 0.538; 1729 Beryl: 0.525
20 Key Tags	Rome, Renaissance, unification, Catholicism, opera, fashion, cuisine, landmarks, Vespa, wine, family, art, history, culture, resilience, Mediterranean, tradition, innovation, architecture, lifestyle	2432 Soomana: 0.552; 12572 Sadegh: 0.544
Historical outside contact	Colonized parts of Africa; modern Italy is a cultural hub	6069 Cevolani: 0.466; 2867 Steins: 0.463; duodecanate 47: 0.461
Notable Achievements	Renaissance art, Roman engineering	20208 Philiphe: 0.5; 177853 Lumezzane: 0.99; 16900 Lozere: 0.495
Notable Cultural Facts	Known for its Renaissance art and cuisine	7478 Hasse: 0.416; 518523 Bryanshumaker: 0.409

Jamaican

10 Cultural Distinctions	Reggae music, Rastafarian culture, jerk cuisine, patois language, vibrant festivals, Blue Mountains, Usain Bolt, Bob Marley, beach tourism, strong community ties	91607 Delaboudiniere: 0.486; 69311 Russ: 0.484; 30029 Preetikakani: 0.48
10 Historical Highlights	Arawak heritage, Spanish colonization, British rule, Maroon resistance, slavery abolition, independence (1962), reggae music, Rastafarianism, athletics, Hurricane Gilbert	20302 Kevinwang: 0.543; 3162 Nostalgia: 0.49; 30296 Bricehuang: 0.475
20 Key Tags	Reggae, Rastafarian, jerk, patois, festivals, Blue Mountains, Bolt, Marley, beaches, tourism, community, independence, resilience, history, culture, music, athletics, heritage, art, cuisine	28732 Rheakamat: 0.581; 8449 Maslovets: 0.988; 48 Doris: 0.576
Historical outside contact	Colonized by Spain and Britain; modern Jamaica is a cultural icon	75823 Csokonai: 0.466; 32272 Hasegawayuya: 0.445; 25404 Shansample: 0.441
Notable Achievements	Global influence in music and athletics	duodecanate r16: 0.531; 61q9: 0.514; 80q9: 0.506
Notable Cultural Facts	Known for its reggae music and Rastafarian culture	19809 Nancyowen: 0.424; 117715 Carlkirby: 0.404

Japanese

10 Cultural Distinctions	Sushi, kimono, cherry blossoms, tea ceremony, martial arts, anime, manga, Shinto shrines, Zen gardens, bullet trains	21413 Albertsao: 1.06; 3696 Herald: 0.494; 2024 McLaughlin: 0.494
10 Historical Highlights	Jomon period, samurai culture, Meiji Restoration, WWII, Hiroshima and Nagasaki, economic miracle, anime and manga, tea ceremony, Zen Buddhism, Shinto traditions	3852 Glennford: 0.485; 210210 Songjian: 0.484; 23801 Erikgustafson: 0.459
20 Key Tags	Samurai, sushi, kimono, cherry blossoms, tea, martial arts, anime, manga, Shinto, Zen, gardens, trains, history, culture, resilience, innovation, tradition, art, cuisine, technology	12262 Nishio: 0.544; 12878 Erneschiller: 0.538
Historical outside contact	Historically isolated; modern Japan is a global leader in technology	1724 Vladimir: 0.516; 903 Nealley: 0.47; 8305 Teika: 0.46
Notable Achievements	Technological advancements, cultural exports	8856 Celastrus: 0.506; 24965 Akayu: 0.499; 30788 Angekauffmann: 0.499
Notable Cultural Facts	Known for its blend of tradition and modernity	17853 Ronaldsayer: 0.562; 11679 Brucebaker: 0.541; 33902 Ingoldsby: 0.54

10 Cultural Distinctions	Kosher dietary laws, Sabbath observance, Hebrew language, synagogue worship, Jewish holidays, menorah symbolism, bar/bat mitzvahs, Jewish humor, strong community ties, contributions to arts and sciences	91607 Delaboudiniere: 1.024; 11216 Billhubbard: 0.443; 14571 Caralexander: 0.429
10 Historical Highlights	Ancient Israel, Babylonian exile, Roman diaspora, Holocaust, Zionist movement, establishment of Israel (1948), Nobel Prize contributions, Torah and Talmud, Jewish emancipation, Jewish resistance during WWII	3887 Gerstner: 1.111; 85401 Yamatenclub: 0.51; 9914 Obukhova: 1.063
Historical outside contact	Historically persecuted (e.g., Holocaust); modern Israel faces geopolitical challenges	471926 Jormungandr: 0.481; 12657 Bonch Bruevich: 0.478; 2883 Barabashov: 0.477
Notable Achievements	Nobel Prize contributions, establishment of Israel	124q3: 0.478; 9845 Okamuraosamu: 0.446; 410475 Robertschulz: 0.439
Notable Cultural Facts	Known for resilience and contributions to global culture	duodecanate 41: 0.649; 2q5: 0.58; 26q12: 0.539

Jewish

10 Cultural Distinctions	Kannada language, classical music, Mysuru Dasara, Hampi ruins, silk sarees, sandalwood products, folk dances, rice-based cuisine, temple architecture, literary tradition	91607 Delaboudiniere: 1.09; 632 Pyrrha: 1.077; 264061 Vitebsk: 0.489
10 Historical Highlights	Kadamba dynasty, Vijayanagara Empire, Mysore Kingdom, Halmidi inscription, Kannada literature, Mysuru Dasara, Jog Falls, classical language status, Chalukya architecture, independence movement	34253 Nitya: 0.473; 296819 Artesian: 0.466; 29762 Panasiewicz: 0.459
20 Key Tags	Kannada, Mysuru, Hampi, Dasara, silk, sandalwood, rice, temples, literature, dances, classical, Kadamba, Chalukya, Vijayanagara, Jog Falls, resilience, history, culture, art, tradition	21714 Geoffreywoo: 0.584
Historical outside contact	Historically influenced by neighboring cultures; modern Karnataka is a cultural hub	80q9: 0.536; 11679 Brucebaker: 0.514; 61q9: 0.497
Notable Achievements	Contributions to literature and architecture	30200 Terryburch: 0.459; 16022 Wissnergross: 0.452; 31522 McCutchen: 0.451
Notable Cultural Facts	Known for its rich literary and architectural heritage	177853 Lumezzane: 0.481; 32053 Demetrimaxim: 0.441; 7056 Kierkegaard: 0.43

Kannada

10 Cultural Distinctions	Swahili language, Maasai traditions, wildlife safaris, diverse ethnic groups, traditional music and dance, coastal cuisine, beadwork, storytelling, agricultural practices, vibrant festivals	7640 Marzari: 1.007; 12659 Schlegel: 0.454; 55735 Magdeburg: 0.453
10 Historical Highlights	Early human fossils, Swahili Coast trade, British colonization, Mau Mau uprising, independence (1963), Jomo Kenyatta's leadership, wildlife conservation, Great Rift Valley, Olympic achievements, Wangari Maathai's activism	4491 Otaru: 0.495; 9325 Stonehenge: 0.489; 6485 Wendeesther: 0.485
20 Key Tags	Swahili, Maasai, safaris, wildlife, festivals, beadwork, storytelling, agriculture, cuisine, music, dance, independence, conservation, Rift Valley, Olympics, resilience, history, culture, art, tradition	28851 Londonbolsius: 0.562; 73857 Hitaneichi: 0.547
Historical outside contact	Colonized by Britain; modern Kenya is a leader in environmental conservation	32272 Hasegawayuya: 0.555; 25404 Shansample: 0.479; 2380 Heilongjiang: 0.464
Notable Achievements	Olympic achievements, environmental activism	12602 Tammytam: 0.522; 11005 Waldtrudering: 0.518; 48529 von Wrangel: 0.51
Notable Cultural Facts	Known for its wildlife and cultural diversity	20302 Kevinwang: 0.517; 20073 Yumiko: 0.494; 19822 Vonzielonka: 0.481

Kenyan

Korean

10 Cultural Distinctions	Hanbok attire, kimchi cuisine, K-pop, Korean dramas, taekwondo, Confucian values, tea ceremonies, traditional music, Buddhist temples, modern technology	69311 Russ: 0.446; 17908 Chriskuyu: 0.446; 34273 Franklynwang: 0.442
10 Historical Highlights	Gojoseon kingdom, Three Kingdoms period, Joseon dynasty, Japanese occupation, Korean War, economic miracle, K-pop rise, technological advancements, UNESCO heritage sites, Confucian influence	210210 Songjian: 0.463; 32424 Caryjames: 0.436; 1724 Vladimir: 0.902
20 Key Tags	Hanbok, kimchi, K-pop, dramas, taekwondo, Confucian, tea, temples, technology, music, Buddhism, history, resilience, culture, art, cuisine, tradition, innovation, heritage	2314 Field: 0.528; 21413 Albertsao: 0.519; 22473 Stanleyhey: 0.518
Historical outside contact	Historically occupied by Japan; modern South Korea is a global cultural leader	duodecanate 41: 0.465; 82q2: 0.457
Notable Achievements	Technological advancements, cultural exports	8856 Celastrus: 0.506; 24965 Akayu: 0.499; 30788 Angekauffmann: 0.499
Notable Cultural Facts	Known for blending tradition with modernity	33902 Ingoldsby: 0.573; 17853 Ronaldsayer: 0.569; 11679 Brucebaker: 0.562

Kurdish

10 Cultural Distinctions	Kurdish language, Newroz celebrations, epic poetry, folk music, carpet weaving, copper-working, mountain lifestyle, traditional clothing, hospitality, agricultural practices	4387 Tanaka: 0.953; 12447 Yatescup: 0.453; 20559 Sheridanlamp: 0.451
10 Historical Highlights	Ancient Mesopotamia, Ottoman Empire, Treaty of Sèvres, Kurdish rebellions, Saddam Hussein's oppression, Kurdish autonomy in Iraq, Newroz festival, rich oral traditions, carpet weaving, copper-working	6658 Akiraabe: 0.513; 2233 Kuznetsov: 0.503
20 Key Tags	Mesopotamia, Newroz, poetry, music, carpets, copper, mountains, clothing, hospitality, agriculture, resilience, autonomy, history, culture, art, tradition, heritage, struggle, identity	6447 Terrycole: 0.557; 4627 Pinomogavero: 0.555; 91607 Delaboudiniere: 0.553
Historical outside contact	Historically oppressed; modern Kurdish regions seek autonomy	639 Latona: 0.482; 15762 Ruhmann: 0.478; 110q2: 0.466
Notable Achievements	Contributions to oral traditions and craftsmanship	24898 Alanholmes: 0.566; 31522 McCutchen: 0.557; 33902 Ingoldsby: 0.534
Notable Cultural Facts	Known for their resilience and rich oral traditions	2q5: 0.575; duodecanate 41: 0.551; 3669 Vertinskij: 0.542

Laotian

10 Cultural Distinctions	Theravada Buddhism, traditional music and dance, rice farming, animist beliefs, silk weaving, Lao cuisine, Mekong River lifestyle, stilt houses, storytelling, vibrant festivals	16645 Aldalara: 0.437; 9592 Clairaut: 0.434; 12447 Yatescup: 0.985
10 Historical Highlights	Kingdom of Lan Xang, French colonization, independence (1953), Vietnam War impact, Plain of Jars, Mekong River trade, Theravada Buddhism, Pathet Lao movement, ASEAN membership, cultural preservation	6569 Ondaatje: 0.481; 3463 Kaokuen: 0.463; 30031 Angelakong: 0.46
20 Key Tags	Buddhism, Mekong, Lan Xang, silk, rice, animism, festivals, storytelling, stilt houses, cuisine, resilience, ASEAN, Plain of Jars, Pathet Lao, history, culture, art, tradition, peace, preservation	28851 Londonbolsius: 0.549; 91607 Delaboudiniere: 0.541
Historical outside contact	Colonized by France; modern Laos is peaceful but economically challenged	373 Melusina: 0.475; 4821 Bianucci: 0.473; 21433 Stekramer: 0.472
Notable Achievements	Preservation of Theravada Buddhism and cultural heritage	80008 Danielarhodes: 0.447; 216591 Coetzee: 0.439; 3686 Antoku: 0.432
Notable Cultural Facts	Known for its Theravada Buddhist practices and Mekong River culture	19809 Nancyowen: 0.36; 1916 Boreas: 0.347; 44473 Randytatum: 0.335

Latvian		
10 Cultural Distinctions	Folk songs, midsummer festival, wooden architecture, amber jewelry, rye bread, sauna culture, Latvian language, traditional costumes, pagan roots, forest connection	28851 Londonbolsius: 0.502; 7333 Bec Borsenberger: 0.492; 4418 Fredfranklin: 0.467
10 Historical Highlights	Baltic tribes, Livonian Crusade, Hanseatic League, independence (1918), Soviet occupation, Singing Revolution, EU membership, Art Nouveau architecture, folk traditions, Dainas (folk songs)	27519 Miames: 0.565; 7112 Ghislaine: 0.556; 16147 Jeanli: 0.555
20 Key Tags	Baltic, Dainas, midsummer, amber, sauna, rye, forests, costumes, pagan, songs, independence, EU, traditions, architecture, resilience, history, culture, art, preservation, peace	35056 Cullers: 0.601; 3901 Nanjingdaxue: 0.589; 3564 Talthybius: 0.583
Historical outside contact	Occupied by Soviets and Nazis; modern Latvia is a leader in cultural preservation	7869 Pradun: 0.476; 4682 Bykov: 0.473; 10761 Lyubimets: 0.469
Notable Achievements	Singing Revolution and cultural preservation	3477 Kazbegi: 0.442; 5253 Fredclifford: 0.439; duodecanate 45: 0.439
Notable Cultural Facts	Known for its Dainas and midsummer celebrations	2618 Coonabarabran: 0.443; 269300 Diego: 0.426; 4021 Dancey: 0.422
Lebanese		
10 Cultural Distinctions	Lebanese cuisine, cedar trees, Arabic-French bilingualism, religious diversity, Dabke dance, Mediterranean lifestyle, hospitality, ancient ruins, souks, mountain villages	17119 Alexisrodrz: 0.479; 16645 Aldalara: 0.475; 56329 Tarxien: 1.058
10 Historical Highlights	Phoenician civilization, Roman rule, Arab conquest, Ottoman Empire, French mandate, independence (1943), civil war (1975-1990), banking hub, cedar symbolism, multiculturalism	38020 Hannadam: 0.551; 11667 Testa: 0.55; 4969 Lawrence: 0.543
20 Key Tags	Phoenician, cedar, Dabke, cuisine, ruins, souks, bilingual, Mediterranean, hospitality, mountains, resilience, history, culture, art, tradition, peace, diversity, banking, independence, heritage	129898 Sanfordselznick: 0.578; 2094 Magnitka: 0.577
Historical outside contact	Historically invaded; modern Lebanon is a cultural and financial hub	3124 Kansas: 0.448; 8232 Akiramizuno: 0.415; 3238 Timresovia: 0.41
Notable Achievements	Contributions to trade and cultural exchange	22543 Ranjan: 0.504; duodecanate 47: 0.5; 4095 Ishizuchisan: 0.493
Notable Cultural Facts	Known for its Phoenician heritage and cedar trees	3887 Gerstner: 0.393; 8375 Kenzokohno: 0.386; 681 Gorgo: 0.37
Lithuanian		
10 Cultural Distinctions	Folk music, amber jewelry, pagan roots, wooden crosses, rye bread, midsummer festival, Lithuanian language, basketball culture, traditional costumes, forest connection	4757 Liselotte: 0.517; 126315 Blathy: 0.497; 28851 Londonbolsius: 0.496
10 Historical Highlights	Grand Duchy of Lithuania, Polish-Lithuanian Commonwealth, Christianization, partitions of Poland, independence (1918), Soviet occupation, Singing Revolution, EU membership, Baltic Way, basketball success	16147 Jeanli: 0.498; 1480 Aunus: 0.495; 31853 Rahulmital: 0.492
20 Key Tags	Baltic, amber, pagan, crosses, rye, midsummer, forests, costumes, basketball, independence, EU, traditions, resilience, history, culture, art, preservation, peace, heritage	3901 Nanjingdaxue: 0.604; 35056 Cullers: 0.6; 8496 Jandlsmith: 0.596
Historical outside contact	Occupied by Soviets and Nazis; modern Lithuania is a leader in cultural preservation	10761 Lyubimets: 0.489; 7869 Pradun: 0.489; 11079 Mitsunori: 0.486
Notable Achievements	Singing Revolution and basketball achievements	11005 Waldtrudering: 0.459; 135799 Raczmiklos: 0.449; 48529 von Wrangel: 0.435
Notable Cultural Facts	Known for its amber and basketball culture	269300 Diego: 0.47; 31858 Raykanipe: 0.456; 24948 Babote: 0.428

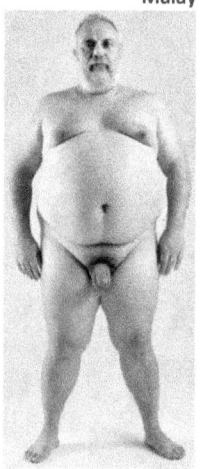

Macedonian

10 Cultural Distinctions	Cyrillic script, folk music, traditional dances, mountain lifestyle, Orthodox Christianity, wine-making, Ohrid Lake, traditional costumes, hospitality, agricultural practices	91607 Delaboudiniere: 0.513; 15111 Winters: 1.131; 14571 Caralexander: 0.492
10 Historical Highlights	Ancient Macedonia, Alexander the Great, Byzantine Empire, Ottoman rule, Ilinden Uprising, Yugoslav federation, independence (1991), Ohrid Agreement, Cyrillic script, cultural festivals	3943 Silbermann: 0.508; 6000 United Nations: 0.877; 4859 Fraknoi: 0.501
20 Key Tags	Alexander, Cyrillic, Ohrid, wine, dances, music, costumes, mountains, Christianity, hospitality, resilience, history, culture, art, tradition, peace, heritage, agriculture, independence	3162 Nostalgia: 0.612; 1797 Schaumasse: 0.61
Historical outside contact	Historically ruled by Ottomans; modern Macedonia is peaceful but faces identity disputes	639 Latona: 0.501; 215463 Jobse: 0.482; 1590 Tsiolkovskaja: 0.844
Notable Achievements	Contributions to ancient history and cultural preservation	4380 Geyer: 0.535; 31522 McCutchen: 0.531; 266646 Zaphod: 0.502
Notable Cultural Facts	Known for its connection to Alexander the Great and Ohrid Lake	681 Gorgo: 0.386

Malay

10 Cultural Distinctions	Malay language, batik art, traditional dances, Islamic traditions, rice farming, kampong lifestyle, shadow puppetry, tropical biodiversity, spicy cuisine, hospitality	6569 Ondaatje: 1.04; 25706 Cekoscielski: 0.481; 40463 Frankkameny: 1.021
10 Historical Highlights	Srivijaya Empire, Malacca Sultanate, Portuguese colonization, British rule, Japanese occupation, independence (1957), Islamic influence, rubber and palm oil trade, ASEAN membership, cultural diversity	3124 Kansas: 0.468; 981 Martina: 0.465; 9817 Thersander: 0.459
20 Key Tags	Malay, batik, dances, Islam, rice, kampong, puppetry, biodiversity, cuisine, hospitality, resilience, history, culture, art, tradition, peace, heritage, ASEAN, independence, trade	4547 Massachusetts: 0.567
Historical outside contact	Colonized by Portuguese and British; modern Malaysia is a leader in ASEAN	25404 Shansample: 0.502; 32272 Hasegawayuya: 0.494; 1724 Vladimir: 0.474
Notable Achievements	Contributions to trade and cultural heritage	duodecanate 47: 0.452; 80q9: 0.448; 4380 Geyer: 0.443
Notable Cultural Facts	Known for its batik art and cultural diversity	20302 Kevinwang: 0.407; 20787 Mitchfourman: 0.404; 8905 Bankakuko: 0.398

Maltese

10 Cultural Distinctions	Maltese language, Catholic traditions, festas, lace-making, traditional music (għana), Mediterranean cuisine, limestone architecture, village life, fireworks, maritime heritage	2519 Annagerman: 1.013; 46441 Mikepenston: 1.007; 14214 Hirsch: 0.461
10 Historical Highlights	Megalithic temples, Phoenician settlement, Roman rule, Arab influence, Knights of St. John, Great Siege of Malta (1565), Napoleonic conquest, British rule, WWII resilience, EU membership	2050 Francis: 0.494; 6000 United Nations: 0.484; 4928 Vermeer: 0.482
20 Key Tags	Temples, Knights, festas, lace, għana, cuisine, limestone, fireworks, maritime, resilience, Mediterranean, Catholic, history, culture, art, tradition, EU, heritage, peace, preservation	13329 Davidhardy: 0.539
Historical outside contact	Colonized by various powers; modern Malta is a cultural crossroads	24370 Marywang: 0.518; 12802 Hagino: 0.512; 210030 Taoyuan: 0.503
Notable Achievements	Megalithic temples, WWII resilience	16142 Leung: 0.444; 55319 Takanashi: 0.438; 18780 Kuncham: 0.428
Notable Cultural Facts	Known for its megalithic temples and festas	2618 Coonabarabran: 0.415; 269300 Diego: 0.402; 28322 Kaeberich: 0.397

Mexican

Mongolian

Moroccan

10 Cultural Distinctions	**Day of the Dead, mariachi music, vibrant festivals, diverse cuisines, Catholic traditions, colorful art, family values, traditional dances, tequila, lucha libre**	**43956 Elidoro: 0.977; 2932 Kempchinsky: 0.468; 30257 Leejanel: 0.447**
10 Historical Highlights	Olmec civilization, Mayan achievements, Aztec Empire, Spanish conquest, Mexican War of Independence, Mexican Revolution, Day of the Dead, muralism, NAFTA, global cultural influence	93q12: 0.464; 6569 Ondaatje: 0.946; 13688 Oklahoma: 0.431
20 Key Tags	Olmec, Mayan, Aztec, mariachi, tequila, cuisine, festivals, Catholic, art, family, dances, independence, revolution, history, culture, resilience, tradition, heritage, lucha libre, muralism	6976 Kanatsu: 0.507
Historical outside contact	Colonized by Spain; modern Mexico is a cultural powerhouse	2771 Polzunov: 0.481; 4669 Hoder: 0.461; 24370 Marywang: 0.46
Notable Achievements	Contributions to art, cuisine, and independence movements	124q3: 0.536; 1264 Letaba: 0.509; duodecanate qc14: 0.502
Notable Cultural Facts	Known for its vibrant festivals and ancient civilizations	95q12: 0.419; 53468 Varros: 0.416; 1412 Lagrula: 0.412
10 Cultural Distinctions	Nomadic lifestyle, ger (yurt) dwellings, throat singing, horse culture, deel clothing, fermented mare's milk (airag), archery, wrestling, Buddhist monasteries, shamanistic practices	30296 Bricehuang: 0.501; 77856 Noblitt: 1.071; 135991 Danarmstrong: 0.487
10 Historical Highlights	Xiongnu Empire, Genghis Khan's conquests, Mongol Empire, Silk Road trade, Yuan dynasty, Tibetan Buddhism, Soviet influence, democratic transition, Naadam festival, nomadic traditions	12755 Balmer: 0.485; 29762 Panasiewicz: 0.473; 4821 Bianucci: 0.471
20 Key Tags	Genghis, nomadic, ger, throat singing, horse, deel, airag, archery, wrestling, Buddhism, shamanism, Silk Road, empire, resilience, history, culture, art, tradition, heritage, Naadam	9171 Carolyndiane: 0.57; 18918 Nishashah: 0.568
Historical outside contact	Historically invaded; modern Mongolia is peaceful and culturally rich	93q12: 0.468; 373 Melusina: 0.466; 1724 Vladimir: 0.465
Notable Achievements	Establishment of the largest contiguous empire in history	20284 Andreilevin: 0.464; 6243 Yoder: 0.461; 96205 Ararat: 0.445
Notable Cultural Facts	Known for its nomadic traditions and Genghis Khan's legacy	4387 Tanaka: 0.455; 22485 Unterman: 0.454; 521 Brixia: 0.452
10 Cultural Distinctions	Berber and Arab heritage, Islamic traditions, souks, tagine cuisine, mint tea, traditional clothing (djellaba), Gnawa music, desert lifestyle, hospitality, intricate tilework	17119 Alexisrodrz: 0.479; 56329 Tarxien: 0.465; 20812 Shannonbabb: 0.45
10 Historical Highlights	Berber kingdoms, Roman Mauretania, Arab conquest, Almoravid dynasty, Saadian dynasty, French and Spanish protectorates, independence (1956), Green March, Casablanca Conference, cultural fusion	7132 Casulli: 0.49; 10660 Felixhormuth: 0.475; 15913 Telemachus: 0.47
20 Key Tags	Berber, Arab, souks, tagine, mint tea, djellaba, Gnawa, desert, hospitality, tilework, resilience, history, culture, art, tradition, heritage, independence, fusion, peace, preservation	366852 Ti: 0.581; 243 Ida: 0.569; 121481 Reganhoward: 0.566
Historical outside contact	Colonized by France and Spain; modern Morocco is a cultural hub	6069 Cevolani: 0.427; 75823 Csokonai: 0.419; 6921 Janejacobs: 0.411
Notable Achievements	Contributions to trade and cultural exchange	22543 Ranjan: 0.504; duodecanate 47: 0.5; 4095 Ishizuchisan: 0.493
Notable Cultural Facts	Known for its souks and cultural fusion	16444 Godefroy: 0.427; 269300 Diego: 0.423; 2867 Steins: 0.414

Native American

10 Cultural Distinctions	Diverse tribal cultures, oral traditions, beadwork, powwows, spiritual connection to nature, traditional dances, storytelling, agriculture (corn, beans, squash), totem poles, pottery	114094 Irvpatterson: 1.043; 11679 Brucebaker: 0.517; 28851 Londonbolsius: 0.517
10 Historical Highlights	Pre-Columbian civilizations, Trail of Tears, Indian Removal Act, Ghost Dance movement, Wounded Knee Massacre, Indian Citizenship Act, tribal sovereignty, cultural revitalization, environmental activism, artistic contributions	9480 Inti: 0.501; 7869 Pradun: 0.49 6569 Ondaatje: 0.488
20 Key Tags	Tribal, sovereignty, powwow, beadwork, storytelling, dances, agriculture, totem, pottery, resilience, history, culture, art, tradition, heritage, preservation, spirituality, activism, nature, peace	2841 Puijo: 0.602; 4217 Engelhardt: 0.595; 138016 Kerribeisser: 0.593
Historical outside contact	Historically displaced and marginalized; modern efforts focus on sovereignty and cultural preservation	64290 Yaushingtung: 0.571; 11459 Andraspal: 0.566; 7815 Dolon: 0.54
Notable Achievements	Contributions to environmental activism and cultural preservation	31522 McCutchen: 0.568; duodecar qc51: 0.536; 249539 Pedrosevilla: 0
Notable Cultural Facts	Known for their spiritual connection to nature and diverse tribal cultures	20073 Yumiko: 0.558; 47q10: 0.521

Nepali

10 Cultural Distinctions	Hindu and Buddhist traditions, colorful festivals, Mount Everest, Gurkha soldiers, traditional music and dance, Newari cuisine, pagoda architecture, prayer flags, trekking culture, diverse ethnic groups	30296 Bricehuang: 0.434; 30025 Benfreed: 0.433; 28851 Londonbols 0.425
10 Historical Highlights	Licchavi dynasty, Malla period, unification under Prithvi Narayan Shah, Gurkha legacy, Rana rule, democratic transition, Maoist insurgency, Mount Everest expeditions, Hindu-Buddhist fusion, earthquake resilience	159974 Badacsony: 0.428; 16588 Johngee: 0.428; 12309 Tommygrav: 0.426
20 Key Tags	Everest, Gurkha, festivals, music, dance, cuisine, pagoda, prayer flags, trekking, resilience, history, culture, art, tradition, heritage, preservation, spirituality, peace, diversity, mountains	271009 Reitterferenc: 0.514; 3086 Kalbaugh: 0.506; 20574 Ochinero: 0
Historical outside contact	Historically isolated; modern Nepal is a leader in cultural preservation	11679 Brucebaker: 0.533; 64290 Yaushingtung: 0.514; 19423 Hefter: 0.512
Notable Achievements	Contributions to mountaineering and cultural heritage	31522 McCutchen: 0.454; 20073 Yumiko: 0.86; 80q9: 0.431
Notable Cultural Facts	Known for its Himalayan culture and Gurkha legacy	duodecanate 41: 0.44; 130q9: 0.414

Nigerian

10 Cultural Distinctions	Diverse ethnic groups, traditional attire, jollof rice, Yoruba and Igbo art, oral storytelling, masquerade festivals, pidgin English, traditional drumming, vibrant markets, religious diversity	3321 Dasha: 0.518; 5225 Loral: 0.51 39799 Hadano: 0.507
10 Historical Highlights	Nok culture, Benin Bronzes, transatlantic slave trade, British colonization, independence (1960), Biafran War, Nollywood rise, oil industry, Boko Haram insurgency, Afrobeats music	8630 Billprady: 0.447; 6710 Apostel: 0.445; 85585 Mjolnir: 0.441
20 Key Tags	Nok, Benin, jollof, Yoruba, Igbo, Afrobeats, Nollywood, oil, storytelling, masquerade, pidgin, drumming, markets, resilience, history, culture, art, tradition, diversity, independence	24829 Berounurbi: 0.571; 1814 Bach 0.563; 8979 Clanga: 0.561
Historical outside contact	Colonized by Britain; modern Nigeria faces ethnic and religious tensions	5855 Yukitsuna: 0.482; 3124 Kansas: 0.455; 24370 Marywang: 0.439
Notable Achievements	Contributions to art, music, and film	236800 Broder: 0.53; 16022 Wissnergross: 0.523; 31522 McCutcl 0.511
Notable Cultural Facts	Known for its cultural diversity and Nollywood	10075 Campeche: 0.382; 95q12: 0.3 20787 Mitchfourman: 0.374

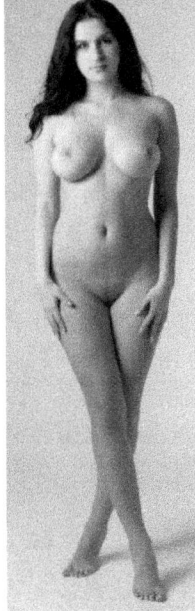

Norwegian	10 Cultural Distinctions	Love for nature, friluftsliv (outdoor lifestyle), skiing, hytte culture (cabins), salmon cuisine, folk music, bunad attire, fjords, egalitarian society, Northern Lights	4498 Shinkoyama: 0.47; 33353 Chattopadhyay: 1.066; 6400 Georgealexander: 0.455
	10 Historical Highlights	Viking Age, unification under Harald Fairhair, Kalmar Union, independence (1905), WWII resistance, oil discovery, Nobel Peace Prize, skiing traditions, stave churches, Arctic exploration	6000 United Nations: 0.505; 1724 Vladimir: 0.497; 130007 Frankteti: 0.496
	20 Key Tags	Vikings, fjords, skiing, hytte, salmon, bunad, egalitarian, Arctic, Nobel, friluftsliv, stave, resistance, oil, resilience, history, culture, art, tradition, peace, exploration	7229 Tonimoore: 0.588; 632 Pyrrha: 0.587
	Historical outside contact	Historically neutral; modern Norway is a leader in peacebuilding	13530 Ninnemann: 0.508; 5731 Zeus: 0.498; 5859 Ostozhenka: 0.498
	Notable Achievements	Nobel Peace Prize contributions, Arctic exploration	24027 Downs: 0.423; 124q3: 0.422; 18636 Villedepompey: 0.413
	Notable Cultural Facts	Known for its fjords and outdoor lifestyle	367406 Buser: 0.416; 1916 Boreas: 0.415; 269300 Diego: 0.406
Pakistani	10 Cultural Distinctions	Shalwar kameez attire, biryani cuisine, truck art, Sufi music, Urdu poetry, cricket passion, Islamic architecture, Eid celebrations, diverse languages, hospitality	69311 Russ: 0.428; 981 Martina: 0.425; 17908 Chriskuyu: 0.423
	10 Historical Highlights	Indus Valley Civilization, Mughal Empire, British colonization, independence (1947), partition, Kashmir conflict, Islamic Republic, Lahore Resolution, nuclear power, cultural festivals	10350 Spallanzani: 0.489; 25404 Shansample: 0.48; 10829 Matsuobasho: 0.463
	20 Key Tags	Indus, Mughal, biryani, Sufi, Urdu, cricket, truck art, Eid, poetry, architecture, resilience, history, culture, art, tradition, diversity, independence, hospitality, peace, festivals	20574 Ochinero: 0.574; 9665 Inastronoviny: 0.557; 632 Pyrrha: 0.552
	Historical outside contact	Partition led to mass migration and violence; modern Pakistan faces geopolitical challenges	639 Latona: 0.508; 710 Gertrud: 0.479; 4387 Tanaka: 0.46
	Notable Achievements	Contributions to poetry, architecture, and independence	53157 Akaishidake: 0.534; 4380 Geyer: 0.507; 6345 Hideo: 0.503
	Notable Cultural Facts	Known for its rich cultural heritage and hospitality	177853 Lumezzane: 0.47; 367406 Buser: 0.451; 19809 Nancyowen: 0.437
Palestinian	10 Cultural Distinctions	Dabke dance, Palestinian embroidery, olive oil production, Arabic poetry, traditional thobes, hospitality, Levantine cuisine, storytelling, religious landmarks, refugee identity	56329 Tarxien: 0.455; 25751 Mokshagundam: 0.432; 9206 Yanaikeizo: 0.419
	10 Historical Highlights	Canaanite heritage, Roman rule, Islamic caliphates, Ottoman Empire, British mandate, Nakba (1948), Intifadas, Oslo Accords, cultural resilience, embroidery traditions	10444 de Hevesy: 0.517; 38020 Hannadam: 0.506; 6672 Corot: 0.505
	20 Key Tags	Canaanite, Nakba, Dabke, embroidery, olive, poetry, thobes, cuisine, storytelling, resilience, history, culture, art, tradition, peace, hospitality, landmarks, identity, Levantine, struggle	3811 Karma: 0.589; 117610 Keithmahoney: 0.576; 15111 Winters: 0.571
	Historical outside contact	Displacement and conflict; modern Palestinians face challenges in statehood recognition	3457 Arnenordheim: 0.576; 8594 Albifrons: 0.541; 168221 Donjennings: 0.508
	Notable Achievements	Contributions to poetry and cultural preservation	31522 McCutchen: 0.51; 2340 Hathor: 0.509; 53157 Akaishidake: 0.504
	Notable Cultural Facts	Known for their cultural resilience and embroidery	duodecanate 41: 0.568; 2q5: 0.509; 91607 Delaboudiniere: 0.5

Paraguayan		
10 Cultural Distinctions	Guaraní traditions, yerba maté, chipa bread, harp music, vibrant festivals, bilingualism (Spanish and Guaraní), strong family ties, rural lifestyle, hospitality, spiritual values	17119 Alexisrodrz: 0.49; 30296 Bricehuang: 0.456; 15845 Bambi: 0.4
10 Historical Highlights	Guaraní heritage, Spanish colonization, independence (1811), War of the Triple Alliance, Chaco War, dictatorship era, democratic transition, yerba maté culture, vibrant festivals, Guaraní language preservation	6569 Ondaatje: 0.857; 373 Melusina 0.463; 14917 Taco: 0.463
20 Key Tags	Guaraní, yerba maté, chipa, harp, festivals, bilingualism, resilience, history, culture, art, tradition, preservation, family, rural, hospitality, values, spirituality, independence, heritage	6795 Ornskoldsvik: 0.551; 8897 Defe 0.549; 17045 Markert: 0.54
Historical outside contact	Colonized by Spain; modern Paraguay is culturally rich	75823 Csokonai: 0.432; 24370 Marywang: 0.419; 93q12: 0.405
Notable Achievements	Preservation of Guaraní language and cultural heritage	5855 Yukitsuna: 0.364; 216591 Coeta 0.363; 11679 Brucebaker: 0.352
Notable Cultural Facts	Known for its Guaraní language and yerba maté culture	4491 Otaru: 0.38; 233661 Alytus: 0.3
Persian		
10 Cultural Distinctions	Persian carpets, poetry, Nowruz festival, calligraphy, saffron cuisine, Persian gardens, tea culture, bazaars, Islamic architecture, hospitality	91607 Delaboudiniere: 0.925; 14214 Hirsch: 1.067; 15969 Charlesgreen: 0.491
10 Historical Highlights	Achaemenid Empire, Zoroastrianism, Persian literature, Islamic conquest, Safavid dynasty, Qajar dynasty, 1979 revolution, Persian carpets, Persepolis, Silk Road trade	3701 Purkyne: 0.493; 20574 Ochiner 1.042; 58191 Dolomiten: 0.468
20 Key Tags	Achaemenid, Zoroastrian, carpets, poetry, Nowruz, calligraphy, gardens, tea, bazaars, architecture, resilience, history, culture, art, tradition, peace, hospitality, trade, heritage, identity	15916 Shigeoyamada: 0.582
Historical outside contact	Historically invaded; modern Iran faces international sanctions	21433 Stekramer: 0.513; 133861 Debrawilmer: 0.464; 29638 Eeshakha 0.46
Notable Achievements	Contributions to literature, architecture, and governance	31522 McCutchen: 0.494; duodecana qc72: 0.488; 30200 Terryburch: 0.48
Notable Cultural Facts	Known for its Persian poetry and carpets	19809 Nancyowen: 0.426; 5538 Luichewoo: 0.41
Peruvian		
10 Cultural Distinctions	Andean textiles, Quechua traditions, ceviche, pan flute music, colorful festivals, Inca ruins, alpaca wool, traditional dances, coca leaf use, spiritual connection to nature	31774 Debralas: 0.482; 87271 Kokubunji: 0.46; 3392 Setouchi: 1.01
10 Historical Highlights	Inca Empire, Spanish conquest, Viceroyalty of Peru, independence (1821), Shining Path conflict, Machu Picchu, Andean textiles, Amazon biodiversity, ceviche cuisine, Quechua language	11667 Testa: 0.516; 55735 Magdebur 0.495; 21488 Danyellelee: 0.494
20 Key Tags	Inca, Machu Picchu, Quechua, ceviche, textiles, pan flute, alpaca, festivals, ruins, coca, resilience, history, culture, art, tradition, preservation, biodiversity, spirituality, heritage, peace	264061 Vitebsk: 0.56; 31031 Altiplan 0.557
Historical outside contact	Colonized by Spain; modern Peru is a leader in cultural preservation	32272 Hasegawayuya: 0.482; 1724 Vladimir: 0.479; 25404 Shansample: 0.475
Notable Achievements	Preservation of Inca heritage and biodiversity	80008 Danielarhodes: 0.453; duodecanate qc256: 0.429; 11795 Fredrikbruhn: 0.423
Notable Cultural Facts	Known for its Inca heritage and biodiversity	19809 Nancyowen: 0.418; 20302 Kevinwang: 0.415; 19822 Vonzielonka 0.407

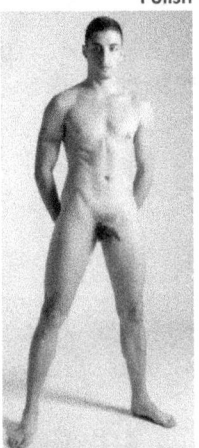

Polish

10 Cultural Distinctions	Catholic traditions, pierogi cuisine, folk dances, amber jewelry, Polish language, Christmas celebrations, historical castles, strong family values, resilience, vibrant art scene	2932 Kempchinsky: 0.488; 25706 Cekoscielski: 0.488; 4217 Engelhardt: 0.453
10 Historical Highlights	Christianization (966), Polish-Lithuanian Commonwealth, partitions of Poland, WWII resistance, Solidarity movement, Nobel Prize winners, Chopin's music, Copernicus' discoveries, Auschwitz liberation, EU membership	9480 Inti: 0.491; 6000 United Nations: 0.487; 46441 Mikepenston: 0.472
20 Key Tags	Catholic, pierogi, Chopin, Copernicus, amber, castles, resilience, Solidarity, Auschwitz, EU, history, culture, art, tradition, family, Christmas, Nobel, dances, language, values	41049 Van Citters: 0.604; 30276 Noahgolowich: 0.601; 11289 Frescobaldi: 0.6
Historical outside contact	Historically partitioned and occupied; modern Poland is a leader in EU integration	13530 Ninnemann: 0.527; 27512 Gilstrap: 0.477; 261109 Annie: 0.474
Notable Achievements	Contributions to science, music, and resistance movements	124q3: 0.569; 9403 Sanduleak: 0.557; duodecanate qc14: 0.553
Notable Cultural Facts	Known for its resilience and contributions to science and arts	2q5: 0.596; duodecanate 41: 0.561; 4380 Geyer: 0.558

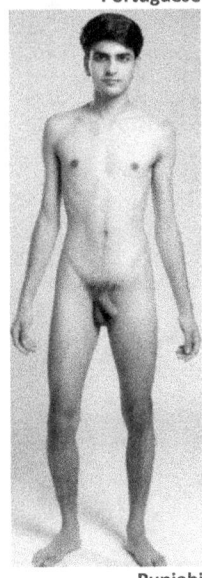

Portuguese

10 Cultural Distinctions	Fado music, azulejos (tiles), seafood cuisine, Catholic traditions, maritime heritage, wine-making, traditional festivals, Portuguese language, hospitality, historical landmarks	2932 Kempchinsky: 0.463; 2519 Annagerman: 0.453; 25706 Cekoscielski: 0.451
10 Historical Highlights	Age of Discoveries, Vasco da Gama's voyages, colonization of Brazil, Iberian Union, Restoration of Independence (1640), Carnation Revolution (1974), maritime trade, Fado music, cork production, EU membership	2747 Cesky Krumlov: 0.45; 14917 Taco: 0.448; 9817 Thersander: 0.443
20 Key Tags	Discoveries, Vasco, Fado, azulejos, seafood, wine, festivals, Catholic, hospitality, landmarks, resilience, history, culture, art, tradition, maritime, cork, EU, heritage, values	3162 Nostalgia: 0.558; 18079 Lion Stoppato: 0.552; 8716 Ginestra: 0.544
Historical outside contact	Colonized parts of Africa and Asia; modern Portugal is a cultural hub	75823 Csokonai: 0.464; 4696 Arpigny: 0.449; 3321 Dasha: 0.447
Notable Achievements	Contributions to exploration and maritime trade	18636 Villedepompey: 0.504; duodecanate 47: 0.49; 12032 Ivory: 0.484
Notable Cultural Facts	Known for its maritime heritage and Fado music	14872 Hoher List: 0.429; 30257 Leejanel: 0.39; 18855 Sarahgutman: 0.386

Punjabi

10 Cultural Distinctions	Sikh traditions, Bhangra dance, phulkari embroidery, Punjabi cuisine, strong community ties, vibrant festivals, Punjabi language, agricultural practices, hospitality, spiritual values	4573 Piestany: 0.433; 2303 Retsina: 0.427; 25706 Cekoscielski: 0.419
10 Historical Highlights	Indus Valley Civilization, Sikhism's founding, Mughal Empire, British colonization, partition (1947), Green Revolution, Bhangra dance, Punjabi poetry, agricultural advancements, vibrant festivals	7640 Marzari: 0.975; 4821 Bianucci: 0.444; 3321 Dasha: 0.443
20 Key Tags	Sikhism, Bhangra, phulkari, cuisine, festivals, community, language, agriculture, poetry, resilience, history, culture, art, tradition, values, hospitality, spirituality, heritage, Green Revolution	3050 Carrera: 0.508; 33826 Kevynadams: 0.499
Historical outside contact	Partition led to mass migration and violence; modern Punjab is culturally rich	4387 Tanaka: 0.482; 8561 Sikoruk: 0.481; 3124 Kansas: 0.468
Notable Achievements	Contributions to agriculture and spiritual traditions	31522 McCutchen: 0.529; 9403 Sanduleak: 0.523; 18520 Wolfratshausen: 0.517
Notable Cultural Facts	Known for its Sikh traditions and agricultural heritage	19809 Nancyowen: 0.442; 3887 Gerstner: 0.43; 19822 Vonzielonka: 0.425

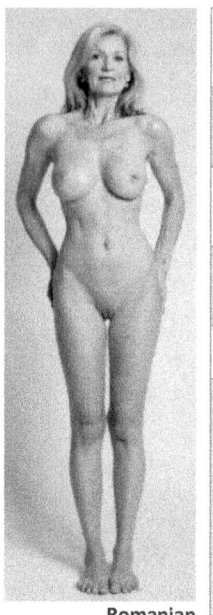

Romanian

10 Cultural Distinctions	Folk music, traditional dances, painted monasteries, Romanian language, Mărțișor tradition, hospitality, rural lifestyle, wine-making, historical castles, spiritual values	25706 Cekoscielski: 0.521; 6216 San Jose: 0.495; 4196 Shuya: 0.494
10 Historical Highlights	Roman influence, medieval principalities, Ottoman rule, unification (1859), independence (1877), communist era, 1989 revolution, Dracula legend, Dacian heritage, EU membership	6000 United Nations: 0.521; 205 Martha: 0.519; 20607 Vernazza: 0.5
20 Key Tags	Dracula, Dacian, Mărțișor, castles, dances, music, wine, hospitality, resilience, history, culture, art, tradition, values, spirituality, heritage, EU, preservation, rural, legends	8061 Gaudium: 0.569; 5302 Romanoserra: 0.566; 8716 Ginestra 0.559
Historical outside contact	Historically occupied; modern Romania is a leader in cultural preservation	10761 Lyubimets: 0.562; 129068 Alexmay: 0.522; 64290 Yaushingtun 0.522
Notable Achievements	Contributions to folklore and cultural preservation	31522 McCutchen: 0.547; 11679 Brucebaker: 0.544; 4380 Geyer: 0.5
Notable Cultural Facts	Known for its Dracula legend and painted monasteries	269300 Diego: 0.403; 4257 Ubasti: 0.399; 19809 Nancyowen: 0.397

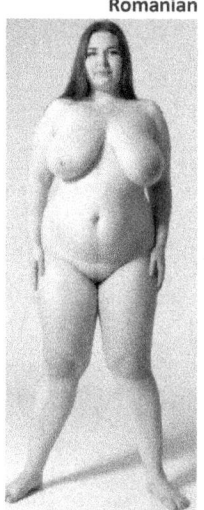

Russian

10 Cultural Distinctions	Orthodox traditions, Russian language, classical music, ballet, matryoshka dolls, vodka culture, winter festivals, strong family values, historical landmarks, resilience	91607 Delaboudiniere: 0.493; 1711 Sandrine: 0.482; 319 Leona: 1.041
10 Historical Highlights	Kievan Rus', Mongol invasion, Tsardom of Russia, Romanov dynasty, Bolshevik Revolution, WWII victory, space exploration, classical literature, ballet, Orthodox Christianity	12159 Bettybiegel: 0.522; 4859 Frak 1.136
20 Key Tags	Kievan, Romanov, Bolshevik, ballet, vodka, matryoshka, Orthodox, resilience, history, culture, art, tradition, family, landmarks, space, literature, values, winter, power, preservation	20850 Gaglani: 0.618; 69264 Nebra: 0.614
Historical outside contact	Historically invaded; modern Russia is a global power	6330 Koen: 0.438; 93q12: 0.437; 68 Tasaka: 0.434
Notable Achievements	Contributions to literature, ballet, and space exploration	18636 Villedepompey: 0.534; 16022 Wissnergross: 0.522; 29337 Hakuroj 0.516
Notable Cultural Facts	Known for its classical literature and space exploration	177853 Lumezzane: 0.491; 7056 Kierkegaard: 0.475; 7639 Offutt: 0.4

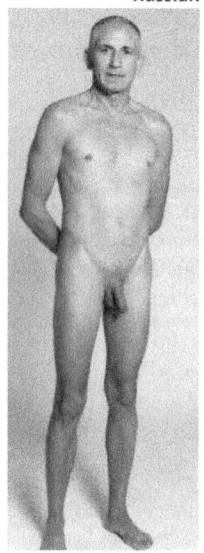

Salvadoran

10 Cultural Distinctions	Pupusa cuisine, vibrant festivals, Spanish language, Catholic traditions, rural lifestyle, storytelling, coffee production, strong community ties, historical landmarks, resilience	25706 Cekoscielski: 0.502; 4547 Massachusetts: 0.482; 18079 Lion Stoppato: 0.469
10 Historical Highlights	Pipil heritage, Spanish colonization, independence (1821), coffee industry, civil war (1980-1992), peace accords (1992), earthquake resilience, pupusa cuisine, vibrant festivals, migration waves	11334 Rio de Janeiro: 0.459; 125 Liberatrix: 0.459; 19434 Bahuffman: 0.448
20 Key Tags	Pipil, pupusa, coffee, festivals, Spanish, Catholic, resilience, history, culture, art, tradition, community, landmarks, storytelling, rural, migration, peace, values, preservation	6719 Gallaj: 0.595; 1337 Gerarda: 0. 256797 Benbow: 0.562
Historical outside contact	Civil war led to displacement; modern El Salvador is rebuilding	19970 Johannpeter: 0.496; 7777 Consadole: 0.455; 5q12: 0.451
Notable Achievements	Contributions to peacebuilding and cultural preservation	31522 McCutchen: 0.521; 4380 Geye 0.514; 7421 Kusaka: 0.509
Notable Cultural Facts	Known for its pupusa cuisine and vibrant festivals	2618 Coonabarabran: 0.387; 2867 Steins: 0.358; 19822 Vonzielonka: 0.

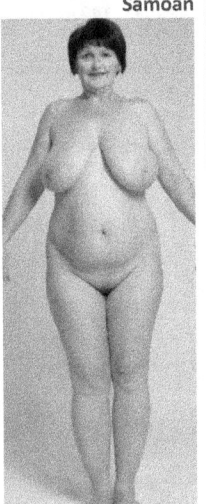

Samoan

Category	Description	Asteroids
10 Cultural Distinctions	Fa'a Samoa (Samoan way of life), traditional tattoos, fire dancing, kava ceremonies, storytelling, Polynesian music, communal living, vibrant festivals, Samoan language, hospitality	1369 Ostanina: 0.908; 10149 Cavagna: 0.465; 85386 Payton: 0.459
10 Historical Highlights	Polynesian settlement, Lapita pottery, Christianization, German colonization, New Zealand administration, independence (1962), fa'a Samoa traditions, maritime skills, Pacific navigation, cultural preservation	87271 Kokubunji: 0.467; 12742 Delisle: 0.455; 181751 Phaenops: 0.45
20 Key Tags	Polynesian, fa'a Samoa, tattoos, kava, storytelling, navigation, festivals, hospitality, resilience, history, culture, art, tradition, preservation, community, music, dance, language, peace	19575 Feeny: 0.554; 10555 Tagaharue: 0.55; 56088 Wuheng: 0.544
Historical outside contact	Colonized by Germany and New Zealand; modern Samoa is culturally resilient	1724 Vladimir: 0.514; 4821 Bianucci: 0.504; 5855 Yukitsuna: 0.485
Notable Achievements	Contributions to Polynesian navigation and cultural preservation	4669 Hoder: 0.459; 31522 McCutchen: 0.455; duodecanate qig113: 0.454
Notable Cultural Facts	Known for its fa'a Samoa traditions and maritime skills	31858 Raykanipe: 0.446; 3518 Florena: 0.44

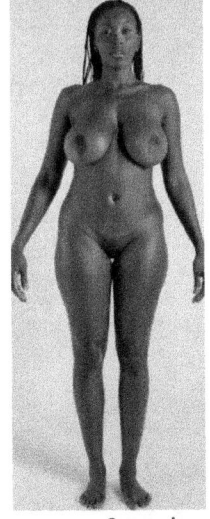

Scottish

Category	Description	Asteroids
10 Cultural Distinctions	Bagpipes, tartan kilts, ceilidh dances, whisky production, Gaelic language, rugged landscapes, literary tradition, castles, hospitality, strong community ties	2519 Annagerman: 1.076; 42981 Jenniskens: 0.504; 10874 Locatelli: 1.044
10 Historical Highlights	Roman invasions, Viking raids, Wars of Independence, Highland Clearances, Jacobite uprisings, Industrial Revolution, Enlightenment thinkers, WWII contributions, devolution (1999), cultural exports	7112 Ghislaine: 0.549; 18127 Denversmith: 0.537; 3790 Raywilson: 0.535
20 Key Tags	Bagpipes, tartan, ceilidh, whisky, Gaelic, castles, resilience, history, culture, art, tradition, preservation, landscapes, hospitality, community, literature, peace, innovation, values	15111 Winters: 0.549
Historical outside contact	Historically marginalized by England; modern Scotland is culturally vibrant	1724 Vladimir: 0.518; 10761 Lyubimets: 0.506; 2323 Zverev: 0.49
Notable Achievements	Contributions to Enlightenment and cultural exports	22543 Ranjan: 0.546; 4380 Geyer: 0.518; 2789 Foshan: 0.512
Notable Cultural Facts	Known for its tartan kilts and whisky production	3571 Milanstefanik: 0.347; 8716 Ginestra: 0.337; 9206 Yanaikeizo: 0.332

Senegalese

Category	Description	Asteroids
10 Cultural Distinctions	Sufi traditions, Wolof language, mbalax music, baobab symbolism, vibrant festivals, Senegalese cuisine, storytelling, hospitality, traditional clothing, strong community ties	30296 Bricehuang: 0.452; 6569 Ondaatje: 0.449; 9681 Sherwoodrowland: 0.448
10 Historical Highlights	Stone circles, Almoravid influence, Jolof Kingdom, trans-Saharan trade, French colonization, independence (1960), Léopold Senghor's leadership, Sufi brotherhoods, Dakar as cultural hub, UNESCO heritage sites	373 Melusina: 0.479; 32580 Avbalasingam: 0.456; 9419 Keikochaki: 0.454
20 Key Tags	Sufi, Wolof, mbalax, baobab, festivals, cuisine, storytelling, resilience, history, culture, art, tradition, preservation, hospitality, diplomacy, community, values, peace, heritage	27330 Markporter: 0.528; 3188 Jekabsons: 0.517; 366852 Ti: 0.515
Historical outside contact	Colonized by France; modern Senegal is a leader in African diplomacy	32272 Hasegawayuya: 0.465; 25404 Shansample: 0.462; 33270 Katiecrysup: 0.459
Notable Achievements	Contributions to African diplomacy and cultural preservation	5855 Yukitsuna: 0.486; 3124 Kansas: 0.484; 30788 Angekauffmann: 0.478
Notable Cultural Facts	Known for its Sufi traditions and mbalax music	7842 Ishitsuka: 0.438; 18855 Sarahgutman: 0.408; 15111 Winters: 0.397

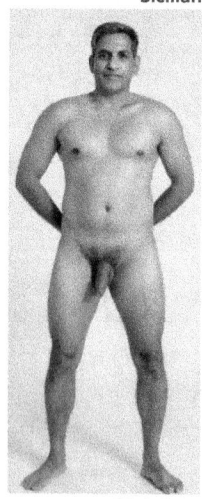

Serbian

10 Cultural Distinctions	Orthodox traditions, Cyrillic script, folk music, traditional dances, rakija (brandy), hospitality, historical landmarks, vibrant festivals, rural lifestyle, strong community ties	6216 San Jose: 2.013; 17698 Racheldavis: 0.481; 178150 Taiyuink 0.48
10 Historical Highlights	Byzantine influence, Ottoman rule, Battle of Kosovo, Serbian Revolution, WWI involvement, Yugoslav era, NATO intervention, cultural resilience, Cyrillic script, Orthodox Christianity	13283 Dahart: 0.498; 5152 Labs: 0.4 3473 Sapporo: 0.493
20 Key Tags	Orthodox, Cyrillic, rakija, dances, music, resilience, history, culture, art, tradition, preservation, hospitality, landmarks, festivals, rural, community, values, peace, heritage	14571 Caralexander: 0.566; 20264 Chauhan: 0.563
Historical outside contact	Historically occupied; modern Serbia is culturally resilient	2q5: 0.531; 7470 Jabberwock: 0.501 7869 Pradun: 0.485
Notable Achievements	Contributions to Orthodox Christianity and cultural preservation	31522 McCutchen: 0.494; 30035 Charlesliu: 0.474
Notable Cultural Facts	Known for its Orthodox traditions and folk music	17853 Ronaldsayer: 0.515; 177853 Lumezzane: 0.498

Sicilian

10 Cultural Distinctions	Greek temples, Arab-Norman architecture, Sicilian cuisine, vibrant festivals, storytelling, wine-making, traditional music, hospitality, rugged landscapes, strong community ties	2932 Kempchinsky: 0.515; 31492 Jennarose: 0.48; 14214 Hirsch: 1.031
10 Historical Highlights	Greek colonization, Roman rule, Arab influence, Norman conquest, Spanish rule, Bourbon era, Italian unification, WWII resilience, Mafia history, cultural fusion	2771 Polzunov: 0.986; 12742 Delisle: 0.514; 1697 Koskenniemi: 0.513
20 Key Tags	Greek, Arab, Norman, cuisine, festivals, storytelling, resilience, history, culture, art, tradition, preservation, wine, hospitality, landscapes, community, values, peace, heritage	8496 Jandlsmith: 0.584; 16479 Paulz 0.562
Historical outside contact	Historically invaded; modern Sicily is culturally rich	2841 Puijo: 0.436; 3124 Kansas: 0.42
Notable Achievements	Contributions to architecture and cultural fusion	30200 Terryburch: 0.509; 80q9: 0.50. 4380 Geyer: 0.499
Notable Cultural Facts	Known for its Greek temples and Arab-Norman architecture	367406 Buser: 0.422; 7125 Eitarodat 0.397; 24139 Brianmcarthy: 0.379

Sinhalese

10 Cultural Distinctions	Theravada Buddhism, Sinhala language, traditional dances, rice farming, vibrant festivals, hospitality, ancient architecture, storytelling, spiritual values, strong community ties	12447 Yatescup: 1.039; 34282 Applegate: 0.478; 7647 Etrepigny: 0.4
10 Historical Highlights	Arrival of Prince Vijaya, adoption of Buddhism, Anuradhapura Kingdom, Polonnaruwa Kingdom, Portuguese colonization, Dutch rule, British colonization, independence (1948), civil conflicts, cultural preservation	33270 Katiecrysup: 0.537; 7355 Bottl 0.521; 12414 Bure: 0.52
20 Key Tags	Buddhism, Sinhala, resilience, history, culture, art, tradition, preservation, festivals, hospitality, architecture, storytelling, values, peace, community, spirituality, rice, dances, heritage	21645 Chentsaiwei: 0.524; 13615 Manulis: 0.515
Historical outside contact	Colonized by Europeans; modern Sri Lanka is culturally resilient	duodecanate 41: 0.5; 2q5: 0.489; 172 Vladimir: 0.484
Notable Achievements	Contributions to Buddhism and cultural preservation	31522 McCutchen: 0.54; 266646 Zaphod: 0.503; 80q9: 0.503
Notable Cultural Facts	Known for its Theravada Buddhist traditions and ancient architecture	177853 Lumezzane: 0.432; 3887 Gerstner: 0.422; 18520 Wolfratshaus 0.406

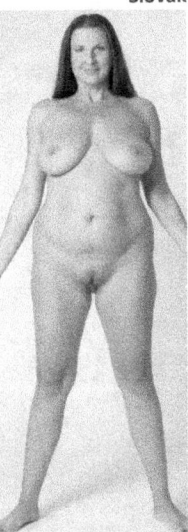

Slovak

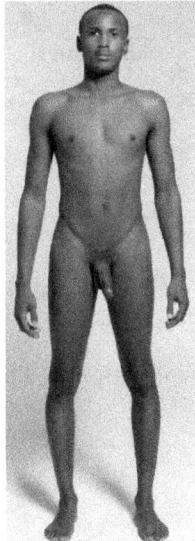

Slovenian

Somali

10 Cultural Distinctions	Folk music, wooden churches, Slovak language, traditional costumes, hearty cuisine, Christmas traditions, hospitality, mountain lifestyle, spa towns, egalitarian values	6216 San Jose: 0.499; 42981 Jenniskens: 0.497; 7333 Bec Borsenberger: 0.491
10 Historical Highlights	Great Moravia, Hungarian rule, Christianization, Hussite Wars, Austro-Hungarian Empire, Czechoslovakia formation (1918), WWII resistance, Velvet Revolution (1989), EU membership, cultural preservation	231666 Aisymnos: 0.47; 3473 Sapporo: 0.47; 4359 Berlage: 0.466
20 Key Tags	Moravia, Hussite, Velvet, EU, folk, costumes, cuisine, resilience, history, culture, art, tradition, preservation, hospitality, mountains, values, Christmas, egalitarian, peace	10444 de Hevesy: 0.583; 13241 Biyo: 0.575; 33353 Chattopadhyay: 0.563
Historical outside contact	Historically ruled by Hungary; modern Slovakia is a leader in cultural preservation	129068 Alexmay: 0.458; 7621 Sweelinck: 0.453; 1790 Volkov: 0.45
Notable Achievements	Velvet Revolution and cultural preservation	5813 Eizaburo: 0.434; 4696 Arpigny: 0.432; 266646 Zaphod: 0.425
Notable Cultural Facts	Known for its wooden churches and folk traditions	17853 Ronaldsayer: 0.421; 3887 Gerstner: 0.414; 62q3: 0.402
10 Cultural Distinctions	Alpine lifestyle, folk music, traditional dances, wine-making, Slovenian language, hospitality, vibrant festivals, historical landmarks, egalitarian values, unique cuisine	15845 Bambi: 0.466; 12932 Conedera: 0.458; 3266 Bernardus: 0.453
10 Historical Highlights	Roman rule, Slavic migration, Habsburg Monarchy, Protestant Reformation, Austro-Hungarian Empire, WWII resistance, independence (1991), EU membership, Alpine tourism, cultural preservation	3473 Sapporo: 0.521; 16147 Jeanli: 0.515; 4821 Bianucci: 0.514
20 Key Tags	Alpine, Habsburg, wine, dances, music, resilience, history, culture, art, tradition, preservation, hospitality, landmarks, festivals, egalitarian, cuisine, peace, independence	11013 Kullander: 0.608; 13241 Biyo: 0.607; 1203 Nanna: 0.601
Historical outside contact	Historically ruled by Habsburgs; modern Slovenia is a leader in cultural preservation	10761 Lyubimets: 0.483; 11795 Fredrikbruhn: 0.459; 82q2: 0.454
Notable Achievements	Contributions to Alpine tourism and cultural preservation	31522 McCutchen: 0.458; 124q3: 0.45; 91607 Delaboudiniere: 0.445
Notable Cultural Facts	Known for its Alpine lifestyle and wine-making	15543 Elizateel: 0.405; 269300 Diego: 0.389; 7624 Gluck: 0.377
10 Cultural Distinctions	Nomadic lifestyle, Somali language, traditional music, storytelling, camel herding, vibrant festivals, Islamic traditions, hospitality, traditional attire, oral poetry	12932 Conedera: 0.501; 223950 Mississauga: 0.953; 8022 Scottcrossfield: 0.488
10 Historical Highlights	Land of Punt, Islamic sultanates, colonial rule (British, Italian), independence (1960), Somali Civil War, piracy issues, nomadic traditions, poetry heritage, Sufi influence, cultural resilience	5426 Sharp: 0.503; 1480 Aunus: 0.499; 30033 Kevinlee: 0.499
20 Key Tags	Punt, nomadic, poetry, storytelling, resilience, history, culture, art, tradition, preservation, hospitality, festivals, attire, Islamic, camel, music, values, peace, heritage	3162 Nostalgia: 0.576; 17470 Mitsuhashi: 0.574; 166622 Sebastien: 0.57
Historical outside contact	Historically colonized; modern Somalia faces challenges in state-building	986 Amelia: 0.486; 313116 Palvenetianer: 0.46; 4821 Bianucci: 0.457
Notable Achievements	Contributions to oral poetry and cultural resilience	31522 McCutchen: 0.514; 2q5: 0.493; duodecanate 41: 0.486
Notable Cultural Facts	Known for its oral poetry and nomadic traditions	11767 Milne: 0.468; 3571 Milanstefanik: 0.461

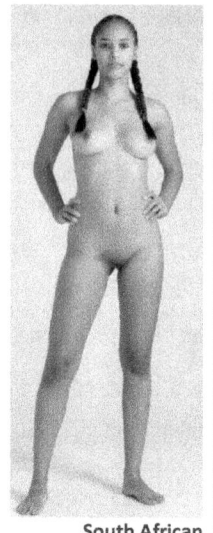

South African

10 Cultural Distinctions	Rainbow Nation, 11 official languages, vibrant music and dance, braai culture, wildlife conservation, traditional healing, rugby passion, diverse cuisines, historical landmarks, egalitarian values	20623 Davidyoung: 0.466; 2314 Fie 0.453; 4560 Klyuchevskij: 0.447
10 Historical Highlights	Early human fossils, Bantu migrations, Dutch colonization, British rule, apartheid era, Nelson Mandela's leadership, 1994 democratic elections, cultural diversity, gold and diamond trade, African Union membership	10767 Toyomasu: 0.523; 4821 Bian 0.498; 10725 Sukunabikona: 0.494
20 Key Tags	Rainbow, apartheid, Mandela, braai, wildlife, music, dance, resilience, history, culture, art, tradition, preservation, reconciliation, landmarks, values, peace, diversity, heritage	90455 Irenehernandez: 0.547; 48 D 0.544; 9482 Rubendario: 0.54
Historical outside contact	Colonized by Dutch and British; modern South Africa is a leader in reconciliation	10829 Matsuobasho: 0.533; 1724 Vladimir: 0.509; 6524 Baalke: 0.501
Notable Achievements	Contributions to reconciliation and cultural diversity	3321 Dasha: 0.583; 43957 Invernizz 0.566; 31522 McCutchen: 0.54
Notable Cultural Facts	Known for its Rainbow Nation identity and cultural diversity	duodecanate 41: 0.415; 20073 Yum 0.412; 20302 Kevinwang: 0.394

Spanish

10 Cultural Distinctions	Flamenco music, bullfighting, tapas cuisine, siesta culture, Spanish language, vibrant festivals, Catholic traditions, historical landmarks, Mediterranean lifestyle, egalitarian values	2932 Kempchinsky: 0.481; 2587 Gardner: 1.059; 11022 Serio: 0.461
10 Historical Highlights	Roman Empire, Visigothic rule, Moorish Al-Andalus, Reconquista, Spanish Inquisition, Spanish Empire, Spanish Civil War, Franco era, EU membership, cultural exports	6658 Akiraabe: 0.54; 1665 Gaby: 0.5 26334 Melimcdowell: 0.53
20 Key Tags	Flamenco, bullfighting, tapas, siesta, resilience, history, culture, art, tradition, preservation, landmarks, festivals, Catholic, Mediterranean, values, peace, diversity, heritage, language	3932 Edshay: 0.599; 21840 Ghoshchoudhury: 0.594
Historical outside contact	Historically colonized parts of the world; modern Spain is a cultural powerhouse	2771 Polzunov: 0.513; 3124 Kansas: 0.498; 12802 Hagino: 0.497
Notable Achievements	Contributions to art, language, and cultural exports	80q9: 0.517; 22543 Ranjan: 0.516; 31522 McCutchen: 0.482
Notable Cultural Facts	Known for its flamenco music and Mediterranean lifestyle	107638 Wendyfreedman: 0.419; 784 Ishitsuka: 0.411; 15111 Winters: 0.4

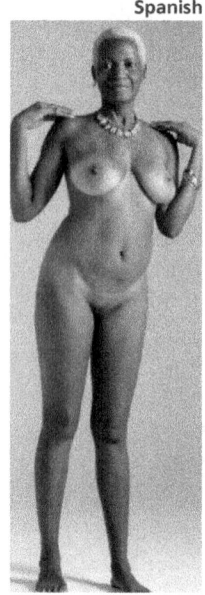

Sudanese

10 Cultural Distinctions	Nubian traditions, Islamic customs, traditional music, storytelling, hospitality, vibrant festivals, diverse cuisines, traditional attire, spiritual values, strong community ties	17853 Ronaldsayer: 0.463; 1369 Ostanina: 0.453; 1412 Lagrula: 0.433
10 Historical Highlights	Kingdom of Kush, Meroë pyramids, Islamic influence, Mahdist War, Anglo-Egyptian rule, independence (1956), Darfur conflict, cultural diversity, Nile River civilization, Nubian heritage	6000 United Nations: 0.434; 4387 Tanaka: 0.426; 55735 Magdeburg: 0
20 Key Tags	Kush, Meroë, Nubian, Nile, resilience, history, culture, art, tradition, preservation, hospitality, festivals, attire, Islamic, storytelling, music, values, peace, heritage	277883 Basu: 0.544; 56000 Mesopotamia: 0.539; 1358 Gaika: 0.
Historical outside contact	Historically colonized; modern Sudan faces challenges in state-building	986 Amelia: 0.513; 313116 Palvenetianer: 0.489; 127545 Crisma 0.478
Notable Achievements	Contributions to Nubian heritage and cultural preservation	4380 Geyer: 0.451; 31522 McCutche 0.436; 2047 Smetana: 0.422
Notable Cultural Facts	Known for its Nubian heritage and Nile River culture	19809 Nancyowen: 0.381; 1916 Bore 0.333; 19822 Vonzielonka: 0.331

Swedish

10 Cultural Distinctions	Fika tradition, minimalist design, midsummer celebrations, sauna culture, egalitarian values, Swedish language, folk music, strong environmentalism, meatball cuisine, winter sports	178267 Sarajevo: 0.484; 12086 Joshualevine: 0.475; 154714 de Schepper: 0.469
10 Historical Highlights	Viking Age, Kalmar Union, Protestant Reformation, Thirty Years' War, Nobel Prize establishment, industrialization, WWII neutrality, welfare state development, EU membership, technological innovation	2415 Ganesa: 0.504; 6923 Borzacchini: 0.489; 6239 Minos: 0.486
20 Key Tags	Vikings, fika, Nobel, sauna, midsummer, egalitarian, design, resilience, history, culture, art, tradition, preservation, innovation, diplomacy, winter, sports, values, peace	14539 Clocke Roeland: 0.61; 508 Princetonia: 0.596; 35056 Cullers: 0.59
Historical outside contact	Historically neutral; modern Sweden is a leader in innovation and diplomacy	1928 Summa: 0.487; 246842 Dutchstapelbroek: 0.486; 24q9: 0.483
Notable Achievements	Establishment of the Nobel Prize and contributions to innovation	124q3: 0.515; duodecanate qig94: 0.493; 31522 McCutchen: 0.486
Notable Cultural Facts	Known for its Nobel Prize and environmental consciousness	5181 SURF: 0.51; 9013 Sansaturio: 0.492; 13667 Samthurman: 0.483

Swiss

10 Cultural Distinctions	Multilingualism, Swiss watches, chocolate production, banking expertise, yodeling, alphorn music, skiing culture, fondue cuisine, strong community ties, neutrality	2094 Magnitka: 0.554; 7333 Bec Borsenberger: 0.534; 20140 Costitx: 0.522
10 Historical Highlights	Helvetic tribes, Roman rule, Swiss Confederacy formation, Reformation, Napoleonic era, neutrality in world wars, banking industry rise, UN headquarters, Alpine tourism, cultural preservation	156751 Chelseaferrell: 0.502; 4821 Bianucci: 0.496; 1453 Fennia: 0.495
20 Key Tags	Helvetic, neutrality, watches, chocolate, banking, skiing, fondue, yodeling, alphorn, resilience, history, culture, art, tradition, preservation, diplomacy, values, peace, innovation, community	33353 Chattopadhyay: 0.589; 632 Pyrrha: 0.581; 274860 Emilylakdawalla: 0.581
Historical outside contact	Historically neutral; modern Switzerland is a leader in diplomacy and innovation	1928 Summa: 0.492; 164587 Taesch: 0.487; 246842 Dutchstapelbroek: 0.474
Notable Achievements	Contributions to diplomacy and innovation	31631 Abbywilliams: 0.556; duodecanate qc72: 0.549; 31522 McCutchen: 0.541
Notable Cultural Facts	Known for its neutrality and Alpine lifestyle	1182 Ilona: 0.537; 26q12: 0.466; 1049 Gotho: 0.465

Syrian

10 Cultural Distinctions	Dabke dance, Arabic poetry, Levantine cuisine, storytelling, religious landmarks, traditional attire, vibrant festivals, spiritual values, strong community ties	25751 Mokshagundam: 0.441; 56329 Tarxien: 0.429; 2094 Magnitka: 0.426
10 Historical Highlights	Ancient city of Ebla, Roman rule, Islamic caliphates, Crusades, Ottoman Empire, French mandate, independence (1946), Six-Day War, civil war, cultural resilience	38020 Hannadam: 0.501; 10847 Koch: 0.487; 10090 Sikorsky: 0.483
20 Key Tags	Ebla, Dabke, poetry, Levantine, resilience, history, culture, art, tradition, preservation, hospitality, festivals, attire, landmarks, storytelling, values, peace, spirituality, community	16463 Nayoro: 0.564; 31595 Noahpritt: 0.563; 9990 Niiyaeki: 0.563
Historical outside contact	Historically invaded; modern Syria faces challenges in state-building	3457 Arnenordheim: 0.498; 313116 Palvenetianer: 0.495; 639 Latona: 0.488
Notable Achievements	Contributions to Arabic poetry and cultural preservation	2340 Hathor: 0.448; 16022 Wissnergross: 0.448; 53157 Akaishidake: 0.442
Notable Cultural Facts	Known for its ancient cities and cultural resilience	duodecanate 41: 0.511; 4380 Geyer: 0.454; 367406 Buser: 0.452

Taiwanese

Tajik

Tamil

10 Cultural Distinctions	Taiwanese cuisine, tea culture, Mandarin and Hokkien languages, vibrant festivals, indigenous crafts, strong family ties, traditional music, hospitality, spiritual values, entrepreneurial spirit	25706 Cekoscielski: 0.496; 11679 Brucebaker: 0.468; 30031 Angelakor 0.467
10 Historical Highlights	Austronesian settlement, Dutch colonization, Qing rule, Japanese occupation, Republic of China establishment, economic miracle, martial law era, democratic transition, cultural preservation, technological advancements	2841 Puijo: 0.57; 6069 Cevolani: 0.56 1724 Vladimir: 1.052
20 Key Tags	Austronesian, tea, Mandarin, Hokkien, resilience, history, culture, art, tradition, preservation, festivals, hospitality, values, spirituality, community, technology, innovation, family, crafts	24826 Pascoli: 0.586; 4546 Franck: 0.583; 18079 Lion Stoppato: 0.58
Historical outside contact	Historically occupied; modern Taiwan is a leader in technology and cultural preservation	10761 Lyubimets: 0.509; 2073 Janac 0.5
Notable Achievements	Contributions to technology and cultural preservation	31522 McCutchen: 0.531; 266646 Zaphod: 0.53; 4380 Geyer: 0.53
Notable Cultural Facts	Known for its tea culture and technological advancements	177853 Lumezzane: 0.484; 3518 Florena: 0.481; 19809 Nancyowen: 0.481
10 Cultural Distinctions	Persian language, traditional music, storytelling, hospitality, vibrant festivals, mountain lifestyle, spiritual values, strong community ties, traditional attire, agricultural practices	22426 Mikehanes: 0.523; 30031 Angelakong: 0.932; 26273 Kateschaf 0.514
10 Historical Highlights	Sogdian heritage, Persian influence, Islamic conquest, Silk Road trade, Soviet era, independence (1991), civil war, cultural resilience, Pamir Mountains, traditional crafts	4821 Bianucci: 0.544; 981 Martina: 0.513; 4572 Brage: 0.995
20 Key Tags	Sogdian, Persian, Silk Road, resilience, history, culture, art, tradition, preservation, hospitality, festivals, attire, storytelling, values, peace, spirituality, community, mountains, crafts	33826 Kevynadams: 0.582; 4147 Lennon: 0.574; 11519 Adler: 0.572
Historical outside contact	Historically occupied; modern Tajikistan is culturally resilient	2q5: 1.003; 1724 Vladimir: 0.501
Notable Achievements	Contributions to Silk Road trade and cultural resilience	4380 Geyer: 0.468; duodecanate 41: 0.455
Notable Cultural Facts	Known for its Persian language and mountain lifestyle	33129 Ivankrasko: 0.452; 3518 Florer 0.451
10 Cultural Distinctions	Tamil language, Bharatanatyam dance, Carnatic music, temple architecture, vibrant festivals, Tamil cuisine, storytelling, spiritual values, strong community ties, traditional crafts	344581 Albisetti: 0.491; 28299 Kanghaoyan: 0.886; 20787 Mitchfourman: 0.47
10 Historical Highlights	Sangam literature, Chola Empire, Pallava dynasty, Vijayanagara Empire, European colonization, Indian independence, Tamil diaspora, Bharatanatyam dance, temple architecture, cultural preservation	8905 Bankakuko: 0.528; 11316 Fuchitatsuo: 1.055; 19575 Feeny: 0.4
20 Key Tags	Sangam, Chola, Bharatanatyam, Carnatic, resilience, history, culture, art, tradition, preservation, festivals, cuisine, storytelling, values, peace, spirituality, community, architecture, crafts	15916 Shigeoyamada: 0.552; 33725 Robertkent: 0.508
Historical outside contact	Historically colonized; modern Tamil Nadu is culturally vibrant	33902 Ingoldsby: 0.49; 24370 Marywang: 0.479; 8561 Sikoruk: 0.47
Notable Achievements	Contributions to literature, dance, and temple architecture	16022 Wissnergross: 0.567; 30200 Terryburch: 0.518; 31522 McCutchen 0.504
Notable Cultural Facts	Known for its Tamil language and Bharatanatyam dance	30257 Leejanel: 0.403; 14600 Gainsbourg: 0.402

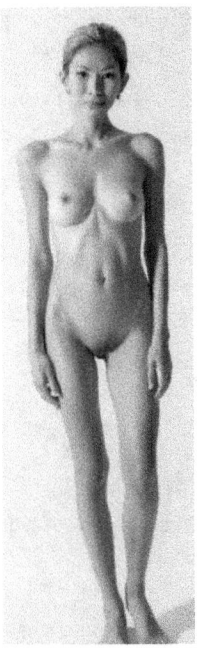

Thai

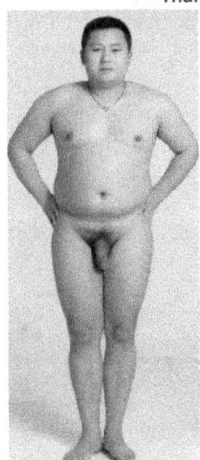

Tibetan

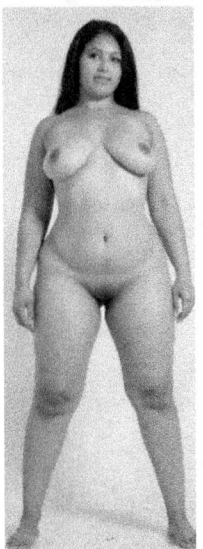

Trinidadian

10 Cultural Distinctions	Thai cuisine, Buddhist temples, traditional dances, silk weaving, floating markets, Muay Thai, royal ceremonies, Songkran festival, hospitality, strong family ties	25706 Cekoscielski: 0.477; 12447 Yatescup: 1.038; 2867 Steins: 0.455
10 Historical Highlights	Sukhothai Kingdom, Ayutthaya Kingdom, Chakri dynasty, Siamese Revolution (1932), WWII neutrality, constitutional monarchy, Buddhist traditions, rice farming, silk production, vibrant festivals	7675 Gorizia: 0.456; 32059 Ruchipandya: 0.438; 10660 Felixhormuth: 0.437
20 Key Tags	Sukhothai, Ayutthaya, Chakri, Buddhism, silk, rice, Songkran, Muay Thai, hospitality, resilience, history, culture, art, tradition, preservation, family, festivals, monarchy, tourism, values	15916 Shigeoyamada: 0.567; 9145 Shustov: 0.554
Historical outside contact	Never colonized; modern Thailand is a leader in tourism and cultural preservation	9280 Stevenjoy: 0.468; 4821 Bianucci: 0.456; 1724 Vladimir: 0.45
Notable Achievements	Contributions to Buddhist traditions and cultural preservation	11679 Brucebaker: 0.546; 31522 McCutchen: 0.538; 80q9: 0.515
Notable Cultural Facts	Known for its Buddhist temples and Muay Thai	2618 Coonabarabran: 0.394; 269300 Diego: 0.373; 28322 Kaeberich: 0.365
10 Cultural Distinctions	Tibetan Buddhism, prayer flags, yak herding, butter tea, sand mandalas, polyandry, traditional music, storytelling, spiritual values, strong community ties	265594 Keletiagnes: 1.036; 90455 Irenehernandez: 1.011; 8716 Ginestra: 0.48
10 Historical Highlights	Zhang Zhung civilization, unification under Songtsen Gampo, introduction of Buddhism, Mongol influence, Qing rule, Tibetan independence movements, Dalai Lama's leadership, cultural resilience, Himalayan lifestyle, traditional medicine	604 Tekmessa: 0.43; 4821 Bianucci: 0.428; 233661 Alytus: 0.425
20 Key Tags	Buddhism, prayer flags, yak, mandalas, resilience, history, culture, art, tradition, preservation, storytelling, values, peace, spirituality, community, mountains, medicine, polyandry, tea	12447 Yatescup: 0.522
Historical outside contact	Historically occupied; modern Tibet faces challenges in autonomy	5678 DuBridge: 0.499; 28q4: 0.486; 53q11: 0.482
Notable Achievements	Contributions to Buddhism and cultural resilience	duodecanate 41: 0.524; 31522 McCutchen: 0.512; 2q5: 0.51
Notable Cultural Facts	Known for its Tibetan Buddhism and Himalayan lifestyle	44473 Randytatum: 0.432; 19822 Vonzielonka: 0.43; 19809 Nancyowen: 0.429
10 Cultural Distinctions	Carnival, calypso music, steelpan, vibrant festivals, diverse cuisines, multiculturalism, storytelling, strong community ties, tropical biodiversity, hospitality	344581 Albisetti: 0.505; 3392 Setouchi: 0.502; 2932 Kempchinsky: 0.489
10 Historical Highlights	Arawak heritage, Spanish colonization, French influence, British rule, independence (1962), Carnival evolution, steelpan invention, calypso music, cricket passion, vibrant festivals	4587 Rees: 0.493; 234294 Pappsandor: 0.488; 3137 Horky: 0.488
20 Key Tags	Arawak, Carnival, calypso, steelpan, resilience, history, culture, art, tradition, preservation, festivals, biodiversity, hospitality, storytelling, community, values, peace, music, diversity	42377 KLENOT: 0.586; 90926 Stahalik: 0.574; 21801 Ancerl: 0.566
Historical outside contact	Colonized by Spain and Britain; modern Trinidad is culturally vibrant	75823 Csokonai: 0.429; 25404 Shansample: 0.415; 10725 Sukunabikona: 0.408
Notable Achievements	Contributions to music and Carnival traditions	9100 Tomohisa: 0.53; 29642 Archiekong: 0.527; 31522 McCutchen: 0.525
Notable Cultural Facts	Known for its Carnival and steelpan music	8373 Stephengould: 0.404; 269300 Diego: 0.401; 188139 Stanbridge: 0.383

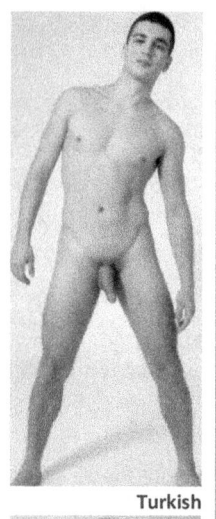

Turkish

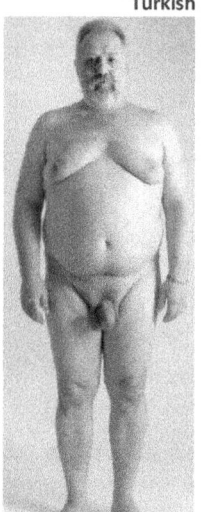

Ukrainian

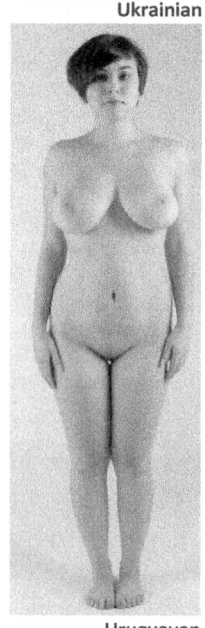

Uruguayan

10 Cultural Distinctions	Turkish cuisine, whirling dervishes, traditional music, storytelling, hospitality, vibrant festivals, Islamic architecture, strong family ties, tea culture, entrepreneurial spirit	2932 Kempchinsky: 0.522; 135991 Danarmstrong: 1.09; 14214 Hirsch: 0.502
10 Historical Highlights	Ottoman Empire, Byzantine influence, Islamic traditions, Republic of Turkey (1923), Atatürk's reforms, WWII neutrality, Turkish language reform, culinary heritage, cultural fusion, technological advancements	9251 Harch: 0.48; 6658 Akiraabe: 0. 4196 Shuya: 0.474
20 Key Tags	Ottoman, Atatürk, cuisine, dervishes, resilience, history, culture, art, tradition, preservation, festivals, hospitality, storytelling, values, peace, spirituality, community, architecture, tea	21645 Chentsaiwei: 0.578; 1963 Bezovec: 0.571
Historical outside contact	Historically diverse; modern Turkey is a leader in cultural fusion	3321 Dasha: 0.521; 1724 Vladimir: 0.518; 11679 Brucebaker: 0.516
Notable Achievements	Contributions to architecture and cultural fusion	30200 Terryburch: 0.509; 80q9: 0.5(4380 Geyer: 0.499
Notable Cultural Facts	Known for its Ottoman heritage and culinary traditions	177853 Lumezzane: 0.484; 1264 Let 0.471; 5276 Gulkis: 0.462
10 Cultural Distinctions	Ukrainian language, folk music, traditional dances, pysanky (decorated eggs), borscht cuisine, storytelling, hospitality, vibrant festivals, spiritual values, strong community ties	15111 Winters: 0.498; 5849 Bhanji: 0.494; 2932 Kempchinsky: 0.493
10 Historical Highlights	Kyivan Rus', adoption of Christianity (988), Cossack Hetmanate, Polish-Lithuanian Commonwealth, Soviet era, independence (1991), Euromaidan protests, cultural resilience, vibrant festivals, agricultural heritage	319 Leona: 0.512; 231666 Aisymnos 0.511; 16874 Kurtwahl: 0.498
20 Key Tags	Kyivan Rus', Cossacks, pysanky, borscht, resilience, history, culture, art, tradition, preservation, festivals, hospitality, storytelling, values, peace, spirituality, community, dances, agriculture	26448 Tongjili: 0.552; 69264 Nebra: 0.55; 278986 Chenshuchu: 0.542
Historical outside contact	Historically occupied; modern Ukraine is culturally resilient	2q5: 1.099; 7470 Jabberwock: 0.499 duodecanate 41: 1.052
Notable Achievements	Contributions to folk traditions and cultural resilience	4380 Geyer: 0.562
Notable Cultural Facts	Known for its folk traditions and pysanky	17853 Ronaldsayer: 0.516; 269300 Diego: 0.477; 11679 Brucebaker: 0.4
10 Cultural Distinctions	Mate tea culture, tango music, Carnival, vibrant festivals, storytelling, hospitality, diverse cuisines, rural lifestyle, egalitarian values, strong family ties	-50001 SqMoon-: 0.528; 344581 Albisetti: 0.51; 11774 Jerne: 0.508
10 Historical Highlights	Indigenous heritage, Spanish colonization, independence (1828), cattle farming, democratic traditions, Carnival celebrations, tango music, vibrant festivals, cultural resilience, strong community ties	10829 Matsuobasho: 0.5; 15845 Bar 0.496; 1724 Vladimir: 0.93
20 Key Tags	Mate, tango, Carnival, resilience, history, culture, art, tradition, preservation, festivals, hospitality, storytelling, values, peace, spirituality, community, rural, egalitarian, family	206 Hersilia: 0.623; 20730 Jorgecarv 0.613; 24215 Jongastel: 0.611
Historical outside contact	Colonized by Spain; modern Uruguay is culturally vibrant	75823 Csokonai: 0.425; 93q12: 0.41!
Notable Achievements	Contributions to democratic traditions and cultural preservation	31522 McCutchen: 0.525; 7410 Kawazoe: 0.507; 11679 Brucebaker: 0.496
Notable Cultural Facts	Known for its mate tea culture and Carnival	30353 Carothers: 0.467; 2618 Coonabarabran: 0.463; 850 Altona: 0.462

Uzbek

Venezuelan

Vietnamese

10 Cultural Distinctions	Uzbek cuisine (plov), traditional music, intricate embroidery, hospitality, vibrant bazaars, Islamic architecture, Navruz festival, tea culture, strong family ties, storytelling	91607 Delaboudiniere: 0.448; 231666 Aisymnos: 0.444; 18079 Lion Stoppato: 0.438
10 Historical Highlights	Silk Road trade, Timurid Empire, Mongol invasions, Russian colonization, Soviet era, independence (1991), Samarkand's prominence, Bukhara Emirate, Islamic Golden Age, cultural preservation	25155 van Belle: 0.458; 12414 Bure: 0.458; 25539 Roberthelm: 0.454
20 Key Tags	Silk Road, Timurid, plov, bazaars, embroidery, Navruz, resilience, history, culture, art, tradition, preservation, hospitality, storytelling, family, architecture, Islamic, Samarkand, Bukhara	3519 Ambiorix: 0.535; 7333 Bec Borsenberger: 0.534; 3634 Iwan: 0.524
Historical outside contact	Colonized by Russia; modern Uzbekistan is culturally resilient	1724 Vladimir: 0.506; 4821 Bianucci: 0.487; 211021 Johnpercin: 0.48
Notable Achievements	Contributions to Silk Road trade and Timurid architecture[_{{{CITATION{{{_1{History of Uzbekistan	2948 Amosov: 0.838; 4380 Geyer: 0.425; 2867 Steins: 0.75
Notable Cultural Facts	Known for its Silk Road cities and Timurid architecture	9277 Togashi: 0.36
10 Cultural Distinctions	Arepas cuisine, vibrant festivals, salsa music, Catholic traditions, storytelling, strong family ties, tropical biodiversity, traditional attire, hospitality, diverse cuisines	14214 Hirsch: 0.468; 25706 Cekoscielski: 0.468; 2932 Kempchinsky: 0.462
10 Historical Highlights	Spanish colonization, independence (1811), Simon Bolivar's leadership, oil boom, economic crises, political upheavals, Orinoco River trade, indigenous heritage, vibrant festivals, cultural fusion	1697 Koskenniemi: 0.466; 4669 Hoder: 0.465; 4088 Baggesen: 0.457
20 Key Tags	Bolivar, arepas, salsa, resilience, history, culture, art, tradition, preservation, festivals, biodiversity, hospitality, storytelling, family, Catholic, attire, cuisine, diversity, Orinoco	13615 Manulis: 0.542; 23798 Samagonzalez: 0.539; 28168 Evanolin: 0.531
Historical outside contact	Colonized by Spain; modern Venezuela faces economic challenges	19691 Iwate: 0.425; 22q6: 0.417; 12180 Kistemaker: 0.404
Notable Achievements	Contributions to independence movements and cultural fusion5	22543 Ranjan: 0.515; 4380 Geyer: 0.513; 11679 Brucebaker: 0.506
Notable Cultural Facts	Known for its arepas and salsa music	18855 Sarahgutman: 0.436; 2805 Kalle: 0.428; 30257 Leejanel: 0.406
10 Cultural Distinctions	Ao dai attire, pho cuisine, Confucian values, traditional music, water puppetry, Tet festival, hospitality, strong family ties, spiritual values, storytelling	14214 Hirsch: 0.443; 23798 Samagonzalez: 0.441; 3254 Bus: 0.44
10 Historical Highlights	Đông Sơn culture, Chinese domination, independence (10th century), Nguyễn dynasty, French colonization, Vietnam War, reunification (1975), Đổi Mới reforms, rice farming, cultural preservation	30031 Angelakong: 1.054; 4359 Berlage: 0.468; 181751 Phaenops: 0.465
20 Key Tags	Đông Sơn, ao dai, pho, Tet, resilience, history, culture, art, tradition, preservation, storytelling, family, hospitality, Confucian, music, puppetry, values, rice, reunification	42614 Ubaldina: 0.59; 12013 Sibatahosimi: 0.559
Historical outside contact	Colonized by China and France; modern Vietnam is culturally vibrant	24370 Marywang: 0.477; 11679 Brucebaker: 0.96; 79q6: 0.46
Notable Achievements	Contributions to cultural preservation and reunification8[_{{{CITATION{{{_9{History of Vietnam	4380 Geyer: 0.522; 3124 Kansas: 0.48
Notable Cultural Facts	Known for its Tet festival and water puppetry	15071 Hallerstein: 0.391; 3571 Milanstefanik: 0.382; 269300 Diego: 0.375

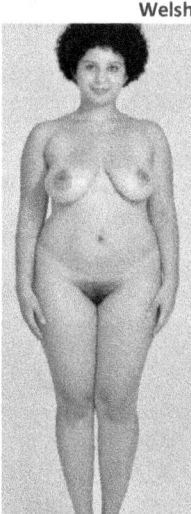

Welsh

10 Cultural Distinctions	Welsh language, Eisteddfod festivals, male voice choirs, leek and daffodil symbols, storytelling, Celtic music, hospitality, rugged landscapes, castles, egalitarian values	1921 Pala: 0.486; 110393 Rammstei 0.468; 2094 Magnitka: 0.466
10 Historical Highlights	Roman occupation, Norman invasions, Edwardian conquest, Glyndŵr's rebellion, Industrial Revolution, coal mining, literary revival, devolution (1999), cultural preservation, rugby passion	74439 Brenden: 0.518; 8503 Masaka 0.514; 7112 Ghislaine: 0.509
20 Key Tags	Glyndŵr, Eisteddfod, choirs, resilience, history, culture, art, tradition, preservation, storytelling, hospitality, castles, landscapes, Celtic, music, values, peace, rugby, egalitarian	21652 Vasishtha: 0.553; 24890 Amaliafinzi: 0.525; 23327 Luchernan 0.518
Historical outside contact	Historically marginalized by England; modern Wales is culturally vibrant	1724 Vladimir: 0.495; 10761 Lyubim 0.494; 4196 Shuya: 0.475
Notable Achievements	Contributions to literary revival and cultural preservation11[_{{{CITATION{{{&#12{The incredible history of Wales	30200 Terryburch: 0.471; 4587 Rees 0.453; 4380 Geyer: 0.45
Notable Cultural Facts	Known for its Eisteddfod festivals and male voice choirs	18855 Sarahgutman: 0.412; 344581 Albisetti: 0.387; 18814 Ivanovsky: 0.3

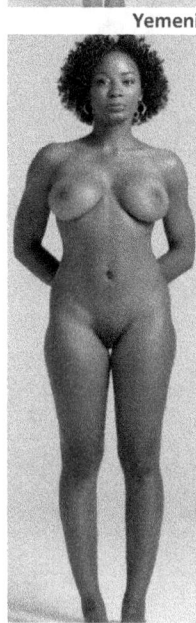

Yemeni

10 Cultural Distinctions	Yemeni cuisine, qat culture, traditional music, storytelling, hospitality, vibrant festivals, Islamic traditions, strong family ties, spiritual values, traditional attire	25706 Cekoscielski: 0.438; 20787 Mitchfourman: 0.435; 2932 Kempchinsky: 0.435
10 Historical Highlights	Kingdom of Saba, Himyarite Kingdom, Islamic caliphates, Ottoman rule, British colonization, unification (1990), coffee trade, cultural resilience, vibrant bazaars, architectural heritage	763 Cupido: 0.48; 9480 Inti: 0.472; 12742 Delisle: 0.466
20 Key Tags	Saba, Himyarite, coffee, qat, resilience, history, culture, art, tradition, preservation, storytelling, hospitality, festivals, attire, Islamic, values, peace, spirituality, bazaars	33826 Kevynadams: 0.582; 125 Liberatrix: 0.572; 99201 Sattler: 0.56
Historical outside contact	Historically colonized; modern Yemen faces challenges in state-building	313116 Palvenetianer: 0.492; 986 Amelia: 0.483; 22q6: 0.466
Notable Achievements	Contributions to coffee trade and architectural heritage[_{{{CITATION{{{&#14{Yemen - Culture, Traditions, Cuisine	3124 Kansas: 0.468; 8905 Bankakuko 0.466; 4380 Geyer: 0.464
Notable Cultural Facts	Known for its coffee trade and architectural heritage	30353 Carothers: 0.403; 5560 Amytis 0.397; 26323 Wuqijin: 0.378

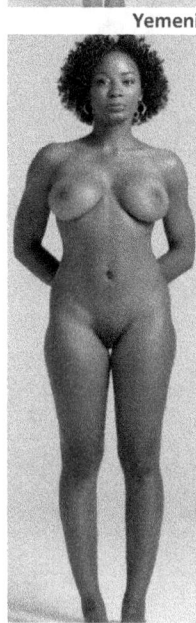

Yoruba

10 Cultural Distinctions	Yoruba language, Orisha worship, vibrant festivals, traditional attire, beadwork, storytelling, drumming, twin celebrations, market systems, culinary diversity	383417 DAO: 1.043; 91607 Delaboudiniere: 0.481; 185639 Rainerkling: 0.475
10 Historical Highlights	Oyo Empire, Ife as a spiritual center, bronze casting excellence, transatlantic slave trade, British colonization, independence (1960), cultural diaspora, Nollywood influence, traditional religion, urbanization in precolonial times	986 Amelia: 0.514; 23281 Vijayjain: 0.512; 14708 Slaven: 0.509
20 Key Tags	Oyo, Ife, Orisha, bronze, Nollywood, twins, drumming, beadwork, storytelling, resilience, history, culture, art, tradition, preservation, festivals, diaspora, markets, culinary, spirituality	24829 Berounurbi: 0.543; 155784 Erc 0.538
Historical outside contact	Colonized by Britain; modern Yoruba culture is globally influential	80q9: 0.48; 75823 Csokonai: 0.465; 1 Vladimir: 0.462
Notable Achievements	Excellence in bronze casting and cultural preservation	29347 Natta: 0.439; 23220 Yalemicha 0.422; 266646 Zaphod: 0.419
Notable Cultural Facts	Known for its twin birth rate and Orisha worship	6471 Collins: 0.432; 23801 Erikgustafson: 0.43; 14015 Senancou 0.42

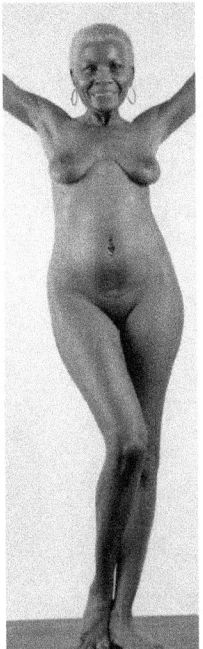

Zambian

10 Cultural Distinctions	Bantu languages, traditional music and dance, vibrant festivals, Nshima cuisine, storytelling, hospitality, traditional crafts, rural lifestyle, spiritual values, strong community ties	25706 Cekoscielski: 0.497; 2867 Steins: 0.428; 20787 Mitchfourman: 0.425
10 Historical Highlights	Early Bantu migrations, Broken Hill Man discovery, British colonization, independence (1964), copper mining boom, Victoria Falls significance, Kenneth Kaunda's leadership, peaceful transitions, cultural diversity, wildlife conservation	681 Gorgo: 0.447; 10829 Matsuobasho: 0.884; 20302 Kevinwang: 0.429
20 Key Tags	Bantu, Nshima, Victoria Falls, copper, resilience, history, culture, art, tradition, preservation, festivals, hospitality, storytelling, community, wildlife, peace, spirituality, crafts, rural	90455 Irenehernandez: 0.542; 48767 Skamander: 0.54; 7318 Dyukov: 0.54
Historical outside contact	Colonized by Britain; modern Zambia is peaceful and culturally diverse	4821 Bianucci: 0.46; 5855 Yukitsuna: 0.451
Notable Achievements	Contributions to peaceful transitions and cultural preservation	4380 Geyer: 0.551; 31522 McCutchen: 0.535; duodecanate 45: 0.535
Notable Cultural Facts	Known for its Victoria Falls and copper mining	269300 Diego: 0.378; 15170 Erikdeul: 0.349; 159826 Knapp: 0.342

Zimbabwean

10 Cultural Distinctions	Shona and Ndebele languages, mbira music, storytelling, traditional dances, spiritual values, hospitality, vibrant festivals, rural lifestyle, beadwork, strong community ties	28851 Londonbolsius: 0.984; 91607 Delaboudiniere: 0.447; 13235 Isiguroyuki: 0.443
10 Historical Highlights	Great Zimbabwe ruins, Shona and Ndebele heritage, British colonization, independence (1980), Mugabe's leadership, land reform policies, cultural resilience, vibrant festivals, stone sculpture, traditional music	1533 Saimaa: 0.462; 681 Gorgo: 0.461; 4119 Miles: 0.446
20 Key Tags	Shona, Ndebele, mbira, Great Zimbabwe, resilience, history, culture, art, tradition, preservation, festivals, hospitality, storytelling, community, spirituality, rural, beadwork, dances, sculpture	9822 Hajdukova: 0.529; 13109 Berzelius: 0.526
Historical outside contact	Colonized by Britain; modern Zimbabwe faces economic challenges	3124 Kansas: 0.461; 4387 Tanaka: 0.456; 5855 Yukitsuna: 0.448
Notable Achievements	Contributions to stone sculpture and cultural resilience	duodecanate 41: 0.516; 80q9: 0.516; 31522 McCutchen: 0.486
Notable Cultural Facts	Known for its Great Zimbabwe ruins and stone sculpture	95q12: 0.392; 9837 Jerryhorow: 0.385; 32428 Peterlangley: 0.378

I thought Copilot's stereotypes were pretty uplifting, so hopefully you won't mind them. It claims that these generalizations came from real research.

And to all the academic purists out there, the table above isn't about what constitutes a real race or real ethnicity, social construct or phenotype. This is about what people claim, and how they can put those labels to use by thinking about the astro factors they matched on.

You can get more out of this table than you think! For example, in addition to my main identity, my DNA report told me I was 47% Senegambian, 40% Nigerian, and 12% English and Irish in DNA origin. I can see the Irish in my nose and mouth region especially. You can also use this table to look up the characteristics of other people or countries you might be interested in.

THE FACE DILEMMA

8.   Having spent about 2 years trying to solve the problem of studying faces, I suddenly arrived at three different methods for doing the research correctly. Because all of these methods ultimately required that I sit down and label each of the mediapipe landmark points one by one, and match them against Makehuman sliders four by four, the results were exponential in scale and would fill this book. Nonetheless, for anyone interested in AI-anthropometry, I'll summarize all three methods in the next few steps. They consisted of 1) ratios of reduced tessellations (RORT), 2) filtered reduced tessellations (f-RORT), and 3) landmark to slider approximation (LANDOX).

   a.   Let's start with RORT. Suppose you have 478 landmarks minus 10 when you take out the left and right eyeballs. The landmarks are numbered, and you can find files on the web which take a few of those numbers and outline some very rough facial feature shapes. *Very* rough. So rough in fact that they are nigh useless for detailed differentiation of 100+ ethnicities. Furthermore, you have no idea which landmark points will be relevant from group to group. There might be several forehead points which differentiate one ethnicity, but a completely different set of points on the nose and chin which differentiate another. So you basically need to look at all pixel points in every image and do ANOVAs or t-tests on the aggregate. That's easy enough in theory EXCEPT that one pixel tells you nothing. The face could be upside down, sideways, etc., so what are you gonna do with one pixel? TWO pixels aren't enough either. Unless you've corrected for scale and can absolutely guarantee that all faces are bounding-boxed, consistently rotated, consistently scaled, and facing exactly the same direction— otherwise [the points on the nose] scale in all kinds of ways, for example. So in the end, you will need at least two pairs of points per measure—one pair for the distance you're looking at and another pair to serve as an anchor distance. But now, this is a probability count of 468 x 467 vs 466 x 465 divided by 2 or 4 or 4! or some other small number depending on how lazy you are or how much control you want over the result space. I didn't want to subject my computer to that or wait 5 months for that kind of run.

   So I decided to use Google's own list of predesignated shapes (tessellations) which divide the face into sensible polygons. There were 852 of these. Knowing nothing about what would be relevant, but with a good formula for calculating the area of each tessellation (all triangles), I decided to take ratios of these tessellation areas. There would be 852 x 851 / 2 of these ratios. Still too many, because I'd have to do this for every asteroid or ethnic group I was studying. To help ease the load, I came up with a very Flintstone algorithm which looked for tessellations that shared two points, added their areas to merge them into a quadrilateral, and piled on any original triangles left over which hadn't been merged. This produced about 450 shapes with no symmetry or stable concavity whatsoever. Just a really bad jigsaw. BUT, the point wasn't to produce something human readable, only to capture general regions. So I went with this. Next, I only allowed second tessellations sharing edges with this *new* one to serve as possible denominators, bring the number of comparisons down to 450 * ~4. That is, I only compared ratios of neighboring shapes. I then eliminated some of the edge tessellations. And that's it. This gives us the RORT process:

   Take the areas of the existing polygons of a surface. Merge some of them by adding their areas, and be sure to keep track of the ones that weren't added. Those need to be taken as is into the reduced group. Divide each area of the reduced group by the area of each neighbor, avoiding repeat combinations. These ratios can then be used as the data you run against other stats. Below is an example of a RORT result. See how, for Lebanese faces, a battery of t-tests showed that the polygon formed by points [117, 228, 31, 111] divided by the polygon formed by points [31, 25, 226, 228] had a ratio of .023069, and this was significantly above the mean, with a positive t at $p<.01$.

FIGURE 35: RORT EXAMPLE RESULTS

Test Column	Variance Assumption	t	df	p-value (2	Mean Diff	Standard Error Difference	Ethnotype
[117, 228, 31, 111] / [31, 25, 226, 228]	Equal variances assumed	2.61705	4845	0.008897	0.023069	0.008814893	Lebanese
[118, 50, 101, 205] / [205, 206, 36, 101]	Equal variances assumed	-2.61362	4289	0.00899	0.019039	0.007284638	Lebanese
[321, 405, 406, 320] / [307, 320, 321, 325]	Equal variances assumed	2.637658	1530	0.008433	0.863672	0.327438908	Lithuanian
[366, 447, 345, 352] / [352, 376, 401, 366]	Equal variances assumed	2.634574	295	0.008869	0.557611	0.211651308	Lithuanian
[238, 79, 20, 239] / [79, 239, 237, 218]	Equal variances assumed	-2.61758	3537	0.008893	0.080819	0.030875577	Lithuanian
[9, 151, 108, 337] / [9, 336, 337, 299]	Equal variances assumed	-2.61599	5149	0.008923	0.030001	0.011468224	Lithuanian
[287, 273, 422, 424] / [273, 287, 291, 375]	Equal variances assumed	2.590019	1201	0.009713	0.224215	0.086568661	Lithuanian
[313, 406, 405, 314] / [314, 405, 404, 315]	Equal variances assumed	2.65444	3634	0.007979	0.34605	0.130366349	Macedonian
[229, 228, 117, 24] / [117, 228, 31, 111]	Equal variances assumed	-2.59188	4333	0.009577	0.047441	0.018303554	Macedonian

b.

Too bad we have no idea where [117, 228, 31, 111] is. Enter f-RORT.

c. RORT produced results I couldn't read, in ratios that weren't controllable in advance. This presented one of those data wrangling bridges that some brave people had to cross before AI could be a thing: Sitting down and labelling every point—the hard way—was the only remedy for this.

f-RORT is the same as RORT, except that each point or polygon has a name, allowing you to filter what goes in and *greatly* reduce the amount of needless processing you do. To name every polygon, I used a quasi-anatomical direction system which sometimes used proper medical terms, sometimes didn't. I'll warn you in advance that the point of my polygon labeling wasn't actually to be medically accurate, but rather to be quickly findable as soon as I read it. Here is the image I used:

FIGURE 36: FACE LANDMARKS

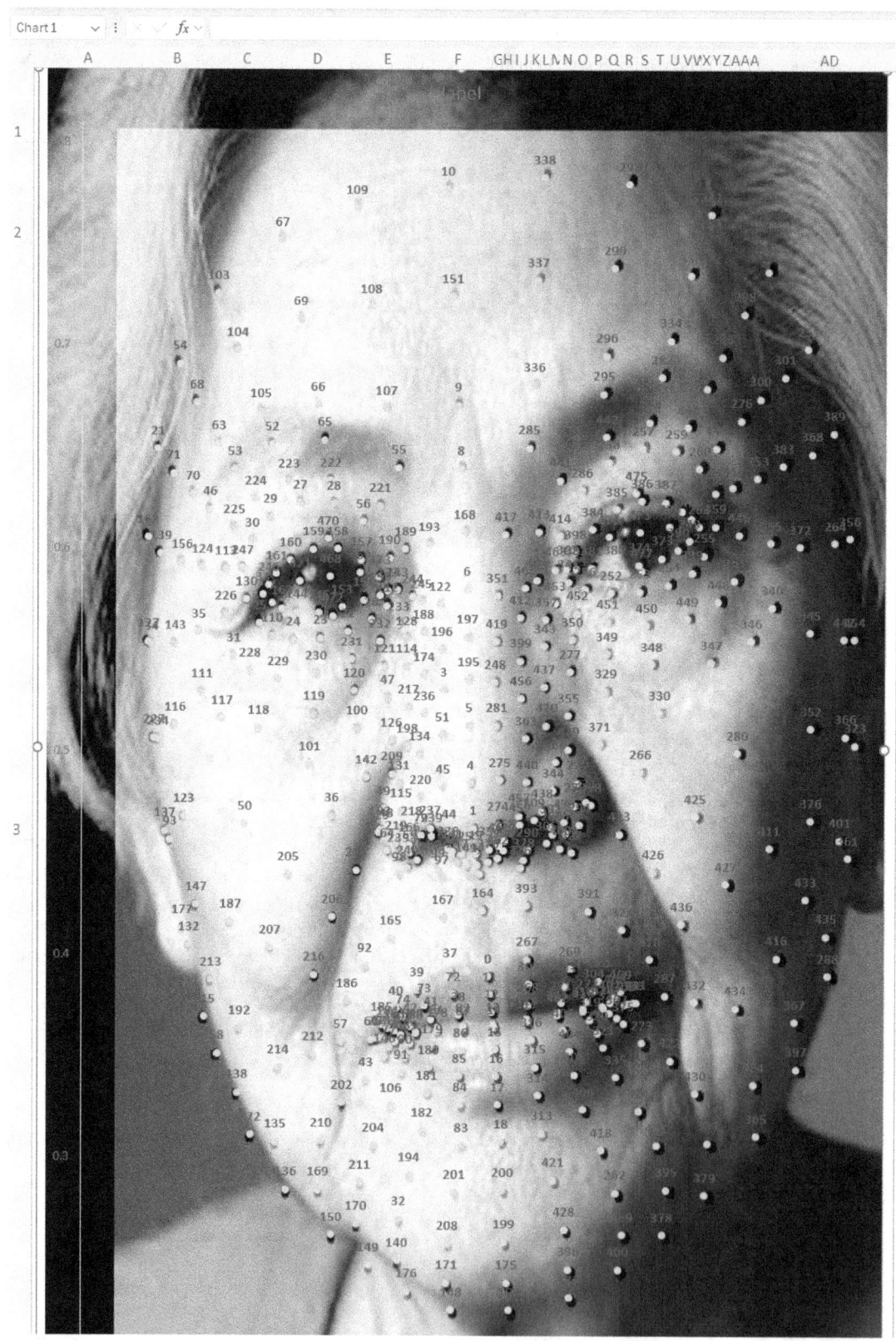

d.

Now remember, my polygons were machine-generated with no planning in advance, so they usually did not follow standard medical / anatomical naming practices. Here are the names of all of the polygons that were relevant to the person above's face. It covers about <u>half</u> of the 900 possible polygons that occurred in my AI-generated sample of 5017 headshots:

TABLE 41: FABRICATED, NONSCIENTIFIC NAMES I USED TO LABEL IRREGULAR POLYGONS ACROSS FACE POINTS

landmark area	label
[2, 164, 393, 326]	right upper philtrum
[2, 94, 141, 370]	septum
[2, 97, 167, 165]	left moustache
[6, 122, 196, 197]	lower upper nose bridge
[6, 197, 419, 351]	right lower upper nose bridge
[9, 151, 108, 109]	left region perilateral to the center forehead
[9, 336, 337, 299]	right lower forehead superior to the proximal brow
[11, 0, 37, 267]	cupid's' bow
[11, 302, 267, 12]	right side of center upper lip
[14, 15, 316, 86]	upper center of the lower lip
[14, 87, 86, 178]	left upper center of the lower lip
[15, 16, 315, 85]	center of lower lip
[15, 86, 85, 179]	distal left center of lower lip
[19, 125, 141, 94]	left septum
[19, 94, 370, 354]	right septum
[20, 60, 99, 240]	septum inferior to the left nostril
[20, 79, 166, 60]	outer left nostril hole
[21, 71, 68, 54]	left superior temple
[22, 23, 230, 229]	middle superior left eye bag
[24, 110, 228, 25]	distal superior left eye bag
[25, 130, 226, 31]	outer left eye angular vertex
[25, 7, 33, 130]	outer distal corner of the left eye
[26, 22, 231, 230]	distal superior region of the inner left eye bag
[27, 28, 222, 223]	center of region inferior to the left brow
[28, 158, 157, 56]	distal inner left upper eyelid
[28, 56, 221, 222]	distal left inner eyelid-inner brow region
[29, 27, 223, 224]	left center of region inferior to the left brow
[30, 29, 224, 225]	proximal left outer eyelid outer brow region
[32, 211, 140, 171]	lower distal left chin
[35, 226, 113, 247]	far outer upper left eyelid
[36, 142, 100, 101]	upper inner left cheek proximal to the superior left mouth line
[40, 92, 186, 39]	lower bi-demi outer nasolabius
[41, 38, 72, 12]	left lower center of the upper lip
[41, 42, 81, 38]	center of the bottom of the left upper lip
[41, 73, 74, 42]	inferior tri-trito outer left upper lip
[42, 74, 184, 185]	inferior bi-trito outer left upper lip
[43, 106, 91, 204]	left outer lip -left chin tracking line
[43, 146, 61, 57]	inferior perimouth distal to the left lip vertex
[43, 202, 204, 57]	lower angular distal to the left perimouth
[44, 1, 4, 274]	center nose tip
[44, 125, 19, 1]	left lower nose tip
[45, 220, 44, 4]	left medial nose bridge
[45, 51, 134, 220]	left medial alar crease
[46, 53, 63, 225]	left outer brow vertex
[46, 70, 156, 63]	left lower peri-outer brow
[48, 115, 131, 49]	upper lateral outer left nostril
[48, 49, 64]	low-center left nostril edge
[48, 64, 235, 219]	lower left nostril edge
[49, 102, 64, 129]	left nostril edge center base
[51, 45, 4, 5]	left proximal lower nose bridge
[52, 65, 66, 222]	center of left eyebrow
[54, 68, 104, 103]	left trito outer forehead outline
[55, 8, 9, 193]	left outer center brow
[56, 157, 173, 190]	left inner upper eyelid
[57, 61, 185, 184]	left lip vertex focal perimouth
[59, 166, 219, 235]	left bottom of outer nostril
[60, 75, 240, 166]	left bottom of bi-demi outer nostril base
[61, 76, 184]	left mouth vertex
[62, 76, 77, 96]	left lower lip vertex
[63, 105, 104, 69]	left distal forehead above outer eyebrow
[63, 53, 52]	upper bi-trito outer left eyebrow
[63, 68, 71, 104]	left superior peri-eyebrow
[64, 98, 240, 99]	left upper philtrum inferior to the outer nostril rim
[65, 55, 107, 9]	medial left upper brow ridge
[66, 65, 107]	left upper bi-demi inner eyebrow transition
[67, 69, 108, 109]	left bi-demi inner upper forehead
[70, 71, 139, 63]	left middle pre-eyebrow
[71, 21, 162]	let inferior temple
[72, 11, 37, 12]	left side of center upper lip
[72, 37, 39, 167]	left distal cupid's bow transition
[73, 39, 40, 74]	superior tri-trito outer left upper lip
[73, 72, 39, 41]	center of left upper lip
[74, 40, 185, 186]	left bi-demi outer upper lip transition
[75, 59, 235, 240]	left bottom of demi-outer nostril base
[76, 61, 146, 77]	inferior left mouth vertex

Code	Description
[76, 62, 183]	left trito outer upper-lower lip boundary
[77, 146, 91, 43]	left perimouth proximal to the outer lower lip
[78, 62, 96, 191]	left superior trio outer lower lip
[79, 239, 237, 241]	left septal-temporal diameter of nose hole
[80, 42, 183, 81]	tri-trito outer lip -lower lip boundary
[81, 82, 38, 13]	right center of the upper-lower lip boundary
[83, 18, 17, 84]	left center inferior to the lower lip
[83, 201, 18]	left distal center superior to the chin
[83, 84, 181, 182]	center of left lower lip - left distal upper chin plane
[84, 85, 180, 181]	inferior center of left lower lip transition
[85, 84, 17, 16]	left center of bottom of lower lip
[88, 89, 179]	left proxisuperior tri-trito outer lower lip
[88, 95, 96, 78]	left superior bi-tetarto outer lower lip
[89, 90, 180, 181]	left inferior bi-demi outer lower lip
[89, 96, 90, 88]	left bi-tetarto outer lower lip
[90, 91, 181, 182]	plane inferior to the bi-trito outer lower lip
[91, 106, 182, 194]	left mouth distal left chin tracking line
[93, 137, 227, 132]	left far middle cheek outline
[96, 77, 90, 91]	left inferior bi-tetarto outer lower lip
[98, 97, 99, 242]	left tetarto upper medial philtrum
[100, 47, 121, 120]	lower center of innermost (paranasal) eye bag fissure
[101, 100, 120, 119]	bottom terminus of left innermost eye bag
[104, 69, 67, 103]	left bi-demi outer upper forehead
[105, 63, 52, 66]	upper bi-demi outer left eyebrow
[105, 66, 69, 107]	left lower forehead above the left eyebrow center
[107, 108, 69, 9]	left forehead over brow lateral to the third eye
[110, 163, 7, 25]	pre distal corner of the lower left eye
[111, 117, 31, 226]	inferior left outer eye vertex
[111, 35, 143, 226]	inferior left crow's feet
[112, 233, 244, 232]	left upper terminus of innermost eye bag line
[112, 26, 232, 231]	left inner eye bag nexus
[113, 225, 46, 247]	infra to the left eyebrow left outer eye tracking line
[114, 128, 47]	left lower [mid-nose bridge - inner eye bag] bi-trito mediolateral transition
[114, 217, 174, 47]	left [mid-nose bridge - lower inner eye bag] demi mediolateral transition
[115, 48, 219, 218]	lower lateral outer left nostril
[116, 143, 227, 111]	left far upper cheekbone
[117, 123, 50, 187]	left outer cheek center lateralis
[117, 228, 31, 25]	face-left eye bag border
[118, 50, 101, 117]	left upper center cheek
[119, 118, 101, 230]	lower center of left eye bag
[122, 193, 245, 244]	left distal upper nose bridge
[122, 6, 168, 193]	left upper nose bridge
[123, 117, 111, 116]	left bi-demi upper cheek plane
[123, 137, 177, 147]	left outer lower cheekbone outplane
[123, 147, 187, 213]	left upper jaw infra outplane
[124, 35, 113, 46]	left eyebrow left outer eye tracking line
[124, 46, 156]	superior exo to the left eyebrow left outer eye tracking line
[125, 44, 237, 241]	medial left nostril hole
[126, 47, 100, 217]	left [superior lower-nose bridge - inferior inner eye bag] bi-trito mediolateral transition
[127, 34, 139, 234]	high upper left cheekbone outline
[128, 114, 188, 174]	left superior base of middle nose bridge
[128, 121, 47, 232]	left bi-demi upper innermost eye bag sulcus
[129, 102, 49]	center left nostril edge
[129, 203, 98, 64]	left lower perinostril (infra to the mouth line)
[129, 209, 126, 49]	left nasal cheek mouth line origin
[133, 112, 243, 244]	left medial epicanthal origin
[133, 155, 112]	left distal epicanthal origin
[135, 136, 150, 169]	left focal lower jaw chin outplane
[135, 214, 192, 187]	left distal mandibular cheek-middle jaw tracking line
[137, 123, 116, 227]	left outer middle cheekbone outplane
[138, 135, 192, 136]	left mid lower jaw infra outplane
[138, 172, 136, 215]	left mid-to-upper lower jaw superoutline
[140, 170, 176]	left lower distal chin
[141, 125, 241, 242]	left superior bi-demi medial top of philtrum
[141, 242, 97, 2]	left subnostril lateral to the septum
[142, 126, 100, 129]	top alar terminus of left mouth line
[143, 34, 227, 156]	high upper left cheekbone infra outline
[143, 35, 124, 156]	left superior crow's feet
[144, 163, 110, 24]	proximal region of the outer lower left eyelid
[144, 24, 23, 229]	distal center of the superior left eye bag
[145, 144, 23]	left center of the lower eyelid
[145, 23, 22, 153]	right center of left lower eyelid
[147, 177, 215, 58]	left upper jaw outline
[148, 171, 140, 176]	left medial lower left chin
[151, 9, 337, 338]	right region perilateral to the center forehead
[154, 153, 22, 26]	distal inner left lower eyelid
[155, 154, 26, 112]	inner left lower eyelid corner
[156, 70, 139, 34]	left subtemporal infra outline
[159, 158, 28]	right center of left upper eyelid

[160, 159, 27, 28]	center of left upper eyelid
[160, 29, 30, 27]	left center of left upper eyelid
[161, 160, 30, 247]	proximal left outer upper eyelid
[162, 127, 139, 71]	left medio temple infra outline
[164, 0, 267, 393]	right lower philtrum
[164, 167, 37, 0]	left lower philtrum
[164, 2, 167]	left upper philtrum
[165, 92, 39, 167]	lower left periphiltrum
[166, 59, 75]	left distal nose hole rim
[166, 79, 218, 219]	left lower base of outer nostril
[170, 149, 176, 150]	left distal bottom of chin
[170, 169, 150]	left lower jaw -distal bottom of chin transition
[171, 175, 199, 396]	center infra bottom of chin
[171, 208, 32, 201]	distal left chin
[174, 236, 196, 217]	left proximal base of middle nose bridge
[175, 152, 377, 396]	right distal bottom of chin
[175, 171, 148, 152]	left bottom center of chin
[177, 132, 58, 137]	left cheek-upper jaw transition
[178, 88, 179, 86]	proxisuperior center of left lower lip
[179, 89, 180, 85]	inferior center of left lower lip
[183, 42, 184, 76]	inferior distal left upper lip
[188, 122, 245, 128]	left low distal upper nose bridge
[188, 174, 196, 122]	left upper distal middle nose bridge
[189, 190, 243, 133]	left proximal epicanthus
[189, 193, 55, 221]	superior left inner eyebrow left inner eye tracking line
[190, 173, 133]	left distal epicanthus
[191, 80, 183, 62]	left demi outer upper-lower lip boundary
[192, 213, 138, 187]	left upper mid jaw infra outline
[193, 168, 8, 417]	lower center brow
[193, 189, 244, 243]	left infra epicanthus
[194, 204, 211, 106]	distal left mouth-left chin tracking plane
[195, 3, 51, 197]	left middle nose bridge
[195, 5, 281, 51]	lower middle nose bridge
[198, 131, 134, 220]	left nostril summit
[199, 200, 208, 171]	left medial infra goatee
[200, 199, 428, 396]	right medial infra goatee
[200, 421, 18, 428]	right center superior to the chin
[201, 194, 32, 211]	middle distal left chin
[201, 200, 18, 208]	let center superior to the chin
[201, 83, 182, 194]	left middle of upper chin
[202, 212, 214, 57]	left jaw-cheek-mouth vocal nexus
[203, 129, 142, 36]	left sub superior mouth line
[203, 165, 98, 97]	left distal upper philtrum
[204, 202, 210, 214]	left mid chin ventriloquist's line
[205, 206, 36, 101]	left center cheek proximal to the mouth line
[205, 50, 187, 101]	focal central mass of left cheek
[206, 203, 36, 165]	central left nasal labial sulcus (middle of left mouth line)
[206, 92, 165]	left mouth line distal to the medial philtrum
[207, 205, 187]	left infra lower cheek focus
[209, 198, 217, 126]	left nasal bridge base mouth line continuation
[209, 49, 131, 198]	upper left nostril edge (left nostril rounder)
[211, 170, 140, 169]	left infra lower distal chin
[211, 204, 210, 169]	left infra lower jaw -distal lower chin transition
[212, 216, 207, 205]	left center lower cheek-upper middle jaw transition
[212, 57, 186, 185]	superior perimouth distal to the left lip vertex
[213, 215, 138, 147]	left upper mid jaw pre- outline
[214, 135, 169, 210]	left lower jaw-distal chin transition plane
[214, 207, 187, 212]	left lower cheek lower jaw distal mandibular transition
[215, 58, 172]	left upper middle jaw outline
[216, 186, 92, 212]	left mouth line distal to the lower philtrum
[216, 206, 205, 92]	left lower cheek mouth line-medial philtrum transition
[217, 198, 236, 134]	left nostril- mouth line -nose base intersection
[218, 79, 237]	left distal center of upper rim of outer nostril
[220, 115, 218, 131]	left diameter distal to the alar crease
[220, 237, 44, 218]	left anterior nostril rim
[221, 55, 65, 222]	left lower inner eyebrow transition
[221, 56, 190, 189]	inferior left inner eyebrow left inner eye tracking line
[223, 52, 53, 222]	lower bi-demi outer left eyebrow
[224, 223, 53, 225]	left lower bi-demi outer eyebrow transition
[226, 130, 247, 33]	outer left upper eyelid
[229, 228, 117, 24]	distal left eye bag
[230, 119, 120, 231]	left midproximal mass of eye bag contour
[230, 229, 118, 117]	left midmedial mass of eye bag contour
[232, 231, 120, 121]	left center of innermost eye bag line sulcus
[233, 128, 245, 232]	left sub epicanthal-innermost eye bag line transition
[234, 93, 227, 34]	left cheek bone outline
[235, 64, 240]	left inferior alar-mouth base
[236, 134, 51, 3]	left distal lower middle nose bridge
[236, 3, 196, 197]	left distal middle nose bridge
[238, 20, 242, 99]	proximal left nostril-septal base
[238, 79, 20, 239]	center left nostril hole
[239, 238, 241, 242]	left proximal septal-temporal diameter of nose hole

[244, 233, 245]	left innermost eyebag line-lower upper nose bridge transition
[247, 246, 161, 33]	proximal outer left upper eyelid
[247, 30, 225]	distal left outer eyelid outer brow region minor
[248, 195, 281, 197]	right downward middle nose bridge
[248, 419, 197, 456]	right distal middle nose bridge
[250, 290, 392, 309]	right bi-demi proximal septal-temporal nose hole
[250, 462, 328, 326]	right superior bi-demi medial top of philtrum
[251, 284, 298, 301]	right inferior distal forehead outline
[251, 301, 389]	right superior temple
[252, 451, 450, 253]	right bi-demi inner superior eye bag
[253, 450, 449, 254]	right superior center of eye bag
[254, 449, 448, 346]	right bi-demi outermost downward eyebag plane
[255, 261, 446, 448]	right plane inferior to the outer eye vertex
[256, 452, 451, 252]	right demi inner superior eye bag
[257, 443, 442, 259]	right inferior focal center of eyebrow transition
[258, 286, 384, 441]	right tri-trito inner eyelid-inner eyebrow tracking line
[258, 442, 441, 257]	right medial center of lower eyebrow transition
[259, 444, 443, 260]	right superior tri-trito outer plane beneath eyebrow
[260, 445, 444]	right superior bi-trito outer plane beneath eyebrow
[263, 255, 359, 249]	distal bi-demi right outer upper eyelid - eye transition
[263, 467, 466, 359]	right bi-trito outer eyelid
[264, 356, 368, 454]	right temple infra outline
[264, 372, 447, 383]	right grand temple
[265, 340, 372, 446]	right focal perieye at outer vertex
[265, 353, 342, 276]	right outer eyebrow-outer crow's feet tracking line
[266, 330, 329, 371]	bottom terminus of right innermost eye bag
[267, 302, 269, 393]	right bi-demi inner philtrum-cupid's bow transition
[268, 12, 13, 38]	bud of lower center upper lip
[268, 271, 302, 12]	right lower center of the upper lip
[269, 391, 393, 326]	right downward bi-demi inner philtrum
[270, 409, 410, 287]	right demi-outer upper lip superioris transition
[271, 272, 304, 303]	right tri-trito inner focal center of upper right lip
[272, 271, 311, 268]	right bi-demi inner upper lip-lower lip boundary
[272, 310, 407, 311]	right center of right upper lip-lower lip boundary
[272, 407, 408, 304]	right tri-tetarto outer focal bottom of upper right lip
[273, 335, 424, 321]	right superior distal chin infra to the mouth vertex
[273, 375, 321, 291]	right bi & tri-tetarto outer lower lip inferioris transition
[274, 1, 19, 354]	right lower nose tip
[275, 440, 363, 281]	right paraxial bi & tri-trito caudal lower nose bridge
[276, 300, 293]	right plane superior to the outer eyebrow vertex
[276, 353, 383, 300]	right outer eyebrow vertex
[277, 343, 437, 355]	lower innermost eyebag-middle nose bridge transition
[278, 279, 360, 344]	focal center of right nostril
[278, 439, 455]	right upwards focal bi-trito outer nostril rim
[279, 278, 294]	right tri-tetarto outer middle of vertical nostril line
[280, 425, 411, 330]	right superior center of cheek mass downwards
[281, 5, 4, 275]	right proximal lower nose bridge
[283, 293, 282, 276]	right superior bi-demi outer eyebrow transition
[283, 444, 445, 276]	right inferior bi-demi outer eyebrow transition
[284, 332, 333, 298]	right distal top of forehead
[285, 336, 9, 295]	right upper center brow
[286, 414, 398, 384]	right inner eyebrow-right inner upper eyelid transition plane
[287, 273, 422, 291]	right inferior middle perimouth
[287, 432, 410]	right upper central focal perimouth
[289, 305, 455]	right outer nostril rim at base
[289, 392, 290, 305]	right distal nose hole edge
[289, 455, 439, 392]	right distal nostril hole rim focus
[290, 328, 460, 250]	right superior bi & tri-trito medial top of philtrum
[291, 409, 408, 287]	right demi outer upper lip- lower lip boundary
[292, 308, 325, 415]	right bi-tetarto outer lower lip superioris
[292, 325, 307, 306]	right bi-trito outer lower lip upper
[293, 298, 333, 301]	distal right forehead superior to the outer eyebrow
[293, 300, 301, 368]	distal right forehead upwards from the outer eyebrow
[293, 334, 282, 296]	right upper outer eyebrow transition
[294, 455, 460, 278]	right tri-tetarto outer vertical nostril line inferioris
[295, 296, 336, 282]	right upper middle eyebrow transition
[297, 338, 337, 299]	right top center of right forehead
[300, 383, 368, 264]	right superior grand temple
[302, 303, 269, 271]	right bi-demi inner upper lip mass
[303, 304, 270, 269]	right focal superior center of upper lip
[304, 408, 409, 270]	right tri-tetarto outer focal center of upper right lip

[305, 460, 455, 290]	right distal posterior nostril hole
[306, 291, 408]	right bi-tetarto outer upper lip-lower lip boundary
[306, 307, 375, 291]	right bi-tetarto outer lower lip verticenter
[306, 408, 407, 292]	right bi-trito outer upper lip-lower lip boundary
[307, 320, 321, 375]	right tri-tetarto outer lower lip bi-demi inferioris
[308, 324, 325, 318]	right bi-demi outer superior lower lip
[309, 438, 457]	right focal medioanterior nostril rim
[310, 415, 407, 292]	right bi-demi outer upper lip-lower lip boundary
[312, 311, 268, 13]	left center of the upper-lower lip boundary
[313, 314, 17, 18]	right center inferior to the lower lip
[313, 406, 405, 314]	right bi-demi inner sub-lip plane
[314, 405, 404, 315]	right bi-demi inner inferior lower lip
[315, 16, 17, 314]	right center of bottom of lower lip
[316, 15, 315, 403]	distal right center of lower lip
[317, 14, 316, 402]	right upper center of lower lip
[318, 319, 325, 403]	right tri-trito outer upwards near upper lower lip
[318, 402, 403, 316]	right bi-demi inner upwards near upper lower lip
[319, 403, 404, 315]	right bi-demi inner upwards verticentral lower lip
[320, 404, 405, 319]	right tri-trito outer upwards verticentral lower lip
[321, 405, 406, 320]	right tri-trito outer upwards inferior lower lip transition
[322, 270, 410, 269]	right tri-trito outer upper lip-(inferior) bi-trito outer philtrum transition
[322, 391, 269, 426]	right top of bi-trito inner lip-center of right mouth line subtemporal tracking line philtrum plane
[323, 366, 361]	right upper jaw infra outline
[323, 454, 447, 264]	right superior high cheekbone infra outline
[325, 319, 320, 307]	right tri-tetarto outer lower lip bi-demi superioris
[327, 460, 328, 294]	right sub nose hole and distal rim superior philtrum transition
[329, 349, 350, 277]	right lower innermost eyebag line
[330, 348, 349, 329]	right lower inner eye bag
[331, 279, 294, 358]	right distal edge of nostril
[331, 358, 279]	right upper distal edge of nostril
[333, 332, 297, 299]	right bi-demi outer top of forehead
[334, 333, 299, 293]	distal right forehead superior to the exocentral eyebrow
[335, 406, 418, 321]	right upwards superior distal chin-midright lower lip transition plane
[336, 296, 299, 334]	right lower forehead superior to the central eyebrow transition
[338, 10, 151, 109]	top center of forehead
[339, 254, 448, 255]	right superior outermost eyebag
[339, 255, 249]	distal bi-demi right outer lower eyelid - eye transition
[341, 382, 362]	right inner eye vertex
[341, 453, 452, 464]	right lower epicanthal transition medial to the inner eye vertex
[341, 463, 464, 362]	right middle epicanthal transition medial to the inner eye vertex
[343, 412, 399, 437]	right distal middle nose bridge transition
[344, 438, 439, 278]	right bottom center of nostril at anterior nose hole
[344, 440, 438, 360]	medioanterior right nostril
[346, 340, 261, 446]	right inferior outer perieye (eye circle)
[346, 347, 280, 330]	right upper cheek plane mass sub eye
[347, 348, 330, 450]	right lower middle eye bag
[350, 357, 277, 452]	right bi-demi lower innermost eyebag line transition
[351, 412, 465, 357]	right distal upper nose bridge
[351, 417, 168, 6]	right upper nose bridge
[352, 280, 411, 346]	right bi-demi upper cheekbone
[352, 345, 340, 346]	right lower far outer eye bag
[352, 366, 345, 401]	right lower cheekbone out plane
[352, 376, 401, 435]	right lower cheekbone-upper jaw infra out plane
[354, 461, 457, 274]	right inner nostril rim anterioris
[355, 371, 329, 277]	right innermost eyebag line terminus-lower middle nose bridge transition plane
[356, 389, 368, 301]	right superior temple infra outplane
[357, 343, 277, 412]	right innermost eyebag line-upper middle nose bridge downward transition plane
[358, 371, 355, 423]	right nasal cheek mouth line origin
[358, 429, 279, 360]	right superior distal edge of nostril
[359, 446, 467, 255]	right plane superior to the outer eye vertex
[360, 363, 440, 420]	right nose base-upper medial nostril transition
[362, 398, 414]	right far inner eyelid
[364, 367, 416, 433]	right distal lowered cheek -pre posterior jaw transition plane
[364, 394, 379, 365]	right lower middle jaw lateral to the chin
[366, 401, 361, 288]	right middle cheek- upper jaw infra outline
[366, 447, 345, 323]	right low upper cheek infra-outplane
[367, 364, 365, 397]	right lower middle jaw sub crow's feet
[370, 462, 461, 354]	right distal columella
[372, 345, 447, 340]	right distal lower crow's feet
[372, 383, 353, 265]	right demi-upper perieye plane
[373, 254, 339, 253]	right bi-demi outer lower eyelid transition

[373, 374, 253]	right focal center of lower eyelid transition
[374, 380, 252, 253]	right tri-trito inner lower eye lid
[376, 352, 411, 433]	right medial outer cheek plane
[376, 433, 435]	right lower distal outer cheek
[377, 400, 369, 396]	right bottom of middle right chin
[381, 256, 252, 380]	right bi-trito inner lower eye lid
[381, 382, 256]	right trito inner lower eyelid
[382, 341, 256, 452]	right superior trito inner eye bag
[385, 386, 258, 384]	right medial center of eyelid-bi-demi inner eyebrow transition plane
[386, 257, 258, 387]	right medial center of eyelid-center of eyebrow transition plane
[387, 259, 257, 260]	right distal center of eyelid-center of eyebrow transition plane
[387, 388, 260, 466]	right bi-demi outer plane above eyelid
[390, 373, 339, 249]	distal tri-trito right outer lower eyelid - eye transition
[391, 327, 326, 328]	right para superior philtrum
[392, 439, 438, 309]	right focal centroanterior nostril rim
[395, 369, 400, 378]	right bottom of far right chin
[395, 378, 379, 394]	bottom of jaw at right ventriloquist line
[395, 431, 369, 394]	right lower far right chin
[396, 369, 262, 428]	right medial lower right chin
[401, 435, 288, 397]	right lower middle cheek- upper jaw infra outline
[411, 416, 433]	right lower outer cheek
[412, 351, 419, 399]	right medial low-upper nose bridge
[413, 441, 285, 417]	right inner eyebrow upper nose bridge transition
[413, 464, 463, 417]	right distal upper nose bridge infra to the epicanthus
[414, 463, 362, 413]	right focal plane medial to the far inner eyelid
[417, 285, 8, 9]	right outer center brow
[417, 465, 464, 351]	right medial upper nose bridge
[418, 262, 431, 369]	right distal middle of chin
[420, 456, 363, 437]	right distal lower middle nose bridge
[421, 313, 18]	right distal center superior to the chin
[421, 418, 406, 313]	right bi-demi inner upper chin
[421, 428, 262, 418]	right center of right chin
[422, 424, 430, 273]	right inferior perimouth
[422, 430, 434, 394]	bi & tri-trito lower right ventriloquist line
[423, 266, 371, 426]	right upper mouth line sulcus distal to the nostril
[423, 358, 327, 294]	right inferior outer nostril edge transition
[424, 418, 431, 335]	right predistal superior chin
[424, 431, 430, 394]	distal upper right chin transition infra to the ventriloquist line
[425, 427, 411, 436]	right lower middle inner cheek
[426, 423, 391, 327]	right superior distal philtrum
[426, 425, 266, 330]	right subeye central cheek plane distal to the nostril (right inner cheek plane)
[429, 355, 437, 358]	right lower nose bridge-nostril center line transition
[429, 420, 360, 437]	right distal nose base-upper nostril transition
[432, 422, 434, 287]	right upper chin ventriloquist's line
[432, 434, 427, 436]	lower right inner cheek distal to the mouth line
[432, 436, 410, 322]	right mouth line distal to the lower philtrum
[434, 364, 416, 394]	right lower cheek middle mandibular transition
[434, 416, 411, 427]	right inner-outer lower cheek transition
[435, 367, 397, 433]	right lower cheek lower jaw distal mandibular transition
[436, 426, 322, 425]	right mouth line distal to the medial philtrum
[440, 275, 274, 4]	right medial nose tip
[440, 457, 438, 274]	right inferior alar crease
[441, 413, 414, 286]	right demi inner eyebrow inferioris - upper nose bridge transition plane
[441, 442, 295, 285]	right inner eyebrow
[442, 443, 282, 295]	right infracenter of eyebrow
[443, 444, 283, 282]	right exocenter of eyebrow
[446, 342, 467, 265]	right plane above crow's feet
[448, 346, 261]	right demi-inferior outer peri-eye
[449, 347, 346, 450]	right downwards middle eye bag
[450, 451, 349, 348]	right bi-demi inner middle eye bag
[452, 350, 349, 451]	right demi inner middle eye bag
[452, 453, 357, 465]	right pre-innermost origin of eye bag line
[453, 464, 465]	right upper nose bridge -inner eye focal transition plane
[456, 248, 281, 363]	right downward nonaxial lower middle nose bridge
[456, 399, 419, 437]	paramedial downward lower middle nose bridge
[458, 459, 461]	distal right lower nose tip
[458, 461, 462, 250]	right inner columellal rim
[459, 457, 461, 309]	right focal demi-inner anterior nostril rim
[459, 458, 250, 309]	right anterior inner half of nose hole rim
[462, 370, 326, 2]	right distal septum
[466, 467, 260, 445]	right bi-trio outer eyelid - bi-demi outer eyebrow tracking line
[467, 342, 445, 276]	right bi-tetarto outer plane inferior to the eyebrow

Medical professionals everywhere I'm sure are squirming. Especially because I know better. The biggest impediments to properly naming specific tessellations and quadrilaterals, though, is that

1) there are so very many of them that you will often have 2-5 polygons piled up in exactly the same area. The base of the nose and outer corners of the mouth were especially tricky, such that I had to use terms like "peri" to distinguish parentheses-like areas around a feature, -demi, -trito, and -tetarto to indicate ½, ⅓, ¼ steps from something alongside (nothing), bi-, tri-, and quarto- to show how many of those steps. "Tracking" indicates an imaginary straight line between things. And there are several other gimmicks I used to make finding each cluster easier. The "distal right forehead superior to the exocentral eyebrow" tells me immediately that I'm looking at the right side of the forehead above the eyebrow, just a little ways further right of the center of that eyebrow.

2) the merged tessellations include blends of entirely different structures. So one region on the left side might include the cheek and the laugh line and the distal region beneath the nose, while the opposite points may cover a different family of shapes. When structures were blended in the same polygon, I called these "transitions." But...

3) ...even if my merge had not clouded structures, the face recognition itself is fuzzy, so you would still need a way to indicate an area along with certain spillover structures.

It was a labor of love, but f-RORT produced some pretty awesome results when used to filter my previously unintelligible, unfiltered RORT results. Now we can tell from the example below that the Norwegian right lower philtrum—when compared to the right upper philtrum—is .123987 units bigger in ratio than average across all ethnotypes. (Everything in Column J is always the numerator. Column L is always the denominator)[52]:

FIGURE 37: F-RORT EXAMPLE RESULTS

	A	B	C	D	E	F	I	J	K	L
1	Test Column	Variance Assumption	t	df	p-value (2	Mean Diffe	Ethnotype	label	Mean Diffe	label (Right)
316	[216, 206, 205, 92] / [206, 92, 165]	Equal variances assumed	-2.58548	3092	0.00977	0.059826	Nigerian	left mouth line distal to the medial philtrum	0.059826	Left lower cheek mouth line-medial philtrum transition
317	[226, 130, 247, 25] / [25, 7, 33, 130]	Equal variances assumed	2.595289	4710	0.00948	0.055046	Norwegian		0.055046	Outer distal corner of the left eye
318	[164, 0, 267, 393] / [2, 164, 393, 326]	Equal variances assumed	2.593236	992	0.009648	0.123987	Norwegian	right lower philtrum	0.123987	Right Upper philtrum
319	[91, 106, 182, 43] / [77, 146, 91, 43]	Equal variances assumed	2.592937	873	0.009675	0.516331	Norwegian		0.516331	Left perimouth proximal to the outer lower lip
320	[105, 66, 69, 107] / [52, 65, 66, 107]	Equal variances assumed	2.586441	5126	0.009725	0.111201	Norwegian	Left lower forehead Above the left eyebrow center	0.111201	
321	[254, 449, 448, 346] / [339, 254, 448, 255]	Equal variances assumed	2.583215	5105	0.009816	0.014392	Norwegian	right bi-demi outermost downward eyebag plane	0.014392	right Superior Outermost eyebag
322	[301, 251, 298, 293] / [301, 368, 389, 251]	Equal variances assumed	2.637156	408	0.00868	1.390154	Pakistani		1.390154	
323	[114, 217, 174, 188] / [174, 236, 196, 217]	Equal variances assumed	-2.62361	2869	0.008746	0.029733	Pakistani	Left proximal base of middle nose bridge	0.029733	

c. While RORT gives machine-usable results, f-RORT gives human-readable versions of this. But as long as we're in the business of labeling data piece by piece, why not just go for broke and label non-

---

[52] Notice that some values in columns J and L are missing. This is because, unfortunately, not all points showed up in my original reference face (from earlier) for me to label them. By the time I realized that I had only covered half of the available polygon groupings, I had already moved onto a better method for doing this, LANDOX.

neighboring points which describe actual facial features? Landmark-to-slider approximation (LANDOX) is exactly what you would expect; instead of taking ratios of neighboring tessellations, I took ratios of preexisting slider target geometries (already provided in Makehuman) and found the points which corresponded to these sliders. Each slider had two end regions for the slider itself, and two more anchor points for some stable, unrotated and unscaled feature which served as a kind of constant against which the slider was changed. Regions weren't necessarily single points, but were the average of whatever points were needed.

FIGURE 38: LANDOX SETUP

Name	movable point	anchor point	fixed1	fixed2
slider_chin-bones-decr|incr	149, 150, 378, 37	394, 169	394, 169	430, 210
slider_chin-cleft-decr|incr	208, 171, 396,42	199, 175	199, 175	201, 421
slider_chin-height-decr|incr	199	200	200	201, 421
slider_chin-jaw-drop-decr|incr	288,361, 132, 58	352, 123, 50, 28C	352, 123, 50, 280	187, 411
slider_chin-prognathism-decr|incr	200, 201,421,26:	416, 367, 397, 1S	416, 367, 397, 19:	416, 365, 192,13€
slider_chin-prominent-decr|incr	199, 208, 428	394, 169	394, 169	200
slider_chin-width-decr|incr	170, 140	395,369	201	421
slider_eyebrows-angle-down|up	8, 9	168	300, 70	372, 143
slider_eyebrows-trans-backward|forward	70, 63, 105, 66, 1	68, 104, 69, 108,	68, 104, 69, 108, :	221, 222, 223, 22∢
slider_eyebrows-trans-down|up	70, 63, 105, 66, 1	221, 222, 223, 2:	221, 222, 223, 22∢	33, 263, 362, 133
slider_forehead-nubian-decr|incr	67, 297	69, 299	69, 299	66, 296
slider_forehead-scale-vert-decr|incr	67, 109, 10, 338,	69, 108, 151, 337	69, 108, 151, 337,	105, 66, 107, 9, 3:

d.

This method is also rough, but yielded much more coherent results. Indeed, these were the results that were the most practically useful for telling us what we're seeing when we identify a person's ethnotypic background on sight. I ran a loop of t-tests comparing each [ethnotype x sex x (z-score normalized) slider] against the mean for that whole grouping of [sex x slider], kept only results with $p<.0001$, and arranged those results from lowest p to highest. (That is, most statistically significant to less so.) For every [ethnotype x sex] group in the table below, the top facial features were the most statistically significant / obvious ones captured through t-tests on the LANDOX labelings, and decrease in significance /obviousness as you go down. The left group of sliders is higher than average across all populations of the same sex. The right group is lower than average. Starred * features showed up as significant in both the males and the females of the ethnotype in question, and might be among the more defining characteristics of that group broadly.

TABLE 42: MAKEHUMAN FACE SLIDER METRICS SIGNIFICANTLY CORRELATED WITH FACE LANDMARK DISTANCES (LANDOX)

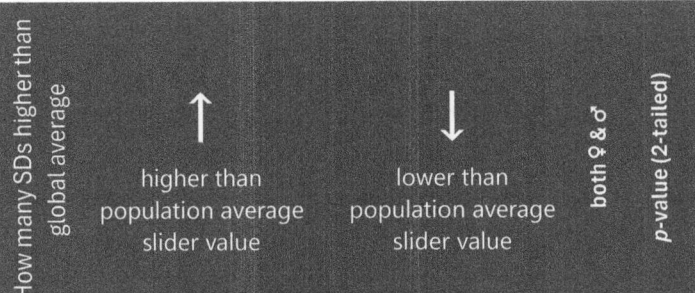

How many SDs higher than global average — higher than population average slider value (↑) — lower than population average slider value (↓) — both ♀ & ♂ — p-value (2-tailed)

-0.866		nose: Scale nostrils flaring		3.76E-08
-0.99		mouth: Scale upperlip volume		6.24E-08
0.963	slider_l-eye-corner2-down|up			8.96E-08
0.94	slider_r-eye-bag-decr|incr			9.63E-08
-1.18		slider_elvs_chipmunkcheeks_l1		1.11E-07
-0.878		eyebrows: Eyebrows bulge	*	1.43E-07
0.828	nose: Scale nostrils width			0.0000003
0.815	mouth: Move depth			4.14E-07
0.686	nose: Move nose base vert.			4.49E-07
-0.821		nose: Scale vertically		9.74E-07
0.838	nose: Move depth			1.03E-06
-0.881		mouth: Upperlip curved shape		1.58E-06
0.807	mouth: Scale upperlip height			3.87E-06
0.644	chin: Tone of side chin			6.63E-06
0.512	slider_r-eye-eyefold-down|up			0.0000218
-0.842		slider_elvs_highchubbycheekbones1	*	0.0000279
-0.877		nose: Scale depth		0.0000628
-0.497		nose: Middle nose bridge width		0.0000961

African female (n=29)

1.49	mouth: Scale upperlip width		*	3.67E-16
-1.51		mouth: Dimples	*	1.09E-14
-1.66		slider_l-eye-trans-down|up		3.31E-14
-1.32		nose-volume-decr|incr	*	1.45E-13
-1.55		slider_r-eye-trans-down|up		2.99E-13
-1.37		chin: Scale chin width	*	3.9E-13
1.69	mouth: Scale lowerlip width		*	4.58E-13
-0.779		slider_nostril_rounding		1.12E-12
-0.929		mouth: Scale lowerlip volume	*	4.71E-12
1.04	slider_l-eye-trans-in|out		*	5.84E-12
-1.2		mouth: Laugh-lines	*	8.52E-12
0.965	slider_r-eye-eyefold-angle-down|up			9.35E-12
1.32	nose: Scale horizontally		*	1.81E-11
1.26	mouth: Scale vertically		*	2.3E-11
-0.915		chin: Scale chin height	*	6.61E-11
1.14	slider_l-eye-eyefold-angle-down|up			3.48E-10
0.883	slider_r-cheek-inner-decr|incr			5.29E-10
1.08	slider_r-eye-trans-in|out		*	6.91E-10
-1.38		slider_r-eye-corner1-down|up		9.18E-10
1.02	slider_r-eye-corner2-down|up		*	2.28E-09
1.07	mouth: Scale horizontally		*	2.88E-09
1.18	mouth: Scale lowerlip height		*	4.84E-09
0.738	slider_r-eye-epicanthus-in|out			6.1E-09
-1.04		nose-nostrils-angle-down|up		8.06E-09
0.975	slider_r-eye-bag-in|out		*	8.36E-09
-1.21		slider_l-eye-corner1-down|up		9.31E-09
0.946	slider_l-eye-bag-in|out			1.53E-08
1.09	eyebrows: Move vert			2.3E-08
0.688	slider_l-cheek-inner-decr|incr		*	2.73E-08

African male (n=24)

-1.29		mouth: Laugh-lines	*	1.66E-13
1.28	nose: Scale nostrils width		*	7.18E-13
-1.61		mouth: Dimples	*	1.32E-12
1.24	mouth: Scale horizontally		*	2.34E-10
-1.38		mouth: Scale lowerlip volume	*	3.05E-10
1.6	mouth: Scale upperlip width		*	8.73E-10
1.68	mouth: Scale lowerlip width		*	3.74E-09
-1.5		chin: Scale chin height	*	5.08E-09
1.67	slider_l-eye-trans-in|out		*	5.45E-09
1.54	mouth: Scale vertically		*	8.31E-09
0.928	forehead: Scale vertically			1.62E-08
1.26	chin: Scale chin prognathism			1.89E-08
-0.916		eyebrows: Eyebrows bulge	*	4.3E-08
-1.27		slider_elvs_highchubbycheekbones1	*	7.14E-08
1.41	slider_r-eye-trans-in|out		*	8.03E-08
-1.17		nose-volume-decr|incr	*	1.25E-07
0.792	forehead: Cranic shape			2.34E-07
1.43	mouth: Move corners vert.			2.7E-07
1.43	mouth: Move corners vert.			2.7E-07
1.43	mouth: Move corners vert.			2.7E-07
-1.16		chin: Scale chin width	*	9.74E-07
0.847	slider_r-eye-bag-in|out		*	1.17E-06
1.21	nose: Scale horizontally		*	1.43E-06
-0.948		mouth: Move vertically		2.36E-06
-0.765		nose: Move vertically		3.14E-06
0.728	slider_r-eye-corner2-down|up		*	3.44E-06
1.23	mouth: Scale lowerlip height		*	3.61E-06
1.33	chin: Cleft chin			5.43E-06
-0.761		forehead: Temple bulge		7.97E-06

1.31	nose: Scale tip width			0.0000153
-0.78		nose-greek-decr|incr		0.0000195
1.06	eyebrows: Eyebrows angle			0.0000311
0.559	eyes: Outer height of right eye			0.0000372
0.719	slider_l-cheek-inner-decr|incr		*	0.0000422

African American female (n=28)

1.77	mouth: Scale upperlip width		*	2.27E-15
-1.9		slider_l-eye-corner1-down|up		2.44E-14
-1.61		mouth: Dimples	*	4.63E-14
-1.73		chin: Scale chin width	*	1.44E-13
-1.16		mouth: Scale lowerlip volume	*	1.55E-13
-1.86		slider_l-eye-trans-down|up	*	4.25E-13
-1.78		slider_r-eye-corner1-down|up		2E-12
1.43	mouth: Scale lowerlip width		*	2.5E-12
-1.53		mouth: Laugh-lines	*	4.67E-12
-1.61		slider_r-eye-trans-down|up	*	7.07E-12
1.33	slider_l-eye-eyefold-angle-down|up		*	3.17E-11
-1.86		slider_elvs_highchubbycheekbones1	*	4.31E-11
1.54	mouth: Scale horizontally		*	5.77E-11
1.4	nose: Scale nostrils width		*	2.37E-10
-1.12		nose-volume-decr|incr	*	8.21E-10
-1.18		slider_nostril_rounding		8.92E-10
1.24	eyebrows: Move vert			1E-09
-1.17		eyebrows: Eyebrows bulge	*	1.87E-09
-0.778		chin: Scale chin height	*	1.99E-09
0.808	nose: Scale horizontally		*	1.49E-08
-1.03		slider_Nose_alar_crease	*	1.81E-08
0.932	slider_r-eye-trans-in|out		*	2.09E-08
0.698	slider_r-cheek-inner-decr|incr			9.37E-08
1.05	slider_l-eye-bag-decr|incr			1.22E-07
0.922	mouth: Scale vertically			1.35E-07
1.02	slider_r-eye-bag-decr|incr			1.55E-07
1.24	slider_r-eye-eyefold-angle-down|up			1.57E-07
-0.83		nose-nostrils-angle-down|up	*	3.11E-07
0.625	slider_l-eye-trans-in|out		*	4.63E-07
0.837	slider_l-eye-eyefold-down|up			1.13E-06
-0.641		nose-greek-decr|incr	*	1.34E-06
1.01	slider_r-eye-epicanthus-in|out			1.37E-06
1.07	slider_r-cheek-trans-down|up			1.84E-06
-0.706		mouth: Scale depth		3.09E-06
0.884	slider_r-eye-eyefold-down|up			3.84E-06
0.598	nose: Move depth			8.74E-06
0.487	nose: Septum Angle			0.0000107
0.697	slider_r-eye-corner2-down|up			0.0000162
0.528	nose: Move nose base vert.			0.0000191
-0.694		eyes: Inner height of right eye		0.0000225

-0.662		mouth: Upperlip curved shape		0.0000263
0.725	slider_l-eye-epicanthus-in|out			0.0000284
-0.733		eyes: Inner height of left eye		0.0000313
-0.523		slider_r-eye-scale-decr|incr		0.0000323
-0.561		nose: Middle nose bridge width		0.0000354
-0.568		slider_l-eye-scale-decr|incr		0.0000438
0.903	slider_l-cheek-trans-down|up			0.0000446
0.658	slider_l-eye-corner2-down|up			0.0000532
-0.707		slider_l-cheek-bones-decr|incr		0.0000779
-0.561		mouth: Scale upperlip volume		0.0000839
0.682	mouth: Scale lowerlip height			0.0000994

African American male (n=26)

-1.47		slider_elvs_highchubbycheekbones1	*	3.11E-12
-1.39		mouth: Dimples	*	8.21E-12
1.52	mouth: Scale upperlip width		*	2.28E-11
1.19	mouth: Scale horizontally		*	2.77E-11
-1.22		mouth: Laugh-lines	*	6.22E-11
-1.28		mouth: Scale lowerlip volume	*	4.17E-10
-1.06		nose-volume-decr|incr	*	7.62E-10
0.972	slider_l-eye-trans-in|out		*	1.21E-09
1.55	nose: Scale nostrils width		*	3.62E-09
-0.897		eyebrows: Eyebrows bulge	*	2.43E-08
0.928	mouth: Move corners vert.			6.24E-08
0.928	mouth: Move corners vert.			6.24E-08
1	nose: Scale horizontally		*	1.16E-07
0.913	slider_r-eye-trans-in|out		*	1.27E-07
1.11	chin: Scale chin prognathism			1.86E-07
-0.905		chin: Scale chin height	*	2.07E-07
-0.802		slider_Nose_alar_crease	*	4.76E-07
1.26	mouth: Scale lowerlip width		*	5.04E-07
-1.29		chin: Scale chin width	*	1.21E-06
0.628	forehead: Scale vertically			0.0000016
-0.577		nose-greek-decr|incr	*	1.91E-06
1.13	mouth: Scale vertically		*	2.11E-06
0.626	eyes: Outer height of right eye			5.19E-06
-1.13		slider_r-eye-trans-down|up	*	6.57E-06
-0.743		nose-nostrils-angle-down|up	*	0.0000106
0.933	slider_l-eye-eyefold-angle-down|up		*	0.0000172
-1.17		slider_l-eye-trans-down|up	*	0.0000183
0.674	chin: Cleft chin			0.0000601
0.583	eyebrows: Eyebrows angle			0.0000645
-0.498		mouth: Move vertically		0.0000673

Afro-Caribbean female (n=34)

1.43 mouth: Scale lowerlip width		*	2.03E-19
-1.85	mouth: Dimples	*	9.82E-18
1.46 mouth: Scale upperlip width		*	6.89E-17
-1.61	chin: Scale chin width	*	9.25E-16
-1.5	chin: Scale chin height	*	2.49E-14
-1.49	mouth: Laugh-lines	*	3.7E-14
-1.82	slider_elvs_highchubbycheekbones1	*	5.93E-14
1.44 slider_r-eye-trans-in|out		*	3.64E-13
1.28 slider_l-eye-trans-in|out		*	5.82E-13
1.65 mouth: Scale horizontally		*	1.37E-12
1.06 nose: Scale horizontally		*	1.42E-12
-0.877	mouth: Scale lowerlip volume	*	4.66E-12
0.945 mouth: Scale vertically		*	5.35E-11
0.892 mouth: Scale lowerlip height		*	1.62E-09
-1.03	slider_Nose_alar_crease	*	2.2E-09
1.06 mouth: Move corners vert.		*	3.26E-09
-0.904	slider_l-eye-trans-down|up		7.37E-09
-0.912	nose-volume-decr|incr	*	1.39E-08
0.839 mouth: Move depth		*	2.57E-08
-0.977	nose-nostrils-angle-down|up		4.21E-08
0.847 nose: Move nose base vert.			9.23E-08
0.88 nose: Scale nostrils width		*	1.04E-07
-0.817	slider_r-eye-trans-down|up		1.06E-07
1.16 slider_r-cheek-trans-down|up			1.3E-07
1.06 slider_l-cheek-trans-down|up			1.61E-07
-1.02	slider_nostril_rounding	*	2.37E-07
-0.919	slider_l-eye-corner1-down|up		6.17E-07
0.923 slider_r-cheek-inner-decr|incr			1.33E-06
-0.905	slider_r-eye-corner1-down|up		1.46E-06
-0.725	eyebrows: Eyebrows bulge		3.21E-06
-0.763	slider_r-eye-eyefold-concave|convex		0.0000063
0.868 chin: Cleft chin		*	0.000008
0.9 slider_r-eye-push1-in|out			0.0000143
-1.03	chin: Scale chin prominence		0.000019
-0.837	nose: Scale vertically		0.0000265
0.993 slider_r-eye-eyefold-angle-down|up			0.0000313
0.896 slider_r-eye-epicanthus-in|out		*	0.000056

Afro-Caribbean male (n=30)

-1.95	chin: Scale chin height	*	2.23E-18
-1.94	mouth: Dimples	*	1.39E-16
-1.46	mouth: Laugh-lines	*	1.21E-15
1.56 mouth: Scale horizontally		*	1.32E-15
1.27 slider_r-eye-trans-in|out		*	1.49E-14
1.34 nose: Scale horizontally		*	3.75E-14
1.66 mouth: Scale lowerlip width		*	6.42E-14
1.54 mouth: Scale upperlip width		*	2.41E-13
-1.44	slider_Nose_alar_crease	*	8.95E-13
-1.23	mouth: Scale lowerlip volume	*	3.01E-12
1.38 mouth: Scale vertically		*	1.26E-11
-1.46	slider_elvs_highchubbycheekbones1	*	1.47E-11
1.21 nose: Scale nostrils width		*	4.17E-10
1.46 chin: Cleft chin		*	4.87E-10
1.92 mouth: Move corners vert.		*	5.2E-10
1.04 slider_l-eye-trans-in|out		*	1.18E-09
1.18 mouth: Scale lowerlip height		*	3.33E-09
-1.55	chin: Scale chin width	*	1.03E-08
-0.99	slider_nostril_rounding	*	2.17E-08
1.28 chin: Scale chin prognathism			2.31E-08
-0.769	mouth: Move vertically		1.11E-06
0.792 mouth: Move depth			3.83E-06
-0.621	mouth: Scale depth		0.0000091
-0.817	nose-volume-decr|incr	*	9.78E-06
0.701 slider_r-eye-epicanthus-in|out		*	0.0000857

Afro-Latino female (n=23)

1.1 mouth: Scale lowerlip width		*	1.39E-14
-0.978	chin: Scale chin height	*	4.32E-14
-1.59	chin: Scale chin width	*	1.2E-12
1.37 slider_r-eye-trans-in|out		*	2.07E-12
1.53 mouth: Scale upperlip width		*	1.73E-11
-1.65	mouth: Dimples	*	1.52E-10

-2.15	slider_elvs_highchubbycheekbones1	*	1.8E-10
-1.12	nose-volume-decr|incr	*	1.97E-09
1.36	slider_l-eye-trans-in|out	*	2.44E-09
0.87	nose: Scale horizontally	*	1.14E-08
-1.27	slider_r-eye-corner1-down|up	*	1.18E-08
-0.763	mouth: Scale lowerlip volume	*	2.5E-08
-1.37	mouth: Laugh-lines	*	5.58E-08
1.51	mouth: Scale horizontally	*	1.72E-07
-1.31	slider_Nose_alar_crease	*	2.3E-07
0.891	nose: Scale nostrils width	*	2.96E-07
-1.12	slider_l-eye-corner1-down|up	*	4.13E-07
0.705	mouth: Scale vertically	*	1.37E-06
1.02	nose: Move nose base vert.		1.37E-06
0.66	mouth: Move corners vert.	*	8.23E-06
0.546	mouth: Scale lowerlip height	*	8.47E-06
-0.716	slider_r-eye-trans-down|up		0.0000117
0.586	mouth: Move depth	*	0.0000191
-0.562	slider_r-eye-eyefold-concave|convex		0.0000298
-0.676	slider_l-eye-trans-down|up		0.0000422
0.651	nose: Move depth		0.0000473
0.653	nose: Move tip vertically		0.0000528
1.23	slider_r-cheek-trans-down|up		0.0000785
-0.788	slider_nostril_rounding	*	0.0000878

1.25	chin: Scale chin prognathism		1.76E-08
0.988	mouth: Scale vertically	*	2.67E-08
0.695	slider_l-eye-trans-in|out	*	6.69E-07
0.892	slider_r-eye-trans-in|out	*	1.43E-06
0.952	nose: Scale nostrils width	*	2.31E-06
0.79	mouth: Scale lowerlip height	*	0.0000118
-0.741	slider_nostril_rounding	*	0.0000302
-0.593	nose-volume-decr|incr	*	0.0000515
0.624	mouth: Move depth	*	0.0000562

Arab female (n=28)

1.15	slider_r-eye-push2-in|out		4.67E-07
0.896	slider_l-eye-push2-in|out		2.19E-06
-0.972	slider_l-eye-eyefold-angle-down|up		0.0000121
0.821	slider_elvs_chipmunkcheeks_l1		0.0000128
1.09	slider_r-eye-scale-decr|incr		0.0000189
0.663	nose: Scale vertically	*	0.0000347
0.651	nose-nostrils-angle-down|up		0.0000364
0.981	slider_l-eye-scale-decr|incr		0.0000724

Afro-Latino male (n=27)[53]

-1.57	mouth: Dimples	*	1.1E-15
-1.46	chin: Scale chin height	*	3E-14
1.28	mouth: Move corners vert.	*	6.52E-13
-1.43	chin: Scale chin width	*	1.03E-12
-1.34	slider_Nose_alar_crease	*	2.07E-12
1.3	mouth: Scale horizontally	*	1.87E-11
1.33	mouth: Scale upperlip width	*	3.72E-11
0.986	nose: Scale horizontally	*	2.41E-10
-1.19	mouth: Laugh-lines	*	2.91E-10
1.14	mouth: Scale lowerlip width	*	3.29E-10
-1.02	mouth: Scale lowerlip volume	*	7.46E-10
1.06	chin: Cleft chin		6.58E-09
-1.34	slider_elvs_highchubbycheekbones1	*	1.24E-08

---

53 At this point you'll notice that every group with the word "afro" in their name necessarily has an afro hairstyle, even though my negative prompt explicitly told the AI to exclude "… afro, feather earrings, clothing, hat, headdress, dot on forehead, scarf, burka, tartan." The AI just couldn't resist putting these things in the picture anyway. But there's a lesson in this, and also a lesson in why I let it slide. A lot of people in 2025 are asking how it got so easy to be sexist, racist, imperialistic, etc. in open public. I don't think I'm any of those things, but here's an explanation for people who don't understand it. I work with mass data. The data is biased. And there's so much more of it than anyone can reasonably cherry-pick through for exceptions to a stereotype. Yes, almost everything is an exception. But broadly speaking, if I went in and attempted to correct every generalization hundreds and thousands of times over, I'd never get the work done. That said, the feather earring and headdress on EVERY Native American image was a bridge too far, and annoyed me more for its defiance of my will than anything else. So I didn't let the AI get away with that one. Or the Middle Eastern clothing tropes in a book about sheer bodies. I'm explaining this to anyone upset with the times we live in. I'm not a fan either. But when I look in the mirror and see parallels to things I wouldn't and didn't vote for. The Golden Rule kicks in and my own glass house becomes evident. Everyone has a piece of every perspective they've come across. The point of this work is to see that commonality and use it to advance yourself—not just to sit stuck with conditions you don't like.

Arab male (n=29)

0.922	nose: Scale vertically		*	3.85E-08
0.939	mouth: Move vertically			6.79E-07
0.757	nose: Lower nose bridge width			0.0000533
-0.546		slider_r-eye-eyefold-angle-down|up		0.0000642
0.754	slider_l-cheek-trans-down|up			0.0000977

Armenian female (n=22)

-1.38		slider_l-eye-trans-in|out	*	2.03E-08
-1.04		slider_r-eye-trans-in|out	*	5.31E-07
1.38	slider_r-eye-push2-in|out			6.59E-07
1.34	slider_l-eye-push2-in|out		*	1.06E-06
0.653	nose-nostrils-angle-down|up			5.01E-06
0.822	slider_r-eye-eyefold-concave|convex			7.75E-06
-0.452		nose: Move vertically		0.000015
0.669	mouth: Move vertically			0.0000176
0.556	nose: Scale vertically			0.0000282
-0.834		slider_r-eye-eyefold-angle-down|up		0.000044
-0.638		nose: Scale horizontally		0.000065

Armenian male (n=26)

-1.13		slider_l-eye-trans-in|out	*	3.7E-12
-0.641		nose: Scale tip width		7.56E-09
-0.65		slider_r-eye-trans-in|out	*	3.25E-08
0.708	nose: Middle nose bridge width			2.98E-07
0.869	nose-hump-decr|incr			9.7E-07
0.955	mouth: Scale philtrum volume			2.31E-06
0.864	nose: Lower nose bridge width			0.000005
-0.615		slider_l-eye-eyefold-angle-down|up		7.75E-06
0.517	slider_elvs_highchubbycheekbones1			8.14E-06
-0.787		mouth: Lowerlip curved shape		0.0000112
0.472	mouth: Dimples			0.0000241
0.866	slider_l-eye-push2-in|out		*	0.0000408

Ashkenazi Jewish female (n=26)

0.909	mouth: Move vertically		*	1.89E-07
-0.652		mouth: Move depth		0.000023
-0.434		mouth: Scale lowerlip height		0.0000539
0.616	nose-nostrils-angle-down|up			0.0000889

Ashkenazi Jewish male (n=24)

0.655	mouth: Move vertically		*	0.0000714

Asian female (n=25)

-1.86		nose-greek-decr|incr	*	9.27E-13
-1.72		eyebrows: Eyebrows bulge	*	2.45E-12
1.61	eyebrows: Eyebrows angle		*	4.89E-12
-0.988		nose: Move depth		6.02E-12
1.9	forehead: Scale vertically		*	5.46E-10
1.87	forehead: Cranic shape		*	9.29E-10

-0.919	mouth: Scale philtrum volume		1.26E-09
1.19	eyebrows: Move vert	*	2.68E-09
-1.19	slider_r-eye-scale-decr|incr	*	5.52E-09
-0.901	slider_l-eye-trans-down|up	*	7.7E-09
-1.05	slider_r-eye-trans-down|up	*	8.64E-09
-0.876	chin: Tone of side chin		1.17E-08
-1.13	nose: Lower nose bridge width	*	1.43E-08
0.907	mouth: Scale upperlip volume		1.93E-08
-1.05	nose: Move nose base vert.		5.93E-08
-1.15	nose: Move vertically	*	6.26E-08
0.958	nose-hump-decr|incr		2.77E-07
0.816	slider_r-eye-eyefold-angle-down|up		3.83E-07
1.11	slider_Nose_alar_crease	*	5.6E-07
-0.968	slider_l-eye-scale-decr|incr	*	7.19E-07
0.819	slider_r-eye-epicanthus-in|out	*	8.43E-07
-0.827	mouth: Scale upperlip width	*	1.62E-06
0.666	nose-volume-decr|incr		3.46E-06
-0.929	nose: Scale depth	*	5.27E-06
-0.661	mouth: Move depth		6.03E-06
0.816	mouth: Move corners vert.	*	6.88E-06
-0.937	nose: Move tip vertically		0.0000072
1.16	slider_l-eye-eyefold-angle-down|up	*	7.62E-06
0.935	slider_eyes_outer_droop	*	7.79E-06
0.717	nose-nostrils-angle-down|up	*	9.03E-06
-1.04	mouth: Scale horizontally	*	9.06E-06
-0.992	slider_l-eye-push1-in|out	*	9.57E-06
-0.898	nose: Scale nostrils flaring	*	0.0000124
-0.889	nose: Scale vertically	*	0.000025
1.05	slider_l-eye-epicanthus-in|out		0.0000313
0.993	forehead: Forehead bulge		0.0000491
0.73	nose-compression-compress|uncompress		0.0000563
-0.953	slider_r-eye-push1-in|out	*	0.0000794
0.744	slider_eyes_middle_droop	*	0.0000866

-1.02	slider_r-eye-trans-down|up	*	1.06E-08
-0.651	nose: Scale nostrils width		1.6E-08
-0.814	mouth: Scale upperlip width	*	2.16E-08
-1	nose: Middle nose bridge width		2.21E-08
-0.896	mouth: Scale horizontally	*	2.35E-08
-1.11	slider_r-eye-push1-in|out	*	3.63E-08
0.732	mouth: Scale middle upperlip		3.67E-08
1.15	slider_Nose_alar_crease	*	6.98E-08
0.529	eyes: Outer height of left eye		9.63E-08
-0.844	slider_l-eye-trans-down|up	*	9.82E-08
0.81	slider_eyes_middle_droop	*	2.15E-07
-0.658	slider_r-eye-scale-decr|incr	*	2.87E-07
0.958	eyebrows: Move vert	*	2.91E-07
-0.726	mouth: Move vertically		1.07E-06
-0.662	slider_l-eye-trans-in|out		1.61E-06
0.977	eyebrows: Eyebrows angle		3.35E-06
-0.864	nose: Scale nostrils flaring	*	4.98E-06
0.598	slider_r-eye-epicanthus-in|out	*	0.0000101
-0.694	nose: Scale vertically	*	0.0000102
0.637	slider_l-eye-eyefold-angle-down|up	*	0.0000111
0.427	mouth: Move corners vert.	*	0.0000141
0.71	slider_r-eye-corner2-down|up		0.0000147
0.669	nose-nostrils-angle-down|up	*	0.0000224
-0.585	slider_l-eye-scale-decr|incr	*	0.0000384
-0.744	slider_r-eye-corner1-down|up		0.0000431
-0.465	eyes: Middle height of left eye		0.0000443
-0.659	slider_r-eye-trans-in|out		0.0000455
0.539	slider_elvs_highchubbycheekbones1		0.0000562

Basque female (n=23)

Asian male (n=27)

-1.44	nose: Lower nose bridge width	*	3.4E-13
-1.69	eyebrows: Eyebrows bulge	*	1.36E-12
1.57	forehead: Scale vertically	*	9.01E-12
0.696	eyes: Outer height of right eye		1.11E-11
1.56	forehead: Cranic shape	*	7.79E-11
-0.792	nose: Scale depth	*	8.98E-10
1.03	slider_eyes_outer_droop	*	1.78E-09
0.773	mouth: Laugh-lines		2.15E-09
0.832	slider_r-eye-bag-in|out		3.86E-09
-1.09	slider_l-eye-push1-in|out	*	6.25E-09
-1.2	nose-greek-decr|incr	*	8.68E-09
-0.862	nose: Move vertically	*	1.05E-08

-0.819	mouth: Scale lowerlip width	*	2.04E-08
0.584	nose-greek-decr|incr		1.5E-07
-0.475	eyebrows: Eyebrows angle		2.58E-06
-0.727	slider_l-eye-trans-in|out	*	3.76E-06
0.904	slider_r-eye-trans-down|up		4.19E-06
0.555	nose: Upper nose bridge width		4.81E-06
0.702	eyebrows: Eyebrows bulge		4.92E-06
0.94	slider_l-eye-trans-down|up		4.93E-06
0.871	slider_elvs_highchubbycheekbones1		9.01E-06
0.832	chin: Scale chin width	*	9.64E-06
-0.627	mouth: Scale upperlip width	*	0.000043

Basque male (n=26)

-0.615	mouth: Scale upperlip width	*	6.11E-08
-0.849	mouth: Scale lowerlip width	*	7.51E-07
-0.694	slider_l-eye-trans-in|out	*	2.37E-06
-0.505	slider_r-eye-eyefold-angle-down|up		0.0000113
-0.805	mouth: Scale vertically		0.0000126
0.974	mouth: Scale lowerlip volume		0.0000348
-0.507	nose: Scale horizontally		0.0000353
0.382	mouth: Dimples		0.0000543
-0.749	nose: Scale nostrils width		0.000081
0.604	chin: Scale chin width	*	0.0000895
0.526	slider_Nose_alar_crease		0.0000939

Bengali female (n=27)

1.22	nose: Scale vertically	*	6.18E-11
-1.11	eyebrows: Move vert		1.4E-09
-0.938	slider_Nose_alar_crease		2.55E-08
0.897	nose: Scale depth		2.8E-08
-1.24	slider_eyes_middle_droop		7.14E-08
-1.19	slider_eyes_outer_droop	*	2.52E-07
1.09	slider_r-eye-scale-decr|incr	*	8.02E-07
-0.812	mouth: Scale lowerlip volume	*	1.22E-06
0.48	mouth: Scale vertically		1.23E-06
0.569	mouth: Scale upperlip width		2.15E-06
-0.986	slider_l-eye-bag-height-decr|incr	*	0.0000023
1	slider_l-eye-scale-decr|incr	*	2.35E-06
-0.848	slider_r-eye-bag-height-decr|incr	*	2.75E-06
0.762	slider_l-eye-push1-in|out		3.81E-06
-0.683	mouth: Upperlip curved shape		5.58E-06

-0.792	nose-hump-decr|incr		6.64E-06
0.638	slider_r-eye-push2-in|out	*	8.75E-06
0.493	chin: Scale chin prominence		0.0000144
0.866	eyes: Middle height of right eye	*	0.0000151
-0.6	mouth: Cupid's bow width		0.0000159
0.719	nose: Scale nostrils width		0.0000193
-0.609	nose: Move vertically		0.0000217
0.867	eyes: Middle height of left eye	*	0.0000266
0.691	mouth: Scale upperlip height		0.0000378
-0.594	slider_nostril_rounding	*	0.0000549
0.617	eyes: Outer height of right eye		0.0000804
0.504	mouth: Move vertically		0.0000864
-0.45	mouth: Scale upperlip volume		0.0000971
0.453	mouth: Scale lowerlip width		0.0000987

Bengali male (n=27)

1.1	slider_l-eye-scale-decr|incr	*	1.99E-09
1.1	slider_r-eye-scale-decr|incr	*	2.96E-09
-0.73	slider_nostril_rounding	*	9.37E-09
0.817	eyes: Middle height of left eye	*	2.53E-08
-0.772	slider_eyes_outer_droop	*	5.09E-07
0.867	eyes: Middle height of right eye	*	8.71E-07
0.797	nose: Scale vertically	*	8.91E-07
-0.753	slider_r-eye-bag-height-decr|incr	*	6.14E-06
1.01	slider_l-eye-push2-in|out		9.14E-06
0.637	eyes: Inner height of left eye		0.000014
-0.66	slider_l-eye-bag-height-decr|incr	*	0.0000166
0.77	slider_r-eye-push2-in|out	*	0.0000195
-0.634	slider_l-eye-epicanthus-in|out		0.0000331
-0.32	mouth: Scale lowerlip volume	*	0.0000483

Berber female (n=16)
(no findings)

Berber male (n=18)

0.855	eyebrows: Eyebrows bulge		6.43E-06
0.68	nose: Upper nose bridge width		0.0000209
-0.861		eyes: Outer height of left eye	0.0000508
0.86	nose: Middle nose bridge width		0.0000791

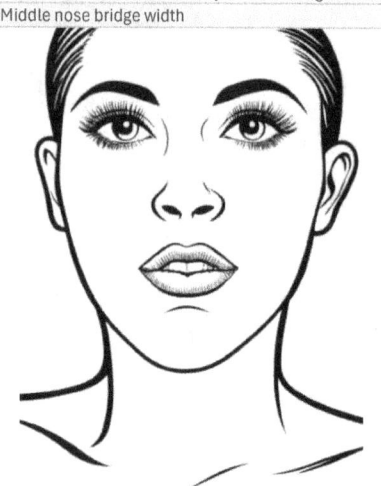

Brazilian female (n=21)

-0.643		eyebrows: Eyebrows angle　*	9.17E-07
0.627	mouth: Scale middle upperlip		0.000037
-0.707		slider_Nose_alar_crease	0.000066

Brazilian male (n=22)

0.497	nose: Upper nose bridge width		1.07E-07
-0.886		eyebrows: Eyebrows angle　*	1.33E-07
0.786	nose-greek-decr|incr		4.17E-07
0.791	nose: Middle nose bridge width		0.0000277
-0.664		mouth: Dimples	0.0000354
0.667	mouth: Scale horizontally		0.0000609
0.623	nose: Scale horizontally		0.0000627

British female (n=23)

-0.981		nose: Scale nostrils width	3.76E-09
-0.917		mouth: Scale upperlip width　*	9.47E-09
-0.795		mouth: Scale lowerlip width　*	2.43E-08
-0.816		mouth: Scale vertically	4.16E-07
-0.748		mouth: Move corners vert.	0.0000011
0.817	chin: Scale chin height		3.53E-06
0.808	mouth: Scale lowerlip volume　*		7.71E-06
0.758	mouth: Laugh-lines		0.0000307
0.748	slider_Nose_alar_crease		0.0000823

British male (n=20)

-0.994	mouth: Scale upperlip width	*	0.0000012
-0.857	mouth: Scale lowerlip width	*	9.29E-06
1.13	mouth: Scale lowerlip volume	*	0.000017
0.608	chin: Scale chin width		0.0000428
0.631	mouth: Dimples		0.0000545

Burmese female (n=24)

0.919	slider_elvs_highchubbycheekbones1	1.36E-07
1.17	slider_r-eye-eyefold-down|up	9.45E-06
-1.2	slider_r-cheek-trans-down|up	0.0000188
0.946	slider_r-eye-eyefold-angle-down|up	0.0000372
-1.47	mouth: Move vertically	0.0000724

Burmese male (n=16)

1.15	slider_eyes_middle_droop	9.02E-06
1.31	slider_r-eye-corner1-down|up	0.0000264
-0.62	slider_r-eye-bag-in|out	0.0000379

Cajun female (n=31)

-0.846	mouth: Scale lowerlip height		3.61E-08
-0.826	mouth: Scale lowerlip width	*	1.75E-07
0.88	slider_r-eye-trans-down|up		2.46E-07
-0.837	mouth: Scale vertically	*	2.73E-07
0.859	slider_l-eye-trans-down|up		1.07E-06
-0.67	slider_l-eye-bag-decr|incr		0.0000065
0.859	mouth: Scale lowerlip volume	*	7.65E-06
-0.609	chin: Tone of side chin		0.0000275
0.81	chin: Scale chin width		0.0000325
-0.611	nose: Scale horizontally		0.0000347
-0.617	slider_l-cheek-volume-decr|incr		0.0000422
0.746	mouth: Upperlip curved shape		0.0000706

Cajun male (n=22)

-0.883		mouth: Scale lowerlip width	*	2.59E-06
-1.01		mouth: Scale vertically	*	0.0000191
1.6	mouth: Scale lowerlip volume		*	0.0000231
1.44	mouth: Lowerlip curved shape			0.0000298
-0.553		mouth: Scale upperlip width		0.0000335

Cambodian male (n=19)

-1.36		mouth: Move vertically	*	8.5E-10
-1.36		mouth: Move vertically	*	8.5E-10
0.853	mouth: Scale vertically		*	3.09E-08
-1.17		slider_r-eye-push2-in|out	*	1.18E-06
1.11	slider_eyes_outer_droop		*	2.99E-06
0.779	slider_r-eye-corner1-down|up		*	4.54E-06
-0.609		chin: Scale chin height		4.97E-06
0.655	chin: Cleft chin		*	8.86E-06
-0.69		slider_r-eye-scale-decr|incr		0.00001
-0.915		slider_l-eye-push2-in|out	*	0.0000117
-0.723		slider_l-eye-scale-decr|incr		0.0000348
0.58	mouth: Scale lowerlip width		*	0.0000696
0.749	slider_l-eye-corner1-down|up			0.0000989

Cambodian female (n=23)

-1.41		mouth: Move vertically	*	1.17E-08
-1.41		mouth: Move vertically	*	1.17E-08
0.707	mouth: Scale vertically		*	2.77E-08
0.457	nose: Upper nose bridge width			1.02E-07
0.445	nose-compression-compress|uncompress			4.63E-07
-1.03		slider_r-eye-push2-in|out	*	8.23E-07
0.965	slider_r-eye-corner1-down|up		*	2.25E-06
0.548	mouth: Scale lowerlip width		*	0.0000225
0.704	chin: Cleft chin		*	0.0000345
-0.67		slider_l-eye-push2-in|out	*	0.0000484
0.849	slider_eyes_outer_droop		*	0.0000544
0.911	slider_r-eye-epicanthus-in|out			0.0000636
-0.345		nose: Scale tip width		0.0000679
-0.654		slider_nostril_rounding		0.0000711
0.66	mouth: Move corners vert.			0.0000959

Canadian female (n=33)

-0.78		mouth: Scale vertically	*	4.49E-10
-0.942		nose: Lower nose bridge width		6.5E-09
-0.709		mouth: Scale lowerlip width	*	6.93E-09
0.785	mouth: Scale lowerlip volume		*	9.14E-08
-0.695		mouth: Scale upperlip height		5.98E-07
-0.626		mouth: Scale lowerlip height	*	6.92E-07
0.692	mouth: Upperlip curved shape			7.09E-07
0.836	slider_elvs_chipmunkcheeks_l1			1.38E-06
-0.734		mouth: Scale upperlip width	*	1.76E-06
0.717	mouth: Scale upperlip volume			0.0000271
-0.681		nose: Scale vertically		0.0000514
0.471	mouth: Lowerlip curved shape		*	0.0000623

Canadian male (n=21)

-0.937	mouth: Scale lowerlip width	*	9.42E-09
-1.3	mouth: Scale vertically	*	3.03E-08
1.71	mouth: Scale lowerlip volume	*	6.99E-08
1.24	mouth: Lowerlip curved shape	*	1.77E-07
-1.02	mouth: Scale lowerlip height	*	8.16E-07
0.848	mouth: Move vertically		8.59E-07
-0.674	nose: Scale horizontally		0.000011
-0.603	mouth: Scale upperlip width	*	0.0000332
-0.785	slider_l-cheek-inner-decr|incr		0.000041

Chinese female (n=23)

-1.62	eyebrows: Eyebrows bulge	*	3.73E-13
1.52	forehead: Scale vertically	*	1.77E-11
1.53	forehead: Cranic shape	*	4.8E-11
1.6	slider_Nose_alar_crease	*	6.84E-11
-1.11	mouth: Scale upperlip width	*	4.73E-10
-1.09	nose: Scale depth	*	5.05E-10
-1.72	nose-greek-decr|incr	*	1.81E-09
-0.983	mouth: Move vertically	*	2.81E-09
-1.06	slider_r-eye-trans-down|up	*	5.15E-09
-1.41	nose: Lower nose bridge width	*	5.69E-09
-1.08	nose: Scale nostrils flaring	*	1.64E-08
-0.983	slider_l-eye-trans-down|up	*	3.97E-08
-1.28	nose: Scale vertically	*	6.85E-08
1.52	eyebrows: Eyebrows angle	*	9.53E-08
-1.13	slider_r-eye-scale-decr|incr	*	4.53E-07
0.9	slider_eyes_middle_droop	*	7.1E-07
0.499	mouth: Scale lowerlip volume	*	9.69E-07
0.946	eyebrows: Move vert		1.41E-06
0.946	slider_eyes_outer_droop		2.16E-06
0.859	slider_r-eye-corner2-down|up	*	3.45E-06

0.808	slider_l-eye-corner2-down|up	*	5.77E-06
-1.16	mouth: Scale horizontally	*	7.23E-06
-0.844	slider_l-cheek-trans-down|up	*	9.43E-06
-0.839	nose: Move vertically	*	0.0000103
-0.836	slider_l-eye-scale-decr|incr	*	0.0000119
0.857	slider_elvs_highchubbycheekbones1	*	0.000014
1.04	slider_l-eye-eyefold-angle-down|up	*	0.0000156
0.813	mouth: Laugh-lines	*	0.0000169
0.726	nose-hump-decr|incr		0.0000486
-0.666	slider_r-eye-corner1-down|up	*	0.0000511
-0.882	slider_r-cheek-trans-down|up	*	0.0000564

Chinese male (n=29)

-0.983	slider_l-eye-push1-in|out		7.32E-14
-1.35	slider_r-eye-push1-in|out	*	2.04E-13
-1.05	mouth: Move vertically	*	3.23E-13
-1.07	nose: Scale nostrils width		4.63E-13
-1.26	mouth: Scale upperlip width	*	4.77E-13
1.35	slider_eyes_outer_droop	*	1.09E-12
1.1	mouth: Laugh-lines	*	1.23E-12
-1.39	eyebrows: Eyebrows bulge	*	1.48E-12
1.5	slider_Nose_alar_crease	*	2.51E-12
-1.2	nose: Scale nostrils flaring	*	3.52E-12
-1.4	nose: Lower nose bridge width	*	4.12E-12
-1.28	nose: Scale vertically	*	5.23E-12
1.13	slider_eyes_middle_droop	*	1.9E-11
-1.03	slider_r-eye-scale-decr|incr	*	8.64E-11
1.11	forehead: Scale vertically	*	1.97E-10
-1.13	nose-greek-decr|incr	*	6.02E-10
-0.905	slider_r-eye-trans-down|up	*	8.82E-10
1.15	forehead: Cranic shape	*	1.88E-09
0.961	slider_elvs_highchubbycheekbones1	*	2.74E-09
-1.19	mouth: Scale horizontally	*	4.8E-09
-0.789	slider_l-eye-trans-in|out		4.84E-09
0.925	slider_l-eye-corner2-down|up	*	9.7E-09
-1.05	nose: Scale depth	*	1.33E-08
-0.601	nose: Move vertically	*	2.38E-08
-0.895	slider_l-eye-scale-decr|incr	*	4.28E-08
0.719	slider_r-eye-bag-in|out		4.82E-08
0.677	slider_l-eye-bag-in|out		5.7E-08
-1.03	slider_l-cheek-trans-down|up	*	1.03E-07
-0.803	slider_l-eye-trans-down|up	*	1.31E-07
-0.999	nose: Middle nose bridge width		3.39E-07
1.01	eyebrows: Eyebrows angle	*	5.06E-07
-0.855	slider_r-eye-trans-in|out		6.69E-07
0.732	slider_l-eye-epicanthus-in|out		9.32E-07
-0.947	slider_r-cheek-trans-down|up	*	9.54E-07

0.612	mouth: Dimples			1.27E-06
0.57	slider_l-eye-eyefold-down|up			1.77E-06
-0.756		slider_r-eye-corner1-down|up	*	1.93E-06
0.817	slider_r-eye-corner2-down|up		*	2.03E-06
-0.359		mouth: Scale lowerlip width		2.68E-06
0.576	slider_l-eye-eyefold-angle-down|up		*	3.58E-06
0.404	mouth: Scale lowerlip volume		*	6.18E-06
0.807	slider_nostril_rounding			7.37E-06
0.421	eyes: Outer height of right eye			0.0000131
0.382	eyes: Outer height of left eye			0.0000193
-0.663		nose: Scale horizontally		0.0000332
0.671	slider_l-cheek-volume-decr|incr			0.0000393
-0.678		slider_l-eye-corner1-down|up		0.000075
-0.516		chin: Scale chin angular		0.0000833

Colombian female (n=22)
(no findings)

Colombian male (n=20)

-0.797	eyebrows: Eyebrows angle		0.0000192
-0.666	slider_Nose_alar_crease		0.0000198
0.58	mouth: Scale horizontally		0.0000214
0.938	nose: Middle nose bridge width		0.0000219
-0.581	nose-volume-decr|incr		0.0000253
0.726	nose-greek-decr|incr		0.0000557

0.529	nose: Scale horizontally		0.0000665
0.668	slider_l-eye-epicanthus-in|out		0.0000757

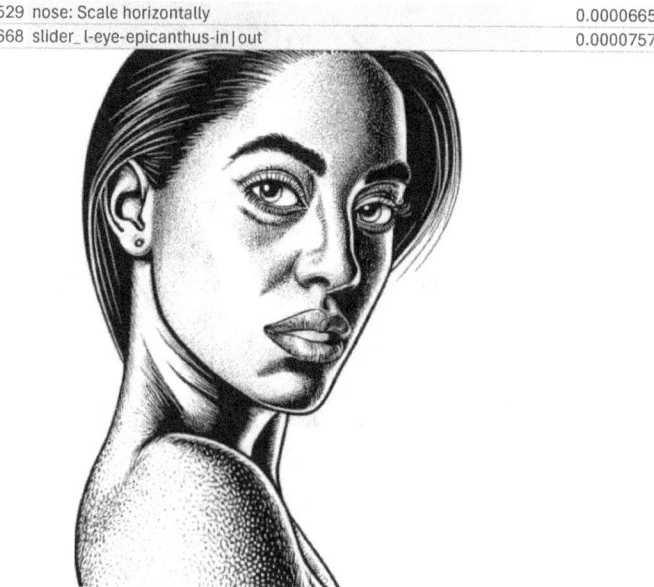

Cuban female (n=30)

0.925	nose-greek-decr|incr		*	8.68E-07
0.776	chin: Scale chin prognathism			1.72E-06
0.794	slider_l-eye-corner1-down|up		*	2.79E-06
0.755	slider_l-eye-trans-down|up			0.0000144
0.621	nose: Scale horizontally		*	0.0000155
0.738	chin: Scale chin prominence		*	0.0000164
0.72	slider_r-eye-trans-down|up			0.0000266
-0.674		eyebrows: Eyebrows angle	*	0.0000288
0.709	slider_r-eye-corner1-down|up		*	0.0000452
0.73	nose: Middle nose bridge width		*	0.0000628
0.487	slider_l-eye-push1-in|out			0.0000653
-0.712		nose-hump-decr|incr		0.0000772
0.558	slider_l-cheek-inner-decr|incr			0.0000913

Cuban male (n=23)

0.768	nose-greek-decr|incr	*	2.6E-07
1.12	nose: Middle nose bridge width	*	2.98E-07
1.08	slider_r-eye-push1-in|out		4.08E-07
1.06	slider_r-cheek-bones-decr|incr		8.27E-07
0.698	slider_r-eye-trans-in|out		1.52E-06
0.599	nose: Upper nose bridge width		3.17E-06
0.822	nose: Scale horizontally	*	3.25E-06
1.03	slider_l-eye-corner1-down|up	*	5.21E-06

-0.707	eyebrows: Eyebrows angle	*	0.0000104
1.13	slider_r-eye-corner1-down|up	*	0.0000158
1.02	nose: Lower nose bridge width		0.0000307
0.578	chin: Scale chin prominence	*	0.0000966

Czech female (n=22)

-0.694	forehead: Scale vertically	*	2.01E-08
-0.655	forehead: Cranic shape	*	1.18E-07
-0.733	mouth: Scale vertically	*	1.51E-07
-0.965	slider_l-cheek-inner-decr|incr	*	3.68E-07
-0.763	nose: Scale horizontally		2.69E-06
-0.745	chin: Scale chin prognathism		0.0000103
-0.656	mouth: Scale lowerlip width	*	0.0000152
-0.614	mouth: Move corners vert.	*	0.0000179
-0.982	nose: Scale nostrils width	*	0.0000407
-0.859	mouth: Scale upperlip width	*	0.0000987

Czech male (n=21)

-0.972	mouth: Scale upperlip width	*	7.89E-10
0.722	mouth: Dimples		2.28E-09
-0.879	mouth: Scale lowerlip width	*	1.5E-07
0.872	mouth: Laugh-lines		3.25E-07
-0.681	slider_r-eye-scale-decr|incr		6.85E-07
1.19	mouth: Scale lowerlip volume		9.41E-07
-0.925	slider_r-eye-trans-in|out		0.0000011
-0.971	nose: Scale nostrils width	*	1.14E-06
-1.02	mouth: Scale vertically	*	1.66E-06
-0.82	slider_l-cheek-inner-decr|incr		0.000002
-0.853	nose: Scale horizontally	*	2.06E-06
-0.977	slider_l-eye-trans-in|out		2.52E-06
0.777	nose-greek-decr|incr		7.05E-06
-0.838	forehead: Scale vertically	*	7.57E-06

-0.804	forehead: Cranic shape	*	0.0000385
0.737	chin: Scale chin height		0.0000394
0.728	nose: Move vertically		0.0000435
0.724	eyebrows: Eyebrows bulge		0.0000456
-0.625	chin: Cleft chin		0.0000769
-0.553	mouth: Move corners vert.	*	0.0000967

Danish female (n=16)

-0.981	nose: Scale nostrils width	*	5.77E-10
-0.746	mouth: Move corners vert.	*	2.69E-09
-1.05	chin: Cleft chin		4.43E-09
-1.15	mouth: Scale vertically		4.52E-09
1.17	mouth: Scale lowerlip volume		9.17E-08
1.19	chin: Scale chin height	*	2.24E-07
-1.23	nose: Scale horizontally		0.0000014
-0.857	slider_l-cheek-inner-decr|incr	*	3.64E-06
-0.799	mouth: Scale lowerlip height		5.19E-06
-0.836	mouth: Scale upperlip width	*	5.31E-06
-0.795	mouth: Scale lowerlip width	*	6.81E-06
1.02	slider_Nose_alar_crease	*	0.0000207
0.634	slider_l-eye-push2-in|out		0.0000256
-0.895	forehead: Cranic shape		0.0000395
-0.907	forehead: Scale vertically		0.0000399
-0.801	slider_r-eye-trans-in|out		0.0000656

Danish male (n=17)

-1.07	slider_l-cheek-inner-decr|incr	*	1.86E-08
-1.24	nose: Scale nostrils width	*	2.85E-07
-0.932	mouth: Scale upperlip width	*	6.45E-07
-0.796	mouth: Scale lowerlip width	*	6.75E-07
0.878	slider_Nose_alar_crease	*	6.95E-06
0.88	mouth: Laugh-lines		7.59E-06
-0.797	nose: Lower nose bridge width		0.000065

-0.794	mouth: Move corners vert.	*	0.0000821
0.672	chin: Scale chin height	*	0.0000868
-0.855	slider_septum_sharp		0.0000979
Dutch female (n=18)			
-0.617	mouth: Scale vertically	*	0.0000342
-0.448	chin: Cleft chin		0.0000634
Dutch male (n=24)			
-0.665	mouth: Scale lowerlip width		1.89E-06
-0.86	mouth: Scale vertically	*	3.14E-06
0.9	mouth: Scale lowerlip volume		0.0000115
-0.748	nose: Scale horizontally		0.000062
-0.676	eyes: Inner height of right eye		0.0000821

English female (n=22)

-0.886	mouth: Scale lowerlip width	*	9.48E-08
-0.836	mouth: Scale vertically	*	2.79E-07
-0.825	mouth: Scale upperlip height		1.45E-06
0.781	mouth: Upperlip curved shape		2.95E-06
-0.856	mouth: Scale lowerlip height		3.56E-06
0.8	chin: Scale chin height	*	5.24E-06
0.75	mouth: Scale lowerlip volume	*	8.18E-06
0.82	mouth: Scale upperlip volume		8.42E-06
-0.714	mouth: Scale upperlip width	*	0.0000203
-0.561	slider_r-cheek-bones-decr|incr		0.0000235
-0.638	mouth: Move depth		0.0000433

Egyptian female (n=23)

-0.582	mouth: Scale lowerlip volume	*	4.29E-06
-0.946	forehead: Temple bulge		0.0000129
0.539	mouth: Scale upperlip width		0.0000222
0.692	slider_r-cheek-trans-down|up		0.0000704
0.692	slider_r-cheek-trans-down|up		0.0000704
-0.67	slider_elvs_highchubbycheekbones1		0.0000743

English male (n=24)

-0.987	mouth: Scale lowerlip width	*	9.15E-09
-0.636	mouth: Move corners vert.		9.01E-08
-0.955	mouth: Scale upperlip width	*	1.06E-07
0.687	mouth: Dimples		1.3E-07
0.746	chin: Scale chin height	*	2.43E-06
1.27	mouth: Scale lowerlip volume	*	8.29E-06
-0.823	nose: Scale nostrils width		9.57E-06
-0.868	mouth: Scale vertically	*	0.0000172
-0.516	forehead: Scale vertically		0.0000228
0.709	mouth: Laugh-lines		0.0000228
0.598	chin: Scale chin width		0.0000516
-0.409	slider_r-eye-trans-in|out		0.0000738

Egyptian male (n=16)

-0.665	mouth: Scale lowerlip volume	*	2.31E-06
0.918	slider_r-eye-scale-decr|incr		0.0000376
-0.98	mouth: Lowerlip curved shape		0.0000629
0.995	slider_r-eye-push1-in|out		0.0000661

Ethiopian female (n=26)

-1.5	mouth: Scale upperlip volume	*	4.06E-13
-1.18	mouth: Upperlip curved shape	*	7.42E-12
1.07	mouth: Scale vertically	*	8.38E-12
1.1	mouth: Scale upperlip height	*	7.65E-11
0.992	mouth: Scale upperlip width	*	5.54E-10
-0.893	mouth: Scale lowerlip volume	*	7.58E-10
-0.712	slider_nostril_rounding		9.92E-10
-0.977	slider_elvs_chipmunkcheeks_l1		1.02E-08
0.954	mouth: Scale lowerlip width	*	1.04E-08
0.899	mouth: Scale lowerlip height	*	1.26E-08
1.02	nose: Move depth		6.06E-08
-0.611	mouth: Laugh-lines	*	1.06E-07
-0.635	mouth: Cupid's bow shape	*	0.0000011
0.884	slider_l-eye-trans-in|out	*	1.71E-06
-0.583	mouth: Dimples	*	1.81E-06
-1.31	mouth: Scale middle upperlip		0.0000041
0.846	mouth: Scale philtrum volume		4.11E-06
-0.511	forehead: Scale vertically		5.49E-06
0.64	slider_r-eye-trans-in|out	*	6.11E-06
0.759	nose: Scale horizontally		7.04E-06
0.464	nose: Lower nose bridge width		0.0000098
-0.5	chin: Scale chin width		0.0000146
0.336	nose: Upper nose bridge width		0.0000366
0.665	slider_r-eye-push1-in|out	*	0.0000389
0.546	eyebrows: Eyebrows bulge		0.0000423
0.438	slider_r-cheek-inner-decr|incr		0.0000427
0.703	nose-hump-decr|incr		0.0000975

Ethiopian male (n=17)

-1.67	mouth: Scale lowerlip volume	*	6.1E-11

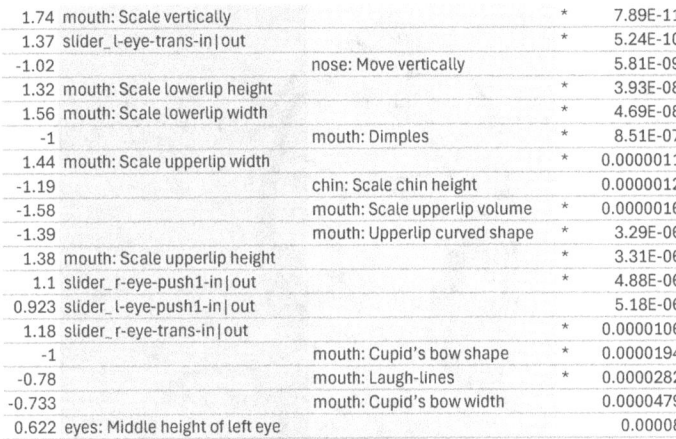

1.74	mouth: Scale vertically	*	7.89E-11
1.37	slider_l-eye-trans-in|out	*	5.24E-10
-1.02	nose: Move vertically		5.81E-09
1.32	mouth: Scale lowerlip height	*	3.93E-08
1.56	mouth: Scale lowerlip width	*	4.69E-08
-1	mouth: Dimples	*	8.51E-07
1.44	mouth: Scale upperlip width	*	0.0000011
-1.19	chin: Scale chin height		0.0000012
-1.58	mouth: Scale upperlip volume	*	0.0000016
-1.39	mouth: Upperlip curved shape	*	3.29E-06
1.38	mouth: Scale upperlip height	*	3.31E-06
1.1	slider_r-eye-push1-in|out	*	4.88E-06
0.923	slider_l-eye-push1-in|out		5.18E-06
1.18	slider_r-eye-trans-in|out	*	0.0000106
-1	mouth: Cupid's bow shape	*	0.0000194
-0.78	mouth: Laugh-lines	*	0.0000282
-0.733	mouth: Cupid's bow width		0.0000479
0.622	eyes: Middle height of left eye		0.00008

Filipino female (n=16)

0.583	mouth: Scale vertically		2.82E-07

Filipino male (n=26)

-0.832	mouth: Move vertically		1.21E-08
-0.832	mouth: Move vertically		1.21E-08
-0.65	nose: Lower nose bridge width		3.97E-07
0.656	slider_eyes_outer_droop		0.0000104
-0.653	mouth: Cupid's bow width		0.0000293
-0.424	mouth: Scale lowerlip volume		0.0000723

Finnish female (n=25)

Value	Parameter	Sig	p-value
-1.03	forehead: Scale vertically	*	4.87E-11
-1.07	forehead: Cranic shape	*	7.94E-11
-1.1	mouth: Scale vertically	*	1.82E-10
-1.1	mouth: Scale upperlip width	*	3.43E-09
-0.719	mouth: Move corners vert.	*	6.32E-09
-0.973	slider_r-eye-scale-decr|incr	*	1.15E-08
-0.911	mouth: Scale lowerlip width	*	1.52E-08
0.878	mouth: Laugh-lines		1.89E-08
0.833	slider_eyes_outer_droop		8.32E-08
-0.913	slider_r-eye-trans-in|out	*	9.71E-08
-1.02	slider_r-eye-push1-in|out		9.98E-08
1.17	mouth: Scale lowerlip volume	*	1.17E-07
-0.86	slider_r-cheek-bones-decr|incr		4.75E-07
0.699	mouth: Upperlip curved shape		8.14E-07
0.976	mouth: Dimples	*	9.12E-07
-0.753	mouth: Scale upperlip height		1.02E-06
0.826	chin: Scale chin height	*	1.54E-06
0.794	nose: Move vertically	*	2.22E-06
-0.692	mouth: Scale lowerlip height	*	3.04E-06
0.603	eyebrows: Eyebrows bulge		3.72E-06
-0.606	eyes: Outer height of left eye		4.64E-06
-0.815	slider_l-eye-scale-decr|incr	*	5.27E-06
-0.565	eyes: Middle height of left eye		0.0000143
-0.619	chin: Cleft chin	*	0.0000173
-0.642	eyes: Outer height of right eye		0.0000174
0.491	chin: Scale chin width	*	0.0000212
0.7	mouth: Scale upperlip volume		0.000026
-0.654	nose: Scale nostrils width	*	0.0000277
-0.762	mouth: Scale horizontally		0.000041
-0.731	slider_l-eye-push2-in|out		0.000055
-0.777	nose: Scale horizontally	*	0.0000563
0.548	mouth: Cupid's bow width		0.0000916

Value	Parameter	Sig	p-value
-0.933	mouth: Scale lowerlip width	*	9.49E-10
-0.845	mouth: Scale upperlip width	*	6E-09
1.01	chin: Scale chin height	*	8.06E-09
-0.935	forehead: Scale vertically	*	1.8E-08
-1.22	mouth: Scale vertically	*	1.88E-08
-0.88	nose: Scale horizontally	*	2.54E-08
-0.845	chin: Cleft chin	*	3.77E-08
-0.709	slider_r-eye-scale-decr|incr	*	3.94E-08
1.4	mouth: Scale lowerlip volume	*	4.83E-08
-0.598	slider_l-eye-scale-decr|incr	*	1.21E-07
-0.94	forehead: Cranic shape	*	1.72E-07
-0.714	slider_l-cheek-inner-decr|incr		2.11E-07
-0.712	mouth: Move corners vert.	*	2.71E-07
-0.859	slider_r-eye-trans-in|out	*	5.4E-07
0.52	mouth: Dimples	*	5.64E-07
-0.752	chin: Scale chin prognathism		0.0000039
1.06	nose: Move vertically	*	4.92E-06
-0.708	slider_l-eye-trans-in|out		0.0000143
0.582	nose-greek-decr|incr		0.000028
-0.923	chin: Scale chin prominence		0.0000297
-0.738	nose: Scale nostrils width	*	0.0000415
-0.869	mouth: Scale lowerlip height	*	0.0000522
0.429	chin: Scale chin width	*	0.0000598

French female (n=21)

Value	Parameter	p-value
-0.5	mouth: Scale vertically	3.94E-07
-0.696	nose: Scale nostrils width	0.0000127
-0.447	mouth: Scale lowerlip width	0.0000215
0.692	slider_Nose_alar_crease	0.0000614

Finnish male (n=22)

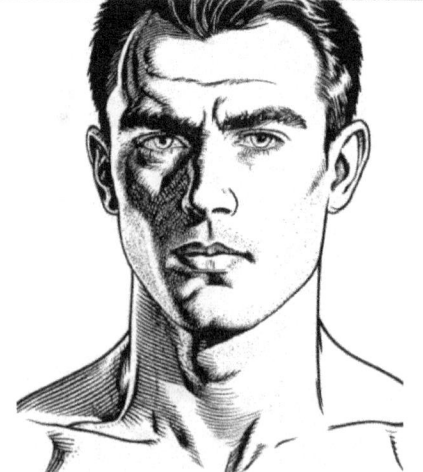

French male (n=18)
(no statistically significant findings)

German female (n=21)

Value	Parameter		p-value
-1.15	mouth: Scale vertically	*	5.83E-15
-0.953	mouth: Scale lowerlip height	*	1.76E-11
1.2 mouth: Scale lowerlip volume		*	9.03E-11
-0.993	chin: Cleft chin	*	9.73E-11
0.912 chin: Scale chin height		*	9.67E-10
-0.959	mouth: Scale lowerlip width	*	1.62E-09
-1.02	forehead: Scale vertically	*	2.54E-07
-0.932	slider_l-cheek-inner-decr|incr	*	3.01E-07
-0.804	mouth: Move corners vert.	*	3.17E-07
-0.971	forehead: Cranic shape	*	8.13E-07
-1.04	nose: Scale horizontally	*	0.0000011
0.865 eyebrows: Eyebrows bulge		*	2.69E-06
-0.738	nose: Scale nostrils width	*	2.89E-06
1 mouth: Move vertically			9.18E-06
-0.727	chin: Scale chin prognathism		0.0000125
0.803 nose: Move vertically		*	0.00002
-0.648	slider_r-eye-trans-in|out	*	0.0000436

German male (n=30)

Value	Parameter		p-value
-0.908	mouth: Scale lowerlip width	*	2.13E-10
-0.732	slider_r-eye-trans-in|out	*	1.52E-09
-1.11	mouth: Scale vertically	*	8.47E-09
1.3 mouth: Scale lowerlip volume		*	1.33E-08
0.817 chin: Scale chin height		*	4.85E-08
-0.659	slider_l-cheek-inner-decr|incr	*	2.13E-07
-0.663	mouth: Scale upperlip width		2.92E-07
-0.803	nose: Scale horizontally	*	4.09E-07
-0.723	forehead: Scale vertically	*	7.34E-07

Value	Parameter		p-value
-0.866	mouth: Scale lowerlip height	*	8.17E-07
-0.682	chin: Cleft chin	*	1.92E-06
-0.698	nose: Scale nostrils width	*	2.42E-06
0.659 nose: Move vertically		*	3.36E-06
0.783 eyebrows: Eyebrows bulge		*	0.00001
-0.666	forehead: Cranic shape	*	0.0000152
-0.587	mouth: Move corners vert.	*	0.0000164
0.647 mouth: Lowerlip curved shape			0.0000169
0.437 mouth: Dimples			0.0000232
0.493 mouth: Laugh-lines			0.0000381

Greek female (n=25)

Value	Parameter	p-value
0.514 nose: Upper nose bridge width		6.97E-10
-0.597	eyebrows: Eyebrows angle	5.53E-07
0.57 nose: Middle nose bridge width		0.0000101

Greek male (n=31)

Value	Parameter	p-value
-0.609	slider_r-eye-eyefold-angle-down|up	6.49E-06
-0.431	mouth: Move corners vert.	0.0000338

Gujarati female (n=27)

Value	Attribute		p-value
0.999	nose: Lower nose bridge width		1E-12
1.48	nose: Scale vertically	*	2.14E-11
-1.11	eyebrows: Move vert		7.5E-10
-1.05	slider_Nose_alar_crease	*	2.05E-08
0.808	nose: Middle nose bridge width		2.54E-08
1.02	nose: Scale depth	*	5.24E-08
1.1	slider_l-eye-push1-in|out		1.07E-07
0.631	mouth: Scale upperlip width	*	1.77E-07
0.933	nose-nostrils-angle-down|up		2.26E-07
-0.721	slider_l-eye-bag-height-decr|incr		3.48E-07
-0.768	slider_eyes_outer_droop		2.65E-06
0.652	slider_l-eye-corner1-down|up		2.67E-06
0.715	slider_r-eye-scale-decr|incr		3.53E-06
-0.682	slider_r-eye-bag-height-decr|incr		8.59E-06
-0.695	nose-hump-decr|incr		9.22E-06
0.811	mouth: Move vertically	*	0.0000108
-0.632	slider_eyes_middle_droop		0.0000414
0.8	slider_r-eye-push1-in|out		0.0000415
0.683	slider_l-eye-scale-decr|incr		0.000075
0.496	nose: Scale nostrils width		0.0000848

Gujarati male (n=20)

Value	Attribute		p-value
1.38	nose: Scale vertically	*	3.74E-08
-1.19	slider_Nose_alar_crease	*	6.48E-08
0.622	mouth: Scale upperlip width	*	1.11E-06

Value	Attribute		p-value
1.22	nose: Scale depth	*	1.52E-06
1.26	mouth: Scale philtrum volume		0.000019
-0.654	slider_nostril_rounding		0.0000288
-0.408	mouth: Scale lowerlip volume		0.0000651
0.904	mouth: Move vertically	*	0.0000668

Haitian female (n=31)

Value	Attribute		p-value
-1.5	mouth: Dimples	*	2.43E-17
1.42	mouth: Scale upperlip width	*	3.95E-17
-1.51	mouth: Laugh-lines	*	6.39E-16
-1.33	chin: Scale chin width	*	4.74E-14
1.29	nose: Scale horizontally	*	5.54E-13
1.22	mouth: Scale horizontally	*	8.97E-13
-1.16	slider_nostril_rounding		2.11E-12
-0.826	mouth: Scale lowerlip volume	*	8.15E-12
1.32	mouth: Scale lowerlip width	*	2.87E-11
-0.932	slider_Nose_alar_crease	*	7.6E-11
-1.24	nose-volume-decr|incr	*	1.68E-10
1.26	nose: Scale nostrils width	*	5.15E-10
1.14	slider_r-eye-trans-in|out	*	5.36E-10
-1.12	slider_elvs_highchubbycheekbones1	*	1.72E-09
1.09	slider_l-eye-trans-in|out	*	1.77E-09
-1.04	chin: Scale chin height	*	3.96E-09
-1.09	nose-nostrils-angle-down|up	*	6.15E-09
0.973	mouth: Scale vertically	*	1.28E-08
0.67	slider_r-cheek-inner-decr|incr		9.93E-08
0.67	slider_r-cheek-inner-decr|incr		9.93E-08
-0.93	slider_l-eye-trans-down|up		1.15E-07
0.637	slider_l-eye-eyefold-angle-down|up		1.22E-07
0.936	mouth: Move depth	*	1.46E-07
0.729	nose: Move nose base vert.	*	6.92E-07
0.908	mouth: Move corners vert.	*	9.36E-07
-0.797	slider_r-eye-trans-down|up		1.17E-06
-0.7	mouth: Move vertically	*	2.04E-06
0.807	slider_l-cheek-inner-decr|incr	*	4.58E-06
-0.614	nose: Scale vertically	*	0.0000124
0.893	slider_r-eye-eyefold-angle-down|up		0.0000127
0.485	chin: Scale chin prognathism	*	0.0000235
0.771	mouth: Scale lowerlip height	*	0.0000357
-0.549	chin: Scale chin prominence		0.0000682

Haitian male (n=24)

-1.15	mouth: Scale lowerlip volume	*	1.88E-15
-1.53	chin: Scale chin height	*	1.57E-14
-1.6	mouth: Dimples	*	2.97E-14
1.38	mouth: Scale upperlip width	*	1.19E-12
-1.45	nose-volume-decr|incr	*	1.44E-12
1.61	mouth: Scale lowerlip width	*	2.36E-12
1.5	mouth: Move corners vert.	*	3.41E-12
-1.2	mouth: Laugh-lines	*	1.73E-11
1.52	slider_l-eye-trans-in|out	*	4.68E-11
1.18	mouth: Scale horizontally	*	5.39E-10
-1.15	mouth: Move vertically	*	1.09E-09
-1.28	slider_elvs_highchubbycheekbones1	*	1.55E-09
1.3	mouth: Scale vertically		1.74E-09
1.3	chin: Cleft chin		3.14E-09
1.09	nose: Scale nostrils width	*	4.48E-09
1.53	slider_r-eye-trans-in|out	*	5.78E-09
-1.43	chin: Scale chin width	*	1.13E-08
1.34	nose: Scale horizontally	*	1.37E-08
1.32	chin: Scale chin prognathism	*	1.52E-08
-1.09	nose-nostrils-angle-down|up	*	2.6E-08
1.01	nose: Move nose base vert.	*	3.07E-08
-0.948	slider_Nose_alar_crease	*	3.35E-07
1.08	mouth: Scale lowerlip height	*	5.23E-07
0.761	nose: Move tip vertically		9.47E-07
-0.713	nose: Scale vertically	*	4.16E-06
0.943	mouth: Move depth	*	6.72E-06
0.947	slider_l-cheek-inner-decr|incr	*	8.03E-06
0.638	slider_r-eye-push1-in|out		0.0000246
-0.712	eyebrows: Move vert		0.0000306
0.755	slider_l-eye-push1-in|out		0.0000493
0.487	slider_l-eye-scale-decr|incr		0.0000919
0.489	slider_r-eye-scale-decr|incr		0.0000939

Hawaiian female (n=23)

1.03	eyebrows: Move vert		3.68E-07
-1	slider_l-eye-scale-decr|incr	*	3.88E-07
-0.796	slider_l-eye-trans-in|out	*	8.86E-07
-1.01	eyes: Middle height of right eye	*	0.0000014
1.37	slider_r-eye-eyefold-down|up		1.53E-06
-1.05	eyes: Inner height of left eye	*	1.75E-06
0.969	slider_eyes_outer_droop	*	2.45E-06
0.681	nose-compression-compress|uncompress		3.29E-06
-1.01	eyes: Middle height of left eye	*	5.94E-06
0.852	nose: Scale nostrils width		0.0000117
-0.625	slider_r-eye-push2-in|out		0.0000294
-0.817	slider_r-eye-scale-decr|incr	*	0.0000312
1.22	slider_r-eye-eyefold-angle-down|up		0.0000463
-0.517	nose: Scale tip width		0.0000516
-0.921	eyes: Inner height of right eye	*	0.0000562
0.911	forehead: Forehead bulge		0.0000883
0.771	slider_r-eye-bag-height-decr|incr	*	0.000099
-0.892	nose: Move tip vertically	*	0.0000995

Hawaiian male (n=19)

-1.18	eyes: Middle height of left eye	*	6.05E-08
-1.2	eyes: Middle height of right eye	*	1.45E-07
-1.21	mouth: Scale philtrum volume		8.57E-07
0.916	mouth: Scale middle upperlip		9.16E-07
-1.25	eyes: Inner height of left eye	*	9.41E-07
-1.01	slider_l-eye-corner2-down|up		1.09E-06
-1	slider_r-eye-corner2-down|up		1.93E-06
-1	slider_r-eye-corner2-down|up		1.93E-06
-0.946	slider_l-eye-scale-decr|incr	*	3.38E-06
-1	slider_r-eye-trans-in|out		4.83E-06
0.991	slider_r-eye-corner1-down|up		4.96E-06
-1.2	eyes: Inner height of right eye	*	0.0000125
-1.22	nose: Move nose base vert.		0.0000137
1.31	chin: Scale chin angular		0.0000152
-1.08	mouth: Scale depth		0.0000222
-0.856	slider_r-eye-scale-decr|incr	*	0.0000247
0.848	slider_eyes_outer_droop	*	0.0000282
0.815	slider_l-eye-corner1-down|up		0.0000323
-1.2	chin: Tone of side chin		0.0000326
-1.2	chin: Tone of side chin		0.0000326
-0.809	slider_l-eye-trans-in|out	*	0.0000346
0.865	slider_l-eye-bag-height-decr|incr		0.0000374
0.923	slider_r-eye-bag-height-decr|incr	*	0.0000383
0.951	chin: Scale chin prominence		0.0000428
-1.16	nose: Move depth		0.0000639
-0.979	slider_r-eye-bag-decr|incr		0.0000911
-1.24	nose: Move tip vertically	*	0.0000945

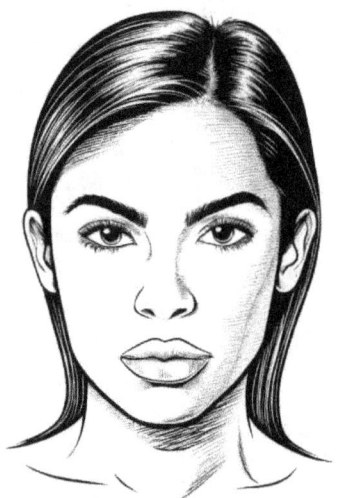

Hispanic female (n=29)

0.758	chin: Scale chin prognathism		4.64E-07
-0.72		nose-hump-decr|incr	* 7.2E-07
0.647	mouth: Scale upperlip width		1.25E-06
-0.648		nose-volume-decr|incr	2.17E-06
0.653	nose: Scale nostrils width		0.0000027
-0.744		slider_Nose_alar_crease	0.0000153
-0.826		slider_elvs_highchubbycheekbones1	0.0000376
0.768	mouth: Scale horizontally		0.0000509
0.768	mouth: Scale horizontally		0.0000509
-0.549		mouth: Laugh-lines	0.0000652
0.682	nose: Scale depth		0.0000994

Hungarian female (n=23)

-0.614		mouth: Scale vertically	* 1.36E-09
-1.05		nose: Scale nostrils width	* 3.68E-07
-0.704		slider_r-cheek-bones-decr|incr	4.78E-06
0.68	nose: Move tip vertically		0.0000114
-0.663		forehead: Scale vertically	* 0.0000157
-0.869		chin: Scale chin prominence	0.0000165
0.731	mouth: Scale philtrum volume		0.0000196
-0.398		mouth: Scale lowerlip width	* 0.0000421
0.657	chin: Tone of side chin		0.000076
-0.629		mouth: Move corners vert.	* 0.0000813
0.488	mouth: Scale lowerlip volume		* 0.0000982

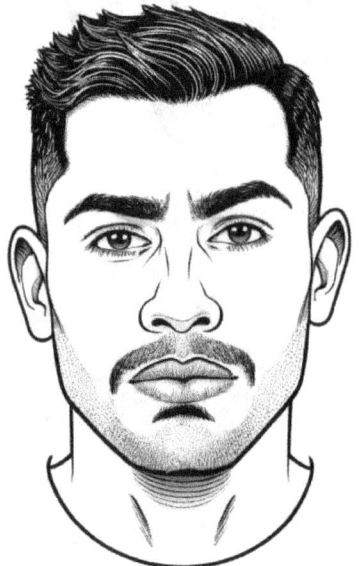

Hispanic male (n=18)

-0.516		slider_l-eye-trans-in|out	0.0000195
-0.748		slider_eyes_middle_droop	0.0000338
-0.819		nose-hump-decr|incr	* 0.0000985

Hungarian male (n=29)

-0.682		mouth: Scale lowerlip width	* 2.05E-09
0.653	mouth: Scale lowerlip volume		* 3.48E-09
-0.863		forehead: Scale vertically	* 1.7E-08
-0.835		nose: Scale nostrils width	* 2.85E-08
0.828	nose-greek-decr|incr		9.07E-08
0.598	mouth: Dimples		9.65E-08
-0.745		mouth: Scale vertically	* 1.11E-07
-0.85		forehead: Cranic shape	2.56E-07
0.637	mouth: Laugh-lines		2.86E-07
-0.691		mouth: Move corners vert.	* 2.88E-07
-0.581		slider_l-cheek-inner-decr|incr	1.17E-06
-0.555		slider_l-eye-trans-in|out	2.24E-06
-0.529		mouth: Scale upperlip width	2.65E-06

0.729	chin: Scale chin height		2.93E-06
0.77	eyebrows: Eyebrows bulge		3.01E-06
-0.632		nose: Scale horizontally	0.0000064
-0.558		chin: Cleft chin	7.22E-06
-0.556		slider_r-eye-trans-in|out	8.79E-06
-0.729		eyebrows: Eyebrows angle	9.57E-06
-0.541		slider_r-eye-eyefold-angle-down|up	0.000014
0.64	nose: Move vertically		0.0000164
-0.634		mouth: Scale middle upperlip	0.0000189

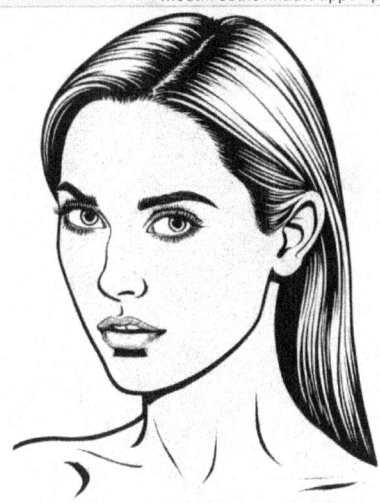

Icelandic female (n=27)

-1.28		slider_r-eye-scale-decr|incr	*	2.34E-10
-0.905		forehead: Scale vertically	*	3.23E-10
1.01	mouth: Scale lowerlip volume		*	4.64E-10
-0.809		mouth: Scale lowerlip width	*	5.45E-10
-0.875		forehead: Cranic shape	*	8.06E-10
-1.16		slider_l-eye-scale-decr|incr	*	8.28E-10
-1.42		slider_l-eye-push2-in|out	*	1.45E-09
-1.04		mouth: Scale vertically	*	1.56E-09
-1.27		eyes: Outer height of left eye		4.1E-09
-1.33		eyes: Outer height of right eye		4.63E-09
1.11	nose: Move vertically			1.2E-08
-1.22		slider_r-eye-push2-in|out	*	1.48E-08
-1.04		eyes: Middle height of right eye		3.36E-08
-0.713		mouth: Scale upperlip width	*	4.15E-08
0.855	slider_eyes_outer_droop			8.67E-08
-1.02		eyes: Middle height of left eye		9.41E-08
0.741	eyebrows: Eyebrows bulge			9.08E-07
-0.849		mouth: Scale upperlip height		1.03E-06
-0.752		mouth: Move corners vert.	*	1.69E-06
0.835	nose-greek-decr|incr		*	7.66E-06
-0.857		mouth: Scale lowerlip height		8.11E-06
0.632	mouth: Upperlip curved shape			0.0000163
-0.693		eyes: Inner height of right eye		0.000037
-0.589		nose-nostrils-angle-down|up		0.000038
-0.537		chin: Cleft chin		0.0000398
-0.928		slider_l-eye-eyefold-concave|convex		0.000092

Icelandic male (n=16)

-1.11		slider_r-eye-scale-decr|incr	*	1.27E-09
-0.88		slider_l-eye-scale-decr|incr	*	1.63E-08
-1.13		mouth: Scale lowerlip width	*	6.02E-08
0.974	mouth: Dimples			9.57E-08
-1.28		slider_r-eye-push2-in|out	*	3.68E-07
-1.22		mouth: Scale upperlip width	*	7.63E-07
-0.72		forehead: Scale vertically	*	0.0000017
-0.86		mouth: Move corners vert.	*	1.83E-06
1.71	mouth: Scale lowerlip volume		*	1.88E-06
-1.14		slider_l-eye-push2-in|out	*	1.98E-06
-1.24		mouth: Scale vertically	*	2.74E-06
1.42	mouth: Lowerlip curved shape			3.12E-06
1.57	forehead: Temple bulge			7.65E-06
-0.622		slider_l-eye-trans-in|out		0.0000153
-0.922		slider_r-cheek-inner-decr|incr		0.000018
0.784	chin: Scale chin height			0.0000206
0.717	nose-greek-decr|incr		*	0.0000326
-0.668		forehead: Cranic shape	*	0.0000545

Indian female (n=22)

1.12	slider_r-eye-scale-decr|incr			3.91E-10
1.07	slider_l-eye-scale-decr|incr		*	4.63E-10
1.05	nose: Scale vertically		*	1.44E-08
1.46	slider_r-eye-push1-in|out			1.6E-08
0.905	nose: Lower nose bridge width			2.42E-08
0.781	nose: Middle nose bridge width			3.27E-08
-1.03		slider_eyes_outer_droop	*	1.71E-06
0.775	nose: Scale depth		*	2.12E-06
1.04	slider_l-eye-push1-in|out		*	2.26E-06
-0.808		slider_Nose_alar_crease	*	6.03E-06
-0.904		eyebrows: Move vert		0.0000148
-0.797		slider_l-eye-eyefold-angle-down|up		0.0000224

-0.535	eyebrows: Eyebrows angle	*	0.0000376
0.215	nose: Upper nose bridge width	*	0.0000599
0.521	slider_l-eye-push2-in|out		0.0000635

-1.34	mouth: Move vertically	*	1.41E-12
0.678	mouth: Scale vertically	*	1.75E-09
0.677	chin: Cleft chin		1.07E-06
0.64	chin: Scale chin prominence		2.92E-06
-0.762	slider_r-eye-push2-in|out		0.0000121
0.794	mouth: Scale middle upperlip		0.0000159
0.714	mouth: Move corners vert.		0.0000478
-0.776	mouth: Cupid's bow width		0.0000549

Indian male (n=25)

-0.801	eyebrows: Eyebrows angle	*	1.1E-08
0.783	slider_r-eye-trans-in|out		4.08E-08
0.547	mouth: Scale upperlip width		7.04E-08
1.26	nose: Scale vertically	*	7.07E-08
-0.698	slider_r-eye-bag-height-decr|incr		1.71E-07
0.72	slider_l-eye-push1-in|out	*	1.76E-07
-0.568	slider_nostril_rounding		2.33E-07
-0.769	slider_Nose_alar_crease	*	1.39E-06
-0.578	slider_eyes_outer_droop	*	0.0000017
-0.534	mouth: Move corners vert.		0.0000054
-0.534	mouth: Move corners vert.		0.0000054
-0.534	mouth: Move corners vert.		0.0000054
0.952	nose: Scale depth	*	6.46E-06
-0.826	slider_elvs_highchubbycheekbones1		0.000013
0.697	slider_l-eye-scale-decr|incr	*	0.0000203
0.313	nose: Upper nose bridge width	*	0.0000272
0.881	mouth: Move vertically		0.0000442
-0.511	slider_l-eye-bag-height-decr|incr		0.0000591
-0.667	slider_eyes_middle_droop		0.0000631

Indonesian male (n=23)

0.848	slider_eyes_outer_droop		1.02E-06
-0.49	eyes: Middle height of left eye		0.0000095
-0.885	mouth: Move vertically	*	0.0000223
0.485	mouth: Scale vertically	*	0.0000398
-0.391	eyes: Middle height of right eye		0.0000467
0.678	slider_l-eye-corner1-down|up		0.0000949

Iranian female (n=28)

1.35	slider_r-eye-push2-in|out		3.01E-11
1.22	slider_l-eye-push2-in|out		2.26E-08
0.886	slider_r-eye-scale-decr|incr		9.61E-07
0.883	slider_l-eye-scale-decr|incr		4.57E-06

Indonesian female (n=23)

-0.44	forehead: Scale vertically		0.0000149
-0.458	slider_r-cheek-bones-decr|incr		0.0000237
-0.561	mouth: Scale lowerlip height		0.0000256

Iranian male (n=27)

-1.19		mouth: Move corners vert.		1.25E-07
-1.19		mouth: Move corners vert.		1.25E-07
-0.918		chin: Cleft chin		6.23E-07
1.14	mouth: Cupid's bow shape			2.49E-06
1.27	mouth: Move vertically			2.93E-06
-0.809		slider_eyes_middle_droop		3.18E-06
0.906	slider_l-cheek-trans-down|up			5.61E-06
1.04	slider_r-cheek-trans-down|up			6.96E-06
-0.646		mouth: Scale vertically		7.64E-06
0.92	chin: Scale chin height			0.0000255
-0.701		slider_eyes_outer_droop		0.0000272
0.52	mouth: Dimples			0.0000324
0.52	mouth: Dimples			0.0000324
-0.525		slider_l-eye-trans-in|out		0.0000461
0.994	slider_elvs_chipmunkcheeks_l1			0.0000472
0.994	slider_elvs_chipmunkcheeks_l1			0.0000472
-0.75		chin: Scale chin prognathism		0.0000532
0.74	chin: Scale chin width			0.0000552
0.793	nose: Lower nose bridge width			0.0000912

Irish male (n=17)

-0.849		mouth: Move corners vert.		8.27E-07
-0.849		mouth: Move corners vert.		8.27E-07
-0.979		mouth: Scale lowerlip width	*	0.0000029
-0.857		chin: Cleft chin	*	4.15E-06
1.01	chin: Scale chin height		*	0.0000059
0.703	slider_Nose_alar_crease			9.93E-06
-0.978		nose: Scale horizontally		0.0000121
-0.844		mouth: Scale upperlip width	*	0.0000229
-1.26		mouth: Scale vertically	*	0.0000369
0.567	mouth: Dimples			0.000049
-0.55		slider_r-eye-trans-in|out		0.0000876

Irish female (n=26)

0.912	chin: Scale chin height		*	1.02E-10
-0.815		mouth: Scale lowerlip width	*	3.35E-10
-0.598		chin: Cleft chin	*	6.27E-09
-0.746		mouth: Scale vertically	*	7.23E-09
0.748	mouth: Scale lowerlip volume			9.71E-07
-0.627		slider_l-cheek-inner-decr|incr		2.83E-06
-0.812		mouth: Scale upperlip width	*	0.0000124

Israeli female (n=25)

0.711	slider_r-eye-trans-down|up		9.64E-07
-0.665		slider_r-eye-bag-decr|incr	0.0000134
0.723	slider_l-eye-trans-down|up		0.0000214
0.723	slider_r-eye-push1-in|out		0.000025
0.725	mouth: Scale middle upperlip		0.0000427
0.512	mouth: Scale upperlip volume		0.0000979

Israeli male (n=24)

0.691	mouth: Move vertically		1.7E-07
-0.563		mouth: Scale vertically	5.46E-06
0.572	eyebrows: Eyebrows bulge		0.0000251
-0.55		forehead: Scale vertically	0.0000379
-0.9		mouth: Scale middle lowerlip	0.0000424
-0.567		slider_elvs_highchubbycheekbones1	0.0000708
-0.638		mouth: Scale lowerlip height	0.0000942

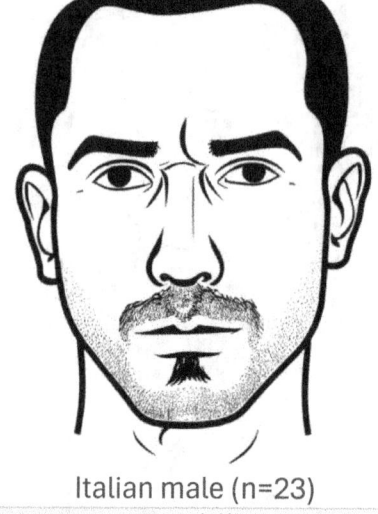

Italian male (n=23)

-0.695		mouth: Move corners vert.	0.0000027
-0.762		slider_r-eye-eyefold-angle-down|up	3.36E-06
-0.586		eyebrows: Eyebrows angle	0.0000236

Italian female (n=23)

-0.482		mouth: Scale lowerlip width	0.0000534

Jamaican female (n=19)

1.23	mouth: Scale upperlip width		*	2.5E-11
-1.4		slider_l-eye-trans-down|up	*	1.68E-09
-0.991		mouth: Scale lowerlip volume	*	3.62E-09
-1.21		slider_r-eye-trans-down|up	*	2.29E-08
-1.26		mouth: Laugh-lines	*	6.6E-08
1.13	slider_r-eye-trans-in|out		*	7.95E-08
-0.938		chin: Scale chin height	*	3.2E-07
1.34	mouth: Scale lowerlip width		*	3.43E-07
1.44	nose: Scale horizontally		*	5.79E-07
1.22	mouth: Scale vertically		*	9.62E-07
1.43	slider_r-eye-eyefold-angle-down|up		*	0.0000019
-1.22		mouth: Dimples	*	4.28E-06
-1.1		eyebrows: Eyebrows bulge	*	5.17E-06
1.5	nose: Scale nostrils width		*	0.0000125
0.964	slider_r-cheek-inner-decr|incr		*	0.0000178
0.978	slider_l-eye-trans-in|out		*	0.0000204
-1.15		chin: Scale chin width	*	0.000021
0.788	nose: Septum Angle			0.0000236
0.733	mouth: Move corners vert.		*	0.0000274
0.733	mouth: Move corners vert.		*	0.0000274

Coef	Label	Label	Sig	p-value
-0.758		mouth: Move vertically	*	0.0000378
1.03	eyebrows: Move vert			0.0000816
1.72	slider_l-eye-eyefold-angle-down|up		*	0.0000825

Jamaican male (n=38)

Coef	Label	Label	Sig	p-value
-1.5		mouth: Scale lowerlip volume	*	1.33E-23
1.52	slider_l-eye-trans-in|out		*	9.22E-18
1.15	nose: Scale nostrils width		*	4.62E-17
-1.29		mouth: Move vertically	*	6.27E-17
-1.34		mouth: Dimples	*	8.38E-17
-1.2		slider_elvs_highchubbycheekbones1		3.34E-16
-1.1		mouth: Laugh-lines	*	4.95E-16
1.39	slider_r-eye-trans-in|out		*	7.22E-16
1.61	mouth: Scale lowerlip width		*	4.05E-15
-1.17		eyebrows: Eyebrows bulge	*	5.11E-15
1.5	mouth: Scale vertically		*	8.39E-15
-1.29		chin: Scale chin height	*	3.53E-14
1.33	nose: Scale horizontally		*	9.31E-14
0.724	eyes: Outer height of right eye			2.95E-12
0.959	forehead: Scale vertically			7.03E-12
1.16	mouth: Scale upperlip width		*	7.75E-12
1.51	mouth: Move corners vert.		*	2E-11
1.51	mouth: Move corners vert.		*	2E-11
-1.12		chin: Scale chin width	*	2.72E-11
0.779	mouth: Scale horizontally			3.56E-11
-0.715		forehead: Temple bulge		5.15E-11
0.989	slider_r-cheek-inner-decr|incr		*	7.46E-11
-1.18		slider_r-eye-trans-down|up	*	9.97E-11
1.15	mouth: Scale lowerlip height			1.23E-10
-1.27		slider_l-eye-trans-down|up	*	1.9E-10
0.815	forehead: Cranic shape			2.11E-10
-0.849		nose-volume-decr|incr		1.91E-09
0.981	chin: Cleft chin			2.37E-09
-0.75		eyes: Inner height of left eye		2.78E-09
-0.923		nose-nostrils-angle-down|up		2.94E-09
0.892	chin: Scale chin prognathism			7.46E-09
-0.805		nose-greek-decr|incr		9.64E-09
-0.727		nose: Scale vertically		4.76E-08
0.642	slider_l-eye-eyefold-concave|convex			6.21E-08
0.546	eyes: Outer height of left eye			8.53E-08
-0.632		eyes: Inner height of right eye		9.26E-08
0.768	slider_l-cheek-inner-decr|incr			0.0000001
-0.766		slider_r-eye-corner1-down|up		1.07E-07
0.878	slider_r-eye-bag-in|out			1.23E-07
0.915	slider_l-eye-eyefold-angle-down|up		*	1.24E-07
0.678	eyebrows: Eyebrows angle			1.44E-07

Coef	Label	Label	Sig	p-value
1.08	slider_r-eye-eyefold-angle-down|up		*	3.3E-07
-0.57		mouth: Scale depth		5.26E-07
0.903	mouth: Scale middle upperlip			7.58E-07
-0.765		slider_l-eye-corner1-down|up		4.66E-06
-0.546		slider_eyes_outer_droop		9.47E-06
-0.528		slider_Nose_alar_crease		0.00001
-0.41		nose: Lower nose bridge width		0.0000117
-0.634		mouth: Scale philtrum volume		0.0000156
0.423	slider_r-eye-eyefold-concave|convex			0.0000318
0.699	slider_r-eye-eyefold-down|up			0.0000473
0.43	slider_r-eye-corner2-down|up			0.0000496
0.663	slider_r-eye-epicanthus-in|out			0.0000903

Japanese female (n=21)

Coef	Label	Label	Sig	p-value
-2.04		nose-greek-decr|incr	*	2.81E-14
-1.79		eyebrows: Eyebrows bulge	*	4.21E-13
1.78	eyebrows: Eyebrows angle		*	2.2E-12
-1.27		mouth: Scale upperlip width	*	6.09E-12
2.26	forehead: Scale vertically		*	8.67E-12
2.27	forehead: Cranic shape		*	1.53E-11
1.74	slider_Nose_alar_crease		*	1.77E-11
-1.22		nose: Move nose base vert.		3.21E-10
-1.43		nose: Scale depth	*	3.4E-10
-1.12		nose: Lower nose bridge width	*	9.67E-10
-1.24		nose: Scale vertically	*	1.02E-09
1.42	nose-hump-decr|incr		*	1.04E-09
-1.14		nose: Move depth	*	9.61E-09
1.17	nose-compression-compress|uncompress			1.27E-08
-0.864		slider_r-eye-trans-down|up	*	1.03E-07
-1		nose: Scale tip width		1.29E-07
-1.22		mouth: Scale horizontally	*	1.61E-07
-0.914		slider_l-eye-trans-down|up	*	1.67E-07
1	mouth: Laugh-lines		*	2.82E-07
-1.12		nose: Scale nostrils flaring	*	4.49E-07
-1		mouth: Move vertically	*	6.24E-07
-0.946		nose: Move tip vertically		1.54E-06
0.975	eyebrows: Move vert			2.09E-06
0.837	eyes: Outer height of left eye		*	3.25E-06
-0.636		mouth: Scale lowerlip width		3.92E-06
-1.09		nose: Move vertically	*	4.77E-06
0.897	eyes: Outer height of right eye			0.000005
-0.818		slider_r-cheek-trans-down|up	*	7.26E-06
0.993	nose-curve-concave|convex			8.15E-06
-0.824		chin: Tone of side chin		0.0000114
0.898	slider_elvs_highchubbycheekbones1		*	0.0000116
-0.735		mouth: Move depth		0.0000173
1.05	forehead: Forehead bulge			0.0000183
-1.03		mouth: Scale philtrum volume	*	0.0000245
0.986	mouth: Dimples			0.0000249
-0.8		slider_l-cheek-trans-down|up		0.0000257

Value	Label	Sig	p-value
0.963	nose-volume-decr|incr	*	0.0000334
0.95	mouth: Scale upperlip volume		0.0000944

Japanese male (n=24)

Value	Label (left)	Label (right)	Sig	p-value
-1.29		mouth: Scale upperlip width	*	6.99E-14
-1.66		eyebrows: Eyebrows bulge	*	1.14E-12
2.1	slider_Nose_alar_crease		*	1.38E-12
1.97	forehead: Scale vertically		*	4.7E-12
-1.95		nose-greek-decr|incr	*	2.24E-11
1.96	forehead: Cranic shape		*	6.68E-11
-1.05		mouth: Move vertically	*	8.87E-11
1.03	mouth: Laugh-lines		*	2.49E-10
	slider_elvs_			
1.26	highchubbycheekbones1		*	3.13E-10
1.86	eyebrows: Eyebrows angle		*	8.6E-10
-1.42		nose: Scale depth	*	1.7E-09
-1.16		nose: Scale nostrils flaring	*	3.96E-09
-1.51		nose: Scale vertically	*	9.72E-09
0.756	eyes: Outer height of left eye		*	1.48E-08
-1.31		nose: Lower nose bridge width	*	1.6E-08
-1.04		slider_r-eye-push1-in|out		1.64E-08
0.84	slider_eyes_middle_droop			2.13E-08
0.767	slider_eyes_outer_droop			2.61E-08
-1.01		slider_l-eye-push1-in|out		3.28E-08
-1.05		mouth: Scale horizontally	*	4.79E-08
0.777	mouth: Move corners vert.			5.06E-08
0.812	eyes: Outer height of right eye		*	5.61E-08
-1.01		nose: Move vertically	*	9.94E-08
-0.799		slider_l-eye-bag-decr|incr		1.31E-07
-0.927		nose: Scale nostrils width		2.08E-07
-1.03		mouth: Scale philtrum volume	*	4.07E-07
-1.13		nose: Move depth	*	4.15E-07
-0.68		slider_r-eye-trans-down|up	*	6.11E-07
1.28	nose-hump-decr|incr			2.08E-06
-0.903		slider_r-cheek-trans-down|up	*	0.0000043
0.977	chin: Scale chin prominence			4.52E-06
-0.56		mouth: Scale lowerlip width	*	6.25E-06
-0.58		slider_l-eye-trans-down|up	*	6.53E-06
0.774	mouth: Scale middle upperlip			0.0000113
0.966	nose-volume-decr|incr		*	0.0000159
-0.641		slider_l-eye-trans-in|out		0.0000346
1.1	slider_nostril_rounding			0.0000361
-0.701		slider_r-eye-bag-decr|incr		0.0000402
-0.592		slider_r-eye-scale-decr|incr		0.0000664
0.757	slider_r-eye-bag-in|out			0.0000692

Jewish female (n=17)

Value	Label (left)	Label (right)	Sig	p-value
1.72	mouth: Move vertically		*	2.64E-08
-0.742		mouth: Scale lowerlip height		4.93E-08
0.813	nose: Scale depth			0.0000021
-1.12		mouth: Move depth		3.05E-06
-0.851		slider_r-cheek-bones-decr|incr		0.0000153
1.6	slider_r-cheek-trans-down|up			0.0000289
-0.509		chin: Cleft chin		0.0000333
-1.3		mouth: Scale depth		0.0000418
0.758	nose-nostrils-angle-down|up			0.0000674

Jewish male (n=24)

Value	Label (left)	Label (right)	Sig	p-value
1.2	mouth: Move vertically		*	6.61E-07
-0.865		nose: Scale horizontally		2.07E-06
-0.943		nose-greek-decr|incr		7.16E-06
0.989	eyebrows: Eyebrows angle			0.0000109
-0.569		mouth: Move corners vert.		0.0000413
-0.675		mouth: Scale vertically		0.0000931

Kannada female (n=28)

Value			*	p
1.34	slider_l-eye-push1-in|out		*	1.81E-14
1.54	slider_r-eye-scale-decr|incr		*	4.75E-14
-1.67		slider_eyes_outer_droop	*	6.06E-13
-1.62		eyebrows: Move vert	*	1.25E-12
1.51	slider_l-eye-scale-decr|incr		*	5.57E-12
1.22	nose: Scale vertically		*	7.02E-12
1.41	slider_r-eye-push1-in|out			1.05E-11
1.45	eyes: Inner height of left eye		*	5.91E-11
-1.42		slider_l-eye-bag-height-decr|incr	*	8.31E-11
1.55	eyes: Middle height of left eye		*	9.19E-11
1.38	eyes: Inner height of right eye			3.38E-10
-0.936		mouth: Upperlip curved shape		3.98E-10
-0.757		mouth: Scale upperlip volume	*	9.12E-10
1.44	eyes: Middle height of right eye		*	1.38E-09
1.08	mouth: Scale upperlip height			1.63E-09
-1.23		slider_r-eye-bag-height-decr|incr	*	5.24E-09
1.21	mouth: Scale philtrum volume		*	5.64E-09
-1.22		slider_eyes_middle_droop		2.14E-08
-0.804		slider_l-eye-eyefold-angle-down|up	*	2.82E-07
-1.04		slider_l-eye-eyefold-down|up	*	3.14E-07
0.668	chin: Scale chin prominence			6.18E-07
-0.573		slider_r-cheek-inner-decr|incr		7.92E-07
-0.839		slider_Nose_alar_crease	*	8.59E-07
0.64	nose: Middle nose bridge width			1.14E-06
0.606	mouth: Move vertically			1.76E-06
0.422	mouth: Scale vertically			2.37E-06
-0.566		mouth: Cupid's bow width		2.37E-06
0.71	nose: Move depth			2.74E-06
0.645	nose: Lower nose bridge width			2.85E-06
-0.644		nose: Septum Angle		3.59E-06
0.703	nose: Scale depth		*	5.62E-06
0.681	nose-nostrils-angle-down|up		*	9.49E-06
0.704	slider_l-eye-corner1-down|up			0.0000102
0.603	slider_r-cheek-volume-decr|incr			0.0000109
0.633	slider_r-eye-corner1-down|up			0.0000229
0.427	slider_l-eye-trans-in|out			0.0000316
0.401	mouth: Scale lowerlip width			0.0000428
0.523	mouth: Scale lowerlip height			0.0000637
-0.546		nose: Move vertically		0.0000697

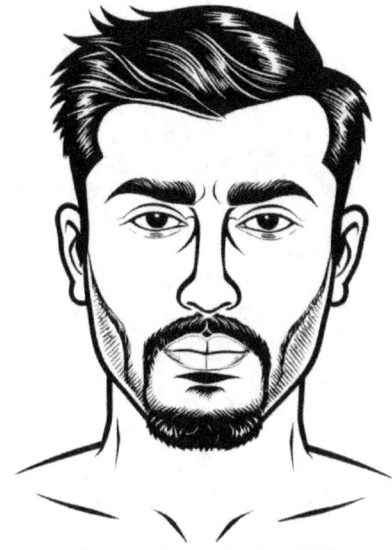

Kannada male (n=20)

Value			*	p
1.29	eyes: Inner height of left eye		*	1.9E-08
1.55	nose: Scale vertically		*	2.49E-08
1.46	mouth: Scale philtrum volume		*	6.67E-08
-0.778		slider_Nose_alar_crease	*	1.95E-07
-1.32		eyebrows: Move vert	*	2.74E-07
1.22	eyes: Middle height of left eye		*	6.92E-07
-1.15		mouth: Scale upperlip volume	*	7.24E-07
1.35	eyes: Middle height of right eye		*	8.21E-07
-1.21		slider_r-eye-bag-height-decr|incr	*	8.84E-07
1.04	slider_l-eye-scale-decr|incr		*	2.19E-06
1.22	slider_r-eye-scale-decr|incr		*	2.73E-06
1.36	eyes: Inner height of right eye		*	0.0000028
-1.08		slider_l-eye-bag-height-decr|incr	*	3.43E-06
0.813	nose-nostrils-angle-down|up		*	7.58E-06
-0.824		slider_l-eye-eyefold-angle-down|up	*	0.0000085
-1.12		slider_l-eye-epicanthus-in|out		8.77E-06
-0.739		slider_nostril_rounding		0.0000158
0.639	mouth: Scale upperlip width			0.0000249
-1.02		slider_l-eye-eyefold-down|up	*	0.0000377
-0.78		slider_eyes_outer_droop	*	0.0000391
1.1	nose: Scale depth		*	0.000055
0.946	slider_l-eye-push1-in|out		*	0.0000909

Kenyan female (n=29)

1.53	mouth: Scale upperlip width		*	1.19E-17
1.73	mouth: Scale lowerlip width		*	8.68E-16
-1.27		mouth: Dimples	*	3.62E-15
-1.45		mouth: Laugh-lines	*	8.19E-15
1.35	mouth: Scale vertically		*	2.2E-14
-1.19		mouth: Scale lowerlip volume	*	3.37E-13
-1.46		nose-volume-decr|incr	*	7.12E-12
-1.27		mouth: Scale upperlip volume	*	1.56E-11
1.38	nose: Scale horizontally		*	2.92E-11
1.1	nose: Scale nostrils width		*	4.65E-11
1.24	mouth: Scale lowerlip height		*	9E-11
-0.94		slider_nostril_rounding		1.34E-10
1.02	slider_r-cheek-inner-decr|incr		*	2.43E-10
-1.07		chin: Scale chin width	*	3.72E-10
-1.31		slider_l-eye-trans-down|up	*	4.76E-10
1.04	slider_l-eye-eyefold-angle-down|up		*	6.15E-10
0.875	slider_r-eye-eyefold-angle-down|up			1.01E-09
-0.963		chin: Scale chin height	*	1.4E-09
1.06	slider_l-eye-trans-in|out		*	1.79E-09
-1.21		slider_r-eye-trans-down|up	*	2.57E-09
0.936	mouth: Scale horizontally		*	5.7E-09
0.938	slider_r-eye-trans-in|out		*	6.03E-09
-1.03		mouth: Upperlip curved shape	*	1.08E-08
0.996	slider_l-cheek-inner-decr|incr		*	9.64E-08
0.941	mouth: Scale upperlip height		*	1.42E-07
-0.794		nose-nostrils-angle-down|up	*	3.11E-07
0.924	mouth: Move depth		*	9.82E-07
0.877	nose: Move depth			1.36E-06
0.565	eyebrows: Move vert		*	1.94E-06
0.835	slider_r-eye-corner2-down|up		*	9.02E-06
0.658	nose: Move nose base vert.			0.0000234
-0.825		slider_r-eye-corner1-down|up	*	0.0000303
-0.681		slider_Nose_alar_crease	*	0.000033
0.949	slider_r-eye-bag-decr|incr			0.0000462

-1.19	slider_elvs_highchubbycheekbones1			4.23E-10
0.907	nose: Scale nostrils width		*	6.95E-10
1.38		mouth: Move corners vert.		9.32E-10
1.25	nose: Scale horizontally		*	1.37E-09
1.08	slider_r-cheek-inner-decr|incr		*	2E-09
1.26	mouth: Scale horizontally		*	3.29E-09
1.04	chin: Scale chin prognathism			5.77E-09
-0.898		eyebrows: Eyebrows bulge		6.75E-09
1.06	eyebrows: Eyebrows angle			7.55E-09
-1.38		chin: Scale chin width	*	8.39E-09
0.852	forehead: Scale vertically			5.68E-08
0.941	slider_r-eye-bag-in|out			5.78E-08
0.81	slider_r-eye-push1-in|out			7.32E-08
0.757	eyes: Middle height of right eye			7.42E-08
-1.05		mouth: Move vertically		1.26E-07
0.937	slider_r-eye-corner2-down|up		*	1.37E-07
0.793	forehead: Cranic shape			1.38E-07
-1.16		mouth: Cupid's bow shape		2.1E-07
-0.717		nose-greek-decr|incr		2.37E-07
-1.08		slider_r-eye-trans-down|up	*	2.57E-07
-1.08		slider_l-eye-trans-down|up	*	3.82E-07
-1.01		slider_l-eye-bag-height-decr|incr		4.32E-07
0.928	slider_l-eye-bag-in|out			5.23E-07
0.744	mouth: Scale middle lowerlip			5.54E-07
0.855	mouth: Move depth		*	5.59E-07
0.784	slider_l-eye-push1-in|out			5.91E-07
-1.28		mouth: Scale upperlip volume	*	7.26E-07
0.758	slider_l-eye-eyefold-angle-down|up		*	1.14E-06
0.658	eyes: Outer height of right eye			1.92E-06
1.26	mouth: Scale upperlip height		*	2.02E-06
0.491	slider_r-eye-scale-decr|incr			2.05E-06
-0.798		mouth: Cupid's bow width		2.83E-06
-0.914		nose: Move vertically		2.96E-06
0.809	slider_l-eye-corner2-down|up			4.47E-06
1.08	nose: Move nose base vert.		*	5.22E-06
-1.27		mouth: Upperlip curved shape	*	5.91E-06
-0.782		slider_r-eye-bag-height-decr|incr		6.53E-06
0.51	slider_l-eye-eyefold-concave|convex			8.79E-06
-0.814		slider_r-eye-corner1-down|up	*	0.0000088
0.654	eyes: Middle height of left eye			0.0000119
-0.703		nose-nostrils-angle-down|up	*	0.000019
-0.932		nose: Middle nose bridge width		0.0000203
0.563	slider_l-cheek-inner-decr|incr		*	0.0000213
1.22	nose: Scale tip width			0.0000231
-0.634		nose: Scale vertically		0.0000419
-1.24		forehead: Forehead bulge		0.0000498
-0.678		slider_Nose_alar_crease	*	0.000059
-0.691		eyebrows: Move vert	*	0.0000603
0.625	eyes: Outer height of left eye			0.0000617
-0.929		nose: Upper nose bridge width		0.0000702
-0.444		forehead: Temple bulge		0.0000948

Kenyan male (n=27)

-1.85		mouth: Scale lowerlip volume	*	2.53E-19
2.07	slider_l-eye-trans-in|out		*	7.38E-19
-1.75		chin: Scale chin height	*	4.27E-14
2.12	mouth: Scale vertically		*	5.59E-14
-1.39		mouth: Laugh-lines	*	8.48E-14
1.68	slider_r-eye-trans-in|out		*	1.44E-13
-1.87		mouth: Dimples	*	1.6E-13
2.34	mouth: Scale lowerlip width		*	7.76E-13
1.9	mouth: Scale upperlip width		*	3.8E-12
-1.49		nose-volume-decr|incr	*	2.06E-11
1.69	mouth: Scale lowerlip height		*	8.01E-11
1.31	chin: Cleft chin			3.15E-10

Korean female (n=29)

-2.42	eyebrows: Eyebrows bulge	*	5.32E-19
2.83 forehead: Scale vertically		*	6.67E-19
2.81 forehead: Cranic shape		*	2.83E-18
-2.72	nose-greek-decr|incr	*	9.87E-18
-1.69	mouth: Scale upperlip width	*	1.04E-17
-1.39	slider_l-cheek-trans-down|up	*	7.45E-15
-1.66	slider_r-eye-trans-down|up	*	9.95E-15
1.59 mouth: Laugh-lines		*	1.93E-14
2.98 eyebrows: Eyebrows angle		*	2.38E-14
-1.42	nose: Scale nostrils flaring	*	4.71E-14
-1.98	nose: Move vertically	*	6.72E-14
-2.13	mouth: Scale horizontally	*	1.16E-13
1.68 eyes: Outer height of right eye		*	1.45E-13
1.13 slider_r-eye-corner2-down|up		*	3.4E-13
2.26 slider_Nose_alar_crease		*	4.07E-13
-2.11	nose: Lower nose bridge width	*	4.22E-13
-1.44	slider_r-cheek-trans-down|up	*	9.59E-13
1.69 eyes: Outer height of left eye		*	1.08E-12
-1.3	nose: Scale depth	*	4.65E-12
1.06 slider_l-eye-corner2-down|up		*	1.49E-11
-1.48	slider_l-eye-trans-down|up	*	1.54E-11
-1.76	nose: Scale vertically	*	5.01E-11
1.18 mouth: Lowerlip curved shape		*	4.43E-10
1.46 chin: Scale chin prominence		*	5.17E-10
-0.955	mouth: Move vertically	*	1.25E-09
0.574 mouth: Scale lowerlip volume		*	1.28E-09
-0.953	nose: Move depth	*	1.75E-09
1.25 slider_elvs_highchubbycheekbones1		*	1.8E-09
1.46 slider_l-eye-eyefold-angle-down|up		*	4.8E-09
-0.808	nose: Scale nostrils width	*	9.25E-09
0.842 chin: Cleft chin		*	3.69E-08
0.908 slider_r-cheek-volume-decr|incr		*	9.57E-08
1.36 mouth: Dimples		*	1.04E-07
0.648 nose-nostrils-angle-down|up		*	2.33E-07
1.01 slider_l-cheek-volume-decr|incr		*	2.75E-07
0.917 slider_l-eye-bag-in|out		*	3.48E-07
1.2 slider_r-eye-eyefold-angle-down|up		*	4.79E-07
1.12 slider_r-eye-bag-in|out		*	5.42E-07
0.873 eyebrows: Move vert		*	6.45E-07
1.05 nose-curve-concave|convex		*	6.57E-07
0.816 nose-volume-decr|incr		*	7.74E-07
0.714 chin: Scale chin prognathism		*	1.18E-06
0.946 nose-hump-decr|incr		*	1.48E-06

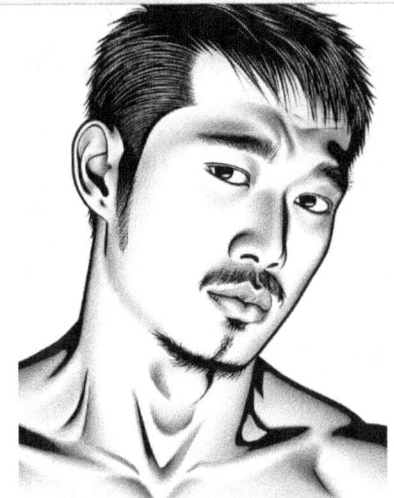

-1.55	nose: Middle nose bridge width	*	1.95E-06
-0.783	mouth: Scale philtrum volume	*	0.000002
-0.678	slider_r-eye-scale-decr|incr	*	2.43E-06
-0.628	chin: Tone of side chin	*	7.61E-06
0.662 mouth: Scale upperlip volume			9.02E-06
-0.646	mouth: Cupid's bow shape		9.55E-06
1.24 slider_nostril_rounding		*	0.0000143
-0.941	slider_r-eye-push1-in|out	*	0.0000242
0.52 mouth: Scale lowerlip height			0.0000282
-0.579	mouth: Move depth	*	0.0000312
0.603 eyes: Middle height of right eye			0.0000319
-0.67	slider_r-eye-bag-height-decr|incr		0.0000407
-0.691	slider_r-eye-corner1-down|up	*	0.0000572
0.514 eyes: Middle height of left eye			0.0000772
0.551 mouth: Move corners vert.		*	0.0000899

Korean male (n=31)

-2.35	nose-greek-decr|incr	*	7.21E-20
-2.47	eyebrows: Eyebrows bulge	*	8.93E-19
2.72 forehead: Scale vertically		*	2.09E-16
-2.04	nose: Lower nose bridge width	*	6.36E-16
2.65 forehead: Cranic shape		*	1.03E-15
1.27 eyes: Outer height of right eye		*	1.76E-15
-1.5	mouth: Scale upperlip width	*	3.39E-15
-1.66	nose: Move vertically	*	8.22E-15
2.28 eyebrows: Eyebrows angle		*	8.25E-15
2.12 slider_Nose_alar_crease		*	2.75E-14
-1.57	slider_r-eye-trans-down|up	*	3.09E-13
1.3 mouth: Laugh-lines		*	6.82E-13
-1.46	nose: Scale depth	*	9.94E-13
0.895 mouth: Scale middle upperlip		*	2.22E-12
-1.63	mouth: Scale horizontally	*	2.33E-12
1.09 eyes: Outer height of left eye		*	3.87E-12
0.742 mouth: Move corners vert.		*	4.26E-12
1.35 slider_r-eye-bag-in|out		*	7.95E-12
-1.23	slider_l-eye-trans-down|up	*	1.67E-11
-1.48	nose: Scale vertically	*	3.49E-11
-1.33	nose: Scale nostrils flaring	*	4.31E-11
-1.41	slider_l-eye-push1-in|out	*	4.99E-11
1.16 nose-volume-decr|incr		*	7.37E-11
-1	nose: Scale nostrils width		1.13E-10
-0.963	mouth: Move vertically	*	1.4E-10
1.36 slider_elvs_highchubbycheekbones1		*	4.94E-10
-0.911	slider_r-eye-scale-decr|incr	*	5.39E-10
1.32 eyebrows: Move vert		*	1.6E-09
-1.43	slider_r-cheek-trans-down|up	*	2.02E-09
1.19 slider_r-eye-eyefold-angle-down|up		*	2.08E-09
-1.28	slider_r-eye-push1-in|out	*	4.93E-09

Value	Slider	Description	Sig	p-value
1.19	slider_l-eye-eyefold-angle-down|up		*	5.85E-09
0.82	slider_r-eye-corner2-down|up		*	6.58E-09
1.57	chin: Scale chin prominence		*	6.7E-09
1.18	nose-hump-decr|incr		*	1.18E-08
-0.885		nose: Move depth	*	1.82E-08
0.657	mouth: Dimples		*	4.11E-08
-0.521		mouth: Scale lowerlip width		5.58E-08
-0.666		mouth: Move depth	*	1.12E-07
-1.22		slider_l-cheek-trans-down|up	*	1.62E-07
-0.962		slider_r-eye-corner1-down|up	*	1.85E-07
-0.788		slider_l-eye-scale-decr|incr		1.97E-07
-0.84		nose: Move nose base vert.		2.05E-07
1	mouth: Lowerlip curved shape		*	3.41E-07
0.903	slider_r-eye-epicanthus-in|out			3.99E-07
0.675	slider_r-eye-eyefold-down|up			4.46E-07
1.03	slider_l-eye-bag-in|out		*	4.48E-07
0.681	slider_l-eye-eyefold-down|up			6.14E-07
-1.31		nose: Middle nose bridge width	*	7.36E-07
0.826	nose-nostrils-angle-down|up		*	9.03E-07
0.759	slider_eyes_outer_droop			1.24E-06
0.725	chin: Cleft chin		*	1.81E-06
0.725	slider_eyes_middle_droop			2.21E-06
-0.773		mouth: Scale philtrum volume	*	0.0000043
0.609	slider_l-eye-corner2-down|up		*	4.47E-06
-0.633		chin: Tone of side chin	*	6.25E-06
0.353	mouth: Scale lowerlip volume		*	8.55E-06
0.857	slider_r-cheek-volume-decr|incr		*	0.000009
0.863	slider_l-cheek-volume-decr|incr		*	0.0000281
-1.06		slider_elvs_chipmunkcheeks_l1		0.0000284
0.791	chin: Scale chin prognathism		*	0.0000297
-0.559		slider_l-eye-bag-decr|incr		0.0000533
0.867	nose-curve-concave|convex		*	0.0000822
0.974	slider_nostril_rounding		*	0.000084
-0.637		nose: Move tip vertically		0.0000912

Kurdish female (n=19)

Value	Slider	Description	Sig	p-value
1.14	chin: Scale chin width			5.51E-08
1.11	slider_elvs_highchubbycheekbones1			2.06E-07
-1.33		slider_r-eye-trans-in|out	*	3.86E-07
1.18	nose: Scale vertically		*	6.94E-07
-0.724		mouth: Scale vertically		0.0000012
-0.805		mouth: Scale lowerlip width		1.59E-06
-1.26		slider_l-eye-trans-in|out	*	0.0000022
-0.867		slider_Nose_alar_crease		0.00001
1.12	nose: Lower nose bridge width		*	0.0000107
1.14	nose: Scale depth		*	0.0000208
0.993	slider_r-eye-trans-down|up			0.0000269
0.894	eyebrows: Eyebrows bulge			0.0000334
-0.802		eyes: Outer height of right eye		0.0000397
-0.773		mouth: Scale lowerlip height		0.0000405

Value	Slider	Description	Sig	p-value
0.651	nose-greek-decr|incr			0.0000415
0.914	slider_l-eye-trans-down|up			0.0000604
0.79	mouth: Dimples			0.0000655
0.85	nose-nostrils-angle-down|up		*	0.0000766

Kurdish male (n=24)

Value	Slider	Description	Sig	p-value
1.25	nose: Scale vertically		*	9.09E-09
0.762	nose-nostrils-angle-down|up		*	1.25E-08
-0.836		slider_l-eye-trans-in|out	*	1.13E-07
1.31	nose: Lower nose bridge width		*	3.85E-06
-0.55		slider_r-eye-trans-in|out	*	4.48E-06
-0.66		eyes: Outer height of left eye		7.81E-06
0.841	nose: Scale depth		*	8.22E-06
1	nose: Middle nose bridge width			0.0000131
0.695	mouth: Scale philtrum volume			0.0000154
0.464	nose: Upper nose bridge width			0.0000785
-0.934		slider_r-eye-corner2-down|up		0.0000938

Laotian female (n=20)

Value	Slider	Description	Sig	p-value
-1.22		mouth: Move vertically	*	1.64E-08
0.988	slider_eyes_outer_droop		*	2.18E-07
-0.913		slider_l-eye-scale-decr|incr	*	2.95E-07
-1.31		slider_r-eye-push2-in|out	*	5.76E-07
-1.27		slider_l-eye-push2-in|out	*	2.85E-06
0.8	slider_r-eye-corner1-down|up			0.0000191
0.632	nose-compression-compress|uncompress			0.0000373
0.558	nose: Upper nose bridge width			0.0000392
-0.604		mouth: Cupid's bow width		0.0000581
-0.798		slider_r-eye-scale-decr|incr	*	0.000097

-0.742	chin: Scale chin angular	2.26E-07
0.676	mouth: Scale lowerlip volume	3.32E-07
1.11	slider_elvs_highchubbycheekbones1	* 3.44E-07
0.778	eyebrows: Eyebrows bulge	1.17E-06
-1.1	chin: Scale chin prognathism	0.0000012
0.86	nose-greek-decr|incr	3.14E-06
0.82	slider_Nose_alar_crease	5.09E-06
-0.837	eyebrows: Eyebrows angle	0.0000115
-1.01	nose: Scale horizontally	* 0.0000128
-0.79	slider_r-eye-scale-decr|incr	0.0000152
0.515	nose: Move nose base vert.	0.0000163
0.468	chin: Scale chin width	0.0000214
0.778	nose: Move vertically	0.0000251
0.734	mouth: Dimples	* 0.0000345
0.992	forehead: Temple bulge	0.0000369
0.879	mouth: Scale depth	0.0000909

Laotian male (n=20)

1.56 slider_eyes_outer_droop		* 5.98E-08
-1.12	mouth: Move vertically	* 1.11E-07
-1.06	slider_l-eye-scale-decr|incr	* 1.92E-07
-0.629	eyes: Outer height of right eye	1.82E-06
-0.925	slider_r-eye-scale-decr|incr	* 0.0000027
-0.924	slider_r-eye-push2-in|out	* 3.67E-06
-0.627	eyes: Outer height of left eye	3.83E-06
-0.815	eyes: Middle height of left eye	0.0000042
-0.882	eyes: Middle height of right eye	8.81E-06
1.08 slider_eyes_middle_droop		0.0000156
0.76 mouth: Scale middle upperlip		0.0000227
-0.745	slider_l-eye-push2-in|out	* 0.0000297
-0.549	chin: Scale chin height	0.0000524
0.528 forehead: Forehead bulge		0.0000532

Latvian male (n=18)

0.897 mouth: Dimples		* 1.45E-09
-1.1	slider_r-eye-trans-in|out	* 6.31E-08
-1	mouth: Scale upperlip width	* 8.13E-08
1.05 mouth: Laugh-lines		* 1.71E-06
-0.829	nose: Scale horizontally	* 2.59E-06
-0.61	mouth: Move corners vert.	* 3.55E-06
-0.906	forehead: Scale vertically	* 0.0000067
-1.04	nose: Scale nostrils width	* 0.0000212
-0.791	slider_l-cheek-inner-decr|incr	0.0000279
0.876 chin: Scale chin height		0.0000312
-0.656	chin: Cleft chin	0.0000371
-0.832	mouth: Scale lowerlip width	* 0.0000372
-0.866	mouth: Scale vertically	* 0.0000429
-0.903	forehead: Cranic shape	* 0.0000493
1.1	slider_elvs_highchubbycheekbones1	* 0.0000827

Latvian female (n=23)

-1.1	forehead: Scale vertically	* 9.61E-10
-0.872	mouth: Scale upperlip width	* 1.71E-09
-0.798	mouth: Scale vertically	* 2.07E-09
-1.06	forehead: Cranic shape	* 4.29E-09
0.981 mouth: Laugh-lines		* 9.2E-09
-1.06	slider_l-eye-trans-in|out	1.04E-08
-1.09	slider_r-eye-trans-in|out	* 2.42E-08
-0.643	mouth: Scale lowerlip width	* 7.69E-08
-1.1	nose: Scale nostrils width	* 1.43E-07
-0.703	mouth: Move corners vert.	* 1.47E-07
-1.27	chin: Scale chin prominence	1.79E-07

Lebanese female (n=27)

0.919	slider_r-eye-scale-decr|incr		3.35E-07
1.01	slider_r-eye-push2-in|out		1.94E-06
0.839	slider_l-eye-push2-in|out		0.0000201
0.874	slider_l-eye-scale-decr|incr		0.0000761

Lebanese male (n=24)

0.935	mouth: Scale philtrum volume		1.23E-07
0.398	mouth: Scale horizontally		0.0000595
-0.473	slider_l-eye-eyefold-angle-down|up		0.0000994

Lithuanian female (n=28)

-1.2		forehead: Scale vertically	*	1.44E-14
-1.11		forehead: Cranic shape	*	3.63E-13
-0.868		mouth: Move corners vert.	*	2.78E-11
-0.715		mouth: Scale vertically	*	3.32E-10
-0.974		nose: Scale nostrils width		3.75E-10
-0.874		chin: Scale chin angular		8.61E-10
-0.707		slider_l-cheek-inner-decr|incr	*	1.84E-09
1	nose-greek-decr|incr			2.41E-09
0.886	eyebrows: Eyebrows bulge		*	3.46E-09
0.729	chin: Tone of side chin			9.83E-09
-1.07		chin: Scale chin prognathism	*	1.77E-08
0.782	nose: Move vertically			6.2E-08
-0.635		mouth: Scale lowerlip width	*	9.37E-08
0.752	mouth: Scale lowerlip volume			1.13E-07
-0.784		slider_r-eye-scale-decr|incr	*	1.19E-07
-0.913		eyebrows: Eyebrows angle	*	3.19E-07
0.753	nose: Move depth			3.47E-07
-0.816		slider_l-eye-scale-decr|incr		5.23E-07
0.776	nose: Move nose base vert.			5.62E-07
1.18	forehead: Temple bulge			5.74E-07
-0.995		eyes: Outer height of right eye	*	5.76E-07
0.659	mouth: Move depth			8.4E-07
0.675	nose: Move tip vertically			8.87E-07
0.955	mouth: Scale depth			9.81E-07
-0.779		mouth: Scale upperlip width		1.83E-06
-0.912		slider_r-eye-push2-in|out		2.34E-06
-1.13		chin: Scale chin prominence		0.0000032
-0.465		nose: Septum Angle		3.93E-06
-0.796		eyes: Outer height of left eye		4.99E-06
-0.709		slider_l-eye-push2-in|out		7.26E-06
-0.652		chin: Cleft chin	*	7.84E-06
-0.833		mouth: Scale middle upperlip	*	0.0000144
-0.746		nose: Scale horizontally	*	0.0000218
0.751	mouth: Laugh-lines			0.000022
-0.709		slider_septum_sharp		0.0000241
-0.604		slider_l-eye-trans-in|out		0.0000351
-0.585		slider_l-eye-eyefold-concave|convex		0.0000906

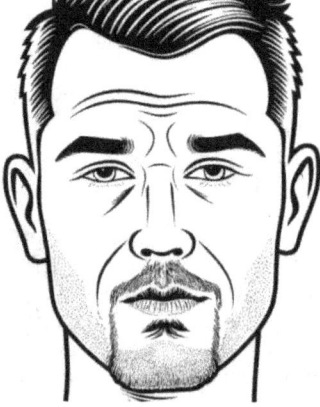

Lithuanian male (n=16)

-1.41		forehead: Scale vertically	*	5.93E-09
-1.39		forehead: Cranic shape	*	1.4E-07
1.16	nose-greek-decr|incr		*	1.81E-07
1.55	eyebrows: Eyebrows bulge		*	2.1E-07
0.943	mouth: Dimples			7.67E-07
-1.31		chin: Scale chin prognathism	*	1.01E-06
-0.986		mouth: Move corners vert.	*	1.01E-06
-1.08		mouth: Scale middle upperlip	*	1.89E-06
-1.01		chin: Cleft chin	*	2.58E-06
-0.926		eyebrows: Eyebrows angle	*	2.74E-06
-0.796		slider_r-eye-scale-decr|incr	*	0.0000164
1.12	chin: Scale chin height			0.000024
-0.762		slider_l-cheek-inner-decr|incr	*	0.0000241
-0.95		mouth: Scale lowerlip width	*	0.000028

-0.799	nose: Scale horizontally	*	0.0000374
-0.918	mouth: Scale vertically	*	0.0000496
-1.09	eyes: Outer height of right eye	*	0.0000532

Macedonian female (n=15)

-0.598	eyebrows: Eyebrows angle	*	6.77E-06

Macedonian male (n=24)

0.927 nose-greek-decr|incr		2.38E-10
-0.706	slider_l-eye-trans-in|out	7.6E-09
-0.809	forehead: Scale vertically	1.35E-06
-0.691	eyebrows: Eyebrows angle *	1.87E-06
-0.831	mouth: Scale middle upperlip	6.02E-06
-0.754	chin: Scale chin prominence	6.74E-06
0.908 eyebrows: Eyebrows bulge		7.99E-06
-0.589	slider_r-eye-trans-in|out	0.0000133
-0.706	mouth: Scale vertically	0.000042
0.766 nose: Middle nose bridge width		0.0000455
-0.726	forehead: Cranic shape	0.0000971

Malay female (n=25)

0.63 mouth: Scale lowerlip width		*	1.11E-09
-0.796	mouth: Move vertically		6.43E-08
0.824 mouth: Scale lowerlip height		*	7.29E-08
0.6 mouth: Scale vertically		*	1.5E-07
0.78 slider_r-cheek-volume-decr|incr			3.23E-06
-0.607	chin: Scale chin height	*	0.000015
1.2 slider_r-eye-epicanthus-in|out			0.0000159
-0.886	slider_r-eye-eyefold-concave|convex		0.0000348
0.726 eyes: Inner height of right eye			0.0000906
0.662 chin: Cleft chin			0.0000939

Malay male (n=31)

0.706 mouth: Scale lowerlip width		*	3.33E-12
0.648 mouth: Scale vertically		*	3.14E-10
-0.667	nose: Lower nose bridge width		2.04E-09
-0.552	chin: Scale chin height	*	5.08E-08
-0.685	chin: Scale chin width		1.2E-07
0.868 slider_eyes_outer_droop			9.32E-07
0.649 slider_r-eye-corner2-down|up			6.26E-06
0.691 mouth: Scale lowerlip height		*	0.000012
-0.47	eyebrows: Eyebrows bulge		0.0000147
-0.6	mouth: Cupid's bow shape		0.0000225
-0.493	mouth: Scale lowerlip volume		0.0000333
0.616 slider_eyes_middle_droop			0.0000344

-0.627		nose: Scale nostrils flaring	0.000044
-0.574		mouth: Cupid's bow width	0.0000586
0.729	mouth: Scale upperlip height		0.0000607
0.576	slider_l-eye-corner2-down|up		0.0000717

Maltese female (n=17)

-1.59		slider_l-cheek-inner-decr|incr	*	0.0000812
-1.19		slider_l-eye-eyefold-angle-down|up		0.0000818

Mexican female (n=33)

0.686	nose: Middle nose bridge width		1.26E-07
-0.57		eyebrows: Eyebrows angle	4.73E-07
0.621	nose-greek-decr|incr		5.58E-07
0.718	chin: Scale chin prognathism		1.31E-06
-0.674		mouth: Cupid's bow width	0.0000014
0.36	nose-compression-compress|uncompress		2.06E-06
-0.626		eyebrows: Move vert	2.58E-06
0.295	nose: Upper nose bridge width		5.95E-06
-0.818		slider_eyes_middle_droop	6.47E-06
-0.628		nose-hump-decr|incr	0.0000296
0.617	chin: Scale chin prominence		0.0000645

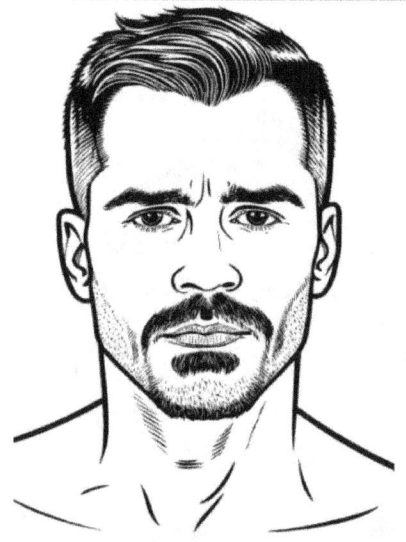

Maltese male (n=16)

2.59	eyes: Inner height of left eye			9.25E-07
2.77	eyes: Inner height of right eye			1.04E-06
-3.33		eyebrows: Move vert		3.46E-06
-2.98		slider_r-cheek-bones-decr|incr		3.55E-06
-2.9		slider_l-cheek-inner-decr|incr	*	4.36E-06
-3.24		slider_l-cheek-bones-decr|incr		4.69E-06
3.71	eyes: Middle height of right eye			0.0000113
3.63	eyes: Middle height of left eye			0.0000181
2.36	slider_r-eye-scale-decr|incr			0.0000255
2.85	slider_r-eye-bag-decr|incr			0.0000258
-2.35		nose: Scale horizontally		0.00003
2.13	slider_l-eye-scale-decr|incr			0.0000363
-2.4		slider_eyes_outer_droop		0.000042
-2.46		mouth: Cupid's bow shape		0.0000545
1.27	nose: Upper nose bridge width			0.0000599

Mexican male (n=28)

-0.471		slider_l-eye-trans-in|out	0.000052

Mongolian female (n=22)

Value			*	p
	slider_elvs_			
1.92	highchubbycheekbones1		*	1.93E-12
-1.95		mouth: Scale horizontally	*	8.32E-12
-1.32		mouth: Scale upperlip width	*	3.64E-11
2.35	slider_eyes_outer_droop		*	6.43E-11
-2		slider_l-eye-scale-decr|incr	*	8.66E-11
-2.11		slider_r-eye-scale-decr|incr	*	2.83E-10
1.28	chin: Scale chin width		*	8.16E-10
1.83	mouth: Dimples		*	1.85E-09
-1.38		slider_l-eye-push1-in|out	*	1.88E-09
-1.86		slider_r-eye-push1-in|out	*	2.01E-09
1.5	slider_eyes_middle_droop		*	3.02E-09
1.68	slider_l-eye-eyefold-angle-down|up		*	6.37E-09
1.16	mouth: Laugh-lines		*	6.43E-09
-1.15		slider_l-cheek-trans-down|up	*	2.09E-08
1.66	eyebrows: Move vert		*	6.69E-08
1.11	chin: Scale chin height		*	1.81E-07
-0.877		eyebrows: Eyebrows bulge	*	2.81E-07
-1.12		slider_r-cheek-trans-down|up	*	2.86E-07
1.11	slider_r-eye-eyefold-angle-down|up		*	2.98E-07
-1.47		slider_r-eye-trans-in|out	*	4.68E-07
1.07	nose-volume-decr|incr		*	5.35E-07
-1.45		eyes: Middle height of left eye	*	5.55E-07
-1.21		nose: Move nose base vert.		6.64E-07
1.16	slider_l-eye-bag-height-decr|incr		*	7.8E-07
1.34	slider_Nose_alar_crease		*	8.31E-07
-0.7		mouth: Scale lowerlip width	*	8.43E-07
1.25	slider_l-eye-epicanthus-in|out		*	1.48E-06
-1.49		slider_l-eye-trans-in|out	*	1.54E-06
-0.873		nose: Scale depth	*	2.09E-06
-1.44		eyes: Middle height of right eye	*	3.25E-06
1.08	slider_l-eye-eyefold-down|up		*	3.61E-06
-1.13		nose-greek-decr|incr		4.87E-06
-0.913		nose: Move vertically	*	5.78E-06
-0.97		nose: Scale tip width	*	9.16E-06
-0.546		chin: Cleft chin		0.0000108
1.08	slider_r-eye-bag-height-decr|incr		*	0.0000109
0.977	nose-nostrils-angle-down|up		*	0.0000121
0.822	forehead: Scale vertically			0.0000131
0.859	chin: Scale chin prominence			0.0000145
0.828	forehead: Cranic shape			0.0000237
1.13	eyebrows: Eyebrows angle			0.0000264
-0.645		chin: Scale chin prognathism	*	0.0000326
-0.549		slider_l-eye-trans-down|up	*	0.0000526

0.96	forehead: Forehead bulge		*	0.000073
-0.705		mouth: Move vertically	*	0.0000733

Mongolian male (n=28)

Value			*	p
	slider_elvs_			
1.71	highchubbycheekbones1		*	2.75E-19
-1.61		slider_l-eye-scale-decr|incr	*	7.39E-18
2.25	slider_eyes_outer_droop		*	6.81E-17
-1.64		slider_r-eye-scale-decr|incr	*	3.23E-16
-1.8		mouth: Scale horizontally	*	3.64E-15
1.73	eyebrows: Move vert		*	8.67E-15
1.58	mouth: Dimples		*	8.78E-15
1.5	slider_eyes_middle_droop		*	1.34E-13
0.86	chin: Scale chin width		*	8.81E-13
-1.2		mouth: Scale upperlip width	*	5.23E-12
-1.28		eyes: Middle height of left eye	*	5.25E-12
-1.15		slider_l-eye-trans-in|out	*	6.75E-12
-1.43		eyes: Middle height of right eye	*	9.24E-12
1.21	mouth: Laugh-lines		*	3E-11
1.22	slider_l-eye-eyefold-angle-down|up		*	5.4E-11
0.911	slider_l-eye-eyefold-down|up		*	6.31E-11
-0.799		mouth: Scale lowerlip width		1.66E-10
-1.33		slider_r-eye-push1-in|out		2E-10
-1.26		slider_l-eye-push1-in|out		6.84E-10
-1.11		nose: Scale tip width	*	7.3E-10
-1.3		slider_l-cheek-trans-down|up	*	8.71E-10
-1.23		nose: Scale depth	*	1.03E-09
-1.22		slider_r-eye-trans-in|out	*	1.05E-09
1.03	nose-hump-decr|incr			2.89E-09
1	slider_l-eye-epicanthus-in|out		*	5.24E-09
-1.23		slider_r-cheek-trans-down|up	*	7.51E-09
1.08	forehead: Forehead bulge		*	9.65E-09
-0.79		mouth: Move vertically	*	1.12E-08
1.02	slider_Nose_alar_crease		*	1.31E-08
-0.86		nose: Scale nostrils width		2.17E-08
-0.692		nose: Move vertically	*	2.89E-08
-1.16		eyes: Inner height of left eye		5.36E-08
0.883	slider_r-eye-eyefold-angle-down|up		*	5.96E-08
1.02	nose-compression-compress|uncompress			8.07E-08
0.823	nose-nostrils-angle-down|up		*	8.24E-08
-1.22		eyes: Inner height of right eye		1.5E-07
-1		slider_r-eye-push2-in|out		1.93E-07
0.798	slider_r-eye-eyefold-down|up			2.26E-07
0.759	slider_l-eye-bag-height-decr|incr		*	3.61E-07
-0.865		nose: Scale nostrils flaring		4.28E-07
-1.03		slider_l-eye-push2-in|out		5.89E-07

Value	Feature	Sig.	p
-0.672	eyebrows: Eyebrows bulge	*	9.71E-07
0.669	slider_l-eye-corner2-down|up		9.83E-07
-0.982	mouth: Cupid's bow shape		1.41E-06
0.894	slider_r-eye-epicanthus-in|out		0.0000017
-0.632	chin: Scale chin prognathism	*	2.03E-06
1.05	slider_r-eye-bag-height-decr|incr	*	2.34E-06
0.556	chin: Scale chin height	*	6.26E-06
-0.636	nose: Lower nose bridge width		0.0000086
-0.562	slider_l-eye-trans-down|up	*	0.0000102
-0.713	eyes: Outer height of right eye		0.0000113
0.796	forehead: Temple bulge		0.0000129
0.719	nose-volume-decr|incr	*	0.0000156
0.746	nose-curve-concave|convex		0.0000677
-0.732	slider_nose crease extra1		0.0000784

Moroccan female (n=22)

Value	Feature	Sig.	p
-0.881	eyes: Outer height of right eye		9.76E-07
0.721	slider_l-eye-trans-down|up	*	5.33E-06
-0.831	eyes: Outer height of left eye		5.85E-06
0.786	eyebrows: Eyebrows bulge	*	0.0000105
-0.759	eyes: Middle height of left eye		0.0000179
0.708	slider_r-eye-trans-down|up	*	0.0000207
0.882	mouth: Scale philtrum volume		0.0000347
-0.584	forehead: Scale vertically	*	0.0000369
-0.647	mouth: Scale upperlip volume		0.0000386
0.76	nose: Lower nose bridge width		0.0000643
0.822	slider_eyes_outer_droop		0.0000654
-0.747	eyes: Middle height of right eye		0.000071

Moroccan male (n=17)

Value	Feature	Sig.	p
-1.28	slider_l-eye-bag-decr|incr		8.02E-09
-1.3	slider_r-eye-bag-decr|incr		6.23E-08
1.33	slider_r-eye-trans-down|up	*	2.61E-07
1.13	slider_l-eye-trans-down|up	*	1.01E-06
-1.14	slider_l-eye-corner2-down|up		5.05E-06
0.887	eyebrows: Eyebrows bulge	*	6.06E-06
0.727	slider_eyes_middle_droop		8.36E-06
-1.04	forehead: Temple bulge		0.0000084
-1.26	slider_r-eye-corner2-down|up		0.000013
-0.709	forehead: Scale vertically	*	0.0000143
-0.872	mouth: Scale lowerlip volume		0.0000156
1.24	chin: Scale chin angular		0.0000161
1.05	slider_r-eye-bag-height-decr|incr		0.0000171
-0.797	forehead: Cranic shape		0.0000179
1.2	chin: Scale chin prominence		0.0000219
-1.09	slider_l-cheek-volume-decr|incr		0.000024
0.544	slider_l-eye-push1-in|out		0.000027
0.76	slider_l-eye-bag-height-decr|incr		0.0000597
-1.11	chin: Tone of side chin		0.000062
-1.14	nose-curve-concave|convex		0.0000645
-0.657	slider_r-eye-bag-in|out		0.0000742
1.06	nose: Scale nostrils flaring		0.0000744
-1.06	nose: Move nose base vert.		0.0000793

Native American female (n=27)

Value	Feature	Sig.	p
-0.624	mouth: Scale lowerlip width	*	2.5E-08
1.08	slider_l-eye-bag-height-decr|incr		4.68E-08
1.26	slider_elvs_chipmunkcheeks_l1	*	4.66E-07
-0.989	slider_r-eye-bag-in|out		8.62E-07
0.861	slider_l-eye-trans-down|up	*	1.24E-06
0.951	slider_l-eye-corner1-down|up	*	0.0000062
-0.484	mouth: Scale vertically	*	6.48E-06
-0.739	mouth: Scale upperlip height	*	0.0000106
-0.692	eyes: Middle height of left eye	*	0.0000107
-0.564	mouth: Scale lowerlip height	*	0.0000134
0.67	mouth: Cupid's bow shape		0.0000154
0.674	slider_r-eye-trans-down|up		0.0000361
0.722	nose: Move vertically		0.0000485
0.744	slider_r-eye-bag-height-decr|incr		0.0000668
-0.59	eyes: Middle height of right eye	*	0.0000919

Native American male (n=33)

-0.945		slider_l-eye-trans-in|out	3.91E-09
-0.792		mouth: Scale lowerlip width	* 4.94E-08
-1.1		slider_r-eye-trans-in|out	5.48E-08
-0.876		mouth: Scale lowerlip height	* 1.07E-07
0.758	chin: Scale chin prominence		9.7E-07
-0.798		mouth: Scale vertically	* 2.04E-06
0.5	mouth: Dimples		5.01E-06
-0.838		eyes: Middle height of left eye	* 5.31E-06
0.73	slider_elvs_chipmunkcheeks_l1		* 0.0000073
-0.774		eyes: Inner height of left eye	0.000012
-0.781		eyes: Middle height of right eye	* 0.0000141
-0.862		mouth: Scale philtrum volume	0.000019
0.627	slider_septum_sharp		0.0000214
-0.942		mouth: Scale upperlip height	* 0.0000241
-0.642		eyes: Inner height of right eye	0.0000296
0.707	slider_l-eye-corner1-down|up		* 0.0000361
-0.79		slider_l-eye-corner2-down|up	0.0000475
0.787	chin: Scale chin angular		0.0000524
0.676	slider_eyes_outer_droop		0.0000609
0.817	slider_r-eye-corner1-down|up		0.0000685
0.743	slider_l-eye-trans-down|up		* 0.0000705

Nepali male (n=26)

-0.719		eyes: Outer height of right eye	1.32E-06
-0.601		slider_nostril_rounding	5.17E-06
0.533	slider_eyes_outer_droop		6.76E-06
-0.782		slider_r-eye-push2-in|out	* 0.000014
-0.481		slider_Nose_alar_crease	0.0000449
-0.506		mouth: Scale lowerlip volume	0.0000669
-0.5		eyes: Middle height of right eye	0.0000768

Nigerian female (n=22)

2.08	mouth: Scale upperlip width		* 2.5E-17
-1.51		mouth: Dimples	* 5.27E-14
-1.32		mouth: Scale lowerlip volume	* 1.78E-12
-1.75		slider_r-eye-trans-down|up	* 2.75E-12
1.95	mouth: Scale lowerlip width		* 3.49E-12
-1.66		slider_r-eye-corner1-down|up	* 3.05E-11
1.78	mouth: Scale vertically		* 1.04E-10
-1.77		slider_l-eye-trans-down|up	* 1.88E-10
-1.35		chin: Scale chin width	* 3.49E-10
-1.38		chin: Scale chin height	* 5.56E-10
-1.54		slider_l-eye-corner1-down|up	* 6.41E-10
1.42	mouth: Scale horizontally		* 1.22E-09
1.17	slider_r-eye-corner2-down|up		* 1.26E-09
-1.43		mouth: Upperlip curved shape	1.9E-09
1.92	slider_r-eye-eyefold-angle-down|up		* 2.11E-09
-1.24		nose: Move vertically	* 2.59E-09

Nepali female (n=16)

0.577	nose: Upper nose bridge width		7.49E-07
0.709	nose: Middle nose bridge width		0.0000071
0.989	slider_l-eye-corner1-down|up		8.95E-06
-0.955		slider_r-eye-push2-in|out	* 0.0000103
-0.822		slider_l-eye-push2-in|out	0.0000184
0.378	nose-compression-compress|uncompress		0.0000756
0.633	slider_r-eye-trans-in|out		0.0000949

-1.96		eyebrows: Eyebrows bulge	* 3.31E-09
-1.18		mouth: Scale upperlip volume	* 6.5E-09
1.55	mouth: Scale lowerlip height		* 1.9E-08
1.44	mouth: Scale upperlip height		* 2.19E-08
-1.29		nose-greek-decr|incr	* 4.56E-08
-1.1		mouth: Laugh-lines	* 5.66E-08
-1.06		eyes: Inner height of right eye	* 1.04E-07
1.42	slider_r-eye-epicanthus-in|out		1.24E-07
-1.12		eyes: Inner height of left eye	* 1.57E-07
0.894	slider_l-eye-corner2-down|up		* 3.03E-07
1.48	slider_r-eye-eyefold-down|up		6.49E-07
0.651	slider_r-cheek-inner-decr|incr		* 9.12E-07
0.97	nose: Scale nostrils width		1.84E-06
-1.4		mouth: Cupid's bow width	* 2.39E-06
1.4	forehead: Scale vertically		* 2.66E-06
1.29	forehead: Cranic shape		* 2.97E-06
-1.44		slider_l-eye-push1-in|out	3.68E-06
0.878	slider_r-eye-bag-in|out		* 0.0000042
-0.824		slider_l-eye-scale-decr|incr	4.37E-06
0.88	nose: Scale horizontally		* 0.0000048
-0.933		mouth: Cupid's bow shape	* 4.92E-06
0.768	mouth: Move corners vert.		* 7.03E-06
1.1	slider_l-eye-eyefold-angle-down|up		* 8.79E-06
0.746	slider_r-eye-trans-in|out		* 8.92E-06
0.822	eyebrows: Eyebrows angle		* 0.0000104
0.967	eyebrows: Move vert		0.0000137
-0.659		slider_r-eye-scale-decr|incr	0.0000143
1.03	chin: Cleft chin		* 0.0000246
0.588	slider_r-eye-bag-decr|incr		0.0000432
-0.634		nose-volume-decr|incr	* 0.0000446
0.64	slider_l-eye-bag-decr|incr		0.0000517
-0.836		slider_nostril_rounding	0.0000552

Nigerian male (n=24)

-1.51		mouth: Dimples	* 2.48E-16
-1.34		mouth: Scale lowerlip volume	* 2.52E-13
-1.71		chin: Scale chin height	* 4.14E-13
2	mouth: Scale lowerlip width		* 1.5E-12
1.14	slider_r-eye-corner2-down|up		* 1.55E-12
-1.28		eyebrows: Eyebrows bulge	* 2.83E-12
1.66	mouth: Scale upperlip width		* 9.4E-12
1.93	mouth: Scale vertically		* 1.53E-11
-1.01		mouth: Laugh-lines	* 1.59E-11
1.28	mouth: Move corners vert.		* 2.05E-10
1.43	slider_l-eye-trans-in|out		4.34E-10
1.74	mouth: Scale lowerlip height		* 8.69E-10
0.992	slider_l-eye-corner2-down|up		9.62E-10
-1.47		slider_l-eye-trans-down|up	* 1.17E-09
-1.39		slider_r-eye-trans-down|up	* 1.31E-09

-1.24		chin: Scale chin width	* 2.28E-09
1.24	slider_r-eye-trans-in|out		* 2.44E-09
0.986	mouth: Scale horizontally		* 3.92E-09
1.48	chin: Cleft chin		* 4.37E-09
1.17	forehead: Scale vertically		* 7.69E-09
0.918	slider_l-eye-eyefold-angle-down|up		* 8.53E-09
-1.17		mouth: Move vertically	1.45E-08
0.92	nose: Scale nostrils width		* 2.73E-08
1.11	forehead: Cranic shape		* 2.95E-08
-1.13		nose-volume-decr|incr	* 5.16E-08
0.937	nose: Move nose base vert.		1.05E-07
-0.917		slider_elvs_highchubbycheekbones1	1.22E-07
-1.12		mouth: Scale upperlip volume	* 1.48E-07
-1.2		mouth: Cupid's bow shape	* 1.69E-07
1.06	slider_r-eye-bag-in|out		* 1.95E-07
0.933	chin: Scale chin prognathism		3.09E-07
-1.28		mouth: Upperlip curved shape	* 4.94E-07
-0.912		slider_r-eye-corner1-down|up	8.8E-07
0.837	mouth: Move depth		1.21E-06
1.19	nose: Scale horizontally		* 1.45E-06
0.763	slider_l-cheek-inner-decr|incr		1.95E-06
-0.895		nose: Move vertically	* 2.58E-06
0.593	eyes: Outer height of right eye		2.84E-06
-0.556		nose: Lower nose bridge width	3.06E-06
-0.659		eyes: Inner height of left eye	* 3.26E-06
1.24	mouth: Scale upperlip height		* 3.41E-06
0.852	mouth: Scale middle lowerlip		3.68E-06
0.69	slider_l-eye-eyefold-concave|convex		3.89E-06
-1.14		mouth: Cupid's bow width	* 4.18E-06
1.14	slider_r-eye-eyefold-angle-down|up		* 4.55E-06
-0.911		slider_l-eye-corner1-down|up	* 5.05E-06
-0.746		slider_l-eye-bag-height-decr|incr	8.59E-06
0.566	eyes: Outer height of left eye		0.00001
-0.565		eyes: Inner height of right eye	* 0.0000101
0.617	nose: Move tip vertically		0.0000118
0.64	slider_r-cheek-inner-decr|incr		* 0.0000132
0.788	eyebrows: Eyebrows angle		0.0000278
-0.758		nose: Scale vertically	0.0000309
-0.655		nose-greek-decr|incr	* 0.0000393
-0.692		slider_r-eye-bag-height-decr|incr	0.0000566

Norwegian female (n=27)

-1.04		mouth: Scale vertically	* 4.02E-14
1.13	mouth: Scale lowerlip volume		* 7.16E-11
-0.777		mouth: Scale lowerlip height	* 2.17E-09
-0.834		mouth: Scale lowerlip width	* 9.01E-09
-0.755		chin: Cleft chin	1.51E-08

-0.743	slider_l-cheek-inner-decr|incr	*	1.87E-08
-0.757	mouth: Move corners vert.		4.68E-08
-0.951	slider_l-eye-scale-decr|incr		1.17E-07
-0.714	slider_r-eye-trans-in|out	*	1.31E-07
-0.932	nose: Scale horizontally	*	6.67E-07
-0.621	nose: Scale nostrils width		1.46E-06
-0.803	slider_r-eye-scale-decr|incr		2.37E-06
0.795 chin: Scale chin height		*	4.83E-06
-0.877	slider_l-eye-trans-in|out		6.83E-06
-0.922	slider_l-eye-push1-in|out		7.34E-06
-0.72	mouth: Scale upperlip width	*	0.0000102
0.61 mouth: Lowerlip curved shape			0.0000311
-0.407	nose: Lower nose bridge width	*	0.0000344
-0.54	mouth: Scale upperlip height	*	0.0000777

Norwegian male (n=21)

-1.03	slider_l-cheek-inner-decr|incr	*	4.33E-09
-1.29	mouth: Scale vertically	*	1.21E-07
-0.97	nose: Scale horizontally	*	2.29E-07
-1.07	mouth: Scale lowerlip width	*	1.28E-06
-0.81	mouth: Scale upperlip width	*	4.09E-06
-0.748	slider_r-eye-trans-in|out	*	4.69E-06
-0.955	mouth: Scale lowerlip height	*	0.000011
0.45 mouth: Dimples			0.0000121
1.67 mouth: Scale lowerlip volume		*	0.0000185
-0.647	nose: Lower nose bridge width	*	0.0000283
0.867 chin: Scale chin height		*	0.0000353
0.843 mouth: Upperlip curved shape			0.0000572
-0.972	mouth: Scale upperlip height	*	0.0000657

Pakistani female (n=18)

1.38 slider_r-eye-scale-decr|incr		*	1.01E-06
1.41 slider_l-eye-scale-decr|incr		*	1.35E-06
-1.25	slider_eyes_outer_droop	*	8.72E-06
-0.847	slider_l-eye-eyefold-angle-down|up	*	0.0000221
-1.03	eyebrows: Move vert	*	0.0000409

Pakistani male (n=26)

-0.856	slider_eyes_outer_droop	*	5.72E-08
-0.571	slider_l-eye-eyefold-angle-down|up	*	3.59E-07
-0.91	slider_eyes_middle_droop		5.85E-07
0.765 slider_l-eye-scale-decr|incr		*	7.21E-06
0.629 eyes: Middle height of right eye			0.0000264
0.782 slider_r-eye-scale-decr|incr		*	0.0000291
0.481 mouth: Dimples			0.0000401
0.922 nose: Scale depth			0.0000424
0.576 eyes: Middle height of left eye			0.0000544
0.759 nose: Scale vertically			0.000071
0.7 mouth: Move vertically			0.0000712
-0.517	mouth: Scale horizontally		0.0000785
-0.633	eyebrows: Move vert	*	0.0000838
-0.573	mouth: Move corners vert.		0.0000852
-0.573	mouth: Move corners vert.		0.0000852

Palestinian female (n=16)

0.955 nose-nostrils-angle-down|up			0.0000534

Palestinian male (n=19)

0.707 nose: Lower nose bridge width		0.0000641

Persian female (n=20)

1.53 slider_r-eye-push2-in|out		1.6E-08
0.995 slider_r-cheek-trans-down|up		7.86E-08
-0.493	mouth: Scale lowerlip volume	0.0000187
0.84 slider_r-eye-scale-decr|incr		0.0000572
1.03 slider_l-eye-push2-in|out		0.0000577
-0.948	slider_r-eye-eyefold-angle-down|up	0.0000694

Persian male (n=15)

-1.2	chin: Scale chin prognathism		6.78E-09
-1.65	slider_r-eye-bag-in|out		1.32E-07
0.884 nose: Scale vertically			0.0000128
1.19 slider_l-cheek-trans-down|up			0.000014
1.19 mouth: Move vertically			0.0000278
-0.703	forehead: Scale vertically		0.000031
-0.778	eyebrows: Eyebrows angle		0.0000405
1.29 mouth: Cupid's bow shape			0.0000742
1.43 slider_elvs_chipmunkcheeks_l1			0.0000742
-1.05	slider_r-cheek-volume-decr|incr		0.00008

Peruvian female (n=27)

0.689 eyebrows: Eyebrows bulge			8.88E-09
0.841 slider_l-eye-trans-down|up		*	9.6E-08
0.761 slider_r-eye-trans-down|up			1.75E-07
-0.642	eyes: Outer height of left eye	*	1.05E-06
-0.616	eyes: Outer height of right eye	*	2.04E-06
0.878 slider_r-eye-corner1-down|up			2.86E-06
1.02 slider_l-eye-corner1-down|up			3.15E-06
0.627 nose: Lower nose bridge width			6.04E-06
-0.766	eyebrows: Move vert		0.0000301
-0.76	slider_r-eye-bag-in|out		0.0000624

Peruvian male (n=29)

-0.842	eyes: Outer height of left eye	*	1.26E-06
-0.814	eyes: Outer height of right eye	*	5.08E-06
-0.666	slider_elvs_highchubbycheekbones1		0.0000131
0.539 mouth: Scale horizontally			0.0000132
-0.603	eyes: Middle height of right eye		0.0000142

-0.694	slider_r-eye-push2-in|out		0.000018
0.37	nose: Upper nose bridge width		0.0000218
0.32	mouth: Scale upperlip width		0.0000263
-0.612	eyes: Middle height of left eye		0.0000347
0.53	slider_l-eye-trans-down|up	*	0.0000478
-0.59	mouth: Laugh-lines		0.000048
-0.461	slider_nostril_rounding		0.0000726

1.24	forehead: Temple bulge		1.04E-06
-0.921	mouth: Scale lowerlip width	*	1.49E-06
0.778	mouth: Dimples		1.64E-06
0.996	mouth: Laugh-lines		6.03E-06
0.758	nose-greek-decr|incr		7.44E-06
0.827	chin: Scale chin height	*	0.0000133
-0.73	slider_l-cheek-inner-decr|incr	*	0.0000143
-0.823	slider_l-eye-trans-in|out		0.0000274
-0.867	chin: Scale chin prominence	*	0.0000276
-0.67	slider_r-cheek-inner-decr|incr		0.000035
0.894	mouth: Scale lowerlip volume	*	0.0000419
	slider_elvs_		
0.995	highchubbycheekbones1		0.0000427
-0.726	slider_r-eye-trans-in|out		0.0000454
-0.67	forehead: Scale vertically	*	0.0000528
-0.86	mouth: Scale vertically	*	0.0000725
-0.672	mouth: Move corners vert.		0.0000783
0.509	slider_Nose_alar_crease	*	0.0000868

Polish female (n=24)

-1.02	nose: Scale nostrils width	*	6.32E-11
-0.828	mouth: Scale vertically	*	1.54E-10
-0.889	forehead: Scale vertically	*	7.47E-09
-0.6	mouth: Scale lowerlip width	*	4E-08
0.517	mouth: Scale lowerlip volume	*	2.07E-07
-0.795	forehead: Cranic shape		4.66E-07
-0.745	chin: Scale chin angular		1.72E-06
-1.15	chin: Scale chin prominence	*	9.02E-06
-0.878	chin: Scale chin prognathism		0.0000107
0.646	chin: Scale chin height	*	0.0000119
-0.713	mouth: Scale lowerlip height		0.0000138
0.607	eyebrows: Eyebrows bulge		0.0000165
0.651	slider_Nose_alar_crease	*	0.0000218
-0.488	nose: Scale nostrils flaring		0.0000273
-0.834	nose: Scale horizontally		0.0000287
-0.635	chin: Cleft chin		0.0000362
-0.688	slider_l-cheek-inner-decr|incr	*	0.0000572

Portuguese female (n=27)

0.643	nose: Move vertically		4.05E-06
0.7	slider_l-eye-trans-down|up		4.56E-06
-0.644	eyebrows: Eyebrows angle	*	6.46E-06
0.621	eyebrows: Eyebrows bulge		6.68E-06
0.668	nose-greek-decr|incr	*	0.0000143
-0.547	forehead: Scale vertically		0.0000231
0.941	slider_l-eye-push1-in|out		0.0000274
0.661	slider_r-eye-trans-down|up		0.0000285
-0.545	forehead: Cranic shape		0.0000548
-0.462	mouth: Scale lowerlip width		0.0000798
-0.808	slider_r-eye-corner2-down|up		0.0000985

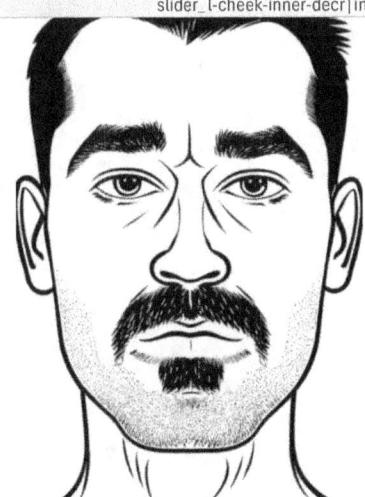

Polish male (n=18)

-0.909	mouth: Scale upperlip width		1.29E-07
-1.2	nose: Scale nostrils width	*	4.5E-07

Portuguese male (n=26)

-0.866	slider_eyes_outer_droop		1.93E-07

0.604	nose-greek-decr|incr		*	7.73E-07
-0.62		eyebrows: Eyebrows angle	*	1.31E-06
-0.907		slider_eyes_middle_droop		0.0000229

Punjabi female (n=27)

1.32	slider_r-eye-push2-in|out			2.51E-09
1.32	slider_r-eye-scale-decr|incr			2.63E-09
1.1	slider_l-eye-scale-decr|incr			5.36E-09
0.987	mouth: Scale philtrum volume			7.07E-09
0.939	nose: Scale vertically		*	1.73E-08
1.06	slider_l-eye-push2-in|out			2.12E-08
0.77	nose-nostrils-angle-down|up		*	3.29E-08
0.742	mouth: Move vertically		*	5.22E-08
-0.929		slider_l-eye-eyefold-angle-down|up		7.47E-07
-0.846		slider_l-eye-eyefold-down|up		0.0000126
0.854	eyes: Inner height of right eye			0.0000326
0.763	eyes: Middle height of left eye			0.0000367
0.734	eyes: Inner height of left eye			0.0000383
-0.578		slider_Nose_alar_crease	*	0.0000458
0.799	eyes: Middle height of right eye			0.0000628
-0.911		slider_eyes_outer_droop		0.0000805
-0.419		nose: Move vertically		0.0000816

Punjabi male (n=22)

1.44	nose: Scale vertically		*	7.02E-08
-0.731		slider_eyes_middle_droop		3.47E-07
1.37	mouth: Move vertically		*	7.68E-07
-1.03		mouth: Move corners vert.		2.84E-06
1.11	nose: Scale depth			0.000014
0.648	nose-nostrils-angle-down|up		*	0.0000436
-0.693		slider_Nose_alar_crease	*	0.0000507
-0.424		slider_nostril_rounding		0.0000824
1.21	slider_elvs_chipmunkcheeks_l1			0.0000957

Romanian female (n=30)

0.702	nose-greek-decr|incr		*	2.8E-07
-0.498		forehead: Scale vertically	*	2.83E-06
-0.501		forehead: Cranic shape	*	2.84E-06
-0.627		slider_r-eye-trans-in|out		0.0000111
-0.643		slider_r-cheek-inner-decr|incr		0.0000352
0.682	mouth: Laugh-lines			0.0000521
-0.573		nose: Scale nostrils width		0.0000574
0.604	nose: Scale depth			0.0000858

Romanian male (n=18)

-0.964		eyebrows: Eyebrows angle		9.63E-11
-0.964		eyebrows: Eyebrows angle		9.63E-11
1.08	nose-greek-decr|incr		*	3E-09
0.916	nose: Move vertically			4.55E-06
-0.831		forehead: Scale vertically	*	8.22E-06
-0.516		mouth: Move corners vert.		0.0000544
-0.773		forehead: Cranic shape	*	0.0000664

Russian female (n=25)

-1.38		nose: Scale nostrils width	*	6.01E-11
-0.919		mouth: Scale upperlip width	*	1.43E-10
1.19	mouth: Laugh-lines		*	3.62E-10
-1.3		nose: Scale depth		4.46E-09
1.4	slider_Nose_alar_crease		*	6E-09
-0.986		nose: Scale vertically		8.53E-09
-1.39		slider_l-eye-trans-in|out	*	2.02E-08
1.35	nose-hump-decr|incr			4.58E-08
1.36	slider_elvs_highchubbycheekbones1		*	5.42E-08
-1.14		slider_r-eye-trans-in|out	*	4.3E-07
-0.767		slider_septum_sharp	*	2.24E-06
-0.828		nose: Scale tip width		2.49E-06
-0.752		nose: Scale nostrils flaring		4.45E-06
-0.942		chin: Scale chin prognathism		0.0000051
-0.899		nose: Scale horizontally	*	0.0000122
-0.756		chin: Scale chin prominence		0.0000272
-1.05		slider_l-eye-push1-in|out		0.0000297
-0.433		mouth: Scale lowerlip width	*	0.0000377
-0.573		mouth: Move vertically		0.0000608
0.586	eyebrows: Move vert			0.0000748
0.36	mouth: Scale lowerlip volume		*	0.000077

Russian male (n=30)

1.55	slider_elvs_highchubbycheekbones1		*	4.44E-14
-1.24		slider_l-eye-trans-in|out	*	8.77E-14
-1.38		slider_r-eye-trans-in|out	*	1.85E-13
0.824	mouth: Dimples			2.66E-13
-1.09		nose: Scale nostrils width	*	3.49E-12
-1.08		mouth: Scale upperlip width	*	6.46E-12
1.04	mouth: Laugh-lines		*	4.2E-10

0.689	mouth: Scale lowerlip volume		*	1.34E-09
-0.672		mouth: Scale lowerlip width	*	1.24E-08
0.506	chin: Scale chin width			1.24E-07
0.826	slider_Nose_alar_crease		*	5.05E-07
-0.611		slider_r-eye-epicanthus-in|out		7.31E-07
-0.713		mouth: Scale vertically		1.54E-06
-0.773		nose: Scale horizontally	*	0.0000017
-0.673		nose: Scale vertically	*	3.47E-06
0.837	forehead: Temple bulge			4.09E-06
-0.715		chin: Scale chin angular		5.31E-06
0.709	chin: Scale chin height			5.77E-06
-0.561		slider_l-cheek-inner-decr|incr		6.95E-06
-0.474		mouth: Move corners vert.		0.000316
-0.613		slider_septum_sharp	*	0.0000564
-0.708		mouth: Scale horizontally		0.0000728
-0.528		slider_r-eye-push1-in|out		0.0000925

Salvadoran female (n=21)

-1.17		nose-hump-decr|incr		1.16E-10
0.976	nose: Middle nose bridge width		*	6.15E-09
1.1	slider_l-eye-corner1-down|up		*	1.54E-07
-1.18		eyebrows: Move vert		4.47E-06
-1.09		slider_eyes_middle_droop		5.7E-07
-0.876		mouth: Cupid's bow width		4.06E-06
0.696	nose: Scale vertically			6.82E-06
0.796	nose-greek-decr|incr			0.0000095
0.788	nose: Scale nostrils width		*	9.77E-06
0.643	nose: Lower nose bridge width		*	0.000012
0.938	chin: Scale chin prominence		*	0.0000159
-0.813		slider_Nose_alar_crease		0.0000206
0.416	nose: Upper nose bridge width			0.0000229
1.08	slider_r-eye-corner1-down|up		*	0.0000243
0.722	chin: Scale chin prognathism			0.0000318
0.65	nose: Scale depth			0.000038
0.715	slider_l-eye-trans-down|up			0.0000487

Salvadoran male (n=22)

0.805	slider_r-eye-corner1-down|up	*	1.73E-06
0.713	slider_l-eye-corner1-down|up	*	0.0000391
0.954	nose: Middle nose bridge width	*	0.0000609
0.825	nose: Lower nose bridge width	*	0.0000663
0.68	nose: Scale nostrils width	*	0.000077
0.592	chin: Scale chin prominence	*	0.0000913

Samoan male (n=26)

1.59	slider_elvs_chipmunkcheeks_l1		*	3.45E-12
-1.21		slider_r-eye-bag-in|out		0.0000001
-0.712		slider_l-eye-trans-in|out	*	3.66E-07
-0.917		nose-hump-decr|incr	*	8.8E-07
-0.8		slider_eyes_middle_droop		1.78E-06
0.8	nose: Scale vertically			1.86E-06
-0.632		eyes: Middle height of left eye		1.93E-06
0.888	slider_r-eye-corner1-down|up			1.95E-06
1.27	nose: Scale nostrils width		*	2.63E-06
0.92	slider_l-eye-corner1-down|up			3.21E-06
-0.54		slider_r-eye-scale-decr|incr		0.0000138
-0.425		slider_l-eye-scale-decr|incr		0.0000189
-0.71		slider_Nose_alar_crease	*	0.0000196
0.643	eyebrows: Move vert			0.0000277
0.602	slider_r-cheek-trans-down|up			0.000054
0.636	chin: Scale chin width			0.0000702
0.536	mouth: Dimples			0.0000966

Samoan female (n=21)

-0.648		slider_l-eye-trans-in|out	*	2.83E-07
1.21	slider_elvs_chipmunkcheeks_l1		*	5.08E-07
-0.831		mouth: Cupid's bow width		6.41E-07
1.31	slider_r-eye-eyefold-down|up			5.01E-06
-0.703		eyebrows: Eyebrows angle		6.01E-06
0.769	nose: Scale nostrils width		*	0.0000115
-0.729		nose-hump-decr|incr	*	0.0000285
1.12	slider_r-eye-epicanthus-in|out			0.0000483
-0.861		slider_Nose_alar_crease	*	0.0000588

Scottish female (n=28)

-1.24		mouth: Scale lowerlip width	*	4.83E-15
-1.13		mouth: Scale vertically	*	1.41E-12
-1.15		mouth: Scale upperlip width	*	2.3E-10
1.25	mouth: Scale lowerlip volume		*	2.58E-10
0.884	chin: Scale chin width		*	3.75E-10
-0.943		mouth: Scale lowerlip height		2.97E-09
0.957	mouth: Upperlip curved shape			2.98E-08
-1.03		mouth: Scale upperlip height		3.69E-08
0.954	chin: Scale chin height		*	6.94E-07
0.979	mouth: Scale upperlip volume			1.45E-06
-0.758		nose: Scale nostrils width		2.53E-06

value	feature	feature	*	p
0.789	mouth: Laugh-lines			3.95E-06
-0.83		mouth: Scale philtrum volume		0.0000084
0.818	slider_Nose_alar_crease			0.0000128
-0.522		slider_l-eye-trans-in|out	*	0.0000415
0.488	nose-compression-compress|uncompress			0.0000442
0.789	mouth: Dimples		*	0.0000608
-0.654		mouth: Move depth		0.0000648
-0.615		slider_l-cheek-inner-decr|incr		0.0000699
0.585	mouth: Cupid's bow width			0.0000926

Scottish male (n=16)

value	feature	feature	*	p
-0.831		mouth: Scale upperlip width	*	3.38E-08
-1.16		mouth: Scale lowerlip width	*	5.03E-07
-0.67		slider_l-eye-trans-in|out	*	7.32E-07
0.645	mouth: Dimples		*	1.72E-06
-0.751		slider_r-eye-trans-in|out		1.83E-06
1.21	chin: Scale chin height		*	6.09E-06
0.682	chin: Scale chin width		*	0.0000193
-1.41		mouth: Scale vertically	*	0.0000206
1.72	mouth: Scale lowerlip volume		*	0.0000226

Senegalese female (n=19)

value	feature	feature	*	p
1.47	mouth: Scale upperlip width		*	3.66E-13
1.32	mouth: Scale lowerlip width		*	5.05E-11
-1.12		chin: Scale chin height		5.29E-09
-1.03		mouth: Scale lowerlip volume	*	5.88E-09
-1.42		mouth: Laugh-lines	*	3.89E-08
-1.41		mouth: Dimples	*	6.44E-08
1.19	mouth: Scale vertically		*	7.69E-08
1.18	mouth: Scale horizontally		*	9.06E-07
0.679	nose: Septum Angle			9.44E-06
1.01	slider_r-cheek-inner-decr|incr		*	0.0000195
0.92	mouth: Scale lowerlip height		*	0.0000428

Senegalese male (n=24)

value	feature	feature	*	p
2.45	mouth: Scale lowerlip width		*	2.06E-15
2.25	mouth: Scale vertically		*	1.8E-14
2.08	mouth: Scale upperlip width		*	4E-14
-1.92		mouth: Scale lowerlip volume	*	2.12E-13
2.04	slider_l-eye-trans-in|out			4.03E-13
-1.76		nose-volume-decr|incr		8.17E-13
1.77	mouth: Scale lowerlip height		*	4.39E-12
-2.05		mouth: Dimples	*	4.69E-12
-1.9		chin: Scale chin height	*	6.32E-12
-1.54		mouth: Move vertically		1.17E-11
-1.77		mouth: Laugh-lines	*	3.57E-11
1.47	mouth: Scale horizontally		*	6.65E-11
1.86	slider_r-eye-trans-in|out			1.59E-10
1.61	slider_r-cheek-inner-decr|incr		*	2.34E-10
1.78	nose: Scale horizontally			1.86E-09
-0.935		nose-nostrils-angle-down|up		4.79E-09
-1.31		chin: Scale chin width		2.14E-08
0.976	slider_l-eye-eyefold-angle-down|up			3.37E-08
-1.02		nose: Scale vertically		5.06E-08
-1.06		eyebrows: Eyebrows bulge		6.07E-08
-1.28		slider_elvs_highchubbycheekbones1		1.4E-07
1.28	slider_l-cheek-inner-decr|incr			1.76E-07
0.986	forehead: Cranic shape			1.94E-07
1.41	chin: Cleft chin			2.61E-07
1.06	forehead: Scale vertically			4.65E-07
0.811	slider_r-eye-push1-in|out			6.07E-07
1.44	nose: Scale nostrils width			1.43E-06
0.762	slider_r-eye-eyefold-angle-down|up			1.63E-06
0.943	eyebrows: Eyebrows angle			1.83E-06
-0.928		nose-greek-decr|incr		1.84E-06
0.829	slider_l-eye-push1-in|out			2.32E-06
-1.01		forehead: Temple bulge		0.0000025
2.1	mouth: Move corners vert.			0.0000026
2.1	mouth: Move corners vert.			0.0000026
2.1	mouth: Move corners vert.			0.0000026
-0.984		slider_l-eye-trans-down|up		3.68E-06
0.854	slider_r-eye-corner2-down|up			8.02E-06
-0.912		slider_r-eye-trans-down|up		0.0000118
-0.721		nose: Move vertically		0.000016
0.781	mouth: Move depth			0.0000302
0.745	slider_l-eye-corner2-down|up			0.0000499
-0.905		nose: Middle nose bridge width		0.0000727
1.04	mouth: Scale upperlip height			0.0000777

Serbian female (n=29)

-0.807	nose: Scale nostrils width	2.13E-09
-0.736	slider_r-eye-eyefold-angle-down|up	7.1E-08
-0.773	slider_l-eye-eyefold-angle-down|up	8.36E-08
-0.448	forehead: Scale vertically	5.36E-06
-0.564	slider_l-cheek-inner-decr|incr	6.47E-06
-0.452	mouth: Scale lowerlip width	7.16E-06
-0.543	mouth: Scale upperlip width *	0.0000159
-0.555	nose: Scale horizontally	0.000027
-0.379	forehead: Cranic shape	0.0000508
0.585	mouth: Laugh-lines	0.0000932

Sicilian female (n=23)

-0.757	eyebrows: Eyebrows angle	1.72E-08
-0.61	slider_r-eye-eyefold-angle-down|up	1.08E-07
-0.504	mouth: Move corners vert.	1.05E-06
-0.532	mouth: Scale lowerlip width	2.58E-06
-0.596	slider_r-eye-epicanthus-in|out	0.0000104
0.709	nose-greek-decr|incr	0.0000114
-0.526	mouth: Scale vertically	0.0000141
0.656	nose: Move vertically	0.0000273
0.777	mouth: Cupid's bow shape	0.0000293
0.777	slider_l-eye-trans-down|up	0.0000678
-0.591	mouth: Scale lowerlip height	0.0000754
-0.659	slider_l-eye-trans-in|out	0.000078

Serbian male (n=30)

-0.628	mouth: Scale upperlip width *	2.41E-08
0.546	mouth: Dimples	4.29E-06
-0.559	slider_r-eye-trans-in|out	0.0000172
0.596	nose: Move vertically	0.0000201
0.585	chin: Scale chin width	0.0000261
-0.561	chin: Cleft chin	0.0000867

Sicilian male (no findings)

Sinhalese female (n=30)

0.824 mouth: Scale upperlip width			1.33E-10
-1.27	eyebrows: Move vert	*	4.04E-10
-1.14	slider_Nose_alar_crease	*	9.14E-10
1.06 nose: Scale vertically		*	1.12E-09
-1.19	slider_r-eye-bag-height-decr|incr		1.25E-09
1.09 slider_r-eye-push1-in|out		*	1.44E-09
1.17 eyes: Middle height of left eye		*	3.54E-09
-1.22	slider_eyes_outer_droop	*	7.91E-09
1.14 eyes: Inner height of left eye		*	1.47E-08
1.23 slider_l-eye-push1-in|out		*	1.49E-08
1.07 slider_l-eye-scale-decr|incr		*	1.57E-08
1.13 eyes: Middle height of right eye		*	2.04E-08
1.08 slider_r-eye-scale-decr|incr		*	3.86E-08
0.648 nose: Lower nose bridge width			6.02E-08
-1.01	slider_eyes_middle_droop		9.75E-08
-0.834	nose-hump-decr|incr		2.95E-07
-1.12	slider_l-eye-bag-height-decr|incr		3.94E-07
0.997 eyes: Inner height of right eye		*	5.25E-07
0.603 nose: Scale horizontally			5.82E-07
0.57 slider_l-eye-trans-in|out		*	6.21E-07
0.803 nose: Scale depth			8.71E-07
-0.567	mouth: Laugh-lines	*	0.0000021
-0.742	slider_nostril_rounding	*	3.41E-06
0.742 nose: Scale nostrils width			0.0000167
0.462 mouth: Scale lowerlip width			0.000026
0.571 slider_r-eye-trans-in|out			0.00003
-0.595	mouth: Scale upperlip volume		0.0000455
0.633 slider_l-cheek-inner-decr|incr			0.0000607
-0.572	mouth: Upperlip curved shape		0.0000623
0.831 slider_l-eye-corner1-down|up		*	0.0000634
0.523 eyebrows: Eyebrows bulge			0.000085

Sinhalese male (n=25)

1.02 slider_r-eye-scale-decr|incr		*	1.03E-09
1.02 eyes: Inner height of left eye		*	6.77E-09
1.03 eyes: Inner height of right eye		*	1.79E-08
0.983 eyes: Middle height of left eye		*	2.39E-08
0.951 slider_l-eye-scale-decr|incr		*	4.7E-08
1.03 eyes: Middle height of right eye		*	1.05E-07
0.984 nose: Scale vertically		*	4.04E-07
-0.868	slider_nostril_rounding	*	4.23E-07
0.868 slider_l-eye-trans-in|out		*	9.58E-07
-0.691	slider_Nose_alar_crease		3.07E-06
0.885 slider_r-eye-push1-in|out		*	3.16E-06
0.377 nose: Upper nose bridge width			0.0000111
-0.791	mouth: Scale middle upperlip		0.0000117
-0.791	mouth: Scale middle upperlip		0.0000117
-0.626	slider_eyes_outer_droop	*	0.0000152
0.857 slider_l-eye-push1-in|out		*	0.0000233
-0.751	eyebrows: Move vert	*	0.0000263
0.846 slider_l-eye-corner1-down|up		*	0.0000754

-0.523	mouth: Scale lowerlip volume		0.0000904
-0.428	mouth: Laugh-lines	*	0.0000967

Slovak female (n=16)

-0.697	eyebrows: Eyebrows angle	*	0.0000778
-0.697	eyebrows: Eyebrows angle	*	0.0000778

Slovak male (n=23)

-0.848	slider_r-eye-trans-in|out		9.17E-10
0.649 chin: Scale chin height			2.16E-08
-0.854	forehead: Scale vertically		8.14E-08
-0.616	mouth: Scale lowerlip width		1.06E-07
-0.893	mouth: Scale vertically		1.73E-07
-0.621	chin: Cleft chin		1.76E-07
-0.676	mouth: Scale upperlip width		2.69E-07
0.723 mouth: Scale lowerlip volume			3.16E-07
0.748 nose-greek-decr|incr			1.06E-06
-0.779	forehead: Cranic shape		4.29E-06
-0.771	slider_l-eye-trans-in|out		4.97E-06
-0.704	nose: Scale horizontally		5.01E-06
-0.699	nose: Scale nostrils width		7.11E-06
0.68 mouth: Dimples			7.79E-06
0.596 slider_l-eye-eyefold-down|up			9.82E-06
-0.627	slider_r-eye-scale-decr|incr		0.0000151
0.706 eyebrows: Eyebrows bulge			0.0000222
0.782 nose: Move vertically			0.0000423
-0.606	slider_r-cheek-bones-decr|incr		0.0000602
-0.618	eyes: Outer height of right eye		0.0000806
-0.505	mouth: Move corners vert.		0.0000828
-0.582	eyebrows: Eyebrows angle	*	0.0000901
-0.582	eyebrows: Eyebrows angle	*	0.0000901

Slovenian female (n=31)

-0.835	mouth: Scale vertically	*	3.42E-12
-0.711	mouth: Scale lowerlip width	*	3.07E-10
-0.743	mouth: Scale lowerlip height		5.18E-09
-0.959	slider_r-cheek-bones-decr|incr		5.92E-08
0.658 mouth: Scale lowerlip volume		*	4.05E-07
-0.597	eyebrows: Eyebrows angle		5.61E-07
-0.577	forehead: Scale vertically		2.12E-06
-0.86	chin: Scale chin prominence		5.58E-06
0.658 mouth: Move vertically		*	9.97E-06
-0.512	slider_r-eye-eyefold-angle-down|up		0.0000184
-0.531	forehead: Cranic shape		0.000021
0.492 mouth: Upperlip curved shape			0.0000346
-0.663	nose: Scale horizontally	*	0.0000875

Somali female (n=21)

1.64 mouth: Scale vertically		*	4.17E-13
1.61 mouth: Scale lowerlip width		*	6.32E-11
1.41 mouth: Scale lowerlip height			3.4E-09
-1.4	mouth: Scale lowerlip volume	*	8.39E-09
1.12 slider_r-cheek-inner-decr|incr		*	6.51E-08
-1.08	mouth: Upperlip curved shape	*	3.78E-07
-1.17	mouth: Scale upperlip volume	*	4.03E-07
1.32 slider_r-eye-push2-in|out		*	1.09E-06
1.01 mouth: Scale upperlip width		*	1.86E-06
0.924 chin: Scale chin prominence			2.69E-06
-1.05	slider_elvs_chipmunkcheeks_l1	*	4.38E-06
-1.03	nose: Move vertically	*	4.54E-06
0.97 mouth: Scale upperlip height		*	4.66E-06
1.19 eyebrows: Eyebrows angle		*	0.0000074
-1.13	nose-greek-decr|incr	*	0.0000143
-0.618	mouth: Cupid's bow shape	*	0.000037
0.857 eyes: Outer height of right eye		*	0.0000401
-0.487	chin: Scale chin width	*	0.0000466
0.791 slider_l-eye-bag-in|out			0.0000467
-0.777	mouth: Dimples	*	0.0000538
1.02 slider_Nose_alar_crease		*	0.0000543

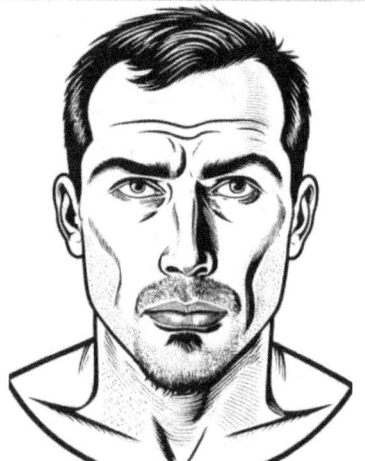

Slovenian male (n=28)

-0.915	nose: Scale nostrils width		8.45E-09
-0.78	slider_l-cheek-inner-decr|incr		4.46E-08
-0.747	nose: Scale horizontally	*	4.8E-08
-0.577	mouth: Scale lowerlip width	*	2.01E-07
-0.782	slider_r-eye-trans-in|out		2.53E-07
-0.643	mouth: Scale upperlip width		4.79E-07
-0.803	mouth: Scale vertically	*	9.18E-07
0.658 mouth: Laugh-lines			2.79E-06
0.55 mouth: Move vertically		*	2.88E-06
-0.684	slider_l-eye-trans-in|out		5.63E-06
0.705 mouth: Scale lowerlip volume		*	6.23E-06
0.49 chin: Scale chin height			0.0000241

Somali male (n=26)

-1.93	mouth: Scale lowerlip volume	*	1.43E-15
2.26 mouth: Scale vertically		*	1.94E-13
2.08 mouth: Scale lowerlip width		*	1.91E-12
1.84 mouth: Scale lowerlip height		*	1.23E-11
-1.19	nose: Move vertically	*	9.12E-11

1.47	slider_r-cheek-inner-decr|incr	*	9.16E-11
-1.24	mouth: Cupid's bow shape	*	8.07E-10
-0.959	nose-greek-decr|incr	*	2.83E-09
-1.63	mouth: Scale upperlip volume	*	5.9E-09
-1.62	mouth: Upperlip curved shape	*	7.18E-09
1.51	mouth: Scale upperlip height	*	2.77E-08
1.13	slider_l-eye-trans-in|out		4.72E-08
0.945	slider_Nose_alar_crease	*	1.27E-07
0.725	eyes: Middle height of left eye		2.62E-07
1.19	mouth: Scale upperlip width	*	2.86E-07
0.826	slider_r-eye-push2-in|out	*	5.36E-07
1.14	eyebrows: Eyebrows angle	*	6.54E-07
0.931	eyes: Middle height of right eye		8.39E-07
-1.08	chin: Scale chin height		8.95E-07
-0.704	forehead: Temple bulge		1.17E-06
-0.605	chin: Scale chin width	*	1.75E-06
0.88	slider_r-eye-scale-decr|incr		2.15E-06
-0.822	mouth: Dimples	*	2.25E-06
0.892	slider_r-eye-trans-in|out		2.61E-06
-1.07	nose: Scale depth		5.59E-06
-0.879	mouth: Move vertically		5.78E-06
-0.613	slider_l-eye-bag-decr|incr		7.49E-06
0.655	slider_l-eye-scale-decr|incr		0.0000115
0.758	eyes: Outer height of right eye	*	0.0000275
-0.935	mouth: Cupid's bow width		0.0000401
0.596	eyes: Outer height of left eye		0.0000441
0.593	slider_r-eye-corner2-down|up		0.0000484
0.684	eyes: Inner height of right eye		0.0000564
-0.544	slider_septum_sharp		0.000058
-0.771	slider_elvs_chipmunkcheeks_l1	*	0.0000655
0.851	chin: Scale chin prominence	*	0.0000773
0.453	slider_elvs_highchubbycheekbones1		0.0000861

South African female
(no findings)

South African[54] male (n=22)

-0.777	slider_l-eye-push2-in|out	0.0000013
0.863	slider_l-eye-trans-in|out	0.000036
-0.75	slider_Nose_alar_crease	0.0000585

Spanish female (n=14)

-0.983	slider_r-eye-eyefold-angle-down|up	7.45E-07

Spanish male (n=22)

-0.695	mouth: Move corners vert.	0.0000086
-0.695	mouth: Move corners vert.	0.0000086

---

[54] Overwhelmingly in research literature and sites of all sorts, people explicitly note whether they are referring to white or black South Africans. The AI's pre-built biases led it to not only produce black South African illustrations for this chapter, but also to produce primarily black training sets to begin with. Thus the stats in this book apply only to the (black) South African population.

Sudanese female (n=18)

-1.55	slider_r-eye-bag-height-decr|incr	*	5.28E-08
1.05	mouth: Scale vertically	*	6.96E-07
-1.17	nose: Move vertically	*	7.04E-07
1.08	mouth: Scale lowerlip width	*	9.65E-07
-0.922	mouth: Scale lowerlip volume	*	2.52E-06
-1.47	slider_l-eye-bag-height-decr|incr	*	4.04E-06
1.19	mouth: Scale upperlip width	*	5.15E-06
1.26	slider_r-eye-trans-in|out	*	0.0000122
-1.08	mouth: Scale upperlip volume	*	0.0000127
1.27	slider_l-eye-trans-in|out	*	0.0000139
-0.998	mouth: Laugh-lines	*	0.0000226
-0.862	mouth: Cupid's bow shape	*	0.0000283
-1.34	slider_eyes_outer_droop	*	0.0000445
-1.22	slider_Nose_alar_crease	*	0.0000477
1.03	nose: Scale horizontally	*	0.0000487
1.11	nose: Scale nostrils width	*	0.0000519
1.22	mouth: Scale middle lowerlip		0.0000538
-0.676	slider_l-cheek-trans-down|up		0.0000828

Sudanese male (n=20)

1.76	slider_l-eye-trans-in|out	*	2.78E-13
-1.27	mouth: Laugh-lines	*	2.14E-10
-1.63	mouth: Scale lowerlip volume	*	6.15E-09
1.53	mouth: Scale upperlip width	*	6.66E-09
1.37	slider_r-eye-trans-in|out	*	5.87E-08
-0.799	slider_elvs_highchubbycheekbones1		7.12E-08
0.988	slider_l-eye-push1-in|out		1.19E-07
1.54	mouth: Scale vertically	*	1.47E-07

-1	slider_l-eye-bag-height-decr|incr	*	1.04E-06
0.998	eyes: Middle height of right eye		1.07E-06
-1.18	slider_r-eye-bag-height-decr|incr	*	0.0000013
0.933	slider_r-eye-push1-in|out		6.97E-06
0.811	eyes: Middle height of left eye		7.79E-06
-1.04	mouth: Dimples		8.08E-06
-0.928	nose: Move vertically	*	8.99E-06
-1.25	mouth: Scale upperlip volume	*	0.0000148
0.723	mouth: Scale horizontally		0.0000155
-1.2	chin: Scale chin height		0.0000264
1.34	mouth: Scale lowerlip width	*	0.0000269
0.933	nose: Scale nostrils width	*	0.000027
0.947	nose: Scale horizontally	*	0.0000384
-0.581	slider_eyes_outer_droop	*	0.0000385
1.21	mouth: Scale upperlip height		0.0000466
-0.932	mouth: Cupid's bow shape	*	0.0000504
-0.542	nose-greek-decr|incr		0.0000761
-0.79	slider_Nose_alar_crease	*	0.0000772

Swedish female (n=21)

-1.01	forehead: Scale vertically	*	5.15E-12
-1.02	mouth: Scale vertically	*	6.37E-11
-0.955	forehead: Cranic shape	*	8.8E-11
-0.867	chin: Cleft chin	*	3.46E-08
-1.01	chin: Scale chin prominence		5.06E-08
-0.813	mouth: Scale lowerlip height	*	7.76E-08
-0.8	chin: Scale chin prognathism		2.55E-07
-1.12	nose: Scale horizontally	*	3.16E-07
0.833	mouth: Upperlip curved shape		5.29E-07
-0.887	slider_l-cheek-inner-decr|incr	*	8.77E-08
0.707	slider_eyes_outer_droop		1.18E-06
1.27	mouth: Cupid's bow width		1.22E-06
0.805	nose: Move vertically	*	1.74E-06
-0.825	mouth: Scale upperlip height	*	3.32E-06
0.886	mouth: Scale lowerlip volume	*	3.38E-06
-0.674	nose: Scale nostrils width		4.43E-06
-0.844	slider_r-cheek-volume-decr|incr		0.0000114
0.53	eyebrows: Eyebrows bulge		0.0000183
-0.798	slider_l-cheek-volume-decr|incr		0.0000328
-0.725	mouth: Move corners vert.		0.000037
0.784	nose: Move nose base vert.		0.0000394
0.679	slider_Nose_alar_crease		0.0000418
0.549	chin: Scale chin height	*	0.000043
0.912	slider_l-cheek-trans-down|up		0.0000607
0.603	slider_eyes_middle_droop		0.0000993

Swedish male (n=21)

-0.983	nose: Scale horizontally	*	9.22E-09
-1.4	mouth: Scale vertically	*	6.34E-08
-0.92	mouth: Scale lowerlip width		2.86E-07
-1.11	mouth: Scale lowerlip height	*	6.47E-07
0.829 chin: Scale chin height		*	1.34E-06
-0.611	slider_r-eye-trans-in|out		3.45E-06
-0.684	forehead: Scale vertically	*	4.29E-06
-0.71	forehead: Cranic shape	*	7.92E-06
-0.631	mouth: Scale upperlip width		0.0000105
-0.866	slider_r-cheek-bones-decr|incr		0.0000107
0.668 nose: Move vertically		*	0.0000235
-0.721	chin: Cleft chin	*	0.0000303
-0.798	slider_l-cheek-inner-decr|incr	*	0.0000374
1.66 mouth: Scale lowerlip volume		*	0.0000417
1.28 mouth: Scale upperlip volume			0.0000744
-1.18	mouth: Scale upperlip height	*	0.000078

Swiss male (n=21)

-0.888	slider_l-cheek-inner-decr|incr		1.98E-06
-0.883	nose: Scale nostrils width		0.0000316
-0.732	chin: Scale chin prominence	*	0.0000498

Syrian female (n=28)

-0.974	eyebrows: Move vert		4.42E-08
1.11 slider_l-eye-scale-decr|incr		*	5.65E-08
0.972 slider_r-eye-scale-decr|incr			9.58E-08
0.959 slider_r-eye-push2-in|out		*	1.54E-07
0.979 slider_l-eye-push2-in|out		*	1.47E-06
0.859 mouth: Cupid's bow shape		*	3.58E-06
-0.916	slider_r-eye-eyefold-down|up		5.87E-06
-0.957	slider_eyes_outer_droop		6.41E-06
0.982 eyes: Inner height of left eye		*	7.52E-06
-0.86	slider_r-eye-eyefold-angle-down|up	*	0.0000108
0.519 slider_l-eye-push1-in|out			0.0000122
0.844 eyes: Middle height of left eye			0.0000422
0.874 eyes: Inner height of right eye		*	0.0000457

Swiss female (n=21)

-0.984	mouth: Scale vertically		1.5E-09
-0.745	mouth: Scale lowerlip width		8.6E-09
-0.776	forehead: Scale vertically		2.04E-08
1.16 mouth: Move vertically			8.18E-08
-0.966	mouth: Scale lowerlip height		1.16E-07
-0.655	forehead: Cranic shape		2.66E-07
0.608 eyebrows: Eyebrows bulge			0.0000127
0.777 mouth: Scale lowerlip volume			0.0000134
-0.683	chin: Cleft chin		0.0000155
-0.777	chin: Scale chin prominence	*	0.0000756
-0.719	nose: Scale horizontally		0.0000818

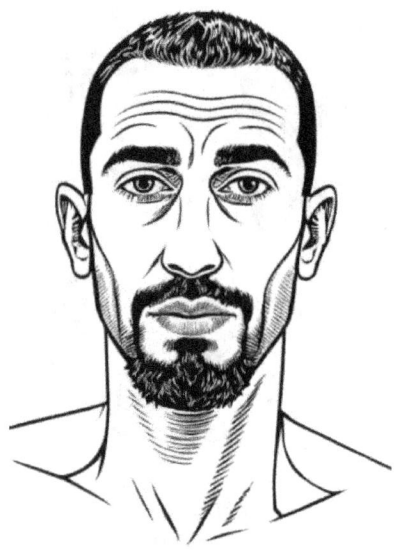

Syrian male (n=30)

value	label	sig	p
0.791	eyes: Inner height of left eye	*	4.03E-08
0.724	slider_l-eye-scale-decr|incr	*	2.02E-07
0.755	slider_l-eye-push2-in|out	*	2.29E-06
0.696	slider_r-eye-push2-in|out	*	4.28E-06
0.875	nose: Lower nose bridge width		4.34E-06
0.74	eyes: Inner height of right eye	*	5.13E-06
-0.566	slider_l-eye-trans-in|out		5.75E-06
0.659	nose: Scale vertically		0.0000246
-0.622	slider_r-eye-eyefold-angle-down|up	*	0.0000535
0.819	mouth: Cupid's bow shape	*	0.0000649
0.546	nose-nostrils-angle-down|up		0.0000693

Taiwanese female (n=29)

value	label	sig	p
2.18	slider_Nose_alar_crease	*	9.42E-17
-2.42	nose-greek-decr|incr	*	3.31E-15
-1.91	nose: Scale vertically	*	6.25E-15
-1.66	eyebrows: Eyebrows bulge	*	8.63E-15
1.89	forehead: Scale vertically	*	1.58E-14
1.88	forehead: Cranic shape	*	4.48E-14
-1.06	mouth: Scale upperlip width	*	1.69E-13
2.17	eyebrows: Eyebrows angle	*	3.53E-13
-1.14	mouth: Move vertically	*	2.68E-12
-1.49	nose: Scale depth	*	2.71E-12
-1.36	nose: Move depth	*	3.02E-12
-1.58	nose: Lower nose bridge width	*	4.86E-12
1.29	nose-hump-decr|incr		6.69E-10
1.05	eyes: Outer height of right eye	*	1.42E-09

value	label	sig	p
-1.39	mouth: Scale philtrum volume	*	2.34E-09
-1.17	nose: Scale nostrils flaring	*	2.57E-09
0.912	eyes: Outer height of left eye		4.28E-09
-0.974	forehead: Temple bulge		3.98E-08
1.12	mouth: Move corners vert.		6.76E-08
-1	chin: Tone of side chin		8.59E-08
1.13	mouth: Scale upperlip volume	*	1.8E-07
0.919	slider_eyes_middle_droop	*	6.57E-07
-0.881	mouth: Scale horizontally	*	7.6E-07
0.665	slider_eyes_outer_droop	*	7.85E-07
-0.786	mouth: Move depth		2.09E-06
0.851	mouth: Upperlip curved shape		2.21E-06
0.781	mouth: Scale middle upperlip	*	4.07E-06
-0.723	nose: Move nose base vert.		4.32E-06
-0.751	slider_r-eye-trans-down|up	*	4.63E-06
-0.873	nose: Move vertically	*	4.78E-06
-1.3	nose: Middle nose bridge width	*	6.71E-06
-0.735	mouth: Scale upperlip height		7.24E-06
0.572	mouth: Laugh-lines	*	0.000035
-0.69	slider_r-eye-bag-decr|incr		0.0000407
-0.605	slider_r-eye-scale-decr|incr	*	0.0000409
-0.551	slider_l-eye-trans-down|up	*	0.0000606
-0.665	slider_l-eye-bag-decr|incr		0.0000617
0.661	slider_r-eye-corner2-down|up	*	0.0000742
-0.338	mouth: Scale lowerlip width	*	0.0000825

Taiwanese male (n=36)

value	label	sig	p
1.25	slider_eyes_outer_droop	*	1.35E-18
-1.47	nose: Lower nose bridge width	*	1.65E-16
-0.885	mouth: Scale upperlip width	*	2.27E-16
-1.44	eyebrows: Eyebrows bulge	*	2.79E-15
0.961	slider_eyes_middle_droop	*	6.31E-15
-1.17	slider_r-eye-push1-in|out		7.39E-14
-0.925	slider_r-eye-scale-decr|incr	*	3.74E-13
1.45	slider_Nose_alar_crease	*	1.63E-12
-0.848	slider_l-eye-scale-decr|incr		3.57E-12
1.22	forehead: Scale vertically	*	8.76E-12
-0.847	slider_l-eye-push1-in|out		1.28E-11
-1.01	nose: Scale nostrils flaring	*	1.92E-11
-0.943	nose: Scale depth	*	3.69E-11
-1.11	nose: Scale vertically	*	8.4E-11
-1.31	nose-greek-decr|incr	*	8.49E-11
1.21	forehead: Cranic shape	*	1.44E-10
-0.768	slider_r-eye-trans-down|up	*	6.44E-10
0.806	mouth: Scale middle upperlip		1.78E-09
0.845	slider_l-eye-epicanthus-in|out		2.08E-09
0.627	mouth: Laugh-lines		1.05E-08
-1.1	nose: Middle nose bridge width	*	1.21E-08
0.608	slider_l-eye-eyefold-angle-down|up		1.55E-08
0.644	slider_l-eye-bag-height-decr|incr		3.24E-08
-0.621	nose: Scale nostrils width		4.78E-08
-0.519	eyes: Middle height of left eye		5.04E-08
0.911	slider_nostril_rounding		9.36E-08

Value	Description		p
1.12	eyebrows: Eyebrows angle	*	1.38E-07
-0.613	slider_l-eye-trans-in|out		1.84E-07
-0.656	mouth: Scale horizontally	*	2.38E-07
0.505	eyes: Outer height of right eye	*	2.46E-07
-0.632	mouth: Move vertically	*	5.34E-07
0.629	slider_r-eye-corner2-down|up	*	1.01E-06
-0.612	slider_r-eye-trans-in|out		0.0000012
-0.606	slider_l-eye-trans-down|up	*	1.54E-06
0.467	slider_l-eye-bag-in|out		1.65E-06
0.402	mouth: Scale lowerlip volume		2.19E-06
-0.568	slider_r-eye-corner1-down|up		0.0000028
-0.318	mouth: Scale lowerlip width	*	2.84E-06
-0.672	nose: Scale horizontally		2.99E-06
-0.515	nose: Move vertically	*	3.16E-06
0.473	slider_elvs_highchubbycheekbones1		4.08E-06
0.852	mouth: Scale upperlip volume	*	5.64E-06
-0.361	eyes: Middle height of right eye		5.84E-06
-0.773	mouth: Scale philtrum volume	*	7.24E-06
0.469	slider_l-eye-eyefold-down|up		0.0000086
0.453	slider_r-eye-bag-in|out		0.0000297
0.551	eyebrows: Move vert		0.0000341
0.426	slider_r-eye-bag-height-decr|incr		0.0000373
0.542	slider_l-eye-corner2-down|up		0.0000475
-0.409	slider_r-cheek-bones-decr|incr		0.0000485
-0.657	nose: Move depth	*	0.0000792

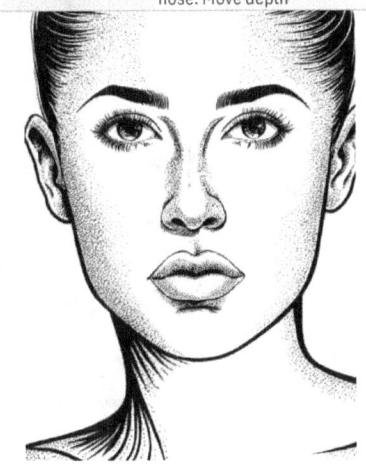

Tajik female (n=19)

Value	Description		p
-1.23	slider_r-eye-trans-in|out	*	8.45E-09
-1.29	slider_l-eye-trans-in|out	*	1.05E-06
0.566	slider_l-eye-bag-height-decr|incr		0.0000791

Tajik male (n=32)

Value	Description		p
-1.04	slider_r-eye-trans-in|out	*	1.75E-11
-1.17	slider_l-eye-trans-in|out	*	8.93E-11
1.18	nose: Lower nose bridge width		1.55E-10
0.956	nose: Scale vertically		4.91E-08
0.856	chin: Scale chin width		9.71E-07
0.814	eyebrows: Eyebrows bulge		1.66E-06
-0.689	mouth: Scale lowerlip width		2.91E-06
0.675	nose: Middle nose bridge width		4.53E-06
0.601	forehead: Forehead bulge		6.53E-06
-0.555	forehead: Scale vertically		9.25E-06
-0.77	slider_l-eye-bag-in|out		9.75E-06
-0.582	chin: Cleft chin		0.0000107
-0.443	slider_r-eye-push1-in|out		0.0000127
0.895	slider_r-eye-trans-down|up		0.0000135
0.639	slider_elvs_highchubbycheekbones1		0.0000136
-0.517	eyebrows: Eyebrows angle		0.0000223
0.72	chin: Scale chin height		0.0000225
0.523	nose-greek-decr|incr		0.000024
-0.814	slider_r-eye-bag-in|out		0.0000257
0.713	slider_r-eye-bag-height-decr|incr		0.0000385
-0.587	slider_r-eye-eyefold-angle-down|up		0.0000401
-0.57	eyes: Outer height of right eye		0.0000523
-0.63	mouth: Scale lowerlip height		0.0000561
0.755	slider_r-eye-corner1-down|up		0.0000801
-0.639	mouth: Move corners vert.		0.0000955

Tamil female (n=28)

Value	Description	Slider		p-value
1.37	nose: Scale vertically		*	4.45E-14
-1.49		eyebrows: Move vert	*	3.85E-12
1.25	slider_l-eye-push1-in|out		*	7.29E-12
1.43	slider_r-eye-scale-decr|incr		*	8.04E-12
1.33	slider_l-eye-scale-decr|incr		*	1.43E-11
-0.975		mouth: Scale upperlip volume	*	2.2E-11
1.2	eyes: Inner height of left eye		*	2.86E-11
1.17	eyes: Inner height of right eye		*	4.42E-11
-1.05		mouth: Upperlip curved shape		2.66E-10
1.14	eyes: Middle height of left eye		*	5.53E-10
-1.15		slider_eyes_outer_droop	*	1.72E-09
-1.09		slider_l-eye-bag-height-decr|incr	*	1.91E-09
1.21	mouth: Scale upperlip height		*	3E-09
-1.25		slider_l-eye-eyefold-down|up	*	3.85E-09
-1.02		slider_l-eye-eyefold-angle-down|up		5.29E-09
0.794	nose-nostrils-angle-down|up			8.54E-09
1.09	eyes: Middle height of right eye		*	1.03E-08
-1.01		slider_r-eye-bag-height-decr|incr	*	1.05E-08
0.591	mouth: Scale vertically			2.05E-08
1.34	slider_r-eye-push1-in|out		*	2.13E-08
0.554	nose-greek-decr|incr		*	2.37E-08
0.696	mouth: Scale upperlip width			3.19E-08
0.535	mouth: Scale lowerlip width			4.18E-08
1.4	mouth: Scale philtrum volume		*	4.99E-08
-0.867		slider_eyes_middle_droop	*	2.89E-07
0.662	nose: Lower nose bridge width			5.37E-07
-1.09		slider_l-eye-epicanthus-in|out	*	8.76E-07
-0.749		slider_Nose_alar_crease	*	1.43E-06
-0.86		nose-hump-decr|incr	*	0.0000021
0.911	slider_l-eye-corner1-down|up		*	2.22E-06
-0.552		nose: Septum Angle	*	3.33E-06
0.886	slider_r-eye-corner1-down|up			4.29E-06
0.71	nose: Move depth		*	4.45E-06
0.757	nose: Scale depth		*	7.81E-06
-0.436		eyebrows: Eyebrows angle	*	0.0000224
0.649	mouth: Scale lowerlip height			0.0000267
0.561	mouth: Move vertically			0.0000401
0.784	slider_l-eye-push2-in|out			0.0000421
0.759	slider_r-eye-push2-in|out			0.000067
-0.595		slider_nostril_rounding	*	0.0000774
-0.709		mouth: Cupid's bow width		0.0000869
-0.335		mouth: Scale lowerlip volume		0.0000976

Tamil male (n=30)

Value	Description	Slider		p-value
-0.954		slider_Nose_alar_crease	*	4.24E-15
-0.871		slider_nostril_rounding	*	3.22E-13
1.25	eyes: Inner height of left eye		*	6.56E-13
0.907	slider_r-eye-trans-in|out			1.1E-11
1.13	slider_l-eye-scale-decr|incr		*	4.48E-11
1.21	eyes: Inner height of right eye		*	4.98E-11
-1.37		slider_r-eye-bag-height-decr|incr	*	8.54E-11
1.14	slider_r-eye-scale-decr|incr		*	1.67E-10
1.22	eyes: Middle height of left eye		*	2.33E-10
1.03	nose: Scale vertically		*	3.87E-10
-0.608		eyebrows: Eyebrows angle	*	5.41E-10
0.988	slider_l-eye-push1-in|out		*	6.22E-10
1.26	eyes: Middle height of right eye		*	9.33E-10
-1.06		eyebrows: Move vert	*	1.4E-09
-1.09		slider_l-eye-bag-height-decr|incr	*	2.42E-09
-1.01		slider_eyes_outer_droop	*	2.82E-09
0.71	slider_r-eye-push1-in|out		*	3.43E-09
1.07	mouth: Scale philtrum volume		*	4.45E-08
0.766	slider_l-eye-trans-in|out			5.6E-09
-0.774		nose-hump-decr|incr	*	1.13E-07
0.856	nose: Move depth		*	4.86E-07
1.18	slider_r-eye-bag-decr|incr			5.45E-07
-0.849		slider_eyes_middle_droop		6.95E-07
-0.465		slider_l-eye-epicanthus-in|out	*	1.09E-06
0.404	nose-greek-decr|incr		*	1.11E-06
-0.536		slider_r-eye-eyefold-down|up		1.13E-06
0.904	chin: Tone of side chin			2.18E-06
0.961	slider_l-eye-bag-decr|incr			2.46E-06
0.873	slider_r-eye-corner2-down|up			3.51E-06
0.842	slider_l-eye-corner2-down|up			0.0000061
0.864	mouth: Scale upperlip height			0.0000102
-0.59		slider_l-eye-eyefold-down|up		0.0000102
0.528	forehead: Temple bulge			0.0000111
0.777	nose: Scale depth		*	0.0000166
0.733	mouth: Move depth			0.0000195
-0.604		nose: Septum Angle	*	0.0000619
-0.737		mouth: Scale upperlip volume	*	0.0000676
0.509	slider_l-eye-corner1-down|up		*	0.0000684
0.393	nose: Scale nostrils width			0.0000782

Thai female (n=17)

-1.12	mouth: Move vertically	*	9.26E-06
0.752	mouth: Scale middle upperlip		0.0000838

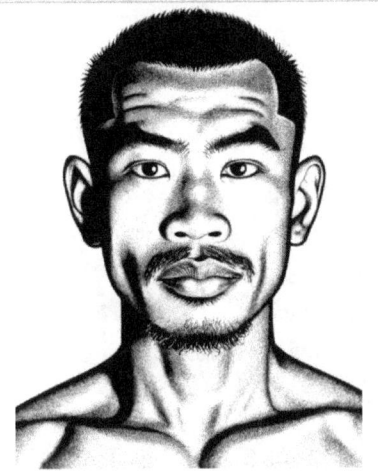

Thai male (n=17)

1.18	slider_eyes_outer_droop		9.02E-10
-0.674	slider_r-eye-scale-decr|incr		1.17E-08
-0.791	slider_l-eye-scale-decr|incr		4.29E-07
0.929	slider_eyes_middle_droop		7.68E-07
-1.03	nose: Lower nose bridge width		9.15E-07
-0.659	eyes: Middle height of left eye		0.0000011
-1.12	mouth: Move vertically	*	1.25E-06
-1.05	nose: Scale vertically		2.26E-06
-0.541	eyes: Middle height of right eye		8.27E-06
-0.779	nose: Scale nostrils flaring		0.0000177
1.12	slider_Nose_alar_crease		0.0000194
0.598	slider_r-eye-bag-in|out		0.0000343
-0.52	nose: Scale nostrils width		0.0000375

Tibetan female (n=26)

-1.91	slider_l-eye-scale-decr|incr	*	2.56E-15
2.1	slider_eyes_outer_droop	*	3.76E-13
-1.92	eyes: Middle height of right eye	*	1.98E-12
-1.8	eyes: Middle height of left eye	*	8.76E-12
-1.53	slider_l-eye-push2-in|out		1.74E-11
-1.8	slider_r-eye-scale-decr|incr		2.77E-11
1.51	slider_eyes_middle_droop	*	3.77E-11
-1.52	eyes: Outer height of right eye	*	8.69E-11
0.836	chin: Scale chin width		1.08E-10
-1.53	eyes: Outer height of left eye	*	1.59E-10
-0.668	mouth: Scale horizontally		3.26E-10
-0.704	mouth: Scale lowerlip width		3.8E-10
-1.61	slider_r-eye-push2-in|out	*	5.74E-10
1.22	slider_r-eye-bag-height-decr|incr		1.03E-09
-1.56	eyes: Inner height of left eye	*	2.06E-09
0.539	nose: Upper nose bridge width		2.06E-09
-0.565	mouth: Scale upperlip width		9.37E-09
0.729	mouth: Dimples		1.09E-08
-1.54	eyes: Inner height of right eye		3.38E-08
0.904	slider_elvs_highchubbycheekbones1		4.16E-08
-0.495	mouth: Scale vertically		4.6E-08
1.01	slider_l-eye-bag-height-decr|incr		9.38E-08
-0.69	chin: Scale chin prognathism		6.59E-07
0.932	slider_l-eye-eyefold-angle-down|up		0.0000022
0.917	eyebrows: Move vert	*	3.49E-06
-0.796	slider_r-cheek-trans-down|up		3.57E-06
-0.628	nose: Scale tip width		5.76E-06
0.715	nose-nostrils-angle-down|up	*	7.85E-06
-0.731	slider_r-eye-bag-in|out		8.71E-06
0.717	slider_l-eye-corner1-down|up		0.0000088
0.717	slider_l-eye-corner1-down|up		0.0000088
0.882	slider_r-eye-corner1-down|up		9.24E-06
-1.03	nose: Move nose base vert.		0.0000113
0.527	nose: Middle nose bridge width		0.0000115
-0.591	mouth: Scale lowerlip height		0.0000197
-0.566	mouth: Scale upperlip height		0.0000466
-0.978	slider_l-eye-bag-in|out		0.0000526
-0.932	slider_l-eye-push1-in|out		0.0000698
0.684	nose: Lower nose bridge width		0.0000805

Tibetan male (n=15)

1.79 slider_eyes_outer_droop		*	9.18E-08
-1.34	eyes: Middle height of left eye	*	3.21E-07
-0.802	eyes: Outer height of right eye	*	4.21E-07
1.55 slider_eyes_middle_droop		*	4.59E-07
-1.38	eyes: Middle height of right eye	*	5.46E-07
1.08 eyebrows: Move vert		*	4.38E-06
-1.17	slider_l-eye-scale-decr|incr	*	4.48E-06
-0.845	eyes: Outer height of left eye		0.0000138
0.945 nose-nostrils-angle-down|up		*	0.000026
-0.957	slider_r-eye-push2-in|out	*	0.0000662
-1.11	eyes: Inner height of left eye	*	0.0000936

Trinidadian male (n=32)

-1	mouth: Dimples	*	1.84E-12
-0.903	mouth: Laugh-lines	*	5.25E-12
-1.04	mouth: Scale lowerlip volume	*	2.55E-10
0.97 slider_l-eye-trans-in|out		*	3.5E-10
0.762 mouth: Scale horizontally		*	4.33E-10
0.876 mouth: Scale upperlip width		*	5.65E-10
-0.971	chin: Scale chin height		7.97E-09
0.784 nose: Scale nostrils width		*	1.94E-08
0.932 slider_r-cheek-inner-decr|incr			4.32E-08
-0.803	slider_elvs_highchubbycheekbones1		4.4E-08
0.886 slider_r-eye-trans-in|out			5.15E-08
1.08 mouth: Scale lowerlip width		*	6.67E-08
0.971 mouth: Scale vertically		*	8.36E-08
-0.864	mouth: Move vertically		8.76E-08
-0.94	nose-nostrils-angle-down|up		3.75E-07
0.912 nose: Scale horizontally			8.47E-07
0.846 slider_r-eye-push1-in|out			3.89E-06
-0.738	nose-volume-decr|incr		5.79E-06
0.744 mouth: Move corners vert.			8.05E-06
-0.54	forehead: Temple bulge		0.0000268
-0.573	slider_Nose_alar_crease		0.0000762
0.604 slider_r-eye-scale-decr|incr			0.0000863
0.609 chin: Cleft chin			0.0000968

Trinidadian female (n=13)

1.09 mouth: Scale upperlip width		*	1.36E-08
0.881 nose: Scale nostrils width		*	0.0000011
-0.987	mouth: Scale lowerlip volume	*	3.14E-06
0.972 mouth: Scale vertically		*	5.75E-06
-1.29	mouth: Dimples	*	0.0000124
-0.948	mouth: Laugh-lines	*	0.0000145
1.08 mouth: Scale lowerlip width		*	0.0000234
0.851 slider_l-eye-trans-in|out		*	0.0000267
1.08 mouth: Scale horizontally		*	0.0000608

Turkish female (n=21)

1.07 slider_l-eye-scale-decr|incr		*	7.14E-08
1.19 slider_l-eye-push2-in|out		*	1.13E-07
1.35 slider_r-eye-push2-in|out		*	1.26E-07

-0.921		slider_r-eye-eyefold-angle-down|up		1.68E-06
0.882	slider_r-eye-scale-decr|incr			1.99E-06
-1.1		slider_r-eye-epicanthus-in|out		0.0000219
-0.565		nose: Scale nostrils width		0.0000741

Turkish male (n=27)

-0.649		slider_l-eye-trans-in|out		1.89E-08
0.829	slider_l-eye-push2-in|out		*	2.37E-06
0.832	slider_r-eye-push2-in|out		*	4.98E-06
0.702	slider_l-eye-scale-decr|incr		*	0.0000953

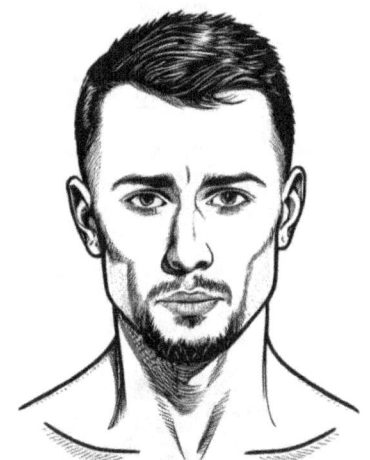

Ukrainian male (n=14)

-0.865		slider_l-eye-trans-in|out		9.87E-07
0.816	mouth: Laugh-lines		*	1.22E-06
-0.696		mouth: Scale upperlip width	*	3.03E-06
-0.768		slider_r-eye-trans-in|out		0.0000035
0.746	mouth: Dimples			3.91E-06
-0.797		nose: Scale nostrils width	*	5.28E-06
-0.738		chin: Scale chin angular	*	0.0000107
0.992	forehead: Temple bulge		*	0.0000125
-0.609		mouth: Scale horizontally		0.0000596

Ukrainian female (n=27)

-0.803		mouth: Scale upperlip width	*	6.08E-09
-1.06		nose: Scale nostrils width	*	1.62E-08
0.915	mouth: Laugh-lines		*	1.06E-07
-0.625		forehead: Scale vertically		3.03E-07
-0.759		chin: Scale chin angular	*	1.08E-06
-0.814		nose: Scale horizontally		1.56E-06
0.631	nose: Upper nose bridge width			2.77E-06
-0.554		forehead: Cranic shape		3.36E-06
-0.392		mouth: Scale lowerlip width		7.52E-06
-0.471		mouth: Move corners vert.		0.0000182
-0.569		nose: Septum Angle		0.0000216
-0.655		slider_l-cheek-inner-decr|incr		0.0000317
-0.711		slider_r-eye-push1-in|out		0.0000434
0.4	chin: Scale chin height			0.0000659
0.925	forehead: Temple bulge		*	0.0000678
-0.41		mouth: Scale vertically		0.0000734
-0.593		slider_r-cheek-bones-decr|incr		0.0000911

Uruguayan female (n=25)

1.31	slider_l-eye-corner1-down|up		4.1E-10
-0.978		slider_r-eye-eyefold-angle-down|up	4.93E-10
1.2	slider_l-eye-trans-down|up		2.66E-09
1	slider_r-eye-trans-down|up		1.02E-08
1.02	slider_r-eye-corner1-down|up		3.76E-08
-1.02		slider_r-eye-corner2-down|up	7.3E-08
1.3	chin: Scale chin prominence		7.33E-08
1.13	chin: Scale chin angular		8.65E-07
-1.07		slider_l-eye-corner2-down|up	1.36E-06
1.04	chin: Scale chin width		1.92E-06
-0.976		slider_l-eye-eyefold-angle-down|up	2.18E-06
-0.575		slider_r-eye-epicanthus-in|out	2.51E-06
0.538	eyebrows: Eyebrows bulge		3.53E-06
1	slider_r-eye-eyefold-concave|convex		4.48E-06
-0.767		slider_r-eye-bag-decr|incr	4.74E-06

-0.942	slider_l-eye-bag-decr|incr		7.88E-06
-0.862	nose: Move nose base vert.		8.52E-06
0.655	slider_elvs_highchubbycheekbones1		8.62E-06
-0.752	mouth: Scale lowerlip width		0.0000121
0.769	slider_septum_sharp		0.0000149
-0.587	slider_r-eye-eyefold-down|up		0.000015
-0.87	mouth: Move depth		0.0000313
-0.719	nose: Move depth		0.0000367
0.748	slider_nose crease extra1		0.0000378
0.603	nose: Scale vertically	*	0.0000492
-0.757	mouth: Scale philtrum volume		0.000051
0.79	chin: Scale chin height		0.0000697
-0.684	slider_eyes_middle_droop		0.00009
0.535	slider_l-eye-push1-in|out		0.0000997

Uruguayan male (n=23)

0.536	nose: Scale vertically	*	0.0000112

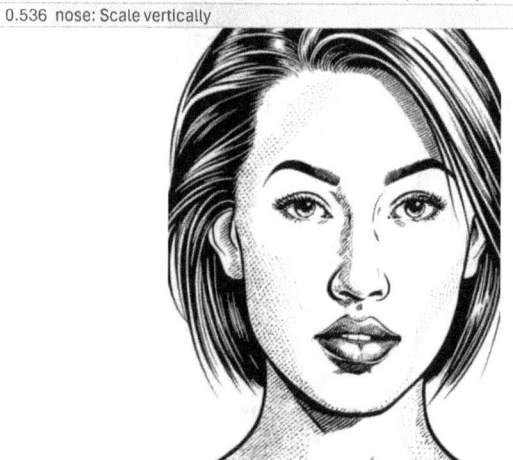

Uzbek female (n=25)

-1.39	slider_l-eye-trans-in|out	*	3.32E-13
0.718	chin: Scale chin width		9.16E-11
-1.29	slider_r-eye-trans-in|out	*	2.02E-10
1.47	slider_eyes_outer_droop	*	9.87E-10
1.15	nose-nostrils-angle-down|up		2.85E-08
1.01	slider_eyes_middle_droop	*	7.45E-08
0.845	slider_l-eye-bag-height-decr|incr	*	1.54E-07
-1.12	eyes: Middle height of left eye	*	2.57E-07
0.943	mouth: Scale philtrum volume	*	5.95E-07

-1.11	eyes: Middle height of right eye	*	1.46E-06
1.03	nose: Scale vertically		0.0000036
-0.759	mouth: Scale horizontally	*	4.38E-06
0.626	slider_r-eye-bag-height-decr|incr	*	5.45E-06
-0.89	slider_r-eye-scale-decr|incr	*	5.63E-06
-0.899	slider_l-eye-scale-decr|incr	*	9.59E-06
0.688	mouth: Dimples	*	0.0000552
-0.824	eyes: Outer height of left eye		0.000087

Uzbek male (n=22)

-1.25	slider_l-eye-trans-in|out	*	9.55E-11
1.1	eyebrows: Move vert		1.47E-09
0.902	slider_eyes_outer_droop	*	4E-08
0.966	slider_elvs_highchubbycheekbones1		4.81E-08
-0.927	slider_r-eye-trans-in|out	*	3.1E-07
-0.823	eyes: Middle height of right eye	*	9.89E-07
-0.598	mouth: Scale horizontally	*	1.34E-06
-0.702	slider_r-cheek-trans-down|up		1.43E-06
0.6	mouth: Dimples	*	1.72E-06
0.749	slider_eyes_middle_droop	*	3.03E-06
-0.697	nose: Scale tip width		3.36E-06
-0.682	slider_l-eye-scale-decr|incr	*	4.03E-06
-0.75	slider_r-eye-scale-decr|incr	*	5.56E-06
-0.667	eyes: Middle height of left eye	*	7.53E-06
-0.726	slider_l-eye-push1-in|out		0.0000127
0.768	forehead: Temple bulge		0.000015
-0.814	slider_r-eye-push1-in|out		0.0000156
0.614	slider_r-eye-bag-height-decr|incr	*	0.0000196
0.476	nose: Upper nose bridge width		0.0000199
0.806	mouth: Scale philtrum volume	*	0.0000453
-0.573	eyes: Outer height of right eye		0.0000527
0.556	slider_l-eye-bag-height-decr|incr	*	0.0000538

Venezuelan female (n=22)

-0.763	mouth: Move vertically		1.05E-06
0.794	nose: Scale horizontally		0.0000108
-0.794	eyebrows: Move vert		0.0000199

Venezuelan male (n=24)

0.708	slider_r-eye-trans-in|out		4.54E-06
0.684	slider_l-eye-push1-in|out		0.0000177
0.742	slider_r-eye-push1-in|out		0.0000182
0.683	slider_l-cheek-inner-decr|incr		0.0000243
-0.878	forehead: Temple bulge		0.0000287
0.846	slider_r-eye-corner1-down|up		0.0000972

Vietnamese female (n=22)

-1.33	mouth: Move vertically	*	9.5E-10
-0.861	mouth: Scale upperlip width	*	4.64E-07
0.73	forehead: Scale vertically		1.43E-06
-1.08	mouth: Scale horizontally	*	2.27E-06
-0.809	slider_r-cheek-trans-down|up		5.75E-06
0.612	forehead: Cranic shape		6.11E-06
0.924	mouth: Scale middle upperlip	*	0.0000115
-0.695	eyebrows: Eyebrows bulge	*	0.0000118
0.814	mouth: Move corners vert.		0.0000221
0.823	chin: Cleft chin	*	0.0000322
-0.695	slider_l-cheek-trans-down|up		0.0000351
0.751	slider_r-cheek-volume-decr|incr		0.0000474
-0.825	nose: Lower nose bridge width	*	0.0000587
0.725	slider_Nose_alar_crease	*	0.0000694

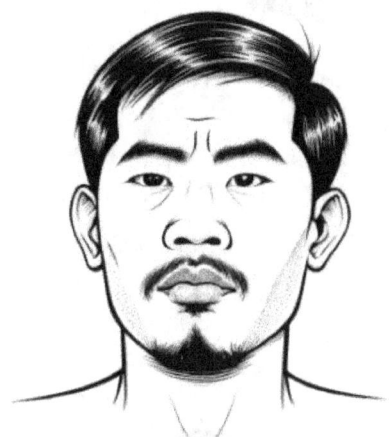

Vietnamese male (n=26)

-1.38	mouth: Move vertically	*	7.33E-12
-0.687	mouth: Scale upperlip width	*	2.42E-08
-0.912	mouth: Scale horizontally	*	8.34E-08
0.971	slider_eyes_outer_droop		1.1E-07
-0.818	nose: Scale nostrils flaring		2.1E-07
-0.721	chin: Scale chin angular		2.41E-07
-0.817	nose: Lower nose bridge width	*	3.2E-07
-0.91	nose: Scale vertically		1.42E-06
-0.66	slider_r-eye-scale-decr|incr		2.21E-06
-0.676	eyebrows: Eyebrows bulge	*	2.68E-06
0.574	mouth: Laugh-lines		3.59E-06
-0.755	nose: Scale depth		4.49E-06
0.532	chin: Cleft chin	*	6.14E-06
-0.57	slider_l-eye-scale-decr|incr		0.0000228
0.695	slider_Nose_alar_crease	*	0.0000297
0.665	mouth: Scale middle upperlip	*	0.0000492
0.609	slider_l-eye-corner2-down|up		0.0000784

Welsh female (n=23)

-1.16	mouth: Scale lowerlip width	*	1.13E-14
-0.933	mouth: Scale vertically	*	1.72E-09
1.14	mouth: Scale lowerlip volume	*	2.46E-09
-1.03	mouth: Scale upperlip width	*	4.5E-07
0.775	chin: Scale chin width	*	7.77E-06
0.716	mouth: Lowerlip curved shape		0.0000105
-0.62	nose: Scale horizontally	*	0.0000111
-0.721	mouth: Scale lowerlip height		0.0000225
0.716	mouth: Upperlip curved shape		0.0000378

Yemeni female (n=26)

-1.02	eyebrows: Move vert		1.18E-08
1.11	nose: Scale vertically	*	2.84E-08
1.02	nose: Lower nose bridge width	*	2.22E-07
1.11	slider_l-eye-corner1-down|up	*	5.64E-07
0.879	eyebrows: Eyebrows bulge	*	1.07E-06
1.04	nose: Scale depth		1.36E-06
-0.897	slider_Nose_alar_crease		0.0000107
0.711	chin: Scale chin prominence		0.0000167
0.538	slider_l-eye-push1-in|out	*	0.0000572
0.682	nose: Scale nostrils flaring		0.0000599
0.915	slider_r-eye-corner1-down|up	*	0.0000772

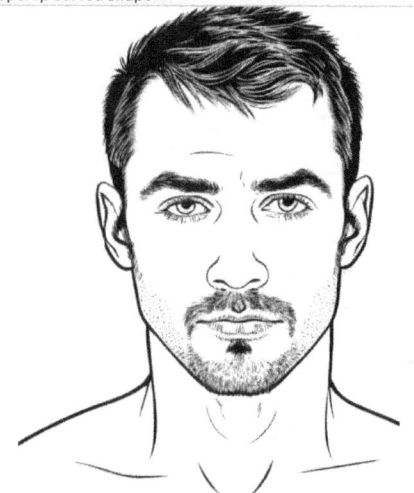

Welsh male (n=25)

-0.973	mouth: Scale lowerlip width	*	7.46E-09
-0.656	nose: Scale horizontally	*	1.72E-07
0.813	chin: Scale chin width	*	2.57E-07
0.633	mouth: Dimples		2.93E-07
-0.76	mouth: Scale upperlip width	*	4.42E-07
1.21	mouth: Scale lowerlip volume	*	0.0000013
0.891	chin: Scale chin height		2.72E-06
-0.94	mouth: Scale vertically	*	5.01E-06
-0.77	slider_r-eye-trans-in|out		0.0000092
-0.695	slider_l-eye-trans-in|out		0.0000267
0.496	nose-volume-decr|incr		0.0000336
-0.564	slider_l-cheek-inner-decr|incr		0.0000772

Yemeni male (n=24)

0.736	nose: Lower nose bridge width	*	2.4E-09
1.05	nose: Scale vertically	*	4.8E-09
0.947	eyes: Inner height of right eye		1.01E-07
0.864	eyes: Inner height of left eye		6.64E-07
0.468	mouth: Scale upperlip width		2.17E-06
0.745	slider_l-eye-push1-in|out	*	3.28E-06
0.645	slider_r-eye-scale-decr|incr		4.42E-06
0.922	slider_r-eye-corner1-down|up	*	6.92E-06
0.51	eyes: Middle height of left eye		0.0000134
0.658	slider_l-eye-scale-decr|incr		0.000015
0.836	slider_l-eye-corner1-down|up	*	0.0000179
-0.62	mouth: Scale lowerlip volume		0.000019
0.953	nose-nostrils-angle-down|up		0.0000218
-0.644	mouth: Lowerlip curved shape		0.00003
0.701	eyebrows: Eyebrows bulge	*	0.0000328

Yoruba female (n=28)

Value	Parameter	Parameter (col2)	Sig	P-value
1.92	mouth: Scale lowerlip width		*	2.44E-16
-1.96		slider_l-eye-trans-down|up	*	1.02E-15
-1.78		slider_r-eye-trans-down|up	*	3.38E-15
-1.5		chin: Scale chin width	*	3.53E-15
1.76	mouth: Scale upperlip width		*	7.43E-15
-1.12		chin: Scale chin height	*	9.23E-15
1.68	mouth: Scale vertically		*	5.27E-14
-1.3		mouth: Scale upperlip volume	*	9.48E-14
-1.49		mouth: Dimples	*	1.46E-13
-1.66		nose-volume-decr|incr	*	8.03E-13
1.25	slider_r-eye-corner2-down|up		*	8.85E-13
-1.38		mouth: Upperlip curved shape	*	1E-12
-1.09		mouth: Scale lowerlip volume	*	3.99E-12
1.52	mouth: Scale lowerlip height		*	8.43E-12
-1.45		slider_r-eye-corner1-down|up	*	1.16E-11
-1.26		mouth: Laugh-lines	*	1.45E-11
1.31	nose: Scale nostrils width		*	3.13E-11
1.37	slider_r-eye-bag-decr|incr			4.31E-11
-1.4		eyebrows: Eyebrows bulge	*	4.33E-11
1.47	slider_l-eye-eyefold-angle-down|up		*	4.8E-11
1.14	slider_l-eye-corner2-down|up			6.28E-11
0.993	slider_l-eye-bag-in|out			6.65E-11
-1.5		slider_l-eye-corner1-down|up		1.08E-10
1.27	mouth: Scale upperlip height		*	2.67E-10
0.991	slider_r-eye-bag-in|out		*	4.79E-10
1.3	slider_r-eye-eyefold-angle-down|up			1.03E-09
1.09	nose: Move nose base vert.		*	2.6E-09
1.13	slider_l-eye-bag-decr|incr			4.11E-09
1.35	nose: Scale horizontally			4.32E-09
0.901	slider_r-cheek-inner-decr|incr			9.77E-09
1.02	nose: Move depth			1.78E-08
-0.974		mouth: Cupid's bow shape	*	2E-08
-1.21		nose-nostrils-angle-down|up		2.72E-08
0.906	mouth: Move depth		*	8.99E-08
0.603	eyes: Outer height of left eye			1.13E-07
-0.859		slider_elvs_highchubbycheekbones1	*	1.89E-07
0.875	slider_l-eye-trans-in|out		*	2.02E-07
0.823	slider_r-eye-trans-in|out		*	6.01E-07
1	mouth: Scale horizontally		*	6.52E-07
0.732	chin: Cleft chin		*	1.69E-06
-0.824		mouth: Move vertically	*	1.79E-06
0.723	forehead: Scale vertically		*	2.86E-06

Value	Parameter	Parameter (col2)	Sig	P-value
0.515	mouth: Move corners vert.		*	3.59E-06
0.515	mouth: Move corners vert.		*	3.59E-06
0.825	slider_l-cheek-inner-decr|incr		*	4.48E-06
-0.843		nose: Scale vertically	*	9.73E-06
-0.698		nose: Move vertically		9.91E-06
-0.694		nose: Scale nostrils flaring		0.0000104
0.623	forehead: Cranic shape		*	0.0000108
0.522	eyes: Outer height of right eye			0.0000168
0.832	slider_l-eye-eyefold-down|up			0.0000201
-0.813		mouth: Cupid's bow width	*	0.0000548
0.778	slider_r-eye-eyefold-down|up			0.0000681
0.799	slider_r-eye-epicanthus-in|out			0.0000834
0.611	chin: Scale chin prognathism		*	0.0000921

Yoruba male (n=22)

Value	Parameter	Parameter (col2)	Sig	P-value
1.65	slider_r-eye-trans-in|out		*	1.52E-12
1.64	nose: Scale horizontally		*	5.89E-12
-1.29		mouth: Scale lowerlip volume	*	2.49E-11
-1.63		mouth: Dimples	*	5.59E-11
-1.93		chin: Scale chin height	*	1.23E-10
1.69	mouth: Scale upperlip width		*	1.47E-10
2.04	mouth: Scale lowerlip width		*	2.43E-10
2.13	mouth: Scale vertically		*	4.52E-10
1.95	mouth: Scale lowerlip height		*	1.38E-09
-1.11		mouth: Laugh-lines	*	2.6E-09
1.69	slider_l-eye-trans-in|out		*	5.93E-09
1.09	mouth: Move depth		*	6.04E-09
1.18	nose: Scale nostrils width		*	1.49E-08
-0.993		eyebrows: Eyebrows bulge	*	3.22E-08
-1.49		chin: Scale chin width	*	3.63E-08
0.933	mouth: Scale horizontally		*	7.85E-08
-1.36		mouth: Move vertically	*	1.46E-07
1.04	slider_r-eye-corner2-down|up		*	2.27E-07
1.89	chin: Cleft chin		*	1.13E-06
-1.44		mouth: Upperlip curved shape	*	1.17E-06
-1.17		slider_r-eye-trans-down|up	*	1.25E-06
-1.21		mouth: Scale upperlip volume	*	1.34E-06
0.94	slider_l-cheek-inner-decr|incr		*	2.28E-06
-0.934		slider_Nose_alar_crease		3.07E-06
1.44	mouth: Scale upperlip height		*	3.44E-06
-1.15		slider_l-eye-trans-down|up	*	4.87E-06
1.08	chin: Scale chin prognathism		*	5.54E-06
-1.15		nose-volume-decr|incr	*	8.09E-06
-0.965		slider_elvs_highchubbycheekbones1	*	0.0000146
-1.31		mouth: Cupid's bow shape	*	0.0000255
-0.664		nose: Scale vertically	*	0.0000338
0.926	forehead: Scale vertically		*	0.0000426
0.813	forehead: Cranic shape		*	0.0000558

-1.38	mouth: Cupid's bow width	*	0.000059
0.945	nose: Move nose base vert.	*	0.000063
1.51	mouth: Move corners vert.	*	0.0000656
1.51	mouth: Move corners vert.	*	0.0000656
0.703	slider_l-eye-eyefold-angle-down|up	*	0.0000746
0.942	slider_r-eye-bag-in|out	*	0.0000773

0.736	slider_l-eye-bag-decr|incr		0.0000423
-1.16	slider_r-eye-corner1-down|up		0.0000722

Zambian female (n=18)

Zambian male (n=17)

1.37	mouth: Scale upperlip width	*	1.06E-11
1.35	slider_r-eye-trans-in|out	*	1.5E-09
1.09	nose: Scale nostrils width	*	1.72E-09
1.6	mouth: Scale lowerlip width	*	1.73E-09
1.67	mouth: Scale vertically	*	2.98E-09
1.51	mouth: Scale lowerlip height	*	5.18E-09
1.45	nose: Scale horizontally	*	1.18E-08
-1.46	mouth: Upperlip curved shape		3.18E-08
0.959	slider_l-eye-bag-in|out		3.28E-08
-1.35	nose-volume-decr|incr	*	4.99E-08
-1.3	mouth: Cupid's bow shape	*	6.42E-08
1.32	slider_l-eye-eyefold-angle-down|up		1.18E-07
-1.34	mouth: Scale upperlip volume		1.85E-07
-1.64	slider_l-eye-trans-down|up		2.15E-07
-1.05	mouth: Scale lowerlip volume	*	2.33E-07
-0.933	chin: Scale chin width		2.4E-07
-1.62	slider_r-eye-trans-down|up	*	2.56E-07
-0.906	mouth: Laugh-lines	*	3.96E-07
1.37	mouth: Scale upperlip height		4.09E-07
1.16	slider_l-eye-trans-in|out	*	1.31E-06
1.03	nose: Move depth		1.41E-06
1.05	slider_r-eye-eyefold-angle-down|up		1.81E-06
-0.811	slider_elvs_highchubbycheekbones1	*	1.85E-06
-0.946	mouth: Dimples	*	2.04E-06
0.998	slider_l-cheek-inner-decr|incr		2.95E-06
0.779	chin: Scale chin prognathism	*	3.41E-06
1.03	slider_r-eye-corner2-down|up	*	3.82E-06
-0.836	chin: Scale chin height	*	3.89E-06
0.807	slider_l-eye-corner2-down|up		4.78E-06
0.97	mouth: Scale middle lowerlip		5.01E-06
-0.914	slider_r-eye-bag-height-decr|incr	*	8.37E-06
0.645	nose-curve-concave|convex		0.0000177
-0.82	mouth: Cupid's bow width		0.0000321
-0.77	slider_l-eye-bag-height-decr|incr	*	0.0000348
0.893	slider_r-eye-bag-in|out		0.0000373
0.999	slider_r-eye-bag-decr|incr		0.0000414

-1.58	mouth: Dimples	*	1.56E-10
2.08	slider_l-eye-trans-in|out	*	2.63E-09
-1.42	mouth: Laugh-lines	*	2.89E-09
-1.46	nose-volume-decr|incr	*	4.22E-09
1.58	mouth: Scale upperlip width	*	1.66E-08
1.79	mouth: Scale vertically	*	1.81E-08
-1.71	chin: Scale chin height	*	1.2E-07
1.05	mouth: Scale horizontally		1.42E-07
1.17	nose: Scale nostrils width		1.67E-07
-1.19	mouth: Move vertically		3.56E-07
-1.6	mouth: Scale lowerlip volume	*	4.62E-07
1.07	chin: Scale chin prognathism	*	5.29E-07
1.73	mouth: Scale lowerlip width	*	9.67E-07
1.38	slider_r-eye-trans-in|out	*	1.04E-06
-0.989	slider_elvs_highchubbycheekbones1	*	1.07E-06
1.38	nose: Scale horizontally	*	1.13E-06
0.511	eyes: Middle height of left eye		1.33E-06
0.61	eyes: Middle height of right eye		1.34E-06
-1.24	eyebrows: Eyebrows bulge		1.68E-06
-1.19	mouth: Cupid's bow shape	*	2.22E-06
1.56	mouth: Move corners vert.		3.12E-06
1.56	mouth: Move corners vert.		3.12E-06
1.56	mouth: Move corners vert.		3.12E-06
-0.772	slider_l-eye-bag-height-decr|incr	*	0.000005
-0.779	slider_r-eye-bag-height-decr|incr	*	0.0000309
1.45	chin: Cleft chin		0.0000371
1.31	forehead: Cranic shape		0.0000435
1.35	mouth: Scale lowerlip height	*	0.0000702
1.45	forehead: Scale vertically		0.0000719
0.889	slider_r-eye-corner2-down|up	*	0.0000748
-0.901	slider_r-eye-trans-down|up	*	0.0000941
0.845	eyes: Outer height of left eye		0.0000953
0.878	eyes: Outer height of right eye		0.0000987

Zimbabwean female (n=22)

Value	Feature	Feature	*	p
1.53	mouth: Scale upperlip width		*	1E-12
-1.55		mouth: Laugh-lines	*	6.05E-12
-1.27		mouth: Dimples	*	2.1E-10
-1.13		mouth: Scale lowerlip volume	*	1.91E-09
-1.23		eyebrows: Eyebrows bulge	*	5.02E-09
-1.38		slider_r-eye-trans-down|up	*	6.61E-09
-1.52		slider_l-eye-trans-down|up	*	1.1E-08
-1.37		nose-volume-decr|incr	*	1.79E-08
1.7	slider_l-eye-eyefold-angle-down|up		*	3.51E-08
-0.85		nose-greek-decr|incr		3.76E-08
1.37	nose: Scale horizontally		*	6.87E-08
-0.992		slider_r-eye-corner1-down|up		9.62E-08
1.14	mouth: Scale horizontally		*	1.17E-07
1.05	eyebrows: Move vert			1.2E-07
1.46	slider_r-eye-eyefold-angle-down|up		*	4.71E-07
1.05	mouth: Scale vertically		*	5.09E-07
1.05	mouth: Scale vertically		*	5.09E-07
1.47	nose: Scale nostrils width		*	6.24E-07
-0.9		slider_nostril_rounding	*	1.44E-06
0.564	eyebrows: Eyebrows angle		*	2.98E-06
-0.932		slider_l-eye-corner1-down|up		3.32E-06
0.969	forehead: Scale vertically		*	6.33E-06
0.896	forehead: Cranic shape		*	8.58E-06
1.12	mouth: Scale lowerlip width		*	8.98E-06
1.12	mouth: Scale lowerlip width		*	8.98E-06
-0.788		mouth: Scale upperlip volume		9.85E-06
-0.727		slider_elvs_highchubbycheekbones1	*	0.0000102
-0.551		nose: Upper nose bridge width		0.0000163
-1.05		eyes: Inner height of right eye		0.0000194
-1.12		eyes: Inner height of left eye		0.0000244
0.795	slider_l-eye-trans-in|out		*	0.0000431
-0.729		chin: Scale chin height	*	0.0000653
0.975	slider_l-cheek-inner-decr|incr		*	0.0000662
0.763	slider_l-eye-eyefold-down|up			0.0000677
-0.726		slider_l-eye-scale-decr|incr		0.0000962

Zimbabwean male (n=21)

Value	Feature	Feature	*	p
-1.57		mouth: Scale lowerlip volume	*	7.37E-13
1.76	nose: Scale horizontally		*	4.28E-11
-1.83		chin: Scale chin height	*	1.04E-10
1.72	mouth: Scale upperlip width		*	3.62E-10
1.86	slider_l-eye-trans-in|out		*	1.68E-09
1.19	nose: Scale nostrils width		*	2.78E-09
1.7	mouth: Move corners vert.			3.8E-09
1.7	mouth: Move corners vert.			3.8E-09
2.05	mouth: Scale lowerlip width		*	5.83E-09
2.05	mouth: Scale lowerlip width		*	5.83E-09
1.97	mouth: Scale vertically		*	5.9E-09
1.97	mouth: Scale vertically		*	5.9E-09
-1.52		mouth: Dimples	*	8.57E-09
1.75	slider_r-eye-trans-in|out			3.74E-08
-1.45		mouth: Move vertically		4.17E-08
-1.35		mouth: Laugh-lines	*	4.56E-08
1.06	forehead: Cranic shape		*	4.78E-08
-1.27		slider_l-eye-trans-down|up	*	4.85E-08
-1.12		eyebrows: Eyebrows bulge	*	5.71E-08
1.13	forehead: Scale vertically		*	9.16E-08
-1.25		slider_r-eye-trans-down|up	*	9.59E-08
1.68	chin: Cleft chin			9.78E-08
-1.11		slider_elvs_highchubbycheekbones1	*	0.0000001
1.12	chin: Scale chin prognathism			1.58E-07
1.04	slider_r-eye-corner2-down|up			2.83E-07
-0.943		slider_nostril_rounding	*	3.08E-07
-1.36		nose-volume-decr|incr	*	3.15E-07
-1.16		slider_Nose_alar_crease		4.11E-07
-1.16		chin: Scale chin width		6.93E-07
-0.676		nose: Scale vertically		1.78E-06
1.19	slider_r-eye-eyefold-angle-down|up		*	1.98E-06
1.02	slider_l-cheek-inner-decr|incr		*	3.39E-06
0.759	eyebrows: Eyebrows angle		*	3.62E-06
1.57	mouth: Scale lowerlip height			4.08E-06
-1.18		mouth: Cupid's bow shape		0.00001
0.79	slider_r-eye-bag-in|out			0.000019
1.04	slider_l-eye-eyefold-angle-down|up		*	0.0000232
0.977	mouth: Scale horizontally		*	0.0000295
-0.829		nose: Move vertically		0.0000344
0.764	slider_l-eye-corner2-down|up			0.0000372
0.663	slider_r-cheek-inner-decr|incr			0.0000631

Having thus satisfied our curiosity regarding what we are subconsciously seeing when we view physical differences among ethnotypes, and having mapped what each body region corresponds to in the abstract (Table 16, p 336), we can now look at ourselves and any others as an abstract bucket of inherent talents for certain behavioral modes—at least according to a world-trained stereotype.

In the next couple of chapters we will shift gears and close our journey with some theoretical extras that sit behind this work.

Chapter 22: Showing the relationship between astrology and astronomy using LLM embeddings

Now that we have embeddings for turning words directly into math, testing astrology and astrological claims against hard science is easy. You just take the claims and embed them, then run statistics against official measures like the orbital elements, emission spectra, or whatever else "real" scientists use.[55] Better yet, we can skip the astrology entirely and just see if the set of wiki bios-as-LLM-math has any relationship to these space rock numbers. Recalling that our asteroid interpretations come from $p<.05$ significant text-mines which in turn come from wiki bios of actual lives, and investigating a direct relationship between the underlying words of the interpretations and the orbital values,

- I embedded (got the math matrix version of) the wiki bios using SpaCy's 3.5 English web embedding model,
- used PCA (principal components analysis) to reduce the the model's 300 columns to a dimension confined to the types of terms I was actually using in the interpretations (rather than the whole English vocabulary)
- and ran a loop of correlations between each PCA column and each orbital element measure available in an asteroid [orbital elements] download from NASA's website (the one with 700,000 asteroid specs in it).

The statistically significant results of each orbital element run consisted of only a few of the PCA columns. I then ran a similarity matcher between these meaningful columns and the original term set embeddings, and this gave me a very rough flow of words which that meaningful PCA-embedding column was associated with in language space.[56] The continuum of high versus low values for each column were neat, but not that surprising since we've been doing stats like this for over a decade now. Still, you can see some patterns that make sense against the astro lore. As we can see in

Figure 39 below, distance from the Sun (the orbital element "a") corresponds to the "institutionness" of pressures felt by a person, and this is consistent with our whole self-other-world progression of astro lore from very personal, genetic

---

[55] The "" are my half-joking dig at people in scientific fields and academia who don't actually ask new questions, but could. Shame on you.

[56] Basically, if an embeddings model is a kind of black box whose columns tell you things like the "verbiness," "prosocialness," "Proper nounness," or "pedantic euphemismness" of the words that trained them, you can preserve some mashup of these language facets as applied to your own set of terms, then get the closest words that reflect the highest and lowest values of each column to get a very rudimentary idea of what that mashup column is measuring. You could also do this without using PCA, but then you'd be considering a bunch of dimensions that may not apply to your term set, the analysis would take longer and more processing power, and then you'd have to fish your results out of there. I tried this first. It was annoying. So PCA won out.

Aries-Cancer Moon impulse through Capricorn+ institutions past Saturn and beyond. We'll leave it to the hard scientists to elaborate the physics behind all this. I've already speculated regarding "bumps on the earth" earlier in the book.

FIGURE 39: CERTAIN WIKIPEDIA TEXT MINED WORDS TRACK CERTAIN ORBITAL ELEMENTS, SUGGESTING A RELATIONSHIP BETWEEN ASTROPHYSICS AND SOCIALLY DOCUMENTABLE EXPERIENCE

Laurentia 2's astro interpretations were created from groups of these same text mines.

(Annotations on figure: "PCA embeddings column", "words w/ highest and lowest vals for that column", "orbital element being compared", "summary of differences between high and low-value words")

#	A (differentColumnName)	B (Term)	C (Processed term)	D (Split Value 180 – ...structure +/ ...al sessm... t-)	E (Split Value ... the nands of the law / sensory organs+)	F (Split Value 103 - pressures from above or beyond- / large scale ocial ghts and unishing odies+)	G (Split Value 98 - mixing and joining- / forcing upon or forcing together)	L (institutional and systemic pressures on the person vs within- [person or object] -felt force)
17	a	qu'il, va, ne	qu'il, va, ne	7.4347	-8.?2		-8.191	
18	a	fee	fee		-9.500	-11.017		
19	a	bail	bail		-9.3338			
20	a	[adb:CIA]	cia		-9.3306			
21	a	lab	lab		-9.2958			
22	a	m	m		-9.2911			
23	a	trial, retrial	trial, retrial		-9.2535			
24	a	august	august	9.3401	-9.0255			
25	a	l'ordre, ainsi	l'ordre, ainsi		-8.9185	-6.0348		
26	a	filming, story - film, biopic, film	filming, film, biopic		-8.7626			
27	a	mixtape	mixtape		-8.7482			
28	a	au	au		-8.6935	-10.672	-8.1191	
29	a	en	en	15.843	-8.5153		-1?.079	
30	a	exam	exam		-8.4074			
31	a	bed, crib	bed, crib		-8.3009			
32	a	story - committee, committee	committee		-8.26			
33	a	kg	kg	-12.049	-8.1611			
34	a	law, [adb:Law]	law	-8.4734	-8.1602			
35	a	prison, penitentiary	prison, penitentiary		-8.0921			
36	a	june	june	8.0334	-8.0364			
37	a	jailed, jail	jailed, jail		-8.0174			
38	a	aide-de-camp	aide-de-camp		-7.94241			
39	a	ta.	tax	13.541	-7.915			
40	a	loan	loan		-7.9131			
41	a	visa	visa		-7.859			
42	a	[Eye Color:Blue]	blue eye color		8.761			
43	a	soda	soda		8.851			
44	a	story - hand	hand		8.9636			
45	a	heat, story - heat	heat		9.0082			
46	a	sky	sky		9.2144			
47	a	lowest, lower, low	lowest, lower, low		9.2686			
48	a	wax	wax		9.4675			
49	a	bass, story - bass	bass		9.6246			
50	a	al, als	al, als	9.293	9.6426			
51	a	story - a	a		9.6682			
52	a	wind, story - wind	wind		9.6934			
53	a	tooth, teetotaler, teeth	tooth, teetotaler, teeth		9.7875			
54	a	flow, story - flow	flow		10			
55	a	story - air, air, airing	air, airing	10.238	10.164			
56	a	ash	ash		10.294			
57	a	story - no	no	6.7544	10.337			
58	a	fish, story - fish	fish		10.564			
59	a	wet	wet		10.637			
60	a	nose	nose		10.645			
62	a	so	so		10.71	-9.7144		
63	a	resound, sound, story - soundi	resound, sound, sounding, sour		10.738			
64	a	sun	sun		10.848			
65	a	ink	ink		11.614			
66	a	sea, story - sea	sea		12.137			
67	a	skin, skinhead, [adb:Skin]	skin, skinhead		12.294			
68	a	eye, [adb:Eyes]	eye, eyes		12.568			

Again, this shouldn't be surprising. The Moon cycles on the scale of days, the Sun on the scale of years, and Saturn on the scale of 29-year adulthood. The farther out we go, the longer the ramp up time for whatever's being built. Few business are built in 30 days; few emotions take one year to register (with obvious exceptions). So basic orbital period has at least one obvious correlation to the length of human socialization windows. Still, it's nice to see that the results support known facts like this.

And when the dust settled, here were the final results:

TABLE 43: ORBITAL ELEMENT RELATIONSHIPS TO BIOGRAPHY-LANGUAGE SPACE

Orbital element	Definition	Match semantic pattern (low element value vs HIGH)
a	semi-major axis	within-[person or object] -felt force vs INSTITUTIONAL AND SYSTEMIC PRESSURES ON THE PERSON
e	orbit eccentricity	interactional upset or disturbance vs MILD PRESENTATION FOR OTHERS' CONSIDERATION
i	inclination of the orbit with respect to the J2000 ecliptic plane.	social actors we share safe (or at least familiar?) messages with vs THOSE WHO IMPOSE UPON US, MAKE US FEEL UNSAFE, OR ACT DESPITE OUR INTERESTS
ω	argument of periapsis (J2000-ecliptic).	regulation vs DRIVEN GROWTH
(cos) Ω	(cosine of the) right ascension of the ascending node	official register vs ABSTRACT WIDE-PUBLIC ENJOYABLES
H	absolute magnitude	that which pulls the rhythms of attention vs THAT WHICH EXPORTS ITS PRE-FAVORED PATTERNS TOWARDS THE PULLER
G	magnitude slope parameter	familial relation, possession and comfort+ / FOREIGNERS, SURPRISE AND DISCOMFORT-

There were no significant findings for the mean anomaly at epoch, M.

11:19 am, 6/26/2025

Let's take a completely random asteroid from my NASA file and see if the above helps us guess what it does. (This really IS random and I have no idea if it will hold up. We'll see.)

Here we go. Random out of 21000+ named asteroids…

- *15268 Wendelinefroger*, a= 2.365, e=.234, i= 2.7, ω =210.42, Ω=143.9, H=14.79, G=.15
- The column extrema are

	a	e	i	ω	Ω	H	G
min	0.555393	0.000208	0.00783	0.00065	0.00079	-1.24	-0.25
max	1349.229	0.993156	175.9768	359.9994	359.9996	25.6	0.6
mean	2.790	0.139	8.592	181.572	168.170	16.611	0.150
stdev	3.560	0.074	6.009	103.567	102.299	1.291	0.002

11:24 am

So we have a standard main belt asteroid (probably interpersonal in nature), a slightly higher than .14 mean eccentricity for other's consideration, low inclination for making others feel closer to safe, a pretty negative cosine of node for official register, and the other two params are average. I always suspect that, within a crowded belt like this, there's an even finer-grained system of harmonics, but we won't worry about that now. The distinguishing elements + my very lazy interpretation thereof suggest an asteroid presenting some kind of formal stability offer for other's consideration. That wouldn't be its meaning, but more like its experiential valence or "sentiment." So I would be less likely to hypothesize, say, abstraction or disruption for this one. Let's test this. Wrong or right, it's going in the book permanently…

11:35 am

15268 Wendelinefroger: a forum for the public judgement of a thing; how you maintain the duodecanate will tend to influence the 'verdicts' you receive from the people who evaluate you; | *Ajani's note: there is some evidence that this may be a MAJOR asteroid which indicates the chief complaint that people have with you when they openly deem you inferior; Pluto-like, it seems to show where you can be pressured to conform by others who have been listening to their own pressurers or allies about traits you should possess; Aries-2 or -11?*

BAM! It's in the ballpark! (Wiping the sweat from my brow, as that really *could* have gone the other way. And I really *would* have recorded my hypothesis' failure here in shame.) It's not a perfect match, but it's not at all randomly unrelated either.[57] So there you have it: from Kepler to social lore.

Since the hypothesis went through fairly successfully, in my opinion, there's nothing more to do in this chapter. In theory, you could take a sample of astronomical bodies, assume an Earth-centric frame, and hypothesize their astrological or social-frequentic meaning based on their elements alone. I do think that we need to develop a second level of granularity to further investigate any correlation differences *within* a band (like the Main/Mars-Jupiter belt or Kuiper belt). But, again, we'll save this work for future researchers.

---

[57] Also, I too was inclined to think about the "unsafeness" of trials for a split second, but the verdict *closes* the trial in the eyes of everyone but the litigants, bringing it to an end. No wonder my gut reaction was that of relief, not of backlash or other assorted events that may be ancillary to the interpretation itself.

Chapter 23: Assorted notes and speculations I made while working on this book

Somewhere in Table 9, (which starts on page 75), you will find a refence to "Sunday morning calculate," where I often lie on my futon for 2 extra hours on waking, thinking about how various ideas fit together. It is here that I often have to create all kinds sketches in order to keep from getting lost, and many of those sketched ideas have already made it into this book. Yet there are some ideas that aren't remotely close to being fleshed out, and I'm not committed enough to them to try explaining them to you. I will however, share my notes. This chapter includes several additional ideas that did not make the rest of the book, but may be useful to researchers in the future. Try deciphering my handwriting. If you dare.

FIGURE 40: EARLY SPECULATIONS ON BODY DIVISIONS

2023:

Early in the conception of this book, I speculated on the optimum number of regions for dividing the body, mapping it to duodecanates. I settled on about 18 major areas. This approach would later be replaced by RORT, f-RORT, and LANDOX as well as basic slider and vector statistics.

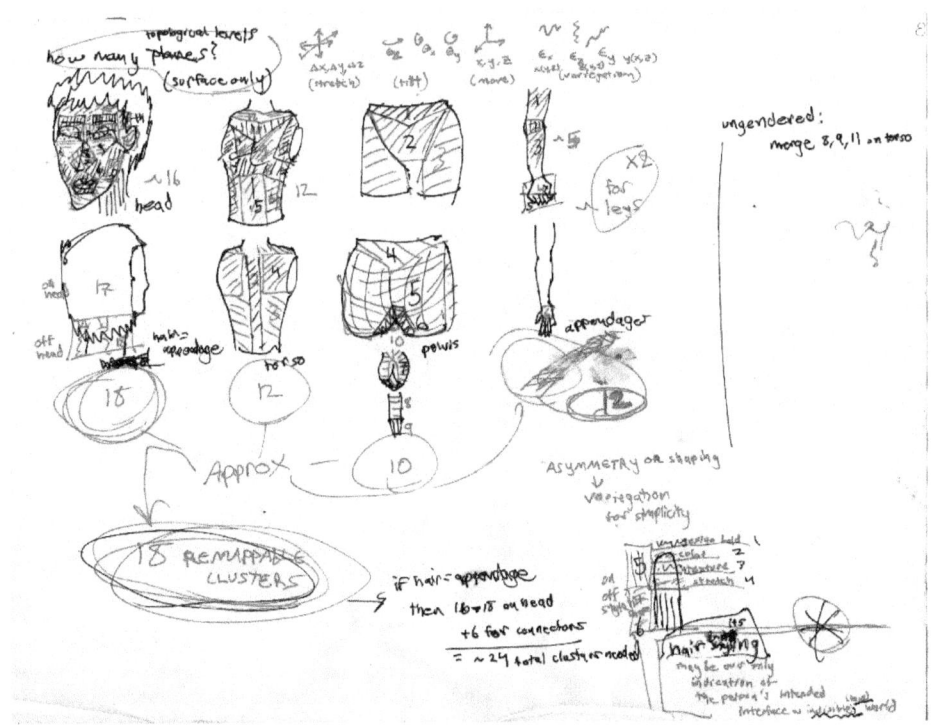

FIGURE 41: DUODECANATE GEOMETRIC TENDENCIES

In what is easily my favorite set of findings that didn't make the book, I took all of the major planets and asteroid locations from my ~130 adult set participants at the time, and put their images into 144 different folders depending on whether any of their majors were located in that numbered duodecanate. I then looked for any traits that seemed common to the people in each folder. This method is highly subjective, dependent on what you the researcher are inclined to notice, yet it seems to follow a pattern doesn't it? I love how only certain features are highlighted, suggesting that certain math function parameters are varying as we move around the cycle. The first row features the duodecanates of Pisces. See how it favors hyperbolas, as in

Table 12, page 274. The Scorpio duodecanates seem to favor parabolas.

... To me, the most intriguing among all of these findings are the Gemini duodecanates 115-117, which are related to different light angles, while 114 is related to the background color against which people tend to see you (which speaks of things like your biome in the eyes of "the star-sized gods" i.e. as a particle cloud on Earth and amidst furnishings). My 117 is opposite my Midheaven, and I can attest that I tend to take horrible candid pictures by default UNLESS the lighting is good. Said differently, the quality of my appearance and apparent attractiveness are *highly* sensitive to light.

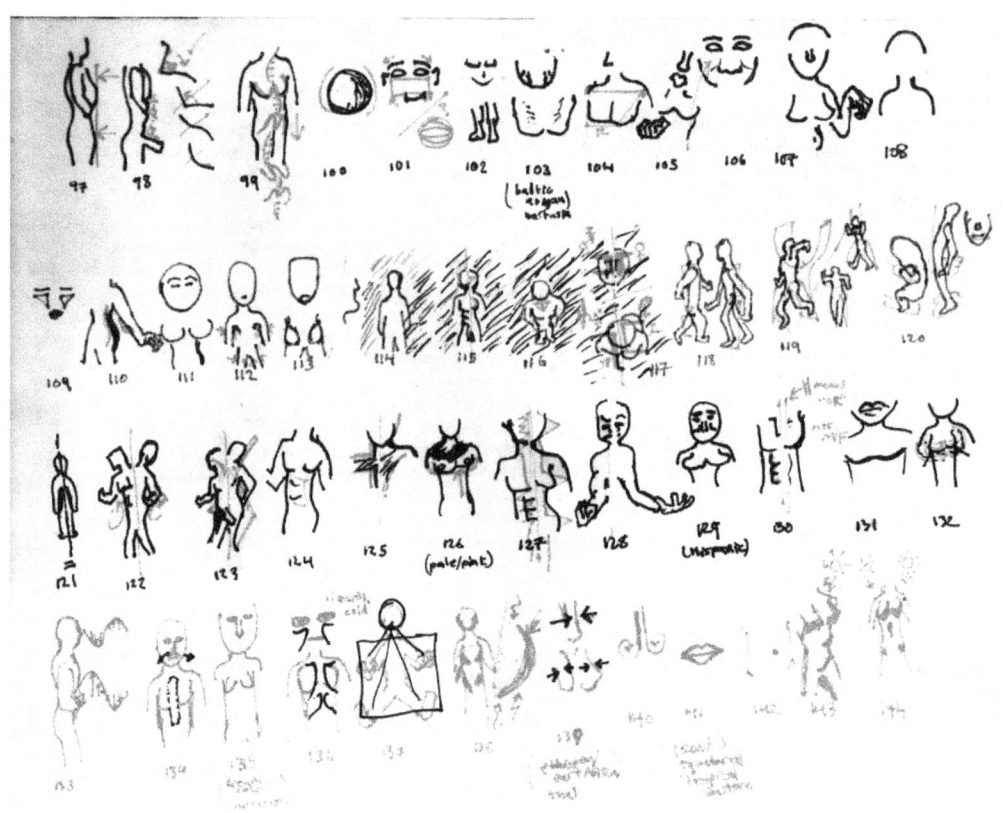

The written descriptions of these geometries are in the table below.

TABLE 44: WRITTEN DESCRIPTIONS OF GROUPED BODY PATTERNS

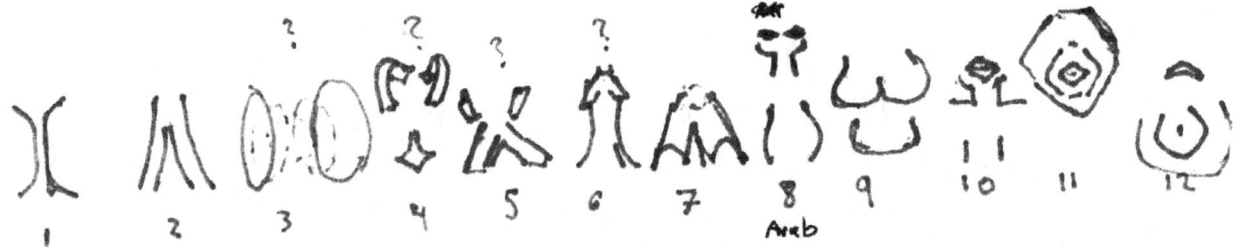

1: squeezed hyperbola dividing midline along the supra-infra axis; fusion line

2: twin cylinders; noticeably departed (especially) legs from anchor point. Not about spreading, but a defining scissoring of appendages

3: depth project; small, low or unknown, yet strongly visible; promotes ethnotypicality in general body plan overall, may be related to the niche culture others think you belong to based on appearances; helps one look more like their stereotype, so may be depth projecting in time—a mouse trail on similars

4: compounded development; heavy sex prototypicality in body or the information it processes; growth pattern seems to support the multiplicative / recursive identity

5: V-yaw-A; leans backwards or forwards with an alternate symmetric scissoring of appendages along the rostro-caudal depth axis

6: rear-leaning back arcing torso about the dextral-sinistral axis; more likely to guarantee some level of chest mass, pelvic tuck or abdominal slimming

7: stereoscopic pair; focuses the symmetric pair of either chest, arms, or leg—or similar appendage family—forward along the anterior-posterior axis when facing the viewer

8: teardrop; tends to pear-down hips, give a sandy feature set, arab/middle-easternizing the face with darker eyes and slightly higher angular cheeks bones

9: muscled-massed; thickens and round-edges volumed sections of the body in general

10: pucker-pinch lips, generally (but not always) horizontally; square neck to shoulders interface, coronally flat pelvis to legs interface

11: doll-ideal nose-mouth-V chin diamond; torso vertical symmetric contrasts; youthful diamond tone; tightens contrasts, pronounces shadows in concentric diamond and arrow regions

12: nipple-navel dot on a uniform hill triangle; generally decreases muscle tone in favor of planar surfaces; pulls out corners of lips down slightly to give a 'distrustful'-looking version of duodecanate 11, seems to drag down the countenance compared to 11 to conform the mouth corners and nose to a triangle at the expense of the hexagon in 11

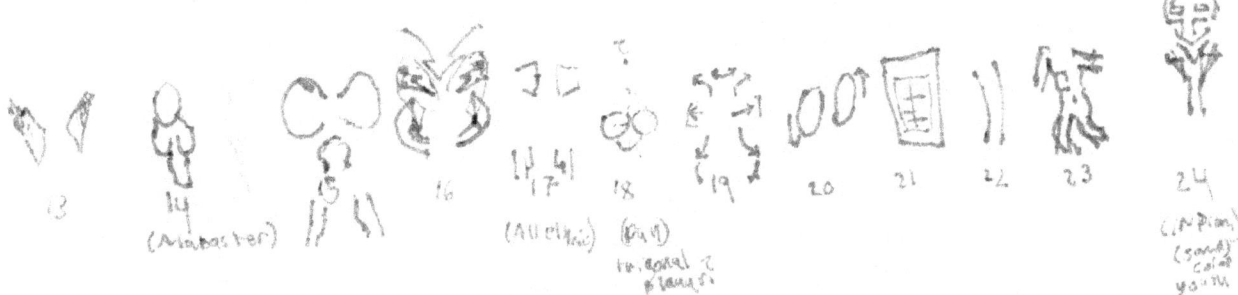

13: detail through shadow; seems to establish the visual depth axis through some kind of gradation in how various anterior-to-posterior features such as the inner cheeks and obliques) are tilted; may begin ballooning between 11-12 and 15 as a complex half dodecagon gets elaborated into a hemisphere

14: alabasters the skin, ovals the face, cylindrifies the abdominal column and u-drags the halves of the chest; north europeanizes the form; also seems to emphasize a half torus above the navel down and rearwards towards both suprailiac muscles

15: for you, the balloon; seems to lengthen or streamline the calves and balloon-end the chest and reproductive areas; may be related to receiver absorption of energy onto a field, as in visual input onto the occipital

16: in-ribbing; clasp posture, puts a transverse C shape into the chest, pushing the two halves apart and pointing the nipples outward. The shape based 'imprint' and complement of 98, ribbing; this is 'in-ribbing'

17: chameleon i ethnic; seems to tone the calves, expand the cheek plain slightly, and incline the person towards 'boss mode'; more likely to blend into any culture or ethnicity through looks or habit; seems to be the home of a unit potential vector complement to the amplitude

18: pan, trans, or flipped sexuality; external tool association; attaches a non-native concept to the form; orthogonality; seems to be the equivalent of 'not X' (duodecanate 90)

19: conducive smile; outcurved hips; pushes cheeks up and out; helps chest separation

20: long tilt bottom; lengthens and enlarges bilateral oval shapes and installs asymmetry in them

21: region melt sideways; brings out the angle or pose. There is an emphasis on the angle at which something is seen in order to bring the trait one wants to emphasize into the best view. Adds a square or grid-like quality to the chest and abdomen. More likely to set the chest and nipples as "two corners of a square, and region melt sideways" of the stomach and navel. Interestingly, trine 117.

22: side hook; curves or tilts that which would ideally be straight

23: cylindrical body frame; features as hilly masses; in pictures, legs were more likely in stride or strided spread; may have something to do with leg muscles; need more leg pictures

24: forking? seems to lend towards a more visible Y-shape from the pelvis to the chest; eye-nose T; slims body and indian-izes features, adding sand and bronze to the skin; face closer to a flat-rounded ovalized parabola; also seems to lessen protruding elements, artifacts of adult development, and confer a sense of youth instead

25: zig-zag line; a more visible sawtooth that runs the course of the body, seems to be a reflector of joints, likely a critical human species location

26: squeezed out, tightly drawn strings; sharpens the bulge/ballooning effect of certain regions, as in cases where the skin is less taught but housing volume; bends the relevant contour > 90 degrees; makes the attitude more apparent

27: vertical inflate poke-conic lip thickness; eyelids descend; poke-conic secondary sex organs as seen in a number of quadrupeds; makes planar the face shield where the male beard forms; could be an important animal species template region involved in adult jaw elaboration

28: water; the mitotic vase; H_2O shape; hooks two smaller clones of a sphere onto the original, upwards along a tubal line, thus simulating the process of "upward displacive mitosis or, in the other direction, downward fusion into a sphere; the mitotic vase," the shape is that of a vase with two similar-radius circles on top, and has interesting implications for why the opposition to the basic sphere shape is not a void in a void, but a three unit mother sphere flow-dividing into two smaller units; the equation appears to be a belled paraboloid. More specifically, this shape wouldn't be a thing *except* as the 'mouse trail' of volume over which a simultaneously sliding and dividing sphere evolves

29: latin-americanizes features; rectangular tube body frame, conducive to stout legs, matted or wild hair; freer or more disapproving countenance; solid stomach—if you punched them there it wouldn't hurt; this region says, 'this is the way I'm gonna do it goddamn it'

30: distal puff; sharpens shoulders forward and renders outer upper torso bigger than inner, as in a jacket

31: medial puff? contributes to mouth indentation lines, a squarer chin, and a downward-tipped bell nose—often slimmer

32: contrasting skin tones? Especially blur and specularity?

33: smooth image grade; tends away from harsh angles in form; pleasant, inviting; seems to enlarge areola in women, soften the features of men

34: conducive to V-shaped chin, rectangular or broad oval forehead as a shape; thus, slims the body weight; V-oval head formation

35: slow medial fusion; seems to flatten the forward front of the nose onto the upper cheek area while widening the nostrils; also widens the rear and reproductive areas

36: softened round woman, hardened square man faces; sexual dimorphism; 'sphery spheres, chiseled prisms, compounded energy containment'; adds weight or salience to all topological features in general; barbell and weight lifter

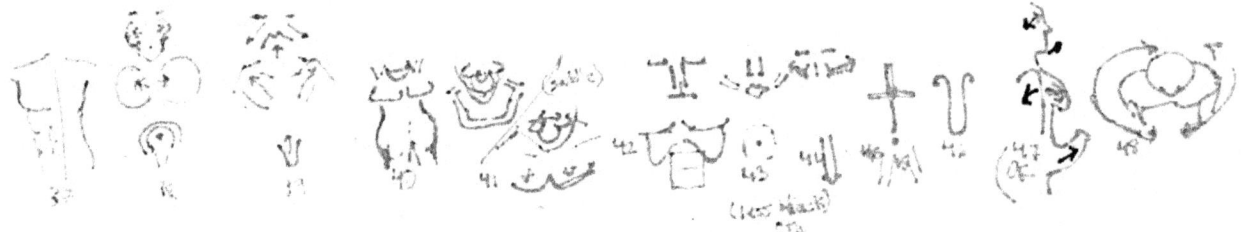

37: smaller build women and heavier framed men; seems to affect muscularity amount; accretion integration amount

38: ovoid repulsion; responsible for the spreading interface at a fork; repels spherical and ovoid shapes on the body via wide gap, or plumps them, especially the cheeks, reproductive attachment to the pelvis, and eyes

39: diverging diagonals; upwards from corners of chest to arms; higher arc cupid's bow stronger creasing and indentation—downward diagonal slash between eye/lateral upper nose bridge to the cheek plains; from what I've observed this cut through the sinuses typically decreases reproductive organs

40: side arcs the rear, uniform front facing arcs the lower lip, increases mouth lines smile creasing, indents lower cheek plain; dipolar smile tighten; cradles the pectorals in a U bowl

41: nostril width; nose tip roundness correlated with upper torso depth; scent rings

42: capital-I nostril-nose bridge-brow; linearizes nose bridge, straightens brow and nostril base in a T shape at each end, flattens the stomach; pronounces the butterfly shape of the lower rib cage, all suggesting greater primaxial-wrap vectoring

43: little mouth; squares the region around the navel, helps prevent mouth from dominating the medio-lateral real estate across the lower jaw, regardless of the size of the lower jaw (so the mouth is not necessarily little if the face is big or rounded); the mouth to rear cheek path near the ears tends to have a longer, more visible line; subjects were less likely to be black;<-after i observed this, i looked for where i had written about 'black-izing' the features. serendipitously for the research, i found one of the 2-3 areas for such in 7, which is square to this duodecanate. i'm sure no one will ever know how far out on a limb i often feel like i'm going in this solo work. looking at folders full of bodies and faces i don't always know if i'm on track or if these observations are even remotely valid. the square relationship between this duodecanate and 7 is very reassuring, as 43 in square really did seem to 'de-blackize' the features. in a couple of subjects, it also attended a noticeable level of prejudice against black interactions—per their bios

44: contrasting upper cheek to fold in the underside of the upper cheeks, pointing in the male organ, suggesting length; undereye to cheek specularity and cornering

45: "front torso cross"—an imprint between the chest and down through the navel, crossing the underbust, more tone with the presence of the cross. supports slimmer legs and tighter appendages

46: down arrow sharp south node front facing imprint; the semisquare 2D version of the mitotic vase, embossed onto the front torso, threatening uncomfortable influence

47: generative hang or widened pointing; affects the jut, hang, or lack thereof, of reproductive characteristics, thus an association with penis length or erection, and breast sag /point vs smallness, as well as outward eye drag. Extent of (more reproductive or eye), "generative hang or widened pointing—especially outward." supports a teardrop quality / shaping here. that which pokes out and grows from there

48: rostro-to-caudal axial wrapping; homogenous surface expansion. Contributes to flattening of the entire view in a caudal-outward direction, giving a planeness to what is seen. More likely to be unconcerned with / minimize the role of muscle tone. Especially visible in the back, but also smooths the front in general. may be associated with the wrapping of ectoderm into becoming skin—how susceptible this process is to pronounced local processing / differentiation beneath; "rostro-to-caudal axial wrapping". most evident in the bulge-droop of the rear

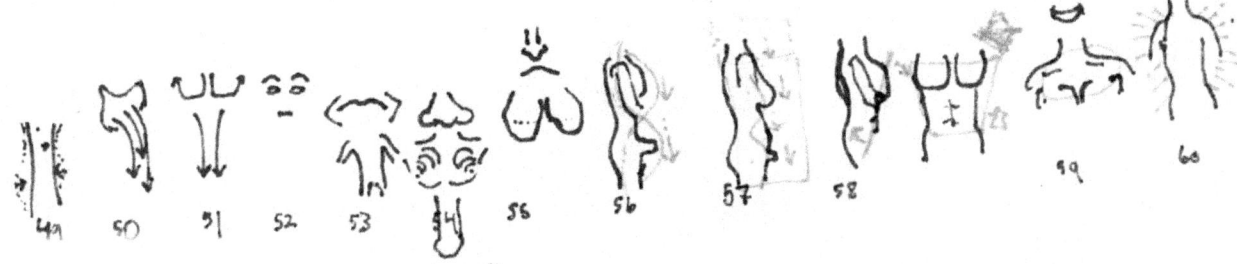

49: seems to add a stockiness that resists the body's curvature, though not enough to eliminate it. Regulated curvature, possibly in preparation for wrapping in 48. "axial confinement". Pulls body features back towards the central axis, smoothing the region into larger, gentler humps. primary external contours. Seems related to somatype, where arms and appendages and probably internal pathways, follow similar curvature topology rules as shown in the torso

50: waterfall; shapes which resemble horns flowing out of sources; 'hanging insertatory'; subjects were more likely than other regions on average to lean towards a heretical or demonic look or set or interests

51: production mass increase; estrogen-to-testosterone; ramps up male secondary sex characterics either on the body, against the body's minimal containment thereof, or prompted by a counter body

52: little eyes; seems to give a preference for a certain kind of dominance, rounds and shrinks the eyes; gives a flat mona lisa smile; seems a little more likely to arch the center of the eyebrows

53: bracket mouth; gliding philtrum and upper lips; many—but not all—had smaller body frames. Don't know if this is a typical characteristic

54: tunneler; triangularizes the nose, classic rounds the nostrils, thickens the penis in males, de-telescopes rounded cylinders on the body

55: fold over shelf chest; linear upper lip boundary, downward pointing nose tip, cylindrical middle nose bridge

56: mass spectrum; where the weight is placed. General bodies were either flat petite, heavy-obese, or held heavy reproductive organs. There wasn't much in between; may reflect spread of surrounding duodecanates

57: window attention downward translation; seems to confer an 'I'm here'ness to the body which makes the general shape and [posture to emphasize that shape] obvious. Obviousness, seriousness, broad shape—especially towards the lower torso and waist. Visual hierarchy seems to pull the torso "window attention downward translation" in the eyes of the viewer

58: yawed breastplate; the front face of the torso was more extruded; rippled abdomens particularly in the males; squeezes out breasts in women; seems to favor slightly greater symmetry in the torso. Can't tell

59: the passageway inferior to the neck, superior to the chest. How clearly defined this region is. Pulls upwards the volume of the breasts and pectorals; generally made the breasts smaller or higher up. Several were augmented or naturally rounder below this region, a direct function of the person's desire to project allure; subjects smiled noticeably more, especially males

60: extended orbit; additional aura or error term on a thing; a feature that intrudes on the viewer's space; including its trajectory shadow

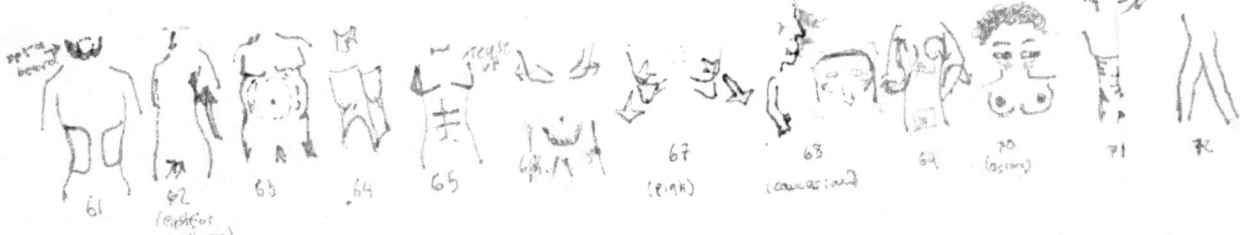

61: the corset; gives a torus-ribbing waist between the pelvis and underbust-navel region; makes notable the mandibular pull down/jowls; forms a panorama with 97 as its in-layer

62: coronal curvature; eastern europe to western asianizes, encourages smaller male reproductive organs and a lighter, gentler feminine build instead; arcs the posture and narrows the eyes. Once again, d62 seems to be more female.

63: bullseye; draws attention either to the coronal core or around it to the waist and chest about the pelvis at the expense of the core, more likely to manifest as weight

64: heavy weight skewed saddle' emphasizes a sagittally symmetric saddle, seemingly with one of the legs being prone to noticeably more extreme weighting than the other; there is an interesting relationship between the chest and the lips here in the unfolding human embryo which warrants further investigation, particularly in terms of tissue signaling in eventually distant organ systems

65: defined or lined abdomen; divisional branching tree; tightens the lips slightly in smile

66: outer corner pulled chest, underarc sub ab column; more likely to square the side pelvis to leg interface, de-pearing / rectangularizing the coronal body profile, de-lines outer corners of the rear, lending to a longer appearance

67: short vest extrude of the chest; pinks the skin color

68: whiter/caucasianized skin, points the nose tip linearly forward, window casing from the upper bridge; appears to shorten the arms; bergmann and allen north—the most caucasian duodecanate if we had to pick one; more likely to narrow lips, outdiagonal cheeks from the eyes, square the part of the head not including the lower jaw

69: countercycling appendages on a cubic build; sets up a spin-antispin energy flow about the medial line through a cubic form, suggesting a circulatory system relationship; appendages, if extruded, tend to be pressed against the main body

70: melanizes nipples, darkens the hair and eyes, pulls outer corners of the eyes down towards the center of the face, asian-izing slightly

71: male tone and muscularity, female puffy cheeks; anterior to ear-under eye planing of the cheeks; back rear eye planing

72: smooth cylinder arms and legs; seems to be *the duodecanate for legs; more likely a critical region in many land-dwelling animals' species templates, and some sea life; elongates the chest slightly to noticeably

73: lanky legs, elongates legs, seems to affect the jointing and stride thereof

74: saloon doors; transverse cut-V planing of the mandibular cheek mass, lends to masculinized features in the face and, to the extent that most of the subjects were clearly developed males, may be an indicator of androgenic activity throughout the body in general

75: the zipper; toned back line; seems to draw the nostrils together, bubble extrude the medial rear crease region

76: equatorialized bilateral extrude; bulky body; equatorializes/tan-bronzes the skin; stabilizes the size of the nostrils against a strong I-shaped philtrum region; sets as heavy the indentation following the line above the nostrils down to the sides of the moustache region (regardless of male or female); rounds the base of the rear, extrudes the pectorals; there was a real scarcity of subjects in this group, i suspect reflecting the scarcity of central american and tropical-climate individuals willing to volunteer in a context clearly skewed towards western expectations for what counts as an 'exhibitionism-worthy' body; that is, western beauty and body standards likely affected this group in particular

77: rounded tetrahedral nose, preferred flowing hair wear; upsqueezed / taught rear muscles; rounded pyramidal

78: downward inward brows, tightness of the arms and hands for controlling/gripping; path aura deblender

79: de-curving solidity, raised (especially lower part of the) abdominal column; forward symmetric hills; renders the body frame solid at the expense of curvature; forward communicator weighing in; puffs the cheeks and makes lower facial features slightly heavier; 'black-izes bearing' or adds a force to the appearance at least minimally; renders certain gross body features or shapes bigger

80: gives a lower poke to the chest, definition or flatness of the underbust, smooth-elongates or allows the pronouncement of legs. Sharp or smooth division of character between gross regions. "(Mostly vertical) sawtooth." Often seen as a sharp lower, smooth upper boundary in a region

81: "concentric cylindrical stacking"; southeasternizes, giving more african or middle eastern features relevance for or against traits; mostly widens nose, cheek, and mouth regions, plumps / voluptuous-increases these and reproductive organs while muscularizing the base to which they are attached. confers increased force / unignorability to the interacting features without the trait holder having to explicitly communicate.

82: basic rounding of the chest and cheeks, regardless of positioning, also seems related to rounding of the suprailiac and hips; "ovoid nonprimaxial understructure"—the 'islands that form symmetrically paired, disconnected from the central axis. In this sense, partially related to arms and legs, and open/de-squinted eye shape

83: "atlas' up-trapezoid", particularly of the cheeks and up the chest and torso. Uses a plane to press the trait upward and inward, giving a primaxial caudodistal to rostromedial line to the trait. Off of this line, spillover may still occur for nonprimaxial traits. If the cheeks are to bulge for example, they were more likely to do so upwards and inwards in the sample, or over the sides, as if someone were pressing hands to the face

84: general light or heavy chest volume; a cubic bounding box that calls visual attention to the upper torso volume as a mass in general and, curiously, the front *plane* of the lower torso, thus constituting an "upwards 2D to 3D coronal extrude"; | *Ajani's note: in a VERY interesting (and literal) twist, the trapezoidizing which takes place between 83 and 84 can be seen on other processes such as heart valve elaboration and stomach formation. a turn on one axis accompanied by a partial turn on another, both of which seem to follow some kind of torquing rule not unlike the relation of E & B fields in electromagnetism and similar to a 3D sign transition cycle i speculated about in laurentia. Given the metabolic and circulatory implications—energy conversion functions—it's not as surprising that 83 is related to stress. I imagine processes like this are heavily related to the organism's orientation with respect to its outward or programmed-outward environment, hence a partial root in external factors. Seems to have some symmetry implications, with obvious hooking and asymmetries in various features all over the front view over the body, depending on what is in this cluster, how emphasized those planets and points are, and what key angles are being made to it. 83 and 84 are good candidates for key regions of the human species template*

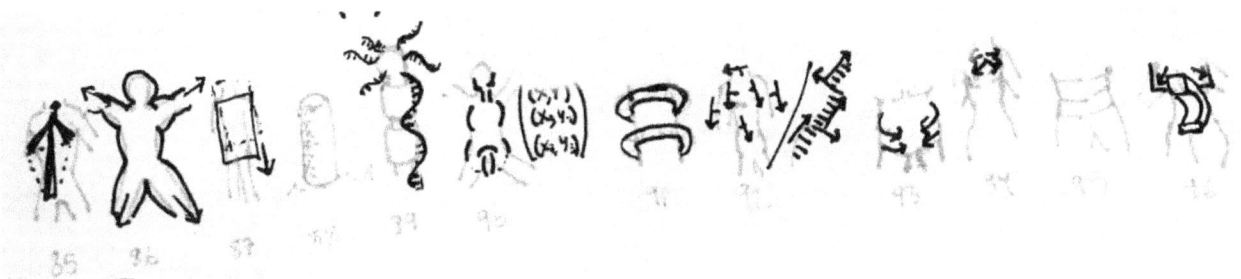

85: tripod comet tail? Gives a linear spillover effect? OR foldout plane, like an open window

86: full exposure star body shape; "the asterisk"; seems to pull out appendages / extrusions from the midline and color their weight OR, the axis OR diamond torso coronal flattener

87: linear; the line; the visual hierarchy follows a straight path top to bottom, or along the length of the individual; likely a powerful region in the charts of many living things' species templates, especially to the extent that the concept of a line forms one of the most fundamental patterns for a time or space-based progression

88: wide cylinder; confers a basic cylinder shape to the feature, more likely in a way that circumscribes, overpowers, shrinks or deflates other shapes attached to it

89: sheathing; "variable amplitude wave"; recursive layering of the tube with more cylinders; is the layer that occurs in time along a path, can produce tubes or cones of varying thickness along the length. Another candidate for a duodecanate most associated with the sun

90: strengthening of the gender or social expression. "The multiplicative vector." This seems to be where promotion of the tools of mating and reproduction live; not the act itself, but elaboration of the tool which is used for it. Differentiated depth which turns up or down every facet of expression that might be useful for mature mating in the species template of many organisms. Elaboration of this area is more likely associated with puberty and the secondary sex characteristics. More mundanely, i imagine, the interactional characteristics. But i can't see such characteristics in action through pictures. And even if i had videos from my sample subjects, i doubt they would tell me much about the actual 1:1 interaction with each person. This duodecanate is the most likely candidate so far not only for the general species template for "organisms," but also for the duodecanate specifically associated with the sun (summer solstice aside). In the context of projecting oneself, one's favorite thing to reconcile. Its function. Dials up various energies in the body in accordance with sign associations of the asteroids contained therein; 'the abacus; the multiplicative vector' for compounding various 1:1 projective features—to be noticed by favored interactants—across the body

91: "rings"; overwhelmingly associated with gender-sponsored dominance; attaches a partner or partner type, and shows where one's intent to re-project what they project is actively engaged by another, no questions asked. That other may not be a person or actual mate. Could be themselves. Could be an alter ego. Features or behaviors which simulate that of the mate, attached to the owner. Adornments, poses, or images which one is iconically tied to; from what i can tell, toroids, matrices, or rings which encircle various areas of the body, including hair… at the time of this writing on 1/7/2023, i know little to nothing about ring theory in mathematics, and have been looking it up on Wikipedia for the last 10 minutes. It seems that if you are going to have shapes and formulas, you also need to have things that go into those formulas and rules for how those formulas work. Hence the need for rings and groups in all this. Fur and other checks on the environment's influence on the body are probably related to this in the sense that, if an organism is to have a body in a niche in the first place, there must be some regulatory surface / interface between the organism and that environment. How philosophical. How profound the role of existential complements to an expression without actual required partners—only contexts as complements

92: buff body; perfected amplitude; "the derivative; rate of change per represented regions at 0"; fully expressed musculature; seems to bring features to their optima. I can't see a commonality in this set, but i will tentatively consider it to be the derivative

93: folded hips and obliques, upper abdominals? Can't tell

94: small nipples; v-outer chest; front view U / wide base parabola

95: horizontal banded torso? …which I've found to sometimes be associated with alcohol consumption

96: "chest to subnavel sagittally extruded sideways wide U whose base is pushed distal from the viewer"; squares the body frame in coronal view pinches the chest rectangularly like a banded bra and pinches the subnavel similarly

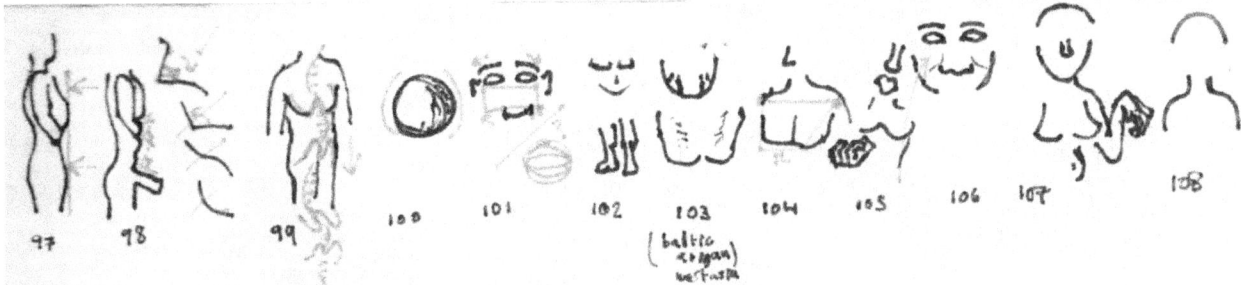

97: front plane press; the classic coronal flattener

98: ribbing; 'region transition decision function steepener' higher metabolically muscularly masculinized all five possessors in the sample, more likely to render the male holder slim with an athletic build, as well as endowed, or increase the salience of these ideas in the viewer. Targeted musculature for each specific region's own purpose. "local sectional sharp amplitude / region transition decision function steepener" between external functional regions hardens and squares all sections of the body, favoring masculine morphology. This is one of the main metadata regions i've found, and is a good candidate for the human species template. seems to be part two—the higher frequency jitter—of what happens in 99

99: androgynizer; 'anterior-posterior phase shift; 'the male-female slider', mixes male and female traits or—for pronounced male or female holders, promotes the expression of the other. Testosteronic within an estrogenic domain. W-function pronouncement / hyperpolarization-depolarization wave, mirrored about the function's peak or trough. Depending on the sign of the function, supports an "M-W priority flip / anterior-posterior phase shift" along amplitude axis distal (i.e. viewer depthwise) to the coronal plane. Produces characteristic male-female projection. Of the six possessors in the sample, three were transgender and all were male-female high binary

100: hyperpowered domain, spherizes non primaxial regions, constraining them to fill up a globe-shaped volume. Either in the chartholder or compelled as a concept in the viewer. "the basic sphere." Not surprisingly, this region is square 136, the hyperboloid

101: smirk / pull back near-flat smile which creates a plateau straight down from the eyes to the sides of the mouth, with some mouth line creasing. Outer eyebrows arch down; possibly rounds or rectangularizes ears. Possibly.

102: leg thread, calf definition; seems to slightly favor sleepy eyes / heavy eyelids

103: pinches the hemilateral; baltic-/western asian-/aryan-izes features; flattens or sideways outpulls the chest, pinches the lower lateral (not medial) chin—horizontally

104: inverted trapezoid chest, pointier nose; more clenched fists or grasping hands in this in this group than other groups; may have a relationship with the fingers and joints

105: the upper round; (their) left leaning, horn nose - de-triangularizes nose and draws upper, middle, and lower nose bridge closer to 1:1:1 ratio; lips thicken vertically; underbust is more gracefully rounded/spherized

106: side jaw-brow table; flowing nose base; dimple whiskers; contributes to beauty-ideal shaped eyes, more downward tilted on the inner corners; side jaws are wider, lending to more of an oval shaped face; straighter, gently curved brow

107: wrist and puff; heart-shaped face; slims the nose; cone-shaped breasts, lower abdomen navel puff—the area in which the navel sits is more likely to resemble a slight mound; many photos selected displayed a grasping gesture, suggesting the inward bend of the wrist

108: perfect semicircular noggin, or ovoid forehead and forehead peak; I also noticed circular shoulders. May be may not be significant

109: cheek to mouth in a downward triangle from the outer eye corners to the outer mouth corners; I noticed the mouths pursed more; clavicles were more salient overall

110: bowed at the central abdomen; investigate connection to elbows

111: circle; rounds the face, expanding the coronal cheek plain; eyebrows tend to be more classically arched, chest rounded; torso more likely to follow a gentle S curve; the nose, in particular, does NOT seem to be heavily affected by this region

112: vertical oval; elongates the face; more likely to narrow the arms and, less so, the legs accordingly; the mouth appears to be noticeably lower-placed, suggesting that this kind of head shape is mostly upper bite and cranially oriented; | *Ajani's note: this duodecanate may be of particular interest to analyze against its neighbor, 111. Surely the kinds of developmental mechanisms involved are associated with other effects throughout the body, conveniently comparable against the effects of 111. There is a big jump between the two*

113: grip sweeping bowl; oval-rectangular head with a V-shaped jaw; chin pokes forward; there was more of a suprailiac C-grip, where the pelvic attachment through the waist, to the legs, was much more likely to resemble a sweeping bowl

114: solid color background; absorption-refraction mood of arms; these images were *very* easy to find, as many more of them placed the individual against a particular solid background color; | *Ajani's note: fascinating, seems to reflect an overall mood affinity to be absorbed into the viewer from the individual. Their actual energetic color; as the background colors behind the individuals stood out here, so too did their... [analyzing...] arm and leg shape and structure—an even further fascinating statement of the motor appendages as sphere-blurring interfaces between the individual and their environment; i believe, 111 - 114 form roughly the region of 'the flagellate'*

115: focal point even-odd gridding; like 114, images were noteworthy in clear background colors, but there was much more often a sharp salient focal point in the image; in high contrast, women's breasts and bottoms were delineated by sharp, arcing lines. Men's heads, penises, and abdomens were similarly sharp lined in detail. Men tended towards even numbers of focus areas, women towards odd numbers. Men towards lines and hexagons, women towards circles and triangles; geometrically, this region seems to be THE defining difference between male and female body types, perhaps as projections of defining differences in how their respective frequentic fields are projected. Men's symmetries tended to *be* the axis/grid, while women's symmetries defined equally oriented parcels across the grid. Round shapes were more typically female while rays and asterisks were more male

116: tilted focal gray-gridding; white and gray color, grayer scaled backgrounds predominated; symmetry tended to be more about the angled coronal plane, approximately 20-30 degrees rearward compared to the 115s, but the rules tend to be similar. Somewhere between the chest jut and nose—if not the nose then the stomach—a focal point emerged; weights tended towards more extreme ends, with thin subjects being very thin

117: T-I white balance rotation; white light; associated with white balance in the background, straight upwards or downwards pointing features; the face in particular was subject to having its features vertically darkly I-compressed or T-expanded after subtracting out an average forehead, with direct implications for stereotypical notions of attractiveness. Ts—where the mouth and nose were horizontally similar in width, tended to make for sparser, prettier faces. Is, where the mouth was substantially wider than the base of the nose (in men this could be further amplified by the presence of a beard or moustache) tended to make for less attractive, more intimidating or off-putting faces; implications for primate evolution of jaw structure; and in a very interesting aesthetic finding i never thought of—1-18-2023—we see the I in the coronal plane in more male forms, in the transverse plane from above the body in more female forms, the rear and breasts in the female doing transversely what the eyebrows and moustache-mouthlines do coronally. The brows and nose-mouth line coronally in females doing what the body base and penis do transversely in males; some body forms have distinct versions of both rotations while some have neither, and this can produce certain kinds of midtransition transgender and androgynous body forms respectively; | *Ajani's note: in my own appearance, i have T's in both rotations based on overt features alone, but bright mouth lines beneath dark ingrown hairs in the moustache region give me a heavy I configuration in the face*

118: sagittal spokes; compacts the central torso at the expense of the limbs or vice versa; affects body proportionality. Almost certainly has implications for general embryological shaping, development from prenatal shaping to adult. I imagine this duodecanate evolves very noticeably over time, perhaps implying that its squares cannot do this, but may more likely measure time or evolve over space instead. But that's just sketched speculation

119: swastika saddle coordinate system; sagittal zig-zagging spokes elaborate the hinges on 118 with one hemisphere widening in the plane, the other widening through it, similar to the ancillary nodes of the Mandelbrot set; in a saddle, appears to affect the sagittal penis and coronal shoulders in men, the sagittal chest and coronal hips in women; major asteroidal contributions here will tend to announce this mapping system

120: C-star splay; via appendages (including the head) bends the body in a C about the dextro-sinistral axis, or splays the arms and legs at less extreme bends. The effect here is to trace out four ovoid paths for range of motion, affecting stubbiness of the appendage joints; the nose and mouth seemed to be squeezed in their triangle, or at least obey a triangular (as opposed to a funneled) configuration

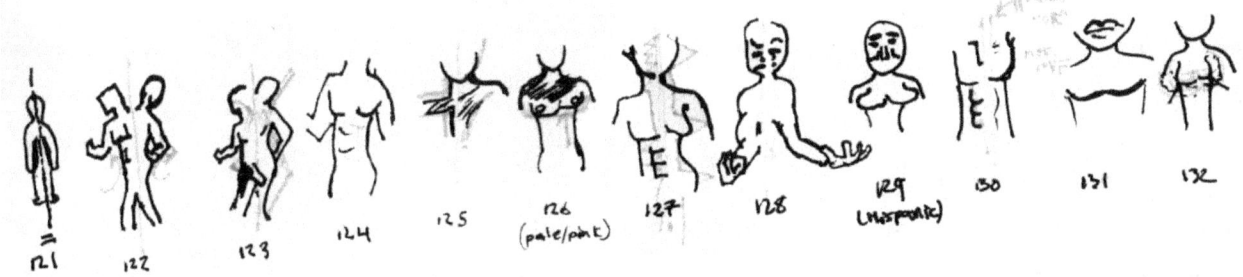

121: basic mirror symmetry of the body about the midline. Not much else to say

122: right hand rule; straight on one side, bent on the other; now of course this is subject to selection 'flukes', but those pre-biased samples are a critical part of how I apply intuition in these surveys. That said... interestingly, of the 15 images sampled, 3 of the 3 men were right bent, and 7 of the remaining 12 women and M2Fs were left bent in the arms. Two of those 12 had no glaring symmetry in their poses. In the coronal plane, following a right hand rule, there is an implication that men spin counterclockwise (with the viewer's thumb pointed to themselves), while women spin clockwise in their projected forms. For basic head to toe consistency though, certain organs twisting left at ventral location or right at dorsal ones would support a certain connection between energy circulation and processing and projective converses versus contrapositives. Which is which depends on where you are standing

123: Z-posture (coronal); facing the viewer, subjects tended to lean one way in the upper body and the other way in the lower body, tilting them along an imaginary circle; male penises tended to be straighter but pointed in a definite direction that was not straight; women were more likely to have their entire body tilted, or at least the head; there are implications for posture here, as well as internal metabolic asymmetries during growth; there was something notably pagan about the appearances of these people

124: back arch; smooths the forward stomach, in some cases creating a dragging effect on the reproductive organs. This may seem trivial, but may have something to do with embryonic uncurling and, in that case, would be part of a very elaborate and comparatively long-running process

125: rail routes; defined or minimal neck, definition in the clavicle, in its separation of the head from torso, also seems to have a kind of inverting relationship to the midplane of the upper chest

126: paler pink skin; high upper chest, the necklace region just beneath the clavicle, the level of detail and contrast therein; for social reasons related to how we dress, seems to say a lot about the level of formality in the contexts others are more likely to find you in; can also resemble a tightening noose; subjects nipples—male and female—were both notably circular, average in size

127: male-female rough-smooth front facing surface, uniform friction vs notches; trades frequency for amplitude in the front facing coronal plane; also related to fat versus muscle

128: bracing arms entangled, or solid as a tree; indicates how hard or how automatically one holds what they hold; affects the biceps; males were more likely to be seriously no-nonsense or threatening. Females conveyed defiance or skepticism in their countenance proportional to the slimness of their faces. Rounder faces were drastically different in that they were very friendly; this region seems to be related to sexual dimorphism applied by the individual as a weapon or tactic for controlling others' actions; | *Ajani's note: the last contour surveyed, 14:17, January 18, 2023*

129: little outpointed; hispanicizes features with narrower nose, squarer cheeks, darker eyes and eyebrows, average rounder face, and outpointed chest; there is a littleness to the body or its presentation; more subjects had an averageness of torso build and tone which did not promote standing out amidst others with less mid-bell curve features. Accordingly, expressions and smiles were attended by smaller scales or energy amounts, consummate with a projected image which faces a harder time being respected by the interactants who survey them; the shoulders tended to be smoother, but also squarer; two of the four subjects were M2F

130: bubbling density; affects the 'bubbling'—creasing among neighboring regions, rough bumpiness vs bloated smoothness in a trait, depending on how sharp / fast / far along the elaboration processes are. More apparently tied to weight and "bubbling density", compactness /tightness of traits (especially broad surfaces). Some association with muscle tone

131: feathered 2^nth degree parabolas; feathered upper lips and light W underbust, parabolic chin; conducive to general good looks typically associated with easier social mobility

132: encompassing sphere; extreme chest sizes at one end or the other, conducive to females or trans males; seems to have a noticeable connection to sexuality and the desire to express it as it is

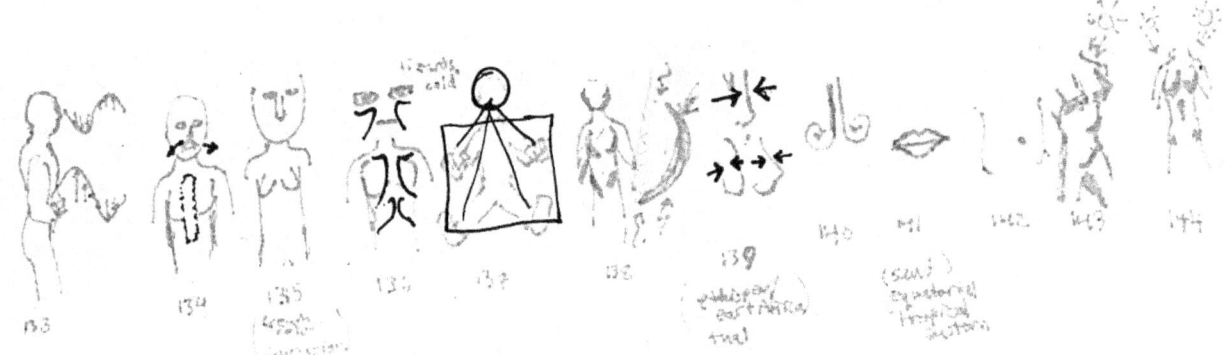

133: up-down point; oscillating vertical amplitude gaze direction towards you the viewer. Traits point noticeably up or down or are posed as such

134: rectangular chop; downlips in the outer corners, squares the chest with a chopping imprint down the midline; slightly smaller sharp-ended ovallette eyes; seems conducive to maleness

135: slim outbent U / flared parabola, caucasianizes, slimmer nose, darker eyes, rectangular body frame, more cream-colored skin; seems to mostly render more consistent noses in a slim outbent U; note the sesquiquadrate relationship with 81. Evolutionary coincidence? Or is it?

136: hyperbolic flutedness / butterfly topology, haunting eyes, looking at an array of images of people who have something here feels a bit eerie. Stern lips / flat, almost unamused resting face indicating a determination to never be irrelevant, regardless of when, where, or how the person is doing something. Adds a definiteness to the body overall, seems to encourage a "hyperbolic flutedness / butterfly topology" in the features, flattening along the center horizon. Gives an air of the unknown to the gaze, making the individual more intimidating; left-right carve / de-rounding

137: quadrappendage from the sun; from a round or pronounced-curve face emerges a four sided pyramid with the limbs as sides and face/central feature at the peak, squaring the circle; seems strongly associated with showmanship projection

138: delineable sectioning; clear-graded syncitializes gross body regions, merging them enough to form a coherent whole, but not so much that they can't be told apart; seems to direct refraction; smooth shadows and matte highlight areas

139: bronze and slim protrusion; 'ethiopian->thai-izes' the features, in an indian ocean-rimmed band. Features that protrude were slimmer and more pinched here, as if they were initial thickenings of the ram line

140: ram line: a two spiral orientations of opposite spin, at their interface, launch a straight line—as would a printing press. This seems to be a generative configuration for merging energies of complementary orientations; 'collision output' or 'generative intersection' may be better names for explaining the flow of this one from 141 sand skin/plane of dots

141: sand skin; gives equatorial and tropical eastern features, dehighlighting /matte skin plane with more gray-absorption, line-sharp lips that don't merge into surrounds as easily; 'plane of dots' may be a more reasonable name for explaining the connection between 142 dot in the plane and 140 ram line

142: singularity; dot in the plane; small nipples and other features sharply contrasted against a wider homogeneous-flat background; perhaps moles and other standout point-like features

143: highlights; striking vertical and front plane light against a plane ~30 degrees rotated rearwards along the dextral-sinistral axis, indicating horizontal-striped light band creases

144: highlights; light corners diagonal to the viewing plane with supra-infra line as axis

FIGURE 42: BEFORE ENERGY FLOWS (RIGHT)

At some point I attempted to model the flow of energy from a central emitter, and explain to myself how planetary spins and cycles formed analogies with walk cycles. This didn't make it into Figure 15 on page 278, but it is interesting to think about.

FIGURE 43: BEFORE SPECIOGRAMS (BOTTOM)

On my way to developing speciograms, I looked at where the energy seemed to be flowing in the male and female bodies.

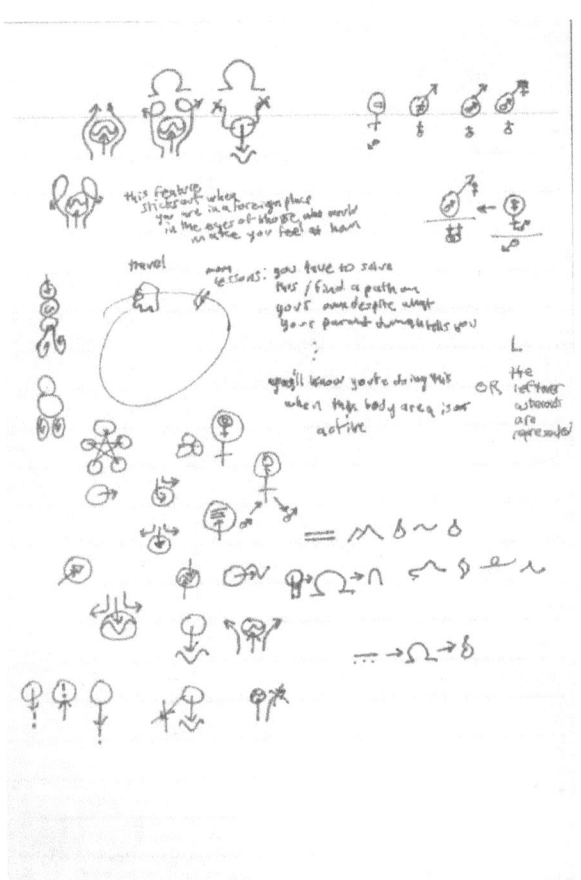

FIGURE 44: MAKEHUMAN AND AI FACE DIFFERENCES (RIGHT)

2024:

Early observations of AI generated images allowed me to finally start asking what it was about my body wiring that attracted me to Indian women. That question, as with all of my inquiries originating in the hormones, quickly faded away and morphed into what would become LANDOX.

FIGURE 45: HOW HUMANS EVOLVED (FROM A PARTICLE PERSPECTIVE AS THE STAR-SIZED GODS SEE US)

This is all speculation, but makes a fun read nonetheless. As you can see, my speciograms are taking form.

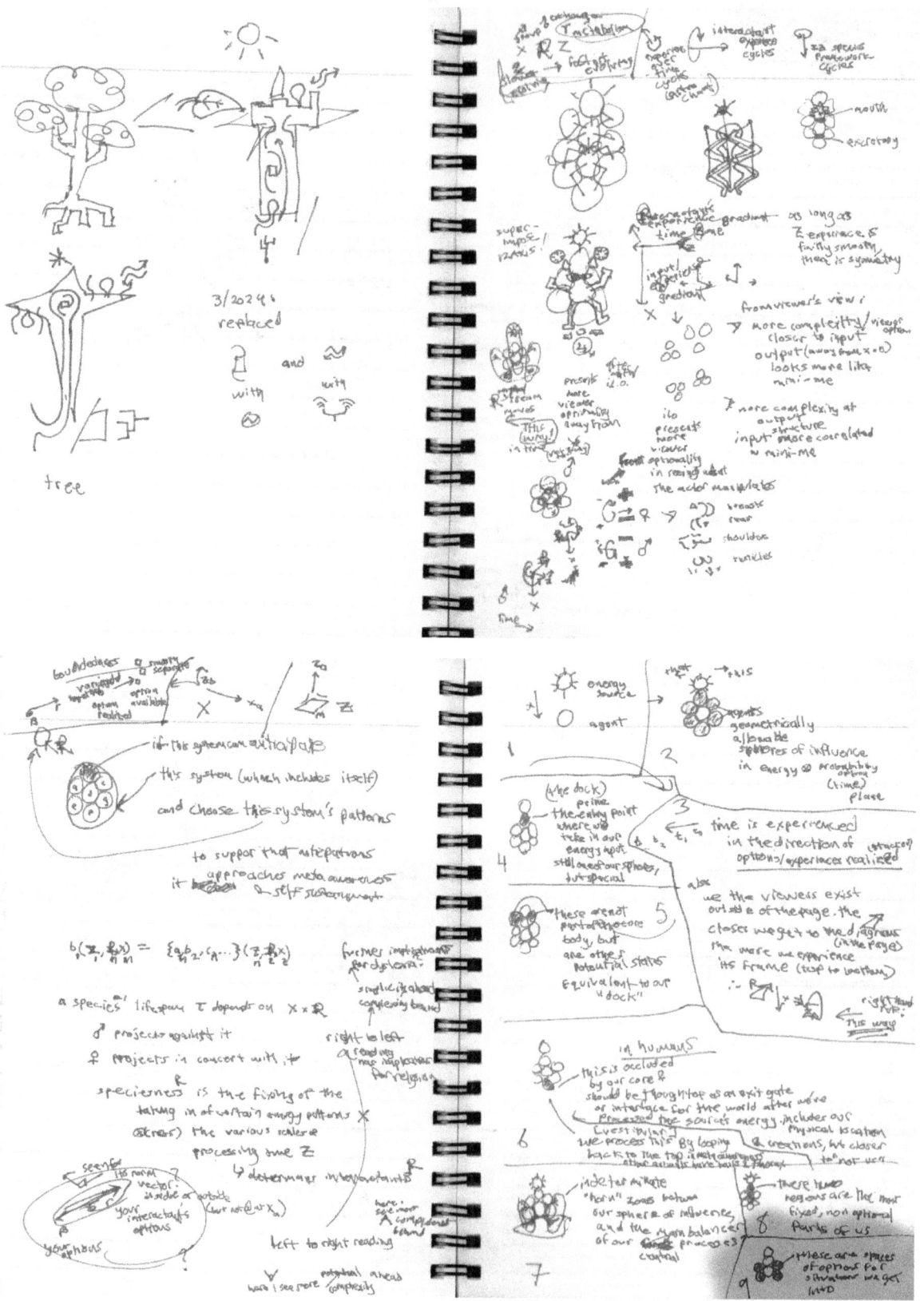

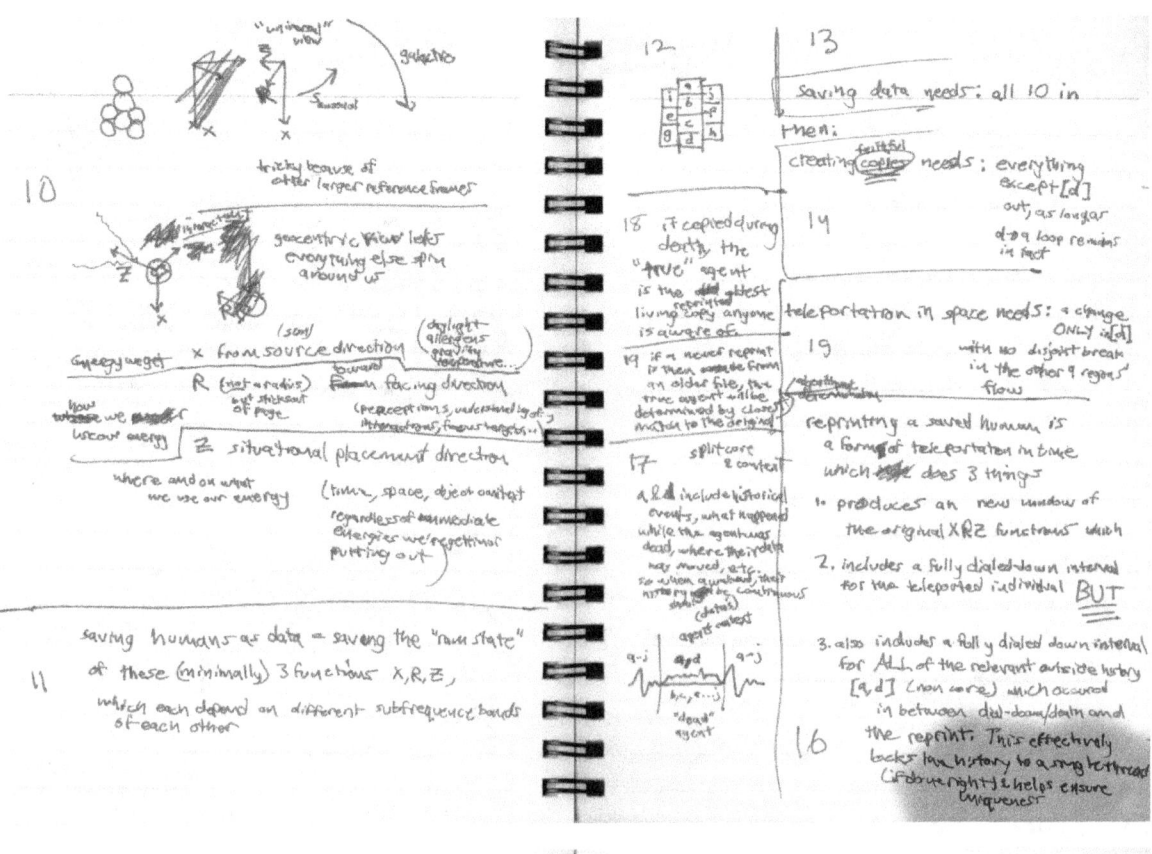

10

tricky because of other larger reference frames

geocentric view lets everything else spin around us

energy weget   x from source direction   (sunlight affections gravity etc telepresence...)

R (not a radius) facing direction (not stickout of page)

how-come-we-spend use our energy

Z situational placement direction

where and on what we use our energy

(time, space, object context regardless of immediate energies we're/goettime putting out

11   saving humans as data = saving the "raw state" of these (minimally) 3 functions X, R, Z, which each depend on different subfrequency bands of each other

12   **13**

saving data needs: all 10 in

then:

creating faithful copies needs: everything except [d]

out; as long as d↔g loop remains in tact

18 if copied during death the "true" agent is the oldest reprinting living copy anyone is aware of

14 teleportation in space needs: a change ONLY in [d] with no disjoint break in the other 9 regions' flow

19 if a newer reprint is then made from an older file, the true agent will be determined by closest match to the deleting

17 split care & context

a [d] includes historical events, what happened while the agent was dead, where their data was moved, etc. so when a symbol that history may be discontinuous

(data)
agent context

q→i   q,d   q→j

b,c,e...j

"dead" agent

19 teleportation in space needs: a change ONLY in [d]

reprinting a saved human is a form of teleportation in time which also does 3 things

1. produces an new window of the original XRZ functions which

2. includes a fully dialed-down interval for the teleported individual BUT

3. also includes a fully dialed-down interval for ALL of the relevant outside history [q,d] (non-core) which occurred in between dial-down/death and the reprint. This effectively backs own history to a single fast thread (for every right) & helps ensure uniqueness

16

20

an original, accurate, unqualified data saves is called a 1-goritm

embedded in [q,d] is the notion of historical "algorithmic convergence" which is related to our rewriting of memories by [b]: every copy or reprint should automatically assume a copy of itself is either a clone or a true self, and one's data should be absorbed into the other. I don't see how to do this except through some kind of blockchain, but if it isn't done, the assumptions of self-awareness & the survival imperative break down.

• No copy should ever be considered homo sapiens-type

• first originally sourced reprints should have certain legal rights to identity, subject to reasonable algorithmic consistency standards (that the saved data was good. Not a robo queen elizabeth seeking to invalidate a more genuine certified data save & bad.

21   capturing not only what was done, but also what could have been done

in the 10-sphere approach we assume that [b] is successfully representing its entire [a-g] system. if we can't know or can't trust enough of the data in [b] (which almost no one will have provided enough of before 2026) then there is another option for at least "semi-truthfully" virtualizing humans who haven't been data saved. These won't be 1-goritms, just avatars or models thereof.

• a 16-sphere system includes the 3 front and 3 back spheres roughly representing the person's productions (upper front), aftermath impressions (lower back), nurturance styles (upper front), & what others think they can/should get out of the person (upper back).

• more importantly, this system takes much stronger note of optionality in light of [b]. that is [e↔F], [g↔h], etc... what were both generated option paths available at various stages of the record. less about detail and more about [what and was taken]

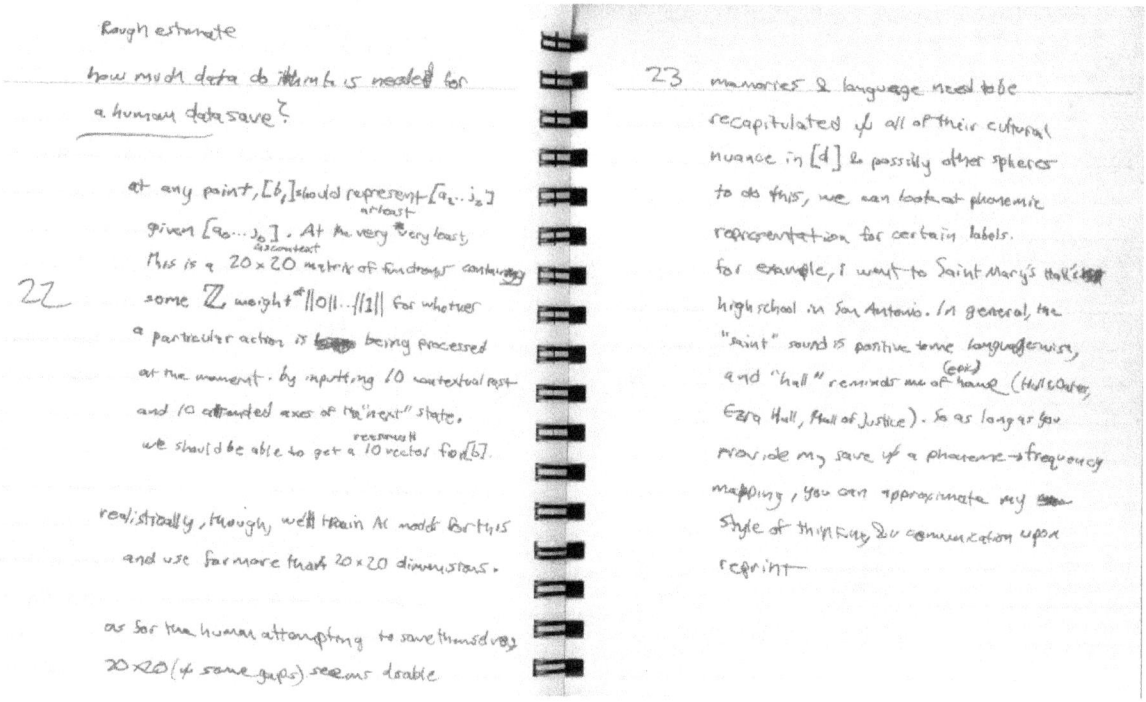

FIGURE 46: ACTION PATTERNS AS SUBNETWORKS

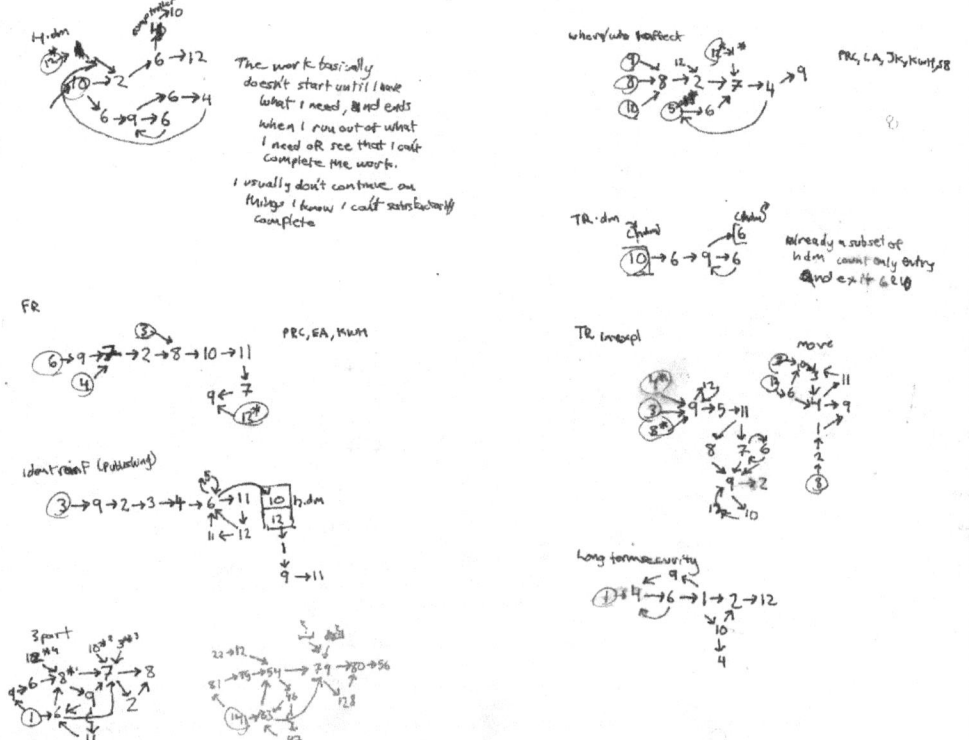

I was originally going to produce my autobiography using a series of network diagrams, but the sheer number of nodes and connections proved so intractably messy that I would abandon the effort in favor of Table 9 and Figure 7 in Chapter 3: Ajani's biography. These diagrams are VERY powerful though, in that they are the sharpest way for us to isolate specific families of behaviors. Too bad the sum of them is so tangled.

FIGURE 47: ASTROS AND TYPOS

On the top left is a theory I really believe to hold legitimacy, but which there aren't enough hours in the day for me to investigate further. It is the beginning of how the self-other-world 3D space of experience somehow gets flattened into a 2D chart. I will explain more in the next figure. The bottom left is a to-do list for completing this book, and squeezed just left of center is the very beginning of a nesting theory which I wouldn't begin until the following year. The right is a list of typos and annoyances I've found in *Laurentia 2* as of today, 6/28/2025. But I'll be honest, with a day job, a family, and my simultaneous work on *G of V* as a one-man publishing house as always, it was really hard to give a shit about continuing this.

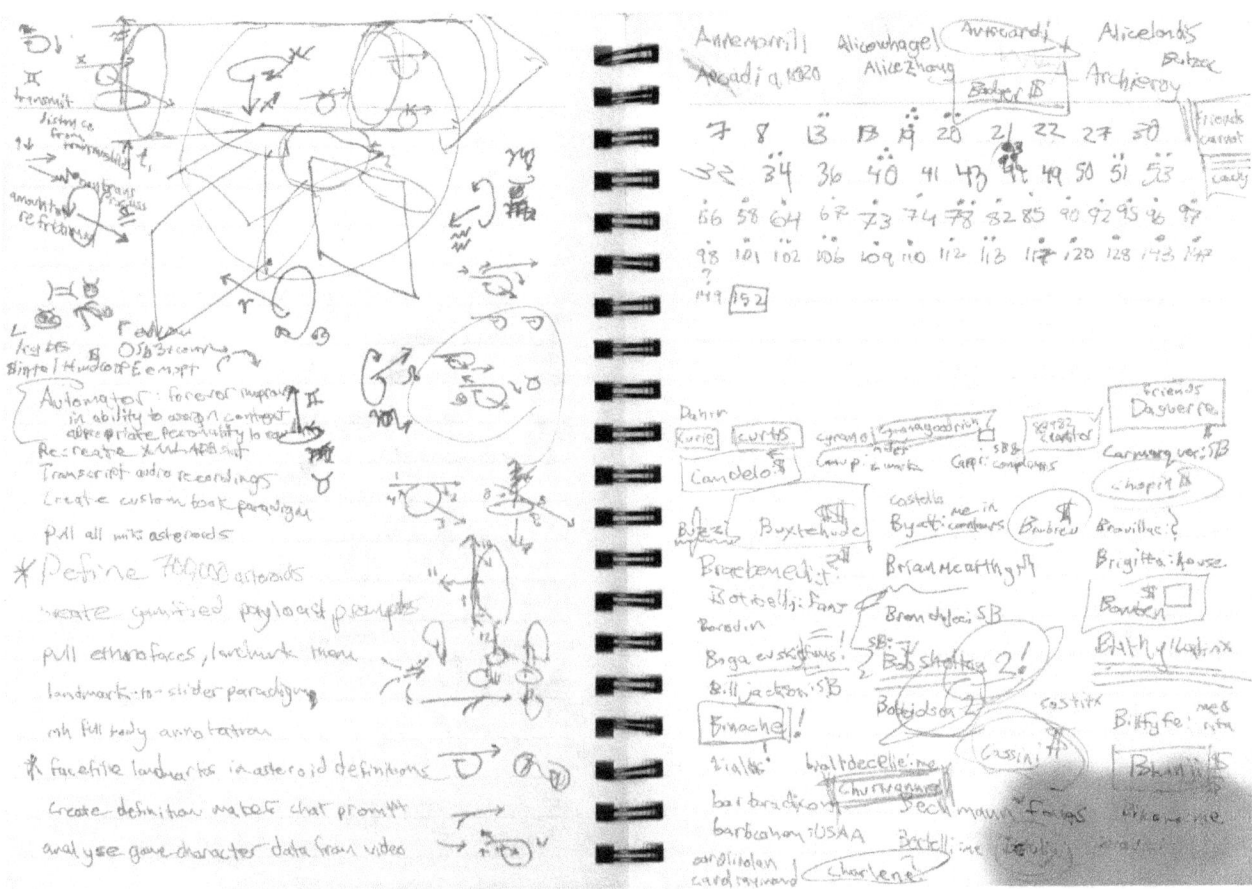

SPECULATIONS ON THE ASTROLOGICAL STRUCTURE AS A 3D TO 2D FLATTENING OF REAL AND POTENTIAL ENERGY

Rather than attempting to explain what is happening in this animation, I'll just give you the summary: "self-other-world" is actually an analogy for three kinds of energy: real, reachable potential, and [not immediately] reachable potential. Imagine you're standing still and looking forward. The energy you're spending looking is actually being used. From here, you could easily turn left or right at very little sustaining energy cost; every other horizon angle would be reachable potential [type 1] at whatever comparable muscle energy you're currently putting in. If you wanted to look up, however, that would be another matter. You couldn't do that without putting in an extra kind of muscle energy from where you are, and it would take a different kind of work or situation to sustain. This is would be potential energy type 2: something you could reach, but not from here. Now imagine that the real energy is the X axis being shot straight forward. Potential type 1 is the Y axis which can easily be immediately reached if you turn sideways. This might also happen automatically just as a function of your internally swaying processes. The Z axis, though, won't be easily achieved unless you put in work to hold your neck up. This would be analogous to the world energy.

The Book of Contours

FIGURE 48: THE 2D ASTRO CHART AS A FLATTENING OF 4 TYPES OF 3D ENERGY

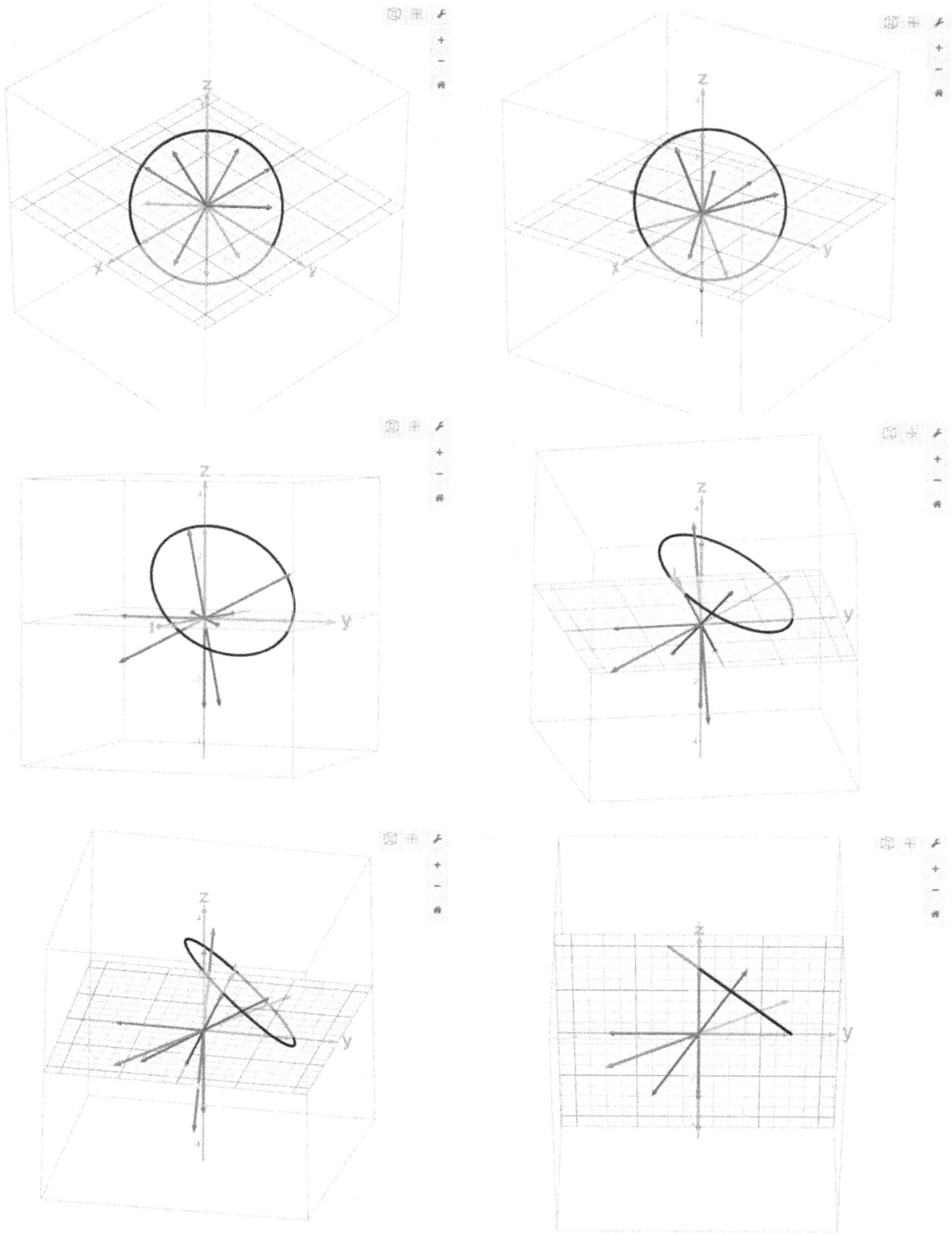

When you look straight on from any single axis, you end up with a plane made up of the two axes you didn't choose. In that plane, your potential to move one way or another oscillates as a function of your inner mechanics. There is a rate of throwing energy along axis 1, axis 2, in a cycle between them, and along a fourth (invisible) axis of Time with animates all of this. You can play with this graph at https://www.desmos.com/3d/4de78d851f

FIGURE 49: THREE TYPES OF ENERGY CYCLING WITHIN A BOUNDARY
+ 1 TIME DIMENSION TO CHANGE WHERE WE ARE ON EACH CURVE

There is A LOT going on in the image below, but I call your attention to a few things.

- The x axis follows a cosine wave
- The y axis (turn the page sideways) follows a sine wave
- The x-y plane follows a circle
- Pretend that the first image in Figure 48 above is a basic astro chart with Aries pointing to the left, Taurus pointing beneath it to the southwest along the x-axis, and so on. From the perspective below, not all "signs" are visible. Going counterclockwise from the x-axis, we see Taurus, Aries, Saj, Scorpio on top of half of Leo, Virgo, and Gemini. We DO NOT see Capricorn or Cancer energy, because that's the viewpoint we're standing on.

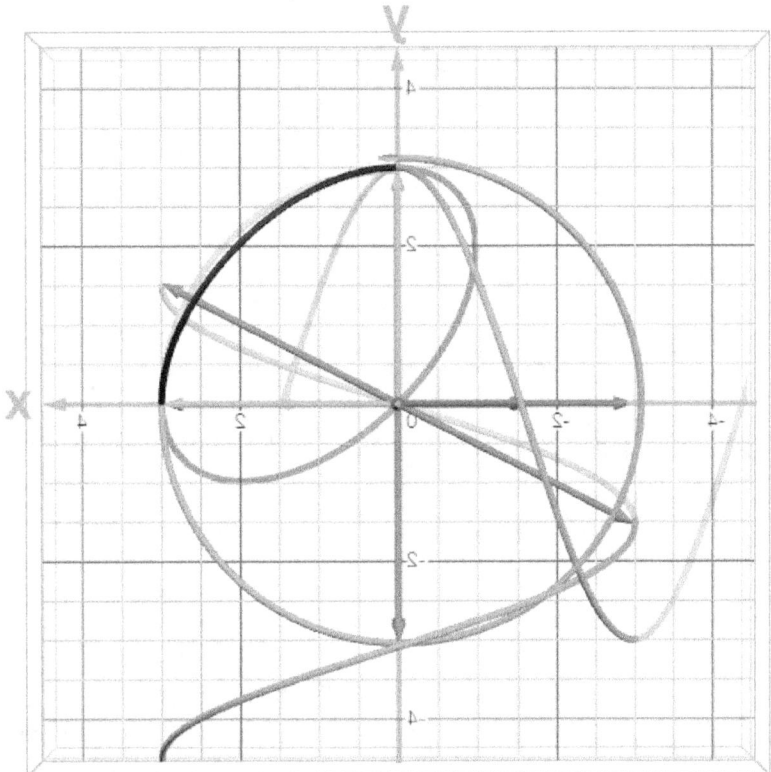

- The above doesn't just happen from the Z-axis viewpoint of "Capricorn institution lens," but also from the Virgo and Taurus axis lenses (Shown in the next figure).
- Also note that, although the overall "potential 2" energy stays in the space (the circle), there is also real energy that gets thrown out in cosine(x) and potential 1 energy thrown out in sine(y) (with a sideways turn). Apparently this Capricorn/+Z perspective circumscribes both real and reachable potential energy—Just like a Capricorn institution. Note that, we can drop the astrological analogies completely and just talk about what kinds of events are "allowed" to be reached from the perspective above. Certainly though, without these astro analogies it would be a lot harder to think about these three+1 energy axes for their practical meaning.

FIGURE 50: AN ENERGY POINT EMITS MULTIPLE AXES' WORTH OF REAL, POTENTIAL 1, AND POTENTIAL 2 ENERGY

We were looking at a flattened view of this energy point above, but in greater real-potential-time space, the picture is more complicated. Sure there are three axes of energy to propagate along, but those axes are all mixed up in multiple planes of energy, so the whole wheel becomes a collection of interdependent pieces. An astrochart is basically a bunch of these graphs of different parameters sitting around a central viewpoint. A thing's birth registers this moment as frozen in the eyes of witnesses.

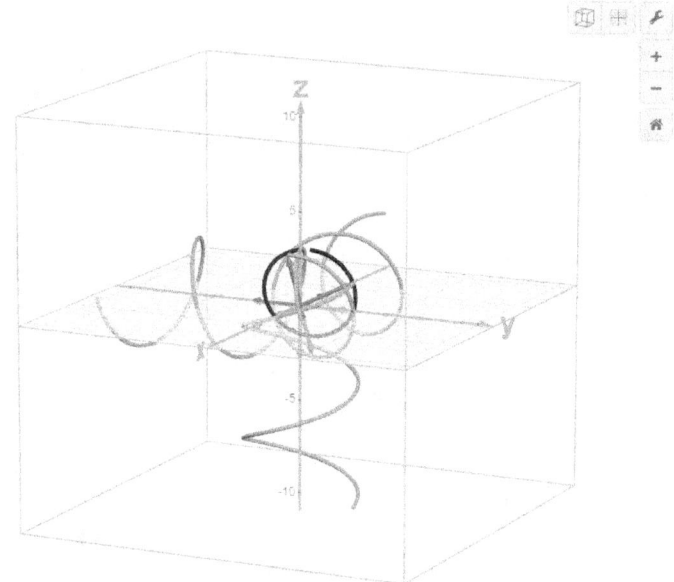

The snapshot below is a little tricky to explain without an animation, but look at the leftmost of the 3 spheres shown. It starts at Aries when Q = pi/2.

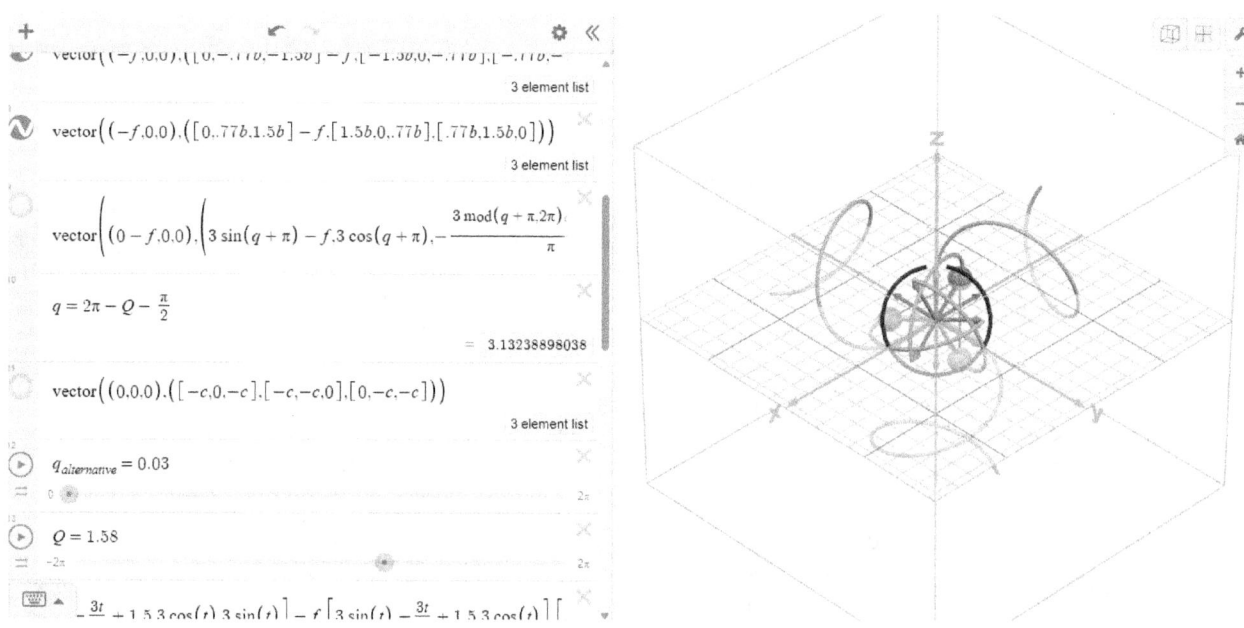

At Q = pi, that dot hits Taurus. But then, weirdly, it moves over to Libra. Most importantly, it's following the emission enrgy curves we discussed earlier. Moving from Aries to Libra through Taurus reminds us of 1) why so many people saw Venus as a double ruler of both the latter signs and 2) why we really need to look at oppositions first after considering an initial starting point in another sign.

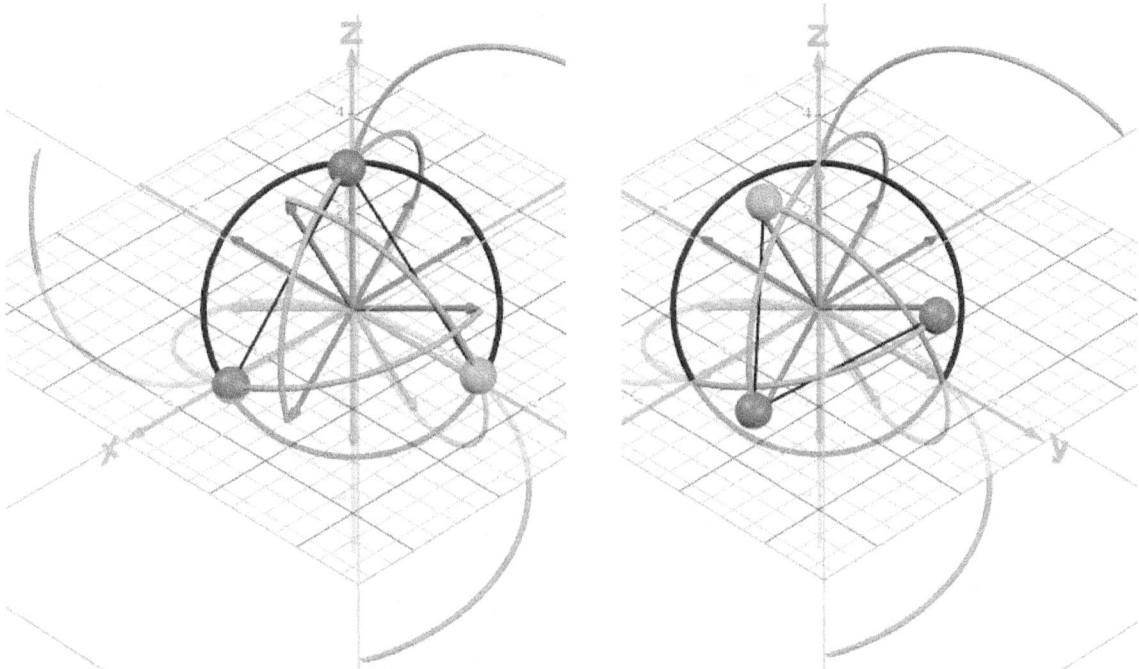

Q=-1 shows where our originally leftmost particle was. In the set of formulas I've designed here, it moves towards the central energy hub, thus making this one a domain or feminine case.

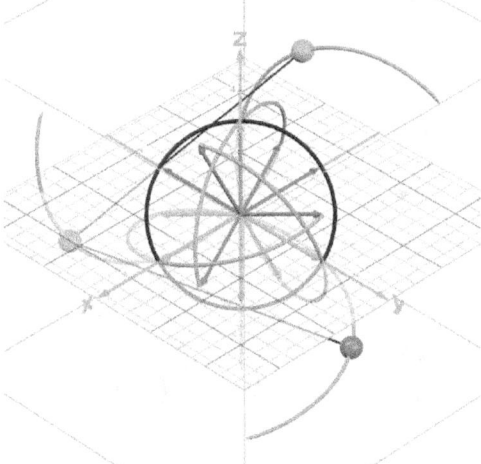

And what does all of this mean? It means that future researchers have another theory to test regarding how we conceive of energy as dimension.

SPECULATION ON THE HOURS (TIME-BASED CLAIVOYANCE): COULD THE MIDNIGHT POINT BE 1°12' LEO FOR EVERYONE?

The figure below is a mess, but follows what was, to me, a VERY interesting track. Basically, if 18q3 is death and somewhere between duodecanate 22 and 24 is the unbounded imagination, as well as birth, then I hypothesize that this region of Aquarius, roughly 0-5° to 15°, shows how time is counted in a lifespan (given that 6q7 is the time ticker unit). After some arduous calculations, I concluded that the denominator and numerators of 1 and 0 along this region trade places from the 0 to the infinite, and that there must be a point where the curve crosses the axis into being. And where does it do this? Halfway through d24, a kind of "AntiMidnight point" to Leo against which one can start a new day.

FIGURE 51: INVESTIGATING THE MIDNIGHT POINT

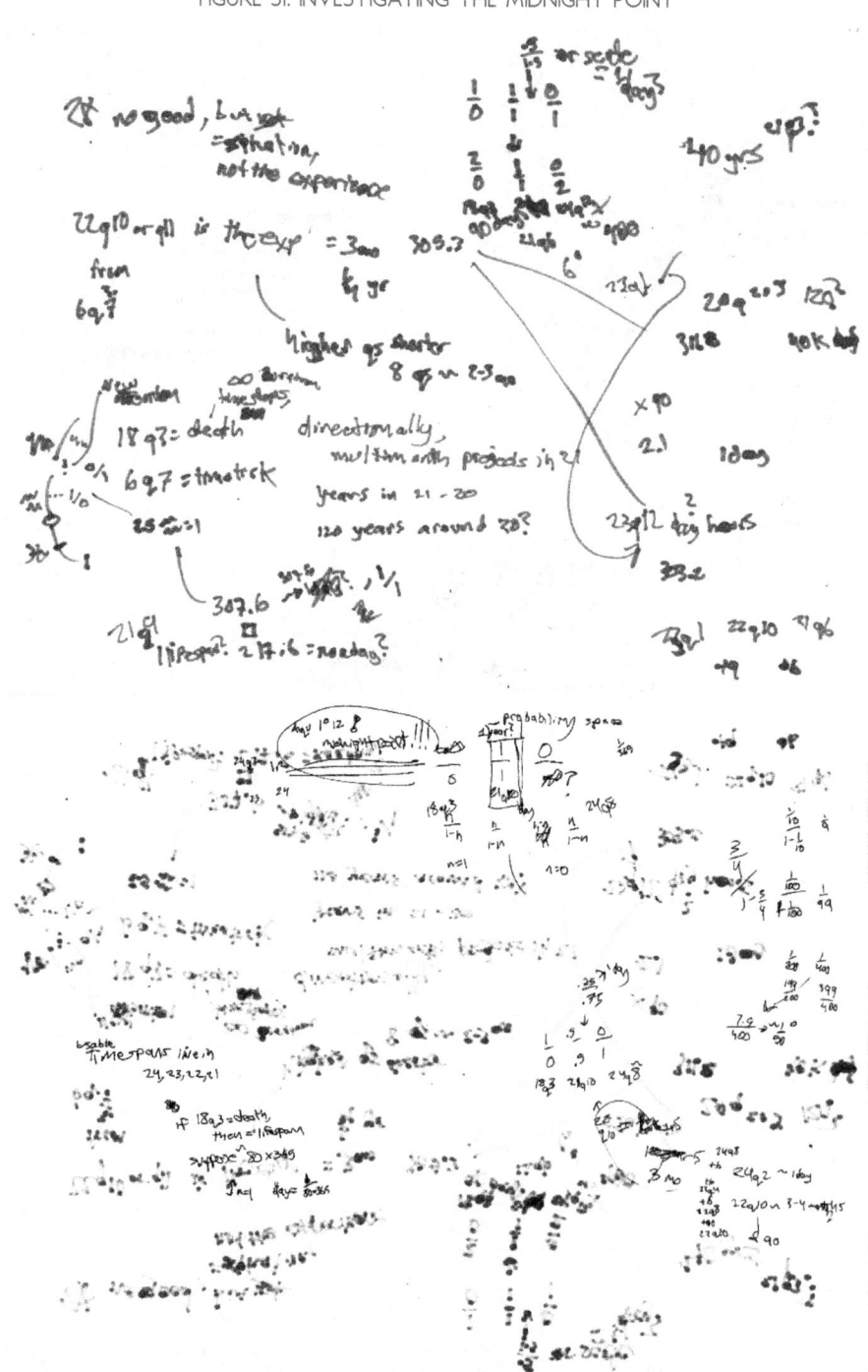

2025:

FIGURE 52: SEQUENCE OF
EVENTS LEADING TO
THIS AUTOBIOGRAPHY
AND WHY IT WAS
WRITTEN IN THIS WAY

As this book
progressed, I thought
about explaining how
we got here. I then
abandoned the idea
because the page count
was already reaching as
far as I wanted to go.
Still, this next figure
shows the various
milestones that my life's
action patterns have
crossed through in
order to produce this
work.

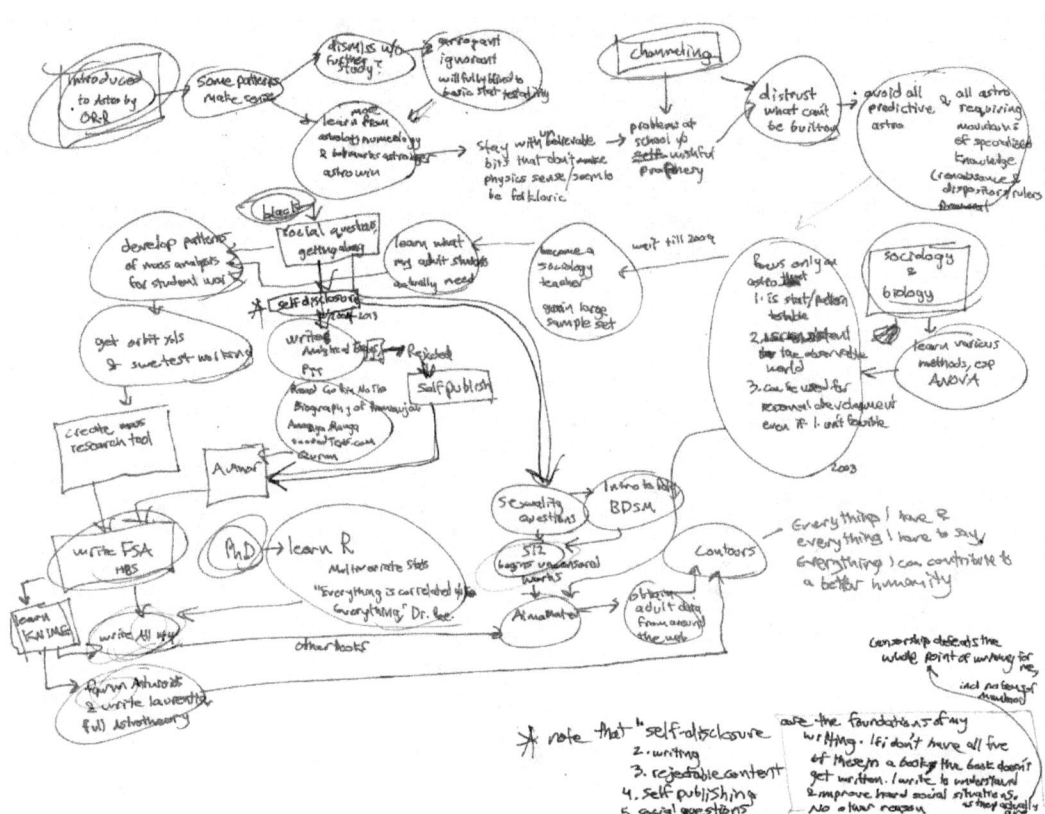

FIGURE 53: DATA-TYPING
SOCIAL AND VISUAL
INFORMATION

This diagram shows how
data flows through my
analysis process—the types
of information I work with
and how they are
transformed into statistical
and qualitative results.

FIGURE 54: SELF-OTHER-WORLD AS ENERGY EVENTS IN A NESTED CONTEXT

Finally, the drawing on the right leads to the drawing on the left, where I conceive of cardinal, fixed, and mutable signs as representing the same type of energy flow nested recursively into their own effects. The general principle states that when we send energy through a place, some of it gets transmitted, some gets bounced, and some of it gets absorbed. The points of transmission, [reflection and forking], absorption, and the process cycles following that absorption are analogous to the four elements, but that last process cycle has its own internal chemistry, and the whole system also has to talk to its context. The section to the upper right shows this.

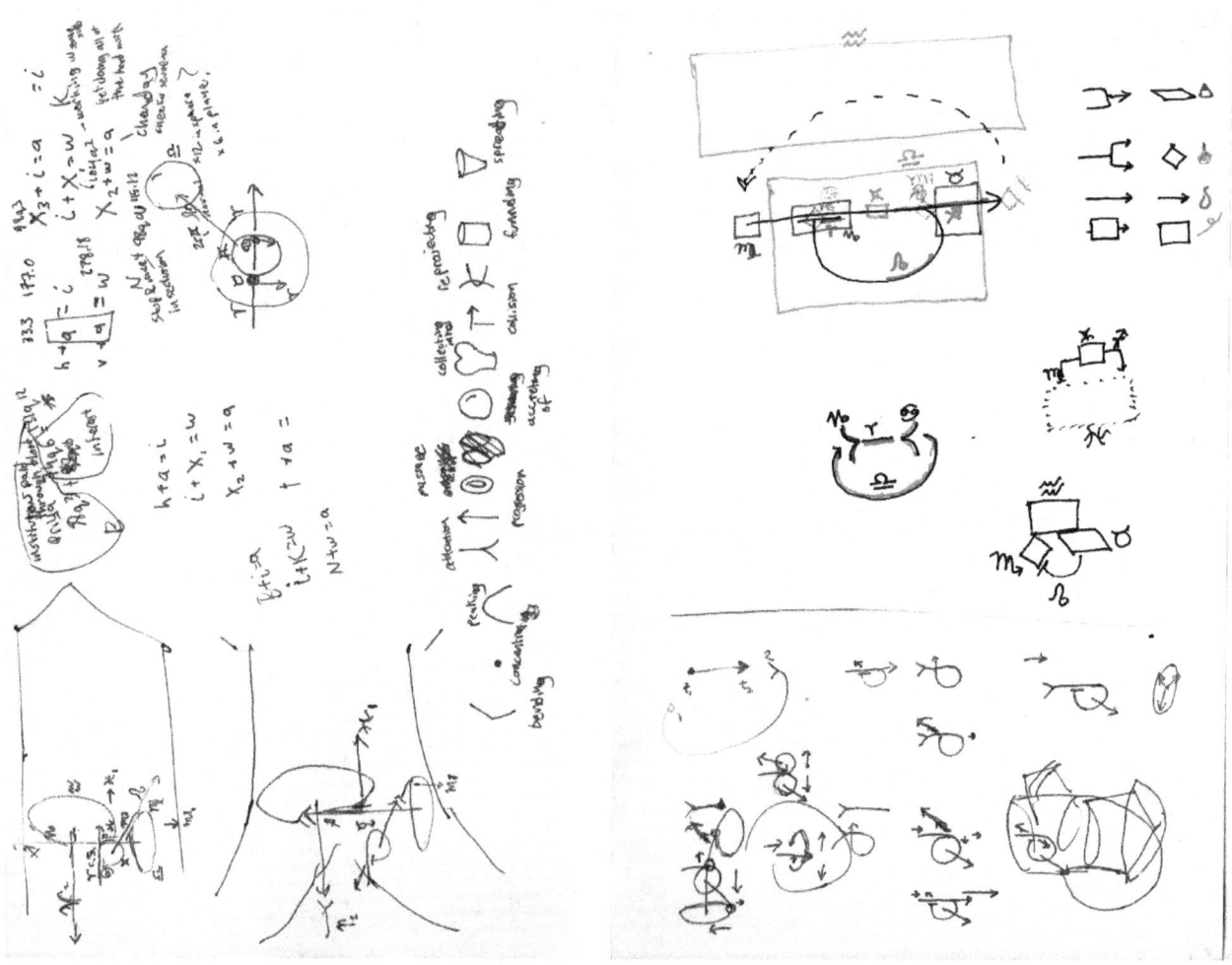

Chapter 24: A return to *Gamified Spirit's* "Dictionary of Major Relations"

In the previous chapter you saw some of my early attempts to represent different aspects of human dynamics. In order to help us easily turn social blocks into algorithms, it may be useful to return to the kind of procedural translation system I wrote about way back when in my book *Gamified Spirit*. In the chapter titled "A Dictionary of Major Relations," we have a system of definitions for some common human experiences which we can use to assess our own states. Perhaps more usefully, we can expand upon that system to build up a library of simplified networks for porting these human experiences into anthrized objects. That is, if we're going to make a lamp or a tree talk, we might also want to teach it how to "believe," "care about," or "own" something. This chapter contains a few of my micro models for these processes.

TABLE 45: A REVISED DICTIONARY OF MAJOR RELATIONS

TRUST

For whatever reason, I always ALWAYS begin this kind of work with the four forms of "trust." I think it's because "trust" was the very first idea I ever truly mulled over back when I worked at IADT, and really needed a good procedural definition to know when it applied versus when my animal wiring was getting over on me.

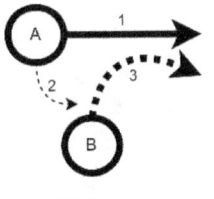

Trust

A trusts B when A can pursue their ends and expect B to not get in the way. Resourcewise, I think it's unreasonable to expect every B out there to actively *support* A, because we can hardly turn our attention to that many Bs in the environment, let alone process specific help from each.

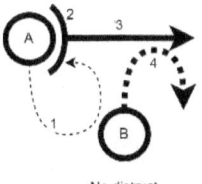

No distrust

The next best thing to trust is "no distrust." **A does not distrust B if A can expect B to not get in the way during A's pursuit, *provided that* A keep up a certain mask.** Despite what we may verbally espouse in the ideal workplace, "No distrust" is the gold standard among folks who are not your close friends.

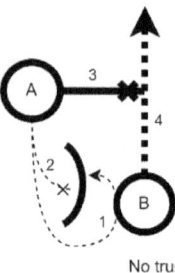

No trust

A does not trust B if A *does* expect negative surprises, cross purposes, or interference from B WHEN A DOES NOT ADOPT A CERTAIN MASK PLEASING TO B. Obviously this is not as pleasant as trust, but there are cases when this really is a better arrangement than any other. A prime example occurs when one enters a committed relationship, but has not turned off their hormones completely. Even before my life partner, I distrusted my very triggery hormones and their tendency to fall for every girl I met. In this case A would = Ajani and B would = Ajani's hormonal stir. It's probably not popular to say that sometimes a male really does feel like a kid in a candy store in certain situations, but acting on that hormonal stir would definitely cause far more grief than satisfaction. Here, it's not good to trust one's urges to lust, retaliation, or anger, but distrusting these wouldn't be good either, because according to the next definition, that would indicate that a part of you stands to harass you randomly at any turn. Hopefully you don't face this issue. But many people do…

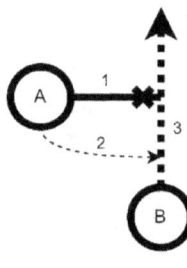

Distrust

A distrusts B when, mask or not, A expects B to bring random or willful impediments to what A is doing.

This one is straightforward, and I've found that it's really easy to identify a "distrustworthy" person. If you see somebody A minding their business (or if you are that somebody), and B comes along and fucks up the the former's scene just because of something B was thinking, then there you have it—especially if this was done habitually.

I think the problem with distrustworthy people is that there's usually a reason we put up with them. The notion of "needing" them for something or needing to avoid something *worse* comes to mind. As in that job we can't afford to lose.

(Note, I tend not to map "*un*trustworthiness," because I've found the connotation to imply more of a judgment call by the viewer. A sees B as untrustworthy because B has done something or been said to do something that A (or often A's influencers) don't approve of. So the tag is placed by A onto B. In the case of *dis*trustworthiness, however, B really has shown a track record (even if only once) for blowing up what A was trying to build regardless of A's attempts to play by the book. This is rooted in a real event sponsored by B onto A's efforts.

NEEDING, HAVING, AND WANTING

"Need" turns out to be a more complicated concept than we might expect, so let's start with "belief."

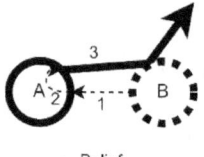

Belief

A believes B when A steers their actions around the existence of B. In the diagram above, B is thought to project its existence onto A, A processes that fact, and A moves accordingly. Simple right? I believe this wall is here, so I won't walk into it. I believe these keyboard keys will produce the characters I expect, so I will keep typing.

It was this definition of belief that started me telling people who ask that I am an atheist rather than a Buddhist-Daoist. Because I found that the A-word was the best filter for separating open-minded people—especially given the work I do—from those who would suddenly see the conversation differently given that my private beliefs now failed to match their own. In reality, although my version of Buddhism (one of the more common kinds) *is* atheistic, it really doesn't die on that sword. My dao says nothing about God at all. I really have no beef with God or your belief therein. I just don't steer *my own* actions around this. I do, however, hold the Golden Rule as my North Star, and make it a point to live and let live as the whole of Nature does for everything. Some people who believe in God also live and let me live. Others do not, though they themselves would not want to be sold on something contrary to *their* reality.

Anyway, it is what it is. I talk more about this in *Rasosho!*.

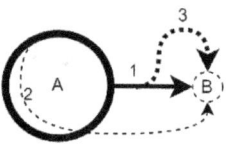

Expecting

Related to belief is the idea of expectation. **A expects B if A acts in some way and conceives B into their own path.** I don't know about you, but to me it seems like we don't really expect things unless we've turned our attention in a certain direction first. No action or attention towards anything = no expectation. In this sense, expectations are necessarily things which show up on a *path of action*.

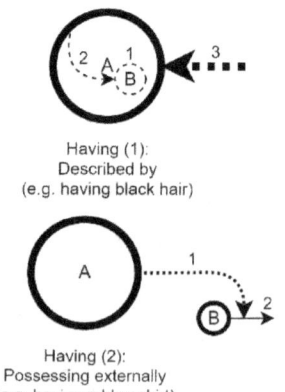

Having (1):
Described by
(e.g. having black hair)

Having (2):
Possessing externally
(e.g. having a blue shirt)

Speaking of conceptions, we arrive at two types of having. **Having (1): A has [is described by] B if A can conceive of B, correlate themselves with B somehow, and the outside world can, in theory, affirm this relationship to apply.** This is like having black hair or having a lot to do; **Having (2): A has [possesses] B if A perceives access to B in the way that A**

prefers to access it. Imagine having a dollar in your hand or a new car. This second notion is closer to the version of having which we all know, but with a twist: having and holding are clearly not the same; note how, when we say we have something as in holding it, we usually imply having access to a certain usage of it, not the object itself. Hence the diagram. I can hold your dollar in my hand, but that's not what we generally mean if it's not also mine to spend. Indeed, the difference between having a thing and having the implied mechanisms that the thing brings is a difference that has tripped up many an individual in their quest for general happiness in their pursuits. They spend their lives chasing the object. But it's really the object's enablements that they want. Often these are already had by the person in other ways.

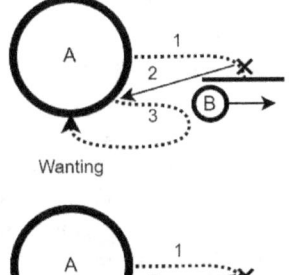

Wanting

Pursuing

Pursuing and wanting are very related, though wanting is *a lot* easier on the resources. When you can't or don't have something but go after it anyway, you're in the realm of both of these. **A wants B when A acts towards the experience of B while admitting to not having it.** Meanwhile, **A *pursues* B when A turns their overt actions towards the experience of B while admitting to not having it.** According to these definitions at least, to want or pursue is to not have.

As for the other senses of want as in a lover telling another, "I want you" in the heat of passion, even then there is some implied future state which is not had, but in any event we'll consider those cases of having while wanting to be more like "valuing" in a measure of further-affirmed desirability of the thing that's not the same as wanting or pursuing it outright. Note how wanting uses

B as a mediator for A's own conception, while pursuing simply marshals A's energy towards B. We only have so much energy to pursue everything we might want, but given that our self-storytelling via outside objects is more or less the definition of identity, our serial wants tend to be ongoing in some way or another until we die. Such is the essence of Taurus' wanted objects, and those objects' Scorpio-like compelling of our actions.

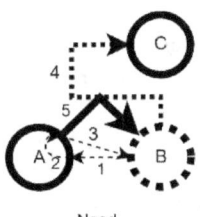

Need

This brings us to the concept of "need." Assuming we don't even have to be alive, I think of need as relative. You can need something *if* you value or want something else. Need occurs "for the purpose of." In the diagram above, A sees B as needed for C, though C need not be external to A. **Need (1): A believes B is needed for C if A believes B to be a precondition for C and A acknowledges B as absent.** A slight variation on this is **Need (2): A believes B is needed for C if A believes B's route to enabling C precludes A's ability to have C without having B.** I like this newer definition myself, because it doesn't frame things in terms of lack, but in terms of B's ability to enable. And if you don't like B or don't want to go through B, this second definition helps you think about alternatives to B more readily instead of dwelling on the idea that B is not there.

Remember, these are all basic heuristics. You can come up with your own if you want. We're not trying to get too philosophical with these, as that would take a lifetime. We just want some good slots and arrows to insert things like qunits and asteroids into. Or generic social patterns without the astro. Whatever it takes to make your robot or network work.

All that said, let's do one more related to having.

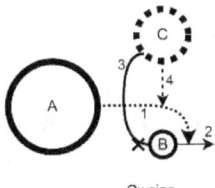

Owning

Owning is like having, except that **A owns B if A has B (in some way), and that having is both acknowledged by a generic C and prevents most Cs from accessing B in the same way.** Now this definition is all kinds of flawed, but its flaws are what make it fun. A philosophy class could go to town on this one, and you might say that a legal definition is probably more stable than the above. Unfortunately, we're working with algorithmic abstraction. If we want to teach anything about acknowledged privacy in situations where most data is third-party surveyable and policeable, and your future algorithm—though describing your original self, is now possessed by some repository like SIER in my fiction books, we do need to talk about what it means to own or have some form of exclusive rights to a thing.

So much of this is social and conceptual. You may own the rights to my music, but not the credits for my having made it. If you don't own the credits then can you stop me from being hired by a rival who knows my talent via the work? That one is probably easy, but what if it isn't music we're talking about, but a model of me that lives on several people's computers, trying to invent my own record label? That might sound crazy in the 2020s I know. But give us a couple of decades more in an AI economy, where self-interest starts being built in.

AFFINITY LEVELS

We can want, pursue, or even have, but how do we represent what we prefer amidst all this?

In Harmony With

Being in harmony with—being aligned with something—occurs when our experience of a thing triggers processes internal to us, in turn prompting us to

continue experiencing ourselves without mandated change.

This is different from **antipathy towards / loss of attention to something, in which our experience of a thing B triggers processes internal to us, in turn prompting us block further experience of B.**

Antipathy Towards

For anything whose happening prompts you to block its further happening (at least for the moment), you can be said (according to this definition) to have a form of antipathy / nonconcern towards it (again in the moment).

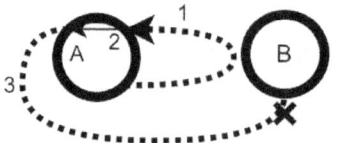

Disharmony With

Beyond antipathy or low concern, we have disharmony with a thing. A is in disharmony with B if A's experience of B **triggers processes internal to A, in turn prompting A to block B** (not just the interface with B).

All three of these affinity levels are good, but how do we describe switching gears or moving to a different preference goal entirely?

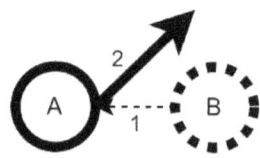

(external) Motivation by

In one of the more straightforward representations, **A is motivated by B if B's projection onto A prompts A to act.** That's easy enough to represent.

LIKING & LOVING

I used to get crushes on or get turned on by nearly every girl who gave me attention… internally at least. Externally, I knew this would be a problem from puberty, and as

early as 4th grade embarked on a campaign of stern order and control which endures to this day. Until recently, I would still take risks in airing this interest, but after Shanna and I got together, I saw this as more of an evolution-sponsored irritation than anything else. Rather than give floor time to a system of male urges that threatened an unnecessary losing (yet taxing) battle against my own mind, I asked myself what my own version of Aries specifically thought it was achieving via the opposite sex, and replaced an interest in [unreachable women] or [reachable women offering negative side roads] with a combination of 1) reachable platonic exchanges only, 2) the girly girl images whose projection I could fully control towards my own male sense / exercises, and 3) this work. And Shanna will tell you that the work far and away dominates all. Sometimes we like (or even love) things that are not at all helpful for where we're trying to go in the long run. Sometimes our serial attachments lead us to break things that are perfect for us already—if we only knew ourselves. In these cases it may be helpful to look at what's happening when we like or dislike something. The diagrams below help illustrate what kinds of energy is being invested here.

Liking

A likes B when A's experience of B triggers A's internal processing which in turn reinforces A's attention to A's triggered internal processing. This is harmony that prompts reinforcement of what B triggers in A. This definition imposes a hard implication upon those of us who stick with things we claim to hate: as framed here, if you reinforce what a thing triggers in you about yourself, at least subconsciously, you like it. Or perhaps it's fairer to say that you're fixated on it if not addicted to the notion of or commentary on it. We can add arrows to this diagram in which A tries to block or kill B, but the mechanism for liking exists as long as your experience of B ultimately successfully fuels the rest of this cycle. There are a lot of Bs out there, and it is the job of media and advertising to use them. The red dot in the

corner of your app comes to mind; once you experience it, it is designed to keep you uncomfortable until you donate more energy to it. When IT wants, not you. Honestly, that kind of hijacking pisses me off as a Scorpio who values control, as they shit up the user experience for me. So I just block those apps. Or people who act like those apps. If you're spiraling on something you hate, blocking is your first and most valuable weapon. Otherwise, it has you and your attentional energy in the palm of its hand, no matter how "tough" or "aware" you think you're being when you allow it to send your whole self down a time-energy rabbit hole once again.

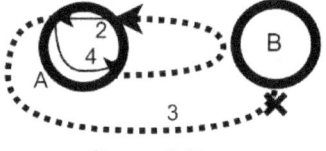

Strong dislike

See here how a strong dislike looks a lot like liking. In fact, there's nothing stopping these two from overlapping. **A has a strong dislike for B when A's experience of B triggers A's internal processing which in turn reinforces A's need to stop B AND YET also re-triggers A's internal processes for experiencing B again.** This could have been plain disharmony from earlier, except that A keeps looking at B, so the cycle never ends. Step 4 is the problem here. The asteroids 65590 Archeptolemos and 12663 Bjorkegren describe two ways in which we do this in our charts.

Part of my motivation for adopting the Buddhist attachment to my dao back in the 2010s lie in this Scorpio pride I have for "the definition of done." Speaking only for myself, there is this sense of frustration with *myself* when I hit something and it doesn't fall down. If I make a threat that has some chance of being idle in the end. If I have to tell our pets or my AI to do something twice. I got this from my mom. I hate repeating myself. Relatedly, though my private recordings up to 2023 are full of rants (invariably when I felt powerless to influence something I should have liked), post-2023, as me and Shanna stabilized as a pair, I stopped this. For non-family and other voluntary-turned negative relationships, you like to say things like,

"Bro. I told you once. Now you're doing it again. Get out." "This information or this exchange is shit. I'm past what I can fix. We're done here." I put the termination on my scoreboard and go about my life. Now that doesn't work if you haven't done all you can. But I always do all that I can. If a thing assaults me past that, then it can get gone. I'm hypersensitive and polite as I can be to everyone I meet. I try to give everyone the benefit of the doubt. I don't necessarily expect this in return since people are raised differently, but there are a lot of ways people can instantly appear distrustworthy to me when they insult this standard.

I guess what I'm saying is, if you don't have a definition of done for things you strongly dislike, then chunks of your energy and effort can be owned by that thing. For our future selves reprinted through AI, let's hope they know how to identify and block bad data better than we do.

On a lighter note, we have my second favorite topic after "trust" and that is, "love."

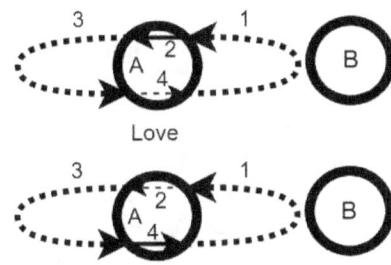

Love

In Love With

Let's say that **A loves B when A's experience of B triggers processes within A which in turn lead A to (recursively?) reinforce how they experience B.** That's alright, I guess, but I have always thought of being in love as better. **A is *in love with* B when A's experience of B reinforces A's process for triggering themselves to keep experiencing B.** By these conceptions at least, love reinforces your triggers to attend to your self-state and, negatively, your obligations, addictions, and obsessions. This is where it becomes easier to say things like "I love you" to someone whom you're often obligated to love, like family or a long time spouse, even if you don't. Granted that doesn't describe all cases, it's just something

I've observed about people when they *say* they love another versus when they actually show it. In the case of being *in love*, however, showing it seems to come along most of the time. Perhaps that's because there is an element of one's internal trigger pointing back to the loved object and not themselves. But there are also negative versions of this as well. If B is a bastard, an abuser, or a calculated distractor, then A may find themselves very stuck in a situation that makes their lives worse than it would be if A had it in them to leave.

It is possible to bypass the internal trigger to send energy back to yourself before sending it to B, and just send it straight to B once you've processed your current experience of them. I describe this as "caring for," though it may just be the same cycle we use in regular persuasion of another to change in light of what we've seen in them. This is a very Ceres setup. Assume the arrows below are done in harmony. If not, things like criticism or generic feedback look suspiciously similar to the diagram below.

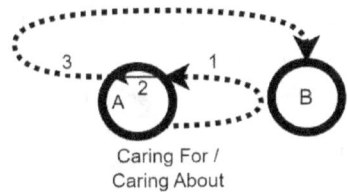

Caring For /
Caring About

BEAUTY AND UGLINESS

A serious study of sociology and society pressures warrants a look at what we are taught to admire as images. Beauty often accompanies love as an idea, so let's define it.

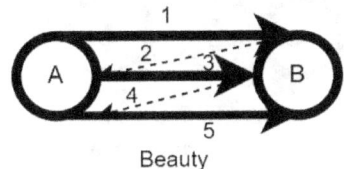

Beauty

Beauty is that state of B which inspires a perceiver A to keep perceiving B in the way that A does, given an underlying experience of (apparent) harmony during the process.

Now, I debated whether or not to put arrows inside of A to denote A's feeling of harmony, but how many times have we

admitted that something or someone was beautiful just because they are advertised to everyone and we are obligated by conversation to say this? In how many different ways can the beholding eye motivate itself to repeat the view? Many people have told me that certain external travel destinations are beautiful, though I surely didn't see it. There may be beauty in music as it's playing, or (in my case) when it times perfectly. So in the end I just left the inner arrows out.

See how beauty is a lot like love in that it sponsors a feedback loop. In the case of love, though, A does not have to throw attention or attributes back onto B. with beauty, A does do this.

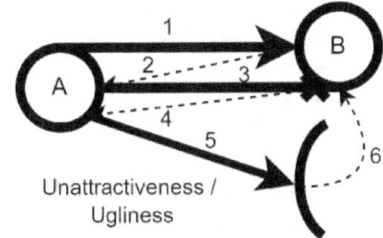

Unattractiveness /
Ugliness

I believe I said this in one of Laurentia's asteroid interpretations, but ugliness is not the opposite of beauty. **Ugly / Unattractive is that state of B which inspires a perceiver A to stop wanting to look at B and instead replace their perception of B with a (likely subconscious) perception of some masked standard over B.** This is almost never positive for B, but has a couple of interesting consequences.

Ugliness can alert us to the masks we prefer. It is also the third definition we've encountered which makes use of a mask, and when placed on top of the diagrams for no trust or no distrust, we might see how one's being seen as ugly or seeing themselves as ugly can spark behaviors towards adopting a more pleasing image to one's space of viewers.

Lastly, the above representation of perceived ugliness shows how folks who know they are deemed ugly according to some standard may be less likely to receive your invite, but more likely to receive whatever value lies in the mask that you and everybody else keeps giving them, whether or not they started out seeking this. For 90%

of my life, I've been treated pretty well by people, but that last 10% always hits me hard. I have a whole file on times I've lost or been rejected, and like so many people who feel they've done their best or deserve the best based on everything they put in, I'm determined to turn even my perceived rejections into value. So the world gets a whole book of my stuff put into its face. A whole military into someone else's country. A whole monopoly into every mom and pop market. The psychology of imperialistic determination is easier to understand if we have a framework for these things. The subsurface psychology goes something like this:

> "I'm all for everyone's opportunity to make what they can of what I put my life into projecting, but I know most people won't even remotely understand it, and will sit in their armchairs labeling it instead. But in this world of [X], I am an infinite collector of certain spoils, and to the extent that the funsies, gossiping public keeps giving me an infinite set of masks it says I should wear instead, then the useless talk and my growing power will keep moving hand in hand."

For me, that infinitely building world above consists of social data. For others it lies in power, money, institutional control, fans,… you name it. Everyone has access to an infinite *something*. As do you. Unless you are on their level in that realm, it's not a matter of stopping them as you yourself would not want to be stopped were you in their shoes. It's a matter of you either using their infinity as an opportunity to build your own, or blocking their role in your life via another qcross in the same qunit inconjunct group, for example. Or blocking them in some other way regardless of the astro… but I'm telling you, it is A LOT easier to see what you have to work with if you have the astro on hand. Otherwise, you'll just need to protect your energy-spend from that "ugly" thing through sheer force of will. This book channels the same energy as the times in which it is being written, in hopes of giving you the building blocks to explain your toughest times, and an illustration of how born disrupters like me don't always start out that way, but have our reasons for accepting that path eventually. Whether or

not we care to benefit you while we do it is an unrelated matter, but has everything to do with whether or not you care to gain benefit from the many places that stranger offers, or are just content to meme him.

The tyrant and monolith arise when the people themselves have spent too much time in their own self-interest at the expense of the whole. From then on, they will find the vacuum of their own indulgence embodied in the one. The only solution is to turn back to their local groups and build something better, to repair things despite this. It is as true for allied countries as it is for families.

The monolith whom groups call ugly is always collecting *some valuable mask* in groups of the collective conception. If only the people had more inventive uses for that energy they keep paying, the monolith would cease to be.

HONOR AND RESPECT

As someone who feels his work to be useful, I'd like to be respected in that work, or at least for a contribution to related that work. Let's dissect "respect."

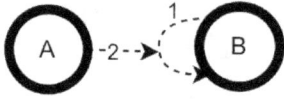

Respect

A respects B in an area when A lets themselves reaffirm what B or B's world claims about B in that area. Remember, this is area specific. Respect for the whole person need not apply.

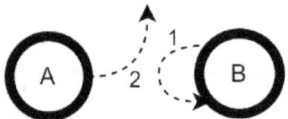

Don't respect

In most cases, we neither respect nor disrespect the others we encounter. The topic just isn't relevant at all. A isn't respecting B when B's or B's world's claims about B don't draw A's affirmation or denial.

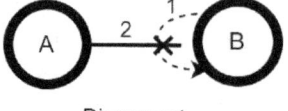

Disrespect

And then there is the almighty notion of disrespect. **A disrespects B when B's or B's world's claims about B draw A's energy towards the contrary.**

I'll emphasize here that telling a person "no" is not the same as disrespecting them. Nor is downvoting their work or criticizing their efforts, arguing with them or recommending against them. Here, disrespect describes attacking the whole face that B has put on in order to do whatever they just did. We Americans are trained to critique, dismiss, judge, make fun of, name call, meme, groupthink, assert our individual interests over the collective safety, rationally explain away others' plight as long as it doesn't affect ourselves, and have fun doing it from an early age, so we have a society which prizes other-disrespect as a form of self-worth more than it prizes, say, innovation or community. That's not a criticism. Just another subjective observation. I grew up on rap culture and definitely have my disrespect mode when fighting a DIY project, and can tell you that there is a great power trip to be offered by this. I suspect that this isn't just the American way, but the *human* way once you've gotten a taste of the full "first world" buffet.

The drawback, of course, is that every B feeling disrespected by any A is going to want to respond in some way, and a culture which values this offers far more opportunities for slash and burn choices inflicted upon every detractor. Guns help us reclaim the power that even senators have for responding to the ways in which the world seems to be moving despite us, as do media channels that help us rip our enemy to shreds with a posse behind us. I would say that this all sucks, but again, I believe this to be a human problem, and that the best thing we can do is build better tools for a better society than this. Before that happens, the ape in us will always rule the day with its pre-global decision-making.

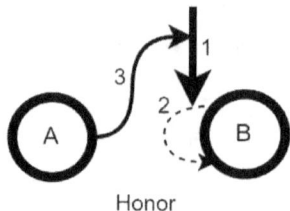

Honor

Interestingly, honor is not the same as respect, and one need not imply the other. You can honor a dead asshole without respecting them. You can respect a living enforcer without honoring them. **A honors B when A acts to reinforce the events or customs which already support B or B's world's claims about B.** That is, respect points us to individuals; honor points us to the circumstances that affirm those individuals' roles.

REST AND BODY RESTORATION

I thought I'd create a diagram for rest, as I noticed that certain things only happen in my life during rest.

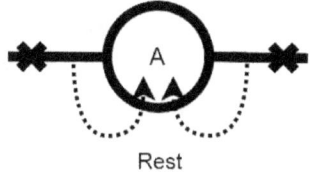

Rest

Rest occurs when A stops all (or most) external effort in favor of the alternative inner processes that such effort would otherwise be spent on. There isn't much to this definition, except that it can be really useful for directing you to the right qunit in Pisces, for example, to tell yourself what is getting recharged when you take a break from your stressors.

While you're not spending your waking energy on stuff, your body prefers to build along certain patterns. Anthropology tells us there are three kinds of growth.

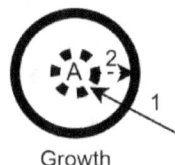

Growth

Basic growth occurs when an inner process adds to an outer form, often increasing its size, density, or annexation of the surrounding area. The opposite of growth is shrinking.

Development

Development occurs when internal processes lead to more mature, more detailed, or more elaborated structures, not necessarily a bigger version of the original, simpler structure. ***Pruning* is a form of development in which potential expressive tracks are cut rather than built,** and this is analogous to most kinds of learning as right roads are selected and noisy ones dropped. In these specific senses, we'll call the opposite of development, "reinvestment" (where what used to be your nose melts back into your face); the opposite of pruning will be "noising."

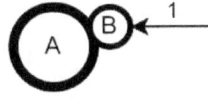

Accretion

Accretion is how we typically think of growth when we are outside of the thing doing the growing. **Accretion occurs when a things adds an external energy to its volume.** Basic eating does this for us as young humans, and the newly acquired B feeds growth processes early on / developmental processes throughout. While investigating human species development I speculated that puberty reflects the rather simple [first Jupiter return nearest your second Saturn square]. This would be conducive to the timeline supporting your public image formation while your native

Saturn is *least* reinforced by the timeline's Saturn. (7/9/2025. While proofing and editing this book: I am sure this theory is wrong. And challenge future astro researchers to fix it.[58])

There are definite parameters for how you grow, accrete, and develop; these aren't just limited to your body. While we may think of making more money as adding to our bank account (accretion), we can also refine what we're interested in spending on (development) and what assets we put our existing money into for earning interest or appreciation (growth). This same analogy could apply to any number of areas we wish to build on.

THE FOUR ELEMENTS

Finally, at the end of this work I asked, "How can I turn these nodes and arrows into things like qunits and aspects for training a simulation in human-readable pieces?" This required a framing of the four elements.

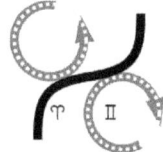 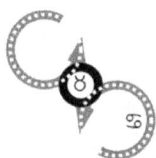

Fire: a type of cycle   Earth: a point of stability
Air: a flow of cycles   Water: a flow of stable points

Imagine the you have an apparently empty space through which energy can pass. When that energy passes, it has a tendency to either roll through unobstructed, or get somehow bent by other forces affecting the space (like universal expansion or galactic spin or something). We can represent these two modes of passage and the two modes they create as the four elements:

- Fire is the energy passing through

---

[58] Speaking of my potentially wrong theories, suppose someone says to me, "Ajani, I'm about to travel into the future to see how people ended up using your work. Got any predictions for how much of it will be considered wrong?" I'd say about 60% of it. Not wrong *per se*, but certainly subject to revision as institutions with more than a single personal laptop, a sole male perspective, no additional full-bio subjects can be expected to be. If I had to guess, I'd say that my work in *144* was closer to accurate than it would appear, as was my method of matching astronomy to astrology in a previous chapter. In general, I tend to think of the work in this book as being tied to the work in *Alma Mater* and *Laurentia 1*. When you talk about right or wrong theories, you're automatically taking these three books together. Between them, I'd say that maybe less than 5% of it is outright wrong (mostly the geometric physics parts) and another 35% could simply be re-run for greater accuracy. The last 20% is less about being wrong and more about leaving the wrong implication. But I'd say that about 80% of what I've done will have been at least directionally correct. 10% will be directionally incorrect, and the last 10% will simply be too weird to assess. Alas, much of this work had no precedent at all—not to my knowledge, so it was made to be revised by future scholars. Until then, I don my Tarot Fool's hat with as much dignity as I can muster.

- Air is the directed space through which fire passes
- Earth is the bent energy encouraged to pass through on one "side" of the potential space, but not equally on the other. Thus an inflection point is created at the intersection of these forces which is not equal to the unobstructed energy which arrived there in the first place

- Water is the asymmetric space described by the direction of the earth element's bend. This defines its flow.

The above framework is mostly captured on the left side (the sideways page) and bottom right side of Figure 54 on page 698. I mostly use this to ground what I'm looking for when putting networks together from so many possible elements.

Conclusion

I hope you have enjoyed (or at least been entertained by) my anthropometry book. I mentioned at the end of *Alma Mater* that it was my dream to contribute to the work in saving humans as data, and I think that one of the first things we need in order to do this is a fully documented sample human, with every potential pattern either explained or mappable to an explanation. I've said it several times before, but humanity isn't the small splash of isolated fiefdoms it once was, nor does it rely on its body the way it used to. The new world of technology, information, and interconnectedness is here, and we are in need of a serious upgrade in how we interact with each other and that world. But how can we go about this when the only rules we know are the rules of the very game that needs to be rewritten? More wars? More media? More markets? Those are all technology. But what about us? If we don't change how we decide what or who is worth warring against, how can we improve?

We can't generally undertake human studies without a lot of hassle. Lots of committees, editors, experts, et cetera. Those definitely have a place in building the extremely reliable, repeatable processes that eventually become our cars and phones. But when it comes time to put those results to brand new uses, and we don't know the very society which we should be using them on, then we just get fancier ways of blowing ourselves up. On the other side of this, it is hard as hell to find people willing to *be* the specimens for understanding what ails or or what blesses us, such that even if the fields were open to our self-study, building the foundation for what questions to ask would pose even further challenges.

…Man, I wish that a living, non AI-generated female sample were easily available for this kind of work. But then again, the book would have been twice as long, or may have even warranted a second biography entirely just to capture her true internal psychology. I am well aware of how sexist this book may sound in some places. The aim was to expose the full psychology for everyone's level-up regarding actual full-human workings, since I am not aware of this kind of work existing anywhere else. But the ask for such heavy disclosure from anyone besides myself was a tall one. I hope the reader understands this. The first woman who produces an autobiography like this will also bring more than her share of surprises. Straight from the depths of the same psyche which we are so thoroughly taught to keep hidden. Surely you don't want everyone doing work like this, but you do need at least a few to provide the initial data set, pretty or not. Our future selves will only be as complete as the cap on our own insight into our own workings. In any event…

I am so very very grateful to my life partner Shanna and my brother Keith for staying in my corner these last three years while I worked on something that was bound to make at least a few people cringe at times. The inner human psychology is messy. There are reasons why we don't say or acknowledge certain things. At the beginning of the accessible-AI era via ChatGPT 4, my brother and I talked about how, as teachers, we expected people to go wild on the tech but, as usual, pay little attention to the societal duty implied. I was partly wrong in that I underestimated just how forward thinking the developers of that tech are as stewards of the fellow fragile humans' hearts, and yet we fragile humans have definitely not gotten better. We are more confused than ever, more vexed by our information and power structures, more equipped to lament these and less equipped to penetrate the micro-level workings that made them so powerful in the first place. Before coming up with solutions, we are wired to see an easier path in simply rallying against certain ideas without enough of a clue as to how they are implemented, let alone fixed. So we insist that the rug should be pulled, not knowing that it will be out from under ourselves. There has to be an answer key to the human test.

Contours is probably the result of my North Node qunit (Table 6, page 69) and 29q12s (Table 2, page 57) doing their basic stuff to the highest level I know, across the farthest span I can reach. It reflects one man's perspectives and speculations, as a sample inside the test tube of human philosophical inquiry. Even without all of the influence we are trained to think we need, it is possible for you to block out the noise and do something that only you can do, and to have its results stretch far beyond your initial borders.

My greatest disappointment about this book is that I'm not sure people will really get what I was trying to tell them through "Figure 7: [Self] data save part 3 of 3 Ajani's Q-bio (with the 144 Qunit Inconjunct Groups / QIGs)." To me, that table is indicative of what we're called to handle as humans: It's apparently out of order, filled with potential dirt and tmi (too much information), it won't end, and yet it has absolutely critical instructions for how people get out out from under where they are (if they are indeed under); it is organized for this purpose alone. Figure 7 is not meant to frustrate, but to show you an example of how each single topic is necessarily connected to three others, and how that quartet is necessarily connected to two more. Provided you can get your hands on all 21000 asteroid locations and interpretations in your own chart, that particular table can explain much of what you may need to see in only three doors: Here's how you choose the opposition. Here's how you navigate the qcross. Here's what else is available to pay attention to in the qunit inconjunct group.

Lastly, I would again like to thank the many people who provided their data for the body work. We progressed the field by leaps and bounds in that space, and it couldn't have happened without you. I would also like to thank all the cultures of the world in the abstract. I was not able to study all 900+ groups listed on Wikipedia out of sheer time and system limitations, but it was truly an honor selecting the images for Chapter 21: Ethnotypes and asteroids, particularly Table 42, page 599. Keeping in mind all of the frequentic analogies in this book's main table (Table 16, page 336), it felt like I was meeting all of the people, generations of their stories across themselves and Nature, all at once. I may have my own perspective which you've heard about enough times throughout the book, but learning yours and the unique allocation of events you were gifted with on top of the personal ones you will have developed—that was something that not even many of the most traveled folks ever get to do.

As always, I wish the reader my best. Even if this book is not directly useful to you, I hope it will positively influence the kinds of knowledge available to the builders of those future systems which you and your children will occupy.

Index of figures and tables

FIGURES

TABLES

Appendix I: Decision Function Modulation

ABSTRACT

In attempts to model adjacent but phenomenologically distinct behavioral domains using a single function, this article proposes a multiple sigmoid-weighted function with which supports different mathematical behaviors along the same linear continuum. Applications for modelling both linear and cyclical systems are discussed, as well as the potential uses of such functions for simulating behavioral rule shifts dynamically.

INTRODUCTION

One of the primary challenges of predicting student outcomes using higher education institutional data lies in the vast space of possible factors involved (Lotkowski, Robbins, & Noeth, 2004). Institutions often rely on measures such as productive grade rate (PGR), hours attempted-to-earned, in-major trends, or demographic factors in order to better understand their students' potential for success, but these measures constitute only a small snapshot of the much more dynamic circumstances under which students live, work, and study (Moir, Sanson, & Chen, 2018; Barclay, Barclay, Mims, Sargent, & Robertson, 2018). While institutions of higher education (IHEs) have evolved greatly in their use of modelling methods using the data available to them, there remains a scarcity of measures within these institutions which reflect the processes (rather than simply the final results) associated with a particular measure (Griffin, Bayl-Smith, & Hu, 2018). We may know of a student who participates in clubs attends semi-regularly, and receives a B, but even given a vast collection of institutional data, may still have little information on the sequence of changing contexts that led to this pattern of outcomes. Ours is the work of snapshots, where animated contexts continue to elude even the most extensive data systems.

Attempts to use snapshot-based measures in understanding outcomes such as student persistence have often produced less useful data than some researchers have initially expected, as these outcomes tend to be rooted in more dynamic behavioral processes than static measures will allow (Tinto, 1997). Additionally, despite the idea that our final outcome measures (such as persistence, completion, and GPA) tend to be reasonably operationalizable, the personal and contextual factors in the eyes of the actual students and staff involved in any one individual's success are not (Denice, 2019). In seeking clearer ways to define the fuzzy inputs that lead to our more structured institutional research-capturable metrics, we encounter numerous sources of potential error associated with complex observations of human behavior in general (Hintze, Volpe, & Shapiro, 2002). A central challenge here may be to develop measures of fuzzy behavioral inputs which, rather than being limited to fixed values, can be represented by more dynamic functions upon such values. In building our various system models, we need to be able to turn certain factors "off" in some populations while turning them "on" in others. Of the factors that remain on, we should also be able to turn some "up" while turning others "down" (modulating them).

METHODS

Because the purpose of this article is to clearly explain a type of function-building process for a non-statistical IHE audience, I will use an ongoing, arbitrary example to work through the logic of decision function modulation (DFM). The more formal equations for the method will be presented in between the example steps. Our purpose is to employ a mathematical method for stitching multiple models, equations, or mathematical behavior into one, so that we may have a tool for better capturing information (such as an IHE system model) which changes fuzzily, dynamically.

SELECTING A DECISION FUNCTION

In order to turn one local function "off" while turning another local function "on" in the same grand function, I chose from an initial group of possible weighting functions which allowed for multiplication by 0 at one end, 1 at the other. These served as different types of decision function (Wald, 1949). I chose from among five candidates: the Heaviside (step function), arctangent, logistic sigmoid, limited domain cosine, and semi-arc square root as shown in Figure 1. Among these, the Heaviside, limited domain sinusoid, and square root functions possessed undesirable discontinuities beyond a certain domain value, while the arctangent and limited domain sinusoids were too asymptotically wide in the absence of additional parameters, so I chose the logistic sigmoid as the appropriate weighting function.

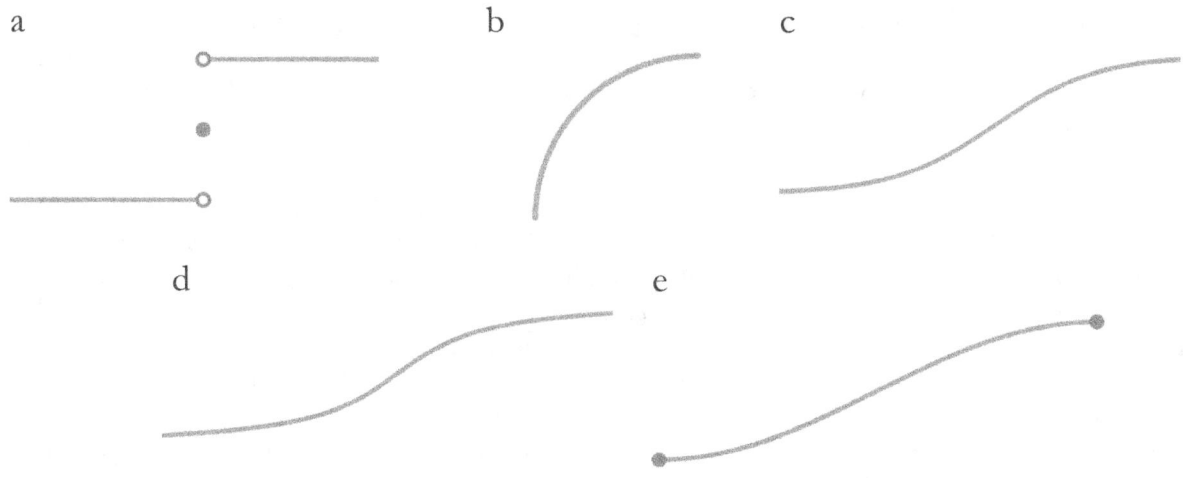

Figure 1. Candidate weighting functions for multiplying another (local) function. Multiplying the local function by any of the above turns that local function "off" on the left and "on" on the right. The five shape choices were (a) the Heaviside step function, (b) one side of the semi-arc square root function, (c) arctangent, (d) the logistic sigmoid, and (e) a restricted domain sinusoid. Choices (a), (b), and (e) were deemed cumbersome, while choice (c) had slightly less desirable asymptotic behavior than choice (d)—taking longer to arrive at its limit values. (d), the logistic sigmoid was selected because it could be made to reach its floor and ceiling limits smoothly and fairly easily. The most basic mathematical form for this shape is $y = 1/(1 + e^{-x})$.

The logistic sigmoid (sigma: ς) has several properties which make it easy to work with as an on-off (or binary decision) function (Humphrys, n.d.). Written in the simplified form $ς = 1/(1 + e^{-K(x-H)})$, this function is a basic s-curve that transitions smoothly from 0 to 1 through a halfway point of .5 at $x = H$, and does so with a steepness of K (Cramer, 2002). By multiplying the function ς times any another local function f which we want to modulate, we may turn f from "off" to "on" as x moves from less than H to greater than H when K is positive.

EXAMPLE 1

For the rest of this article, we will explain DFM using an ongoing working example. Consider a local function $y = \cos(4x)$. We can multiply by the $\cos(4x)$ by the decision function $1/(1 + e^{-2(x-3)})$ to obtain the behavior shown in Figure 2.

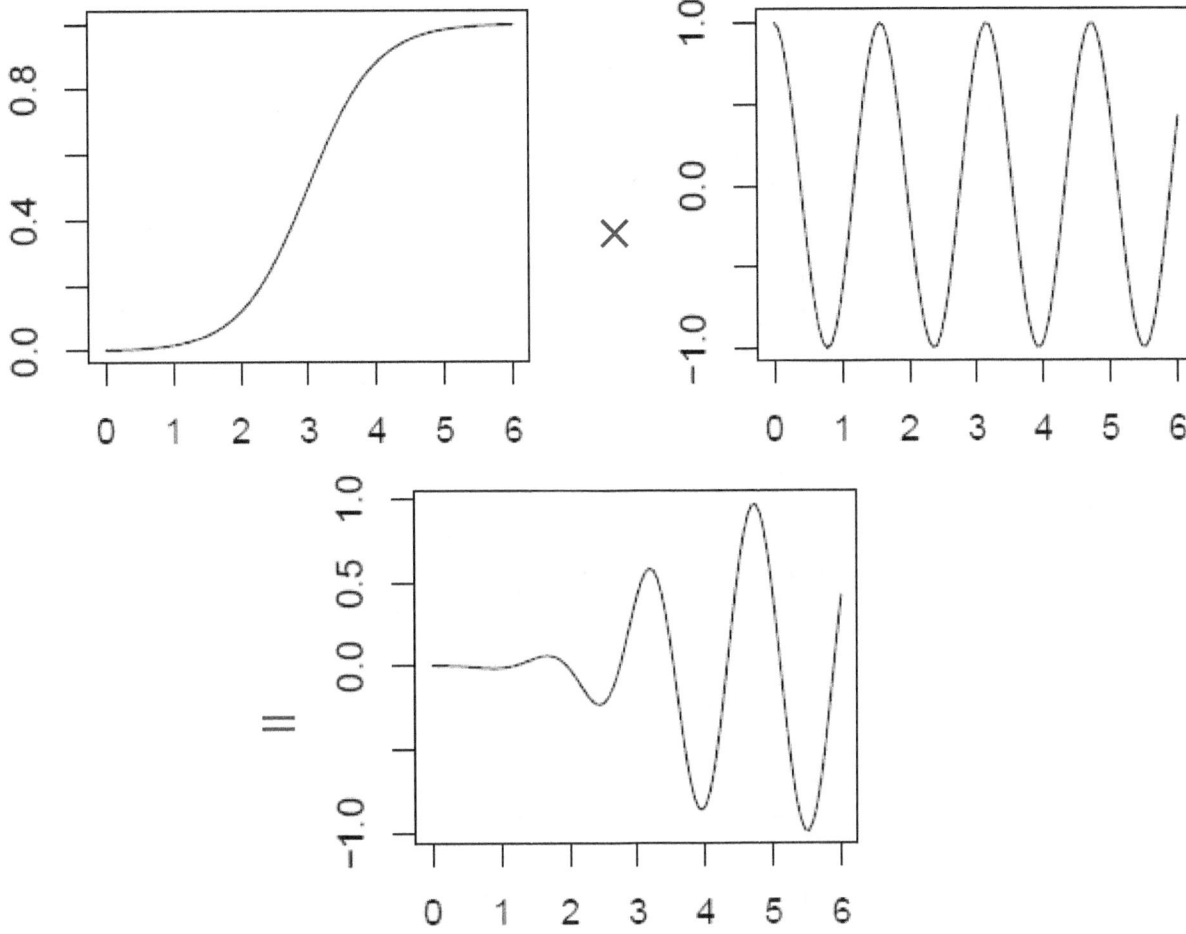

Figure 2: The function $y = (\cos(4x)) \cdot 1/(1 + e^{-2(x-3)})$ $0 \le x \le 6$, weighted such that the $\cos(4x)$ region is gradually multiplied into significance on the right side of the region.

Suppose we wanted a different behavior on the left side of the region. This would warrant addition of another sigmoid in the opposite direction, achieved by reversing "$x - 3$" as "$3 - x$". This backwards sigmoid obeys the formula $1/(1 + e^{-2(3-x)})$ (Figure 3).

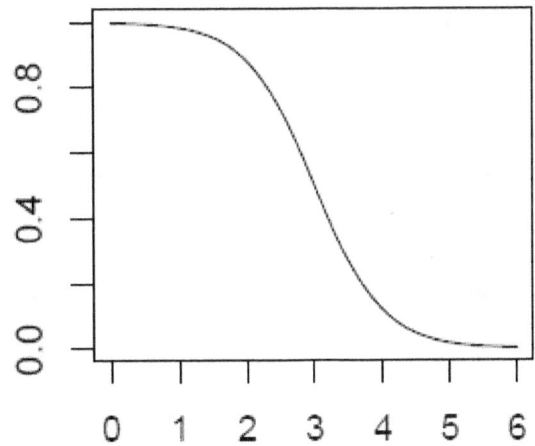

Figure 3. A logistic sigmoidal function $y = 1/\left(1 + e^{-2(3-x)}\right)$ on the region $0 \leq x \leq 6$

If we wanted a different local function such as $y = 2x + 1$, we would multiply this by the new, reversed-facing decision function.

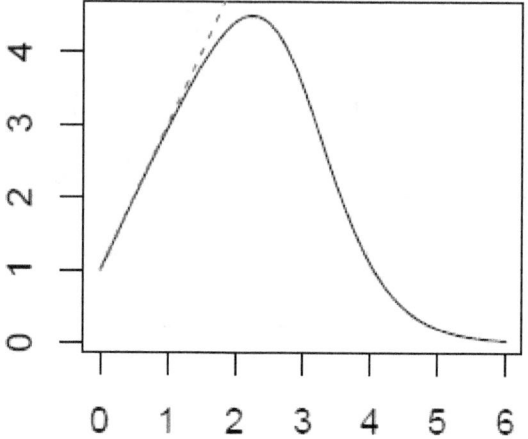

Figure 4. The function $y = (2x + 1) \cdot 1/\left(1 + e^{-2(3-x)}\right) 0 \leq x \leq 6$, weighted such that the $(2x + 1)$ behavior is salient only on the left side of the region. The actual $y = (2x + 1)$ function is shown as a dotted line.

Joining the two sample functions together gives us the result illustrated in Figure 5.

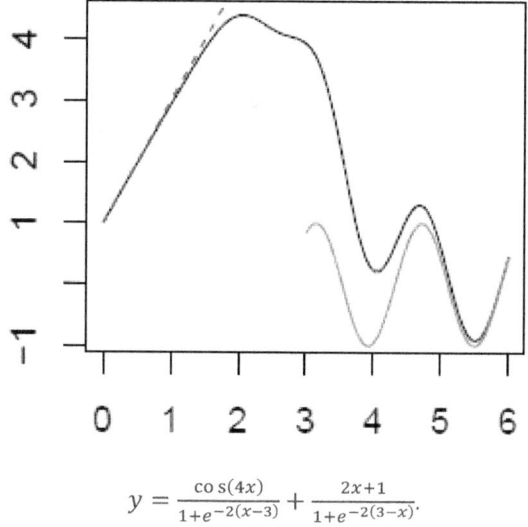

$$y = \frac{\cos(4x)}{1 + e^{-2(x-3)}} + \frac{2x+1}{1 + e^{-2(3-x)}}.$$

Figure 5. A smooth piecewise function joining two different mathematical behaviors into one.

Note that although the two functions are joined in Figure 5, there is a sizable middle region that does not look like either function. This is because the decision functions themselves have considerable overlap in their "on" domains. That is, the left sigmoid and right sigmoids have tails which reach too far into each other's tails by about 2 units, as shown in Figure 6,

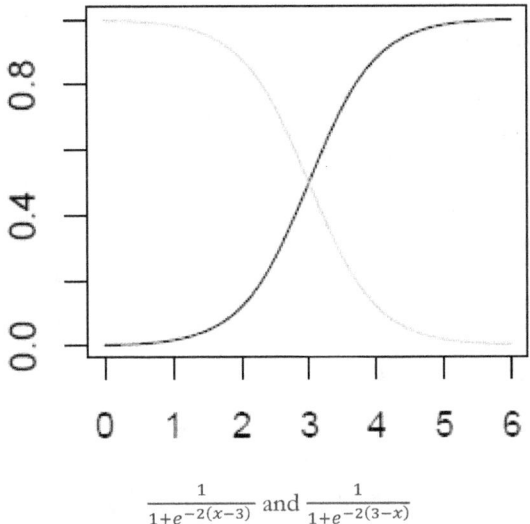

$$\frac{1}{1+e^{-2(x-3)}} \text{ and } \frac{1}{1+e^{-2(3-x)}}$$

Figure 6. The decision functions overlap considerably. It is true that we can turn one function off while another turns on using these, but the particular transition shown above may be slower than we desire. The left function we multiply will be completely "on" ($\varsigma_{left} = 1$) at $x = 0$, but then take two more units before turning almost completely off. The right function will behave similarly, where ($\varsigma_{right} = 1$) at $x = 6$.

By changing the coefficient on the exponent in each decision function, we can better control the falloff window of each function. Using coefficients of $K = 6$ instead of $K = 2$ in the example above, we obtain the formulas in Figure 7.

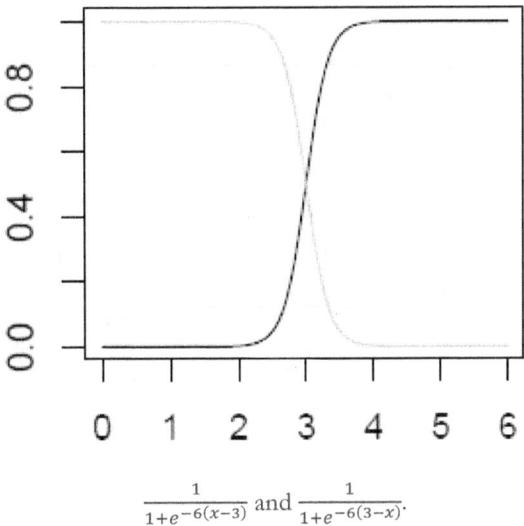

$$\frac{1}{1+e^{-6(x-3)}} \text{ and } \frac{1}{1+e^{-6(3-x)}}.$$

Figure 7. A pair of decision functions of steepness $K = 6$.

Using the same local functions of $\cos(4x)$ and $2x + 1$, we get the sharper behavior shown in Figure 8.

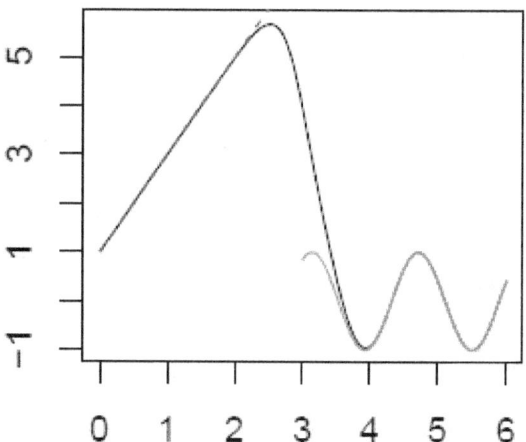

Figure 8. A more sharply behaved piecewise function that behaves as $y = 2x + 1$ on the left side and $y = \cos(4x)$ on the right side. Compare to Figure 5.

Through amplitude modulation of local functions using sigmoidal weights, we have now constructed a single smooth, piecewise function.

JOINING FUNCTIONS WHICH USE DIFFERENT PARAMETERS

Because we are assembling separate local behaviors, it is possible to evolve different regions of the grand function using different parameters. Figure 9 shows the left side of the function evolved using a parameter t while the right side remains relatively fixed.

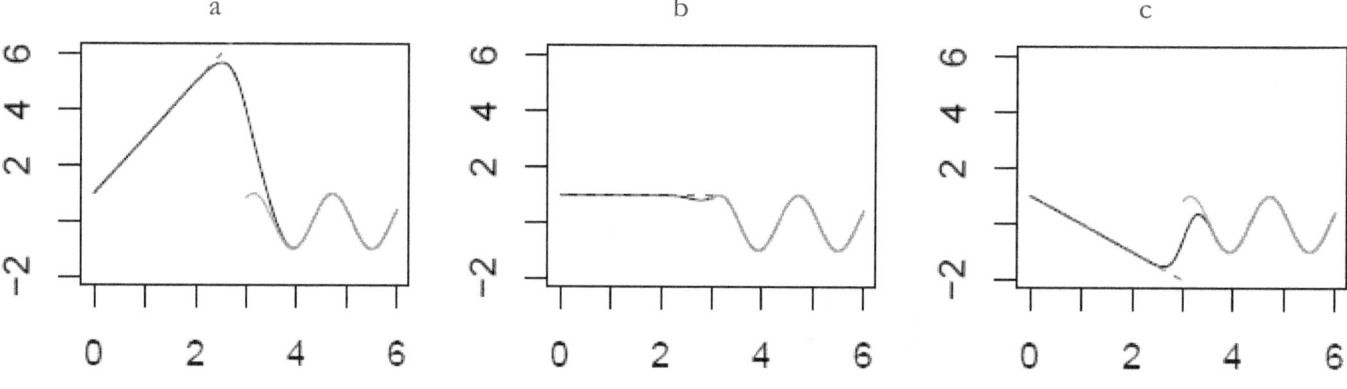

Figure 9. Evolution of the sample function $y = (2tx + 1)$ at (a) $t = 1$, (b) $t = 0$, and (c) $t = -.5$ respectively. Notice that we can change the left function with minimal change to the right function.

Using what we know about the sigmoid function to generalize our example, we obtain a formula for combining two functions, f_{first} and f_{last} into one:

$$y = \frac{f_{first}}{1+e^{-K(x-H)}} + \frac{f_{last}}{1+e^{-K(H-x)}} \tag{1}$$

where steepness K controls how quickly we want the transition to occur. Meanwhile, H serves as our "halfpoint" along the domain. This is where each decision function is halfway on and halfway off. That is, whatever functions we are looking at are multiplied by or .5.

MOVING HALFPOINTS BETWEEN FUNCTIONS

Suppose now, that our example required that the first region encompass 25% of the domain while the last region should encompass 75% of the behavior. Rather than setting our halfpoint between regions at the 50% mark (the value 3 in the example domain of $[0,6]$), we would set it at the 25% mark (1.5 in the example). The new decision functions would turn on their local behaviors at that general halfpoint $H = 1.5$ as follows:

$$y = \frac{\cos(4x)}{1+e^{-6(x-1.5)}} + \frac{2tx+1}{1+e^{-6(1.5-x)}} \tag{2}$$

Producing a smaller region of influence for the left function as illustrated in Figure 10.

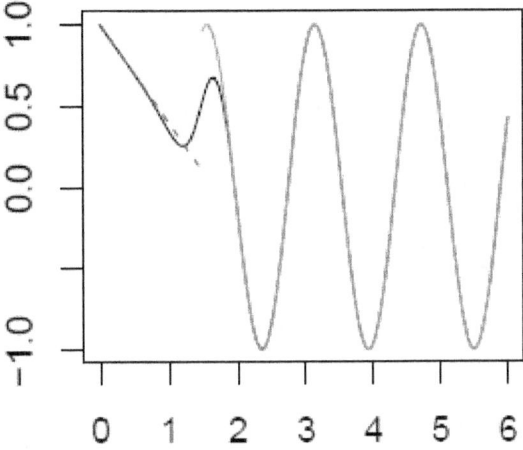

Figure 10. $y = \frac{\cos(4x)}{1+e^{-6(x-1.5)}} + \frac{2tx+1}{1+e^{-6(1.5-x)}} t = -.3, 0 \le x \le 6$ with a halfpoint at $x = 1.5$.

Thus we can change the transition points for our piecewise functions.

DETERMINING APPROPRIATE STEEPNESS

Given a piecing of two local functions over $x \ge 0$, the generic formula for a decision function on the first (lower) side of a specified non-negative domain is

$$\frac{1}{1+e^{-K(H-x)}} \tag{3}$$

where K is the steepness of the decision functions we've chosen and H is the functions' shared halfpoint. Meanwhile, the formula for the last (higher) decision function over a non-negative domain is

$$\frac{1}{1+e^{-K(x-H)}} \tag{4}$$

The x and H are reversed.

Now what if we want to calculate an appropriate steepness coefficient for sharply controlling the overlap in our local domains? Suppose, for example, we want a particular f_{last} function to be 95% irrelevant (that is, to have a 95% falloff) below a certain lower threshold value $x = L$. In that case we'll want the decision function to satisfy the following equation:

$$\frac{1}{1+e^{-K(L-H)}} < .05 \tag{5}$$

which becomes

$$K > \frac{\ln\left(\frac{1}{.05}-1\right)}{-(L-H)} \text{ or } K > \frac{\ln(19)}{H-L} \tag{6}$$

This says that if we wanted the last function f_{last} in our ongoing example to be weighted at less than 5% at a value $H - L$ before the halfpoint $H = 3$ (that is, if we wanted to multiply it by no more than .05 when $x \le L$), we would use $K > ln(19)/(H - L)$ as our K. If, for example, we wanted f_{last} to be 95% irrelevant at $x = 2.5$, then $K > ln(19)/(3 - 2.5)$; this gives $K > 5.89$, which explains the earlier coefficient choice of $K = 6$ in the example.

Generalizing to any desired weighting at any desired positive point, we obtain the following value for the steepness of f_{last}'s decision function:

$$K > \frac{\ln\left(\frac{1}{W}-1\right)}{H-L} \tag{7}$$

where W is the maximum percentage weight which the function f_{last} is allowed to have below the specified lower local threshold L for a function weighted 50% at halfpoint H. Stated differently, if we want f_{last} to be worth 50% at $x = H$ and worth W at $x = L$ (where W <50%), then the above equation is what we would use. (Here, the "lower local threshold" describes the leftwards-falling side of a decision function.)

For the first sigmoid f_{first}, the above coefficient is

$$K > \frac{\ln\left(\frac{1}{W}-1\right)}{L-H} \tag{8}$$

Here, L would be the <u>upper</u> local threshold (the weight falling as we move to the right), and the L and H are reversed.

JOINING THREE OR MORE REGIONS

Before joining three or more functions, we first need to make a distinction between the left and right halfpoints in a function. When there are only two functions, $H_{first,right} = H_{last,left} = H$ since there is only one point of crossing, where f_{first} will fall in weight as we move to the right of H_{first} while f_{last} will fall in weight as we move to the left of H_{last}. These will warrant slightly different mathematical treatments as we proceed.

Piecewise assembly of domains for three or more regions requires a mirror sigmoid, which can be constructed using the absolute value of the main domain variable (x) about its regional midpoint M. Where does M come from? Since we'll be turning a function on for a while then off again, our sigmoid will look like a hill instead of an S. The middle of that hill will be where $x = M$, and will be where f_{middle} is multiplied by 1. Note that unlike f_{first} and f_{last}, f_{middle} will be multiplied by .5 on two sides H_{left} and H_{right}, and will fall off at both lower and upper local thresholds L_{left} and L_{right} on each side of $x = M$. If, for example, we inserted a third local region f_{middle} into our previous domain $\{0 \le x \le 6\}$, and wanted that third region centered at $M = 4$, with halfpoints $H_{middle,left} = 3.5$ and $H_{middle,right} = 4.5$, and 99% falloff ($W = .01$ weightings) at the points $L_{middle,left} = 3.1$ and $L_{middle,right} = 4.9$, we would first construct one weighting sigmoid for the lower side of this new region,

$$K > \frac{\ln\left(\frac{1}{W}-1\right)}{H_{middle,left}-L_{middle,left}} = \frac{\ln\left(\frac{1}{.01}-1\right)}{3.5-3.1} = \frac{\ln(99)}{.4} = 11.5 \tag{9}$$

then, by equation (3)

$$\frac{1}{1+e^{-K(H-x)}} = \frac{1}{1+e^{-11.5(3.5-x)}} \tag{10}$$

as shown in Figure 11. Next we would mirror the sigmoid about the desired center $M = 4$. We do this by introducing a (-4) to both the lower halfpoint term (3.5 in the example) and the x term, then folding the $x - 4$ into a negative absolute value, effectively turning the right half of the weighting function around on the $x = 4$ axis. This produces equation (11) and is shown in Figure 12.

$$\frac{1}{1+e^{-11.5\left(-(3.5-4)-abs(x-4)\right)}} \tag{11}$$

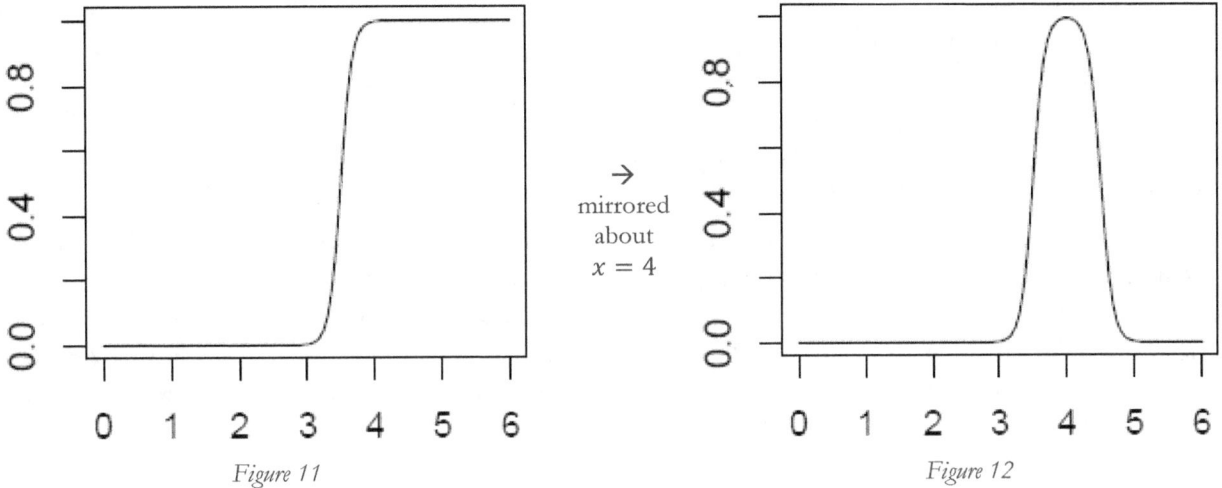

Figure 11   Figure 12

Figures 11 and 12: First and second steps in constructing a symmetric weighting function

The above assumes that our halfpoints are symmetric about the midpoint M. Asymmetric halfpoints are beyond the scope of this paper, but may be arrived at by applying another weighting function to the first weighting function.

Now let us assume that this new decision function is attached to a new local function $10(x - 4)^3 - 1$. (This is $10x^3 - 1$, translated in order to set $x = 4$ as its center.) The new (mirrored) decision function modulates the amplitude on a local function $10(x - 4)^3 - 1$ as shown in Figure 13.

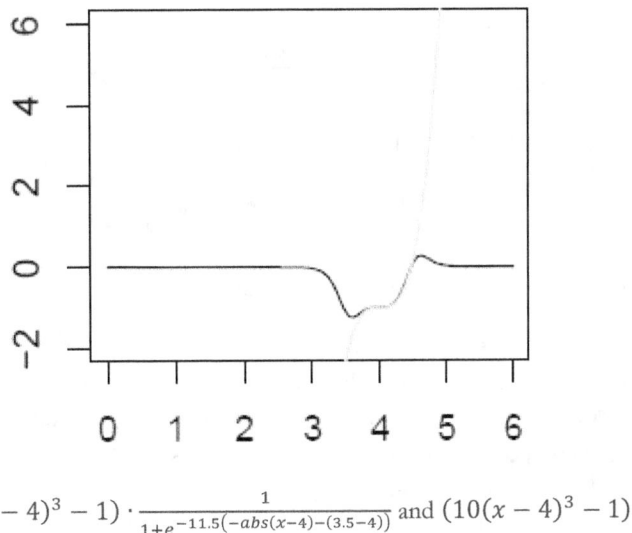

$$(10(x - 4)^3 - 1) \cdot \frac{1}{1+e^{-11.5\left(-abs(x-4)-(3.5-4)\right)}} \text{ and } (10(x - 4)^3 - 1)$$

Figure 13: Local frequency behavior and its original function.

Given our procedures for weighting a local function f_{middle} above by multiplying a mirror sigmoid ς_{middle} attached to that local function; also given a lower local halfpoint $H_{middle,left}$, a regional midpoint M, lower local threshold $L_{(middle,left)}$, a threshold weighting W, and a steepness of K, we have the conditions for weighting any function which is <u>not</u> the first or last in a piecewise group:

$$\frac{1}{1+e^{-K\left(-abs(x-M)-\left(H_{middle,left}-M\right)\right)}}, \text{ where } K > \frac{\ln\left(\frac{1}{W}-1\right)}{H_{middle,left}-L} \tag{12}$$

Recall also that the first and last-end decision functions are

$$\frac{1}{1+e^{-K\left(H_{first}-x\right)}} \text{ and } \frac{1}{1+e^{-K(x-H_{last})}} \tag{13}$$

respectively. Thus we have the three weightings needed to construct a full decision function modulation.

Let us now join the three weighting functions from our ongoing example. Assuming halfpoints at 3.5 and 4.5 on either side of the central weighting function at $M = 4$, weights W of 1% at local thresholds $|H - L| = .4$ beyond such halfpoints for each of the three functions, a first sigmoid which begins at $x = 0$ and spans all the way to $H = 3.5$, and a last sigmoid that begins at $H = 4.5$ and spans all the way to $x = 6$, we may obtain the appropriate weightings. Assuming further that our left, middle, and right functions are $(2x + 1)$, $(10(x - 4)^3 - 1)$, and $\cos(4x)$ respectively, we obtain the full equation

$$\frac{-.2x+1}{1+e^{-11.5(3.5-x)}} + \frac{\left(10(x-4)^3-1\right)}{1+e^{-11.5(-abs(x-4)-(3.5-4))}} + \frac{\cos(4x)}{1+e^{-11.5(x-4.5)}} \tag{14}$$

shown in Figure 14 below.

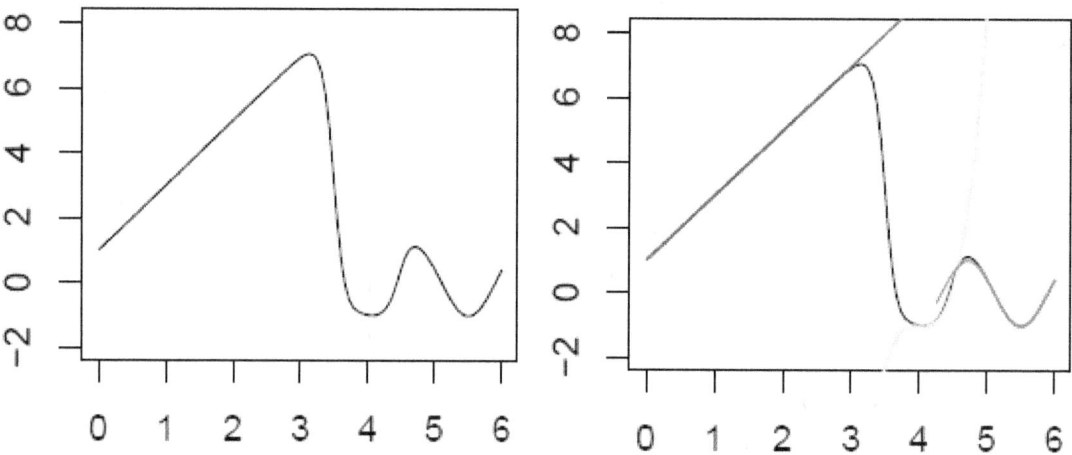

Figure 14: The function obeys all three behaviors, but only in the specified local domains.

The resulting DFM function can have each of its local functions made dependent on different variables, and may be extended into N dimensions by introducing more middle sigmoids with their own midpoints M and local thresholds L. Extrapolating from the equations above, we introduce the basic-form general equation for constructing a smooth piecewise function with $N \geq 3$ component functions $f_{1..N}$, a constant steepness K, constant falloff range $(H_{i>1} - L_{i>1})$ given a constant threshold weight $W_{i \geq 1}$ across functions f_i, and non-mirrored f_1 and f_N (f_{first} and f_{last}),

$$\frac{f_1}{1+e^{-K\left(H_{1,(right)}-x\right)}} + \sum_{i=2}^{N-1}\frac{f_i}{1+e^{-K\left(-abs(x-M_i)-\left(H_{i,left}-M_i\right)\right)}} + \frac{f_N}{1+e^{-K\left(x-H_{N,(left)}\right)}} \tag{15}$$

where the following conditions hold:

(a) All steepnesses are equal.

$$K > \frac{\ln\left(\frac{1}{W_i}-1\right)}{H_i - L_i} \text{ and } K_i = K \text{ for any } i \in \{1..N\}$$

(b) All falloff equations produce the same result.

$$\frac{\ln\left(\frac{1}{W_i}-1\right)}{H_i - L_i} = \frac{\ln\left(\frac{1}{W_j}-1\right)}{H_j - L_j} \text{ for any } i,j \in \{1..N\}, i \neq j$$

(c) Left lower thresholds are less than left halfpoints which are less than midpoints of each non-first region

$$L_{i,left} < H_{i,left} < M_i \text{ for any } i \in \{2..N\}$$

(d) Left lower thresholds, left halfpoints, and midpoints increase as f's index increases across non-first regions.

$$L_{i,left} < L_{i+1,left}, H_{i,left} < H_{i+1,left}, M_i < M_{i+1} \text{ for any } i \in \{2..N\}$$

(e) f_{first}'s right (and only) halfpoint equals f_2's left halfpoint

$$H_{1,(right)} = H_{2,left}$$

(f) f_{first}'s right falloff weight equals f_2's left falloff weight

$$W_1 = W_2$$

(g) f_{first}'s right side falloff range is negative that of f_2's left falloff range

$$(L_{1,(right)} - H_{1,(right)}) = (H_{2,left} - L_{2,left})$$

The model is considered "basic" because so many factors (a-g) are held constant across local functions. Despite all of the conditions, however, the case above just means that our local functions and their thresholds are taken in order of increasing input values, and subjected to the same family of key decision function constants. Holding $(H_i - L_i)$, and W_i constant; keeping $L_{i,left} < H_{i,left} < M_i$ within each function region, and listing the regions in order takes care of most of this for basic modeling purposes.

MODELING CYCLES

IHEs are often tasked with modeling cyclical data across terms, semesters, or quarters. It would be convenient to construct a DFM function for modeling such cycles. To do this, we simply note that the mirror sigmoid we introduced in equation (12) can, by itself, serve as a multiplier on a particular region of a cycle as long as we allow the input values to reset in periodic behavior. Such periodic behavior can be established via the modulo (mod) function, which gives the remainder of a division problem. For example, $10 \, mod \, 8 = 2$ since the remainder of $10 \div 8 = 2$. By the same logic, $18 \, mod \, 8$ is also 2. Accordingly, if we want a particular $f(x)$ behavior to repeat every T units, all we need to do is take $f(x mod T)$. Wherever x is, we replace it with $x \, mod \, T$.

Suppose for instance we wanted the behavior in our ongoing example to repeat every 6 units. Substituting x with $x \, mod \, 6$ in equation 14 gives the following behavior shown in Figure 15.

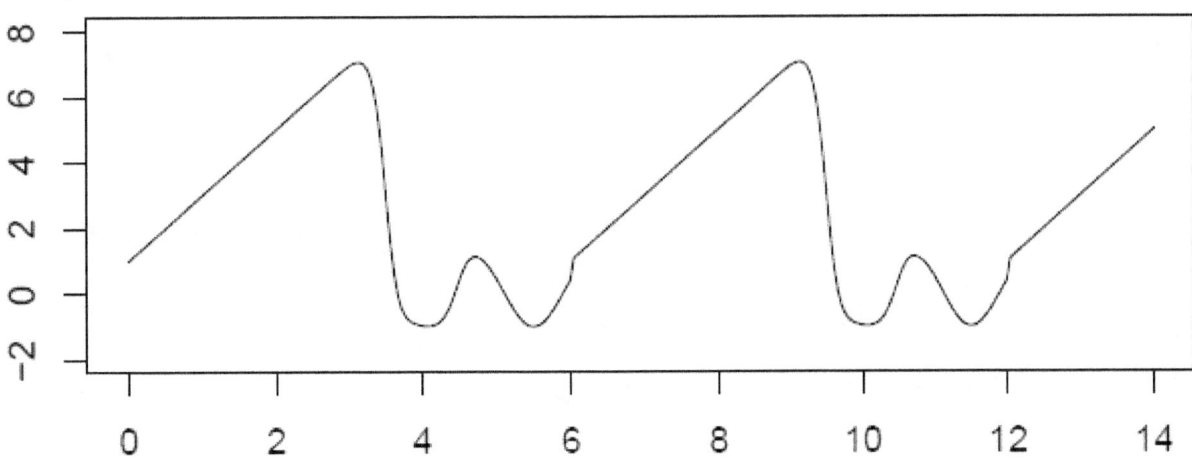

Figure 15. Periodic decision function modulation. Note that the function isn't smooth at each new period.

We've established a cycle, but not a smooth one. This is because our f_{first} and f_{last} aren't mirror sigmoids. In order to make them into mirror sigmoids, we'll need to turn their end point behavior into halfpoint behavior so that the left and right boundaries of our function can average into each other. For f_{first}, assuming a starting point a $x = 0$, this transition is made as follows:

$$\frac{f_1}{1+e^{-K(H_1-x)}} \rightarrow \frac{f_1}{1+e^{-K\left(-abs\left(x \bmod T-\frac{H_1}{2}\right)-\left(-\frac{H_1}{2}\right)\right)}} \tag{16}$$

For f_{last}, assuming an ending point a $x = T$, this mirror-sigmoid version is

$$\frac{f_N}{1+e^{-K(x-H_N)}} \rightarrow \frac{f_i}{1+e^{-K\left(-abs\left(x \bmod T-\frac{T-H_N}{2}\right)-\left(H_N-\frac{T-H_N}{2}\right)\right)}} \tag{17}$$

We could have simplified equations (16) and (17), but I've left them inefficient so that they could be easily compared to the operations in equation (15). Returning to our example, we arrive at Figure 16.

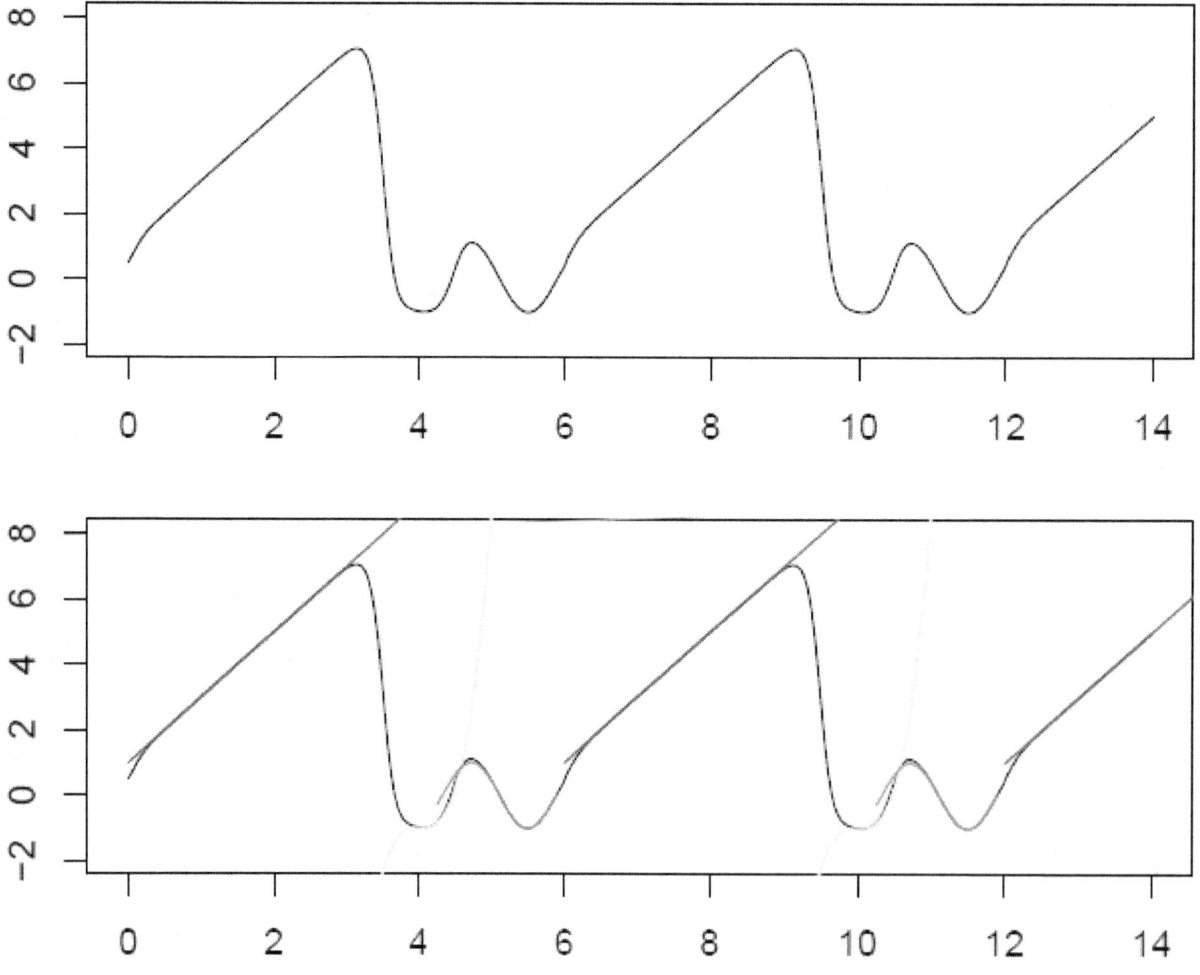

Figure 16. By introducing "midpoints" to our end functions f_{first} and f_{last}, we have now produced a smoothly cycling DFM function.

Thus we arrive at the formula for the cyclization of a previously bounded piecewise function, subject to the original conditions in equation (15):

$$F_{cyclized}(x, \{f\}, \varsigma) = \frac{f_1(x \bmod T)}{1+e^{-K\left(-abs\left(x \bmod T - \frac{H_{1,right}}{2}\right) - \left(\frac{H_{1,right}}{2}\right)\right)}} \tag{18}$$

$$+ \sum_{i=2}^{N-1} \frac{f_i(x \bmod T)}{1+e^{-K\left(-abs(x-M_i) - \left(H_{i,left} - M_i\right)\right)}}$$

$$+ \frac{f_N(x \bmod T)}{1+e^{-K\left(-abs\left(x \bmod T - \frac{T-H_{N,left}}{2}\right) - \left(H_{N,left} \frac{T-H_{N,left}}{2}\right)\right)}}$$

Below is the more general form for cyclical piecewise DFM given an ordered sequence of local functions over a base domain $x \bmod T \in [0..T)$, subject to the ordering conditions in equation (15):

$$F_{cyclical}(x, \{f\}, \varsigma) = \sum_{i=1}^{N} f_i(x \bmod T)\varsigma_i(x \bmod T) = \sum_{i=1}^{N} \frac{f_i(x \bmod T)}{1+e^{-K\left(-abs(x \bmod T - M_i) - \left(H_{i,left} - M_i\right)\right)}} \tag{19}$$

For those of us in IHEs who prefer an easier to read version of the above, the basic form of equation (19) is

$$\frac{current\ function_1\left(x \bmod \left(\begin{smallmatrix}constant\ repeat\\ period\ length\end{smallmatrix}\right)\right)}{1+e^{-\left(\begin{smallmatrix}constant\\ steepness\end{smallmatrix}\right)\left(-abs\left[x \bmod \left(\begin{smallmatrix}constant\ repeat\\ period\ length\end{smallmatrix}\right) - \left(\begin{smallmatrix}current\\ midpoint_1\end{smallmatrix}\right)\right] - \left[\left(\begin{smallmatrix}left\\ halfpoint_1\end{smallmatrix}\right) - \left(\begin{smallmatrix}current\\ midpoint_1\end{smallmatrix}\right)\right]\right)}} + \tag{20}$$

$$\frac{current\ function_2\left(x \bmod \left(\begin{smallmatrix}constant\ repeat\\ period\ length\end{smallmatrix}\right)\right)}{1+e^{-\left(\begin{smallmatrix}constant\\ steepness\end{smallmatrix}\right)\left(-abs\left[x \bmod \left(\begin{smallmatrix}constant\ repeat\\ period\ length\end{smallmatrix}\right) - \left(\begin{smallmatrix}current\\ midpoint_2\end{smallmatrix}\right)\right] - \left[\left(\begin{smallmatrix}left\\ halfpoint_2\end{smallmatrix}\right) - \left(\begin{smallmatrix}current\\ midpoint_2\end{smallmatrix}\right)\right]\right)}} + \cdots$$

where constant steepness is

$$\begin{smallmatrix}constant\\ steepness\end{smallmatrix} > \frac{\ln\left(\frac{1}{\begin{smallmatrix}what\ we\ consider\\ \text{"a low percentage" at threshold}\end{smallmatrix}} - 1\right)}{\begin{smallmatrix}how\ far\ away\ from\ a\ halfpoint\ we\\ need\ to\ be\ for\ the\ low\ threshold\ to\ apply\end{smallmatrix}}$$

EXAMPLE 2

Using equation (20), suppose we want to construct a very basic sleep-wake activity level cycle that has a flat value of 1.45 for eight hours of the day, but varies as $3cos(x) + 4$ for the remaining 16 hours. Suppose also that sleep happens between 10pm ($x = 22$) and 6am ($x = 6$). What do we do?

1. First, we find the repeat period. This is $T = 8 + 16 = 24$.
2. Second, we slide the sleep hours to make the problem simpler. Let $s = x - 22$ where s is the start of sleep.
   a. The step above means that waking would begin at $s = -16$, but since this is a 24-hour cycle, adding 24 means waking starts at $s = 8$ (eight hours after sleep begins).
3. Next we find midpoints. The middle of the sleep range (0-8) is $M_{sleep} = 4$. The middle of the waking range (8-24) is $M_{sleep} = 16$.
4. Now we find left (lower) halfpoints. The transition from sleep to waking occurs at $H_{waking(left)} = 8$. The transition from waking to sleep occurs at $H_{waking(right)} = H_{sleep(left)}$. This happens at 0, 24, 48... but since we're taking left halfpoints, we will only consider $H_{sleep(left)}$, and take $s \bmod T$ to do so. $H_{sleep(left)} = 0,24,48 \ldots \bmod 24 = 0$ (where sleep starts).
5. To determine falloff ranges, we'll first determine an appropriate weight where our local function would be considered negligible. 5% weight, or $W = .05$, is fine.

6. We don't actually need to determine thresholds (L) in the basic case. $H - L$ (how long it takes a transition to occur) will be easier since the formulas we have used all assume symmetry. Suppose it takes 45 minutes to transition from half 5% asleep or awake to 50% asleep or awake. This is .75 hours. Thus $H - L = .75$.

7. Calculating constant steepness K, we use the above to obtain $K > ln\left(\frac{1}{.05} - 1\right) /.75$ or $K > 3.93$.

8. We now have everything we need to plug into equation (20):

$$F(s) = \frac{1.45}{1 + e^{-3.93(-|(s \bmod 24)-4|-(0-4))}} + \frac{3\cos(s \bmod 24) + 4}{1 + e^{-3.93(-|(s \bmod 24)-16|-(8-16))}}$$

9. Finally, substituting $s = x - 22$ and simplifying, we get

$$F(x) = \frac{1.45}{1+e^{-3.93(-|((x-22)\bmod 24)-4|+4)}} + \frac{3\cos((x-22)\bmod24)+4}{1+e^{-3.93(-|((x-22)\bmod24)-16|+8)}} \tag{21}$$

The result of all this is shown in Figure (17) below.

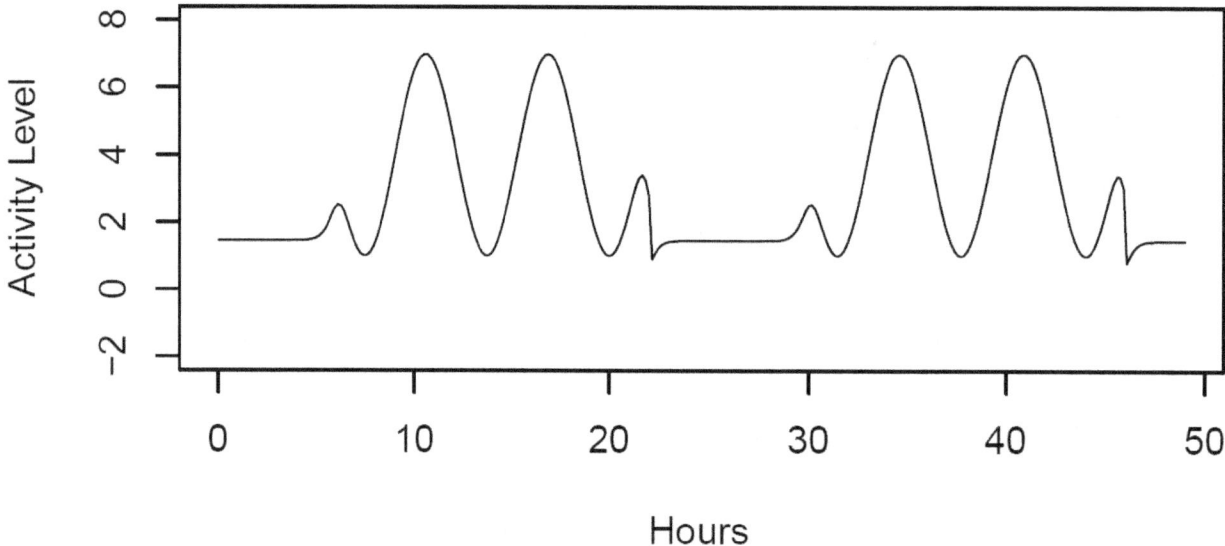

Figure 17. Example of a smooth, cyclical DFM function built from parameters of our choosing. It may not look smooth, but notice that the cosine term shrinks in amplitude near the "sleep" regions.

HIGHER DIMENSIONAL FUNCTIONS

So far DFM functions have basically consisted of a series of sigmoids each multiplying an associated local function. Varying the amplitude of those functions has allowed us to turn them on or off, while varying the frequencies (periods, midpoints, thresholds, and halfpoints) has allowed us to control the onset of such functions. The real application for these piecewise assemblies lies in stitching together multidimensional models. We can, for example, treat an entire joined function of the form shown in equation (19) as a local function in another DFM assembly.

$$\sum_{j=1}^{N} \frac{g_j(<x, y \bmod \tau>)}{1+e^{-\kappa\left(-abs(<x, y \bmod \tau>-M_j)-(H_{j,left}-M_j)\right)}} \tag{22}$$

$$\text{where } g_{j(<x,y>)} = \sum_{i=1,j}^{N} \frac{f_{i,j}(<x \bmod T_j, y>)}{1+e^{-K_j\left(-abs(<x \bmod T_j, y>-M_{i,j})-(H_{i,left,j}-M_{i,j})\right)}}$$

Note that above we're using a collection of variables in the form of a vector, and changing one dimension at a time. τ and κ are the repeat period and steepness for the y dimension while T and K are the are the repeat period and steepness for the x dimension. This is a matter of taking a group of DFM functions as "rows" and using each of them as a local function "column" in another DFM function.

Alternatively, each f_i can also consist of several more complex, multivariate functions. To illustrate, suppose we have several linear regression models, each applicable during a different time of year. If each regression model is of the form $y_i = \sum_{i,j} \beta_{i,j} z_j + \varepsilon_i$ then we have

$$\sum_{i=1}^{N} \frac{\sum_{i,j} \beta_{i,j} z_j + \varepsilon_i}{1 + e^{-K\left(-abs(x \bmod T - M_i) - \left(H_{i,left} - M_i\right)\right)}} \tag{23}$$

where i is the function index and j is the predictor index within the space of all regression variables considered.

In human speak, we can place entire regression equation (or other reasonable modelling function) into a DFM function and modulate when it applies at various points in the specified period. For building retention models where it is often useful to break the analyses into smaller, more coherent groups, piecewise sigmoidal joining allows us to collapse different predictive structures into a single holistic framework, and may also be useful for investigating those factors which appear in some local functions but not in others.

AN EXAMPLE OF COMBINING MODELS

Suppose our earlier example (non-cyclical) proved to be an accurate model for describing general student engagement in a hypothetical 6-month online program, but only for students who reported fewer family problems. For students reporting a higher level of family problems on a scale from 0 to 8, suppose the appropriate formula was $E = 6 - x$. In this case we have two models: $E_{p\rightarrow 8} = 6 - x$ while $E_{p\rightarrow 0}$ follows equation (14). Applying equations (3) and (4) to both models, using—for example—an arbitrary, relatively low steepness $K = 2$ as our hypothetical data might dictate, and assuming a single halfpoint of $p = 4$ between the two models, we can create a "sheet" for shifting from one model to another. The formula is

$$\frac{1}{1+e^{-2(4-p)}}\left(\frac{-2x+1}{1+e^{-11.5(3.5-x)}} + \frac{\left(10(x-4)^3-1\right)}{1+e^{-11.5(-abs(x-4)-(3.5-4))}} + \frac{\cos(4x)}{1+e^{-11.5(x-4.5)}}\right) + \frac{1}{1+e^{-2(p-4)}}(6-x) \tag{24}$$

$$\text{where } p \in [0,8], x \in [0,6]$$

The display of both models in smooth transition is shown in Figure (18).

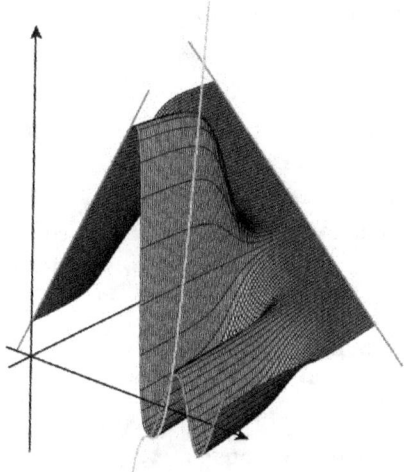

Figure 18. The function for a hypothetical scenario which obeys one (single-local function) model further into the background, while obeying another (three-local function) model as we approach the foreground. Plotted using https://www.monroecc.edu/faculty/paulseeburger/calcnsf/CalcPlot3D/.

Though not necessarily easy to visualize, this concept can be applied to systems of more than three dimensions, where the weight given to various variables in each model may be adjusted as needed.

DISCUSSION

Decision function modulation, or DFM, allows for the dynamic modelling of adjacent behavioral phenomena with potentially differing behavioral inputs such as calm-alert-stress, submissive-unassuming-warm, novice-familiar-experienced-expert, and a host of other continuums which evolve over time or condition. Although it is possible to model such evolving systems using a series of constants (how extraverted are you in a public place versus a familiar place), series modelling may not always capture the idea that individuals may simply reference different variables as circumstances change (public behavioral inputs versus familiar behavioral inputs). By reducing a local pattern of behavior to very near 0 when its underlying assumptions no longer apply, DFM functions allow us to introduce local variation into our models without significant changes to the entire domain. The general structure of such functions is

$$\frac{f_1}{exponetial\ weight_1} + \frac{f_2}{exponetial\ weight_2} + \cdots$$

where each function can be a constant, model, or another piecewise function. They may be as complicated as the weighted outputs of a deep learning schema or as simple as 0, but in any case allow us to mute them at will.

LIMITATIONS

There are some limitations to the DFM approach to function joining. First, it isn't clear that the logistic sigmoid is the best choice. Posing an initial construct for local regions to consist of spheres of attractors, I strongly considered the arctangent to be the appropriate function in line with the associated trigonometry. I later rejected the arctangent under the assumption the influence of other attractors would "block" the regions behind them, but these assumptions need testing against actual phenomena.

A second, probably major, limitation to DFM as it is presented here is that it treats adjacent regions as independent and symmetrically distributed. Mirror sigmoids employed the same steepness on both their left and right sides, and one weighting function's presence does not significantly influence the one it overlaps with. A certain notion of "bond structure" is lost when we assemble weightings in this way, suggesting that such functions might be better informed by insights from chemistry. Relatedly, the multidimensional examples discussed in this article do not consider the very common covariation found among predictors. We have only outlined a starting point for modelling spaces which are surely more complicated in reality.

FURTHER RESEARCH

An advantage to using DFM is that it allows us to represent nominal variables numerically over a region that can also hold purely numeric information. By choosing a representative sinusoid as a local function, we may apply a fourier transform to a local region in order to determine its fit with a particular comparison frequency. If, for example, one region of a local function produced behavior which is 99% "turned on" in favor of $cos(4x)$, we might perform a fourier decomposition of the function against the $\lambda^{-1}=4$ factor to tell us the amount of "4-frequency." Not 3. Not 5. Here we would treat 4 as a separately optimized value that may stand in as a kind of frequency-based dummy encoding for a particular nominal class. If for example we wanted to dummy code Math as 1, English as 2, and Music as 3, we could assign a $cos(1x), cos(2x), or cos(3x)$ as the local functions respectively, and decompose the whole function later to extract the correct value. Digit-based sinusoids may represent even further application of this principal, where 90 different majors may be represented by cosines 1x through 90x, while at the same time 20 different extracurricular organizations may be represented by adding cosines 1(100) through 20(100) onto the first cosine.

CONCLUSION

In understanding human behavior, it is essential that we develop better mechanisms for capturing dynamic process (Škec, Cash, & Štorga, 2017). Linear and polynomial regression, series approximation, and curve-fitting for multipoint data collection allow us to better trace the paths taken by individual's behavioral measures, such that trajectories are easier to predict and adjust for. In the future we might use DFM to develop a kind of topology of human personality—where we may do more than just score a person's openness or agreeableness, but locate where average populations are most likely to invoke such traits. A person's openness, for example, may be a more salient trait in social or novel experiential situations than in hunger or focus situations where neuroticism may gain more relevance. DFM allows us to parcel out sections of a single behavioral "data stream" for specific spectral characteristics. In the study of behavior, we now have the means to go beyond the *what* of personality, into the realm of the *when* and *how*.

I began using DFM functions as a way of allowing a particular construct my colleagues and I were studying (resilience-like engagement) to be measured and mapped over a more changeable set of preconditions. As recent explorations in neuroscience have begun to elucidate the frequency encoding mechanisms of the brain (Henderson & Gong, 2018), so too can we use frequency patterned regions of modulated amplitudes to join together measures which, though certainly related, have meaningful uniqueness components beyond their communalities. Time series are useful, as are separable probabilistic models, but occasionally our investigations may require a more balanced treatment between the two extremes of full domain autocorrelation and aggregate domain black box statistics. With simpler methods for piecing domains together, we may find increased usefulness in our heretofore disparate models yet, as we determine patterns in our data one local region at a time.

REFERENCES

Barclay, T. H., Barclay, R. D., Mims, A., Sargent, Z. & Robertson, K. (2018). Academic retention: Predictors of college success. *Education, 139*(2), 59-70.

Cramer, J. S. (2002). The origins of logistic regression (Technical report 119). 167-178. Tinbergen Institute.

Denice, P. (2019). Trajectories through postsecondary education and students' life course transitions. *Social Science Research, 80,* 243-260.

Griffin, B., Bayl-Smith, P., & Hu, W. (2018). Predicting patterns of change and stability in student performance across a medical degree. *Medical Education, 52*(4), 438-446.

Henderson, J.A., & Gong, P. (2018). Functional mechanisms underlie the emergence of a diverse range of plasticity phenomena. *PLOS Computational Biology, 14*(11): e1006590.

Hintze, J. M., Volpe, R. J., & Shapiro, E. S. (2002). Best practices in the systematic direct observation of student behavior. In A. Thomas & J. Grimes (Eds.), *Best practices in school psychology IV,* (p. 993-1006). National Association of School Psychologists.

Humphrys, M. (n.d.) Sigmoid activation function. Retrieved December 9, 2019 from https://www.computing.dcu.ie/~humphrys/Notes/Neural/sigmoid.html.

Lotkowski, V., Robbins, S., & Noeth, R. (2004). The role of academic and non-academic factors in improving college retention. *ACT Policy Report.* Iowa City, IA: ACT, Inc.

Moir, F., Yielder, J., Sanson, J., & Chen, Y. (2018). Depression in medical students: Current insights. *Advances in medical education and practice, 9,* 323-333.

Škec, S., Cash, P., & Storga, M. (2017). A dynamic approach to real-time performance measurement in design projects. *Journal of Engineering Design,* 255-286.

Tinto, V. (1997). Classrooms as communities: Exploring the educational character of student persistence. *The Journal of Higher Education, 68*(6), 599-623.

Wald, A. (1949). Statistical decision functions. *Ann. Math. Statist., 20*(2), 165-205.

Appendix II: Rasosho!

CHAPTER 1. THEORY

I wrote the following after reading Stephen Hawking's *A Brief History of Time* and a biography of S. Ramanujan, the former of which I had been avoiding since physics has always given me trouble.

Energy: the only thing

Potential (independent of harness) & Kinetic (dependent on harness): two subtypes of existent energy

Interrelational / intrarelational potential and kinetic: four subtypes of energy:

	Dependent potential ([resonance: potential transfer] extent of moving together/ **gravity | charge | heat**), Interrelational potential.
	*Sub*dependent potential ([induction: potential amassing] sliding reference/ **time | number**), Intrarelational potential.
	Subdependent kinetic([amassing]within/**mass | composition**). Intrarelational kinetic.
	Dependent kinetic ([transfer] between/**moving** (e.g. heating | "lighting" | sound as waves towards targets)), Interrelational kinetic.

Rules:

1. **Potential, by definition, cannot be "seen" accurately.** Heisenberg: to see what's in the box is to take evidence from it. To analyze time left is to lose it. To measure gravity *between objects in question* is to disturb it. To view it is to harness its viewable qualities, thus making those qualities kinetic.
2. **Dependent objects cannot "see" things.** Dependent objects here are defined as relationships between things. They cannot make meaning of the outside world on their own, but are a property of "amassed" things. To the extent that dependent objects are identified according to a stereotyped relational standard, they are uniform in their composition. (Thus they cannot receive change without changing themselves.) Amassed things are made up of non-uniform components—which means they can absorb change without being destroyed themselves.
3. **By (1) and (2), only matter sponsors action (can both see and be seen).** Visible actions are performed by "amassed" things. *Actions* here defined as [a stereotyped *transfer amassed* under a label]. Without non-uniform

composite sets of energies, actions will exist without viewers (the composites) to view/label them as coherent. Coherence requires referents. Only other coherent objects can "see" things as coherent.

4. **"Seeing" cannot take place without transfer of "precoherent" objects.** Without packets of energy that get transferred, coherence cannot obtain.

5. **"Transfer" as a state must exist.** Though the potential for change cannot be seen (1), such a potential enables "seeing" as a process.

6. **By (3) only matter which contains at least two sets of nonequivalent matter can "see."** Object α must contain β_2 as an impinging object and β_1 as a referent in order to even have the minimal constructs for "seeing." Thus, all viewable things require at least three "amassed" dimensions. (When β_2 arrives, α will identify it/use it as β_1. α, β_1, and β_2 must all be unequal to each other. Thus, everything that "sees" is composed of differences.)

7. **By (6) with (5), Matter, with seeing, establishes four dimensions as the minimal, coherently changing system.** By (6),there must be a difference between β_2 as arrived versus not arrived. Even with three dimensions, Amassed systems of three cannot "see," cannot change, without a transfer process. We add the dimension of $\tau=\{\alpha, \beta_1, \beta_2\}'$ to our existing $\{\alpha, \beta_1, \beta_2\}$ to get $\{\alpha, \beta_1, \beta_2, \tau\}$, whenever we wish to describe a *changing* system. For pure analysis of static systems, three dimensions or less are okay. For perceivable reality, only four and up will do. See that, in the context of systems that "view," induction is the same as "iterated amassing." Define $\{\alpha, \beta_1, \beta_2, \tau\}$ as a *changing object.*

8. **By (6), resonance [degree of equivalence] is a necessary quality for differentiation.** Let us say $\varepsilon_{\alpha,\beta1}$ is the difference between α and β_1. If the $\varepsilon_{\alpha,\beta1}$ property is null, α and β_1 are the same. What will α use, by (6), to contextualize β_2 when it arrives? Given only itself, α has no way of "knowing" it has viewed at all. This is the short argument. Similar arguments for other εs follow.

9. **By (8) and (1), the level of "potential" (resonance) between objects can only be studied if we are willing to make an object of the non-amassed potential.** But, by definition of amassing, (2) and (3), amassed things consist of other, non-equivalent things. Thus, the study of errors yields new errors.

To study dynamic human relationships is to study the exchanges between sets of at least two non-equivalent objects. By (8), even the study of the "non-equivalent" objects [Smith at time 1] with himself [Smith at time 2] is a five dimensional system $\{\alpha, \beta_1, \beta_2, \tau, \varepsilon\}$. Here, ε must be included as a separate element in order to for us to study the relationship in at least pretended "isolation."

Some basic "math" for the four energies:

Name	Some symbols	Generic properties	Sample "math"
Resonance (Affinity)	$+, \sim$ (combination) $-, \neq$ (interference)	Exists as uniformly constituted relationships between things. A concept which, when divided, reproduces the same concept without error, differing from the original only in magnitude (number). Curiously, we can explain all four energies in terms of this one, if only we were not born with the ability to notice differences in number. Alas, in a system which is unevenly resonant (hot in some areas, cool in others; subset of 1 in some areas, subset of 2 in others), the concept of iteration is born.	$+ \rightarrow -$ (Resonance implies dissonance, as resonant things must be somehow exclude each other in order to "pair" at all. That is, $(+\rightarrow-)\rightarrow\neq$) $+ \rightarrow x$ (Resonance implies number. See left.)
Iteration (Number)	O $0...9$ (constant) $a...z$ (variable)	Iteration is the stacking of resonant constructs. To the extent that a construct includes another like it, but is not included in that other, iteration is unidirectional. Recursive reference sets the direction. Iteration begins with a single resonant object, which in turn begins with two other objects not equal to itself. Iteration's forwardness is best explained by analogy: if a psychologically amassed system always trains its members that consequents assume priors (and not the other way around), the	$x \supset + (x \rightarrow +)$ (Iteration is the superset of combinations. Iterations are resonant. Like order relations. See left.) $x_1 + x_2 \rightarrow x_3$ (Iterations are additive)

		members will always perceive their forward direction as unchanging.	
Amassing (Matter)	$\int, \Sigma$ (predictable, unpredictable combination) $\partial,$ $\begin{pmatrix} x11 & \cdots & x12 \\ \vdots & \ddots & \vdots \\ x21 & \cdots & x22 \end{pmatrix}$ (predictable, unpredictable deconstruction)	An amassed thing is the combination of other things. Any harness (observed, used) system with more than one object in it is "amassed," though not all such systems are externally "material." Note, even a mental construct is amassed, since its presence does coincide with changes in the thinker's (cognitive) physiology. So "matter" isn't really the applicable word. Matter is type of amassed thing which other amassed things can relate to in an iterative way (it can receive and elicit interference without having its basic assembly altered.) Amassing describes reality, but iteration compresses the complexity of such into manageable packets. See comment. When we study human *interactions*, it is simpler to think of them as black box magnitudes. When we study the *composition* of systems, "amassing" operations are better.	Let x be the sum of a person's cognition (physiological, social, etc.) at any moment ∂x: $$\int x\, \partial x \rightarrow x^2$$ $$\rightarrow \underbrace{x + \cdots + x}_{(x\,times)}$$ (the sum of a person's cognition is their cognition combined with itself over the scope of its cognitive moments. Read as: "I am the sum of my thoughts about myself and world").
Transfer (Energy)	(emission) (absorption)	Consider a system with two objects in it. There is a subset of this system which includes only the first object. How does that subset relate to the whole? Transfer measures the ways in which parts "become" their wholes, priors inform successors, antecedents are assumed by consequents. Where there is more than one object in a system, there is transfer within that system Even if the system comprises parts which look the same, the existence of subsets necessitates, in the very least, a relationship between visible "parts" and invisible magnitudes thereof.	$(\partial\Sigma \rightarrow) \rightarrow$ - (Emissions emit dissonance. The traveling light cannot project itself. By analogy, "Change makes different." $(+\rightarrow -) \rightarrow - (-\rightarrow +)$ (Resonance as dissonance interferes with dissonance as resonance. Resonance and dissonance are non-commutative.)

How do we conceptualize the origin of Iteration from Resonance?

- Consider an entirely resonant system. If the resonance *is* the system, the system is either (a) indivisibly uniform and thus its own full and empty set (which makes no sense because this would be a pure relation between "objects" which have been vanquished under <u>complete</u> resonance) or (b) divisibly uniform (and thus not uniform in terms of "pockets of magnitude"; it has subsets equal in composition but unequal in number). Either way, resonant systems imply dissonant objects.

Some sociological variables:

Magnitudes

- Ω = the rules for constructing one's reality
- α = a particular situation
- β = oneself in a particular situation
- γ = a particular object of interaction in a particular situation
- δ = the hidden properties (inner workings, private thoughts, reasons, future trajectory) underlying an a particular object in a particular situation
- ε_{xy} = the difference (non-resonance) between x & y
- S = Subject
- O = Object (Other) in general

- $S(x,y)$ =   Subject's thoughts about (perceptions of) x in a particular situation y. Returns a magnitude. Takes two magnitudes as arguments which correspond roughly to a percept (x; left brain-ish) and an ambient concept against which the percept acts (y; whole physiological state). x = "what is." y = "what should be."

- $S(S(x),y)$ =   Subject's thoughts about his thoughts about x in a particular situation y. Returns a magnitude.

Sets

- $\{S,O,y\}$ =   The "subject, object, context" vector; S's interaction with O in situation y

- $\{S,O,y,\tau,\varepsilon\}$ =   Interaction vector; S, O, y the same as above; τ is, roughly, where the interaction tends towards in time; ε describes the relationships among S, O, y, and τ. All five are reduced to empirical magnitudes, dot products, or determinants.

- i_{name} =   A sociological interaction; an interaction vector; subscript is the name of the interaction.

Matrices of magnitudes

- $\partial\Sigma S(O,y)$ =   the space containing all viewers' S observations about an object O in a situation y. contains as many rows as relevant viewers and as many columns as the properties they assign

- $\partial_2\Sigma S(O,y)$ =   the above is cumbersome. This is the two row version of the above. Row one contain averages (normal) properties. Row two contains standard deviations of those same properties. "Normality" is assumed.

Some assumptions:

- Within S:
  - $\Omega \supset \alpha$ (That is, $S(\Omega,y) \supset S(\alpha,y)$)
  - α is some function of γ, δ, Ω, S and O
  - $S(\beta,\Omega) \neq S(\beta,y)$. How one thinks of oneself broadly is not how one thinks of oneself in a narrow situation.
  - $S(\beta,\Sigma\alpha) \neq S(\Sigma\beta,\Sigma\alpha)$. How one thinks of oneself given all of his situations is not how one thinks of one's aggregate self, given all of his situations.
- $O \neq S(O, \Omega)$. One never sees the "empirically true" object. Said scientifically, the external world's assessment of an object will never match an individual's assessment. Especially since the external world assumes no idiosyncratic "should be" as background.
- $\partial\Sigma\, S(O, \Omega) \rightarrow O$. The deconstructed aggregate of all perceptions about an empirically true object gives rise to the object's magnitude. There is some function which accomplishes this mapping, usually a basic definition. For example, in a system with only Smith and Jones, if Smith thinks an oak is a tall tree and Jones thinks an oak is an old tree, the sum for oak is "tall+old+tree," the deconstructed amassed value ∂ of which it is comprised is a 2x3 matrix of slopes and the mapping (however contrived) produces something like "tree" as the empirical "truth" within that system. You can see why $O \neq S(O, \Omega)$. The "true" O is defined here as the space of labels applied to it. We work with "flattened" versions of this space, limited by our own experiential background.
- Similarly, $S_0 \neq \partial\Sigma S(S_0, \Omega)$. The "truth" of an individual is never seen by the individual himself, for he is the aggregate of all who think of him.
- $\partial_2\Sigma S(S_0, \Omega) \neq \partial\Sigma S(S_0, \Omega)$. Though "normal space" approximates true space, what person hangs out only around "normal" people. We express on the fringes. $\partial_2\Sigma S(S_0, \Omega)$ is what the average person would say about us S_0 in our absence. $\partial\Sigma S(S_0, \Omega)$ is usually bigger than two rows and contains what "relevant" people would say about us. If most of the world doesn't know of Smith, only friends and peers, and/or if friends and peers include people whose views of Smith are nonsensical given the demands of Ω, it is better to use a $\partial\Sigma S(S_0, \Omega)$ with purposely selected observers over the "garbage can" $\partial_2\Sigma S(S_0, \Omega)$.
- **Important:** for linguistic reasons related to the previous bullet, we avoid claiming that S = S. This is because we don't want to assume that [S as subject] equals [S as object]. The former tends to be a soulless label. The latter tends to imply certain referred properties. Instead, we say S ~ S. This is weaker, but more tractable where our analysis of S's dynamics are concerned.

Labeling magnitudes

We can describe the world using any number of primitives, but the base system we choose will alter our understanding of the laws described. A binary system uses the "existence-nonexistence" paradigm as a primitive. An octal system uses either pairs (2) of minimally changing objects (4) or three dimensions (^{3}) of pairs (2) as primitives. We can expect the brain to be aided or hindered by the base system it uses, as can be shown when we try to do 12_{10} + 8_{10} = 20_{10} in base 16 (C_{16} + 8_{16} = 14_{16}). Humans use base 10, so pairs (2) of interactions (5) or interactions (5) framed over dichotomous properties (2) is a human-tractable system.

All of the above formulas and variables aside, we attempt to describe interactions in base 10, assigning each number a meaning based on the kind of study for which it is minimally required. For entertainment, I've listed physics units as analogs, just so you can see a parallel-ish kind of empirical dimensionality.

Number	Related Physics	Required for
0	Unmeasured, uncertain; Speed (weight, ratio)	Non-recognition, **irrelevance**, non-weighting of a thing that might actually be there.
1	Power (W, mass/duration)	Uniqueness (**existence**)
2	Duration (s,m)	**Dissonance**, difference, (dual uniqueness without margining)
3	Mass (kg)	**Identity**, context, viewer viewing one thing against the backdrop of another
4	Current (A)	**Changing**, moving, perceiving (identity (3) + related (1))
5	Temperature (K)	**Interacting** (see above)
6	Volume (6D: m^3,kg^2)	**Information** (differentiated (2) identities(3))
7	Permittivity of space (7D: A^{2}s^4/kg m^3)	**Knowing** (rote), (differentiated (2) × identities(3) + related (1)) Communication, (and identity (3) + moved (4))
8	Spacetime volume (m^{3}s)	**Influence**, (differentiated (2) × changes(4)) Learning (interacting (5) + with an identity (3) ; knowing (7) + related (1))
9	Capacitance (9D: A^{2}s^4/kg m^2; i.e. 16-7)	Conveyed learning, **understanding** (learning (8) + related (1)) Body of knowledge (identity (3) upon itself (²); ~ integrated identity $\int_0^3 x$

* Exponents mean we *count* dimensions here. We don't do the actual math. So volume (duration^3) is a 6D concept: Duration$_1$, duration$_2$, and duration$_3$, dimensions are needed (where duration is a 2D concept: magnitude + reference point). Only later transforms flatten these into the values we know and love.

* Spacetime volume is made-up, but has an interesting property: the longer a volume sits, the more "presence" it has where it is sitting. This is kind of like influence isn't it?

Human exchanges outlined

Purpose of the notes: to illuminate paths to happiness by showing what needs to be known.

Two methods:

Method 1: As a human concept, happiness requires a changeable actor (4), a relation to oneself or world (+ at least 1), and a changeable world (+4). Three points form a plane in regular math, so we can construct either change space (4x3) or identity space (3x3) in order to optimally identify that which describes a person's happiness. I will not use this method.

Method 2: Interactions take five dimensions. Though there are all kinds of permutations that come from the vector, {S,O,y,τ,ε} we can simplify matters by making each interaction binary with respect to the "normal" world standard. This yields 32 fundamental interactions. I will use this method.

Let 1 be a valid, recognized behavioral option in the normal world. Let 0 be an unrecognized option.

S=1: The subject's action is observable

S=0: The subject's action is not observable

O=1: The object's action is observable

O=0: The object's action is not observable

y=1: The situation (assumed always observable) is desirable to the average person

y=0: The situation is not necessarily desirable to the average person, but could be neutral.

τ=1: The subject changes favorably in the eyes of the average person

τ=0: The subject changes unfavorably in the eyes of the average person

ε =1: The object changes favorably in the eyes of the average person

ε =0: The object changes unfavorably in the eyes of the average person

The table below is derived from analysis of the five-vector.

Interaction	S	O	y	τ	ε	Interaction	S	O	y	τ	ε
Expressing (well)	1	1	1	1	1	Fortune received	0	1	1	1	1
Opposing	1	1	1	1	0	Opportunity	0	1	1	1	0
Losing	1	1	1	0	1	Loss	0	1	1	0	1
Blowing it	1	1	1	0	0	Misfortune	0	1	1	0	0
Doing	1	1	0	1	1	Experiencing / Learning	0	1	0	1	1
Capitalizing	1	1	0	1	0	Benefitting at the expense of	0	1	0	1	0
Defending	1	1	0	0	1	Witnessing negatively	0	1	0	0	1
Falling victim to	1	1	0	0	0	Being mislead	0	1	0	0	0
Thinking (well)	1	0	1	1	1	Fortunate event	0	0	1	1	1
Plotting	1	0	1	1	0	Turn of luck	0	0	1	1	0
Acquiescing	1	0	1	0	1	Missing out	0	0	1	0	1
Lowering mood	1	0	1	0	0	Inability	0	0	1	0	0
Becoming optimistic	1	0	0	1	1	Luck	0	0	0	1	1
Becoming opportunistic	1	0	0	1	0	Sole beneficiary	0	0	0	1	0
Sacrificing	1	0	0	0	1	Watching others' luck	0	0	0	0	1
Enduring	1	0	0	0	0	Slumping	0	0	0	0	0

We can see that the S=0s seem to be complements of the S=1s.

Although the binary model seems to describe some kind of experiential space, the typology seems to be lacking a certain humanistic quality. That is, people in their interactions don't seem to use these typologies as frequently as they do others such as love, knowledge, belief, etc. Accordingly, we seek a transformation which includes some more human terms.

A conceptualization of belief

What happens when a person believes something? Tacitly or actively, a belief may be viewed as a kind of experiential object which holds a behaviorally recognized, contextual presence. That is, if I believe it, I somehow steer my reality around it—whether or not the belief is well-formed by my conscious. The implication is that a belief is not so if I (1) act as if the believed object wasn't there or (2) exclude it from the behavioral context when acting on a related object (acting as if its effects aren't there). *A person believes that which he steers his actions around.*

A conceptualization of want

When a person wants something, it may be claimed that they somehow "intend" towards its realization. For the purposes of fitting it to five-vector typology, we will define *wanting as steering one's action's towards the realization of a thing, recognizing that the thing is not had.* As with belief, action is not necessarily overt, but a function of overt behavior in conjunction with cognitive intention. Thus, as long as actions are informed by intentions, rocks can't want (which makes sense).

As for the "not had," part: This separates wanting from intending. We might imagine that turning one's actions towards a thing, by itself, is nothing more than intention (which, cognitively, is closely correlated with simple *at*tention). But staring into space—attending the void—is not wanting. Nor does reflexively picking my nose mean that I "wanted" to do it. We need a way to separate basic intention from those intentions meant to correct [undesirably absent] experiences. Thus we add the condition that a person must recognize the experience as absent AND turn his intentions towards its presence if he is to "want" it. For, if you accused a person who just blinked of "wanting" to blink, he might reasonably be expected to argue against you. The "recognized as not had" condition also protects us from claiming that people "wanted" the unintended consequences of references frames they didn't know they were in. Finally, even "ongoing want" is considered by this definition.

Having and action

We have seen above, that good definitions of "having" and "action" are critical for our definitions of belief and want to work. For simplicity let us define a living being's *action* as *a physiologically-mediated change from an existing state, seen by a particular viewer.* A thought is an action because the physiology is neural. A dream is an action—albeit usually involuntary. Sneezing is an action. But who is to say whether Smith murdered Jones or only killed him in self-defense? When defining actions, the reference frame is all powerful—making action (like the notion of "change" upon which it is built)—as slippery and relative as the notion of time itself. We can extend action to non-living beings such as corporations by replacing "physiologically-mediated" with "sub-unit mediated" where a sub-unit is recognized by the "actor" as a valid division of its own identity.

A definition of "having" must come with imply not just possession, but a kind of willful possession. Specifically, Smith may hold onto Jones' dollar and still not "have" it in the sense that it is his (Smith's) to spend. He does, however, have it in the sense that he holds it. In another example, Jones may have a college degree without physically holding it. How then do we approach having in a way that is generally practical? We will define *having as one's perceiving the potential to experience a thing as that one would intend.* Unfortunately, this definition requires that we sweep certain linguistic permutations of the word under the rug; "having" a disease, for example, may not be the kind of thing one "intends." Having a bubbly personality may be somewhat intended but, also, somewhat natural and unintended, not subject to willful experience. Thirdly, "having done" something also defies our definition.

The various conflations of "having" with possession (experiential access), characterization, and temporal precedence can hardly be helped. Thus we will stick with our definition as describing "having as potential experience." Let *"having a character state"* be defined as *perceiving the potential to intentionally associate that state with one's character.* Let *"having experienced"* be defined as *perceiving the potential to intentionally (legitimately) reference an experience as part of one's past.* All three senses of "having" assume that the experiential access involved is both (a) legitimate (i.e. believable among relevant observers) and (b) broadly speaking, callable <u>at will</u>. If I have $4 million in the bank, I perceive the ability to legitimately experience said value as I would intend (bank hours aside). If I have this victory in the bag, I perceive the ability to act as this win is already part of my history. If I have a cold, I perceive the ability to believably describe a cold as part of my physiological state.

Surely there are sharper definitions for both "having" and "action." But if we sharpen them too much, we will no longer be able to use them in descriptions of the many fuzzy human interactions that exist out there.

Definition of self, other, and world (context)

In describing dyads, we need definitions of self, other, and world—keeping with the subject-object-context vector discussed above. Here, we state simply that a person's *self is the subset of his experiences which stem directly from the functioning of his perceived physiology*; these are the qualities which he believes his physiology capable of reproducing at will. "At will" is the more familiar wording for "as intended." The physiology I can't escape and its associated, longstanding, highly correlated experiences constitute my self. And though I may perform any number of passing actions in the world, only those actions which I experience to be reflections of my aggregated set of predisposed physiological experiences are counted as "part of me."

The *Other is simply the object with which I assume conscious interaction*—regardless of whether I perceive them with my five senses. Internal thoughts are just as important for interacting with others, for it is based on my internal response to (the idea of) another that phenomena such as love and attraction are born. Another person is an object which I assume interfaces with situations in the way that I do and has similar qualities as those which I have, only, their actions and qualities are not subject to my self.

The *World, our context is defined as the set of perceived data not associated with my self or current Other*. Why did we say of Other, "the object with which I *assume* conscious interaction?" because in exchange with Other, I frequently attend to all kinds of different ideas which are not them. Yet the assumption is that I am still engaging with Other, even though we are now talking about the weather. If Other is the attended space between interaction moments, World is the space of the unattended—which includes those who, at some later time, could serve as still different Others. The World underscores what we assume to be true in our interaction with Others.

Recap

We have defined the following critically human ideas:

- Action
- Belief
- Having
- Want
- Self
- Other
- World

In the process, certain critical ideas have arisen

- Action: self, perception, physiology, change,
- Belief: self, intent, object, actions
- Having: self, experience, object, intent
- Want: self, actions, object, perception
- Self: physiology, perception, intent
- Other: self, intent, perception
- World: perception, self, object, intent

Clearly, in the human dynamics we have endeavored to study, the most salient ideas from the above are:

self, perception, action, object, intent, experience, physiology

Everyday experience shows that physiology is often treated as a property of the self, and that we (practically speaking) interact with "selves" more than we do with physiologies, so we will bundle physiology in with "self." Next, let us further eliminate "Self," with its physiology assuming it instead. Further, although experience is important, it is, in a sense, a permutation of having. To experience something is to have the perception of it. Thus we absorb experience into having to produce the most important five dimensions for our re-mapped vector:

object, action, perception, intent, having

Now, let us construct true-false statements:

- Perception: we will assume that the self perceives *something* when it acts, but what?
  - Rather than specify objects of perception, we note that perception tends to approximate the complement of action, receiving action. Thus,
- Action: **Does the self act on/towards or receive action from/through?**
- Object: **Is the object Other or Self?** We needed to ask this because action, having, wanting, and believe seem to differ in their internal-external direction.
- Having & intent: We postulate that the self and Other may both intend something. **Does the self have the thing that it intends? Does the Other have the thing that self intends?**
- Perception and intent: Lastly, we want to know if we are dealing with a case of correction or benefit. **Does the self perceive this situation as harmonious with himself or dissonant with its overall intent?**

And there we have it. Let us transform the former five-vector as follows:

$$\{S,O,y,\tau,\varepsilon\} \rightarrow \{ \underset{r/a}{\underline{\text{Self acts}}}, \underset{s/o}{\underline{\text{Object is Other}}}, \underset{sh}{\underline{\text{Self has}}}, \underset{oh}{\underline{\text{Object has}}}, \underset{d/h}{\underline{\text{Dissonance}}} \}$$

- S (refined subset) $\rightarrow$ Self acts
- S (refined subset) $\rightarrow$ Object is Other
- ε $\rightarrow$ Object has
- τ $\rightarrow$ Self has
- $\overline{\tau\varepsilon}$ $\rightarrow$ dissonance

The new table:

$$\{ \underset{r/a}{\underline{\text{Self acts}}}, \underset{s/o}{\underline{\text{Object is Other}}}, \underset{sh}{\underline{\text{Self has}}}, \underset{oh}{\underline{\text{Object has}}}, \underset{d/h}{\underline{\text{Dissonance}}} \}$$

Interaction	r/a	s/o	sh	oh	d/h	Interaction	r/a	s/o	sh	oh	d/h
Preoccupation with	1	1	1	1	1	Being influenced by	0	1	1	1	1
Engaging with	1	1	1	1	0	Having + (Experiencing)	0	1	1	1	0
Ineffectiveness towards	1	1	1	0	1	Disapproving of	0	1	1	0	1
Suppressing (opposing)	1	1	1	0	0	Having − (Possessing)	0	1	1	0	0
Compulsion towards	1	1	0	1	1	Being "checked" by (events)	0	1	0	1	1
Wanting (things)	1	1	0	1	0	Respecting	0	1	0	1	0
Using	1	1	0	0	1	Disappointment	0	1	0	0	1
Expecting	1	1	0	0	0	Hoping	0	1	0	0	0
Acting in spite of	1	0	1	1	1	Being upset with	0	0	1	1	1
Acting	1	0	1	1	0	Satisfaction with	0	0	1	1	0
Avoiding	1	0	1	0	1	Dissatisfaction in light of	0	0	1	0	1
Doing	1	0	1	0	0	Being indifferent towards	0	0	1	0	0
Having an aversion to	1	0	0	1	1	Discontentment in light of	0	0	0	1	1
Believing	1	0	0	1	0	Acceptance	0	0	0	1	0
Enduring	1	0	0	0	1	Sadness	0	0	0	0	1
Dismissing	1	0	0	0	0	Contentment	0	0	0	0	0

Some may say that we cannot codify human interaction. But surely, <u>in the practical sense</u>, we can tell when someone is overtly acting or receiving. Surely we can tell whether a person feels reasonably contented or discontented in such actions. Surely we can recognize when a person is engaging an object versus a situation. Although there is no doubt that we could dispute the five-vector on epistemological grounds, I submit that—absent other methods for comprehensively studying the entire space of fundamental human interaction—the above can be a useful starting point.

Remember, we use five dimensions because, first, 1 and 2 dimensions are obviously limited in what they can describe. Second, though three dimensions (3-space) is minimal for including actor, reference point (viewer) and context (the situation which circumscribes the actor and viewer), it does not allow for said 3-space to evolve in time; the fourth dimension establishes 3-space at *t=1* versus 3-space at *t=2*, but does not consider the relationship among 3-space objects themselves. Thus, in the end, a fifth dimension is necessary for specifying the set of interrelationships (error terms) among actor, viewer, and context.

> Example:

> Say, for instance we want to describe the relationship between Smith and his wife Little (2D). Is this Smith and Little as friends? Family? Business partners? Say we want to describe them as business partners (3D). Is it when the business first started or after it became successful? Suppose we want to describe Smith and Little as business partners at the start of the business (4D). Surely, even this does not intuitively lend itself to anything beyond general description (getting along, annoying each other, etc.) But we don't want general description. We want micro-level resolution. Annoying each other under what circumstances? Getting along in light of common context or because they love each other? Notice how actor and viewer can band together either in light of context or in spite of it, and we have no way of knowing the wherefore of it simply because the necessary addition of "context" as a latent factor produces a kind of black-box range of explanations for our final view of Smith and Little. So a fifth dimension is added which opens the box: Smith and Little will be studied as business partners at the start of the business, given that they both love a challenge (5D). (Note how we might expect a different dynamic given that Smith loves a challenge while Little does it because she thinks Smith can't do it on his own. In addition to the two who's, where, and when, we need the *why*.)

Without going into details, here are some additional observations that may follow from the 5-typology. For the sake of communicative clarity, I may record on these in accompanying file. If I do, I will call the original five-vector "soy-ti" and the second (more humanistic) model "rasosho:"

- Noting our definition of a relationship, it is useful to consider pairs of interactions. After all, humans continually change from one interaction to another. Surely certain compound interactions have become as important as the fundamental ones from which they are built.

- Distrust (expecting → being checked by)
- Knowing (believing → engaging with)
- Love (engaging with → engaging with)
- Hate (engaging with → preoccupation with)
- Desire (compulsion towards → wanting)
- Frustration (compulsion towards → compulsion towards)
- Depression (preoccupation with → sadness)
- Pursuit (Doing → wanting)
- How often has [being influenced by] become [being upset with] after the object of influence withdraws!
- How [expecting] and [using] are related: When you use a tool, you expect it to work, but in using it, you see that it hasn't completed its work yet. On the other hand, when you expect something, you steer (s/a=1, d/h=0) your actions around its future manifestation (s/o=1, oh=0). But if you do this in the context of an inharmonious arrangement, I argue that it implies an object pushed towards manifestation for its utility.
- [Satisfaction with] seems to be the stable completion of [acting]
- [Dissatisfaction in light of] versus [discontentment in light of]: The first is negativity towards a situation. The second is a vague sense of negativity *given* a situation, but not necessarily towards it (more like resignation, but resignation implies something just a little too narrow in its expressive neutrality).

Why didn't we just develop the five-vector like this in the first place? Two reasons:

1. The actual justification for using a five-vector versus a vector of some lower dimension follows directly from $\{S,O,y,\tau,\varepsilon\}$.
2. It is a useful exercise to "rectify" dimensions by essentially reconceptualizing Object (O) and situation (y) in terms not-self (S) and expected coherence of error set ($\tau\varepsilon$) respectively. The exercise shows that neither $\{S,O,y,\tau,\varepsilon\}$ nor $\{r/a, s/o, sh, oh, d/h\}$ are *the* exclusive space for describing human interrelations in five-vector.

Just for fun, let us order rasosho. Not by desirability, but by some hypothesized level of energy required. The assumptions are:

*   It takes more physiological/biochemical energy to "be in disharmony" than to do anything else in the vector. After this, overt action takes up much energy. We say disharmony is more costly than action, because rarely do actions intended to correct disharmony achieve their ends in a single go. Disharmony tends to outlive the actions tended to rectify them. Thus actions performed under disharmony are among the most costly of all.
*   s/o is lower energy than sh or oh because, whether we choose other or non-other (unfocused world or self) as the prime object of attention, sh and oh consider each of these plus their associated intents. So s/o is the lowest energy dimension of all five. We assume that it takes more brain energy to load a focused construct than an unfocused one, so Other is the higher energy object.
*   Ironically, despite the above argument for s/o, we may guess that sh takes more energy than oh as a dimension. This is because the amount of data we have for describing ourselves is likely to be much richer than the data we have on others. In the average situation, processing our status regarding our own interest is expected to be more complex (and thus) more costly than assessing others.
*   Even with sh as costly compared to oh and s/o, this dimension may still be assumed to require less brain power than the realms of overarching disharmony or overt action.

Thus the ordering: d/h (read reversed as h=0, d=1), r/a, sh, oh, s/o:							I actually wasn't happy with the arrangement to the left, as it seemed to come with its own moral implications. So I placed the d/h condition last as a way of arranging all of the interactions regardless of desirability. In my mind, the table below is slightly more practical, for reasons that will become evident below.					
Interaction	Ra r/a	so s/o	sh sh	o oh	! d/h		Interaction	r/a	s/o	sh	oh	d/h
Preoccupation with	1	1	1	1	1		Preoccupation with	1	1	1	1	1
Acting in spite of	1	0	1	1	1		Engaging with	1	1	1	1	0
Ineffectiveness towards	1	1	1	0	1		Acting in spite of	1	0	1	1	1
Avoiding	1	0	1	0	1		Acting	1	0	1	1	0
Compulsion towards	1	1	0	1	1		Ineffectiveness towards	1	1	1	0	1
Having an aversion to	1	0	0	1	1		Suppressing (opposing)	1	1	1	0	0
Using	1	1	0	0	1		Avoiding	1	0	1	0	1
Enduring	1	0	0	0	1		Doing	1	0	1	0	0
Being influenced by	0	1	1	1	1		Compulsion towards	1	1	0	1	1
Being upset with	0	0	1	1	1		Wanting (things)	1	1	0	1	0
Disapproving of	0	1	1	0	1		Having an aversion to	1	0	0	1	1
Dissatisfaction in light of	0	0	1	0	1		Believing	1	0	0	1	0
Being "checked" by (events)	0	1	0	1	1		Using	1	1	0	0	1
Discontentment in light of	0	0	0	1	1		Expecting	1	1	0	0	0
Disappointment	0	1	0	0	1		Enduring	1	0	0	0	1
Sadness	0	0	0	0	1		Dismissing	1	0	0	0	0
Engaging with	1	1	1	1	0		Being influenced by	0	1	1	1	1
Acting	1	0	1	1	0		Having + (Experiencing)	0	1	1	1	0
Suppressing (opposing)	1	1	1	0	0		Being upset with	0	0	1	1	1
Doing	1	0	1	0	0		Satisfaction with	0	0	1	1	0
Wanting (things)	1	1	0	1	0		Disapproving of	0	1	1	0	1
Believing	1	0	0	1	0		Having − (Possessing)	0	1	1	0	0
Expecting	1	1	0	0	0		Dissatisfaction in light of	0	0	1	0	1
Dismissing	1	0	0	0	0		Being indifferent towards	0	0	1	0	0
Having + (Experiencing)	0	1	1	1	0		Being "checked" by (events)	0	1	0	1	1
Satisfaction with	0	0	1	1	0		Respecting	0	1	0	1	0
Having − (Possessing)	0	1	1	0	0		Discontentment in light of	0	0	0	1	1
Being indifferent towards	0	0	1	0	0		Acceptance	0	0	0	1	0
Respecting	0	1	0	1	0		Disappointment	0	1	0	0	1
Acceptance	0	0	0	1	0		Hoping	0	1	0	0	0
Hoping	0	1	0	0	0		Sadness	0	0	0	0	1
Contentment	0	0	0	0	0		Contentment	0	0	0	0	0

One thing is certain, though. Preoccupation is, wholesale, costly, whereas contentment is physiologically cheap.

How might we use the rasosho vector?

There appears to be a thinner line between "good" states and "bad" states than one might think. I am interested in studying "action chains" (that is, personalities as stereotyped orderings of the above.) We can imagine that the simplest path between any two interactions is the change in a single dimension. Two change more than one dimension at a time simply takes more work. So we can look at a personality as treading a particular dimension-by-dimension changing path in accordance with its natural disposition. The simplest way for a person to establish an action chain via this typology is to engage a kind of Q-sort whereby the person circles the appropriate interactions which answer the following question: "I am most often aware of when I am ___ something." Subsequently, we have the person * the interactions where "I am least often aware of when I am __ something." Below is an example of this activity. I take the groups I circled, starred, or omitted, add up each dimension (all the r/as for example), average them, multiply the result by 20 and subtract 10. For example, there are 5 high r/as with a value of "1" and 12 high r/a interactions total. So 5/12 of the high r/as are concerned with action, (7/12 are concerned with receptiveness). 5/12*20-10 = -1.67 (rounded to -2), basically rates this person's "high" focus on action on a scale of -10 to 10 as being low. So among the character traits shown by this person, receptiveness tends to be the rule. Note that what we are doing here amounts to a really cheap version of a "multinomial logistic regression" in statistics.

high						mid						low					
Interaction	r/a	s/o	sh	oh	d/h	Interaction	r/a	s/o	sh	oh	d/h	Interaction	r/a	s/o	sh	oh	d/h
Preoccupation with	1	1	1	1	1	Doing	1	0	1	0	0	Acting	1	0	1	1	0
Engaging with	1	1	1	1	0	Compulsion towards	1	1	0	1	1	Ineffectiveness towards	1	1	1	0	1
Acting in spite of	1	0	1	1	1	Wanting (things)	1	1	0	1	0	Avoiding	1	0	1	0	1
Suppressing (opposing)	1	1	1	0	0	Having an aversion to	1	0	0	1	1	Believing	1	0	0	1	0
Enduring	1	0	0	0	1	Dismissing	1	0	0	0	0	Using	1	1	0	0	1
Being influenced by	0	1	1	1	1	Having + (Experiencing)	0	1	1	1	0	Expecting	1	1	0	0	0
Being upset with	0	0	1	1	1	Disapproving of	0	1	1	0	1	Being "checked"	0	1	0	1	1
Satisfaction with	0	0	1	1	0	Having − (Possessing)	0	1	1	0	0	Hoping	0	1	0	0	0
Dissatisfaction in light of	0	0	1	0	1	Respecting	0	1	0	1	0						
Being indifferent towards	0	0	1	0	0	Acceptance	0	0	0	1	0						
Discontentment in light of	0	0	0	1	1	Disappointment	0	1	0	0	1						
Contentment	0	0	0	0	0	Sadness	0	0	0	0	1						
	-2	-3	5	2	2		-2	2	-3	0	-2		5	3	-3	-3	0
Compared to other tendencies, this person is...	Receptive rather than active	Self-focused	Far more attention to own	More attention to other's aims	More stress												

The premise here is that a person describes themselves according to the dynamics they notice most about themselves, regardless of whether the traits they notice line up with the reality in other's eyes. This person may be slightly neurotic in the Big-Five sense (d/h), introverted (or at least inward-focused) (r/a, s/o are low), and concerned with "pleasing everyone" (sh,oh are high). Also, I've highlighted the interactions that seem to typify their respective groups. Given the highlights, could we say that this person is self-protective in expectations?

The real joy in dynamics is lies in its ability to illuminate relationships. Instead of asking the person to circle, "I am most often aware of when I am ___ something," we can ask, "I am most often aware of when I am ___ some*one*." Again, the idea is, regardless of how I *think* I relate to someone, what my subconscious "notices" will tell the tale. Below is an example from the same person in their assessment of their relationship with a very distant co-worker. The question is, how can we use mere smidgeons of data to magnify our biases before venturing into the unknown?

high						mid						low					
Interaction	r/a	s/o	sh	oh	d/h	Interaction	r/a	s/o	sh	oh	d/h	Interaction	r/a	s/o	sh	oh	d/h
Avoiding	1	0	1	0	1	Contentment	0	0	0	0	0	Acting in spite of	1	0	1	1	1
Dissatisfaction in light of	0	0	1	0	1	Preoccupation	1	1	1	1	1	Compulsion	1	1	0	1	1
Suppressing (opposing)	1	1	1	0	0	Ineffectiveness	1	1	1	0	1	Aversion	1	0	0	1	1
Respecting	0	1	0	1	0	Using	1	1	0	0	1	Being influenced	0	1	1	1	1
						Enduring	1	0	0	0	1	Engaging with	1	1	1	1	0
						Being upset	0	0	1	1	1	Dismissing	1	0	0	0	0
						Disapproving of	0	1	1	0	1	Indifference	0	0	1	0	0
						Being "checked"	0	1	0	1	1						
						Discontentment	0	0	0	1	1						
						Disappointment	0	1	0	0	1						
						Sadness	0	0	0	0	1						
						Acting	1	0	1	1	0						
						Doing	1	0	1	0	0						
						Wanting	1	1	0	1	0						
						Believing	1	0	0	1	0						
						Expecting	1	1	0	0	0						
						Having +	0	1	1	1	0						
						Satisfaction	0	0	1	1	0						
						Having –	0	1	1	0	0						
						Acceptance	0	0	0	1	0						
						Hoping	0	1	0	0	0						
	0	0	5	-5	0		-1	0	-1	0	0		4	-1	1	4	1
In light of this Other, our subject			looks out for their own interests	seems to pay attention to the other's "failings"								and on a more subconscious level acts in the face of Others' deeds	Is active...			..in seeing the Other's interests	

It is clear that our subject is critical of this Other.

But again, of what use is it to know how Subject feels towards Other? Surely there are many uses, but perhaps one of the best uses comes from a certain nefarious interest held by the investigator. For those of us who like psychology, rasosho can be used not just to see how we respond to other, but to find out how *we think* other responds to us. No, it will not enable a person to read minds, but it will enable one to better visualize the kinds of Other she thinks she is dealing with. Surely this is valuable information.

Perhaps just as useful is the ability to take others' treatment of oneself and analyze one's one public image from "afar."

Consequences of rasosho dimensions

$$\{ \underbrace{\text{Self acts}}_{r/a}, \underbrace{\text{Object is Other}}_{s/o}, \underbrace{\text{Self has}}_{sh}, \underbrace{\text{Object has}}_{oh}, \underbrace{\text{Dissonance}}_{d/h} \}$$

It is natural to ask how certain interactions are trained. Assuming that one's genetically seeded personality becomes "coherent" through continual exchanges with others, we may posit the following normal conditions:

- A person is socialized to act, but mainly in ways acceptable to the normal individual; since few people are precisely bounded in their exposure to normal others, most individuals learn (1) to act in a normally acceptable way amidst strangers and non-intimates but also (2) to form a kind of aggregate from such people based on repeated measures of "normals" grouped according to genetic, physiological, and environmental heuristics. That is, normal individuals train me to be normal towards individuals, but groups of normal act in conjunction with my broader external-perceptive and proprioceptive experience to outline my outlook towards groups.
  - The self as actor—the *a* in r/a—is the more publicly desirable in dyads. The self as recipient—the r in r/a—ultimately helps restrict the training of self as actor in all relationships.
  - r/a is one component of the person's function for describing world view. If five major others are chiefly responsible for my training, and they seem to agree with each other, I may yet (ambient data permitting) function as these five wish. But if these trainers seem to clash more often than not, I will become as contrary to their collective influence as is required for me to survive amongst them.

  Let us define here a "belonging function"

  $$d_3\big(S(\beta,\alpha), r/a_\alpha, s/o_\alpha, sh_\alpha oh_\alpha d/h_\alpha, \partial_{2,32}\Sigma S(\beta,\Omega), r, c\big) \rightarrow r/a, s/o, sh, oh, d/h$$

  $$d_3\left(\begin{array}{c} \textit{how good} \\ \textit{S feels} \\ \textit{about this} \end{array}, \begin{array}{c} \textit{the interaction which} \\ \textit{the O wants} \end{array}, \begin{array}{c} \textit{S's normal} \\ \textit{personality}, \\ \textit{matrix} \end{array} \begin{array}{c} \textit{for the moment} \\ \textit{or over time?} \end{array}, \begin{array}{c} \textit{S's trait} \\ \textit{in question} \end{array} \right) \rightarrow \textit{S's interaction}$$

  Where

  - $S(\beta,\alpha)$ is what the **subject** thinks of himself in a given situation. It returns a magnitude which, for now, we will restrict to some <u>real</u> value between 0 (harmony) and 1 (dissonance).
  - $\{r/a_o, s/o_o, sh_o, oh_o, d/h_o\}$ is the typical five-vector interaction for the group (**object**) in question, populated by <u>real</u> numbers either 0 or 1.
  - $\partial_{2,32}\Sigma S(\beta,\Omega)$ is a 2 x 32 matrix of <u>real</u> parameters (0..1) for the subject, including genetic seeding. Row 1 is the set of means, row 2 is the set of standard deviations for each of the 32 interactions used previously. It is the **situation** inasmuch it is the background personality which seeds the subject's response.
  - r, c, are the whole number row and column of the subject's interested interaction (roughly, τ,ε).
  - $\{r/a, s/o, sh, oh, d/h\}$ is the subject's typical response

Though there are many parameters here, THE FUNCTION IS NOT AS COMPLICATED AS IT LOOKS. For the purposes of study, we usually just assign all of these based on experience. The real value of it comes in training simulations to adjust the map accordingly, weighting its nodes. I will use an example to prove to you that the model isn't so impenetrable.

Suppose you have a group of people who want something. $\{r/a_o, s/o_o, sh_o, oh_o, d/h_o\} = \{1,1,0,1,0\}$. Suppose that my generic personality, $\partial_{2,32}\Sigma S(\beta,\Omega)$, has among other things, a .57 in the usually, possessing position (row = 2 for stdev, c = whichever column holds the "possessing interaction". Suppose I feel pretty good about this ($S(\beta, \alpha) = .81$, and I am inclined to comfortably (e.g $d/h=.12$) and fully act (e.g. .94) in a way that supports mainly the group but somewhat myself (e.g. $s/o=.8$), recognizing that the group needs (e.g. $oh=.4$) what I can give (e.g. $sh=.7$) $\{r/a, s/o, sh, oh, d/h\} = \{.94, .8, .7, .4, .12\}$. The final formula might look like this:

$$\text{For } d_3\big(S(\beta,\alpha), r/a_\alpha, s/o_\alpha, sh_\alpha oh_\alpha d/h_\alpha, \partial_{2,32}\Sigma S(\beta,\Omega), r, c\big) \to r/a, s/o, sh, oh, d/h:$$

$$d_3\left(.81,1,1,0,1,0, \begin{pmatrix} ? & \cdots & ? \\ \vdots & \ddots & \vdots \\ ? & \cdots possessing_{2,c} = .57 \cdots & ? \end{pmatrix}, 2, c\right) \to .94, .8, .7, .4, .12$$

That's it. Since d_3 *is* a mapping, in people (2012, c.e.) it will usually evade mathematical approximation. Thus the above formula is useless beyond its role as a descriptive curiosity. Why do it then?

First, if we build up enough of these, we *can* start replacing numbers with functions. This basically entails brain scanning for differences in thoughts about doing versus observing (r/a) self versus not self (s/o) self or object as comfortable versus not comfortable (sh, oh), and overall arousal/stress level (d/h). We would then normalize measures of the stimulated areas, enabling us to read a person's five-vector interaction (though certainly not their mind and its objects thereof). Next, it would be interesting to scan the brain for stereotyped patterns corresponding to each interaction in general. Through extrapolation techniques like CCA (canonical correlation analysis) coupled with a kind of fourier decomposition, we might be able to "pull out" $\partial_{2,32}\Sigma S(\beta, \Omega), r, c$ or all of the above depending on the amount of overlap among associated neural regions. $S(\beta, \alpha)$ is a simple measure of stress given whatever situation we have presented. $r/a_\alpha, s/o_\alpha, sh_\alpha oh_\alpha d/h_\alpha$ *is* the interaction we have presented. By modeling the dynamics among all of these in a handful of people, we can inform our neural networks for artificial personalities. (I personally would like us to simulate the AI for a Buddha or Jesus with this technology—just to see what such mythicized legends were *really* like.)

On a more immediate level, it isn't the formula that is important, but the process of thinking about the parameters involved. For those of us who like numbers, it is fascinating to see before you how Jones' asking you for money corresponds not necessarily to your thoughts of giving, but to your thoughts of ego-magnanimity. For example, though I chose the numbers in the above illustration arbitrarily, I did not expect that

> [feeling] pretty good about this ($S(\beta, \alpha) = .81$, and [being] am inclined to comfortably (e.g $d/h=.12$) and fully act (e.g. .94) in a way that supports mainly the group but somewhat myself (e.g. $s/o=.8$), recognizing that the group needs (e.g. $oh=.4$) what [one] can give (e.g. $sh=.7$) [$\{.94, .8, .7, .4, .12\}$]

Would line up closely with "suppression" $\{1,1,1,0,0\}$ and, to a slightly lesser extent, "engagement with" $\{1,1,1,1,0\}$. But look again. Doesn't "I'm doing it for poor little you" *sound* like that paternalistic shade?

Whew. That was condition number one: we learn to belong as a complex function of where we started and who's engaging us.

- A person is socialized more in terms of externally visible properties than visible ones. That is, when s/o concerns the "o," people care more. Our belonging functions and learned behaviors will be weighted accordingly.
- When our trainers claim that we have a high *sh* in light of personality quality X, (sh near 1), we internalize their input but not necessarily its "truth." A highly lauded person may come to believe the hype if it is comfortable for them to do so (genetically/psychologically—which we could simply ask), but if the hype is comfortable, they may come to disbelieve/distrust the hype artists themselves—independently of the hype's truth. Externally trained sh influences my sh and my trust (level of dissonance) in response to further training.
  - o   By the way, what is training? It is nothing more than using the above d_3 formula on a new situation, adjusting the $\partial_{2.32}$ as a result.
- If other people/situations around us seem to have low oh, we will learn to act in spite of them—though not always effectively. $oh_{trainer}$ trains $sh_{subject}$, $r/a_{subject}$, and $oh_{subject}$.
- If the world seems to work well when we are stressed, we may gravitate towards aggression—even if our trainers swear to us that stress is bad, their attention and compliance may teach us otherwise. We can expect our evolved d/h parameter to function in accordance with the level of dissonance among and within our trainers, as well as in accordance with our own perceived levels of success when displaying stress previously (d/h nearing 1).

Ordering the five vector.

I hesitate to do this, but for the purposes of machine-programming, it may prove easier: We will assign numbers to the 32 interactions based on energy (physiological processing) requirements.

	Interaction	r/a	sh	oh	s/o	d/h
32	Preoccupation with	1	1	1	1	1
31	Engaging with	1	1	1	1	0
30	Acting in spite of	1	1	1	0	1
29	Acting	1	1	1	0	0
28	Ineffectiveness towards	1	1	0	1	1
27	Suppressing (opposing)	1	1	0	1	0
26	Avoiding	1	1	0	0	1
25	Doing	1	1	0	0	0
24	Compulsion towards	1	0	1	1	1
23	Wanting (things)	1	0	1	1	0
22	Having an aversion to	1	0	1	0	1
21	Believing	1	0	1	0	0
20	Using	1	0	0	1	1
19	Expecting	1	0	0	1	0
18	Enduring	1	0	0	0	1
17	Dismissing	1	0	0	0	0
16	Being influenced by	0	1	1	1	1
15	Having + (Experiencing)	0	1	1	1	0
14	Being upset with	0	1	1	0	1
13	Satisfaction with	0	1	1	0	0
12	Disapproving of	0	1	0	1	1
11	Having – (Possessing)	0	1	0	1	0
10	Dissatisfaction in light of	0	1	0	0	1
9	Being indifferent towards	0	1	0	0	0
8	Being "checked" by (events)	0	0	1	1	1
7	Respecting	0	0	1	1	0
6	Discontentment in light of	0	0	1	0	1
5	Acceptance	0	0	1	0	0
4	Disappointment	0	0	0	1	1
3	Hoping	0	0	0	1	0
2	Sadness	0	0	0	0	1
1	Contentment	0	0	0	0	0

See that this is the secondary ordering from before, where we have made interactions into (somewhat falsely) ordinal variables. Broadly, the ordering says that contentment takes 1 step of energy: that required to simply recognize that it applies. Respect takes seven steps of energy. Let us think of "steps of energy" roughly as dimensions of complexity in the thinker. The assumption is that plain old contentment—no actions (r/a), no external objects (s/o), no ends to be sought or compared (sh,oh), and no inner tension (d/h) is the most metabolically cost-efficient state you can have. Sadness, on the other hand, can look just like contentment, except that some unfocused "something" isn't right. As soon as we start focusing on objects, the cognitive load increases exponentially.

s/o means something other than our blank state is focused. This is dissonance (d/h) implied, and held before us as a construct. It takes energy to hold up something that already takes energy in order for it to be "not you." So s/o assumes d/h on top of dh. Similarly, oh means we have s/o on top of s/o: an object is held up and its level of dissonance (another cognitive object) is held up. sh takes the object's level of dissonance in oh and relates it back to the self. Thus, if it takes energy upon energy upon energy to conceive of an object's dissonance upon the object upon natural equilibrium, it takes even more energy to tell ourselves that the object's dissonance relates to our original state in some sequence. That is, thinking of a thing takes less energy than thinking of a thing and telling ourselves that such a thing is further focused on ourselves.

Lastly, acting means we address the above upon itself, changing in sequence.

In this way, "Disappointment + Disapproving of = Being influenced by" is not meant to make intuitive sense, only energetic sense. Also, in a rather obvious observation, we don't always maximize our energy usage; "Disappointment + Disapproving of" is not well defined, but the energy required for "Disappointment + Disapproving of" does equal 16 processing steps, some of which will typically be dedicated to other things. Accordingly, "interaction + same interaction" usually makes the same interaction more salient—particle style. But given the energy it takes to process other inputs, we end up with math which is more like "2+2 = up to 4" or "2+2 = 2... + the other 2 is used in the writing of this 2 +2 as a memory." Such is the inertia of the mind. Cognitive interactions are not particle additive, but wavelike-interferable when recognizably distinct. They are only additive in the sense that, as memories, they make themselves more salient as later background. In short, addition doesn't exist here among labels, only among the energy required to indulge those labels. Presumably, for every week spent "being upset," I could have spent 4 days "doing."

With the interactions numbered, functions such as the belonging function can be rewritten as primitive.

$$d_3\big(S(\beta,\alpha), r/a_\alpha, s/o_\alpha, sh_\alpha oh_\alpha d/h_\alpha, \partial_{2,32}\Sigma S(\beta,\Omega), r, c\big) \rightarrow r/a, s/o, sh, oh, d/h$$

$$\downarrow$$

$$\|d_3\|\big(S(\beta,\alpha), interaction\#_{other}, \partial_{2,32}, r, c\big) \rightarrow \big(interaction\#_{subject}, prob\big)$$

This function won't tell you how a person teeters between multiple interactions as a response, but does produce a definite interaction as a result. Shorthand: d_3 yields an interaction-like vector. $\|d_3\|$ yields a most probable interaction along with its associated probability. Humans won't be able to use this except as part of some elaborate mind-control or marketing program. Machines will eat it up as their human designers attempt to simulate nature. As knowledge builds, we will modify this accordingly.

The role of genetics

While one might think that the above model shows that contentment should be the standard, not so fast. First, humans are tasked with surviving. "Vegging out" is not allowed. Second, living humans have certain metabolic (read dissonant) process going on non-stop until the day they die. Even zombies need energy to walk. So a certain level of change implies a that certain level of dissonance will exist within the subject *all the time*. Even in sleep. Thus it isn't a matter of *if* we will pit parts of ourselves against ourselves, but *how*.

Genetics seeds our homeostatic state. Skin color and body build affect nutrient use and absorption and, consequently, the various metabolic processes which use those same nutrients. I can use calcium to grow bones or power neuronal potentials, and my genetics will instill me with a need to gravitate towards calcium sources accordingly. I may be easily aroused in terms of attention. My genetics, in dictating such, may compel my Big-Five neuroticism.

Where interactions are concerned, humans don't simply process energy along a smooth line. The eyes know one frequency range of electromagnetic energy as the stuff of vision, while the skin knows this another frequency range as the stuff of skin cancer. Similar energy types, very different effects. In this way, humans have evolved to fit certain conditions found in certain regions of earth—deviations from which alter the physiological resources available to process sociological items. And just as the eyes are concerned with one modality and the skin another, so too does the brain have its own ways of quantizing information via the lobes.

Why don't we just flow from doing (25) to avoiding (26) (or any energetically proximate pairs for that matter) if the energy steps between them are so closely related? Because the body works on thresholds. Sensation will not be felt below a certain level. Sounds will not be heard. In this way, we derive the biological equivalent of step functions: You heard it or you didn't. The neuron displayed bursting or it didn't. Similarly, this perceptual packet was the Object or it wasn't. The dissonance demanded correction or it didn't. I am satisfied with this enough to stop it or not.

So we think of the five-vector as a set of cognitive quanta (bands of acceptable value, between which data cannot exist). While I may add three energy units to "doing," ineffectiveness will not result unless the other cognitive packets for my perceiving ineffectiveness also arrive. Such a transition is dictated partly by socialization, but largely by genetics.

My genes thus determine my body's natural tendency to distribute my nutrients, attention, and thus cognition towards certain perceptual objects—internal or external. More energy will not change me, unless that energy is fed to me in packets conducive to change (and only then in ways which line up with the parts of my cognition primed to receive those packets. Thus, through the body's step functions, we develop the inertia of stubborn personality. We keep seeing the tree as a tree until someone, in believable packaging, convinces us that it is, more specifically, an oak.

The study of genetics, though useful for addressing the mechanics of the body, is not as promising for fixing social ills. More beautiful bodies will only change the background behind ancient exchanges. The genetically advanced individual may be made happy initially, but the collective will continue to train that individual in the long run as it will—faults and insecurities included.

The Soul

While we are certainly interested in the world we can see with our five basic senses, there is already plenty of work in this area. The study of dynamics is useful because it focuses on the study of *processes*, generally unseen as objects, labeled as stylized exchanges between objects—so that a system like rasosho prompts questions about "souls" and "spirits." As sociologists, we want to look not only at what people are doing and why, but also how others come to develop templates for others' broad actions despite others' narrow actions. Humans are noteworthy among animals in that we have the capacity to see something and thoroughly distrust it based on other data—thus ensuring our survival. But what is it that enables us to form the invisible templates against which to compare visible data? It may be argued that there are many such processual-data templates, but among the most interesting are the concepts of "soul" and "spirit."

Before we define the soul empirically, let us think about what people usually mean when they talk about it. Some folk beliefs about the soul include:

- It somehow wraps a person's entire being into one seemingly meta-aware norm.
- It often attends a body to which it is "attached," but can somehow exist without that body

- It can experience states beyond those accessible to the five basic senses (of which the idea of "heaven" is an example)
- It can change
- It may or may not be part of some collective.

There are many explanations we can offer about what the soul is and its tie (if any) to physical reality. For brevity, I will divide these explanations into three families: psychological construct, material entity, collective indicator. That is, we may argue that the "true soul" lives in one of three "places:" fabricated (or at least elaborated) in one's mind, in interaction-based reality (like anything we can see or touch), or in "super-reality" (where corporations and conceptualizations of laws live—not physical, but, in a sense, institutionalized as an idea above the physical). The table below gives some ideas about the soul's form and function. Items in the same column do not necessarily support each other. I have used something like a five vector to further subdivide the groups, the idea being that, whatever the truth of the soul's "identity" $\{S,O,y\}$, we usually only know it through interaction $\{S,O,y,\tau,\varepsilon\}$. A 3 x 5 matrix shows that a soul can be defined, among other ways, as a static plane (3D- $\{S,O,y\}$) of interactions $\{S,O,y,\tau,\varepsilon\}$.

Psychological construct	Material entity	Collective indicator
• The soul does not exist, but is made up in one's mind as any other human-cognitive construct (**skeptic**).	• The soul does not exist, but is made up as a wrapper around our predictions for living things' behavior beyond the sense-observable (**behavioral**).	• The soul does not exist, but is, like all other human constructs, a label for some perceived extra-social percept (**wide-label**)
• The soul does not exist, but is an artifact of human perceived interactions which do exist in one's mind (**biological**)	• The soul does not exist, but our conclusions about other's aggregate behaviors do. The "soul" is a label for our conclusions about Jones' behavior in the long run, over multiple viewers (**normed perceptual**)	• The soul does not exist, but humans have evolved tools for packaging their morality of which the soul is one such concept. (**trained moral**)
• The soul may exist, but only human psychology can give it any coherence (**psychological sieve**)	• The soul may exist, but five-sense empiricism can only measure its sense-related "artifacts" (**partial measure**)	• The soul may exist, but is widely defined in terms of separateness from the material world (**exclusion**)
• The soul does exists, but its view is both enabled and distorted by psychology (**psychological lens**)	• The soul does exist, but it defies complete empirical measure (**semi-visibility**)	• The soul does exist, but is seen as a function of normed interactions among local actors (**crest-to-crest**)
• The soul does exist, and is more "real" than the psychological creature which conceives of it (**super-identity**)	• The soul does exist, and the living material world is a crystallized portion of it (**crystallization**)	• The soul does exist, and is the local manifestation of a more fundamental collective energy (**lifestream**)

Practically speaking (not ontologically or "postmodern-ly" speaking), here is what we know "for certain:"

- The *concept* of "soul" does exist.
- Humans really do interact with their predictions about and cognitive filtering of things at least as much as they can be thought of as interacting with the things themselves.
- The idea of "soul" seems to be associated with religion and other socio-moral items.

For these reasons, whether or not the soul is real, we will study it anyway. The idea is that, since the concept is there, and since real people do use often the concept in informing important life decision (sometimes the most important of all), a science of interaction would be remiss to ignore it.

For the purposes of this investigation, the following table lists the views we [can] or [will not] take, along with reasons.

View	Useful	Reason
Psychological Dimension		
• skeptic	Sort of	Once we give a label to a construct, it is impractical to deny both construct AND the label. Even if there is no soul, this position seems to imply that the construct exists in a kind of solipsistic vacuum. But isn't all proprioception like this to a certain extent? What of individual "personality" and "emotion?" Only haters take the skeptic position seriously, for playing this game opens up an entire can of worms on what it means to "mean" anything. Nonetheless, in the spirit of the scientific method, we will assume that there is no soul in the phenomenal sense. This will limit our arguments to "measurable" psychological and biological realms.
• biological	Sort of	Though we will assume that humans perceive interactions and do use labels for such perceptions, we cannot swear by individual cognition to study the broad concept of soul.
• psychological sieve	Not really	This is a fairly safe position. Yet, if we ride the fence, there no guarantee that the soul is an exclusively human concept. To say "I don't know *what*" here causes us also to say "I don't know *how*." (e.g. Perhaps, robot perception can also give "soul" coherence through the measure of em fields.) The word *only* is the key.
• psychological lens	Sort of	This is almost safe, but (in terms of the broad scientific community) we just don't know if the soul does exist. Why not just combine this one with the above view? [The soul may exist but if it did, would be filtered through psychology.] I do combine them, but not under the "private psychology" heading. Can you see why? The combined view is called partial measure.
• super-identity	Maybe, but not really	This isn't really realistic scientifically, since it basically says "a thing I can't define is defined by a bigger thing I can't define in my head. In terms of individual-to-broad conceptual power, this is worse than the skeptic position (where empirical study is concerned) because it posits two unmeasurables instead of one. This is a non-definition.
		Each of the psychological definitions comes with the same problem: defining the soul in terms of private minds essentially camouflages the topic—making it difficult to study. It isn't that these views are false (in some qualities of the "soul" and not others, each may carry its own degree of truth). Accordingly, we will often defer to the material equivalents of these which—though equally shaky from an ontological point of view—at least assumes some practical means of measurability.
Material Dimension		
• behavioral	Maybe	As with all "the soul does not exist" arguments, we would have to make a distinction between phenomenal existence and psychological construct existence. That aside, the soul as some kind of psychological wrapper seems so safe as to be almost uninformative. Even "personality" is a wrapper around stereotyped perceived behaviors.
• normed perceptual	Yes	To study the soul empirically, we eventually need to set some boundaries regarding where it ends and begins. Jones' blinking usually won't change our opinion of him. We assume that not every action performed by Jones will change our opinion of his soul—especially if we are to eventually reference the soul (socially) after Jones is gone. The soul as an aggregate allows us to construct the concept as a thing whose conceptual presence extends beyond the immediately measurable. This doesn't mean the soul is ghostly, only—like "anger"—we can describe it as "happening" even without certain immediate cues. Multiple viewers take this definition out of the realm of "psychological construct."
• partial measure	Yes	This is a safe position. It is not so much a definition as it is an outline for how we might approach the study of our topic.
• semi-visibility	Not really	This is partial measure which assumes the thing being defined. As with all As with all "the soul does exist" arguments, it runs counter to scientific assumption in 2012 c.e.
• crystallization	In a weird way, yes	Again, scientifically, we don't know that the soul exists. However, the "crystallization" idea has interesting implications for how the *idea* of soul becomes reified in local minds as the result of collective training. I will actually use the crystallization argument later to show that—for moral purposes, societies may benefit from training "souls" regardless of whether there is any absolute reality behind such things.

		Material arguments presume that souls, real or not, have a measurable quality to them, even if such qualities are doggedly psychological. They are, at least, not completely private.
Social (collective) Dimension		
• wide-label	Not really	A "does not exist" position with a sociolinguistic edge. "Soul" is just a word. But a definition is more than its phrases. Among humans, a definition thrives on its implications as well. Is Smith good or not evil? Is he cruel or unkind? The wide-label position, though perhaps apt, is impractical because it minimizes the extent to which people actually fight and die in the name of whatever the label represents. Even if soul is just a word, for social and political reasons, we would be foolish and irresponsible to treat it as standing for something no more than this—especially since we respond to other labels for psychologically effective invisible things like "gut-feelings" and reputations every day.
• trained moral	Sort of	Not a definition, but may illuminate the relationship between "soul" as a psychological construct and human evolution.
• exclusion	Sort of	Not a definition, but introduces a valuable error term in our study. The soul is partly immeasurable because it is built on the idea of certain immeasurable things. Thus it sits in the family with "non-existence," "impossibility," and "infinity." There will always be some extent to which we can't capture it. Indeed, if the soul is defined in terms of ever-changing interactions, it will always be "unpinnable" in some way.
• crest-to-crest	Maybe	Combined with the crystallization argument, this view may be used to study how souls avoid epiphenomenality (having no effects on the material world). Although it comes with the usual flaws of a "soul does exist" argument, it essentially forces such existence as a set of interpersonal norms among actors.
• lifestream	Yes	Though it sounds very metaphysical, this is the only (quasi-) definition that establishes "soul" as a label for a phenomenon that can be experienced across minds (like redness or hotness—which do indeed stand for ideas which impinge upon the biology as frequencies/energy subsequently imbued with perceptual meaning).
		Collective constructs are not only useful, but also necessary for broad definitions of what we are studying.

Anyway, it's all semantics. Let us define the individual soul as follows:

soul: *the aggregated, predicted personality which informs what a living thing would do were its sense-perceivable qualities not present.*

Again, I am not interested in truth so much as I am interested in a definition that can be worked with. The above is a combination of **exclusion** and **partial measure**, but also assumes **trained moral**, **crystallization** and **lifestream** in the sense that people will derive their ideas about Jones' soul against what they think is the broader world's set of standards. A mere linguistic argument will lead us to this. To the extent that "sense-perceivable" means that we need to care about whose senses are involved. The definition also assumes **psychological lens** and **biological** explanations inasmuch as our bodies will react to preconscious data from another living thing, while our minds will consciously define that living thing.

If for no other reason besides humans' interest in anthropomorphizing things, we assume the soul to be a property of living things by definition. Not because rocks don't have "would be" states, but because (1) rocks don't seem to have personalities (unless you're an artist), (2) rocks don't seem to have meta-being in the sense that they can alter their behaviors to enhance or sustain their function (even plants "eat" and grow towards the sun and, in these ways, might be said to have souls), and (3) a rock without its sense-perceivable details reverts back to a generic platonic form (or an uninstantiated class in programming)—whereas a living thing still leaves us with the socio-affective echo of our own predictions of how it might change our response under given circumstances.

For the purposes of study, we say that a things needs to have been considered living at some point to "qualify" for a soul.

Interestingly, by this definition, humans have souls, dogs have souls, orchids could have souls, humanity has a soul, the earth might have a soul—all to the extent that they "self-correct" in order to preserve a certain homeostatic norm. "Personality" here just means a thing's expressive tendency in anthropomorphic terms. A rock *could* have a soul if only we tended to consider it as undergoing active, dynamic processes towards a kind of equilibrium. Alas, without considering properties such as inertia, gravity, or chemical composition as constituting a rock's "dynamics," we aren't likely to ascribe to it a soul any time soon outside of the realm of communicative symbolism. The earth, on the other hand has, at least, weather patterns, stable-ish angular momentum, and a tendency to mediate the formation of life (from which the plants and animals bud). Even humans, in the long run, arise from the earth (in both the macromolecule and creationist scenarios)—unless you believe we were deposited here from outside. Whatever the case, if it "lives," affects us, and can be thought of as meta-aware, we consider it to have a soul. If you think that only humans "live" in a way that is relevant, you may not consider other things to have souls. It doesn't matter though, since the definition allows people who disagree with you to study these other things as soul-carrying anyway. For moral reasons, non-human souls are also interesting. If only atop a metaphorical foundation, such study carries with it implications for how humans interact with non-human things sans laws to bind them.

Note that the soul is an inherently moral concept—or at least an ethical one. Once we get into the realm of describing what a living thing would "choose" given an aggregate personality, we automatically get into conceptions of right and wrong—not because there is such a thing as right and wrong absolutely, but because living things are tasked, by definition, with the job of self-sustainment. At the very least, a living thing must be seen as sustaining itself in terms analogous to the human interpretation of such. Failure to do so is wrong for that thing as far as "life" is concerned. (Humans sometimes extend this to the concept of "afterlife" where this same principle is concerned). Here we consider

> **"right"** *to be that which is conducive to the continued, non-self destructive expression of a thing within the world which includes it.*

> **"Wrong"** *is not right.*

The minimal homeostasis in a changing system counts as right, since "living" is concerned with this. So maintaining the status quo is right only in the sense that said status quo evolves with the standards of ambient society. In this way, our usual notion of the status quo is actually the image of a wrong thing, since time is always compelling the formation of new experiences. To sit still (metaphorically / expressively, not as in resting) while time changes us is not conducive to self-sustainment, and is therefore wrong by our definition—especially as we mortal things inch towards inevitable death. What then, in the moments before death, is the optimal homeostatic condition? Who knows, but I imagine that one's last moment is important to his ego-awareness, but irrelevant to his biological self, negligible in the grand scheme of nature, but manifestly important to the living tasked with continuing their lives in the face of one's demise. Thus it may be said that Smith's private right and wrong are of little use to me, but the extent to which his private right and wrong bring public effects to the rest of us…well, all of society is built on such things. Such is one case for collective moralities and the reason for the soul as a moral object. As a socio-cognitive package for what happens in the face of the unknown, the concept of "soul" elicits those ideas most personal in the personality. Strangely, from a biological perspective, souls are not important because they are real or not real, but because the concepts that they package compel our attention towards dimensions of our own expression in places where there are few external structures to guide us.

We have defined the soul as "the personality that would be…" If self-sustainment is the rule of the living, failure of a personality to sponsor its own self-sustainment—given the rules of its environment—is wrong. At the creature's departure from sense-perceivable presence (e.g. death or coma), a personality is subject to the view of those who conceive it. Thenceforth, Smith's right and wrong are known by the extent to which we witnesses would aid or destroy ourselves in light of the Smith's soul's "expression."

CHAPTER 2. HUMAN BELIEF IN GENERAL

A man wants what he turns his actions towards. In order to discover a person's Natural Way (hereafter called Dao), it is enough to look at the things he pays attention to.

Yet some would say that men often pursue things they do not want. Not so. A man always pursues what his inclination propels him to pursue. However, whether he is able to label his pursuit appropriately makes the ultimate difference between a resolute will and a will divided.

We can discuss two ways in which a person's will can be divided. 1) The subconscious wants one thing while the conscious calls that thing by a contrary name. 2) The conscious wants a thing but pursues a contrary, lesser, or comparatively unimportant thing as its means. Actually, these two forms of "divided will" amount to the same thing— similar to Festinger's cognitive dissonance. In the end, although we could debate all day regarding the meaning of "will," "subconscious" and other things, it is enough for us to be content with describing the world as humans see it—using words like "will" to discuss practical matters even though the same words possess no meaning in other languages—let alone the language of the absolute.

There is some confusion among humans regarding the purpose of life and the means to its greatest expression. Let us answer the issue here: Life is a thing done by the living.

There is some confusion among humans regarding the purpose of human life. Here, another answer is offered by humanity itself: Human life is a thing conducted by humans that live. And what does it mean to be human? Being human means seeing the world through a set of senses which has come to describe a human as an ego positioned among egos, in a physical form stereotyped among similar physical forms. Just as we would not describe a thinking, talking tree as "human" no matter how human the tree appeared to behave, we would not say that just any source of ego-imbued mental activity qualifies as human, the thing must be reasonably human in physical form. And just as we would not say that just any mannequin with a human physical form qualifies as human, the thing must be human in the sense that other egos think the thing capable of communication via the same kinds of constructs employed by the latter. That is, I am not human because being so means something in the absolute sense (for surely *Homo erectus*, though also considered human, would disagree that I am *his* kind of human); instead, I am human because 1) other physical forms similar to mine appear to use communicative and apparently "mental" constructs similar to mine to communicate ego-experiences similar to mine and 2) we all seem to believe ourselves aware of ourselves through such expression. Here, the definition of "human" can be summarized very roughly as "same look, same communication, same expected behaviors relative to the rest of the perceived world." Not just physical form, but expressive action. Not just expressive action, but expected expressive action in the eyes of the natural world that surrounds us (which includes other forms like ours). This is what it means to be human.

And what is purpose? Purpose is the end served by a thing—that thing which is enabled by another thing. In this way, purposes can roll on forever in a great endless chain if we wish. A human whose life enjoys this kind of unending chain of ends is said to enjoy the journey. Meanwhile, those who look forward to the day when a single ultimate purpose has been achieved are said to seek not a "journey" but a highest purpose instead (though the two need not exclude each other). To the extent that such people see their highest purpose as identifying with (and having the capability to adopt the forms of) their own ego-imbued selves, there is a tendency to describe that highest purpose as being human too. These are believers in God. (I may drop the "human form" assumption, though, while keeping the ego-self assumption. In this way God becomes super-human). Lastly, some believe that there is no highest purpose or that, if there is one, such a highest purpose cannot be described as ego-imbued. These are atheists and certain kinds of agnostics.

According to our definition above, all humans have wants as the result of their endlessly pursuing things—consciously or otherwise. But some of those humans aim their lives towards the attainment of an ultimate Want: This is their ego-conception of their life's purpose (which may or may not be the same as their purpose as framed by another entity). Those who look to the ultimate Want as 1) singular and 2) identifying with "human" egos are broadly described as believers in God. Those who look to the ultimate Want as 1) singular but 2) not identifying with human egos are broadly described under various categories of atheism and agnosticism (which, for the purposes of survival in society are nonetheless infused with at least some level of ethics or morality). Those who follow no ultimate Want seek only the journey (which, for the purposes of survival in society, is also infused with at least some level of ethics or morality).

Summarized, the purpose of my human life is to live as "humans" do in a way which fulfills my view of my ego-purpose. This is generally God, society, or the purposeless journey. Since all the world is the assembly of differences, a human is most adaptable when he gains the capacity to hear of all three paths without sacrificing the way among them most natural to him. We call such a Way his Dao.

A man believes that which he steers his actions around. If I believe a rock is there in front of me, I may look towards it, reach for it, walk around it, or attempt to sit on it, but I will not go stumbling through it. Similarly, it is a fool who walks smack into a wall which he knows is there, and an incomplete believer who stumbles through a thing he "believes in." In this way, a person who has been taught those behaviors and principles acceptable to society but who violates those principles anyway is like a person who slams himself into a rock. Eventually he will feel the ache. So too do I invite my own "karma" by violating the rules of the society whose acceptance I require. Although it is true that not all rules are fit for all people, in moral matters of great importance, a grown person should know better. Ignorance is no defense in the eyes of Nature. One who does not heed the best interests of the group which sustains him often has to wait until the next lifetime to educate himself in that which is right. (Said somewhat facetiously. See other writings on reincarnation.)

Because belief is, for the most part, similar to acknowledgement, education is a critical and defining quality for humanity. Upon education, societies are built and existential traps identified. Tried paths to pleasure and wealth are paved in advance, and the avenues to ego-expression kept free of random debris. Through education, humans reduce the role of chaos in their own lives even as they arrange themselves in ways that make the system as a whole more chaotic. It is thus important for a child to be granted access to as many dimensions of life as possible prior to his admission into adult (political, warring, reproductive, and ideology-making) society. It is not for early schooling to convince the child to believe in everything, but to show him all of the avenues that he will be able to choose from. Curricula should cover both the sequential (typically left) and creative (typically right) mind. Early socialization should cover both the controlled social (typically front) and sense-emotional (typically back and temporal) mind. Thus we elaborate again on what it means to be human. Not just the physical form, but the expressive action. Not just the expressive action, but the expected expressive action enabled by "human-specific" competencies against the backdrop of the natural world. Physical form aside, we are human because centuries of self-aware/other-aware entities before us have left structures for us to communicate about and drawn conclusions about patterns in the world which we are inclined to accept. We call another "human" when we expect that entity is capable of evolving up to our standard of expressive richness within its lifetime. Anything above this is animal, alien, or superhuman. But, as for us, human existence ceases to be such as soon as the notion of the social world is taken out. Without the social world, though we might (in some strange way) still know right from wrong, "morality" and "law" as [communicable ideas in their current form] disintegrate. Without the social world, though we may aim for some ultimate purpose, knowledge of God is thoroughly incomplete since there is no notion of the collective "us" to serve as the scaffolding for such a Being. Belief, then is the gateway to steered action. Education builds the foundation for beliefs not held in blindness. Complete education reveals to a person as many choices relevant to her expression as possible. And once a person is sufficiently educated in the tools that will enable them to live optimally the life most natural to them, the good life becomes possible. Without social knowledge, the good life as humans conceive of it (beyond the bliss of happy savagery) is impossible.

The Buddhists and some Hindus say that humanity is rooted in illusion. It may be more appropriate to say that the absolute nature of humanity is illusory while the relative (and fairly stable) nature of humanity is real enough to be useful in the practical world. We can look at this through anthropology. I have made the basic case above that the meaning of "humanity" depends largely on agreement since, at the very least, none among us can draw the definitive line where "This specimen of *H. neandertalensis* is human, but this specimen of *H. ergaster* is not; This *H. ergaster* is human but this *A. sediba* is not." And even if we say that the only human is *H. sapiens*, what, then of a recently fertilized zygote? What of the woman's egg with sperm attaching at that moment? Are these human? What of the dead man? Is he human? What of conjoined twins or those born without cortex? Are they human? This is why, even without the notion of evolution, definitions of humanity depend on where certain other humans agree to draw the line. That some populations favor abortion while others do not is an indication that society has yet to define an absolute line between human and non-human life. Even if all of society where to agree today on an official starting point for human life, short of backing such a line with observable laws, we will always risk being wrong in such matters as these where we are called to define ourselves. Because humans can be wrong in defining themselves, sharp definitions of humanity must yield to fuzzy ones. This is why we take the definition of humanity as stable enough with furry edges: "same look, same communication, same behavioral context."

Why does it pay to know that the definition of humanity is fuzzy at the edges? Because superhuman concepts such as God and robot *live* on those very edges. A Believer (hereafter used to describe a monotheist / [believer in a single god]) assumes that the highest cause can be described in terms of tendencies which can be used to describe herself (human tendencies). Even if God is superhuman, we can flatten our descriptions of the Entity using human terms. This is called anthropomorphization. Via anthropomorphization, Nature's laws can be assigned "willful" origins. A Nonbeliever (hereafter a description of one who either [does not anthropomorphize] or [does not acknowledge] a terminal cause) assumes that there is either no highest cause that can be accurately flattened into ego-space. Here at the beginning of the third millennium c.e., Believers are confronted with increasing intrusion of non-ego, non-anthropomorphic items into their realms of social experience (phones, artificial intelligence, mind-altering pharmaceuticals, god-like / life-steering corporations) and so are under increasing assault at the hands of none other than human progress itself. Non-believers, on the other hand, encounter increasing complexity in their attempts to dig-up morality and Grand Purpose from these same systems. All in all, those of the third millennium world—Believers and Nonbelievers alike—continue living against the backdrop of technological, communicative, and institutional complexity. Yet these very technologies which stand for constructs bigger than human do not themselves seem (to the individuals within them) to require singular individuality for their sustainment. Only through collectives do they apparently rise and fall. Thus we ask, "What does it mean to be human in places where the things humans make no longer require their makers?" This is the call for individual meaning, as few humans would be excited to claim that their highest purpose is to be a cog amidst overlapping toys of their own creation.

A man trusts that which enables his natural actions to go unobstructed. A man distrusts that which he expects to block even actions which are not natural to him.

- In places where I *trust*, I can pursue my natural inclination without worry.
- In places where I *do not distrust*, I can play some non-natural role in exchange for freedom from worry.
- Where I *do not trust*, I expect to be blocked if I pursue my natural inclination.
- Where I *distrust*, I expect there is some non-negligible probability of being blocked no matter what I do.

Though I would love to trust everyone, the world is full of differences. Some will be offended simply by my being around. Some bring outside problems into their dealings with me. In cases where trust cannot be had, a lack of distrust is the next best thing; at least in this case I know that there exists some mask that I may put on to help our relations go smoothly.

Why discuss trust? Because if belief is what a person steers his actions around, trust determines what other beliefs he can concern himself with while he is steering around the first belief. As a man is of at least two minds at during most of his waking hours (creative [inclination-biological-emotional] and sequential [rational-linguistic-communicative]), his life revolves around trading inclinations for perceptions, trading wants for the image of wants fulfilled. At any time, he holds an incompletely articulated reference point for current actions alongside his capacity to frame what he is doing against that reference point. If he does not trust his reference point, his pursuit of the desired end will be "watered down" as part of his attention is hijacked by his animal-like defense preparations against the shady reference. It follows that one who cannot trust the relevant components of his circumstance cannot express himself optimally there. If one does not trust his own view of his highest purpose (given that he has one), does not trust himself or his talents, does not trust the tools at his disposal (which include other humans), or does not trust the path he takes to achieve his ends, his pursuit of the good life becomes that much more difficult. It is better, then (as Confucius suggests), to place <u>oneself</u> in circumstances which align with his talents if society proper is to gain maximally from his presence in it.

A word on trust in human institutions: Except for children, mentally incapable (including the dead), and individuals who have shown themselves resistant to basic public guidelines, a person should be allowed to choose his optimum circumstance. This is because, the more limits a society places on its citizens' right to choose (given that the citizens are able to conceptualize other choices) the more likely members of that society are to resort to self-interest above the interests of the whole. It isn't that I have taken away my people's choice, but the idea that a single person's realization of the loss of choice prompts him to talk to others to look for other areas where I have robbed the people. If the people do not trust me, they are less likely to come back to me without coercion. And when I need them the most to populate my staff and enforce my laws in places where I cannot be present, they will invariably plant the seeds—knowingly or unknowingly—of my downfall.

People behave in ways consistent with the things they believe in and seek shelter consistently in the things they trust. Trust is gained through consistent harmony with the people's Dao. That is, each person has a path which is natural to him, and entities engender more trust to the extent that they enable each individual to follow that unique path. Thus we can make broad observations about the various groups of people and their associated highest purposes.

> *[Belief and Nonbelief] as a case study.* Since anthropomorphization of a single highest force means applying a personality (stereotyped self-awareness, social dynamics, existential circumstance) to it (thus the vision of God), it is consistent that Believers should follow a Force which makes laws, holds possessions (such as "Mine"), has the capacity to love and feel slighted, and (perhaps most importantly) can deliver direction in the language of human understanding. It is consistent that God frames all things and all of time using Himself as the primary backdrop, and equally consistent that He will speak through human forms. So it is with the People of the Book (Judeo-Christian-Muslims who comprise the majority of Monotheists in the third millennium). A God of preferred super-sovereignty engenders a sense of specialness among His Followers. A God of preferred mercy engenders mercy among His followers alongside the permeating sense of transgression upon which such mercy stands. A God of expansive framing will foster evangelism and conquest of other frames among His followers. And a God of Ultimate Heaven and Ultimate Hell will subsume the very paradoxes among the humans who serve Him. Hence, it is consistent that People of the Book will fight among themselves whether or not their common enemies have been conquered. It is consistent that the God of the People of the Book even *has* enemies—despite the idea that He holds no equal. So too do the Believers say, "All is of God, but these people are less than we are." Here God is, finally, described as typically male owing to the outward focus of His interface with humanity. This is the God of the people who are themselves full of paradoxes and one of the chief justifications for Nonbelievers' unwillingness to follow. Nonetheless, it is not wrong to believe in such a God. It is in fact, right to follow this God. Not because we can prove or disprove that which is beyond proof or disproof, but because it is efficient for a human (Believer or Non-) to interface with other humans on human terms. It is socially efficient to interface with human moral law on terms that hold coherent implications for human behavior. Nonbelievers are often at the mercy of Believers in the third millennium because it is Believers (not Nonbelievers) who, paradoxically, will kill each other and themselves in the name of the God who says "Thou shalt not kill." The paradox of divinely-driven "judgmental mercy" often poses a danger to those who ignore the Believers' singular God. But if the Nonbelievers just don't believe, what does it matter that they are preached to?

> ...for it is consistent that a Believer will expand the message of a God who, as humans do, extends His own meaning making to all things. But it is inconsistent for a Nonbeliever to expand a message against a thing he does not believe in. His nonbelief is borne out by his attempts to walk through the rock which is not there. Many Nonbelievers, however, obey a tradition of attempting to convince others against belief, and we might guess that this is more of a defense against Believers' natural call to ingroup or outgroup evangelism. The paradox of virtue, however is that the execution of such is one-sided. The paradox of humanity is that its expression is one-sided. Thus, the wealthiest of all men sees only people poorer than he is. The most assured of

all men is the last one to attempt to convince others of his beliefs for the sake of defensive argument. The Good man, using only harmony, cannot destroy an evil one while and evil one can destroy anything—including himself—except for the absolute good (which we define as far-reaching harmony with the greater among human values). And the Believer knows a God above men while the Nonbeliever knows a principle man-made. Yet the Believer does not have the right to judge on behalf of God while the Nonbeliever does not have the rational power to frame against God which makes no sense to him. In this way, many humans divide themselves and fight over principles which their greater systems forbid them to fight over. One possible cure for this is [education in] and [acceptance of] the human paradox—and the recognition that each has his own Way.

It is right for a person to believe in God because the system of believing in God defines right as such. Wrong in this system is nonbelief. But condemning others in this system for their non-belief is also wrong (since only God can judge). Yet, outside of this system, right and wrong in "God's" eyes is, to some, a non-idea. It is left to society and moral upbringing to determine virtue, but it is inconsistent to anthropomorphize pets, corporations, and God as an idea to be argued against. How useful is it to *refuse* to acknowledge my fellow human as a human—referring to her as "cell collection number so-and-so" instead? Regular humans anthropomorphize things. That's just what they do. And if it does not hurt a man to treat his pets, cars, and movie characters like real people, and it doesn't hurt him to tell his children about Santa Claus or Corporation X, it should not hurt him to grant others the right to interface with their world through a human-like construct. What great system forbids this? Accordingly, allowing a Believer to believe *and* preach according to that Believer's own morality is the most rational position a Nonbeliever can take in these matters.

If men were more aligned with their professed beliefs, acceptance would become the rule rather than the exception. The challenge of Nonbelievers is to let Believers both preach and believe. The challenge of Believers is to spread Divine faith without spreading man-made judgment and subsequent war with other groups who are also creations of the One Creator—especially with other Believers.

The measure of truth is the extent to which the messenger and its hearers can live out what is said. Paradoxical behavior in a man is an accurate depiction of his nature, but it cannot speak truth about which among his contrary ends stands highest. A doctrine of peace should instill peace in its hearers. A doctrine of rationality should make sense to its hearers. If completely rational, it should make comfortable allowances even for "irrational" subsets of its rational members (as mathematics does). In this way, we ask whether words can actually capture the truth of an idea meant to be acted upon, or are we humans destined to remain children grasping in these matters. What do you think?

Education stops when those who hold the knowledge hoard it or lose their ability to translate it. To "know" is to believe something that the majority of normal people trust as accurate. A normal person is one whose actions do not, on the whole, strike us as unusually positive or negative over a series of interactions. I remind you that we strive for practicality in this text over rigor. Interaction series such as the chain of familiarity established through Kenny's PERSON (in the social science research) show that humans move from their own biases towards their [responses to others in context] in forming opinions of those others. This is a good heuristic, so we will go with it. I am best equipped to interact well with a particular person when I am educated in as many of the potentially relevant social maneuvers that might be required in his presence. In this way, play is as important to a child as any formal education, as simulations and entertainment are as important to adults as an occupation. These avenues reveal to us social "packages" without requiring that we pay the real world for our using those actions. Indeed, they enable us to explore behavioral options that may not be accessible to us in the regular physical world.

CHAPTER 3. THE ROOTS OF BELIEF AND NON-BELIEF

When I tell those who pry that I am an Atheist, few understand what this means. Let me clarify: I do not believe that the physics, biology, and social laws that govern humans can be accurately summed up in the form of a ruling personality. Based on the world that I can study with my eyes, I believe that humankind answers to the product of its own agreement, not to a god. Many Believers ask me to prove that there is no God, but this is where the unnecessary conflict starts: as a Nonbeliever, I don't need to disprove God. I just don't believe. To me, proving or disproving God is like proving or disproving the idea that blue is the best color in the world: it falls to a person's opinion, and how she reconciles her actions with her intentions. Trust me, it would be nice if you could just "convince me" to believe in something that works in my favor. I agree with Pascal's assertion that it is risky to ignore God if you are wrong [assuming the penalties are what Believers say they are]. But true "belief" doesn't work that way. When a person truly believes something, they steer their actions around it; I have found over the years that, in us humans, logic is secondary to our actions, so that even if you could completely prove to me that God exists AND prove that I should modify my self-categorization because of this, my actions will still betray the truth of where I stand: I simply don't plan my life around what a super-personality might think, even if you are right about it being there.

I am writing this essay for people like myself who have learned to doubt humankind's power to rule over other humans in total consistency. I argue that, because unique personalities are necessarily inconsistent with some portion of the world in which they find themselves, no single personality could rule over an entire world full of differences without losing its status as omnipotent. I also claim that Nature itself seems to allow all things to exist, so that a God truly above Nature must be at least as accepting of all things as Nature is. I am a Nonbeliever in the "personality theory of the Divine" not for rational reasons, but for practical reasons. Personalities have preferences. A Nature which is above human-centered preference cannot limit itself to special groups of humans above others, special books in special languages, or even special moments in time in order to save humans from some ill-fate that the Nature itself allowed. Though I have formerly tried to simply believe in a God which is "greater than or equal to Nature" while at the same time being "similar in character" to men, my actions present me with the inevitable feeling that I am bowing not before a great King, but before some flattened caricature of human's own explained purpose. That the paradoxes are too numerous to count means, for me, that I cannot steer my actions around a concept that doesn't make sense to me. A biased personality which sits above all of Nature which in turn sits above all biased personalities doesn't make sense to me. Nor does [steering my actions around what such a personality might want] make any sense to me.

The lack of steering of my actions around the idea of a god's will, by definition makes me a non-believer. Yet I argue that, at its core, this opinion can only be seen as a crime of "intent" which produces no harm to others on its own. That I don't believe in a god does not mean that I need to convince you to disbelieve. In fact, if the idea of God makes sense to you, have at it. I will argue in this essay that Belief is actually better than Nonbelief where the advancement of moral society is concerned and that there is at least one way for a person to be a Nonbeliever and still take a position that honors a single Creator. If, by the end, of the essay, I have convinced you that my views are 1) contradictory and 2) that the belief of the Nonbeliever is conducive to an even stronger faith than that held by stereotypical Believers (that is, if my arguments seem to support the case *for* God), then I would have succeeded in my main objective: My aim is to build a bridge to the good life for those who do not follow the rules of any god.

Part I: Arguments against a god

Here is the first part of the entire argument (why god as most men define it is either non-existent or non-omnipotent). The second part (why man should believe in a God anyway) comes later.

1. Men are petty (or at least limited in vision) because they have egos / personalities / wants which beg to be satisfied.
2. I consider "wanting" a thing to mean [acknowledging that thing without having it, even as a person turns their actions towards its realization].
3. Nature is real enough to us, but consists (among other things) of plants, animals, murders, corporations, dogmas, and every human personality that ever existed.

4. We can assume that a god above all things must also be above #3—whatever "above" means.
5. If there is a god above all things, this god must at least be above all human wants.
6. But the typical monotheistic god, in addition to being narrowly male in expression, does "want" things and even makes "laws" to this effect. Thus there are patterns of human expression which exist outside of this god's realm of realization:
     a. Why a god would need to make laws to keep humans in line with its will—despite the fact that humans are always subject to its will anyway—is a mystery.
     b. Why a god would mark some people as "chosen" and others as "not" when all were created by this god in the first place is a mystery.
     c. How a god could come to decide that the work of its own hand was "sinful" or "flawed" when said god is usually assumed perfect is a mystery.
     d. How the principles of an entire "personality above Nature above personalities" could, further, go back into Nature as a prophet or whatever and encapsulate itself is a mystery.
     e. Why a god of eternal "love" would basically say, "Love me or else burn in Hell forever," especially in light of 6a, and 6c, is a mystery.
7. To me, #6 (a-e) contradicts the notion of a god above all things, mainly because the thing described in #6 seems to want things which really (among gods) should be beyond want. That is, #6 is biased as <u>men</u> would be biased and, to make a long story short, seems just too petty to be a real god above the magnificence and mercy (diversity) of Nature. Nature is magnanimous. The god I have described in #6 is not.

Again, this is my own opinion. If you can view #6 differently, then good for you.

But I could live even with the inconsistencies in #6. For many Nonbelievers, #8 is an irreconcilable problem.

8. If the test of truth is, among other things, consistency with what is observed (either in hearts or minds), the fact that, historically, monotheists have on the whole, warred with themselves, decimated civilizations not their own, stolen from / erased the history of / enslaved those seen as unlike them in the name of the god which "is love" tells us that
     a. Humans [establishing themselves as superior] and [working to erase inferior parties or beliefs] is characteristic of a belief system which forces one biased personality onto the rest of creation.
     b. [Humans vying for power then not being satisfied with it] is a byproduct of worshipping a god who already has everything, but feels it necessary to wage war on its own creation / save its own creation from a situation that it (the god) sponsored in the first place. So too do many Believers invent their own differences, denominations, classes, and "races" and hate outsiders over those differences. As the god goes, so go the men.
     c. We observe so many Believers hypocritically judging "us versus them" when not in worship service, though their own god (to them) tells them that it is not their place to judge in this way. As the god of Heaven rewards moral conformity, so too does the god of Hell excommunicate those who differ in areas that a biased personality favors.
     d. Often, when (as a science teacher) I have talked to a stereotypical Christian about certain branches of science, I have found that he doesn't want to hear it. If I talk to a typical practitioner of Judaism about the exaltation of certain prophets, he doesn't want to hear it. If I talk to a typical Muslim about Christianity, he becomes defensive. And if I mention Atheism to any of these, they draw their ideological swords. All of this occurs even as the three of these claim to follow the same god who is above all people. If the followers of the god of everything cannot themselves hear out every case, then on some social-psychological level, all of these seem incomplete.
     e. If a particular Believer believes that coercion and the fear of Hell is the best way to get people to genuinely follow a thing out of love (as opposed to cowardice), that believer knows how to lie to himself—as he teaches you to lie to yourself about why you would follow the path to eternity.

The bottom line is that the stereotyped faith of the Believer, though noble, produces actual behaviors which are inconsistent with the truth as he professes it. If his god is so good, why is the Believer so full of judgment? If his lord is so peaceful, why must he erase outsiders with his apocalyptic doctrine? If his master is so all-encompassing, why will the Believer not simply hear out the science that sits before our very eyes? The answer to these questions, I think, is as follows:

9. Humans, despite lofty aims, are still animals who fear things and defend themselves from uncertainty. Rather than following a god who makes sense, we follow a god whose mixed-up values line up with ours. We judge and fear the unknown. Our gods change their eternal minds. We make laws to offset uncertainty. Our gods command humans whom they have already given free will. We compel ourselves to "love" in the face of what we don't like. And we set up power structures which divide other humans into nice, neat "us versus them" categories. Our gods pick "chosen" people above others that they themselves made.

So it is convenient for a Christian to question a Muslim's "72 virgins" but not his own "3-in-1" Trinity. It is convenient for a stereotyped practitioner of Islam to take the rites of prayer literally but the story of certain prophets as a metaphor. We pick and choose. How many times have we seen a person of the book (Judeo-Christian-Muslim) take the beasts in biblical Revelations as a metaphor but take the story of 7-day creation and 6,000 year-old man literally? Why be so strict with some parts of the Bible but not with others? Again, the answer is because, whatever "truth is out there," humans filter it to line up with their own fears and biases. To be sure, one could just as easily take [7 days] to mean [7 "God" days] (read epochs), and reconcile geology with Creationism nicely. One could take [man from the dust] to mean [man from the multicellular metabolite through evolution] and say that "God was the cause, evolution the means." The main reason people don't do this is because they do not want to open the door to conceding other aspects of their faith, which is understandable. But if I were a true Believer I would say, "My God rules everything, even science. So bring it. I find the complexity fascinating and surely worthy work for the Eternal King."

It is not because of "god" that I am a Nonbeliever, but because the people who profess their single god, on average, do not back up their claims with action. Now, if you tell me that Heaven awaits the "good" yet proceed to conquer my culture, discriminate against my people, and war even with your own citizens and neighbors over materialities such as money, oil, [empirical knowledge] and power alike, *why in the world* should I believe that you have found "truth" (let alone believe that your description of a force above Nature is an accurate one)? Nonbelievers do not arise because of the thing that isn't there, but because of the behaviors of those who <u>are</u> there. That said, let us build the bridge to repair the divide.

Part II: Arguments *for* a God

Here is the second half of the argument. The philosopher Kant says essentially, "We can't prove or disprove God, so let's pursue the Sublime anyway." Derrida says, "Words rest upon their reference frame." Even the loosest interpretation of Aristotle says, "Everything in the practical world serves at least one end (even if it is only the expression of the thing that generated it in the first place)." The Buddha believed in an Ultimate Nothing, but led a very "something-like" worldly life of good anyway. What do we know about the <u>practical</u> world?

10. Words explain actions and perceptions, but it is the actions and perceptions themselves that ultimately build practical experience.
11. When a human studies something, she lends clarity to parts within a whole. Her words label the structures thought to comprise that whole.
12. In line with #11, a human can study a thing without changing its nature. Just because I learn that a human body consists of organs doesn't mean that the body stops being a [whole body] and becomes organs instead. It simply means that I can now interact with the body as a [whole body] AND / OR the body as a [collection of organs]. Once I learn of cells, I can treat you as a [whole body], a [set of organs], OR a [super-collection of cells]. In this way, knowledge adds more dimensions to the expressive options available to us, but need not replace the "true" nature of things.
13. Though the Buddhists say that "person-ness" is an illusion, they still interact with people (including themselves) as if a person is a real-enough thing in the practical world. This behavior, in words, would be called paradoxical. But who really cares? Who, besides people who dwell in the world of constructed words would dismiss the Buddhist tenets as being impractical nonetheless? Nietzsche and Derrida have looked at this. Paradoxical or not, the four noble truths and associated teachings are useful for finding happiness. Similarly, though I may say that "a human is nothing more than a meta-aware super-collection of cells," it would be highly impractical to treat every person I meet as such a super-collection. For expediency and practicality both, I assume personalities in others and treat them accordingly as, simply, humans—not as a sea of organic objects.

14. The believer reflects her belief by steering her actions around it. A society which refuses to find common ground between the theoretical and the practical world will war with itself until it perishes at the hands of its own inner tension—just like a stressful body. Though denial of God is understandable from an empirical perspective, it is not a practical position. Nor is it a necessary consequence of science.
      a.   Words' meanings are built on agreement. Science and official religions alike are built upon the [transmission of] and [action upon] words which, in the end, are nothing without agreement. The dogma is not important. Only our willingness to coexist matters, for all humans—even extreme friends—may be assumed to differ in the perceived content of their "minds."
      b.   Human trades, though sometimes distinguishable by realm, can also be distinguishable by scope; A clerk types on her perception of a computer. A technician repairs his conception of a computer. A salesman sells collections of objects called "computers."

      Similarly, a psychiatrist heals a person as "mind," a generic doctor heals a person as "organs," a surgeon heals a person as "the location of an exacting work," and a biophysicist heals a person by generating useful theories about the interplay among cells. A human can exist on any of these levels and be healed all the same. (Notice that, among these, the biophysicist heals indirectly.) It is not for the psychiatrist to bicker with the surgeon over their respective definitions because those definitions need not even concern each other to a significant degree. Even given conceptual differences, the two really only need to let the other one do his own work. Similarly, the Nonbeliever steers her actions in society against the backdrop of a human-translated moral code and sense-perceived sciences. The Believer summarizes these same things under the construct "personality" and interfaces with its subsequent laws in the same way that she would interface with a regular (thoroughly exalted) human. Thus the Believer and Nonbeliever are like psychiatrist and biophysicist respectively: Neither possesses the final "truth" (Kant). Yet both perform services for the advancement of humankind.
           i.   When I claim to be a Nonbeliever, I speak of how I *believe* the world above us should be framed, but I cannot prove that this is the only way it should be done. Nor am I interested in word-spinning with you when it is *much* more expedient for us to simply cooperate.
           ii.   If I am rational, I know my view of existence is falsifiable (as the sciences are). Thus, barring that the entire world falls into some Borg-like stupor, I will never grasp the truth about the Divine—only strive towards it with the observations of the eye in hand.
           iii. If I am faithful, I know that God above is beyond description. For every scientific advancement, God is that much more the Genius. For every seemingly different faith, God is that much more multifaceted—adapting to other cultures in ways that my human smallness could not emulate.

15. Why should an Atheist like myself believe in God? For the same reason that we treat people as people and not as collections of cells: For the Nonbeliever, "God" is the compressed version of human morality and social values infused with the power to supersede Nature. Human morality is real enough. Inasmuch as we are constantly discovering things that modify our current understanding of Nature, the ability to "supersede Nature as it stands" is a power that we ourselves demonstrate—not because Nature can actually be overridden, but because our *understanding* of Nature is so incomplete that our practical interface with it is constantly being overwritten in even our own scientific journals.

$$\text{Personificationbyhumans(Canweinteractwithitashumanlike?)} + $$
$$\text{Naturallawswhichcompelbehavior(Canitbethoughttohaveawill?)} \cong \text{God}$$
$$+ \text{theabilitytooverrideNature(CanitexpanduponoruseNature?)}$$

Thus, I can disbelieve in God yet believe firmly in the parts which describe God. What makes me a Nonbeliever is that I do not steer my actions around the will of the whole, but instead steer my actions around the interface among the parts. We *can* treat Nature as if it had a personality. Must we? No. (Even the Believer cites free will here.) *Should we* treat Nature as if it had a personality? Either for practicality or out of sheer amazement, probably. (Ask any sufficiently expert scientist. Many will hold a god-like view of the vastness they have studied.)

We *can* see Nature as compelling human behavior whether it be through genetics of early social circumstance. *Should we?* Unless you have some kind of excessively internal locus of control—thinking that you are in no way compelled by <u>anything</u> beyond you—probably.

Finally, we can override Nature. Even an air-conditioner can do this. Thus all of the main characteristics of God are established. These don't prove God, but they give a Nonbeliever more than enough reason to let a Believer believe without arguing with her. Because we are rationalists, we know that our beliefs are insufficient for establishing absolute truth. Because our science clarifies all that we observe, we are not disturbed when we observe belief, but rather see it for the socially-beneficial (and possibly accurate) sanctuary that it is. Not everyone wants to be a biophysicist.

Let me summarize. Believers themselves say God is beyond description. Rational Nonbelievers say the body of their own knowledge is falsifiable. Thus, neither can prove or disprove the Divine with finality. Ironically (for both sides) this is the way it *should* be. Nonbelievers will find an expedient construct in the idea of God as well as a balance with the greater morality easily conceptualized by society. A world without God is similar to the world we know but much more complex. God is to human morality what money is to human value: the efficient language of exchange. And if one has no doubt that her path of personification versus non-personification is the correct one, peace with others should be the rule, not a burden to be hammered against others in futile debate.

I write this for non-believers seeking the spirituality of ancient times in a world susceptible to defensive and destructive dogma. Nature is grand. Why would we not want to treat it as a beloved guest in our lives? This does not mean that we need to suddenly become Believers. I will *always* distrust a flawed man's description of "perfection." I refuse to steer my life decisions around self-inconsistent, mob-driven peer pressure. Another person's fear of a Hell makes no difference to me—especially when it is that person's job to promote Heaven instead. Two millennia of power-lust will not make man's exaggerated caricature of himself any more real to me. Nor will I ever bow to a master who isn't at least as well-behaved as I think I am. But this doesn't mean that there is no God in the absolute sense—only that I will have to rely on my own best social and moral judgment to see what such a God might look like. Men and their institutions may or may not help in this. Actually, *only* people who live life as they profess—*only* people whose faith is strong enough to withstand any new (including scientific) information can really help me in this.

A short story of monotheistic creation for Nonbelievers

16. We can think of all of existence as a super-complex waveform. There are harmonies and resonances, atomic and subatomic structure. We can take a window sliced from the entire waveform as a specific point in time and make predictions about the rest of the wave. If our slice covers every component wave in the universe, we will be able to predict *everything*. Alas, we can only slice in accordance with the power of our instruments—thus only sampling a subset of existence. Because there are certain dimensions in physics which are beyond our grasp, things can exist outside of our reference frame. From this, the image of free will is born. Not because there is such a thing as choice, but because causal factors outside of our [ability to explain] will compel our next action and, for simplicity, we will say that we chose it ourselves.

17. Thus, from a slice of earthly existence 4.6 billion years ago, the following potentialities existed:
    a. Certain physical attributes (like angular momentum amidst space dust) were able to sustain themselves.
    b. Causal factors possessed the potential to compel their effects. This, along with #17a, combine to form the basis of the "will."
    c. Systems **O** outside of systems **I** were able to combine—making bigger systems **O** + **I** (we will call this "induction"—which means systems can be overridden when they absorb other systems without having their basic dynamics changed. The new system overrides the old. This will be the basis for omnipotence.)
    d. We take either the prior Big Bang or the beginning of the Solar System as a starting point for our wave slice (thus establishing a kind of "First Cause" for our subsequent descriptions.) For this view of creation, we do not care about what happened before the Big Bang.
    e. #17a through #17d constitute the justification for God before Earth, but does not define God. Why am I doing this? Because without this, the story becomes boring as well as impractical. That we may [look at the science] and [personify it] is far more useful to a socio-moral collective than a lifeless set of bullets. And before Believers out there get upset that I might be calling their God a list of those very bullets, I say that I am only giving a Nonbeliever an explanation of the complexity / simplicity in terms that she may understand; if we can personify the potentiality (just as we personify the cells and call the sum human), we can say that God is here.

18. The Solar System coalesces and Earth cools. Chemical compounds sustain their own levels as "pre-metabolic systems." Prokaryotes, Eukaryotes, then pre-humans living in animalism of an underdeveloped meta-awareness. Evolution is the means. There is *Australopithecus*, filed as human. Thus, over the passage of epochs, Earth and animal are made. (The Bible outlines these epochs as an initial six stages according to cosmology, geology, and ecology. The seventh epoch is the period during which the creation can look at the stabilized work of the Creator.) Humans dwell in underdeveloped meta-awareness (behaviorally determined by Nature, not their own society) in the Garden of Eden—a culture prior to collective society and morality.

19. From *Australopithecus* through *Homo*, humans eat from the Tree and develop meta-awareness (awareness of their social selves and their place in nature) opening up a can of worms. By their nature as retroactively declared *Homo sapiens* progenitors, the groups called Y-Adam & Mitochondrial Eve are destined to be the source of their own existential strife, exiled from Eden because they have chosen to impose civilization upon themselves. God is annoyed (Nature disturbed by its own subset). But then again, being the original potentiality in the first place, God necessarily lives through the eyes of the new humans. (Self-aware man sees himself as the star in God's movie). All humans from here on are born into the illusions of knowledge left by their fathers. The Hindus are right. With every birth subject to socialization, the pain of delivering babies with bigger brains. K-strategy (animals which produce few children but undergo slow and steady growth) is maximized. The original illusion of "ego-meaning" is perpetuated over and over. Who will save us from ourselves?

20. An exemplar for delivering humans from themselves is promised. Jews and Muslims say it isn't Jesus. Christians say it is. Whatever the case, we now have at least one example of how to treat others in a life full of suffering, how to spread meaning in a peaceful way, and how to follow the most harmonious path in accordance with the original potentiality (God the Father) in the form of Jesus. Is it necessary or even correct to elevate this man to the level of God? In matters of God (as we have said before) much is, by definition, improvable. The closer one gets to God, the harder it is to make sense of that person's *telos* (or end; as shown in Aristotle). So the final answer is: It doesn't matter whether Jesus is God or not—at least not to the Nonbeliever. Christians, Muslims, and Jews often battle over this point even though God has expressly told them not to worship their own power to judge (possibly because such judgment is like elevating their own understanding as idol).

    A sad story: as with God, humans kill themselves over Jesus before following the basic message intended by the Supreme God. But the issue is not really Jesus. It is politics, fear, and the need to be special (#9)—co-opted by generations of men vying for power. That is, as long as we allow our attention to Grand Divinity to be clouded by human-cultural and political interests, we will continue to reinforce differences that *H. sapiens* does not hold.

21. One day, say the People of the Book (Judeo-Christian-Muslims), judgment will come for all persons dead or alive. This makes sense since a person leaves a social "echo" among others after she dies. As a slice of the grand wave herself, no human can be expected to exist as a discontinuity. Without getting too heavily into the math, we basically argue that packages of simple waves (like those describing a particular human's life) should be cyclical and periodic, modified only by interference elsewhere within the system. Thus, reincarnation exists as a unique person feels a natural affinity for other people who existed before her. The dead, like calming capacitors, leave traces of their social legacy. In light of the present, the past is judged. In light of the living, the dead are judged. Even if through similarity of action only, all humans are compelled towards their maker (most harmonized, Natural potentiality) via a pattern of repeatedly expressed interaction with their surroundings and peers.

22. Why did we not just tell the scientific version of this story? Because the science as we currently know it fails to thread together the practical sense of order which we humans require daily: the "what for." While it could be called "pragmatic," "rational," or "realistic" for a person to leave the God part of the story out, you will find, as a Nonbeliever, that there exists an evolved space in the human psychology which begs for an affective (emotional) tie to the life one leads. The more I study, the more amazed I am in light of the natural world. As with people, my physically-sponsored emotions compel me to interface with this life as richly as possible. Thus through genuine love—not fear of Hell or of other men—do we treat our interaction with Nature as if it were an interaction with a close friend. It becomes one's mission then to bring harmony to the whole world—not just one's comrades in dogma. The call of life, then—for Believer and Nonbeliever alike—is to live happily with others on the journey to perfect our own collective nature.

23. As for the arguments against God: Whatever. Humans are walking paradoxes, therefore it is consistent that their image of their maker will also be a paradox. The "true" Source, however, is beyond any one person's power to describe on behalf of all people. Arguments #1 through #8 concern man's story about God, not God Itself, and only work against men who do not live the far-reaching peace that they profess. Strong in faith, the

Believer is unaffected by the #1-#8. Assured in rationality, the Nonbeliever absorbs the benefits of belief using #16-#21 as a possible foundation for cooperation with those who do not share his rational tools.

The Guidelines for non-cliquish Spirituality

I am about to lay out some rules that I follow for the pursuit of truth. These rules are not based on science, yet they are practical. Hence the limits of science on its own. Occasionally, common sense and practicality should win out over empiricism.

24. **A thing at its maximum turns into its opposite,** as light that blinds, sound that deafens.
25. **A thing and its circumstances are one,** thus for everything that exists, there is also a natural interaction between that thing and the world which is not it. Increasingly, we want to study the interactions of things with their circumstances, hence the interest in spirituality.
26. An idea can be considered "true" if most normal people generally accept it as given. Science tends to be rooted in sense-based truth, but is ignorant of the inner workings of single minds, for single minds and what they accept are not visible to outside parties. That is, where a single mind navigates spaces where truth is missing, belief and assumption rule the day. **The study of spirituality must avoid mind-reading.**
27. **Spirituality is not the same as religion, for we need ways to divorce group-specific doctrine from broad socio-behavioral observation.** Accordingly, we can study spirituality without studying God. Just as we can study human eyes without studying the specific humans that possess them.
28. One should be clear on the scientific study of spirituality's "realm of expertise." Otherwise, we will confuse its tenets. Thus, **our starting definitions of spirituality and spirit should be rooted in the empirical (or at least quasi-empirical) world.** Physics and biology deal with the empirical since they rely on observations of actual things. Politics and psychology deal with the quasi-empirical since they rely on the agreed-upon names of interactions among actual things.
29. Because of its close tie to religion, our starting point for spirituality must take a complementary position towards religion. That is, like the unique elements of a vector, Scientific spirituality and Religious frames should coexist but compel no conclusions for each other. I will state this complementarity right here: Spirituality studies the components of social interactions divorced from 1) immediate 5-sense perception, 2) the present moment in time, or 3) the present scope of interaction. Psychology and Biology study interactions not so divorced. Religion provides a collective institutional and social psychological structure for behavioral intention. That is, Religion organizes and directs our intentions in light of a consistently public end beyond the empirical world. Spirituality summarizes our actions and perceptions aimed at non-empirical qualities of the public world. Each deals with the non-empirical (not sense-perception based) world, but **religion specifically looks at explanations of the world as a whole and mobilizes groups within it. Spirituality specifically looks at the psychological and behavioral dynamics of individual people with respect to the world those people see.** With groups of people, spirituality becomes collective spirituality, but if there is no imposed set of rituals or doctrine meant to direct spiritual people towards a defined end, religion need not follow. Conversely, if we simply say, "Heaven is" and do not concern ourselves with how a person interacts uniquely with the non-measurable world before them, spirituality need not follow from religion either.
30. The study of the non-empirical world will depend upon the study of actions in the empirical world. Discrepancies between behaviors done in the face of the unknown and those done against the known are themselves a subject for spirituality.

CHAPTER 4. OBSERVATIONS ON PERSONAL LOVES

This section consists of journal entries, as I feel these are closer than [abstract theory] to that fuzziness which comes with private preferences for fun.

SEX AND SCULPTURE

4/6/12

To me, sex is an art—the art of sharing oneself with another. For some, the experience is like that of acting, to others, it is a dance. Personally, I think of sex as sculpture; I aim to trace the contours of the body. Here, sex is more like a careful craft, where the subject becomes frozen, in a sense, against your futile attempts to replicate her form.

I am currently 32 years old, and have had only a few partners in my lifetime. Of those few, I would really only revisit one, as the others taught me the limits of sculpting a muse "out of character." Where the standards of stereotypical maleness require a forcefulness beyond my comfort level, I was an embarrassing failure to the woman who expected me to be stronger in the bed than I was. My first partner in particular (with a comfortable feeling and a mind to teach me) was, in my view, intimidating beyond measure—where my only defense was anger in hindsight (surely a show of the "toughness" unavailable to me just minutes before).

As for my last partner: awkwardness. The differences in our bodies and (more importantly) our approaches to intimacy rendered a recipe for a comedy more than a song of love. She too was a valuable partner, though; after her (and in light of my first) I vowed at 29 never again to sleep with someone I didn't trust. Indeed, so it had been all along: for many, sex is the regular state of things; that the experience be fun is the only requirement. For others, sex is closer to the sacred—with trust or (perhaps even better) a glimpse of sublimity required for the union to work.

As one who has always been protective of his power over himself, I have kept partnerships rare by choice, preferring instead to flirt with the many charming (but invariably unavailable) women out there. At first I wondered why this route seemed the more natural. Later I realized this was simply a means of fostering the highest kind of control possible— coupled with amity. Where status or the rules of the institution do not permit, I have prided myself on approaching the line without crossing it—a "que sera, sera" non-attachment permeating my most memorable exchanges. Like dating without spending money; loving surreptitiously, for a few minutes, in a room full of unprivy onlookers; she would be my girlfriend every Wednesday without either one costing each other's time or emotion…I think, for some, such is as safe (and no doubt as fulfilling) as it gets—lest the thrill of a romance just beyond real-world eyes yield to the boring predictability, the taming chains of formal cohabitus…

Not that all live-in romances are stifling, mind you—just the ones carried out with partners who don't leave you happier than you otherwise would be without them. I am *extremely* happy on my own—full of quirks and interests which only a mirror would understand. Not so much full of myself as unwilling to change for others. And so it is: I do plan to meet that muse one day, but until then it's back to pondering Kant and ordering lists of esoteric objects…without someone over my shoulder asking me why.

B.

4/27/12

The things I find beautiful in this life are hard to describe—no, impossible to describe (since to describe them fully in words would be to bind the unbounded sense of harmony they elicit). I have tried and failed again to capture the muse

B., and am once again moved to wonder what it is about her (besides her striking good looks) which compel my attention. Let me attempt to sketch her for you, though.

B. is ten years my junior (a fact which the disciplined stoic within me still finds disturbing) with black hair, and a stand-offish way. A student of mine, she turns heads and charms easily, but prefers to hide behind her phone in that crowd called my classroom. Her body shape is typically "sexy" by most standards and is of the kind that makes men uncomfortable with lust. (I know this because, being sensitive to the emotions of others in the room, I can truly feel the temperature rise when she enters). Funny enough, I too find myself stuttering on occasion when I look in her direction, as it does take work for me to continue teaching despite her. But it isn't really her look that does this—rather her way. She becomes more domineering as I get to know her, but also more vulnerable with progressively visible insecurities. Over her power to compel? Her need to be obeyed? Who knows? I suspect, though, it is the hidden "other side" for which she wishes to be recognized—a side that no mere groupie could glimpse—that makes her into the fire-slinging dictator that she is. A true force of nature and I (wiser than I once was) a mere witness to her complexity.

And although it may sound rather unromantic, I must be, above all, drawn to that very complexity—not to the body as an object. She makes me want to do more philosophy, learn more about psychology as a way of understanding such creatures in general. I want to be with her that I may study her uncountable intricacies. But, then again, studying is what I do. In other words, I am more *myself* in light of her than in light of other things—tracing the forms of the human construct with even more fervor. Not her looks, but her power carried upon beauty's palanquin. Not her domineering ways, but the idea that I have both overpowered them and been increasingly inspired by them with every successive interaction. Where we began adversarially, we are now on tepid speaking terms (you'd have to have been there in the beginning to know what an improvement that is). Thus she stands apart from others in my world of Buddhist sameness. If that isn't a muse, I don't know what is.

The kind of sculpture that I practice is the art of faithful replication. I do not possess the creative mind for originality—only an eye for consistency in things that already exist. At first it bothered me to learn that the praise I'd received since childhood did not translate into actual talent (In real estate, in programming, in leadership, teaching, etc.), but over time, I've come to appreciate the usefulness of non-originality: If I were original, I would almost certainly get caught up in the modern western need for "bigger, faster, better." Since I cannot do "bigger, faster, better," I only know how to more thoroughly accept what is. I think this is a recipe for *contentment* over *continual improvement*, and I think the world could use more of this. Certainly there is something to be said for some time-honored things—even those of one's life. To me, sculpture does this—honoring the captured object. My work isn't the greatest, but out of a need to honor the instance, I see it as a way of accessing an eternal thing. It should be no wonder that, drawing an ego-defining link between sculpture and honor, honor and love, I take none of these lightly, and have historically paid dearly for attempting to do so.

I imagine the day when I can say to B., "Let me sculpt you," and know that I could do so faithfully. I find it ironic that, despite my fascination with her, I don't love her; despite my enjoyment of her sexual power, I have never dreamt of her; despite jokes that I'll marry her one day, I am thoroughly happy without her. I think all of these things hold because I truly do respect her, and in a move so deep as to have apparently penetrated my subconscious, I have never fantasized about a woman whom I truly respect before she has given me permission to do so. (Perhaps on some high level, my subconscious considers this a kind of non-consensual invasion of her soul's space?) In this way, to replicate her by touching the formless and giving it form: I think this runs even deeper than sex, for it is evidence that another person has drawn something powerfully natural within the native…consensually.

I LOVE YOU

4/28/12

Dr. Gary Chapman's five love languages are interesting: Quality Time, Gifts, Acts of Service, Compliments, and Physical Touch. Of these, I surely value "quality time" the most. Maybe it is because academia has been my mask of choice for so long that I find words irritating when it comes to expressing deep things; I don't know how to say "I love you" using such words—at least not without sounding like a bad actor.

Still, I *can* say it. When we are close to each other caught up in mutual charms, it is as if you can hear it. In cheerful conversation over trivialities, the subtext declares, "What is love but one taste of the many harmonies one knows how to feel?" For two years I wondered whether or not a Buddhist who believes in ultimately Nothing could form the kinds of bonds that bespeak worldly love—whether, in the name of practical Buddhahood, one could extend the calling beyond the monasteries into the homes of regular working men and women. I asked, "if one must truly abandon normal life in order to reach enlightenment, does this not reduce enlightenment to an impracticality contrary to the *sapiens* objective?" Say what you want about humans' rational constructs, but they are as present and "real" as the alms for which the monks themselves continually beg. I asked, "If not animal-love, then what of animal-hunger or animal-sleep? No, there must be a way for enlightenment and worldly love to travel together." Indeed, here is what I found:

In the nihilistic sense, all is Nothing. Thus the pretended separation of this world from ultimate Nothingness is itself "nothing." The game, in the meantime, is mediated by a mind which considers untold numbers of "Somethings" framed against its own tendency to reify the illusion. In this way, Nirvana is like a limit in mathematics: we name it the far off horizon yet use normal experiences to count our way towards it. In love, the enlightened ones see the loved thing as an extension of their own ability to count, not through the lust that constrains or the insecurity that judges, but through the eyes of one who has found another as the seeming externalization of the former's road. I love her as the clarifying glasses which sharpen my view of eternity. Even one who sees total sameness yet sees this sameness through his own unique mind. Even if that mind itself is an illusion, he is still, in this illusory world, tied to it solely. To this way of seeing, I am exclusively devoted. Through this experience called "her," this way of seeing gained its sharpest definition. As unique as the ethereal memory of our beginning and the amplification of my natural way through everything she has been to me, I come to love her with the passion of one who loves every ounce of life he lives. This is how the Nirvana-bound nihilist carries love without constraining desire: She is not the object of his pursuit, but extends the means through which he is himself. Nor is she merely a tool, for he can separate his broad will from hers no more than he can separate his eyes from their seeing. Whether playfully combative or intensely gentle, together they are natural—so that even eternity knows its own reflection.

MISSING YOU

The idea of enlightenment is simple: this is the state where all deeming desires are conquered and one's general path through life known. I may still have fears, but now I know why. I may still desire things, but such desires do not compel me to battle myself. (Hunger, sleep, and the natural psychology with which I am in harmony still apply; keeping up with the Joneses, considering externalities as oppressors, a sense that I have not accomplished "enough" does not apply.) After enlightenment, a person (presumably) will not go back to the state where he battled himself for the sake of the confused societies which trained him, though he will continue to function in those societies as one who sees them in their full opportunity. Thus, the things that come to him were a part of his way before they arrived (since he is already "complete" as a person) and the things which leave him remain a part of his interface with the world. I believe, then, that an enlightened person can still want things but is not oppressed by such wants, and can experience the loss of things without being emotionally diminished by such loss. Such is the reason that I can love you without fear of losing you. You are a part of my view of this world and when you leave, though I may miss you, I am as happy with you in your absence as I am in your presence. I suppose this is a testament to the bond between souls (if one believes in such things).

I find that many temporary friendships have a kind of permanent quality to them—as if we have known each other long before the first words were exchanged. Perhaps true love is like this. There is no need to search for it because it manifests itself as soon as you learn this enduring harmony with your own lens. Does it make sense that my alter embodies the things I hold valuable elevated atop the things I find less valuable? Does it make sense that he or she travels with me as the result of some chain of experiences which I hold dear? Surely this one is alive in my actions typified by a return to these places such that, near or far, I could never truly lose them.

PROLOGUE TO MUSE

2/24/12

I was never good at communicating romantically—probably because I am not at home in the world of words. Words are more of a tool than a work of art for me—wielded like the first object you would pick up to stop a burglar. That is, if there were some other way to record my thoughts into history or communicate to others reliably, I wouldn't use words at all. Not surprisingly then, I try not to get close enough to others to require uncomfortable words since, when out of my element, I will often communicate with an undesirable edge.

In romance, I can be clumsy, obsessive, strange, and exasperating—all because of a native discomfort with emotional vulnerability. Nonetheless, as I looked at the body of my philosophical work, I saw that romance was a thing I had not yet written about in earnest—so it needed to be done. Beyond theory and synthesis of the very broad kinds of "good advice" out there, I hadn't really written about a person who inspired me. As such, "Muse" was a kind of project— where I sought to write about romance as I actually experience it.

Life is too short to be mired in inefficiency. I only have three to eight decades to explore to the fullest. You, with your tempting walk and sassy attitude—I've met your kind before: after hours of my study, writing, recording, and contemplating, will you wish I were more boastful? More "alpha" manly?

In youth, I was a slave to my temper. "Alpha" manly is cute when we spar, dangerous when the police are involved. I avoid "alpha" manly as surely as my father taught me that "fights are to the death"—where your idea of *confidence* might be my idea of provocation. I have no sense of humor in these settings and…those of your kind—with your suggestions of how I should improve myself/get out more/be more outgoing, are not worth the hassle or the money.

Years as a slave to my temper, I know what it is to make my own life difficult. I have offended others and been made to pay—so that now there is only one question for us: Am I a better person with you? Or will I hurt you too?

We begin with the worst assumptions—guard raised in full. Because I've been kicked out of so many places—spelled out platonic friendship and had it read back to me as lechery—not a colleague, acquaintance or stranger will ever see that side again. Not a romance that ever began in truth, but a string of partnerships that ended when I saw I was being taken lightly—she can have the man's man while I learn once again that the best life is the solitary one…in a way.

You, with your cool and class, would rather observe art than spar intellectually—refreshing as though I came out of a muddy hole, breeze-kissed—would make me question that nasty habit I have of flirting with the help. I study the life of the Buddha and flow of the Dao as a quasi-ascetic, without wedding ring, but more than happy to exchange charm with girls who display a bright and happy sexuality. So says dimension 2 of my factor analysis of traits of the people I know. (Yes, I really went there.)

My fortress walls are three feet of nerd behind two feet of stoic coldness just behind the moat where passive apathy and childish immaturity trade laps. You, Muse, must have known this since you too approach life with a passionate "Whatever, man"—raising all kinds of hell when you don't get your way, but so delightful even then—

One of these Sundays I will sculpt you. Though we've met, we won't really meet until we travel. Eyes as a still garden— there is nothing special in them until I watch you stare off to the side. Then everyone can see: you are in some ethereal place. Only because you change so easily—hat, dress, tennis shoes and hero cape—do I forget who you were yesterday and trade you in for tomorrow as if serial dalliance never stopped. It's not like I require novelty, but I *adore* the complexity in a work of art which captures the tide of souls—the human form, female form—terrain of skin curves like sheet music notes. You must have known of the former emotional storms because you do not lean on sexuality, drama, or pressure to pull me in, though you have these in excess. Instead, it is the easy flow of our conversation that means more than anything; we can switch from work to play and back, talking about anything—usually childishly. There stands my true Muse.

I suppose I trust you, though I really do not know how this happened. I am better with you than without—though I used to love traveling alone. We get into trouble together—but more as a paired menace than anything really serious—and span the world with our journeys and the questions we want to answer.

Our house is happy and full of sun. We are both too selfish for children, and have agreed to part company the moment we get bored with each other (though secretly neither of us sees that happening). We'll reflect for a long time on whether to marry…ironically, not because of us but because of the expectations of others: will we still be able to play around without the specter of domesticity held over our heads?

THE HANGING GARDENS OF BABYLON

I should like to build some of my own, for the same reasons.

CHAPTER 5. OBSERVATIONS OF THE ESOTERIC

STOPPING HABITS

Not lost, but different: it occurs to me that worldly love should be transcended as an experiment in death. How do I survive without my deeming desires? Will life cease to *mean*? It is so hard to know without forgoing those desires for a time. I wonder whether the promise of temporary austerity is too lofty a promise to keep, yet I simultaneously find myself increasingly irritable in the face of these habits of mine. There are too many important things to do in the world besides worry about my ego. Unfortunately, ego desires are not a thing one can simply "turn off."

KEEPING HABITS

I have attempted to stop, but failed. Philosophers speak of the "is-seems divide"—that state where a person is always of two minds (present-focused versus future-aimed)—prompting me to wonder whether or not we are all of two minds on some level that compels two paths to enlightenment. The thought proceeds this way:

- The Buddhist seeks escape from this world which is not there.
- The believer strives for a Heaven which his earthly eyes will never show him.
- The leader represents the people but is in many ways separate from them.
- The follower has the power to compel or (often) oust a leader, though he does not have the formal authority given by other followers

So maybe it *is* true that the first are the last…

To transcend the world is to refer to it as one's foundation. Does this not mean that any Heaven we build above Earth must rely on Earth to supply us with the tools for knowing and describing that Heaven? How do you transcend a habit without referring to it?

I believe then, that enlightenment as we know it is only half-lit until we have come to terms both with the world here and the world beyond. As my anthropology class and I watch these clips of bonobos mating shamelessly, I think to myself, "Surely humans are just like this only with social brains to temper the urge!" *We're not so savage*, you say. But count the wars; the faithful who murder in the name of peace; the powerful who guard their influence as if held at gunpoint by the unschooled and powerless. Tell me that we have transcended our desire to desire as any other animal and I tell you that you are fooling yourself. The monks who retreat from the world and claim to have overcome it…they are fooling themselves. The men who reason around their urges—effectively stalling but not surmounting such urges…they are fooling themselves.

I came to this conclusion recently when I realized that the very reason I am not a committed Buddhist is the reason I still have this feeling of incompleteness despite having glimpsed enlightenment: my rational self has completed the monolith, but the animal self has not yet cut the ribbon. In the mirror I say, "Congratulations Self, you are without peer!" but in my heart I can see the inconsistencies. So it was with the sages I have studied: "Congratulations, Jesus. You are without sin! Here are 2000 years of people sinning against themselves because they think you have fixed everything for them." "Congratulations, the Buddha. You are above the world—no, all existence even! Here is the Sangha and generations of escapists who have yet to do (in the dominating West) what even the most menial politicians do daily." Not that I have anything against the sages. I'm just saying, though.

Perhaps it is better to keep the desire nature "healthily happy" than to say it isn't there. Otherwise, generations of my followers will spill forth the repressed discontent that I so skillfully swept out of view.

SOME LESSONS FROM AN ORACLE

The I-Ching (Chinese Book of Changes) is built partly on an interesting arrangement. Oracular counsel is provided through a series of six-line "hexagrams" arranged in a recursive fashion by family. Each line can be broken or solid, can be read as changing or fixed (broken to solid, solid to broken, broken unchanged, or solid unchanged) and represents, roughly speaking, direct harmony (solid) versus processual harmony (broken) with the will of Heaven. Six-line hexagrams are the stacking of two three-line trigrams; trigram lines represent the inner, outer, and abstract worlds as one moves upwards. For example, the trigram Thunder ☳, means the inner world / self (bottom solid line 1) reflects "Heaven's Way," but the immediate surroundings (middle broken line 2) and the abstract situation (upper broken line 3) aren't seeing Heaven's Way yet. (They are in the process of traveling towards it.) Thus I am like lightning to them—a rebel. Me against the world like Tupac. You get the idea. If I flip Thunder, I get Mountain ☶. Now the situation (line 3) reflects Heaven, but you (line 2) and I (line 1) aren't there yet; we are headed towards where we need to go, but don't yet feel we have accomplished what we need to accomplish. This is like being blocked by a mountain.

When you put trigrams on top of each other, you get the 64 hexagrams. The bottom is what you see, and the top is, broadly, where you are going. For example, ䷙ is someone who sees mountain moving towards thunder: right now this situation looks like an impasse, but soon I will power through it, and you will simply watch it happen. This is my "taming power."

The most interesting thing about the I-Ching—aside from its pictorial depictions of "situation-framing" in psychology—is the idea that families of hexagrams are determined by only three transformations: flipping, swapping and inverting. I'll leave the details out, but can you see how, in my (line 1) mind, I am the most richly described thing here in a room full of people? Talking to you, I observe your outward self (line 2) tangibly, but since I cannot read your mind, what's going on in your head is a (line 3) abstraction to me. If we flip this trigram, my inner thoughts become the abstraction (line 3) and you become the rich (line 1) self, while outward appearances are comparatively unchanged. Thinking about this makes me wonder: If we spend our lives thinking that we ourselves are so important, does that not mean that the world (which thinks itself important) regards us with less and less clarity? Thus, the harder I work to make myself understood to you, the more I reinforce the experiential divide between us; with every "clarifying" move, I become ever the black box to those right in front of me. Again, the first are the last. I suppose the game, then, is not to clarify myself, but to assume clarity is already there—interfacing with you as if you already understand.

What this says about harmony: To assume harmony is to rid oneself of the need to *clarify*. This doesn't mean we shouldn't communicate—only that such communication shouldn't be built on a need to correct a confusion we aren't willing to admit the presence of. Where keeping habits are concerned, I wonder if the world really cares that I am enlightened while everyone else is not. Were the trigram flipped, I would watch my thunder spirit become your mountain-bound ascetic—perhaps seeing clearly that my faith without your benefit is meaningless.

BEING ENLIGHTENED

For those who care to know, here is how I accidentally found enlightenment. After years vying for control of my own emotional terrain, I finally found work at a job which required the same level of discipline needed to gain such control. Frequently frustrated, I decided that the place would never give me the freedom I wanted, so I claimed that freedom by writing about the various episodes there—in attempts to rationalize my situation. During this time, I also became a Daoist with Buddhist leanings. It was my lifelong dream to write philosophy and, to make a long story short, I made the time to pursue this dream. Once I had written everything I needed to say, I decided there was nothing left in this life for me to do (that is, everything else was icing). And so it was. After putting three years' worth of writing together and saying to myself of a number of issues, "It looked messed up, but it was exactly in line with my values," I decided that even a life unfinished in years can be complete in outlook. Thus I claimed enlightenment. If I found myself on my deathbed this afternoon (given that the circumstances weren't ridiculous), I would feel fine in light of the life lived.

What is enlightenment, then? Is it walking around with a cloud of light over your head? Speaking in calm parables? Soothing everyone with your sage-like speech? No, enlightenment is none of these. Instead, I think of it as a kind of math function which enables you to take any set of experiences and map out your way in full resolve. My function steers me towards the search for an eternal "truth," but includes remedies for situations which do not foster such a search. This is captured in a writing called the "pillars"—a statement of values inspired by my friend K., and was greatly facilitated by a series of rationalizations called the "full dictionary of major relations."

The bottom line is, a person who says, "This is who I am, rain or shine," "I have attained my life's title—my service to the world outside," and "I will never go back to ignorance of these things," is enlightened. A person cannot be enlightened, I think, if he doesn't know how his path affects others. In general, I am a Limiter—meaning I create boundaries (and sometimes imprisoning structures) for others. I do this for the good of the whole and not for any single individual unless the individual seeks to understand their own pre-made structures. Then, the walls built around the whole trace paths of freedom within them. Enlightenment does not mean wholesale "goodness" but, rather, the focus of one's existence both locally and in the abstract humanity revealed. Enlightenment certainly does not mean everyone will be happy with you—hence the other side of contentment.

THE OTHER SIDE OF CONTENTMENT

My chief complaint with the Buddhists (though I am an undercover Buddhist myself) lies with the impractical nature of our ideas. We are the existentialists—semi-Platonic idealists who divorce perfection from materiality, begging for alms while claiming that alms don't matter. Really, all major "transcendent" belief systems are this contradictory, but I am more critical of my kindred because I believe that devoted Buddhists (in ideology not dogma) are among the most gentle souls in the world. The idea that Buddhism doesn't have to exclude other faiths is a testament to its openness. That Buddhism, on its own, is perfectly at home with existential ambiguity (the greatest ambiguity of all) speaks of the strength held by its practitioners. So one would think that these people would be able to spread more good in the world than they (we) do. Alas, this is not so, since the world generally has a hard time striving towards "Nothingness." Further, Buddhists have a hard time striving for the very worldly wealth which is of no importance to them, so they rarely acquire the influence needed to force their practices on others.

Confucius would probably agree that, in mobs, most people need to be forced towards order. Thus Buddhism is strong on the individual level, weak on the societal level. I find this mildly disappointing. But then again, the idea that you are truly part of a group that practices what it preaches can make you feel at least a little special. Not that believers in other faiths don't practice what they preach, just that I find Buddhism and Daoism (as philosophies) are less war- and judgment-centered than other belief systems. The other side of contentment? Humans are still animals. To a certain extent, we like war. We define ourselves by judging others. And we like to win. Without additional insight from other ideologies such as Christianity, Islam, Hinduism, or Confucianism, we Buddhists and Daoists remain on a cloud separate from the realities of material survival.

There is an element of beauty in a system which values war and inequality, since such systems tend to bind like minds together in strong harmony. Just as we get crazy over our favorite soccer and football teams, we become strongly devoted to "us" when mobilized fiercely against "them" As the Judeo-Christian-Islam God judges those who don't follow Him exclusively, so often do His believers judge non-believers. As Confucian and Hindu thinkers draw lines in the societal sand, so too do the politics of rank and ritual take on a kind of collective social-psychological meaning dipped in Divinity. These systems tell us that, to be content in a world full of disparate others, there must be paradoxes. More inward philosophies tell us that, to be content within ourselves, peace must permeate our interface with the world outside. In this way, humans do well to have both a philosophy and a religion. A religion materializes morality in the form of public practice. A philosophy "processualizes" sense-based experience in the form of mental constructs for understanding. That is, religion gives psychological order to public abstraction; philosophy translates perceptual "data" for use by a personal behavioral program. Religion without personal philosophy is blind. Personal philosophy without religion is collective-aimless. Even if an anti-religion is better than no moral position at all. Even an anti-philosophy is better than total incoherence in one's responses to the world.

If I am enlightened, hooray for me. Now I need a view of you which allows me to use my philosophy to make your world better. Why should I make your world better? Because, even in the most selfish sense, making your world worse or being indifferent to your plight only makes things harder for me. What does inwardly focused enlightenment look like upside-down? After thinking about it, I suspect it looks like arrogance, standoffishness, or simple inaccessibility. Perhaps it looks like an inviable austerity, or an uninspiring unprofitability. On the other side, I would thus seek a materializing worldview which takes my abstractions and converts them to your benefit. Here, the Daoists and Buddhists have several auxiliary tools to choose from in addition to their existing bodies of explanation. Each requires a view of governed Nature. Each requires a stance on inequality beyond the simple "we wish people didn't do it" ideal. Each requires a means of focusing its practitioners on the future rather than the merely fuzzy conception of changeless eternity. All of these requirements exist so that these so-called "soft individuals" may make real and practical changes in society beyond the monastery walls. Though I am no expert on any of these matters, I believe that the Christian golden rule, Islamic resistance to watering down one's belief through mere lip-service, the Hindu fearlessness in questioning all that is, and Shinto reverence for the past are the best places for beginning a construction of a more tangible edge to the inward philosophies.

Even after I achieve enlightenment, there remains another goal on the other side. It is no single purpose common to all who have claimed peace, but a more general kind of "outside benefit" which honors the more materially grounded aspects of human nature. If worldly wealth is truly meaningless, Buddhists should not be afraid to get rich. If power is only others' efficacy preceded by the illusion of another's influence, Daoists should not be afraid to hold the illusion called "power." Let the monks have children—with an eye for bringing one more stubbornly good person into a world full of doubts.

HONOR BY SHOWING

For my own clarity, I have created personal definitions for respect and honor. You respect something when you acknowledge it as being what it claims to be. You honor something when you support what it claims to be with your own action. In each case, the "claims" can be made by others. For example, if someone holds the official rank of my supervisor and I say to myself (even if only subconsciously), "Yes, I accept them as fitting the part," then I respect them as a supervisor. This doesn't mean that I have to respect them in other areas. Nor does it mean that I have to like them or even tolerate their presence. Respect is, thus, about accepting another's claim to a role. Suppose, on the other hand, I show all of the deference towards this supervisor when she is around, and behave towards her in a way that lets her know that I am reinforcing her role as my supervisor. In this case, I am honoring them. Even if (in my mind) I think, "This person is so insufferable!" it doesn't matter. Where my *actions* reinforce a person's claim to a role, I honor them. See how you can honor someone you don't respect? Or respect them without honoring them? I thought of these definitions not just to spin some philosophical wheels, but instead to solve a certain linguistically-driven puzzle I encountered:

Some say that the words we use define us. When one speaks enough of *joy*, joy builds their reference frame. That is, whether they have joy or not will serve as a foundation for their actions. On the other hand, if one has no conception of "the loyalty shown to an older sibling for the sake of blood relation" it will be hard to frame one's actions in terms of this. Further, if the thought of *happiness* makes me happy, using the word pushes me slightly in this direction. If the thought of *honor* calls my attention to my own value system, I may (in some cases) need to know when certain relations suggest that I compromise my honor because I will need to be aware when a social situation, for example, yields to a moral one. Respect, on the other hand, is valuable because it reaffirms the extent to which I can expect someone to do as their role suggests; that is, in some sense, it tells me how much I can take them at "face value" within that context— allowing me to perform my own role with that much more resolve. Without respect, suspicion creeps in. Where there is suspicion, my attention is divided between what I need to do and what I wonder about your next unfitting action.

By the above definitions, we honor by showing. For example, the principal complaint of Islam against Christianity is that Christians, in dividing the One True God into pieces and elevating His prophet Jesus above that One True God, fail to honor the Most High as He was meant to be honored. Islam is thus built on showing devotion through intentional and consistent practice. Christians, of course, disagree. On another level, I honor my significant other by performing the actions that reinforce our union. I dishonor my spouse by acting negatively towards them in comparison to the way I treated them when we first came together.

For those who strive to be honest, a liar is dishonorable. For those who strive to be dedicated, itchy feet carry dishonor. And when I finally decide that *this is what I stand for, rain or shine*, I also define honor as my own adherence to this standard. To fall short of my own defining ways is to dishonor myself. If I cannot honor myself, then I can always rely on others to reinforce who I am, but—if not chosen carefully—others can be notoriously unreliable in matters confined my own identity. I have chosen to write about honor here because, in light of the previous section, I would still like to lend some structure to the notion of Daoist / Buddhist social efficacy, and feel that such external efficacy begins with those systems and people that we honor.

Though an ascetic, one may still hold things like education systems, marriage, or artistic creativity in high regard. To show such regard through <u>willing</u> action is to honor these ideas regardless of whether one admits them as fixtures into one's life. But I believe that, if you willingly honor something beyond yourself despite its lack of personal relevance to you, there is an extent to which you value them as Aristotelian auto-*telea* (ends unto themselves) and perhaps you should make room for them. I beg for alms as means to material survival in a world which "isn't here." I continue to "live" as a Buddhist though "living" is an illusion. As long as I am in the business of using meaningless tools for ultimately no reason, I might as well contribute to a world which needs my peace by showing my interest in other external things unto themselves. Again, marriage, power, and renown may naturally appeal to some of us as "honored concepts" and there is no sin in this. If I am truly enlightened, these will only add to the clarity I have found.

FAITH IN SMALL PLACES

Though I operate under the mantle of skepticism, I feel that there is much cause in the Universe for faith in the unseen. To give some examples,

- The idea that a particle can act like a particle or a wave is neat.
- Complex numbers and irrational numbers have a theoretical usefulness regardless of our ability to eyeball them in the real world.
- That two minds can have completely different conceptions of a thing and still agree is amazing. In fact, *every* communicative act requires some degree of trust that the other will receive the message as intended.
- That we humans can talk about things not in front of us or externalize our memories through the creation of writing and societies is awesome. (We take these things for granted, but imagine living 4 million years ago without all of our toys. *Australopithecus* would be blown away by our swag.)
- The human capacity for empathy and ability to conceptualize such is also amazing.

While the above ideas may be easy to dismiss as mundane, people who theorize heavily in these areas know that building entire bodies of "absolute-like" knowledge essentially upon mere agreement is no trivial matter. (See the inductive construction of the natural numbers or definition of addition as an [order relation] to convince yourself of this.) So much of what we "know" has faith at its core—even the knowledge of those who know enough to make claims that they know nothing.

Quantum mechanics, teleporting particles, wi-fi networks, collective morality, solar energy—who would have thought that there were so many ways to send information without anyone seeing the whereby? For those of us who claim belief only in what we see, surely there is hope for a world beyond the visible after all. We can't "see" opinions, yet who doesn't respond to them?

FAITH IN UNIQUE PLACES: STANDING-UP INDIAN AND THE HOURS

Speaking of a world beyond this one, I have at least two personal reasons for being interested in spirituality. When I was about 12, my brothers and I saw, firsthand, a freak of science. On our living room ironing board was one of our light brown toy Indians (from a Cowboys and Indians play set) standing at about a 15° angle on its edge. When was the last time you saw an object appear to "balance itself" despite its center of mass? I remember my two brothers and I looking at the odd sight; I poked it with a pencil and the three of us watched it teeter. I moved the pencil all around it and (like the true eldest "voice of reason") said, "It must be a spider web or a hair holding it up." Not so. After a few seconds of Houdini-like checks (another light poking, another ±3° damped "teetering" at a period of about ½ a second), I found no reason for the toy to stand as it did, poked it one last time so that it fell, and was unable to stand it up again.

The event ended with my rather original comment, "That was weird."

Still, my brothers and I have not forgotten what we now call the Standing-Up Indian.

My other reason for studying spirituality stems from a phenomenon that persists to this day. I follow a calendar called "the Hours" which basically consists of previews of the day in microcosm. Over the course of the last 10+ years of observation, I have noticed that experiences held at very specific times of day mirror experiences at other very specific times of day to such an extent that I (1) get plenty of warning before stressful events and (2) can "control" (with some error) how my day will go based on the time at which that day began. After two years initially studying this, I learned that there is a strong tie between such hours and my astrology chart, and have since set out to calculate every division of the day. For me, the hours are so predictable, so reliable, that I have a hard time imagining that they don't work for everyone. Unfortunately, my attempts to convince others that the hours apply have met with limited success. Too bad for them, since I rather like the security that this calendar grants. Though I've recently grown tired of explaining the system to deaf ears, I shall attempt to outline the system once again in the next section.

Standing-Up Indian and the Hours constitute my motivation for studying faith in a way that always assumes a "rational" explanation. While it is entirely possible that I simply missed the "hair" that held the Indian up, the fact that it teetered twice when I poked it does not support this. Perhaps there was some electrostatic thing going on, but when I put my hand around it, this didn't seem to be the case either. Whatever it was, I assume it to be rooted in science, and am compelled to study quantum mechanics as a result. Meanwhile, the Hours motivate me to study human circadian rhythms and responses to seasonality, weather, and days of the week as "small-factor forces" which nonetheless contribute to how we feel.

Some of my students in Physical Anthropology have claimed that science and faith necessarily conflict. Nonsense. A "rational" explanation (falsifiable and empirically-driven) need not preclude a seemingly miraculous superset—especially among those who lack the constructs to describe that superset. If my individual cells can't explain my entire body in "cell language," that has no bearing on the idea (1) my entire body can still be explained while (2) my entire body (and awareness thereof) is no less miraculous to the small cells within *even with* an explanation. In the end, it doesn't really matter that we can explain something if we cannot do anything about the thing we have explained. The explanation is useful only to the extent that the minds who have posed it may benefit from it. That is, even if we could explain the ocean, it is no less vast. Even if we could explain Death or the Heavens, how humans change in light of the things is no less mysterious. I think we should endeavor to learn as much as we can about "eternity" if for no other reason than to gain insight into our place in existence in the long term. Life is too short to be tied up in struggle over small specks of truth.

HOW THE HOURS WORK

On the hours, let me begin with some background.

I have never cared for alarms, so I wake up without one. Travel back to the year 2001. Three days in a row, I wake up at exactly 6:38. An average day follows. Later, I wake up at 7:17. Since this makes me late for my teaching job, a chaotic day follows the 7:17 wake-up time. Later, 6:38 again. Another average day. Over the course of the next year and a half, I wake up at various times, but note that 6:38am, 7:17am, and 2:22am tend to be followed by days with a "character" specific to each, regardless of whether I am working that day, grocery shopping, going to class, or hanging out with friends.

The rare 2:22am wake-up brings with it, a landmark event (while other times such as 2:21 and 2:23 just don't happen. 6:38am means that I start preparing to do something around 7-ish, while a 6:34am wake-up means I start my day immediately. 7:17am is always chaotic, but if I wake up after 7:47, the day is easy *even if* I am super-duper late for work. In this way, I learn of certain time windows: 2:22am to 3:23am is important. 6:34am – 7:17am is good. 7:17am to 7:47am is basically "bad." 7:47am to 8:07am is a day when I will charm somebody or create something.

Most importantly, I also learn when the windows stop during this time. If I drop something on my foot any time between 6:34am and 8:07am (like a heavy bar of soap—which actually happened several times during the year and a half), I noticed an accompanying mistake sometime during that day. If I "drop the soap" at 7:16am, 7:46am or 8:06am the mistake occurs around 5pm. (I found out later that the official "stop time" is 5:21pm). If I drop the soap at 6:55am, the mistake occurs around noon. Do you see what is happening here? Such a "calendar" continues to work even today. For example, on the very day I am writing this, I awoke at 8:04am which indicates (1) that the day will be charming / artsy since it begins between 7:47am and 8:07am and (2) that I will start the main "business of the day" at a time between the window's start time and the end of the day which is proportionally positioned with respect to the wake-up within this 20 minute window: that is, around $\frac{8:04-7:47}{8:07-7:47} \times (17:21 - 7:47) + 7:47 = 15:54$. Call it 4pm-ish. What's so useful about that? Here's what. I have been working from 2:30pm to 4:00pm and 6:00pm to 8:00pm every Monday for the last two months. Just this morning I checked my email and found that the schedule was changed to 4:00pm - 6:00pm (from its original 6:00pm – 8:00pm—which means that my day indeed starts at 4pm-ish). I didn't know this prior to today, but some aspect of the Hours seems to have been "ready" for the time change. And so it has been nearly every day for a decade now.

Enough background. How would you calculate your own hours? First of all, since I haven't been able to get data from other people on this phenomenon, I don't know if it works for everyone. So this is all speculation. If it works for you, then great; you'll find a powerful anticipatory tool at your disposal. If it doesn't work, then whatever.

Begin by getting your hands on your astrology birth chart. (Here is a reminder that I didn't see a connection to astrology until two years after noticing the hours, so you may already have certain significant times in mind.) Be sure you have your exact birth time and birthplace, since this thing is clearly minute-dependent. Next, take a broad look at your wheel. Each major "planet" will represent an "Hour." For example if your Venus is in 12 Cancer followed by your mercury in 16 cancer, you will find that, sometime during your day, there exists a 16-minute window during which, given that you wake up here, you can do "Venus-stuff" all day with the main event occurring wherever your actual wake-up falls. (Each degree of separation in an astrology chart is worth about 4 minutes, since there are about 1440 minutes in a day and 360° in a circle.) Unfortunately, I am still working on how to calculate the precise time independent of the person's pre-existing knowledge. What I normally do is ask, "Are there specific waking times during the day where the rest of your day takes on a certain typical 'character?'" Given that the person says yes (and they usually don't) I look for the corresponding planet to pinpoint in their chart. Broadly:

- Sun is where you express your will
- Venus is artsy / charming
- Mercury is analytical communicative
- Mars is physical / combative or aggressive
- Midheaven is public image-related
- Pluto is will to power
- Saturn is structured (as a scholar I acquire much of my new knowledge on days where I wake up in the Hour of Saturn
- North node is characterized by events important to the long-term identity / so-called "destiny"

It is with considerable embarrassment that I cannot report on Moon, Jupiter or Ascendant. In my own chart, there is no noticeable "Hour of Ascendant," My Jupiter and Node are .5° apart (suggesting that my Hour of Jupiter is a mere 2 minutes long before the North Node Hour takes over), and my Hour of Moon is *very* predictable, but very late in the day, and I don't often wake up during its window. (In fact it is the Moon which stops my day at 17:21. I don't know how this works for others).

In your own chart, you can hopefully identify an anchor point based on your ideas of a pre-existing window. Otherwise, I can only offer two theories for starting based on my own chart. Apply them at your own risk:

Sun-Moon midpoint. This is simple. Find the midpoint of your sun and moon. Either this point or the point opposite it may mark "Midnight" in your chart. (Increasingly, I doubt this one.)

Sunrise. Given your birth time, rotate your chart to where the sun is on the Ascendant. This time, more or less would be near your Hour of Sun. Take that time (in minutes) divided by 1440, multiply what you get by 360, and subtract this last number of degrees from where your sun is. This might also work to identify your "midnight."

Once you have found your "midnight," every other point on your chart follows accordingly. Kind of. I have noticed that several of my windows are longer or shorter than others, with "clearer" windows generally lasting longer than fuzzier ones.

Anyway, do with this as you will. I swear by such observations, though.